A2 ALTITUDE CORRECTION TABLES 10°–90°—SUN, STARS, PLANETS

OCT.—MAR. SUN APR.—SEPT.

App. Alt.	Lower Limb	Upper Limb	App. Alt.	Lower Limb	Upper Limb
9 33	+10·8	−21·5	9 39	+10·6	−21·2
9 45	+10·9	−21·4	9 50	+10·7	−21·1
9 56	+11·0	−21·3	10 02	+10·8	−21·0
10 08	+11·1	−21·2	10 14	+10·9	−20·9
10 20	+11·2	−21·1	10 27	+11·0	−20·8
10 33	+11·3	−21·0	10 40	+11·1	−20·7
10 46	+11·4	−20·9	10 53	+11·2	−20·6
11 00	+11·5	−20·8	11 07	+11·3	−20·5
11 15	+11·6	−20·7	11 22	+11·4	−20·4
11 30	+11·7	−20·6	11 37	+11·5	−20·3
11 45	+11·8	−20·5	11 53	+11·6	−20·2
12 01	+11·9	−20·4	12 10	+11·7	−20·1
12 18	+12·0	−20·3	12 27	+11·8	−20·0
12 36	+12·1	−20·2	12 45	+11·9	−19·9
12 54	+12·2	−20·1	13 04	+12·0	−19·8
13 14	+12·3	−20·0	13 24	+12·1	−19·7
13 34	+12·4	−19·9	13 44	+12·2	−19·6
13 55	+12·5	−19·8	14 06	+12·3	−19·5
14 17	+12·6	−19·7	14 29	+12·4	−19·4
14 41	+12·7	−19·6	14 53	+12·5	−19·3
15 05	+12·8	−19·5	15 18	+12·6	−19·2
15 31	+12·9	−19·4	15 45	+12·7	−19·1
15 59	+13·0	−19·3	16 13	+12·8	−19·0
16 27	+13·1	−19·2	16 43	+12·9	−18·9
16 58	+13·2	−19·1	17 14	+13·0	−18·8
17 30	+13·3	−19·0	17 47	+13·1	−18·7
18 05	+13·4	−18·9	18 23	+13·2	−18·6
18 41	+13·5	−18·8	19 00	+13·3	−18·5
19 20	+13·6	−18·7	19 41	+13·4	−18·4
20 02	+13·7	−18·6	20 24	+13·5	−18·3
20 46	+13·8	−18·5	21 10	+13·6	−18·2
21 34	+13·9	−18·4	21 59	+13·7	−18·1
22 25	+14·0	−18·3	22 52	+13·8	−18·0
23 20	+14·1	−18·2	23 49	+13·9	−17·9
24 20	+14·2	−18·1	24 51	+14·0	−17·8
25 24	+14·3	−18·0	25 58	+14·1	−17·7
26 34	+14·4	−17·9	27 11	+14·2	−17·6
27 50	+14·5	−17·8	28 31	+14·3	−17·5
29 13	+14·6	−17·7	29 58	+14·4	−17·4
30 44	+14·7	−17·6	31 33	+14·5	−17·3
32 24	+14·8	−17·5	33 18	+14·6	−17·2
34 15	+14·9	−17·4	35 15	+14·7	−17·1
36 17	+15·0	−17·3	37 24	+14·8	−17·0
38 34	+15·1	−17·2	39 48	+14·9	−16·9
41 06	+15·2	−17·1	42 28	+15·0	−16·8
43 56	+15·3	−17·0	45 29	+15·1	−16·7
47 07	+15·4	−16·9	48 52	+15·2	−16·6
50 43	+15·5	−16·8	52 41	+15·3	−16·5
54 46	+15·6	−16·7	56 59	+15·4	−16·4
59 21	+15·7	−16·6	61 50	+15·5	−16·3
64 28	+15·8	−16·5	67 15	+15·6	−16·2
70 10	+15·9	−16·4	73 14	+15·7	−16·1
76 24	+16·0	−16·3	79 42	+15·8	−16·0
83 05	+16·1	−16·2	86 31	+15·9	−15·9
90 00			90 00		

STARS AND PLANETS

App. Alt.	Corrⁿ
9 55	−5·3
10 07	−5·2
10 20	−5·1
10 32	−5·0
10 46	−4·9
10 59	−4·8
11 14	−4·7
11 29	−4·6
11 44	−4·5
12 00	−4·4
12 17	−4·3
12 35	−4·2
12 53	−4·1
13 12	−4·0
13 32	−3·9
13 53	−3·8
14 16	−3·7
14 39	−3·6
15 03	−3·5
15 29	−3·4
15 56	−3·3
16 25	−3·2
16 55	−3·1
17 27	−3·0
18 01	−2·9
18 37	−2·8
19 16	−2·7
19 56	−2·6
20 40	−2·5
21 27	−2·4
22 17	−2·3
23 11	−2·2
24 09	−2·1
25 12	−2·0
26 20	−1·9
27 34	−1·8
28 54	−1·7
30 22	−1·6
31 58	−1·5
33 43	−1·4
35 38	−1·3
37 45	−1·2
40 06	−1·1
42 42	−1·0
45 34	−0·9
48 45	−0·8
52 16	−0·7
56 09	−0·6
60 26	−0·5
65 06	−0·4
70 09	−0·3
75 32	−0·2
81 12	−0·1
87 03	0·0
90 00	

Additional Corrⁿ — 2020

VENUS

Jan. 1–Feb. 17
Sept. 18–Dec. 31

App. Alt. °	Additional Corrⁿ '
0	+0·1
60	

Feb. 18–Apr. 9
July 29–Sept. 17

App. Alt. °	Additional Corrⁿ '
0	+0·2
41	+0·1
76	

Apr. 10–May 2
July 6–July 28

App. Alt. °	Additional Corrⁿ '
0	+0·3
34	+0·2
60	+0·1
80	

May 3–May 18
June 20–July 5

App. Alt. °	Additional Corrⁿ '
0	+0·4
29	+0·3
51	+0·2
68	+0·1
83	

May 19–June 19

App. Alt. °	Additional Corrⁿ '
0	+0·5
26	+0·4
46	+0·3
60	+0·2
73	+0·1
84	

MARS

Jan. 1–June 5

App. Alt. °	Additional Corrⁿ '
0	+0·1
60	

June 6–Aug. 11
Nov. 24–Dec. 31

App. Alt. °	Additional Corrⁿ '
0	+0·2
41	+0·1
76	

Aug. 12–Sept. 29
Oct. 14–Nov. 23

App. Alt. °	Additional Corrⁿ '
0	+0·3
34	+0·2
60	+0·1
80	

Sept. 30–Oct. 13

App. Alt. °	Additional Corrⁿ '
0	+0·4
29	+0·3
51	+0·2
68	+0·1
83	

DIP

Ht. of Eye (m)	Corrⁿ	Ht. of Eye (ft.)
2·4	−2·8	8·0
2·6	−2·9	8·6
2·8	−3·0	9·2
3·0	−3·1	9·8
3·2	−3·2	10·5
3·4	−3·3	11·2
3·6	−3·4	11·9
3·8	−3·5	12·6
4·0	−3·6	13·3
4·3	−3·7	14·1
4·5	−3·8	14·9
4·7	−3·9	15·7
5·0	−4·0	16·5
5·2	−4·1	17·4
5·5	−4·2	18·3
5·8	−4·3	19·1
6·1	−4·4	20·1
6·3	−4·5	21·0
6·6	−4·6	22·0
6·9	−4·7	22·9
7·2	−4·8	23·9
7·5	−4·9	24·9
7·9	−5·0	26·0
8·2	−5·1	27·1
8·5	−5·2	28·1
8·8	−5·3	29·2
9·2	−5·4	30·4
9·5	−5·5	31·5
9·9	−5·6	32·7
10·3	−5·7	33·9
10·6	−5·8	35·1
11·0	−5·9	36·3
11·4	−6·0	37·6
11·8	−6·1	38·9
12·2	−6·2	40·1
12·6	−6·3	41·5
13·0	−6·4	42·8
13·4	−6·5	44·2
13·8	−6·6	45·5
14·2	−6·7	46·9
14·7	−6·8	48·4
15·1	−6·9	49·8
15·5	−7·0	51·3
16·0	−7·1	52·8
16·5	−7·2	54·3
16·9	−7·3	55·8
17·4	−7·4	57·4
17·9	−7·5	58·9
18·4	−7·6	60·5
18·8	−7·7	62·1
19·3	−7·8	63·8
19·8	−7·9	65·4
20·4	−8·0	67·1
20·9	−8·1	68·8
21·4		70·5

DIP — supplementary (Ht. of Eye / Corrⁿ)

Ht. of Eye (m)	Corrⁿ
1·0	−1·8
1·5	−2·2
2·0	−2·5
2·5	−2·8
3·0	−3·0

See table ←

Ht. of Eye (m)	Corrⁿ
20	−7·9
22	−8·3
24	−8·6
26	−9·0
28	−9·3
30	−9·6
32	−10·0
34	−10·3
36	−10·6
38	−10·8
40	−11·1
42	−11·4
44	−11·7
46	−12·0
48	−12·2

Ht. of Eye (ft.)	Corrⁿ
2	−1·4
4	−1·9
6	−2·4
8	−2·7
10	−3·1

See table ←

Ht. of Eye (ft.)	Corrⁿ
70	−8·1
75	−8·4
80	−8·7
85	−8·9
90	−9·2
95	−9·5
100	−9·7
105	−9·9
110	−10·2
115	−10·4
120	−10·6
125	−10·8
130	−11·1
135	−11·3
140	−11·5
145	−11·7
150	−11·9
155	−12·1

App. Alt. = Apparent altitude = Sextant altitude corrected for index error and dip.

App. Alt.	OCT.—MAR. SUN APR.—SEPT.				STARS PLANETS	App. Alt.	OCT.—MAR. SUN APR.—SEPT.				STARS PLANETS
	Lower Limb	Upper Limb	Lower Limb	Upper Limb			Lower Limb	Upper Limb	Lower Limb	Upper Limb	
° ′	′	′	′	′	′	° ′	′	′	′	′	′
0 00	−17·5	−49·8	−17·8	−49·6	−33·8	3 30	+3·4	−28·9	+3·1	−28·7	−12·9
0 03	16·9	49·2	17·2	49·0	33·2	3 35	3·6	28·7	3·3	28·5	12·7
0 06	16·3	48·6	16·6	48·4	32·6	3 40	3·8	28·5	3·6	28·2	12·5
0 09	15·7	48·0	16·0	47·8	32·0	3 45	4·0	28·3	3·8	28·0	12·3
0 12	15·2	47·5	15·4	47·2	31·5	3 50	4·2	28·1	4·0	27·8	12·1
0 15	14·6	46·9	14·8	46·6	30·9	3 55	4·4	27·9	4·1	27·7	11·9
0 18	−14·1	−46·4	−14·3	−46·1	−30·4	4 00	+4·6	−27·7	+4·3	−27·5	−11·7
0 21	13·5	45·8	13·8	45·6	29·8	4 05	4·8	27·5	4·5	27·3	11·5
0 24	13·0	45·3	13·3	45·1	29·3	4 10	4·9	27·4	4·7	27·1	11·4
0 27	12·5	44·8	12·8	44·6	28·8	4 15	5·1	27·2	4·9	26·9	11·2
0 30	12·0	44·3	12·3	44·1	28·3	4 20	5·3	27·0	5·0	26·8	11·0
0 33	11·6	43·9	11·8	43·6	27·9	4 25	5·4	26·9	5·2	26·6	10·9
0 36	−11·1	−43·4	−11·3	−43·1	−27·4	4 30	+5·6	−26·7	+5·3	−26·5	−10·7
0 39	10·6	42·9	10·9	42·7	26·9	4 35	5·7	26·6	5·5	26·3	10·6
0 42	10·2	42·5	10·5	42·3	26·5	4 40	5·9	26·4	5·6	26·2	10·4
0 45	9·8	42·1	10·0	41·8	26·1	4 45	6·0	26·3	5·8	26·0	10·3
0 48	9·4	41·7	9·6	41·4	25·7	4 50	6·2	26·1	5·9	25·9	10·1
0 51	9·0	41·3	9·2	41·0	25·3	4 55	6·3	26·0	6·1	25·7	10·0
0 54	−8·6	−40·9	−8·8	−40·6	−24·9	5 00	+6·4	−25·9	+6·2	−25·6	−9·8
0 57	8·2	40·5	8·4	40·2	24·5	5 05	6·6	25·7	6·3	25·5	9·7
1 00	7·8	40·1	8·0	39·8	24·1	5 10	6·7	25·6	6·5	25·3	9·6
1 03	7·4	39·7	7·7	39·5	23·7	5 15	6·8	25·5	6·6	25·2	9·5
1 06	7·1	39·4	7·3	39·1	23·4	5 20	7·0	25·3	6·7	25·1	9·3
1 09	6·7	39·0	7·0	38·8	23·0	5 25	7·1	25·2	6·8	25·0	9·2
1 12	−6·4	−38·7	−6·6	−38·4	−22·7	5 30	+7·2	−25·1	+6·9	−24·9	−9·1
1 15	6·0	38·3	6·3	38·1	22·3	5 35	7·3	25·0	7·1	24·7	9·0
1 18	5·7	38·0	6·0	37·8	22·0	5 40	7·4	24·9	7·2	24·6	8·9
1 21	5·4	37·7	5·7	37·5	21·7	5 45	7·5	24·8	7·3	24·5	8·8
1 24	5·1	37·4	5·3	37·1	21·4	5 50	7·6	24·7	7·4	24·4	8·7
1 27	4·8	37·1	5·0	36·8	21·1	5 55	7·7	24·6	7·5	24·3	8·6
1 30	−4·5	−36·8	−4·7	−36·5	−20·8	6 00	+7·8	−24·5	+7·6	−24·2	−8·5
1 35	4·0	36·3	4·3	36·1	20·3	6 10	8·0	24·3	7·8	24·0	8·3
1 40	3·6	35·9	3·8	35·6	19·9	6 20	8·2	24·1	8·0	23·8	8·1
1 45	3·1	35·4	3·4	35·2	19·4	6 30	8·4	23·9	8·2	23·6	7·9
1 50	2·7	35·0	2·9	34·7	19·0	6 40	8·6	23·7	8·3	23·5	7·7
1 55	2·3	34·6	2·5	34·3	18·6	6 50	8·7	23·6	8·5	23·3	7·6
2 00	−1·9	−34·2	−2·1	−33·9	−18·2	7 00	+8·9	−23·4	+8·7	−23·1	−7·4
2 05	1·5	33·8	1·7	33·5	17·8	7 10	9·1	23·2	8·8	23·0	7·2
2 10	1·1	33·4	1·4	33·2	17·4	7 20	9·2	23·1	9·0	22·8	7·1
2 15	0·8	33·1	1·0	32·8	17·1	7 30	9·3	23·0	9·1	22·7	6·9
2 20	0·4	32·7	0·7	32·5	16·7	7 40	9·5	22·8	9·2	22·6	6·8
2 25	−0·1	32·4	−0·3	32·1	16·4	7 50	9·6	22·7	9·4	22·4	6·7
2 30	+0·2	−32·1	0·0	−31·8	−16·1	8 00	+9·7	−22·6	+9·5	−22·3	−6·6
2 35	0·5	31·8	+0·3	31·5	15·8	8 10	9·9	22·4	9·6	22·2	6·4
2 40	0·8	31·5	0·6	31·2	15·4	8 20	10·0	22·3	9·7	22·1	6·3
2 45	1·1	31·2	0·9	30·9	15·2	8 30	10·1	22·2	9·9	21·9	6·2
2 50	1·4	30·9	1·2	30·6	14·9	8 40	10·2	22·1	10·0	21·8	6·1
2 55	1·7	30·6	1·4	30·4	14·6	8 50	10·3	22·0	10·1	21·7	6·0
3 00	+2·0	−30·3	+1·7	−30·1	−14·3	9 00	+10·4	−21·9	+10·2	−21·6	−5·9
3 05	2·2	30·1	2·0	29·8	14·1	9 10	10·5	21·8	10·3	21·5	5·8
3 10	2·5	29·8	2·2	29·6	13·8	9 20	10·6	21·7	10·4	21·4	5·7
3 15	2·7	29·6	2·5	29·3	13·6	9 30	10·7	21·6	10·5	21·3	5·6
3 20	2·9	29·4	2·7	29·1	13·4	9 40	10·8	21·5	10·6	21·2	5·5
3 25	3·2	29·1	2·9	28·9	13·1	9 50	10·9	21·4	10·6	21·2	5·4
3 30	+3·4	−28·9	+3·1	−28·7	−12·9	10 00	+11·0	−21·3	+10·7	−21·1	−5·3

Additional corrections for temperature and pressure are given on the following page.

For bubble sextant observations ignore dip and use the star corrections for Sun, planets and stars.

ADDITIONAL REFRACTION CORRECTIONS FOR NON-STANDARD CONDITIONS

Temperature in Fahrenheit

−20°F −10° 0° +10° 20° 30° 40° 50° 60° 70° 80° 90° 100°F

Pressure in millibars: 1050 1040 1030 1020 1010 1000 990 980 970

Pressure in inches: 31.0 30.5 30.0 29.5 29.0

Zone letters: A B C D E F G H J K L M N P

Temperature in Celsius

−30°C −20° −10° 0° +10° 20° 30° 40°C

App. Alt.	A	B	C	D	E	F	G	H	J	K	L	M	N	P	App. Alt.
° ′	′	′	′	′	′	′	′	′	′	′	′	′	′	′	° ′
00 00	−7·3	−5·9	−4·6	−3·4	−2·2	−1·1	0·0	+1·0	+2·0	+3·0	+4·0	+4·9	+5·9	+6·9	00 00
00 30	5·5	4·5	3·5	2·6	1·7	0·8	0·0	0·8	1·6	2·3	3·1	3·8	4·5	5·3	00 30
01 00	4·4	3·5	2·8	2·0	1·3	0·7	0·0	0·6	1·2	1·8	2·4	3·0	3·6	4·2	01 00
01 30	3·5	2·9	2·2	1·7	1·1	0·5	0·0	0·5	1·0	1·5	2·0	2·5	2·9	3·4	01 30
02 00	2·9	2·4	1·9	1·4	0·9	0·4	0·0	0·4	0·8	1·3	1·7	2·0	2·4	2·8	02 00
02 30	−2·5	−2·0	−1·6	−1·2	−0·8	−0·4	0·0	+0·4	+0·7	+1·1	+1·4	+1·7	+2·1	+2·4	02 30
03 00	2·1	1·7	1·4	1·0	0·7	0·3	0·0	0·3	0·6	0·9	1·2	1·5	1·8	2·1	03 00
03 30	1·9	1·5	1·2	0·9	0·6	0·3	0·0	0·3	0·5	0·8	1·1	1·3	1·6	1·8	03 30
04 00	1·6	1·3	1·1	0·8	0·5	0·3	0·0	0·2	0·5	0·7	0·9	1·2	1·4	1·6	04 00
04 30	1·5	1·2	0·9	0·7	0·5	0·2	0·0	0·2	0·4	0·6	0·8	1·0	1·3	1·5	04 30
05 00	−1·3	−1·1	−0·9	−0·6	−0·4	−0·2	0·0	+0·2	+0·4	+0·6	+0·8	+0·9	+1·1	+1·3	05 00
06	1·1	0·9	0·7	0·5	0·3	0·2	0·0	0·2	0·3	0·5	0·6	0·8	0·9	1·1	06
07	1·0	0·8	0·6	0·5	0·3	0·1	0·0	0·1	0·3	0·4	0·5	0·7	0·8	0·9	07
08	0·8	0·7	0·5	0·4	0·3	0·1	0·0	0·1	0·2	0·4	0·5	0·6	0·7	0·8	08
09	0·7	0·6	0·5	0·4	0·2	0·1	0·0	0·1	0·2	0·3	0·4	0·5	0·6	0·7	09
10 00	−0·7	−0·5	−0·4	−0·3	−0·2	−0·1	0·0	+0·1	+0·2	+0·3	+0·4	+0·5	+0·6	+0·7	10 00
12	0·6	0·5	0·4	0·3	0·2	0·1	0·0	0·1	0·2	0·2	0·3	0·4	0·5	0·5	12
14	0·5	0·4	0·3	0·2	0·1	0·1	0·0	0·1	0·1	0·2	0·3	0·3	0·4	0·5	14
16	0·4	0·3	0·3	0·2	0·1	0·1	0·0	0·1	0·1	0·2	0·2	0·3	0·3	0·4	16
18	0·4	0·3	0·2	0·2	0·1	−0·1	0·0	+0·1	0·1	0·2	0·2	0·3	0·3	0·4	18
20 00	−0·3	−0·3	−0·2	−0·2	−0·1	0·0	0·0	0·0	+0·1	+0·1	+0·2	+0·2	+0·3	+0·3	20 00
25	0·3	0·2	0·2	0·1	0·1	0·0	0·0	0·0	0·1	0·1	0·1	0·2	0·2	0·2	25
30	0·2	0·2	0·1	0·1	0·1	0·0	0·0	0·0	+0·1	0·1	0·1	0·1	0·2	0·2	30
35	0·2	0·1	0·1	0·1	−0·1	0·0	0·0	0·0	0·0	0·1	0·1	0·1	0·1	0·2	35
40	0·1	0·1	0·1	−0·1	0·0	0·0	0·0	0·0	0·0	+0·1	0·1	0·1	0·1	0·1	40
50 00	−0·1	−0·1	−0·1	0·0	0·0	0·0	0·0	0·0	0·0	0·0	+0·1	+0·1	+0·1	+0·1	50 00

The graph is entered with arguments temperature and pressure to find a zone letter; using as arguments this zone letter and apparent altitude (sextant altitude corrected for index error and dip), a correction is taken from the table. This correction is to be applied to the sextant altitude in addition to the corrections for standard conditions (for the Sun, stars and planets from page A2-A3 and for the Moon from pages xxxiv and xxxv).

2020
Nautical Almanac
COMMERCIAL EDITION

PUBLISHED BY:

Paradise Cay Publications, Inc.
PO Box 29
Arcata, CA 95518-0029
Tel: 1-707-822-9063
Fax: 1-707-822-9163
www.paracay.com

ISBN: 9781951116033

Printed and distributed with permissions by Paradise Cay Publications

NOTE

Every care is taken to prevent errors in the production of this publication. As a final precaution it is recommended that the sequence of pages in this copy be examined on receipt. If faulty, it should be returned for replacement.

PREFACE

The first three sections of this book are a complete and accurate duplications from *The Nautical Almanac* produced jointly by Her Majesty's Nautical Almanac Office, United Kingdom Hydrographic Office, Admiralty Way, Taunton, Somerset, TA1 2DN, United Kingdom and the Nautical Almanac Office of the US Naval Observatory.

The following United States government work is excerpted from the above notice and no copyright is claimed for it in the United States: pages 6 and 7, and pages 286-317.

The UK Hydrographic Office makes the accompanying 2019 Nautical Almanac data available to Paradise Cay Publications Inc for use in accordance with Licence agreement GB CS-001-Paradise Cay Publications.

We gratefully acknowledge the United Kingdom Hydrographic Office and the United States Naval Observatory for permission to use the material contained in the almanac section of this publication.

CONDITIONS OF RELEASE

DISCLAIMER

Whilst the UK Hydrographic Office has endeavoured to ensure that the material supplied is suitable for the purpose, it accepts no liability (to the maximum extent permitted by law) for any damage or loss of any nature arising from its use. The material supplied is used entirely at the Recipient's own risk.

THE NAUTICAL ALMANAC 2020
Commercial Edition

LIST OF CONTENTS

CALENDAR, 2020

RELIGIOUS CALENDARS

Epiphany	Jan. 6	Low Sunday	Apr. 19
Septuagesima Sunday	Feb. 9	Rogation Sunday	May 17
Quinquagesima Sunday	Feb. 23	Ascension Day—Holy Thursday	May 21
Ash Wednesday	Feb. 26	Whit Sunday—Pentecost	May 31
Quadragesima Sunday	Mar. 1	Trinity Sunday	June 7
Palm Sunday	Apr. 5	Corpus Christi	June 11
Good Friday	Apr. 10	First Sunday in Advent	Nov. 29
Easter Day	Apr. 12	Christmas Day (Friday)	Dec. 25
First Day of Passover (Pesach)	Apr. 9	Day of Atonement (Yom Kippur)	Sept. 28
Feast of Weeks (Shavuot)	May 29	First day of Tabernacles (Succoth)	Oct. 3
Jewish New Year 5781 (Rosh Hashanah)	Sept. 19		
Ramadân, First day of (tabular)	Apr. 24	Islamic New Year (1442)	Aug. 20

The Jewish and Islamic dates above are tabular dates, which begin at sunset on the previous evening and end at sunset on the date tabulated. In practice, the dates of Islamic fasts and festivals are determined by an actual sighting of the appropriate new moon.

CIVIL CALENDAR—UNITED KINGDOM

Accession of Queen Elizabeth II	Feb. 6	Birthday of Prince Philip, Duke of Edinburgh	June 10
St David (Wales)	Mar. 1		
Commonwealth Day	Mar. 9	The Queen's Official Birthday†	June 13
St Patrick (Ireland)	Mar. 17	Remembrance Sunday	Nov. 8
Birthday of Queen Elizabeth II	Apr. 21	Birthday of the Prince of Wales	Nov. 14
St George (England)	Apr. 23	St Andrew (Scotland)	Nov. 30
Coronation Day	June 2		

PUBLIC HOLIDAYS

England and Wales—Jan. 1†, Apr. 10, Apr. 13, May 4†, May 25, Aug. 31, Dec. 25, Dec. 28

Northern Ireland—Jan. 1†, Mar. 17, Apr. 10, Apr. 13, May 4†, May 25, July 13†, Aug. 31, Dec. 25, Dec. 28

Scotland—Jan. 1, Jan. 2, Apr. 10, May 4, May 25†, Aug. 3, Dec. 25, Dec. 28†

CIVIL CALENDAR—UNITED STATES OF AMERICA

New Year's Day	Jan. 1	Labor Day	Sept. 7
Martin Luther King's Birthday	Jan. 20	Columbus Day	Oct. 12
Washington's Birthday	Feb. 17	General Election Day	Nov. 3
Memorial Day	May 25	Veterans Day	Nov. 11
Independence Day	July 4	Thanksgiving Day	Nov. 26

†Dates subject to confirmation

PHASES OF THE MOON

New Moon				First Quarter				Full Moon				Last Quarter			
	d	h	m		d	h	m		d	h	m		d	h	m
				Jan.	3	04	45	Jan.	10	19	21	Jan.	17	12	58
Jan.	24	21	42	Feb.	2	01	42	Feb.	9	07	33	Feb.	15	22	17
Feb.	23	15	32	Mar.	2	19	57	Mar.	9	17	48	Mar.	16	09	34
Mar.	24	09	28	Apr.	1	10	21	Apr.	8	02	35	Apr.	14	22	56
Apr.	23	02	26	Apr.	30	20	38	May	7	10	45	May	14	14	03
May	22	17	39	May	30	03	30	June	5	19	12	June	13	06	24
June	21	06	41	June	28	08	16	July	5	04	44	July	12	23	29
July	20	17	33	July	27	12	33	Aug.	3	15	59	Aug.	11	16	45
Aug.	19	02	42	Aug.	25	17	58	Sept.	2	05	22	Sept.	10	09	26
Sept.	17	11	00	Sept.	24	01	55	Oct.	1	21	05	Oct.	10	00	40
Oct.	16	19	31	Oct.	23	13	23	Oct.	31	14	49	Nov.	8	13	46
Nov.	15	05	07	Nov.	22	04	45	Nov.	30	09	30	Dec.	8	00	37
Dec.	14	16	17	Dec.	21	23	41	Dec.	30	03	28				

DAYS OF THE WEEK AND DAYS OF THE YEAR

	JAN.		FEB.		MAR.		APR.		MAY		JUNE		JULY		AUG.		SEPT.		OCT.		NOV.		DEC.	
Day	Wk	Yr	Wk	Yr	Wk	Yr	Wk	Yr	Wk	Yr	Wk	Yr	Wk	Yr	Wk	Yr	Wk	Yr	Wk	Yr	Wk	Yr	Wk	Yr
1	W.	1	Sa.	32	Su.	61	W.	92	F.	122	M.	153	W.	183	Sa.	214	Tu.	245	Th.	275	Su.	306	Tu.	336
2	Th.	2	Su.	33	M.	62	Th.	93	Sa.	123	Tu.	154	Th.	184	Su.	215	W.	246	F.	276	M.	307	W.	337
3	F.	3	M.	34	Tu.	63	F.	94	Su.	124	W.	155	F.	185	M.	216	Th.	247	Sa.	277	Tu.	308	Th.	338
4	Sa.	4	Tu.	35	W.	64	Sa.	95	M.	125	Th.	156	Sa.	186	Tu.	217	F.	248	Su.	278	W.	309	F.	339
5	Su.	5	W.	36	Th.	65	Su.	96	Tu.	126	F.	157	Su.	187	W.	218	Sa.	249	M.	279	Th.	310	Sa.	340
6	M.	6	Th.	37	F.	66	M.	97	W.	127	Sa.	158	M.	188	Th.	219	Su.	250	Tu.	280	F.	311	Su.	341
7	Tu.	7	F.	38	Sa.	67	Tu.	98	Th.	128	Su.	159	Tu.	189	F.	220	M.	251	W.	281	Sa.	312	M.	342
8	W.	8	Sa.	39	Su.	68	W.	99	F.	129	M.	160	W.	190	Sa.	221	Tu.	252	Th.	282	Su.	313	Tu.	343
9	Th.	9	Su.	40	M.	69	Th.	100	Sa.	130	Tu.	161	Th.	191	Su.	222	W.	253	F.	283	M.	314	W.	344
10	F.	10	M.	41	Tu.	70	F.	101	Su.	131	W.	162	F.	192	M.	223	Th.	254	Sa.	284	Tu.	315	Th.	345
11	Sa.	11	Tu.	42	W.	71	Sa.	102	M.	132	Th.	163	Sa.	193	Tu.	224	F.	255	Su.	285	W.	316	F.	346
12	Su.	12	W.	43	Th.	72	Su.	103	Tu.	133	F.	164	Su.	194	W.	225	Sa.	256	M.	286	Th.	317	Sa.	347
13	M.	13	Th.	44	F.	73	M.	104	W.	134	Sa.	165	M.	195	Th.	226	Su.	257	Tu.	287	F.	318	Su.	348
14	Tu.	14	F.	45	Sa.	74	Tu.	105	Th.	135	Su.	166	Tu.	196	F.	227	M.	258	W.	288	Sa.	319	M.	349
15	W.	15	Sa.	46	Su.	75	W.	106	F.	136	M.	167	W.	197	Sa.	228	Tu.	259	Th.	289	Su.	320	Tu.	350
16	Th.	16	Su.	47	M.	76	Th.	107	Sa.	137	Tu.	168	Th.	198	Su.	229	W.	260	F.	290	M.	321	W.	351
17	F.	17	M.	48	Tu.	77	F.	108	Su.	138	W.	169	F.	199	M.	230	Th.	261	Sa.	291	Tu.	322	Th.	352
18	Sa.	18	Tu.	49	W.	78	Sa.	109	M.	139	Th.	170	Sa.	200	Tu.	231	F.	262	Su.	292	W.	323	F.	353
19	Su.	19	W.	50	Th.	79	Su.	110	Tu.	140	F.	171	Su.	201	W.	232	Sa.	263	M.	293	Th.	324	Sa.	354
20	M.	20	Th.	51	F.	80	M.	111	W.	141	Sa.	172	M.	202	Th.	233	Su.	264	Tu.	294	F.	325	Su.	355
21	Tu.	21	F.	52	Sa.	81	Tu.	112	Th.	142	Su.	173	Tu.	203	F.	234	M.	265	W.	295	Sa.	326	M.	356
22	W.	22	Sa.	53	Su.	82	W.	113	F.	143	M.	174	W.	204	Sa.	235	Tu.	266	Th.	296	Su.	327	Tu.	357
23	Th.	23	Su.	54	M.	83	Th.	114	Sa.	144	Tu.	175	Th.	205	Su.	236	W.	267	F.	297	M.	328	W.	358
24	F.	24	M.	55	Tu.	84	F.	115	Su.	145	W.	176	F.	206	M.	237	Th.	268	Sa.	298	Tu.	329	Th.	359
25	Sa.	25	Tu.	56	W.	85	Sa.	116	M.	146	Th.	177	Sa.	207	Tu.	238	F.	269	Su.	299	W.	330	F.	360
26	Su.	26	W.	57	Th.	86	Su.	117	Tu.	147	F.	178	Su.	208	W.	239	Sa.	270	M.	300	Th.	331	Sa.	361
27	M.	27	Th.	58	F.	87	M.	118	W.	148	Sa.	179	M.	209	Th.	240	Su.	271	Tu.	301	F.	332	Su.	362
28	Tu.	28	F.	59	Sa.	88	Tu.	119	Th.	149	Su.	180	Tu.	210	F.	241	M.	272	W.	302	Sa.	333	M.	363
29	W.	29	Sa.	60	Su.	89	W.	120	F.	150	M.	181	W.	211	Sa.	242	Tu.	273	Th.	303	Su.	334	Tu.	364
30	Th.	30			M.	90	Th.	121	Sa.	151	Tu.	182	Th.	212	Su.	243	W.	274	F.	304	M.	335	W.	365
31	F.	31			Tu.	91			Su.	152			F.	213	M.	244			Sa.	305			Th.	366

ECLIPSES

There are two eclipses of the Sun.

1. *An annular eclipse of the Sun,* June 21. See map on page 6. The eclipse begins at $03^h 46^m$ and ends at $09^h 34^m$; the annular phase begins at $04^h 48^m$ and ends at $08^h 32^m$. The maximum duration of annularity is $1^m 18^s$.

2. *A total eclipse of the Sun,* December 14. See map on page 7. The eclipse begins at $13^h 34^m$ and ends at $18^h 53^m$; the total phase begins at $14^h 33^m$ and ends at $17^h 54^m$. The maximum duration of totality is $2^m 14^s$.

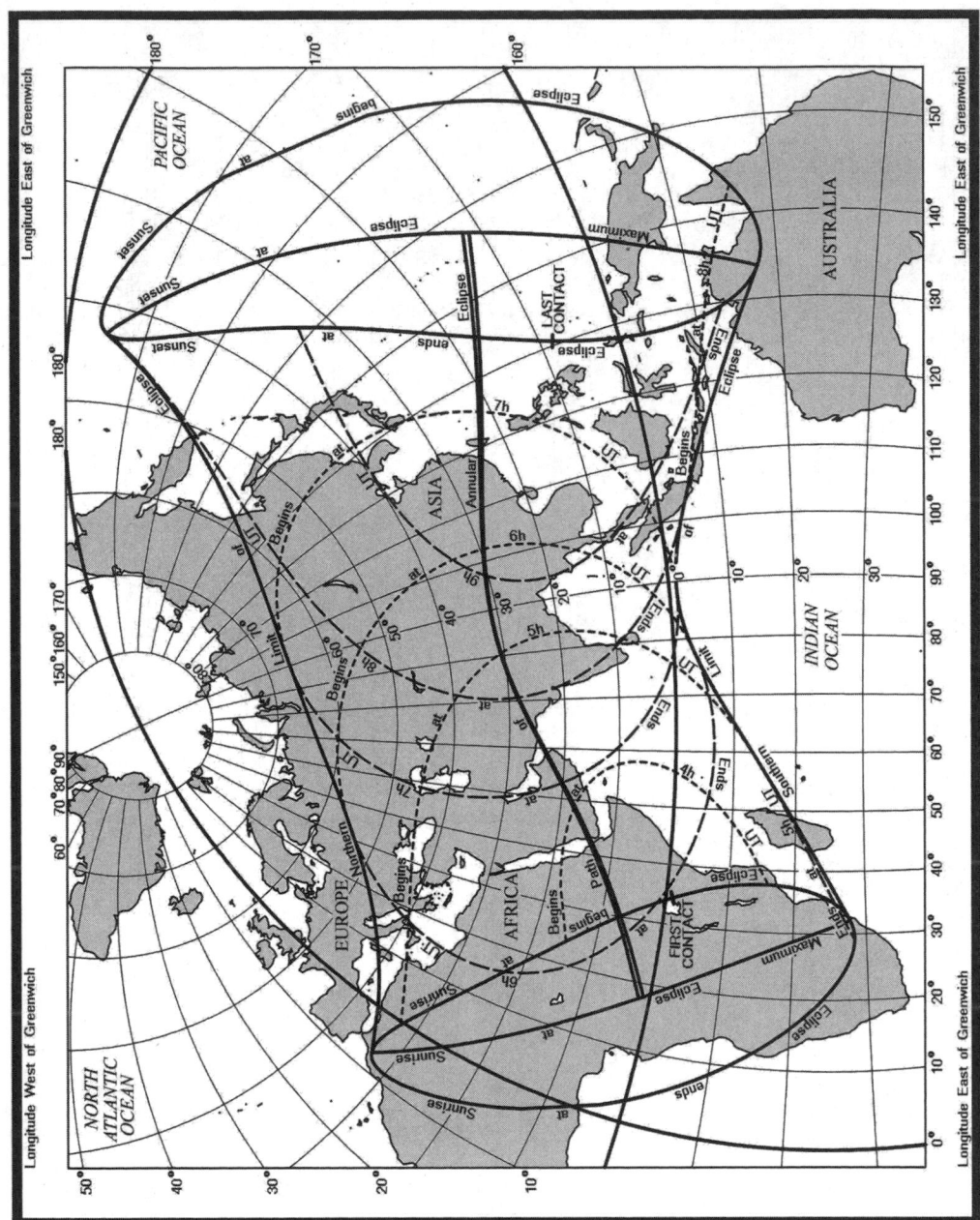

SOLAR ECLIPSE DIAGRAMS

The principal features shown on the above diagrams are: the paths of
total and annular eclipses; the northern and southern limits of partial
eclipse; the sunrise and sunset curves; dashed lines which show the
times of beginning and end of partial eclipse at hourly intervals.

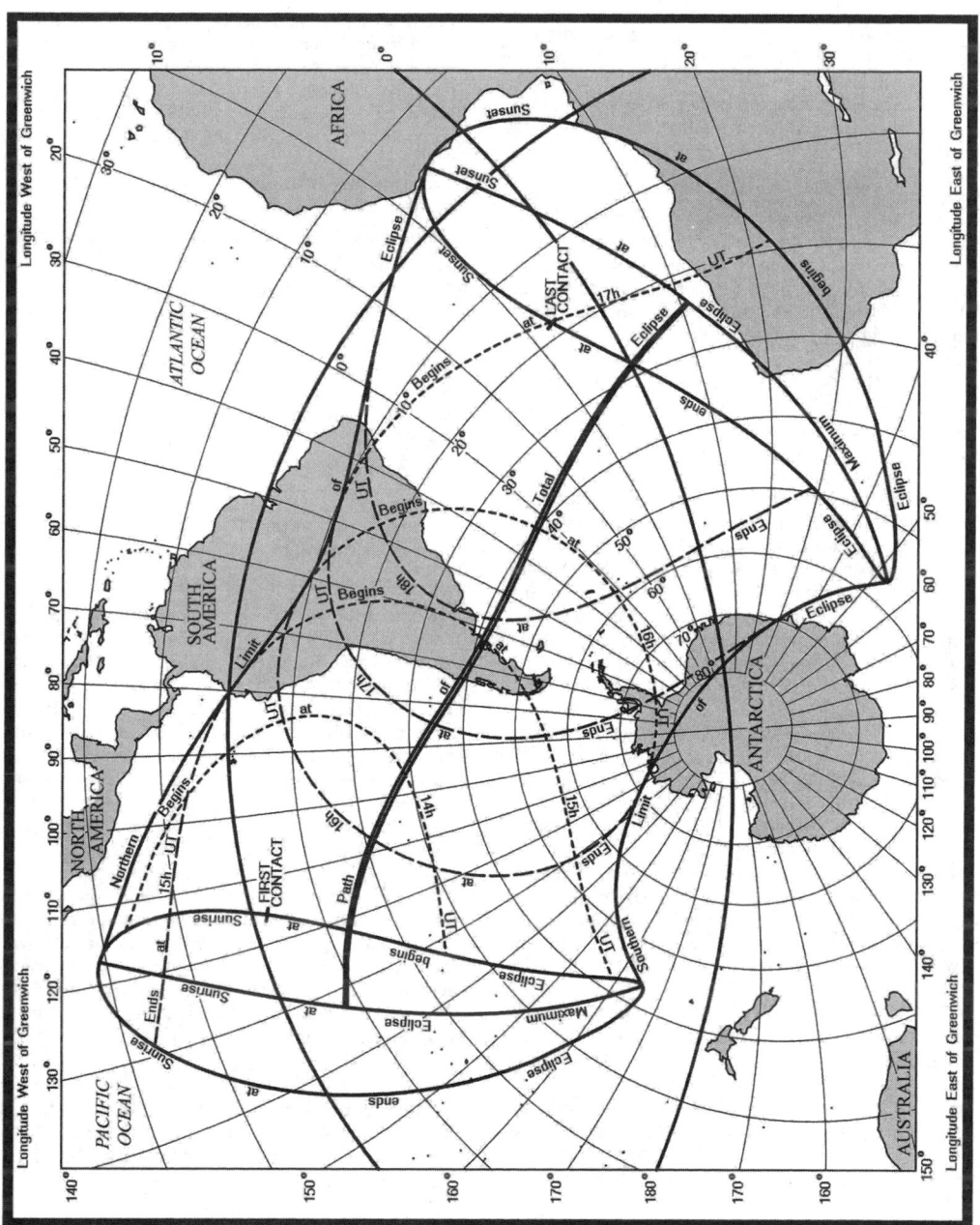

SOLAR ECLIPSE DIAGRAMS

Further details of the paths and times of central eclipse are given in
The Astronomical Almanac.

VISIBILITY OF PLANETS

VENUS is a brilliant object in the evening sky from the beginning of the year until late May when it becomes too close to the Sun for observation. In the second week of June it reappears in the morning sky where it stays until the end of the year. Venus is in conjunction with Mercury on May 22.

MARS rises well before sunrise in Libra at the beginning of the year, when it can only be seen in the morning sky. Its westward elongation gradually increases as it moves through Scorpius, Ophiuchus (passing 5° N of *Antares* on January 17), Sagittarius, Capricornus, Aquarius, and into Pisces in late June, when it can be seen for more than half the night. In early July it moves into Cetus and late that month returns to Pisces, in which constellation it remains for the rest of the year. Mars is at opposition on October 13, when it can be seen throughout the night. Mars is in conjunction with Jupiter on March 20 and with Saturn on March 31.

JUPITER can be seen in the second week of January just before sunrise in Sagittarius. Its westward elongation gradually increases and from late April it can be seen for more than half the night. It is at opposition on July 14 when it is visible throughout the night. Its eastward elongation then decreases and from mid-October it can only be seen in the evening sky passing into Capricornus in late December. Jupiter is in conjunction with Mars on March 20 and with Saturn on December 21.

SATURN can be seen at the end of January just before sunrise in Sagittarius. Its westward elongation gradually increases, passing into Capricornus during the second half of March, and from the end of April can be seen for more than half the night. It returns to Sagittarius in early July and is at opposition on July 20 when it is visible throughout the night. Its eastward elongation then decreases and from late October it can only be seen in the evening sky, passing again into Capricornus in mid-December. Saturn is in conjunction with Mars on March 31 and with Jupiter on December 21.

MERCURY can only be seen low in the east before sunrise, or low in the west after sunset (about the time of beginning or end of civil twilight). It is visible in the mornings between the following approximate dates: March 4 (+2·4) to April 27 (−1·2), July 10 (+2·9) to August 9 (−1·4) and November 1 (+1·6) to December 3 (−0·8); the planet is brighter at the end of each period. It is visible in the evenings between the following approximate dates: January 24 (−1·1) to February 19 (+1·6), May 12 (−1·5) to June 22 (+3·2) and August 27 (−1·0) to October 20 (+2·3); the planet is brighter at the beginning of each period. The figures in parentheses are the magnitudes.

PLANET DIAGRAM

General Description. The diagram on the opposite page shows, in graphical form for any date during the year, the local mean time of meridian passage of the Sun, of the five planets Mercury, Venus, Mars, Jupiter, and Saturn, and of each 30° of SHA; intermediate lines corresponding to particular stars, may be drawn in by the user if desired. It is intended to provide a general picture of the availability of planets and stars for observation.

On each side of the line marking the time of meridian passage of the Sun a band, 45^m wide, is shaded to indicate that planets and most stars crossing the meridian within 45^m of the Sun are too close to the Sun for observation.

Method of use and interpretation. For any date, the diagram provides immediately the local mean times of meridian passage of the Sun, planets and stars, and thus the following information:

(a) whether a planet or star is too close to the Sun for observation;

(b) some indication of its position in the sky, especially during twilight;

(c) the proximity of other planets.

When the meridian passage of an outer planet occurs at midnight, the body is in opposition to the Sun and is visible all night; a planet may then be observable during both morning and evening twilights. As the time of meridian passage decreases, the body eventually ceases to be observable in the morning, but its altitude above the eastern horizon at sunset gradually increases; this continues until the body is on the meridian during evening twilight. From then onwards, the body is observable above the western horizon and its altitude at sunset gradually decreases; eventually the body becomes too close to the Sun for observation. When the body again becomes visible it is seen low in the east during morning twilight; its altitude at sunrise increases until meridian passage occurs during morning twilight. Then, as the time of meridian passage decreases to 0^h, the body is observable in the west during morning twilight with a gradually decreasing altitude, until it once again reaches opposition.

DO NOT CONFUSE

Jupiter with Mars in the second half of March, with Saturn in late April to early June and early November to the end of December; on all occasions Jupiter is the brighter object.

Mars with Saturn from late March to early April when Saturn is the brighter object.

Mercury with Venus in the fourth week of May when Venus is the brighter object.

LOCAL MEAN TIME OF MERIDIAN PASSAGE

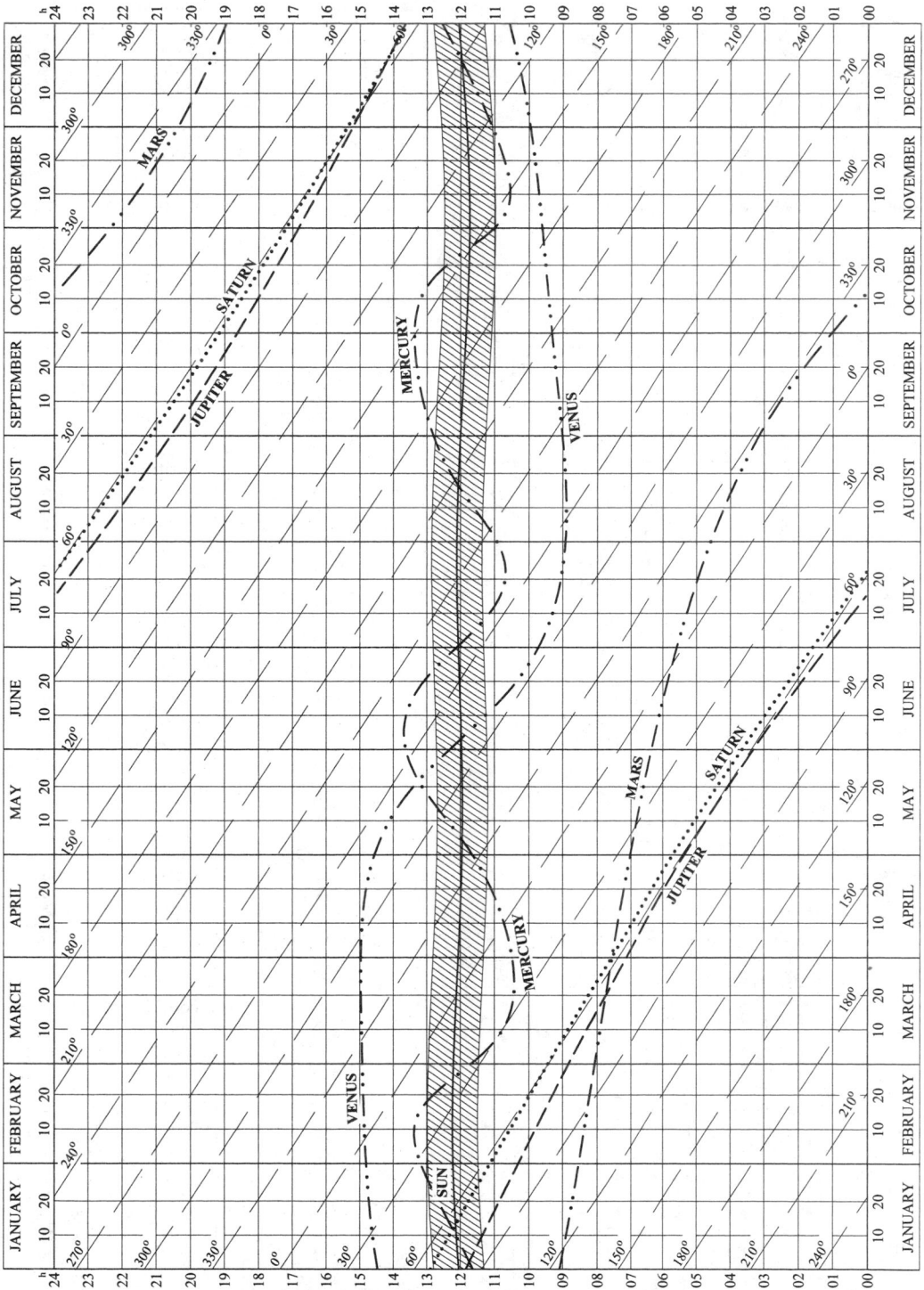

LOCAL MEAN TIME OF MERIDIAN PASSAGE

UT	ARIES GHA	VENUS −4.0 GHA	Dec	MARS +1.6 GHA	Dec	JUPITER −1.8 GHA	Dec	SATURN +0.5 GHA	Dec	STARS Name	SHA	Dec
1 00	100 07.1	142 40.9	S18 15.9	223 53.5	S19 26.7	182 51.5	S23 10.8	167 00.2	S21 41.1	Acamar	315 14.7	S40 13.8
01	115 09.5	157 40.3	15.0	238 54.2	27.1	197 53.3	10.8	182 02.3	41.0	Achernar	335 23.2	S57 08.5
02	130 12.0	172 39.6	14.1	253 54.9	27.5	212 55.2	10.7	197 04.5	41.0	Acrux	173 04.2	S63 12.2
03	145 14.4	187 39.0	.. 13.2	268 55.7	.. 27.9	227 57.0	.. 10.7	212 06.6	.. 40.9	Adhara	255 08.6	S29 00.0
04	160 16.9	202 38.4	12.2	283 56.4	28.3	242 58.9	10.7	227 08.8	40.9	Aldebaran	290 43.9	N16 32.8
05	175 19.4	217 37.8	11.3	298 57.1	28.7	258 00.7	10.7	242 10.9	40.8			
W 06	190 21.8	232 37.2	S18 10.4	313 57.9	S19 29.1	273 02.5	S23 10.6	257 13.1	S21 40.8	Alioth	166 16.7	N55 50.9
E 07	205 24.3	247 36.6	09.5	328 58.6	29.5	288 04.4	10.6	272 15.2	40.8	Alkaid	152 55.5	N49 12.7
D 08	220 26.8	262 36.0	08.6	343 59.3	29.9	303 06.2	10.6	287 17.4	40.7	Alnair	27 38.4	S46 52.1
N 09	235 29.2	277 35.4	.. 07.6	359 00.0	.. 30.3	318 08.1	.. 10.6	302 19.5	.. 40.7	Alnilam	275 41.5	S 1 11.5
E 10	250 31.7	292 34.8	06.7	14 00.8	30.6	333 09.9	10.5	317 21.7	40.6	Alphard	217 51.4	S 8 44.7
S 11	265 34.2	307 34.2	05.8	29 01.5	31.0	348 11.7	10.5	332 23.8	40.6			
D 12	280 36.6	322 33.6	S18 04.9	44 02.2	S19 31.4	3 13.6	S23 10.5	347 26.0	S21 40.5	Alphecca	126 07.5	N26 38.9
A 13	295 39.1	337 33.0	03.9	59 03.0	31.8	18 15.4	10.5	2 28.1	40.5	Alpheratz	357 38.9	N29 12.1
Y 14	310 41.6	352 32.3	03.0	74 03.7	32.2	33 17.2	10.4	17 30.3	40.5	Altair	62 04.2	N 8 55.3
15	325 44.0	7 31.7	.. 02.1	89 04.4	.. 32.6	48 19.1	.. 10.4	32 32.5	.. 40.4	Ankaa	353 11.3	S42 12.2
16	340 46.5	22 31.1	01.1	104 05.2	33.0	63 20.9	10.4	47 34.6	40.4	Antares	112 21.1	S26 28.4
17	355 48.9	37 30.5	18 00.2	119 05.9	33.4	78 22.8	10.4	62 36.8	40.3			
18	10 51.4	52 29.9	S17 59.3	134 06.6	S19 33.8	93 24.6	S23 10.3	77 38.9	S21 40.3	Arcturus	145 51.8	N19 04.7
19	25 53.9	67 29.3	58.3	149 07.3	34.2	108 26.4	10.3	92 41.1	40.2	Atria	107 19.4	S69 03.5
20	40 56.3	82 28.7	57.4	164 08.1	34.6	123 28.3	10.3	107 43.2	40.2	Avior	234 15.6	S59 34.3
21	55 58.8	97 28.1	.. 56.5	179 08.8	.. 35.0	138 30.1	.. 10.2	122 45.4	.. 40.2	Bellatrix	278 26.9	N 6 21.9
22	71 01.3	112 27.5	55.5	194 09.5	35.3	153 31.9	10.2	137 47.5	40.1	Betelgeuse	270 56.1	N 7 24.5
23	86 03.7	127 26.9	54.6	209 10.2	35.7	168 33.8	10.2	152 49.7	40.1			
2 00	101 06.2	142 26.3	S17 53.7	224 11.0	S19 36.1	183 35.6	S23 10.2	167 51.8	S21 40.0	Canopus	263 53.6	S52 42.5
01	116 08.7	157 25.7	52.7	239 11.7	36.5	198 37.5	10.1	182 54.0	40.0	Capella	280 27.3	N46 01.0
02	131 11.1	172 25.1	51.8	254 12.4	36.9	213 39.3	10.1	197 56.1	39.9	Deneb	49 28.9	N45 21.2
03	146 13.6	187 24.5	.. 50.8	269 13.2	.. 37.3	228 41.1	.. 10.1	212 58.3	.. 39.9	Denebola	182 29.0	N14 27.6
04	161 16.1	202 24.0	49.9	284 13.9	37.7	243 43.0	10.1	228 00.4	39.9	Diphda	348 51.4	S17 52.9
05	176 18.5	217 23.4	49.0	299 14.6	38.1	258 44.8	10.0	243 02.6	39.8			
T 06	191 21.0	232 22.8	S17 48.0	314 15.3	S19 38.5	273 46.7	S23 10.0	258 04.7	S21 39.8	Dubhe	193 45.9	N61 38.4
H 07	206 23.4	247 22.2	47.1	329 16.1	38.8	288 48.5	10.0	273 06.9	39.7	Elnath	278 06.6	N28 37.3
U 08	221 25.9	262 21.6	46.1	344 16.8	39.2	303 50.3	10.0	288 09.0	39.7	Eltanin	90 44.6	N51 29.2
R 09	236 28.4	277 21.0	.. 45.2	359 17.5	.. 39.6	318 52.2	.. 09.9	303 11.2	.. 39.6	Enif	33 43.0	N 9 58.0
S 10	251 30.8	292 20.4	44.2	14 18.2	40.0	333 54.0	09.9	318 13.3	39.6	Fomalhaut	15 19.2	S29 31.2
D 11	266 33.3	307 19.8	43.3	29 19.0	40.4	348 55.8	09.9	333 15.5	39.5			
A 12	281 35.8	322 19.2	S17 42.3	44 19.7	S19 40.8	3 57.7	S23 09.9	348 17.6	S21 39.5	Gacrux	171 55.9	S57 13.1
Y 13	296 38.2	337 18.6	41.4	59 20.4	41.2	18 59.5	09.8	3 19.8	39.5	Gienah	175 47.6	S17 39.0
14	311 40.7	352 18.0	40.4	74 21.1	41.6	34 01.4	09.8	18 22.0	39.4	Hadar	148 41.8	S60 27.7
15	326 43.2	7 17.4	.. 39.5	89 21.9	.. 41.9	49 03.2	.. 09.8	33 24.1	.. 39.4	Hamal	327 55.5	N23 33.4
16	341 45.6	22 16.9	38.5	104 22.6	42.3	64 05.0	09.7	48 26.3	39.3	Kaus Aust.	83 38.3	S34 22.4
17	356 48.1	37 16.3	37.6	119 23.3	42.7	79 06.9	09.7	63 28.4	39.3			
18	11 50.5	52 15.7	S17 36.6	134 24.0	S19 43.1	94 08.7	S23 09.7	78 30.6	S21 39.2	Kochab	137 20.7	N74 04.2
19	26 53.0	67 15.1	35.7	149 24.8	43.5	109 10.6	09.7	93 32.7	39.2	Markab	13 34.0	N15 18.7
20	41 55.5	82 14.5	34.7	164 25.5	43.9	124 12.4	09.6	108 34.9	39.2	Menkar	314 10.1	N 4 09.9
21	56 57.9	97 13.9	.. 33.8	179 26.2	.. 44.2	139 14.2	.. 09.6	123 37.0	.. 39.1	Menkent	148 02.4	S36 27.8
22	72 00.4	112 13.3	32.8	194 26.9	44.6	154 16.1	09.6	138 39.2	39.1	Miaplacidus	221 38.0	S69 47.7
23	87 02.9	127 12.8	31.9	209 27.7	45.0	169 17.9	09.6	153 41.3	39.0			
3 00	102 05.3	142 12.2	S17 30.9	224 28.4	S19 45.4	184 19.8	S23 09.5	168 43.5	S21 39.0	Mirfak	308 33.6	N49 55.9
01	117 07.8	157 11.6	30.0	239 29.1	45.8	199 21.6	09.5	183 45.6	38.9	Nunki	75 53.1	S26 16.2
02	132 10.3	172 11.0	29.0	254 29.8	46.2	214 23.4	09.5	198 47.8	38.9	Peacock	53 12.7	S56 40.3
03	147 12.7	187 10.4	.. 28.0	269 30.5	.. 46.5	229 25.3	.. 09.5	213 49.9	.. 38.9	Pollux	243 21.9	N27 58.5
04	162 15.2	202 09.8	27.1	284 31.3	46.9	244 27.1	09.4	228 52.1	38.8	Procyon	244 54.7	N 5 10.3
05	177 17.7	217 09.3	26.1	299 32.0	47.3	259 28.9	09.4	243 54.2	38.8			
F 06	192 20.1	232 08.7	S17 25.2	314 32.7	S19 47.7	274 30.8	S23 09.4	258 56.4	S21 38.7	Rasalhague	96 02.6	N12 32.8
R 07	207 22.6	247 08.1	24.2	329 33.4	48.1	289 32.6	09.3	273 58.5	38.7	Regulus	207 38.5	N11 52.1
I 08	222 25.0	262 07.5	23.2	344 34.2	48.5	304 34.5	09.3	289 00.7	38.6	Rigel	281 07.4	S 8 10.9
D 09	237 27.5	277 07.0	.. 22.3	359 34.9	.. 48.8	319 36.3	.. 09.3	304 02.8	.. 38.6	Rigil Kent.	139 46.0	S60 54.6
A 10	252 30.0	292 06.4	21.3	14 35.6	49.2	334 38.1	09.3	319 05.0	38.6	Sabik	102 07.7	S15 44.8
Y 11	267 32.4	307 05.8	20.3	29 36.3	49.6	349 40.0	09.2	334 07.1	38.5			
12	282 34.9	322 05.2	S17 19.4	44 37.0	S19 50.0	4 41.8	S23 09.2	349 09.3	S21 38.5	Schedar	349 35.4	N56 39.0
13	297 37.4	337 04.7	18.4	59 37.8	50.4	19 43.7	09.2	4 11.4	38.4	Shaula	96 16.2	S37 06.9
14	312 39.8	352 04.1	17.4	74 38.5	50.7	34 45.5	09.2	19 13.6	38.4	Sirius	258 29.4	S16 44.7
15	327 42.3	7 03.5	.. 16.5	89 39.2	.. 51.1	49 47.3	.. 09.1	34 15.7	.. 38.3	Spica	158 26.6	S11 15.8
16	342 44.8	22 02.9	15.5	104 39.9	51.5	64 49.2	09.1	49 17.9	38.3	Suhail	222 48.8	S43 30.7
17	357 47.2	37 02.4	14.5	119 40.6	51.9	79 51.0	09.1	64 20.0	38.2			
18	12 49.7	52 01.8	S17 13.5	134 41.4	S19 52.2	94 52.9	S23 09.0	79 22.2	S21 38.2	Vega	80 36.4	N38 48.2
19	27 52.1	67 01.2	12.6	149 42.1	52.6	109 54.7	09.0	94 24.4	38.2	Zuben'ubi	137 00.6	S16 07.3
20	42 54.6	82 00.7	11.6	164 42.8	53.0	124 56.5	09.0	109 26.5	38.1			
21	57 57.1	97 00.1	.. 10.6	179 43.5	.. 53.4	139 58.4	.. 09.0	124 28.7	.. 38.1			
22	72 59.5	111 59.5	09.7	194 44.2	53.8	155 00.2	08.9	139 30.8	38.0			
23	88 02.0	126 58.9	08.7	209 45.0	54.1	170 02.0	08.9	154 33.0	38.0			
Mer. Pass. 17ʰ 12.8ᵐ		v −0.6	d 0.9	v 0.7	d 0.4	v 1.8	d 0.0	v 2.2	d 0.0			

	SHA	Mer. Pass.
Venus	41 20.1	14ʰ 31ᵐ
Mars	123 04.8	9 03
Jupiter	82 29.4	11 44
Saturn	66 45.6	12 47

UT	SUN GHA	SUN Dec	MOON GHA	MOON v	MOON Dec	MOON d	MOON HP
d h	° ′	° ′	° ′	′	° ′	′	′
1 00	179 13.6	S23 03.5	110 56.9	15.4	S 9 58.5	10.7	54.3
01	194 13.3	03.3	125 31.3	15.4	9 47.8	10.7	54.3
02	209 13.0	03.1	140 05.7	15.4	9 37.1	10.8	54.3
03	224 12.7	.. 03.0	154 40.1	15.5	9 26.3	10.8	54.3
04	239 12.4	02.8	169 14.6	15.5	9 15.5	10.8	54.3
05	254 12.1	02.6	183 49.1	15.6	9 04.7	10.9	54.3
06	269 11.8	S23 02.4	198 23.7	15.6	S 8 53.8	10.9	54.3
W 07	284 11.5	02.2	212 58.3	15.6	8 42.9	10.9	54.2
E 08	299 11.2	02.0	227 32.9	15.6	8 32.0	11.0	54.2
D 09	314 10.9	.. 01.8	242 07.5	15.7	8 21.0	11.0	54.2
N 10	329 10.6	01.6	256 42.2	15.7	8 10.0	11.0	54.2
E 11	344 10.3	01.4	271 16.9	15.8	7 59.0	11.0	54.2
S 12	359 10.0	S23 01.2	285 51.7	15.8	S 7 48.0	11.1	54.2
D 13	14 09.7	01.0	300 26.5	15.8	7 36.9	11.1	54.2
A 14	29 09.4	00.8	315 01.3	15.8	7 25.8	11.1	54.2
Y 15	44 09.1	.. 00.6	329 36.1	15.9	7 14.7	11.2	54.2
16	59 08.8	00.4	344 11.0	15.9	7 03.5	11.2	54.2
17	74 08.5	00.2	358 45.9	15.9	6 52.3	11.2	54.2
18	89 08.2	S23 00.0	13 20.8	15.9	S 6 41.1	11.2	54.2
19	104 07.9	22 59.7	27 55.7	16.0	6 29.9	11.2	54.2
20	119 07.6	59.5	42 30.7	16.0	6 18.7	11.3	54.2
21	134 07.3	.. 59.3	57 05.7	16.0	6 07.4	11.3	54.2
22	149 07.1	59.1	71 40.7	16.0	5 56.1	11.3	54.2
23	164 06.8	58.9	86 15.7	16.1	5 44.8	11.4	54.2
2 00	179 06.5	S22 58.7	100 50.8	16.0	S 5 33.4	11.3	54.2
01	194 06.2	58.5	115 25.8	16.1	5 22.1	11.4	54.2
02	209 05.9	58.3	130 00.9	16.1	5 10.7	11.4	54.2
03	224 05.6	.. 58.1	144 36.0	16.2	4 59.3	11.4	54.2
04	239 05.3	57.9	159 11.2	16.1	4 47.9	11.4	54.2
05	254 05.0	57.6	173 46.3	16.1	4 36.5	11.5	54.2
06	269 04.7	S22 57.4	188 21.4	16.2	S 4 25.0	11.5	54.2
T 07	284 04.4	57.2	202 56.6	16.2	4 13.5	11.4	54.2
H 08	299 04.1	57.0	217 31.8	16.2	4 02.1	11.5	54.2
U 09	314 03.8	.. 56.8	232 07.0	16.2	3 50.6	11.6	54.2
R 10	329 03.5	56.6	246 42.2	16.2	3 39.0	11.5	54.2
S 11	344 03.2	56.3	261 17.4	16.2	3 27.5	11.5	54.2
D 12	359 02.9	S22 56.1	275 52.6	16.2	S 3 16.0	11.6	54.2
A 13	14 02.6	55.9	290 27.8	16.3	3 04.4	11.6	54.2
Y 14	29 02.4	55.7	305 03.1	16.2	2 52.8	11.5	54.2
15	44 02.1	.. 55.5	319 38.3	16.2	2 41.3	11.6	54.2
16	59 01.8	55.2	334 13.5	16.2	2 29.7	11.6	54.2
17	74 01.5	55.0	348 48.8	16.2	2 18.1	11.6	54.2
18	89 01.2	S22 54.8	3 24.0	16.3	S 2 06.5	11.7	54.2
19	104 00.9	54.6	17 59.3	16.3	1 54.8	11.6	54.2
20	119 00.6	54.3	32 34.6	16.2	1 43.2	11.6	54.3
21	134 00.3	.. 54.1	47 09.8	16.3	1 31.6	11.7	54.3
22	149 00.0	53.9	61 45.1	16.2	1 19.9	11.7	54.3
23	163 59.7	53.7	76 20.3	16.3	1 08.2	11.6	54.3
3 00	178 59.4	S22 53.4	90 55.6	16.2	S 0 56.6	11.7	54.3
01	193 59.1	53.2	105 30.8	16.3	0 44.9	11.7	54.3
02	208 58.9	53.0	120 06.1	16.2	0 33.2	11.7	54.3
03	223 58.6	.. 52.7	134 41.3	16.2	0 21.5	11.6	54.3
04	238 58.3	52.5	149 16.5	16.2	S 0 09.9	11.7	54.3
05	253 58.0	52.3	163 51.7	16.3	N 0 01.8	11.7	54.3
06	268 57.7	S22 52.0	178 27.0	16.2	N 0 13.5	11.7	54.3
F 07	283 57.4	51.8	193 02.2	16.2	0 25.2	11.7	54.3
R 08	298 57.1	51.6	207 37.4	16.1	0 36.9	11.7	54.3
I 09	313 56.8	.. 51.3	222 12.5	16.2	0 48.6	11.7	54.4
D 10	328 56.5	51.1	236 47.7	16.2	1 00.3	11.7	54.4
A 11	343 56.3	50.8	251 22.9	16.1	1 12.0	11.7	54.4
Y 12	358 56.0	S22 50.6	265 58.0	16.1	N 1 23.7	11.7	54.4
13	13 55.7	50.4	280 33.1	16.1	1 35.4	11.7	54.4
14	28 55.4	50.1	295 08.2	16.1	1 47.1	11.7	54.4
15	43 55.1	.. 49.9	309 43.3	16.1	1 58.8	11.7	54.4
16	58 54.8	49.6	324 18.4	16.1	2 10.5	11.7	54.4
17	73 54.5	49.4	338 53.5	16.0	2 22.2	11.7	54.4
18	88 54.2	S22 49.2	353 28.5	16.0	N 2 33.9	11.7	54.4
19	103 53.9	48.9	8 03.5	16.0	2 45.6	11.7	54.5
20	118 53.7	48.7	22 38.5	16.0	2 57.3	11.6	54.5
21	133 53.4	.. 48.4	37 13.5	15.9	3 09.0	11.6	54.5
22	148 53.1	48.2	51 48.4	15.9	3 20.6	11.7	54.5
23	163 52.8	47.9	66 23.3	15.9	N 3 32.3	11.7	54.5
	SD 16.3	d 0.2	SD 14.8		14.8		14.8

Lat.	Twilight Naut.	Twilight Civil	Sunrise	Moonrise 1	Moonrise 2	Moonrise 3	Moonrise 4
°	h m	h m	h m	h m	h m	h m	h m
N 72	08 23	10 41	■	12 37	12 18	12 00	11 42
N 70	08 05	09 49	■	12 26	12 14	12 02	11 50
68	07 50	09 16	■	12 17	12 10	12 03	11 57
66	07 37	08 53	10 27	12 09	12 07	12 04	12 02
64	07 26	08 34	09 49	12 03	12 04	12 06	12 07
62	07 17	08 18	09 23	11 57	12 02	12 06	12 11
60	07 09	08 05	09 02	11 52	12 00	12 07	12 15
N 58	07 02	07 54	08 45	11 48	11 58	12 08	12 18
56	06 55	07 44	08 31	11 44	11 57	12 09	12 21
54	06 50	07 35	08 19	11 40	11 55	12 09	12 24
52	06 44	07 28	08 08	11 37	11 54	12 10	12 26
50	06 39	07 20	07 58	11 34	11 53	12 10	12 28
45	06 28	07 05	07 38	11 28	11 50	12 11	12 33
N 40	06 18	06 52	07 22	11 23	11 48	12 12	12 37
35	06 08	06 40	07 08	11 18	11 46	12 13	12 41
30	06 00	06 30	06 56	11 14	11 44	12 14	12 44
20	05 44	06 11	06 35	11 07	11 41	12 15	12 49
N 10	05 28	05 54	06 17	11 01	11 39	12 16	12 54
0	05 11	05 38	06 00	10 55	11 36	12 17	12 58
S 10	04 53	05 20	05 43	10 49	11 34	12 18	13 03
20	04 31	05 00	05 24	10 43	11 31	12 19	13 08
30	04 02	04 35	05 03	10 36	11 28	12 21	13 13
35	03 44	04 20	04 50	10 32	11 27	12 21	13 17
40	03 21	04 03	04 35	10 27	11 25	12 22	13 20
45	02 52	03 41	04 18	10 22	11 22	12 23	13 25
S 50	02 08	03 12	03 56	10 15	11 20	12 24	13 30
52	01 42	02 57	03 45	10 12	11 19	12 25	13 32
54	01 02	02 40	03 33	10 09	11 17	12 26	13 35
56	////	02 19	03 19	10 05	11 16	12 26	13 38
58	////	01 51	03 03	10 01	11 14	12 27	13 41
S 60	////	01 07	02 44	09 56	11 12	12 28	13 45

Lat.	Sunset	Twilight Civil	Twilight Naut.	Moonset 1	Moonset 2	Moonset 3	Moonset 4
°	h m	h m	h m	h m	h m	h m	h m
N 72	■	13 27	15 45	21 57	23 42	25 27	01 27
N 70	■	14 19	16 03	22 06	23 44	25 22	01 22
68	■	14 52	16 18	22 13	23 45	25 17	01 17
66	13 41	15 15	16 31	22 19	23 46	25 13	01 13
64	14 19	15 34	16 41	22 25	23 47	25 10	01 10
62	14 45	15 49	16 51	22 30	23 48	25 07	01 07
60	15 06	16 02	16 59	22 33	23 48	25 05	01 05
N 58	15 23	16 14	17 06	22 36	23 49	25 02	01 02
56	15 37	16 24	17 12	22 39	23 50	25 01	01 01
54	15 49	16 32	17 18	22 42	23 50	24 59	00 59
52	16 00	16 40	17 24	22 44	23 50	24 57	00 57
50	16 09	16 47	17 29	22 46	23 51	24 56	00 56
45	16 29	17 03	17 40	22 51	23 52	24 53	00 53
N 40	16 46	17 16	17 50	22 55	23 52	24 50	00 50
35	17 00	17 28	17 59	22 58	23 53	24 48	00 48
30	17 12	17 38	18 08	23 01	23 53	24 46	00 46
20	17 32	17 56	18 24	23 06	23 54	24 43	00 43
N 10	17 50	18 13	18 40	23 11	23 55	24 40	00 40
0	18 08	18 30	18 56	23 15	23 56	24 37	00 37
S 10	18 25	18 48	19 15	23 19	23 57	24 34	00 34
20	18 43	19 08	19 37	23 24	23 57	24 31	00 31
30	19 05	19 32	20 05	23 28	23 58	24 28	00 28
35	19 17	19 47	20 23	23 31	23 58	24 26	00 26
40	19 32	20 05	20 46	23 34	23 59	24 23	00 23
45	19 50	20 27	21 15	23 38	24 00	00 00	00 21
S 50	20 11	20 55	21 59	23 42	24 00	00 00	00 18
52	20 22	21 10	22 24	23 44	24 01	00 01	00 17
54	20 34	21 27	23 03	23 47	24 01	00 01	00 15
56	20 48	21 48	////	23 49	24 01	00 01	00 13
58	21 04	22 16	////	23 52	24 02	00 02	00 12
S 60	21 23	22 58	////	23 55	24 02	00 02	00 09

Day	SUN Eqn. of Time 00h	SUN Eqn. of Time 12h	SUN Mer. Pass.	MOON Mer. Pass. Upper	MOON Mer. Pass. Lower	Age	Phase
d	m s	m s	h m	h m	h m	d	%
1	03 05	03 19	12 03	17 05	04 44	06	34
2	03 34	03 48	12 04	17 46	05 26	07	44
3	04 02	04 16	12 04	18 27	06 06	08	53

UT	ARIES	VENUS −4.0		MARS +1.5		JUPITER −1.8		SATURN +0.5		STARS		
d h	GHA	GHA	Dec	GHA	Dec	GHA	Dec	GHA	Dec	Name	SHA	Dec
4 00	103 04.5	141 58.4	S17 07.7	224 45.7	S19 54.5	185 03.9	S23 08.9	169 35.1	S21 37.9	Acamar	315 14.7	S40 13.8
01	118 06.9	156 57.8	06.7	239 46.4	54.9	200 05.7	08.8	184 37.3	37.9	Achernar	335 23.3	S57 08.6
02	133 09.4	171 57.2	05.7	254 47.1	55.3	215 07.6	08.8	199 39.4	37.9	Acrux	173 04.2	S63 12.2
03	148 11.9	186 56.7	.. 04.8	269 47.8	.. 55.6	230 09.4	.. 08.8	214 41.6	.. 37.8	Adhara	255 08.6	S29 00.1
04	163 14.3	201 56.1	03.8	284 48.6	56.0	245 11.2	08.8	229 43.7	37.8	Aldebaran	290 43.9	N16 32.8
05	178 16.8	216 55.6	02.8	299 49.3	56.4	260 13.1	08.7	244 45.9	37.7			
06	193 19.3	231 55.0	S17 01.8	314 50.0	S19 56.8	275 14.9	S23 08.7	259 48.0	S21 37.7	Alioth	166 16.7	N55 50.9
07	208 21.7	246 54.4	17 00.8	329 50.7	57.1	290 16.8	08.7	274 50.2	37.6	Alkaid	152 55.4	N49 12.7
08	223 24.2	261 53.9	16 59.9	344 51.4	57.5	305 18.6	08.6	289 52.3	37.6	Alnair	27 38.4	S46 52.1
09	238 26.6	276 53.3	.. 58.9	359 52.1	.. 57.9	320 20.4	.. 08.6	304 54.5	.. 37.6	Alnilam	275 41.5	S 1 11.5
10	253 29.1	291 52.7	57.9	14 52.9	58.3	335 22.3	08.6	319 56.6	37.5	Alphard	217 51.4	S 8 44.7
11	268 31.6	306 52.2	56.9	29 53.6	58.6	350 24.1	08.6	334 58.8	37.5			
12	283 34.0	321 51.6	S16 55.9	44 54.3	S19 59.0	5 26.0	S23 08.5	350 00.9	S21 37.4	Alphecca	126 07.4	N26 38.8
13	298 36.5	336 51.1	54.9	59 55.0	59.4	20 27.8	08.5	5 03.1	37.4	Alpheratz	357 38.9	N29 12.1
14	313 39.0	351 50.5	53.9	74 55.7	19 59.8	35 29.6	08.5	20 05.2	37.3	Altair	62 04.2	N 8 55.3
15	328 41.4	6 49.9	.. 53.0	89 56.4	20 00.1	50 31.5	.. 08.4	35 07.4	.. 37.3	Ankaa	353 11.3	S42 12.2
16	343 43.9	21 49.4	52.0	104 57.2	00.5	65 33.3	08.4	50 09.5	37.2	Antares	112 21.0	S26 28.4
17	358 46.4	36 48.8	51.0	119 57.9	00.9	80 35.2	08.4	65 11.7	37.2			
18	13 48.8	51 48.3	S16 50.0	134 58.6	S20 01.2	95 37.0	S23 08.4	80 13.8	S21 37.2	Arcturus	145 51.8	N19 04.7
19	28 51.3	66 47.7	49.0	149 59.3	01.6	110 38.8	08.3	95 16.0	37.1	Atria	107 19.3	S69 03.5
20	43 53.8	81 47.2	48.0	165 00.0	02.0	125 40.7	08.3	110 18.1	37.1	Avior	234 15.6	S59 34.3
21	58 56.2	96 46.6	.. 47.0	180 00.7	.. 02.4	140 42.5	.. 08.3	125 20.3	.. 37.0	Bellatrix	278 26.9	N 6 21.9
22	73 58.7	111 46.1	46.0	195 01.5	02.7	155 44.4	08.2	140 22.4	37.0	Betelgeuse	270 56.1	N 7 24.5
23	89 01.1	126 45.5	45.0	210 02.2	03.1	170 46.2	08.2	155 24.6	36.9			
5 00	104 03.6	141 45.0	S16 44.0	225 02.9	S20 03.5	185 48.0	S23 08.2	170 26.7	S21 36.9	Canopus	263 53.6	S52 42.5
01	119 06.1	156 44.4	43.0	240 03.6	03.8	200 49.9	08.2	185 28.9	36.8	Capella	280 27.3	N46 01.0
02	134 08.5	171 43.9	42.0	255 04.3	04.2	215 51.7	08.1	200 31.0	36.8	Deneb	49 28.9	N45 21.2
03	149 11.0	186 43.3	.. 41.0	270 05.0	.. 04.6	230 53.6	.. 08.1	215 33.2	.. 36.8	Denebola	182 29.0	N14 27.6
04	164 13.5	201 42.8	40.0	285 05.7	04.9	245 55.4	08.1	230 35.3	36.7	Diphda	348 51.4	S17 52.9
05	179 15.9	216 42.2	39.0	300 06.5	05.3	260 57.2	08.0	245 37.5	36.7			
06	194 18.4	231 41.7	S16 38.0	315 07.2	S20 05.7	275 59.1	S23 08.0	260 39.6	S21 36.6	Dubhe	193 45.8	N61 38.4
07	209 20.9	246 41.1	37.0	330 07.9	06.1	291 00.9	08.0	275 41.8	36.6	Elnath	278 06.6	N28 37.3
08	224 23.3	261 40.6	36.0	345 08.6	06.4	306 02.8	08.0	290 43.9	36.5	Eltanin	90 44.6	N51 29.2
09	239 25.8	276 40.0	.. 35.0	0 09.3	.. 06.8	321 04.6	.. 07.9	305 46.1	.. 36.5	Enif	33 43.0	N 9 58.0
10	254 28.2	291 39.5	34.0	15 10.0	07.2	336 06.4	07.9	320 48.2	36.5	Fomalhaut	15 19.2	S29 31.2
11	269 30.7	306 38.9	33.0	30 10.7	07.5	351 08.3	07.9	335 50.4	36.4			
12	284 33.2	321 38.4	S16 32.0	45 11.4	S20 07.9	6 10.1	S23 07.8	350 52.5	S21 36.4	Gacrux	171 55.9	S57 13.1
13	299 35.6	336 37.8	31.0	60 12.2	08.3	21 12.0	07.8	5 54.7	36.3	Gienah	175 47.6	S17 39.0
14	314 38.1	351 37.3	30.0	75 12.9	08.6	36 13.8	07.8	20 56.8	36.3	Hadar	148 41.7	S60 27.7
15	329 40.6	6 36.7	.. 29.0	90 13.6	.. 09.0	51 15.6	.. 07.7	35 59.0	.. 36.2	Hamal	327 55.6	N23 33.4
16	344 43.0	21 36.2	28.0	105 14.3	09.4	66 17.5	07.7	51 01.1	36.2	Kaus Aust.	83 38.3	S34 22.4
17	359 45.5	36 35.7	27.0	120 15.0	09.7	81 19.3	07.7	66 03.3	36.1			
18	14 48.0	51 35.1	S16 26.0	135 15.7	S20 10.1	96 21.2	S23 07.7	81 05.4	S21 36.1	Kochab	137 20.7	N74 04.2
19	29 50.4	66 34.6	25.0	150 16.4	10.5	111 23.0	07.6	96 07.6	36.1	Markab	13 34.0	N15 18.7
20	44 52.9	81 34.0	24.0	165 17.1	10.8	126 24.8	07.6	111 09.7	36.0	Menkar	314 10.2	N 4 09.9
21	59 55.4	96 33.5	.. 23.0	180 17.9	.. 11.2	141 26.7	.. 07.6	126 11.9	.. 36.0	Menkent	148 02.4	S36 27.8
22	74 57.8	111 33.0	21.9	195 18.6	11.5	156 28.5	07.5	141 14.1	35.9	Miaplacidus	221 38.0	S69 47.8
23	90 00.3	126 32.4	20.9	210 19.3	11.9	171 30.4	07.5	156 16.2	35.9			
6 00	105 02.7	141 31.9	S16 19.9	225 20.0	S20 12.3	186 32.2	S23 07.5	171 18.4	S21 35.8	Mirfak	308 33.6	N49 55.9
01	120 05.2	156 31.4	18.9	240 20.7	12.6	201 34.0	07.5	186 20.5	35.8	Nunki	75 53.1	S26 16.2
02	135 07.7	171 30.8	17.9	255 21.4	13.0	216 35.9	07.4	201 22.7	35.7	Peacock	53 12.7	S56 40.3
03	150 10.1	186 30.3	.. 16.9	270 22.1	.. 13.4	231 37.7	.. 07.4	216 24.8	.. 35.7	Pollux	243 21.9	N27 58.5
04	165 12.6	201 29.8	15.9	285 22.8	13.7	246 39.6	07.4	231 27.0	35.7	Procyon	244 54.7	N 5 10.3
05	180 15.1	216 29.2	14.8	300 23.5	14.1	261 41.4	07.3	246 29.1	35.6			
06	195 17.5	231 28.7	S16 13.8	315 24.2	S20 14.4	276 43.2	S23 07.3	261 31.3	S21 35.6	Rasalhague	96 02.6	N12 32.8
07	210 20.0	246 28.2	12.8	330 25.0	14.8	291 45.1	07.3	276 33.4	35.5	Regulus	207 38.5	N11 52.1
08	225 22.5	261 27.6	11.8	345 25.7	15.2	306 46.9	07.2	291 35.6	35.5	Rigel	281 07.4	S 8 10.9
09	240 24.9	276 27.1	.. 10.8	0 26.4	.. 15.5	321 48.8	.. 07.2	306 37.7	.. 35.4	Rigil Kent.	139 45.9	S60 54.0
10	255 27.4	291 26.6	09.7	15 27.1	15.9	336 50.6	07.2	321 39.9	35.4	Sabik	102 07.7	S15 44.8
11	270 29.9	306 26.0	08.7	30 27.8	16.2	351 52.4	07.1	336 42.0	35.3			
12	285 32.3	321 25.5	S16 07.7	45 28.5	S20 16.6	6 54.3	S23 07.1	351 44.2	S21 35.3	Schedar	349 35.4	N56 39.0
13	300 34.8	336 25.0	06.7	60 29.2	17.0	21 56.1	07.1	6 46.3	35.3	Shaula	96 16.2	S37 06.9
14	315 37.2	351 24.4	05.7	75 29.9	17.3	36 58.0	07.1	21 48.5	35.2	Sirius	258 29.4	S16 44.7
15	330 39.7	6 23.9	.. 04.6	90 30.6	.. 17.7	51 59.8	.. 07.0	36 50.6	.. 35.2	Spica	158 26.6	S11 15.8
16	345 42.2	21 23.4	03.6	105 31.3	18.0	67 01.6	07.0	51 52.8	35.1	Suhail	222 48.8	S43 30.7
17	0 44.6	36 22.9	02.6	120 32.0	18.4	82 03.5	07.0	66 54.9	35.1			
18	15 47.1	51 22.3	S16 01.6	135 32.7	S20 18.8	97 05.3	S23 06.9	81 57.1	S21 35.0	Vega	80 36.4	N38 48.2
19	30 49.6	66 21.8	16 00.5	150 33.5	19.1	112 07.2	06.9	96 59.2	35.0	Zuben'ubi	137 00.6	S16 07.3
20	45 52.0	81 21.3	15 59.5	165 34.2	19.5	127 09.0	06.9	112 01.4	34.9		SHA	Mer. Pass.
21	60 54.5	96 20.8	.. 58.5	180 34.9	.. 19.8	142 10.8	.. 06.8	127 03.5	.. 34.9		° '	h m
22	75 57.0	111 20.2	57.4	195 35.6	20.2	157 12.7	06.8	142 05.7	34.9	Venus	37 41.3	14 34
23	90 59.4	126 19.7	56.4	210 36.3	20.6	172 14.5	06.8	157 07.8	34.8	Mars	120 59.3	8 59
	h m									Jupiter	81 44.4	11 35
Mer. Pass.	17 01.0	v −0.5	d 1.0	v 0.7	d 0.4	v 1.8	d 0.0	v 2.2	d 0.0	Saturn	66 23.1	12 36

Day	UT (d h)	SUN GHA (° ′)	SUN Dec (° ′)	MOON GHA (° ′)	v (′)	MOON Dec (° ′)	d (′)	HP (′)
	4 00	178 52.5	S22 47.7	80 58.2	15.9	N 3 44.0	11.6	54.5
	01	193 52.2	47.4	95 33.1	15.8	3 55.6	11.7	54.5
	02	208 51.9	47.2	110 07.9	15.8	4 07.3	11.6	54.6
	03	223 51.6	. . 46.9	124 42.7	15.8	4 18.9	11.6	54.6
	04	238 51.4	46.7	139 17.5	15.7	4 30.5	11.6	54.6
	05	253 51.1	46.4	153 52.2	15.7	4 42.1	11.6	54.6
	06	268 50.8	S22 46.2	168 26.9	15.7	N 4 53.7	11.6	54.6
S	07	283 50.5	45.9	183 01.6	15.6	5 05.3	11.6	54.6
A	08	298 50.2	45.7	197 36.2	15.6	5 16.9	11.5	54.7
T	09	313 49.9	. . 45.4	212 10.8	15.6	5 28.4	11.6	54.7
U	10	328 49.7	45.2	226 45.4	15.6	5 40.0	11.5	54.7
R	11	343 49.4	44.9	241 20.0	15.4	5 51.5	11.5	54.7
D	12	358 49.1	S22 44.6	255 54.4	15.5	N 6 03.0	11.5	54.7
A	13	13 48.8	44.4	270 28.9	15.4	6 14.5	11.5	54.7
Y	14	28 48.5	44.1	285 03.3	15.4	6 26.0	11.5	54.8
	15	43 48.2	. . 43.9	299 37.7	15.3	6 37.5	11.5	54.8
	16	58 47.9	43.6	314 12.0	15.3	6 49.0	11.4	54.8
	17	73 47.7	43.3	328 46.3	15.3	7 00.4	11.4	54.8
	18	88 47.4	S22 43.1	343 20.6	15.2	N 7 11.8	11.4	54.8
	19	103 47.1	42.8	357 54.8	15.1	7 23.2	11.4	54.9
	20	118 46.8	42.6	12 28.9	15.1	7 34.6	11.3	54.9
	21	133 46.5	. . 42.3	27 03.0	15.1	7 45.9	11.3	54.9
	22	148 46.2	42.0	41 37.1	15.0	7 57.2	11.3	54.9
	23	163 46.0	41.8	56 11.1	15.0	8 08.5	11.3	54.9
	5 00	178 45.7	S22 41.5	70 45.1	14.9	N 8 19.8	11.3	55.0
	01	193 45.4	41.2	85 19.0	14.8	8 31.1	11.2	55.0
	02	208 45.1	41.0	99 52.8	14.8	8 42.3	11.2	55.0
	03	223 44.8	. . 40.7	114 26.6	14.8	8 53.5	11.2	55.0
	04	238 44.6	40.4	129 00.4	14.7	9 04.7	11.1	55.0
	05	253 44.3	40.1	143 34.1	14.6	9 15.8	11.1	55.1
	06	268 44.0	S22 39.9	158 07.7	14.6	N 9 26.9	11.1	55.1
	07	283 43.7	39.6	172 41.3	14.5	9 38.0	11.1	55.1
	08	298 43.4	39.3	187 14.8	14.5	9 49.1	11.0	55.1
S	09	313 43.1	. . 39.1	201 48.3	14.4	10 00.1	11.0	55.2
U	10	328 42.9	38.8	216 21.7	14.4	10 11.1	11.0	55.2
N	11	343 42.6	38.5	230 55.1	14.2	10 22.1	10.9	55.2
D	12	358 42.3	S22 38.2	245 28.3	14.3	N10 33.0	10.9	55.2
A	13	13 42.0	37.9	260 01.6	14.1	10 43.9	10.9	55.2
Y	14	28 41.7	37.7	274 34.7	14.1	10 54.8	10.8	55.3
	15	43 41.5	. . 37.4	289 07.8	14.1	11 05.6	10.8	55.3
	16	58 41.2	37.1	303 40.9	13.9	11 16.4	10.7	55.3
	17	73 40.9	36.8	318 13.8	13.9	11 27.1	10.8	55.3
	18	88 40.6	S22 36.6	332 46.7	13.9	N11 37.9	10.6	55.4
	19	103 40.3	36.3	347 19.6	13.7	11 48.5	10.7	55.4
	20	118 40.1	36.0	1 52.3	13.7	11 59.2	10.5	55.4
	21	133 39.8	. . 35.7	16 25.0	13.7	12 09.7	10.6	55.5
	22	148 39.5	35.4	30 57.7	13.5	12 20.3	10.5	55.5
	23	163 39.2	35.1	45 30.2	13.5	12 30.8	10.5	55.5
	6 00	178 39.0	S22 34.8	60 02.7	13.4	N12 41.3	10.4	55.5
	01	193 38.7	34.6	74 35.1	13.4	12 51.7	10.3	55.6
	02	208 38.4	34.3	89 07.5	13.2	13 02.0	10.4	55.6
	03	223 38.1	. . 34.0	103 39.7	13.2	13 12.4	10.2	55.6
	04	238 37.8	33.7	118 11.9	13.1	13 22.6	10.3	55.6
	05	253 37.6	33.4	132 44.0	13.1	13 32.9	10.1	55.7
	06	268 37.3	S22 33.1	147 16.1	12.9	N13 43.0	10.1	55.7
	07	283 37.0	32.8	161 48.0	12.9	13 53.1	10.1	55.7
	08	298 36.7	32.5	176 19.9	12.8	14 03.2	10.0	55.8
M	09	313 36.5	. . 32.2	190 51.7	12.8	14 13.2	10.0	55.8
O	10	328 36.2	31.9	205 23.5	12.6	14 23.2	9.9	55.8
N	11	343 35.9	31.7	219 55.1	12.6	14 33.1	9.8	55.8
D	12	358 35.6	S22 31.4	234 26.7	12.5	N14 42.9	9.8	55.9
A	13	13 35.4	31.1	248 58.2	12.4	14 52.7	9.8	55.9
Y	14	28 35.1	30.8	263 29.6	12.3	15 02.5	9.6	55.9
	15	43 34.8	. . 30.5	278 00.9	12.2	15 12.1	9.7	56.0
	16	58 34.5	30.2	292 32.1	12.2	15 21.8	9.5	56.0
	17	73 34.3	29.9	307 03.3	12.1	15 31.3	9.5	56.0
	18	88 34.0	S22 29.6	321 34.4	11.9	N15 40.8	9.4	56.0
	19	103 33.7	29.3	336 05.3	11.9	15 50.2	9.4	56.1
	20	118 33.4	29.0	350 36.2	11.9	15 59.6	9.3	56.1
	21	133 33.2	. . 28.7	5 07.1	11.7	16 08.9	9.2	56.1
	22	148 32.9	28.4	19 37.8	11.6	16 18.1	9.2	56.2
	23	163 32.6	28.1	34 08.4	11.6	N16 27.3	9.1	56.2
		SD 16.3	*d* 0.3	SD 14.9		15.0		15.2

Lat. (°)	Twilight Naut. (h m)	Twilight Civil (h m)	Sunrise (h m)	Moonrise 4 (h m)	Moonrise 5 (h m)	Moonrise 6 (h m)	Moonrise 7 (h m)
N 72	08 20	10 31	■	11 42	11 21	10 51	09 33
N 70	08 02	09 44	■	11 50	11 37	11 20	10 53
68	07 47	09 13	11 33	11 57	11 50	11 42	11 32
66	07 35	08 50	10 21	12 02	12 00	11 59	11 59
64	07 25	08 32	09 45	12 07	12 09	12 13	12 20
62	07 16	08 17	09 20	12 11	12 17	12 25	12 37
60	07 08	08 04	09 00	12 15	12 24	12 35	12 51
N 58	07 01	07 53	08 44	12 18	12 30	12 44	13 03
56	06 55	07 43	08 30	12 21	12 35	12 52	13 14
54	06 49	07 35	08 18	12 24	12 40	12 59	13 23
52	06 44	07 27	08 07	12 26	12 44	13 05	13 32
50	06 39	07 20	07 58	12 28	12 48	13 11	13 39
45	06 28	07 05	07 38	12 33	12 57	13 24	13 56
N 40	06 18	06 52	07 22	12 37	13 04	13 34	14 09
35	06 09	06 41	07 08	12 41	13 10	13 43	14 20
30	06 01	06 30	06 57	12 44	13 16	13 51	14 30
20	05 45	06 12	06 36	12 49	13 25	14 04	14 47
N 10	05 29	05 56	06 18	12 54	13 34	14 16	15 02
0	05 13	05 39	06 01	12 58	13 42	14 27	15 17
S 10	04 55	05 22	05 44	13 03	13 50	14 39	15 31
20	04 33	05 02	05 26	13 08	13 58	14 51	15 46
30	04 05	04 38	05 05	13 13	14 08	15 05	16 04
35	03 47	04 23	04 52	13 17	14 14	15 13	16 14
40	03 24	04 05	04 38	13 20	14 20	15 22	16 26
45	02 55	03 44	04 21	13 25	14 28	15 33	16 40
S 50	02 13	03 15	03 59	13 30	14 37	15 46	16 57
52	01 48	03 01	03 49	13 32	14 41	15 53	17 05
54	01 11	02 44	03 37	13 35	14 46	16 00	17 14
56	////	02 24	03 24	13 38	14 51	16 07	17 25
58	////	01 57	03 08	13 41	14 57	16 16	17 36
S 60	////	01 17	02 49	13 45	15 04	16 26	17 50

Lat. (°)	Sunset (h m)	Twilight Civil (h m)	Twilight Naut. (h m)	Moonset 4 (h m)	Moonset 5 (h m)	Moonset 6 (h m)	Moonset 7 (h m)
N 72	■	13 40	15 51	01 27	03 17	05 20	08 19
N 70	■	14 27	16 09	01 22	03 03	04 53	07 00
68	12 38	14 58	16 23	01 17	02 52	04 32	06 22
66	13 50	15 21	16 35	01 13	02 42	04 16	05 56
64	14 25	15 39	16 46	01 10	02 35	04 03	05 35
62	14 51	15 54	16 55	01 07	02 28	03 52	05 19
60	15 11	16 07	17 02	01 05	02 22	03 43	05 05
N 58	15 27	16 17	17 09	01 02	02 17	03 34	04 54
56	15 41	16 27	17 16	01 01	02 13	03 27	04 44
54	15 53	16 36	17 21	00 59	02 09	03 21	04 35
52	16 03	16 43	17 27	00 57	02 05	03 15	04 27
50	16 13	16 51	17 32	00 56	02 02	03 10	04 20
45	16 32	17 06	17 43	00 53	01 55	02 59	04 05
N 40	16 48	17 19	17 53	00 50	01 49	02 50	03 53
35	17 02	17 30	18 01	00 48	01 44	02 42	03 42
30	17 14	17 40	18 10	00 46	01 40	02 35	03 33
20	17 34	17 58	18 26	00 43	01 32	02 23	03 17
N 10	17 52	18 15	18 41	00 40	01 25	02 13	03 03
0	18 09	18 31	18 57	00 37	01 19	02 03	02 51
S 10	18 26	18 49	19 16	00 34	01 13	01 54	02 38
20	18 44	19 08	19 37	00 31	01 06	01 43	02 24
30	19 05	19 32	20 05	00 28	00 58	01 32	02 09
35	19 18	19 47	20 23	00 26	00 54	01 25	02 00
40	19 32	20 05	20 45	00 23	00 49	01 17	01 49
45	19 49	20 26	21 14	00 21	00 43	01 08	01 37
S 50	20 11	20 54	21 57	00 18	00 37	00 58	01 23
52	20 21	21 08	22 21	00 17	00 34	00 53	01 16
54	20 33	21 25	22 57	00 15	00 30	00 47	01 09
56	20 46	21 45	////	00 13	00 26	00 41	01 00
58	21 02	22 12	////	00 12	00 22	00 35	00 51
S 60	21 20	22 50	////	00 09	00 17	00 27	00 40

Day	SUN Eqn. of Time 00^h	SUN Eqn. of Time 12^h	SUN Mer. Pass.	MOON Mer. Pass. Upper	MOON Mer. Pass. Lower	MOON Age	MOON Phase
d	m s	m s	h m	h m	h m	d	%
4	04 29	04 43	12 05	19 09	06 48	09	62
5	04 57	05 10	12 05	19 52	07 30	10	72
6	05 24	05 37	12 06	20 39	08 15	11	80

2020 JANUARY 7, 8, 9 (TUES., WED., THURS.)

UT	ARIES GHA	VENUS −4.0 GHA	Dec	MARS +1.5 GHA	Dec	JUPITER −1.8 GHA	Dec	SATURN +0.5 GHA	Dec	STARS Name	SHA	Dec
7 00	106 01.9	141 19.2	S15 55.4	225 37.0	S20 20.9	187 16.4	S23 06.7	172 10.0	S21 34.8	Acamar	315 14.7	S40 13.8
01	121 04.4	156 18.7	54.3	240 37.7	21.3	202 18.2	06.7	187 12.1	34.7	Achernar	335 23.3	S57 08.6
02	136 06.8	171 18.2	53.3	255 38.4	21.6	217 20.1	06.7	202 14.3	34.7	Acrux	173 04.1	S63 12.2
03	151 09.3	186 17.6 ..	52.3	270 39.1 ..	22.0	232 21.9 ..	06.7	217 16.4 ..	34.6	Adhara	255 08.6	S29 00.1
04	166 11.7	201 17.1	51.2	285 39.8	22.3	247 23.7	06.6	232 18.6	34.6	Aldebaran	290 43.9	N16 32.8
05	181 14.2	216 16.6	50.2	300 40.5	22.7	262 25.6	06.6	247 20.7	34.5			
06	196 16.7	231 16.1	S15 49.2	315 41.2	S20 23.0	277 27.4	S23 06.6	262 22.9	S21 34.5	Alioth	166 16.7	N55 50.9
07	211 19.1	246 15.6	48.1	330 41.9	23.4	292 29.3	06.5	277 25.0	34.5	Alkaid	152 55.4	N49 12.7
T 08	226 21.6	261 15.0	47.1	345 42.6	23.8	307 31.1	06.5	292 27.2	34.4	Alnair	27 38.4	S46 52.1
U 09	241 24.1	276 14.5 ..	46.1	0 43.3 ..	24.1	322 32.9 ..	06.5	307 29.3 ..	34.4	Alnilam	275 41.5	S 1 11.5
E 10	256 26.5	291 14.0	45.0	15 44.0	24.5	337 34.8	06.4	322 31.5	34.3	Alphard	217 51.4	S 8 44.7
S 11	271 29.0	306 13.5	44.0	30 44.8	24.8	352 36.6	06.4	337 33.6	34.3			
D 12	286 31.5	321 13.0	S15 43.0	45 45.5	S20 25.2	7 38.5	S23 06.4	352 35.8	S21 34.2	Alphecca	126 07.4	N26 38.8
A 13	301 33.9	336 12.5	41.9	60 46.2	25.5	22 40.3	06.3	7 37.9	34.2	Alpheratz	357 38.9	N29 12.1
Y 14	316 36.4	351 12.0	40.9	75 46.9	25.9	37 42.1	06.3	22 40.1	34.1	Altair	62 04.2	N 8 55.3
15	331 38.8	6 11.4 ..	39.8	90 47.6 ..	26.2	52 44.0 ..	06.3	37 42.2 ..	34.1	Ankaa	353 11.3	S42 12.2
16	346 41.3	21 10.9	38.8	105 48.3	26.6	67 45.8	06.2	52 44.4	34.1	Antares	112 21.0	S26 28.4
17	1 43.8	36 10.4	37.7	120 49.0	26.9	82 47.7	06.2	67 46.5	34.0			
18	16 46.2	51 09.9	S15 36.7	135 49.7	S20 27.3	97 49.5	S23 06.2	82 48.7	S21 34.0	Arcturus	145 51.7	N19 04.7
19	31 48.7	66 09.4	35.7	150 50.4	27.6	112 51.4	06.2	97 50.8	33.9	Atria	107 19.3	S69 03.5
20	46 51.2	81 08.9	34.6	165 51.1	28.0	127 53.2	06.1	112 53.0	33.9	Avior	234 15.6	S59 34.3
21	61 53.6	96 08.4 ..	33.6	180 51.8 ..	28.3	142 55.0 ..	06.1	127 55.1 ..	33.8	Bellatrix	278 26.9	N 6 21.9
22	76 56.1	111 07.9	32.5	195 52.5	28.7	157 56.9	06.1	142 57.3	33.8	Betelgeuse	270 56.1	N 7 24.5
23	91 58.6	126 07.4	31.5	210 53.2	29.0	172 58.7	06.0	157 59.4	33.7			
8 00	107 01.0	141 06.9	S15 30.4	225 53.9	S20 29.4	188 00.6	S23 06.0	173 01.6	S21 33.7	Canopus	263 53.6	S52 42.5
01	122 03.5	156 06.4	29.4	240 54.6	29.7	203 02.4	06.0	188 03.7	33.7	Capella	280 27.3	N46 01.0
02	137 06.0	171 05.8	28.3	255 55.3	30.1	218 04.2	05.9	203 05.9	33.6	Deneb	49 28.9	N45 21.2
03	152 08.4	186 05.3 ..	27.3	270 56.0 ..	30.4	233 06.1 ..	05.9	218 08.0 ..	33.6	Denebola	182 29.0	N14 27.6
04	167 10.9	201 04.8	26.2	285 56.7	30.8	248 07.9	05.9	233 10.2	33.5	Diphda	348 51.4	S17 52.9
05	182 13.3	216 04.3	25.2	300 57.4	31.1	263 09.8	05.8	248 12.3	33.5			
06	197 15.8	231 03.8	S15 24.1	315 58.1	S20 31.5	278 11.6	S23 05.8	263 14.5	S21 33.4	Dubhe	193 45.8	N61 38.4
W 07	212 18.3	246 03.3	23.1	330 58.8	31.8	293 13.5	05.8	278 16.6	33.4	Elnath	278 06.6	N28 37.3
E 08	227 20.7	261 02.8	22.0	345 59.5	32.2	308 15.3	05.7	293 18.8	33.3	Eltanin	90 44.6	N51 29.2
D 09	242 23.2	276 02.3 ..	21.0	1 00.2 ..	32.5	323 17.1 ..	05.7	308 20.9 ..	33.3	Enif	33 43.0	N 9 58.0
N 10	257 25.7	291 01.8	19.9	16 00.9	32.9	338 19.0	05.7	323 23.1	33.2	Fomalhaut	15 19.2	S29 31.2
E 11	272 28.1	306 01.3	18.8	31 01.6	33.2	353 20.8	05.6	338 25.2	33.2			
S 12	287 30.6	321 00.8	S15 17.8	46 02.3	S20 33.6	8 22.7	S23 05.6	353 27.4	S21 33.2	Gacrux	171 55.8	S57 13.1
D 13	302 33.1	336 00.3	16.7	61 03.0	33.9	23 24.5	05.6	8 29.5	33.1	Gienah	175 47.6	S17 39.0
A 14	317 35.5	350 59.8	15.7	76 03.7	34.3	38 26.3	05.5	23 31.7	33.1	Hadar	148 41.7	S60 27.7
Y 15	332 38.0	5 59.3 ..	14.6	91 04.4 ..	34.6	53 28.2 ..	05.5	38 33.8 ..	33.0	Hamal	327 55.6	N23 33.4
16	347 40.5	20 58.8	13.6	106 05.1	34.9	68 30.0	05.5	53 36.0	33.0	Kaus Aust.	83 38.2	S34 22.4
17	2 42.9	35 58.3	12.5	121 05.8	35.3	83 31.9	05.4	68 38.1	32.9			
18	17 45.4	50 57.8	S15 11.4	136 06.5	S20 35.6	98 33.7	S23 05.4	83 40.3	S21 32.9	Kochab	137 20.6	N74 04.2
19	32 47.8	65 57.3	10.4	151 07.2	36.0	113 35.6	05.4	98 42.4	32.8	Markab	13 34.0	N15 18.7
20	47 50.3	80 56.9	09.3	166 07.9	36.3	128 37.4	05.4	113 44.6	32.8	Menkar	314 10.2	N 4 09.9
21	62 52.8	95 56.4 ..	08.3	181 08.6 ..	36.7	143 39.2 ..	05.3	128 46.7 ..	32.8	Menkent	148 02.4	S36 27.8
22	77 55.2	110 55.9	07.2	196 09.3	37.0	158 41.1	05.3	143 48.9	32.7	Miaplacidus	221 38.0	S69 47.8
23	92 57.7	125 55.4	06.1	211 10.0	37.4	173 42.9	05.3	158 51.0	32.7			
9 00	108 00.2	140 54.9	S15 05.1	226 10.7	S20 37.7	188 44.8	S23 05.2	173 53.2	S21 32.6	Mirfak	308 33.6	N49 55.9
01	123 02.6	155 54.4	04.0	241 11.4	38.0	203 46.6	05.2	188 55.3	32.6	Nunki	75 53.1	S26 16.2
02	138 05.1	170 53.9	02.9	256 12.1	38.4	218 48.5	05.2	203 57.5	32.5	Peacock	53 12.7	S56 40.3
03	153 07.6	185 53.4 ..	01.9	271 12.8 ..	38.7	233 50.3 ..	05.1	218 59.6 ..	32.5	Pollux	243 21.9	N27 58.5
04	168 10.0	200 52.9	15 00.8	286 13.5	39.1	248 52.1	05.1	234 01.8	32.4	Procyon	244 54.7	N 5 10.3
05	183 12.5	215 52.4	14 59.7	301 14.2	39.4	263 54.0	05.1	249 03.9	32.4			
06	198 15.0	230 51.9	S14 58.7	316 14.9	S20 39.8	278 55.8	S23 05.0	264 06.1	S21 32.3	Rasalhague	96 02.6	N12 32.8
07	213 17.4	245 51.5	57.6	331 15.6	40.1	293 57.7	05.0	279 08.2	32.3	Regulus	207 38.5	N11 52.1
T 08	228 19.9	260 51.0	56.5	346 16.3	40.4	308 59.5	05.0	294 10.4	32.3	Rigel	281 07.4	S 8 10.9
H 09	243 22.3	275 50.5 ..	55.5	1 17.0 ..	40.8	324 01.4 ..	04.9	309 12.5 ..	32.2	Rigil Kent.	139 45.9	S60 54.6
U 10	258 24.8	290 50.0	54.4	16 17.7	41.1	339 03.2	04.9	324 14.7	32.2	Sabik	102 07.7	S15 44.8
R 11	273 27.3	305 49.5	53.3	31 18.4	41.5	354 05.0	04.9	339 16.8	32.1			
S 12	288 29.7	320 49.0	S14 52.2	46 19.1	S20 41.8	9 06.9	S23 04.8	354 19.0	S21 32.1	Schedar	349 35.5	N56 39.0
D 13	303 32.2	335 48.5	51.2	61 19.8	42.1	24 08.7	04.8	9 21.1	32.0	Shaula	96 16.2	S37 06.9
A 14	318 34.7	350 48.1	50.1	76 20.5	42.5	39 10.6	04.8	24 23.3	32.0	Sirius	258 29.4	S16 44.8
Y 15	333 37.1	5 47.6 ..	49.0	91 21.2 ..	42.8	54 12.4 ..	04.7	39 25.4 ..	31.9	Spica	158 26.5	S11 15.8
16	348 39.6	20 47.1	47.9	106 21.9	43.2	69 14.3	04.7	54 27.6	31.9	Suhail	222 48.8	S43 30.7
17	3 42.1	35 46.6	46.9	121 22.5	43.5	84 16.1	04.7	69 29.7	31.8			
18	18 44.5	50 46.1	S14 45.8	136 23.2	S20 43.8	99 17.9	S23 04.6	84 31.9	S21 31.8	Vega	80 36.3	N38 48.2
19	33 47.0	65 45.7	44.7	151 23.9	44.2	114 19.8	04.6	99 34.0	31.8	Zuben'ubi	137 00.6	S16 07.3
20	48 49.5	80 45.2	43.6	166 24.6	44.5	129 21.6	04.6	114 36.2	31.7		SHA	Mer. Pass.
21	63 51.9	95 44.7 ..	42.6	181 25.3 ..	44.8	144 23.5 ..	04.5	129 38.3 ..	31.7	Venus	34 05.8	14 36
22	78 54.4	110 44.2	41.5	196 26.0	45.2	159 25.3	04.5	144 40.5	31.6	Mars	118 52.9	8 56
23	93 56.8	125 43.7	40.4	211 26.7	45.5	174 27.2	04.5	159 42.6	31.6	Jupiter	80 59.5	11 27
Mer. Pass. 16 49.2		v −0.5 d 1.1		v 0.7 d 0.3		v 1.8 d 0.0		v 2.1 d 0.0		Saturn	66 00.5	12 26

UT	SUN GHA	SUN Dec	MOON GHA	v	MOON Dec	d	HP
d h	° ′	° ′	° ′	′	° ′	′	′
7 00	178 32.3	S22 27.8	48 39.0	11.5	N16 36.4	9.0	56.2
01	193 32.1	27.5	63 09.5	11.3	16 45.4	8.9	56.3
02	208 31.8	27.1	77 39.8	11.3	16 54.3	8.9	56.3
03	223 31.5 ..	26.8	92 10.1	11.2	17 03.2	8.8	56.3
04	238 31.3	26.5	106 40.3	11.1	17 12.0	8.7	56.3
05	253 31.0	26.2	121 10.4	11.0	17 20.7	8.7	56.4
06	268 30.7	S22 25.9	135 40.4	11.0	N17 29.4	8.5	56.4
07	283 30.4	25.6	150 10.4	10.8	17 37.9	8.5	56.4
08	298 30.2	25.3	164 40.2	10.8	17 46.4	8.4	56.5
09	313 29.9 ..	25.0	179 10.0	10.6	17 54.8	8.4	56.5
10	328 29.6	24.7	193 39.6	10.6	18 03.2	8.2	56.5
11	343 29.4	24.4	208 09.2	10.5	18 11.4	8.2	56.6
12	358 29.1	S22 24.0	222 38.7	10.3	N18 19.6	8.1	56.6
13	13 28.8	23.7	237 08.0	10.3	18 27.7	8.0	56.6
14	28 28.6	23.4	251 37.3	10.2	18 35.7	7.9	56.7
15	43 28.3 ..	23.1	266 06.5	10.1	18 43.6	7.8	56.7
16	58 28.0	22.8	280 35.6	10.0	18 51.4	7.7	56.7
17	73 27.7	22.5	295 04.6	10.0	18 59.1	7.6	56.8
18	88 27.5	S22 22.2	309 33.6	9.8	N19 06.7	7.6	56.8
19	103 27.2	21.8	324 02.4	9.7	19 14.3	7.4	56.8
20	118 26.9	21.5	338 31.1	9.7	19 21.7	7.4	56.9
21	133 26.7 ..	21.2	352 59.8	9.5	19 29.1	7.2	56.9
22	148 26.4	20.9	7 28.3	9.5	19 36.3	7.2	56.9
23	163 26.1	20.5	21 56.8	9.3	19 43.5	7.1	57.0
8 00	178 25.9	S22 20.2	36 25.1	9.3	N19 50.6	6.9	57.0
01	193 25.6	19.9	50 53.4	9.2	19 57.5	6.9	57.0
02	208 25.3	19.6	65 21.6	9.1	20 04.4	6.8	57.1
03	223 25.1 ..	19.3	79 49.7	9.0	20 11.2	6.6	57.1
04	238 24.8	18.9	94 17.7	8.9	20 17.8	6.6	57.1
05	253 24.5	18.6	108 45.6	8.8	20 24.4	6.4	57.2
06	268 24.3	S22 18.3	123 13.4	8.7	N20 30.8	6.3	57.2
07	283 24.0	17.9	137 41.1	8.7	20 37.1	6.3	57.2
08	298 23.7	17.6	152 08.8	8.5	20 43.4	6.1	57.3
09	313 23.5 ..	17.3	166 36.3	8.5	20 49.5	6.0	57.3
10	328 23.2	17.0	181 03.8	8.3	20 55.5	5.9	57.3
11	343 22.9	16.6	195 31.1	8.3	21 01.4	5.8	57.4
12	358 22.7	S22 16.3	209 58.4	8.2	N21 07.2	5.7	57.4
13	13 22.4	16.0	224 25.6	8.1	21 12.9	5.5	57.4
14	28 22.1	15.6	238 52.7	8.0	21 18.4	5.5	57.4
15	43 21.9 ..	15.3	253 19.7	7.9	21 23.9	5.3	57.5
16	58 21.6	15.0	267 46.6	7.9	21 29.2	5.2	57.5
17	73 21.3	14.6	282 13.5	7.7	21 34.4	5.1	57.5
18	88 21.1	S22 14.3	296 40.2	7.7	N21 39.5	4.9	57.6
19	103 20.8	14.0	311 06.9	7.6	21 44.4	4.8	57.6
20	118 20.6	13.6	325 33.5	7.5	21 49.2	4.8	57.6
21	133 20.3 ..	13.3	340 00.0	7.4	21 54.0	4.5	57.7
22	148 20.0	12.9	354 26.4	7.4	21 58.5	4.5	57.7
23	163 19.8	12.6	8 52.8	7.3	22 03.0	4.3	57.7
9 00	178 19.5	S22 12.3	23 19.1	7.1	N22 07.3	4.2	57.8
01	193 19.2	11.9	37 45.2	7.2	22 11.5	4.1	57.8
02	208 19.0	11.6	52 11.4	7.0	22 15.6	4.0	57.9
03	223 18.7 ..	11.2	66 37.4	6.9	22 19.6	3.8	57.9
04	238 18.5	10.9	81 03.3	6.9	22 23.4	3.7	57.9
05	253 18.2	10.5	95 29.2	6.8	22 27.1	3.5	57.9
06	268 17.9	S22 10.2	109 55.0	6.8	N22 30.6	3.4	58.0
07	283 17.7	09.8	124 20.8	6.6	22 34.0	3.3	58.0
08	298 17.4	09.5	138 46.4	6.6	22 37.3	3.1	58.0
09	313 17.2 ..	09.2	153 12.0	6.6	22 40.4	3.0	58.1
10	328 16.9	08.8	167 37.6	6.4	22 43.4	2.9	58.1
11	343 16.6	08.5	182 03.0	6.4	22 46.3	2.7	58.1
12	358 16.4	S22 08.1	196 28.4	6.3	N22 49.0	2.6	58.1
13	13 16.1	07.8	210 53.7	6.3	22 51.6	2.4	58.2
14	28 15.9	07.4	225 19.0	6.2	22 54.0	2.3	58.2
15	43 15.6 ..	07.1	239 44.2	6.1	22 56.3	2.2	58.2
16	58 15.3	06.7	254 09.3	6.1	22 58.5	2.0	58.3
17	73 15.1	06.3	268 34.4	6.0	23 00.5	1.9	58.3
18	88 14.8	S22 06.0	282 59.4	6.0	N23 02.4	1.7	58.3
19	103 14.6	05.6	297 24.4	5.9	23 04.1	1.6	58.4
20	118 14.3	05.3	311 49.3	5.9	23 05.7	1.4	58.4
21	133 14.1 ..	04.9	326 14.2	5.8	23 07.1	1.3	58.4
22	148 13.8	04.6	340 39.0	5.8	23 08.4	1.1	58.4
23	163 13.5	04.2	355 03.8	5.7	N23 09.5	1.0	58.5
	SD 16.3	d 0.3	SD 15.4		15.6		15.8

Days: TUESDAY (7), WEDNESDAY (8), THURSDAY (9)

Twilight / Sunrise / Moonrise

Lat.	Naut.	Civil	Sunrise	7	8	9	10
°	h m	h m	h m	h m	h m	h m	h m
N 72	08 16	10 21	■	09 33	□	□	□
N 70	07 58	09 37	■	10 53	□	□	□
68	07 44	09 08	11 12	11 32	11 14	□	□
66	07 33	08 46	10 14	11 59	12 02	12 15	13 03
64	07 23	08 29	09 41	12 20	12 33	13 00	13 53
62	07 14	08 15	09 16	12 37	12 56	13 30	14 25
60	07 07	08 02	08 57	12 51	13 15	13 52	14 48
N 58	07 00	07 52	08 42	13 03	13 31	14 10	15 07
56	06 54	07 42	08 28	13 14	13 44	14 26	15 23
54	06 48	07 34	08 16	13 23	13 56	14 39	15 37
52	06 43	07 26	08 06	13 32	14 06	14 51	15 49
50	06 38	07 19	07 57	13 39	14 15	15 01	15 59
45	06 28	07 04	07 38	13 56	14 35	15 23	16 21
N 40	06 18	06 52	07 22	14 09	14 50	15 40	16 39
35	06 09	06 41	07 09	14 20	15 04	15 55	16 54
30	06 01	06 31	06 57	14 30	15 16	16 08	17 07
20	05 46	06 13	06 37	14 47	15 36	16 30	17 29
N 10	05 30	05 57	06 19	15 02	15 53	16 49	17 48
0	05 14	05 40	06 03	15 17	16 10	17 07	18 06
S 10	04 56	05 23	05 46	15 31	16 26	17 24	18 24
20	04 35	05 04	05 28	15 46	16 44	17 44	18 43
30	04 07	04 40	05 07	16 04	17 05	18 06	19 05
35	03 50	04 26	04 55	16 14	17 17	18 19	19 18
40	03 28	04 08	04 41	16 26	17 31	18 34	19 33
45	02 59	03 47	04 24	16 40	17 47	18 52	19 51
S 50	02 18	03 20	04 03	16 57	18 08	19 14	20 13
52	01 54	03 06	03 53	17 05	18 17	19 25	20 23
54	01 21	02 49	03 41	17 14	18 28	19 37	20 35
56	////	02 30	03 28	17 25	18 41	19 51	20 49
58	////	02 04	03 13	17 36	18 55	20 07	21 04
S 60	////	01 28	02 55	17 50	19 12	20 26	21 23

Sunset / Twilight / Moonset

Lat.	Sunset	Civil	Naut.	7	8	9	10
°	h m	h m	h m	h m	h m	h m	h m
N 72	■	13 53	15 58	08 19	□	□	□
N 70	■	14 36	16 15	07 00	□	□	□
68	13 01	15 05	16 29	06 22	08 28	□	□
66	14 00	15 27	16 41	05 56	07 40	09 24	10 39
64	14 33	15 44	16 50	05 35	07 10	08 39	09 48
62	14 57	15 59	16 59	05 19	06 47	08 10	09 17
60	15 16	16 11	17 07	05 05	06 29	07 47	08 53
N 58	15 32	16 22	17 13	04 54	06 14	07 29	08 34
56	15 45	16 31	17 19	04 44	06 01	07 14	08 18
54	15 57	16 39	17 25	04 35	05 50	07 01	08 05
52	16 07	16 47	17 30	04 27	05 40	06 50	07 53
50	16 16	16 54	17 35	04 20	05 31	06 39	07 42
45	16 36	17 09	17 46	04 05	05 12	06 18	07 20
N 40	16 51	17 21	17 55	03 53	04 57	06 01	07 02
35	17 05	17 32	18 04	03 42	04 44	05 47	06 47
30	17 16	17 42	18 12	03 33	04 33	05 34	06 34
20	17 36	18 00	18 27	03 17	04 14	05 13	06 12
N 10	17 54	18 16	18 42	03 03	03 57	04 54	05 53
0	18 10	18 33	18 59	02 51	03 42	04 37	05 35
S 10	18 27	18 50	19 16	02 38	03 26	04 19	05 17
20	18 45	19 09	19 38	02 24	03 10	04 01	04 57
30	19 05	19 33	20 05	02 09	02 51	03 39	04 35
35	19 17	19 47	20 23	02 00	02 40	03 27	04 22
40	19 32	20 04	20 45	01 49	02 27	03 12	04 07
45	19 49	20 25	21 13	01 37	02 12	02 55	03 49
S 50	20 10	20 53	21 54	01 23	01 54	02 34	03 26
52	20 20	21 06	22 17	01 16	01 46	02 24	03 15
54	20 31	21 23	22 50	01 09	01 36	02 13	03 03
56	20 44	21 42	////	01 00	01 26	02 00	02 49
58	20 59	22 07	////	00 51	01 13	01 46	02 33
S 60	21 17	22 42	////	00 40	00 59	01 28	02 14

SUN and MOON

Day	Eqn. of Time 00h	Eqn. of Time 12h	Mer. Pass.	Mer. Pass. Upper	Mer. Pass. Lower	Age	Phase
d	m s	m s	h m	h m	h m	d	%
7	05 50	06 03	12 06	21 29	09 03	12	88
8	06 16	06 29	12 06	22 23	09 56	13	94
9	06 41	06 54	12 07	23 21	10 51	14	98 ○

UT	ARIES GHA	VENUS −4.0 GHA	Dec	MARS +1.5 GHA	Dec	JUPITER −1.8 GHA	Dec	SATURN +0.5 GHA	Dec
10 00	108 59.3	140 43.3	S14 39.3	226 27.4	S20 45.8	189 29.0	S23 04.4	174 44.8	S21 31.5
01	124 01.8	155 42.8	38.2	241 28.1	46.2	204 30.8	04.4	189 46.9	31.5
02	139 04.2	170 42.3	37.2	256 28.8	46.5	219 32.7	04.4	204 49.1	31.4
03	154 06.7	185 41.8 ..	36.1	271 29.5 ..	46.9	234 34.5 ..	04.3	219 51.2 ..	31.4
04	169 09.2	200 41.4	35.0	286 30.2	47.2	249 36.4	04.3	234 53.4	31.3
05	184 11.6	215 40.9	33.9	301 30.9	47.5	264 38.2	04.3	249 55.5	31.3
06	199 14.1	230 40.4	S14 32.8	316 31.6	S20 47.9	279 40.1	S23 04.2	264 57.7	S21 31.3
07	214 16.6	245 39.9	31.7	331 32.3	48.2	294 41.9	04.2	279 59.8	31.2
08	229 19.0	260 39.5	30.6	346 33.0	48.5	309 43.7	04.2	295 02.0	31.2
F 09	244 21.5	275 39.0 ..	29.6	1 33.7 ..	48.9	324 45.6 ..	04.1	310 04.1 ..	31.1
R 10	259 24.0	290 38.5	28.5	16 34.3	49.2	339 47.4	04.1	325 06.3	31.1
I 11	274 26.4	305 38.1	27.4	31 35.0	49.5	354 49.3	04.0	340 08.4	31.0
D 12	289 28.9	320 37.6	S14 26.3	46 35.7	S20 49.9	9 51.1	S23 04.0	355 10.6	S21 31.0
A 13	304 31.3	335 37.1	25.2	61 36.4	50.2	24 53.0	04.0	10 12.7	30.9
Y 14	319 33.8	350 36.6	24.1	76 37.1	50.5	39 54.8	03.9	25 14.9	30.9
15	334 36.3	5 36.2 ..	23.0	91 37.8 ..	50.9	54 56.7 ..	03.9	40 17.0 ..	30.8
16	349 38.7	20 35.7	21.9	106 38.5	51.2	69 58.5	03.9	55 19.2	30.8
17	4 41.2	35 35.2	20.8	121 39.2	51.5	85 00.3	03.8	70 21.3	30.8
18	19 43.7	50 34.8	S14 19.8	136 39.9	S20 51.9	100 02.2	S23 03.8	85 23.5	S21 30.7
19	34 46.1	65 34.3	18.7	151 40.6	52.2	115 04.0	03.8	100 25.6	30.7
20	49 48.6	80 33.8	17.6	166 41.3	52.5	130 05.9	03.7	115 27.8	30.6
21	64 51.1	95 33.4 ..	16.5	181 42.0 ..	52.8	145 07.7 ..	03.7	130 29.9 ..	30.6
22	79 53.5	110 32.9	15.4	196 42.6	53.2	160 09.6	03.7	145 32.1	30.5
23	94 56.0	125 32.5	14.3	211 43.3	53.5	175 11.4	03.6	160 34.2	30.5
11 00	109 58.5	140 32.0	S14 13.2	226 44.0	S20 53.8	190 13.3	S23 03.6	175 36.4	S21 30.4
01	125 00.9	155 31.5	12.1	241 44.7	54.2	205 15.1	03.6	190 38.5	30.4
02	140 03.4	170 31.1	11.0	256 45.4	54.5	220 16.9	03.5	205 40.7	30.3
03	155 05.8	185 30.6 ..	09.9	271 46.1 ..	54.8	235 18.8 ..	03.5	220 42.8 ..	30.3
04	170 08.3	200 30.1	08.8	286 46.8	55.1	250 20.6	03.5	235 45.0	30.3
05	185 10.8	215 29.7	07.7	301 47.5	55.5	265 22.5	03.4	250 47.1	30.2
06	200 13.2	230 29.2	S14 06.6	316 48.2	S20 55.8	280 24.3	S23 03.4	265 49.2	S21 30.2
07	215 15.7	245 28.8	05.5	331 48.9	56.1	295 26.2	03.4	280 51.4	30.1
S 08	230 18.2	260 28.3	04.4	346 49.5	56.5	310 28.0	03.3	295 53.5	30.1
A 09	245 20.6	275 27.9 ..	03.3	1 50.2 ..	56.8	325 29.9 ..	03.3	310 55.7 ..	30.0
T 10	260 23.1	290 27.4	02.2	16 50.9	57.1	340 31.7	03.3	325 57.8	30.0
U 11	275 25.6	305 26.9	01.1	31 51.6	57.4	355 33.5	03.2	341 00.0	29.9
R 12	290 28.0	320 26.5	S14 00.0	46 52.3	S20 57.8	10 35.4	S23 03.2	356 02.1	S21 29.9
D 13	305 30.5	335 26.0	13 58.9	61 53.0	58.1	25 37.2	03.1	11 04.3	29.8
A 14	320 32.9	350 25.6	57.8	76 53.7	58.4	40 39.1	03.1	26 06.4	29.8
Y 15	335 35.4	5 25.1 ..	56.7	91 54.4 ..	58.7	55 40.9 ..	03.1	41 08.6 ..	29.8
16	350 37.9	20 24.7	55.6	106 55.0	59.1	70 42.8	03.0	56 10.7	29.7
17	5 40.3	35 24.2	54.5	121 55.7	59.4	85 44.6	03.0	71 12.9	29.7
18	20 42.8	50 23.8	S13 53.4	136 56.4	S20 59.7	100 46.5	S23 03.0	86 15.0	S21 29.6
19	35 45.3	65 23.3	52.3	151 57.1	21 00.0	115 48.3	02.9	101 17.2	29.6
20	50 47.7	80 22.9	51.1	166 57.8	00.4	130 50.1	02.9	116 19.3	29.5
21	65 50.2	95 22.4 ..	50.0	181 58.5 ..	00.7	145 52.0 ..	02.9	131 21.5 ..	29.5
22	80 52.7	110 22.0	48.9	196 59.2	01.0	160 53.8	02.8	146 23.6	29.4
23	95 55.1	125 21.5	47.8	211 59.9	01.3	175 55.7	02.8	161 25.8	29.4
12 00	110 57.6	140 21.1	S13 46.7	227 00.5	S21 01.6	190 57.5	S23 02.8	176 27.9	S21 29.3
01	126 00.1	155 20.6	45.6	242 01.2	02.0	205 59.4	02.7	191 30.1	29.3
02	141 02.5	170 20.2	44.5	257 01.9	02.2	221 01.2	02.7	206 32.2	29.2
03	156 05.0	185 19.7 ..	43.4	272 02.6 ..	02.6	236 03.1 ..	02.7	221 34.4 ..	29.2
04	171 07.4	200 19.3	42.3	287 03.3	02.9	251 04.9	02.6	236 36.5	29.2
05	186 09.9	215 18.8	41.1	302 04.0	03.3	266 06.7	02.6	251 38.7	29.1
06	201 12.4	230 18.4	S13 40.0	317 04.7	S21 03.6	281 08.6	S23 02.5	266 40.8	S21 29.1
07	216 14.8	245 17.9	38.9	332 05.3	03.9	296 10.4	02.5	281 43.0	29.0
08	231 17.3	260 17.5	37.8	347 06.0	04.2	311 12.3	02.5	296 45.1	29.0
S 09	246 19.8	275 17.1 ..	36.7	2 06.7 ..	04.5	326 14.1 ..	02.4	311 47.3 ..	28.9
U 10	261 22.2	290 16.6	35.6	17 07.4	04.9	341 16.0	02.4	326 49.4	28.9
N 11	276 24.7	305 16.2	34.4	32 08.1	05.2	356 17.8	02.4	341 51.6	28.8
D 12	291 27.2	320 15.7	S13 33.3	47 08.8	S21 05.5	11 19.7	S23 02.3	356 53.7	S21 28.8
A 13	306 29.6	335 15.3	32.2	62 09.4	05.8	26 21.5	02.3	11 55.9	28.7
Y 14	321 32.1	350 14.8	31.1	77 10.1	06.1	41 23.4	02.3	26 58.0	28.7
15	336 34.6	5 14.4 ..	30.0	92 10.8 ..	06.4	56 25.2 ..	02.2	42 00.2 ..	28.7
16	351 37.0	20 14.0	28.9	107 11.5	06.8	71 27.0	02.2	57 02.3	28.6
17	6 39.5	35 13.5	27.7	122 12.2	07.1	86 28.9	02.1	72 04.5	28.6
18	21 41.9	50 13.1	S13 26.6	137 12.9	S21 07.4	101 30.7	S23 02.1	87 06.6	S21 28.5
19	36 44.4	65 12.7	25.5	152 13.5	07.7	116 32.6	02.1	102 08.8	28.5
20	51 46.9	80 12.2	24.4	167 14.2	08.0	131 34.4	02.0	117 10.9	28.4
21	66 49.3	95 11.8 ..	23.2	182 14.9 ..	08.3	146 36.3 ..	02.0	132 13.1 ..	28.4
22	81 51.8	110 11.3	22.1	197 15.6	08.7	161 38.1	02.0	147 15.2	28.3
23	96 54.3	125 10.9	21.0	212 16.3	09.0	176 40.0	01.9	162 17.4	28.3
Mer. Pass. 16 37.4		v −0.5	d 1.1	v 0.7	d 0.3	v 1.8	d 0.0	v 2.1	d 0.0

STARS

Name	SHA	Dec
Acamar	315 14.7	S40 13.8
Achernar	335 23.3	S57 08.6
Acrux	173 04.1	S63 12.2
Adhara	255 08.6	S29 00.1
Aldebaran	290 43.9	N16 32.8
Alioth	166 16.6	N55 50.9
Alkaid	152 55.4	N49 12.6
Alnair	27 38.4	S46 52.1
Alnilam	275 41.5	S 1 11.5
Alphard	217 51.4	S 8 44.7
Alphecca	126 07.4	N26 38.8
Alpheratz	357 38.9	N29 12.1
Altair	62 04.2	N 8 55.3
Ankaa	353 11.3	S42 12.2
Antares	112 21.0	S26 28.4
Arcturus	145 51.7	N19 04.7
Atria	107 19.2	S69 03.5
Avior	234 15.6	S59 34.4
Bellatrix	278 26.9	N 6 21.9
Betelgeuse	270 56.1	N 7 24.5
Canopus	263 53.6	S52 42.5
Capella	280 27.3	N46 01.0
Deneb	49 28.9	N45 21.2
Denebola	182 28.9	N14 27.6
Diphda	348 51.4	S17 52.9
Dubhe	193 45.7	N61 38.4
Elnath	278 06.6	N28 37.3
Eltanin	90 44.6	N51 29.1
Enif	33 43.0	N 9 58.0
Fomalhaut	15 19.2	S29 31.2
Gacrux	171 55.8	S57 13.1
Gienah	175 47.6	S17 39.0
Hadar	148 41.6	S60 27.7
Hamal	327 55.6	N23 33.4
Kaus Aust.	83 38.2	S34 22.4
Kochab	137 20.6	N74 04.2
Markab	13 34.0	N15 18.7
Menkar	314 10.2	N 4 09.9
Menkent	148 02.3	S36 27.8
Miaplacidus	221 38.0	S69 47.8
Mirfak	308 33.6	N49 56.0
Nunki	75 53.1	S26 16.2
Peacock	53 12.7	S56 40.3
Pollux	243 21.8	N27 58.5
Procyon	244 54.7	N 5 10.3
Rasalhague	96 02.6	N12 32.8
Regulus	207 38.5	N11 52.1
Rigel	281 07.4	S 8 10.9
Rigil Kent.	139 45.8	S60 54.6
Sabik	102 07.7	S15 44.8
Schedar	349 35.5	N56 39.0
Shaula	96 16.2	S37 06.9
Sirius	258 29.4	S16 44.8
Spica	158 26.5	S11 15.8
Suhail	222 48.7	S43 30.7
Vega	80 36.3	N38 48.1
Zuben'ubi	137 00.6	S16 07.3

	SHA	Mer. Pass.
Venus	30 33.5	14 38
Mars	116 45.6	8 53
Jupiter	80 14.8	11 18
Saturn	65 37.9	12 16

SUN / MOON

UT	SUN GHA	SUN Dec	MOON GHA	v	MOON Dec	d	HP
d h	° ′	° ′	° ′	′	° ′	′	′
10 00	178 13.3	S22 03.9	9 28.5	5.6	N23 10.5	0.9	58.5
01	193 13.0	03.5	23 53.1	5.6	23 11.4	0.7	58.5
02	208 12.8	03.1	38 17.7	5.6	23 12.1	0.5	58.6
03	223 12.5	.. 02.8	52 42.3	5.6	23 12.6	0.4	58.6
04	238 12.3	02.4	67 06.9	5.4	23 13.0	0.2	58.6
05	253 12.0	02.0	81 31.3	5.5	23 13.2	0.1	58.6
06	268 11.7	S22 01.7	95 55.8	5.4	N23 13.3	0.1	58.7
07	283 11.5	01.3	110 20.2	5.4	23 13.2	0.2	58.7
F 08	298 11.2	01.0	124 44.6	5.4	23 13.0	0.4	58.7
R 09	313 11.0	.. 00.6	139 09.0	5.3	23 12.6	0.5	58.8
I 10	328 10.7	22 00.2	153 33.3	5.3	23 12.1	0.7	58.8
D 11	343 10.5	21 59.9	167 57.6	5.2	23 11.4	0.8	58.8
A 12	358 10.2	S21 59.5	182 21.8	5.3	N23 10.6	1.0	58.8
Y 13	13 10.0	59.1	196 46.1	5.2	23 09.6	1.2	58.9
14	28 09.7	58.7	211 10.3	5.2	23 08.4	1.3	58.9
15	43 09.5	.. 58.4	225 34.5	5.2	23 07.1	1.4	58.9
16	58 09.2	58.0	239 58.7	5.1	23 05.7	1.6	58.9
17	73 09.0	57.6	254 22.8	5.2	23 04.1	1.8	59.0
18	88 08.7	S21 57.3	268 47.0	5.1	N23 02.3	1.9	59.0
19	103 08.4	56.9	283 11.1	5.1	23 00.4	2.1	59.0
20	118 08.2	56.5	297 35.2	5.1	22 58.3	2.2	59.0
21	133 07.9	.. 56.1	311 59.3	5.1	22 56.1	2.4	59.1
22	148 07.7	55.8	326 23.4	5.1	22 53.7	2.6	59.1
23	163 07.4	55.4	340 47.5	5.1	22 51.1	2.7	59.1
11 00	178 07.2	S21 55.0	355 11.6	5.0	N22 48.4	2.8	59.1
01	193 06.9	54.6	9 35.6	5.1	22 45.6	3.0	59.1
02	208 06.7	54.3	23 59.7	5.1	22 42.6	3.2	59.2
03	223 06.4	.. 53.9	38 23.8	5.1	22 39.4	3.3	59.2
04	238 06.2	53.5	52 47.9	5.1	22 36.1	3.5	59.2
05	253 05.9	53.1	67 12.0	5.1	22 32.6	3.6	59.2
06	268 05.7	S21 52.7	81 36.1	5.1	N22 29.0	3.8	59.3
S 07	283 05.4	52.4	96 00.2	5.1	22 25.2	4.0	59.3
A 08	298 05.2	52.0	110 24.3	5.1	22 21.2	4.1	59.3
T 09	313 04.9	.. 51.6	124 48.4	5.1	22 17.1	4.2	59.3
U 10	328 04.7	51.2	139 12.5	5.2	22 12.9	4.3	59.3
R 11	343 04.4	50.8	153 36.7	5.1	22 08.5	4.5	59.4
D 12	358 04.2	S21 50.4	168 00.8	5.2	N22 04.0	4.7	59.4
A 13	13 04.0	50.0	182 25.0	5.2	21 59.3	4.9	59.4
Y 14	28 03.7	49.7	196 49.2	5.2	21 54.4	5.0	59.4
15	43 03.5	.. 49.3	211 13.4	5.3	21 49.4	5.1	59.4
16	58 03.2	48.9	225 37.7	5.2	21 44.3	5.3	59.5
17	73 03.0	48.5	240 01.9	5.3	21 39.0	5.5	59.5
18	88 02.7	S21 48.1	254 26.2	5.4	N21 33.5	5.6	59.5
19	103 02.5	47.7	268 50.6	5.3	21 27.9	5.7	59.5
20	118 02.2	47.3	283 14.9	5.4	21 22.2	5.9	59.5
21	133 02.0	.. 46.9	297 39.3	5.4	21 16.3	6.1	59.5
22	148 01.7	46.5	312 03.7	5.4	21 10.2	6.1	59.6
23	163 01.5	46.1	326 28.1	5.5	21 04.1	6.4	59.6
12 00	178 01.2	S21 45.8	340 52.6	5.6	N20 57.7	6.4	59.6
01	193 01.0	45.4	355 17.2	5.5	20 51.3	6.7	59.6
02	208 00.8	45.0	9 41.7	5.6	20 44.6	6.7	59.6
03	223 00.5	.. 44.6	24 06.3	5.6	20 37.9	6.9	59.6
04	238 00.3	44.2	38 30.9	5.7	20 31.0	7.0	59.7
05	253 00.0	43.8	52 55.6	5.7	20 24.0	7.2	59.7
06	267 59.8	S21 43.4	67 20.3	5.8	N20 16.8	7.3	59.7
07	282 59.5	43.0	81 45.1	5.8	20 09.5	7.5	59.7
S 08	297 59.3	42.6	96 09.9	5.9	20 02.0	7.5	59.7
U 09	312 59.1	.. 42.2	110 34.8	5.9	19 54.5	7.7	59.7
N 10	327 58.8	41.8	124 59.7	5.9	19 46.8	7.9	59.7
D 11	342 58.6	41.4	139 24.6	6.0	19 38.9	8.0	59.7
A 12	357 58.3	S21 41.0	153 49.6	6.1	N19 30.9	8.1	59.7
Y 13	12 58.1	40.6	168 14.7	6.1	19 22.8	8.2	59.8
14	27 57.8	40.2	182 39.8	6.1	19 14.6	8.3	59.8
15	42 57.6	.. 39.7	197 04.9	6.2	19 06.2	8.5	59.8
16	57 57.4	39.3	211 30.1	6.3	18 57.7	8.6	59.8
17	72 57.1	38.9	225 55.4	6.3	18 49.1	8.7	59.8
18	87 56.9	S21 38.5	240 20.7	6.4	N18 40.3	8.8	59.8
19	102 56.6	38.1	254 46.1	6.4	18 31.5	9.0	59.8
20	117 56.4	37.7	269 11.5	6.5	18 22.5	9.1	59.8
21	132 56.2	.. 37.3	283 37.0	6.6	18 13.4	9.3	59.8
22	147 55.9	36.9	298 02.6	6.6	18 04.1	9.3	59.8
23	162 55.7	36.5	312 28.2	6.6	N17 54.8	9.5	59.8
	SD 16.3	d 0.4	SD 16.0		16.2		16.3

Twilight / Moonrise

Lat.	Naut.	Civil	Sunrise	Moonrise 10	11	12	13
°	h m	h m	h m	h m	h m	h m	h m
N 72	08 10	10 09	■	□	□	□	17 19
N 70	07 54	09 30	■	□	□	15 11	17 52
68	07 41	09 03	10 55	□	13 24	16 05	18 16
66	07 30	08 42	10 06	13 03	14 41	16 37	18 34
64	07 20	08 25	09 35	13 53	15 18	17 01	18 49
62	07 12	08 12	09 12	14 25	15 44	17 20	19 01
60	07 05	08 00	08 54	14 48	16 05	17 35	19 12
N 58	06 58	07 49	08 39	15 07	16 22	17 48	19 21
56	06 52	07 40	08 26	15 23	16 36	18 00	19 28
54	06 47	07 32	08 14	15 37	16 48	18 10	19 35
52	06 42	07 25	08 05	15 49	16 59	18 18	19 42
50	06 37	07 18	07 56	15 59	17 09	18 26	19 47
45	06 27	07 04	07 37	16 21	17 29	18 43	20 00
N 40	06 18	06 51	07 21	16 39	17 45	18 56	20 10
35	06 09	06 41	07 08	16 54	17 59	19 08	20 18
30	06 01	06 31	06 57	17 07	18 11	19 18	20 26
20	05 46	06 14	06 37	17 29	18 31	19 35	20 38
N 10	05 32	05 58	06 20	17 48	18 49	19 50	20 50
0	05 16	05 42	06 04	18 06	19 06	20 04	21 00
S 10	04 58	05 25	05 48	18 24	19 22	20 18	21 11
20	04 37	05 06	05 30	18 43	19 40	20 33	21 22
30	04 10	04 43	05 10	19 05	20 00	20 50	21 34
35	03 53	04 29	04 58	19 18	20 12	21 00	21 42
40	03 31	04 12	04 44	19 33	20 25	21 11	21 50
45	03 04	03 51	04 27	19 51	20 41	21 24	22 00
S 50	02 24	03 24	04 07	20 13	21 01	21 40	22 11
52	02 02	03 11	03 57	20 23	21 10	21 47	22 17
54	01 31	02 55	03 46	20 35	21 21	21 56	22 23
56	00 25	02 36	03 33	20 49	21 33	22 05	22 29
58	////	02 12	03 18	21 04	21 46	22 15	22 36
S 60	////	01 39	03 01	21 23	22 02	22 27	22 45

Sunset / Twilight / Moonset

Lat.	Sunset	Civil	Naut.	Moonset 10	11	12	13
°	h m	h m	h m	h m	h m	h m	h m
N 72	■	14 07	16 06	□	□	□	12 34
N 70	■	14 46	16 22	□	□	12 41	11 59
68	13 21	15 13	16 35	□	12 24	11 46	11 34
66	14 10	15 34	16 46	10 39	11 06	11 13	11 14
64	14 41	15 50	16 56	09 48	10 28	10 48	10 58
62	15 04	16 04	17 04	09 17	10 02	10 29	10 45
60	15 22	16 16	17 11	08 53	09 41	10 13	10 34
N 58	15 37	16 26	17 18	08 34	09 24	09 59	10 24
56	15 50	16 35	17 23	08 18	09 09	09 47	10 15
54	16 01	16 44	17 29	08 05	08 57	09 37	10 07
52	16 11	16 51	17 34	07 53	08 46	09 28	10 00
50	16 20	16 58	17 38	07 42	08 36	09 19	09 54
45	16 39	17 12	17 49	07 20	08 15	09 02	09 41
N 40	16 54	17 24	17 58	07 02	07 58	08 47	09 29
35	17 07	17 35	18 06	06 47	07 44	08 35	09 20
30	17 19	17 45	18 14	06 34	07 31	08 24	09 11
20	17 38	18 02	18 29	06 12	07 10	08 05	08 56
N 10	17 55	18 18	18 44	05 53	06 52	07 49	08 43
0	18 11	18 34	19 00	05 35	06 34	07 34	08 31
S 10	18 28	18 50	19 17	05 17	06 17	07 18	08 19
20	18 45	19 09	19 38	04 57	05 58	07 02	08 05
30	19 05	19 32	20 05	04 35	05 37	06 42	07 50
35	19 17	19 47	20 22	04 22	05 24	06 31	07 41
40	19 31	20 03	20 43	04 07	05 09	06 18	07 31
45	19 48	20 24	21 11	03 49	04 52	06 03	07 19
S 50	20 08	20 50	21 50	03 26	04 30	05 44	07 04
52	20 18	21 04	22 12	03 15	04 20	05 35	06 57
54	20 29	21 19	22 42	03 03	04 08	05 25	06 50
56	20 41	21 38	23 39	02 49	03 55	05 14	06 41
58	20 56	22 01	////	02 33	03 39	05 01	06 31
S 60	21 13	22 34	////	02 14	03 20	04 45	06 20

SUN / MOON

Day	SUN Eqn. of Time 00h	SUN Eqn. of Time 12h	Mer. Pass.	MOON Mer. Pass. Upper	MOON Mer. Pass. Lower	Age	Phase
d	m s	m s	h m	h m	h m	d	%
10	07 06	07 19	12 07	24 20	11 50	15	100
11	07 31	07 43	12 08	00 20	12 50	16	99
12	07 55	08 06	12 08	01 20	13 49	17	96

UT	ARIES	VENUS −4·0		MARS +1·5		JUPITER −1·8		SATURN +0·5		STARS		
d h	GHA	GHA	Dec	GHA	Dec	GHA	Dec	GHA	Dec	Name	SHA	Dec
	° ′	° ′	° ′	° ′	° ′	° ′	° ′	° ′	° ′		° ′	° ′
13 00	111 56.7	140 10.5	S13 19.9	227 17.0	S21 09.3	191 41.8	S23 01.9	177 19.5	S21 28.2	Acamar	315 14.7	S40 13.8
01	126 59.2	155 10.0	18.7	242 17.6	09.6	206 43.7	01.9	192 21.7	28.2	Achernar	335 23.3	S57 08.6
02	142 01.7	170 09.6	17.6	257 18.3	09.9	221 45.5	01.8	207 23.8	28.1	Acrux	173 04.1	S63 12.2
03	157 04.1	185 09.2	.. 16.5	272 19.0	.. 10.2	236 47.4	.. 01.8	222 26.0	.. 28.1	Adhara	255 08.6	S29 00.1
04	172 06.6	200 08.7	15.4	287 19.7	10.5	251 49.2	01.7	237 28.1	28.0	Aldebaran	290 43.9	N16 32.8
05	187 09.1	215 08.3	14.2	302 20.4	10.9	266 51.0	01.7	252 30.3	28.0			
06	202 11.5	230 07.9	S13 13.1	317 21.0	S21 11.2	281 52.9	S23 01.7	267 32.4	S21 28.0	Alioth	166 16.6	N55 50.9
07	217 14.0	245 07.5	12.0	332 21.7	11.5	296 54.7	01.6	282 34.6	27.9	Alkaid	152 55.3	N49 12.6
08	232 16.4	260 07.0	10.8	347 22.4	11.8	311 56.6	01.6	297 36.7	27.9	Alnair	27 38.4	S46 52.1
09	247 18.9	275 06.6	.. 09.7	2 23.1	.. 12.1	326 58.4	.. 01.6	312 38.9	.. 27.8	Alnilam	275 41.5	S 1 11.5
10	262 21.4	290 06.2	08.6	17 23.8	12.4	342 00.3	01.5	327 41.0	27.8	Alphard	217 51.4	S 8 44.7
11	277 23.8	305 05.7	07.5	32 24.4	12.7	357 02.1	01.5	342 43.1	27.7			
12	292 26.3	320 05.3	S13 06.3	47 25.1	S21 13.0	12 04.0	S23 01.5	357 45.3	S21 27.7	Alphecca	126 07.4	N26 38.8
13	307 28.8	335 04.9	05.2	62 25.8	13.4	27 05.8	01.4	12 47.4	27.6	Alpheratz	357 39.0	N29 12.1
14	322 31.2	350 04.5	04.1	77 26.5	13.7	42 07.7	01.4	27 49.5	27.5	Altair	62 04.2	N 8 55.3
15	337 33.7	5 04.0	.. 02.9	92 27.2	.. 14.0	57 09.5	.. 01.3	42 51.8	.. 27.4	Ankaa	353 11.3	S42 12.2
16	352 36.2	20 03.6	01.8	107 27.8	14.3	72 11.4	01.3	57 54.1	27.4	Antares	112 21.0	S26 28.4
17	7 38.6	35 03.2	13 00.7	122 28.5	14.6	87 13.2	01.3	72 56.2	27.4			
18	22 41.1	50 02.8	S12 59.5	137 29.2	S21 14.9	102 15.1	S23 01.2	87 58.3	S21 27.4	Arcturus	145 51.7	N19 04.7
19	37 43.5	65 02.3	58.4	152 29.9	15.2	117 16.9	01.2	103 00.4	27.4	Atria	107 19.2	S69 03.5
20	52 46.0	80 01.9	57.2	167 30.6	15.5	132 18.7	01.2	118 02.6	27.3	Avior	234 15.6	S59 34.4
21	67 48.5	95 01.5	.. 56.1	182 31.2	.. 15.8	147 20.6	.. 01.1	133 04.7	.. 27.3	Bellatrix	278 26.9	N 6 21.9
22	82 50.9	110 01.1	55.0	197 31.9	16.1	162 22.4	01.1	148 06.9	27.2	Betelgeuse	270 56.1	N 7 24.5
23	97 53.4	125 00.6	53.8	212 32.6	16.5	177 24.3	01.0	163 09.0	27.2			
14 00	112 55.9	140 00.2	S12 52.7	227 33.3	S21 16.8	192 26.1	S23 01.0	178 11.2	S21 27.1	Canopus	263 53.6	S52 42.6
01	127 58.3	154 59.8	51.6	242 34.0	17.1	207 28.0	01.0	193 13.3	27.1	Capella	280 27.3	N46 01.0
02	143 00.8	169 59.4	50.4	257 34.6	17.4	222 29.8	00.9	208 15.4	27.0	Deneb	49 28.9	N45 21.2
03	158 03.3	184 59.0	.. 49.3	272 35.3	.. 17.7	237 31.7	.. 00.9	223 17.6	.. 27.0	Denebola	182 28.9	N14 27.6
04	173 05.7	199 58.5	48.1	287 36.0	18.0	252 33.5	00.9	238 19.7	26.9	Diphda	348 51.4	S17 52.9
05	188 08.2	214 58.1	47.0	302 36.7	18.3	267 35.4	00.8	253 21.9	26.9			
06	203 10.7	229 57.7	S12 45.9	317 37.3	S21 18.6	282 37.2	S23 00.8	268 24.0	S21 26.9	Dubhe	193 45.7	N61 38.4
07	218 13.1	244 57.3	44.7	332 38.0	18.9	297 39.1	00.7	283 26.2	26.8	Elnath	278 06.6	N28 37.3
08	233 15.6	259 56.9	43.6	347 38.7	19.2	312 40.9	00.7	298 28.3	26.8	Eltanin	90 44.5	N51 29.1
09	248 18.0	274 56.5	.. 42.4	2 39.4	.. 19.5	327 42.8	.. 00.7	313 30.5	.. 26.7	Enif	33 43.0	N 9 58.0
10	263 20.5	289 56.0	41.3	17 40.0	19.8	342 44.6	00.6	328 32.6	26.7	Fomalhaut	15 19.2	S29 31.2
11	278 23.0	304 55.6	40.1	32 40.7	20.1	357 46.5	00.6	343 34.8	26.6			
12	293 25.4	319 55.2	S12 39.0	47 41.4	S21 20.4	12 48.3	S23 00.6	358 36.9	S21 26.6	Gacrux	171 55.7	S57 13.2
13	308 27.9	334 54.8	37.8	62 42.1	20.7	27 50.2	00.5	13 39.1	26.5	Gienah	175 47.5	S17 39.0
14	323 30.4	349 54.4	36.7	77 42.8	21.0	42 52.0	00.5	28 41.2	26.5	Hadar	148 41.6	S60 27.7
15	338 32.8	4 54.0	.. 35.6	92 43.4	.. 21.3	57 53.8	.. 00.4	43 43.4	.. 26.4	Hamal	327 55.6	N23 33.4
16	353 35.3	19 53.6	34.4	107 44.1	21.6	72 55.7	00.4	58 45.5	26.4	Kaus Aust.	83 38.2	S34 22.4
17	8 37.8	34 53.2	33.3	122 44.8	22.0	87 57.5	00.4	73 47.7	26.3			
18	23 40.2	49 52.8	S12 32.1	137 45.5	S21 22.3	102 59.4	S23 00.3	88 49.8	S21 26.3	Kochab	137 20.5	N74 04.2
19	38 42.7	64 52.3	31.0	152 46.1	22.6	118 01.2	00.3	103 52.0	26.2	Markab	13 34.0	N15 18.7
20	53 45.2	79 51.9	29.8	167 46.8	22.9	133 03.1	00.3	118 54.1	26.2	Menkar	314 10.2	N 4 09.9
21	68 47.6	94 51.5	.. 28.7	182 47.5	.. 23.2	148 04.9	.. 00.2	133 56.3	.. 26.2	Menkent	148 02.3	S36 27.8
22	83 50.1	109 51.1	27.5	197 48.2	23.5	163 06.8	00.2	148 58.4	26.1	Miaplacidus	221 37.9	S69 47.8
23	98 52.5	124 50.7	26.4	212 48.8	23.8	178 08.6	00.1	164 00.6	26.1			
15 00	113 55.0	139 50.3	S12 25.2	227 49.5	S21 24.1	193 10.5	S23 00.1	179 02.7	S21 26.0	Mirfak	308 33.6	N49 56.0
01	128 57.5	154 49.9	24.1	242 50.2	24.4	208 12.3	00.1	194 04.9	26.0	Nunki	75 53.1	S26 16.2
02	143 59.9	169 49.5	22.9	257 50.8	24.7	223 14.2	00.0	209 07.0	25.9	Peacock	53 12.7	S56 44.3
03	159 02.4	184 49.1	.. 21.7	272 51.5	.. 25.0	238 16.0	23 00.0	224 09.2	.. 25.9	Pollux	243 21.8	N27 58.5
04	174 04.9	199 48.7	20.6	287 52.2	25.3	253 17.9	22 59.9	239 11.3	25.8	Procyon	244 54.7	N 5 10.3
05	189 07.3	214 48.3	19.4	302 52.9	25.6	268 19.7	59.9	254 13.5	25.8			
06	204 09.8	229 47.9	S12 18.3	317 53.5	S21 25.9	283 21.6	S22 59.9	269 15.6	S21 25.7	Rasalhague	96 02.6	N12 32.8
07	219 12.3	244 47.5	17.1	332 54.2	26.2	298 23.4	59.8	284 17.8	25.7	Regulus	207 38.4	N11 52.1
08	234 14.7	259 47.1	16.0	347 54.9	26.5	313 25.3	59.8	299 19.9	25.6	Rigel	281 07.4	S 8 10.9
09	249 17.2	274 46.7	.. 14.8	2 55.6	.. 26.8	328 27.1	.. 59.8	314 22.1	.. 25.6	Rigil Kent.	139 45.8	S60 54.6
10	264 19.6	289 46.3	13.7	17 56.2	27.1	343 29.0	59.7	329 24.2	25.5	Sabik	102 07.6	S15 44.8
11	279 22.1	304 45.9	12.5	32 56.9	27.3	358 30.8	59.7	344 26.4	25.5			
12	294 24.6	319 45.5	S12 11.3	47 57.6	S21 27.6	13 32.7	S22 59.6	359 28.5	S21 25.5	Schedar	349 35.5	N56 39.0
13	309 27.0	334 45.1	10.2	62 58.3	27.9	28 34.5	59.6	14 30.7	25.4	Shaula	96 16.1	S37 06.9
14	324 29.5	349 44.7	09.0	77 58.9	28.2	43 36.4	59.6	29 32.8	25.4	Sirius	258 29.4	S16 44.8
15	339 32.0	4 44.3	.. 07.9	92 59.6	.. 28.5	58 38.2	.. 59.5	44 35.0	.. 25.3	Spica	158 26.5	S11 15.8
16	354 34.4	19 43.9	06.7	108 00.3	28.8	73 40.1	59.5	59 37.1	25.3	Suhail	222 48.7	S43 30.7
17	9 36.9	34 43.5	05.5	123 00.9	29.1	88 41.9	59.4	74 39.3	25.2			
18	24 39.4	49 43.1	S12 04.4	138 01.6	S21 29.4	103 43.8	S22 59.4	89 41.4	S21 25.2	Vega	80 36.3	N38 48.1
19	39 41.8	64 42.7	03.2	153 02.3	29.7	118 45.6	59.4	104 43.6	25.1	Zuben'ubi	137 00.5	S16 07.3
20	54 44.3	79 42.3	02.1	168 03.0	30.0	133 47.5	59.3	119 45.7	25.1		SHA	Mer. Pass.
21	69 46.8	94 41.9	12 00.9	183 03.6	.. 30.3	148 49.3	.. 59.3	134 47.9	.. 25.0		° ′	h m
22	84 49.2	109 41.5	11 59.7	198 04.3	30.6	163 51.2	59.3	149 50.0	25.0	Venus	27 04.4	14 40
23	99 51.7	124 41.1	S11 58.6	213 05.0	30.9	178 53.0	59.2	164 52.2	24.9	Mars	114 37.4	8 49
	h m									Jupiter	79 30.3	11 09
Mer. Pass.	16 25.6	v −0.4	d 1.1	v 0.7	d 0.3	v 1.8	d 0.0	v 2.1	d 0.0	Saturn	65 15.3	12 06

MONDAY   TUESDAY   WEDNESDAY

UT	SUN GHA	SUN Dec	MOON GHA	v	MOON Dec	d	HP
13 00	177 55.4	S21 36.1	326 53.8	6.7	N17 45.3	9.6	59.8
01	192 55.2	35.7	341 19.5	6.8	17 35.7	9.7	59.9
02	207 55.0	35.2	355 45.3	6.8	17 26.0	9.8	59.9
03	222 54.7 ..	34.8	10 11.1	6.9	17 16.2	9.9	59.9
04	237 54.5	34.4	24 37.0	7.0	17 06.3	10.1	59.9
05	252 54.3	34.0	39 03.0	7.0	16 56.2	10.1	59.9
M 06	267 54.0	S21 33.6	53 29.0	7.1	N16 46.1	10.3	59.9
O 07	282 53.8	33.2	67 55.1	7.2	16 35.8	10.3	59.9
N 08	297 53.5	32.7	82 21.3	7.2	16 25.5	10.5	59.9
D 09	312 53.3 ..	32.3	96 47.5	7.2	16 15.0	10.6	59.9
A 10	327 53.1	31.9	111 13.7	7.4	16 04.4	10.6	59.9
Y 11	342 52.8	31.5	125 40.1	7.4	15 53.8	10.8	59.9
12	357 52.6	S21 31.1	140 06.5	7.4	N15 43.0	10.9	59.9
13	12 52.4	30.6	154 32.9	7.6	15 32.1	10.9	59.9
14	27 52.1	30.2	168 59.5	7.5	15 21.2	11.1	59.9
15	42 51.9 ..	29.8	183 26.0	7.7	15 10.1	11.2	59.9
16	57 51.7	29.4	197 52.7	7.7	14 58.9	11.2	59.9
17	72 51.4	29.0	212 19.4	7.8	14 47.7	11.3	59.9
18	87 51.2	S21 28.5	226 46.2	7.8	N14 36.4	11.5	59.9
19	102 51.0	28.1	241 13.0	7.9	14 24.9	11.5	59.9
20	117 50.7	27.7	255 39.9	8.0	14 13.4	11.6	59.9
21	132 50.5 ..	27.2	270 06.9	8.0	14 01.8	11.7	59.9
22	147 50.3	26.8	284 33.9	8.1	13 50.1	11.8	59.9
23	162 50.0	26.4	299 01.0	8.2	13 38.3	11.8	59.9
14 00	177 49.8	S21 26.0	313 28.2	8.2	N13 26.5	12.0	59.9
01	192 49.6	25.5	327 55.4	8.3	13 14.5	12.0	59.9
02	207 49.3	25.1	342 22.7	8.3	13 02.5	12.1	59.9
03	222 49.1 ..	24.7	356 50.0	8.4	12 50.4	12.1	59.9
04	237 48.9	24.2	11 17.4	8.5	12 38.3	12.3	59.9
05	252 48.6	23.8	25 44.9	8.5	12 26.0	12.3	59.9
06	267 48.4	S21 23.4	40 12.4	8.6	N12 13.7	12.4	59.9
07	282 48.2	22.9	54 40.0	8.6	12 01.3	12.4	59.9
T 08	297 48.0	22.5	69 07.6	8.8	11 48.9	12.6	59.9
U 09	312 47.7 ..	22.1	83 35.4	8.7	11 36.3	12.5	59.9
E 10	327 47.5	21.6	98 03.1	8.8	11 23.8	12.7	59.9
S 11	342 47.3	21.2	112 30.9	8.9	11 11.1	12.7	59.9
D 12	357 47.0	S21 20.8	126 58.8	9.0	N10 58.4	12.8	59.9
A 13	12 46.8	20.3	141 26.8	9.0	10 45.6	12.9	59.9
Y 14	27 46.6	19.9	155 54.8	9.0	10 32.7	12.9	59.9
15	42 46.3 ..	19.4	170 22.8	9.1	10 19.8	12.9	59.9
16	57 46.1	19.0	184 50.9	9.2	10 06.9	13.0	59.9
17	72 45.9	18.6	199 19.1	9.2	9 53.9	13.1	59.9
18	87 45.7	S21 18.1	213 47.3	9.3	N 9 40.8	13.1	59.8
19	102 45.4	17.7	228 15.6	9.3	9 27.7	13.2	59.8
20	117 45.2	17.2	242 43.9	9.4	9 14.5	13.2	59.8
21	132 45.0 ..	16.8	257 12.3	9.4	9 01.3	13.3	59.8
22	147 44.8	16.3	271 40.7	9.5	8 48.0	13.3	59.8
23	162 44.5	15.9	286 09.2	9.6	8 34.7	13.4	59.8
15 00	177 44.3	S21 15.4	300 37.8	9.6	N 8 21.3	13.4	59.8
01	192 44.1	15.0	315 06.4	9.6	8 07.9	13.4	59.8
02	207 43.9	14.5	329 35.0	9.7	7 54.5	13.5	59.8
03	222 43.6 ..	14.1	344 03.7	9.7	7 41.0	13.5	59.8
04	237 43.4	13.7	358 32.4	9.8	7 27.5	13.6	59.8
05	252 43.2	13.2	13 01.2	9.8	7 13.9	13.6	59.8
06	267 43.0	S21 12.8	27 30.0	9.9	N 7 00.3	13.6	59.8
W 07	282 42.7	12.3	41 58.9	9.9	6 46.7	13.7	59.7
E 08	297 42.5	11.8	56 27.8	10.0	6 33.0	13.7	59.7
D 09	312 42.3 ..	11.4	70 56.8	10.0	6 19.3	13.7	59.7
N 10	327 42.1	10.9	85 25.8	10.0	6 05.6	13.8	59.7
E 11	342 41.8	10.5	99 54.8	10.1	5 51.8	13.8	59.7
S 12	357 41.6	S21 10.0	114 23.9	10.1	N 5 38.0	13.8	59.7
D 13	12 41.4	09.6	128 53.0	10.2	5 24.2	13.8	59.7
A 14	27 41.2	09.1	143 22.2	10.2	5 10.4	13.9	59.7
Y 15	42 41.0 ..	08.7	157 51.4	10.3	4 56.5	13.9	59.7
16	57 40.7	08.2	172 20.7	10.2	4 42.6	13.9	59.6
17	72 40.5	07.7	186 49.9	10.4	4 28.7	13.9	59.6
18	87 40.3	S21 07.3	201 19.3	10.3	N 4 14.8	13.9	59.6
19	102 40.1	06.8	215 48.6	10.4	4 00.9	14.0	59.6
20	117 39.9	06.4	230 18.0	10.4	3 46.9	14.0	59.6
21	132 39.6 ..	05.9	244 47.4	10.5	3 32.9	14.0	59.6
22	147 39.4	05.4	259 16.9	10.5	3 18.9	13.9	59.6
23	162 39.2	05.0	273 46.4	10.5	N 3 05.0	14.1	59.6
	SD 16.3	d 0.4	SD 16.3		16.3		16.3

Lat.	Twilight Naut.	Twilight Civil	Sunrise	Moonrise 13	14	15	16
°	h m	h m	h m	h m	h m	h m	h m
N 72	08 04	09 58	■■	17 19	19 50	22 04	24 12
N 70	07 49	09 22	■■	17 52	20 05	22 09	24 08
68	07 36	08 57	10 40	18 16	20 17	22 12	24 04
66	07 26	08 37	09 57	18 34	20 27	22 16	24 02
64	07 17	08 21	09 29	18 49	20 35	22 18	23 59
62	07 09	08 08	09 07	19 01	20 42	22 20	23 57
60	07 02	07 57	08 50	19 12	20 48	22 22	23 55
N 58	06 56	07 47	08 35	19 21	20 53	22 24	23 54
56	06 51	07 38	08 23	19 28	20 58	22 26	23 52
54	06 45	07 30	08 12	19 35	21 02	22 27	23 51
52	06 41	07 23	08 02	19 42	21 06	22 28	23 50
50	06 36	07 17	07 54	19 47	21 09	22 30	23 49
45	06 26	07 03	07 35	20 00	21 16	22 32	23 46
N 40	06 17	06 51	07 21	20 10	21 22	22 34	23 45
35	06 09	06 40	07 08	20 18	21 28	22 36	23 43
30	06 01	06 31	06 57	20 26	21 32	22 38	23 42
20	05 47	06 14	06 38	20 38	21 40	22 40	23 39
N 10	05 32	05 58	06 21	20 50	21 47	22 43	23 37
0	05 17	05 43	06 05	21 00	21 54	22 45	23 35
S 10	05 00	05 27	05 49	21 11	22 00	22 47	23 33
20	04 39	05 08	05 32	21 22	22 07	22 50	23 31
30	04 13	04 45	05 12	21 34	22 15	22 53	23 29
35	03 56	04 32	05 00	21 42	22 19	22 54	23 28
40	03 35	04 15	04 47	21 50	22 25	22 56	23 26
45	03 08	03 55	04 31	22 00	22 30	22 58	23 25
S 50	02 30	03 29	04 11	22 11	22 37	23 01	23 23
52	02 09	03 16	04 02	22 17	22 41	23 02	23 22
54	01 41	03 01	03 51	22 23	22 44	23 03	23 21
56	00 53	02 43	03 39	22 29	22 48	23 04	23 20
58	////	02 20	03 24	22 36	22 52	23 06	23 18
S 60	////	01 50	03 08	22 45	22 57	23 08	23 17

Lat.	Sunset	Twilight Civil	Twilight Naut.	Moonset 13	14	15	16
°	h m	h m	h m	h m	h m	h m	h m
N 72	■■	14 21	16 15	12 34	11 56	11 31	11 10
N 70	■■	14 56	16 30	11 59	11 39	11 24	11 10
68	13 38	15 22	16 42	11 34	11 25	11 17	11 10
66	14 21	15 41	16 52	11 14	11 14	11 12	11 10
64	14 49	15 57	17 01	10 58	11 04	11 07	11 10
62	15 11	16 10	17 09	10 45	10 56	11 04	11 10
60	15 28	16 22	17 16	10 34	10 49	11 00	11 10
N 58	15 43	16 31	17 22	10 24	10 42	10 57	11 10
56	15 55	16 40	17 28	10 15	10 37	10 54	11 10
54	16 06	16 48	17 33	10 07	10 32	10 52	11 10
52	16 16	16 56	17 38	10 00	10 27	10 49	11 10
50	16 24	17 01	17 42	09 54	10 23	10 47	11 10
45	16 43	17 15	17 52	09 41	10 14	10 43	11 10
N 40	16 57	17 27	18 01	09 29	10 06	10 39	11 10
35	17 10	17 38	18 09	09 20	09 59	10 35	11 09
30	17 21	17 47	18 16	09 11	09 54	10 33	11 09
20	17 40	18 04	18 31	08 56	09 43	10 27	11 09
N 10	17 57	18 19	18 45	08 43	09 34	10 23	11 09
0	18 13	18 35	19 01	08 31	09 26	10 18	11 09
S 10	18 28	18 51	19 18	08 19	09 17	10 14	11 09
20	18 45	19 10	19 38	08 05	09 08	10 09	11 08
30	19 05	19 32	20 04	07 50	08 58	10 04	11 08
35	19 17	19 46	20 21	07 41	08 51	10 00	11 08
40	19 30	20 02	20 42	07 31	08 44	09 57	11 08
45	19 46	20 22	21 08	07 19	08 36	09 52	11 08
S 50	20 06	20 48	21 46	07 04	08 26	09 47	11 07
52	20 15	21 01	22 07	06 57	08 21	09 45	11 07
54	20 26	21 15	22 34	06 50	08 16	09 42	11 07
56	20 38	21 33	23 19	06 41	08 11	09 40	11 07
58	20 52	21 55	////	06 31	08 04	09 36	11 07
S 60	21 09	22 25	////	06 20	07 57	09 33	11 06

Day	SUN Eqn. of Time 00ʰ	SUN Eqn. of Time 12ʰ	SUN Mer. Pass.	MOON Mer. Pass. Upper	MOON Mer. Pass. Lower	Age	Phase
d	m s	m s	h m	h m	h m	d	%
13	08 18	08 29	12 08	02 18	14 46	18	90
14	08 40	08 51	12 09	03 13	15 40	19	82
15	09 02	09 13	12 09	04 06	16 32	20	73

UT	ARIES GHA	VENUS −4·0 GHA	Dec	MARS +1·5 GHA	Dec	JUPITER −1·8 GHA	Dec	SATURN +0·5 GHA	Dec	Name	SHA	Dec
16 00	114 54.1	139 40.7	S11 57.4	228 05.6	S21 31.2	193 54.9	S22 59.2	179 54.3	S21 24.9	Acamar	315 14.7	S40 13.9
01	129 56.6	154 40.3	56.2	243 06.3	31.5	208 56.7	59.1	194 56.5	24.8	Achernar	335 23.3	S57 08.6
02	144 59.1	169 39.9	55.1	258 07.0	31.8	223 58.6	59.1	209 58.6	24.8	Acrux	173 04.0	S63 12.2
03	160 01.5	184 39.5 ..	53.9	273 07.6 ..	32.1	239 00.4 ..	59.1	225 00.8 ..	24.8	Adhara	255 08.6	S29 00.1
04	175 04.0	199 39.1	52.7	288 08.3	32.4	254 02.3	59.0	240 02.9	24.7	Aldebaran	290 43.9	N16 32.8
05	190 06.5	214 38.7	51.6	303 09.0	32.6	269 04.1	59.0	255 05.1	24.7			
06	205 08.9	229 38.3	S11 50.4	318 09.7	S21 32.9	284 06.0	S22 58.9	270 07.2	S21 24.6	Alioth	166 16.5	N55 50.9
07	220 11.4	244 38.0	49.2	333 10.3	33.2	299 07.8	58.9	285 09.4	24.6	Alkaid	152 55.3	N49 12.6
T 08	235 13.9	259 37.6	48.1	348 11.0	33.5	314 09.7	58.9	300 11.5	24.5	Alnair	27 38.4	S46 52.1
H 09	250 16.3	274 37.2 ..	46.9	3 11.7 ..	33.8	329 11.5 ..	58.8	315 13.7 ..	24.5	Alnilam	275 41.5	S 1 11.5
U 10	265 18.8	289 36.8	45.7	18 12.3	34.1	344 13.4	58.8	330 15.8	24.4	Alphard	217 51.3	S 8 44.7
R 11	280 21.3	304 36.4	44.6	33 13.0	34.4	359 15.2	58.7	345 18.0	24.4			
S 12	295 23.7	319 36.0	S11 43.4	48 13.7	S21 34.7	14 17.1	S22 58.7	0 20.1	S21 24.3	Alphecca	126 07.3	N26 38.8
D 13	310 26.2	334 35.6	42.2	63 14.3	35.0	29 18.9	58.7	15 22.3	24.3	Alpheratz	357 39.0	N29 12.1
A 14	325 28.6	349 35.2	41.0	78 15.0	35.3	44 20.8	58.6	30 24.4	24.2	Altair	62 04.2	N 8 55.3
Y 15	340 31.1	4 34.9 ..	39.9	93 15.7 ..	35.6	59 22.6 ..	58.6	45 26.6 ..	24.2	Ankaa	353 11.3	S42 12.2
16	355 33.6	19 34.5	38.7	108 16.3	35.8	74 24.5	58.5	60 28.7	24.1	Antares	112 21.0	S26 28.4
17	10 36.0	34 34.1	37.5	123 17.0	36.1	89 26.3	58.5	75 30.9	24.1			
18	25 38.5	49 33.7	S11 36.3	138 17.7	S21 36.4	104 28.2	S22 58.5	90 33.0	S21 24.0	Arcturus	145 51.6	N19 04.7
19	40 41.0	64 33.3	35.2	153 18.3	36.7	119 30.0	58.4	105 35.2	24.0	Atria	107 19.1	S69 03.4
20	55 43.4	79 32.9	34.0	168 19.0	37.0	134 31.9	58.4	120 37.3	24.0	Avior	234 15.6	S59 34.4
21	70 45.9	94 32.6 ..	32.8	183 19.7 ..	37.3	149 33.7 ..	58.3	135 39.5 ..	23.9	Bellatrix	278 26.9	N 6 21.9
22	85 48.4	109 32.2	31.6	198 20.3	37.6	164 35.6	58.3	150 41.6	23.9	Betelgeuse	270 56.1	N 7 24.5
23	100 50.8	124 31.8	30.5	213 21.0	37.8	179 37.4	58.3	165 43.8	23.8			
17 00	115 53.3	139 31.4	S11 29.3	228 21.7	S21 38.1	194 39.3	S22 58.2	180 45.9	S21 23.8	Canopus	263 53.6	S52 42.6
01	130 55.7	154 31.0	28.1	243 22.3	38.4	209 41.1	58.2	195 48.1	23.7	Capella	280 27.4	N46 01.0
02	145 58.2	169 30.6	26.9	258 23.0	38.7	224 43.0	58.1	210 50.2	23.7	Deneb	49 28.9	N45 21.1
03	161 00.7	184 30.3 ..	25.8	273 23.7 ..	39.0	239 44.8 ..	58.1	225 52.4 ..	23.6	Denebola	182 28.9	N14 27.6
04	176 03.1	199 29.9	24.6	288 24.3	39.3	254 46.7	58.1	240 54.5	23.6	Diphda	348 51.4	S17 52.9
05	191 05.6	214 29.5	23.4	303 25.0	39.6	269 48.5	58.0	255 56.7	23.5			
06	206 08.1	229 29.1	S11 22.2	318 25.7	S21 39.8	284 50.4	S22 58.0	270 58.8	S21 23.5	Dubhe	193 45.7	N61 38.4
07	221 10.5	244 28.8	21.0	333 26.3	40.1	299 52.2	57.9	286 01.0	23.4	Elnath	278 06.6	N28 37.3
F 08	236 13.0	259 28.4	19.9	348 27.0	40.4	314 54.1	57.9	301 03.1	23.4	Eltanin	90 44.5	N51 29.1
R 09	251 15.5	274 28.0 ..	18.7	3 27.7 ..	40.7	329 55.9 ..	57.9	316 05.3 ..	23.3	Enif	33 43.0	N 9 58.0
I 10	266 17.9	289 27.6	17.5	18 28.3	41.0	344 57.8	57.8	331 07.4	23.3	Fomalhaut	15 19.2	S29 31.2
D 11	281 20.4	304 27.3	16.3	33 29.0	41.3	359 59.6	57.8	346 09.6	23.2			
A 12	296 22.9	319 26.9	S11 15.1	48 29.7	S21 41.5	15 01.5	S22 57.7	1 11.7	S21 23.2	Gacrux	171 55.7	S57 13.2
Y 13	311 25.3	334 26.5	14.0	63 30.3	41.8	30 03.3	57.7	16 13.9	23.2	Gienah	175 47.5	S17 39.0
14	326 27.8	349 26.1	12.8	78 31.0	42.1	45 05.2	57.7	31 16.0	23.1	Hadar	148 41.6	S60 27.8
15	341 30.2	4 25.8 ..	11.6	93 31.6 ..	42.4	60 07.0 ..	57.6	46 18.2 ..	23.1	Hamal	327 55.6	N23 33.4
16	356 32.7	19 25.4	10.4	108 32.3	42.7	75 08.9	57.6	61 20.3	23.0	Kaus Aust.	83 38.2	S34 22.4
17	11 35.2	34 25.0	09.2	123 33.0	42.9	90 10.7	57.5	76 22.5	23.0			
18	26 37.6	49 24.6	S11 08.0	138 33.6	S21 43.2	105 12.6	S22 57.5	91 24.6	S21 22.9	Kochab	137 20.4	N74 04.2
19	41 40.1	64 24.3	06.8	153 34.3	43.5	120 14.4	57.5	106 26.8	22.9	Markab	13 34.0	N15 18.7
20	56 42.6	79 23.9	05.7	168 35.0	43.8	135 16.3	57.4	121 28.9	22.8	Menkar	314 10.2	N 4 09.9
21	71 45.0	94 23.5 ..	04.5	183 35.6 ..	44.1	150 18.1 ..	57.4	136 31.1 ..	22.8	Menkent	148 02.3	S36 27.8
22	86 47.5	109 23.2	03.3	198 36.3	44.3	165 20.0	57.3	151 33.2	22.7	Miaplacidus	221 37.9	S69 47.8
23	101 50.0	124 22.8	02.1	213 37.0	44.6	180 21.8	57.3	166 35.4	22.7			
18 00	116 52.4	139 22.4	S11 00.9	228 37.6	S21 44.9	195 23.7	S22 57.3	181 37.5	S21 22.6	Mirfak	308 33.6	N49 56.0
01	131 54.9	154 22.1	10 59.7	243 38.3	45.2	210 25.5	57.2	196 39.7	22.6	Nunki	75 53.1	S26 16.2
02	146 57.4	169 21.7	58.5	258 38.9	45.5	225 27.4	57.2	211 41.8	22.5	Peacock	53 12.7	S56 40.3
03	161 59.8	184 21.3 ..	57.3	273 39.6 ..	45.7	240 29.2 ..	57.1	226 44.0 ..	22.5	Pollux	243 21.8	N27 58.5
04	177 02.3	199 21.0	56.1	288 40.3	46.0	255 31.1	57.1	241 46.1	22.4	Procyon	244 54.7	N 5 10.3
05	192 04.7	214 20.6	55.0	303 40.9	46.3	270 32.9	57.0	256 48.3	22.4			
06	207 07.2	229 20.2	S10 53.8	318 41.6	S21 46.6	285 34.8	S22 57.0	271 50.4	S21 22.4	Rasalhague	96 02.5	N12 32.7
07	222 09.7	244 19.9	52.6	333 42.3	46.8	300 36.7	57.0	286 52.6	22.3	Regulus	207 38.4	N11 52.1
S 08	237 12.1	259 19.5	51.4	348 42.9	47.1	315 38.5	56.9	301 54.7	22.3	Rigel	281 07.4	S 8 10.9
A 09	252 14.6	274 19.1 ..	50.2	3 43.6 ..	47.4	330 40.4 ..	56.9	316 56.9 ..	22.2	Rigil Kent.	139 45.8	S60 54.6
T 10	267 17.1	289 18.8	49.0	18 44.2	47.7	345 42.2	56.8	331 59.0	22.2	Sabik	102 07.6	S15 44.8
U 11	282 19.5	304 18.4	47.8	33 44.9	47.9	0 44.1	56.8	347 01.2	22.1			
R 12	297 22.0	319 18.0	S10 46.6	48 45.6	S21 48.2	15 45.9	S22 56.8	2 03.3	S21 22.1	Schedar	349 35.5	N56 38.9
D 13	312 24.5	334 17.7	45.4	63 46.2	48.5	30 47.8	56.7	17 05.5	22.0	Shaula	96 16.1	S37 06.9
A 14	327 26.9	349 17.3	44.2	78 46.9	48.8	45 49.6	56.7	32 07.6	22.0	Sirius	258 29.4	S16 44.8
Y 15	342 29.4	4 17.0 ..	43.0	93 47.5 ..	49.0	60 51.5 ..	56.6	47 09.8 ..	21.9	Spica	158 26.5	S11 15.8
16	357 31.8	19 16.6	41.8	108 48.2	49.3	75 53.3	56.6	62 11.9	21.9	Suhail	222 48.7	S43 30.7
17	12 34.3	34 16.2	40.6	123 48.9	49.6	90 55.2	56.6	77 14.1	21.8			
18	27 36.8	49 15.9	S10 39.4	138 49.5	S21 49.9	105 57.0	S22 56.5	92 16.2	S21 21.8	Vega	80 36.3	N38 48.1
19	42 39.2	64 15.5	38.2	153 50.2	50.1	120 58.9	56.5	107 18.4	21.7	Zuben'ubi	137 00.5	S16 07.3
20	57 41.7	79 15.2	37.0	168 50.8	50.4	136 00.7	56.4	122 20.5	21.7			
21	72 44.2	94 14.8 ..	35.8	183 51.5 ..	50.7	151 02.6 ..	56.4	137 22.7 ..	21.6		SHA	Mer. Pass.
22	87 46.6	109 14.5	34.6	198 52.2	51.0	166 04.4	56.3	152 24.8	21.6	Venus	23 38.1	14 42
23	102 49.1	124 14.1	33.4	213 52.8	51.2	181 06.3	56.3	167 27.0	21.5	Mars	112 28.4	8 46
Mer. Pass. 16 13.8		v −0.4	d 1.2	v 0.7	d 0.3	v 1.9	d 0.0	v 2.2	d 0.0	Jupiter	78 46.0	11 00
										Saturn	64 52.6	11 55

SUN / MOON

UT	SUN GHA	SUN Dec	MOON GHA	v	MOON Dec	d	HP
d h	° '	° '	° '	'	° '	'	'
16 00	177 39.0	S21 04.5	288 15.9	10.5	N 2 50.9	14.0	59.5
01	192 38.8	04.1	302 45.4	10.6	2 36.9	14.0	59.5
02	207 38.5	03.6	317 15.0	10.6	2 22.9	14.0	59.5
03	222 38.3 ..	03.1	331 44.6	10.6	2 08.9	14.0	59.5
04	237 38.1	02.7	346 14.2	10.7	1 54.9	14.1	59.5
05	252 37.9	02.2	0 43.9	10.7	1 40.8	14.0	59.5
06	267 37.7	S21 01.7	15 13.6	10.7	N 1 26.8	14.0	59.5
07	282 37.4	01.3	29 43.3	10.7	1 12.8	14.1	59.5
08	297 37.2	00.8	44 13.0	10.7	0 58.7	14.0	59.4
09	312 37.0	21 00.3	58 42.7	10.8	0 44.7	14.0	59.4
10	327 36.8	20 59.8	73 12.5	10.8	0 30.7	14.1	59.4
11	342 36.6	59.4	87 42.3	10.8	0 16.6	14.0	59.4
12	357 36.4	S20 58.9	102 12.1	10.8	N 0 02.6	14.0	59.4
13	12 36.2	58.4	116 41.9	10.9	S 0 11.4	14.0	59.4
14	27 35.9	58.0	131 11.8	10.8	0 25.4	14.0	59.3
15	42 35.7 ..	57.5	145 41.6	10.9	0 39.4	14.0	59.3
16	57 35.5	57.0	160 11.5	10.9	0 53.4	14.0	59.3
17	72 35.3	56.5	174 41.4	10.9	1 07.4	13.9	59.3
18	87 35.1	S20 56.1	189 11.3	10.9	S 1 21.3	14.0	59.3
19	102 34.9	55.6	203 41.2	10.9	1 35.3	13.9	59.3
20	117 34.7	55.1	218 11.1	10.9	1 49.2	13.9	59.2
21	132 34.4 ..	54.6	232 41.0	11.0	2 03.1	13.9	59.2
22	147 34.2	54.1	247 11.0	10.9	2 17.0	13.8	59.2
23	162 34.0	53.7	261 40.9	11.0	2 30.8	13.9	59.2
17 00	177 33.8	S20 53.2	276 10.9	11.0	S 2 44.7	13.8	59.2
01	192 33.6	52.7	290 40.9	10.9	2 58.5	13.8	59.2
02	207 33.4	52.2	305 10.8	11.0	3 12.3	13.8	59.2
03	222 33.2 ..	51.7	319 40.8	11.0	3 26.1	13.7	59.1
04	237 33.0	51.3	334 10.8	11.0	3 39.8	13.8	59.1
05	252 32.7	50.8	348 40.8	11.0	3 53.6	13.6	59.1
06	267 32.5	S20 50.3	3 10.7	11.0	S 4 07.2	13.7	59.1
07	282 32.3	49.8	17 40.7	11.0	4 20.9	13.6	59.1
08	297 32.1	49.3	32 10.7	11.0	4 34.5	13.6	59.1
09	312 31.9 ..	48.8	46 40.7	11.0	4 48.1	13.6	59.0
10	327 31.7	48.4	61 10.7	10.9	5 01.7	13.5	59.0
11	342 31.5	47.9	75 40.6	11.0	5 15.2	13.5	59.0
12	357 31.3	S20 47.4	90 10.6	11.0	S 5 28.7	13.5	59.0
13	12 31.1	46.9	104 40.6	10.9	5 42.2	13.4	59.0
14	27 30.9	46.4	119 10.5	11.0	5 55.6	13.4	58.9
15	42 30.7 ..	45.9	133 40.5	10.9	6 09.0	13.3	58.9
16	57 30.5	45.4	148 10.4	11.0	6 22.3	13.3	58.9
17	72 30.2	44.9	162 40.4	10.9	6 35.6	13.3	58.9
18	87 30.0	S20 44.4	177 10.3	10.9	S 6 48.9	13.2	58.9
19	102 29.8	43.9	191 40.2	10.9	7 02.1	13.1	58.9
20	117 29.6	43.4	206 10.1	10.9	7 15.2	13.1	58.8
21	132 29.4 ..	42.9	220 40.0	10.9	7 28.3	13.1	58.8
22	147 29.2	42.5	235 09.9	10.9	7 41.4	13.0	58.8
23	162 29.0	42.0	249 39.8	10.8	7 54.4	13.0	58.8
18 00	177 28.8	S20 41.5	264 09.6	10.8	S 8 07.4	12.9	58.8
01	192 28.6	41.0	278 39.4	10.9	8 20.3	12.9	58.7
02	207 28.4	40.5	293 09.3	10.8	8 33.2	12.8	58.7
03	222 28.2 ..	40.0	307 39.1	10.8	8 46.0	12.8	58.7
04	237 28.0	39.5	322 08.9	10.7	8 58.8	12.7	58.7
05	252 27.8	39.0	336 38.6	10.8	9 11.5	12.6	58.7
06	267 27.6	S20 38.5	351 08.4	10.7	S 9 24.1	12.6	58.7
07	282 27.4	38.0	5 38.1	10.7	9 36.7	12.5	58.6
08	297 27.2	37.5	20 07.8	10.7	9 49.2	12.5	58.6
09	312 27.0 ..	37.0	34 37.5	10.7	10 01.7	12.4	58.6
10	327 26.8	36.5	49 07.2	10.7	10 14.1	12.3	58.6
11	342 26.6	36.0	63 36.9	10.6	10 26.4	12.3	58.6
12	357 26.4	S20 35.4	78 06.5	10.6	S10 38.7	12.2	58.5
13	12 26.2	34.9	92 36.1	10.6	10 50.9	12.2	58.5
14	27 26.0	34.4	107 05.7	10.5	11 03.1	12.0	58.5
15	42 25.8 ..	33.9	121 35.2	10.5	11 15.1	12.1	58.5
16	57 25.6	33.4	136 04.7	10.5	11 27.2	11.9	58.5
17	72 25.4	32.9	150 34.2	10.5	11 39.1	11.9	58.4
18	87 25.2	S20 32.4	165 03.7	10.5	S11 51.0	11.8	58.4
19	102 25.0	31.9	179 33.2	10.4	12 02.8	11.7	58.4
20	117 24.8	31.4	194 02.6	10.4	12 14.5	11.7	58.4
21	132 24.6 ..	30.9	208 32.0	10.3	12 26.2	11.6	58.4
22	147 24.4	30.4	223 01.3	10.4	12 37.8	11.5	58.3
23	162 24.2	29.9	237 30.7	10.3	S12 49.3	11.4	58.3
	SD 16.3	d 0.5	SD 16.2		16.1		15.9

Twilight / Moonrise

Lat.	Twilight Naut.	Twilight Civil	Sunrise	Moonrise 16	Moonrise 17	Moonrise 18	Moonrise 19
°	h m	h m	h m	h m	h m	h m	h m
N 72	07 57	09 45	■■■	24 12	00 12	02 22	04 43
N 70	07 43	09 13	11 54	24 08	00 08	02 07	04 13
68	07 31	08 50	10 26	24 04	00 04	01 56	03 51
66	07 21	08 31	09 48	24 02	00 02	01 47	03 34
64	07 13	08 16	09 22	23 59	25 39	01 39	03 20
62	07 06	08 04	09 02	23 57	25 33	01 33	03 08
60	06 59	07 53	08 45	23 55	25 27	01 27	02 58
N 58	06 53	07 44	08 31	23 54	25 22	01 22	02 50
56	06 48	07 35	08 19	23 52	25 18	01 18	02 42
54	06 43	07 28	08 09	23 51	25 14	01 14	02 36
52	06 39	07 21	08 00	23 50	25 10	01 10	02 30
50	06 34	07 15	07 51	23 49	25 07	01 07	02 24
45	06 25	07 01	07 34	23 46	25 00	01 00	02 13
N 40	06 16	06 50	07 19	23 45	24 54	00 54	02 03
35	06 09	06 40	07 07	23 43	24 49	00 49	01 55
30	06 01	06 31	06 56	23 42	24 45	00 45	01 48
20	05 47	06 14	06 38	23 39	24 37	00 37	01 36
N 10	05 33	05 59	06 22	23 37	24 31	00 31	01 25
0	05 18	05 44	06 06	23 35	24 25	00 25	01 15
S 10	05 02	05 28	05 51	23 33	24 19	00 19	01 05
20	04 42	05 10	05 34	23 31	24 12	00 12	00 55
30	04 16	04 48	05 15	23 29	24 05	00 05	00 43
35	04 00	04 35	05 03	23 28	24 01	00 01	00 36
40	03 39	04 19	04 50	23 26	23 57	24 29	00 29
45	03 13	03 59	04 35	23 25	23 51	24 20	00 20
S 50	02 37	03 34	04 16	23 23	23 45	24 09	00 09
52	02 17	03 22	04 06	23 22	23 42	24 04	00 04
54	01 51	03 07	03 56	23 21	23 39	23 59	24 23
56	01 12	02 50	03 44	23 20	23 35	23 53	24 14
58	////	02 29	03 31	23 18	23 31	23 46	24 05
S 60	////	02 01	03 15	23 17	23 27	23 39	23 54

Sunset / Twilight / Moonset

Lat.	Sunset	Twilight Civil	Twilight Naut.	Moonset 16	Moonset 17	Moonset 18	Moonset 19
°	h m	h m	h m	h m	h m	h m	h m
N 72	■■■	14 35	16 24	11 10	10 50	10 26	09 51
N 70	12 26	15 07	16 38	11 10	10 57	10 42	10 23
68	13 55	15 31	16 49	11 10	11 03	10 55	10 46
66	14 32	15 49	16 59	11 10	11 08	11 06	11 05
64	14 58	16 04	17 07	11 10	11 12	11 15	11 20
62	15 19	16 17	17 15	11 10	11 16	11 23	11 32
60	15 35	16 27	17 21	11 10	11 20	11 30	11 43
N 58	15 49	16 37	17 27	11 10	11 22	11 36	11 52
56	16 01	16 45	17 32	11 10	11 25	11 42	12 01
54	16 11	16 53	17 37	11 10	11 28	11 46	12 08
52	16 20	16 59	17 42	11 10	11 30	11 51	12 15
50	16 29	17 06	17 46	11 10	11 32	11 55	12 21
45	16 46	17 19	17 55	11 10	11 36	12 03	12 34
N 40	17 01	17 30	18 04	11 10	11 40	12 11	12 44
35	17 13	17 40	18 11	11 09	11 43	12 17	12 54
30	17 24	17 49	18 19	11 09	11 46	12 23	13 02
20	17 42	18 06	18 33	11 09	11 50	12 32	13 16
N 10	17 58	18 21	18 47	11 09	11 55	12 41	13 28
0	18 14	18 36	19 01	11 09	11 59	12 49	13 40
S 10	18 29	18 52	19 18	11 09	12 03	12 57	13 51
20	18 46	19 10	19 38	11 08	12 07	13 05	14 04
30	19 05	19 31	20 03	11 08	12 12	13 15	14 18
35	19 16	19 45	20 20	11 08	12 15	13 21	14 26
40	19 29	20 00	20 40	11 08	12 18	13 27	14 36
45	19 44	20 20	21 05	11 08	12 22	13 35	14 47
S 50	20 03	20 45	21 41	11 07	12 26	13 44	15 00
52	20 13	20 57	22 01	11 07	12 28	13 48	15 07
54	20 23	21 11	22 26	11 07	12 30	13 53	15 14
56	20 34	21 28	23 03	11 07	12 33	13 58	15 22
58	20 48	21 49	////	11 07	12 36	14 04	15 30
S 60	21 03	22 16	////	11 06	12 39	14 10	15 41

SUN / MOON

Day	SUN Eqn. of Time 00ʰ	SUN Eqn. of Time 12ʰ	SUN Mer. Pass.	MOON Mer. Pass. Upper	MOON Mer. Pass. Lower	Age	Phase
d	m s	m s	h m	h m	h m	d %	
16	09 24	09 34	12 10	04 57	17 22	21 62	
17	09 44	09 54	12 10	05 47	18 12	22 51	
18	10 04	10 14	12 10	06 37	19 02	23 39	

UT	ARIES	VENUS −4.0		MARS +1.4		JUPITER −1.9		SATURN +0.5		STARS		
	GHA	GHA	Dec	GHA	Dec	GHA	Dec	GHA	Dec	Name	SHA	Dec
d h	° ′	° ′	° ′	° ′	° ′	° ′	° ′	° ′	° ′		° ′	° ′
19 00	117 51.6	139 13.7	S10 32.2	228 53.5	S21 51.5	196 08.2	S22 56.3	182 29.1	S21 21.5	Acamar	315 14.7	S40 13.9
01	132 54.0	154 13.4	31.0	243 54.1	51.8	211 10.0	56.2	197 31.3	21.5	Achernar	335 23.4	S57 08.6
02	147 56.5	169 13.0	29.8	258 54.8	52.0	226 11.9	56.2	212 33.4	21.4	Acrux	173 04.0	S63 12.2
03	162 59.0	184 12.7	.. 28.6	273 55.5	.. 52.2	241 13.7	.. 56.1	227 35.6	.. 21.4	Adhara	255 08.6	S29 00.1
04	178 01.4	199 12.3	27.4	288 56.1	52.6	256 15.6	56.1	242 37.7	21.3	Aldebaran	290 43.9	N16 32.8
05	193 03.9	214 12.0	26.2	303 56.8	52.8	271 17.4	56.1	257 39.9	21.3			
06	208 06.3	229 11.6	S10 25.0	318 57.4	S21 53.1	286 19.3	S22 56.0	272 42.0	S21 21.2	Alioth	166 16.5	N55 50.9
07	223 08.8	244 11.3	23.8	333 58.1	53.4	301 21.1	56.0	287 44.2	21.2	Alkaid	152 55.3	N49 12.6
08	238 11.3	259 10.9	22.6	348 58.7	53.7	316 23.0	55.9	302 46.3	21.1	Alnair	27 38.4	S46 52.1
S 09	253 13.7	274 10.6	.. 21.4	3 59.4	.. 53.9	331 24.8	.. 55.9	317 48.5	.. 21.1	Alnilam	275 41.5	S 1 11.5
U 10	268 16.2	289 10.2	20.2	19 00.1	54.2	346 26.7	55.8	332 50.7	21.0	Alphard	217 51.3	S 8 44.8
N 11	283 18.7	304 09.9	19.0	34 00.7	54.5	1 28.5	55.8	347 52.8	21.0			
D 12	298 21.1	319 09.5	S10 17.8	49 01.4	S21 54.7	16 30.4	S22 55.8	2 55.0	S21 20.9	Alphecca	126 07.3	N26 38.8
A 13	313 23.6	334 09.2	16.6	64 02.0	55.0	31 32.2	55.7	17 57.1	20.9	Alpheratz	357 39.0	N29 12.0
Y 14	328 26.1	349 08.8	15.4	79 02.7	55.3	46 34.1	55.7	32 59.3	20.8	Altair	62 04.2	N 8 55.3
15	343 28.5	4 08.5	.. 14.2	94 03.3	.. 55.5	61 36.0	.. 55.6	48 01.4	.. 20.8	Ankaa	353 11.3	S42 12.2
16	358 31.0	19 08.1	13.0	109 04.0	55.8	76 37.8	55.6	63 03.6	20.7	Antares	112 20.9	S26 28.4
17	13 33.5	34 07.8	11.8	124 04.7	56.1	91 39.7	55.5	78 05.7	20.7			
18	28 35.9	49 07.4	S10 10.6	139 05.3	S21 56.3	106 41.5	S22 55.5	93 07.9	S21 20.6	Arcturus	145 51.6	N19 04.7
19	43 38.4	64 07.1	09.4	154 06.0	56.6	121 43.4	55.5	108 10.0	20.6	Atria	107 19.1	S69 03.4
20	58 40.8	79 06.7	08.2	169 06.6	56.8	136 45.2	55.4	123 12.2	20.5	Avior	234 15.6	S59 34.4
21	73 43.3	94 06.4	.. 07.0	184 07.3	.. 57.1	151 47.1	.. 55.4	138 14.3	.. 20.5	Bellatrix	278 26.9	N 6 21.9
22	88 45.8	109 06.0	05.7	199 07.9	57.4	166 48.9	55.3	153 16.5	20.5	Betelgeuse	270 56.1	N 7 24.5
23	103 48.2	124 05.7	04.5	214 08.6	57.6	181 50.8	55.3	168 18.6	20.4			
20 00	118 50.7	139 05.4	S10 03.3	229 09.2	S21 57.9	196 52.6	S22 55.2	183 20.8	S21 20.4	Canopus	263 53.6	S52 42.6
01	133 53.2	154 05.0	02.1	244 09.9	58.2	211 54.5	55.2	198 22.9	20.3	Capella	280 27.4	N46 01.0
02	148 55.6	169 04.7	10 00.9	259 10.6	58.4	226 56.4	55.2	213 25.1	20.3	Deneb	49 28.9	N45 21.1
03	163 58.1	184 04.3	9 59.7	274 11.2	.. 58.7	241 58.2	.. 55.1	228 27.2	.. 20.2	Denebola	182 28.9	N14 27.6
04	179 00.6	199 04.0	58.5	289 11.9	59.0	257 00.1	55.1	243 29.4	20.2	Diphda	348 51.4	S17 52.9
05	194 03.0	214 03.6	57.3	304 12.5	59.2	272 01.9	55.0	258 31.5	20.1			
06	209 05.5	229 03.3	S 9 56.1	319 13.2	S21 59.5	287 03.8	S22 55.0	273 33.7	S21 20.1	Dubhe	193 45.6	N61 38.4
07	224 07.9	244 03.0	54.8	334 13.8	21 59.7	302 05.6	54.9	288 35.8	20.0	Elnath	278 06.6	N28 37.3
08	239 10.4	259 02.6	53.6	349 14.5	22 00.0	317 07.5	54.9	303 38.0	20.0	Eltanin	90 44.5	N51 29.1
M 09	254 12.9	274 02.3	.. 52.4	4 15.1	.. 00.3	332 09.3	.. 54.9	318 40.1	.. 19.9	Enif	33 43.0	N 9 58.0
O 10	269 15.3	289 01.9	51.2	19 15.8	00.5	347 11.2	54.8	333 42.3	19.9	Fomalhaut	15 19.2	S29 31.2
N 11	284 17.8	304 01.6	50.0	34 16.4	00.8	2 13.1	54.8	348 44.4	19.8			
D 12	299 20.3	319 01.3	S 9 48.8	49 17.1	S22 01.0	17 14.9	S22 54.7	3 46.6	S21 19.8	Gacrux	171 55.7	S57 13.2
A 13	314 22.7	334 00.9	47.6	64 17.8	01.3	32 16.8	54.7	18 48.7	19.7	Gienah	175 47.5	S17 39.1
Y 14	329 25.2	349 00.6	46.3	79 18.4	01.6	47 18.6	54.6	33 50.9	19.7	Hadar	148 41.5	S60 27.8
15	344 27.7	4 00.3	.. 45.1	94 19.1	.. 01.8	62 20.5	.. 54.6	48 53.0	.. 19.6	Hamal	327 55.6	N23 33.4
16	359 30.1	18 59.9	43.9	109 19.7	02.1	77 22.3	54.6	63 55.2	19.6	Kaus Aust.	83 38.2	S34 22.4
17	14 32.6	33 59.6	42.7	124 20.4	02.3	92 24.2	54.5	78 57.3	19.5			
18	29 35.1	48 59.3	S 9 41.5	139 21.0	S22 02.6	107 26.0	S22 54.5	93 59.5	S21 19.5	Kochab	137 20.4	N74 04.2
19	44 37.5	63 58.9	40.3	154 21.7	02.9	122 27.9	54.4	109 01.6	19.4	Markab	13 34.0	N15 18.7
20	59 40.0	78 58.6	39.0	169 22.3	03.1	137 29.8	54.4	124 03.8	19.4	Menkar	314 10.2	N 4 09.9
21	74 42.4	93 58.3	.. 37.8	184 23.0	.. 03.4	152 31.6	.. 54.3	139 05.9	.. 19.4	Menkent	148 02.3	S36 27.8
22	89 44.9	108 57.9	36.6	199 23.6	03.6	167 33.5	54.3	154 08.1	19.3	Miaplacidus	221 37.9	S69 47.8
23	104 47.4	123 57.6	35.4	214 24.3	03.9	182 35.3	54.3	169 10.2	19.3			
21 00	119 49.8	138 57.3	S 9 34.2	229 24.9	S22 04.1	197 37.2	S22 54.2	184 12.4	S21 19.2	Mirfak	308 33.6	N49 56.0
01	134 52.3	153 56.9	32.9	244 25.6	04.4	212 39.0	54.2	199 14.5	19.2	Nunki	75 53.1	S26 16.2
02	149 54.8	168 56.6	31.7	259 26.2	04.6	227 40.9	54.1	214 16.7	19.1	Peacock	53 12.7	S56 40.3
03	164 57.2	183 56.3	.. 30.5	274 26.9	.. 04.9	242 42.7	.. 54.1	229 18.8	.. 19.1	Pollux	243 21.8	N27 58.5
04	179 59.7	198 55.9	29.3	289 27.5	05.2	257 44.6	54.0	244 21.0	19.0	Procyon	244 54.7	N 5 10.3
05	195 02.2	213 55.6	28.0	304 28.2	05.4	272 46.5	54.0	259 23.2	19.0			
06	210 04.6	228 55.3	S 9 26.8	319 28.8	S22 05.7	287 48.3	S22 54.0	274 25.3	S21 18.9	Rasalhague	96 02.5	N12 32.7
07	225 07.1	243 54.9	25.6	334 29.5	05.9	302 50.2	53.9	289 27.5	18.9	Regulus	207 38.4	N11 52.1
T 08	240 09.6	258 54.6	24.4	349 30.1	06.2	317 52.0	53.9	304 29.6	18.8	Rigel	281 07.4	S 8 10.9
U 09	255 12.0	273 54.3	.. 23.2	4 30.8	.. 06.4	332 53.9	.. 53.8	319 31.8	.. 18.8	Rigil Kent.	139 45.7	S60 54.6
E 10	270 14.5	288 54.0	21.9	19 31.4	06.7	347 55.7	53.8	334 33.9	18.7	Sabik	102 07.6	S15 44.8
S 11	285 16.9	303 53.6	20.7	34 32.1	06.9	2 57.6	53.7	349 36.1	18.7			
D 12	300 19.4	318 53.3	S 9 19.5	49 32.7	S22 07.2	17 59.5	S22 53.7	4 38.2	S21 18.6	Schedar	349 35.6	N56 38.9
A 13	315 21.9	333 53.0	18.3	64 33.4	07.4	33 01.3	53.7	19 40.4	18.6	Shaula	96 16.1	S37 06.9
Y 14	330 24.3	348 52.7	17.0	79 34.0	07.7	48 03.2	53.6	34 42.5	18.5	Sirius	258 29.4	S16 44.8
15	345 26.8	3 52.3	.. 15.8	94 34.7	.. 07.9	63 05.0	.. 53.6	49 44.7	.. 18.5	Spica	158 26.4	S11 15.8
16	0 29.3	18 52.0	14.6	109 35.3	08.2	78 06.9	53.5	64 46.8	18.4	Suhail	222 48.7	S43 30.8
17	15 31.7	33 51.7	13.4	124 36.0	08.4	93 08.7	53.5	79 49.0	18.4			
18	30 34.2	48 51.4	S 9 12.1	139 36.6	S22 08.7	108 10.6	S22 53.4	94 51.1	S21 18.3	Vega	80 36.3	N38 48.1
19	45 36.7	63 51.0	10.9	154 37.3	08.9	123 12.5	53.4	109 53.3	18.3	Zuben'ubi	137 00.5	S16 07.3
20	60 39.1	78 50.7	09.7	169 37.9	09.2	138 14.3	53.3	124 55.4	18.3		SHA	Mer.Pass.
21	75 41.6	93 50.4	.. 08.4	184 38.6	.. 09.4	153 16.2	.. 53.3	139 57.6	.. 18.2		° ′	h m
22	90 44.1	108 50.1	07.2	199 39.2	09.7	168 18.0	53.3	154 59.7	18.2	Venus	20 14.7	14 44
23	105 46.5	123 49.8	06.0	214 39.9	09.9	183 19.9	53.2	170 01.9	18.1	Mars	110 18.5	8 43
	h m									Jupiter	78 01.9	10 51
Mer.Pass. 16 02.0		v −0.3	d 1.2	v 0.7	d 0.3	v 1.9	d 0.0	v 2.2	d 0.0	Saturn	64 30.1	11 45

	UT	SUN GHA	SUN Dec	MOON GHA	*v*	MOON Dec	*d*	HP
	d h	° ′	° ′	° ′	′	° ′	′	′
	19 00	177 24.0	S20 29.3	252 00.0	10.2	S13 00.7	11.4	58.3
	01	192 23.8	28.8	266 29.2	10.3	13 12.1	11.2	58.3
	02	207 23.6	28.3	280 58.5	10.2	13 23.3	11.2	58.3
	03	222 23.4	. . 27.8	295 27.7	10.2	13 34.5	11.1	58.2
	04	237 23.2	27.3	309 56.9	10.1	13 45.6	11.1	58.2
	05	252 23.0	26.8	324 26.0	10.1	13 56.7	10.9	58.2
	06	267 22.8	S20 26.2	338 55.1	10.1	S14 07.6	10.9	58.2
	07	282 22.6	25.7	353 24.2	10.1	14 18.5	10.8	58.2
	08	297 22.4	25.2	7 53.3	10.0	14 29.3	10.7	58.1
S	09	312 22.2	. . 24.7	22 22.3	10.0	14 40.0	10.6	58.1
U	10	327 22.0	24.2	36 51.3	9.9	14 50.6	10.5	58.1
N	11	342 21.8	23.7	51 20.2	9.9	15 01.1	10.5	58.1
D	12	357 21.6	S20 23.1	65 49.1	9.9	S15 11.6	10.3	58.1
A	13	12 21.4	22.6	80 18.0	9.9	15 21.9	10.3	58.0
Y	14	27 21.2	22.1	94 46.9	9.8	15 32.2	10.1	58.0
	15	42 21.0	. . 21.6	109 15.7	9.8	15 42.3	10.1	58.0
	16	57 20.8	21.0	123 44.5	9.7	15 52.4	10.0	58.0
	17	72 20.7	20.5	138 13.2	9.7	16 02.4	9.9	58.0
	18	87 20.5	S20 20.0	152 41.9	9.7	S16 12.3	9.8	57.9
	19	102 20.3	19.5	167 10.6	9.6	16 22.1	9.7	57.9
	20	117 20.1	18.9	181 39.2	9.6	16 31.8	9.6	57.9
	21	132 19.9	. . 18.4	196 07.8	9.6	16 41.4	9.5	57.9
	22	147 19.7	17.9	210 36.4	9.5	16 50.9	9.4	57.9
	23	162 19.5	17.4	225 04.9	9.5	17 00.3	9.3	57.8
	20 00	177 19.3	S20 16.8	239 33.4	9.5	S17 09.6	9.2	57.8
	01	192 19.1	16.3	254 01.9	9.4	17 18.8	9.1	57.8
	02	207 18.9	15.8	268 30.3	9.4	17 27.9	9.0	57.8
	03	222 18.7	. . 15.2	282 58.7	9.3	17 36.9	8.9	57.8
	04	237 18.6	14.7	297 27.0	9.4	17 45.8	8.8	57.7
	05	252 18.4	14.2	311 55.4	9.2	17 54.6	8.6	57.7
	06	267 18.2	S20 13.6	326 23.6	9.3	S18 03.2	8.6	57.7
	07	282 18.0	13.1	340 51.9	9.2	18 11.8	8.5	57.7
	08	297 17.8	12.6	355 20.1	9.2	18 20.3	8.4	57.7
M	09	312 17.6	. . 12.0	9 48.3	9.1	18 28.7	8.2	57.6
O	10	327 17.4	11.5	24 16.4	9.1	18 36.9	8.2	57.6
N	11	342 17.2	11.0	38 44.5	9.1	18 45.1	8.0	57.6
D	12	357 17.1	S20 10.4	53 12.6	9.1	S18 53.1	7.9	57.6
A	13	12 16.9	09.9	67 40.7	9.0	19 01.0	7.9	57.6
Y	14	27 16.7	09.4	82 08.7	9.0	19 08.9	7.7	57.5
	15	42 16.5	. . 08.8	96 36.7	8.9	19 16.6	7.6	57.5
	16	57 16.3	08.3	111 04.6	8.9	19 24.2	7.4	57.5
	17	72 16.1	07.7	125 32.5	8.9	19 31.6	7.4	57.5
	18	87 15.9	S20 07.2	140 00.4	8.8	S19 39.0	7.3	57.5
	19	102 15.8	06.7	154 28.2	8.9	19 46.3	7.1	57.4
	20	117 15.6	06.1	168 56.1	8.8	19 53.4	7.0	57.4
	21	132 15.4	. . 05.6	183 23.9	8.7	20 00.4	6.9	57.4
	22	147 15.2	05.0	197 51.6	8.7	20 07.3	6.8	57.4
	23	162 15.0	04.5	212 19.3	8.7	20 14.1	6.7	57.4
	21 00	177 14.8	S20 03.9	226 47.0	8.7	S20 20.8	6.5	57.3
	01	192 14.7	03.4	241 14.7	8.7	20 27.3	6.4	57.3
	02	207 14.5	02.8	255 42.4	8.6	20 33.7	6.3	57.3
	03	222 14.3	. . 02.3	270 10.0	8.6	20 40.0	6.2	57.3
	04	237 14.1	01.7	284 37.6	8.6	20 46.2	6.1	57.3
	05	252 13.9	01.2	299 05.2	8.5	20 52.3	5.9	57.2
	06	267 13.7	S20 00.7	313 32.7	8.5	S20 58.2	5.9	57.2
	07	282 13.6	20 00.1	328 00.2	8.5	21 04.1	5.7	57.2
T	08	297 13.4	19 59.6	342 27.7	8.5	21 09.8	5.5	57.2
U	09	312 13.2	. . 59.0	356 55.2	8.4	21 15.3	5.5	57.2
E	10	327 13.0	58.5	11 22.6	8.5	21 20.8	5.3	57.1
S	11	342 12.8	57.9	25 50.1	8.4	21 26.1	5.2	57.1
D	12	357 12.7	S19 57.3	40 17.5	8.4	S21 31.3	5.1	57.1
A	13	12 12.5	56.8	54 44.9	8.4	21 36.4	4.9	57.1
Y	14	27 12.3	56.2	69 12.3	8.3	21 41.3	4.9	57.1
	15	42 12.1	. . 55.7	83 39.6	8.3	21 46.2	4.7	57.0
	16	57 12.0	55.1	98 06.9	8.4	21 50.9	4.5	57.0
	17	72 11.8	54.6	112 34.3	8.3	21 55.4	4.5	57.0
	18	87 11.6	S19 54.0	127 01.6	8.3	S21 59.9	4.3	57.0
	19	102 11.4	53.5	141 28.9	8.3	22 04.2	4.2	57.0
	20	117 11.2	52.9	155 56.2	8.2	22 08.4	4.0	56.9
	21	132 11.1	. . 52.3	170 23.4	8.3	22 12.4	4.0	56.9
	22	147 10.9	51.8	184 50.7	8.2	22 16.4	3.8	56.9
	23	162 10.7	51.2	199 17.9	8.3	S22 20.2	3.6	56.9
		SD 16.3	*d* 0.5	SD 15.8		15.7		15.6

Lat.	Twilight Naut.	Twilight Civil	Sunrise	Moonrise 19	Moonrise 20	Moonrise 21	Moonrise 22
°	h m	h m	h m	h m	h m	h m	h m
N 72	07 49	09 33	■	04 43	■	■	■
N 70	07 36	09 04	11 10	04 13	06 36	■	■
68	07 25	08 42	10 12	03 51	05 51	08 10	■
66	07 16	08 25	09 39	03 34	05 22	07 11	08 53
64	07 09	08 11	09 15	03 20	05 00	06 37	08 03
62	07 02	07 59	08 56	03 08	04 42	06 13	07 32
60	06 56	07 49	08 40	02 58	04 28	05 53	07 09
N 58	06 50	07 40	08 27	02 50	04 16	05 37	06 50
56	06 45	07 32	08 16	02 42	04 05	05 24	06 34
54	06 41	07 25	08 06	02 36	03 56	05 12	06 21
52	06 36	07 18	07 57	02 30	03 47	05 02	06 09
50	06 32	07 12	07 49	02 24	03 40	04 52	05 59
45	06 23	06 59	07 32	02 13	03 24	04 33	05 37
N 40	06 15	06 48	07 18	02 03	03 11	04 17	05 20
35	06 08	06 39	07 06	01 55	03 00	04 04	05 05
30	06 01	06 30	06 56	01 48	02 51	03 52	04 52
20	05 47	06 14	06 38	01 36	02 34	03 33	04 30
N 10	05 34	06 00	06 22	01 25	02 20	03 16	04 12
0	05 20	05 45	06 07	01 15	02 07	03 00	03 54
S 10	05 03	05 30	05 52	01 05	01 54	02 44	03 37
20	04 44	05 12	05 36	00 55	01 40	02 27	03 18
30	04 19	04 51	05 17	00 43	01 24	02 08	02 57
35	04 03	04 38	05 06	00 36	01 15	01 57	02 44
40	03 44	04 23	04 54	00 29	01 04	01 44	02 30
45	03 19	04 04	04 39	00 20	00 52	01 29	02 13
S 50	02 44	03 40	04 20	00 09	00 37	01 11	01 52
52	02 25	03 28	04 11	00 04	00 30	01 02	01 42
54	02 02	03 14	04 02	24 23	00 23	00 52	01 30
56	01 28	02 58	03 50	24 14	00 14	00 42	01 18
58	////	02 38	03 38	24 05	00 05	00 29	01 03
S 60	////	02 12	03 22	23 54	24 15	00 15	00 45

Lat.	Sunset	Twilight Civil	Twilight Naut.	Moonset 19	Moonset 20	Moonset 21	Moonset 22
°	h m	h m	h m	h m	h m	h m	h m
N 72	■	14 50	16 34	09 51	■	■	■
N 70	13 13	15 19	16 47	10 23	09 48	■	■
68	14 10	15 40	16 57	10 46	10 34	10 07	■
66	14 44	15 57	17 06	11 05	11 04	11 06	11 18
64	15 08	16 11	17 14	11 20	11 27	11 41	12 08
62	15 27	16 23	17 21	11 32	11 45	12 06	12 39
60	15 42	16 34	17 27	11 43	12 00	12 26	13 03
N 58	15 55	16 42	17 32	11 52	12 13	12 42	13 22
56	16 07	16 50	17 37	12 01	12 25	12 56	13 37
54	16 17	16 57	17 42	12 08	12 34	13 08	13 51
52	16 25	17 04	17 46	12 15	12 43	13 19	14 03
50	16 33	17 10	17 50	12 21	12 51	13 28	14 13
45	16 50	17 23	17 59	12 34	13 08	13 48	14 35
N 40	17 04	17 34	18 07	12 44	13 22	14 05	14 53
35	17 16	17 43	18 14	12 54	13 34	14 18	15 08
30	17 26	17 52	18 21	13 02	13 44	14 30	15 21
20	17 44	18 08	18 34	13 16	14 02	14 51	15 43
N 10	18 00	18 22	18 48	13 28	14 17	15 09	16 02
0	18 14	18 37	19 02	13 40	14 32	15 26	16 20
S 10	18 29	18 52	19 18	13 51	14 47	15 43	16 38
20	18 45	19 09	19 38	14 04	15 02	16 01	16 57
30	19 04	19 30	20 02	14 18	15 20	16 21	17 19
35	19 15	19 43	20 18	14 26	15 31	16 33	17 32
40	19 27	19 59	20 37	14 36	15 43	16 47	17 47
45	19 42	20 17	21 02	14 47	15 57	17 04	18 05
S 50	20 01	20 41	21 36	15 00	16 15	17 24	18 27
52	20 09	20 53	21 54	15 07	16 23	17 34	18 37
54	20 19	21 06	22 17	15 14	16 32	17 45	18 49
56	20 30	21 22	22 50	15 22	16 43	17 58	19 03
58	20 43	21 42	////	15 30	16 55	18 12	19 19
S 60	20 58	22 06	////	15 41	17 08	18 29	19 38

Day	SUN Eqn. of Time 00^h	SUN Eqn. of Time 12^h	SUN Mer. Pass.	MOON Mer. Pass. Upper	MOON Mer. Pass. Lower	MOON Age	MOON Phase
d	m s	m s	h m	h m	h m	d	%
19	10 24	10 33	12 11	07 27	19 53	24	29
20	10 42	10 51	12 11	08 19	20 46	25	20
21	11 00	11 09	12 11	09 13	21 40	26	12

UT	ARIES GHA	VENUS −4.1 GHA	Dec	MARS +1.4 GHA	Dec	JUPITER −1.9 GHA	Dec	SATURN +0.6 GHA	Dec	Name	SHA	Dec
22 00	120 49.0	138 49.4	S 9 04.8	229 40.5	S22 10.2	198 21.7	S22 53.2	185 04.0	S21 18.1	Acamar	315 14.8	S40 13.9
01	135 51.4	153 49.1	03.5	244 41.2	10.4	213 23.6	53.1	200 06.2	18.0	Achernar	335 23.4	S57 08.6
02	150 53.9	168 48.8	02.3	259 41.8	10.7	228 25.5	53.1	215 08.3	18.0	Acrux	173 03.9	S63 12.3
03	165 56.4	183 48.5	9 01.1	274 42.5 ..	10.9	243 27.3 ..	53.0	230 10.5 ..	17.9	Adhara	255 08.6	S29 00.1
04	180 58.8	198 48.2	8 59.8	289 43.1	11.2	258 29.2	53.0	245 12.6	17.9	Aldebaran	290 43.9	N16 32.8
05	196 01.3	213 47.8	58.6	304 43.8	11.4	273 31.0	52.9	260 14.8	17.8			
06	211 03.8	228 47.5	S 8 57.4	319 44.4	S22 11.7	288 32.9	S22 52.9	275 16.9	S21 17.8	Alioth	166 16.5	N55 50.9
W 07	226 06.2	243 47.2	56.1	334 45.1	11.9	303 34.8	52.9	290 19.1	17.7	Alkaid	152 55.2	N49 12.6
E 08	241 08.7	258 46.9	54.9	349 45.7	12.1	318 36.6	52.8	305 21.2	17.7	Alnair	27 38.4	S46 52.0
D 09	256 11.2	273 46.6 ..	53.7	4 46.4 ..	12.4	333 38.5 ..	52.8	320 23.4 ..	17.6	Alnilam	275 41.5	S 1 11.5
N 10	271 13.6	288 46.3	52.4	19 47.0	12.6	348 40.3	52.7	335 25.6	17.6	Alphard	217 51.3	S 8 44.8
E 11	286 16.1	303 45.9	51.2	34 47.7	12.9	3 42.2	52.7	350 27.7	17.5			
S 12	301 18.6	318 45.6	S 8 50.0	49 48.3	S22 13.1	18 44.0	S22 52.6	5 29.9	S21 17.5	Alphecca	126 07.3	N26 38.8
D 13	316 21.0	333 45.3	48.7	64 48.9	13.4	33 45.9	52.6	20 32.0	17.4	Alpheratz	357 39.0	N29 12.0
A 14	331 23.5	348 45.0	47.5	79 49.6	13.6	48 47.8	52.5	35 34.2	17.4	Altair	62 04.1	N 8 55.2
Y 15	346 25.9	3 44.7 ..	46.3	94 50.2 ..	13.9	63 49.6 ..	52.5	50 36.3 ..	17.3	Ankaa	353 11.4	S42 12.2
16	1 28.4	18 44.4	45.0	109 50.9	14.1	78 51.5	52.5	65 38.5	17.3	Antares	112 20.9	S26 28.4
17	16 30.9	33 44.1	43.8	124 51.5	14.3	93 53.3	52.4	80 40.6	17.2			
18	31 33.3	48 43.7	S 8 42.6	139 52.2	S22 14.6	108 55.2	S22 52.4	95 42.8	S21 17.2	Arcturus	145 51.6	N19 04.6
19	46 35.8	63 43.4	41.3	154 52.8	14.8	123 57.1	52.3	110 44.9	17.1	Atria	107 19.0	S69 03.4
20	61 38.3	78 43.1	40.1	169 53.5	15.1	138 58.9	52.3	125 47.1	17.1	Avior	234 15.5	S59 34.4
21	76 40.7	93 42.8 ..	38.8	184 54.1 ..	15.3	154 00.8 ..	52.2	140 49.2 ..	17.1	Bellatrix	278 26.9	N 6 21.9
22	91 43.2	108 42.5	37.6	199 54.8	15.6	169 02.6	52.2	155 51.4	17.0	Betelgeuse	270 56.1	N 7 24.5
23	106 45.7	123 42.2	36.4	214 55.4	15.8	184 04.5	52.1	170 53.5	17.0			
23 00	121 48.1	138 41.9	S 8 35.1	229 56.1	S22 16.0	199 06.4	S22 52.1	185 55.7	S21 16.9	Canopus	263 53.6	S52 42.6
01	136 50.6	153 41.6	33.9	244 56.7	16.3	214 08.2	52.1	200 57.8	16.9	Capella	280 27.4	N46 01.0
02	151 53.1	168 41.3	32.7	259 57.3	16.5	229 10.1	52.0	216 00.0	16.8	Deneb	49 28.9	N45 21.1
03	166 55.5	183 41.0 ..	31.4	274 58.0 ..	16.8	244 11.9 ..	52.0	231 02.1 ..	16.8	Denebola	182 28.8	N14 27.6
04	181 58.0	198 40.7	30.2	289 58.6	17.0	259 13.8	51.9	246 04.3	16.7	Diphda	348 51.4	S17 52.9
05	197 00.4	213 40.3	28.9	304 59.3	17.2	274 15.7	51.9	261 06.4	16.7			
06	212 02.9	228 40.0	S 8 27.7	319 59.9	S22 17.5	289 17.5	S22 51.8	276 08.6	S21 16.6	Dubhe	193 45.6	N61 38.4
T 07	227 05.4	243 39.7	26.5	335 00.6	17.7	304 19.4	51.8	291 10.8	16.6	Elnath	278 06.6	N28 37.4
H 08	242 07.8	258 39.4	25.2	350 01.2	17.9	319 21.2	51.7	306 12.9	16.5	Eltanin	90 44.5	N51 29.1
U 09	257 10.3	273 39.1 ..	24.0	5 01.9 ..	18.2	334 23.1 ..	51.7	321 15.1 ..	16.5	Enif	33 43.0	N 9 57.9
R 10	272 12.8	288 38.8	22.7	20 02.5	18.4	349 25.0	51.6	336 17.2	16.4	Fomalhaut	15 19.2	S29 31.2
S 11	287 15.2	303 38.5	21.5	35 03.1	18.7	4 26.8	51.6	351 19.4	16.4			
D 12	302 17.7	318 38.2	S 8 20.2	50 03.8	S22 18.9	19 28.7	S22 51.6	6 21.5	S21 16.3	Gacrux	171 55.6	S57 13.2
A 13	317 20.2	333 37.9	19.0	65 04.4	19.1	34 30.5	51.5	21 23.7	16.3	Gienah	175 47.5	S17 39.1
Y 14	332 22.6	348 37.6	17.8	80 05.1	19.4	49 32.4	51.5	36 25.8	16.2	Hadar	148 41.5	S60 27.8
15	347 25.1	3 37.3 ..	16.5	95 05.7 ..	19.6	64 34.3 ..	51.4	51 28.0 ..	16.2	Hamal	327 55.6	N23 33.3
16	2 27.5	18 37.0	15.3	110 06.4	19.9	79 36.1	51.4	66 30.1	16.1	Kaus Aust.	83 38.1	S34 22.4
17	17 30.0	33 36.7	14.0	125 07.0	20.1	94 38.0	51.3	81 32.3	16.1			
18	32 32.5	48 36.4	S 8 12.8	140 07.6	S22 20.3	109 39.8	S22 51.3	96 34.4	S21 16.0	Kochab	137 20.3	N74 04.2
19	47 34.9	63 36.1	11.5	155 08.3	20.5	124 41.7	51.2	111 36.6	16.0	Markab	13 34.0	N15 18.7
20	62 37.4	78 35.8	10.3	170 08.9	20.8	139 43.6	51.2	126 38.7	15.9	Menkar	314 10.2	N 4 09.9
21	77 39.9	93 35.5 ..	09.0	185 09.6 ..	21.0	154 45.4 ..	51.1	141 40.9 ..	15.9	Menkent	148 02.2	S36 27.8
22	92 42.3	108 35.2	07.8	200 10.2	21.2	169 47.3	51.1	156 43.0	15.8	Miaplacidus	221 37.9	S69 47.9
23	107 44.8	123 34.9	06.5	215 10.9	21.5	184 49.1	51.1	171 45.2	15.8			
24 00	122 47.3	138 34.6	S 8 05.3	230 11.5	S22 21.7	199 51.0	S22 51.0	186 47.3	S21 15.7	Mirfak	308 33.6	N49 56.0
01	137 49.7	153 34.3	04.1	245 12.1	21.9	214 52.9	51.0	201 49.5	15.7	Nunki	75 53.0	S26 16.2
02	152 52.2	168 34.0	02.8	260 12.8	22.2	229 54.7	50.9	216 51.7	15.7	Peacock	53 12.7	S56 40.3
03	167 54.7	183 33.7 ..	01.6	275 13.4 ..	22.4	244 56.6 ..	50.9	231 53.8 ..	15.6	Pollux	243 21.8	N27 58.5
04	182 57.1	198 33.4	8 00.3	290 14.1	22.6	259 58.5	50.8	246 56.0	15.6	Procyon	244 54.6	N 5 10.3
05	197 59.6	213 33.1	7 59.1	305 14.7	22.9	275 00.3	50.8	261 58.1	15.5			
06	213 02.0	228 32.8	S 7 57.8	320 15.3	S22 23.1	290 02.2	S22 50.7	277 00.3	S21 15.5	Rasalhague	96 02.5	N12 32.7
07	228 04.5	243 32.5	56.6	335 16.0	23.3	305 04.0	50.7	292 02.4	15.4	Regulus	207 38.4	N11 52.1
08	243 07.0	258 32.2	55.3	350 16.6	23.6	320 05.9	50.6	307 04.6	15.4	Rigel	281 07.4	S 8 10.9
F 09	258 09.4	273 31.9 ..	54.1	5 17.3 ..	23.8	335 07.8 ..	50.6	322 06.7 ..	15.3	Rigil Kent.	139 45.7	S60 54.6
R 10	273 11.9	288 31.6	52.8	20 17.9	24.0	350 09.6	50.5	337 08.9	15.3	Sabik	102 07.6	S15 44.9
I 11	288 14.4	303 31.4	51.6	35 18.5	24.2	5 11.5	50.5	352 11.0	15.2			
D 12	303 16.8	318 31.1	S 7 50.3	50 19.2	S22 24.5	20 13.3	S22 50.5	7 13.2	S21 15.2	Schedar	349 35.6	N56 38.9
A 13	318 19.3	333 30.8	49.1	65 19.8	24.7	35 15.2	50.4	22 15.3	15.1	Shaula	96 16.1	S37 06.9
Y 14	333 21.8	348 30.5	47.8	80 20.5	24.9	50 17.1	50.4	37 17.5	15.1	Sirius	258 29.4	S16 44.8
15	348 24.2	3 30.2 ..	46.6	95 21.1 ..	25.2	65 18.9 ..	50.3	52 19.6 ..	15.0	Spica	158 26.4	S11 15.8
16	3 26.7	18 29.9	45.3	110 21.7	25.4	80 20.8	50.3	67 21.8	15.0	Suhail	222 48.7	S43 30.8
17	18 29.2	33 29.6	44.1	125 22.4	25.6	95 22.7	50.2	82 24.0	14.9			
18	33 31.6	48 29.3	S 7 42.8	140 23.0	S22 25.8	110 24.5	S22 50.2	97 26.1	S21 14.9	Vega	80 36.3	N38 48.1
19	48 34.1	63 29.0	41.5	155 23.7	26.1	125 26.4	50.1	112 28.3	14.8	Zuben'ubi	137 00.5	S16 07.3
20	63 36.5	78 28.7	40.3	170 24.3	26.3	140 28.2	50.1	127 30.4	14.8		SHA	Mer. Pass.
21	78 39.0	93 28.4 ..	39.0	185 24.9 ..	26.5	155 30.1 ..	50.0	142 32.6 ..	14.7	Venus	16 53.8	14 46
22	93 41.5	108 28.2	37.8	200 25.6	26.7	170 32.0	50.0	157 34.7	14.7	Mars	108 07.9	8 40
23	108 43.9	123 27.9	36.5	215 26.2	27.0	185 33.8	49.9	172 36.9	14.6	Jupiter	77 18.2	10 42
Mer. Pass. 15 50.2		v −0.3 d 1.2		v 0.6 d 0.2		v 1.9 d 0.0		v 2.2 d 0.0		Saturn	64 07.6	11 35

SUN and MOON

UT	SUN GHA	SUN Dec	MOON GHA	v	MOON Dec	d	HP
d h	° ′	° ′	° ′	′	° ′	′	′
22 00	177 10.5	S19 50.7	213 45.2	8.2	S22 23.8	3.6	56.9
01	192 10.4	50.1	228 12.4	8.2	22 27.4	3.4	56.8
02	207 10.2	49.5	242 39.6	8.2	22 30.8	3.3	56.8
03	222 10.0	.. 49.0	257 06.8	8.2	22 34.1	3.1	56.8
04	237 09.8	48.4	271 34.0	8.3	22 37.2	3.0	56.8
05	252 09.7	47.9	286 01.3	8.2	22 40.2	2.9	56.8
06	267 09.5	S19 47.3	300 28.5	8.2	S22 43.1	2.8	56.7
W 07	282 09.3	46.7	314 55.7	8.2	22 45.9	2.6	56.7
E 08	297 09.2	46.2	329 22.9	8.2	22 48.5	2.5	56.7
D 09	312 09.0	.. 45.6	343 50.1	8.2	22 51.0	2.4	56.7
N 10	327 08.8	45.0	358 17.3	8.2	22 53.4	2.2	56.7
E 11	342 08.6	44.5	12 44.5	8.2	22 55.6	2.1	56.6
S 12	357 08.5	S19 43.9	27 11.7	8.2	S22 57.7	2.0	56.6
D 13	12 08.3	43.3	41 38.9	8.2	22 59.7	1.8	56.6
A 14	27 08.1	42.8	56 06.1	8.3	23 01.5	1.7	56.6
Y 15	42 08.0	.. 42.2	70 33.4	8.2	23 03.2	1.6	56.6
16	57 07.8	41.6	85 00.6	8.2	23 04.8	1.4	56.5
17	72 07.6	41.0	99 27.8	8.3	23 06.2	1.4	56.5
18	87 07.4	S19 40.5	113 55.1	8.3	S23 07.6	1.1	56.5
19	102 07.3	39.9	128 22.4	8.3	23 08.7	1.1	56.5
20	117 07.1	39.3	142 49.7	8.3	23 09.8	0.9	56.5
21	132 06.9	.. 38.7	157 17.0	8.3	23 10.7	0.8	56.4
22	147 06.8	38.2	171 44.3	8.3	23 11.5	0.7	56.4
23	162 06.6	37.6	186 11.6	8.4	23 12.2	0.5	56.4
23 00	177 06.4	S19 37.0	200 39.0	8.3	S23 12.7	0.4	56.4
01	192 06.3	36.4	215 06.3	8.4	23 13.1	0.3	56.4
02	207 06.1	35.9	229 33.7	8.4	23 13.4	0.1	56.3
03	222 05.9	.. 35.3	244 01.1	8.4	23 13.5	0.0	56.3
04	237 05.8	34.7	258 28.5	8.5	23 13.5	0.1	56.3
05	252 05.6	34.1	272 56.0	8.5	23 13.4	0.3	56.3
06	267 05.4	S19 33.6	287 23.5	8.5	S23 13.1	0.3	56.3
T 07	282 05.3	33.0	301 51.0	8.5	23 12.8	0.5	56.2
H 08	297 05.1	32.4	316 18.5	8.6	23 12.3	0.7	56.2
U 09	312 05.0	.. 31.8	330 46.1	8.6	23 11.6	0.7	56.2
R 10	327 04.8	31.2	345 13.7	8.6	23 10.9	0.9	56.2
S 11	342 04.6	30.7	359 41.3	8.6	23 10.0	1.0	56.2
D 12	357 04.5	S19 30.1	14 08.9	8.7	S23 09.0	1.2	56.1
A 13	12 04.4	29.5	28 36.6	8.7	23 07.8	1.3	56.1
Y 14	27 04.1	28.9	43 04.3	8.8	23 06.5	1.4	56.1
15	42 04.0	.. 28.3	57 32.1	8.8	23 05.1	1.5	56.1
16	57 03.8	27.7	71 59.9	8.8	23 03.6	1.6	56.1
17	72 03.6	27.1	86 27.7	8.9	23 02.0	1.8	56.0
18	87 03.5	S19 26.6	100 55.6	8.9	S23 00.2	1.9	56.0
19	102 03.3	26.0	115 23.5	8.9	22 58.3	2.0	56.0
20	117 03.2	25.4	129 51.4	9.0	22 56.3	2.2	56.0
21	132 03.0	.. 24.8	144 19.4	9.0	22 54.1	2.2	56.0
22	147 02.8	24.2	158 47.4	9.1	22 51.9	2.4	55.9
23	162 02.7	23.6	173 15.5	9.1	22 49.5	2.5	55.9
24 00	177 02.5	S19 23.0	187 43.6	9.1	S22 47.0	2.6	55.9
01	192 02.4	22.4	202 11.7	9.3	22 44.4	2.8	55.9
02	207 02.2	21.8	216 40.0	9.2	22 41.6	2.9	55.9
03	222 02.1	.. 21.2	231 08.2	9.3	22 38.7	3.0	55.8
04	237 01.9	20.7	245 36.5	9.3	22 35.7	3.1	55.8
05	252 01.7	20.1	260 04.8	9.4	22 32.6	3.2	55.8
06	267 01.6	S19 19.5	274 33.2	9.5	S22 29.4	3.3	55.8
07	282 01.4	18.9	289 01.7	9.5	22 26.1	3.5	55.8
08	297 01.3	18.3	303 30.2	9.5	22 22.6	3.6	55.7
F 09	312 01.1	.. 17.7	317 58.7	9.6	22 19.0	3.6	55.7
R 10	327 01.0	17.1	332 27.3	9.7	22 15.4	3.9	55.7
I 11	342 00.8	16.5	346 56.0	9.7	22 11.5	3.9	55.7
D 12	357 00.6	S19 15.9	1 24.7	9.7	S22 07.6	4.0	55.7
A 13	12 00.5	15.3	15 53.4	9.8	22 03.6	4.1	55.6
Y 14	27 00.3	14.7	30 22.2	9.9	21 59.5	4.3	55.6
15	42 00.2	.. 14.1	44 51.1	9.9	21 55.2	4.4	55.6
16	57 00.0	13.5	59 20.0	10.0	21 50.8	4.4	55.6
17	71 59.9	12.9	73 49.0	10.1	21 46.4	4.6	55.6
18	86 59.7	S19 12.3	88 18.1	10.1	S21 41.8	4.7	55.5
19	101 59.6	11.7	102 47.2	10.1	21 37.1	4.8	55.5
20	116 59.4	11.1	117 16.3	10.3	21 32.3	4.9	55.5
21	131 59.3	.. 10.5	131 45.6	10.2	21 27.4	5.0	55.5
22	146 59.1	09.9	146 14.8	10.4	21 22.4	5.2	55.5
23	161 59.0	09.3	160 44.2	10.4	S21 17.2	5.2	55.5
	SD 16.3	d 0.6	SD 15.4		15.3		15.2

Twilight · Sunrise · Moonrise

Lat.	Naut.	Civil	Sunrise	Moonrise 22	23	24	25
°	h m	h m	h m	h m	h m	h m	h m
N 72	07 41	09 20	■	■	■	■	■
N 70	07 29	08 54	10 45	■	■	■	■
68	07 19	08 34	09 59	■	■	■	11 05
66	07 11	08 18	09 29	08 53	10 00	10 20	10 25
64	07 04	08 05	09 07	08 03	09 05	09 40	09 57
62	06 57	07 54	08 49	07 32	08 33	09 12	09 36
60	06 52	07 44	08 34	07 09	08 08	08 50	09 18
N 58	06 47	07 36	08 22	06 50	07 49	08 33	09 04
56	06 42	07 28	08 11	06 34	07 33	08 18	08 51
54	06 38	07 21	08 01	06 21	07 19	08 05	08 40
52	06 34	07 15	07 53	06 09	07 07	07 54	08 31
50	06 30	07 10	07 46	05 59	06 56	07 44	08 22
45	06 22	06 57	07 29	05 37	06 34	07 23	08 04
N 40	06 14	06 47	07 16	05 20	06 16	07 06	07 48
35	06 07	06 38	07 05	05 05	06 01	06 51	07 36
30	06 00	06 29	06 55	04 52	05 48	06 39	07 24
20	05 47	06 14	06 38	04 30	05 26	06 18	07 05
N 10	05 34	06 00	06 22	04 12	05 06	05 59	06 48
0	05 21	05 46	06 08	03 54	04 48	05 42	06 33
S 10	05 05	05 31	05 54	03 37	04 30	05 24	06 17
20	04 46	05 14	05 38	03 18	04 11	05 06	06 00
30	04 22	04 54	05 20	02 57	03 49	04 44	05 41
35	04 07	04 41	05 10	02 44	03 36	04 32	05 29
40	03 48	04 26	04 57	02 30	03 21	04 17	05 16
45	03 24	04 08	04 43	02 13	03 03	04 00	05 01
S 50	02 51	03 45	04 25	01 52	02 41	03 39	04 42
52	02 34	03 34	04 17	01 42	02 31	03 28	04 33
54	02 12	03 21	04 07	01 30	02 19	03 17	04 23
56	01 42	03 05	03 57	01 18	02 05	03 04	04 11
58	00 49	02 47	03 45	01 03	01 49	02 49	03 58
S 60	////	02 24	03 30	00 45	01 30	02 30	03 43

Sunset · Twilight · Moonset

Lat.	Sunset	Civil	Naut.	Moonset 22	23	24	25
°	h m	h m	h m	h m	h m	h m	h m
N 72	■	15 04	16 44	■	■	■	■
N 70	13 40	15 30	16 56	■	■	■	■
68	14 26	15 50	17 05	■	■	■	14 35
66	14 55	16 06	17 14	11 18	12 04	13 34	15 14
64	15 17	16 19	17 21	12 08	12 59	14 14	15 41
62	15 35	16 30	17 27	12 39	13 31	14 41	16 02
60	15 50	16 40	17 32	13 03	13 55	15 03	16 19
N 58	16 02	16 48	17 37	13 22	14 15	15 20	16 33
56	16 13	16 56	17 42	13 37	14 31	15 35	16 45
54	16 22	17 03	17 46	13 51	14 45	15 47	16 56
52	16 31	17 09	17 50	14 03	14 57	15 58	17 05
50	16 38	17 14	17 54	14 13	15 07	16 08	17 13
45	16 53	17 26	18 02	14 34	15 29	16 29	17 31
N 40	17 08	17 37	18 10	14 53	15 47	16 45	17 45
35	17 19	17 46	18 17	15 08	16 02	16 59	17 57
30	17 29	17 54	18 23	15 21	16 15	17 11	18 08
20	17 46	18 09	18 36	15 43	16 37	17 32	18 26
N 10	18 01	18 23	18 49	16 02	16 56	17 50	18 42
0	18 15	18 37	19 03	16 20	17 14	18 07	18 56
S 10	18 30	18 52	19 19	16 38	17 32	18 23	19 11
20	18 45	19 09	19 37	16 57	17 51	18 41	19 27
30	19 03	19 29	20 01	17 19	18 13	19 01	19 44
35	19 13	19 42	20 16	17 32	18 26	19 13	19 54
40	19 25	19 56	20 35	17 47	18 40	19 27	20 06
45	19 40	20 14	20 58	18 05	18 58	19 43	20 20
S 50	19 57	20 37	21 31	18 27	19 20	20 02	20 37
52	20 06	20 48	21 48	18 37	19 30	20 12	20 44
54	20 15	21 01	22 09	18 49	19 41	20 22	20 53
56	20 25	21 16	22 37	19 03	19 55	20 34	21 03
58	20 37	21 34	23 25	19 19	20 10	20 47	21 14
S 60	20 51	21 57	////	19 38	20 29	21 03	21 27

SUN and MOON data

Day	Eqn. of Time 00h	12h	Mer. Pass.	Mer. Pass. Upper	Lower	Age	Phase
d	m s	m s	h m	h m	h m	d	%
22	11 17	11 26	12 11	22 34	10 07	27	6
23	11 34	11 42	12 12	11 01	23 28	28	2
24	11 50	11 57	12 12	11 54	24 20	29	0

UT	ARIES GHA	VENUS −4·1 GHA	Dec	MARS +1·4 GHA	Dec	JUPITER −1·9 GHA	Dec	SATURN +0·6 GHA	Dec	STARS Name	SHA	Dec
25 00	123 46.4	138 27.6	S 7 35.3	230 26.9	S22 27.2	200 35.7	S22 49.9	187 39.0	S21 14.6	Acamar	315 14.8	S40 13.9
01	138 48.9	153 27.3	34.0	245 27.5	27.4	215 37.6	49.9	202 41.2	14.5	Achernar	335 23.4	S57 08.5
02	153 51.3	168 27.0	32.8	260 28.1	27.6	230 39.4	49.8	217 43.3	14.5	Acrux	173 03.9	S63 12.3
03	168 53.8	183 26.7	.. 31.5	275 28.8	.. 27.9	245 41.3	.. 49.8	232 45.5	.. 14.4	Adhara	255 08.6	S29 00.1
04	183 56.3	198 26.4	30.3	290 29.4	28.1	260 43.2	49.7	247 47.6	14.4	Aldebaran	290 43.9	N16 32.8
05	198 58.7	213 26.1	29.0	305 30.0	28.3	275 45.0	49.7	262 49.8	14.3			
06	214 01.2	228 25.9	S 7 27.7	320 30.7	S22 28.5	290 46.9	S22 49.6	277 52.0	S21 14.3	Alioth	166 16.4	N55 50.9
07	229 03.7	243 25.6	26.5	335 31.3	28.8	305 48.7	49.6	292 54.1	14.2	Alkaid	152 55.2	N49 12.6
S 08	244 06.1	258 25.3	25.2	350 32.0	29.0	320 50.6	49.5	307 56.3	14.2	Alnair	27 38.4	S46 52.0
A 09	259 08.6	273 25.0	.. 24.0	5 32.6	.. 29.2	335 52.5	.. 49.5	322 58.4	.. 14.2	Alnilam	275 41.5	S 1 11.6
T 10	274 11.0	288 24.7	22.7	20 33.2	29.4	350 54.3	49.4	338 00.6	14.1	Alphard	217 51.3	S 8 44.8
U 11	289 13.5	303 24.4	21.4	35 33.9	29.6	5 56.2	49.4	353 02.7	14.1			
R 12	304 16.0	318 24.2	S 7 20.2	50 34.5	S22 29.9	20 58.1	S22 49.3	8 04.9	S21 14.0	Alphecca	126 07.3	N26 38.8
D 13	319 18.4	333 23.9	18.9	65 35.1	30.1	35 59.9	49.3	23 07.0	14.0	Alpheratz	357 39.0	N29 12.0
A 14	334 20.9	348 23.6	17.7	80 35.8	30.3	51 01.8	49.2	38 09.2	13.9	Altair	62 04.1	N 8 55.2
Y 15	349 23.4	3 23.3	.. 16.4	95 36.4	.. 30.5	66 03.7	.. 49.2	53 11.3	.. 13.9	Ankaa	353 11.4	S42 12.2
16	4 25.8	18 23.0	15.2	110 37.1	30.7	81 05.5	49.2	68 13.5	13.8	Antares	112 20.9	S26 28.4
17	19 28.3	33 22.8	13.9	125 37.7	31.0	96 07.4	49.1	83 15.6	13.8			
18	34 30.8	48 22.5	S 7 12.6	140 38.3	S22 31.2	111 09.2	S22 49.1	98 17.8	S21 13.7	Arcturus	145 51.6	N19 04.6
19	49 33.2	63 22.2	11.4	155 39.0	31.4	126 11.1	49.0	113 20.0	13.7	Atria	107 19.0	S69 03.4
20	64 35.7	78 21.9	10.1	170 39.6	31.6	141 13.0	49.0	128 22.1	13.6	Avior	234 15.5	S59 34.5
21	79 38.1	93 21.6	.. 08.9	185 40.2	.. 31.8	156 14.8	.. 48.9	143 24.3	.. 13.6	Bellatrix	278 26.9	N 6 21.9
22	94 40.6	108 21.4	07.6	200 40.9	32.0	171 16.7	48.9	158 26.4	13.5	Betelgeuse	270 56.1	N 7 24.5
23	109 43.1	123 21.1	06.3	215 41.5	32.3	186 18.6	48.8	173 28.6	13.5			
26 00	124 45.5	138 20.8	S 7 05.1	230 42.1	S22 32.5	201 20.4	S22 48.8	188 30.7	S21 13.4	Canopus	263 53.6	S52 42.6
01	139 48.0	153 20.5	03.8	245 42.8	32.7	216 22.3	48.7	203 32.9	13.4	Capella	280 27.4	N46 01.0
02	154 50.5	168 20.3	02.5	260 43.4	32.9	231 24.2	48.7	218 35.0	13.3	Deneb	49 28.9	N45 21.1
03	169 52.9	183 20.0	.. 01.3	275 44.1	.. 33.1	246 26.0	.. 48.6	233 37.2	.. 13.3	Denebola	182 28.8	N14 27.5
04	184 55.4	198 19.7	7 00.0	290 44.7	33.3	261 27.9	48.6	248 39.3	13.2	Diphda	348 51.4	S17 52.9
05	199 57.9	213 19.4	6 58.7	305 45.3	33.6	276 29.8	48.5	263 41.5	13.2			
06	215 00.3	228 19.2	S 6 57.5	320 46.0	S22 33.8	291 31.6	S22 48.5	278 43.7	S21 13.1	Dubhe	193 45.6	N61 38.4
07	230 02.8	243 18.9	56.2	335 46.6	34.0	306 33.5	48.4	293 45.8	13.1	Elnath	278 06.6	N28 37.4
S 08	245 05.3	258 18.6	55.0	350 47.2	34.2	321 35.4	48.4	308 48.0	13.0	Eltanin	90 44.5	N51 29.1
U 09	260 07.7	273 18.3	.. 53.7	5 47.9	.. 34.4	336 37.2	.. 48.3	323 50.1	.. 13.0	Enif	33 43.0	N 9 57.9
N 10	275 10.2	288 18.1	52.4	20 48.5	34.6	351 39.1	48.3	338 52.3	12.9	Fomalhaut	15 19.2	S29 31.2
11	290 12.6	303 17.8	51.2	35 49.1	34.8	6 41.0	48.3	353 54.4	12.9			
D 12	305 15.1	318 17.5	S 6 49.9	50 49.8	S22 35.1	21 42.8	S22 48.2	8 56.6	S21 12.8	Gacrux	171 55.6	S57 13.2
A 13	320 17.6	333 17.2	48.6	65 50.4	35.3	36 44.7	48.2	23 58.7	12.8	Gienah	175 47.4	S17 39.1
Y 14	335 20.0	348 17.0	47.4	80 51.0	35.5	51 46.6	48.1	39 00.9	12.7	Hadar	148 41.4	S60 27.8
15	350 22.5	3 16.7	.. 46.1	95 51.7	.. 35.7	66 48.4	.. 48.1	54 03.0	.. 12.7	Hamal	327 55.6	N23 33.3
16	5 25.0	18 16.4	44.8	110 52.3	35.9	81 50.3	48.0	69 05.2	12.6	Kaus Aust.	83 38.1	S34 22.4
17	20 27.4	33 16.2	43.6	125 52.9	36.1	96 52.2	48.0	84 07.4	12.6			
18	35 29.9	48 15.9	S 6 42.3	140 53.6	S22 36.3	111 54.0	S22 47.9	99 09.5	S21 12.5	Kochab	137 20.2	N74 04.2
19	50 32.4	63 15.6	41.0	155 54.2	36.5	126 55.9	47.9	114 11.7	12.5	Markab	13 34.1	N15 18.7
20	65 34.8	78 15.3	39.8	170 54.8	36.7	141 57.7	47.8	129 13.8	12.5	Menkar	314 10.2	N 4 09.9
21	80 37.3	93 15.1	.. 38.5	185 55.5	.. 37.0	156 59.6	.. 47.8	144 16.0	.. 12.4	Menkent	148 02.2	S36 27.8
22	95 39.8	108 14.8	37.2	200 56.1	37.2	172 01.5	47.7	159 18.1	12.4	Miaplacidus	221 37.9	S69 47.9
23	110 42.2	123 14.5	36.0	215 56.7	37.4	187 03.3	47.7	174 20.3	12.3			
27 00	125 44.7	138 14.3	S 6 34.7	230 57.4	S22 37.6	202 05.2	S22 47.6	189 22.4	S21 12.3	Mirfak	308 33.7	N49 56.0
01	140 47.1	153 14.0	33.4	245 58.0	37.8	217 07.1	47.6	204 24.6	12.2	Nunki	75 53.0	S26 16.2
02	155 49.6	168 13.7	32.1	260 58.6	38.0	232 09.0	47.5	219 26.7	12.2	Peacock	53 12.7	S56 40.2
03	170 52.1	183 13.5	.. 30.9	275 59.3	.. 38.2	247 10.8	.. 47.5	234 28.9	.. 12.1	Pollux	243 21.8	N27 58.5
04	185 54.5	198 13.2	29.6	290 59.9	38.4	262 12.7	47.4	249 31.1	12.1	Procyon	244 54.6	N 5 10.3
05	200 57.0	213 12.9	28.3	306 00.5	38.6	277 14.6	47.4	264 33.2	12.0			
06	215 59.5	228 12.7	S 6 27.1	321 01.2	S22 38.8	292 16.4	S22 47.3	279 35.4	S21 12.0	Rasalhague	96 02.5	N12 32.7
07	231 01.9	243 12.4	25.8	336 01.8	39.0	307 18.3	47.3	294 37.5	11.9	Regulus	207 38.4	N11 52.1
M 08	246 04.4	258 12.2	24.5	351 02.4	39.2	322 20.2	47.2	309 39.7	11.9	Rigel	281 07.4	S 8 10.9
O 09	261 06.9	273 11.9	.. 23.3	6 03.0	.. 39.4	337 22.0	.. 47.2	324 41.8	.. 11.8	Rigil Kent.	139 45.6	S60 54.6
N 10	276 09.3	288 11.6	22.0	21 03.7	39.6	352 23.9	47.2	339 44.0	11.8	Sabik	102 07.6	S15 44.9
11	291 11.8	303 11.4	20.7	36 04.3	39.9	7 25.8	47.1	354 46.1	11.7			
D 12	306 14.2	318 11.1	S 6 19.4	51 04.9	S22 40.1	22 27.6	S22 47.1	9 48.3	S21 11.7	Schedar	349 35.6	N56 38.9
A 13	321 16.7	333 10.8	18.2	66 05.6	40.3	37 29.5	47.0	24 50.5	11.6	Shaula	96 16.0	S37 06.9
Y 14	336 19.2	348 10.6	16.9	81 06.2	40.5	52 31.4	47.0	39 52.6	11.6	Sirius	258 29.4	S16 44.8
15	351 21.6	3 10.3	.. 15.6	96 06.8	.. 40.7	67 33.2	.. 46.9	54 54.8	.. 11.5	Spica	158 26.4	S11 15.8
16	6 24.1	18 10.1	14.3	111 07.5	40.9	82 35.1	46.9	69 56.9	11.5	Suhail	222 48.7	S43 30.8
17	21 26.6	33 09.8	13.1	126 08.1	41.1	97 37.0	46.8	84 59.1	11.4			
18	36 29.0	48 09.5	S 6 11.8	141 08.7	S22 41.3	112 38.8	S22 46.8	100 01.2	S21 11.4	Vega	80 36.3	N38 48.1
19	51 31.5	63 09.3	10.5	156 09.4	41.5	127 40.7	46.7	115 03.4	11.3	Zuben'ubi	137 00.4	S16 07.3
20	66 34.0	78 09.0	09.3	171 10.0	41.7	142 42.6	46.7	130 05.5	11.3		SHA	Mer. Pass.
21	81 36.4	93 08.8	.. 08.0	186 10.6	.. 41.9	157 44.4	.. 46.6	145 07.7	.. 11.2	Venus	13 35.3	14 47
22	96 38.9	108 08.5	06.7	201 11.2	42.1	172 46.3	46.6	160 09.9	11.2	Mars	105 56.6	8 37
23	111 41.4	123 08.2	05.4	216 11.9	42.3	187 48.2	46.5	175 12.0	11.1	Jupiter	76 34.9	10 33
Mer. Pass. 15 38.4		v −0.3 d 1.3		v 0.6 d 0.2		v 1.9 d 0.0		v 2.2 d 0.0		Saturn	63 45.2	11 24

UT	SUN		MOON					Lat.	Twilight		Sunrise	Moonrise			
									Naut.	Civil		25	26	27	28
	GHA	Dec	GHA	v	Dec	d	HP	°	h m	h m	h m	h m	h m	h m	h m
d h	° '	° '	° '	'	° '	'	'	N 72	07 31	09 07	11 53	▬	12 15	11 24	10 57
25 00	176 58.8	S19 08.7	175 13.6	10.5	S21 12.0	5.3	55.4	N 70	07 21	08 44	10 24	▬	11 22	10 59	10 43
01	191 58.7	08.1	189 43.1	10.5	21 06.7	5.4	55.4	68	07 12	08 25	09 45	11 05	10 49	10 39	10 31
02	206 58.5	07.4	204 12.6	10.6	21 01.3	5.6	55.4	66	07 05	08 11	09 19	10 25	10 25	10 24	10 22
03	221 58.4 ..	06.8	218 42.2	10.6	20 55.7	5.6	55.4	64	06 58	07 59	08 59	09 57	10 06	10 11	10 13
04	236 58.2	06.2	233 11.8	10.7	20 50.1	5.7	55.4	62	06 52	07 48	08 42	09 36	09 50	10 00	10 06
05	251 58.1	05.6	247 41.5	10.8	20 44.4	5.9	55.3	60	06 47	07 39	08 28	09 18	09 37	09 50	10 00
06	266 57.9	S19 05.0	262 11.3	10.9	S20 38.5	5.9	55.3	N 58	06 43	07 31	08 17	09 04	09 26	09 42	09 55
07	281 57.8	04.4	276 41.2	10.9	20 32.6	6.0	55.3	56	06 38	07 24	08 07	08 51	09 16	09 35	09 50
S 08	296 57.6	03.8	291 11.1	11.0	20 26.6	6.2	55.3	54	06 34	07 18	07 58	08 40	09 07	09 29	09 46
A 09	311 57.5 ..	03.2	305 41.1	11.0	20 20.4	6.2	55.3	52	06 31	07 12	07 50	08 31	09 00	09 23	09 42
T 10	326 57.3	02.6	320 11.1	11.1	20 14.2	6.3	55.2	50	06 27	07 07	07 42	08 22	08 52	09 17	09 38
U 11	341 57.2	02.0	334 41.2	11.2	20 07.9	6.4	55.2	45	06 19	06 55	07 27	08 04	08 37	09 06	09 31
R 12	356 57.0	S19 01.3	349 11.4	11.2	S20 01.5	6.5	55.2	N 40	06 12	06 45	07 14	07 48	08 25	08 56	09 24
D 13	11 56.9	00.7	3 41.6	11.3	19 55.0	6.6	55.2	35	06 06	06 36	07 03	07 36	08 14	08 48	09 19
A 14	26 56.7	19 00.1	18 11.9	11.4	19 48.4	6.7	55.2	30	05 59	06 28	06 54	07 24	08 05	08 41	09 14
Y 15	41 56.6	18 59.5	32 42.3	11.4	19 41.7	6.8	55.2	20	05 47	06 14	06 37	07 05	07 49	08 28	09 05
16	56 56.4	58.9	47 12.7	11.5	19 34.9	6.8	55.1	N 10	05 35	06 00	06 23	06 48	07 35	08 17	08 57
17	71 56.3	58.3	61 43.2	11.6	19 28.1	7.0	55.1	0	05 22	05 47	06 09	06 33	07 21	08 07	08 50
18	86 56.2	S18 57.7	76 13.8	11.6	S19 21.1	7.0	55.1	S 10	05 07	05 33	05 55	06 17	07 08	07 57	08 43
19	101 56.0	57.0	90 44.4	11.7	19 14.1	7.2	55.1	20	04 48	05 16	05 40	06 00	06 54	07 45	08 36
20	116 55.9	56.4	105 15.1	11.8	19 06.9	7.2	55.1	30	04 25	04 57	05 23	05 41	06 37	07 33	08 27
21	131 55.7 ..	55.8	119 45.9	11.8	18 59.7	7.3	55.1	35	04 10	04 45	05 13	05 29	06 28	07 25	08 22
22	146 55.6	55.2	134 16.7	11.9	18 52.4	7.4	55.0	40	03 52	04 30	05 01	05 16	06 17	07 17	08 16
23	161 55.4	54.6	148 47.6	12.0	18 45.0	7.4	55.0	45	03 29	04 13	04 47	05 01	06 04	07 07	08 09
26 00	176 55.3	S18 53.9	163 18.6	12.0	S18 37.6	7.6	55.0	S 50	02 58	03 51	04 30	04 42	05 48	06 55	08 01
01	191 55.1	53.3	177 49.6	12.2	18 30.0	7.6	55.0	52	02 42	03 40	04 22	04 33	05 41	06 49	07 57
02	206 55.0	52.7	192 20.8	12.1	18 22.4	7.8	55.0	54	02 22	03 28	04 13	04 23	05 33	06 43	07 53
03	221 54.9 ..	52.1	206 51.9	12.3	18 14.6	7.7	55.0	56	01 56	03 13	04 03	04 11	05 23	06 36	07 49
04	236 54.7	51.5	221 23.2	12.3	18 06.9	7.9	54.9	58	01 16	02 56	03 52	03 58	05 13	06 29	07 44
05	251 54.6	50.8	235 54.5	12.3	17 59.0	8.0	54.9	S 60	////	02 35	03 38	03 43	05 01	06 20	07 38

	SUN		MOON					Lat.	Sunset	Twilight		Moonset			
										Civil	Naut.	25	26	27	28
06	266 54.4	S18 50.2	250 25.8	12.5	S17 51.0	8.0	54.9	°	h m	h m	h m	h m	h m	h m	h m
07	281 54.3	49.6	264 57.3	12.5	17 43.0	8.1	54.9	N 72	12 33	15 19	16 55	▬	15 06	17 31	19 27
08	296 54.2	49.0	279 28.8	12.6	17 34.9	8.2	54.9	N 70	14 02	15 42	17 05	▬	15 58	17 55	19 39
S 09	311 54.0 ..	48.3	294 00.4	12.6	17 26.7	8.2	54.9	68	14 40	16 00	17 14	14 35	16 30	18 13	19 49
U 10	326 53.9	47.7	308 32.0	12.7	17 18.5	8.4	54.8	66	15 07	16 15	17 21	15 14	16 53	18 27	19 57
N 11	341 53.7	47.1	323 03.7	12.8	17 10.1	8.4	54.8	64	15 27	16 27	17 28	15 41	17 11	18 39	20 04
D 12	356 53.6	S18 46.5	337 35.5	12.8	S17 01.7	8.4	54.8	62	15 43	16 38	17 33	16 02	17 26	18 49	20 10
A 13	11 53.5	45.8	352 07.3	12.9	16 53.3	8.6	54.8	60	15 57	16 47	17 38	16 19	17 38	18 57	20 15
Y 14	26 53.3	45.2	6 39.2	13.0	16 44.7	8.6	54.8	N 58	16 09	16 54	17 43	16 33	17 49	19 05	20 19
15	41 53.2 ..	44.6	21 11.2	13.0	16 36.1	8.7	54.8	56	16 19	17 01	17 47	16 45	17 58	19 11	20 23
16	56 53.1	43.9	35 43.2	13.1	16 27.4	8.7	54.7	54	16 28	17 08	17 51	16 56	18 06	19 17	20 27
17	71 52.9	43.3	50 15.3	13.1	16 18.7	8.8	54.7	52	16 36	17 14	17 55	17 05	18 14	19 22	20 30
18	86 52.8	S18 42.7	64 47.4	13.2	S16 09.9	8.9	54.7	50	16 43	17 19	17 58	17 13	18 20	19 27	20 33
19	101 52.6	42.0	79 19.6	13.3	16 01.0	9.0	54.7	45	16 58	17 30	18 06	17 31	18 34	19 37	20 39
20	116 52.5	41.4	93 51.9	13.4	15 52.0	9.0	54.7	N 40	17 11	17 40	18 13	17 45	18 46	19 46	20 44
21	131 52.4 ..	40.8	108 24.3	13.4	15 43.0	9.1	54.7	35	17 22	17 49	18 20	17 57	18 56	19 53	20 49
22	146 52.2	40.2	122 56.7	13.5	15 33.9	9.1	54.7	30	17 31	17 57	18 28	18 08	19 04	19 59	20 52
23	161 52.1	39.5	137 29.2	13.5	15 24.8	9.2	54.6	20	17 48	18 11	18 38	18 26	19 19	20 10	20 59
27 00	176 52.0	S18 38.9	152 01.7	13.6	S15 15.6	9.2	54.6	N 10	18 02	18 24	18 50	18 42	19 32	20 19	21 05
01	191 51.8	38.2	166 34.3	13.6	15 06.4	9.4	54.6	0	18 16	18 38	19 03	18 56	19 44	20 28	21 11
02	206 51.7	37.6	181 06.9	13.7	14 57.0	9.3	54.6	S 10	18 30	18 52	19 18	19 11	19 55	20 37	21 16
03	221 51.6 ..	37.0	195 39.6	13.8	14 47.7	9.5	54.6	20	18 45	19 08	19 36	19 27	20 08	20 46	21 22
04	236 51.4	36.3	210 12.4	13.9	14 38.2	9.5	54.6	30	19 02	19 28	19 59	19 44	20 22	20 57	21 28
05	251 51.3	35.7	224 45.3	13.8	14 28.7	9.5	54.6	35	19 12	19 40	20 14	19 54	20 31	21 03	21 32
06	266 51.2	S18 35.1	239 18.1	14.0	S14 19.2	9.6	54.5	40	19 23	19 54	20 32	20 06	20 40	21 10	21 36
07	281 51.0	34.4	253 51.1	14.0	14 09.6	9.7	54.5	45	19 37	20 11	20 54	20 20	20 51	21 18	21 41
08	296 50.9	33.8	268 24.1	14.1	13 59.9	9.7	54.5	S 50	19 54	20 33	21 25	20 37	21 04	21 27	21 47
M 09	311 50.8 ..	33.1	282 57.2	14.1	13 50.2	9.8	54.5	52	20 02	20 43	21 41	20 44	21 10	21 31	21 50
O 10	326 50.6	32.5	297 30.3	14.2	13 40.4	9.8	54.5	54	20 10	20 56	22 00	20 53	21 17	21 36	21 52
N 11	341 50.5	31.9	312 03.5	14.2	13 30.6	9.9	54.5	56	20 20	21 10	22 26	21 03	21 25	21 42	21 56
D 12	356 50.4	S18 31.2	326 36.7	14.3	S13 20.7	9.9	54.5	58	20 32	21 27	23 03	21 14	21 33	21 47	21 59
A 13	11 50.3	30.6	341 10.0	14.4	13 10.8	10.0	54.5	S 60	20 45	21 47	////	21 27	21 43	21 54	22 03
Y 14	26 50.1	29.9	355 43.4	14.4	13 00.8	10.0	54.4								
15	41 50.0 ..	29.3	10 16.8	14.4	12 50.8	10.1	54.4		SUN			MOON			
16	56 49.9	28.7	24 50.2	14.5	12 40.7	10.1	54.4	Day	Eqn. of Time		Mer.	Mer. Pass.		Age	Phase
17	71 49.7	28.0	39 23.7	14.6	12 30.6	10.1	54.4		00ʰ	12ʰ	Pass.	Upper	Lower		
18	86 49.6	S18 27.4	53 57.3	14.6	S12 20.5	10.3	54.4	d	m s	m s	h m	h m	h m	d	%
19	101 49.5	26.7	68 30.9	14.7	12 10.2	10.3	54.4	25	12 04	12 12	12 12	12 45	00 20	01	0	⬤
20	116 49.4	26.1	83 04.6	14.7	12 00.0	10.3	54.4	26	12 19	12 25	12 12	13 33	01 09	02	3	
21	131 49.2 ..	25.4	97 38.3	14.7	11 49.7	10.4	54.4	27	12 32	12 38	12 13	14 18	01 55	03	7	
22	146 49.1	24.8	112 12.0	14.9	11 39.3	10.3	54.4								
23	161 49.0	24.1	126 45.9	14.8	S11 29.0	10.5	54.3								
	SD 16.3	d 0.6	SD 15.0		14.9		14.8									

UT	ARIES GHA	VENUS −4.1 GHA	Dec	MARS +1.4 GHA	Dec	JUPITER −1.9 GHA	Dec	SATURN +0.6 GHA	Dec	STARS Name	SHA	Dec
28 00	126 43.8	138 08.0	S 6 04.2	231 12.5	S22 42.5	202 50.0	S22 46.5	190 14.2	S21 11.1	Acamar	315 14.8	S40 13.9
01	141 46.3	153 07.7	02.9	246 13.1	42.7	217 51.9	46.4	205 16.3	11.0	Achernar	335 23.4	S57 08.5
02	156 48.7	168 07.5	01.6	261 13.8	42.9	232 53.8	46.4	220 18.5	11.0	Acrux	173 03.9	S63 12.3
03	171 51.2	183 07.2	6 00.3	276 14.4	.. 43.1	247 55.7	.. 46.3	235 20.6	.. 10.9	Adhara	255 08.6	S29 00.2
04	186 53.7	198 07.0	5 59.0	291 15.0	43.3	262 57.5	46.3	250 22.8	10.9	Aldebaran	290 44.0	N16 32.8
05	201 56.1	213 06.7	57.8	306 15.7	43.5	277 59.4	46.2	265 24.9	10.8			
06	216 58.6	228 06.5	S 5 56.5	321 16.3	S22 43.7	293 01.3	S22 46.2	280 27.1	S21 10.8	Alioth	166 16.4	N55 50.9
07	232 01.1	243 06.2	55.2	336 16.9	43.9	308 03.1	46.1	295 29.3	10.7	Alkaid	152 55.2	N49 12.6
08	247 03.5	258 05.9	53.9	351 17.5	44.1	323 05.0	46.1	310 31.4	10.7	Alnair	27 38.4	S46 52.0
09	262 06.0	273 05.7	.. 52.7	6 18.2	.. 44.3	338 06.9	.. 46.0	325 33.6	.. 10.7	Alnilam	275 41.5	S 1 11.6
10	277 08.5	288 05.4	51.4	21 18.8	44.5	353 08.7	46.0	340 35.7	10.6	Alphard	217 51.3	S 8 44.8
11	292 10.9	303 05.2	50.1	36 19.4	44.7	8 10.6	45.9	355 37.9	10.6			
12	307 13.4	318 04.9	S 5 48.8	51 20.1	S22 44.9	23 12.5	S22 45.9	10 40.0	S21 10.5	Alphecca	126 07.2	N26 38.7
13	322 15.9	333 04.7	47.6	66 20.7	45.1	38 14.3	45.8	25 42.2	10.5	Alpheratz	357 39.0	N29 12.0
14	337 18.3	348 04.4	46.3	81 21.3	45.3	53 16.2	45.8	40 44.4	10.4	Altair	62 04.1	N 8 55.2
15	352 20.8	3 04.2	.. 45.0	96 21.9	.. 45.5	68 18.1	.. 45.7	55 46.5	.. 10.4	Ankaa	353 11.4	S42 12.2
16	7 23.2	18 03.9	43.7	111 22.6	45.7	83 20.0	45.7	70 48.7	10.3	Antares	112 20.9	S26 28.4
17	22 25.7	33 03.7	42.4	126 23.2	45.8	98 21.8	45.6	85 50.8	10.3			
18	37 28.2	48 03.4	S 5 41.2	141 23.8	S22 46.0	113 23.7	S22 45.6	100 53.0	S21 10.2	Arcturus	145 51.5	N19 04.6
19	52 30.6	63 03.2	39.9	156 24.4	46.2	128 25.6	45.5	115 55.1	10.2	Atria	107 18.9	S69 03.4
20	67 33.1	78 02.9	38.6	171 25.1	46.4	143 27.4	45.5	130 57.3	10.1	Avior	234 15.6	S59 34.5
21	82 35.6	93 02.7	.. 37.3	186 25.7	.. 46.6	158 29.3	.. 45.4	145 59.4	.. 10.1	Bellatrix	278 26.9	N 6 21.9
22	97 38.0	108 02.4	36.0	201 26.3	46.8	173 31.2	45.4	161 01.6	10.0	Betelgeuse	270 56.1	N 7 24.5
23	112 40.5	123 02.2	34.8	216 27.0	47.0	188 33.1	45.3	176 03.8	10.0			
29 00	127 43.0	138 01.9	S 5 33.5	231 27.6	S22 47.2	203 34.9	S22 45.3	191 05.9	S21 09.9	Canopus	263 53.7	S52 42.6
01	142 45.4	153 01.7	32.2	246 28.2	47.4	218 36.8	45.2	206 08.1	09.9	Capella	280 27.4	N46 01.1
02	157 47.9	168 01.4	30.9	261 28.8	47.6	233 38.7	45.2	221 10.2	09.8	Deneb	49 28.9	N45 21.1
03	172 50.3	183 01.2	.. 29.6	276 29.5	.. 47.8	248 40.5	.. 45.1	236 12.4	.. 09.8	Denebola	182 28.8	N14 27.5
04	187 52.8	198 00.9	28.3	291 30.1	48.0	263 42.4	45.1	251 14.5	09.7	Diphda	348 51.4	S17 52.9
05	202 55.3	213 00.7	27.1	306 30.7	48.2	278 44.3	45.0	266 16.7	09.7			
06	217 57.7	228 00.4	S 5 25.8	321 31.3	S22 48.4	293 46.2	S22 45.0	281 18.9	S21 09.6	Dubhe	193 45.5	N61 38.4
07	233 00.2	243 00.2	24.5	336 32.0	48.5	308 48.0	44.9	296 21.0	09.6	Elnath	278 06.6	N28 37.4
08	248 02.7	258 00.0	23.2	351 32.6	48.7	323 49.9	44.9	311 23.2	09.5	Eltanin	90 44.4	N51 29.0
09	263 05.1	272 59.7	.. 21.9	6 33.2	.. 48.9	338 51.8	.. 44.8	326 25.3	.. 09.5	Enif	33 43.0	N 9 57.9
10	278 07.6	287 59.5	20.7	21 33.8	49.1	353 53.6	44.8	341 27.5	09.4	Fomalhaut	15 19.2	S29 31.2
11	293 10.1	302 59.2	19.4	36 34.5	49.3	8 55.5	44.7	356 29.6	09.4			
12	308 12.5	317 59.0	S 5 18.1	51 35.1	S22 49.5	23 57.4	S22 44.7	11 31.8	S21 09.3	Gacrux	171 55.6	S57 13.2
13	323 15.0	332 58.7	16.8	66 35.7	49.7	38 59.3	44.6	26 34.0	09.3	Gienah	175 47.4	S17 39.1
14	338 17.5	347 58.5	15.5	81 36.3	49.9	54 01.1	44.6	41 36.1	09.2	Hadar	148 41.4	S60 27.8
15	353 19.9	2 58.3	.. 14.2	96 37.0	.. 50.1	69 03.0	.. 44.6	56 38.3	.. 09.2	Hamal	327 55.6	N23 33.3
16	8 22.4	17 58.0	12.9	111 37.6	50.2	84 04.9	44.5	71 40.4	09.1	Kaus Aust.	83 38.1	S34 22.4
17	23 24.8	32 57.8	11.7	126 38.2	50.4	99 06.7	44.5	86 42.6	09.1			
18	38 27.3	47 57.5	S 5 10.4	141 38.8	S22 50.6	114 08.6	S22 44.4	101 44.7	S21 09.0	Kochab	137 20.2	N74 04.1
19	53 29.8	62 57.3	09.1	156 39.5	50.8	129 10.5	44.4	116 46.9	09.0	Markab	13 34.1	N15 18.7
20	68 32.2	77 57.0	07.8	171 40.1	51.0	144 12.4	44.3	131 49.1	08.9	Menkar	314 10.2	N 4 09.9
21	83 34.7	92 56.8	.. 06.5	186 40.7	.. 51.2	159 14.2	.. 44.3	146 51.2	.. 08.9	Menkent	148 02.2	S36 27.8
22	98 37.2	107 56.6	05.2	201 41.3	51.4	174 16.1	44.2	161 53.4	08.8	Miaplacidus	221 37.9	S69 47.9
23	113 39.6	122 56.3	03.9	216 42.0	51.5	189 18.0	44.2	176 55.5	08.8			
30 00	128 42.1	137 56.1	S 5 02.7	231 42.6	S22 51.7	204 19.9	S22 44.1	191 57.7	S21 08.7	Mirfak	308 33.7	N49 56.0
01	143 44.6	152 55.8	01.4	246 43.2	51.9	219 21.7	44.1	206 59.8	08.7	Nunki	75 53.0	S26 16.2
02	158 47.0	167 55.6	5 00.1	261 43.8	52.1	234 23.6	44.0	222 02.0	08.6	Peacock	53 12.6	S56 40.2
03	173 49.5	182 55.4	4 58.8	276 44.5	.. 52.3	249 25.5	.. 43.9	237 04.2	.. 08.6	Pollux	243 21.8	N27 58.5
04	188 51.9	197 55.1	57.5	291 45.1	52.5	264 27.3	43.9	252 06.3	08.6	Procyon	244 54.6	N 5 10.3
05	203 54.4	212 54.9	56.2	306 45.7	52.6	279 29.2	43.8	267 08.5	08.5			
06	218 56.9	227 54.7	S 4 54.9	321 46.3	S22 52.8	294 31.1	S22 43.8	282 10.6	S21 08.5	Rasalhague	96 02.5	N12 32.7
07	233 59.3	242 54.4	53.7	336 47.0	53.0	309 33.0	43.7	297 12.8	08.4	Regulus	207 38.4	N11 52.1
08	249 01.8	257 54.2	52.4	351 47.6	53.2	324 34.8	43.7	312 15.0	08.4	Rigel	281 07.4	S 8 10.9
09	264 04.3	272 54.0	.. 51.1	6 48.2	.. 53.4	339 36.7	.. 43.6	327 17.1	.. 08.3	Rigil Kent.	139 45.6	S60 54.6
10	279 06.7	287 53.7	49.8	21 48.8	53.5	354 38.6	43.6	342 19.3	08.3	Sabik	102 07.5	S15 44.9
11	294 09.2	302 53.5	48.5	36 49.4	53.7	9 40.5	43.5	357 21.4	08.2			
12	309 11.7	317 53.3	S 4 47.2	51 50.1	S22 53.9	24 42.3	S22 43.5	12 23.6	S21 08.1	Schedar	349 35.6	N56 38.9
13	324 14.1	332 53.0	45.9	66 50.7	54.1	39 44.2	43.4	27 25.7	08.1	Shaula	96 16.0	S37 06.9
14	339 16.6	347 52.8	44.6	81 51.3	54.3	54 46.1	43.4	42 27.9	08.1	Sirius	258 29.4	S16 44.8
15	354 19.1	2 52.5	.. 43.3	96 51.9	.. 54.4	69 48.0	.. 43.3	57 30.1	.. 08.0	Spica	158 26.4	S11 15.8
16	9 21.5	17 52.3	42.1	111 52.6	54.6	84 49.8	43.3	72 32.2	08.0	Suhail	222 48.7	S43 30.8
17	24 24.0	32 52.1	40.8	126 53.2	54.8	99 51.7	43.2	87 34.4	07.9			
18	39 26.4	47 51.9	S 4 39.5	141 53.8	S22 55.0	114 53.6	S22 43.2	102 36.5	S21 07.9	Vega	80 36.3	N38 48.0
19	54 28.9	62 51.6	38.2	156 54.4	55.2	129 55.5	43.1	117 38.7	07.8	Zuben'ubi	137 00.4	S16 07.3
20	69 31.4	77 51.4	36.9	171 55.0	55.3	144 57.3	43.1	132 40.8	07.8		SHA	Mer.Pass.
21	84 33.8	92 51.2	.. 35.6	186 55.7	.. 55.5	159 59.2	.. 43.0	147 43.0	.. 07.7	Venus	10 19.0	14 48
22	99 36.3	107 50.9	34.3	201 56.3	55.7	175 01.1	43.0	162 45.2	07.7	Mars	103 44.6	8 34
23	114 38.8	122 50.7	33.0	216 56.9	55.9	190 03.0	42.9	177 47.3	07.6	Jupiter	75 52.0	10 24
Mer. Pass.	15 26.6	v −0.2	d 1.3	v 0.6	d 0.2	v 1.9	d 0.0	v 2.2	d 0.0	Saturn	63 23.0	11 14

UT	SUN GHA	SUN Dec	MOON GHA	v	MOON Dec	d	HP
d h	° ′	° ′	° ′	′	° ′	′	′
28 00	176 48.9	S18 23.5	141 19.7	14.9	S11 18.5	10.4	54.3
01	191 48.7	22.8	155 53.6	15.0	11 08.1	10.5	54.3
02	206 48.6	22.2	170 27.6	15.0	10 57.6	10.5	54.3
03	221 48.5	.. 21.5	185 01.6	15.0	10 47.0	10.6	54.3
04	236 48.4	20.9	199 35.6	15.1	10 36.4	10.6	54.3
05	251 48.2	20.2	214 09.7	15.2	10 25.8	10.7	54.3
06	266 48.1	S18 19.6	228 43.9	15.2	S10 15.1	10.7	54.3
07	281 48.0	18.9	243 18.1	15.2	10 04.4	10.7	54.3
T 08	296 47.9	18.3	257 52.3	15.3	9 53.7	10.8	54.3
U 09	311 47.7	.. 17.6	272 26.6	15.3	9 42.9	10.8	54.2
E 10	326 47.6	17.0	287 00.9	15.3	9 32.1	10.8	54.2
S 11	341 47.5	16.3	301 35.2	15.4	9 21.3	10.9	54.2
D 12	356 47.4	S18 15.7	316 09.6	15.5	S 9 10.4	10.9	54.2
A 13	11 47.2	15.0	330 44.1	15.4	8 59.5	10.9	54.2
Y 14	26 47.1	14.3	345 18.5	15.5	8 48.6	11.0	54.2
15	41 47.0	.. 13.7	359 53.0	15.6	8 37.6	11.0	54.2
16	56 46.9	13.0	14 27.6	15.6	8 26.6	11.0	54.2
17	71 46.8	12.4	29 02.2	15.6	8 15.6	11.0	54.2
18	86 46.6	S18 11.7	43 36.8	15.6	S 8 04.6	11.1	54.2
19	101 46.5	11.1	58 11.4	15.7	7 53.5	11.1	54.2
20	116 46.4	10.4	72 46.1	15.7	7 42.4	11.2	54.2
21	131 46.3	.. 09.7	87 20.8	15.8	7 31.2	11.1	54.2
22	146 46.2	09.1	101 55.6	15.8	7 20.1	11.2	54.2
23	161 46.1	08.4	116 30.4	15.8	7 08.9	11.2	54.2
29 00	176 45.9	S18 07.8	131 05.2	15.8	S 6 57.7	11.2	54.1
01	191 45.8	07.1	145 40.0	15.9	6 46.5	11.3	54.1
02	206 45.7	06.4	160 14.9	15.9	6 35.2	11.3	54.1
03	221 45.6	.. 05.8	174 49.8	15.9	6 23.9	11.3	54.1
04	236 45.5	05.1	189 24.7	16.0	6 12.6	11.3	54.1
05	251 45.4	04.4	203 59.7	16.0	6 01.3	11.3	54.1
06	266 45.2	S18 03.8	218 34.7	16.0	S 5 50.0	11.4	54.1
W 07	281 45.1	03.1	233 09.7	16.0	5 38.6	11.4	54.1
E 08	296 45.0	02.4	247 44.7	16.1	5 27.2	11.4	54.1
D 09	311 44.9	.. 01.8	262 19.8	16.1	5 15.8	11.4	54.1
N 10	326 44.8	01.1	276 54.9	16.1	5 04.4	11.4	54.1
E 11	341 44.7	18 00.4	291 30.0	16.1	4 53.0	11.5	54.1
S 12	356 44.6	S17 59.8	306 05.1	16.1	S 4 41.5	11.4	54.1
D 13	11 44.4	59.1	320 40.2	16.2	4 30.1	11.5	54.1
A 14	26 44.3	58.4	335 15.4	16.2	4 18.6	11.5	54.1
Y 15	41 44.2	.. 57.8	349 50.6	16.2	4 07.1	11.5	54.1
16	56 44.1	57.1	4 25.8	16.2	3 55.6	11.5	54.1
17	71 44.0	56.4	19 01.0	16.2	3 44.1	11.6	54.1
18	86 43.9	S17 55.7	33 36.2	16.2	S 3 32.5	11.5	54.1
19	101 43.8	55.1	48 11.4	16.3	3 21.0	11.6	54.1
20	116 43.7	54.4	62 46.7	16.3	3 09.4	11.5	54.1
21	131 43.6	.. 53.7	77 22.0	16.2	2 57.9	11.6	54.1
22	146 43.5	53.0	91 57.2	16.3	2 46.3	11.6	54.1
23	161 43.3	52.4	106 32.5	16.3	2 34.7	11.6	54.1
30 00	176 43.2	S17 51.7	121 07.8	16.3	S 2 23.1	11.6	54.1
01	191 43.1	51.0	135 43.1	16.4	2 11.5	11.6	54.1
02	206 43.0	50.3	150 18.5	16.3	1 59.9	11.6	54.1
03	221 42.9	.. 49.7	164 53.8	16.3	1 48.3	11.6	54.1
04	236 42.8	49.0	179 29.1	16.4	1 36.7	11.7	54.1
05	251 42.7	48.3	194 04.5	16.3	1 25.0	11.6	54.1
06	266 42.6	S17 47.6	208 39.8	16.4	S 1 13.4	11.7	54.1
T 07	281 42.5	47.0	223 15.2	16.3	1 01.7	11.6	54.1
H 08	296 42.4	46.3	237 50.5	16.4	0 50.1	11.7	54.1
U 09	311 42.3	.. 45.6	252 25.9	16.3	0 38.4	11.6	54.1
R 10	326 42.2	44.9	267 01.2	16.4	0 26.8	11.7	54.1
S 11	341 42.1	44.2	281 36.6	16.3	0 15.1	11.6	54.1
D 12	356 42.0	S17 43.5	296 11.9	16.4	S 0 03.5	11.7	54.1
A 13	11 41.9	42.9	310 47.3	16.3	N 0 08.2	11.6	54.1
Y 14	26 41.8	42.2	325 22.6	16.4	0 19.8	11.7	54.1
15	41 41.6	.. 41.5	339 58.0	16.3	0 31.5	11.6	54.1
16	56 41.5	40.8	354 33.3	16.4	0 43.1	11.7	54.1
17	71 41.4	40.1	9 08.7	16.3	0 54.8	11.7	54.1
18	86 41.3	S17 39.4	23 44.0	16.3	N 1 06.5	11.7	54.2
19	101 41.2	38.8	38 19.3	16.3	1 18.1	11.7	54.2
20	116 41.1	38.1	52 54.6	16.3	1 29.8	11.6	54.2
21	131 41.0	.. 37.4	67 29.9	16.3	1 41.4	11.6	54.2
22	146 40.9	36.7	82 05.2	16.3	1 53.0	11.7	54.2
23	161 40.8	36.0	96 40.5	16.3	N 2 04.7	11.6	54.2
	SD 16.3	d 0.7	SD 14.8		14.7		14.7

Lat.	Twilight Naut.	Twilight Civil	Sunrise	Moonrise 28	29	30	31
°	h m	h m	h m	h m	h m	h m	h m
N 72	07 22	08 54	11 01	10 57	10 36	10 18	10 00
N 70	07 12	08 33	10 05	10 43	10 30	10 18	10 06
68	07 05	08 16	09 32	10 31	10 24	10 17	10 11
66	06 58	08 03	09 09	10 22	10 19	10 17	10 14
64	06 52	07 52	08 50	10 13	10 15	10 16	10 18
62	06 47	07 42	08 35	10 06	10 12	10 16	10 21
60	06 42	07 34	08 22	10 00	10 08	10 16	10 23
N 58	06 38	07 26	08 11	09 55	10 06	10 16	10 25
56	06 34	07 20	08 01	09 50	10 05	10 15	10 27
54	06 31	07 14	07 53	09 46	10 01	10 15	10 29
52	06 27	07 08	07 45	09 42	09 59	10 15	10 31
50	06 24	07 03	07 38	09 38	09 57	10 15	10 32
45	06 17	06 52	07 24	09 31	09 53	10 14	10 36
N 40	06 10	06 43	07 12	09 24	09 50	10 14	10 38
35	06 04	06 35	07 01	09 19	09 47	10 14	10 41
30	05 58	06 27	06 52	09 14	09 44	10 14	10 43
20	05 47	06 13	06 36	09 05	09 40	10 13	10 47
N 10	05 35	06 01	06 23	08 57	09 36	10 13	10 50
0	05 22	05 48	06 09	08 50	09 32	10 13	10 53
S 10	05 08	05 34	05 56	08 43	09 28	10 12	10 57
20	04 51	05 18	05 42	08 36	09 24	10 12	11 00
30	04 28	04 59	05 25	08 27	09 20	10 12	11 04
35	04 14	04 48	05 16	08 22	09 17	10 12	11 06
40	03 57	04 34	05 05	08 16	09 14	10 11	11 09
45	03 35	04 18	04 52	08 09	09 10	10 11	11 12
S 50	03 06	03 57	04 35	08 01	09 06	10 11	11 15
52	02 50	03 46	04 28	07 57	09 04	10 11	11 17
54	02 32	03 35	04 19	07 53	09 02	10 11	11 19
56	02 08	03 21	04 10	07 49	09 00	10 10	11 21
58	01 35	03 05	03 59	07 44	08 57	10 10	11 23
S 60	////	02 46	03 47	07 38	08 54	10 10	11 26

Lat.	Sunset	Twilight Civil	Twilight Naut.	Moonset 28	29	30	31
°	h m	h m	h m	h m	h m	h m	h m
N 72	13 26	15 33	17 06	19 27	21 14	22 58	24 44
N 70	14 22	15 54	17 15	19 39	21 18	22 55	24 33
68	14 55	16 11	17 23	19 49	21 21	22 52	24 25
66	15 18	16 24	17 29	19 57	21 24	22 51	24 18
64	15 37	16 35	17 35	20 04	21 27	22 49	24 12
62	15 52	16 45	17 40	2O 10	21 29	22 48	24 07
60	16 05	16 53	17 45	20 15	21 31	22 46	24 02
N 58	16 16	17 01	17 49	20 19	21 32	22 45	23 59
56	16 25	17 07	17 53	20 23	21 34	22 44	23 55
54	16 34	17 13	17 56	20 27	21 35	22 43	23 52
52	16 41	17 18	17 59	20 30	21 36	22 43	23 49
50	16 48	17 23	18 01	20 33	21 37	22 42	23 47
45	17 03	17 34	18 10	20 39	21 40	22 40	23 41
N 40	17 15	17 44	18 16	20 44	21 42	22 39	23 37
35	17 25	17 52	18 22	20 49	21 43	22 38	23 33
30	17 34	17 59	18 28	20 52	21 45	22 37	23 29
20	17 50	18 13	18 39	20 59	21 47	22 35	23 23
N 10	18 04	18 26	18 51	21 05	21 50	22 34	23 18
0	18 17	18 38	19 04	21 11	21 52	22 32	23 13
S 10	18 30	18 52	19 18	21 16	21 54	22 31	23 08
20	18 44	19 07	19 35	21 22	21 56	22 29	23 03
30	19 00	19 26	19 57	21 28	21 58	22 27	22 57
35	19 10	19 38	20 11	21 32	22 00	22 26	22 54
40	19 21	19 51	20 28	21 36	22 01	22 25	22 50
45	19 34	20 07	20 50	21 41	22 03	22 24	22 46
S 50	19 50	20 28	21 19	21 47	22 05	22 22	22 40
52	19 57	20 38	21 34	21 50	22 06	22 22	22 38
54	20 05	20 50	21 52	21 52	22 07	22 21	22 35
56	20 15	21 03	22 14	21 56	22 08	22 20	22 32
58	20 25	21 19	22 46	21 59	22 09	22 19	22 29
S 60	20 38	21 38	23 50	22 03	22 11	22 18	22 25

Day	SUN Eqn. of Time 00h	SUN Eqn. of Time 12h	SUN Mer. Pass.	MOON Mer. Pass. Upper	MOON Mer. Pass. Lower	Age	Phase
d	m s	m s	h m	h m	h m	d	%
28	12 44	12 50	12 13	15 00	02 39	04	12
29	12 56	13 02	12 13	15 42	03 21	05	19
30	13 07	13 12	12 13	16 22	04 02	06	27

UT	ARIES GHA	VENUS −4.1 GHA	Dec	MARS +1.4 GHA	Dec	JUPITER −1.9 GHA	Dec	SATURN +0.6 GHA	Dec	STARS Name	SHA	Dec
31 00	129 41.2	137 50.5	S 4 31.7	231 57.5	S22 56.0	205 04.8	S22 42.9	192 49.5	S21 07.6	Acamar	315 14.8	S40 13.9
01	144 43.7	152 50.2	30.4	246 58.2	56.2	220 06.7	42.8	207 51.6	07.5	Achernar	335 23.5	S57 08.5
02	159 46.2	167 50.0	29.2	261 58.8	56.4	235 08.6	42.8	222 53.8	07.5	Acrux	173 03.8	S63 12.3
03	174 48.6	182 49.8	.. 27.9	276 59.4	.. 56.6	250 10.5	.. 42.7	237 56.0	.. 07.4	Adhara	255 08.6	S29 00.2
04	189 51.1	197 49.5	26.6	292 00.0	56.7	265 12.3	42.7	252 58.1	07.4	Aldebaran	290 44.0	N16 32.8
05	204 53.6	212 49.3	25.3	307 00.6	56.9	280 14.2	42.6	268 00.3	07.3			
06	219 56.0	227 49.1	S 4 24.0	322 01.3	S22 57.1	295 16.1	S22 42.6	283 02.4	S21 07.3	Alioth	166 16.4	N55 50.9
07	234 58.5	242 48.9	22.7	337 01.9	57.3	310 18.0	42.5	298 04.6	07.2	Alkaid	152 55.1	N49 12.6
08	250 00.9	257 48.6	21.4	352 02.5	57.4	325 19.8	42.5	313 06.8	07.2	Alnair	27 38.4	S46 52.0
F 09	265 03.4	272 48.4	.. 20.1	7 03.1	.. 57.6	340 21.7	.. 42.4	328 08.9	.. 07.1	Alnilam	275 41.5	S 1 11.6
R 10	280 05.9	287 48.2	18.8	22 03.7	57.8	355 23.6	42.4	343 11.1	07.1	Alphard	217 51.3	S 8 44.8
I 11	295 08.3	302 48.0	17.5	37 04.4	58.0	10 25.5	42.3	358 13.2	07.0			
D 12	310 10.8	317 47.7	S 4 16.2	52 05.0	S22 58.1	25 27.3	S22 42.3	13 15.4	S21 07.0	Alphecca	126 07.2	N26 38.7
A 13	325 13.3	332 47.5	14.9	67 05.6	58.3	40 29.2	42.2	28 17.5	06.9	Alpheratz	357 39.0	N29 12.0
Y 14	340 15.7	347 47.3	13.6	82 06.2	58.5	55 31.1	42.2	43 19.7	06.9	Altair	62 04.1	N 8 55.2
15	355 18.2	2 47.1	.. 12.3	97 06.8	.. 58.6	70 33.0	.. 42.1	58 21.9	.. 06.8	Ankaa	353 11.4	S42 12.2
16	10 20.7	17 46.8	11.1	112 07.5	58.8	85 34.9	42.1	73 24.0	06.8	Antares	112 20.8	S26 28.4
17	25 23.1	32 46.6	09.8	127 08.1	59.0	100 36.7	42.0	88 26.2	06.7			
18	40 25.6	47 46.4	S 4 08.5	142 08.7	S22 59.2	115 38.6	S22 42.0	103 28.3	S21 06.7	Arcturus	145 51.5	N19 04.6
19	55 28.0	62 46.2	07.2	157 09.3	59.3	130 40.5	41.9	118 30.5	06.6	Atria	107 18.9	S69 03.4
20	70 30.5	77 45.9	05.9	172 09.9	59.5	145 42.4	41.9	133 32.7	06.6	Avior	234 15.6	S59 34.5
21	85 33.0	92 45.7	.. 04.6	187 10.6	.. 59.7	160 44.2	.. 41.8	148 34.8	.. 06.5	Bellatrix	278 26.9	N 6 21.9
22	100 35.4	107 45.5	03.3	202 11.2	22 59.8	175 46.1	41.8	163 37.0	06.5	Betelgeuse	270 56.1	N 7 24.5
23	115 37.9	122 45.3	02.0	217 11.8	23 00.0	190 48.0	41.7	178 39.1	06.4			
1 00	130 40.4	137 45.1	S 4 00.7	232 12.4	S23 00.2	205 49.9	S22 41.7	193 41.3	S21 06.4	Canopus	263 53.7	S52 42.6
01	145 42.8	152 44.8	3 59.4	247 13.0	00.3	220 51.8	41.6	208 43.5	06.3	Capella	280 27.4	N46 01.1
02	160 45.3	167 44.6	58.1	262 13.6	00.5	235 53.6	41.6	223 45.6	06.3	Deneb	49 28.9	N45 21.1
03	175 47.8	182 44.4	.. 56.8	277 14.3	.. 00.7	250 55.5	.. 41.5	238 47.8	.. 06.2	Denebola	182 28.8	N14 27.5
04	190 50.2	197 44.2	55.5	292 14.9	00.8	265 57.4	41.5	253 49.9	06.2	Diphda	348 51.5	S17 52.9
05	205 52.7	212 43.9	54.2	307 15.5	01.0	280 59.3	41.4	268 52.1	06.1			
06	220 55.2	227 43.7	S 3 52.9	322 16.1	S23 01.2	296 01.1	S22 41.4	283 54.3	S21 06.1	Dubhe	193 45.5	N61 38.4
07	235 57.6	242 43.5	51.6	337 16.7	01.3	311 03.0	41.3	298 56.4	06.0	Elnath	278 06.6	N28 37.4
S 08	251 00.1	257 43.3	50.3	352 17.4	01.5	326 04.9	41.2	313 58.6	06.0	Eltanin	90 44.4	N51 29.0
A 09	266 02.5	272 43.1	.. 49.0	7 18.0	.. 01.7	341 06.8	.. 41.2	329 00.7	.. 06.0	Enif	33 43.0	N 9 57.9
T 10	281 05.0	287 42.9	47.7	22 18.6	01.8	356 08.7	41.1	344 02.9	05.9	Fomalhaut	15 19.2	S29 31.2
U 11	296 07.5	302 42.6	46.4	37 19.2	02.0	11 10.5	41.1	359 05.1	05.9			
R 12	311 09.9	317 42.4	S 3 45.1	52 19.8	S23 02.2	26 12.4	S22 41.0	14 07.2	S21 05.8	Gacrux	171 55.5	S57 13.2
D 13	326 12.4	332 42.2	43.8	67 20.4	02.3	41 14.3	41.0	29 09.4	05.8	Gienah	175 47.4	S17 39.1
A 14	341 14.9	347 42.0	42.6	82 21.1	02.5	56 16.2	40.9	44 11.5	05.7	Hadar	148 41.3	S60 27.8
Y 15	356 17.3	2 41.8	.. 41.3	97 21.7	.. 02.7	71 18.1	.. 40.9	59 13.7	.. 05.7	Hamal	327 55.7	N23 33.3
16	11 19.8	17 41.6	40.0	112 22.3	02.8	86 19.9	40.8	74 15.9	05.6	Kaus Aust.	83 38.1	S34 22.4
17	26 22.3	32 41.3	38.7	127 22.9	03.0	101 21.8	40.8	89 18.0	05.6			
18	41 24.7	47 41.1	S 3 37.4	142 23.5	S23 03.1	116 23.7	S22 40.7	104 20.2	S21 05.5	Kochab	137 20.1	N74 04.1
19	56 27.2	62 40.9	36.1	157 24.1	03.3	131 25.6	40.7	119 22.3	05.5	Markab	13 34.1	N15 18.7
20	71 29.7	77 40.7	34.8	172 24.8	03.5	146 27.4	40.6	134 24.5	05.4	Menkar	314 10.2	N 4 09.9
21	86 32.1	92 40.5	.. 33.5	187 25.4	.. 03.6	161 29.3	.. 40.6	149 26.7	.. 05.4	Menkent	148 02.2	S36 27.8
22	101 34.6	107 40.3	32.2	202 26.0	03.8	176 31.2	40.5	164 28.8	05.3	Miaplacidus	221 37.9	S69 47.9
23	116 37.0	122 40.1	30.9	217 26.6	03.9	191 33.1	40.5	179 31.0	05.3			
2 00	131 39.5	137 39.8	S 3 29.6	232 27.2	S23 04.1	206 35.0	S22 40.4	194 33.1	S21 05.2	Mirfak	308 33.7	N49 56.0
01	146 42.0	152 39.6	28.3	247 27.8	04.3	221 36.8	40.4	209 35.3	05.2	Nunki	75 53.0	S26 16.2
02	161 44.4	167 39.4	27.0	262 28.5	04.4	236 38.7	40.3	224 37.5	05.1	Peacock	53 12.6	S56 40.2
03	176 46.9	182 39.2	.. 25.7	277 29.1	.. 04.6	251 40.6	.. 40.3	239 39.6	.. 05.1	Pollux	243 21.8	N27 58.6
04	191 49.4	197 39.0	24.4	292 29.7	04.7	266 42.5	40.2	254 41.8	05.0	Procyon	244 54.6	N 5 10.3
05	206 51.8	212 38.8	23.1	307 30.3	04.9	281 44.4	40.2	269 43.9	05.0			
06	221 54.3	227 38.6	S 3 21.8	322 30.9	S23 05.1	296 46.2	S22 40.1	284 46.1	S21 04.9	Rasalhague	96 02.5	N12 32.7
07	236 56.8	242 38.4	20.5	337 31.5	05.2	311 48.1	40.1	299 48.3	04.9	Regulus	207 38.4	N11 52.1
08	251 59.2	257 38.1	19.2	352 32.2	05.4	326 50.0	40.0	314 50.4	04.8	Rigel	281 07.5	S 8 11.0
S 09	267 01.7	272 37.9	.. 17.9	7 32.8	.. 05.5	341 51.9	.. 39.9	329 52.6	.. 04.8	Rigil Kent.	139 45.6	S60 54.7
U 10	282 04.1	287 37.7	16.6	22 33.4	05.7	356 53.8	39.9	344 54.8	04.7	Sabik	102 07.5	S15 44.9
N 11	297 06.6	302 37.5	15.3	37 34.0	05.8	11 55.7	39.8	359 56.9	04.7			
D 12	312 09.1	317 37.3	S 3 14.0	52 34.6	S23 06.0	26 57.5	S22 39.8	14 59.1	S21 04.6	Schedar	349 35.6	N56 38.9
A 13	327 11.5	332 37.1	12.7	67 35.2	06.1	41 59.4	39.7	30 01.2	04.6	Shaula	96 16.0	S37 06.9
Y 14	342 14.0	347 36.9	11.4	82 35.8	06.3	57 01.3	39.7	45 03.4	04.5	Sirius	258 29.4	S16 44.8
15	357 16.5	2 36.7	.. 10.1	97 36.5	.. 06.4	72 03.2	.. 39.6	60 05.6	.. 04.5	Spica	158 26.3	S11 15.9
16	12 18.9	17 36.5	08.8	112 37.1	06.6	87 05.1	39.6	75 07.7	04.4	Suhail	222 48.7	S43 30.8
17	27 21.4	32 36.3	07.5	127 37.7	06.8	102 06.9	39.5	90 09.9	04.4			
18	42 23.9	47 36.1	S 3 06.2	142 38.3	S23 06.9	117 08.8	S22 39.5	105 12.0	S21 04.3	Vega	80 36.2	N38 48.0
19	57 26.3	62 35.9	04.9	157 38.9	07.1	132 10.7	39.4	120 14.2	04.3	Zuben'ubi	137 00.4	S16 07.4
20	72 28.8	77 35.6	03.6	172 39.5	07.2	147 12.6	39.4	135 16.4	04.2		SHA	Mer. Pass.
21	87 31.3	92 35.4	.. 02.3	187 40.1	.. 07.4	162 14.5	.. 39.3	150 18.5	.. 04.2		° ′	h m
22	102 33.7	107 35.2	3 01.0	202 40.8	07.5	177 16.4	39.3	165 20.7	04.1	Venus	7 04.7	14 49
23	117 36.2	122 35.0	S 2 59.7	217 41.4	07.7	192 18.2	39.2	180 22.8	04.1	Mars	101 32.0	8 31
Mer. Pass.	h m 15 14.8	v −0.2	d 1.3	v 0.6	d 0.2	v 1.9	d 0.1	v 2.2	d 0.0	Jupiter Saturn	75 09.5 63 00.9	10 15 11 04

UT	SUN		MOON					Lat.	Twilight		Sunrise	Moonrise			
									Naut.	Civil		31	1	2	3
	GHA	Dec	GHA	v	Dec	d	HP								
d h	° ′	° ′	° ′	′	° ′	′	′	°	h m	h m	h m	h m	h m	h m	h m
31 00	176 40.7	S17 35.3	111 15.8	16.3	N 2 16.3	11.6	54.2	N 72	07 11	08 41	10 32	10 00	09 41	09 16	08 33
01	191 40.6	34.6	125 51.1	16.2	2 27.9	11.6	54.2	N 70	07 03	08 22	09 48	10 06	09 53	09 38	09 18
02	206 40.5	33.9	140 26.3	16.2	2 39.5	11.7	54.2	68	06 56	08 07	09 20	10 11	10 04	09 56	09 47
03	221 40.4 ..	33.2	155 01.5	16.3	2 51.2	11.6	54.2	66	06 51	07 55	08 58	10 14	10 12	10 10	10 07
04	236 40.3	32.6	169 36.8	16.2	3 02.8	11.6	54.2	64	06 46	07 44	08 41	10 18	10 19	10 22	10 27
05	251 40.2	31.9	184 12.0	16.2	3 14.4	11.5	54.2	62	06 41	07 35	08 27	10 21	10 26	10 32	10 42
06	266 40.1	S17 31.2	198 47.2	16.1	N 3 25.9	11.6	54.2	60	06 37	07 28	08 15	10 23	10 31	10 41	10 54
07	281 40.0	30.5	213 22.3	16.2	3 37.5	11.6	54.2	N 58	06 33	07 21	08 05	10 25	10 36	10 49	11 05
F 08	296 39.9	29.8	227 57.5	16.1	3 49.1	11.5	54.3	56	06 30	07 15	07 56	10 27	10 40	10 55	11 14
R 09	311 39.9 ..	29.1	242 32.6	16.1	4 00.6	11.6	54.3	54	06 26	07 09	07 48	10 29	10 44	11 02	11 23
I 10	326 39.8	28.4	257 07.7	16.1	4 12.2	11.5	54.3	52	06 23	07 04	07 41	10 31	10 48	11 07	11 30
D 11	341 39.7	27.7	271 42.8	16.0	4 23.7	11.5	54.3	50	06 21	06 59	07 34	10 32	10 51	11 12	11 37
A 12	356 39.6	S17 27.0	286 17.8	16.1	N 4 35.2	11.5	54.3	45	06 14	06 49	07 21	10 36	10 58	11 23	11 51
Y 13	11 39.5	26.3	300 52.9	16.0	4 46.7	11.5	54.3	N 40	06 08	06 40	07 09	10 38	11 04	11 32	12 04
14	26 39.4	25.6	315 27.9	16.0	4 58.2	11.5	54.3	35	06 02	06 33	06 59	10 41	11 09	11 40	12 14
15	41 39.3 ..	24.9	330 02.9	15.9	5 09.7	11.5	54.3	30	05 57	06 26	06 51	10 43	11 14	11 46	12 23
16	56 39.2	24.2	344 37.8	15.9	5 21.2	11.4	54.3	20	05 46	06 13	06 36	10 47	11 21	11 58	12 39
17	71 39.1	23.5	359 12.7	15.9	5 32.6	11.4	54.3	N 10	05 35	06 01	06 22	10 50	11 28	12 09	12 52
18	86 39.0	S17 22.8	13 47.6	15.9	N 5 44.0	11.4	54.4	0	05 23	05 48	06 10	10 53	11 35	12 19	13 05
19	101 38.9	22.1	28 22.5	15.8	5 55.4	11.4	54.4	S 10	05 09	05 35	05 57	10 57	11 42	12 29	13 18
20	116 38.8	21.4	42 57.3	15.9	6 06.8	11.4	54.4	20	04 53	05 20	05 44	11 00	11 49	12 39	13 32
21	131 38.7 ..	20.7	57 32.2	15.7	6 18.2	11.4	54.4	30	04 31	05 02	05 28	11 04	11 57	12 52	13 48
22	146 38.6	20.0	72 06.9	15.8	6 29.6	11.3	54.4	35	04 18	04 51	05 19	11 06	12 02	12 59	13 58
23	161 38.5	19.3	86 41.7	15.7	6 40.9	11.3	54.4	40	04 01	04 38	05 08	11 09	12 07	13 07	14 08
1 00	176 38.4	S17 18.6	101 16.4	15.6	N 6 52.2	11.3	54.4	45	03 41	04 22	04 56	11 12	12 13	13 16	14 21
01	191 38.4	17.9	115 51.0	15.7	7 03.5	11.3	54.5	S 50	03 13	04 03	04 41	11 15	12 21	13 28	14 37
02	206 38.3	17.2	130 25.7	15.6	7 14.8	11.2	54.5	52	02 58	03 53	04 34	11 17	12 24	13 33	14 44
03	221 38.2 ..	16.5	145 00.3	15.5	7 26.0	11.3	54.5	54	02 41	03 42	04 26	11 19	12 28	13 39	14 52
04	236 38.1	15.8	159 34.8	15.5	7 37.3	11.2	54.5	56	02 20	03 29	04 17	11 21	12 33	13 46	15 01
05	251 38.0	15.1	174 09.3	15.5	7 48.5	11.1	54.5	58	01 52	03 14	04 07	11 23	12 37	13 53	15 12
06	266 37.9	S17 14.4	188 43.8	15.5	N 7 59.6	11.2	54.5	S 60	01 05	02 56	03 55	11 26	12 43	14 02	15 24
07	281 37.8	13.7	203 18.3	15.4	8 10.8	11.1	54.6								

								Lat.	Sunset	Twilight		Moonset			
										Civil	Naut.	31	1	2	3
S 08	296 37.7	S17 13.0	217 52.7	15.3	N 8 21.9	11.1	54.6								
A 09	311 37.6 ..	12.3	232 27.0	15.3	8 33.0	11.1	54.6	°	h m	h m	h m	h m	h m	h m	h m
T 10	326 37.6	11.6	247 01.3	15.3	8 44.1	11.0	54.6	N 72	13 57	15 48	17 17	24 44	00 44	02 38	04 55
U 11	341 37.5	10.9	261 35.6	15.2	8 55.1	11.1	54.6	N 70	14 40	16 06	17 25	24 33	00 33	02 17	04 12
R 12	356 37.4	S17 10.2	276 09.8	15.2	N 9 06.2	11.0	54.6	68	15 09	16 21	17 32	24 25	00 25	02 01	03 44
D 13	11 37.3	09.5	290 44.0	15.1	9 17.2	10.9	54.7	66	15 30	16 34	17 38	24 18	00 18	01 48	03 23
A 14	26 37.2	08.8	305 18.1	15.0	9 28.1	10.9	54.7	64	15 47	16 44	17 43	24 12	00 12	01 37	03 06
Y 15	41 37.1 ..	08.0	319 52.1	15.1	9 39.0	10.9	54.7	62	16 01	16 53	17 47	24 07	00 07	01 28	02 52
16	56 37.0	07.3	334 26.2	14.9	9 49.9	10.9	54.7	60	16 13	17 00	17 51	24 02	00 02	01 20	02 40
17	71 36.9	06.6	349 00.1	14.9	10 00.8	10.8	54.7	N 58	16 23	17 07	17 55	23 59	25 13	01 13	02 30
18	86 36.9	S17 05.9	3 34.0	14.9	N10 11.6	10.8	54.8	56	16 32	17 13	17 58	23 55	25 07	01 07	02 22
19	101 36.8	05.2	18 07.9	14.8	10 22.4	10.8	54.8	54	16 40	17 19	18 01	23 52	25 02	01 02	02 14
20	116 36.7	04.5	32 41.7	14.8	10 33.2	10.7	54.8	52	16 47	17 24	18 04	23 49	24 57	00 57	02 07
21	131 36.6 ..	03.8	47 15.5	14.7	10 43.9	10.7	54.8	50	16 53	17 28	18 07	23 47	24 53	00 53	02 01
22	146 36.5	03.1	61 49.2	14.6	10 54.6	10.7	54.8	45	17 07	17 38	18 13	23 41	24 43	00 43	01 47
23	161 36.4	02.3	76 22.8	14.6	11 05.3	10.6	54.8	N 40	17 18	17 47	18 19	23 37	24 36	00 36	01 36
2 00	176 36.4	S17 01.6	90 56.4	14.6	N11 15.9	10.6	54.9	35	17 28	17 55	18 25	23 33	24 29	00 29	01 27
01	191 36.3	00.9	105 30.0	14.4	11 26.5	10.5	54.9	30	17 37	18 02	18 30	23 29	24 23	00 23	01 19
02	206 36.2	17 00.2	120 03.4	14.4	11 37.0	10.5	54.9	20	17 52	18 15	18 41	23 23	24 13	00 13	01 04
03	221 36.1	16 59.5	134 36.8	14.3	11 47.5	10.5	54.9	N 10	18 05	18 27	18 52	23 18	24 04	00 04	00 52
04	236 36.0	58.8	149 10.2	14.3	11 58.0	10.4	55.0	0	18 17	18 39	19 04	23 13	23 56	24 41	00 41
05	251 36.0	58.1	163 43.5	14.2	12 08.4	10.4	55.0	S 10	18 30	18 52	19 17	23 08	23 47	24 29	00 29
06	266 35.9	S16 57.3	178 16.7	14.2	N12 18.8	10.3	55.0	20	18 43	19 06	19 34	23 03	23 39	24 17	00 17
07	281 35.8	56.6	192 49.9	14.1	12 29.1	10.3	55.0	30	18 59	19 24	19 55	22 57	23 29	24 03	00 03
08	296 35.7	55.9	207 23.0	14.0	12 39.4	10.2	55.1	35	19 08	19 35	20 08	22 54	23 23	23 55	24 32
S 09	311 35.6 ..	55.2	221 56.0	14.0	12 49.6	10.2	55.1	40	19 18	19 48	20 25	22 50	23 16	23 46	24 20
U 10	326 35.6	54.5	236 29.0	13.9	12 59.8	10.2	55.1	45	19 30	20 04	20 45	22 46	23 09	23 35	24 06
N 11	341 35.5	53.7	251 01.9	13.8	13 10.0	10.1	55.1	S 50	19 45	20 23	21 13	22 40	23 00	23 22	23 50
D 12	356 35.4	S16 53.0	265 34.7	13.8	N13 20.1	10.0	55.2	52	19 52	20 33	21 27	22 38	22 56	23 16	23 42
A 13	11 35.3	52.3	280 07.5	13.7	13 30.1	10.1	55.2	54	20 00	20 43	21 43	22 35	22 51	23 10	23 34
Y 14	26 35.2	51.6	294 40.2	13.6	13 40.2	9.9	55.2	56	20 09	20 56	22 04	22 32	22 46	23 03	23 24
15	41 35.2 ..	50.9	309 12.8	13.5	13 50.1	9.9	55.2	58	20 19	21 10	22 31	22 29	22 40	22 54	23 13
16	56 35.1	50.1	323 45.3	13.5	14 00.0	9.9	55.3	S 60	20 30	21 28	23 13	22 25	22 34	22 45	23 00
17	71 35.0	49.4	338 17.8	13.4	14 09.9	9.8	55.3								

									SUN			MOON			
18	86 34.9	S16 48.7	352 50.2	13.4	N14 19.7	9.7	55.3	Day	Eqn. of Time		Mer.	Mer. Pass.		Age	Phase
19	101 34.9	48.0	7 22.6	13.2	14 29.4	9.7	55.3		00h	12h	Pass.	Upper	Lower		
20	116 34.8	47.2	21 54.8	13.2	14 39.1	9.7	55.4	d	m s	m s	h m	h m	h m	d %	
21	131 34.7 ..	46.5	36 27.0	13.1	14 48.8	9.5	55.4	31	13 17	13 22	12 13	17 03	04 43	07 35	
22	146 34.6	45.8	50 59.1	13.1	14 58.3	9.6	55.4	1	13 26	13 30	12 14	17 45	05 24	08 45	
23	161 34.6	45.1	65 31.2	12.9	N15 07.9	9.4	55.4	2	13 34	13 38	12 14	18 30	06 07	09 54	
	SD 16.3	d 0.7	SD 14.8		14.9		15.0									

UT	ARIES GHA	VENUS −4.1 GHA	Dec	MARS +1.3 GHA	Dec	JUPITER −1.9 GHA	Dec	SATURN +0.6 GHA	Dec	STARS Name	SHA	Dec
3 00	132 38.6	137 34.8	S 2 58.4	232 42.0	S23 07.8	207 20.1	S22 39.2	195 25.0	S21 04.0	Acamar	315 14.8	S40 13.9
01	147 41.1	152 34.6	57.1	247 42.6	08.0	222 22.0	39.1	210 27.2	04.0	Achernar	335 23.5	S57 08.5
02	162 43.6	167 34.4	55.8	262 43.2	08.1	237 23.9	39.1	225 29.3	03.9	Acrux	173 03.8	S63 12.3
03	177 46.0	182 34.2	.. 54.5	277 43.8	.. 08.3	252 25.8	.. 39.0	240 31.5	.. 03.9	Adhara	255 08.6	S29 00.2
04	192 48.5	197 34.0	53.1	292 44.4	08.4	267 27.6	38.9	255 33.7	03.8	Aldebaran	290 44.0	N16 32.8
05	207 51.0	212 33.8	51.8	307 45.0	08.6	282 29.5	38.9	270 35.8	03.8			
06	222 53.4	227 33.6	S 2 50.5	322 45.7	S23 08.7	297 31.4	S22 38.8	285 38.0	S21 03.7	Alioth	166 16.3	N55 50.9
07	237 55.9	242 33.4	49.2	337 46.3	08.9	312 33.3	38.8	300 40.1	03.7	Alkaid	152 55.1	N49 12.6
M 08	252 58.4	257 33.2	47.9	352 46.9	09.0	327 35.2	38.7	315 42.3	03.6	Alnair	27 38.4	S46 52.0
O 09	268 00.8	272 33.0	.. 46.6	7 47.5	.. 09.2	342 37.1	.. 38.7	330 44.5	.. 03.6	Alnilam	275 41.5	S 1 11.6
N 10	283 03.3	287 32.8	45.3	22 48.1	09.3	357 38.9	38.6	345 46.6	03.5	Alphard	217 51.3	S 8 44.8
D 11	298 05.8	302 32.6	44.0	37 48.7	09.5	12 40.8	38.6	0 48.8	03.5			
A 12	313 08.2	317 32.4	S 2 42.7	52 49.3	S23 09.6	27 42.7	S22 38.5	15 51.0	S21 03.4	Alphecca	126 07.2	N26 38.7
Y 13	328 10.7	332 32.2	41.4	67 50.0	09.8	42 44.6	38.5	30 53.1	03.4	Alpheratz	357 39.0	N29 12.0
14	343 13.1	347 32.0	40.1	82 50.6	09.9	57 46.5	38.4	45 55.3	03.3	Altair	62 04.1	N 8 55.2
15	358 15.6	2 31.8	.. 38.8	97 51.2	.. 10.1	72 48.4	.. 38.4	60 57.4	.. 03.3	Ankaa	353 11.4	S42 12.2
16	13 18.1	17 31.6	37.5	112 51.8	10.2	87 50.2	38.3	75 59.6	03.2	Antares	112 20.8	S26 28.4
17	28 20.5	32 31.4	36.2	127 52.4	10.4	102 52.1	38.3	91 01.8	03.2			
18	43 23.0	47 31.2	S 2 34.9	142 53.0	S23 10.5	117 54.0	S22 38.2	106 03.9	S21 03.1	Arcturus	145 51.5	N19 04.6
19	58 25.5	62 31.0	33.6	157 53.6	10.6	132 55.9	38.2	121 06.1	03.1	Atria	107 18.8	S69 03.4
20	73 27.9	77 30.8	32.3	172 54.2	10.7	147 57.8	38.1	136 08.3	03.0	Avior	234 15.6	S59 34.5
21	88 30.4	92 30.6	.. 31.0	187 54.8	.. 10.9	162 59.7	.. 38.0	151 10.4	.. 03.0	Bellatrix	278 26.9	N 6 21.9
22	103 32.9	107 30.4	29.7	202 55.5	11.1	178 01.6	38.0	166 12.6	03.0	Betelgeuse	270 56.1	N 7 24.5
23	118 35.3	122 30.2	28.4	217 56.1	11.2	193 03.4	37.9	181 14.7	02.9			
4 00	133 37.8	137 30.0	S 2 27.1	232 56.7	S23 11.4	208 05.3	S22 37.9	196 16.9	S21 02.9	Canopus	263 53.7	S52 42.7
01	148 40.2	152 29.8	25.8	247 57.3	11.5	223 07.2	37.8	211 19.1	02.8	Capella	280 27.4	N46 01.1
02	163 42.7	167 29.6	24.5	262 57.9	11.6	238 09.1	37.8	226 21.2	02.8	Deneb	49 28.9	N45 21.0
03	178 45.2	182 29.4	.. 23.2	277 58.5	.. 11.8	253 11.0	.. 37.7	241 23.4	.. 02.7	Denebola	182 28.8	N14 27.5
04	193 47.6	197 29.2	21.9	292 59.1	11.9	268 12.9	37.7	256 25.6	02.7	Diphda	348 51.5	S17 52.9
05	208 50.1	212 29.0	20.6	307 59.7	12.1	283 14.8	37.6	271 27.7	02.6			
06	223 52.6	227 28.8	S 2 19.2	323 00.3	S23 12.2	298 16.6	S22 37.6	286 29.9	S21 02.6	Dubhe	193 45.5	N61 38.4
07	238 55.0	242 28.6	17.9	338 01.0	12.4	313 18.5	37.5	301 32.0	02.5	Elnath	278 06.6	N28 37.4
T 08	253 57.5	257 28.4	16.6	353 01.6	12.5	328 20.4	37.5	316 34.2	02.5	Eltanin	90 44.4	N51 29.0
U 09	269 00.0	272 28.2	.. 15.3	8 02.2	.. 12.6	343 22.3	.. 37.4	331 36.4	.. 02.4	Enif	33 43.0	N 9 57.9
E 10	284 02.4	287 28.0	14.0	23 02.8	12.8	358 24.2	37.4	346 38.5	02.4	Fomalhaut	15 19.2	S29 31.2
S 11	299 04.9	302 27.8	12.7	38 03.4	12.9	13 26.1	37.3	1 40.7	02.3			
D 12	314 07.4	317 27.6	S 2 11.4	53 04.0	S23 13.1	28 28.0	S22 37.2	16 42.9	S21 02.3	Gacrux	171 55.5	S57 13.2
A 13	329 09.8	332 27.4	10.1	68 04.6	13.2	43 29.8	37.2	31 45.0	02.2	Gienah	175 47.4	S17 39.1
Y 14	344 12.3	347 27.3	08.8	83 05.2	13.3	58 31.7	37.1	46 47.2	02.2	Hadar	148 41.3	S60 27.8
15	359 14.7	2 27.1	.. 07.5	98 05.8	.. 13.5	73 33.6	.. 37.1	61 49.4	.. 02.1	Hamal	327 55.7	N23 33.3
16	14 17.2	17 26.9	06.2	113 06.4	13.6	88 35.5	37.0	76 51.5	02.1	Kaus Aust.	83 38.1	S34 22.4
17	29 19.7	32 26.7	04.9	128 07.1	13.7	103 37.4	37.0	91 53.7	02.0			
18	44 22.1	47 26.5	S 2 03.6	143 07.7	S23 13.9	118 39.3	S22 36.9	106 55.8	S21 02.0	Kochab	137 20.0	N74 04.1
19	59 24.6	62 26.3	02.3	158 08.3	14.0	133 41.2	36.9	121 58.0	01.9	Markab	13 34.1	N15 18.7
20	74 27.1	77 26.1	2 01.0	173 08.9	14.2	148 43.0	36.8	137 00.2	01.9	Menkar	314 10.2	N 4 09.9
21	89 29.5	92 25.9	1 59.7	188 09.5	.. 14.3	163 44.9	.. 36.8	152 02.3	.. 01.8	Menkent	148 02.1	S36 27.9
22	104 32.0	107 25.7	58.4	203 10.1	14.4	178 46.8	36.7	167 04.5	01.8	Miaplacidus	221 37.9	S69 47.9
23	119 34.5	122 25.5	57.0	218 10.7	14.6	193 48.7	36.7	182 06.7	01.7			
5 00	134 36.9	137 25.3	S 1 55.7	233 11.3	S23 14.7	208 50.6	S22 36.6	197 08.8	S21 01.7	Mirfak	308 33.7	N49 56.0
01	149 39.4	152 25.1	54.4	248 11.9	14.8	223 52.5	36.5	212 11.0	01.6	Nunki	75 53.0	S26 16.2
02	164 41.9	167 25.0	53.1	263 12.5	15.0	238 54.4	36.5	227 13.2	01.6	Peacock	53 12.6	S56 40.2
03	179 44.3	182 24.8	.. 51.8	278 13.1	.. 15.1	253 56.3	.. 36.4	242 15.3	.. 01.5	Pollux	243 21.8	N27 58.6
04	194 46.8	197 24.6	50.5	293 13.8	15.2	268 58.1	36.4	257 17.5	01.5	Procyon	244 54.6	N 5 10.3
05	209 49.2	212 24.4	49.2	308 14.4	15.4	284 00.0	36.3	272 19.6	01.4			
06	224 51.7	227 24.2	S 1 47.9	323 15.0	S23 15.5	299 01.9	S22 36.3	287 21.8	S21 01.4	Rasalhague	96 02.4	N12 32.7
W 07	239 54.2	242 24.0	46.6	338 15.6	15.6	314 03.8	36.2	302 24.0	01.3	Regulus	207 38.3	N11 52.1
E 08	254 56.6	257 23.8	45.3	353 16.2	15.8	329 05.7	36.2	317 26.1	01.3	Rigel	281 07.5	S 8 11.0
D 09	269 59.1	272 23.6	.. 44.0	8 16.8	.. 15.9	344 07.6	.. 36.1	332 28.3	.. 01.2	Rigil Kent.	139 45.5	S60 54.7
N 10	285 01.6	287 23.4	42.7	23 17.4	16.0	359 09.5	36.1	347 30.5	01.2	Sabik	102 07.5	S15 44.9
E 11	300 04.0	302 23.3	41.4	38 18.0	16.2	14 11.4	36.0	2 32.6	01.1			
S 12	315 06.5	317 23.1	S 1 40.1	53 18.6	S23 16.3	29 13.2	S22 35.9	17 34.8	S21 01.1	Schedar	349 35.7	N56 38.9
D 13	330 09.0	332 22.9	38.7	68 19.2	16.4	44 15.1	35.9	32 37.0	01.0	Shaula	96 16.0	S37 06.9
A 14	345 11.4	347 22.7	37.4	83 19.8	16.5	59 17.0	35.8	47 39.1	01.0	Sirius	258 29.4	S16 44.8
Y 15	0 13.9	2 22.5	.. 36.1	98 20.4	.. 16.7	74 18.9	.. 35.8	62 41.3	.. 00.9	Spica	158 26.3	S11 15.9
16	15 16.4	17 22.3	34.8	113 21.1	16.8	89 20.8	35.7	77 43.5	00.9	Suhail	222 48.7	S43 30.9
17	30 18.8	32 22.1	33.5	128 21.7	16.9	104 22.7	35.7	92 45.6	00.8			
18	45 21.3	47 22.0	S 1 32.2	143 22.3	S23 17.1	119 24.6	S22 35.6	107 47.8	S21 00.8	Vega	80 36.2	N38 48.0
19	60 23.7	62 21.8	30.9	158 22.9	17.2	134 26.5	35.6	122 50.0	00.7	Zuben'ubi	137 00.4	S16 07.4
20	75 26.2	77 21.6	29.6	173 23.5	17.3	149 28.4	35.5	137 52.1	00.7		SHA	Mer.Pass.
21	90 28.7	92 21.4	.. 28.3	188 24.1	.. 17.4	164 30.3	.. 35.5	152 54.3	.. 00.6	Venus	3 52.2	14 50
22	105 31.1	107 21.2	27.0	203 24.7	17.6	179 32.1	35.4	167 56.4	00.6	Mars	99 18.9	8 28
23	120 33.6	122 21.0	25.7	218 25.3	17.7	194 34.0	35.4	182 58.6	00.5	Jupiter	74 27.5	10 06
Mer.Pass. 15 03.0		v −0.2	d 1.3	v 0.6	d 0.1	v 1.9	d 0.1	v 2.2	d 0.0	Saturn	62 39.1	10 53

UT	SUN GHA	SUN Dec	MOON GHA	v	MOON Dec	d	HP
d h	° ′	° ′	° ′	′	° ′	′	′
3 00	176 34.5	S16 44.3	80 03.1	12.9	N15 17.3	9.5	55.5
01	191 34.4	43.6	94 35.0	12.8	15 26.8	9.3	55.5
02	206 34.3	42.9	109 06.8	12.7	15 36.1	9.3	55.5
03	221 34.3 ..	42.2	123 38.5	12.7	15 45.4	9.2	55.6
04	236 34.2	41.4	138 10.2	12.5	15 54.6	9.2	55.6
05	251 34.1	40.7	152 41.7	12.5	16 03.8	9.1	55.6
06	266 34.1	S16 40.0	167 13.2	12.4	N16 12.9	9.0	55.6
07	281 34.0	39.2	181 44.6	12.3	16 21.9	9.0	55.7
M 08	296 33.9	38.5	196 15.9	12.3	16 30.9	8.9	55.7
O 09	311 33.8 ..	37.8	210 47.2	12.1	16 39.8	8.8	55.7
N 10	326 33.8	37.0	225 18.3	12.1	16 48.6	8.8	55.8
D 11	341 33.7	36.3	239 49.4	12.0	16 57.4	8.7	55.8
A 12	356 33.6	S16 35.6	254 20.4	11.9	N17 06.1	8.6	55.8
Y 13	11 33.6	34.9	268 51.3	11.8	17 14.7	8.5	55.9
14	26 33.5	34.1	283 22.1	11.7	17 23.2	8.5	55.9
15	41 33.4 ..	33.4	297 52.8	11.6	17 31.7	8.4	55.9
16	56 33.4	32.7	312 23.4	11.6	17 40.1	8.3	56.0
17	71 33.3	31.9	326 54.0	11.4	17 48.4	8.3	56.0
18	86 33.2	S16 31.2	341 24.4	11.4	N17 56.7	8.1	56.0
19	101 33.2	30.4	355 54.8	11.3	18 04.8	8.1	56.1
20	116 33.1	29.7	10 25.1	11.2	18 12.9	8.1	56.1
21	131 33.0 ..	29.0	24 55.3	11.1	18 21.0	7.9	56.1
22	146 33.0	28.2	39 25.4	11.0	18 28.9	7.8	56.2
23	161 32.9	27.5	53 55.4	10.9	18 36.7	7.8	56.2
4 00	176 32.8	S16 26.8	68 25.3	10.8	N18 44.5	7.7	56.2
01	191 32.8	26.0	82 55.1	10.8	18 52.2	7.6	56.3
02	206 32.7	25.3	97 24.9	10.6	18 59.8	7.5	56.3
03	221 32.6 ..	24.5	111 54.5	10.6	19 07.3	7.4	56.3
04	236 32.6	23.8	126 24.1	10.4	19 14.7	7.3	56.4
05	251 32.5	23.1	140 53.5	10.4	19 22.0	7.3	56.4
06	266 32.4	S16 22.3	155 22.9	10.3	N19 29.3	7.1	56.4
07	281 32.4	21.6	169 52.2	10.2	19 36.4	7.1	56.5
T 08	296 32.3	20.8	184 21.4	10.1	19 43.5	7.0	56.5
U 09	311 32.3 ..	20.1	198 50.5	10.0	19 50.5	6.8	56.5
E 10	326 32.2	19.3	213 19.5	9.9	19 57.3	6.8	56.6
S 11	341 32.1	18.6	227 48.4	9.8	20 04.1	6.7	56.6
D 12	356 32.1	S16 17.9	242 17.2	9.7	N20 10.8	6.6	56.6
A 13	11 32.0	17.1	256 45.9	9.7	20 17.4	6.4	56.7
Y 14	26 32.0	16.4	271 14.6	9.5	20 23.8	6.4	56.7
15	41 31.9 ..	15.6	285 43.1	9.4	20 30.2	6.3	56.7
16	56 31.8	14.9	300 11.5	9.4	20 36.5	6.2	56.8
17	71 31.8	14.1	314 39.9	9.3	20 42.7	6.0	56.8
18	86 31.7	S16 13.4	329 08.2	9.1	N20 48.7	6.0	56.9
19	101 31.7	12.6	343 36.3	9.1	20 54.7	5.9	56.9
20	116 31.6	11.9	358 04.4	9.0	21 00.6	5.7	56.9
21	131 31.5 ..	11.1	12 32.4	8.9	21 06.3	5.7	57.0
22	146 31.5	10.4	27 00.3	8.8	21 12.0	5.5	57.0
23	161 31.4	09.6	41 28.1	8.7	21 17.5	5.4	57.0
5 00	176 31.4	S16 08.9	55 55.8	8.6	N21 22.9	5.3	57.1
01	191 31.3	08.1	70 23.4	8.5	21 28.2	5.2	57.1
02	206 31.3	07.4	84 50.9	8.5	21 33.4	5.1	57.2
03	221 31.2 ..	06.6	99 18.4	8.3	21 38.5	5.0	57.2
04	236 31.1	05.9	113 45.7	8.3	21 43.5	4.8	57.2
05	251 31.1	05.1	128 13.0	8.1	21 48.3	4.7	57.3
06	266 31.0	S16 04.4	142 40.1	8.1	N21 53.0	4.7	57.3
W 07	281 31.0	03.6	157 07.2	8.0	21 57.7	4.5	57.3
E 08	296 30.9	02.9	171 34.2	7.9	22 02.2	4.3	57.4
D 09	311 30.9 ..	02.1	186 01.1	7.8	22 06.5	4.3	57.4
N 10	326 30.8	01.4	200 27.9	7.8	22 10.8	4.1	57.5
E 11	341 30.8	16 00.6	214 54.7	7.6	22 14.9	4.0	57.5
S 12	356 30.7	S15 59.8	229 21.3	7.6	N22 18.9	3.9	57.5
D 13	11 30.7	59.1	243 47.9	7.5	22 22.8	3.7	57.6
A 14	26 30.6	58.3	258 14.4	7.4	22 26.5	3.6	57.6
Y 15	41 30.6 ..	57.6	272 40.8	7.3	22 30.1	3.5	57.7
16	56 30.5	56.8	287 07.1	7.2	22 33.6	3.4	57.7
17	71 30.5	56.1	301 33.3	7.2	22 37.0	3.2	57.7
18	86 30.4	S15 55.3	315 59.5	7.0	N22 40.2	3.1	57.8
19	101 30.4	54.5	330 25.5	7.0	22 43.3	2.9	57.8
20	116 30.3	53.8	344 51.5	6.9	22 46.2	2.9	57.8
21	131 30.3 ..	53.0	359 17.4	6.9	22 49.1	2.7	57.9
22	146 30.2	52.3	13 43.3	6.8	22 51.8	2.5	57.9
23	161 30.2	51.5	28 09.1	6.6	N22 54.3	2.4	58.0
	SD 16.3	d 0.7	SD 15.2	15.4			15.7

Lat.	Twilight Naut.	Twilight Civil	Sunrise	Moonrise 3	4	5	6
°	h m	h m	h m	h m	h m	h m	h m
N 72	07 01	08 27	10 08	08 33	□	□	□
N 70	06 54	08 10	09 32	09 18	08 28	□	□
68	06 48	07 57	09 07	09 47	09 34	08 49	□
66	06 43	07 46	08 47	10 09	10 10	10 16	10 42
64	06 39	07 37	08 32	10 27	10 36	10 55	11 33
62	06 35	07 28	08 19	10 42	10 57	11 22	12 04
60	06 31	07 21	08 08	10 54	11 13	11 43	12 28
N 58	06 28	07 15	07 58	11 05	11 27	12 00	12 47
56	06 25	07 09	07 50	11 14	11 39	12 14	13 03
54	06 22	07 04	07 43	11 23	11 50	12 27	13 17
52	06 19	07 00	07 36	11 30	12 00	12 38	13 29
50	06 17	06 55	07 30	11 37	12 08	12 48	13 39
45	06 11	06 46	07 17	11 51	12 26	13 09	14 01
N 40	06 05	06 38	07 06	12 04	12 41	13 26	14 19
35	06 00	06 30	06 57	12 14	12 53	13 40	14 34
30	05 55	06 24	06 49	12 23	13 04	13 52	14 47
20	05 45	06 12	06 35	12 39	13 23	14 14	15 10
N 10	05 35	06 00	06 22	12 52	13 40	14 32	15 29
0	05 24	05 49	06 10	13 05	13 55	14 49	15 47
S 10	05 11	05 36	05 58	13 18	14 11	15 07	16 05
20	04 55	05 22	05 46	13 32	14 28	15 26	16 25
30	04 34	05 05	05 31	13 48	14 47	15 47	16 47
35	04 22	04 55	05 22	13 58	14 58	16 00	17 00
40	04 06	04 42	05 12	14 08	15 11	16 15	17 15
45	03 46	04 27	05 00	14 21	15 27	16 32	17 33
S 50	03 20	04 08	04 46	14 37	15 46	16 54	17 56
52	03 07	03 59	04 39	14 44	15 55	17 04	18 07
54	02 51	03 49	04 32	14 52	16 05	17 16	18 19
56	02 32	03 37	04 23	15 01	16 17	17 29	18 33
58	02 07	03 23	04 14	15 12	16 30	17 45	18 49
S 60	01 31	03 07	04 03	15 24	16 46	18 03	19 09

Lat.	Sunset	Twilight Civil	Twilight Naut.	Moonset 3	4	5	6
°	h m	h m	h m	h m	h m	h m	h m
N 72	14 21	16 02	17 29	04 55	□	□	□
N 70	14 57	16 19	17 36	04 12	06 44	□	□
68	15 22	16 32	17 41	03 44	05 39	08 14	□
66	15 41	16 43	17 46	03 23	05 03	06 47	08 20
64	15 57	16 52	17 50	03 06	04 38	06 09	07 30
62	16 10	17 00	17 54	02 52	04 18	05 43	06 58
60	16 21	17 07	17 58	02 40	04 02	05 22	06 34
N 58	16 30	17 13	18 01	02 30	03 49	05 05	06 15
56	16 38	17 19	18 04	02 22	03 37	04 51	05 59
54	16 46	17 24	18 07	02 14	03 27	04 39	05 34
52	16 52	17 29	18 09	02 07	03 18	04 28	05 34
50	16 58	17 33	18 12	02 01	03 10	04 18	05 23
45	17 11	17 42	18 17	01 47	02 52	03 58	05 01
N 40	17 22	17 50	18 23	01 36	02 38	03 42	04 44
35	17 31	17 58	18 28	01 27	02 27	03 28	04 29
30	17 39	18 04	18 33	01 19	02 16	03 16	04 16
20	17 53	18 16	18 43	01 04	01 59	02 55	03 54
N 10	18 06	18 27	18 53	00 52	01 43	02 37	03 35
0	18 18	18 39	19 04	00 41	01 29	02 21	03 17
S 10	18 29	18 51	19 17	00 29	01 14	02 04	02 59
20	18 42	19 05	19 32	00 17	00 59	01 46	02 40
30	18 57	19 22	19 53	00 03	00 42	01 26	02 17
35	19 05	19 33	20 05	24 32	00 32	01 14	02 04
40	19 15	19 45	20 21	24 20	00 20	01 01	01 50
45	19 27	19 59	20 40	24 06	00 06	00 45	01 32
S 50	19 41	20 18	21 06	23 50	24 15	00 25	01 10
52	19 47	20 27	21 19	23 42	24 15	00 15	00 59
54	19 55	20 37	21 34	23 34	24 05	00 05	00 47
56	20 03	20 49	21 53	23 24	23 53	24 34	00 34
58	20 12	21 02	22 17	23 13	23 39	24 18	00 18
S 60	20 23	21 18	22 51	23 00	23 23	23 59	24 55

Day	SUN Eqn. of Time 00h	SUN Eqn. of Time 12h	SUN Mer. Pass.	MOON Mer. Pass. Upper	MOON Mer. Pass. Lower	Age	Phase
d	m s	m s	h m	h m	h m	d	%
3	13 42	13 45	12 14	19 17	06 53	10	64
4	13 49	13 52	12 14	20 08	07 42	11	73
5	13 54	13 57	12 14	21 03	08 35	12	82

UT	ARIES	VENUS −4·1		MARS +1·3		JUPITER −1·9		SATURN +0·6		STARS		
d h	GHA	GHA	Dec	GHA	Dec	GHA	Dec	GHA	Dec	Name	SHA	Dec
6 00	135 36.1	137 20.9	S 1 24.4	233 25.9	S23 17.8	209 35.9	S22 35.3	198 00.8	S21 00.5	Acamar	315 14.8	S40 13.9
01	150 38.5	152 20.7	23.1	248 26.5	17.9	224 37.8	35.2	213 02.9	00.4	Achernar	335 23.5	S57 08.5
02	165 41.0	167 20.5	21.7	263 27.1	18.1	239 39.7	35.2	228 05.1	00.4	Acrux	173 03.8	S63 12.3
03	180 43.5	182 20.3	.. 20.4	278 27.7	.. 18.2	254 41.6	.. 35.1	243 07.3	.. 00.3	Adhara	255 08.6	S29 00.2
04	195 45.9	197 20.1	19.1	293 28.3	18.3	269 43.5	35.1	258 09.4	00.3	Aldebaran	290 44.0	N16 32.8
05	210 48.4	212 19.9	17.8	308 28.9	18.4	284 45.4	35.0	273 11.6	00.2			
06	225 50.9	227 19.8	S 1 16.5	323 29.5	S23 18.6	299 47.3	S22 35.0	288 13.8	S21 00.2	Alioth	166 16.3	N55 50.9
07	240 53.3	242 19.6	15.2	338 30.2	18.7	314 49.2	34.9	303 15.9	00.1	Alkaid	152 55.1	N49 12.6
08	255 55.8	257 19.4	13.9	353 30.8	18.8	329 51.0	34.9	318 18.1	00.1	Alnair	27 38.4	S46 52.0
09	270 58.2	272 19.2	.. 12.6	8 31.4	.. 18.9	344 52.9	.. 34.8	333 20.3	.. 00.0	Alnilam	275 41.5	S 1 11.6
10	286 00.7	287 19.0	11.3	23 32.0	19.1	359 54.8	34.8	348 22.4	21 00.0	Alphard	217 51.3	S 8 44.8
11	301 03.2	302 18.9	10.0	38 32.6	19.2	14 56.7	34.7	3 24.6	20 59.9			
12	316 05.6	317 18.7	S 1 08.7	53 33.2	S23 19.3	29 58.6	S22 34.6	18 26.8	S20 59.9	Alphecca	126 07.2	N26 38.7
13	331 08.1	332 18.5	07.3	68 33.8	19.4	45 00.5	34.6	33 28.9	59.8	Alpheratz	357 39.0	N29 12.0
14	346 10.6	347 18.3	06.0	83 34.4	19.6	60 02.4	34.5	48 31.1	59.8	Altair	62 04.1	N 8 55.2
15	1 13.0	2 18.1	.. 04.7	98 35.0	.. 19.7	75 04.3	.. 34.5	63 33.3	.. 59.8	Ankaa	353 11.4	S42 12.2
16	16 15.5	17 18.0	03.4	113 35.6	19.8	90 06.2	34.4	78 35.4	59.7	Antares	112 20.8	S26 28.4
17	31 18.0	32 17.8	02.1	128 36.2	19.9	105 08.1	34.4	93 37.6	59.7			
18	46 20.4	47 17.6	S 1 00.8	143 36.8	S23 20.0	120 10.0	S22 34.3	108 39.8	S20 59.6	Arcturus	145 51.5	N19 04.6
19	61 22.9	62 17.4	0 59.5	158 37.4	20.2	135 11.9	34.3	123 41.9	59.6	Atria	107 18.8	S69 03.4
20	76 25.3	77 17.2	58.2	173 38.0	20.3	150 13.7	34.2	138 44.1	59.5	Avior	234 15.6	S59 34.5
21	91 27.8	92 17.1	.. 56.9	188 38.6	.. 20.4	165 15.6	.. 34.1	153 46.3	.. 59.5	Bellatrix	278 26.9	N 6 21.9
22	106 30.3	107 16.9	55.6	203 39.2	20.5	180 17.5	34.1	168 48.4	59.4	Betelgeuse	270 56.1	N 7 24.5
23	121 32.7	122 16.7	54.3	218 39.8	20.6	195 19.4	34.0	183 50.6	59.4			
7 00	136 35.2	137 16.5	S 0 52.9	233 40.4	S23 20.7	210 21.3	S22 34.0	198 52.8	S20 59.3	Canopus	263 53.7	S52 42.7
01	151 37.7	152 16.4	51.6	248 41.0	20.9	225 23.2	33.9	213 54.9	59.3	Capella	280 27.4	N46 01.1
02	166 40.1	167 16.2	50.3	263 41.6	21.0	240 25.1	33.9	228 57.1	59.2	Deneb	49 28.9	N45 21.0
03	181 42.6	182 16.0	.. 49.0	278 42.3	.. 21.1	255 27.0	.. 33.8	243 59.3	.. 59.2	Denebola	182 28.7	N14 27.5
04	196 45.1	197 15.8	47.7	293 42.9	21.2	270 28.9	33.8	259 01.4	59.1	Diphda	348 51.5	S17 52.9
05	211 47.5	212 15.7	46.4	308 43.5	21.3	285 30.8	33.7	274 03.6	59.1			
06	226 50.0	227 15.5	S 0 45.1	323 44.1	S23 21.4	300 32.7	S22 33.7	289 05.8	S20 59.0	Dubhe	193 45.4	N61 38.4
07	241 52.5	242 15.3	43.8	338 44.7	21.6	315 34.6	33.6	304 07.9	59.0	Elnath	278 06.6	N28 37.4
08	256 54.9	257 15.1	42.5	353 45.3	21.7	330 36.5	33.5	319 10.1	58.9	Eltanin	90 44.4	N51 29.0
09	271 57.4	272 15.0	.. 41.2	8 45.9	.. 21.8	345 38.4	.. 33.5	334 12.3	.. 58.9	Enif	33 43.0	N 9 57.9
10	286 59.8	287 14.8	39.8	23 46.5	21.9	0 40.2	33.4	349 14.4	58.8	Fomalhaut	15 19.2	S29 31.2
11	302 02.3	302 14.6	38.5	38 47.1	22.0	15 42.1	33.4	4 16.6	58.8			
12	317 04.8	317 14.4	S 0 37.2	53 47.7	S23 22.1	30 44.0	S22 33.3	19 18.8	S20 58.7	Gacrux	171 55.5	S57 13.3
13	332 07.2	332 14.3	35.9	68 48.3	22.2	45 45.9	33.3	34 20.9	58.7	Gienah	175 47.4	S17 39.1
14	347 09.7	347 14.1	34.6	83 48.9	22.4	60 47.8	33.2	49 23.1	58.6	Hadar	148 41.3	S60 27.8
15	2 12.2	2 13.9	.. 33.3	98 49.5	.. 22.5	75 49.7	.. 33.2	64 25.3	.. 58.6	Hamal	327 55.7	N23 33.3
16	17 14.6	17 13.7	32.0	113 50.1	22.6	90 51.6	33.1	79 27.4	58.5	Kaus Aust.	83 38.0	S34 22.4
17	32 17.1	32 13.6	30.7	128 50.7	22.7	105 53.5	33.0	94 29.6	58.5			
18	47 19.6	47 13.4	S 0 29.4	143 51.3	S23 22.8	120 55.4	S22 33.0	109 31.8	S20 58.4	Kochab	137 20.0	N74 04.1
19	62 22.0	62 13.2	28.1	158 51.9	22.9	135 57.3	32.9	124 33.9	58.4	Markab	13 34.1	N15 18.7
20	77 24.5	77 13.1	26.8	173 52.5	23.0	150 59.2	32.9	139 36.1	58.3	Menkar	314 10.3	N 4 09.9
21	92 27.0	92 12.9	.. 25.4	188 53.1	.. 23.1	166 01.1	.. 32.8	154 38.3	.. 58.3	Menkent	148 02.1	S36 27.9
22	107 29.4	107 12.7	24.1	203 53.7	23.3	181 03.0	32.8	169 40.4	58.2	Miaplacidus	221 37.9	S69 48.0
23	122 31.9	122 12.5	22.8	218 54.3	23.4	196 04.9	32.7	184 42.6	58.2			
8 00	137 34.3	137 12.4	S 0 21.5	233 54.9	S23 23.5	211 06.8	S22 32.7	199 44.8	S20 58.1	Mirfak	308 33.7	N49 56.0
01	152 36.8	152 12.2	20.2	248 55.5	23.6	226 08.7	32.6	214 46.9	58.1	Nunki	75 53.0	S26 16.2
02	167 39.3	167 12.0	18.9	263 56.1	23.7	241 10.6	32.5	229 49.1	58.0	Peacock	53 12.6	S56 40.2
03	182 41.7	182 11.9	.. 17.6	278 56.7	.. 23.8	256 12.5	.. 32.5	244 51.3	.. 58.0	Pollux	243 21.8	N27 58.6
04	197 44.2	197 11.7	16.3	293 57.3	23.9	271 14.4	32.4	259 53.4	57.9	Procyon	244 54.6	N 5 10.3
05	212 46.7	212 11.5	15.0	308 57.9	24.0	286 16.2	32.4	274 55.6	57.9			
06	227 49.1	227 11.4	S 0 13.6	323 58.5	S23 24.1	301 18.1	S22 32.3	289 57.8	S20 57.8	Rasalhague	96 02.4	N12 32.7
07	242 51.6	242 11.2	12.3	338 59.1	24.2	316 20.0	32.3	304 59.9	57.8	Regulus	207 38.3	N11 52.1
08	257 54.1	257 11.0	11.0	353 59.7	24.3	331 21.9	32.2	320 02.1	57.7	Rigel	281 07.5	S 8 11.0
09	272 56.5	272 10.9	.. 09.7	9 00.3	.. 24.4	346 23.8	.. 32.2	335 04.3	.. 57.7	Rigil Kent.	139 45.5	S60 54.7
10	287 59.0	287 10.7	08.4	24 00.9	24.5	1 25.7	32.1	350 06.5	57.6	Sabik	102 07.5	S15 44.9
11	303 01.5	302 10.5	07.1	39 01.5	24.7	16 27.6	32.0	5 08.6	57.6			
12	318 03.9	317 10.4	S 0 05.8	54 02.1	S23 24.8	31 29.5	S22 32.0	20 10.8	S20 57.5	Schedar	349 35.7	N56 38.9
13	333 06.4	332 10.2	04.5	69 02.7	24.9	46 31.4	31.9	35 13.0	57.5	Shaula	96 15.9	S37 06.9
14	348 08.8	347 10.0	03.2	84 03.3	25.0	61 33.3	31.9	50 15.1	57.4	Sirius	258 29.4	S16 44.9
15	3 11.3	2 09.8	.. 01.9	99 03.9	.. 25.1	76 35.2	.. 31.8	65 17.3	.. 57.4	Spica	158 26.3	S11 15.9
16	18 13.8	17 09.7	S 00.5	114 04.5	25.2	91 37.1	31.8	80 19.5	57.3	Suhail	222 48.7	S43 30.9
17	33 16.2	32 09.5	N 00.8	129 05.1	25.3	106 39.0	31.7	95 21.6	57.3			
18	48 18.7	47 09.4	N 0 02.1	144 05.7	S23 25.4	121 40.9	S22 31.7	110 23.8	S20 57.2	Vega	80 36.2	N38 48.0
19	63 21.2	62 09.2	03.4	159 06.3	25.5	136 42.8	31.6	125 26.0	57.2	Zuben'ubi	137 00.3	S16 07.4
20	78 23.6	77 09.0	04.7	174 06.9	25.6	151 44.7	31.5	140 28.1	57.1		SHA	Mer.Pass.
21	93 26.1	92 08.9	.. 06.0	189 07.6	.. 25.7	166 46.6	.. 31.5	155 30.3	.. 57.1		° ′	h m
22	108 28.6	107 08.7	07.3	204 08.2	25.8	181 48.5	31.4	170 32.5	57.0	Venus	0 41.3	14 51
23	123 31.0	122 08.5	08.6	219 08.8	25.9	196 50.4	31.4	185 34.6	57.0	Mars	97 05.2	8 25
Mer. Pass. 14 51.2		v −0.2	d 1.3	v 0.6	d 0.1	v 1.9	d 0.1	v 2.2	d 0.0	Jupiter	73 46.1	9 57
										Saturn	62 17.6	10 43

UT	SUN GHA	SUN Dec	MOON GHA	v	Dec	d	HP
d h	° ′	° ′	° ′	′	° ′	′	′
6 00	176 30.1	S15 50.7	42 34.7	6.7	N22 56.7	2.3	58.0
01	191 30.1	50.0	57 00.4	6.5	22 59.0	2.1	58.0
02	206 30.0	49.2	71 25.9	6.5	23 01.1	2.0	58.1
03	221 30.0	.. 48.5	85 51.4	6.4	23 03.1	1.9	58.1
04	236 29.9	47.7	100 16.8	6.3	23 05.0	1.7	58.2
05	251 29.9	46.9	114 42.1	6.3	23 06.7	1.6	58.2
06	266 29.8	S15 46.2	129 07.4	6.2	N23 08.3	1.4	58.2
T 07	281 29.8	45.4	143 32.6	6.1	23 09.7	1.3	58.3
H 08	296 29.8	44.6	157 57.7	6.1	23 11.0	1.1	58.3
U 09	311 29.7	.. 43.9	172 22.8	6.0	23 12.1	1.0	58.3
R 10	326 29.7	43.1	186 47.8	6.0	23 13.1	0.9	58.4
S 11	341 29.6	42.3	201 12.8	5.9	23 14.0	0.7	58.4
D 12	356 29.6	S15 41.6	215 37.7	5.8	N23 14.7	0.5	58.5
A 13	11 29.5	40.8	230 02.5	5.8	23 15.2	0.4	58.5
Y 14	26 29.5	40.0	244 27.3	5.7	23 15.6	0.3	58.5
15	41 29.4	.. 39.3	258 52.0	5.7	23 15.9	0.1	58.6
16	56 29.4	38.5	273 16.7	5.6	23 16.0	0.1	58.6
17	71 29.4	37.7	287 41.3	5.6	23 15.9	0.2	58.6
18	86 29.3	S15 37.0	302 05.9	5.5	N23 15.7	0.4	58.7
19	101 29.3	36.2	316 30.4	5.5	23 15.3	0.5	58.7
20	116 29.2	35.4	330 54.9	5.4	23 14.8	0.6	58.8
21	131 29.2	.. 34.6	345 19.3	5.4	23 14.2	0.8	58.8
22	146 29.2	33.9	359 43.7	5.4	23 13.4	1.0	58.8
23	161 29.1	33.1	14 08.1	5.3	23 12.4	1.1	58.9
7 00	176 29.1	S15 32.3	28 32.4	5.3	N23 11.3	1.3	58.9
01	191 29.0	31.5	42 56.7	5.2	23 10.0	1.5	58.9
02	206 29.0	30.8	57 20.9	5.2	23 08.5	1.6	59.0
03	221 29.0	.. 30.0	71 45.1	5.2	23 06.9	1.7	59.0
04	236 28.9	29.2	86 09.3	5.1	23 05.2	1.9	59.0
05	251 28.9	28.5	100 33.4	5.1	23 03.3	2.1	59.1
06	266 28.8	S15 27.7	114 57.5	5.1	N23 01.2	2.2	59.1
F 07	281 28.8	26.9	129 21.6	5.0	22 59.0	2.4	59.2
R 08	296 28.8	26.1	143 45.6	5.1	22 56.6	2.5	59.2
I 09	311 28.7	.. 25.3	158 09.7	5.0	22 54.1	2.7	59.2
D 10	326 28.7	24.6	172 33.7	4.9	22 51.4	2.8	59.3
A 11	341 28.7	23.8	186 57.6	5.0	22 48.6	3.1	59.3
Y 12	356 28.6	S15 23.0	201 21.6	5.0	N22 45.5	3.1	59.4
13	11 28.6	22.2	215 45.6	4.9	22 42.4	3.3	59.4
14	26 28.6	21.5	230 09.5	4.9	22 39.1	3.5	59.4
15	41 28.5	.. 20.7	244 33.4	4.9	22 35.6	3.7	59.4
16	56 28.5	19.9	258 57.3	4.9	22 31.9	3.8	59.5
17	71 28.5	19.1	273 21.2	4.9	22 28.1	3.9	59.5
18	86 28.4	S15 18.3	287 45.1	4.9	N22 24.2	4.1	59.5
19	101 28.4	17.6	302 09.0	4.9	22 20.1	4.3	59.6
20	116 28.4	16.8	316 32.9	4.8	22 15.8	4.4	59.6
21	131 28.3	.. 16.0	330 56.7	4.9	22 11.4	4.6	59.6
22	146 28.3	15.2	345 20.6	4.9	22 06.8	4.8	59.7
23	161 28.3	14.4	359 44.5	4.9	22 02.0	4.8	59.7
8 00	176 28.2	S15 13.6	14 08.4	4.8	N21 57.2	5.1	59.7
01	191 28.2	12.9	28 32.2	4.9	21 52.1	5.2	59.7
02	206 28.2	12.1	42 56.1	4.9	21 46.9	5.4	59.8
03	221 28.1	.. 11.3	57 20.0	4.9	21 41.5	5.5	59.8
04	236 28.1	10.5	71 43.9	4.9	21 36.0	5.7	59.8
05	251 28.1	09.7	86 07.8	4.9	21 30.3	5.8	59.9
06	266 28.1	S15 08.9	100 31.7	5.0	N21 24.5	6.0	59.9
S 07	281 28.0	08.1	114 55.7	4.9	21 18.5	6.1	59.9
A 08	296 28.0	07.4	129 19.6	5.0	21 12.4	6.3	59.9
T 09	311 28.0	.. 06.6	143 43.6	5.0	21 06.1	6.4	60.0
U 10	326 27.9	05.8	158 07.6	5.0	20 59.7	6.6	60.0
R 11	341 27.9	05.0	172 31.6	5.0	20 53.1	6.7	60.0
D 12	356 27.9	S15 04.2	186 55.6	5.1	N20 46.4	6.9	60.1
A 13	11 27.9	03.4	201 19.7	5.1	20 39.5	7.0	60.1
Y 14	26 27.8	02.6	215 43.8	5.1	20 32.5	7.2	60.1
15	41 27.8	.. 01.8	230 07.9	5.1	20 25.3	7.3	60.1
16	56 27.8	01.0	244 32.0	5.1	20 18.0	7.5	60.2
17	71 27.8	15 00.3	258 56.1	5.2	20 10.5	7.6	60.2
18	86 27.7	S14 59.5	273 20.3	5.3	N20 02.9	7.8	60.2
19	101 27.7	58.7	287 44.6	5.2	19 55.1	7.9	60.2
20	116 27.7	57.9	302 08.8	5.3	19 47.2	8.0	60.3
21	131 27.7	.. 57.1	316 33.1	5.3	19 39.2	8.2	60.3
22	146 27.6	56.3	330 57.4	5.4	19 31.0	8.3	60.3
23	161 27.6	55.5	345 21.8	5.4	N19 22.7	8.5	60.3
	SD 16.2	d 0.8	SD 15.9		16.2		16.4

Lat.	Twilight Naut.	Civil	Sunrise	Moonrise 6	7	8	9
°	h m	h m	h m	h m	h m	h m	h m
N 72	06 49	08 14	09 46	□	□	□	13 58
N 70	06 44	07 59	09 16	□	□	□	14 54
68	06 39	07 47	08 54	□	□	13 04	15 27
66	06 35	07 37	08 37	10 42	11 57	13 50	15 51
64	06 31	07 28	08 23	11 33	12 43	14 20	16 10
62	06 28	07 21	08 11	12 04	13 12	14 43	16 25
60	06 25	07 15	08 01	12 28	13 35	15 01	16 37
N 58	06 22	07 09	07 52	12 47	13 53	15 16	16 48
56	06 20	07 04	07 44	13 03	14 08	15 29	16 58
54	06 17	06 59	07 37	13 17	14 22	15 40	17 06
52	06 15	06 55	07 31	13 29	14 33	15 50	17 14
50	06 13	06 51	07 25	13 39	14 43	15 58	17 20
45	06 08	06 42	07 13	14 01	15 05	16 17	17 35
N 40	06 03	06 35	07 03	14 19	15 22	16 32	17 46
35	05 58	06 28	06 54	14 34	15 36	16 45	17 57
30	05 54	06 22	06 47	14 47	15 49	16 56	18 05
20	05 44	06 11	06 33	15 10	16 11	17 15	18 20
N 10	05 35	06 00	06 22	15 29	16 29	17 31	18 33
0	05 24	05 49	06 11	15 47	16 47	17 47	18 46
S 10	05 12	05 37	05 59	16 05	17 04	18 02	18 58
20	04 57	05 24	05 47	16 25	17 23	18 19	19 11
30	04 38	05 08	05 33	16 47	17 44	18 37	19 26
35	04 25	04 58	05 25	17 00	17 57	18 48	19 34
40	04 10	04 46	05 16	17 15	18 11	19 01	19 44
45	03 52	04 32	05 05	17 33	18 28	19 16	19 55
S 50	03 27	04 14	04 51	17 56	18 50	19 33	20 09
52	03 15	04 06	04 45	18 07	19 00	19 42	20 15
54	03 00	03 56	04 38	18 19	19 11	19 51	20 22
56	02 43	03 45	04 30	18 33	19 24	20 02	20 30
58	02 21	03 32	04 21	18 49	19 39	20 14	20 39
S 60	01 51	03 17	04 11	19 09	19 56	20 28	20 49

Lat.	Sunset	Twilight Civil	Naut.	Moonset 6	7	8	9
°	h m	h m	h m	h m	h m	h m	h m
N 72	14 43	16 16	17 41	□	□	□	11 22
N 70	15 13	16 31	17 46	□	□	□	10 25
68	15 35	16 43	17 51	□	□	10 09	09 50
66	15 53	16 52	17 55	08 20	09 09	09 22	09 25
64	16 07	17 01	17 58	07 30	08 23	08 52	09 06
62	16 18	17 08	18 01	06 58	07 54	08 29	08 49
60	16 29	17 14	18 04	06 34	07 31	08 10	08 36
N 58	16 37	17 20	18 07	06 15	07 12	07 54	08 24
56	16 45	17 25	18 09	05 59	06 57	07 41	08 14
54	16 52	17 30	18 12	05 46	06 43	07 30	08 05
52	16 58	17 34	18 14	05 34	06 32	07 19	07 57
50	17 04	17 38	18 16	05 23	06 21	07 10	07 50
45	17 16	17 46	18 21	05 01	06 00	06 51	07 34
N 40	17 26	17 54	18 26	04 44	05 42	06 35	07 21
35	17 34	18 00	18 31	04 29	05 27	06 21	07 10
30	17 42	18 07	18 35	04 16	05 14	06 10	07 00
20	17 55	18 18	18 44	03 54	04 52	05 50	06 44
N 10	18 07	18 28	18 53	03 35	04 33	05 32	06 29
0	18 18	18 39	19 04	03 17	04 15	05 15	06 15
S 10	18 29	18 51	19 16	02 59	03 57	04 59	06 01
20	18 41	19 04	19 31	02 40	03 38	04 41	05 46
30	18 54	19 20	19 50	02 17	03 16	04 20	05 29
35	19 03	19 30	20 02	02 04	03 03	04 08	05 19
40	19 12	19 41	20 17	01 50	02 48	03 54	05 07
45	19 23	19 55	20 35	01 32	02 30	03 38	04 53
S 50	19 36	20 13	20 59	01 10	02 07	03 17	04 36
52	19 42	20 21	21 12	00 59	01 57	03 07	04 28
54	19 49	20 30	21 26	00 47	01 44	02 56	04 19
56	19 56	20 41	21 43	00 34	01 31	02 44	04 09
58	20 05	20 54	22 04	00 18	01 14	02 29	03 58
S 60	20 15	21 08	22 32	24 55	00 55	02 12	03 45

Day	SUN Eqn. of Time 00h	12h	Mer. Pass.	MOON Mer. Pass. Upper	Lower	Age	Phase
d	m s	m s	h m	h m	h m	d	%
6	13 59	14 02	12 14	22 01	09 32	13	90
7	14 04	14 05	12 14	23 01	10 31	14	95
8	14 07	14 08	12 14	24 01	11 31	15	99

UT	ARIES GHA	VENUS −4.2 GHA	VENUS Dec	MARS +1.3 GHA	MARS Dec	JUPITER −1.9 GHA	JUPITER Dec	SATURN +0.6 GHA	SATURN Dec	STARS Name	SHA	Dec
9 00	138 33.5	137 08.4	N 0 09.9	234 09.4	S23 26.0	211 52.3	S22 31.3	200 36.8	S20 56.9	Acamar	315 14.9	S40 13.9
01	153 35.9	152 08.2	11.2	249 10.0	26.1	226 54.2	31.3	215 39.0	56.9	Achernar	335 23.5	S57 08.5
02	168 38.4	167 08.0	12.6	264 10.6	26.2	241 56.1	31.2	230 41.2	56.8	Acrux	173 03.7	S63 12.4
03	183 40.9	182 07.9	.. 13.9	279 11.2	.. 26.3	256 58.0	.. 31.1	245 43.3	.. 56.8	Adhara	255 08.6	S29 00.2
04	198 43.3	197 07.7	15.2	294 11.8	26.4	271 59.9	31.1	260 45.5	56.7	Aldebaran	290 44.0	N16 32.8
05	213 45.8	212 07.5	16.5	309 12.4	26.5	287 01.8	31.0	275 47.7	56.7			
06	228 48.3	227 07.4	N 0 17.8	324 13.0	S23 26.6	302 03.7	S22 31.0	290 49.8	S20 56.7	Alioth	166 16.3	N55 50.9
07	243 50.7	242 07.2	19.1	339 13.6	26.7	317 05.6	30.9	305 52.0	56.6	Alkaid	152 55.0	N49 12.6
08	258 53.2	257 07.1	20.4	354 14.2	26.8	332 07.5	30.9	320 54.2	56.6	Alnair	27 38.4	S46 52.0
S 09	273 55.7	272 06.9	.. 21.7	9 14.8	.. 26.9	347 09.4	.. 30.8	335 56.3	.. 56.5	Alnilam	275 41.5	S 1 11.6
U 10	288 58.1	287 06.7	23.0	24 15.3	27.0	2 11.3	30.8	350 58.5	56.5	Alphard	217 51.3	S 8 44.8
N 11	304 00.6	302 06.6	24.3	39 15.9	27.1	17 13.2	30.7	6 00.7	56.4			
D 12	319 03.1	317 06.4	N 0 25.7	54 16.5	S23 27.2	32 15.1	S22 30.6	21 02.9	S20 56.4	Alphecca	126 07.1	N26 38.7
A 13	334 05.5	332 06.2	27.0	69 17.1	27.3	47 17.0	30.6	36 05.0	56.3	Alpheratz	357 39.0	N29 12.0
Y 14	349 08.0	347 06.1	28.3	84 17.7	27.4	62 18.9	30.5	51 07.2	56.3	Altair	62 04.1	N 8 55.2
15	4 10.4	2 05.9	.. 29.6	99 18.3	.. 27.5	77 20.8	.. 30.5	66 09.4	.. 56.2	Ankaa	353 11.4	S42 12.2
16	19 12.9	17 05.8	30.9	114 18.9	27.6	92 22.7	30.4	81 11.5	56.2	Antares	112 20.7	S26 28.4
17	34 15.4	32 05.6	32.2	129 19.5	27.7	107 24.6	30.4	96 13.7	56.1			
18	49 17.8	47 05.4	N 0 33.5	144 20.1	S23 27.8	122 26.5	S22 30.3	111 15.9	S20 56.1	Arcturus	145 51.4	N19 04.6
19	64 20.3	62 05.3	34.8	159 20.7	27.8	137 28.4	30.2	126 18.0	56.0	Atria	107 18.7	S69 03.4
20	79 22.8	77 05.1	36.1	174 21.3	27.9	152 30.3	30.2	141 20.2	56.0	Avior	234 15.6	S59 34.5
21	94 25.2	92 05.0	.. 37.4	189 21.9	.. 28.0	167 32.2	.. 30.1	156 22.4	.. 55.9	Bellatrix	278 26.9	N 6 21.9
22	109 27.7	107 04.8	38.8	204 22.5	28.1	182 34.1	30.1	171 24.6	55.9	Betelgeuse	270 56.1	N 7 24.5
23	124 30.2	122 04.6	40.1	219 23.1	28.2	197 36.0	30.0	186 26.7	55.8			
10 00	139 32.6	137 04.5	N 0 41.4	234 23.7	S23 28.3	212 37.9	S22 30.0	201 28.9	S20 55.8	Canopus	263 53.7	S52 42.7
01	154 35.1	152 04.3	42.7	249 24.3	28.4	227 39.8	29.9	216 31.1	55.7	Capella	280 27.4	N46 01.1
02	169 37.6	167 04.2	44.0	264 24.9	28.5	242 41.7	29.9	231 33.2	55.7	Deneb	49 28.8	N45 21.0
03	184 40.0	182 04.0	.. 45.3	279 25.5	.. 28.6	257 43.6	.. 29.8	246 35.4	.. 55.6	Denebola	182 28.7	N14 27.5
04	199 42.5	197 03.9	46.6	294 26.1	28.7	272 45.5	29.7	261 37.6	55.6	Diphda	348 51.5	S17 52.9
05	214 44.9	212 03.7	47.9	309 26.7	28.8	287 47.4	29.7	276 39.8	55.5			
06	229 47.4	227 03.5	N 0 49.2	324 27.3	S23 28.9	302 49.3	S22 29.6	291 41.9	S20 55.5	Dubhe	193 45.4	N61 38.4
07	244 49.9	242 03.4	50.5	339 27.9	29.0	317 51.2	29.6	306 44.1	55.4	Elnath	278 06.6	N28 37.4
08	259 52.3	257 03.2	51.8	354 28.5	29.0	332 53.1	29.5	321 46.3	55.4	Eltanin	90 44.3	N51 29.0
M 09	274 54.8	272 03.1	.. 53.2	9 29.1	.. 29.1	347 55.0	.. 29.5	336 48.4	.. 55.3	Enif	33 43.0	N 9 57.9
O 10	289 57.3	287 02.9	54.5	24 29.7	29.2	2 56.9	29.4	351 50.6	55.3	Fomalhaut	15 19.2	S29 31.2
N 11	304 59.7	302 02.8	55.8	39 30.3	29.3	17 58.8	29.3	6 52.8	55.2			
D 12	320 02.2	317 02.6	N 0 57.1	54 30.9	S23 29.4	33 00.7	S22 29.3	21 54.9	S20 55.2	Gacrux	171 55.4	S57 13.3
A 13	335 04.7	332 02.4	58.4	69 31.5	29.5	48 02.6	29.2	36 57.1	55.1	Gienah	175 47.3	S17 39.1
Y 14	350 07.1	347 02.3	0 59.7	84 32.1	29.6	63 04.5	29.2	51 59.3	55.1	Hadar	148 41.2	S60 27.8
15	5 09.6	2 02.1	1 01.0	99 32.7	.. 29.7	78 06.4	.. 29.1	67 01.5	.. 55.0	Hamal	327 55.7	N23 33.3
16	20 12.0	17 02.0	02.3	114 33.3	29.7	93 08.3	29.1	82 03.6	55.0	Kaus Aust.	83 38.0	S34 22.4
17	35 14.5	32 01.8	03.6	129 33.9	29.8	108 10.2	29.0	97 05.8	54.9			
18	50 17.0	47 01.7	N 1 04.9	144 34.5	S23 29.8	123 12.1	S22 28.9	112 08.0	S20 54.9	Kochab	137 19.9	N74 04.1
19	65 19.4	62 01.5	06.2	159 35.1	30.0	138 14.0	28.9	127 10.1	54.8	Markab	13 34.1	N15 18.7
20	80 21.9	77 01.4	07.6	174 35.7	30.1	153 15.9	28.8	142 12.3	54.8	Menkar	314 10.3	N 4 09.9
21	95 24.4	92 01.2	.. 08.9	189 36.3	.. 30.2	168 17.8	.. 28.8	157 14.5	.. 54.7	Menkent	148 02.1	S36 27.9
22	110 26.8	107 01.1	10.2	204 36.9	30.3	183 19.7	28.7	172 16.7	54.7	Miaplacidus	221 37.9	S69 48.0
23	125 29.3	122 00.9	11.5	219 37.5	30.3	198 21.6	28.7	187 18.8	54.6			
11 00	140 31.8	137 00.8	N 1 12.8	234 38.1	S23 30.4	213 23.5	S22 28.6	202 21.0	S20 54.6	Mirfak	308 33.8	N49 56.0
01	155 34.2	152 00.6	14.1	249 38.7	30.5	228 25.4	28.5	217 23.2	54.5	Nunki	75 52.9	S26 16.2
02	170 36.7	167 00.4	15.4	264 39.3	30.6	243 27.3	28.5	232 25.4	54.5	Peacock	53 12.6	S56 40.2
03	185 39.2	182 00.3	.. 16.7	279 39.9	.. 30.7	258 29.3	.. 28.4	247 27.5	.. 54.4	Pollux	243 21.8	N27 58.6
04	200 41.6	197 00.1	18.0	294 40.5	30.8	273 31.2	28.4	262 29.7	54.4	Procyon	244 54.6	N 5 10.3
05	215 44.1	212 00.0	19.3	309 41.0	30.8	288 33.1	28.3	277 31.9	54.3			
06	230 46.5	226 59.8	N 1 20.6	324 41.6	S23 30.9	303 35.0	S22 28.3	292 34.0	S20 54.3	Rasalhague	96 02.4	N12 32.7
07	245 49.0	241 59.7	22.0	339 42.2	31.0	318 36.9	28.2	307 36.2	54.2	Regulus	207 38.3	N11 52.1
08	260 51.5	256 59.5	23.3	354 42.8	31.1	333 38.8	28.1	322 38.4	54.2	Rigel	281 07.5	S 8 11.0
T 09	275 53.9	271 59.4	.. 24.6	9 43.4	.. 31.2	348 40.7	.. 28.1	337 40.6	.. 54.1	Rigil Kent.	139 45.4	S60 54.7
U 10	290 56.4	286 59.2	25.9	24 44.0	31.2	3 42.6	28.0	352 42.7	54.1	Sabik	102 07.4	S15 44.9
E 11	305 58.9	301 59.1	27.2	39 44.6	31.3	18 44.5	28.0	7 44.9	54.1			
S 12	321 01.3	316 58.9	N 1 28.5	54 45.2	S23 31.4	33 46.4	S22 27.9	22 47.1	S20 54.0	Schedar	349 35.7	N56 38.9
D 13	336 03.8	331 58.8	29.8	69 45.8	31.5	48 48.3	27.8	37 49.3	54.0	Shaula	96 15.9	S37 06.9
A 14	351 06.3	346 58.6	31.1	84 46.4	31.6	63 50.2	27.8	52 51.4	53.9	Sirius	258 29.4	S16 44.9
Y 15	6 08.7	1 58.5	.. 32.4	99 47.0	.. 31.6	78 52.1	.. 27.7	67 53.6	.. 53.9	Spica	158 26.3	S11 15.9
16	21 11.2	16 58.3	33.7	114 47.6	31.7	93 54.0	27.7	82 55.8	53.8	Suhail	222 48.7	S43 30.9
17	36 13.7	31 58.2	35.0	129 48.2	31.8	108 55.9	27.6	97 57.9	53.8			
18	51 16.1	46 58.0	N 1 36.3	144 48.8	S23 31.9	123 57.8	S22 27.6	113 00.1	S20 53.7	Vega	80 36.2	N38 48.0
19	66 18.6	61 57.9	37.7	159 49.4	32.0	138 59.7	27.5	128 02.3	53.7	Zuben'ubi	137 00.3	S16 07.4
20	81 21.0	76 57.7	39.0	174 50.0	32.0	154 01.6	27.5	143 04.5	53.6			
21	96 23.5	91 57.6	.. 40.3	189 50.6	.. 32.1	169 03.5	.. 27.4	158 06.6	.. 53.6		SHA	Mer. Pass.
22	111 26.0	106 57.4	41.6	204 51.2	32.2	184 05.5	27.3	173 08.8	53.5	Venus	357 31.9	14 52
23	126 28.4	121 57.3	42.9	219 51.8	32.3	199 07.4	27.3	188 11.0	53.5	Mars	94 51.1	8 22
Mer. Pass. 14 39.4		v −0.2	d 1.3	v 0.6	d 0.1	v 1.9	d 0.1	v 2.2	d 0.0	Jupiter	73 05.3	9 48
										Saturn	61 56.3	10 33

UT	SUN GHA	SUN Dec	MOON GHA	v	MOON Dec	d	HP
d h	° ′	° ′	° ′	′	° ′	′	′
9 00	176 27.6	S14 54.7	359 46.2	5.4	N19 14.2	8.6	60.3
01	191 27.6	53.9	14 10.6	5.5	19 05.6	8.7	60.4
02	206 27.5	53.1	28 35.1	5.5	18 56.9	8.9	60.4
03	221 27.5	.. 52.3	42 59.6	5.5	18 48.0	9.0	60.4
04	236 27.5	51.5	57 24.1	5.6	18 39.0	9.1	60.4
05	251 27.5	50.7	71 48.7	5.7	18 29.9	9.3	60.4
06	266 27.5	S14 49.9	86 13.4	5.7	N18 20.6	9.4	60.5
07	281 27.4	49.1	100 38.1	5.7	18 11.2	9.5	60.5
08	296 27.4	48.3	115 02.8	5.8	18 01.7	9.7	60.5
S 09	311 27.4	.. 47.5	129 27.6	5.8	17 52.0	9.7	60.5
U 10	326 27.4	46.7	143 52.4	5.9	17 42.3	10.0	60.5
N 11	341 27.4	45.9	158 17.3	5.9	17 32.3	10.0	60.6
D 12	356 27.3	S14 45.1	172 42.2	6.0	N17 22.3	10.1	60.6
A 13	11 27.3	44.3	187 07.2	6.0	17 12.2	10.3	60.6
Y 14	26 27.3	43.5	201 32.2	6.0	17 01.9	10.4	60.6
15	41 27.3	.. 42.7	215 57.2	6.2	16 51.5	10.5	60.6
16	56 27.3	41.9	230 22.4	6.1	16 41.0	10.6	60.6
17	71 27.3	41.1	244 47.5	6.3	16 30.4	10.8	60.6
18	86 27.2	S14 40.3	259 12.8	6.2	N16 19.6	10.8	60.7
19	101 27.2	39.5	273 38.0	6.4	16 08.8	11.0	60.7
20	116 27.2	38.7	288 03.4	6.4	15 57.8	11.1	60.7
21	131 27.2	.. 37.9	302 28.8	6.4	15 46.7	11.2	60.7
22	146 27.2	37.1	316 54.2	6.5	15 35.5	11.3	60.7
23	161 27.2	36.3	331 19.7	6.6	15 24.2	11.4	60.7
10 00	176 27.1	S14 35.5	345 45.3	6.6	N15 12.8	11.5	60.7
01	191 27.1	34.7	0 10.9	6.6	15 01.3	11.6	60.7
02	206 27.1	33.9	14 36.5	6.7	14 49.7	11.7	60.7
03	221 27.1	.. 33.1	29 02.2	6.8	14 38.0	11.8	60.8
04	236 27.1	32.3	43 28.0	6.8	14 26.2	11.9	60.8
05	251 27.1	31.5	57 53.8	6.9	14 14.3	12.0	60.8
06	266 27.1	S14 30.7	72 19.7	7.0	N14 02.3	12.1	60.8
07	281 27.1	29.9	86 45.7	7.0	13 50.2	12.2	60.8
08	296 27.0	29.1	101 11.7	7.0	13 38.0	12.3	60.8
M 09	311 27.0	.. 28.3	115 37.7	7.2	13 25.7	12.3	60.8
O 10	326 27.0	27.4	130 03.9	7.1	13 13.4	12.5	60.8
N 11	341 27.0	26.6	144 30.0	7.3	13 00.9	12.5	60.8
D 12	356 27.0	S14 25.8	158 56.3	7.2	N12 48.4	12.6	60.8
A 13	11 27.0	25.0	173 22.5	7.4	12 35.8	12.8	60.8
Y 14	26 27.0	24.2	187 48.9	7.4	12 23.0	12.7	60.8
15	41 27.0	.. 23.4	202 15.3	7.4	12 10.3	12.9	60.8
16	56 27.0	22.6	216 41.7	7.5	11 57.4	12.9	60.8
17	71 27.0	21.8	231 08.2	7.6	11 44.5	13.1	60.8
18	86 26.9	S14 21.0	245 34.8	7.6	N11 31.4	13.1	60.8
19	101 26.9	20.1	260 01.4	7.7	11 18.3	13.1	60.8
20	116 26.9	19.3	274 28.1	7.7	11 05.2	13.3	60.8
21	131 26.9	.. 18.5	288 54.8	7.8	10 51.9	13.3	60.8
22	146 26.9	17.7	303 21.6	7.9	10 38.6	13.3	60.8
23	161 26.9	16.9	317 48.5	7.9	10 25.3	13.5	60.8
11 00	176 26.9	S14 16.1	332 15.4	7.9	N10 11.8	13.4	60.8
01	191 26.9	15.3	346 42.3	8.0	9 58.4	13.6	60.8
02	206 26.9	14.4	1 09.3	8.1	9 44.8	13.6	60.8
03	221 26.9	.. 13.6	15 36.4	8.1	9 31.2	13.7	60.8
04	236 26.9	12.8	30 03.5	8.2	9 17.5	13.7	60.8
05	251 26.9	12.0	44 30.7	8.2	9 03.8	13.8	60.8
06	266 26.9	S14 11.2	58 57.9	8.3	N 8 50.0	13.8	60.8
07	281 26.9	10.4	73 25.2	8.3	8 36.2	13.9	60.8
T 08	296 26.9	09.5	87 52.5	8.4	8 22.3	14.0	60.8
U 09	311 26.9	.. 08.7	102 19.9	8.4	8 08.3	13.9	60.8
E 10	326 26.9	07.9	116 47.3	8.4	7 54.4	14.1	60.8
S 11	341 26.8	07.1	131 14.7	8.6	7 40.3	14.0	60.8
D 12	356 26.8	S14 06.3	145 42.3	8.5	N 7 26.3	14.1	60.8
A 13	11 26.8	05.5	160 09.8	8.6	7 12.2	14.2	60.8
Y 14	26 26.8	04.6	174 37.4	8.7	6 58.0	14.2	60.8
15	41 26.8	.. 03.8	189 05.1	8.7	6 43.8	14.2	60.7
16	56 26.8	03.0	203 32.8	8.8	6 29.6	14.3	60.7
17	71 26.8	02.2	218 00.6	8.8	6 15.3	14.2	60.7
18	86 26.8	S14 01.3	232 28.4	8.8	N 6 01.1	14.4	60.7
19	101 26.8	14 00.5	246 56.2	8.9	5 46.7	14.3	60.7
20	116 26.8	13 59.7	261 24.1	8.9	5 32.4	14.4	60.7
21	131 26.8	.. 58.9	275 52.0	9.0	5 18.0	14.4	60.7
22	146 26.8	58.1	290 20.0	9.0	5 03.6	14.4	60.7
23	161 26.8	57.2	304 48.0	9.1	N 4 49.2	14.5	60.7
	SD 16.2	d 0.8	SD 16.5		16.6		16.6

Lat.	Twilight Naut.	Twilight Civil	Sunrise	Moonrise 9	Moonrise 10	Moonrise 11	Moonrise 12
°	h m	h m	h m	h m	h m	h m	h m
N 72	06 37	08 00	09 27	13 58	16 59	19 24	21 39
N 70	06 33	07 47	09 01	14 54	17 20	19 32	21 38
68	06 30	07 36	08 41	15 27	17 37	19 39	21 37
66	06 26	07 28	08 26	15 51	17 50	19 45	21 36
64	06 23	07 20	08 13	16 10	18 01	19 49	21 35
62	06 21	07 14	08 02	16 25	18 10	19 53	21 35
60	06 18	07 08	07 53	16 37	18 18	19 57	21 34
N 58	06 16	07 03	07 45	16 48	18 24	20 00	21 34
56	06 14	06 58	07 38	16 58	18 30	20 03	21 33
54	06 12	06 54	07 31	17 06	18 36	20 05	21 33
52	06 10	06 50	07 26	17 14	18 41	20 07	21 33
50	06 08	06 46	07 20	17 20	18 45	20 09	21 32
45	06 04	06 39	07 09	17 35	18 54	20 14	21 32
N 40	06 00	06 32	07 00	17 46	19 02	20 17	21 31
35	05 56	06 26	06 52	17 57	19 09	20 21	21 31
30	05 52	06 20	06 45	18 05	19 15	20 23	21 30
20	05 43	06 09	06 32	18 20	19 25	20 28	21 30
N 10	05 34	05 59	06 21	18 33	19 34	20 32	21 29
0	05 25	05 49	06 11	18 46	19 42	20 36	21 29
S 10	05 13	05 38	06 00	18 58	19 50	20 40	21 28
20	04 59	05 26	05 49	19 11	19 59	20 45	21 28
30	04 40	05 11	05 36	19 26	20 09	20 49	21 27
35	04 29	05 01	05 28	19 34	20 15	20 52	21 27
40	04 15	04 50	05 19	19 44	20 21	20 55	21 27
45	03 57	04 37	05 09	19 55	20 29	20 59	21 26
S 50	03 34	04 20	04 57	20 09	20 38	21 03	21 26
52	03 23	04 12	04 51	20 15	20 42	21 05	21 26
54	03 09	04 03	04 44	20 22	20 47	21 07	21 26
56	02 53	03 53	04 37	20 30	20 52	21 10	21 26
58	02 33	03 41	04 29	20 39	20 57	21 12	21 25
S 60	02 08	03 27	04 20	20 49	21 04	21 15	21 25

Lat.	Sunset	Twilight Civil	Twilight Naut.	Moonset 9	Moonset 10	Moonset 11	Moonset 12
°	h m	h m	h m	h m	h m	h m	h m
N 72	15 03	16 30	17 53	11 22	10 21	09 52	09 29
N 70	15 29	16 43	17 57	10 25	09 58	09 41	09 26
68	15 48	16 53	18 00	09 50	09 40	09 31	09 24
66	16 04	17 02	18 03	09 25	09 25	09 24	09 22
64	16 17	17 09	18 06	09 06	09 13	09 17	09 20
62	16 27	17 16	18 09	08 49	09 03	09 12	09 19
60	16 36	17 22	18 11	08 36	08 54	09 07	09 17
N 58	16 44	17 27	18 13	08 24	08 46	09 02	09 16
56	16 52	17 31	18 15	08 14	08 39	08 58	09 15
54	16 58	17 35	18 17	08 05	08 32	08 55	09 14
52	17 04	17 39	18 19	07 57	08 27	08 52	09 13
50	17 09	17 43	18 21	07 50	08 22	08 49	09 13
45	17 20	17 50	18 25	07 34	08 11	08 42	09 11
N 40	17 29	17 57	18 29	07 21	08 01	08 37	09 09
35	17 37	18 03	18 33	07 10	07 53	08 32	09 08
30	17 44	18 09	18 37	07 00	07 46	08 28	09 07
20	17 57	18 19	18 45	06 44	07 34	08 21	09 05
N 10	18 07	18 29	18 54	06 29	07 23	08 14	09 03
0	18 18	18 39	19 04	06 15	07 13	08 08	09 01
S 10	18 28	18 50	19 15	06 01	07 02	08 02	09 00
20	18 39	19 02	19 29	05 46	06 51	07 55	08 58
30	18 52	19 17	19 47	05 29	06 38	07 48	08 55
35	19 00	19 27	19 59	05 19	06 31	07 43	08 54
40	19 08	19 37	20 13	05 07	06 22	07 38	08 53
45	19 18	19 51	20 30	04 53	06 12	07 32	08 51
S 50	19 31	20 07	20 53	04 36	06 00	07 25	08 49
52	19 36	20 15	21 04	04 28	05 55	07 22	08 48
54	19 43	20 24	21 17	04 19	05 48	07 18	08 47
56	19 50	20 34	21 33	04 09	05 41	07 14	08 46
58	19 58	20 45	21 52	03 58	05 33	07 10	08 44
S 60	20 07	20 59	22 16	03 45	05 24	07 04	08 43

	SUN			MOON			
Day	Eqn. of Time 00h	Eqn. of Time 12h	Mer. Pass.	Mer. Pass. Upper	Mer. Pass. Lower	Age	Phase
d	m s	m s	h m	h m	h m	d	%
9	14 10	14 11	12 14	00 01	12 30	16	100
10	14 11	14 12	12 14	00 59	13 28	17	98
11	14 12	14 13	12 14	01 55	14 22	18	93

UT	ARIES GHA	VENUS −4·2 GHA	Dec	MARS +1·3 GHA	Dec	JUPITER −1·9 GHA	Dec	SATURN +0·6 GHA	Dec
12 00	141 30.9	136 57.1	N 1 44.2	234 52.4	S23 32.3	214 09.3	S22 27.2	203 13.2	S20 53.4
01	156 33.4	151 57.0	.. 45.5	249 53.0	32.4	229 11.2	27.2	218 15.3	53.4
02	171 35.8	166 56.8	46.8	264 53.5	32.5	244 13.1	27.1	233 17.5	53.3
03	186 38.3	181 56.7	.. 48.1	279 54.1	.. 32.6	259 15.0	.. 27.1	248 19.7	.. 53.3
04	201 40.8	196 56.5	49.4	294 54.7	32.6	274 16.9	27.0	263 21.9	53.2
05	216 43.2	211 56.4	50.7	309 55.3	32.7	289 18.8	26.9	278 24.0	53.2
W 06	231 45.7	226 56.3	N 1 52.0	324 55.9	S23 32.8	304 20.7	S22 26.9	293 26.2	S20 53.1
E 07	246 48.1	241 56.1	53.3	339 56.5	32.9	319 22.6	26.8	308 28.4	53.1
D 08	261 50.6	256 56.0	54.6	354 57.1	32.9	334 24.5	26.8	323 30.5	53.0
N 09	276 53.1	271 55.8	.. 56.0	9 57.7	.. 33.0	349 26.4	.. 26.7	338 32.7	.. 53.0
E 10	291 55.5	286 55.7	57.3	24 58.3	33.1	4 28.3	26.7	353 34.9	52.9
S 11	306 58.0	301 55.5	58.6	39 58.9	33.1	19 30.2	26.6	8 37.1	52.9
D 12	322 00.5	316 55.4	N 1 59.9	54 59.5	S23 33.2	34 32.2	S22 26.5	23 39.2	S20 52.8
A 13	337 02.9	331 55.2	2 01.2	70 00.1	33.3	49 34.1	26.5	38 41.4	52.8
Y 14	352 05.4	346 55.1	02.5	85 00.7	33.4	64 36.0	26.4	53 43.6	52.7
15	7 07.9	1 54.9	.. 03.8	100 01.3	.. 33.4	79 37.9	.. 26.4	68 45.8	.. 52.7
16	22 10.3	16 54.8	05.1	115 01.9	33.5	94 39.8	26.3	83 47.9	52.6
17	37 12.8	31 54.6	06.4	130 02.5	33.6	109 41.7	26.2	98 50.1	52.6
18	52 15.3	46 54.5	N 2 07.7	145 03.0	S23 33.6	124 43.6	S22 26.2	113 52.3	S20 52.5
19	67 17.7	61 54.4	09.0	160 03.6	33.7	139 45.5	26.1	128 54.5	52.5
20	82 20.2	76 54.2	10.3	175 04.2	33.8	154 47.4	26.1	143 56.6	52.4
21	97 22.6	91 54.1	.. 11.6	190 04.8	.. 33.8	169 49.3	.. 26.0	158 58.8	.. 52.4
22	112 25.1	106 53.9	12.9	205 05.4	33.9	184 51.2	26.0	174 01.0	52.3
23	127 27.6	121 53.8	14.2	220 06.0	34.0	199 53.2	25.9	189 03.2	52.3
13 00	142 30.0	136 53.6	N 2 15.5	235 06.6	S23 34.0	214 55.1	S22 25.8	204 05.3	S20 52.2
01	157 32.5	151 53.5	16.9	250 07.2	34.1	229 57.0	25.8	219 07.5	52.2
02	172 35.0	166 53.4	18.2	265 07.8	34.2	244 58.9	25.7	234 09.7	52.1
03	187 37.4	181 53.2	.. 19.5	280 08.4	.. 34.2	260 00.8	.. 25.7	249 11.9	.. 52.1
04	202 39.9	196 53.1	20.8	295 09.0	34.3	275 02.7	25.6	264 14.0	52.0
05	217 42.4	211 52.9	22.1	310 09.6	34.4	290 04.6	25.6	279 16.2	52.0
T 06	232 44.8	226 52.8	N 2 23.4	325 10.2	S23 34.4	305 06.5	S22 25.5	294 18.4	S20 51.9
H 07	247 47.3	241 52.6	24.7	340 10.8	34.5	320 08.4	25.4	309 20.6	51.9
U 08	262 49.7	256 52.5	26.0	355 11.3	34.6	335 10.3	25.4	324 22.7	51.8
R 09	277 52.2	271 52.4	.. 27.3	10 11.9	.. 34.6	350 12.3	.. 25.3	339 24.9	.. 51.8
S 10	292 54.7	286 52.2	28.6	25 12.5	34.7	5 14.2	25.3	354 27.1	51.7
D 11	307 57.1	301 52.1	29.9	40 13.1	34.7	20 16.1	25.2	9 29.3	51.7
A 12	322 59.6	316 51.9	N 2 31.2	55 13.7	S23 34.8	35 18.0	S22 25.1	24 31.4	S20 51.7
Y 13	338 02.1	331 51.8	32.5	70 14.3	34.9	50 19.9	25.1	39 33.6	51.6
14	353 04.5	346 51.7	33.8	85 14.9	34.9	65 21.8	25.0	54 35.8	51.6
15	8 07.0	1 51.5	.. 35.1	100 15.5	.. 35.0	80 23.7	.. 25.0	69 38.0	.. 51.5
16	23 09.5	16 51.4	36.4	115 16.1	35.1	95 25.6	24.9	84 40.2	51.5
17	38 11.9	31 51.2	37.7	130 16.7	35.1	110 27.5	24.9	99 42.3	51.4
18	53 14.4	46 51.1	N 2 39.0	145 17.3	S23 35.2	125 29.5	S22 24.8	114 44.5	S20 51.4
19	68 16.9	61 51.0	40.3	160 17.9	35.2	140 31.4	24.7	129 46.7	51.3
20	83 19.3	76 50.8	41.6	175 18.4	35.3	155 33.3	24.7	144 48.9	51.3
21	98 21.8	91 50.7	.. 42.9	190 19.0	.. 35.4	170 35.2	.. 24.6	159 51.0	.. 51.2
22	113 24.2	106 50.5	44.3	205 19.6	35.4	185 37.1	24.6	174 53.2	51.2
23	128 26.7	121 50.4	45.6	220 20.2	35.5	200 39.0	24.5	189 55.4	51.1
14 00	143 29.2	136 50.3	N 2 46.9	235 20.8	S23 35.5	215 40.9	S22 24.4	204 57.6	S20 51.1
01	158 31.6	151 50.1	48.2	250 21.4	35.6	230 42.8	24.4	219 59.7	51.0
02	173 34.1	166 50.0	49.5	265 22.0	35.6	245 44.8	24.3	235 01.9	51.0
03	188 36.6	181 49.8	.. 50.8	280 22.6	.. 35.7	260 46.7	.. 24.3	250 04.1	.. 50.9
04	203 39.0	196 49.7	52.1	295 23.2	35.8	275 48.6	24.2	265 06.3	50.9
05	218 41.5	211 49.6	53.4	310 23.8	35.8	290 50.5	24.2	280 08.4	50.8
F 06	233 44.0	226 49.4	N 2 54.7	325 24.4	S23 35.9	305 52.4	S22 24.1	295 10.6	S20 50.8
R 07	248 46.4	241 49.3	56.0	340 25.0	35.9	320 54.3	24.0	310 12.8	50.7
I 08	263 48.9	256 49.1	57.3	355 25.5	36.0	335 56.2	24.0	325 15.0	50.7
D 09	278 51.4	271 49.0	.. 58.6	10 26.1	.. 36.0	350 58.2	.. 23.9	340 17.2	.. 50.6
A 10	293 53.9	286 48.9	2 59.9	25 26.7	36.1	6 00.1	23.9	355 19.3	50.6
Y 11	308 56.3	301 48.7	3 01.2	40 27.3	36.1	21 02.0	23.8	10 21.5	50.5
12	323 58.7	316 48.6	N 3 02.5	55 27.9	S23 36.2	36 03.9	S22 23.7	25 23.7	S20 50.5
13	339 01.2	331 48.5	03.8	70 28.5	36.3	51 05.8	23.7	40 25.9	50.4
14	354 03.7	346 48.3	05.1	85 29.1	36.3	66 07.7	23.6	55 28.0	50.4
15	9 06.1	1 48.2	.. 06.4	100 29.7	.. 36.4	81 09.6	.. 23.6	70 30.2	.. 50.3
16	24 08.6	16 48.1	07.7	115 30.3	36.4	96 11.6	23.5	85 32.4	50.3
17	39 11.1	31 47.9	09.0	130 30.9	36.5	111 13.5	23.5	100 34.6	50.2
18	54 13.5	46 47.8	N 3 10.3	145 31.4	S23 36.5	126 15.4	S22 23.4	115 36.8	S20 50.2
19	69 16.0	61 47.6	11.6	160 32.0	36.6	141 17.3	23.3	130 38.9	50.1
20	84 18.5	76 47.5	12.9	175 32.6	36.6	156 19.2	23.3	145 41.1	50.1
21	99 20.9	91 47.4	.. 14.2	190 33.2	.. 36.7	171 21.1	.. 23.2	160 43.3	.. 50.0
22	114 23.4	106 47.2	15.5	205 33.8	36.7	186 23.1	23.2	175 45.5	50.0
23	129 25.8	121 47.1	16.8	220 34.4	36.8	201 25.0	23.1	190 47.6	49.9
Mer. Pass.	14 27.6	v −0.1	d 1.3	v 0.6	d 0.1	v 1.9	d 0.1	v 2.2	d 0.0

STARS

Name	SHA	Dec
Acamar	315 14.9	S40 13.9
Achernar	335 23.6	S57 08.5
Acrux	173 03.7	S63 12.4
Adhara	255 08.6	S29 00.2
Aldebaran	290 44.0	N16 32.8
Alioth	166 16.2	N55 50.9
Alkaid	152 55.0	N49 12.6
Alnair	27 38.4	S46 52.0
Alnilam	275 41.5	S 1 11.6
Alphard	217 51.3	S 8 44.8
Alphecca	126 07.1	N26 38.7
Alpheratz	357 39.0	N29 12.0
Altair	62 04.1	N 8 55.2
Ankaa	353 11.4	S42 12.1
Antares	112 20.7	S26 28.4
Arcturus	145 51.4	N19 04.6
Atria	107 18.7	S69 03.4
Avior	234 15.6	S59 34.6
Bellatrix	278 26.9	N 6 21.9
Betelgeuse	270 56.1	N 7 24.5
Canopus	263 53.7	S52 42.7
Capella	280 27.4	N46 01.1
Deneb	49 28.8	N45 21.0
Denebola	182 28.7	N14 27.5
Diphda	348 51.5	S17 52.9
Dubhe	193 45.4	N61 38.5
Elnath	278 06.6	N28 37.4
Eltanin	90 44.3	N51 29.0
Enif	33 43.0	N 9 57.9
Fomalhaut	15 19.2	S29 31.2
Gacrux	171 55.4	S57 13.3
Gienah	175 47.3	S17 39.1
Hadar	148 41.2	S60 27.8
Hamal	327 55.7	N23 33.3
Kaus Aust.	83 38.0	S34 22.4
Kochab	137 19.8	N74 04.1
Markab	13 34.1	N15 18.7
Menkar	314 10.3	N 4 09.9
Menkent	148 02.0	S36 27.9
Miaplacidus	221 37.9	S69 48.0
Mirfak	308 33.8	N49 56.0
Nunki	75 52.9	S26 16.2
Peacock	53 12.6	S56 40.2
Pollux	243 21.8	N27 58.6
Procyon	244 54.7	N 5 10.3
Rasalhague	96 02.4	N12 32.7
Regulus	207 38.3	N11 52.1
Rigel	281 07.5	S 8 11.0
Rigil Kent.	139 45.4	S60 54.7
Sabik	102 07.4	S15 44.9
Schedar	349 35.7	N56 38.9
Shaula	96 15.9	S37 06.9
Sirius	258 29.4	S16 44.9
Spica	158 26.3	S11 15.9
Suhail	222 48.7	S43 30.9
Vega	80 36.2	N38 48.0
Zuben'ubi	137 00.3	S16 07.4

	SHA	Mer. Pass.
Venus	354 23.6	14 53
Mars	92 36.6	8 19
Jupiter	72 25.0	9 39
Saturn	61 35.3	10 22

UT	SUN		MOON					Lat.	Twilight		Sunrise	Moonrise			
									Naut.	Civil		12	13	14	15
	GHA	Dec	GHA	v	Dec	d	HP								
d h	° ′	° ′	° ′	′	° ′	′	′	°	h m	h m	h m	h m	h m	h m	h m
								N 72	06 25	07 46	09 09	21 39	23 52	26 12	02 12
12 00	176 26.8	S13 56.4	319 16.1	9.1	N 4 34.7	14.4	60.7	N 70	06 22	07 35	08 46	21 38	23 41	25 47	01 47
01	191 26.8	55.6	333 44.2	9.1	4 20.3	14.5	60.6	68	06 20	07 26	08 29	21 37	23 32	25 29	01 29
02	206 26.8	54.8	348 12.3	9.2	4 05.8	14.5	60.6	66	06 17	07 18	08 15	21 36	23 25	25 14	01 14
03	221 26.8 . .	53.9	2 40.5	9.2	3 51.3	14.6	60.6	64	06 15	07 11	08 03	21 35	23 19	25 02	01 02
04	236 26.8	53.1	17 08.7	9.2	3 36.7	14.5	60.6	62	06 13	07 06	07 53	21 35	23 14	24 52	00 52
05	251 26.9	52.3	31 36.9	9.3	3 22.2	14.5	60.6	60	06 12	07 01	07 45	21 34	23 10	24 43	00 43
06	266 26.9	S13 51.5	46 05.2	9.3	N 3 07.7	14.6	60.6	N 58	06 10	06 56	07 38	21 34	23 06	24 36	00 36
W 07	281 26.9	50.6	60 33.5	9.4	2 53.1	14.6	60.6	56	06 08	06 52	07 31	21 33	23 02	24 29	00 29
E 08	296 26.9	49.8	75 01.9	9.4	2 38.5	14.5	60.5	54	06 07	06 48	07 25	21 33	22 59	24 23	00 23
D 09	311 26.9 . .	49.0	89 30.3	9.4	2 24.0	14.6	60.5	52	06 05	06 45	07 20	21 33	22 56	24 18	00 18
N 10	326 26.9	48.1	103 58.7	9.4	2 09.4	14.6	60.5	50	06 04	06 42	07 15	21 32	22 54	24 13	00 13
E 11	341 26.9	47.3	118 27.1	9.5	1 54.8	14.6	60.5	45	06 00	06 34	07 05	21 32	22 48	24 03	00 03
S 12	356 26.9	S13 46.5	132 55.6	9.5	N 1 40.2	14.6	60.5	N 40	05 56	06 28	06 56	21 31	22 43	23 54	25 04
D 13	11 26.9	45.7	147 24.1	9.6	1 25.6	14.6	60.5	35	05 53	06 23	06 49	21 31	22 40	23 47	24 54
A 14	26 26.9	44.8	161 52.7	9.6	1 11.0	14.6	60.4	30	05 49	06 18	06 42	21 30	22 36	23 41	24 45
Y 15	41 26.9 . .	44.0	176 21.3	9.6	0 56.4	14.5	60.4	20	05 42	06 08	06 31	21 30	22 30	23 30	24 29
16	56 26.9	43.2	190 49.9	9.6	0 41.9	14.6	60.4	N 10	05 34	05 59	06 20	21 29	22 25	23 20	24 16
17	71 26.9	42.3	205 18.5	9.6	0 27.3	14.6	60.4	0	05 25	05 50	06 11	21 29	22 20	23 12	24 04
18	86 26.9	S13 41.5	219 47.1	9.7	N 0 12.7	14.5	60.4	S 10	05 14	05 39	06 01	21 28	22 15	23 03	23 51
19	101 26.9	40.7	234 15.8	9.7	S 0 01.8	14.6	60.3	20	05 01	05 28	05 50	21 28	22 10	22 54	23 38
20	116 26.9	39.8	248 44.5	9.8	0 16.4	14.5	60.3	30	04 43	05 13	05 38	21 27	22 05	22 43	23 23
21	131 26.9 . .	39.0	263 13.3	9.7	0 30.9	14.5	60.3	35	04 32	05 04	05 31	21 27	22 02	22 37	23 15
22	146 26.9	38.2	277 42.0	9.8	0 45.4	14.5	60.3	40	04 19	04 54	05 23	21 27	21 58	22 30	23 05
23	161 27.0	37.3	292 10.8	9.8	0 59.9	14.5	60.3	45	04 03	04 42	05 13	21 26	21 54	22 22	22 54
13 00	176 27.0	S13 36.5	306 39.6	9.8	S 1 14.4	14.5	60.2	S 50	03 41	04 26	05 02	21 26	21 49	22 13	22 40
01	191 27.0	35.7	321 08.4	9.8	1 28.9	14.4	60.2	52	03 30	04 19	04 57	21 26	21 47	22 09	22 33
02	206 27.0	34.8	335 37.2	9.9	1 43.3	14.5	60.2	54	03 18	04 10	04 51	21 26	21 44	22 04	22 26
03	221 27.0 . .	34.0	350 06.1	9.8	1 57.8	14.4	60.2	56	03 03	04 01	04 44	21 25	21 41	21 58	22 19
04	236 27.0	33.2	4 34.9	9.9	2 12.2	14.3	60.2	58	02 45	03 50	04 36	21 25	21 38	21 53	22 10
05	251 27.0	32.3	19 03.8	9.9	2 26.5	14.4	60.1	S 60	02 23	03 37	04 28	21 25	21 35	21 46	22 00
06	266 27.0	S13 31.5	33 32.7	9.9	S 2 40.9	14.3	60.1								
T 07	281 27.0	30.7	48 01.6	10.0	2 55.2	14.3	60.1	Lat.	Sunset	Twilight		Moonset			
H 08	296 27.1	29.8	62 30.6	9.9	3 09.5	14.3	60.1			Civil	Naut.	12	13	14	15
U 09	311 27.1 . .	29.0	76 59.5	10.0	3 23.8	14.2	60.0								
R 10	326 27.1	28.1	91 28.5	9.9	3 38.0	14.3	60.0	°	h m	h m	h m	h m	h m	h m	h m
S 11	341 27.1	27.3	105 57.4	10.0	3 52.3	14.1	60.0	N 72	15 21	16 44	18 05	09 29	09 08	08 44	08 13
D 12	356 27.1	S13 26.5	120 26.4	10.0	S 4 06.4	14.2	60.0	N 70	15 44	16 55	18 08	09 26	09 12	08 58	08 40
A 13	11 27.1	25.6	134 55.4	10.0	4 20.6	14.1	59.9	68	16 01	17 04	18 10	09 24	09 16	09 09	09 00
Y 14	26 27.1	24.8	149 24.4	10.0	4 34.7	14.0	59.9	66	16 15	17 12	18 12	09 22	09 20	09 18	09 16
15	41 27.1 . .	24.0	163 53.4	10.0	4 48.7	14.0	59.9	64	16 26	17 18	18 14	09 20	09 23	09 25	09 29
16	56 27.2	23.1	178 22.4	10.1	5 02.7	14.0	59.9	62	16 36	17 24	18 16	09 19	09 25	09 32	09 40
17	71 27.2	22.3	192 51.5	10.0	5 16.7	14.0	59.8	60	16 44	17 29	18 18	09 17	09 27	09 38	09 50
18	86 27.2	S13 21.4	207 20.5	10.0	S 5 30.7	13.9	59.8	N 58	16 52	17 33	18 20	09 16	09 29	09 43	09 58
19	101 27.2	20.6	221 49.5	10.0	5 44.6	13.8	59.8	56	16 58	17 37	18 21	09 15	09 31	09 47	10 06
20	116 27.2	19.8	236 18.5	10.1	5 58.4	13.8	59.8	54	17 04	17 41	18 23	09 14	09 33	09 51	10 12
21	131 27.2 . .	18.9	250 47.6	10.0	6 12.2	13.8	59.7	52	17 09	17 44	18 24	09 13	09 34	09 55	10 18
22	146 27.2	18.1	265 16.6	10.1	6 26.0	13.7	59.7	50	17 14	17 48	18 26	09 13	09 35	09 59	10 24
23	161 27.3	17.2	279 45.7	10.0	6 39.7	13.6	59.7	45	17 24	17 55	18 29	09 11	09 38	10 06	10 36
14 00	176 27.3	S13 16.4	294 14.7	10.1	S 6 53.3	13.6	59.7	N 40	17 33	18 01	18 33	09 09	09 41	10 12	10 46
01	191 27.3	15.5	308 43.8	10.0	7 06.9	13.6	59.6	35	17 40	18 06	18 36	09 08	09 43	10 18	10 54
02	206 27.3	14.7	323 12.8	10.0	7 20.5	13.5	59.6	30	17 47	18 11	18 39	09 07	09 45	10 22	11 01
03	221 27.3 . .	13.9	337 41.8	10.1	7 34.0	13.4	59.6	20	17 58	18 21	18 47	09 05	09 48	10 30	11 14
04	236 27.3	13.0	352 10.9	10.0	7 47.4	13.4	59.5	N 10	18 08	18 30	18 55	09 03	09 51	10 38	11 26
05	251 27.4	12.2	6 39.9	10.0	8 00.8	13.3	59.5	0	18 18	18 39	19 04	09 01	09 53	10 45	11 36
06	266 27.4	S13 11.3	21 09.0	10.0	S 8 14.1	13.3	59.5	S 10	18 27	18 49	19 14	09 00	09 56	10 51	11 47
07	281 27.4	10.5	35 38.0	10.0	8 27.4	13.2	59.5	20	18 38	19 00	19 27	08 58	09 59	10 59	11 58
08	296 27.4	09.6	50 07.0	10.0	8 40.6	13.1	59.4	30	18 50	19 15	19 44	08 55	10 02	11 07	12 11
F 09	311 27.4 . .	08.8	64 36.0	10.0	8 53.7	13.1	59.4	35	18 57	19 23	19 55	08 54	10 04	11 12	12 19
R 10	326 27.5	07.9	79 05.0	10.1	9 06.8	13.0	59.4	40	19 05	19 33	20 08	08 53	10 06	11 17	12 28
I 11	341 27.5	07.1	93 34.1	10.0	9 19.8	13.0	59.3	45	19 14	19 46	20 25	08 51	10 08	11 24	12 38
D 12	356 27.5	S13 06.2	108 03.1	9.9	S 9 32.8	12.9	59.3	S 50	19 25	20 01	20 46	08 49	10 11	11 32	12 50
A 13	11 27.5	05.4	122 32.0	10.0	9 45.7	12.8	59.3	52	19 31	20 08	20 56	08 48	10 12	11 35	12 56
Y 14	26 27.5	04.5	137 01.0	10.0	9 58.5	12.7	59.3	54	19 37	20 17	21 08	08 47	10 14	11 39	13 02
15	41 27.6 . .	03.7	151 30.0	10.0	10 11.2	12.7	59.2	56	19 43	20 26	21 23	08 46	10 15	11 43	13 10
16	56 27.6	02.8	165 59.0	9.9	10 23.9	12.6	59.2	58	19 50	20 36	21 40	08 44	10 17	11 48	13 18
17	71 27.6	02.0	180 27.9	9.9	10 36.5	12.6	59.2	S 60	19 59	20 49	22 01	08 43	10 19	11 54	13 27
18	86 27.6	S13 01.1	194 56.8	10.0	S10 49.1	12.4	59.1								
19	101 27.7	13 00.3	209 25.8	9.9	11 01.5	12.4	59.1			SUN			MOON		
20	116 27.7	12 59.4	223 54.7	9.9	11 13.9	12.3	59.1	Day	Eqn. of Time		Mer.	Mer. Pass.		Age	Phase
21	131 27.7 . .	58.6	238 23.6	9.9	11 26.2	12.3	59.1		00ʰ	12ʰ	Pass.	Upper	Lower		
22	146 27.7	57.7	252 52.5	9.9	11 38.5	12.1	59.0	d	m s	m s	h m	h m	h m	d	%
23	161 27.7	56.9	267 21.4	9.8	S11 50.6	12.1	59.0	12	14 13	14 12	12 14	02 49	15 15	19	86
								13	14 12	14 12	12 14	03 41	16 07	20	76
	SD 16.2	d 0.8	SD 16.5		16.3		16.2	14	14 11	14 10	12 14	04 32	16 58	21	66

UT	ARIES GHA	VENUS −4·2 GHA	Dec	MARS +1·2 GHA	Dec	JUPITER −1·9 GHA	Dec	SATURN +0·6 GHA	Dec	STARS Name	SHA	Dec
15 00	144 28.3	136 47.0	N 3 18.1	235 35.0	S23 36.8	216 26.9	S22 23.0	205 49.8	S20 49.9	Acamar	315 14.9	S40 13.9
01	159 30.8	151 46.8	19.4	250 35.6	36.9	231 28.8	23.0	220 52.0	49.8	Achernar	335 23.6	S57 08.5
02	174 33.2	166 46.7	20.7	265 36.2	36.9	246 30.7	22.9	235 54.2	49.8	Acrux	173 03.7	S63 12.4
03	189 35.7	181 46.6	.. 22.0	280 36.8	.. 37.0	261 32.6	.. 22.9	250 56.4	.. 49.7	Adhara	255 08.6	S29 00.2
04	204 38.2	196 46.4	23.3	295 37.3	37.0	276 34.5	22.8	265 58.5	49.7	Aldebaran	290 44.0	N16 32.8
05	219 40.6	211 46.3	24.6	310 37.9	37.1	291 36.5	22.7	281 00.7	49.6			
06	234 43.1	226 46.2	N 3 25.9	325 38.5	S23 37.1	306 38.4	S22 22.7	296 02.9	S20 49.6	Alioth	166 16.2	N55 50.9
07	249 45.6	241 46.0	27.2	340 39.1	37.2	321 40.3	22.6	311 05.1	49.6	Alkaid	152 55.0	N49 12.6
S 08	264 48.0	256 45.9	28.5	355 39.7	37.2	336 42.2	22.6	326 07.3	49.5	Alnair	27 38.4	S46 52.0
A 09	279 50.5	271 45.8	.. 29.8	10 40.3	.. 37.2	351 44.1	.. 22.5	341 09.4	.. 49.5	Alnilam	275 41.5	S 1 11.6
T 10	294 53.0	286 45.6	31.1	25 40.9	37.3	6 46.0	22.5	356 11.6	49.4	Alphard	217 51.3	S 8 44.8
U 11	309 55.4	301 45.5	32.4	40 41.5	37.3	21 48.0	22.4	11 13.8	49.4			
R 12	324 57.9	316 45.4	N 3 33.7	55 42.1	S23 37.4	36 49.9	S22 22.3	26 16.0	S20 49.3	Alphecca	126 07.1	N26 38.7
D 13	340 00.3	331 45.2	35.0	70 42.6	37.4	51 51.8	22.3	41 18.2	49.3	Alpheratz	357 39.1	N29 12.0
A 14	355 02.8	346 45.1	36.3	85 43.2	37.5	66 53.7	22.2	56 20.3	49.2	Altair	62 04.1	N 8 55.2
Y 15	10 05.3	1 45.0	.. 37.6	100 43.8	.. 37.5	81 55.6	.. 22.2	71 22.5	.. 49.2	Ankaa	353 11.4	S42 12.1
16	25 07.7	16 44.8	38.9	115 44.4	37.6	96 57.6	22.1	86 24.7	49.1	Antares	112 20.7	S26 28.4
17	40 10.2	31 44.7	40.2	130 45.0	37.6	111 59.5	22.0	101 26.9	49.1			
18	55 12.7	46 44.6	N 3 41.5	145 45.6	S23 37.6	127 01.4	S22 22.0	116 29.0	S20 49.0	Arcturus	145 51.4	N19 04.6
19	70 15.1	61 44.4	42.8	160 46.2	37.7	142 03.3	21.9	131 31.2	49.0	Atria	107 18.6	S69 03.4
20	85 17.6	76 44.3	44.1	175 46.8	37.7	157 05.2	21.9	146 33.4	48.9	Avior	234 15.6	S59 34.6
21	100 20.1	91 44.2	.. 45.4	190 47.4	.. 37.8	172 07.1	.. 21.8	161 35.6	.. 48.9	Bellatrix	278 26.9	N 6 21.9
22	115 22.5	106 44.0	46.7	205 47.9	37.8	187 09.1	21.7	176 37.8	48.8	Betelgeuse	270 56.1	N 7 24.5
23	130 25.0	121 43.9	48.0	220 48.5	37.9	202 11.0	21.7	191 39.9	48.8			
16 00	145 27.5	136 43.8	N 3 49.3	235 49.1	S23 37.9	217 12.9	S22 21.6	206 42.1	S20 48.7	Canopus	263 53.8	S52 42.7
01	160 29.9	151 43.6	50.6	250 49.7	37.9	232 14.8	21.6	221 44.3	48.7	Capella	280 27.5	N46 01.1
02	175 32.4	166 43.5	51.9	265 50.3	38.0	247 16.7	21.5	236 46.5	48.6	Deneb	49 28.8	N45 21.0
03	190 34.8	181 43.4	.. 53.2	280 50.9	.. 38.0	262 18.7	.. 21.4	251 48.7	.. 48.6	Denebola	182 28.7	N14 27.5
04	205 37.3	196 43.2	54.5	295 51.5	38.1	277 20.6	21.4	266 50.8	48.5	Diphda	348 51.5	S17 52.9
05	220 39.8	211 43.1	55.8	310 52.1	38.1	292 22.5	21.3	281 53.0	48.5			
06	235 42.2	226 43.0	N 3 57.1	325 52.6	S23 38.1	307 24.4	S22 21.3	296 55.2	S20 48.4	Dubhe	193 45.4	N61 38.5
07	250 44.7	241 42.9	58.4	340 53.2	38.2	322 26.3	21.2	311 57.4	48.4	Elnath	278 06.6	N28 37.4
S 08	265 47.2	256 42.7	3 59.7	355 53.8	38.2	337 28.3	21.2	326 59.6	48.3	Eltanin	90 44.3	N51 29.0
U 09	280 49.6	271 42.6	4 01.0	10 54.4	.. 38.2	352 30.2	.. 21.1	342 01.8	.. 48.3	Enif	33 42.9	N 9 57.9
N 10	295 52.1	286 42.5	02.3	25 55.0	38.3	7 32.1	21.0	357 03.9	48.2	Fomalhaut	15 19.2	S29 31.2
D 11	310 54.6	301 42.3	03.6	40 55.6	38.3	22 34.0	21.0	12 06.1	48.2			
A 12	325 57.0	316 42.2	N 4 04.9	55 56.2	S23 38.4	37 35.9	S22 20.9	27 08.3	S20 48.1	Gacrux	171 55.4	S57 13.3
Y 13	340 59.5	331 42.1	06.1	70 56.8	38.4	52 37.9	20.9	42 10.5	48.1	Gienah	175 47.3	S17 39.2
14	356 01.9	346 41.9	07.4	85 57.4	38.4	67 39.8	20.8	57 12.7	48.0	Hadar	148 41.1	S60 27.8
15	11 04.4	1 41.8	.. 08.7	100 57.9	.. 38.5	82 41.7	.. 20.7	72 14.8	.. 48.0	Hamal	327 55.7	N23 33.3
16	26 06.9	16 41.7	10.0	115 58.5	38.5	97 43.6	20.7	87 17.0	47.9	Kaus Aust.	83 38.0	S34 22.4
17	41 09.3	31 41.6	11.3	130 59.1	38.5	112 45.5	20.6	102 19.2	47.9			
18	56 11.8	46 41.4	N 4 12.6	145 59.7	S23 38.6	127 47.5	S22 20.6	117 21.4	S20 47.8	Kochab	137 19.8	N74 04.1
19	71 14.3	61 41.3	13.9	161 00.3	38.6	142 49.4	20.5	132 23.6	47.8	Markab	13 34.1	N15 18.7
20	86 16.7	76 41.2	15.2	176 00.9	38.6	157 51.3	20.4	147 25.7	47.8	Menkar	314 10.3	N 4 09.9
21	101 19.2	91 41.0	.. 16.5	191 01.5	.. 38.7	172 53.2	.. 20.4	162 27.9	.. 47.7	Menkent	148 02.0	S36 27.9
22	116 21.7	106 40.9	17.8	206 02.1	38.7	187 55.2	20.3	177 30.1	47.7	Miaplacidus	221 37.9	S69 48.0
23	131 24.1	121 40.8	19.1	221 02.6	38.7	202 57.1	20.3	192 32.3	47.6			
17 00	146 26.6	136 40.7	N 4 20.4	236 03.2	S23 38.8	217 59.0	S22 20.2	207 34.5	S20 47.6	Mirfak	308 33.8	N49 56.0
01	161 29.1	151 40.5	21.7	251 03.8	38.8	233 00.9	20.1	222 36.7	47.5	Nunki	75 52.9	S26 16.2
02	176 31.5	166 40.4	23.0	266 04.4	38.8	248 02.8	20.1	237 38.8	47.5	Peacock	53 12.5	S56 40.2
03	191 34.0	181 40.3	.. 24.3	281 05.0	.. 38.9	263 04.8	.. 20.0	252 41.0	.. 47.4	Pollux	243 21.8	N27 58.6
04	206 36.4	196 40.2	25.6	296 05.6	38.9	278 06.7	20.0	267 43.2	47.4	Procyon	244 54.7	N 5 10.3
05	221 38.9	211 40.0	26.9	311 06.2	38.9	293 08.6	19.9	282 45.4	47.3			
06	236 41.4	226 39.9	N 4 28.2	326 06.7	S23 39.0	308 10.5	S22 19.8	297 47.6	S20 47.3	Rasalhague	96 02.3	N12 32.7
07	251 43.8	241 39.8	29.4	341 07.3	39.0	323 12.5	19.8	312 49.7	47.2	Regulus	207 38.3	N11 52.1
08	266 46.3	256 39.6	30.7	356 07.9	39.0	338 14.4	19.7	327 51.9	47.2	Rigel	281 07.5	S 8 11.0
M 09	281 48.8	271 39.5	.. 32.0	11 08.5	.. 39.0	353 16.3	.. 19.7	342 54.1	.. 47.1	Rigil Kent.	139 45.3	S60 54.7
O 10	296 51.2	286 39.4	33.3	26 09.1	39.1	8 18.2	19.6	357 56.3	47.1	Sabik	102 07.4	S15 44.9
N 11	311 53.7	301 39.3	34.6	41 09.7	39.1	23 20.2	19.5	12 58.5	47.0			
D 12	326 56.2	316 39.1	N 4 35.9	56 10.3	S23 39.1	38 22.1	S22 19.5	28 00.7	S20 47.0	Schedar	349 35.7	N56 38.9
A 13	341 58.6	331 39.0	37.2	71 10.9	39.2	53 24.0	19.4	43 02.8	46.9	Shaula	96 15.9	S37 06.9
Y 14	357 01.1	346 38.9	38.5	86 11.4	39.2	68 25.9	19.4	58 05.0	46.9	Sirius	258 29.4	S16 44.9
15	12 03.6	1 38.8	.. 39.8	101 12.0	.. 39.2	83 27.9	.. 19.3	73 07.2	.. 46.8	Spica	158 26.2	S11 15.9
16	27 06.0	16 38.6	41.1	116 12.6	39.2	98 29.8	19.2	88 09.4	46.8	Suhail	222 48.7	S43 30.9
17	42 08.5	31 38.5	42.4	131 13.2	39.3	113 31.7	19.2	103 11.6	46.7			
18	57 10.9	46 38.4	N 4 43.7	146 13.8	S23 39.3	128 33.6	S22 19.1	118 13.8	S20 46.7	Vega	80 36.1	N38 48.0
19	72 13.4	61 38.3	44.9	161 14.4	39.3	143 35.6	19.1	133 15.9	46.6	Zuben'ubi	137 00.3	S16 07.4
20	87 15.9	76 38.1	46.2	176 15.0	39.3	158 37.5	19.0	148 18.1	46.6		SHA	Mer. Pass.
21	102 18.3	91 38.0	.. 47.5	191 15.5	.. 39.4	173 39.4	.. 18.9	163 20.3	.. 46.5	Venus	351 16.3	14 53
22	117 20.8	106 37.9	48.8	206 16.1	39.4	188 41.3	18.9	178 22.5	46.5	Mars	90 21.7	8 16
23	132 23.3	121 37.8	50.1	221 16.7	39.4	203 43.3	18.8	193 24.7	46.4	Jupiter	71 45.5	9 30
Mer. Pass. 14 15.8		v −0.1	d 1.3	v 0.6	d 0.0	v 1.9	d 0.1	v 2.2	d 0.0	Saturn	61 14.7	10 12

UT	SUN GHA	SUN Dec	MOON GHA	v	Dec	d	HP
d h	° ′	° ′	° ′	′	° ′	′	′
15 00	176 27.8	S12 56.0	281 50.2	9.9	S12 02.7	12.0	59.0
01	191 27.8	55.2	296 19.1	9.8	12 14.7	12.0	58.9
02	206 27.8	54.3	310 47.9	9.8	12 26.7	11.8	58.9
03	221 27.8 ..	53.5	325 16.7	9.8	12 38.5	11.8	58.9
04	236 27.9	52.6	339 45.5	9.8	12 50.3	11.6	58.8
05	251 27.9	51.8	354 14.3	9.7	13 01.9	11.6	58.8
06	266 27.9	S12 50.9	8 43.0	9.8	S13 13.5	11.5	58.8
07	281 27.9	50.1	23 11.8	9.7	13 25.0	11.4	58.8
08	296 28.0	49.2	37 40.5	9.7	13 36.4	11.4	58.7
09	311 28.0 ..	48.4	52 09.2	9.7	13 47.8	11.2	58.7
10	326 28.0	47.5	66 37.9	9.7	13 59.0	11.2	58.7
11	341 28.1	46.6	81 06.6	9.6	14 10.2	11.0	58.6
12	356 28.1	S12 45.8	95 35.2	9.6	S14 21.2	11.0	58.6
13	11 28.1	44.9	110 03.8	9.6	14 32.2	10.9	58.6
14	26 28.1	44.1	124 32.4	9.6	14 43.1	10.8	58.5
15	41 28.2 ..	43.2	139 01.0	9.6	14 53.9	10.7	58.5
16	56 28.2	42.4	153 29.6	9.5	15 04.6	10.5	58.5
17	71 28.2	41.5	167 58.1	9.6	15 15.1	10.5	58.5
18	86 28.3	S12 40.6	182 26.7	9.5	S15 25.6	10.4	58.4
19	101 28.3	39.8	196 55.2	9.4	15 36.0	10.4	58.4
20	116 28.3	38.9	211 23.6	9.5	15 46.4	10.2	58.4
21	131 28.3 ..	38.1	225 52.1	9.4	15 56.6	10.1	58.3
22	146 28.4	37.2	240 20.5	9.4	16 06.7	10.0	58.3
23	161 28.4	36.3	254 48.9	9.4	16 16.7	9.9	58.3
16 00	176 28.4	S12 35.5	269 17.3	9.4	S16 26.6	9.8	58.2
01	191 28.5	34.6	283 45.7	9.3	16 36.4	9.7	58.2
02	206 28.5	33.8	298 14.0	9.4	16 46.1	9.6	58.2
03	221 28.5 ..	32.9	312 42.4	9.3	16 55.7	9.5	58.2
04	236 28.6	32.0	327 10.7	9.2	17 05.2	9.4	58.1
05	251 28.6	31.2	341 38.9	9.3	17 14.6	9.2	58.1
06	266 28.6	S12 30.3	356 07.2	9.2	S17 23.8	9.2	58.1
07	281 28.7	29.4	10 35.4	9.2	17 33.0	9.1	58.0
08	296 28.7	28.6	25 03.6	9.2	17 42.1	8.9	58.0
09	311 28.7 ..	27.7	39 31.8	9.2	17 51.0	8.9	58.0
10	326 28.8	26.9	54 00.0	9.1	17 59.9	8.7	57.9
11	341 28.8	26.0	68 28.1	9.1	18 08.6	8.7	57.9
12	356 28.8	S12 25.1	82 56.2	9.1	S18 17.3	8.5	57.9
13	11 28.9	24.3	97 24.3	9.1	18 25.8	8.4	57.9
14	26 28.9	23.4	111 52.4	9.1	18 34.2	8.3	57.8
15	41 29.0 ..	22.5	126 20.5	9.0	18 42.5	8.2	57.8
16	56 29.0	21.7	140 48.5	9.0	18 50.7	8.1	57.8
17	71 29.0	20.8	155 16.5	9.0	18 58.8	7.9	57.7
18	86 29.1	S12 19.9	169 44.5	9.0	S19 06.7	7.8	57.7
19	101 29.1	19.1	184 12.5	8.9	19 14.5	7.8	57.7
20	116 29.1	18.2	198 40.4	8.9	19 22.3	7.6	57.7
21	131 29.2 ..	17.3	213 08.3	8.9	19 29.9	7.5	57.6
22	146 29.2	16.5	227 36.3	8.8	19 37.4	7.3	57.6
23	161 29.2	15.6	242 04.1	8.9	19 44.7	7.3	57.6
17 00	176 29.3	S12 14.7	256 32.0	8.9	S19 52.0	7.1	57.5
01	191 29.3	13.9	270 59.9	8.8	19 59.1	7.1	57.5
02	206 29.4	13.0	285 27.7	8.8	20 06.2	6.9	57.5
03	221 29.4 ..	12.1	299 55.5	8.8	20 13.1	6.7	57.4
04	236 29.4	11.2	314 23.3	8.8	20 19.8	6.7	57.4
05	251 29.5	10.4	328 51.1	8.7	20 26.5	6.5	57.4
06	266 29.5	S12 09.5	343 18.8	8.8	S20 33.0	6.5	57.3
07	281 29.6	08.6	357 46.6	8.7	20 39.5	6.3	57.3
08	296 29.6	07.8	12 14.3	8.7	20 45.8	6.1	57.3
09	311 29.6 ..	06.9	26 42.0	8.7	20 51.9	6.1	57.3
10	326 29.7	06.0	41 09.7	8.7	20 58.0	5.9	57.3
11	341 29.7	05.1	55 37.4	8.7	21 03.9	5.8	57.2
12	356 29.8	S12 04.3	70 05.1	8.6	S21 09.7	5.7	57.2
13	11 29.8	03.4	84 32.7	8.7	21 15.4	5.6	57.2
14	26 29.9	02.5	99 00.4	8.6	21 21.0	5.4	57.1
15	41 29.9 ..	01.6	113 28.0	8.6	21 26.4	5.3	57.1
16	56 29.9	12 00.8	127 55.6	8.6	21 31.7	5.2	57.1
17	71 30.0	11 59.9	142 23.2	8.6	21 36.9	5.0	57.1
18	86 30.0	S11 59.0	156 50.8	8.6	S21 41.9	5.0	57.0
19	101 30.1	58.1	171 18.4	8.6	21 46.9	4.8	57.0
20	116 30.1	57.3	185 46.0	8.5	21 51.7	4.6	57.0
21	131 30.2 ..	56.4	200 13.6	8.5	21 56.3	4.6	56.9
22	146 30.2	55.5	214 41.1	8.6	22 00.9	4.4	56.9
23	161 30.3	54.6	229 08.7	8.6	S22 05.3	4.3	56.9
	SD 16.2	d 0.9	SD 16.0		15.8		15.6

Twilight / Sunrise / Moonrise

Lat.	Twilight Naut.	Twilight Civil	Sunrise	Moonrise 15	16	17	18
°	h m	h m	h m	h m	h m	h m	h m
N 72	06 13	07 32	08 51	02 12	05 14	▬▬	▬▬
N 70	06 11	07 23	08 31	01 47	04 06	▬▬	▬▬
68	06 10	07 15	08 16	01 29	03 29	05 42	▬▬
66	06 08	07 08	08 04	01 14	03 04	04 54	06 40
64	06 07	07 03	07 53	01 02	02 44	04 24	05 54
62	06 06	06 58	07 45	00 55	02 28	04 01	05 24
60	06 05	06 53	07 37	00 43	02 15	03 43	05 01
N 58	06 03	06 49	07 30	00 36	02 04	03 28	04 43
56	06 02	06 46	07 24	00 29	01 54	03 15	04 28
54	06 01	06 42	07 19	00 23	01 45	03 03	04 14
52	06 00	06 39	07 14	00 18	01 38	02 54	04 03
50	05 59	06 36	07 10	00 13	01 31	02 45	03 53
45	05 56	06 30	07 00	00 03	01 16	02 26	03 31
N 40	05 53	06 25	06 52	25 04	01 04	02 11	03 14
35	05 50	06 20	06 46	24 54	00 54	01 58	03 00
30	05 47	06 15	06 40	24 45	00 45	01 47	02 47
20	05 41	06 06	06 29	24 29	00 29	01 28	02 26
N 10	05 33	05 58	06 20	24 16	00 16	01 12	02 07
0	05 25	05 50	06 11	24 04	00 04	00 56	01 50
S 10	05 15	05 40	06 02	23 51	24 41	00 41	01 33
20	05 02	05 29	05 52	23 38	24 25	00 25	01 15
30	04 46	05 16	05 41	23 23	24 07	00 07	00 54
35	04 36	05 08	05 34	23 15	23 56	24 41	00 41
40	04 23	04 58	05 27	23 05	23 44	24 27	00 27
45	04 08	04 46	05 18	22 54	23 29	24 11	00 11
S 50	03 48	04 32	05 07	22 40	23 12	23 50	24 37
52	03 38	04 25	05 02	22 33	23 03	23 40	24 26
54	03 26	04 17	04 57	22 26	22 54	23 29	24 14
56	03 13	04 08	04 51	22 19	22 44	23 17	24 01
58	02 57	03 58	04 44	22 10	22 32	23 03	23 45
S 60	02 37	03 47	04 36	22 00	22 19	22 46	23 26

Sunset / Twilight / Moonset

Lat.	Sunset	Twilight Civil	Twilight Naut.	Moonset 15	16	17	18
°	h m	h m	h m	h m	h m	h m	h m
N 72	15 39	16 58	18 18	08 13	07 02	▬▬	▬▬
N 70	15 58	17 07	18 19	08 40	08 11	▬▬	▬▬
68	16 13	17 15	18 20	09 00	08 48	08 27	▬▬
66	16 26	17 21	18 21	09 16	09 14	09 15	09 21
64	16 36	17 27	18 23	09 29	09 35	09 46	10 08
62	16 45	17 32	18 24	09 40	09 52	10 09	10 38
60	16 52	17 36	18 25	09 50	10 06	10 28	11 01
N 58	16 59	17 40	18 26	09 58	10 18	10 44	11 19
56	17 05	17 44	18 27	10 06	10 28	10 57	11 35
54	17 10	17 47	18 28	10 12	10 37	11 09	11 48
52	17 15	17 50	18 29	10 18	10 46	11 19	12 00
50	17 19	17 52	18 30	10 24	10 53	11 28	12 10
45	17 28	17 59	18 33	10 36	11 09	11 47	12 32
N 40	17 36	18 04	18 36	10 46	11 22	12 03	12 50
35	17 43	18 09	18 39	10 54	11 33	12 17	13 04
30	17 49	18 13	18 42	11 01	11 43	12 28	13 17
20	17 59	18 22	18 48	11 14	12 00	12 48	13 39
N 10	18 09	18 30	18 55	11 26	12 15	13 06	13 58
0	18 17	18 39	19 03	11 36	12 29	13 22	14 16
S 10	18 26	18 48	19 13	11 47	12 43	13 38	14 34
20	18 36	18 59	19 25	11 58	12 58	13 56	14 53
30	18 47	19 12	19 41	12 11	13 15	14 16	15 15
35	18 53	19 19	19 52	12 19	13 25	14 28	15 28
40	19 01	19 29	20 04	12 28	13 36	14 42	15 42
45	19 09	19 41	20 19	12 38	13 50	14 58	16 00
S 50	19 20	19 55	20 39	12 50	14 06	15 18	16 22
52	19 25	20 02	20 49	12 56	14 14	15 27	16 32
54	19 30	20 09	21 00	13 02	14 23	15 38	16 44
56	19 36	20 18	21 13	13 10	14 33	15 50	16 58
58	19 43	20 28	21 28	13 18	14 44	16 04	17 13
S 60	19 50	20 39	21 48	13 27	14 57	16 20	17 32

SUN / MOON

Day	SUN Eqn. of Time 00h	SUN Eqn. of Time 12h	SUN Mer. Pass.	MOON Mer. Pass. Upper	MOON Mer. Pass. Lower	Age	Phase
d	m s	m s	h m	h m	h m	d	%
15	14 09	14 08	12 14	05 24	17 50	22	55
16	14 06	14 05	12 14	06 16	18 43	23	44
17	14 03	14 01	12 14	07 09	19 36	24	33

UT	ARIES	VENUS −4.2		MARS +1.2		JUPITER −1.9		SATURN +0.6		STARS		
	GHA	GHA	Dec	GHA	Dec	GHA	Dec	GHA	Dec	Name	SHA	Dec
d h	° ′	° ′	° ′	° ′	° ′	° ′	° ′	° ′	° ′		° ′	° ′
18 00	147 25.7	136 37.6	N 4 51.4	236 17.3	S23 39.4	218 45.2	S22 18.8	208 26.9	S20 46.4	Acamar	315 14.9	S40 13.9
01	162 28.2	151 37.5	52.7	251 17.9	39.5	233 47.1	18.7	223 29.0	46.3	Achernar	335 23.6	S57 08.5
02	177 30.7	166 37.4	54.0	266 18.5	39.5	248 49.0	18.7	238 31.2	46.3	Acrux	173 03.6	S63 12.4
03	192 33.1	181 37.3	.. 55.3	281 19.1	.. 39.5	263 51.0	.. 18.6	253 33.4	.. 46.2	Adhara	255 08.6	S29 00.2
04	207 35.6	196 37.1	56.6	296 19.6	39.5	278 52.9	18.5	268 35.6	46.2	Aldebaran	290 44.0	N16 32.8
05	222 38.1	211 37.0	57.8	311 20.2	39.5	293 54.8	18.5	283 37.8	46.2			
06	237 40.5	226 36.9	N 4 59.1	326 20.8	S23 39.6	308 56.7	S22 18.4	298 40.0	S20 46.1	Alioth	166 16.2	N55 50.9
07	252 43.0	241 36.8	5 00.4	341 21.4	39.6	323 58.7	18.4	313 42.1	46.1	Alkaid	152 55.0	N49 12.6
T 08	267 45.4	256 36.6	01.7	356 22.0	39.6	339 00.6	18.3	328 44.3	46.0	Alnair	27 38.4	S46 51.9
U 09	282 47.9	271 36.5	.. 03.0	11 22.6	.. 39.6	354 02.5	.. 18.2	343 46.5	.. 46.0	Alnilam	275 41.5	S 1 11.6
E 10	297 50.4	286 36.4	04.3	26 23.2	39.7	9 04.4	18.2	358 48.7	45.9	Alphard	217 51.3	S 8 44.9
S 11	312 52.8	301 36.3	05.6	41 23.7	39.7	24 06.4	18.1	13 50.9	45.9			
D 12	327 55.3	316 36.2	N 5 06.9	56 24.3	S23 39.7	39 08.3	S22 18.1	28 53.1	S20 45.8	Alphecca	126 07.1	N26 38.7
A 13	342 57.8	331 36.0	08.2	71 24.9	39.7	54 10.2	18.0	43 55.2	45.8	Alpheratz	357 39.1	N29 12.0
Y 14	358 00.2	346 35.9	09.4	86 25.5	39.7	69 12.2	17.9	58 57.4	45.7	Altair	62 04.0	N 8 55.2
15	13 02.7	1 35.8	.. 10.7	101 26.1	.. 39.7	84 14.1	.. 17.9	73 59.6	.. 45.7	Ankaa	353 11.4	S42 12.1
16	28 05.2	16 35.7	12.0	116 26.7	39.8	99 16.0	17.8	89 01.8	45.6	Antares	112 20.7	S26 28.4
17	43 07.6	31 35.5	13.3	131 27.3	39.8	114 17.9	17.8	104 04.0	45.6			
18	58 10.1	46 35.4	N 5 14.6	146 27.8	S23 39.8	129 19.9	S22 17.7	119 06.2	S20 45.5	Arcturus	145 51.4	N19 04.6
19	73 12.5	61 35.3	15.9	161 28.4	39.8	144 21.8	17.6	134 08.4	45.5	Atria	107 18.5	S69 03.4
20	88 15.0	76 35.2	17.2	176 29.0	39.8	159 23.7	17.6	149 10.5	45.4	Avior	234 15.6	S59 34.6
21	103 17.5	91 35.1	.. 18.4	191 29.6	.. 39.8	174 25.7	.. 17.5	164 12.7	.. 45.4	Bellatrix	278 26.9	N 6 21.9
22	118 19.9	106 34.9	19.7	206 30.2	39.9	189 27.6	17.5	179 14.9	45.3	Betelgeuse	270 56.1	N 7 24.5
23	133 22.4	121 34.8	21.0	221 30.8	39.9	204 29.5	17.4	194 17.1	45.3			
19 00	148 24.9	136 34.7	N 5 22.3	236 31.4	S23 39.9	219 31.4	S22 17.3	209 19.3	S20 45.2	Canopus	263 53.8	S52 42.7
01	163 27.3	151 34.6	23.6	251 31.9	39.9	234 33.4	17.3	224 21.5	45.2	Capella	280 27.5	N46 01.1
02	178 29.8	166 34.4	24.9	266 32.5	39.9	249 35.3	17.2	239 23.7	45.1	Deneb	49 28.8	N45 21.0
03	193 32.3	181 34.3	.. 26.2	281 33.1	.. 39.9	264 37.2	.. 17.2	254 25.8	.. 45.1	Denebola	182 28.7	N14 27.5
04	208 34.7	196 34.2	27.4	296 33.7	39.9	279 39.2	17.1	269 28.0	45.0	Diphda	348 51.5	S17 52.9
05	223 37.2	211 34.1	28.7	311 34.3	40.0	294 41.1	17.0	284 30.2	45.0			
06	238 39.7	226 34.0	N 5 30.0	326 34.9	S23 40.0	309 43.0	S22 17.0	299 32.4	S20 44.9	Dubhe	193 45.4	N61 38.5
W 07	253 42.1	241 33.8	31.3	341 35.4	40.0	324 44.9	16.9	314 34.6	44.9	Elnath	278 06.6	N28 37.4
E 08	268 44.6	256 33.7	32.6	356 36.0	40.0	339 46.9	16.8	329 36.8	44.8	Eltanin	90 44.3	N51 29.0
D 09	283 47.0	271 33.6	.. 33.9	11 36.6	.. 40.0	354 48.8	.. 16.8	344 39.0	.. 44.8	Enif	33 42.9	N 9 57.9
N 10	298 49.5	286 33.5	35.1	26 37.2	40.0	9 50.7	16.7	359 41.1	44.8	Fomalhaut	15 19.2	S29 31.2
E 11	313 52.0	301 33.4	36.4	41 37.8	40.0	24 52.7	16.7	14 43.3	44.7			
S 12	328 54.4	316 33.2	N 5 37.7	56 38.4	S23 40.0	39 54.6	S22 16.6	29 45.5	S20 44.7	Gacrux	171 55.4	S57 13.3
D 13	343 56.9	331 33.1	39.0	71 39.0	40.1	54 56.5	16.5	44 47.7	44.6	Gienah	175 47.3	S17 39.2
A 14	358 59.4	346 33.0	40.3	86 39.5	40.1	69 58.5	16.5	59 49.9	44.6	Hadar	148 41.1	S60 27.9
Y 15	14 01.8	1 32.9	.. 41.6	101 40.1	.. 40.1	85 00.4	.. 16.4	74 52.1	.. 44.5	Hamal	327 55.7	N23 33.3
16	29 04.3	16 32.8	42.8	116 40.7	40.1	100 02.3	16.4	89 54.3	44.5	Kaus Aust.	83 37.9	S34 22.3
17	44 06.8	31 32.6	44.1	131 41.3	40.1	115 04.3	16.3	104 56.4	44.4			
18	59 09.2	46 32.5	N 5 45.4	146 41.9	S23 40.1	130 06.2	S22 16.2	119 58.6	S20 44.4	Kochab	137 19.7	N74 04.1
19	74 11.7	61 32.4	46.7	161 42.5	40.1	145 08.1	16.2	135 00.8	44.3	Markab	13 34.1	N15 18.6
20	89 14.2	76 32.3	48.0	176 43.0	40.1	160 10.1	16.1	150 03.0	44.3	Menkar	314 10.3	N 4 09.9
21	104 16.6	91 32.2	.. 49.2	191 43.6	.. 40.1	175 12.0	.. 16.1	165 05.2	.. 44.2	Menkent	148 02.0	S36 27.9
22	119 19.1	106 32.0	50.5	206 44.2	40.1	190 13.9	16.0	180 07.4	44.2	Miaplacidus	221 37.9	S69 48.0
23	134 21.5	121 31.9	51.8	221 44.8	40.1	205 15.8	15.9	195 09.6	44.1			
20 00	149 24.0	136 31.8	N 5 53.1	236 45.4	S23 40.1	220 17.8	S22 15.9	210 11.8	S20 44.1	Mirfak	308 33.8	N49 56.0
01	164 26.5	151 31.7	54.4	251 46.0	40.1	235 19.7	15.8	225 13.9	44.0	Nunki	75 52.9	S26 16.2
02	179 28.9	166 31.6	55.7	266 46.6	40.2	250 21.6	15.8	240 16.1	44.0	Peacock	53 12.5	S56 40.1
03	194 31.4	181 31.4	.. 56.9	281 47.1	.. 40.2	265 23.6	.. 15.7	255 18.3	.. 43.9	Pollux	243 21.8	N27 58.6
04	209 33.9	196 31.3	58.2	296 47.7	40.2	280 25.5	15.6	270 20.5	43.9	Procyon	244 54.7	N 5 10.2
05	224 36.3	211 31.2	5 59.5	311 48.3	40.2	295 27.4	15.6	285 22.7	43.8			
06	239 38.8	226 31.1	N 6 00.8	326 48.9	S23 40.2	310 29.4	S22 15.5	300 24.9	S20 43.8	Rasalhague	96 02.3	N12 32.6
07	254 41.3	241 31.0	02.0	341 49.5	40.2	325 31.3	15.5	315 27.1	43.7	Regulus	207 38.3	N11 52.1
T 08	269 43.7	256 30.9	03.3	356 50.1	40.2	340 33.2	15.4	330 29.3	43.7	Rigel	281 07.5	S 8 11.0
H 09	284 46.2	271 30.7	.. 04.6	11 50.6	.. 40.2	355 35.2	.. 15.3	345 31.4	.. 43.6	Rigil Kent.	139 45.3	S60 54.7
U 10	299 48.7	286 30.6	05.9	26 51.2	40.2	10 37.1	15.3	0 33.6	43.6	Sabik	102 07.4	S15 44.9
R 11	314 51.1	301 30.5	07.2	41 51.8	40.2	25 39.0	15.2	15 35.8	43.5			
S 12	329 53.6	316 30.4	N 6 08.4	56 52.4	S23 40.2	40 41.0	S22 15.2	30 38.0	S20 43.5	Schedar	349 35.8	N56 38.9
D 13	344 56.0	331 30.3	09.7	71 53.0	40.2	55 42.9	15.1	45 40.2	43.5	Shaula	96 15.8	S37 06.9
A 14	359 58.5	346 30.1	11.0	86 53.6	40.2	70 44.9	15.0	60 42.4	43.4	Sirius	258 29.4	S16 44.9
Y 15	15 01.0	1 30.0	.. 12.3	101 54.1	.. 40.2	85 46.8	.. 15.0	75 44.6	.. 43.4	Spica	158 26.2	S11 15.9
16	30 03.4	16 29.9	13.5	116 54.7	40.2	100 48.7	14.9	90 46.8	43.3	Suhail	222 48.7	S43 30.9
17	45 05.9	31 29.8	14.8	131 55.3	40.2	115 50.7	14.9	105 48.9	43.3			
18	60 08.4	46 29.7	N 6 16.1	146 55.9	S23 40.2	130 52.6	S22 14.8	120 51.1	S20 43.2	Vega	80 36.1	N38 48.0
19	75 10.8	61 29.6	17.4	161 56.5	40.2	145 54.5	14.7	135 53.3	43.2	Zuben'ubi	137 00.2	S16 07.4
20	90 13.3	76 29.4	18.7	176 57.1	40.2	160 56.5	14.7	150 55.5	43.1		SHA	Mer. Pass.
21	105 15.8	91 29.3	.. 19.9	191 57.6	.. 40.2	175 58.4	.. 14.6	165 57.7	.. 43.1		° ′	h m
22	120 18.2	106 29.2	21.2	206 58.2	40.2	191 00.3	14.6	180 59.9	43.0	Venus	348 09.8	14 54
23	135 20.7	121 29.1	22.5	221 58.8	40.2	206 02.3	14.5	196 02.1	43.0	Mars	88 06.5	8 14
	h m									Jupiter	71 06.6	9 21
Mer. Pass.	14 04.0	v −0.1	d 1.3	v 0.6	d 0.0	v 1.9	d 0.1	v 2.2	d 0.0	Saturn	60 54.4	10 01

UT	SUN GHA	Dec	MOON GHA	v	Dec	d	HP
d h	° ′	° ′	° ′	′	° ′	′	′
18 00	176 30.3	S11 53.8	243 36.3	8.5	S22 09.6	4.2	56.9
01	191 30.4	52.9	258 03.8	8.6	22 13.8	4.0	56.8
02	206 30.4	52.0	272 31.4	8.5	22 17.8	3.9	56.8
03	221 30.4	.. 51.1	286 58.9	8.5	22 21.7	3.8	56.8
04	236 30.5	50.3	301 26.4	8.6	22 25.5	3.7	56.8
05	251 30.5	49.4	315 54.0	8.5	22 29.2	3.5	56.7
06	266 30.6	S11 48.5	330 21.5	8.6	S22 32.7	3.4	56.7
T 07	281 30.6	47.6	344 49.1	8.5	22 36.1	3.2	56.7
U 08	296 30.7	46.7	359 16.6	8.5	22 39.3	3.2	56.7
E 09	311 30.7	.. 45.9	13 44.1	8.6	22 42.5	3.0	56.6
S 10	326 30.8	45.0	28 11.7	8.5	22 45.5	2.9	56.6
D 11	341 30.8	44.1	42 39.2	8.6	22 48.4	2.7	56.6
A 12	356 30.9	S11 43.2	57 06.8	8.6	S22 51.1	2.6	56.6
Y 13	11 30.9	42.3	71 34.4	8.5	22 53.7	2.5	56.5
14	26 31.0	41.5	86 01.9	8.6	22 56.2	2.4	56.5
15	41 31.0	.. 40.6	100 29.5	8.6	22 58.6	2.2	56.5
16	56 31.1	39.7	114 57.1	8.6	23 00.8	2.1	56.5
17	71 31.1	38.8	129 24.7	8.6	23 02.9	2.0	56.4
18	86 31.2	S11 37.9	143 52.3	8.6	S23 04.9	1.9	56.4
19	101 31.2	37.0	158 19.9	8.6	23 06.8	1.7	56.4
20	116 31.3	36.2	172 47.5	8.6	23 08.5	1.6	56.4
21	131 31.3	.. 35.3	187 15.1	8.7	23 10.1	1.4	56.3
22	146 31.4	34.4	201 42.8	8.6	23 11.5	1.4	56.3
23	161 31.4	33.5	216 10.4	8.7	23 12.9	1.2	56.3
19 00	176 31.5	S11 32.6	230 38.1	8.7	S23 14.1	1.0	56.3
01	191 31.5	31.7	245 05.8	8.7	23 15.1	1.0	56.2
02	206 31.6	30.8	259 33.5	8.7	23 16.1	0.8	56.2
03	221 31.7	.. 30.0	274 01.2	8.8	23 16.9	0.7	56.2
04	236 31.7	29.1	288 29.0	8.8	23 17.6	0.5	56.2
05	251 31.8	28.2	302 56.8	8.8	23 18.1	0.5	56.2
06	266 31.8	S11 27.3	317 24.6	8.8	S23 18.6	0.3	56.1
W 07	281 31.9	26.4	331 52.4	8.8	23 18.9	0.2	56.1
E 08	296 31.9	25.5	346 20.2	8.9	23 19.1	0.2	56.1
D 09	311 32.0	.. 24.6	0 48.1	8.8	23 19.1	0.1	56.1
N 10	326 32.0	23.8	15 15.9	9.0	23 19.0	0.2	56.0
E 11	341 32.1	22.9	29 43.9	8.9	23 18.8	0.3	56.0
S 12	356 32.1	S11 22.0	44 11.8	9.0	S23 18.5	0.5	56.0
D 13	11 32.2	21.1	58 39.8	9.0	23 18.0	0.5	56.0
A 14	26 32.3	20.2	73 07.8	9.0	23 17.5	0.7	55.9
Y 15	41 32.3	.. 19.3	87 35.8	9.0	23 16.8	0.9	55.9
16	56 32.4	18.4	102 03.8	9.1	23 15.9	0.9	55.9
17	71 32.4	17.5	116 31.9	9.1	23 15.0	1.1	55.9
18	86 32.5	S11 16.6	131 00.0	9.2	S23 13.9	1.2	55.9
19	101 32.6	15.7	145 28.2	9.2	23 12.7	1.3	55.8
20	116 32.6	14.9	159 56.4	9.2	23 11.4	1.5	55.8
21	131 32.7	.. 14.0	174 24.6	9.3	23 09.9	1.6	55.8
22	146 32.7	13.1	188 52.9	9.3	23 08.3	1.7	55.8
23	161 32.8	12.2	203 21.2	9.3	23 06.6	1.8	55.8
20 00	176 32.8	S11 11.3	217 49.5	9.4	S23 04.8	1.9	55.7
01	191 32.9	10.4	232 17.9	9.4	23 02.9	2.1	55.7
02	206 33.0	09.5	246 46.3	9.4	23 00.8	2.1	55.7
03	221 33.0	.. 08.6	261 14.7	9.5	22 58.7	2.3	55.7
04	236 33.1	07.7	275 43.2	9.5	22 56.4	2.5	55.7
05	251 33.1	06.8	290 11.7	9.6	22 53.9	2.5	55.6
06	266 33.2	S11 05.9	304 40.3	9.6	S22 51.4	2.6	55.6
T 07	281 33.3	05.0	319 08.9	9.7	22 48.8	2.8	55.6
H 08	296 33.3	04.1	333 37.6	9.7	22 46.0	2.9	55.6
U 09	311 33.4	.. 03.2	348 06.3	9.7	22 43.1	3.0	55.6
R 10	326 33.5	02.4	2 35.0	9.8	22 40.1	3.1	55.5
S 11	341 33.5	01.5	17 03.8	9.9	22 37.0	3.3	55.5
D 12	356 33.6	S11 00.6	31 32.7	9.9	S22 33.7	3.3	55.5
A 13	11 33.6	10 59.7	46 01.6	9.9	22 30.4	3.5	55.5
Y 14	26 33.7	58.8	60 30.5	10.0	22 26.9	3.6	55.5
15	41 33.8	.. 57.9	74 59.5	10.0	22 23.3	3.6	55.4
16	56 33.8	57.0	89 28.5	10.1	22 19.7	3.8	55.4
17	71 33.9	56.1	103 57.6	10.2	22 15.9	4.0	55.4
18	86 34.0	S10 55.2	118 26.8	10.2	S22 11.9	4.0	55.4
19	101 34.0	54.3	132 56.0	10.2	22 07.9	4.1	55.4
20	116 34.1	53.4	147 25.2	10.3	22 03.8	4.3	55.3
21	131 34.2	.. 52.5	161 54.5	10.3	21 59.5	4.3	55.3
22	146 34.2	51.6	176 23.8	10.4	21 55.2	4.5	55.3
23	161 34.3	50.7	190 53.2	10.5	S21 50.7	4.5	55.3
	SD 16.2 d 0.9		SD 15.4		15.3		15.1

Lat.	Naut.	Civil	Sunrise	Moonrise 18	19	20	21
°	h m	h m	h m	h m	h m	h m	h m
N 72	05 59	07 18	08 34	▬	▬	▬	▬
N 70	05 59	07 10	08 17	▬	▬	▬	▬
68	05 59	07 04	08 04	▬	▬	▬	09 27
66	05 59	06 58	07 53	06 40	08 02	08 31	08 37
64	05 58	06 53	07 43	05 54	07 03	07 45	08 05
62	05 58	06 49	07 36	05 24	06 30	07 15	07 42
60	05 57	06 45	07 29	05 01	06 05	06 52	07 23
N 58	05 56	06 42	07 23	04 43	05 45	06 33	07 07
56	05 56	06 39	07 17	04 28	05 29	06 18	06 54
54	05 55	06 36	07 13	04 14	05 15	06 04	06 42
52	05 54	06 34	07 08	04 03	05 03	05 53	06 32
50	05 54	06 31	07 04	03 53	04 52	05 42	06 23
45	05 52	06 26	06 56	03 31	04 30	05 21	06 03
N 40	05 49	06 21	06 48	03 14	04 12	05 03	05 47
35	05 47	06 17	06 42	03 00	03 57	04 48	05 34
30	05 44	06 12	06 37	02 47	03 44	04 35	05 22
20	05 39	06 05	06 27	02 26	03 21	04 14	05 02
N 10	05 32	05 57	06 19	02 07	03 02	03 55	04 44
0	05 25	05 49	06 10	01 50	02 44	03 37	04 28
S 10	05 16	05 41	06 02	01 33	02 26	03 19	04 12
20	05 04	05 31	05 53	01 15	02 07	03 00	03 54
30	04 49	05 18	05 43	00 54	01 44	02 38	03 34
35	04 39	05 11	05 37	00 41	01 31	02 25	03 22
40	04 28	05 02	05 30	00 27	01 16	02 10	03 08
45	04 13	04 51	05 22	00 11	00 59	01 53	02 52
S 50	03 54	04 38	05 12	24 37	00 37	01 31	02 32
52	03 45	04 31	05 08	24 26	00 26	01 21	02 22
54	03 34	04 24	05 03	24 14	00 14	01 09	02 12
56	03 22	04 16	04 57	24 00	00 00	00 55	02 00
58	03 08	04 07	04 51	23 45	24 40	00 40	01 46
S 60	02 50	03 56	04 44	23 26	24 21	00 21	01 29

Lat.	Sunset	Civil	Naut.	Moonset 18	19	20	21
°	h m	h m	h m	h m	h m	h m	h m
N 72	15 56	17 11	18 31	▬	▬	▬	▬
N 70	16 12	17 19	18 30	▬	▬	▬	▬
68	16 26	17 25	18 31	▬	▬	▬	12 02
66	16 36	17 31	18 31	09 21	09 52	11 12	12 51
64	16 46	17 36	18 31	10 08	10 50	11 58	13 22
62	16 53	17 40	18 31	10 38	11 24	12 28	13 46
60	17 00	17 43	18 32	11 01	11 48	12 51	14 04
N 58	17 06	17 47	18 32	11 19	12 08	13 09	14 19
56	17 11	17 50	18 33	11 35	12 24	13 24	14 32
54	17 16	17 52	18 34	11 48	12 38	13 37	14 44
52	17 20	17 55	18 34	12 00	12 50	13 49	14 54
50	17 24	17 57	18 35	12 10	13 01	13 59	15 03
45	17 33	18 03	18 37	12 32	13 23	14 20	15 21
N 40	17 40	18 07	18 39	12 50	13 41	14 38	15 37
35	17 46	18 12	18 41	13 04	13 57	14 52	15 50
30	17 51	18 16	18 44	13 17	14 10	15 05	16 01
20	18 01	18 23	18 49	13 39	14 32	15 26	16 20
N 10	18 09	18 31	18 55	13 58	14 51	15 44	16 36
0	18 17	18 38	19 03	14 16	15 09	16 02	16 52
S 10	18 25	18 47	19 12	14 34	15 27	16 19	17 07
20	18 34	18 57	19 23	14 53	15 47	16 37	17 24
30	18 44	19 09	19 38	15 15	16 09	16 58	17 42
35	18 50	19 16	19 48	15 28	16 22	17 11	17 53
40	18 57	19 25	19 59	15 42	16 37	17 25	18 06
45	19 05	19 36	20 13	16 00	16 55	17 41	18 20
S 50	19 14	19 49	20 32	16 22	17 17	18 02	18 38
52	19 19	19 55	20 41	16 32	17 27	18 12	18 46
54	19 23	20 02	20 51	16 44	17 39	18 23	18 56
56	19 29	20 10	21 03	16 58	17 53	18 35	19 06
58	19 35	20 19	21 17	17 13	18 09	18 49	19 18
S 60	19 42	20 29	21 34	17 32	18 28	19 06	19 32

Day	SUN Eqn. of Time 00h	12h	Mer. Pass.	MOON Mer. Pass. Upper	Lower	Age	Phase
d	m s	m s	h m	h m	h m	d	%
18	13 59	13 57	12 14	08 03	20 30	25	24
19	13 54	13 52	12 14	08 57	21 23	26	16
20	13 49	13 46	12 14	09 49	22 15	27	9

UT (d h)	ARIES GHA	VENUS −4·2 GHA	Dec	MARS +1·2 GHA	Dec	JUPITER −1·9 GHA	Dec	SATURN +0·6 GHA	Dec	STARS Name	SHA	Dec
21 00	150 23.1	136 29.0	N 6 23.8	236 59.4	S23 40.2	221 04.2	S22 14.4	211 04.3	S20 42.9	Acamar	315 14.9	S40 13.9
01	165 25.6	151 28.9	25.0	252 00.0	40.2	236 06.1	14.4	226 06.5	42.9	Achernar	335 23.6	S57 08.5
02	180 28.1	166 28.7	26.3	267 00.6	40.2	251 08.1	14.3	241 08.6	42.8	Acrux	173 03.6	S63 12.4
03	195 30.5	181 28.6 ..	27.6	282 01.1 ..	40.2	266 10.0 ..	14.3	256 10.8 ..	42.8	Adhara	255 08.7	S29 00.2
04	210 33.0	196 28.5	28.9	297 01.7	40.2	281 12.0	14.2	271 13.0	42.7	Aldebaran	290 44.0	N16 32.8
05	225 35.5	211 28.4	30.1	312 02.3	40.2	296 13.9	14.1	286 15.2	42.7			
06	240 37.9	226 28.3	N 6 31.4	327 02.9	S23 40.2	311 15.8	S22 14.1	301 17.4	S20 42.6	Alioth	166 16.1	N55 50.9
07	255 40.4	241 28.2	32.7	342 03.5	40.2	326 17.8	14.0	316 19.6	42.6	Alkaid	152 54.9	N49 12.6
F 08	270 42.9	256 28.1	33.9	357 04.1	40.1	341 19.7	13.9	331 21.8	42.5	Alnair	27 38.4	S46 51.9
R 09	285 45.3	271 27.9 ..	35.2	12 04.6 ..	40.1	356 21.6 ..	13.9	346 24.0 ..	42.5	Alnilam	275 41.6	S 1 11.6
I 10	300 47.8	286 27.8	36.5	27 05.2	40.1	11 23.6	13.8	1 26.2	42.4	Alphard	217 51.2	S 8 44.9
D 11	315 50.3	301 27.7	37.8	42 05.8	40.1	26 25.5	13.8	16 28.4	42.4			
A 12	330 52.7	316 27.6	N 6 39.0	57 06.4	S23 40.1	41 27.5	S22 13.7	31 30.5	S20 42.4	Alphecca	126 07.0	N26 38.7
Y 13	345 55.2	331 27.5	40.3	72 07.0	40.1	56 29.4	13.6	46 32.7	42.3	Alpheratz	357 39.1	N29 12.0
14	0 57.6	346 27.4	41.6	87 07.6	40.1	71 31.3	13.6	61 34.9	42.3	Altair	62 04.0	N 8 55.2
15	16 00.1	1 27.2 ..	42.8	102 08.1 ..	40.1	86 33.3 ..	13.5	76 37.1 ..	42.2	Ankaa	353 11.4	S42 12.1
16	31 02.6	16 27.1	44.1	117 08.7	40.1	101 35.2	13.5	91 39.3	42.2	Antares	112 20.6	S26 28.4
17	46 05.0	31 27.0	45.4	132 09.3	40.1	116 37.1	13.4	106 41.5	42.1			
18	61 07.5	46 26.9	N 6 46.7	147 09.9	S23 40.1	131 39.1	S22 13.3	121 43.7	S20 42.1	Arcturus	145 51.4	N19 04.6
19	76 10.0	61 26.8	47.9	162 10.5	40.1	146 41.0	13.3	136 45.9	42.0	Atria	107 18.5	S69 03.4
20	91 12.4	76 26.7	49.2	177 11.1	40.1	161 43.0	13.2	151 48.1	42.0	Avior	234 15.6	S59 34.6
21	106 14.9	91 26.6 ..	50.5	192 11.6 ..	40.0	176 44.9 ..	13.2	166 50.3 ..	41.9	Bellatrix	278 26.9	N 6 21.9
22	121 17.4	106 26.4	51.7	207 12.2	40.0	191 46.8	13.1	181 52.5	41.9	Betelgeuse	270 56.2	N 7 24.5
23	136 19.8	121 26.3	53.0	222 12.8	40.0	206 48.8	13.0	196 54.6	41.8			
22 00	151 22.3	136 26.2	N 6 54.3	237 13.4	S23 40.0	221 50.7	S22 13.0	211 56.8	S20 41.8	Canopus	263 53.8	S52 42.7
01	166 24.8	151 26.1	55.5	252 14.0	40.0	236 52.7	12.9	226 59.0	41.7	Capella	280 27.5	N46 01.1
02	181 27.2	166 26.0	56.8	267 14.6	40.0	251 54.6	12.9	242 01.2	41.7	Deneb	49 28.8	N45 21.0
03	196 29.7	181 25.9 ..	58.1	282 15.1 ..	40.0	266 56.5 ..	12.8	257 03.4 ..	41.6	Denebola	182 28.7	N14 27.5
04	211 32.1	196 25.8	6 59.4	297 15.7	40.0	281 58.5	12.7	272 05.6	41.6	Diphda	348 51.5	S17 52.9
05	226 34.6	211 25.7	7 00.6	312 16.3	40.0	297 00.4	12.7	287 07.8	41.5			
06	241 37.1	226 25.5	N 7 01.9	327 16.9	S23 39.9	312 02.4	S22 12.6	302 10.0	S20 41.5	Dubhe	193 45.3	N61 38.5
S 07	256 39.5	241 25.4	03.2	342 17.5	39.9	327 04.3	12.5	317 12.2	41.4	Elnath	278 06.7	N28 37.4
A 08	271 42.0	256 25.3	04.4	357 18.1	39.9	342 06.2	12.5	332 14.4	41.4	Eltanin	90 44.2	N51 28.9
T 09	286 44.5	271 25.2 ..	05.7	12 18.6 ..	39.9	357 08.2 ..	12.4	347 16.6 ..	41.3	Enif	33 42.9	N 9 57.9
U 10	301 46.9	286 25.1	07.0	27 19.2	39.9	12 10.1	12.4	2 18.8	41.3	Fomalhaut	15 19.2	S29 31.1
R 11	316 49.4	301 25.0	08.2	42 19.8	39.9	27 12.1	12.3	17 20.9	41.3			
D 12	331 51.9	316 24.9	N 7 09.5	57 20.4	S23 39.8	42 14.0	S22 12.2	32 23.1	S20 41.2	Gacrux	171 55.3	S57 13.3
A 13	346 54.3	331 24.7	10.8	72 21.0	39.8	57 16.0	12.2	47 25.3	41.2	Gienah	175 47.3	S17 39.2
Y 14	1 56.8	346 24.6	12.0	87 21.5	39.8	72 17.9	12.1	62 27.5	41.1	Hadar	148 41.1	S60 27.9
15	16 59.2	1 24.5 ..	13.3	102 22.1 ..	39.8	87 19.8 ..	12.1	77 29.7 ..	41.1	Hamal	327 55.7	N23 33.3
16	32 01.7	16 24.4	14.5	117 22.7	39.8	102 21.8	12.0	92 31.9	41.0	Kaus Aust.	83 37.9	S34 22.3
17	47 04.2	31 24.3	15.8	132 23.3	39.8	117 23.7	11.9	107 34.1	41.0			
18	62 06.6	46 24.2	N 7 17.1	147 23.9	S23 39.7	132 25.7	S22 11.9	122 36.3	S20 40.9	Kochab	137 19.6	N74 04.1
19	77 09.1	61 24.1	18.3	162 24.5	39.7	147 27.6	11.8	137 38.5	40.9	Markab	13 34.1	N15 18.6
20	92 11.6	76 24.0	19.6	177 25.0	39.7	162 29.6	11.8	152 40.7	40.8	Menkar	314 10.3	N 4 09.9
21	107 14.0	91 23.8 ..	20.9	192 25.6 ..	39.7	177 31.5 ..	11.7	167 42.9 ..	40.8	Menkent	148 02.0	S36 27.9
22	122 16.5	106 23.7	22.1	207 26.2	39.7	192 33.4	11.6	182 45.1	40.7	Miaplacidus	221 37.9	S69 48.1
23	137 19.0	121 23.6	23.4	222 26.8	39.7	207 35.4	11.6	197 47.3	40.7			
23 00	152 21.4	136 23.5	N 7 24.7	237 27.4	S23 39.6	222 37.3	S22 11.5	212 49.5	S20 40.6	Mirfak	308 33.8	N49 56.0
01	167 23.9	151 23.4	25.9	252 28.0	39.6	237 39.3	11.5	227 51.6	40.6	Nunki	75 52.8	S26 16.2
02	182 26.4	166 23.3	27.2	267 28.5	39.6	252 41.2	11.4	242 53.8	40.5	Peacock	53 12.5	S56 40.1
03	197 28.8	181 23.2 ..	28.4	282 29.1 ..	39.6	267 43.2 ..	11.3	257 56.0 ..	40.5	Pollux	243 21.8	N27 58.6
04	212 31.3	196 23.1	29.7	297 29.7	39.6	282 45.1	11.3	272 58.2	40.4	Procyon	244 54.7	N 5 10.2
05	227 33.7	211 23.0	31.0	312 30.3	39.6	297 47.0	11.2	288 00.4	40.4			
06	242 36.2	226 22.8	N 7 32.2	327 30.9	S23 39.5	312 49.0	S22 11.1	303 02.6	S20 40.4	Rasalhague	96 02.3	N12 32.6
07	257 38.7	241 22.7	33.5	342 31.5	39.5	327 50.9	11.1	318 04.8	40.3	Regulus	207 38.3	N11 52.0
08	272 41.1	256 22.6	34.7	357 32.0	39.5	342 52.9	11.0	333 07.0	40.3	Rigel	281 07.5	S 8 11.0
S 09	287 43.6	271 22.5 ..	36.0	12 32.6 ..	39.4	357 54.8 ..	11.0	348 09.2 ..	40.2	Rigil Kent.	139 45.3	S60 54.7
U 10	302 46.1	286 22.4	37.3	27 33.2	39.4	12 56.8	10.9	3 11.4	40.2	Sabik	102 07.3	S15 44.9
N 11	317 48.5	301 22.3	38.5	42 33.8	39.4	27 58.7	10.8	18 13.6	40.1			
D 12	332 51.0	316 22.2	N 7 39.8	57 34.4	S23 39.4	43 00.7	S22 10.8	33 15.8	S20 40.1	Schedar	349 35.8	N56 38.9
A 13	347 53.5	331 22.1	41.0	72 34.9	39.3	58 02.6	10.7	48 18.0	40.0	Shaula	96 15.8	S37 06.2
Y 14	2 55.9	346 22.0	42.3	87 35.5	39.3	73 04.6	10.7	63 20.2	40.0	Sirius	258 29.5	S16 44.9
15	17 58.4	1 21.8 ..	43.6	102 36.1 ..	39.3	88 06.5 ..	10.6	78 22.4 ..	39.9	Spica	158 26.2	S11 15.9
16	33 00.9	16 21.7	44.8	117 36.7	39.3	103 08.4	10.5	93 24.6	39.9	Suhail	222 48.7	S43 30.9
17	48 03.3	31 21.6	46.1	132 37.3	39.2	118 10.4	10.5	108 26.7	39.8			
18	63 05.8	46 21.5	N 7 47.3	147 37.9	S23 39.2	133 12.3	S22 10.4	123 28.9	S20 39.8	Vega	80 36.1	N38 47.9
19	78 08.2	61 21.4	48.6	162 38.4	39.2	148 14.3	10.4	138 31.1	39.7	Zuben'ubi	137 00.2	S16 07.4
20	93 10.7	76 21.3	49.8	177 39.0	39.2	163 16.2	10.3	153 33.3	39.7		SHA	Mer. Pass.
21	108 13.2	91 21.2 ..	51.1	192 39.6 ..	39.1	178 18.2 ..	10.2	168 35.5 ..	39.6		° '	h m
22	123 15.6	106 21.1	52.4	207 40.2	39.1	193 20.1	10.2	183 37.7	39.6	Venus	345 03.9	14 54
23	138 18.1	121 21.0	53.6	222 40.8	39.1	208 22.1	10.1	198 39.9	39.5	Mars	85 51.1	8 11
Mer. Pass. 13 52.2		v −0.1	d 1.3	v 0.6	d 0.0	v 1.9	d 0.1	v 2.2	d 0.0	Jupiter	70 28.4	9 11
										Saturn	60 34.5	9 51

INDEX TO SELECTED STARS, 2020

Name	No	Mag	SHA	Dec
Acamar	7	3·2	315	S 40
Achernar	5	0·5	335	S 57
Acrux	30	1·3	173	S 63
Adhara	19	1·5	255	S 29
Aldebaran	10	0·9	291	N 17
Alioth	32	1·8	166	N 56
Alkaid	34	1·9	153	N 49
Alnair	55	1·7	28	S 47
Alnilam	15	1·7	276	S 1
Alphard	25	2·0	218	S 9
Alphecca	41	2·2	126	N 27
Alpheratz	1	2·1	358	N 29
Altair	51	0·8	62	N 9
Ankaa	2	2·4	353	S 42
Antares	42	1·0	112	S 26
Arcturus	37	0·0	146	N 19
Atria	43	1·9	107	S 69
Avior	22	1·9	234	S 60
Bellatrix	13	1·6	278	N 6
Betelgeuse	16	Var.*	271	N 7
Canopus	17	−0·7	264	S 53
Capella	12	0·1	280	N 46
Deneb	53	1·3	49	N 45
Denebola	28	2·1	182	N 14
Diphda	4	2·0	349	S 18
Dubhe	27	1·8	194	N 62
Elnath	14	1·7	278	N 29
Eltanin	47	2·2	91	N 51
Enif	54	2·4	34	N 10
Fomalhaut	56	1·2	15	S 30
Gacrux	31	1·6	172	S 57
Gienah	29	2·6	176	S 18
Hadar	35	0·6	149	S 60
Hamal	6	2·0	328	N 24
Kaus Australis	48	1·9	84	S 34
Kochab	40	2·1	137	N 74
Markab	57	2·5	14	N 15
Menkar	8	2·5	314	N 4
Menkent	36	2·1	148	S 36
Miaplacidus	24	1·7	222	S 70
Mirfak	9	1·8	309	N 50
Nunki	50	2·0	76	S 26
Peacock	52	1·9	53	S 57
Pollux	21	1·1	243	N 28
Procyon	20	0·4	245	N 5
Rasalhague	46	2·1	96	N 13
Regulus	26	1·4	208	N 12
Rigel	11	0·1	281	S 8
Rigil Kentaurus	38	−0·3	140	S 61
Sabik	44	2·4	102	S 16
Schedar	3	2·2	350	N 57
Shaula	45	1·6	96	S 37
Sirius	18	−1·5	258	S 17
Spica	33	1·0	158	S 11
Suhail	23	2·2	223	S 44
Vega	49	0·0	81	N 39
Zubenelgenubi	39	2·8	137	S 16

No	Name	Mag	SHA	Dec
1	Alpheratz	2·1	358	N 29
2	Ankaa	2·4	353	S 42
3	Schedar	2·2	350	N 57
4	Diphda	2·0	349	S 18
5	Achernar	0·5	335	S 57
6	Hamal	2·0	328	N 24
7	Acamar	3·2	315	S 40
8	Menkar	2·5	314	N 4
9	Mirfak	1·8	309	N 50
10	Aldebaran	0·9	291	N 17
11	Rigel	0·1	281	S 8
12	Capella	0·1	280	N 46
13	Bellatrix	1·6	278	N 6
14	Elnath	1·7	278	N 29
15	Alnilam	1·7	276	S 1
16	Betelgeuse	Var.*	271	N 7
17	Canopus	−0·7	264	S 53
18	Sirius	−1·5	258	S 17
19	Adhara	1·5	255	S 29
20	Procyon	0·4	245	N 5
21	Pollux	1·1	243	N 28
22	Avior	1·9	234	S 60
23	Suhail	2·2	223	S 44
24	Miaplacidus	1·7	222	S 70
25	Alphard	2·0	218	S 9
26	Regulus	1·4	208	N 12
27	Dubhe	1·8	194	N 62
28	Denebola	2·1	182	N 14
29	Gienah	2·6	176	S 18
30	Acrux	1·3	173	S 63
31	Gacrux	1·6	172	S 57
32	Alioth	1·8	166	N 56
33	Spica	1·0	158	S 11
34	Alkaid	1·9	153	N 49
35	Hadar	0·6	149	S 60
36	Menkent	2·1	148	S 36
37	Arcturus	0·0	146	N 19
38	Rigil Kentaurus	−0·3	140	S 61
39	Zubenelgenubi	2·8	137	S 16
40	Kochab	2·1	137	N 74
41	Alphecca	2·2	126	N 27
42	Antares	1·0	112	S 26
43	Atria	1·9	107	S 69
44	Sabik	2·4	102	S 16
45	Shaula	1·6	96	S 37
46	Rasalhague	2·1	96	N 13
47	Eltanin	2·2	91	N 51
48	Kaus Australis	1·9	84	S 34
49	Vega	0·0	81	N 39
50	Nunki	2·0	76	S 26
51	Altair	0·8	62	N 9
52	Peacock	1·9	53	S 57
53	Deneb	1·3	49	N 45
54	Enif	2·4	34	N 10
55	Alnair	1·7	28	S 47
56	Fomalhaut	1·2	15	S 30
57	Markab	2·5	14	N 15

*0·1 — 1·2

ALTITUDE CORRECTION TABLES 10°-90°—SUN, STARS, PLANETS

OCT.—MAR. SUN APR.—SEPT.

App. Alt.	Lower Limb	Upper Limb	App. Alt.	Lower Limb	Upper Limb
9 33	+10.8	−21.5	9 39	+10.6	−21.2
9 45	+10.9	−21.4	9 50	+10.7	−21.1
9 56	+11.0	−21.3	10 02	+10.8	−21.0
10 08	+11.1	−21.2	10 14	+10.9	−20.9
10 20	+11.2	−21.1	10 27	+11.0	−20.8
10 33	+11.3	−21.0	10 40	+11.1	−20.7
10 46	+11.4	−20.9	10 53	+11.2	−20.6
11 00	+11.5	−20.8	11 07	+11.3	−20.5
11 15	+11.6	−20.7	11 22	+11.4	−20.4
11 30	+11.7	−20.6	11 37	+11.5	−20.3
11 45	+11.8	−20.5	11 53	+11.6	−20.2
12 01	+11.9	−20.4	12 10	+11.7	−20.1
12 18	+12.0	−20.3	12 27	+11.8	−20.0
12 36	+12.1	−20.2	12 45	+11.9	−19.9
12 54	+12.2	−20.1	13 04	+12.0	−19.8
13 14	+12.3	−20.0	13 24	+12.1	−19.7
13 34	+12.4	−19.9	13 44	+12.2	−19.6
13 55	+12.5	−19.8	14 06	+12.3	−19.5
14 17	+12.6	−19.7	14 29	+12.4	−19.4
14 41	+12.7	−19.6	14 53	+12.5	−19.3
15 05	+12.8	−19.5	15 18	+12.6	−19.2
15 31	+12.9	−19.4	15 45	+12.7	−19.1
15 59	+13.0	−19.3	16 13	+12.8	−19.0
16 27	+13.1	−19.2	16 43	+12.9	−18.9
16 58	+13.2	−19.1	17 14	+13.0	−18.8
17 30	+13.3	−19.0	17 47	+13.1	−18.7
18 05	+13.4	−18.9	18 23	+13.2	−18.6
18 41	+13.5	−18.8	19 00	+13.3	−18.5
19 20	+13.6	−18.7	19 41	+13.4	−18.4
20 02	+13.7	−18.6	20 24	+13.5	−18.3
20 46	+13.8	−18.5	21 10	+13.6	−18.2
21 34	+13.9	−18.4	21 59	+13.7	−18.1
22 25	+14.0	−18.3	22 52	+13.8	−18.0
23 20	+14.1	−18.2	23 49	+13.9	−17.9
24 20	+14.2	−18.1	24 51	+14.0	−17.8
25 24	+14.3	−18.0	25 58	+14.1	−17.7
26 34	+14.4	−17.9	27 11	+14.2	−17.6
27 50	+14.5	−17.8	28 31	+14.3	−17.5
29 13	+14.6	−17.7	29 58	+14.4	−17.4
30 44	+14.7	−17.6	31 33	+14.5	−17.3
32 24	+14.8	−17.5	33 18	+14.6	−17.2
34 15	+14.9	−17.4	35 15	+14.7	−17.1
36 17	+15.0	−17.3	37 24	+14.8	−17.0
38 34	+15.1	−17.2	39 48	+14.9	−16.9
41 06	+15.2	−17.1	42 28	+15.0	−16.8
43 56	+15.3	−17.0	45 29	+15.1	−16.7
47 07	+15.4	−16.9	48 52	+15.2	−16.6
50 43	+15.5	−16.8	52 41	+15.3	−16.5
54 46	+15.6	−16.7	56 59	+15.4	−16.4
59 21	+15.7	−16.6	61 50	+15.5	−16.3
64 28	+15.8	−16.5	67 15	+15.6	−16.2
70 10	+15.9	−16.4	73 14	+15.7	−16.1
76 24	+16.0	−16.3	79 42	+15.8	−16.0
83 05	+16.1	−16.2	86 31	+15.9	−15.9
90 00			90 00		

STARS AND PLANETS

App Alt.	Corrn		App. Alt.	Additional Corrn
9 55	−5.3			**2020**
10 07	−5.2			**VENUS**
10 20	−5.1			Jan. 1–Feb. 17
10 32	−5.1			Sept. 18–Dec. 31
10 46	−5.0		° '	
10 59	−4.9		60	+0.1
11 14	−4.8			
11 29	−4.7		Feb. 18–Apr. 9	
11 44	−4.6		July 29–Sept. 17	
12 00	−4.5		° '	
12 17	−4.4		41	+0.2
12 35	−4.3		76	+0.1
12 53	−4.2			
13 12	−4.1		Apr. 10–May 2	
13 32	−4.0		July 6–July 28	
13 53	−3.9		° '	
14 16	−3.8		0	+0.3
14 39	−3.7		34	+0.2
15 03	−3.6		60	+0.1
15 29	−3.5		80	
15 56	−3.4			
16 25	−3.3		May 3–May 18	
16 55	−3.2		June 20–July 5	
17 27	−3.1		° '	
18 01	−3.0		0	+0.4
18 37	−2.9		29	+0.3
19 16	−2.8		51	+0.2
19 56	−2.7		68	+0.1
20 40	−2.6		83	
21 27	−2.5			
22 17	−2.4		May 19–June 19	
23 11	−2.3		° '	
24 09	−2.2		0	+0.5
25 12	−2.1		26	+0.4
26 20	−2.0		46	+0.3
27 34	−1.9		60	+0.2
28 54	−1.8		73	+0.1
30 22	−1.7		84	
31 58	−1.6			
33 43	−1.5		**MARS**	
35 38	−1.4		Jan. 1–June 5	
37 45	−1.3		° '	
40 06	−1.2		0	+0.1
42 42	−1.1		60	
45 34	−1.0			
48 45	−0.9		June 6–Aug. 11	
52 16	−0.8		Nov. 24–Dec. 31	
56 09	−0.7		° '	
60 26	−0.6		0	+0.2
65 06	−0.5		41	+0.1
70 09	−0.4		76	
75 32	−0.3		Aug. 12–Sept. 29	
81 12	−0.2		Oct. 14–Nov. 23	
87 03	−0.1		° '	
90 00	0.0		0	+0.3
			34	+0.2
			60	+0.1
			80	
			Sept. 30–Oct. 13	
			° '	
			0	+0.4
			29	+0.3
			51	+0.2
			68	+0.1
			83	

DIP

Ht. of Eye (m)	Corrn	Ht. of Eye (ft)	Ht. of Eye (m)	Corrn
2.4	−2.8	8.0	1.0	−1.8
2.6	−2.9	8.6	1.5	−2.2
2.8	−3.0	9.2	2.0	−2.5
3.0	−3.1	9.8	2.5	−2.8
3.2	−3.2	10.5	3.0	−3.0
3.4	−3.3	11.2		
3.6	−3.4	11.9	See table ←	
3.8	−3.5	12.6		
4.0	−3.6	13.3	m '	
4.3	−3.7	14.1	20	−7.9
4.5	−3.8	14.9	22	−8.3
4.7	−3.9	15.7	24	−8.6
5.0	−4.0	16.5	26	−9.0
5.2	−4.1	17.4	28	−9.3
5.5	−4.2	18.3	30	−9.6
5.8	−4.3	19.1	32	−10.0
6.1	−4.4	20.1	34	−10.3
6.3	−4.5	21.0	36	−10.6
6.6	−4.6	22.0	38	−10.8
6.9	−4.7	22.9		
7.2	−4.8	23.9	40	−11.1
7.5	−4.9	24.9	42	−11.4
7.9	−5.0	26.0	44	−11.7
8.2	−5.1	27.1	46	−11.9
8.5	−5.2	28.1	48	−12.2
8.8	−5.3	29.2		
9.2	−5.4	30.4	ft '	
9.5	−5.5	31.5	2	−1.4
9.9	−5.6	32.7	4	−1.9
10.3	−5.7	33.9	6	−2.4
10.6	−5.8	35.1	8	−2.7
11.0	−5.9	36.3	10	−3.1
11.4	−6.0	37.6		
11.8	−6.1	38.9	See table ←	
12.2	−6.2	40.1		
12.6	−6.3	41.5	ft '	
13.0	−6.4	42.8	70	−8.1
13.4	−6.5	44.2	75	−8.4
13.8	−6.6	45.5	80	−8.7
14.2	−6.7	46.9	85	−8.9
14.7	−6.8	48.4	90	−9.2
15.1	−6.9	49.8	95	−9.5
15.5	−7.0	51.3	100	−9.7
16.0	−7.1	52.8	105	−9.9
16.5	−7.2	54.3	110	−10.2
16.9	−7.3	55.8	115	−10.4
17.4	−7.4	57.4	120	−10.6
17.9	−7.5	58.9	125	−10.8
18.4	−7.6	60.5		
18.8	−7.7	62.1	130	−11.1
19.3	−7.8	63.8	135	−11.3
19.8	−7.9	65.4	140	−11.5
20.4	−8.0	67.1	145	−11.7
20.9	−8.1	68.8	150	−11.9
21.4		70.5	155	−12.1

App. Alt. = Apparent altitude = Sextant altitude corrected for index error and dip.

UT	SUN		MOON					Lat.	Twilight		Sunrise	Moonrise			
	GHA	Dec	GHA	v	Dec	d	HP		Naut.	Civil		21	22	23	24
d h	° '	° '	° '	'	° '	'	'	°	h m	h m	h m	h m	h m	h m	h m
21 00	176 34.4	S10 49.8	205 22.7	10.5	S21 46.2	4.7	55.3	N 72	05 46	07 04	08 17	■	■	09 49	09 17
01	191 34.4	48.9	219 52.2	10.6	21 41.5	4.8	55.3	N 70	05 47	06 58	08 03	■	09 47	09 17	08 59
02	206 34.5	48.0	234 21.8	10.6	21 36.7	4.9	55.2	68	05 48	06 53	07 51	09 27	09 06	08 54	08 45
03	221 34.6	.. 47.1	248 51.4	10.7	21 31.8	5.0	55.2	66	05 49	06 48	07 41	08 37	08 37	08 36	08 34
04	236 34.6	46.2	263 21.1	10.7	21 26.8	5.1	55.2	64	05 49	06 44	07 33	08 05	08 16	08 21	08 24
05	251 34.7	45.3	277 50.8	10.8	21 21.7	5.2	55.2	62	05 49	06 41	07 26	07 42	07 58	08 09	08 16
06	266 34.8	S10 44.4	292 20.6	10.8	S21 16.5	5.3	55.2	60	05 49	06 38	07 20	07 23	07 44	07 58	08 09
07	281 34.8	43.5	306 50.4	10.9	21 11.2	5.4	55.1	N 58	05 49	06 35	07 15	07 07	07 31	07 49	08 02
08	296 34.9	42.6	321 20.3	11.0	21 05.8	5.5	55.1	56	05 49	06 32	07 10	06 54	07 21	07 41	07 57
F 09	311 35.0	.. 41.7	335 50.3	11.0	21 00.3	5.6	55.1	54	05 49	06 30	07 06	06 42	07 11	07 33	07 52
R 10	326 35.0	40.8	350 20.3	11.1	20 54.7	5.7	55.1	52	05 49	06 28	07 02	06 32	07 02	07 27	07 47
I 11	341 35.1	39.9	4 50.4	11.1	20 49.0	5.8	55.1	50	05 48	06 26	06 59	06 23	06 55	07 21	07 43
D 12	356 35.2	S10 39.0	19 20.5	11.2	S20 43.2	5.9	55.1	45	05 47	06 21	06 51	06 03	06 38	07 08	07 34
A 13	11 35.3	38.1	33 50.7	11.3	20 37.3	6.0	55.0	N 40	05 45	06 17	06 44	05 47	06 25	06 58	07 26
Y 14	26 35.3	37.2	48 21.0	11.3	20 31.3	6.1	55.0	35	05 44	06 13	06 39	05 34	06 14	06 49	07 20
15	41 35.4	.. 36.3	62 51.3	11.3	20 25.2	6.1	55.0	30	05 42	06 10	06 34	05 22	06 03	06 41	07 14
16	56 35.5	35.4	77 21.6	11.5	20 19.1	6.3	55.0	20	05 37	06 03	06 25	05 02	05 46	06 27	07 04
17	71 35.5	34.4	91 52.1	11.5	20 12.8	6.4	55.0	N 10	05 32	05 56	06 18	04 44	05 31	06 15	06 55
18	86 35.6	S10 33.5	106 22.6	11.5	S20 06.4	6.5	55.0	0	05 25	05 49	06 10	04 28	05 17	06 03	06 47
19	101 35.7	32.6	120 53.1	11.6	19 59.9	6.5	54.9	S 10	05 16	05 41	06 03	04 12	05 03	05 52	06 39
20	116 35.8	31.7	135 23.7	11.6	19 53.4	6.7	54.9	20	05 06	05 32	05 55	03 54	04 47	05 39	06 30
21	131 35.8	.. 30.8	149 54.4	11.7	19 46.7	6.7	54.9	30	04 52	05 21	05 45	03 34	04 30	05 25	06 20
22	146 35.9	29.9	164 25.1	11.8	19 40.0	6.8	54.9	35	04 43	05 14	05 40	03 22	04 21	05 17	06 14
23	161 36.0	29.0	178 55.9	11.9	19 33.2	7.0	54.9	40	04 32	05 06	05 34	03 08	04 08	05 08	06 07
22 00	176 36.0	S10 28.1	193 26.8	11.9	S19 26.2	7.0	54.9	45	04 18	04 56	05 26	02 52	03 54	04 57	05 59
01	191 36.1	27.2	207 57.7	12.0	19 19.2	7.1	54.9	S 50	04 01	04 43	05 18	02 32	03 37	04 43	05 50
02	206 36.2	26.3	222 28.7	12.0	19 12.1	7.1	54.8	52	03 52	04 37	05 14	02 22	03 29	04 37	05 45
03	221 36.3	.. 25.4	236 59.7	12.1	19 05.0	7.3	54.8	54	03 42	04 31	05 09	02 12	03 20	04 30	05 41
04	236 36.3	24.5	251 30.8	12.2	18 57.7	7.3	54.8	56	03 31	04 23	05 04	02 00	03 10	04 23	05 35
05	251 36.4	23.6	266 02.0	12.2	18 50.4	7.5	54.8	58	03 18	04 15	04 59	01 46	02 58	04 14	05 29
06	266 36.5	S10 22.7	280 33.2	12.3	S18 42.9	7.5	54.8	S 60	03 02	04 05	04 52	01 29	02 45	04 04	05 22

UT	SUN		MOON					Lat.	Sunset	Twilight		Moonset			
	GHA	Dec	GHA	v	Dec	d	HP			Civil	Naut.	21	22	23	24
d h	° '	° '	° '	'	° '	'	'	°	h m	h m	h m	h m	h m	h m	h m
22 07	281 36.6	S10 21.8	295 04.5	12.4	S18 35.4	7.6	54.8	N 72	16 12	17 25	18 44	■	■	14 58	17 00
S 08	296 36.6	20.8	309 35.9	12.4	18 27.8	7.7	54.8	N 70	16 26	17 31	18 42	■	13 23	15 27	17 15
A 09	311 36.7	.. 19.9	324 07.3	12.4	18 20.1	7.7	54.7	68	16 38	17 36	18 41	12 02	14 03	15 49	17 28
T 10	326 36.8	19.0	338 38.7	12.6	18 12.4	7.9	54.7	66	16 47	17 41	18 40	12 51	14 31	16 06	17 38
U 11	341 36.9	18.1	353 10.3	12.5	18 04.5	7.9	54.7	64	16 55	17 44	18 40	13 22	14 52	16 20	17 46
R 12	356 36.9	S10 17.2	7 41.8	12.7	S17 56.6	8.0	54.7	62	17 02	17 48	18 39	13 46	15 08	16 32	17 53
D 13	11 37.0	16.3	22 13.5	12.7	17 48.6	8.1	54.7	60	17 08	17 51	18 39	14 04	15 22	16 41	18 00
A 14	26 37.1	15.4	36 45.2	12.8	17 40.5	8.1	54.7	N 58	17 13	17 53	18 39	14 19	15 34	16 50	18 05
Y 15	41 37.2	.. 14.5	51 17.0	12.8	17 32.4	8.2	54.7	56	17 18	17 56	18 39	14 32	15 44	16 57	18 10
16	56 37.3	13.6	65 48.8	12.9	17 24.2	8.3	54.6	54	17 22	17 58	18 39	14 44	15 53	17 04	18 14
17	71 37.3	12.7	80 20.7	13.0	17 15.9	8.4	54.6	52	17 26	18 00	18 39	14 54	16 01	17 10	18 18
18	86 37.4	S10 11.7	94 52.7	13.0	S17 07.5	8.4	54.6	50	17 29	18 02	18 40	15 03	16 09	17 15	18 22
19	101 37.5	10.8	109 24.7	13.1	16 59.1	8.6	54.6	45	17 37	18 07	18 41	15 21	16 24	17 27	18 29
20	116 37.6	09.9	123 56.8	13.1	16 50.5	8.5	54.6	N 40	17 43	18 11	18 42	15 37	16 37	17 36	18 35
21	131 37.6	.. 09.0	138 28.9	13.2	16 42.0	8.7	54.6	35	17 49	18 14	18 44	15 50	16 47	17 45	18 41
22	146 37.7	08.1	153 01.1	13.2	16 33.3	8.7	54.6	30	17 54	18 18	18 46	16 01	16 57	17 52	18 46
23	161 37.8	07.2	167 33.3	13.3	16 24.6	8.8	54.5	20	18 02	18 24	18 50	16 20	17 13	18 04	18 54
23 00	176 37.9	S10 06.3	182 05.6	13.4	S16 15.8	8.9	54.5	N 10	18 10	18 31	18 56	16 36	17 27	18 15	19 01
01	191 38.0	05.4	196 38.0	13.4	16 06.9	8.9	54.5	0	18 17	18 38	19 02	16 52	17 39	18 25	19 08
02	206 38.0	04.4	211 10.4	13.5	15 58.0	9.0	54.5	S 10	18 24	18 46	19 11	17 07	17 52	18 34	19 14
03	221 38.1	.. 03.5	225 42.9	13.6	15 49.0	9.1	54.5	20	18 32	18 55	19 21	17 24	18 06	18 45	19 21
04	236 38.2	02.6	240 15.5	13.6	15 39.9	9.1	54.5	30	18 41	19 06	19 35	17 42	18 22	18 57	19 29
05	251 38.3	01.7	254 48.1	13.6	15 30.8	9.2	54.5	35	18 47	19 13	19 44	17 53	18 31	19 04	19 34
06	266 38.4	S10 00.8	269 20.7	13.7	S15 21.6	9.2	54.5	40	18 53	19 21	19 54	18 06	18 41	19 11	19 39
07	281 38.4	9 59.9	283 53.4	13.8	15 12.4	9.3	54.5	45	19 00	19 30	20 08	18 20	18 53	19 20	19 45
08	296 38.5	59.0	298 26.2	13.8	15 03.1	9.4	54.4	S 50	19 08	19 43	20 25	18 38	19 07	19 31	19 52
S 09	311 38.6	.. 58.0	312 59.0	13.9	14 53.7	9.4	54.4	52	19 12	19 48	20 33	18 46	19 14	19 36	19 55
U 10	326 38.7	57.1	327 31.9	13.9	14 44.3	9.5	54.4	54	19 17	19 55	20 43	18 56	19 21	19 42	19 59
N 11	341 38.8	56.2	342 04.8	14.0	14 34.8	9.6	54.4	56	19 22	20 02	20 54	19 06	19 30	19 48	20 02
D 12	356 38.9	S 9 55.3	356 37.8	14.1	S14 25.2	9.6	54.4	58	19 27	20 10	21 06	19 18	19 39	19 55	20 07
A 13	11 38.9	54.4	11 10.9	14.0	14 15.6	9.6	54.4	S 60	19 33	20 20	21 22	19 32	19 50	20 02	20 12
Y 14	26 39.0	53.5	25 43.9	14.2	14 06.0	9.8	54.4								
15	41 39.1	.. 52.5	40 17.1	14.2	13 56.2	9.7	54.4								
16	56 39.2	51.6	54 50.3	14.3	13 46.5	9.9	54.3								
17	71 39.3	50.7	69 23.6	14.3	13 36.6	9.8	54.3								

UT	SUN		MOON					Day	SUN			MOON			
	GHA	Dec	GHA	v	Dec	d	HP		Eqn. of Time 00h	Eqn. of Time 12h	Mer. Pass.	Mer. Pass. Upper	Lower	Age	Phase
d h	° '	° '	° '	'	° '	'	'	d	m s	m s	h m	h m	h m	d	%
23 18	86 39.4	S 9 49.8	83 56.9	14.3	S13 26.8	10.0	54.3	21	13 43	13 39	12 14	10 40	23 04	28	4
19	101 39.4	48.9	98 30.2	14.4	13 16.8	10.0	54.3	22	13 36	13 32	12 14	11 28	23 51	29	1
20	116 39.5	48.0	113 03.6	14.5	13 06.8	10.0	54.3	23	13 29	13 25	12 13	12 14	24 36	30	0
21	131 39.6	.. 47.0	127 37.1	14.5	12 56.8	10.1	54.3								
22	146 39.7	46.1	142 10.6	14.6	12 46.7	10.1	54.3								
23	161 39.8	45.2	156 44.2	14.6	S12 36.6	10.2	54.3								
	SD 16.2	d 0.9	SD 15.0		14.9		14.8									

UT	ARIES	VENUS −4.3		MARS +1.2		JUPITER −2.0		SATURN +0.7		STARS		
d h	GHA	GHA	Dec	GHA	Dec	GHA	Dec	GHA	Dec	Name	SHA	Dec
24 00	153 20.6	136 20.9	N 7 54.9	237 41.3	S23 39.0	223 24.0	S22 10.0	213 42.1	S20 39.5	Acamar	315 14.9	S40 13.9
01	168 23.0	151 20.7	. . 56.1	252 41.9	. . 39.0	238 26.0	. . 10.0	228 44.3	. . 39.5	Achernar	335 23.6	S57 08.5
02	183 25.5	166 20.6	57.4	267 42.5	39.0	253 27.9	09.9	243 46.5	39.4	Acrux	173 03.6	S63 12.4
03	198 28.0	181 20.5	. . 58.6	282 43.1	. . 39.0	268 29.9	. . 09.9	258 48.7	. . 39.4	Adhara	255 08.7	S29 00.2
04	213 30.4	196 20.4	7 59.9	297 43.7	38.9	283 31.8	09.8	273 50.9	39.3	Aldebaran	290 44.1	N16 32.8
05	228 32.9	211 20.3	8 01.1	312 44.3	38.9	298 33.8	09.7	288 53.1	39.3			
M 06	243 35.3	226 20.2	N 8 02.4	327 44.8	S23 38.9	313 35.7	S22 09.7	303 55.3	S20 39.2	Alioth	166 16.1	N55 50.9
O 07	258 37.8	241 20.1	03.7	342 45.4	38.8	328 37.7	09.6	318 57.5	39.2	Alkaid	152 54.9	N49 12.6
N 08	273 40.3	256 20.0	04.9	357 46.0	38.8	343 39.6	09.6	333 59.7	39.1	Alnair	27 38.4	S46 51.9
D 09	288 42.7	271 19.9	. . 06.2	12 46.6	. . 38.8	358 41.6	. . 09.5	349 01.9	. . 39.1	Alnilam	275 41.6	S 1 11.6
A 10	303 45.2	286 19.8	07.4	27 47.2	38.7	13 43.5	09.4	4 04.1	39.0	Alphard	217 51.3	S 8 44.9
Y 11	318 47.7	301 19.7	08.7	42 47.8	38.7	28 45.4	09.4	19 06.3	39.0			
12	333 50.1	316 19.5	N 8 09.9	57 48.3	S23 38.7	43 47.4	S22 09.3	34 08.5	S20 38.9	Alphecca	126 07.0	N26 38.7
13	348 52.6	331 19.4	11.2	72 48.9	38.6	58 49.3	09.2	49 10.7	38.9	Alpheratz	357 39.1	N29 12.0
14	3 55.1	346 19.3	12.4	87 49.5	38.6	73 51.3	09.2	64 12.9	38.8	Altair	62 04.0	N 8 55.2
15	18 57.5	1 19.2	. . 13.7	102 50.1	. . 38.6	88 53.2	. . 09.1	79 15.1	. . 38.8	Ankaa	353 11.5	S42 12.1
16	34 00.0	16 19.1	14.9	117 50.7	38.5	103 55.2	09.1	94 17.3	38.7	Antares	112 20.6	S26 28.4
17	49 02.5	31 19.0	16.2	132 51.2	38.5	118 57.1	09.0	109 19.4	38.7			
18	64 04.9	46 18.9	N 8 17.4	147 51.8	S23 38.5	133 59.1	S22 08.9	124 21.6	S20 38.7	Arcturus	145 51.3	N19 04.6
19	79 07.4	61 18.8	18.7	162 52.4	38.4	149 01.0	08.9	139 23.8	38.6	Atria	107 18.4	S69 03.4
20	94 09.8	76 18.7	19.9	177 53.0	38.4	164 03.0	08.8	154 26.0	38.6	Avior	234 15.6	S59 34.6
21	109 12.3	91 18.6	. . 21.2	192 53.6	. . 38.4	179 04.9	. . 08.8	169 28.2	. . 38.5	Bellatrix	278 27.0	N 6 21.9
22	124 14.8	106 18.5	22.4	207 54.2	38.3	194 06.9	08.7	184 30.4	38.5	Betelgeuse	270 56.2	N 7 24.5
23	139 17.2	121 18.4	23.7	222 54.7	38.3	209 08.9	08.6	199 32.6	38.4			
25 00	154 19.7	136 18.2	N 8 24.9	237 55.3	S23 38.3	224 10.8	S22 08.6	214 34.8	S20 38.4	Canopus	263 53.8	S52 42.7
01	169 22.2	151 18.1	26.2	252 55.9	38.2	239 12.8	08.5	229 37.0	38.3	Capella	280 27.5	N46 01.1
02	184 24.6	166 18.0	27.4	267 56.5	38.2	254 14.7	08.5	244 39.2	38.3	Deneb	49 28.8	N45 20.9
03	199 27.1	181 17.9	. . 28.7	282 57.1	. . 38.1	269 16.7	. . 08.4	259 41.4	. . 38.2	Denebola	182 28.7	N14 27.5
04	214 29.6	196 17.8	29.9	297 57.6	38.1	284 18.6	08.3	274 43.6	38.2	Diphda	348 51.5	S17 52.9
05	229 32.0	211 17.7	31.2	312 58.2	38.1	299 20.6	08.3	289 45.8	38.1			
T 06	244 34.5	226 17.6	N 8 32.4	327 58.8	S23 38.0	314 22.5	S22 08.2	304 48.0	S20 38.1	Dubhe	193 45.3	N61 38.5
U 07	259 36.9	241 17.5	33.6	342 59.4	38.0	329 24.5	08.1	319 50.2	38.0	Elnath	278 06.7	N28 37.4
E 08	274 39.4	256 17.4	34.9	358 00.0	37.9	344 26.4	08.1	334 52.4	38.0	Eltanin	90 44.2	N51 28.9
S 09	289 41.9	271 17.3	. . 36.1	13 00.6	. . 37.9	359 28.4	. . 08.0	349 54.6	. . 37.9	Enif	33 42.9	N 9 57.9
D 10	304 44.3	286 17.2	37.4	28 01.1	37.9	14 30.3	08.0	4 56.8	37.9	Fomalhaut	15 19.2	S29 31.1
A 11	319 46.8	301 17.1	38.6	43 01.7	37.8	29 32.3	07.9	19 59.0	37.9			
Y 12	334 49.3	316 17.0	N 8 39.9	58 02.3	S23 37.8	44 34.2	S22 07.8	35 01.2	S20 37.8	Gacrux	171 55.3	S57 13.4
13	349 51.7	331 16.9	41.1	73 02.9	37.7	59 36.2	07.8	50 03.4	37.8	Gienah	175 47.3	S17 39.2
14	4 54.2	346 16.7	42.4	88 03.5	37.7	74 38.1	07.7	65 05.6	37.7	Hadar	148 41.0	S60 27.9
15	19 56.7	1 16.6	. . 43.6	103 04.0	. . 37.6	89 40.1	. . 07.7	80 07.8	. . 37.7	Hamal	327 55.7	N23 33.3
16	34 59.1	16 16.5	44.8	118 04.6	37.6	104 42.0	07.6	95 10.0	37.6	Kaus Aust.	83 37.9	S34 22.3
17	50 01.6	31 16.4	46.1	133 05.2	37.6	119 44.0	07.5	110 12.2	37.6			
18	65 04.1	46 16.3	N 8 47.3	148 05.8	S23 37.5	134 46.0	S22 07.5	125 14.4	S20 37.5	Kochab	137 19.6	N74 04.1
19	80 06.5	61 16.2	48.6	163 06.4	37.5	149 47.9	07.4	140 16.6	37.5	Markab	13 34.1	N15 18.6
20	95 09.0	76 16.1	49.8	178 07.0	37.4	164 49.9	07.3	155 18.8	37.4	Menkar	314 10.3	N 4 09.9
21	110 11.4	91 16.0	. . 51.1	193 07.5	. . 37.4	179 51.8	. . 07.3	170 21.0	. . 37.4	Menkent	148 01.9	S36 27.9
22	125 13.9	106 15.9	52.3	208 08.1	37.3	194 53.8	07.2	185 23.2	37.3	Miaplacidus	221 37.9	S69 48.1
23	140 16.4	121 15.8	53.5	223 08.7	37.3	209 55.7	07.2	200 25.4	37.3			
26 00	155 18.8	136 15.7	N 8 54.8	238 09.3	S23 37.2	224 57.7	S22 07.1	215 27.6	S20 37.2	Mirfak	308 33.9	N49 56.0
01	170 21.3	151 15.6	56.0	253 09.9	37.2	239 59.6	07.0	230 29.8	37.2	Nunki	75 52.8	S26 16.2
02	185 23.8	166 15.5	57.3	268 10.4	37.2	255 01.6	07.0	245 32.0	37.1	Peacock	53 12.5	S56 40.1
03	200 26.2	181 15.4	. . 58.5	283 11.0	. . 37.1	270 03.5	. . 06.9	260 34.2	. . 37.1	Pollux	243 21.8	N27 58.6
04	215 28.7	196 15.3	8 59.7	298 11.6	37.1	285 05.5	06.9	275 36.4	37.1	Procyon	244 54.7	N 5 10.2
05	230 31.2	211 15.2	9 01.0	313 12.2	37.0	300 07.5	06.8	290 38.6	37.0			
W 06	245 33.6	226 15.1	N 9 02.2	328 12.8	S23 37.0	315 09.4	S22 06.7	305 40.8	S20 37.0	Rasalhague	96 02.3	N12 32.6
E 07	260 36.1	241 14.9	03.5	343 13.4	36.9	330 11.4	06.7	320 43.0	36.9	Regulus	207 38.3	N11 52.1
D 08	275 38.5	256 14.8	04.7	358 13.9	36.9	345 13.3	06.6	335 45.2	36.9	Rigel	281 07.5	S 8 11.0
N 09	290 41.0	271 14.7	. . 05.9	13 14.5	. . 36.8	0 15.3	. . 06.5	350 47.4	. . 36.8	Rigil Kent.	139 45.2	S60 54.7
E 10	305 43.5	286 14.6	07.2	28 15.1	36.8	15 17.2	06.5	5 49.6	36.8	Sabik	102 07.3	S15 44.9
S 11	320 45.9	301 14.5	08.4	43 15.7	36.7	30 19.2	06.4	20 51.8	36.7			
D 12	335 48.4	316 14.4	N 9 09.6	58 16.3	S23 36.7	45 21.2	S22 06.4	35 54.0	S20 36.7	Schedar	349 35.8	N56 38.8
A 13	350 50.9	331 14.3	10.9	73 16.8	36.6	60 23.1	06.3	50 56.2	36.6	Shaula	96 15.8	S37 06.9
Y 14	5 53.3	346 14.2	12.1	88 17.4	36.6	75 25.1	06.2	65 58.4	36.6	Sirius	258 29.5	S16 44.9
15	20 55.8	1 14.1	. . 13.3	103 18.0	. . 36.5	90 27.0	. . 06.2	81 00.6	. . 36.5	Spica	158 26.2	S11 15.9
16	35 58.3	16 14.0	14.6	118 18.6	36.5	105 29.0	06.1	96 02.8	36.5	Suhail	222 48.7	S43 31.0
17	51 00.7	31 13.9	15.8	133 19.2	36.4	120 30.9	06.1	111 05.0	36.4			
18	66 03.2	46 13.8	N 9 17.0	148 19.8	S23 36.4	135 32.9	S22 06.0	126 07.2	S20 36.4	Vega	80 36.1	N38 47.9
19	81 05.7	61 13.7	18.3	163 20.3	36.3	150 34.9	05.9	141 09.4	36.4	Zuben'ubi	137 00.2	S16 07.4
20	96 08.1	76 13.6	19.5	178 20.9	36.2	165 36.8	05.9	156 11.6	36.3		SHA	Mer. Pass.
21	111 10.6	91 13.5	. . 20.7	193 21.5	. . 36.2	180 38.8	. . 05.8	171 13.8	. . 36.3		° ′	h m
22	126 13.0	106 13.4	22.0	208 22.1	36.1	195 40.7	05.7	186 16.0	36.2	Venus	341 58.5	14 55
23	141 15.5	121 13.3	23.2	223 22.7	36.1	210 42.7	05.7	201 18.2	36.2	Mars	83 35.6	8 08
	h m									Jupiter	69 51.1	9 02
Mer. Pass.	13 40.4	v −0.1	d 1.2	v 0.6	d 0.0	v 2.0	d 0.1	v 2.2	d 0.0	Saturn	60 15.1	9 40

UT	SUN		MOON					Lat.	Twilight		Sunrise	Moonrise			
									Naut.	Civil		24	25	26	27
	GHA	Dec	GHA	v	Dec	d	HP	°	h m	h m	h m	h m	h m	h m	h m
d h	° ′	° ′	° ′	′	° ′	′	′	N 72	05 32	06 50	08 01	09 17	08 54	08 35	08 17
24 00	176 39.9	S 9 44.3	171 17.8	14.6	S12 26.4	10.2	54.3	N 70	05 35	06 45	07 49	08 59	08 45	08 33	08 21
01	191 40.0	43.4	185 51.4	14.7	12 16.2	10.3	54.3	68	05 37	06 41	07 38	08 45	08 38	08 30	08 23
02	206 40.0	42.4	200 25.1	14.8	12 05.9	10.3	54.3	66	05 38	06 38	07 30	08 34	08 31	08 29	08 26
03	221 40.1 ..	41.5	214 58.9	14.8	11 55.6	10.4	54.2	64	05 40	06 34	07 23	08 24	08 26	08 27	08 28
04	236 40.2	40.6	229 32.7	14.8	11 45.2	10.4	54.2	62	05 41	06 32	07 17	08 16	08 21	08 26	08 30
05	251 40.3	39.7	244 06.5	14.9	11 34.8	10.5	54.2	60	05 41	06 29	07 12	08 09	08 17	08 24	08 31
06	266 40.4	S 9 38.8	258 40.4	14.9	S11 24.3	10.4	54.2	N 58	05 42	06 27	07 07	08 02	08 13	08 23	08 33
07	281 40.5	37.8	273 14.3	15.0	11 13.9	10.6	54.2	56	05 42	06 25	07 03	07 57	08 10	08 22	08 34
08	296 40.6	36.9	287 48.3	15.0	11 03.3	10.6	54.2	54	05 42	06 23	06 59	07 52	08 07	08 21	08 35
M 09	311 40.7 ..	36.0	302 22.3	15.1	10 52.7	10.6	54.2	52	05 43	06 22	06 56	07 47	08 05	08 21	08 36
O 10	326 40.8	35.1	316 56.4	15.1	10 42.1	10.7	54.2	50	05 43	06 20	06 53	07 43	08 02	08 20	08 37
N 11	341 40.8	34.2	331 30.5	15.2	10 31.4	10.7	54.2	45	05 42	06 16	06 46	07 34	07 57	08 18	08 39
D 12	356 40.9	S 9 33.2	346 04.7	15.2	S10 20.7	10.7	54.2	N 40	05 41	06 13	06 40	07 26	07 52	08 17	08 41
A 13	11 41.0	32.3	0 38.9	15.2	10 10.0	10.8	54.2	35	05 40	06 10	06 35	07 20	07 49	08 16	08 43
Y 14	26 41.1	31.4	15 13.1	15.3	9 59.2	10.8	54.2	30	05 39	06 07	06 31	07 14	07 45	08 15	08 44
15	41 41.2 ..	30.5	29 47.4	15.3	9 48.4	10.8	54.1	20	05 35	06 01	06 23	07 04	07 39	08 13	08 46
16	56 41.3	29.5	44 21.7	15.3	9 37.6	10.9	54.1	N 10	05 31	05 55	06 16	06 55	07 34	08 12	08 49
17	71 41.4	28.6	58 56.0	15.4	9 26.7	10.9	54.1	0	05 25	05 49	06 10	06 47	07 29	08 10	08 51
18	86 41.5	S 9 27.7	73 30.4	15.4	S 9 15.8	11.0	54.1	S 10	05 17	05 42	06 03	06 39	07 24	08 09	08 53
19	101 41.6	26.8	88 04.8	15.5	9 04.8	11.0	54.1	20	05 07	05 34	05 56	06 30	07 19	08 07	08 55
20	116 41.7	25.8	102 39.3	15.5	8 53.8	11.0	54.1	30	04 54	05 23	05 48	06 20	07 13	08 05	08 57
21	131 41.7 ..	24.9	117 13.8	15.5	8 42.8	11.0	54.1	35	04 46	05 17	05 43	06 14	07 09	08 04	08 59
22	146 41.8	24.0	131 48.3	15.6	8 31.8	11.1	54.1	40	04 36	05 09	05 37	06 07	07 05	08 03	09 00
23	161 41.9	23.1	146 22.9	15.6	8 20.7	11.1	54.1	45	04 23	05 00	05 31	05 59	07 01	08 02	09 02
25 00	176 42.0	S 9 22.1	160 57.5	15.7	S 8 09.6	11.1	54.1	S 50	04 07	04 49	05 23	05 50	06 55	08 00	09 05
01	191 42.1	21.2	175 32.2	15.6	7 58.5	11.2	54.1	52	03 59	04 43	05 19	05 45	06 53	07 59	09 06
02	206 42.2	20.3	190 06.8	15.7	7 47.3	11.2	54.1	54	03 50	04 37	05 15	05 41	06 50	07 59	09 07
03	221 42.3 ..	19.4	204 41.5	15.8	7 36.1	11.2	54.1	56	03 40	04 31	05 11	05 35	06 47	07 58	09 08
04	236 42.4	18.4	219 16.3	15.7	7 24.9	11.3	54.1	58	03 28	04 23	05 06	05 29	06 44	07 57	09 10
05	251 42.5	17.5	233 51.0	15.8	7 13.6	11.2	54.1	S 60	03 14	04 14	05 00	05 22	06 40	07 56	09 11
06	266 42.6	S 9 16.6	248 25.8	15.9	S 7 02.4	11.3	54.1								

07	281 42.7	15.7	263 00.7	15.8	6 51.1	11.4	54.0	Lat.	Sunset	Twilight		Moonset			
08	296 42.8	14.7	277 35.5	15.9	6 39.7	11.3	54.0			Civil	Naut.	24	25	26	27
T 09	311 42.9 ..	13.8	292 10.4	15.9	6 28.4	11.4	54.0								
U 10	326 43.0	12.9	306 45.3	15.9	6 17.0	11.3	54.0	°	h m	h m	h m	h m	h m	h m	h m
E 11	341 43.1	11.9	321 20.2	16.0	6 05.7	11.5	54.0	N 72	16 27	17 39	18 57	17 00	18 49	20 34	22 19
S 12	356 43.1	S 9 11.0	335 55.2	16.0	S 5 54.2	11.4	54.0	N 70	16 39	17 43	18 54	17 15	18 56	20 33	22 11
D 13	11 43.2	10.1	350 30.2	16.0	5 42.8	11.4	54.0	68	16 49	17 47	18 51	17 28	19 01	20 33	22 05
A 14	26 43.3	09.2	5 05.2	16.0	5 31.4	11.5	54.0	66	16 58	17 50	18 50	17 38	19 06	20 33	22 00
Y 15	41 43.4 ..	08.2	19 40.2	16.1	5 19.9	11.5	54.0	64	17 04	17 53	18 48	17 46	19 10	20 33	21 55
16	56 43.5	07.3	34 15.3	16.1	5 08.4	11.5	54.0	62	17 10	17 56	18 47	17 53	19 13	20 32	21 51
17	71 43.6	06.4	48 50.4	16.1	4 56.9	11.5	54.0	60	17 16	17 58	18 46	18 00	19 16	20 32	21 48
18	86 43.7	S 9 05.4	63 25.5	16.1	S 4 45.4	11.5	54.0	N 58	17 20	18 00	18 46	18 05	19 19	20 32	21 45
19	101 43.8	04.5	78 00.6	16.1	4 33.9	11.6	54.0	56	17 24	18 02	18 45	18 10	19 21	20 32	21 42
20	116 43.9	03.6	92 35.7	16.2	4 22.3	11.6	54.0	54	17 28	18 04	18 45	18 14	19 23	20 32	21 40
21	131 44.0 ..	02.7	107 10.9	16.2	4 10.7	11.5	54.0	52	17 31	18 06	18 45	18 18	19 25	20 31	21 38
22	146 44.1	01.7	121 46.1	16.2	3 59.2	11.6	54.0	50	17 34	18 07	18 45	18 22	19 27	20 31	21 36
23	161 44.2	9 00.8	136 21.3	16.2	3 47.6	11.6	54.0	45	17 41	18 11	18 45	18 29	19 30	20 31	21 32
26 00	176 44.3	S 8 59.9	150 56.5	16.2	S 3 36.0	11.7	54.0	N 40	17 47	18 14	18 45	18 35	19 33	20 31	21 28
01	191 44.4	58.9	165 31.7	16.3	3 24.3	11.6	54.0	35	17 51	18 17	18 46	18 41	19 36	20 31	21 25
02	206 44.5	58.0	180 07.0	16.2	3 12.7	11.6	54.0	30	17 56	18 20	18 48	18 46	19 38	20 30	21 23
03	221 44.6 ..	57.1	194 42.2	16.3	3 01.1	11.7	54.0	20	18 03	18 26	18 51	18 54	19 42	20 30	21 18
04	236 44.7	56.1	209 17.5	16.3	2 49.4	11.6	54.0	N 10	18 10	18 31	18 56	19 01	19 46	20 30	21 14
05	251 44.8	55.2	223 52.8	16.3	2 37.8	11.7	54.0	0	18 16	18 37	19 02	19 08	19 49	20 30	21 10
06	266 44.9	S 8 54.3	238 28.1	16.3	S 2 26.1	11.7	54.0	S 10	18 23	18 44	19 09	19 14	19 52	20 29	21 06
W 07	281 45.0	53.3	253 03.4	16.3	2 14.4	11.7	54.0	20	18 30	18 52	19 19	19 21	19 56	20 29	21 02
E 08	296 45.1	52.4	267 38.7	16.3	2 02.7	11.7	54.0	30	18 38	19 03	19 31	19 29	19 59	20 29	20 58
D 09	311 45.2 ..	51.5	282 14.0	16.1	1 51.0	11.7	54.0	35	18 43	19 09	19 40	19 34	20 01	20 28	20 55
N 10	326 45.3	50.5	296 49.4	16.3	1 39.3	11.7	54.0	40	18 48	19 16	19 50	19 39	20 04	20 28	20 52
E 11	341 45.4	49.6	311 24.7	16.3	1 27.6	11.7	54.0	45	18 55	19 25	20 02	19 45	20 07	20 28	20 49
S 12	356 45.5	S 8 48.7	326 00.0	16.4	S 1 15.9	11.7	54.0	S 50	19 02	19 36	20 18	19 52	20 10	20 28	20 45
D 13	11 45.6	47.7	340 35.4	16.4	1 04.2	11.7	54.0	52	19 06	19 41	20 25	19 55	20 12	20 27	20 43
A 14	26 45.7	46.8	355 10.8	16.3	0 52.5	11.7	54.0	54	19 10	19 47	20 34	19 59	20 13	20 27	20 41
Y 15	41 45.8 ..	45.9	9 46.1	16.4	0 40.8	11.7	54.0	56	19 14	19 54	20 44	20 02	20 15	20 27	20 39
16	56 45.9	44.9	24 21.5	16.4	0 29.1	11.8	54.0	58	19 19	20 01	20 56	20 07	20 17	20 27	20 36
17	71 46.0	44.0	38 56.9	16.4	0 17.3	11.7	54.0	S 60	19 24	20 10	21 10	20 12	20 19	20 27	20 34
18	86 46.1	S 8 43.1	53 32.3	16.3	S 0 05.6	11.7	54.0								

19	101 46.2	42.1	68 07.6	16.4	N 0 06.1	11.7	54.0		SUN			MOON			
20	116 46.3	41.2	82 43.0	16.4	0 17.8	11.7	54.0	Day	Eqn. of Time		Mer.	Mer. Pass.		Age	Phase
21	131 46.4 ..	40.3	97 18.4	16.4	0 29.5	11.8	54.0		00ʰ	12ʰ	Pass.	Upper	Lower		
22	146 46.5	39.3	111 53.8	16.3	0 41.3	11.7	54.0	d	m s	m s	h m	h m	h m	d	%
23	161 46.7	38.4	126 29.1	16.4	N 0 53.0	11.7	54.0	24	13 21	13 16	12 13	12 57	00 36	01	1
								25	13 12	13 08	12 13	13 39	01 18	02	3
	SD 16.2	d 0.9	SD 14.8		14.7		14.7	26	13 03	12 58	12 13	14 20	02 00	03	7

UT	ARIES GHA	VENUS −4.3 GHA	Dec	MARS +1.1 GHA	Dec	JUPITER −2.0 GHA	Dec	SATURN +0.7 GHA	Dec	STARS Name	SHA	Dec
27 00	156 18.0	136 13.2	N 9 24.4	238 23.2	S23 36.0	225 44.7	S22 05.6	216 20.4	S20 36.1	Acamar	315 15.0	S40 13.9
01	171 20.4	151 13.1	25.7	253 23.8	36.0	240 46.6	05.6	231 22.6	36.1	Achernar	335 23.7	S57 08.5
02	186 22.9	166 13.0	26.9	268 24.4	35.9	255 48.6	05.5	246 24.8	36.0	Acrux	173 03.6	S63 12.5
03	201 25.4	181 12.9 ..	28.1	283 25.0 ..	35.9	270 50.5 ..	05.4	261 27.0 ..	36.0	Adhara	255 08.7	S29 00.2
04	216 27.8	196 12.7	29.4	298 25.6	35.8	285 52.5	05.4	276 29.2	35.9	Aldebaran	290 44.1	N16 32.8
05	231 30.3	211 12.6	30.6	313 26.2	35.8	300 54.5	05.3	291 31.4	35.9			
06	246 32.8	226 12.5	N 9 31.8	328 26.7	S23 35.7	315 56.4	S22 05.2	306 33.6	S20 35.8	Alioth	166 16.1	N55 50.9
07	261 35.2	241 12.4	33.1	343 27.3	35.6	330 58.4	05.2	321 35.8	35.8	Alkaid	152 54.9	N49 12.6
T 08	276 37.7	256 12.3	34.3	358 27.9	35.6	346 00.3	05.1	336 38.0	35.7	Alnair	27 38.4	S46 51.9
H 09	291 40.2	271 12.2 ..	35.5	13 28.5 ..	35.5	1 02.3 ..	05.1	351 40.2 ..	35.7	Alnilam	275 41.6	S 1 11.6
U 10	306 42.6	286 12.1	36.7	28 29.1	35.5	16 04.3	05.0	6 42.4	35.7	Alphard	217 51.3	S 8 44.9
R 11	321 45.1	301 12.0	38.0	43 29.6	35.4	31 06.2	04.9	21 44.6	35.6			
S 12	336 47.5	316 11.9	N 9 39.2	58 30.2	S23 35.3	46 08.2	S22 04.9	36 46.8	S20 35.6	Alphecca	126 07.0	N26 38.7
D 13	351 50.0	331 11.8	40.4	73 30.8	35.3	61 10.1	04.8	51 49.0	35.5	Alpheratz	357 39.1	N29 11.9
A 14	6 52.5	346 11.7	41.7	88 31.4	35.2	76 12.1	04.8	66 51.2	35.5	Altair	62 04.0	N 8 55.2
Y 15	21 54.9	1 11.6 ..	42.9	103 32.0 ..	35.2	91 14.1 ..	04.7	81 53.5 ..	35.4	Ankaa	353 11.5	S42 12.1
16	36 57.4	16 11.5	44.1	118 32.6	35.1	106 16.0	04.6	96 55.7	35.4	Antares	112 20.6	S26 28.4
17	51 59.9	31 11.4	45.3	133 33.1	35.0	121 18.0	04.6	111 57.9	35.3			
18	67 02.3	46 11.3	N 9 46.6	148 33.7	S23 35.0	136 19.9	S22 04.5	127 00.1	S20 35.3	Arcturus	145 51.3	N19 04.6
19	82 04.8	61 11.2	47.8	163 34.3	34.9	151 21.9	04.4	142 02.3	35.2	Atria	107 18.4	S69 03.4
20	97 07.3	76 11.1	49.0	178 34.9	34.9	166 23.9	04.4	157 04.5	35.2	Avior	234 15.7	S59 34.6
21	112 09.7	91 11.0 ..	50.2	193 35.5 ..	34.8	181 25.8 ..	04.3	172 06.7 ..	35.1	Bellatrix	278 27.0	N 6 21.9
22	127 12.2	106 10.9	51.5	208 36.0	34.7	196 27.8	04.3	187 08.9	35.1	Betelgeuse	270 56.2	N 7 24.5
23	142 14.6	121 10.8	52.7	223 36.6	34.7	211 29.8	04.2	202 11.1	35.1			
28 00	157 17.1	136 10.7	N 9 53.9	238 37.2	S23 34.6	226 31.7	S22 04.1	217 13.3	S20 35.0	Canopus	263 53.9	S52 42.7
01	172 19.6	151 10.6	55.1	253 37.8	34.5	241 33.7	04.1	232 15.5	35.0	Capella	280 27.5	N46 01.1
02	187 22.0	166 10.5	56.4	268 38.4	34.5	256 35.7	04.0	247 17.7	34.9	Deneb	49 28.8	N45 20.9
03	202 24.5	181 10.4 ..	57.6	283 39.0 ..	34.4	271 37.6 ..	04.0	262 19.9 ..	34.9	Denebola	182 28.6	N14 27.5
04	217 27.0	196 10.3	9 58.8	298 39.5	34.4	286 39.6	03.9	277 22.1	34.8	Diphda	348 51.5	S17 52.9
05	232 29.4	211 10.2	10 00.0	313 40.1	34.3	301 41.5	03.8	292 24.3	34.8			
06	247 31.9	226 10.1	N10 01.2	328 40.7	S23 34.2	316 43.5	S22 03.8	307 26.5	S20 34.7	Dubhe	193 45.3	N61 38.5
07	262 34.4	241 10.0	02.5	343 41.3	34.2	331 45.5	03.7	322 28.7	34.7	Elnath	278 06.7	N28 37.4
08	277 36.8	256 09.9	03.7	358 41.9	34.1	346 47.4	03.6	337 30.9	34.6	Eltanin	90 44.2	N51 28.9
F 09	292 39.3	271 09.8 ..	04.9	13 42.4 ..	34.0	1 49.4 ..	03.6	352 33.1 ..	34.6	Enif	33 42.9	N 9 57.9
R 10	307 41.8	286 09.7	06.1	28 43.0	34.0	16 51.4	03.5	7 35.3	34.5	Fomalhaut	15 19.2	S29 31.1
I 11	322 44.2	301 09.6	07.3	43 43.6	33.9	31 53.3	03.5	22 37.5	34.5			
D 12	337 46.7	316 09.5	N10 08.6	58 44.2	S23 33.8	46 55.3	S22 03.4	37 39.7	S20 34.5	Gacrux	171 55.3	S57 13.4
A 13	352 49.1	331 09.4	09.8	73 44.8	33.8	61 57.3	03.3	52 41.9	34.4	Gienah	175 47.3	S17 39.2
Y 14	7 51.6	346 09.3	11.0	88 45.4	33.7	76 59.2	03.3	67 44.2	34.4	Hadar	148 41.0	S60 27.9
15	22 54.1	1 09.2 ..	12.2	103 45.9 ..	33.6	92 01.2 ..	03.2	82 46.4 ..	34.3	Hamal	327 55.8	N23 33.3
16	37 56.5	16 09.1	13.4	118 46.5	33.5	107 03.2	03.1	97 48.6	34.3	Kaus Aust.	83 37.9	S34 22.3
17	52 59.0	31 08.9	14.7	133 47.1	33.5	122 05.1	03.1	112 50.8	34.2			
18	68 01.5	46 08.8	N10 15.9	148 47.7	S23 33.4	137 07.1	S22 03.0	127 53.0	S20 34.2	Kochab	137 19.5	N74 04.2
19	83 03.9	61 08.7	17.1	163 48.3	33.3	152 09.1	03.0	142 55.2	34.1	Markab	13 34.1	N15 18.6
20	98 06.4	76 08.6	18.3	178 48.9	33.3	167 11.0	02.9	157 57.4	34.1	Menkar	314 10.3	N 4 09.9
21	113 08.9	91 08.5 ..	19.5	193 49.4 ..	33.2	182 13.0 ..	02.8	172 59.6 ..	34.0	Menkent	148 01.9	S36 27.9
22	128 11.3	106 08.4	20.7	208 50.0	33.1	197 15.0	02.8	188 01.8	34.0	Miaplacidus	221 38.0	S69 48.1
23	143 13.8	121 08.3	21.9	223 50.6	33.1	212 16.9	02.7	203 04.0	33.9			
29 00	158 16.2	136 08.2	N10 23.2	238 51.2	S23 33.0	227 18.9	S22 02.7	218 06.2	S20 33.9	Mirfak	308 33.9	N49 56.0
01	173 18.7	151 08.1	24.4	253 51.8	32.9	242 20.9	02.6	233 08.4	33.9	Nunki	75 52.8	S26 16.2
02	188 21.2	166 08.0	25.6	268 52.3	32.8	257 22.8	02.5	248 10.6	33.8	Peacock	53 12.4	S56 40.1
03	203 23.6	181 07.9 ..	26.8	283 52.9 ..	32.8	272 24.8 ..	02.5	263 12.8 ..	33.8	Pollux	243 21.8	N27 58.6
04	218 26.1	196 07.8	28.0	298 53.5	32.7	287 26.8	02.4	278 15.0	33.7	Procyon	244 54.7	N 5 10.2
05	233 28.6	211 07.7	29.2	313 54.1	32.7	302 28.7	02.3	293 17.2	33.7			
06	248 31.0	226 07.6	N10 30.4	328 54.7	S23 32.5	317 30.7	S22 02.3	308 19.5	S20 33.6	Rasalhague	96 02.3	N12 32.6
07	263 33.5	241 07.5	31.6	343 55.3	32.5	332 32.7	02.2	323 21.7	33.6	Regulus	207 38.3	N11 52.1
S 08	278 36.0	256 07.4	32.9	358 55.8	32.4	347 34.6	02.2	338 23.9	33.5	Rigel	281 07.6	S 8 11.0
A 09	293 38.4	271 07.3 ..	34.1	13 56.4 ..	32.3	2 36.6 ..	02.1	353 26.1 ..	33.5	Rigil Kent.	139 45.2	S60 54.7
T 10	308 40.9	286 07.2	35.3	28 57.0	32.2	17 38.6	02.0	8 28.3	33.4	Sabik	102 07.3	S15 44.9
U 11	323 43.4	301 07.1	36.5	43 57.6	32.2	32 40.5	02.0	23 30.5	33.4			
R 12	338 45.8	316 07.0	N10 37.7	58 58.2	S23 32.1	47 42.5	S22 01.9	38 32.7	S20 33.3	Schedar	349 35.8	N56 38.8
D 13	353 48.3	331 06.9	38.9	73 58.7	32.0	62 44.5	01.8	53 34.9	33.3	Shaula	96 15.8	S37 06.9
A 14	8 50.7	346 06.8	40.1	88 59.3	31.9	77 46.5	01.8	68 37.1	33.3	Sirius	258 29.5	S16 44.9
Y 15	23 53.2	1 06.7 ..	41.3	103 59.9 ..	31.9	92 48.4 ..	01.7	83 39.3 ..	33.2	Spica	158 26.2	S11 15.9
16	38 55.7	16 06.6	42.5	119 00.5	31.8	107 50.4	01.7	98 41.5	33.2	Suhail	222 48.7	S43 31.0
17	53 58.1	31 06.5	43.7	134 01.1	31.7	122 52.4	01.6	113 43.7	33.1			
18	69 00.6	46 06.4	N10 44.9	149 01.7	S23 31.6	137 54.3	S22 01.5	128 45.9	S20 33.1	Vega	80 36.1	N38 47.9
19	84 03.1	61 06.3	46.2	164 02.2	31.5	152 56.3	01.5	143 48.2	33.0	Zuben'ubi	137 00.2	S16 07.4
20	99 05.5	76 06.2	47.4	179 02.8	31.5	167 58.3	01.4	158 50.4	33.0		SHA	Mer.Pass.
21	114 08.0	91 06.1 ..	48.6	194 03.4 ..	31.4	183 00.3 ..	01.4	173 52.6 ..	32.9	Venus	338 53.6	14 55
22	129 10.5	106 06.0	49.8	209 04.0	31.3	198 02.2	01.3	188 54.8	32.9	Mars	81 20.1	8 05
23	144 12.3	121 05.9	51.0	224 04.6	31.2	213 04.2	01.2	203 57.0	32.8	Jupiter	69 14.6	8 53
Mer.Pass. 13 28.6	v −0.1 d 1.2	v 0.6	d 0.1	v 2.0	d 0.1	v 2.2	d 0.0			Saturn	59 56.2	9 30

UT	SUN GHA	SUN Dec	MOON GHA	MOON v	MOON Dec	MOON d	MOON HP
d h	° ′	° ′	° ′	′	° ′	′	′
27 00	176 46.8	S 8 37.4	141 04.5	16.4	N 1 04.7	11.7	54.0
01	191 46.9	36.5	155 39.9	16.4	1 16.4	11.7	54.0
02	206 47.0	35.6	170 15.3	16.3	1 28.1	11.7	54.0
03	221 47.1	.. 34.6	184 50.6	16.4	1 39.8	11.7	54.0
04	236 47.2	33.7	199 26.0	16.3	1 51.5	11.7	54.0
05	251 47.3	32.8	214 01.3	16.4	2 03.2	11.7	54.0
06	266 47.4	S 8 31.8	228 36.7	16.3	N 2 14.9	11.6	54.0
07	281 47.5	30.9	243 12.0	16.3	2 26.5	11.7	54.0
T 08	296 47.6	29.9	257 47.3	16.3	2 38.2	11.7	54.0
H 09	311 47.7	.. 29.0	272 22.6	16.3	2 49.9	11.6	54.0
U 10	326 47.8	28.1	286 57.9	16.3	3 01.5	11.7	54.0
R 11	341 47.9	27.1	301 33.2	16.3	3 13.2	11.6	54.0
S 12	356 48.0	S 8 26.2	316 08.5	16.2	N 3 24.8	11.6	54.0
D 13	11 48.1	25.2	330 43.7	16.3	3 36.4	11.6	54.0
A 14	26 48.2	24.3	345 19.0	16.2	3 48.0	11.6	54.0
Y 15	41 48.4	.. 23.4	359 54.2	16.2	3 59.6	11.6	54.0
16	56 48.5	22.4	14 29.4	16.2	4 11.2	11.5	54.1
17	71 48.6	21.5	29 04.6	16.2	4 22.7	11.6	54.1
18	86 48.7	S 8 20.5	43 39.8	16.2	N 4 34.3	11.5	54.1
19	101 48.8	19.6	58 15.0	16.1	4 45.8	11.5	54.1
20	116 48.9	18.7	72 50.1	16.2	4 57.3	11.5	54.1
21	131 49.0	.. 17.7	87 25.3	16.1	5 08.8	11.5	54.1
22	146 49.1	16.8	102 00.4	16.1	5 20.3	11.5	54.1
23	161 49.2	15.8	116 35.5	16.0	5 31.8	11.5	54.1
28 00	176 49.3	S 8 14.9	131 10.5	16.0	N 5 43.3	11.4	54.1
01	191 49.4	14.0	145 45.5	16.1	5 54.7	11.4	54.1
02	206 49.6	13.0	160 20.6	15.9	6 06.1	11.4	54.1
03	221 49.7	.. 12.1	174 55.5	16.0	6 17.5	11.3	54.1
04	236 49.8	11.1	189 30.5	15.9	6 28.8	11.4	54.1
05	251 49.9	10.2	204 05.4	15.9	6 40.2	11.3	54.2
06	266 50.0	S 8 09.2	218 40.3	15.9	N 6 51.5	11.3	54.2
07	281 50.1	08.3	233 15.2	15.9	7 02.8	11.3	54.2
F 08	296 50.2	07.4	247 50.1	15.8	7 14.1	11.2	54.2
R 09	311 50.3	.. 06.4	262 24.9	15.8	7 25.3	11.3	54.2
I 10	326 50.5	05.5	276 59.7	15.7	7 36.6	11.2	54.2
11	341 50.6	04.5	291 34.4	15.7	7 47.8	11.2	54.2
D 12	356 50.7	S 8 03.6	306 09.1	15.7	N 7 59.0	11.1	54.2
A 13	11 50.8	02.6	320 43.8	15.7	8 10.1	11.1	54.2
Y 14	26 50.9	01.7	335 18.5	15.6	8 21.2	11.1	54.2
15	41 51.0	8 00.8	349 53.1	15.6	8 32.3	11.1	54.3
16	56 51.1	7 59.8	4 27.7	15.5	8 43.4	11.0	54.3
17	71 51.2	58.9	19 02.2	15.5	8 54.4	11.0	54.3
18	86 51.4	S 7 57.9	33 36.7	15.5	N 9 05.4	11.0	54.3
19	101 51.5	57.0	48 11.2	15.4	9 16.4	10.9	54.3
20	116 51.6	56.0	62 45.6	15.4	9 27.3	10.9	54.3
21	131 51.7	.. 55.1	77 20.0	15.3	9 38.2	10.9	54.3
22	146 51.8	54.1	91 54.3	15.3	9 49.1	10.8	54.3
23	161 51.9	53.2	106 28.6	15.3	9 59.9	10.8	54.4
29 00	176 52.1	S 7 52.2	121 02.9	15.2	N10 10.7	10.8	54.4
01	191 52.2	51.3	135 37.1	15.2	10 21.5	10.7	54.4
02	206 52.3	50.3	150 11.3	15.1	10 32.2	10.7	54.4
03	221 52.4	.. 49.4	164 45.4	15.1	10 42.9	10.7	54.4
04	236 52.5	48.4	179 19.5	15.0	10 53.6	10.6	54.4
05	251 52.6	47.5	193 53.5	15.0	11 04.2	10.6	54.4
06	266 52.8	S 7 46.6	208 27.5	14.9	N11 14.8	10.5	54.5
07	281 52.9	45.6	223 01.4	14.9	11 25.3	10.5	54.5
S 08	296 53.0	44.7	237 35.3	14.9	11 35.8	10.5	54.5
A 09	311 53.1	.. 43.7	252 09.2	14.7	11 46.3	10.4	54.5
T 10	326 53.2	42.8	266 42.9	14.8	11 56.7	10.4	54.5
U 11	341 53.3	41.8	281 16.7	14.7	12 07.1	10.3	54.5
R 12	356 53.5	S 7 40.9	295 50.4	14.6	N12 17.4	10.3	54.6
D 13	11 53.6	39.9	310 24.0	14.6	12 27.7	10.2	54.6
A 14	26 53.7	39.0	324 57.6	14.5	12 37.9	10.2	54.6
Y 15	41 53.8	.. 38.0	339 31.1	14.4	12 48.1	10.2	54.6
16	56 53.9	37.1	354 04.5	14.4	12 58.3	10.1	54.6
17	71 54.1	36.1	8 37.9	14.4	13 08.4	10.0	54.6
18	86 54.2	S 7 35.2	23 11.3	14.3	N13 18.4	10.0	54.7
19	101 54.3	34.2	37 44.6	14.2	13 28.4	10.0	54.7
20	116 54.4	33.3	52 17.8	14.2	13 38.4	9.9	54.7
21	131 54.5	.. 32.3	66 51.0	14.1	13 48.3	9.9	54.7
22	146 54.7	31.4	81 24.1	14.0	13 58.2	9.8	54.7
23	161 54.8	30.4	95 57.1	14.0	N14 08.0	9.7	54.8
	SD 16.2	d 0.9	SD 14.7		14.8		14.9

Twilight / Moonrise

Lat.	Naut.	Civil	Sunrise	Moonrise 27	28	29	1
°	h m	h m	h m	h m	h m	h m	h m
N 72	05 18	06 35	07 45	08 17	07 58	07 35	07 01
N 70	05 22	06 32	07 34	08 21	08 08	07 54	07 35
68	05 25	06 29	07 26	08 23	08 16	08 09	08 00
66	05 28	06 27	07 19	08 26	08 23	08 21	08 19
64	05 30	06 25	07 13	08 28	08 29	08 31	08 35
62	05 32	06 23	07 08	08 30	08 34	08 40	08 48
60	05 33	06 21	07 03	08 31	08 39	08 47	08 59
N 58	05 34	06 20	06 59	08 33	08 43	08 54	09 08
56	05 35	06 18	06 55	08 34	08 46	09 00	09 17
54	05 36	06 17	06 52	08 35	08 50	09 05	09 24
52	05 36	06 15	06 49	08 36	08 52	09 10	09 31
50	05 37	06 14	06 47	08 37	08 55	09 15	09 37
45	05 37	06 11	06 41	08 39	09 01	09 24	09 51
N 40	05 37	06 09	06 36	08 41	09 06	09 32	10 02
35	05 37	06 06	06 32	08 43	09 10	09 39	10 11
30	05 36	06 04	06 28	08 44	09 14	09 45	10 19
20	05 33	05 59	06 21	08 46	09 20	09 56	10 34
N 10	05 29	05 54	06 15	08 49	09 26	10 05	10 47
0	05 24	05 48	06 09	08 51	09 32	10 14	10 58
S 10	05 17	05 42	06 03	08 53	09 37	10 23	11 10
20	05 09	05 35	05 57	08 55	09 43	10 32	11 23
30	04 57	05 25	05 50	08 57	09 50	10 43	11 38
35	04 49	05 20	05 45	08 59	09 54	10 50	11 47
40	04 40	05 13	05 41	09 00	09 58	10 57	11 57
45	04 28	05 05	05 35	09 02	10 03	11 05	12 08
S 50	04 13	04 54	05 28	09 05	10 10	11 16	12 23
52	04 06	04 49	05 25	09 06	10 13	11 20	12 29
54	03 58	04 44	05 21	09 07	10 16	11 26	12 37
56	03 48	04 38	05 17	09 08	10 19	11 31	12 45
58	03 37	04 31	05 13	09 10	10 23	11 38	12 54
S 60	03 25	04 23	05 08	09 11	10 28	11 45	13 05

Twilight / Moonset

Lat.	Sunset	Civil	Naut.	Moonset 27	28	29	1
°	h m	h m	h m	h m	h m	h m	h m
N 72	16 42	17 52	19 10	22 19	24 09	00 09	02 14
N 70	16 53	17 55	19 06	22 11	23 52	25 42	01 42
68	17 01	17 58	19 02	22 05	23 39	25 18	01 18
66	17 08	18 00	18 59	22 00	23 28	25 00	01 00
64	17 14	18 02	18 57	21 55	23 19	24 46	00 46
62	17 19	18 04	18 55	21 51	23 11	24 33	00 33
60	17 23	18 05	18 54	21 48	23 05	24 23	00 23
N 58	17 27	18 07	18 52	21 45	22 59	24 14	00 14
56	17 31	18 08	18 51	21 42	22 54	24 06	00 06
54	17 34	18 10	18 51	21 40	22 49	23 59	25 11
52	17 37	18 11	18 50	21 38	22 45	23 53	25 02
50	17 39	18 12	18 49	21 36	22 41	23 47	24 55
45	17 45	18 15	18 49	21 32	22 33	23 35	24 39
N 40	17 50	18 17	18 49	21 28	22 26	23 25	24 26
35	17 54	18 20	18 49	21 25	22 21	23 17	24 15
30	17 58	18 22	18 50	21 23	22 15	23 10	24 05
20	18 04	18 27	18 52	21 18	22 07	22 57	23 49
N 10	18 10	18 32	18 56	21 14	21 59	22 46	23 34
0	18 16	18 37	19 01	21 10	21 52	22 35	23 21
S 10	18 22	18 43	19 08	21 06	21 45	22 25	23 07
20	18 28	18 50	19 16	21 02	21 37	22 14	22 53
30	18 35	18 59	19 28	20 58	21 28	22 01	22 37
35	18 39	19 05	19 35	20 55	21 23	21 54	22 27
40	18 44	19 12	19 45	20 52	21 18	21 45	22 17
45	18 50	19 20	19 56	20 49	21 11	21 36	22 04
S 50	18 56	19 30	20 11	20 45	21 03	21 24	21 49
52	18 59	19 35	20 18	20 43	21 00	21 19	21 42
54	19 03	19 40	20 26	20 41	20 56	21 13	21 34
56	19 07	19 46	20 35	20 39	20 52	21 06	21 25
58	19 11	19 52	20 45	20 36	20 47	20 59	21 15
S 60	19 15	20 00	20 58	20 34	20 41	20 51	21 04

Day	SUN Eqn. of Time 00ʰ	12ʰ	SUN Mer. Pass.	MOON Mer. Pass. Upper	Lower	Age	Phase
d	m s	m s	h m	h m	h m	d	%
27	12 53	12 48	12 13	15 00	02 40	04	13
28	12 43	12 38	12 13	15 42	03 21	05	20
29	12 32	12 26	12 12	16 24	04 03	06	28

UT	ARIES GHA	VENUS −4.3 GHA	Dec	MARS +1.1 GHA	Dec	JUPITER −2.0 GHA	Dec	SATURN +0.7 GHA	Dec	STARS Name	SHA	Dec
1 00	159 15.4	136 05.8	N10 52.2	239 05.2	S23 31.1	228 06.2	S22 01.2	218 59.2	S20 32.8	Acamar	315 15.0	S40 13.8
01	174 17.9	151 05.7	53.4	254 05.7	31.1	243 08.1	01.1	234 01.4	32.8	Achernar	335 23.7	S57 08.5
02	189 20.3	166 05.6	54.6	269 06.3	31.0	258 10.1	01.0	249 03.6	32.7	Acrux	173 03.6	S63 12.5
03	204 22.8	181 05.5 ..	55.8	284 06.9 ..	30.9	273 12.1 ..	01.0	264 05.8 ..	32.7	Adhara	255 08.7	S29 00.3
04	219 25.2	196 05.4	57.0	299 07.5	30.8	288 14.1	00.9	279 08.0	32.6	Aldebaran	290 44.1	N16 32.8
05	234 27.7	211 05.3	58.2	314 08.1	30.7	303 16.0	00.9	294 10.2	32.6			
06	249 30.2	226 05.2	N10 59.4	329 08.7	S23 30.6	318 18.0	S22 00.8	309 12.5	S20 32.5	Alioth	166 16.1	N55 50.9
07	264 32.6	241 05.1	11 00.6	344 09.2	30.6	333 20.0	00.7	324 14.7	32.5	Alkaid	152 54.9	N49 12.6
08	279 35.1	256 05.0	01.8	359 09.8	30.5	348 21.9	00.7	339 16.9	32.4	Alnair	27 38.4	S46 51.9
S 09	294 37.6	271 04.9 ..	03.0	14 10.4 ..	30.4	3 23.9 ..	00.6	354 19.1 ..	32.4	Alnilam	275 41.6	S 1 11.6
U 10	309 40.0	286 04.8	04.2	29 11.0	30.3	18 25.9	00.5	9 21.3	32.3	Alphard	217 51.3	S 8 44.9
N 11	324 42.5	301 04.7	05.4	44 11.6	30.2	33 27.9	00.5	24 23.5	32.3			
D 12	339 45.0	316 04.6	N11 06.6	59 12.1	S23 30.1	48 29.8	S22 00.4	39 25.7	S20 32.3	Alphecca	126 07.0	N26 38.7
A 13	354 47.4	331 04.5	07.8	74 12.7	30.0	63 31.8	00.4	54 27.9	32.2	Alpheratz	357 39.1	N29 11.9
Y 14	9 49.9	346 04.4	09.0	89 13.3	30.0	78 33.8	00.3	69 30.1	32.2	Altair	62 04.0	N 8 55.2
15	24 52.3	1 04.3 ..	10.2	104 13.9 ..	29.9	93 35.8 ..	00.2	84 32.3 ..	32.1	Ankaa	353 11.5	S42 12.1
16	39 54.8	16 04.3	11.4	119 14.5	29.8	108 37.7	00.2	99 34.6	32.1	Antares	112 20.6	S26 28.4
17	54 57.3	31 04.2	12.6	134 15.1	29.7	123 39.7	00.1	114 36.8	32.0			
18	69 59.7	46 04.1	N11 13.8	149 15.6	S23 29.6	138 41.7	S22 00.1	129 39.0	S20 32.0	Arcturus	145 51.3	N19 04.6
19	85 02.2	61 04.0	15.0	164 16.2	29.5	153 43.7	22 00.0	144 41.2	31.9	Atria	107 18.3	S69 03.4
20	100 04.7	76 03.9	16.2	179 16.8	29.4	168 45.6	21 59.9	159 43.4	31.9	Avior	234 15.7	S59 34.7
21	115 07.1	91 03.8 ..	17.4	194 17.4 ..	29.4	183 47.6 ..	59.9	174 45.6 ..	31.8	Bellatrix	278 27.0	N 6 21.9
22	130 09.6	106 03.7	18.6	209 18.0	29.3	198 49.6	59.8	189 47.8	31.8	Betelgeuse	270 56.2	N 7 24.5
23	145 12.1	121 03.6	19.8	224 18.6	29.2	213 51.6	59.7	204 50.0	31.8			
2 00	160 14.5	136 03.5	N11 21.0	239 19.1	S23 29.1	228 53.5	S21 59.7	219 52.2	S20 31.7	Canopus	263 53.9	S52 42.7
01	175 17.0	151 03.4	22.2	254 19.7	29.0	243 55.5	59.6	234 54.5	31.7	Capella	280 27.6	N46 01.1
02	190 19.5	166 03.3	23.4	269 20.3	28.9	258 57.5	59.6	249 56.7	31.6	Deneb	49 28.8	N45 20.9
03	205 21.9	181 03.2 ..	24.5	284 20.9 ..	28.8	273 59.5 ..	59.5	264 58.9 ..	31.6	Denebola	182 28.6	N14 27.5
04	220 24.4	196 03.1	25.7	299 21.5	28.7	289 01.4	59.4	280 01.1	31.5	Diphda	348 51.5	S17 52.9
05	235 26.8	211 03.0	26.9	314 22.1	28.6	304 03.4	59.4	295 03.3	31.5			
06	250 29.3	226 02.9	N11 28.1	329 22.6	S23 28.5	319 05.4	S21 59.3	310 05.5	S20 31.4	Dubhe	193 45.3	N61 38.5
07	265 31.8	241 02.8	29.3	344 23.2	28.5	334 07.4	59.2	325 07.7	31.4	Elnath	278 06.7	N28 37.4
08	280 34.2	256 02.7	30.5	359 23.8	28.4	349 09.4	59.2	340 09.9	31.3	Eltanin	90 44.2	N51 28.9
M 09	295 36.7	271 02.6 ..	31.7	14 24.4 ..	28.3	4 11.3 ..	59.1	355 12.1 ..	31.3	Enif	33 42.9	N 9 57.9
O 10	310 39.2	286 02.5	32.9	29 25.0	28.2	19 13.3	59.1	10 14.4	31.3	Fomalhaut	15 19.2	S29 31.1
N 11	325 41.6	301 02.4	34.1	44 25.6	28.1	34 15.3	59.0	25 16.6	31.2			
D 12	340 44.1	316 02.3	N11 35.3	59 26.1	S23 28.0	49 17.3	S21 58.9	40 18.8	S20 31.2	Gacrux	171 55.3	S57 13.4
A 13	355 46.6	331 02.2	36.5	74 26.7	27.9	64 19.2	58.9	55 21.0	31.1	Gienah	175 47.3	S17 39.2
Y 14	10 49.0	346 02.1	37.6	89 27.3	27.8	79 21.2	58.8	70 23.2	31.1	Hadar	148 41.0	S60 27.9
15	25 51.5	1 02.0 ..	38.8	104 27.9 ..	27.7	94 23.2 ..	58.8	85 25.4 ..	31.0	Hamal	327 55.8	N23 33.3
16	40 54.0	16 01.9	40.0	119 28.5	27.6	109 25.2	58.7	100 27.6	31.0	Kaus Aust.	83 37.9	S34 22.3
17	55 56.4	31 01.8	41.2	134 29.1	27.5	124 27.2	58.6	115 29.8	30.9			
18	70 58.9	46 01.7	N11 42.4	149 29.6	S23 27.4	139 29.1	S21 58.6	130 32.1	S20 30.9	Kochab	137 19.5	N74 04.2
19	86 01.3	61 01.6	43.6	164 30.2	27.3	154 31.1	58.5	145 34.3	30.8	Markab	13 34.1	N15 18.6
20	101 03.8	76 01.5	44.8	179 30.8	27.2	169 33.1	58.4	160 36.5	30.8	Menkar	314 10.3	N 4 09.9
21	116 06.3	91 01.4 ..	46.0	194 31.4 ..	27.1	184 35.1 ..	58.4	175 38.7 ..	30.8	Menkent	148 01.9	S36 28.0
22	131 08.7	106 01.3	47.1	209 32.0	27.0	199 37.1	58.3	190 40.9	30.7	Miaplacidus	221 38.0	S69 48.1
23	146 11.2	121 01.2	48.3	224 32.6	26.9	214 39.0	58.3	205 43.1	30.7			
3 00	161 13.7	136 01.1	N11 49.5	239 33.1	S23 26.8	229 41.0	S21 58.2	220 45.3	S20 30.6	Mirfak	308 33.9	N49 56.0
01	176 16.1	151 01.0	50.7	254 33.7	26.7	244 43.0	58.1	235 47.6	30.6	Nunki	75 52.8	S26 16.2
02	191 18.6	166 00.9	51.9	269 34.3	26.6	259 45.0	58.1	250 49.8	30.5	Peacock	53 12.4	S56 40.1
03	206 21.1	181 00.8 ..	53.1	284 34.9 ..	26.5	274 47.0 ..	58.0	265 52.0 ..	30.5	Pollux	243 21.8	N27 58.6
04	221 23.5	196 00.7	54.2	299 35.5	26.4	289 48.9	57.9	280 54.2	30.4	Procyon	244 54.7	N 5 10.2
05	236 26.0	211 00.7	55.4	314 36.1	26.3	304 50.9	57.9	295 56.4	30.4			
06	251 28.4	226 00.6	N11 56.6	329 36.6	S23 26.2	319 52.9	S21 57.8	310 58.6	S20 30.3	Rasalhague	96 02.2	N12 32.6
07	266 30.9	241 00.5	57.8	344 37.2	26.1	334 54.9	57.8	326 00.8	30.3	Regulus	207 38.3	N11 52.1
08	281 33.4	256 00.4	11 59.0	359 37.8	26.0	349 56.9	57.7	341 03.1	30.3	Rigel	281 07.6	S 8 11.0
T 09	296 35.8	271 00.3	12 00.1	14 38.4 ..	25.9	4 58.8 ..	57.6	356 05.3 ..	30.2	Rigil Kent.	139 45.2	S60 54.8
U 10	311 38.3	286 00.2	01.3	29 39.0	25.8	20 00.8	57.6	11 07.5	30.2	Sabik	102 07.3	S15 44.9
E 11	326 40.8	301 00.1	02.5	44 39.6	25.7	35 02.8	57.5	26 09.7	30.1			
S 12	341 43.2	316 00.0	N12 03.7	59 40.1	S23 25.6	50 04.8	S21 57.5	41 11.9	S20 30.1	Schedar	349 35.8	N56 38.8
D 13	356 45.7	330 59.9	04.9	74 40.7	25.5	65 06.8	57.4	56 14.1	30.0	Shaula	96 15.7	S37 06.9
A 14	11 48.2	345 59.8	06.0	89 41.3	25.4	80 08.8	57.3	71 16.3	30.0	Sirius	258 29.5	S16 44.9
Y 15	26 50.6	0 59.7 ..	07.2	104 41.9 ..	25.3	95 10.7 ..	57.3	86 18.6 ..	29.9	Spica	158 26.1	S11 15.9
16	41 53.1	15 59.6	08.4	119 42.5	25.2	110 12.7	57.2	101 20.8	29.9	Suhail	222 48.7	S43 31.0
17	56 55.6	30 59.5	09.6	134 43.1	25.1	125 14.7	57.1	116 23.0	29.9			
18	71 58.0	45 59.4	N12 10.7	149 43.6	S23 25.0	140 16.7	S21 57.1	131 25.2	S20 29.8	Vega	80 36.0	N38 47.9
19	87 00.5	60 59.3	11.9	164 44.2	24.9	155 18.7	57.0	146 27.4	29.8	Zuben'ubi	137 00.2	S16 07.4
20	102 02.9	75 59.2	13.1	179 44.8	24.8	170 20.7	57.0	161 29.6	29.7		SHA	Mer. Pass.
21	117 05.4	90 59.1 ..	14.3	194 45.4 ..	24.7	185 22.6 ..	56.9	176 31.9 ..	29.7	Venus	335 48.9	14 56
22	132 07.9	105 59.0	15.4	209 46.0	24.6	200 24.6	56.8	191 34.1	29.6	Mars	79 04.6	8 02
23	147 10.3	120 58.9	16.6	224 46.6	24.5	215 26.6	56.8	206 36.3	29.6	Jupiter	68 39.0	8 43
Mer. Pass. 13 16.8		v −0.1	d 1.2	v 0.6	d 0.1	v 2.0	d 0.1	v 2.2	d 0.0	Saturn	59 37.7	9 19

UT	SUN GHA	SUN Dec	MOON GHA	v	Dec	d	HP
d h	° ′	° ′	° ′	′	° ′	′	′
1 00	176 54.9	S 7 29.5	110 30.1	13.9	N14 17.7	9.7	54.8
01	191 55.0	28.5	125 03.0	13.9	14 27.4	9.6	54.8
02	206 55.2	27.6	139 35.9	13.8	14 37.0	9.6	54.8
03	221 55.3	.. 26.6	154 08.7	13.7	14 46.6	9.5	54.8
04	236 55.4	25.7	168 41.4	13.7	14 56.1	9.5	54.9
05	251 55.5	24.7	183 14.1	13.6	15 05.6	9.4	54.9
06	266 55.6	S 7 23.8	197 46.7	13.5	N15 15.0	9.4	54.9
07	281 55.8	22.8	212 19.2	13.5	15 24.4	9.3	54.9
08	296 55.9	21.8	226 51.7	13.4	15 33.7	9.2	54.9
S 09	311 56.0	.. 20.9	241 24.1	13.3	15 42.9	9.2	55.0
U 10	326 56.1	19.9	255 56.4	13.3	15 52.1	9.1	55.0
N 11	341 56.3	19.0	270 28.7	13.2	16 01.2	9.0	55.0
D 12	356 56.4	S 7 18.0	285 00.9	13.1	N16 10.2	9.0	55.0
A 13	11 56.5	17.1	299 33.0	13.1	16 19.2	8.9	55.1
Y 14	26 56.6	16.1	314 05.1	12.9	16 28.1	8.9	55.1
15	41 56.8	.. 15.2	328 37.0	12.9	16 37.0	8.8	55.1
16	56 56.9	14.2	343 08.9	12.9	16 45.8	8.7	55.1
17	71 57.0	13.3	357 40.8	12.7	16 54.5	8.6	55.2
18	86 57.1	S 7 12.3	12 12.5	12.7	N17 03.1	8.6	55.2
19	101 57.3	11.4	26 44.2	12.6	17 11.7	8.5	55.2
20	116 57.4	10.4	41 15.8	12.6	17 20.2	8.4	55.2
21	131 57.5	.. 09.4	55 47.4	12.4	17 28.6	8.4	55.3
22	146 57.6	08.5	70 18.8	12.4	17 37.0	8.3	55.3
23	161 57.8	07.5	84 50.2	12.3	17 45.3	8.2	55.3
2 00	176 57.9	S 7 06.6	99 21.5	12.2	N17 53.5	8.1	55.3
01	191 58.0	05.6	113 52.7	12.2	18 01.6	8.1	55.4
02	206 58.1	04.7	128 23.9	12.1	18 09.7	8.0	55.4
03	221 58.3	.. 03.7	142 55.0	12.0	18 17.7	7.9	55.4
04	236 58.4	02.8	157 26.0	11.9	18 25.6	7.8	55.5
05	251 58.5	01.8	171 56.9	11.8	18 33.4	7.8	55.5
06	266 58.7	S 7 00.8	186 27.7	11.8	N18 41.2	7.7	55.5
07	281 58.8	6 59.9	200 58.5	11.6	18 48.9	7.6	55.5
08	296 58.9	58.9	215 29.1	11.6	18 56.5	7.5	55.6
M 09	311 59.0	.. 58.0	229 59.7	11.6	19 04.0	7.4	55.6
O 10	326 59.2	57.0	244 30.3	11.4	19 11.4	7.3	55.6
N 11	341 59.3	56.1	259 00.7	11.3	19 18.7	7.3	55.7
D 12	356 59.4	S 6 55.1	273 31.0	11.3	N19 26.0	7.1	55.7
A 13	11 59.6	54.1	288 01.3	11.2	19 33.1	7.1	55.7
Y 14	26 59.7	53.2	302 31.5	11.1	19 40.2	7.0	55.7
15	41 59.8	.. 52.2	317 01.6	11.0	19 47.2	6.9	55.8
16	57 00.0	51.3	331 31.6	11.0	19 54.1	6.8	55.8
17	72 00.1	50.3	346 01.6	10.8	20 00.9	6.7	55.8
18	87 00.2	S 6 49.4	0 31.4	10.8	N20 07.6	6.7	55.9
19	102 00.3	48.4	15 01.2	10.7	20 14.3	6.5	55.9
20	117 00.5	47.4	29 30.9	10.6	20 20.8	6.4	55.9
21	132 00.6	.. 46.5	44 00.5	10.5	20 27.2	6.4	56.0
22	147 00.7	45.5	58 30.0	10.5	20 33.6	6.2	56.0
23	162 00.9	44.6	72 59.5	10.3	20 39.8	6.2	56.0
3 00	177 01.0	S 6 43.6	87 28.8	10.3	N20 46.0	6.0	56.1
01	192 01.1	42.6	101 58.1	10.2	20 52.0	6.0	56.1
02	207 01.3	41.7	116 27.3	10.1	20 58.0	5.8	56.1
03	222 01.4	.. 40.7	130 56.4	10.0	21 03.8	5.8	56.2
04	237 01.5	39.8	145 25.4	10.0	21 09.6	5.6	56.2
05	252 01.7	38.8	159 54.4	9.8	21 15.2	5.5	56.2
06	267 01.8	S 6 37.8	174 23.2	9.8	N21 20.7	5.5	56.3
07	282 01.9	36.9	188 52.0	9.7	21 26.2	5.3	56.3
T 08	297 02.1	35.9	203 20.7	9.6	21 31.5	5.2	56.3
U 09	312 02.2	.. 35.0	217 49.3	9.5	21 36.7	5.1	56.4
E 10	327 02.3	34.0	232 17.8	9.5	21 41.8	5.0	56.4
S 11	342 02.5	33.0	246 46.3	9.4	21 46.8	4.9	56.4
D 12	357 02.6	S 6 32.1	261 14.7	9.2	N21 51.7	4.8	56.5
A 13	12 02.7	31.1	275 42.9	9.2	21 56.5	4.7	56.5
Y 14	27 02.9	30.1	290 11.1	9.1	22 01.2	4.5	56.5
15	42 03.0	.. 29.2	304 39.2	9.1	22 05.7	4.5	56.6
16	57 03.1	28.2	319 07.3	8.9	22 10.2	4.3	56.6
17	72 03.3	27.3	333 35.2	8.9	22 14.5	4.2	56.6
18	87 03.4	S 6 26.3	348 03.1	8.8	N22 18.7	4.1	56.7
19	102 03.5	25.3	2 30.9	8.7	22 22.8	4.0	56.7
20	117 03.7	24.4	16 58.6	8.6	22 26.8	3.8	56.8
21	132 03.8	.. 23.4	31 26.2	8.6	22 30.6	3.8	56.8
22	147 04.0	22.4	45 53.8	8.5	22 34.4	3.6	56.8
23	162 04.1	21.5	60 21.3	8.4	N22 38.0	3.5	56.9
	SD 16.2	d 1.0	SD 15.0		15.2		15.4

Lat.	Twilight Naut.	Twilight Civil	Sunrise	Moonrise 1	2	3	4
°	h m	h m	h m	h m	h m	h m	h m
N 72	05 03	06 21	07 29	07 01	□	□	□
N 70	05 09	06 19	07 21	07 35	07 02	□	□
68	05 13	06 17	07 13	08 00	07 48	07 24	□
66	05 17	06 16	07 08	08 19	08 18	08 20	08 31
64	05 20	06 15	07 03	08 35	08 41	08 53	09 19
62	05 23	06 14	06 58	08 48	08 59	09 18	09 50
60	05 25	06 13	06 54	08 59	09 14	09 37	10 14
N 58	05 26	06 12	06 51	09 08	09 27	09 54	10 32
56	05 28	06 11	06 48	09 17	09 38	10 07	10 48
54	05 29	06 10	06 45	09 24	09 48	10 19	11 02
52	05 30	06 09	06 43	09 31	09 57	10 30	11 13
50	05 31	06 08	06 40	09 37	10 05	10 40	11 24
45	05 32	06 06	06 36	09 51	10 22	10 59	11 46
N 40	05 33	06 04	06 31	10 02	10 36	11 16	12 04
35	05 33	06 02	06 28	10 11	10 47	11 29	12 19
30	05 33	06 00	06 24	10 19	10 58	11 41	12 32
20	05 31	05 57	06 19	10 34	11 16	12 02	12 54
N 10	05 28	05 53	06 14	10 47	11 31	12 20	13 13
0	05 24	05 48	06 09	10 58	11 46	12 37	13 31
S 10	05 18	05 43	06 04	11 10	12 01	12 54	13 49
20	05 10	05 36	05 58	11 23	12 17	13 12	14 09
30	04 59	05 28	05 52	11 38	12 35	13 33	14 31
35	04 52	05 22	05 48	11 47	12 46	13 45	14 44
40	04 44	05 16	05 44	11 57	12 58	13 59	14 59
45	04 33	05 09	05 39	12 08	13 12	14 16	15 18
S 50	04 19	05 00	05 33	12 23	13 30	14 37	15 40
52	04 13	04 55	05 30	12 29	13 39	14 47	15 51
54	04 05	04 50	05 27	12 37	13 48	14 58	16 03
56	03 56	04 45	05 24	12 45	13 59	15 11	16 17
58	03 47	04 39	05 20	12 54	14 11	15 26	16 34
S 60	03 35	04 32	05 16	13 05	14 25	15 44	16 54

Lat.	Sunset	Twilight Civil	Twilight Naut.	Moonset 1	2	3	4
°	h m	h m	h m	h m	h m	h m	h m
N 72	16 57	18 06	19 24	02 14	□	□	□
N 70	17 05	18 07	19 18	01 42	03 51	□	□
68	17 12	18 09	19 13	01 18	03 06	05 14	□
66	17 18	18 10	19 09	01 00	02 37	04 19	05 59
64	17 23	18 11	19 06	00 46	02 15	03 46	05 11
62	17 27	18 12	19 03	00 33	01 57	03 22	04 40
60	17 31	18 13	19 01	00 23	01 43	03 02	04 17
N 58	17 34	18 14	18 59	00 14	01 31	02 47	03 58
56	17 37	18 15	18 58	00 06	01 20	02 33	03 43
54	17 40	18 15	18 56	25 11	01 11	02 22	03 29
52	17 42	18 16	18 55	25 02	01 02	02 11	03 18
50	17 44	18 17	18 54	24 55	00 55	02 02	03 07
45	17 49	18 19	18 53	24 39	00 39	01 43	02 46
N 40	17 53	18 20	18 52	24 26	00 26	01 27	02 28
35	17 57	18 22	18 52	24 15	00 15	01 14	02 13
30	18 00	18 24	18 52	24 05	00 05	01 03	02 01
20	18 06	18 28	18 53	23 49	24 43	00 43	01 39
N 10	18 11	18 32	18 56	23 34	24 26	00 26	01 20
0	18 15	18 36	19 00	23 21	24 10	00 10	01 02
S 10	18 20	18 41	19 06	23 07	23 54	24 45	00 45
20	18 26	18 48	19 14	22 53	23 37	24 26	00 26
30	18 32	18 56	19 24	22 37	23 18	24 04	00 04
35	18 35	19 01	19 31	22 27	23 06	23 52	24 45
40	18 39	19 07	19 40	22 17	22 53	23 37	24 29
45	18 44	19 14	19 50	22 04	22 38	23 20	24 11
S 50	18 50	19 23	20 03	21 49	22 19	22 58	23 48
52	18 53	19 27	20 10	21 42	22 11	22 48	23 38
54	18 56	19 32	20 17	21 34	22 01	22 37	23 25
56	18 59	19 38	20 26	21 25	21 50	22 24	23 11
58	19 02	19 44	20 35	21 15	21 37	22 08	22 55
S 60	19 07	19 51	20 47	21 04	21 22	21 50	22 35

Day	SUN Eqn. of Time 00ʰ	SUN Eqn. of Time 12ʰ	SUN Mer. Pass.	MOON Mer. Pass. Upper	MOON Mer. Pass. Lower	Age	Phase
d	m s	m s	h m	h m	h m	d	%
1	12 21	12 15	12 12	17 10	04 47	07	37
2	12 09	12 03	12 12	17 58	05 33	08	47
3	11 56	11 50	12 12	18 50	06 23	09	57

UT	ARIES GHA	VENUS −4.3 GHA	VENUS Dec	MARS +1.1 GHA	MARS Dec	JUPITER −2.0 GHA	JUPITER Dec	SATURN +0.7 GHA	SATURN Dec	STARS Name	SHA	Dec
4 00	162 12.8	135 58.8	N12 17.8	239 47.1	S23 24.4	230 28.6	S21 56.7	221 38.5	S20 29.5	Acamar	315 15.0	S40 13.8
01	177 15.3	150 58.7	19.0	254 47.7	24.3	245 30.6	56.6	236 40.7	29.5	Achernar	335 23.7	S57 08.4
02	192 17.7	165 58.6	20.1	269 48.3	24.2	260 32.6	56.6	251 42.9	29.5	Acrux	173 03.5	S63 12.5
03	207 20.2	180 58.6 ..	21.3	284 48.9 ..	24.1	275 34.5 ..	56.5	266 45.2 ..	29.4	Adhara	255 08.7	S29 00.3
04	222 22.7	195 58.5	22.5	299 49.5	24.0	290 36.5	56.5	281 47.4	29.4	Aldebaran	290 44.1	N16 32.8
05	237 25.1	210 58.4	23.6	314 50.1	23.8	305 38.5	56.4	296 49.6	29.3			
06	252 27.6	225 58.3	N12 24.8	329 50.6	S23 23.7	320 40.5	S21 56.3	311 51.8	S20 29.3	Alioth	166 16.1	N55 50.9
W 07	267 30.1	240 58.2	26.0	344 51.2	23.6	335 42.5	56.3	326 54.0	29.2	Alkaid	152 54.8	N49 12.6
E 08	282 32.5	255 58.1	27.2	359 51.8	23.5	350 44.5	56.2	341 56.2	29.2	Alnair	27 38.3	S46 51.9
D 09	297 35.0	270 58.0 ..	28.3	14 52.4 ..	23.4	5 46.5 ..	56.2	356 58.5 ..	29.1	Alnilam	275 41.6	S 1 11.6
N 10	312 37.4	285 57.9	29.5	29 53.0	23.3	20 48.4	56.1	12 00.7	29.1	Alphard	217 51.3	S 8 44.9
E 11	327 39.9	300 57.8	30.7	44 53.6	23.2	35 50.4	56.0	27 02.9	29.0			
S 12	342 42.4	315 57.7	N12 31.8	59 54.2	S23 23.1	50 52.4	S21 56.0	42 05.1	S20 29.0	Alphecca	126 06.9	N26 38.7
D 13	357 44.8	330 57.6	33.0	74 54.7	23.0	65 54.4	55.9	57 07.3	29.0	Alpheratz	357 39.1	N29 11.9
A 14	12 47.3	345 57.5	34.2	89 55.3	22.9	80 56.4	55.8	72 09.5	28.9	Altair	62 04.0	N 8 55.2
Y 15	27 49.8	0 57.4 ..	35.3	104 55.9 ..	22.7	95 58.4 ..	55.8	87 11.8 ..	28.9	Ankaa	353 11.5	S42 12.1
16	42 52.2	15 57.3	36.5	119 56.5	22.6	111 00.4	55.7	102 14.0	28.8	Antares	112 20.5	S26 28.4
17	57 54.7	30 57.2	37.7	134 57.1	22.5	126 02.4	55.7	117 16.2	28.8			
18	72 57.2	45 57.1	N12 38.8	149 57.7	S23 22.4	141 04.3	S21 55.6	132 18.4	S20 28.7	Arcturus	145 51.3	N19 04.6
19	87 59.6	60 57.0	40.0	164 58.2	22.3	156 06.3	55.5	147 20.6	28.7	Atria	107 18.2	S69 03.4
20	103 02.1	75 57.0	41.1	179 58.8	22.2	171 08.3	55.5	162 22.8	28.6	Avior	234 15.7	S59 34.7
21	118 04.6	90 56.9 ..	42.3	194 59.4 ..	22.1	186 10.3 ..	55.4	177 25.1 ..	28.6	Bellatrix	278 27.0	N 6 21.9
22	133 07.0	105 56.8	43.5	210 00.0	21.9	201 12.3	55.4	192 27.3	28.6	Betelgeuse	270 56.2	N 7 24.5
23	148 09.5	120 56.7	44.6	225 00.6	21.8	216 14.3	55.3	207 29.5	28.5			
5 00	163 11.9	135 56.6	N12 45.8	240 01.2	S23 21.7	231 16.3	S21 55.2	222 31.7	S20 28.5	Canopus	263 53.9	S52 42.7
01	178 14.4	150 56.5	47.0	255 01.8	21.6	246 18.3	55.2	237 33.9	28.4	Capella	280 27.6	N46 01.1
02	193 16.9	165 56.4	48.1	270 02.3	21.5	261 20.3	55.1	252 36.2	28.4	Deneb	49 28.7	N45 20.9
03	208 19.3	180 56.3 ..	49.3	285 02.9 ..	21.4	276 22.2 ..	55.0	267 38.4 ..	28.3	Denebola	182 28.6	N14 27.5
04	223 21.8	195 56.2	50.4	300 03.5	21.3	291 24.2	55.0	282 40.6	28.3	Diphda	348 51.5	S17 52.8
05	238 24.3	210 56.1	51.6	315 04.1	21.1	306 26.2	54.9	297 42.8	28.2			
06	253 26.7	225 56.0	N12 52.8	330 04.7	S23 21.0	321 28.2	S21 54.9	312 45.0	S20 28.2	Dubhe	193 45.3	N61 38.5
T 07	268 29.2	240 55.9	53.9	345 05.3	20.9	336 30.2	54.8	327 47.3	28.2	Elnath	278 06.7	N28 37.4
H 08	283 31.7	255 55.8	55.1	0 05.8	20.8	351 32.2	54.7	342 49.5	28.1	Eltanin	90 44.1	N51 28.9
U 09	298 34.1	270 55.7 ..	56.2	15 06.4 ..	20.7	6 34.2 ..	54.7	357 51.7 ..	28.1	Enif	33 42.9	N 9 57.9
R 10	313 36.6	285 55.7	57.4	30 07.0	20.5	21 36.2	54.6	12 53.9	28.0	Fomalhaut	15 19.2	S29 31.1
S 11	328 39.0	300 55.6	58.5	45 07.6	20.4	36 38.2	54.5	27 56.1	28.0			
D 12	343 41.5	315 55.5	N12 59.7	60 08.2	S23 20.3	51 40.2	S21 54.5	42 58.4	S20 27.9	Gacrux	171 55.3	S57 13.4
A 13	358 44.0	330 55.4	13 00.8	75 08.8	20.2	66 42.2	54.4	58 00.6	27.9	Gienah	175 47.2	S17 39.2
Y 14	13 46.4	345 55.3	02.0	90 09.4	20.1	81 44.1	54.4	73 02.8	27.8	Hadar	148 40.9	S60 27.9
15	28 48.9	0 55.2 ..	03.2	105 09.9 ..	19.9	96 46.1 ..	54.3	88 05.0 ..	27.8	Hamal	327 55.8	N23 33.3
16	43 51.4	15 55.1	04.3	120 10.5	19.8	111 48.1	54.2	103 07.2	27.8	Kaus Aust.	83 37.8	S34 22.3
17	58 53.8	30 55.0	05.5	135 11.1	19.7	126 50.1	54.2	118 09.5	27.7			
18	73 56.3	45 54.9	N13 06.6	150 11.7	S23 19.6	141 52.1	S21 54.1	133 11.7	S20 27.7	Kochab	137 19.4	N74 04.2
19	88 58.8	60 54.8	07.8	165 12.3	19.5	156 54.1	54.1	148 13.9	27.6	Markab	13 34.1	N15 18.6
20	104 01.2	75 54.7	08.9	180 12.9	19.3	171 56.1	54.0	163 16.1	27.6	Menkar	314 10.4	N 4 09.9
21	119 03.7	90 54.6 ..	10.1	195 13.5 ..	19.2	186 58.1 ..	53.9	178 18.3 ..	27.5	Menkent	148 01.9	S36 28.0
22	134 06.2	105 54.5	11.2	210 14.0	19.1	202 00.1	53.9	193 20.6	27.5	Miaplacidus	221 38.0	S69 48.1
23	149 08.6	120 54.5	12.4	225 14.6	19.0	217 02.1	53.8	208 22.8	27.5			
6 00	164 11.1	135 54.4	N13 13.5	240 15.2	S23 18.8	232 04.1	S21 53.7	223 25.0	S20 27.4	Mirfak	308 33.9	N49 55.9
01	179 13.5	150 54.3	14.7	255 15.8	18.7	247 06.1	53.7	238 27.2	27.4	Nunki	75 52.8	S26 16.2
02	194 16.0	165 54.2	15.8	270 16.4	18.5	262 08.1	53.6	253 29.4	27.3	Peacock	53 12.4	S56 40.1
03	209 18.5	180 54.1 ..	17.0	285 17.0 ..	18.5	277 10.1 ..	53.6	268 31.7 ..	27.3	Pollux	243 21.8	N27 58.6
04	224 20.9	195 54.0	18.1	300 17.5	18.3	292 12.0	53.5	283 33.9	27.2	Procyon	244 54.7	N 5 10.2
05	239 23.4	210 53.9	19.3	315 18.1	18.2	307 14.0	53.4	298 36.1	27.2			
06	254 25.9	225 53.8	N13 20.4	330 18.7	S23 18.1	322 16.0	S21 53.4	313 38.3	S20 27.1	Rasalhague	96 02.2	N12 32.6
F 07	269 28.3	240 53.7	21.6	345 19.3	18.0	337 18.0	53.3	328 40.6	27.1	Regulus	207 38.3	N11 52.0
R 08	284 30.8	255 53.6	22.7	0 19.9	17.8	352 20.0	53.3	343 42.8	27.1	Rigel	281 07.6	S 8 11.0
I 09	299 33.3	270 53.5 ..	23.8	15 20.5 ..	17.7	7 22.0 ..	53.2	358 45.0 ..	27.0	Rigil Kent.	139 45.1	S60 54.8
D 10	314 35.7	285 53.4	25.0	30 21.1	17.6	22 24.0	53.1	13 47.2	27.0	Sabik	102 07.3	S15 44.9
A 11	329 38.2	300 53.4	26.1	45 21.6	17.5	37 26.0	53.1	28 49.4	26.9			
Y 12	344 40.7	315 53.3	N13 27.3	60 22.2	S23 17.3	52 28.0	S21 53.0	43 51.7	S20 26.9	Schedar	349 35.8	N56 38.8
13	359 43.1	330 53.2	28.4	75 22.8	17.2	67 30.0	52.9	58 53.9	26.8	Shaula	96 15.7	S37 06.9
14	14 45.6	345 53.1	29.6	90 23.4	17.1	82 32.0	52.9	73 56.1	26.8	Sirius	258 29.5	S16 44.9
15	29 48.0	0 53.0 ..	30.7	105 24.0 ..	16.9	97 34.0 ..	52.8	88 58.3 ..	26.8	Spica	158 26.1	S11 16.0
16	44 50.5	15 52.9	31.8	120 24.6	16.8	112 36.0	52.8	104 00.6	26.7	Suhail	222 48.7	S43 31.0
17	59 53.0	30 52.8	33.0	135 25.2	16.7	127 38.0	52.7	119 02.8	26.7			
18	74 55.4	45 52.7	N13 34.1	150 25.7	S23 16.6	142 40.0	S21 52.6	134 05.0	S20 26.6	Vega	80 36.0	N38 47.9
19	89 57.9	60 52.6	35.3	165 26.3	16.4	157 42.0	52.6	149 07.2	26.6	Zuben'ubi	137 00.1	S16 07.4
20	105 00.4	75 52.5	36.4	180 26.9	16.3	172 44.0	52.5	164 09.5	26.5		SHA	Mer. Pass.
21	120 02.8	90 52.5 ..	37.5	195 27.5 ..	16.2	187 46.0 ..	52.5	179 11.7 ..	26.5			
22	135 05.3	105 52.4	38.7	210 28.1	16.0	202 48.0	52.4	194 13.9	26.4	Venus	332 44.6	14 56
23	150 07.8	120 52.3	39.8	225 28.7	15.9	217 50.0	52.3	209 16.1	26.4	Mars	76 49.2	8 00
Mer. Pass. 13 05.1		v −0.1	d 1.2	v 0.6	d 0.1	v 2.0	d 0.1	v 2.2	d 0.0	Jupiter	68 04.3	8 34
										Saturn	59 19.8	9 09

UT	SUN GHA	SUN Dec	MOON GHA	v	MOON Dec	d	HP
d h	° ′	° ′	° ′	′	° ′	′	′
4 00	177 04.2	S 6 20.5	74 48.7	8.3	N22 41.5	3.4	56.9
01	192 04.4	19.6	89 16.0	8.2	22 44.9	3.2	56.9
02	207 04.5	18.6	103 43.2	8.2	22 48.1	3.1	57.0
03	222 04.6	.. 17.6	118 10.4	8.1	22 51.2	3.0	57.0
04	237 04.8	16.7	132 37.5	8.0	22 54.2	2.9	57.1
05	252 04.9	15.7	147 04.5	8.0	22 57.1	2.7	57.1
06	267 05.1	S 6 14.7	161 31.5	7.8	N22 59.8	2.7	57.1
W 07	282 05.2	13.8	175 58.3	7.8	23 02.5	2.4	57.2
E 08	297 05.3	12.8	190 25.1	7.8	23 04.9	2.4	57.2
D 09	312 05.5	.. 11.8	204 51.9	7.6	23 07.3	2.2	57.3
N 10	327 05.6	10.9	219 18.5	7.6	23 09.5	2.1	57.3
E 11	342 05.7	09.9	233 45.1	7.5	23 11.6	2.0	57.3
S 12	357 05.9	S 6 08.9	248 11.6	7.5	N23 13.6	1.8	57.4
D 13	12 06.0	08.0	262 38.1	7.4	23 15.4	1.7	57.4
A 14	27 06.2	07.0	277 04.5	7.3	23 17.1	1.5	57.4
Y 15	42 06.3	.. 06.1	291 30.8	7.2	23 18.6	1.4	57.5
16	57 06.4	05.1	305 57.0	7.2	23 20.0	1.3	57.5
17	72 06.6	04.1	320 23.2	7.1	23 21.3	1.2	57.6
18	87 06.7	S 6 03.2	334 49.3	7.1	N23 22.5	1.0	57.6
19	102 06.9	02.2	349 15.4	7.0	23 23.5	0.8	57.6
20	117 07.0	01.2	3 41.4	6.9	23 24.3	0.7	57.7
21	132 07.2	6 00.3	18 07.3	6.9	23 25.0	0.6	57.7
22	147 07.3	5 59.3	32 33.2	6.8	23 25.6	0.5	57.8
23	162 07.4	58.3	46 59.0	6.8	23 26.1	0.3	57.8
5 00	177 07.6	S 5 57.4	61 24.8	6.7	N23 26.4	0.1	57.9
01	192 07.7	56.4	75 50.5	6.6	23 26.5	0.0	57.9
02	207 07.9	55.4	90 16.1	6.6	23 26.5	0.1	57.9
03	222 08.0	.. 54.5	104 41.7	6.6	23 26.4	0.3	58.0
04	237 08.1	53.5	119 07.3	6.5	23 26.1	0.4	58.0
05	252 08.3	52.5	133 32.8	6.4	23 25.7	0.6	58.1
06	267 08.4	S 5 51.6	147 58.2	6.4	N23 25.1	0.7	58.1
T 07	282 08.6	50.6	162 23.6	6.4	23 24.4	0.9	58.1
H 08	297 08.7	49.6	176 49.0	6.3	23 23.5	1.0	58.2
U 09	312 08.9	.. 48.7	191 14.3	6.2	23 22.5	1.1	58.2
R 10	327 09.0	47.7	205 39.5	6.3	23 21.4	1.4	58.3
S 11	342 09.1	46.7	220 04.8	6.1	23 20.0	1.4	58.3
D 12	357 09.3	S 5 45.7	234 29.9	6.2	N23 18.6	1.6	58.3
A 13	12 09.4	44.8	248 55.1	6.1	23 17.0	1.8	58.4
Y 14	27 09.6	43.8	263 20.2	6.0	23 15.2	1.9	58.4
15	42 09.7	.. 42.8	277 45.2	6.0	23 13.3	2.0	58.5
16	57 09.9	41.9	292 10.2	6.0	23 11.3	2.3	58.5
17	72 10.0	40.9	306 35.2	6.0	23 09.0	2.3	58.5
18	87 10.2	S 5 39.9	321 00.2	5.9	N23 06.7	2.5	58.6
19	102 10.3	39.0	335 25.1	5.9	23 04.2	2.7	58.6
20	117 10.4	38.0	349 50.0	5.8	23 01.5	2.8	58.7
21	132 10.6	.. 37.0	4 14.8	5.8	22 58.7	3.0	58.7
22	147 10.7	36.1	18 39.6	5.8	22 55.7	3.1	58.7
23	162 10.9	35.1	33 04.4	5.8	22 52.6	3.3	58.8
6 00	177 11.0	S 5 34.1	47 29.2	5.8	N22 49.3	3.4	58.8
01	192 11.2	33.1	61 54.0	5.7	22 45.9	3.6	58.9
02	207 11.3	32.2	76 18.7	5.7	22 42.3	3.7	58.9
03	222 11.5	.. 31.2	90 43.4	5.7	22 38.6	3.9	59.0
04	237 11.6	30.2	105 08.1	5.7	22 34.7	4.1	59.0
05	252 11.8	29.3	119 32.8	5.6	22 30.6	4.2	59.0
06	267 11.9	S 5 28.3	133 57.4	5.7	N22 26.4	4.3	59.1
07	282 12.1	27.3	148 22.1	5.6	22 22.1	4.5	59.1
08	297 12.2	26.4	162 46.7	5.6	22 17.6	4.7	59.2
F 09	312 12.4	.. 25.4	177 11.3	5.6	22 12.9	4.8	59.2
R 10	327 12.5	24.4	191 35.9	5.6	22 08.1	4.9	59.2
I 11	342 12.7	23.4	206 00.5	5.6	22 03.2	5.2	59.3
D 12	357 12.8	S 5 22.5	220 25.1	5.6	N21 58.0	5.2	59.3
A 13	12 12.9	21.5	234 49.7	5.5	21 52.8	5.4	59.3
Y 14	27 13.1	20.5	249 14.2	5.5	21 47.4	5.6	59.4
15	42 13.2	.. 19.6	263 38.8	5.6	21 41.8	5.7	59.4
16	57 13.4	18.6	278 03.4	5.5	21 36.1	5.9	59.5
17	72 13.5	17.6	292 27.9	5.6	21 30.2	6.0	59.5
18	87 13.7	S 5 16.6	306 52.5	5.6	N21 24.2	6.2	59.5
19	102 13.8	15.7	321 17.1	5.5	21 18.0	6.3	59.6
20	117 14.0	14.7	335 41.6	5.6	21 11.7	6.5	59.6
21	132 14.1	.. 13.7	350 06.2	5.6	21 05.2	6.6	59.7
22	147 14.3	12.7	4 30.8	5.6	20 58.6	6.8	59.7
23	162 14.4	11.8	18 55.4	5.6	N20 51.8	6.9	59.7
	SD 16.1	d 1.0	SD 15.6		15.9		16.2

Lat.	Twilight Naut.	Twilight Civil	Sunrise	Moonrise 4	5	6	7
°	h m	h m	h m	h m	h m	h m	h m
N 72	04 47	06 06	07 13	□	□	□	□
N 70	04 55	06 06	07 07	□	□	□	11 26
68	05 01	06 05	07 01	□	□	□	12 23
66	05 06	06 05	06 56	08 31	09 17	10 58	12 57
64	05 10	06 05	06 52	09 19	10 12	11 36	13 21
62	05 13	06 04	06 49	09 50	10 44	12 03	13 40
60	05 16	06 04	06 46	10 14	11 09	12 24	13 56
N 58	05 18	06 04	06 43	10 32	11 28	12 41	14 09
56	05 20	06 03	06 40	10 48	11 44	12 56	14 20
54	05 22	06 03	06 38	11 02	11 58	13 08	14 30
52	05 23	06 02	06 36	11 13	12 10	13 19	14 39
50	05 25	06 02	06 34	11 24	12 20	13 29	14 47
45	05 27	06 01	06 30	11 46	12 43	13 49	15 04
N 40	05 28	06 00	06 27	12 04	13 01	14 06	15 18
35	05 29	05 59	06 24	12 19	13 16	14 20	15 29
30	05 30	05 57	06 21	12 32	13 29	14 32	15 39
20	05 29	05 54	06 16	12 54	13 51	14 52	15 57
N 10	05 27	05 51	06 12	13 13	14 10	15 10	16 12
0	05 23	05 47	06 08	13 31	14 28	15 27	16 26
S 10	05 18	05 43	06 04	13 49	14 46	15 44	16 40
20	05 11	05 37	05 59	14 09	15 06	16 02	16 55
30	05 01	05 30	05 54	14 31	15 28	16 22	17 12
35	04 55	05 25	05 51	14 44	15 41	16 34	17 22
40	04 47	05 20	05 47	14 59	15 56	16 48	17 33
45	04 37	05 13	05 43	15 18	16 14	17 04	17 47
S 50	04 25	05 05	05 38	15 40	16 36	17 24	18 03
52	04 19	05 01	05 36	15 51	16 47	17 33	18 10
54	04 12	04 57	05 33	16 03	16 59	17 44	18 19
56	04 04	04 52	05 30	16 17	17 13	17 56	18 28
58	03 55	04 46	05 27	16 34	17 29	18 10	18 39
S 60	03 45	04 40	05 24	16 54	17 48	18 26	18 51

Lat.	Sunset	Twilight Civil	Twilight Naut.	Moonset 4	5	6	7
°	h m	h m	h m	h m	h m	h m	h m
N 72	17 11	18 19	19 39	□	□	□	□
N 70	17 18	18 19	19 31	□	□	□	09 10
68	17 24	18 19	19 24	□	□	□	08 12
66	17 28	18 19	19 19	05 59	07 11	07 33	07 37
64	17 32	18 20	19 15	05 11	06 16	06 54	07 12
62	17 36	18 20	19 11	04 40	05 44	06 26	06 52
60	17 38	18 20	19 08	04 17	05 19	06 05	06 36
N 58	17 41	18 20	19 06	03 58	05 00	05 48	06 22
56	17 44	18 21	19 04	03 43	04 44	05 33	06 10
54	17 46	18 21	19 02	03 29	04 30	05 20	06 00
52	17 48	18 21	19 00	03 18	04 18	05 09	05 50
50	17 49	18 22	18 59	03 07	04 07	04 59	05 42
45	17 53	18 22	18 57	02 46	03 45	04 38	05 24
N 40	17 57	18 24	18 55	02 28	03 27	04 21	05 09
35	17 59	18 25	18 54	02 13	03 12	04 07	04 57
30	18 02	18 26	18 54	02 01	02 58	03 54	04 46
20	18 07	18 29	18 54	01 39	02 36	03 33	04 27
N 10	18 11	18 32	18 56	01 20	02 16	03 14	04 11
0	18 15	18 35	19 00	01 02	01 58	02 56	03 55
S 10	18 19	18 40	19 04	00 45	01 40	02 39	03 40
20	18 23	18 45	19 11	00 26	01 20	02 20	03 23
30	18 28	18 52	19 21	00 04	00 58	01 58	03 04
35	18 31	18 57	19 27	24 45	00 45	01 45	02 52
40	18 35	19 02	19 35	24 29	00 29	01 30	02 39
45	18 39	19 09	19 44	24 11	00 11	01 13	02 24
S 50	18 44	19 17	19 56	23 48	24 51	00 51	02 05
52	18 46	19 20	20 02	23 38	24 40	00 40	01 55
54	18 48	19 25	20 09	23 25	24 28	00 28	01 45
56	18 51	19 29	20 17	23 11	24 15	00 15	01 34
58	18 54	19 35	20 25	22 55	23 59	25 05	01 20
S 60	18 58	19 41	20 35	22 35	23 40	25 05	01 05

	SUN Eqn. of Time 00h	12h	SUN Mer. Pass.	MOON Mer. Pass. Upper	Lower	Age	Phase
Day	m s	m s	h m	h m	h m	d %	
4	11 43	11 37	12 12	19 45	07 17	10 67	
5	11 30	11 23	12 11	20 42	08 13	11 77	◗
6	11 16	11 09	12 11	21 41	09 12	12 85	

UT	ARIES	VENUS −4.3		MARS +1.0		JUPITER −2.0		SATURN +0.7		STARS		
d h	GHA	GHA	Dec	GHA	Dec	GHA	Dec	GHA	Dec	Name	SHA	Dec
7 00	165 10.2	135 52.2	N13 41.0	240 29.3	S23 15.8	232 52.0	S21 52.3	224 18.3	S20 26.4	Acamar	315 15.0	S40 13.8
01	180 12.7	150 52.1	42.1	255 29.9	15.6	247 54.0	52.2	239 20.6	26.3	Achernar	335 23.7	S57 08.4
02	195 15.2	165 52.0	43.2	270 30.4	15.5	262 56.0	52.1	254 22.8	26.3	Acrux	173 03.5	S63 12.5
03	210 17.6	180 51.9	.. 44.4	285 31.0	.. 15.4	277 58.0	.. 52.1	269 25.0	.. 26.2	Adhara	255 08.7	S29 00.3
04	225 20.1	195 51.8	45.5	300 31.6	15.2	293 00.0	52.0	284 27.2	26.2	Aldebaran	290 44.1	N16 32.8
05	240 22.5	210 51.7	46.6	315 32.2	15.1	308 02.0	52.0	299 29.5	26.1			
06	255 25.0	225 51.6	N13 47.8	330 32.8	S23 15.0	323 04.0	S21 51.9	314 31.7	S20 26.1	Alioth	166 16.0	N55 50.9
07	270 27.5	240 51.6	48.9	345 33.4	14.8	338 06.0	51.8	329 33.9	26.1	Alkaid	152 54.8	N49 12.6
S 08	285 29.9	255 51.5	50.0	0 34.0	14.7	353 08.0	51.8	344 36.1	26.0	Alnair	27 38.3	S46 51.9
A 09	300 32.4	270 51.4	.. 51.2	15 34.5	.. 14.6	8 10.0	.. 51.7	359 38.4	.. 26.0	Alnilam	275 41.6	S 1 11.6
T 10	315 34.9	285 51.3	52.3	30 35.1	14.4	23 12.0	51.7	14 40.6	25.9	Alphard	217 51.3	S 8 44.9
U 11	330 37.3	300 51.2	53.4	45 35.7	14.3	38 14.0	51.6	29 42.8	25.9			
R 12	345 39.8	315 51.1	N13 54.6	60 36.3	S23 14.2	53 16.0	S21 51.5	44 45.0	S20 25.8	Alphecca	126 06.9	N26 38.7
D 13	0 42.3	330 51.0	55.7	75 36.9	14.0	68 18.0	51.5	59 47.3	25.8	Alpheratz	357 39.1	N29 11.9
A 14	15 44.7	345 50.9	56.8	90 37.5	13.9	83 20.0	51.4	74 49.5	25.7	Altair	62 03.9	N 8 55.2
Y 15	30 47.2	0 50.8	.. 58.0	105 38.1	.. 13.7	98 22.0	.. 51.3	89 51.7	.. 25.7	Ankaa	353 11.5	S42 12.1
16	45 49.6	15 50.8	13 59.1	120 38.6	13.5	113 24.0	51.3	104 53.9	25.7	Antares	112 20.5	S26 28.4
17	60 52.1	30 50.7	14 00.2	135 39.2	13.5	128 26.0	51.2	119 56.2	25.6			
18	75 54.6	45 50.6	N14 01.3	150 39.8	S23 13.3	143 28.0	S21 51.2	134 58.4	S20 25.6	Arcturus	145 51.3	N19 04.6
19	90 57.0	60 50.5	02.5	165 40.4	13.2	158 30.0	51.1	150 00.6	25.5	Atria	107 18.2	S69 03.4
20	105 59.5	75 50.4	03.6	180 41.0	13.1	173 32.0	51.0	165 02.8	25.5	Avior	234 15.7	S59 34.7
21	121 02.0	90 50.3	.. 04.7	195 41.6	.. 12.9	188 34.0	.. 51.0	180 05.1	.. 25.4	Bellatrix	278 27.0	N 6 21.9
22	136 04.4	105 50.2	05.8	210 42.2	12.8	203 36.0	50.9	195 07.3	25.4	Betelgeuse	270 56.2	N 7 24.5
23	151 06.9	120 50.1	07.0	225 42.8	12.6	218 38.0	50.9	210 09.5	25.4			
8 00	166 09.4	135 50.1	N14 08.1	240 43.3	S23 12.5	233 40.0	S21 50.8	225 11.8	S20 25.3	Canopus	263 53.9	S52 42.8
01	181 11.8	150 50.0	09.2	255 43.9	12.4	248 42.0	50.7	240 14.0	25.3	Capella	280 27.6	N46 01.1
02	196 14.3	165 49.9	10.3	270 44.5	12.2	263 44.0	50.7	255 16.2	25.2	Deneb	49 28.7	N45 20.9
03	211 16.8	180 49.8	.. 11.5	285 45.1	.. 12.1	278 46.0	.. 50.6	270 18.4	.. 25.2	Denebola	182 28.6	N14 27.5
04	226 19.2	195 49.7	12.6	300 45.7	11.9	293 48.0	50.5	285 20.7	25.1	Diphda	348 51.5	S17 52.8
05	241 21.7	210 49.6	13.7	315 46.3	11.8	308 50.0	50.5	300 22.9	25.1			
06	256 24.1	225 49.5	N14 14.8	330 46.9	S23 11.6	323 52.0	S21 50.4	315 25.1	S20 25.0	Dubhe	193 45.3	N61 38.5
07	271 26.6	240 49.4	16.0	345 47.5	11.5	338 54.0	50.4	330 27.3	25.0	Elnath	278 06.7	N28 37.4
08	286 29.1	255 49.4	17.1	0 48.0	11.4	353 56.0	50.3	345 29.6	25.0	Eltanin	90 44.1	N51 28.9
S 09	301 31.5	270 49.3	.. 18.2	15 48.6	.. 11.2	8 58.0	.. 50.2	0 31.8	.. 24.9	Enif	33 42.9	N 9 57.9
U 10	316 34.0	285 49.2	19.3	30 49.2	11.1	24 00.0	50.2	15 34.0	24.9	Fomalhaut	15 19.2	S29 31.1
N 11	331 36.5	300 49.1	20.4	45 49.8	10.9	39 02.0	50.1	30 36.3	24.8			
D 12	346 38.9	315 49.0	N14 21.5	60 50.4	S23 10.8	54 04.0	S21 50.1	45 38.5	S20 24.8	Gacrux	171 55.3	S57 13.4
A 13	1 41.4	330 48.9	22.7	75 51.0	10.6	69 06.0	50.0	60 40.7	24.8	Gienah	175 47.2	S17 39.2
Y 14	16 43.9	345 48.8	23.8	90 51.6	10.5	84 08.0	49.9	75 42.9	24.7	Hadar	148 40.9	S60 27.9
15	31 46.3	0 48.7	.. 24.9	105 52.2	.. 10.3	99 10.1	.. 49.9	90 45.2	.. 24.7	Hamal	327 55.8	N23 33.3
16	46 48.8	15 48.7	26.0	120 52.7	10.2	114 12.1	49.8	105 47.4	24.6	Kaus Aust.	83 37.8	S34 22.3
17	61 51.3	30 48.6	27.1	135 53.3	10.1	129 14.1	49.8	120 49.6	24.6			
18	76 53.7	45 48.5	N14 28.2	150 53.9	S23 09.9	144 16.1	S21 49.7	135 51.9	S20 24.5	Kochab	137 19.4	N74 04.2
19	91 56.2	60 48.4	29.4	165 54.5	09.8	159 18.1	49.6	150 54.1	24.5	Markab	13 34.1	N15 18.6
20	106 58.6	75 48.3	30.5	180 55.1	09.6	174 20.1	49.6	165 56.3	24.5	Menkar	314 10.4	N 4 09.9
21	122 01.1	90 48.2	.. 31.6	195 55.7	.. 09.5	189 22.1	.. 49.5	180 58.5	.. 24.4	Menkent	148 01.9	S36 28.0
22	137 03.6	105 48.1	32.7	210 56.3	09.3	204 24.1	49.4	196 00.8	24.4	Miaplacidus	221 38.0	S69 48.1
23	152 06.0	120 48.0	33.8	225 56.9	09.2	219 26.1	49.4	211 03.0	24.3			
9 00	167 08.5	135 48.0	N14 34.9	240 57.4	S23 09.0	234 28.1	S21 49.3	226 05.2	S20 24.3	Mirfak	308 33.9	N49 55.9
01	182 11.0	150 47.9	36.0	255 58.0	08.9	249 30.1	49.3	241 07.5	24.2	Nunki	75 52.7	S26 16.2
02	197 13.4	165 47.8	37.1	270 58.6	08.7	264 32.1	49.2	256 09.7	24.2	Peacock	53 12.4	S56 40.1
03	212 15.9	180 47.7	.. 38.2	285 59.2	.. 08.6	279 34.1	.. 49.1	271 11.9	.. 24.2	Pollux	243 21.8	N27 58.6
04	227 18.4	195 47.6	39.4	300 59.8	08.4	294 36.1	49.1	286 14.1	24.1	Procyon	244 54.7	N 5 10.2
05	242 20.8	210 47.5	40.5	316 00.4	08.3	309 38.2	49.0	301 16.4	24.1			
06	257 23.3	225 47.4	N14 41.6	331 01.0	S23 08.1	324 40.2	S21 49.0	316 18.6	S20 24.0	Rasalhague	96 02.2	N12 32.6
07	272 25.7	240 47.4	42.7	346 01.6	08.0	339 42.2	48.9	331 20.8	24.0	Regulus	207 38.3	N11 52.0
08	287 28.2	255 47.3	43.8	1 02.1	07.8	354 44.2	48.8	346 23.1	23.9	Rigel	281 07.6	S 8 11.0
M 09	302 30.7	270 47.2	.. 44.9	16 02.7	.. 07.7	9 46.2	.. 48.8	1 25.3	.. 23.9	Rigil Kent.	139 45.1	S60 54.8
O 10	317 33.1	285 47.1	46.0	31 03.3	07.5	24 48.2	48.7	16 27.5	23.9	Sabik	102 07.2	S15 44.9
N 11	332 35.6	300 47.0	47.1	46 03.9	07.4	39 50.2	48.6	31 29.8	23.8			
D 12	347 38.1	315 46.9	N14 48.2	61 04.5	S23 07.2	54 52.2	S21 48.6	46 32.0	S20 23.8	Schedar	349 35.8	N56 38.8
A 13	2 40.5	330 46.9	49.3	76 05.1	07.0	69 54.2	48.5	61 34.2	23.7	Shaula	96 15.7	S37 06.9
Y 14	17 43.0	345 46.8	50.4	91 05.7	06.9	84 56.2	48.5	76 36.4	23.7	Sirius	258 29.5	S16 44.9
15	32 45.5	0 46.7	.. 51.5	106 06.3	.. 06.7	99 58.2	.. 48.4	91 38.7	.. 23.6	Spica	158 26.1	S11 16.0
16	47 47.9	15 46.6	52.6	121 06.9	06.6	115 00.3	48.3	106 40.9	23.6	Suhail	222 48.7	S43 31.0
17	62 50.4	30 46.5	53.7	136 07.4	06.4	130 02.3	48.3	121 43.1	23.6			
18	77 52.9	45 46.4	N14 54.8	151 08.0	S23 06.3	145 04.3	S21 48.2	136 45.4	S20 23.5	Vega	80 36.0	N38 47.9
19	92 55.3	60 46.3	55.9	166 08.6	06.1	160 06.3	48.2	151 47.6	23.5	Zuben'ubi	137 00.1	S16 07.4
20	107 57.8	75 46.3	57.0	181 09.2	06.0	175 08.3	48.1	166 49.8	23.4		SHA	Mer. Pass.
21	123 00.2	90 46.2	.. 58.1	196 09.8	.. 05.8	190 10.3	.. 48.0	181 52.1	.. 23.4		° ′	h m
22	138 02.7	105 46.1	14 59.2	211 10.4	05.6	205 12.3	48.0	196 54.3	23.3	Venus	329 40.7	14 57
23	153 05.2	120 46.0	N15 00.3	226 11.0	05.5	220 14.3	47.9	211 56.5	23.3	Mars	74 34.0	7 57
	h m									Jupiter	67 30.6	8 24
Mer. Pass.	12 53.3	v −0.1	d 1.1	v 0.6	d 0.1	v 2.0	d 0.1	v 2.2	d 0.0	Saturn	59 02.4	8 58

SUN / MOON

UT (d h)	SUN GHA	SUN Dec	MOON GHA	v	Dec	d	HP
7 00	177 14.6	S 5 10.8	33 20.0	5.6	N20 44.9	7.1	59.8
01	192 14.7	09.8	47 44.6	5.6	20 37.8	7.2	59.8
02	207 14.9	08.9	62 09.2	5.6	20 30.6	7.4	59.8
03	222 15.0	.. 07.9	76 33.8	5.7	20 23.2	7.5	59.9
04	237 15.2	06.9	90 58.5	5.6	20 15.7	7.6	59.9
05	252 15.3	05.9	105 23.1	5.7	20 08.1	7.8	59.9
06	267 15.5	S 5 05.0	119 47.8	5.7	N20 00.3	8.0	60.0
07	282 15.7	04.0	134 12.5	5.7	19 52.3	8.0	60.0
S 08	297 15.8	03.0	148 37.2	5.7	19 44.3	8.3	60.1
A 09	312 16.0	.. 02.0	163 01.9	5.7	19 36.0	8.3	60.1
T 10	327 16.1	01.1	177 26.6	5.8	19 27.7	8.5	60.1
U 11	342 16.3	5 00.1	191 51.4	5.7	19 19.2	8.7	60.2
R 12	357 16.4	S 4 59.1	206 16.1	5.8	N19 10.5	8.8	60.2
D 13	12 16.6	58.1	220 40.9	5.9	19 01.7	8.9	60.2
A 14	27 16.7	57.2	235 05.8	5.8	18 52.8	9.0	60.3
Y 15	42 16.9	.. 56.2	249 30.6	5.9	18 43.8	9.2	60.3
16	57 17.0	55.2	263 55.5	5.9	18 34.6	9.4	60.3
17	72 17.2	54.2	278 20.4	5.9	18 25.2	9.4	60.4
18	87 17.3	S 4 53.3	292 45.3	6.0	N18 15.8	9.6	60.4
19	102 17.5	52.3	307 10.3	5.9	18 06.2	9.8	60.4
20	117 17.6	51.3	321 35.2	6.1	17 56.4	9.8	60.4
21	132 17.8	.. 50.3	336 00.3	6.0	17 46.6	10.0	60.5
22	147 17.9	49.4	350 25.3	6.1	17 36.6	10.1	60.5
23	162 18.1	48.4	4 50.4	6.1	17 26.5	10.3	60.5
8 00	177 18.3	S 4 47.4	19 15.5	6.1	N17 16.2	10.3	60.6
01	192 18.4	46.4	33 40.6	6.2	17 05.9	10.5	60.6
02	207 18.6	45.5	48 05.8	6.2	16 55.4	10.7	60.6
03	222 18.7	.. 44.5	62 31.0	6.2	16 44.7	10.7	60.6
04	237 18.9	43.5	76 56.2	6.3	16 34.0	10.9	60.7
05	252 19.0	42.5	91 21.5	6.3	16 23.1	10.9	60.7
06	267 19.2	S 4 41.6	105 46.8	6.3	N16 12.2	11.1	60.7
07	282 19.3	40.6	120 12.1	6.4	16 01.1	11.2	60.7
S 08	297 19.5	39.6	134 37.5	6.4	15 49.9	11.4	60.8
U 09	312 19.7	.. 38.6	149 02.9	6.5	15 38.5	11.4	60.8
N 10	327 19.8	37.7	163 28.4	6.4	15 27.1	11.6	60.8
D 11	342 20.0	36.7	177 53.8	6.6	15 15.5	11.6	60.9
A 12	357 20.1	S 4 35.7	192 19.4	6.5	N15 03.9	11.8	60.9
Y 13	12 20.3	34.7	206 44.9	6.6	14 52.1	11.9	60.9
14	27 20.4	33.8	221 10.5	6.7	14 40.2	12.0	60.9
15	42 20.6	.. 32.8	235 36.2	6.6	14 28.2	12.1	60.9
16	57 20.8	31.8	250 01.8	6.7	14 16.1	12.2	61.0
17	72 20.9	30.8	264 27.5	6.8	14 03.9	12.3	61.0
18	87 21.1	S 4 29.8	278 53.3	6.8	N13 51.6	12.4	61.0
19	102 21.2	28.9	293 19.1	6.8	13 39.2	12.5	61.0
20	117 21.4	27.9	307 44.9	6.9	13 26.7	12.6	61.1
21	132 21.5	.. 26.9	322 10.8	6.9	13 14.1	12.7	61.1
22	147 21.7	25.9	336 36.7	6.9	13 01.4	12.8	61.1
23	162 21.9	25.0	351 02.6	7.0	12 48.6	12.8	61.1
9 00	177 22.0	S 4 24.0	5 28.6	7.1	N12 35.8	13.0	61.1
01	192 22.2	23.0	19 54.7	7.0	12 22.8	13.1	61.1
02	207 22.3	22.0	34 20.7	7.1	12 09.7	13.1	61.2
03	222 22.5	.. 21.0	48 46.8	7.2	11 56.6	13.3	61.2
04	237 22.6	20.1	63 13.0	7.2	11 43.3	13.3	61.2
05	252 22.8	19.1	77 39.2	7.2	11 30.0	13.4	61.2
06	267 23.0	S 4 18.1	92 05.4	7.3	N11 16.6	13.4	61.2
07	282 23.1	17.1	106 31.7	7.3	11 03.2	13.6	61.2
M 08	297 23.3	16.2	120 58.0	7.3	10 49.6	13.6	61.3
O 09	312 23.4	.. 15.2	135 24.3	7.4	10 36.0	13.7	61.3
N 10	327 23.6	14.2	149 50.7	7.4	10 22.3	13.8	61.3
D 11	342 23.8	13.2	164 17.1	7.5	10 08.5	13.9	61.3
A 12	357 23.9	S 4 12.2	178 43.6	7.4	N 9 54.6	13.9	61.3
Y 13	12 24.1	11.3	193 10.0	7.6	9 40.7	14.0	61.3
14	27 24.2	10.3	207 36.6	7.6	9 26.7	14.0	61.3
15	42 24.4	.. 09.3	222 03.2	7.6	9 12.7	14.1	61.3
16	57 24.6	08.3	236 29.8	7.6	8 58.6	14.2	61.3
17	72 24.7	07.3	250 56.4	7.7	8 44.4	14.2	61.3
18	87 24.9	S 4 06.4	265 23.1	7.7	N 8 30.2	14.3	61.4
19	102 25.1	05.4	279 49.8	7.8	8 15.9	14.4	61.4
20	117 25.2	04.4	294 16.6	7.7	8 01.5	14.4	61.4
21	132 25.4	.. 03.4	308 43.3	7.9	7 47.1	14.5	61.4
22	147 25.5	02.4	323 10.2	7.8	7 32.6	14.5	61.4
23	162 25.7	01.5	337 37.0	7.9	N 7 18.1	14.5	61.4
	SD 16.1	d 1.0	SD 16.4		16.6		16.7

Twilight / Sunrise / Moonrise

Lat.	Naut.	Civil	Sunrise	7	8	9	10
N 72	04 31	05 51	06 58	▭	13 42	16 22	18 45
N 70	04 41	05 52	06 53	11 26	14 16	16 37	18 49
68	04 48	05 53	06 48	12 23	14 40	16 48	18 51
66	04 54	05 53	06 45	12 57	14 58	16 57	18 54
64	04 59	05 54	06 42	13 21	15 13	17 05	18 55
62	05 03	05 55	06 39	13 40	15 25	17 11	18 57
60	05 07	05 55	06 37	13 56	15 35	17 17	18 58
N 58	05 10	05 55	06 34	14 09	15 44	17 22	19 00
56	05 13	05 56	06 33	14 20	15 52	17 26	19 01
54	05 15	05 56	06 31	14 30	15 59	17 30	19 02
52	05 17	05 56	06 29	14 39	16 05	17 34	19 03
50	05 18	05 56	06 28	14 47	16 11	17 37	19 03
45	05 22	05 56	06 25	15 04	16 23	17 44	19 05
N 40	05 24	05 55	06 22	15 18	16 33	17 50	19 07
35	05 25	05 55	06 20	15 29	16 42	17 55	19 08
30	05 26	05 54	06 18	15 39	16 49	17 59	19 09
20	05 26	05 52	06 14	15 57	17 02	18 07	19 11
N 10	05 25	05 50	06 11	16 12	17 13	18 14	19 13
0	05 23	05 47	06 07	16 26	17 24	18 20	19 15
S 10	05 18	05 43	06 04	16 40	17 34	18 26	19 16
20	05 12	05 38	06 00	16 55	17 45	18 33	19 18
30	05 04	05 32	05 56	17 12	17 58	18 40	19 20
35	04 58	05 28	05 53	17 22	18 05	18 45	19 21
40	04 51	05 23	05 51	17 33	18 14	18 49	19 23
45	04 42	05 17	05 47	17 47	18 23	18 55	19 24
S 50	04 31	05 10	05 43	18 03	18 35	19 02	19 26
52	04 25	05 07	05 41	18 10	18 40	19 05	19 27
54	04 19	05 03	05 39	18 19	18 46	19 08	19 28
56	04 12	04 59	05 37	18 28	18 52	19 12	19 29
58	04 04	04 54	05 34	18 39	19 00	19 16	19 30
S 60	03 54	04 48	05 31	18 51	19 08	19 21	19 31

Sunset / Twilight / Moonset

Lat.	Sunset	Civil	Naut.	7	8	9	10
N 72	17 26	18 33	19 54	▭	08 57	08 17	07 51
N 70	17 31	18 31	19 44	09 10	08 22	08 00	07 44
68	17 35	18 30	19 36	08 12	07 57	07 47	07 38
66	17 38	18 29	19 29	07 37	07 37	07 36	07 34
64	17 41	18 29	19 24	07 12	07 22	07 27	07 30
62	17 44	18 28	19 20	06 52	07 08	07 19	07 26
60	17 46	18 28	19 16	06 36	06 57	07 12	07 23
N 58	17 48	18 27	19 13	06 22	06 47	07 05	07 20
56	17 50	18 27	19 10	06 10	06 38	07 00	07 18
54	17 51	18 27	19 08	06 00	06 30	06 55	07 16
52	17 53	18 27	19 06	05 50	06 23	06 50	07 14
50	17 54	18 27	19 04	05 42	06 17	06 46	07 12
45	17 57	18 27	19 01	05 24	06 03	06 37	07 08
N 40	18 00	18 27	18 58	05 09	05 52	06 30	07 04
35	18 02	18 27	18 57	04 57	05 42	06 23	07 01
30	18 04	18 28	18 56	04 46	05 34	06 18	06 59
20	18 08	18 30	18 55	04 27	05 19	06 08	06 54
N 10	18 11	18 32	18 56	04 11	05 06	05 59	06 50
0	18 14	18 35	18 59	03 55	04 54	05 51	06 46
S 10	18 17	18 38	19 03	03 40	04 41	05 42	06 42
20	18 21	18 43	19 09	03 23	04 28	05 33	06 38
30	18 25	18 49	19 17	03 04	04 12	05 23	06 33
35	18 27	18 53	19 23	02 52	04 03	05 17	06 30
40	18 30	18 57	19 30	02 39	03 53	05 10	06 27
45	18 33	19 03	19 38	02 24	03 41	05 01	06 23
S 50	18 37	19 10	19 49	02 05	03 26	04 52	06 18
52	18 39	19 13	19 55	01 55	03 19	04 47	06 16
54	18 41	19 17	20 01	01 45	03 11	04 42	06 14
56	18 43	19 21	20 08	01 34	03 03	04 36	06 11
58	18 46	19 26	20 15	01 20	02 53	04 30	06 08
S 60	18 49	19 31	20 25	01 05	02 41	04 23	06 05

SUN / MOON

Day	SUN Eqn. of Time 00h	SUN Eqn. of Time 12h	SUN Mer. Pass.	MOON Mer. Pass. Upper	MOON Mer. Pass. Lower	Age	Phase %
	m s	m s	h m	h m	h m	d	%
7	11 02	10 55	12 11	22 40	10 11	13	93
8	10 47	10 40	12 11	23 37	11 09	14	98
9	10 32	10 25	12 10	24 33	12 05	15	100

UT	ARIES GHA	VENUS −4.4 GHA	Dec	MARS +1.0 GHA	Dec	JUPITER −2.0 GHA	Dec	SATURN +0.7 GHA	Dec
10 TUESDAY									
00	168 07.6	135 45.9	N15 01.4	241 11.6	S23 05.3	235 16.4	S21 47.9	226 58.8	S20 23.3
01	183 10.1	150 45.8	02.5	256 12.2	05.2	250 18.4	47.8	242 01.0	23.2
02	198 12.6	165 45.8	03.6	271 12.7	05.0	265 20.4	47.7	257 03.2	23.2
03	213 15.0	180 45.7	.. 04.7	286 13.3	.. 04.9	280 22.4	.. 47.7	272 05.5	.. 23.1
04	228 17.5	195 45.6	05.8	301 13.9	04.7	295 24.4	47.7	287 07.7	23.1
05	243 20.0	210 45.5	06.9	316 14.5	04.5	310 26.4	47.6	302 09.9	23.0
06	258 22.4	225 45.4	N15 08.0	331 15.1	S23 04.4	325 28.4	S21 47.5	317 12.2	S20 23.0
07	273 24.9	240 45.3	09.1	346 15.7	04.2	340 30.4	47.4	332 14.4	23.0
08	288 27.3	255 45.3	10.2	1 16.3	04.1	355 32.5	47.4	347 16.6	22.9
09	303 29.8	270 45.2	.. 11.3	16 16.9	.. 03.9	10 34.5	.. 47.3	2 18.9	.. 22.9
10	318 32.3	285 45.1	12.4	31 17.5	03.7	25 36.5	47.2	17 21.1	22.8
11	333 34.7	300 45.0	13.5	46 18.1	03.6	40 38.5	47.2	32 23.3	22.8
12	348 37.2	315 44.9	N15 14.5	61 18.6	S23 03.4	55 40.5	S21 47.1	47 25.6	S20 22.8
13	3 39.7	330 44.8	15.6	76 19.2	03.3	70 42.5	47.1	62 27.8	22.7
14	18 42.1	345 44.8	16.7	91 19.8	03.1	85 44.5	47.0	77 30.0	22.7
15	33 44.6	0 44.7	.. 17.8	106 20.4	.. 02.9	100 46.6	.. 46.9	92 32.3	.. 22.6
16	48 47.1	15 44.6	18.9	121 21.0	02.8	115 48.6	46.9	107 34.5	22.6
17	63 49.5	30 44.5	20.0	136 21.6	02.6	130 50.6	46.8	122 36.7	22.5
18	78 52.0	45 44.4	N15 21.1	151 22.2	S23 02.4	145 52.6	S21 46.8	137 39.0	S20 22.5
19	93 54.5	60 44.3	22.2	166 22.8	02.3	160 54.6	46.7	152 41.2	22.5
20	108 56.9	75 44.3	23.3	181 23.4	02.1	175 56.6	46.6	167 43.4	22.4
21	123 59.4	90 44.2	.. 24.3	196 23.9	.. 01.9	190 58.7	.. 46.6	182 45.7	.. 22.4
22	139 01.8	105 44.1	25.4	211 24.5	01.8	206 00.7	46.5	197 47.9	22.3
23	154 04.3	120 44.0	26.5	226 25.1	01.6	221 02.7	46.5	212 50.1	22.3
11 WEDNESDAY									
00	169 06.8	135 43.9	N15 27.6	241 25.7	S23 01.4	236 04.7	S21 46.4	227 52.4	S20 22.2
01	184 09.2	150 43.9	28.7	256 26.3	01.3	251 06.7	46.3	242 54.6	22.2
02	199 11.7	165 43.8	29.8	271 26.9	01.1	266 08.7	46.3	257 56.8	22.2
03	214 14.2	180 43.7	.. 30.8	286 27.5	.. 00.9	281 10.8	.. 46.2	272 59.1	.. 22.1
04	229 16.6	195 43.6	31.9	301 28.1	00.7	296 12.8	46.2	288 01.3	22.1
05	244 19.1	210 43.5	33.0	316 28.7	00.6	311 14.8	46.1	303 03.5	22.0
06	259 21.6	225 43.4	N15 34.1	331 29.3	S23 00.4	326 16.8	S21 46.0	318 05.8	S20 22.0
07	274 24.0	240 43.4	35.2	346 29.9	00.3	341 18.8	46.0	333 08.0	22.0
08	289 26.5	255 43.3	36.2	1 30.4	23 00.1	356 20.8	45.9	348 10.2	21.9
09	304 28.9	270 43.2	.. 37.3	16 31.0	22 59.9	11 22.9	.. 45.8	3 12.5	.. 21.9
10	319 31.4	285 43.1	38.4	31 31.6	59.8	26 24.9	45.8	18 14.7	21.8
11	334 33.9	300 43.0	39.5	46 32.2	59.6	41 26.9	45.7	33 17.0	21.8
12	349 36.3	315 43.0	N15 40.5	61 32.8	S22 59.4	56 28.9	S21 45.7	48 19.2	S20 21.7
13	4 38.8	330 42.9	41.6	76 33.4	59.3	71 30.9	45.6	63 21.4	21.7
14	19 41.3	345 42.8	42.7	91 34.0	59.1	86 33.0	45.5	78 23.7	21.7
15	34 43.7	0 42.7	.. 43.8	106 34.6	.. 58.9	101 35.0	.. 45.5	93 25.9	.. 21.6
16	49 46.2	15 42.6	44.8	121 35.2	58.7	116 37.0	45.4	108 28.1	21.6
17	64 48.7	30 42.6	45.9	136 35.8	58.6	131 39.0	45.4	123 30.4	21.5
18	79 51.1	45 42.5	N15 47.0	151 36.3	S22 58.4	146 41.0	S21 45.3	138 32.6	S20 21.5
19	94 53.6	60 42.4	48.1	166 36.9	58.2	161 43.1	45.2	153 34.8	21.4
20	109 56.1	75 42.3	49.1	181 37.5	58.1	176 45.1	45.2	168 37.1	21.4
21	124 58.5	90 42.2	.. 50.2	196 38.1	.. 57.9	191 47.1	.. 45.1	183 39.3	.. 21.4
22	140 01.0	105 42.2	51.3	211 38.7	57.7	206 49.1	45.1	198 41.6	21.3
23	155 03.4	120 42.1	52.3	226 39.3	57.5	221 51.2	45.0	213 43.8	21.3
12 THURSDAY									
00	170 05.9	135 42.0	N15 53.4	241 39.9	S22 57.4	236 53.2	S21 44.9	228 46.0	S20 21.2
01	185 08.4	150 41.9	54.5	256 40.5	57.2	251 55.2	44.9	243 48.3	21.2
02	200 10.8	165 41.8	55.6	271 41.1	57.0	266 57.2	44.8	258 50.5	21.2
03	215 13.3	180 41.8	.. 56.6	286 41.7	.. 56.8	281 59.2	.. 44.8	273 52.7	.. 21.1
04	230 15.8	195 41.7	57.7	301 42.3	56.7	297 01.3	44.7	288 55.0	21.1
05	245 18.2	210 41.6	58.8	316 42.9	56.5	312 03.3	44.6	303 57.2	21.0
06	260 20.7	225 41.5	N15 59.8	331 43.4	S22 56.3	327 05.3	S21 44.6	318 59.5	S20 21.0
07	275 23.2	240 41.4	16 00.9	346 44.0	56.1	342 07.3	44.5	334 01.7	21.0
08	290 25.6	255 41.4	02.0	1 44.6	56.0	357 09.4	44.5	349 03.9	20.9
09	305 28.1	270 41.3	.. 03.0	16 45.2	.. 55.8	12 11.4	.. 44.4	4 06.2	.. 20.9
10	320 30.5	285 41.2	04.1	31 45.8	55.6	27 13.4	44.3	19 08.4	20.8
11	335 33.0	300 41.1	05.1	46 46.4	55.4	42 15.4	44.3	34 10.6	20.8
12	350 35.5	315 41.1	N16 06.2	61 47.0	S22 55.2	57 17.5	S21 44.2	49 12.9	S20 20.7
13	5 37.9	330 41.0	07.3	76 47.6	55.1	72 19.5	44.1	64 15.1	20.7
14	20 40.4	345 40.9	08.3	91 48.2	54.9	87 21.5	44.1	79 17.4	20.7
15	35 42.9	0 40.8	.. 09.4	106 48.8	.. 54.7	102 23.5	.. 44.0	94 19.6	.. 20.6
16	50 45.3	15 40.7	10.4	121 49.4	54.5	117 25.5	44.0	109 21.8	20.6
17	65 47.8	30 40.7	11.5	136 50.0	54.3	132 27.6	43.9	124 24.1	20.5
18	80 50.3	45 40.6	N16 12.6	151 50.5	S22 54.2	147 29.6	S21 43.8	139 26.3	S20 20.5
19	95 52.7	60 40.5	13.6	166 51.1	54.0	162 31.6	43.8	154 28.6	20.5
20	110 55.2	75 40.4	14.7	181 51.7	53.8	177 33.7	43.7	169 30.8	20.4
21	125 57.7	90 40.4	.. 15.7	196 52.3	.. 53.6	192 35.7	.. 43.7	184 33.0	.. 20.4
22	141 00.1	105 40.3	16.8	211 52.9	53.4	207 37.7	43.6	199 35.3	20.3
23	156 02.6	120 40.2	17.8	226 53.5	53.3	222 39.7	· 43.5	214 37.5	20.3
Mer. Pass.	12 41.5	v −0.1	d 1.1	v 0.6	d 0.2	v 2.0	d 0.1	v 2.2	d 0.0

STARS

Name	SHA	Dec
Acamar	315 15.0	S40 13.8
Achernar	335 23.7	S57 08.4
Acrux	173 03.5	S63 12.5
Adhara	255 08.7	S29 00.3
Aldebaran	290 44.1	N16 32.8
Alioth	166 16.0	N55 51.0
Alkaid	152 54.8	N49 12.6
Alnair	27 38.3	S46 51.9
Alnilam	275 41.6	S 1 11.6
Alphard	217 51.3	S 8 44.9
Alphecca	126 06.9	N26 38.7
Alpheratz	357 39.1	N29 11.9
Altair	62 03.9	N 8 55.2
Ankaa	353 11.5	S42 12.1
Antares	112 20.5	S26 28.4
Arcturus	145 51.3	N19 04.6
Atria	107 18.1	S69 03.4
Avior	234 15.8	S59 34.7
Bellatrix	278 27.0	N 6 21.9
Betelgeuse	270 56.2	N 7 24.5
Canopus	263 54.0	S52 42.8
Capella	280 27.6	N46 01.1
Deneb	49 28.7	N45 20.9
Denebola	182 28.6	N14 27.5
Diphda	348 51.5	S17 52.8
Dubhe	193 45.3	N61 38.6
Elnath	278 06.8	N28 37.4
Eltanin	90 44.1	N51 28.9
Enif	33 42.9	N 9 57.9
Fomalhaut	15 19.2	S29 31.1
Gacrux	171 55.3	S57 13.4
Gienah	175 47.2	S17 39.2
Hadar	148 40.9	S60 28.0
Hamal	327 55.8	N23 33.3
Kaus Aust.	83 37.8	S34 22.3
Kochab	137 19.3	N74 04.2
Markab	13 34.1	N15 18.6
Menkar	314 10.4	N 4 09.9
Menkent	148 01.8	S36 28.0
Miaplacidus	221 38.1	S69 48.2
Mirfak	308 34.0	N49 55.9
Nunki	75 52.7	S26 16.2
Peacock	53 12.3	S56 40.1
Pollux	243 21.9	N27 58.6
Procyon	244 54.7	N 5 10.2
Rasalhague	96 02.2	N12 32.6
Regulus	207 38.3	N11 52.1
Rigel	281 07.6	S 8 11.0
Rigil Kent.	139 45.1	S60 54.8
Sabik	102 07.2	S15 44.9
Schedar	349 35.8	N56 38.8
Shaula	96 15.6	S37 06.9
Sirius	258 29.5	S16 44.9
Spica	158 26.1	S11 16.0
Suhail	222 48.7	S43 31.0
Vega	80 36.0	N38 47.9
Zuben'ubi	137 00.1	S16 07.5

	SHA	Mer. Pass.
Venus	326 37.2	14 57
Mars	72 18.9	7 54
Jupiter	66 57.9	8 15
Saturn	58 45.6	8 47

UT	SUN GHA	SUN Dec	MOON GHA	v	MOON Dec	d	HP
d h	o '	o '	o '	'	o '	'	'
10 00	177 25.9	S 4 00.5	352 03.9	7.9	N 7 03.6	14.6	61.4
01	192 26.0	3 59.5	6 30.8	8.0	6 49.0	14.7	61.4
02	207 26.2	58.5	20 57.8	8.0	6 34.3	14.7	61.4
03	222 26.3	.. 57.5	35 24.8	8.0	6 19.6	14.7	61.4
04	237 26.5	56.6	49 51.8	8.0	6 04.9	14.8	61.4
05	252 26.7	55.6	64 18.8	8.1	5 50.1	14.8	61.4
06	267 26.8	S 3 54.6	78 45.9	8.1	N 5 35.3	14.9	61.4
07	282 27.0	53.6	93 13.0	8.2	5 20.4	14.8	61.4
T 08	297 27.2	52.6	107 40.2	8.2	5 05.6	15.0	61.4
U 09	312 27.3	.. 51.7	122 07.4	8.2	4 50.6	14.9	61.4
E 10	327 27.5	50.7	136 34.6	8.2	4 35.7	15.0	61.4
S 11	342 27.6	49.7	151 01.8	8.2	4 20.7	15.0	61.4
D 12	357 27.8	S 3 48.7	165 29.0	8.3	N 4 05.7	15.0	61.4
A 13	12 28.0	47.7	179 56.3	8.3	3 50.7	15.0	61.4
Y 14	27 28.1	46.8	194 23.6	8.4	3 35.7	15.1	61.4
15	42 28.3	.. 45.8	208 51.0	8.3	3 20.6	15.1	61.4
16	57 28.5	44.8	223 18.3	8.4	3 05.5	15.1	61.4
17	72 28.6	43.8	237 45.7	8.4	2 50.4	15.1	61.4
18	87 28.8	S 3 42.8	252 13.1	8.4	N 2 35.3	15.1	61.4
19	102 29.0	41.8	266 40.5	8.5	2 20.2	15.2	61.4
20	117 29.1	40.9	281 08.0	8.5	2 05.0	15.1	61.3
21	132 29.3	.. 39.9	295 35.5	8.5	1 49.9	15.1	61.3
22	147 29.5	38.9	310 03.0	8.5	1 34.8	15.2	61.3
23	162 29.6	37.9	324 30.5	8.5	1 19.6	15.2	61.3
11 00	177 29.8	S 3 36.9	338 58.0	8.6	N 1 04.4	15.1	61.3
01	192 30.0	36.0	353 25.6	8.5	0 49.3	15.2	61.3
02	207 30.1	35.0	7 53.1	8.6	0 34.1	15.2	61.3
03	222 30.3	.. 34.0	22 20.7	8.6	0 18.9	15.1	61.3
04	237 30.4	33.0	36 48.3	8.7	N 0 03.8	15.2	61.3
05	252 30.6	32.0	51 16.0	8.6	S 0 11.4	15.1	61.3
06	267 30.8	S 3 31.0	65 43.6	8.7	S 0 26.5	15.1	61.2
W 07	282 30.9	30.1	80 11.3	8.6	0 41.6	15.2	61.2
E 08	297 31.1	29.1	94 38.9	8.7	0 56.8	15.1	61.2
D 09	312 31.3	.. 28.1	109 06.6	8.7	1 11.9	15.1	61.2
N 10	327 31.4	27.1	123 34.3	8.7	1 27.0	15.0	61.2
E 11	342 31.6	26.1	138 02.0	8.7	1 42.0	15.1	61.2
S 12	357 31.8	S 3 25.2	152 29.7	8.7	S 1 57.1	15.0	61.2
D 13	12 31.9	24.2	166 57.4	8.8	2 12.1	15.0	61.1
A 14	27 32.1	23.2	181 25.2	8.7	2 27.1	15.0	61.1
Y 15	42 32.3	.. 22.2	195 52.9	8.8	2 42.1	15.0	61.1
16	57 32.4	21.2	210 20.7	8.7	2 57.1	14.9	61.1
17	72 32.6	20.2	224 48.4	8.8	3 12.0	14.9	61.1
18	87 32.8	S 3 19.3	239 16.2	8.8	S 3 26.9	14.9	61.0
19	102 32.9	18.3	253 44.0	8.8	3 41.8	14.8	61.0
20	117 33.1	17.3	268 11.8	8.8	3 56.6	14.9	61.0
21	132 33.3	.. 16.3	282 39.6	8.7	4 11.5	14.7	61.0
22	147 33.5	15.3	297 07.3	8.8	4 26.2	14.8	61.0
23	162 33.6	14.3	311 35.1	8.8	4 41.0	14.7	60.9
12 00	177 33.8	S 3 13.4	326 02.9	8.8	S 4 55.7	14.6	60.9
01	192 34.0	12.4	340 30.7	8.8	5 10.3	14.6	60.9
02	207 34.1	11.4	354 58.5	8.8	5 24.9	14.6	60.9
03	222 34.3	.. 10.4	9 26.3	8.8	5 39.5	14.5	60.8
04	237 34.5	09.4	23 54.1	8.8	5 54.0	14.5	60.8
05	252 34.6	08.4	38 21.9	8.8	6 08.5	14.4	60.8
06	267 34.8	S 3 07.4	52 49.7	8.8	S 6 22.9	14.4	60.8
07	282 35.0	06.5	67 17.5	8.8	6 37.3	14.3	60.7
T 08	297 35.1	05.5	81 45.3	8.8	6 51.6	14.3	60.7
H 09	312 35.3	.. 04.5	96 13.1	8.8	7 05.9	14.2	60.7
U 10	327 35.5	03.5	110 40.9	8.8	7 20.1	14.1	60.7
R 11	342 35.6	02.5	125 08.7	8.8	7 34.2	14.1	60.6
S 12	357 35.8	S 3 01.5	139 36.5	8.8	S 7 48.3	14.0	60.6
D 13	12 36.0	3 00.6	154 04.3	8.7	8 02.3	14.0	60.6
A 14	27 36.2	2 59.6	168 32.0	8.8	8 16.3	13.9	60.6
Y 15	42 36.3	.. 58.6	182 59.8	8.8	8 30.2	13.9	60.5
16	57 36.5	57.6	197 27.6	8.7	8 44.1	13.7	60.5
17	72 36.7	56.6	211 55.3	8.8	8 57.8	13.7	60.5
18	87 36.8	S 2 55.6	226 23.1	8.7	S 9 11.5	13.7	60.4
19	102 37.0	54.6	240 50.8	8.7	9 25.2	13.6	60.4
20	117 37.2	53.7	255 18.5	8.7	9 38.8	13.4	60.4
21	132 37.3	.. 52.7	269 46.2	8.7	9 52.2	13.5	60.4
22	147 37.5	51.7	284 13.9	8.7	10 05.7	13.3	60.3
23	162 37.7	50.7	298 41.6	8.7	S10 19.0	13.3	60.3
	SD 16.1	d 1.0	SD 16.7		16.7		16.5

Twilight / Sunrise / Moonrise

Lat.	Naut.	Civil	Sunrise	Moonrise 10	11	12	13
o	h m	h m	h m	h m	h m	h m	h m
N 72	04 14	05 36	06 42	18 45	21 04	23 27	26 11
N 70	04 26	05 38	06 39	18 49	20 58	23 08	25 27
68	04 35	05 41	06 36	18 51	20 52	22 54	24 59
66	04 42	05 43	06 33	18 54	20 48	22 42	24 37
64	04 48	05 44	06 31	18 55	20 44	22 33	24 20
62	04 53	05 45	06 29	18 57	20 41	22 24	24 06
60	04 58	05 46	06 28	18 58	20 39	22 17	23 55
N 58	05 02	05 47	06 26	19 00	20 36	22 11	23 44
56	05 05	05 48	06 25	19 01	20 34	22 06	23 36
54	05 07	05 48	06 24	19 02	20 32	22 01	23 28
52	05 10	05 49	06 23	19 03	20 30	21 57	23 21
50	05 12	05 49	06 22	19 03	20 29	21 53	23 15
45	05 16	05 50	06 19	19 05	20 25	21 44	23 01
N 40	05 19	05 50	06 17	19 07	20 23	21 37	22 50
35	05 21	05 51	06 16	19 08	20 20	21 31	22 41
30	05 23	05 51	06 14	19 09	20 18	21 26	22 33
20	05 24	05 50	06 12	19 11	20 14	21 17	22 19
N 10	05 24	05 48	06 09	19 13	20 11	21 09	22 07
0	05 22	05 46	06 07	19 15	20 08	21 02	21 55
S 10	05 19	05 43	06 04	19 16	20 05	20 54	21 44
20	05 13	05 39	06 01	19 18	20 02	20 47	21 32
30	05 06	05 34	05 58	19 19	19 59	20 38	21 19
35	05 01	05 31	05 56	19 21	19 57	20 33	21 11
40	04 54	05 27	05 54	19 23	19 54	20 27	21 02
45	04 46	05 22	05 51	19 24	19 52	20 21	20 52
S 50	04 36	05 15	05 48	19 26	19 49	20 13	20 40
52	04 31	05 12	05 46	19 27	19 48	20 10	20 34
54	04 26	05 09	05 45	19 28	19 46	20 06	20 28
56	04 19	05 05	05 43	19 29	19 45	20 02	20 21
58	04 12	05 01	05 41	19 30	19 43	19 57	20 13
S 60	04 04	04 56	05 39	19 31	19 41	19 52	20 04

Sunset / Twilight / Moonset

Lat.	Sunset	Civil	Naut.	Moonset 10	11	12	13
o	h m	h m	h m	h m	h m	h m	h m
N 72	17 40	18 47	20 09	07 51	07 28	07 05	06 36
N 70	17 43	18 44	19 57	07 44	07 29	07 14	06 56
68	17 46	18 41	19 48	07 38	07 30	07 22	07 13
66	17 48	18 39	19 40	07 34	07 31	07 29	07 26
64	17 50	18 37	19 33	07 30	07 32	07 34	07 37
62	17 52	18 36	19 28	07 26	07 33	07 39	07 47
60	17 53	18 35	19 24	07 23	07 33	07 43	07 55
N 58	17 55	18 34	19 20	07 20	07 34	07 47	08 02
56	17 56	18 33	19 17	07 18	07 34	07 51	08 08
54	17 57	18 32	19 14	07 16	07 35	07 54	08 14
52	17 58	18 32	19 11	07 14	07 35	07 56	08 19
50	17 59	18 31	19 09	07 12	07 35	07 59	08 24
45	18 01	18 31	19 05	07 08	07 36	08 04	08 34
N 40	18 03	18 30	19 01	07 04	07 37	08 09	08 43
35	18 05	18 30	18 59	07 01	07 37	08 13	08 50
30	18 06	18 30	18 58	06 59	07 38	08 17	08 57
20	18 09	18 31	18 56	06 54	07 39	08 23	09 08
N 10	18 11	18 32	18 56	06 50	07 39	08 28	09 18
0	18 13	18 34	18 58	06 46	07 40	08 33	09 27
S 10	18 16	18 37	19 01	06 42	07 41	08 39	09 36
20	18 18	18 40	19 06	06 38	07 41	08 44	09 46
30	18 21	18 45	19 13	06 33	07 42	08 50	09 58
35	18 23	18 49	19 18	06 30	07 42	08 53	10 05
40	18 25	18 52	19 25	06 27	07 43	08 58	10 12
45	18 28	18 57	19 32	06 23	07 43	09 03	10 21
S 50	18 31	19 03	19 42	06 18	07 44	09 09	10 32
52	18 32	19 06	19 47	06 16	07 44	09 11	10 37
54	18 34	19 10	19 53	06 14	07 45	09 14	10 42
56	18 35	19 13	19 59	06 11	07 45	09 17	10 48
58	18 37	19 17	20 06	06 08	07 45	09 21	10 55
S 60	18 40	19 22	20 14	06 05	07 46	09 25	11 03

SUN and MOON

Day	Eqn. of Time 00h	Eqn. of Time 12h	Mer. Pass.	Mer. Pass. Upper	Mer. Pass. Lower	Age	Phase
d	m s	m s	h m	h m	h m	d	%
10	10 17	10 09	12 10	00 33	13 00	16	99
11	10 01	09 53	12 10	01 27	13 54	17	95
12	09 45	09 37	12 10	02 21	14 48	18	89

UT	ARIES	VENUS −4.4		MARS +1.0		JUPITER −2.0		SATURN +0.7		STARS		
	GHA	GHA	Dec	GHA	Dec	GHA	Dec	GHA	Dec	Name	SHA	Dec
d h	° ′	° ′	° ′	° ′	° ′	° ′	° ′	° ′	° ′		° ′	° ′
13 00	171 05.0	135 40.1	N16 18.9	241 54.1	S22 53.1	237 41.8	S21 43.5	229 39.8	S20 20.2	Acamar	315 15.0	S40 13.8
01	186 07.5	150 40.0	20.0	256 54.7	52.9	252 43.8	43.4	244 42.0	20.2	Achernar	335 23.7	S57 08.4
02	201 10.0	165 40.0	21.0	271 55.3	52.7	267 45.8	43.4	259 44.2	20.2	Acrux	173 03.5	S63 12.5
03	216 12.4	180 39.9 ..	22.1	286 55.9 ..	52.5	282 47.8 ..	43.3	274 46.5 ..	20.1	Adhara	255 08.8	S29 00.3
04	231 14.9	195 39.8	23.1	301 56.5	52.3	297 49.9	43.2	289 48.7	20.1	Aldebaran	290 44.1	N16 32.8
05	246 17.4	210 39.7	24.2	316 57.1	52.2	312 51.9	43.2	304 51.0	20.0			
06	261 19.8	225 39.7	N16 25.2	331 57.7	S22 52.0	327 53.9	S21 43.1	319 53.2	S20 20.0	Alioth	166 16.0	N55 51.0
07	276 22.3	240 39.6	26.3	346 58.3	51.8	342 56.0	43.1	334 55.4	20.0	Alkaid	152 54.8	N49 12.7
08	291 24.8	255 39.5	27.3	1 58.8	51.6	357 58.0	43.0	349 57.7	19.9	Alnair	27 38.3	S46 51.9
F 09	306 27.2	270 39.4 ..	28.4	16 59.4 ..	51.4	13 00.0 ..	42.9	4 59.9 ..	19.9	Alnilam	275 41.7	S 1 11.6
R 10	321 29.7	285 39.4	29.4	32 00.0	51.2	28 02.0	42.9	20 02.2	19.8	Alphard	217 51.3	S 8 44.9
I 11	336 32.2	300 39.3	30.5	47 00.6	51.0	43 04.1	42.8	35 04.4	19.8			
D 12	351 34.6	315 39.2	N16 31.5	62 01.2	S22 50.9	58 06.1	S21 42.8	50 06.7	S20 19.8	Alphecca	126 06.9	N26 38.7
A 13	6 37.1	330 39.1	32.6	77 01.8	50.7	73 08.1	42.7	65 08.9	19.7	Alpheratz	357 39.1	N29 11.9
Y 14	21 39.5	345 39.1	33.6	92 02.4	50.5	88 10.2	42.6	80 11.1	19.7	Altair	62 03.9	N 8 55.2
15	36 42.0	0 39.0 ..	34.6	107 03.0 ..	50.3	103 12.2 ..	42.6	95 13.4 ..	19.6	Ankaa	353 11.5	S42 12.0
16	51 44.5	15 38.9	35.7	122 03.6	50.1	118 14.2	42.5	110 15.6	19.6	Antares	112 20.5	S26 28.5
17	66 46.9	30 38.8	36.7	137 04.2	49.9	133 16.2	42.5	125 17.9	19.6			
18	81 49.4	45 38.8	N16 37.8	152 04.8	S22 49.7	148 18.3	S21 42.4	140 20.1	S20 19.5	Arcturus	145 51.2	N19 04.6
19	96 51.9	60 38.7	38.8	167 05.4	49.5	163 20.3	42.3	155 22.4	19.5	Atria	107 18.1	S69 03.4
20	111 54.3	75 38.6	39.9	182 06.0	49.3	178 22.3	42.3	170 24.6	19.4	Avior	234 15.8	S59 34.7
21	126 56.8	90 38.5 ..	40.9	197 06.6 ..	49.2	193 24.4 ..	42.2	185 26.8 ..	19.4	Bellatrix	278 27.0	N 6 21.9
22	141 59.3	105 38.5	41.9	212 07.2	49.0	208 26.4	42.2	200 29.1	19.3	Betelgeuse	270 56.2	N 7 24.5
23	157 01.7	120 38.4	43.0	227 07.7	48.8	223 28.4	42.1	215 31.3	19.3			
14 00	172 04.2	135 38.3	N16 44.0	242 08.3	S22 48.6	238 30.5	S21 42.0	230 33.6	S20 19.3	Canopus	263 54.0	S52 42.8
01	187 06.6	150 38.2	45.1	257 08.9	48.4	253 32.5	42.0	245 35.8	19.2	Capella	280 27.6	N46 01.1
02	202 09.1	165 38.2	46.1	272 09.5	48.2	268 34.5	41.9	260 38.1	19.2	Deneb	49 28.7	N45 20.9
03	217 11.6	180 38.1 ..	47.1	287 10.1 ..	48.0	283 36.6 ..	41.9	275 40.3 ..	19.1	Denebola	182 06.8	N14 27.5
04	232 14.0	195 38.0	48.2	302 10.7	47.8	298 38.6	41.8	290 42.5	19.1	Diphda	348 51.5	S17 52.8
05	247 16.5	210 37.9	49.2	317 11.3	47.6	313 40.6	41.7	305 44.8	19.1			
06	262 19.0	225 37.9	N16 50.2	332 11.9	S22 47.4	328 42.7	S21 41.7	320 47.0	S20 19.0	Dubhe	193 45.3	N61 38.6
07	277 21.4	240 37.8	51.3	347 12.5	47.2	343 44.7	41.6	335 49.3	19.0	Elnath	278 06.8	N28 37.4
S 08	292 23.9	255 37.7	52.3	2 13.1	47.0	358 46.7	41.6	350 51.5	18.9	Eltanin	90 44.0	N51 28.9
A 09	307 26.4	270 37.6 ..	53.3	17 13.7 ..	46.9	13 48.8 ..	41.5	5 53.8 ..	18.9	Enif	33 42.9	N 9 57.9
T 10	322 28.8	285 37.5	54.4	32 14.3	46.7	28 50.8	41.4	20 56.0	18.9	Fomalhaut	15 19.2	S29 31.1
U 11	337 31.3	300 37.5	55.4	47 14.9	46.5	43 52.8	41.4	35 58.3	18.8			
R 12	352 33.8	315 37.4	N16 56.4	62 15.5	S22 46.3	58 54.9	S21 41.3	51 00.5	S20 18.8	Gacrux	171 55.2	S57 13.5
D 13	7 36.2	330 37.4	57.5	77 16.1	46.1	73 56.9	41.3	66 02.7	18.7	Gienah	175 47.2	S17 39.2
A 14	22 38.7	345 37.3	58.5	92 16.7	45.9	88 58.9	41.2	81 05.0	18.7	Hadar	148 40.9	S60 28.0
Y 15	37 41.1	0 37.2	16 59.5	107 17.3 ..	45.7	104 01.0 ..	41.1	96 07.2 ..	18.7	Hamal	327 55.8	N23 33.3
16	52 43.6	15 37.1	17 00.6	122 17.9	45.5	119 03.0	41.1	111 09.5	18.6	Kaus Aust.	83 37.7	S34 22.3
17	67 46.1	30 37.1	01.6	137 18.4	45.3	134 05.0	41.0	126 11.7	18.6			
18	82 48.5	45 37.0	N17 02.6	152 19.0	S22 45.1	149 07.1	S21 41.0	141 14.0	S20 18.5	Kochab	137 19.3	N74 04.2
19	97 51.0	60 36.9	03.6	167 19.6	44.9	164 09.1	40.9	156 16.2	18.5	Markab	13 34.0	N15 18.6
20	112 53.5	75 36.8	04.7	182 20.2	44.7	179 11.1	40.8	171 18.5	18.5	Menkar	314 10.4	N 4 09.9
21	127 55.9	90 36.8 ..	05.7	197 20.8 ..	44.5	194 13.2 ..	40.8	186 20.7 ..	18.4	Menkent	148 01.8	S36 28.0
22	142 58.4	105 36.7	06.7	212 21.4	44.3	209 15.2	40.7	201 22.9	18.4	Miaplacidus	221 38.1	S69 48.2
23	158 00.9	120 36.6	07.8	227 22.0	44.1	224 17.3	40.7	216 25.2	18.3			
15 00	173 03.3	135 36.6	N17 08.8	242 22.6	S22 43.9	239 19.3	S21 40.6	231 27.4	S20 18.3	Mirfak	308 34.0	N49 55.9
01	188 05.8	150 36.5	09.8	257 23.2	43.7	254 21.3	40.5	246 29.7	18.3	Nunki	75 52.7	S26 16.2
02	203 08.3	165 36.4	10.8	272 23.8	43.5	269 23.4	40.5	261 31.9	18.2	Peacock	53 12.3	S56 40.1
03	218 10.7	180 36.3 ..	11.8	287 24.4 ..	43.3	284 25.4 ..	40.4	276 34.2 ..	18.2	Pollux	243 21.9	N27 58.6
04	233 13.2	195 36.3	12.9	302 25.0	43.1	299 27.4	40.4	291 36.4	18.1	Procyon	244 54.7	N 5 10.2
05	248 15.6	210 36.2	13.9	317 25.6	42.9	314 29.5	40.3	306 38.7	18.1			
06	263 18.1	225 36.1	N17 14.9	332 26.2	S22 42.7	329 31.5	S21 40.2	321 40.9	S20 18.1	Rasalhague	96 02.1	N12 32.6
07	278 20.6	240 36.1	15.9	347 26.8	42.5	344 33.6	40.2	336 43.2	18.0	Regulus	207 38.3	N11 52.1
08	293 23.0	255 36.0	16.9	2 27.4	42.3	359 35.6	40.1	351 45.4	18.0	Rigel	281 07.6	S 8 11.0
S 09	308 25.5	270 35.9 ..	18.0	17 28.0 ..	42.1	14 37.6 ..	40.1	6 47.7 ..	17.9	Rigil Kent.	139 45.0	S60 54.8
U 10	323 28.0	285 35.9	19.0	32 28.6	41.9	29 39.7	40.0	21 49.9	17.9	Sabik	102 07.2	S15 44.9
N 11	338 30.4	300 35.8	20.0	47 29.2	41.7	44 41.7	39.9	36 52.2	17.9			
D 12	353 32.9	315 35.7	N17 21.0	62 29.8	S22 41.5	59 43.8	S21 39.9	51 54.4	S20 17.8	Schedar	349 35.8	N56 38.8
A 13	8 35.4	330 35.6	22.0	77 30.4	41.3	74 45.8	39.8	66 56.7	17.8	Shaula	96 15.6	S37 06.9
Y 14	23 37.8	345 35.6	23.0	92 31.0	41.1	89 47.8	39.8	81 58.9	17.7	Sirius	258 29.5	S16 44.9
15	38 40.3	0 35.5 ..	24.1	107 31.6 ..	40.9	104 49.9 ..	39.7	97 01.1 ..	17.7	Spica	158 26.1	S11 16.0
16	53 42.8	15 35.4	25.1	122 32.1	40.7	119 51.9	39.6	112 03.4	17.7	Suhail	222 48.7	S43 31.0
17	68 45.2	30 35.4	26.1	137 32.7	40.5	134 54.0	39.6	127 05.6	17.6			
18	83 47.7	45 35.3	N17 27.1	152 33.3	S22 40.3	149 56.0	S21 39.5	142 07.9	S20 17.6	Vega	80 35.9	N38 47.9
19	98 50.1	60 35.2	28.1	167 33.9	40.1	164 58.0	39.5	157 10.1	17.5	Zuben'ubi	137 00.1	S16 07.5
20	113 52.6	75 35.2	29.1	182 34.5	39.8	180 00.1	39.4	172 12.4	17.5		SHA	Mer. Pass.
21	128 55.1	90 35.1 ..	30.1	197 35.1 ..	39.6	195 02.1 ..	39.4	187 14.6 ..	17.5		° ′	h m
22	143 57.5	105 35.0	31.1	212 35.7	39.4	210 04.2	39.3	202 16.9	17.4	Venus	323 34.1	14 58
23	159 00.0	120 35.0	32.1	227 36.3	39.2	225 06.2	39.2	217 19.1	17.4	Mars	70 04.2	7 51
	h m									Jupiter	66 26.3	8 05
Mer. Pass. 12 29.7		v −0.1	d 1.0	v 0.6	d 0.2	v 2.0	d 0.1	v 2.2	d 0.0	Saturn	58 29.4	8 36

SUN / MOON

UT	SUN GHA	SUN Dec	MOON GHA	v	MOON Dec	d	HP
d h	° ′	° ′	° ′	′	° ′	′	′
13 00	177 37.9	S 2 49.7	313 09.3	8.7	S10 32.3	13.2	60.3
01	192 38.0	48.7	327 37.0	8.7	10 45.5	13.1	60.2
02	207 38.2	47.8	342 04.7	8.6	10 58.6	13.0	60.2
03	222 38.4	.. 46.8	356 32.3	8.7	11 11.6	13.0	60.2
04	237 38.5	45.8	11 00.0	8.6	11 24.6	12.8	60.1
05	252 38.7	44.8	25 27.6	8.6	11 37.4	12.8	60.1
06	267 38.9	S 2 43.8	39 55.2	8.6	S11 50.2	12.7	60.1
07	282 39.1	42.8	54 22.8	8.6	12 02.9	12.6	60.0
08	297 39.2	41.8	68 50.4	8.6	12 15.5	12.6	60.0
F 09	312 39.4	.. 40.9	83 18.0	8.5	12 28.1	12.4	60.0
R 10	327 39.6	39.9	97 45.5	8.6	12 40.5	12.3	59.9
I 11	342 39.7	38.9	112 13.1	8.5	12 52.8	12.3	59.9
D 12	357 39.9	S 2 37.9	126 40.6	8.5	S13 05.1	12.2	59.9
A 13	12 40.1	36.9	141 08.1	8.5	13 17.3	12.0	59.8
Y 14	27 40.3	35.9	155 35.6	8.5	13 29.3	12.0	59.8
15	42 40.4	.. 34.9	170 03.1	8.5	13 41.3	11.9	59.8
16	57 40.6	34.0	184 30.6	8.4	13 53.2	11.7	59.7
17	72 40.8	33.0	198 58.0	8.5	14 04.9	11.7	59.7
18	87 41.0	S 2 32.0	213 25.5	8.4	S14 16.6	11.6	59.7
19	102 41.1	31.0	227 52.9	8.4	14 28.2	11.5	59.6
20	117 41.3	30.0	242 20.3	8.4	14 39.7	11.4	59.6
21	132 41.5	.. 29.0	256 47.7	8.4	14 51.1	11.2	59.6
22	147 41.6	28.0	271 15.1	8.3	15 02.3	11.2	59.5
23	162 41.8	27.1	285 42.4	8.3	15 13.5	11.1	59.5
14 00	177 42.0	S 2 26.1	300 09.7	8.4	S15 24.6	10.9	59.4
01	192 42.2	25.1	314 37.1	8.3	15 35.5	10.9	59.4
02	207 42.3	24.1	329 04.4	8.3	15 46.4	10.7	59.4
03	222 42.5	.. 23.1	343 31.7	8.2	15 57.1	10.6	59.3
04	237 42.7	22.1	357 58.9	8.3	16 07.7	10.6	59.3
05	252 42.9	21.1	12 26.2	8.2	16 18.3	10.4	59.3
06	267 43.0	S 2 20.1	26 53.4	8.3	S16 28.7	10.3	59.2
S 07	282 43.2	19.2	41 20.7	8.2	16 39.0	10.2	59.2
A 08	297 43.4	18.2	55 47.9	8.2	16 49.2	10.0	59.1
T 09	312 43.6	.. 17.2	70 15.1	8.1	16 59.2	10.0	59.1
U 10	327 43.7	16.2	84 42.2	8.2	17 09.2	9.9	59.1
R 11	342 43.9	15.2	99 09.4	8.1	17 19.1	9.7	59.0
D 12	357 44.1	S 2 14.2	113 36.5	8.2	S17 28.8	9.6	59.0
A 13	12 44.3	13.2	128 03.7	8.1	17 38.4	9.5	59.0
Y 14	27 44.4	12.3	142 30.8	8.1	17 47.9	9.4	58.9
15	42 44.6	.. 11.3	156 57.9	8.1	17 57.3	9.2	58.9
16	57 44.8	10.3	171 25.0	8.0	18 06.5	9.2	58.8
17	72 45.0	09.3	185 52.0	8.1	18 15.7	9.0	58.8
18	87 45.1	S 2 08.3	200 19.1	8.0	S18 24.7	8.9	58.8
19	102 45.3	07.3	214 46.1	8.0	18 33.6	8.8	58.7
20	117 45.5	06.3	229 13.1	8.1	18 42.4	8.6	58.7
21	132 45.7	.. 05.3	243 40.2	8.0	18 51.0	8.5	58.7
22	147 45.8	04.4	258 07.2	7.9	18 59.5	8.4	58.6
23	162 46.0	03.4	272 34.1	8.0	19 07.9	8.3	58.6
15 00	177 46.2	S 2 02.4	287 01.1	8.0	S19 16.2	8.2	58.5
01	192 46.4	01.4	301 28.1	7.9	19 24.4	8.0	58.5
02	207 46.5	2 00.4	315 55.0	8.0	19 32.4	7.9	58.5
03	222 46.7	1 59.4	330 22.0	7.9	19 40.3	7.8	58.4
04	237 46.9	58.4	344 48.9	7.9	19 48.1	7.6	58.4
05	252 47.1	57.4	359 15.8	7.9	19 55.7	7.6	58.4
06	267 47.2	S 1 56.5	13 42.7	7.9	S20 03.3	7.4	58.3
07	282 47.4	55.5	28 09.6	7.9	20 10.7	7.2	58.3
08	297 47.6	54.5	42 36.5	7.9	20 17.9	7.2	58.2
S 09	312 47.8	.. 53.5	57 03.4	7.9	20 25.1	7.0	58.2
U 10	327 47.9	52.5	71 30.3	7.9	20 32.1	6.9	58.2
N 11	342 48.1	51.5	85 57.2	7.8	20 39.0	6.7	58.1
D 12	357 48.3	S 1 50.5	100 24.0	7.9	S20 45.7	6.6	58.1
A 13	12 48.5	49.5	114 50.9	7.9	20 52.3	6.5	58.1
Y 14	27 48.7	48.6	129 17.8	7.8	20 58.8	6.3	58.0
15	42 48.8	.. 47.6	143 44.6	7.9	21 05.1	6.3	58.0
16	57 49.0	46.6	158 11.5	7.8	21 11.4	6.1	57.9
17	72 49.2	45.6	172 38.3	7.9	21 17.5	5.9	57.9
18	87 49.4	S 1 44.6	187 05.2	7.8	S21 23.4	5.8	57.9
19	102 49.5	43.6	201 32.0	7.9	21 29.2	5.7	57.8
20	117 49.7	42.6	215 58.9	7.8	21 34.9	5.6	57.8
21	132 49.9	.. 41.6	230 25.7	7.8	21 40.5	5.4	57.8
22	147 50.1	40.7	244 52.5	7.9	21 45.9	5.3	57.7
23	162 50.3	39.7	259 19.4	7.8	S21 51.2	5.1	57.7
	SD 16.1	d 1.0	SD 16.3		16.1		15.8

Twilight / Sunrise / Moonrise

Lat.	Naut.	Civil	Sunrise	Moonrise 13	14	15	16
°	h m	h m	h m	h m	h m	h m	h m
N 72	03 57	05 20	06 27	26 11	02 11	■■	■■
N 70	04 11	05 25	06 25	25 27	01 27	■■	■■
68	04 21	05 28	06 23	24 59	00 59	03 12	■■
66	04 30	05 31	06 22	24 37	00 37	02 33	04 27
64	04 37	05 34	06 21	24 20	00 20	02 05	03 43
62	04 43	05 36	06 20	24 06	00 06	01 45	03 15
60	04 48	05 37	06 19	23 55	25 28	01 28	02 52
N 58	04 53	05 39	06 18	23 44	25 14	01 14	02 35
56	04 57	05 40	06 17	23 36	25 01	01 01	02 20
54	05 00	05 41	06 16	23 28	24 51	00 51	02 07
52	05 03	05 42	06 16	23 21	24 41	00 41	01 55
50	05 05	05 43	06 15	23 15	24 33	00 33	01 45
45	05 10	05 45	06 14	23 01	24 15	00 15	01 25
N 40	05 14	05 46	06 13	22 50	24 01	00 01	01 08
35	05 17	05 46	06 12	22 41	23 49	24 23	00 53
30	05 19	05 47	06 11	22 33	23 38	24 41	00 41
20	05 21	05 47	06 09	22 19	23 20	24 20	00 20
N 10	05 22	05 46	06 07	22 07	23 05	24 02	00 02
0	05 21	05 45	06 06	21 55	22 50	23 45	24 40
S 10	05 19	05 43	06 04	21 44	22 35	23 28	24 22
20	05 14	05 40	06 02	21 32	22 20	23 10	24 02
30	05 08	05 36	06 00	21 19	22 02	22 49	23 40
35	05 03	05 33	05 59	21 11	21 52	22 37	23 27
40	04 58	05 30	05 57	21 02	21 41	22 24	23 12
45	04 51	05 26	05 55	20 51	21 27	22 07	22 54
S 50	04 42	05 20	05 53	20 40	21 11	21 48	22 32
52	04 37	05 18	05 52	20 34	21 03	21 38	22 22
54	04 32	05 15	05 51	20 28	20 54	21 27	22 10
56	04 26	05 12	05 49	20 21	20 45	21 16	21 56
58	04 20	05 08	05 48	20 13	20 34	21 02	21 40
S 60	04 12	05 04	05 46	20 04	20 21	20 46	21 21

Sunset / Twilight / Moonset

Lat.	Sunset	Civil	Naut.	Moonset 13	14	15	16
°	h m	h m	h m	h m	h m	h m	h m
N 72	17 53	19 01	20 25	06 36	05 46	■■	■■
N 70	17 55	18 56	20 11	06 56	06 31	■■	■■
68	17 57	18 52	20 00	07 13	07 01	06 42	■■
66	17 58	18 49	19 51	07 26	07 24	07 22	07 23
64	17 59	18 46	19 43	07 37	07 42	07 50	08 07
62	18 00	18 44	19 37	07 47	07 57	08 12	08 36
60	18 01	18 42	19 31	07 55	08 09	08 29	08 58
N 58	18 02	18 41	19 27	08 02	08 20	08 44	09 17
56	18 02	18 39	19 23	08 08	08 30	08 56	09 32
54	18 03	18 38	19 20	08 14	08 38	09 07	09 45
52	18 03	18 37	19 17	08 19	08 46	09 17	09 57
50	18 04	18 36	19 14	08 24	08 52	09 26	10 07
45	18 05	18 34	19 09	08 34	09 07	09 45	10 28
N 40	18 06	18 33	19 05	08 43	09 19	10 00	10 46
35	18 07	18 32	19 02	08 50	09 30	10 13	11 00
30	18 08	18 32	19 00	08 57	09 39	10 24	11 13
20	18 09	18 31	18 57	09 08	09 55	10 43	11 35
N 10	18 11	18 32	18 56	09 18	10 08	11 00	11 54
0	18 12	18 33	18 57	09 27	10 21	11 16	12 11
S 10	18 14	18 35	18 59	09 36	10 34	11 32	12 29
20	18 16	18 38	19 03	09 46	10 48	11 49	12 48
30	18 18	18 42	19 10	09 58	11 04	12 09	13 10
35	18 19	18 44	19 14	10 05	11 14	12 20	13 22
40	18 21	18 48	19 19	10 12	11 24	12 33	13 37
45	18 22	18 52	19 26	10 21	11 37	12 49	13 55
S 50	18 24	18 57	19 35	10 32	11 52	13 08	14 16
52	18 25	18 59	19 40	10 37	12 00	13 17	14 27
54	18 26	19 02	19 44	10 42	12 08	13 27	14 39
56	18 28	19 05	19 50	10 48	12 17	13 39	14 52
58	18 29	19 08	19 56	10 55	12 27	13 52	15 08
S 60	18 30	19 12	20 04	11 03	12 39	14 08	15 26

SUN / MOON

Day	Eqn. of Time 00ʰ	12ʰ	Mer. Pass.	Mer. Pass. Upper	Lower	Age	Phase
d	m s	m s	h m	h m	h m	d	%
13	09 29	09 21	12 09	03 14	15 41	19	80
14	09 12	09 04	12 09	04 08	16 36	20	70
15	08 56	08 47	12 09	05 03	17 31	21	60

UT	ARIES GHA	VENUS −4.4 GHA	Dec	MARS +0.9 GHA	Dec	JUPITER −2.1 GHA	Dec	SATURN +0.7 GHA	Dec	STARS Name	SHA	Dec
16 00	174 02.5	135 34.9	N17 33.2	242 36.9	S22 39.0	240 08.2	S21 39.2	232 21.4	S20 17.3	Acamar	315 15.1	S40 13.8
01	189 04.9	150 34.8	34.2	257 37.5	38.8	255 10.3	39.1	247 23.6	17.3	Achernar	335 23.7	S57 08.4
02	204 07.4	165 34.7	35.2	272 38.1	38.6	270 12.3	39.1	262 25.9	17.3	Acrux	173 03.5	S63 12.6
03	219 09.9	180 34.7	.. 36.2	287 38.7	.. 38.4	285 14.4	.. 39.0	277 28.1	.. 17.2	Adhara	255 08.8	S29 00.3
04	234 12.3	195 34.6	37.2	302 39.3	38.2	300 16.4	38.9	292 30.4	17.2	Aldebaran	290 44.1	N16 32.8
05	249 14.8	210 34.5	38.2	317 39.9	38.0	315 18.5	38.9	307 32.6	17.1			
06	264 17.2	225 34.5	N17 39.2	332 40.5	S22 37.8	330 20.5	S21 38.8	322 34.9	S20 17.1	Alioth	166 16.0	N55 51.0
07	279 19.7	240 34.4	40.2	347 41.1	37.6	345 22.5	38.8	337 37.1	17.1	Alkaid	152 54.8	N49 12.7
08	294 22.2	255 34.3	41.2	2 41.7	37.4	0 24.6	38.7	352 39.4	17.0	Alnair	27 38.3	S46 51.8
M 09	309 24.6	270 34.3	.. 42.2	17 42.3	.. 37.1	15 26.6	.. 38.6	7 41.6	.. 17.0	Alnilam	275 41.7	S 1 11.6
O 10	324 27.1	285 34.2	43.2	32 42.9	36.9	30 28.7	38.6	22 43.9	16.9	Alphard	217 51.3	S 8 44.9
N 11	339 29.6	300 34.1	44.2	47 43.5	36.7	45 30.7	38.5	37 46.1	16.9			
D 12	354 32.0	315 34.1	N17 45.2	62 44.1	S22 36.5	60 32.8	S21 38.5	52 48.4	S20 16.9	Alphecca	126 06.9	N26 38.7
A 13	9 34.5	330 34.0	46.2	77 44.7	36.3	75 34.8	38.4	67 50.6	16.8	Alpheratz	357 39.1	N29 11.9
Y 14	24 37.0	345 33.9	47.2	92 45.3	36.1	90 36.9	38.3	82 52.9	16.8	Altair	62 03.9	N 8 55.2
15	39 39.4	0 33.9	.. 48.2	107 45.9	.. 35.9	105 38.9	.. 38.3	97 55.1	.. 16.7	Ankaa	353 11.5	S42 12.0
16	54 41.9	15 33.8	49.2	122 46.5	35.7	120 40.9	38.2	112 57.4	16.7	Antares	112 20.4	S26 28.5
17	69 44.4	30 33.7	50.2	137 47.1	35.4	135 43.0	38.2	127 59.6	16.7			
18	84 46.8	45 33.7	N17 51.2	152 47.7	S22 35.2	150 45.0	S21 38.1	143 01.9	S20 16.6	Arcturus	145 51.2	N19 04.6
19	99 49.3	60 33.6	52.2	167 48.3	35.0	165 47.1	38.0	158 04.1	16.6	Atria	107 18.0	S69 03.4
20	114 51.7	75 33.5	53.2	182 48.9	34.8	180 49.1	38.0	173 06.4	16.5	Avior	234 15.8	S59 34.7
21	129 54.2	90 33.5	.. 54.2	197 49.5	.. 34.6	195 51.2	.. 37.9	188 08.6	.. 16.5	Bellatrix	278 27.1	N 6 21.9
22	144 56.7	105 33.4	55.2	212 50.1	34.4	210 53.2	37.9	203 10.9	16.5	Betelgeuse	270 56.3	N 7 24.5
23	159 59.1	120 33.4	56.2	227 50.7	34.2	225 55.3	37.8	218 13.1	16.4			
17 00	175 01.6	135 33.3	N17 57.2	242 51.3	S22 33.9	240 57.3	S21 37.8	233 15.4	S20 16.4	Canopus	263 54.0	S52 42.8
01	190 04.1	150 33.2	58.1	257 51.9	33.7	255 59.4	37.7	248 17.7	16.3	Capella	280 27.6	N46 01.1
02	205 06.5	165 33.2	17 59.1	272 52.5	33.5	271 01.4	37.6	263 19.9	16.3	Deneb	49 28.7	N45 20.9
03	220 09.0	180 33.1	18 00.1	287 53.1	.. 33.3	286 03.5	.. 37.6	278 22.2	.. 16.3	Denebola	182 38.6	N14 27.5
04	235 11.5	195 33.0	01.1	302 53.7	33.1	301 05.5	37.5	293 24.4	16.2	Diphda	348 51.5	S17 52.8
05	250 13.9	210 33.0	02.1	317 54.3	32.9	316 07.6	37.5	308 26.7	16.2			
06	265 16.4	225 32.9	N18 03.1	332 54.9	S22 32.6	331 09.6	S21 37.4	323 28.9	S20 16.1	Dubhe	193 45.3	N61 38.6
07	280 18.9	240 32.8	04.1	347 55.5	32.4	346 11.7	37.3	338 31.2	16.1	Elnath	278 06.8	N28 37.4
T 08	295 21.3	255 32.8	05.1	2 56.1	32.2	1 13.7	37.3	353 33.4	16.1	Eltanin	90 44.5	N51 28.9
U 09	310 23.8	270 32.7	.. 06.1	17 56.7	.. 32.0	16 15.8	.. 37.2	8 35.7	.. 16.0	Enif	33 42.8	N 9 57.9
E 10	325 26.2	285 32.6	07.0	32 57.3	31.8	31 17.8	37.2	23 37.9	16.0	Fomalhaut	15 19.2	S29 31.1
S 11	340 28.7	300 32.6	08.0	47 57.9	31.6	46 19.9	37.1	38 40.2	16.0			
D 12	355 31.2	315 32.5	N18 09.0	62 58.5	S22 31.3	61 21.9	S21 37.0	53 42.4	S20 15.9	Gacrux	171 55.2	S57 13.5
A 13	10 33.6	330 32.5	10.0	77 59.1	31.1	76 24.0	37.0	68 44.7	15.9	Gienah	175 47.2	S17 39.2
Y 14	25 36.1	345 32.4	11.0	92 59.7	30.9	91 26.0	36.9	83 46.9	15.8	Hadar	148 40.8	S60 28.0
15	40 38.6	0 32.3	.. 12.0	108 00.3	.. 30.7	106 28.1	.. 36.9	98 49.2	.. 15.8	Hamal	327 55.8	N23 33.3
16	55 41.0	15 32.3	12.9	123 00.9	30.5	121 30.1	36.8	113 51.4	15.8	Kaus Aust.	83 37.7	S34 22.3
17	70 43.5	30 32.2	13.9	138 01.5	30.2	136 32.2	36.8	128 53.7	15.7			
18	85 46.0	45 32.1	N18 14.9	153 02.1	S22 30.0	151 34.2	S21 36.7	143 56.0	S20 15.7	Kochab	137 19.2	N74 04.2
19	100 48.4	60 32.1	15.9	168 02.7	29.8	166 36.3	36.6	158 58.2	15.6	Markab	13 34.0	N15 18.6
20	115 50.9	75 32.0	16.9	183 03.3	29.6	181 38.3	36.6	174 00.5	15.6	Menkar	314 10.4	N 4 09.9
21	130 53.4	90 32.0	.. 17.8	198 03.9	.. 29.3	196 40.4	.. 36.5	189 02.7	.. 15.6	Menkent	148 01.8	S36 28.0
22	145 55.8	105 31.9	18.8	213 04.5	29.1	211 42.4	36.5	204 05.0	15.5	Miaplacidus	221 38.1	S69 48.2
23	160 58.3	120 31.8	19.8	228 05.1	28.9	226 44.5	36.4	219 07.2	15.5			
18 00	176 00.7	135 31.8	N18 20.8	243 05.7	S22 28.7	241 46.5	S21 36.3	234 09.5	S20 15.4	Mirfak	308 34.0	N49 55.9
01	191 03.2	150 31.7	21.7	258 06.3	28.5	256 48.6	36.3	249 11.7	15.4	Nunki	75 52.7	S26 16.2
02	206 05.7	165 31.7	22.7	273 06.9	28.2	271 50.6	36.2	264 14.0	15.4	Peacock	53 12.3	S56 40.0
03	221 08.1	180 31.6	.. 23.7	288 07.5	.. 28.0	286 52.7	.. 36.2	279 16.3	.. 15.3	Pollux	243 21.9	N27 58.6
04	236 10.6	195 31.5	24.7	303 08.1	27.8	301 54.7	36.1	294 18.5	15.3	Procyon	244 54.7	N 5 10.2
05	251 13.1	210 31.5	25.7	318 08.7	27.6	316 56.8	36.1	309 20.8	15.3			
06	266 15.5	225 31.4	N18 26.6	333 09.3	S22 27.3	331 58.8	S21 36.0	324 23.0	S20 15.2	Rasalhague	96 02.1	N12 32.6
W 07	281 18.0	240 31.4	27.6	348 09.9	27.1	347 00.9	35.9	339 25.3	15.2	Regulus	207 38.3	N11 52.1
E 08	296 20.5	255 31.3	28.5	3 10.5	26.9	2 02.9	35.9	354 27.5	15.1	Rigel	281 07.6	S 8 11.0
D 09	311 22.9	270 31.2	.. 29.5	18 11.1	.. 26.6	17 05.0	.. 35.8	9 29.8	.. 15.1	Rigil Kent.	139 45.0	S60 54.8
N 10	326 25.4	285 31.2	30.5	33 11.7	26.4	32 07.1	35.8	24 32.0	15.1	Sabik	102 07.2	S15 44.9
E 11	341 27.8	300 31.1	31.4	48 12.3	26.2	47 09.1	35.7	39 34.3	15.0			
S 12	356 30.3	315 31.1	N18 32.4	63 12.9	S22 26.0	62 11.2	S21 35.6	54 36.6	S20 15.0	Schedar	349 35.8	N56 38.8
D 13	11 32.8	330 31.0	33.4	78 13.5	25.7	77 13.2	35.6	69 38.8	14.9	Shaula	96 15.6	S37 06.9
A 14	26 35.2	345 30.9	34.3	93 14.1	25.5	92 15.3	35.5	84 41.1	14.9	Sirius	258 29.6	S16 44.9
Y 15	41 37.7	0 30.9	.. 35.3	108 14.7	.. 25.3	107 17.3	.. 35.5	99 43.3	.. 14.9	Spica	158 26.1	S11 16.0
16	56 40.2	15 30.8	36.3	123 15.3	25.1	122 19.4	35.4	114 45.6	14.8	Suhail	222 48.7	S43 31.0
17	71 42.6	30 30.8	37.2	138 15.9	24.8	137 21.4	35.4	129 47.8	14.8			
18	86 45.1	45 30.7	N18 38.2	153 16.5	S22 24.6	152 23.5	S21 35.3	144 50.1	S20 14.8	Vega	80 35.9	N38 47.9
19	101 47.6	60 30.7	39.2	168 17.1	24.4	167 25.6	35.2	159 52.4	14.7	Zuben'ubi	137 00.1	S16 07.5
20	116 50.0	75 30.6	40.1	183 17.7	24.1	182 27.6	35.2	174 54.6	14.7		SHA	Mer. Pass.
21	131 52.5	90 30.5	.. 41.1	198 18.3	.. 23.9	197 29.7	.. 35.1	189 56.9	.. 14.6	Venus	320 31.7	14 58
22	146 55.0	105 30.5	42.1	213 18.9	23.7	212 31.7	35.1	204 59.1	14.6	Mars	67 49.7	7 48
23	161 57.4	120 30.4	43.0	228 19.5	23.4	227 33.8	35.0	220 01.4	14.6	Jupiter	65 55.7	7 55
Mer. Pass. 12 17.9		v −0.1	d 1.0	v 0.6	d 0.2	v 2.1	d 0.1	v 2.3	d 0.0	Saturn	58 13.8	8 26

UT	SUN GHA	SUN Dec	MOON GHA	v	Dec	d	HP
d h	° ′	° ′	° ′	′	° ′	′	′
16 00	177 50.4	S 1 38.7	273 46.2	7.9	S21 56.3	5.1	57.6
01	192 50.6	37.7	288 13.1	7.9	22 01.4	4.8	57.6
02	207 50.8	36.7	302 40.0	7.8	22 06.2	4.8	57.6
03	222 51.0	.. 35.7	317 06.8	7.9	22 11.0	4.6	57.5
04	237 51.1	34.7	331 33.7	7.9	22 15.6	4.5	57.5
05	252 51.3	33.7	346 00.6	7.8	22 20.1	4.3	57.5
06	267 51.5	S 1 32.7	0 27.4	7.9	S22 24.4	4.2	57.4
07	282 51.7	31.8	14 54.3	7.9	22 28.6	4.1	57.4
08	297 51.9	30.8	29 21.2	7.9	22 32.7	4.0	57.4
M 09	312 52.0	.. 29.8	43 48.1	7.9	22 36.7	3.8	57.3
O 10	327 52.2	28.8	58 15.0	8.0	22 40.5	3.6	57.3
N 11	342 52.4	27.8	72 42.0	7.9	22 44.1	3.6	57.3
D 12	357 52.6	S 1 26.8	87 08.9	8.0	S22 47.7	3.4	57.2
A 13	12 52.8	25.8	101 35.9	7.9	22 51.1	3.2	57.2
Y 14	27 52.9	24.8	116 02.8	8.0	22 54.3	3.2	57.1
15	42 53.1	.. 23.9	130 29.8	8.0	22 57.5	2.9	57.1
16	57 53.3	22.9	144 56.8	8.1	23 00.4	2.9	57.1
17	72 53.5	21.9	159 23.9	8.0	23 03.3	2.7	57.0
18	87 53.6	S 1 20.9	173 50.9	8.0	S23 06.0	2.6	57.0
19	102 53.8	19.9	188 17.9	8.1	23 08.6	2.5	57.0
20	117 54.0	18.9	202 45.0	8.1	23 11.1	2.3	56.9
21	132 54.2	.. 17.9	217 12.1	8.1	23 13.4	2.2	56.9
22	147 54.4	16.9	231 39.2	8.2	23 15.6	2.0	56.9
23	162 54.5	15.9	246 06.4	8.1	23 17.6	1.9	56.8
17 00	177 54.7	S 1 15.0	260 33.5	8.2	S23 19.5	1.8	56.8
01	192 54.9	14.0	275 00.7	8.2	23 21.3	1.7	56.8
02	207 55.1	13.0	289 27.9	8.3	23 23.0	1.5	56.7
03	222 55.3	.. 12.0	303 55.2	8.2	23 24.5	1.4	56.7
04	237 55.4	11.0	318 22.4	8.3	23 25.9	1.2	56.7
05	252 55.6	10.0	332 49.7	8.4	23 27.1	1.1	56.6
06	267 55.8	S 1 09.0	347 17.1	8.3	S23 28.2	1.0	56.6
07	282 56.0	08.0	1 44.4	8.4	23 29.2	0.9	56.6
T 08	297 56.2	07.1	16 11.8	8.4	23 30.1	0.6	56.5
U 09	312 56.3	.. 06.1	30 39.2	8.5	23 30.8	0.6	56.5
E 10	327 56.5	05.1	45 06.7	8.4	23 31.4	0.4	56.5
S 11	342 56.7	04.1	59 34.1	8.5	23 31.8	0.4	56.4
D 12	357 56.9	S 1 03.1	74 01.6	8.6	S23 32.2	0.2	56.4
A 13	12 57.1	02.1	88 29.2	8.6	23 32.4	0.0	56.4
Y 14	27 57.2	01.1	102 56.8	8.6	23 32.4	0.2	56.4
15	42 57.4	1 00.1	117 24.4	8.7	23 32.4	0.2	56.3
16	57 57.6	0 59.1	131 52.1	8.7	23 32.2	0.4	56.3
17	72 57.8	58.2	146 19.8	8.7	23 31.8	0.4	56.3
18	87 58.0	S 0 57.2	160 47.5	8.8	S23 31.4	0.6	56.2
19	102 58.2	56.2	175 15.3	8.8	23 30.8	0.7	56.2
20	117 58.3	55.2	189 43.1	8.8	23 30.1	0.8	56.2
21	132 58.5	.. 54.2	204 10.9	8.9	23 29.3	1.0	56.1
22	147 58.7	53.2	218 38.8	9.0	23 28.3	1.1	56.1
23	162 58.9	52.2	233 06.8	9.0	23 27.2	1.2	56.1
18 00	177 59.1	S 0 51.2	247 34.8	9.0	S23 26.0	1.3	56.1
01	192 59.2	50.2	262 02.8	9.1	23 24.7	1.5	56.0
02	207 59.4	49.3	276 30.9	9.1	23 23.2	1.6	56.0
03	222 59.6	.. 48.3	290 59.0	9.2	23 21.6	1.7	56.0
04	237 59.8	47.3	305 27.2	9.2	23 19.9	1.8	55.9
05	253 00.0	46.3	319 55.4	9.3	23 18.1	1.9	55.9
06	268 00.1	S 0 45.3	334 23.7	9.3	S23 16.2	2.1	55.9
W 07	283 00.3	44.3	348 52.0	9.3	23 14.1	2.2	55.9
E 08	298 00.5	43.3	3 20.3	9.4	23 11.9	2.3	55.8
D 09	313 00.7	.. 42.3	17 48.7	9.5	23 09.6	2.5	55.8
N 10	328 00.9	41.3	32 17.2	9.5	23 07.1	2.5	55.8
E 11	343 01.1	40.4	46 45.7	9.6	23 04.6	2.7	55.8
S 12	358 01.2	S 0 39.4	61 14.3	9.6	S23 01.9	2.8	55.7
D 13	13 01.4	38.4	75 42.9	9.7	22 59.1	2.9	55.7
A 14	28 01.6	37.4	90 11.6	9.7	22 56.2	3.0	55.7
Y 15	43 01.8	.. 36.4	104 40.3	9.8	22 53.2	3.1	55.6
16	58 02.0	35.4	119 09.1	9.8	22 50.1	3.3	55.6
17	73 02.2	34.4	133 37.9	9.9	22 46.8	3.4	55.6
18	88 02.3	S 0 33.4	148 06.8	10.0	S22 43.4	3.4	55.6
19	103 02.5	32.4	162 35.8	10.0	22 40.0	3.6	55.5
20	118 02.7	31.5	177 04.8	10.1	22 36.4	3.7	55.5
21	133 02.9	.. 30.5	191 33.9	10.1	22 32.7	3.9	55.5
22	148 03.1	29.5	206 03.0	10.2	22 28.8	3.9	55.5
23	163 03.2	28.5	220 32.2	10.2	S22 24.9	4.0	55.5
	SD 16.1	d 1.0	SD 15.6		15.4		15.2

Moonrise

Lat.	Twilight Naut.	Twilight Civil	Sunrise	Moonrise 16	17	18	19
°	h m	h m	h m	h m	h m	h m	h m
N 72	03 38	05 04	06 12	■	■	■	■
N 70	03 55	05 10	06 11	■	■	■	■
68	04 07	05 15	06 11	■	■	■	08 07
66	04 17	05 19	06 10	04 27	06 06	06 48	06 53
64	04 26	05 23	06 10	03 43	05 03	05 52	06 16
62	04 33	05 26	06 10	03 15	04 28	05 19	05 50
60	04 39	05 28	06 10	02 52	04 03	04 55	05 29
N 58	04 44	05 30	06 09	02 35	03 43	04 35	05 12
56	04 48	05 32	06 09	02 20	03 26	04 19	04 58
54	04 52	05 34	06 09	02 07	03 12	04 05	04 46
52	04 56	05 35	06 09	01 55	03 00	03 53	04 35
50	04 59	05 36	06 09	01 45	02 49	03 42	04 25
45	05 05	05 39	06 08	01 25	02 26	03 20	04 05
N 40	05 09	05 41	06 08	01 08	02 08	03 02	03 48
35	05 13	05 42	06 07	00 53	01 53	02 47	03 34
30	05 15	05 43	06 07	00 41	01 40	02 34	03 22
20	05 19	05 44	06 06	00 20	01 17	02 11	03 01
N 10	05 20	05 45	06 06	00 02	00 58	01 52	02 42
0	05 20	05 44	06 05	24 40	00 40	01 33	02 25
S 10	05 19	05 43	06 04	24 22	00 22	01 15	02 08
20	05 15	05 41	06 03	24 02	00 02	00 56	01 50
30	05 10	05 38	06 02	23 40	24 34	00 34	01 29
35	05 06	05 36	06 01	23 27	24 20	00 20	01 16
40	05 01	05 33	06 00	23 12	24 05	00 05	01 02
45	04 55	05 30	05 59	22 54	23 47	24 45	00 45
S 50	04 47	05 25	05 58	22 32	23 25	24 24	00 24
52	04 43	05 23	05 57	22 22	23 14	24 14	00 14
54	04 38	05 21	05 56	22 10	23 02	24 03	00 03
56	04 33	05 18	05 55	21 56	22 48	23 50	24 59
58	04 28	05 15	05 55	21 40	22 32	23 35	24 47
S 60	04 21	05 12	05 54	21 21	22 12	23 18	24 32

Moonset

Lat.	Sunset	Twilight Civil	Twilight Naut.	Moonset 16	17	18	19
°	h m	h m	h m	h m	h m	h m	h m
N 72	18 07	19 15	20 43	■	■	■	■
N 70	18 07	19 09	20 25	■	■	■	■
68	18 08	19 03	20 12	■	■	■	09 16
66	18 08	18 59	20 02	07 23	07 38	08 48	10 29
64	18 08	18 55	19 53	08 07	08 42	09 43	11 06
62	18 08	18 52	19 46	08 36	09 16	10 16	11 31
60	18 08	18 50	19 39	08 58	09 42	10 40	11 52
N 58	18 08	18 48	19 34	09 17	10 02	11 00	12 08
56	18 08	18 46	19 30	09 32	10 18	11 16	12 22
54	18 09	18 44	19 26	09 45	10 32	11 30	12 34
52	18 09	18 42	19 22	09 57	10 45	11 42	12 45
50	18 09	18 41	19 19	10 07	10 56	11 52	12 54
45	18 09	18 38	19 13	10 28	11 18	12 14	13 14
N 40	18 09	18 36	19 08	10 46	11 37	12 32	13 30
35	18 10	18 35	19 04	11 00	11 52	12 47	13 44
30	18 10	18 34	19 01	11 13	12 05	13 00	13 56
20	18 10	18 32	18 58	11 35	12 28	13 22	14 16
N 10	18 11	18 32	18 56	11 54	12 47	13 41	14 33
0	18 11	18 32	18 56	12 11	13 06	13 59	14 49
S 10	18 12	18 33	18 58	12 29	13 24	14 16	15 06
20	18 13	18 35	19 01	12 48	13 44	14 35	15 23
30	18 14	18 38	19 06	13 10	14 06	14 57	15 42
35	18 15	18 40	19 10	13 22	14 19	15 10	15 54
40	18 16	18 43	19 14	13 37	14 35	15 24	16 07
45	18 17	18 46	19 20	13 55	14 53	15 42	16 23
S 50	18 18	18 50	19 28	14 16	15 15	16 03	16 41
52	18 18	18 52	19 32	14 27	15 26	16 13	16 50
54	18 19	18 54	19 36	14 39	15 38	16 25	17 00
56	18 20	18 57	19 41	14 52	15 52	16 38	17 12
58	18 20	19 00	19 47	15 08	16 08	16 53	17 25
S 60	18 21	19 03	19 53	15 26	16 28	17 11	17 40

Day	SUN Eqn. of Time 00h	12h	Mer. Pass.	MOON Mer. Pass. Upper	Lower	Age	Phase
d	m s	m s	h m	h m	h m	d	%
16	08 39	08 30	12 08	05 58	18 26	22	49
17	08 21	08 13	12 08	06 53	19 20	23	39
18	08 04	07 55	12 08	07 46	20 12	24	29

UT	ARIES	VENUS −4.4		MARS +0.9		JUPITER −2.1		SATURN +0.7		STARS		
	GHA	GHA	Dec	GHA	Dec	GHA	Dec	GHA	Dec	Name	SHA	Dec
d h	° ′	° ′	° ′	° ′	° ′	° ′	° ′	° ′	° ′		° ′	° ′
19 00	176 59.9	135 30.4	N18 44.0	243 20.1	S22 23.2	242 35.8	S21 34.9	235 03.6	S20 14.5	Acamar	315 15.1	S40 13.8
01	192 02.3	150 30.3	44.9	258 20.7	23.0	257 37.9	34.9	250 05.9	14.5	Achernar	335 23.7	S57 08.4
02	207 04.8	165 30.3	45.9	273 21.3	22.7	272 40.0	34.8	265 08.2	14.5	Acrux	173 03.5	S63 12.6
03	222 07.3	180 30.2 ..	46.8	288 21.9 ..	22.5	287 42.0 ..	34.8	280 10.4 ..	14.4	Adhara	255 08.8	S29 00.3
04	237 09.7	195 30.2	47.8	303 22.5	22.3	302 44.1	34.7	295 12.7	14.4	Aldebaran	290 44.2	N16 32.8
05	252 12.2	210 30.1	48.8	318 23.1	22.0	317 46.1	34.7	310 14.9	14.3			
06	267 14.7	225 30.0	N18 49.7	333 23.7	S22 21.8	332 48.2	S21 34.6	325 17.2	S20 14.3	Alioth	166 16.0	N55 51.0
07	282 17.1	240 30.0	50.7	348 24.3	21.6	347 50.3	34.5	340 19.5	14.3	Alkaid	152 54.7	N49 12.7
T 08	297 19.6	255 29.9	51.6	3 24.9	21.3	2 52.3	34.5	355 21.7	14.2	Alnair	27 38.3	S46 51.8
H 09	312 22.1	270 29.9 ..	52.6	18 25.5 ..	21.1	17 54.4 ..	34.4	10 24.0 ..	14.2	Alnilam	275 41.7	S 1 11.6
U 10	327 24.5	285 29.8	53.5	33 26.1	20.9	32 56.4	34.4	25 26.2	14.1	Alphard	217 51.3	S 8 44.9
R 11	342 27.0	300 29.8	54.5	48 26.7	20.6	47 58.5	34.3	40 28.5	14.1			
S 12	357 29.5	315 29.7	N18 55.4	63 27.4	S22 20.4	63 00.6	S21 34.2	55 30.8	S20 14.1	Alphecca	126 06.8	N26 38.7
D 13	12 31.9	330 29.7	56.4	78 28.0	20.2	78 02.6	34.2	70 33.0	14.0	Alpheratz	357 39.1	N29 11.9
A 14	27 34.4	345 29.6	57.3	93 28.6	19.9	93 04.7	34.1	85 35.3	14.0	Altair	62 03.9	N 8 55.2
Y 15	42 36.8	0 29.5 ..	58.3	108 29.2 ..	19.7	108 06.7 ..	34.1	100 37.5 ..	14.0	Ankaa	353 11.5	S42 12.0
16	57 39.3	15 29.5	18 59.2	123 29.8	19.5	123 08.8	34.0	115 39.8	13.9	Antares	112 20.4	S26 28.5
17	72 41.8	30 29.4	19 00.2	138 30.4	19.2	138 10.9	34.0	130 42.1	13.9			
18	87 44.2	45 29.4	N19 01.1	153 31.0	S22 19.0	153 12.9	S21 33.9	145 44.3	S20 13.8	Arcturus	145 51.2	N19 04.6
19	102 46.7	60 29.3	02.1	168 31.6	18.7	168 15.0	33.8	160 46.6	13.8	Atria	107 17.9	S69 03.4
20	117 49.2	75 29.3	03.0	183 32.2	18.5	183 17.1	33.8	175 48.8	13.8	Avior	234 15.8	S59 34.7
21	132 51.6	90 29.2 ..	03.9	198 32.8 ..	18.3	198 19.1 ..	33.7	190 51.1 ..	13.7	Bellatrix	278 27.1	N 6 21.9
22	147 54.1	105 29.2	04.9	213 33.4	18.0	213 21.2	33.7	205 53.4	13.7	Betelgeuse	270 56.3	N 7 24.5
23	162 56.6	120 29.1	05.8	228 34.0	17.8	228 23.2	33.6	220 55.6	13.7			
20 00	177 59.0	135 29.1	N19 06.8	243 34.6	S22 17.6	243 25.3	S21 33.6	235 57.9	S20 13.6	Canopus	263 54.0	S52 42.8
01	193 01.5	150 29.0	07.7	258 35.2	17.3	258 27.4	33.5	251 00.1	13.6	Capella	280 27.7	N46 01.1
02	208 03.9	165 29.0	08.6	273 35.8	17.1	273 29.4	33.4	266 02.4	13.5	Deneb	49 28.6	N45 20.9
03	223 06.4	180 28.9 ..	09.6	288 36.4 ..	16.8	288 31.5 ..	33.4	281 04.7 ..	13.5	Denebola	182 28.6	N14 27.5
04	238 08.9	195 28.9	10.5	303 37.0	16.6	303 33.6	33.3	296 06.9	13.5	Diphda	348 51.5	S17 52.8
05	253 11.3	210 28.8	11.5	318 37.6	16.4	318 35.6	33.3	311 09.2	13.4			
06	268 13.8	225 28.8	N19 12.4	333 38.2	S22 16.1	333 37.7	S21 33.2	326 11.5	S20 13.4	Dubhe	193 45.3	N61 38.6
07	283 16.3	240 28.7	13.3	348 38.8	15.9	348 39.8	33.2	341 13.7	13.4	Elnath	278 06.8	N28 37.4
08	298 18.7	255 28.7	14.3	3 39.4	15.6	3 41.8	33.1	356 16.0	13.3	Eltanin	90 44.0	N51 28.9
F 09	313 21.2	270 28.6 ..	15.2	18 40.1 ..	15.4	18 43.9 ..	33.0	11 18.2 ..	13.3	Enif	33 42.8	N 9 57.9
R 10	328 23.7	285 28.6	16.1	33 40.7	15.1	33 46.0	33.0	26 20.5	13.2	Fomalhaut	15 19.2	S29 31.1
I 11	343 26.1	300 28.5	17.1	48 41.3	14.9	48 48.0	32.9	41 22.8	13.2			
D 12	358 28.6	315 28.5	N19 18.0	63 41.9	S22 14.7	63 50.1	S21 32.9	56 25.0	S20 13.2	Gacrux	171 55.2	S57 13.5
A 13	13 31.1	330 28.4	18.9	78 42.5	14.4	78 52.2	32.8	71 27.3	13.1	Gienah	175 47.2	S17 39.3
Y 14	28 33.5	345 28.4	19.9	93 43.1	14.2	93 54.2	32.8	86 29.6	13.1	Hadar	148 40.8	S60 28.0
15	43 36.0	0 28.3 ..	20.8	108 43.7 ..	13.9	108 56.3 ..	32.7	101 31.8 ..	13.1	Hamal	327 55.8	N23 33.3
16	58 38.4	15 28.3	21.7	123 44.3	13.7	123 58.4	32.7	116 34.1	13.0	Kaus Aust.	83 37.7	S34 22.3
17	73 40.9	30 28.2	22.7	138 44.9	13.4	139 00.4	32.6	131 36.3	13.0			
18	88 43.4	45 28.2	N19 23.6	153 45.5	S22 13.2	154 02.5	S21 32.5	146 38.6	S20 12.9	Kochab	137 19.2	N74 04.2
19	103 45.8	60 28.1	24.5	168 46.1	12.9	169 04.6	32.5	161 40.9	12.9	Markab	13 34.0	N15 18.6
20	118 48.3	75 28.1	25.4	183 46.7	12.7	184 06.6	32.4	176 43.1	12.9	Menkar	314 10.4	N 4 09.9
21	133 50.8	90 28.0 ..	26.4	198 47.3 ..	12.4	199 08.7 ..	32.4	191 45.4 ..	12.8	Menkent	148 01.8	S36 28.0
22	148 53.2	105 28.0	27.3	213 47.9	12.2	214 10.8	32.3	206 47.7	12.8	Miaplacidus	221 38.2	S69 48.2
23	163 55.7	120 27.9	28.2	228 48.5	12.0	229 12.8	32.2	221 49.9	12.8			
21 00	178 58.2	135 27.9	N19 29.2	243 49.1	S22 11.7	244 14.9	S21 32.2	236 52.2	S20 12.7	Mirfak	308 34.0	N49 55.9
01	194 00.6	150 27.9	30.1	258 49.8	11.5	259 17.0	32.1	251 54.5	12.7	Nunki	75 52.6	S26 16.2
02	209 03.1	165 27.8	31.0	273 50.4	11.2	274 19.0	32.1	266 56.7	12.6	Peacock	53 12.2	S56 40.0
03	224 05.6	180 27.8 ..	31.9	288 51.0 ..	11.0	289 21.1 ..	32.0	281 59.0 ..	12.6	Pollux	243 21.9	N27 58.6
04	239 08.0	195 27.7	32.8	303 51.6	10.7	304 23.2	32.0	297 01.3	12.6	Procyon	244 54.7	N 5 10.2
05	254 10.5	210 27.7	33.8	318 52.2	10.5	319 25.3	31.9	312 03.5	12.5			
06	269 12.9	225 27.6	N19 34.7	333 52.8	S22 10.2	334 27.3	S21 31.8	327 05.8	S20 12.5	Rasalhague	96 02.1	N12 32.6
07	284 15.4	240 27.6	35.6	348 53.4	10.0	349 29.4	31.8	342 08.0	12.5	Regulus	207 38.3	N11 52.1
S 08	299 17.9	255 27.5	36.5	3 54.0	09.7	4 31.5	31.7	357 10.3	12.4	Rigel	281 07.6	S 8 11.0
A 09	314 20.3	270 27.5 ..	37.4	18 54.6 ..	09.5	19 33.5 ..	31.7	12 12.6 ..	12.4	Rigil Kent.	139 45.0	S60 54.8
T 10	329 22.8	285 27.4	38.4	33 55.2	09.2	34 35.6	31.6	27 14.8	12.4	Sabik	102 07.1	S15 44.9
U 11	344 25.3	300 27.4	39.3	48 55.8	09.0	49 37.7	31.6	42 17.1	12.3			
R 12	359 27.7	315 27.4	N19 40.2	63 56.4	S22 08.7	64 39.7	S21 31.5	57 19.4	S20 12.3	Schedar	349 35.8	N56 38.7
D 13	14 30.2	330 27.3	41.1	78 57.0	08.5	79 41.8	31.4	72 21.6	12.2	Shaula	96 15.6	S37 06.9
A 14	29 32.7	345 27.3	42.0	93 57.7	08.2	94 43.9	31.4	87 23.9	12.2	Sirius	258 29.6	S16 44.9
Y 15	44 35.1	0 27.2 ..	42.9	108 58.3 ..	08.0	109 46.0 ..	31.3	102 26.2 ..	12.2	Spica	158 26.1	S11 16.0
16	59 37.6	15 27.2	43.8	123 58.9	07.7	124 48.0	31.3	117 28.4	12.1	Suhail	222 48.8	S43 31.1
17	74 40.0	30 27.1	44.7	138 59.5	07.5	139 50.1	31.2	132 30.7	12.1			
18	89 42.5	45 27.1	N19 45.7	154 00.1	S22 07.2	154 52.2	S21 31.2	147 33.0	S20 12.1	Vega	80 35.9	N38 47.9
19	104 45.0	60 27.1	46.6	169 00.7	06.9	169 54.3	31.1	162 35.2	12.0	Zuben'ubi	137 00.0	S16 07.5
20	119 47.4	75 27.0	47.5	184 01.3	06.7	184 56.3	31.0	177 37.5	12.0		SHA	Mer. Pass.
21	134 49.9	90 27.0 ..	48.4	199 01.9 ..	06.4	199 58.4 ..	31.0	192 39.8 ..	11.9		° ′	h m
22	149 52.4	105 26.9	49.3	214 02.5	06.2	215 00.5	30.9	207 42.0	11.9	Venus	317 30.1	14 58
23	164 54.8	120 26.9	50.2	229 03.1	05.9	230 02.6	30.9	222 44.3	11.9	Mars	65 35.6	7 45
	h m									Jupiter	65 26.3	7 45
Mer. Pass. 12 06.1		v 0.0	d 0.9	v 0.6	d 0.2	v 2.1	d 0.1	v 2.3	d 0.0	Saturn	57 58.9	8 15

SUN and MOON

UT	SUN GHA	SUN Dec	MOON GHA	v	MOON Dec	d	HP
d h	° ′	° ′	° ′	′	° ′	′	′
19 00	178 03.4	S 0 27.5	235 01.4	10.3	S22 20.9	4.2	55.4
01	193 03.6	26.5	249 30.7	10.3	22 16.7	4.3	55.4
02	208 03.8	25.5	264 00.0	10.5	22 12.4	4.3	55.4
03	223 04.0	.. 24.5	278 29.5	10.4	22 08.1	4.5	55.4
04	238 04.2	23.6	292 58.9	10.6	22 03.6	4.6	55.3
05	253 04.3	22.6	307 28.5	10.6	21 59.0	4.7	55.3
06	268 04.5	S 0 21.6	321 58.1	10.6	S21 54.3	4.8	55.3
T 07	283 04.7	20.6	336 27.7	10.7	21 49.5	4.9	55.3
H 08	298 04.9	19.6	350 57.4	10.8	21 44.6	5.0	55.2
U 09	313 05.1	.. 18.6	5 27.2	10.8	21 39.6	5.1	55.2
R 10	328 05.3	17.6	19 57.0	10.9	21 34.5	5.2	55.2
S 11	343 05.4	16.6	34 26.9	11.0	21 29.3	5.3	55.2
D 12	358 05.6	S 0 15.6	48 56.9	11.0	S21 24.0	5.4	55.2
A 13	13 05.8	14.7	63 26.9	11.1	21 18.6	5.5	55.1
Y 14	28 06.0	13.7	77 57.0	11.2	21 13.1	5.6	55.1
15	43 06.2	.. 12.7	92 27.2	11.2	21 07.5	5.7	55.1
16	58 06.4	11.7	106 57.4	11.3	21 01.8	5.9	55.1
17	73 06.5	10.7	121 27.7	11.3	20 55.9	5.9	55.1
18	88 06.7	S 0 09.7	135 58.0	11.4	S20 50.0	6.0	55.0
19	103 06.9	08.7	150 28.4	11.5	20 44.0	6.1	55.0
20	118 07.1	07.7	164 58.9	11.5	20 37.9	6.1	55.0
21	133 07.3	.. 06.7	179 29.4	11.6	20 31.8	6.3	55.0
22	148 07.5	05.8	194 00.0	11.6	20 25.5	6.4	55.0
23	163 07.7	04.8	208 30.6	11.8	20 19.1	6.5	54.9
20 00	178 07.8	S 0 03.8	223 01.4	11.7	S20 12.6	6.5	54.9
01	193 08.0	02.8	237 32.1	11.9	20 06.1	6.7	54.9
02	208 08.2	01.8	252 03.0	11.9	19 59.4	6.7	54.9
03	223 08.4	S 00.8	266 33.9	12.0	19 52.7	6.8	54.9
04	238 08.6	N 00.2	281 04.9	12.0	19 45.9	7.0	54.8
05	253 08.8	01.2	295 35.9	12.1	19 38.9	7.0	54.8
06	268 08.9	N 0 02.1	310 07.0	12.2	S19 31.9	7.1	54.8
F 07	283 09.1	03.1	324 38.2	12.2	19 24.8	7.1	54.8
R 08	298 09.3	04.1	339 09.4	12.3	19 17.7	7.3	54.8
I 09	313 09.5	.. 05.1	353 40.7	12.3	19 10.4	7.3	54.8
D 10	328 09.7	06.1	8 12.0	12.4	19 03.1	7.5	54.7
A 11	343 09.9	07.1	22 43.4	12.5	18 55.6	7.5	54.7
Y 12	358 10.1	N 0 08.1	37 14.9	12.5	S18 48.1	7.6	54.7
13	13 10.2	09.1	51 46.4	12.6	18 40.5	7.6	54.7
14	28 10.4	10.1	66 18.0	12.7	18 32.9	7.8	54.7
15	43 10.6	.. 11.0	80 49.7	12.7	18 25.1	7.8	54.7
16	58 10.8	12.0	95 21.4	12.8	18 17.3	7.9	54.6
17	73 11.0	13.0	109 53.2	12.9	18 09.4	8.0	54.6
18	88 11.2	N 0 14.0	124 25.1	12.9	S18 01.4	8.1	54.6
19	103 11.3	15.0	138 57.0	12.9	17 53.3	8.1	54.6
20	118 11.5	16.0	153 28.9	13.1	17 45.2	8.2	54.6
21	133 11.7	.. 17.0	168 01.0	13.0	17 37.0	8.3	54.6
22	148 11.9	18.0	182 33.0	13.2	17 28.7	8.4	54.5
23	163 12.1	18.9	197 05.2	13.2	17 20.3	8.4	54.5
21 00	178 12.3	N 0 19.9	211 37.4	13.3	S17 11.9	8.5	54.5
01	193 12.5	20.9	226 09.7	13.3	17 03.4	8.6	54.5
02	208 12.6	21.9	240 42.0	13.4	16 54.8	8.6	54.5
03	223 12.8	.. 22.9	255 14.4	13.4	16 46.2	8.8	54.5
04	238 13.0	23.9	269 46.8	13.5	16 37.4	8.7	54.5
05	253 13.2	24.9	284 19.3	13.6	16 28.7	8.9	54.4
06	268 13.4	N 0 25.9	298 51.9	13.6	S16 19.8	8.9	54.4
S 07	283 13.6	26.8	313 24.5	13.7	16 10.9	9.0	54.4
A 08	298 13.8	27.8	327 57.2	13.7	16 01.9	9.0	54.4
T 09	313 13.9	.. 28.8	342 29.9	13.8	15 52.9	9.2	54.4
U 10	328 14.1	29.8	357 02.7	13.9	15 43.7	9.1	54.4
R 11	343 14.3	30.8	11 35.6	13.9	15 34.6	9.3	54.4
D 12	358 14.5	N 0 31.8	26 08.5	13.9	S15 25.3	9.3	54.4
A 13	13 14.7	32.8	40 41.4	14.0	15 16.0	9.3	54.3
Y 14	28 14.9	33.8	55 14.4	14.1	15 06.7	9.5	54.3
15	43 15.1	.. 34.7	69 47.5	14.1	14 57.2	9.4	54.3
16	58 15.2	35.7	84 20.6	14.2	14 47.8	9.6	54.3
17	73 15.4	36.7	98 53.8	14.2	14 38.2	9.6	54.3
18	88 15.6	N 0 37.7	113 27.0	14.3	S14 28.6	9.6	54.3
19	103 15.8	38.7	128 00.3	14.4	14 19.0	9.8	54.3
20	118 16.0	39.7	142 33.6	14.4	14 09.2	9.7	54.3
21	133 16.2	.. 40.7	157 07.0	14.4	13 59.5	9.9	54.3
22	148 16.4	41.6	171 40.4	14.5	13 49.6	9.8	54.2
23	163 16.5	42.6	186 13.9	14.5	S13 39.8	10.0	54.2
	SD 16.1	d 1.0	SD 15.0		14.9		14.8

Twilight, Sunrise and Moonrise

Lat.	Naut.	Civil	Sunrise	Moonrise 19	20	21	22
°	h m	h m	h m	h m	h m	h m	h m
N 72	03 18	04 48	05 56	■	■	08 19	07 39
N 70	03 38	04 56	05 57	■	08 23	07 39	07 18
68	03 53	05 02	05 58	08 07	07 26	07 11	07 01
66	04 04	05 08	05 59	06 53	06 52	06 50	06 48
64	04 14	05 12	06 00	06 16	06 28	06 33	06 36
62	04 22	05 16	06 00	05 50	06 08	06 19	06 27
60	04 29	05 19	06 00	05 29	05 52	06 07	06 18
N 58	04 35	05 22	06 01	05 12	05 39	05 57	06 11
56	04 40	05 24	06 01	04 58	05 27	05 48	06 05
54	04 44	05 26	06 02	04 46	05 16	05 40	05 59
52	04 48	05 28	06 02	04 35	05 07	05 33	05 54
50	04 52	05 30	06 02	04 25	04 59	05 26	05 49
45	04 59	05 33	06 03	04 05	04 41	05 12	05 39
N 40	05 04	05 36	06 03	03 48	04 27	05 01	05 30
35	05 09	05 38	06 03	03 34	04 15	04 51	05 23
30	05 12	05 40	06 03	03 22	04 04	04 42	05 16
20	05 16	05 42	06 04	03 01	03 46	04 27	05 05
N 10	05 19	05 43	06 04	02 42	03 30	04 14	04 55
0	05 19	05 43	06 04	02 25	03 15	04 01	04 46
S 10	05 19	05 43	06 04	02 08	03 00	03 49	04 36
20	05 16	05 42	06 04	01 50	02 43	03 35	04 26
30	05 12	05 40	06 04	01 29	02 25	03 20	04 15
35	05 09	05 38	06 03	01 16	02 14	03 11	04 08
40	05 05	05 36	06 03	01 02	02 01	03 01	04 00
45	04 59	05 34	06 03	00 45	01 47	02 49	03 51
S 50	04 52	05 30	06 02	00 24	01 28	02 34	03 41
52	04 49	05 28	06 02	00 14	01 20	02 28	03 36
54	04 45	05 27	06 02	00 03	01 10	02 20	03 30
56	04 40	05 24	06 02	24 59	00 59	02 11	03 17
58	04 35	05 22	06 01	24 47	00 47	02 02	03 17
S 60	04 29	05 19	06 01	24 32	00 32	01 51	03 09

Sunset, Twilight and Moonset

Lat.	Sunset	Civil	Naut.	Moonset 19	20	21	22
°	h m	h m	h m	h m	h m	h m	h m
N 72	18 21	19 30	21 01	■	■	12 23	14 34
N 70	18 20	19 21	20 41	■	10 42	13 01	14 53
68	18 19	19 15	20 25	09 16	11 38	13 28	15 08
66	18 18	19 09	20 13	10 29	12 11	13 48	15 20
64	18 17	19 05	20 03	11 06	12 35	14 04	15 31
62	18 16	19 01	19 55	11 31	12 54	14 17	15 39
60	18 16	18 57	19 48	11 52	13 09	14 28	15 46
N 58	18 15	18 54	19 41	12 08	13 22	14 38	15 53
56	18 15	18 52	19 36	12 22	13 33	14 46	15 59
54	18 14	18 50	19 32	12 34	13 43	14 54	16 04
52	18 14	18 48	19 28	12 45	13 52	15 00	16 08
50	18 14	18 46	19 24	12 54	14 00	15 06	16 12
45	18 13	18 44	19 17	13 14	14 16	15 19	16 21
N 40	18 12	18 39	19 11	13 30	14 30	15 30	16 29
35	18 12	18 37	19 07	13 44	14 42	15 39	16 35
30	18 12	18 36	19 03	13 56	14 52	15 47	16 41
20	18 11	18 33	18 59	14 16	15 09	16 00	16 50
N 10	18 11	18 32	18 56	14 33	15 24	16 12	16 58
0	18 11	18 31	18 55	14 49	15 37	16 23	17 06
S 10	18 10	18 31	18 56	15 06	15 51	16 34	17 14
20	18 10	18 32	18 58	15 23	16 06	16 45	17 22
30	18 11	18 34	19 02	15 42	16 23	16 59	17 31
35	18 11	18 36	19 05	15 54	16 32	17 06	17 37
40	18 11	18 38	19 09	16 07	16 43	17 15	17 43
45	18 11	18 40	19 15	16 23	16 56	17 25	17 50
S 50	18 11	18 44	19 21	16 41	17 12	17 37	17 58
52	18 11	18 45	19 25	16 50	17 19	17 42	18 02
54	18 12	18 47	19 29	17 00	17 27	17 49	18 06
56	18 12	18 49	19 33	17 12	17 37	17 55	18 11
58	18 12	18 51	19 39	17 25	17 47	18 03	18 16
S 60	18 12	18 54	19 44	17 40	17 59	18 12	18 21

SUN and MOON

Day	Eqn. of Time 00h	Eqn. of Time 12h	Mer. Pass.	Mer. Pass. Upper	Mer. Pass. Lower	Age	Phase
d	m s	m s	h m	h m	h m	d %	
19	07 47	07 38	12 08	08 37	21 02	25 21	
20	07 29	07 20	12 07	09 26	21 49	26 13	
21	07 11	07 02	12 07	10 12	22 34	27 8	

UT	ARIES	VENUS −4·5		MARS +0·9		JUPITER −2·1		SATURN +0·7		STARS		
	GHA	GHA	Dec	GHA	Dec	GHA	Dec	GHA	Dec	Name	SHA	Dec
d h	° ′	° ′	° ′	° ′	° ′	° ′	° ′	° ′	° ′		° ′	° ′
22 00	179 57.3	135 26.9	N19 51.1	244 03.7	S22 05.7	245 04.6	S21 30.8	237 46.6	S20 11.8	Acamar	315 15.1	S40 13.8
01	194 59.8	150 26.8	52.0	259 04.4	05.4	260 06.7	30.8	252 48.9	11.8	Achernar	335 23.8	S57 08.3
02	210 02.2	165 26.8	52.9	274 05.0	05.2	275 08.8	30.7	267 51.1	11.8	Acrux	173 03.5	S63 12.6
03	225 04.7	180 26.7	.. 53.8	289 05.6	.. 04.9	290 10.9	.. 30.6	282 53.4	.. 11.7	Adhara	255 08.8	S29 00.3
04	240 07.2	195 26.7	54.7	304 06.2	04.6	305 12.9	30.6	297 55.7	11.7	Aldebaran	290 44.2	N16 32.8
05	255 09.6	210 26.7	55.6	319 06.8	04.4	320 15.0	30.5	312 57.9	11.7			
06	270 12.1	225 26.6	N19 56.5	334 07.4	S22 04.1	335 17.1	S21 30.5	328 00.2	S20 11.6	Alioth	166 16.0	N55 51.0
07	285 14.5	240 26.6	57.4	349 08.0	03.9	350 19.2	30.4	343 02.5	11.6	Alkaid	152 54.7	N49 12.7
08	300 17.0	255 26.5	58.3	4 08.6	03.6	5 21.2	30.4	358 04.7	11.5	Alnair	27 38.2	S46 51.8
S 09	315 19.5	270 26.5	19 59.2	19 09.2	.. 03.4	20 23.3	.. 30.3	13 07.0	.. 11.5	Alnilam	275 41.7	S 1 11.6
U 10	330 21.9	285 26.5	20 00.1	34 09.8	03.1	35 25.4	30.3	28 09.3	11.5	Alphard	217 51.3	S 8 44.9
N 11	345 24.4	300 26.4	01.0	49 10.5	02.8	50 27.5	30.2	43 11.5	11.4			
D 12	0 26.9	315 26.4	N20 01.9	64 11.1	S22 02.6	65 29.5	S21 30.1	58 13.8	S20 11.4	Alphecca	126 06.8	N26 38.7
A 13	15 29.3	330 26.3	02.8	79 11.7	02.3	80 31.6	30.1	73 16.1	11.4	Alpheratz	357 39.1	N29 11.9
Y 14	30 31.8	345 26.3	03.7	94 12.3	02.1	95 33.7	30.0	88 18.3	11.3	Altair	62 03.8	N 8 55.1
15	45 34.3	0 26.3	.. 04.6	109 12.9	.. 01.8	110 35.8	.. 30.0	103 20.6	.. 11.3	Ankaa	353 11.5	S42 12.0
16	60 36.7	15 26.2	05.5	124 13.5	01.5	125 37.9	29.9	118 22.9	11.3	Antares	112 20.4	S26 28.5
17	75 39.2	30 26.2	06.4	139 14.1	01.3	140 39.9	29.9	133 25.2	11.2			
18	90 41.6	45 26.2	N20 07.3	154 14.7	S22 01.0	155 42.0	S21 29.8	148 27.4	S20 11.2	Arcturus	145 51.2	N19 04.6
19	105 44.1	60 26.1	08.2	169 15.3	00.8	170 44.1	29.7	163 29.7	11.1	Atria	107 17.9	S69 03.5
20	120 46.6	75 26.1	09.1	184 16.0	00.5	185 46.2	29.7	178 32.0	11.1	Avior	234 15.9	S59 34.7
21	135 49.0	90 26.1	.. 10.0	199 16.6	.. 00.2	200 48.3	.. 29.6	193 34.2	.. 11.1	Bellatrix	278 27.1	N 6 21.9
22	150 51.5	105 26.0	10.9	214 17.2	22 00.0	215 50.3	29.6	208 36.5	11.0	Betelgeuse	270 56.3	N 7 24.5
23	165 54.0	120 26.0	11.7	229 17.8	21 59.7	230 52.4	29.5	223 38.8	11.0			
23 00	180 56.4	135 26.0	N20 12.6	244 18.4	S21 59.4	245 54.5	S21 29.5	238 41.0	S20 11.0	Canopus	263 54.1	S52 42.8
01	195 58.9	150 25.9	13.5	259 19.0	59.2	260 56.6	29.4	253 43.3	10.9	Capella	280 27.7	N46 01.1
02	211 01.4	165 25.9	14.4	274 19.6	58.9	275 58.7	29.4	268 45.6	10.9	Deneb	49 28.6	N45 20.9
03	226 03.8	180 25.9	.. 15.3	289 20.2	.. 58.7	291 00.7	.. 29.3	283 47.9	.. 10.9	Denebola	182 28.6	N14 27.5
04	241 06.3	195 25.8	16.2	304 20.8	58.4	306 02.8	29.2	298 50.1	10.8	Diphda	348 51.5	S17 52.8
05	256 08.8	210 25.8	17.1	319 21.5	58.1	321 04.9	29.2	313 52.4	10.8			
06	271 11.2	225 25.8	N20 17.9	334 22.1	S21 57.9	336 07.0	S21 29.1	328 54.7	S20 10.8	Dubhe	193 45.3	N61 38.6
07	286 13.7	240 25.7	18.8	349 22.7	57.6	351 09.1	29.1	343 56.9	10.7	Elnath	278 06.8	N28 37.4
08	301 16.1	255 25.7	19.7	4 23.3	57.3	6 11.1	29.0	358 59.2	10.7	Eltanin	90 43.9	N51 28.9
M 09	316 18.6	270 25.7	.. 20.6	19 23.9	.. 57.1	21 13.2	.. 29.0	14 01.5	.. 10.6	Enif	33 42.8	N 9 57.9
O 10	331 21.1	285 25.6	21.5	34 24.5	56.8	36 15.3	28.9	29 03.8	10.6	Fomalhaut	15 19.2	S29 31.1
N 11	346 23.5	300 25.6	22.4	49 25.1	56.5	51 17.4	28.9	44 06.0	10.6			
D 12	1 26.0	315 25.6	N20 23.2	64 25.7	S21 56.3	66 19.5	S21 28.8	59 08.3	S20 10.5	Gacrux	171 55.2	S57 13.5
A 13	16 28.5	330 25.5	24.1	79 26.4	56.0	81 21.6	28.7	74 10.6	10.5	Gienah	175 47.2	S17 39.3
Y 14	31 30.9	345 25.5	25.0	94 27.0	55.7	96 23.6	28.7	89 12.9	10.5	Hadar	148 40.8	S60 28.0
15	46 33.4	0 25.5	.. 25.9	109 27.6	.. 55.5	111 25.7	.. 28.6	104 15.1	.. 10.4	Hamal	327 55.8	N23 33.3
16	61 35.9	15 25.4	26.7	124 28.2	55.2	126 27.8	28.6	119 17.4	10.4	Kaus Aust.	83 37.7	S34 22.3
17	76 38.3	30 25.4	27.6	139 28.8	54.9	141 29.9	28.5	134 19.7	10.4			
18	91 40.8	45 25.4	N20 28.5	154 29.4	S21 54.7	156 32.0	S21 28.5	149 22.0	S20 10.3	Kochab	137 19.1	N74 04.2
19	106 43.2	60 25.4	29.4	169 30.0	54.4	171 34.1	28.4	164 24.2	10.3	Markab	13 34.0	N15 18.6
20	121 45.7	75 25.3	30.2	184 30.7	54.1	186 36.1	28.3	179 26.5	10.3	Menkar	314 10.4	N 4 09.9
21	136 48.2	90 25.3	.. 31.1	199 31.3	.. 53.8	201 38.2	.. 28.3	194 28.8	.. 10.2	Menkent	148 01.8	S36 28.0
22	151 50.6	105 25.3	32.0	214 31.9	53.6	216 40.3	28.2	209 31.0	10.2	Miaplacidus	221 38.2	S69 48.2
23	166 53.1	120 25.2	32.9	229 32.5	53.3	231 42.4	28.2	224 33.3	10.1			
24 00	181 55.6	135 25.2	N20 33.7	244 33.1	S21 53.0	246 44.5	S21 28.1	239 35.6	S20 10.1	Mirfak	308 34.0	N49 55.9
01	196 58.0	150 25.2	34.6	259 33.7	52.8	261 46.6	28.1	254 37.9	10.1	Nunki	75 52.6	S26 16.2
02	212 00.5	165 25.2	35.5	274 34.3	52.5	276 48.7	28.0	269 40.1	10.0	Peacock	53 12.2	S56 40.0
03	227 03.0	180 25.1	.. 36.3	289 35.0	.. 52.2	291 50.8	.. 28.0	284 42.4	.. 10.0	Pollux	243 21.9	N27 58.6
04	242 05.4	195 25.1	37.2	304 35.6	51.9	306 52.8	27.9	299 44.7	10.0	Procyon	244 54.8	N 5 10.2
05	257 07.9	210 25.1	38.1	319 36.2	51.7	321 54.9	27.9	314 47.0	09.9			
06	272 10.4	225 25.1	N20 38.9	334 36.8	S21 51.4	336 57.0	S21 27.8	329 49.2	S20 09.9	Rasalhague	96 02.1	N12 32.6
07	287 12.8	240 25.0	39.8	349 37.4	51.1	351 59.1	27.7	344 51.5	09.9	Regulus	207 38.3	N11 52.1
T 08	302 15.3	255 25.0	40.7	4 38.0	50.9	7 01.2	27.7	359 53.8	09.8	Rigel	281 07.7	S 8 11.0
U 09	317 17.7	270 25.0	.. 41.5	19 38.6	.. 50.6	22 03.3	.. 27.6	14 56.1	.. 09.8	Rigil Kent.	139 44.9	S60 54.8
E 10	332 20.2	285 25.0	42.4	34 39.3	50.3	37 05.4	27.6	29 58.3	09.8	Sabik	102 07.1	S15 44.9
S 11	347 22.7	300 24.9	43.2	49 39.9	50.0	52 07.5	27.5	45 00.6	09.7			
D 12	2 25.1	315 24.9	N20 44.1	64 40.5	S21 49.8	67 09.5	S21 27.5	60 02.9	S20 09.7	Schedar	349 35.8	N56 38.7
A 13	17 27.6	330 24.9	45.0	79 41.1	49.5	82 11.6	27.4	75 05.2	09.7	Shaula	96 15.5	S37 06.9
Y 14	32 30.1	345 24.9	45.8	94 41.7	49.2	97 13.7	27.4	90 07.4	09.6	Sirius	258 29.6	S16 44.9
15	47 32.5	0 24.8	.. 46.7	109 42.3	.. 48.9	112 15.8	.. 27.3	105 09.7	.. 09.6	Spica	158 26.0	S11 16.0
16	62 35.0	15 24.8	47.5	124 43.0	48.7	127 17.9	27.2	120 12.0	09.6	Suhail	222 48.8	S43 31.1
17	77 37.5	30 24.8	48.4	139 43.6	48.4	142 20.0	27.2	135 14.3	09.5			
18	92 39.9	45 24.8	N20 49.2	154 44.2	S21 48.1	157 22.1	S21 27.1	150 16.6	S20 09.5	Vega	80 35.9	N38 47.9
19	107 42.4	60 24.8	50.1	169 44.8	47.8	172 24.2	27.1	165 18.8	09.4	Zuben'ubi	137 00.0	S16 07.5
20	122 44.9	75 24.7	51.0	184 45.4	47.6	187 26.3	27.0	180 21.1	09.4		SHA	Mer. Pass.
21	137 47.3	90 24.7	.. 51.8	199 46.0	.. 47.3	202 28.4	.. 27.0	195 23.4	.. 09.4		° ′	h m
22	152 49.8	105 24.7	52.7	214 46.7	47.0	217 30.4	26.9	210 25.7	09.3	Venus	314 29.5	14 58
23	167 52.2	120 24.7	53.5	229 47.3	46.7	232 32.5	26.9	225 27.9	09.3	Mars	63 22.0	7 42
	h m									Jupiter	64 58.1	7 35
Mer. Pass. 11 54.3		v 0.0	d 0.9	v 0.6	d 0.3	v 2.1	d 0.1	v 2.3	d 0.0	Saturn	57 44.6	8 04

UT (d h)	SUN GHA	SUN Dec	MOON GHA	v	MOON Dec	d	HP
	° ′	° ′	° ′	′	° ′	′	′
22 00	178 16.7	N 0 43.6	200 47.4	14.6	S13 29.8	10.0	54.2
01	193 16.9	44.6	215 21.0	14.6	13 19.8	10.0	54.2
02	208 17.1	45.6	229 54.6	14.7	13 09.8	10.1	54.2
03	223 17.3	.. 46.6	244 28.3	14.7	12 59.7	10.1	54.2
04	238 17.5	47.6	259 02.0	14.7	12 49.6	10.2	54.2
05	253 17.7	48.6	273 35.7	14.8	12 39.4	10.3	54.2
06	268 17.8	N 0 49.5	288 09.5	14.9	S12 29.1	10.2	54.2
07	283 18.0	50.5	302 43.4	14.9	12 18.9	10.4	54.2
08	298 18.2	51.5	317 17.3	15.0	12 08.5	10.3	54.2
09	313 18.4	.. 52.5	331 51.3	14.9	11 58.2	10.5	54.1
10	328 18.6	53.5	346 25.2	15.1	11 47.7	10.4	54.1
11	343 18.8	54.5	0 59.3	15.1	11 37.3	10.6	54.1
12	358 19.0	N 0 55.5	15 33.4	15.1	S11 26.7	10.5	54.1
13	13 19.2	56.4	30 07.5	15.1	11 16.2	10.6	54.1
14	28 19.3	57.4	44 41.6	15.2	11 05.6	10.7	54.1
15	43 19.5	.. 58.4	59 15.8	15.3	10 54.9	10.6	54.1
16	58 19.7	0 59.4	73 50.1	15.3	10 44.3	10.8	54.1
17	73 19.9	1 00.4	88 24.4	15.3	10 33.5	10.7	54.1
18	88 20.1	N 1 01.4	102 58.7	15.3	S10 22.8	10.8	54.1
19	103 20.3	02.4	117 33.0	15.4	10 12.0	10.9	54.1
20	118 20.5	03.4	132 07.4	15.5	10 01.1	10.8	54.1
21	133 20.6	.. 04.3	146 41.9	15.4	9 50.3	11.0	54.1
22	148 20.8	05.3	161 16.3	15.5	9 39.3	10.9	54.0
23	163 21.0	06.3	175 50.8	15.6	9 28.4	11.0	54.0
23 00	178 21.2	N 1 07.3	190 25.4	15.5	S 9 17.4	11.0	54.0
01	193 21.4	08.3	204 59.9	15.6	9 06.4	11.1	54.0
02	208 21.6	09.3	219 34.5	15.7	8 55.3	11.1	54.0
03	223 21.8	.. 10.3	234 09.2	15.7	8 44.2	11.1	54.0
04	238 22.0	11.2	248 43.9	15.7	8 33.1	11.1	54.0
05	253 22.1	12.2	263 18.6	15.7	8 22.0	11.2	54.0
06	268 22.3	N 1 13.2	277 53.3	15.8	S 8 10.8	11.2	54.0
07	283 22.5	14.2	292 28.1	15.8	7 59.6	11.3	54.0
08	298 22.7	15.2	307 02.9	15.8	7 48.3	11.2	54.0
09	313 22.9	.. 16.2	321 37.7	15.8	7 37.1	11.3	54.0
10	328 23.1	17.1	336 12.5	15.9	7 25.8	11.4	54.0
11	343 23.3	18.1	350 47.4	15.9	7 14.4	11.3	54.0
12	358 23.5	N 1 19.1	5 22.3	16.0	S 7 03.1	11.4	54.0
13	13 23.6	20.1	19 57.3	15.9	6 51.7	11.4	54.0
14	28 23.8	21.1	34 32.2	16.0	6 40.3	11.4	54.0
15	43 24.0	.. 22.1	49 07.2	16.0	6 28.9	11.5	54.0
16	58 24.2	23.1	63 42.2	16.0	6 17.4	11.5	54.0
17	73 24.4	24.0	78 17.2	16.1	6 05.9	11.5	54.0
18	88 24.6	N 1 25.0	92 52.3	16.1	S 5 54.4	11.5	54.0
19	103 24.8	26.0	107 27.4	16.1	5 42.9	11.5	53.9
20	118 25.0	27.0	122 02.5	16.1	5 31.4	11.6	53.9
21	133 25.1	.. 28.0	136 37.6	16.1	5 19.8	11.6	53.9
22	148 25.3	29.0	151 12.7	16.2	5 08.2	11.6	53.9
23	163 25.5	30.0	165 47.9	16.1	4 56.6	11.6	53.9
24 00	178 25.7	N 1 30.9	180 23.0	16.2	S 4 45.0	11.6	53.9
01	193 25.9	31.9	194 58.2	16.2	4 33.4	11.7	53.9
02	208 26.1	32.9	209 33.4	16.3	4 21.7	11.6	53.9
03	223 26.3	.. 33.9	224 08.7	16.2	4 10.1	11.7	53.9
04	238 26.5	34.9	238 43.9	16.2	3 58.4	11.7	53.9
05	253 26.6	35.9	253 19.1	16.3	3 46.7	11.7	53.9
06	268 26.8	N 1 36.8	267 54.4	16.3	S 3 35.0	11.7	53.9
07	283 27.0	37.8	282 29.7	16.3	3 23.3	11.8	53.9
08	298 27.2	38.8	297 05.0	16.3	3 11.5	11.7	53.9
09	313 27.4	.. 39.8	311 40.3	16.3	2 59.8	11.8	53.9
10	328 27.6	40.8	326 15.6	16.3	2 48.0	11.8	53.9
11	343 27.8	41.8	340 50.9	16.4	2 36.2	11.7	53.9
12	358 28.0	N 1 42.7	355 26.3	16.3	S 2 24.5	11.8	53.9
13	13 28.1	43.7	10 01.6	16.4	2 12.7	11.8	53.9
14	28 28.3	44.7	24 37.0	16.3	2 00.9	11.8	53.9
15	43 28.5	.. 45.7	39 12.3	16.4	1 49.1	11.9	53.9
16	58 28.7	46.7	53 47.7	16.3	1 37.2	11.8	53.9
17	73 28.9	47.7	68 23.0	16.4	1 25.4	11.8	53.9
18	88 29.1	N 1 48.6	82 58.4	16.4	S 1 13.6	11.8	53.9
19	103 29.3	49.6	97 33.8	16.4	1 01.8	11.9	53.9
20	118 29.5	50.6	112 09.2	16.4	0 49.9	11.8	53.9
21	133 29.6	.. 51.6	126 44.6	16.4	0 38.1	11.8	53.9
22	148 29.8	52.6	141 20.0	16.3	0 26.3	11.9	53.9
23	163 30.0	53.6	155 55.3	16.4	S 0 14.4	11.8	53.9
	SD 16.1	d 1.0	SD 14.7	14.7	14.7		

Day column letters: SUNDAY (22), MONDAY (23), TUESDAY (24)

Twilight / Moonrise

Lat.	Twilight Naut.	Twilight Civil	Sunrise	Moonrise 22	23	24	25
N 72	02 57	04 32	05 41	07 39	07 14	06 53	06 34
N 70	03 20	04 41	05 43	07 18	07 02	06 49	06 36
68	03 37	04 49	05 46	07 01	06 53	06 45	06 37
66	03 51	04 56	05 47	06 48	06 45	06 41	06 38
64	04 02	05 01	05 49	06 36	06 38	06 39	06 39
62	04 11	05 06	05 50	06 27	06 32	06 36	06 40
60	04 19	05 10	05 51	06 18	06 27	06 34	06 41
N 58	04 26	05 13	05 52	06 11	06 22	06 32	06 41
56	04 32	05 16	05 53	06 05	06 18	06 31	06 42
54	04 37	05 19	05 54	05 59	06 15	06 29	06 42
52	04 41	05 21	05 55	05 54	06 12	06 28	06 43
50	04 45	05 23	05 56	05 49	06 09	06 26	06 43
45	04 53	05 28	05 57	05 39	06 02	06 24	06 44
N 40	04 59	05 31	05 58	05 30	05 57	06 21	06 45
35	05 04	05 34	05 59	05 23	05 52	06 19	06 46
30	05 08	05 36	06 00	05 16	05 48	06 17	06 46
20	05 14	05 39	06 01	05 05	05 40	06 14	06 48
N 10	05 17	05 41	06 02	04 55	05 34	06 12	06 49
0	05 19	05 43	06 03	04 46	05 28	06 09	06 49
S 10	05 19	05 43	06 04	04 36	05 22	06 06	06 50
20	05 17	05 43	06 05	04 26	05 15	06 04	06 51
30	05 14	05 42	06 05	04 15	05 08	06 01	06 53
35	05 11	05 41	06 06	04 08	05 04	05 59	06 53
40	05 08	05 39	06 06	04 00	04 59	05 57	06 54
45	05 03	05 37	06 07	03 51	04 53	05 54	06 55
S 50	04 57	05 35	06 07	03 41	04 46	05 51	06 56
52	04 54	05 34	06 07	03 36	04 43	05 50	06 57
54	04 51	05 32	06 08	03 30	04 40	05 49	06 57
56	04 47	05 31	06 08	03 24	04 36	05 47	06 58
58	04 42	05 29	06 08	03 17	04 32	05 45	06 59
S 60	04 37	05 27	06 08	03 09	04 27	05 43	06 59

Sunset / Twilight / Moonset

Lat.	Sunset	Twilight Civil	Naut.	Moonset 22	23	24	25
N 72	18 35	19 45	21 21	14 34	16 26	18 13	19 58
N 70	18 32	19 34	20 57	14 53	16 36	18 15	19 52
68	18 29	19 26	20 39	15 08	16 44	18 16	19 48
66	18 27	19 19	20 25	15 21	16 50	18 17	19 44
64	18 26	19 14	20 13	15 31	16 55	18 18	19 41
62	18 24	19 09	20 04	15 39	17 00	18 19	19 38
60	18 23	19 05	19 56	15 46	17 04	18 20	19 36
N 58	18 22	19 01	19 49	15 53	17 07	18 21	19 34
56	18 21	18 58	19 43	15 59	17 10	18 21	19 32
54	18 20	18 55	19 38	16 04	17 13	18 22	19 30
52	18 19	18 53	19 33	16 08	17 16	18 22	19 29
50	18 18	18 51	19 29	16 12	17 18	18 23	19 27
45	18 17	18 47	19 21	16 21	17 23	18 24	19 25
N 40	18 15	18 43	19 14	16 29	17 27	18 24	19 22
35	18 14	18 40	19 09	16 35	17 30	18 25	19 20
30	18 13	18 37	19 05	16 41	17 33	18 26	19 18
20	18 12	18 34	19 00	16 50	17 39	18 27	19 15
N 10	18 11	18 32	18 56	16 58	17 43	18 28	19 12
0	18 10	18 30	18 54	17 06	17 48	18 29	19 09
S 10	18 09	18 30	18 54	17 14	17 52	18 29	19 06
20	18 08	18 30	18 55	17 22	17 57	18 30	19 04
30	18 07	18 31	18 59	17 31	18 02	18 31	19 00
35	18 06	18 32	19 01	17 37	18 05	18 32	18 58
40	18 06	18 33	19 04	17 43	18 08	18 32	18 56
45	18 05	18 35	19 09	17 50	18 12	18 33	18 54
S 50	18 05	18 37	19 15	17 58	18 17	18 34	18 51
52	18 05	18 38	19 18	18 02	18 19	18 34	18 50
54	18 04	18 39	19 21	18 06	18 21	18 35	18 48
56	18 04	18 41	19 25	18 11	18 23	18 35	18 46
58	18 04	18 43	19 29	18 16	18 26	18 36	18 45
S 60	18 03	18 45	19 34	18 21	18 29	18 36	18 43

SUN / MOON

Day	Eqn. of Time 00ʰ	Eqn. of Time 12ʰ	Mer. Pass.	Mer. Pass. Upper	Mer. Pass. Lower	Age	Phase
	m s	m s	h m	h m	h m	d	%
22	06 53	06 45	12 07	10 56	23 17	28	3
23	06 36	06 27	12 06	11 38	23 58	29	1
24	06 18	06 09	12 06	12 19	24 39	00	0

UT (d h)	ARIES GHA	VENUS −4.5 GHA	VENUS Dec	MARS +0.8 GHA	MARS Dec	JUPITER −2.1 GHA	JUPITER Dec	SATURN +0.7 GHA	SATURN Dec	STARS Name	SHA	Dec
25 00	182 54.7	135 24.7	N20 54.4	244 47.9	S21 46.4	247 34.6	S21 26.8	240 30.2	S20 09.3	Acamar	315 15.1	S40 13.8
01	197 57.2	150 24.6	55.2	259 48.5	46.2	262 36.7	26.7	255 32.5	09.2	Achernar	335 23.8	S57 08.3
02	212 59.6	165 24.6	56.1	274 49.1	45.9	277 38.8	26.7	270 34.8	09.2	Acrux	173 03.5	S63 12.6
03	228 02.1	180 24.6	.. 56.9	289 49.7	.. 45.6	292 40.9	.. 26.6	285 37.1	.. 09.2	Adhara	255 08.8	S29 00.3
04	243 04.6	195 24.6	57.8	304 50.4	45.3	307 43.0	26.6	300 39.3	09.1	Aldebaran	290 44.2	N16 32.8
05	258 07.0	210 24.6	58.6	319 51.0	45.0	322 45.1	26.5	315 41.6	09.1			
06	273 09.5	225 24.5	N20 59.5	334 51.6	S21 44.8	337 47.2	S21 26.5	330 43.9	S20 09.1	Alioth	166 16.0	N55 51.0
W 07	288 12.0	240 24.5	21 00.3	349 52.2	44.5	352 49.3	26.4	345 46.2	09.0	Alkaid	152 54.7	N49 12.7
E 08	303 14.4	255 24.5	01.1	4 52.8	44.2	7 51.4	26.4	0 48.4	09.0	Alnair	27 38.2	S46 51.8
D 09	318 16.9	270 24.5	.. 02.0	19 53.4	.. 43.9	22 53.5	.. 26.3	15 50.7	.. 09.0	Alnilam	275 41.7	S 1 11.6
N 10	333 19.3	285 24.5	02.8	34 54.1	43.6	37 55.6	26.3	30 53.0	08.9	Alphard	217 51.3	S 8 44.9
E 11	348 21.8	300 24.5	03.7	49 54.7	43.4	52 57.7	26.2	45 55.3	08.9			
S 12	3 24.3	315 24.5	N21 04.5	64 55.3	S21 43.1	67 59.8	S21 26.1	60 57.6	S20 08.9	Alphecca	126 06.8	N26 38.7
D 13	18 26.7	330 24.4	05.4	79 55.9	42.8	83 01.9	26.1	75 59.8	08.8	Alpheratz	357 39.1	N29 11.9
A 14	33 29.2	345 24.4	06.2	94 56.5	42.5	98 03.9	26.0	91 02.1	08.8	Altair	62 03.8	N 8 55.1
Y 15	48 31.7	0 24.4	.. 07.0	109 57.2	.. 42.2	113 06.0	.. 26.0	106 04.4	.. 08.8	Ankaa	353 11.5	S42 12.0
16	63 34.1	15 24.4	07.9	124 57.8	41.9	128 08.1	25.9	121 06.7	08.7	Antares	112 20.4	S26 28.5
17	78 36.6	30 24.4	08.7	139 58.4	41.7	143 10.2	25.9	136 09.0	08.7			
18	93 39.1	45 24.4	N21 09.6	154 59.0	S21 41.4	158 12.3	S21 25.8	151 11.2	S20 08.7	Arcturus	145 51.2	N19 04.6
19	108 41.5	60 24.4	10.4	169 59.6	41.1	173 14.4	25.8	166 13.5	08.6	Atria	107 17.8	S69 03.5
20	123 44.0	75 24.3	11.2	185 00.3	40.8	188 16.5	25.7	181 15.8	08.6	Avior	234 15.9	S59 34.7
21	138 46.5	90 24.3	.. 12.1	200 00.9	.. 40.5	203 18.6	.. 25.7	196 18.1	.. 08.5	Bellatrix	278 27.1	N 6 21.9
22	153 48.9	105 24.3	12.9	215 01.5	40.2	218 20.7	25.6	211 20.4	08.5	Betelgeuse	270 56.3	N 7 24.5
23	168 51.4	120 24.3	13.7	230 02.1	39.9	233 22.8	25.5	226 22.6	08.5			
26 00	183 53.8	135 24.3	N21 14.6	245 02.7	S21 39.7	248 24.9	S21 25.5	241 24.9	S20 08.4	Canopus	263 54.1	S52 42.8
01	198 56.3	150 24.3	15.4	260 03.3	39.4	263 27.0	25.4	256 27.2	08.4	Capella	280 27.7	N46 01.1
02	213 58.8	165 24.3	16.2	275 04.0	39.1	278 29.1	25.4	271 29.5	08.4	Deneb	49 28.6	N45 20.8
03	229 01.2	180 24.3	.. 17.0	290 04.6	.. 38.8	293 31.2	.. 25.3	286 31.8	.. 08.3	Denebola	182 28.6	N14 27.5
04	244 03.7	195 24.3	17.9	305 05.2	38.5	308 33.3	25.3	301 34.0	08.3	Diphda	348 51.5	S17 52.8
05	259 06.2	210 24.2	18.7	320 05.8	38.2	323 35.4	25.2	316 36.3	08.3			
06	274 08.6	225 24.2	N21 19.5	335 06.4	S21 37.9	338 37.5	S21 25.2	331 38.6	S20 08.2	Dubhe	193 45.3	N61 38.6
T 07	289 11.1	240 24.2	20.4	350 07.1	37.6	353 39.6	25.1	346 40.9	08.2	Elnath	278 06.8	N28 37.4
H 08	304 13.6	255 24.2	21.2	5 07.7	37.4	8 41.7	25.1	1 43.2	08.2	Eltanin	90 43.9	N51 28.9
U 09	319 16.0	270 24.2	.. 22.0	20 08.3	.. 37.1	23 43.8	.. 25.0	16 45.5	.. 08.1	Enif	33 42.8	N 9 57.8
R 10	334 18.5	285 24.2	22.8	35 08.9	36.8	38 45.9	25.0	31 47.7	08.1	Fomalhaut	15 19.2	S29 31.0
S 11	349 20.9	300 24.2	23.7	50 09.6	36.5	53 48.0	24.9	46 50.0	08.1			
D 12	4 23.4	315 24.2	N21 24.5	65 10.2	S21 36.2	68 50.1	S21 24.8	61 52.3	S20 08.0	Gacrux	171 55.2	S57 13.5
A 13	19 25.9	330 24.2	25.3	80 10.8	35.9	83 52.2	24.8	76 54.6	08.0	Gienah	175 47.2	S17 39.3
Y 14	34 28.3	345 24.2	26.1	95 11.4	35.6	98 54.3	24.7	91 56.9	08.0	Hadar	148 42.8	S60 28.0
15	49 30.8	0 24.2	.. 26.9	110 12.0	.. 35.3	113 56.4	.. 24.7	106 59.2	.. 07.9	Hamal	327 55.8	N23 33.3
16	64 33.3	15 24.2	27.8	125 12.7	35.0	128 58.5	24.6	122 01.4	07.9	Kaus Aust.	83 37.6	S34 22.3
17	79 35.7	30 24.2	28.6	140 13.3	34.7	144 00.6	24.6	137 03.7	07.9			
18	94 38.2	45 24.2	N21 29.4	155 13.9	S21 34.5	159 02.7	S21 24.5	152 06.0	S20 07.8	Kochab	137 19.1	N74 04.2
19	109 40.7	60 24.2	30.2	170 14.5	34.2	174 04.8	24.5	167 08.3	07.8	Markab	13 34.0	N15 18.6
20	123 43.1	75 24.2	31.0	185 15.1	33.9	189 06.9	24.4	182 10.6	07.8	Menkar	314 10.4	N 4 09.9
21	139 45.6	90 24.2	.. 31.8	200 15.8	.. 33.6	204 09.0	.. 24.4	197 12.9	.. 07.7	Menkent	148 01.8	S36 28.0
22	154 48.1	105 24.2	32.7	215 16.4	33.3	219 11.1	24.3	212 15.1	07.7	Miaplacidus	221 38.2	S69 48.2
23	169 50.5	120 24.2	33.5	230 17.0	33.0	234 13.2	24.3	227 17.4	07.7			
27 00	184 53.0	135 24.2	N21 34.3	245 17.6	S21 32.7	249 15.3	S21 24.2	242 19.7	S20 07.6	Mirfak	308 34.1	N49 55.9
01	199 55.4	150 24.2	35.1	260 18.3	32.4	264 17.4	24.1	257 22.0	07.6	Nunki	75 52.6	S26 16.2
02	214 57.9	165 24.1	35.9	275 18.9	32.1	279 19.5	24.1	272 24.3	07.6	Peacock	53 12.2	S56 40.0
03	230 00.4	180 24.1	.. 36.7	290 19.5	.. 31.8	294 21.7	.. 24.0	287 26.6	.. 07.5	Pollux	243 21.9	N27 58.6
04	245 02.8	195 24.1	37.5	305 20.1	31.5	309 23.8	24.0	302 28.8	07.5	Procyon	244 54.8	N 5 10.2
05	260 05.3	210 24.1	38.3	320 20.7	31.2	324 25.9	23.9	317 31.1	07.5			
06	275 07.8	225 24.2	N21 39.1	335 21.4	S21 30.9	339 28.0	S21 23.9	332 33.4	S20 07.4	Rasalhague	96 02.1	N12 32.6
07	290 10.2	240 24.2	40.0	350 22.0	30.6	354 30.1	23.8	347 35.7	07.4	Regulus	207 38.3	N11 52.1
F 08	305 12.7	255 24.2	40.8	5 22.6	30.3	9 32.2	23.8	2 38.0	07.4	Rigel	281 07.7	S 8 11.0
R 09	320 15.2	270 24.2	.. 41.6	20 23.2	.. 30.0	24 34.3	.. 23.7	17 40.3	.. 07.3	Rigil Kent.	139 44.9	S60 54.9
I 10	335 17.6	285 24.2	42.4	35 23.9	29.7	39 36.4	23.7	32 42.6	07.3	Sabik	102 07.1	S15 44.9
D 11	350 20.1	300 24.2	43.2	50 24.5	29.5	54 38.5	23.6	47 44.8	07.3			
A 12	5 22.5	315 24.2	N21 44.0	65 25.1	S21 29.2	69 40.6	S21 23.6	62 47.1	S20 07.2	Schedar	349 35.9	N56 38.7
Y 13	20 25.0	330 24.2	44.8	80 25.7	28.9	84 42.7	23.5	77 49.4	07.2	Shaula	96 15.5	S37 06.9
14	35 27.5	345 24.2	45.6	95 26.4	28.6	99 44.8	23.5	92 51.7	07.2	Sirius	258 29.6	S16 44.9
15	50 29.9	0 24.2	.. 46.4	110 27.0	.. 28.3	114 46.9	.. 23.4	107 54.0	.. 07.1	Spica	158 26.0	S11 16.0
16	65 32.4	15 24.2	47.2	125 27.6	28.0	129 49.0	23.3	122 56.3	07.1	Suhail	222 48.8	S43 31.1
17	80 34.9	30 24.2	48.0	140 28.2	27.7	144 51.1	23.3	137 58.6	07.1			
18	95 37.3	45 24.2	N21 48.8	155 28.9	S21 27.4	159 53.3	S21 23.2	153 00.9	S20 07.0	Vega	80 35.8	N38 47.9
19	110 39.8	60 24.2	49.6	170 29.5	27.1	174 55.4	23.2	168 03.1	07.0	Zuben'ubi	137 00.0	S16 07.5
20	125 42.3	75 24.2	50.4	185 30.1	26.8	189 57.5	23.1	183 05.4	07.0			
21	140 44.7	90 24.2	.. 51.2	200 30.7	.. 26.5	204 59.6	.. 23.1	198 07.7	.. 06.9		SHA	Mer. Pass.
22	155 47.2	105 24.2	52.0	215 31.4	26.2	220 01.7	23.0	213 10.0	06.9	Venus	311 30.5	14 58
23	170 49.7	120 24.2	52.8	230 32.0	25.9	235 03.8	23.0	228 12.3	06.9	Mars	61 08.9	7 40
Mer. Pass. 11 42.5		v 0.0 d 0.8		v 0.6 d 0.3		v 2.1 d 0.1		v 2.3 d 0.0		Jupiter	64 31.1	7 25
										Saturn	57 31.1	7 53

UT	SUN GHA	SUN Dec	MOON GHA	v	MOON Dec	d	HP
d h	° ′	° ′	° ′	′	° ′	′	′
25 00	178 30.2	N 1 54.5	170 30.7	16.4	S 0 02.6	11.9	53.9
01	193 30.4	55.5	185 06.1	16.4	N 0 09.3	11.8	53.9
02	208 30.6	56.5	199 41.5	16.4	0 21.1	11.9	53.9
03	223 30.8	.. 57.5	214 16.9	16.4	0 33.0	11.8	53.9
04	238 31.0	58.5	228 52.3	16.4	0 44.8	11.9	53.9
05	253 31.1	1 59.5	243 27.7	16.3	0 56.7	11.8	53.9
06	268 31.3	N 2 00.4	258 03.0	16.4	N 1 08.5	11.8	53.9
W 07	283 31.5	01.4	272 38.4	16.4	1 20.3	11.9	53.9
E 08	298 31.7	02.4	287 13.8	16.3	1 32.2	11.8	53.9
D 09	313 31.9	.. 03.4	301 49.1	16.4	1 44.0	11.8	53.9
N 10	328 32.1	04.4	316 24.5	16.3	1 55.8	11.8	53.9
E 11	343 32.3	05.3	330 59.8	16.3	2 07.6	11.8	53.9
S 12	358 32.5	N 2 06.3	345 35.1	16.4	N 2 19.4	11.8	53.9
D 13	13 32.6	07.3	0 10.5	16.3	2 31.2	11.8	54.0
A 14	28 32.8	08.3	14 45.8	16.3	2 43.0	11.8	54.0
Y 15	43 33.0	.. 09.3	29 21.1	16.3	2 54.8	11.8	54.0
16	58 33.2	10.3	43 56.4	16.2	3 06.6	11.8	54.0
17	73 33.4	11.2	58 31.6	16.3	3 18.4	11.7	54.0
18	88 33.6	N 2 12.2	73 06.9	16.3	N 3 30.1	11.8	54.0
19	103 33.8	13.2	87 42.2	16.2	3 41.9	11.7	54.0
20	118 34.0	14.2	102 17.4	16.2	3 53.6	11.7	54.0
21	133 34.2	.. 15.2	116 52.6	16.2	4 05.3	11.7	54.0
22	148 34.3	16.1	131 27.8	16.2	4 17.0	11.7	54.0
23	163 34.5	17.1	146 03.0	16.2	4 28.7	11.7	54.0
26 00	178 34.7	N 2 18.1	160 38.2	16.1	N 4 40.4	11.7	54.0
01	193 34.9	19.1	175 13.3	16.1	4 52.1	11.6	54.0
02	208 35.1	20.1	189 48.4	16.1	5 03.7	11.6	54.0
03	223 35.3	.. 21.0	204 23.5	16.1	5 15.3	11.7	54.0
04	238 35.5	22.0	218 58.6	16.1	5 27.0	11.6	54.0
05	253 35.7	23.0	233 33.7	16.0	5 38.6	11.5	54.0
06	268 35.8	N 2 24.0	248 08.7	16.1	N 5 50.1	11.6	54.0
T 07	283 36.0	25.0	262 43.8	16.0	6 01.7	11.5	54.0
H 08	298 36.2	25.9	277 18.8	15.9	6 13.2	11.5	54.0
U 09	313 36.4	.. 26.9	291 53.7	16.0	6 24.7	11.5	54.1
R 10	328 36.6	27.9	306 28.7	15.9	6 36.2	11.5	54.1
11	343 36.8	28.9	321 03.6	15.9	6 47.7	11.4	54.1
S 12	358 37.0	N 2 29.9	335 38.5	15.8	N 6 59.1	11.4	54.1
D 13	13 37.2	30.8	350 13.3	15.9	7 10.5	11.4	54.1
A 14	28 37.3	31.8	4 48.2	15.8	7 21.9	11.4	54.1
Y 15	43 37.5	.. 32.8	19 23.0	15.8	7 33.3	11.4	54.1
16	58 37.7	33.8	33 57.8	15.7	7 44.7	11.3	54.1
17	73 37.9	34.8	48 32.5	15.7	7 56.0	11.3	54.1
18	88 38.1	N 2 35.7	63 07.2	15.7	N 8 07.3	11.2	54.1
19	103 38.3	36.7	77 41.9	15.7	8 18.5	11.3	54.1
20	118 38.5	37.7	92 16.6	15.6	8 29.8	11.2	54.1
21	133 38.7	.. 38.7	106 51.2	15.6	8 41.0	11.1	54.1
22	148 38.9	39.7	121 25.8	15.5	8 52.1	11.2	54.2
23	163 39.0	40.6	136 00.3	15.5	9 03.3	11.1	54.2
27 00	178 39.2	N 2 41.6	150 34.8	15.5	N 9 14.4	11.1	54.2
01	193 39.4	42.6	165 09.3	15.4	9 25.5	11.0	54.2
02	208 39.6	43.6	179 43.7	15.4	9 36.5	11.0	54.2
03	223 39.8	.. 44.6	194 18.1	15.4	9 47.5	11.0	54.2
04	238 40.0	45.5	208 52.5	15.3	9 58.5	10.9	54.2
05	253 40.2	46.5	223 26.8	15.3	10 09.4	10.9	54.2
06	268 40.4	N 2 47.5	238 01.1	15.2	N10 20.3	10.9	54.2
07	283 40.5	48.5	252 35.3	15.2	10 31.2	10.8	54.2
08	298 40.7	49.4	267 09.5	15.2	10 42.0	10.8	54.2
F 09	313 40.9	.. 50.4	281 43.7	15.1	10 52.8	10.7	54.3
R 10	328 41.1	51.4	296 17.8	15.0	11 03.5	10.7	54.3
I 11	343 41.3	52.4	310 51.8	15.1	11 14.2	10.7	54.3
D 12	358 41.5	N 2 53.4	325 25.9	14.9	N11 24.9	10.6	54.3
A 13	13 41.7	54.3	339 59.8	15.0	11 35.5	10.6	54.3
Y 14	28 41.9	55.3	354 33.8	14.8	11 46.1	10.6	54.3
15	43 42.0	.. 56.3	9 07.6	14.9	11 56.7	10.5	54.3
16	58 42.2	57.3	23 41.5	14.8	12 07.2	10.4	54.3
17	73 42.4	58.2	38 15.3	14.7	12 17.6	10.4	54.4
18	88 42.6	N 2 59.2	52 49.0	14.7	N12 28.0	10.4	54.4
19	103 42.8	3 00.2	67 22.7	14.7	12 38.4	10.3	54.4
20	118 43.0	01.2	81 56.4	14.5	12 48.7	10.2	54.4
21	133 43.2	.. 02.2	96 29.9	14.6	12 58.9	10.3	54.4
22	148 43.4	03.1	111 03.5	14.5	13 09.2	10.1	54.4
23	163 43.6	04.1	125 37.0	14.4	N13 19.3	10.1	54.4
	SD 16.1	d 1.0	SD 14.7		14.7		14.8

Lat.	Naut. (Twilight)	Civil (Twilight)	Sunrise	Moonrise 25	26	27	28
°	h m	h m	h m	h m	h m	h m	h m
N 72	02 33	04 15	05 25	06 34	06 15	05 53	05 22
N 70	03 01	04 26	05 29	06 36	06 23	06 09	05 51
68	03 21	04 36	05 33	06 37	06 30	06 22	06 12
66	03 37	04 44	05 36	06 38	06 35	06 32	06 29
64	03 50	04 50	05 38	06 39	06 40	06 41	06 43
62	04 00	04 56	05 40	06 40	06 44	06 49	06 55
60	04 09	05 00	05 42	06 41	06 48	06 55	07 05
N 58	04 16	05 04	05 44	06 41	06 51	07 01	07 14
56	04 23	05 08	05 45	06 42	06 54	07 06	07 22
54	04 29	05 11	05 47	06 42	06 56	07 11	07 29
52	04 34	05 14	05 48	06 43	06 59	07 15	07 35
50	04 38	05 17	05 49	06 43	07 01	07 19	07 40
45	04 47	05 22	05 51	06 44	07 05	07 28	07 53
N 40	04 54	05 26	05 53	06 45	07 09	07 35	08 03
35	05 00	05 30	05 55	06 46	07 13	07 41	08 12
30	05 04	05 32	05 56	06 47	07 16	07 46	08 19
20	05 11	05 37	05 59	06 48	07 21	07 56	08 33
N 10	05 15	05 40	06 01	06 49	07 26	08 04	08 45
0	05 18	05 42	06 02	06 49	07 30	08 12	08 56
S 10	05 19	05 43	06 04	06 50	07 35	08 20	09 07
20	05 18	05 44	06 06	06 51	07 40	08 28	09 19
30	05 16	05 43	06 07	06 53	07 45	08 38	09 33
35	05 14	05 43	06 08	06 53	07 48	08 44	09 41
40	05 11	05 42	06 09	06 54	07 52	08 50	09 50
45	05 07	05 41	06 11	06 55	07 56	08 58	10 01
S 50	05 02	05 40	06 12	06 56	08 01	09 07	10 14
52	04 59	05 39	06 13	06 57	08 04	09 11	10 20
54	04 57	05 38	06 13	06 57	08 06	09 16	10 27
56	04 53	05 37	06 14	06 58	08 09	09 21	10 34
58	04 49	05 36	06 15	06 59	08 12	09 27	10 43
S 60	04 45	05 34	06 16	06 59	08 16	09 33	10 53

Lat.	Sunset	Civil (Twilight)	Naut. (Twilight)	Moonset 25	26	27	28
°	h m	h m	h m	h m	h m	h m	h m
N 72	18 49	20 00	21 44	19 58	21 47	23 47	26 33
N 70	18 44	19 48	21 15	19 52	21 33	23 20	25 22
68	18 40	19 38	20 54	19 48	21 22	23 00	24 45
66	18 37	19 30	20 37	19 44	21 13	22 44	24 20
64	18 35	19 23	20 24	19 41	21 05	22 31	24 00
62	18 32	19 17	20 13	19 38	20 58	22 20	23 44
60	18 30	19 12	20 04	19 34	20 53	22 11	23 31
N 58	18 28	19 08	19 57	19 34	20 48	22 03	23 19
56	18 27	19 04	19 50	19 32	20 43	21 56	23 09
54	18 26	19 01	19 44	19 30	20 40	21 50	23 01
52	18 24	18 58	19 39	19 29	20 36	21 44	22 53
50	18 23	18 56	19 34	19 27	20 33	21 39	22 46
45	18 21	18 50	19 25	19 25	20 26	21 28	22 31
N 40	18 19	18 46	19 18	19 22	20 20	21 19	22 19
35	18 17	18 42	19 12	19 20	20 15	21 11	22 08
30	18 15	18 39	19 07	19 18	20 11	21 04	21 59
20	18 13	18 35	19 01	19 15	20 03	20 53	21 44
N 10	18 11	18 32	18 56	19 12	19 56	20 42	21 30
0	18 09	18 29	18 54	19 09	19 50	20 33	21 18
S 10	18 07	18 28	18 52	19 06	19 44	20 23	21 05
20	18 05	18 27	18 53	19 04	19 38	20 13	20 51
30	18 03	18 27	18 55	19 00	19 30	20 02	20 36
35	18 02	18 27	18 57	18 58	19 26	19 55	20 27
40	18 01	18 28	18 59	18 56	19 21	19 48	20 17
45	18 00	18 29	19 03	18 54	19 15	19 39	20 05
S 50	17 58	18 30	19 08	18 51	19 09	19 28	19 51
52	17 58	18 31	19 10	18 50	19 06	19 23	19 44
54	17 57	18 32	19 13	18 48	19 02	19 18	19 37
56	17 56	18 33	19 16	18 46	18 59	19 12	19 29
58	17 55	18 34	19 20	18 45	18 54	19 06	19 20
S 60	17 54	18 35	19 24	18 43	18 50	18 58	19 09

Day	Eqn. of Time 00ʰ	Eqn. of Time 12ʰ	SUN Mer. Pass.	MOON Mer. Pass. Upper	MOON Mer. Pass. Lower	Age	Phase
d	m s	m s	h m	h m	h m	d	%
25	06 00	05 51	12 06	12 59	00 39	01	1
26	05 42	05 32	12 06	13 40	01 20	02	4
27	05 23	05 14	12 05	14 22	02 01	03	9

UT	ARIES GHA	VENUS −4.5 GHA	Dec	MARS +0.8 GHA	Dec	JUPITER −2.1 GHA	Dec	SATURN +0.7 GHA	Dec	STARS Name	SHA	Dec
28 00	185 52.1	135 24.2	N21 53.6	245 32.6	S21 25.6	250 05.9	S21 22.9	243 14.6	S20 06.8	Acamar	315 15.1	S40 13.8
01	200 54.6	150 24.3	54.3	260 33.2	25.3	265 08.0	22.9	258 16.9	06.8	Achernar	335 23.8	S57 08.3
02	215 57.0	165 24.3	55.1	275 33.9	25.0	280 10.1	22.8	273 19.2	06.8	Acrux	173 03.5	S63 12.6
03	230 59.5	180 24.3 ..	55.9	290 34.5 ..	24.7	295 12.2 ..	22.8	288 21.4 ..	06.7	Adhara	255 08.8	S29 00.3
04	246 02.0	195 24.3	56.7	305 35.1	24.4	310 14.4	22.7	303 23.7	06.7	Aldebaran	290 44.2	N16 32.8
05	261 04.4	210 24.3	57.5	320 35.7	24.0	325 16.5	22.7	318 26.0	06.7			
06	276 06.9	225 24.3	N21 58.3	335 36.4	S21 23.7	340 18.6	S21 22.6	333 28.3	S20 06.6	Alioth	166 16.0	N55 51.0
07	291 09.4	240 24.3	59.1	350 37.0	23.4	355 20.7	22.6	348 30.6	06.6	Alkaid	152 54.7	N49 12.7
S 08	306 11.8	255 24.3	21 59.9	5 37.6	23.1	10 22.8	22.5	3 32.9	06.6	Alnair	27 38.2	S46 51.8
A 09	321 14.3	270 24.3	22 00.7	20 38.2 ..	22.8	25 24.9 ..	22.4	18 35.2 ..	06.5	Alnilam	275 41.7	S 1 11.6
T 10	336 16.8	285 24.4	01.4	35 38.9	22.5	40 27.0	22.4	33 37.5	06.5	Alphard	217 51.3	S 8 44.9
U 11	351 19.2	300 24.4	02.2	50 39.5	22.2	55 29.1	22.3	48 39.8	06.5			
R 12	6 21.7	315 24.4	N22 03.0	65 40.1	S21 21.9	70 31.2	S21 22.3	63 42.0	S20 06.4	Alphecca	126 06.8	N26 38.7
D 13	21 24.2	330 24.4	03.8	80 40.7	21.6	85 33.4	22.2	78 44.3	06.4	Alpheratz	357 39.1	N29 11.9
A 14	36 26.6	345 24.4	04.6	95 41.4	21.3	100 35.5	22.2	93 46.6	06.4	Altair	62 03.8	N 8 55.2
Y 15	51 29.1	0 24.4 ..	05.4	110 42.0 ..	21.0	115 37.6 ..	22.1	108 48.9 ..	06.3	Ankaa	353 11.5	S42 12.0
16	66 31.5	15 24.4	06.1	125 42.6	20.7	130 39.7	22.1	123 51.2	06.3	Antares	112 20.4	S26 28.5
17	81 34.0	30 24.5	06.9	140 43.3	20.4	145 41.8	22.0	138 53.5	06.3			
18	96 36.5	45 24.5	N22 07.7	155 43.9	S21 20.1	160 43.9	S21 22.0	153 55.8	S20 06.3	Arcturus	145 51.2	N19 04.6
19	111 38.9	60 24.5	08.5	170 44.5	19.8	175 46.0	21.9	168 58.1	06.2	Atria	107 17.8	S69 03.5
20	126 41.4	75 24.5	09.2	185 45.1	19.5	190 48.2	21.9	184 00.4	06.2	Avior	234 15.9	S59 34.7
21	141 43.9	90 24.5 ..	10.0	200 45.8 ..	19.2	205 50.3 ..	21.8	199 02.7 ..	06.2	Bellatrix	278 27.1	N 6 21.9
22	156 46.3	105 24.5	10.8	215 46.4	18.9	220 52.4	21.8	214 04.9	06.1	Betelgeuse	270 56.3	N 7 24.5
23	171 48.8	120 24.6	11.6	230 47.0	18.5	235 54.5	21.7	229 07.2	06.1			
29 00	186 51.3	135 24.6	N22 12.3	245 47.6	S21 18.2	250 56.6	S21 21.7	244 09.5	S20 06.1	Canopus	263 54.1	S52 42.8
01	201 53.7	150 24.6	13.1	260 48.3	17.9	265 58.7	21.6	259 11.8	06.0	Capella	280 27.7	N46 01.1
02	216 56.2	165 24.6	13.9	275 48.9	17.6	281 00.9	21.6	274 14.1	06.0	Deneb	49 28.6	N45 20.8
03	231 58.6	180 24.7 ..	14.7	290 49.5 ..	17.3	296 03.0 ..	21.5	289 16.4 ..	06.0	Denebola	182 28.6	N14 27.5
04	247 01.1	195 24.7	15.4	305 50.2	17.0	311 05.1	21.5	304 18.7	05.9	Diphda	348 51.5	S17 52.8
05	262 03.6	210 24.7	16.2	320 50.8	16.7	326 07.2	21.4	319 21.0	05.9			
06	277 06.0	225 24.7	N22 17.0	335 51.4	S21 16.4	341 09.3	S21 21.4	334 23.3	S20 05.9	Dubhe	193 45.3	N61 38.6
07	292 08.5	240 24.7	17.7	350 52.1	16.1	356 11.4	21.3	349 25.6	05.8	Elnath	278 06.8	N28 37.4
S 08	307 11.0	255 24.8	18.5	5 52.7	15.8	11 13.6	21.2	4 27.9	05.8	Eltanin	90 43.9	N51 28.9
U 09	322 13.4	270 24.8 ..	19.3	20 53.3 ..	15.5	26 15.7 ..	21.2	19 30.2 ..	05.8	Enif	33 42.8	N 9 57.8
N 10	337 15.9	285 24.8	20.0	35 53.9	15.1	41 17.8	21.1	34 32.5	05.7	Fomalhaut	15 19.1	S29 31.0
11	352 18.4	300 24.8	20.8	50 54.6	14.8	56 19.9	21.1	49 34.7	05.7			
D 12	7 20.8	315 24.9	N22 21.6	65 55.2	S21 14.5	71 22.0	S21 21.0	64 37.0	S20 05.7	Gacrux	171 55.2	S57 13.5
A 13	22 23.3	330 24.9	22.3	80 55.8	14.2	86 24.2	21.0	79 39.3	05.6	Gienah	175 47.2	S17 39.3
Y 14	37 25.8	345 24.9	23.1	95 56.5	13.9	101 26.3	20.9	94 41.6	05.6	Hadar	148 40.7	S60 28.0
15	52 28.2	0 24.9 ..	23.8	110 57.1 ..	13.6	116 28.4 ..	20.9	109 43.9 ..	05.6	Hamal	327 55.8	N23 33.3
16	67 30.7	15 25.0	24.6	125 57.7	13.3	131 30.5	20.8	124 46.2	05.5	Kaus Aust.	83 37.6	S34 22.3
17	82 33.1	30 25.0	25.4	140 58.3	12.9	146 32.6	20.8	139 48.5	05.5			
18	97 35.6	45 25.0	N22 26.1	155 59.0	S21 12.6	161 34.8	S21 20.7	154 50.8	S20 05.5	Kochab	137 19.0	N74 04.2
19	112 38.1	60 25.1	26.9	170 59.6	12.3	176 36.9	20.7	169 53.1	05.4	Markab	13 34.0	N15 18.6
20	127 40.5	75 25.1	27.6	186 00.2	12.0	191 39.0	20.6	184 55.4	05.4	Menkar	314 10.4	N 4 09.9
21	142 43.0	90 25.1 ..	28.4	201 00.9 ..	11.7	206 41.1 ..	20.6	199 57.7 ..	05.4	Menkent	148 01.7	S36 28.1
22	157 45.5	105 25.2	29.1	216 01.5	11.4	221 43.2	20.5	215 00.0	05.4	Miaplacidus	221 38.3	S69 48.2
23	172 47.9	120 25.2	29.9	231 02.1	11.1	236 45.4	20.5	230 02.3	05.3			
30 00	187 50.4	135 25.2	N22 30.7	246 02.8	S21 10.7	251 47.5	S21 20.4	245 04.6	S20 05.3	Mirfak	308 34.1	N49 55.9
01	202 52.9	150 25.2	31.4	261 03.4	10.4	266 49.6	20.4	260 06.9	05.3	Nunki	75 52.6	S26 16.2
02	217 55.3	165 25.3	32.2	276 04.0	10.1	281 51.7	20.3	275 09.2	05.2	Peacock	53 12.1	S56 40.0
03	232 57.8	180 25.3 ..	32.9	291 04.7 ..	09.8	296 53.9 ..	20.3	290 11.5 ..	05.2	Pollux	243 21.9	N27 58.6
04	248 00.3	195 25.3	33.7	306 05.3	09.5	311 56.0	20.2	305 13.7	05.2	Procyon	244 54.8	N 5 10.2
05	263 02.7	210 25.4	34.4	321 05.9	09.2	326 58.1	20.2	320 16.0	05.1			
06	278 05.2	225 25.4	N22 35.2	336 06.6	S21 08.8	342 00.2	S21 20.1	335 18.3	S20 05.1	Rasalhague	96 02.0	N12 32.6
07	293 07.6	240 25.5	35.9	351 07.2	08.5	357 02.3	20.1	350 20.6	05.1	Regulus	207 38.3	N11 52.1
M 08	308 10.1	255 25.5	36.7	6 07.8	08.2	12 04.5	20.0	5 22.9	05.0	Rigel	281 07.7	S 8 11.0
O 09	323 12.6	270 25.5 ..	37.4	21 08.4 ..	07.9	27 06.6 ..	20.0	20 25.2 ..	05.0	Rigil Kent.	139 44.9	S60 54.9
N 10	338 15.0	285 25.6	38.1	36 09.1	07.6	42 08.7	19.9	35 27.5	05.0	Sabik	102 07.1	S15 44.9
11	353 17.5	300 25.6	38.9	51 09.7	07.3	57 10.8	19.9	50 29.8	04.9			
D 12	8 20.0	315 25.6	N22 39.6	66 10.3	S21 06.9	72 13.0	S21 19.8	65 32.1	S20 04.9	Schedar	349 35.8	N56 38.7
A 13	23 22.4	330 25.7	40.4	81 11.0	06.6	87 15.1	19.8	80 34.4	04.9	Shaula	96 15.5	S37 06.9
Y 14	38 24.9	345 25.7	41.1	96 11.6	06.3	102 17.2	19.7	95 36.7	04.9	Sirius	258 29.6	S16 44.9
15	53 27.4	0 25.8 ..	41.9	111 12.2 ..	06.0	117 19.4 ..	19.7	110 39.0 ..	04.8	Spica	158 26.0	S11 16.0
16	68 29.8	15 25.8	42.6	126 12.9	05.7	132 21.5	19.6	125 41.3	04.8	Suhail	222 48.8	S43 31.1
17	83 32.3	30 25.8	43.3	141 13.5	05.3	147 23.6	19.6	140 43.6	04.8			
18	98 34.7	45 25.9	N22 44.1	156 14.1	S21 05.0	162 25.7	S21 19.5	155 45.9	S20 04.7	Vega	80 35.8	N38 47.9
19	113 37.2	60 25.9	44.8	171 14.8	04.7	177 27.9	19.4	170 48.2	04.7	Zuben'ubi	137 00.0	S16 07.5
20	128 39.7	75 26.0	45.5	186 15.4	04.4	192 30.0	19.4	185 50.5	04.7		SHA	Mer.Pass.
21	143 42.1	90 26.0 ..	46.3	201 16.0 ..	04.0	207 32.1 ..	19.3	200 52.8 ..	04.6	Venus	308 33.3	14 58
22	158 44.6	105 26.1	47.0	216 16.7	03.7	222 34.2	19.3	215 55.1	04.6	Mars	58 56.4	7 37
23	173 47.1	120 26.1	47.8	231 17.3	03.4	237 36.4	19.2	230 57.4	04.6	Jupiter	64 05.4	7 15
Mer.Pass. 11 30.7		v 0.0	d 0.8	v 0.6	d 0.3	v 2.1	d 0.1	v 2.3	d 0.0	Saturn	57 18.3	7 42

UT	SUN GHA	SUN Dec	MOON GHA	v	Dec	d	HP
d h	° ′	° ′	° ′	′	° ′	′	′
28 00	178 43.7	N 3 05.1	140 10.4	14.4	N13 29.4	10.1	54.4
01	193 43.9	06.1	154 43.8	14.3	13 39.5	10.0	54.5
02	208 44.1	07.0	169 17.1	14.3	13 49.5	10.0	54.5
03	223 44.3 ..	08.0	183 50.4	14.2	13 59.5	9.9	54.5
04	238 44.5	09.0	198 23.6	14.2	14 09.4	9.8	54.5
05	253 44.7	10.0	212 56.8	14.1	14 19.2	9.8	54.5
06	268 44.9 N 3 10.9		227 29.9	14.1	N14 29.0	9.8	54.5
S 07	283 45.1	11.9	242 03.0	14.0	14 38.8	9.6	54.5
A 08	298 45.2	12.9	256 36.0	13.9	14 48.4	9.7	54.6
T 09	313 45.4 ..	13.9	271 08.9	13.9	14 58.1	9.5	54.6
U 10	328 45.6	14.8	285 41.8	13.8	15 07.6	9.5	54.6
R 11	343 45.8	15.8	300 14.6	13.8	15 17.1	9.5	54.6
D 12	358 46.0 N 3 16.8		314 47.4	13.7	N15 26.6	9.4	54.6
A 13	13 46.2	17.8	329 20.1	13.6	15 36.0	9.3	54.6
Y 14	28 46.4	18.7	343 52.7	13.6	15 45.3	9.2	54.7
15	43 46.6 ..	19.7	358 25.3	13.5	15 54.5	9.2	54.7
16	58 46.7	20.7	12 57.8	13.5	16 03.7	9.2	54.7
17	73 46.9	21.7	27 30.3	13.4	16 12.9	9.0	54.7
18	88 47.1 N 3 22.6		42 02.7	13.3	N16 21.9	9.1	54.7
19	103 47.3	23.6	56 35.0	13.3	16 31.0	8.9	54.7
20	118 47.5	24.6	71 07.3	13.2	16 39.9	8.9	54.8
21	133 47.7 ..	25.6	85 39.5	13.1	16 48.8	8.8	54.8
22	148 47.9	26.5	100 11.6	13.1	16 57.6	8.7	54.8
23	163 48.1	27.5	114 43.7	13.0	17 06.3	8.6	54.8
29 00	178 48.2 N 3 28.5		129 15.7	13.0	N17 14.9	8.6	54.8
01	193 48.4	29.5	143 47.7	12.8	17 23.5	8.5	54.9
02	208 48.6	30.4	158 19.5	12.9	17 32.0	8.5	54.9
03	223 48.8 ..	31.4	172 51.4	12.7	17 40.5	8.4	54.9
04	238 49.0	32.4	187 23.1	12.7	17 48.9	8.3	54.9
05	253 49.2	33.3	201 54.8	12.6	17 57.2	8.2	54.9
06	268 49.4 N 3 34.3		216 26.4	12.5	N18 05.4	8.1	54.9
S 07	283 49.6	35.3	230 57.9	12.5	18 13.5	8.1	55.0
U 08	298 49.7	36.3	245 29.4	12.4	18 21.6	8.0	55.0
N 09	313 49.9 ..	37.2	260 00.8	12.4	18 29.6	7.9	55.0
D 10	328 50.1	38.2	274 32.2	12.2	18 37.5	7.8	55.0
A 11	343 50.3	39.2	289 03.4	12.2	18 45.3	7.8	55.1
Y 12	358 50.5 N 3 40.2		303 34.6	12.2	N18 53.1	7.6	55.1
13	13 50.7	41.1	318 05.8	12.0	19 00.7	7.6	55.1
14	28 50.9	42.1	332 36.8	12.0	19 08.3	7.5	55.1
15	43 51.1 ..	43.1	347 07.8	11.9	19 15.8	7.4	55.1
16	58 51.2	44.0	1 38.7	11.9	19 23.2	7.4	55.2
17	73 51.4	45.0	16 09.6	11.8	19 30.6	7.2	55.2
18	88 51.6 N 3 46.0		30 40.4	11.7	N19 37.8	7.2	55.2
19	103 51.8	47.0	45 11.1	11.6	19 45.0	7.0	55.2
20	118 52.0	47.9	59 41.7	11.6	19 52.0	7.0	55.2
21	133 52.2 ..	48.9	74 12.3	11.5	19 59.0	6.9	55.3
22	148 52.4	49.9	88 42.8	11.4	20 05.9	6.8	55.3
23	163 52.6	50.8	103 13.2	11.4	20 12.7	6.7	55.3
30 00	178 52.7 N 3 51.8		117 43.6	11.3	N20 19.4	6.6	55.3
01	193 52.9	52.8	132 13.9	11.2	20 26.0	6.6	55.4
02	208 53.1	53.8	146 44.1	11.1	20 32.6	6.4	55.4
03	223 53.3 ..	54.7	161 14.2	11.1	20 39.0	6.3	55.4
04	238 53.5	55.7	175 44.3	11.0	20 45.3	6.3	55.4
05	253 53.7	56.7	190 14.3	10.9	20 51.6	6.1	55.5
06	268 53.9 N 3 57.6		204 44.2	10.8	N20 57.7	6.0	55.5
M 07	283 54.1	58.6	219 14.0	10.8	21 03.7	6.0	55.5
O 08	298 54.2	3 59.6	233 43.8	10.7	21 09.7	5.8	55.5
N 09	313 54.4 ..	4 00.5	248 13.5	10.7	21 15.5	5.8	55.6
10	328 54.6	01.5	262 43.2	10.5	21 21.3	5.6	55.6
11	343 54.8	02.5	277 12.7	10.5	21 26.9	5.6	55.6
D 12	358 55.0 N 4 03.5		291 42.2	10.5	N21 32.5	5.4	55.6
A 13	13 55.2	04.4	306 11.7	10.3	21 37.9	5.3	55.7
Y 14	28 55.4	05.4	320 41.0	10.3	21 43.2	5.3	55.7
15	43 55.5 ..	06.4	335 10.3	10.2	21 48.5	5.1	55.7
16	58 55.7	07.3	349 39.5	10.1	21 53.6	5.0	55.8
17	73 55.9	08.3	4 08.6	10.1	21 58.6	4.9	55.8
18	88 56.1 N 4 09.3		18 37.7	10.0	N22 03.5	4.8	55.8
19	103 56.3	10.2	33 06.7	10.0	22 08.3	4.7	55.8
20	118 56.5	11.2	47 35.7	9.8	22 13.0	4.6	55.9
21	133 56.7 ..	12.2	62 04.5	9.8	22 17.6	4.5	55.9
22	148 56.8	13.1	76 33.3	9.7	22 22.1	4.3	55.9
23	163 57.0	14.1	91 02.0	9.7	N22 26.4	4.3	56.0
	SD 16.0	d 1.0	SD 14.9		15.0		15.2

Twilight — Sunrise — Moonrise

Lat.	Naut.	Civil	Sunrise	Moonrise 28	29	30	31
°	h m	h m	h m	h m	h m	h m	h m
N 72	02 06	03 57	05 10	05 22	04 11	▢	▢
N 70	02 40	04 11	05 15	05 51	05 23	▢	▢
68	03 04	04 22	05 20	06 12	06 06	05 39	
66	03 22	04 31	05 24	06 29	06 27	06 26	06 28
64	03 37	04 39	05 28	06 43	06 48	06 56	07 14
62	03 49	04 45	05 31	06 55	07 04	07 19	07 44
60	03 58	04 51	05 33	07 05	07 18	07 38	08 07
N 58	04 07	04 56	05 35	07 14	07 30	07 53	08 26
56	04 14	05 00	05 38	07 22	07 41	08 06	08 41
54	04 20	05 04	05 39	07 29	07 50	08 18	08 54
52	04 26	05 07	05 41	07 35	07 58	08 28	09 06
50	04 31	05 10	05 42	07 40	08 06	08 37	09 16
45	04 41	05 16	05 46	07 53	08 22	08 56	09 38
N 40	04 49	05 21	05 48	08 03	08 35	09 12	09 56
35	04 55	05 25	05 51	08 12	08 46	09 25	10 11
30	05 01	05 29	05 53	08 19	08 56	09 37	10 23
20	05 08	05 34	05 56	08 33	09 13	09 57	10 45
N 10	05 13	05 38	05 59	08 45	09 28	10 14	11 05
0	05 17	05 41	06 01	08 56	09 42	10 31	11 23
S 10	05 18	05 43	06 04	09 07	09 56	10 47	11 41
20	05 19	05 44	06 06	09 19	10 11	11 05	12 00
30	05 17	05 45	06 09	09 33	10 28	11 25	12 22
35	05 16	05 45	06 11	09 41	10 38	11 37	12 35
40	05 14	05 45	06 12	09 50	10 50	11 51	12 50
45	05 11	05 45	06 14	10 01	11 04	12 07	13 08
S 50	05 07	05 44	06 17	10 14	11 21	12 27	13 31
52	05 05	05 44	06 18	10 20	11 29	12 37	13 42
54	05 02	05 44	06 19	10 27	11 38	12 48	13 54
56	05 00	05 43	06 20	10 34	11 48	13 00	14 08
58	04 56	05 42	06 21	10 43	11 59	13 15	14 24
S 60	04 53	05 41	06 23	10 53	12 13	13 32	14 44

Sunset — Twilight — Moonset

Lat.	Sunset	Civil	Naut.	Moonset 28	29	30	31
°	h m	h m	h m	h m	h m	h m	h m
N 72	19 03	20 16	22 11	26 33	02 33	▢	▢
N 70	18 56	20 02	21 34	25 22	01 22	▢	▢
68	18 51	19 50	21 09	24 45	00 45	02 46	
66	18 47	19 40	20 50	24 20	00 20	02 00	03 44
64	18 43	19 33	20 35	24 00	00 00	01 31	02 58
62	18 40	19 26	20 23	23 44	25 08	01 08	02 29
60	18 38	19 20	20 13	23 31	24 50	00 50	02 06
N 58	18 35	19 15	20 04	23 19	24 35	00 35	01 48
56	18 33	19 11	19 57	23 09	24 22	00 22	01 33
54	18 31	19 07	19 50	23 01	24 11	00 11	01 20
52	18 29	19 04	19 45	22 53	24 02	00 02	01 08
50	18 28	19 01	19 40	22 46	23 53	24 58	00 58
45	18 24	18 54	19 29	22 31	23 34	24 37	00 37
N 40	18 22	18 49	19 21	22 19	23 19	24 19	00 19
35	18 19	18 45	19 15	22 08	23 07	24 05	00 05
30	18 17	18 41	19 09	21 59	22 56	23 52	24 49
20	18 14	18 36	19 01	21 44	22 37	23 31	24 26
N 10	18 11	18 32	18 56	21 30	22 20	23 13	24 07
0	18 08	18 29	18 53	21 18	22 05	22 55	23 48
S 10	18 05	18 26	18 51	21 05	21 50	22 38	23 30
20	18 03	18 25	18 50	20 51	21 33	22 19	23 10
30	18 00	18 24	18 51	20 36	21 15	21 58	22 48
35	17 58	18 23	18 53	20 27	21 04	21 46	22 34
40	17 56	18 23	18 55	20 17	20 51	21 31	22 19
45	17 54	18 23	18 57	20 05	20 37	21 15	22 01
S 50	17 52	18 24	19 01	19 51	20 19	20 54	21 38
52	17 51	18 24	19 03	19 44	20 10	20 44	21 27
54	17 49	18 25	19 06	19 37	20 01	20 33	21 15
56	17 48	18 25	19 08	19 29	19 51	20 20	21 01
58	17 47	18 26	19 11	19 20	19 39	20 05	20 44
S 60	17 45	18 26	19 15	19 09	19 25	19 48	20 24

SUN — MOON

Day	Eqn. of Time 00h	12h	Mer. Pass.	Mer. Pass. Upper	Lower	Age	Phase
d	m s	m s	h m	h m	h m	d	%
28	05 05	04 56	12 05	15 07	02 44	04	15
29	04 47	04 38	12 05	15 53	03 29	05	22
30	04 29	04 20	12 04	16 43	04 18	06	31

2020 MAR. 31, APR. 1, 2 (TUES., WED., THURS.)

UT	ARIES	VENUS −4.6		MARS +0.8		JUPITER −2.1		SATURN +0.7		STARS		
d h	GHA	GHA	Dec	GHA	Dec	GHA	Dec	GHA	Dec	Name	SHA	Dec
31 00	188 49.5	135 26.1	N22 48.5	246 17.9	S21 03.1	252 38.5	S21 19.2	245 59.7	S20 04.5	Acamar	315 15.1	S40 13.8
01	203 52.0	150 26.2	49.2	261 18.6	02.8	267 40.6	19.1	261 02.0	04.5	Achernar	335 23.8	S57 08.3
02	218 54.5	165 26.2	49.9	276 19.2	02.4	282 42.8	19.1	276 04.3	04.5	Acrux	173 03.5	S63 12.6
03	233 56.9	180 26.3	.. 50.7	291 19.9	.. 02.1	297 44.9	.. 19.0	291 06.6	.. 04.4	Adhara	255 08.9	S29 00.3
04	248 59.4	195 26.3	51.4	306 20.5	01.8	312 47.0	19.0	306 08.9	04.4	Aldebaran	290 44.2	N16 32.8
05	264 01.9	210 26.4	52.1	321 21.1	01.5	327 49.1	18.9	321 11.2	04.4			
06	279 04.3	225 26.4	N22 52.9	336 21.8	S21 01.1	342 51.3	S21 18.9	336 13.5	S20 04.4	Alioth	166 16.0	N55 51.0
07	294 06.8	240 26.5	53.6	351 22.4	00.8	357 53.4	18.8	351 15.8	04.3	Alkaid	152 54.7	N49 12.7
08	309 09.2	255 26.5	54.3	6 23.0	00.5	12 55.5	18.8	6 18.1	04.3	Alnair	27 38.2	S46 51.8
T 09	324 11.7	270 26.6	.. 55.0	21 23.7	21 00.2	27 57.7	.. 18.7	21 20.4	.. 04.3	Alnilam	275 41.7	S 1 11.6
U 10	339 14.2	285 26.6	55.8	36 24.3	20 59.8	42 59.8	18.7	36 22.7	04.2	Alphard	217 51.3	S 8 44.9
E 11	354 16.6	300 26.7	56.5	51 24.9	59.5	58 01.9	18.6	51 25.0	04.2			
S 12	9 19.1	315 26.7	N22 57.2	66 25.6	S20 59.2	73 04.1	S21 18.6	66 27.3	S20 04.2	Alphecca	126 06.8	N26 38.7
D 13	24 21.6	330 26.8	57.9	81 26.2	58.8	88 06.2	18.5	81 29.6	04.1	Alpheratz	357 39.0	N29 11.9
A 14	39 24.0	345 26.8	58.7	96 26.8	58.5	103 08.3	18.5	96 31.9	04.1	Altair	62 03.8	N 8 55.2
Y 15	54 26.5	0 26.9	22 59.4	111 27.5	.. 58.2	118 10.5	.. 18.4	111 34.2	.. 04.1	Ankaa	353 11.5	S42 12.0
16	69 29.0	15 26.9	23 00.1	126 28.1	57.9	133 12.6	18.4	126 36.5	04.1	Antares	112 20.3	S26 28.5
17	84 31.4	30 27.0	00.8	141 28.7	57.5	148 14.7	18.3	141 38.8	04.0			
18	99 33.9	45 27.1	N23 01.5	156 29.4	S20 57.2	163 16.9	S21 18.3	156 41.1	S20 04.0	Arcturus	145 51.2	N19 04.6
19	114 36.4	60 27.1	02.3	171 30.0	56.9	178 19.0	18.2	171 43.4	04.0	Atria	107 17.7	S69 03.5
20	129 38.8	75 27.2	03.0	186 30.7	56.6	193 21.1	18.2	186 45.7	03.9	Avior	234 15.9	S59 34.8
21	144 41.3	90 27.2	.. 03.7	201 31.3	.. 56.2	208 23.3	.. 18.1	201 48.0	.. 03.9	Bellatrix	278 27.1	N 6 21.9
22	159 43.7	105 27.3	04.4	216 31.9	55.9	223 25.4	18.1	216 50.3	03.9	Betelgeuse	270 56.3	N 7 24.5
23	174 46.2	120 27.3	05.1	231 32.6	55.6	238 27.5	18.0	231 52.6	03.8			
1 00	189 48.7	135 27.4	N23 05.8	246 33.2	S20 55.2	253 29.7	S21 18.0	246 54.9	S20 03.8	Canopus	263 54.1	S52 42.8
01	204 51.1	150 27.5	06.5	261 33.8	54.9	268 31.8	17.9	261 57.2	03.8	Capella	280 27.7	N46 01.1
02	219 53.6	165 27.5	07.2	276 34.5	54.6	283 33.9	17.9	276 59.5	03.7	Deneb	49 28.5	N45 20.8
03	234 56.1	180 27.6	.. 08.0	291 35.1	.. 54.2	298 36.1	.. 17.8	292 01.8	.. 03.7	Denebola	182 28.6	N14 27.5
04	249 58.5	195 27.7	08.7	306 35.8	53.9	313 38.2	17.8	307 04.1	03.7	Diphda	348 51.5	S17 52.8
05	265 01.0	210 27.7	09.4	321 36.4	53.6	328 40.3	17.7	322 06.4	03.7			
06	280 03.5	225 27.8	N23 10.1	336 37.0	S20 53.2	343 42.5	S21 17.7	337 08.7	S20 03.6	Dubhe	193 45.3	N61 38.7
W 07	295 05.9	240 27.8	10.8	351 37.7	52.9	358 44.6	17.6	352 11.0	03.6	Elnath	278 06.9	N28 37.4
E 08	310 08.4	255 27.9	11.5	6 38.3	52.6	13 46.7	17.6	7 13.3	03.6	Eltanin	90 43.9	N51 28.9
D 09	325 10.9	270 28.0	.. 12.2	21 38.9	.. 52.2	28 48.9	.. 17.5	22 15.6	.. 03.5	Enif	33 42.8	N 9 57.9
N 10	340 13.3	285 28.0	12.9	36 39.6	51.9	43 51.0	17.5	37 17.9	03.5	Fomalhaut	15 19.1	S29 31.0
E 11	355 15.8	300 28.1	13.6	51 40.2	51.6	58 53.2	17.4	52 20.2	03.5			
S 12	10 18.2	315 28.2	N23 14.3	66 40.9	S20 51.2	73 55.3	S21 17.4	67 22.5	S20 03.4	Gacrux	171 55.2	S57 13.6
D 13	25 20.7	330 28.2	15.0	81 41.5	50.9	88 57.4	17.3	82 24.8	03.4	Gienah	175 47.2	S17 39.3
A 14	40 23.2	345 28.3	15.7	96 42.1	50.6	103 59.6	17.3	97 27.1	03.4	Hadar	148 40.7	S60 28.1
Y 15	55 25.6	0 28.4	.. 16.4	111 42.8	.. 50.2	119 01.7	.. 17.2	112 29.4	.. 03.4	Hamal	327 55.8	N23 33.3
16	70 28.1	15 28.4	17.1	126 43.4	49.9	134 03.9	17.2	127 31.7	03.3	Kaus Aust.	83 37.6	S34 22.3
17	85 30.6	30 28.5	17.8	141 44.1	49.6	149 06.0	17.1	142 34.0	03.3			
18	100 33.0	45 28.6	N23 18.5	156 44.7	S20 49.2	164 08.1	S21 17.1	157 36.4	S20 03.3	Kochab	137 19.0	N74 04.3
19	115 35.5	60 28.7	19.2	171 45.3	48.9	179 10.3	17.1	172 38.7	03.2	Markab	13 34.0	N15 18.6
20	130 38.0	75 28.7	19.9	186 46.0	48.6	194 12.4	17.0	187 41.0	03.2	Menkar	314 10.4	N 4 09.9
21	145 40.4	90 28.8	.. 20.6	201 46.6	.. 48.2	209 14.5	.. 17.0	202 43.3	.. 03.2	Menkent	148 01.7	S36 28.1
22	160 42.9	105 28.9	21.3	216 47.3	47.9	224 16.7	16.9	217 45.6	03.2	Miaplacidus	221 38.3	S69 48.2
23	175 45.3	120 29.0	22.0	231 47.9	47.6	239 18.8	16.9	232 47.9	03.1			
2 00	190 47.8	135 29.0	N23 22.7	246 48.5	S20 47.2	254 21.0	S21 16.8	247 50.2	S20 03.1	Mirfak	308 34.1	N49 55.9
01	205 50.3	150 29.1	23.4	261 49.2	46.9	269 23.1	16.8	262 52.5	03.1	Nunki	75 52.5	S26 16.2
02	220 52.7	165 29.2	24.1	276 49.8	46.5	284 25.3	16.7	277 54.8	03.0	Peacock	53 12.1	S56 40.0
03	235 55.2	180 29.3	.. 24.7	291 50.5	.. 46.2	299 27.4	.. 16.7	292 57.1	.. 03.0	Pollux	243 22.0	N27 58.6
04	250 57.7	195 29.3	25.4	306 51.1	45.9	314 29.5	16.6	307 59.4	03.0	Procyon	244 54.8	N 5 10.2
05	266 00.1	210 29.4	26.1	321 51.7	45.5	329 31.7	16.6	323 01.7	02.9			
06	281 02.6	225 29.5	N23 26.8	336 52.4	S20 45.2	344 33.8	S21 16.5	338 04.0	S20 02.9	Rasalhague	96 02.0	N12 32.6
T 07	296 05.1	240 29.6	27.5	351 53.0	44.8	359 36.0	16.5	353 06.3	02.9	Regulus	207 38.3	N11 52.1
H 08	311 07.5	255 29.7	28.2	6 53.7	44.5	14 38.1	16.4	8 08.6	02.9	Rigel	281 07.7	S 8 11.0
U 09	326 10.0	270 29.7	.. 28.9	21 54.3	.. 44.2	29 40.3	.. 16.4	23 10.9	.. 02.8	Rigil Kent.	139 44.9	S60 54.9
R 10	341 12.5	285 29.8	29.5	36 54.9	43.8	44 42.4	16.3	38 13.2	02.8	Sabik	102 07.1	S15 44.9
S 11	356 14.9	300 29.9	30.2	51 55.6	43.5	59 44.5	16.3	53 15.6	02.8			
D 12	11 17.4	315 30.0	N23 30.9	66 56.2	S20 43.1	74 46.7	S21 16.2	68 17.9	S20 02.7	Schedar	349 35.8	N56 38.7
A 13	26 19.8	330 30.1	31.6	81 56.9	42.8	89 48.8	16.2	83 20.2	02.7	Shaula	96 15.5	S37 06.9
Y 14	41 22.3	345 30.1	32.3	96 57.5	42.5	104 51.0	16.1	98 22.5	02.7	Sirius	258 29.6	S16 44.9
15	56 24.8	0 30.2	.. 32.9	111 58.2	.. 42.1	119 53.1	.. 16.1	113 24.8	.. 02.7	Spica	158 26.0	S11 16.0
16	71 27.2	15 30.3	33.6	126 58.8	41.8	134 55.3	16.0	128 27.1	02.6	Suhail	222 48.8	S43 31.1
17	86 29.7	30 30.4	34.3	141 59.4	41.4	149 57.4	16.0	143 29.4	02.6			
18	101 32.2	45 30.5	N23 35.0	157 00.1	S20 41.1	164 59.6	S21 15.9	158 31.7	S20 02.6	Vega	80 35.8	N38 47.9
19	116 34.6	60 30.6	35.7	172 00.7	40.8	180 01.7	15.9	173 34.0	02.5	Zuben'ubi	137 00.0	S16 07.5
20	131 37.1	75 30.7	36.3	187 01.4	40.4	195 03.9	15.8	188 36.3	02.5		SHA	Mer. Pass.
21	146 39.6	90 30.8	.. 37.0	202 02.0	.. 40.1	210 06.0	.. 15.8	203 38.6	.. 02.5		° ′	h m
22	161 42.0	105 30.9	37.7	217 02.7	39.7	225 08.1	15.7	218 40.9	02.5	Venus	305 38.7	14 58
23	176 44.5	120 30.9	38.3	232 03.3	39.4	240 10.3	15.7	233 43.3	02.4	Mars	56 44.5	7 33
	h m									Jupiter	63 41.0	7 05
Mer. Pass.	11 18.9	v 0.1	d 0.7	v 0.6	d 0.3	v 2.1	d 0.0	v 2.3	d 0.0	Saturn	57 06.2	7 31

UT	SUN GHA	SUN Dec	MOON GHA	v	MOON Dec	d	HP
d h	° ′	° ′	° ′	′	° ′	′	′
31 00	178 57.2	N 4 15.1	105 30.7	9.6	N22 30.7	4.1	56.0
01	193 57.4	16.0	119 59.3	9.5	22 34.8	4.0	56.0
02	208 57.6	17.0	134 27.8	9.5	22 38.8	3.9	56.0
03	223 57.8	.. 18.0	148 56.3	9.4	22 42.7	3.8	56.1
04	238 58.0	18.9	163 24.7	9.3	22 46.5	3.7	56.1
05	253 58.2	19.9	177 53.0	9.2	22 50.2	3.5	56.1
06	268 58.3	N 4 20.9	192 21.2	9.2	N22 53.7	3.5	56.2
07	283 58.5	21.8	206 49.4	9.2	22 57.2	3.3	56.2
08	298 58.7	22.8	221 17.6	9.0	23 00.5	3.2	56.2
09	313 58.9	.. 23.8	235 45.6	9.0	23 03.7	3.0	56.2
10	328 59.1	24.7	250 13.6	9.0	23 06.7	3.0	56.3
11	343 59.3	25.7	264 41.6	8.8	23 09.7	2.8	56.3
12	358 59.5	N 4 26.7	279 09.4	8.8	N23 12.5	2.7	56.3
13	13 59.6	27.6	293 37.2	8.8	23 15.2	2.6	56.4
14	28 59.8	28.6	308 05.0	8.7	23 17.8	2.5	56.4
15	44 00.0	.. 29.6	322 32.7	8.6	23 20.3	2.3	56.4
16	59 00.2	30.5	337 00.3	8.6	23 22.6	2.2	56.5
17	74 00.4	31.5	351 27.9	8.5	23 24.8	2.1	56.5
18	89 00.6	N 4 32.5	5 55.4	8.5	N23 26.9	1.9	56.5
19	104 00.8	33.4	20 22.9	8.4	23 28.8	1.9	56.6
20	119 00.9	34.4	34 50.3	8.3	23 30.7	1.7	56.6
21	134 01.1	.. 35.4	49 17.6	8.3	23 32.4	1.5	56.6
22	149 01.3	36.3	63 44.9	8.3	23 33.9	1.5	56.7
23	164 01.5	37.3	78 12.2	8.1	23 35.4	1.3	56.7
1 00	179 01.7	N 4 38.3	92 39.3	8.2	N23 36.7	1.1	56.7
01	194 01.9	39.2	107 06.5	8.1	23 37.8	1.1	56.8
02	209 02.1	40.2	121 33.6	8.0	23 38.9	0.9	56.8
03	224 02.2	.. 41.1	136 00.6	8.0	23 39.8	0.8	56.8
04	239 02.4	42.1	150 27.6	7.9	23 40.6	0.6	56.9
05	254 02.6	43.1	164 54.5	7.9	23 41.2	0.5	56.9
06	269 02.8	N 4 44.0	179 21.4	7.8	N23 41.7	0.4	56.9
07	284 03.0	45.0	193 48.2	7.8	23 42.1	0.2	57.0
08	299 03.2	46.0	208 15.0	7.7	23 42.3	0.1	57.0
09	314 03.4	.. 46.9	222 41.7	7.7	23 42.4	0.0	57.0
10	329 03.5	47.9	237 08.4	7.7	23 42.4	0.2	57.1
11	344 03.7	48.8	251 35.1	7.6	23 42.2	0.3	57.1
12	359 03.9	N 4 49.8	266 01.7	7.6	N23 41.9	0.5	57.2
13	14 04.1	50.8	280 28.3	7.5	23 41.4	0.6	57.2
14	29 04.3	51.7	294 54.8	7.5	23 40.8	0.7	57.2
15	44 04.5	.. 52.7	309 21.3	7.4	23 40.1	0.9	57.3
16	59 04.6	53.7	323 47.7	7.5	23 39.2	1.0	57.3
17	74 04.8	54.6	338 14.2	7.3	23 38.2	1.1	57.3
18	89 05.0	N 4 55.6	352 40.5	7.4	N23 37.1	1.3	57.4
19	104 05.2	56.5	7 06.9	7.3	23 35.8	1.5	57.4
20	119 05.4	57.5	21 33.2	7.3	23 34.3	1.5	57.4
21	134 05.6	.. 58.5	35 59.5	7.2	23 32.8	1.7	57.5
22	149 05.8	4 59.4	50 25.7	7.2	23 31.1	1.9	57.5
23	164 05.9	5 00.4	64 51.9	7.2	23 29.2	2.0	57.6
2 00	179 06.1	N 5 01.3	79 18.1	7.2	N23 27.2	2.1	57.6
01	194 06.3	02.3	93 44.3	7.1	23 25.1	2.3	57.6
02	209 06.5	03.3	108 10.4	7.1	23 22.8	2.5	57.7
03	224 06.7	.. 04.2	122 36.5	7.1	23 20.3	2.5	57.7
04	239 06.9	05.2	137 02.6	7.0	23 17.8	2.7	57.7
05	254 07.0	06.1	151 28.6	7.0	23 15.1	2.9	57.8
06	269 07.2	N 5 07.1	165 54.6	7.0	N23 12.2	3.0	57.8
07	284 07.4	08.1	180 20.6	7.0	23 09.2	3.1	57.9
08	299 07.6	09.0	194 46.6	7.0	23 06.1	3.3	57.9
09	314 07.8	.. 10.0	209 12.6	6.9	23 02.8	3.5	57.9
10	329 08.0	10.9	223 38.5	7.0	22 59.3	3.6	58.0
11	344 08.1	11.9	238 04.5	6.9	22 55.7	3.7	58.0
12	359 08.3	N 5 12.9	252 30.4	6.9	N22 52.0	3.9	58.0
13	14 08.5	13.8	266 56.3	6.8	22 48.1	4.0	58.1
14	29 08.7	14.8	281 22.1	6.9	22 44.1	4.1	58.1
15	44 08.9	.. 15.7	295 48.0	6.9	22 40.0	4.3	58.2
16	59 09.1	16.7	310 13.9	6.8	22 35.7	4.5	58.2
17	74 09.2	17.7	324 39.7	6.9	22 31.2	4.6	58.2
18	89 09.4	N 5 18.6	339 05.6	6.8	N22 26.6	4.7	58.3
19	104 09.6	19.6	353 31.4	6.8	22 21.9	4.9	58.3
20	119 09.8	20.5	7 57.2	6.8	22 17.0	5.0	58.4
21	134 10.0	.. 21.5	22 23.0	6.8	22 12.0	5.2	58.4
22	149 10.2	22.4	36 48.8	6.8	22 06.8	5.3	58.4
23	164 10.3	23.4	51 14.6	6.8	N22 01.5	5.4	58.5
	SD 16.0	d 1.0	SD 15.4		15.6		15.8

Day side labels: TUESDAY, WEDNESDAY, THURSDAY

Lat.	Twilight Naut.	Twilight Civil	Sunrise	Moonrise 31	1	2	3
°	h m	h m	h m	h m	h m	h m	h m
N 72	01 33	03 39	04 54	▭	▭	▭	▭
N 70	02 18	03 55	05 01	▭	▭	▭	▭
68	02 46	04 08	05 08	▭	▭	▭	09 17
66	03 07	04 19	05 13	06 28	06 50	08 13	10 08
64	03 23	04 27	05 17	07 14	07 53	09 03	10 39
62	03 37	04 35	05 21	07 44	08 27	09 34	11 02
60	03 48	04 41	05 24	08 07	08 53	09 58	11 21
N 58	03 57	04 47	05 27	08 26	09 13	10 17	11 36
56	04 05	04 52	05 30	08 41	09 29	10 32	11 50
54	04 12	04 56	05 32	08 54	09 43	10 46	12 01
52	04 18	05 00	05 34	09 06	09 56	10 58	12 11
50	04 24	05 03	05 36	09 16	10 06	11 08	12 20
45	04 35	05 10	05 40	09 38	10 29	11 30	12 39
N 40	04 44	05 16	05 44	09 56	10 48	11 47	12 54
35	04 51	05 21	05 46	10 11	11 03	12 02	13 07
30	04 57	05 25	05 49	10 23	11 16	12 15	13 19
20	05 05	05 31	05 53	10 45	11 39	12 37	13 38
N 10	05 11	05 36	05 57	11 05	11 59	12 56	13 55
0	05 16	05 40	06 00	11 23	12 17	13 13	14 10
S 10	05 18	05 43	06 04	11 41	12 36	13 31	14 26
20	05 20	05 45	06 07	12 00	12 55	13 50	14 43
30	05 19	05 47	06 11	12 22	13 18	14 12	15 02
35	05 18	05 48	06 13	12 35	13 32	14 24	15 13
40	05 17	05 48	06 15	12 50	13 47	14 39	15 25
45	05 15	05 49	06 18	13 08	14 05	14 56	15 40
S 50	05 12	05 49	06 21	13 31	14 28	15 18	15 59
52	05 10	05 49	06 23	13 42	14 39	15 28	16 07
54	05 08	05 49	06 24	13 54	14 52	15 40	16 17
56	05 06	05 49	06 26	14 08	15 06	15 53	16 28
58	05 03	05 49	06 28	14 24	15 23	16 08	16 40
S 60	05 00	05 49	06 30	14 44	15 43	16 26	16 54

Lat.	Sunset	Twilight Civil	Twilight Naut.	Moonset 31	1	2	3
°	h m	h m	h m	h m	h m	h m	h m
N 72	19 17	20 33	22 47	▭	▭	▭	▭
N 70	19 09	20 16	21 57	▭	▭	▭	▭
68	19 02	20 02	21 26	▭	▭	▭	06 44
66	18 57	19 51	21 04	03 44	05 15	05 48	05 53
64	18 52	19 42	20 47	02 58	04 12	04 58	05 21
62	18 48	19 35	20 33	02 29	03 37	04 27	04 57
60	18 45	19 28	20 22	02 06	03 12	04 03	04 38
N 58	18 42	19 22	20 12	01 48	02 52	03 44	04 22
56	18 39	19 17	20 04	01 33	02 36	03 28	04 09
54	18 37	19 13	19 57	01 20	02 22	03 15	03 57
52	18 35	19 09	19 51	01 08	02 09	03 03	03 46
50	18 33	19 05	19 45	00 58	01 59	02 52	03 37
45	18 28	18 58	19 33	00 37	01 36	02 30	03 17
N 40	18 25	18 52	19 24	00 19	01 18	02 12	03 01
35	18 22	18 47	19 17	00 05	01 02	01 57	02 47
30	18 19	18 43	19 11	24 49	00 49	01 44	02 36
20	18 14	18 37	19 02	24 26	00 26	01 21	02 15
N 10	18 11	18 32	18 56	24 07	00 07	01 02	01 57
0	18 07	18 28	18 52	23 48	24 44	00 44	01 41
S 10	18 04	18 25	18 49	23 30	24 26	00 26	01 24
20	18 00	18 22	18 48	23 10	24 06	00 06	01 06
30	17 56	18 20	18 48	22 48	23 43	24 45	00 45
35	17 54	18 19	18 48	22 34	23 30	24 32	00 32
40	17 51	18 18	18 50	22 19	23 15	24 18	00 18
45	17 49	18 18	18 52	22 01	22 56	24 01	00 01
S 50	17 45	18 18	18 55	21 38	22 34	23 41	24 57
52	17 44	18 17	18 56	21 27	22 23	23 31	24 48
54	17 42	18 17	18 58	21 15	22 10	23 19	24 39
56	17 40	18 17	19 00	21 01	21 56	23 07	24 29
58	17 38	18 17	19 03	20 44	21 39	22 52	24 17
S 60	17 36	18 18	19 06	20 24	21 19	22 34	24 04

Day	SUN Eqn. of Time 00h	SUN Eqn. of Time 12h	SUN Mer. Pass.	MOON Mer. Pass. Upper	MOON Mer. Pass. Lower	Age	Phase
d	m s	m s	h m	h m	h m	d	%
31	04 11	04 03	12 04	17 35	05 09	07	41
1	03 54	03 45	12 04	18 30	06 03	08	51
2	03 36	03 27	12 03	19 27	06 59	09	61

2020 APRIL 3, 4, 5 (FRI., SAT., SUN.)

UT	ARIES GHA	VENUS −4·6 GHA	VENUS Dec	MARS +0·7 GHA	MARS Dec	JUPITER −2·2 GHA	JUPITER Dec	SATURN +0·7 GHA	SATURN Dec	STARS Name	SHA	Dec
3 00	191 47.0	135 31.0	N23 39.0	247 03.9	S20 39.0	255 12.4	S21 15.6	248 45.6	S20 02.4	Acamar	315 15.1	S40 13.7
01	206 49.4	150 31.1	39.7	262 04.6	38.7	270 14.6	15.6	263 47.9	02.4	Achernar	335 23.8	S57 08.3
02	221 51.9	165 31.2	40.4	277 05.2	38.3	285 16.7	15.5	278 50.2	02.3	Acrux	173 03.5	S63 12.7
03	236 54.3	180 31.3 ..	41.0	292 05.9 ..	38.0	300 18.9 ..	15.5	293 52.5 ..	02.3	Adhara	255 08.9	S29 00.3
04	251 56.8	195 31.4	41.7	307 06.5	37.7	315 21.0	15.4	308 54.8	02.3	Aldebaran	290 44.2	N16 32.8
05	266 59.3	210 31.5	42.4	322 07.2	37.3	330 23.2	15.4	323 57.1	02.2			
06	282 01.7	225 31.6	N23 43.0	337 07.8	S20 37.0	345 25.3	S21 15.4	338 59.4	S20 02.2	Alioth	166 15.9	N55 51.1
07	297 04.2	240 31.7	43.7	352 08.5	36.6	0 27.5	15.3	354 01.7	02.2	Alkaid	152 54.7	N49 12.7
08	312 06.7	255 31.8	44.4	7 09.1	36.3	15 29.6	15.3	9 04.0	02.2	Alnair	27 38.2	S46 51.8
F 09	327 09.1	270 31.9 ..	45.0	22 09.7 ..	35.9	30 31.8 ..	15.2	24 06.4 ..	02.1	Alnilam	275 41.7	S 1 11.6
R 10	342 11.6	285 32.0	45.7	37 10.4	35.6	45 33.9	15.2	39 08.7	02.1	Alphard	217 51.3	S 8 44.9
I 11	357 14.1	300 32.1	46.3	52 11.0	35.2	60 36.1	15.1	54 11.0	02.1			
D 12	12 16.5	315 32.2	N23 47.0	67 11.7	S20 34.9	75 38.2	S21 15.1	69 13.3	S20 02.1	Alphecca	126 06.8	N26 38.7
A 13	27 19.0	330 32.3	47.7	82 12.3	34.5	90 40.4	15.0	84 15.6	02.0	Alpheratz	357 39.0	N29 11.9
Y 14	42 21.5	345 32.4	48.3	97 13.0	34.2	105 42.5	15.0	99 17.9	02.0	Altair	62 03.7	N 8 55.2
15	57 23.9	0 32.5 ..	49.0	112 13.6 ..	33.8	120 44.7 ..	14.9	114 20.2 ..	02.0	Ankaa	353 11.4	S42 11.9
16	72 26.4	15 32.6	49.6	127 14.3	33.5	135 46.8	14.9	129 22.5	01.9	Antares	112 20.3	S26 28.5
17	87 28.8	30 32.7	50.3	142 14.9	33.1	150 49.0	14.8	144 24.8	01.9			
18	102 31.3	45 32.8	N23 50.9	157 15.6	S20 32.8	165 51.1	S21 14.8	159 27.2	S20 01.9	Arcturus	145 51.1	N19 04.6
19	117 33.8	60 32.9	51.6	172 16.2	32.4	180 53.3	14.7	174 29.5	01.9	Atria	107 17.7	S69 03.5
20	132 36.2	75 33.0	52.3	187 16.8	32.1	195 55.4	14.7	189 31.8	01.8	Avior	234 16.0	S59 34.8
21	147 38.7	90 33.1 ..	52.9	202 17.5 ..	31.7	210 57.6 ..	14.6	204 34.1 ..	01.8	Bellatrix	278 27.1	N 6 21.9
22	162 41.2	105 33.2	53.6	217 18.1	31.4	225 59.8	14.6	219 36.4	01.8	Betelgeuse	270 56.3	N 7 24.5
23	177 43.6	120 33.3	54.2	232 18.8	31.0	241 01.9	14.5	234 38.7	01.7			
4 00	192 46.1	135 33.5	N23 54.9	247 19.4	S20 30.7	256 04.1	S21 14.5	249 41.0	S20 01.7	Canopus	263 54.2	S52 42.8
01	207 48.6	150 33.6	55.5	262 20.1	30.3	271 06.2	14.4	264 43.3	01.7	Capella	280 27.7	N46 01.1
02	222 51.0	165 33.7	56.2	277 20.7	30.0	286 08.4	14.4	279 45.7	01.7	Deneb	49 28.5	N45 20.8
03	237 53.5	180 33.8 ..	56.8	292 21.4 ..	29.6	301 10.5 ..	14.4	294 48.0 ..	01.6	Denebola	182 28.6	N14 27.5
04	252 55.9	195 33.9	57.5	307 22.0	29.3	316 12.7	14.3	309 50.3	01.6	Diphda	348 51.5	S17 52.8
05	267 58.4	210 34.0	58.1	322 22.7	28.9	331 14.8	14.3	324 52.6	01.6			
06	283 00.9	225 34.1	N23 58.7	337 23.3	S20 28.6	346 17.0	S21 14.2	339 54.9	S20 01.5	Dubhe	193 45.3	N61 38.7
07	298 03.3	240 34.2	23 59.4	352 24.0	28.2	1 19.1	14.2	354 57.2	01.5	Elnath	278 06.9	N28 37.4
S 08	313 05.8	255 34.4	24 00.0	7 24.6	27.9	16 21.3	14.1	9 59.5	01.5	Eltanin	90 43.8	N51 28.9
A 09	328 08.3	270 34.5 ..	00.7	22 25.3 ..	27.5	31 23.5 ..	14.1	25 01.8 ..	01.5	Enif	33 42.8	N 9 57.9
T 10	343 10.7	285 34.6	01.3	37 25.9	27.2	46 25.6	14.0	40 04.2	01.4	Fomalhaut	15 19.1	S29 31.0
U 11	358 13.2	300 34.7	02.0	52 26.5	26.8	61 27.8	14.0	55 06.5	01.4			
R 12	13 15.7	315 34.8	N24 02.6	67 27.2	S20 26.4	76 29.9	S21 13.9	70 08.8	S20 01.4	Gacrux	171 55.2	S57 13.6
D 13	28 18.1	330 35.0	03.2	82 27.8	26.1	91 32.1	13.9	85 11.1	01.3	Gienah	175 47.2	S17 39.3
A 14	43 20.6	345 35.1	03.9	97 28.5	25.7	106 34.2	13.8	100 13.4	01.3	Hadar	148 40.7	S60 28.1
Y 15	58 23.1	0 35.2 ..	04.5	112 29.1 ..	25.4	121 36.4 ..	13.8	115 15.7 ..	01.3	Hamal	327 55.8	N23 33.3
16	73 25.5	15 35.3	05.1	127 29.8	25.0	136 38.6	13.7	130 18.1	01.3	Kaus Aust.	83 37.5	S34 22.3
17	88 28.0	30 35.4	05.8	142 30.4	24.7	151 40.7	13.7	145 20.4	01.2			
18	103 30.4	45 35.6	N24 06.4	157 31.1	S20 24.3	166 42.9	S21 13.7	160 22.7	S20 01.2	Kochab	137 19.0	N74 04.3
19	118 32.9	60 35.7	07.0	172 31.7	24.0	181 45.0	13.6	175 25.0	01.2	Markab	13 34.0	N15 18.6
20	133 35.4	75 35.8	07.7	187 32.4	23.6	196 47.2	13.6	190 27.3	01.2	Menkar	314 10.4	N 4 09.9
21	148 37.8	90 35.9 ..	08.3	202 33.0 ..	23.2	211 49.4 ..	13.5	205 29.6 ..	01.1	Menkent	148 01.7	S36 28.1
22	163 40.3	105 36.1	08.9	217 33.7	22.9	226 51.5	13.5	220 31.9	01.1	Miaplacidus	221 38.4	S69 48.3
23	178 42.8	120 36.2	09.6	232 34.3	22.5	241 53.7	13.4	235 34.3	01.1			
5 00	193 45.2	135 36.3	N24 10.2	247 35.0	S20 22.2	256 55.8	S21 13.4	250 36.6	S20 01.0	Mirfak	308 34.1	N49 55.9
01	208 47.7	150 36.5	10.8	262 35.6	21.8	271 58.0	13.3	265 38.9	01.0	Nunki	75 52.5	S26 16.2
02	223 50.2	165 36.6	11.5	277 36.3	21.5	287 00.2	13.3	280 41.2	01.0	Peacock	53 12.1	S56 40.0
03	238 52.6	180 36.7 ..	12.1	292 36.9 ..	21.1	302 02.3 ..	13.2	295 43.5 ..	01.0	Pollux	243 22.0	N27 58.6
04	253 55.1	195 36.8	12.7	307 37.6	20.7	317 04.5	13.2	310 45.8	00.9	Procyon	244 54.8	N 5 10.2
05	268 57.6	210 37.0	13.3	322 38.2	20.4	332 06.6	13.1	325 48.2	00.9			
06	284 00.0	225 37.1	N24 13.9	337 38.9	S20 20.0	347 08.8	S21 13.1	340 50.5	S20 00.9	Rasalhague	96 02.0	N12 32.6
07	299 02.5	240 37.3	14.6	352 39.5	19.7	2 11.0	13.1	355 52.8	00.9	Regulus	207 38.3	N11 52.1
08	314 04.9	255 37.4	15.2	7 40.2	19.3	17 13.1	13.0	10 55.1	00.8	Rigel	281 07.7	S 8 11.0
S 09	329 07.4	270 37.5 ..	15.8	22 40.8 ..	18.9	32 15.3 ..	13.0	25 57.4 ..	00.8	Rigil Kent.	139 44.9	S60 54.9
U 10	344 09.9	285 37.7	16.4	37 41.5	18.6	47 17.5	12.9	40 59.8	00.8	Sabik	102 07.0	S15 44.9
N 11	359 12.3	300 37.8	17.1	52 42.1	18.2	62 19.6	12.9	56 02.1	00.7			
D 12	14 14.8	315 37.9	N24 17.7	67 42.8	S20 17.9	77 21.8	S21 12.8	71 04.4	S20 00.7	Schedar	349 35.8	N56 38.7
A 13	29 17.3	330 38.1	18.3	82 43.4	17.5	92 23.9	12.8	86 06.7	00.7	Shaula	96 15.4	S37 06.9
Y 14	44 19.7	345 38.2	18.9	97 44.1	17.1	107 26.1	12.7	101 09.0	00.7	Sirius	258 29.6	S16 44.9
15	59 22.2	0 38.4 ..	19.5	112 44.8 ..	16.8	122 28.3 ..	12.7	116 11.3 ..	00.6	Spica	158 26.0	S11 16.0
16	74 24.7	15 38.5	20.1	127 45.4	16.4	137 30.4	12.6	131 13.7	00.6	Suhail	222 48.8	S43 31.1
17	89 27.1	30 38.6	20.7	142 46.1	16.0	152 32.6	12.6	146 16.0	00.6			
18	104 29.6	45 38.8	N24 21.4	157 46.7	S20 15.7	167 34.8	S21 12.5	161 18.3	S20 00.6	Vega	80 35.8	N38 47.9
19	119 32.0	60 38.9	22.0	172 47.4	15.3	182 36.9	12.5	176 20.6	00.5	Zuben'ubi	137 00.0	S16 07.5
20	134 34.5	75 39.0	22.6	187 48.0	15.0	197 39.1	12.5	191 22.9	00.5		SHA	Mer.Pass.
21	149 37.0	90 39.2 ..	23.2	202 48.7 ..	14.6	212 41.3 ..	12.4	206 25.3 ..	00.5	Venus	302 47.4	14 58
22	164 39.4	105 39.4	23.8	217 49.3	14.2	227 43.4	12.4	221 27.6	00.5	Mars	54 33.3	7 30
23	179 41.9	120 39.5	24.4	232 50.0	13.9	242 45.6	12.3	236 29.9	00.4	Jupiter	63 18.0	6 55
Mer. Pass. 11 07.1		v 0.1	d 0.6	v 0.6	d 0.4	v 2.2	d 0.0	v 2.3	d 0.0	Saturn	56 54.9	7 20

UT	SUN GHA	SUN Dec	MOON GHA	v	MOON Dec	d	HP	Lat.	Twilight Naut.	Twilight Civil	Sunrise	Moonrise 3	Moonrise 4	Moonrise 5	Moonrise 6
	o '	o '	o '	'	o '	'	'	o	h m	h m	h m	h m	h m	h m	h m
d h								N 72	00 37	03 19	04 38	▭	10 00	13 12	15 40
3 00	179 10.5	N 5 24.4	65 40.4	6.8	N21 56.1	5.6	58.5	N 70	01 51	03 39	04 47	▭	11 06	13 34	15 49
01	194 10.7	25.3	80 06.2	6.8	21 50.5	5.8	58.5	68	02 26	03 54	04 55	09 17	11 41	13 51	15 56
02	209 10.9	26.3	94 32.0	6.8	21 44.7	5.9	58.6	66	02 51	04 06	05 01	10 08	12 07	14 05	16 02
03	224 11.1 ..	27.2	108 57.8	6.8	21 38.8	6.0	58.6	64	03 10	04 16	05 06	10 39	12 26	14 17	16 07
04	239 11.3	28.2	123 23.6	6.8	21 32.8	6.2	58.7	62	03 25	04 24	05 11	11 02	12 42	14 26	16 11
05	254 11.4	29.1	137 49.4	6.8	21 26.6	6.3	58.7	60	03 37	04 32	05 15	11 21	12 55	14 34	16 15
06	269 11.6	N 5 30.1	152 15.2	6.8	N21 20.3	6.4	58.7	N 58	03 47	04 38	05 19	11 36	13 06	14 41	16 18
07	284 11.8	31.0	166 41.0	6.8	21 13.9	6.6	58.8	56	03 56	04 43	05 22	11 50	13 16	14 48	16 21
F 08	299 12.0	32.0	181 06.8	6.8	21 07.3	6.7	58.8	54	04 04	04 48	05 25	12 01	13 25	14 53	16 24
R 09	314 12.2 ..	33.0	195 32.6	6.8	21 00.6	6.9	58.9	52	04 11	04 53	05 27	12 11	13 32	14 58	16 26
I 10	329 12.4	33.9	209 58.4	6.8	20 53.7	7.0	58.9	50	04 17	04 56	05 30	12 20	13 39	15 03	16 28
11	344 12.5	34.9	224 24.2	6.8	20 46.7	7.2	58.9	45	04 29	05 05	05 35	12 39	13 54	15 13	16 33
D 12	359 12.7	N 5 35.8	238 50.0	6.9	N20 39.5	7.3	59.0	N 40	04 39	05 11	05 39	12 54	14 06	15 21	16 37
A 13	14 12.9	36.8	253 15.9	6.8	20 32.2	7.4	59.0	35	04 47	05 17	05 42	13 07	14 16	15 28	16 40
Y 14	29 13.1	37.7	267 41.7	6.9	20 24.8	7.6	59.0	30	04 53	05 21	05 45	13 19	14 25	15 34	16 43
15	44 13.3 ..	38.7	282 07.6	6.8	20 17.2	7.7	59.1	20	05 03	05 29	05 51	13 38	14 41	15 44	16 48
16	59 13.5	39.6	296 33.4	6.9	20 09.5	7.8	59.1	N 10	05 10	05 34	05 55	13 55	14 54	15 54	16 53
17	74 13.6	40.6	310 59.3	6.9	20 01.7	8.0	59.2	0	05 15	05 39	06 00	14 10	15 07	16 02	16 57
18	89 13.8	N 5 41.5	325 25.2	6.9	N19 53.7	8.1	59.2	S 10	05 18	05 43	06 04	14 26	15 19	16 11	17 01
19	104 14.0	42.5	339 51.1	6.9	19 45.6	8.3	59.2	20	05 20	05 46	06 08	14 43	15 33	16 20	17 05
20	119 14.2	43.4	354 17.0	6.9	19 37.3	8.3	59.3	30	05 21	05 49	06 13	15 02	15 48	16 30	17 10
21	134 14.4 ..	44.4	8 42.9	7.0	19 29.0	8.6	59.3	35	05 21	05 50	06 15	15 13	15 56	16 36	17 13
22	149 14.5	45.4	23 08.9	6.9	19 20.4	8.6	59.4	40	05 20	05 51	06 18	15 25	16 06	16 43	17 17
23	164 14.7	46.3	37 34.8	7.0	19 11.8	8.8	59.4	45	05 18	05 52	06 22	15 40	16 18	16 51	17 20
4 00	179 14.9	N 5 47.3	52 00.8	7.0	N19 03.0	8.9	59.4	S 50	05 16	05 54	06 26	15 59	16 32	17 00	17 25
01	194 15.1	48.2	66 26.8	7.0	18 54.1	9.0	59.5	52	05 15	05 54	06 28	16 07	16 39	17 05	17 27
02	209 15.3	49.2	80 52.8	7.0	18 45.1	9.2	59.5	54	05 14	05 54	06 30	16 17	16 46	17 09	17 29
03	224 15.4 ..	50.1	95 18.8	7.1	18 35.9	9.3	59.5	56	05 12	05 55	06 32	16 28	16 54	17 14	17 32
04	239 15.6	51.1	109 44.9	7.0	18 26.6	9.5	59.6	58	05 10	05 55	06 35	16 40	17 03	17 20	17 34
05	254 15.8	52.0	124 10.9	7.1	18 17.1	9.5	59.6	S 60	05 07	05 56	06 37	16 54	17 13	17 27	17 38
06	269 16.0	N 5 53.0	138 37.0	7.1	N18 07.6	9.7	59.6	Lat.	Sunset	Twilight Civil	Twilight Naut.	Moonset 3	Moonset 4	Moonset 5	Moonset 6
07	284 16.2	53.9	153 03.1	7.1	17 57.9	9.8	59.7								
S 08	299 16.4	54.9	167 29.2	7.2	17 48.1	9.9	59.7								
A 09	314 16.5 ..	55.8	181 55.4	7.1	17 38.2	10.1	59.8	o	h m	h m	h m	h m	h m	h m	h m
T 10	329 16.7	56.8	196 21.5	7.2	17 28.1	10.2	59.8	N 72	19 31	20 51	////	▭	08 02	06 49	06 17
U 11	344 16.9	57.7	210 47.7	7.2	17 17.9	10.3	59.8	N 70	19 21	20 31	22 23	▭	06 56	06 25	06 05
R 12	359 17.1	N 5 58.7	225 13.9	7.3	N17 07.6	10.4	59.9	68	19 13	20 15	21 45	06 44	06 19	06 06	05 55
D 13	14 17.3	5 59.6	239 40.2	7.2	16 57.2	10.5	59.9	66	19 07	20 02	21 19	05 53	05 52	05 50	05 47
A 14	29 17.4	6 00.6	254 06.4	7.3	16 46.7	10.7	59.9	64	19 01	19 52	20 59	05 21	05 32	05 38	05 41
Y 15	44 17.6 ..	01.5	268 32.7	7.3	16 36.0	10.8	60.0	62	18 56	19 43	20 44	04 57	05 15	05 27	05 35
16	59 17.8	02.5	282 59.0	7.3	16 25.2	10.9	60.0	60	18 52	19 36	20 31	04 38	05 01	05 17	05 29
17	74 18.0	03.4	297 25.3	7.4	16 14.3	11.0	60.0	N 58	18 49	19 29	20 21	04 22	04 49	05 09	05 25
18	89 18.2	N 6 04.4	311 51.7	7.3	N16 03.3	11.1	60.1	56	18 45	19 24	20 11	04 09	04 39	05 02	05 21
19	104 18.3	05.3	326 18.0	7.4	15 52.2	11.3	60.1	54	18 42	19 19	20 04	03 57	04 30	04 56	05 17
20	119 18.5	06.3	340 44.4	7.4	15 40.9	11.3	60.1	52	18 40	19 14	19 57	03 46	04 21	04 50	05 14
21	134 18.7 ..	07.2	355 10.8	7.5	15 29.6	11.5	60.2	50	18 37	19 10	19 50	03 37	04 14	04 44	05 11
22	149 18.9	08.2	9 37.3	7.5	15 18.1	11.5	60.2	45	18 32	19 02	19 38	03 17	03 58	04 33	05 04
23	164 19.1	09.1	24 03.8	7.4	15 06.6	11.7	60.2	N 40	18 28	18 55	19 28	03 01	03 45	04 23	04 58
5 00	179 19.2	N 6 10.1	38 30.2	7.6	N14 54.9	11.8	60.3	35	18 24	18 50	19 20	02 47	03 33	04 15	04 53
01	194 19.4	11.0	52 56.8	7.5	14 43.1	11.9	60.3	30	18 21	18 45	19 13	02 36	03 24	04 08	04 49
02	209 19.6	12.0	67 23.3	7.6	14 31.2	12.0	60.3	20	18 15	18 37	19 03	02 15	03 06	03 55	04 41
03	224 19.8 ..	12.9	81 49.9	7.6	14 19.2	12.1	60.4	N 10	18 10	18 32	18 56	01 57	02 51	03 44	04 35
04	239 20.0	13.9	96 16.5	7.6	14 07.1	12.2	60.4	0	18 06	18 27	18 52	01 41	02 37	03 33	04 28
05	254 20.1	14.8	110 43.1	7.6	13 54.9	12.3	60.4	S 10	18 02	18 23	18 47	01 24	02 23	03 23	04 22
06	269 20.3	N 6 15.7	125 09.7	7.7	N13 42.6	12.4	60.5	20	17 57	18 20	18 45	01 06	02 08	03 11	04 15
07	284 20.5	16.7	139 36.4	7.7	13 30.2	12.5	60.5	30	17 53	18 17	18 44	00 45	01 50	02 58	04 07
08	299 20.7	17.6	154 03.1	7.7	13 17.7	12.6	60.5	35	17 50	18 15	18 44	00 32	01 40	02 50	04 02
S 09	314 20.9 ..	18.6	168 29.8	7.7	13 05.1	12.7	60.5	40	17 47	18 14	18 45	00 18	01 28	02 41	03 57
U 10	329 21.0	19.5	182 56.5	7.8	12 52.4	12.8	60.6	45	17 43	18 12	18 46	00 01	01 14	02 31	03 51
N 11	344 21.2	20.5	197 23.3	7.8	12 39.6	12.8	60.6	S 50	17 39	18 11	18 49	24 57	00 57	02 18	03 43
D 12	359 21.4	N 6 21.4	211 50.1	7.8	N12 26.8	13.0	60.6	52	17 37	18 11	18 50	24 48	00 48	02 13	03 40
A 13	14 21.6	22.4	226 16.9	7.8	12 13.8	13.1	60.7	54	17 35	18 10	18 51	24 39	00 39	02 06	03 36
Y 14	29 21.8	23.3	240 43.7	7.9	12 00.7	13.1	60.7	56	17 33	18 10	18 53	24 29	00 29	01 59	03 32
15	44 21.9 ..	24.3	255 10.6	7.9	11 47.6	13.3	60.7	58	17 30	18 09	18 55	24 17	00 17	01 51	03 27
16	59 22.1	25.2	269 37.5	7.9	11 34.3	13.3	60.7	S 60	17 27	18 09	18 57	24 04	00 04	01 41	03 22
17	74 22.3	26.1	284 04.4	7.9	11 21.0	13.4	60.8								
18	89 22.5	N 6 27.1	298 31.3	8.0	N11 07.6	13.5	60.8		SUN			MOON			
19	104 22.6	28.0	312 58.3	7.9	10 54.1	13.6	60.8	Day	Eqn. of Time 00h	Eqn. of Time 12h	Mer. Pass.	Mer. Pass. Upper	Mer. Pass. Lower	Age	Phase
20	119 22.8	29.0	327 25.2	8.0	10 40.6	13.7	60.8								
21	134 23.0 ..	29.9	341 52.2	8.1	10 26.9	13.7	60.9	d	m s	m s	h m	h m	h m	d	%
22	149 23.2	30.9	356 19.3	8.0	10 13.2	13.8	60.9	3	03 18	03 09	12 03	20 24	07 55	10	72
23	164 23.4	31.8	10 46.3	8.1	N 9 59.4	13.9	60.9	4	03 01	02 52	12 03	21 20	08 52	11	82
	SD 16.0	d 1.0	SD 16.1		16.3		16.5	5	02 43	02 35	12 03	22 15	09 48	12	90

UT	ARIES GHA	VENUS −4.6 GHA	Dec	MARS +0.7 GHA	Dec	JUPITER −2.2 GHA	Dec	SATURN +0.6 GHA	Dec
6 00	194 44.4	135 39.7	N24 25.0	247 50.6	S20 13.5	257 47.8	S21 12.3	251 32.2	S20 00.4
01	209 46.8	150 39.8	25.6	262 51.3	13.1	272 49.9	12.2	266 34.5	00.4
02	224 49.3	165 40.0	26.2	277 51.9	12.8	287 52.1	12.2	281 36.9	00.3
03	239 51.8	180 40.1 ..	26.8	292 52.6 ..	12.4	302 54.3 ..	12.1	296 39.2 ..	00.3
04	254 54.2	195 40.3	27.4	307 53.2	12.0	317 56.4	12.1	311 41.5	00.3
05	269 56.7	210 40.4	28.0	322 53.9	11.7	332 58.6	12.0	326 43.8	00.3
M 06	284 59.2	225 40.6	N24 28.6	337 54.5	S20 11.3	348 00.8	S21 12.0	341 46.1	S20 00.2
O 07	300 01.6	240 40.7	29.2	352 55.2	10.9	3 02.9	12.0	356 48.5	00.2
N 08	315 04.1	255 40.9	29.8	7 55.9	10.6	18 05.1	11.9	11 50.8	00.2
D 09	330 06.5	270 41.1 ..	30.4	22 56.5 ..	10.2	33 07.3 ..	11.9	26 53.1 ..	00.2
A 10	345 09.0	285 41.2	31.0	37 57.2	09.8	48 09.5	11.8	41 55.4	00.1
Y 11	0 11.5	300 41.4	31.6	52 57.8	09.5	63 11.6	11.8	56 57.8	00.1
12	15 13.9	315 41.5	N24 32.2	67 58.5	S20 09.1	78 13.8	S21 11.7	72 00.1	S20 00.1
13	30 16.4	330 41.7	32.8	82 59.1	08.7	93 16.0	11.7	87 02.4	00.1
14	45 18.9	345 41.9	33.4	97 59.8	08.4	108 18.1	11.6	102 04.7	00.0
15	60 21.3	0 42.0 ..	34.0	113 00.4 ..	08.0	123 20.3 ..	11.6	117 07.0 ..	00.0
16	75 23.8	15 42.2	34.6	128 01.1	07.6	138 22.5	11.6	132 09.4	00.0
17	90 26.3	30 42.4	35.2	143 01.7	07.2	153 24.7	11.5	147 11.7	20 00.0
18	105 28.7	45 42.5	N24 35.8	158 02.4	S20 06.9	168 26.8	S21 11.5	162 14.0	S19 59.9
19	120 31.2	60 42.7	36.4	173 03.1	06.5	183 29.0	11.4	177 16.3	59.9
20	135 33.6	75 42.9	37.0	188 03.7	06.1	198 31.2	11.4	192 18.7	59.9
21	150 36.1	90 43.0 ..	37.6	203 04.4 ..	05.8	213 33.3 ..	11.3	207 21.0 ..	59.9
22	165 38.6	105 43.2	38.2	218 05.0	05.4	228 35.5	11.3	222 23.3	59.8
23	180 41.0	120 43.4	38.7	233 05.7	05.0	243 37.7	11.2	237 25.6	59.8
7 00	195 43.5	135 43.5	N24 39.3	248 06.3	S20 04.7	258 39.9	S21 11.2	252 28.0	S19 59.8
01	210 46.0	150 43.7	39.9	263 07.0	04.3	273 42.0	11.2	267 30.3	59.7
02	225 48.4	165 43.9	40.5	278 07.6	03.9	288 44.2	11.1	282 32.6	59.7
03	240 50.9	180 44.1 ..	41.1	293 08.3 ..	03.5	303 46.4 ..	11.1	297 34.9 ..	59.7
04	255 53.4	195 44.2	41.7	308 09.0	03.2	318 48.6	11.0	312 37.2	59.7
05	270 55.8	210 44.4	42.2	323 09.6	02.8	333 50.7	11.0	327 39.6	59.6
T 06	285 58.3	225 44.6	N24 42.8	338 10.3	S20 02.4	348 52.9	S21 10.9	342 41.9	S19 59.6
U 07	301 00.8	240 44.8	43.4	353 10.9	02.0	3 55.1	10.9	357 44.2	59.6
E 08	316 03.2	255 44.9	44.0	8 11.6	01.7	18 57.3	10.8	12 46.5	59.6
S 09	331 05.7	270 45.1 ..	44.6	23 12.2 ..	01.3	33 59.4 ..	10.8	27 48.9 ..	59.5
D 10	346 08.1	285 45.3	45.1	38 12.9	00.9	49 01.6	10.8	42 51.2	59.5
A 11	1 10.6	300 45.5	45.7	53 13.6	00.5	64 03.8	10.7	57 53.5	59.5
Y 12	16 13.1	315 45.7	N24 46.3	68 14.2	S20 00.2	79 06.0	S21 10.7	72 55.9	S19 59.5
13	31 15.5	330 45.9	46.9	83 14.9	19 59.8	94 08.1	10.6	87 58.2	59.4
14	46 18.0	345 46.0	47.4	98 15.5	59.4	109 10.3	10.6	103 00.5	59.4
15	61 20.5	0 46.2 ..	48.0	113 16.2 ..	59.0	124 12.5 ..	10.5	118 02.8 ..	59.4
16	76 22.9	15 46.4	48.6	128 16.9	58.7	139 14.7	10.5	133 05.2	59.4
17	91 25.4	30 46.6	49.1	143 17.5	58.3	154 16.9	10.4	148 07.5	59.3
18	106 27.9	45 46.8	N24 49.7	158 18.2	S19 57.9	169 19.0	S21 10.4	163 09.8	S19 59.3
19	121 30.3	60 47.0	50.3	173 18.8	57.5	184 21.2	10.4	178 12.1	59.3
20	136 32.8	75 47.2	50.9	188 19.5	57.2	199 23.4	10.3	193 14.5	59.3
21	151 35.2	90 47.4 ..	51.4	203 20.1 ..	56.8	214 25.6 ..	10.3	208 16.8 ..	59.2
22	166 37.7	105 47.6	52.0	218 20.8	56.4	229 27.8	10.2	223 19.1	59.2
23	181 40.2	120 47.7	52.6	233 21.5	56.0	244 29.9	10.2	238 21.4	59.2
8 00	196 42.6	135 47.9	N24 53.1	248 22.1	S19 55.6	259 32.1	S21 10.1	253 23.8	S19 59.2
01	211 45.1	150 48.1	53.7	263 22.8	55.3	274 34.3	10.1	268 26.1	59.1
02	226 47.6	165 48.3	54.2	278 23.4	54.9	289 36.5	10.1	283 28.4	59.1
03	241 50.0	180 48.5 ..	54.8	293 24.1 ..	54.5	304 38.7 ..	10.0	298 30.8 ..	59.1
04	256 52.5	195 48.7	55.4	308 24.8	54.1	319 40.8	10.0	313 33.1	59.1
05	271 55.0	210 48.9	55.9	323 25.4	53.8	334 43.0	09.9	328 35.4	59.0
W 06	286 57.4	225 49.1	N24 56.5	338 26.1	S19 53.4	349 45.2	S21 09.9	343 37.7	S19 59.0
E 07	301 59.9	240 49.3	57.0	353 26.7	53.0	4 47.4	09.8	358 40.1	59.0
D 08	317 02.4	255 49.5	57.6	8 27.4	52.6	19 49.6	09.8	13 42.4	59.0
N 09	332 04.8	270 49.7 ..	58.2	23 28.1 ..	52.2	34 51.8 ..	09.8	28 44.7 ..	58.9
E 10	347 07.3	285 49.9	58.7	38 28.7	51.9	49 53.9	09.7	43 47.1	58.9
S 11	2 09.7	300 50.2	59.3	53 29.4	51.5	64 56.1	09.7	58 49.4	58.9
D 12	17 12.2	315 50.4	N24 59.8	68 30.1	S19 51.1	79 58.3	S21 09.6	73 51.7	S19 58.9
A 13	32 14.7	330 50.6	25 00.4	83 30.7	50.7	95 00.5	09.6	88 54.0	58.8
Y 14	47 17.1	345 50.8	00.9	98 31.4	50.3	110 02.7	09.5	103 56.4	58.8
15	62 19.6	0 51.0 ..	01.5	113 32.0 ..	49.9	125 04.9 ..	09.5	118 58.7 ..	58.8
16	77 22.1	15 51.2	02.0	128 32.7	49.6	140 07.0	09.5	134 01.0	58.8
17	92 24.5	30 51.4	02.6	143 33.4	49.2	155 09.2	09.4	149 03.4	58.7
18	107 27.0	45 51.6	N25 03.1	158 34.0	S19 48.8	170 11.4	S21 09.4	164 05.7	S19 58.7
19	122 29.5	60 51.8	03.7	173 34.7	48.4	185 13.6	09.3	179 08.0	58.7
20	137 31.9	75 52.1	04.2	188 35.3	48.0	200 15.8	09.3	194 10.4	58.7
21	152 34.4	90 52.3 ..	04.8	203 36.0 ..	47.6	215 18.0 ..	09.2	209 12.7 ..	58.6
22	167 36.8	105 52.5	05.3	218 36.7	47.3	230 20.2	09.2	224 15.0	58.6
23	182 39.3	120 52.7	05.8	233 37.3	46.9	245 22.3	09.2	239 17.4	58.6
Mer. Pass.	h m 10 55.3	v 0.2	d 0.6	v 0.7	d 0.4	v 2.2	d 0.0	v 2.3	d 0.0

STARS

Name	SHA	Dec
Acamar	315 15.1	S40 13.7
Achernar	335 23.8	S57 08.3
Acrux	173 03.5	S63 12.7
Adhara	255 08.9	S29 00.3
Aldebaran	290 44.2	N16 32.8
Alioth	166 15.9	N55 51.1
Alkaid	152 54.7	N49 12.7
Alnair	27 38.1	S46 51.7
Alnilam	275 41.8	S 1 11.6
Alphard	217 51.3	S 8 44.9
Alphecca	126 06.7	N26 38.7
Alpheratz	357 39.0	N29 11.9
Altair	62 03.7	N 8 55.2
Ankaa	353 11.4	S42 11.9
Antares	112 20.3	S26 28.5
Arcturus	145 51.1	N19 04.6
Atria	107 17.6	S69 03.5
Avior	234 16.0	S59 34.8
Bellatrix	278 27.1	N 6 21.9
Betelgeuse	270 56.4	N 7 24.5
Canopus	263 54.2	S52 42.8
Capella	280 27.8	N46 01.1
Deneb	49 28.5	N45 20.8
Denebola	182 28.6	N14 27.5
Diphda	348 51.5	S17 52.8
Dubhe	193 45.3	N61 38.7
Elnath	278 06.9	N28 37.4
Eltanin	90 43.8	N51 28.9
Enif	33 42.7	N 9 57.9
Fomalhaut	15 19.1	S29 31.0
Gacrux	171 55.2	S57 13.6
Gienah	175 47.2	S17 39.3
Hadar	148 40.7	S60 28.1
Hamal	327 55.8	N23 33.3
Kaus Aust.	83 37.5	S34 22.3
Kochab	137 18.9	N74 04.3
Markab	13 34.0	N15 18.6
Menkar	314 10.4	N 4 09.9
Menkent	148 01.7	S36 28.1
Miaplacidus	221 38.4	S69 48.3
Mirfak	308 34.1	N49 55.9
Nunki	75 52.5	S26 16.2
Peacock	53 12.0	S56 40.8
Pollux	243 22.0	N27 58.6
Procyon	244 54.8	N 5 10.2
Rasalhague	96 02.0	N12 32.6
Regulus	207 38.3	N11 52.1
Rigel	281 07.7	S 8 11.0
Rigil Kent.	139 44.8	S60 54.9
Sabik	102 07.0	S15 44.9
Schedar	349 35.8	N56 38.7
Shaula	96 15.4	S37 06.9
Sirius	258 29.7	S16 44.9
Spica	158 26.0	S11 16.0
Suhail	222 48.9	S43 31.1
Vega	80 35.7	N38 47.9
Zuben'ubi	137 00.0	S16 07.5

	SHA	Mer. Pass.
Venus	300 00.0	h m 14 57
Mars	52 22.8	7 27
Jupiter	62 56.4	6 44
Saturn	56 44.4	7 09

UT	SUN GHA	Dec	MOON GHA	v	Dec	d	HP
d h	° ′	° ′	° ′	′	° ′	′	′
6 00	179 23.5	N 6 32.8	25 13.4	8.0	N 9 45.5	13.9	60.9
01	194 23.7	33.7	39 40.4	8.1	9 31.6	14.0	61.0
02	209 23.9	34.6	54 07.5	8.2	9 17.6	14.1	61.0
03	224 24.1 ..	35.6	68 34.7	8.1	9 03.5	14.1	61.0
04	239 24.2	36.5	83 01.8	8.2	8 49.4	14.3	61.0
05	254 24.4	37.5	97 29.0	8.1	8 35.1	14.2	61.0
06	269 24.6	N 6 38.4	111 56.1	8.2	N 8 20.9	14.4	61.1
07	284 24.8	39.4	126 23.3	8.2	8 06.5	14.4	61.1
M 08	299 25.0	40.3	140 50.5	8.3	7 52.1	14.5	61.1
O 09	314 25.1 ..	41.2	155 17.8	8.2	7 37.6	14.5	61.1
N 10	329 25.3	42.2	169 45.0	8.3	7 23.1	14.6	61.1
D 11	344 25.5	43.1	184 12.3	8.3	7 08.5	14.6	61.2
A 12	359 25.7	N 6 44.1	198 39.6	8.3	N 6 53.9	14.7	61.2
Y 13	14 25.8	45.0	213 06.9	8.3	6 39.2	14.7	61.2
14	29 26.0	45.9	227 34.2	8.3	6 24.5	14.8	61.2
15	44 26.2 ..	46.9	242 01.5	8.3	6 09.7	14.8	61.2
16	59 26.4	47.8	256 28.8	8.4	5 54.9	14.9	61.2
17	74 26.5	48.8	270 56.2	8.3	5 40.0	14.9	61.3
18	89 26.7	N 6 49.7	285 23.5	8.4	N 5 25.1	15.0	61.3
19	104 26.9	50.6	299 50.9	8.4	5 10.1	15.0	61.3
20	119 27.1	51.6	314 18.3	8.4	4 55.1	15.0	61.3
21	134 27.3 ..	52.5	328 45.7	8.4	4 40.1	15.1	61.3
22	149 27.4	53.5	343 13.1	8.4	4 25.0	15.1	61.3
23	164 27.6	54.4	357 40.5	8.4	4 09.9	15.1	61.3
7 00	179 27.8	N 6 55.3	12 07.9	8.4	N 3 54.8	15.2	61.3
01	194 28.0	56.3	26 35.3	8.5	3 39.6	15.2	61.3
02	209 28.1	57.2	41 02.8	8.4	3 24.4	15.2	61.4
03	224 28.3 ..	58.2	55 30.2	8.5	3 09.2	15.3	61.4
04	239 28.5	6 59.1	69 57.7	8.4	2 53.9	15.2	61.4
05	254 28.7	7 00.0	84 25.1	8.5	2 38.7	15.3	61.4
06	269 28.8	N 7 01.0	98 52.6	8.5	N 2 23.4	15.3	61.4
07	284 29.0	01.9	113 20.1	8.4	2 08.1	15.4	61.4
T 08	299 29.2	02.8	127 47.5	8.5	1 52.7	15.3	61.4
U 09	314 29.4 ..	03.8	142 15.0	8.5	1 37.4	15.4	61.4
E 10	329 29.5	04.7	156 42.5	8.4	1 22.0	15.4	61.4
S 11	344 29.7	05.6	171 09.9	8.5	1 06.6	15.3	61.4
D 12	359 29.9	N 7 06.6	185 37.4	8.5	N 0 51.3	15.4	61.4
A 13	14 30.1	07.5	200 04.9	8.5	0 35.9	15.4	61.4
Y 14	29 30.2	08.5	214 32.4	8.4	0 20.5	15.4	61.4
15	44 30.4 ..	09.4	228 59.8	8.5	N 0 05.1	15.4	61.4
16	59 30.6	10.3	243 27.3	8.5	S 0 10.3	15.4	61.4
17	74 30.8	11.3	257 54.8	8.4	0 25.7	15.4	61.4
18	89 30.9	N 7 12.2	272 22.2	8.5	S 0 41.1	15.4	61.4
19	104 31.1	13.1	286 49.7	8.4	0 56.5	15.4	61.4
20	119 31.3	14.1	301 17.1	8.5	1 11.9	15.4	61.4
21	134 31.4 ..	15.0	315 44.6	8.4	1 27.3	15.4	61.4
22	149 31.6	15.9	330 12.0	8.5	1 42.7	15.3	61.4
23	164 31.8	16.9	344 39.5	8.4	1 58.0	15.4	61.4
8 00	179 32.0	N 7 17.8	359 06.9	8.4	S 2 13.4	15.3	61.4
01	194 32.1	18.7	13 34.3	8.4	2 28.7	15.3	61.4
02	209 32.3	19.7	28 01.7	8.4	2 44.0	15.3	61.4
03	224 32.5 ..	20.6	42 29.1	8.4	2 59.3	15.3	61.4
04	239 32.7	21.5	56 56.5	8.4	3 14.6	15.3	61.4
05	254 32.8	22.5	71 23.9	8.4	3 29.9	15.2	61.4
06	269 33.0	N 7 23.4	85 51.3	8.3	S 3 45.1	15.2	61.4
W 07	284 33.2	24.3	100 18.6	8.4	4 00.3	15.2	61.4
E 08	299 33.4	25.3	114 46.0	8.3	4 15.5	15.1	61.4
D 09	314 33.5 ..	26.2	129 13.3	8.3	4 30.6	15.1	61.4
N 10	329 33.7	27.1	143 40.6	8.3	4 45.7	15.0	61.4
E 11	344 33.9	28.1	158 07.9	8.3	5 00.8	15.0	61.4
S 12	359 34.0	N 7 29.0	172 35.2	8.3	S 5 15.8	15.1	61.3
D 13	14 34.2	29.9	187 02.5	8.3	5 30.9	14.9	61.3
A 14	29 34.4	30.8	201 29.7	8.3	5 45.8	14.9	61.3
Y 15	44 34.6 ..	31.8	215 57.0	8.2	6 00.7	14.9	61.3
16	59 34.7	32.7	230 24.2	8.2	6 15.6	14.9	61.3
17	74 34.9	33.6	244 51.4	8.2	6 30.5	14.7	61.3
18	89 35.1	N 7 34.6	259 18.6	8.2	S 6 45.2	14.8	61.3
19	104 35.3	35.5	273 45.8	8.1	7 00.0	14.7	61.2
20	119 35.4	36.4	288 12.9	8.2	7 14.7	14.6	61.2
21	134 35.6 ..	37.4	302 40.0	8.1	7 29.3	14.6	61.2
22	149 35.8	38.3	317 07.1	8.1	7 43.9	14.5	61.2
23	164 35.9	39.2	331 34.2	8.1	S 7 58.4	14.5	61.2
	SD 16.0	d 0.9	SD 16.7		16.7		16.7

Lat.	Twilight Naut.	Civil	Sunrise	Moonrise 6	7	8	9
°	h m	h m	h m	h m	h m	h m	h m
N 72	////	02 59	04 22	15 40	18 01	20 24	22 59
N 70	01 17	03 22	04 33	15 49	18 00	20 12	22 31
68	02 04	03 39	04 42	15 56	17 59	20 03	22 10
66	02 34	03 53	04 49	16 02	17 58	19 55	21 53
64	02 55	04 04	04 56	16 07	17 58	19 48	21 40
62	03 12	04 14	05 01	16 11	17 57	19 43	21 29
60	03 26	04 22	05 06	16 15	17 56	19 38	21 19
N 58	03 37	04 29	05 10	16 18	17 56	19 34	21 11
56	03 47	04 35	05 14	16 21	17 56	19 30	21 04
54	03 55	04 41	05 17	16 24	17 55	19 27	20 58
52	04 03	04 45	05 20	16 26	17 55	19 24	20 52
50	04 09	04 50	05 23	16 28	17 55	19 21	20 47
45	04 23	04 59	05 29	16 33	17 54	19 15	20 36
N 40	04 34	05 06	05 34	16 37	17 53	19 10	20 26
35	04 42	05 13	05 38	16 40	17 53	19 06	20 18
30	04 49	05 18	05 42	16 43	17 53	19 02	20 12
20	05 00	05 26	05 48	16 48	17 52	18 56	20 00
N 10	05 08	05 33	05 54	16 53	17 51	18 50	19 50
0	05 14	05 38	05 59	16 57	17 51	18 45	19 40
S 10	05 18	05 43	06 04	17 01	17 50	18 40	19 31
20	05 21	05 47	06 09	17 05	17 50	18 35	19 21
30	05 23	05 50	06 15	17 10	17 49	18 29	19 09
35	05 23	05 52	06 18	17 13	17 49	18 25	19 03
40	05 23	05 54	06 21	17 17	17 49	18 21	18 56
45	05 22	05 56	06 26	17 20	17 49	18 17	18 47
S 50	05 21	05 58	06 31	17 25	17 48	18 12	18 37
52	05 20	05 59	06 33	17 27	17 48	18 09	18 32
54	05 19	06 00	06 35	17 29	17 48	18 07	18 27
56	05 18	06 01	06 38	17 32	17 48	18 04	18 22
58	05 16	06 02	06 41	17 34	17 47	18 00	18 15
S 60	05 15	06 03	06 45	17 38	17 47	17 57	18 08

Lat.	Sunset	Twilight Civil	Naut.	Moonset 6	7	8	9
°	h m	h m	h m	h m	h m	h m	h m
N 72	19 46	21 10	////	06 17	05 52	05 28	05 02
N 70	19 34	20 46	23 00	06 05	05 49	05 33	05 16
68	19 25	20 28	22 06	05 55	05 46	05 37	05 28
66	19 17	20 14	21 35	05 47	05 44	05 41	05 38
64	19 10	20 02	21 13	05 41	05 42	05 44	05 46
62	19 04	19 52	20 55	05 35	05 41	05 47	05 53
60	19 00	19 44	20 41	05 29	05 39	05 49	05 59
N 58	18 55	19 37	20 29	05 25	05 38	05 51	06 05
56	18 51	19 30	20 19	05 21	05 37	05 53	06 10
54	18 48	19 25	20 10	05 17	05 36	05 55	06 14
52	18 45	19 20	20 03	05 14	05 35	05 56	06 18
50	18 42	19 15	19 57	05 11	05 34	05 57	06 22
45	18 36	19 06	19 42	05 04	05 33	06 01	06 30
N 40	18 31	18 58	19 31	04 58	05 31	06 03	06 36
35	18 26	18 52	19 23	04 53	05 30	06 05	06 42
30	18 23	18 47	19 15	04 49	05 28	06 07	06 47
20	18 16	18 38	19 04	04 41	05 26	06 11	06 56
N 10	18 10	18 32	18 56	04 35	05 24	06 14	07 04
0	18 05	18 26	18 50	04 28	05 22	06 16	07 11
S 10	18 00	18 21	18 46	04 22	05 21	06 19	07 18
20	17 55	18 17	18 43	04 15	05 18	06 22	07 26
30	17 49	18 13	18 41	04 07	05 16	06 26	07 35
35	17 46	18 11	18 40	04 02	05 15	06 28	07 40
40	17 42	18 09	18 40	03 57	05 13	06 30	07 46
45	17 38	18 07	18 41	03 51	05 11	06 32	07 53
S 50	17 33	18 05	18 42	03 43	05 09	06 35	08 02
52	17 30	18 04	18 43	03 40	05 08	06 37	08 05
54	17 28	18 03	18 44	03 36	05 07	06 38	08 10
56	17 25	18 02	18 45	03 32	05 06	06 40	08 14
58	17 22	18 01	18 46	03 27	05 04	06 42	08 20
S 60	17 18	18 00	18 48	03 22	05 03	06 44	08 26

Day	SUN Eqn. of Time 00h	12h	Mer. Pass.	MOON Mer. Pass. Upper	Lower	Age	Phase
d	m s	m s	h m	h m	h m	d	%
6	02 26	02 18	12 02	23 10	10 43	13	96
7	02 09	02 01	12 02	24 04	11 37	14	99
8	01 52	01 44	12 02	00 04	12 31	15	100

UT	ARIES	VENUS −4·6		MARS +0·7		JUPITER −2·2		SATURN +0·6		STARS		
d h	GHA	GHA	Dec	GHA	Dec	GHA	Dec	GHA	Dec	Name	SHA	Dec
9 00	197 41.8	135 52.9	N25 06.4	248 38.0	S19 46.5	260 24.5	S21 09.1	254 19.7	S19 58.6	Acamar	315 15.1	S40 13.7
01	212 44.2	150 53.1	06.9	263 38.7	46.1	275 26.7	09.1	269 22.0	58.5	Achernar	335 23.8	S57 08.2
02	227 46.7	165 53.4	07.5	278 39.3	45.7	290 28.9	09.0	284 24.3	58.5	Acrux	173 03.5	S63 12.7
03	242 49.2	180 53.6 ..	08.0	293 40.0 ..	45.3	305 31.1 ..	09.0	299 26.7 ..	58.5	Adhara	255 08.9	S29 00.3
04	257 51.6	195 53.8	08.5	308 40.6	44.9	320 33.3	08.9	314 29.0	58.5	Aldebaran	290 44.2	N16 32.8
05	272 54.1	210 54.0	09.1	323 41.3	44.6	335 35.5	08.9	329 31.3	58.4			
06	287 56.6	225 54.3	N25 09.6	338 42.0	S19 44.2	350 37.7	S21 08.9	344 33.7	S19 58.4	Alioth	166 15.9	N55 51.1
T 07	302 59.0	240 54.5	10.2	353 42.6	43.8	5 39.8	08.9	359 36.0	58.4	Alkaid	152 54.7	N49 12.8
H 08	318 01.5	255 54.7	10.7	8 43.3	43.4	20 42.0	08.8	14 38.3	58.4	Alnair	27 38.1	S46 51.7
U 09	333 04.0	270 55.0 ..	11.2	23 44.0 ..	43.0	35 44.2 ..	08.7	29 40.7 ..	58.4	Alnilam	275 41.8	S 1 11.6
R 10	348 06.4	285 55.2	11.8	38 44.6	42.6	50 46.4	08.7	44 43.0	58.3	Alphard	217 51.4	S 8 44.9
S 11	3 08.9	300 55.4	12.3	53 45.3	42.2	65 48.6	08.6	59 45.3	58.3			
D 12	18 11.3	315 55.7	N25 12.8	68 46.0	S19 41.9	80 50.8	S21 08.6	74 47.7	S19 58.3	Alphecca	126 06.7	N26 38.7
A 13	33 13.8	330 55.9	13.4	83 46.6	41.5	95 53.0	08.6	89 50.0	58.3	Alpheratz	357 39.0	N29 11.9
Y 14	48 16.3	345 56.1	13.9	98 47.3	41.1	110 55.2	08.5	104 52.3	58.2	Altair	62 03.7	N 8 55.2
15	63 18.7	0 56.4 ..	14.4	113 48.0 ..	40.7	125 57.4 ..	08.5	119 54.7 ..	58.2	Ankaa	353 11.4	S42 11.9
16	78 21.2	15 56.6	14.9	128 48.6	40.3	140 59.6	08.4	134 57.0	58.2	Antares	112 20.3	S26 28.5
17	93 23.7	30 56.8	15.5	143 49.3	39.9	156 01.8	08.4	149 59.3	58.2			
18	108 26.1	45 57.1	N25 16.0	158 50.0	S19 39.5	171 03.9	S21 08.4	165 01.7	S19 58.1	Arcturus	145 51.1	N19 04.6
19	123 28.6	60 57.3	16.5	173 50.6	39.1	186 06.1	08.3	180 04.0	58.1	Atria	107 17.6	S69 03.5
20	138 31.1	75 57.6	17.0	188 51.3	38.7	201 08.3	08.3	195 06.3	58.1	Avior	234 16.0	S59 34.8
21	153 33.5	90 57.8 ..	17.6	203 51.9 ..	38.3	216 10.5 ..	08.2	210 08.7 ..	58.1	Bellatrix	278 27.2	N 6 21.9
22	168 36.0	105 58.0	18.1	218 52.6	38.0	231 12.7	08.2	225 11.0	58.0	Betelgeuse	270 56.4	N 7 24.5
23	183 38.5	120 58.3	18.6	233 53.3	37.6	246 14.9	08.1	240 13.3	58.0			
10 00	198 40.9	135 58.5	N25 19.1	248 53.9	S19 37.2	261 17.1	S21 08.1	255 15.7	S19 58.0	Canopus	263 54.2	S52 42.8
01	213 43.4	150 58.8	19.7	263 54.6	36.8	276 19.3	08.1	270 18.0	58.0	Capella	280 27.8	N46 01.1
02	228 45.8	165 59.0	20.2	278 55.3	36.4	291 21.5	08.0	285 20.4	57.9	Deneb	49 28.5	N45 20.8
03	243 48.3	180 59.3 ..	20.7	293 55.9 ..	36.0	306 23.7 ..	08.0	300 22.7 ..	57.9	Denebola	182 28.6	N14 27.6
04	258 50.8	195 59.5	21.2	308 56.6	35.6	321 25.9	07.9	315 25.0	57.9	Diphda	348 51.5	S17 52.8
05	273 53.2	210 59.8	21.7	323 57.3	35.2	336 28.1	07.9	330 27.4	57.9			
06	288 55.7	226 00.0	N25 22.2	338 57.9	S19 34.8	351 30.3	S21 07.9	345 29.7	S19 57.9	Dubhe	193 45.4	N61 38.7
07	303 58.2	241 00.3	22.8	353 58.6	34.4	6 32.5	07.8	0 32.0	57.8	Elnath	278 06.9	N28 37.4
F 08	319 00.6	256 00.5	23.3	8 59.3	34.0	21 34.7	07.8	15 34.4	57.8	Eltanin	90 43.8	N51 28.9
R 09	334 03.1	271 00.8 ..	23.8	23 59.9 ..	33.6	36 36.9 ..	07.7	30 36.7 ..	57.8	Enif	33 42.7	N 9 57.9
I 10	349 05.6	286 01.1	24.3	39 00.6	33.2	51 39.1	07.7	45 39.0	57.8	Fomalhaut	15 19.1	S29 31.0
D 11	4 08.0	301 01.3	24.8	54 01.3	32.9	66 41.3	07.7	60 41.4	57.7			
A 12	19 10.5	316 01.6	N25 25.3	69 01.9	S19 32.5	81 43.5	S21 07.6	75 43.7	S19 57.7	Gacrux	171 55.2	S57 13.6
Y 13	34 12.9	331 01.8	25.8	84 02.6	32.1	96 45.7	07.6	90 46.1	57.7	Gienah	175 47.2	S17 39.3
14	49 15.4	346 02.1	26.3	99 03.3	31.7	111 47.9	07.5	105 48.4	57.7	Hadar	148 40.7	S60 28.1
15	64 17.9	1 02.4 ..	26.8	114 04.0 ..	31.3	126 50.1 ..	07.5	120 50.7 ..	57.6	Hamal	327 55.8	N23 33.2
16	79 20.3	16 02.6	27.3	129 04.6	30.9	141 52.3	07.4	135 53.1	57.6	Kaus Aust.	83 37.5	S34 22.3
17	94 22.8	31 02.9	27.8	144 05.3	30.5	156 54.4	07.4	150 55.4	57.6			
18	109 25.3	46 03.2	N25 28.4	159 06.0	S19 30.1	171 56.6	S21 07.4	165 57.7	S19 57.6	Kochab	137 18.9	N74 04.3
19	124 27.7	61 03.4	28.9	174 06.6	29.7	186 58.8	07.3	181 00.1	57.6	Markab	13 34.0	N15 18.6
20	139 30.2	76 03.7	29.4	189 07.3	29.3	202 01.0	07.3	196 02.4	57.5	Menkar	314 10.4	N 4 09.9
21	154 32.7	91 04.0 ..	29.9	204 08.0 ..	28.9	217 03.2 ..	07.2	211 04.8 ..	57.5	Menkent	148 01.7	S36 28.1
22	169 35.1	106 04.2	30.4	219 08.6	28.5	232 05.4	07.2	226 07.1	57.5	Miaplacidus	221 38.4	S69 48.3
23	184 37.6	121 04.5	30.9	234 09.3	28.1	247 07.6	07.2	241 09.4	57.5			
11 00	199 40.1	136 04.8	N25 31.4	249 10.0	S19 27.7	262 09.8	S21 07.1	256 11.8	S19 57.4	Mirfak	308 34.1	N49 55.9
01	214 42.5	151 05.1	31.9	264 10.6	27.3	277 12.1	07.1	271 14.1	57.4	Nunki	75 52.5	S26 16.2
02	229 45.0	166 05.3	32.4	279 11.3	26.9	292 14.3	07.0	286 16.5	57.4	Peacock	53 12.0	S56 40.0
03	244 47.4	181 05.6 ..	32.9	294 12.0 ..	26.5	307 16.5 ..	07.0	301 18.8 ..	57.4	Pollux	243 22.0	N27 58.6
04	259 49.9	196 05.9	33.3	309 12.7	26.1	322 18.7	07.0	316 21.1	57.3	Procyon	244 54.8	N 5 10.2
05	274 52.4	211 06.2	33.8	324 13.3	25.7	337 20.9	06.9	331 23.5	57.3			
06	289 54.8	226 06.5	N25 34.3	339 14.0	S19 25.3	352 23.1	S21 06.9	346 25.8	S19 57.3	Rasalhague	96 02.0	N12 32.6
07	304 57.3	241 06.7	34.8	354 14.7	24.9	7 25.3	06.8	1 28.2	57.3	Regulus	207 38.3	N11 52.1
S 08	319 59.8	256 07.0	35.3	9 15.3	24.5	22 27.5	06.8	16 30.5	57.3	Rigel	281 07.7	S 8 11.0
A 09	335 02.2	271 07.3 ..	35.8	24 16.0 ..	24.1	37 29.7 ..	06.8	31 32.8 ..	57.2	Rigil Kent.	139 44.8	S60 54.9
T 10	350 04.7	286 07.6	36.3	39 16.7	23.7	52 31.9	06.7	46 35.2	57.2	Sabik	102 07.0	S15 44.9
U 11	5 07.2	301 07.9	36.8	54 17.3	23.3	67 34.1	06.7	61 37.5	57.2			
R 12	20 09.6	316 08.2	N25 37.3	69 18.0	S19 22.9	82 36.3	S21 06.6	76 39.9	S19 57.2	Schedar	349 35.8	N56 38.7
D 13	35 12.1	331 08.5	37.8	84 18.7	22.5	97 38.5	06.6	91 42.2	57.1	Shaula	96 15.4	S37 06.9
A 14	50 14.6	346 08.7	38.3	99 19.4	22.1	112 40.7	06.6	106 44.5	57.1	Sirius	258 29.7	S16 44.9
Y 15	65 17.0	1 09.0 ..	38.7	114 20.0 ..	21.7	127 42.9 ..	06.5	121 46.9 ..	57.1	Spica	158 26.0	S11 16.0
16	80 19.5	16 09.3	39.2	129 20.7	21.3	142 45.1	06.5	136 49.2	57.1	Suhail	222 48.9	S43 31.1
17	95 21.9	31 09.6	39.7	144 21.4	20.9	157 47.3	06.4	151 51.6	57.1			
18	110 24.4	46 09.9	N25 40.2	159 22.0	S19 20.5	172 49.5	S21 06.4	166 53.9	S19 57.0	Vega	80 35.7	N38 47.9
19	125 26.9	61 10.2	40.7	174 22.7	20.1	187 51.7	06.4	181 56.2	57.0	Zuben'ubi	136 59.5	S16 07.5
20	140 29.3	76 10.5	41.2	189 23.4	19.7	202 53.9	06.3	196 58.6	57.0		SHA	Mer.Pass.
21	155 31.8	91 10.8 ..	41.6	204 24.1 ..	19.3	217 56.1 ..	06.3	212 00.9 ..	57.0		° '	h m
22	170 34.3	106 11.1	42.1	219 24.7	18.9	232 58.3	06.2	227 03.3	56.9	Venus	297 17.6	14 56
23	185 36.7	121 11.4	42.6	234 25.4	18.5	248 00.5	06.2	242 05.6	56.9	Mars	50 13.0	7 24
	h m									Jupiter	62 36.2	6 34
Mer. Pass.	10 43.5	v 0.3	d 0.5	v 0.7	d 0.4	v 2.2	d 0.0	v 2.3	d 0.0	Saturn	56 34.8	6 58

UT	SUN GHA	SUN Dec	MOON GHA	v	MOON Dec	d	HP
d h	° ′	° ′	° ′	′	° ′	′	′
9 00	179 36.1	N 7 40.1	346 01.3	8.0	S 8 12.9	14.4	61.2
01	194 36.3	41.1	0 28.3	8.1	8 27.3	14.3	61.2
02	209 36.4	42.0	14 55.4	8.0	8 41.6	14.3	61.1
03	224 36.6	.. 42.9	29 22.4	7.9	8 55.9	14.2	61.1
04	239 36.8	43.8	43 49.3	8.0	9 10.1	14.2	61.1
05	254 37.0	44.8	58 16.3	7.9	9 24.3	14.1	61.1
06	269 37.1	N 7 45.7	72 43.2	7.9	S 9 38.4	14.0	61.1
07	284 37.3	46.6	87 10.1	7.9	9 52.4	13.9	61.0
T 08	299 37.5	47.6	101 37.0	7.9	10 06.3	13.9	61.0
H 09	314 37.6	.. 48.5	116 03.9	7.8	10 20.2	13.8	61.0
U 10	329 37.8	49.4	130 30.7	7.8	10 34.0	13.7	61.0
R 11	344 38.0	50.3	144 57.5	7.8	10 47.7	13.6	61.0
S 12	359 38.1	N 7 51.3	159 24.3	7.7	S11 01.3	13.6	60.9
D 13	14 38.3	52.2	173 51.0	7.7	11 14.9	13.4	60.9
A 14	29 38.5	53.1	188 17.7	7.7	11 28.3	13.4	60.9
Y 15	44 38.6	.. 54.0	202 44.4	7.7	11 41.7	13.3	60.9
16	59 38.8	55.0	217 11.1	7.7	11 55.0	13.3	60.8
17	74 39.0	55.9	231 37.8	7.6	12 08.3	13.1	60.8
18	89 39.2	N 7 56.8	246 04.4	7.6	S12 21.4	13.0	60.8
19	104 39.3	57.7	260 31.0	7.6	12 34.4	13.0	60.8
20	119 39.5	58.7	274 57.6	7.5	12 47.4	12.8	60.7
21	134 39.7	7 59.6	289 24.1	7.5	13 00.2	12.8	60.7
22	149 39.8	8 00.5	303 50.6	7.5	13 13.0	12.7	60.7
23	164 40.0	01.4	318 17.1	7.4	13 25.7	12.5	60.6
10 00	179 40.2	N 8 02.3	332 43.5	7.5	S13 38.2	12.5	60.6
01	194 40.3	03.3	347 10.0	7.4	13 50.7	12.4	60.6
02	209 40.5	04.2	1 36.4	7.4	14 03.1	12.2	60.6
03	224 40.7	.. 05.1	16 02.8	7.3	14 15.3	12.2	60.5
04	239 40.8	06.0	30 29.1	7.3	14 27.5	12.1	60.5
05	254 41.0	07.0	44 55.4	7.3	14 39.6	11.9	60.5
06	269 41.2	N 8 07.9	59 21.7	7.3	S14 51.5	11.9	60.4
07	284 41.3	08.8	73 48.0	7.2	15 03.4	11.7	60.4
F 08	299 41.5	09.7	88 14.2	7.2	15 15.1	11.6	60.4
R 09	314 41.7	.. 10.6	102 40.4	7.2	15 26.7	11.6	60.3
I 10	329 41.8	11.6	117 06.6	7.2	15 38.3	11.4	60.3
D 11	344 42.0	12.5	131 32.8	7.1	15 49.7	11.3	60.3
A 12	359 42.2	N 8 13.4	145 58.9	7.1	S16 01.0	11.1	60.2
Y 13	14 42.3	14.3	160 25.0	7.1	16 12.1	11.1	60.2
14	29 42.5	15.2	174 51.1	7.1	16 23.2	11.0	60.2
15	44 42.7	.. 16.2	189 17.2	7.0	16 34.2	10.8	60.1
16	59 42.8	17.1	203 43.2	7.0	16 45.0	10.7	60.1
17	74 43.0	18.0	218 09.2	7.0	16 55.7	10.6	60.1
18	89 43.2	N 8 18.9	232 35.2	7.0	S17 06.3	10.4	60.0
19	104 43.3	19.8	247 01.2	6.9	17 16.7	10.4	60.0
20	119 43.5	20.8	261 27.1	6.9	17 27.1	10.2	60.0
21	134 43.7	.. 21.7	275 53.0	6.9	17 37.3	10.1	59.9
22	149 43.8	22.6	290 18.9	6.9	17 47.4	10.0	59.9
23	164 44.0	23.5	304 44.8	6.8	17 57.4	9.8	59.9
11 00	179 44.2	N 8 24.4	319 10.6	6.8	S18 07.2	9.7	59.8
01	194 44.3	25.3	333 36.4	6.8	18 16.9	9.6	59.8
02	209 44.5	26.3	348 02.2	6.8	18 26.5	9.5	59.8
03	224 44.6	.. 27.2	2 28.0	6.8	18 36.0	9.3	59.7
04	239 44.8	28.1	16 53.8	6.8	18 45.3	9.2	59.7
05	254 45.0	29.0	31 19.6	6.7	18 54.5	9.1	59.6
06	269 45.1	N 8 29.9	45 45.3	6.7	S19 03.6	8.9	59.6
07	284 45.3	30.8	60 11.0	6.7	19 12.5	8.8	59.6
S 08	299 45.5	31.7	74 36.7	6.7	19 21.3	8.7	59.5
A 09	314 45.6	.. 32.7	89 02.4	6.7	19 30.0	8.5	59.5
T 10	329 45.8	33.6	103 28.1	6.6	19 38.5	8.4	59.5
U 11	344 46.0	34.5	117 53.7	6.7	19 46.9	8.2	59.4
R 12	359 46.1	N 8 35.4	132 19.4	6.6	S19 55.1	8.2	59.4
D 13	14 46.3	36.3	146 45.0	6.6	20 03.3	7.9	59.3
A 14	29 46.4	37.2	161 10.6	6.6	20 11.2	7.9	59.3
Y 15	44 46.6	.. 38.1	175 36.2	6.6	20 19.1	7.7	59.3
16	59 46.8	39.1	190 01.8	6.6	20 26.8	7.6	59.2
17	74 46.9	40.0	204 27.4	6.6	20 34.4	7.4	59.2
18	89 47.1	N 8 40.9	218 53.0	6.5	S20 41.8	7.3	59.1
19	104 47.3	41.8	233 18.5	6.6	20 49.1	7.1	59.1
20	119 47.4	42.7	247 44.1	6.6	20 56.2	7.0	59.1
21	134 47.6	.. 43.6	262 09.7	6.5	21 03.2	6.8	59.0
22	149 47.7	44.5	276 35.2	6.5	21 10.0	6.8	59.0
23	164 47.9	45.4	291 00.8	6.5	S21 16.8	6.5	58.9
	SD 16.0	d 0.9	SD 16.6		16.4		16.2

Moonrise

Lat.	Naut.	Civil	Sunrise	9	10	11	12
°	h m	h m	h m	h m	h m	h m	h m
N 72	////	02 37	04 05	22 59	■	■	■
N 70	////	03 04	04 18	22 31	25 13	01 13	■
68	01 39	03 24	04 29	22 10	24 25	00 25	03 21
66	02 15	03 40	04 38	21 53	23 55	25 57	01 57
64	02 40	03 53	04 45	21 40	23 32	25 20	01 20
62	02 59	04 03	04 52	21 29	23 14	24 53	00 53
60	03 14	04 12	04 57	21 19	22 59	24 33	00 33
N 58	03 27	04 20	05 02	21 11	22 47	24 16	00 16
56	03 38	04 27	05 06	21 04	22 36	24 02	00 02
54	03 47	04 33	05 10	20 58	22 26	23 49	25 03
52	03 55	04 38	05 14	20 52	22 18	23 39	24 50
50	04 02	04 43	05 17	20 47	22 10	23 29	24 39
45	04 17	04 53	05 24	20 36	21 54	23 09	24 17
N 40	04 29	05 02	05 29	20 26	21 41	22 53	23 59
35	04 38	05 08	05 34	20 18	21 30	22 39	23 43
30	04 45	05 14	05 38	20 12	21 20	22 27	23 30
20	04 57	05 23	05 46	20 00	21 04	22 07	23 08
N 10	05 06	05 31	05 52	19 50	20 50	21 50	22 48
0	05 13	05 37	05 58	19 40	20 36	21 33	22 30
S 10	05 18	05 42	06 04	19 31	20 23	21 17	22 12
20	05 22	05 47	06 10	19 21	20 09	21 00	21 53
30	05 24	05 52	06 16	19 09	19 53	20 40	21 31
35	05 25	05 55	06 20	19 03	19 44	20 29	21 18
40	05 26	05 57	06 24	18 56	19 33	20 16	21 03
45	05 26	06 00	06 29	18 47	19 21	20 00	20 44
S 50	05 25	06 03	06 35	18 37	19 06	19 41	20 24
52	05 25	06 04	06 38	18 32	18 59	19 32	20 14
54	05 24	06 05	06 41	18 27	18 52	19 22	20 02
56	05 24	06 07	06 44	18 22	18 43	19 11	19 49
58	05 23	06 08	06 48	18 15	18 34	18 58	19 33
S 60	05 21	06 10	06 52	18 08	18 23	18 43	19 15

Moonset

Lat.	Sunset	Civil	Naut.	9	10	11	12
°	h m	h m	h m	h m	h m	h m	h m
N 72	20 01	21 32	////	05 02	04 23	■	■
N 70	19 47	21 03	////	05 16	04 54	04 11	■
68	19 36	20 42	22 32	05 28	05 16	04 59	04 03
66	19 27	20 26	21 53	05 38	05 34	05 31	05 28
64	19 19	20 12	21 26	05 46	05 49	05 54	06 06
62	19 13	20 01	21 07	05 53	06 01	06 13	06 33
60	19 07	19 52	20 51	05 59	06 12	06 29	06 54
N 58	19 02	19 44	20 38	06 05	06 21	06 42	07 11
56	18 57	19 37	20 27	06 10	06 29	06 53	07 26
54	18 53	19 31	20 17	06 14	06 36	07 03	07 38
52	18 50	19 25	20 09	06 18	06 43	07 12	07 49
50	18 47	19 20	20 02	06 22	06 49	07 20	07 59
45	18 40	19 10	19 46	06 30	07 01	07 38	08 20
N 40	18 34	19 02	19 35	06 36	07 12	07 52	08 37
35	18 29	18 55	19 25	06 42	07 21	08 04	08 51
30	18 24	18 49	19 18	06 47	07 29	08 14	09 04
20	18 17	18 39	19 05	06 56	07 43	08 33	09 25
N 10	18 10	18 32	18 56	07 04	07 55	08 48	09 43
0	18 04	18 25	18 50	07 11	08 07	09 03	10 01
S 10	17 59	18 20	18 44	07 18	08 18	09 18	10 18
20	17 53	18 15	18 40	07 26	08 30	09 34	10 36
30	17 46	18 10	18 38	07 35	08 45	09 53	10 58
35	17 42	18 07	18 37	07 40	08 53	10 03	11 10
40	17 37	18 05	18 36	07 46	09 02	10 16	11 25
45	17 32	18 02	18 36	07 53	09 13	10 30	11 42
S 50	17 26	17 59	18 36	08 02	09 27	10 48	12 03
52	17 24	17 58	18 37	08 05	09 33	10 57	12 13
54	17 21	17 56	18 37	08 10	09 40	11 06	12 25
56	17 17	17 55	18 38	08 14	09 48	11 17	12 38
58	17 14	17 53	18 38	08 20	09 56	11 29	12 53
S 60	17 10	17 52	18 40	08 26	10 06	11 44	13 11

	SUN			MOON			
Day	Eqn. of Time 00h	12h	Mer. Pass.	Mer. Pass. Upper	Lower	Age	Phase
d	m s	m s	h m	h m	h m	d	%
9	01 36	01 28	12 01	00 58	13 26	16	97
10	01 20	01 12	12 01	01 53	14 21	17	92
11	01 04	00 56	12 01	02 50	15 18	18	84

UT	ARIES	VENUS −4·7		MARS +0·6		JUPITER −2·2		SATURN +0·6		STARS		
	GHA	GHA	Dec	GHA	Dec	GHA	Dec	GHA	Dec	Name	SHA	Dec
d h	° ′	° ′	° ′	° ′	° ′	° ′	° ′	° ′	° ′		° ′	° ′
12 00	200 39.2	136 11.7	N25 43.1	249 26.1	S19 18.1	263 02.8	S21 06.2	257 08.0	S19 56.9	Acamar	315 15.1	S40 13.7
01	215 41.7	151 12.0	43.5	264 26.8	17.7	278 05.0	06.1	272 10.3	56.9	Achernar	335 23.8	S57 08.2
02	230 44.1	166 12.3	44.0	279 27.4	17.3	293 07.2	06.1	287 12.6	56.9	Acrux	173 03.5	S63 12.7
03	245 46.6	181 12.6 ..	44.5	294 28.1 ..	16.9	308 09.4 ..	06.0	302 15.0 ..	56.8	Adhara	255 08.9	S29 00.3
04	260 49.1	196 13.0	45.0	309 28.8	16.5	323 11.6	06.0	317 17.3	56.8	Aldebaran	290 44.2	N16 32.8
05	275 51.5	211 13.3	45.4	324 29.5	16.1	338 13.8	06.0	332 19.7	56.8			
06	290 54.0	226 13.6	N25 45.9	339 30.1	S19 15.6	353 16.0	S21 05.9	347 22.0	S19 56.8	Alioth	166 15.9	N55 51.1
07	305 56.4	241 13.9	46.4	354 30.8	15.2	8 18.2	05.9	2 24.4	56.7	Alkaid	152 54.7	N49 12.8
08	320 58.9	256 14.2	46.9	9 31.5	14.8	23 20.4	05.9	17 26.7	56.7	Alnair	27 38.1	S46 51.7
S 09	336 01.4	271 14.5 ..	47.3	24 32.1 ..	14.4	38 22.6 ..	05.8	32 29.1 ..	56.7	Alnilam	275 41.8	S 1 11.6
U 10	351 03.8	286 14.8	47.8	39 32.8	14.0	53 24.8	05.8	47 31.4	56.7	Alphard	217 51.4	S 8 44.9
N 11	6 06.3	301 15.2	48.3	54 33.5	13.6	68 27.1	05.7	62 33.7	56.7			
D 12	21 08.8	316 15.5	N25 48.7	69 34.2	S19 13.2	83 29.3	S21 05.7	77 36.1	S19 56.6	Alphecca	126 06.7	N26 38.7
A 13	36 11.2	331 15.8	49.2	84 34.8	12.8	98 31.5	05.7	92 38.4	56.6	Alpheratz	357 39.0	N29 11.9
Y 14	51 13.7	346 16.1	49.7	99 35.5	12.4	113 33.7	05.6	107 40.8	56.6	Altair	62 03.7	N 8 55.2
15	66 16.2	1 16.4 ..	50.1	114 36.2 ..	12.0	128 35.9 ..	05.6	122 43.1 ..	56.6	Ankaa	353 11.4	S42 11.9
16	81 18.6	16 16.8	50.6	129 36.9	11.6	143 38.1	05.5	137 45.5	56.6	Antares	112 20.3	S26 28.5
17	96 21.1	31 17.1	51.0	144 37.5	11.2	158 40.3	05.5	152 47.8	56.5			
18	111 23.5	46 17.4	N25 51.5	159 38.2	S19 10.8	173 42.5	S21 05.5	167 50.2	S19 56.5	Arcturus	145 51.1	N19 04.6
19	126 26.0	61 17.7	52.0	174 38.9	10.4	188 44.8	05.4	182 52.5	56.5	Atria	107 17.5	S69 03.5
20	141 28.5	76 18.1	52.4	189 39.6	09.9	203 47.0	05.4	197 54.9	56.5	Avior	234 16.1	S59 34.8
21	156 30.9	91 18.4 ..	52.9	204 40.2 ..	09.5	218 49.2 ..	05.4	212 57.2 ..	56.4	Bellatrix	278 27.2	N 6 21.9
22	171 33.4	106 18.7	53.3	219 40.9	09.1	233 51.4	05.3	227 59.5	56.4	Betelgeuse	270 56.4	N 7 24.5
23	186 35.9	121 19.1	53.8	234 41.6	08.7	248 53.6	05.3	243 01.9	56.4			
13 00	201 38.3	136 19.4	N25 54.2	249 42.3	S19 08.3	263 55.8	S21 05.2	258 04.2	S19 56.4	Canopus	263 54.3	S52 42.7
01	216 40.8	151 19.7	54.7	264 43.0	07.9	278 58.0	05.2	273 06.6	56.4	Capella	280 27.8	N46 01.1
02	231 43.3	166 20.1	55.2	279 43.7	07.5	294 00.3	05.2	288 08.9	56.3	Deneb	49 28.4	N45 20.8
03	246 45.7	181 20.4 ..	55.6	294 44.3 ..	07.1	309 02.5 ..	05.1	303 11.3 ..	56.3	Denebola	182 28.6	N14 27.6
04	261 48.2	196 20.8	56.1	309 45.0	06.7	324 04.7	05.1	318 13.6	56.3	Diphda	348 51.5	S17 52.7
05	276 50.7	211 21.1	56.5	324 45.7	06.2	339 06.9	05.0	333 16.0	56.3			
06	291 53.1	226 21.4	N25 57.0	339 46.3	S19 05.8	354 09.1	S21 05.0	348 18.3	S19 56.3	Dubhe	193 45.4	N61 38.7
07	306 55.6	241 21.8	57.4	354 47.0	05.4	9 11.3	05.0	3 20.7	56.2	Elnath	278 06.9	N28 37.4
08	321 58.0	256 22.1	57.9	9 47.7	05.0	24 13.6	04.9	18 23.0	56.2	Eltanin	90 43.7	N51 28.9
M 09	337 00.5	271 22.5 ..	58.3	24 48.4 ..	04.6	39 15.8 ..	04.9	33 25.4 ..	56.2	Enif	33 42.7	N 9 57.9
O 10	352 03.0	286 22.8	58.8	39 49.1	04.2	54 18.0	04.9	48 27.7	56.2	Fomalhaut	15 19.1	S29 31.0
N 11	7 05.4	301 23.2	59.2	54 49.7	03.8	69 20.2	04.8	63 30.1	56.1			
D 12	22 07.9	316 23.5	N25 59.6	69 50.4	S19 03.4	84 22.4	S21 04.8	78 32.4	S19 56.1	Gacrux	171 55.2	S57 13.6
A 13	37 10.4	331 23.9	26 00.1	84 51.1	02.9	99 24.6	04.7	93 34.8	56.1	Gienah	175 47.2	S17 39.3
Y 14	52 12.8	346 24.2	00.5	99 51.8	02.5	114 26.9	04.7	108 37.1	56.1	Hadar	148 40.7	S60 28.1
15	67 15.3	1 24.6 ..	01.0	114 52.4 ..	02.1	129 29.1 ..	04.7	123 39.5 ..	56.1	Hamal	327 55.8	N23 33.2
16	82 17.8	16 24.9	01.4	129 53.1	01.7	144 31.3	04.6	138 41.8	56.0	Kaus Aust.	83 37.5	S34 22.3
17	97 20.2	31 25.3	01.9	144 53.8	01.3	159 33.5	04.6	153 44.2	56.0			
18	112 22.7	46 25.7	N26 02.3	159 54.5	S19 00.9	174 35.7	S21 04.6	168 46.5	S19 56.0	Kochab	137 18.9	N74 04.3
19	127 25.2	61 26.0	02.7	174 55.2	00.5	189 38.0	04.5	183 48.9	56.0	Markab	13 33.9	N15 18.6
20	142 27.6	76 26.4	03.2	189 55.8	19 00.0	204 40.2	04.5	198 51.2	56.0	Menkar	314 10.4	N 4 09.9
21	157 30.1	91 26.8 ..	03.6	204 56.5	18 59.6	219 42.4 ..	04.4	213 53.6 ..	55.9	Menkent	148 01.7	S36 28.1
22	172 32.5	106 27.1	04.0	219 57.2	59.2	234 44.6	04.4	228 55.9	55.9	Miaplacidus	221 38.5	S69 48.3
23	187 35.0	121 27.5	04.5	234 57.9	58.8	249 46.9	04.4	243 58.3	55.9			
14 00	202 37.5	136 27.9	N26 04.9	249 58.6	S18 58.4	264 49.1	S21 04.3	259 00.6	S19 55.9	Mirfak	308 34.1	N49 55.9
01	217 39.9	151 28.2	05.3	264 59.2	58.0	279 51.3	04.3	274 03.0	55.9	Nunki	75 52.4	S26 16.2
02	232 42.4	166 28.6	05.8	279 59.9	57.6	294 53.5	04.3	289 05.3	55.8	Peacock	53 11.9	S56 40.0
03	247 44.9	181 29.0 ..	06.2	295 00.6 ..	57.1	309 55.7 ..	04.2	304 07.7 ..	55.8	Pollux	243 22.0	N27 58.6
04	262 47.3	196 29.3	06.6	310 01.3	56.7	324 58.0	04.2	319 10.0	55.8	Procyon	244 54.9	N 5 10.2
05	277 49.8	211 29.7	07.1	325 02.0	56.3	340 00.2	04.1	334 12.4	55.8			
06	292 52.3	226 30.1	N26 07.5	340 02.6	S18 55.9	355 02.4	S21 04.1	349 14.7	S19 55.8	Rasalhague	96 01.9	N12 32.6
07	307 54.7	241 30.5	07.9	355 03.3	55.5	10 04.6	04.1	4 17.1	55.7	Regulus	207 38.3	N11 52.1
T 08	322 57.2	256 30.8	08.3	10 04.0	55.0	25 06.9	04.0	19 19.4	55.7	Rigel	281 07.7	S 8 11.0
U 09	337 59.7	271 31.2 ..	08.8	25 04.7 ..	54.6	40 09.1 ..	04.0	34 21.8 ..	55.7	Rigil Kent.	139 44.8	S60 54.9
E 10	353 02.1	286 31.6	09.2	40 05.4	54.2	55 11.3	04.0	49 24.1	55.7	Sabik	102 07.0	S15 44.9
S 11	8 04.6	301 32.0	09.6	55 06.0	53.8	70 13.5	03.9	64 26.5	55.7			
D 12	23 07.0	316 32.4	N26 10.0	70 06.7	S18 53.4	85 15.8	S21 03.9	79 28.8	S19 55.6	Schedar	349 35.8	N56 38.6
A 13	38 09.5	331 32.8	10.5	85 07.4	52.9	100 18.0	03.9	94 31.2	55.6	Shaula	96 15.3	S37 06.9
Y 14	53 12.0	346 33.2	10.9	100 08.1	52.5	115 20.2	03.8	109 33.5	55.6	Sirius	258 29.7	S16 44.9
15	68 14.4	1 33.5 ..	11.3	115 08.8 ..	52.1	130 22.4 ..	03.8	124 35.9 ..	55.6	Spica	158 26.0	S11 16.0
16	83 16.9	16 33.9	11.7	130 09.5	51.7	145 24.7	03.7	139 38.2	55.6	Suhail	222 48.9	S43 31.1
17	98 19.4	31 34.3	12.1	145 10.1	51.3	160 26.9	03.7	154 40.6	55.5			
18	113 21.8	46 34.7	N26 12.6	160 10.8	S18 50.8	175 29.1	S21 03.7	169 42.9	S19 55.5	Vega	80 35.7	N38 47.9
19	128 24.3	61 35.1	13.0	175 11.5	50.4	190 31.3	03.6	184 45.3	55.5	Zuben'ubi	136 59.9	S16 07.5
20	143 26.8	76 35.5	13.4	190 12.2	50.0	205 33.6	03.6	199 47.7	55.5		SHA	Mer. Pass.
21	158 29.2	91 35.9 ..	13.8	205 12.9 ..	49.6	220 35.8 ..	03.6	214 50.0 ..	55.5		° ′	h m
22	173 31.7	106 36.3	14.2	220 13.6	49.2	235 38.0	03.5	229 52.4	55.4	Venus	294 41.1	14 54
23	188 34.1	121 36.7	14.6	235 14.2	48.7	250 40.3	03.5	244 54.7	55.4	Mars	48 03.9	7 21
	h m									Jupiter	62 17.5	6 23
Mer. Pass. 10 31.7		v 0.4	d 0.4	v 0.7	d 0.4	v 2.2	d 0.0	v 2.3	d 0.0	Saturn	56 25.9	6 47

SUN / MOON

UT	SUN GHA	SUN Dec	MOON GHA	v	MOON Dec	d	HP
d h	° ′	° ′	° ′	′	° ′	′	′
12 00	179 48.1	N 8 46.4	305 26.3	6.6	S21 23.3	6.4	58.9
01	194 48.2	47.3	319 51.9	6.5	21 29.7	6.3	58.9
02	209 48.4	48.2	334 17.4	6.6	21 36.0	6.2	58.8
03	224 48.6	.. 49.1	348 43.0	6.5	21 42.2	6.0	58.8
04	239 48.7	50.0	3 08.5	6.6	21 48.2	5.8	58.7
05	254 48.9	50.9	17 34.1	6.5	21 54.0	5.7	58.7
06	269 49.0	N 8 51.8	31 59.6	6.6	S21 59.7	5.6	58.7
07	284 49.2	52.7	46 25.2	6.6	22 05.3	5.4	58.6
S 08	299 49.4	53.6	60 50.8	6.5	22 10.7	5.2	58.6
U 09	314 49.5	.. 54.5	75 16.3	6.6	22 15.9	5.2	58.5
N 10	329 49.7	55.5	89 41.9	6.6	22 21.1	4.9	58.5
D 11	344 49.8	56.4	104 07.5	6.6	22 26.0	4.8	58.5
A 12	359 50.0	N 8 57.3	118 33.1	6.6	S22 30.8	4.7	58.4
Y 13	14 50.2	58.2	132 58.7	6.7	22 35.5	4.6	58.4
14	29 50.3	8 59.1	147 24.4	6.6	22 40.1	4.3	58.3
15	44 50.5	9 00.0	161 50.0	6.7	22 44.4	4.3	58.3
16	59 50.6	00.9	176 15.7	6.6	22 48.7	4.1	58.2
17	74 50.8	01.8	190 41.3	6.7	22 52.8	3.9	58.2
18	89 51.0	N 9 02.7	205 07.0	6.7	S22 56.7	3.8	58.2
19	104 51.1	03.6	219 32.7	6.7	23 00.5	3.7	58.1
20	119 51.3	04.5	233 58.4	6.8	23 04.2	3.5	58.1
21	134 51.4	.. 05.4	248 24.2	6.8	23 07.7	3.3	58.0
22	149 51.6	06.3	262 50.0	6.8	23 11.0	3.2	58.0
23	164 51.7	07.2	277 15.8	6.8	23 14.2	3.1	58.0
13 00	179 51.9	N 9 08.1	291 41.6	6.8	S23 17.3	2.9	57.9
01	194 52.1	09.1	306 07.4	6.9	23 20.2	2.8	57.9
02	209 52.2	10.0	320 33.3	6.9	23 23.0	2.6	57.8
03	224 52.4	.. 10.9	334 59.2	6.9	23 25.6	2.5	57.8
04	239 52.5	11.8	349 25.1	7.0	23 28.1	2.4	57.8
05	254 52.7	12.7	3 51.1	7.0	23 30.5	2.2	57.7
06	269 52.8	N 9 13.6	18 17.1	7.0	S23 32.7	2.0	57.7
07	284 53.0	14.5	32 43.1	7.1	23 34.7	1.9	57.6
08	299 53.2	15.4	47 09.2	7.1	23 36.6	1.8	57.6
M 09	314 53.3	.. 16.3	61 35.3	7.1	23 38.4	1.6	57.6
O 10	329 53.5	17.2	76 01.4	7.2	23 40.0	1.5	57.5
N 11	344 53.6	18.1	90 27.6	7.2	23 41.5	1.3	57.5
D 12	359 53.8	N 9 19.0	104 53.8	7.2	S23 42.8	1.2	57.4
A 13	14 53.9	19.9	119 20.0	7.3	23 44.0	1.0	57.4
Y 14	29 54.1	20.8	133 46.3	7.3	23 45.0	1.0	57.4
15	44 54.3	.. 21.7	148 12.6	7.4	23 46.0	0.7	57.3
16	59 54.4	22.6	162 39.0	7.4	23 46.7	0.6	57.3
17	74 54.6	23.5	177 05.4	7.5	23 47.3	0.5	57.2
18	89 54.7	N 9 24.4	191 31.9	7.5	S23 47.8	0.4	57.2
19	104 54.9	25.3	205 58.4	7.5	23 48.2	0.2	57.2
20	119 55.0	26.2	220 24.9	7.6	23 48.4	0.1	57.1
21	134 55.2	.. 27.1	234 51.5	7.7	23 48.5	0.1	57.1
22	149 55.3	28.0	249 18.2	7.7	23 48.4	0.2	57.1
23	164 55.5	28.9	263 44.9	7.7	23 48.2	0.4	57.0
14 00	179 55.7	N 9 29.8	278 11.6	7.8	S23 47.8	0.4	57.0
01	194 55.8	30.7	292 38.4	7.9	23 47.4	0.7	56.9
02	209 56.0	31.6	307 05.3	7.9	23 46.7	0.7	56.9
03	224 56.1	.. 32.5	321 32.2	7.9	23 46.0	0.9	56.9
04	239 56.3	33.4	335 59.1	8.1	23 45.1	1.0	56.8
05	254 56.4	34.3	350 26.2	8.0	23 44.1	1.2	56.8
06	269 56.6	N 9 35.2	4 53.2	8.2	S23 42.9	1.2	56.8
07	284 56.7	36.1	19 20.4	8.2	23 41.7	1.5	56.7
T 08	299 56.9	37.0	33 47.6	8.2	23 40.2	1.5	56.7
U 09	314 57.0	.. 37.9	48 14.8	8.3	23 38.7	1.7	56.7
E 10	329 57.2	38.8	62 42.1	8.4	23 37.0	1.8	56.6
S 11	344 57.3	39.7	77 09.5	8.4	23 35.2	1.9	56.6
D 12	359 57.5	N 9 40.5	91 36.9	8.5	S23 33.3	2.1	56.5
A 13	14 57.6	41.4	106 04.4	8.6	23 31.2	2.2	56.5
Y 14	29 57.8	42.3	120 32.0	8.6	23 29.0	2.3	56.5
15	44 57.9	.. 43.2	134 59.6	8.7	23 26.7	2.4	56.4
16	59 58.1	44.1	149 27.3	8.7	23 24.3	2.6	56.4
17	74 58.3	45.0	163 55.0	8.8	23 21.7	2.7	56.4
18	89 58.4	N 9 45.9	178 22.8	8.9	S23 19.0	2.8	56.3
19	104 58.6	46.8	192 50.7	9.0	23 16.2	2.9	56.3
20	119 58.7	47.7	207 18.7	9.0	23 13.3	3.1	56.3
21	134 58.9	.. 48.6	221 46.7	9.1	23 10.2	3.2	56.2
22	149 59.0	49.5	236 14.8	9.1	23 07.0	3.3	56.2
23	164 59.2	50.4	250 42.9	9.2	S23 03.7	3.4	56.2
	SD 16.0	d 0.9	SD 15.9		15.7		15.4

Twilight / Moonrise

Lat.	Naut.	Civil	Sunrise	Moonrise 12	13	14	15
°	h m	h m	h m	h m	h m	h m	h m
N 72	////	02 12	03 48	■■	■■	■■	■■
N 70	////	02 45	04 04	■■	■■	■■	■■
68	01 05	03 08	04 16	03 21	■■	■■	■■
66	01 54	03 26	04 26	01 57	03 58	05 12	05 13
64	02 24	03 41	04 35	01 20	02 53	03 57	04 28
62	02 45	03 52	04 42	00 53	02 19	03 20	03 58
60	03 02	04 03	04 48	00 33	01 53	02 54	03 35
N 58	03 16	04 11	04 54	00 16	01 33	02 34	03 17
56	03 28	04 19	04 59	00 02	01 17	02 17	03 01
54	03 38	04 25	05 03	25 03	01 03	02 02	02 48
52	03 47	04 31	05 07	24 50	00 50	01 50	02 36
50	03 55	04 37	05 11	24 39	00 39	01 39	02 26
45	04 11	04 48	05 18	24 17	00 17	01 15	02 04
N 40	04 23	04 57	05 25	23 59	24 57	00 57	01 47
35	04 33	05 04	05 30	23 43	24 41	00 41	01 32
30	04 42	05 11	05 35	23 30	24 28	00 28	01 19
20	04 55	05 21	05 43	23 08	24 05	00 05	00 57
N 10	05 04	05 29	05 50	22 48	23 45	24 38	00 38
0	05 12	05 36	05 57	22 30	23 27	24 20	00 20
S 10	05 18	05 42	06 04	22 12	23 08	24 03	00 03
20	05 22	05 48	06 10	21 53	22 48	23 44	24 38
30	05 26	05 54	06 18	21 31	22 25	23 22	24 18
35	05 27	05 57	06 22	21 18	22 12	23 09	24 07
40	05 29	06 00	06 27	21 03	21 57	22 54	23 54
45	05 29	06 03	06 33	20 46	21 38	22 36	23 38
S 50	05 30	06 07	06 40	20 24	21 15	22 14	23 18
52	05 30	06 09	06 43	20 14	21 04	22 04	23 09
54	05 29	06 10	06 46	20 02	20 52	21 52	22 59
56	05 29	06 12	06 50	19 49	20 38	21 38	22 47
58	05 29	06 14	06 54	19 33	20 21	21 22	22 33
S 60	05 28	06 16	06 59	19 15	20 01	21 03	22 17

Sunset / Twilight / Moonset

Lat.	Sunset	Civil	Naut.	Moonset 12	13	14	15
°	h m	h m	h m	h m	h m	h m	h m
N 72	20 16	21 56	////	■■	■■	■■	■■
N 70	20 00	21 21	////	■■	04 03	■■	■■
68	19 47	20 56	23 10	04 03	05 27	06 10	07 59
66	19 37	20 38	22 13	05 28	06 31	07 24	08 44
64	19 28	20 23	21 42	06 06	06 31...	08 01	09 14
62	19 21	20 11	21 19	06 33	07 06	08 01	09 14
60	19 14	20 00	21 01	06 54	07 32	08 27	09 36
N 58	19 09	19 51	20 47	07 11	07 52	08 47	09 54
56	19 04	19 44	20 35	07 26	08 09	09 04	10 09
54	18 59	19 37	20 24	07 38	08 23	09 18	10 23
52	18 55	19 31	20 15	07 49	08 35	09 31	10 34
50	18 51	19 25	20 07	07 59	08 46	09 42	10 44
45	18 43	19 14	19 51	08 20	09 09	10 05	11 05
N 40	18 37	19 05	19 38	08 37	09 28	10 23	11 22
35	18 31	18 57	19 28	08 51	09 43	10 39	11 36
30	18 26	18 51	19 19	09 04	09 56	10 52	11 49
20	18 18	18 40	19 07	09 25	10 19	11 15	12 10
N 10	18 10	18 32	18 57	09 43	10 39	11 34	12 28
0	18 01	18 25	18 43	10 01	10 58	11 53	12 45
S 10	17 57	18 18	18 43	10 18	11 16	12 11	13 02
20	17 50	18 12	18 38	10 36	11 36	12 31	13 20
30	17 42	18 06	18 34	10 58	11 58	12 53	13 41
35	17 38	18 03	18 33	11 10	12 12	13 06	13 53
40	17 33	18 00	18 32	11 25	12 27	13 21	14 07
45	17 27	17 57	18 31	11 42	12 46	13 39	14 24
S 50	17 20	17 53	18 30	12 03	13 08	14 02	14 44
52	17 17	17 51	18 30	12 13	13 19	14 12	14 53
54	17 14	17 49	18 30	12 25	13 32	14 24	15 04
56	17 10	17 48	18 30	12 38	13 46	14 38	15 16
58	17 06	17 45	18 31	12 53	14 03	14 54	15 30
S 60	17 01	17 43	18 31	13 11	14 23	15 14	15 47

SUN / MOON

	SUN		SUN	MOON			
Day	Eqn. of Time 00h	12h	Mer. Pass.	Mer. Pass. Upper	Lower	Age	Phase
d	m s	m s	h m	h m	h m	d	%
12	00 48	00 40	12 01	03 47	16 16	19	75
13	00 33	00 25	12 00	04 44	17 12	20	65
14	00 18	00 10	12 00	05 40	18 07	21	55

UT	ARIES GHA	VENUS −4·7 GHA	Dec	MARS +0·6 GHA	Dec	JUPITER −2·2 GHA	Dec	SATURN +0·6 GHA	Dec
15 00	203 36.6	136 37.1	N26 15.0	250 14.9	S18 48.3	265 42.5	S21 03.5	259 57.1	S19 55.4
01	218 39.1	151 37.5	15.5	265 15.6	47.9	280 44.7	03.4	274 59.4	55.4
02	233 41.5	166 37.9	15.9	280 16.3	47.5	295 46.9	03.4	290 01.8	55.4
03	248 44.0	181 38.3 ..	16.3	295 17.0 ..	47.0	310 49.2 ..	03.4	305 04.1 ..	55.3
04	263 46.5	196 38.7	16.7	310 17.7	46.6	325 51.4	03.3	320 06.5	55.3
05	278 48.9	211 39.1	17.1	325 18.3	46.2	340 53.6	03.3	335 08.9	55.3
06	293 51.4	226 39.6	N26 17.5	340 19.0	S18 45.8	355 55.9	S21 03.2	350 11.2	S19 55.3
W 07	308 53.9	241 40.0	17.9	355 19.7	45.4	10 58.1	03.2	5 13.6	55.3
E 08	323 56.3	256 40.4	18.3	10 20.4	44.9	26 00.3	03.2	20 15.9	55.2
D 09	338 58.8	271 40.8 ..	18.7	25 21.1 ..	44.5	41 02.6 ..	03.1	35 18.3 ..	55.2
N 10	354 01.3	286 41.2	19.1	40 21.8	44.1	56 04.8	03.1	50 20.6	55.2
E 11	9 03.7	301 41.6	19.5	55 22.5	43.7	71 07.0	03.1	65 23.0	55.2
S 12	24 06.2	316 42.1	N26 19.9	70 23.1	S18 43.2	86 09.3	S21 03.0	80 25.3	S19 55.2
D 13	39 08.6	331 42.5	20.3	85 23.8	42.8	101 11.5	03.0	95 27.7	55.2
A 14	54 11.1	346 42.9	20.7	100 24.5	42.4	116 13.7	03.0	110 30.1	55.1
Y 15	69 13.6	1 43.3 ..	21.1	115 25.2 ..	42.0	131 16.0 ..	02.9	125 32.4 ..	55.1
16	84 16.0	16 43.8	21.5	130 25.9	41.5	146 18.2	02.9	140 34.8	55.1
17	99 18.5	31 44.2	21.9	145 26.6	41.1	161 20.4	02.9	155 37.1	55.1
18	114 21.0	46 44.6	N26 22.3	160 27.3	S18 40.7	176 22.7	S21 02.8	170 39.5	S19 55.1
19	129 23.4	61 45.1	22.7	175 27.9	40.2	191 24.9	02.8	185 41.8	55.0
20	144 25.9	76 45.5	23.1	190 28.6	39.8	206 27.1	02.8	200 44.2	55.0
21	159 28.4	91 45.9 ..	23.5	205 29.3 ..	39.4	221 29.4 ..	02.7	215 46.6 ..	55.0
22	174 30.8	106 46.4	23.9	220 30.0	39.0	236 31.6	02.7	230 48.9	55.0
23	189 33.3	121 46.8	24.3	235 30.7	38.5	251 33.8	02.6	245 51.3	55.0
16 00	204 35.8	136 47.2	N26 24.7	250 31.4	S18 38.1	266 36.1	S21 02.6	260 53.6	S19 54.9
01	219 38.2	151 47.7	25.0	265 32.1	37.7	281 38.3	02.6	275 56.0	54.9
02	234 40.7	166 48.1	25.4	280 32.8	37.3	296 40.6	02.5	290 58.4	54.9
03	249 43.1	181 48.6 ..	25.8	295 33.4 ..	36.8	311 42.8 ..	02.5	306 00.7 ..	54.9
04	264 45.6	196 49.0	26.2	310 34.1	36.4	326 45.0	02.5	321 03.1	54.9
05	279 48.1	211 49.5	26.6	325 34.8	36.0	341 47.3	02.4	336 05.4	54.8
06	294 50.5	226 49.9	N26 27.0	340 35.5	S18 35.5	356 49.5	S21 02.4	351 07.8	S19 54.8
T 07	309 53.0	241 50.4	27.4	355 36.2	35.1	11 51.7	02.4	6 10.1	54.8
H 08	324 55.5	256 50.8	27.7	10 36.9	34.7	26 54.0	02.3	21 12.5	54.8
U 09	339 57.9	271 51.3 ..	28.1	25 37.6 ..	34.2	41 56.2 ..	02.3	36 14.9 ..	54.8
R 10	355 00.4	286 51.7	28.5	40 38.3	33.8	56 58.5	02.2	51 17.2	54.8
S 11	10 02.9	301 52.2	28.9	55 39.0	33.4	72 00.7	02.2	66 19.6	54.7
D 12	25 05.3	316 52.6	N26 29.3	70 39.6	S18 33.0	87 02.9	S21 02.2	81 22.0	S19 54.7
A 13	40 07.8	331 53.1	29.6	85 40.3	32.5	102 05.2	02.2	96 24.3	54.7
Y 14	55 10.3	346 53.6	30.0	100 41.0	32.1	117 07.4	02.1	111 26.7	54.7
15	70 12.7	1 54.0 ..	30.4	115 41.7 ..	31.7	132 09.7 ..	02.1	126 29.0 ..	54.7
16	85 15.2	16 54.5	30.8	130 42.4	31.2	147 11.9	02.1	141 31.4	54.6
17	100 17.6	31 55.0	31.1	145 43.1	30.8	162 14.1	02.0	156 33.8	54.6
18	115 20.1	46 55.4	N26 31.5	160 43.8	S18 30.4	177 16.4	S21 02.0	171 36.1	S19 54.6
19	130 22.6	61 55.9	31.9	175 44.5	29.9	192 18.6	02.0	186 38.5	54.6
20	145 25.0	76 56.4	32.3	190 45.2	29.5	207 20.9	01.9	201 40.8	54.6
21	160 27.5	91 56.8 ..	32.6	205 45.9 ..	29.1	222 23.1 ..	01.9	216 43.2 ..	54.6
22	175 30.0	106 57.3	33.0	220 46.5	28.6	237 25.4	01.9	231 45.6	54.5
23	190 32.4	121 57.8	33.4	235 47.2	28.2	252 27.6	01.8	246 47.9	54.5
17 00	205 34.9	136 58.3	N26 33.7	250 47.9	S18 27.8	267 29.8	S21 01.8	261 50.3	S19 54.5
01	220 37.4	151 58.7	34.1	265 48.6	27.3	282 32.1	01.8	276 52.7	54.5
02	235 39.8	166 59.2	34.5	280 49.3	26.9	297 34.3	01.7	291 55.0	54.5
03	250 42.3	181 59.7 ..	34.8	295 50.0 ..	26.5	312 36.6 ..	01.7	306 57.4 ..	54.5
04	265 44.7	197 00.2	35.2	310 50.7	26.0	327 38.8	01.7	321 59.7	54.4
05	280 47.2	212 00.7	35.6	325 51.4	25.6	342 41.1	01.6	337 02.1	54.4
06	295 49.7	227 01.2	N26 35.9	340 52.1	S18 25.2	357 43.3	S21 01.6	352 04.5	S19 54.4
07	310 52.1	242 01.7	36.3	355 52.8	24.7	12 45.6	01.6	7 06.8	54.4
08	325 54.6	257 02.2	36.7	10 53.5	24.3	27 47.8	01.5	22 09.2	54.4
F 09	340 57.1	272 02.6 ..	37.0	25 54.2 ..	23.8	42 50.0 ..	01.5	37 11.6 ..	54.3
R 10	355 59.5	287 03.1	37.4	40 54.8	23.4	57 52.3	01.5	52 13.9	54.3
I 11	11 02.0	302 03.6	37.7	55 55.5	23.0	72 54.5	01.4	67 16.3	54.3
D 12	26 04.5	317 04.1	N26 38.1	70 56.2	S18 22.5	87 56.8	S21 01.4	82 18.7	S19 54.3
A 13	41 06.9	332 04.6	38.5	85 56.9	22.1	102 59.0	01.4	97 21.0	54.3
Y 14	56 09.4	347 05.1	38.8	100 57.6	21.7	118 01.3	01.3	112 23.4	54.3
15	71 11.9	2 05.6 ..	39.2	115 58.3 ..	21.2	133 03.5 ..	01.3	127 25.7 ..	54.2
16	86 14.3	17 06.2	39.5	130 59.0	20.8	148 05.8	01.3	142 28.1	54.2
17	101 16.8	32 06.7	39.9	145 59.7	20.3	163 08.0	01.2	157 30.5	54.2
18	116 19.2	47 07.2	N26 40.2	161 00.4	S18 19.9	178 10.3	S21 01.2	172 32.8	S19 54.2
19	131 21.7	62 07.7	40.6	176 01.1	19.5	193 12.5	01.2	187 35.2	54.2
20	146 24.2	77 08.2	40.9	191 01.8	19.0	208 14.8	01.1	202 37.6	54.2
21	161 26.6	92 08.7 ..	41.3	206 02.5 ..	18.6	223 17.0 ..	01.1	217 39.9 ..	54.1
22	176 29.1	107 09.2	41.6	221 03.2	18.2	238 19.3	01.1	232 42.3	54.1
23	191 31.6	122 09.7	42.0	236 03.9	17.7	253 21.5	01.0	247 44.7	54.1
Mer. Pass. 10ʰ 19.9ᵐ		v 0.5	d 0.4	v 0.7	d 0.4	v 2.2	d 0.0	v 2.4	d 0.0

STARS

Name	SHA	Dec
Acamar	315 15.1	S40 13.7
Achernar	335 23.8	S57 08.2
Acrux	173 03.5	S63 12.7
Adhara	255 08.9	S29 00.3
Aldebaran	290 44.2	N16 32.8
Alioth	166 15.9	N55 51.1
Alkaid	152 54.6	N49 12.8
Alnair	27 38.1	S46 51.7
Alnilam	275 41.8	S 1 11.6
Alphard	217 51.4	S 8 44.9
Alphecca	126 06.7	N26 38.7
Alpheratz	357 39.0	N29 11.9
Altair	62 03.7	N 8 55.2
Ankaa	353 11.4	S42 11.9
Antares	112 20.2	S26 28.5
Arcturus	145 51.1	N19 04.6
Atria	107 17.5	S69 03.5
Avior	234 16.1	S59 34.8
Bellatrix	278 27.2	N 6 21.9
Betelgeuse	270 56.4	N 7 24.5
Canopus	263 54.3	S52 42.7
Capella	280 27.8	N46 01.1
Deneb	49 28.4	N45 20.8
Denebola	182 28.6	N14 27.6
Diphda	348 51.5	S17 52.7
Dubhe	193 45.4	N61 38.7
Elnath	278 06.9	N28 37.4
Eltanin	90 43.7	N51 28.9
Enif	33 42.7	N 9 57.9
Fomalhaut	15 19.0	S29 31.0
Gacrux	171 55.2	S57 13.6
Gienah	175 47.2	S17 39.3
Hadar	148 40.6	S60 28.1
Hamal	327 55.8	N23 33.2
Kaus Aust.	83 37.4	S34 22.3
Kochab	137 18.9	N74 04.3
Markab	13 33.9	N15 18.6
Menkar	314 10.4	N 4 09.9
Menkent	148 01.7	S36 28.1
Miaplacidus	221 38.5	S69 48.3
Mirfak	308 34.1	N49 55.8
Nunki	75 52.4	S26 16.2
Peacock	53 11.9	S56 40.0
Pollux	243 22.0	N27 58.6
Procyon	244 54.9	N 5 10.2
Rasalhague	96 01.9	N12 32.6
Regulus	207 38.3	N11 52.1
Rigel	281 07.7	S 8 11.0
Rigil Kent.	139 44.8	S60 55.0
Sabik	102 06.9	S15 44.9
Schedar	349 35.8	N56 38.6
Shaula	96 15.3	S37 06.9
Sirius	258 29.7	S16 44.9
Spica	158 26.0	S11 16.0
Suhail	222 48.9	S43 31.1
Vega	80 35.7	N38 47.9
Zuben'ubi	136 59.9	S16 07.5

	SHA	Mer. Pass.
Venus	292 11.5	14ʰ 52ᵐ
Mars	45 55.6	7 18
Jupiter	62 00.3	6 13
Saturn	56 17.9	6 35

UT	SUN GHA	SUN Dec	MOON GHA	v	MOON Dec	d	HP
15 00	179 59.3	N 9 51.3	265 11.1	9.3	S23 00.3	3.5	56.1
01	194 59.5	52.2	279 39.4	9.4	22 56.8	3.7	56.1
02	209 59.6	53.1	294 07.8	9.4	22 53.1	3.7	56.1
03	224 59.8	.. 53.9	308 36.2	9.5	22 49.4	3.9	56.0
04	239 59.9	54.8	323 04.7	9.6	22 45.5	4.0	56.0
05	255 00.1	55.7	337 33.3	9.6	22 41.5	4.1	56.0
W 06	270 00.2	N 9 56.6	352 01.9	9.7	S22 37.4	4.3	55.9
E 07	285 00.4	57.5	6 30.6	9.8	22 33.1	4.3	55.9
D 08	300 00.5	58.4	20 59.4	9.9	22 28.8	4.5	55.9
N 09	315 00.7	9 59.3	35 28.3	9.9	22 24.3	4.5	55.8
E 10	330 00.8	10 00.2	49 57.2	10.0	22 19.8	4.7	55.8
S 11	345 01.0	01.1	64 26.2	10.1	22 15.1	4.8	55.8
D 12	0 01.1	N10 02.0	78 55.3	10.2	S22 10.3	4.9	55.8
A 13	15 01.3	02.8	93 24.5	10.2	22 05.4	5.0	55.7
Y 14	30 01.4	03.7	107 53.7	10.3	22 00.4	5.1	55.7
15	45 01.6	.. 04.6	122 23.0	10.4	21 55.3	5.2	55.7
16	60 01.7	05.5	136 52.4	10.4	21 50.1	5.3	55.6
17	75 01.8	06.4	151 21.8	10.5	21 44.8	5.4	55.6
18	90 02.0	N10 07.3	165 51.3	10.6	S21 39.4	5.5	55.6
19	105 02.1	08.2	180 20.9	10.7	21 33.9	5.7	55.6
20	120 02.3	09.1	194 50.6	10.8	21 28.2	5.7	55.5
21	135 02.4	.. 09.9	209 20.4	10.8	21 22.5	5.8	55.5
22	150 02.6	10.8	223 50.2	10.9	21 16.7	5.9	55.5
23	165 02.7	11.7	238 20.1	11.0	21 10.8	6.0	55.4
16 00	180 02.9	N10 12.6	252 50.1	11.0	S21 04.8	6.1	55.4
01	195 03.0	13.5	267 20.1	11.1	20 58.7	6.3	55.4
02	210 03.2	14.4	281 50.2	11.2	20 52.4	6.3	55.4
03	225 03.3	.. 15.2	296 20.4	11.3	20 46.1	6.4	55.3
04	240 03.5	16.1	310 50.7	11.3	20 39.7	6.5	55.3
05	255 03.6	17.0	325 21.0	11.5	20 33.2	6.5	55.3
T 06	270 03.8	N10 17.9	339 51.5	11.5	S20 26.7	6.7	55.3
H 07	285 03.9	18.8	354 22.0	11.5	20 20.0	6.8	55.2
U 08	300 04.0	19.7	8 52.5	11.7	20 13.2	6.9	55.2
R 09	315 04.2	.. 20.5	23 23.2	11.7	20 06.3	6.9	55.2
S 10	330 04.3	21.4	37 53.9	11.8	19 59.4	7.0	55.2
D 11	345 04.5	22.3	52 24.7	11.8	19 52.4	7.2	55.1
A 12	0 04.6	N10 23.2	66 55.5	12.0	S19 45.2	7.2	55.1
Y 13	15 04.8	24.1	81 26.5	12.0	19 38.0	7.3	55.1
14	30 04.9	25.0	95 57.5	12.1	19 30.7	7.4	55.1
15	45 05.1	.. 25.8	110 28.6	12.1	19 23.3	7.4	55.0
16	60 05.2	26.7	124 59.7	12.2	19 15.9	7.6	55.0
17	75 05.3	27.6	139 30.9	12.3	19 08.3	7.6	55.0
18	90 05.5	N10 28.5	154 02.2	12.4	S19 00.7	7.7	55.0
19	105 05.6	29.4	168 33.6	12.4	18 53.0	7.8	54.9
20	120 05.8	30.2	183 05.0	12.6	18 45.2	7.9	54.9
21	135 05.9	.. 31.1	197 36.6	12.5	18 37.3	7.9	54.9
22	150 06.1	32.0	212 08.1	12.7	18 29.4	8.1	54.9
23	165 06.2	32.9	226 39.8	12.7	18 21.3	8.1	54.9
17 00	180 06.3	N10 33.8	241 11.5	12.8	S18 13.2	8.1	54.8
01	195 06.5	34.6	255 43.3	12.9	18 05.1	8.3	54.8
02	210 06.6	35.5	270 15.2	12.9	17 56.8	8.3	54.8
03	225 06.8	.. 36.4	284 47.1	13.0	17 48.5	8.4	54.8
04	240 06.9	37.3	299 19.1	13.1	17 40.1	8.5	54.8
05	255 07.1	38.1	313 51.2	13.1	17 31.6	8.6	54.7
F 06	270 07.2	N10 39.0	328 23.3	13.2	S17 23.0	8.6	54.7
R 07	285 07.3	39.9	342 55.5	13.3	17 14.4	8.7	54.7
I 08	300 07.5	40.8	357 27.8	13.3	17 05.7	8.7	54.7
D 09	315 07.6	.. 41.6	12 00.1	13.4	16 57.0	8.8	54.7
A 10	330 07.8	42.5	26 32.5	13.4	16 48.2	8.9	54.6
Y 11	345 07.9	43.4	41 04.9	13.6	16 39.3	9.0	54.6
12	0 08.0	N10 44.3	55 37.5	13.6	S16 30.3	9.0	54.6
13	15 08.2	45.1	70 10.1	13.6	16 21.3	9.1	54.6
14	30 08.3	46.0	84 42.7	13.7	16 12.2	9.2	54.6
15	45 08.5	.. 46.9	99 15.4	13.8	16 03.0	9.2	54.6
16	60 08.6	47.8	113 48.2	13.8	15 53.8	9.3	54.5
17	75 08.7	48.6	128 21.0	13.9	15 44.5	9.3	54.5
18	90 08.9	N10 49.5	142 53.9	14.0	S15 35.2	9.4	54.5
19	105 09.0	50.4	157 26.9	14.0	15 25.8	9.5	54.5
20	120 09.2	51.2	171 59.9	14.1	15 16.3	9.5	54.5
21	135 09.3	.. 52.1	186 33.0	14.1	15 06.8	9.6	54.5
22	150 09.4	53.0	201 06.1	14.2	14 57.2	9.6	54.4
23	165 09.6	53.9	215 39.3	14.3	S14 47.6	9.7	54.4
	SD 16.0	d 0.9	SD 15.2		15.0		14.9

Lat.	Naut.	Civil	Sunrise	Moonrise 15	16	17	18
N 72	////	01 43	03 31	■■	■■	07 04	06 05
N 70	////	02 25	03 49	■■	■■	06 06	05 39
68	////	02 52	04 03		05 53	05 32	05 19
66	01 29	03 12	04 14	05 13	05 10	05 07	05 03
64	02 06	03 28	04 24	04 28	04 41	04 47	04 50
62	02 31	03 42	04 32	03 58	04 19	04 31	04 39
60	02 50	03 53	04 39	03 35	04 01	04 18	04 29
N 58	03 06	04 02	04 46	03 17	03 46	04 06	04 21
56	03 19	04 11	04 51	03 01	03 33	03 56	04 14
54	03 30	04 18	04 56	02 48	03 22	03 47	04 07
52	03 39	04 24	05 00	02 36	03 12	03 39	04 01
50	03 48	04 30	05 04	02 26	03 03	03 32	03 56
45	04 05	04 42	05 13	02 04	02 44	03 17	03 44
N 40	04 18	04 52	05 20	01 47	02 29	03 04	03 34
35	04 29	05 00	05 26	01 32	02 16	02 53	03 26
30	04 38	05 07	05 32	01 19	02 04	02 44	03 19
20	04 52	05 18	05 41	00 57	01 45	02 27	03 06
N 10	05 03	05 28	05 49	00 38	01 27	02 13	02 55
0	05 11	05 35	05 56	00 20	01 11	01 59	02 44
S 10	05 18	05 42	06 04	00 03	00 55	01 46	02 34
20	05 23	05 49	06 11	24 38	00 38	01 31	02 23
30	05 28	05 56	06 20	24 18	00 18	01 15	02 10
35	05 30	05 59	06 25	24 07	00 07	01 05	02 02
40	05 31	06 03	06 30	23 54	24 54	00 54	01 54
45	05 33	06 07	06 37	23 38	24 41	00 41	01 43
S 50	05 34	06 12	06 44	23 18	24 25	00 25	01 31
52	05 34	06 14	06 48	23 09	24 17	00 17	01 26
54	05 35	06 16	06 52	22 59	24 09	00 09	01 19
56	05 35	06 18	06 56	22 47	23 59	25 12	01 12
58	05 35	06 21	07 01	22 33	23 48	25 04	01 04
S 60	05 35	06 23	07 06	22 17	23 36	24 55	00 55

Lat.	Sunset	Civil	Naut.	Moonset 15	16	17	18
N 72	20 33	22 25	////	■■	■■	09 34	12 05
N 70	20 14	21 41	////	■■	■■	10 30	12 29
68	19 59	21 12	////	■■	09 04	11 03	12 48
66	19 47	20 50	22 38	07 59	09 46	11 27	13 02
64	19 37	20 34	21 59	08 44	10 15	11 46	13 14
62	19 29	20 20	21 32	09 14	10 36	12 01	13 24
60	19 22	20 09	21 12	09 36	10 54	12 14	13 33
N 58	19 15	19 59	20 56	09 54	11 08	12 25	13 41
56	19 10	19 50	20 43	10 09	11 21	12 34	13 47
54	19 05	19 43	20 31	10 23	11 32	12 42	13 53
52	19 00	19 36	20 22	10 34	11 41	12 50	13 58
50	18 56	19 30	20 13	10 44	11 50	12 57	14 03
45	18 47	19 18	19 56	11 05	12 08	13 11	14 13
N 40	18 40	19 08	19 42	11 22	12 22	13 23	14 22
35	18 34	19 00	19 31	11 36	12 35	13 33	14 29
30	18 28	18 53	19 22	11 49	12 46	13 41	14 36
20	18 19	18 41	19 08	12 10	13 04	13 56	14 47
N 10	18 11	18 32	18 57	12 28	13 20	14 09	14 56
0	18 03	18 24	18 48	12 45	13 35	14 21	15 05
S 10	17 56	18 17	18 42	13 02	13 50	14 33	15 14
20	17 48	18 10	18 36	13 20	14 06	14 46	15 24
30	17 39	18 03	18 31	13 41	14 24	15 01	15 34
35	17 34	18 00	18 29	13 53	14 34	15 09	15 40
40	17 28	17 56	18 27	14 07	14 46	15 19	15 47
45	17 22	17 52	18 26	14 24	15 00	15 30	15 55
S 50	17 14	17 47	18 25	14 44	15 17	15 43	16 05
52	17 11	17 45	18 24	14 53	15 25	15 49	16 09
54	17 07	17 43	18 24	15 04	15 34	15 56	16 14
56	17 02	17 40	18 23	15 16	15 44	16 04	16 20
58	16 58	17 38	18 23	15 30	15 55	16 13	16 26
S 60	16 52	17 35	18 23	15 47	16 08	16 22	16 32

	SUN			MOON			
Day	Eqn. of Time 00ʰ	12ʰ	Mer. Pass.	Mer. Pass. Upper	Lower	Age	Phase
d	m s	m s	h m	h m	h m	d	%
15	00 03	00 04	12 00	06 33	18 59	22	45
16	00 11	00 18	12 00	07 23	19 47	23	35
17	00 25	00 32	11 59	08 10	20 33	24	26

UT	ARIES	VENUS −4.7		MARS +0.6		JUPITER −2.3		SATURN +0.6		STARS		
	GHA	GHA	Dec	GHA	Dec	GHA	Dec	GHA	Dec	Name	SHA	Dec
d h	° ′	° ′	° ′	° ′	° ′	° ′	° ′	° ′	° ′		° ′	° ′
18 00	206 34.0	137 10.3	N26 42.3	251 04.6	S18 17.3	268 23.8	S21 01.0	262 47.0	S19 54.1	Acamar	315 15.1	S40 13.7
01	221 36.5	152 10.8	42.7	266 05.3	16.8	283 26.0	01.0	277 49.4	54.1	Achernar	335 23.8	S57 08.2
02	236 39.0	167 11.3	43.0	281 06.0	16.4	298 28.3	00.9	292 51.8	54.1	Acrux	173 03.5	S63 12.7
03	251 41.4	182 11.8 . .	43.3	296 06.7 . .	16.0	313 30.5 . .	00.9	307 54.1 . .	54.0	Adhara	255 09.0	S29 00.3
04	266 43.9	197 12.4	43.7	311 07.3	15.5	328 32.8	00.9	322 56.5	54.0	Aldebaran	290 44.3	N16 32.8
05	281 46.3	212 12.9	44.0	326 08.0	15.1	343 35.0	00.8	337 58.9	54.0			
06	296 48.8	227 13.4	N26 44.4	341 08.7	S18 14.6	358 37.3	S21 00.8	353 01.2	S19 54.0	Alioth	166 15.9	N55 51.1
07	311 51.3	242 13.9	44.7	356 09.4	14.2	13 39.5	00.8	8 03.6	54.0	Alkaid	152 54.6	N49 12.8
S 08	326 53.7	257 14.5	45.1	11 10.1	13.8	28 41.8	00.8	23 06.0	54.0	Alnair	27 38.0	S46 51.7
A 09	341 56.2	272 15.0 . .	45.4	26 10.8 . .	13.3	43 44.1 . .	00.7	38 08.3 . .	53.9	Alnilam	275 41.8	S 1 11.6
T 10	356 58.7	287 15.5	45.7	41 11.5	12.9	58 46.3	00.7	53 10.7	53.9	Alphard	217 51.4	S 8 44.9
U 11	12 01.1	302 16.1	46.1	56 12.2	12.4	73 48.6	00.7	68 13.1	53.9			
R 12	27 03.6	317 16.6	N26 46.4	71 12.9	S18 12.0	88 50.8	S21 00.6	83 15.5	S19 53.9	Alphecca	126 06.7	N26 38.8
D 13	42 06.1	332 17.2	46.7	86 13.6	11.5	103 53.1	00.6	98 17.8	53.9	Alpheratz	357 39.0	N29 11.8
A 14	57 08.5	347 17.7	47.1	101 14.3	11.1	118 55.3	00.6	113 20.2	53.9	Altair	62 03.6	N 8 55.2
Y 15	72 11.0	2 18.3 . .	47.4	116 15.0 . .	10.7	133 57.6 . .	00.5	128 22.6 . .	53.8	Ankaa	353 11.4	S42 11.9
16	87 13.5	17 18.8	47.7	131 15.7	10.2	148 59.8	00.5	143 24.9	53.8	Antares	112 20.2	S26 28.5
17	102 15.9	32 19.4	48.1	146 16.4	09.8	164 02.1	00.5	158 27.3	53.8			
18	117 18.4	47 19.9	N26 48.4	161 17.1	S18 09.3	179 04.3	S21 00.4	173 29.7	S19 53.8	Arcturus	145 51.1	N19 04.6
19	132 20.8	62 20.5	48.7	176 17.8	08.9	194 06.6	00.4	188 32.0	53.8	Atria	107 17.4	S69 03.5
20	147 23.3	77 21.0	49.1	191 18.5	08.4	209 08.9	00.4	203 34.4	53.8	Avior	234 16.1	S59 34.8
21	162 25.8	92 21.6 . .	49.4	206 19.2 . .	08.0	224 11.1 . .	00.3	218 36.8 . .	53.7	Bellatrix	278 27.2	N 6 21.9
22	177 28.2	107 22.1	49.7	221 19.9	07.5	239 13.4	00.3	233 39.2	53.7	Betelgeuse	270 56.4	N 7 24.5
23	192 30.7	122 22.7	50.0	236 20.6	07.1	254 15.6	00.3	248 41.5	53.7			
19 00	207 33.2	137 23.3	N26 50.4	251 21.3	S18 06.7	269 17.9	S21 00.2	263 43.9	S19 53.7	Canopus	263 54.3	S52 42.7
01	222 35.6	152 23.8	50.7	266 22.0	06.2	284 20.2	00.2	278 46.3	53.7	Capella	280 27.8	N46 01.1
02	237 38.1	167 24.4	51.0	281 22.7	05.8	299 22.4	00.2	293 48.6	53.7	Deneb	49 28.4	N45 20.8
03	252 40.6	182 25.0 . .	51.3	296 23.4 . .	05.3	314 24.7 . .	00.2	308 51.0 . .	53.6	Denebola	182 28.6	N14 27.6
04	267 43.0	197 25.5	51.7	311 24.1	04.9	329 26.9	00.1	323 53.4	53.6	Diphda	348 51.5	S17 52.7
05	282 45.5	212 26.1	52.0	326 24.8	04.4	344 29.2	00.1	338 55.7	53.6			
06	297 48.0	227 26.7	N26 52.3	341 25.5	S18 04.0	359 31.5	S21 00.1	353 58.1	S19 53.6	Dubhe	193 45.4	N61 38.7
07	312 50.4	242 27.2	52.6	356 26.2	03.5	14 33.7	00.0	9 00.5	53.6	Elnath	278 06.9	N28 37.4
S 08	327 52.9	257 27.8	52.9	11 26.9	03.1	29 36.0	00.0	24 02.9	53.6	Eltanin	90 43.7	N51 28.9
U 09	342 55.3	272 28.4 . .	53.2	26 27.6 . .	02.6	44 38.2	21 00.0	39 05.2 . .	53.5	Enif	33 42.7	N 9 57.9
N 10	357 57.8	287 29.0	53.6	41 28.3	02.2	59 40.5	20 59.9	54 07.6	53.5	Fomalhaut	15 19.0	S29 31.0
D 11	13 00.3	302 29.6	53.9	56 29.0	01.7	74 42.8	59.9	69 10.0	53.5			
A 12	28 02.7	317 30.2	N26 54.2	71 29.7	S18 01.3	89 45.0	S20 59.9	84 12.4	S19 53.5	Gacrux	171 55.2	S57 13.6
Y 13	43 05.2	332 30.7	54.5	86 30.4	00.8	104 47.3	59.8	99 14.7	53.5	Gienah	175 47.2	S17 39.3
14	58 07.7	347 31.3	54.8	101 31.1	18 00.4	119 49.5	59.8	114 17.1	53.5	Hadar	148 40.6	S60 28.1
15	73 10.1	2 31.9 . .	55.1	116 31.8	17 59.9	134 51.8 . .	59.8	129 19.5 . .	53.4	Hamal	327 55.8	N23 33.2
16	88 12.6	17 32.5	55.4	131 32.5	59.5	149 54.1	59.8	144 21.8	53.4	Kaus Aust.	83 37.4	S34 22.3
17	103 15.1	32 33.1	55.7	146 33.2	59.1	164 56.3	59.7	159 24.2	53.4			
18	118 17.5	47 33.7	N26 56.1	161 33.9	S17 58.6	179 58.6	S20 59.7	174 26.6	S19 53.4	Kochab	137 18.9	N74 04.3
19	133 20.0	62 34.3	56.4	176 34.6	58.2	195 00.9	59.7	189 29.0	53.4	Markab	13 33.9	N15 18.6
20	148 22.4	77 34.9	56.7	191 35.3	57.7	210 03.1	59.6	204 31.3	53.4	Menkar	314 10.4	N 4 09.9
21	163 24.9	92 35.5 . .	57.0	206 36.0 . .	57.3	225 05.4 . .	59.6	219 33.7 . .	53.4	Menkent	148 01.7	S36 28.1
22	178 27.4	107 36.1	57.3	221 36.7	56.8	240 07.7	59.6	234 36.1	53.3	Miaplacidus	221 38.6	S69 48.3
23	193 29.8	122 36.7	57.6	236 37.4	56.4	255 09.9	59.5	249 38.5	53.3			
20 00	208 32.3	137 37.3	N26 57.9	251 38.1	S17 55.9	270 12.2	S20 59.5	264 40.8	S19 53.3	Mirfak	308 34.1	N49 55.8
01	223 34.8	152 37.9	58.2	266 38.8	55.4	285 14.5	59.5	279 43.2	53.3	Nunki	75 52.4	S26 16.2
02	238 37.2	167 38.5	58.5	281 39.5	55.0	300 16.7	59.5	294 45.6	53.3	Peacock	53 11.9	S56 40.0
03	253 39.7	182 39.2 . .	58.8	296 40.2 . .	54.5	315 19.0 . .	59.4	309 48.0 . .	53.3	Pollux	243 22.0	N27 58.6
04	268 42.2	197 39.8	59.1	311 40.9	54.1	330 21.3	59.4	324 50.3	53.2	Procyon	244 54.9	N 5 10.3
05	283 44.6	212 40.4	59.4	326 41.6	53.6	345 23.5	59.4	339 52.7	53.2			
06	298 47.1	227 41.0	N26 59.7	341 42.3	S17 53.2	0 25.8	S20 59.3	354 55.1	S19 53.2	Rasalhague	96 01.9	N12 32.6
07	313 49.6	242 41.6	27 00.0	356 43.1	52.7	15 28.1	59.3	9 57.5	53.2	Regulus	207 38.4	N11 52.1
08	328 52.0	257 42.2	00.3	11 43.8	52.3	30 30.3	59.3	24 59.8	53.2	Rigel	281 07.8	S 8 10.9
M 09	343 54.5	272 42.9 . .	00.6	26 44.5 . .	51.8	45 32.6 . .	59.3	40 02.2 . .	53.2	Rigil Kent.	139 44.8	S60 55.0
O 10	358 56.9	287 43.5	00.9	41 45.2	51.4	60 34.9	59.2	55 04.6	53.2	Sabik	102 06.9	S15 44.9
N 11	13 59.4	302 44.1	01.2	56 45.9	50.9	75 37.1	59.2	70 07.0	53.1			
D 12	29 01.9	317 44.8	N27 01.5	71 46.6	S17 50.5	90 39.4	S20 59.2	85 09.3	S19 53.1	Schedar	349 35.8	N56 38.6
A 13	44 04.3	332 45.4	01.8	86 47.3	50.0	105 41.7	59.1	100 11.7	53.1	Shaula	96 15.3	S37 06.9
Y 14	59 06.8	347 46.0	02.0	101 48.0	49.6	120 43.9	59.1	115 14.1	53.1	Sirius	258 29.7	S16 44.9
15	74 09.3	2 46.7 . .	02.3	116 48.7 . .	49.1	135 46.2 . .	59.1	130 16.5 . .	53.1	Spica	158 26.0	S11 16.0
16	89 11.7	17 47.3	02.6	131 49.4	48.7	150 48.5	59.1	145 18.9	53.1	Suhail	222 48.9	S43 31.1
17	104 14.2	32 48.0	02.9	146 50.1	48.2	165 50.8	59.0	160 21.2	53.1			
18	119 16.7	47 48.6	N27 03.2	161 50.8	S17 47.7	180 53.0	S20 59.0	175 23.6	S19 53.0	Vega	80 35.6	N38 47.9
19	134 19.1	62 49.2	03.5	176 51.5	47.3	195 55.3	59.0	190 26.0	53.0	Zuben'ubi	136 59.9	S16 07.5
20	149 21.6	77 49.9	03.8	191 52.2	46.8	210 57.6	58.9	205 28.4	53.0		SHA	Mer. Pass.
21	164 24.0	92 50.5 . .	04.1	206 52.9 . .	46.4	225 59.8 . .	58.9	220 30.7 . .	53.0		° ′	h m
22	179 26.5	107 51.2	04.3	221 53.6	45.9	241 02.1	58.9	235 33.1	53.0	Venus	289 50.1	14 50
23	194 29.0	122 51.8	04.6	236 54.3	45.5	256 04.4	58.9	250 35.5	53.0	Mars	43 48.1	7 14
	h m									Jupiter	61 44.7	6 02
Mer. Pass. 10 08.1		v 0.6	d 0.3	v 0.7	d 0.4	v 2.3	d 0.0	v 2.4	d 0.0	Saturn	56 10.7	6 24

UT	SUN GHA	SUN Dec	MOON GHA	v	MOON Dec	d	HP
d h	° ′	° ′	° ′	′	° ′	′	′
18 00	180 09.7	N10 54.7	230 12.6	14.3	S14 37.9	9.8	54.4
01	195 09.9	55.6	244 45.9	14.3	14 28.1	9.8	54.4
02	210 10.0	56.5	259 19.2	14.5	14 18.3	9.8	54.4
03	225 10.1	.. 57.3	273 52.7	14.4	14 08.5	10.0	54.4
04	240 10.3	58.2	288 26.1	14.6	13 58.5	9.9	54.4
05	255 10.4	10 59.1	302 59.7	14.5	13 48.6	10.1	54.3
06	270 10.5	N11 00.0	317 33.2	14.7	S13 38.5	10.0	54.3
07	285 10.7	00.8	332 06.9	14.7	13 28.5	10.2	54.3
S 08	300 10.8	01.7	346 40.6	14.7	13 18.3	10.1	54.3
A 09	315 10.9	.. 02.6	1 14.3	14.8	13 08.2	10.3	54.3
T 10	330 11.1	03.4	15 48.1	14.8	12 57.9	10.2	54.3
U 11	345 11.2	04.3	30 21.9	14.9	12 47.7	10.4	54.3
R 12	0 11.4	N11 05.2	44 55.8	14.9	S12 37.3	10.3	54.3
D 13	15 11.5	06.0	59 29.7	15.0	12 27.0	10.4	54.2
A 14	30 11.6	06.9	74 03.7	15.0	12 16.6	10.5	54.2
Y 15	45 11.8	.. 07.8	88 37.7	15.1	12 06.1	10.5	54.2
16	60 11.9	08.6	103 11.8	15.1	11 55.6	10.6	54.2
17	75 12.0	09.5	117 45.9	15.2	11 45.0	10.6	54.2
18	90 12.2	N11 10.4	132 20.1	15.2	S11 34.4	10.6	54.2
19	105 12.3	11.2	146 54.3	15.3	11 23.8	10.7	54.2
20	120 12.4	12.1	161 28.6	15.3	11 13.1	10.7	54.2
21	135 12.6	.. 12.9	176 02.9	15.3	11 02.4	10.8	54.2
22	150 12.7	13.8	190 37.2	15.4	10 51.6	10.8	54.1
23	165 12.8	14.7	205 11.6	15.4	10 40.8	10.8	54.1
19 00	180 13.0	N11 15.5	219 46.0	15.5	S10 30.0	10.9	54.1
01	195 13.1	16.4	234 20.5	15.5	10 19.1	10.9	54.1
02	210 13.2	17.3	248 55.0	15.5	10 08.2	11.0	54.1
03	225 13.4	.. 18.1	263 29.5	15.6	9 57.2	11.0	54.1
04	240 13.5	19.0	278 04.1	15.6	9 46.2	11.0	54.1
05	255 13.6	19.8	292 38.7	15.6	9 35.2	11.0	54.1
06	270 13.8	N11 20.7	307 13.3	15.7	S 9 24.2	11.1	54.1
07	285 13.9	21.6	321 48.0	15.7	9 13.1	11.2	54.1
S 08	300 14.0	22.4	336 22.7	15.8	9 01.9	11.1	54.1
U 09	315 14.2	.. 23.3	350 57.5	15.7	8 50.8	11.2	54.1
N 10	330 14.3	24.2	5 32.2	15.9	8 39.6	11.3	54.1
D 11	345 14.4	25.0	20 07.1	15.8	8 28.3	11.2	54.0
A 12	0 14.6	N11 25.9	34 41.9	15.9	S 8 17.1	11.3	54.0
Y 13	15 14.7	26.7	49 16.8	15.9	8 05.8	11.3	54.0
14	30 14.8	27.6	63 51.7	15.9	7 54.5	11.4	54.0
15	45 15.0	.. 28.4	78 26.6	16.0	7 43.1	11.4	54.0
16	60 15.1	29.3	93 01.6	16.0	7 31.7	11.4	54.0
17	75 15.2	30.2	107 36.6	16.0	7 20.3	11.4	54.0
18	90 15.4	N11 31.0	122 11.6	16.0	S 7 08.9	11.4	54.0
19	105 15.5	31.9	136 46.6	16.1	6 57.5	11.5	54.0
20	120 15.6	32.7	151 21.7	16.1	6 46.0	11.5	54.0
21	135 15.7	.. 33.6	165 56.8	16.1	6 34.5	11.6	54.0
22	150 15.9	34.4	180 31.9	16.1	6 22.9	11.5	54.0
23	165 16.0	35.3	195 07.0	16.2	6 11.4	11.6	54.0
20 00	180 16.1	N11 36.2	209 42.2	16.2	S 5 59.8	11.6	54.0
01	195 16.3	37.0	224 17.4	16.2	5 48.2	11.6	54.0
02	210 16.4	37.9	238 52.6	16.2	5 36.6	11.7	54.0
03	225 16.5	.. 38.7	253 27.8	16.2	5 24.9	11.6	54.0
04	240 16.7	39.6	268 03.0	16.3	5 13.3	11.7	54.0
05	255 16.8	40.4	282 38.3	16.3	5 01.6	11.7	54.0
06	270 16.9	N11 41.3	297 13.6	16.2	S 4 49.9	11.7	54.0
07	285 17.0	42.1	311 48.8	16.3	4 38.2	11.8	54.0
08	300 17.2	43.0	326 24.1	16.4	4 26.4	11.7	54.0
M 09	315 17.3	.. 43.8	340 59.5	16.3	4 14.7	11.8	54.0
O 10	330 17.4	44.7	355 34.8	16.3	4 02.9	11.8	54.0
N 11	345 17.5	45.5	10 10.1	16.4	3 51.1	11.8	54.0
D 12	0 17.7	N11 46.4	24 45.5	16.3	S 3 39.3	11.8	54.0
A 13	15 17.8	47.2	39 20.9	16.3	3 27.5	11.8	54.0
Y 14	30 17.9	48.1	53 56.2	16.4	3 15.7	11.9	53.9
15	45 18.1	.. 48.9	68 31.6	16.4	3 03.8	11.9	53.9
16	60 18.2	49.8	83 07.0	16.4	2 52.0	11.9	53.9
17	75 18.3	50.6	97 42.4	16.4	2 40.1	11.8	53.9
18	90 18.4	N11 51.5	112 17.8	16.5	S 2 28.3	11.9	53.9
19	105 18.6	52.3	126 53.3	16.4	2 16.4	11.9	53.9
20	120 18.7	53.2	141 28.7	16.4	2 04.5	11.9	53.9
21	135 18.8	.. 54.0	156 04.1	16.5	1 52.6	11.9	53.9
22	150 18.9	54.9	170 39.6	16.4	1 40.7	12.0	53.9
23	165 19.1	55.7	185 15.0	16.4	S 1 28.7	11.9	53.9
	SD 15.9	d 0.9	SD 14.8		14.7		14.7

Lat.	Twilight Naut.	Twilight Civil	Sunrise	Moonrise 18	19	20	21
°	h m	h m	h m	h m	h m	h m	h m
N 72	////	01 05	03 13	06 05	05 35	05 13	04 54
N 70	////	02 02	03 34	05 39	05 21	05 06	04 53
68	////	02 34	03 50	05 19	05 09	05 01	04 53
66	00 56	02 58	04 03	05 03	05 00	04 56	04 52
64	01 46	03 16	04 14	04 50	04 51	04 52	04 52
62	02 16	03 31	04 23	04 39	04 44	04 48	04 52
60	02 38	03 43	04 31	04 29	04 38	04 45	04 51
N 58	02 55	03 53	04 38	04 21	04 33	04 42	04 51
56	03 09	04 02	04 44	04 14	04 28	04 40	04 51
54	03 21	04 10	04 49	04 07	04 23	04 38	04 51
52	03 32	04 17	04 54	04 01	04 19	04 36	04 51
50	03 41	04 24	04 58	03 56	04 16	04 34	04 51
45	03 59	04 37	05 08	03 44	04 08	04 30	04 50
N 40	04 13	04 48	05 16	03 34	04 01	04 26	04 50
35	04 25	04 56	05 23	03 26	03 55	04 23	04 50
30	04 35	05 04	05 29	03 19	03 51	04 21	04 50
20	04 50	05 16	05 39	03 06	03 42	04 16	04 49
N 10	05 01	05 26	05 48	02 55	03 34	04 12	04 49
0	05 10	05 35	05 56	02 44	03 27	04 08	04 49
S 10	05 18	05 42	06 04	02 34	03 20	04 05	04 49
20	05 24	05 50	06 12	02 23	03 12	04 01	04 48
30	05 29	05 57	06 22	02 10	03 03	03 56	04 48
35	05 32	06 01	06 27	02 02	02 58	03 53	04 48
40	05 34	06 06	06 33	01 54	02 52	03 50	04 48
45	05 36	06 11	06 41	01 43	02 46	03 47	04 48
S 50	05 38	06 16	06 49	01 31	02 37	03 43	04 47
52	05 39	06 18	06 53	01 26	02 34	03 41	04 47
54	05 40	06 21	06 57	01 19	02 29	03 39	04 47
56	05 40	06 24	07 02	01 12	02 25	03 36	04 47
58	05 41	06 27	07 07	01 04	02 20	03 34	04 47
S 60	05 41	06 30	07 13	00 55	02 14	03 31	04 47

Lat.	Sunset	Twilight Civil	Twilight Naut.	Moonset 18	19	20	21
°	h m	h m	h m	h m	h m	h m	h m
N 72	20 50	23 09	////	12 05	14 02	15 50	17 36
N 70	20 28	22 03	////	12 29	14 15	15 55	17 33
68	20 11	21 28	////	12 48	14 25	15 58	17 30
66	19 58	21 04	23 16	13 02	14 33	16 01	17 28
64	19 47	20 45	22 18	13 14	14 40	16 03	17 26
62	19 37	20 30	21 46	13 24	14 46	16 05	17 25
60	19 29	20 17	21 24	13 33	14 51	16 07	17 24
N 58	19 22	20 07	21 06	13 41	14 55	16 09	17 22
56	19 16	19 57	20 51	13 47	14 59	16 10	17 21
54	19 10	19 49	20 39	13 53	15 03	16 12	17 20
52	19 05	19 42	20 28	13 58	15 06	16 13	17 20
50	19 01	19 36	20 19	14 03	15 09	16 14	17 19
45	18 51	19 22	20 00	14 13	15 15	16 16	17 17
N 40	18 43	19 11	19 46	14 22	15 20	16 18	17 16
35	18 36	19 02	19 34	14 29	15 25	16 20	17 15
30	18 30	18 55	19 24	14 36	15 29	16 21	17 13
20	18 20	18 42	19 09	14 47	15 36	16 24	17 12
N 10	18 11	18 32	18 57	14 56	15 42	16 26	17 10
0	18 02	18 23	18 48	15 05	15 47	16 28	17 08
S 10	17 54	18 16	18 40	15 14	15 53	16 30	17 07
20	17 46	18 08	18 34	15 24	15 59	16 32	17 05
30	17 36	18 00	18 28	15 34	16 05	16 34	17 03
35	17 30	17 56	18 26	15 40	16 09	16 36	17 02
40	17 24	17 52	18 23	15 47	16 13	16 37	17 01
45	17 17	17 47	18 21	15 55	16 18	16 39	17 00
S 50	17 08	17 41	18 19	16 05	16 24	16 41	16 59
52	17 04	17 39	18 18	16 09	16 27	16 42	16 57
54	17 00	17 36	18 17	16 14	16 30	16 43	16 56
56	16 55	17 33	18 17	16 20	16 33	16 44	16 55
58	16 50	17 30	18 16	16 26	16 36	16 46	16 54
S 60	16 44	17 27	18 15	16 32	16 40	16 47	16 53

	SUN			MOON			
Day	Eqn. of Time 00h	12h	Mer. Pass.	Mer. Pass. Upper	Lower	Age	Phase
d	m s	m s	h m	h m	h m	d	%
18	00 39	00 45	11 59	08 55	21 16	25	18
19	00 52	00 58	11 59	09 37	21 58	26	11
20	01 04	01 10	11 59	10 18	22 38	27	6

2020 APRIL 21, 22, 23 (TUES., WED., THURS.)

UT	ARIES	VENUS −4·7		MARS +0·5		JUPITER −2·3		SATURN +0·6		STARS		
	GHA	GHA	Dec	GHA	Dec	GHA	Dec	GHA	Dec	Name	SHA	Dec
d h	° ′	° ′	° ′	° ′	° ′	° ′	° ′	° ′	° ′		° ′	° ′
21 00	209 31.4	137 52.5	N27 04.9	251 55.0	S17 45.0	271 06.7	S20 58.8	265 37.9	S19 53.0	Acamar	315 15.2	S40 13.7
01	224 33.9	152 53.2	05.2	266 55.8	44.6	286 08.9	58.8	280 40.3	52.9	Achernar	335 23.8	S57 08.2
02	239 36.4	167 53.8	05.5	281 56.5	44.1	301 11.2	58.8	295 42.6	52.9	Acrux	173 03.5	S63 12.8
03	254 38.8	182 54.5	.. 05.7	296 57.2	.. 43.6	316 13.5	.. 58.7	310 45.0	.. 52.9	Adhara	255 09.0	S29 00.3
04	269 41.3	197 55.1	06.0	311 57.9	43.2	331 15.8	58.7	325 47.4	52.9	Aldebaran	290 44.3	N16 32.8
05	284 43.8	212 55.8	06.3	326 58.6	42.7	346 18.0	58.7	340 49.8	52.9			
06	299 46.2	227 56.5	N27 06.6	341 59.3	S17 42.3	1 20.3	S20 58.6	355 52.2	S19 52.9	Alioth	166 15.9	N55 51.1
07	314 48.7	242 57.1	06.8	357 00.0	41.8	16 22.6	58.6	10 54.5	52.9	Alkaid	152 54.6	N49 12.8
08	329 51.2	257 57.8	07.1	12 00.7	41.4	31 24.9	58.6	25 56.9	52.8	Alnair	27 38.0	S46 51.7
09	344 53.6	272 58.5	.. 07.4	27 01.4	.. 40.9	46 27.1	.. 58.5	40 59.3	.. 52.8	Alnilam	275 41.8	S 1 11.6
10	359 56.1	287 59.2	07.7	42 02.1	40.4	61 29.4	58.5	56 01.7	52.8	Alphard	217 51.4	S 8 44.9
11	14 58.5	302 59.8	07.9	57 02.8	40.0	76 31.7	58.5	71 04.1	52.8			
12	30 01.0	318 00.5	N27 08.2	72 03.5	S17 39.5	91 34.0	S20 58.5	86 06.4	S19 52.8	Alphecca	126 06.7	N26 38.8
13	45 03.5	333 01.2	08.5	87 04.3	39.1	106 36.2	58.5	101 08.8	52.8	Alpheratz	357 39.0	N29 11.8
14	60 05.9	348 01.9	08.7	102 05.0	38.6	121 38.5	58.4	116 11.2	52.8	Altair	62 03.6	N 8 55.2
15	75 08.4	3 02.6	.. 09.0	117 05.7	.. 38.1	136 40.8	.. 58.4	131 13.6	.. 52.7	Ankaa	353 11.4	S42 11.8
16	90 10.9	18 03.3	09.3	132 06.4	37.7	151 43.1	58.4	146 16.0	52.7	Antares	112 20.2	S26 28.5
17	105 13.3	33 04.0	09.6	147 07.1	37.2	166 45.4	58.3	161 18.3	52.7			
18	120 15.8	48 04.7	N27 09.8	162 07.8	S17 36.8	181 47.6	S20 58.3	176 20.7	S19 52.7	Arcturus	145 51.1	N19 04.6
19	135 18.3	63 05.3	10.1	177 08.5	36.3	196 49.9	58.3	191 23.1	52.7	Atria	107 17.4	S69 03.5
20	150 20.7	78 06.0	10.3	192 09.2	35.8	211 52.2	58.3	206 25.5	52.7	Avior	234 16.2	S59 34.8
21	165 23.2	93 06.7	.. 10.6	207 09.9	.. 35.4	226 54.5	.. 58.2	221 27.9	.. 52.7	Bellatrix	278 27.2	N 6 21.9
22	180 25.6	108 07.4	10.9	222 10.7	34.9	241 56.8	58.2	236 30.3	52.6	Betelgeuse	270 56.4	N 7 24.5
23	195 28.1	123 08.2	11.1	237 11.4	34.5	256 59.0	58.2	251 32.6	52.6			
22 00	210 30.6	138 08.9	N27 11.4	252 12.1	S17 34.0	272 01.3	S20 58.2	266 35.0	S19 52.6	Canopus	263 54.3	S52 42.7
01	225 33.0	153 09.6	11.6	267 12.8	33.5	287 03.6	58.1	281 37.4	52.6	Capella	280 27.8	N46 01.0
02	240 35.5	168 10.3	11.9	282 13.5	33.1	302 05.9	58.1	296 39.8	52.6	Deneb	49 28.4	N45 20.8
03	255 38.0	183 11.0	.. 12.2	297 14.2	.. 32.6	317 08.2	.. 58.1	311 42.2	.. 52.6	Denebola	182 28.6	N14 27.6
04	270 40.4	198 11.7	12.4	312 14.9	32.2	332 10.5	58.0	326 44.6	52.6	Diphda	348 51.5	S17 52.7
05	285 42.9	213 12.4	12.7	327 15.6	31.7	347 12.7	58.0	341 46.9	52.5			
06	300 45.4	228 13.1	N27 12.9	342 16.3	S17 31.2	2 15.0	S20 58.0	356 49.3	S19 52.5	Dubhe	193 45.4	N61 38.7
07	315 47.8	243 13.9	13.2	357 17.1	30.8	17 17.3	58.0	11 51.7	52.5	Elnath	278 06.9	N28 37.4
08	330 50.3	258 14.6	13.4	12 17.8	30.3	32 19.6	57.9	26 54.1	52.5	Eltanin	90 43.7	N51 29.0
09	345 52.8	273 15.3	.. 13.7	27 18.5	.. 29.8	47 21.9	.. 57.9	41 56.5	.. 52.5	Enif	33 42.6	N 9 57.9
10	0 55.2	288 16.0	13.9	42 19.2	29.4	62 24.2	57.9	56 58.9	52.5	Fomalhaut	15 19.0	S29 30.9
11	15 57.7	303 16.8	14.2	57 19.9	28.9	77 26.4	57.9	72 01.2	52.5			
12	31 00.1	318 17.5	N27 14.4	72 20.6	S17 28.5	92 28.7	S20 57.8	87 03.6	S19 52.5	Gacrux	171 55.2	S57 13.7
13	46 02.6	333 18.2	14.7	87 21.3	28.0	107 31.0	57.8	102 06.0	52.4	Gienah	175 47.2	S17 39.3
14	61 05.1	348 19.0	14.9	102 22.0	27.5	122 33.3	57.8	117 08.4	52.4	Hadar	148 40.6	S60 28.2
15	76 07.5	3 19.7	.. 15.2	117 22.8	.. 27.1	137 35.6	.. 57.8	132 10.8	.. 52.4	Hamal	327 55.8	N23 33.2
16	91 10.0	18 20.4	15.4	132 23.5	26.6	152 37.9	57.7	147 13.2	52.4	Kaus Aust.	83 37.4	S34 22.3
17	106 12.5	33 21.2	15.7	147 24.2	26.1	167 40.2	57.7	162 15.6	52.4			
18	121 14.9	48 21.9	N27 15.9	162 24.9	S17 25.7	182 42.4	S20 57.7	177 17.9	S19 52.4	Kochab	137 18.8	N74 04.4
19	136 17.4	63 22.7	16.2	177 25.6	25.2	197 44.7	57.7	192 20.3	52.4	Markab	13 33.9	N15 18.6
20	151 19.9	78 23.4	16.4	192 26.3	24.7	212 47.0	57.6	207 22.7	52.4	Menkar	314 10.5	N 4 09.9
21	166 22.3	93 24.2	.. 16.6	207 27.0	.. 24.3	227 49.3	.. 57.6	222 25.1	.. 52.3	Menkent	148 01.7	S36 28.1
22	181 24.8	108 24.9	16.9	222 27.8	23.8	242 51.6	57.6	237 27.5	52.3	Miaplacidus	221 38.6	S69 48.3
23	196 27.3	123 25.7	17.1	237 28.5	23.3	257 53.9	57.5	252 29.9	52.3			
23 00	211 29.7	138 26.5	N27 17.4	252 29.2	S17 22.9	272 56.2	S20 57.5	267 32.3	S19 52.3	Mirfak	308 34.1	N49 55.8
01	226 32.2	153 27.2	17.6	267 29.9	22.4	287 58.5	57.5	282 34.7	52.3	Nunki	75 52.4	S26 16.2
02	241 34.6	168 28.0	17.8	282 30.6	21.9	303 00.7	57.5	297 37.0	52.3	Peacock	53 11.8	S56 40.0
03	256 37.1	183 28.7	.. 18.1	297 31.3	.. 21.5	318 03.0	.. 57.4	312 39.4	.. 52.3	Pollux	243 22.1	N27 58.6
04	271 39.6	198 29.5	18.3	312 32.1	21.0	333 05.3	57.4	327 41.8	52.2	Procyon	244 54.9	N 5 10.3
05	286 42.0	213 30.3	18.5	327 32.8	20.5	348 07.6	57.4	342 44.2	52.2			
06	301 44.5	228 31.1	N27 18.8	342 33.5	S17 20.1	3 09.9	S20 57.4	357 46.6	S19 52.2	Rasalhague	96 01.9	N12 32.6
07	316 47.0	243 31.8	19.0	357 34.2	19.6	18 12.2	57.3	12 49.0	52.2	Regulus	207 38.4	N11 52.1
08	331 49.4	258 32.6	19.2	12 34.9	19.1	33 14.5	57.3	27 51.4	52.2	Rigel	281 07.8	S 8 10.9
09	346 51.9	273 33.4	.. 19.5	27 35.6	.. 18.7	48 16.8	.. 57.3	42 53.8	.. 52.2	Rigil Kent.	139 44.8	S60 55.0
10	1 54.4	288 34.2	19.7	42 36.4	18.2	63 19.1	57.3	57 56.1	52.2	Sabik	102 06.9	S15 44.9
11	16 56.8	303 34.9	19.9	57 37.1	17.7	78 21.4	57.2	72 58.5	52.2			
12	31 59.3	318 35.7	N27 20.2	72 37.8	S17 17.3	93 23.7	S20 57.2	88 00.9	S19 52.1	Schedar	349 35.8	N56 38.6
13	47 01.7	333 36.5	20.4	87 38.5	16.8	108 25.9	57.2	103 03.3	52.1	Shaula	96 15.3	S37 06.9
14	62 04.2	348 37.3	20.6	102 39.2	16.3	123 28.2	57.2	118 05.7	52.1	Sirius	258 29.7	S16 44.9
15	77 06.7	3 38.1	.. 20.8	117 39.9	.. 15.8	138 30.5	.. 57.1	133 08.1	.. 52.1	Spica	158 26.0	S11 16.0
16	92 09.1	18 38.9	21.1	132 40.7	15.4	153 32.8	57.1	148 10.5	52.1	Suhail	222 48.9	S43 31.1
17	107 11.6	33 39.7	21.3	147 41.4	14.9	168 35.1	57.1	163 12.9	52.1			
18	122 14.1	48 40.5	N27 21.5	162 42.1	S17 14.4	183 37.4	S20 57.1	178 15.3	S19 52.1	Vega	80 35.6	N38 47.9
19	137 16.5	63 41.3	21.7	177 42.8	14.0	198 39.7	57.0	193 17.7	52.1	Zuben'ubi	136 59.9	S16 07.5
20	152 19.0	78 42.1	21.9	192 43.5	13.5	213 42.0	57.0	208 20.0	52.1		SHA	Mer. Pass.
21	167 21.5	93 42.9	.. 22.2	207 44.3	.. 13.0	228 44.3	.. 57.0	223 22.4	.. 52.0		° ′	h m
22	182 23.9	108 43.7	22.4	222 45.0	12.6	243 46.6	57.0	238 24.8	52.0	Venus	287 38.3	14 47
23	197 26.4	123 44.5	22.6	237 45.7	12.1	258 48.9	56.9	253 27.2	52.0	Mars	41 41.5	7 11
Mer. Pass. h m 9 56.3		v 0.7	d 0.2	v 0.7	d 0.5	v 2.3	d 0.0	v 2.4	d 0.0	Jupiter	61 30.7	5 51
										Saturn	56 04.4	6 13

UT	SUN GHA	SUN Dec	MOON GHA	v	MOON Dec	d	HP
d h	° ′	° ′	° ′	′	° ′	′	′
21 00	180 19.2	N11 56.6	199 50.4	16.5	S 1 16.8	11.9	53.9
01	195 19.3	57.4	214 25.9	16.4	1 04.9	12.0	54.0
02	210 19.4	58.3	229 01.3	16.5	0 52.9	11.9	54.0
03	225 19.6	11 59.1	243 36.8	16.4	0 41.0	11.9	54.0
04	240 19.7	12 00.0	258 12.2	16.4	0 29.1	12.0	54.0
05	255 19.8	00.8	272 47.6	16.5	0 17.1	12.0	54.0
06	270 19.9	N12 01.7	287 23.1	16.4	S 0 05.1	11.9	54.0
07	285 20.1	02.5	301 58.5	16.4	N 0 06.8	12.0	54.0
08	300 20.2	03.4	316 33.9	16.5	0 18.8	11.9	54.0
09	315 20.3 ..	04.2	331 09.4	16.4	0 30.7	12.0	54.0
10	330 20.4	05.0	345 44.8	16.4	0 42.7	11.9	54.0
11	345 20.5	05.9	0 20.2	16.4	0 54.6	12.0	54.0
12	0 20.7	N12 06.7	14 55.6	16.4	N 1 06.6	12.0	54.0
13	15 20.8	07.6	29 31.0	16.4	1 18.6	11.9	54.0
14	30 20.9	08.4	44 06.4	16.4	1 30.5	12.0	54.0
15	45 21.0 ..	09.3	58 41.8	16.4	1 42.5	11.9	54.0
16	60 21.2	10.1	73 17.2	16.3	1 54.4	11.9	54.0
17	75 21.3	10.9	87 52.5	16.4	2 06.3	12.0	54.0
18	90 21.4	N12 11.8	102 27.9	16.3	N 2 18.3	11.9	54.0
19	105 21.5	12.6	117 03.2	16.3	2 30.2	11.9	54.0
20	120 21.6	13.5	131 38.5	16.3	2 42.1	12.0	54.0
21	135 21.8 ..	14.3	146 13.8	16.3	2 54.1	11.9	54.0
22	150 21.9	15.1	160 49.1	16.3	3 06.0	11.9	54.0
23	165 22.0	16.0	175 24.4	16.3	3 17.9	11.8	54.0
22 00	180 22.1	N12 16.8	189 59.7	16.2	N 3 29.7	11.9	54.0
01	195 22.2	17.7	204 34.9	16.2	3 41.6	11.9	54.0
02	210 22.4	18.5	219 10.1	16.2	3 53.5	11.9	54.0
03	225 22.5 ..	19.3	233 45.3	16.2	4 05.4	11.8	54.0
04	240 22.6	20.2	248 20.5	16.2	4 17.2	11.8	54.0
05	255 22.7	21.0	262 55.7	16.1	4 29.0	11.8	54.0
06	270 22.8	N12 21.9	277 30.8	16.2	N 4 40.8	11.9	54.1
07	285 23.0	22.7	292 06.0	16.1	4 52.7	11.7	54.1
08	300 23.1	23.5	306 41.1	16.0	5 04.4	11.8	54.1
09	315 23.2 ..	24.4	321 16.1	16.1	5 16.2	11.8	54.1
10	330 23.3	25.2	335 51.2	16.0	5 28.0	11.7	54.1
11	345 23.4	26.0	350 26.2	16.0	5 39.7	11.7	54.1
12	0 23.6	N12 26.9	5 01.2	16.0	N 5 51.4	11.7	54.1
13	15 23.7	27.7	19 36.2	16.0	6 03.1	11.7	54.1
14	30 23.8	28.5	34 11.2	15.9	6 14.8	11.7	54.1
15	45 23.9 ..	29.4	48 46.1	15.9	6 26.5	11.6	54.1
16	60 24.0	30.2	63 21.0	15.8	6 38.1	11.6	54.1
17	75 24.1	31.0	77 55.8	15.9	6 49.7	11.6	54.1
18	90 24.3	N12 31.9	92 30.7	15.8	N 7 01.3	11.6	54.1
19	105 24.4	32.7	107 05.5	15.7	7 12.9	11.6	54.1
20	120 24.5	33.5	121 40.2	15.8	7 24.5	11.5	54.1
21	135 24.6 ..	34.4	136 15.0	15.7	7 36.0	11.5	54.1
22	150 24.7	35.2	150 49.7	15.7	7 47.5	11.5	54.2
23	165 24.8	36.0	165 24.4	15.6	7 59.0	11.4	54.2
23 00	180 25.0	N12 36.9	179 59.0	15.6	N 8 10.4	11.4	54.2
01	195 25.1	37.7	194 33.6	15.6	8 21.8	11.4	54.2
02	210 25.2	38.5	209 08.2	15.5	8 33.2	11.4	54.2
03	225 25.3 ..	39.3	223 42.7	15.5	8 44.6	11.3	54.2
04	240 25.4	40.2	238 17.2	15.4	8 55.9	11.3	54.2
05	255 25.5	41.0	252 51.6	15.4	9 07.2	11.3	54.2
06	270 25.6	N12 41.8	267 26.0	15.4	N 9 18.5	11.2	54.2
07	285 25.8	42.7	282 00.4	15.4	9 29.7	11.2	54.2
08	300 25.9	43.5	296 34.8	15.2	9 40.9	11.2	54.3
09	315 26.0 ..	44.3	311 09.0	15.3	9 52.1	11.1	54.3
10	330 26.1	45.1	325 43.3	15.2	10 03.2	11.1	54.3
11	345 26.2	46.0	340 17.5	15.2	10 14.3	11.1	54.3
12	0 26.3	N12 46.8	354 51.7	15.1	N10 25.4	11.0	54.3
13	15 26.4	47.6	9 25.8	15.1	10 36.4	11.0	54.3
14	30 26.5	48.4	23 59.9	15.0	10 47.4	10.9	54.3
15	45 26.7 ..	49.3	38 33.9	15.0	10 58.3	10.9	54.3
16	60 26.8	50.1	53 07.9	15.0	11 09.2	10.9	54.3
17	75 26.9	50.9	67 41.9	14.8	11 20.1	10.8	54.3
18	90 27.0	N12 51.7	82 15.7	14.9	N11 30.9	10.8	54.4
19	105 27.1	52.6	96 49.6	14.8	11 41.7	10.8	54.4
20	120 27.2	53.4	111 23.4	14.8	11 52.5	10.7	54.4
21	135 27.3 ..	54.2	125 57.2	14.7	12 03.2	10.6	54.4
22	150 27.4	55.0	140 30.9	14.6	12 13.8	10.6	54.4
23	165 27.5	55.9	155 04.5	14.6	N12 24.4	10.6	54.4
	SD 15.9	d 0.8	SD 14.7		14.7		14.8

Days: TUESDAY (21), WEDNESDAY (22), THURSDAY (23)

Twilight / Sunrise / Moonrise

Lat.	Naut.	Civil	Sunrise	Moonrise 21	22	23	24
°	h m	h m	h m	h m	h m	h m	h m
N 72	////	////	02 54	04 54	04 34	04 12	03 44
N 70	////	01 35	03 18	04 53	04 40	04 25	04 08
68	////	02 16	03 36	04 53	04 45	04 36	04 27
66	////	02 43	03 51	04 52	04 49	04 45	04 41
64	01 23	03 03	04 03	04 52	04 52	04 53	04 54
62	02 00	03 20	04 13	04 52	04 55	04 59	05 04
60	02 25	03 33	04 22	04 51	04 58	05 05	05 13
N 58	02 44	03 45	04 30	04 51	05 00	05 10	05 21
56	02 59	03 54	04 36	04 51	05 02	05 14	05 28
54	03 12	04 03	04 42	04 51	05 04	05 18	05 35
52	03 24	04 11	04 48	04 51	05 06	05 22	05 40
50	03 33	04 17	04 52	04 51	05 07	05 25	05 45
45	03 53	04 32	05 03	04 50	05 11	05 33	05 56
N 40	04 09	04 43	05 12	04 50	05 14	05 39	06 06
35	04 21	04 53	05 19	04 50	05 16	05 44	06 14
30	04 31	05 01	05 25	04 50	05 19	05 49	06 21
20	04 47	05 14	05 37	04 49	05 23	05 57	06 33
N 10	04 59	05 25	05 46	04 49	05 26	06 04	06 44
0	05 09	05 34	05 55	04 49	05 29	06 11	06 54
S 10	05 18	05 42	06 04	04 49	05 33	06 18	07 04
20	05 25	05 51	06 13	04 48	05 36	06 25	07 15
30	05 31	05 59	06 24	04 48	05 41	06 34	07 28
35	05 34	06 04	06 30	04 48	05 43	06 39	07 35
40	05 37	06 09	06 36	04 48	05 46	06 44	07 44
45	05 40	06 14	06 44	04 48	05 49	06 51	07 54
S 50	05 42	06 20	06 54	04 47	05 53	06 58	08 05
52	05 44	06 23	06 58	04 47	05 54	07 02	08 11
54	05 45	06 26	07 03	04 47	05 56	07 06	08 17
56	05 46	06 29	07 08	04 47	05 58	07 11	08 24
58	05 47	06 33	07 14	04 47	06 01	07 16	08 32
S 60	05 48	06 37	07 21	04 47	06 03	07 21	08 41

Sunset / Twilight / Moonset

Lat.	Sunset	Civil	Naut.	Moonset 21	22	23	24
°	h m	h m	h m	h m	h m	h m	h m
N 72	21 07	////	////	17 36	19 24	21 21	23 44
N 70	20 42	22 30	////	17 33	19 13	20 58	22 56
68	20 23	21 46	////	17 30	19 04	20 41	22 26
66	20 08	21 18	////	17 28	18 57	20 28	22 03
64	19 56	20 57	22 41	17 26	18 50	20 17	21 46
62	19 46	20 40	22 02	17 25	18 45	20 07	21 31
60	19 37	20 26	21 36	17 24	18 41	19 59	21 19
N 58	19 29	20 14	21 16	17 22	18 37	19 52	21 09
56	19 22	20 04	21 00	17 21	18 33	19 46	21 00
54	19 16	19 55	20 46	17 20	18 30	19 40	20 52
52	19 10	19 48	20 35	17 20	18 27	19 35	20 44
50	19 05	19 41	20 25	17 19	18 24	19 31	20 38
45	18 55	19 26	20 05	17 17	18 19	19 21	20 24
N 40	18 46	19 15	19 49	17 16	18 14	19 13	20 13
35	18 38	19 05	19 37	17 15	18 10	19 06	20 03
30	18 32	18 57	19 26	17 13	18 06	19 00	19 55
20	18 21	18 43	19 10	17 12	18 00	18 49	19 40
N 10	18 11	18 32	18 58	17 10	17 54	18 40	19 27
0	18 02	18 23	18 48	17 08	17 49	18 31	19 16
S 10	17 53	18 14	18 39	17 07	17 44	18 23	19 04
20	17 43	18 06	18 32	17 05	17 39	18 14	18 51
30	17 33	17 57	18 25	17 03	17 33	18 04	18 37
35	17 27	17 53	18 22	17 02	17 29	17 58	18 29
40	17 20	17 48	18 19	17 01	17 25	17 51	18 19
45	17 12	17 42	18 16	17 00	17 21	17 43	18 08
S 50	17 03	17 36	18 14	16 58	17 15	17 34	17 55
52	16 58	17 33	18 12	16 57	17 13	17 29	17 49
54	16 53	17 30	18 11	16 56	17 10	17 25	17 42
56	16 48	17 27	18 10	16 55	17 07	17 20	17 35
58	16 42	17 23	18 09	16 54	17 03	17 14	17 26
S 60	16 35	17 19	18 08	16 53	17 00	17 07	17 17

SUN / MOON

Day	Eqn. of Time 00ʰ	Eqn. of Time 12ʰ	Mer. Pass.	Mer. Pass. Upper	Mer. Pass. Lower	Age	Phase
d	m s	m s	h m	h m	h m	d	%
21	01 16	01 22	11 59	10 59	23 19	28	3
22	01 28	01 34	11 58	11 39	24 00	29	0
23	01 40	01 45	11 58	12 21	00 00	00	0

UT	ARIES	VENUS −4·7		MARS +0·5		JUPITER −2·3		SATURN +0·6		STARS		
	GHA	GHA	Dec	GHA	Dec	GHA	Dec	GHA	Dec	Name	SHA	Dec
d h	° ′	° ′	° ′	° ′	° ′	° ′	° ′	° ′	° ′		° ′	° ′
24 00	212 28.9	138 45.3	N27 22.8	252 46.4	S17 11.6	273 51.2	S20 56.9	268 29.6	S19 52.0	Acamar	315 15.2	S40 13.6
01	227 31.3	153 46.2	23.0	267 47.1	11.1	288 53.5	56.9	283 32.0	52.0	Achernar	335 23.8	S57 08.2
02	242 33.8	168 47.0	23.3	282 47.9	10.7	303 55.8	56.9	298 34.4	52.0	Acrux	173 03.5	S63 12.8
03	257 36.2	183 47.8 · ·	23.5	297 48.6 · ·	10.2	318 58.1 · ·	56.8	313 36.8 · ·	52.0	Adhara	255 09.0	S29 00.3
04	272 38.7	198 48.6	23.7	312 49.3	09.7	334 00.4	56.8	328 39.2	52.0	Aldebaran	290 44.3	N16 32.8
05	287 41.2	213 49.4	23.9	327 50.0	09.2	349 02.7	56.8	343 41.6	51.9			
06	302 43.6	228 50.3	N27 24.1	342 50.7	S17 08.8	4 05.0	S20 56.8	358 44.0	S19 51.9	Alioth	166 16.0	N55 51.2
07	317 46.1	243 51.1	24.3	357 51.5	08.3	19 07.3	56.7	13 46.4	51.9	Alkaid	152 54.6	N49 12.8
08	332 48.6	258 51.9	24.5	12 52.2	07.8	34 09.6	56.7	28 48.7	51.9	Alnair	27 38.0	S46 51.7
F 09	347 51.0	273 52.8 · ·	24.7	27 52.9 · ·	07.4	49 11.9 · ·	56.7	43 51.1 · ·	51.9	Alnilam	275 41.8	S 1 11.6
R 10	2 53.5	288 53.6	24.9	42 53.6	06.9	64 14.2	56.7	58 53.5	51.9	Alphard	217 51.4	S 8 44.9
I 11	17 56.0	303 54.5	25.2	57 54.3	06.4	79 16.5	56.7	73 55.9	51.9			
D 12	32 58.4	318 55.3	N27 25.4	72 55.1	S17 05.9	94 18.8	S20 56.6	88 58.3	S19 51.9	Alphecca	126 06.7	N26 38.8
A 13	48 00.9	333 56.1	25.6	87 55.8	05.5	109 21.1	56.6	104 00.7	51.9	Alpheratz	357 39.0	N29 11.8
Y 14	63 03.4	348 57.0	25.8	102 56.5	05.0	124 23.4	56.6	119 03.1	51.8	Altair	62 03.6	N 8 55.2
15	78 05.8	3 57.8 · ·	26.0	117 57.2 · ·	04.5	139 25.7 · ·	56.6	134 05.5 · ·	51.8	Ankaa	353 11.4	S42 11.8
16	93 08.3	18 58.7	26.2	132 58.0	04.0	154 28.0	56.5	149 07.9	51.8	Antares	112 20.2	S26 28.5
17	108 10.7	33 59.5	26.4	147 58.7	03.6	169 30.3	56.5	164 10.3	51.8			
18	123 13.2	49 00.4	N27 26.6	162 59.4	S17 03.1	184 32.6	S20 56.5	179 12.7	S19 51.8	Arcturus	145 51.1	N19 04.6
19	138 15.7	64 01.3	26.8	178 00.1	02.6	199 34.9	56.5	194 15.1	51.8	Atria	107 17.4	S69 03.5
20	153 18.1	79 02.1	27.0	193 00.8	02.1	214 37.2	56.4	209 17.5	51.8	Avior	234 16.2	S59 34.6
21	168 20.6	94 03.0 · ·	27.2	208 01.6 · ·	01.7	229 39.5 · ·	56.4	224 19.9 · ·	51.8	Bellatrix	278 27.2	N 6 21.9
22	183 23.1	109 03.9	27.4	223 02.3	01.2	244 41.8	56.4	239 22.3	51.8	Betelgeuse	270 56.4	N 7 24.5
23	198 25.5	124 04.7	27.6	238 03.0	00.7	259 44.1	56.4	254 24.7	51.7			
25 00	213 28.0	139 05.6	N27 27.8	253 03.7	S17 00.2	274 46.4	S20 56.3	269 27.0	S19 51.7	Canopus	263 54.3	S52 42.7
01	228 30.5	154 06.5	28.0	268 04.5	16 59.8	289 48.7	56.3	284 29.4	51.7	Capella	280 27.9	N46 01.0
02	243 32.9	169 07.4	28.2	283 05.2	59.3	304 51.0	56.3	299 31.8	51.7	Deneb	49 28.3	N45 20.8
03	258 35.4	184 08.2 · ·	28.3	298 05.9 · ·	58.8	319 53.3 · ·	56.3	314 34.2 · ·	51.7	Denebola	182 28.6	N14 27.6
04	273 37.8	199 09.1	28.5	313 06.6	58.3	334 55.6	56.3	329 36.6	51.7	Diphda	348 51.5	S17 52.7
05	288 40.3	214 10.0	28.7	328 07.4	57.8	349 57.9	56.2	344 39.0	51.7			
06	303 42.8	229 10.9	N27 28.9	343 08.1	S16 57.4	5 00.2	S20 56.2	359 41.4	S19 51.7	Dubhe	193 45.5	N61 38.7
07	318 45.2	244 11.8	29.1	358 08.8	56.9	20 02.5	56.2	14 43.8	51.7	Elnath	278 06.9	N28 37.4
S 08	333 47.7	259 12.7	29.3	13 09.5	56.4	35 04.8	56.2	29 46.2	51.6	Eltanin	90 43.6	N51 29.0
A 09	348 50.2	274 13.6 · ·	29.5	28 10.3 · ·	55.9	50 07.2 · ·	56.1	44 48.6 · ·	51.6	Enif	33 42.6	N 9 57.9
T 10	3 52.6	289 14.5	29.7	43 11.0	55.5	65 09.5	56.1	59 51.0	51.6	Fomalhaut	15 19.0	S29 30.9
U 11	18 55.1	304 15.4	29.9	58 11.7	55.0	80 11.8	56.1	74 53.4	51.6			
R 12	33 57.6	319 16.3	N27 30.0	73 12.4	S16 54.5	95 14.1	S20 56.1	89 55.8	S19 51.6	Gacrux	171 55.2	S57 13.7
D 13	49 00.0	334 17.2	30.2	88 13.2	54.0	110 16.4	56.1	104 58.2	51.6	Gienah	175 47.2	S17 39.3
A 14	64 02.5	349 18.1	30.4	103 13.9	53.5	125 18.7	56.0	120 00.6	51.6	Hadar	148 40.6	S60 28.2
Y 15	79 05.0	4 19.0 · ·	30.6	118 14.6 · ·	53.1	140 21.0 · ·	56.0	135 03.0 · ·	51.6	Hamal	327 55.8	N23 33.2
16	94 07.4	19 19.9	30.8	133 15.3	52.6	155 23.3	56.0	150 05.4	51.6	Kaus Aust.	83 37.4	S34 22.3
17	109 09.9	34 20.8	31.0	148 16.1	52.1	170 25.6	56.0	165 07.8	51.6			
18	124 12.3	49 21.7	N27 31.1	163 16.8	S16 51.6	185 27.9	S20 55.9	180 10.2	S19 51.5	Kochab	137 18.8	N74 04.4
19	139 14.8	64 22.6	31.3	178 17.5	51.1	200 30.2	55.9	195 12.6	51.5	Markab	13 33.9	N15 18.6
20	154 17.3	79 23.6	31.5	193 18.3	50.7	215 32.6	55.9	210 15.0	51.5	Menkar	314 10.5	N 4 09.9
21	169 19.7	94 24.5 · ·	31.7	208 19.0 · ·	50.2	230 34.9 · ·	55.9	225 17.4 · ·	51.5	Menkent	148 01.7	S36 28.1
22	184 22.2	109 25.4	31.8	223 19.7	49.7	245 37.2	55.9	240 19.8	51.5	Miaplacidus	221 38.7	S69 48.3
23	199 24.7	124 26.3	32.0	238 20.4	49.2	260 39.5	55.8	255 22.2	51.5			
26 00	214 27.1	139 27.3	N27 32.2	253 21.2	S16 48.7	275 41.8	S20 55.8	270 24.6	S19 51.5	Mirfak	308 34.1	N49 55.8
01	229 29.6	154 28.2	32.4	268 21.9	48.2	290 44.1	55.8	285 27.0	51.5	Nunki	75 52.3	S26 16.2
02	244 32.1	169 29.2	32.5	283 22.6	47.8	305 46.4	55.8	300 29.4	51.5	Peacock	53 11.8	S56 40.0
03	259 34.5	184 30.1 · ·	32.7	298 23.3 · ·	47.3	320 48.7 · ·	55.7	315 31.8 · ·	51.4	Pollux	243 22.1	N27 58.6
04	274 37.0	199 31.0	32.9	313 24.1	46.8	335 51.1	55.7	330 34.2	51.4	Procyon	244 54.9	N 5 10.3
05	289 39.5	214 32.0	33.0	328 24.8	46.3	350 53.4	55.7	345 36.6	51.4			
06	304 41.9	229 32.9	N27 33.2	343 25.5	S16 45.8	5 55.7	S20 55.7	0 39.0	S19 51.4	Rasalhague	96 01.9	N12 32.7
07	319 44.4	244 33.9	33.4	358 26.3	45.4	20 58.0	55.7	15 41.4	51.4	Regulus	207 38.4	N11 52.1
08	334 46.8	259 34.8	33.6	13 27.0	44.9	36 00.3	55.6	30 43.8	51.4	Rigel	281 07.8	S 8 10.9
S 09	349 49.3	274 35.8 · ·	33.7	28 27.7 · ·	44.4	51 02.6 · ·	55.6	45 46.2 · ·	51.4	Rigil Kent.	139 44.7	S60 55.0
U 10	4 51.8	289 36.8	33.9	43 28.5	43.9	66 04.9	55.6	60 48.6	51.4	Sabik	102 06.9	S15 44.9
N 11	19 54.2	304 37.7	34.0	58 29.2	43.4	81 07.3	55.6	75 51.0	51.4			
D 12	34 56.7	319 38.7	N27 34.2	73 29.9	S16 42.9	96 09.6	S20 55.6	90 53.4	S19 51.4	Schedar	349 35.7	N56 38.6
A 13	49 59.2	334 39.6	34.4	88 30.6	42.5	111 11.9	55.5	105 55.8	51.4	Shaula	96 15.3	S37 06.9
Y 14	65 01.6	349 40.6	34.5	103 31.4	42.0	126 14.2	55.5	120 58.2	51.3	Sirius	258 29.7	S16 44.9
15	80 04.1	4 41.6 · ·	34.7	118 32.1 · ·	41.5	141 16.5 · ·	55.5	136 00.6 · ·	51.3	Spica	158 26.0	S11 16.0
16	95 06.6	19 42.6	34.9	133 32.8	41.0	156 18.8	55.5	151 03.0	51.3	Suhail	222 49.0	S43 31.1
17	110 09.0	34 43.5	35.0	148 33.6	40.5	171 21.2	55.5	166 05.4	51.3			
18	125 11.5	49 44.5	N27 35.2	163 34.3	S16 40.0	186 23.5	S20 55.4	181 07.8	S19 51.3	Vega	80 35.6	N38 47.9
19	140 13.9	64 45.5	35.3	178 35.0	39.5	201 25.8	55.4	196 10.2	51.3	Zuben'ubi	136 59.9	S16 07.5
20	155 16.4	79 46.5	35.5	193 35.8	39.1	216 28.1	55.4	211 12.6	51.3		SHA	Mer. Pass.
21	170 18.9	94 47.5 · ·	35.6	208 36.5 · ·	38.6	231 30.4 · ·	55.4	226 15.0 · ·	51.3		° ′	h m
22	185 21.3	109 48.5	35.8	223 37.2	38.1	246 32.7	55.3	241 17.4	51.3	Venus	285 37.6	14 43
23	200 23.8	124 49.5	35.9	238 38.0	37.6	261 35.1	55.3	256 19.8	51.3	Mars	39 35.7	7 07
	h m									Jupiter	61 18.4	5 40
Mer. Pass. 9 44.5		v 0.9	d 0.2	v 0.7	d 0.5	v 2.3	d 0.0	v 2.4	d 0.0	Saturn	55 59.1	6 01

UT	SUN GHA	Dec	MOON GHA	v	Dec	d	HP
24 00	180 27.7	N12 56.7	169 38.1	14.6	N12 35.0	10.5	54.4
01	195 27.8	57.5	184 11.7	14.5	12 45.5	10.5	54.4
02	210 27.9	58.3	198 45.2	14.4	12 56.0	10.4	54.4
03	225 28.0	12 59.1	213 18.6	14.4	13 06.4	10.3	54.5
04	240 28.1	13 00.0	227 52.0	14.4	13 16.7	10.4	54.5
05	255 28.2	00.8	242 25.4	14.2	13 27.1	10.2	54.5
06	270 28.3	N13 01.6	256 58.6	14.3	N13 37.3	10.2	54.5
07	285 28.4	02.4	271 31.9	14.2	13 47.5	10.2	54.5
08	300 28.5	03.2	286 05.1	14.1	13 57.7	10.1	54.5
F 09	315 28.6 ..	04.1	300 38.2	14.0	14 07.8	10.1	54.5
R 10	330 28.8	04.9	315 11.2	14.1	14 17.9	10.0	54.5
I 11	345 28.9	05.7	329 44.3	13.9	14 27.9	9.9	54.6
D 12	0 29.0	N13 06.5	344 17.2	13.9	N14 37.8	9.9	54.6
A 13	15 29.1	07.3	358 50.1	13.8	14 47.7	9.8	54.6
Y 14	30 29.2	08.1	13 22.9	13.8	14 57.5	9.8	54.6
15	45 29.3 ..	09.0	27 55.7	13.7	15 07.3	9.7	54.6
16	60 29.4	09.8	42 28.4	13.7	15 17.0	9.6	54.6
17	75 29.5	10.6	57 01.1	13.6	15 26.6	9.6	54.6
18	90 29.6	N13 11.4	71 33.7	13.6	N15 36.2	9.6	54.7
19	105 29.7	12.2	86 06.3	13.4	15 45.8	9.4	54.7
20	120 29.8	13.0	100 38.7	13.5	15 55.2	9.4	54.7
21	135 29.9 ..	13.9	115 11.2	13.3	16 04.6	9.3	54.7
22	150 30.0	14.7	129 43.5	13.3	16 13.9	9.3	54.7
23	165 30.1	15.5	144 15.8	13.2	16 23.2	9.2	54.7
25 00	180 30.3	N13 16.3	158 48.0	13.2	N16 32.4	9.1	54.7
01	195 30.4	17.1	173 20.2	13.1	16 41.5	9.1	54.8
02	210 30.5	17.9	187 52.3	13.1	16 50.6	9.0	54.8
03	225 30.6 ..	18.7	202 24.4	13.0	16 59.6	8.9	54.8
04	240 30.7	19.5	216 56.4	12.9	17 08.5	8.8	54.8
05	255 30.8	20.4	231 28.3	12.8	17 17.3	8.8	54.8
06	270 30.9	N13 21.2	246 00.1	12.8	N17 26.1	8.7	54.8
S 07	285 31.0	22.0	260 31.9	12.8	17 34.8	8.6	54.9
A 08	300 31.1	22.8	275 03.7	12.6	17 43.4	8.6	54.9
T 09	315 31.2 ..	23.6	289 35.3	12.6	17 52.0	8.5	54.9
U 10	330 31.3	24.4	304 06.9	12.5	18 00.5	8.4	54.9
R 11	345 31.4	25.2	318 38.4	12.5	18 08.9	8.3	54.9
D 12	0 31.5	N13 26.0	333 09.9	12.4	N18 17.2	8.2	54.9
A 13	15 31.6	26.8	347 41.3	12.3	18 25.4	8.2	54.9
Y 14	30 31.7	27.6	2 12.6	12.3	18 33.6	8.1	55.0
15	45 31.8 ..	28.4	16 43.9	12.2	18 41.7	8.0	55.0
16	60 31.9	29.2	31 15.1	12.1	18 49.7	7.9	55.0
17	75 32.0	30.1	45 46.2	12.1	18 57.6	7.8	55.0
18	90 32.1	N13 30.9	60 17.3	12.0	N19 05.4	7.8	55.0
19	105 32.2	31.7	74 48.3	11.9	19 13.2	7.7	55.1
20	120 32.3	32.5	89 19.2	11.9	19 20.9	7.6	55.1
21	135 32.4 ..	33.3	103 50.1	11.8	19 28.5	7.4	55.1
22	150 32.5	34.1	118 20.9	11.7	19 35.9	7.5	55.1
23	165 32.6	34.9	132 51.6	11.7	19 43.4	7.3	55.1
26 00	180 32.7	N13 35.7	147 22.3	11.6	N19 50.7	7.2	55.1
01	195 32.8	36.5	161 52.9	11.5	19 57.9	7.1	55.2
02	210 32.9	37.3	176 23.4	11.5	20 05.0	7.1	55.2
03	225 33.0 ..	38.1	190 53.9	11.4	20 12.1	6.9	55.2
04	240 33.1	38.9	205 24.3	11.3	20 19.0	6.9	55.2
05	255 33.2	39.7	219 54.6	11.3	20 25.9	6.8	55.2
06	270 33.3	N13 40.5	234 24.9	11.2	N20 32.7	6.6	55.2
07	285 33.4	41.3	248 55.1	11.1	20 39.3	6.6	55.3
08	300 33.5	42.1	263 25.2	11.1	20 45.9	6.5	55.3
S 09	315 33.6 ..	42.9	277 55.3	11.0	20 52.4	6.4	55.3
U 10	330 33.7	43.7	292 25.3	10.9	20 58.8	6.3	55.3
N 11	345 33.8	44.5	306 55.2	10.9	21 05.1	6.1	55.3
D 12	0 33.9	N13 45.3	321 25.1	10.8	N21 11.2	6.1	55.4
A 13	15 34.0	46.1	335 54.9	10.7	21 17.3	6.0	55.4
Y 14	30 34.1	46.9	350 24.6	10.7	21 23.3	5.9	55.4
15	45 34.2 ..	47.7	4 54.3	10.6	21 29.2	5.8	55.4
16	60 34.3	48.5	19 23.9	10.5	21 35.0	5.6	55.4
17	75 34.4	49.3	33 53.4	10.5	21 40.6	5.6	55.5
18	90 34.5	N13 50.1	48 22.9	10.4	N21 46.2	5.5	55.5
19	105 34.6	50.9	62 52.3	10.4	21 51.7	5.3	55.5
20	120 34.7	51.7	77 21.7	10.3	21 57.0	5.3	55.5
21	135 34.8 ..	52.5	91 51.0	10.2	22 02.3	5.1	55.5
22	150 34.9	53.3	106 20.2	10.1	22 07.4	5.1	55.6
23	165 35.0	54.1	120 49.3	10.1	N22 12.5	4.9	55.6
	SD 15.9	d 0.8	SD 14.9		15.0		15.1

Lat.	Twilight Naut.	Twilight Civil	Sunrise	Moonrise 24	25	26	27
°	h m	h m	h m	h m	h m	h m	h m
N 72	////	////	02 34	03 44	02 54	▢	▢
N 70	////	01 01	03 02	04 08	03 43	▢	▢
68	////	01 55	03 23	04 27	04 15	03 56	▢
66	////	02 27	03 39	04 41	04 38	04 35	04 33
64	00 53	02 50	03 53	04 54	04 57	05 03	05 16
62	01 42	03 08	04 04	05 04	05 12	05 24	05 44
60	02 11	03 23	04 13	05 13	05 25	05 41	06 06
N 58	02 32	03 36	04 22	05 21	05 36	05 56	06 24
56	02 49	03 46	04 29	05 28	05 46	06 08	06 40
54	03 04	03 56	04 36	05 35	05 54	06 19	06 53
52	03 16	04 04	04 41	05 40	06 02	06 29	07 04
50	03 26	04 11	04 47	05 45	06 09	06 38	07 14
45	03 48	04 26	04 58	05 56	06 24	06 56	07 36
N 40	04 04	04 39	05 07	06 06	06 36	07 11	07 53
35	04 17	04 49	05 15	06 14	06 47	07 24	08 07
30	04 28	04 57	05 22	06 21	06 56	07 36	08 20
20	04 45	05 12	05 34	06 33	07 12	07 55	08 42
N 10	04 58	05 23	05 45	06 44	07 26	08 12	09 01
0	05 09	05 33	05 55	06 54	07 40	08 28	09 19
S 10	05 18	05 43	06 04	07 04	07 53	08 44	09 36
20	05 26	05 52	06 14	07 15	08 07	09 01	09 56
30	05 33	06 01	06 25	07 28	08 24	09 21	10 18
35	05 36	06 06	06 32	07 35	08 33	09 32	10 31
40	05 40	06 11	06 39	07 44	08 44	09 45	10 46
45	05 43	06 18	06 48	07 54	08 57	10 01	11 03
S 50	05 47	06 25	06 58	08 05	09 13	10 21	11 26
52	05 48	06 28	07 03	08 11	09 21	10 30	11 36
54	05 49	06 31	07 08	08 17	09 29	10 41	11 48
56	05 51	06 35	07 14	08 24	09 39	10 52	12 02
58	05 53	06 39	07 20	08 32	09 49	11 06	12 18
S 60	05 54	06 43	07 28	08 41	10 02	11 22	12 38

Lat.	Sunset	Twilight Civil	Twilight Naut.	Moonset 24	25	26	27
°	h m	h m	h m	h m	h m	h m	h m
N 72	21 27	////	////	23 44	▢	▢	▢
N 70	20 58	23 10	////	22 56	▢	▢	▢
68	20 36	22 07	////	22 26	24 23	00 23	▢
66	20 19	21 33	////	22 03	23 44	00 23	01 30
64	20 05	21 09	23 16	21 46	23 17	24 48	00 48
62	19 54	20 50	22 20	21 31	22 57	24 20	00 20
60	19 44	20 35	21 49	21 19	22 40	23 58	25 08
N 58	19 36	20 22	21 26	21 09	22 26	23 41	24 48
56	19 28	20 11	21 09	21 00	22 14	23 26	24 32
54	19 21	20 02	20 54	20 52	22 03	23 13	24 18
52	19 15	19 53	20 42	20 44	21 54	23 02	24 05
50	19 10	19 46	20 31	20 38	21 46	22 52	23 54
45	18 59	19 34	20 09	20 24	21 28	22 31	23 32
N 40	18 49	19 18	19 53	20 13	21 14	22 14	23 13
35	18 41	19 08	19 40	20 03	21 02	22 00	22 58
30	18 34	18 59	19 29	19 55	20 51	21 48	22 45
20	18 22	18 44	19 11	19 40	20 33	21 27	22 22
N 10	18 11	18 33	18 58	19 27	20 17	21 09	22 02
0	18 01	18 23	18 47	19 16	20 02	20 52	21 44
S 10	17 52	18 13	18 38	19 04	19 48	20 35	21 26
20	17 41	18 04	18 30	18 51	19 32	20 17	21 06
30	17 30	17 55	18 23	18 37	19 14	19 56	20 43
35	17 23	17 49	18 19	18 29	19 04	19 44	20 30
40	17 16	17 44	18 16	18 19	18 52	19 30	20 15
45	17 07	17 38	18 12	18 08	18 38	19 14	19 57
S 50	16 57	17 31	18 08	17 55	18 21	18 53	19 34
52	16 52	17 27	18 07	17 49	18 13	18 44	19 23
54	16 47	17 24	18 05	17 42	18 04	18 33	19 11
56	16 41	17 20	18 04	17 35	17 54	18 21	18 57
58	16 34	17 16	18 02	17 26	17 43	18 07	18 41
S 60	16 27	17 12	18 00	17 17	17 30	17 50	18 21

	SUN			MOON			
Day	Eqn. of Time 00ʰ	12ʰ	Mer. Pass.	Mer. Pass. Upper	Lower	Age	Phase
d	m s	m s	h m	h m	h m	d	%
24	01 50	01 56	11 58	13 05	00 43	01	2
25	02 01	02 06	11 58	13 51	01 28	02	5
26	02 11	02 15	11 58	14 40	02 15	03	11

UT	ARIES GHA	VENUS −4.7 GHA	Dec	MARS +0.4 GHA	Dec	JUPITER −2.3 GHA	Dec	SATURN +0.6 GHA	Dec	STARS Name	SHA	Dec
27 00	215 26.3	139 50.5	N27 36.1	253 38.7	S16 37.1	276 37.4	S20 55.3	271 22.2	S19 51.2	Acamar	315 15.2	S40 13.6
01	230 28.7	154 51.5	36.3	268 39.4	36.6	291 39.7	55.3	286 24.6	51.2	Achernar	335 23.8	S57 08.1
02	245 31.2	169 52.5	36.4	283 40.2	36.1	306 42.0	55.3	301 27.0	51.2	Acrux	173 03.5	S63 12.8
03	260 33.7	184 53.5	.. 36.6	298 40.9	.. 35.7	321 44.3	.. 55.2	316 29.4	.. 51.2	Adhara	255 09.0	S29 00.3
04	275 36.1	199 54.5	36.7	313 41.6	35.2	336 46.7	55.2	331 31.8	51.2	Aldebaran	290 44.3	N16 32.8
05	290 38.6	214 55.5	36.9	328 42.4	34.7	351 49.0	55.2	346 34.2	51.2			
06	305 41.1	229 56.5	N27 37.0	343 43.1	S16 34.2	6 51.3	S20 55.2	1 36.7	S19 51.2	Alioth	166 16.0	N55 51.2
07	320 43.5	244 57.5	37.1	358 43.8	33.7	21 53.6	55.2	16 39.1	51.2	Alkaid	152 54.6	N49 12.8
08	335 46.0	259 58.5	37.3	13 44.6	33.2	36 56.0	55.1	31 41.5	51.2	Alnair	27 38.0	S46 51.7
M 09	350 48.4	274 59.6	.. 37.4	28 45.3	.. 32.7	51 58.3	.. 55.1	46 43.9	.. 51.2	Alnilam	275 41.8	S 1 11.6
O 10	5 50.9	290 00.6	37.6	43 46.0	32.2	67 00.6	55.1	61 46.3	51.2	Alphard	217 51.4	S 8 44.9
N 11	20 53.4	305 01.6	37.7	58 46.8	31.8	82 02.9	55.1	76 48.7	51.1			
D 12	35 55.8	320 02.6	N27 37.9	73 47.5	S16 31.3	97 05.3	S20 55.1	91 51.1	S19 51.1	Alphecca	126 06.6	N26 38.8
A 13	50 58.3	335 03.7	38.0	88 48.2	30.8	112 07.6	55.0	106 53.5	51.1	Alpheratz	357 38.9	N29 11.8
Y 14	66 00.8	350 04.7	38.1	103 49.0	30.3	127 09.9	55.0	121 55.9	51.1	Altair	62 03.6	N 8 55.2
15	81 03.2	5 05.7	.. 38.3	118 49.7	.. 29.8	142 12.2	.. 55.0	136 58.3	.. 51.1	Ankaa	353 11.4	S42 11.8
16	96 05.7	20 06.8	38.4	133 50.4	29.3	157 14.6	55.0	152 00.7	51.1	Antares	112 20.2	S26 28.5
17	111 08.2	35 07.8	38.6	148 51.2	28.8	172 16.9	55.0	167 03.1	51.1			
18	126 10.6	50 08.9	N27 38.7	163 51.9	S16 28.3	187 19.2	S20 55.0	182 05.5	S19 51.1	Arcturus	145 51.1	N19 04.7
19	141 13.1	65 09.9	38.8	178 52.6	27.8	202 21.5	54.9	197 07.9	51.1	Atria	107 17.3	S69 03.6
20	156 15.6	80 11.0	39.0	193 53.4	27.4	217 23.9	54.9	212 10.3	51.1	Avior	234 16.2	S59 34.8
21	171 18.0	95 12.0	.. 39.1	208 54.1	.. 26.9	232 26.2	.. 54.9	227 12.7	.. 51.1	Bellatrix	278 27.2	N 6 21.9
22	186 20.5	110 13.1	39.2	223 54.8	26.4	247 28.5	54.9	242 15.2	51.1	Betelgeuse	270 56.4	N 7 24.5
23	201 22.9	125 14.1	39.4	238 55.6	25.9	262 30.8	54.9	257 17.6	51.0			
28 00	216 25.4	140 15.2	N27 39.5	253 56.3	S16 25.4	277 33.2	S20 54.8	272 20.0	S19 51.0	Canopus	263 54.4	S52 42.7
01	231 27.9	155 16.3	39.6	268 57.1	24.9	292 35.5	54.8	287 22.4	51.0	Capella	280 27.9	N46 01.0
02	246 30.3	170 17.3	39.8	283 57.8	24.4	307 37.8	54.8	302 24.8	51.0	Deneb	49 28.3	N45 20.8
03	261 32.8	185 18.4	.. 39.9	298 58.5	.. 23.9	322 40.1	.. 54.8	317 27.2	.. 51.0	Denebola	182 28.6	N14 27.6
04	276 35.3	200 19.5	40.0	313 59.3	23.4	337 42.5	54.8	332 29.6	51.0	Diphda	348 51.4	S17 52.7
05	291 37.7	215 20.6	40.1	329 00.0	22.9	352 44.8	54.7	347 32.0	51.0			
06	306 40.2	230 21.7	N27 40.3	344 00.7	S16 22.4	7 47.1	S20 54.7	2 34.4	S19 51.0	Dubhe	193 45.5	N61 38.8
07	321 42.7	245 22.7	40.4	359 01.5	22.0	22 49.5	54.7	17 36.8	51.0	Elnath	278 06.9	N28 37.4
T 08	336 45.1	260 23.8	40.5	14 02.2	21.5	37 51.8	54.7	32 39.2	51.0	Eltanin	90 43.6	N51 29.0
U 09	351 47.6	275 24.9	.. 40.6	29 03.0	.. 21.0	52 54.1	.. 54.7	47 41.6	.. 51.0	Enif	33 42.6	N 9 57.9
E 10	6 50.1	290 26.0	40.8	44 03.7	20.5	67 56.5	54.7	62 44.1	51.0	Fomalhaut	15 19.0	S29 30.9
S 11	21 52.5	305 27.1	40.9	59 04.4	20.0	82 58.8	54.6	77 46.5	51.0			
D 12	36 55.0	320 28.2	N27 41.0	74 05.2	S16 19.5	98 01.1	S20 54.6	92 48.9	S19 50.9	Gacrux	171 55.2	S57 13.7
A 13	51 57.4	335 29.3	41.1	89 05.9	19.0	113 03.5	54.6	107 51.3	50.9	Gienah	175 47.2	S17 39.3
Y 14	66 59.9	350 30.4	41.2	104 06.6	18.5	128 05.8	54.6	122 53.7	50.9	Hadar	148 40.6	S60 28.2
15	82 02.4	5 31.5	.. 41.4	119 07.4	.. 18.0	143 08.1	.. 54.6	137 56.1	.. 50.9	Hamal	327 55.8	N23 33.2
16	97 04.8	20 32.6	41.5	134 08.1	17.5	158 10.5	54.5	152 58.5	50.9	Kaus Aust.	83 37.3	S34 22.3
17	112 07.3	35 33.7	41.6	149 08.9	17.0	173 12.8	54.5	168 00.9	50.9			
18	127 09.8	50 34.8	N27 41.7	164 09.6	S16 16.5	188 15.1	S20 54.5	183 03.3	S19 50.9	Kochab	137 18.8	N74 04.4
19	142 12.2	65 36.0	41.8	179 10.3	16.0	203 17.5	54.5	198 05.8	50.9	Markab	13 33.8	N15 18.6
20	157 14.7	80 37.1	41.9	194 11.1	15.5	218 19.8	54.5	213 08.2	50.9	Menkar	314 10.4	N 4 09.9
21	172 17.2	95 38.2	.. 42.0	209 11.8	.. 15.0	233 22.1	.. 54.5	228 10.6	.. 50.9	Menkent	148 01.6	S36 28.1
22	187 19.6	110 39.3	42.2	224 12.6	14.6	248 24.5	54.4	243 13.0	50.9	Miaplacidus	221 38.7	S69 48.3
23	202 22.1	125 40.5	42.3	239 13.3	14.1	263 26.8	54.4	258 15.4	50.9			
29 00	217 24.6	140 41.6	N27 42.4	254 14.0	S16 13.6	278 29.1	S20 54.4	273 17.8	S19 50.9	Mirfak	308 34.1	N49 55.8
01	232 27.0	155 42.7	42.5	269 14.8	13.1	293 31.5	54.4	288 20.2	50.8	Nunki	75 52.3	S26 16.2
02	247 29.5	170 43.9	42.6	284 15.5	12.6	308 33.8	54.4	303 22.6	50.8	Peacock	53 11.8	S56 39.9
03	262 31.9	185 45.0	.. 42.7	299 16.3	.. 12.1	323 36.1	.. 54.4	318 25.0	.. 50.8	Pollux	243 22.1	N27 58.6
04	277 34.4	200 46.2	42.8	314 17.0	11.6	338 38.5	54.3	333 27.5	50.8	Procyon	244 54.9	N 5 10.3
05	292 36.9	215 47.3	42.9	329 17.8	11.1	353 40.8	54.3	348 29.9	50.8			
06	307 39.3	230 48.5	N27 43.0	344 18.5	S16 10.6	8 43.1	S20 54.3	3 32.3	S19 50.8	Rasalhague	96 01.8	N12 32.7
W 07	322 41.8	245 49.6	43.1	359 19.2	10.1	23 45.5	54.3	18 34.7	50.8	Regulus	207 38.4	N11 52.1
E 08	337 44.3	260 50.8	43.2	14 20.0	09.6	38 47.8	54.3	33 37.1	50.8	Rigel	281 07.8	S 8 10.9
D 09	352 46.7	275 51.9	.. 43.3	29 20.7	.. 09.1	53 50.2	.. 54.2	48 39.5	.. 50.8	Rigil Kent.	139 44.7	S60 55.0
N 10	7 49.2	290 53.1	43.4	44 21.5	08.6	68 52.5	54.2	63 41.9	50.8	Sabik	102 06.9	S15 44.9
E 11	22 51.7	305 54.3	43.5	59 22.2	08.1	83 54.8	54.2	78 44.4	50.8			
S 12	37 54.1	320 55.4	N27 43.6	74 23.0	S16 07.6	98 57.2	S20 54.2	93 46.8	S19 50.8	Schedar	349 35.7	N56 38.6
D 13	52 56.6	335 56.6	43.7	89 23.7	07.1	113 59.5	54.2	108 49.2	50.8	Shaula	96 15.2	S37 06.9
A 14	67 59.0	350 57.8	43.8	104 24.4	06.6	129 01.9	54.2	123 51.6	50.8	Sirius	258 29.8	S16 44.9
Y 15	83 01.5	5 59.0	.. 43.9	119 25.2	.. 06.1	144 04.2	.. 54.1	138 54.0	.. 50.7	Spica	158 26.0	S11 16.0
16	98 04.0	21 00.1	44.0	134 25.9	05.6	159 06.5	54.1	153 56.4	50.7	Suhail	222 49.0	S43 31.1
17	113 06.4	36 01.3	44.1	149 26.7	05.1	174 08.9	54.1	168 58.8	50.7			
18	128 08.9	51 02.5	N27 44.2	164 27.4	S16 04.6	189 11.2	S20 54.1	184 01.3	S19 50.7	Vega	80 35.6	N38 47.9
19	143 11.4	66 03.7	44.3	179 28.2	04.1	204 13.6	54.1	199 03.7	50.7	Zuben'ubi	136 59.9	S16 07.5
20	158 13.8	81 04.9	44.4	194 28.9	03.6	219 15.9	54.1	214 06.1	50.7			
21	173 16.3	96 06.1	.. 44.5	209 29.6	.. 03.1	234 18.3	.. 54.1	229 08.5	.. 50.7	Venus	283 49.8	14 38
22	188 18.8	111 07.3	44.6	224 30.4	02.6	249 20.6	54.0	244 10.9	50.7	Mars	37 30.9	7 04
23	203 21.2	126 08.5	44.7	239 31.1	02.1	264 22.9	54.0	259 13.3	50.7	Jupiter	61 07.8	5 29
Mer. Pass. 9 32.7		v 1.1	d 0.1	v 0.7	d 0.5	v 2.3	d 0.0	v 2.4	d 0.0	Saturn	55 54.6	5 50

Stars column footer: SHA / Mer. Pass.

UT	SUN GHA	SUN Dec	MOON GHA	v	MOON Dec	d	HP
d h	° ′	° ′	° ′	′	° ′	′	′
27 00	180 35.1	N13 54.9	135 18.4	10.1	N22 17.4	4.8	55.6
01	195 35.2	55.7	149 47.5	10.0	22 22.2	4.7	55.6
02	210 35.3	56.4	164 16.5	9.9	22 26.9	4.6	55.7
03	225 35.4 ..	57.2	178 45.4	9.8	22 31.5	4.5	55.7
04	240 35.4	58.0	193 14.2	9.8	22 36.0	4.3	55.7
05	255 35.5	58.8	207 43.0	9.8	22 40.3	4.3	55.7
06	270 35.6	N13 59.6	222 11.8	9.6	N22 44.6	4.1	55.7
07	285 35.7	14 00.4	236 40.4	9.6	22 48.7	4.1	55.8
M 08	300 35.8	01.2	251 09.0	9.6	22 52.8	3.9	55.8
O 09	315 35.9 ..	02.0	265 37.6	9.5	22 56.7	3.7	55.8
N 10	330 36.0	02.8	280 06.1	9.5	23 00.4	3.7	55.8
D 11	345 36.1	03.6	294 34.6	9.4	23 04.1	3.6	55.9
A 12	0 36.2	N14 04.4	309 03.0	9.3	N23 07.7	3.4	55.9
Y 13	15 36.3	05.1	323 31.3	9.3	23 11.1	3.3	55.9
14	30 36.4	05.9	337 59.6	9.2	23 14.4	3.2	55.9
15	45 36.5 ..	06.7	352 27.8	9.2	23 17.6	3.1	55.9
16	60 36.6	07.5	6 56.0	9.1	23 20.7	2.9	56.0
17	75 36.7	08.3	21 24.1	9.1	23 23.6	2.8	56.0
18	90 36.8	N14 09.1	35 52.2	9.0	N23 26.4	2.7	56.0
19	105 36.8	09.9	50 20.2	9.0	23 29.1	2.6	56.0
20	120 36.9	10.7	64 48.2	8.9	23 31.7	2.5	56.1
21	135 37.0 ..	11.4	79 16.1	8.9	23 34.2	2.3	56.1
22	150 37.1	12.2	93 44.0	8.8	23 36.5	2.2	56.1
23	165 37.2	13.0	108 11.8	8.8	23 38.7	2.1	56.1
28 00	180 37.3	N14 13.8	122 39.6	8.7	N23 40.8	1.9	56.2
01	195 37.4	14.6	137 07.3	8.7	23 42.7	1.9	56.2
02	210 37.5	15.4	151 35.0	8.6	23 44.6	1.6	56.2
03	225 37.6 ..	16.1	166 02.6	8.7	23 46.2	1.6	56.2
04	240 37.7	16.9	180 30.3	8.5	23 47.8	1.4	56.3
05	255 37.7	17.7	194 57.8	8.5	23 49.2	1.3	56.3
06	270 37.8	N14 18.5	209 25.3	8.5	N23 50.5	1.2	56.3
07	285 37.9	19.3	223 52.8	8.5	23 51.7	1.1	56.3
T 08	300 38.0	20.1	238 20.3	8.4	23 52.8	0.9	56.4
U 09	315 38.1 ..	20.8	252 47.7	8.3	23 53.7	0.8	56.4
E 10	330 38.2	21.6	267 15.0	8.3	23 54.5	0.6	56.4
S 11	345 38.3	22.4	281 42.3	8.3	23 55.1	0.5	56.4
D 12	0 38.4	N14 23.2	296 09.6	8.3	N23 55.6	0.4	56.5
A 13	15 38.4	24.0	310 36.9	8.2	23 56.0	0.3	56.5
Y 14	30 38.5	24.7	325 04.1	8.2	23 56.3	0.1	56.5
15	45 38.6 ..	25.5	339 31.3	8.2	23 56.4	0.0	56.6
16	60 38.7	26.3	353 58.5	8.1	23 56.4	0.2	56.6
17	75 38.8	27.1	8 25.6	8.1	23 56.2	0.3	56.6
18	90 38.9	N14 27.8	22 52.7	8.1	N23 55.9	0.4	56.6
19	105 39.0	28.6	37 19.8	8.0	23 55.5	0.6	56.7
20	120 39.1	29.4	51 46.8	8.0	23 54.9	0.7	56.7
21	135 39.1 ..	30.2	66 13.8	8.0	23 54.2	0.8	56.7
22	150 39.2	31.0	80 40.8	8.0	23 53.4	1.0	56.7
23	165 39.3	31.7	95 07.8	7.9	23 52.4	1.1	56.8
29 00	180 39.4	N14 32.5	109 34.7	8.0	N23 51.3	1.2	56.8
01	195 39.5	33.3	124 01.7	7.9	23 50.1	1.4	56.8
02	210 39.6	34.0	138 28.6	7.8	23 48.7	1.5	56.9
03	225 39.7 ..	34.8	152 55.4	7.9	23 47.2	1.6	56.9
04	240 39.7	35.6	167 22.3	7.8	23 45.6	1.8	56.9
05	255 39.8	36.4	181 49.1	7.9	23 43.8	2.0	56.9
06	270 39.9	N14 37.1	196 16.0	7.8	N23 41.8	2.0	57.0
W 07	285 40.0	37.9	210 42.8	7.8	23 39.8	2.2	57.0
E 08	300 40.1	38.7	225 09.6	7.8	23 37.6	2.4	57.0
D 09	315 40.2 ..	39.5	239 36.4	7.7	23 35.2	2.4	57.1
N 10	330 40.2	40.2	254 03.1	7.8	23 32.8	2.7	57.1
E 11	345 40.3	41.0	268 29.9	7.7	23 30.1	2.7	57.1
S 12	0 40.4	N14 41.8	282 56.6	7.8	N23 27.4	2.9	57.1
D 13	15 40.5	42.5	297 23.4	7.7	23 24.5	3.0	57.2
A 14	30 40.6	43.3	311 50.1	7.7	23 21.5	3.2	57.2
Y 15	45 40.6 ..	44.1	326 16.8	7.7	23 18.3	3.3	57.2
16	60 40.7	44.8	340 43.5	7.7	23 15.0	3.5	57.3
17	75 40.8	45.6	355 10.2	7.7	23 11.5	3.5	57.3
18	90 40.9	N14 46.4	9 36.9	7.7	N23 08.0	3.8	57.3
19	105 41.0	47.1	24 03.6	7.7	23 04.2	3.8	57.4
20	120 41.1	47.9	38 30.3	7.7	23 00.4	4.0	57.4
21	135 41.1 ..	48.7	52 57.0	7.7	22 56.4	4.1	57.4
22	150 41.2	49.4	67 23.7	7.7	22 52.3	4.3	57.4
23	165 41.3	50.2	81 50.4	7.7	N22 48.0	4.4	57.5
	SD 15.9	d 0.8	SD 15.2		15.4		15.6

Twilight / Sunrise / Moonrise

Lat.	Naut.	Civil	Sunrise	Moonrise 27	28	29	30
°	h m	h m	h m	h m	h m	h m	h m
N 72	////	////	02 13	☐	☐	☐	☐
N 70	////	////	02 46	☐	☐	☐	☐
68	////	01 32	03 09	☐	☐	☐	☐
66	////	02 11	03 28	04 33	04 38	05 39	07 32
64	////	02 37	03 42	05 16	05 45	06 43	08 11
62	01 21	02 57	03 55	05 44	06 20	07 18	08 38
60	01 56	03 13	04 05	06 06	06 46	07 43	08 59
N 58	02 21	03 27	04 14	06 24	07 06	08 03	09 16
56	02 39	03 38	04 22	06 40	07 23	08 20	09 31
54	02 55	03 48	04 29	06 53	07 37	08 34	09 43
52	03 08	03 57	04 35	07 04	07 49	08 46	09 54
50	03 19	04 05	04 41	07 14	08 00	08 57	10 04
45	03 42	04 21	04 53	07 36	08 23	09 20	10 24
N 40	03 59	04 34	05 03	07 53	08 42	09 38	10 41
35	04 13	04 45	05 12	08 07	08 57	09 53	10 55
30	04 24	04 54	05 20	08 20	09 11	10 06	11 07
20	04 43	05 10	05 33	08 42	09 33	10 29	11 28
N 10	04 57	05 22	05 44	09 01	09 53	10 49	11 45
0	05 08	05 33	05 54	09 19	10 12	11 07	12 02
S 10	05 18	05 43	06 04	09 36	10 31	11 25	12 19
20	05 26	05 52	06 15	09 56	10 51	11 45	12 37
30	05 34	06 03	06 27	10 18	11 14	12 07	12 57
35	05 38	06 08	06 34	10 31	11 27	12 20	13 09
40	05 42	06 14	06 42	10 46	11 43	12 36	13 23
45	05 46	06 21	06 52	11 03	12 02	12 54	13 39
S 50	05 51	06 29	07 03	11 26	12 25	13 16	13 59
52	05 52	06 32	07 08	11 36	12 36	13 27	14 08
54	05 54	06 36	07 14	11 48	12 49	13 39	14 19
56	05 56	06 40	07 20	12 02	13 03	13 53	14 30
58	05 58	06 45	07 27	12 18	13 21	14 09	14 44
S 60	06 00	06 50	07 35	12 38	13 42	14 29	15 00

Sunset / Twilight / Moonset

Lat.	Sunset	Civil	Naut.	Moonset 27	28	29	30
°	h m	h m	h m	h m	h m	h m	h m
N 72	21 48	////	////	☐	☐	☐	☐
N 70	21 13	////	////	☐	☐	☐	☐
68	20 49	22 31	////	☐	☐	☐	☐
66	20 30	21 49	////	01 30	03 16	04 08	04 11
64	20 15	21 21	////	00 48	02 09	03 04	03 32
62	20 02	21 00	22 41	00 34	01 34	02 29	03 04
60	19 52	20 44	22 03	25 08	01 08	02 04	02 43
N 58	19 42	20 30	21 38	24 48	00 48	01 44	02 25
56	19 34	20 18	21 18	24 32	00 32	01 27	02 10
54	19 27	20 08	21 02	24 18	00 18	01 13	01 58
52	19 21	19 59	20 49	24 05	00 05	01 01	01 46
50	19 15	19 51	20 37	23 54	24 50	00 50	01 36
45	19 02	19 34	20 14	23 32	24 27	00 27	01 15
N 40	18 52	19 21	19 57	23 13	24 08	00 08	00 58
35	18 43	19 10	19 43	22 58	23 53	24 44	00 44
30	18 36	19 01	19 31	22 45	23 39	24 31	00 31
20	18 23	18 46	19 13	22 22	23 17	24 10	00 10
N 10	18 11	18 33	18 59	22 02	22 57	23 51	24 44
0	18 01	18 22	18 47	21 44	22 38	23 33	24 28
S 10	17 50	18 12	18 37	21 26	22 20	23 16	24 13
20	17 40	18 02	18 28	21 06	22 00	22 57	23 56
30	17 27	17 52	18 20	20 43	21 36	22 35	23 37
35	17 20	17 46	18 16	20 30	21 23	22 22	23 26
40	17 12	17 40	18 12	20 15	21 07	22 07	23 13
45	17 03	17 33	18 08	19 57	20 49	21 49	22 57
S 50	16 51	17 25	18 04	19 34	20 25	21 27	22 38
52	16 46	17 22	18 02	19 23	20 14	21 17	22 29
54	16 41	17 18	18 00	19 11	20 01	21 05	22 19
56	16 34	17 14	17 58	18 57	19 47	20 51	22 08
58	16 27	17 09	17 56	18 41	19 29	20 35	21 54
S 60	16 19	17 04	17 53	18 21	19 08	20 16	21 39

SUN / MOON

Day	Eqn. of Time 00h	12h	Mer. Pass.	Mer. Pass. Upper	Lower	Age	Phase
d	m s	m s	h m	h m	h m	d	%
27	02 20	02 25	11 58	15 31	03 05	04	18
28	02 29	02 33	11 57	16 25	03 58	05	26
29	02 37	02 41	11 57	17 20	04 52	06	36

UT	ARIES GHA	VENUS −4.7 GHA	Dec	MARS +0.4 GHA	Dec	JUPITER −2.4 GHA	Dec	SATURN +0.6 GHA	Dec	STARS Name	SHA	Dec
30 00	218 23.7	141 09.7	N27 44.7	254 31.9	S16 01.6	279 25.3	S20 54.0	274 15.8	S19 50.7	Acamar	315 15.1	S40 13.6
01	233 26.2	156 10.9	.. 44.8	269 32.6	.. 01.1	294 27.6	.. 54.0	289 18.2	.. 50.7	Achernar	335 23.7	S57 08.1
02	248 28.6	171 12.1	44.9	284 33.4	00.6	309 30.0	54.0	304 20.6	50.7	Acrux	173 03.5	S63 12.8
03	263 31.1	186 13.3	.. 45.0	299 34.1	16 00.1	324 32.3	.. 54.0	319 23.0	.. 50.7	Adhara	255 09.0	S29 00.3
04	278 33.5	201 14.5	45.1	314 34.9	15 59.6	339 34.7	53.9	334 25.4	50.7	Aldebaran	290 44.3	N16 32.8
05	293 36.0	216 15.8	45.2	329 35.6	59.1	354 37.0	53.9	349 27.8	50.7			
06	308 38.5	231 17.0	N27 45.3	344 36.4	S15 58.6	9 39.4	S20 53.9	4 30.3	S19 50.6	Alioth	166 16.0	N55 51.2
T 07	323 40.9	246 18.2	45.3	359 37.1	58.1	24 41.7	53.9	19 32.7	50.6	Alkaid	152 54.6	N49 12.8
H 08	338 43.4	261 19.5	45.4	14 37.8	57.6	39 44.0	53.9	34 35.1	50.6	Alnair	27 37.9	S46 51.7
U 09	353 45.9	276 20.7	.. 45.5	29 38.6	.. 57.1	54 46.4	.. 53.9	49 37.5	.. 50.6	Alnilam	275 41.8	S 1 11.5
R 10	8 48.3	291 21.9	45.6	44 39.3	56.6	69 48.7	53.8	64 39.9	50.6	Alphard	217 51.4	S 8 44.9
S 11	23 50.8	306 23.2	45.7	59 40.1	56.1	84 51.1	53.8	79 42.3	50.6			
D 12	38 53.3	321 24.4	N27 45.7	74 40.8	S15 55.6	99 53.4	S20 53.8	94 44.8	S19 50.6	Alphecca	126 06.6	N26 38.8
A 13	53 55.7	336 25.7	45.8	89 41.6	55.1	114 55.8	53.8	109 47.2	50.6	Alpheratz	357 38.9	N29 11.8
Y 14	68 58.2	351 26.9	45.9	104 42.3	54.6	129 58.1	53.8	124 49.6	50.6	Altair	62 03.5	N 8 55.2
15	84 00.7	6 28.2	.. 46.0	119 43.1	.. 54.1	145 00.5	.. 53.8	139 52.0	.. 50.6	Ankaa	353 11.3	S42 11.8
16	99 03.1	21 29.4	46.0	134 43.8	53.6	160 02.8	53.8	154 54.4	50.6	Antares	112 20.1	S26 28.5
17	114 05.6	36 30.7	46.1	149 44.6	53.1	175 05.2	53.7	169 56.9	50.6			
18	129 08.0	51 31.9	N27 46.2	164 45.3	S15 52.6	190 07.5	S20 53.7	184 59.3	S19 50.6	Arcturus	145 51.1	N19 04.7
19	144 10.5	66 33.2	46.2	179 46.1	52.1	205 09.9	53.7	200 01.7	50.6	Atria	107 17.3	S69 03.6
20	159 13.0	81 34.5	46.3	194 46.8	51.6	220 12.2	53.7	215 04.1	50.6	Avior	234 16.3	S59 34.8
21	174 15.4	96 35.7	.. 46.4	209 47.6	.. 51.1	235 14.6	.. 53.7	230 06.5	.. 50.6	Bellatrix	278 27.2	N 6 21.9
22	189 17.9	111 37.0	46.5	224 48.3	50.6	250 16.9	53.7	245 09.0	50.6	Betelgeuse	270 56.4	N 7 24.5
23	204 20.4	126 38.3	46.5	239 49.1	50.1	265 19.3	53.7	260 11.4	50.5			
1 00	219 22.8	141 39.6	N27 46.6	254 49.8	S15 49.6	280 21.6	S20 53.6	275 13.8	S19 50.5	Canopus	263 54.4	S52 42.7
01	234 25.3	156 40.9	46.7	269 50.6	49.1	295 24.0	53.6	290 16.2	50.5	Capella	280 27.9	N46 01.0
02	249 27.8	171 42.1	46.7	284 51.3	48.6	310 26.3	53.6	305 18.6	50.5	Deneb	49 28.3	N45 20.8
03	264 30.2	186 43.4	.. 46.8	299 52.1	.. 48.1	325 28.7	.. 53.6	320 21.1	.. 50.5	Denebola	182 28.6	N14 27.6
04	279 32.7	201 44.7	46.8	314 52.8	47.6	340 31.0	53.6	335 23.5	50.5	Diphda	348 51.4	S17 52.7
05	294 35.2	216 46.0	46.9	329 53.6	47.1	355 33.4	53.6	350 25.9	50.5			
06	309 37.6	231 47.3	N27 47.0	344 54.3	S15 46.6	10 35.7	S20 53.5	5 28.3	S19 50.5	Dubhe	193 45.5	N61 38.8
07	324 40.1	246 48.6	47.0	359 55.1	46.0	25 38.1	53.5	20 30.7	50.5	Elnath	278 06.9	N28 37.4
F 08	339 42.5	261 49.9	47.1	14 55.8	45.5	40 40.5	53.5	35 33.2	50.5	Eltanin	90 43.6	N51 29.0
R 09	354 45.0	276 51.3	.. 47.1	29 56.6	.. 45.0	55 42.8	.. 53.5	50 35.6	.. 50.5	Enif	33 42.6	N 9 57.9
10	9 47.5	291 52.6	47.2	44 57.3	44.5	70 45.2	53.5	65 38.0	50.5	Fomalhaut	15 18.9	S29 30.9
11	24 49.9	306 53.9	47.3	59 58.1	44.0	85 47.5	53.5	80 40.4	50.5			
D 12	39 52.4	321 55.2	N27 47.3	74 58.8	S15 43.5	100 49.9	S20 53.5	95 42.9	S19 50.5	Gacrux	171 55.2	S57 13.7
A 13	54 54.9	336 56.5	47.4	89 59.6	43.0	115 52.2	53.5	110 45.3	50.5	Gienah	175 47.2	S17 39.3
Y 14	69 57.3	351 57.9	47.4	105 00.3	42.5	130 54.6	53.4	125 47.7	50.5	Hadar	148 40.6	S60 28.2
15	84 59.8	6 59.2	.. 47.5	120 01.1	.. 42.0	145 56.9	.. 53.4	140 50.1	.. 50.5	Hamal	327 55.8	N23 33.2
16	100 02.3	22 00.5	47.5	135 01.8	41.5	160 59.3	53.4	155 52.5	50.5	Kaus Aust.	83 37.3	S34 22.3
17	115 04.7	37 01.9	47.6	150 02.6	41.0	176 01.7	53.4	170 55.0	50.5			
18	130 07.2	52 03.2	N27 47.6	165 03.3	S15 40.5	191 04.0	S20 53.4	185 57.4	S19 50.5	Kochab	137 18.8	N74 04.4
19	145 09.6	67 04.5	47.7	180 04.1	40.0	206 06.4	53.4	200 59.8	50.4	Markab	13 33.8	N15 18.6
20	160 12.1	82 05.9	47.7	195 04.8	39.5	221 08.7	53.4	216 02.2	50.4	Menkar	314 10.4	N 4 09.9
21	175 14.6	97 07.2	.. 47.8	210 05.6	.. 39.0	236 11.1	.. 53.3	231 04.7	.. 50.4	Menkent	148 01.6	S36 28.2
22	190 17.0	112 08.6	47.8	225 06.3	38.5	251 13.4	53.3	246 07.1	50.4	Miaplacidus	221 38.7	S69 48.3
23	205 19.5	127 10.0	47.9	240 07.1	37.9	266 15.8	53.3	261 09.5	50.4			
2 00	220 22.0	142 11.3	N27 47.9	255 07.9	S15 37.4	281 18.2	S20 53.3	276 11.9	S19 50.4	Mirfak	308 34.1	N49 55.8
01	235 24.4	157 12.7	48.0	270 08.6	36.9	296 20.5	53.3	291 14.4	50.4	Nunki	75 52.3	S26 16.2
02	250 26.9	172 14.0	48.0	285 09.4	36.4	311 22.9	53.3	306 16.8	50.4	Peacock	53 11.7	S56 39.9
03	265 29.4	187 15.4	.. 48.0	300 10.1	.. 35.9	326 25.2	.. 53.3	321 19.2	.. 50.4	Pollux	243 22.1	N27 58.6
04	280 31.8	202 16.8	48.1	315 10.9	35.4	341 27.6	53.3	336 21.6	50.4	Procyon	244 54.9	N 5 10.3
05	295 34.3	217 18.2	48.1	330 11.6	34.9	356 30.0	53.2	351 24.1	50.4			
06	310 36.8	232 19.6	N27 48.2	345 12.4	S15 34.4	11 32.3	S20 53.2	6 26.5	S19 50.4	Rasalhague	96 01.8	N12 32.7
07	325 39.2	247 20.9	48.2	0 13.1	33.9	26 34.7	53.2	21 28.9	50.4	Regulus	207 38.4	N11 52.1
S 08	340 41.7	262 22.3	48.2	15 13.9	33.4	41 37.1	53.2	36 31.3	50.4	Rigel	281 07.8	S 8 10.9
A 09	355 44.1	277 23.7	.. 48.3	30 14.6	.. 32.9	56 39.4	.. 53.2	51 33.8	.. 50.4	Rigil Kent.	139 44.7	S60 55.0
T 10	10 46.6	292 25.1	48.3	45 15.4	32.3	71 41.8	53.2	66 36.2	50.4	Sabik	102 06.8	S15 44.9
U 11	25 49.1	307 26.5	48.3	60 16.2	31.8	86 44.1	53.2	81 38.6	50.4			
R 12	40 51.5	322 27.9	N27 48.4	75 16.9	S15 31.3	101 46.5	S20 53.2	96 41.0	S19 50.4	Schedar	349 35.7	N56 38.6
D 13	55 54.0	337 29.3	48.4	90 17.7	30.8	116 48.9	53.1	111 43.5	50.4	Shaula	96 15.2	S37 06.9
A 14	70 56.5	352 30.7	48.4	105 18.4	30.3	131 51.2	53.1	126 45.9	50.4	Sirius	258 29.8	S16 44.9
Y 15	85 58.9	7 32.1	.. 48.5	120 19.2	.. 29.8	146 53.6	.. 53.1	141 48.3	.. 50.4	Spica	158 26.0	S11 16.0
16	101 01.4	22 33.5	48.5	135 19.9	29.3	161 56.0	53.1	156 50.8	50.4	Suhail	222 49.0	S43 31.1
17	116 03.9	37 35.0	48.5	150 20.7	28.8	176 58.3	53.1	171 53.2	50.4			
18	131 06.3	52 36.4	N27 48.6	165 21.4	S15 28.3	192 00.7	S20 53.1	186 55.6	S19 50.3	Vega	80 35.5	N38 48.0
19	146 08.8	67 37.8	48.6	180 22.2	27.8	207 03.1	53.1	201 58.0	50.3	Zuben'ubi	136 59.9	S16 07.5
20	161 11.3	82 39.2	48.6	195 23.0	27.2	222 05.4	53.1	217 00.5	50.3		SHA	Mer.Pass.
21	176 13.7	97 40.7	.. 48.6	210 23.7	.. 26.7	237 07.8	.. 53.1	232 02.9	.. 50.3	Venus	282 16.7	14 32
22	191 16.2	112 42.1	48.7	225 24.5	26.2	252 10.2	53.0	247 05.3	50.3	Mars	35 27.0	7 00
23	206 18.6	127 43.5	48.7	240 25.2	25.7	267 12.5	53.0	262 07.8	50.3	Jupiter	60 58.8	5 18
Mer. Pass.	h m 9 20.9	v 1.3	d 0.1	v 0.8	d 0.5	v 2.4	d 0.0	v 2.4	d 0.0	Saturn	55 51.0	5 38

UT	SUN GHA	SUN Dec	MOON GHA	v	MOON Dec	d	HP
d h	° ′	° ′	° ′	′	° ′	′	′
30 00	180 41.4	N14 51.0	96 17.1	7.7	N22 43.6	4.6	57.5
01	195 41.5	51.7	110 43.8	7.7	22 39.0	4.7	57.5
02	210 41.5	52.5	125 10.5	7.7	22 34.3	4.8	57.6
03	225 41.6 ..	53.3	139 37.2	7.7	22 29.5	4.9	57.6
04	240 41.7	54.0	154 03.9	7.8	22 24.6	5.1	57.6
05	255 41.8	54.8	168 30.7	7.7	22 19.5	5.3	57.7
06	270 41.8	N14 55.5	182 57.4	7.7	N22 14.2	5.3	57.7
T 07	285 41.9	56.3	197 24.1	7.7	22 08.9	5.5	57.7
H 08	300 42.0	57.1	211 50.8	7.8	22 03.4	5.7	57.7
U 09	315 42.1 ..	57.8	226 17.6	7.7	21 57.7	5.7	57.8
R 10	330 42.2	58.6	240 44.3	7.8	21 52.0	5.9	57.8
S 11	345 42.2	14 59.3	255 11.1	7.8	21 46.1	6.1	57.8
D 12	0 42.3	N15 00.1	269 37.9	7.8	N21 40.0	6.1	57.9
A 13	15 42.4	00.9	284 04.7	7.8	21 33.9	6.4	57.9
Y 14	30 42.5	01.6	298 31.5	7.8	21 27.5	6.4	57.9
15	45 42.5 ..	02.4	312 58.3	7.8	21 21.1	6.6	58.0
16	60 42.6	03.1	327 25.1	7.9	21 14.5	6.7	58.0
17	75 42.7	03.9	341 52.0	7.8	21 07.8	6.8	58.0
18	90 42.8	N15 04.6	356 18.8	7.9	N21 01.0	7.0	58.1
19	105 42.8	05.4	10 45.7	7.9	20 54.0	7.1	58.1
20	120 42.9	06.2	25 12.6	7.9	20 46.9	7.2	58.1
21	135 43.0 ..	06.9	39 39.5	7.9	20 39.7	7.3	58.2
22	150 43.1	07.7	54 06.4	8.0	20 32.4	7.5	58.2
23	165 43.1	08.4	68 33.4	7.9	20 24.9	7.5	58.2
1 00	180 43.2	N15 09.2	83 00.3	8.0	N20 17.3	7.8	58.3
01	195 43.3	09.9	97 27.3	8.0	20 09.5	7.8	58.3
02	210 43.4	10.7	111 54.3	8.1	20 01.7	8.0	58.3
03	225 43.4 ..	11.4	126 21.4	8.0	19 53.7	8.1	58.4
04	240 43.5	12.2	140 48.4	8.1	19 45.6	8.3	58.4
05	255 43.6	12.9	155 15.5	8.1	19 37.3	8.4	58.4
06	270 43.7	N15 13.7	169 42.6	8.1	N19 28.9	8.4	58.4
F 07	285 43.7	14.4	184 09.7	8.1	19 20.5	8.7	58.5
R 08	300 43.8	15.2	198 36.8	8.2	19 11.8	8.7	58.5
I 09	315 43.9 ..	15.9	213 04.0	8.2	19 03.1	8.9	58.5
D 10	330 44.0	16.7	227 31.2	8.2	18 54.2	8.9	58.6
A 11	345 44.0	17.4	241 58.4	8.2	18 45.3	9.1	58.6
Y 12	0 44.1	N15 18.2	256 25.6	8.2	N18 36.2	9.3	58.6
13	15 44.2	18.9	270 52.8	8.3	18 26.9	9.3	58.7
14	30 44.2	19.7	285 20.1	8.3	18 17.6	9.4	58.7
15	45 44.3 ..	20.4	299 47.4	8.3	18 08.2	9.6	58.7
16	60 44.4	21.2	314 14.7	8.4	17 58.6	9.7	58.8
17	75 44.4	21.9	328 42.1	8.4	17 48.9	9.8	58.8
18	90 44.5	N15 22.7	343 09.5	8.4	N17 39.1	9.9	58.8
19	105 44.6	23.4	357 36.9	8.4	17 29.2	10.1	58.9
20	120 44.7	24.2	12 04.3	8.4	17 19.1	10.1	58.9
21	135 44.7 ..	24.9	26 31.7	8.5	17 09.0	10.3	58.9
22	150 44.8	25.7	40 59.2	8.5	16 58.7	10.3	59.0
23	165 44.9	26.4	55 26.7	8.5	16 48.4	10.5	59.0
2 00	180 44.9	N15 27.1	69 54.2	8.6	N16 37.9	10.6	59.0
01	195 45.0	27.9	84 21.8	8.6	16 27.3	10.7	59.1
02	210 45.1	28.6	98 49.4	8.6	16 16.6	10.8	59.1
03	225 45.1 ..	29.4	113 17.0	8.6	16 05.8	10.9	59.1
04	240 45.2	30.1	127 44.6	8.6	15 54.9	11.0	59.1
05	255 45.3	30.9	142 12.2	8.7	15 43.9	11.1	59.2
06	270 45.3	N15 31.6	156 39.9	8.7	N15 32.8	11.2	59.2
S 07	285 45.4	32.3	171 07.6	8.8	15 21.6	11.4	59.2
A 08	300 45.5	33.1	185 35.4	8.7	15 10.2	11.4	59.3
T 09	315 45.5 ..	33.8	200 03.1	8.8	14 58.8	11.5	59.3
U 10	330 45.6	34.6	214 30.9	8.8	14 47.3	11.6	59.3
R 11	345 45.7	35.3	228 58.7	8.8	14 35.7	11.7	59.4
D 12	0 45.7	N15 36.0	243 26.5	8.9	N14 24.0	11.9	59.4
A 13	15 45.8	36.8	257 54.4	8.8	14 12.1	11.9	59.4
Y 14	30 45.9	37.5	272 22.2	8.9	14 00.2	12.0	59.5
15	45 45.9 ..	38.2	286 50.1	9.0	13 48.2	12.1	59.5
16	60 46.0	39.0	301 18.1	8.9	13 36.1	12.2	59.5
17	75 46.1	39.7	315 46.0	9.0	13 23.9	12.2	59.5
18	90 46.1	N15 40.4	330 14.0	8.9	N13 11.7	12.4	59.6
19	105 46.2	41.2	344 41.9	9.1	12 59.3	12.5	59.6
20	120 46.3	41.9	359 10.0	9.0	12 46.8	12.5	59.6
21	135 46.3 ..	42.6	13 38.0	9.0	12 34.3	12.7	59.7
22	150 46.4	43.4	28 06.0	9.1	12 21.6	12.7	59.7
23	165 46.5	44.1	42 34.1	9.1	N12 08.9	12.8	59.7
	SD 15.9	d 0.7	SD 15.8		16.0		16.2

Lat.	Twilight Naut.	Twilight Civil	Sunrise	Moonrise 30	1	2	3
°	h m	h m	h m	h m	h m	h m	h m
N 72	////	////	01 49	▭	▭	10 09	12 43
N 70	////	////	02 28	▭	07 59	10 42	12 58
68	////	01 02	02 55	▭	08 56	11 06	13 09
66	////	01 53	03 16	07 32	09 29	11 25	13 19
64	////	02 23	03 32	08 11	09 53	11 39	13 27
62	00 55	02 46	03 46	08 38	10 12	11 52	13 33
60	01 40	03 04	03 57	08 59	10 28	12 02	13 39
N 58	02 08	03 18	04 07	09 16	10 41	12 11	13 44
56	02 29	03 31	04 15	09 31	10 52	12 19	13 49
54	02 46	03 41	04 23	09 43	11 02	12 26	13 53
52	03 00	03 51	04 30	09 54	11 11	12 32	13 57
50	03 12	03 59	04 36	10 04	11 19	12 38	14 00
45	03 36	04 16	04 49	10 24	11 35	12 50	14 07
N 40	03 55	04 30	05 00	10 41	11 49	13 00	14 13
35	04 09	04 42	05 09	10 55	12 01	13 09	14 18
30	04 21	04 52	05 17	11 07	12 11	13 16	14 23
20	04 40	05 08	05 31	11 28	12 28	13 29	14 31
N 10	04 55	05 21	05 43	11 45	12 43	13 40	14 37
0	05 07	05 32	05 54	12 02	12 57	13 51	14 44
S 10	05 18	05 43	06 05	12 19	13 11	14 01	14 50
20	05 27	05 53	06 16	12 37	13 26	14 12	14 57
30	05 36	06 04	06 29	12 57	13 43	14 25	15 05
35	05 40	06 10	06 37	13 09	13 53	14 32	15 09
40	05 45	06 17	06 45	13 23	14 04	14 41	15 14
45	05 50	06 24	06 55	13 39	14 17	14 50	15 20
S 50	05 55	06 33	07 07	13 59	14 33	15 02	15 27
52	05 57	06 37	07 13	14 08	14 41	15 07	15 30
54	05 59	06 41	07 19	14 19	14 49	15 13	15 33
56	06 01	06 46	07 26	14 30	14 58	15 20	15 37
58	06 04	06 51	07 33	14 44	15 09	15 27	15 41
S 60	06 06	06 56	07 42	15 00	15 21	15 35	15 46

Lat.	Sunset	Twilight Civil	Twilight Naut.	Moonset 30	1	2	3
°	h m	h m	h m	h m	h m	h m	h m
N 72	22 13	////	////	▭	▭	05 26	04 45
N 70	21 30	////	////	▭	05 41	04 51	04 28
68	21 02	23 04	////	▭	04 44	04 28	04 14
66	20 41	22 07	////	04 11	04 09	04 06	04 03
64	20 24	21 35	////	03 32	03 44	03 50	03 53
62	20 11	21 11	23 10	03 04	03 25	03 37	03 45
60	19 59	20 53	22 19	02 43	03 08	03 26	03 38
N 58	19 49	20 38	21 49	02 25	02 55	03 16	03 32
56	19 40	20 25	21 28	02 10	02 43	03 07	03 26
54	19 33	20 14	21 10	01 58	02 32	02 59	03 21
52	19 26	20 05	20 56	01 46	02 23	02 52	03 17
50	19 19	19 56	20 43	01 36	02 15	02 46	03 12
45	19 06	19 39	20 19	01 15	01 57	02 32	03 03
N 40	18 55	19 25	20 00	00 58	01 42	02 21	02 56
35	18 46	19 13	19 46	00 44	01 30	02 11	02 49
30	18 38	19 03	19 33	00 31	01 19	02 03	02 43
20	18 24	18 47	19 14	00 10	01 00	01 48	02 33
N 10	18 12	18 34	18 59	24 44	00 44	01 35	02 24
0	18 00	18 22	18 47	24 28	00 28	01 23	02 16
S 10	17 49	18 11	18 36	24 13	00 13	01 10	02 08
20	17 38	18 01	18 27	23 56	24 57	00 57	01 58
30	17 25	17 49	18 18	23 37	24 42	00 42	01 48
35	17 17	17 43	18 13	23 26	24 33	00 33	01 42
40	17 08	17 37	18 09	23 13	24 23	00 23	01 35
45	16 58	17 29	18 04	22 57	24 10	00 10	01 26
S 50	16 46	17 20	17 59	22 38	23 56	25 17	01 17
52	16 41	17 17	17 57	22 29	23 49	25 12	01 12
54	16 34	17 12	17 54	22 19	23 41	25 07	01 07
56	16 28	17 08	17 52	22 08	23 32	25 01	01 01
58	16 20	17 03	17 49	21 54	23 23	24 55	00 55
S 60	16 11	16 57	17 47	21 39	23 11	24 48	00 48

	SUN			MOON			
Day	Eqn. of Time 00h	Eqn. of Time 12h	Mer. Pass.	Mer. Pass. Upper	Mer. Pass. Lower	Age	Phase
d	m s	m s	h m	h m	h m	d	%
30	02 45	02 49	11 57	18 15	05 48	07	46
1	02 53	02 56	11 57	19 10	06 43	08	57
2	03 00	03 03	11 57	20 03	07 37	09	68

UT	ARIES	VENUS −4.7		MARS +0.4		JUPITER −2.4		SATURN +0.6		STARS		
	GHA	GHA	Dec	GHA	Dec	GHA	Dec	GHA	Dec	Name	SHA	Dec
d h	° ′	° ′	° ′	° ′	° ′	° ′	° ′	° ′	° ′		° ′	° ′
3 00	221 21.1	142 45.0	N27 48.7	255 26.0	S15 25.2	282 14.9	S20 53.0	277 10.2	S19 50.3	Acamar	315 15.1	S40 13.6
01	236 23.6	157 46.4	48.7	270 26.8	24.7	297 17.3	53.0	292 12.6	50.3	Achernar	335 23.7	S57 08.1
02	251 26.0	172 47.9	48.8	285 27.5	24.2	312 19.6	53.0	307 15.0	50.3	Acrux	173 03.5	S63 12.8
03	266 28.5	187 49.3 ..	48.8	300 28.3 ..	23.7	327 22.0 ..	53.0	322 17.5 ..	50.3	Adhara	255 09.0	S29 00.2
04	281 31.0	202 50.8	48.8	315 29.0	23.1	342 24.4	53.0	337 19.9	50.3	Aldebaran	290 44.3	N16 32.8
05	296 33.4	217 52.3	48.8	330 29.8	22.6	357 26.7	53.0	352 22.3	50.3			
06	311 35.9	232 53.7	N27 48.8	345 30.5	S15 22.1	12 29.1	S20 53.0	7 24.8	S19 50.3	Alioth	166 16.0	N55 51.2
07	326 38.4	247 55.2	48.8	0 31.3	21.6	27 31.5	52.9	22 27.2	50.3	Alkaid	152 54.6	N49 12.9
S 08	341 40.8	262 56.7	48.9	15 32.1	21.1	42 33.8	52.9	37 29.6	50.3	Alnair	27 37.9	S46 51.6
U 09	356 43.3	277 58.1 ..	48.9	30 32.8 ..	20.6	57 36.2 ..	52.9	52 32.0 ..	50.3	Alnilam	275 41.8	S 1 11.5
N 10	11 45.7	292 59.6	48.9	45 33.6	20.1	72 38.6	52.9	67 34.5	50.3	Alphard	217 51.4	S 8 44.9
D 11	26 48.2	308 01.1	48.9	60 34.3	19.5	87 41.0	52.9	82 36.9	50.3			
A 12	41 50.7	323 02.6	N27 48.9	75 35.1	S15 19.0	102 43.3	S20 52.9	97 39.3	S19 50.3	Alphecca	126 06.6	N26 38.8
Y 13	56 53.1	338 04.1	48.9	90 35.9	18.5	117 45.7	52.9	112 41.8	50.3	Alpheratz	357 38.9	N29 11.8
14	71 55.6	353 05.6	48.9	105 36.6	18.0	132 48.1	52.9	127 44.2	50.3	Altair	62 03.5	N 8 55.2
15	86 58.1	8 07.1 ..	48.9	120 37.4 ..	17.5	147 50.5 ..	52.9	142 46.6 ..	50.3	Ankaa	353 11.3	S42 11.8
16	102 00.5	23 08.6	48.9	135 38.2	17.0	162 52.8	52.8	157 49.1	50.3	Antares	112 20.1	S26 28.5
17	117 03.0	38 10.1	49.0	150 38.9	16.5	177 55.2	52.8	172 51.5	50.3			
18	132 05.5	53 11.6	N27 49.0	165 39.7	S15 15.9	192 57.6	S20 52.8	187 53.9	S19 50.3	Arcturus	145 51.1	N19 04.7
19	147 07.9	68 13.1	49.0	180 40.4	15.4	207 59.9	52.8	202 56.4	50.3	Atria	107 17.2	S69 03.6
20	162 10.4	83 14.6	49.0	195 41.2	14.9	223 02.3	52.8	217 58.8	50.3	Avior	234 16.3	S59 34.8
21	177 12.9	98 16.1 ..	49.0	210 41.9 ..	14.4	238 04.7 ..	52.8	233 01.2 ..	50.3	Bellatrix	278 27.2	N 6 21.9
22	192 15.3	113 17.6	49.0	225 42.7	13.9	253 07.1	52.8	248 03.7	50.3	Betelgeuse	270 56.4	N 7 24.5
23	207 17.8	128 19.2	49.0	240 43.5	13.4	268 09.4	52.8	263 06.1	50.3			
4 00	222 20.2	143 20.7	N27 49.0	255 44.2	S15 12.9	283 11.8	S20 52.8	278 08.5	S19 50.2	Canopus	263 54.4	S52 42.7
01	237 22.7	158 22.2	49.0	270 45.0	12.3	298 14.2	52.8	293 11.0	50.2	Capella	280 27.9	N46 01.0
02	252 25.2	173 23.7	49.0	285 45.8	11.8	313 16.6	52.7	308 13.4	50.2	Deneb	49 28.3	N45 20.9
03	267 27.6	188 25.3 ..	49.0	300 46.5 ..	11.3	328 18.9 ..	52.7	323 15.8 ..	50.2	Denebola	182 28.6	N14 27.6
04	282 30.1	203 26.8	49.0	315 47.3	10.8	343 21.3	52.7	338 18.3	50.2	Diphda	348 51.4	S17 52.7
05	297 32.6	218 28.4	49.0	330 48.0	10.3	358 23.7	52.7	353 20.7	50.2			
06	312 35.0	233 29.9	N27 49.0	345 48.8	S15 09.8	13 26.1	S20 52.7	8 23.1	S19 50.2	Dubhe	193 45.5	N61 38.8
07	327 37.5	248 31.5	49.0	0 49.6	09.2	28 28.5	52.7	23 25.6	50.2	Elnath	278 07.0	N28 37.4
M 08	342 40.0	263 33.0	48.9	15 50.3	08.7	43 30.8	52.7	38 28.0	50.2	Eltanin	90 43.6	N51 29.0
O 09	357 42.4	278 34.6 ..	48.9	30 51.1 ..	08.2	58 33.2 ..	52.7	53 30.4 ..	50.2	Enif	33 42.6	N 9 57.9
N 10	12 44.9	293 36.2	48.9	45 51.9	07.7	73 35.6	52.7	68 32.9	50.2	Fomalhaut	15 18.9	S29 30.9
D 11	27 47.3	308 37.7	48.9	60 52.6	07.2	88 38.0	52.7	83 35.3	50.2			
A 12	42 49.8	323 39.3	N27 48.9	75 53.4	S15 06.6	103 40.4	S20 52.6	98 37.7	S19 50.2	Gacrux	171 55.2	S57 13.7
Y 13	57 52.3	338 40.9	48.9	90 54.2	06.1	118 42.7	52.6	113 40.2	50.2	Gienah	175 47.2	S17 39.3
14	72 54.7	353 42.5	48.9	105 54.9	05.6	133 45.1	52.6	128 42.6	50.2	Hadar	148 40.6	S60 28.2
15	87 57.2	8 44.0 ..	48.9	120 55.7 ..	05.1	148 47.5 ..	52.6	143 45.0 ..	50.2	Hamal	327 55.8	N23 33.2
16	102 59.7	23 45.6	48.9	135 56.5	04.6	163 49.9	52.6	158 47.5	50.2	Kaus Aust.	83 37.3	S34 22.3
17	118 02.1	38 47.2	48.8	150 57.2	04.1	178 52.3	52.6	173 49.9	50.2			
18	133 04.6	53 48.8	N27 48.8	165 58.0	S15 03.5	193 54.6	S20 52.6	188 52.4	S19 50.2	Kochab	137 18.8	N74 04.4
19	148 07.1	68 50.4	48.8	180 58.7	03.0	208 57.0	52.6	203 54.8	50.2	Markab	13 33.8	N15 18.6
20	163 09.5	83 52.0	48.8	195 59.5	02.5	223 59.4	52.6	218 57.2	50.2	Menkar	314 10.4	N 4 09.9
21	178 12.0	98 53.6 ..	48.8	211 00.3 ..	02.0	239 01.8 ..	52.6	233 59.7 ..	50.2	Menkent	148 01.6	S36 28.2
22	193 14.5	113 55.2	48.8	226 01.0	01.5	254 04.2	52.5	249 02.1	50.2	Miaplacidus	221 38.8	S69 48.3
23	208 16.9	128 56.8	48.7	241 01.8	00.9	269 06.6	52.5	264 04.5	50.2			
5 00	223 19.4	143 58.4	N27 48.7	256 02.6	S15 00.4	284 08.9	S20 52.5	279 07.0	S19 50.2	Mirfak	308 34.1	N49 55.8
01	238 21.8	159 00.1	48.7	271 03.3	14 59.9	299 11.3	52.5	294 09.4	50.2	Nunki	75 52.3	S26 16.2
02	253 24.3	174 01.7	48.7	286 04.1	59.4	314 13.7	52.5	309 11.8	50.2	Peacock	53 11.7	S56 39.9
03	268 26.8	189 03.3 ..	48.6	301 04.9 ..	58.9	329 16.1 ..	52.5	324 14.3 ..	50.2	Pollux	243 22.1	N27 58.6
04	283 29.2	204 05.0	48.6	316 05.6	58.3	344 18.5	52.5	339 16.7	50.2	Procyon	244 54.9	N 5 10.3
05	298 31.7	219 06.6	48.6	331 06.4	57.8	359 20.9	52.5	354 19.2	50.2			
06	313 34.2	234 08.2	N27 48.6	346 07.2	S14 57.3	14 23.2	S20 52.5	9 21.6	S19 50.2	Rasalhague	96 01.8	N12 32.7
07	328 36.6	249 09.9	48.5	1 07.9	56.8	29 25.6	52.5	24 24.0	50.2	Regulus	207 38.4	N11 52.1
T 08	343 39.1	264 11.5	48.5	16 08.7	56.3	44 28.0	52.5	39 26.5	50.2	Rigel	281 07.8	S 8 10.9
U 09	358 41.6	279 13.2 ..	48.5	31 09.5 ..	55.7	59 30.4 ..	52.5	54 28.9 ..	50.2	Rigil Kent.	139 44.5	S60 55.0
E 10	13 44.0	294 14.8	48.4	46 10.2	55.2	74 32.8	52.5	69 31.4	50.2	Sabik	102 06.8	S15 44.9
S 11	28 46.5	309 16.5	48.4	61 11.0	54.7	89 35.2	52.5	84 33.8	50.2			
D 12	43 49.0	324 18.1	N27 48.4	76 11.8	S14 54.2	104 37.6	S20 52.4	99 36.2	S19 50.2	Schedar	349 35.7	N56 38.6
A 13	58 51.4	339 19.8	48.3	91 12.6	53.6	119 40.0	52.4	114 38.7	50.2	Shaula	96 15.2	S37 06.9
Y 14	73 53.9	354 21.5	48.3	106 13.3	53.1	134 42.3	52.4	129 41.1	50.2	Sirius	258 29.8	S16 44.9
15	88 56.3	9 23.1 ..	48.3	121 14.1 ..	52.6	149 44.7 ..	52.4	144 43.6 ..	50.2	Spica	158 26.0	S11 16.0
16	103 58.8	24 24.8	48.2	136 14.9	52.1	164 47.1	52.4	159 46.0	50.2	Suhail	222 49.0	S43 31.1
17	119 01.3	39 26.5	48.2	151 15.6	51.6	179 49.5	52.4	174 48.4	50.2			
18	134 03.7	54 28.2	N27 48.2	166 16.4	S14 51.0	194 51.9	S20 52.4	189 50.9	S19 50.2	Vega	80 35.5	N38 48.0
19	149 06.2	69 29.9	48.1	181 17.2	50.5	209 54.3	52.4	204 53.3	50.2	Zuben'ubi	136 59.9	S16 07.5
20	164 08.7	84 31.6	48.1	196 17.9	50.0	224 56.7	52.4	219 55.8	50.2		SHA	Mer. Pass.
21	179 11.1	99 33.3 ..	48.0	211 18.7 ..	49.5	239 59.1 ..	52.4	234 58.2 ..	50.2		° ′	h m
22	194 13.6	114 35.0	48.0	226 19.5	48.9	255 01.5	52.4	250 00.6	50.2	Venus	281 00.4	14 25
23	209 16.1	129 36.7	47.9	241 20.2	48.4	270 03.9	52.4	265 03.1	50.2	Mars	33 24.0	6 57
	h m									Jupiter	60 51.6	5 06
Mer. Pass. 9 09.1	v 1.6 d 0.0		v 0.8 d 0.5		v 2.4 d 0.0		v 2.4 d 0.0		Saturn	55 48.3	5 27

UT	SUN GHA	SUN Dec	MOON GHA	v	MOON Dec	d	HP
d h	° ′	° ′	° ′	′	° ′	′	′
3 00	180 46.5	N15 44.8	57 02.2	9.1	N11 56.1	12.9	59.7
01	195 46.6	45.6	71 30.3	9.1	11 43.2	12.9	59.8
02	210 46.6	46.3	85 58.4	9.2	11 30.3	13.1	59.8
03	225 46.7	.. 47.0	100 26.6	9.2	11 17.2	13.1	59.8
04	240 46.8	47.8	114 54.8	9.1	11 04.1	13.2	59.9
05	255 46.8	48.5	129 22.9	9.2	10 50.9	13.3	59.9
06	270 46.9	N15 49.2	143 51.1	9.3	N10 37.6	13.3	59.9
07	285 47.0	50.0	158 19.4	9.2	10 24.3	13.5	59.9
S 08	300 47.0	50.7	172 47.6	9.3	10 10.8	13.5	60.0
U 09	315 47.1	.. 51.4	187 15.9	9.2	9 57.3	13.5	60.0
N 10	330 47.1	52.1	201 44.1	9.3	9 43.8	13.7	60.0
D 11	345 47.2	52.9	216 12.4	9.3	9 30.1	13.7	60.0
A 12	0 47.3	N15 53.6	230 40.7	9.3	N 9 16.4	13.8	60.1
Y 13	15 47.3	54.3	245 09.0	9.3	9 02.6	13.8	60.1
14	30 47.4	55.1	259 37.3	9.4	8 48.8	13.9	60.1
15	45 47.4	.. 55.8	274 05.7	9.3	8 34.9	14.0	60.1
16	60 47.5	56.5	288 34.0	9.3	8 20.9	14.0	60.2
17	75 47.6	57.2	303 02.3	9.4	8 06.9	14.1	60.2
18	90 47.6	N15 58.0	317 30.7	9.4	N 7 52.8	14.2	60.2
19	105 47.7	58.7	331 59.1	9.4	7 38.6	14.2	60.2
20	120 47.7	15 59.4	346 27.5	9.4	7 24.4	14.2	60.3
21	135 47.8	16 00.1	0 55.9	9.4	7 10.2	14.3	60.3
22	150 47.9	00.8	15 24.3	9.4	6 55.9	14.4	60.3
23	165 47.9	01.6	29 52.7	9.3	6 41.5	14.4	60.3
4 00	180 48.0	N16 02.3	44 21.1	9.4	N 6 27.1	14.5	60.4
01	195 48.0	03.0	58 49.5	9.4	6 12.6	14.5	60.4
02	210 48.1	03.7	73 17.9	9.4	5 58.1	14.6	60.4
03	225 48.1	.. 04.4	87 46.3	9.4	5 43.5	14.6	60.4
04	240 48.2	05.2	102 14.7	9.5	5 28.9	14.6	60.4
05	255 48.3	05.9	116 43.2	9.4	5 14.3	14.7	60.5
06	270 48.3	N16 06.6	131 11.6	9.4	N 4 59.6	14.7	60.5
07	285 48.4	07.3	145 40.0	9.5	4 44.9	14.8	60.5
M 08	300 48.4	08.0	160 08.5	9.4	4 30.1	14.8	60.5
O 09	315 48.5	.. 08.8	174 36.9	9.4	4 15.3	14.9	60.5
N 10	330 48.5	09.5	189 05.3	9.4	4 00.4	14.8	60.5
D 11	345 48.6	10.2	203 33.7	9.4	3 45.6	15.0	60.6
A 12	0 48.7	N16 10.9	218 02.1	9.5	N 3 30.6	14.9	60.6
Y 13	15 48.7	11.6	232 30.6	9.4	3 15.7	15.0	60.6
14	30 48.8	12.3	246 59.0	9.4	3 00.7	15.0	60.6
15	45 48.8	.. 13.1	261 27.4	9.4	2 45.7	15.0	60.7
16	60 48.9	13.8	275 55.8	9.4	2 30.7	15.0	60.7
17	75 48.9	14.5	290 24.2	9.3	2 15.7	15.1	60.7
18	90 49.0	N16 15.2	304 52.5	9.4	N 2 00.6	15.1	60.7
19	105 49.0	15.9	319 20.9	9.4	1 45.5	15.1	60.7
20	120 49.1	16.6	333 49.3	9.3	1 30.4	15.1	60.7
21	135 49.1	.. 17.3	348 17.6	9.4	1 15.3	15.2	60.7
22	150 49.2	18.0	2 46.0	9.3	1 00.1	15.1	60.8
23	165 49.2	18.8	17 14.3	9.3	0 45.0	15.2	60.8
5 00	180 49.3	N16 19.5	31 42.6	9.3	N 0 29.8	15.2	60.8
01	195 49.3	20.2	46 10.9	9.3	N 0 14.6	15.2	60.8
02	210 49.4	20.9	60 39.2	9.2	S 0 00.6	15.2	60.8
03	225 49.4	.. 21.6	75 07.4	9.3	0 15.8	15.2	60.8
04	240 49.5	22.3	89 35.7	9.2	0 31.0	15.2	60.8
05	255 49.6	23.0	104 03.9	9.3	0 46.2	15.2	60.8
06	270 49.6	N16 23.7	118 32.2	9.1	S 1 01.4	15.2	60.9
07	285 49.7	24.4	133 00.3	9.2	1 16.6	15.2	60.9
T 08	300 49.7	25.1	147 28.5	9.2	1 31.8	15.2	60.9
U 09	315 49.8	.. 25.8	161 56.7	9.1	1 47.0	15.2	60.9
E 10	330 49.8	26.5	176 24.8	9.1	2 02.2	15.2	60.9
S 11	345 49.9	27.2	190 52.9	9.1	2 17.4	15.2	60.9
D 12	0 49.9	N16 27.9	205 21.0	9.1	S 2 32.6	15.1	60.9
A 13	15 49.9	28.6	219 49.1	9.0	2 47.7	15.2	60.9
Y 14	30 50.0	29.4	234 17.1	9.0	3 02.9	15.1	60.9
15	45 50.0	.. 30.1	248 45.1	9.0	3 18.0	15.2	60.9
16	60 50.1	30.8	263 13.1	8.9	3 33.2	15.1	60.9
17	75 50.1	31.5	277 41.1	8.9	3 48.3	15.1	60.9
18	90 50.2	N16 32.2	292 09.0	8.9	S 4 03.4	15.0	60.9
19	105 50.2	32.9	306 36.9	8.9	4 18.4	15.1	61.0
20	120 50.3	33.6	321 04.8	8.9	4 33.5	15.0	61.0
21	135 50.3	.. 34.3	335 32.7	8.8	4 48.5	15.0	61.0
22	150 50.4	35.0	350 00.5	8.8	5 03.5	15.0	61.0
23	165 50.4	35.7	4 28.3	8.7	S 5 18.5	14.9	61.0
	SD 15.9 d 0.7		SD 16.4		16.5		16.6

Twilight / Moonrise

Lat.	Twilight Naut.	Twilight Civil	Sunrise	Moonrise 3	4	5	6
°	h m	h m	h m	h m	h m	h m	h m
N 72	////	////	01 20	12 43	15 02	17 21	19 46
N 70	////	////	02 10	12 58	15 06	17 15	19 28
68	////	////	02 41	13 09	15 09	17 10	19 14
66	////	01 33	03 04	13 19	15 12	17 06	19 02
64	////	02 09	03 22	13 27	15 14	17 02	18 53
62	////	02 34	03 37	13 33	15 16	16 59	18 45
60	01 22	02 54	03 49	13 39	15 17	16 57	18 38
N 58	01 55	03 10	03 59	13 44	15 19	16 55	18 32
56	02 19	03 23	04 09	13 49	15 20	16 53	18 26
54	02 37	03 34	04 17	13 53	15 21	16 51	18 22
52	02 53	03 44	04 24	13 57	15 22	16 49	18 17
50	03 05	03 53	04 31	14 00	15 23	16 48	18 13
45	03 31	04 12	04 45	14 07	15 25	16 45	18 05
N 40	03 50	04 26	04 56	14 13	15 27	16 42	17 58
35	04 06	04 39	05 06	14 18	15 29	16 40	17 52
30	04 18	04 49	05 14	14 23	15 30	16 38	17 47
20	04 38	05 06	05 29	14 31	15 32	16 34	17 38
N 10	04 54	05 20	05 42	14 37	15 34	16 32	17 30
0	05 07	05 32	05 53	14 44	15 36	16 29	17 23
S 10	05 18	05 43	06 05	14 50	15 38	16 26	17 16
20	05 28	05 54	06 17	14 57	15 40	16 23	17 08
30	05 38	06 06	06 31	15 05	15 42	16 20	16 59
35	05 43	06 13	06 39	15 09	15 44	16 18	16 54
40	05 48	06 20	06 48	15 14	15 45	16 16	16 49
45	05 53	06 28	06 59	15 20	15 47	16 14	16 43
S 50	05 59	06 37	07 12	15 27	15 49	16 11	16 35
52	06 01	06 41	07 18	15 30	15 50	16 10	16 31
54	06 04	06 46	07 24	15 33	15 51	16 09	16 28
56	06 06	06 51	07 31	15 37	15 52	16 07	16 23
58	06 09	06 56	07 40	15 41	15 54	16 06	16 19
S 60	06 12	07 03	07 49	15 46	15 55	16 04	16 14

Sunset / Twilight / Moonset

Lat.	Sunset	Twilight Civil	Twilight Naut.	Moonset 3	4	5	6
°	h m	h m	h m	h m	h m	h m	h m
N 72	22 44	////	////	04 45	04 17	03 53	03 28
N 70	21 49	////	////	04 28	04 10	03 54	03 37
68	21 16	////	////	04 14	04 04	03 55	03 45
66	20 52	22 27	////	04 03	03 59	03 55	03 51
64	20 34	21 49	////	03 53	03 55	03 56	03 57
62	20 19	21 22	////	03 45	03 51	03 56	04 01
60	20 06	21 02	22 37	03 38	03 48	03 57	04 06
N 58	19 56	20 46	22 02	03 32	03 45	03 57	04 09
56	19 46	20 32	21 37	03 26	03 42	03 57	04 13
54	19 38	20 21	21 18	03 21	03 40	03 58	04 16
52	19 31	20 10	21 03	03 17	03 38	03 58	04 18
50	19 24	20 01	20 50	03 12	03 36	03 58	04 21
45	19 10	19 43	20 24	03 03	03 32	03 59	04 26
N 40	18 58	19 28	20 04	02 56	03 28	03 59	04 31
35	18 48	19 16	19 49	02 49	03 25	03 59	04 34
30	18 40	19 05	19 36	02 43	03 22	04 00	04 38
20	18 25	18 48	19 15	02 33	03 17	04 00	04 44
N 10	18 12	18 34	19 00	02 24	03 13	04 01	04 49
0	18 00	18 22	18 47	02 16	03 09	04 01	04 54
S 10	17 48	18 10	18 36	02 08	03 04	04 01	04 59
20	17 36	17 59	18 25	01 58	03 00	04 02	05 04
30	17 22	17 47	18 15	01 48	02 55	04 02	05 11
35	17 14	17 40	18 11	01 42	02 52	04 02	05 14
40	17 05	17 33	18 05	01 35	02 48	04 03	05 18
45	16 54	17 25	18 00	01 26	02 44	04 03	05 23
S 50	16 41	17 16	17 54	01 17	02 39	04 03	05 28
52	16 35	17 12	17 52	01 12	02 37	04 03	05 31
54	16 29	17 07	17 49	01 07	02 35	04 04	05 34
56	16 21	17 02	17 46	01 01	02 32	04 04	05 37
58	16 13	16 56	17 43	00 55	02 29	04 04	05 40
S 60	16 04	16 50	17 40	00 48	02 25	04 04	05 44

Day	SUN Eqn. of Time 00h	12h	SUN Mer. Pass.	MOON Mer. Pass. Upper	Lower	Age	Phase
d	m s	m s	h m	h m	h m	d	%
3	03 06	03 09	11 57	20 56	08 30	10	78
4	03 12	03 14	11 57	21 49	09 22	11	87
5	03 17	03 20	11 57	22 41	10 15	12	94

UT	ARIES	VENUS −4.7		MARS +0.3		JUPITER −2.4		SATURN +0.5		STARS		
d h	GHA	GHA	Dec	GHA	Dec	GHA	Dec	GHA	Dec	Name	SHA	Dec
6 00	224 18.5	144 38.4	N27 47.9	256 21.0	S14 47.9	285 06.2	S20 52.4	280 05.5	S19 50.2	Acamar	315 15.1	S40 13.6
01	239 21.0	159 40.1	47.9	271 21.8	47.4	300 08.6	52.3	295 08.0	50.2	Achernar	335 23.7	S57 08.1
02	254 23.4	174 41.8	47.8	286 22.6	46.8	315 11.0	52.3	310 10.4	50.2	Acrux	173 03.5	S63 12.8
03	269 25.9	189 43.5 ..	47.8	301 23.3 ..	46.3	330 13.4 ..	52.3	325 12.8 ..	50.2	Adhara	255 09.0	S29 00.2
04	284 28.4	204 45.2	47.7	316 24.1	45.8	345 15.8	52.3	340 15.3	50.2	Aldebaran	290 44.3	N16 32.8
05	299 30.8	219 47.0	47.7	331 24.9	45.3	0 18.2	52.3	355 17.7	50.2			
W 06	314 33.3	234 48.7	N27 47.6	346 25.6	S14 44.7	15 20.6	S20 52.3	10 20.2	S19 50.2	Alioth	166 16.0	N55 51.2
E 07	329 35.8	249 50.4	47.6	1 26.4	44.2	30 23.0	52.3	25 22.6	50.2	Alkaid	152 54.7	N49 12.9
D 08	344 38.2	264 52.2	47.5	16 27.2	43.7	45 25.4	52.3	40 25.1	50.2	Alnair	27 37.9	S46 51.6
N 09	359 40.7	279 53.9 ..	47.5	31 28.0 ..	43.2	60 27.8 ..	52.3	55 27.5 ..	50.2	Alnilam	275 41.8	S 1 11.5
E 10	14 43.2	294 55.7	47.4	46 28.7	42.6	75 30.2	52.3	70 29.9	50.2	Alphard	217 51.4	S 8 44.9
S 11	29 45.6	309 57.4	47.4	61 29.5	42.1	90 32.6	52.3	85 32.4	50.2			
D 12	44 48.1	324 59.2	N27 47.3	76 30.3	S14 41.6	105 35.0	S20 52.3	100 34.8	S19 50.2	Alphecca	126 06.6	N26 38.8
A 13	59 50.6	340 00.9	47.2	91 31.0	41.1	120 37.4	52.3	115 37.3	50.2	Alpheratz	357 38.9	N29 11.8
Y 14	74 53.0	355 02.7	47.2	106 31.8	40.5	135 39.8	52.3	130 39.7	50.2	Altair	62 03.5	N 8 55.2
15	89 55.5	10 04.5 ..	47.1	121 32.6 ..	40.0	150 42.2 ..	52.3	145 42.2 ..	50.2	Ankaa	353 11.3	S42 11.8
16	104 57.9	25 06.2	47.1	136 33.4	39.5	165 44.6	52.3	160 44.6	50.1	Antares	112 20.1	S26 28.5
17	120 00.4	40 08.0	47.0	151 34.1	39.0	180 47.0	52.2	175 47.1	50.1			
18	135 02.9	55 09.8	N27 46.9	166 34.9	S14 38.4	195 49.4	S20 52.2	190 49.5	S19 50.1	Arcturus	145 51.1	N19 04.7
19	150 05.3	70 11.6	46.9	181 35.7	37.9	210 51.8	52.2	205 51.9	50.1	Atria	107 17.2	S69 03.6
20	165 07.8	85 13.3	46.8	196 36.5	37.4	225 54.2	52.2	220 54.4	50.1	Avior	234 16.3	S59 34.8
21	180 10.3	100 15.1 ..	46.7	211 37.2 ..	36.9	240 56.6 ..	52.2	235 56.8 ..	50.1	Bellatrix	278 27.2	N 6 21.9
22	195 12.2	115 16.9	46.7	226 38.0	36.3	255 59.0	52.2	250 59.3	50.1	Betelgeuse	270 56.4	N 7 24.5
23	210 15.2	130 18.7	46.6	241 38.8	35.8	271 01.4	52.2	266 01.7	50.1			
7 00	225 17.7	145 20.5	N27 46.5	256 39.6	S14 35.3	286 03.8	S20 52.2	281 04.2	S19 50.1	Canopus	263 54.4	S52 42.7
01	240 20.1	160 22.3	46.5	271 40.3	34.7	301 06.2	52.2	296 06.6	50.1	Capella	280 27.9	N46 01.0
02	255 22.6	175 24.1	46.4	286 41.1	34.2	316 08.6	52.2	311 09.1	50.1	Deneb	49 28.2	N45 20.9
03	270 25.0	190 25.9 ..	46.3	301 41.9 ..	33.7	331 11.0 ..	52.2	326 11.5 ..	50.1	Denebola	182 28.6	N14 27.6
04	285 27.5	205 27.8	46.3	316 42.7	33.2	346 13.4	52.2	341 14.0	50.1	Diphda	348 51.4	S17 52.7
05	300 30.0	220 29.6	46.2	331 43.4	32.6	1 15.8	52.2	356 16.4	50.1			
T 06	315 32.4	235 31.4	N27 46.1	346 44.2	S14 32.1	16 18.2	S20 52.2	11 18.8	S19 50.1	Dubhe	193 45.5	N61 38.8
H 07	330 34.9	250 33.2	46.0	1 45.0	31.6	31 20.6	52.2	26 21.3	50.1	Elnath	278 07.0	N28 37.3
U 08	345 37.4	265 35.1	46.0	16 45.8	31.0	46 23.0	52.2	41 23.7	50.1	Eltanin	90 43.5	N51 29.0
R 09	0 39.8	280 36.9 ..	45.9	31 46.5 ..	30.5	61 25.4 ..	52.2	56 26.2 ..	50.1	Enif	33 42.5	N 9 57.9
S 10	15 42.3	295 38.8	45.8	46 47.3	30.0	76 27.8	52.2	71 28.6	50.1	Fomalhaut	15 18.9	S29 30.9
D 11	30 44.8	310 40.6	45.7	61 48.1	29.5	91 30.2	52.2	86 31.1	50.2			
A 12	45 47.2	325 42.5	N27 45.7	76 48.9	S14 28.9	106 32.6	S20 52.1	101 33.5	S19 50.2	Gacrux	171 55.2	S57 13.7
Y 13	60 49.7	340 44.3	45.6	91 49.6	28.4	121 35.0	52.1	116 36.0	50.2	Gienah	175 47.2	S17 39.3
14	75 52.2	355 46.2	45.5	106 50.4	27.9	136 37.4	52.1	131 38.4	50.2	Hadar	148 40.6	S60 28.2
15	90 54.6	10 48.0 ..	45.4	121 51.2 ..	27.3	151 39.8 ..	52.1	146 40.9 ..	50.2	Hamal	327 55.8	N23 33.2
16	105 57.1	25 49.9	45.3	136 52.0	26.8	166 42.2	52.1	161 43.3	50.2	Kaus Aust.	83 37.3	S34 22.3
17	120 59.5	40 51.8	45.3	151 52.8	26.3	181 44.6	52.1	176 45.8	50.2			
18	136 02.0	55 53.6	N27 45.2	166 53.5	S14 25.8	196 47.0	S20 52.1	191 48.2	S19 50.2	Kochab	137 18.8	N74 04.4
19	151 04.5	70 55.5	45.1	181 54.3	25.2	211 49.4	52.1	206 50.7	50.2	Markab	13 33.8	N15 18.6
20	166 06.9	85 57.4	45.0	196 55.1	24.7	226 51.8	52.1	221 53.1	50.2	Menkar	314 10.4	N 4 09.9
21	181 09.4	100 59.3 ..	44.9	211 55.9 ..	24.2	241 54.2 ..	52.1	236 55.6 ..	50.2	Menkent	148 01.6	S36 28.2
22	196 11.9	116 01.2	44.8	226 56.6	23.6	256 56.6	52.1	251 58.0	50.2	Miaplacidus	221 38.8	S69 48.3
23	211 14.3	131 03.1	44.7	241 57.4	23.1	271 59.0	52.1	267 00.5	50.2			
8 00	226 16.8	146 05.0	N27 44.6	256 58.2	S14 22.6	287 01.5	S20 52.1	282 02.9	S19 50.2	Mirfak	308 34.1	N49 55.8
01	241 19.3	161 06.9	44.5	271 59.0	22.0	302 03.9	52.1	297 05.4	50.2	Nunki	75 52.3	S26 16.2
02	256 21.7	176 08.8	44.5	286 59.8	21.5	317 06.3	52.1	312 07.8	50.2	Peacock	53 11.6	S56 39.9
03	271 24.2	191 10.7 ..	44.4	302 00.5 ..	21.0	332 08.7 ..	52.1	327 10.3 ..	50.2	Pollux	243 21.6	N27 58.6
04	286 26.7	206 12.6	44.3	317 01.3	20.4	347 11.1	52.1	342 12.7	50.2	Procyon	244 54.9	N 5 10.3
05	301 29.1	221 14.5	44.2	332 02.1	19.9	2 13.5	52.1	357 15.2	50.2			
F 06	316 31.6	236 16.4	N27 44.1	347 02.9	S14 19.4	17 15.9	S20 52.1	12 17.6	S19 50.2	Rasalhague	96 01.8	N12 32.7
R 07	331 34.0	251 18.4	44.0	2 03.7	18.8	32 18.3	52.1	27 20.1	50.2	Regulus	207 38.4	N11 52.1
I 08	346 36.5	266 20.3	43.9	17 04.4	18.3	47 20.7	52.1	42 22.5	50.2	Rigel	281 07.8	S 8 10.9
D 09	1 39.0	281 22.2 ..	43.8	32 05.2 ..	17.8	62 23.1 ..	52.1	57 25.0 ..	50.2	Rigil Kent.	139 44.7	S60 55.1
A 10	16 41.4	296 24.2	43.7	47 06.0	17.2	77 25.6	52.1	72 27.4	50.2	Sabik	102 06.8	S15 44.9
Y 11	31 43.9	311 26.1	43.6	62 06.8	16.7	92 28.0	52.1	87 29.9	50.2			
12	46 46.4	326 28.1	N27 43.5	77 07.6	S14 16.2	107 30.4	S20 52.1	102 32.3	S19 50.2	Schedar	349 35.7	N56 38.6
13	61 48.8	341 30.0	43.4	92 08.3	15.7	122 32.8	52.0	117 34.8	50.2	Shaula	96 15.2	S37 06.9
14	76 51.3	356 32.0	43.3	107 09.1	15.1	137 35.2	52.0	132 37.2	50.2	Sirius	258 29.8	S16 44.9
15	91 53.8	11 33.9 ..	43.2	122 09.9 ..	14.6	152 37.6 ..	52.0	147 39.7 ..	50.2	Spica	158 26.0	S11 16.0
16	106 56.2	26 35.9	43.1	137 10.7	14.1	167 40.0	52.0	162 42.1	50.2	Suhail	222 49.0	S43 31.1
17	121 58.7	41 37.9	42.9	152 11.5	13.5	182 42.4	52.0	177 44.6	50.2			
18	137 01.2	56 39.8	N27 42.8	167 12.2	S14 13.0	197 44.9	S20 52.0	192 47.0	S19 50.2	Vega	80 35.5	N38 48.0
19	152 03.6	71 41.8	42.7	182 13.0	12.4	212 47.3	52.0	207 49.5	50.2	Zuben'ubi	136 59.9	S16 07.5
20	167 06.1	86 43.8	42.6	197 13.8	11.9	227 49.7	52.0	222 51.9	50.2		SHA	Mer. Pass.
21	182 08.5	101 45.8 ..	42.5	212 14.6 ..	11.4	242 52.1 ..	52.0	237 54.4 ..	50.2		° '	h m
22	197 11.0	116 47.8	42.4	227 15.4	10.8	257 54.5	52.0	252 56.9	50.2	Venus	280 02.9	14 17
23	212 13.5	131 49.8	42.3	242 16.2	10.3	272 56.9	52.0	267 59.3	50.2	Mars	31 21.9	6 53
	h m									Jupiter	60 46.1	4 55
Mer. Pass.	8 57.4	v 1.9	d 0.1	v 0.8	d 0.5	v 2.4	d 0.0	v 2.4	d 0.0	Saturn	55 46.5	5 15

SUN and MOON

UT	SUN GHA	SUN Dec	MOON GHA	v	MOON Dec	d	HP
d h	° ′	° ′	° ′	′	° ′	′	′
6 00	180 50.5	N16 36.4	18 56.0	8.8	S 5 33.4	14.9	61.0
01	195 50.5	37.1	33 23.8	8.7	5 48.3	14.9	61.0
02	210 50.6	37.8	47 51.5	8.6	6 03.2	14.8	61.0
03	225 50.6 ..	38.5	62 19.1	8.6	6 18.0	14.8	61.0
04	240 50.7	39.2	76 46.7	8.6	6 32.8	14.8	61.0
05	255 50.7	39.8	91 14.3	8.6	6 47.6	14.7	61.0
06	270 50.7	N16 40.5	105 41.9	8.5	S 7 02.3	14.7	61.0
W 07	285 50.8	41.2	120 09.4	8.5	7 17.0	14.6	61.0
E 08	300 50.8	41.9	134 36.9	8.4	7 31.6	14.6	61.0
D 09	315 50.9 ..	42.6	149 04.3	8.4	7 46.2	14.5	61.0
N 10	330 50.9	43.3	163 31.7	8.4	8 00.7	14.5	61.0
E 11	345 51.0	44.0	177 59.1	8.3	8 15.2	14.5	61.0
S 12	0 51.0	N16 44.7	192 26.4	8.3	S 8 29.7	14.3	60.9
D 13	15 51.1	45.4	206 53.7	8.2	8 44.0	14.4	60.9
A 14	30 51.1	46.1	221 20.9	8.2	8 58.4	14.2	60.9
Y 15	45 51.1 ..	46.8	235 48.1	8.2	9 12.6	14.2	60.9
16	60 51.2	47.5	250 15.3	8.1	9 26.8	14.2	60.9
17	75 51.2	48.2	264 42.4	8.1	9 41.0	14.1	60.9
18	90 51.3	N16 48.9	279 09.5	8.0	S 9 55.1	14.0	60.9
19	105 51.3	49.5	293 36.5	8.0	10 09.1	13.9	60.9
20	120 51.4	50.2	308 03.5	8.0	10 23.0	13.9	60.9
21	135 51.4 ..	50.9	322 30.5	7.9	10 36.9	13.8	60.9
22	150 51.4	51.6	336 57.4	7.8	10 50.7	13.8	60.9
23	165 51.5	52.3	351 24.2	7.9	11 04.5	13.6	60.9
7 00	180 51.5	N16 53.0	5 51.1	7.7	S11 18.1	13.6	60.9
01	195 51.6	53.7	20 17.8	7.8	11 31.7	13.5	60.9
02	210 51.6	54.4	34 44.6	7.6	11 45.2	13.5	60.8
03	225 51.6 ..	55.0	49 11.2	7.7	11 58.7	13.3	60.8
04	240 51.7	55.7	63 37.9	7.6	12 12.0	13.3	60.8
05	255 51.7	56.4	78 04.5	7.5	12 25.3	13.2	60.8
06	270 51.8	N16 57.1	92 31.0	7.5	S12 38.5	13.1	60.8
T 07	285 51.8	57.8	106 57.5	7.5	12 51.6	13.0	60.8
H 08	300 51.8	58.5	121 24.0	7.4	13 04.6	12.9	60.8
U 09	315 51.9 ..	59.1	135 50.4	7.4	13 17.5	12.8	60.7
R 10	330 51.9	16 59.8	150 16.8	7.3	13 30.3	12.8	60.7
S 11	345 51.9	17 00.5	164 43.1	7.3	13 43.1	12.6	60.7
D 12	0 52.0	N17 01.2	179 09.4	7.2	S13 55.7	12.6	60.7
A 13	15 52.0	01.9	193 35.6	7.2	14 08.3	12.4	60.7
Y 14	30 52.1	02.6	208 01.8	7.1	14 20.7	12.4	60.7
15	45 52.1 ..	03.2	222 27.9	7.1	14 33.1	12.3	60.6
16	60 52.1	03.9	236 54.0	7.1	14 45.4	12.1	60.6
17	75 52.2	04.6	251 20.1	7.0	14 57.5	12.1	60.6
18	90 52.2	N17 05.3	265 46.1	6.9	S15 09.6	11.9	60.6
19	105 52.2	05.9	280 12.0	7.0	15 21.5	11.8	60.6
20	120 52.3	06.6	294 38.0	6.8	15 33.3	11.8	60.5
21	135 52.3 ..	07.3	309 03.8	6.9	15 45.1	11.6	60.5
22	150 52.3	08.0	323 29.7	6.7	15 56.7	11.5	60.5
23	165 52.4	08.6	337 55.4	6.8	16 08.2	11.4	60.5
8 00	180 52.4	N17 09.3	352 21.2	6.7	S16 19.6	11.3	60.5
01	195 52.4	10.0	6 46.9	6.6	16 30.9	11.1	60.4
02	210 52.5	10.7	21 12.5	6.6	16 42.0	11.1	60.4
03	225 52.5 ..	11.3	35 38.1	6.6	16 53.1	10.9	60.4
04	240 52.6	12.0	50 03.7	6.5	17 04.0	10.8	60.4
05	255 52.6	12.7	64 29.2	6.5	17 14.8	10.7	60.3
06	270 52.6	N17 13.4	78 54.7	6.5	S17 25.5	10.6	60.3
07	285 52.7	14.0	93 20.2	6.4	17 36.1	10.4	60.3
08	300 52.7	14.7	107 45.6	6.3	17 46.5	10.3	60.3
F 09	315 52.7 ..	15.4	122 10.9	6.3	17 56.8	10.2	60.2
R 10	330 52.7	16.0	136 36.2	6.3	18 07.0	10.1	60.2
I 11	345 52.8	16.7	151 01.5	6.3	18 17.1	9.9	60.2
D 12	0 52.8	N17 17.4	165 26.8	6.2	S18 27.0	9.8	60.2
A 13	15 52.8	18.1	179 52.0	6.2	18 36.8	9.7	60.1
Y 14	30 52.9	18.7	194 17.2	6.1	18 46.5	9.5	60.1
15	45 52.9 ..	19.4	208 42.3	6.1	18 56.0	9.4	60.1
16	60 52.9	20.1	223 07.4	6.1	19 05.4	9.3	60.0
17	75 53.0	20.7	237 32.5	6.1	19 14.7	9.1	60.0
18	90 53.0	N17 21.4	251 57.6	6.0	S19 23.8	9.0	60.0
19	105 53.0	22.1	266 22.6	6.0	19 32.8	8.9	60.0
20	120 53.1	22.7	280 47.6	5.9	19 41.7	8.7	59.9
21	135 53.1 ..	23.4	295 12.5	6.0	19 50.4	8.6	59.9
22	150 53.1	24.1	309 37.5	5.8	19 59.0	8.5	59.9
23	165 53.1	24.7	324 02.3	5.9	S20 07.5	8.3	59.8
SD	15.9	d 0.7	SD 16.6		16.5		16.4

Twilight, Sunrise and Moonrise

Lat.	Twilight Naut.	Twilight Civil	Sunrise	Moonrise 6	7	8	9
°	h m	h m	h m	h m	h m	h m	h m
N 72	////	////	00 38	19 46	22 43	■■	■■
N 70	////	////	01 50	19 28	21 56	■■	■■
68	////	////	02 27	19 14	21 26	23 54	■■
66	////	01 09	02 52	19 02	21 03	23 09	25 19
64	////	01 54	03 12	18 53	20 46	22 40	24 26
62	////	02 22	03 28	18 45	20 32	22 17	23 54
60	01 01	02 44	03 41	18 38	20 20	21 59	23 30
N 58	01 42	03 01	03 52	18 32	20 09	21 44	23 11
56	02 08	03 15	04 02	18 26	20 00	21 32	22 55
54	02 28	03 28	04 11	18 22	19 52	21 21	22 42
52	02 45	03 38	04 19	18 17	19 45	21 11	22 30
50	02 59	03 48	04 26	18 13	19 39	21 02	22 20
45	03 26	04 07	04 40	18 05	19 25	20 44	21 58
N 40	03 46	04 23	04 53	17 58	19 14	20 29	21 40
35	04 02	04 35	05 03	17 52	19 05	20 17	21 25
30	04 16	04 46	05 12	17 47	18 56	20 06	21 13
20	04 37	05 04	05 27	17 38	18 42	19 47	20 51
N 10	04 53	05 19	05 41	17 30	18 30	19 31	20 32
0	05 06	05 31	05 53	17 23	18 18	19 16	20 14
S 10	05 18	05 43	06 05	17 16	18 07	19 01	19 57
20	05 29	05 55	06 18	17 08	17 55	18 45	19 38
30	05 39	06 08	06 33	16 59	17 41	18 27	19 17
35	05 45	06 15	06 42	16 54	17 33	18 16	19 05
40	05 50	06 23	06 51	16 49	17 24	18 04	18 50
45	05 56	06 31	07 02	16 43	17 14	17 50	18 34
S 50	06 02	06 41	07 16	16 35	17 02	17 33	18 13
52	06 05	06 46	07 22	16 31	16 56	17 25	18 03
54	06 08	06 51	07 29	16 28	16 49	17 17	17 52
56	06 11	06 56	07 37	16 23	16 42	17 07	17 39
58	06 14	07 02	07 46	16 19	16 35	16 55	17 25
S 60	06 18	07 09	07 56	16 14	16 26	16 42	17 08

Sunset, Twilight and Moonset

Lat.	Sunset	Twilight Civil	Twilight Naut.	Moonset 6	7	8	9
°	h m	h m	h m	h m	h m	h m	h m
N 72	23 47	////	////	03 28	02 57	01 59	■■
N 70	22 09	////	////	03 37	03 18	02 48	■■
68	21 30	////	////	03 45	03 34	03 20	02 52
66	21 04	22 53	////	03 51	03 47	03 43	03 38
64	20 44	22 04	////	03 57	03 58	04 02	04 09
62	20 27	21 34	////	04 01	04 08	04 17	04 32
60	20 14	21 12	23 00	04 06	04 16	04 30	04 50
N 58	20 02	20 54	22 15	04 09	04 23	04 41	05 06
56	19 52	20 39	21 48	04 13	04 30	04 51	05 19
54	19 43	20 27	21 27	04 16	04 35	05 00	05 30
52	19 36	20 16	21 10	04 18	04 41	05 07	05 41
50	19 28	20 06	20 56	04 21	04 45	05 14	05 50
45	19 13	19 47	20 28	04 26	04 56	05 29	06 09
N 40	19 01	19 31	20 08	04 31	05 04	05 42	06 25
35	18 51	19 18	19 52	04 34	05 12	05 52	06 38
30	18 42	19 07	19 38	04 38	05 18	06 02	06 50
20	18 26	18 49	19 17	04 44	05 29	06 18	07 10
N 10	18 12	18 35	19 00	04 49	05 39	06 32	07 27
0	18 00	18 22	18 47	04 54	05 49	06 45	07 44
S 10	17 48	18 10	18 35	04 59	05 58	06 59	08 00
20	17 35	17 58	18 24	05 04	06 08	07 13	08 18
30	17 20	17 45	18 13	05 11	06 20	07 29	08 38
35	17 11	17 38	18 08	05 14	06 26	07 39	08 50
40	17 01	17 30	18 02	05 18	06 34	07 50	09 03
45	16 50	17 21	17 57	05 23	06 43	08 03	09 20
S 50	16 36	17 11	17 50	05 28	06 54	08 19	09 40
52	16 30	17 07	17 47	05 31	06 59	08 26	09 49
54	16 23	17 02	17 44	05 34	07 04	08 34	10 00
56	16 16	16 56	17 41	05 37	07 11	08 44	10 12
58	16 06	16 50	17 38	05 40	07 18	08 54	10 26
S 60	15 56	16 43	17 34	05 44	07 26	09 07	10 43

SUN and MOON (notes)

Day	Eqn. of Time 00h	Eqn. of Time 12h	Mer. Pass.	Mer. Pass. Upper	Mer. Pass. Lower	Age	Phase
d	m s	m s	h m	h m	h m	d	%
6	03 22	03 24	11 57	23 36	11 08	13	99
7	03 26	03 28	11 57	24 32	12 04	14	100
8	03 30	03 31	11 56	00 32	13 01	15	98

UT	ARIES GHA	VENUS −4.7 GHA	Dec	MARS +0.3 GHA	Dec	JUPITER −2.4 GHA	Dec	SATURN +0.5 GHA	Dec	STARS Name	SHA	Dec
d h	° ′	° ′	° ′	° ′	° ′	° ′	° ′	° ′	° ′		° ′	° ′
9 00	227 15.9	146 51.8	N27 42.2	257 16.9	S14 09.8	287 59.3	S20 52.0	283 01.8	S19 50.2	Acamar	315 15.1	S40 13.6
01	242 18.4	161 53.8	42.0	272 17.7	09.2	303 01.8	52.0	298 04.2	50.2	Achernar	335 23.7	S57 08.1
02	257 20.9	176 55.8	41.9	287 18.5	08.7	318 04.2	52.0	313 06.7	50.2	Acrux	173 03.6	S63 12.8
03	272 23.3	191 57.8	41.8	302 19.3	08.2	333 06.6	52.0	328 09.1	50.2	Adhara	255 09.0	S29 00.2
04	287 25.8	206 59.8	41.7	317 20.1	07.6	348 09.0	52.0	343 11.6	50.2	Aldebaran	290 44.3	N16 32.8
05	302 28.3	222 01.8	41.6	332 20.9	07.1	3 11.4	52.0	358 14.0	50.2			
06	317 30.7	237 03.8	N27 41.5	347 21.6	S14 06.6	18 13.9	S20 52.0	13 16.5	S19 50.2	Alioth	166 16.0	N55 51.2
07	332 33.2	252 05.9	41.3	2 22.4	06.0	33 16.3	52.0	28 18.9	50.2	Alkaid	152 54.7	N49 12.9
S 08	347 35.6	267 07.9	41.2	17 23.2	05.5	48 18.7	52.0	43 21.4	50.2	Alnair	27 37.8	S46 51.6
A 09	2 38.1	282 09.9	41.1	32 24.0	05.0	63 21.1	52.0	58 23.9	50.2	Alnilam	275 41.8	S 1 11.5
T 10	17 40.6	297 12.0	41.0	47 24.8	04.4	78 23.5	52.0	73 26.3	50.2	Alphard	217 51.5	S 8 44.9
U 11	32 43.0	312 14.0	40.8	62 25.6	03.9	93 25.9	52.0	88 28.8	50.2			
R 12	47 45.5	327 16.0	N27 40.7	77 26.3	S14 03.4	108 28.4	S20 52.0	103 31.2	S19 50.2	Alphecca	126 06.6	N26 38.8
D 13	62 48.0	342 18.1	40.6	92 27.1	02.8	123 30.8	52.0	118 33.7	50.2	Alpheratz	357 38.9	N29 11.8
A 14	77 50.4	357 20.2	40.5	107 27.9	02.3	138 33.2	52.0	133 36.1	50.2	Altair	62 03.5	N 8 55.2
Y 15	92 52.9	12 22.2	40.3	122 28.7	01.7	153 35.6	52.0	148 38.6	50.2	Ankaa	353 11.3	S42 11.8
16	107 55.4	27 24.3	40.2	137 29.5	01.2	168 38.1	52.0	163 41.1	50.2	Antares	112 20.1	S26 28.5
17	122 57.8	42 26.4	40.1	152 30.3	00.7	183 40.5	52.0	178 43.5	50.2			
18	138 00.3	57 28.4	N27 39.9	167 31.1	S14 00.1	198 42.9	S20 52.0	193 46.0	S19 50.2	Arcturus	145 51.1	N19 04.7
19	153 02.8	72 30.5	39.8	182 31.8	13 59.6	213 45.3	52.0	208 48.4	50.2	Atria	107 17.2	S69 03.6
20	168 05.2	87 32.6	39.7	197 32.6	59.1	228 47.7	52.0	223 50.9	50.2	Avior	234 16.3	S59 34.8
21	183 07.7	102 34.7	39.5	212 33.4	58.5	243 50.2	52.0	238 53.3	50.2	Bellatrix	278 27.2	N 6 21.9
22	198 10.1	117 36.8	39.4	227 34.2	58.0	258 52.6	52.0	253 55.8	50.2	Betelgeuse	270 56.4	N 7 24.5
23	213 12.6	132 38.9	39.3	242 35.0	57.4	273 55.0	52.0	268 58.3	50.2			
10 00	228 15.1	147 41.0	N27 39.1	257 35.8	S13 56.9	288 57.4	S20 52.0	284 00.7	S19 50.2	Canopus	263 54.4	S52 42.7
01	243 17.5	162 43.1	39.0	272 36.6	56.4	303 59.9	52.0	299 03.2	50.2	Capella	280 27.9	N46 01.0
02	258 20.0	177 45.2	38.8	287 37.4	55.8	319 02.3	52.0	314 05.6	50.2	Deneb	49 28.2	N45 20.9
03	273 22.5	192 47.3	38.7	302 38.1	55.3	334 04.7	52.0	329 08.1	50.3	Denebola	182 28.6	N14 27.6
04	288 24.9	207 49.4	38.6	317 38.9	54.8	349 07.1	52.0	344 10.5	50.3	Diphda	348 51.4	S17 52.6
05	303 27.4	222 51.5	38.4	332 39.7	54.2	4 09.6	52.0	359 13.0	50.3			
06	318 29.9	237 53.6	N27 38.3	347 40.5	S13 53.7	19 12.0	S20 52.0	14 15.5	S19 50.3	Dubhe	193 45.6	N61 38.8
07	333 32.3	252 55.8	38.1	2 41.3	53.1	34 14.4	52.0	29 17.9	50.3	Elnath	278 07.0	N28 37.3
S 08	348 34.8	267 57.9	38.0	17 42.1	52.6	49 16.8	52.0	44 20.4	50.3	Eltanin	90 43.5	N51 29.0
U 09	3 37.3	283 00.0	37.8	32 42.9	52.1	64 19.3	52.0	59 22.8	50.3	Enif	33 42.5	N 9 57.9
N 10	18 39.7	298 02.2	37.7	47 43.7	51.5	79 21.7	52.0	74 25.3	50.3	Fomalhaut	15 18.9	S29 30.9
11	33 42.2	313 04.3	37.5	62 44.5	51.0	94 24.1	52.0	89 27.8	50.3			
D 12	48 44.6	328 06.5	N27 37.4	77 45.2	S13 50.4	109 26.6	S20 52.0	104 30.2	S19 50.3	Gacrux	171 55.3	S57 13.7
A 13	63 47.1	343 08.6	37.2	92 46.0	49.9	124 29.0	52.0	119 32.7	50.3	Gienah	175 47.2	S17 39.3
Y 14	78 49.6	358 10.8	37.1	107 46.8	49.4	139 31.4	52.0	134 35.1	50.3	Hadar	148 40.6	S60 28.2
15	93 52.0	13 13.0	36.9	122 47.6	48.8	154 33.8	52.0	149 37.6	50.3	Hamal	327 55.8	N23 33.2
16	108 54.5	28 15.1	36.8	137 48.4	48.3	169 36.3	52.0	164 40.1	50.3	Kaus Aust.	83 37.2	S34 22.3
17	123 57.0	43 17.3	36.6	152 49.2	47.7	184 38.7	52.0	179 42.5	50.3			
18	138 59.4	58 19.5	N27 36.4	167 50.0	S13 47.2	199 41.1	S20 52.0	194 45.0	S19 50.3	Kochab	137 18.8	N74 04.5
19	154 01.9	73 21.7	36.3	182 50.8	46.7	214 43.6	52.0	209 47.5	50.3	Markab	13 33.8	N15 18.6
20	169 04.4	88 23.8	36.1	197 51.6	46.1	229 46.0	52.0	224 49.9	50.3	Menkar	314 10.4	N 4 09.9
21	184 06.8	103 26.0	36.0	212 52.4	45.6	244 48.4	52.0	239 52.4	50.3	Menkent	148 01.6	S36 28.2
22	199 09.3	118 28.2	35.8	227 53.1	45.0	259 50.9	52.0	254 54.8	50.3	Miaplacidus	221 38.9	S69 48.3
23	214 11.8	133 30.4	35.6	242 53.9	44.5	274 53.3	52.0	269 57.3	50.3			
11 00	229 14.2	148 32.6	N27 35.5	257 54.7	S13 44.0	289 55.7	S20 52.0	284 59.8	S19 50.3	Mirfak	308 34.1	N49 55.8
01	244 16.7	163 34.8	35.3	272 55.5	43.4	304 58.2	52.0	300 02.2	50.3	Nunki	75 52.2	S26 16.2
02	259 19.1	178 37.0	35.2	287 56.3	42.9	320 00.6	52.0	315 04.7	50.3	Peacock	53 11.6	S56 39.9
03	274 21.6	193 39.3	35.0	302 57.1	42.3	335 03.0	52.0	330 07.2	50.3	Pollux	243 22.1	N27 58.6
04	289 24.1	208 41.5	34.8	317 57.9	41.8	350 05.5	52.0	345 09.6	50.3	Procyon	244 54.9	N 5 10.3
05	304 26.5	223 43.7	34.7	332 58.7	41.2	5 07.9	52.0	0 12.1	50.3			
06	319 29.0	238 45.9	N27 34.5	347 59.5	S13 40.7	20 10.3	S20 52.0	15 14.5	S19 50.3	Rasalhague	96 01.8	N12 32.7
07	334 31.5	253 48.2	34.3	3 00.3	40.2	35 12.8	52.0	30 17.0	50.3	Regulus	207 38.4	N11 52.1
08	349 33.9	268 50.4	34.1	18 01.1	39.6	50 15.2	52.0	45 19.5	50.4	Rigel	281 07.8	S 8 10.9
M 09	4 36.4	283 52.6	34.0	33 01.9	39.1	65 17.6	52.0	60 21.9	50.4	Rigil Kent.	139 44.7	S60 55.1
O 10	19 38.9	298 54.9	33.8	48 02.6	38.5	80 20.1	52.0	75 24.4	50.4	Sabik	102 06.8	S15 44.9
N 11	34 41.3	313 57.1	33.6	63 03.4	38.0	95 22.5	52.0	90 26.9	50.4			
D 12	49 43.8	328 59.4	N27 33.4	78 04.2	S13 37.5	110 24.9	S20 52.0	105 29.3	S19 50.4	Schedar	349 35.6	N56 38.6
A 13	64 46.3	344 01.7	33.3	93 05.0	36.9	125 27.4	52.0	120 31.8	50.4	Shaula	96 15.1	S37 06.9
Y 14	79 48.7	359 03.9	33.1	108 05.8	36.4	140 29.8	52.0	135 34.3	50.4	Sirius	258 29.8	S16 44.9
15	94 51.2	14 06.2	32.9	123 06.6	35.8	155 32.3	52.0	150 36.7	50.4	Spica	158 26.0	S11 16.0
16	109 53.6	29 08.5	32.7	138 07.4	35.3	170 34.7	52.0	165 39.2	50.4	Suhail	222 49.0	S43 31.1
17	124 56.1	44 10.7	32.6	153 08.2	34.7	185 37.1	52.0	180 41.7	50.4			
18	139 58.6	59 13.0	N27 32.4	168 09.0	S13 34.2	200 39.6	S20 52.0	195 44.1	S19 50.4	Vega	80 35.5	N38 48.0
19	155 01.0	74 15.3	32.2	183 09.8	33.6	215 42.0	52.0	210 46.6	50.4	Zuben'ubi	136 59.8	S16 07.5
20	170 03.5	89 17.6	32.0	198 10.6	33.1	230 44.5	52.0	225 49.1	50.4		SHA	Mer.Pass.
21	185 06.0	104 19.9	31.8	213 11.4	32.6	245 46.9	52.0	240 51.5	50.4	Venus	279 25.9	14 07
22	200 08.4	119 22.2	31.6	228 12.2	32.0	260 49.3	52.0	255 54.0	50.4	Mars	29 20.7	6 49
23	215 10.9	134 24.5	31.4	243 13.0	31.5	275 51.8	52.0	270 56.4	50.4	Jupiter	60 42.4	4 43
Mer. Pass.	h m 8 45.6	v 2.2	d 0.2	v 0.8	d 0.5	v 2.4	d 0.0	v 2.5	d 0.0	Saturn	55 45.6	5 03

UT	SUN		MOON					Lat.	Twilight		Sunrise	Moonrise			
									Naut.	Civil		9	10	11	12
	GHA	Dec	GHA	v	Dec	d	HP	°	h m	h m	h m	h m	h m	h m	h m
d h	° ′	° ′	° ′	′	° ′	′	′	N 72	▭	▭	▭	▬	▬	▬	▬
9 00	180 53.2	N17 25.4	338 27.2	5.9	S20 15.8	8.1	59.8	N 70	////	////	01 28	▬	▬	▬	▬
01	195 53.2	26.0	352 52.1	5.8	20 23.9	8.0	59.8	68	////	////	02 12	▬	▬	▬	▬
02	210 53.2	26.7	7 16.9	5.8	20 31.9	7.9	59.7	66	////	00 35	02 40	25 19	01 19	▬	03 36
03	225 53.3	. . 27.4	21 41.7	5.8	20 39.8	7.7	59.7	64	////	01 37	03 02	24 26	00 26	01 50	02 34
04	240 53.3	28.0	36 06.5	5.7	20 47.5	7.6	59.7	62	////	02 10	03 19	23 54	25 11	01 11	02 00
05	255 53.3	28.7	50 31.2	5.8	20 55.1	7.5	59.6	60	00 31	02 34	03 33	23 30	24 44	00 44	01 35
06	270 53.3	N17 29.3	64 56.0	5.7	S21 02.6	7.2	59.6	N 58	01 27	02 53	03 46	23 11	24 23	00 23	01 15
07	285 53.4	30.0	79 20.7	5.7	21 09.8	7.2	59.6	56	01 58	03 08	03 56	22 55	24 05	00 05	00 58
S 08	300 53.4	30.7	93 45.4	5.7	21 17.0	7.0	59.5	54	02 20	03 21	04 05	22 42	23 51	24 44	00 44
A 09	315 53.4	. . 31.3	108 10.1	5.6	21 24.0	6.8	59.5	52	02 37	03 33	04 14	22 30	23 38	24 32	00 32
T 10	330 53.5	32.0	122 34.7	5.7	21 30.8	6.7	59.5	50	02 52	03 42	04 21	22 20	23 27	24 21	00 21
U 11	345 53.5	32.6	136 59.4	5.7	21 37.5	6.6	59.4	45	03 21	04 03	04 37	21 58	23 03	23 58	24 43
R 12	0 53.5	N17 33.3	151 24.1	5.6	S21 44.1	6.4	59.4	N 40	03 42	04 19	04 49	21 40	22 44	23 40	24 26
D 13	15 53.5	34.0	165 48.7	5.6	21 50.5	6.2	59.4	35	03 59	04 33	05 00	21 25	22 29	23 24	24 12
A 14	30 53.5	34.6	180 13.3	5.6	21 56.7	6.1	59.3	30	04 13	04 44	05 10	21 13	22 15	23 11	24 00
Y 15	45 53.6	. . 35.3	194 37.9	5.7	22 02.8	5.9	59.3	20	04 35	05 02	05 26	20 51	21 52	22 48	23 39
16	60 53.6	35.9	209 02.6	5.6	22 08.7	5.8	59.3	N 10	04 52	05 18	05 40	20 32	21 32	22 28	23 21
17	75 53.6	36.6	223 27.2	5.6	22 14.5	5.6	59.2	0	05 06	05 31	05 53	20 14	21 13	22 10	23 04
18	90 53.6	N17 37.2	237 51.8	5.6	S22 20.1	5.5	59.2	S 10	05 18	05 44	06 06	19 57	20 54	21 52	22 47
19	105 53.7	37.9	252 16.4	5.6	22 25.6	5.3	59.2	20	05 30	05 56	06 19	19 38	20 35	21 32	22 29
20	120 53.7	38.5	266 41.0	5.6	22 30.9	5.2	59.1	30	05 41	06 10	06 35	19 17	20 12	21 09	22 08
21	135 53.7	. . 39.2	281 05.6	5.6	22 36.1	5.0	59.1	35	05 47	06 17	06 44	19 05	19 58	20 56	21 55
22	150 53.7	39.8	295 30.2	5.6	22 41.1	4.9	59.1	40	05 53	06 25	06 54	18 50	19 43	20 40	21 41
23	165 53.8	40.5	309 54.8	5.6	S20 46.0	4.7	59.0	45	05 59	06 34	07 06	18 34	19 24	20 22	21 24
10 00	180 53.8	N17 41.1	324 19.4	5.6	S22 50.7	4.5	59.0	S 50	06 06	06 45	07 20	18 13	19 01	19 59	21 03
01	195 53.8	41.8	338 44.0	5.7	22 55.2	4.4	58.9	52	06 09	06 50	07 27	18 03	18 50	19 48	20 53
02	210 53.8	42.4	353 08.7	5.6	22 59.6	4.3	58.9	54	06 12	06 55	07 34	17 52	18 38	19 35	20 42
03	225 53.9	. . 43.1	7 33.3	5.7	23 03.9	4.1	58.9	56	06 16	07 01	07 43	17 39	18 24	19 21	20 29
04	240 53.9	43.7	21 58.0	5.6	23 08.0	3.9	58.8	58	06 19	07 08	07 52	17 25	18 07	19 04	20 14
05	255 53.9	44.4	36 22.6	5.7	23 11.9	3.8	58.8	S 60	06 24	07 15	08 03	17 08	17 47	18 44	19 56

UT	SUN		MOON					Lat.	Sunset	Twilight		Moonset			
										Civil	Naut.	9	10	11	12
								°	h m	h m	h m	h m	h m	h m	h m
06	270 53.9	N17 45.0	50 47.3	5.7	S23 15.7	3.6	58.8	N 72	▭	▭	▭	▬	▬	▬	▬
07	285 53.9	45.7	65 12.0	5.7	23 19.3	3.5	58.7	N 70	22 32	////	////	▬	▬	▬	▬
08	300 54.0	46.3	79 36.7	5.7	23 22.8	3.3	58.7	68	21 45	////	////	02 52	▬	▬	▬
S 09	315 54.0	. . 47.0	94 01.5	5.7	23 26.1	3.1	58.6	66	21 16	23 40	////	03 38	03 32	▬	05 15
U 10	330 54.0	47.6	108 26.2	5.8	23 29.2	3.0	58.6	64	20 53	22 21	////	04 09	04 25	05 04	06 16
N 11	345 54.0	48.3	122 51.0	5.8	23 32.2	2.9	58.6	62	20 36	21 46	////	04 32	04 57	05 42	06 50
D 12	0 54.0	N17 48.9	137 15.8	5.8	S23 35.1	2.7	58.5	60	20 21	21 21	23 41	04 50	05 21	06 09	07 15
A 13	15 54.1	49.6	151 40.6	5.9	23 37.8	2.5	58.5	N 58	20 09	21 02	22 30	05 06	05 41	06 31	07 35
Y 14	30 54.1	50.2	166 05.5	5.9	23 40.3	2.4	58.5	56	19 58	20 46	21 58	05 19	05 57	06 48	07 52
15	45 54.1	. . 50.8	180 30.4	5.9	23 42.7	2.2	58.4	54	19 49	20 33	21 35	05 30	06 11	07 03	08 05
16	60 54.1	51.5	194 55.3	5.9	23 44.9	2.1	58.4	52	19 40	20 22	21 17	05 41	06 23	07 16	08 18
17	75 54.1	52.1	209 20.2	6.0	23 47.0	1.9	58.3	50	19 33	20 11	21 02	05 50	06 34	07 27	08 28
18	90 54.1	N17 52.8	223 45.2	6.0	S23 48.9	1.8	58.3	45	19 17	19 51	20 33	06 09	06 56	07 50	08 51
19	105 54.2	53.4	238 10.2	6.1	23 50.7	1.6	58.3	N 40	19 04	19 34	20 12	06 25	07 14	08 09	09 09
20	120 54.2	54.1	252 35.3	6.1	23 52.3	1.4	58.2	35	18 53	19 21	19 55	06 38	07 29	08 25	09 24
21	135 54.2	. . 54.7	267 00.4	6.1	23 53.7	1.3	58.2	30	18 43	19 09	19 40	06 50	07 42	08 39	09 37
22	150 54.2	55.3	281 25.5	6.2	23 55.0	1.2	58.1	20	18 27	18 51	19 18	07 10	08 05	09 02	09 59
23	165 54.2	56.0	295 50.7	6.2	23 56.2	1.0	58.1	N 10	18 13	18 35	19 01	07 27	08 24	09 22	10 18
11 00	180 54.3	N17 56.6	310 15.9	6.2	S23 57.2	0.9	58.1	0	18 00	18 22	18 47	07 44	08 43	09 41	10 36
01	195 54.3	57.3	324 41.1	6.3	23 58.1	0.7	58.0	S 10	17 47	18 09	18 34	08 00	09 01	09 59	10 54
02	210 54.3	57.9	339 06.4	6.4	23 58.8	0.5	58.0	20	17 33	17 56	18 23	08 18	09 20	10 19	11 13
03	225 54.3	. . 58.5	353 31.8	6.4	23 59.3	0.4	57.9	30	17 18	17 43	18 12	08 38	09 43	10 42	11 35
04	240 54.3	59.2	7 57.2	6.4	23 59.7	0.3	57.9	35	17 09	17 35	18 06	08 50	09 56	10 56	11 48
05	255 54.3	17 59.8	22 22.6	6.5	24 00.0	0.1	57.9	40	16 58	17 27	18 00	09 03	10 11	11 11	12 03
06	270 54.3	N18 00.4	36 48.1	6.6	S24 00.1	0.0	57.8	45	16 46	17 18	17 53	09 20	10 30	11 30	12 20
07	285 54.4	01.1	51 13.7	6.6	24 00.1	0.2	57.8	S 50	16 32	17 07	17 46	09 40	10 52	11 53	12 41
08	300 54.4	01.7	65 39.3	6.6	23 59.9	0.4	57.8	52	16 25	17 02	17 43	09 49	11 03	12 04	12 52
M 09	315 54.4	. . 02.3	80 04.9	6.7	23 59.5	0.4	57.7	54	16 18	16 57	17 40	10 00	11 15	12 17	13 03
O 10	330 54.4	03.0	94 30.6	6.8	23 59.1	0.7	57.7	56	16 09	16 51	17 36	10 12	11 29	12 31	13 16
N 11	345 54.4	03.6	108 56.4	6.8	23 58.4	0.7	57.6	58	16 00	16 44	17 33	10 26	11 46	12 48	13 32
D 12	0 54.4	N18 04.2	123 22.2	6.9	S23 57.7	0.9	57.6	S 60	15 49	16 37	17 28	10 43	12 06	13 08	13 50
A 13	15 54.4	04.9	137 48.1	7.0	23 56.8	1.1	57.6								
Y 14	30 54.5	05.5	152 14.1	7.0	23 55.7	1.2	57.5								
15	45 54.5	. . 06.1	166 40.1	7.0	23 54.5	1.3	57.5			SUN			MOON		
16	60 54.5	06.8	181 06.1	7.2	23 53.2	1.5	57.4								
17	75 54.5	07.4	195 32.3	7.2	23 51.7	1.6	57.4	Day	Eqn. of Time		Mer.	Mer. Pass.		Age	Phase
18	90 54.5	N18 08.0	209 58.5	7.3	S23 50.1	1.7	57.4		00h	12h	Pass.	Upper	Lower		
19	105 54.5	08.6	224 24.8	7.3	23 48.4	1.9	57.3	d	m s	m s	h m	h m	h m	d	%
20	120 54.5	09.3	238 51.1	7.4	23 46.5	2.1	57.3	9	03 33	03 34	11 56	01 30	13 59	16	94
21	135 54.5	. . 09.9	253 17.5	7.5	23 44.4	2.1	57.3	10	03 35	03 36	11 56	02 29	14 58	17	88
22	150 54.5	10.5	267 44.0	7.5	23 42.3	2.3	57.2	11	03 37	03 38	11 56	03 27	15 55	18	80
23	165 54.6	11.2	282 10.5	7.6	S23 40.0	2.5	57.2								
	SD 15.9	d 0.6	SD 16.2		15.9		15.7									

UT (d h)	ARIES GHA	VENUS −4·6 GHA	Dec	MARS +0·2 GHA	Dec	JUPITER −2·4 GHA	Dec	SATURN +0·5 GHA	Dec	STARS Name	SHA	Dec
12 00	230 13.4	149 26.8	N27 31.3	258 13.8	S13 30.9	290 54.2	S20 52.0	285 58.9	S19 50.4	Acamar	315 15.1	S40 13.5
01	245 15.8	164 29.1	31.1	273 14.6	30.4	305 56.7	52.0	301 01.4	50.4	Achernar	335 23.7	S57 08.0
02	260 18.3	179 31.4	30.9	288 15.4	29.8	320 59.1	52.0	316 03.8	50.4	Acrux	173 03.6	S63 12.8
03	275 20.8	194 33.8	.. 30.7	303 16.2	.. 29.3	336 01.5	.. 52.0	331 06.3	.. 50.4	Adhara	255 09.1	S29 00.2
04	290 23.2	209 36.1	30.5	318 17.0	28.8	351 04.0	52.0	346 08.8	50.4	Aldebaran	290 44.3	N16 32.8
05	305 25.7	224 38.4	30.3	333 17.7	28.2	6 06.4	52.0	1 11.3	50.4			
06	320 28.1	239 40.8	N27 30.1	348 18.5	S13 27.7	21 08.9	S20 52.0	16 13.7	S19 50.4	Alioth	166 16.0	N55 51.2
07	335 30.6	254 43.1	29.9	3 19.3	27.1	36 11.3	52.0	31 16.2	50.5	Alkaid	152 54.7	N49 12.9
T 08	350 33.1	269 45.4	29.7	18 20.1	26.6	51 13.8	52.0	46 18.7	50.5	Alnair	27 37.8	S46 51.6
U 09	5 35.5	284 47.8	.. 29.5	33 20.9	.. 26.0	66 16.2	.. 52.0	61 21.1	.. 50.5	Alnilam	275 41.8	S 1 11.5
E 10	20 38.0	299 50.1	29.3	48 21.7	25.5	81 18.6	52.0	76 23.6	50.5	Alphard	217 51.5	S 8 44.9
S 11	35 40.5	314 52.5	29.1	63 22.5	24.9	96 21.1	52.0	91 26.1	50.5			
D 12	50 42.9	329 54.9	N27 28.9	78 23.3	S13 24.4	111 23.5	S20 52.0	106 28.5	S19 50.5	Alphecca	126 06.6	N26 38.8
A 13	65 45.4	344 57.2	28.7	93 24.1	23.8	126 26.0	52.1	121 31.0	50.5	Alpheratz	357 38.8	N29 11.8
Y 14	80 47.9	359 59.6	28.5	108 24.9	23.3	141 28.4	52.1	136 33.5	50.5	Altair	62 03.5	N 8 55.2
15	95 50.3	15 02.0	.. 28.3	123 25.7	.. 22.8	156 30.9	.. 52.1	151 35.9	.. 50.5	Ankaa	353 11.3	S42 11.7
16	110 52.8	30 04.3	28.1	138 26.5	22.2	171 33.3	52.1	166 38.4	50.5	Antares	112 20.1	S26 28.5
17	125 55.2	45 06.7	27.9	153 27.3	21.7	186 35.8	52.1	181 40.9	50.5			
18	140 57.7	60 09.1	N27 27.7	168 28.1	S13 21.1	201 38.2	S20 52.1	196 43.3	S19 50.5	Arcturus	145 51.1	N19 04.7
19	156 00.2	75 11.5	27.5	183 28.9	20.6	216 40.7	52.1	211 45.8	50.5	Atria	107 17.1	S69 03.6
20	171 02.6	90 13.9	27.3	198 29.7	20.0	231 43.1	52.1	226 48.3	50.5	Avior	234 16.4	S59 34.8
21	186 05.1	105 16.3	.. 27.1	213 30.5	.. 19.5	246 45.6	.. 52.1	241 50.8	.. 50.5	Bellatrix	278 27.2	N 6 21.9
22	201 07.6	120 18.7	26.8	228 31.3	18.9	261 48.0	52.1	256 53.2	50.5	Betelgeuse	270 56.4	N 7 24.5
23	216 10.0	135 21.1	26.6	243 32.1	18.4	276 50.5	52.1	271 55.7	50.5			
13 00	231 12.5	150 23.5	N27 26.4	258 32.9	S13 17.8	291 52.9	S20 52.1	286 58.2	S19 50.5	Canopus	263 54.5	S52 42.7
01	246 15.0	165 26.0	26.2	273 33.7	17.3	306 55.4	52.1	302 00.6	50.5	Capella	280 27.9	N46 01.0
02	261 17.4	180 28.4	26.0	288 34.5	16.7	321 57.8	52.1	317 03.1	50.6	Deneb	49 28.2	N45 20.9
03	276 19.9	195 30.8	.. 25.8	303 35.3	.. 16.2	337 00.3	.. 52.1	332 05.6	.. 50.6	Denebola	182 28.6	N14 27.6
04	291 22.4	210 33.3	25.6	318 36.1	15.6	352 02.7	52.1	347 08.1	50.6	Diphda	348 51.4	S17 52.6
05	306 24.8	225 35.7	25.3	333 36.9	15.1	7 05.2	52.1	2 10.5	50.6			
06	321 27.3	240 38.1	N27 25.1	348 37.7	S13 14.5	22 07.6	S20 52.1	17 13.0	S19 50.6	Dubhe	193 45.6	N61 38.8
W 07	336 29.7	255 40.6	24.9	3 38.5	14.0	37 10.1	52.1	32 15.5	50.6	Elnath	278 07.0	N28 37.3
E 08	351 32.2	270 43.0	24.7	18 39.3	13.4	52 12.5	52.1	47 17.9	50.6	Eltanin	90 43.5	N51 29.0
D 09	6 34.7	285 45.5	.. 24.4	33 40.1	.. 12.9	67 15.0	.. 52.1	62 20.4	.. 50.6	Enif	33 42.5	N 9 57.9
N 10	21 37.1	300 48.0	24.2	48 40.9	12.4	82 17.4	52.1	77 22.9	50.6	Fomalhaut	15 18.9	S29 30.0
E 11	36 39.6	315 50.4	24.0	63 41.7	11.8	97 19.9	52.1	92 25.4	50.6			
S 12	51 42.1	330 52.9	N27 23.8	78 42.5	S13 11.3	112 22.3	S20 52.1	107 27.8	S19 50.6	Gacrux	171 55.3	S57 13.7
D 13	66 44.5	345 55.4	23.5	93 43.3	10.7	127 24.8	52.1	122 30.3	50.6	Gienah	175 47.2	S17 39.3
A 14	81 47.0	0 57.8	23.3	108 44.1	10.2	142 27.2	52.2	137 32.8	50.6	Hadar	148 40.6	S60 28.3
Y 15	96 49.5	16 00.3	.. 23.1	123 44.9	.. 09.6	157 29.7	.. 52.2	152 35.3	.. 50.6	Hamal	327 55.7	N23 33.2
16	111 51.9	31 02.8	22.8	138 45.7	09.1	172 32.1	52.2	167 37.7	50.6	Kaus Aust.	83 37.2	S34 22.3
17	126 54.4	46 05.3	22.6	153 46.5	08.5	187 34.6	52.2	182 40.2	50.6			
18	141 56.9	61 07.8	N27 22.4	168 47.3	S13 08.0	202 37.0	S20 52.2	197 42.7	S19 50.6	Kochab	137 18.8	N74 04.5
19	156 59.3	76 10.3	22.1	183 48.2	07.4	217 39.5	52.2	212 45.1	50.7	Markab	13 33.7	N15 18.6
20	172 01.8	91 12.8	21.9	198 49.0	06.9	232 42.0	52.2	227 47.6	50.7	Menkar	314 10.4	N 4 09.9
21	187 04.2	106 15.3	.. 21.7	213 49.8	.. 06.3	247 44.4	.. 52.2	242 50.1	.. 50.7	Menkent	148 01.6	S36 28.2
22	202 06.7	121 17.8	21.4	228 50.6	05.8	262 46.9	52.2	257 52.6	50.7	Miaplacidus	221 38.9	S69 48.3
23	217 09.2	136 20.4	21.2	243 51.4	05.2	277 49.3	52.2	272 55.0	50.7			
14 00	232 11.6	151 22.9	N27 21.0	258 52.2	S13 04.7	292 51.8	S20 52.2	287 57.5	S19 50.7	Mirfak	308 34.1	N49 55.8
01	247 14.1	166 25.4	20.7	273 53.0	04.1	307 54.2	52.2	303 00.0	50.7	Nunki	75 52.2	S26 16.2
02	262 16.6	181 27.9	20.5	288 53.8	03.6	322 56.7	52.2	318 02.5	50.7	Peacock	53 11.6	S56 39.9
03	277 19.0	196 30.5	.. 20.2	303 54.6	.. 03.0	337 59.2	.. 52.2	333 04.9	.. 50.7	Pollux	243 22.1	N27 58.6
04	292 21.5	211 33.0	20.0	318 55.4	02.5	353 01.6	52.2	348 07.4	50.7	Procyon	244 55.0	N 5 10.3
05	307 24.0	226 35.6	19.7	333 56.2	02.0	8 04.1	52.2	3 09.9	50.7			
06	322 26.4	241 38.1	N27 19.5	348 57.0	S13 01.4	23 06.5	S20 52.2	18 12.4	S19 50.7	Rasalhague	96 01.8	N12 32.7
07	337 28.9	256 40.7	19.2	3 57.8	00.8	38 09.0	52.2	33 14.9	50.7	Regulus	207 38.4	N11 52.1
T 08	352 31.4	271 43.2	19.0	18 58.6	13 00.3	53 11.5	52.2	48 17.3	50.7	Rigel	281 07.8	S 8 10.9
H 09	7 33.8	286 45.8	.. 18.7	33 59.4	12 59.7	68 13.9	.. 52.3	63 19.8	.. 50.7	Rigil Kent.	139 44.7	S60 55.1
U 10	22 36.3	301 48.4	18.5	49 00.2	59.2	83 16.4	52.3	78 22.3	50.8	Sabik	102 06.8	S15 44.9
R 11	37 38.7	316 51.0	18.2	64 01.0	58.6	98 18.8	52.3	93 24.8	50.8			
S 12	52 41.2	331 53.5	N27 18.0	79 01.8	S12 58.1	113 21.3	S20 52.3	108 27.2	S19 50.8	Schedar	349 35.6	N56 38.6
D 13	67 43.7	346 56.1	17.7	94 02.6	57.5	128 23.8	52.3	123 29.7	50.8	Shaula	96 15.1	S37 07.0
A 14	82 46.1	1 58.7	17.5	109 03.5	56.9	143 26.2	52.3	138 32.2	50.8	Sirius	258 29.8	S16 44.9
Y 15	97 48.6	17 01.3	.. 17.2	124 04.3	.. 56.4	158 28.7	.. 52.3	153 34.7	.. 50.8	Spica	158 26.0	S11 16.0
16	112 51.1	32 03.9	17.0	139 05.1	55.8	173 31.2	52.3	168 37.1	50.8	Suhail	222 49.1	S43 31.1
17	127 53.5	47 06.5	16.7	154 05.9	55.3	188 33.6	52.3	183 39.6	50.8			
18	142 56.0	62 09.1	N27 16.4	169 06.7	S12 54.7	203 36.1	S20 52.3	198 42.1	S19 50.8	Vega	80 35.4	N38 48.0
19	157 58.5	77 11.7	16.2	184 07.5	54.2	218 38.5	52.3	213 44.6	50.8	Zuben'ubi	136 59.8	S16 07.5
20	173 00.9	92 14.3	15.9	199 08.3	53.6	233 41.0	52.3	228 47.1	50.8		SHA	Mer. Pass.
21	188 03.4	107 17.0	.. 15.7	214 09.1	.. 53.1	248 43.5	.. 52.3	243 49.5	.. 50.8	Venus	279 11.1	13 56
22	203 05.8	122 19.6	15.4	229 09.9	52.5	263 45.9	52.3	258 52.0	50.8	Mars	27 20.4	6 45
23	218 08.3	137 22.2	15.1	244 10.7	52.0	278 48.4	52.3	273 54.5	50.8	Jupiter	60 40.4	4 32
Mer. Pass. 8 33.8		v 2.5	d 0.2	v 0.8	d 0.5	v 2.5	d 0.0	v 2.5	d 0.0	Saturn	55 45.7	4 51

UT	SUN GHA	SUN Dec	MOON GHA	v	MOON Dec	d	HP
d h	° ′	° ′	° ′	′	° ′	′	′
12 00	180 54.6	N18 11.8	296 37.1	7.7	S23 37.5	2.5	57.1
01	195 54.6	12.4	311 03.8	7.8	23 35.0	2.7	57.1
02	210 54.6	13.0	325 30.6	7.8	23 32.3	2.9	57.1
03	225 54.6 ..	13.7	339 57.4	8.0	23 29.4	2.9	57.0
04	240 54.6	14.3	354 24.4	7.9	23 26.5	3.1	57.0
05	255 54.6	14.9	8 51.3	8.1	23 23.4	3.2	57.0
06	270 54.6	N18 15.5	23 18.4	8.2	S23 20.2	3.4	56.9
07	285 54.6	16.2	37 45.6	8.2	23 16.8	3.4	56.9
T 08	300 54.6	16.8	52 12.8	8.3	23 13.4	3.6	56.8
U 09	315 54.7 ..	17.4	66 40.1	8.4	23 09.8	3.8	56.8
E 10	330 54.7	18.0	81 07.5	8.4	23 06.0	3.8	56.8
S 11	345 54.7	18.6	95 34.9	8.6	23 02.2	4.0	56.7
D 12	0 54.7	N18 19.3	110 02.5	8.6	S22 58.2	4.1	56.7
A 13	15 54.7	19.9	124 30.1	8.7	22 54.1	4.2	56.7
Y 14	30 54.7	20.5	138 57.8	8.8	22 49.9	4.3	56.6
15	45 54.7 ..	21.1	153 25.6	8.8	22 45.6	4.5	56.6
16	60 54.7	21.7	167 53.4	9.0	22 41.1	4.5	56.6
17	75 54.7	22.3	182 21.4	9.0	22 36.6	4.7	56.5
18	90 54.7	N18 23.0	196 49.4	9.1	S22 31.9	4.8	56.5
19	105 54.7	23.6	211 17.5	9.2	22 27.1	4.9	56.4
20	120 54.7	24.2	225 45.7	9.3	22 22.2	5.1	56.4
21	135 54.7 ..	24.8	240 14.0	9.4	22 17.1	5.1	56.4
22	150 54.7	25.4	254 42.4	9.4	22 12.0	5.2	56.3
23	165 54.7	26.0	269 10.8	9.6	22 06.8	5.4	56.3
13 00	180 54.7	N18 26.6	283 39.4	9.6	S22 01.4	5.5	56.3
01	195 54.7	27.3	298 08.0	9.7	21 55.9	5.6	56.2
02	210 54.8	27.9	312 36.7	9.8	21 50.3	5.6	56.2
03	225 54.8 ..	28.5	327 05.5	9.9	21 44.7	5.8	56.2
04	240 54.8	29.1	341 34.4	10.0	21 38.9	5.9	56.1
05	255 54.8	29.7	356 03.4	10.1	21 33.0	6.0	56.1
06	270 54.8	N18 30.3	10 32.5	10.1	S21 27.0	6.1	56.1
W 07	285 54.8	30.9	25 01.6	10.2	21 20.9	6.2	56.0
E 08	300 54.8	31.5	39 30.8	10.3	21 14.7	6.3	56.0
D 09	315 54.8 ..	32.1	54 00.1	10.5	21 08.4	6.5	56.0
N 10	330 54.8	32.8	68 29.6	10.4	21 01.9	6.5	55.9
E 11	345 54.8	33.4	82 59.0	10.6	20 55.4	6.6	55.9
S 12	0 54.8	N18 34.0	97 28.6	10.7	S20 48.8	6.7	55.9
D 13	15 54.8	34.6	111 58.3	10.7	20 42.1	6.7	55.9
A 14	30 54.8	35.2	126 28.0	10.9	20 35.4	6.9	55.8
Y 15	45 54.8 ..	35.8	140 57.9	10.9	20 28.5	7.0	55.8
16	60 54.8	36.4	155 27.8	11.0	20 21.5	7.1	55.8
17	75 54.8	37.0	169 57.8	11.1	20 14.4	7.2	55.7
18	90 54.8	N18 37.6	184 27.9	11.2	S20 07.2	7.2	55.7
19	105 54.8	38.2	198 58.1	11.2	20 00.0	7.4	55.7
20	120 54.8	38.8	213 28.3	11.4	19 52.6	7.4	55.6
21	135 54.8 ..	39.4	227 58.7	11.4	19 45.2	7.5	55.6
22	150 54.8	40.0	242 29.1	11.5	19 37.7	7.6	55.6
23	165 54.8	40.6	256 59.6	11.6	19 30.1	7.7	55.6
14 00	180 54.8	N18 41.2	271 30.2	11.7	S19 22.4	7.8	55.5
01	195 54.8	41.8	286 00.9	11.8	19 14.6	7.8	55.5
02	210 54.8	42.4	300 31.7	11.8	19 06.8	8.0	55.5
03	225 54.8 ..	43.0	315 02.5	12.0	18 58.8	8.0	55.5
04	240 54.8	43.6	329 33.5	12.0	18 50.8	8.1	55.4
05	255 54.8	44.2	344 04.5	12.1	18 42.7	8.2	55.4
06	270 54.8	N18 44.8	358 35.6	12.2	S18 34.5	8.2	55.4
07	285 54.7	45.4	13 06.8	12.2	18 26.3	8.4	55.3
T 08	300 54.7	46.0	27 38.0	12.4	18 17.9	8.4	55.3
H 09	315 54.7 ..	46.6	42 09.4	12.4	18 09.5	8.5	55.3
U 10	330 54.7	47.2	56 40.8	12.5	18 01.0	8.5	55.3
R 11	345 54.7	47.8	71 12.3	12.6	17 52.5	8.7	55.2
S 12	0 54.7	N18 48.4	85 43.9	12.6	S17 43.8	8.7	55.2
D 13	15 54.7	49.0	100 15.5	12.7	17 35.1	8.7	55.2
A 14	30 54.7	49.5	114 47.2	12.9	17 26.4	8.9	55.1
Y 15	45 54.7 ..	50.1	129 19.1	12.8	17 17.5	8.9	55.1
16	60 54.7	50.7	143 50.9	13.0	17 08.6	9.0	55.1
17	75 54.7	51.3	158 22.9	13.0	16 59.6	9.1	55.1
18	90 54.7	N18 51.9	172 54.9	13.1	S16 50.5	9.1	55.1
19	105 54.7	52.5	187 27.0	13.2	16 41.4	9.2	55.0
20	120 54.7	53.1	201 59.2	13.3	16 32.2	9.3	55.0
21	135 54.7 ..	53.7	216 31.5	13.3	16 23.0	9.3	55.0
22	150 54.7	54.3	231 03.8	13.4	16 13.7	9.4	55.0
23	165 54.7	54.9	245 36.2	13.5	S16 04.3	9.4	54.9
	SD 15.9	d 0.6	SD 15.4		15.2		15.0

Moonrise

Lat.	Twilight Naut.	Twilight Civil	Sunrise	12	13	14	15
°	h m	h m	h m	h m	h m	h m	h m
N 72	□	□	□	■	■	■	04 37
N 70	////	////	01 00	■	■	04 42	04 03
68	////	////	01 56		04 35	03 55	03 38
66	////	////	02 28	03 36	03 29	03 24	03 19
64	////	01 19	02 52	02 34	02 53	03 01	03 04
62	////	01 58	03 11	02 00	02 27	02 42	02 51
60	////	02 24	03 26	01 35	02 07	02 27	02 40
N 58	01 11	02 45	03 39	01 15	01 50	02 14	02 30
56	01 46	03 01	03 50	00 58	01 36	02 03	02 22
54	02 11	03 15	04 00	00 44	01 24	01 53	02 14
52	02 30	03 27	04 09	00 32	01 13	01 44	02 08
50	02 46	03 37	04 16	00 21	01 03	01 36	02 01
45	03 16	03 59	04 33	24 43	00 43	01 19	01 48
N 40	03 38	04 16	04 46	24 26	00 26	01 05	01 37
35	03 56	04 30	04 58	24 12	00 12	00 53	01 28
30	04 10	04 42	05 08	24 00	00 00	00 43	01 20
20	04 33	05 01	05 25	23 39	24 25	00 25	01 05
N 10	04 51	05 17	05 39	23 21	24 09	00 09	00 53
0	05 06	05 31	05 53	23 04	23 54	24 41	00 41
S 10	05 19	05 44	06 06	22 47	23 40	24 29	00 29
20	05 31	05 57	06 21	22 29	23 24	24 17	00 17
30	05 43	06 11	06 37	22 08	23 06	24 02	00 02
35	05 49	06 19	06 46	21 55	22 55	23 54	24 51
40	05 55	06 28	06 57	21 41	22 43	23 44	24 44
45	06 02	06 38	07 09	21 24	22 28	23 33	24 36
S 50	06 10	06 49	07 25	21 03	22 11	23 19	24 26
52	06 13	06 54	07 32	20 53	22 02	23 12	24 21
54	06 16	07 00	07 39	20 42	21 53	23 05	24 16
56	06 20	07 06	07 48	20 29	21 42	22 57	24 11
58	06 24	07 13	07 58	20 14	21 30	22 48	24 05
S 60	06 29	07 21	08 10	19 56	21 16	22 38	23 58

Moonset

Lat.	Sunset	Twilight Civil	Twilight Naut.	12	13	14	15
°	h m	h m	h m	h m	h m	h m	h m
N 72	□	□	□	■	■	■	09 26
N 70	23 04	////	////	■	■	07 43	09 58
68	22 02	////	////		06 07	08 30	10 21
66	21 27	////	////	05 15	07 13	09 00	10 39
64	21 03	22 40	////	06 16	07 48	09 22	10 54
62	20 44	21 58	////	06 50	08 13	09 40	11 06
60	20 28	21 31	////	07 15	08 33	09 55	11 16
N 58	20 15	21 10	22 47	07 35	08 49	10 07	11 25
56	20 04	20 53	22 10	07 52	09 03	10 18	11 33
54	19 54	20 39	21 44	08 05	09 15	10 27	11 39
52	19 45	20 27	21 25	08 18	09 26	10 36	11 46
50	19 37	20 16	21 09	08 28	09 35	10 43	11 51
45	19 21	19 55	20 38	08 51	09 55	10 59	12 03
N 40	19 07	19 37	20 15	09 09	10 11	11 12	12 13
35	18 55	19 23	19 57	09 24	10 24	11 23	12 21
30	18 45	19 12	19 43	09 37	10 36	11 33	12 29
20	18 28	18 52	19 20	09 59	10 55	11 50	12 41
N 10	18 14	18 36	19 02	10 18	11 13	12 04	12 52
0	18 00	18 22	18 47	10 36	11 29	12 17	13 03
S 10	17 46	18 08	18 34	10 54	11 44	12 30	13 13
20	17 32	17 55	18 22	11 13	12 01	12 45	13 24
30	17 16	17 41	18 10	11 35	12 21	13 01	13 36
35	17 06	17 33	18 04	11 48	12 32	13 10	13 43
40	16 55	17 24	17 57	12 03	12 45	13 21	13 51
45	16 43	17 15	17 50	12 20	13 00	13 33	14 00
S 50	16 28	17 03	17 43	12 41	13 19	13 48	14 11
52	16 21	16 58	17 39	12 52	13 28	13 55	14 16
54	16 13	16 52	17 36	13 03	13 37	14 03	14 22
56	16 04	16 46	17 32	13 16	13 48	14 11	14 28
58	15 54	16 39	17 28	13 32	14 01	14 21	14 35
S 60	15 42	16 31	17 23	13 50	14 15	14 32	14 43

Day	SUN Eqn. of Time 00ʰ	SUN Eqn. of Time 12ʰ	SUN Mer. Pass.	MOON Mer. Pass. Upper	MOON Mer. Pass. Lower	Age	Phase
d	m s	m s	h m	h m	h m	d	%
12	03 38	03 39	11 56	04 23	16 50	19	71
13	03 39	03 39	11 56	05 16	17 42	20	61
14	03 39	03 39	11 56	06 06	18 29	21	51

UT	ARIES	VENUS −4·5		MARS +0·2		JUPITER −2·5		SATURN +0·5		STARS		
d h	GHA ° ′	GHA ° ′	Dec ° ′	GHA ° ′	Dec ° ′	GHA ° ′	Dec ° ′	GHA ° ′	Dec ° ′	Name	SHA ° ′	Dec ° ′
15 00	233 10.8	152 24.8	N27 14.9	259 11.5	S12 51.4	293 50.9	S20 52.4	288 57.0	S19 50.8	Acamar	315 15.1	S40 13.5
01	248 13.2	167 27.5	14.6	274 12.3	50.9	308 53.3	52.4	303 59.5	50.9	Achernar	335 23.7	S57 08.0
02	263 15.7	182 30.1	14.3	289 13.1	50.3	323 55.8	52.4	319 01.9	50.9	Acrux	173 03.6	S63 12.9
03	278 18.2	197 32.8	. . 14.0	304 14.0	. . 49.8	338 58.3	. . 52.4	334 04.4	. . 50.9	Adhara	255 09.1	S29 00.2
04	293 20.6	212 35.4	13.8	319 14.8	49.2	354 00.7	52.4	349 06.9	50.9	Aldebaran	290 44.3	N16 32.8
05	308 23.1	227 38.1	13.5	334 15.6	48.7	9 03.2	52.4	4 09.4	50.9			
06	323 25.6	242 40.7	N27 13.2	349 16.4	S12 48.1	24 05.7	S20 52.4	19 11.9	S19 50.9	Alioth	166 16.0	N55 51.2
07	338 28.0	257 43.4	13.0	4 17.2	47.6	39 08.1	52.4	34 14.3	50.9	Alkaid	152 54.7	N49 12.9
08	353 30.5	272 46.1	12.7	19 18.0	47.0	54 10.6	52.4	49 16.8	50.9	Alnair	27 37.8	S46 51.6
F 09	8 33.0	287 48.8	. . 12.4	34 18.8	. . 46.4	69 13.1	. . 52.4	64 19.3	. . 50.9	Alnilam	275 41.8	S 1 11.5
R 10	23 35.4	302 51.4	12.1	49 19.6	45.9	84 15.6	52.4	79 21.8	50.9	Alphard	217 51.5	S 8 44.9
I 11	38 37.9	317 54.1	11.8	64 20.4	45.3	99 18.0	52.4	94 24.3	50.9			
D 12	53 40.3	332 56.8	N27 11.6	79 21.3	S12 44.8	114 20.5	S20 52.4	109 26.7	S19 50.9	Alphecca	126 06.6	N26 38.8
A 13	68 42.8	347 59.5	11.3	94 22.1	44.2	129 23.0	52.5	124 29.2	50.9	Alpheratz	357 38.8	N29 11.9
Y 14	83 45.3	3 02.2	11.0	109 22.9	43.7	144 25.4	52.5	139 31.7	51.0	Altair	62 03.4	N 8 55.2
15	98 47.7	18 04.9	. . 10.7	124 23.7	. . 43.1	159 27.9	. . 52.5	154 34.2	. . 51.0	Ankaa	353 11.2	S42 11.7
16	113 50.2	33 07.6	10.4	139 24.5	42.6	174 30.4	52.5	169 36.7	51.0	Antares	112 20.1	S26 28.5
17	128 52.7	48 10.3	10.1	154 25.3	42.0	189 32.8	52.5	184 39.2	51.0			
18	143 55.1	63 13.0	N27 09.9	169 26.1	S12 41.5	204 35.3	S20 52.5	199 41.6	S19 51.0	Arcturus	145 51.1	N19 04.7
19	158 57.6	78 15.8	09.6	184 26.9	40.9	219 37.8	52.5	214 44.1	51.0	Atria	107 17.1	S69 03.6
20	174 00.1	93 18.5	09.3	199 27.7	40.3	234 40.3	52.5	229 46.6	51.0	Avior	234 16.4	S59 34.8
21	189 02.5	108 21.2	. . 09.0	214 28.6	. . 39.8	249 42.7	. . 52.5	244 49.1	. . 51.0	Bellatrix	278 27.2	N 6 21.9
22	204 05.0	123 24.0	08.7	229 29.4	39.2	264 45.2	52.5	259 51.6	51.0	Betelgeuse	270 56.4	N 7 24.5
23	219 07.5	138 26.7	08.4	244 30.2	38.7	279 47.7	52.5	274 54.0	51.0			
16 00	234 09.9	153 29.4	N27 08.1	259 31.0	S12 38.1	294 50.2	S20 52.5	289 56.5	S19 51.0	Canopus	263 54.5	S52 42.6
01	249 12.4	168 32.2	07.8	274 31.8	37.6	309 52.6	52.6	304 59.0	51.0	Capella	280 27.9	N46 01.0
02	264 14.8	183 35.0	07.5	289 32.6	37.0	324 55.1	52.6	320 01.5	51.1	Deneb	49 28.1	N45 20.9
03	279 17.3	198 37.7	. . 07.2	304 33.4	. . 36.5	339 57.6	. . 52.6	335 04.0	. . 51.1	Denebola	182 28.7	N14 27.6
04	294 19.8	213 40.5	06.9	319 34.3	35.9	355 00.1	52.6	350 06.5	51.1	Diphda	348 51.3	S17 52.6
05	309 22.2	228 43.2	06.6	334 35.1	35.4	10 02.5	52.6	5 09.0	51.1			
06	324 24.7	243 46.0	N27 06.3	349 35.9	S12 34.8	25 05.0	S20 52.6	20 11.4	S19 51.1	Dubhe	193 45.6	N61 38.8
07	339 27.2	258 48.8	06.0	4 36.7	34.2	40 07.5	52.6	35 13.9	51.1	Elnath	278 07.0	N28 37.3
S 08	354 29.6	273 51.6	05.7	19 37.5	33.7	55 10.0	52.6	50 16.4	51.1	Eltanin	90 43.5	N51 29.1
A 09	9 32.1	288 54.4	. . 05.4	34 38.3	. . 33.1	70 12.4	. . 52.6	65 18.9	. . 51.1	Enif	33 42.5	N 9 57.9
T 10	24 34.6	303 57.1	05.1	49 39.1	32.6	85 14.9	52.6	80 21.4	51.1	Fomalhaut	15 18.8	S29 30.9
U 11	39 37.0	318 59.9	04.8	64 40.0	32.0	100 17.4	52.6	95 23.9	51.1			
R 12	54 39.5	334 02.7	N27 04.5	79 40.8	S12 31.5	115 19.9	S20 52.6	110 26.3	S19 51.1	Gacrux	171 55.3	S57 13.8
D 13	69 41.9	349 05.5	04.2	94 41.6	30.9	130 22.4	52.7	125 28.8	51.1	Gienah	175 47.2	S17 39.3
A 14	84 44.4	4 08.4	03.9	109 42.4	30.3	145 24.8	52.7	140 31.3	51.2	Hadar	148 40.6	S60 28.3
Y 15	99 46.9	19 11.2	. . 03.5	124 43.2	. . 29.8	160 27.3	. . 52.7	155 33.8	. . 51.2	Hamal	327 55.7	N23 33.2
16	114 49.3	34 14.0	03.2	139 44.0	29.2	175 29.8	52.7	170 36.3	51.2	Kaus Aust.	83 37.2	S34 22.3
17	129 51.8	49 16.8	02.9	154 44.9	28.7	190 32.3	52.7	185 38.8	51.2			
18	144 54.3	64 19.6	N27 02.6	169 45.7	S12 28.1	205 34.8	S20 52.7	200 41.3	S19 51.2	Kochab	137 18.8	N74 04.5
19	159 56.7	79 22.5	02.3	184 46.5	27.6	220 37.2	52.7	215 43.7	51.2	Markab	13 33.7	N15 18.6
20	174 59.2	94 25.3	02.0	199 47.3	27.0	235 39.7	52.7	230 46.2	51.2	Menkar	314 10.4	N 4 09.5
21	190 01.7	109 28.1	. . 01.6	214 48.1	. . 26.4	250 42.2	. . 52.7	245 48.7	. . 51.2	Menkent	148 01.6	S36 28.2
22	205 04.1	124 31.0	01.3	229 48.9	25.9	265 44.7	52.7	260 51.2	51.2	Miaplacidus	221 39.0	S69 48.3
23	220 06.6	139 33.8	01.0	244 49.8	25.3	280 47.2	52.8	275 53.7	51.2			
17 00	235 09.1	154 36.7	N27 00.7	259 50.6	S12 24.8	295 49.6	S20 52.8	290 56.2	S19 51.2	Mirfak	308 34.1	N49 55.8
01	250 11.5	169 39.6	00.4	274 51.4	24.2	310 52.1	52.8	305 58.7	51.3	Nunki	75 52.2	S26 16.2
02	265 14.0	184 42.4	27 00.0	289 52.2	23.7	325 54.6	52.8	321 01.2	51.3	Peacock	53 11.5	S56 39.9
03	280 16.4	199 45.3	26 59.7	304 53.0	. . 23.1	340 57.1	. . 52.8	336 03.7	. . 51.3	Pollux	243 22.1	N27 58.6
04	295 18.9	214 48.2	59.4	319 53.8	22.5	355 59.6	52.8	351 06.1	51.3	Procyon	244 55.0	N 5 10.3
05	310 21.4	229 51.0	59.0	334 54.7	22.0	11 02.1	52.8	6 08.6	51.3			
06	325 23.8	244 53.9	N26 58.7	349 55.5	S12 21.4	26 04.5	S20 52.8	21 11.1	S19 51.3	Rasalhague	96 01.7	N12 32.7
07	340 26.3	259 56.8	58.4	4 56.3	20.9	41 07.0	52.8	36 13.6	51.3	Regulus	207 38.4	N11 52.1
08	355 28.8	274 59.7	58.0	19 57.1	20.3	56 09.5	52.9	51 16.1	51.3	Rigel	281 07.8	S 8 10.9
S 09	10 31.2	290 02.6	. . 57.7	34 57.9	. . 19.7	71 12.0	. . 52.9	66 18.6	. . 51.3	Rigil Kent.	139 44.7	S60 55.1
U 10	25 33.7	305 05.5	57.4	49 58.8	19.2	86 14.5	52.9	81 21.1	51.3	Sabik	102 06.8	S15 44.9
N 11	40 36.2	320 08.4	57.0	64 59.6	18.6	101 17.0	52.9	96 23.6	51.4			
D 12	55 38.6	335 11.3	N26 56.7	80 00.4	S12 18.1	116 19.5	S20 52.9	111 26.1	S19 51.4	Schedar	349 35.6	N56 38.6
A 13	70 41.1	350 14.2	56.4	95 01.2	17.5	131 21.9	52.9	126 28.5	51.4	Shaula	96 15.1	S37 07.0
Y 14	85 43.5	5 17.1	56.0	110 02.0	17.0	146 24.4	52.9	141 31.0	51.4	Sirius	258 29.8	S16 44.8
15	100 46.0	20 20.1	. . 55.7	125 02.9	. . 16.4	161 26.9	. . 52.9	156 33.5	. . 51.4	Spica	158 26.0	S11 16.0
16	115 48.5	35 23.0	55.3	140 03.7	15.8	176 29.4	52.9	171 36.0	51.4	Suhail	222 49.1	S43 31.1
17	130 50.9	50 25.9	55.0	155 04.5	15.3	191 31.9	53.0	186 38.5	51.4			
18	145 53.4	65 28.9	N26 54.7	170 05.3	S12 14.7	206 34.4	S20 53.0	201 41.0	S19 51.4	Vega	80 35.4	N38 48.0
19	160 55.9	80 31.8	54.3	185 06.2	14.2	221 36.9	53.0	216 43.5	51.4	Zuben'ubi	136 59.8	S16 07.5
20	175 58.3	95 34.8	54.0	200 07.0	13.6	236 39.4	53.0	231 46.0	51.4		SHA	Mer. Pass.
21	191 00.8	110 37.7	. . 53.6	215 07.8	. . 13.0	251 41.9	. . 53.0	246 48.5	. . 51.4		° ′	h m
22	206 03.3	125 40.7	53.3	230 08.6	12.5	266 44.3	53.0	261 51.0	51.5	Venus	279 19.5	13 44
23	221 05.7	140 43.6	52.9	245 09.4	11.9	281 46.8	53.0	276 53.5	51.5	Mars	25 21.1	6 42
	h m									Jupiter	60 40.2	4 20
Mer. Pass.	8 22.0	v 2.8	d 0.3	v 0.8	d 0.6	v 2.5	d 0.0	v 2.5	d 0.0	Saturn	55 46.6	4 39

UT	SUN GHA	SUN Dec	MOON GHA	v	MOON Dec	d	HP
d h	° ′	° ′	° ′	′	° ′	′	′
15 00	180 54.6	N18 55.4	260 08.7	13.5	S15 54.9	9.5	54.9
01	195 54.6	56.0	274 41.2	13.7	15 45.4	9.6	54.9
02	210 54.6	56.6	289 13.9	13.6	15 35.8	9.6	54.9
03	225 54.6 ..	57.2	303 46.5	13.8	15 26.2	9.7	54.9
04	240 54.6	57.8	318 19.3	13.8	15 16.5	9.8	54.8
05	255 54.6	58.4	332 52.1	13.9	15 06.7	9.8	54.8
06	270 54.6	N18 59.0	347 25.0	14.0	S14 56.9	9.8	54.8
07	285 54.6	18 59.5	1 58.0	14.0	14 47.1	9.9	54.8
08	300 54.6	19 00.1	16 31.0	14.1	14 37.2	10.0	54.7
F 09	315 54.6 ..	00.7	31 04.1	14.1	14 27.2	10.0	54.7
R 10	330 54.6	01.3	45 37.2	14.2	14 17.2	10.1	54.7
I 11	345 54.5	01.9	60 10.4	14.3	14 07.1	10.1	54.7
D 12	0 54.5	N19 02.4	74 43.7	14.3	S13 57.0	10.2	54.7
A 13	15 54.5	03.0	89 17.0	14.4	13 46.8	10.2	54.7
Y 14	30 54.5	03.6	103 50.4	14.5	13 36.6	10.3	54.6
15	45 54.5 ..	04.2	118 23.9	14.5	13 26.3	10.3	54.6
16	60 54.5	04.8	132 57.4	14.6	13 16.0	10.3	54.6
17	75 54.5	05.3	147 31.0	14.6	13 05.7	10.5	54.6
18	90 54.5	N19 05.9	162 04.6	14.7	S12 55.2	10.4	54.6
19	105 54.4	06.5	176 38.3	14.7	12 44.8	10.5	54.6
20	120 54.4	07.1	191 12.0	14.8	12 34.3	10.6	54.5
21	135 54.4 ..	07.6	205 45.8	14.9	12 23.7	10.6	54.5
22	150 54.4	08.2	220 19.7	14.9	12 13.1	10.6	54.5
23	165 54.4	08.8	234 53.6	15.0	12 02.5	10.7	54.5
16 00	180 54.4	N19 09.4	249 27.6	15.0	S11 51.8	10.7	54.5
01	195 54.4	09.9	264 01.6	15.0	11 41.1	10.8	54.5
02	210 54.4	10.5	278 35.6	15.1	11 30.3	10.8	54.4
03	225 54.3 ..	11.1	293 09.7	15.2	11 19.5	10.9	54.4
04	240 54.3	11.7	307 43.9	15.2	11 08.6	10.9	54.4
05	255 54.3	12.2	322 18.1	15.3	10 57.7	10.9	54.4
06	270 54.3	N19 12.8	336 52.4	15.3	S10 46.8	11.0	54.4
S 07	285 54.3	13.4	351 26.7	15.3	10 35.8	11.0	54.4
A 08	300 54.3	13.9	6 01.0	15.4	10 24.8	11.0	54.4
T 09	315 54.2 ..	14.5	20 35.4	15.5	10 13.8	11.1	54.3
U 10	330 54.2	15.1	35 09.9	15.4	10 02.7	11.1	54.3
R 11	345 54.2	15.6	49 44.3	15.6	9 51.6	11.1	54.3
D 12	0 54.2	N19 16.2	64 18.9	15.5	S 9 40.5	11.2	54.3
A 13	15 54.2	16.8	78 53.4	15.6	9 29.3	11.2	54.3
Y 14	30 54.2	17.3	93 28.0	15.7	9 18.1	11.3	54.3
15	45 54.1 ..	17.9	108 02.7	15.7	9 06.8	11.2	54.3
16	60 54.1	18.5	122 37.4	15.7	8 55.6	11.3	54.3
17	75 54.1	19.0	137 12.1	15.7	8 44.3	11.4	54.3
18	90 54.1	N19 19.6	151 46.8	15.8	S 8 32.9	11.3	54.2
19	105 54.1	20.2	166 21.6	15.9	8 21.6	11.4	54.2
20	120 54.0	20.7	180 56.5	15.8	8 10.2	11.4	54.2
21	135 54.0 ..	21.3	195 31.3	15.9	7 58.8	11.5	54.2
22	150 54.0	21.8	210 06.2	16.0	7 47.3	11.5	54.2
23	165 54.0	22.4	224 41.2	15.9	7 35.8	11.5	54.2
17 00	180 54.0	N19 23.0	239 16.1	16.0	S 7 24.3	11.5	54.2
01	195 54.0	23.5	253 51.1	16.0	7 12.8	11.5	54.2
02	210 53.9	24.1	268 26.1	16.1	7 01.3	11.6	54.2
03	225 53.9 ..	24.6	283 01.2	16.1	6 49.7	11.6	54.2
04	240 53.9	25.2	297 36.3	16.1	6 38.1	11.6	54.2
05	255 53.9	25.8	312 11.4	16.1	6 26.5	11.7	54.2
06	270 53.8	N19 26.3	326 46.5	16.1	S 6 14.8	11.6	54.1
07	285 53.8	26.9	341 21.6	16.2	6 03.2	11.7	54.1
08	300 53.8	27.4	355 56.8	16.2	5 51.5	11.7	54.1
S 09	315 53.8 ..	28.0	10 32.0	16.2	5 39.8	11.8	54.1
U 10	330 53.8	28.5	25 07.2	16.3	5 28.0	11.7	54.1
N 11	345 53.7	29.1	39 42.5	16.3	5 16.3	11.8	54.1
D 12	0 53.7	N19 29.6	54 17.8	16.2	S 5 04.5	11.8	54.1
A 13	15 53.7	30.2	68 53.0	16.3	4 52.7	11.8	54.1
Y 14	30 53.7	30.7	83 28.3	16.4	4 40.9	11.8	54.1
15	45 53.6 ..	31.3	98 03.7	16.3	4 29.1	11.8	54.1
16	60 53.6	31.9	112 39.0	16.4	4 17.3	11.8	54.1
17	75 53.6	32.4	127 14.4	16.3	4 05.5	11.9	54.1
18	90 53.6	N19 33.0	141 49.7	16.4	S 3 53.6	11.9	54.1
19	105 53.5	33.5	156 25.1	16.4	3 41.7	11.9	54.1
20	120 53.5	34.0	171 00.5	16.4	3 29.8	11.9	54.1
21	135 53.5 ..	34.6	185 35.9	16.4	3 17.9	11.9	54.1
22	150 53.5	35.1	200 11.3	16.5	3 06.0	11.9	54.1
23	165 53.4	35.7	214 46.8	16.4	S 2 54.1	12.0	54.1
	SD 15.8	d 0.6	SD 14.9		14.8		14.7

Lat.	Twilight Naut.	Twilight Civil	Sunrise	Moonrise 15	Moonrise 16	Moonrise 17	Moonrise 18
°	h m	h m	h m	h m	h m	h m	h m
N 72	☐	☐	☐	04 37	04 00	03 35	03 14
N 70	////	////	00 04	04 03	03 42	03 26	03 12
68	////	////	01 39	03 38	03 27	03 18	03 09
66	////	////	02 16	03 19	03 15	03 11	03 07
64	////	00 57	02 43	03 04	03 05	03 06	03 06
62	////	01 45	03 03	02 51	02 57	03 01	03 04
60	////	02 15	03 19	02 40	02 49	02 57	03 03
N 58	00 51	02 37	03 33	02 30	02 43	02 53	03 02
56	01 35	02 54	03 45	02 22	02 37	02 49	03 01
54	02 02	03 09	03 55	02 14	02 32	02 46	03 00
52	02 23	03 22	04 04	02 08	02 27	02 44	02 59
50	02 40	03 33	04 12	02 01	02 23	02 41	02 58
45	03 11	03 55	04 30	01 48	02 13	02 36	02 56
N 40	03 35	04 13	04 44	01 37	02 06	02 31	02 55
35	03 53	04 27	04 55	01 28	01 59	02 27	02 54
30	04 08	04 40	05 06	01 20	01 53	02 23	02 53
20	04 32	05 00	05 23	01 05	01 43	02 17	02 51
N 10	04 50	05 16	05 39	00 53	01 34	02 12	02 49
0	05 06	05 31	05 53	00 41	01 25	02 07	02 47
S 10	05 19	05 45	06 07	00 29	01 16	02 02	02 46
20	05 32	05 58	06 22	00 17	01 07	01 56	02 44
30	05 44	06 13	06 39	00 02	00 57	01 50	02 42
35	05 51	06 21	06 48	24 51	00 51	01 46	02 41
40	05 58	06 30	07 00	24 44	00 44	01 42	02 40
45	06 05	06 41	07 13	24 36	00 36	01 38	02 39
S 50	06 13	06 53	07 29	24 26	00 26	01 32	02 37
52	06 17	06 58	07 36	24 21	00 21	01 29	02 36
54	06 21	07 04	07 44	24 16	00 16	01 26	02 35
56	06 25	07 11	07 54	24 11	00 11	01 23	02 34
58	06 29	07 18	08 04	24 05	00 05	01 20	02 33
S 60	06 34	07 26	08 16	23 58	25 15	01 15	02 32

Lat.	Sunset	Twilight Civil	Twilight Naut.	Moonset 15	Moonset 16	Moonset 17	Moonset 18
°	h m	h m	h m	h m	h m	h m	h m
N 72	☐	☐	☐	09 26	11 33	13 24	15 10
N 70	☐	////	☐	09 58	11 49	13 31	15 10
68	22 19	////	////	10 21	12 02	13 37	15 10
66	21 40	////	////	10 39	12 12	13 42	15 09
64	21 13	23 04	////	10 54	12 21	13 46	15 09
62	20 52	22 11	////	11 06	12 29	13 49	15 09
60	20 35	21 41	////	11 16	12 35	13 52	15 09
N 58	20 21	21 18	23 09	11 25	12 41	13 55	15 09
56	20 09	21 00	22 21	11 33	12 46	13 57	15 09
54	19 59	20 45	21 53	11 39	12 50	14 00	15 08
52	19 50	20 32	21 32	11 46	12 54	14 02	15 08
50	19 41	20 21	21 15	11 51	12 58	14 03	15 08
45	19 24	19 58	20 42	12 03	13 06	14 07	15 08
N 40	19 10	19 41	20 19	12 13	13 12	14 10	15 08
35	18 58	19 26	20 00	12 21	13 18	14 13	15 08
30	18 47	19 14	19 45	12 29	13 23	14 15	15 08
20	18 30	18 53	19 21	12 41	13 31	14 20	15 07
N 10	18 14	18 37	19 03	12 52	13 38	14 23	15 07
0	18 00	18 22	18 47	13 03	13 45	14 26	15 07
S 10	17 46	18 08	18 34	13 13	13 52	14 30	15 07
20	17 31	17 54	18 21	13 24	13 59	14 33	15 06
30	17 14	17 39	18 08	13 36	14 08	14 37	15 06
35	17 04	17 31	18 02	13 43	14 12	14 40	15 06
40	16 53	17 22	17 55	13 51	14 18	14 42	15 06
45	16 40	17 12	17 47	14 00	14 24	14 45	15 05
S 50	16 24	17 00	17 39	14 11	14 31	14 49	15 05
52	16 16	16 54	17 36	14 16	14 34	14 50	15 05
54	16 08	16 48	17 32	14 22	14 38	14 52	15 05
56	15 59	16 41	17 27	14 28	14 42	14 54	15 05
58	15 48	16 34	17 23	14 35	14 47	14 56	15 05
S 60	15 36	16 26	17 18	14 43	14 52	14 58	15 04

	SUN			MOON			
Day	Eqn. of Time 00ʰ	Eqn. of Time 12ʰ	Mer. Pass.	Mer. Pass. Upper	Mer. Pass. Lower	Age	Phase
d	m s	m s	h m	h m	h m	d	%
15	03 39	03 38	11 56	06 52	19 14	22	41
16	03 38	03 37	11 56	07 35	19 56	23	32
17	03 36	03 35	11 56	08 17	20 37	24	24

UT	ARIES GHA	VENUS −4·4 GHA	Dec	MARS +0·2 GHA	Dec	JUPITER −2·5 GHA	Dec	SATURN +0·5 GHA	Dec	STARS Name	SHA	Dec
18 00	236 08.2	155 46.6	N26 52.6	260 10.3	S12 11.4	296 49.3	S20 53.0	291 55.9	S19 51.5	Acamar	315 15.1	S40 13.5
01	251 10.7	170 49.6	52.2	275 11.1	10.8	311 51.8	53.0	306 58.4	51.5	Achernar	335 23.6	S57 08.0
02	266 13.1	185 52.5	51.9	290 11.9	10.2	326 54.3	53.1	322 00.9	51.5	Acrux	173 03.6	S63 12.9
03	281 15.6	200 55.5 ..	51.5	305 12.7 ..	09.7	341 56.8 ..	53.1	337 03.4 ..	51.5	Adhara	255 09.1	S29 00.2
04	296 18.0	215 58.5	51.1	320 13.6	09.1	356 59.3	53.1	352 05.9	51.5	Aldebaran	290 44.3	N16 32.8
05	311 20.5	231 01.5	50.8	335 14.4	08.6	12 01.8	53.1	7 08.4	51.5			
M 06	326 23.0	246 04.5	N26 50.4	350 15.2	S12 08.0	27 04.3	S20 53.1	22 10.9	S19 51.5	Alioth	166 16.0	N55 51.2
O 07	341 25.4	261 07.5	50.1	5 16.0	07.4	42 06.8	53.1	37 13.4	51.5	Alkaid	152 54.7	N49 12.9
N 08	356 27.9	276 10.5	49.7	20 16.8	06.9	57 09.3	53.1	52 15.9	51.6	Alnair	27 37.7	S46 51.6
D 09	11 30.4	291 13.5 ..	49.3	35 17.7 ..	06.3	72 11.8 ..	53.1	67 18.4 ..	51.6	Alnilam	275 41.9	S 1 11.5
A 10	26 32.8	306 16.5	49.0	50 18.5	05.7	87 14.3	53.2	82 20.9	51.6	Alphard	217 51.5	S 8 44.9
Y 11	41 35.3	321 19.5	48.6	65 19.3	05.2	102 16.7	53.2	97 23.4	51.6			
12	56 37.8	336 22.5	N26 48.3	80 20.1	S12 04.6	117 19.2	S20 53.2	112 25.9	S19 51.6	Alphecca	126 06.6	N26 38.9
13	71 40.2	351 25.6	47.9	95 21.0	04.1	132 21.7	53.2	127 28.4	51.6	Alpheratz	357 38.8	N29 11.9
14	86 42.7	6 28.6	47.5	110 21.8	03.5	147 24.2	53.2	142 30.8	51.6	Altair	62 03.4	N 8 55.2
15	101 45.2	21 31.6 ..	47.1	125 22.6 ..	02.9	162 26.7 ..	53.2	157 33.3 ..	51.6	Ankaa	353 11.2	S42 11.7
16	116 47.6	36 34.7	46.8	140 23.4	02.4	177 29.2	53.2	172 35.8	51.6	Antares	112 20.1	S26 28.5
17	131 50.1	51 37.7	46.4	155 24.3	01.8	192 31.7	53.2	187 38.3	51.7			
18	146 52.5	66 40.7	N26 46.0	170 25.1	S12 01.3	207 34.2	S20 53.3	202 40.8	S19 51.7	Arcturus	145 51.1	N19 04.7
19	161 55.0	81 43.8	45.7	185 25.9	00.7	222 36.7	53.3	217 43.3	51.7	Atria	107 17.1	S69 03.6
20	176 57.5	96 46.8	45.3	200 26.8	12 00.1	237 39.2	53.3	232 45.8	51.7	Avior	234 16.4	S59 34.8
21	191 59.9	111 49.9 ..	44.9	215 27.6	11 59.6	252 41.7 ..	53.3	247 48.3 ..	51.7	Bellatrix	278 27.2	N 6 21.9
22	207 02.4	126 53.0	44.5	230 28.4	59.0	267 44.2	53.3	262 50.8	51.7	Betelgeuse	270 56.5	N 7 24.5
23	222 04.9	141 56.0	44.1	245 29.2	58.4	282 46.7	53.3	277 53.3	51.7			
19 00	237 07.3	156 59.1	N26 43.8	260 30.1	S11 57.9	297 49.2	S20 53.3	292 55.8	S19 51.7	Canopus	263 54.5	S52 42.6
01	252 09.8	172 02.2	43.4	275 30.9	57.3	312 51.7	53.3	307 58.3	51.7	Capella	280 27.9	N46 01.0
02	267 12.3	187 05.3	43.0	290 31.7	56.8	327 54.2	53.4	323 00.8	51.8	Deneb	49 28.1	N45 20.9
03	282 14.7	202 08.4 ..	42.6	305 32.5 ..	56.2	342 56.7 ..	53.4	338 03.3 ..	51.8	Denebola	182 28.7	N14 27.6
04	297 17.2	217 11.5	42.2	320 33.4	55.6	357 59.2	53.4	353 05.8	51.8	Diphda	348 51.3	S17 52.6
05	312 19.6	232 14.6	41.8	335 34.2	55.1	13 01.7	53.4	8 08.3	51.8			
T 06	327 22.1	247 17.7	N26 41.4	350 35.0	S11 54.5	28 04.2	S20 53.4	23 10.8	S19 51.8	Dubhe	193 45.6	N61 38.8
U 07	342 24.6	262 20.8	41.1	5 35.9	53.9	43 06.7	53.4	38 13.3	51.8	Elnath	278 07.0	N28 37.3
E 08	357 27.0	277 23.9	40.7	20 36.7	53.4	58 09.2	53.4	53 15.8	51.8	Eltanin	90 43.5	N51 29.1
S 09	12 29.5	292 27.0 ..	40.3	35 37.5 ..	52.8	73 11.7 ..	53.5	68 18.3 ..	51.8	Enif	33 42.4	N 9 57.9
D 10	27 32.0	307 30.1	39.9	50 38.3	52.3	88 14.2	53.5	83 20.8	51.9	Fomalhaut	15 18.8	S29 30.8
A 11	42 34.4	322 33.2	39.5	65 39.2	51.7	103 16.7	53.5	98 23.3	51.9			
Y 12	57 36.9	337 36.4	N26 39.1	80 40.0	S11 51.1	118 19.2	S20 53.5	113 25.8	S19 51.9	Gacrux	171 55.3	S57 13.8
13	72 39.4	352 39.5	38.7	95 40.8	50.6	133 21.7	53.5	128 28.3	51.9	Gienah	175 47.2	S17 39.3
14	87 41.8	7 42.6	38.3	110 41.7	50.0	148 24.2	53.5	143 30.8	51.9	Hadar	148 40.6	S60 28.3
15	102 44.3	22 45.8 ..	37.9	125 42.5 ..	49.4	163 26.7 ..	53.5	158 33.3 ..	51.9	Hamal	327 55.7	N23 33.2
16	117 46.8	37 48.9	37.5	140 43.3	48.9	178 29.2	53.6	173 35.8	51.9	Kaus Aust.	83 37.2	S34 22.3
17	132 49.2	52 52.1	37.1	155 44.2	48.3	193 31.8	53.6	188 38.3	51.9			
18	147 51.7	67 55.2	N26 36.7	170 45.0	S11 47.7	208 34.3	S20 53.6	203 40.8	S19 51.9	Kochab	137 18.9	N74 04.5
19	162 54.1	82 58.4	36.3	185 45.8	47.2	223 36.8	53.6	218 43.3	51.9	Markab	13 33.7	N15 18.6
20	177 56.6	98 01.5	35.9	200 46.6	46.6	238 39.3	53.6	233 45.8	52.0	Menkar	314 10.4	N 4 09.9
21	192 59.1	113 04.7 ..	35.5	215 47.5 ..	46.1	253 41.8 ..	53.6	248 48.3 ..	52.0	Menkent	148 01.6	S36 28.2
22	208 01.5	128 07.9	35.1	230 48.3	45.5	268 44.3	53.6	263 50.8	52.0	Miaplacidus	221 39.0	S69 48.3
23	223 04.0	143 11.1	34.6	245 49.1	44.9	283 46.8	53.7	278 53.3	52.0			
20 00	238 06.5	158 14.2	N26 34.2	260 50.0	S11 44.4	298 49.3	S20 53.7	293 55.8	S19 52.0	Mirfak	308 34.1	N49 55.8
01	253 08.9	173 17.4	33.8	275 50.8	43.8	313 51.8	53.7	308 58.3	52.0	Nunki	75 52.2	S26 16.2
02	268 11.4	188 20.6	33.4	290 51.6	43.2	328 54.3	53.7	324 00.8	52.0	Peacock	53 11.5	S56 39.9
03	283 13.9	203 23.8 ..	33.0	305 52.5 ..	42.7	343 56.8 ..	53.7	339 03.3 ..	52.0	Pollux	243 22.1	N27 58.6
04	298 16.3	218 27.0	32.6	320 53.3	42.1	358 59.3	53.7	354 05.8	52.1	Procyon	244 55.0	N 5 10.3
05	313 18.8	233 30.2	32.2	335 54.1	41.5	14 01.8	53.7	9 08.3	52.1			
W 06	328 21.2	248 33.4	N26 31.7	350 55.0	S11 41.0	29 04.3	S20 53.8	24 10.8	S19 52.1	Rasalhague	96 01.7	N12 32.7
E 07	343 23.7	263 36.6	31.3	5 55.8	40.4	44 06.9	53.8	39 13.3	52.1	Regulus	207 38.5	N11 52.1
D 08	358 26.2	278 39.8	30.9	20 56.6	39.8	59 09.4	53.8	54 15.8	52.1	Rigel	281 07.8	S 8 10.9
N 09	13 28.6	293 43.1 ..	30.5	35 57.5 ..	39.3	74 11.9 ..	53.8	69 18.3 ..	52.1	Rigil Kent.	139 44.7	S60 55.1
E 10	28 31.1	308 46.3	30.1	50 58.3	38.7	89 14.4	53.8	84 20.8	52.1	Sabik	102 06.8	S15 44.9
S 11	43 33.6	323 49.5	29.6	65 59.1	38.1	104 16.9	53.8	99 23.3	52.1			
D 12	58 36.0	338 52.7	N26 29.2	81 00.0	S11 37.6	119 19.4	S20 53.9	114 25.8	S19 52.1	Schedar	349 35.5	N56 38.6
A 13	73 38.5	353 56.0	28.8	96 00.8	37.0	134 21.9	53.9	129 28.3	52.2	Shaula	96 15.1	S37 07.0
Y 14	88 41.0	8 59.2	28.4	111 01.6	36.5	149 24.4	53.9	144 30.8	52.2	Sirius	258 29.8	S16 44.8
15	103 43.4	24 02.5 ..	27.9	126 02.5 ..	35.9	164 26.9 ..	53.9	159 33.3 ..	52.2	Spica	158 26.0	S11 16.0
16	118 45.9	39 05.7	27.5	141 03.3	35.3	179 29.5	53.9	174 35.8	52.2	Suhail	222 49.1	S43 31.1
17	133 48.4	54 09.0	27.1	156 04.1	34.8	194 32.0	53.9	189 38.3	52.2			
18	148 50.8	69 12.2	N26 26.6	171 05.0	S11 34.2	209 34.5	S20 53.9	204 40.8	S19 52.2	Vega	80 35.4	N38 48.0
19	163 53.3	84 15.5	26.2	186 05.8	33.6	224 37.0	54.0	219 43.3	52.2	Zuben'ubi	136 59.8	S16 07.5
20	178 55.7	99 18.8	25.8	201 06.6	33.1	239 39.5	54.0	234 45.8	52.2		SHA	Mer.Pass.
21	193 58.2	114 22.0 ..	25.3	216 07.5 ..	32.5	254 42.0 ..	54.0	249 48.3 ..	52.3		° ′	h m
22	209 00.7	129 25.3	24.9	231 08.3	31.9	269 44.5	54.0	264 50.8	52.3	Venus	279 51.8	13 29
23	224 03.1	144 28.6	24.4	246 09.2	31.4	284 47.1	54.0	279 53.3	52.3	Mars	23 22.7	6 38
	h m									Jupiter	60 41.9	4 08
Mer. Pass. 8 10.2		*v* 3.1 *d* 0.4		*v* 0.8 *d* 0.6		*v* 2.5 *d* 0.0		*v* 2.5 *d* 0.0		Saturn	55 48.5	4 28

UT	SUN GHA	Dec	MOON GHA	v	Dec	d	HP
d h	° ′	° ′	° ′	′	° ′	′	′
18 00	180 53.4	N19 36.2	229 22.2	16.4	S 2 42.1	11.9	54.1
01	195 53.4	36.8	243 57.6	16.5	2 30.2	12.0	54.1
02	210 53.4	37.3	258 33.1	16.5	2 18.2	11.9	54.1
03	225 53.3 ..	37.9	273 08.6	16.4	2 06.3	12.0	54.1
04	240 53.3	38.4	287 44.0	16.5	1 54.3	12.0	54.1
05	255 53.3	39.0	302 19.5	16.5	1 42.3	12.0	54.1
06	270 53.3	N19 39.5	316 55.0	16.5	S 1 30.3	12.0	54.1
07	285 53.2	40.0	331 30.5	16.4	1 18.3	12.0	54.1
M 08	300 53.2	40.6	346 05.9	16.5	1 06.3	12.0	54.1
O 09	315 53.2 ..	41.1	0 41.4	16.5	0 54.3	12.0	54.1
N 10	330 53.1	41.7	15 16.9	16.5	0 42.3	12.0	54.1
D 11	345 53.1	42.2	29 52.4	16.5	S 0 30.3	12.0	54.1
A 12	0 53.1	N19 42.7	44 27.9	16.5	S 0 18.3	12.0	54.1
Y 13	15 53.1	43.3	59 03.4	16.4	S 0 06.3	12.1	54.1
14	30 53.0	43.8	73 38.8	16.5	N 0 05.8	12.0	54.1
15	45 53.0 ..	44.4	88 14.3	16.5	0 17.8	12.0	54.1
16	60 53.0	44.9	102 49.8	16.4	0 29.8	12.0	54.1
17	75 52.9	45.4	117 25.2	16.5	0 41.8	12.1	54.1
18	90 52.9	N19 46.0	132 00.7	16.4	N 0 53.9	12.0	54.1
19	105 52.9	46.5	146 36.1	16.5	1 05.9	12.0	54.1
20	120 52.8	47.0	161 11.6	16.4	1 17.9	12.0	54.1
21	135 52.8 ..	47.6	175 47.0	16.4	1 29.9	12.0	54.1
22	150 52.8	48.1	190 22.4	16.4	1 41.9	12.1	54.1
23	165 52.8	48.6	204 57.8	16.4	1 54.0	12.0	54.1
19 00	180 52.7	N19 49.2	219 33.2	16.4	N 2 06.0	12.0	54.1
01	195 52.7	49.7	234 08.6	16.4	2 18.0	12.0	54.1
02	210 52.7	50.2	248 44.0	16.3	2 30.0	12.0	54.1
03	225 52.6 ..	50.8	263 19.3	16.4	2 42.0	11.9	54.1
04	240 52.6	51.3	277 54.7	16.3	2 53.9	12.0	54.1
05	255 52.6	51.8	292 30.0	16.3	3 05.9	12.0	54.1
06	270 52.5	N19 52.4	307 05.3	16.3	N 3 17.9	12.0	54.1
07	285 52.5	52.9	321 40.6	16.3	3 29.9	11.9	54.1
T 08	300 52.5	53.4	336 15.9	16.2	3 41.8	12.0	54.1
U 09	315 52.4 ..	53.9	350 51.1	16.2	3 53.8	11.9	54.1
E 10	330 52.4	54.5	5 26.3	16.3	4 05.7	11.9	54.1
S 11	345 52.4	55.0	20 01.6	16.1	4 17.6	11.9	54.1
D 12	0 52.3	N19 55.5	34 36.7	16.2	N 4 29.5	11.9	54.2
A 13	15 52.3	56.0	49 11.9	16.1	4 41.4	11.9	54.2
Y 14	30 52.3	56.5	63 47.0	16.1	4 53.3	11.8	54.2
15	45 52.2 ..	57.1	78 22.1	16.1	5 05.1	11.9	54.2
16	60 52.2	57.6	92 57.2	16.1	5 17.0	11.8	54.2
17	75 52.1	58.1	107 32.3	16.0	5 28.8	11.8	54.2
18	90 52.1	N19 58.7	122 07.3	16.0	N 5 40.6	11.8	54.2
19	105 52.1	59.2	136 42.3	16.0	5 52.4	11.8	54.2
20	120 52.0	19 59.7	151 17.3	15.9	6 04.2	11.8	54.2
21	135 52.0	20 00.2	165 52.2	15.9	6 16.0	11.7	54.2
22	150 52.0	00.7	180 27.1	15.9	6 27.7	11.8	54.2
23	165 51.9	01.3	195 02.0	15.9	6 39.5	11.7	54.2
20 00	180 51.9	N20 01.8	209 36.9	15.8	N 6 51.2	11.7	54.2
01	195 51.8	02.3	224 11.7	15.8	7 02.9	11.6	54.3
02	210 51.8	02.8	238 46.5	15.7	7 14.5	11.6	54.3
03	225 51.8 ..	03.3	253 21.2	15.7	7 26.1	11.7	54.3
04	240 51.7	03.8	267 55.9	15.7	7 37.8	11.5	54.3
05	255 51.7	04.4	282 30.6	15.6	7 49.3	11.6	54.3
06	270 51.7	N20 04.9	297 05.2	15.6	N 8 00.9	11.5	54.3
W 07	285 51.6	05.4	311 39.8	15.6	8 12.4	11.6	54.3
E 08	300 51.6	05.9	326 14.4	15.5	8 24.0	11.4	54.3
D 09	315 51.5 ..	06.4	340 48.9	15.5	8 35.4	11.5	54.3
N 10	330 51.5	06.9	355 23.4	15.4	8 46.9	11.4	54.3
E 11	345 51.5	07.4	9 57.8	15.4	8 58.3	11.4	54.3
S 12	0 51.4	N20 07.9	24 32.2	15.4	N 9 09.7	11.4	54.4
D 13	15 51.4	08.5	39 06.6	15.3	9 21.1	11.3	54.4
A 14	30 51.3	09.0	53 40.9	15.2	9 32.4	11.3	54.4
Y 15	45 51.3 ..	09.5	68 15.1	15.3	9 43.7	11.3	54.4
16	60 51.3	10.0	82 49.4	15.1	9 55.0	11.2	54.4
17	75 51.2	10.5	97 23.5	15.2	10 06.2	11.2	54.4
18	90 51.2	N20 11.0	111 57.7	15.1	N10 17.4	11.2	54.4
19	105 51.1	11.5	126 31.8	15.0	10 28.6	11.1	54.4
20	120 51.1	12.0	141 05.8	15.0	10 39.7	11.1	54.5
21	135 51.0 ..	12.5	155 39.8	14.9	10 50.8	11.1	54.5
22	150 51.0	13.0	170 13.7	14.9	11 01.9	11.0	54.5
23	165 51.0	13.5	184 47.6	14.8	N11 12.9	10.9	54.5
	SD 15.8	d 0.5	SD 14.7		14.8		14.8

Twilight / Sunrise / Moonrise

Lat.	Twilight Naut.	Civil	Sunrise	Moonrise 18	19	20	21
°	h m	h m	h m	h m	h m	h m	h m
N 72	☐	☐	☐	03 14	02 55	02 34	02 08
N 70	☐	☐	☐	03 12	02 58	02 44	02 28
68	////	////	01 20	03 09	03 01	02 52	02 43
66	////	////	02 04	03 07	03 03	02 59	02 55
64	////	00 24	02 33	03 06	03 05	03 05	03 06
62	////	01 32	02 55	03 04	03 07	03 11	03 15
60	////	02 05	03 12	03 03	03 09	03 15	03 23
N 58	00 22	02 29	03 27	03 02	03 10	03 19	03 30
56	01 23	02 48	03 39	03 01	03 11	03 23	03 36
54	01 53	03 03	03 50	03 00	03 13	03 26	03 41
52	02 16	03 17	04 00	02 59	03 14	03 29	03 46
50	02 34	03 28	04 08	02 58	03 15	03 32	03 51
45	03 07	03 52	04 26	02 56	03 17	03 38	04 01
N 40	03 31	04 10	04 41	02 55	03 18	03 43	04 09
35	03 50	04 25	04 53	02 54	03 20	03 47	04 16
30	04 06	04 38	05 04	02 53	03 21	03 51	04 22
20	04 30	04 59	05 22	02 51	03 24	03 57	04 33
N 10	04 50	05 16	05 38	02 49	03 26	04 03	04 42
0	05 05	05 31	05 53	02 47	03 28	04 09	04 51
S 10	05 19	05 45	06 08	02 46	03 30	04 14	05 01
20	05 33	06 00	06 23	02 44	03 32	04 21	05 10
30	05 46	06 15	06 41	02 42	03 35	04 27	05 22
35	05 53	06 23	06 51	02 41	03 36	04 31	05 28
40	06 00	06 33	07 02	02 40	03 38	04 36	05 35
45	06 08	06 44	07 16	02 39	03 40	04 41	05 44
S 50	06 16	06 56	07 33	02 37	03 42	04 48	05 55
52	06 20	07 02	07 40	02 36	03 43	04 51	06 00
54	06 24	07 08	07 49	02 35	03 44	04 54	06 05
56	06 29	07 15	07 59	02 34	03 46	04 58	06 11
58	06 34	07 23	08 10	02 33	03 47	05 02	06 18
S 60	06 39	07 32	08 23	02 32	03 49	05 06	06 25

Sunset / Twilight / Moonset

Lat.	Sunset	Twilight Civil	Naut.	Moonset 18	19	20	21
°	h m	h m	h m	h m	h m	h m	h m
N 72	☐	☐	☐	15 10	16 57	18 50	21 01
N 70	☐	☐	☐	15 10	16 49	18 33	20 26
68	22 39	////	////	15 10	16 43	18 19	20 02
66	21 52	////	////	15 09	16 37	18 08	19 43
64	21 22	////	////	15 09	16 33	17 59	19 27
62	21 00	22 25	////	15 09	16 29	17 51	19 15
60	20 42	21 51	////	15 09	16 26	17 44	19 04
N 58	20 27	21 26	////	15 09	16 23	17 38	18 55
56	20 15	21 07	22 34	15 09	16 20	17 33	18 47
54	20 04	20 51	22 02	15 08	16 18	17 28	18 40
52	19 54	20 38	21 39	15 08	16 15	17 24	18 33
50	19 45	20 26	21 21	15 08	16 14	17 20	18 27
45	19 27	20 02	20 47	15 08	16 09	17 11	18 15
N 40	19 12	19 44	20 22	15 08	16 06	17 05	18 05
35	19 00	19 28	20 03	15 08	16 03	16 59	17 56
30	18 49	19 16	19 48	15 08	16 00	16 53	17 48
20	18 31	18 55	19 23	15 07	15 55	16 43	17 35
N 10	18 15	18 37	19 04	15 07	15 51	16 37	17 24
0	18 00	18 22	18 48	15 07	15 47	16 29	17 13
S 10	17 45	18 08	18 33	15 07	15 44	16 22	17 02
20	17 30	17 53	18 20	15 06	15 40	16 14	16 51
30	17 12	17 38	18 07	15 06	15 35	16 05	16 38
35	17 02	17 29	18 00	15 06	15 32	16 00	16 30
40	16 50	17 20	17 53	15 06	15 29	15 54	16 22
45	16 37	17 09	17 45	15 05	15 26	15 48	16 12
S 50	16 20	16 56	17 36	15 05	15 22	15 40	16 00
52	16 12	16 50	17 32	15 05	15 20	15 36	15 55
54	16 03	16 44	17 28	15 05	15 18	15 32	15 48
56	15 54	16 37	17 24	15 05	15 16	15 28	15 42
58	15 43	16 29	17 19	15 05	15 13	15 23	15 34
S 60	15 30	16 21	17 13	15 04	15 10	15 17	15 26

Day	SUN Eqn. of Time 00ʰ	12ʰ	Mer. Pass.	MOON Mer. Pass. Upper	Lower	Age	Phase
d	m s	m s	h m	h m	h m	d	%
18	03 34	03 32	11 56	21 17	08 57	25	16
19	03 31	03 29	11 57	21 58	09 38	26	10
20	03 28	03 26	11 57	22 40	10 19	27	5

UT	ARIES	VENUS −4.3		MARS +0.1		JUPITER −2.5		SATURN +0.5		STARS		
	GHA	GHA	Dec	GHA	Dec	GHA	Dec	GHA	Dec	Name	SHA	Dec
d h	° ′	° ′	° ′	° ′	° ′	° ′	° ′	° ′	° ′		° ′	° ′
21 00	239 05.6	159 31.9	N26 24.0	261 10.0	S11 30.8	299 49.6	S20 54.0	294 55.8	S19 52.3	Acamar	315 15.1	S40 13.5
01	254 08.1	174 35.2	23.6	276 10.8	30.2	314 52.1	54.1	309 58.3	52.3	Achernar	335 23.6	S57 08.0
02	269 10.5	189 38.5	23.1	291 11.7	29.7	329 54.6	54.1	325 00.8	52.3	Acrux	173 03.6	S63 12.9
03	284 13.0	204 41.8 ..	22.7	306 12.5 ..	29.1	344 57.1 ..	54.1	340 03.3 ..	52.3	Adhara	255 09.1	S29 00.2
04	299 15.5	219 45.1	22.2	321 13.3	28.5	359 59.6	54.1	355 05.8	52.4	Aldebaran	290 44.3	N16 32.8
05	314 17.9	234 48.4	21.8	336 14.2	28.0	15 02.2	54.1	10 08.3	52.4			
06	329 20.4	249 51.7	N26 21.3	351 15.0	S11 27.4	30 04.7	S20 54.1	25 10.8	S19 52.4	Alioth	166 16.1	N55 51.3
07	344 22.9	264 55.0	20.9	6 15.9	26.8	45 07.2	54.2	40 13.3	52.4	Alkaid	152 54.7	N49 12.9
T 08	359 25.3	279 58.3	20.4	21 16.7	26.3	60 09.7	54.2	55 15.8	52.4	Alnair	27 37.7	S46 51.6
H 09	14 27.8	295 01.7 ..	20.0	36 17.5 ..	25.7	75 12.2 ..	54.2	70 18.4 ..	52.4	Alnilam	275 41.9	S 1 11.5
U 10	29 30.2	310 05.0	19.5	51 18.4	25.1	90 14.8	54.2	85 20.9	52.4	Alphard	217 51.5	S 8 44.9
R 11	44 32.7	325 08.3	19.1	66 19.2	24.6	105 17.3	54.2	100 23.4	52.4			
S 12	59 35.2	340 11.7	N26 18.6	81 20.0	S11 24.0	120 19.8	S20 54.2	115 25.9	S19 52.5	Alphecca	126 06.6	N26 38.9
D 13	74 37.6	355 15.0	18.1	96 20.9	23.4	135 22.3	54.3	130 28.4	52.5	Alpheratz	357 38.8	N29 11.9
A 14	89 40.1	10 18.3	17.7	111 21.7	22.9	150 24.8	54.3	145 30.9	52.5	Altair	62 03.4	N 8 55.3
Y 15	104 42.6	25 21.7 ..	17.2	126 22.6 ..	22.3	165 27.4 ..	54.3	160 33.4 ..	52.5	Ankaa	353 11.2	S42 11.7
16	119 45.0	40 25.0	16.8	141 23.4	21.7	180 29.9	54.3	175 35.9	52.5	Antares	112 20.1	S26 28.5
17	134 47.5	55 28.4	16.3	156 24.2	21.2	195 32.4	54.3	190 38.4	52.5			
18	149 50.0	70 31.8	N26 15.8	171 25.1	S11 20.6	210 34.9	S20 54.3	205 40.9	S19 52.5	Arcturus	145 51.1	N19 04.7
19	164 52.4	85 35.1	15.4	186 25.9	20.0	225 37.4	54.4	220 43.4	52.5	Atria	107 17.1	S69 03.7
20	179 54.9	100 38.5	14.9	201 26.8	19.5	240 40.0	54.4	235 45.9	52.6	Avior	234 16.4	S59 34.8
21	194 57.3	115 41.9 ..	14.4	216 27.6 ..	18.9	255 42.5 ..	54.4	250 48.4 ..	52.6	Bellatrix	278 27.2	N 6 21.9
22	209 59.8	130 45.3	14.0	231 28.4	18.3	270 45.0	54.4	265 50.9	52.6	Betelgeuse	270 56.5	N 7 24.5
23	225 02.3	145 48.6	13.5	246 29.3	17.7	285 47.5	54.4	280 53.5	52.6			
22 00	240 04.7	160 52.0	N26 13.0	261 30.1	S11 17.2	300 50.1	S20 54.5	295 56.0	S19 52.6	Canopus	263 54.5	S52 42.6
01	255 07.2	175 55.4	12.5	276 31.0	16.6	315 52.6	54.5	310 58.5	52.6	Capella	280 27.9	N46 01.0
02	270 09.7	190 58.8	12.1	291 31.8	16.0	330 55.1	54.5	326 01.0	52.6	Deneb	49 28.1	N45 20.9
03	285 12.1	206 02.2 ..	11.6	306 32.7 ..	15.5	345 57.6 ..	54.5	341 03.5 ..	52.7	Denebola	182 28.7	N14 27.6
04	300 14.6	221 05.6	11.1	321 33.5	14.9	1 00.2	54.5	356 06.0	52.7	Diphda	348 51.3	S17 52.6
05	315 17.1	236 09.0	10.6	336 34.3	14.3	16 02.7	54.5	11 08.5	52.7			
06	330 19.5	251 12.4	N26 10.2	351 35.2	S11 13.8	31 05.2	S20 54.6	26 11.0	S19 52.7	Dubhe	193 45.7	N61 38.8
07	345 22.0	266 15.9	09.7	6 36.0	13.2	46 07.7	54.6	41 13.5	52.7	Elnath	278 07.0	N28 37.3
08	0 24.5	281 19.3	09.2	21 36.9	12.6	61 10.3	54.6	56 16.0	52.7	Eltanin	90 43.4	N51 29.1
F 09	15 26.9	296 22.7 ..	08.7	36 37.7 ..	12.1	76 12.8 ..	54.6	71 18.5 ..	52.7	Enif	33 42.4	N 9 57.9
R 10	30 29.4	311 26.1	08.2	51 38.6	11.5	91 15.3	54.6	86 21.1	52.8	Fomalhaut	15 18.8	S29 30.8
I 11	45 31.8	326 29.6	07.7	66 39.4	10.9	106 17.8	54.7	101 23.6	52.8			
D 12	60 34.3	341 33.0	N26 07.3	81 40.2	S11 10.4	121 20.4	S20 54.7	116 26.1	S19 52.8	Gacrux	171 55.3	S57 13.8
A 13	75 36.8	356 36.4	06.8	96 41.1	09.8	136 22.9	54.7	131 28.6	52.8	Gienah	175 47.2	S17 39.3
Y 14	90 39.2	11 39.9	06.3	111 41.9	09.2	151 25.4	54.7	146 31.1	52.8	Hadar	148 40.6	S60 28.3
15	105 41.7	26 43.3 ..	05.8	126 42.8 ..	08.6	166 28.0 ..	54.7	161 33.6 ..	52.8	Hamal	327 55.7	N23 33.2
16	120 44.2	41 46.8	05.3	141 43.6	08.1	181 30.5	54.8	176 36.1	52.8	Kaus Aust.	83 37.2	S34 22.3
17	135 46.6	56 50.3	04.8	156 44.5	07.5	196 33.0	54.8	191 38.6	52.9			
18	150 49.1	71 53.7	N26 04.3	171 45.3	S11 06.9	211 35.6	S20 54.8	206 41.1	S19 52.9	Kochab	137 18.9	N74 04.5
19	165 51.6	86 57.2	03.8	186 46.2	06.4	226 38.1	54.8	221 43.7	52.9	Markab	13 33.7	N15 18.7
20	180 54.0	102 00.7	03.3	201 47.0	05.8	241 40.6	54.8	236 46.2	52.9	Menkar	314 10.4	N 4 10.0
21	195 56.5	117 04.1 ..	02.8	216 47.8 ..	05.2	256 43.1 ..	54.8	251 48.7 ..	52.9	Menkent	148 01.6	S36 28.2
22	210 59.0	132 07.6	02.3	231 48.7	04.7	271 45.7	54.9	266 51.2	52.9	Miaplacidus	221 39.1	S69 48.3
23	226 01.4	147 11.1	01.8	246 49.5	04.1	286 48.2	54.9	281 53.7	52.9			
23 00	241 03.9	162 14.6	N26 01.3	261 50.4	S11 03.5	301 50.7	S20 54.9	296 56.2	S19 53.0	Mirfak	308 34.1	N49 55.7
01	256 06.3	177 18.1	00.8	276 51.2	03.0	316 53.3	54.9	311 58.7	53.0	Nunki	75 52.1	S26 16.2
02	271 08.8	192 21.6	26 00.3	291 52.1	02.4	331 55.8	54.9	327 01.2	53.0	Peacock	53 11.5	S56 39.9
03	286 11.3	207 25.0	25 59.8	306 52.9 ..	01.8	346 58.3 ..	55.0	342 03.8 ..	53.0	Pollux	243 22.2	N27 58.6
04	301 13.7	222 28.6	59.3	321 53.8	01.2	2 00.9	55.0	357 06.3	53.0	Procyon	244 55.0	N 5 10.3
05	316 16.2	237 32.1	58.8	336 54.6	00.7	17 03.4	55.0	12 08.8	53.0			
06	331 18.7	252 35.6	N25 58.3	351 55.5	S11 00.1	32 05.9	S20 55.0	27 11.3	S19 53.0	Rasalhague	96 01.7	N12 32.7
07	346 21.1	267 39.1	57.8	6 56.3	10 59.5	47 08.5	55.0	42 13.8	53.1	Regulus	207 38.5	N11 52.1
S 08	1 23.6	282 42.6	57.2	21 57.2	59.0	62 11.0	55.1	57 16.3	53.1	Rigel	281 07.8	S 8 10.9
A 09	16 26.1	297 46.1 ..	56.7	36 58.0 ..	58.4	77 13.5 ..	55.1	72 18.8 ..	53.1	Rigil Kent.	139 44.7	S60 55.1
T 10	31 28.5	312 49.6	56.2	51 58.9	57.8	92 16.1	55.1	87 21.3	53.1	Sabik	102 06.7	S15 44.9
U 11	46 31.0	327 53.2	55.7	66 59.7	57.3	107 18.6	55.1	102 23.9	53.1			
R 12	61 33.5	342 56.7	N25 55.2	82 00.6	S10 56.7	122 21.2	S20 55.1	117 26.4	S19 53.1	Schedar	349 35.5	N56 38.6
D 13	76 35.9	358 00.2	54.7	97 01.4	56.1	137 23.7	55.2	132 28.9	53.1	Shaula	96 15.1	S37 07.0
A 14	91 38.4	13 03.8	54.1	112 02.3	55.5	152 26.2	55.2	147 31.4	53.2	Sirius	258 29.8	S16 44.8
Y 15	106 40.8	28 07.3 ..	53.6	127 03.1 ..	55.0	167 28.8 ..	55.2	162 33.9 ..	53.2	Spica	158 26.0	S11 16.0
16	121 43.3	43 10.9	53.1	142 04.0	54.4	182 31.3	55.2	177 36.4	53.2	Suhail	222 49.1	S43 31.1
17	136 45.8	58 14.4	52.6	157 04.8	53.8	197 33.8	55.2	192 39.0	53.2			
18	151 48.2	73 18.0	N25 52.0	172 05.7	S10 53.3	212 36.4	S20 55.3	207 41.5	S19 53.2	Vega	80 35.4	N38 48.0
19	166 50.7	88 21.5	51.5	187 06.5	52.7	227 38.9	55.3	222 44.0	53.2	Zuben'ubi	136 59.8	S16 07.5
20	181 53.2	103 25.1	51.0	202 07.4	52.1	242 41.5	55.3	237 46.5	53.2		SHA	Mer.Pass.
21	196 55.6	118 28.7 ..	50.5	217 08.2 ..	51.5	257 44.0 ..	55.3	252 49.0 ..	53.3		° ′	h m
22	211 58.1	133 32.2	49.9	232 09.1	51.0	272 46.5	55.3	267 51.5	53.3	Venus	280 47.3	13 14
23	227 00.6	148 35.8	49.4	247 09.9	50.4	287 49.1	55.4	282 54.0	53.3	Mars	21 25.4	6 34
	h m									Jupiter	60 45.3	3 56
Mer.Pass.	7 58.4	v 3.4	d 0.5	v 0.8	d 0.6	v 2.5	d 0.0	v 2.5	d 0.0	Saturn	55 51.2	4 16

UT	SUN GHA	SUN Dec	MOON GHA	v	MOON Dec	d	HP
d h	° ′	° ′	° ′	′	° ′	′	′
21 00	180 50.9	N20 14.0	199 21.4	14.8	N11 23.8	11.0	54.5
01	195 50.9	14.5	213 55.2	14.7	11 34.8	10.9	54.5
02	210 50.8	15.0	228 28.9	14.7	11 45.7	10.8	54.5
03	225 50.8 ..	15.5	243 02.6	14.6	11 56.5	10.8	54.5
04	240 50.7	16.0	257 36.2	14.6	12 07.3	10.8	54.6
05	255 50.7	16.5	272 09.8	14.5	12 18.1	10.7	54.6
06	270 50.7	N20 17.0	286 43.3	14.5	N12 28.8	10.7	54.6
07	285 50.6	17.5	301 16.8	14.4	12 39.5	10.6	54.6
08	300 50.6	18.0	315 50.2	14.3	12 50.1	10.6	54.6
09	315 50.5 ..	18.5	330 23.5	14.3	13 00.7	10.5	54.6
10	330 50.5	19.0	344 56.8	14.3	13 11.2	10.5	54.6
11	345 50.4	19.5	359 30.1	14.1	13 21.7	10.4	54.6
12	0 50.4	N20 20.0	14 03.2	14.1	N13 32.1	10.4	54.7
13	15 50.3	20.5	28 36.3	14.1	13 42.5	10.3	54.7
14	30 50.3	21.0	43 09.4	14.0	13 52.8	10.3	54.7
15	45 50.2 ..	21.5	57 42.4	13.9	14 03.1	10.2	54.7
16	60 50.2	22.0	72 15.3	13.9	14 13.3	10.2	54.7
17	75 50.1	22.5	86 48.2	13.8	14 23.5	10.1	54.7
18	90 50.1	N20 23.0	101 21.0	13.8	N14 33.6	10.1	54.7
19	105 50.1	23.5	115 53.8	13.6	14 43.7	10.0	54.8
20	120 50.0	24.0	130 26.4	13.7	14 53.7	9.9	54.8
21	135 50.0 ..	24.5	144 59.1	13.5	15 03.6	9.9	54.8
22	150 49.9	25.0	159 31.6	13.5	15 13.5	9.8	54.8
23	165 49.9	25.5	174 04.1	13.5	15 23.3	9.8	54.8
22 00	180 49.8	N20 25.9	188 36.6	13.3	N15 33.1	9.7	54.8
01	195 49.8	26.4	203 08.9	13.3	15 42.8	9.6	54.9
02	210 49.7	26.9	217 41.2	13.3	15 52.4	9.6	54.9
03	225 49.7 ..	27.4	232 13.5	13.1	16 02.0	9.5	54.9
04	240 49.6	27.9	246 45.6	13.1	16 11.5	9.4	54.9
05	255 49.6	28.4	261 17.7	13.1	16 20.9	9.4	54.9
06	270 49.5	N20 28.9	275 49.8	12.9	N16 30.3	9.3	54.9
07	285 49.5	29.4	290 21.7	12.9	16 39.6	9.3	54.9
08	300 49.4	29.8	304 53.6	12.9	16 48.9	9.1	55.0
09	315 49.4 ..	30.3	319 25.5	12.7	16 58.0	9.1	55.0
10	330 49.3	30.8	333 57.2	12.7	17 07.1	9.1	55.0
11	345 49.3	31.3	348 28.9	12.6	17 16.2	8.9	55.0
12	0 49.2	N20 31.8	3 00.5	12.6	N17 25.1	8.9	55.0
13	15 49.2	32.3	17 32.1	12.5	17 34.0	8.8	55.0
14	30 49.1	32.7	32 03.6	12.4	17 42.8	8.7	55.1
15	45 49.1 ..	33.2	46 35.0	12.3	17 51.5	8.7	55.1
16	60 49.0	33.7	61 06.3	12.3	18 00.2	8.6	55.1
17	75 48.9	34.2	75 37.6	12.2	18 08.8	8.5	55.1
18	90 48.9	N20 34.7	90 08.8	12.2	N18 17.3	8.4	55.1
19	105 48.8	35.1	104 40.0	12.0	18 25.7	8.3	55.2
20	120 48.8	35.6	119 11.0	12.0	18 34.0	8.3	55.2
21	135 48.7 ..	36.1	133 42.0	11.9	18 42.3	8.1	55.2
22	150 48.7	36.6	148 12.9	11.9	18 50.4	8.1	55.2
23	165 48.6	37.0	162 43.8	11.8	18 58.5	8.0	55.2
23 00	180 48.6	N20 37.5	177 14.6	11.7	N19 06.5	8.0	55.2
01	195 48.5	38.0	191 45.3	11.6	19 14.5	7.8	55.3
02	210 48.5	38.5	206 15.9	11.6	19 22.3	7.8	55.3
03	225 48.4 ..	38.9	220 46.5	11.5	19 30.1	7.6	55.3
04	240 48.4	39.4	235 17.0	11.4	19 37.7	7.6	55.3
05	255 48.3	39.9	249 47.4	11.4	19 45.3	7.5	55.3
06	270 48.2	N20 40.3	264 17.8	11.3	N19 52.8	7.4	55.3
07	285 48.2	40.8	278 48.1	11.2	20 00.2	7.3	55.4
08	300 48.1	41.3	293 18.3	11.1	20 07.5	7.2	55.4
09	315 48.1 ..	41.8	307 48.4	11.1	20 14.7	7.1	55.4
10	330 48.0	42.2	322 18.5	11.0	20 21.8	7.0	55.4
11	345 48.0	42.7	336 48.5	10.9	20 28.8	6.9	55.4
12	0 47.9	N20 43.2	351 18.4	10.9	N20 35.7	6.8	55.5
13	15 47.8	43.6	5 48.3	10.8	20 42.5	6.8	55.5
14	30 47.8	44.1	20 18.1	10.7	20 49.3	6.6	55.5
15	45 47.7 ..	44.6	34 47.8	10.7	20 55.9	6.5	55.5
16	60 47.7	45.0	49 17.5	10.6	21 02.4	6.4	55.5
17	75 47.6	45.5	63 47.0	10.6	21 08.8	6.4	55.6
18	90 47.6	N20 46.0	78 16.6	10.4	N21 15.2	6.2	55.6
19	105 47.5	46.4	92 46.0	10.4	21 21.4	6.1	55.6
20	120 47.4	46.9	107 15.4	10.3	21 27.5	6.0	55.6
21	135 47.4 ..	47.3	121 44.7	10.2	21 33.5	5.9	55.6
22	150 47.3	47.8	136 13.9	10.2	21 39.4	5.8	55.6
23	165 47.3	48.3	150 43.1	10.1	N21 45.2	5.7	55.7
	SD 15.8 d 0.5		SD 14.9	15.0			15.1

(Left column day labels: THURSDAY for 21, FRIDAY for 22, SATURDAY for 23)

Twilight / Sunrise / Moonrise

Lat.	Naut.	Civil	Sunrise	21	22	23	24
°	h m	h m	h m	h m	h m	h m	h m
N 72	▢	▢	▢	02 08	01 29	▢	▢
N 70	▢	▢	▢	02 28	02 06	01 22	▢
68	////	////	00 58	02 43	02 32	02 15	01 28
66	////	////	01 52	02 55	02 52	02 48	02 44
64	////	////	02 24	03 06	03 08	03 12	03 22
62	////	01 17	02 48	03 15	03 21	03 31	03 48
60	////	01 55	03 06	03 23	03 33	03 47	04 09
N 58	////	02 21	03 22	03 30	03 43	04 01	04 26
56	01 10	02 41	03 35	03 36	03 52	04 12	04 40
54	01 45	02 58	03 46	03 41	03 59	04 23	04 53
52	02 09	03 12	03 56	03 46	04 06	04 32	05 04
50	02 28	03 24	04 05	03 51	04 13	04 40	05 14
45	03 03	03 48	04 24	04 01	04 27	04 57	05 34
N 40	03 28	04 07	04 39	04 09	04 38	05 12	05 51
35	03 48	04 23	04 52	04 16	04 48	05 24	06 05
30	04 04	04 36	05 03	04 22	04 56	05 34	06 18
20	04 29	04 58	05 22	04 33	05 11	05 53	06 39
N 10	04 49	05 15	05 38	04 42	05 24	06 09	06 57
0	05 05	05 31	05 53	04 51	05 36	06 24	07 15
S 10	05 20	05 46	06 08	05 01	05 49	06 39	07 32
20	05 34	06 01	06 24	05 10	06 02	06 56	07 51
30	05 47	06 17	06 42	05 22	06 17	07 14	08 12
35	05 55	06 26	06 53	05 28	06 26	07 25	08 25
40	06 02	06 35	07 05	05 35	06 36	07 38	08 40
45	06 10	06 47	07 19	05 44	06 48	07 53	08 57
S 50	06 20	07 00	07 36	05 55	07 03	08 12	09 19
52	06 24	07 06	07 45	06 00	07 10	08 20	09 29
54	06 28	07 12	07 54	06 05	07 17	08 30	09 41
56	06 33	07 20	08 04	06 11	07 26	08 41	09 54
58	06 38	07 28	08 15	06 18	07 36	08 54	10 10
S 60	06 44	07 37	08 29	06 25	07 47	09 09	10 29

Sunset / Twilight / Moonset

Lat.	Sunset	Civil	Naut.	21	22	23	24
°	h m	h m	h m	h m	h m	h m	h m
N 72	▢	▢	▢	21 01	▢	▢	▢
N 70	▢	▢	▢	20 26	22 47	▢	▢
68	23 03	////	////	20 02	21 55	24 26	00 26
66	22 05	////	////	19 43	21 23	23 10	25 02
64	21 32	////	////	19 27	21 00	22 33	24 01
62	21 08	22 41	////	19 15	20 41	22 07	23 27
60	20 49	22 01	////	19 04	20 26	21 47	23 02
N 58	20 33	21 34	////	18 55	20 13	21 30	22 42
56	20 20	21 14	22 48	18 47	20 02	21 16	22 26
54	20 08	20 57	22 11	18 40	19 52	21 04	22 12
52	19 58	20 43	21 46	18 33	19 44	20 53	21 59
50	19 49	20 30	21 27	18 27	19 36	20 44	21 49
45	19 30	20 06	20 51	18 15	19 19	20 24	21 26
N 40	19 15	19 47	20 26	18 05	19 06	20 08	21 08
35	19 02	19 31	20 06	17 56	18 55	19 54	20 53
30	18 51	19 19	19 50	17 48	18 45	19 42	20 40
20	18 32	18 56	19 24	17 35	18 28	19 22	20 18
N 10	18 16	18 38	19 05	17 24	18 13	19 04	19 58
0	18 00	18 22	18 48	17 13	17 59	18 48	19 40
S 10	17 45	18 08	18 33	17 02	17 45	18 32	19 22
20	17 29	17 53	18 20	16 51	17 30	18 14	19 03
30	17 11	17 37	18 06	16 38	17 14	17 54	18 40
35	17 00	17 28	17 59	16 30	17 04	17 43	18 27
40	16 48	17 18	17 51	16 22	16 53	17 29	18 12
45	16 34	17 07	17 43	16 12	16 40	17 13	17 54
S 50	16 17	16 53	17 33	16 00	16 24	16 54	17 32
52	16 08	16 47	17 29	15 55	16 17	16 45	17 22
54	15 59	16 41	17 25	15 48	16 09	16 35	17 10
56	15 49	16 33	17 20	15 42	15 59	16 23	16 56
58	15 37	16 25	17 15	15 34	15 49	16 10	16 40
S 60	15 24	16 16	17 09	15 26	15 37	15 54	16 21

SUN and MOON

Day	Eqn. of Time 00h	Eqn. of Time 12h	Mer. Pass.	Mer. Pass. Upper	Mer. Pass. Lower	Age	Phase
d	m s	m s	h m	h m	h m	d	%
21	03 24	03 22	11 57	11 02	23 24	28	2
22	03 19	03 17	11 57	11 48	24 11	29	0
23	03 14	03 12	11 57	12 36	00 11	01	1

UT	ARIES GHA	VENUS −4.1 GHA	Dec	MARS +0.1 GHA	Dec	JUPITER −2.5 GHA	Dec	SATURN +0.5 GHA	Dec	STARS Name	SHA	Dec
24 00	242 03.0	163 39.4	N25 48.9	262 10.8	S10 49.8	302 51.6	S20 55.4	297 56.6	S19 53.3	Acamar	315 15.1	S40 13.5
01	257 05.5	178 43.0	48.3	277 11.6	49.3	317 54.2	55.4	312 59.1	53.3	Achernar	335 23.6	S57 08.0
02	272 07.9	193 46.6	47.8	292 12.5	48.7	332 56.7	55.4	328 01.6	53.3	Acrux	173 03.6	S63 12.9
03	287 10.4	208 50.2 ..	47.3	307 13.3 ..	48.1	347 59.2 ..	55.5	343 04.1 ..	53.4	Adhara	255 09.1	S29 00.2
04	302 12.9	223 53.7	46.7	322 14.2	47.5	3 01.8	55.5	358 06.6	53.4	Aldebaran	290 44.3	N16 32.8
05	317 15.3	238 57.3	46.2	337 15.0	47.0	18 04.3	55.5	13 09.2	53.4			
06	332 17.8	254 00.9	N25 45.6	352 15.9	S10 46.4	33 06.9	S20 55.5	28 11.7	S19 53.4	Alioth	166 16.1	N55 51.3
07	347 20.3	269 04.6	45.1	7 16.7	45.8	48 09.4	55.5	43 14.2	53.4	Alkaid	152 54.7	N49 13.0
S 08	2 22.7	284 08.2	44.5	22 17.6	45.3	63 12.0	55.6	58 16.7	53.4	Alnair	27 37.7	S46 51.6
U 09	17 25.2	299 11.8 ..	44.0	37 18.4 ..	44.7	78 14.5 ..	55.6	73 19.2 ..	53.4	Alnilam	275 41.8	S 1 11.5
N 10	32 27.7	314 15.4	43.5	52 19.3	44.1	93 17.0	55.6	88 21.7	53.5	Alphard	217 51.5	S 8 44.9
D 11	47 30.1	329 19.0	42.9	67 20.1	43.5	108 19.6	55.6	103 24.3	53.5			
A 12	62 32.6	344 22.6	N25 42.4	82 21.0	S10 43.0	123 22.1	S20 55.6	118 26.8	S19 53.5	Alphecca	126 06.6	N26 38.9
Y 13	77 35.1	359 26.3	41.8	97 21.8	42.4	138 24.7	55.7	133 29.3	53.5	Alpheratz	357 38.7	N29 11.9
14	92 37.5	14 29.9	41.3	112 22.7	41.8	153 27.2	55.7	148 31.8	53.5	Altair	62 03.4	N 8 55.3
15	107 40.0	29 33.5 ..	40.7	127 23.5 ..	41.3	168 29.8 ..	55.7	163 34.3 ..	53.5	Ankaa	353 11.2	S42 11.7
16	122 42.4	44 37.2	40.2	142 24.4	40.7	183 32.3	55.7	178 36.9	53.6	Antares	112 20.0	S26 28.5
17	137 44.9	59 40.8	39.6	157 25.3	40.1	198 34.9	55.8	193 39.4	53.6			
18	152 47.4	74 44.4	N25 39.0	172 26.1	S10 39.5	213 37.4	S20 55.8	208 41.9	S19 53.6	Arcturus	145 51.1	N19 04.7
19	167 49.8	89 48.1	38.5	187 27.0	39.0	228 40.0	55.8	223 44.4	53.6	Atria	107 17.0	S69 03.7
20	182 52.3	104 51.7	37.9	202 27.8	38.4	243 42.5	55.8	238 46.9	53.6	Avior	234 16.5	S59 34.7
21	197 54.8	119 55.4 ..	37.4	217 28.7 ..	37.8	258 45.1 ..	55.8	253 49.5 ..	53.6	Bellatrix	278 27.2	N 6 21.9
22	212 57.2	134 59.1	36.8	232 29.5	37.2	273 47.6	55.9	268 52.0	53.7	Betelgeuse	270 56.4	N 7 24.5
23	227 59.7	150 02.7	36.2	247 30.4	36.7	288 50.1	55.9	283 54.5	53.7			
25 00	243 02.2	165 06.4	N25 35.7	262 31.2	S10 36.1	303 52.7	S20 55.9	298 57.0	S19 53.7	Canopus	263 54.5	S52 42.6
01	258 04.6	180 10.1	35.1	277 32.1	35.5	318 55.2	55.9	313 59.5	53.7	Capella	280 27.9	N46 01.0
02	273 07.1	195 13.7	34.6	292 33.0	35.0	333 57.8	56.0	329 02.1	53.7	Deneb	49 28.1	N45 20.9
03	288 09.6	210 17.4 ..	34.0	307 33.8 ..	34.4	349 00.3 ..	56.0	344 04.6 ..	53.7	Denebola	182 28.7	N14 27.6
04	303 12.0	225 21.1	33.4	322 34.7	33.8	4 02.9	56.0	359 07.1	53.8	Diphda	348 51.3	S17 52.6
05	318 14.5	240 24.8	32.8	337 35.5	33.2	19 05.4	56.0	14 09.6	53.8			
06	333 16.9	255 28.5	N25 32.3	352 36.4	S10 32.6	34 08.0	S20 56.0	29 12.1	S19 53.8	Dubhe	193 45.7	N61 38.8
07	348 19.4	270 32.2	31.7	7 37.2	32.1	49 10.5	56.1	44 14.7	53.8	Elnath	278 07.0	N28 37.3
M 08	3 21.9	285 35.8	31.1	22 38.1	31.5	64 13.1	56.1	59 17.2	53.8	Eltanin	90 43.4	N51 29.1
O 09	18 24.3	300 39.5 ..	30.6	37 39.0 ..	30.9	79 15.7 ..	56.1	74 19.7 ..	53.8	Enif	33 42.4	N 9 58.0
N 10	33 26.8	315 43.2	30.0	52 39.8	30.4	94 18.2	56.1	89 22.2	53.9	Fomalhaut	15 18.8	S29 30.8
D 11	48 29.3	330 47.0	29.4	67 40.7	29.8	109 20.8	56.2	104 24.7	53.9			
A 12	63 31.7	345 50.7	N25 28.8	82 41.5	S10 29.2	124 23.3	S20 56.2	119 27.3	S19 53.9	Gacrux	171 55.3	S57 13.8
Y 13	78 34.2	0 54.4	28.2	97 42.4	28.7	139 25.9	56.2	134 29.8	53.9	Gienah	175 47.2	S17 39.3
14	93 36.7	15 58.1	27.7	112 43.2	28.1	154 28.4	56.2	149 32.3	53.9	Hadar	148 40.6	S60 28.3
15	108 39.1	31 01.8 ..	27.1	127 44.1 ..	27.5	169 31.0 ..	56.3	164 34.8 ..	53.9	Hamal	327 55.7	N23 33.2
16	123 41.6	46 05.5	26.5	142 45.0	26.9	184 33.5	56.3	179 37.4	54.0	Kaus Aust.	83 37.1	S34 22.3
17	138 44.1	61 09.3	25.9	157 45.8	26.4	199 36.1	56.3	194 39.9	54.0			
18	153 46.5	76 13.0	N25 25.3	172 46.7	S10 25.8	214 38.6	S20 56.3	209 42.4	S19 54.0	Kochab	137 18.9	N74 04.5
19	168 49.0	91 16.7	24.7	187 47.5	25.2	229 41.2	56.4	224 44.9	54.0	Markab	13 33.7	N15 18.7
20	183 51.4	106 20.4	24.1	202 48.4	24.6	244 43.7	56.4	239 47.5	54.0	Menkar	314 10.4	N 4 10.0
21	198 53.9	121 24.2 ..	23.6	217 49.3 ..	24.1	259 46.3 ..	56.4	254 50.0 ..	54.0	Menkent	148 01.6	S36 28.2
22	213 56.4	136 27.9	23.0	232 50.1	23.5	274 48.9	56.4	269 52.5	54.1	Miaplacidus	221 39.1	S69 48.3
23	228 58.8	151 31.7	22.4	247 51.0	22.9	289 51.4	56.4	284 55.0	54.1			
26 00	244 01.3	166 35.4	N25 21.8	262 51.8	S10 22.3	304 54.0	S20 56.5	299 57.6	S19 54.1	Mirfak	308 34.0	N49 55.7
01	259 03.8	181 39.2	21.2	277 52.7	21.8	319 56.5	56.5	315 00.1	54.1	Nunki	75 52.1	S26 16.2
02	274 06.2	196 42.9	20.6	292 53.6	21.2	334 59.1	56.5	330 02.6	54.1	Peacock	53 11.4	S56 39.9
03	289 08.7	211 46.7 ..	20.0	307 54.4 ..	20.6	350 01.6 ..	56.5	345 05.1 ..	54.1	Pollux	243 22.2	N27 58.6
04	304 11.2	226 50.4	19.4	322 55.3	20.0	5 04.2	56.6	0 07.7	54.2	Procyon	244 55.0	N 5 10.3
05	319 13.6	241 54.2	18.8	337 56.2	19.5	20 06.8	56.6	15 10.2	54.2			
06	334 16.1	256 58.0	N25 18.2	352 57.0	S10 18.9	35 09.3	S20 56.6	30 12.7	S19 54.2	Rasalhague	96 01.7	N12 32.7
07	349 18.6	272 01.7	17.6	7 57.9	18.3	50 11.9	56.6	45 15.2	54.2	Regulus	207 38.5	N11 52.1
T 08	4 21.0	287 05.5	17.0	22 58.7	17.7	65 14.4	56.7	60 17.8	54.2	Rigel	281 07.8	S 8 10.9
U 09	19 23.5	302 09.3 ..	16.4	37 59.6 ..	17.2	80 17.0 ..	56.7	75 20.3 ..	54.2	Rigil Kent.	139 44.7	S60 55.1
E 10	34 25.9	317 13.1	15.8	53 00.5	16.6	95 19.6	56.7	90 22.8	54.3	Sabik	102 06.7	S15 44.9
S 11	49 28.4	332 16.9	15.2	68 01.3	16.0	110 22.1	56.7	105 25.3	54.3			
D 12	64 30.9	347 20.6	N25 14.6	83 02.2	S10 15.4	125 24.7	S20 56.8	120 27.9	S19 54.3	Schedar	349 35.5	N56 38.6
A 13	79 33.3	2 24.4	14.0	98 03.1	14.9	140 27.2	56.8	135 30.4	54.3	Shaula	96 15.0	S37 07.0
Y 14	94 35.8	17 28.2	13.3	113 03.9	14.3	155 29.8	56.8	150 32.9	54.3	Sirius	258 29.8	S16 44.8
15	109 38.3	32 32.0 ..	12.7	128 04.8 ..	13.7	170 32.4 ..	56.8	165 35.4 ..	54.3	Spica	158 26.0	S11 16.0
16	124 40.7	47 35.8	12.1	143 05.6	13.2	185 34.9	56.9	180 38.0	54.4	Suhail	222 49.1	S43 31.1
17	139 43.2	62 39.6	11.5	158 06.5	12.6	200 37.5	56.9	195 40.5	54.4			
18	154 45.7	77 43.4	N25 10.9	173 07.4	S10 12.0	215 40.0	S20 56.9	210 43.0	S19 54.4	Vega	80 35.4	N38 48.1
19	169 48.1	92 47.2	10.3	188 08.2	11.4	230 42.6	56.9	225 45.6	54.4	Zuben'ubi	136 59.8	S16 07.5
20	184 50.6	107 51.0	09.7	203 09.1	10.9	245 45.2	57.0	240 48.1	54.4		SHA	Mer. Pass.
21	199 53.1	122 54.8 ..	09.0	218 10.0 ..	10.3	260 47.7 ..	57.0	255 50.6 ..	54.5	Venus	282 04.2	12 56
22	214 55.5	137 58.7	08.4	233 10.8	09.7	275 50.3	57.0	270 53.1	54.5	Mars	19 29.1	6 30
23	229 58.0	153 02.5	07.8	248 11.7	09.1	290 52.9	57.0	285 55.7	54.5	Jupiter	60 50.5	3 44
Mer. Pass. 7 46.6		v 3.7 d 0.6		v 0.9 d 0.6		v 2.6 d 0.0		v 2.5 d 0.0		Saturn	55 54.8	4 04

UT	SUN GHA	SUN Dec	MOON GHA	v	MOON Dec	d	HP
d h	° ′	° ′	° ′	′	° ′	′	′
24 00	180 47.2	N20 48.7	165 12.2	10.1	N21 50.9	5.6	55.7
01	195 47.1	49.2	179 41.3	10.0	21 56.5	5.5	55.7
02	210 47.1	49.6	194 10.3	9.9	22 02.0	5.4	55.7
03	225 47.0	.. 50.1	208 39.2	9.8	22 07.4	5.2	55.7
04	240 47.0	50.6	223 08.0	9.8	22 12.6	5.2	55.8
05	255 46.9	51.0	237 36.8	9.7	22 17.8	5.0	55.8
06	270 46.8	N20 51.5	252 05.5	9.7	N22 22.8	4.9	55.8
07	285 46.8	51.9	266 34.2	9.6	22 27.7	4.8	55.8
08	300 46.7	52.4	281 02.8	9.5	22 32.5	4.7	55.8
S 09	315 46.7	.. 52.8	295 31.3	9.5	22 37.2	4.6	55.9
U 10	330 46.6	53.3	309 59.8	9.4	22 41.8	4.4	55.9
N 11	345 46.5	53.7	324 28.2	9.4	22 46.2	4.4	55.9
D 12	0 46.5	N20 54.2	338 56.6	9.3	N22 50.6	4.2	55.9
A 13	15 46.4	54.6	353 24.9	9.2	22 54.8	4.1	55.9
Y 14	30 46.4	55.1	7 53.1	9.2	22 58.9	4.0	56.0
15	45 46.3	.. 55.5	22 21.3	9.1	23 02.9	3.9	56.0
16	60 46.2	56.0	36 49.4	9.1	23 06.8	3.7	56.0
17	75 46.2	56.4	51 17.5	9.0	23 10.5	3.6	56.0
18	90 46.1	N20 56.9	65 45.5	9.0	N23 14.1	3.5	56.0
19	105 46.0	57.3	80 13.5	8.9	23 17.6	3.4	56.1
20	120 46.0	57.8	94 41.4	8.9	23 21.0	3.2	56.1
21	135 45.9	.. 58.2	109 09.3	8.8	23 24.2	3.2	56.1
22	150 45.8	58.7	123 37.1	8.7	23 27.4	3.0	56.1
23	165 45.8	59.1	138 04.8	8.7	23 30.4	2.8	56.1
25 00	180 45.7	N20 59.6	152 32.5	8.7	N23 33.2	2.8	56.2
01	195 45.7	21 00.0	167 00.2	8.6	23 36.0	2.6	56.2
02	210 45.6	00.5	181 27.8	8.6	23 38.6	2.5	56.2
03	225 45.5	.. 00.9	195 55.4	8.5	23 41.1	2.4	56.2
04	240 45.5	01.3	210 22.9	8.5	23 43.5	2.2	56.3
05	255 45.4	01.8	224 50.4	8.4	23 45.7	2.1	56.3
06	270 45.3	N21 02.2	239 17.8	8.4	N23 47.8	2.0	56.3
07	285 45.3	02.7	253 45.2	8.4	23 49.8	1.8	56.3
08	300 45.2	03.1	268 12.6	8.3	23 51.6	1.7	56.3
M 09	315 45.1	.. 03.6	282 39.9	8.2	23 53.3	1.6	56.4
O 10	330 45.1	04.0	297 07.1	8.3	23 54.9	1.4	56.4
N 11	345 45.0	04.4	311 34.4	8.2	23 56.3	1.4	56.4
D 12	0 44.9	N21 04.9	326 01.6	8.2	N23 57.7	1.1	56.4
A 13	15 44.9	05.3	340 28.8	8.1	23 58.8	1.1	56.4
Y 14	30 44.8	05.7	354 55.9	8.1	23 59.9	0.9	56.5
15	45 44.7	.. 06.2	9 23.0	8.0	24 00.8	0.8	56.5
16	60 44.7	06.6	23 50.0	8.1	24 01.6	0.6	56.5
17	75 44.6	07.0	38 17.1	8.0	24 02.2	0.4	56.5
18	90 44.5	N21 07.5	52 44.1	8.0	N24 02.7	0.4	56.5
19	105 44.5	07.9	67 11.1	7.9	24 03.1	0.2	56.6
20	120 44.4	08.3	81 38.0	7.9	24 03.3	0.1	56.6
21	135 44.3	.. 08.8	96 04.9	7.9	24 03.4	0.0	56.6
22	150 44.2	09.2	110 31.8	7.9	24 03.4	0.2	56.6
23	165 44.2	09.6	124 58.7	7.8	24 03.2	0.3	56.7
26 00	180 44.1	N21 10.1	139 25.6	7.8	N24 02.9	0.5	56.7
01	195 44.0	10.5	153 52.4	7.8	24 02.4	0.5	56.7
02	210 44.0	10.9	168 19.2	7.8	24 01.9	0.8	56.7
03	225 43.9	.. 11.3	182 46.0	7.8	24 01.1	0.8	56.7
04	240 43.8	11.8	197 12.8	7.8	24 00.3	1.0	56.8
05	255 43.8	12.2	211 39.6	7.7	23 59.3	1.2	56.8
06	270 43.7	N21 12.6	226 06.3	7.8	N23 58.1	1.3	56.8
07	285 43.6	13.1	240 33.0	7.8	23 56.8	1.4	56.8
T 08	300 43.5	13.5	254 59.8	7.7	23 55.4	1.5	56.8
U 09	315 43.5	.. 13.9	269 26.5	7.7	23 53.9	1.7	56.9
E 10	330 43.4	14.3	283 53.2	7.7	23 52.2	1.9	56.9
S 11	345 43.3	14.7	298 19.9	7.6	23 50.3	1.9	56.9
D 12	0 43.3	N21 15.2	312 46.5	7.7	N23 48.4	2.1	56.9
A 13	15 43.2	15.6	327 13.2	7.7	23 46.3	2.3	57.0
Y 14	30 43.1	16.0	341 39.9	7.7	23 44.0	2.4	57.0
15	45 43.0	.. 16.4	356 06.6	7.6	23 41.6	2.5	57.0
16	60 43.0	16.9	10 33.2	7.7	23 39.1	2.7	57.0
17	75 42.9	17.3	24 59.9	7.7	23 36.4	2.8	57.0
18	90 42.8	N21 17.7	39 26.6	7.6	N23 33.6	2.9	57.1
19	105 42.8	18.1	53 53.2	7.7	23 30.7	3.1	57.1
20	120 42.7	18.5	68 19.9	7.7	23 27.6	3.2	57.1
21	135 42.6	.. 18.9	82 46.6	7.7	23 24.4	3.4	57.1
22	150 42.5	19.4	97 13.3	7.6	23 21.0	3.5	57.2
23	165 42.5	19.8	111 39.9	7.7	N23 17.5	3.6	57.2
	SD 15.8	d 0.4	SD 15.2		15.4		15.5

Twilight / Sunrise / Moonrise

Lat.	Naut.	Civil	Sunrise	Moonrise 24	25	26	27
°	h m	h m	h m	h m	h m	h m	h m
N 72	□	□	□	□	□	□	□
N 70	□	□	□	□	□	□	□
68	////	////	00 27	01 28	□	□	□
66	////	////	01 40	02 44	02 42	03 12	05 05
64	////	////	02 15	03 22	03 44	04 32	05 52
62	////	01 02	02 41	03 48	04 18	05 09	06 23
60	////	01 46	03 00	04 09	04 43	05 35	06 46
N 58	////	02 14	03 17	04 26	05 03	05 55	07 04
56	00 56	02 36	03 30	04 40	05 19	06 12	07 20
54	01 36	02 53	03 42	04 53	05 34	06 27	07 33
52	02 03	03 08	03 52	05 04	05 46	06 39	07 44
50	02 23	03 20	04 02	05 14	05 57	06 51	07 55
45	03 00	03 46	04 21	05 34	06 20	07 14	08 16
N 40	03 26	04 05	04 37	05 51	06 38	07 32	08 33
35	03 46	04 21	04 50	06 05	06 53	07 48	08 48
30	04 02	04 35	05 01	06 18	07 07	08 01	09 01
20	04 28	04 57	05 21	06 39	07 30	08 24	09 22
N 10	04 49	05 15	05 38	06 57	07 49	08 44	09 41
0	05 05	05 31	05 53	07 15	08 08	09 03	09 58
S 10	05 21	05 46	06 09	07 32	08 27	09 22	10 16
20	05 35	06 02	06 25	07 51	08 47	09 41	10 34
30	05 49	06 18	06 44	08 12	09 10	10 04	10 56
35	05 56	06 27	06 55	08 25	09 23	10 18	11 08
40	06 04	06 38	07 07	08 40	09 39	10 34	11 22
45	06 13	06 49	07 22	08 57	09 58	10 52	11 39
S 50	06 23	07 03	07 40	09 19	10 21	11 15	12 00
52	06 27	07 09	07 48	09 29	10 32	11 26	12 10
54	06 32	07 16	07 58	09 41	10 45	11 39	12 22
56	06 37	07 24	08 08	09 54	11 00	11 53	12 34
58	06 42	07 32	08 21	10 10	11 17	12 10	12 49
S 60	06 48	07 42	08 35	10 29	11 38	12 31	13 06

Sunset / Twilight / Moonset

Lat.	Sunset	Civil	Naut.	Moonset 24	25	26	27
°	h m	h m	h m	h m	h m	h m	h m
N 72	□	□	□	□	□	□	□
N 70	□	□	□	□	□	□	□
68	□	□	□	00 26	□	□	□
66	22 18	////	////	25 02	01 02	02 26	02 29
64	21 41	////	////	24 01	00 01	01 06	01 41
62	21 15	22 58	////	23 27	24 30	00 30	01 10
60	20 55	22 11	////	23 02	24 03	00 03	00 47
N 58	20 39	21 42	////	22 42	23 43	24 28	00 28
56	20 25	21 20	23 03	22 26	23 25	24 13	00 13
54	20 13	21 02	22 20	22 12	23 11	23 59	24 37
52	20 02	20 48	21 53	21 59	22 58	23 47	24 27
50	19 53	20 35	21 33	21 49	22 47	23 37	24 18
45	19 34	20 09	20 55	21 26	22 24	23 15	23 58
N 40	19 18	19 49	20 29	21 08	22 05	22 57	23 43
35	19 04	19 33	20 09	20 53	21 50	22 42	23 30
30	18 53	19 20	19 52	20 40	21 36	22 29	23 18
20	18 33	18 57	19 26	20 18	21 13	22 07	22 58
N 10	18 16	18 39	19 06	19 58	20 53	21 48	22 41
0	18 01	18 23	18 49	19 40	20 34	21 29	22 24
S 10	17 45	18 07	18 33	19 22	20 15	21 11	22 08
20	17 29	17 52	18 19	19 03	19 55	20 52	21 50
30	17 10	17 36	18 05	18 40	19 32	20 29	21 30
35	16 59	17 26	17 57	18 27	19 18	20 16	21 18
40	16 46	17 16	17 49	18 12	19 03	20 00	21 04
45	16 32	17 04	17 41	17 54	18 44	19 42	20 48
S 50	16 14	16 51	17 31	17 32	18 20	19 19	20 28
52	16 05	16 44	17 27	17 22	18 09	19 08	20 18
54	15 56	16 37	17 22	17 10	17 56	18 56	20 07
56	15 45	16 30	17 17	16 56	17 42	18 42	19 55
58	15 33	16 21	17 11	16 40	17 24	18 25	19 41
S 60	15 19	16 11	17 05	16 21	17 03	18 05	19 24

SUN and MOON

Day	SUN Eqn. of Time 00h	12h	SUN Mer. Pass.	MOON Mer. Pass. Upper	Lower	Age	Phase
d	m s	m s	h m	h m	h m	d	%
24	03 09	03 06	11 57	13 27	01 01	02	3
25	03 03	03 00	11 57	14 21	01 54	03	8
26	02 57	02 53	11 57	15 16	02 49	04	14

UT	ARIES	VENUS −4.1		MARS +0.0		JUPITER −2.5		SATURN +0.4		STARS		
	GHA	GHA	Dec	GHA	Dec	GHA	Dec	GHA	Dec	Name	SHA	Dec
d h	° ′	° ′	° ′	° ′	° ′	° ′	° ′	° ′	° ′		° ′	° ′
27 00	245 00.4	168 06.3	N25 07.2	263 12.6	S10 08.6	305 55.4	S20 57.1	300 58.2	S19 54.5	Acamar	315 15.1	S40 13.5
01	260 02.9	183 10.1	06.6	278 13.4	08.0	320 58.0	57.1	316 00.7	54.5	Achernar	335 23.6	S57 08.0
02	275 05.4	198 14.0	05.9	293 14.3	07.4	336 00.6	57.1	331 03.3	54.5	Acrux	173 03.7	S63 12.9
03	290 07.8	213 17.8 ..	05.3	308 15.2 ..	06.8	351 03.1 ..	57.1	346 05.8 ..	54.6	Adhara	255 09.1	S29 00.2
04	305 10.3	228 21.6	04.7	323 16.0	06.3	6 05.7	57.2	1 08.3	54.6	Aldebaran	290 44.2	N16 32.8
05	320 12.8	243 25.5	04.0	338 16.9	05.7	21 08.3	57.2	16 10.8	54.6			
06	335 15.2	258 29.3	N25 03.4	353 17.8	S10 05.1	36 10.8	S20 57.2	31 13.4	S19 54.6	Alioth	166 16.1	N55 51.3
W 07	350 17.7	273 33.1	02.8	8 18.6	04.5	51 13.4	57.2	46 15.9	54.6	Alkaid	152 54.7	N49 13.0
E 08	5 20.2	288 37.0	02.2	23 19.5	03.9	66 16.0	57.3	61 18.4	54.7	Alnair	27 37.6	S46 51.6
D 09	20 22.6	303 40.8 ..	01.5	38 20.4 ..	03.4	81 18.5 ..	57.3	76 21.0 ..	54.7	Alnilam	275 41.8	S 1 11.5
N 10	35 25.1	318 44.7	00.9	53 21.2	02.8	96 21.1	57.3	91 23.5	54.7	Alphard	217 51.5	S 8 44.9
E 11	50 27.5	333 48.5	25 00.3	68 22.1	02.2	111 23.7	57.3	106 26.0	54.7			
S 12	65 30.0	348 52.4	N24 59.6	83 23.0	S10 01.6	126 26.2	S20 57.4	121 28.5	S19 54.7	Alphecca	126 06.6	N26 38.9
D 13	80 32.5	3 56.2	59.0	98 23.8	01.1	141 28.8	57.4	136 31.1	54.7	Alpheratz	357 38.7	N29 11.9
A 14	95 34.9	19 00.1	58.3	113 24.7	10 00.5	156 31.4	57.4	151 33.6	54.8	Altair	62 03.4	N 8 55.3
Y 15	110 37.4	34 04.0 ..	57.7	128 25.6	9 59.9	171 33.9 ..	57.5	166 36.1 ..	54.8	Ankaa	353 11.1	S42 11.7
16	125 39.9	49 07.8	57.0	143 26.5	59.3	186 36.5	57.5	181 38.7	54.8	Antares	112 20.0	S26 28.5
17	140 42.3	64 11.7	56.4	158 27.3	58.8	201 39.1	57.5	196 41.2	54.8			
18	155 44.8	79 15.6	N24 55.8	173 28.2	S 9 58.2	216 41.7	S20 57.5	211 43.7	S19 54.8	Arcturus	145 51.1	N19 04.7
19	170 47.3	94 19.5	55.1	188 29.1	57.6	231 44.2	57.6	226 46.3	54.9	Atria	107 17.0	S69 03.7
20	185 49.7	109 23.3	54.5	203 29.9	57.0	246 46.8	57.6	241 48.8	54.9	Avior	234 16.5	S59 34.7
21	200 52.2	124 27.2 ..	53.8	218 30.8 ..	56.5	261 49.4 ..	57.6	256 51.3 ..	54.9	Bellatrix	278 27.2	N 6 21.9
22	215 54.7	139 31.1	53.2	233 31.7	55.9	276 51.9	57.6	271 53.9	54.9	Betelgeuse	270 56.4	N 7 24.5
23	230 57.1	154 35.0	52.5	248 32.5	55.3	291 54.5	57.7	286 56.4	54.9			
28 00	245 59.6	169 38.9	N24 51.9	263 33.4	S 9 54.7	306 57.1	S20 57.7	301 58.9	S19 55.0	Canopus	263 54.5	S52 42.6
01	261 02.0	184 42.8	51.2	278 34.3	54.2	321 59.7	57.7	317 01.5	55.0	Capella	280 27.9	N46 01.0
02	276 04.5	199 46.7	50.6	293 35.2	53.6	337 02.2	57.7	332 04.0	55.0	Deneb	49 28.0	N45 20.9
03	291 07.0	214 50.6 ..	49.9	308 36.0 ..	53.0	352 04.8 ..	57.8	347 06.5 ..	55.0	Denebola	182 28.7	N14 27.6
04	306 09.4	229 54.5	49.3	323 36.9	52.4	7 07.4	57.8	2 09.1	55.0	Diphda	348 51.3	S17 52.6
05	321 11.9	244 58.4	48.6	338 37.8	51.9	22 10.0	57.8	17 11.6	55.0			
06	336 14.4	260 02.3	N24 48.0	353 38.6	S 9 51.3	37 12.5	S20 57.9	32 14.1	S19 55.1	Dubhe	193 45.7	N61 38.8
T 07	351 16.8	275 06.2	47.3	8 39.5	50.7	52 15.1	57.9	47 16.7	55.1	Elnath	278 07.0	N28 37.3
H 08	6 19.3	290 10.1	46.6	23 40.4	50.1	67 17.7	57.9	62 19.2	55.1	Eltanin	90 43.4	N51 29.1
U 09	21 21.8	305 14.0 ..	46.0	38 41.3 ..	49.5	82 20.3 ..	57.9	77 21.7 ..	55.1	Enif	33 42.4	N 9 58.0
R 10	36 24.2	320 17.9	45.3	53 42.1	49.0	97 22.8	58.0	92 24.3	55.1	Fomalhaut	15 18.7	S29 30.8
S 11	51 26.7	335 21.8	44.7	68 43.0	48.4	112 25.4	58.0	107 26.8	55.2			
D 12	66 29.2	350 25.7	N24 44.0	83 43.9	S 9 47.8	127 28.0	S20 58.0	122 29.3	S19 55.2	Gacrux	171 55.3	S57 13.8
A 13	81 31.6	5 29.6	43.3	98 44.7	47.2	142 30.6	58.1	137 31.9	55.2	Gienah	175 47.2	S17 39.3
Y 14	96 34.1	20 33.6	42.7	113 45.6	46.7	157 33.1	58.1	152 34.4	55.2	Hadar	148 40.6	S60 28.3
15	111 36.5	35 37.5 ..	42.0	128 46.5 ..	46.1	172 35.7 ..	58.1	167 36.9 ..	55.2	Hamal	327 55.7	N23 33.2
16	126 39.0	50 41.4	41.3	143 47.4	45.5	187 38.3	58.1	182 39.5	55.3	Kaus Aust.	83 37.1	S34 22.3
17	141 41.5	65 45.4	40.7	158 48.2	44.9	202 40.9	58.2	197 42.0	55.3			
18	156 43.9	80 49.3	N24 40.0	173 49.1	S 9 44.4	217 43.5	S20 58.2	212 44.5	S19 55.3	Kochab	137 18.9	N74 04.5
19	171 46.4	95 53.2	39.3	188 50.0	43.8	232 46.0	58.2	227 47.1	55.3	Markab	13 33.6	N15 18.7
20	186 48.9	110 57.2	38.7	203 50.9	43.2	247 48.6	58.2	242 49.6	55.3	Menkar	314 10.4	N 4 10.0
21	201 51.3	126 01.1 ..	38.0	218 51.7 ..	42.6	262 51.2 ..	58.3	257 52.1 ..	55.4	Menkent	148 01.6	S36 28.2
22	216 53.8	141 05.0	37.3	233 52.6	42.1	277 53.8	58.3	272 54.7	55.4	Miaplacidus	221 39.1	S69 48.3
23	231 56.3	156 09.0	36.6	248 53.5	41.5	292 56.4	58.3	287 57.2	55.4			
29 00	246 58.7	171 12.9	N24 36.0	263 54.4	S 9 40.9	307 58.9	S20 58.4	302 59.8	S19 55.4	Mirfak	308 34.0	N49 55.7
01	262 01.2	186 16.9	35.3	278 55.2	40.3	323 01.5	58.4	318 02.3	55.4	Nunki	75 52.1	S26 16.2
02	277 03.7	201 20.8	34.6	293 56.1	39.7	338 04.1	58.4	333 04.8	55.5	Peacock	53 11.4	S56 39.9
03	292 06.1	216 24.8 ..	33.9	308 57.0 ..	39.2	353 06.7 ..	58.4	348 07.4 ..	55.5	Pollux	243 22.2	N27 58.6
04	307 08.6	231 28.7	33.2	323 57.9	38.6	8 09.3	58.5	3 09.9	55.5	Procyon	244 55.0	N 5 10.3
05	322 11.0	246 32.7	32.6	338 58.8	38.0	23 11.8	58.5	18 12.4	55.5			
06	337 13.5	261 36.6	N24 31.9	353 59.6	S 9 37.4	38 14.4	S20 58.5	33 15.0	S19 55.5	Rasalhague	96 01.7	N12 32.7
07	352 16.0	276 40.6	31.2	9 00.5	36.9	53 17.0	58.6	48 17.5	55.6	Regulus	207 38.5	N11 52.1
F 08	7 18.4	291 44.6	30.5	24 01.4	36.3	68 19.6	58.6	63 20.1	55.6	Rigel	281 07.8	S 8 10.9
R 09	22 20.9	306 48.5 ..	29.8	39 02.3 ..	35.7	83 22.2 ..	58.6	78 22.6 ..	55.6	Rigil Kent.	139 44.7	S60 55.1
I 10	37 23.4	321 52.5	29.1	54 03.1	35.1	98 24.8	58.6	93 25.1	55.6	Sabik	102 06.7	S15 44.9
D 11	52 25.8	336 56.5	28.4	69 04.0	34.5	113 27.4	58.7	108 27.7	55.6			
A 12	67 28.3	352 00.4	N24 27.8	84 04.9	S 9 34.0	128 29.9	S20 58.7	123 30.2	S19 55.7	Schedar	349 35.4	N56 38.6
Y 13	82 30.8	7 04.4	27.1	99 05.8	33.4	143 32.5	58.7	138 32.7	55.7	Shaula	96 15.0	S37 07.0
14	97 33.2	22 08.4	26.4	114 06.6	32.8	158 35.1	58.8	153 35.3	55.7	Sirius	258 29.8	S16 44.8
15	112 35.7	37 12.4 ..	25.7	129 07.5 ..	32.2	173 37.7 ..	58.8	168 37.8 ..	55.7	Spica	158 26.0	S11 16.0
16	127 38.1	52 16.4	25.0	144 08.4	31.7	188 40.3	58.8	183 40.4	55.7	Suhail	222 49.1	S43 31.1
17	142 40.6	67 20.3	24.3	159 09.3	31.1	203 42.9	58.9	198 42.9	55.8			
18	157 43.1	82 24.3	N24 23.6	174 10.2	S 9 30.5	218 45.5	S20 58.9	213 45.4	S19 55.8	Vega	80 35.4	N38 48.1
19	172 45.5	97 28.3	22.9	189 11.0	29.9	233 48.0	58.9	228 48.0	55.8	Zuben'ubi	136 59.8	S16 07.5
20	187 48.0	112 32.3	22.2	204 11.9	29.3	248 50.6	58.9	243 50.5	55.8			
21	202 50.5	127 36.3 ..	21.5	219 12.8 ..	28.8	263 53.2 ..	59.0	258 53.1 ..	55.8		SHA	Mer. Pass.
22	217 52.9	142 40.3	20.8	234 13.7	28.2	278 55.8	59.0	273 55.6	55.9	Venus	283 39.3	12 38
23	232 55.4	157 44.3	20.1	249 14.6	27.6	293 58.4	59.0	288 58.1	55.9	Mars	17 33.8	6 25
	h m									Jupiter	60 57.5	3 32
Mer. Pass.	7 34.8	v 3.9	d 0.7	v 0.9	d 0.6	v 2.6	d 0.0	v 2.5	d 0.0	Saturn	55 59.3	3 51

UT	SUN GHA	SUN Dec	MOON GHA	v	Dec	d	HP
d h	° ′	° ′	° ′	′	° ′	′	′
27 00	180 42.4	N21 20.2	126 06.6	7.7	N23 13.9	3.8	57.2
01	195 42.3	20.6	140 33.3	7.7	23 10.1	3.9	57.2
02	210 42.2	21.0	155 00.0	7.7	23 06.2	4.0	57.2
03	225 42.2 . .	21.4	169 26.7	7.8	23 02.2	4.2	57.3
04	240 42.1	21.8	183 53.5	7.7	22 58.0	4.3	57.3
05	255 42.0	22.2	198 20.2	7.8	22 53.7	4.5	57.3
W 06	270 41.9	N21 22.7	212 47.0	7.7	N22 49.2	4.6	57.3
E 07	285 41.9	23.1	227 13.7	7.8	22 44.6	4.7	57.4
D 08	300 41.8	23.5	241 40.5	7.8	22 39.9	4.9	57.4
N 09	315 41.7 . .	23.9	256 07.3	7.8	22 35.0	5.0	57.4
E 10	330 41.6	24.3	270 34.1	7.9	22 30.0	5.1	57.4
S 11	345 41.6	24.7	285 01.0	7.8	22 24.9	5.2	57.5
D 12	0 41.5	N21 25.1	299 27.8	7.9	N22 19.7	5.4	57.5
A 13	15 41.4	25.5	313 54.7	7.9	22 14.3	5.6	57.5
Y 14	30 41.3	25.9	328 21.6	7.9	22 08.7	5.6	57.5
15	45 41.2 . .	26.3	342 48.5	7.9	22 03.1	5.8	57.5
16	60 41.2	26.7	357 15.4	8.0	21 57.3	5.9	57.6
17	75 41.1	27.1	11 42.4	8.0	21 51.4	6.1	57.6
18	90 41.0	N21 27.5	26 09.4	8.0	N21 45.3	6.2	57.6
19	105 40.9	27.9	40 36.4	8.0	21 39.1	6.3	57.6
20	120 40.9	28.3	55 03.4	8.1	21 32.8	6.4	57.7
21	135 40.8 . .	28.7	69 30.5	8.1	21 26.4	6.6	57.7
22	150 40.7	29.1	83 57.6	8.1	21 19.8	6.7	57.7
23	165 40.6	29.5	98 24.7	8.1	21 13.1	6.8	57.7
28 00	180 40.5	N21 29.9	112 51.8	8.2	N21 06.3	7.0	57.7
01	195 40.5	30.3	127 19.0	8.2	20 59.3	7.1	57.8
02	210 40.4	30.7	141 46.2	8.2	20 52.2	7.2	57.8
03	225 40.3 . .	31.1	156 13.4	8.3	20 45.0	7.3	57.8
04	240 40.2	31.5	170 40.7	8.3	20 37.7	7.5	57.8
05	255 40.1	31.9	185 08.0	8.3	20 30.2	7.5	57.9
T 06	270 40.1	N21 32.3	199 35.3	8.3	N20 22.7	7.7	57.9
H 07	285 40.0	32.7	214 02.6	8.4	20 15.0	7.9	57.9
U 08	300 39.9	33.1	228 30.0	8.5	20 07.1	7.9	57.9
R 09	315 39.8 . .	33.5	242 57.5	8.4	19 59.2	8.1	58.0
S 10	330 39.7	33.9	257 24.9	8.5	19 51.1	8.2	58.0
D 11	345 39.7	34.3	271 52.4	8.5	19 42.9	8.3	58.0
A 12	0 39.6	N21 34.7	286 19.9	8.6	N19 34.6	8.4	58.0
Y 13	15 39.5	35.1	300 47.5	8.6	19 26.2	8.5	58.0
14	30 39.4	35.5	315 15.1	8.6	19 17.7	8.7	58.1
15	45 39.3 . .	35.8	329 42.7	8.7	19 09.0	8.8	58.1
16	60 39.3	36.2	344 10.4	8.7	19 00.2	8.8	58.1
17	75 39.2	36.6	358 38.1	8.7	18 51.4	9.0	58.1
18	90 39.1	N21 37.0	13 05.8	8.8	N18 42.4	9.2	58.2
19	105 39.0	37.4	27 33.6	8.8	18 33.2	9.2	58.2
20	120 38.9	37.8	42 01.4	8.8	18 24.0	9.3	58.2
21	135 38.8 . .	38.2	56 29.2	8.9	18 14.7	9.5	58.2
22	150 38.8	38.6	70 57.1	8.9	18 05.2	9.5	58.2
23	165 38.7	38.9	85 25.0	9.0	17 55.7	9.7	58.3
29 00	180 38.6	N21 39.3	99 53.0	9.0	N17 46.0	9.8	58.3
01	195 38.5	39.7	114 21.0	9.0	17 36.2	9.8	58.3
02	210 38.4	40.1	128 49.0	9.1	17 26.4	10.0	58.3
03	225 38.3 . .	40.5	143 17.1	9.1	17 16.4	10.1	58.4
04	240 38.3	40.8	157 45.2	9.1	17 06.3	10.2	58.4
05	255 38.2	41.2	172 13.3	9.2	16 56.1	10.3	58.4
F 06	270 38.1	N21 41.6	186 41.5	9.2	N16 45.8	10.4	58.4
R 07	285 38.0	42.0	201 09.7	9.2	16 35.4	10.5	58.5
I 08	300 37.9	42.4	215 37.9	9.3	16 24.9	10.6	58.5
D 09	315 37.8 . .	42.7	230 06.2	9.4	16 14.3	10.7	58.5
A 10	330 37.8	43.1	244 34.6	9.3	16 03.6	10.8	58.5
Y 11	345 37.7	43.5	259 02.9	9.4	15 52.8	10.9	58.5
12	0 37.6	N21 43.9	273 31.3	9.4	N15 41.9	11.0	58.6
13	15 37.5	44.2	287 59.7	9.5	15 30.9	11.1	58.6
14	30 37.4	44.6	302 28.2	9.5	15 19.8	11.2	58.6
15	45 37.3 . .	45.0	316 56.7	9.5	15 08.6	11.2	58.6
16	60 37.2	45.4	331 25.2	9.6	14 57.4	11.4	58.7
17	75 37.2	45.7	345 53.8	9.6	14 46.0	11.4	58.7
18	90 37.1	N21 46.1	0 22.4	9.6	N14 34.6	11.6	58.7
19	105 37.0	46.5	14 51.0	9.7	14 23.0	11.6	58.7
20	120 36.9	46.8	29 19.7	9.7	14 11.4	11.7	58.7
21	135 36.8 . .	47.2	43 48.4	9.7	13 59.7	11.9	58.8
22	150 36.7	47.6	58 17.1	9.8	13 47.8	11.8	58.8
23	165 36.6	48.0	72 45.9	9.8	N13 36.0	12.0	58.8
	SD 15.8	d 0.4	SD 15.7		15.8		16.0

Twilight / Moonrise

Lat.	Naut.	Civil	Sunrise	Moonrise 27	28	29	30
°	h m	h m	h m	h m	h m	h m	h m
N 72	☐	☐	☐	☐	☐	07 16	10 02
N 70	☐	☐	☐	☐	08 05	10 22	
68	☐	☐	☐	06 20	08 35	10 38	
66	////	////	01 27	05 05	07 03	08 58	10 50
64	////	////	02 07	05 52	07 31	09 16	11 00
62	////	00 43	02 34	06 23	07 53	09 30	11 09
60	////	01 37	02 55	06 46	08 11	09 42	11 16
N 58	////	02 08	03 12	07 04	08 25	09 53	11 23
56	00 39	02 30	03 26	07 20	08 38	10 02	11 29
54	01 28	02 48	03 38	07 33	08 49	10 10	11 34
52	01 57	03 04	03 49	07 44	08 58	10 17	11 39
50	02 18	03 17	03 59	07 55	09 07	10 24	11 43
45	02 56	03 43	04 19	08 16	09 25	10 37	11 52
N 40	03 23	04 03	04 35	08 33	09 40	10 49	11 59
35	03 44	04 20	04 49	08 48	09 52	10 59	12 06
30	04 01	04 34	05 00	09 01	10 03	11 07	12 11
20	04 28	04 56	05 20	09 22	10 22	11 22	12 21
N 10	04 48	05 15	05 38	09 41	10 38	11 34	12 30
0	05 06	05 32	05 54	09 58	10 53	11 46	12 38
S 10	05 21	05 47	06 10	10 16	11 08	11 58	12 46
20	05 36	06 03	06 27	10 34	11 24	12 10	12 54
30	05 50	06 20	06 46	10 56	11 42	12 25	13 04
35	05 58	06 29	06 57	11 08	11 53	12 33	13 09
40	06 06	06 40	07 10	11 22	12 05	12 42	13 15
45	06 15	06 52	07 25	11 39	12 19	12 53	13 23
S 50	06 26	07 06	07 43	12 00	12 37	13 06	13 31
52	06 30	07 13	07 52	12 10	12 45	13 13	13 35
54	06 35	07 20	08 02	12 22	12 54	13 19	13 40
56	06 40	07 28	08 13	12 34	13 04	13 27	13 45
58	06 46	07 37	08 26	12 49	13 16	13 35	13 50
S 60	06 52	07 47	08 40	13 06	13 29	13 45	13 56

Sunset / Twilight / Moonset

Lat.	Sunset	Civil	Naut.	Moonset 27	28	29	30
°	h m	h m	h m	h m	h m	h m	h m
N 72	☐	☐	☐	☐	☐	04 08	03 12
N 70	☐	☐	☐	☐	03 18	02 50	
68	☐	☐	☐	03 09	02 46	02 32	
66	22 31	////	////	02 29	02 26	02 22	02 18
64	21 50	////	////	01 41	01 56	02 03	02 07
62	21 22	23 19	////	01 10	01 34	01 48	01 57
60	21 01	22 21	////	00 47	01 16	01 35	01 48
N 58	20 44	21 49	////	00 28	01 01	01 24	01 40
56	20 29	21 26	23 23	00 13	00 48	01 14	01 34
54	20 17	21 07	22 24	24 37	00 37	01 05	01 28
52	20 06	20 52	22 00	24 27	00 27	00 57	01 22
50	19 57	20 39	21 38	24 18	00 18	00 50	01 17
45	19 36	20 12	20 59	23 58	24 35	00 35	01 07
N 40	19 20	19 52	20 32	23 43	24 23	00 23	00 58
35	19 06	19 35	20 11	23 30	24 12	00 12	00 50
30	18 55	19 21	19 54	23 18	24 02	00 02	00 43
20	18 34	18 59	19 27	22 58	23 46	24 31	00 31
N 10	18 17	18 40	19 07	22 41	23 32	24 21	00 21
0	18 01	18 23	18 49	22 24	23 18	24 11	00 11
S 10	17 45	18 08	18 34	22 08	23 05	24 01	00 01
20	17 28	17 52	18 19	21 50	22 50	23 50	24 50
30	17 09	17 35	18 04	21 30	22 33	23 38	24 42
35	16 58	17 25	17 56	21 18	22 24	23 31	24 38
40	16 45	17 15	17 48	21 04	22 12	23 22	24 33
45	16 30	17 03	17 39	20 48	21 59	23 13	24 28
S 50	16 11	16 48	17 29	20 28	21 43	23 01	24 21
52	16 02	16 42	17 24	20 18	21 35	22 56	24 18
54	15 52	16 34	17 19	20 07	21 26	22 49	24 14
56	15 41	16 27	17 14	19 55	21 17	22 43	24 10
58	15 29	16 18	17 08	19 41	21 06	22 35	24 06
S 60	15 14	16 08	17 02	19 24	20 53	22 26	24 01

SUN / MOON

Day	SUN Eqn. of Time 00h	12h	Mer. Pass.	MOON Mer. Pass. Upper	Lower	Age	Phase
d	m s	m s	h m	h m	h m	d	%
27	02 50	02 46	11 57	16 11	03 44	05	22
28	02 42	02 38	11 57	17 06	04 39	06	32
29	02 35	02 30	11 57	17 58	05 32	07	43

UT	ARIES GHA	VENUS −4·2 GHA	Dec	MARS +0·0 GHA	Dec	JUPITER −2·6 GHA	Dec	SATURN +0·4 GHA	Dec	STARS Name	SHA	Dec
30 00	247 57.9	172 48.3	N24 19.4	264 15.4	S 9 27.0	309 01.0	S20 59.1	304 00.7	S19 55.9	Acamar	315 15.1	S40 13.4
01	263 00.3	187 52.2	18.7	279 16.3	26.5	324 03.6	59.1	319 03.2	55.9	Achernar	335 23.6	S57 07.9
02	278 02.8	202 56.2	18.0	294 17.2	25.9	339 06.2	59.1	334 05.8	55.9	Acrux	173 03.7	S63 12.9
03	293 05.3	218 00.2	.. 17.3	309 18.1	.. 25.3	354 08.7	.. 59.2	349 08.3	.. 56.0	Adhara	255 09.1	S29 00.2
04	308 07.7	233 04.2	16.6	324 19.0	24.7	9 11.3	59.2	4 10.8	56.0	Aldebaran	290 44.2	N16 32.8
05	323 10.2	248 08.2	15.9	339 19.9	24.1	24 13.9	59.2	19 13.4	56.0			
S 06	338 12.6	263 12.3	N24 15.2	354 20.7	S 9 23.6	39 16.5	S20 59.2	34 15.9	S19 56.0	Alioth	166 16.1	N55 51.3
A 07	353 15.1	278 16.3	14.5	9 21.6	23.0	54 19.1	59.3	49 18.5	56.0	Alkaid	152 54.7	N49 13.0
T 08	8 17.6	293 20.3	13.8	24 22.5	22.4	69 21.7	59.3	64 21.0	56.1	Alnair	27 37.6	S46 51.6
U 09	23 20.0	308 24.3	.. 13.1	39 23.4	.. 21.8	84 24.3	.. 59.3	79 23.5	.. 56.1	Alnilam	275 41.8	S 1 11.5
R 10	38 22.5	323 28.3	12.4	54 24.3	21.3	99 26.9	59.4	94 26.1	56.1	Alphard	217 51.5	S 8 44.9
D 11	53 25.0	338 32.3	11.6	69 25.1	20.7	114 29.5	59.4	109 28.6	56.1			
A 12	68 27.4	353 36.3	N24 10.9	84 26.0	S 9 20.1	129 32.1	S20 59.4	124 31.2	S19 56.1	Alphecca	126 06.6	N26 38.9
Y 13	83 29.9	8 40.3	10.2	99 26.9	19.5	144 34.7	59.5	139 33.7	56.2	Alpheratz	357 38.7	N29 11.9
14	98 32.4	23 44.4	09.5	114 27.8	18.9	159 37.3	59.5	154 36.3	56.2	Altair	62 03.3	N 8 55.3
15	113 34.8	38 48.4	.. 08.8	129 28.7	.. 18.4	174 39.9	.. 59.5	169 38.8	.. 56.2	Ankaa	353 11.1	S42 11.7
16	128 37.3	53 52.4	08.1	144 29.6	17.8	189 42.4	59.5	184 41.3	56.2	Antares	112 20.0	S26 28.5
17	143 39.8	68 56.4	07.4	159 30.4	17.2	204 45.0	59.6	199 43.9	56.2			
18	158 42.2	84 00.4	N24 06.6	174 31.3	S 9 16.6	219 47.6	S20 59.6	214 46.4	S19 56.3	Arcturus	145 51.1	N19 04.7
19	173 44.7	99 04.5	05.9	189 32.2	16.1	234 50.2	59.6	229 49.0	56.3	Atria	107 17.0	S69 03.7
20	188 47.1	114 08.5	05.2	204 33.1	15.5	249 52.8	59.7	244 51.5	56.3	Avior	234 16.5	S59 34.7
21	203 49.6	129 12.5	.. 04.5	219 34.0	.. 14.9	264 55.4	.. 59.7	259 54.1	.. 56.3	Bellatrix	278 27.2	N 6 21.9
22	218 52.1	144 16.5	03.8	234 34.9	14.3	279 58.0	59.7	274 56.6	56.4	Betelgeuse	270 56.4	N 7 24.5
23	233 54.5	159 20.6	03.0	249 35.8	13.7	295 00.6	59.8	289 59.1	56.4			
31 00	248 57.0	174 24.6	N24 02.3	264 36.6	S 9 13.2	310 03.2	S20 59.8	305 01.7	S19 56.4	Canopus	263 54.5	S52 42.6
01	263 59.5	189 28.6	01.6	279 37.5	12.6	325 05.8	59.8	320 04.2	56.4	Capella	280 27.9	N46 01.0
02	279 01.9	204 32.7	00.9	294 38.4	12.0	340 08.4	59.9	335 06.8	56.4	Deneb	49 28.0	N45 20.9
03	294 04.4	219 36.7	24 00.1	309 39.3	.. 11.4	355 11.0	.. 59.9	350 09.3	.. 56.5	Denebola	182 28.7	N14 27.6
04	309 06.9	234 40.8	23 59.4	324 40.2	10.8	10 13.6	20 59.9	5 11.9	56.5	Diphda	348 51.2	S17 52.6
05	324 09.3	249 44.8	58.7	339 41.1	10.3	25 16.2	21 00.0	20 14.4	56.5			
S 06	339 11.8	264 48.8	N23 58.0	354 42.0	S 9 09.7	40 18.8	S21 00.0	35 17.0	S19 56.5	Dubhe	193 45.7	N61 38.8
U 07	354 14.2	279 52.9	57.2	9 42.8	09.1	55 21.4	00.0	50 19.5	56.5	Elnath	278 06.9	N28 37.3
N 08	9 16.7	294 56.9	56.5	24 43.7	08.5	70 24.0	00.0	65 22.0	56.6	Eltanin	90 43.4	N51 29.1
D 09	24 19.2	310 01.0	.. 55.8	39 44.6	.. 08.0	85 26.6	.. 00.1	80 24.6	.. 56.6	Enif	33 42.3	N 9 58.0
A 10	39 21.6	325 05.0	55.0	54 45.5	07.4	100 29.2	00.1	95 27.1	56.6	Fomalhaut	15 18.7	S29 30.8
Y 11	54 24.1	340 09.1	54.3	69 46.4	06.8	115 31.8	00.1	110 29.7	56.6			
12	69 26.6	355 13.1	N23 53.6	84 47.3	S 9 06.2	130 34.4	S21 00.2	125 32.2	S19 56.7	Gacrux	171 55.4	S57 13.8
13	84 29.0	10 17.2	52.8	99 48.2	05.6	145 37.0	00.2	140 34.8	56.7	Gienah	175 47.3	S17 39.3
14	99 31.5	25 21.2	52.1	114 49.1	05.1	160 39.6	00.2	155 37.3	56.7	Hadar	148 40.6	S60 28.3
15	114 34.0	40 25.3	.. 51.4	129 49.9	.. 04.5	175 42.2	.. 00.3	170 39.9	.. 56.7	Hamal	327 55.6	N23 33.3
16	129 36.4	55 29.3	50.6	144 50.8	03.9	190 44.8	00.3	185 42.4	56.7	Kaus Aust.	83 37.1	S34 22.3
17	144 38.9	70 33.4	49.9	159 51.7	03.3	205 47.4	00.3	200 45.0	56.8			
18	159 41.4	85 37.4	N23 49.2	174 52.6	S 9 02.7	220 50.0	S21 00.4	215 47.5	S19 56.8	Kochab	137 18.9	N74 04.6
19	174 43.8	100 41.5	48.4	189 53.5	02.2	235 52.6	00.4	230 50.1	56.8	Markab	13 33.6	N15 18.7
20	189 46.3	115 45.5	47.7	204 54.4	01.6	250 55.2	00.4	245 52.6	56.8	Menkar	314 10.3	N 4 10.0
21	204 48.7	130 49.6	.. 46.9	219 55.3	.. 01.0	265 57.8	.. 00.5	260 55.1	.. 56.9	Menkent	148 01.6	S36 28.2
22	219 51.2	145 53.6	46.2	234 56.2	9 00.4	281 00.4	00.5	275 57.7	56.9	Miaplacidus	221 39.2	S69 48.3
23	234 53.7	160 57.7	45.5	249 57.1	8 59.8	296 03.0	00.5	291 00.2	56.9			
1 00	249 56.1	176 01.8	N23 44.7	264 58.0	S 8 59.3	311 05.6	S21 00.6	306 02.8	S19 56.9	Mirfak	308 34.0	N49 55.7
01	264 58.6	191 05.8	44.0	279 58.8	58.7	326 08.2	00.6	321 05.3	56.9	Nunki	75 52.1	S26 16.2
02	280 01.1	206 09.9	43.2	294 59.7	58.1	341 10.8	00.6	336 07.9	57.0	Peacock	53 11.3	S56 39.9
03	295 03.5	221 14.0	.. 42.5	310 00.6	.. 57.5	356 13.4	.. 00.7	351 10.4	.. 57.0	Pollux	243 22.2	N27 58.6
04	310 06.0	236 18.0	41.7	325 01.5	57.0	11 16.0	00.7	6 13.0	57.0	Procyon	244 55.0	N 5 10.3
05	325 08.5	251 22.1	41.0	340 02.4	56.4	26 18.6	00.7	21 15.5	57.0			
M 06	340 10.9	266 26.1	N23 40.2	355 03.3	S 8 55.8	41 21.3	S21 00.8	36 18.1	S19 57.0	Rasalhague	96 01.7	N12 32.8
O 07	355 13.4	281 30.2	39.5	10 04.2	55.2	56 23.9	00.8	51 20.6	57.1	Regulus	207 38.5	N11 52.1
N 08	10 15.9	296 34.3	38.8	25 05.1	54.6	71 26.5	00.8	66 23.2	57.1	Rigel	281 07.8	S 8 10.8
D 09	25 18.3	311 38.3	.. 38.0	40 06.0	.. 54.1	86 29.1	.. 00.9	81 25.7	.. 57.1	Rigil Kent.	139 44.7	S60 55.2
A 10	40 20.8	326 42.4	37.3	55 06.9	53.5	101 31.7	00.9	96 28.3	57.1	Sabik	102 06.7	S15 44.9
Y 11	55 23.2	341 46.5	36.5	70 07.8	52.9	116 34.3	00.9	111 30.8	57.2			
12	70 25.7	356 50.6	N23 35.8	85 08.7	S 8 52.3	131 36.9	S21 01.0	126 33.4	S19 57.2	Schedar	349 35.4	N56 38.6
13	85 28.2	11 54.6	35.0	100 09.5	51.7	146 39.5	01.0	141 35.9	57.2	Shaula	96 15.0	S37 07.0
14	100 30.6	26 58.7	34.2	115 10.4	51.2	161 42.1	01.0	156 38.5	57.2	Sirius	258 29.8	S16 44.8
15	115 33.1	42 02.8	.. 33.5	130 11.3	.. 50.6	176 44.7	.. 01.1	171 41.0	.. 57.3	Spica	158 26.0	S11 16.0
16	130 35.6	57 06.8	32.7	145 12.2	50.0	191 47.3	01.1	186 43.6	57.3	Suhail	222 49.2	S43 31.1
17	145 38.0	72 10.9	32.0	160 13.1	49.4	206 49.9	01.1	201 46.1	57.3			
18	160 40.5	87 15.0	N23 31.2	175 14.0	S 8 48.8	221 52.6	S21 01.2	216 48.7	S19 57.3	Vega	80 35.3	N38 48.1
19	175 43.0	102 19.1	30.5	190 14.9	48.3	236 55.2	01.2	231 51.2	57.3	Zuben'ubi	136 59.8	S16 07.5
20	190 45.4	117 23.1	29.7	205 15.8	47.7	251 57.8	01.2	246 53.8	57.4		SHA	Mer. Pass.
21	205 47.9	132 27.2	.. 29.0	220 16.7	.. 47.1	267 00.4	.. 01.3	261 56.3	.. 57.4			
22	220 50.3	147 31.3	28.2	235 17.6	46.5	282 03.0	01.3	276 58.9	57.4	Venus	285 27.6	12 19
23	235 52.8	162 35.4	27.4	250 18.5	45.9	297 05.6	01.3	292 01.4	57.4	Mars	15 39.6	6 21
Mer. Pass.	7 23.0	v 4.0	d 0.7	v 0.9	d 0.6	v 2.6	d 0.0	v 2.5	d 0.0	Jupiter	61 06.2	3 19
										Saturn	56 04.7	3 39

UT	SUN		MOON				Lat.	Twilight		Sunrise	Moonrise			
								Naut.	Civil		30	31	1	2
	GHA	Dec	GHA	v	Dec	d	HP							
d h	° ′	° ′	° ′	′	° ′	′	′	°	h m	h m	h m	h m	h m	h m	h m
30 00	180 36.5	N21 48.3	87 14.7	9.8	N13 24.0	12.1	58.8	N 72	▢	▢	▢	10 02	12 20	14 33	16 50
01	195 36.5	48.7	101 43.5	9.9	13 11.9	12.1	58.9	N 70	▢	▢	▢	10 22	12 28	14 32	16 38
02	210 36.4	49.1	116 12.4	9.9	12 59.8	12.2	58.9	68	▢	▢	▢	10 38	12 35	14 30	16 29
03	225 36.3 . .	49.4	130 41.3	9.9	12 47.6	12.3	58.9	66	////	////	01 15	10 50	12 40	14 29	16 21
04	240 36.2	49.8	145 10.2	10.0	12 35.3	12.4	58.9	64	////	////	01 59	11 00	12 44	14 28	16 14
05	255 36.1	50.1	159 39.2	10.0	12 22.9	12.5	58.9	62	////	00 12	02 28	11 09	12 48	14 27	16 09
06	270 36.0	N21 50.5	174 08.2	10.0	N12 10.4	12.5	59.0	60	////	01 28	02 50	11 16	12 51	14 27	16 04
07	285 35.9	50.9	188 37.2	10.0	11 57.9	12.6	59.0	N 58	////	02 01	03 08	11 23	12 54	14 26	16 00
S 08	300 35.8	51.2	203 06.2	10.1	11 45.3	12.7	59.0	56	00 11	02 25	03 23	11 29	12 57	14 26	15 56
A 09	315 35.7 . .	51.6	217 35.3	10.0	11 32.6	12.8	59.0	54	01 20	02 44	03 35	11 34	12 59	14 25	15 52
T 10	330 35.7	52.0	232 04.3	10.2	11 19.8	12.8	59.0	52	01 51	03 00	03 46	11 39	13 01	14 25	15 49
U 11	345 35.6	52.3	246 33.5	10.1	11 07.0	12.9	59.1	50	02 14	03 14	03 56	11 43	13 03	14 24	15 47
R 12	0 35.5	N21 52.7	261 02.6	10.2	N10 54.1	13.0	59.1	45	02 53	03 41	04 17	11 52	13 07	14 23	15 41
D 13	15 35.4	53.0	275 31.8	10.1	10 41.1	13.0	59.1	N 40	03 21	04 01	04 34	11 59	13 11	14 23	15 36
A 14	30 35.3	53.4	290 00.9	10.3	10 28.1	13.1	59.1	35	03 43	04 18	04 47	12 06	13 14	14 22	15 31
Y 15	45 35.2 . .	53.8	304 30.2	10.2	10 15.0	13.2	59.1	30	04 00	04 33	05 00	12 11	13 16	14 21	15 28
16	60 35.1	54.1	318 59.4	10.2	10 01.8	13.2	59.2	20	04 27	04 56	05 20	12 21	13 21	14 21	15 21
17	75 35.0	54.5	333 28.6	10.3	9 48.6	13.3	59.2	N 10	04 48	05 15	05 38	12 30	13 25	14 20	15 16
18	90 34.9	N21 54.8	347 57.9	10.3	N 9 35.3	13.4	59.2	0	05 06	05 32	05 54	12 38	13 28	14 19	15 10
19	105 34.8	55.2	2 27.2	10.3	9 21.9	13.4	59.2	S 10	05 22	05 48	06 10	12 46	13 32	14 18	15 05
20	120 34.8	55.5	16 56.5	10.4	9 08.5	13.5	59.3	20	05 37	06 04	06 28	12 54	13 36	14 18	15 00
21	135 34.7 . .	55.9	31 25.9	10.3	8 55.0	13.5	59.3	30	05 52	06 21	06 47	13 04	13 41	14 17	14 54
22	150 34.6	56.2	45 55.2	10.4	8 41.5	13.6	59.3	35	06 00	06 31	06 59	13 09	13 43	14 16	14 50
23	165 34.5	56.6	60 24.6	10.4	8 27.9	13.6	59.3	40	06 18	06 54	07 28	13 23	13 50	14 15	14 42
31 00	180 34.4	N21 56.9	74 54.0	10.4	N 8 14.3	13.7	59.3	S 50	06 28	07 09	07 47	13 31	13 54	14 15	14 37
01	195 34.3	57.3	89 23.4	10.4	8 00.6	13.8	59.3	52	06 33	07 16	07 56	13 35	13 55	14 14	14 34
02	210 34.2	57.6	103 52.8	10.4	7 46.8	13.8	59.4	54	06 38	07 23	08 06	13 40	13 57	14 14	14 31
03	225 34.1 . .	58.0	118 22.2	10.5	7 33.0	13.9	59.4	56	06 43	07 31	08 17	13 45	14 00	14 14	14 28
04	240 34.0	58.3	132 51.7	10.4	7 19.1	13.9	59.4	58	06 49	07 41	08 30	13 50	14 02	14 13	14 25
05	255 33.9	58.7	147 21.1	10.5	7 05.2	13.9	59.4	S 60	06 56	07 51	08 46	13 56	14 05	14 13	14 22

	SUN		MOON				Lat.	Sunset	Twilight		Moonset			
									Civil	Naut.	30	31	1	2
d h	° ′	° ′	° ′	′	° ′	′	′	°	h m	h m	h m	h m	h m	h m	h m
06	270 33.8	N21 59.0	161 50.6	10.5	N 6 51.3	14.0	59.4	N 72	▢	▢	▢	03 12	02 41	02 16	01 53
07	285 33.7	59.4	176 20.1	10.4	6 37.3	14.1	59.5	N 70	▢	▢	▢	02 50	02 30	02 14	01 58
08	300 33.6	21 59.7	190 49.5	10.5	6 23.2	14.1	59.5	68	▢	▢	▢	02 32	02 22	02 12	02 02
S 09	315 33.6	22 00.1	205 19.0	10.5	6 09.1	14.1	59.5	66	22 45	////	////	02 18	02 14	02 10	02 06
U 10	330 33.5	00.4	219 48.5	10.6	5 55.0	14.2	59.5	64	21 58	////	////	02 07	02 08	02 09	02 09
N 11	345 33.4	00.8	234 18.1	10.5	5 40.8	14.2	59.5	62	21 29	////	////	01 57	02 03	02 08	02 12
D 12	0 33.3	N22 01.1	248 47.6	10.5	N 5 26.6	14.3	59.6	60	21 07	22 30	////	01 48	01 58	02 06	02 15
A 13	15 33.2	01.5	263 17.1	10.5	5 12.3	14.3	59.6	N 58	20 49	21 56	////	01 40	01 54	02 05	02 17
Y 14	30 33.1	01.8	277 46.6	10.5	4 58.0	14.3	59.6	56	20 34	21 31	////	01 34	01 50	02 04	02 19
15	45 33.0 . .	02.1	292 16.1	10.6	4 43.7	14.3	59.6	54	20 21	21 12	22 38	01 28	01 47	02 04	02 22
16	60 32.9	02.5	306 45.7	10.5	4 29.4	14.4	59.6	52	20 10	20 56	22 06	01 22	01 44	02 03	02 22
17	75 32.8	02.8	321 15.2	10.5	4 15.0	14.5	59.6	50	20 00	20 43	21 43	01 17	01 41	02 02	02 23
18	90 32.7	N22 03.2	335 44.7	10.6	N 4 00.5	14.4	59.7	45	19 39	20 15	21 03	01 07	01 35	02 01	02 27
19	105 32.6	03.5	350 14.3	10.5	3 46.1	14.5	59.7	N 40	19 22	19 54	20 35	00 58	01 29	01 59	02 29
20	120 32.5	03.8	4 43.8	10.5	3 31.6	14.5	59.7	35	19 08	19 38	20 13	00 50	01 25	01 58	02 32
21	135 32.4 . .	04.2	19 13.3	10.6	3 17.1	14.6	59.7	30	18 56	19 23	19 56	00 43	01 21	01 57	02 34
22	150 32.3	04.5	33 42.9	10.5	3 02.5	14.6	59.7	20	18 36	19 00	19 29	00 31	01 14	01 55	02 37
23	165 32.2	04.8	48 12.4	10.5	2 47.9	14.6	59.7	N 10	18 18	18 41	19 07	00 21	01 08	01 54	02 40
1 00	180 32.1	N22 05.2	62 41.9	10.5	N 2 33.3	14.6	59.8	0	18 01	18 24	18 50	00 11	01 02	01 52	02 43
01	195 32.0	05.5	77 11.4	10.5	2 18.7	14.6	59.8	S 10	17 45	18 08	18 34	00 01	00 56	01 51	02 46
02	210 31.9	05.8	91 40.9	10.5	2 04.1	14.7	59.8	20	17 28	17 52	18 19	24 50	00 50	01 49	02 49
03	225 31.9 . .	06.2	106 10.4	10.5	1 49.4	14.6	59.8	30	17 08	17 34	18 04	24 42	00 42	01 47	02 53
04	240 31.8	06.5	120 39.9	10.5	1 34.8	14.7	59.8	35	16 56	17 24	17 56	24 38	00 38	01 46	02 55
05	255 31.7	06.8	135 09.4	10.4	1 20.1	14.7	59.8	40	16 43	17 13	17 47	24 33	00 33	01 45	02 57
06	270 31.6	N22 07.2	149 38.8	10.5	N 1 05.4	14.8	59.8	45	16 28	17 01	17 38	24 28	00 28	01 43	03 00
07	285 31.5	07.5	164 08.3	10.4	0 50.6	14.7	59.9	S 50	16 09	16 46	17 27	24 21	00 21	01 41	03 03
08	300 31.4	07.8	178 37.7	10.5	0 35.9	14.7	59.9	52	16 00	16 39	17 22	24 18	00 18	01 41	03 05
M 09	315 31.3 . .	08.2	193 07.2	10.4	0 21.2	14.8	59.9	54	15 50	16 32	17 17	24 14	00 14	01 40	03 06
O 10	330 31.2	08.5	207 36.6	10.4	N 0 06.4	14.8	59.9	56	15 38	16 24	17 12	24 10	00 10	01 39	03 08
N 11	345 31.1	08.8	222 06.0	10.3	S 0 08.4	14.7	59.9	58	15 25	16 16	17 06	24 06	00 06	01 37	03 10
D 12	0 31.0	N22 09.2	236 35.3	10.4	S 0 23.1	14.8	59.9	S 60	15 10	16 04	16 59	24 01	00 01	01 36	03 12
A 13	15 30.9	09.5	251 04.7	10.3	0 37.9	14.8	59.9								
Y 14	30 30.8	09.8	265 34.0	10.4	0 52.7	14.8	59.9			SUN			MOON		
15	45 30.7 . .	10.1	280 03.4	10.3	1 07.5	14.7	60.0	Day	Eqn. of Time		Mer.	Mer. Pass.		Age	Phase
16	60 30.6	10.5	294 32.7	10.2	1 22.2	14.8	60.0		00ʰ	12ʰ	Pass.	Upper	Lower		
17	75 30.5	10.8	309 01.9	10.3	1 37.0	14.8	60.0	d	m s	m s	h m	h m	h m	d %	
18	90 30.4	N22 11.1	323 31.2	10.2	S 1 51.8	14.8	60.0	30	02 26	02 22	11 58	18 50	06 24	08 54	
19	105 30.3	11.4	338 00.4	10.2	2 06.6	14.7	60.0	31	02 18	02 13	11 58	19 40	07 15	09 65	
20	120 30.2	11.7	352 29.6	10.2	2 21.3	14.8	60.0	1	02 09	02 04	11 58	20 31	08 06	10 76	
21	135 30.1 . .	12.1	6 58.8	10.2	2 36.1	14.7	60.0								
22	150 30.0	12.4	21 28.0	10.1	2 50.8	14.8	60.0								
23	165 29.9	12.7	35 57.1	10.1	S 3 05.6	14.7	60.0								
	SD 15.8	d 0.3	SD 16.1		16.2		16.3								

UT	ARIES GHA	VENUS −4.2 GHA	Dec	MARS −0.1 GHA	Dec	JUPITER −2.6 GHA	Dec	SATURN +0.4 GHA	Dec	STARS Name	SHA	Dec
2 00	250 55.3	177 39.4	N23 26.7	265 19.4	S 8 45.4	312 08.2	S21 01.4	307 04.0	S19 57.5	Acamar	315 15.1	S40 13.4
01	265 57.7	192 43.5	25.9	280 20.3	44.8	327 10.8	01.4	322 06.5	57.5	Achernar	335 23.5	S57 07.9
02	281 00.2	207 47.6	25.2	295 21.2	44.2	342 13.4	01.4	337 09.1	57.5	Acrux	173 03.7	S63 12.9
03	296 02.7	222 51.7 ..	24.4	310 22.1 ..	43.6	357 16.1 ..	01.5	352 11.6 ..	57.5	Adhara	255 09.1	S29 00.2
04	311 05.1	237 55.8	23.6	325 23.0	43.0	12 18.7	01.5	7 14.2	57.5	Aldebaran	290 44.2	N16 32.8
05	326 07.6	252 59.8	22.9	340 23.9	42.5	27 21.3	01.5	22 16.7	57.6			
06	341 10.1	268 03.9	N23 22.1	355 24.8	S 8 41.9	42 23.9	S21 01.6	37 19.3	S19 57.6	Alioth	166 16.1	N55 51.3
07	356 12.5	283 08.0	21.3	10 25.7	41.3	57 26.5	01.6	52 21.8	57.6	Alkaid	152 54.7	N49 13.0
08	11 15.0	298 12.1	20.6	25 26.5	40.7	72 29.1	01.6	67 24.4	57.6	Alnair	27 37.6	S46 51.6
09	26 17.5	313 16.2 ..	19.8	40 27.4 ..	40.1	87 31.7 ..	01.7	82 27.0 ..	57.7	Alnilam	275 41.8	S 1 11.5
10	41 19.9	328 20.2	19.0	55 28.3	39.6	102 34.4	01.7	97 29.5	57.7	Alphard	217 51.5	S 8 44.9
11	56 22.4	343 24.3	18.3	70 29.2	39.0	117 37.0	01.7	112 32.1	57.7			
12	71 24.8	358 28.4	N23 17.5	85 30.1	S 8 38.4	132 39.6	S21 01.8	127 34.6	S19 57.7	Alphecca	126 06.6	N26 38.9
13	86 27.3	13 32.5	16.7	100 31.0	37.8	147 42.2	01.8	142 37.2	57.8	Alpheratz	357 38.7	N29 11.9
14	101 29.8	28 36.6	16.0	115 31.9	37.2	162 44.8	01.8	157 39.7	57.8	Altair	62 03.3	N 8 55.3
15	116 32.2	43 40.7 ..	15.2	130 32.8 ..	36.7	177 47.4 ..	01.9	172 42.3 ..	57.8	Ankaa	353 11.1	S42 11.6
16	131 34.7	58 44.7	14.4	145 33.7	36.1	192 50.1	01.9	187 44.8	57.8	Antares	112 20.0	S26 28.5
17	146 37.2	73 48.8	13.7	160 34.6	35.5	207 52.7	01.9	202 47.4	57.8			
18	161 39.6	88 52.9	N23 12.9	175 35.5	S 8 34.9	222 55.3	S21 02.0	217 49.9	S19 57.9	Arcturus	145 51.1	N19 04.7
19	176 42.1	103 57.0	12.1	190 36.4	34.3	237 57.9	02.0	232 52.5	57.9	Atria	107 17.0	S69 03.7
20	191 44.6	119 01.1	11.3	205 37.3	33.8	253 00.5	02.1	247 55.0	57.9	Avior	234 16.5	S59 34.7
21	206 47.0	134 05.1 ..	10.6	220 38.2 ..	33.2	268 03.1 ..	02.1	262 57.6 ..	57.9	Bellatrix	278 27.2	N 6 21.9
22	221 49.5	149 09.2	09.8	235 39.1	32.6	283 05.8	02.1	278 00.2	58.0	Betelgeuse	270 56.4	N 7 24.5
23	236 51.9	164 13.3	09.0	250 40.0	32.0	298 08.4	02.2	293 02.7	58.0			
3 00	251 54.4	179 17.4	N23 08.2	265 40.9	S 8 31.5	313 11.0	S21 02.2	308 05.3	S19 58.0	Canopus	263 54.5	S52 42.6
01	266 56.9	194 21.5	07.5	280 41.8	30.9	328 13.6	02.2	323 07.8	58.0	Capella	280 27.9	N46 01.0
02	281 59.3	209 25.5	06.7	295 42.7	30.3	343 16.2	02.3	338 10.4	58.1	Deneb	49 28.0	N45 20.9
03	297 01.8	224 29.6 ..	05.9	310 43.6 ..	29.7	358 18.9 ..	02.3	353 12.9 ..	58.1	Denebola	182 28.7	N14 27.6
04	312 04.3	239 33.7	05.1	325 44.5	29.1	13 21.5	02.3	8 15.5	58.1	Diphda	348 51.2	S17 52.6
05	327 06.7	254 37.8	04.3	340 45.4	28.5	28 24.1	02.4	23 18.0	58.1			
06	342 09.2	269 41.8	N23 03.5	355 46.3	S 8 28.0	43 26.7	S21 02.4	38 20.6	S19 58.2	Dubhe	193 45.8	N61 38.8
07	357 11.7	284 45.9	02.8	10 47.2	27.4	58 29.4	02.4	53 23.2	58.2	Elnath	278 06.9	N28 37.3
08	12 14.1	299 50.0	02.0	25 48.1	26.8	73 32.0	02.5	68 25.7	58.2	Eltanin	90 43.4	N51 29.1
09	27 16.6	314 54.1 ..	01.2	40 49.0 ..	26.2	88 34.6 ..	02.5	83 28.3 ..	58.2	Enif	33 42.3	N 9 58.0
10	42 19.1	329 58.1	23 00.4	55 49.9	25.6	103 37.2	02.5	98 30.8	58.3	Fomalhaut	15 18.7	S29 30.8
11	57 21.5	345 02.2	22 59.6	70 50.8	25.1	118 39.8	02.6	113 33.4	58.3			
12	72 24.0	0 06.2	N22 58.8	85 51.7	S 8 24.5	133 42.5	S21 02.6	128 35.9	S19 58.3	Gacrux	171 55.4	S57 13.8
13	87 26.4	15 10.3	58.0	100 52.6	23.9	148 45.1	02.7	143 38.5	58.3	Gienah	175 47.3	S17 39.3
14	102 28.9	30 14.3	57.2	115 53.5	23.3	163 47.7	02.7	158 41.1	58.3	Hadar	148 40.6	S60 28.3
15	117 31.4	45 18.4 ..	56.5	130 54.5 ..	22.7	178 50.3 ..	02.7	173 43.6 ..	58.4	Hamal	327 55.6	N23 33.3
16	132 33.8	60 22.4	55.7	145 55.4	22.2	193 53.0	02.8	188 46.2	58.4	Kaus Aust.	83 37.1	S34 22.3
17	147 36.3	75 26.4	54.9	160 56.3	21.6	208 55.6	02.8	203 48.7	58.4			
18	162 38.8	90 30.5	N22 54.1	175 57.2	S 8 21.0	223 58.2	S21 02.8	218 51.3	S19 58.4	Kochab	137 19.0	N74 04.6
19	177 41.2	105 34.5	53.3	190 58.1	20.4	239 00.8	02.9	233 53.8	58.5	Markab	13 33.6	N15 18.7
20	192 43.7	120 38.5	52.6	205 59.0	19.8	254 03.5	02.9	248 56.4	58.5	Menkar	314 10.3	N 4 10.0
21	207 46.2	135 42.5 ..	51.8	220 59.9 ..	19.3	269 06.1 ..	02.9	263 59.0 ..	58.5	Menkent	148 01.6	S36 28.2
22	222 48.6	150 46.6	51.1	236 00.8	18.7	284 08.7	03.0	279 01.5	58.5	Miaplacidus	221 39.2	S69 48.3
23	237 51.1	165 50.6	50.3	251 01.7	18.1	299 11.3	03.0	294 04.1	58.6			
4 00	252 53.6	180 54.7	N22 49.6	266 02.6	S 8 17.5	314 14.0	S21 03.1	309 06.6	S19 58.6	Mirfak	308 34.0	N49 55.7
01	267 56.0	195 58.7	48.8	281 03.5	16.9	329 16.6	03.1	324 09.2	58.6	Nunki	75 52.1	S26 16.2
02	282 58.5	211 02.8	48.1	296 04.4	16.4	344 19.2	03.1	339 11.8	58.6	Peacock	53 11.3	S56 39.9
03	298 00.9	226 06.9 ..	47.3	311 05.3 ..	15.8	359 21.9 ..	03.2	354 14.3 ..	58.7	Pollux	243 22.2	N27 58.6
04	313 03.4	241 10.9	46.5	326 06.2	15.2	14 24.5	03.2	9 16.9	58.7	Procyon	244 55.0	N 5 10.3
05	328 05.9	256 15.0	45.8	341 07.1	14.6	29 27.1	03.2	24 19.4	58.7			
06	343 08.3	271 19.1	N22 45.0	356 08.0	S 8 14.0	44 29.7	S21 03.3	39 22.0	S19 58.7	Rasalhague	96 01.7	N12 32.8
07	358 10.8	286 23.1	44.2	11 08.9	13.5	59 32.4	03.3	54 24.6	58.8	Regulus	207 38.5	N11 52.1
08	13 13.3	301 27.2	43.5	26 09.8	12.9	74 35.0	03.4	69 27.1	58.8	Rigel	281 07.8	S 8 10.8
09	28 15.7	316 31.3 ..	42.7	41 10.7 ..	12.3	89 37.6 ..	03.4	84 29.7 ..	58.8	Rigil Kent.	139 44.7	S60 55.2
10	43 18.2	331 35.4	41.9	56 11.6	11.7	104 40.3	03.4	99 32.2	58.8	Sabik	102 06.7	S15 44.9
11	58 20.7	346 39.4	41.2	71 12.6	11.1	119 42.9	03.5	114 34.8	58.9			
12	73 23.1	1 43.5	N22 40.4	86 13.5	S 8 10.6	134 45.5	S21 03.5	129 37.4	S19 58.9	Schedar	349 35.4	N56 38.5
13	88 25.6	16 47.6	39.6	101 14.4	10.0	149 48.1	03.5	144 39.9	58.9	Shaula	96 15.0	S37 07.0
14	103 28.1	31 51.6	38.8	116 15.3	09.4	164 50.8	03.6	159 42.5	58.9	Sirius	258 29.8	S16 44.8
15	118 30.5	46 55.7 ..	38.1	131 16.2 ..	08.8	179 53.4 ..	03.6	174 45.0 ..	59.0	Spica	158 26.0	S11 16.0
16	133 33.0	61 59.8	37.3	146 17.1	08.2	194 56.0	03.6	189 47.6	59.0	Suhail	222 49.2	S43 31.1
17	148 35.4	77 03.9	36.5	161 18.0	07.7	209 58.7	03.7	204 50.2	59.0			
18	163 37.9	92 07.9	N22 35.7	176 18.9	S 8 07.1	225 01.3	S21 03.7	219 52.7	S19 59.0	Vega	80 35.3	N38 48.1
19	178 40.4	107 12.0	34.9	191 19.8	06.5	240 03.9	03.8	234 55.3	59.1	Zuben'ubi	136 59.8	S16 07.5
20	193 42.8	122 16.1	34.1	206 20.7	05.9	255 06.6	03.8	249 57.8	59.1		SHA	Mer. Pass.
21	208 45.3	137 20.1 ..	33.4	221 21.6 ..	05.3	270 09.2 ..	03.8	265 00.4 ..	59.1	Venus	287 23.0	12 00
22	223 47.8	152 24.2	32.6	236 22.5	04.8	285 11.8	03.9	280 03.0	59.1	Mars	13 46.5	6 17
23	238 50.2	167 28.3	31.8	251 23.5	04.2	300 14.5	03.9	295 05.5	59.2	Jupiter	61 16.6	3 07
Mer. Pass.	7 11.2	v 4.1	d 0.8	v 0.9	d 0.6	v 2.6	d 0.0	v 2.6	d 0.0	Saturn	56 10.9	3 27

UT (d h)	SUN GHA	SUN Dec	MOON GHA	v	MOON Dec	d	HP
	° '	° '	° '	'	° '	'	'
2 00	180 29.8	N22 13.0	50 26.2	10.1	S 3 20.3	14.7	60.0
01	195 29.7	13.3	64 55.3	10.0	3 35.0	14.7	60.1
02	210 29.6	13.7	79 24.3	10.1	3 49.7	14.7	60.1
03	225 29.5 ..	14.0	93 53.4	9.9	4 04.4	14.7	60.1
04	240 29.4	14.3	108 22.3	10.0	4 19.1	14.6	60.1
05	255 29.3	14.6	122 51.3	9.9	4 33.7	14.6	60.1
06	270 29.2 N22	14.9	137 20.2	9.9	S 4 48.3	14.6	60.1
07	285 29.1	15.2	151 49.1	9.8	5 02.9	14.6	60.1
08	300 29.0	15.6	166 17.9	9.8	5 17.5	14.6	60.1
09	315 28.9 ..	15.9	180 46.7	9.8	5 32.1	14.5	60.1
10	330 28.8	16.2	195 15.5	9.7	5 46.6	14.5	60.1
11	345 28.7	16.5	209 44.2	9.7	6 01.1	14.5	60.1
12	0 28.6 N22	16.8	224 12.9	9.7	S 6 15.6	14.4	60.1
13	15 28.5	17.1	238 41.6	9.6	6 30.0	14.4	60.1
14	30 28.4	17.4	253 10.2	9.6	6 44.4	14.4	60.1
15	45 28.3 ..	17.7	267 38.8	9.5	6 58.8	14.3	60.2
16	60 28.2	18.0	282 07.3	9.5	7 13.1	14.3	60.2
17	75 28.1	18.4	296 35.8	9.4	7 27.4	14.2	60.2
18	90 28.0 N22	18.7	311 04.2	9.4	S 7 41.6	14.2	60.2
19	105 27.9	19.0	325 32.6	9.4	7 55.8	14.2	60.2
20	120 27.8	19.3	340 01.0	9.3	8 10.0	14.1	60.2
21	135 27.7 ..	19.6	354 29.3	9.3	8 24.1	14.1	60.2
22	150 27.6	19.9	8 57.6	9.2	8 38.2	14.0	60.2
23	165 27.5	20.2	23 25.8	9.2	8 52.2	14.0	60.2
3 00	180 27.4 N22	20.5	37 54.0	9.1	S 9 06.2	13.9	60.2
01	195 27.3	20.8	52 22.1	9.1	9 20.1	13.8	60.2
02	210 27.2	21.1	66 50.2	9.0	9 33.9	13.9	60.2
03	225 27.1 ..	21.4	81 18.2	9.0	9 47.8	13.7	60.2
04	240 27.0	21.7	95 46.2	8.9	10 01.5	13.7	60.2
05	255 26.8	22.0	110 14.1	8.8	10 15.2	13.6	60.2
06	270 26.7 N22	22.3	124 41.9	8.9	S10 28.8	13.6	60.2
07	285 26.6	22.6	139 09.8	8.7	10 42.4	13.5	60.2
08	300 26.5	22.9	153 37.5	8.7	10 55.9	13.5	60.2
09	315 26.4 ..	23.2	168 05.2	8.7	11 09.4	13.3	60.2
10	330 26.3	23.5	182 32.9	8.6	11 22.7	13.4	60.2
11	345 26.2	23.8	197 00.5	8.6	11 36.1	13.2	60.2
12	0 26.1 N22	24.1	211 28.1	8.5	S11 49.3	13.2	60.2
13	15 26.0	24.4	225 55.6	8.4	12 02.5	13.1	60.2
14	30 25.9	24.7	240 23.0	8.4	12 15.6	13.0	60.2
15	45 25.8 ..	25.0	254 50.4	8.3	12 28.6	12.9	60.2
16	60 25.7	25.3	269 17.7	8.3	12 41.5	12.9	60.2
17	75 25.6	25.5	283 45.0	8.2	12 54.4	12.8	60.1
18	90 25.5 N22	25.8	298 12.2	8.2	S13 07.2	12.7	60.1
19	105 25.4	26.1	312 39.4	8.1	13 19.9	12.6	60.1
20	120 25.3	26.4	327 06.5	8.0	13 32.5	12.5	60.1
21	135 25.2 ..	26.7	341 33.5	8.0	13 45.0	12.5	60.1
22	150 25.1	27.0	356 00.5	7.9	13 57.5	12.3	60.1
23	165 25.0	27.3	10 27.4	7.9	14 09.8	12.3	60.1
4 00	180 24.8 N22	27.6	24 54.3	7.8	S14 22.1	12.2	60.1
01	195 24.7	27.9	39 21.1	7.8	14 34.3	12.1	60.1
02	210 24.6	28.1	53 47.9	7.7	14 46.4	12.0	60.1
03	225 24.5 ..	28.4	68 14.6	7.6	14 58.4	11.9	60.1
04	240 24.4	28.7	82 41.2	7.6	15 10.3	11.8	60.1
05	255 24.3	29.0	97 07.8	7.6	15 22.1	11.7	60.1
06	270 24.2 N22	29.3	111 34.4	7.4	S15 33.8	11.6	60.0
07	285 24.1	29.6	126 00.8	7.4	15 45.4	11.5	60.0
08	300 24.0	29.8	140 27.2	7.4	15 56.9	11.4	60.0
09	315 23.9 ..	30.1	154 53.6	7.3	16 08.3	11.3	60.0
10	330 23.8	30.4	169 19.9	7.2	16 19.6	11.1	60.0
11	345 23.7	30.7	183 46.1	7.2	16 30.7	11.1	60.0
12	0 23.6 N22	31.0	198 12.3	7.2	S16 41.8	11.0	60.0
13	15 23.4	31.2	212 38.5	7.0	16 52.8	10.8	60.0
14	30 23.3	31.5	227 04.5	7.0	17 03.6	10.8	60.0
15	45 23.2 ..	31.8	241 30.5	7.0	17 14.4	10.6	59.9
16	60 23.1	32.1	255 56.5	6.9	17 25.0	10.5	59.9
17	75 23.0	32.3	270 22.4	6.9	17 35.5	10.4	59.9
18	90 22.9 N22	32.6	284 48.3	6.8	S17 45.9	10.3	59.9
19	105 22.8	32.9	299 14.1	6.7	17 56.2	10.2	59.9
20	120 22.7	33.2	313 39.8	6.7	18 06.4	10.0	59.9
21	135 22.6 ..	33.4	328 05.5	6.6	18 16.4	9.9	59.9
22	150 22.5	33.7	342 31.1	6.6	18 26.3	9.8	59.8
23	165 22.4	34.0	356 56.7	6.6	S18 36.1	9.7	59.8
	SD 15.8 d 0.3		SD 16.4	16.4			16.3

(Rows d h: 2 = TUESDAY, 3 = WEDNESDAY, 4 = THURSDAY)

Twilight / Moonrise

Lat.	Naut.	Civil	Sunrise	Moonrise 2	3	4	5
°	h m	h m	h m	h m	h m	h m	h m
N 72	☐	☐	☐	16 50	19 22	■	■
N 70	☐	☐	☐	16 38	18 54	21 37	■
68	☐	☐	☐	16 29	18 33	20 49	■
66	////	////	01 02	16 21	18 17	20 18	22 26
64	////	////	01 52	16 14	18 03	19 55	21 47
62	////	////	02 23	16 09	17 52	19 37	21 20
60	////	01 19	02 46	16 04	17 43	19 23	20 59
N 58	////	01 56	03 04	16 00	17 35	19 10	20 42
56	////	02 21	03 20	15 56	17 27	18 59	20 27
54	01 12	02 41	03 33	15 52	17 21	18 50	20 15
52	01 46	02 57	03 44	15 49	17 15	18 41	20 04
50	02 10	03 11	03 54	15 47	17 10	18 34	19 54
45	02 51	03 39	04 15	15 41	16 59	18 17	19 34
N 40	03 19	04 00	04 32	15 36	16 50	18 04	19 17
35	03 41	04 17	04 47	15 31	16 42	17 53	19 03
30	03 59	04 32	04 59	15 28	16 35	17 43	18 51
20	04 27	04 56	05 20	15 21	16 23	17 27	18 31
N 10	04 48	05 15	05 38	15 16	16 13	17 13	18 13
0	05 06	05 32	05 55	15 10	16 04	16 59	17 57
S 10	05 22	05 49	06 11	15 05	15 54	16 46	17 41
20	05 38	06 05	06 29	15 00	15 44	16 32	17 23
30	05 53	06 23	06 49	14 54	15 33	16 16	17 03
35	06 01	06 33	07 01	14 50	15 26	16 07	16 52
40	06 10	06 44	07 14	14 46	15 19	15 56	16 38
45	06 20	06 57	07 30	14 42	15 11	15 44	16 23
S 50	06 31	07 12	07 49	14 37	15 01	15 29	16 04
52	06 35	07 19	07 59	14 34	14 56	15 22	15 55
54	06 41	07 26	08 09	14 31	14 51	15 14	15 45
56	06 46	07 35	08 21	14 28	14 45	15 06	15 33
58	06 52	07 44	08 34	14 25	14 39	14 56	15 20
S 60	06 59	07 55	08 50	14 22	14 32	14 45	15 05

Sunset / Twilight / Moonset

Lat.	Sunset	Civil	Naut.	Moonset 2	3	4	5
°	h m	h m	h m	h m	h m	h m	h m
N 72	☐	☐	☐	01 53	01 26	00 47	■
N 70	☐	☐	☐	01 58	01 40	01 17	00 31
68	☐	☐	☐	02 02	01 52	01 40	01 21
66	22 59	////	////	02 06	02 02	01 57	01 53
64	22 06	////	////	02 09	02 10	02 12	02 16
62	21 35	////	////	02 12	02 17	02 24	02 35
60	21 12	22 40	////	02 15	02 24	02 35	02 51
N 58	20 53	22 02	////	02 17	02 29	02 44	03 04
56	20 38	21 37	////	02 19	02 34	02 52	03 16
54	20 24	21 17	22 47	02 20	02 38	02 59	03 26
52	20 13	21 00	22 12	02 22	02 42	03 06	03 35
50	20 03	20 46	21 48	02 23	02 46	03 12	03 43
45	19 42	20 18	21 06	02 27	02 54	03 25	04 00
N 40	19 24	19 57	20 38	02 29	03 01	03 35	04 15
35	19 10	19 39	20 16	02 32	03 06	03 44	04 27
30	18 58	19 25	19 58	02 34	03 11	03 52	04 37
20	18 37	19 01	19 30	02 37	03 20	04 06	04 56
N 10	18 19	18 42	19 08	02 40	03 28	04 18	05 11
0	18 02	18 24	18 50	02 43	03 35	04 30	05 26
S 10	17 45	18 08	18 34	02 46	03 43	04 41	05 41
20	17 28	17 51	18 19	02 49	03 51	04 53	05 57
30	17 07	17 34	18 03	02 53	04 00	05 08	06 16
35	16 56	17 24	17 55	02 55	04 05	05 16	06 27
40	16 42	17 12	17 46	02 57	04 11	05 25	06 39
45	16 26	17 00	17 37	03 00	04 18	05 36	06 54
S 50	16 07	16 45	17 26	03 03	04 26	05 50	07 12
52	15 58	16 38	17 21	03 05	04 30	05 56	07 21
54	15 47	16 30	17 16	03 06	04 34	06 03	07 30
56	15 35	16 22	17 10	03 08	04 39	06 11	07 41
58	15 22	16 12	17 04	03 10	04 44	06 19	07 53
S 60	15 06	16 01	16 57	03 12	04 50	06 29	08 08

SUN and MOON

Day	SUN Eqn. of Time 00h	12h	Mer. Pass.	MOON Mer. Pass. Upper	Lower	Age	Phase
d	m s	m s	h m	h m	h m	d	%
2	01 59	01 55	11 58	21 23	08 57	11	85
3	01 50	01 45	11 58	22 17	09 49	12	93
4	01 40	01 34	11 58	23 13	10 44	13	98

UT	ARIES GHA	VENUS −4·2 GHA	Dec	MARS −0·1 GHA	Dec	JUPITER −2·6 GHA	Dec	SATURN +0·4 GHA	Dec	STARS Name	SHA	Dec
5 00	253 52.7	182 32.3	N22 31.0	266 24.4	S 8 03.6	315 17.1	S21 04.0	310 08.1	S19 59.2	Acamar	315 15.0	S40 13.4
01	268 55.2	197 36.4	30.2	281 25.3	03.0	330 19.7	04.0	325 10.7	59.2	Achernar	335 23.5	S57 07.9
02	283 57.6	212 40.5	29.4	296 26.2	02.4	345 22.4	04.0	340 13.2	59.2	Acrux	173 03.7	S63 12.9
03	299 00.1	227 44.5	.. 28.7	311 27.1	.. 01.9	0 25.0	.. 04.1	355 15.8	.. 59.3	Adhara	255 09.1	S29 00.1
04	314 02.5	242 48.6	27.9	326 28.0	01.3	15 27.7	04.1	10 18.3	59.3	Aldebaran	290 44.2	N16 32.8
05	329 05.0	257 52.6	27.1	341 28.9	00.7	30 30.3	04.1	25 20.9	59.3			
06	344 07.5	272 56.7	N22 26.3	356 29.8	S 8 00.1	45 32.9	S21 04.2	40 23.5	S19 59.3	Alioth	166 16.1	N55 51.3
07	359 09.9	288 00.8	25.5	11 30.7	7 59.5	60 35.6	04.2	55 26.0	59.4	Alkaid	152 54.7	N49 13.0
F 08	14 12.4	303 04.8	24.7	26 31.7	59.0	75 38.2	04.3	70 28.6	59.4	Alnair	27 37.5	S46 51.6
R 09	29 14.9	318 08.9	.. 23.9	41 32.6	.. 58.4	90 40.8	.. 04.3	85 31.2	.. 59.4	Alnilam	275 41.8	S 1 11.5
I 10	44 17.3	333 12.9	23.2	56 33.5	57.8	105 43.5	04.3	100 33.7	59.4	Alphard	217 51.5	S 8 44.9
D 11	59 19.8	348 17.0	22.4	71 34.4	57.2	120 46.1	04.4	115 36.3	59.5			
A 12	74 22.3	3 21.0	N22 21.6	86 35.3	S 7 56.6	135 48.7	S21 04.4	130 38.9	S19 59.5	Alphecca	126 06.6	N26 38.9
Y 13	89 24.7	18 25.1	20.8	101 36.2	56.1	150 51.4	04.4	145 41.4	59.5	Alpheratz	357 38.7	N29 11.9
14	104 27.2	33 29.1	20.0	116 37.1	55.5	165 54.0	04.5	160 44.0	59.5	Altair	62 03.3	N 8 55.3
15	119 29.7	48 33.2	.. 19.2	131 38.0	.. 54.9	180 56.7	.. 04.5	175 46.6	.. 59.6	Ankaa	353 11.1	S42 11.6
16	134 32.1	63 37.2	18.4	146 39.0	54.3	195 59.3	04.6	190 49.1	59.6	Antares	112 20.0	S26 28.5
17	149 34.6	78 41.3	17.7	161 39.9	53.7	211 01.9	04.6	205 51.7	59.6			
18	164 37.0	93 45.3	N22 16.9	176 40.8	S 7 53.2	226 04.6	S21 04.7	220 54.2	S19 59.6	Arcturus	145 51.1	N19 04.8
19	179 39.5	108 49.4	16.1	191 41.7	52.6	241 07.2	04.7	235 56.8	59.7	Atria	107 16.9	S69 03.7
20	194 42.0	123 53.4	15.3	206 42.6	52.0	256 09.9	04.7	250 59.4	59.7	Avior	234 16.6	S59 33.4
21	209 44.4	138 57.5	.. 14.5	221 43.5	.. 51.4	271 12.5	.. 04.8	266 01.9	.. 59.7	Bellatrix	278 27.2	N 6 21.9
22	224 46.9	154 01.5	13.7	236 44.4	50.8	286 15.1	04.8	281 04.5	59.7	Betelgeuse	270 56.4	N 7 24.5
23	239 49.4	169 05.5	12.9	251 45.4	50.2	301 17.8	04.8	296 07.1	59.8			
6 00	254 51.8	184 09.6	N22 12.1	266 46.3	S 7 49.7	316 20.4	S21 04.9	311 09.6	S19 59.8	Canopus	263 54.6	S52 42.6
01	269 54.3	199 13.6	11.4	281 47.2	49.1	331 23.1	04.9	326 12.2	59.8	Capella	280 27.8	N46 01.0
02	284 56.8	214 17.6	10.6	296 48.1	48.5	346 25.7	05.0	341 14.8	59.8	Deneb	49 28.0	N45 21.0
03	299 59.2	229 21.7	.. 09.8	311 49.0	.. 47.9	1 28.4	.. 05.0	356 17.3	.. 59.9	Denebola	182 28.7	N14 27.6
04	315 01.7	244 25.7	09.0	326 49.9	47.3	16 31.0	05.0	11 19.9	59.9	Diphda	348 51.2	S17 52.5
05	330 04.2	259 29.7	08.2	341 50.8	46.8	31 33.6	05.1	26 22.5	59.9			
06	345 06.6	274 33.8	N22 07.4	356 51.8	S 7 46.2	46 36.3	S21 05.1	41 25.0	S19 59.9	Dubhe	193 45.8	N61 38.8
S 07	0 09.1	289 37.8	06.6	11 52.7	45.6	61 38.9	05.1	56 27.6	20 00.0	Elnath	278 06.9	N28 37.3
A 08	15 11.5	304 41.8	05.8	26 53.6	45.0	76 41.6	05.2	71 30.2	00.0	Eltanin	90 43.4	N51 29.2
T 09	30 14.0	319 45.9	.. 05.0	41 54.5	.. 44.4	91 44.2	.. 05.2	86 32.7	.. 00.0	Enif	33 42.3	N 9 58.0
U 10	45 16.5	334 49.9	04.3	56 55.4	43.9	106 46.9	05.3	101 35.3	00.1	Fomalhaut	15 18.6	S29 30.8
R 11	60 18.9	349 53.9	03.5	71 56.3	43.3	121 49.5	05.3	116 37.9	00.1			
D 12	75 21.4	4 57.9	N22 02.7	86 57.3	S 7 42.7	136 52.2	S21 05.3	131 40.4	S20 00.1	Gacrux	171 55.4	S57 13.8
A 13	90 23.9	20 02.0	01.9	101 58.2	42.1	151 54.8	05.4	146 43.0	00.1	Gienah	175 47.3	S17 39.3
Y 14	105 26.3	35 06.0	01.1	116 59.1	41.5	166 57.4	05.4	161 45.6	00.2	Hadar	148 40.6	S60 28.4
15	120 28.8	50 10.0	22 00.3	132 00.0	.. 41.0	182 00.1	.. 05.5	176 48.1	.. 00.2	Hamal	327 55.6	N23 33.3
16	135 31.3	65 14.0	21 59.5	147 00.9	40.4	197 02.7	05.5	191 50.7	00.2	Kaus Aust.	83 37.1	S34 22.3
17	150 33.7	80 18.0	58.7	162 01.9	39.8	212 05.4	05.5	206 53.3	00.2			
18	165 36.2	95 22.0	N21 58.0	177 02.8	S 7 39.2	227 08.0	S21 05.6	221 55.9	S20 00.3	Kochab	137 19.0	N74 04.6
19	180 38.7	110 26.0	57.2	192 03.7	38.6	242 10.7	05.6	236 58.4	00.3	Markab	13 33.6	N15 18.7
20	195 41.1	125 30.1	56.4	207 04.6	38.1	257 13.3	05.7	252 01.0	00.3	Menkar	314 10.3	N 4 10.0
21	210 43.6	140 34.1	.. 55.6	222 05.5	.. 37.5	272 16.0	.. 05.7	267 03.6	.. 00.3	Menkent	148 01.6	S36 28.2
22	225 46.0	155 38.1	54.8	237 06.4	36.9	287 18.6	05.7	282 06.1	00.4	Miaplacidus	221 39.3	S69 48.3
23	240 48.5	170 42.1	54.0	252 07.4	36.3	302 21.3	05.8	297 08.7	00.4			
7 00	255 51.0	185 46.1	N21 53.2	267 08.3	S 7 35.7	317 23.9	S21 05.8	312 11.3	S20 00.4	Mirfak	308 34.0	N49 55.7
01	270 53.4	200 50.1	52.5	282 09.2	35.2	332 26.6	05.9	327 13.8	00.4	Nunki	75 52.0	S26 16.2
02	285 55.9	215 54.1	51.7	297 10.1	34.6	347 29.2	05.9	342 16.4	00.5	Peacock	53 11.3	S56 39.9
03	300 58.4	230 58.1	.. 50.9	312 11.0	.. 34.0	2 31.9	.. 06.0	357 19.0	.. 00.5	Pollux	243 22.2	N27 58.6
04	316 00.8	246 02.1	50.1	327 12.0	33.4	17 34.5	06.0	12 21.6	00.5	Procyon	244 55.0	N 5 10.3
05	331 03.3	261 06.1	49.3	342 12.9	32.8	32 37.2	06.0	27 24.1	00.6			
06	346 05.8	276 10.1	N21 48.5	357 13.8	S 7 32.3	47 39.8	S21 06.1	42 26.7	S20 00.6	Rasalhague	96 01.7	N12 32.8
07	1 08.2	291 14.0	47.7	12 14.7	31.7	62 42.5	06.1	57 29.3	00.6	Regulus	207 38.5	N11 52.1
S 08	16 10.7	306 18.0	47.0	27 15.7	31.1	77 45.1	06.2	72 31.8	00.6	Rigel	281 07.8	S 8 10.8
U 09	31 13.2	321 22.0	.. 46.2	42 16.6	.. 30.5	92 47.8	.. 06.2	87 34.4	.. 00.7	Rigil Kent.	139 44.7	S60 55.2
N 10	46 15.6	336 26.0	45.4	57 17.5	29.9	107 50.4	06.2	102 37.0	00.7	Sabik	102 06.7	S15 44.9
D 11	61 18.1	351 30.0	44.6	72 18.4	29.4	122 53.1	06.3	117 39.5	00.7			
A 12	76 20.5	6 34.0	N21 43.8	87 19.3	S 7 28.8	137 55.7	S21 06.3	132 42.1	S20 00.7	Schedar	349 35.3	N56 38.6
Y 13	91 23.0	21 37.9	43.0	102 20.3	28.2	152 58.4	06.4	147 44.7	00.8	Shaula	96 15.0	S37 07.0
14	106 25.5	36 41.9	42.2	117 21.2	27.6	168 01.0	06.4	162 47.3	00.8	Sirius	258 29.8	S16 44.8
15	121 27.9	51 45.9	.. 41.5	132 22.1	.. 27.0	183 03.7	.. 06.4	177 49.8	.. 00.8	Spica	158 26.0	S11 16.0
16	136 30.4	66 49.9	40.7	147 23.0	26.5	198 06.3	06.5	192 52.4	00.8	Suhail	222 49.2	S43 31.1
17	151 32.9	81 53.8	39.9	162 24.0	25.9	213 09.0	06.5	207 55.0	00.9			
18	166 35.3	96 57.8	N21 39.1	177 24.9	S 7 25.3	228 11.7	S21 06.6	222 57.5	S20 00.9	Vega	80 35.3	N38 48.1
19	181 37.8	112 01.8	38.3	192 25.8	24.7	243 14.3	06.6	238 00.1	00.9	Zuben'ubi	136 59.8	S16 07.5
20	196 40.3	127 05.7	37.6	207 26.7	24.1	258 17.0	06.6	253 02.7	01.0			
21	211 42.7	142 09.7	.. 36.8	222 27.6	.. 23.6	273 19.6	.. 06.7	268 05.3	.. 01.0		SHA	Mer. Pass.
22	226 45.2	157 13.7	36.0	237 28.6	23.0	288 22.3	06.7	283 07.8	01.0	Venus	289 17.7	11 40
23	241 47.7	172 17.6	35.2	252 29.5	22.4	303 24.9	06.8	298 10.4	01.0	Mars	11 54.4	6 13
Mer. Pass.	6 59.4	v 4.0	d 0.8	v 0.9	d 0.6	v 2.6	d 0.0	v 2.6	d 0.0	Jupiter	61 28.6	2 54
										Saturn	56 17.8	3 15

UT	SUN GHA	SUN Dec	MOON GHA	v	Dec	d	HP
d h	° ′	° ′	° ′	′	° ′	′	′
5 00	180 22.2	N22 34.2	11 22.3	6.5	S18 45.8	9.5	59.8
01	195 22.1	34.5	25 47.8	6.4	18 55.3	9.4	59.8
02	210 22.0	34.8	40 13.2	6.4	19 04.7	9.3	59.8
03	225 21.9	.. 35.0	54 38.6	6.3	19 14.0	9.2	59.8
04	240 21.8	35.3	69 03.9	6.3	19 23.2	9.0	59.7
05	255 21.7	35.6	83 29.2	6.3	19 32.2	8.9	59.7
06	270 21.6	N22 35.8	97 54.5	6.2	S19 41.1	8.8	59.7
07	285 21.5	36.1	112 19.7	6.1	19 49.9	8.6	59.7
F 08	300 21.4	36.4	126 44.8	6.1	19 58.5	8.5	59.7
R 09	315 21.2	.. 36.6	141 09.9	6.1	20 07.0	8.4	59.6
I 10	330 21.1	36.9	155 35.0	6.0	20 15.4	8.2	59.6
D 11	345 21.0	37.2	170 00.0	6.0	20 23.6	8.0	59.6
A 12	0 20.9	N22 37.4	184 25.0	6.0	S20 31.6	8.0	59.6
Y 13	15 20.8	37.7	198 50.0	5.9	20 39.6	7.8	59.6
14	30 20.7	38.0	213 14.9	5.9	20 47.4	7.6	59.5
15	45 20.6	.. 38.2	227 39.8	5.8	20 55.0	7.6	59.5
16	60 20.5	38.5	242 04.6	5.8	21 02.6	7.3	59.5
17	75 20.4	38.7	256 29.4	5.8	21 09.9	7.3	59.5
18	90 20.2	N22 39.0	270 54.2	5.7	S21 17.2	7.0	59.5
19	105 20.1	39.2	285 18.9	5.7	21 24.2	7.0	59.4
20	120 20.0	39.5	299 43.6	5.7	21 31.2	6.8	59.4
21	135 19.9	.. 39.8	314 08.3	5.6	21 38.0	6.6	59.4
22	150 19.8	40.0	328 32.9	5.6	21 44.6	6.5	59.4
23	165 19.7	40.3	342 57.5	5.6	21 51.1	6.3	59.3
6 00	180 19.6	N22 40.5	357 22.1	5.6	S21 57.4	6.2	59.3
01	195 19.5	40.8	11 46.7	5.6	22 03.6	6.1	59.3
02	210 19.3	41.0	26 11.3	5.5	22 09.7	5.9	59.3
03	225 19.2	.. 41.3	40 35.8	5.5	22 15.6	5.7	59.2
04	240 19.1	41.5	55 00.3	5.5	22 21.3	5.6	59.2
05	255 19.0	41.8	69 24.8	5.5	22 26.9	5.4	59.2
06	270 18.9	N22 42.0	83 49.3	5.4	S22 32.3	5.3	59.2
S 07	285 18.8	42.3	98 13.7	5.5	22 37.6	5.1	59.1
A 08	300 18.7	42.5	112 38.2	5.4	22 42.7	5.0	59.1
T 09	315 18.5	.. 42.8	127 02.6	5.4	22 47.7	4.8	59.1
U 10	330 18.4	43.0	141 27.0	5.5	22 52.5	4.7	59.0
R 11	345 18.3	43.3	155 51.5	5.4	22 57.2	4.5	59.0
D 12	0 18.2	N22 43.5	170 15.9	5.4	S23 01.7	4.3	59.0
A 13	15 18.1	43.8	184 40.3	5.4	23 06.0	4.2	59.0
Y 14	30 18.0	44.0	199 04.7	5.4	23 10.2	4.1	58.9
15	45 17.9	.. 44.2	213 29.1	5.4	23 14.3	3.8	58.9
16	60 17.7	44.5	227 53.5	5.4	23 18.1	3.8	58.9
17	75 17.6	44.7	242 17.9	5.4	23 21.9	3.5	58.9
18	90 17.5	N22 45.0	256 42.3	5.4	S23 25.4	3.4	58.8
19	105 17.4	45.2	271 06.7	5.4	23 28.8	3.3	58.8
20	120 17.3	45.5	285 31.1	5.4	23 32.1	3.1	58.8
21	135 17.2	.. 45.7	299 55.5	5.5	23 35.2	2.9	58.7
22	150 17.0	45.9	314 20.0	5.4	23 38.1	2.8	58.7
23	165 16.9	46.2	328 44.4	5.5	23 40.9	2.6	58.7
7 00	180 16.8	N22 46.4	343 08.9	5.5	S23 43.5	2.5	58.6
01	195 16.7	46.6	357 33.4	5.5	23 46.0	2.3	58.6
02	210 16.6	46.9	11 57.9	5.5	23 48.3	2.2	58.6
03	225 16.5	.. 47.1	26 22.4	5.6	23 50.5	2.0	58.5
04	240 16.3	47.4	40 47.0	5.5	23 52.5	1.8	58.5
05	255 16.2	47.6	55 11.5	5.6	23 54.3	1.7	58.5
06	270 16.1	N22 47.8	69 36.1	5.6	S23 56.0	1.5	58.5
07	285 16.0	48.1	84 00.7	5.7	23 57.5	1.4	58.4
08	300 15.9	48.3	98 25.4	5.7	23 58.9	1.2	58.4
S 09	315 15.8	.. 48.5	112 50.1	5.7	24 00.1	1.0	58.4
U 10	330 15.6	48.7	127 14.8	5.7	24 01.1	0.9	58.3
N 11	345 15.5	49.0	141 39.5	5.8	24 02.0	0.8	58.3
D 12	0 15.4	N22 49.2	156 04.3	5.8	S24 02.8	0.6	58.3
A 13	15 15.3	49.4	170 29.1	5.9	24 03.4	0.3	58.2
Y 14	30 15.2	49.7	184 54.0	5.9	24 03.8	0.3	58.2
15	45 15.1	.. 49.9	199 18.9	5.9	24 04.1	0.1	58.2
16	60 14.9	50.1	213 43.8	6.0	24 04.2	0.0	58.1
17	75 14.8	50.3	228 08.8	6.0	24 04.2	0.1	58.1
18	90 14.7	N22 50.6	242 33.8	6.1	S24 04.1	0.4	58.1
19	105 14.6	50.8	256 58.9	6.1	24 03.7	0.4	58.1
20	120 14.5	51.0	271 24.0	6.2	24 03.3	0.7	58.0
21	135 14.3	.. 51.2	285 49.2	6.2	24 02.6	0.7	58.0
22	150 14.2	51.5	300 14.4	6.3	24 01.9	0.9	57.9
23	165 14.1	51.7	314 39.7	6.3	S24 01.0	1.1	57.9
	SD 15.8	d 0.2	SD 16.2		16.1		15.9

Lat.	Naut.	Civil	Sunrise	Moonrise 5	6	7	8
°	h m	h m	h m	h m	h m	h m	h m
N 72	▭	▭	▭	▬	▬	▬	▬
N 70	▭	▭	▭	▬	▬	▬	▬
68	▭	▭	▭	▬	▬	▬	▬
66	////	////	00 48	22 26	24 47	00 47	▬
64	////	////	01 46	21 47	23 26	24 32	00 32
62	////	////	02 18	21 20	22 49	23 53	24 30
60	////	01 11	02 42	20 59	22 23	23 26	24 07
N 58	////	01 51	03 01	20 42	22 02	23 05	23 49
56	////	02 17	03 17	20 27	21 45	22 48	23 33
54	01 05	02 38	03 31	20 15	21 31	22 33	23 20
52	01 42	02 55	03 42	20 04	21 18	22 20	23 08
50	02 06	03 09	03 53	19 54	21 07	22 09	22 58
45	02 49	03 37	04 14	19 34	20 44	21 45	22 36
N 40	03 18	03 59	04 31	19 17	20 26	21 26	22 18
35	03 40	04 17	04 46	19 03	20 10	21 11	22 03
30	03 58	04 31	04 59	18 51	19 57	20 57	21 51
20	04 26	04 55	05 20	18 31	19 34	20 34	21 28
N 10	04 48	05 15	05 38	18 13	19 14	20 14	21 09
0	05 07	05 33	05 55	17 57	18 56	19 55	20 51
S 10	05 23	05 49	06 12	17 41	18 38	19 36	20 34
20	05 39	06 06	06 30	17 23	18 18	19 16	20 14
30	05 54	06 24	06 50	17 03	17 56	18 53	19 52
35	06 03	06 34	07 02	16 52	17 43	18 39	19 39
40	06 12	06 46	07 16	16 38	17 28	18 23	19 24
45	06 22	06 59	07 32	16 23	17 10	18 05	19 06
S 50	06 33	07 14	07 52	16 04	16 48	17 41	18 44
52	06 38	07 21	08 01	15 55	16 37	17 30	18 33
54	06 43	07 29	08 12	15 45	16 25	17 18	18 21
56	06 49	07 38	08 24	15 33	16 12	17 03	18 08
58	06 55	07 47	08 38	15 20	15 56	16 46	17 52
S 60	07 02	07 58	08 54	15 05	15 37	16 25	17 32

Lat.	Sunset	Twilight Civil	Naut.	Moonset 5	6	7	8
°	h m	h m	h m	h m	h m	h m	h m
N 72	▭	▭	▭	▬	▬	▬	▬
N 70	▭	▭	▭	00 31	▬	▬	▬
68	▭	▭	▭	01 21	▬	▬	▬
66	23 15	////	////	01 53	01 47	01 30	▬
64	22 14	////	////	02 16	02 26	02 51	03 48
62	21 40	////	////	02 35	02 54	03 28	04 26
60	21 16	22 49	////	02 51	03 15	03 55	04 53
N 58	20 57	22 08	////	03 04	03 33	04 15	05 14
56	20 41	21 41	////	03 16	03 48	04 32	05 31
54	20 28	21 21	22 55	03 26	04 01	04 47	05 46
52	20 16	21 03	22 17	03 35	04 12	05 00	05 58
50	20 05	20 49	21 52	03 43	04 22	05 11	06 10
45	19 44	20 21	21 09	04 00	04 43	05 34	06 33
N 40	19 26	19 59	20 40	04 15	05 00	05 53	06 52
35	19 12	19 41	20 18	04 27	05 15	06 09	07 07
30	18 59	19 24	20 00	04 37	05 27	06 22	07 21
20	18 38	19 02	19 31	04 56	05 49	06 46	07 44
N 10	18 19	18 42	19 09	05 11	06 08	07 06	08 04
0	18 02	18 25	18 51	05 26	06 25	07 24	08 22
S 10	17 46	18 08	18 34	05 41	06 43	07 43	08 41
20	17 28	17 51	18 19	05 57	07 01	08 03	09 01
30	17 07	17 33	18 03	06 16	07 23	08 26	09 23
35	16 55	17 23	17 55	06 27	07 36	08 40	09 37
40	16 41	17 12	17 46	06 39	07 50	08 55	09 52
45	16 25	16 59	17 36	06 54	08 08	09 14	10 10
S 50	16 05	16 43	17 25	07 12	08 29	09 37	10 33
52	15 56	16 36	17 20	07 21	08 40	09 48	10 43
54	15 45	16 28	17 14	07 30	08 51	10 01	10 56
56	15 33	16 20	17 08	07 41	09 05	10 16	11 10
58	15 19	16 10	17 02	07 53	09 20	10 33	11 26
S 60	15 03	15 59	16 55	08 08	09 39	10 53	11 46

Day	SUN Eqn. of Time 00h	12h	Mer. Pass.	MOON Mer. Pass. Upper	Lower	Age	Phase
d	m s	m s	h m	h m	h m	d	%
5	01 29	01 24	11 59	24 11	11 42	14	100
6	01 18	01 13	11 59	00 11	12 41	15	99
7	01 07	01 02	11 59	01 10	13 40	16	96

UT	ARIES	VENUS −4·1		MARS −0·1		JUPITER −2·6		SATURN +0·4		STARS		
	GHA	GHA	Dec	GHA	Dec	GHA	Dec	GHA	Dec	Name	SHA	Dec
d h	° ′	° ′	° ′	° ′	° ′	° ′	° ′	° ′	° ′		° ′	° ′
8 00	256 50.1	187 21.6 N21 34.4		267 30.4 S 7 21.8		318 27.6 S21 06.8		313 13.0 S20 01.1		Acamar	315 15.0 S40 13.4	
01	271 52.6	202 25.5	33.6	282 31.3	21.2	333 30.2	06.9	328 15.6	01.1	Achernar	335 23.5 S57 07.9	
02	286 55.0	217 29.5	32.9	297 32.3	20.7	348 32.9	06.9	343 18.1	01.1	Acrux	173 03.8 S63 12.9	
03	301 57.5	232 33.4 . .	32.1	312 33.2 . .	20.1	3 35.6 . .	06.9	358 20.7 . .	01.1	Adhara	255 09.1 S29 00.1	
04	317 00.0	247 37.4	31.3	327 34.1	19.5	18 38.2	07.0	13 23.3	01.2	Aldebaran	290 44.2 N16 32.8	
05	332 02.4	262 41.3	30.5	342 35.1	18.9	33 40.9	07.0	28 25.9	01.2			
06	347 04.9	277 45.3 N21 29.8		357 36.0 S 7 18.3		48 43.5 S21 07.1		43 28.4 S20 01.2		Alioth	166 16.2 N55 51.3	
07	2 07.4	292 49.2	29.0	12 36.9	17.8	63 46.2	07.1	58 31.0	01.3	Alkaid	152 54.7 N49 13.0	
08	17 09.8	307 53.2	28.2	27 37.8	17.2	78 48.9	07.1	73 33.6	01.3	Alnair	27 37.5 S46 51.6	
M 09	32 12.3	322 57.1 . .	27.4	42 38.8 . .	16.6	93 51.5 . .	07.2	88 36.1 . .	01.3	Alnilam	275 41.8 S 1 11.5	
O 10	47 14.8	338 01.0	26.6	57 39.7	16.0	108 54.2	07.2	103 38.7	01.3	Alphard	217 51.5 S 8 44.9	
N 11	62 17.2	353 05.0	25.9	72 40.6	15.4	123 56.8	07.3	118 41.3	01.4			
D 12	77 19.7	8 08.9 N21 25.1		87 41.5 S 7 14.9		138 59.5 S21 07.3		133 43.9 S20 01.4		Alphecca	126 06.6 N26 38.9	
A 13	92 22.2	23 12.8	24.3	102 42.5	14.3	154 02.1	07.4	148 46.4	01.4	Alpheratz	357 38.6 N29 11.9	
Y 14	107 24.6	38 16.7	23.5	117 43.4	13.7	169 04.8	07.4	163 49.0	01.5	Altair	62 03.3 N 8 55.3	
15	122 27.1	53 20.7 . .	22.8	132 44.3 . .	13.1	184 07.5 . .	07.4	178 51.6 . .	01.5	Ankaa	353 11.0 S42 11.6	
16	137 29.5	68 24.6	22.0	147 45.3	12.5	199 10.1	07.5	193 54.2	01.5	Antares	112 20.0 S26 28.5	
17	152 32.0	83 28.5	21.2	162 46.2	12.0	214 12.8	07.5	208 56.7	01.5			
18	167 34.5	98 32.4 N21 20.4		177 47.1 S 7 11.4		229 15.5 S21 07.6		223 59.3 S20 01.6		Arcturus	145 51.1 N19 04.8	
19	182 36.9	113 36.3	19.7	192 48.0	10.8	244 18.1	07.6	239 01.9	01.6	Atria	107 16.9 S69 03.7	
20	197 39.4	128 40.2	18.9	207 49.0	10.2	259 20.8	07.7	254 04.5	01.6	Avior	234 16.6 S59 34.7	
21	212 41.9	143 44.2 . .	18.1	222 49.9 . .	09.6	274 23.4 . .	07.7	269 07.1 . .	01.6	Bellatrix	278 27.2 N 6 21.9	
22	227 44.3	158 48.1	17.4	237 50.8	09.1	289 26.1	07.7	284 09.6	01.7	Betelgeuse	270 56.4 N 7 24.5	
23	242 46.8	173 52.0	16.6	252 51.8	08.5	304 28.8	07.8	299 12.2	01.7			
9 00	257 49.3	188 55.9 N21 15.8		267 52.7 S 7 07.9		319 31.4 S21 07.8		314 14.8 S20 01.7		Canopus	263 54.6 S52 42.5	
01	272 51.7	203 59.8	15.0	282 53.6	07.3	334 34.1	07.9	329 17.4	01.8	Capella	280 27.8 N46 00.9	
02	287 54.2	219 03.7	14.3	297 54.5	06.7	349 36.8	07.9	344 19.9	01.8	Deneb	49 27.9 N45 21.0	
03	302 56.6	234 07.6 . .	13.5	312 55.5 . .	06.2	4 39.4 . .	08.0	359 22.5 . .	01.8	Denebola	182 28.7 N14 27.6	
04	317 59.1	249 11.5	12.7	327 56.4	05.6	19 42.1	08.0	14 25.1	01.8	Diphda	348 51.2 S17 52.5	
05	333 01.6	264 15.3	12.0	342 57.3	05.0	34 44.7	08.0	29 27.7	01.9			
06	348 04.0	279 19.2 N21 11.2		357 58.3 S 7 04.4		49 47.4 S21 08.1		44 30.2 S20 01.9		Dubhe	193 45.8 N61 38.8	
07	3 06.5	294 23.1	10.4	12 59.2	03.8	64 50.1	08.1	59 32.8	01.9	Elnath	278 06.9 N28 37.3	
08	18 09.0	309 27.0	09.7	28 00.1	03.3	79 52.7	08.2	74 35.4	02.0	Eltanin	90 43.4 N51 29.2	
T 09	33 11.4	324 30.9 . .	08.9	43 01.1 . .	02.7	94 55.4 . .	08.2	89 38.0 . .	02.0	Enif	33 42.3 N 9 58.0	
U 10	48 13.9	339 34.7	08.1	58 02.0	02.1	109 58.1	08.3	104 40.6	02.0	Fomalhaut	15 18.6 S29 30.8	
E 11	63 16.4	354 38.6	07.4	73 02.9	01.5	125 00.7	08.3	119 43.1	02.0			
S 12	78 18.8	9 42.5 N21 06.6		88 03.9 S 7 00.9		140 03.4 S21 08.3		134 45.7 S20 02.1		Gacrux	171 55.4 S57 13.8	
D 13	93 21.3	24 46.4	05.8	103 04.8	7 00.4	155 06.1	08.4	149 48.3	02.1	Gienah	175 47.3 S17 39.3	
A 14	108 23.8	39 50.2	05.1	118 05.7	6 59.8	170 08.7	08.4	164 50.9	02.1	Hadar	148 40.6 S60 28.4	
Y 15	123 26.2	54 54.1 . .	04.3	133 06.7 . .	59.2	185 11.4 . .	08.5	179 53.4 . .	02.2	Hamal	327 55.6 N23 33.3	
16	138 28.7	69 58.0	03.6	148 07.6	58.6	200 14.1	08.5	194 56.0	02.2	Kaus Aust.	83 37.0 S34 22.4	
17	153 31.1	85 01.8	02.8	163 08.5	58.0	215 16.7	08.6	209 58.6	02.2			
18	168 33.6	100 05.7 N21 02.0		178 09.5 S 6 57.5		230 19.4 S21 08.6		225 01.2 S20 02.2		Kochab	137 19.0 N74 04.6	
19	183 36.1	115 09.5	01.3	193 10.4	56.9	245 22.1	08.6	240 03.8	02.3	Markab	13 33.5 N15 18.7	
20	198 38.5	130 13.4	21 00.5	208 11.3	56.3	260 24.8	08.7	255 06.3	02.3	Menkar	314 10.3 N 4 10.0	
21	213 41.0	145 17.2	20 59.7	223 12.3 . .	55.7	275 27.4 . .	08.7	270 08.9 . .	02.3	Menkent	148 01.6 S36 28.2	
22	228 43.5	160 21.1	59.0	238 13.2	55.1	290 30.1	08.8	285 11.5	02.4	Miaplacidus	221 39.3 S69 48.3	
23	243 45.9	175 24.9	58.2	253 14.1	54.6	305 32.8	08.8	300 14.1	02.4			
10 00	258 48.4	190 28.7 N20 57.5		268 15.1 S 6 54.0		320 35.4 S21 08.9		315 16.7 S20 02.4		Mirfak	308 33.9 N49 55.7	
01	273 50.9	205 32.6	56.7	283 16.0	53.4	335 38.1	08.9	330 19.2	02.4	Nunki	75 52.0 S26 16.2	
02	288 53.3	220 36.4	56.0	298 16.9	52.8	350 40.8	09.0	345 21.8	02.5	Peacock	53 11.2 S56 39.9	
03	303 55.8	235 40.2 . .	55.2	313 17.9 . .	52.2	5 43.4 . .	09.0	0 24.4 . .	02.5	Pollux	243 22.2 N27 58.6	
04	318 58.3	250 44.1	54.5	328 18.8	51.7	20 46.1	09.0	15 27.0	02.5	Procyon	244 55.0 N 5 10.3	
05	334 00.7	265 47.9	53.7	343 19.7	51.1	35 48.8	09.1	30 29.6	02.6			
06	349 03.2	280 51.7 N20 53.0		358 20.7 S 6 50.5		50 51.5 S21 09.1		45 32.1 S20 02.6		Rasalhague	96 01.6 N12 32.8	
W 07	4 05.6	295 55.5	52.2	13 21.6	49.9	65 54.1	09.2	60 34.7	02.6	Regulus	207 38.5 N11 52.1	
E 08	19 08.1	310 59.3	51.4	28 22.6	49.4	80 56.8	09.2	75 37.3	02.6	Rigel	281 07.8 S 8 10.8	
D 09	34 10.6	326 03.2 . .	50.7	43 23.5 . .	48.8	95 59.5 . .	09.3	90 39.9 . .	02.7	Rigil Kent.	139 44.7 S60 55.2	
N 10	49 13.0	341 07.0	49.9	58 24.4	48.2	111 02.2	09.3	105 42.5	02.7	Sabik	102 06.7 S15 44.9	
E 11	64 15.5	356 10.8	49.2	73 25.4	47.6	126 04.8	09.4	120 45.0	02.7			
S 12	79 18.0	11 14.6 N20 48.4		88 26.3 S 6 47.0		141 07.5 S21 09.4		135 47.6 S20 02.8		Schedar	349 35.3 N56 38.6	
D 13	94 20.4	26 18.4	47.7	103 27.2	46.5	156 10.2	09.4	150 50.2	02.8	Shaula	96 15.0 S37 07.0	
A 14	109 22.9	41 22.2	47.0	118 28.2	45.9	171 12.9	09.5	165 52.8	02.8	Sirius	258 29.8 S16 44.8	
Y 15	124 25.4	56 26.0 . .	46.2	133 29.1 . .	45.3	186 15.5 . .	09.5	180 55.4 . .	02.8	Spica	158 26.0 S11 16.0	
16	139 27.8	71 29.8	45.5	148 30.1	44.7	201 18.2	09.6	195 58.0	02.9	Suhail	222 49.2 S43 31.1	
17	154 30.3	86 33.6	44.7	163 31.0	44.1	216 20.9	09.6	211 00.5	02.9			
18	169 32.8	101 37.3 N20 44.0		178 31.9 S 6 43.6		231 23.6 S21 09.7		226 03.1 S20 02.9		Vega	80 35.3 N38 48.1	
19	184 35.2	116 41.1	43.2	193 32.9	43.0	246 26.2	09.7	241 05.7	03.0	Zuben'ubi	136 59.8 S16 07.5	
20	199 37.7	131 44.9	42.5	208 33.8	42.4	261 28.9	09.8	256 08.3	03.0		SHA	Mer. Pass.
21	214 40.1	146 48.7 . .	41.7	223 34.8 . .	41.8	276 31.6 . .	09.8	271 10.9 . .	03.0		° ′	h m
22	229 42.6	161 52.5	41.0	238 35.7	41.3	291 34.3	09.8	286 13.5	03.0	Venus	291 06.6	11 21
23	244 45.1	176 56.2	40.3	253 36.6	40.7	306 36.9	09.9	301 16.0	03.1	Mars	10 03.4	6 08
	h m									Jupiter	61 42.2	2 41
Mer. Pass. 6 47.6		v 3.9 d 0.8		v 0.9 d 0.6		v 2.7 d 0.0		v 2.6 d 0.0		Saturn	56 25.5	3 02

SUN and MOON — GHA / Dec

UT	SUN GHA	SUN Dec	MOON GHA	v	MOON Dec	d	HP
8 00	180 14.0	N22 51.9	329 05.0	6.4	S23 59.9	1.2	57.9
01	195 13.9	52.1	343 30.4	6.4	23 58.7	1.4	57.8
02	210 13.7	52.3	357 55.8	6.5	23 57.3	1.5	57.8
03	225 13.6 ..	52.6	12 21.3	6.6	23 55.8	1.7	57.8
04	240 13.5	52.8	26 46.9	6.6	23 54.1	1.7	57.7
05	255 13.4	53.0	41 12.5	6.7	23 52.4	2.0	57.7
06	270 13.3	N22 53.2	55 38.2	6.8	S23 50.4	2.1	57.7
07	285 13.1	53.4	70 04.0	6.8	23 48.3	2.2	57.6
M 08	300 13.0	53.6	84 29.8	6.9	23 46.1	2.4	57.6
O 09	315 12.9 ..	53.8	98 55.7	7.0	23 43.7	2.5	57.6
N 10	330 12.8	54.1	113 21.7	7.0	23 41.2	2.6	57.5
D 11	345 12.7	54.3	127 47.7	7.1	23 38.6	2.8	57.5
A 12	0 12.5	N22 54.5	142 13.8	7.2	S23 35.8	2.9	57.5
Y 13	15 12.4	54.7	156 40.0	7.2	23 32.9	3.1	57.4
14	30 12.3	54.9	171 06.2	7.3	23 29.8	3.2	57.4
15	45 12.2 ..	55.1	185 32.5	7.4	23 26.6	3.3	57.4
16	60 12.1	55.3	199 58.9	7.5	23 23.3	3.4	57.3
17	75 11.9	55.5	214 25.4	7.5	23 19.9	3.6	57.3
18	90 11.8	N22 55.7	228 51.9	7.6	S23 16.3	3.8	57.3
19	105 11.7	56.0	243 18.5	7.7	23 12.5	3.8	57.2
20	120 11.6	56.2	257 45.2	7.8	23 08.7	4.0	57.2
21	135 11.5 ..	56.4	272 12.0	7.9	23 04.7	4.1	57.2
22	150 11.3	56.6	286 38.9	7.9	23 00.6	4.2	57.1
23	165 11.2	56.8	301 05.8	8.1	22 56.4	4.4	57.1
9 00	180 11.1	N22 57.0	315 32.9	8.1	S22 52.0	4.5	57.1
01	195 11.0	57.2	330 00.0	8.2	22 47.5	4.6	57.0
02	210 10.8	57.4	344 27.2	8.2	22 42.9	4.7	57.0
03	225 10.7 ..	57.6	358 54.4	8.4	22 38.2	4.9	57.0
04	240 10.6	57.8	13 21.8	8.5	22 33.3	5.0	56.9
05	255 10.5	58.0	27 49.3	8.5	22 28.3	5.1	56.9
06	270 10.4	N22 58.2	42 16.8	8.6	S22 23.2	5.2	56.9
07	285 10.2	58.4	56 44.4	8.7	22 18.0	5.3	56.8
T 08	300 10.1	58.6	71 12.1	8.8	22 12.7	5.5	56.8
U 09	315 10.0 ..	58.8	85 39.9	8.9	22 07.2	5.5	56.8
E 10	330 09.9	59.0	100 07.8	9.0	22 01.7	5.7	56.7
S 11	345 09.7	59.2	114 35.8	9.0	21 56.0	5.8	56.7
D 12	0 09.6	N22 59.4	129 03.8	9.2	S21 50.2	5.9	56.7
A 13	15 09.5	59.6	143 32.0	9.2	21 44.3	6.0	56.6
Y 14	30 09.4	22 59.8	158 00.2	9.4	21 38.3	6.1	56.6
15	45 09.2	23 00.0	172 28.6	9.4	21 32.2	6.2	56.6
16	60 09.1	00.1	186 57.0	9.5	21 26.0	6.4	56.5
17	75 09.0	00.3	201 25.5	9.6	21 19.6	6.4	56.5
18	90 08.9	N23 00.5	215 54.1	9.7	S21 13.2	6.5	56.5
19	105 08.8	00.7	230 22.8	9.8	21 06.7	6.7	56.4
20	120 08.6	00.9	244 51.6	9.9	21 00.0	6.7	56.4
21	135 08.5 ..	01.1	259 20.5	9.9	20 53.3	6.9	56.4
22	150 08.4	01.3	273 49.4	10.1	20 46.4	6.9	56.3
23	165 08.3	01.5	288 18.5	10.1	20 39.5	7.1	56.3
10 00	180 08.1	N23 01.7	302 47.6	10.3	S20 32.4	7.1	56.3
01	195 08.0	01.8	317 16.9	10.3	20 25.3	7.2	56.2
02	210 07.9	02.0	331 46.2	10.4	20 18.1	7.4	56.2
03	225 07.8 ..	02.2	346 15.6	10.5	20 10.7	7.4	56.2
04	240 07.6	02.4	0 45.1	10.7	20 03.3	7.5	56.1
05	255 07.5	02.6	15 14.8	10.6	19 55.8	7.6	56.1
06	270 07.4	N23 02.8	29 44.4	10.8	S19 48.2	7.7	56.1
W 07	285 07.3	03.0	44 14.2	10.9	19 40.5	7.8	56.0
E 08	300 07.1	03.1	58 44.1	11.0	19 32.7	7.9	56.0
D 09	315 07.0 ..	03.3	73 14.1	11.0	19 24.8	8.0	56.0
N 10	330 06.9	03.5	87 44.1	11.2	19 16.8	8.0	56.0
E 11	345 06.8	03.7	102 14.3	11.2	19 08.8	8.2	55.9
S 12	0 06.6	N23 03.9	116 44.5	11.3	S19 00.6	8.2	55.9
D 13	15 06.5	04.0	131 14.8	11.5	18 52.4	8.3	55.9
A 14	30 06.4	04.2	145 45.3	11.5	18 44.1	8.4	55.8
Y 15	45 06.3 ..	04.4	160 15.8	11.5	18 35.7	8.4	55.8
16	60 06.1	04.6	174 46.3	11.7	18 27.3	8.6	55.8
17	75 06.0	04.7	189 17.0	11.8	18 18.7	8.6	55.8
18	90 05.9	N23 04.9	203 47.8	11.8	S18 10.1	8.7	55.7
19	105 05.7	05.1	218 18.6	12.0	18 01.4	8.8	55.7
20	120 05.6	05.3	232 49.6	12.0	17 52.6	8.8	55.7
21	135 05.5 ..	05.4	247 20.6	12.1	17 43.8	8.9	55.6
22	150 05.4	05.6	261 51.7	12.2	17 34.9	9.0	55.6
23	165 05.2	05.8	276 22.9	12.3	S17 25.9	9.1	55.6
	SD 15.8	d 0.2	SD 15.7		15.4		15.2

Twilight, Sunrise and Moonrise

Lat.	Naut.	Civil	Sunrise	Moonrise 8	9	10	11
N 72	□	□	□	■■	■■	■■	03 19
N 70	□	□	□	■■	■■	■■	02 30
68	□	□	□	■■	■■	02 21	01 58
66	////	////	00 32	■■	01 47	01 40	01 35
64	////	////	01 40	00 32	01 00	01 12	01 16
62	////	////	02 15	24 30	00 30	00 50	01 01
60	////	01 04	02 40	24 07	00 07	00 32	00 48
N 58	////	01 47	02 59	23 49	24 18	00 18	00 37
56	////	02 14	03 15	23 33	24 05	00 05	00 28
54	00 58	02 36	03 29	23 20	23 54	24 19	00 19
52	01 38	02 53	03 41	23 08	23 44	24 11	00 11
50	02 04	03 07	03 51	22 58	23 35	24 04	00 04
45	02 47	03 36	04 13	22 36	23 17	23 49	24 17
N 40	03 17	03 58	04 31	22 18	23 01	23 37	24 07
35	03 40	04 16	04 46	22 03	22 48	23 26	23 59
30	03 58	04 31	04 58	21 51	22 37	23 17	23 53
20	04 26	04 55	05 20	21 28	22 18	23 01	23 41
N 10	04 49	05 15	05 38	21 09	22 01	22 47	23 30
0	05 07	05 33	05 56	20 51	21 45	22 34	23 20
S 10	05 24	05 50	06 13	20 34	21 29	22 21	23 10
20	05 40	06 07	06 31	20 14	21 12	22 07	22 59
30	05 56	06 25	06 52	19 52	20 52	21 51	22 47
35	06 04	06 36	07 04	19 39	20 40	21 41	22 40
40	06 13	06 47	07 18	19 24	20 27	21 30	22 32
45	06 23	07 00	07 34	19 06	20 12	21 17	22 22
S 50	06 35	07 16	07 54	18 44	19 52	21 02	22 11
52	06 40	07 23	08 04	18 33	19 43	20 55	22 05
54	06 45	07 31	08 15	18 21	19 33	20 46	22 00
56	06 51	07 40	08 27	18 08	19 21	20 37	21 53
58	06 58	07 50	08 41	17 52	19 07	20 27	21 46
S 60	07 05	08 01	08 58	17 32	18 51	20 15	21 37

Sunset, Twilight and Moonset

Lat.	Sunset	Civil	Naut.	Moonset 8	9	10	11
N 72	□	□	□	■■	■■	■■	06 30
N 70	□	□	□	■■	■■	■■	07 17
68	□	□	□	■■	■■	05 45	07 48
66	23 33	////	////	■■	04 30	06 15	08 10
64	22 20	////	////	03 48	05 15	06 52	08 28
62	21 45	////	////	04 26	05 45	07 13	08 42
60	21 20	22 57	////	04 53	06 08	07 30	08 54
N 58	21 00	22 13	////	05 14	06 26	07 45	09 04
56	20 44	21 45	////	05 31	06 41	07 57	09 13
54	20 30	21 24	23 02	05 46	06 54	08 08	09 21
52	20 18	21 06	22 22	05 58	07 06	08 17	09 29
50	20 08	20 52	21 56	06 10	07 16	08 25	09 35
45	19 46	20 23	21 12	06 33	07 37	08 43	09 49
N 40	19 28	20 01	20 42	06 52	07 54	08 58	10 00
35	19 13	19 43	20 19	07 07	08 08	09 10	10 10
30	19 01	19 28	20 01	07 21	08 21	09 20	10 18
20	18 39	19 03	19 32	07 44	08 42	09 38	10 32
N 10	18 20	18 43	19 10	08 04	09 00	09 54	10 45
0	18 03	18 25	18 52	08 22	09 17	10 09	10 57
S 10	17 46	18 09	18 35	08 41	09 34	10 23	11 08
20	17 28	17 52	18 19	09 01	09 53	10 39	11 20
30	17 07	17 33	18 03	09 23	10 13	10 57	11 34
35	16 55	17 23	17 54	09 37	10 25	11 07	11 42
40	16 41	17 11	17 45	09 52	10 39	11 19	11 52
45	16 25	16 58	17 35	10 10	10 56	11 32	12 02
S 50	16 04	16 42	17 24	10 33	11 16	11 49	12 15
52	15 55	16 35	17 19	10 43	11 25	11 57	12 21
54	15 44	16 27	17 13	10 56	11 36	12 05	12 28
56	15 32	16 18	17 07	11 10	11 48	12 15	12 35
58	15 17	16 09	17 01	11 26	12 02	12 26	12 43
S 60	15 01	15 57	16 53	11 46	12 18	12 39	12 52

SUN and MOON

Day	SUN Eqn. of Time 00h	12h	Mer. Pass.	MOON Mer. Pass. Upper	Lower	Age	Phase
d	m s	m s	h m	h m	h m	d %	
8	00 56	00 50	11 59	02 09	14 37	17 91	
9	00 45	00 39	11 59	03 05	15 31	18 84	
10	00 33	00 27	12 00	03 57	16 22	19 76	◑

UT	ARIES	VENUS −4.1		MARS −0.2		JUPITER −2.6		SATURN +0.3		STARS		
	GHA	GHA	Dec	GHA	Dec	GHA	Dec	GHA	Dec	Name	SHA	Dec
d h	° ′	° ′	° ′	° ′	° ′	° ′	° ′	° ′	° ′		° ′	° ′
11 00	259 47.5	192 00.0	N20 39.5	268 37.6	S 6 40.1	321 39.6	S21 09.9	316 18.6	S20 03.1	Acamar	315 15.0	S40 13.4
01	274 50.0	207 03.8	38.8	283 38.5	39.5	336 42.3	10.0	331 21.2	03.1	Achernar	335 23.4	S57 07.9
02	289 52.5	222 07.5	38.0	298 39.5	38.9	351 45.0	10.0	346 23.8	03.2	Acrux	173 03.8	S63 12.9
03	304 54.9	237 11.3	.. 37.3	313 40.4	.. 38.4	6 47.6	.. 10.1	1 26.4	.. 03.2	Adhara	255 09.1	S29 00.1
04	319 57.4	252 15.0	36.6	328 41.3	37.8	21 50.3	10.1	16 29.0	03.2	Aldebaran	290 44.2	N16 32.8
05	334 59.9	267 18.8	35.8	343 42.3	37.2	36 53.0	10.2	31 31.5	03.3			
06	350 02.3	282 22.5	N20 35.1	358 43.2	S 6 36.6	51 55.7	S21 10.2	46 34.1	S20 03.3	Alioth	166 16.2	N55 51.3
07	5 04.8	297 26.3	34.4	13 44.2	36.0	66 58.4	10.3	61 36.7	03.3	Alkaid	152 54.8	N49 13.0
T 08	20 07.2	312 30.0	33.6	28 45.1	35.5	82 01.0	10.3	76 39.3	03.3	Alnair	27 37.5	S46 51.5
H 09	35 09.7	327 33.8	.. 32.9	43 46.1	.. 34.9	97 03.7	.. 10.3	91 41.9	.. 03.4	Alnilam	275 41.8	S 1 11.5
U 10	50 12.2	342 37.5	32.2	58 47.0	34.3	112 06.4	10.4	106 44.5	03.4	Alphard	217 51.5	S 8 44.9
R 11	65 14.6	357 41.2	31.4	73 47.9	33.7	127 09.1	10.4	121 47.0	03.4			
S 12	80 17.1	12 45.0	N20 30.7	88 48.9	S 6 33.2	142 11.8	S21 10.5	136 49.6	S20 03.5	Alphecca	126 06.6	N26 38.9
D 13	95 19.6	27 48.7	30.0	103 49.8	32.6	157 14.4	10.5	151 52.2	03.5	Alpheratz	357 38.6	N29 11.9
A 14	110 22.0	42 52.4	29.3	118 50.8	32.0	172 17.1	10.6	166 54.8	03.5	Altair	62 03.3	N 8 55.3
Y 15	125 24.5	57 56.1	.. 28.5	133 51.7	.. 31.4	187 19.8	.. 10.6	181 57.4	.. 03.6	Ankaa	353 11.0	S42 11.6
16	140 27.0	72 59.9	27.8	148 52.7	30.8	202 22.5	10.7	197 00.0	03.6	Antares	112 20.0	S26 28.5
17	155 29.4	88 03.6	27.1	163 53.6	30.3	217 25.2	10.7	212 02.6	03.6			
18	170 31.9	103 07.3	N20 26.3	178 54.6	S 6 29.7	232 27.8	S21 10.8	227 05.1	S20 03.6	Arcturus	145 51.1	N19 04.8
19	185 34.4	118 11.0	25.6	193 55.5	29.1	247 30.5	10.8	242 07.7	03.7	Atria	107 16.9	S69 03.8
20	200 36.8	133 14.7	24.9	208 56.4	28.5	262 33.2	10.8	257 10.3	03.7	Avior	234 16.6	S59 34.7
21	215 39.3	148 18.4	.. 24.2	223 57.4	.. 28.0	277 35.9	.. 10.9	272 12.9	.. 03.7	Bellatrix	278 27.2	N 6 22.0
22	230 41.7	163 22.1	23.5	238 58.3	27.4	292 38.6	10.9	287 15.5	03.8	Betelgeuse	270 56.4	N 7 24.5
23	245 44.2	178 25.8	22.7	253 59.3	26.8	307 41.3	11.0	302 18.1	03.8			
12 00	260 46.7	193 29.5	N20 22.0	269 00.2	S 6 26.2	322 43.9	S21 11.0	317 20.7	S20 03.8	Canopus	263 54.6	S52 42.5
01	275 49.1	208 33.2	21.3	284 01.2	25.6	337 46.6	11.1	332 23.2	03.9	Capella	280 27.8	N46 00.9
02	290 51.6	223 36.9	20.6	299 02.1	25.1	352 49.3	11.1	347 25.8	03.9	Deneb	49 27.9	N45 21.0
03	305 54.1	238 40.5	.. 19.9	314 03.1	.. 24.5	7 52.0	.. 11.2	2 28.4	.. 03.9	Denebola	182 28.7	N14 27.6
04	320 56.5	253 44.2	19.2	329 04.0	23.9	22 54.7	11.2	17 31.0	03.9	Diphda	348 51.2	S17 52.5
05	335 59.0	268 47.9	18.4	344 05.0	23.3	37 57.4	11.3	32 33.6	04.0			
06	351 01.5	283 51.6	N20 17.7	359 05.9	S 6 22.8	53 00.1	S21 11.3	47 36.2	S20 04.0	Dubhe	193 45.8	N61 38.8
07	6 03.9	298 55.2	17.0	14 06.9	22.2	68 02.7	11.4	62 38.8	04.0	Elnath	278 06.9	N28 37.3
08	21 06.4	313 58.9	16.3	29 07.8	21.6	83 05.4	11.4	77 41.4	04.1	Eltanin	90 43.4	N51 29.2
F 09	36 08.9	329 02.6	.. 15.6	44 08.7	.. 21.0	98 08.1	.. 11.4	92 43.9	.. 04.1	Enif	33 42.3	N 9 58.0
R 10	51 11.3	344 06.2	14.9	59 09.7	20.4	113 10.8	11.5	107 46.5	04.1	Fomalhaut	15 18.6	S29 30.8
I 11	66 13.8	359 09.9	14.2	74 10.6	19.9	128 13.5	11.5	122 49.1	04.2			
D 12	81 16.2	14 13.5	N20 13.5	89 11.6	S 6 19.3	143 16.2	S21 11.6	137 51.7	S20 04.2	Gacrux	171 55.4	S57 13.8
A 13	96 18.7	29 17.2	12.8	104 12.5	18.7	158 18.9	11.6	152 54.3	04.2	Gienah	175 47.3	S17 39.3
Y 14	111 21.2	44 20.8	12.1	119 13.5	18.1	173 21.6	11.7	167 56.9	04.2	Hadar	148 40.7	S60 28.4
15	126 23.6	59 24.5	.. 11.4	134 14.4	.. 17.6	188 24.2	.. 11.7	182 59.5	.. 04.3	Hamal	327 55.6	N23 33.3
16	141 26.1	74 28.1	10.7	149 15.4	17.0	203 26.9	11.8	198 02.1	04.3	Kaus Aust.	83 37.0	S34 22.4
17	156 28.6	89 31.7	10.0	164 16.3	16.4	218 29.6	11.8	213 04.7	04.3			
18	171 31.0	104 35.4	N20 09.2	179 17.3	S 6 15.8	233 32.3	S21 11.9	228 07.2	S20 04.4	Kochab	137 19.1	N74 04.6
19	186 33.5	119 39.0	08.5	194 18.2	15.2	248 35.0	11.9	243 09.8	04.4	Markab	13 33.5	N15 18.7
20	201 36.0	134 42.6	07.9	209 19.2	14.7	263 37.7	12.0	258 12.4	04.4	Menkar	314 10.3	N 4 10.0
21	216 38.4	149 46.2	.. 07.2	224 20.1	.. 14.1	278 40.4	.. 12.0	273 15.0	.. 04.5	Menkent	148 01.6	S36 28.2
22	231 40.9	164 49.8	06.5	239 21.1	13.5	293 43.1	12.1	288 17.6	04.5	Miaplacidus	221 39.3	S69 48.3
23	246 43.3	179 53.4	05.8	254 22.0	12.9	308 45.8	12.1	303 20.2	04.5			
13 00	261 45.8	194 57.1	N20 05.1	269 23.0	S 6 12.4	323 48.4	S21 12.2	318 22.8	S20 04.6	Mirfak	308 33.9	N49 55.7
01	276 48.3	210 00.7	04.4	284 24.0	11.8	338 51.1	12.2	333 25.4	04.6	Nunki	75 52.0	S26 16.2
02	291 50.7	225 04.3	03.7	299 24.9	11.2	353 53.8	12.2	348 28.0	04.6	Peacock	53 11.2	S56 39.9
03	306 53.2	240 07.9	.. 03.0	314 25.9	.. 10.6	8 56.5	.. 12.3	3 30.5	.. 04.6	Pollux	243 22.2	N27 58.6
04	321 55.7	255 11.5	02.3	329 26.8	10.1	23 59.2	12.3	18 33.1	04.7	Procyon	244 55.0	N 5 10.3
05	336 58.1	270 15.0	01.6	344 27.8	09.5	39 01.9	12.4	33 35.7	04.7			
06	352 00.5	285 18.6	N20 00.9	359 28.7	S 6 08.9	54 04.6	S21 12.4	48 38.3	S20 04.7	Rasalhague	96 01.6	N12 32.8
07	7 03.1	300 22.2	20 00.2	14 29.7	08.3	69 07.3	12.5	63 40.9	04.8	Regulus	207 38.5	N11 52.1
S 08	22 05.5	315 25.8	19 59.5	29 30.6	07.8	84 10.0	12.5	78 43.5	04.8	Rigel	281 07.8	S 8 10.8
A 09	37 08.0	330 29.4	.. 58.9	44 31.6	.. 07.2	99 12.7	.. 12.6	93 46.1	.. 04.8	Rigil Kent.	139 44.7	S60 55.2
T 10	52 10.5	345 32.9	58.2	59 32.5	06.6	114 15.4	12.6	108 48.7	04.9	Sabik	102 06.7	S15 44.9
U 11	67 12.9	0 36.5	57.5	74 33.5	06.0	129 18.1	12.7	123 51.3	04.9			
R 12	82 15.4	15 40.1	N19 56.8	89 34.4	S 6 05.4	144 20.8	S21 12.7	138 53.9	S20 04.9	Schedar	349 35.3	N56 38.6
D 13	97 17.8	30 43.6	56.1	104 35.4	04.9	159 23.4	12.8	153 56.5	05.0	Shaula	96 15.0	S37 07.0
A 14	112 20.3	45 47.2	55.4	119 36.3	04.3	174 26.1	12.8	168 59.1	05.0	Sirius	258 29.8	S16 44.8
Y 15	127 22.8	60 50.8	.. 54.8	134 37.3	.. 03.7	189 28.8	.. 12.9	184 01.6	.. 05.0	Spica	158 26.0	S11 16.0
16	142 25.2	75 54.3	54.1	149 38.3	03.1	204 31.5	12.9	199 04.2	05.0	Suhail	222 49.2	S43 31.1
17	157 27.7	90 57.9	53.4	164 39.2	02.6	219 34.2	13.0	214 06.8	05.1			
18	172 30.2	106 01.4	N19 52.7	179 40.2	S 6 02.0	234 36.9	S21 13.0	229 09.4	S20 05.1	Vega	80 35.3	N38 48.1
19	187 32.6	121 04.9	52.1	194 41.1	01.4	249 39.6	13.1	244 12.0	05.1	Zuben'ubi	136 59.8	S16 07.5
20	202 35.1	136 08.5	51.4	209 42.1	00.8	264 42.3	13.1	259 14.6	05.2		SHA	Mer. Pass.
21	217 37.6	151 12.0	.. 50.7	224 43.0	6 00.3	279 45.0	.. 13.2	274 17.2	.. 05.2	Venus	292 42.8	11 03
22	232 40.0	166 15.5	50.1	239 44.0	5 59.7	294 47.7	13.2	289 19.8	05.2	Mars	8 13.5	6 04
23	247 42.5	181 19.1	49.4	254 45.0	5 59.1	309 50.4	13.3	304 22.4	05.3	Jupiter	61 57.3	2 29
Mer. Pass.	h m 6 35.8	v 3.6	d 0.7	v 0.9	d 0.6	v 2.7	d 0.0	v 2.6	d 0.0	Saturn	56 34.0	2 50

UT	SUN GHA	SUN Dec	MOON GHA	v	MOON Dec	d	HP
d h	° ′	° ′	° ′	′	° ′	′	′
11 00	180 05.1	N23 05.9	290 54.2	12.3	S17 16.8	9.1	55.6
01	195 05.0	06.1	305 25.5	12.5	17 07.7	9.2	55.5
02	210 04.9	06.3	319 57.0	12.5	16 58.5	9.3	55.5
03	225 04.7 ..	06.4	334 28.5	12.6	16 49.2	9.4	55.5
04	240 04.6	06.6	349 00.1	12.7	16 39.8	9.4	55.5
05	255 04.5	06.8	3 31.8	12.8	16 30.4	9.4	55.4
06	270 04.4	N23 06.9	18 03.6	12.8	S16 21.0	9.6	55.4
07	285 04.2	07.1	32 35.4	12.9	16 11.4	9.6	55.4
T 08	300 04.1	07.3	47 07.3	13.0	16 01.8	9.7	55.4
H 09	315 04.0 ..	07.4	61 39.3	13.1	15 52.1	9.7	55.3
U 10	330 03.8	07.6	76 11.4	13.2	15 42.4	9.8	55.3
R 11	345 03.7	07.8	90 43.6	13.2	15 32.6	9.8	55.3
S 12	0 03.6	N23 07.9	105 15.8	13.4	S15 22.8	9.9	55.3
D 13	15 03.5	08.1	119 48.2	13.3	15 12.9	10.0	55.2
A 14	30 03.3	08.2	134 20.5	13.5	15 02.9	10.0	55.2
Y 15	45 03.2 ..	08.4	148 53.0	13.5	14 52.9	10.1	55.2
16	60 03.1	08.6	163 25.5	13.7	14 42.8	10.1	55.2
17	75 02.9	08.7	177 58.2	13.6	14 32.7	10.2	55.1
18	90 02.8	N23 08.9	192 30.8	13.8	S14 22.5	10.2	55.1
19	105 02.7	09.0	207 03.6	13.8	14 12.3	10.3	55.1
20	120 02.6	09.2	221 36.4	13.9	14 02.0	10.3	55.1
21	135 02.4 ..	09.3	236 09.3	14.0	13 51.7	10.4	55.0
22	150 02.3	09.5	250 42.3	14.0	13 41.3	10.5	55.0
23	165 02.2	09.7	265 15.3	14.1	13 30.8	10.5	55.0
12 00	180 02.0	N23 09.8	279 48.4	14.2	S13 20.3	10.5	55.0
01	195 01.9	10.0	294 21.6	14.2	13 09.8	10.5	55.0
02	210 01.8	10.1	308 54.8	14.3	12 59.2	10.6	54.9
03	225 01.7 ..	10.3	323 28.1	14.4	12 48.6	10.7	54.9
04	240 01.5	10.4	338 01.5	14.4	12 37.9	10.7	54.9
05	255 01.4	10.6	352 34.9	14.5	12 27.2	10.8	54.9
06	270 01.3	N23 10.7	7 08.4	14.6	S12 16.4	10.8	54.9
07	285 01.1	10.9	21 41.9	14.6	12 05.6	10.8	54.8
F 08	300 01.0	11.0	36 15.5	14.7	11 54.8	10.9	54.8
R 09	315 00.9 ..	11.2	50 49.2	14.7	11 43.9	10.9	54.8
I 10	330 00.8	11.3	65 22.9	14.8	11 33.0	11.0	54.8
D 11	345 00.6	11.4	79 56.7	14.8	11 22.0	11.0	54.8
A 12	0 00.5	N23 11.6	94 30.5	14.9	S11 11.0	11.0	54.7
Y 13	15 00.4	11.7	109 04.4	14.9	11 00.0	11.1	54.7
14	30 00.2	11.9	123 38.3	15.0	10 48.9	11.1	54.7
15	45 00.1 ..	12.0	138 12.3	15.1	10 37.8	11.2	54.7
16	60 00.0	12.2	152 46.4	15.1	10 26.6	11.2	54.7
17	74 59.8	12.3	167 20.5	15.2	10 15.4	11.2	54.7
18	89 59.7	N23 12.4	181 54.7	15.2	S10 04.2	11.2	54.6
19	104 59.6	12.6	196 28.9	15.2	9 53.0	11.3	54.6
20	119 59.4	12.7	211 03.1	15.3	9 41.7	11.3	54.6
21	134 59.3 ..	12.9	225 37.4	15.4	9 30.4	11.4	54.6
22	149 59.2	13.0	240 11.8	15.4	9 19.0	11.4	54.6
23	164 59.1	13.1	254 46.2	15.4	9 07.6	11.4	54.6
13 00	179 58.9	N23 13.3	269 20.6	15.5	S 8 56.2	11.4	54.5
01	194 58.8	13.4	283 55.1	15.5	8 44.8	11.5	54.5
02	209 58.7	13.5	298 29.6	15.6	8 33.3	11.5	54.5
03	224 58.5 ..	13.7	313 04.2	15.6	8 21.8	11.5	54.5
04	239 58.4	13.8	327 38.8	15.7	8 10.3	11.5	54.5
05	254 58.3	13.9	342 13.5	15.7	7 58.8	11.6	54.5
06	269 58.1	N23 14.1	356 48.2	15.7	S 7 47.2	11.6	54.5
07	284 58.0	14.2	11 22.9	15.8	7 35.6	11.6	54.5
S 08	299 57.9	14.3	25 57.7	15.8	7 24.0	11.7	54.4
A 09	314 57.7 ..	14.5	40 32.5	15.8	7 12.3	11.6	54.4
T 10	329 57.6	14.6	55 07.3	15.9	7 00.7	11.7	54.4
U 11	344 57.5	14.7	69 42.2	15.9	6 49.0	11.7	54.4
R 12	359 57.4	N23 14.9	84 17.1	16.0	S 6 37.3	11.7	54.4
D 13	14 57.2	15.0	98 52.1	15.9	6 25.6	11.8	54.4
A 14	29 57.1	15.1	113 27.0	16.0	6 13.8	11.8	54.4
Y 15	44 57.0 ..	15.2	128 02.0	16.1	6 02.0	11.7	54.4
16	59 56.8	15.4	142 37.1	16.0	5 50.3	11.8	54.4
17	74 56.7	15.5	157 12.1	16.1	5 38.5	11.9	54.3
18	89 56.6	N23 15.6	171 47.2	16.2	S 5 26.6	11.8	54.3
19	104 56.5	15.7	186 22.4	16.1	5 14.8	11.9	54.3
20	119 56.3	15.8	200 57.5	16.2	5 02.9	11.8	54.3
21	134 56.2 ..	16.0	215 32.7	16.2	4 51.1	11.9	54.3
22	149 56.0	16.1	230 07.9	16.2	4 39.2	11.9	54.3
23	164 55.9	16.2	244 43.1	16.2	S 4 27.3	11.9	54.3
	SD 15.8	d 0.1	SD 15.1		14.9		14.8

Lat.	Naut.	Civil	Sunrise	Moonrise 11	12	13	14
°	h m	h m	h m	h m	h m	h m	h m
N 72	☐	☐	☐	03 19	02 26	01 58	01 36
N 70	☐	☐	☐	02 30	02 03	01 45	01 30
68	☐	☐	☐	01 58	01 45	01 35	01 26
66	////	////	00 04	01 35	01 30	01 26	01 22
64	////	////	01 36	01 16	01 18	01 19	01 19
62	////	////	02 12	01 01	01 08	01 12	01 16
60	////	00 58	02 37	00 48	00 59	01 07	01 13
N 58	////	01 44	02 57	00 37	00 51	01 02	01 11
56	////	02 12	03 14	00 28	00 44	00 58	01 09
54	00 53	02 34	03 28	00 19	00 38	00 54	01 08
52	01 35	02 52	03 40	00 11	00 33	00 50	01 06
50	02 02	03 06	03 51	00 04	00 27	00 47	01 04
45	02 46	03 36	04 13	24 17	00 17	00 40	01 01
N 40	03 16	03 58	04 31	24 07	00 07	00 34	00 59
35	03 39	04 16	04 45	23 59	24 29	00 29	00 56
30	03 58	04 31	04 58	23 53	24 24	00 24	00 54
20	04 26	04 56	05 20	23 41	24 17	00 17	00 51
N 10	04 49	05 16	05 39	23 30	24 10	00 10	00 47
0	05 08	05 34	05 56	23 20	24 03	00 03	00 44
S 10	05 24	05 51	06 14	23 10	23 57	24 41	00 41
20	05 40	06 08	06 32	22 59	23 50	24 38	00 38
30	05 57	06 27	06 53	22 47	23 42	24 35	00 35
35	06 05	06 37	07 05	22 40	23 37	24 32	00 32
40	06 15	06 49	07 19	22 32	23 32	24 30	00 30
45	06 25	07 02	07 36	22 22	23 26	24 27	00 27
S 50	06 36	07 18	07 56	22 11	23 18	24 24	00 24
52	06 42	07 25	08 06	22 05	23 15	24 23	00 23
54	06 47	07 33	08 17	22 00	23 11	24 21	00 21
56	06 53	07 42	08 29	21 53	23 07	24 19	00 19
58	07 00	07 52	08 44	21 46	23 02	24 17	00 17
S 60	07 07	08 04	09 01	21 37	22 57	24 15	00 15

Lat.	Sunset	Civil	Naut.	Moonset 11	12	13	14
°	h m	h m	h m	h m	h m	h m	h m
N 72	☐	☐	☐	06 30	08 56	10 53	12 41
N 70	☐	☐	☐	07 17	09 17	11 04	12 44
68	☐	☐	☐	07 48	09 34	11 12	12 46
66	☐	☐	☐	08 10	09 47	11 19	12 48
64	22 25	////	////	08 28	09 58	11 25	12 49
62	21 49	////	////	08 42	10 08	11 30	12 50
60	21 23	23 04	////	08 54	10 16	11 34	12 51
N 58	21 03	22 17	////	09 04	10 22	11 38	12 52
56	20 47	21 48	////	09 13	10 29	11 42	12 53
54	20 32	21 27	23 09	09 21	10 34	11 45	12 54
52	20 20	21 09	22 26	09 29	10 39	11 48	12 55
50	20 10	20 54	21 59	09 35	10 43	11 50	12 55
45	19 47	20 25	21 14	09 49	10 53	11 55	12 57
N 40	19 29	20 02	20 44	10 00	11 01	12 00	12 58
35	19 15	19 44	20 21	10 10	11 08	12 04	12 59
30	19 02	19 29	20 02	10 18	11 14	12 07	13 00
20	18 40	19 04	19 34	10 32	11 24	12 13	13 01
N 10	18 21	18 44	19 11	10 45	11 33	12 18	13 03
0	18 04	18 26	18 52	10 57	11 41	12 23	13 04
S 10	17 46	18 09	18 35	11 08	11 49	12 28	13 05
20	17 28	17 52	18 19	11 20	11 58	12 33	13 06
30	17 07	17 33	18 03	11 34	12 08	12 39	13 08
35	16 55	17 23	17 55	11 42	12 14	12 42	13 08
40	16 41	17 11	17 45	11 52	12 20	12 45	13 09
45	16 24	16 58	17 35	12 02	12 27	12 50	13 10
S 50	16 04	16 42	17 23	12 15	12 36	12 55	13 12
52	15 54	16 35	17 18	12 21	12 40	12 57	13 12
54	15 43	16 27	17 13	12 28	12 45	13 00	13 13
56	15 30	16 18	17 07	12 35	12 50	13 02	13 13
58	15 16	16 08	17 00	12 43	12 55	13 05	13 14
S 60	14 59	15 56	16 53	12 52	13 02	13 09	13 15

Day	SUN Eqn. of Time 00h	SUN Eqn. of Time 12h	SUN Mer. Pass.	MOON Mer. Pass. Upper	MOON Mer. Pass. Lower	Age	Phase
d	m s	m s	h m	h m	h m	d	%
11	00 21	00 15	12 00	04 45	17 08	20	67
12	00 08	00 02	12 00	05 31	17 52	21	57
13	00 04	00 10	12 00	06 13	18 34	22	48

UT	ARIES	VENUS −4·3		MARS −0·2		JUPITER −2·7		SATURN +0·3		STARS		
	GHA	GHA	Dec	GHA	Dec	GHA	Dec	GHA	Dec	Name	SHA	Dec
d h	° ′	° ′	° ′	° ′	° ′	° ′	° ′	° ′	° ′		° ′	° ′
14 00	262 45.0	196 22.6	N19 48.7	269 45.9	S 5 58.5	324 53.1	S21 13.3	319 25.0	S20 05.3	Acamar	315 15.0	S40 13.4
01	277 47.4	211 26.1	48.0	284 46.9	58.0	339 55.8	13.3	334 27.6	05.3	Achernar	335 23.4	S57 07.9
02	292 49.9	226 29.6	47.4	299 47.8	57.4	354 58.5	13.4	349 30.2	05.4	Acrux	173 03.8	S63 12.9
03	307 52.3	241 33.1	.. 46.7	314 48.8	.. 56.8	10 01.2	.. 13.4	4 32.8	.. 05.4	Adhara	255 09.1	S29 00.1
04	322 54.8	256 36.6	46.1	329 49.7	56.2	25 03.9	13.5	19 35.3	05.4	Aldebaran	290 44.2	N16 32.8
05	337 57.3	271 40.1	45.4	344 50.7	55.7	40 06.6	13.5	34 37.9	05.5			
06	352 59.7	286 43.6	N19 44.7	359 51.7	S 5 55.1	55 09.3	S21 13.6	49 40.5	S20 05.5	Alioth	166 16.2	N55 51.3
07	8 02.2	301 47.1	44.1	14 52.6	54.5	70 12.0	13.6	64 43.1	05.5	Alkaid	152 54.8	N49 13.0
08	23 04.7	316 50.6	43.4	29 53.6	53.9	85 14.7	13.7	79 45.7	05.5	Alnair	27 37.5	S46 51.5
S 09	38 07.1	331 54.1	.. 42.8	44 54.5	.. 53.3	100 17.4	.. 13.7	94 48.3	.. 05.6	Alnilam	275 41.8	S 1 11.5
U 10	53 09.6	346 57.6	42.1	59 55.5	52.8	115 20.1	13.8	109 50.9	05.6	Alphard	217 51.6	S 8 44.9
N 11	68 12.1	2 01.1	41.4	74 56.5	52.2	130 22.8	13.8	124 53.5	05.6			
D 12	83 14.5	17 04.5	N19 40.8	89 57.4	S 5 51.6	145 25.5	S21 13.9	139 56.1	S20 05.7	Alphecca	126 06.6	N26 39.0
A 13	98 17.0	32 08.0	40.1	104 58.4	51.1	160 28.2	13.9	154 58.7	05.7	Alpheratz	357 38.6	N29 11.9
Y 14	113 19.4	47 11.5	39.5	119 59.3	50.5	175 30.9	14.0	170 01.3	05.7	Altair	62 03.3	N 8 55.3
15	128 21.9	62 14.9	.. 38.8	135 00.3	.. 49.9	190 33.6	.. 14.0	185 03.9	.. 05.8	Ankaa	353 11.0	S42 11.6
16	143 24.4	77 18.4	38.2	150 01.3	49.3	205 36.3	14.1	200 06.5	05.8	Antares	112 20.0	S26 28.5
17	158 26.8	92 21.9	37.5	165 02.2	48.8	220 39.0	14.1	215 09.1	05.8			
18	173 29.3	107 25.3	N19 36.9	180 03.2	S 5 48.2	235 41.7	S21 14.2	230 11.7	S20 05.9	Arcturus	145 51.1	N19 04.8
19	188 31.8	122 28.8	36.2	195 04.1	47.6	250 44.4	14.2	245 14.3	05.9	Atria	107 16.9	S69 03.8
20	203 34.2	137 32.2	35.6	210 05.1	47.0	265 47.1	14.3	260 16.9	05.9	Avior	234 16.6	S59 34.7
21	218 36.7	152 35.6	.. 35.0	225 06.1	.. 46.5	280 49.8	.. 14.3	275 19.5	.. 06.0	Bellatrix	278 27.2	N 6 22.0
22	233 39.2	167 39.1	34.3	240 07.0	45.9	295 52.5	14.4	290 22.1	06.0	Betelgeuse	270 56.4	N 7 24.5
23	248 41.6	182 42.5	33.7	255 08.0	45.3	310 55.2	14.4	305 24.7	06.0			
15 00	263 44.1	197 45.9	N19 33.0	270 09.0	S 5 44.7	325 57.9	S21 14.5	320 27.2	S20 06.1	Canopus	263 54.6	S52 42.5
01	278 46.6	212 49.4	32.4	285 09.9	44.2	341 00.6	14.5	335 29.8	06.1	Capella	280 27.8	N46 00.9
02	293 49.0	227 52.8	31.8	300 10.9	43.6	356 03.3	14.6	350 32.4	06.1	Deneb	49 27.9	N45 21.0
03	308 51.5	242 56.2	.. 31.1	315 11.8	.. 43.0	11 06.0	.. 14.6	5 35.0	.. 06.1	Denebola	182 28.7	N14 27.6
04	323 53.9	257 59.6	30.5	330 12.8	42.4	26 08.7	14.7	20 37.6	06.2	Diphda	348 51.1	S17 52.5
05	338 56.4	273 03.0	29.9	345 13.8	41.9	41 11.4	14.7	35 40.2	06.2			
06	353 58.9	288 06.4	N19 29.2	0 14.7	S 5 41.3	56 14.1	S21 14.8	50 42.8	S20 06.2	Dubhe	193 45.8	N61 38.8
07	9 01.3	303 09.8	28.6	15 15.7	40.7	71 16.8	14.8	65 45.4	06.3	Elnath	278 06.9	N28 37.3
08	24 03.8	318 13.2	28.0	30 16.7	40.1	86 19.6	14.9	80 48.0	06.3	Eltanin	90 43.4	N51 29.2
M 09	39 06.3	333 16.6	.. 27.3	45 17.6	.. 39.6	101 22.3	.. 14.9	95 50.6	.. 06.3	Enif	33 42.2	N 9 58.0
O 10	54 08.7	348 20.0	26.7	60 18.6	39.0	116 25.0	15.0	110 53.2	06.4	Fomalhaut	15 18.6	S29 30.8
N 11	69 11.2	3 23.4	26.1	75 19.6	38.4	131 27.7	15.0	125 55.8	06.4			
D 12	84 13.7	18 26.8	N19 25.5	90 20.5	S 5 37.8	146 30.4	S21 15.1	140 58.4	S20 06.4	Gacrux	171 55.5	S57 13.8
A 13	99 16.1	33 30.2	24.9	105 21.5	37.3	161 33.1	15.1	156 01.0	06.5	Gienah	175 47.3	S17 39.3
Y 14	114 18.6	48 33.5	24.2	120 22.5	36.7	176 35.8	15.2	171 03.6	06.5	Hadar	148 40.7	S60 28.4
15	129 21.1	63 36.9	.. 23.6	135 23.4	.. 36.1	191 38.5	.. 15.2	186 06.2	.. 06.5	Hamal	327 55.5	N23 33.3
16	144 23.5	78 40.3	23.0	150 24.4	35.5	206 41.2	15.3	201 08.8	06.6	Kaus Aust.	83 37.0	S34 22.4
17	159 26.0	93 43.6	22.4	165 25.4	35.0	221 43.9	15.3	216 11.4	06.6			
18	174 28.4	108 47.0	N19 21.8	180 26.3	S 5 34.4	236 46.6	S21 15.4	231 14.0	S20 06.6	Kochab	137 19.1	N74 04.6
19	189 30.9	123 50.4	21.1	195 27.3	33.8	251 49.3	15.4	246 16.6	06.7	Markab	13 33.5	N15 18.7
20	204 33.4	138 53.7	20.5	210 28.3	33.3	266 52.0	15.5	261 19.2	06.7	Menkar	314 10.3	N 4 10.0
21	219 35.8	153 57.1	.. 19.9	225 29.2	.. 32.7	281 54.7	.. 15.5	276 21.8	.. 06.7	Menkent	148 01.7	S36 28.2
22	234 38.3	169 00.4	19.3	240 30.2	32.1	296 57.5	15.6	291 24.4	06.8	Miaplacidus	221 39.4	S69 48.3
23	249 40.8	184 03.7	18.7	255 31.2	31.5	312 00.2	15.6	306 27.0	06.8			
16 00	264 43.2	199 07.1	N19 18.1	270 32.1	S 5 31.0	327 02.9	S21 15.7	321 29.6	S20 06.8	Mirfak	308 33.9	N49 55.7
01	279 45.7	214 10.4	17.5	285 33.1	30.4	342 05.6	15.7	336 32.2	06.9	Nunki	75 52.0	S26 16.2
02	294 48.2	229 13.7	16.9	300 34.1	29.8	357 08.3	15.8	351 34.8	06.9	Peacock	53 11.2	S56 39.9
03	309 50.6	244 17.1	.. 16.3	315 35.0	.. 29.2	12 11.0	.. 15.8	6 37.4	.. 06.9	Pollux	243 22.2	N27 58.6
04	324 53.1	259 20.4	15.7	330 36.0	28.7	27 13.7	15.9	21 40.0	07.0	Procyon	244 55.0	N 5 10.3
05	339 55.5	274 23.7	15.1	345 37.0	28.1	42 16.4	15.9	36 42.6	07.0			
06	354 58.0	289 27.0	N19 14.5	0 38.0	S 5 27.5	57 19.1	S21 16.0	51 45.2	S20 07.0	Rasalhague	96 01.6	N12 32.8
07	10 00.5	304 30.3	13.9	15 38.9	27.0	72 21.9	16.0	66 47.8	07.1	Regulus	207 38.5	N11 52.1
T 08	25 02.9	319 33.6	13.3	30 39.9	26.4	87 24.6	16.1	81 50.4	07.1	Rigel	281 07.8	S 8 10.8
U 09	40 05.4	334 36.9	.. 12.7	45 40.9	.. 25.8	102 27.3	.. 16.1	96 53.0	.. 07.1	Rigil Kent.	139 44.8	S60 55.2
E 10	55 07.9	349 40.2	12.1	60 41.8	25.2	117 30.0	16.2	111 55.6	07.2	Sabik	102 06.7	S15 44.9
S 11	70 10.3	4 43.5	11.5	75 42.8	24.7	132 32.7	16.2	126 58.2	07.2			
D 12	85 12.8	19 46.8	N19 10.9	90 43.8	S 5 24.1	147 35.4	S21 16.3	142 00.8	S20 07.2	Schedar	349 35.2	N56 38.6
A 13	100 15.3	34 50.1	10.3	105 44.8	23.5	162 38.1	16.3	157 03.4	07.3	Shaula	96 14.9	S37 07.0
Y 14	115 17.7	49 53.3	09.7	120 45.7	22.9	177 40.8	16.4	172 06.0	07.3	Sirius	258 29.8	S16 44.8
15	130 20.2	64 56.6	.. 09.1	135 46.7	.. 22.4	192 43.6	.. 16.4	187 08.6	.. 07.3	Spica	158 26.0	S11 16.0
16	145 22.7	79 59.9	08.6	150 47.7	21.8	207 46.3	16.5	202 11.2	07.3	Suhail	222 49.2	S43 31.1
17	160 25.1	95 03.1	08.0	165 48.7	21.2	222 49.0	16.5	217 13.8	07.4			
18	175 27.6	110 06.4	N19 07.4	180 49.6	S 5 20.7	237 51.7	S21 16.6	232 16.4	S20 07.4	Vega	80 35.3	N38 48.2
19	190 30.0	125 09.7	06.8	195 50.6	20.1	252 54.4	16.6	247 19.0	07.4	Zuben'ubi	136 59.8	S16 07.5
20	205 32.5	140 12.9	06.2	210 51.6	19.5	267 57.1	16.7	262 21.6	07.5		SHA	Mer.Pass.
21	220 35.0	155 16.2	.. 05.6	225 52.5	.. 18.9	282 59.8	.. 16.7	277 24.2	.. 07.5		° ′	h m
22	235 37.4	170 19.4	05.1	240 53.5	18.4	298 02.6	16.8	292 26.8	07.5	Venus	294 01.9	10 46
23	250 39.9	185 22.7	04.5	255 54.5	17.8	313 05.3	16.8	307 29.4	07.6	Mars	6 24.9	5 59
	h m									Jupiter	62 13.8	2 16
Mer.Pass. 6 24.0		v 3.4	d 0.6	v 1.0	d 0.6	v 2.7	d 0.0	v 2.6	d 0.0	Saturn	56 43.2	2 38

UT	SUN GHA	SUN Dec	MOON GHA	MOON v	MOON Dec	MOON d	MOON HP
d h	° ′	° ′	° ′	′	° ′	′	′
14 00	179 55.8	N23 16.3	259 18.3	16.3	S 4 15.4	12.0	54.3
01	194 55.6	16.4	273 53.6	16.3	4 03.4	11.9	54.3
02	209 55.5	16.6	288 28.9	16.3	3 51.5	11.9	54.3
03	224 55.4	.. 16.7	303 04.2	16.3	3 39.6	12.0	54.3
04	239 55.2	16.8	317 39.5	16.3	3 27.6	12.0	54.3
05	254 55.1	16.9	332 14.8	16.3	3 15.6	12.0	54.3
06	269 55.0	N23 17.0	346 50.1	16.4	S 3 03.6	12.0	54.2
07	284 54.8	17.1	1 25.5	16.4	2 51.6	12.0	54.2
08	299 54.7	17.3	16 00.9	16.4	2 39.6	12.0	54.2
S 09	314 54.6	.. 17.4	30 36.3	16.4	2 27.6	12.0	54.2
U 10	329 54.4	17.5	45 11.7	16.4	2 15.6	12.0	54.2
N 11	344 54.3	17.6	59 47.1	16.4	2 03.6	12.0	54.2
D 12	359 54.2	N23 17.7	74 22.5	16.4	S 1 51.6	12.1	54.2
A 13	14 54.0	17.8	88 57.9	16.5	1 39.5	12.0	54.2
Y 14	29 53.9	17.9	103 33.4	16.4	1 27.5	12.0	54.2
15	44 53.8	.. 18.0	118 08.8	16.5	1 15.5	12.1	54.2
16	59 53.6	18.1	132 44.3	16.4	1 03.4	12.0	54.2
17	74 53.5	18.2	147 19.7	16.5	0 51.4	12.1	54.2
18	89 53.4	N23 18.4	161 55.2	16.5	S 0 39.3	12.1	54.2
19	104 53.2	18.5	176 30.7	16.4	0 27.2	12.0	54.2
20	119 53.1	18.6	191 06.1	16.5	0 15.2	12.1	54.2
21	134 53.0	.. 18.7	205 41.6	16.4	S 0 03.1	12.0	54.2
22	149 52.8	18.8	220 17.0	16.5	N 0 08.9	12.1	54.2
23	164 52.7	18.9	234 52.5	16.5	0 21.0	12.0	54.2
15 00	179 52.6	N23 19.0	249 28.0	16.4	N 0 33.0	12.1	54.2
01	194 52.4	19.1	264 03.4	16.5	0 45.1	12.0	54.2
02	209 52.3	19.2	278 38.9	16.4	0 57.2	12.0	54.2
03	224 52.2	.. 19.3	293 14.3	16.5	1 09.2	12.1	54.2
04	239 52.0	19.4	307 49.8	16.4	1 21.3	12.0	54.2
05	254 51.9	19.5	322 25.2	16.5	1 33.3	12.0	54.2
06	269 51.8	N23 19.6	337 00.7	16.4	N 1 45.3	12.1	54.2
07	284 51.6	19.7	351 36.1	16.4	1 57.4	12.0	54.2
08	299 51.5	19.8	6 11.5	16.4	2 09.4	12.0	54.2
M 09	314 51.4	.. 19.9	20 46.9	16.4	2 21.4	12.0	54.2
O 10	329 51.2	20.0	35 22.3	16.4	2 33.4	12.0	54.2
N 11	344 51.1	20.0	49 57.7	16.3	2 45.4	12.0	54.2
D 12	359 51.0	N23 20.1	64 33.0	16.4	N 2 57.4	12.0	54.2
A 13	14 50.8	20.2	79 08.4	16.3	3 09.4	12.0	54.2
Y 14	29 50.7	20.3	93 43.7	16.3	3 21.4	12.0	54.2
15	44 50.6	.. 20.4	108 19.0	16.3	3 33.4	11.9	54.2
16	59 50.4	20.5	122 54.3	16.3	3 45.3	12.0	54.2
17	74 50.3	20.6	137 29.6	16.3	3 57.3	11.9	54.2
18	89 50.1	N23 20.7	152 04.9	16.2	N 4 09.2	12.0	54.2
19	104 50.0	20.8	166 40.1	16.2	4 21.2	11.9	54.2
20	119 49.9	20.9	181 15.3	16.2	4 33.1	11.9	54.2
21	134 49.7	.. 21.0	195 50.5	16.2	4 45.0	11.8	54.3
22	149 49.6	21.0	210 25.7	16.1	4 56.8	11.9	54.3
23	164 49.5	21.1	225 00.8	16.2	5 08.7	11.9	54.3
16 00	179 49.3	N23 21.2	239 36.0	16.1	N 5 20.6	11.8	54.3
01	194 49.2	21.3	254 11.1	16.0	5 32.4	11.8	54.3
02	209 49.1	21.4	268 46.1	16.1	5 44.2	11.8	54.3
03	224 48.9	.. 21.5	283 21.2	16.0	5 56.0	11.8	54.3
04	239 48.8	21.5	297 56.2	16.0	6 07.8	11.8	54.3
05	254 48.7	21.6	312 31.2	15.9	6 19.6	11.7	54.3
06	269 48.5	N23 21.7	327 06.1	15.9	N 6 31.3	11.7	54.3
07	284 48.4	21.8	341 41.0	15.9	6 43.0	11.7	54.3
T 08	299 48.3	21.9	356 15.9	15.9	6 54.7	11.7	54.3
U 09	314 48.1	.. 21.9	10 50.8	15.8	7 06.4	11.7	54.3
E 10	329 48.0	22.0	25 25.6	15.8	7 18.1	11.6	54.3
S 11	344 47.8	22.1	40 00.4	15.8	7 29.7	11.6	54.4
D 12	359 47.7	N23 22.2	54 35.2	15.7	N 7 41.3	11.6	54.4
A 13	14 47.6	22.2	69 09.9	15.6	7 52.9	11.5	54.4
Y 14	29 47.4	22.3	83 44.5	15.7	8 04.4	11.6	54.4
15	44 47.3	.. 22.4	98 19.2	15.6	8 16.0	11.5	54.4
16	59 47.2	22.5	112 53.8	15.5	8 27.5	11.5	54.4
17	74 47.0	22.5	127 28.3	15.6	8 39.0	11.4	54.4
18	89 46.9	N23 22.6	142 02.9	15.4	N 8 50.4	11.4	54.4
19	104 46.8	22.7	156 37.3	15.5	9 01.8	11.4	54.4
20	119 46.6	22.8	171 11.8	15.3	9 13.2	11.4	54.4
21	134 46.5	.. 22.8	185 46.1	15.4	9 24.6	11.3	54.5
22	149 46.4	22.9	200 20.5	15.3	9 35.9	11.3	54.5
23	164 46.2	23.0	214 54.8	15.2	N 9 47.2	11.3	54.5
	SD 15.8	d 0.1	SD 14.8		14.8		14.8

Lat.	Twilight Naut.	Twilight Civil	Sunrise	Moonrise 14	Moonrise 15	Moonrise 16	Moonrise 17
°	h m	h m	h m	h m	h m	h m	h m
N 72	☐	☐	☐	01 36	01 15	00 55	00 32
N 70	☐	☐	☐	01 30	01 16	01 03	00 47
68	☐	☐	☐	01 26	01 17	01 09	01 00
66	☐	☐	☐	01 22	01 18	01 14	01 10
64	////	////	01 33	01 19	01 18	01 18	01 18
62	////	////	02 10	01 16	01 19	01 22	01 26
60	////	00 53	02 36	01 13	01 19	01 25	01 32
N 58	////	01 41	02 56	01 11	01 20	01 28	01 38
56	////	02 11	03 13	01 09	01 20	01 31	01 43
54	00 48	02 33	03 27	01 08	01 20	01 34	01 48
52	01 33	02 51	03 39	01 06	01 21	01 36	01 52
50	02 01	03 06	03 50	01 04	01 21	01 38	01 56
45	02 46	03 35	04 13	01 01	01 22	01 42	02 04
N 40	03 16	03 58	04 31	00 59	01 22	01 46	02 11
35	03 39	04 16	04 46	00 56	01 23	01 49	02 17
30	03 58	04 31	04 59	00 54	01 23	01 52	02 22
20	04 27	04 56	05 21	00 51	01 24	01 57	02 31
N 10	04 49	05 16	05 39	00 47	01 24	02 01	02 40
0	05 08	05 34	05 57	00 44	01 25	02 05	02 47
S 10	05 25	05 51	06 14	00 41	01 25	02 10	02 55
20	05 41	06 09	06 33	00 38	01 26	02 14	03 03
30	05 58	06 28	06 54	00 35	01 27	02 19	03 13
35	06 06	06 38	07 06	00 32	01 27	02 22	03 18
40	06 16	06 50	07 20	00 30	01 28	02 26	03 25
45	06 26	07 03	07 37	00 27	01 28	02 30	03 32
S 50	06 38	07 19	07 58	00 24	01 29	02 35	03 41
52	06 43	07 27	08 08	00 23	01 30	02 37	03 45
54	06 49	07 35	08 19	00 21	01 30	02 39	03 50
56	06 55	07 44	08 31	00 19	01 30	02 42	03 55
58	07 02	07 54	08 46	00 17	01 31	02 45	04 00
S 60	07 09	08 06	09 03	00 15	01 31	02 48	04 07

Lat.	Sunset	Twilight Civil	Twilight Naut.	Moonset 14	Moonset 15	Moonset 16	Moonset 17
°	h m	h m	h m	h m	h m	h m	h m
N 72	☐	☐	☐	12 41	14 27	16 17	18 19
N 70	☐	☐	☐	12 44	14 23	16 04	17 53
68	☐	☐	☐	12 46	14 19	15 53	17 33
66	☐	☐	☐	12 48	14 15	15 45	17 17
64	22 29	////	////	12 49	14 13	15 37	17 05
62	21 52	////	////	12 50	14 10	15 31	16 54
60	21 26	23 10	////	12 51	14 08	15 26	16 45
N 58	21 05	22 20	////	12 52	14 06	15 21	16 37
56	20 48	21 51	////	12 53	14 05	15 17	16 30
54	20 34	21 29	23 14	12 54	14 03	15 13	16 24
52	20 22	21 11	22 29	12 55	14 02	15 09	16 18
50	20 11	20 56	22 01	12 55	14 01	15 06	16 13
45	19 49	20 26	21 16	12 57	13 58	15 00	16 02
N 40	19 31	20 04	20 45	12 58	13 56	14 54	15 54
35	19 16	19 45	20 22	12 59	13 54	14 49	15 46
30	19 03	19 30	20 04	13 00	13 52	14 45	15 39
20	18 41	19 05	19 35	13 01	13 49	14 38	15 28
N 10	18 22	18 45	19 12	13 03	13 47	14 31	15 18
0	18 04	18 27	18 53	13 04	13 44	14 25	15 08
S 10	17 47	18 10	18 36	13 05	13 42	14 19	14 59
20	17 28	17 52	18 20	13 06	13 39	14 13	14 49
30	17 07	17 34	18 03	13 08	13 36	14 06	14 37
35	16 55	17 23	17 55	13 08	13 35	14 02	14 31
40	16 41	17 11	17 45	13 09	13 33	13 57	14 23
45	16 24	16 58	17 35	13 10	13 31	13 52	14 15
S 50	16 03	16 42	17 23	13 12	13 28	13 45	14 04
52	15 54	16 34	17 18	13 12	13 27	13 42	14 00
54	15 42	16 26	17 12	13 13	13 26	13 39	13 54
56	15 30	16 17	17 06	13 13	13 24	13 36	13 49
58	15 15	16 07	17 00	13 14	13 23	13 32	13 42
S 60	14 58	15 55	16 52	13 15	13 21	13 27	13 35

Day	SUN Eqn. of Time 00ʰ	SUN Eqn. of Time 12ʰ	SUN Mer. Pass.	MOON Mer. Pass. Upper	MOON Mer. Pass. Lower	Age	Phase
d	m s	m s	h m	h m	h m	d %	
14	00 17	00 23	12 00	06 54	19 14	23 38	
15	00 29	00 36	12 01	07 35	19 55	24 29	
16	00 42	00 49	12 01	08 15	20 36	25 21	

UT	ARIES GHA	VENUS −4.4 GHA	VENUS Dec	MARS −0.3 GHA	MARS Dec	JUPITER −2.7 GHA	JUPITER Dec	SATURN +0.3 GHA	SATURN Dec	STARS Name	SHA	Dec
17 00	265 42.4	200 25.9	N19 03.9	270 55.5	S 5 17.2	328 08.0	S21 16.9	322 32.0	S20 07.6	Acamar	315 15.0	S40 13.4
01	280 44.8	215 29.1	03.3	285 56.4	16.7	343 10.7	16.9	337 34.6	07.6	Achernar	335 23.4	S57 07.9
02	295 47.3	230 32.4	02.8	300 57.4	16.1	358 13.4	17.0	352 37.2	07.7	Acrux	173 03.8	S63 12.9
03	310 49.8	245 35.6 ..	02.2	315 58.4 ..	15.5	13 16.1 ..	17.0	7 39.8 ..	07.7	Adhara	255 09.1	S29 00.1
04	325 52.2	260 38.8	01.6	330 59.4	14.9	28 18.9	17.1	22 42.4	07.7	Aldebaran	290 44.2	N16 32.8
05	340 54.7	275 42.0	01.1	346 00.3	14.4	43 21.6	17.1	37 45.0	07.8			
W 06	355 57.2	290 45.2	N19 00.5	1 01.3	S 5 13.8	58 24.3	S21 17.2	52 47.6	S20 07.8	Alioth	166 16.2	N55 51.3
E 07	10 59.6	305 48.4	18 59.9	16 02.3	13.2	73 27.0	17.2	67 50.2	07.8	Alkaid	152 54.8	N49 13.0
D 08	26 02.1	320 51.6	59.4	31 03.3	12.7	88 29.7	17.3	82 52.8	07.9	Alnair	27 37.4	S46 51.5
N 09	41 04.5	335 54.8 ..	58.8	46 04.3 ..	12.1	103 32.4 ..	17.3	97 55.4 ..	07.9	Alnilam	275 41.8	S 1 11.4
E 10	56 07.0	350 58.0	58.3	61 05.2	11.5	118 35.2	17.4	112 58.0	07.9	Alphard	217 51.6	S 8 44.9
S 11	71 09.5	6 01.2	57.7	76 06.2	10.9	133 37.9	17.4	128 00.6	08.0			
D 12	86 11.9	21 04.4	N18 57.1	91 07.2	S 5 10.4	148 40.6	S21 17.5	143 03.3	S20 08.0	Alphecca	126 06.6	N26 39.0
A 13	101 14.4	36 07.6	56.6	106 08.2	09.8	163 43.3	17.5	158 05.9	08.0	Alpheratz	357 38.6	N29 11.9
Y 14	116 16.9	51 10.8	56.0	121 09.1	09.2	178 46.0	17.6	173 08.5	08.1	Altair	62 03.2	N 8 55.3
15	131 19.3	66 14.0 ..	55.5	136 10.1 ..	08.7	193 48.8 ..	17.6	188 11.1 ..	08.1	Ankaa	353 11.0	S42 11.6
16	146 21.8	81 17.1	54.9	151 11.1	08.1	208 51.5	17.7	203 13.7	08.1	Antares	112 20.0	S26 28.5
17	161 24.3	96 20.3	54.4	166 12.1	07.5	223 54.2	17.7	218 16.3	08.2			
18	176 26.7	111 23.5	N18 53.8	181 13.1	S 5 06.9	238 56.9	S21 17.8	233 18.9	S20 08.2	Arcturus	145 51.1	N19 04.8
19	191 29.2	126 26.6	53.3	196 14.0	06.4	253 59.6	17.8	248 21.5	08.2	Atria	107 16.9	S69 03.8
20	206 31.6	141 29.8	52.7	211 15.0	05.8	269 02.4	17.9	263 24.1	08.3	Avior	234 16.6	S59 34.7
21	221 34.1	156 32.9 ..	52.2	226 16.0 ..	05.2	284 05.1 ..	17.9	278 26.7 ..	08.3	Bellatrix	278 27.2	N 6 22.0
22	236 36.6	171 36.1	51.6	241 17.0	04.7	299 07.8	18.0	293 29.3	08.3	Betelgeuse	270 56.4	N 7 24.5
23	251 39.0	186 39.2	51.1	256 18.0	04.1	314 10.5	18.0	308 31.9	08.4			
18 00	266 41.5	201 42.4	N18 50.6	271 18.9	S 5 03.5	329 13.2	S21 18.1	323 34.5	S20 08.4	Canopus	263 54.6	S52 42.5
01	281 44.0	216 45.5	50.0	286 19.9	03.0	344 16.0	18.2	338 37.1	08.4	Capella	280 27.8	N46 00.9
02	296 46.4	231 48.6	49.5	301 20.9	02.4	359 18.7	18.2	353 39.7	08.5	Deneb	49 27.9	N45 21.0
03	311 48.9	246 51.7 ..	49.0	316 21.9 ..	01.8	14 21.4 ..	18.3	8 42.3 ..	08.5	Denebola	182 28.7	N14 27.7
04	326 51.4	261 54.9	48.4	331 22.9	01.2	29 24.1	18.3	23 44.9	08.5	Diphda	348 51.1	S17 52.5
05	341 53.8	276 58.0	47.9	346 23.9	00.7	44 26.9	18.4	38 47.5	08.6			
T 06	356 56.3	292 01.1	N18 47.4	1 24.8	S 5 00.1	59 29.6	S21 18.4	53 50.1	S20 08.6	Dubhe	193 45.9	N61 38.8
H 07	11 58.8	307 04.2	46.8	16 25.8	4 59.5	74 32.3	18.5	68 52.7	08.6	Elnath	278 06.9	N28 37.3
U 08	27 01.2	322 07.3	46.3	31 26.8	59.0	89 35.0	18.5	83 55.4	08.7	Eltanin	90 43.4	N51 29.2
R 09	42 03.7	337 10.4 ..	45.8	46 27.8 ..	58.4	104 37.8 ..	18.6	98 58.0 ..	08.7	Enif	33 42.2	N 9 58.0
S 10	57 06.1	352 13.5	45.2	61 28.8	57.8	119 40.5	18.6	114 00.6	08.7	Fomalhaut	15 18.5	S29 30.8
D 11	72 08.6	7 16.6	44.7	76 29.8	57.3	134 43.2	18.7	129 03.2	08.8			
A 12	87 11.1	22 19.7	N18 44.2	91 30.7	S 4 56.7	149 45.9	S21 18.7	144 05.8	S20 08.8	Gacrux	171 55.5	S57 13.8
Y 13	102 13.5	37 22.8	43.7	106 31.7	56.1	164 48.6	18.8	159 08.4	08.9	Gienah	175 47.3	S17 39.3
14	117 16.0	52 25.9	43.2	121 32.7	55.6	179 51.4	18.8	174 11.0	08.9	Hadar	148 40.7	S60 28.4
15	132 18.5	67 28.9 ..	42.6	136 33.7 ..	55.0	194 54.1 ..	18.9	189 13.6 ..	08.9	Hamal	327 55.5	N23 33.3
16	147 20.9	82 32.0	42.1	151 34.7	54.4	209 56.8	18.9	204 16.2	09.0	Kaus Aust.	83 37.0	S34 22.4
17	162 23.4	97 35.1	41.6	166 35.7	53.8	224 59.6	19.0	219 18.8	09.0			
18	177 25.9	112 38.1	N18 41.1	181 36.6	S 4 53.3	240 02.3	S21 19.0	234 21.4	S20 09.0	Kochab	137 19.1	N74 04.6
19	192 28.3	127 41.2	40.6	196 37.6	52.7	255 05.0	19.1	249 24.0	09.1	Markab	13 33.5	N15 18.7
20	207 30.8	142 44.3	40.1	211 38.6	52.1	270 07.7	19.1	264 26.6	09.1	Menkar	314 10.3	N 4 10.0
21	222 33.3	157 47.3 ..	39.6	226 39.6 ..	51.6	285 10.5 ..	19.2	279 29.2 ..	09.1	Menkent	148 01.7	S36 28.2
22	237 35.7	172 50.3	39.1	241 40.6	51.0	300 13.2	19.2	294 31.9	09.2	Miaplacidus	221 39.4	S69 48.3
23	252 38.2	187 53.4	38.6	256 41.6	50.4	315 15.9	19.3	309 34.5	09.2			
19 00	267 40.6	202 56.4	N18 38.1	271 42.6	S 4 49.9	330 18.6	S21 19.4	324 37.1	S20 09.2	Mirfak	308 33.9	N49 55.7
01	282 43.1	217 59.5	37.5	286 43.6	49.3	345 21.4	19.4	339 39.7	09.3	Nunki	75 52.0	S26 16.2
02	297 45.6	233 02.5	37.0	301 44.5	48.7	0 24.1	19.5	354 42.3	09.3	Peacock	53 11.1	S56 39.9
03	312 48.0	248 05.5 ..	36.5	316 45.5 ..	48.2	15 26.8 ..	19.5	9 44.9 ..	09.3	Pollux	243 22.2	N27 58.6
04	327 50.5	263 08.5	36.0	331 46.5	47.6	30 29.6	19.6	24 47.5	09.4	Procyon	244 55.0	N 5 10.3
05	342 53.0	278 11.6	35.6	346 47.0	47.0	45 32.3	19.6	39 50.1	09.4			
F 06	357 55.4	293 14.6	N18 35.1	1 48.5	S 4 46.5	60 35.0	S21 19.7	54 52.7	S20 09.4	Rasalhague	96 01.6	N12 32.8
R 07	12 57.9	308 17.6	34.6	16 49.5	45.9	75 37.7	19.7	69 55.3	09.5	Regulus	207 38.5	N11 52.1
I 08	28 00.4	323 20.6	34.1	31 50.5	45.3	90 40.5	19.8	84 57.9	09.5	Rigel	281 07.8	S 8 10.8
D 09	43 02.8	338 23.6 ..	33.6	46 51.5 ..	44.8	105 43.2 ..	19.8	100 00.5 ..	09.5	Rigil Kent.	139 44.8	S60 55.2
A 10	58 05.3	353 26.6	33.1	61 52.5	44.2	120 45.9	19.9	115 03.2	09.6	Sabik	102 06.7	S15 44.9
Y 11	73 07.8	8 29.6	32.6	76 53.4	43.6	135 48.7	19.9	130 05.8	09.6			
12	88 10.2	23 32.6	N18 32.1	91 54.4	S 4 43.1	150 51.4	S21 20.0	145 08.4	S20 09.6	Schedar	349 35.2	N56 38.6
13	103 12.7	38 35.5	31.6	106 55.4	42.5	165 54.1	20.0	160 11.0	09.7	Shaula	96 14.9	S37 07.0
14	118 15.1	53 38.5	31.1	121 56.4	41.9	180 56.9	20.1	175 13.6	09.7	Sirius	258 29.8	S16 44.7
15	133 17.6	68 41.5 ..	30.7	136 57.4 ..	41.4	195 59.6 ..	20.1	190 16.2 ..	09.7	Spica	158 26.0	S11 16.0
16	148 20.1	83 44.5	30.2	151 58.4	40.8	211 02.3	20.2	205 18.8	09.8	Suhail	222 49.2	S43 31.1
17	163 22.5	98 47.4	29.7	166 59.4	40.2	226 05.0	20.3	220 21.4	09.8			
18	178 25.0	113 50.4	N18 29.2	182 00.4	S 4 39.7	241 07.8	S21 20.3	235 24.0	S20 09.8	Vega	80 35.3	N38 48.2
19	193 27.5	128 53.4	28.8	197 01.4	39.1	256 10.5	20.4	250 26.6	09.9	Zuben'ubi	136 59.8	S16 07.5
20	208 29.9	143 56.3	28.3	212 02.4	38.5	271 13.2	20.4	265 29.3	09.9		SHA	Mer.Pass.
21	223 32.4	158 59.3 ..	27.8	227 03.4 ..	38.0	286 16.0 ..	20.5	280 31.9 ..	09.9		° ′	h m
22	238 34.9	174 02.2	27.3	242 04.4	37.4	301 18.7	20.5	295 34.5	10.0	Venus	295 00.9	10 31
23	253 37.3	189 05.2	26.9	257 05.4	36.8	316 21.4	20.6	310 37.1	10.0	Mars	4 37.4	5 54
Mer. Pass.	6 12.2	v 3.1	d 0.5	v 1.0	d 0.6	v 2.7	d 0.1	v 2.6	d 0.0	Jupiter	62 31.7	2 03
										Saturn	56 53.0	2 25

UT	SUN GHA	SUN Dec	MOON GHA	v	Dec	d	HP
d h	° ′	° ′	° ′	′	° ′	′	′
17 00	179 46.1	N23 23.0	229 29.0	15.2	N 9 58.5	11.2	54.5
01	194 45.9	23.1	244 03.2	15.2	10 09.7	11.2	54.5
02	209 45.8	23.2	258 37.4	15.1	10 20.9	11.1	54.5
03	224 45.7	.. 23.2	273 11.5	15.0	10 32.0	11.2	54.5
04	239 45.5	23.3	287 45.5	15.0	10 43.2	11.1	54.5
05	254 45.4	23.4	302 19.5	15.0	10 54.3	11.0	54.6
06	269 45.3	N23 23.4	316 53.5	14.9	N11 05.3	11.0	54.6
W 07	284 45.1	23.5	331 27.4	14.8	11 16.3	11.0	54.6
E 08	299 45.0	23.5	346 01.2	14.8	11 27.3	10.9	54.6
D 09	314 44.9	.. 23.6	0 35.0	14.8	11 38.2	10.9	54.6
N 10	329 44.7	23.7	15 08.8	14.7	11 49.1	10.9	54.6
E 11	344 44.6	23.7	29 42.5	14.6	12 00.0	10.8	54.6
S 12	359 44.4	N23 23.8	44 16.1	14.6	N12 10.8	10.7	54.7
D 13	14 44.3	23.8	58 49.7	14.5	12 21.5	10.8	54.7
A 14	29 44.2	23.9	73 23.2	14.4	12 32.3	10.6	54.7
Y 15	44 44.0	.. 24.0	87 56.6	14.4	12 42.9	10.7	54.7
16	59 43.9	24.0	102 30.0	14.3	12 53.6	10.6	54.7
17	74 43.8	24.1	117 03.3	14.3	13 04.2	10.5	54.7
18	89 43.6	N23 24.1	131 36.6	14.2	N13 14.7	10.5	54.7
19	104 43.5	24.2	146 09.8	14.2	13 25.2	10.4	54.8
20	119 43.4	24.2	160 43.0	14.1	13 35.6	10.4	54.8
21	134 43.2	.. 24.3	175 16.1	14.0	13 46.0	10.3	54.8
22	149 43.1	24.3	189 49.1	13.9	13 56.3	10.3	54.8
23	164 42.9	24.4	204 22.0	13.9	14 06.6	10.3	54.8
18 00	179 42.8	N23 24.4	218 54.9	13.9	N14 16.9	10.1	54.8
01	194 42.7	24.5	233 27.8	13.7	14 27.0	10.2	54.9
02	209 42.5	24.5	248 00.5	13.7	14 37.2	10.0	54.9
03	224 42.4	.. 24.6	262 33.2	13.7	14 47.2	10.0	54.9
04	239 42.3	24.6	277 05.9	13.5	14 57.2	10.0	54.9
05	254 42.1	24.7	291 38.4	13.5	15 07.2	9.9	54.9
06	269 42.0	N23 24.7	306 10.9	13.4	N15 17.1	9.8	54.9
T 07	284 41.9	24.8	320 43.3	13.4	15 26.9	9.8	55.0
H 08	299 41.7	24.8	335 15.7	13.3	15 36.7	9.7	55.0
U 09	314 41.6	.. 24.9	349 48.0	13.2	15 46.4	9.7	55.0
R 10	329 41.4	24.9	4 20.2	13.1	15 56.1	9.6	55.0
S 11	344 41.3	24.9	18 52.3	13.1	16 05.7	9.5	55.0
D 12	359 41.2	N23 25.0	33 24.4	13.0	N16 15.2	9.4	55.1
A 13	14 41.0	25.0	47 56.4	12.9	16 24.6	9.4	55.1
Y 14	29 40.9	25.1	62 28.3	12.9	16 34.0	9.4	55.1
15	44 40.8	.. 25.1	77 00.2	12.7	16 43.4	9.2	55.1
16	59 40.6	25.1	91 31.9	12.8	16 52.6	9.2	55.1
17	74 40.5	25.2	106 03.7	12.6	17 01.8	9.1	55.2
18	89 40.3	N23 25.2	120 35.3	12.5	N17 10.9	9.1	55.2
19	104 40.2	25.3	135 06.8	12.5	17 20.0	8.9	55.2
20	119 40.1	25.3	149 38.3	12.4	17 28.9	8.9	55.2
21	134 39.9	.. 25.3	164 09.7	12.4	17 37.8	8.9	55.2
22	149 39.8	25.4	178 41.1	12.2	17 46.7	8.7	55.3
23	164 39.7	25.4	193 12.3	12.2	17 55.4	8.7	55.3
19 00	179 39.5	N23 25.4	207 43.5	12.1	N18 04.1	8.6	55.3
01	194 39.4	25.5	222 14.6	12.0	18 12.7	8.5	55.3
02	209 39.3	25.5	236 45.6	12.0	18 21.2	8.5	55.3
03	224 39.1	.. 25.5	251 16.6	11.8	18 29.7	8.3	55.4
04	239 39.0	25.6	265 47.4	11.8	18 38.0	8.3	55.4
05	254 38.8	25.6	280 18.2	11.8	18 46.3	8.2	55.4
06	269 38.7	N23 25.6	294 49.0	11.6	N18 54.5	8.1	55.4
07	284 38.6	25.6	309 19.6	11.6	19 02.6	8.0	55.4
08	299 38.4	25.7	323 50.2	11.4	19 10.6	8.0	55.5
F 09	314 38.3	.. 25.7	338 20.6	11.4	19 18.6	7.9	55.5
R 10	329 38.2	25.7	352 51.0	11.4	19 26.5	7.7	55.5
I 11	344 38.0	25.8	7 21.4	11.2	19 34.2	7.7	55.5
D 12	359 37.9	N23 25.8	21 51.6	11.2	N19 41.9	7.6	55.5
A 13	14 37.7	25.8	36 21.8	11.1	19 49.5	7.5	55.6
Y 14	29 37.6	25.8	50 51.9	11.0	19 57.0	7.4	55.6
15	44 37.5	.. 25.9	65 21.9	10.9	20 04.4	7.3	55.6
16	59 37.3	25.9	79 51.8	10.9	20 11.7	7.2	55.6
17	74 37.2	25.9	94 21.7	10.8	20 18.9	7.2	55.7
18	89 37.1	N23 25.9	108 51.5	10.7	N20 26.1	7.0	55.7
19	104 36.9	25.9	123 21.2	10.6	20 33.1	6.9	55.7
20	119 36.8	26.0	137 50.8	10.5	20 40.0	6.9	55.7
21	134 36.6	.. 26.0	152 20.3	10.5	20 46.9	6.7	55.7
22	149 36.5	26.0	166 49.8	10.4	20 53.6	6.7	55.8
23	164 36.4	26.0	181 19.2	10.3	N21 00.3	6.5	55.8
	SD 15.8	d 0.0	SD 14.9		15.0		15.1

Lat.	Twilight Naut.	Twilight Civil	Sunrise	Moonrise 17	Moonrise 18	Moonrise 19	Moonrise 20
°	h m	h m	h m	h m	h m	h m	h m
N 72	▭	▭	▭	00 32	00 22 00 00 44	▭	▭
N 70	▭	▭	▭	00 47	00 23 00 57	▭	▭
68	▭	▭	▭	01 00	00 49	00 35	▭
66	▭	▭	▭	01 10	01 06	01 02	00 58
64	////	////	01 31	01 18	01 20	01 23	01 30
62	////	////	02 09	01 26	01 31	01 40	01 53
60	////	00 50	02 36	01 32	01 41	01 54	02 12
N 58	////	01 40	02 56	01 38	01 50	02 06	02 28
56	////	02 10	03 13	01 43	01 58	02 16	02 41
54	00 46	02 33	03 27	01 48	02 05	02 26	02 53
52	01 32	02 51	03 39	01 52	02 11	02 34	03 03
50	02 00	03 06	03 50	01 56	02 16	02 41	03 13
45	02 46	03 35	04 13	02 04	02 29	02 57	03 32
N 40	03 16	03 58	04 31	02 11	02 39	03 11	03 48
35	03 39	04 16	04 46	02 17	02 47	03 22	04 01
30	03 58	04 31	04 59	02 22	02 55	03 32	04 13
20	04 27	04 56	05 21	02 31	03 08	03 49	04 34
N 10	04 50	05 17	05 40	02 40	03 20	04 04	04 51
0	05 09	05 36	05 58	02 47	03 31	04 18	05 08
S 10	05 26	05 52	06 15	02 55	03 42	04 32	05 24
20	05 42	06 10	06 34	03 03	03 54	04 47	05 42
30	05 59	06 28	06 55	03 13	04 08	05 05	06 03
35	06 07	06 39	07 07	03 18	04 16	05 15	06 15
40	06 17	06 51	07 21	03 25	04 25	05 27	06 29
45	06 27	07 04	07 38	03 32	04 36	05 41	06 46
S 50	06 39	07 20	07 59	03 41	04 49	05 58	07 06
52	06 44	07 28	08 09	03 45	04 55	06 06	07 16
54	06 50	07 36	08 20	03 50	05 02	06 15	07 27
56	06 56	07 45	08 33	03 55	05 09	06 25	07 40
58	07 03	07 55	08 47	04 00	05 18	06 37	07 55
S 60	07 10	08 07	09 05	04 07	05 27	06 50	08 12

Lat.	Sunset	Twilight Civil	Twilight Naut.	Moonset 17	Moonset 18	Moonset 19	Moonset 20
°	h m	h m	h m	h m	h m	h m	h m
N 72	▭	▭	▭	18 19	21 11	▭	▭
N 70	▭	▭	▭	17 53	19 58	▭	▭
68	▭	▭	▭	17 33	19 22	21 30	▭
66	▭	▭	▭	17 17	18 56	20 41	22 33
64	22 32	////	////	17 05	18 36	20 10	21 43
62	21 54	////	////	16 54	18 20	19 47	21 11
60	21 27	23 13	////	16 45	18 06	19 29	20 48
N 58	21 07	22 22	////	16 37	17 55	19 14	20 29
56	20 50	21 52	////	16 30	17 45	19 01	20 13
54	20 36	21 24	23 18	16 24	17 36	18 49	20 00
52	20 23	21 12	22 31	16 18	17 29	18 39	19 48
50	20 12	20 57	22 03	16 13	17 22	18 31	19 38
45	19 50	20 27	21 17	16 02	17 07	18 12	19 16
N 40	19 32	20 05	20 46	15 54	16 55	17 57	18 59
35	19 17	19 46	20 23	15 46	16 44	17 44	18 44
30	19 04	19 31	20 04	15 39	16 35	17 33	18 31
20	18 42	19 06	19 35	15 28	16 19	17 14	18 09
N 10	18 23	18 46	19 13	15 18	16 06	16 57	17 51
0	18 05	18 27	18 54	15 08	15 53	16 41	17 33
S 10	17 47	18 10	18 37	14 59	15 41	16 26	17 15
20	17 29	17 53	18 20	14 49	15 27	16 10	16 57
30	17 08	17 34	18 04	14 37	15 12	15 51	16 35
35	16 55	17 23	17 55	14 31	15 03	15 40	16 22
40	16 41	17 12	17 46	14 23	14 53	15 27	16 08
45	16 24	16 58	17 35	14 15	14 41	15 12	15 51
S 50	16 04	16 42	17 24	14 04	14 27	14 54	15 29
52	15 54	16 35	17 18	14 00	14 20	14 46	15 19
54	15 43	16 26	17 13	13 54	14 13	14 36	15 08
56	15 30	16 17	17 06	13 49	14 05	14 26	14 55
58	15 15	16 07	17 00	13 42	13 55	14 14	14 40
S 60	14 58	15 55	16 52	13 35	13 45	14 00	14 22

	SUN			MOON			
Day	Eqn. of Time 00ʰ	Eqn. of Time 12ʰ	Mer. Pass.	Mer. Pass. Upper	Mer. Pass. Lower	Age	Phase
d	m s	m s	h m	h m	h m	d	%
17	00 55	01 02	12 01	08 58	21 20	26	14
18	01 08	01 15	12 01	09 42	22 05	27	8
19	01 22	01 28	12 01	10 30	22 55	28	3

2020 JUNE 20, 21, 22 (SAT., SUN., MON.)

UT	ARIES	VENUS −4·5		MARS −0·3		JUPITER −2·7		SATURN +0·3		STARS		
d h	GHA	GHA	Dec	GHA	Dec	GHA	Dec	GHA	Dec	Name	SHA	Dec
20 00	268 39.8	204 08.1	N18 26.4	272 06.3	S 4 36.3	331 24.2	S21 20.6	325 39.7	S20 10.1	Acamar	315 14.9	S40 13.3
01	283 42.2	219 11.0	25.9	287 07.3	35.7	346 26.9	20.7	340 42.3	10.1	Achernar	335 23.4	S57 07.8
02	298 44.7	234 14.0	25.5	302 08.3	35.1	1 29.6	20.7	355 44.9	10.1	Acrux	173 03.9	S63 12.9
03	313 47.2	249 16.9 ..	25.0	317 09.3 ..	34.6	16 32.4 ..	20.8	10 47.5 ..	10.2	Adhara	255 09.1	S29 00.1
04	328 49.6	264 19.8	24.5	332 10.3	34.0	31 35.1	20.8	25 50.1	10.2	Aldebaran	290 44.2	N16 32.8
05	343 52.1	279 22.7	24.1	347 11.3	33.4	46 37.8	20.9	40 52.8	10.2			
06	358 54.6	294 25.6	N18 23.6	2 12.3	S 4 32.9	61 40.6	S21 20.9	55 55.4	S20 10.3	Alioth	166 16.2	N55 51.3
S 07	13 57.0	309 28.5	23.2	17 13.3	32.3	76 43.3	21.0	70 58.0	10.3	Alkaid	152 54.8	N49 13.0
A 08	28 59.5	324 31.4	22.7	32 14.3	31.7	91 46.0	21.1	86 00.6	10.3	Alnair	27 37.4	S46 51.5
T 09	44 02.0	339 34.3 ..	22.3	47 15.3 ..	31.2	106 48.8 ..	21.1	101 03.2 ..	10.4	Alnilam	275 41.8	S 1 11.4
U 10	59 04.4	354 37.2	21.8	62 16.3	30.6	121 51.5	21.2	116 05.8	10.4	Alphard	217 51.6	S 8 44.8
R 11	74 06.9	9 40.1	21.4	77 17.3	30.0	136 54.3	21.2	131 08.4	10.4			
D 12	89 09.4	24 43.0	N18 20.9	92 18.3	S 4 29.5	151 57.0	S21 21.3	146 11.0	S20 10.5	Alphecca	126 06.6	N26 39.0
A 13	104 11.8	39 45.9	20.5	107 19.3	28.9	166 59.7	21.3	161 13.7	10.5	Alpheratz	357 38.5	N29 11.9
Y 14	119 14.3	54 48.8	20.0	122 20.3	28.3	182 02.5	21.4	176 16.3	10.5	Altair	62 03.2	N 8 55.4
15	134 16.7	69 51.7 ..	19.6	137 21.3 ..	27.8	197 05.2 ..	21.4	191 18.9 ..	10.6	Ankaa	353 10.9	S42 11.6
16	149 19.2	84 54.5	19.1	152 22.3	27.2	212 07.9	21.5	206 21.5	10.6	Antares	112 20.0	S26 28.6
17	164 21.7	99 57.4	18.7	167 23.3	26.6	227 10.7	21.5	221 24.1	10.6			
18	179 24.1	115 00.3	N18 18.2	182 24.3	S 4 26.1	242 13.4	S21 21.6	236 26.7	S20 10.7	Arcturus	145 51.1	N19 04.8
19	194 26.6	130 03.1	17.8	197 25.3	25.5	257 16.1	21.6	251 29.3	10.7	Atria	107 16.9	S69 03.8
20	209 29.1	145 06.0	17.4	212 26.3	25.0	272 18.9	21.7	266 31.9	10.8	Avior	234 16.7	S59 34.7
21	224 31.5	160 08.8 ..	16.9	227 27.3 ..	24.4	287 21.6 ..	21.8	281 34.6 ..	10.8	Bellatrix	278 27.2	N 6 22.0
22	239 34.0	175 11.7	16.5	242 28.3	23.8	302 24.4	21.8	296 37.2	10.8	Betelgeuse	270 56.4	N 7 24.5
23	254 36.5	190 14.5	16.1	257 29.3	23.3	317 27.1	21.9	311 39.8	10.9			
21 00	269 38.9	205 17.3	N18 15.6	272 30.3	S 4 22.7	332 29.8	S21 21.9	326 42.4	S20 10.9	Canopus	263 54.6	S52 42.5
01	284 41.4	220 20.2	15.2	287 31.3	22.1	347 32.6	22.0	341 45.0	10.9	Capella	280 27.8	N46 00.9
02	299 43.9	235 23.0	14.8	302 32.3	21.6	2 35.3	22.0	356 47.6	11.0	Deneb	49 27.9	N45 21.0
03	314 46.3	250 25.8 ..	14.4	317 33.3 ..	21.0	17 38.1 ..	22.1	11 50.2 ..	11.0	Denebola	182 28.7	N14 27.7
04	329 48.8	265 28.6	13.9	332 34.3	20.4	32 40.8	22.1	26 52.9	11.0	Diphda	348 51.1	S17 52.5
05	344 51.2	280 31.5	13.5	347 35.3	19.9	47 43.5	22.2	41 55.5	11.1			
06	359 53.7	295 34.3	N18 13.1	2 36.3	S 4 19.3	62 46.3	S21 22.2	56 58.1	S20 11.1	Dubhe	193 45.9	N61 38.8
07	14 56.2	310 37.1	12.7	17 37.3	18.7	77 49.0	22.3	72 00.7	11.1	Elnath	278 06.9	N28 37.3
08	29 58.6	325 39.9	12.2	32 38.3	18.2	92 51.8	22.3	87 03.3	11.2	Eltanin	90 43.3	N51 29.2
S 09	45 01.1	340 42.7 ..	11.8	47 39.3 ..	17.6	107 54.5 ..	22.4	102 05.9 ..	11.2	Enif	33 42.2	N 9 58.0
U 10	60 03.6	355 45.5	11.4	62 40.3	17.1	122 57.2	22.5	117 08.5	11.2	Fomalhaut	15 18.5	S29 30.7
N 11	75 06.0	10 48.3	11.0	77 41.3	16.5	138 00.0	22.5	132 11.2	11.3			
D 12	90 08.5	25 51.1	N18 10.6	92 42.3	S 4 15.9	153 02.7	S21 22.6	147 13.8	S20 11.3	Gacrux	171 55.5	S57 13.8
A 13	105 11.0	40 53.8	10.2	107 43.3	15.4	168 05.5	22.6	162 16.4	11.4	Gienah	175 47.3	S17 39.3
Y 14	120 13.4	55 56.6	09.8	122 44.3	14.8	183 08.2	22.7	177 19.0	11.4	Hadar	148 40.7	S60 28.4
15	135 15.9	70 59.4 ..	09.4	137 45.3 ..	14.2	198 10.9 ..	22.7	192 21.6 ..	11.4	Hamal	327 55.5	N23 33.3
16	150 18.4	86 02.2	09.0	152 46.3	13.7	213 13.7	22.8	207 24.2	11.5	Kaus Aust.	83 37.0	S34 22.4
17	165 20.8	101 04.9	08.6	167 47.3	13.1	228 16.4	22.8	222 26.8	11.5			
18	180 23.3	116 07.7	N18 08.1	182 48.3	S 4 12.6	243 19.2	S21 22.9	237 29.5	S20 11.5	Kochab	137 19.2	N74 04.6
19	195 25.7	131 10.5	07.7	197 49.3	12.0	258 21.9	22.9	252 32.1	11.6	Markab	13 33.4	N15 18.8
20	210 28.2	146 13.2	07.3	212 50.3	11.4	273 24.7	23.0	267 34.7	11.6	Menkar	314 10.2	N 4 10.0
21	225 30.7	161 16.0 ..	06.9	227 51.3 ..	10.9	288 27.4 ..	23.1	282 37.3 ..	11.6	Menkent	148 01.7	S36 28.3
22	240 33.1	176 18.7	06.6	242 52.3	10.3	303 30.1	23.1	297 39.9	11.7	Miaplacidus	221 39.4	S69 48.3
23	255 35.6	191 21.4	06.2	257 53.4	09.7	318 32.9	23.2	312 42.5	11.7			
22 00	270 38.1	206 24.2	N18 05.8	272 54.4	S 4 09.2	333 35.6	S21 23.2	327 45.2	S20 11.7	Mirfak	308 33.8	N49 55.7
01	285 40.5	221 26.9	05.4	287 55.4	08.6	348 38.4	23.3	342 47.8	11.8	Nunki	75 52.0	S26 16.2
02	300 43.0	236 29.6	05.0	302 56.4	08.1	3 41.1	23.3	357 50.4	11.8	Peacock	53 11.1	S56 40.0
03	315 45.5	251 32.4 ..	04.6	317 57.4 ..	07.5	18 43.9 ..	23.4	12 53.0 ..	11.9	Pollux	243 22.2	N27 58.6
04	330 47.9	266 35.1	04.2	332 58.4	06.9	33 46.6	23.4	27 55.6	11.9	Procyon	244 55.0	N 5 10.3
05	345 50.4	281 37.8	03.8	347 59.4	06.4	48 49.4	23.5	42 58.2	11.9			
06	0 52.9	296 40.5	N18 03.4	3 00.4	S 4 05.8	63 52.1	S21 23.5	58 00.9	S20 12.0	Rasalhague	96 01.6	N12 32.8
07	15 55.3	311 43.2	03.0	18 01.4	05.3	78 54.8	23.6	73 03.5	12.0	Regulus	207 38.5	N11 52.1
08	30 57.8	326 45.9	02.7	33 02.4	04.7	93 57.6	23.7	88 06.1	12.0	Rigel	281 07.7	S 8 10.8
M 09	46 00.2	341 48.6 ..	02.3	48 03.4 ..	04.1	109 00.3 ..	23.7	103 08.7 ..	12.1	Rigil Kent.	139 44.8	S60 55.2
O 10	61 02.7	356 51.3	01.9	63 04.4	03.6	124 03.1	23.8	118 11.3	12.1	Sabik	102 06.6	S15 44.9
N 11	76 05.2	11 54.0	01.5	78 05.5	03.0	139 05.8	23.8	133 13.9	12.1			
D 12	91 07.6	26 56.7	N18 01.2	93 06.5	S 4 02.4	154 08.6	S21 23.9	148 16.6	S20 12.2	Schedar	349 35.2	N56 38.6
A 13	106 10.1	41 59.4	00.8	108 07.5	01.9	169 11.3	23.9	163 19.2	12.2	Shaula	96 14.9	S37 07.0
Y 14	121 12.6	57 02.1	00.4	123 08.5	01.3	184 14.1	24.0	178 21.8	12.2	Sirius	258 29.8	S16 44.7
15	136 15.0	72 04.7	18 00.0	138 09.5 ..	00.8	199 16.8 ..	24.0	193 24.4 ..	12.3	Spica	158 26.0	S11 16.0
16	151 17.5	87 07.4	17 59.7	153 10.5	S 4 00.2	214 19.6	24.1	208 27.0	12.3	Suhail	222 49.2	S43 31.0
17	166 20.0	102 10.1	59.3	168 11.5	3 59.6	229 22.3	24.2	223 29.7	12.4			
18	181 22.4	117 12.7	N17 58.9	183 12.5	S 3 59.1	244 25.1	S21 24.2	238 32.3	S20 12.4	Vega	80 35.3	N38 48.2
19	196 24.9	132 15.4	58.6	198 13.5	58.5	259 27.8	24.3	253 34.9	12.4	Zuben'ubi	136 59.8	S16 07.5
20	211 27.4	147 18.1	58.2	213 14.6	58.0	274 30.6	24.3	268 37.5	12.5		SHA	Mer.Pass.
21	226 29.8	162 20.7 ..	57.9	228 15.6 ..	57.4	289 33.3 ..	24.4	283 40.1 ..	12.5		° ′	h m
22	241 32.3	177 23.3	57.5	243 16.6	56.8	304 36.0	24.4	298 42.7	12.5	Venus	295 38.4	10 17
23	256 34.7	192 26.0	57.1	258 17.6	56.3	319 38.8	24.5	313 45.4	12.6	Mars	2 51.3	5 50
	h m									Jupiter	62 50.9	1 50
Mer. Pass.	6 00.4	v 2.8	d 0.4	v 1.0	d 0.6	v 2.7	d 0.1	v 2.6	d 0.0	Saturn	57 03.5	2 13

SUN / MOON

UT	SUN GHA	SUN Dec	MOON GHA	v	Dec	d	HP
d h	° ′	° ′	° ′	′	° ′	′	′
20 00	179 36.2	N23 26.0	195 48.5	10.3	N21 06.8	6.4	55.8
01	194 36.1	26.0	210 17.8	10.1	21 13.2	6.4	55.8
02	209 36.0	26.0	224 46.9	10.1	21 19.6	6.2	55.9
03	224 35.8 ..	26.1	239 16.0	10.0	21 25.8	6.1	55.9
04	239 35.7	26.1	253 45.0	10.0	21 31.9	6.0	55.9
05	254 35.6	26.1	268 14.0	9.8	21 37.9	5.9	55.9
06	269 35.4	N23 26.1	282 42.8	9.8	N21 43.8	5.8	55.9
S 07	284 35.3	26.1	297 11.6	9.7	21 49.6	5.7	56.0
A 08	299 35.1	26.1	311 40.3	9.7	21 55.3	5.6	56.0
T 09	314 35.0 ..	26.1	326 09.0	9.5	22 00.9	5.5	56.0
U 10	329 34.9	26.1	340 37.5	9.5	22 06.4	5.3	56.0
R 11	344 34.7	26.1	355 06.0	9.5	22 11.7	5.3	56.1
D 12	359 34.6	N23 26.2	9 34.5	9.3	N22 17.0	5.1	56.1
A 13	14 34.5	26.2	24 02.8	9.3	22 22.1	5.0	56.1
Y 14	29 34.3	26.2	38 31.1	9.2	22 27.1	4.9	56.1
15	44 34.2 ..	26.2	52 59.3	9.2	22 32.0	4.8	56.2
16	59 34.0	26.2	67 27.5	9.0	22 36.8	4.7	56.2
17	74 33.9	26.2	81 55.5	9.1	22 41.5	4.5	56.2
18	89 33.8	N23 26.2	96 23.6	8.9	N22 46.0	4.4	56.2
19	104 33.6	26.2	110 51.5	8.9	22 50.4	4.3	56.2
20	119 33.5	26.2	125 19.4	8.8	22 54.7	4.2	56.3
21	134 33.4 ..	26.2	139 47.2	8.7	22 58.9	4.1	56.3
22	149 33.2	26.2	154 14.9	8.7	23 03.0	3.9	56.3
23	164 33.1	26.2	168 42.6	8.6	23 06.9	3.8	56.3
21 00	179 32.9	N23 26.2	183 10.2	8.6	N23 10.7	3.7	56.4
01	194 32.8	26.2	197 37.8	8.5	23 14.4	3.6	56.4
02	209 32.7	26.2	212 05.3	8.4	23 18.0	3.4	56.4
03	224 32.5 ..	26.2	226 32.7	8.4	23 21.4	3.3	56.4
04	239 32.4	26.2	241 00.1	8.4	23 24.7	3.2	56.5
05	254 32.3	26.2	255 27.5	8.2	23 27.9	3.1	56.5
06	269 32.1	N23 26.2	269 54.7	8.2	N23 31.0	2.9	56.5
07	284 32.0	26.2					
08	299 31.9	26.2					
S 09	314 31.7 ..	26.1					
U 10	329 31.6	26.1	An annular eclipse of				
N 11	344 31.4	26.1	the Sun occurs on this				
D 12	359 31.3	N23 26.1	date. See page 5.				
A 13	14 31.2	26.1	11 04.1	7.9	N23 48.7	2.0	56.7
Y 14	29 31.0	26.1	25 31.0	7.8	23 50.7	1.8	56.7
15	44 30.9 ..	26.1	39 57.8	7.7	23 52.5	1.8	56.7
16	59 30.8	26.1	54 24.5	7.7	23 54.3	1.6	56.7
17	74 30.6	26.1	68 51.2	7.7	23 55.9	1.4	56.8
18	89 30.5	N23 26.0	83 17.9	7.7	N23 57.3	1.3	56.8
19	104 30.3	26.0	97 44.6	7.6	23 58.6	1.2	56.8
20	119 30.2	26.0	112 11.2	7.5	23 59.8	1.0	56.8
21	134 30.1 ..	26.0	126 37.7	7.5	24 00.8	0.9	56.8
22	149 29.9	26.0	141 04.2	7.5	24 01.7	0.8	56.9
23	164 29.8	26.0	155 30.7	7.5	24 02.5	0.6	56.9
22 00	179 29.7	N23 25.9	169 57.2	7.4	N24 03.1	0.5	56.9
01	194 29.5	25.9	184 23.6	7.4	24 03.6	0.3	56.9
02	209 29.4	25.9	198 50.0	7.3	24 03.9	0.2	57.0
03	224 29.3 ..	25.9	213 16.3	7.4	24 04.1	0.1	57.0
04	239 29.1	25.9	227 42.7	7.3	24 04.2	0.1	57.0
05	254 29.0	25.8	242 09.0	7.2	24 04.1	0.2	57.0
06	269 28.8	N23 25.8	256 35.2	7.3	N24 03.9	0.4	57.1
07	284 28.7	25.8	271 01.5	7.2	24 03.5	0.5	57.1
08	299 28.6	25.8	285 27.7	7.2	24 03.0	0.6	57.1
M 09	314 28.4 ..	25.7	299 53.9	7.2	24 02.4	0.8	57.1
O 10	329 28.3	25.7	314 20.1	7.2	24 01.6	1.0	57.1
N 11	344 28.2	25.7	328 46.3	7.1	24 00.6	1.1	57.2
D 12	359 28.0	N23 25.7	343 12.4	7.2	N23 59.5	1.2	57.2
A 13	14 27.9	25.6	357 38.6	7.1	23 58.3	1.3	57.2
Y 14	29 27.8	25.6	12 04.7	7.1	23 57.0	1.6	57.2
15	44 27.6 ..	25.6	26 30.8	7.1	23 55.4	1.6	57.2
16	59 27.5	25.6	40 56.9	7.1	23 53.8	1.8	57.3
17	74 27.4	25.5	55 23.0	7.1	23 52.0	2.0	57.3
18	89 27.2	N23 25.5	69 49.1	7.0	N23 50.0	2.0	57.3
19	104 27.1	25.5	84 15.1	7.1	23 48.0	2.3	57.3
20	119 26.9	25.4	98 41.2	7.0	23 45.7	2.3	57.4
21	134 26.8 ..	25.4	113 07.2	7.1	23 43.4	2.6	57.4
22	149 26.7	25.4	127 33.3	7.1	23 40.8	2.6	57.4
23	164 26.5	25.3	141 59.4	7.0	N23 38.2	2.8	57.4
	SD 15.8	d 0.0	SD 15.3		15.4		15.6

Twilight / Sunrise / Moonrise

Lat.	Naut.	Civil	Sunrise	Moonrise 20	21	22	23
°	h m	h m	h m	h m	h m	h m	h m
N 72	□	□	□	□	□	□	□
N 70	□	□	□	□	□	□	□
68	□	□	□	□	00 09	□	□
66	□	□	□	00 58	00 55	01 00	02 38
64	////	////	01 31	01 30	01 46	02 23	03 35
62	////	////	02 09	01 53	02 17	03 00	04 08
60	////	00 49	02 36	02 12	02 41	03 27	04 33
N 58	////	01 40	02 56	02 28	03 00	03 48	04 52
56	////	02 11	03 13	02 41	03 16	04 05	05 08
54	00 45	02 33	03 28	02 53	03 30	04 19	05 22
52	01 32	02 51	03 40	03 03	03 42	04 32	05 34
50	02 00	03 06	03 51	03 13	03 52	04 43	05 45
45	02 46	03 36	04 13	03 32	04 15	05 06	06 07
N 40	03 17	03 59	04 31	03 48	04 33	05 25	06 25
35	03 40	04 17	04 46	04 01	04 48	05 41	06 40
30	03 59	04 32	05 00	04 13	05 01	05 54	06 53
20	04 28	04 57	05 22	04 34	05 23	06 17	07 15
N 10	04 50	05 18	05 41	04 51	05 43	06 38	07 35
0	05 09	05 36	05 58	05 08	06 01	06 56	07 53
S 10	05 26	05 53	06 16	05 24	06 19	07 15	08 11
20	05 43	06 10	06 34	05 42	06 39	07 35	08 30
30	05 59	06 29	06 56	06 03	07 02	07 58	08 52
35	06 08	06 40	07 08	06 15	07 15	08 12	09 05
40	06 17	06 52	07 22	06 29	07 30	08 28	09 20
45	06 28	07 05	07 39	06 46	07 49	08 47	09 38
S 50	06 40	07 21	08 00	07 06	08 12	09 10	09 59
52	06 45	07 29	08 10	07 16	08 23	09 22	10 10
54	06 51	07 37	08 21	07 27	08 35	09 34	10 22
56	06 57	07 46	08 33	07 40	08 50	09 49	10 35
58	07 04	07 56	08 48	07 55	09 07	10 06	10 51
S 60	07 11	08 08	09 06	08 12	09 27	10 28	11 09

Sunset / Twilight / Moonset

Lat.	Sunset	Civil	Naut.	Moonset 20	21	22	23
°	h m	h m	h m	h m	h m	h m	h m
N 72	□	□	□	□	□	□	□
N 70	□	□	□	□	□	□	□
68	□	□	□	□	□	□	□
66	□	□	□	22 33	24 23	00 23	00 43
64	22 33	////	////	21 43	23 00	23 45	24 06
62	21 54	////	////	21 11	22 22	23 12	23 41
60	21 28	23 14	////	20 48	21 56	22 47	23 21
N 58	21 07	22 23	////	20 29	21 35	22 27	23 05
56	20 51	21 53	////	20 13	21 18	22 11	22 51
54	20 36	21 31	23 19	20 00	21 04	21 57	22 39
52	20 24	21 13	22 31	19 48	20 51	21 45	22 28
50	20 13	20 58	22 03	19 38	20 40	21 34	22 18
45	19 50	20 28	21 18	19 16	20 17	21 11	21 58
N 40	19 32	20 05	20 47	18 59	19 58	20 53	21 42
35	19 17	19 47	20 24	18 44	19 43	20 38	21 28
30	19 04	19 32	20 05	18 31	19 29	20 24	21 16
20	18 42	19 07	19 36	18 09	19 06	20 02	20 55
N 10	18 23	18 46	19 13	17 51	18 46	19 42	20 37
0	18 06	18 28	18 54	17 33	18 27	19 23	20 20
S 10	17 48	18 11	18 37	17 15	18 09	19 05	20 02
20	17 30	17 54	18 21	16 57	17 49	18 45	19 44
30	17 08	17 35	18 05	16 35	17 25	18 22	19 23
35	16 56	17 24	17 56	16 22	17 12	18 08	19 10
40	16 42	17 12	17 46	16 08	16 56	17 53	18 56
45	16 25	16 59	17 36	15 51	16 38	17 34	18 39
S 50	16 04	16 43	17 24	15 29	16 14	17 11	18 17
52	15 54	16 35	17 19	15 19	16 03	16 59	18 07
54	15 43	16 27	17 13	15 08	15 51	16 47	17 56
56	15 30	16 18	17 07	14 55	15 36	16 32	17 43
58	15 16	16 08	17 00	14 40	15 19	16 15	17 27
S 60	14 58	15 56	16 53	14 22	14 58	15 54	17 09

SUN / MOON

Day	Eqn. of Time 00h	Eqn. of Time 12h	Mer. Pass.	Mer. Pass. Upper	Mer. Pass. Lower	Age	Phase
d	m s	m s	h m	h m	h m	d	%
20	01 35	01 41	12 02	11 20	23 47	29	1
21	01 48	01 55	12 02	12 14	24 42	00	0
22	02 01	02 08	12 02	13 10	00 42	01	2

2020 JUNE 23, 24, 25 (TUES., WED., THURS.)

UT	ARIES GHA	VENUS −4·6 GHA	Dec	MARS −0·4 GHA	Dec	JUPITER −2·7 GHA	Dec	SATURN +0·3 GHA	Dec	STARS Name	SHA	Dec
23 00	271 37.2	207 28.6	N17 56.8	273 18.6	S 3 55.7	334 41.5	S21 24.5	328 48.0	S20 12.6	Acamar	315 14.9	S40 13.3
01	286 39.7	222 31.3	56.4	288 19.6	55.2	349 44.3	24.6	343 50.6	12.6	Achernar	335 23.3	S57 07.8
02	301 42.1	237 33.9	56.1	303 20.6	54.6	4 47.0	24.7	358 53.2	12.7	Acrux	173 03.9	S63 12.9
03	316 44.6	252 36.5 ..	55.7	318 21.6 ..	54.0	19 49.8 ..	24.7	13 55.8 ..	12.7	Adhara	255 09.1	S29 00.1
04	331 47.1	267 39.1	55.4	333 22.7	53.5	34 52.5	24.8	28 58.5	12.8	Aldebaran	290 44.1	N16 32.9
05	346 49.5	282 41.8	55.0	348 23.7	52.9	49 55.3	24.8	44 01.1	12.8			
06	1 52.0	297 44.4	N17 54.7	3 24.7	S 3 52.3	64 58.0	S21 24.9	59 03.7	S20 12.8	Alioth	166 16.2	N55 51.3
07	16 54.5	312 47.0	54.3	18 25.7	51.8	80 00.8	24.9	74 06.3	12.9	Alkaid	152 54.8	N49 13.0
T 08	31 56.9	327 49.6	54.0	33 26.7	51.3	95 03.5	25.0	89 08.9	12.9	Alnair	27 37.4	S46 51.5
U 09	46 59.4	342 52.2 ..	53.6	48 27.7 ..	50.7	110 06.3 ..	25.0	104 11.6 ..	12.9	Alnilam	275 41.8	S 1 11.4
E 10	62 01.8	357 54.8	53.3	63 28.8	50.1	125 09.0	25.1	119 14.2	13.0	Alphard	217 51.6	S 8 44.8
S 11	77 04.3	12 57.4	53.0	78 29.8	49.6	140 11.8	25.2	134 16.8	13.0			
D 12	92 06.8	28 00.0	N17 52.6	93 30.8	S 3 49.0	155 14.5	S21 25.2	149 19.4	S20 13.0	Alphecca	126 06.6	N26 39.0
A 13	107 09.2	43 02.5	52.3	108 31.8	48.5	170 17.3	25.3	164 22.0	13.1	Alpheratz	357 38.5	N29 11.9
Y 14	122 11.7	58 05.1	51.9	123 32.8	47.9	185 20.1	25.3	179 24.7	13.1	Altair	62 03.2	N 8 55.4
15	137 14.2	73 07.7 ..	51.6	138 33.8 ..	47.3	200 22.8 ..	25.4	194 27.3 ..	13.2	Ankaa	353 10.9	S42 11.6
16	152 16.6	88 10.3	51.3	153 34.9	46.8	215 25.6	25.4	209 29.9	13.2	Antares	112 20.0	S26 28.6
17	167 19.1	103 12.8	50.9	168 35.9	46.2	230 28.3	25.5	224 32.5	13.2			
18	182 21.6	118 15.4	N17 50.6	183 36.9	S 3 45.7	245 31.1	S21 25.5	239 35.1	S20 13.3	Arcturus	145 51.1	N19 04.8
19	197 24.0	133 18.0	50.3	198 37.9	45.1	260 33.8	25.6	254 37.8	13.3	Atria	107 16.9	S69 03.8
20	212 26.5	148 20.5	50.0	213 38.9	44.6	275 36.6	25.7	269 40.4	13.3	Avior	234 16.7	S59 34.6
21	227 29.0	163 23.1 ..	49.6	228 40.0 ..	44.0	290 39.3 ..	25.7	284 43.0 ..	13.4	Bellatrix	278 27.1	N 6 22.0
22	242 31.4	178 25.6	49.3	243 41.0	43.4	305 42.1	25.8	299 45.6	13.4	Betelgeuse	270 56.4	N 7 24.6
23	257 33.9	193 28.2	49.0	258 42.0	42.9	320 44.8	25.8	314 48.2	13.4			
24 00	272 36.3	208 30.7	N17 48.7	273 43.0	S 3 42.3	335 47.6	S21 25.9	329 50.9	S20 13.5	Canopus	263 54.6	S52 42.5
01	287 38.8	223 33.2	48.4	288 44.0	41.8	350 50.3	25.9	344 53.5	13.5	Capella	280 27.8	N46 00.9
02	302 41.3	238 35.8	48.0	303 45.1	41.2	5 53.1	26.0	359 56.1	13.6	Deneb	49 27.8	N45 21.0
03	317 43.7	253 38.3 ..	47.7	318 46.1 ..	40.7	20 55.8 ..	26.0	14 58.7 ..	13.6	Denebola	182 28.8	N14 27.7
04	332 46.2	268 40.8	47.4	333 47.1	40.1	35 58.6	26.1	30 01.4	13.6	Diphda	348 51.1	S17 52.5
05	347 48.7	283 43.3	47.1	348 48.1	39.5	51 01.4	26.2	45 04.0	13.7			
06	2 51.1	298 45.9	N17 46.8	3 49.1	S 3 39.0	66 04.1	S21 26.2	60 06.6	S20 13.7	Dubhe	193 45.9	N61 38.8
W 07	17 53.6	313 48.4	46.5	18 50.2	38.4	81 06.9	26.3	75 09.2	13.7	Elnath	278 06.9	N28 37.3
E 08	32 56.1	328 50.9	46.2	33 51.2	37.9	96 09.6	26.3	90 11.8	13.8	Eltanin	90 43.3	N51 29.3
D 09	47 58.5	343 53.4 ..	45.9	48 52.2 ..	37.3	111 12.4 ..	26.4	105 14.5 ..	13.8	Enif	33 42.2	N 9 58.1
N 10	63 01.0	358 55.9	45.6	63 53.2	36.8	126 15.1	26.4	120 17.1	13.8	Fomalhaut	15 18.5	S29 30.7
E 11	78 03.5	13 58.4	45.3	78 54.3	36.2	141 17.9	26.5	135 19.7	13.9			
S 12	93 05.9	29 00.9	N17 45.0	93 55.3	S 3 35.7	156 20.6	S21 26.6	150 22.3	S20 13.9	Gacrux	171 55.5	S57 15.8
D 13	108 08.4	44 03.4	44.7	108 56.3	35.1	171 23.4	26.6	165 25.0	14.0	Gienah	175 47.3	S17 39.3
A 14	123 10.8	59 05.8	44.4	123 57.3	34.5	186 26.2	26.7	180 27.6	14.0	Hadar	148 40.7	S60 28.4
Y 15	138 13.3	74 08.3 ..	44.1	138 58.4 ..	34.0	201 28.9 ..	26.7	195 30.2 ..	14.0	Hamal	327 55.5	N23 33.3
16	153 15.8	89 10.8	43.8	153 59.4	33.4	216 31.7	26.8	210 32.8	14.1	Kaus Aust.	83 37.0	S34 22.4
17	168 18.2	104 13.3	43.5	169 00.4	32.9	231 34.4	26.8	225 35.4	14.1			
18	183 20.7	119 15.7	N17 43.2	184 01.4	S 3 32.3	246 37.2	S21 26.9	240 38.1	S20 14.1	Kochab	137 19.2	N74 04.6
19	198 23.2	134 18.2	42.9	199 02.5	31.8	261 39.9	27.0	255 40.7	14.2	Markab	13 33.4	N15 18.8
20	213 25.6	149 20.6	42.6	214 03.5	31.2	276 42.7	27.0	270 43.3	14.2	Menkar	314 10.2	N 4 10.0
21	228 28.1	164 23.1 ..	42.3	229 04.5 ..	30.7	291 45.5 ..	27.1	285 45.9 ..	14.3	Menkent	148 01.7	S36 28.3
22	243 30.6	179 25.6	42.0	244 05.5	30.1	306 48.2	27.1	300 48.6	14.3	Miaplacidus	221 39.5	S69 48.2
23	258 33.0	194 28.0	41.7	259 06.6	29.5	321 51.0	27.2	315 51.2	14.3			
25 00	273 35.5	209 30.4	N17 41.5	274 07.6	S 3 29.0	336 53.7	S21 27.2	330 53.8	S20 14.4	Mirfak	308 33.8	N49 55.7
01	288 38.0	224 32.9	41.2	289 08.6	28.4	351 56.5	27.3	345 56.4	14.4	Nunki	75 51.9	S26 16.2
02	303 40.4	239 35.3	40.9	304 09.6	27.9	6 59.2	27.3	0 59.1	14.4	Peacock	53 11.1	S56 44.0
03	318 42.9	254 37.7 ..	40.6	319 10.7 ..	27.3	22 02.0 ..	27.4	16 01.7 ..	14.5	Pollux	243 22.2	N27 58.6
04	333 45.3	269 40.2	40.3	334 11.7	26.8	37 04.8	27.5	31 04.3	14.5	Procyon	244 55.0	N 5 10.3
05	348 47.8	284 42.6	40.1	349 12.7	26.2	52 07.5	27.5	46 06.9	14.6			
06	3 50.3	299 45.0	N17 39.8	4 13.8	S 3 25.7	67 10.3	S21 27.6	61 09.6	S20 14.6	Rasalhague	96 01.6	N12 32.8
07	18 52.7	314 47.4	39.5	19 14.8	25.1	82 13.0	27.6	76 12.2	14.6	Regulus	207 38.5	N11 52.1
T 08	33 55.2	329 49.8	39.2	34 15.8	24.6	97 15.8	27.7	91 14.8	14.7	Rigel	281 07.7	S 8 10.8
H 09	48 57.7	344 52.3 ..	39.0	49 16.8 ..	24.0	112 18.6 ..	27.7	106 17.4 ..	14.7	Rigil Kent.	139 44.8	S60 55.2
U 10	64 00.1	359 54.7	38.7	64 17.9	23.5	127 21.3	27.8	121 20.1	14.7	Sabik	102 06.6	S15 44.9
R 11	79 02.6	14 57.1	38.4	79 18.9	22.9	142 24.1	27.9	136 22.7	14.8			
S 12	94 05.1	29 59.4	N17 38.2	94 19.9	S 3 22.3	157 26.8	S21 27.9	151 25.3	S20 14.8	Schedar	349 35.1	N56 38.6
D 13	109 07.5	45 01.8	37.9	109 21.0	21.8	172 29.6	28.0	166 27.9	14.8	Shaula	96 14.9	S37 07.0
A 14	124 10.0	60 04.2	37.6	124 22.0	21.2	187 32.4	28.0	181 30.6	14.9	Sirius	258 29.8	S16 44.7
Y 15	139 12.5	75 06.6 ..	37.4	139 23.0 ..	20.7	202 35.1 ..	28.1	196 33.2 ..	14.9	Spica	158 26.0	S11 16.0
16	154 14.9	90 09.0	37.1	154 24.1	20.1	217 37.9	28.1	211 35.8	15.0	Suhail	222 49.3	S43 31.0
17	169 17.4	105 11.4	36.9	169 25.1	19.6	232 40.7	28.2	226 38.4	15.0			
18	184 19.8	120 13.7	N17 36.6	184 26.1	S 3 19.0	247 43.4	S21 28.3	241 41.1	S20 15.0	Vega	80 35.2	N38 48.2
19	199 22.3	135 16.1	36.4	199 27.2	18.5	262 46.2	28.3	256 43.7	15.1	Zuben'ubi	136 59.8	S16 07.5
20	214 24.8	150 18.5	36.1	214 28.2	17.9	277 48.9	28.4	271 46.3	15.1		SHA	Mer. Pass.
21	229 27.2	165 20.8 ..	35.8	229 29.2 ..	17.4	292 51.7 ..	28.4	286 48.9 ..	15.1			
22	244 29.7	180 23.2	35.6	244 30.3	16.8	307 54.5	28.5	301 51.6	15.2	Venus	295 54.4	10 04
23	259 32.2	195 25.5	35.3	259 31.3	16.3	322 57.2	28.5	316 54.2	15.2	Mars	1 06.7	5 45
Mer.Pass. 5 48.6		v 2.5	d 0.3	v 1.0	d 0.6	v 2.8	d 0.1	v 2.6	d 0.0	Jupiter	63 11.2	1 37
										Saturn	57 14.5	2 00

SUN and MOON

UT	SUN GHA	SUN Dec	MOON GHA	v	MOON Dec	d	HP
d h	° ′	° ′	° ′	′	° ′	′	′
23 00	179 26.4	N23 25.3	156 25.4	7.1	N23 35.4	3.0	57.4
01	194 26.3	25.3	170 51.5	7.0	23 32.4	3.1	57.5
02	209 26.1	25.2	185 17.5	7.1	23 29.3	3.2	57.5
03	224 26.0	.. 25.2	199 43.6	7.1	23 26.1	3.4	57.5
04	239 25.9	25.1	214 09.7	7.1	23 22.7	3.5	57.5
05	254 25.7	25.1	228 35.8	7.1	23 19.2	3.7	57.5
06	269 25.6	N23 25.1	243 01.9	7.1	N23 15.5	3.8	57.6
07	284 25.5	25.0	257 28.0	7.1	23 11.7	3.9	57.6
08	299 25.3	25.0	271 54.1	7.1	23 07.8	4.1	57.6
09	314 25.2	.. 24.9	286 20.2	7.1	23 03.7	4.2	57.6
10	329 25.0	24.9	300 46.3	7.2	22 59.5	4.4	57.6
11	344 24.9	24.8	315 12.5	7.2	22 55.1	4.5	57.7
12	359 24.8	N23 24.8	329 38.7	7.1	N22 50.6	4.7	57.7
13	14 24.6	24.8	344 04.8	7.3	22 45.9	4.8	57.7
14	29 24.5	24.7	358 31.1	7.2	22 41.1	4.9	57.7
15	44 24.4	.. 24.7	12 57.3	7.2	22 36.2	5.1	57.7
16	59 24.2	24.6	27 23.5	7.3	22 31.1	5.2	57.8
17	74 24.1	24.6	41 49.8	7.3	22 25.9	5.3	57.8
18	89 24.0	N23 24.5	56 16.1	7.3	N22 20.6	5.5	57.8
19	104 23.8	24.5	70 42.4	7.4	22 15.1	5.6	57.8
20	119 23.7	24.4	85 08.8	7.3	22 09.5	5.8	57.8
21	134 23.6	.. 24.4	99 35.1	7.4	22 03.7	5.8	57.9
22	149 23.4	24.3	114 01.5	7.5	21 57.9	6.1	57.9
23	164 23.3	24.3	128 28.0	7.4	21 51.8	6.1	57.9
24 00	179 23.2	N23 24.2	142 54.4	7.5	N21 45.7	6.3	57.9
01	194 23.0	24.2	157 20.9	7.5	21 39.4	6.4	57.9
02	209 22.9	24.1	171 47.4	7.6	21 33.0	6.6	58.0
03	224 22.8	.. 24.1	186 14.0	7.6	21 26.4	6.7	58.0
04	239 22.6	24.0	200 40.6	7.6	21 19.7	6.8	58.0
05	254 22.5	23.9	215 07.2	7.6	21 12.9	6.9	58.0
06	269 22.4	N23 23.9	229 33.8	7.7	N21 06.0	7.1	58.0
07	284 22.2	23.8	244 00.5	7.8	20 58.9	7.2	58.1
08	299 22.1	23.8	258 27.3	7.7	20 51.7	7.4	58.1
09	314 21.9	.. 23.7	272 54.0	7.9	20 44.3	7.4	58.1
10	329 21.8	23.7	287 20.9	7.8	20 36.9	7.6	58.1
11	344 21.7	23.6	301 47.7	7.9	20 29.3	7.7	58.1
12	359 21.5	N23 23.5	316 14.6	7.9	N20 21.6	7.8	58.1
13	14 21.4	23.5	330 41.5	8.0	20 13.8	8.0	58.2
14	29 21.3	23.4	345 08.5	8.0	20 05.8	8.1	58.2
15	44 21.1	.. 23.3	359 35.5	8.1	19 57.7	8.2	58.2
16	59 21.0	23.3	14 02.6	8.1	19 49.5	8.3	58.2
17	74 20.9	23.2	28 29.7	8.1	19 41.2	8.4	58.2
18	89 20.7	N23 23.1	42 56.8	8.2	N19 32.8	8.6	58.2
19	104 20.6	23.1	57 24.0	8.2	19 24.2	8.7	58.3
20	119 20.5	23.0	71 51.2	8.3	19 15.5	8.8	58.3
21	134 20.3	.. 22.9	86 18.5	8.3	19 06.7	8.9	58.3
22	149 20.2	22.9	100 45.8	8.3	18 57.8	9.0	58.3
23	164 20.1	22.8	115 13.2	8.4	18 48.8	9.1	58.3
25 00	179 19.9	N23 22.7	129 40.6	8.4	N18 39.7	9.3	58.3
01	194 19.8	22.7	144 08.0	8.5	18 30.4	9.3	58.4
02	209 19.7	22.6	158 35.5	8.6	18 21.1	9.5	58.4
03	224 19.5	.. 22.5	173 03.1	8.6	18 11.6	9.6	58.4
04	239 19.4	22.4	187 30.7	8.6	18 02.0	9.7	58.4
05	254 19.3	22.4	201 58.3	8.7	17 52.3	9.8	58.4
06	269 19.1	N23 22.3	216 26.0	8.8	N17 42.5	9.9	58.4
07	284 19.0	22.2	230 53.8	8.8	17 32.6	10.0	58.5
08	299 18.9	22.1	245 21.6	8.8	17 22.6	10.1	58.5
09	314 18.7	.. 22.1	259 49.4	8.9	17 12.5	10.2	58.5
10	329 18.6	22.0	274 17.3	8.9	17 02.3	10.4	58.5
11	344 18.5	21.9	288 45.2	9.0	16 51.9	10.4	58.5
12	359 18.4	N23 21.8	303 13.2	9.0	N16 41.5	10.5	58.5
13	14 18.2	21.8	317 41.2	9.1	16 31.0	10.6	58.6
14	29 18.1	21.7	332 09.3	9.1	16 20.4	10.7	58.6
15	44 18.0	.. 21.6	346 37.4	9.2	16 09.7	10.8	58.6
16	59 17.8	21.5	1 05.6	9.2	15 58.9	10.9	58.6
17	74 17.7	21.4	15 33.8	9.3	15 48.0	11.0	58.6
18	89 17.6	N23 21.4	30 02.1	9.3	N15 37.0	11.1	58.6
19	104 17.4	21.3	44 30.4	9.3	15 25.9	11.2	58.6
20	119 17.3	21.2	58 58.7	9.4	15 14.7	11.3	58.7
21	134 17.2	.. 21.1	73 27.1	9.5	15 03.4	11.4	58.7
22	149 17.0	21.0	87 55.6	9.5	14 52.0	11.4	58.7
23	164 16.9	20.9	102 24.1	9.5	N14 40.6	11.6	58.7
SD	15.8	d 0.1	SD 15.7		15.8		15.9

Left column day labels: T U E S D A Y (23), W E D N E S D A Y (24), T H U R S D A Y (25)

Twilight, Sunrise and Moonrise

Lat.	Naut.	Civil	Sunrise	23	24	25	26
°	h m	h m	h m	h m	h m	h m	h m
N 72	□	□	□	□	□	03 54	07 30
N 70	□	□	□	□	05 29	07 55	
68	□	□	□	03 41	06 09	08 14	
66	□	□	□	02 38	04 38	06 36	08 29
64	////	////	01 33	03 35	05 12	06 56	08 42
62	////	////	02 11	04 08	05 36	07 13	08 52
60	////	00 51	02 37	04 33	05 55	07 27	09 01
N 58	////	01 42	02 57	04 52	06 11	07 38	09 08
56	////	02 12	03 14	05 08	06 25	07 49	09 15
54	00 47	02 34	03 28	05 22	06 37	07 58	09 21
52	01 34	02 52	03 41	05 34	06 47	08 05	09 27
50	02 01	03 07	03 52	05 45	06 56	08 13	09 32
45	02 47	03 37	04 14	06 07	07 15	08 28	09 42
N 40	03 18	03 59	04 32	06 25	07 31	08 40	09 51
35	03 41	04 18	04 47	06 40	07 44	08 51	09 58
30	03 59	04 33	05 00	06 53	07 56	09 00	10 05
20	04 29	04 58	05 22	07 15	08 16	09 16	10 16
N 10	04 51	05 18	05 41	07 35	08 33	09 30	10 26
0	05 10	05 36	05 59	07 53	08 49	09 43	10 35
S 10	05 27	05 53	06 16	08 11	09 04	09 56	10 44
20	05 43	06 11	06 35	08 30	09 21	10 09	10 54
30	06 00	06 30	06 56	08 52	09 41	10 25	11 05
35	06 09	06 40	07 08	09 05	09 52	10 34	11 11
40	06 18	06 52	07 23	09 20	10 05	10 44	11 19
45	06 28	07 06	07 39	09 38	10 20	10 56	11 27
S 50	06 40	07 22	08 00	09 59	10 39	11 11	11 37
52	06 45	07 29	08 10	10 10	10 48	11 18	11 42
54	06 51	07 37	08 21	10 22	10 58	11 25	11 47
56	06 57	07 46	08 34	10 35	11 09	11 34	11 52
58	07 04	07 57	08 48	10 51	11 21	11 43	11 59
S 60	07 11	08 08	09 06	11 09	11 36	11 54	12 06

Sunset, Twilight and Moonset

Lat.	Sunset	Civil	Naut.	23	24	25	26
°	h m	h m	h m	h m	h m	h m	h m
N 72	□	□	□	□	□	03 22	01 37
N 70	□	□	□	□	01 45	01 10	
68	□	□	□	01 38	01 04	00 49	
66	□	□	□	00 43	00 40	00 36	00 32
64	22 32	////	////	24 06	00 06	00 15	00 19
62	21 54	////	////	23 41	23 57	24 07	00 07
60	21 28	23 13	////	23 21	23 43	23 57	24 08
N 58	21 07	22 23	////	23 05	23 30	23 49	24 03
56	20 51	21 53	////	22 51	23 20	23 41	23 58
54	20 37	21 31	23 17	22 39	23 10	23 34	23 54
52	20 24	21 13	22 31	22 28	23 01	23 28	23 50
50	20 13	20 58	22 03	22 18	22 54	23 23	23 47
45	19 51	20 28	21 18	21 58	22 37	23 10	23 39
N 40	19 33	20 06	20 47	21 42	22 24	23 00	23 33
35	19 18	19 48	20 24	21 28	22 12	22 52	23 27
30	19 05	19 32	20 06	21 16	22 02	22 44	23 22
20	18 43	19 07	19 37	20 55	21 45	22 31	23 14
N 10	18 24	18 47	19 14	20 37	21 29	22 19	23 06
0	18 06	18 29	18 55	20 20	21 15	22 08	22 59
S 10	17 49	18 12	18 38	20 02	21 00	21 57	22 52
20	17 30	17 54	18 22	19 44	20 45	21 45	22 44
30	17 09	17 35	18 05	19 23	20 26	21 31	22 36
35	16 57	17 25	17 57	19 10	20 16	21 23	22 30
40	16 43	17 13	17 47	18 56	20 04	21 14	22 24
45	16 26	17 00	17 37	18 39	19 49	21 03	22 18
S 50	16 05	16 44	17 25	18 17	19 32	20 50	22 09
52	15 55	16 36	17 20	18 07	19 23	20 44	22 05
54	15 44	16 28	17 14	17 56	19 14	20 37	22 01
56	15 31	16 19	17 08	17 43	19 03	20 29	21 56
58	15 17	16 09	17 01	17 27	18 51	20 21	21 51
S 60	14 59	15 57	16 54	17 09	18 37	20 11	21 45

SUN and MOON data

Day	Eqn. of Time 00h	Eqn. of Time 12h	Mer. Pass.	Mer. Pass. Upper	Mer. Pass. Lower	Age	Phase
d	m s	m s	h m	h m	h m	d	%
23	02 14	02 21	12 02	14 06	01 38	02	6
24	02 27	02 34	12 03	15 02	02 34	03	12
25	02 40	02 46	12 03	15 55	03 29	04	20

UT (d h)	ARIES GHA	VENUS −4·6 GHA	Dec	MARS −0·4 GHA	Dec	JUPITER −2·7 GHA	Dec	SATURN +0·2 GHA	Dec	Star Name	SHA	Dec
26 00	274 34.6	210 27.9	N17 35.1	274 32.3	S 3 15.7	338 00.0	S21 28.6	331 56.8	S20 15.3	Acamar	315 14.9	S40 13.3
01	289 37.1	225 30.2	34.9	289 33.4	15.2	353 02.8	28.7	346 59.4	15.3	Achernar	335 23.3	S57 07.8
02	304 39.6	240 32.6	34.6	304 34.4	14.6	8 05.5	28.7	2 02.1	15.3	Acrux	173 03.9	S63 12.9
03	319 42.0	255 34.9 ..	34.4	319 35.4 ..	14.1	23 08.3 ..	28.8	17 04.7 ..	15.4	Adhara	255 09.1	S29 00.1
04	334 44.5	270 37.2	34.1	334 36.5	13.5	38 11.0	28.8	32 07.3	15.4	Aldebaran	290 44.1	N16 32.9
05	349 46.9	285 39.6	33.9	349 37.5	13.0	53 13.8	28.9	47 10.0	15.4			
06	4 49.4	300 41.9	N17 33.6	4 38.5	S 3 12.6	68 16.6	S21 28.9	62 12.6	S20 15.5	Alioth	166 16.3	N55 51.3
07	19 51.9	315 44.2	33.4	19 39.6	11.9	83 19.3	29.0	77 15.2	15.5	Alkaid	152 54.8	N49 13.0
08	34 54.3	330 46.5	33.2	34 40.6	11.3	98 22.1	29.1	92 17.8	15.6	Alnair	27 37.3	S46 51.5
F 09	49 56.8	345 48.8 ..	32.9	49 41.6 ..	10.8	113 24.9 ..	29.1	107 20.5 ..	15.6	Alnilam	275 41.8	S 1 11.4
R 10	64 59.3	0 51.1	32.7	64 42.7	10.2	128 27.6	29.2	122 23.1	15.6	Alphard	217 51.6	S 8 44.8
I 11	80 01.7	15 53.5	32.5	79 43.7	09.7	143 30.4	29.2	137 25.7	15.7			
D 12	95 04.2	30 55.8	N17 32.2	94 44.8	S 3 09.1	158 33.2	S21 29.3	152 28.3	S20 15.7	Alphecca	126 06.6	N26 39.0
A 13	110 06.7	45 58.1	32.0	109 45.8	08.6	173 35.9	29.3	167 31.0	15.8	Alpheratz	357 38.5	N29 11.9
Y 14	125 09.1	61 00.3	31.8	124 46.8	08.0	188 38.7	29.4	182 33.6	15.8	Altair	62 03.2	N 8 55.4
15	140 11.6	76 02.6 ..	31.6	139 47.9 ..	07.5	203 41.5 ..	29.5	197 36.2 ..	15.8	Ankaa	353 10.9	S42 11.6
16	155 14.1	91 04.9	31.3	154 48.9	06.9	218 44.2	29.5	212 38.9	15.9	Antares	112 20.0	S26 28.6
17	170 16.5	106 07.2	31.1	169 50.0	06.4	233 47.0	29.6	227 41.5	15.9			
18	185 19.0	121 09.5	N17 30.9	184 51.0	S 3 05.8	248 49.8	S21 29.6	242 44.1	S20 15.9	Arcturus	145 51.1	N19 04.8
19	200 21.4	136 11.8	30.7	199 52.0	05.3	263 52.5	29.7	257 46.7	16.0	Atria	107 16.9	S69 03.8
20	215 23.9	151 14.0	30.4	214 53.1	04.7	278 55.3	29.7	272 49.4	16.0	Avior	234 16.7	S59 34.6
21	230 26.4	166 16.3 ..	30.2	229 54.1 ..	04.2	293 58.1 ..	29.8	287 52.0 ..	16.1	Bellatrix	278 27.1	N 6 22.0
22	245 28.8	181 18.6	30.0	244 55.2	03.6	309 00.8	29.9	302 54.6	16.1	Betelgeuse	270 56.4	N 7 24.6
23	260 31.3	196 20.8	29.8	259 56.2	03.1	324 03.6	29.9	317 57.2	16.1			
27 00	275 33.8	211 23.1	N17 29.6	274 57.2	S 3 02.5	339 06.4	S21 30.0	332 59.9	S20 16.2	Canopus	263 54.6	S52 42.4
01	290 36.2	226 25.3	29.4	289 58.3	02.0	354 09.1	30.0	348 02.5	16.2	Capella	280 27.7	N46 00.9
02	305 38.7	241 27.6	29.2	304 59.3	01.4	9 11.9	30.1	3 05.1	16.2	Deneb	49 27.8	N45 21.1
03	320 41.2	256 29.8 ..	29.0	320 00.4 ..	00.9	24 14.7 ..	30.1	18 07.8 ..	16.3	Denebola	182 28.8	N14 27.7
04	335 43.6	271 32.0	28.7	335 01.4	3 00.3	39 17.4	30.2	33 10.4	16.3	Diphda	348 51.0	S17 52.5
05	350 46.1	286 34.3	28.5	350 02.4	2 59.8	54 20.2	30.3	48 13.0	16.4			
06	5 48.6	301 36.5	N17 28.3	5 03.5	S 2 59.2	69 23.0	S21 30.3	63 15.6	S20 16.4	Dubhe	193 45.9	N61 38.8
07	20 51.0	316 38.7	28.1	20 04.5	58.7	84 25.7	30.4	78 18.3	16.4	Elnath	278 06.9	N28 37.3
S 08	35 53.5	331 41.0	27.9	35 05.6	58.1	99 28.5	30.4	93 20.9	16.5	Eltanin	90 43.3	N51 29.3
A 09	50 55.9	346 43.2 ..	27.7	50 06.6 ..	57.6	114 31.3 ..	30.5	108 23.5 ..	16.5	Enif	33 42.1	N 9 58.1
T 10	65 58.4	1 45.4	27.5	65 07.7	57.0	129 34.0	30.6	123 26.2	16.5	Fomalhaut	15 18.5	S29 30.7
U 11	81 00.9	16 47.6	27.3	80 08.7	56.5	144 36.8	30.6	138 28.8	16.6			
R 12	96 03.3	31 49.8	N17 27.1	95 09.7	S 2 55.9	159 39.6	S21 30.7	153 31.4	S20 16.6	Gacrux	171 55.5	S57 13.8
D 13	111 05.8	46 52.0	26.9	110 10.8	55.4	174 42.3	30.7	168 34.1	16.7	Gienah	175 47.3	S17 39.3
A 14	126 08.3	61 54.2	26.7	125 11.8	54.8	189 45.1	30.8	183 36.7	16.7	Hadar	148 40.7	S60 28.4
Y 15	141 10.7	76 56.4 ..	26.6	140 12.9 ..	54.3	204 47.9 ..	30.8	198 39.3 ..	16.7	Hamal	327 55.4	N23 33.3
16	156 13.2	91 58.6	26.4	155 13.9	53.7	219 50.6	30.9	213 41.9	16.8	Kaus Aust.	83 37.0	S34 22.4
17	171 15.7	107 00.8	26.2	170 15.0	53.2	234 53.4	31.0	228 44.6	16.8			
18	186 18.1	122 03.0	N17 26.0	185 16.0	S 2 52.7	249 56.2	S21 31.0	243 47.2	S20 16.9	Kochab	137 19.3	N74 04.6
19	201 20.6	137 05.2	25.8	200 17.1	52.1	264 59.0	31.1	258 49.8	16.9	Markab	13 33.4	N15 18.8
20	216 23.0	152 07.4	25.6	215 18.1	51.6	280 01.7	31.1	273 52.5	16.9	Menkar	314 10.2	N 4 10.1
21	231 25.5	167 09.5 ..	25.4	230 19.2 ..	51.0	295 04.5 ..	31.2	288 55.1 ..	17.0	Menkent	148 01.7	S36 28.3
22	246 28.0	182 11.7	25.3	245 20.2	50.5	310 07.3	31.2	303 57.7	17.0	Miaplacidus	221 39.5	S69 48.2
23	261 30.4	197 13.9	25.1	260 21.3	49.9	325 10.0	31.3	319 00.4	17.0			
28 00	276 32.9	212 16.0	N17 24.9	275 22.3	S 2 49.4	340 12.8	S21 31.4	334 03.0	S20 17.1	Mirfak	308 33.8	N49 55.7
01	291 35.4	227 18.2	24.7	290 23.4	48.8	355 15.6	31.4	349 05.6	17.1	Nunki	75 51.9	S26 16.2
02	306 37.8	242 20.3	24.5	305 24.4	48.3	10 18.4	31.5	4 08.2	17.2	Peacock	53 11.0	S56 44.0
03	321 40.3	257 22.5 ..	24.4	320 25.5 ..	47.7	25 21.1 ..	31.5	19 10.9 ..	17.2	Pollux	243 22.2	N27 58.6
04	336 42.8	272 24.6	24.2	335 26.5	47.2	40 23.9	31.6	34 13.5	17.2	Procyon	244 55.0	N 5 10.3
05	351 45.2	287 26.8	24.0	350 27.6	46.6	55 26.7	31.7	49 16.1	17.3			
06	6 47.7	302 28.9	N17 23.8	5 28.6	S 2 46.1	70 29.4	S21 31.7	64 18.8	S20 17.3	Rasalhague	96 01.6	N12 32.8
07	21 50.2	317 31.1	23.7	20 29.7	45.6	85 32.2	31.8	79 21.4	17.4	Regulus	207 38.5	N11 52.1
08	36 52.6	332 33.2	23.5	35 30.7	45.0	100 35.0	31.8	94 24.0	17.4	Rigel	281 07.7	S 8 10.8
S 09	51 55.1	347 35.3 ..	23.3	50 31.8 ..	44.5	115 37.8 ..	31.9	109 26.7 ..	17.4	Rigil Kent.	139 44.8	S60 55.2
U 10	66 57.5	2 37.5	23.2	65 32.8	43.9	130 40.5	31.9	124 29.3	17.5	Sabik	102 06.6	S15 44.9
N 11	82 00.0	17 39.6	23.0	80 33.9	43.4	145 43.3	32.0	139 31.9	17.5			
D 12	97 02.5	32 41.7	N17 22.9	95 34.9	S 2 42.8	160 46.1	S21 32.1	154 34.6	S20 17.5	Schedar	349 35.1	N56 38.6
A 13	112 04.9	47 43.8	22.7	110 36.0	42.3	175 48.9	32.1	169 37.2	17.6	Shaula	96 14.9	S37 07.0
Y 14	127 07.4	62 45.9	22.5	125 37.0	41.7	190 51.6	32.2	184 39.8	17.6	Sirius	258 29.8	S16 44.7
15	142 09.9	77 48.0 ..	22.4	140 38.1 ..	41.2	205 54.4 ..	32.2	199 42.5 ..	17.7	Spica	158 26.0	S11 16.0
16	157 12.3	92 50.1	22.2	155 39.1	40.7	220 57.2	32.3	214 45.1	17.7	Suhail	222 49.3	S43 31.0
17	172 14.8	107 52.2	22.1	170 40.2	40.1	235 59.9	32.3	229 47.7	17.7			
18	187 17.3	122 54.3	N17 21.9	185 41.2	S 2 39.6	251 02.7	S21 32.4	244 50.4	S20 17.8	Vega	80 35.2	N38 48.2
19	202 19.7	137 56.4	21.8	200 42.3	39.0	266 05.5	32.5	259 53.0	17.8	Zuben'ubi	136 59.8	S16 07.5
20	217 22.2	152 58.5	21.6	215 43.3	38.5	281 08.3	32.5	274 55.6	17.9			
21	232 24.6	168 00.6 ..	21.4	230 44.4 ..	37.9	296 11.0 ..	32.6	289 58.3 ..	17.9			
22	247 27.1	183 02.7	21.3	245 45.4	37.4	311 13.8	32.6	305 00.9	17.9			
23	262 29.6	198 04.8	21.2	260 46.5	36.9	326 16.6	32.7	320 03.5	18.0			
Mer. Pass. 5 36.8		v 2.2	d 0.2	v 1.0	d 0.5	v 2.8	d 0.1	v 2.6	d 0.0			

	SHA	Mer. Pass.
Venus	295 49.3	9 53
Mars	359 23.5	5 40
Jupiter	63 32.6	1 23
Saturn	57 26.1	1 48

UT	SUN GHA	SUN Dec	MOON GHA	v	MOON Dec	d	HP
26 00	179 16.8	N23 20.8	116 52.6	9.6	N14 29.0	11.6	58.7
01	194 16.6	20.8	131 21.2	9.6	14 17.4	11.7	58.7
02	209 16.5	20.7	145 49.8	9.7	14 05.7	11.8	58.7
03	224 16.4	.. 20.6	160 18.5	9.7	13 53.9	11.9	58.7
04	239 16.2	20.5	174 47.2	9.8	13 42.0	11.9	58.8
05	254 16.1	20.4	189 16.0	9.8	13 30.1	12.0	58.8
06	269 16.0	N23 20.3	203 44.8	9.9	N13 18.1	12.2	58.8
07	284 15.8	20.2	218 13.7	9.9	13 05.9	12.1	58.8
08	299 15.7	20.1	232 42.6	9.9	12 53.8	12.3	58.8
F 09	314 15.6	.. 20.0	247 11.5	10.0	12 41.5	12.4	58.8
R 10	329 15.5	19.9	261 40.5	10.0	12 29.1	12.4	58.8
I 11	344 15.3	19.8	276 09.5	10.1	12 16.7	12.5	58.8
D 12	359 15.2	N23 19.7	290 38.6	10.1	N12 04.2	12.5	58.9
A 13	14 15.1	19.6	305 07.7	10.1	11 51.7	12.6	58.9
Y 14	29 14.9	19.5	319 36.8	10.2	11 39.1	12.7	58.9
15	44 14.8	.. 19.4	334 06.0	10.2	11 26.4	12.8	58.9
16	59 14.7	19.4	348 35.2	10.2	11 13.6	12.8	58.9
17	74 14.5	19.3	3 04.4	10.3	11 00.8	12.9	58.9
18	89 14.4	N23 19.2	17 33.7	10.4	N10 47.9	13.0	58.9
19	104 14.3	19.1	32 03.1	10.3	10 34.9	13.0	58.9
20	119 14.2	18.9	46 32.4	10.4	10 21.9	13.1	59.0
21	134 14.0	.. 18.8	61 01.8	10.4	10 08.8	13.1	59.0
22	149 13.9	18.7	75 31.2	10.5	9 55.7	13.2	59.0
23	164 13.8	18.6	90 00.7	10.5	9 42.5	13.2	59.0
27 00	179 13.6	N23 18.5	104 30.2	10.5	N 9 29.3	13.4	59.0
01	194 13.5	18.4	118 59.7	10.6	9 15.9	13.3	59.0
02	209 13.4	18.3	133 29.3	10.6	9 02.6	13.4	59.0
03	224 13.2	.. 18.2	147 58.9	10.6	8 49.2	13.5	59.0
04	239 13.1	18.1	162 28.5	10.7	8 35.7	13.5	59.0
05	254 13.0	18.0	176 58.2	10.6	8 22.2	13.6	59.1
06	269 12.9	N23 17.9	191 27.8	10.7	N 8 08.6	13.6	59.1
S 07	284 12.7	17.8	205 57.5	10.7	7 55.0	13.7	59.1
A 08	299 12.6	17.7	220 27.3	10.7	7 41.3	13.7	59.1
T 09	314 12.5	.. 17.6	234 57.0	10.8	7 27.6	13.7	59.1
U 10	329 12.3	17.5	249 26.8	10.8	7 13.9	13.8	59.1
R 11	344 12.2	17.3	263 56.6	10.8	7 00.1	13.9	59.1
D 12	359 12.1	N23 17.2	278 26.4	10.9	N 6 46.2	13.8	59.1
A 13	14 12.0	17.1	292 56.3	10.8	6 32.4	14.0	59.1
Y 14	29 11.8	17.0	307 26.1	10.9	6 18.4	13.9	59.1
15	44 11.7	.. 16.9	321 56.0	10.9	6 04.5	14.0	59.1
16	59 11.6	16.8	336 25.9	11.0	5 50.5	14.0	59.2
17	74 11.4	16.7	350 55.9	10.9	5 36.5	14.1	59.2
18	89 11.3	N23 16.5	5 25.8	11.0	N 5 22.4	14.1	59.2
19	104 11.2	16.4	19 55.8	10.9	5 08.3	14.1	59.2
20	119 11.1	16.3	34 25.7	11.0	4 54.2	14.1	59.2
21	134 10.9	.. 16.2	48 55.7	11.0	4 40.1	14.2	59.2
22	149 10.8	16.1	63 25.7	11.0	4 25.9	14.2	59.2
23	164 10.7	15.9	77 55.7	11.1	4 11.7	14.3	59.2
28 00	179 10.5	N23 15.8	92 25.8	11.0	N 3 57.4	14.2	59.2
01	194 10.4	15.7	106 55.8	11.0	3 43.2	14.3	59.2
02	209 10.3	15.6	121 25.8	11.1	3 28.9	14.3	59.2
03	224 10.2	.. 15.5	135 55.9	11.0	3 14.6	14.3	59.2
04	239 10.0	15.3	150 25.9	11.1	3 00.3	14.4	59.3
05	254 09.9	15.2	164 56.0	11.1	2 45.9	14.4	59.3
06	269 09.8	N23 15.1	179 26.1	11.1	N 2 31.5	14.3	59.3
07	284 09.7	15.0	193 56.2	11.0	2 17.2	14.4	59.3
08	299 09.5	14.8	208 26.2	11.1	2 02.8	14.4	59.3
S 09	314 09.4	.. 14.7	222 56.3	11.1	1 48.4	14.5	59.3
U 10	329 09.3	14.6	237 26.4	11.1	1 33.9	14.4	59.3
N 11	344 09.2	14.4	251 56.5	11.1	1 19.5	14.4	59.3
D 12	359 09.0	N23 14.3	266 26.6	11.0	N 1 05.1	14.5	59.3
A 13	14 08.9	14.2	280 56.6	11.1	0 50.6	14.5	59.3
Y 14	29 08.8	14.0	295 26.7	11.0	0 36.1	14.4	59.3
15	44 08.6	.. 13.9	309 56.8	11.1	0 21.7	14.5	59.3
16	59 08.5	13.8	324 26.9	11.0	N 0 07.2	14.5	59.3
17	74 08.4	13.7	338 56.9	11.1	S 0 07.3	14.4	59.3
18	89 08.3	N23 13.5	353 27.0	11.0	S 0 21.7	14.5	59.3
19	104 08.1	13.4	7 57.0	11.1	0 36.2	14.5	59.3
20	119 08.0	13.2	22 27.1	11.0	0 50.7	14.5	59.4
21	134 07.9	.. 13.1	36 57.1	11.0	1 05.2	14.4	59.4
22	149 07.8	13.0	51 27.1	11.0	1 19.6	14.5	59.4
23	164 07.6	12.8	65 57.1	11.0	S 1 34.1	14.5	59.4
SD	15.8	d 0.1	SD 16.0		16.1		16.2

Twilight / Sunrise / Moonrise

Lat.	Naut.	Civil	Sunrise	Moonrise 26	27	28	29
N 72	□	□	□	07 30	09 52	12 03	14 14
N 70	□	□	□	07 55	10 03	12 04	14 06
68	□	□	□	08 14	10 12	12 06	14 00
66	□	□	□	08 29	10 19	12 06	13 54
64	////	////	01 36	08 42	10 25	12 07	13 50
62	////	////	02 13	08 52	10 30	12 08	13 46
60	////	00 56	02 39	09 01	10 35	12 08	13 42
N 58	////	01 44	02 59	09 08	10 39	12 09	13 40
56	////	02 14	03 16	09 15	10 42	12 09	13 37
54	00 51	02 36	03 30	09 21	10 46	12 10	13 35
52	01 36	02 53	03 42	09 27	10 48	12 10	13 32
50	02 03	03 08	03 53	09 32	10 51	12 11	13 30
45	02 48	03 38	04 15	09 42	10 57	12 11	13 26
N 40	03 19	04 00	04 33	09 51	11 01	12 12	13 23
35	03 42	04 19	04 48	09 58	11 05	12 12	13 20
30	04 00	04 34	05 01	10 05	11 09	12 13	13 17
20	04 29	04 59	05 23	10 16	11 15	12 14	13 13
N 10	04 52	05 19	05 42	10 26	11 21	12 15	13 09
0	05 11	05 37	06 00	10 35	11 26	12 15	13 05
S 10	05 28	05 54	06 17	10 44	11 31	12 16	13 02
20	05 44	06 11	06 35	10 54	11 36	12 17	12 58
30	06 00	06 30	06 56	11 05	11 42	12 18	12 53
35	06 09	06 41	07 09	11 11	11 46	12 18	12 51
40	06 18	06 52	07 23	11 19	11 50	12 19	12 48
45	06 29	07 06	07 40	11 27	11 54	12 20	12 45
S 50	06 40	07 22	08 00	11 37	12 00	12 21	12 41
52	06 45	07 29	08 10	11 42	12 02	12 21	12 40
54	06 51	07 37	08 21	11 47	12 05	12 21	12 38
56	06 57	07 46	08 34	11 52	12 08	12 22	12 36
58	07 04	07 56	08 48	11 59	12 11	12 22	12 34
S 60	07 11	08 08	09 05	12 06	12 15	12 23	12 31

Sunset / Twilight / Moonset

Lat.	Sunset	Civil	Naut.	Moonset 26	27	28	29
N 72	□	□	□	01 37	01 02	00 37	(00 14 / 23 49)
N 70	□	□	□	01 10	00 49	00 32	00 16
68	□	□	□	00 49	00 38	00 28	00 18
66	□	□	□	00 32	00 28	00 24	00 20
64	22 30	////	////	00 19	00 21	00 22	00 22
62	21 53	////	////	00 07	00 14	00 19	00 23
60	21 27	23 09	////	24 08	00 08	00 17	00 25
N 58	21 07	22 21	////	24 03	00 03	00 15	00 26
56	20 50	21 52	////	23 58	24 13	00 13	00 27
54	20 36	21 30	23 14	23 54	24 11	00 11	00 27
52	20 24	21 13	22 30	23 50	24 10	00 10	00 28
50	20 13	20 58	22 03	23 47	24 08	00 08	00 29
45	19 51	20 28	21 18	23 39	24 05	00 05	00 31
N 40	19 33	20 06	20 47	23 33	24 03	00 03	00 32
35	19 18	19 48	20 24	23 27	24 01	00 01	00 33
30	19 05	19 33	20 06	23 22	23 59	24 34	00 34
20	18 43	19 08	19 37	23 14	23 55	24 36	00 36
N 10	18 24	18 47	19 14	23 06	23 52	24 37	00 37
0	18 07	18 29	18 56	22 59	23 49	24 39	00 39
S 10	17 50	18 12	18 39	22 52	23 46	24 40	00 40
20	17 31	17 55	18 23	22 44	23 43	24 42	00 42
30	17 10	17 36	18 06	22 36	23 40	24 44	00 44
35	16 58	17 26	17 58	22 30	23 37	24 44	00 44
40	16 44	17 14	17 48	22 24	23 35	24 46	00 46
45	16 27	17 01	17 38	22 18	23 32	24 47	00 47
S 50	16 06	16 45	17 26	22 09	23 29	24 48	00 48
52	15 57	16 37	17 21	22 05	23 27	24 49	00 49
54	15 46	16 29	17 15	22 01	23 25	24 50	00 50
56	15 33	16 20	17 09	21 56	23 24	24 51	00 51
58	15 18	16 10	17 03	21 51	23 21	24 52	00 52
S 60	15 01	15 59	16 55	21 45	23 19	24 53	00 53

SUN and MOON

Day	SUN Eqn. of Time 00h	12h	Mer. Pass.	MOON Mer. Pass. Upper	Lower	Age	Phase
	m s	m s	h m	h m	h m	d	%
26	02 53	02 59	12 03	16 47	04 22	05	30
27	03 05	03 11	12 03	17 38	05 13	06	40
28	03 18	03 24	12 03	18 27	06 02	07	52

UT	ARIES GHA	VENUS −4.7 GHA	Dec	MARS −0.5 GHA	Dec	JUPITER −2.7 GHA	Dec	SATURN +0.2 GHA	Dec
29 00	277 32.0	213 06.8	N17 21.0	275 47.6	S 2 36.3	341 19.4	S21 32.8	335 06.2	S20 18.0
01	292 34.5	228 08.9	20.9	290 48.6	35.8	356 22.1	32.8	350 08.8	18.0
02	307 37.0	243 11.0	20.7	305 49.7	35.2	11 24.9	32.9	5 11.4	18.1
03	322 39.4	258 13.0 ..	20.6	320 50.7 ..	34.7	26 27.7 ..	32.9	20 14.0 ..	18.1
04	337 41.9	273 15.1	20.4	335 51.8	34.1	41 30.5	33.0	35 16.7	18.2
05	352 44.4	288 17.2	20.3	350 52.8	33.6	56 33.2	33.0	50 19.3	18.2
M 06	7 46.8	303 19.2	N17 20.2	5 53.9	S 2 33.1	71 36.0	S21 33.1	65 21.9	S20 18.2
O 07	22 49.3	318 21.3	20.0	20 55.0	32.5	86 38.8	33.2	80 24.6	18.3
N 08	37 51.8	333 23.3	19.9	35 56.0	32.0	101 41.6	33.2	95 27.2	18.3
D 09	52 54.2	348 25.3 ..	19.7	50 57.1 ..	31.4	116 44.3 ..	33.3	110 29.8 ..	18.4
A 10	67 56.7	3 27.4	19.6	65 58.1	30.9	131 47.1	33.3	125 32.5	18.4
Y 11	82 59.1	18 29.4	19.5	80 59.2	30.4	146 49.9	33.4	140 35.1	18.4
12	98 01.6	33 31.4	N17 19.4	96 00.3	S 2 29.8	161 52.7	S21 33.5	155 37.8	S20 18.5
13	113 04.1	48 33.5	19.2	111 01.3	29.3	176 55.5	33.5	170 40.4	18.5
14	128 06.5	63 35.5	19.1	126 02.4	28.7	191 58.2	33.6	185 43.0	18.5
15	143 09.0	78 37.5 ..	19.0	141 03.4 ..	28.2	207 01.0 ..	33.6	200 45.7 ..	18.6
16	158 11.5	93 39.5	18.8	156 04.5	27.6	222 03.8	33.7	215 48.3	18.6
17	173 13.9	108 41.5	18.7	171 05.6	27.1	237 06.6	33.8	230 50.9	18.7
18	188 16.4	123 43.5	N17 18.6	186 06.6	S 2 26.6	252 09.3	S21 33.8	245 53.6	S20 18.7
19	203 18.9	138 45.6	18.5	201 07.7	26.0	267 12.1	33.9	260 56.2	18.7
20	218 21.3	153 47.6	18.4	216 08.7	25.5	282 14.9	33.9	275 58.8	18.8
21	233 23.8	168 49.5 ..	18.2	231 09.8 ..	24.9	297 17.7 ..	34.0	291 01.5 ..	18.8
22	248 26.3	183 51.5	18.1	246 10.9	24.4	312 20.5	34.0	306 04.1	18.9
23	263 28.7	198 53.5	18.0	261 11.9	23.9	327 23.2	34.1	321 06.7	18.9
30 00	278 31.2	213 55.5	N17 17.9	276 13.0	S 2 23.3	342 26.0	S21 34.2	336 09.4	S20 18.9
01	293 33.6	228 57.5	17.8	291 14.0	22.8	357 28.8	34.2	351 12.0	19.0
02	308 36.1	243 59.5	17.7	306 15.1	22.2	12 31.6	34.3	6 14.6	19.0
03	323 38.6	259 01.5 ..	17.6	321 16.2 ..	21.7	27 34.3 ..	34.3	21 17.3 ..	19.1
04	338 41.0	274 03.4	17.4	336 17.2	21.2	42 37.1	34.4	36 19.9	19.1
05	353 43.5	289 05.4	17.3	351 18.3	20.6	57 39.9	34.5	51 22.5	19.1
T 06	8 46.0	304 07.4	N17 17.2	6 19.4	S 2 20.1	72 42.7	S21 34.5	66 25.2	S20 19.2
U 07	23 48.4	319 09.3	17.1	21 20.4	19.5	87 45.5	34.6	81 27.8	19.2
E 08	38 50.9	334 11.3	17.0	36 21.5	19.0	102 48.2	34.6	96 30.4	19.2
S 09	53 53.4	349 13.2 ..	16.9	51 22.6 ..	18.5	117 51.0 ..	34.7	111 33.1 ..	19.3
D 10	68 55.8	4 15.2	16.8	66 23.6	17.9	132 53.8	34.7	126 35.7	19.3
A 11	83 58.3	19 17.1	16.7	81 24.7	17.4	147 56.6	34.8	141 38.4	19.4
Y 12	99 00.7	34 19.1	N17 16.6	96 25.8	S 2 16.9	162 59.4	S21 34.9	156 41.0	S20 19.4
13	114 03.2	49 21.0	16.5	111 26.8	16.3	178 02.1	34.9	171 43.6	19.4
14	129 05.7	64 23.0	16.4	126 27.9	15.8	193 04.9	35.0	186 46.3	19.5
15	144 08.1	79 24.9 ..	16.3	141 29.0 ..	15.2	208 07.7 ..	35.0	201 48.9 ..	19.5
16	159 10.6	94 26.8	16.2	156 30.0	14.7	223 10.5	35.1	216 51.5	19.6
17	174 13.1	109 28.8	16.1	171 31.1	14.2	238 13.3	35.2	231 54.2	19.6
18	189 15.5	124 30.7	N17 16.0	186 32.2	S 2 13.6	253 16.0	S21 35.2	246 56.8	S20 19.6
19	204 18.0	139 32.6	16.0	201 33.2	13.1	268 18.8	35.3	261 59.4	19.7
20	219 20.5	154 34.5	15.9	216 34.3	12.6	283 21.6	35.3	277 02.1	19.7
21	234 22.9	169 36.4 ..	15.8	231 35.4 ..	12.0	298 24.4 ..	35.4	292 04.7 ..	19.8
22	249 25.4	184 38.3	15.7	246 36.4	11.5	313 27.2	35.5	307 07.3	19.8
23	264 27.9	199 40.2	15.6	261 37.5	10.9	328 30.0	35.5	322 10.0	19.8
1 00	279 30.3	214 42.1	N17 15.5	276 38.6	S 2 10.4	343 32.7	S21 35.6	337 12.6	S20 19.9
01	294 32.8	229 44.0	15.4	291 39.7	09.9	358 35.5	35.6	352 15.3	19.9
02	309 35.2	244 45.9	15.4	306 40.7	09.3	13 38.3	35.7	7 17.9	20.0
03	324 37.7	259 47.8 ..	15.3	321 41.8 ..	08.8	28 41.1 ..	35.7	22 20.5 ..	20.0
04	339 40.2	274 49.7	15.2	336 42.9	08.3	43 43.9	35.8	37 23.2	20.0
05	354 42.6	289 51.6	15.1	351 43.9	07.7	58 46.6	35.9	52 25.8	20.1
W 06	9 45.1	304 53.5	N17 15.0	6 45.0	S 2 07.2	73 49.4	S21 35.9	67 28.4	S20 20.1
E 07	24 47.6	319 55.4	15.0	21 46.1	06.7	88 52.2	36.0	82 31.1	20.1
D 08	39 50.0	334 57.2	14.9	36 47.2	06.1	103 55.0	36.0	97 33.7	20.2
N 09	54 52.5	349 59.1 ..	14.8	51 48.2 ..	05.6	118 57.8 ..	36.1	112 36.4 ..	20.2
E 10	69 55.0	5 01.0	14.8	66 49.3	05.1	134 00.6	36.2	127 39.0	20.3
S 11	84 57.4	20 02.8	14.7	81 50.4	04.5	149 03.3	36.2	142 41.6	20.3
D 12	99 59.9	35 04.7	N17 14.6	96 51.5	S 2 04.0	164 06.1	S21 36.3	157 44.3	S20 20.3
A 13	115 02.4	50 06.6	14.5	111 52.5	03.4	179 08.9	36.3	172 46.9	20.4
Y 14	130 04.8	65 08.4	14.5	126 53.6	02.9	194 11.7	36.4	187 49.5	20.4
15	145 07.3	80 10.3 ..	14.4	141 54.7 ..	02.4	209 14.5 ..	36.5	202 52.2 ..	20.5
16	160 09.7	95 12.1	14.3	156 55.8	01.8	224 17.3	36.5	217 54.8	20.5
17	175 12.2	110 13.9	14.3	171 56.8	01.3	239 20.1	36.6	232 57.5	20.5
18	190 14.7	125 15.8	N17 14.2	186 57.9	S 2 00.8	254 22.8	S21 36.6	248 00.1	S20 20.6
19	205 17.1	140 17.6	14.2	201 59.0	S 2 00.2	269 25.6	36.7	263 02.7	20.6
20	220 19.6	155 19.5	14.1	217 00.1	1 59.7	284 28.4	36.7	278 05.4	20.7
21	235 22.1	170 21.3 ..	14.0	232 01.1 ..	59.2	299 31.2 ..	36.8	293 08.0 ..	20.7
22	250 24.5	185 23.1	14.0	247 02.2	58.6	314 34.0	36.9	308 10.6	20.7
23	265 27.0	200 24.9	13.9	262 03.3	58.1	329 36.8	36.9	323 13.3	20.8
Mer. Pass.	5 25.0	v 1.9	d 0.1	v 1.1	d 0.5	v 2.8	d 0.1	v 2.6	d 0.0

STARS

Name	SHA	Dec
Acamar	315 14.9	S40 13.3
Achernar	335 23.2	S57 07.8
Acrux	173 03.9	S63 12.9
Adhara	255 09.1	S29 00.0
Aldebaran	290 44.1	N16 32.9
Alioth	166 16.3	N55 51.3
Alkaid	152 54.8	N49 13.0
Alnair	27 37.3	S46 51.5
Alnilam	275 41.8	S 1 11.4
Alphard	217 51.6	S 8 44.8
Alphecca	126 06.6	N26 39.0
Alpheratz	357 38.4	N29 12.0
Altair	62 03.2	N 8 55.4
Ankaa	353 10.8	S42 11.6
Antares	112 20.0	S26 28.6
Arcturus	145 51.1	N19 04.8
Atria	107 16.9	S69 03.8
Avior	234 16.7	S59 34.6
Bellatrix	278 27.1	N 6 22.0
Betelgeuse	270 56.4	N 7 24.6
Canopus	263 54.6	S52 42.4
Capella	280 27.7	N46 00.9
Deneb	49 27.8	N45 21.1
Denebola	182 28.8	N14 27.7
Diphda	348 51.0	S17 52.5
Dubhe	193 46.0	N61 38.8
Elnath	278 06.8	N28 37.3
Eltanin	90 43.3	N51 29.3
Enif	33 42.1	N 9 58.1
Fomalhaut	15 18.4	S29 30.7
Gacrux	171 55.6	S57 13.8
Gienah	175 47.3	S17 39.3
Hadar	148 40.8	S60 28.4
Hamal	327 55.4	N23 33.3
Kaus Aust.	83 37.0	S34 22.4
Kochab	137 19.3	N74 04.7
Markab	13 33.4	N15 18.8
Menkar	314 10.2	N 4 10.1
Menkent	148 01.7	S36 28.3
Miaplacidus	221 39.5	S69 48.2
Mirfak	308 33.8	N49 55.7
Nunki	75 51.9	S26 16.2
Peacock	53 11.0	S56 44.0
Pollux	243 22.2	N27 58.6
Procyon	244 55.0	N 5 10.3
Rasalhague	96 01.6	N12 32.8
Regulus	207 38.6	N11 52.2
Rigel	281 07.7	S 8 10.8
Rigil Kent.	139 44.8	S60 55.2
Sabik	102 06.6	S15 44.9
Schedar	349 35.1	N56 38.6
Shaula	96 14.9	S37 07.0
Sirius	258 29.8	S16 44.7
Spica	158 26.1	S11 16.0
Suhail	222 49.3	S43 31.0
Vega	80 35.2	N38 48.2
Zuben'ubi	136 59.8	S16 07.5

	SHA	Mer. Pass.
Venus	295 24.3	9 43
Mars	357 41.8	5 35
Jupiter	63 54.8	1 10
Saturn	57 38.2	1 35

UT	SUN GHA	SUN Dec	MOON GHA	v	MOON Dec	d	HP
d h	° ′	° ′	° ′	′	° ′	′	′
29 00	179 07.5	N23 12.7	80 27.1	11.0	S 1 48.6	14.4	59.4
01	194 07.4	12.6	94 57.1	11.0	2 03.0	14.5	59.4
02	209 07.3	12.4	109 27.1	10.9	2 17.5	14.4	59.4
03	224 07.1	.. 12.3	123 57.0	10.9	2 31.9	14.4	59.4
04	239 07.0	12.1	138 26.9	11.0	2 46.3	14.5	59.4
05	254 06.9	12.0	152 56.9	10.8	3 00.8	14.4	59.4
06	269 06.8	N23 11.9	167 26.7	10.9	S 3 15.2	14.3	59.4
07	284 06.6	11.7	181 56.6	10.9	3 29.5	14.4	59.4
M 08	299 06.5	11.6	196 26.5	10.8	3 43.9	14.3	59.4
O 09	314 06.4	.. 11.4	210 56.3	10.8	3 58.2	14.4	59.4
N 10	329 06.3	11.3	225 26.1	10.8	4 12.6	14.3	59.4
D 11	344 06.2	11.1	239 55.9	10.7	4 26.9	14.3	59.4
A 12	359 06.0	N23 11.0	254 25.6	10.8	S 4 41.2	14.2	59.4
Y 13	14 05.9	10.8	268 55.4	10.7	4 55.4	14.3	59.4
14	29 05.8	10.7	283 25.1	10.7	5 09.7	14.2	59.4
15	44 05.7	.. 10.5	297 54.8	10.6	5 23.9	14.2	59.4
16	59 05.5	10.4	312 24.4	10.6	5 38.1	14.1	59.4
17	74 05.4	10.2	326 54.0	10.6	5 52.2	14.1	59.4
18	89 05.3	N23 10.1	341 23.6	10.5	S 6 06.3	14.1	59.4
19	104 05.2	09.9	355 53.1	10.6	6 20.4	14.1	59.4
20	119 05.0	09.8	10 22.7	10.5	6 34.5	14.0	59.4
21	134 04.9	.. 09.6	24 52.2	10.4	6 48.5	14.0	59.4
22	149 04.8	09.5	39 21.6	10.4	7 02.5	13.9	59.4
23	164 04.7	09.3	53 51.0	10.4	7 16.4	14.0	59.4
30 00	179 04.6	N23 09.2	68 20.4	10.3	S 7 30.4	13.8	59.4
01	194 04.4	09.0	82 49.7	10.3	7 44.2	13.8	59.4
02	209 04.3	08.9	97 19.0	10.3	7 58.0	13.8	59.4
03	224 04.2	.. 08.7	111 48.3	10.2	8 11.8	13.8	59.4
04	239 04.1	08.5	126 17.5	10.2	8 25.6	13.7	59.4
05	254 03.9	08.4	140 46.7	10.2	8 39.3	13.6	59.4
06	269 03.8	N23 08.2	155 15.9	10.1	S 8 52.9	13.6	59.4
07	284 03.7	08.1	169 45.0	10.0	9 06.5	13.6	59.4
T 08	299 03.6	07.9	184 14.0	10.0	9 20.1	13.4	59.4
U 09	314 03.5	.. 07.7	198 43.0	10.0	9 33.5	13.5	59.4
E 10	329 03.3	07.6	213 12.0	9.9	9 47.0	13.4	59.4
S 11	344 03.2	07.4	227 40.9	9.9	10 00.4	13.3	59.4
D 12	359 03.1	N23 07.2	242 09.8	9.8	S10 13.7	13.3	59.4
A 13	14 03.0	07.1	256 38.6	9.8	10 27.0	13.2	59.4
Y 14	29 02.8	06.9	271 07.4	9.7	10 40.2	13.1	59.4
15	44 02.7	.. 06.8	285 36.1	9.7	10 53.3	13.1	59.4
16	59 02.6	06.6	300 04.8	9.7	11 06.4	13.1	59.4
17	74 02.5	06.4	314 33.5	9.5	11 19.5	12.9	59.4
18	89 02.4	N23 06.3	329 02.0	9.6	S11 32.4	12.9	59.4
19	104 02.2	06.1	343 30.6	9.5	11 45.3	12.9	59.4
20	119 02.1	05.9	357 59.1	9.4	11 58.2	12.7	59.4
21	134 02.0	.. 05.7	12 27.5	9.4	12 10.9	12.7	59.4
22	149 01.9	05.6	26 55.9	9.3	12 23.6	12.6	59.4
23	164 01.8	05.4	41 24.2	9.3	12 36.2	12.6	59.4
1 00	179 01.6	N23 05.2	55 52.5	9.2	S12 48.8	12.5	59.4
01	194 01.5	05.1	70 20.7	9.2	13 01.3	12.3	59.4
02	209 01.4	04.9	84 48.9	9.1	13 13.6	12.4	59.4
03	224 01.3	.. 04.7	99 17.0	9.0	13 26.0	12.2	59.4
04	239 01.2	04.5	113 45.0	9.0	13 38.2	12.2	59.4
05	254 01.1	04.4	128 13.0	9.0	13 50.4	12.0	59.4
06	269 00.9	N23 04.2	142 41.0	8.9	S14 02.4	12.0	59.4
W 07	284 00.8	04.0	157 08.9	8.8	14 14.4	11.9	59.3
E 08	299 00.7	03.8	171 36.7	8.8	14 26.3	11.9	59.3
D 09	314 00.6	.. 03.7	186 04.5	8.7	14 38.2	11.7	59.3
N 10	329 00.5	03.5	200 32.2	8.6	14 49.9	11.6	59.3
E 11	344 00.3	03.3	214 59.8	8.6	15 01.5	11.6	59.3
S 12	359 00.2	N23 03.1	229 27.4	8.6	S15 13.1	11.5	59.3
D 13	14 00.1	02.9	243 55.0	8.5	15 24.6	11.3	59.3
A 14	29 00.0	02.7	258 22.5	8.4	15 35.9	11.3	59.3
Y 15	43 59.9	.. 02.6	272 49.9	8.3	15 47.2	11.2	59.3
16	58 59.8	02.4	287 17.2	8.4	15 58.4	11.1	59.3
17	73 59.6	02.2	301 44.6	8.2	16 09.5	11.0	59.3
18	88 59.5	N23 02.0	316 11.8	8.2	S16 20.5	10.8	59.3
19	103 59.4	01.8	330 39.0	8.1	16 31.3	10.8	59.3
20	118 59.3	01.6	345 06.1	8.1	16 42.1	10.7	59.3
21	133 59.2	.. 01.5	359 33.2	8.0	16 52.8	10.6	59.2
22	148 59.0	01.3	14 00.2	8.0	17 03.4	10.5	59.2
23	163 58.9	01.1	28 27.2	7.9	S17 13.9	10.3	59.2
	SD 15.8	d 0.2	SD 16.2		16.2		16.2

Twilight / Moonrise

Lat.	Naut.	Civil	Sunrise	Moonrise 29	30	1	2
°	h m	h m	h m	h m	h m	h m	h m
N 72	□	□	□	14 14	16 34	19 30	■
N 70	□	□	□	14 06	16 14	18 37	■
68	□	□	□	14 00	15 58	18 04	20 31
66	////	////	00 12	13 54	15 45	17 41	19 42
64	////	////	01 40	13 50	15 34	17 22	19 12
62	////	////	02 16	13 46	15 26	17 07	18 49
60	////	01 02	02 42	13 42	15 18	16 55	18 30
N 58	////	01 48	03 01	13 40	15 11	16 44	18 15
56	////	02 16	03 18	13 37	15 05	16 35	18 02
54	00 57	02 38	03 32	13 35	15 00	16 26	17 51
52	01 39	02 56	03 44	13 32	14 55	16 19	17 41
50	02 06	03 10	03 55	13 30	14 51	16 12	17 32
45	02 50	03 40	04 17	13 26	14 42	15 58	17 14
N 40	03 20	04 02	04 35	13 23	14 34	15 47	16 59
35	03 43	04 20	04 49	13 20	14 28	15 37	16 46
30	04 02	04 35	05 02	13 17	14 22	15 28	16 35
20	04 30	05 00	05 24	13 13	14 12	15 14	16 16
N 10	04 53	05 20	05 43	13 09	14 04	15 01	15 59
0	05 11	05 38	06 00	13 05	13 56	14 49	15 44
S 10	05 28	05 55	06 17	13 02	13 48	14 37	15 29
20	05 44	06 12	06 36	12 58	13 40	14 25	15 13
30	06 00	06 30	06 57	12 53	13 30	14 10	14 55
35	06 09	06 41	07 09	12 51	13 25	14 02	14 44
40	06 18	06 52	07 23	12 48	13 19	13 53	14 32
45	06 28	07 06	07 39	12 45	13 12	13 42	14 18
S 50	06 40	07 21	08 00	12 41	13 04	13 29	14 00
52	06 45	07 29	08 09	12 40	13 00	13 23	13 52
54	06 51	07 37	08 20	12 38	12 56	13 17	13 43
56	06 57	07 46	08 33	12 36	12 51	13 09	13 33
58	07 03	07 56	08 47	12 34	12 46	13 01	13 21
S 60	07 11	08 07	09 04	12 31	12 40	12 52	13 08

Sunset / Twilight / Moonset

Lat.	Sunset	Civil	Naut.	Moonset 29	30	1	2
°	h m	h m	h m	h m	h m	h m	h m
N 72	□	□	□	(00 14 / 23 49)	23 17	22 13	■
N 70	□	□	□	00 16	(00 23 / 23 40)	23 09	■
68	□	□	□	00 18	(00 09 / 23 57)	23 42	23 13
66	23 44	////	////	00 20	00 16	00 12	00 07
64	22 26	////	////	00 22	00 22	00 24	00 27
62	21 51	////	////	00 23	00 28	00 34	00 43
60	21 25	23 04	////	00 25	00 33	00 43	00 56
N 58	21 06	22 19	////	00 26	00 37	00 50	01 07
56	20 49	21 50	////	00 27	00 41	00 57	01 18
54	20 35	21 25	23 09	00 27	00 44	01 03	01 26
52	20 23	21 12	22 27	00 28	00 47	01 09	01 34
50	20 13	20 57	22 01	00 29	00 50	01 14	01 42
45	19 51	20 28	21 17	00 31	00 56	01 25	01 57
N 40	19 33	20 06	20 47	00 32	01 02	01 34	02 10
35	19 18	19 48	20 24	00 33	01 06	01 42	02 21
30	19 05	19 33	20 06	00 34	01 10	01 48	02 31
20	18 43	19 08	19 37	00 36	01 17	02 00	02 47
N 10	18 25	18 48	19 15	00 37	01 23	02 11	03 01
0	18 07	18 30	18 56	00 39	01 29	02 21	03 15
S 10	17 50	18 13	18 39	00 40	01 35	02 31	03 29
20	17 32	17 56	18 23	00 42	01 41	02 41	03 43
30	17 11	17 37	18 07	00 44	01 48	02 54	04 00
35	16 59	17 27	17 59	00 44	01 52	03 01	04 10
40	16 45	17 15	17 49	00 46	01 57	03 09	04 21
45	16 28	17 02	17 39	00 47	02 02	03 18	04 34
S 50	16 08	16 46	17 28	00 48	02 09	03 30	04 50
52	15 58	16 39	17 23	00 49	02 12	03 35	04 58
54	15 47	16 31	17 17	00 50	02 15	03 41	05 07
56	15 35	16 22	17 11	00 51	02 19	03 47	05 16
58	15 21	16 12	17 04	00 52	02 23	03 53	05 27
S 60	15 04	16 01	16 57	00 53	02 27	04 03	05 40

SUN and MOON

Day	Eqn. of Time 00h	12h	Mer. Pass.	Mer. Pass. Upper	Lower	Age	Phase
d	m s	m s	h m	h m	h m	d	%
29	03 30	03 36	12 04	19 17	06 52	08	63
30	03 42	03 47	12 04	20 08	07 42	09	74
1	03 53	03 59	12 04	21 02	08 35	10	83

UT (d h)	ARIES GHA	VENUS −4·7 GHA	Dec	MARS −0·5 GHA	Dec	JUPITER −2·7 GHA	Dec	SATURN +0·2 GHA	Dec	STARS Name	SHA	Dec
2 00	280 29.5	215 26.7	N17 13.9	277 04.4	S 1 57.6	344 39.5	S21 37.0	338 15.9	S20 20.8	Acamar	315 14.9	S40 13.3
01	295 31.9	230 28.6	13.8	292 05.4	57.0	359 42.3	37.0	353 18.6	20.9	Achernar	335 23.2	S57 07.8
02	310 34.4	245 30.4	13.8	307 06.5	56.5	14 45.1	37.1	8 21.2	20.9	Acrux	173 04.0	S63 12.9
03	325 36.9	260 32.2 ..	13.7	322 07.6 ..	56.0	29 47.9 ..	37.2	23 23.8 ..	20.9	Adhara	255 09.1	S29 00.0
04	340 39.3	275 34.0	13.7	337 08.7	55.4	44 50.7	37.2	38 26.5	21.0	Aldebaran	290 44.1	N16 32.9
05	355 41.8	290 35.8	13.6	352 09.8	54.9	59 53.5	37.3	53 29.1	21.0			
06	10 44.2	305 37.6	N17 13.5	7 10.8	S 1 54.4	74 56.3	S21 37.3	68 31.8	S20 21.1	Alioth	166 16.3	N55 51.3
07	25 46.7	320 39.4	13.5	22 11.9	53.8	89 59.0	37.4	83 34.4	21.1	Alkaid	152 54.9	N49 13.1
T 08	40 49.2	335 41.2	13.5	37 13.0	53.3	105 01.8	37.5	98 37.0	21.1	Alnair	27 37.3	S46 51.5
H 09	55 51.6	350 43.0 ..	13.4	52 14.1 ..	52.8	120 04.6 ..	37.5	113 39.7 ..	21.2	Alnilam	275 41.8	S 1 11.4
U 10	70 54.1	5 44.8	13.4	67 15.2	52.3	135 07.4	37.6	128 42.3	21.2	Alphard	217 51.6	S 8 44.8
R 11	85 56.6	20 46.5	13.4	82 16.2	51.7	150 10.2	37.6	143 45.0	21.3			
S 12	100 59.0	35 48.3	N17 13.3	97 17.3	S 1 51.2	165 13.0	S21 37.7	158 47.6	S20 21.3	Alphecca	126 06.6	N26 39.0
D 13	116 01.5	50 50.1	13.3	112 18.4	50.7	180 15.8	37.8	173 50.2	21.3	Alpheratz	357 38.4	N29 12.0
A 14	131 04.0	65 51.9	13.2	127 19.5	50.1	195 18.5	37.8	188 52.9	21.4	Altair	62 03.2	N 8 55.4
Y 15	146 06.4	80 53.6 ..	13.2	142 20.6 ..	49.6	210 21.3 ..	37.9	203 55.5 ..	21.4	Ankaa	353 10.8	S42 11.5
16	161 08.9	95 55.4	13.2	157 21.7	49.1	225 24.1	37.9	218 58.2	21.5	Antares	112 20.0	S26 28.6
17	176 11.3	110 57.2	13.1	172 22.7	48.5	240 26.9	38.0	234 00.8	21.5			
18	191 13.8	125 58.9	N17 13.1	187 23.8	S 1 48.0	255 29.7	S21 38.1	249 03.4	S20 21.5	Arcturus	145 51.1	N19 04.8
19	206 16.3	141 00.7	13.1	202 24.9	47.5	270 32.5	38.1	264 06.1	21.6	Atria	107 16.9	S69 03.8
20	221 18.7	156 02.4	13.0	217 26.0	46.9	285 35.3	38.2	279 08.7	21.6	Avior	234 16.7	S59 34.6
21	236 21.2	171 04.2 ..	13.0	232 27.1 ..	46.4	300 38.1 ..	38.2	294 11.4 ..	21.7	Bellatrix	278 27.1	N 6 22.0
22	251 23.7	186 05.9	13.0	247 28.2	45.9	315 40.8	38.3	309 14.0	21.7	Betelgeuse	270 56.4	N 7 24.6
23	266 26.1	201 07.7	12.9	262 29.2	45.4	330 43.6	38.3	324 16.6	21.7			
3 00	281 28.6	216 09.4	N17 12.9	277 30.3	S 1 44.8	345 46.4	S21 38.4	339 19.3	S20 21.8	Canopus	263 54.5	S52 42.4
01	296 31.1	231 11.1	12.9	292 31.4	44.3	0 49.2	38.5	354 21.9	21.8	Capella	280 27.7	N46 00.9
02	311 33.5	246 12.9	12.9	307 32.5	43.8	15 52.0	38.5	9 24.6	21.8	Deneb	49 27.8	N45 21.1
03	326 36.0	261 14.6 ..	12.8	322 33.6 ..	43.2	30 54.8 ..	38.6	24 27.2 ..	21.9	Denebola	182 28.8	N14 27.7
04	341 38.5	276 16.3	12.8	337 34.7	42.7	45 57.6	38.6	39 29.8	21.9	Diphda	348 51.0	S17 52.4
05	356 40.9	291 18.0	12.8	352 35.8	42.2	61 00.4	38.7	54 32.5	22.0			
06	11 43.4	306 19.8	N17 12.8	7 36.8	S 1 41.6	76 03.2	S21 38.8	69 35.1	S20 22.0	Dubhe	193 46.0	N61 38.8
07	26 45.8	321 21.5	12.8	22 37.9	41.1	91 05.9	38.8	84 37.8	22.0	Elnath	278 06.8	N28 37.3
F 08	41 48.3	336 23.2	12.7	37 39.0	40.6	106 08.7	38.9	99 40.4	22.1	Eltanin	90 43.3	N51 29.3
R 09	56 50.8	351 24.9 ..	12.7	52 40.1 ..	40.1	121 11.5 ..	38.9	114 43.0 ..	22.1	Enif	33 42.1	N 9 58.1
I 10	71 53.2	6 26.6	12.7	67 41.2	39.5	136 14.3	39.0	129 45.7	22.1	Fomalhaut	15 18.4	S29 30.7
D 11	86 55.7	21 28.3	12.7	82 42.3	39.0	151 17.1	39.1	144 48.3	22.2			
A 12	101 58.2	36 30.0	N17 12.7	97 43.4	S 1 38.5	166 19.9	S21 39.1	159 51.0	S20 22.2	Gacrux	171 55.6	S57 13.8
Y 13	117 00.6	51 31.7	12.7	112 44.5	37.9	181 22.7	39.2	174 53.6	22.3	Gienah	175 47.3	S17 39.3
14	132 03.1	66 33.4	12.7	127 45.6	37.4	196 25.5	39.2	189 56.2	22.3	Hadar	148 45.8	S60 28.4
15	147 05.6	81 35.1 ..	12.6	142 46.6 ..	36.9	211 28.3 ..	39.3	204 58.9 ..	22.4	Hamal	327 55.4	N23 33.3
16	162 08.0	96 36.8	12.6	157 47.7	36.4	226 31.0	39.4	220 01.5	22.4	Kaus Aust.	83 36.9	S34 22.4
17	177 10.5	111 38.4	12.6	172 48.8	35.8	241 33.8	39.4	235 04.2	22.4			
18	192 13.0	126 40.1	N17 12.6	187 49.9	S 1 35.3	256 36.6	S21 39.5	250 06.8	S20 22.5	Kochab	137 19.4	N74 04.7
19	207 15.4	141 41.8	12.6	202 51.0	34.8	271 39.4	39.5	265 09.5	22.5	Markab	13 33.3	N15 18.8
20	222 17.9	156 43.5	12.6	217 52.1	34.3	286 42.2	39.6	280 12.1	22.6	Menkar	314 10.1	N 4 10.1
21	237 20.3	171 45.1 ..	12.6	232 53.2 ..	33.7	301 45.0 ..	39.7	295 14.7 ..	22.6	Menkent	148 01.7	S36 28.3
22	252 22.8	186 46.8	12.6	247 54.3	33.2	316 47.8	39.7	310 17.4	22.6	Miaplacidus	221 39.6	S69 48.2
23	267 25.3	201 48.5	12.6	262 55.4	32.7	331 50.6	39.8	325 20.0	22.7			
4 00	282 27.7	216 50.1	N17 12.6	277 56.5	S 1 32.2	346 53.4	S21 39.8	340 22.7	S20 22.7	Mirfak	308 33.7	N49 55.7
01	297 30.2	231 51.8	12.6	292 57.6	31.6	1 56.2	39.9	355 25.3	22.8	Nunki	75 51.9	S26 16.2
02	312 32.7	246 53.4	12.6	307 58.7	31.1	16 58.9	39.9	10 27.9	22.8	Peacock	53 11.0	S56 40.0
03	327 35.1	261 55.1 ..	12.6	322 59.8 ..	30.6	32 01.7 ..	40.0	25 30.6 ..	22.8	Pollux	243 22.2	N27 58.6
04	342 37.6	276 56.7	12.6	338 00.9	30.1	47 04.5	40.1	40 33.2	22.9	Procyon	244 55.0	N 5 10.3
05	357 40.1	291 58.4	12.6	353 01.9	29.5	62 07.3	40.1	55 35.9	22.9			
06	12 42.5	307 00.0	N17 12.6	8 03.0	S 1 29.0	77 10.1	S21 40.2	70 38.5	S20 23.0	Rasalhague	96 01.6	N12 32.9
07	27 45.0	322 01.7	12.6	23 04.1	28.5	92 12.9	40.2	85 41.2	23.0	Regulus	207 38.6	N11 52.2
S 08	42 47.5	337 03.3	12.6	38 05.2	28.0	107 15.7	40.3	100 43.8	23.0	Rigel	281 07.7	S 8 10.7
A 09	57 49.9	352 04.9 ..	12.6	53 06.3 ..	27.4	122 18.5 ..	40.4	115 46.4 ..	23.1	Rigil Kent.	139 44.9	S60 55.2
T 10	72 52.4	7 06.6	12.7	68 07.4	26.9	137 21.3	40.4	130 49.1	23.1	Sabik	102 06.6	S15 44.9
U 11	87 54.8	22 08.2	12.7	83 08.5	26.4	152 24.1	40.5	145 51.7	23.2			
R 12	102 57.3	37 09.8	N17 12.7	98 09.6	S 1 25.9	167 26.9	S21 40.5	160 54.4	S20 23.2	Schedar	349 35.0	N56 38.6
D 13	117 59.8	52 11.4	12.7	113 10.7	25.3	182 29.7	40.6	175 57.0	23.2	Shaula	96 14.9	S37 07.0
A 14	133 02.2	67 13.0	12.7	128 11.8	24.8	197 32.4	40.7	190 59.7	23.3	Sirius	258 29.8	S16 44.7
Y 15	148 04.7	82 14.7 ..	12.7	143 12.9 ..	24.3	212 35.2 ..	40.7	206 02.3 ..	23.3	Spica	158 26.1	S11 16.0
16	163 07.2	97 16.3	12.7	158 14.0	23.8	227 38.0	40.8	221 04.9	23.4	Suhail	222 49.3	S43 31.0
17	178 09.6	112 17.9	12.8	173 15.1	23.2	242 40.8	40.8	236 07.6	23.4			
18	193 12.1	127 19.5	N17 12.8	188 16.2	S 1 22.7	257 43.6	S21 40.9	251 10.2	S20 23.5	Vega	80 35.2	N38 48.2
19	208 14.6	142 21.1	12.8	203 17.3	22.2	272 46.4	41.0	266 12.9	23.5	Zuben'ubi	136 59.8	S16 07.5
20	223 17.0	157 22.7	12.8	218 18.4	21.7	287 49.2	41.0	281 15.5	23.5		SHA	Mer.Pass.
21	238 19.5	172 24.3 ..	12.8	233 19.5 ..	21.1	302 52.0 ..	41.1	296 18.2 ..	23.6		° '	h m
22	253 22.0	187 25.9	12.9	248 20.6	20.6	317 54.8	41.1	311 20.8	23.6	Venus	294 40.8	9 34
23	268 24.4	202 27.4	12.9	263 21.7	20.1	332 57.6	41.2	326 23.4	23.7	Mars	356 01.7	5 30
	h m									Jupiter	64 17.8	0 57
Mer. Pass.	5 13.2	v 1.7	d 0.0	v 1.1	d 0.5	v 2.8	d 0.1	v 2.6	d 0.0	Saturn	57 50.7	1 22

UT	SUN GHA	SUN Dec	MOON GHA	v	Dec	d	HP
d h	° ′	° ′	° ′	′	° ′	′	′
2 00	178 58.8	N23 00.9	42 54.1	7.8	S17 24.2	10.3	59.2
01	193 58.7	00.7	57 20.9	7.8	17 34.5	10.1	59.2
02	208 58.6	00.5	71 47.7	7.8	17 44.6	10.1	59.2
03	223 58.5	.. 00.3	86 14.5	7.6	17 54.7	9.9	59.2
04	238 58.4	23 00.1	100 41.1	7.6	18 04.6	9.8	59.2
05	253 58.2	22 59.9	115 07.7	7.6	18 14.4	9.7	59.2
06	268 58.1	N22 59.7	129 34.3	7.5	S18 24.1	9.6	59.2
07	283 58.0	59.5	144 00.8	7.4	18 33.7	9.5	59.1
T 08	298 57.9	59.4	158 27.2	7.4	18 43.2	9.3	59.1
H 09	313 57.8	.. 59.2	172 53.6	7.4	18 52.5	9.2	59.1
U 10	328 57.7	59.0	187 20.0	7.3	19 01.7	9.2	59.1
R 11	343 57.5	58.8	201 46.3	7.2	19 10.9	8.9	59.1
S 12	358 57.4	N22 58.6	216 12.5	7.2	S19 19.8	8.9	59.1
D 13	13 57.3	58.4	230 38.7	7.1	19 28.7	8.8	59.1
A 14	28 57.2	58.2	245 04.8	7.1	19 37.5	8.6	59.1
Y 15	43 57.1	.. 58.0	259 30.9	7.0	19 46.1	8.5	59.0
16	58 57.0	57.8	273 56.9	6.9	19 54.6	8.3	59.0
17	73 56.9	57.6	288 22.8	7.0	20 02.9	8.3	59.0
18	88 56.7	N22 57.4	302 48.8	6.8	S20 11.2	8.1	59.0
19	103 56.6	57.2	317 14.6	6.8	20 19.3	7.9	59.0
20	118 56.5	57.0	331 40.4	6.8	20 27.2	7.9	59.0
21	133 56.4	.. 56.8	346 06.2	6.7	20 35.1	7.7	59.0
22	148 56.3	56.6	0 31.9	6.7	20 42.8	7.6	58.9
23	163 56.2	56.4	14 57.6	6.7	20 50.4	7.4	58.9
3 00	178 56.1	N22 56.1	29 23.3	6.6	S20 57.8	7.3	58.9
01	193 55.9	55.9	43 48.9	6.5	21 05.1	7.2	58.9
02	208 55.8	55.7	58 14.4	6.5	21 12.3	7.0	58.9
03	223 55.7	.. 55.5	72 39.9	6.5	21 19.3	6.9	58.9
04	238 55.6	55.3	87 05.4	6.4	21 26.2	6.8	58.9
05	253 55.5	55.1	101 30.8	6.4	21 33.0	6.6	58.8
06	268 55.4	N22 54.9	115 56.2	6.3	S21 39.6	6.5	58.8
07	283 55.3	54.7	130 21.5	6.4	21 46.1	6.3	58.8
F 08	298 55.2	54.5	144 46.9	6.2	21 52.4	6.2	58.8
R 09	313 55.0	.. 54.3	159 12.1	6.3	21 58.6	6.1	58.8
I 10	328 54.9	54.1	173 37.4	6.2	22 04.7	5.9	58.8
D 11	343 54.8	53.8	188 02.6	6.2	22 10.6	5.7	58.7
A 12	358 54.7	N22 53.6	202 27.8	6.1	S22 16.3	5.6	58.7
Y 13	13 54.6	53.4	216 52.9	6.2	22 21.9	5.5	58.7
14	28 54.5	53.2	231 18.1	6.1	22 27.4	5.3	58.7
15	43 54.4	.. 53.0	245 43.2	6.0	22 32.7	5.2	58.7
16	58 54.3	52.8	260 08.2	6.1	22 37.9	5.0	58.6
17	73 54.2	52.5	274 33.3	6.0	22 42.9	4.9	58.6
18	88 54.0	N22 52.3	288 58.3	6.0	S22 47.8	4.8	58.6
19	103 53.9	52.1	303 23.3	6.0	22 52.6	4.5	58.6
20	118 53.8	51.9	317 48.3	6.0	22 57.1	4.5	58.6
21	133 53.7	.. 51.7	332 13.3	5.9	23 01.6	4.2	58.6
22	148 53.6	51.5	346 38.2	6.0	23 05.8	4.2	58.5
23	163 53.5	51.2	1 03.2	5.9	23 10.0	4.0	58.5
4 00	178 53.4	N22 51.0	15 28.1	5.9	S23 14.0	3.8	58.5
01	193 53.3	50.8	29 53.0	5.9	23 17.8	3.7	58.5
02	208 53.2	50.6	44 17.9	5.9	23 21.5	3.5	58.5
03	223 53.0	.. 50.3	58 42.8	5.9	23 25.0	3.4	58.4
04	238 52.9	50.1	73 07.7	5.8	23 28.4	3.2	58.4
05	253 52.8	49.9	87 32.5	5.9	23 31.6	3.1	58.4
06	268 52.7	N22 49.7	101 57.4	5.9	S23 34.7	2.9	58.4
07	283 52.6	49.4	116 22.3	5.9	23 37.6	2.7	58.3
S 08	298 52.5	49.2	130 47.2	5.8	23 40.3	2.7	58.3
A 09	313 52.4	.. 49.0	145 12.0	5.9	23 43.0	2.4	58.3
T 10	328 52.3	48.7	159 36.9	5.9	23 45.4	2.3	58.3
U 11	343 52.2	48.5	174 01.8	5.9	23 47.7	2.2	58.3
R 12	358 52.1	N22 48.3	188 26.7	5.9	S23 49.9	2.0	58.2
D 13	13 52.0	48.1	202 51.6	5.9	23 51.9	1.8	58.2
A 14	28 51.9	47.8	217 16.5	5.9	23 53.7	1.7	58.2
Y 15	43 51.7	.. 47.6	231 41.4	5.9	23 55.4	1.5	58.2
16	58 51.6	47.4	246 06.3	6.0	23 56.9	1.4	58.1
17	73 51.5	47.1	260 31.3	6.0	23 58.3	1.2	58.1
18	88 51.4	N22 46.9	274 56.3	5.9	S23 59.5	1.1	58.1
19	103 51.3	46.7	289 21.2	6.0	24 00.6	0.9	58.1
20	118 51.2	46.4	303 46.2	6.1	24 01.5	0.8	58.0
21	133 51.1	.. 46.2	318 11.3	6.0	24 02.3	0.6	58.0
22	148 51.0	45.9	332 36.3	6.1	24 02.9	0.5	58.0
23	163 50.9	45.7	347 01.4	6.1	S24 03.4	0.3	58.0
	SD 15.8	d 0.2	SD 16.1		16.0		15.9

Twilight / Sunrise / Moonrise

Lat.	Naut.	Civil	Sunrise	Moonrise 2	3	4	5
°	h m	h m	h m	h m	h m	h m	h m
N 72	☐	☐	☐	■	■	■	■
N 70	☐	☐	☐	■	■	■	■
68	☐	☐	☐	20 31	■	■	■
66	////	////	00 38	19 42	21 51	■	■
64	////	////	01 46	19 12	20 56	22 19	23 02
62	////	////	02 20	18 49	20 23	21 39	22 28
60	////	01 09	02 45	18 30	19 59	21 12	22 03
N 58	////	01 52	03 04	18 15	19 40	20 51	21 43
56	////	02 20	03 21	18 02	19 24	20 33	21 26
54	01 04	02 41	03 34	17 51	19 10	20 18	21 12
52	01 43	02 58	03 46	17 41	18 58	20 05	21 00
50	02 09	03 13	03 57	17 32	18 48	19 54	20 49
45	02 53	03 42	04 19	17 14	18 26	19 31	20 26
N 40	03 22	04 04	04 36	16 59	18 08	19 12	20 07
35	03 45	04 21	04 51	16 46	17 53	18 56	19 52
30	04 03	04 36	05 03	16 35	17 40	18 42	19 39
20	04 31	05 01	05 25	16 16	17 18	18 19	19 16
N 10	04 54	05 21	05 44	15 59	16 59	17 59	18 56
0	05 12	05 38	06 01	15 44	16 42	17 40	18 38
S 10	05 29	05 55	06 18	15 29	16 24	17 21	18 19
20	05 44	06 12	06 36	15 13	16 05	17 01	17 59
30	06 01	06 30	06 57	14 55	15 44	16 38	17 37
35	06 09	06 41	07 09	14 44	15 31	16 25	17 23
40	06 18	06 52	07 22	14 32	15 17	16 09	17 08
45	06 28	07 05	07 39	14 18	15 00	15 51	16 49
S 50	06 39	07 21	07 59	14 00	14 39	15 28	16 26
52	06 44	07 28	08 08	13 52	14 29	15 17	16 15
54	06 50	07 36	08 19	13 43	14 18	15 04	16 03
56	06 56	07 45	08 31	13 33	14 05	14 50	15 49
58	07 02	07 54	08 45	13 21	13 50	14 33	15 32
S 60	07 09	08 06	09 02	13 08	13 33	14 13	15 11

Sunset / Twilight / Moonset

Lat.	Sunset	Civil	Naut.	Moonset 2	3	4	5
°	h m	h m	h m	h m	h m	h m	h m
N 72	☐	☐	☐	■	■	■	■
N 70	☐	☐	☐	■	■	■	■
68	☐	☐	☐	23 13	■	■	■
66	23 25	////	////	00 07	{00 02 / 23 54}	■	■
64	22 21	////	////	00 27	00 33	00 49	01 29
62	21 47	////	////	00 43	00 57	01 22	02 08
60	21 23	22 57	////	00 56	01 16	01 47	02 36
N 58	21 04	22 15	////	01 07	01 31	02 06	02 57
56	20 48	21 48	////	01 18	01 45	02 23	03 15
54	20 34	21 27	23 03	01 26	01 57	02 37	03 29
52	20 22	21 10	22 24	01 34	02 07	02 49	03 42
50	20 12	20 55	21 59	01 42	02 16	03 00	03 54
45	19 50	20 27	21 16	01 57	02 36	03 22	04 17
N 40	19 32	20 05	20 46	02 10	02 52	03 40	04 36
35	19 18	19 47	20 24	02 21	03 05	03 56	04 52
30	19 05	19 32	20 05	02 30	03 17	04 09	05 06
20	18 44	19 08	19 37	02 47	03 37	04 32	05 29
N 10	18 25	18 48	19 15	03 01	03 55	04 51	05 49
0	18 08	18 30	18 57	03 15	04 11	05 10	06 08
S 10	17 51	18 14	18 40	03 29	04 28	05 28	06 27
20	17 33	17 57	18 24	03 43	04 46	05 48	06 47
30	17 12	17 39	18 08	04 00	05 06	06 10	07 10
35	17 00	17 28	18 00	04 10	05 18	06 24	07 23
40	16 46	17 17	17 51	04 21	05 32	06 39	07 39
45	16 30	17 04	17 41	04 34	05 48	06 57	07 58
S 50	16 10	16 48	17 29	04 50	06 09	07 20	08 21
52	16 01	16 41	17 24	04 58	06 18	07 31	08 32
54	15 50	16 33	17 19	05 07	06 29	07 43	08 44
56	15 38	16 24	17 13	05 16	06 41	07 57	08 59
58	15 24	16 15	17 07	05 27	06 56	08 14	09 16
S 60	15 07	16 03	16 59	05 40	07 13	08 34	09 36

SUN / MOON

Day	Eqn. of Time 00h	12h	Mer. Pass.	Mer. Pass. Upper	Lower	Age	Phase
d	m s	m s	h m	h m	h m	d	%
2	04 05	04 10	12 04	21 58	09 30	11	91
3	04 16	04 21	12 04	22 56	10 27	12	96
4	04 26	04 32	12 05	23 54	11 25	13	99

Phase: ◯

UT	ARIES GHA	VENUS −4.7 GHA	Dec	MARS −0.6 GHA	Dec	JUPITER −2.7 GHA	Dec	SATURN +0.2 GHA	Dec	STARS Name	SHA	Dec
5 00	283 26.9	217 29.0	N17 12.9	278 22.8	S 1 19.6	348 00.4	S21 41.3	341 26.1	S20 23.7	Acamar	315 14.8	S40 13.3
01	298 29.3	232 30.6	12.9	293 23.9	19.1	3 03.2	41.3	356 28.7	23.7	Achernar	335 23.2	S57 07.8
02	313 31.8	247 32.2	13.0	308 25.0	18.5	18 06.0	41.4	11 31.4	23.8	Acrux	173 04.0	S63 12.9
03	328 34.3	262 33.8 ..	13.0	323 26.1 ..	18.0	33 08.8 ..	41.4	26 34.0 ..	23.8	Adhara	255 09.1	S29 00.0
04	343 36.7	277 35.3	13.0	338 27.2	17.5	48 11.6	41.5	41 36.7	23.9	Aldebaran	290 44.1	N16 32.9
05	358 39.2	292 36.9	13.1	353 28.3	17.0	63 14.3	41.6	56 39.3	23.9			
06	13 41.7	307 38.5	N17 13.1	8 29.4	S 1 16.4	78 17.1	S21 41.6	71 42.0	S20 23.9	Alioth	166 16.3	N55 51.3
07	28 44.1	322 40.0	13.1	23 30.5	15.9	93 19.9	41.7	86 44.6	24.0	Alkaid	152 54.9	N49 13.1
08	43 46.6	337 41.6	13.2	38 31.6	15.4	108 22.7	41.7	101 47.2	24.0	Alnair	27 37.2	S46 51.5
S 09	58 49.1	352 43.1 ..	13.2	53 32.7 ..	14.9	123 25.5 ..	41.8	116 49.9 ..	24.1	Alnilam	275 41.7	S 1 11.4
U 10	73 51.5	7 44.7	13.2	68 33.8	14.4	138 28.3	41.8	131 52.5	24.1	Alphard	217 51.6	S 8 44.8
N 11	88 54.0	22 46.2	13.3	83 34.9	13.8	153 31.1	41.9	146 55.2	24.1			
D 12	103 56.5	37 47.8	N17 13.3	98 36.1	S 1 13.3	168 33.9	S21 42.0	161 57.8	S20 24.2	Alphecca	126 06.6	N26 39.0
A 13	118 58.9	52 49.3	13.3	113 37.2	12.8	183 36.7	42.0	177 00.5	24.2	Alpheratz	357 38.4	N29 12.0
Y 14	134 01.4	67 50.9	13.4	128 38.3	12.3	198 39.5	42.1	192 03.1	24.3	Altair	62 03.2	N 8 55.4
15	149 03.8	82 52.4 ..	13.4	143 39.4 ..	11.8	213 42.3 ..	42.2	207 05.8 ..	24.3	Ankaa	353 10.8	S42 11.5
16	164 06.3	97 53.9	13.5	158 40.5	11.2	228 45.1	42.2	222 08.4	24.3	Antares	112 20.0	S26 28.6
17	179 08.8	112 55.5	13.5	173 41.6	10.7	243 47.9	42.3	237 11.0	24.4			
18	194 11.2	127 57.0	N17 13.5	188 42.7	S 1 10.2	258 50.7	S21 42.3	252 13.7	S20 24.4	Arcturus	145 51.1	N19 04.8
19	209 13.7	142 58.5	13.6	203 43.8	09.7	273 53.5	42.4	267 16.3	24.5	Atria	107 16.9	S69 03.9
20	224 16.2	158 00.0	13.6	218 44.9	09.2	288 56.3	42.4	282 19.0	24.5	Avior	234 16.7	S59 34.6
21	239 18.6	173 01.6 ..	13.7	233 46.0 ..	08.6	303 59.1 ..	42.5	297 21.6 ..	24.5	Bellatrix	278 27.1	N 6 22.0
22	254 21.1	188 03.1	13.7	248 47.1	08.1	319 01.9	42.6	312 24.3	24.6	Betelgeuse	270 56.3	N 7 24.6
23	269 23.6	203 04.6	13.8	263 48.2	07.6	334 04.6	42.6	327 26.9	24.6			
6 00	284 26.0	218 06.1	N17 13.8	278 49.3	S 1 07.1	349 07.4	S21 42.7	342 29.6	S20 24.7	Canopus	263 54.5	S52 42.4
01	299 28.5	233 07.6	13.9	293 50.4	06.6	4 10.2	42.7	357 32.2	24.7	Capella	280 27.7	N46 00.9
02	314 31.0	248 09.1	13.9	308 51.6	06.0	19 13.0	42.8	12 34.8	24.7	Deneb	49 27.8	N45 21.1
03	329 33.4	263 10.6 ..	14.0	323 52.7 ..	05.5	34 15.8 ..	42.9	27 37.5 ..	24.8	Denebola	182 28.8	N14 27.7
04	344 35.9	278 12.1	14.0	338 53.8	05.0	49 18.6	42.9	42 40.1	24.8	Diphda	348 51.0	S17 52.4
05	359 38.3	293 13.6	14.1	353 54.9	04.5	64 21.4	43.0	57 42.8	24.9			
06	14 40.8	308 15.1	N17 14.1	8 56.0	S 1 04.0	79 24.2	S21 43.0	72 45.4	S20 24.9	Dubhe	193 46.0	N61 38.8
07	29 43.3	323 16.6	14.2	23 57.1	03.5	94 27.0	43.1	87 48.1	24.9	Elnath	278 06.8	N28 37.3
08	44 45.7	338 18.1	14.2	38 58.2	02.9	109 29.8	43.2	102 50.7	25.0	Eltanin	90 43.3	N51 29.3
M 09	59 48.2	353 19.6 ..	14.3	53 59.3 ..	02.4	124 32.6 ..	43.2	117 53.4 ..	25.0	Enif	33 42.1	N 9 58.1
O 10	74 50.7	8 21.0	14.4	69 00.5	01.9	139 35.4	43.3	132 56.0	25.1	Fomalhaut	15 18.4	S29 30.7
N 11	89 53.1	23 22.5	14.4	84 01.6	01.4	154 38.2	43.3	147 58.7	25.1			
D 12	104 55.6	38 24.0	N17 14.5	99 02.7	S 1 00.9	169 41.0	S21 43.4	163 01.3	S20 25.1	Gacrux	171 55.6	S57 13.8
A 13	119 58.1	53 25.5	14.5	114 03.8	1 00.4	184 43.8	43.5	178 03.9	25.2	Gienah	175 47.4	S17 39.3
Y 14	135 00.5	68 26.9	14.6	129 04.9	0 59.8	199 46.6	43.5	193 06.6	25.2	Hadar	148 40.8	S60 28.4
15	150 03.0	83 28.4 ..	14.7	144 06.0 ..	59.3	214 49.4 ..	43.6	208 09.2 ..	25.3	Hamal	327 55.4	N23 33.3
16	165 05.4	98 29.9	14.7	159 07.1	58.8	229 52.2	43.6	223 11.9	25.3	Kaus Aust.	83 36.9	S34 22.4
17	180 07.9	113 31.3	14.8	174 08.3	58.3	244 55.0	43.7	238 14.5	25.4			
18	195 10.4	128 32.8	N17 14.9	189 09.4	S 0 57.8	259 57.8	S21 43.8	253 17.2	S20 25.4	Kochab	137 19.4	N74 04.7
19	210 12.8	143 34.2	14.9	204 10.5	57.3	275 00.6	43.8	268 19.8	25.4	Markab	13 33.3	N15 18.8
20	225 15.3	158 35.7	15.0	219 11.6	56.7	290 03.4	43.9	283 22.5	25.5	Menkar	314 10.1	N 4 10.1
21	240 17.8	173 37.1 ..	15.1	234 12.7 ..	56.2	305 06.2 ..	43.9	298 25.1 ..	25.5	Menkent	148 01.7	S36 28.3
22	255 20.2	188 38.6	15.1	249 13.8	55.7	320 09.0	44.0	313 27.8	25.6	Miaplacidus	221 39.6	S69 48.2
23	270 22.7	203 40.0	15.2	264 14.9	55.2	335 11.8	44.1	328 30.4	25.6			
7 00	285 25.2	218 41.4	N17 15.3	279 16.1	S 0 54.7	350 14.6	S21 44.1	343 33.1	S20 25.6	Mirfak	308 33.7	N49 55.7
01	300 27.6	233 42.9	15.3	294 17.2	54.2	5 17.4	44.2	358 35.7	25.7	Nunki	75 51.9	S26 16.2
02	315 30.1	248 44.3	15.4	309 18.3	53.7	20 20.2	44.2	13 38.3	25.7	Peacock	53 11.0	S56 40.0
03	330 32.6	263 45.7 ..	15.5	324 19.4 ..	53.1	35 23.0 ..	44.3	28 41.0 ..	25.8	Pollux	243 22.1	N27 58.6
04	345 35.0	278 47.2	15.6	339 20.5	52.6	50 25.8	44.4	43 43.6	25.8	Procyon	244 55.0	N 5 10.3
05	0 37.5	293 48.6	15.6	354 21.7	52.1	65 28.6	44.4	58 46.3	25.8			
06	15 39.9	308 50.0	N17 15.7	9 22.8	S 0 51.6	80 31.4	S21 44.5	73 48.9	S20 25.9	Rasalhague	96 01.6	N12 32.9
07	30 42.4	323 51.4	15.8	24 23.9	51.1	95 34.2	44.5	88 51.6	25.9	Regulus	207 38.6	N11 52.2
08	45 44.9	338 52.8	15.9	39 25.0	50.6	110 36.9	44.6	103 54.2	26.0	Rigel	281 07.7	S 8 10.7
T 09	60 47.3	353 54.3 ..	15.9	54 26.1 ..	50.1	125 39.7 ..	44.7	118 56.9 ..	26.0	Rigil Kent.	139 44.9	S60 55.3
U 10	75 49.8	8 55.7	16.0	69 27.3	49.5	140 42.5	44.7	133 59.5	26.0	Sabik	102 06.6	S15 44.9
E 11	90 52.3	23 57.1	16.1	84 28.4	49.0	155 45.3	44.8	149 02.2	26.1			
S 12	105 54.7	38 58.5	N17 16.2	99 29.5	S 0 48.5	170 48.1	S21 44.8	164 04.8	S20 26.1	Schedar	349 35.0	N56 38.6
D 13	120 57.2	53 59.9	16.3	114 30.6	48.0	185 50.9	44.9	179 07.5	26.2	Shaula	96 14.9	S37 07.0
A 14	135 59.7	69 01.3	16.4	129 31.8	47.5	200 53.7	45.0	194 10.1	26.2	Sirius	258 29.8	S16 44.7
Y 15	151 02.1	84 02.7 ..	16.4	144 32.9 ..	47.0	215 56.5 ..	45.0	209 12.8 ..	26.2	Spica	158 26.1	S11 16.0
16	166 04.6	99 04.1	16.5	159 34.0	46.5	230 59.3	45.1	224 15.4	26.3	Suhail	222 49.3	S43 31.0
17	181 07.1	114 05.4	16.6	174 35.1	46.0	246 02.1	45.1	239 18.1	26.3			
18	196 09.5	129 06.8	N17 16.7	189 36.2	S 0 45.4	261 04.9	S21 45.2	254 20.7	S20 26.4	Vega	80 35.2	N38 48.3
19	211 12.0	144 08.2	16.8	204 37.4	44.9	276 07.7	45.3	269 23.3	26.4	Zuben'ubi	136 59.8	S16 07.5
20	226 14.4	159 09.6	16.9	219 38.5	44.4	291 10.5	45.3	284 26.0	26.5		SHA	Mer.Pass.
21	241 16.9	174 11.0 ..	17.0	234 39.6 ..	43.9	306 13.3 ..	45.4	299 28.6 ..	26.5			
22	256 19.4	189 12.4	17.1	249 40.7	43.4	321 16.1	45.4	314 31.3	26.5	Venus	293 40.1	9 27
23	271 21.8	204 13.7	17.1	264 41.9	42.9	336 18.9	45.5	329 33.9	26.6	Mars	354 23.3	5 24
Mer.Pass.	5 01.4	v 1.5	d 0.1	v 1.1	d 0.5	v 2.8	d 0.1	v 2.6	d 0.0	Jupiter	64 41.4	0 43
										Saturn	58 03.5	1 10

SUN / MOON

UT	SUN GHA	SUN Dec	MOON GHA	v	MOON Dec	d	HP
5 00	178 50.8	N22 45.5	1 26.5	6.1	S24 03.7	0.2	58.0
01	193 50.7	45.2	15 51.6	6.2	24 03.9	0.0	57.9
02	208 50.6	45.0	30 16.8	6.2	24 03.9	0.1	57.9
03	223 50.5	.. 44.8	44 42.0	6.2	24 03.8	0.3	57.9
04	238 50.4	44.5	59 07.2	6.3	24 03.5	0.5	57.9
05	253 50.3	44.3	73 32.5	6.3	24 03.0	0.6	57.8
06	268 50.1	N22 44.0	87 57.8	6.3	S24 02.4	0.7	57.8
07	283 50.0	43.8	102 23.1	6.4	24 01.7	0.9	57.8
08	298 49.9	43.5	116 48.5	6.4	24 00.8	1.0	57.8
S 09	313 49.8	.. 43.3	131 13.9	6.5	23 59.8	1.2	57.7
U 10	328 49.7	43.0	145 39.4	6.5	23 58.6	1.3	57.7
N 11	343 49.6	42.8	160 04.9	6.6	23 57.3	1.5	57.7
D 12	358 49.5	N22 42.6	174 30.5	6.6	S23 55.8	1.6	57.6
A 13	13 49.4	42.3	188 56.1	6.6	23 54.2	1.8	57.6
Y 14	28 49.3	42.1	203 21.7	6.8	23 52.4	1.9	57.6
15	43 49.2	.. 41.8	217 47.5	6.7	23 50.5	2.0	57.6
16	58 49.1	41.6	232 13.2	6.8	23 48.5	2.2	57.5
17	73 49.0	41.3	246 39.0	6.9	23 46.3	2.3	57.5
18	88 48.9	N22 41.1	261 04.9	6.9	S23 44.0	2.5	57.5
19	103 48.8	40.8	275 30.8	7.0	23 41.5	2.6	57.5
20	118 48.7	40.6	289 56.8	7.1	23 38.9	2.8	57.4
21	133 48.6	.. 40.3	304 22.9	7.1	23 36.1	2.9	57.4
22	148 48.5	40.0	318 49.0	7.1	23 33.2	3.0	57.4
23	163 48.4	39.8	333 15.1	7.3	23 30.2	3.2	57.4
6 00	178 48.3	N22 39.5	347 41.4	7.3	S23 27.0	3.3	57.3
01	193 48.2	39.3	2 07.7	7.3	23 23.7	3.4	57.3
02	208 48.1	39.0	16 34.0	7.5	23 20.3	3.6	57.3
03	223 48.0	.. 38.8	31 00.5	7.5	23 16.7	3.7	57.2
04	238 47.9	38.5	45 27.0	7.5	23 13.0	3.8	57.2
05	253 47.8	38.3	59 53.5	7.7	23 09.2	4.0	57.2
06	268 47.7	N22 38.0	74 20.2	7.7	S23 05.2	4.1	57.2
07	283 47.6	37.7	88 46.9	7.8	23 01.1	4.2	57.1
08	298 47.5	37.5	103 13.7	7.8	22 56.9	4.4	57.1
M 09	313 47.4	.. 37.2	117 40.5	8.0	22 52.5	4.5	57.1
O 10	328 47.3	37.0	132 07.5	8.0	22 48.0	4.6	57.1
N 11	343 47.2	36.7	146 34.5	8.1	22 43.4	4.7	57.0
D 12	358 47.1	N22 36.4	161 01.6	8.1	S22 38.7	4.9	57.0
A 13	13 47.0	36.2	175 28.7	8.3	22 33.8	5.0	57.0
Y 14	28 46.9	35.9	189 56.0	8.3	22 28.8	5.1	56.9
15	43 46.8	.. 35.6	204 23.3	8.4	22 23.7	5.2	56.9
16	58 46.6	35.4	218 50.7	8.5	22 18.5	5.4	56.9
17	73 46.5	35.1	233 18.2	8.5	22 13.1	5.4	56.9
18	88 46.4	N22 34.8	247 45.7	8.6	S22 07.7	5.6	56.8
19	103 46.4	34.6	262 13.3	8.8	22 02.1	5.7	56.8
20	118 46.3	34.3	276 41.1	8.8	21 56.4	5.9	56.8
21	133 46.2	.. 34.0	291 08.9	8.9	21 50.5	5.9	56.7
22	148 46.1	33.8	305 36.8	8.9	21 44.6	6.0	56.7
23	163 46.0	33.5	320 04.7	9.1	21 38.6	6.2	56.7
7 00	178 45.9	N22 33.2	334 32.8	9.1	S21 32.4	6.3	56.7
01	193 45.8	32.9	349 00.9	9.2	21 26.1	6.3	56.6
02	208 45.7	32.7	3 29.1	9.4	21 19.8	6.5	56.6
03	223 45.6	.. 32.4	17 57.5	9.3	21 13.3	6.6	56.6
04	238 45.5	32.1	32 25.8	9.5	21 06.7	6.7	56.6
05	253 45.4	31.8	46 54.3	9.6	21 00.0	6.8	56.5
06	268 45.3	N22 31.6	61 22.9	9.7	S20 53.2	6.9	56.5
07	283 45.2	31.3	75 51.6	9.7	20 46.3	7.1	56.5
T 08	298 45.1	31.0	90 20.3	9.8	20 39.2	7.1	56.4
U 09	313 45.0	.. 30.7	104 49.1	9.9	20 32.1	7.2	56.4
E 10	328 44.9	30.5	119 18.0	10.0	20 24.9	7.3	56.4
S 11	343 44.8	30.2	133 47.0	10.1	20 17.6	7.4	56.4
D 12	358 44.7	N22 29.9	148 16.1	10.2	S20 10.2	7.5	56.3
A 13	13 44.6	29.6	162 45.3	10.3	20 02.7	7.6	56.3
Y 14	28 44.5	29.3	177 14.6	10.3	19 55.1	7.7	56.3
15	43 44.4	.. 29.1	191 43.9	10.5	19 47.4	7.8	56.3
16	58 44.3	28.8	206 13.4	10.5	19 39.6	7.9	56.2
17	73 44.2	28.5	220 42.9	10.6	19 31.7	8.0	56.2
18	88 44.1	N22 28.2	235 12.5	10.7	S19 23.7	8.1	56.2
19	103 44.0	27.9	249 42.2	10.8	19 15.6	8.1	56.1
20	118 43.9	27.6	264 12.0	10.9	19 07.5	8.3	56.1
21	133 43.8	.. 27.4	278 41.9	11.0	18 59.2	8.3	56.1
22	148 43.7	27.1	293 11.9	11.0	18 50.9	8.4	56.1
23	163 43.6	26.8	307 41.9	11.2	S18 42.5	8.5	56.0
	SD 15.8	d 0.3	SD 15.7		15.5		15.3

Twilight / Sunrise / Moonrise

Lat.	Naut.	Civil	Sunrise	Moonrise 5	6	7	8
N 72	□	□	□	■	■	■	■
N 70	□	□	□	■	■		01 02
68	□	□		■	■	00 56	00 18
66	////	////	00 55	■	(00 04 / 23 54)	23 49	23 44
64	////	////	01 53	23 02	23 20	23 27	23 30
62	////	////	02 25	22 28	22 54	23 09	23 17
60	////	01 18	02 49	22 03	22 34	22 54	23 07
N 58	////	01 57	03 08	21 43	22 18	22 41	22 58
56	////	02 24	03 24	21 26	22 04	22 30	22 50
54	01 12	02 44	03 37	21 12	21 52	22 21	22 42
52	01 48	03 01	03 49	21 00	21 41	22 12	22 36
50	02 13	03 15	03 59	20 49	21 31	22 04	22 30
45	02 55	03 44	04 21	20 26	21 11	21 47	22 17
N 40	03 24	04 05	04 38	20 07	20 55	21 34	22 07
35	03 47	04 23	04 52	19 52	20 41	21 22	21 58
30	04 05	04 38	05 05	19 39	20 29	21 12	21 50
20	04 33	05 02	05 26	19 16	20 08	20 54	21 36
N 10	04 54	05 21	05 44	18 56	19 50	20 39	21 24
0	05 13	05 39	06 01	18 38	19 33	20 25	21 13
S 10	05 29	05 55	06 18	18 19	19 16	20 10	21 01
20	05 45	06 12	06 36	17 59	18 58	19 55	20 49
30	06 00	06 30	06 56	17 37	18 37	19 37	20 35
35	06 09	06 40	07 08	17 23	18 24	19 26	20 27
40	06 18	06 51	07 22	17 08	18 10	19 14	20 17
45	06 27	07 04	07 38	16 49	17 54	19 00	20 06
S 50	06 38	07 20	07 58	16 26	17 33	18 43	19 53
52	06 43	07 27	08 07	16 15	17 23	18 35	19 47
54	06 49	07 34	08 17	16 03	17 12	18 25	19 40
56	06 55	07 43	08 29	15 49	16 59	18 15	19 32
58	07 01	07 53	08 43	15 32	16 44	18 03	19 24
S 60	07 08	08 04	08 59	15 11	16 26	17 49	19 14

Sunset / Twilight / Moonset

Lat.	Sunset	Civil	Naut.	Moonset 5	6	7	8
N 72	□	□	□	■	■	■	■
N 70	□	□	□	■	■	■	04 26
68	□	□	□	■	■	02 46	05 09
66	23 10	////	////	■	01 44	03 46	05 37
64	22 15	////	////	01 29	02 45	04 20	05 58
62	21 43	////	////	02 08	03 19	04 45	06 15
60	21 20	22 49	////	02 36	03 44	05 05	06 29
N 58	21 01	22 11	////	02 57	04 04	05 21	06 41
56	20 45	21 45	////	03 15	04 20	05 34	06 52
54	20 32	21 21	22 56	03 29	04 34	05 46	07 01
52	20 20	21 08	22 20	03 42	04 46	05 56	07 09
50	20 10	20 54	21 56	03 54	04 57	06 06	07 16
45	19 49	20 26	21 14	04 17	05 19	06 25	07 32
N 40	19 32	20 04	20 45	04 36	05 37	06 41	07 45
35	19 17	19 47	20 23	04 52	05 52	06 54	07 55
30	19 05	19 32	20 05	05 06	06 05	07 06	08 05
20	18 44	19 08	19 37	05 29	06 27	07 25	08 21
N 10	18 25	18 48	19 15	05 49	06 47	07 42	08 35
0	18 09	18 31	18 57	06 08	07 04	07 58	08 48
S 10	17 52	18 14	18 41	06 27	07 22	08 14	09 01
20	17 34	17 58	18 25	06 47	07 41	08 31	09 15
30	17 14	17 40	18 09	07 10	08 03	08 50	09 30
35	17 02	17 30	18 01	07 23	08 16	09 01	09 39
40	16 48	17 18	17 52	07 39	08 31	09 14	09 50
45	16 32	17 06	17 43	07 58	08 48	09 29	10 02
S 50	16 12	16 50	17 31	08 21	09 09	09 47	10 16
52	16 03	16 43	17 27	08 32	09 20	09 56	10 23
54	15 53	16 36	17 21	08 44	09 31	10 05	10 30
56	15 41	16 27	17 15	08 57	09 44	10 16	10 39
58	15 27	16 17	17 09	09 16	09 59	10 28	10 48
S 60	15 11	16 06	17 02	09 36	10 17	10 43	10 59

SUN / MOON

Day	Eqn. of Time 00h	Eqn. of Time 12h	Mer. Pass.	Mer. Pass. Upper	Mer. Pass. Lower	Age	Phase
5	04 37	04 42	12 05	24 51	12 23	14	100
6	04 47	04 52	12 05	00 51	13 19	15	98
7	04 56	05 01	12 05	01 46	14 11	16	94

Phase: ○ (Full Moon)

2020 JULY 8, 9, 10 (WED., THURS., FRI.)

UT d h	ARIES GHA	VENUS −4.7 GHA	Dec	MARS −0.6 GHA	Dec	JUPITER −2.7 GHA	Dec	SATURN +0.2 GHA	Dec	STARS Name	SHA	Dec
8 00	286 24.3	219 15.1	N17 17.2	279 43.0	S 0 42.4	351 21.7	S21 45.5	344 36.6	S20 26.6	Acamar	315 14.8	S40 13.3
01	301 26.8	234 16.5	17.3	294 44.1	41.9	6 24.5	45.6	359 39.2	26.7	Achernar	335 23.1	S57 07.8
02	316 29.2	249 17.8	17.4	309 45.3	41.4	21 27.3	45.7	14 41.9	26.7	Acrux	173 04.0	S63 12.9
03	331 31.7	264 19.2 ..	17.5	324 46.4 ..	40.9	36 30.1 ..	45.7	29 44.5 ..	26.7	Adhara	255 09.1	S29 00.0
04	346 34.2	279 20.5	17.6	339 47.5	40.3	51 32.9	45.8	44 47.2	26.8	Aldebaran	290 44.0	N16 32.9
05	1 36.6	294 21.9	17.7	354 48.6	39.8	66 35.7	45.8	59 49.8	26.8			
06	16 39.1	309 23.2	N17 17.8	9 49.8	S 0 39.3	81 38.5	S21 45.9	74 52.5	S20 26.9	Alioth	166 16.3	N55 51.3
W 07	31 41.6	324 24.6	17.9	24 50.9	38.8	96 41.3	46.0	89 55.1	26.9	Alkaid	152 54.9	N49 13.1
E 08	46 44.0	339 25.9	18.0	39 52.0	38.3	111 44.1	46.0	104 57.8	26.9	Alnair	27 37.2	S46 51.5
D 09	61 46.5	354 27.3 ..	18.1	54 53.1 ..	37.8	126 46.9 ..	46.1	120 00.4 ..	27.0	Alnilam	275 41.7	S 1 11.4
N 10	76 48.9	9 28.6	18.2	69 54.3	37.3	141 49.7	46.1	135 03.1	27.0	Alphard	217 51.6	S 8 44.8
E 11	91 51.4	24 30.0	18.3	84 55.4	36.8	156 52.5	46.2	150 05.7	27.1			
S 12	106 53.9	39 31.3	N17 18.4	99 56.5	S 0 36.3	171 55.3	S21 46.3	165 08.4	S20 27.1	Alphecca	126 06.6	N26 39.0
D 13	121 56.3	54 32.6	18.5	114 57.7	35.8	186 58.1	46.3	180 11.0	27.1	Alpheratz	357 38.4	N29 12.0
A 14	136 58.8	69 34.0	18.6	129 58.8	35.3	202 00.9	46.4	195 13.7	27.2	Altair	62 03.1	N 8 55.4
Y 15	152 01.3	84 35.3 ..	18.7	144 59.9 ..	34.7	217 03.7 ..	46.4	210 16.3 ..	27.2	Ankaa	353 10.7	S42 11.5
16	167 03.7	99 36.6	18.8	160 01.1	34.2	232 06.5	46.5	225 19.0	27.3	Antares	112 20.0	S26 28.6
17	182 06.2	114 37.9	18.9	175 02.2	33.7	247 09.3	46.6	240 21.6	27.3			
18	197 08.7	129 39.2	N17 19.0	190 03.3	S 0 33.2	262 12.1	S21 46.6	255 24.3	S20 27.4	Arcturus	145 51.2	N19 04.8
19	212 11.1	144 40.6	19.1	205 04.5	32.7	277 14.9	46.7	270 26.9	27.4	Atria	107 16.9	S69 03.9
20	227 13.6	159 41.9	19.3	220 05.6	32.2	292 17.7	46.7	285 29.6	27.4	Avior	234 16.7	S59 34.6
21	242 16.0	174 43.2 ..	19.4	235 06.7 ..	31.7	307 20.5 ..	46.8	300 32.2 ..	27.5	Bellatrix	278 27.1	N 6 22.0
22	257 18.5	189 44.5	19.5	250 07.9	31.2	322 23.3	46.9	315 34.9	27.5	Betelgeuse	270 56.3	N 7 24.6
23	272 21.0	204 45.8	19.6	265 09.0	30.7	337 26.1	46.9	330 37.5	27.6			
9 00	287 23.4	219 47.1	N17 19.7	280 10.1	S 0 30.2	352 28.9	S21 47.0	345 40.2	S20 27.6	Canopus	263 54.5	S52 42.4
01	302 25.9	234 48.4	19.8	295 11.3	29.7	7 31.7	47.0	0 42.8	27.6	Capella	280 27.7	N46 00.9
02	317 28.4	249 49.7	19.9	310 12.4	29.2	22 34.5	47.1	15 45.5	27.7	Deneb	49 27.8	N45 21.1
03	332 30.8	264 51.0 ..	20.0	325 13.5 ..	28.7	37 37.3 ..	47.2	30 48.1 ..	27.7	Denebola	182 28.8	N14 27.7
04	347 33.3	279 52.3	20.1	340 14.7	28.2	52 40.1	47.2	45 50.8	27.8	Diphda	348 50.9	S17 52.4
05	2 35.8	294 53.6	20.3	355 15.8	27.7	67 42.9	47.3	60 53.4	27.8			
06	17 38.2	309 54.8	N17 20.4	10 17.0	S 0 27.1	82 45.7	S21 47.3	75 56.0	S20 27.8	Dubhe	193 46.0	N61 38.8
T 07	32 40.7	324 56.1	20.5	25 18.1	26.6	97 48.6	47.4	90 58.7	27.9	Elnath	278 06.8	N28 37.3
H 08	47 43.2	339 57.4	20.6	40 19.2	26.1	112 51.4	47.5	106 01.3	27.9	Eltanin	90 43.4	N51 29.3
U 09	62 45.6	354 58.7 ..	20.7	55 20.4 ..	25.6	127 54.2 ..	47.5	121 04.0 ..	28.0	Enif	33 42.1	N 9 58.1
R 10	77 48.1	10 00.0	20.9	70 21.5	25.1	142 57.0	47.6	136 06.6	28.0	Fomalhaut	15 18.4	S29 30.7
S 11	92 50.5	25 01.2	21.0	85 22.6	24.6	157 59.8	47.6	151 09.3	28.1			
D 12	107 53.0	40 02.5	N17 21.1	100 23.8	S 0 24.1	173 02.6	S21 47.7	166 11.9	S20 28.1	Gacrux	171 55.6	S57 13.8
A 13	122 55.5	55 03.8	21.2	115 24.9	23.6	188 05.4	47.7	181 14.6	28.1	Gienah	175 47.4	S17 39.3
Y 14	137 57.9	70 05.0	21.3	130 26.1	23.1	203 08.2	47.8	196 17.2	28.2	Hadar	148 40.8	S60 28.4
15	153 00.4	85 06.3 ..	21.5	145 27.2 ..	22.6	218 11.0 ..	47.9	211 19.9 ..	28.2	Hamal	327 55.3	N23 33.3
16	168 02.9	100 07.5	21.6	160 28.3	22.1	233 13.8	47.9	226 22.5	28.3	Kaus Aust.	83 36.9	S34 22.4
17	183 05.3	115 08.8	21.7	175 29.5	21.6	248 16.6	48.0	241 25.2	28.3			
18	198 07.8	130 10.1	N17 21.8	190 30.6	S 0 21.1	263 19.4	S21 48.0	256 27.8	S20 28.3	Kochab	137 19.5	N74 04.7
19	213 10.3	145 11.3	22.0	205 31.8	20.6	278 22.2	48.1	271 30.5	28.4	Markab	13 33.3	N15 18.8
20	228 12.7	160 12.6	22.1	220 32.9	20.1	293 25.0	48.2	286 33.1	28.4	Menkar	314 10.1	N 4 10.1
21	243 15.2	175 13.8 ..	22.2	235 34.1 ..	19.6	308 27.8 ..	48.2	301 35.8 ..	28.5	Menkent	148 01.7	S36 28.3
22	258 17.7	190 15.0	22.3	250 35.2	19.1	323 30.6	48.3	316 38.4	28.5	Miaplacidus	221 39.6	S69 48.2
23	273 20.1	205 16.3	22.5	265 36.3	18.6	338 33.4	48.3	331 41.1	28.5			
10 00	288 22.6	220 17.5	N17 22.6	280 37.5	S 0 18.1	353 36.2	S21 48.4	346 43.7	S20 28.6	Mirfak	308 33.7	N49 55.7
01	303 25.0	235 18.7	22.7	295 38.6	17.6	8 39.0	48.5	1 46.4	28.6	Nunki	75 51.9	S26 16.2
02	318 27.5	250 20.0	22.9	310 39.8	17.1	23 41.8	48.5	16 49.0	28.7	Peacock	53 10.9	S56 44.0
03	333 30.0	265 21.2 ..	23.0	325 40.9 ..	16.6	38 44.6 ..	48.6	31 51.7 ..	28.7	Pollux	243 22.1	N27 58.6
04	348 32.4	280 22.4	23.1	340 42.1	16.1	53 47.4	48.6	46 54.4	28.8	Procyon	244 55.0	N 5 10.3
05	3 34.9	295 23.7	23.3	355 43.2	15.6	68 50.2	48.7	61 57.0	28.8			
06	18 37.4	310 24.9	N17 23.4	10 44.4	S 0 15.1	83 53.0	S21 48.8	76 59.7	S20 28.8	Rasalhague	96 01.6	N12 32.9
F 07	33 39.8	325 26.1	23.5	25 45.5	14.6	98 55.8	48.8	92 02.3	28.9	Regulus	207 38.6	N11 52.2
R 08	48 42.3	340 27.3	23.7	40 46.7	14.1	113 58.6	48.9	107 05.0	28.9	Rigel	281 07.7	S 8 10.7
I 09	63 44.8	355 28.5 ..	23.8	55 47.8 ..	13.6	129 01.4 ..	48.9	122 07.6 ..	29.0	Rigil Kent.	139 44.9	S60 55.3
D 10	78 47.2	10 29.7	23.9	70 49.0	13.1	144 04.2	49.0	137 10.3	29.0	Sabik	102 06.6	S15 44.9
A 11	93 49.7	25 30.9	24.1	85 50.1	12.6	159 07.0	49.1	152 12.9	29.0			
Y 12	108 52.1	40 32.1	N17 24.2	100 51.3	S 0 12.1	174 09.8	S21 49.1	167 15.6	S20 29.1	Schedar	349 34.9	N56 38.6
13	123 54.6	55 33.3	24.3	115 52.4	11.6	189 12.6	49.2	182 18.2	29.1	Shaula	96 14.9	S37 07.0
14	138 57.1	70 34.5	24.5	130 53.6	11.1	204 15.4	49.2	197 20.9	29.2	Sirius	258 29.8	S16 44.7
15	153 59.5	85 35.7 ..	24.6	145 54.7 ..	10.6	219 18.2 ..	49.3	212 23.5 ..	29.2	Spica	158 26.1	S11 16.0
16	169 02.0	100 36.9	24.8	160 55.9	10.1	234 21.0	49.4	227 26.2	29.2	Suhail	222 49.3	S43 31.0
17	184 04.5	115 38.1	24.9	175 57.0	09.6	249 23.8	49.4	242 28.8	29.3			
18	199 06.9	130 39.3	N17 25.0	190 58.2	S 0 09.1	264 26.6	S21 49.5	257 31.5	S20 29.3	Vega	80 35.2	N38 48.3
19	214 09.4	145 40.5	25.2	205 59.3	08.6	279 29.4	49.5	272 34.1	29.4	Zuben'ubi	136 59.9	S16 07.5
20	229 11.9	160 41.7	25.3	221 00.5	08.1	294 32.2	49.6	287 36.8	29.4		SHA	Mer. Pass.
21	244 14.3	175 42.9 ..	25.5	236 01.6 ..	07.6	309 35.1 ..	49.6	302 39.4 ..	29.5		° ′	h m
22	259 16.8	190 44.0	25.6	251 02.8	07.1	324 37.9	49.7	317 42.1	29.5	Venus	292 23.7	9 20
23	274 19.3	205 45.2	25.8	266 03.9	06.6	339 40.7	49.8	332 44.7	29.5	Mars	352 46.7	5 19
	h m									Jupiter	65 05.5	0 30
Mer. Pass.	4 49.6	v 1.3	d 0.1	v 1.1	d 0.5	v 2.8	d 0.1	v 2.6	d 0.0	Saturn	58 16.7	0 57

UT	SUN GHA	SUN Dec	MOON GHA	v	MOON Dec	d	HP
d h	o ′	o ′	o ′	′	o ′	′	′
8 00	178 43.5	N22 26.5	322 12.1	11.2	S18 34.0	8.6	56.0
01	193 43.4	26.2	336 42.3	11.3	18 25.4	8.7	56.0
02	208 43.3	25.9	351 12.6	11.4	18 16.7	8.7	56.0
03	223 43.2 ..	25.6	5 43.0	11.5	18 08.0	8.8	55.9
04	238 43.1	25.3	20 13.5	11.6	17 59.2	8.9	55.9
05	253 43.1	25.1	34 44.1	11.6	17 50.3	9.0	55.9
06	268 43.0	N22 24.8	49 14.7	11.8	S17 41.3	9.1	55.9
W 07	283 42.9	24.5	63 45.5	11.8	17 32.2	9.1	55.8
E 08	298 42.8	24.2	78 16.3	11.9	17 23.1	9.2	55.8
D 09	313 42.7 ..	23.9	92 47.2	12.0	17 13.9	9.3	55.8
N 10	328 42.6	23.6	107 18.2	12.1	17 04.6	9.3	55.7
E 11	343 42.5	23.3	121 49.3	12.2	16 55.3	9.4	55.7
S 12	358 42.4	N22 23.0	136 20.5	12.2	S16 45.9	9.5	55.7
D 13	13 42.3	22.7	150 51.7	12.4	16 36.4	9.6	55.7
A 14	28 42.2	22.4	165 23.1	12.4	16 26.8	9.6	55.6
Y 15	43 42.1 ..	22.1	179 54.5	12.5	16 17.2	9.7	55.6
16	58 42.0	21.8	194 26.0	12.5	16 07.5	9.8	55.6
17	73 41.9	21.5	208 57.5	12.7	15 57.7	9.8	55.6
18	88 41.8	N22 21.2	223 29.2	12.7	S15 47.9	9.9	55.6
19	103 41.8	20.9	238 00.9	12.8	15 38.0	9.9	55.5
20	118 41.7	20.6	252 32.7	12.9	15 28.1	10.0	55.5
21	133 41.6 ..	20.3	267 04.6	13.0	15 18.1	10.1	55.5
22	148 41.5	20.0	281 36.6	13.0	15 08.0	10.1	55.5
23	163 41.4	19.7	296 08.6	13.1	14 57.9	10.2	55.4
9 00	178 41.3	N22 19.4	310 40.7	13.2	S14 47.7	10.2	55.4
01	193 41.2	19.1	325 12.9	13.3	14 37.5	10.3	55.4
02	208 41.1	18.8	339 45.2	13.3	14 27.2	10.3	55.4
03	223 41.0 ..	18.5	354 17.5	13.5	14 16.9	10.4	55.3
04	238 40.9	18.2	8 50.0	13.4	14 06.5	10.5	55.3
05	253 40.8	17.9	23 22.4	13.6	13 56.0	10.5	55.3
06	268 40.8	N22 17.6	37 55.0	13.6	S13 45.5	10.6	55.3
T 07	283 40.7	17.3	52 27.6	13.7	13 34.9	10.6	55.2
H 08	298 40.6	16.9	67 00.3	13.8	13 24.3	10.6	55.2
U 09	313 40.5 ..	16.6	81 33.1	13.9	13 13.7	10.7	55.2
R 10	328 40.4	16.3	96 06.0	13.9	13 03.0	10.8	55.2
S 11	343 40.3	16.0	110 38.9	13.9	12 52.2	10.8	55.2
D 12	358 40.2	N22 15.7	125 11.8	14.1	S12 41.4	10.8	55.1
A 13	13 40.1	15.4	139 44.9	14.1	12 30.6	10.9	55.1
Y 14	28 40.0	15.1	154 18.0	14.2	12 19.7	10.9	55.1
15	43 40.0 ..	14.8	168 51.2	14.2	12 08.8	11.0	55.1
16	58 39.9	14.5	183 24.4	14.3	11 57.8	11.0	55.1
17	73 39.8	14.1	197 57.7	14.4	11 46.8	11.0	55.0
18	88 39.7	N22 13.8	212 31.1	14.4	S11 35.8	11.1	55.0
19	103 39.6	13.5	227 04.5	14.5	11 24.7	11.2	55.0
20	118 39.5	13.2	241 38.0	14.5	11 13.5	11.1	55.0
21	133 39.4 ..	12.9	256 11.5	14.6	11 02.4	11.3	55.0
22	148 39.3	12.6	270 45.1	14.7	10 51.2	11.3	54.9
23	163 39.3	12.2	285 18.8	14.7	10 39.9	11.3	54.9
10 00	178 39.2	N22 11.9	299 52.5	14.8	S10 28.6	11.3	54.9
01	193 39.1	11.6	314 26.3	14.8	10 17.3	11.3	54.9
02	208 39.0	11.3	329 00.1	14.9	10 06.0	11.4	54.9
03	223 38.9 ..	11.0	343 34.0	15.0	9 54.6	11.4	54.8
04	238 38.8	10.6	358 08.0	15.0	9 43.2	11.4	54.8
05	253 38.7	10.3	12 42.0	15.0	9 31.8	11.5	54.8
06	268 38.7	N22 10.0	27 16.0	15.1	S 9 20.3	11.5	54.8
07	283 38.6	09.7	41 50.1	15.2	9 08.8	11.5	54.8
08	298 38.5	09.3	56 24.3	15.2	8 57.3	11.6	54.8
F 09	313 38.4 ..	09.0	70 58.5	15.2	8 45.7	11.6	54.7
R 10	328 38.3	08.7	85 32.7	15.3	8 34.1	11.6	54.7
I 11	343 38.2	08.4	100 07.0	15.3	8 22.5	11.6	54.7
D 12	358 38.1	N22 08.0	114 41.3	15.4	S 8 10.9	11.7	54.7
A 13	13 38.1	07.7	129 15.7	15.5	7 59.2	11.7	54.7
Y 14	28 38.0	07.4	143 50.2	15.4	7 47.5	11.7	54.7
15	43 37.9 ..	07.0	158 24.6	15.6	7 35.8	11.7	54.6
16	58 37.8	06.7	172 59.2	15.5	7 24.1	11.8	54.6
17	73 37.7	06.4	187 33.7	15.6	7 12.3	11.7	54.6
18	88 37.6	N22 06.0	202 08.3	15.7	S 7 00.6	11.8	54.6
19	103 37.5	05.7	216 43.0	15.6	6 48.8	11.9	54.6
20	118 37.5	05.4	231 17.6	15.7	6 36.9	11.8	54.6
21	133 37.4 ..	05.1	245 52.3	15.8	6 25.1	11.8	54.6
22	148 37.3	04.7	260 27.1	15.8	6 13.3	11.9	54.6
23	163 37.2	04.4	275 01.9	15.8	S 6 01.4	11.9	54.5
	SD 15.8	d 0.3	SD 15.2		15.0		14.9

Twilight / Sunrise / Moonrise

Lat.	Naut.	Civil	Sunrise	Moonrise 8	9	10	11
o	h m	h m	h m	h m	h m	h m	h m
N 72	▯	▯	▯	■■	00 55	(00 20 / 23 56)	23 35
N 70	▯	▯	▯	01 02	00 25	(00 04 / 23 48)	23 34
68	▯	▯	▯	23 44	(00 02 / 23 51)	23 41	23 33
66	////	////	01 10	23 44	23 40	23 36	23 31
64	////	////	02 00	23 30	23 31	23 31	23 30
62	////	////	02 31	23 17	23 23	23 27	23 30
60	////	01 27	02 54	23 07	23 16	23 23	23 29
N 58	////	02 03	03 12	22 58	23 10	23 20	23 28
56	////	02 29	03 27	22 50	23 04	23 17	23 28
54	01 20	02 48	03 40	22 42	23 00	23 14	23 27
52	01 54	03 05	03 52	22 36	22 55	23 12	23 27
50	02 17	03 19	04 02	22 30	22 51	23 09	23 26
45	02 58	03 46	04 23	22 17	22 42	23 05	23 25
N 40	03 27	04 07	04 40	22 07	22 35	23 01	23 25
35	03 49	04 25	04 54	21 58	22 29	22 57	23 24
30	04 06	04 39	05 06	21 50	22 23	22 54	23 23
20	04 34	05 03	05 27	21 36	22 14	22 49	23 22
N 10	04 55	05 22	05 45	21 24	22 05	22 44	23 21
0	05 13	05 39	06 02	21 13	21 57	22 40	23 21
S 10	05 29	05 56	06 18	21 01	21 49	22 35	23 20
20	05 45	06 12	06 36	20 49	21 41	22 31	23 19
30	06 00	06 30	06 56	20 35	21 31	22 25	23 18
35	06 08	06 41	07 07	20 27	21 25	22 22	23 17
40	06 17	06 51	07 21	20 17	21 19	22 18	23 17
45	06 26	07 03	07 37	20 06	21 11	22 14	23 16
S 50	06 37	07 18	07 56	19 53	21 02	22 09	23 15
52	06 42	07 25	08 05	19 47	20 58	22 07	23 15
54	06 47	07 33	08 15	19 40	20 53	22 05	23 14
56	06 53	07 41	08 27	19 32	20 48	22 02	23 14
58	06 59	07 50	08 40	19 24	20 42	21 59	23 13
S 60	07 06	08 01	08 56	19 14	20 36	21 55	23 13

Sunset / Twilight / Moonset

Lat.	Sunset	Civil	Naut.	Moonset 8	9	10	11
o	h m	h m	h m	h m	h m	h m	h m
N 72	▯	▯	▯	■■	06 12	08 18	10 10
N 70	▯	▯	▯	04 26	06 41	08 33	10 16
68	▯	▯	▯	05 09	07 02	08 44	10 20
66	22 57	////	////	05 37	07 19	08 54	10 24
64	22 09	////	////	05 58	07 32	09 02	10 27
62	21 38	////	////	06 15	07 44	09 08	10 30
60	21 16	22 41	////	06 29	07 53	09 14	10 32
N 58	20 58	22 06	////	06 41	08 02	09 19	10 35
56	20 43	21 41	////	06 52	08 09	09 24	10 37
54	20 30	21 21	22 48	07 01	08 15	09 28	10 38
52	20 18	21 05	22 16	07 09	08 21	09 31	10 40
50	20 08	20 51	21 52	07 16	08 27	09 35	10 41
45	19 47	20 24	21 12	07 32	08 38	09 42	10 44
N 40	19 31	20 03	20 43	07 45	08 47	09 48	10 47
35	19 16	19 46	20 22	07 55	08 55	09 53	10 49
30	19 04	19 31	20 04	08 05	09 02	09 57	10 51
20	18 43	19 08	19 37	08 21	09 14	10 05	10 54
N 10	18 26	18 48	19 15	08 35	09 25	10 12	10 57
0	18 09	18 31	18 57	08 48	09 34	10 18	10 59
S 10	17 52	18 15	18 41	09 01	09 44	10 24	11 02
20	17 35	17 59	18 26	09 15	09 54	10 31	11 05
30	17 15	17 41	18 11	09 30	10 06	10 38	11 08
35	17 03	17 31	18 03	09 39	10 13	10 42	11 10
40	16 50	17 20	17 54	09 50	10 20	10 47	11 12
45	16 34	17 08	17 44	10 02	10 29	10 53	11 14
S 50	16 15	16 53	17 34	10 16	10 40	10 59	11 17
52	16 06	16 46	17 29	10 23	10 45	11 02	11 18
54	15 56	16 38	17 24	10 30	10 50	11 06	11 19
56	15 44	16 30	17 18	10 39	10 56	11 09	11 21
58	15 31	16 21	17 12	10 48	11 02	11 13	11 23
S 60	15 15	16 10	17 05	10 59	11 10	11 18	11 24

SUN / MOON

Day	SUN Eqn. of Time 00h	SUN Eqn. of Time 12h	SUN Mer. Pass.	MOON Mer. Pass. Upper	MOON Mer. Pass. Lower	Age	Phase
d	m s	m s	h m	h m	h m	d	%
8	05 06	05 10	12 05	02 36	15 00	17	88
9	05 15	05 19	12 05	03 24	15 46	18	81
10	05 23	05 27	12 05	04 08	16 29	19	73

UT	ARIES GHA	VENUS GHA	VENUS Dec	MARS GHA	MARS Dec	JUPITER GHA	JUPITER Dec	SATURN GHA	SATURN Dec	STARS Name	SHA	Dec
11 00	289 21.7	220 46.4	N17 25.9	281 05.1	S 0 06.1	354 43.5	S21 49.8	347 47.4	S20 29.6	Acamar	315 14.8	S40 13.2
01	304 24.2	235 47.6	26.1	296 06.2	05.6	9 46.3	49.9	2 50.0	29.6	Achernar	335 23.1	S57 07.8
02	319 26.6	250 48.7	26.2	311 07.4	05.1	24 49.1	49.9	17 52.7	29.7	Acrux	173 04.1	S63 12.9
03	334 29.1	265 49.9 ..	26.4	326 08.5 ..	04.6	39 51.9 ..	50.0	32 55.3 ..	29.7	Adhara	255 09.1	S29 00.0
04	349 31.6	280 51.1	26.5	341 09.7	04.1	54 54.7	50.1	47 58.0	29.7	Aldebaran	290 44.0	N16 32.9
05	4 34.0	295 52.2	26.7	356 10.8	03.6	69 57.5	50.1	63 00.6	29.8			
06	19 36.5	310 53.4	N17 26.8	11 12.0	S 0 03.1	85 00.3	S21 50.2	78 03.3	S20 29.8	Alioth	166 16.4	N55 51.3
S 07	34 39.0	325 54.5	27.0	26 13.2	02.6	100 03.1	50.2	93 05.9	29.9	Alkaid	152 54.9	N49 13.1
A 08	49 41.4	340 55.7	27.1	41 14.3	02.1	115 05.9	50.3	108 08.6	29.9	Alnair	27 37.2	S46 51.5
T 09	64 43.9	355 56.8 ..	27.3	56 15.5 ..	01.6	130 08.7 ..	50.4	123 11.2 ..	29.9	Alnilam	275 41.7	S 1 11.4
U 10	79 46.4	10 58.0	27.4	71 16.6	01.1	145 11.5	50.4	138 13.9	30.0	Alphard	217 51.6	S 8 44.8
R 11	94 48.8	25 59.1	27.6	86 17.8	00.6	160 14.3	50.5	153 16.5	30.0			
D 12	109 51.3	41 00.3	N17 27.7	101 18.9	S 0 00.1	175 17.1	S21 50.5	168 19.2	S20 30.1	Alphecca	126 06.6	N26 39.0
A 13	124 53.7	56 01.4	27.9	116 20.1	N 00.3	190 19.9	50.6	183 21.8	30.1	Alpheratz	357 38.3	N29 12.0
Y 14	139 56.2	71 02.6	28.0	131 21.3	00.8	205 22.7	50.7	198 24.5	30.2	Altair	62 03.1	N 8 55.4
15	154 58.7	86 03.7 ..	28.2	146 22.4 ..	01.3	220 25.5 ..	50.7	213 27.1 ..	30.2	Ankaa	353 10.7	S42 11.5
16	170 01.1	101 04.8	28.3	161 23.6	01.8	235 28.3	50.8	228 29.8	30.2	Antares	112 20.0	S26 28.6
17	185 03.6	116 06.0	28.5	176 24.7	02.3	250 31.1	50.8	243 32.5	30.3			
18	200 06.1	131 07.1	N17 28.7	191 25.9	N 0 02.8	265 33.9	S21 50.9	258 35.1	S20 30.3	Arcturus	145 51.2	N19 04.8
19	215 08.5	146 08.2	28.8	206 27.1	03.3	280 36.7	50.9	273 37.8	30.4	Atria	107 16.9	S69 03.9
20	230 11.0	161 09.3	29.0	221 28.2	03.8	295 39.5	51.0	288 40.4	30.4	Avior	234 16.7	S59 34.6
21	245 13.5	176 10.4 ..	29.1	236 29.4 ..	04.3	310 42.4 ..	51.1	303 43.1 ..	30.4	Bellatrix	278 27.1	N 6 22.0
22	260 15.9	191 11.6	29.3	251 30.5	04.8	325 45.2	51.1	318 45.7	30.5	Betelgeuse	270 56.3	N 7 24.6
23	275 18.4	206 12.7	29.5	266 31.7	05.3	340 48.0	51.2	333 48.4	30.5			
12 00	290 20.9	221 13.8	N17 29.6	281 32.9	N 0 05.8	355 50.8	S21 51.2	348 51.0	S20 30.6	Canopus	263 54.5	S52 42.4
01	305 23.3	236 14.9	29.8	296 34.0	06.3	10 53.6	51.3	3 53.7	30.6	Capella	280 27.6	N46 00.9
02	320 25.8	251 16.0	29.9	311 35.2	06.8	25 56.4	51.4	18 56.3	30.7	Deneb	49 27.7	N45 21.1
03	335 28.2	266 17.1 ..	30.1	326 36.4 ..	07.3	40 59.2 ..	51.4	33 59.0 ..	30.7	Denebola	182 28.8	N14 27.7
04	350 30.7	281 18.2	30.3	341 37.5	07.7	56 02.0	51.5	49 01.6	30.7	Diphda	348 50.9	S17 52.4
05	5 33.2	296 19.3	30.4	356 38.7	08.2	71 04.8	51.5	64 04.3	30.8			
06	20 35.6	311 20.4	N17 30.6	11 39.9	N 0 08.7	86 07.6	S21 51.6	79 06.9	S20 30.8	Dubhe	193 46.0	N61 38.8
07	35 38.1	326 21.5	30.8	26 41.0	09.2	101 10.4	51.7	94 09.6	30.9	Elnath	278 06.8	N28 37.3
08	50 40.6	341 22.6	30.9	41 42.2	09.7	116 13.2	51.7	109 12.2	30.9	Eltanin	90 43.4	N51 29.3
S 09	65 43.0	356 23.7 ..	31.1	56 43.4 ..	10.2	131 16.0 ..	51.8	124 14.9 ..	30.9	Enif	33 42.1	N 9 58.1
U 10	80 45.5	11 24.8	31.3	71 44.5	10.7	146 18.8	51.8	139 17.5	31.0	Fomalhaut	15 18.3	S29 30.7
N 11	95 48.0	26 25.9	31.4	86 45.7	11.2	161 21.6	51.9	154 20.2	31.0			
D 12	110 50.4	41 26.9	N17 31.6	101 46.9	N 0 11.7	176 24.4	S21 52.0	169 22.8	S20 31.1	Gacrux	171 55.6	S57 13.8
A 13	125 52.9	56 28.0	31.8	116 48.0	12.2	191 27.2	52.0	184 25.5	31.1	Gienah	175 47.4	S17 39.3
Y 14	140 55.4	71 29.1	31.9	131 49.2	12.7	206 30.0	52.1	199 28.2	31.1	Hadar	148 40.9	S60 28.4
15	155 57.8	86 30.2 ..	32.1	146 50.4 ..	13.1	221 32.8 ..	52.1	214 30.8 ..	31.2	Hamal	327 55.3	N23 33.3
16	171 00.3	101 31.3	32.3	161 51.5	13.6	236 35.6	52.2	229 33.5	31.2	Kaus Aust.	83 36.9	S34 22.4
17	186 02.7	116 32.3	32.4	176 52.7	14.1	251 38.5	52.2	244 36.1	31.3			
18	201 05.2	131 33.4	N17 32.6	191 53.9	N 0 14.6	266 41.3	S21 52.3	259 38.8	S20 31.3	Kochab	137 19.5	N74 04.7
19	216 07.7	146 34.5	32.8	206 55.0	15.1	281 44.1	52.4	274 41.4	31.4	Markab	13 33.3	N15 18.8
20	231 10.1	161 35.5	33.0	221 56.2	15.6	296 46.9	52.4	289 44.1	31.4	Menkar	314 10.1	N 4 10.1
21	246 12.6	176 36.6 ..	33.1	236 57.4 ..	16.1	311 49.7 ..	52.5	304 46.7 ..	31.4	Menkent	148 01.7	S36 28.3
22	261 15.1	191 37.6	33.3	251 58.6	16.6	326 52.5	52.5	319 49.4	31.5	Miaplacidus	221 39.6	S69 48.2
23	276 17.5	206 38.7	33.5	266 59.7	17.1	341 55.3	52.6	334 52.0	31.5			
13 00	291 20.0	221 39.8	N17 33.7	282 00.9	N 0 17.5	356 58.1	S21 52.7	349 54.7	S20 31.6	Mirfak	308 33.6	N49 55.7
01	306 22.5	236 40.8	33.8	297 02.1	18.0	12 00.9	52.7	4 57.3	31.6	Nunki	75 51.9	S26 16.2
02	321 24.9	251 41.9	34.0	312 03.3	18.5	27 03.7	52.8	20 00.0	31.6	Peacock	53 10.9	S56 40.0
03	336 27.4	266 42.9 ..	34.2	327 04.4 ..	19.0	42 06.5 ..	52.8	35 02.6 ..	31.7	Pollux	243 22.1	N27 58.6
04	351 29.8	281 43.9	34.4	342 05.6	19.5	57 09.3	52.9	50 05.3	31.7	Procyon	244 55.0	N 5 10.4
05	6 32.3	296 45.0	34.5	357 06.8	20.0	72 12.1	52.9	65 08.0	31.8			
06	21 34.8	311 46.0	N17 34.7	12 08.0	N 0 20.5	87 14.9	S21 53.0	80 10.6	S20 31.8	Rasalhague	96 01.6	N12 32.9
07	36 37.2	326 47.1	34.9	27 09.1	21.0	102 17.7	53.1	95 13.3	31.9	Regulus	207 38.6	N11 52.2
08	51 39.7	341 48.1	35.1	42 10.3	21.4	117 20.5	53.1	110 15.9	31.9	Rigel	281 07.6	S 8 10.7
M 09	66 42.2	356 49.1 ..	35.3	57 11.5 ..	21.9	132 23.3 ..	53.2	125 18.6 ..	31.9	Rigil Kent.	139 44.9	S60 55.3
O 10	81 44.6	11 50.2	35.4	72 12.7	22.4	147 26.1	53.2	140 21.2	32.0	Sabik	102 06.6	S15 44.9
N 11	96 47.1	26 51.2	35.6	87 13.8	22.9	162 28.9	53.3	155 23.9	32.0			
D 12	111 49.6	41 52.2	N17 35.8	102 15.0	N 0 23.4	177 31.8	S21 53.4	170 26.5	S20 32.1	Schedar	349 34.9	N56 38.6
A 13	126 52.0	56 53.2	36.0	117 16.2	23.9	192 34.6	53.4	185 29.2	32.1	Shaula	96 14.9	S37 07.0
Y 14	141 54.5	71 54.2	36.2	132 17.4	24.4	207 37.4	53.5	200 31.8	32.1	Sirius	258 29.8	S16 44.7
15	156 57.0	86 55.3 ..	36.3	147 18.6 ..	24.8	222 40.2 ..	53.5	215 34.5 ..	32.2	Spica	158 26.1	S11 16.0
16	171 59.4	101 56.3	36.5	162 19.7	25.3	237 43.0	53.6	230 37.1	32.2	Suhail	222 49.3	S43 31.0
17	187 01.9	116 57.3	36.7	177 20.9	25.8	252 45.8	53.7	245 39.8	32.3			
18	202 04.3	131 58.3	N17 36.9	192 22.1	N 0 26.3	267 48.6	S21 53.7	260 42.5	S20 32.3	Vega	80 35.2	N38 48.3
19	217 06.8	146 59.3	37.1	207 23.3	26.8	282 51.4	53.8	275 45.1	32.4	Zuben'ubi	136 59.9	S16 07.5
20	232 09.3	162 00.3	37.3	222 24.5	27.3	297 54.2	53.8	290 47.8	32.4		SHA	Mer. Pass.
21	247 11.7	177 01.3 ..	37.5	237 25.6 ..	27.7	312 57.0 ..	53.9	305 50.4 ..	32.4	Venus	290 52.9	9 14
22	262 14.2	192 02.3	37.6	252 26.8	28.2	327 59.8	53.9	320 53.1	32.5	Mars	351 12.0	5 13
23	277 16.7	207 03.3	37.8	267 28.0	28.7	343 02.6	54.0	335 55.7	32.5	Jupiter	65 29.9	0 17
Mer. Pass. 4 37.8		v 1.1	d 0.2	v 1.2	d 0.5	v 2.8	d 0.1	v 2.7	d 0.0	Saturn	58 30.2	0 44

SUN / MOON

UT	SUN GHA	Dec	MOON GHA	v	Dec	d	HP
11 00	178 37.1	N22 04.0	289 36.7	15.9	S 5 49.5	11.9	54.5
01	193 37.1	03.7	304 11.6	15.8	5 37.6	11.9	54.5
02	208 37.0	03.4	318 46.4	16.0	5 25.7	12.0	54.5
03	223 36.9	.. 03.0	333 21.4	15.9	5 13.7	11.9	54.5
04	238 36.8	02.7	347 56.3	16.0	5 01.8	12.0	54.5
05	253 36.7	02.4	2 31.3	16.0	4 49.8	11.9	54.5
06	268 36.7	N22 02.0	17 06.3	16.1	S 4 37.9	12.0	54.5
S 07	283 36.6	01.7	31 41.4	16.0	4 25.9	12.0	54.4
A 08	298 36.5	01.3	46 16.4	16.1	4 13.9	12.0	54.4
T 09	313 36.4	.. 01.0	60 51.5	16.1	4 01.9	12.1	54.4
U 10	328 36.3	00.7	75 26.6	16.2	3 49.8	12.0	54.4
R 11	343 36.3	00.3	90 01.8	16.1	3 37.8	12.0	54.4
D 12	358 36.2	N22 00.0	104 36.9	16.2	S 3 25.8	12.1	54.4
A 13	13 36.1	21 59.6	119 12.1	16.2	3 13.7	12.0	54.4
Y 14	28 36.0	59.3	133 47.3	16.2	3 01.7	12.1	54.4
15	43 35.9	.. 58.9	148 22.5	16.3	2 49.6	12.1	54.4
16	58 35.9	58.6	162 57.8	16.3	2 37.5	12.0	54.4
17	73 35.8	58.2	177 33.1	16.2	2 25.5	12.1	54.4
18	88 35.7	N21 57.9	192 08.3	16.3	S 2 13.4	12.1	54.3
19	103 35.6	57.6	206 43.6	16.3	2 01.3	12.1	54.3
20	118 35.5	57.2	221 18.9	16.4	1 49.2	12.1	54.3
21	133 35.5	.. 56.9	235 54.3	16.3	1 37.1	12.1	54.3
22	148 35.4	56.5	250 29.6	16.4	1 25.0	12.1	54.3
23	163 35.3	56.2	265 05.0	16.3	1 12.9	12.1	54.3
12 00	178 35.2	N21 55.8	279 40.3	16.4	S 1 00.8	12.1	54.3
01	193 35.2	55.4	294 15.7	16.4	0 48.7	12.1	54.3
02	208 35.1	55.1	308 51.1	16.4	0 36.6	12.1	54.3
03	223 35.0	.. 54.7	323 26.5	16.4	0 24.5	12.0	54.3
04	238 34.9	54.4	338 01.9	16.4	0 12.5	12.1	54.3
05	253 34.8	54.0	352 37.3	16.4	S 0 00.4	12.1	54.3
06	268 34.8	N21 53.7	7 12.7	16.4	N 0 11.7	12.1	54.3
S 07	283 34.7	53.3	21 48.1	16.4	0 23.8	12.1	54.3
U 08	298 34.6	53.0	36 23.5	16.4	0 35.9	12.1	54.3
N 09	313 34.5	.. 52.6	50 58.9	16.4	0 48.0	12.1	54.3
D 10	328 34.5	52.3	65 34.3	16.4	1 00.1	12.0	54.3
A 11	343 34.4	51.9	80 09.7	16.5	1 12.1	12.1	54.3
Y 12	358 34.3	N21 51.5	94 45.2	16.4	N 1 24.2	12.1	54.3
13	13 34.2	51.2	109 20.6	16.4	1 36.3	12.0	54.3
14	28 34.2	50.8	123 56.0	16.4	1 48.3	12.1	54.3
15	43 34.1	.. 50.5	138 31.4	16.4	2 00.4	12.0	54.2
16	58 34.0	50.1	153 06.8	16.4	2 12.4	12.0	54.2
17	73 33.9	49.7	167 42.2	16.4	2 24.4	12.1	54.2
18	88 33.9	N21 49.4	182 17.6	16.4	N 2 36.5	12.0	54.2
19	103 33.8	49.0	196 53.0	16.3	2 48.5	12.0	54.2
20	118 33.7	48.6	211 28.3	16.4	3 00.5	12.0	54.2
21	133 33.7	.. 48.3	226 03.7	16.3	3 12.5	11.9	54.2
22	148 33.6	47.9	240 39.0	16.4	3 24.4	12.0	54.2
23	163 33.5	47.5	255 14.4	16.3	3 36.4	12.0	54.3
13 00	178 33.4	N21 47.2	269 49.7	16.3	N 3 48.4	11.9	54.3
01	193 33.4	46.8	284 25.0	16.3	4 00.3	11.9	54.3
02	208 33.3	46.4	299 00.3	16.3	4 12.2	11.9	54.3
03	223 33.2	.. 46.1	313 35.6	16.3	4 24.1	11.9	54.3
04	238 33.1	45.7	328 10.9	16.2	4 36.0	11.9	54.3
05	253 33.1	45.3	342 46.1	16.2	4 47.9	11.9	54.3
06	268 33.0	N21 45.0	357 21.3	16.2	N 4 59.8	11.8	54.3
07	283 32.9	44.6	11 56.5	16.2	5 11.6	11.8	54.3
08	298 32.9	44.2	26 31.7	16.2	5 23.4	11.8	54.3
M 09	313 32.8	.. 43.8	41 06.9	16.1	5 35.2	11.8	54.3
O 10	328 32.7	43.5	55 42.0	16.2	5 47.0	11.8	54.3
N 11	343 32.6	43.1	70 17.2	16.0	5 58.8	11.7	54.3
D 12	358 32.6	N21 42.7	84 52.2	16.1	N 6 10.5	11.8	54.3
A 13	13 32.5	42.4	99 27.3	16.1	6 22.3	11.7	54.3
Y 14	28 32.4	42.0	114 02.4	16.0	6 34.0	11.6	54.3
15	43 32.4	.. 41.6	128 37.4	16.0	6 45.6	11.7	54.3
16	58 32.3	41.2	143 12.4	15.9	6 57.3	11.6	54.3
17	73 32.2	40.8	157 47.3	15.9	7 08.9	11.7	54.3
18	88 32.2	N21 40.5	172 22.2	15.9	N 7 20.6	11.5	54.3
19	103 32.1	40.1	186 57.1	15.9	7 32.1	11.6	54.3
20	118 32.0	39.7	201 32.0	15.8	7 43.7	11.5	54.3
21	133 31.9	.. 39.3	216 06.8	15.8	7 55.2	11.6	54.3
22	148 31.9	38.9	230 41.6	15.8	8 06.8	11.4	54.4
23	163 31.8	38.6	245 16.4	15.7	N 8 18.2	11.5	54.4
	SD 15.8	d 0.4	SD 14.8		14.8		14.8

Twilight / Moonrise

Lat.	Naut.	Civil	Sunrise	Moonrise 11	12	13	14
N 72	☐	☐	☐	23 35	23 15	22 54	22 27
N 70	☐	☐	☐	23 34	23 20	23 05	22 48
68	☐	☐	☐	23 33	23 24	23 15	23 05
66	////	////	01 24	23 31	23 27	23 23	23 19
64	////	////	02 08	23 30	23 30	23 30	23 31
62	////	00 23	02 37	23 30	23 33	23 36	23 41
60	////	01 37	02 59	23 29	23 35	23 41	23 49
N 58	////	02 10	03 16	23 28	23 37	23 46	23 57
56	00 21	02 34	03 31	23 28	23 39	23 50	24 03
54	01 29	02 53	03 44	23 27	23 40	23 54	24 09
52	02 00	03 09	03 55	23 27	23 42	23 57	24 15
50	02 22	03 22	04 05	23 26	23 43	24 00	00 00
45	03 02	03 49	04 25	23 25	23 46	24 07	00 07
N 40	03 29	04 10	04 42	23 25	23 48	24 13	00 13
35	03 51	04 27	04 56	23 24	23 50	24 17	00 17
30	04 08	04 41	05 08	23 23	23 52	24 22	00 22
20	04 35	05 04	05 28	23 22	23 55	24 29	00 29
N 10	04 56	05 23	05 46	23 21	23 58	24 36	00 36
0	05 14	05 40	06 02	23 21	24 01	00 01	00 42
S 10	05 30	05 56	06 18	23 20	24 04	00 04	00 48
20	05 45	06 12	06 35	23 19	24 07	00 07	00 55
30	06 00	06 29	06 55	23 18	24 10	00 10	01 03
35	06 07	06 39	07 06	23 17	24 12	00 12	01 08
40	06 16	06 50	07 20	23 17	24 15	00 15	01 13
45	06 25	07 02	07 35	23 16	24 17	00 17	01 19
S 50	06 36	07 16	07 54	23 15	24 20	00 20	01 26
52	06 40	07 23	08 03	23 15	24 22	00 22	01 29
54	06 45	07 30	08 13	23 14	24 23	00 23	01 33
56	06 51	07 39	08 24	23 14	24 25	00 25	01 37
58	06 57	07 48	08 37	23 13	24 27	00 27	01 42
S 60	07 03	07 58	08 52	23 13	24 29	00 29	01 47

Sunset / Twilight / Moonset

Lat.	Sunset	Civil	Naut.	Moonset 11	12	13	14
N 72	☐	☐	☐	10 10	11 57	13 44	15 39
N 70	☐	☐	☐	10 16	11 55	13 35	15 19
68	☐	☐	☐	10 20	11 54	13 27	15 04
66	22 44	////	////	10 24	11 52	13 21	14 51
64	22 01	////	////	10 27	11 51	13 15	14 41
62	21 33	23 36	////	10 30	11 50	13 10	14 32
60	21 11	22 32	////	10 32	11 49	13 06	14 24
N 58	20 54	22 00	////	10 35	11 49	13 03	14 18
56	20 39	21 36	23 39	10 37	11 48	13 00	14 12
54	20 27	21 17	22 40	10 38	11 48	12 57	14 07
52	20 16	21 02	22 10	10 40	11 47	12 54	14 02
50	20 06	20 49	21 48	10 41	11 47	12 52	13 58
45	19 46	20 22	21 09	10 44	11 45	12 47	13 49
N 40	19 29	20 01	20 41	10 47	11 45	12 43	13 41
35	19 15	19 45	20 20	10 49	11 44	12 39	13 35
30	19 03	19 30	20 03	10 51	11 43	12 36	13 29
20	18 43	19 07	19 36	10 54	11 42	12 30	13 19
N 10	18 26	18 48	19 15	10 57	11 41	12 25	13 10
0	18 09	18 32	18 58	10 59	11 40	12 21	13 02
S 10	17 53	18 16	18 42	11 02	11 39	12 16	12 54
20	17 36	18 00	18 27	11 05	11 38	12 11	12 46
30	17 17	17 43	18 12	11 08	11 37	12 06	12 36
35	17 05	17 33	18 04	11 10	11 36	12 03	12 31
40	16 52	17 22	17 56	11 12	11 35	11 59	12 24
45	16 37	17 10	17 47	11 14	11 34	11 55	12 17
S 50	16 18	16 55	17 36	11 17	11 33	11 50	12 08
52	16 09	16 49	17 32	11 18	11 33	11 48	12 04
54	15 59	16 41	17 27	11 19	11 32	11 45	12 00
56	15 48	16 33	17 21	11 21	11 32	11 43	11 55
58	15 35	16 24	17 15	11 23	11 31	11 40	11 49
S 60	15 20	16 14	17 09	11 24	11 30	11 36	11 43

SUN / MOON

Day	Eqn. of Time 00h	12h	Mer. Pass.	Mer. Pass. Upper	Lower	Age	Phase
	m s	m s	h m	h m	h m	d	%
11	05 31	05 35	12 06	04 50	17 10	20	64
12	05 39	05 43	12 06	05 30	17 51	21	55
13	05 46	05 50	12 06	06 11	18 31	22	45

UT d h	ARIES GHA	VENUS −4.7 GHA	Dec	MARS −0.8 GHA	Dec	JUPITER −2.8 GHA	Dec	SATURN +0.1 GHA	Dec	Name	SHA	Dec
14 00	292 19.1	222 04.3	N17 38.0	282 29.2	N 0 29.2	358 05.4	S21 54.1	350 58.4	S20 32.6	Acamar	315 14.8	S40 13.2
01	307 21.6	237 05.3	38.2	297 30.4	29.7	13 08.2	54.1	6 01.0	32.6	Achernar	335 23.1	S57 07.8
02	322 24.1	252 06.3	38.4	312 31.6	30.2	28 11.0	54.2	21 03.7	32.6	Acrux	173 04.1	S63 12.9
03	337 26.5	267 07.3 ..	38.6	327 32.7 ..	30.6	43 13.8 ..	54.2	36 06.3 ..	32.7	Adhara	255 09.1	S29 00.0
04	352 29.0	282 08.3	38.8	342 33.9	31.1	58 16.6	54.3	51 09.0	32.7	Aldebaran	290 44.0	N16 32.9
05	7 31.5	297 09.3	39.0	357 35.1	31.6	73 19.5	54.4	66 11.6	32.8			
06	22 33.9	312 10.2	N17 39.2	12 36.3	N 0 32.1	88 22.3	S21 54.4	81 14.3	S20 32.8	Alioth	166 16.4	N55 51.3
07	37 36.4	327 11.2	39.3	27 37.5	32.6	103 25.1	54.5	96 17.0	32.8	Alkaid	152 54.9	N49 13.1
08	52 38.8	342 12.2	39.5	42 38.7	33.0	118 27.9	54.5	111 19.6	32.9	Alnair	27 37.2	S46 51.5
09	67 41.3	357 13.2 ..	39.7	57 39.9 ..	33.5	133 30.7 ..	54.6	126 22.3 ..	32.9	Alnilam	275 41.7	S 1 11.4
10	82 43.8	12 14.2	39.9	72 41.0	34.0	148 33.5	54.6	141 24.9	33.0	Alphard	217 51.6	S 8 44.8
11	97 46.2	27 15.1	40.1	87 42.2	34.5	163 36.3	54.7	156 27.6	33.0			
12	112 48.7	42 16.1	N17 40.3	102 43.4	N 0 35.0	178 39.1	S21 54.8	171 30.2	S20 33.1	Alphecca	126 06.6	N26 39.0
13	127 51.2	57 17.1	40.5	117 44.6	35.5	193 41.9	54.8	186 32.9	33.1	Alpheratz	357 38.3	N29 12.0
14	142 53.6	72 18.0	40.7	132 45.8	35.9	208 44.7	54.9	201 35.5	33.1	Altair	62 03.1	N 8 55.4
15	157 56.1	87 19.0 ..	40.9	147 47.0 ..	36.4	223 47.5 ..	54.9	216 38.2 ..	33.2	Ankaa	353 10.7	S42 11.5
16	172 58.6	102 19.9	41.1	162 48.2	36.9	238 50.3	55.0	231 40.8	33.2	Antares	112 20.0	S26 28.6
17	188 01.0	117 20.9	41.3	177 49.4	37.4	253 53.1	55.1	246 43.5	33.3			
18	203 03.5	132 21.9	N17 41.5	192 50.6	N 0 37.8	268 55.9	S21 55.1	261 46.2	S20 33.3	Arcturus	145 51.2	N19 04.8
19	218 05.9	147 22.8	41.7	207 51.7	38.3	283 58.7	55.2	276 48.8	33.3	Atria	107 17.0	S69 03.9
20	233 08.4	162 23.8	41.9	222 52.9	38.8	299 01.5	55.2	291 51.5	33.4	Avior	234 16.7	S59 34.5
21	248 10.9	177 24.7 ..	42.1	237 54.1 ..	39.3	314 04.3 ..	55.3	306 54.1 ..	33.4	Bellatrix	278 27.0	N 6 22.0
22	263 13.3	192 25.7	42.3	252 55.3	39.8	329 07.2	55.3	321 56.8	33.5	Betelgeuse	270 56.3	N 7 24.6
23	278 15.8	207 26.6	42.5	267 56.5	40.2	344 10.0	55.4	336 59.4	33.5			
15 00	293 18.3	222 27.5	N17 42.7	282 57.7	N 0 40.7	359 12.8	S21 55.5	352 02.1	S20 33.6	Canopus	263 54.5	S52 42.3
01	308 20.7	237 28.5	42.9	297 58.9	41.2	14 15.6	55.5	7 04.7	33.6	Capella	280 27.6	N46 00.9
02	323 23.2	252 29.4	43.1	313 00.1	41.7	29 18.4	55.6	22 07.4	33.6	Deneb	49 27.7	N45 21.2
03	338 25.7	267 30.4 ..	43.3	328 01.3 ..	42.2	44 21.2 ..	55.6	37 10.0 ..	33.7	Denebola	182 28.8	N14 27.7
04	353 28.1	282 31.3	43.5	343 02.5	42.6	59 24.0	55.7	52 12.7	33.7	Diphda	348 50.9	S17 52.4
05	8 30.6	297 32.2	43.7	358 03.7	43.1	74 26.8	55.7	67 15.4	33.8			
06	23 33.1	312 33.1	N17 43.9	13 04.9	N 0 43.6	89 29.6	S21 55.8	82 18.0	S20 33.8	Dubhe	193 46.0	N61 38.8
07	38 35.5	327 34.1	44.1	28 06.1	44.1	104 32.4	55.9	97 20.7	33.8	Elnath	278 06.8	N28 37.3
08	53 38.0	342 35.0	44.3	43 07.3	44.5	119 35.2	55.9	112 23.3	33.9	Eltanin	90 43.4	N51 29.4
09	68 40.4	357 35.9 ..	44.5	58 08.5 ..	45.0	134 38.0 ..	56.0	127 26.0 ..	33.9	Enif	33 42.0	N 9 58.1
10	83 42.9	12 36.8	44.7	73 09.7	45.5	149 40.8	56.0	142 28.6	34.0	Fomalhaut	15 18.3	S29 30.7
11	98 45.4	27 37.7	44.9	88 10.9	46.0	164 43.6	56.1	157 31.3	34.0			
12	113 47.8	42 38.7	N17 45.1	103 12.1	N 0 46.4	179 46.4	S21 56.2	172 33.9	S20 34.1	Gacrux	171 55.7	S57 13.8
13	128 50.3	57 39.6	45.3	118 13.3	46.9	194 49.2	56.2	187 36.6	34.1	Gienah	175 47.4	S17 39.3
14	143 52.8	72 40.5	45.5	133 14.5	47.4	209 52.0	56.3	202 39.3	34.1	Hadar	148 40.9	S60 28.4
15	158 55.2	87 41.4 ..	45.7	148 15.7 ..	47.9	224 54.9 ..	56.3	217 41.9 ..	34.2	Hamal	327 55.3	N23 33.3
16	173 57.7	102 42.3	45.9	163 16.9	48.3	239 57.7	56.4	232 44.6	34.2	Kaus Aust.	83 36.9	S34 22.4
17	189 00.2	117 43.2	46.1	178 18.1	48.8	255 00.5	56.4	247 47.2	34.3			
18	204 02.6	132 44.1	N17 46.3	193 19.3	N 0 49.3	270 03.3	S21 56.5	262 49.9	S20 34.3	Kochab	137 19.6	N74 04.7
19	219 05.1	147 45.0	46.5	208 20.5	49.8	285 06.1	56.6	277 52.5	34.3	Markab	13 33.3	N15 18.8
20	234 07.6	162 45.9	46.7	223 21.7	50.2	300 08.9	56.6	292 55.2	34.4	Menkar	314 10.1	N 4 10.1
21	249 10.0	177 46.8 ..	46.9	238 22.9 ..	50.7	315 11.7 ..	56.7	307 57.8 ..	34.4	Menkent	148 01.8	S36 28.3
22	264 12.5	192 47.7	47.1	253 24.1	51.2	330 14.5	56.7	323 00.5	34.5	Miaplacidus	221 39.7	S69 48.2
23	279 14.9	207 48.6	47.3	268 25.3	51.6	345 17.3	56.8	338 03.2	34.5			
16 00	294 17.4	222 49.5	N17 47.6	283 26.5	N 0 52.1	0 20.1	S21 56.8	353 05.8	S20 34.6	Mirfak	308 33.6	N49 55.7
01	309 19.9	237 50.4	47.8	298 27.7	52.6	15 22.9	56.9	8 08.5	34.6	Nunki	75 51.9	S26 16.2
02	324 22.3	252 51.2	48.0	313 28.9	53.1	30 25.7	57.0	23 11.1	34.6	Peacock	53 10.9	S56 40.0
03	339 24.8	267 52.1 ..	48.2	328 30.1 ..	53.5	45 28.5 ..	57.0	38 13.8 ..	34.7	Pollux	243 22.1	N27 58.6
04	354 27.3	282 53.0	48.4	343 31.3	54.0	60 31.3	57.1	53 16.4	34.7	Procyon	244 55.0	N 5 10.4
05	9 29.7	297 53.9	48.6	358 32.5	54.5	75 34.1	57.1	68 19.1	34.8			
06	24 32.2	312 54.8	N17 48.8	13 33.7	N 0 55.0	90 36.9	S21 57.2	83 21.7	S20 34.8	Rasalhague	96 01.6	N12 32.9
07	39 34.7	327 55.6	49.0	28 34.9	55.4	105 39.7	57.3	98 24.4	34.8	Regulus	207 38.6	N11 52.2
08	54 37.1	342 56.5	49.2	43 36.1	55.9	120 42.6	57.3	113 27.1	34.9	Rigel	281 07.6	S 8 10.7
09	69 39.6	357 57.4 ..	49.4	58 37.4 ..	56.4	135 45.4 ..	57.4	128 29.7 ..	34.9	Rigil Kent.	139 44.9	S60 55.3
10	84 42.0	12 58.2	49.7	73 38.6	56.8	150 48.2	57.4	143 32.4	35.0	Sabik	102 06.6	S15 44.9
11	99 44.5	27 59.1	49.9	88 39.8	57.3	165 51.0	57.5	158 35.0	35.0			
12	114 47.0	43 00.0	N17 50.1	103 41.0	N 0 57.8	180 53.8	S21 57.5	173 37.7	S20 35.0	Schedar	349 34.9	N56 38.6
13	129 49.4	58 00.8	50.3	118 42.2	58.2	195 56.6	57.6	188 40.3	35.1	Shaula	96 14.9	S37 07.0
14	144 51.9	73 01.7	50.5	133 43.4	58.7	210 59.4	57.7	203 43.0	35.1	Sirius	258 29.8	S16 44.6
15	159 54.4	88 02.5 ..	50.7	148 44.6 ..	59.2	226 02.2 ..	57.7	218 45.6 ..	35.2	Spica	158 26.1	S11 16.0
16	174 56.8	103 03.4	50.9	163 45.8	0 59.7	241 05.0	57.8	233 48.3	35.2	Suhail	222 49.3	S43 31.0
17	189 59.3	118 04.2	51.2	178 47.0	1 00.1	256 07.8	57.8	248 51.0	35.3			
18	205 01.8	133 05.1	N17 51.4	193 48.3	N 1 00.6	271 10.6	S21 57.9	263 53.6	S20 35.3	Vega	80 35.2	N38 48.3
19	220 04.2	148 05.9	51.6	208 49.5	01.1	286 13.4	57.9	278 56.3	35.3	Zuben'ubi	136 59.9	S16 07.5
20	235 06.7	163 06.8	51.8	223 50.7	01.5	301 16.2	58.0	293 58.9	35.4		SHA	Mer. Pass.
21	250 09.2	178 07.6 ..	52.0	238 51.9 ..	02.0	316 19.0 ..	58.1	309 01.6 ..	35.4			h m
22	265 11.6	193 08.5	52.2	253 53.1	02.5	331 21.8	58.1	324 04.2	35.5	Venus	289 09.3	9 10
23	280 14.1	208 09.3	52.4	268 54.3	02.9	346 24.6	58.2	339 06.9	35.5	Mars	349 39.4	5 08
Mer. Pass.	h m 4 26.1	v 0.9	d 0.2	v 1.2	d 0.5	v 2.8	d 0.1	v 2.7	d 0.0	Jupiter	65 54.5	0 03
										Saturn	58 43.8	0 32

UT	SUN GHA	SUN Dec	MOON GHA	v	MOON Dec	d	HP
d h	° ′	° ′	° ′	′	° ′	′	′
14 00	178 31.7	N21 38.2	259 51.1	15.7	N 8 29.7	11.4	54.4
01	193 31.7	37.8	274 25.8	15.6	8 41.1	11.4	54.4
02	208 31.6	37.4	289 00.4	15.6	8 52.5	11.4	54.4
03	223 31.5	.. 37.0	303 35.0	15.6	9 03.9	11.3	54.4
04	238 31.5	36.6	318 09.6	15.5	9 15.2	11.3	54.4
05	253 31.4	36.3	332 44.1	15.5	9 26.5	11.3	54.4
06	268 31.3	N21 35.9	347 18.6	15.5	N 9 37.8	11.2	54.4
07	283 31.3	35.5	1 53.1	15.4	9 49.0	11.2	54.4
T 08	298 31.2	35.1	16 27.5	15.3	10 00.2	11.2	54.4
U 09	313 31.1	.. 34.7	31 01.8	15.3	10 11.4	11.1	54.5
E 10	328 31.1	34.3	45 36.1	15.3	10 22.5	11.1	54.5
S 11	343 31.0	33.9	60 10.4	15.2	10 33.6	11.1	54.5
D 12	358 30.9	N21 33.5	74 44.6	15.2	N10 44.7	11.0	54.5
A 13	13 30.9	33.2	89 18.8	15.1	10 55.7	11.0	54.5
Y 14	28 30.8	32.8	103 52.9	15.0	11 06.7	10.9	54.5
15	43 30.8	.. 32.4	118 26.9	15.1	11 17.6	10.9	54.5
16	58 30.7	32.0	133 01.0	14.9	11 28.5	10.9	54.5
17	73 30.6	31.6	147 34.9	14.9	11 39.4	10.8	54.6
18	88 30.6	N21 31.2	162 08.8	14.9	N11 50.2	10.8	54.6
19	103 30.5	30.8	176 42.7	14.8	12 01.0	10.8	54.6
20	118 30.4	30.4	191 16.5	14.7	12 11.8	10.7	54.6
21	133 30.4	.. 30.0	205 50.2	14.7	12 22.5	10.6	54.6
22	148 30.3	29.6	220 23.9	14.7	12 33.1	10.6	54.6
23	163 30.2	29.2	234 57.6	14.6	12 43.7	10.6	54.6
15 00	178 30.2	N21 28.8	249 31.2	14.5	N12 54.3	10.5	54.7
01	193 30.1	28.4	264 04.7	14.4	13 04.8	10.5	54.7
02	208 30.1	28.0	278 38.1	14.4	13 15.3	10.4	54.7
03	223 30.0	.. 27.6	293 11.5	14.4	13 25.7	10.4	54.7
04	238 29.9	27.2	307 44.9	14.3	13 36.1	10.3	54.7
05	253 29.9	26.8	322 18.2	14.2	13 46.4	10.3	54.7
06	268 29.8	N21 26.4	336 51.4	14.1	N13 56.7	10.2	54.8
W 07	283 29.7	26.0	351 24.5	14.1	14 06.9	10.2	54.8
E 08	298 29.7	25.6	5 57.6	14.0	14 17.1	10.1	54.8
D 09	313 29.6	.. 25.2	20 30.6	14.0	14 27.2	10.0	54.8
N 10	328 29.6	24.8	35 03.6	13.9	14 37.2	10.0	54.8
E 11	343 29.5	24.4	49 36.5	13.8	14 47.2	10.0	54.8
S 12	358 29.4	N21 24.0	64 09.3	13.8	N14 57.2	9.9	54.9
D 13	13 29.4	23.6	78 42.1	13.7	15 07.1	9.8	54.9
A 14	28 29.3	23.2	93 14.8	13.6	15 16.9	9.8	54.9
Y 15	43 29.3	.. 22.8	107 47.4	13.6	15 26.7	9.7	54.9
16	58 29.2	22.4	122 20.0	13.4	15 36.4	9.7	54.9
17	73 29.1	22.0	136 52.4	13.4	15 46.1	9.6	55.0
18	88 29.1	N21 21.6	151 24.8	13.4	N15 55.7	9.5	55.0
19	103 29.0	21.1	165 57.2	13.3	16 05.2	9.5	55.0
20	118 29.0	20.7	180 29.5	13.2	16 14.7	9.4	55.0
21	133 28.9	.. 20.3	195 01.7	13.1	16 24.1	9.3	55.0
22	148 28.8	19.9	209 33.8	13.0	16 33.4	9.3	55.1
23	163 28.8	19.5	224 05.8	13.0	16 42.7	9.2	55.1
16 00	178 28.7	N21 19.1	238 37.8	12.9	N16 51.9	9.2	55.1
01	193 28.7	18.7	253 09.7	12.8	17 01.1	9.0	55.1
02	208 28.6	18.3	267 41.5	12.8	17 10.1	9.0	55.1
03	223 28.6	.. 17.8	282 13.3	12.6	17 19.1	8.9	55.2
04	238 28.5	17.4	296 44.9	12.6	17 28.1	8.8	55.2
05	253 28.4	17.0	311 16.5	12.5	17 36.9	8.8	55.2
06	268 28.4	N21 16.6	325 48.0	12.5	N17 45.7	8.7	55.2
T 07	283 28.3	16.2	340 19.5	12.3	17 54.4	8.7	55.2
H 08	298 28.3	15.8	354 50.8	12.3	18 03.1	8.6	55.3
U 09	313 28.2	.. 15.3	9 22.1	12.2	18 11.7	8.4	55.3
R 10	328 28.2	14.9	23 53.3	12.1	18 20.1	8.5	55.3
S 11	343 28.1	14.5	38 24.4	12.1	18 28.6	8.3	55.3
D 12	358 28.1	N21 14.1	52 55.5	11.9	N18 36.9	8.3	55.4
A 13	13 28.0	13.7	67 26.4	11.9	18 45.2	8.1	55.4
Y 14	28 27.9	13.2	81 57.3	11.8	18 53.3	8.1	55.4
15	43 27.9	.. 12.8	96 28.1	11.7	19 01.4	8.0	55.4
16	58 27.8	12.4	110 58.8	11.7	19 09.4	8.0	55.5
17	73 27.8	12.0	125 29.5	11.5	19 17.4	7.8	55.5
18	88 27.7	N21 11.6	140 00.0	11.5	N19 25.2	7.8	55.5
19	103 27.6	11.1	154 30.5	11.4	19 33.0	7.6	55.5
20	118 27.6	10.7	169 00.9	11.3	19 40.6	7.6	55.6
21	133 27.6	.. 10.3	183 31.2	11.2	19 48.2	7.5	55.6
22	148 27.5	09.8	198 01.4	11.2	19 55.7	7.4	55.6
23	163 27.5	09.4	212 31.6	11.0	N20 03.1	7.3	55.6
SD	15.8	d 0.4	SD 14.8		14.9		15.1

Lat.	Twilight Naut.	Twilight Civil	Sunrise	Moonrise 14	15	16	17
°	h m	h m	h m	h m	h m	h m	h m
N 72	□	□	□	22 27	21 41	□	□
N 70	□	□	□	22 48	22 24	21 25	□
68	□	□	□	23 05	22 53	22 35	□
66	////	////	01 37	23 19	23 15	23 12	23 08
64	////	////	02 17	23 31	23 33	23 38	23 49
62	////	00 53	02 44	23 41	23 47	23 58	24 17
60	////	01 46	03 04	23 49	24 00	00 00	00 15
N 58	////	02 17	03 21	23 57	24 10	00 10	00 29
56	00 49	02 40	03 35	24 03	00 03	00 20	00 42
54	01 37	02 58	03 48	24 09	00 09	00 28	00 52
52	02 06	03 13	03 58	24 15	00 15	00 35	01 02
50	02 27	03 26	04 08	00 00	00 19	00 42	01 10
45	03 05	03 52	04 28	00 07	00 30	00 57	01 28
N 40	03 32	04 12	04 44	00 13	00 39	01 09	01 43
35	03 53	04 29	04 58	00 17	00 46	01 19	01 56
30	04 10	04 42	05 09	00 22	00 53	01 28	02 07
20	04 36	05 05	05 29	00 29	01 05	01 43	02 26
N 10	04 57	05 24	05 46	00 36	01 15	01 57	02 43
0	05 14	05 40	06 02	00 42	01 25	02 10	02 58
S 10	05 30	05 56	06 18	00 48	01 35	02 23	03 14
20	05 44	06 11	06 35	00 55	01 45	02 37	03 31
30	05 59	06 28	06 54	01 03	01 57	02 53	03 50
35	06 07	06 38	07 05	01 08	02 04	03 02	04 02
40	06 15	06 48	07 18	01 13	02 12	03 13	04 15
45	06 24	07 00	07 33	01 19	02 21	03 26	04 31
S 50	06 34	07 14	07 51	01 26	02 33	03 41	04 50
52	06 38	07 21	08 00	01 29	02 38	03 48	04 59
54	06 43	07 28	08 10	01 33	02 44	03 56	05 09
56	06 48	07 36	08 21	01 37	02 50	04 05	05 21
58	06 54	07 44	08 33	01 42	02 58	04 16	05 34
S 60	07 00	07 54	08 48	01 47	03 06	04 28	05 50

Lat.	Sunset	Twilight Civil	Twilight Naut.	Moonset 14	15	16	17
°	h m	h m	h m	h m	h m	h m	h m
N 72	□	□	□	15 39	17 57	□	□
N 70	□	□	□	15 19	17 15	19 53	□
68	□	□	□	15 04	16 47	18 44	□
66	22 31	////	////	14 51	16 26	18 08	19 57
64	21 53	////	////	14 41	16 10	17 43	19 17
62	21 27	23 13	////	14 32	15 56	17 23	18 49
60	21 06	22 23	////	14 24	15 45	17 06	18 27
N 58	20 50	21 53	////	14 18	15 35	16 53	18 10
56	20 36	21 31	23 18	14 12	15 26	16 41	17 55
54	20 24	21 13	22 32	14 07	15 18	16 31	17 43
52	20 13	20 58	22 04	14 02	15 11	16 22	17 32
50	20 03	20 45	21 44	13 58	15 05	16 14	17 22
45	19 44	20 19	21 06	13 49	14 52	15 57	17 01
N 40	19 28	19 59	20 39	13 41	14 41	15 43	16 45
35	19 14	19 43	20 18	13 35	14 32	15 31	16 31
30	19 02	19 29	20 02	13 29	14 24	15 20	16 18
20	18 43	19 07	19 35	13 19	14 10	15 03	15 58
N 10	18 26	18 48	19 15	13 10	13 58	14 47	15 40
0	18 10	18 32	18 58	13 02	13 46	14 33	15 23
S 10	17 54	18 16	18 42	12 54	13 35	14 18	15 06
20	17 37	18 01	18 28	12 46	13 23	14 03	14 48
30	17 18	17 44	18 13	12 36	13 09	13 46	14 28
35	17 07	17 35	18 06	12 31	13 01	13 36	14 15
40	16 54	17 24	17 58	12 24	12 52	13 24	14 02
45	16 39	17 12	17 49	12 17	12 42	13 10	13 45
S 50	16 21	16 58	17 39	12 08	12 29	12 54	13 25
52	16 12	16 52	17 34	12 04	12 23	12 46	13 16
54	16 03	16 45	17 30	12 00	12 17	12 38	13 05
56	15 52	16 37	17 24	11 55	12 09	12 28	12 53
58	15 39	16 28	17 19	11 49	12 01	12 17	12 39
S 60	15 25	16 18	17 13	11 43	11 52	12 04	12 23

Day	SUN Eqn. of Time 00h	SUN Eqn. of Time 12h	Mer. Pass.	MOON Mer. Pass. Upper	MOON Mer. Pass. Lower	Age	Phase
d	m s	m s	h m	h m	h m	d	%
14	05 53	05 56	12 06	06 52	19 14	23	36
15	05 59	06 02	12 06	07 35	19 58	24	27
16	06 05	06 08	12 06	08 21	20 45	25	19

UT	ARIES GHA	VENUS −4·7 GHA	VENUS Dec	MARS −0·8 GHA	MARS Dec	JUPITER −2·7 GHA	JUPITER Dec	SATURN +0·1 GHA	SATURN Dec	STARS Name	SHA	Dec
17 00	295 16.5	223 10.1	N17 52.7	283 55.5	N 1 03.4	1 27.4	S21 58.2	354 09.5	S20 35.5	Acamar	315 14.7	S40 13.2
01	310 19.0	238 11.0	52.9	298 56.8	03.9	16 30.3	58.3	9 12.2	35.6	Achernar	335 23.0	S57 07.8
02	325 21.5	253 11.8	53.1	313 58.0	04.3	31 33.1	58.3	24 14.9	35.6	Acrux	173 04.1	S63 12.9
03	340 23.9	268 12.6 ..	53.3	328 59.2 ..	04.8	46 35.9 ..	58.4	39 17.5 ..	35.7	Adhara	255 09.1	S29 00.0
04	355 26.4	283 13.5	53.5	344 00.4	05.3	61 38.7	58.5	54 20.2	35.7	Aldebaran	290 44.0	N16 32.9
05	10 28.9	298 14.3	53.8	359 01.6	05.7	76 41.5	58.5	69 22.8	35.8			
06	25 31.3	313 15.1	N17 54.0	14 02.8	N 1 06.2	91 44.3	S21 58.6	84 25.5	S20 35.8	Alioth	166 16.4	N55 51.3
07	40 33.8	328 15.9	54.2	29 04.1	06.7	106 47.1	58.6	99 28.1	35.8	Alkaid	152 54.9	N49 13.1
08	55 36.3	343 16.8	54.4	44 05.3	07.1	121 49.9 ·	58.7	114 30.8	35.9	Alnair	27 37.1	S46 51.5
F 09	70 38.7	358 17.6 ..	54.6	59 06.5 ..	07.6	136 52.7 ..	58.7	129 33.4 ..	35.9	Alnilam	275 41.7	S 1 11.4
R 10	85 41.2	13 18.4	54.9	74 07.7	08.1	151 55.5	58.8	144 36.1	36.0	Alphard	217 51.6	S 8 44.8
I 11	100 43.7	28 19.2	55.1	89 08.9	08.5	166 58.3	58.9	159 38.8	36.0			
D 12	115 46.1	43 20.0	N17 55.3	104 10.2	N 1 09.0	182 01.1	S21 58.9	174 41.4	S20 36.0	Alphecca	126 06.6	N26 39.0
A 13	130 48.6	58 20.8	55.5	119 11.4	09.4	197 03.9	59.0	189 44.1	36.1	Alpheratz	357 38.3	N29 12.0
Y 14	145 51.0	73 21.6	55.7	134 12.6	09.9	212 06.7	59.0	204 46.7	36.1	Altair	62 03.1	N 8 55.4
15	160 53.5	88 22.4 ..	56.0	149 13.8 ..	10.4	227 09.5 ..	59.1	219 49.4 ..	36.2	Ankaa	353 10.7	S42 11.5
16	175 56.0	103 23.2	56.2	164 15.1	10.8	242 12.3	59.1	234 52.0	36.2	Antares	112 20.0	S26 28.6
17	190 58.4	118 24.0	56.4	179 16.3	11.3	257 15.1	59.2	249 54.7	36.3			
18	206 00.9	133 24.8	N17 56.6	194 17.5	N 1 11.8	272 17.9	S21 59.3	264 57.4	S20 36.3	Arcturus	145 51.2	N19 04.8
19	221 03.4	148 25.6	56.8	209 18.7	12.2	287 20.8	59.3	280 00.0	36.3	Atria	107 17.0	S69 03.9
20	236 05.8	163 26.4	57.1	224 19.9	12.7	302 23.6	59.4	295 02.7	36.4	Avior	234 16.7	S59 34.5
21	251 08.3	178 27.2 ..	57.3	239 21.2 ..	13.2	317 26.4 ..	59.4	310 05.3 ..	36.4	Bellatrix	278 27.0	N 6 22.0
22	266 10.8	193 28.0	57.5	254 22.4	13.6	332 29.2	59.5	325 08.0	36.5	Betelgeuse	270 56.3	N 7 24.6
23	281 13.2	208 28.8	57.7	269 23.6	14.1	347 32.0	59.5	340 10.6	36.5			
18 00	296 15.7	223 29.6	N17 58.0	284 24.9	N 1 14.5	2 34.8	S21 59.6	355 13.3	S20 36.5	Canopus	263 54.5	S52 42.3
01	311 18.2	238 30.4	58.2	299 26.1	15.0	17 37.6	59.7	10 15.9	36.6	Capella	280 27.6	N46 00.9
02	326 20.6	253 31.2	58.4	314 27.3	15.5	32 40.4	59.7	25 18.6	36.6	Deneb	49 27.7	N45 21.2
03	341 23.1	268 31.9 ..	58.6	329 28.5 ..	15.9	47 43.2 ..	59.8	40 21.3 ..	36.7	Denebola	182 28.8	N14 27.7
04	356 25.5	283 32.7	58.9	344 29.8	16.4	62 46.0	59.8	55 23.9	36.7	Diphda	348 50.9	S17 52.4
05	11 28.0	298 33.5	59.1	359 31.0	16.9	77 48.8	59.9	70 26.6	36.7			
06	26 30.5	313 34.3	N17 59.3	14 32.2	N 1 17.3	92 51.6	S21 59.9	85 29.2	S20 36.8	Dubhe	193 46.1	N61 38.8
07	41 32.9	328 35.0	59.5	29 33.5	17.8	107 54.4	22 00.0	100 31.9	36.8	Elnath	278 06.7	N28 37.3
S 08	56 35.4	343 35.8	17 59.8	44 34.7	18.2	122 57.2	00.1	115 34.5	36.9	Eltanin	90 43.4	N51 29.4
A 09	71 37.9	358 36.6	18 00.0	59 35.9 ..	18.7	138 00.0 ..	00.1	130 37.2 ..	36.9	Enif	33 42.0	N 9 58.1
T 10	86 40.3	13 37.3	00.2	74 37.1	19.1	153 02.8	00.1	145 39.9	37.0	Fomalhaut	15 18.3	S29 30.7
U 11	101 42.8	28 38.1	00.4	89 38.4	19.6	168 05.6	00.2	160 42.5	37.0			
R 12	116 45.3	43 38.9	N18 00.7	104 39.6	N 1 20.1	183 08.4	S22 00.3	175 45.2	S20 37.0	Gacrux	171 55.7	S57 13.8
D 13	131 47.7	58 39.6	00.9	119 40.8	20.5	198 11.2	00.3	190 47.8	37.1	Gienah	175 47.4	S17 39.3
A 14	146 50.2	73 40.4	01.1	134 42.1	21.0	213 14.0	00.4	205 50.5	37.1	Hadar	148 40.9	S60 28.4
Y 15	161 52.7	88 41.2 ..	01.4	149 43.3 ..	21.4	228 16.8 ..	00.4	220 53.1 ..	37.2	Hamal	327 55.3	N23 33.4
16	176 55.1	103 41.9	01.6	164 44.5	21.9	243 19.7	00.5	235 55.8	37.2	Kaus Aust.	83 36.9	S34 22.4
17	191 57.6	118 42.7	01.8	179 45.8	22.4	258 22.5	00.6	250 58.5	37.2			
18	207 00.0	133 43.4	N18 02.0	194 47.0	N 1 22.8	273 25.3	S22 00.6	266 01.1	S20 37.3	Kochab	137 19.6	N74 04.7
19	222 02.5	148 44.2	02.3	209 48.3	23.3	288 28.1	00.7	281 03.8	37.3	Markab	13 33.2	N15 18.9
20	237 05.0	163 44.9	02.5	224 49.5	23.7	303 30.9	00.7	296 06.4	37.4	Menkar	314 10.0	N 4 10.1
21	252 07.4	178 45.7 ..	02.7	239 50.7 ..	24.2	318 33.7 ..	00.8	311 09.1 ..	37.4	Menkent	148 01.8	S36 28.3
22	267 09.9	193 46.4	03.0	254 52.0	24.6	333 36.5	00.8	326 11.7	37.5	Miaplacidus	221 39.7	S69 48.1
23	282 12.4	208 47.1	03.2	269 53.2	25.1	348 39.3	00.9	341 14.4	37.5			
19 00	297 14.8	223 47.9	N18 03.4	284 54.4	N 1 25.5	3 42.1	S22 01.0	356 17.0	S20 37.5	Mirfak	308 33.6	N49 55.7
01	312 17.3	238 48.6	03.7	299 55.7	26.0	18 44.9	01.0	11 19.7	37.6	Nunki	75 51.9	S26 16.2
02	327 19.8	253 49.3	03.9	314 56.9	26.5	33 47.7	01.1	26 22.4	37.6	Peacock	53 10.9	S56 40.0
03	342 22.2	268 50.1 ..	04.1	329 58.2 ..	26.9	48 50.5 ..	01.1	41 25.0 ..	37.7	Pollux	243 22.1	N27 58.6
04	357 24.7	283 50.8	04.4	344 59.4	27.4	63 53.3	01.2	56 27.7	37.7	Procyon	244 54.9	N 5 10.4
05	12 27.2	298 51.5	04.6	0 00.6	27.8	78 56.1	01.2	71 30.3	37.7			
06	27 29.6	313 52.3	N18 04.8	15 01.9	N 1 28.3	93 58.9	S22 01.3	86 33.0	S20 37.8	Rasalhague	96 01.6	N12 32.9
07	42 32.1	328 53.0	05.0	30 03.1	28.7	109 01.7	01.3	101 35.6	37.8	Regulus	207 38.6	N11 52.2
08	57 34.5	343 53.7	05.3	45 04.4	29.2	124 04.5	01.4	116 38.3	37.9	Rigel	281 07.6	S 8 10.7
S 09	72 37.0	358 54.4 ..	05.5	60 05.6 ..	29.6	139 07.3 ..	01.5	131 41.0 ..	37.9	Rigil Kent.	139 45.0	S60 55.3
U 10	87 39.5	13 55.2	05.7	75 06.9	30.1	154 10.1	01.5	146 43.6	38.0	Sabik	102 06.6	S15 44.9
N 11	102 41.9	28 55.9	06.0	90 08.1	30.5	169 12.9	01.6	161 46.3	38.0			
D 12	117 44.4	43 56.6	N18 06.2	105 09.3	N 1 31.0	184 15.7	S22 01.6	176 48.9	S20 38.0	Schedar	349 34.8	N56 38.6
A 13	132 46.9	58 57.3	06.4	120 10.6	31.5	199 18.5	01.7	191 51.6	38.1	Shaula	96 14.9	S37 07.1
Y 14	147 49.3	73 58.0	06.7	135 11.8	31.9	214 21.3	01.7	206 54.2	38.1	Sirius	258 29.7	S16 44.6
15	162 51.8	88 58.7 ..	06.9	150 13.1 ..	32.4	229 24.1 ..	01.8	221 56.9 ..	38.2	Spica	158 26.1	S11 16.0
16	177 54.3	103 59.4	07.1	165 14.3	32.8	244 27.0	01.9	236 59.6	38.2	Suhail	222 49.3	S43 30.9
17	192 56.7	119 00.1	07.4	180 15.6	33.3	259 29.8	01.9	252 02.2	38.2			
18	207 59.2	134 00.8	N18 07.6	195 16.8	N 1 33.7	274 32.6	S22 02.0	267 04.9	S20 38.3	Vega	80 35.2	N38 48.3
19	223 01.6	149 01.5	07.8	210 18.1	34.2	289 35.4	02.0	282 07.5	38.3	Zuben'ubi	136 59.9	S16 07.5
20	238 04.1	164 02.2	08.1	225 19.3	34.6	304 38.2	02.1	297 10.2	38.4		SHA	Mer. Pass.
21	253 06.6	179 02.9 ..	08.3	240 20.6 ..	35.1	319 41.0 ..	02.1	312 12.8 ..	38.4			h m
22	268 09.0	194 03.6	08.5	255 21.8	35.5	334 43.8	02.2	327 15.5	38.4	Venus	287 13.9	9 06
23	283 11.5	209 04.3	08.8	270 23.1	36.0	349 46.6	02.2	342 18.2	38.5	Mars	348 09.2	5 02
Mer. Pass.	h m 4 14.3	v 0.8	d 0.2	v 1.2	d 0.5	v 2.8	d 0.1	v 2.7	d 0.0	Jupiter	66 19.1	23 45
										Saturn	58 57.6	0 19

SUN / MOON

UT	SUN GHA	SUN Dec	MOON GHA	v	MOON Dec	d	HP
d h	° ′	° ′	° ′	′	° ′	′	′
17 00	178 27.4	N21 09.0	227 01.6	11.0	N20 10.4	7.2	55.7
01	193 27.4	08.6	241 31.6	10.9	20 17.6	7.2	55.7
02	208 27.3	08.1	256 01.5	10.8	20 24.8	7.0	55.7
03	223 27.3 ..	07.7	270 31.3	10.8	20 31.8	6.9	55.7
04	238 27.2	07.3	285 01.1	10.6	20 38.7	6.9	55.8
05	253 27.2	06.8	299 30.7	10.6	20 45.6	6.7	55.8
06	268 27.1	N21 06.4	314 00.3	10.5	N20 52.3	6.7	55.8
07	283 27.0	06.0	328 29.8	10.4	20 59.0	6.5	55.8
08	298 27.0	05.6	342 59.2	10.3	21 05.5	6.4	55.9
F 09	313 26.9 ..	05.1	357 28.5	10.2	21 11.9	6.4	55.9
R 10	328 26.9	04.7	11 57.7	10.2	21 18.3	6.2	55.9
I 11	343 26.8	04.2	26 26.9	10.0	21 24.5	6.2	55.9
D 12	358 26.8	N21 03.8	40 55.9	10.0	N21 30.7	6.0	56.0
A 13	13 26.7	03.4	55 24.9	9.9	21 36.7	5.9	56.0
Y 14	28 26.7	02.9	69 53.8	9.9	21 42.6	5.8	56.0
15	43 26.7 ..	02.5	84 22.7	9.7	21 48.4	5.8	56.1
16	58 26.6	02.1	98 51.4	9.7	21 54.2	5.6	56.1
17	73 26.6	01.6	113 20.1	9.6	21 59.8	5.5	56.1
18	88 26.5	N21 01.2	127 48.7	9.5	N22 05.3	5.3	56.1
19	103 26.5	00.7	142 17.2	9.4	22 10.6	5.3	56.2
20	118 26.4	21 00.3	156 45.6	9.3	22 15.9	5.2	56.2
21	133 26.4	20 59.9	171 13.9	9.3	22 21.1	5.0	56.2
22	148 26.3	59.4	185 42.2	9.2	22 26.1	4.9	56.2
23	163 26.3	59.0	200 10.4	9.1	22 31.0	4.9	56.3
18 00	178 26.2	N20 58.5	214 38.5	9.1	N22 35.9	4.6	56.3
01	193 26.2	58.1	229 06.6	8.9	22 40.5	4.6	56.3
02	208 26.1	57.7	243 34.5	8.9	22 45.1	4.5	56.4
03	223 26.1 ..	57.2	258 02.4	8.8	22 49.6	4.3	56.4
04	238 26.0	56.8	272 30.2	8.8	22 53.9	4.2	56.4
05	253 26.0	56.3	286 58.0	8.6	22 58.1	4.1	56.4
06	268 25.9	N20 55.9	301 25.6	8.6	N23 02.2	4.0	56.5
S 07	283 25.9	55.4	315 53.2	8.5	23 06.2	3.9	56.5
A 08	298 25.9	55.0	330 20.7	8.5	23 10.1	3.7	56.5
T 09	313 25.8 ..	54.5	344 48.2	8.4	23 13.8	3.6	56.6
U 10	328 25.8	54.1	359 15.6	8.3	23 17.4	3.4	56.6
R 11	343 25.7	53.6	13 42.9	8.2	23 20.8	3.4	56.6
D 12	358 25.7	N20 53.2	28 10.1	8.2	N23 24.2	3.2	56.6
A 13	13 25.6	52.7	42 37.3	8.1	23 27.4	3.1	56.7
Y 14	28 25.6	52.3	57 04.4	8.1	23 30.5	2.9	56.7
15	43 25.5 ..	51.8	71 31.5	7.9	23 33.4	2.9	56.7
16	58 25.5	51.4	85 58.4	8.0	23 36.3	2.7	56.8
17	73 25.5	50.9	100 25.4	7.8	23 39.0	2.5	56.8
18	88 25.4	N20 50.5	114 52.2	7.8	N23 41.5	2.4	56.8
19	103 25.4	50.0	129 19.0	7.7	23 43.9	2.3	56.8
20	118 25.3	49.6	143 45.7	7.7	23 46.2	2.2	56.9
21	133 25.3 ..	49.1	158 12.4	7.6	23 48.4	2.0	56.9
22	148 25.2	48.7	172 39.0	7.6	23 50.4	1.9	56.9
23	163 25.2	48.2	187 05.6	7.5	23 52.3	1.7	57.0
19 00	178 25.2	N20 47.7	201 32.1	7.5	N23 54.0	1.7	57.0
01	193 25.1	47.3	215 58.6	7.4	23 55.7	1.4	57.0
02	208 25.1	46.8	230 25.0	7.3	23 57.1	1.4	57.0
03	223 25.0 ..	46.4	244 51.3	7.3	23 58.5	1.2	57.1
04	238 25.0	45.9	259 17.6	7.2	23 59.7	1.0	57.1
05	253 25.0	45.0	273 43.8	7.3	24 00.7	0.9	57.1
06	268 24.9	N20 45.0	288 10.1	7.1	N24 01.6	0.8	57.2
07	283 24.9	44.5	302 36.2	7.1	24 02.4	0.6	57.2
08	298 24.8	44.1	317 02.3	7.1	24 03.0	0.5	57.2
S 09	313 24.8 ..	43.6	331 28.4	7.0	24 03.5	0.3	57.2
U 10	328 24.8	43.1	345 54.4	7.0	24 03.8	0.2	57.3
N 11	343 24.7	42.7	0 20.4	6.9	24 04.0	0.1	57.3
D 12	358 24.7	N20 42.2	14 46.3	7.0	N24 04.1	0.1	57.3
A 13	13 24.6	41.7	29 12.3	6.8	24 04.0	0.3	57.4
Y 14	28 24.6	41.3	43 38.1	6.9	24 03.7	0.3	57.4
15	43 24.6 ..	40.8	58 04.0	6.8	24 03.4	0.6	57.4
16	58 24.5	40.3	72 29.8	6.7	24 02.8	0.6	57.4
17	73 24.5	39.9	86 55.5	6.8	24 02.2	0.9	57.5
18	88 24.5	N20 39.4	101 21.3	6.7	N24 01.3	0.9	57.5
19	103 24.4	38.9	115 47.0	6.7	24 00.4	1.2	57.5
20	118 24.4	38.5	130 12.7	6.7	23 59.2	1.2	57.6
21	133 24.3 ..	38.0	144 38.4	6.6	23 58.0	1.4	57.6
22	148 24.3	37.5	159 04.0	6.6	23 56.6	1.6	57.6
23	163 24.3	37.1	173 29.6	6.6	N23 55.0	1.7	57.6
	SD 15.8	d 0.5	SD 15.2		15.4		15.6

Twilight / Sunrise / Moonrise

Lat.	Twilight Naut.	Civil	Sunrise	Moonrise 17	18	19	20
°	h m	h m	h m	h m	h m	h m	h m
N 72	□	□	□	□	□	□	□
N 70	□	□	□	□	□	□	□
68	////	////	00 38	□	□	□	□
66	////	////	01 50	23 08	23 07	24 03	00 03
64	////	////	02 26	23 49	24 16	00 16	01 14
62	////	01 12	02 51	24 17	00 17	00 52	01 50
60	////	01 56	03 10	00 15	00 39	01 17	02 16
N 58	////	02 24	03 26	00 29	00 57	01 38	02 36
56	01 06	02 46	03 40	00 42	01 12	01 55	02 53
54	01 46	03 03	03 52	00 52	01 25	02 09	03 07
52	02 13	03 17	04 02	01 02	01 36	02 22	03 20
50	02 33	03 30	04 11	01 10	01 46	02 33	03 31
45	03 09	03 55	04 31	01 28	02 08	02 56	03 54
N 40	03 35	04 15	04 46	01 43	02 25	03 14	04 12
35	03 56	04 31	05 00	01 56	02 39	03 30	04 28
30	04 12	04 44	05 11	02 07	02 52	03 43	04 41
20	04 38	05 06	05 30	02 26	03 14	04 06	05 04
N 10	04 58	05 25	05 47	02 43	03 32	04 26	05 24
0	05 15	05 41	06 03	02 58	03 50	04 45	05 42
S 10	05 30	05 56	06 18	03 14	04 08	05 04	06 00
20	05 44	06 11	06 34	03 31	04 27	05 24	06 20
30	05 58	06 27	06 53	03 50	04 49	05 47	06 43
35	06 05	06 36	07 04	04 02	05 02	06 01	06 56
40	06 13	06 47	07 16	04 15	05 17	06 17	07 12
45	06 22	06 58	07 31	04 31	05 35	06 35	07 30
S 50	06 31	07 12	07 48	04 50	05 57	06 59	07 53
52	06 36	07 18	07 57	04 59	06 08	07 10	08 04
54	06 40	07 25	08 06	05 09	06 20	07 23	08 16
56	06 45	07 32	08 17	05 21	06 33	07 38	08 30
58	06 51	07 41	08 29	05 34	06 50	07 55	08 47
S 60	06 56	07 50	08 43	05 50	07 09	08 17	09 07

Sunset / Twilight / Moonset

Lat.	Sunset	Twilight Civil	Naut.	Moonset 17	18	19	20
°	h m	h m	h m	h m	h m	h m	h m
N 72	□	□	□	□	□	□	□
N 70	□	□	□	□	□	□	□
68	23 22	////	////	□	□	□	□
66	22 19	////	////	19 57	21 51	22 53	22 53
64	21 45	////	////	19 17	20 42	21 42	22 11
62	21 20	22 56	////	18 49	20 07	21 06	21 43
60	21 01	22 14	////	18 27	19 41	20 40	21 21
N 58	20 45	21 46	////	18 10	19 21	20 20	21 03
56	20 31	21 25	23 02	17 55	19 04	20 03	20 48
54	20 20	21 08	22 24	17 43	18 50	19 49	20 35
52	20 10	20 54	21 58	17 32	18 38	19 36	20 24
50	20 00	20 42	21 38	17 22	18 27	19 25	20 14
45	19 41	20 17	21 02	17 01	18 04	19 02	19 53
N 40	19 26	19 57	20 37	16 45	17 46	18 43	19 35
35	19 13	19 41	20 16	16 31	17 30	18 28	19 21
30	19 01	19 28	20 00	16 18	17 17	18 14	19 08
20	18 42	19 06	19 34	15 58	16 54	17 51	18 46
N 10	18 25	18 48	19 14	15 40	16 35	17 31	18 27
0	18 10	18 32	18 58	15 23	16 16	17 12	18 09
S 10	17 55	18 17	18 43	15 06	15 58	16 53	17 52
20	17 38	18 02	18 29	14 48	15 38	16 33	17 32
30	17 20	17 45	18 15	14 28	15 15	16 10	17 10
35	17 09	17 36	18 07	14 15	15 02	15 56	16 57
40	16 57	17 26	18 00	14 02	14 47	15 40	16 42
45	16 42	17 15	17 51	13 45	14 29	15 22	16 24
S 50	16 24	17 01	17 42	13 25	14 06	14 58	16 02
52	16 16	16 55	17 37	13 16	13 55	14 47	15 51
54	16 07	16 48	17 33	13 05	13 43	14 34	15 39
56	15 56	16 41	17 28	12 53	13 29	14 19	15 25
58	15 44	16 32	17 23	12 39	13 13	14 02	15 09
S 60	15 30	16 23	17 17	12 23	12 53	13 40	14 49

SUN / MOON

Day	Eqn. of Time 00h	12h	Mer. Pass.	Mer. Pass. Upper	Lower	Age	Phase
	m s	m s	h m	h m	h m	d	%	
17	06 10	06 13	12 06	09 10	21 36	26	11
18	06 15	06 17	12 06	10 03	22 31	27	6
19	06 19	06 21	12 06	10 59	23 27	28	2

UT	ARIES	VENUS −4·6		MARS −0·9		JUPITER −2·7		SATURN +0·1		STARS		
	GHA	GHA	Dec	GHA	Dec	GHA	Dec	GHA	Dec	Name	SHA	Dec
d h	° ′	° ′	° ′	° ′	° ′	° ′	° ′	° ′	° ′		° ′	° ′
20 00	298 14.0	224 05.0	N18 09.0	285 24.3	N 1 36.4	4 49.4	S22 02.3	357 20.8	S20 38.5	Acamar	315 14.7	S40 13.2
01	313 16.4	239 05.7	09.3	300 25.6	36.9	19 52.2	02.4	12 23.5	38.6	Achernar	335 23.0	S57 07.8
02	328 18.9	254 06.4	09.5	315 26.8	37.3	34 55.0	02.4	27 26.1	38.6	Acrux	173 04.1	S63 12.9
03	343 21.4	269 07.1	.. 09.7	330 28.1	.. 37.8	49 57.8	.. 02.5	42 28.8	.. 38.7	Adhara	255 09.0	S29 00.0
04	358 23.8	284 07.8	10.0	345 29.3	38.2	65 00.6	02.5	57 31.4	38.7	Aldebaran	290 44.0	N16 32.9
05	13 26.3	299 08.5	10.2	0 30.6	38.7	80 03.4	02.6	72 34.1	38.7			
06	28 28.8	314 09.1	N18 10.4	15 31.8	N 1 39.1	95 06.2	S22 02.6	87 36.8	S20 38.8	Alioth	166 16.4	N55 51.3
07	43 31.2	329 09.8	10.7	30 33.1	39.6	110 09.0	02.7	102 39.4	38.8	Alkaid	152 55.0	N49 13.1
08	58 33.7	344 10.5	10.9	45 34.3	40.0	125 11.8	02.7	117 42.1	38.9	Alnair	27 37.1	S46 51.5
M 09	73 36.1	359 11.2	.. 11.1	60 35.6	.. 40.5	140 14.6	.. 02.8	132 44.7	.. 38.9	Alnilam	275 41.7	S 1 11.4
O 10	88 38.6	14 11.8	11.4	75 36.9	40.9	155 17.4	02.8	147 47.4	38.9	Alphard	217 51.6	S 8 44.8
N 11	103 41.1	29 12.5	11.6	90 38.1	41.4	170 20.2	02.9	162 50.0	39.0			
D 12	118 43.5	44 13.2	N18 11.9	105 39.4	N 1 41.8	185 23.0	S22 03.0	177 52.7	S20 39.0	Alphecca	126 06.7	N26 39.0
A 13	133 46.0	59 13.8	12.1	120 40.6	42.3	200 25.8	03.0	192 55.3	39.1	Alpheratz	357 38.3	N29 12.0
Y 14	148 48.5	74 14.5	12.3	135 41.9	42.7	215 28.6	03.1	207 58.0	39.1	Altair	62 03.1	N 8 55.4
15	163 50.9	89 15.2	.. 12.6	150 43.1	.. 43.1	230 31.4	.. 03.1	223 00.7	.. 39.2	Ankaa	353 10.6	S42 11.5
16	178 53.4	104 15.8	12.8	165 44.4	43.6	245 34.2	03.2	238 03.3	39.2	Antares	112 20.0	S26 28.6
17	193 55.9	119 16.5	13.0	180 45.7	44.0	260 37.0	03.2	253 06.0	39.2			
18	208 58.3	134 17.2	N18 13.3	195 46.9	N 1 44.5	275 39.8	S22 03.3	268 08.6	S20 39.3	Arcturus	145 51.2	N19 04.8
19	224 00.8	149 17.8	13.5	210 48.2	44.9	290 42.6	03.4	283 11.3	39.3	Atria	107 17.0	S69 03.9
20	239 03.3	164 18.5	13.8	225 49.4	45.4	305 45.4	03.4	298 13.9	39.4	Avior	234 16.7	S59 34.5
21	254 05.7	179 19.1	.. 14.0	240 50.7	.. 45.8	320 48.2	.. 03.5	313 16.6	.. 39.4	Bellatrix	278 27.0	N 6 22.0
22	269 08.2	194 19.8	14.2	255 52.0	46.3	335 51.0	03.5	328 19.3	39.4	Betelgeuse	270 56.3	N 7 24.6
23	284 10.6	209 20.4	14.5	270 53.2	46.7	350 53.8	03.5	343 21.9	39.5			
21 00	299 13.1	224 21.1	N18 14.7	285 54.5	N 1 47.2	5 56.6	S22 03.6	358 24.6	S20 39.5	Canopus	263 54.5	S52 42.3
01	314 15.6	239 21.7	15.0	300 55.8	47.6	20 59.4	03.7	13 27.2	39.6	Capella	280 27.6	N46 00.9
02	329 18.0	254 22.4	15.2	315 57.0	48.0	36 02.2	03.7	28 29.9	39.6	Deneb	49 27.7	N45 21.2
03	344 20.5	269 23.0	.. 15.4	330 58.3	.. 48.5	51 05.0	.. 03.8	43 32.5	.. 39.6	Denebola	182 28.8	N14 27.7
04	359 23.0	284 23.6	15.7	345 59.5	48.9	66 07.8	03.9	58 35.2	39.7	Diphda	348 50.8	S17 52.4
05	14 25.4	299 24.3	15.9	1 00.8	49.4	81 10.6	03.9	73 37.9	39.7			
06	29 27.9	314 24.9	N18 16.2	16 02.1	N 1 49.8	96 13.4	S22 04.0	88 40.5	S20 39.8	Dubhe	193 46.1	N61 38.7
07	44 30.4	329 25.6	16.4	31 03.3	50.3	111 16.2	04.0	103 43.2	39.8	Elnath	278 06.7	N28 37.3
08	59 32.8	344 26.2	16.6	46 04.6	50.7	126 19.0	04.1	118 45.8	39.9	Eltanin	90 43.4	N51 29.4
T 09	74 35.3	359 26.8	.. 16.9	61 05.9	.. 51.1	141 21.8	.. 04.1	133 48.5	.. 39.9	Enif	33 42.0	N 9 58.2
U 10	89 37.8	14 27.4	17.1	76 07.2	51.6	156 24.7	04.2	148 51.1	39.9	Fomalhaut	15 18.3	S29 30.7
E 11	104 40.2	29 28.1	17.4	91 08.4	52.0	171 27.5	04.2	163 53.8	40.0			
S 12	119 42.7	44 28.7	N18 17.6	106 09.7	N 1 52.5	186 30.3	S22 04.3	178 56.5	S20 40.0	Gacrux	171 55.7	S57 13.8
D 13	134 45.1	59 29.3	17.8	121 11.0	52.9	201 33.1	04.4	193 59.1	40.1	Gienah	175 47.4	S17 39.3
A 14	149 47.6	74 29.9	18.1	136 12.2	53.3	216 35.9	04.4	209 01.8	40.1	Hadar	148 40.9	S60 28.4
Y 15	164 50.1	89 30.6	.. 18.3	151 13.5	.. 53.8	231 38.7	.. 04.5	224 04.4	.. 40.1	Hamal	327 55.2	N23 33.4
16	179 52.5	104 31.2	18.6	166 14.8	54.2	246 41.5	04.5	239 07.1	40.2	Kaus Aust.	83 36.9	S34 22.4
17	194 55.0	119 31.8	18.8	181 16.0	54.7	261 44.3	04.6	254 09.7	40.2			
18	209 57.5	134 32.4	N18 19.0	196 17.3	N 1 55.1	276 47.1	S22 04.6	269 12.4	S20 40.3	Kochab	137 19.7	N74 04.7
19	224 59.9	149 33.0	19.3	211 18.6	55.6	291 49.9	04.7	284 15.1	40.3	Markab	13 33.2	N15 17.4
20	240 02.4	164 33.6	19.5	226 19.9	56.0	306 52.7	04.7	299 17.7	40.3	Menkar	314 10.0	N 4 10.1
21	255 04.9	179 34.2	.. 19.8	241 21.1	.. 56.4	321 55.5	.. 04.8	314 20.4	.. 40.4	Menkent	148 01.8	S36 28.3
22	270 07.3	194 34.9	20.0	256 22.4	56.9	336 58.3	04.8	329 23.0	40.4	Miaplacidus	221 39.7	S69 48.1
23	285 09.8	209 35.5	20.3	271 23.7	57.3	352 01.1	04.9	344 25.7	40.5			
22 00	300 12.3	224 36.1	N18 20.5	286 25.0	N 1 57.7	7 03.9	S22 05.0	359 28.3	S20 40.5	Mirfak	308 33.5	N49 55.7
01	315 14.7	239 36.7	20.7	301 26.2	58.2	22 06.7	05.0	14 31.0	40.6	Nunki	75 51.9	S26 16.2
02	330 17.2	254 37.3	21.0	316 27.5	58.6	37 09.5	05.1	29 33.7	40.6	Peacock	53 10.9	S56 44.0
03	345 19.6	269 37.9	.. 21.2	331 28.8	.. 59.1	52 12.3	.. 05.1	44 36.3	.. 40.6	Pollux	243 22.1	N27 58.6
04	0 22.1	284 38.5	21.5	346 30.1	59.5	67 15.1	05.2	59 39.0	40.7	Procyon	244 54.9	N 5 10.4
05	15 24.6	299 39.1	21.7	1 31.3	1 59.9	82 17.9	05.2	74 41.6	40.7			
06	30 27.0	314 39.6	N18 21.9	16 32.6	N 2 00.4	97 20.7	S22 05.3	89 44.3	S20 40.8	Rasalhague	96 01.6	N12 32.9
W 07	45 29.5	329 40.2	22.2	31 33.9	00.8	112 23.5	05.3	104 46.9	40.8	Regulus	207 38.6	N11 52.2
E 08	60 32.0	344 40.8	22.4	46 35.2	01.2	127 26.3	05.4	119 49.6	40.8	Rigel	281 07.6	S 8 10.7
D 09	75 34.4	359 41.4	.. 22.7	61 36.5	.. 01.7	142 29.1	.. 05.5	134 52.3	.. 40.9	Rigil Kent.	139 45.0	S60 55.3
N 10	90 36.9	14 42.0	22.9	76 37.7	02.1	157 31.9	05.5	149 54.9	40.9	Sabik	102 06.6	S15 44.9
E 11	105 39.4	29 42.6	23.2	91 39.0	02.5	172 34.7	05.6	164 57.6	41.0			
S 12	120 41.8	44 43.2	N18 23.4	106 40.3	N 2 03.0	187 37.5	S22 05.6	180 00.2	S20 41.0	Schedar	349 34.8	N56 38.7
D 13	135 44.3	59 43.8	23.6	121 41.6	03.4	202 40.3	05.7	195 02.9	41.0	Shaula	96 14.9	S37 07.1
A 14	150 46.7	74 44.3	23.9	136 42.9	03.8	217 43.1	05.7	210 05.5	41.1	Sirius	258 29.7	S16 44.6
Y 15	165 49.2	89 44.9	.. 24.1	151 44.2	.. 04.3	232 45.9	.. 05.8	225 08.2	.. 41.1	Spica	158 26.1	S11 16.0
16	180 51.7	104 45.5	24.4	166 45.4	04.7	247 48.7	05.8	240 10.9	41.2	Suhail	222 49.3	S43 30.9
17	195 54.1	119 46.1	24.6	181 46.7	05.1	262 51.5	05.9	255 13.5	41.2			
18	210 56.6	134 46.6	N18 24.9	196 48.0	N 2 05.6	277 54.3	S22 05.9	270 16.2	S20 41.3	Vega	80 35.2	N38 48.3
19	225 59.1	149 47.2	25.1	211 49.3	06.0	292 57.1	06.0	285 18.8	41.3	Zuben'ubi	136 59.9	S16 07.5
20	241 01.5	164 47.8	25.3	226 50.6	06.4	307 59.8	06.0	300 21.5	41.3		SHA	Mer. Pass.
21	256 04.0	179 48.3	.. 25.6	241 51.9	.. 06.9	323 02.6	.. 06.1	315 24.1	.. 41.4		° ′	h m
22	271 06.5	194 48.9	25.8	256 53.2	07.3	338 05.4	06.2	330 26.8	41.4	Venus	285 08.0	9 02
23	286 08.9	209 49.5	26.1	271 54.4	07.7	353 08.2	06.2	345 29.4	41.5	Mars	346 41.4	4 56
	h m									Jupiter	66 43.5	23 32
Mer. Pass. 4 02.5		v 0.6	d 0.2	v 1.3	d 0.4	v 2.8	d 0.1	v 2.7	d 0.0	Saturn	59 11.5	0 06

UT	SUN GHA	Dec	MOON GHA	v	Dec	d	HP
d h	° ′	° ′	° ′	′	° ′	′	′
20 00	178 24.2	N20 36.6	187 55.2	6.6	N23 53.3	1.9	57.7
01	193 24.2	36.1	202 20.8	6.6	23 51.4	2.0	57.7
02	208 24.2	35.6	216 46.4	6.5	23 49.4	2.1	57.7
03	223 24.1 ..	35.2	231 11.9	6.5	23 47.3	2.3	57.8
04	238 24.1	34.7	245 37.4	6.6	23 45.0	2.5	57.8
05	253 24.1	34.2	260 03.0	6.5	23 42.5	2.6	57.8
06	268 24.0	N20 33.7	274 28.5	6.5	N23 39.9	2.7	57.8
M 07	283 24.0	33.3	288 54.0	6.5	23 37.2	2.9	57.9
O 08	298 24.0	32.8	303 19.5	6.4	23 34.3	3.1	57.9
N 09	313 23.9 ..	32.3	317 44.9	6.5	23 31.2	3.2	57.9
D 10	328 23.9	31.8	332 10.4	6.5	23 28.0	3.3	57.9
A 11	343 23.9	31.3	346 35.9	6.5	23 24.7	3.5	58.0
Y 12	358 23.8	N20 30.9	1 01.4	6.4	N23 21.2	3.7	58.0
13	13 23.8	30.4	15 26.8	6.5	23 17.5	3.7	58.0
14	28 23.8	29.9	29 52.3	6.5	23 13.8	4.0	58.0
15	43 23.7 ..	29.4	44 17.8	6.5	23 09.8	4.1	58.1
16	58 23.7	28.9	58 43.3	6.5	23 05.7	4.2	58.1
17	73 23.7	28.5	73 08.8	6.5	23 01.5	4.4	58.1
18	88 23.6	N20 28.0	87 34.3	6.5	N22 57.1	4.5	58.1
19	103 23.6	27.5	101 59.8	6.5	22 52.6	4.7	58.2
20	118 23.6	27.0	116 25.3	6.5	22 47.9	4.8	58.2
21	133 23.5 ..	26.5	130 50.8	6.5	22 43.1	5.0	58.2
22	148 23.5	26.0	145 16.3	6.6	22 38.1	5.1	58.2
23	163 23.5	25.6	159 41.9	6.6	22 33.0	5.2	58.3
21 00	178 23.5	N20 25.1	174 07.5	6.6	N22 27.8	5.4	58.3
01	193 23.4	24.6	188 33.1	6.6	22 22.4	5.6	58.3
02	208 23.4	24.1	202 58.7	6.6	22 16.8	5.7	58.3
03	223 23.4 ..	23.6	217 24.3	6.6	22 11.1	5.8	58.4
04	238 23.3	23.1	231 49.9	6.7	22 05.3	6.0	58.4
05	253 23.3	22.6	246 15.6	6.7	21 59.3	6.1	58.4
06	268 23.3	N20 22.1	260 41.3	6.7	N21 53.2	6.2	58.4
T 07	283 23.3	21.7	275 07.0	6.8	21 47.0	6.4	58.5
U 08	298 23.2	21.2	289 32.8	6.7	21 40.6	6.6	58.5
E 09	313 23.2 ..	20.7	303 58.5	6.8	21 34.0	6.6	58.5
S 10	328 23.2	20.2	318 24.3	6.9	21 27.4	6.8	58.5
D 11	343 23.1	19.7	332 50.2	6.8	21 20.6	7.0	58.5
A 12	358 23.1	N20 19.2	347 16.0	6.9	N21 13.6	7.1	58.6
Y 13	13 23.1	18.7	1 41.9	7.0	21 06.5	7.2	58.6
14	28 23.1	18.2	16 07.9	6.9	20 59.3	7.3	58.6
15	43 23.0 ..	17.7	30 33.8	7.0	20 52.0	7.5	58.6
16	58 23.0	17.2	44 59.8	7.0	20 44.5	7.7	58.7
17	73 23.0	16.7	59 25.8	7.1	20 36.8	7.7	58.7
18	88 23.0	N20 16.2	73 51.9	7.1	N20 29.1	7.9	58.7
19	103 22.9	15.7	88 18.0	7.2	20 21.2	8.0	58.7
20	118 22.9	15.2	102 44.2	7.1	20 13.2	8.2	58.7
21	133 22.9 ..	14.7	117 10.3	7.3	20 05.0	8.2	58.8
22	148 22.9	14.2	131 36.6	7.2	19 56.8	8.4	58.8
23	163 22.8	13.7	146 02.8	7.3	19 48.4	8.6	58.8
22 00	178 22.8	N20 13.2	160 29.1	7.4	N19 39.8	8.6	58.8
01	193 22.8	12.7	174 55.5	7.4	19 31.2	8.8	58.8
02	208 22.8	12.2	189 21.9	7.4	19 22.4	8.9	58.8
03	223 22.7 ..	11.7	203 48.3	7.5	19 13.5	9.0	58.9
04	238 22.7	11.2	218 14.8	7.6	19 04.5	9.2	58.9
05	253 22.7	10.7	232 41.4	7.5	18 55.3	9.3	58.9
06	268 22.7	N20 10.2	247 07.9	7.6	N18 46.0	9.3	58.9
W 07	283 22.7	09.7	261 34.5	7.7	18 36.7	9.6	58.9
E 08	298 22.6	09.2	276 01.2	7.7	18 27.1	9.6	59.0
D 09	313 22.6 ..	08.7	290 27.9	7.8	18 17.5	9.7	59.0
N 10	328 22.6	08.2	304 54.7	7.8	18 07.8	9.9	59.0
E 11	343 22.6	07.7	319 21.5	7.9	17 57.9	9.9	59.0
S 12	358 22.5	N20 07.2	333 48.4	7.9	N17 48.0	10.1	59.0
D 13	13 22.5	06.7	348 15.3	7.9	17 37.9	10.2	59.0
A 14	28 22.5	06.2	2 42.2	8.1	17 27.7	10.3	59.1
Y 15	43 22.5 ..	05.7	17 09.3	8.0	17 17.4	10.4	59.1
16	58 22.5	05.1	31 36.3	8.1	17 07.0	10.5	59.1
17	73 22.4	04.6	46 03.4	8.2	16 56.5	10.7	59.1
18	88 22.4	N20 04.1	60 30.6	8.2	N16 45.8	10.7	59.1
19	103 22.4	03.6	74 57.8	8.3	16 35.1	10.8	59.1
20	118 22.4	03.1	89 25.1	8.3	16 24.3	11.0	59.1
21	133 22.4 ..	02.6	103 52.4	8.3	16 13.3	11.0	59.2
22	148 22.4	02.1	118 19.7	8.5	16 02.3	11.1	59.2
23	163 22.3	01.6	132 47.2	8.4	N15 51.2	11.3	59.2
	SD 15.8	d 0.5	SD 15.8		16.0		16.1

Twilight / Moonrise

Lat.	Naut.	Civil	Sunrise	Moonrise 20	21	22	23
°	h m	h m	h m	h m	h m	h m	h m
N 72	□	□	□	□	□	□	04 49
N 70	□	□	□	□	□	02 34	05 22
68	////	////	01 10	□	□	03 32	05 46
66	////	////	02 03	00 03	02 04	04 06	06 04
64	////	////	02 35	01 14	02 45	04 31	06 19
62	////	01 28	02 58	01 50	03 13	04 50	06 31
60	////	02 06	03 17	02 16	03 34	05 05	06 41
N 58	////	02 32	03 32	02 36	03 52	05 19	06 50
56	01 20	02 52	03 45	02 53	04 06	05 30	06 58
54	01 55	03 08	03 56	03 07	04 19	05 40	07 05
52	02 19	03 22	04 06	03 20	04 30	05 49	07 12
50	02 38	03 34	04 15	03 31	04 40	05 57	07 17
45	03 13	03 59	04 34	03 54	05 01	06 14	07 29
N 40	03 39	04 18	04 49	04 12	05 17	06 27	07 39
35	03 58	04 33	05 02	04 28	05 31	06 39	07 48
30	04 14	04 46	05 13	04 41	05 44	06 49	07 55
20	04 39	05 08	05 32	05 04	06 04	07 06	08 08
N 10	04 59	05 25	05 48	05 24	06 23	07 22	08 19
0	05 15	05 41	06 03	05 42	06 39	07 36	08 30
S 10	05 30	05 55	06 18	06 00	06 56	07 50	08 40
20	05 43	06 10	06 34	06 20	07 14	08 05	08 51
30	05 57	06 26	06 52	06 43	07 35	08 22	09 04
35	06 04	06 35	07 02	06 56	07 47	08 32	09 11
40	06 11	06 45	07 14	07 12	08 01	08 43	09 20
45	06 20	06 56	07 28	07 30	08 17	08 56	09 29
S 50	06 29	07 09	07 45	07 53	08 37	09 12	09 41
52	06 33	07 15	07 53	08 04	08 46	09 20	09 46
54	06 37	07 21	08 02	08 16	08 57	09 28	09 52
56	06 42	07 29	08 12	08 30	09 09	09 37	09 59
58	06 47	07 37	08 24	08 47	09 23	09 48	10 06
S 60	06 52	07 46	08 37	09 07	09 39	10 00	10 14

Sunset / Twilight / Moonset

Lat.	Sunset	Civil	Naut.	Moonset 20	21	22	23
°	h m	h m	h m	h m	h m	h m	h m
N 72	□	□	□	□	□	□	(00 05 / 23 23)
N 70	□	□	□	□	□	(00 23 / 23 30)	23 06
68	22 56	////	////	□	23 24	23 05	22 53
66	22 07	////	////	22 53	22 49	22 45	22 41
64	21 36	////	////	22 11	22 24	22 29	22 32
62	21 13	22 40	////	21 43	22 04	22 16	22 24
60	20 55	22 04	////	21 21	21 48	22 05	22 17
N 58	20 40	21 39	////	21 03	21 34	21 55	22 11
56	20 27	21 19	22 48	20 48	21 22	21 46	22 05
54	20 16	21 03	22 15	20 35	21 11	21 38	22 00
52	20 06	20 50	21 52	20 24	21 02	21 31	21 55
50	19 57	20 38	21 33	20 14	20 53	21 25	21 51
45	19 39	20 14	20 59	19 53	20 36	21 12	21 42
N 40	19 24	19 55	20 34	19 35	20 21	21 00	21 35
35	19 11	19 39	20 14	19 21	20 08	20 50	21 28
30	19 00	19 24	19 58	19 08	19 57	20 42	21 22
20	18 41	19 05	19 33	18 46	19 38	20 27	21 12
N 10	18 25	18 48	19 14	18 27	19 22	20 14	21 03
0	18 09	18 33	18 58	18 09	19 06	20 02	20 55
S 10	17 55	18 17	18 43	17 52	18 51	19 49	20 47
20	17 39	18 03	18 30	17 32	18 34	19 36	20 37
30	17 21	17 47	18 16	17 10	18 15	19 21	20 27
35	17 11	17 38	18 09	16 57	18 03	19 12	20 21
40	16 59	17 29	18 02	16 42	17 50	19 01	20 14
45	16 45	17 18	17 54	16 24	17 35	18 49	20 06
S 50	16 28	17 05	17 45	16 02	17 15	18 35	19 56
52	16 20	16 59	17 41	15 51	17 06	18 28	19 51
54	16 11	16 52	17 36	15 39	16 56	18 20	19 46
56	16 01	16 45	17 32	15 25	16 45	18 11	19 40
58	15 50	16 37	17 27	15 09	16 31	18 01	19 34
S 60	15 36	16 28	17 21	14 49	16 15	17 50	19 27

SUN / MOON

Day	SUN Eqn. of Time 00ʰ	12ʰ	Mer. Pass.	MOON Mer. Pass. Upper	Lower	Age	Phase
d	m s	m s	h m	h m	h m	d	%
20	06 23	06 25	12 06	11 56	24 24	29	0
21	06 26	06 27	12 06	12 53	00 24	01	1
22	06 29	06 30	12 06	13 49	01 21	02	4 ●

2020 JULY 23, 24, 25 (THURS., FRI., SAT.)

UT	ARIES	VENUS −4·6		MARS −0·9		JUPITER −2·7		SATURN +0·1		STARS		
	GHA	GHA	Dec	GHA	Dec	GHA	Dec	GHA	Dec	Name	SHA	Dec
d h	° ′	° ′	° ′	° ′	° ′	° ′	° ′	° ′	° ′		° ′	° ′
23 00	301 11.4	224 50.0	N18 26.3	286 55.7	N 2 08.2	8 11.0	S22 06.3	0 32.1	S20 41.5	Acamar	315 14.7	S40 13.2
01	316 13.9	239 50.6	26.6	301 57.0	08.6	23 13.8	06.3	15 34.8	41.5	Achernar	335 23.0	S57 07.8
02	331 16.3	254 51.1	26.8	316 58.3	09.0	38 16.6	06.4	30 37.4	41.6	Acrux	173 04.2	S63 12.9
03	346 18.8	269 51.7 ..	27.0	331 59.6 ..	09.5	53 19.4 ..	06.4	45 40.1 ..	41.6	Adhara	255 09.0	S28 59.9
04	1 21.2	284 52.3	27.3	347 00.9	09.9	68 22.2	06.5	60 42.7	41.7	Aldebaran	290 43.9	N16 32.9
05	16 23.7	299 52.8	27.5	2 02.2	10.3	83 25.0	06.5	75 45.4	41.7			
06	31 26.2	314 53.4	N18 27.8	17 03.5	N 2 10.8	98 27.8	S22 06.6	90 48.0	S20 41.7	Alioth	166 16.4	N55 51.3
07	46 28.6	329 53.9	28.0	32 04.8	11.2	113 30.6	06.6	105 50.7	41.8	Alkaid	152 55.0	N49 13.1
T 08	61 31.1	344 54.5	28.3	47 06.1	11.6	128 33.4	06.7	120 53.4	41.8	Alnair	27 37.1	S46 51.6
H 09	76 33.6	359 55.0 ..	28.5	62 07.4 ..	12.1	143 36.2 ..	06.8	135 56.0 ..	41.9	Alnilam	275 41.6	S 1 11.3
U 10	91 36.0	14 55.6	28.8	77 08.7	12.5	158 39.0	06.8	150 58.7	41.9	Alphard	217 51.6	S 8 44.8
R 11	106 38.5	29 56.1	29.0	92 09.9	12.9	173 41.8	06.9	166 01.3	42.0			
S 12	121 41.0	44 56.6	N18 29.2	107 11.2	N 2 13.3	188 44.6	S22 06.9	181 04.0	S20 42.0	Alphecca	126 06.7	N26 39.0
D 13	136 43.4	59 57.2	29.5	122 12.5	13.8	203 47.4	07.0	196 06.6	42.0	Alpheratz	357 38.3	N29 12.0
A 14	151 45.9	74 57.7	29.7	137 13.8	14.2	218 50.2	07.0	211 09.3	42.1	Altair	62 03.1	N 8 55.5
Y 15	166 48.4	89 58.3 ..	30.0	152 15.1 ..	14.6	233 53.0 ..	07.1	226 12.0 ..	42.1	Ankaa	353 10.6	S42 11.5
16	181 50.8	104 58.8	30.2	167 16.4	15.1	248 55.8	07.1	241 14.6	42.2	Antares	112 20.0	S26 28.6
17	196 53.3	119 59.3	30.5	182 17.7	15.5	263 58.6	07.2	256 17.3	42.2			
18	211 55.7	134 59.8	N18 30.7	197 19.0	N 2 15.9	279 01.4	S22 07.2	271 19.9	S20 42.2	Arcturus	145 51.2	N19 04.8
19	226 58.2	150 00.4	30.9	212 20.3	16.3	294 04.2	07.3	286 22.6	42.3	Atria	107 17.0	S69 03.9
20	242 00.7	165 00.9	31.2	227 21.6	16.8	309 07.0	07.3	301 25.2	42.3	Avior	234 16.7	S59 34.5
21	257 03.1	180 01.4 ..	31.4	242 22.9 ..	17.2	324 09.8 ..	07.4	316 27.9 ..	42.3	Bellatrix	278 27.0	N 6 22.0
22	272 05.6	195 02.0	31.7	257 24.2	17.6	339 12.6	07.4	331 30.6	42.4	Betelgeuse	270 56.3	N 7 24.6
23	287 08.1	210 02.5	31.9	272 25.5	18.0	354 15.4	07.5	346 33.2	42.4			
24 00	302 10.5	225 03.0	N18 32.2	287 26.8	N 2 18.5	9 18.2	S22 07.6	1 35.9	S20 42.5	Canopus	263 54.5	S52 42.3
01	317 13.0	240 03.5	32.4	302 28.1	18.9	24 21.0	07.6	16 38.5	42.5	Capella	280 27.5	N46 00.9
02	332 15.5	255 04.0	32.7	317 29.4	19.3	39 23.8	07.7	31 41.2	42.6	Deneb	49 27.7	N45 21.2
03	347 17.9	270 04.6 ..	32.9	332 30.7 ..	19.7	54 26.6 ..	07.7	46 43.8 ..	42.6	Denebola	182 28.8	N14 27.7
04	2 20.4	285 05.1	33.1	347 32.0	20.2	69 29.4	07.8	61 46.5	42.6	Diphda	348 50.8	S17 52.4
05	17 22.8	300 05.6	33.4	2 33.3	20.6	84 32.2	07.8	76 49.2	42.7			
06	32 25.3	315 06.1	N18 33.6	17 34.7	N 2 21.0	99 35.0	S22 07.9	91 51.8	S20 42.7	Dubhe	193 46.1	N61 38.7
07	47 27.8	330 06.6	33.9	32 36.0	21.4	114 37.7	07.9	106 54.5	42.8	Elnath	278 06.7	N28 37.3
08	62 30.2	345 07.1	34.1	47 37.3	21.9	129 40.5	08.0	121 57.1	42.8	Eltanin	90 43.4	N51 29.4
F 09	77 32.7	0 07.6 ..	34.4	62 38.6 ..	22.3	144 43.3 ..	08.0	136 59.8 ..	42.9	Enif	33 42.0	N 9 58.2
R 10	92 35.2	15 08.1	34.6	77 39.9	22.7	159 46.1	08.1	152 02.4	42.9	Fomalhaut	15 18.3	S29 30.7
I 11	107 37.6	30 08.6	34.9	92 41.2	23.1	174 48.9	08.1	167 05.1	42.9			
D 12	122 40.1	45 09.1	N18 35.1	107 42.5	N 2 23.6	189 51.7	S22 08.2	182 07.7	S20 43.0	Gacrux	171 55.7	S57 13.8
A 13	137 42.6	60 09.6	35.3	122 43.8	24.0	204 54.5	08.2	197 10.4	43.0	Gienah	175 47.4	S17 39.3
Y 14	152 45.0	75 10.1	35.6	137 45.1	24.4	219 57.3	08.3	212 13.1	43.1	Hadar	148 40.9	S60 28.4
15	167 47.5	90 10.6 ..	35.8	152 46.4 ..	24.8	235 00.1 ..	08.4	227 15.7 ..	43.1	Hamal	327 55.2	N23 33.4
16	182 50.0	105 11.1	36.1	167 47.7	25.2	250 02.9	08.4	242 18.4	43.1	Kaus Aust.	83 36.9	S34 22.4
17	197 52.4	120 11.6	36.3	182 49.0	25.7	265 05.7	08.5	257 21.0	43.2			
18	212 54.9	135 12.1	N18 36.6	197 50.4	N 2 26.1	280 08.5	S22 08.5	272 23.7	S20 43.2	Kochab	137 19.7	N74 04.7
19	227 57.3	150 12.6	36.8	212 51.7	26.5	295 11.3	08.6	287 26.3	43.3	Markab	13 33.2	N15 18.9
20	242 59.8	165 13.1	37.0	227 53.0	26.9	310 14.1	08.6	302 29.0	43.3	Menkar	314 10.0	N 4 10.1
21	258 02.3	180 13.6 ..	37.3	242 54.3 ..	27.3	325 16.9 ..	08.7	317 31.7 ..	43.3	Menkent	148 01.8	S36 28.3
22	273 04.7	195 14.0	37.5	257 55.6	27.8	340 19.7	08.7	332 34.3	43.4	Miaplacidus	221 39.7	S69 48.1
23	288 07.2	210 14.5	37.8	272 56.9	28.2	355 22.5	08.8	347 37.0	43.4			
25 00	303 09.7	225 15.0	N18 38.0	287 58.2	N 2 28.6	10 25.3	S22 08.8	2 39.6	S20 43.5	Mirfak	308 33.5	N49 55.7
01	318 12.1	240 15.5	38.3	302 59.6	29.0	25 28.1	08.9	17 42.3	43.5	Nunki	75 51.9	S26 16.2
02	333 14.6	255 16.0	38.5	318 00.9	29.4	40 30.8	08.9	32 44.9	43.5	Peacock	53 10.9	S56 40.0
03	348 17.1	270 16.4 ..	38.7	333 02.2 ..	29.9	55 33.6 ..	09.0	47 47.6 ..	43.6	Pollux	243 22.1	N27 58.6
04	3 19.5	285 16.9	39.0	348 03.5	30.3	70 36.4	09.0	62 50.2	43.6	Procyon	244 54.9	N 5 10.4
05	18 22.0	300 17.4	39.2	3 04.8	30.7	85 39.2	09.1	77 52.9	43.7			
06	33 24.4	315 17.9	N18 39.5	18 06.1	N 2 31.1	100 42.0	S22 09.1	92 55.6	S20 43.7	Rasalhague	96 01.6	N12 32.9
07	48 26.9	330 18.3	39.7	33 07.5	31.5	115 44.8	09.2	107 58.2	43.7	Regulus	207 38.6	N11 52.2
S 08	63 29.4	345 18.8	40.0	48 08.8	32.0	130 47.6	09.3	123 00.9	43.8	Rigel	281 07.6	S 8 10.7
A 09	78 31.8	0 19.3 ..	40.2	63 10.1 ..	32.4	145 50.4 ..	09.3	138 03.5 ..	43.8	Rigil Kent.	139 45.0	S60 55.3
T 10	93 34.3	15 19.7	40.5	78 11.4	32.8	160 53.2	09.4	153 06.2	43.9	Sabik	102 06.6	S15 44.9
U 11	108 36.8	30 20.2	40.7	93 12.7	33.2	175 56.0	09.4	168 08.8	43.9			
R 12	123 39.2	45 20.7	N18 40.9	108 14.1	N 2 33.6	190 58.8	S22 09.5	183 11.5	S20 44.0	Schedar	349 34.8	N56 38.7
D 13	138 41.7	60 21.1	41.2	123 15.4	34.0	206 01.6	09.5	198 14.2	44.0	Shaula	96 14.9	S37 07.1
A 14	153 44.2	75 21.6	41.4	138 16.7	34.4	221 04.4	09.6	213 16.8	44.0	Sirius	258 29.7	S16 44.6
Y 15	168 46.6	90 22.0 ..	41.7	153 18.0 ..	34.9	236 07.2 ..	09.6	228 19.5 ..	44.1	Spica	158 26.1	S11 16.0
16	183 49.1	105 22.5	41.9	168 19.4	35.3	251 09.9	09.7	243 22.1	44.1	Suhail	222 49.3	S43 30.9
17	198 51.6	120 23.0	42.2	183 20.7	35.7	266 12.7	09.7	258 24.8	44.2			
18	213 54.0	135 23.4	N18 42.4	198 22.0	N 2 36.1	281 15.5	S22 09.8	273 27.4	S20 44.2	Vega	80 35.2	N38 48.3
19	228 56.5	150 23.9	42.6	213 23.3	36.5	296 18.3	09.8	288 30.1	44.2	Zuben'ubi	136 59.9	S16 07.5
20	243 58.9	165 24.3	42.9	228 24.7	36.9	311 21.1	09.9	303 32.7	44.3		SHA	Mer.Pass.
21	259 01.4	180 24.8 ..	43.1	243 26.0 ..	37.4	326 23.9 ..	09.9	318 35.4 ..	44.3		° ′	h m
22	274 03.9	195 25.2	43.4	258 27.3	37.8	341 26.7	10.0	333 38.1	44.4	Venus	282 52.5	8 59
23	289 06.3	210 25.6	43.6	273 28.7	38.2	356 29.5	10.0	348 40.7	44.4	Mars	345 16.3	4 50
	h m									Jupiter	67 07.6	23 18
Mer. Pass.	3 50.7	v 0.5	d 0.2	v 1.3	d 0.4	v 2.8	d 0.1	v 2.7	d 0.0	Saturn	59 25.3	23 49

UT	SUN GHA	SUN Dec	MOON GHA	v	Dec	d	HP
d h	° ′	° ′	° ′	′	° ′	′	′
23 00	178 22.3	N20 01.0	147 14.6	8.6	N15 39.9	11.3	59.2
01	193 22.3	00.5	161 42.2	8.5	15 28.6	11.4	59.2
02	208 22.3	20 00.0	176 09.7	8.6	15 17.2	11.5	59.2
03	223 22.3	19 59.5	190 37.3	8.7	15 05.7	11.6	59.2
04	238 22.3	59.0	205 05.0	8.7	14 54.1	11.7	59.2
05	253 22.2	58.5	219 32.7	8.8	14 42.4	11.8	59.3
06	268 22.2	N19 57.9	234 00.5	8.8	N14 30.6	11.9	59.3
07	283 22.2	57.4	248 28.3	8.9	14 18.7	12.0	59.3
08	298 22.2	56.9	262 56.2	8.9	14 06.7	12.0	59.3
09	313 22.2 ..	56.4	277 24.1	9.0	13 54.7	12.2	59.3
10	328 22.2	55.9	291 52.1	9.0	13 42.5	12.2	59.3
11	343 22.1	55.3	306 20.1	9.1	13 30.3	12.3	59.3
12	358 22.1	N19 54.8	320 48.2	9.2	N13 18.0	12.4	59.3
13	13 22.1	54.3	335 16.4	9.1	13 05.6	12.5	59.3
14	28 22.1	53.8	349 44.5	9.2	12 53.1	12.5	59.3
15	43 22.1 ..	53.3	4 12.7	9.3	12 40.6	12.6	59.4
16	58 22.1	52.7	18 41.0	9.3	12 28.0	12.7	59.4
17	73 22.1	52.2	33 09.3	9.4	12 15.3	12.8	59.4
18	88 22.0	N19 51.7	47 37.7	9.4	N12 02.5	12.8	59.4
19	103 22.0	51.2	62 06.1	9.5	11 49.7	12.9	59.4
20	118 22.0	50.6	76 34.6	9.5	11 36.8	13.0	59.4
21	133 22.0 ..	50.1	91 03.1	9.5	11 23.8	13.1	59.4
22	148 22.0	49.6	105 31.6	9.6	11 10.7	13.1	59.4
23	163 22.0	49.1	120 00.2	9.7	10 57.6	13.1	59.4
24 00	178 22.0	N19 48.5	134 28.9	9.7	N10 44.5	13.3	59.4
01	193 22.0	48.0	148 57.6	9.7	10 31.2	13.3	59.4
02	208 22.0	47.5	163 26.3	9.8	10 17.9	13.3	59.4
03	223 21.9 ..	46.9	177 55.1	9.8	10 04.6	13.5	59.5
04	238 21.9	46.4	192 23.9	9.8	9 51.1	13.4	59.5
05	253 21.9	45.9	206 52.7	9.9	9 37.7	13.6	59.5
06	268 21.9	N19 45.3	221 21.6	10.0	N 9 24.1	13.6	59.5
07	283 21.9	44.8	235 50.6	9.9	9 10.5	13.6	59.5
08	298 21.9	44.3	250 19.5	10.1	8 56.9	13.7	59.5
09	313 21.9 ..	43.7	264 48.6	10.0	8 43.2	13.7	59.5
10	328 21.9	43.2	279 17.6	10.1	8 29.5	13.8	59.5
11	343 21.9	42.7	293 46.7	10.1	8 15.7	13.9	59.5
12	358 21.9	N19 42.1	308 15.8	10.2	N 8 01.8	13.8	59.5
13	13 21.9	41.6	322 45.0	10.2	7 48.0	14.0	59.5
14	28 21.8	41.1	337 14.2	10.2	7 34.0	13.9	59.5
15	43 21.8 ..	40.5	351 43.4	10.3	7 20.1	14.0	59.5
16	58 21.8	40.0	6 12.7	10.3	7 06.1	14.1	59.5
17	73 21.8	39.5	20 42.0	10.3	6 52.0	14.1	59.5
18	88 21.8	N19 38.9	35 11.3	10.4	N 6 37.9	14.1	59.5
19	103 21.8	38.4	49 40.7	10.4	6 23.8	14.2	59.5
20	118 21.8	37.8	64 10.1	10.4	6 09.6	14.2	59.5
21	133 21.8 ..	37.3	78 39.5	10.4	5 55.4	14.2	59.5
22	148 21.8	36.8	93 08.9	10.5	5 41.2	14.3	59.5
23	163 21.8	36.2	107 38.4	10.5	5 26.9	14.2	59.5
25 00	178 21.8	N19 35.7	122 07.9	10.6	N 5 12.7	14.4	59.5
01	193 21.8	35.1	136 37.5	10.5	4 58.3	14.3	59.5
02	208 21.8	34.6	151 07.0	10.6	4 44.0	14.4	59.5
03	223 21.8 ..	34.1	165 36.6	10.6	4 29.6	14.4	59.5
04	238 21.8	33.5	180 06.2	10.6	4 15.2	14.4	59.5
05	253 21.8	33.0	194 35.8	10.7	4 00.8	14.4	59.5
06	268 21.8	N19 32.4	209 05.5	10.6	N 3 46.4	14.5	59.5
07	283 21.8	31.9	223 35.1	10.7	3 31.9	14.5	59.5
08	298 21.8	31.3	238 04.8	10.7	3 17.4	14.4	59.5
09	313 21.7 ..	30.8	252 34.5	10.8	3 03.0	14.6	59.5
10	328 21.7	30.2	267 04.3	10.7	2 48.4	14.5	59.5
11	343 21.7	29.7	281 34.0	10.8	2 33.9	14.5	59.5
12	358 21.7	N19 29.1	296 03.8	10.7	N 2 19.4	14.5	59.5
13	13 21.7	28.6	310 33.5	10.8	2 04.8	14.5	59.5
14	28 21.7	28.0	325 03.3	10.8	1 50.3	14.6	59.5
15	43 21.7 ..	27.5	339 33.1	10.8	1 35.7	14.5	59.5
16	58 21.7	26.9	354 02.9	10.8	1 21.2	14.6	59.5
17	73 21.7	26.4	8 32.7	10.9	1 06.6	14.6	59.5
18	88 21.7	N19 25.8	23 02.6	10.8	N 0 52.0	14.6	59.5
19	103 21.7	25.3	37 32.4	10.9	0 37.4	14.6	59.5
20	118 21.7	24.7	52 02.3	10.8	0 22.8	14.5	59.5
21	133 21.7 ..	24.2	66 32.1	10.9	N 0 08.3	14.6	59.5
22	148 21.7	23.6	81 02.0	10.8	S 0 06.3	14.6	59.5
23	163 21.7	23.1	95 31.8	10.9	S 0 20.9	14.6	59.5
	SD 15.8	d 0.5	SD 16.2		16.2		16.2

Rows labelled: THURSDAY (23), FRIDAY (24), SATURDAY (25)

Twilight / Sunrise / Moonrise

Lat.	Naut.	Civil	Sunrise	Moonrise 23	24	25	26
°	h m	h m	h m	h m	h m	h m	h m
N 72	□	□	□	04 49	07 22	09 37	11 48
N 70	□	□	□	05 22	07 36	09 41	11 43
68	////	////	01 31	05 46	07 48	09 44	11 39
66	////	////	02 15	06 04	07 57	09 47	11 35
64	////	00 36	02 44	06 19	08 05	09 49	11 32
62	////	01 43	03 06	06 31	08 12	09 51	11 30
60	////	02 16	03 23	06 41	08 18	09 53	11 28
N 58	00 33	02 40	03 38	06 50	08 23	09 55	11 26
56	01 34	02 58	03 50	06 58	08 27	09 56	11 24
54	02 04	03 14	04 01	07 05	08 32	09 57	11 22
52	02 26	03 27	04 10	07 12	08 35	09 58	11 21
50	02 44	03 39	04 19	07 17	08 38	09 59	11 20
45	03 18	04 02	04 37	07 29	08 46	10 01	11 17
N 40	03 42	04 20	04 51	07 39	08 52	10 03	11 14
35	04 01	04 35	05 04	07 48	08 57	10 05	11 12
30	04 16	04 48	05 14	07 55	09 01	10 06	11 11
20	04 41	05 09	05 33	08 08	09 09	10 09	11 08
N 10	05 00	05 26	05 48	08 19	09 16	10 11	11 05
0	05 15	05 41	06 03	08 30	09 22	10 13	11 03
S 10	05 29	05 55	06 17	08 40	09 28	10 15	11 00
20	05 43	06 09	06 33	08 51	09 35	10 17	10 58
30	05 56	06 25	06 50	09 04	09 43	10 19	10 55
35	06 02	06 33	07 00	09 11	09 47	10 21	10 53
40	06 10	06 43	07 12	09 20	09 52	10 22	10 52
45	06 17	06 53	07 25	09 29	09 58	10 24	10 50
S 50	06 26	07 06	07 42	09 41	10 05	10 26	10 47
52	06 30	07 11	07 49	09 46	10 08	10 27	10 46
54	06 34	07 18	07 58	09 52	10 11	10 29	10 45
56	06 38	07 24	08 08	09 59	10 15	10 30	10 44
58	06 43	07 32	08 19	10 06	10 19	10 31	10 42
S 60	06 48	07 41	08 31	10 14	10 24	10 33	10 41

Sunset / Twilight / Moonset

Lat.	Sunset	Civil	Naut.	Moonset 23	24	25	26
°	h m	h m	h m	h m	h m	h m	h m
N 72	□	□	□	{00 05 / 23 23}	22 56	22 32	22 08
N 70	□	□	□	23 06	22 48	22 33	22 16
68	22 36	////	////	22 53	22 42	22 33	22 23
66	21 54	////	////	22 41	22 37	22 33	22 29
64	21 27	23 24	////	22 32	22 33	22 34	22 34
62	21 05	22 27	////	22 24	22 29	22 34	22 38
60	20 48	21 55	////	22 17	22 26	22 34	22 42
N 58	20 34	21 32	23 29	22 11	22 23	22 34	22 45
56	20 22	21 13	22 36	22 05	22 20	22 34	22 48
54	20 11	20 58	22 07	22 00	22 18	22 35	22 51
52	20 02	20 45	21 45	21 55	22 16	22 35	22 54
50	19 53	20 34	21 27	21 51	22 14	22 35	22 56
45	19 36	20 10	20 54	21 42	22 10	22 35	23 01
N 40	19 21	19 52	20 30	21 35	22 06	22 35	23 05
35	19 09	19 37	20 12	21 28	22 03	22 36	23 08
30	18 58	19 25	19 56	21 22	22 00	22 36	23 12
20	18 40	19 04	19 32	21 12	21 55	22 36	23 17
N 10	18 25	18 47	19 13	21 03	21 51	22 36	23 22
0	18 10	18 32	18 58	20 55	21 46	22 36	23 26
S 10	17 56	18 18	18 44	20 47	21 42	22 37	23 31
20	17 40	18 04	18 31	20 37	21 38	22 37	23 36
30	17 23	17 49	18 18	20 27	21 32	22 37	23 41
35	17 13	17 40	18 11	20 21	21 29	22 37	23 45
40	17 02	17 31	18 04	20 14	21 26	22 37	23 48
45	16 48	17 20	17 56	20 06	21 22	22 37	23 52
S 50	16 32	17 08	17 48	19 56	21 17	22 37	23 58
52	16 24	17 02	17 44	19 51	21 15	22 37	24 00
54	16 16	16 56	17 40	19 46	21 12	22 37	24 02
56	16 06	16 49	17 36	19 40	21 09	22 38	24 05
58	15 55	16 42	17 31	19 34	21 06	22 38	24 08
S 60	15 42	16 33	17 26	19 27	21 03	22 38	24 12

SUN and MOON

Day	SUN Eqn. of Time 00h	SUN Eqn. of Time 12h	SUN Mer. Pass.	MOON Mer. Pass. Upper	MOON Mer. Pass. Lower	Age	Phase
d	m s	m s	h m	h m	h m	d %	
23	06 31	06 31	12 07	14 43	02 16	03 10	
24	06 32	06 33	12 07	15 34	03 09	04 18	
25	06 33	06 33	12 07	16 25	04 00	05 28	

UT	ARIES GHA	VENUS −4·6 GHA	Dec	MARS −1·0 GHA	Dec	JUPITER −2·7 GHA	Dec	SATURN +0·1 GHA	Dec	STARS Name	SHA	Dec
26 00	304 08.8	225 26.1	N18 43.8	288 30.0	N 2 38.6	11 32.3	S22 10.1	3 43.4	S20 44.4	Acamar	315 14.6	S40 13.2
01	319 11.3	240 26.5	44.1	303 31.3	39.0	26 35.1	10.1	18 46.0	44.5	Achernar	335 22.9	S57 07.7
02	334 13.7	255 27.0	44.3	318 32.6	39.4	41 37.9	10.2	33 48.7	44.5	Acrux	173 04.2	S63 12.9
03	349 16.2	270 27.4 ..	44.6	333 34.0 ..	39.8	56 40.7 ..	10.2	48 51.3 ..	44.6	Adhara	255 09.0	S28 59.9
04	4 18.7	285 27.8	44.8	348 35.3	40.2	71 43.4	10.3	63 54.0	44.6	Aldebaran	290 43.9	N16 32.9
05	19 21.1	300 28.3	45.1	3 36.6	40.7	86 46.2	10.3	78 56.6	44.6			
S 06	34 23.6	315 28.7	N18 45.3	18 38.0	N 2 41.1	101 49.0	S22 10.4	93 59.3	S20 44.7	Alioth	166 16.5	N55 51.3
U 07	49 26.1	330 29.2	45.5	33 39.3	41.5	116 51.8	10.4	109 02.0	44.7	Alkaid	152 55.0	N49 13.1
N 08	64 28.5	345 29.6	45.8	48 40.6	41.9	131 54.6	10.5	124 04.6	44.8	Alnair	27 37.1	S46 51.6
D 09	79 31.0	0 30.0 ..	46.0	63 42.0 ..	42.3	146 57.4 ..	10.6	139 07.3 ..	44.8	Alnilam	275 41.6	S 1 11.3
A 10	94 33.4	15 30.4	46.3	78 43.3	42.7	162 00.2	10.6	154 09.9	44.8	Alphard	217 51.6	S 8 44.8
Y 11	109 35.9	30 30.9	46.5	93 44.6	43.1	177 03.0	10.7	169 12.6	44.9			
12	124 38.4	45 31.3	N18 46.7	108 46.0	N 2 43.5	192 05.8	S22 10.7	184 15.2	S20 44.9	Alphecca	126 06.7	N26 39.1
13	139 40.8	60 31.7	47.0	123 47.3	43.9	207 08.6	10.8	199 17.9	45.0	Alpheratz	357 38.2	N29 12.1
14	154 43.3	75 32.1	47.2	138 48.6	44.3	222 11.3	10.8	214 20.5	45.0	Altair	62 03.1	N 8 55.5
15	169 45.8	90 32.6 ..	47.5	153 50.0 ..	44.8	237 14.1 ..	10.9	229 23.2 ..	45.0	Ankaa	353 10.6	S42 11.5
16	184 48.2	105 33.0	47.7	168 51.3	45.2	252 16.9	10.9	244 25.9	45.1	Antares	112 20.0	S26 28.6
17	199 50.7	120 33.4	47.9	183 52.7	45.6	267 19.7	11.0	259 28.5	45.1			
18	214 53.2	135 33.8	N18 48.2	198 54.0	N 2 46.0	282 22.5	S22 11.0	274 31.2	S20 45.2	Arcturus	145 51.2	N19 04.8
19	229 55.6	150 34.2	48.4	213 55.3	46.4	297 25.3	11.1	289 33.8	45.2	Atria	107 17.0	S69 03.9
20	244 58.1	165 34.6	48.7	228 56.7	46.8	312 28.1	11.1	304 36.5	45.2	Avior	234 16.7	S59 34.5
21	260 00.5	180 35.0 ..	48.9	243 58.0 ..	47.2	327 30.9 ..	11.2	319 39.1 ..	45.3	Bellatrix	278 27.0	N 6 22.0
22	275 03.0	195 35.5	49.2	258 59.4	47.6	342 33.7	11.2	334 41.8	45.3	Betelgeuse	270 56.2	N 7 24.6
23	290 05.5	210 35.9	49.4	274 00.7	48.0	357 36.4	11.3	349 44.4	45.4			
27 00	305 07.9	225 36.3	N18 49.6	289 02.1	N 2 48.4	12 39.2	S22 11.3	4 47.1	S20 45.4	Canopus	263 54.5	S52 42.3
01	320 10.4	240 36.7	49.9	304 03.4	48.8	27 42.0	11.4	19 49.8	45.4	Capella	280 27.5	N46 00.9
02	335 12.9	255 37.1	50.1	319 04.7	49.2	42 44.8	11.4	34 52.4	45.5	Deneb	49 27.7	N45 21.2
03	350 15.3	270 37.5 ..	50.3	334 06.1 ..	49.6	57 47.6 ..	11.5	49 55.1 ..	45.5	Denebola	182 28.8	N14 27.7
04	5 17.8	285 37.9	50.6	349 07.4	50.0	72 50.4	11.5	64 57.7	45.6	Diphda	348 50.8	S17 52.4
05	20 20.3	300 38.3	50.8	4 08.8	50.4	87 53.2	11.6	80 00.4	45.6			
M 06	35 22.7	315 38.7	N18 51.1	19 10.1	N 2 50.9	102 56.0	S22 11.6	95 03.0	S20 45.6	Dubhe	193 46.1	N61 38.7
O 07	50 25.2	330 39.1	51.3	34 11.5	51.3	117 58.8	11.7	110 05.7	45.7	Elnath	278 06.7	N28 37.3
N 08	65 27.7	345 39.5	51.5	49 12.8	51.7	133 01.5	11.7	125 08.3	45.7	Eltanin	90 43.4	N51 29.4
D 09	80 30.1	0 39.9 ..	51.8	64 14.2 ..	52.1	148 04.3 ..	11.8	140 11.0 ..	45.8	Enif	33 42.0	N 9 58.2
A 10	95 32.6	15 40.2	52.0	79 15.5	52.5	163 07.1	11.8	155 13.7	45.8	Fomalhaut	15 18.2	S29 30.7
Y 11	110 35.0	30 40.6	52.3	94 16.9	52.9	178 09.9	11.9	170 16.3	45.9			
12	125 37.5	45 41.0	N18 52.5	109 18.2	N 2 53.3	193 12.7	S22 11.9	185 19.0	S20 45.9	Gacrux	171 55.7	S57 13.8
13	140 40.0	60 41.4	52.7	124 19.6	53.7	208 15.5	12.0	200 21.6	45.9	Gienah	175 47.4	S17 39.3
14	155 42.4	75 41.8	53.0	139 20.9	54.1	223 18.3	12.0	215 24.3	46.0	Hadar	148 41.0	S60 28.4
15	170 44.9	90 42.2 ..	53.2	154 22.3 ..	54.5	238 21.0 ..	12.1	230 26.9 ..	46.0	Hamal	327 55.2	N23 33.4
16	185 47.4	105 42.6	53.4	169 23.6	54.9	253 23.8	12.1	245 29.6	46.1	Kaus Aust.	83 36.9	S34 22.4
17	200 49.8	120 42.9	53.7	184 25.0	55.3	268 26.6	12.2	260 32.2	46.1			
18	215 52.3	135 43.3	N18 53.9	199 26.3	N 2 55.7	283 29.4	S22 12.2	275 34.9	S20 46.1	Kochab	137 19.8	N74 04.7
19	230 54.8	150 43.7	54.2	214 27.7	56.1	298 32.2	12.3	290 37.6	46.2	Markab	13 33.2	N15 18.9
20	245 57.2	165 44.1	54.4	229 29.0	56.5	313 35.0	12.3	305 40.2	46.2	Menkar	314 10.0	N 4 10.1
21	260 59.7	180 44.4 ..	54.6	244 30.4 ..	56.9	328 37.8 ..	12.4	320 42.9 ..	46.3	Menkent	148 01.8	S36 28.3
22	276 02.2	195 44.8	54.9	259 31.8	57.3	343 40.5	12.4	335 45.5	46.3	Miaplacidus	221 39.7	S69 48.1
23	291 04.6	210 45.2	55.1	274 33.1	57.7	358 43.3	12.5	350 48.2	46.3			
28 00	306 07.1	225 45.6	N18 55.3	289 34.5	N 2 58.1	13 46.1	S22 12.6	5 50.8	S20 46.4	Mirfak	308 33.5	N49 55.7
01	321 09.5	240 45.9	55.6	304 35.8	58.5	28 48.9	12.6	20 53.5	46.4	Nunki	75 51.9	S26 16.2
02	336 12.0	255 46.3	55.8	319 37.2	58.9	43 51.7	12.7	35 56.1	46.5	Peacock	53 10.9	S56 40.0
03	351 14.5	270 46.7 ..	56.1	334 38.5 ..	59.3	58 54.5 ..	12.7	50 58.8 ..	46.5	Pollux	243 22.1	N27 58.6
04	6 16.9	285 47.0	56.3	349 39.9	2 59.7	73 57.3	12.8	66 01.4	46.5	Procyon	244 54.9	N 5 10.4
05	21 19.4	300 47.4	56.5	4 41.3	3 00.1	89 00.0	12.8	81 04.1	46.6			
T 06	36 21.9	315 47.7	N18 56.8	19 42.6	N 3 00.5	104 02.8	S22 12.9	96 06.8	S20 46.6	Rasalhague	96 01.6	N12 32.9
U 07	51 24.3	330 48.1	57.0	34 44.0	00.9	119 05.6	12.9	111 09.4	46.7	Regulus	207 38.6	N11 52.2
E 08	66 26.8	345 48.5	57.2	49 45.4	01.3	134 08.4	13.0	126 12.1	46.7	Rigel	281 07.6	S 8 10.7
S 09	81 29.3	0 48.8 ..	57.5	64 46.7 ..	01.7	149 11.2 ..	13.0	141 14.7 ..	46.8	Rigil Kent.	139 45.0	S60 55.3
D 10	96 31.7	15 49.2	57.7	79 48.1	02.1	164 14.0	13.1	156 17.4	46.8	Sabik	102 06.6	S15 44.9
A 11	111 34.2	30 49.5	57.9	94 49.4	02.5	179 16.7	13.1	171 20.0	46.8			
Y 12	126 36.6	45 49.9	N18 58.2	109 50.8	N 3 02.9	194 19.5	S22 13.2	186 22.7	S20 46.9	Schedar	349 34.7	N56 38.7
13	141 39.1	60 50.2	58.4	124 52.2	03.3	209 22.3	13.2	201 25.3	46.9	Shaula	96 14.9	S37 07.1
14	156 41.6	75 50.6	58.6	139 53.5	03.7	224 25.1	13.3	216 28.0	46.9	Sirius	258 29.7	S16 44.6
15	171 44.0	90 50.9 ..	58.9	154 54.9 ..	04.1	239 27.9 ..	13.3	231 30.6 ..	47.0	Spica	158 26.1	S11 16.0
16	186 46.5	105 51.3	59.1	169 56.3	04.5	254 30.7	13.4	246 33.3	47.0	Suhail	222 49.3	S43 30.9
17	201 49.0	120 51.6	59.3	184 57.6	04.8	269 33.4	13.4	261 36.0	47.1			
18	216 51.4	135 52.0	N18 59.6	199 59.0	N 3 05.2	284 36.2	S22 13.5	276 38.6	S20 47.1	Vega	80 35.2	N38 48.4
19	231 53.9	150 52.3	18 59.8	215 00.4	05.6	299 39.0	13.5	291 41.3	47.1	Zuben'ubi	136 59.9	S16 07.5
20	246 56.4	165 52.7	19 00.0	230 01.7	06.0	314 41.8	13.6	306 43.9	47.2		SHA	Mer.Pass.
21	261 58.8	180 53.0 ..	00.3	245 03.1 ..	06.4	329 44.6 ..	13.6	321 46.6 ..	47.2			h m
22	277 01.3	195 53.3	00.5	260 04.5	06.8	344 47.4	13.7	336 49.2	47.3	Venus	280 28.3	8 57
23	292 03.8	210 53.7	00.7	275 05.9	07.2	359 50.1	13.7	351 51.9	47.3	Mars	343 54.1	4 43
	h m									Jupiter	67 31.3	23 05
Mer. Pass.	3 38.9	v 0.4	d 0.2	v 1.4	d 0.4	v 2.8	d 0.1	v 2.7	d 0.0	Saturn	59 39.2	23 37

SUN and MOON

UT	SUN GHA	SUN Dec	MOON GHA	v	Dec	d	HP
d h	° ′	° ′	° ′	′	° ′	′	′
26 00	178 21.7	N19 22.5	110 01.7	10.9	S 0 35.5	14.6	59.5
01	193 21.7	22.0	124 31.6	10.8	0 50.1	14.5	59.5
02	208 21.7	21.4	139 01.4	10.9	1 04.6	14.6	59.5
03	223 21.7 ..	20.8	153 31.3	10.9	1 19.2	14.5	59.5
04	238 21.7	20.3	168 01.2	10.9	1 33.7	14.5	59.5
05	253 21.8	19.7	182 31.1	10.8	1 48.2	14.6	59.5
06	268 21.8	N19 19.2	197 00.9	10.9	S 2 02.8	14.5	59.5
07	283 21.8	18.6	211 30.8	10.9	2 17.3	14.5	59.5
S 08	298 21.8	18.0	226 00.7	10.8	2 31.8	14.4	59.5
U 09	313 21.8 ..	17.5	240 30.5	10.9	2 46.2	14.5	59.4
N 10	328 21.8	16.9	255 00.4	10.8	3 00.7	14.4	59.4
D 11	343 21.8	16.4	269 30.2	10.8	3 15.1	14.5	59.4
A 12	358 21.8	N19 15.8	284 00.0	10.9	S 3 29.6	14.3	59.4
Y 13	13 21.8	15.2	298 29.9	10.8	3 43.9	14.4	59.4
14	28 21.8	14.7	312 59.7	10.8	3 58.3	14.4	59.4
15	43 21.8 ..	14.1	327 29.5	10.8	4 12.7	14.3	59.4
16	58 21.8	13.5	341 59.3	10.8	4 27.0	14.3	59.4
17	73 21.8	13.0	356 29.1	10.7	4 41.3	14.2	59.4
18	88 21.8	N19 12.4	10 58.8	10.8	S 4 55.5	14.3	59.4
19	103 21.8	11.9	25 28.6	10.7	5 09.8	14.2	59.4
20	118 21.8	11.3	39 58.3	10.7	5 24.0	14.1	59.4
21	133 21.8 ..	10.7	54 28.0	10.7	5 38.1	14.2	59.4
22	148 21.8	10.2	68 57.7	10.7	5 52.3	14.1	59.4
23	163 21.8	09.6	83 27.4	10.7	6 06.4	14.0	59.4
27 00	178 21.9	N19 09.0	97 57.1	10.6	S 6 20.4	14.1	59.3
01	193 21.9	08.4	112 26.7	10.6	6 34.5	13.9	59.3
02	208 21.9	07.9	126 56.3	10.6	6 48.4	14.0	59.3
03	223 21.9 ..	07.3	141 25.9	10.6	7 02.4	13.9	59.3
04	238 21.9	06.7	155 55.5	10.6	7 16.3	13.9	59.3
05	253 21.9	06.2	170 25.1	10.5	7 30.2	13.8	59.3
06	268 21.9	N19 05.6	184 54.6	10.5	S 7 44.0	13.7	59.3
07	283 21.9	05.0	199 24.1	10.5	7 57.7	13.8	59.3
M 08	298 21.9	04.4	213 53.6	10.4	8 11.5	13.6	59.3
O 09	313 21.9 ..	03.9	228 23.0	10.4	8 25.1	13.6	59.3
N 10	328 21.9	03.3	242 52.4	10.4	8 38.7	13.6	59.3
D 11	343 22.0	02.7	257 21.8	10.4	8 52.3	13.5	59.3
A 12	358 22.0	N19 02.1	271 51.2	10.3	S 9 05.8	13.5	59.2
Y 13	13 22.0	01.6	286 20.5	10.3	9 19.3	13.4	59.2
14	28 22.0	01.0	300 49.8	10.2	9 32.7	13.3	59.2
15	43 22.0	19 00.4	315 19.0	10.3	9 46.0	13.3	59.2
16	58 22.0	18 59.8	329 48.3	10.2	9 59.3	13.3	59.2
17	73 22.0	59.3	344 17.5	10.1	10 12.6	13.1	59.2
18	88 22.0	N18 58.7	358 46.6	10.1	S10 25.7	13.1	59.2
19	103 22.1	58.1	13 15.7	10.1	10 38.8	13.1	59.2
20	118 22.1	57.5	27 44.8	10.1	10 51.9	13.0	59.2
21	133 22.1 ..	56.9	42 13.9	10.0	11 04.9	12.9	59.2
22	148 22.1	56.4	56 42.9	10.0	11 17.8	12.8	59.2
23	163 22.1	55.8	71 11.9	9.9	11 30.6	12.8	59.1
28 00	178 22.1	N18 55.2	85 40.8	9.9	S11 43.4	12.7	59.1
01	193 22.1	54.6	100 09.7	9.8	11 56.1	12.7	59.1
02	208 22.2	54.0	114 38.5	9.8	12 08.8	12.5	59.1
03	223 22.2 ..	53.5	129 07.3	9.8	12 21.3	12.5	59.1
04	238 22.2	52.9	143 36.1	9.7	12 33.8	12.4	59.1
05	253 22.2	52.3	158 04.8	9.7	12 46.2	12.4	59.1
06	268 22.2	N18 51.7	172 33.5	9.7	S12 58.6	12.3	59.1
07	283 22.2	51.1	187 02.2	9.6	13 10.9	12.1	59.0
T 08	298 22.2	50.5	201 30.8	9.5	13 23.0	12.2	59.0
U 09	313 22.3 ..	49.9	215 59.3	9.5	13 35.2	12.0	59.0
E 10	328 22.3	49.4	230 27.8	9.5	13 47.2	11.9	59.0
S 11	343 22.3	48.8	244 56.3	9.4	13 59.1	11.9	59.0
D 12	358 22.3	N18 48.2	259 24.7	9.4	S14 11.0	11.8	59.0
A 13	13 22.3	47.6	273 53.1	9.3	14 22.8	11.6	59.0
Y 14	28 22.4	47.0	288 21.4	9.3	14 34.4	11.6	59.0
15	43 22.4 ..	46.4	302 49.7	9.2	14 46.0	11.6	58.9
16	58 22.4	45.8	317 17.9	9.2	14 57.6	11.4	58.9
17	73 22.4	45.2	331 46.1	9.2	15 09.0	11.3	58.9
18	88 22.4	N18 44.6	346 14.3	9.0	S15 20.3	11.3	58.9
19	103 22.4	44.1	0 43.3	9.1	15 31.6	11.1	58.9
20	118 22.5	43.5	15 10.4	9.0	15 42.7	11.1	58.9
21	133 22.5 ..	42.9	29 38.4	8.9	15 53.8	10.9	58.9
22	148 22.5	42.3	44 06.3	8.9	16 04.7	10.9	58.9
23	163 22.5	41.7	58 34.2	8.9	S16 15.6	10.7	58.8
	SD 15.8	d 0.6	SD 16.2		16.1		16.1

Twilight, Sunrise and Moonrise

Lat.	Naut.	Civil	Sunrise	Moonrise 26	27	28	29
°	h m	h m	h m	h m	h m	h m	h m
N 72	☐	☐	☐	11 48	14 04	16 40	■
N 70	////	////	00 17	11 43	13 48	16 03	19 06
68	////	////	01 50	11 39	13 35	15 37	17 51
66	////	////	02 27	11 35	13 25	15 17	17 14
64	////	01 08	02 54	11 32	13 16	15 01	16 48
62	////	01 56	03 14	11 30	13 08	14 48	16 28
60	////	02 25	03 30	11 28	13 02	14 37	16 12
N 58	01 02	02 47	03 44	11 26	12 57	14 28	15 58
56	01 46	03 05	03 55	11 24	12 52	14 20	15 46
54	02 13	03 20	04 06	11 22	12 47	14 12	15 36
52	02 34	03 32	04 15	11 21	12 43	14 06	15 27
50	02 50	03 43	04 23	11 20	12 40	14 00	15 19
45	03 22	04 06	04 40	11 17	12 32	13 47	15 02
N 40	03 45	04 23	04 54	11 14	12 25	13 37	14 48
35	04 04	04 38	05 06	11 12	12 20	13 28	14 36
30	04 19	04 50	05 16	11 11	12 15	13 20	14 25
20	04 42	05 10	05 34	11 08	12 07	13 07	14 08
N 10	05 00	05 27	05 49	11 05	12 00	12 55	13 52
0	05 16	05 41	06 03	11 03	11 53	12 45	13 38
S 10	05 29	05 55	06 17	11 00	11 46	12 34	13 24
20	05 42	06 08	06 32	10 58	11 39	12 23	13 09
30	05 54	06 23	06 48	10 55	11 31	12 10	12 52
35	06 01	06 31	06 58	10 53	11 27	12 02	12 42
40	06 07	06 40	07 09	10 52	11 22	11 54	12 30
45	06 15	06 50	07 22	10 50	11 16	11 44	12 17
S 50	06 23	07 02	07 38	10 47	11 09	11 33	12 01
52	06 26	07 08	07 45	10 46	11 06	11 27	11 54
54	06 30	07 13	07 53	10 45	11 02	11 21	11 45
56	06 34	07 20	08 03	10 44	10 58	11 15	11 36
58	06 38	07 27	08 13	10 42	10 54	11 08	11 26
S 60	06 43	07 35	08 25	10 41	10 49	10 59	11 14

Sunset, Twilight and Moonset

Lat.	Sunset	Civil	Naut.	Moonset 26	27	28	29
°	h m	h m	h m	h m	h m	h m	h m
N 72	☐	☐	☐	22 08	21 39	20 53	■
N 70	23 29	////	////	22 16	21 58	21 32	20 22
68	22 18	////	////	22 23	22 13	21 59	21 37
66	21 42	////	////	22 29	22 25	22 22	22 15
64	21 17	22 58	////	22 34	22 35	22 37	22 42
62	20 57	22 13	////	22 38	22 44	22 51	23 03
60	20 41	21 45	////	22 42	22 51	23 03	23 20
N 58	20 28	21 24	23 05	22 45	22 58	23 13	23 34
56	20 16	21 06	22 24	22 48	23 04	23 22	23 46
54	20 06	20 52	21 58	22 51	23 09	23 30	23 57
52	19 57	20 40	21 38	22 54	23 14	23 38	24 07
50	19 49	20 29	21 21	22 56	23 18	23 44	24 16
45	19 32	20 06	20 50	23 01	23 28	23 58	24 34
N 40	19 18	19 49	20 27	23 05	23 36	24 10	00 10
35	19 07	19 35	20 09	23 08	23 43	24 20	00 20
30	18 56	19 23	19 54	23 12	23 49	24 29	00 29
20	18 39	19 03	19 31	23 17	23 59	24 44	00 44
N 10	18 24	18 46	19 12	23 22	24 09	00 09	00 57
0	18 10	18 32	18 57	23 26	24 17	00 17	01 10
S 10	17 56	18 18	18 44	23 31	24 26	00 26	01 22
20	17 42	18 05	18 32	23 36	24 35	00 35	01 36
30	17 25	17 50	18 19	23 41	24 46	00 46	01 51
35	17 15	17 42	18 13	23 45	24 52	00 52	02 00
40	17 04	17 33	18 06	23 48	24 59	00 59	02 11
45	16 51	17 23	17 59	23 52	25 08	01 08	02 23
S 50	16 36	17 11	17 51	23 58	25 18	01 18	02 37
52	16 28	17 06	17 47	24 00	00 00	01 22	02 44
54	16 20	17 00	17 44	24 02	00 02	01 27	02 52
56	16 11	16 54	17 40	24 05	00 05	01 33	03 01
58	16 01	16 47	17 35	24 08	00 08	01 40	03 11
S 60	15 49	16 38	17 31	24 12	00 12	01 47	03 22

SUN and MOON

Day	SUN Eqn. of Time 00h	12h	Mer. Pass.	MOON Mer. Pass. Upper	Lower	Age	Phase
d	m s	m s	h m	h m	h m	d	%
26	06 33	06 33	12 07	17 15	04 50	06	38
27	06 33	06 32	12 07	18 05	05 40	07	50
28	06 32	06 31	12 07	18 57	06 31	08	61

UT	ARIES	VENUS −4·6		MARS −1·1		JUPITER −2·7		SATURN +0·1		STARS		
	GHA	GHA	Dec	GHA	Dec	GHA	Dec	GHA	Dec	Name	SHA	Dec
d h	° ′	° ′	° ′	° ′	° ′	° ′	° ′	° ′	° ′		° ′	° ′
29 00	307 06.2	225 54.0	N19 01.0	290 07.2	N 3 07.6	14 52.9	S22 13.8	6 54.5	S20 47.3	Acamar	315 14.6	S40 13.2
01	322 08.7	240 54.3	01.2	305 08.6	08.0	29 55.7	13.8	21 57.2	47.4	Achernar	335 22.9	S57 07.7
02	337 11.1	255 54.7	01.4	320 10.0	08.4	44 58.5	13.9	36 59.8	47.4	Acrux	173 04.2	S63 12.9
03	352 13.6	270 55.0 ..	01.7	335 11.4 ..	08.8	60 01.3 ..	13.9	52 02.5 ..	47.4	Adhara	255 09.0	S28 59.9
04	7 16.1	285 55.3	01.9	350 12.7	09.2	75 04.1	14.0	67 05.1	47.5	Aldebaran	290 43.9	N16 33.1
05	22 18.5	300 55.7	02.1	5 14.1	09.6	90 06.8	14.0	82 07.8	47.5			
06	37 21.0	315 56.0	N19 02.4	20 15.5	N 3 10.0	105 09.6	S22 14.1	97 10.5	S20 47.6	Alioth	166 16.5	N55 51.3
W 07	52 23.5	330 56.3	02.6	35 16.9	10.3	120 12.4	14.1	112 13.1	47.6	Alkaid	152 55.0	N49 13.1
E 08	67 25.9	345 56.6	02.8	50 18.2	10.7	135 15.2	14.2	127 15.8	47.6	Alnair	27 37.1	S46 51.6
D 09	82 28.4	0 57.0 ..	03.1	65 19.6 ..	11.1	150 18.0 ..	14.2	142 18.4 ..	47.7	Alnilam	275 41.6	S 1 11.3
N 10	97 30.9	15 57.3	03.3	80 21.0	11.5	165 20.7	14.2	157 21.1	47.7	Alphard	217 51.6	S 8 44.8
E 11	112 33.3	30 57.6	03.5	95 22.4	11.9	180 23.5	14.3	172 23.7	47.8			
S 12	127 35.8	45 57.9	N19 03.7	110 23.7	N 3 12.3	195 26.3	S22 14.3	187 26.4	S20 47.8	Alphecca	126 06.7	N26 39.1
D 13	142 38.3	60 58.2	04.0	125 25.1	12.7	210 29.1	14.4	202 29.0	47.8	Alpheratz	357 38.2	N29 12.1
A 14	157 40.7	75 58.5	04.2	140 26.5	13.1	225 31.9	14.4	217 31.7	47.9	Altair	62 03.1	N 8 55.5
Y 15	172 43.2	90 58.9 ..	04.4	155 27.9 ..	13.5	240 34.6 ..	14.5	232 34.3 ..	47.9	Ankaa	353 10.6	S42 11.5
16	187 45.6	105 59.2	04.7	170 29.3	13.9	255 37.4	14.5	247 37.0	48.0	Antares	112 20.0	S26 28.6
17	202 48.1	120 59.5	04.9	185 30.7	14.2	270 40.2	14.6	262 39.6	48.0			
18	217 50.6	135 59.8	N19 05.1	200 32.0	N 3 14.6	285 43.0	S22 14.6	277 42.3	S20 48.0	Arcturus	145 51.2	N19 04.8
19	232 53.0	151 00.1	05.3	215 33.4	15.0	300 45.8	14.7	292 44.9	48.1	Atria	107 17.0	S69 03.9
20	247 55.5	166 00.4	05.6	230 34.8	15.4	315 48.5	14.7	307 47.6	48.1	Avior	234 16.7	S59 34.5
21	262 58.0	181 00.7 ..	05.8	245 36.2 ..	15.8	330 51.3 ..	14.8	322 50.3 ..	48.2	Bellatrix	278 27.0	N 6 22.0
22	278 00.4	196 01.0	06.0	260 37.6	16.2	345 54.1	14.8	337 52.9	48.2	Betelgeuse	270 56.2	N 7 24.6
23	293 02.9	211 01.3	06.3	275 39.0	16.6	0 56.9	14.9	352 55.6	48.2			
30 00	308 05.4	226 01.6	N19 06.5	290 40.4	N 3 17.0	15 59.7	S22 14.9	7 58.2	S20 48.3	Canopus	263 54.4	S52 42.3
01	323 07.8	241 01.9	06.7	305 41.7	17.3	31 02.4	15.0	23 00.9	48.3	Capella	280 27.5	N46 00.9
02	338 10.3	256 02.2	06.9	320 43.1	17.7	46 05.2	15.0	38 03.5	48.4	Deneb	49 27.7	N45 21.2
03	353 12.8	271 02.5 ..	07.2	335 44.5 ..	18.1	61 08.0 ..	15.1	53 06.2 ..	48.4	Denebola	182 28.8	N14 27.7
04	8 15.2	286 02.8	07.4	350 45.9	18.5	76 10.8	15.1	68 08.8	48.4	Diphda	348 50.8	S17 52.4
05	23 17.7	301 03.1	07.6	5 47.3	18.9	91 13.5	15.2	83 11.5	48.5			
06	38 20.1	316 03.4	N19 07.8	20 48.7	N 3 19.3	106 16.3	S22 15.2	98 14.1	S20 48.5	Dubhe	193 46.1	N61 38.7
T 07	53 22.6	331 03.7	08.1	35 50.1	19.7	121 19.1	15.3	113 16.8	48.6	Elnath	278 06.7	N28 37.3
H 08	68 25.1	346 04.0	08.3	50 51.5	20.0	136 21.9	15.3	128 19.4	48.6	Eltanin	90 43.4	N51 29.4
U 09	83 27.5	1 04.3 ..	08.5	65 52.9 ..	20.4	151 24.7 ..	15.4	143 22.1 ..	48.6	Enif	33 42.0	N 9 58.2
R 10	98 30.0	16 04.5	08.7	80 54.3	20.8	166 27.4	15.4	158 24.7	48.7	Fomalhaut	15 18.2	S29 30.7
S 11	113 32.5	31 04.8	09.0	95 55.7	21.2	181 30.2	15.5	173 27.4	48.7			
D 12	128 34.9	46 05.1	N19 09.2	110 57.0	N 3 21.6	196 33.0	S22 15.5	188 30.1	S20 48.8	Gacrux	171 55.8	S57 13.8
A 13	143 37.4	61 05.4	09.4	125 58.4	22.0	211 35.8	15.6	203 32.7	48.8	Gienah	175 47.4	S17 39.3
Y 14	158 39.9	76 05.7	09.6	140 59.8	22.3	226 38.5	15.6	218 35.4	48.8	Hadar	148 41.0	S60 28.4
15	173 42.3	91 06.0 ..	09.9	156 01.2 ..	22.7	241 41.3 ..	15.7	233 38.0 ..	48.9	Hamal	327 55.2	N23 33.4
16	188 44.8	106 06.2	10.1	171 02.6	23.1	256 44.1	15.7	248 40.7	48.9	Kaus Aust.	83 36.9	S34 22.4
17	203 47.2	121 06.5	10.3	186 04.0	23.5	271 46.9	15.8	263 43.3	49.0			
18	218 49.7	136 06.8	N19 10.5	201 05.4	N 3 23.9	286 49.6	S22 15.8	278 46.0	S20 49.0	Kochab	137 19.8	N74 04.7
19	233 52.2	151 07.1	10.8	216 06.8	24.2	301 52.4	15.9	293 48.6	49.0	Markab	13 33.2	N15 18.9
20	248 54.6	166 07.3	11.0	231 08.2	24.6	316 55.2	15.9	308 51.3	49.1	Menkar	314 09.9	N 4 10.1
21	263 57.1	181 07.6 ..	11.2	246 09.6 ..	25.0	331 58.0 ..	16.0	323 53.9 ..	49.1	Menkent	148 01.8	S36 28.3
22	278 59.6	196 07.9	11.4	261 11.0	25.4	347 00.7	16.0	338 56.6	49.1	Miaplacidus	221 39.7	S69 48.1
23	294 02.0	211 08.2	11.7	276 12.4	25.8	2 03.5	16.1	353 59.2	49.2			
31 00	309 04.5	226 08.4	N19 11.9	291 13.8	N 3 26.1	17 06.3	S22 16.1	9 01.9	S20 49.2	Mirfak	308 33.4	N49 55.7
01	324 07.0	241 08.7	12.1	306 15.2	26.5	32 09.1	16.1	24 04.5	49.3	Nunki	75 51.9	S26 16.2
02	339 09.4	256 09.0	12.3	321 16.6	26.9	47 11.8	16.2	39 07.2	49.3	Peacock	53 10.8	S56 40.1
03	354 11.9	271 09.2 ..	12.5	336 18.0 ..	27.3	62 14.6 ..	16.2	54 09.8 ..	49.3	Pollux	243 22.1	N27 58.6
04	9 14.4	286 09.5	12.8	351 19.5	27.7	77 17.4	16.3	69 12.5	49.4	Procyon	244 54.9	N 5 10.4
05	24 16.8	301 09.7	13.0	6 20.9	28.0	92 20.2	16.3	84 15.1	49.4			
06	39 19.3	316 10.0	N19 13.2	21 22.3	N 3 28.4	107 22.9	S22 16.4	99 17.8	S20 49.5	Rasalhague	96 01.6	N12 32.9
07	54 21.7	331 10.3	13.4	36 23.7	28.8	122 25.7	16.4	114 20.4	49.5	Regulus	207 38.6	N11 52.2
08	69 24.2	346 10.5	13.6	51 25.1	29.2	137 28.5	16.5	129 23.1	49.5	Rigel	281 07.5	S 8 10.7
F 09	84 26.7	1 10.8 ..	13.9	66 26.5 ..	29.6	152 31.3 ..	16.5	144 25.8 ..	49.6	Rigil Kent.	139 45.1	S60 55.3
R 10	99 29.1	16 11.0	14.1	81 27.9	29.9	167 34.0	16.6	159 28.4	49.6	Sabik	102 06.7	S15 44.9
I 11	114 31.6	31 11.3	14.3	96 29.3	30.3	182 36.8	16.6	174 31.1	49.7			
D 12	129 34.1	46 11.5	N19 14.5	111 30.7	N 3 30.7	197 39.6	S22 16.7	189 33.7	S20 49.7	Schedar	349 34.7	N56 38.7
A 13	144 36.5	61 11.8	14.7	126 32.1	31.1	212 42.3	16.7	204 36.4	49.7	Shaula	96 14.9	S37 07.1
Y 14	159 39.0	76 12.0	14.9	141 33.5	31.4	227 45.1	16.8	219 39.0	49.8	Sirius	258 29.7	S16 44.6
15	174 41.5	91 12.3 ..	15.2	156 35.0 ..	31.8	242 47.9 ..	16.8	234 41.7 ..	49.8	Spica	158 26.1	S11 16.0
16	189 43.9	106 12.5	15.4	171 36.4	32.2	257 50.7	16.9	249 44.3	49.9	Suhail	222 49.3	S43 30.9
17	204 46.4	121 12.8	15.6	186 37.8	32.6	272 53.4	16.9	264 47.0	49.9			
18	219 48.9	136 13.0	N19 15.8	201 39.2	N 3 32.9	287 56.2	S22 17.0	279 49.6	S20 49.9	Vega	80 35.2	N38 48.4
19	234 51.3	151 13.3	16.0	216 40.6	33.3	302 59.0	17.0	294 52.3	50.0	Zuben'ubi	136 59.9	S16 07.5
20	249 53.8	166 13.5	16.2	231 42.0	33.7	318 01.8	17.1	309 54.9	50.0			
21	264 56.2	181 13.7 ..	16.5	246 43.4 ..	34.1	333 04.5 ..	17.1	324 57.6 ..	50.0		SHA	Mer.Pass.
22	279 58.7	196 14.0	16.7	261 44.9	34.4	348 07.3	17.1	340 00.2	50.1	Venus	277 56.3	h m 8 56
23	295 01.2	211 14.2	16.9	276 46.3	34.8	3 10.1	17.2	355 02.9	50.1	Mars	342 35.0	4 37
	h m									Jupiter	67 54.3	22 52
Mer. Pass. 3 27.1		v 0.3	d 0.2	v 1.4	d 0.4	v 2.8	d 0.0	v 2.7	d 0.0	Saturn	59 52.9	23 24

UT	SUN GHA	SUN Dec	MOON GHA	v	Dec	d	HP
	° ′	° ′	° ′	′	° ′	′	′
29 00	178 22.6	N18 41.1	73 02.1	8.7	S16 26.3	10.7	58.8
01	193 22.6	40.5	87 29.8	8.8	16 37.0	10.6	58.8
02	208 22.6	39.9	101 57.6	8.7	16 47.6	10.4	58.8
03	223 22.6 ..	39.3	116 25.3	8.6	16 58.0	10.4	58.8
04	238 22.6	38.7	130 52.9	8.6	17 08.4	10.2	58.8
05	253 22.7	38.1	145 20.5	8.6	17 18.6	10.2	58.8
06	268 22.7	N18 37.5	159 48.1	8.5	S17 28.8	10.0	58.7
W 07	283 22.7	36.9	174 15.6	8.4	17 38.8	10.0	58.7
E 08	298 22.7	36.3	188 43.0	8.4	17 48.8	9.8	58.7
D 09	313 22.8 ..	35.7	203 10.4	8.4	17 58.6	9.7	58.7
N 10	328 22.8	35.1	217 37.8	8.3	18 08.3	9.6	58.7
E 11	343 22.8	34.5	232 05.1	8.2	18 17.9	9.5	58.7
S 12	358 22.8	N18 33.9	246 32.3	8.2	S18 27.4	9.4	58.7
D 13	13 22.8	33.3	260 59.5	8.2	18 36.8	9.3	58.6
A 14	28 22.9	32.7	275 26.7	8.1	18 46.1	9.1	58.6
Y 15	43 22.9 ..	32.1	289 53.8	8.0	18 55.2	9.1	58.6
16	58 22.9	31.5	304 20.8	8.0	19 04.3	8.9	58.6
17	73 22.9	30.9	318 47.8	8.0	19 13.2	8.8	58.6
18	88 23.0	N18 30.3	333 14.8	7.9	S19 22.0	8.7	58.6
19	103 23.0	29.7	347 41.7	7.9	19 30.7	8.5	58.6
20	118 23.0	29.1	2 08.6	7.8	19 39.2	8.5	58.5
21	133 23.1 ..	28.5	16 35.4	7.8	19 47.7	8.3	58.5
22	148 23.1	27.9	31 02.2	7.7	19 56.0	8.2	58.5
23	163 23.1	27.3	45 28.9	7.7	20 04.2	8.1	58.5
30 00	178 23.1	N18 26.7	59 55.6	7.6	S20 12.3	7.9	58.5
01	193 23.2	26.1	74 22.2	7.6	20 20.2	7.8	58.5
02	208 23.2	25.4	88 48.8	7.6	20 28.0	7.7	58.4
03	223 23.2 ..	24.8	103 15.4	7.5	20 35.7	7.6	58.4
04	238 23.2	24.2	117 41.9	7.5	20 43.3	7.4	58.4
05	253 23.3	23.6	132 08.4	7.4	20 50.7	7.3	58.4
06	268 23.3	N18 23.0	146 34.8	7.4	S20 58.0	7.2	58.4
T 07	283 23.3	22.4	161 01.2	7.3	21 05.2	7.1	58.4
H 08	298 23.4	21.8	175 27.5	7.3	21 12.3	6.9	58.3
U 09	313 23.4 ..	21.2	189 53.8	7.3	21 19.2	6.8	58.3
R 10	328 23.4	20.6	204 20.1	7.2	21 26.0	6.6	58.3
S 11	343 23.5	19.9	218 46.3	7.2	21 32.6	6.6	58.3
D 12	358 23.5	N18 19.3	233 12.5	7.2	S21 39.2	6.3	58.3
A 13	13 23.5	18.7	247 38.7	7.1	21 45.5	6.3	58.3
Y 14	28 23.5	18.1	262 04.8	7.1	21 51.8	6.1	58.2
15	43 23.6 ..	17.5	276 30.9	7.1	21 57.9	6.0	58.2
16	58 23.6	16.9	290 57.0	7.0	22 03.9	5.8	58.2
17	73 23.6	16.3	305 23.0	7.0	22 09.7	5.7	58.2
18	88 23.7	N18 15.6	319 49.0	6.9	S22 15.4	5.6	58.2
19	103 23.7	15.0	334 14.9	7.0	22 21.0	5.4	58.2
20	118 23.7	14.4	348 40.9	6.9	22 26.4	5.3	58.1
21	133 23.8 ..	13.8	3 06.8	6.9	22 31.7	5.1	58.1
22	148 23.8	13.2	17 32.7	6.8	22 36.8	5.0	58.1
23	163 23.8	12.6	31 58.5	6.9	22 41.8	4.9	58.1
31 00	178 23.9	N18 11.9	46 24.4	6.8	S22 46.7	4.7	58.1
01	193 23.9	11.3	60 50.2	6.8	22 51.4	4.6	58.1
02	208 23.9	10.7	75 16.0	6.7	22 56.0	4.4	58.0
03	223 24.0 ..	10.1	89 41.7	6.8	23 00.4	4.3	58.0
04	238 24.0	09.5	104 07.5	6.7	23 04.7	4.1	58.0
05	253 24.0	08.8	118 33.2	6.7	23 08.8	4.0	58.0
06	268 24.1	N18 08.2	132 58.9	6.7	S23 12.8	3.9	58.0
F 07	283 24.1	07.6	147 24.6	6.7	23 16.7	3.7	57.9
R 08	298 24.2	07.0	161 50.3	6.7	23 20.4	3.5	57.9
I 09	313 24.2 ..	06.3	176 16.0	6.7	23 23.9	3.4	57.9
D 10	328 24.2	05.7	190 41.7	6.6	23 27.3	3.3	57.9
A 11	343 24.3	05.1	205 07.3	6.7	23 30.6	3.1	57.9
Y 12	358 24.3	N18 04.5	219 33.0	6.6	S23 33.7	3.0	57.8
13	13 24.3	03.8	233 58.6	6.6	23 36.7	2.8	57.8
14	28 24.4	03.2	248 24.2	6.6	23 39.5	2.7	57.8
15	43 24.4 ..	02.6	262 49.8	6.7	23 42.2	2.6	57.8
16	58 24.5	02.0	277 15.5	6.6	23 44.8	2.4	57.8
17	73 24.5	01.3	291 41.1	6.6	23 47.2	2.2	57.8
18	88 24.5	N18 00.7	306 06.7	6.6	S23 49.4	2.1	57.7
19	103 24.6	18 00.1	320 32.3	6.7	23 51.5	1.9	57.7
20	118 24.6	17 59.4	334 58.0	6.6	23 53.4	1.8	57.7
21	133 24.6 ..	58.8	349 23.6	6.6	23 55.2	1.7	57.7
22	148 24.7	58.2	3 49.2	6.7	23 56.9	1.5	57.7
23	163 24.7	57.5	18 14.9	6.6	S23 58.4	1.4	57.6
	SD 15.8	d 0.6	SD 16.0		15.9		15.8

Twilight / Sunrise / Moonrise

Lat.	Naut.	Civil	Sunrise	Moonrise 29	30	31	1
°	h m	h m	h m	h m	h m	h m	h m
N 72	—	—	—	■	■	■	■
N 70	////	////	01 11	19 06	■	■	■
68	////	////	02 07	17 51	■	■	■
66	////	////	02 39	17 14	19 18	■	22 33
64	////	01 30	03 03	16 48	18 34	20 05	21 02
62	////	02 09	03 22	16 28	18 04	19 26	20 24
60	////	02 35	03 37	16 12	17 42	19 00	19 57
N 58	01 22	02 55	03 50	15 58	17 24	18 39	19 37
56	01 57	03 12	04 01	15 46	17 09	18 21	19 19
54	02 22	03 26	04 11	15 36	16 56	18 07	19 05
52	02 41	03 38	04 19	15 27	16 45	17 54	18 52
50	02 56	03 48	04 27	15 19	16 34	17 43	18 41
45	03 26	04 09	04 43	15 02	16 13	17 20	18 17
N 40	03 49	04 26	04 57	14 48	15 56	17 01	17 59
35	04 06	04 40	05 08	14 36	15 42	16 45	17 43
30	04 21	04 52	05 18	14 25	15 30	16 32	17 29
20	04 43	05 11	05 35	14 08	15 09	16 09	17 06
N 10	05 01	05 27	05 49	13 52	14 50	15 49	16 46
0	05 16	05 41	06 03	13 38	14 34	15 30	16 27
S 10	05 29	05 54	06 16	13 24	14 17	15 12	16 09
20	05 41	06 07	06 30	13 09	13 59	14 52	15 49
30	05 52	06 21	06 47	12 52	13 38	14 30	15 25
35	05 58	06 29	06 56	12 42	13 26	14 16	15 12
40	06 05	06 37	07 06	12 30	13 12	14 01	14 56
45	06 12	06 47	07 19	12 17	12 56	13 43	14 38
S 50	06 19	06 58	07 34	12 01	12 36	13 20	14 14
52	06 22	07 03	07 41	11 54	12 27	13 09	14 03
54	06 26	07 09	07 49	11 45	12 16	12 57	13 50
56	06 30	07 15	07 57	11 36	12 04	12 43	13 36
58	06 34	07 22	08 07	11 26	11 51	12 27	13 19
S 60	06 38	07 30	08 18	11 14	11 35	12 08	12 58

Sunset / Twilight / Moonset

Lat.	Sunset	Civil	Naut.	Moonset 29	30	31	1
°	h m	h m	h m	h m	h m	h m	h m
N 72	—	—	—	■	■	■	■
N 70	22 53	////	////	20 22	■	■	■
68	22 02	////	////	21 37	■	■	■
66	21 30	////	////	22 15	22 08	■	22 52
64	21 07	22 37	////	22 42	22 53	23 21	24 23
62	20 49	22 01	////	23 03	23 23	24 00	00 00
60	20 34	21 35	////	23 20	23 46	24 27	00 27
N 58	20 22	21 16	22 46	23 34	24 04	00 04	00 48
56	20 11	20 59	22 13	23 46	24 20	00 20	01 05
54	20 01	20 46	21 49	23 57	24 33	00 33	01 20
52	19 53	20 34	21 30	24 07	00 07	00 44	01 33
50	19 45	20 24	21 15	24 16	00 16	00 55	01 44
45	19 29	20 03	20 45	24 34	00 34	01 17	02 07
N 40	19 15	19 46	20 23	00 10	00 49	01 34	02 26
35	19 04	19 32	20 06	00 20	01 02	01 49	02 42
30	18 54	19 20	19 52	00 29	01 13	02 02	02 56
20	18 38	19 01	19 29	00 44	01 32	02 24	03 19
N 10	18 23	18 46	19 12	00 57	01 49	02 43	03 39
0	18 10	18 32	18 57	01 10	02 04	03 01	03 58
S 10	17 57	18 19	18 44	01 22	02 20	03 19	04 17
20	17 43	18 06	18 32	01 36	02 37	03 38	04 37
30	17 27	17 52	18 21	01 51	02 56	04 00	05 00
35	17 17	17 44	18 15	02 00	03 08	04 13	05 13
40	17 07	17 36	18 08	02 11	03 21	04 28	05 29
45	16 55	17 26	18 02	02 23	03 36	04 45	05 48
S 50	16 40	17 15	17 54	02 37	03 55	05 08	06 11
52	16 33	17 10	17 51	02 44	04 04	05 18	06 22
54	16 25	17 04	17 48	02 52	04 14	05 30	06 35
56	16 16	16 58	17 44	03 01	04 26	05 44	06 50
58	16 06	16 52	17 40	03 11	04 39	06 00	07 07
S 60	15 55	16 44	17 36	03 22	04 55	06 19	07 28

SUN / MOON

Day	Eqn. of Time 00h	12h	Mer. Pass.	Mer. Pass. Upper	Lower	Age	Phase
d	m s	m s	h m	h m	h m	d	%
29	06 30	06 29	12 06	19 51	07 24	09	72
30	06 28	06 26	12 06	20 47	08 19	10	81
31	06 25	06 23	12 06	21 44	09 16	11	89

UT	ARIES GHA	VENUS −4.5 GHA	Dec	MARS −1.1 GHA	Dec	JUPITER −2.7 GHA	Dec	SATURN +0.2 GHA	Dec	STARS Name	SHA	Dec
d h	° ′	° ′	° ′	° ′	° ′	° ′	° ′	° ′	° ′		° ′	° ′
1 00	310 03.6	226 14.4	N19 17.1	291 47.7	N 3 35.2	18 12.8	S22 17.2	10 05.5	S20 50.2	Acamar	315 14.6	S40 13.2
01	325 06.1	241 14.7	17.3	306 49.1	35.5	33 15.6	17.3	25 08.2	50.2	Achernar	335 22.9	S57 07.7
02	340 08.6	256 14.9	17.5	321 50.5	35.9	48 18.4	17.3	40 10.8	50.2	Acrux	173 04.2	S63 12.9
03	355 11.0	271 15.1 . .	17.8	336 52.0 . .	36.3	63 21.1 . .	17.4	55 13.5 . .	50.3	Adhara	255 09.0	S28 59.9
04	10 13.5	286 15.4	18.0	351 53.4	36.7	78 23.9	17.4	70 16.1	50.3	Aldebaran	290 43.9	N16 32.1
05	25 16.0	301 15.6	18.2	6 54.8	37.0	93 26.7	17.5	85 18.8	50.4			
06	40 18.4	316 15.8	N19 18.4	21 56.2	N 3 37.4	108 29.5	S22 17.5	100 21.4	S20 50.4	Alioth	166 16.5	N55 51.3
07	55 20.9	331 16.1	18.6	36 57.6	37.8	123 32.2	17.6	115 24.1	50.4	Alkaid	152 55.0	N49 13.1
S 08	70 23.4	346 16.3	18.8	51 59.1	38.1	138 35.0	17.6	130 26.7	50.5	Alnair	27 37.0	S46 51.6
A 09	85 25.8	1 16.5 . .	19.0	67 00.5 . .	38.5	153 37.8 . .	17.7	145 29.4 . .	50.5	Alnilam	275 41.6	S 1 11.3
T 10	100 28.3	16 16.7	19.2	82 01.9	38.9	168 40.5	17.7	160 32.0	50.6	Alphard	217 51.6	S 8 44.8
U 11	115 30.7	31 17.0	19.5	97 03.3	39.3	183 43.3	17.8	175 34.7	50.6			
R 12	130 33.2	46 17.2	N19 19.7	112 04.8	N 3 39.6	198 46.1	S22 17.8	190 37.3	S20 50.6	Alphecca	126 06.7	N26 39.1
D 13	145 35.7	61 17.4	19.9	127 06.2	40.0	213 48.8	17.9	205 40.0	50.7	Alpheratz	357 38.2	N29 12.1
A 14	160 38.1	76 17.6	20.1	142 07.6	40.4	228 51.6	17.9	220 42.6	50.7	Altair	62 03.1	N 8 55.5
Y 15	175 40.6	91 17.8 . .	20.3	157 09.0 . .	40.7	243 54.4 . .	17.9	235 45.3 . .	50.7	Ankaa	353 10.5	S42 11.5
16	190 43.1	106 18.0	20.5	172 10.5	41.1	258 57.1	18.0	250 47.9	50.8	Antares	112 20.0	S26 28.6
17	205 45.5	121 18.3	20.7	187 11.9	41.5	273 59.9	18.0	265 50.6	50.8			
18	220 48.0	136 18.5	N19 20.9	202 13.3	N 3 41.8	289 02.7	S22 18.1	280 53.2	S20 50.9	Arcturus	145 51.2	N19 04.8
19	235 50.5	151 18.7	21.1	217 14.8	42.2	304 05.5	18.1	295 55.9	50.9	Atria	107 17.1	S69 03.9
20	250 52.9	166 18.9	21.3	232 16.2	42.6	319 08.2	18.2	310 58.5	50.9	Avior	234 16.7	S59 34.4
21	265 55.4	181 19.1 . .	21.6	247 17.6 . .	42.9	334 11.0 . .	18.2	326 01.2 . .	51.0	Bellatrix	278 26.9	N 6 22.1
22	280 57.9	196 19.3	21.8	262 19.1	43.3	349 13.8	18.3	341 03.8	51.0	Betelgeuse	270 56.2	N 7 24.6
23	296 00.3	211 19.5	22.0	277 20.5	43.7	4 16.5	18.3	356 06.5	51.1			
2 00	311 02.8	226 19.7	N19 22.2	292 21.9	N 3 44.0	19 19.3	S22 18.4	11 09.1	S20 51.1	Canopus	263 54.4	S52 42.2
01	326 05.2	241 19.9	22.4	307 23.4	44.4	34 22.1	18.4	26 11.8	51.1	Capella	280 27.5	N46 00.9
02	341 07.7	256 20.1	22.6	322 24.8	44.8	49 24.8	18.5	41 14.4	51.2	Deneb	49 27.7	N45 21.3
03	356 10.2	271 20.3 . .	22.8	337 26.2 . .	45.1	64 27.6 . .	18.5	56 17.1 . .	51.2	Denebola	182 28.8	N14 27.7
04	11 12.6	286 20.5	23.0	352 27.7	45.5	79 30.4	18.6	71 19.7	51.3	Diphda	348 50.7	S17 52.4
05	26 15.1	301 20.7	23.2	7 29.1	45.8	94 33.1	18.6	86 22.4	51.3			
06	41 17.6	316 20.9	N19 23.4	22 30.6	N 3 46.2	109 35.9	S22 18.6	101 25.0	S20 51.3	Dubhe	193 46.1	N61 38.7
07	56 20.0	331 21.1	23.6	37 32.0	46.6	124 38.6	18.7	116 27.7	51.4	Elnath	278 06.6	N28 37.3
08	71 22.5	346 21.3	23.8	52 33.4	46.9	139 41.4	18.7	131 30.3	51.4	Eltanin	90 43.4	N51 29.4
S 09	86 25.0	1 21.5 . .	24.0	67 34.9 . .	47.3	154 44.2 . .	18.8	146 33.0 . .	51.4	Enif	33 42.0	N 9 58.2
U 10	101 27.4	16 21.7	24.2	82 36.3	47.7	169 46.9	18.8	161 35.6	51.5	Fomalhaut	15 18.2	S29 30.7
N 11	116 29.9	31 21.9	24.4	97 37.8	48.0	184 49.7	18.9	176 38.3	51.5			
D 12	131 32.3	46 22.1	N19 24.6	112 39.2	N 3 48.4	199 52.5	S22 18.9	191 40.9	S20 51.6	Gacrux	171 55.8	S57 13.8
A 13	146 34.8	61 22.3	24.8	127 40.6	48.8	214 55.2	19.0	206 43.6	51.6	Gienah	175 47.4	S17 39.3
Y 14	161 37.3	76 22.4	25.1	142 42.1	49.1	229 58.0	19.0	221 46.2	51.6	Hadar	148 41.0	S60 28.4
15	176 39.7	91 22.6 . .	25.3	157 43.5 . .	49.5	245 00.8 . .	19.1	236 48.9 . .	51.7	Hamal	327 55.1	N23 33.4
16	191 42.2	106 22.8	25.5	172 45.0	49.8	260 03.5	19.1	251 51.5	51.7	Kaus Aust.	83 36.9	S34 22.4
17	206 44.7	121 23.0	25.7	187 46.4	50.2	275 06.3	19.1	266 54.2	51.8			
18	221 47.1	136 23.2	N19 25.9	202 47.9	N 3 50.6	290 09.1	S22 19.2	281 56.8	S20 51.8	Kochab	137 19.9	N74 04.7
19	236 49.6	151 23.4	26.1	217 49.3	50.9	305 11.8	19.2	296 59.5	51.8	Markab	13 33.2	N15 18.9
20	251 52.1	166 23.5	26.3	232 50.8	51.3	320 14.6	19.3	312 02.1	51.9	Menkar	314 09.9	N 4 10.2
21	266 54.5	181 23.7 . .	26.5	247 52.2 . .	51.6	335 17.3 . .	19.3	327 04.8 . .	51.9	Menkent	148 01.8	S36 28.3
22	281 57.0	196 23.9	26.7	262 53.7	52.0	350 20.1	19.4	342 07.4	51.9	Miaplacidus	221 39.7	S69 48.1
23	296 59.5	211 24.1	26.9	277 55.1	52.4	5 22.9	19.4	357 10.1	52.0			
3 00	312 01.9	226 24.2	N19 27.1	292 56.6	N 3 52.7	20 25.6	S22 19.5	12 12.7	S20 52.0	Mirfak	308 33.4	N49 55.7
01	327 04.4	241 24.4	27.3	307 58.0	53.1	35 28.4	19.5	27 15.4	52.1	Nunki	75 51.9	S26 16.2
02	342 06.8	256 24.6	27.5	322 59.5	53.4	50 31.2	19.6	42 18.0	52.1	Peacock	53 10.8	S56 40.1
03	357 09.3	271 24.8 . .	27.7	338 00.9 . .	53.8	65 33.9 . .	19.6	57 20.7 . .	52.1	Pollux	243 22.1	N27 58.6
04	12 11.8	286 24.9	27.9	353 02.4	54.1	80 36.7	19.7	72 23.3	52.2	Procyon	244 54.9	N 5 10.4
05	27 14.2	301 25.1	28.1	8 03.8	54.5	95 39.4	19.7	87 26.0	52.2			
06	42 16.7	316 25.3	N19 28.2	23 05.3	N 3 54.9	110 42.2	S22 19.7	102 28.6	S20 52.3	Rasalhague	96 01.6	N12 32.9
07	57 19.2	331 25.4	28.4	38 06.7	55.2	125 45.0	19.8	117 31.3	52.3	Regulus	207 38.6	N11 52.2
08	72 21.6	346 25.6	28.6	53 08.2	55.6	140 47.7	19.8	132 33.9	52.3	Rigel	281 07.5	S 8 10.6
M 09	87 24.1	1 25.8 . .	28.8	68 09.7 . .	55.9	155 50.5 . .	19.9	147 36.6 . .	52.4	Rigil Kent.	139 45.1	S60 55.3
O 10	102 26.6	16 25.9	29.0	83 11.1	56.3	170 53.2	19.9	162 39.2	52.4	Sabik	102 06.7	S15 44.9
N 11	117 29.0	31 26.1	29.2	98 12.6	56.6	185 56.0	20.0	177 41.9	52.4			
D 12	132 31.5	46 26.2	N19 29.4	113 14.0	N 3 57.0	200 58.8	S22 20.0	192 44.5	S20 52.5	Schedar	349 34.7	N56 38.7
A 13	147 34.0	61 26.4	29.6	128 15.5	57.3	216 01.5	20.1	207 47.2	52.5	Shaula	96 14.9	S37 07.1
Y 14	162 36.4	76 26.5	29.8	143 17.0	57.7	231 04.3	20.1	222 49.8	52.6	Sirius	258 29.7	S16 44.6
15	177 38.9	91 26.7 . .	30.0	158 18.4 . .	58.1	246 07.0 . .	20.1	237 52.5 . .	52.6	Spica	158 26.1	S11 16.0
16	192 41.3	106 26.9	30.2	173 19.9	58.4	261 09.8	20.2	252 55.1	52.6	Suhail	222 49.3	S43 30.9
17	207 43.8	121 27.0	30.4	188 21.3	58.8	276 12.6	20.2	267 57.8	52.7			
18	222 46.3	136 27.2	N19 30.6	203 22.8	N 3 59.1	291 15.3	S22 20.3	283 00.4	S20 52.7	Vega	80 35.3	N38 48.4
19	237 48.7	151 27.3	30.8	218 24.3	59.5	306 18.1	20.3	298 03.1	52.7	Zuben'ubi	136 59.9	S16 07.5
20	252 51.2	166 27.5	31.0	233 25.7	3 59.8	321 20.8	20.4	313 05.7	52.8		SHA	Mer. Pass.
21	267 53.7	181 27.6 . .	31.2	248 27.2	4 00.2	336 23.6 . .	20.4	328 08.3 . .	52.8		° ′	h m
22	282 56.1	196 27.8	31.4	263 28.7	00.5	351 26.4	20.5	343 11.0	52.9	Venus	275 16.9	4 55
23	297 58.6	211 27.9	31.5	278 30.1	00.9	6 29.1	20.5	358 13.6	52.9	Mars	341 19.2	4 30
	h m									Jupiter	68 16.5	22 39
Mer. Pass. 3 15.3		v 0.2	d 0.2	v 1.4	d 0.4	v 2.8	d 0.0	v 2.6	d 0.0	Saturn	60 06.4	23 11

SUN and MOON

UT	SUN GHA	SUN Dec	MOON GHA	v	MOON Dec	d	HP
1 00	178 24.8	N17 56.9	32 40.5	6.7	S23 59.8	1.2	57.6
01	193 24.8	56.3	47 06.2	6.7	24 01.0	1.0	57.6
02	208 24.8	55.6	61 31.9	6.7	24 02.0	0.9	57.6
03	223 24.9	.. 55.0	75 57.6	6.7	24 02.9	0.8	57.6
04	238 24.9	54.4	90 23.3	6.7	24 03.7	0.6	57.5
05	253 25.0	53.7	104 49.0	6.7	24 04.3	0.5	57.5
S 06	268 25.0	N17 53.1	119 14.7	6.8	S24 04.8	0.3	57.5
A 07	283 25.1	52.5	133 40.5	6.8	24 05.1	0.2	57.5
T 08	298 25.1	51.8	148 06.3	6.8	24 05.3	0.0	57.5
U 09	313 25.1	.. 51.2	162 32.1	6.8	24 05.3	0.1	57.4
R 10	328 25.2	50.6	176 57.9	6.9	24 05.2	0.2	57.4
D 11	343 25.2	49.9	191 23.8	6.8	24 05.0	0.4	57.4
A 12	358 25.3	N17 49.3	205 49.6	7.0	S24 04.6	0.6	57.4
Y 13	13 25.3	48.7	220 15.6	6.9	24 04.0	0.7	57.4
14	28 25.4	48.0	234 41.5	7.0	24 03.3	0.8	57.3
15	43 25.4	.. 47.4	249 07.5	7.0	24 02.5	1.0	57.3
16	58 25.5	46.7	263 33.5	7.0	24 01.5	1.1	57.3
17	73 25.5	46.1	277 59.5	7.1	24 00.4	1.3	57.3
18	88 25.5	N17 45.5	292 25.6	7.1	S23 59.1	1.4	57.2
19	103 25.6	44.8	306 51.7	7.1	23 57.7	1.5	57.2
20	118 25.6	44.2	321 17.8	7.2	23 56.2	1.7	57.2
21	133 25.7	.. 43.5	335 44.0	7.3	23 54.5	1.8	57.2
22	148 25.7	42.9	350 10.3	7.2	23 52.7	2.0	57.2
23	163 25.8	42.2	4 36.5	7.4	23 50.7	2.1	57.1
2 00	178 25.8	N17 41.6	19 02.9	7.3	S23 48.6	2.3	57.1
01	193 25.9	41.0	33 29.2	7.4	23 46.3	2.4	57.1
02	208 25.9	40.3	47 55.6	7.5	23 43.9	2.5	57.1
03	223 26.0	.. 39.7	62 22.1	7.5	23 41.4	2.6	57.1
04	238 26.0	39.0	76 48.6	7.6	23 38.8	2.8	57.0
05	253 26.1	38.4	91 15.2	7.6	23 36.0	3.0	57.0
S 06	268 26.1	N17 37.7	105 41.8	7.6	S23 33.0	3.0	57.0
U 07	283 26.2	37.1	120 08.4	7.8	23 30.0	3.2	57.0
N 08	298 26.2	36.4	134 35.2	7.7	23 26.8	3.4	56.9
D 09	313 26.3	.. 35.8	149 01.9	7.9	23 23.4	3.5	56.9
A 10	328 26.3	35.1	163 28.8	7.9	23 19.9	3.6	56.9
Y 11	343 26.3	34.5	177 55.7	7.9	23 16.3	3.7	56.9
12	358 26.4	N17 33.8	192 22.6	8.0	S23 12.6	3.9	56.9
13	13 26.4	33.2	206 49.6	8.1	23 08.7	3.9	56.8
14	28 26.5	32.5	221 16.7	8.1	23 04.8	4.2	56.8
15	43 26.6	.. 31.9	235 43.8	8.2	23 00.6	4.2	56.8
16	58 26.6	31.2	250 11.0	8.2	22 56.4	4.4	56.8
17	73 26.7	30.6	264 38.2	8.4	22 52.0	4.5	56.8
18	88 26.7	N17 29.9	279 05.6	8.3	S22 47.5	4.6	56.7
19	103 26.8	29.3	293 32.9	8.5	22 42.9	4.8	56.7
20	118 26.8	28.6	308 00.4	8.5	22 38.1	4.8	56.7
21	133 26.9	.. 28.0	322 27.9	8.6	22 33.3	5.0	56.7
22	148 26.9	27.3	336 55.5	8.7	22 28.3	5.1	56.6
23	163 27.0	26.7	351 23.2	8.7	22 23.2	5.3	56.6
3 00	178 27.0	N17 26.0	5 50.9	8.8	S22 17.9	5.3	56.6
01	193 27.1	25.3	20 18.7	8.8	22 12.6	5.5	56.6
02	208 27.1	24.7	34 46.5	9.0	22 07.1	5.6	56.6
03	223 27.2	.. 24.0	49 14.5	9.0	22 01.5	5.7	56.5
04	238 27.2	23.4	63 42.5	9.1	21 55.8	5.8	56.5
05	253 27.3	22.7	78 10.6	9.1	21 50.0	5.9	56.5
M 06	268 27.3	N17 22.1	92 38.7	9.3	S21 44.0	6.0	56.5
O 07	283 27.4	21.4	107 07.0	9.3	21 38.0	6.2	56.4
N 08	298 27.5	20.7	121 35.3	9.4	21 31.8	6.3	56.4
D 09	313 27.5	.. 20.1	136 03.7	9.4	21 25.6	6.4	56.4
A 10	328 27.6	19.4	150 32.1	9.6	21 19.2	6.5	56.4
Y 11	343 27.6	18.8	165 00.7	9.6	21 12.7	6.6	56.4
12	358 27.7	N17 18.1	179 29.3	9.7	S21 06.1	6.7	56.3
13	13 27.7	17.4	193 58.0	9.7	20 59.4	6.8	56.3
14	28 27.8	16.8	208 26.7	9.9	20 52.6	7.0	56.3
15	43 27.8	.. 16.1	222 55.6	9.9	20 45.6	7.0	56.3
16	58 27.9	15.4	237 24.5	10.0	20 38.6	7.1	56.2
17	73 28.0	14.8	251 53.5	10.1	20 31.5	7.2	56.2
18	88 28.0	N17 14.1	266 22.6	10.1	S20 24.3	7.4	56.2
19	103 28.1	13.4	280 51.7	10.3	20 16.9	7.4	56.2
20	118 28.1	12.8	295 21.0	10.3	20 09.5	7.5	56.2
21	133 28.2	.. 12.1	309 50.3	10.4	20 02.0	7.6	56.1
22	148 28.3	11.4	324 19.7	10.4	19 54.4	7.7	56.1
23	163 28.3	10.8	338 49.1	10.6	S19 46.7	7.8	56.1
	SD 15.8	d 0.7	SD 15.6		15.5		15.3

Twilight, Sunrise, Moonrise

Lat.	Twilight Naut.	Twilight Civil	Sunrise	Moonrise 1	2	3	4
N 72	▭	▭	▭	■	■	■	23 29
N 70	////	////	01 38	■	■	23 51	22 48
68	////	////	02 22	■	■	22 40	22 19
66	////	00 45	02 51	22 33	22 09	22 02	21 57
64	////	01 48	03 13	21 02	21 26	21 36	21 40
62	////	02 21	03 30	20 24	20 57	21 15	21 26
60	00 41	02 45	03 44	19 57	20 35	20 59	21 14
N 58	01 38	03 03	03 56	19 37	20 17	20 44	21 03
56	02 08	03 19	04 07	19 19	20 02	20 32	20 54
54	02 30	03 32	04 16	19 05	19 49	20 21	20 46
52	02 48	03 43	04 24	18 52	19 37	20 12	20 38
50	03 02	03 53	04 31	18 41	19 27	20 03	20 32
45	03 31	04 13	04 47	18 17	19 06	19 45	20 17
N 40	03 52	04 29	05 00	17 59	18 48	19 30	20 05
35	04 09	04 43	05 10	17 43	18 34	19 18	19 55
30	04 23	04 54	05 20	17 29	18 21	19 07	19 46
20	04 45	05 13	05 36	17 06	17 59	18 48	19 31
N 10	05 02	05 28	05 50	16 46	17 40	18 31	19 18
0	05 16	05 41	06 03	16 27	17 23	18 16	19 05
S 10	05 28	05 54	06 16	16 09	17 05	18 00	18 52
20	05 40	06 06	06 29	15 49	16 46	17 43	18 39
30	05 51	06 19	06 44	15 25	16 24	17 24	18 23
35	05 56	06 27	06 53	15 12	16 11	17 13	18 14
40	06 02	06 35	07 03	14 56	15 57	17 00	18 03
45	06 08	06 44	07 15	14 38	15 39	16 45	17 51
S 50	06 15	06 54	07 29	14 14	15 17	16 26	17 36
52	06 18	06 59	07 36	14 03	15 07	16 17	17 29
54	06 21	07 04	07 43	13 50	14 55	16 07	17 21
56	06 25	07 10	07 52	13 36	14 41	15 55	17 13
58	06 28	07 16	08 01	13 19	14 25	15 42	17 03
S 60	06 32	07 23	08 11	12 58	14 07	15 27	16 51

Sunset, Twilight, Moonset

Lat.	Sunset	Twilight Civil	Twilight Naut.	Moonset 1	2	3	4
N 72	▭	▭	▭	■	■	■	
N 70	22 27	////	////	■	■	■	01 18
68	21 46	////	////	■	■	■	02 28
66	21 19	23 15	////	22 52	25 10	01 10	03 05
64	20 58	22 20	////	24 23	00 23	01 53	03 30
62	20 41	21 49	////	00 00	01 00	02 21	03 50
60	20 27	21 25	23 20	00 27	01 27	02 43	04 06
N 58	20 15	21 07	22 31	00 48	01 47	03 00	04 20
56	20 05	20 52	22 02	01 05	02 04	03 15	04 32
54	19 56	20 39	21 40	01 20	02 19	03 28	04 42
52	19 48	20 28	21 23	01 33	02 32	03 39	04 51
50	19 40	20 18	21 08	01 44	02 43	03 49	04 59
45	19 25	19 58	20 40	02 07	03 06	04 10	05 16
N 40	19 12	19 42	20 19	02 26	03 24	04 27	05 30
35	19 02	19 29	20 03	02 42	03 40	04 41	05 42
30	18 52	19 18	19 49	02 56	03 53	04 53	05 53
20	18 36	19 00	19 27	03 19	04 16	05 14	06 10
N 10	18 23	18 45	19 11	03 39	04 36	05 32	06 25
0	18 10	18 31	18 57	03 58	04 54	05 49	06 40
S 10	17 57	18 19	18 44	04 17	05 13	06 05	06 54
20	17 44	18 07	18 33	04 37	05 32	06 23	07 09
30	17 28	17 54	18 22	05 00	05 55	06 43	07 26
35	17 20	17 46	18 17	05 13	06 08	06 55	07 36
40	17 10	17 38	18 11	05 29	06 23	07 09	07 47
45	16 58	17 29	18 05	05 48	06 41	07 25	08 01
S 50	16 44	17 19	17 58	06 11	07 03	07 45	08 18
52	16 37	17 14	17 55	06 22	07 14	07 54	08 24
54	16 30	17 09	17 52	06 35	07 26	08 04	08 32
56	16 22	17 03	17 48	06 50	07 40	08 16	08 42
58	16 12	16 57	17 45	07 07	07 56	08 30	08 52
S 60	16 02	16 50	17 41	07 28	08 15	08 45	09 04

SUN and MOON

	SUN Eqn. of Time 00ʰ	SUN Eqn. of Time 12ʰ	SUN Mer. Pass.	MOON Mer. Pass. Upper	MOON Mer. Pass. Lower	Age	Phase
Day	m s	m s	h m	h m	h m	d	%
1	06 21	06 19	12 06	22 41	10 13	12	95
2	06 17	06 15	12 06	23 36	11 09	13	98
3	06 12	06 09	12 06	24 28	12 02	14	100

UT	ARIES	VENUS −4·5		MARS −1·2		JUPITER −2·7		SATURN +0·2		STARS		
	GHA	GHA	Dec	GHA	Dec	GHA	Dec	GHA	Dec	Name	SHA	Dec
d h	° ′	° ′	° ′	° ′	° ′	° ′	° ′	° ′	° ′		° ′	° ′
4 00	313 01.1	226 28.0 N19 31.7		293 31.6 N 4 01.2		21 31.9 S22 20.5		13 16.3 S20 52.9		Acamar	315 14.6	S40 13.2
01	328 03.5	241 28.2	31.9	308 33.1	01.6	36 34.6	20.6	28 18.9	53.0	Achernar	335 22.8	S57 07.7
02	343 06.0	256 28.3	32.1	323 34.5	01.9	51 37.4	20.6	43 21.6	53.0	Acrux	173 04.3	S63 12.9
03	358 08.5	271 28.5 . .	32.3	338 36.0 . .	02.3	66 40.1 . .	20.7	58 24.2 . .	53.1	Adhara	255 09.0	S28 59.9
04	13 10.9	286 28.6	32.5	353 37.5	02.6	81 42.9	20.7	73 26.9	53.1	Aldebaran	290 43.9	N16 32.7
05	28 13.4	301 28.8	32.7	8 39.0	03.0	96 45.7	20.8	88 29.5	53.1			
06	43 15.8	316 28.9 N19 32.9		23 40.4 N 4 03.3		111 48.4 S22 20.8		103 32.2 S20 53.2		Alioth	166 16.5	N55 51.3
07	58 18.3	331 29.0	33.1	38 41.9	03.7	126 51.2	20.9	118 34.8	53.2	Alkaid	152 55.0	N49 13.0
08	73 20.8	346 29.2	33.2	53 43.4	04.0	141 53.9	20.9	133 37.5	53.2	Alnair	27 37.0	S46 51.6
T 09	88 23.2	1 29.3 . .	33.4	68 44.9 . .	04.4	156 56.7 . .	20.9	148 40.1 . .	53.3	Alnilam	275 41.6	S 1 11.3
U 10	103 25.7	16 29.4	33.6	83 46.3	04.7	171 59.4	21.0	163 42.8	53.3	Alphard	217 51.6	S 8 44.8
E 11	118 28.2	31 29.6	33.8	98 47.8	05.1	187 02.2	21.0	178 45.4	53.4			
S 12	133 30.6	46 29.7 N19 34.0		113 49.3 N 4 05.4		202 05.0 S22 21.1		193 48.1 S20 53.4		Alphecca	126 06.7	N26 39.1
D 13	148 33.1	61 29.8	34.2	128 50.8	05.8	217 07.7	21.1	208 50.7	53.4	Alpheratz	357 38.2	N29 12.1
A 14	163 35.6	76 29.9	34.4	143 52.2	06.1	232 10.5	21.2	223 53.4	53.5	Altair	62 03.1	N 8 55.5
Y 15	178 38.0	91 30.1 . .	34.5	158 53.7 . .	06.5	247 13.2 . .	21.2	238 56.0 . .	53.5	Ankaa	353 10.5	S42 11.5
16	193 40.5	106 30.2	34.7	173 55.2	06.8	262 16.0	21.3	253 58.6	53.5	Antares	112 20.0	S26 28.6
17	208 42.9	121 30.3	34.9	188 56.7	07.1	277 18.7	21.3	269 01.3	53.6			
18	223 45.4	136 30.4 N19 35.1		203 58.2 N 4 07.5		292 21.5 S22 21.3		284 03.9 S20 53.6		Arcturus	145 51.2	N19 04.8
19	238 47.9	151 30.6	35.3	218 59.6	07.8	307 24.2	21.4	299 06.6	53.7	Atria	107 17.1	S69 04.0
20	253 50.3	166 30.7	35.5	234 01.1	08.2	322 27.0	21.4	314 09.2	53.7	Avior	234 16.7	S59 34.4
21	268 52.8	181 30.8 . .	35.6	249 02.6 . .	08.5	337 29.7 . .	21.5	329 11.9 . .	53.7	Bellatrix	278 26.9	N 6 22.1
22	283 55.3	196 30.9	35.8	264 04.1	08.9	352 32.5	21.5	344 14.5	53.8	Betelgeuse	270 56.2	N 7 24.6
23	298 57.7	211 31.0	36.0	279 05.6	09.2	7 35.3	21.6	359 17.2	53.8			
5 00	314 00.2	226 31.2 N19 36.2		294 07.1 N 4 09.6		22 38.0 S22 21.6		14 19.8 S20 53.8		Canopus	263 54.4	S52 42.2
01	329 02.7	241 31.3	36.4	309 08.5	09.9	37 40.8	21.7	29 22.5	53.9	Capella	280 27.4	N46 00.9
02	344 05.1	256 31.4	36.5	324 10.0	10.2	52 43.5	21.7	44 25.1	53.9	Deneb	49 27.7	N45 21.3
03	359 07.6	271 31.5 . .	36.7	339 11.5 . .	10.6	67 46.3 . .	21.7	59 27.8 . .	54.0	Denebola	182 28.8	N14 27.7
04	14 10.1	286 31.6	36.9	354 13.0	10.9	82 49.0	21.8	74 30.4	54.0	Diphda	348 50.7	S17 52.4
05	29 12.5	301 31.7	37.1	9 14.5	11.3	97 51.8	21.8	89 33.1	54.0			
06	44 15.0	316 31.8 N19 37.3		24 16.0 N 4 11.6		112 54.5 S22 21.9		104 35.7 S20 54.1		Dubhe	193 46.1	N61 38.7
W 07	59 17.4	331 31.9	37.4	39 17.5	11.9	127 57.3	21.9	119 38.3	54.1	Elnath	278 06.6	N28 37.3
E 08	74 19.9	346 32.1	37.6	54 19.0	12.3	143 00.0	22.0	134 41.0	54.1	Eltanin	90 43.4	N51 29.5
D 09	89 22.4	1 32.2 . .	37.8	69 20.5 . .	12.6	158 02.8 . .	22.0	149 43.6 . .	54.2	Enif	33 42.0	N 9 58.2
N 10	104 24.8	16 32.3	38.0	84 22.0	13.0	173 05.5	22.0	164 46.3	54.2	Fomalhaut	15 18.2	S29 30.7
E 11	119 27.3	31 32.4	38.1	99 23.4	13.3	188 08.3	22.1	179 48.9	54.3			
S 12	134 29.8	46 32.5 N19 38.3		114 24.9 N 4 13.7		203 11.0 S22 22.1		194 51.6 S20 54.3		Gacrux	171 55.8	S57 13.8
D 13	149 32.2	61 32.6	38.5	129 26.4	14.0	218 13.8	22.2	209 54.2	54.3	Gienah	175 47.4	S17 39.3
A 14	164 34.7	76 32.7	38.7	144 27.9	14.3	233 16.5	22.2	224 56.9	54.4	Hadar	148 41.0	S60 28.4
Y 15	179 37.2	91 32.8 . .	38.8	159 29.4 . .	14.7	248 19.3 . .	22.3	239 59.5 . .	54.4	Hamal	327 55.1	N23 33.4
16	194 39.6	106 32.9	39.0	174 30.9	15.0	263 22.0	22.3	255 02.2	54.4	Kaus Aust.	83 36.9	S34 22.4
17	209 42.1	121 33.0	39.2	189 32.4	15.4	278 24.8	22.3	270 04.8	54.5			
18	224 44.6	136 33.1 N19 39.4		204 33.9 N 4 15.7		293 27.5 S22 22.4		285 07.4 S20 54.5		Kochab	137 20.0	N74 04.7
19	239 47.0	151 33.1	39.5	219 35.4	16.0	308 30.3	22.4	300 10.1	54.6	Markab	13 33.1	N15 18.9
20	254 49.5	166 33.2	39.7	234 36.9	16.4	323 33.0	22.5	315 12.7	54.6	Menkar	314 09.9	N 4 10.2
21	269 51.9	181 33.3 . .	39.9	249 38.4 . .	16.7	338 35.8 . .	22.5	330 15.4 . .	54.6	Menkent	148 01.8	S36 28.3
22	284 54.4	196 33.4	40.1	264 39.9	17.0	353 38.5	22.6	345 18.0	54.7	Miaplacidus	221 39.7	S69 48.1
23	299 56.9	211 33.5	40.2	279 41.4	17.4	8 41.3	22.6	0 20.7	54.7			
6 00	314 59.3	226 33.6 N19 40.4		294 42.9 N 4 17.7		23 44.0 S22 22.6		15 23.3 S20 54.7		Mirfak	308 33.4	N49 55.7
01	330 01.8	241 33.7	40.6	309 44.4	18.0	38 46.8	22.7	30 26.0	54.8	Nunki	75 51.9	S26 16.2
02	345 04.3	256 33.8	40.7	324 45.9	18.4	53 49.5	22.7	45 28.6	54.8	Peacock	53 10.8	S56 40.1
03	0 06.7	271 33.9 . .	40.9	339 47.5 . .	18.7	68 52.3 . .	22.8	60 31.3 . .	54.9	Pollux	243 22.0	N27 58.6
04	15 09.2	286 33.9	41.1	354 49.0	19.1	83 55.0	22.8	75 33.9	54.9	Procyon	244 54.9	N 5 10.4
05	30 11.7	301 34.0	41.2	9 50.5	19.4	98 57.8	22.9	90 36.5	54.9			
06	45 14.1	316 34.1 N19 41.4		24 52.0 N 4 19.7		114 00.5 S22 22.9		105 39.2 S20 55.0		Rasalhague	96 01.6	N12 32.9
07	60 16.6	331 34.2	41.6	39 53.5	20.1	129 03.3	22.9	120 41.8	55.0	Regulus	207 38.6	N11 52.2
T 08	75 19.0	346 34.3	41.7	54 55.0	20.4	144 06.0	23.0	135 44.5	55.0	Rigel	281 07.5	S 8 10.6
H 09	90 21.5	1 34.3 . .	41.9	69 56.5 . .	20.7	159 08.7 . .	23.0	150 47.1 . .	55.1	Rigil Kent.	139 45.1	S60 55.3
U 10	105 24.0	16 34.4	42.1	84 58.0	21.1	174 11.5	23.1	165 49.8	55.1	Sabik	102 06.7	S15 44.9
R 11	120 26.4	31 34.5	42.2	99 59.5	21.4	189 14.2	23.1	180 52.4	55.2			
S 12	135 28.9	46 34.6 N19 42.4		115 01.0 N 4 21.7		204 17.0 S22 23.2		195 55.1 S20 55.2		Schedar	349 34.6	N56 38.7
D 13	150 31.4	61 34.7	42.6	130 02.6	22.1	219 19.7	23.2	210 57.7	55.2	Shaula	96 14.9	S37 07.1
A 14	165 33.8	76 34.7	42.7	145 04.1	22.4	234 22.5	23.2	226 00.3	55.3	Sirius	258 29.7	S16 44.6
Y 15	180 36.3	91 34.8 . .	42.9	160 05.6 . .	22.7	249 25.2 . .	23.3	241 03.0 . .	55.3	Spica	158 26.2	S11 16.0
16	195 38.8	106 34.9	43.1	175 07.1	23.0	264 28.0	23.3	256 05.6	55.3	Suhail	222 49.3	S43 30.9
17	210 41.2	121 34.9	43.2	190 08.6	23.4	279 30.7	23.4	271 08.3	55.4			
18	225 43.7	136 35.0 N19 43.4		205 10.1 N 4 23.7		294 33.5 S22 23.4		286 10.9 S20 55.4		Vega	80 35.3	N38 48.4
19	240 46.2	151 35.1	43.5	220 11.6	24.0	309 36.2	23.4	301 13.6	55.4	Zuben'ubi	136 59.9	S16 07.5
20	255 48.6	166 35.1	43.7	235 13.2	24.4	324 38.9	23.5	316 16.2	55.5		SHA	Mer. Pass.
21	270 51.1	181 35.2 . .	43.9	250 14.7 . .	24.7	339 41.7 . .	23.5	331 18.8 . .	55.5		° ′	h m
22	285 53.5	196 35.3	44.0	265 16.2	25.0	354 44.4	23.6	346 21.5	55.6	Venus	272 31.0	8 54
23	300 56.0	211 35.3	44.2	280 17.7	25.4	9 47.2	23.6	1 24.1	55.6	Mars	340 06.9	4 23
	h m									Jupiter	68 37.8	22 25
Mer. Pass. 3 03.5		v 0.1 d 0.2		v 1.5 d 0.3		v 2.8 d 0.0		v 2.6 d 0.0		Saturn	60 19.6	22 59

UT	SUN GHA	SUN Dec	MOON GHA	v	MOON Dec	d	HP
d h	° ′	° ′	° ′	′	° ′	′	′
4 00	178 28.4	N17 10.1	353 18.7	10.6	S19 38.9	7.9	56.1
01	193 28.4	09.4	7 48.3	10.8	19 31.0	8.0	56.0
02	208 28.5	08.8	22 18.1	10.8	19 23.0	8.1	56.0
03	223 28.6	.. 08.1	36 47.9	10.8	19 14.9	8.2	56.0
04	238 28.6	07.4	51 17.7	11.0	19 06.7	8.3	56.0
05	253 28.7	06.8	65 47.7	11.0	18 58.4	8.3	56.0
06	268 28.7	N17 06.1	80 17.7	11.1	S18 50.1	8.5	55.9
07	283 28.8	05.4	94 47.8	11.2	18 41.6	8.5	55.9
08	298 28.9	04.8	109 18.0	11.3	18 33.1	8.6	55.9
09	313 28.9	.. 04.1	123 48.3	11.4	18 24.5	8.7	55.9
10	328 29.0	03.4	138 18.7	11.4	18 15.8	8.8	55.8
11	343 29.0	02.7	152 49.1	11.5	18 07.0	8.8	55.8
12	358 29.1	N17 02.1	167 19.6	11.6	S17 58.2	8.9	55.8
13	13 29.2	01.4	181 50.2	11.7	17 49.3	9.1	55.8
14	28 29.2	00.7	196 20.9	11.8	17 40.2	9.1	55.8
15	43 29.3	17 00.0	210 51.7	11.8	17 31.1	9.1	55.7
16	58 29.4	16 59.4	225 22.5	11.9	17 22.0	9.3	55.7
17	73 29.4	58.7	239 53.4	12.0	17 12.7	9.3	55.7
18	88 29.5	N16 58.0	254 24.4	12.1	S17 03.4	9.4	55.7
19	103 29.6	57.3	268 55.5	12.1	16 54.0	9.5	55.7
20	118 29.6	56.7	283 26.6	12.2	16 44.5	9.5	55.6
21	133 29.7	.. 56.0	297 57.8	12.3	16 35.0	9.6	55.6
22	148 29.7	55.3	312 29.1	12.4	16 25.4	9.7	55.6
23	163 29.8	54.6	327 00.5	12.4	16 15.7	9.7	55.6
5 00	178 29.9	N16 54.0	341 31.9	12.6	S16 06.0	9.8	55.5
01	193 29.9	53.3	356 03.5	12.6	15 56.2	9.9	55.5
02	208 30.0	52.6	10 35.1	12.6	15 46.3	10.0	55.5
03	223 30.1	.. 51.9	25 06.7	12.8	15 36.3	10.0	55.5
04	238 30.1	51.2	39 38.5	12.8	15 26.3	10.0	55.5
05	253 30.2	50.6	54 10.3	12.9	15 16.3	10.2	55.4
06	268 30.3	N16 49.9	68 42.2	13.0	S15 06.1	10.1	55.4
07	283 30.3	49.2	83 14.2	13.0	14 56.0	10.3	55.4
08	298 30.4	48.5	97 46.2	13.1	14 45.7	10.3	55.4
09	313 30.5	.. 47.8	112 18.3	13.2	14 35.4	10.4	55.4
10	328 30.5	47.1	126 50.5	13.3	14 25.0	10.4	55.3
11	343 30.6	46.5	141 22.8	13.3	14 14.6	10.5	55.3
12	358 30.7	N16 45.8	155 55.1	13.4	S14 04.1	10.5	55.3
13	13 30.8	45.1	170 27.5	13.5	13 53.6	10.6	55.3
14	28 30.8	44.4	185 00.0	13.5	13 43.0	10.6	55.3
15	43 30.9	.. 43.7	199 32.5	13.6	13 32.4	10.7	55.2
16	58 31.0	43.0	214 05.1	13.7	13 21.7	10.7	55.2
17	73 31.0	42.3	228 37.8	13.7	13 11.0	10.8	55.2
18	88 31.1	N16 41.7	243 10.5	13.8	S13 00.2	10.9	55.2
19	103 31.2	41.0	257 43.3	13.9	12 49.3	10.9	55.2
20	118 31.2	40.3	272 16.2	13.9	12 38.4	10.9	55.1
21	133 31.3	.. 39.6	286 49.1	14.0	12 27.5	11.0	55.1
22	148 31.4	38.9	301 22.1	14.0	12 16.5	11.0	55.1
23	163 31.5	38.2	315 55.1	14.1	12 05.5	11.0	55.1
6 00	178 31.5	N16 37.5	330 28.2	14.2	S11 54.5	11.2	55.1
01	193 31.6	36.8	345 01.4	14.3	11 43.3	11.1	55.1
02	208 31.7	36.1	359 34.7	14.3	11 32.2	11.2	55.0
03	223 31.7	.. 35.5	14 08.0	14.3	11 21.0	11.2	55.0
04	238 31.8	34.8	28 41.3	14.4	11 09.8	11.3	55.0
05	253 31.9	34.1	43 14.7	14.5	10 58.5	11.3	55.0
06	268 32.0	N16 33.4	57 48.2	14.5	S10 47.2	11.3	55.0
07	283 32.0	32.7	72 21.7	14.6	10 35.9	11.4	54.9
08	298 32.1	32.0	86 55.3	14.7	10 24.5	11.4	54.9
09	313 32.2	.. 31.3	101 29.0	14.7	10 13.1	11.5	54.9
10	328 32.3	30.6	116 02.7	14.7	10 01.6	11.5	54.9
11	343 32.3	29.9	130 36.4	14.8	9 50.1	11.5	54.8
12	358 32.4	N16 29.2	145 10.2	14.9	S 9 38.6	11.5	54.9
13	13 32.5	28.5	159 44.1	14.9	9 27.1	11.6	54.9
14	28 32.6	27.8	174 18.0	15.0	9 15.5	11.6	54.8
15	43 32.6	.. 27.1	188 52.0	15.0	9 03.9	11.6	54.8
16	58 32.7	26.4	203 26.0	15.0	8 52.3	11.7	54.8
17	73 32.8	25.7	218 00.0	15.1	8 40.6	11.7	54.8
18	88 32.9	N16 25.0	232 34.1	15.2	S 8 28.9	11.7	54.8
19	103 32.9	24.3	247 08.3	15.2	8 17.2	11.8	54.7
20	118 33.0	23.6	261 42.5	15.2	8 05.4	11.7	54.7
21	133 33.1	.. 22.9	276 16.7	15.3	7 53.7	11.8	54.7
22	148 33.2	22.2	290 51.0	15.4	7 41.9	11.8	54.7
23	163 33.3	21.5	305 25.4	15.4	S 7 30.1	11.9	54.7
	SD 15.8	d 0.7	SD 15.2		15.1		14.9

Left margin day labels: TUESDAY, WEDNESDAY, THURSDAY

Lat.	Twilight Naut.	Twilight Civil	Sunrise	Moonrise 4	5	6	7
°	h m	h m	h m	h m	h m	h m	h m
N 72	////	////	00 47	23 29	22 44	22 16	21 54
N 70	////	////	02 00	22 48	22 23	22 05	21 50
68	////	////	02 37	22 19	22 06	21 56	21 47
66	////	01 19	03 02	21 57	21 53	21 48	21 44
64	////	02 04	03 22	21 40	21 42	21 42	21 42
62	////	02 32	03 38	21 26	21 32	21 36	21 40
60	01 11	02 54	03 51	21 14	21 24	21 31	21 38
N 58	01 52	03 11	04 02	21 03	21 17	21 27	21 36
56	02 18	03 25	04 12	20 54	21 10	21 23	21 35
54	02 38	03 38	04 21	20 46	21 04	21 20	21 33
52	02 55	03 48	04 29	20 38	20 59	21 17	21 32
50	03 09	03 58	04 36	20 32	20 54	21 14	21 31
45	03 36	04 17	04 50	20 17	20 44	21 07	21 29
N 40	03 56	04 33	05 02	20 05	20 36	21 02	21 27
35	04 12	04 45	05 13	19 55	20 28	20 58	21 25
30	04 25	04 56	05 22	19 46	20 22	20 54	21 23
20	04 46	05 14	05 37	19 31	20 10	20 47	21 21
N 10	05 02	05 28	05 50	19 18	20 00	20 40	21 18
0	05 16	05 41	06 03	19 05	19 51	20 35	21 16
S 10	05 27	05 53	06 15	18 52	19 42	20 29	21 14
20	05 38	06 05	06 28	18 39	19 32	20 22	21 12
30	05 49	06 17	06 42	18 23	19 20	20 15	21 09
35	05 54	06 24	06 51	18 14	19 13	20 11	21 07
40	05 59	06 32	07 00	18 03	19 06	20 07	21 06
45	06 05	06 40	07 11	17 51	18 57	20 01	21 04
S 50	06 11	06 50	07 25	17 36	18 46	19 55	21 01
52	06 14	06 54	07 31	17 29	18 41	19 51	21 00
54	06 17	06 59	07 38	17 21	18 36	19 48	20 59
56	06 20	07 05	07 46	17 13	18 29	19 44	20 57
58	06 23	07 10	07 54	17 03	18 23	19 40	20 56
S 60	06 26	07 17	08 04	16 51	18 15	19 36	20 54

Lat.	Sunset	Twilight Civil	Twilight Naut.	Moonset 4	5	6	7
°	h m	h m	h m	h m	h m	h m	h m
N 72	23 08	////	////	▬	03 22	05 42	07 39
N 70	22 06	////	////	01 18	04 02	06 01	07 48
68	21 31	////	////	02 28	04 29	06 16	07 55
66	21 07	22 46	////	03 05	04 50	06 28	08 01
64	20 48	22 04	////	03 30	05 06	06 38	08 06
62	20 32	21 37	////	03 50	05 20	06 46	08 10
60	20 19	21 16	22 54	04 06	05 31	06 54	08 14
N 58	20 08	20 59	22 16	04 20	05 41	07 00	08 17
56	19 58	20 45	21 51	04 32	05 49	07 06	08 20
54	19 50	20 33	21 31	04 42	05 57	07 11	08 22
52	19 42	20 22	21 15	04 51	06 04	07 15	08 25
50	19 35	20 13	21 02	04 59	06 10	07 19	08 27
45	19 21	19 54	20 35	05 16	06 23	07 28	08 31
N 40	19 09	19 39	20 15	05 30	06 34	07 35	08 35
35	18 59	19 26	19 59	05 42	06 43	07 42	08 38
30	18 50	19 16	19 46	05 53	06 51	07 47	08 41
20	18 35	18 58	19 25	06 10	07 04	07 56	08 46
N 10	18 22	18 44	19 09	06 25	07 16	08 05	08 51
0	18 09	18 31	18 56	06 40	07 27	08 12	08 55
S 10	17 57	18 19	18 45	06 54	07 39	08 20	08 59
20	17 45	18 08	18 34	07 09	07 50	08 28	09 03
30	17 30	17 55	18 24	07 26	08 03	08 37	09 08
35	17 22	17 48	18 19	07 36	08 11	08 42	09 10
40	17 12	17 41	18 13	07 47	08 20	08 48	09 14
45	17 01	17 32	18 08	08 01	08 30	08 55	09 17
S 50	16 48	17 23	18 01	08 17	08 42	09 03	09 21
52	16 42	17 18	17 59	08 24	08 48	09 07	09 23
54	16 35	17 13	17 56	08 32	08 54	09 11	09 25
56	16 28	17 08	17 53	08 42	09 01	09 15	09 28
58	16 18	17 02	17 50	08 52	09 08	09 20	09 30
S 60	16 09	16 56	17 46	09 04	09 17	09 26	09 33

	SUN			MOON			
Day	Eqn. of Time 00ʰ	Eqn. of Time 12ʰ	Mer. Pass.	Mer. Pass. Upper	Mer. Pass. Lower	Age	Phase
d	m s	m s	h m	h m	h m	d	%
4	06 07	06 04	12 06	00 28	12 52	15	99
5	06 01	05 57	12 06	01 16	13 39	16	96
6	05 54	05 51	12 06	02 02	14 23	17	92

UT	ARIES GHA	VENUS −4.5 GHA	VENUS Dec	MARS −1.2 GHA	MARS Dec	JUPITER −2.7 GHA	JUPITER Dec	SATURN +0.2 GHA	SATURN Dec	STARS Name	SHA	Dec
7 00	315 58.5	226 35.4	N19 44.4	295 19.3	N 4 25.7	24 49.9	S22 23.7	16 26.8	S20 55.6	Acamar	315 14.5	S40 13.2
01	331 00.9	241 35.5	44.5	310 20.8	26.0	39 52.7	23.7	31 29.4	55.7	Achernar	335 22.8	S57 07.7
02	346 03.4	256 35.5	44.7	325 22.3	26.3	54 55.4	23.7	46 32.1	55.7	Acrux	173 04.3	S63 12.9
03	1 05.9	271 35.6 ..	44.8	340 23.8 ..	26.7	69 58.1 ..	23.8	61 34.7 ..	55.7	Adhara	255 09.0	S28 59.9
04	16 08.3	286 35.6	45.0	355 25.3	27.0	85 00.9	23.8	76 37.4	55.8	Aldebaran	290 43.8	N16 32.9
05	31 10.8	301 35.7	45.1	10 26.9	27.3	100 03.6	23.9	91 40.0	55.8			
06	46 13.3	316 35.7	N19 45.3	25 28.4	N 4 27.6	115 06.4	S22 23.9	106 42.6	S20 55.9	Alioth	166 16.5	N55 51.3
07	61 15.7	331 35.8	45.5	40 29.9	28.0	130 09.1	23.9	121 45.3	55.9	Alkaid	152 55.1	N49 13.0
08	76 18.2	346 35.8	45.6	55 31.5	28.3	145 11.9	24.0	136 47.9	55.9	Alnair	27 37.0	S46 51.6
F 09	91 20.6	1 35.9 ..	45.8	70 33.0 ..	28.6	160 14.6 ..	24.0	151 50.6 ..	56.0	Alnilam	275 41.5	S 1 11.3
R 10	106 23.1	16 35.9	45.9	85 34.5	29.0	175 17.3	24.1	166 53.2	56.0	Alphard	217 51.6	S 8 44.7
I 11	121 25.6	31 36.0	46.1	100 36.0	29.3	190 20.1	24.1	181 55.9	56.0			
D 12	136 28.0	46 36.0	N19 46.2	115 37.6	N 4 29.6	205 22.8	S22 24.2	196 58.5	S20 56.1	Alphecca	126 06.7	N26 39.1
A 13	151 30.5	61 36.1	46.4	130 39.1	29.9	220 25.6	24.2	212 01.1	56.1	Alpheratz	357 38.2	N29 12.1
Y 14	166 33.0	76 36.1	46.5	145 40.6	30.3	235 28.3	24.2	227 03.8	56.1	Altair	62 03.1	N 8 55.5
15	181 35.4	91 36.2 ..	46.7	160 42.2 ..	30.6	250 31.0 ..	24.3	242 06.4 ..	56.2	Ankaa	353 10.5	S42 11.5
16	196 37.9	106 36.2	46.8	175 43.7	30.9	265 33.8	24.3	257 09.1	56.2	Antares	112 20.0	S26 28.6
17	211 40.4	121 36.3	47.0	190 45.2	31.2	280 36.5	24.4	272 11.7	56.3			
18	226 42.8	136 36.3	N19 47.1	205 46.8	N 4 31.5	295 39.3	S22 24.4	287 14.4	S20 56.3	Arcturus	145 51.3	N19 04.8
19	241 45.3	151 36.4	47.3	220 48.3	31.9	310 42.0	24.4	302 17.0	56.3	Atria	107 17.1	S69 04.0
20	256 47.8	166 36.4	47.4	235 49.9	32.2	325 44.7	24.5	317 19.6	56.4	Avior	234 16.7	S59 34.4
21	271 50.2	181 36.4 ..	47.6	250 51.4 ..	32.5	340 47.5 ..	24.5	332 22.3 ..	56.4	Bellatrix	278 26.9	N 6 22.1
22	286 52.7	196 36.5	47.7	265 52.9	32.8	355 50.2	24.6	347 24.9	56.4	Betelgeuse	270 56.2	N 7 24.6
23	301 55.1	211 36.5	47.9	280 54.5	33.2	10 52.9	24.6	2 27.6	56.5			
8 00	316 57.6	226 36.5	N19 48.0	295 56.0	N 4 33.5	25 55.7	S22 24.6	17 30.2	S20 56.5	Canopus	263 54.4	S52 42.2
01	332 00.1	241 36.6	48.2	310 57.6	33.8	40 58.4	24.7	32 32.8	56.5	Capella	280 27.4	N46 00.9
02	347 02.5	256 36.6	48.3	325 59.1	34.1	56 01.2	24.7	47 35.5	56.6	Deneb	49 27.7	N45 21.3
03	2 05.0	271 36.7 ..	48.5	341 00.6 ..	34.4	71 03.9 ..	24.8	62 38.1 ..	56.6	Denebola	182 28.8	N14 27.7
04	17 07.5	286 36.7	48.6	356 02.2	34.8	86 06.6	24.8	77 40.8	56.7	Diphda	348 50.7	S17 52.4
05	32 09.9	301 36.7	48.8	11 03.7	35.1	101 09.4	24.8	92 43.4	56.7			
06	47 12.4	316 36.7	N19 48.9	26 05.3	N 4 35.4	116 12.1	S22 24.9	107 46.1	S20 56.7	Dubhe	193 46.1	N61 38.7
07	62 14.9	331 36.8	49.0	41 06.8	35.7	131 14.8	24.9	122 48.7	56.8	Elnath	278 06.6	N28 37.3
S 08	77 17.3	346 36.8	49.2	56 08.4	36.0	146 17.6	25.0	137 51.3	56.8	Eltanin	90 43.5	N51 29.5
A 09	92 19.8	1 36.8 ..	49.3	71 09.9 ..	36.3	161 20.3 ..	25.0	152 54.0 ..	56.8	Enif	33 41.9	N 9 58.2
T 10	107 22.3	16 36.9	49.5	86 11.5	36.7	176 23.1	25.0	167 56.6	56.9	Fomalhaut	15 18.2	S29 30.7
U 11	122 24.7	31 36.9	49.6	101 13.0	37.0	191 25.8	25.1	182 59.3	56.9			
R 12	137 27.2	46 36.9	N19 49.8	116 14.6	N 4 37.3	206 28.5	S22 25.1	198 01.9	S20 56.9	Gacrux	171 55.8	S57 13.8
D 13	152 29.6	61 36.9	49.9	131 16.1	37.6	221 31.3	25.2	213 04.5	57.0	Gienah	175 47.4	S17 39.2
A 14	167 32.1	76 36.9	50.0	146 17.7	37.9	236 34.0	25.2	228 07.2	57.0	Hadar	148 41.1	S60 28.4
Y 15	182 34.6	91 37.0 ..	50.2	161 19.2 ..	38.2	251 36.7 ..	25.3	243 09.8 ..	57.1	Hamal	327 55.1	N23 33.4
16	197 37.0	106 37.0	50.3	176 20.8	38.6	266 39.5	25.3	258 12.5	57.1	Kaus Aust.	83 36.9	S34 22.4
17	212 39.5	121 37.0	50.5	191 22.3	38.9	281 42.2	25.3	273 15.1	57.1			
18	227 42.0	136 37.0	N19 50.6	206 23.9	N 4 39.2	296 44.9	S22 25.4	288 17.7	S20 57.2	Kochab	137 20.0	N74 04.7
19	242 44.4	151 37.0	50.7	221 25.5	39.5	311 47.7	25.4	303 20.4	57.2	Markab	13 33.1	N15 18.9
20	257 46.9	166 37.0	50.9	236 27.0	39.8	326 50.4	25.5	318 23.0	57.2	Menkar	314 09.9	N 4 10.2
21	272 49.4	181 37.1 ..	51.0	251 28.6 ..	40.1	341 53.1 ..	25.5	333 25.7 ..	57.3	Menkent	148 01.9	S36 28.2
22	287 51.8	196 37.1	51.1	266 30.1	40.4	356 55.9	25.5	348 28.3	57.3	Miaplacidus	221 39.7	S69 48.0
23	302 54.3	211 37.1	51.3	281 31.7	40.8	11 58.6	25.6	3 30.9	57.3			
9 00	317 56.7	226 37.1	N19 51.4	296 33.3	N 4 41.1	27 01.3	S22 25.6	18 33.6	S20 57.4	Mirfak	308 33.3	N49 55.7
01	332 59.2	241 37.1	51.6	311 34.8	41.4	42 04.1	25.6	33 36.2	57.4	Nunki	75 51.9	S26 16.2
02	348 01.7	256 37.1	51.7	326 36.4	41.7	57 06.8	25.7	48 38.9	57.5	Peacock	53 10.8	S56 40.1
03	3 04.1	271 37.1 ..	51.8	341 37.9 ..	42.0	72 09.5 ..	25.7	63 41.5 ..	57.5	Pollux	243 22.0	N27 58.6
04	18 06.6	286 37.1	52.0	356 39.5	42.3	87 12.3	25.8	78 44.1	57.5	Procyon	244 54.9	N 5 10.4
05	33 09.1	301 37.1	52.1	11 41.1	42.6	102 15.0	25.8	93 46.8	57.6			
06	48 11.5	316 37.1	N19 52.2	26 42.6	N 4 42.9	117 17.7	S22 25.8	108 49.4	S20 57.6	Rasalhague	96 01.6	N12 32.9
07	63 14.0	331 37.1	52.4	41 44.2	43.3	132 20.4	25.9	123 52.1	57.6	Regulus	207 38.6	N11 52.2
08	78 16.5	346 37.1	52.5	56 45.8	43.6	147 23.2	25.9	138 54.7	57.7	Rigel	281 07.5	S 8 10.6
S 09	93 18.9	1 37.1 ..	52.6	71 47.3 ..	43.9	162 25.9 ..	26.0	153 57.3 ..	57.7	Rigil Kent.	139 45.1	S60 55.3
U 10	108 21.4	16 37.0	52.7	86 48.9	44.2	177 28.6	26.0	169 00.0	57.7	Sabik	102 06.7	S15 44.9
N 11	123 23.9	31 37.0	52.9	101 50.5	44.5	192 31.4	26.0	184 02.6	57.8			
D 12	138 26.3	46 37.1	N19 53.0	116 52.0	N 4 44.8	207 34.1	S22 26.1	199 05.3	S20 57.8	Schedar	349 34.6	N56 38.7
A 13	153 28.8	61 37.1	53.1	131 53.6	45.1	222 36.8	26.1	214 07.9	57.8	Shaula	96 14.9	S37 07.1
Y 14	168 31.2	76 37.1	53.3	146 55.2	45.4	237 39.6	26.2	229 10.5	57.9	Sirius	258 29.6	S16 44.6
15	183 33.7	91 37.1 ..	53.4	161 56.8 ..	45.7	252 42.3 ..	26.2	244 13.2 ..	57.9	Spica	158 26.2	S11 16.0
16	198 36.2	106 37.1	53.5	176 58.3	46.0	267 45.0	26.2	259 15.8	58.0	Suhail	222 49.3	S43 30.8
17	213 38.6	121 37.1	53.6	191 59.9	46.3	282 47.7	26.3	274 18.5	58.0			
18	228 41.1	136 37.1	N19 53.8	207 01.5	N 4 46.6	297 50.5	S22 26.3	289 21.1	S20 58.0	Vega	80 35.3	N38 48.4
19	243 43.6	151 37.1	53.9	222 03.1	47.0	312 53.2	26.4	304 23.7	58.1	Zuben'ubi	136 59.9	S16 07.5
20	258 46.0	166 37.1	54.0	237 04.6	47.3	327 55.9	26.4	319 26.4	58.1		SHA	Mer. Pass.
21	273 48.5	181 37.1 ..	54.1	252 06.2 ..	47.6	342 58.7 ..	26.4	334 29.0 ..	58.1	Venus	269 58.9	8 54
22	288 51.0	196 37.1	54.3	267 07.8	47.9	358 01.4	26.5	349 31.7	58.2	Mars	338 58.4	4 16
23	303 53.4	211 37.1	54.4	282 09.4	48.2	13 04.1	26.5	4 34.3	58.2	Jupiter	68 58.1	22 12
Mer. Pass. h m 2 51.7		v 0.0 d 0.1		v 1.6 d 0.3		v 2.7 d 0.0		v 2.6 d 0.0		Saturn	60 32.6	22 46

UT	SUN GHA	SUN Dec	MOON GHA	v	MOON Dec	d	HP
d h	° ′	° ′	° ′	′	° ′	′	′
7 00	178 33.3	N16 20.8	319 59.8	15.4	S 7 18.2	11.8	54.7
01	193 33.4	20.1	334 34.2	15.4	7 06.4	11.9	54.7
02	208 33.5	19.4	349 08.6	15.5	6 54.5	11.9	54.6
03	223 33.6	.. 18.7	3 43.1	15.6	6 42.6	11.9	54.6
04	238 33.6	18.0	18 17.7	15.6	6 30.7	12.0	54.6
05	253 33.7	17.3	32 52.3	15.6	6 18.7	11.9	54.6
06	268 33.8	N16 16.6	47 26.9	15.6	S 6 06.8	12.0	54.6
07	283 33.9	15.9	62 01.5	15.7	5 54.8	12.0	54.6
08	298 34.0	15.2	76 36.2	15.8	5 42.8	12.0	54.6
F 09	313 34.0	.. 14.5	91 11.0	15.7	5 30.8	12.0	54.5
R 10	328 34.1	13.8	105 45.7	15.8	5 18.8	12.1	54.5
I 11	343 34.2	13.1	120 20.5	15.8	5 06.7	12.0	54.5
D 12	358 34.3	N16 12.4	134 55.3	15.9	S 4 54.7	12.1	54.5
A 13	13 34.4	11.7	149 30.2	15.9	4 42.6	12.1	54.5
Y 14	28 34.4	11.0	164 05.1	15.9	4 30.5	12.1	54.5
15	43 34.5	.. 10.3	178 40.0	16.0	4 18.4	12.1	54.5
16	58 34.6	09.5	193 15.0	15.9	4 06.3	12.1	54.5
17	73 34.7	08.8	207 49.9	16.0	3 54.2	12.1	54.5
18	88 34.8	N16 08.1	222 24.9	16.1	S 3 42.1	12.1	54.4
19	103 34.9	07.4	237 00.0	16.0	3 30.0	12.1	54.4
20	118 34.9	06.7	251 35.0	16.1	3 17.9	12.2	54.4
21	133 35.0	.. 06.0	266 10.1	16.1	3 05.7	12.1	54.4
22	148 35.1	05.3	280 45.2	16.1	2 53.6	12.2	54.4
23	163 35.2	04.6	295 20.3	16.2	2 41.4	12.1	54.4
8 00	178 35.3	N16 03.9	309 55.5	16.1	S 2 29.3	12.2	54.4
01	193 35.4	03.2	324 30.6	16.2	2 17.1	12.1	54.4
02	208 35.4	02.4	339 05.8	16.2	2 05.0	12.2	54.4
03	223 35.5	.. 01.7	353 41.0	16.2	1 52.8	12.2	54.3
04	238 35.6	01.0	8 16.2	16.3	1 40.6	12.2	54.3
05	253 35.7	16 00.3	22 51.5	16.2	1 28.4	12.1	54.3
06	268 35.8	N15 59.6	37 26.7	16.3	S 1 16.3	12.2	54.3
07	283 35.9	58.9	52 02.0	16.3	1 04.1	12.2	54.3
S 08	298 36.0	58.2	66 37.3	16.3	0 51.9	12.1	54.3
A 09	313 36.0	.. 57.4	81 12.6	16.3	0 39.8	12.2	54.3
T 10	328 36.1	56.7	95 47.9	16.3	0 27.6	12.2	54.3
U 11	343 36.2	56.0	110 23.2	16.3	0 15.4	12.1	54.3
R 12	358 36.3	N15 55.3	124 58.5	16.4	S 0 03.3	12.2	54.3
D 13	13 36.4	54.6	139 33.9	16.3	N 0 08.9	12.2	54.3
A 14	28 36.5	53.8	154 09.2	16.4	0 21.1	12.1	54.3
Y 15	43 36.6	.. 53.1	168 44.6	16.3	0 33.2	12.1	54.3
16	58 36.6	52.4	183 19.9	16.4	0 45.3	12.2	54.3
17	73 36.7	51.7	197 55.3	16.4	0 57.5	12.1	54.2
18	88 36.8	N15 51.0	212 30.7	16.4	N 1 09.6	12.1	54.2
19	103 36.9	50.3	227 06.1	16.3	1 21.7	12.2	54.2
20	118 37.0	49.5	241 41.4	16.4	1 33.9	12.1	54.2
21	133 37.1	.. 48.8	256 16.8	16.4	1 46.0	12.1	54.2
22	148 37.2	48.1	270 52.2	16.4	1 58.1	12.0	54.2
23	163 37.3	47.4	285 27.6	16.3	2 10.1	12.1	54.2
9 00	178 37.4	N15 46.6	300 02.9	16.4	N 2 22.2	12.1	54.2
01	193 37.4	45.9	314 38.3	16.4	2 34.3	12.0	54.2
02	208 37.5	45.2	329 13.7	16.4	2 46.3	12.1	54.2
03	223 37.6	.. 44.5	343 49.1	16.3	2 58.4	12.0	54.2
04	238 37.7	43.7	358 24.4	16.4	3 10.4	12.0	54.2
05	253 37.8	43.0	12 59.8	16.3	3 22.4	12.0	54.2
06	268 37.9	N15 42.3	27 35.1	16.4	N 3 34.4	12.0	54.2
07	283 38.0	41.6	42 10.5	16.3	3 46.4	12.0	54.2
08	298 38.1	40.8	56 45.8	16.3	3 58.4	11.9	54.2
S 09	313 38.2	.. 40.1	71 21.1	16.4	4 10.3	12.0	54.2
U 10	328 38.3	39.4	85 56.5	16.3	4 22.3	11.9	54.2
N 11	343 38.4	38.7	100 31.8	16.3	4 34.2	11.9	54.2
D 12	358 38.5	N15 37.9	115 07.1	16.2	N 4 46.1	11.9	54.2
A 13	13 38.5	37.2	129 42.3	16.3	4 58.0	11.8	54.2
Y 14	28 38.6	36.5	144 17.6	16.2	5 09.8	11.9	54.2
15	43 38.7	.. 35.7	158 52.8	16.3	5 21.7	11.8	54.2
16	58 38.8	35.0	173 28.1	16.2	5 33.5	11.8	54.2
17	73 38.9	34.3	188 03.3	16.2	5 45.3	11.8	54.2
18	88 39.0	N15 33.6	202 38.5	16.2	N 5 57.1	11.8	54.2
19	103 39.1	32.8	217 13.7	16.1	6 08.9	11.7	54.2
20	118 39.2	32.1	231 48.8	16.2	6 20.6	11.7	54.2
21	133 39.3	.. 31.4	246 24.0	16.1	6 32.3	11.7	54.2
22	148 39.4	30.6	260 59.1	16.1	6 44.0	11.7	54.2
23	163 39.5	29.9	275 34.2	16.0	N 6 55.7	11.6	54.2
	SD 15.8	d 0.7	SD 14.9		14.8		14.8

Lat.	Twilight Naut.	Twilight Civil	Sunrise	Moonrise 7	Moonrise 8	Moonrise 9	Moonrise 10
°	h m	h m	h m	h m	h m	h m	h m
N 72	////	////	01 29	21 54	21 34	21 13	20 48
N 70	////	////	02 20	21 50	21 36	21 22	21 06
68	////	////	02 51	21 47	21 38	21 29	21 20
66	////	01 42	03 14	21 44	21 40	21 36	21 31
64	////	02 18	03 31	21 42	21 41	21 41	21 41
62	////	02 43	03 46	21 40	21 42	21 46	21 49
60	01 31	03 03	03 58	21 38	21 44	21 50	21 57
N 58	02 05	03 19	04 09	21 36	21 45	21 53	22 03
56	02 28	03 32	04 18	21 35	21 45	21 56	22 09
54	02 47	03 44	04 26	21 33	21 46	21 59	22 14
52	03 02	03 54	04 33	21 32	21 47	22 02	22 18
50	03 15	04 03	04 40	21 31	21 48	22 04	22 22
45	03 40	04 21	04 54	21 29	21 49	22 10	22 32
N 40	03 59	04 36	05 05	21 27	21 50	22 14	22 39
35	04 15	04 48	05 15	21 25	21 51	22 18	22 46
30	04 27	04 58	05 23	21 23	21 52	22 21	22 52
20	04 47	05 15	05 38	21 21	21 54	22 27	23 02
N 10	05 03	05 29	05 51	21 18	21 55	22 32	23 11
0	05 16	05 41	06 02	21 16	21 57	22 37	23 19
S 10	05 27	05 52	06 14	21 14	21 58	22 42	23 28
20	05 37	06 03	06 26	21 12	22 00	22 48	23 37
30	05 46	06 15	06 40	21 09	22 02	22 54	23 47
35	05 51	06 21	06 48	21 07	22 03	22 58	23 53
40	05 56	06 28	06 57	21 06	22 04	23 02	24 00
45	06 01	06 36	07 07	21 04	22 05	23 06	24 08
S 50	06 07	06 45	07 20	21 01	22 08	23 12	24 18
52	06 09	06 49	07 26	21 00	22 08	23 15	24 23
54	06 12	06 54	07 32	20 59	22 08	23 18	24 28
56	06 14	06 59	07 39	20 57	22 09	23 21	24 33
58	06 17	07 04	07 47	20 56	22 10	23 24	24 39
S 60	06 20	07 10	07 57	20 54	22 11	23 29	24 47

Lat.	Sunset	Twilight Civil	Twilight Naut.	Moonset 7	Moonset 8	Moonset 9	Moonset 10
°	h m	h m	h m	h m	h m	h m	h m
N 72	22 33	////	////	07 39	09 28	11 15	13 06
N 70	21 47	////	////	07 48	09 29	11 08	12 50
68	21 17	23 32	////	07 55	09 29	11 03	12 38
66	20 55	22 23	////	08 01	09 30	10 58	12 28
64	20 37	21 49	////	08 06	09 31	10 54	12 19
62	20 23	21 25	23 36	08 10	09 31	10 51	12 12
60	20 11	21 06	22 34	08 14	09 31	10 48	12 06
N 58	20 01	20 50	22 03	08 17	09 32	10 46	12 00
56	19 52	20 37	21 40	08 20	09 32	10 44	11 55
54	19 44	20 26	21 22	08 22	09 32	10 42	11 51
52	19 37	20 16	21 08	08 25	09 33	10 40	11 47
50	19 30	20 07	20 55	08 27	09 33	10 38	11 44
45	19 17	19 49	20 30	08 31	09 33	10 35	11 36
N 40	19 05	19 35	20 11	08 35	09 34	10 32	11 30
35	18 56	19 23	19 56	08 38	09 34	10 29	11 24
30	18 47	19 13	19 43	08 41	09 34	10 27	11 20
20	18 33	18 56	19 23	08 46	09 35	10 23	11 11
N 10	18 21	18 42	19 08	08 51	09 35	10 20	11 04
0	18 09	18 30	18 55	08 55	09 36	10 16	10 57
S 10	17 58	18 19	18 45	08 59	09 36	10 13	10 51
20	17 46	18 08	18 35	09 03	09 37	10 10	10 43
30	17 32	17 57	18 25	09 08	09 37	10 06	10 35
35	17 24	17 50	18 20	09 10	09 37	10 04	10 31
40	17 15	17 43	18 16	09 14	09 38	10 01	10 25
45	17 05	17 36	18 11	09 17	09 38	09 58	10 19
S 50	16 52	17 27	18 05	09 21	09 38	09 55	10 12
52	16 46	17 22	18 03	09 23	09 38	09 53	10 09
54	16 40	17 18	18 00	09 25	09 39	09 51	10 05
56	16 33	17 13	17 58	09 28	09 39	09 49	10 01
58	16 25	17 08	17 55	09 30	09 39	09 47	09 56
S 60	16 15	17 02	17 52	09 33	09 39	09 45	09 51

Day	SUN Eqn. of Time 00h	SUN Eqn. of Time 12h	SUN Mer. Pass.	MOON Mer. Pass. Upper	MOON Mer. Pass. Lower	Age	Phase %
d	m s	m s	h m	h m	h m	d	%
7	05 47	05 43	12 06	02 45	15 05	18	86
8	05 39	05 35	12 06	03 26	15 46	19	79
9	05 31	05 26	12 05	04 07	16 27	20	70

UT	ARIES	VENUS −4.4		MARS −1.3		JUPITER −2.7		SATURN +0.2		STARS		
d h	GHA	GHA	Dec	GHA	Dec	GHA	Dec	GHA	Dec	Name	SHA	Dec
10 00	318 55.9	226 37.1	N19 54.5	297 11.0	N 4 48.5	28 06.8	S22 26.6	19 36.9	S20 58.2	Acamar	315 14.5	S40 13.2
01	333 58.3	241 37.0	54.6	312 12.5	48.8	43 09.6	26.6	34 39.6	58.3	Achernar	335 22.8	S57 07.7
02	349 00.8	256 37.0	54.7	327 14.1	49.1	58 12.3	26.6	49 42.2	58.3	Acrux	173 04.3	S63 12.9
03	4 03.3	271 37.0 ..	54.9	342 15.7 ..	49.4	73 15.0 ..	26.7	64 44.8 ..	58.3	Adhara	255 09.0	S28 59.9
04	19 05.7	286 37.0	55.0	357 17.3	49.7	88 17.7	26.7	79 47.5	58.4	Aldebaran	290 43.8	N16 32.9
05	34 08.2	301 37.0	55.1	12 18.9	50.0	103 20.5	26.7	94 50.1	58.4			
06	49 10.7	316 37.0	N19 55.2	27 20.5	N 4 50.3	118 23.2	S22 26.8	109 52.8	S20 58.5	Alioth	166 16.6	N55 51.3
07	64 13.1	331 36.9	55.3	42 22.1	50.6	133 25.9	26.8	124 55.4	58.5	Alkaid	152 55.1	N49 13.0
08	79 15.6	346 36.9	55.5	57 23.6	50.9	148 28.6	26.9	139 58.0	58.5	Alnair	27 37.0	S46 51.6
M 09	94 18.1	1 36.9 ..	55.6	72 25.2 ..	51.2	163 31.4 ..	26.9	155 00.7 ..	58.6	Alnilam	275 41.5	S 1 11.3
O 10	109 20.5	16 36.9	55.7	87 26.8	51.5	178 34.1	26.9	170 03.3	58.6	Alphard	217 51.6	S 8 44.7
N 11	124 23.0	31 36.8	55.8	102 28.4	51.8	193 36.8	27.0	185 05.9	58.6			
D 12	139 25.5	46 36.8	N19 55.9	117 30.0	N 4 52.1	208 39.5	S22 27.0	200 08.6	S20 58.7	Alphecca	126 06.7	N26 39.1
A 13	154 27.9	61 36.8	56.0	132 31.6	52.4	223 42.3	27.0	215 11.2	58.7	Alpheratz	357 38.1	N29 12.1
Y 14	169 30.4	76 36.8	56.2	147 33.2	52.7	238 45.0	27.1	230 13.9	58.7	Altair	62 03.1	N 8 55.5
15	184 32.8	91 36.7 ..	56.3	162 34.8 ..	53.0	253 47.7 ..	27.1	245 16.5 ..	58.8	Ankaa	353 10.5	S42 11.5
16	199 35.3	106 36.7	56.4	177 36.4	53.3	268 50.4	27.2	260 19.1	58.8	Antares	112 20.1	S26 28.6
17	214 37.8	121 36.7	56.5	192 38.0	53.6	283 53.2	27.2	275 21.8	58.8			
18	229 40.2	136 36.6	N19 56.6	207 39.6	N 4 53.9	298 55.9	S22 27.2	290 24.4	S20 58.9	Arcturus	145 51.3	N19 04.8
19	244 42.7	151 36.6	56.7	222 41.2	54.2	313 58.6	27.3	305 27.0	58.9	Atria	107 17.2	S69 04.0
20	259 45.2	166 36.6	56.8	237 42.8	54.5	329 01.3	27.3	320 29.7	58.9	Avior	234 16.7	S59 34.4
21	274 47.6	181 36.5 ..	56.9	252 44.4 ..	54.8	344 04.0 ..	27.4	335 32.3 ..	59.0	Bellatrix	278 26.9	N 6 22.1
22	289 50.1	196 36.5	57.1	267 46.0	55.1	359 06.8	27.4	350 35.0	59.0	Betelgeuse	270 56.2	N 7 24.6
23	304 52.6	211 36.5	57.2	282 47.6	55.4	14 09.5	27.4	5 37.6	59.1			
11 00	319 55.0	226 36.4	N19 57.3	297 49.2	N 4 55.7	29 12.2	S22 27.5	20 40.2	S20 59.1	Canopus	263 54.4	S52 42.2
01	334 57.5	241 36.4	57.4	312 50.8	56.0	44 14.9	27.5	35 42.9	59.1	Capella	280 27.4	N46 00.9
02	350 00.0	256 36.4	57.5	327 52.4	56.3	59 17.6	27.5	50 45.5	59.2	Deneb	49 27.7	N45 21.3
03	5 02.4	271 36.3 ..	57.6	342 54.0 ..	56.6	74 20.4 ..	27.6	65 48.1 ..	59.2	Denebola	182 28.9	N14 27.7
04	20 04.9	286 36.3	57.7	357 55.6	56.9	89 23.1	27.6	80 50.8	59.2	Diphda	348 50.7	S17 52.4
05	35 07.3	301 36.2	57.8	12 57.2	57.2	104 25.8	27.7	95 53.4	59.3			
06	50 09.8	316 36.2	N19 57.9	27 58.8	N 4 57.5	119 28.5	S22 27.7	110 56.0	S20 59.3	Dubhe	193 46.1	N61 38.7
07	65 12.3	331 36.2	58.0	43 00.4	57.8	134 31.2	27.7	125 58.7	59.3	Elnath	278 06.6	N28 37.3
T 08	80 14.7	346 36.1	58.1	58 02.0	58.1	149 34.0	27.8	141 01.3	59.4	Eltanin	90 43.5	N51 29.5
U 09	95 17.2	1 36.1 ..	58.2	73 03.6 ..	58.3	164 36.7 ..	27.8	156 03.9 ..	59.4	Enif	33 41.9	N 9 58.2
E 10	110 19.7	16 36.0	58.3	88 05.2	58.6	179 39.4	27.8	171 06.6	59.4	Fomalhaut	15 18.2	S29 30.7
S 11	125 22.1	31 36.0	58.4	103 06.8	58.9	194 42.1	27.9	186 09.2	59.5			
D 12	140 24.6	46 35.9	N19 58.5	118 08.5	N 4 59.2	209 44.8	S22 27.9	201 11.9	S20 59.5	Gacrux	171 55.8	S57 13.7
A 13	155 27.1	61 35.9	58.6	133 10.1	59.5	224 47.6	28.0	216 14.5	59.5	Gienah	175 47.5	S17 39.2
Y 14	170 29.5	76 35.8	58.7	148 11.7	4 59.8	239 50.3	28.0	231 17.1	59.6	Hadar	148 41.1	S60 28.4
15	185 32.0	91 35.8 ..	58.8	163 13.3	5 00.1	254 53.0 ..	28.0	246 19.8 ..	59.6	Hamal	327 55.1	N23 33.4
16	200 34.4	106 35.7	58.9	178 14.9	00.4	269 55.7	28.1	261 22.4	59.6	Kaus Aust.	83 36.9	S34 22.4
17	215 36.9	121 35.7	59.0	193 16.5	00.7	284 58.4	28.1	276 25.0	59.7			
18	230 39.4	136 35.6	N19 59.1	208 18.2	N 5 01.0	300 01.1	S22 28.1	291 27.7	S20 59.7	Kochab	137 20.1	N74 04.7
19	245 41.8	151 35.6	59.2	223 19.8	01.3	315 03.9	28.2	306 30.3	59.8	Markab	13 33.1	N15 18.9
20	260 44.3	166 35.5	59.3	238 21.4	01.6	330 06.6	28.2	321 32.9	59.8	Menkar	314 09.9	N 4 10.2
21	275 46.8	181 35.5 ..	59.4	253 23.0 ..	01.8	345 09.3 ..	28.2	336 35.6 ..	59.8	Menkent	148 01.9	S36 28.2
22	290 49.2	196 35.4	59.5	268 24.6	02.1	0 12.0	28.3	351 38.2	59.9	Miaplacidus	221 39.7	S69 48.0
23	305 51.7	211 35.3	59.6	283 26.3	02.4	15 14.7	28.3	6 40.8	59.9			
12 00	320 54.2	226 35.3	N19 59.7	298 27.9	N 5 02.7	30 17.4	S22 28.4	21 43.5	S20 59.9	Mirfak	308 33.3	N49 55.7
01	335 56.6	241 35.2	59.8	313 29.5	03.0	45 20.2	28.4	36 46.1	21 00.0	Nunki	75 51.9	S26 16.2
02	350 59.1	256 35.2	19 59.9	328 31.1	03.3	60 22.9	28.4	51 48.7	00.0	Peacock	53 10.8	S56 40.1
03	6 01.6	271 35.1	20 00.0	343 32.8 ..	03.6	75 25.6 ..	28.5	66 51.4 ..	00.0	Pollux	243 22.0	N27 58.6
04	21 04.0	286 35.0	00.1	358 34.4	03.9	90 28.3	28.5	81 54.0	00.1	Procyon	244 54.9	N 5 10.4
05	36 06.5	301 35.0	00.2	13 36.0	04.1	105 31.0	28.5	96 56.6	00.1			
06	51 08.9	316 34.9	N20 00.3	28 37.6	N 5 04.4	120 33.7	S22 28.6	111 59.3	S21 00.1	Rasalhague	96 01.7	N12 32.9
W 07	66 11.4	331 34.8	00.4	43 39.3	04.7	135 36.4	28.6	127 01.9	00.2	Regulus	207 38.6	N11 52.2
E 08	81 13.9	346 34.8	00.4	58 40.9	05.0	150 39.1	28.6	142 04.5	00.2	Rigel	281 07.5	S 8 10.6
D 09	96 16.3	1 34.7 ..	00.5	73 42.5 ..	05.3	165 41.9 ..	28.7	157 07.2 ..	00.2	Rigil Kent.	139 45.2	S60 55.3
N 10	111 18.8	16 34.6	00.6	88 44.2	05.6	180 44.6	28.7	172 09.8	00.3	Sabik	102 06.7	S15 44.9
E 11	126 21.3	31 34.6	00.7	103 45.8	05.9	195 47.3	28.8	187 12.4	00.3			
S 12	141 23.7	46 34.5	N20 00.8	118 47.4	N 5 06.1	210 50.0	S22 28.8	202 15.1	S21 00.3	Schedar	349 34.6	N56 38.7
D 13	156 26.2	61 34.4	00.9	133 49.1	06.4	225 52.7	28.8	217 17.7	00.4	Shaula	96 14.9	S37 07.1
A 14	171 28.7	76 34.4	01.0	148 50.7	06.7	240 55.4	28.9	232 20.3	00.4	Sirius	258 29.6	S16 44.6
Y 15	186 31.1	91 34.3 ..	01.1	163 52.3 ..	07.0	255 58.1 ..	28.9	247 23.0 ..	00.4	Spica	158 26.2	S11 16.0
16	201 33.6	106 34.2	01.1	178 54.0	07.3	271 00.8	28.9	262 25.6	00.5	Suhail	222 49.3	S43 30.8
17	216 36.1	121 34.1	01.2	193 55.6	07.6	286 03.6	29.0	277 28.2	00.5			
18	231 38.5	136 34.1	N20 01.3	208 57.2	N 5 07.8	301 06.3	S22 29.0	292 30.9	S21 00.5	Vega	80 35.3	N38 48.4
19	246 41.0	151 34.0	01.4	223 58.9	08.1	316 09.0	29.0	307 33.5	00.6	Zuben'ubi	137 00.0	S16 07.5
20	261 43.4	166 33.9	01.5	239 00.5	08.4	331 11.7	29.1	322 36.1	00.6		SHA	Mer. Pass.
21	276 45.9	181 33.8 ..	01.6	254 02.2 ..	08.7	346 14.4 ..	29.1	337 38.8 ..	00.6		° ′	h m
22	291 48.4	196 33.8	01.6	269 03.8	09.0	1 17.1	29.2	352 41.4	00.7	Venus	266 41.4	8 54
23	306 50.8	211 33.7	01.7	284 05.5	09.2	16 19.8	29.2	7 44.0	00.7	Mars	337 54.1	4 08
Mer. Pass. 2 39.9		v 0.0	d 0.1	v 1.6	d 0.3	v 2.7	d 0.0	v 2.6	d 0.0	Jupiter	69 17.2	21 59
										Saturn	60 45.2	22 33

UT (d h)	SUN GHA	SUN Dec	MOON GHA	v	MOON Dec	d	HP
MONDAY							
10 00	178 39.6	N15 29.2	290 09.2	16.1	N 7 07.3	11.6	54.2
01	193 39.7	28.4	304 44.3	16.0	7 18.9	11.6	54.2
02	208 39.8	27.7	319 19.3	16.0	7 30.5	11.5	54.2
03	223 39.9	.. 27.0	333 54.3	16.0	7 42.0	11.6	54.2
04	238 40.0	26.2	348 29.3	15.9	7 53.6	11.5	54.2
05	253 40.1	25.5	3 04.2	15.9	8 05.1	11.4	54.2
06	268 40.2	N15 24.8	17 39.1	15.9	N 8 16.5	11.5	54.2
07	283 40.3	24.0	32 14.0	15.8	8 28.0	11.4	54.2
08	298 40.4	23.3	46 48.8	15.8	8 39.4	11.4	54.2
09	313 40.5	.. 22.5	61 23.6	15.8	8 50.8	11.3	54.2
10	328 40.6	21.8	75 58.4	15.8	9 02.1	11.3	54.2
11	343 40.7	21.1	90 33.2	15.7	9 13.4	11.3	54.3
12	358 40.8	N15 20.3	105 07.9	15.7	N 9 24.7	11.3	54.3
13	13 40.8	19.6	119 42.6	15.6	9 36.0	11.2	54.3
14	28 40.9	18.9	134 17.2	15.6	9 47.2	11.1	54.3
15	43 41.0	.. 18.1	148 51.8	15.6	9 58.3	11.2	54.3
16	58 41.1	17.4	163 26.4	15.5	10 09.5	11.1	54.3
17	73 41.2	16.6	178 00.9	15.5	10 20.6	11.1	54.3
18	88 41.3	N15 15.9	192 35.4	15.4	N10 31.7	11.0	54.3
19	103 41.4	15.2	207 09.8	15.4	10 42.7	11.0	54.3
20	118 41.5	14.4	221 44.2	15.4	10 53.7	10.9	54.3
21	133 41.6	.. 13.7	236 18.6	15.3	11 04.6	10.9	54.3
22	148 41.7	12.9	250 52.9	15.3	11 15.5	10.9	54.3
23	163 41.8	12.2	265 27.2	15.2	11 26.4	10.8	54.3
TUESDAY							
11 00	178 42.0	N15 11.4	280 01.4	15.2	N11 37.2	10.8	54.4
01	193 42.1	10.7	294 35.6	15.1	11 48.0	10.8	54.4
02	208 42.2	10.0	309 09.7	15.1	11 58.8	10.7	54.4
03	223 42.3	.. 09.2	323 43.8	15.0	12 09.5	10.6	54.4
04	238 42.4	08.5	338 17.8	15.0	12 20.1	10.6	54.4
05	253 42.5	07.7	352 51.8	15.0	12 30.7	10.6	54.4
06	268 42.6	N15 07.0	7 25.8	14.8	N12 41.3	10.5	54.4
07	283 42.7	06.2	21 59.6	14.9	12 51.8	10.5	54.4
08	298 42.8	05.5	36 33.5	14.7	13 02.3	10.4	54.4
09	313 42.9	.. 04.7	51 07.2	14.8	13 12.7	10.4	54.5
10	328 43.0	04.0	65 41.0	14.6	13 23.1	10.3	54.5
11	343 43.1	03.2	80 14.6	14.7	13 33.4	10.3	54.5
12	358 43.2	N15 02.5	94 48.3	14.5	N13 43.7	10.2	54.5
13	13 43.3	01.7	109 21.8	14.5	13 53.9	10.2	54.5
14	28 43.4	01.0	123 55.3	14.5	14 04.1	10.1	54.5
15	43 43.5	15 00.2	138 28.8	14.4	14 14.2	10.1	54.5
16	58 43.6	14 59.5	153 02.2	14.3	14 24.3	10.0	54.6
17	73 43.7	58.7	167 35.5	14.3	14 34.3	10.0	54.6
18	88 43.8	N14 58.0	182 08.8	14.2	N14 44.3	9.9	54.6
19	103 43.9	57.2	196 42.0	14.1	14 54.2	9.8	54.6
20	118 44.0	56.5	211 15.1	14.1	15 04.0	9.8	54.6
21	133 44.1	.. 55.7	225 48.2	14.0	15 13.8	9.8	54.6
22	148 44.2	55.0	240 21.2	14.0	15 23.6	9.6	54.6
23	163 44.3	54.2	254 54.2	13.9	15 33.2	9.6	54.7
WEDNESDAY							
12 00	178 44.5	N14 53.5	269 27.1	13.8	N15 42.8	9.6	54.7
01	193 44.6	52.7	283 59.9	13.7	15 52.4	9.5	54.7
02	208 44.7	52.0	298 32.6	13.7	16 01.9	9.4	54.7
03	223 44.8	.. 51.2	313 05.3	13.7	16 11.3	9.4	54.7
04	238 44.9	50.5	327 38.0	13.5	16 20.7	9.3	54.7
05	253 45.0	49.7	342 10.5	13.5	16 30.0	9.2	54.8
06	268 45.1	N14 48.9	356 43.0	13.4	N16 39.2	9.2	54.8
07	283 45.2	48.2	11 15.4	13.4	16 48.4	9.1	54.8
08	298 45.3	47.4	25 47.8	13.3	16 57.5	9.1	54.8
09	313 45.4	.. 46.7	40 20.1	13.2	17 06.6	8.9	54.8
10	328 45.5	45.9	54 52.3	13.1	17 15.5	8.9	54.9
11	343 45.6	45.2	69 24.4	13.1	17 24.4	8.9	54.9
12	358 45.8	N14 44.4	83 56.5	13.0	N17 33.3	8.7	54.9
13	13 45.9	43.6	98 28.5	12.9	17 42.0	8.7	54.9
14	28 46.0	42.9	113 00.4	12.8	17 50.7	8.6	54.9
15	43 46.1	.. 42.1	127 32.2	12.8	17 59.3	8.5	55.0
16	58 46.2	41.4	142 04.0	12.7	18 07.9	8.4	55.0
17	73 46.3	40.6	156 35.7	12.6	18 16.3	8.4	55.0
18	88 46.4	N14 39.8	171 07.3	12.6	N18 24.7	8.4	55.0
19	103 46.5	39.1	185 38.9	12.4	18 33.1	8.2	55.1
20	118 46.6	38.3	200 10.3	12.4	18 41.3	8.2	55.1
21	133 46.8	.. 37.6	214 41.7	12.4	18 49.5	8.1	55.1
22	148 46.9	36.8	229 13.1	12.2	18 57.6	8.0	55.1
23	163 47.0	36.0	243 44.3	12.2	N19 05.6	7.9	55.1
	SD 15.8	d 0.7	SD 14.8		14.8		15.0

Twilight / Sunrise / Moonrise

Lat.	Naut.	Civil	Sunrise	Moonrise 10	11	12	13
N 72	////	////	01 57	20 48	20 13	☐	☐
N 70	////	////	02 37	21 06	20 45	20 09	☐
68	////	01 10	03 04	21 20	21 09	20 53	20 20
66	////	02 01	03 24	21 31	21 27	21 23	21 19
64	////	02 32	03 41	21 41	21 42	21 45	21 53
62	01 02	02 54	03 54	21 49	21 55	22 03	22 18
60	01 48	03 12	04 06	21 57	22 06	22 18	22 38
N 58	02 17	03 27	04 15	22 03	22 15	22 31	22 54
56	02 38	03 39	04 24	22 09	22 23	22 42	23 08
54	02 55	03 50	04 31	22 14	22 31	22 52	23 20
52	03 09	03 59	04 38	22 18	22 37	23 01	23 31
50	03 21	04 08	04 44	22 22	22 43	23 09	23 40
45	03 45	04 25	04 57	22 32	22 56	23 25	24 00
N 40	04 03	04 39	05 08	22 39	23 07	23 39	24 17
35	04 18	04 50	05 17	22 46	23 16	23 51	24 31
30	04 30	05 00	05 25	22 52	23 24	24 01	00 01
20	04 49	05 16	05 39	23 02	23 39	24 19	00 19
N 10	05 03	05 29	05 51	23 11	23 51	24 34	00 34
0	05 15	05 40	06 02	23 19	24 03	00 03	00 49
S 10	05 26	05 51	06 13	23 28	24 15	00 14	01 04
20	05 35	06 01	06 24	23 37	24 27	00 27	01 19
30	05 44	06 12	06 37	23 47	24 42	00 42	01 38
35	05 48	06 18	06 44	23 53	24 50	00 50	01 48
40	05 53	06 25	06 53	24 00	00 00	01 00	02 01
45	05 57	06 32	07 03	24 08	00 08	01 11	02 15
S 50	06 02	06 40	07 15	24 18	00 18	01 25	02 33
52	06 04	06 44	07 20	24 23	00 23	01 32	02 41
54	06 06	06 48	07 26	24 28	00 28	01 39	02 51
56	06 09	06 53	07 33	24 33	00 33	01 47	03 01
58	06 11	06 58	07 40	24 39	00 39	01 56	03 14
S 60	06 14	07 03	07 49	24 47	00 47	02 06	03 28

Sunset / Twilight / Moonset

Lat.	Sunset	Civil	Naut.	Moonset 10	11	12	13
N 72	22 06	////	////	13 06	15 10	☐	☐
N 70	21 29	////	////	12 50	14 40	16 50	☐
68	21 03	22 51	////	12 38	14 17	16 07	18 22
66	20 43	22 04	////	12 28	14 00	15 38	17 23
64	20 27	21 35	////	12 19	13 46	15 17	16 50
62	20 14	21 13	22 59	12 12	13 34	14 59	16 25
60	20 03	20 56	22 17	12 06	13 24	14 45	16 06
N 58	19 53	20 42	21 50	12 00	13 16	14 33	15 50
56	19 45	20 29	21 30	11 55	13 08	14 22	15 36
54	19 38	20 19	21 14	11 51	13 02	14 13	15 24
52	19 31	20 10	21 00	11 47	12 56	14 05	15 14
50	19 25	20 01	20 48	11 44	12 50	13 57	15 05
45	19 12	19 44	20 24	11 36	12 38	13 42	14 46
N 40	19 02	19 31	20 06	11 30	12 29	13 29	14 30
35	18 52	19 19	19 52	11 24	12 20	13 18	14 17
30	18 45	19 10	19 40	11 20	12 13	13 08	14 05
20	18 31	18 54	19 21	11 11	12 01	12 52	13 45
N 10	18 19	18 41	19 07	11 04	11 50	12 38	13 28
0	18 09	18 30	18 55	10 57	11 40	12 25	13 12
S 10	17 58	18 19	18 45	10 51	11 30	12 11	12 56
20	17 46	18 09	18 35	10 43	11 19	11 57	12 40
30	17 34	17 58	18 27	10 35	11 07	11 41	12 20
35	17 26	17 52	18 22	10 31	11 00	11 32	12 09
40	17 18	17 46	18 18	10 25	10 52	11 21	11 56
45	17 08	17 39	18 14	10 19	10 42	11 09	11 40
S 50	16 56	17 30	18 09	10 12	10 31	10 54	11 22
52	16 51	17 27	18 07	10 09	10 26	10 47	11 13
54	16 45	17 23	18 05	10 05	10 20	10 39	11 03
56	16 38	17 18	18 02	10 01	10 14	10 30	10 52
58	16 31	17 13	18 00	09 56	10 07	10 21	10 39
S 60	16 22	17 08	17 58	09 51	09 59	10 09	10 25

SUN and MOON

Day	SUN Eqn. of Time 00h	12h	Mer. Pass.	MOON Mer. Pass. Upper	Lower	Age	Phase
10	05 22	05 17	12 05	04 47	17 08	21	61
11	05 12	05 07	12 05	05 29	17 51	22	52
12	05 02	04 57	12 05	06 14	18 37	23	42

UT	ARIES	VENUS −4.4		MARS −1.4		JUPITER −2.7		SATURN +0.2		STARS		
d h	GHA	GHA	Dec	GHA	Dec	GHA	Dec	GHA	Dec	Name	SHA	Dec
13 00	321 53.3	226 33.6	N20 01.8	299 07.1	N 5 09.5	31 22.5	S22 29.2	22 46.7	S21 00.8	Acamar	315 14.5	S40 13.2
01	336 55.8	241 33.5	01.9	314 08.7	09.8	46 25.2	29.3	37 49.3	00.8	Achernar	335 22.7	S57 07.7
02	351 58.2	256 33.4	02.0	329 10.4	10.1	61 27.9	29.3	52 51.9	00.8	Acrux	173 04.3	S63 12.9
03	7 00.7	271 33.3 ..	02.0	344 12.0 ..	10.4	76 30.6 ..	29.3	67 54.6 ..	00.9	Adhara	255 08.9	S28 59.9
04	22 03.2	286 33.3	02.1	359 13.7	10.6	91 33.4	29.4	82 57.2	00.9	Aldebaran	290 43.8	N16 32.9
05	37 05.6	301 33.2	02.2	14 15.3	10.9	106 36.1	29.4	97 59.8	00.9			
06	52 08.1	316 33.1	N20 02.3	29 17.0	N 5 11.2	121 38.8	S22 29.4	113 02.5	S21 01.0	Alioth	166 16.6	N55 51.3
07	67 10.5	331 33.0	02.3	44 18.6	11.5	136 41.5	29.5	128 05.1	01.0	Alkaid	152 55.1	N49 13.0
T 08	82 13.0	346 32.9	02.4	59 20.3	11.7	151 44.2	29.5	143 07.7	01.0	Alnair	27 37.0	S46 51.6
H 09	97 15.5	1 32.8 ..	02.5	74 22.0 ..	12.0	166 46.9 ..	29.5	158 10.4 ..	01.1	Alnilam	275 41.5	S 1 11.3
U 10	112 17.9	16 32.7	02.6	89 23.6	12.3	181 49.6	29.6	173 13.0	01.1	Alphard	217 51.6	S 8 44.7
R 11	127 20.4	31 32.6	02.6	104 25.3	12.6	196 52.3	29.6	188 15.6	01.1			
S 12	142 22.9	46 32.6	N20 02.7	119 26.9	N 5 12.9	211 55.0	S22 29.6	203 18.3	S21 01.2	Alphecca	126 06.8	N26 39.1
D 13	157 25.3	61 32.5	02.8	134 28.6	13.1	226 57.7	29.7	218 20.9	01.2	Alpheratz	357 38.1	N29 12.1
A 14	172 27.8	76 32.4	02.8	149 30.2	13.4	242 00.4	29.7	233 23.5	01.2	Altair	62 03.1	N 8 55.5
Y 15	187 30.3	91 32.3 ..	02.9	164 31.9 ..	13.7	257 03.1 ..	29.8	248 26.2 ..	01.3	Ankaa	353 10.4	S42 11.5
16	202 32.7	106 32.2	03.0	179 33.6	14.0	272 05.8	29.8	263 28.8	01.3	Antares	112 20.1	S26 28.6
17	217 35.2	121 32.1	03.1	194 35.2	14.2	287 08.5	29.8	278 31.4	01.3			
18	232 37.7	136 32.0	N20 03.1	209 36.9	N 5 14.5	302 11.2	S22 29.9	293 34.0	S21 01.4	Arcturus	145 51.3	N19 04.8
19	247 40.1	151 31.9	03.2	224 38.5	14.8	317 13.9	29.9	308 36.7	01.4	Atria	107 17.2	S69 04.0
20	262 42.6	166 31.8	03.3	239 40.2	15.0	332 16.6	29.9	323 39.3	01.4	Avior	234 16.7	S59 34.4
21	277 45.0	181 31.7 ..	03.3	254 41.9 ..	15.3	347 19.3 ..	30.0	338 41.9 ..	01.5	Bellatrix	278 26.9	N 6 22.1
22	292 47.5	196 31.6	03.4	269 43.5	15.6	2 22.0	30.0	353 44.6	01.5	Betelgeuse	270 56.1	N 7 24.6
23	307 50.0	211 31.5	03.5	284 45.2	15.9	17 24.8	30.0	8 47.2	01.5			
14 00	322 52.4	226 31.4	N20 03.5	299 46.9	N 5 16.1	32 27.5	S22 30.1	23 49.8	S21 01.6	Canopus	263 54.3	S52 42.2
01	337 54.9	241 31.3	03.6	314 48.5	16.4	47 30.2	30.1	38 52.5	01.6	Capella	280 27.3	N46 00.9
02	352 57.4	256 31.2	03.7	329 50.2	16.7	62 32.9	30.1	53 55.1	01.6	Deneb	49 27.7	N45 21.3
03	7 59.8	271 31.1 ..	03.7	344 51.9 ..	16.9	77 35.6 ..	30.2	68 57.7 ..	01.7	Denebola	182 28.9	N14 27.7
04	23 02.3	286 31.0	03.8	359 53.5	17.2	92 38.3	30.2	84 00.3	01.7	Diphda	348 50.7	S17 52.4
05	38 04.8	301 30.9*	03.8	14 55.2	17.5	107 41.0	30.2	99 03.0	01.7			
06	53 07.2	316 30.8	N20 03.9	29 56.9	N 5 17.8	122 43.7	S22 30.3	114 05.6	S21 01.8	Dubhe	193 46.1	N61 38.6
07	68 09.7	331 30.7	04.0	44 58.6	18.0	137 46.4	30.3	129 08.2	01.8	Elnath	278 06.5	N28 37.3
08	83 12.2	346 30.6	04.0	60 00.2	18.3	152 49.1	30.3	144 10.9	01.8	Eltanin	90 43.5	N51 29.5
F 09	98 14.6	1 30.4 ..	04.1	75 01.9 ..	18.6	167 51.8 ..	30.4	159 13.5 ..	01.9	Enif	33 41.9	N 9 58.2
R 10	113 17.1	16 30.3	04.1	90 03.6	18.8	182 54.5	30.4	174 16.1	01.9	Fomalhaut	15 18.1	S29 30.7
I 11	128 19.5	31 30.2	04.2	105 05.3	19.1	197 57.2	30.4	189 18.8	01.9			
D 12	143 22.0	46 30.1	N20 04.2	120 06.9	N 5 19.4	212 59.9	S22 30.5	204 21.4	S21 02.0	Gacrux	171 55.9	S57 13.7
A 13	158 24.5	61 30.0	04.3	135 08.6	19.6	228 02.6	30.5	219 24.0	02.0	Gienah	175 47.5	S17 39.2
Y 14	173 26.9	76 29.9	04.4	150 10.3	19.9	243 05.3	30.5	234 26.6	02.0	Hadar	148 41.1	S60 28.4
15	188 29.4	91 29.8 ..	04.4	165 12.0 ..	20.2	258 08.0 ..	30.6	249 29.3 ..	02.1	Hamal	327 55.1	N23 33.4
16	203 31.9	106 29.7	04.5	180 13.7	20.4	273 10.7	30.6	264 31.9	02.1	Kaus Aust.	83 36.9	S34 22.4
17	218 34.3	121 29.5	04.5	195 15.4	20.7	288 13.4	30.6	279 34.5	02.1			
18	233 36.8	136 29.4	N20 04.6	210 17.0	N 5 21.0	303 16.1	S22 30.7	294 37.2	S21 02.2	Kochab	137 20.1	N74 04.7
19	248 39.3	151 29.3	04.6	225 18.7	21.2	318 18.7	30.7	309 39.8	02.2	Markab	13 33.1	N15 19.0
20	263 41.7	166 29.2	04.7	240 20.4	21.5	333 21.4	30.7	324 42.4	02.2	Menkar	314 09.8	N 4 10.2
21	278 44.2	181 29.1 ..	04.7	255 22.1 ..	21.8	348 24.1 ..	30.8	339 45.0 ..	02.3	Menkent	148 01.9	S36 28.2
22	293 46.7	196 29.0	04.8	270 23.8	22.0	3 26.8	30.8	354 47.7	02.3	Miaplacidus	221 39.7	S69 48.0
23	308 49.1	211 28.8	04.8	285 25.5	22.3	18 29.5	30.9	9 50.3	02.3			
15 00	323 51.6	226 28.7	N20 04.9	300 27.2	N 5 22.5	33 32.2	S22 30.9	24 52.9	S21 02.4	Mirfak	308 33.3	N49 55.7
01	338 54.0	241 28.6	04.9	315 28.9	22.8	48 34.9	30.9	39 55.6	02.4	Nunki	75 51.9	S26 16.2
02	353 56.5	256 28.5	05.0	330 30.6	23.1	63 37.6	31.0	54 58.2	02.4	Peacock	53 10.8	S56 40.1
03	8 59.0	271 28.3 ..	05.0	345 32.3 ..	23.3	78 40.3 ..	31.0	70 00.8 ..	02.5	Pollux	243 22.0	N27 58.6
04	24 01.4	286 28.2	05.1	0 33.9	23.6	93 43.0	31.0	85 03.4	02.5	Procyon	244 54.8	N 5 10.4
05	39 03.9	301 28.1	05.1	15 35.6	23.8	108 45.7	31.1	100 06.1	02.5			
06	54 06.4	316 28.0	N20 05.2	30 37.3	N 5 24.1	123 48.4	S22 31.1	115 08.7	S21 02.6	Rasalhague	96 01.7	N12 32.9
07	69 08.8	331 27.8	05.2	45 39.0	24.4	138 51.1	31.1	130 11.3	02.6	Regulus	207 38.6	N11 52.2
S 08	84 11.3	346 27.7	05.3	60 40.7	24.6	153 53.8	31.2	145 13.9	02.6	Rigel	281 07.4	S 8 10.6
A 09	99 13.8	1 27.6 ..	05.3	75 42.4 ..	24.9	168 56.5 ..	31.2	160 16.6 ..	02.7	Rigil Kent.	139 45.2	S60 55.3
T 10	114 16.2	16 27.5	05.3	90 44.1	25.1	183 59.2	31.2	175 19.2	02.7	Sabik	102 06.7	S15 44.9
U 11	129 18.7	31 27.3	05.4	105 45.8	25.4	199 01.9	31.3	190 21.8	02.7			
R 12	144 21.1	46 27.2	N20 05.4	120 47.5	N 5 25.7	214 04.6	S22 31.3	205 24.5	S21 02.8	Schedar	349 34.6	N56 38.8
D 13	159 23.6	61 27.1	05.5	135 49.2	25.9	229 07.3	31.3	220 27.1	02.8	Shaula	96 15.0	S37 07.1
A 14	174 26.1	76 26.9	05.5	150 50.9	26.2	244 09.9	31.3	235 29.7	02.8	Sirius	258 29.6	S16 44.6
Y 15	189 28.5	91 26.8 ..	05.5	165 52.7 ..	26.4	259 12.6 ..	31.4	250 32.3 ..	02.9	Spica	158 26.2	S11 16.0
16	204 31.0	106 26.7	05.6	180 54.4	26.7	274 15.3	31.4	265 35.0	02.9	Suhail	222 49.3	S43 30.8
17	219 33.5	121 26.5	05.6	195 56.1	27.0	289 18.0	31.4	280 37.6	02.9			
18	234 35.9	136 26.4	N20 05.7	210 57.8	N 5 27.2	304 20.7	S22 31.5	295 40.2	S21 03.0	Vega	80 35.3	N38 48.4
19	249 38.4	151 26.3	05.7	225 59.5	27.5	319 23.4	31.5	310 42.8	03.0	Zuben'ubi	137 00.0	S16 07.5
20	264 40.9	166 26.1	05.7	241 01.2	27.7	334 26.1	31.5	325 45.5	03.0		SHA	Mer.Pass.
21	279 43.3	181 26.0 ..	05.8	256 02.9 ..	28.0	349 28.8 ..	31.6	340 48.1 ..	03.1		° '	h m
22	294 45.8	196 25.8	05.8	271 04.6	28.2	4 31.5	31.6	355 50.7	03.1	Venus	263 39.0	8 54
23	309 48.3	211 25.7	05.8	286 06.3	28.5	19 34.2	31.6	10 53.3	03.1	Mars	336 54.4	4 00
										Jupiter	69 35.0	21 46
Mer.Pass. 2 28.1		v −0.1	d 0.1	v 1.7	d 0.3	v 2.7	d 0.0	v 2.6	d 0.0	Saturn	60 57.4	22 21

UT	SUN GHA	SUN Dec	MOON GHA	v	MOON Dec	d	HP
d h	° ′	° ′	° ′	′	° ′	′	′
13 00	178 47.1	N14 35.3	258 15.5	12.0	N19 13.5	7.8	55.2
01	193 47.2	34.5	272 46.5	12.0	19 21.3	7.8	55.2
02	208 47.3	33.7	287 17.5	12.0	19 29.1	7.7	55.2
03	223 47.4 ..	33.0	301 48.5	11.8	19 36.8	7.5	55.2
04	238 47.5	32.2	316 19.3	11.8	19 44.3	7.5	55.3
05	253 47.7	31.4	330 50.1	11.7	19 51.8	7.5	55.3
06	268 47.8	N14 30.7	345 20.8	11.6	N19 59.3	7.3	55.3
T 07	283 47.9	29.9	359 51.4	11.5	20 06.6	7.2	55.3
H 08	298 48.0	29.2	14 21.9	11.5	20 13.8	7.2	55.4
U 09	313 48.1 ..	28.4	28 52.4	11.3	20 21.0	7.1	55.4
R 10	328 48.2	27.6	43 22.7	11.3	20 28.1	6.9	55.4
S 11	343 48.3	26.8	57 53.0	11.2	20 35.0	6.9	55.4
D 12	358 48.5	N14 26.1	72 23.2	11.1	N20 41.9	6.8	55.5
A 13	13 48.6	25.3	86 53.3	11.1	20 48.7	6.7	55.5
Y 14	28 48.7	24.5	101 23.4	10.9	20 55.4	6.6	55.5
15	43 48.8 ..	23.8	115 53.3	10.9	21 02.0	6.5	55.6
16	58 48.9	23.0	130 23.2	10.8	21 08.5	6.4	55.6
17	73 49.0	22.2	144 53.0	10.7	21 14.9	6.3	55.6
18	88 49.2	N14 21.5	159 22.7	10.7	N21 21.2	6.2	55.6
19	103 49.3	20.7	173 52.4	10.5	21 27.4	6.1	55.7
20	118 49.4	19.9	188 21.9	10.5	21 33.5	6.0	55.7
21	133 49.5 ..	19.1	202 51.4	10.4	21 39.5	5.9	55.7
22	148 49.6	18.4	217 20.8	10.3	21 45.4	5.8	55.7
23	163 49.7	17.6	231 50.1	10.2	21 51.2	5.6	55.8
14 00	178 49.9	N14 16.8	246 19.3	10.1	N21 56.8	5.6	55.8
01	193 50.0	16.1	260 48.4	10.1	22 02.4	5.5	55.8
02	208 50.1	15.3	275 17.5	10.0	22 07.9	5.4	55.9
03	223 50.2 ..	14.5	289 46.5	9.9	22 13.3	5.2	55.9
04	238 50.3	13.7	304 15.4	9.8	22 18.5	5.2	55.9
05	253 50.5	13.0	318 44.2	9.8	22 23.7	5.0	56.0
06	268 50.6	N14 12.2	333 13.0	9.6	N22 28.7	5.0	56.0
07	283 50.7	11.4	347 41.6	9.6	22 33.7	4.8	56.0
08	298 50.8	10.6	2 10.2	9.5	22 38.5	4.7	56.0
F 09	313 50.9 ..	09.9	16 38.7	9.5	22 43.2	4.6	56.1
R 10	328 51.1	09.1	31 07.2	9.3	22 47.8	4.4	56.1
I 11	343 51.2	08.3	45 35.5	9.3	22 52.2	4.4	56.1
D 12	358 51.3	N14 07.5	60 03.8	9.2	N22 56.6	4.2	56.2
A 13	13 51.4	06.7	74 32.0	9.1	23 00.8	4.2	56.2
Y 14	28 51.5	06.0	89 00.1	9.0	23 05.0	4.0	56.2
15	43 51.7 ..	05.2	103 28.1	9.0	23 09.0	3.8	56.3
16	58 51.8	04.4	117 56.1	8.9	23 12.8	3.8	56.3
17	73 51.9	03.6	132 24.0	8.8	23 16.6	3.6	56.3
18	88 52.0	N14 02.9	146 51.8	8.8	N23 20.2	3.5	56.4
19	103 52.1	02.1	161 19.6	8.6	23 23.7	3.4	56.4
20	118 52.3	01.3	175 47.2	8.6	23 27.1	3.3	56.4
21	133 52.4	14 00.5	190 14.8	8.6	23 30.4	3.1	56.5
22	148 52.5	13 59.7	204 42.4	8.4	23 33.5	3.1	56.5
23	163 52.6	58.9	219 09.8	8.4	23 36.6	2.8	56.5
15 00	178 52.8	N13 58.2	233 37.2	8.3	N23 39.4	2.8	56.6
01	193 52.9	57.4	248 04.5	8.3	23 42.2	2.6	56.6
02	208 53.0	56.6	262 31.8	8.2	23 44.8	2.5	56.6
03	223 53.1 ..	55.8	276 59.0	8.1	23 47.3	2.4	56.7
04	238 53.3	55.0	291 26.1	8.0	23 49.7	2.2	56.7
05	253 53.4	54.2	305 53.1	8.0	23 51.9	2.1	56.7
06	268 53.5	N13 53.5	320 20.1	7.9	N23 54.0	2.0	56.8
S 07	283 53.6	52.7	334 47.0	7.9	23 56.0	1.8	56.8
A 08	298 53.8	51.9	349 13.9	7.8	23 57.8	1.7	56.8
T 09	313 53.9 ..	51.1	3 40.7	7.7	23 59.5	1.6	56.9
U 10	328 54.0	50.3	18 07.4	7.7	24 01.1	1.4	56.9
R 11	343 54.1	49.5	32 34.1	7.6	24 02.5	1.3	56.9
D 12	358 54.3	N13 48.7	47 00.7	7.6	N24 03.8	1.1	57.0
A 13	13 54.4	48.0	61 27.3	7.5	24 04.9	1.1	57.0
Y 14	28 54.5	47.2	75 53.8	7.4	24 06.0	0.8	57.0
15	43 54.6 ..	46.4	90 20.2	7.4	24 06.8	0.8	57.1
16	58 54.8	45.6	104 46.6	7.4	24 07.6	0.6	57.1
17	73 54.9	44.8	119 13.0	7.3	24 08.2	0.4	57.1
18	88 55.0	N13 44.0	133 39.3	7.2	N24 08.6	0.3	57.2
19	103 55.1	43.2	148 05.5	7.2	24 08.9	0.2	57.2
20	118 55.3	42.4	162 31.7	7.1	24 09.1	0.0	57.2
21	133 55.4 ..	41.6	176 57.8	7.1	24 09.1	0.1	57.3
22	148 55.5	40.9	191 23.9	7.1	24 09.0	0.3	57.3
23	163 55.7	40.1	205 50.0	7.0	N24 08.7	0.4	57.3
SD 15.8	d 0.8		SD 15.1		15.3		15.5

Lat.	Twilight Naut.	Twilight Civil	Sunrise	Moonrise 13	Moonrise 14	Moonrise 15	Moonrise 16
°	h m	h m	h m	h m	h m	h m	h m
N 72	////	////	02 20	☐	☐	☐	☐
N 70	////	////	02 53	☐	☐	☐	☐
68	////	01 39	03 17	20 20	☐	☐	☐
66	////	02 18	03 35	21 19	21 14	☐	23 17
64	////	02 44	03 50	21 53	22 10	22 52	24 11
62	01 28	03 05	04 02	22 18	22 44	23 30	24 43
60	02 03	03 21	04 13	22 38	23 08	23 57	25 07
N 58	02 28	03 34	04 22	22 54	23 28	24 18	00 18
56	02 47	03 46	04 30	23 08	23 44	24 35	00 35
54	03 02	03 56	04 37	23 20	23 58	24 50	00 50
52	03 15	04 05	04 43	23 31	24 10	00 10	01 02
50	03 27	04 13	04 49	23 40	24 21	00 21	01 14
45	03 49	04 29	05 01	24 00	00 00	00 44	01 37
N 40	04 07	04 42	05 11	24 17	00 17	01 02	01 56
35	04 20	04 53	05 20	24 31	00 31	01 17	02 12
30	04 32	05 02	05 27	00 01	00 43	01 31	02 25
20	04 50	05 17	05 40	00 19	01 03	01 53	02 48
N 10	05 04	05 29	05 51	00 34	01 22	02 13	03 09
0	05 15	05 40	06 01	00 49	01 39	02 32	03 27
S 10	05 25	05 50	06 11	01 04	01 56	02 50	03 46
20	05 33	05 59	06 22	01 19	02 14	03 10	04 06
30	05 41	06 10	06 34	01 38	02 35	03 33	04 30
35	05 45	06 15	06 41	01 48	02 48	03 46	04 43
40	05 49	06 21	06 49	02 01	03 02	04 02	04 59
45	05 53	06 26	06 58	02 15	03 19	04 21	05 18
S 50	05 57	06 35	07 09	02 33	03 40	04 44	05 41
52	05 59	06 39	07 14	02 41	03 50	04 55	05 53
54	06 01	06 43	07 20	02 51	04 02	05 08	06 06
56	06 03	06 47	07 26	03 01	04 15	05 23	06 20
58	06 05	06 51	07 33	03 14	04 30	05 40	06 38
S 60	06 07	06 56	07 41	03 28	04 48	06 01	06 59

Lat.	Sunset	Twilight Civil	Twilight Naut.	Moonset 13	Moonset 14	Moonset 15	Moonset 16
°	h m	h m	h m	h m	h m	h m	h m
N 72	21 43	////	////	☐	☐	☐	☐
N 70	21 12	23 52	////	☐	☐	☐	☐
68	20 49	22 23	////	18 22	☐	☐	☐
66	20 31	21 47	////	17 23	19 16	☐	21 08
64	20 17	21 21	23 53	16 50	18 20	19 33	20 14
62	20 05	21 02	22 35	16 25	17 47	18 55	19 41
60	19 55	20 46	22 02	16 06	17 23	18 28	19 17
N 58	19 46	20 33	21 38	15 50	17 03	18 07	18 58
56	19 38	20 22	21 20	15 36	16 47	17 50	18 41
54	19 31	20 12	21 05	15 24	16 33	17 36	18 28
52	19 25	20 03	20 52	15 14	16 21	17 23	18 15
50	19 19	19 56	20 41	15 05	16 11	17 12	18 05
45	19 07	19 39	20 19	14 46	15 49	16 48	17 42
N 40	18 58	19 27	20 02	14 30	15 31	16 30	17 24
35	18 49	19 16	19 48	14 17	15 16	16 14	17 09
30	18 42	19 07	19 37	14 05	15 03	16 00	16 56
20	18 29	18 52	19 19	13 45	14 41	15 37	16 33
N 10	18 18	18 40	19 05	13 28	14 22	15 17	16 13
0	18 08	18 29	18 54	13 12	14 04	14 58	15 55
S 10	17 58	18 20	18 45	12 56	13 46	14 39	15 36
20	17 47	18 10	18 36	12 40	13 27	14 19	15 16
30	17 35	18 00	18 28	12 20	13 05	13 56	14 53
35	17 28	17 55	18 24	12 09	12 52	13 42	14 40
40	17 21	17 49	18 21	11 56	12 37	13 26	14 24
45	17 12	17 42	18 17	11 40	12 19	13 07	14 06
S 50	17 01	17 35	18 13	11 22	11 58	12 44	13 42
52	16 56	17 31	18 11	11 13	11 47	12 33	13 31
54	16 50	17 27	18 09	11 03	11 36	12 20	13 18
56	16 44	17 23	18 07	10 52	11 22	12 05	13 04
58	16 37	17 19	18 05	10 39	11 07	11 48	12 47
S 60	16 29	17 14	18 03	10 25	10 48	11 26	12 26

Day	SUN Eqn. of Time 00ʰ	SUN Eqn. of Time 12ʰ	SUN Mer. Pass.	MOON Mer. Pass. Upper	MOON Mer. Pass. Lower	Age	Phase
d	m s	m s	h m	h m	h m	d	%
13	04 52	04 46	12 05	07 01	19 25	24	33
14	04 41	04 35	12 05	07 51	20 17	25	24
15	04 29	04 23	12 04	08 45	21 13	26	16

UT	ARIES	VENUS −4·4		MARS −1·5		JUPITER −2·6		SATURN +0·2		STARS		
	GHA	GHA	Dec	GHA	Dec	GHA	Dec	GHA	Dec	Name	SHA	Dec
d h	° ′	° ′	° ′	° ′	° ′	° ′	° ′	° ′	° ′		° ′	° ′
16 00	324 50.7	226 25.6	N20 05.9	301 08.0	N 5 28.7	34 36.9	S22 31.7	25 56.0	S21 03.2	Acamar	315 14.5	S40 13.1
01	339 53.2	241 25.4	05.9	316 09.8	29.0	49 39.5	31.7	40 58.6	03.2	Achernar	335 22.7	S57 07.7
02	354 55.6	256 25.3	05.9	331 11.5	29.2	64 42.2	31.7	56 01.2	03.2	Acrux	173 04.3	S63 12.8
03	9 58.1	271 25.1 . .	06.0	346 13.2 . .	29.5	79 44.9 . .	31.8	71 03.8 . .	03.3	Adhara	255 08.9	S28 59.8
04	25 00.6	286 25.0	06.0	1 14.9	29.7	94 47.6	31.8	86 06.5	03.3	Aldebaran	290 43.8	N16 32.9
05	40 03.0	301 24.8	06.0	16 16.6	30.0	109 50.3	31.8	101 09.1	03.3			
06	55 05.5	316 24.7	N20 06.0	31 18.4	N 5 30.3	124 53.0	S22 31.9	116 11.7	S21 03.4	Alioth	166 16.6	N55 51.3
07	70 08.0	331 24.6	06.1	46 20.1	30.5	139 55.7	31.9	131 14.3	03.4	Alkaid	152 55.1	N49 13.0
08	85 10.4	346 24.4	06.1	61 21.8	30.8	154 58.4	31.9	146 17.0	03.4	Alnair	27 37.0	S46 51.6
S 09	100 12.9	1 24.3 . .	06.1	76 23.5 . .	31.0	170 01.0 . .	32.0	161 19.6 . .	03.5	Alnilam	275 41.5	S 1 11.3
U 10	115 15.4	16 24.1	06.2	91 25.2	31.3	185 03.7	32.0	176 22.2	03.5	Alphard	217 51.5	S 8 44.7
N 11	130 17.8	31 24.0	06.2	106 27.0	31.5	200 06.4	32.0	191 24.8	03.5			
D 12	145 20.3	46 23.8	N20 06.2	121 28.7	N 5 31.8	215 09.1	S22 32.1	206 27.5	S21 03.5	Alphecca	126 06.8	N26 39.1
A 13	160 22.8	61 23.7	06.2	136 30.4	32.0	230 11.8	32.1	221 30.1	03.6	Alpheratz	357 38.1	N29 12.1
Y 14	175 25.2	76 23.5	06.2	151 32.2	32.3	245 14.5	32.1	236 32.7	03.6	Altair	62 03.1	N 8 55.5
15	190 27.7	91 23.4 . .	06.3	166 33.9 . .	32.5	260 17.2 . .	32.2	251 35.3 . .	03.6	Ankaa	353 10.4	S42 11.5
16	205 30.1	106 23.2	06.3	181 35.6	32.7	275 19.8	32.2	266 38.0	03.7	Antares	112 20.1	S26 28.6
17	220 32.6	121 23.1	06.3	196 37.3	33.0	290 22.5	32.2	281 40.6	03.7			
18	235 35.1	136 22.9	N20 06.3	211 39.1	N 5 33.2	305 25.2	S22 32.3	296 43.2	S21 03.7	Arcturus	145 51.3	N19 04.8
19	250 37.5	151 22.7	06.4	226 40.8	33.5	320 27.9	32.3	311 45.8	03.8	Atria	107 17.2	S69 04.0
20	265 40.0	166 22.6	06.4	241 42.5	33.7	335 30.6	32.3	326 48.5	03.8	Avior	234 16.7	S59 34.4
21	280 42.5	181 22.4 . .	06.4	256 44.3 . .	34.0	350 33.3 . .	32.3	341 51.1 . .	03.8	Bellatrix	278 26.8	N 6 22.1
22	295 44.9	196 22.3	06.4	271 46.0	34.2	5 35.9	32.4	356 53.7	03.9	Betelgeuse	270 56.1	N 7 24.6
23	310 47.4	211 22.1	06.4	286 47.8	34.5	20 38.6	32.4	11 56.3	03.9			
17 00	325 49.9	226 22.0	N20 06.4	301 49.5	N 5 34.7	35 41.3	S22 32.4	26 59.0	S21 03.9	Canopus	263 54.3	S52 42.2
01	340 52.3	241 21.8	06.5	316 51.2	35.0	50 44.0	32.5	42 01.6	04.0	Capella	280 27.3	N46 00.9
02	355 54.8	256 21.6	06.5	331 53.0	35.2	65 46.7	32.5	57 04.2	04.0	Deneb	49 27.7	N45 21.3
03	10 57.3	271 21.5 . .	06.5	346 54.7 . .	35.5	80 49.4 . .	32.5	72 06.8 . .	04.0	Denebola	182 28.9	N14 27.7
04	25 59.7	286 21.3	06.5	1 56.5	35.7	95 52.0	32.6	87 09.4	04.1	Diphda	348 50.6	S17 52.3
05	41 02.2	301 21.2	06.5	16 58.2	35.9	110 54.7	32.6	102 12.1	04.1			
06	56 04.6	316 21.0	N20 06.5	31 59.9	N 5 36.2	125 57.4	S22 32.6	117 14.7	S21 04.1	Dubhe	193 46.1	N61 38.6
07	71 07.1	331 20.8	06.5	47 01.7	36.4	141 00.1	32.7	132 17.3	04.2	Elnath	278 06.5	N28 37.3
08	86 09.6	346 20.7	06.5	62 03.4	36.7	156 02.8	32.7	147 19.9	04.2	Eltanin	90 43.5	N51 29.5
M 09	101 12.0	1 20.5 . .	06.6	77 05.2 . .	36.9	171 05.4 . .	32.7	162 22.6 . .	04.2	Enif	33 41.9	N 9 58.2
O 10	116 14.5	16 20.3	06.6	92 06.9	37.1	186 08.1	32.8	177 25.2	04.3	Fomalhaut	15 18.1	S29 30.7
N 11	131 17.0	31 20.2	06.6	107 08.7	37.4	201 10.8	32.8	192 27.8	04.3			
D 12	146 19.4	46 20.0	N20 06.6	122 10.4	N 5 37.6	216 13.5	S22 32.8	207 30.4	S21 04.3	Gacrux	171 55.9	S57 13.7
A 13	161 21.9	61 19.8	06.6	137 12.2	37.9	231 16.2	32.8	222 33.1	04.4	Gienah	175 47.5	S17 39.2
Y 14	176 24.4	76 19.7	06.6	152 13.9	38.1	246 18.8	32.9	237 35.7	04.4	Hadar	148 41.1	S60 28.4
15	191 26.8	91 19.5 . .	06.6	167 15.7 . .	38.3	261 21.5 . .	32.9	252 38.3 . .	04.4	Hamal	327 55.0	N23 33.4
16	206 29.3	106 19.3	06.6	182 17.5	38.6	276 24.2	32.9	267 40.9	04.4	Kaus Aust.	83 36.9	S34 22.4
17	221 31.8	121 19.1	06.6	197 19.2	38.8	291 26.9	33.0	282 43.5	04.5			
18	236 34.2	136 19.0	N20 06.6	212 21.0	N 5 39.1	306 29.5	S22 33.0	297 46.2	S21 04.5	Kochab	137 20.2	N74 04.7
19	251 36.7	151 18.8	06.6	227 22.7	39.3	321 32.2	33.0	312 48.8	04.5	Markab	13 33.1	N15 19.0
20	266 39.1	166 18.6	06.6	242 24.5	39.5	336 34.9	33.1	327 51.4	04.6	Menkar	314 09.8	N 4 10.2
21	281 41.6	181 18.5 . .	06.6	257 26.2 . .	39.8	351 37.6 . .	33.1	342 54.0 . .	04.6	Menkent	148 01.9	S36 28.2
22	296 44.1	196 18.3	06.6	272 28.0	40.0	6 40.3	33.1	357 56.6	04.6	Miaplacidus	221 39.7	S69 48.0
23	311 46.5	211 18.1	06.6	287 29.8	40.3	21 42.9	33.2	12 59.3	04.7			
18 00	326 49.0	226 17.9	N20 06.6	302 31.5	N 5 40.5	36 45.6	S22 33.2	28 01.9	S21 04.7	Mirfak	308 33.2	N49 55.7
01	341 51.5	241 17.7	06.6	317 33.3	40.7	51 48.3	33.2	43 04.5	04.7	Nunki	75 51.9	S26 16.2
02	356 53.9	256 17.6	06.6	332 35.1	41.0	66 51.0	33.2	58 07.1	04.8	Peacock	53 10.8	S56 40.1
03	11 56.4	271 17.4 . .	06.6	347 36.8 . .	41.2	81 53.6 . .	33.3	73 09.7 . .	04.8	Pollux	243 22.0	N27 58.6
04	26 58.9	286 17.2	06.6	2 38.6	41.4	96 56.3	33.3	88 12.4	04.8	Procyon	244 54.8	N 5 10.4
05	42 01.3	301 17.0	06.6	17 40.4	41.7	111 59.0	33.3	103 15.0	04.9			
06	57 03.8	316 16.9	N20 06.6	32 42.1	N 5 41.9	127 01.7	S22 33.4	118 17.6	S21 04.9	Rasalhague	96 01.7	N12 33.0
07	72 06.2	331 16.7	06.6	47 43.9	42.1	142 04.3	33.4	133 20.2	04.9	Regulus	207 38.5	N11 52.2
08	87 08.7	346 16.5	06.6	62 45.7	42.4	157 07.0	33.4	148 22.8	05.0	Rigel	281 07.4	S 8 10.6
T 09	102 11.2	1 16.3 . .	06.6	77 47.5 . .	42.6	172 09.7 . .	33.5	163 25.5 . .	05.0	Rigil Kent.	139 45.2	S60 55.3
U 10	117 13.6	16 16.1	06.6	92 49.2	42.8	187 12.3	33.5	178 28.1	05.0	Sabik	102 06.7	S15 44.9
E 11	132 16.1	31 15.9	06.6	107 51.0	43.1	202 15.0	33.5	193 30.7	05.0			
S 12	147 18.6	46 15.8	N20 06.6	122 52.8	N 5 43.3	217 17.7	S22 33.5	208 33.3	S21 05.1	Schedar	349 34.5	N56 38.8
D 13	162 21.0	61 15.6	06.6	137 54.6	43.5	232 20.4	33.6	223 35.9	05.1	Shaula	96 15.0	S37 07.1
A 14	177 23.5	76 15.4	06.5	152 56.3	43.8	247 23.0	33.6	238 38.6	05.1	Sirius	258 29.6	S16 44.5
Y 15	192 26.0	91 15.2 . .	06.5	167 58.1 . .	44.0	262 25.7 . .	33.6	253 41.2 . .	05.2	Spica	158 26.2	S11 16.0
16	207 28.4	106 15.0	06.5	182 59.9	44.2	277 28.4	33.7	268 43.8	05.2	Suhail	222 49.3	S43 30.8
17	222 30.9	121 14.8	06.5	198 01.7	44.4	292 31.0	33.7	283 46.4	05.2			
18	237 33.4	136 14.6	N20 06.5	213 03.5	N 5 44.7	307 33.7	S22 33.7	298 49.0	S21 05.3	Vega	80 35.3	N38 48.4
19	252 35.8	151 14.4	06.5	228 05.2	44.9	322 36.4	33.8	313 51.7	05.3	Zuben'ubi	137 00.0	S16 07.5
20	267 38.3	166 14.3	06.5	243 07.0	45.1	337 39.1	33.8	328 54.3	05.3		SHA	Mer. Pass.
21	282 40.7	181 14.1 . .	06.4	258 08.8 . .	45.4	352 41.7 . .	33.8	343 56.9 . .	05.4		° ′	h m
22	297 43.2	196 13.9	06.4	273 10.6	45.6	7 44.4	33.8	358 59.5	05.4	Venus	260 32.1	8 55
23	312 45.7	211 13.7	06.4	288 12.4	45.8	22 47.1	33.9	14 02.1	05.4	Mars	335 59.6	3 52
	h m									Jupiter	69 51.5	21 33
Mer. Pass. 2 16.3		v −0.2	d 0.0	v 1.8	d 0.2	v 2.7	d 0.0	v 2.6	d 0.0	Saturn	61 09.1	22 08

UT	SUN GHA	SUN Dec	MOON GHA	v	MOON Dec	d	HP
d h	° ′	° ′	° ′	′	° ′	′	′
16 00	178 55.8	N13 39.3	220 16.0	7.0	N24 08.3	0.6	57.4
01	193 55.9	38.5	234 42.0	6.9	24 07.7	0.7	57.4
02	208 56.0	37.7	249 07.9	6.9	24 07.0	0.8	57.5
03	223 56.2	.. 36.9	263 33.8	6.8	24 06.2	1.0	57.5
04	238 56.3	36.1	277 59.6	6.8	24 05.2	1.1	57.5
05	253 56.4	35.3	292 25.4	6.8	24 04.1	1.3	57.6
06	268 56.6	N13 34.5	306 51.2	6.7	N24 02.8	1.5	57.6
07	283 56.7	33.7	321 16.9	6.7	24 01.3	1.6	57.6
08	298 56.8	32.9	335 42.6	6.7	23 59.7	1.7	57.7
S 09	313 57.0	.. 32.1	350 08.3	6.7	23 58.0	1.9	57.7
U 10	328 57.1	31.3	4 34.0	6.6	23 56.1	2.0	57.7
N 11	343 57.2	30.5	18 59.6	6.6	23 54.1	2.2	57.8
D 12	358 57.4	N13 29.7	33 25.2	6.5	N23 51.9	2.3	57.8
A 13	13 57.5	29.0	47 50.7	6.6	23 49.6	2.5	57.8
Y 14	28 57.6	28.2	62 16.3	6.5	23 47.1	2.6	57.9
15	43 57.7	.. 27.4	76 41.8	6.5	23 44.5	2.8	57.9
16	58 57.9	26.6	91 07.3	6.5	23 41.7	2.9	57.9
17	73 58.0	25.8	105 32.8	6.4	23 38.8	3.1	58.0
18	88 58.1	N13 25.0	119 58.2	6.5	N23 35.7	3.3	58.0
19	103 58.3	24.2	134 23.7	6.4	23 32.4	3.3	58.0
20	118 58.4	23.4	148 49.1	6.4	23 29.1	3.6	58.1
21	133 58.5	.. 22.6	163 14.5	6.4	23 25.5	3.7	58.1
22	148 58.7	21.8	177 39.9	6.4	23 21.8	3.8	58.1
23	163 58.8	21.0	192 05.3	6.4	23 18.0	4.0	58.2
17 00	178 58.9	N13 20.2	206 30.7	6.3	N23 14.0	4.1	58.2
01	193 59.1	19.4	220 56.0	6.4	23 09.9	4.3	58.2
02	208 59.2	18.6	235 21.4	6.4	23 05.6	4.4	58.3
03	223 59.3	.. 17.8	249 46.8	6.3	23 01.2	4.6	58.3
04	238 59.5	17.0	264 12.1	6.4	22 56.6	4.8	58.3
05	253 59.6	16.2	278 37.5	6.3	22 51.8	4.8	58.4
06	268 59.8	N13 15.4	293 02.8	6.4	N22 47.0	5.1	58.4
07	283 59.9	14.6	307 28.2	6.4	22 41.9	5.2	58.4
08	299 00.0	13.7	321 53.6	6.3	22 36.7	5.3	58.5
M 09	314 00.2	.. 12.9	336 18.9	6.4	22 31.4	5.5	58.5
O 10	329 00.3	12.1	350 44.3	6.4	22 25.9	5.6	58.5
N 11	344 00.4	11.3	5 09.7	6.3	22 20.3	5.8	58.6
D 12	359 00.6	N13 10.5	19 35.0	6.4	N22 14.5	5.9	58.6
A 13	14 00.7	09.7	34 00.4	6.4	22 08.6	6.1	58.6
Y 14	29 00.8	08.9	48 25.8	6.4	22 02.5	6.2	58.7
15	44 01.0	.. 08.1	62 51.2	6.5	21 56.3	6.4	58.7
16	59 01.1	07.3	77 16.7	6.4	21 49.9	6.5	58.7
17	74 01.3	06.5	91 42.1	6.5	21 43.4	6.6	58.8
18	89 01.4	N13 05.7	106 07.6	6.4	N21 36.8	6.8	58.8
19	104 01.5	04.9	120 33.0	6.5	21 30.0	7.0	58.8
20	119 01.7	04.1	134 58.5	6.5	21 23.0	7.0	58.9
21	134 01.8	.. 03.3	149 24.0	6.6	21 16.0	7.3	58.9
22	149 01.9	02.5	163 49.6	6.5	21 08.7	7.3	58.9
23	164 02.1	01.7	178 15.1	6.6	21 01.4	7.5	59.0
18 00	179 02.2	N13 00.8	192 40.7	6.6	N20 53.9	7.7	59.0
01	194 02.4	13 00.0	207 06.3	6.6	20 46.2	7.8	59.0
02	209 02.5	12 59.2	221 31.9	6.6	20 38.4	7.9	59.0
03	224 02.6	.. 58.4	235 57.5	6.7	20 30.5	8.1	59.1
04	239 02.8	57.6	250 23.2	6.7	20 22.4	8.2	59.1
05	254 02.9	56.8	264 48.9	6.7	20 14.2	8.3	59.1
06	269 03.1	N12 56.0	279 14.6	6.8	N20 05.9	8.5	59.2
07	284 03.2	55.2	293 40.4	6.8	19 57.4	8.6	59.2
T 08	299 03.3	54.4	308 06.2	6.8	19 48.8	8.7	59.2
U 09	314 03.5	.. 53.5	322 32.0	6.9	19 40.1	8.9	59.2
E 10	329 03.6	52.7	336 57.9	6.8	19 31.2	9.0	59.3
S 11	344 03.8	51.9	351 23.7	7.0	19 22.2	9.1	59.3
D 12	359 03.9	N12 51.1	5 49.7	6.9	N19 13.1	9.3	59.3
A 13	14 04.1	50.3	20 15.6	7.0	19 03.8	9.4	59.4
Y 14	29 04.2	49.5	34 41.6	7.0	18 54.4	9.5	59.4
15	44 04.3	.. 48.7	49 07.6	7.1	18 44.9	9.6	59.4
16	59 04.5	47.9	63 33.7	7.1	18 35.3	9.8	59.4
17	74 04.6	47.0	77 59.8	7.1	18 25.5	9.9	59.5
18	89 04.8	N12 46.2	92 25.9	7.2	N18 15.6	10.0	59.5
19	104 04.9	45.4	106 52.1	7.2	18 05.6	10.2	59.5
20	119 05.1	44.6	121 18.3	7.3	17 55.4	10.2	59.5
21	134 05.2	.. 43.8	135 44.6	7.3	17 45.2	10.4	59.6
22	149 05.3	43.0	150 10.9	7.3	17 34.8	10.5	59.6
23	164 05.5	42.1	164 37.2	7.4	N17 24.3	10.6	59.6
	SD 15.8	d 0.8	SD 15.7		16.0		16.2

Lat.	Twilight Naut.	Twilight Civil	Sunrise	Moonrise 16	Moonrise 17	Moonrise 18	Moonrise 19
°	h m	h m	h m	h m	h m	h m	h m
N 72	////	////	02 40	☐	☐	☐	01 35
N 70	////	01 05	03 09	☐	☐	00 34	02 29
68	////	02 01	03 29	☐	☐	00 34	03 02
66	////	02 33	03 46	23 17	25 23	01 23	03 25
64	00 57	02 57	03 59	24 11	00 11	01 53	03 44
62	01 47	03 15	04 10	24 43	00 43	02 16	03 59
60	02 17	03 30	04 20	25 07	01 07	02 35	04 12
N 58	02 38	03 42	04 28	00 18	01 26	02 50	04 22
56	02 56	03 53	04 36	00 35	01 42	03 03	04 32
54	03 10	04 02	04 42	00 50	01 56	03 14	04 40
52	03 22	04 10	04 48	01 02	02 08	03 24	04 47
50	03 33	04 17	04 53	01 14	02 18	03 33	04 54
45	03 54	04 33	05 04	01 37	02 40	03 52	05 08
N 40	04 10	04 45	05 14	01 56	02 58	04 07	05 20
35	04 23	04 55	05 22	02 12	03 13	04 20	05 30
30	04 34	05 04	05 29	02 25	03 26	04 31	05 39
20	04 51	05 18	05 41	02 48	03 48	04 50	05 53
N 10	05 04	05 29	05 51	03 09	04 07	05 07	06 06
0	05 15	05 39	06 01	03 27	04 25	05 22	06 18
S 10	05 24	05 49	06 10	03 46	04 43	05 38	06 31
20	05 31	05 57	06 20	04 06	05 02	05 54	06 43
30	05 39	06 07	06 31	04 30	05 23	06 13	06 58
35	05 42	06 12	06 38	04 43	05 36	06 24	07 06
40	05 45	06 17	06 45	04 59	05 51	06 36	07 16
45	05 49	06 23	06 53	05 18	06 08	06 51	07 27
S 50	05 52	06 30	07 04	05 41	06 30	07 09	07 41
52	05 54	06 33	07 08	05 53	06 40	07 18	07 47
54	05 55	06 37	07 13	06 06	06 52	07 27	07 54
56	05 57	06 40	07 19	06 20	07 05	07 38	08 02
58	05 58	06 44	07 26	06 38	07 20	07 50	08 10
S 60	06 00	06 49	07 33	06 59	07 38	08 04	08 20

Lat.	Sunset	Twilight Civil	Twilight Naut.	Moonset 16	Moonset 17	Moonset 18	Moonset 19
°	h m	h m	h m	h m	h m	h m	h m
N 72	21 22	////	////	☐	☐	22 54	21 49
N 70	20 55	22 51	////	☐	☐	21 58	21 26
68	20 35	22 01	////	☐	21 52	21 24	21 09
66	20 20	21 31	////	21 08	21 03	20 59	20 54
64	20 07	21 08	23 00	20 14	20 32	20 39	20 42
62	19 56	20 51	22 15	19 41	20 08	20 23	20 32
60	19 46	20 36	21 47	19 17	19 49	20 10	20 24
N 58	19 38	20 24	21 27	18 58	19 33	19 58	20 16
56	19 31	20 14	21 10	18 41	19 20	19 48	20 09
54	19 25	20 04	20 56	18 28	19 08	19 39	20 03
52	19 19	19 56	20 44	18 15	18 58	19 31	19 57
50	19 14	19 49	20 34	18 05	18 48	19 24	19 52
45	19 03	19 34	20 13	17 42	18 29	19 08	19 41
N 40	18 53	19 22	19 57	17 24	18 13	18 55	19 32
35	18 46	19 12	19 44	17 09	17 59	18 44	19 24
30	18 39	19 04	19 33	16 56	17 47	18 34	19 17
20	18 27	18 50	19 17	16 33	17 27	18 18	19 05
N 10	18 17	18 38	19 04	16 13	17 09	18 03	18 55
0	18 07	18 29	18 53	15 55	16 52	17 49	18 45
S 10	17 58	18 19	18 44	15 36	16 35	17 35	18 34
20	17 48	18 11	18 37	15 16	16 17	17 20	18 23
30	17 37	18 02	18 30	14 53	15 56	17 03	18 11
35	17 31	17 57	18 26	14 40	15 44	16 53	18 04
40	17 23	17 51	18 23	14 24	15 30	16 41	17 55
45	17 15	17 45	18 20	14 06	15 13	16 28	17 45
S 50	17 05	17 39	18 17	13 42	14 52	16 11	17 33
52	17 00	17 36	18 15	13 31	14 42	16 03	17 28
54	16 55	17 32	18 14	13 18	14 31	15 54	17 22
56	16 50	17 29	18 12	13 04	14 18	15 44	17 15
58	16 43	17 25	18 11	12 47	14 03	15 32	17 07
S 60	16 36	17 20	18 09	12 26	13 46	15 19	16 58

Day	SUN Eqn. of Time 00ʰ	SUN Eqn. of Time 12ʰ	SUN Mer. Pass.	MOON Mer. Pass. Upper	MOON Mer. Pass. Lower	Age	Phase
d	m s	m s	h m	h m	h m	d	%
16	04 17	04 11	12 04	09 41	22 10	27	9
17	04 04	03 58	12 04	10 39	23 07	28	4
18	03 51	03 45	12 04	11 36	24 04	29	1

UT	ARIES GHA	VENUS −4.4 GHA	Dec	MARS −1.5 GHA	Dec	JUPITER −2.6 GHA	Dec	SATURN +0.2 GHA	Dec	STARS Name	SHA	Dec
d h	° ′	° ′	° ′	° ′	° ′	° ′	° ′	° ′	° ′		° ′	° ′
19 00	327 48.1	226 13.5	N20 06.4	303 14.2	N 5 46.0	37 49.7	S22 33.9	29 04.8	S21 05.5	Acamar	315 14.4	S40 13.1
01	342 50.6	241 13.3	06.4	318 16.0	46.3	52 52.4	33.9	44 07.4	05.5	Achernar	335 22.6	S57 07.7
02	357 53.1	256 13.1	06.4	333 17.8	46.5	67 55.1	34.0	59 10.0	05.5	Acrux	173 04.4	S63 12.8
03	12 55.5	271 12.9	.. 06.3	348 19.6	.. 46.7	82 57.7	.. 34.0	74 12.6	.. 05.5	Adhara	255 08.9	S28 59.8
04	27 58.0	286 12.7	06.3	3 21.3	46.9	98 00.4	34.0	89 15.2	05.6	Aldebaran	290 43.7	N16 32.9
05	43 00.5	301 12.5	06.3	18 23.1	47.2	113 03.1	34.0	104 17.8	05.6			
06	58 02.9	316 12.3	N20 06.3	33 24.9	N 5 47.4	128 05.7	S22 34.1	119 20.5	S21 05.6	Alioth	166 16.6	N55 51.2
W 07	73 05.4	331 12.1	06.2	48 26.7	47.6	143 08.4	34.1	134 23.1	05.7	Alkaid	152 55.1	N49 13.0
E 08	88 07.9	346 11.9	06.2	63 28.5	47.8	158 11.1	34.1	149 25.7	05.7	Alnair	27 37.0	S46 51.6
D 09	103 10.3	1 11.7	.. 06.2	78 30.3	.. 48.1	173 13.7	.. 34.2	164 28.3	.. 05.7	Alnilam	275 41.5	S 1 11.3
N 10	118 12.8	16 11.5	06.2	93 32.1	48.3	188 16.4	34.2	179 30.9	05.8	Alphard	217 51.5	S 8 44.7
E 11	133 15.2	31 11.3	06.1	108 33.9	48.5	203 19.1	34.2	194 33.5	05.8			
S 12	148 17.7	46 11.1	N20 06.1	123 35.7	N 5 48.7	218 21.7	S22 34.2	209 36.2	S21 05.8	Alphecca	126 06.8	N26 39.1
D 13	163 20.2	61 10.9	06.1	138 37.5	49.0	233 24.4	34.3	224 38.8	05.9	Alpheratz	357 38.1	N29 12.2
A 14	178 22.6	76 10.7	06.1	153 39.3	49.2	248 27.1	34.3	239 41.4	05.9	Altair	62 03.1	N 8 55.5
Y 15	193 25.1	91 10.5	.. 06.0	168 41.1	.. 49.4	263 29.7	.. 34.3	254 44.0	.. 05.9	Ankaa	353 10.4	S42 11.5
16	208 27.6	106 10.3	06.0	183 43.0	49.6	278 32.4	34.4	269 46.6	05.9	Antares	112 20.1	S26 28.6
17	223 30.0	121 10.1	06.0	198 44.8	49.8	293 35.0	34.4	284 49.2	06.0			
18	238 32.5	136 09.9	N20 05.9	213 46.6	N 5 50.1	308 37.7	S22 34.4	299 51.9	S21 06.0	Arcturus	145 51.3	N19 04.8
19	253 35.0	151 09.7	05.9	228 48.4	50.3	323 40.4	34.4	314 54.5	06.0	Atria	107 17.3	S69 04.0
20	268 37.4	166 09.5	05.9	243 50.2	50.5	338 43.0	34.5	329 57.1	06.1	Avior	234 16.7	S59 34.4
21	283 39.9	181 09.3	.. 05.8	258 52.0	.. 50.7	353 45.7	.. 34.5	344 59.7	.. 06.1	Bellatrix	278 26.8	N 6 22.1
22	298 42.3	196 09.1	05.8	273 53.8	50.9	8 48.4	34.5	0 02.3	06.1	Betelgeuse	270 56.1	N 7 24.7
23	313 44.8	211 08.9	05.8	288 55.6	51.2	23 51.0	34.6	15 04.9	06.2			
20 00	328 47.3	226 08.7	N20 05.7	303 57.4	N 5 51.4	38 53.7	S22 34.6	30 07.6	S21 06.2	Canopus	263 54.3	S52 42.2
01	343 49.7	241 08.5	05.7	318 59.3	51.6	53 56.3	34.6	45 10.2	06.2	Capella	280 27.3	N46 00.9
02	358 52.2	256 08.2	05.7	334 01.1	51.8	68 59.0	34.6	60 12.8	06.3	Deneb	49 27.7	N45 21.4
03	13 54.7	271 08.0	.. 05.6	349 02.9	.. 52.0	84 01.7	.. 34.7	75 15.4	.. 06.3	Denebola	182 28.9	N14 27.7
04	28 57.1	286 07.8	05.6	4 04.7	52.2	99 04.3	34.7	90 18.0	06.3	Diphda	348 50.6	S17 52.3
05	43 59.6	301 07.6	05.5	19 06.5	52.5	114 07.0	34.7	105 20.6	06.3			
06	59 02.1	316 07.4	N20 05.5	34 08.4	N 5 52.7	129 09.6	S22 34.8	120 23.2	S21 06.4	Dubhe	193 46.1	N61 38.6
T 07	74 04.5	331 07.2	05.5	49 10.2	52.9	144 12.3	34.8	135 25.9	06.4	Elnath	278 06.5	N28 37.3
H 08	89 07.0	346 07.0	05.4	64 12.0	53.1	159 15.0	34.8	150 28.5	06.4	Eltanin	90 43.5	N51 29.5
U 09	104 09.5	1 06.8	.. 05.4	79 13.8	.. 53.3	174 17.6	.. 34.8	165 31.1	.. 06.5	Enif	33 41.9	N 9 58.2
R 10	119 11.9	16 06.5	05.3	94 15.7	53.5	189 20.3	34.9	180 33.7	06.5	Fomalhaut	15 18.1	S29 30.7
S 11	134 14.4	31 06.3	05.3	109 17.5	53.7	204 22.9	34.9	195 36.3	06.5			
D 12	149 16.8	46 06.1	N20 05.2	124 19.3	N 5 54.0	219 25.6	S22 34.9	210 38.9	S21 06.6	Gacrux	171 55.9	S57 13.7
A 13	164 19.3	61 05.9	05.2	139 21.1	54.2	234 28.2	35.0	225 41.5	06.6	Gienah	175 47.5	S17 39.2
Y 14	179 21.8	76 05.7	05.2	154 23.0	54.4	249 30.9	35.0	240 44.2	06.6	Hadar	148 41.2	S60 28.4
15	194 24.2	91 05.5	.. 05.1	169 24.8	.. 54.6	264 33.6	.. 35.0	255 46.8	.. 06.6	Hamal	327 55.0	N23 33.5
16	209 26.7	106 05.2	05.1	184 26.6	54.8	279 36.2	35.0	270 49.4	06.7	Kaus Aust.	83 37.0	S34 22.4
17	224 29.2	121 05.0	05.0	199 28.5	55.0	294 38.9	35.1	285 52.0	06.7			
18	239 31.6	136 04.8	N20 05.0	214 30.3	N 5 55.2	309 41.5	S22 35.1	300 54.6	S21 06.7	Kochab	137 20.2	N74 04.7
19	254 34.1	151 04.6	04.9	229 32.1	55.4	324 44.2	35.1	315 57.2	06.8	Markab	13 33.1	N15 19.0
20	269 36.6	166 04.4	04.9	244 34.0	55.6	339 46.8	35.1	330 59.8	06.8	Menkar	314 09.8	N 4 10.2
21	284 39.0	181 04.1	.. 04.8	259 35.8	.. 55.9	354 49.5	.. 35.2	346 02.5	.. 06.8	Menkent	148 01.9	S36 28.2
22	299 41.5	196 03.9	04.8	274 37.7	56.1	9 52.1	35.2	1 05.1	06.9	Miaplacidus	221 39.7	S69 48.0
23	314 43.9	211 03.7	04.7	289 39.5	56.3	24 54.8	35.2	16 07.7	06.9			
21 00	329 46.4	226 03.5	N20 04.7	304 41.3	N 5 56.5	39 57.5	S22 35.3	31 10.3	S21 06.9	Mirfak	308 33.2	N49 55.8
01	344 48.9	241 03.2	04.6	319 43.2	56.7	55 00.1	35.3	46 12.9	06.9	Nunki	75 51.9	S26 16.2
02	359 51.3	256 03.0	04.5	334 45.0	56.9	70 02.8	35.3	61 15.5	07.0	Peacock	53 10.8	S56 40.1
03	14 53.8	271 02.8	.. 04.5	349 46.9	.. 57.1	85 05.4	.. 35.3	76 18.1	.. 07.0	Pollux	243 22.0	N27 58.6
04	29 56.3	286 02.6	04.4	4 48.7	57.3	100 08.1	35.4	91 20.7	07.0	Procyon	244 54.8	N 5 10.4
05	44 58.7	301 02.3	04.4	19 50.6	57.5	115 10.7	35.4	106 23.4	07.1			
06	60 01.2	316 02.1	N20 04.3	34 52.4	N 5 57.7	130 13.4	S22 35.4	121 26.0	S21 07.1	Rasalhague	96 01.7	N12 33.0
07	75 03.7	331 01.9	04.3	49 54.3	57.9	145 16.0	35.4	136 28.6	07.1	Regulus	207 38.5	N11 52.2
08	90 06.1	346 01.7	04.2	64 56.1	58.1	160 18.7	35.5	151 31.2	07.2	Rigel	281 07.4	S 8 10.6
F 09	105 08.6	1 01.4	.. 04.1	79 58.0	.. 58.3	175 21.3	.. 35.5	166 33.8	.. 07.2	Rigil Kent.	139 45.3	S60 55.3
R 10	120 11.1	16 01.2	04.1	94 59.8	58.5	190 24.0	35.5	181 36.4	07.2	Sabik	102 06.7	S15 44.9
I 11	135 13.5	31 01.0	04.0	110 01.7	58.8	205 26.6	35.6	196 39.0	07.2			
D 12	150 16.0	46 00.7	N20 03.9	125 03.5	N 5 59.0	220 29.3	S22 35.6	211 41.6	S21 07.3	Schedar	349 34.5	N56 38.8
A 13	165 18.4	61 00.5	03.9	140 05.4	59.2	235 31.9	35.6	226 44.2	07.3	Shaula	96 15.0	S37 07.1
Y 14	180 20.9	76 00.3	03.8	155 07.2	59.4	250 34.6	35.6	241 46.9	07.3	Sirius	258 29.6	S16 44.5
15	195 23.4	91 00.0	.. 03.8	170 09.1	.. 59.6	265 37.2	.. 35.7	256 49.5	.. 07.4	Spica	158 26.2	S11 16.0
16	210 25.8	105 59.8	03.7	185 11.0	5 59.8	280 39.9	35.7	271 52.1	07.4	Suhail	222 49.3	S43 30.8
17	225 28.3	120 59.6	03.6	200 12.8	6 00.0	295 42.5	35.7	286 54.7	07.4			
18	240 30.8	135 59.3	N20 03.5	215 14.7	N 6 00.2	310 45.2	S22 35.7	301 57.3	S21 07.5	Vega	80 35.3	N38 48.4
19	255 33.2	150 59.1	03.5	230 16.5	00.4	325 47.8	35.8	316 59.9	07.5	Zuben'ubi	137 00.0	S16 07.5
20	270 35.7	165 58.9	03.4	245 18.4	00.6	340 50.5	35.8	332 02.5	07.5		SHA	Mer. Pass.
21	285 38.2	180 58.6	.. 03.3	260 20.3	.. 00.8	355 53.1	.. 35.8	347 05.1	.. 07.5		° ′	h m
22	300 40.6	195 58.4	03.3	275 22.1	01.0	10 55.8	35.8	2 07.7	07.6	Venus	257 21.4	8 56
23	315 43.1	210 58.2	03.2	290 24.0	01.2	25 58.4	35.9	17 10.4	07.6	Mars	335 10.2	3 44
	h m									Jupiter	70 06.4	21 21
Mer. Pass.	2 04.5	v −0.2	d 0.0	v 1.8	d 0.2	v 2.7	d 0.0	v 2.6	d 0.0	Saturn	61 20.3	21 56

UT	SUN GHA	SUN Dec	MOON GHA	v	MOON Dec	d	HP
d h	° ′	° ′	° ′	′	° ′	′	′
19 00	179 05.6	N12 41.3	179 03.6	7.4	N17 13.7	10.7	59.6
01	194 05.8	40.5	193 30.0	7.4	17 03.0	10.9	59.6
02	209 05.9	39.7	207 56.4	7.5	16 52.1	11.0	59.7
03	224 06.1 ..	38.9	222 22.9	7.6	16 41.1	11.0	59.7
04	239 06.2	38.0	236 49.5	7.6	16 30.1	11.2	59.7
05	254 06.4	37.2	251 16.1	7.6	16 18.9	11.3	59.7
06	269 06.5	N12 36.4	265 42.7	7.7	N16 07.6	11.4	59.8
W 07	284 06.6	35.6	280 09.4	7.7	15 56.2	11.5	59.8
E 08	299 06.8	34.8	294 36.1	7.8	15 44.7	11.6	59.8
D 09	314 06.9 ..	33.9	309 02.9	7.8	15 33.1	11.7	59.8
N 10	329 07.1	33.1	323 29.7	7.8	15 21.4	11.8	59.8
E 11	344 07.2	32.3	337 56.5	7.9	15 09.6	11.9	59.9
S 12	359 07.4	N12 31.5	352 23.4	8.0	N14 57.7	12.1	59.9
D 13	14 07.5	30.7	6 50.4	7.9	14 45.6	12.1	59.9
A 14	29 07.7	29.8	21 17.3	8.1	14 33.5	12.2	59.9
Y 15	44 07.8 ..	29.0	35 44.4	8.0	14 21.3	12.3	59.9
16	59 08.0	28.2	50 11.4	8.2	14 09.0	12.4	59.9
17	74 08.1	27.4	64 38.6	8.2	13 56.6	12.5	60.0
18	89 08.3	N12 26.5	79 05.7	8.2	N13 44.1	12.6	60.0
19	104 08.4	25.7	93 32.9	8.3	13 31.5	12.6	60.0
20	119 08.6	24.9	108 00.2	8.3	13 18.9	12.8	60.0
21	134 08.7 ..	24.1	122 27.5	8.3	13 06.1	12.8	60.0
22	149 08.9	23.2	136 54.8	8.4	12 53.3	13.0	60.0
23	164 09.0	22.4	151 22.2	8.4	12 40.3	13.0	60.1
20 00	179 09.2	N12 21.6	165 49.6	8.5	N12 27.3	13.1	60.1
01	194 09.3	20.8	180 17.1	8.5	12 14.2	13.1	60.1
02	209 09.5	19.9	194 44.6	8.5	12 01.1	13.3	60.1
03	224 09.6 ..	19.1	209 12.1	8.6	11 47.8	13.3	60.1
04	239 09.8	18.3	223 39.7	8.7	11 34.5	13.4	60.1
05	254 09.9	17.5	238 07.4	8.7	11 21.1	13.5	60.1
06	269 10.1	N12 16.6	252 35.1	8.7	N11 07.6	13.5	60.2
T 07	284 10.2	15.8	267 02.8	8.7	10 54.1	13.6	60.2
H 08	299 10.4	15.0	281 30.5	8.9	10 40.5	13.7	60.2
U 09	314 10.5 ..	14.1	295 58.4	8.8	10 26.8	13.8	60.2
R 10	329 10.7	13.3	310 26.2	8.9	10 13.0	13.8	60.2
S 11	344 10.8	12.5	324 54.1	8.9	9 59.2	13.9	60.2
D 12	359 11.0	N12 11.7	339 22.0	9.0	N 9 45.3	13.9	60.2
A 13	14 11.1	10.8	353 50.0	9.0	9 31.4	14.0	60.2
Y 14	29 11.3	10.0	8 18.0	9.0	9 17.4	14.1	60.2
15	44 11.4 ..	09.2	22 46.0	9.1	9 03.3	14.1	60.2
16	59 11.6	08.3	37 14.1	9.1	8 49.2	14.2	60.2
17	74 11.7	07.5	51 42.2	9.2	8 35.0	14.2	60.3
18	89 11.9	N12 06.7	66 10.4	9.1	N 8 20.8	14.3	60.3
19	104 12.0	05.8	80 38.5	9.3	8 06.5	14.3	60.3
20	119 12.2	05.0	95 06.8	9.2	7 52.2	14.4	60.3
21	134 12.3 ..	04.2	109 35.0	9.3	7 37.8	14.4	60.3
22	149 12.5	03.3	124 03.3	9.3	7 23.4	14.5	60.3
23	164 12.6	02.5	138 31.6	9.4	7 08.9	14.5	60.3
21 00	179 12.8	N12 01.7	153 00.0	9.4	N 6 54.4	14.5	60.3
01	194 13.0	00.8	167 28.4	9.4	6 39.9	14.6	60.3
02	209 13.1	12 00.0	181 56.8	9.5	6 25.3	14.7	60.3
03	224 13.3	11 59.2	196 25.3	9.4	6 10.6	14.6	60.3
04	239 13.4	58.3	210 53.7	9.5	5 56.0	14.7	60.3
05	254 13.6	57.5	225 22.2	9.6	5 41.3	14.8	60.3
06	269 13.7	N11 56.7	239 50.8	9.5	N 5 26.5	14.8	60.3
07	284 13.9	55.8	254 19.3	9.6	5 11.7	14.8	60.3
08	299 14.0	55.0	268 47.9	9.7	4 56.9	14.8	60.3
F 09	314 14.2 ..	54.1	283 16.6	9.6	4 42.1	14.9	60.3
R 10	329 14.4	53.3	297 45.2	9.7	4 27.2	14.8	60.3
I 11	344 14.5	52.5	312 13.9	9.7	4 12.4	14.9	60.3
D 12	359 14.7	N11 51.6	326 42.6	9.7	N 3 57.5	15.0	60.3
A 13	14 14.8	50.8	341 11.3	9.7	3 42.5	14.9	60.3
Y 14	29 15.0	50.0	355 40.0	9.8	3 27.6	15.0	60.3
15	44 15.1 ..	49.1	10 08.8	9.7	3 12.6	15.0	60.3
16	59 15.3	48.3	24 37.5	9.8	2 57.6	15.0	60.3
17	74 15.5	47.4	39 06.3	9.9	2 42.6	15.0	60.3
18	89 15.6	N11 46.6	53 35.2	9.8	N 2 27.6	15.0	60.3
19	104 15.8	45.8	68 04.0	9.8	2 12.6	15.1	60.3
20	119 15.9	44.9	82 32.9	9.8	1 57.5	15.0	60.3
21	134 16.1 ..	44.1	97 01.7	9.9	1 42.5	15.1	60.3
22	149 16.2	43.2	111 30.6	9.9	1 27.4	15.0	60.3
23	164 16.4	42.4	125 59.5	9.9	N 1 12.4	15.1	60.3
	SD 15.8	d 0.8	SD 16.3		16.4		16.4

Lat.	Twilight Naut.	Twilight Civil	Sunrise	Moonrise 19	Moonrise 20	Moonrise 21	Moonrise 22
°	h m	h m	h m	h m	h m	h m	h m
N 72	////	////	02 59	01 35	04 35	07 00	09 16
N 70	////	01 39	03 23	02 29	04 56	07 07	09 14
68	////	02 20	03 42	03 03	05 11	07 14	09 12
66	////	02 48	03 56	03 25	05 24	07 19	09 11
64	01 27	03 08	04 08	03 44	05 34	07 23	09 10
62	02 04	03 25	04 18	03 59	05 43	07 27	09 08
60	02 29	03 38	04 27	04 12	05 51	07 30	09 08
N 58	02 49	03 50	04 35	04 22	05 57	07 33	09 07
56	03 04	03 59	04 41	04 32	06 03	07 35	09 06
54	03 17	04 08	04 47	04 40	06 09	07 37	09 05
52	03 29	04 16	04 53	04 47	06 13	07 39	09 05
50	03 38	04 22	04 58	04 54	06 17	07 41	09 04
45	03 58	04 37	05 08	05 08	06 27	07 45	09 03
N 40	04 14	04 48	05 17	05 20	06 34	07 48	09 02
35	04 26	04 58	05 24	05 30	06 41	07 51	09 01
30	04 36	05 06	05 30	05 39	06 46	07 54	09 01
20	04 52	05 19	05 42	05 53	06 56	07 58	08 59
N 10	05 04	05 30	05 51	06 06	07 05	08 02	08 58
0	05 14	05 39	06 00	06 18	07 13	08 06	08 57
S 10	05 22	05 47	06 09	06 31	07 21	08 09	08 56
20	05 29	05 55	06 18	06 43	07 29	08 13	08 55
30	05 36	06 04	06 28	06 58	07 39	08 17	08 54
35	05 39	06 08	06 34	07 06	07 45	08 20	08 54
40	05 42	06 13	06 41	07 16	07 51	08 23	08 53
45	05 44	06 19	06 49	07 27	07 58	08 26	08 52
S 50	05 47	06 25	06 58	07 41	08 07	08 30	08 51
52	05 48	06 27	07 02	07 47	08 11	08 32	08 51
54	05 49	06 30	07 07	07 54	08 15	08 34	08 51
56	05 50	06 33	07 12	08 02	08 20	08 36	08 50
58	05 51	06 37	07 18	08 10	08 26	08 38	08 50
S 60	05 52	06 41	07 24	08 20	08 32	08 41	08 49

Lat.	Sunset	Twilight Civil	Twilight Naut.	Moonset 19	Moonset 20	Moonset 21	Moonset 22
°	h m	h m	h m	h m	h m	h m	h m
N 72	21 03	////	////	21 49	21 16	20 51	20 27
N 70	20 40	22 19	////	21 26	21 06	20 49	20 32
68	20 22	21 41	////	21 09	20 57	20 47	20 37
66	20 08	21 15	////	20 54	20 50	20 46	20 41
64	19 56	20 55	22 32	20 42	20 44	20 44	20 45
62	19 46	20 39	21 58	20 32	20 39	20 43	20 48
60	19 38	20 26	21 34	20 24	20 34	20 42	20 50
N 58	19 30	20 15	21 15	20 16	20 30	20 41	20 53
56	19 24	20 05	21 00	20 09	20 26	20 41	20 55
54	19 18	19 57	20 47	20 03	20 23	20 40	20 57
52	19 13	19 50	20 36	19 57	20 20	20 39	20 58
50	19 08	19 43	20 27	19 52	20 17	20 39	21 00
45	18 58	19 29	20 07	19 41	20 11	20 37	21 03
N 40	18 49	19 18	19 52	19 32	20 05	20 36	21 06
35	18 42	19 08	19 40	19 24	20 01	20 35	21 09
30	18 36	19 00	19 30	19 17	19 57	20 34	21 11
20	18 25	18 47	19 14	19 05	19 50	20 33	21 15
N 10	18 15	18 37	19 02	18 55	19 44	20 32	21 18
0	18 07	18 28	18 52	18 45	19 38	20 30	21 22
S 10	17 58	18 19	18 44	18 34	19 32	20 29	21 25
20	17 49	18 11	18 37	18 23	19 26	20 27	21 28
30	17 39	18 03	18 31	18 11	19 19	20 26	21 32
35	17 33	17 59	18 28	18 04	19 14	20 25	21 34
40	17 26	17 54	18 26	17 55	19 10	20 24	21 37
45	17 19	17 49	18 23	17 45	19 04	20 22	21 40
S 50	17 09	17 43	18 20	17 33	18 57	20 21	21 43
52	17 05	17 40	18 19	17 28	18 54	20 20	21 45
54	17 00	17 37	18 18	17 22	18 50	20 19	21 47
56	16 55	17 34	18 17	17 15	18 47	20 18	21 49
58	16 50	17 31	18 17	17 07	18 42	20 17	21 51
S 60	16 43	17 27	18 16	16 58	18 37	20 16	21 53

	SUN			MOON			
Day	Eqn. of Time 00h	Eqn. of Time 12h	Mer. Pass.	Mer. Pass. Upper	Mer. Pass. Lower	Age	Phase
d	m s	m s	h m	h m	h m	d	%
19	03 38	03 31	12 04	12 32	00 04	00	0
20	03 24	03 16	12 03	13 26	00 59	01	3
21	03 09	03 02	12 03	14 18	01 52	02	8

UT	ARIES GHA	VENUS −4·3 GHA	Dec	MARS −1·6 GHA	Dec	JUPITER −2·6 GHA	Dec	SATURN +0·3 GHA	Dec	STARS Name	SHA	Dec
22 00	330 45.6	225 57.9	N20 03.1	305 25.9	N 6 01.4	41 01.1	S22 35.9	32 13.0	S21 07.6	Acamar	315 14.4	S40 13.1
01	345 48.0	240 57.7	03.1	320 27.7	01.6	56 03.7	35.9	47 15.6	07.7	Achernar	335 22.6	S57 07.8
02	0 50.5	255 57.4	03.0	335 29.6	01.8	71 06.3	35.9	62 18.2	07.7	Acrux	173 04.4	S63 12.8
03	15 52.9	270 57.2 ..	02.9	350 31.5 ..	02.0	86 09.0 ..	36.0	77 20.8 ..	07.7	Adhara	255 08.9	S28 59.8
04	30 55.4	285 57.0	02.8	5 33.4	02.2	101 11.6	36.0	92 23.4	07.7	Aldebaran	290 43.7	N16 33.0
05	45 57.9	300 56.7	02.8	20 35.2	02.4	116 14.3	36.0	107 26.0	07.8			
06	61 00.3	315 56.5	N20 02.7	35 37.1	N 6 02.6	131 16.9	S22 36.0	122 28.6	S21 07.8	Alioth	166 16.6	N55 51.2
07	76 02.8	330 56.2	02.6	50 39.0	02.8	146 19.6	36.1	137 31.2	07.8	Alkaid	152 55.2	N49 13.0
S 08	91 05.3	345 56.0	02.5	65 40.9	03.0	161 22.2	36.1	152 33.8	07.9	Alnair	27 37.0	S46 51.6
A 09	106 07.7	0 55.7 ..	02.4	80 42.7 ..	03.2	176 24.9 ..	36.1	167 36.4 ..	07.9	Alnilam	275 41.5	S 1 11.3
T 10	121 10.2	15 55.5	02.4	95 44.6	03.3	191 27.5	36.2	182 39.1	07.9	Alphard	217 51.5	S 8 44.7
U 11	136 12.7	30 55.3	02.3	110 46.5	03.5	206 30.1	36.2	197 41.7	07.9			
R 12	151 15.1	45 55.0	N20 02.2	125 48.4	N 6 03.7	221 32.8	S22 36.2	212 44.3	S21 08.0	Alphecca	126 06.8	N26 39.1
D 13	166 17.6	60 54.8	02.1	140 50.3	03.9	236 35.4	36.2	227 46.9	08.0	Alpheratz	357 38.1	N29 12.2
A 14	181 20.0	75 54.5	02.0	155 52.2	04.1	251 38.1	36.3	242 49.5	08.0	Altair	62 03.1	N 8 55.5
Y 15	196 22.5	90 54.3 ..	01.9	170 54.0 ..	04.3	266 40.7 ..	36.3	257 52.1 ..	08.1	Ankaa	353 10.4	S42 11.5
16	211 25.0	105 54.0	01.9	185 55.9	04.5	281 43.4	36.3	272 54.7	08.1	Antares	112 20.1	S26 28.6
17	226 27.4	120 53.8	01.8	200 57.8	04.7	296 46.0	36.3	287 57.3	08.1			
18	241 29.9	135 53.5	N20 01.7	215 59.7	N 6 04.9	311 48.6	S22 36.4	302 59.9	S21 08.2	Arcturus	145 51.3	N19 04.8
19	256 32.4	150 53.3	01.6	231 01.6	05.1	326 51.3	36.4	318 02.5	08.2	Atria	107 17.3	S69 04.0
20	271 34.8	165 53.0	01.5	246 03.5	05.3	341 53.9	36.4	333 05.1	08.2	Avior	234 16.7	S59 34.3
21	286 37.3	180 52.8 ..	01.4	261 05.4 ..	05.5	356 56.6 ..	36.4	348 07.7 ..	08.2	Bellatrix	278 26.8	N 6 22.1
22	301 39.8	195 52.5	01.3	276 07.3	05.7	11 59.2	36.5	3 10.4	08.3	Betelgeuse	270 56.1	N 7 24.7
23	316 42.2	210 52.3	01.2	291 09.2	05.9	27 01.8	36.5	18 13.0	08.3			
23 00	331 44.7	225 52.0	N20 01.2	306 11.1	N 6 06.0	42 04.5	S22 36.5	33 15.6	S21 07.6	Canopus	263 54.3	S52 42.2
01	346 47.2	240 51.8	01.1	321 13.0	06.2	57 07.1	36.5	48 18.2	08.4	Capella	280 27.3	N46 00.9
02	1 49.6	255 51.5	01.0	336 14.9	06.4	72 09.7	36.6	63 20.8	08.4	Deneb	49 27.7	N45 21.4
03	16 52.1	270 51.3 ..	00.9	351 16.8 ..	06.6	87 12.4 ..	36.6	78 23.4 ..	08.4	Denebola	182 28.9	N14 27.7
04	31 54.5	285 51.0	00.8	6 18.7	06.8	102 15.0	36.6	93 26.0	08.4	Diphda	348 50.6	S17 52.3
05	46 57.0	300 50.8	00.7	21 20.6	07.0	117 17.7	36.6	108 28.6	08.5			
06	61 59.5	315 50.5	N20 00.6	36 22.5	N 6 07.2	132 20.3	S22 36.7	123 31.2	S21 08.5	Dubhe	193 46.1	N61 38.6
07	77 01.9	330 50.2	00.5	51 24.4	07.4	147 22.9	36.7	138 33.8	08.5	Elnath	278 06.5	N28 37.3
08	92 04.4	345 50.0	00.4	66 26.3	07.5	162 25.6	36.7	153 36.4	08.6	Eltanin	90 43.6	N51 29.5
S 09	107 06.9	0 49.7 ..	00.3	81 28.2 ..	07.7	177 28.2 ..	36.7	168 39.0 ..	08.6	Enif	33 41.9	N 9 58.2
U 10	122 09.3	15 49.5	00.2	96 30.1	07.9	192 30.8	36.7	183 41.6	08.6	Fomalhaut	15 18.1	S29 30.7
N 11	137 11.8	30 49.2	00.1	111 32.0	08.1	207 33.5	36.8	198 44.2	08.6			
D 12	152 14.3	45 49.0	N20 00.0	126 33.9	N 6 08.3	222 36.1	S22 36.8	213 46.8	S21 08.7	Gacrux	171 55.9	S57 13.7
A 13	167 16.7	60 48.7	19 59.9	141 35.8	08.5	237 38.7	36.8	228 49.4	08.7	Gienah	175 47.5	S17 39.2
Y 14	182 19.2	75 48.4	59.8	156 37.7	08.7	252 41.4	36.8	243 52.1	08.7	Hadar	148 41.2	S60 28.4
15	197 21.6	90 48.2 ..	59.7	171 39.6 ..	08.8	267 44.0 ..	36.9	258 54.7 ..	08.8	Hamal	327 55.0	N23 33.5
16	212 24.1	105 47.9	59.6	186 41.6	09.0	282 46.6	36.9	273 57.3	08.8	Kaus Aust.	83 37.0	S34 22.4
17	227 26.6	120 47.7	59.5	201 43.5	09.2	297 49.3	36.9	288 59.9	08.8			
18	242 29.0	135 47.4	N19 59.4	216 45.4	N 6 09.4	312 51.9	S22 36.9	304 02.5	S21 08.8	Kochab	137 20.3	N74 04.7
19	257 31.5	150 47.1	59.3	231 47.3	09.6	327 54.5	37.0	319 05.1	08.9	Markab	13 33.1	N15 19.0
20	272 34.0	165 46.9	59.2	246 49.2	09.8	342 57.2	37.0	334 07.7	08.9	Menkar	314 09.8	N 4 10.2
21	287 36.4	180 46.6 ..	59.1	261 51.1 ..	09.9	357 59.8 ..	37.0	349 10.3 ..	08.9	Menkent	148 01.9	S36 28.2
22	302 38.9	195 46.3	58.9	276 53.1	10.1	13 02.4	37.0	4 12.9	08.9	Miaplacidus	221 39.7	S69 48.0
23	317 41.4	210 46.1	58.8	291 55.0	10.3	28 05.1	37.1	19 15.5	09.0			
24 00	332 43.8	225 45.8	N19 58.7	306 56.9	N 6 10.5	43 07.7	S22 37.1	34 18.1	S21 09.0	Mirfak	308 33.2	N49 55.8
01	347 46.3	240 45.6	58.6	321 58.8	10.7	58 10.3	37.1	49 20.7	09.0	Nunki	75 51.9	S26 16.2
02	2 48.8	255 45.3	58.5	337 00.8	10.8	73 13.0	37.1	64 23.3	09.1	Peacock	53 10.8	S56 40.1
03	17 51.2	270 45.0 ..	58.4	352 02.7 ..	11.0	88 15.6 ..	37.2	79 25.9 ..	09.1	Pollux	243 22.0	N27 58.6
04	32 53.7	285 44.8	58.3	7 04.6	11.2	103 18.2	37.2	94 28.5	09.1	Procyon	244 54.8	N 5 10.4
05	47 56.1	300 44.5	58.2	22 06.6	11.4	118 20.9	37.2	109 31.1	09.1			
06	62 58.6	315 44.2	N19 58.0	37 08.5	N 6 11.6	133 23.5	S22 37.2	124 33.7	S21 09.2	Rasalhague	96 01.7	N12 33.0
07	78 01.1	330 44.0	57.9	52 10.4	11.7	148 26.1	37.3	139 36.3	09.2	Regulus	207 38.5	N11 52.2
08	93 03.5	345 43.7	57.8	67 12.3	11.9	163 28.7	37.3	154 38.9	09.2	Rigel	281 07.4	S 8 10.6
M 09	108 06.0	0 43.4 ..	57.7	82 14.3 ..	12.1	178 31.4 ..	37.3	169 41.5 ..	09.3	Rigil Kent.	139 45.3	S60 55.3
O 10	123 08.5	15 43.1	57.6	97 16.2	12.3	193 34.0	37.3	184 44.1	09.3	Sabik	102 06.7	S15 44.9
N 11	138 10.9	30 42.9	57.5	112 18.2	12.4	208 36.6	37.3	199 46.7	09.3			
D 12	153 13.4	45 42.6	N19 57.3	127 20.1	N 6 12.6	223 39.2	S22 37.4	214 49.3	S21 09.3	Schedar	349 34.5	N56 38.8
A 13	168 15.9	60 42.3	57.2	142 22.0	12.8	238 41.9	37.4	229 51.9	09.4	Shaula	96 15.0	S37 07.1
Y 14	183 18.3	75 42.1	57.1	157 24.0	13.0	253 44.5	37.4	244 54.5	09.4	Sirius	258 29.6	S16 44.5
15	198 20.8	90 41.8 ..	57.0	172 25.9 ..	13.2	268 47.1 ..	37.4	259 57.1 ..	09.4	Spica	158 26.2	S11 15.9
16	213 23.3	105 41.5	56.9	187 27.9	13.3	283 49.8	37.5	274 59.7	09.5	Suhail	222 49.3	S43 30.8
17	228 25.7	120 41.2	56.7	202 29.8	13.5	298 52.4	37.5	290 02.3	09.5			
18	243 28.2	135 41.0	N19 56.6	217 31.7	N 6 13.7	313 55.0	S22 37.5	305 05.0	S21 09.5	Vega	80 35.3	N38 48.4
19	258 30.6	150 40.7	56.5	232 33.7	13.8	328 57.6	37.5	320 07.6	09.5	Zuben'ubi	137 00.0	S16 07.5
20	273 33.1	165 40.4	56.4	247 35.6	14.0	344 00.3	37.6	335 10.2	09.6		SHA	Mer. Pass.
21	288 35.6	180 40.1 ..	56.2	262 37.6 ..	14.2	359 02.9 ..	37.6	350 12.8 ..	09.6	Venus	254 07.3	8 57
22	303 38.0	195 39.9	56.1	277 39.5	14.4	14 05.5	37.6	5 15.4	09.6	Mars	334 26.4	3 15
23	318 40.5	210 39.6	56.0	292 41.5	14.5	29 08.1	37.6	20 18.0	09.6	Jupiter	70 19.8	21 08
Mer. Pass. 1 52.7		v −0.3	d 0.1	v 1.9	d 0.2	v 2.6	d 0.0	v 2.6	d 0.0	Saturn	61 30.9	21 43

UT	SUN GHA	SUN Dec	MOON GHA	v	MOON Dec	d	HP
d h	° ′	° ′	° ′	′	° ′	′	′
22 00	179 16.6	N11 41.6	140 28.4	9.9	N 0 57.3	15.0	60.3
01	194 16.7	40.7	154 57.3	10.0	0 42.3	15.1	60.3
02	209 16.9	39.9	169 26.3	9.9	0 27.2	15.1	60.3
03	224 17.0 ..	39.0	183 55.2	10.0	N 0 12.1	15.0	60.3
04	239 17.2	38.2	198 24.2	10.0	S 0 02.9	15.1	60.3
05	254 17.4	37.3	212 53.2	9.9	0 18.0	15.0	60.3
06	269 17.5 N11 36.5		227 22.1	10.0	S 0 33.0	15.1	60.3
07	284 17.7	35.7	241 51.1	10.0	0 48.1	15.0	60.2
08	299 17.8	34.8	256 20.1	10.0	1 03.1	15.0	60.2
09	314 18.0 ..	34.0	270 49.1	10.0	1 18.1	15.1	60.2
10	329 18.2	33.1	285 18.1	10.0	1 33.2	15.0	60.2
11	344 18.3	32.3	299 47.1	10.0	1 48.2	14.9	60.2
12	359 18.5 N11 31.4		314 16.1	10.0	S 2 03.1	15.0	60.2
13	14 18.6	30.6	328 45.1	10.0	2 18.1	15.0	60.2
14	29 18.8	29.7	343 14.1	10.1	2 33.1	14.9	60.2
15	44 19.0 ..	28.9	357 43.2	10.0	2 48.0	14.9	60.2
16	59 19.1	28.0	12 12.2	10.0	3 02.9	14.9	60.2
17	74 19.3	27.2	26 41.2	10.0	3 17.8	14.8	60.2
18	89 19.5 N11 26.3		41 10.2	10.0	S 3 32.6	14.8	60.1
19	104 19.6	25.5	55 39.2	10.0	3 47.5	14.8	60.1
20	119 19.8	24.7	70 08.2	10.0	4 02.3	14.7	60.1
21	134 19.9 ..	23.8	84 37.2	10.0	4 17.0	14.8	60.1
22	149 20.1	23.0	99 06.2	10.0	4 31.8	14.7	60.1
23	164 20.3	22.1	113 35.2	9.9	4 46.5	14.7	60.1
23 00	179 20.4 N11 21.3		128 04.1	10.0	S 5 01.2	14.6	60.1
01	194 20.6	20.4	142 33.1	10.0	5 15.8	14.6	60.1
02	209 20.8	19.6	157 02.1	9.9	5 30.4	14.6	60.0
03	224 20.9 ..	18.7	171 31.0	10.0	5 45.0	14.5	60.0
04	239 21.1	17.9	186 00.0	9.9	5 59.5	14.5	60.0
05	254 21.3	17.0	200 28.9	9.9	6 14.0	14.4	60.0
06	269 21.4 N11 16.2		214 57.8	9.9	S 6 28.4	14.4	60.0
07	284 21.6	15.3	229 26.7	9.9	6 42.8	14.4	60.0
08	299 21.8	14.5	243 55.6	9.8	6 57.2	14.3	60.0
09	314 21.9 ..	13.6	258 24.4	9.9	7 11.5	14.2	59.9
10	329 22.1	12.7	272 53.3	9.8	7 25.7	14.2	59.9
11	344 22.3	11.9	287 22.1	9.9	7 39.9	14.2	59.9
12	359 22.4 N11 11.0		301 51.0	9.8	S 7 54.1	14.1	59.9
13	14 22.6	10.2	316 19.8	9.7	8 08.2	14.0	59.9
14	29 22.8	09.3	330 48.5	9.8	8 22.2	14.0	59.9
15	44 22.9 ..	08.5	345 17.3	9.7	8 36.2	14.0	59.8
16	59 23.1	07.6	359 46.0	9.8	8 50.2	13.8	59.8
17	74 23.3	06.8	14 14.8	9.7	9 04.0	13.8	59.8
18	89 23.4 N11 05.9		28 43.5	9.6	S 9 17.8	13.8	59.8
19	104 23.6	05.1	43 12.1	9.7	9 31.6	13.7	59.8
20	119 23.8	04.2	57 40.8	9.6	9 45.3	13.6	59.8
21	134 23.9 ..	03.3	72 09.4	9.6	9 58.9	13.6	59.7
22	149 24.1	02.5	86 38.0	9.6	10 12.5	13.5	59.7
23	164 24.3	01.6	101 06.6	9.6	10 26.0	13.4	59.7
24 00	179 24.4 N11 00.8		115 35.2	9.5	S10 39.4	13.3	59.7
01	194 24.6	10 59.9	130 03.7	9.5	10 52.7	13.3	59.7
02	209 24.8	59.1	144 32.2	9.5	11 06.0	13.2	59.7
03	224 24.9 ..	58.2	159 00.7	9.4	11 19.2	13.2	59.6
04	239 25.1	57.4	173 29.1	9.4	11 32.4	13.0	59.6
05	254 25.3	56.5	187 57.5	9.4	11 45.4	13.0	59.6
06	269 25.4 N10 55.6		202 25.9	9.3	S11 58.4	12.9	59.6
07	284 25.6	54.8	216 54.2	9.4	12 11.3	12.8	59.5
08	299 25.8	53.9	231 22.6	9.3	12 24.1	12.8	59.5
09	314 26.0 ..	53.1	245 50.9	9.2	12 36.9	12.7	59.5
10	329 26.1	52.2	260 19.1	9.2	12 49.6	12.5	59.5
11	344 26.3	51.3	274 47.3	9.2	13 02.1	12.5	59.5
12	359 26.5 N10 50.5		289 15.5	9.2	S13 14.6	12.5	59.5
13	14 26.6	49.6	303 43.7	9.1	13 27.1	12.3	59.4
14	29 26.8	48.8	318 11.8	9.1	13 39.4	12.2	59.4
15	44 27.0 ..	47.9	332 39.9	9.1	13 51.6	12.2	59.4
16	59 27.2	47.0	347 08.0	9.0	14 03.8	12.0	59.4
17	74 27.3	46.2	1 36.0	9.0	14 15.8	12.0	59.3
18	89 27.5 N10 45.3		16 04.0	9.0	S14 27.8	11.9	59.3
19	104 27.7	44.4	30 32.0	8.9	14 39.7	11.8	59.3
20	119 27.8	43.6	44 59.9	8.9	14 51.5	11.6	59.3
21	134 28.0 ..	42.7	59 27.8	8.8	15 03.1	11.6	59.3
22	149 28.2	41.9	73 55.6	8.8	15 14.7	11.5	59.2
23	164 28.4	41.0	88 23.4	8.8	S15 26.2	11.4	59.2
	SD 15.8	d 0.9	SD 16.4		16.3		16.2

(Left day labels: SATURDAY for 22, SUNDAY for 23, MONDAY for 24.)

Lat.	Twilight Naut.	Twilight Civil	Sunrise	Moonrise 22	23	24	25
°	h m	h m	h m	h m	h m	h m	h m
N 72	////	01 06	03 16	09 16	11 34	14 04	▬
N 70	////	02 04	03 37	09 14	11 21	13 35	16 15
68	////	02 38	03 53	09 12	11 11	13 13	15 25
66	00 57	03 01	04 07	09 11	11 03	12 57	14 54
64	01 49	03 19	04 17	09 10	10 56	12 43	14 31
62	02 19	03 34	04 27	09 08	10 50	12 32	14 13
60	02 41	03 47	04 34	09 08	10 45	12 22	13 58
N 58	02 58	03 57	04 41	09 07	10 40	12 14	13 46
56	03 13	04 06	04 47	09 06	10 36	12 06	13 35
54	03 25	04 14	04 53	09 05	10 33	12 00	13 25
52	03 35	04 21	04 58	09 05	10 30	11 54	13 17
50	03 44	04 27	05 02	09 04	10 27	11 49	13 09
45	04 03	04 41	05 12	09 03	10 20	11 37	12 53
N 40	04 17	04 51	05 20	09 02	10 15	11 28	12 40
35	04 29	05 00	05 26	09 01	10 11	11 20	12 29
30	04 38	05 07	05 32	09 01	10 07	11 13	12 19
20	04 53	05 20	05 42	08 59	10 00	11 01	12 02
N 10	05 05	05 30	05 51	08 58	09 54	10 50	11 48
0	05 14	05 38	05 59	08 57	09 49	10 41	11 34
S 10	05 21	05 46	06 07	08 56	09 43	10 31	11 21
20	05 27	05 53	06 16	08 55	09 38	10 21	11 07
30	05 33	06 01	06 25	08 54	09 31	10 10	10 51
35	05 35	06 05	06 30	08 54	09 28	10 03	10 41
40	05 37	06 09	06 37	08 53	09 23	09 55	10 31
45	05 40	06 14	06 44	08 52	09 19	09 47	10 18
S 50	05 41	06 19	06 52	08 51	09 13	09 36	10 03
52	05 42	06 21	06 56	08 51	09 10	09 32	09 56
54	05 43	06 24	07 00	08 51	09 08	09 26	09 49
56	05 43	06 27	07 05	08 50	09 04	09 21	09 40
58	05 44	06 30	07 10	08 50	09 01	09 14	09 31
S 60	05 45	06 33	07 16	08 49	08 57	09 07	09 19

Lat.	Sunset	Twilight Civil	Twilight Naut.	Moonset 22	23	24	25
°	h m	h m	h m	h m	h m	h m	h m
N 72	20 44	22 46	////	20 27	19 59	19 19	▬
N 70	20 24	21 54	////	20 32	20 14	19 50	19 04
68	20 09	21 23	////	20 37	20 26	20 13	19 54
66	19 56	21 00	22 56	20 41	20 37	20 32	20 26
64	19 46	20 43	22 11	20 45	20 45	20 47	20 50
62	19 37	20 28	21 42	20 48	20 53	20 59	21 09
60	19 29	20 16	21 21	20 50	20 59	21 10	21 25
N 58	19 22	20 06	21 04	20 53	21 05	21 19	21 38
56	19 16	19 57	20 50	20 55	21 10	21 27	21 50
54	19 11	19 50	20 38	20 57	21 14	21 35	22 00
52	19 06	19 43	20 28	20 58	21 19	21 41	22 09
50	19 02	19 36	20 19	21 00	21 22	21 47	22 17
45	18 53	19 24	20 01	21 03	21 30	22 00	22 34
N 40	18 45	19 13	19 47	21 06	21 37	22 11	22 48
35	18 38	19 04	19 36	21 09	21 43	22 20	23 01
30	18 32	18 57	19 26	21 11	21 49	22 28	23 11
20	18 22	18 45	19 11	21 15	21 58	22 42	23 29
N 10	18 14	18 35	19 00	21 18	22 06	22 54	23 45
0	18 06	18 27	18 51	21 22	22 13	23 06	24 00
S 10	17 58	18 19	18 44	21 25	22 21	23 18	24 15
20	17 50	18 12	18 38	21 28	22 29	23 30	24 31
30	17 40	18 05	18 33	21 32	22 38	23 44	24 50
35	17 35	18 01	18 30	21 34	22 44	23 53	25 01
40	17 29	17 57	18 28	21 37	22 50	24 02	00 02
45	17 22	17 52	18 26	21 40	22 57	24 13	00 13
S 50	17 14	17 47	18 24	21 43	23 06	24 27	00 27
52	17 10	17 45	18 24	21 45	23 10	24 33	00 33
54	17 06	17 42	18 23	21 47	23 14	24 40	00 40
56	17 01	17 39	18 23	21 49	23 19	24 48	00 48
58	16 56	17 36	18 22	21 51	23 24	24 57	00 57
S 60	16 50	17 33	18 22	21 53	23 31	25 07	01 07

Day	SUN Eqn. of Time 00h	SUN Eqn. of Time 12h	SUN Mer. Pass.	MOON Mer. Pass. Upper	MOON Mer. Pass. Lower	Age	Phase
d	m s	m s	h m	h m	h m	d	%
22	02 54	02 46	12 03	15 09	02 44	03	16
23	02 39	02 31	12 03	16 01	03 35	04	25
24	02 23	02 14	12 02	16 53	04 27	05	36

UT	ARIES	VENUS −4.3		MARS −1.7		JUPITER −2.6		SATURN +0.3		STARS		
	GHA	GHA	Dec	GHA	Dec	GHA	Dec	GHA	Dec	Name	SHA	Dec
d h	° ′	° ′	° ′	° ′	° ′	° ′	° ′	° ′	° ′		° ′	° ′
25 00	333 43.0	225 39.3	N19 55.8	307 43.4	N 6 14.7	44 10.7	S22 37.6	35 20.6	S21 09.7	Acamar	315 14.4	S40 13.1
01	348 45.4	240 39.0	55.7	322 45.4	14.9	59 13.4	37.7	50 23.2	09.7	Achernar	335 22.6	S57 07.8
02	3 47.9	255 38.8	55.6	337 47.4	15.0	74 16.0	37.7	65 25.8	09.7	Acrux	173 04.4	S63 12.8
03	18 50.4	270 38.5	.. 55.4	352 49.3	.. 15.2	89 18.6	.. 37.7	80 28.4	.. 09.8	Adhara	255 08.9	S28 59.8
04	33 52.8	285 38.2	55.3	7 51.3	15.4	104 21.2	37.7	95 31.0	09.8	Aldebaran	290 43.7	N16 33.0
05	48 55.3	300 37.9	55.2	22 53.2	15.6	119 23.9	37.8	110 33.6	09.8			
06	63 57.7	315 37.6	N19 55.0	37 55.2	N 6 15.7	134 26.5	S22 37.8	125 36.2	S21 09.8	Alioth	166 16.6	N55 51.2
07	79 00.2	330 37.4	54.9	52 57.1	15.9	149 29.1	37.8	140 38.8	09.9	Alkaid	152 55.2	N49 13.0
T 08	94 02.7	345 37.1	54.8	67 59.1	16.1	164 31.7	37.8	155 41.4	09.9	Alnair	27 37.0	S46 51.6
U 09	109 05.1	0 36.8	.. 54.6	83 01.1	.. 16.2	179 34.3	.. 37.8	170 44.0	.. 09.9	Alnilam	275 41.4	S 1 11.3
E 10	124 07.6	15 36.5	54.5	98 03.0	16.4	194 37.0	37.9	185 46.6	09.9	Alphard	217 51.5	S 8 44.7
S 11	139 10.1	30 36.2	54.4	113 05.0	16.6	209 39.6	37.9	200 49.2	10.0			
D 12	154 12.5	45 35.9	N19 54.2	128 07.0	N 6 16.7	224 42.2	S22 37.9	215 51.8	S21 10.0	Alphecca	126 06.8	N26 39.1
A 13	169 15.0	60 35.7	54.1	143 08.9	16.9	239 44.8	37.9	230 54.4	10.0	Alpheratz	357 38.1	N29 12.2
Y 14	184 17.5	75 35.4	53.9	158 10.9	17.1	254 47.4	38.0	245 57.0	10.1	Altair	62 03.1	N 8 55.5
15	199 19.9	90 35.1	.. 53.8	173 12.9	.. 17.2	269 50.1	.. 38.0	260 59.6	.. 10.1	Ankaa	353 10.4	S42 11.5
16	214 22.4	105 34.8	53.7	188 14.8	17.4	284 52.7	38.0	276 02.2	10.1	Antares	112 20.1	S26 28.6
17	229 24.9	120 34.5	53.5	203 16.8	17.6	299 55.3	38.0	291 04.8	10.1			
18	244 27.3	135 34.2	N19 53.4	218 18.8	N 6 17.7	314 57.9	S22 38.0	306 07.4	S21 10.2	Arcturus	145 51.3	N19 04.8
19	259 29.8	150 34.0	53.2	233 20.8	17.9	330 00.5	38.1	321 10.0	10.2	Atria	107 17.3	S69 04.0
20	274 32.2	165 33.7	53.1	248 22.7	18.1	345 03.1	38.1	336 12.6	10.2	Avior	234 16.6	S59 34.3
21	289 34.7	180 33.4	.. 52.9	263 24.7	.. 18.2	0 05.8	.. 38.1	351 15.2	.. 10.2	Bellatrix	278 26.8	N 6 22.1
22	304 37.2	195 33.1	52.8	278 26.7	18.4	15 08.4	38.1	6 17.7	10.3	Betelgeuse	270 56.0	N 7 24.7
23	319 39.6	210 32.8	52.6	293 28.7	18.5	30 11.0	38.2	21 20.3	10.3			
26 00	334 42.1	225 32.5	N19 52.5	308 30.7	N 6 18.7	45 13.6	S22 38.2	36 22.9	S21 10.3	Canopus	263 54.2	S52 42.1
01	349 44.6	240 32.2	52.3	323 32.6	18.9	60 16.2	38.2	51 25.5	10.3	Capella	280 27.2	N46 00.9
02	4 47.0	255 31.9	52.2	338 34.6	19.0	75 18.8	38.2	66 28.1	10.4	Deneb	49 27.7	N45 21.4
03	19 49.5	270 31.6	.. 52.0	353 36.6	.. 19.2	90 21.4	.. 38.2	81 30.7	.. 10.4	Denebola	182 28.9	N14 27.7
04	34 52.0	285 31.4	51.9	8 38.6	19.3	105 24.1	38.3	96 33.3	10.4	Diphda	348 50.6	S17 52.3
05	49 54.4	300 31.1	51.7	23 40.6	19.5	120 26.7	38.3	111 35.9	10.5			
06	64 56.9	315 30.8	N19 51.6	38 42.6	N 6 19.7	135 29.3	S22 38.3	126 38.5	S21 10.5	Dubhe	193 46.1	N61 38.6
W 07	79 59.4	330 30.5	51.4	53 44.6	19.8	150 31.9	38.3	141 41.1	10.5	Elnath	278 06.4	N28 37.3
E 08	95 01.8	345 30.2	51.3	68 46.6	20.0	165 34.5	38.3	156 43.7	10.5	Eltanin	90 43.6	N51 29.5
D 09	110 04.3	0 29.9	.. 51.1	83 48.6	.. 20.1	180 37.1	.. 38.4	171 46.3	.. 10.6	Enif	33 41.9	N 9 58.3
N 10	125 06.7	15 29.6	51.0	98 50.5	20.3	195 39.7	38.4	186 48.9	10.6	Fomalhaut	15 18.1	S29 30.7
E 11	140 09.2	30 29.3	50.8	113 52.5	20.5	210 42.4	38.4	201 51.5	10.6			
S 12	155 11.7	45 29.0	N19 50.6	128 54.5	N 6 20.6	225 45.0	S22 38.4	216 54.1	S21 10.6	Gacrux	171 55.9	S57 13.7
D 13	170 14.1	60 28.7	50.5	143 56.5	20.8	240 47.6	38.5	231 56.7	10.7	Gienah	175 47.5	S17 39.2
A 14	185 16.6	75 28.4	50.3	158 58.5	20.9	255 50.2	38.5	246 59.3	10.7	Hadar	148 41.2	S60 28.4
Y 15	200 19.1	90 28.1	.. 50.2	174 00.5	.. 21.1	270 52.8	.. 38.5	262 01.9	.. 10.7	Hamal	327 55.0	N23 33.5
16	215 21.5	105 27.8	50.0	189 02.5	21.2	285 55.4	38.5	277 04.5	10.7	Kaus Aust.	83 37.0	S34 22.5
17	230 24.0	120 27.5	49.8	204 04.5	21.4	300 58.0	38.5	292 07.1	10.8			
18	245 26.5	135 27.2	N19 49.7	219 06.5	N 6 21.6	316 00.6	S22 38.6	307 09.7	S21 10.8	Kochab	137 20.3	N74 04.6
19	260 28.9	150 26.9	49.5	234 08.5	21.7	331 03.2	38.6	322 12.3	10.8	Markab	13 33.1	N15 19.0
20	275 31.4	165 26.6	49.3	249 10.5	21.9	346 05.8	38.6	337 14.9	10.9	Menkar	314 09.7	N 4 10.2
21	290 33.8	180 26.3	.. 49.2	264 12.6	.. 22.0	1 08.4	.. 38.6	352 17.5	.. 10.9	Menkent	148 01.9	S36 28.2
22	305 36.3	195 26.0	49.0	279 14.6	22.2	16 11.1	38.6	7 20.1	10.9	Miaplacidus	221 39.7	S69 47.9
23	320 38.8	210 25.7	48.8	294 16.6	22.3	31 13.7	38.7	22 22.7	10.9			
27 00	335 41.2	225 25.4	N19 48.7	309 18.6	N 6 22.5	46 16.3	S22 38.7	37 25.3	S21 11.0	Mirfak	308 33.1	N49 55.8
01	350 43.7	240 25.1	48.5	324 20.6	22.6	61 18.9	38.7	52 27.8	11.0	Nunki	75 51.9	S26 16.2
02	5 46.2	255 24.8	48.3	339 22.6	22.8	76 21.5	38.7	67 30.4	11.0	Peacock	53 10.8	S56 40.1
03	20 48.6	270 24.5	.. 48.2	354 24.6	.. 22.9	91 24.1	.. 38.7	82 33.0	.. 11.0	Pollux	243 21.9	N27 58.6
04	35 51.1	285 24.2	48.0	9 26.6	23.1	106 26.7	38.8	97 35.6	11.1	Procyon	244 54.8	N 5 10.4
05	50 53.6	300 23.9	47.8	24 28.7	23.2	121 29.3	38.8	112 38.2	11.1			
06	65 56.0	315 23.6	N19 47.6	39 30.7	N 6 23.4	136 31.9	S22 38.8	127 40.8	S21 11.1	Rasalhague	96 01.7	N12 33.0
07	80 58.5	330 23.3	47.5	54 32.7	23.5	151 34.5	38.8	142 43.4	11.1	Regulus	207 38.5	N11 52.2
T 08	96 01.0	345 23.0	47.3	69 34.7	23.7	166 37.1	38.8	157 46.0	11.2	Rigel	281 07.4	S 8 10.6
H 09	111 03.4	0 22.7	.. 47.1	84 36.7	.. 23.8	181 39.7	.. 38.9	172 48.6	.. 11.2	Rigil Kent.	139 45.3	S60 55.2
U 10	126 05.9	15 22.4	46.9	99 38.8	24.0	196 42.3	38.9	187 51.2	11.2	Sabik	102 06.7	S15 44.9
R 11	141 08.3	30 22.1	46.8	114 40.8	24.1	211 44.9	38.9	202 53.8	11.2			
S 12	156 10.8	45 21.8	N19 46.6	129 42.8	N 6 24.3	226 47.5	S22 38.9	217 56.4	S21 11.3	Schedar	349 34.5	N56 38.8
D 13	171 13.3	60 21.5	46.4	144 44.8	24.4	241 50.1	38.9	232 59.0	11.3	Shaula	96 15.0	S37 07.1
A 14	186 15.7	75 21.2	46.2	159 46.9	24.6	256 52.7	39.0	248 01.6	11.3	Sirius	258 29.5	S16 44.5
Y 15	201 18.2	90 20.9	.. 46.0	174 48.9	.. 24.7	271 55.3	.. 39.0	263 04.2	.. 11.3	Spica	158 26.2	S11 15.9
16	216 20.7	105 20.6	45.8	189 50.9	24.9	286 57.9	39.0	278 06.8	11.4	Suhail	222 49.3	S43 30.8
17	231 23.1	120 20.3	45.7	204 53.0	25.0	302 00.5	39.0	293 09.3	11.4			
18	246 25.6	135 20.0	N19 45.5	219 55.0	N 6 25.2	317 03.1	S22 39.0	308 11.9	S21 11.4	Vega	80 35.3	N38 48.5
19	261 28.1	150 19.7	45.3	234 57.0	25.3	332 05.7	39.1	323 14.5	11.5	Zuben'ubi	137 00.0	S16 07.5
20	276 30.5	165 19.3	45.1	249 59.1	25.4	347 08.3	39.1	338 17.1	11.5		SHA	Mer. Pass.
21	291 33.0	180 19.0	.. 44.9	265 01.1	.. 25.6	2 10.9	.. 39.1	353 19.7	.. 11.5		° ′	h m
22	306 35.5	195 18.7	44.7	280 03.1	25.7	17 13.5	39.1	8 22.3	11.5	Venus	250 50.4	8 58
23	321 38.0	210 18.4	44.6	295 05.2	25.9	32 16.1	39.1	23 24.9	11.6	Mars	333 48.6	3 26
Mer. Pass.	h m 1 40.9	v −0.3	d 0.2	v 2.0	d 0.2	v 2.6	d 0.0	v 2.6	d 0.0	Jupiter	70 31.5	20 55
										Saturn	61 40.8	21 31

UT	SUN GHA	SUN Dec	MOON GHA	v	MOON Dec	d	HP
25 00	179 28.5	N10 40.1	102 51.2	8.7	S15 37.6	11.3	59.2
01	194 28.7	39.3	117 18.9	8.7	15 48.9	11.2	59.2
02	209 28.9	38.4	131 46.6	8.7	16 00.1	11.1	59.1
03	224 29.1	.. 37.5	146 14.3	8.6	16 11.2	11.0	59.1
04	239 29.2	36.7	160 41.9	8.6	16 22.2	10.9	59.1
05	254 29.4	35.8	175 09.5	8.5	16 33.1	10.8	59.1
06	269 29.6	N10 34.9	189 37.0	8.5	S16 43.9	10.6	59.1
07	284 29.7	34.1	204 04.5	8.5	16 54.5	10.6	59.0
08	299 29.9	33.2	218 32.0	8.4	17 05.1	10.5	59.0
09	314 30.1	.. 32.3	232 59.4	8.4	17 15.6	10.3	59.0
10	329 30.3	31.5	247 26.8	8.4	17 25.9	10.3	59.0
11	344 30.4	30.6	261 54.2	8.3	17 36.2	10.1	58.9
12	359 30.6	N10 29.7	276 21.5	8.3	S17 46.3	10.0	58.9
13	14 30.8	28.9	290 48.8	8.2	17 56.3	9.9	58.9
14	29 31.0	28.0	305 16.0	8.2	18 06.2	9.8	58.9
15	44 31.1	.. 27.1	319 43.2	8.2	18 16.0	9.7	58.8
16	59 31.3	26.3	334 10.4	8.1	18 25.7	9.5	58.8
17	74 31.5	25.4	348 37.5	8.1	18 35.2	9.4	58.8
18	89 31.7	N10 24.5	3 04.6	8.1	S18 44.6	9.4	58.8
19	104 31.9	23.7	17 31.7	8.0	18 54.0	9.2	58.8
20	119 32.0	22.8	31 58.7	8.0	19 03.2	9.0	58.7
21	134 32.2	.. 21.9	46 25.7	8.0	19 12.2	9.0	58.7
22	149 32.4	21.1	60 52.7	7.9	19 21.2	8.8	58.7
23	164 32.6	20.2	75 19.6	7.8	19 30.0	8.7	58.7
26 00	179 32.7	N10 19.3	89 46.4	7.9	S19 38.7	8.6	58.6
01	194 32.9	18.4	104 13.3	7.8	19 47.3	8.5	58.6
02	209 33.1	17.6	118 40.1	7.8	19 55.8	8.3	58.6
03	224 33.3	.. 16.7	133 06.9	7.7	20 04.1	8.2	58.6
04	239 33.5	15.8	147 33.6	7.7	20 12.3	8.1	58.5
05	254 33.6	15.0	162 00.3	7.7	20 20.4	8.0	58.5
06	269 33.8	N10 14.1	176 27.0	7.6	S20 28.4	7.8	58.5
07	284 34.0	13.2	190 53.6	7.6	20 36.2	7.7	58.5
08	299 34.2	12.3	205 20.2	7.6	20 43.9	7.6	58.4
09	314 34.3	.. 11.5	219 46.8	7.6	20 51.5	7.4	58.4
10	329 34.5	10.6	234 13.4	7.5	20 58.9	7.3	58.4
11	344 34.7	09.7	248 39.9	7.5	21 06.2	7.2	58.4
12	359 34.9	N10 08.8	263 06.4	7.4	S21 13.4	7.0	58.3
13	14 35.1	08.0	277 32.8	7.5	21 20.4	6.9	58.3
14	29 35.2	07.1	291 59.3	7.4	21 27.3	6.8	58.3
15	44 35.4	.. 06.2	306 25.7	7.3	21 34.1	6.7	58.3
16	59 35.6	05.3	320 52.0	7.4	21 40.8	6.5	58.2
17	74 35.8	04.5	335 18.4	7.3	21 47.3	6.3	58.2
18	89 36.0	N10 03.6	349 44.7	7.3	S21 53.6	6.3	58.2
19	104 36.1	02.7	4 11.0	7.3	21 59.9	6.0	58.2
20	119 36.3	01.8	18 37.3	7.2	22 05.9	6.0	58.1
21	134 36.5	.. 01.0	33 03.5	7.3	22 11.9	5.8	58.1
22	149 36.7	10 00.1	47 29.8	7.2	22 17.7	5.7	58.1
23	164 36.9	9 59.2	61 56.0	7.2	22 23.4	5.5	58.1
27 00	179 37.0	N 9 58.3	76 22.2	7.2	S22 28.9	5.4	58.0
01	194 37.2	57.5	90 48.4	7.1	22 34.3	5.3	58.0
02	209 37.4	56.6	105 14.5	7.2	22 39.6	5.1	58.0
03	224 37.6	.. 55.7	119 40.7	7.1	22 44.7	5.0	58.0
04	239 37.8	54.8	134 06.8	7.1	22 49.7	4.8	58.0
05	254 38.0	53.9	148 32.9	7.1	22 54.5	4.7	57.9
06	269 38.1	N 9 53.1	162 59.0	7.1	S22 59.2	4.6	57.9
07	284 38.3	52.2	177 25.1	7.1	23 03.8	4.4	57.9
08	299 38.5	51.3	191 51.2	7.0	23 08.2	4.2	57.8
09	314 38.7	.. 50.4	206 17.2	7.1	23 12.4	4.2	57.8
10	329 38.9	49.5	220 43.3	7.0	23 16.6	3.9	57.8
11	344 39.1	48.7	235 09.3	7.0	23 20.5	3.9	57.8
12	359 39.2	N 9 47.8	249 35.3	7.1	S23 24.4	3.7	57.8
13	14 39.4	46.9	264 01.4	7.0	23 28.1	3.5	57.7
14	29 39.6	46.0	278 27.4	7.0	23 31.6	3.4	57.7
15	44 39.8	.. 45.1	292 53.4	7.0	23 35.0	3.3	57.7
16	59 40.0	44.3	307 19.4	7.1	23 38.3	3.1	57.7
17	74 40.2	43.4	321 45.5	7.0	23 41.4	3.0	57.6
18	89 40.3	N 9 42.5	336 11.5	7.0	S23 44.4	2.8	57.6
19	104 40.5	41.6	350 37.5	7.0	23 47.2	2.7	57.6
20	119 40.7	40.7	5 03.5	7.1	23 49.9	2.5	57.6
21	134 40.9	.. 39.8	19 29.6	7.0	23 52.4	2.4	57.5
22	149 41.1	39.0	33 55.6	7.0	23 54.8	2.2	57.5
23	164 41.3	38.1	48 21.6	7.1	S23 57.0	2.1	57.5
	SD 15.9	d 0.9	SD 16.1		15.9		15.7

Twilight / Moonrise

Lat.	Naut.	Civil	Sunrise	25	26	27	28
N 72	////	01 44	03 33	■	■	■	■
N 70	////	02 26	03 51	16 15	■	■	■
68	////	02 53	04 05	15 25	■	▬	■
66	01 29	03 14	04 17	14 54	16 57	19 20	■
64	02 07	03 30	04 26	14 31	16 19	17 56	19 03
62	02 33	03 44	04 34	14 13	15 51	17 19	18 23
60	02 52	03 55	04 42	13 58	15 31	16 52	17 56
N 58	03 08	04 04	04 48	13 46	15 13	16 32	17 34
56	03 21	04 13	04 53	13 35	14 59	16 15	17 16
54	03 32	04 20	04 58	13 25	14 47	16 00	17 01
52	03 41	04 26	05 03	13 17	14 36	15 48	16 48
50	03 50	04 32	05 07	13 09	14 26	15 36	16 37
45	04 07	04 44	05 15	12 53	14 06	15 13	16 13
N 40	04 20	04 54	05 22	12 40	13 49	14 55	15 54
35	04 31	05 02	05 29	12 29	13 36	14 40	15 38
30	04 40	05 09	05 34	12 19	13 24	14 26	15 24
20	04 54	05 21	05 43	12 02	13 03	14 03	15 01
N 10	05 05	05 30	05 51	11 48	12 46	13 44	14 41
0	05 13	05 37	05 58	11 34	12 29	13 25	14 22
S 10	05 20	05 44	06 06	11 21	12 13	13 07	14 03
20	05 25	05 51	06 13	11 07	11 56	12 48	13 43
30	05 30	05 58	06 22	10 51	11 36	12 25	13 19
35	05 32	06 01	06 27	10 41	11 24	12 12	13 06
40	05 33	06 05	06 32	10 31	11 11	11 57	12 50
45	05 35	06 09	06 38	10 18	10 55	11 39	12 31
S 50	05 36	06 13	06 46	10 03	10 36	11 17	12 08
52	05 36	06 15	06 49	09 56	10 27	11 07	11 56
54	05 36	06 17	06 53	09 49	10 17	10 55	11 44
56	05 36	06 20	06 57	09 40	10 06	10 41	11 29
58	05 37	06 22	07 02	09 31	09 53	10 25	11 12
S 60	05 37	06 25	07 07	09 19	09 38	10 06	10 50

Sunset / Twilight / Moonset

Lat.	Sunset	Civil	Naut.	25	26	27	28
N 72	20 27	22 11	////	■	■	■	■
N 70	20 09	21 32	////	19 04	■	■	■
68	19 56	21 06	23 50	19 54	■	■	■
66	19 44	20 46	22 26	20 26	20 19	19 54	■
64	19 35	20 30	21 52	20 50	20 58	21 19	22 08
62	19 27	20 17	21 27	21 09	21 26	21 56	22 48
60	19 18	20 07	21 08	21 25	21 47	22 22	23 16
N 58	19 14	19 57	20 53	21 38	22 05	22 43	23 37
56	19 09	19 49	20 41	21 50	22 19	23 00	23 55
54	19 04	19 42	20 30	22 00	22 32	23 15	24 10
52	19 00	19 36	20 20	22 09	22 43	23 28	24 23
50	18 56	19 30	20 12	22 17	22 53	23 39	24 34
45	18 47	19 18	19 55	22 34	23 14	24 02	00 02
N 40	18 40	19 08	19 42	22 48	23 32	24 21	00 21
35	18 34	19 00	19 31	23 01	23 46	24 37	00 37
30	18 29	18 54	19 23	23 11	23 58	24 50	00 50
20	18 20	18 42	19 09	23 29	24 20	00 20	01 14
N 10	18 12	18 34	18 58	23 45	24 39	00 39	01 34
0	18 05	18 26	18 50	24 00	00 00	00 56	01 53
S 10	17 58	18 19	18 44	24 15	00 15	01 14	02 11
20	17 50	18 13	18 38	24 31	00 31	01 32	02 31
30	17 42	18 06	18 34	24 50	00 50	01 54	02 55
35	17 37	18 03	18 32	25 01	01 01	02 07	03 08
40	17 32	17 59	18 31	00 02	01 13	02 21	03 24
45	17 26	17 55	18 29	00 13	01 28	02 39	03 43
S 50	17 18	17 51	18 29	00 27	01 46	03 00	04 06
52	17 15	17 49	18 28	00 33	01 55	03 10	04 17
54	17 11	17 47	18 28	00 40	02 04	03 22	04 30
56	17 07	17 45	18 28	00 48	02 15	03 35	04 45
58	17 02	17 42	18 28	00 57	02 27	03 51	05 02
S 60	16 57	17 40	18 28	01 07	02 42	04 10	05 23

SUN / MOON

Day	Eqn. of Time 00h	Eqn. of Time 12h	Mer. Pass.	Mer. Pass. Upper	Mer. Pass. Lower	Age	Phase
d	m s	m s	h m	h m	h m	d	%
25	02 06	01 58	12 02	17 47	05 20	06	47
26	01 49	01 41	12 02	18 43	06 15	07	58
27	01 32	01 23	12 01	19 39	07 11	08	69

UT	ARIES GHA	VENUS −4.3 GHA	Dec	MARS −1.7 GHA	Dec	JUPITER −2.6 GHA	Dec	SATURN +0.3 GHA	Dec	STARS Name	SHA	Dec
28 00	336 40.4	225 18.1	N19 44.4	310 07.2	N 6 26.0	47 18.7	S22 39.2	38 27.5	S21 11.6	Acamar	315 14.4	S40 13.1
01	351 42.8	240 17.8	44.2	325 09.3	26.2	62 21.3	39.2	53 30.1	11.6	Achernar	335 22.6	S57 07.8
02	6 45.3	255 17.5	44.0	340 11.3	26.3	77 23.9	39.2	68 32.7	11.6	Acrux	173 04.4	S63 12.8
03	21 47.8	270 17.2 ..	43.8	355 13.3 ..	26.5	92 26.5 ..	39.2	83 35.3 ..	11.7	Adhara	255 08.8	S28 59.8
04	36 50.2	285 16.9	43.6	10 15.4	26.6	107 29.1	39.2	98 37.9	11.7	Aldebaran	290 43.7	N16 33.0
05	51 52.7	300 16.6	43.4	25 17.4	26.7	122 31.7	39.3	113 40.4	11.7			
06	66 55.2	315 16.2	N19 43.2	40 19.5	N 6 26.9	137 34.3	S22 39.3	128 43.0	S21 11.7	Alioth	166 16.6	N55 51.2
07	81 57.6	330 15.9	43.0	55 21.5	27.0	152 36.9	39.3	143 45.6	11.8	Alkaid	152 55.2	N49 13.0
08	97 00.1	345 15.6	42.8	70 23.6	27.2	167 39.5	39.3	158 48.2	11.8	Alnair	27 36.9	S46 51.6
F 09	112 02.6	0 15.3 ..	42.6	85 25.6 ..	27.3	182 42.1 ..	39.3	173 50.8 ..	11.8	Alnilam	275 41.4	S 1 11.3
R 10	127 05.0	15 15.0	42.4	100 27.7	27.4	197 44.7	39.4	188 53.4	11.8	Alphard	217 51.5	S 8 44.7
I 11	142 07.5	30 14.7	42.2	115 29.7	27.6	212 47.3	39.4	203 56.0	11.9			
D 12	157 10.0	45 14.4	N19 42.0	130 31.8	N 6 27.7	227 49.9	S22 39.4	218 58.6	S21 11.9	Alphecca	126 06.8	N26 39.1
A 13	172 12.4	60 14.0	41.8	145 33.8	27.9	242 52.5	39.4	234 01.2	11.9	Alpheratz	357 38.0	N29 12.2
Y 14	187 14.9	75 13.7	41.6	160 35.9	28.0	257 55.1	39.4	249 03.8	11.9	Altair	62 03.1	N 8 55.5
15	202 17.3	90 13.4 ..	41.4	175 38.0 ..	28.1	272 57.7 ..	39.4	264 06.3 ..	12.0	Ankaa	353 10.3	S42 11.5
16	217 19.8	105 13.1	41.2	190 40.0	28.3	288 00.3	39.5	279 08.9	12.0	Antares	112 20.1	S26 28.6
17	232 22.3	120 12.8	41.0	205 42.1	28.4	303 02.9	39.5	294 11.5	12.0			
18	247 24.7	135 12.5	N19 40.8	220 44.2	N 6 28.5	318 05.5	S22 39.5	309 14.1	S21 12.0	Arcturus	145 51.3	N19 04.8
19	262 27.2	150 12.1	40.6	235 46.2	28.7	333 08.1	39.5	324 16.7	12.1	Atria	107 17.4	S69 04.0
20	277 29.7	165 11.8	40.4	250 48.3	28.8	348 10.7	39.5	339 19.3	12.1	Avior	234 16.6	S59 34.3
21	292 32.1	180 11.5 ..	40.2	265 50.4 ..	28.9	3 13.2 ..	39.6	354 21.9 ..	12.1	Bellatrix	278 26.7	N 6 22.1
22	307 34.6	195 11.2	40.0	280 52.4	29.1	18 15.8	39.6	9 24.5	12.1	Betelgeuse	270 56.0	N 7 24.7
23	322 37.1	210 10.9	39.8	295 54.5	29.2	33 18.4	39.6	24 27.1	12.2			
29 00	337 39.5	225 10.5	N19 39.6	310 56.6	N 6 29.3	48 21.0	S22 39.6	39 29.6	S21 12.2	Canopus	263 54.2	S52 42.1
01	352 42.0	240 10.2	39.4	325 58.6	29.5	63 23.6	39.6	54 32.2	12.2	Capella	280 27.2	N46 00.9
02	7 44.5	255 09.9	39.2	341 00.7	29.6	78 26.2	39.6	69 34.8	12.2	Deneb	49 27.7	N45 21.4
03	22 46.9	270 09.6 ..	38.9	356 02.8 ..	29.7	93 28.8 ..	39.7	84 37.4 ..	12.3	Denebola	182 28.9	N14 27.6
04	37 49.4	285 09.2	38.7	11 04.9	29.9	108 31.4	39.7	99 40.0	12.3	Diphda	348 50.6	S17 52.3
05	52 51.8	300 08.9	38.5	26 06.9	30.0	123 34.0	39.7	114 42.6	12.3			
06	67 54.3	315 08.6	N19 38.3	41 09.0	N 6 30.1	138 36.6	S22 39.7	129 45.2	S21 12.3	Dubhe	193 46.1	N61 38.6
07	82 56.8	330 08.3	38.1	56 11.1	30.3	153 39.2	39.7	144 47.8	12.4	Elnath	278 06.4	N28 37.3
S 08	97 59.2	345 08.0	37.9	71 13.2	30.4	168 41.7	39.8	159 50.3	12.4	Eltanin	90 43.6	N51 29.5
A 09	113 01.7	0 07.6 ..	37.7	86 15.3 ..	30.5	183 44.3 ..	39.8	174 52.9 ..	12.4	Enif	33 41.9	N 9 58.3
T 10	128 04.2	15 07.3	37.4	101 17.3	30.7	198 46.9	39.8	189 55.5	12.4	Fomalhaut	15 18.1	S29 30.7
U 11	143 06.6	30 07.0	37.2	116 19.4	30.8	213 49.5	39.8	204 58.1	12.5			
R 12	158 09.1	45 06.7	N19 37.0	131 21.5	N 6 30.9	228 52.1	S22 39.8	220 00.7	S21 12.5	Gacrux	171 55.9	S57 13.7
D 13	173 11.6	60 06.3	36.8	146 23.6	31.0	243 54.7	39.8	235 03.3	12.5	Gienah	175 47.5	S17 39.2
A 14	188 14.0	75 06.0	36.6	161 25.7	31.2	258 57.3	39.9	250 05.9	12.5	Hadar	148 41.2	S60 28.4
Y 15	203 16.5	90 05.7 ..	36.3	176 27.8 ..	31.3	273 59.8 ..	39.9	265 08.4 ..	12.6	Hamal	327 54.9	N23 33.5
16	218 18.9	105 05.4	36.1	191 29.9	31.4	289 02.4	39.9	280 11.0	12.6	Kaus Aust.	83 37.0	S34 22.5
17	233 21.4	120 05.0	35.9	206 32.0	31.6	304 05.0	39.9	295 13.6	12.6			
18	248 23.9	135 04.7	N19 35.7	221 34.1	N 6 31.7	319 07.6	S22 39.9	310 16.2	S21 12.6	Kochab	137 20.4	N74 04.6
19	263 26.3	150 04.4	35.4	236 36.1	31.8	334 10.2	40.0	325 18.8	12.7	Markab	13 33.1	N15 19.0
20	278 28.8	165 04.0	35.2	251 38.2	31.9	349 12.8	40.0	340 21.4	12.7	Menkar	314 09.7	N 4 10.2
21	293 31.3	180 03.7 ..	35.0	266 40.3 ..	32.1	4 15.4 ..	40.0	355 24.0 ..	12.7	Menkent	148 01.9	S36 28.2
22	308 33.7	195 03.4	34.8	281 42.4	32.2	19 17.9	40.0	10 26.5	12.7	Miaplacidus	221 39.7	S69 47.9
23	323 36.2	210 03.1	34.5	296 44.5	32.3	34 20.5	40.0	25 29.1	12.7			
30 00	338 38.7	225 02.7	N19 34.3	311 46.6	N 6 32.4	49 23.1	S22 40.0	40 31.7	S21 12.8	Mirfak	308 33.1	N49 55.8
01	353 41.1	240 02.4	34.1	326 48.7	32.6	64 25.7	40.1	55 34.3	12.8	Nunki	75 51.9	S26 16.2
02	8 43.6	255 02.1	33.9	341 50.9	32.7	79 28.3	40.1	70 36.9	12.8	Peacock	53 10.8	S56 40.2
03	23 46.1	270 01.7 ..	33.6	356 53.0 ..	32.8	94 30.9 ..	40.1	85 39.5 ..	12.8	Pollux	243 21.9	N27 58.6
04	38 48.5	285 01.4	33.4	11 55.1	32.9	109 33.4	40.1	100 42.1	12.9	Procyon	244 54.8	N 5 10.4
05	53 51.0	300 01.1	33.2	26 57.2	33.1	124 36.0	40.1	115 44.6	12.9			
06	68 53.4	315 00.7	N19 32.9	41 59.3	N 6 33.2	139 38.6	S22 40.1	130 47.2	S21 12.9	Rasalhague	96 01.7	N12 33.0
07	83 55.9	330 00.4	32.7	57 01.4	33.3	154 41.2	40.2	145 49.8	12.9	Regulus	207 38.5	N11 52.2
08	98 58.4	345 00.1	32.4	72 03.5	33.4	169 43.8	40.2	160 52.4	13.0	Rigel	281 07.3	S 8 10.6
S 09	114 00.8	359 59.7 ..	32.2	87 05.6 ..	33.5	184 46.3 ..	40.2	175 55.0 ..	13.0	Rigil Kent.	139 45.3	S60 55.2
U 10	129 03.3	14 59.4	32.0	102 07.7	33.7	199 48.9	40.2	190 57.6	13.0	Sabik	102 06.7	S15 44.9
N 11	144 05.8	29 59.1	31.7	117 09.8	33.8	214 51.5	40.2	206 00.1	13.0			
D 12	159 08.2	44 58.7	N19 31.5	132 12.0	N 6 33.9	229 54.1	S22 40.2	221 02.7	S21 13.1	Schedar	349 34.4	N56 38.8
A 13	174 10.7	59 58.4	31.3	147 14.1	34.0	244 56.7	40.3	236 05.3	13.1	Shaula	96 15.0	S37 07.1
Y 14	189 13.2	74 58.1	31.0	162 16.2	34.1	259 59.2	40.3	251 07.9	13.1	Sirius	258 29.5	S16 44.5
15	204 15.6	89 57.7 ..	30.8	177 18.3 ..	34.3	275 01.8 ..	40.3	266 10.5 ..	13.1	Spica	158 26.2	S11 15.9
16	219 18.1	104 57.4	30.5	192 20.4	34.4	290 04.4	40.3	281 13.1	13.2	Suhail	222 49.2	S43 30.8
17	234 20.6	119 57.1	30.3	207 22.6	34.5	305 07.0	40.3	296 15.6	13.2			
18	249 23.0	134 56.7	N19 30.0	222 24.7	N 6 34.6	320 09.5	S22 40.3	311 18.2	S21 13.2	Vega	80 35.4	N38 48.5
19	264 25.5	149 56.4	29.8	237 26.8	34.7	335 12.1	40.4	326 20.8	13.2	Zuben'ubi	137 00.0	S16 07.5
20	279 27.9	164 56.1	29.5	252 29.0	34.8	350 14.7	40.4	341 23.4	13.3			
21	294 30.4	179 55.7 ..	29.3	267 31.1 ..	35.0	5 17.3 ..	40.4	356 26.0 ..	13.3			
22	309 32.9	194 55.4	29.1	282 33.2	35.1	20 19.8	40.4	11 28.5	13.3			
23	324 35.3	209 55.0	28.8	297 35.3	35.2	35 22.4	40.4	26 31.1	13.3			

Name	SHA	Mer. Pass.
	° ′	h m
Venus	247 31.0	8 59
Mars	333 17.0	3 16
Jupiter	70 41.5	20 43
Saturn	61 50.1	21 18

	h m				
Mer. Pass.	1 29.1	v −0.3 d 0.2	v 2.1 d 0.1	v 2.6 d 0.0	v 2.6 d 0.0

UT	SUN GHA	SUN Dec	MOON GHA	v	MOON Dec	d	HP
d h	° ′	° ′	° ′	′	° ′	′	′
28 00	179 41.5	N 9 37.2	62 47.7	7.0	S23 59.1	2.0	57.5
01	194 41.6	36.3	77 13.7	7.1	24 01.1	1.8	57.4
02	209 41.8	35.4	91 39.8	7.0	24 02.9	1.7	57.4
03	224 42.0	. . 34.5	106 05.8	7.1	24 04.6	1.5	57.4
04	239 42.2	33.7	120 31.9	7.1	24 06.1	1.4	57.4
05	254 42.4	32.8	134 58.0	7.2	24 07.5	1.2	57.4
06	269 42.6	N 9 31.9	149 24.2	7.1	S24 08.7	1.1	57.3
07	284 42.8	31.0	163 50.3	7.1	24 09.8	0.9	57.3
08	299 42.9	30.1	178 16.4	7.2	24 10.7	0.8	57.3
F 09	314 43.1	. . 29.2	192 42.6	7.2	24 11.5	0.7	57.3
R 10	329 43.3	28.3	207 08.8	7.2	24 12.2	0.5	57.2
I 11	344 43.5	27.5	221 35.0	7.2	24 12.7	0.5	57.2
D 12	359 43.7	N 9 26.6	236 01.2	7.3	S24 13.1	0.2	57.2
A 13	14 43.9	25.7	250 27.5	7.3	24 13.3	0.1	57.2
Y 14	29 44.1	24.8	264 53.8	7.3	24 13.4	0.1	57.1
15	44 44.3	. . 23.9	279 20.1	7.3	24 13.3	0.2	57.1
16	59 44.4	23.0	293 46.4	7.4	24 13.1	0.3	57.1
17	74 44.6	22.1	308 12.8	7.4	24 12.8	0.5	57.1
18	89 44.8	N 9 21.2	322 39.2	7.4	S24 12.3	0.7	57.0
19	104 45.0	20.4	337 05.6	7.5	24 11.6	0.7	57.0
20	119 45.2	19.5	351 32.1	7.5	24 10.9	0.9	57.0
21	134 45.4	. . 18.6	5 58.6	7.5	24 10.0	1.1	57.0
22	149 45.6	17.7	20 25.1	7.6	24 08.9	1.2	57.0
23	164 45.8	16.8	34 51.7	7.6	24 07.7	1.3	56.9
29 00	179 46.0	N 9 15.9	49 18.3	7.6	S24 06.4	1.5	56.9
01	194 46.1	15.0	63 44.9	7.7	24 04.9	1.6	56.9
02	209 46.3	14.1	78 11.6	7.7	24 03.3	1.7	56.9
03	224 46.5	. . 13.2	92 38.3	7.8	24 01.6	1.9	56.8
04	239 46.7	12.3	107 05.1	7.8	23 59.7	2.0	56.8
05	254 46.9	11.5	121 31.9	7.8	23 57.7	2.2	56.8
06	269 47.1	N 9 10.6	135 58.7	7.9	S23 55.5	2.3	56.8
07	284 47.3	09.7	150 25.6	8.0	23 53.2	2.4	56.8
S 08	299 47.5	08.8	164 52.6	8.0	23 50.8	2.5	56.7
A 09	314 47.7	. . 07.9	179 19.6	8.0	23 48.3	2.7	56.7
T 10	329 47.9	07.0	193 46.6	8.1	23 45.6	2.9	56.7
U 11	344 48.1	06.1	208 13.7	8.2	23 42.7	2.9	56.7
R 12	359 48.2	N 9 05.2	222 40.9	8.2	S23 39.8	3.1	56.6
D 13	14 48.4	04.3	237 08.1	8.2	23 36.7	3.2	56.6
A 14	29 48.6	03.4	251 35.3	8.3	23 33.5	3.4	56.6
Y 15	44 48.8	. . 02.5	266 02.6	8.4	23 30.1	3.4	56.6
16	59 49.0	01.6	280 30.0	8.4	23 26.7	3.6	56.6
17	74 49.2	9 00.7	294 57.4	8.5	23 23.1	3.8	56.5
18	89 49.4	N 8 59.8	309 24.9	8.5	S23 19.3	3.8	56.5
19	104 49.6	59.0	323 52.4	8.6	23 15.5	4.0	56.5
20	119 49.8	58.1	338 20.0	8.6	23 11.5	4.1	56.5
21	134 50.0	. . 57.2	352 47.6	8.7	23 07.4	4.3	56.4
22	149 50.2	56.3	7 15.3	8.8	23 03.1	4.3	56.4
23	164 50.4	55.4	21 43.1	8.8	22 58.8	4.5	56.4
30 00	179 50.5	N 8 54.5	36 10.9	8.9	S22 54.3	4.6	56.4
01	194 50.7	53.6	50 38.8	9.0	22 49.7	4.7	56.4
02	209 50.9	52.7	65 06.8	9.0	22 45.0	4.9	56.3
03	224 51.1	. . 51.8	79 34.8	9.1	22 40.1	4.9	56.3
04	239 51.3	50.9	94 02.9	9.1	22 35.2	5.1	56.3
05	254 51.5	50.0	108 31.0	9.2	22 30.1	5.2	56.3
06	269 51.7	N 8 49.1	122 59.2	9.3	S22 24.9	5.3	56.3
07	284 51.9	48.2	137 27.5	9.3	22 19.6	5.5	56.2
08	299 52.1	47.3	151 55.8	9.5	22 14.1	5.5	56.2
S 09	314 52.3	. . 46.4	166 24.3	9.4	22 08.6	5.7	56.2
U 10	329 52.5	45.5	180 52.7	9.6	22 02.9	5.8	56.2
N 11	344 52.7	44.6	195 21.3	9.6	21 57.1	5.9	56.2
D 12	359 52.9	N 8 43.7	209 49.9	9.7	S21 51.2	6.0	56.1
A 13	14 53.1	42.8	224 18.6	9.8	21 45.2	6.1	56.1
Y 14	29 53.3	41.9	238 47.4	9.8	21 39.1	6.2	56.1
15	44 53.5	. . 41.0	253 16.2	9.9	21 32.9	6.3	56.1
16	59 53.7	40.1	267 45.1	10.0	21 26.6	6.4	56.0
17	74 53.9	39.2	282 14.1	10.0	21 20.2	6.6	56.0
18	89 54.0	N 8 38.3	296 43.1	10.1	S21 13.6	6.6	56.0
19	104 54.2	37.4	311 12.2	10.2	21 07.0	6.8	56.0
20	119 54.4	36.5	325 41.4	10.3	21 00.2	6.8	56.0
21	134 54.6	. . 35.6	340 10.7	10.3	20 53.4	7.0	55.9
22	149 54.8	34.7	354 40.0	10.4	20 46.4	7.1	55.9
23	164 55.0	33.8	9 09.4	10.5	S20 39.3	7.1	55.9
	SD 15.9	d 0.9	SD 15.6		15.4		15.3

Twilight and Moonrise:

Lat.	Naut.	Civil	Sunrise	Moonrise 28	29	30	31
°	h m	h m	h m	h m	h m	h m	h m
N 72	////	02 11	03 48	■	■	■	22 18
N 70	////	02 45	04 04	■	■	21 06	21 14
68	01 01	03 08	04 16	■	20 28	20 38	20 38
66	01 53	03 26	04 27	■	20 28	20 18	20 12
64	02 23	03 41	04 35	19 03	19 35	19 47	19 51
62	02 45	03 53	04 42	18 23	19 02	19 23	19 35
60	03 02	04 03	04 49	17 56	18 38	19 04	19 21
N 58	03 17	04 12	04 54	17 34	18 19	18 49	19 09
56	03 28	04 19	04 59	17 16	18 03	18 36	18 59
54	03 39	04 26	05 04	17 01	17 49	18 24	18 50
52	03 48	04 32	05 07	16 48	17 37	18 14	18 42
50	03 55	04 37	05 11	16 37	17 26	18 04	18 34
45	04 11	04 48	05 19	16 13	17 04	17 45	18 19
N 40	04 24	04 57	05 25	15 54	16 46	17 29	18 06
35	04 34	05 05	05 31	15 38	16 30	17 16	17 55
30	04 42	05 11	05 36	15 24	16 17	17 04	17 45
20	04 55	05 21	05 44	15 01	15 55	16 44	17 28
N 10	05 05	05 30	05 51	14 41	15 35	16 26	17 13
0	05 12	05 37	05 57	14 22	15 17	16 10	17 00
S 10	05 18	05 43	06 04	14 03	14 59	15 53	16 46
20	05 23	05 49	06 11	13 43	14 39	15 36	16 31
30	05 26	05 54	06 18	13 19	14 17	15 15	16 14
35	05 28	05 57	06 23	13 06	14 03	15 03	16 04
40	05 29	06 00	06 28	12 50	13 48	14 50	15 53
45	05 30	06 04	06 33	12 31	13 30	14 33	15 39
S 50	05 30	06 07	06 40	12 08	13 07	14 13	15 23
52	05 30	06 09	06 43	11 56	12 56	14 04	15 15
54	05 30	06 11	06 46	11 44	12 44	13 53	15 06
56	05 29	06 12	06 50	11 29	12 30	13 41	14 57
58	05 29	06 14	06 54	11 12	12 13	13 27	14 46
S 60	05 28	06 16	06 59	10 50	11 53	13 10	14 33

Twilight and Moonset:

Lat.	Sunset	Civil	Naut.	Moonset 28	29	30	31
°	h m	h m	h m	h m	h m	h m	h m
N 72	20 10	21 44	////	■	■	■	■
N 70	19 55	21 12	////	■	■	23 49	26 00
68	19 43	20 50	22 48	■	■	23 49	26 00
66	19 33	20 32	22 03	■	22 38	24 37	00 37
64	19 24	20 18	21 34	22 08	23 31	25 07	01 07
62	19 17	20 07	21 13	22 48	24 03	00 03	01 30
60	19 11	19 57	20 56	23 16	24 27	00 27	01 48
N 58	19 06	19 48	20 43	23 37	24 46	00 46	02 03
56	19 01	19 41	20 31	23 55	25 02	01 02	02 16
54	18 57	19 34	20 21	24 10	00 10	01 15	02 28
52	18 53	19 29	20 12	24 23	00 23	01 27	02 37
50	18 50	19 23	20 05	24 34	00 34	01 38	02 46
45	18 42	19 12	19 49	00 02	00 58	02 00	03 05
N 40	18 36	19 04	19 37	00 21	01 17	02 17	03 20
35	18 30	18 56	19 27	00 37	01 33	02 32	03 33
30	18 26	18 50	19 19	00 50	01 46	02 45	03 44
20	18 18	18 40	19 06	01 14	02 10	03 06	04 03
N 10	18 11	18 32	18 57	01 34	02 30	03 25	04 19
0	18 04	18 25	18 49	01 53	02 48	03 43	04 34
S 10	17 58	18 19	18 44	02 11	03 07	04 00	04 49
20	17 51	18 13	18 39	02 31	03 27	04 19	05 05
30	17 44	18 08	18 36	02 55	03 50	04 40	05 24
35	17 39	18 05	18 34	03 08	04 04	04 53	05 35
40	17 35	18 02	18 33	03 24	04 19	05 07	05 47
45	17 29	17 59	18 33	03 43	04 38	05 24	06 01
S 50	17 23	17 55	18 33	04 06	05 01	05 45	06 19
52	17 19	17 54	18 33	04 17	05 12	05 54	06 27
54	17 16	17 52	18 33	04 30	05 24	06 06	06 36
56	17 13	17 50	18 33	04 45	05 39	06 18	06 46
58	17 08	17 48	18 34	05 02	05 55	06 33	06 58
S 60	17 04	17 46	18 35	05 23	06 16	06 50	07 11

	SUN			MOON			
Day	Eqn. of Time 00ʰ	Eqn. of Time 12ʰ	Mer. Pass.	Mer. Pass. Upper	Mer. Pass. Lower	Age	Phase
d	m s	m s	h m	h m	h m	d	%
28	01 15	01 06	12 01	20 35	08 07	09	78
29	00 57	00 47	12 01	21 30	09 03	10	86
30	00 38	00 29	12 00	22 22	09 56	11	93

UT	ARIES GHA	VENUS −4·3 GHA	Dec	MARS −1·8 GHA	Dec	JUPITER −2·6 GHA	Dec	SATURN +0·3 GHA	Dec	STARS Name	SHA	Dec
31 00	339 37.8	224 54.7	N19 28.6	312 37.5	N 6 35.3	50 25.0	S22 40.4	41 33.7	S21 13.3	Acamar	315 14.3	S40 13.1
01	354 40.3	239 54.4	28.3	327 39.6	35.4	65 27.6	40.5	56 36.3	13.4	Achernar	335 22.5	S57 07.8
02	9 42.7	254 54.0	28.1	342 41.7	35.5	80 30.1	40.5	71 38.9	13.4	Acrux	173 04.4	S63 12.8
03	24 45.2	269 53.7 ..	27.8	357 43.9 ..	35.6	95 32.7 ..	40.5	86 41.5 ..	13.4	Adhara	255 08.8	S28 59.8
04	39 47.7	284 53.4	27.5	12 46.0	35.8	110 35.3	40.5	101 44.0	13.4	Aldebaran	290 43.6	N16 33.0
05	54 50.1	299 53.0	27.3	27 48.2	35.9	125 37.9	40.5	116 46.6	13.5			
M 06	69 52.6	314 52.7	N19 27.0	42 50.3	N 6 36.0	140 40.4	S22 40.6	131 49.2	S21 13.5	Alioth	166 16.6	N55 51.2
O 07	84 55.1	329 52.3	26.8	57 52.4	36.1	155 43.0	40.6	146 51.8	13.5	Alkaid	152 55.2	N49 13.0
N 08	99 57.5	344 52.0	26.5	72 54.6	36.2	170 45.6	40.6	161 54.4	13.5	Alnair	27 36.9	S46 51.6
D 09	115 00.0	359 51.6 ..	26.3	87 56.7 ..	36.3	185 48.2 ..	40.6	176 56.9 ..	13.6	Alnilam	275 41.4	S 1 11.3
A 10	130 02.4	14 51.3	26.0	102 58.9	36.4	200 50.7	40.6	191 59.5	13.6	Alphard	217 51.5	S 8 44.7
Y 11	145 04.9	29 51.0	25.8	118 01.0	36.5	215 53.3	40.6	207 02.1	13.6			
12	160 07.4	44 50.6	N19 25.5	133 03.2	N 6 36.6	230 55.9	S22 40.6	222 04.7	S21 13.6	Alphecca	126 06.8	N26 39.1
13	175 09.8	59 50.3	25.2	148 05.3	36.8	245 58.4	40.6	237 07.3	13.7	Alpheratz	357 38.0	N29 12.2
14	190 12.3	74 49.9	25.0	163 07.5	36.9	261 01.0	40.7	252 09.8	13.7	Altair	62 03.1	N 8 55.5
15	205 14.8	89 49.6 ..	24.7	178 09.6 ..	37.0	276 03.6 ..	40.7	267 12.4 ..	13.7	Ankaa	353 10.3	S42 11.5
16	220 17.2	104 49.2	24.4	193 11.8	37.1	291 06.1	40.7	282 15.0	13.7	Antares	112 20.1	S26 28.6
17	235 19.7	119 48.9	24.2	208 13.9	37.2	306 08.7	40.7	297 17.6	13.7			
18	250 22.2	134 48.6	N19 23.9	223 16.1	N 6 37.3	321 11.3	S22 40.7	312 20.1	S21 13.8	Arcturus	145 51.3	N19 04.8
19	265 24.6	149 48.2	23.6	238 18.3	37.4	336 13.8	40.7	327 22.7	13.8	Atria	107 17.4	S69 04.0
20	280 27.1	164 47.9	23.4	253 20.4	37.5	351 16.4	40.8	342 25.3	13.8	Avior	234 16.6	S59 34.3
21	295 29.5	179 47.5 ..	23.1	268 22.6 ..	37.6	6 19.0 ..	40.8	357 27.9 ..	13.8	Bellatrix	278 26.7	N 6 22.1
22	310 32.0	194 47.2	22.8	283 24.7	37.7	21 21.6	40.8	12 30.5	13.9	Betelgeuse	270 56.0	N 7 24.7
23	325 34.5	209 46.8	22.6	298 26.9	37.8	36 24.1	40.8	27 33.0	13.9			
1 00	340 36.9	224 46.5	N19 22.3	313 29.1	N 6 37.9	51 26.7	S22 40.8	42 35.6	S21 13.9	Canopus	263 54.2	S52 42.1
01	355 39.4	239 46.1	22.0	328 31.2	38.0	66 29.3	40.8	57 38.2	13.9	Capella	280 27.2	N46 00.9
02	10 41.9	254 45.8	21.8	343 33.4	38.1	81 31.8	40.8	72 40.8	14.0	Deneb	49 27.7	N45 21.4
03	25 44.3	269 45.4 ..	21.5	358 35.6 ..	38.3	96 34.4 ..	40.9	87 43.4 ..	14.0	Denebola	182 28.9	N14 27.6
04	40 46.8	284 45.1	21.2	13 37.7	38.4	111 36.9	40.9	102 45.9	14.0	Diphda	348 50.6	S17 52.3
05	55 49.3	299 44.7	20.9	28 39.9	38.5	126 39.5	40.9	117 48.5	14.0			
T 06	70 51.7	314 44.4	N19 20.7	43 42.1	N 6 38.6	141 42.1	S22 40.9	132 51.1	S21 14.0	Dubhe	193 46.1	N61 38.6
U 07	85 54.2	329 44.0	20.4	58 44.3	38.7	156 44.6	40.9	147 53.7	14.1	Elnath	278 06.4	N28 37.4
E 08	100 56.7	344 43.7	20.1	73 46.4	38.8	171 47.2	40.9	162 56.2	14.1	Eltanin	90 43.6	N51 29.5
S 09	115 59.1	359 43.4 ..	19.8	88 48.6 ..	38.9	186 49.8 ..	40.9	177 58.8 ..	14.1	Enif	33 41.9	N 9 58.3
D 10	131 01.6	14 43.0	19.6	103 50.8	39.0	201 52.3	41.0	193 01.4	14.1	Fomalhaut	15 18.1	S29 30.7
A 11	146 04.0	29 42.7	19.3	118 53.0	39.1	216 54.9	41.0	208 04.0	14.2			
Y 12	161 06.5	44 42.3	N19 19.0	133 55.2	N 6 39.2	231 57.5	S22 41.0	223 06.5	S21 14.2	Gacrux	171 55.9	S57 13.7
13	176 09.0	59 42.0	18.7	148 57.3	39.3	247 00.0	41.0	238 09.1	14.2	Gienah	175 47.5	S17 39.2
14	191 11.4	74 41.6	18.4	163 59.5	39.4	262 02.6	41.0	253 11.7	14.2	Hadar	148 41.3	S60 28.4
15	206 13.9	89 41.2 ..	18.1	179 01.7 ..	39.5	277 05.1 ..	41.0	268 14.3 ..	14.2	Hamal	327 54.9	N23 33.5
16	221 16.4	104 40.9	17.9	194 03.9	39.6	292 07.7	41.0	283 16.8	14.3	Kaus Aust.	83 37.0	S34 22.5
17	236 18.8	119 40.5	17.6	209 06.1	39.7	307 10.3	41.1	298 19.4	14.3			
18	251 21.3	134 40.2	N19 17.3	224 08.3	N 6 39.8	322 12.8	S22 41.1	313 22.0	S21 14.3	Kochab	137 20.5	N74 04.6
19	266 23.8	149 39.8	17.0	239 10.5	39.9	337 15.4	41.1	328 24.6	14.3	Markab	13 33.0	N15 19.0
20	281 26.2	164 39.5	16.7	254 12.6	40.0	352 17.9	41.1	343 27.1	14.4	Menkar	314 09.7	N 4 10.2
21	296 28.7	179 39.1 ..	16.4	269 14.8 ..	40.1	7 20.5 ..	41.1	358 29.7 ..	14.4	Menkent	148 01.9	S36 28.2
22	311 31.1	194 38.8	16.1	284 17.0	40.2	22 23.1	41.1	13 32.3	14.4	Miaplacidus	221 39.7	S69 47.9
23	326 33.6	209 38.4	15.9	299 19.2	40.2	37 25.6	41.1	28 34.9	14.4			
2 00	341 36.1	224 38.1	N19 15.6	314 21.4	N 6 40.3	52 28.2	S22 41.2	43 37.4	S21 14.5	Mirfak	308 33.1	N49 55.8
01	356 38.5	239 37.7	15.3	329 23.6	40.4	67 30.7	41.2	58 40.0	14.5	Nunki	75 51.9	S26 16.2
02	11 41.0	254 37.4	15.0	344 25.8	40.5	82 33.3	41.2	73 42.6	14.5	Peacock	53 10.8	S56 40.2
03	26 43.5	269 37.0 ..	14.7	359 28.0 ..	40.6	97 35.8 ..	41.2	88 45.2 ..	14.5	Pollux	243 21.9	N27 58.6
04	41 45.9	284 36.7	14.4	14 30.2	40.7	112 38.4	41.2	103 47.7	14.5	Procyon	244 54.7	N 5 10.4
05	56 48.4	299 36.3	14.1	29 32.4	40.8	127 41.0	41.2	118 50.3	14.6			
W 06	71 50.9	314 35.9	N19 13.8	44 34.6	N 6 40.9	142 43.5	S22 41.2	133 52.9	S21 14.6	Rasalhague	96 01.7	N12 33.0
E 07	86 53.3	329 35.6	13.5	59 36.8	41.0	157 46.1	41.3	148 55.5	14.6	Regulus	207 38.5	N11 52.1
D 08	101 55.8	344 35.2	13.2	74 39.1	41.1	172 48.6	41.3	163 58.0	14.6	Rigel	281 07.3	S 8 10.6
N 09	116 58.3	359 34.9 ..	12.9	89 41.3 ..	41.2	187 51.2 ..	41.3	179 00.6 ..	14.7	Rigil Kent.	139 45.4	S60 55.2
E 10	132 00.7	14 34.5	12.6	104 43.5	41.3	202 53.7	41.3	194 03.2	14.7	Sabik	102 06.8	S15 44.9
S 11	147 03.2	29 34.2	12.3	119 45.7	41.4	217 56.3	41.3	209 05.8	14.7			
D 12	162 05.6	44 33.8	N19 12.0	134 47.9	N 6 41.5	232 58.8	S22 41.3	224 08.3	S21 14.7	Schedar	349 34.4	N56 38.9
A 13	177 08.1	59 33.4	11.7	149 50.1	41.5	248 01.4	41.3	239 10.9	14.7	Shaula	96 15.0	S37 07.1
Y 14	192 10.6	74 33.1	11.4	164 52.3	41.6	263 04.0	41.4	254 13.5	14.8	Sirius	258 29.5	S16 44.5
15	207 13.0	89 32.7 ..	11.1	179 54.6 ..	41.7	278 06.5 ..	41.4	269 16.0 ..	14.8	Spica	158 26.2	S11 15.9
16	222 15.5	104 32.4	10.8	194 56.8	41.8	293 09.1	41.4	284 18.6	14.8	Suhail	222 49.2	S43 30.7
17	237 18.0	119 32.0	10.5	209 59.0	41.9	308 11.6	41.4	299 21.2	14.8			
18	252 20.4	134 31.6	N19 10.2	225 01.2	N 6 42.0	323 14.2	S22 41.4	314 23.8	S21 14.8	Vega	80 35.4	N38 48.5
19	267 22.9	149 31.3	09.9	240 03.4	42.1	338 16.7	41.4	329 26.3	14.9	Zuben'ubi	137 00.0	S16 07.5
20	282 25.4	164 30.9	09.6	255 05.7	42.2	353 19.3	41.4	344 28.9	14.9		SHA	Mer.Pass.
21	297 27.8	179 30.6 ..	09.2	270 07.9 ..	42.3	8 21.8 ..	41.4	359 31.5 ..	14.9		° '	h m
22	312 30.3	194 30.2	08.9	285 10.1	42.3	23 24.4	41.5	14 34.0	14.9	Venus	244 09.5	9 01
23	327 32.8	209 29.8	08.6	300 12.3	42.4	38 26.9	41.5	29 36.6	15.0	Mars	332 52.1	3 06
	h m									Jupiter	70 49.7	20 31
Mer.Pass. 1 17.3	v −0.4 d 0.3			v 2.2 d 0.1		v 2.6 d 0.0		v 2.6 d 0.0		Saturn	61 58.7	21 06

SUN and MOON

UT	SUN GHA	SUN Dec	MOON GHA	v	MOON Dec	d	HP
31 00	179 55.2	N 8 32.9	23 38.9	10.5	S20 32.2	7.3	55.9
01	194 55.4	32.0	38 08.4	10.6	20 24.9	7.3	55.9
02	209 55.6	31.1	52 38.0	10.7	20 17.6	7.5	55.8
03	224 55.8	.. 30.2	67 07.7	10.8	20 10.1	7.5	55.8
04	239 56.0	29.3	81 37.5	10.9	20 02.6	7.7	55.8
05	254 56.2	28.4	96 07.4	10.9	19 54.9	7.7	55.8
M 06	269 56.4	N 8 27.5	110 37.3	11.0	S19 47.2	7.9	55.8
O 07	284 56.6	26.6	125 07.3	11.0	19 39.3	7.9	55.7
N 08	299 56.8	25.7	139 37.3	11.2	19 31.4	8.0	55.7
D 09	314 57.0	.. 24.8	154 07.5	11.2	19 23.4	8.1	55.7
A 10	329 57.2	23.9	168 37.7	11.3	19 15.3	8.2	55.7
Y 11	344 57.4	23.0	183 08.0	11.3	19 07.1	8.3	55.7
12	359 57.6	N 8 22.1	197 38.3	11.5	S18 58.8	8.4	55.7
13	14 57.8	21.2	212 08.8	11.5	18 50.4	8.4	55.6
14	29 58.0	20.3	226 39.3	11.6	18 42.0	8.6	55.6
15	44 58.2	.. 19.4	241 09.9	11.6	18 33.4	8.6	55.6
16	59 58.4	18.4	255 40.5	11.8	18 24.8	8.7	55.6
17	74 58.6	17.5	270 11.3	11.8	18 16.1	8.8	55.6
18	89 58.8	N 8 16.6	284 42.1	11.8	S18 07.3	8.9	55.5
19	104 59.0	15.7	299 12.9	12.0	17 58.4	8.9	55.5
20	119 59.2	14.8	313 43.9	12.0	17 49.5	9.1	55.5
21	134 59.4	.. 13.9	328 14.9	12.1	17 40.4	9.1	55.5
22	149 59.6	13.0	342 46.0	12.2	17 31.3	9.2	55.5
23	164 59.8	12.1	357 17.2	12.2	17 22.1	9.2	55.4
1 00	180 00.0	N 8 11.2	11 48.4	12.3	S17 12.9	9.4	55.4
01	195 00.2	10.3	26 19.7	12.4	17 03.5	9.4	55.4
02	210 00.4	09.4	40 51.1	12.5	16 54.1	9.5	55.4
03	225 00.6	.. 08.5	55 22.6	12.5	16 44.6	9.5	55.4
04	240 00.8	07.6	69 54.1	12.6	16 35.1	9.6	55.3
05	255 01.0	06.7	84 25.7	12.7	16 25.5	9.7	55.3
T 06	270 01.2	N 8 05.7	98 57.4	12.7	S16 15.8	9.8	55.3
U 07	285 01.4	04.8	113 29.1	12.8	16 06.0	9.8	55.3
E 08	300 01.6	03.9	128 00.9	12.9	15 56.2	9.9	55.3
S 09	315 01.8	.. 03.0	142 32.8	12.9	15 46.3	10.0	55.3
D 10	330 02.0	02.1	157 04.7	13.0	15 36.3	10.0	55.2
A 11	345 02.2	01.2	171 36.7	13.1	15 26.3	10.1	55.2
Y 12	0 02.4	N 8 00.3	186 08.8	13.2	S15 16.2	10.1	55.2
13	15 02.6	7 59.4	200 41.0	13.2	15 06.1	10.3	55.2
14	30 02.8	58.5	215 13.2	13.3	14 55.8	10.2	55.2
15	45 03.0	.. 57.6	229 45.5	13.3	14 45.6	10.4	55.2
16	60 03.2	56.7	244 17.8	13.4	14 35.2	10.4	55.1
17	75 03.4	55.7	258 50.2	13.5	14 24.8	10.4	55.1
18	90 03.6	N 7 54.8	273 22.7	13.5	S14 14.4	10.5	55.1
19	105 03.8	53.9	287 55.2	13.6	14 03.9	10.6	55.1
20	120 04.0	53.0	302 27.8	13.7	13 53.3	10.6	55.1
21	135 04.2	.. 52.1	317 00.5	13.7	13 42.7	10.6	55.0
22	150 04.4	51.2	331 33.2	13.8	13 32.1	10.8	55.0
23	165 04.6	50.3	346 06.0	13.9	13 21.3	10.7	55.0
2 00	180 04.8	N 7 49.4	0 38.9	13.9	S13 10.6	10.9	55.0
01	195 05.0	48.4	15 11.8	14.0	12 59.7	10.8	55.0
02	210 05.2	47.5	29 44.8	14.0	12 48.9	11.0	55.0
03	225 05.4	.. 46.6	44 17.8	14.1	12 37.9	10.9	55.0
04	240 05.6	45.7	58 50.9	14.1	12 27.0	11.0	54.9
05	255 05.8	44.8	73 24.0	14.2	12 16.0	11.1	54.9
W 06	270 06.0	N 7 43.9	87 57.2	14.3	S12 04.9	11.1	54.9
E 07	285 06.2	43.0	102 30.5	14.3	11 53.8	11.2	54.9
D 08	300 06.4	42.0	117 03.8	14.4	11 42.6	11.2	54.9
N 09	315 06.6	.. 41.1	131 37.2	14.5	11 31.4	11.2	54.9
E 10	330 06.8	40.2	146 10.7	14.4	11 20.2	11.3	54.8
S 11	345 07.0	39.3	160 44.1	14.6	11 08.9	11.3	54.8
D 12	0 07.2	N 7 38.4	175 17.7	14.6	S10 57.6	11.3	54.8
A 13	15 07.5	37.5	189 51.3	14.6	10 46.3	11.4	54.8
Y 14	30 07.7	36.6	204 24.9	14.7	10 34.9	11.5	54.8
15	45 07.9	.. 35.6	218 58.6	14.8	10 23.4	11.4	54.8
16	60 08.1	34.7	233 32.4	14.8	10 12.0	11.5	54.8
17	75 08.3	33.8	248 06.2	14.8	10 00.5	11.6	54.8
18	90 08.5	N 7 32.9	262 40.0	14.9	S 9 48.9	11.6	54.7
19	105 08.7	32.0	277 14.9	15.0	9 37.3	11.6	54.7
20	120 08.9	31.1	291 47.9	15.0	9 25.7	11.6	54.7
21	135 09.1	.. 30.1	306 21.9	15.0	9 14.1	11.7	54.7
22	150 09.3	29.2	320 55.9	15.1	9 02.4	11.7	54.7
23	165 09.5	28.3	335 30.0	15.1	S 8 50.7	11.7	54.7
	SD 15.9	d 0.9	SD 15.2		15.0		14.9

Twilight, Sunrise, Moonrise

Lat.	Twilight Naut.	Twilight Civil	Sunrise	Moonrise 31	1	2	3
N 72	////	02 34	04 03	22 18	21 08	20 37	20 13
N 70	////	03 02	04 17	21 14	20 42	20 22	20 06
68	01 35	03 22	04 28	20 38	20 22	20 11	20 01
66	02 12	03 38	04 36	20 12	20 06	20 01	19 57
64	02 38	03 51	04 44	19 51	19 53	19 53	19 53
62	02 57	04 02	04 50	19 35	19 42	19 46	19 50
60	03 12	04 11	04 56	19 21	19 32	19 40	19 47
N 58	03 25	04 19	05 01	19 09	19 24	19 35	19 44
56	03 36	04 26	05 05	18 59	19 17	19 30	19 42
54	03 45	04 32	05 09	18 50	19 10	19 26	19 40
52	03 54	04 37	05 12	18 42	19 04	19 22	19 38
50	04 01	04 42	05 16	18 34	18 58	19 19	19 36
45	04 16	04 52	05 22	18 19	18 47	19 11	19 32
N 40	04 27	05 00	05 28	18 06	18 37	19 04	19 29
35	04 36	05 07	05 33	17 55	18 29	18 59	19 27
30	04 44	05 13	05 37	17 45	18 21	18 54	19 24
20	04 56	05 22	05 44	17 28	18 08	18 45	19 20
N 10	05 05	05 30	05 51	17 13	17 57	18 38	19 16
0	05 11	05 36	05 57	17 00	17 46	18 31	19 13
S 10	05 17	05 41	06 02	16 46	17 36	18 23	19 09
20	05 20	05 46	06 08	16 31	17 24	18 16	19 05
30	05 23	05 51	06 15	16 14	17 11	18 07	19 01
35	05 24	05 53	06 19	16 04	17 04	18 02	18 59
40	05 24	05 56	06 23	15 53	16 55	17 56	18 56
45	05 24	05 58	06 28	15 39	16 45	17 50	18 53
S 50	05 24	06 01	06 34	15 23	16 33	17 42	18 49
52	05 23	06 02	06 36	15 15	16 27	17 38	18 47
54	05 23	06 04	06 39	15 06	16 21	17 34	18 45
56	05 22	06 05	06 42	14 57	16 14	17 29	18 43
58	05 21	06 06	06 46	14 46	16 06	17 24	18 40
S 60	05 20	06 08	06 50	14 33	15 56	17 18	18 38

Sunset, Twilight, Moonset

Lat.	Sunset	Twilight Civil	Twilight Naut.	Moonset 31	1	2	3
N 72	19 53	21 20	////	■	00 21	03 07	05 10
N 70	19 40	20 54	23 30	■	01 25	03 32	05 22
68	19 30	20 34	22 17	26 00	02 00	03 50	05 31
66	19 21	20 19	21 42	00 37	02 25	04 05	05 39
64	19 14	20 06	21 18	01 07	02 44	04 17	05 46
62	19 08	19 56	21 00	01 30	03 00	04 27	05 52
60	19 02	19 47	20 45	01 48	03 13	04 36	05 57
N 58	18 58	19 39	20 32	02 03	03 24	04 43	06 01
56	18 53	19 33	20 22	02 16	03 33	04 50	06 05
54	18 50	19 27	20 13	02 28	03 42	04 56	06 08
52	18 46	19 21	20 05	02 37	03 49	05 01	06 11
50	18 43	19 17	19 58	02 46	03 56	05 06	06 14
45	18 36	19 07	19 43	03 05	04 11	05 16	06 20
N 40	18 31	18 59	19 32	03 20	04 23	05 25	06 25
35	18 26	18 52	19 23	03 33	04 33	05 32	06 30
30	18 22	18 46	19 15	03 44	04 42	05 39	06 33
20	18 15	18 37	19 03	04 03	04 57	05 50	06 40
N 10	18 09	18 30	18 55	04 19	05 10	05 59	06 46
0	18 03	18 24	18 48	04 34	05 23	06 08	06 51
S 10	17 58	18 19	18 43	04 49	05 35	06 17	06 56
20	17 52	18 14	18 40	05 05	05 48	06 26	07 02
30	17 45	18 09	18 37	05 24	06 03	06 37	07 08
35	17 42	18 07	18 36	05 35	06 11	06 43	07 12
40	17 37	18 05	18 36	05 47	06 21	06 50	07 16
45	17 33	18 02	18 36	06 01	06 32	06 58	07 21
S 50	17 27	17 59	18 37	06 19	06 46	07 08	07 26
52	17 24	17 58	18 37	06 27	06 52	07 12	07 29
54	17 21	17 57	18 38	06 36	06 59	07 17	07 32
56	17 18	17 56	18 39	06 46	07 07	07 22	07 35
58	17 15	17 54	18 40	06 58	07 15	07 28	07 38
S 60	17 11	17 53	18 41	07 11	07 25	07 35	07 42

SUN and MOON

Day	Eqn. of Time 00h	Eqn. of Time 12h	Mer. Pass.	Mer. Pass. Upper	Mer. Pass. Lower	Age	Phase
	m s	m s	h m	h m	h m	d	%
31	00 19	00 10	12 00	23 11	10 47	12	97
1	00 00	00 09	12 00	23 57	11 35	13	99
2	00 19	00 29	12 00	24 41	12 19	14	100

UT	ARIES GHA	VENUS −4·3 GHA	Dec	MARS −1·9 GHA	Dec	JUPITER −2·5 GHA	Dec	SATURN +0·3 GHA	Dec	STARS Name	SHA	Dec
3 00	342 35.2	224 29.5	N19 08.3	315 14.6	N 6 42.5	53 29.5	S22 41.5	44 39.2	S21 15.0	Acamar	315 14.3	S40 13.1
01	357 37.7	239 29.1	08.0	330 16.8	42.6	68 32.0	41.5	59 41.8	15.0	Achernar	335 22.5	S57 07.8
02	12 40.1	254 28.8	07.7	345 19.0	42.7	83 34.6	41.5	74 44.3	15.0	Acrux	173 04.4	S63 12.8
03	27 42.6	269 28.4	.. 07.4	0 21.3	.. 42.8	98 37.1	.. 41.5	89 46.9	.. 15.0	Adhara	255 08.8	S28 59.8
04	42 45.1	284 28.0	07.1	15 23.5	42.9	113 39.7	41.5	104 49.5	15.1	Aldebaran	290 43.6	N16 33.0
05	57 47.5	299 27.7	06.7	30 25.7	42.9	128 42.2	41.5	119 52.0	15.1			
06	72 50.0	314 27.3	N19 06.4	45 28.0	N 6 43.0	143 44.8	S22 41.6	134 54.6	S21 15.1	Alioth	166 16.7	N55 51.2
07	87 52.5	329 26.9	06.1	60 30.2	43.1	158 47.3	41.6	149 57.2	15.1	Alkaid	152 55.2	N49 13.0
T 08	102 54.9	344 26.6	05.8	75 32.5	43.2	173 49.9	41.6	164 59.8	15.1	Alnair	27 36.9	S46 51.7
H 09	117 57.4	359 26.2	.. 05.5	90 34.7	.. 43.3	188 52.4	.. 41.6	180 02.3	.. 15.2	Alnilam	275 41.4	S 1 11.3
U 10	132 59.9	14 25.9	05.2	105 37.0	43.4	203 54.9	41.6	195 04.9	15.2	Alphard	217 51.5	S 8 44.7
R 11	148 02.3	29 25.5	04.8	120 39.2	43.4	218 57.5	41.6	210 07.5	15.2			
S 12	163 04.8	44 25.1	N19 04.5	135 41.4	N 6 43.5	234 00.0	S22 41.6	225 10.0	S21 15.2	Alphecca	126 06.9	N26 39.1
D 13	178 07.2	59 24.8	04.2	150 43.7	43.6	249 02.6	41.6	240 12.6	15.3	Alpheratz	357 38.0	N29 12.2
A 14	193 09.7	74 24.4	03.9	165 45.9	43.7	264 05.1	41.7	255 15.2	15.3	Altair	62 03.1	N 8 55.5
Y 15	208 12.2	89 24.0	.. 03.5	180 48.2	.. 43.8	279 07.7	.. 41.7	270 17.7	.. 15.3	Ankaa	353 10.3	S42 11.5
16	223 14.6	104 23.7	03.2	195 50.4	43.8	294 10.2	41.7	285 20.3	15.3	Antares	112 20.2	S26 28.6
17	238 17.1	119 23.3	02.9	210 52.7	43.9	309 12.8	41.7	300 22.9	15.3			
18	253 19.6	134 22.9	N19 02.6	225 55.0	N 6 44.0	324 15.3	S22 41.7	315 25.4	S21 15.4	Arcturus	145 51.4	N19 04.8
19	268 22.0	149 22.6	02.2	240 57.2	44.1	339 17.8	41.7	330 28.0	15.4	Atria	107 17.5	S69 04.0
20	283 24.5	164 22.2	01.9	255 59.5	44.1	354 20.4	41.7	345 30.6	15.4	Avior	234 16.6	S59 34.3
21	298 27.0	179 21.8	.. 01.6	271 01.7	.. 44.2	9 22.9	.. 41.7	0 33.1	.. 15.4	Bellatrix	278 26.7	N 6 22.1
22	313 29.4	194 21.5	01.2	286 04.0	44.3	24 25.5	41.8	15 35.7	15.4	Betelgeuse	270 56.0	N 7 24.7
23	328 31.9	209 21.1	00.9	301 06.3	44.3	39 28.0	41.8	30 38.3	15.5			
4 00	343 34.4	224 20.7	N19 00.6	316 08.5	N 6 44.5	54 30.6	S22 41.8	45 40.8	S21 15.5	Canopus	263 54.2	S52 42.1
01	358 36.8	239 20.4	19 00.2	331 10.8	44.5	69 33.1	41.8	60 43.4	15.5	Capella	280 27.1	N46 00.9
02	13 39.3	254 20.0	18 59.9	346 13.0	44.6	84 35.6	41.8	75 46.0	15.5	Deneb	49 27.7	N45 21.4
03	28 41.7	269 19.6	.. 59.6	1 15.3	.. 44.7	99 38.2	.. 41.8	90 48.5	.. 15.6	Denebola	182 28.9	N14 27.6
04	43 44.2	284 19.3	59.2	16 17.6	44.8	114 40.7	41.8	105 51.1	15.6	Diphda	348 50.6	S17 52.3
05	58 46.7	299 18.9	58.9	31 19.9	44.8	129 43.3	41.8	120 53.7	15.6			
06	73 49.1	314 18.5	N18 58.6	46 22.1	N 6 44.9	144 45.8	S22 41.9	135 56.2	S21 15.6	Dubhe	193 46.1	N61 38.5
07	88 51.6	329 18.2	58.2	61 24.4	45.0	159 48.3	41.9	150 58.8	15.6	Elnath	278 06.4	N28 37.4
F 08	103 54.1	344 17.8	57.9	76 26.7	45.1	174 50.9	41.9	166 01.4	15.7	Eltanin	90 43.7	N51 29.5
R 09	118 56.5	359 17.4	.. 57.5	91 29.0	.. 45.1	189 53.4	.. 41.9	181 03.9	.. 15.7	Enif	33 41.9	N 9 58.3
I 10	133 59.0	14 17.0	57.2	106 31.2	45.2	204 56.0	41.9	196 06.5	15.7	Fomalhaut	15 18.1	S29 30.7
D 11	149 01.5	29 16.7	56.9	121 33.5	45.3	219 58.5	41.9	211 09.1	15.7			
A 12	164 03.9	44 16.3	N18 56.5	136 35.8	N 6 45.3	235 01.0	S22 41.9	226 11.6	S21 15.7	Gacrux	171 56.0	S57 13.7
Y 13	179 06.4	59 15.9	56.2	151 38.1	45.4	250 03.6	41.9	241 14.2	15.8	Gienah	175 47.5	S37 19.2
14	194 08.8	74 15.6	55.8	166 40.4	45.5	265 06.1	41.9	256 16.8	15.8	Hadar	148 41.3	S60 28.4
15	209 11.3	89 15.2	.. 55.5	181 42.6	.. 45.6	280 08.6	.. 42.0	271 19.3	.. 15.8	Hamal	327 54.9	N23 33.5
16	224 13.8	104 14.8	55.1	196 44.9	45.6	295 11.2	42.0	286 21.9	15.8	Kaus Aust.	83 37.0	S34 22.5
17	239 16.2	119 14.4	54.8	211 47.2	45.7	310 13.7	42.0	301 24.5	15.8			
18	254 18.7	134 14.1	N18 54.4	226 49.5	N 6 45.8	325 16.2	S22 42.0	316 27.0	S21 15.9	Kochab	137 20.5	N74 04.6
19	269 21.2	149 13.7	54.1	241 51.8	45.8	340 18.8	42.0	331 29.6	15.9	Markab	13 33.0	N15 19.0
20	284 23.6	164 13.3	53.7	256 54.1	45.9	355 21.3	42.0	346 32.2	15.9	Menkar	314 09.7	N 4 10.2
21	299 26.1	179 13.0	.. 53.4	271 56.4	.. 46.0	10 23.8	.. 42.0	1 34.7	.. 15.9	Menkent	148 02.0	S36 28.2
22	314 28.6	194 12.6	53.0	286 58.7	46.0	25 26.4	42.0	16 37.3	15.9	Miaplacidus	221 39.7	S69 47.9
23	329 31.0	209 12.2	52.7	302 01.0	46.1	40 28.9	42.0	31 39.9	16.0			
5 00	344 33.5	224 11.8	N18 52.3	317 03.3	N 6 46.2	55 31.4	S22 42.0	46 42.4	S21 16.0	Mirfak	308 33.1	N49 55.8
01	359 36.0	239 11.5	52.0	332 05.6	46.2	70 34.0	42.1	61 45.0	16.0	Nunki	75 51.9	S26 16.2
02	14 38.4	254 11.1	51.6	347 07.9	46.3	85 36.5	42.1	76 47.5	16.0	Peacock	53 10.8	S56 40.2
03	29 40.9	269 10.7	.. 51.3	2 10.2	.. 46.4	100 39.0	.. 42.1	91 50.1	.. 16.0	Pollux	243 21.9	N27 58.6
04	44 43.3	284 10.3	50.9	17 12.5	46.4	115 41.6	42.1	106 52.7	16.1	Procyon	244 54.7	N 5 10.4
05	59 45.8	299 10.0	50.5	32 14.8	46.5	130 44.1	42.1	121 55.2	16.1			
06	74 48.3	314 09.6	N18 50.2	47 17.1	N 6 46.6	145 46.6	S22 42.1	136 57.8	S21 16.1	Rasalhague	96 01.7	N12 33.0
07	89 50.7	329 09.2	49.8	62 19.4	46.6	160 49.2	42.1	152 00.4	16.1	Regulus	207 38.5	N11 52.1
S 08	104 53.2	344 08.8	49.5	77 21.7	46.7	175 51.7	42.1	167 02.9	16.1	Rigel	281 07.3	S 8 10.6
A 09	119 55.7	359 08.5	.. 49.1	92 24.0	.. 46.7	190 54.2	.. 42.1	182 05.5	.. 16.2	Rigil Kent.	139 45.4	S60 55.2
T 10	134 58.1	14 08.1	48.7	107 26.3	46.8	205 56.8	42.2	197 08.0	16.2	Sabik	102 06.8	S15 44.9
U 11	150 00.6	29 07.7	48.4	122 28.6	46.9	220 59.3	42.2	212 10.6	16.2			
R 12	165 03.1	44 07.3	N18 48.0	137 30.9	N 6 46.9	236 01.8	S22 42.2	227 13.2	S21 16.2	Schedar	349 34.4	N56 38.9
D 13	180 05.5	59 07.0	47.7	152 33.3	47.0	251 04.3	42.2	242 15.7	16.2	Shaula	96 15.0	S37 07.1
A 14	195 08.0	74 06.6	47.3	167 35.6	47.1	266 06.9	42.2	257 18.3	16.3	Sirius	258 29.5	S16 44.5
Y 15	210 10.4	89 06.2	.. 46.9	182 37.9	.. 47.1	281 09.4	.. 42.2	272 20.9	.. 16.3	Spica	158 26.2	S11 15.9
16	225 12.9	104 05.8	46.6	197 40.2	47.2	296 11.9	42.2	287 23.4	16.3	Suhail	222 49.2	S43 30.7
17	240 15.4	119 05.5	46.2	212 42.5	47.2	311 14.5	42.2	302 26.0	16.3			
18	255 17.8	134 05.1	N18 45.8	227 44.9	N 6 47.3	326 17.0	S22 42.2	317 28.5	S21 16.3	Vega	80 35.4	N38 48.5
19	270 20.3	149 04.7	45.4	242 47.2	47.3	341 19.5	42.2	332 31.1	16.4	Zuben'ubi	137 00.0	S16 07.5
20	285 22.8	164 04.3	45.1	257 49.5	47.4	356 22.0	42.3	347 33.7	16.4		SHA	Mer.Pass.
21	300 25.2	179 03.9	.. 44.7	272 51.8	.. 47.5	11 24.6	.. 42.3	2 36.2	.. 16.4	Venus	240 46.4	9 03
22	315 27.7	194 03.6	44.3	287 54.2	47.5	26 27.1	42.3	17 38.8	16.4	Mars	332 34.2	2 55
23	330 30.2	209 03.2	44.0	302 56.5	47.6	41 29.6	42.3	32 41.3	16.4	Jupiter	70 56.2	20 19
Mer. Pass. 1 05.5		v −0.4 d 0.3		v 2.3 d 0.1		v 2.5 d 0.0		v 2.6 d 0.0		Saturn	62 06.5	20 54

SUN and MOON

UT	SUN GHA	SUN Dec	MOON GHA	v	Dec	d	HP
d h	° ′	° ′	° ′	′	° ′	′	′
3 00	180 09.7	N 7 27.4	350 04.1	15.2	S 8 39.0	11.8	54.7
01	195 09.9	26.5	4 39.3	15.2	8 27.2	11.8	54.6
02	210 10.1	25.6	19 12.5	15.3	8 15.4	11.8	54.6
03	225 10.3	.. 24.6	33 46.8	15.3	8 03.6	11.8	54.6
04	240 10.5	23.7	48 21.1	15.3	7 51.8	11.9	54.6
05	255 10.7	22.8	62 55.4	15.4	7 39.9	11.9	54.6
06	270 10.9	N 7 21.9	77 29.8	15.5	S 7 28.0	11.9	54.6
07	285 11.1	21.0	92 04.3	15.4	7 16.1	11.9	54.6
T 08	300 11.4	20.0	106 38.7	15.5	7 04.2	12.0	54.5
H 09	315 11.6	.. 19.1	121 13.2	15.6	6 52.2	12.0	54.5
U 10	330 11.8	18.2	135 47.8	15.6	6 40.2	12.0	54.5
R 11	345 12.0	17.3	150 22.4	15.6	6 28.2	12.0	54.5
S 12	0 12.2	N 7 16.4	164 57.0	15.6	S 6 16.2	12.1	54.5
D 13	15 12.4	15.4	179 31.6	15.7	6 04.1	12.0	54.5
A 14	30 12.6	14.5	194 06.3	15.7	5 52.1	12.1	54.5
Y 15	45 12.8	.. 13.6	208 41.0	15.8	5 40.0	12.1	54.5
16	60 13.0	12.7	223 15.8	15.8	5 27.9	12.1	54.5
17	75 13.2	11.8	237 50.6	15.8	5 15.8	12.1	54.4
18	90 13.4	N 7 10.8	252 25.4	15.8	S 5 03.7	12.2	54.4
19	105 13.6	09.9	267 00.2	15.9	4 51.5	12.1	54.4
20	120 13.8	09.0	281 35.1	15.9	4 39.4	12.2	54.4
21	135 14.0	.. 08.1	296 10.0	15.9	4 27.2	12.2	54.4
22	150 14.3	07.2	310 44.9	16.0	4 15.0	12.2	54.4
23	165 14.5	06.2	325 19.9	16.0	4 02.8	12.2	54.4
4 00	180 14.7	N 7 05.3	339 54.9	16.0	S 3 50.6	12.3	54.4
01	195 14.9	04.4	354 29.9	16.0	3 38.4	12.2	54.4
02	210 15.1	03.5	9 04.9	16.1	3 26.2	12.2	54.3
03	225 15.3	.. 02.5	23 40.0	16.0	3 14.0	12.2	54.3
04	240 15.5	01.6	38 15.0	16.2	3 01.8	12.3	54.3
05	255 15.7	7 00.7	52 50.2	16.1	2 49.5	12.2	54.3
06	270 15.9	N 6 59.8	67 25.3	16.1	S 2 37.3	12.3	54.3
07	285 16.1	58.8	82 00.4	16.2	2 25.0	12.3	54.3
08	300 16.3	57.9	96 35.6	16.2	2 12.8	12.3	54.3
F 09	315 16.5	.. 57.0	111 10.8	16.2	2 00.5	12.3	54.3
R 10	330 16.8	56.1	125 46.0	16.2	1 48.2	12.2	54.3
I 11	345 17.0	55.1	140 21.2	16.2	1 36.0	12.3	54.3
D 12	0 17.2	N 6 54.2	154 56.4	16.3	S 1 23.7	12.3	54.2
A 13	15 17.4	53.3	169 31.7	16.2	1 11.4	12.2	54.2
Y 14	30 17.6	52.4	184 06.9	16.3	0 59.2	12.3	54.2
15	45 17.8	.. 51.4	198 42.2	16.3	0 46.9	12.3	54.2
16	60 18.0	50.5	213 17.5	16.3	0 34.6	12.2	54.2
17	75 18.2	49.6	227 52.8	16.3	0 22.4	12.3	54.2
18	90 18.4	N 6 48.7	242 28.1	16.3	S 0 10.1	12.3	54.2
19	105 18.6	47.7	257 03.4	16.3	N 0 02.2	12.2	54.2
20	120 18.8	46.8	271 38.7	16.4	0 14.4	12.3	54.2
21	135 19.1	.. 45.9	286 14.1	16.3	0 26.7	12.3	54.2
22	150 19.3	45.0	300 49.4	16.4	0 38.9	12.3	54.2
23	165 19.5	44.0	315 24.8	16.3	0 51.2	12.2	54.2
5 00	180 19.7	N 6 43.1	330 00.1	16.4	N 1 03.4	12.2	54.2
01	195 19.9	42.2	344 35.5	16.4	1 15.6	12.2	54.1
02	210 20.1	41.3	359 10.9	16.3	1 27.8	12.2	54.1
03	225 20.3	.. 40.3	13 46.2	16.4	1 40.0	12.1	54.1
04	240 20.5	39.4	28 21.6	16.4	1 52.1	12.2	54.1
05	255 20.7	38.5	42 57.0	16.3	2 04.4	12.2	54.1
06	270 21.0	N 6 37.5	57 32.3	16.4	N 2 16.6	12.2	54.1
07	285 21.2	36.6	72 07.7	16.4	2 28.8	12.1	54.1
S 08	300 21.4	35.7	86 43.1	16.4	2 40.9	12.2	54.1
A 09	315 21.6	.. 34.8	101 18.5	16.3	2 53.1	12.1	54.1
T 10	330 21.8	33.8	115 53.8	16.4	3 05.2	12.1	54.1
U 11	345 22.0	32.9	130 29.2	16.4	3 17.3	12.1	54.1
R 12	0 22.2	N 6 32.0	145 04.6	16.3	N 3 29.4	12.1	54.1
D 13	15 22.4	31.0	159 39.9	16.4	3 41.5	12.1	54.1
A 14	30 22.6	30.1	174 15.3	16.3	3 53.6	12.0	54.1
Y 15	45 22.9	.. 29.2	188 50.6	16.4	4 05.6	12.1	54.1
16	60 23.1	28.2	203 26.0	16.3	4 17.7	12.0	54.1
17	75 23.3	27.3	218 01.3	16.3	4 29.7	12.0	54.1
18	90 23.5	N 6 26.4	232 36.6	16.3	N 4 41.7	11.9	54.1
19	105 23.7	25.5	247 11.9	16.3	4 53.6	12.0	54.1
20	120 23.9	24.5	261 47.2	16.3	5 05.6	11.9	54.1
21	135 24.1	.. 23.6	276 22.5	16.3	5 17.5	12.0	54.1
22	150 24.3	22.7	290 57.8	16.2	5 29.5	11.9	54.1
23	165 24.5	21.7	305 33.0	16.3	N 5 41.4	11.8	54.1
	SD 15.9	d 0.9	SD 14.8		14.8		14.7

Twilight, Sunrise and Moonrise

Lat.	Naut.	Civil	Sunrise	Moonrise 3	4	5	6
°	h m	h m	h m	h m	h m	h m	h m
N 72	////	02 54	04 18	20 13	19 52	19 31	19 07
N 70	01 09	03 18	04 29	20 06	19 52	19 37	19 22
68	01 59	03 35	04 39	20 01	19 52	19 43	19 33
66	02 29	03 49	04 46	19 57	19 52	19 48	19 43
64	02 51	04 01	04 53	19 53	19 52	19 52	19 51
62	03 08	04 10	04 58	19 50	19 52	19 55	19 58
60	03 22	04 19	05 03	19 47	19 52	19 58	20 04
N 58	03 34	04 26	05 07	19 44	19 53	20 01	20 10
56	03 43	04 32	05 11	19 42	19 53	20 03	20 15
54	03 52	04 37	05 14	19 40	19 53	20 05	20 19
52	03 59	04 42	05 17	19 38	19 53	20 07	20 23
50	04 06	04 47	05 20	19 36	19 53	20 09	20 26
45	04 20	04 56	05 26	19 32	19 53	20 13	20 34
N 40	04 30	05 03	05 31	19 29	19 53	20 16	20 41
35	04 39	05 09	05 35	19 27	19 53	20 19	20 46
30	04 46	05 15	05 39	19 24	19 53	20 22	20 51
20	04 57	05 23	05 45	19 20	19 53	20 26	21 00
N 10	05 05	05 29	05 51	19 16	19 53	20 30	21 08
0	05 11	05 35	05 56	19 13	19 54	20 34	21 15
S 10	05 15	05 39	06 00	19 09	19 54	20 38	21 23
20	05 18	05 43	06 06	19 05	19 54	20 42	21 30
30	05 20	05 47	06 11	19 01	19 54	20 47	21 39
35	05 20	05 49	06 15	18 59	19 54	20 49	21 45
40	05 20	05 51	06 18	18 56	19 54	20 53	21 51
45	05 19	05 53	06 22	18 53	19 55	20 56	21 58
S 50	05 18	05 55	06 27	18 49	19 55	21 00	22 06
52	05 17	05 56	06 30	18 47	19 55	21 02	22 10
54	05 16	05 57	06 32	18 45	19 55	21 05	22 14
56	05 15	05 57	06 35	18 43	19 55	21 07	22 19
58	05 13	05 58	06 38	18 40	19 55	21 10	22 24
S 60	05 11	05 59	06 41	18 38	19 56	21 13	22 30

Sunset, Twilight and Moonset

Lat.	Sunset	Civil	Naut.	Moonset 3	4	5	6
°	h m	h m	h m	h m	h m	h m	h m
N 72	19 36	20 58	////	05 10	07 01	08 48	10 38
N 70	19 26	20 36	22 37	05 22	07 05	08 45	10 26
68	19 17	20 19	21 52	05 31	07 07	08 41	10 16
66	19 09	20 06	21 24	05 39	07 10	08 39	10 08
64	19 03	19 55	21 03	05 46	07 12	08 36	10 01
62	18 58	19 45	20 47	05 52	07 14	08 34	09 55
60	18 53	19 37	20 33	05 57	07 15	08 33	09 50
N 58	18 49	19 30	20 22	06 01	07 17	08 31	09 46
56	18 46	19 24	20 12	06 05	07 18	08 30	09 42
54	18 42	19 19	20 04	06 09	07 19	08 29	09 38
52	18 39	19 14	19 57	06 11	07 20	08 28	09 35
50	18 37	19 10	19 50	06 14	07 21	08 27	09 32
45	18 31	19 01	19 37	06 20	07 23	08 24	09 26
N 40	18 26	18 54	19 26	06 25	07 24	08 23	09 21
35	18 22	18 48	19 18	06 30	07 26	08 21	09 16
30	18 18	18 43	19 11	06 33	07 27	08 20	09 12
20	18 12	18 35	19 01	06 40	07 29	08 17	09 05
N 10	18 07	18 28	18 53	06 46	07 31	08 15	08 59
0	18 02	18 23	18 47	06 51	07 32	08 13	08 54
S 10	17 57	18 18	18 43	06 56	07 34	08 11	08 48
20	17 52	18 15	18 40	07 02	07 36	08 09	08 42
30	17 47	18 11	18 39	07 08	07 38	08 07	08 36
35	17 44	18 09	18 38	07 12	07 39	08 05	08 32
40	17 40	18 07	18 39	07 16	07 40	08 04	08 27
45	17 36	18 06	18 40	07 21	07 42	08 02	08 22
S 50	17 31	18 04	18 41	07 26	07 43	08 00	08 16
52	17 29	18 03	18 42	07 29	07 44	07 59	08 14
54	17 27	18 02	18 43	07 32	07 45	07 58	08 11
56	17 24	18 01	18 44	07 35	07 46	07 57	08 07
58	17 21	18 01	18 46	07 38	07 47	07 55	08 04
S 60	17 18	18 00	18 48	07 42	07 48	07 54	08 00

SUN and MOON data

Day	Eqn. of Time 00ʰ	12ʰ	Mer. Pass.	Mer. Pass. Upper	Lower	Age	Phase
d	m s	m s	h m	h m	h m	d	%
3	00 38	00 48	11 59	13 02	00 41	15	98
4	00 58	01 08	11 59	13 43	01 23	16	95
5	01 18	01 28	11 59	14 24	02 03	17	90

UT	ARIES GHA	VENUS −4·2 GHA	VENUS Dec	MARS −2·0 GHA	MARS Dec	JUPITER −2·5 GHA	JUPITER Dec	SATURN +0·3 GHA	SATURN Dec	STARS Name	SHA	Dec
d h	° ′	° ′	° ′	° ′	° ′	° ′	° ′	° ′	° ′		° ′	° ′
6 00	345 32.6	224 02.8	N18 43.6	317 58.8	N 6 47.6	56 32.1	S22 42.3	47 43.9	S21 16.5	Acamar	315 14.3	S40 13.1
01	0 35.1	239 02.4	43.2	333 01.2	47.7	71 34.7	42.3	62 46.5	16.5	Achernar	335 22.5	S57 07.8
02	15 37.6	254 02.0	42.8	348 03.5	47.7	86 37.2	42.3	77 49.0	16.5	Acrux	173 04.5	S63 12.8
03	30 40.0	269 01.7 ..	42.5	3 05.8 ..	47.8	101 39.7 ..	42.3	92 51.6 ..	16.5	Adhara	255 08.8	S28 59.8
04	45 42.5	284 01.3	42.1	18 08.2	47.9	116 42.2	42.3	107 54.1	16.5	Aldebaran	290 43.6	N16 33.0
05	60 44.9	299 00.9	41.7	33 10.5	47.9	131 44.7	42.3	122 56.7	16.6			
06	75 47.4	314 00.5	N18 41.3	48 12.9	N 6 48.0	146 47.3	S22 42.3	137 59.3	S21 16.6	Alioth	166 16.7	N55 51.2
07	90 49.9	329 00.1	40.9	63 15.2	48.0	161 49.8	42.4	153 01.8	16.6	Alkaid	152 55.2	N49 13.0
08	105 52.3	343 59.8	40.6	78 17.5	48.1	176 52.3	42.4	168 04.4	16.6	Alnair	27 36.9	S46 51.7
S 09	120 54.8	358 59.4 ..	40.2	93 19.9 ..	48.1	191 54.8 ..	42.4	183 06.9 ..	16.6	Alnilam	275 41.3	S 1 11.3
U 10	135 57.3	13 59.0	39.8	108 22.2	48.2	206 57.4	42.4	198 09.5	16.6	Alphard	217 51.5	S 8 44.7
N 11	150 59.7	28 58.6	39.4	123 24.6	48.2	221 59.9	42.4	213 12.0	16.7			
D 12	166 02.2	43 58.2	N18 39.0	138 26.9	N 6 48.3	237 02.4	S22 42.4	228 14.6	S21 16.7	Alphecca	126 06.9	N26 39.1
A 13	181 04.7	58 57.9	38.6	153 29.3	48.3	252 04.9	42.4	243 17.2	16.7	Alpheratz	357 38.0	N29 12.2
Y 14	196 07.1	73 57.5	38.2	168 31.6	48.4	267 07.4	42.4	258 19.7	16.7	Altair	62 03.1	N 8 55.5
15	211 09.6	88 57.1 ..	37.9	183 34.0 ..	48.4	282 10.0 ..	42.4	273 22.3 ..	16.7	Ankaa	353 10.3	S42 11.6
16	226 12.0	103 56.7	37.5	198 36.3	48.5	297 12.5	42.4	288 24.8	16.8	Antares	112 20.2	S26 28.6
17	241 14.5	118 56.3	37.1	213 38.7	48.5	312 15.0	42.4	303 27.4	16.8			
18	256 17.0	133 55.9	N18 36.7	228 41.1	N 6 48.6	327 17.5	S22 42.5	318 30.0	S21 16.8	Arcturus	145 51.4	N19 04.8
19	271 19.4	148 55.6	36.3	243 43.4	48.6	342 20.0	42.5	333 32.5	16.8	Atria	107 17.5	S69 04.0
20	286 21.9	163 55.2	35.9	258 45.8	48.7	357 22.5	42.5	348 35.1	16.8	Avior	234 16.6	S59 34.3
21	301 24.4	178 54.8 ..	35.5	273 48.1 ..	48.7	12 25.1 ..	42.5	3 37.6 ..	16.9	Bellatrix	278 26.7	N 6 22.1
22	316 26.8	193 54.4	35.1	288 50.5	48.8	27 27.6	42.5	18 40.2	16.9	Betelgeuse	270 56.0	N 7 24.7
23	331 29.3	208 54.0	34.7	303 52.9	48.8	42 30.1	42.5	33 42.7	16.9			
7 00	346 31.8	223 53.6	N18 34.3	318 55.2	N 6 48.9	57 32.6	S22 42.5	48 45.3	S21 16.9	Canopus	263 54.1	S52 42.1
01	1 34.2	238 53.3	33.9	333 57.6	48.9	72 35.1	42.5	63 47.8	16.9	Capella	280 27.1	N46 00.9
02	16 36.7	253 52.9	33.5	349 00.0	49.0	87 37.6	42.5	78 50.4	16.9	Deneb	49 27.8	N45 21.4
03	31 39.2	268 52.5 ..	33.1	4 02.3 ..	49.0	102 40.2 ..	42.5	93 53.0 ..	17.0	Denebola	182 28.9	N14 27.6
04	46 41.6	283 52.1	32.7	19 04.7	49.1	117 42.7	42.5	108 55.5	17.0	Diphda	348 50.5	S17 52.3
05	61 44.1	298 51.7	32.3	34 07.1	49.1	132 45.2	42.5	123 58.1	17.0			
06	76 46.5	313 51.3	N18 31.9	49 09.5	N 6 49.1	147 47.7	S22 42.6	139 00.6	S21 17.0	Dubhe	193 46.1	N61 38.5
07	91 49.0	328 51.0	31.5	64 11.8	49.2	162 50.2	42.6	154 03.2	17.0	Elnath	278 06.3	N28 37.4
08	106 51.5	343 50.6	31.1	79 14.2	49.2	177 52.7	42.6	169 05.7	17.1	Eltanin	90 43.7	N51 29.5
M 09	121 53.9	358 50.2 ..	30.7	94 16.6 ..	49.3	192 55.2 ..	42.6	184 08.3 ..	17.1	Enif	33 41.9	N 9 58.3
O 10	136 56.4	13 49.8	30.3	109 19.0	49.3	207 57.8	42.6	199 10.8	17.1	Fomalhaut	15 18.1	S29 30.7
N 11	151 58.9	28 49.4	29.9	124 21.4	49.4	223 00.3	42.6	214 13.4	17.1			
D 12	167 01.3	43 49.0	N18 29.5	139 23.7	N 6 49.4	238 02.8	S22 42.6	229 16.0	S21 17.1	Gacrux	171 56.0	S57 13.7
A 13	182 03.8	58 48.6	29.1	154 26.1	49.4	253 05.3	42.6	244 18.5	17.2	Gienah	175 47.5	S17 39.2
Y 14	197 06.3	73 48.3	28.7	169 28.5	49.5	268 07.8	42.6	259 21.1	17.2	Hadar	148 41.3	S60 28.4
15	212 08.7	88 47.9 ..	28.3	184 30.9 ..	49.5	283 10.3 ..	42.6	274 23.6 ..	17.2	Hamal	327 54.9	N23 33.5
16	227 11.2	103 47.5	27.9	199 33.3	49.6	298 12.8	42.6	289 26.2	17.2	Kaus Aust.	83 37.0	S34 22.5
17	242 13.7	118 47.1	27.5	214 35.7	49.6	313 15.3	42.6	304 28.7	17.2			
18	257 16.1	133 46.7	N18 27.1	229 38.1	N 6 49.6	328 17.8	S22 42.7	319 31.3	S21 17.2	Kochab	137 20.6	N74 04.6
19	272 18.6	148 46.3	26.7	244 40.5	49.7	343 20.3	42.7	334 33.8	17.3	Markab	13 33.0	N15 19.0
20	287 21.0	163 45.9	26.2	259 42.9	49.7	358 22.9	42.7	349 36.4	17.3	Menkar	314 09.7	N 4 10.2
21	302 23.5	178 45.5 ..	25.8	274 45.3 ..	49.8	13 25.4 ..	42.7	4 38.9 ..	17.3	Menkent	148 02.0	S36 28.2
22	317 26.0	193 45.2	25.4	289 47.7	49.8	28 27.9	42.7	19 41.5	17.3	Miaplacidus	221 39.6	S69 47.9
23	332 28.4	208 44.8	25.0	304 50.1	49.8	43 30.4	42.7	34 44.0	17.3			
8 00	347 30.9	223 44.4	N18 24.6	319 52.5	N 6 49.9	58 32.9	S22 42.7	49 46.6	S21 17.4	Mirfak	308 33.0	N49 55.8
01	2 33.4	238 44.0	24.2	334 54.9	49.9	73 35.4	42.7	64 49.1	17.4	Nunki	75 51.9	S26 16.2
02	17 35.8	253 43.6	23.7	349 57.3	49.9	88 37.9	42.7	79 51.7	17.4	Peacock	53 10.9	S56 40.2
03	32 38.3	268 43.2 ..	23.3	4 59.7 ..	50.0	103 40.4 ..	42.7	94 54.3 ..	17.4	Pollux	243 21.9	N27 58.6
04	47 40.8	283 42.8	22.9	20 02.1	50.0	118 42.9	42.7	109 56.8	17.4	Procyon	244 54.7	N 5 10.4
05	62 43.2	298 42.4	22.5	35 04.5	50.1	133 45.4	42.7	124 59.4	17.4			
06	77 45.7	313 42.1	N18 22.1	50 06.9	N 6 50.1	148 47.9	S22 42.7	140 01.9	S21 17.5	Rasalhague	96 01.8	N12 33.0
07	92 48.1	328 41.7	21.6	65 09.3	50.1	163 50.4	42.7	155 04.5	17.5	Regulus	207 38.5	N11 52.1
08	107 50.6	343 41.3	21.2	80 11.7	50.2	178 52.9	42.8	170 07.0	17.5	Rigel	281 07.3	S 8 10.6
T 09	122 53.1	358 40.9 ..	20.8	95 14.1 ..	50.2	193 55.4 ..	42.8	185 09.6 ..	17.5	Rigil Kent.	139 45.4	S60 55.2
U 10	137 55.5	13 40.5	20.4	110 16.6	50.2	208 57.9	42.8	200 12.1	17.5	Sabik	102 06.8	S15 44.9
E 11	152 58.0	28 40.1	19.9	125 19.0	50.3	224 00.4	42.8	215 14.7	17.5			
S 12	168 00.5	43 39.7	N18 19.5	140 21.4	N 6 50.3	239 02.9	S22 42.8	230 17.2	S21 17.6	Schedar	349 34.4	N56 38.9
D 13	183 02.9	58 39.3	19.1	155 23.8	50.3	254 05.5	42.8	245 19.8	17.6	Shaula	96 15.1	S37 07.1
A 14	198 05.4	73 38.9	18.7	170 26.2	50.4	269 08.0	42.8	260 22.3	17.6	Sirius	258 29.5	S16 44.5
Y 15	213 07.9	88 38.5 ..	18.2	185 28.7 ..	50.4	284 10.5 ..	42.8	275 24.9 ..	17.6	Spica	158 26.2	S11 15.9
16	228 10.3	103 38.2	17.8	200 31.1	50.4	299 13.0	42.8	290 27.4	17.6	Suhail	222 49.2	S43 30.7
17	243 12.8	118 37.8	17.4	215 33.5	50.4	314 15.5	42.8	305 30.0	17.7			
18	258 15.3	133 37.4	N18 16.9	230 35.9	N 6 50.5	329 18.0	S22 42.8	320 32.5	S21 17.7	Vega	80 35.4	N38 48.5
19	273 17.7	148 37.0	16.5	245 38.4	50.5	344 20.5	42.8	335 35.1	17.7	Zuben'ubi	137 00.1	S16 07.5
20	288 20.2	163 36.6	16.1	260 40.8	50.5	359 23.0	42.8	350 37.6	17.7		SHA	Mer. Pass.
21	303 22.6	178 36.2 ..	15.6	275 43.2 ..	50.6	14 25.5 ..	42.8	5 40.2 ..	17.7		° ′	h m
22	318 25.1	193 35.8	15.2	290 45.7	50.6	29 28.0	42.8	20 42.7	17.7	Venus	237 21.9	9 05
23	333 27.6	208 35.4	14.8	305 48.1	50.6	44 30.5	42.9	35 45.3	17.8	Mars	332 23.5	2 44
	h m									Jupiter	71 00.8	20 06
Mer. Pass. 0 53.7		v −0.4 d 0.4		v 2.4 d 0.0		v 2.5 d 0.0		v 2.6 d 0.0		Saturn	62 13.5	20 41

UT	SUN GHA	SUN Dec	MOON GHA	v	MOON Dec	d	HP
d h	° ′	° ′	° ′	′	° ′	′	′
SUNDAY							
6 00	180 24.8	N 6 20.8	320 08.3	16.2	N 5 53.2	11.9	54.1
01	195 25.0	19.9	334 43.5	16.2	6 05.1	11.8	54.1
02	210 25.2	18.9	349 18.7	16.2	6 16.9	11.8	54.1
03	225 25.4 ..	18.0	3 53.9	16.2	6 28.7	11.8	54.1
04	240 25.6	17.1	18 29.1	16.1	6 40.5	11.7	54.1
05	255 25.8	16.1	33 04.2	16.2	6 52.2	11.7	54.1
06	270 26.0	N 6 15.2	47 39.4	16.1	N 7 03.9	11.7	54.1
07	285 26.3	14.3	62 14.5	16.1	7 15.6	11.7	54.1
08	300 26.5	13.3	76 49.6	16.0	7 27.3	11.6	54.1
09	315 26.7 ..	12.4	91 24.6	16.1	7 38.9	11.6	54.1
10	330 26.9	11.5	105 59.7	16.0	7 50.5	11.6	54.1
11	345 27.1	10.5	120 34.7	16.0	8 02.1	11.6	54.1
12	0 27.3	N 6 09.6	135 09.7	16.0	N 8 13.7	11.5	54.1
13	15 27.5	08.7	149 44.7	15.9	8 25.2	11.5	54.1
14	30 27.7	07.7	164 19.6	16.0	8 36.7	11.4	54.1
15	45 28.0 ..	06.8	178 54.6	15.9	8 48.1	11.4	54.1
16	60 28.2	05.9	193 29.5	15.8	8 59.5	11.4	54.1
17	75 28.4	04.9	208 04.3	15.9	9 10.9	11.4	54.1
18	90 28.6	N 6 04.0	222 39.2	15.8	N 9 22.3	11.3	54.1
19	105 28.8	03.1	237 14.0	15.8	9 33.6	11.3	54.1
20	120 29.0	02.1	251 48.8	15.7	9 44.9	11.2	54.1
21	135 29.2 ..	01.2	266 23.5	15.7	9 56.1	11.2	54.1
22	150 29.5	6 00.3	280 58.2	15.7	10 07.3	11.2	54.1
23	165 29.7	5 59.3	295 32.9	15.6	10 18.5	11.1	54.1
MONDAY							
7 00	180 29.9	N 5 58.4	310 07.5	15.6	N10 29.6	11.1	54.1
01	195 30.1	57.4	324 42.1	15.6	10 40.7	11.0	54.1
02	210 30.3	56.5	339 16.7	15.5	10 51.7	11.0	54.1
03	225 30.5 ..	55.6	353 51.2	15.5	11 02.7	11.0	54.1
04	240 30.7	54.6	8 25.7	15.5	11 13.7	10.9	54.1
05	255 31.0	53.7	23 00.2	15.4	11 24.6	10.9	54.1
06	270 31.2	N 5 52.8	37 34.6	15.4	N11 35.5	10.9	54.1
07	285 31.4	51.8	52 09.0	15.3	11 46.4	10.7	54.1
08	300 31.6	50.9	66 43.3	15.3	11 57.1	10.8	54.1
09	315 31.8 ..	49.9	81 17.6	15.3	12 07.9	10.7	54.1
10	330 32.0	49.0	95 51.9	15.2	12 18.6	10.7	54.2
11	345 32.2	48.1	110 26.1	15.2	12 29.3	10.6	54.2
12	0 32.5	N 5 47.1	125 00.3	15.1	N12 39.9	10.5	54.2
13	15 32.7	46.2	139 34.4	15.1	12 50.4	10.5	54.2
14	30 32.9	45.3	154 08.5	15.0	13 00.9	10.5	54.2
15	45 33.1 ..	44.3	168 42.5	15.0	13 11.4	10.4	54.2
16	60 33.3	43.4	183 16.5	14.9	13 21.8	10.4	54.2
17	75 33.5	42.4	197 50.4	14.9	13 32.2	10.3	54.2
18	90 33.8	N 5 41.5	212 24.3	14.9	N13 42.5	10.3	54.2
19	105 34.0	40.6	226 58.2	14.7	13 52.8	10.2	54.2
20	120 34.2	39.6	241 31.9	14.8	14 03.0	10.1	54.2
21	135 34.4 ..	38.7	256 05.7	14.7	14 13.1	10.1	54.2
22	150 34.6	37.7	270 39.4	14.6	14 23.2	10.1	54.3
23	165 34.8	36.8	285 13.0	14.6	14 33.3	10.0	54.3
TUESDAY							
8 00	180 35.0	N 5 35.9	299 46.6	14.5	N14 43.3	9.9	54.3
01	195 35.3	34.9	314 20.1	14.5	14 53.2	9.9	54.3
02	210 35.5	34.0	328 53.6	14.4	15 03.1	9.8	54.3
03	225 35.7 ..	33.0	343 27.0	14.4	15 12.9	9.8	54.3
04	240 35.9	32.1	358 00.4	14.3	15 22.7	9.7	54.3
05	255 36.1	31.2	12 33.7	14.3	15 32.4	9.6	54.3
06	270 36.3	N 5 30.2	27 07.0	14.3	N15 42.0	9.6	54.3
07	285 36.6	29.3	41 40.2	14.1	15 51.6	9.5	54.3
08	300 36.8	28.3	56 13.3	14.1	16 01.1	9.5	54.4
09	315 37.0 ..	27.4	70 46.4	14.0	16 10.6	9.4	54.4
10	330 37.2	26.5	85 19.4	14.0	16 20.0	9.3	54.4
11	345 37.4	25.5	99 52.4	13.9	16 29.3	9.3	54.4
12	0 37.6	N 5 24.6	114 25.3	13.8	N16 38.6	9.2	54.4
13	15 37.9	23.6	128 58.1	13.8	16 47.8	9.1	54.4
14	30 38.1	22.7	143 30.9	13.7	16 56.9	9.0	54.4
15	45 38.3 ..	21.7	158 03.6	13.7	17 05.9	9.0	54.5
16	60 38.5	20.8	172 36.3	13.6	17 14.9	9.0	54.5
17	75 38.7	19.9	187 09.9	13.5	17 23.9	8.8	54.5
18	90 38.9	N 5 18.9	201 41.4	13.5	N17 32.7	8.8	54.5
19	105 39.2	18.0	216 13.9	13.4	17 41.5	8.7	54.5
20	120 39.4	17.0	230 46.3	13.3	17 50.2	8.7	54.6
21	135 39.6 ..	16.1	245 18.6	13.3	17 58.9	8.6	54.6
22	150 39.8	15.1	259 50.9	13.2	18 07.5	8.5	54.6
23	165 40.0	14.2	274 23.1	13.1	N18 16.0	8.4	54.6
	SD 15.9	d 0.9	SD 14.7		14.8		14.8

Twilight / Sunrise / Moonrise

Lat.	Naut.	Civil	Sunrise	Moonrise 6	7	8	9
°	h m	h m	h m	h m	h m	h m	h m
N 72	00 11	03 13	04 32	19 07	18 37	17 34	▭
N 70	01 43	03 33	04 42	19 22	19 03	18 33	▭
68	02 19	03 48	04 49	19 33	19 22	19 08	18 43
66	02 45	04 00	04 56	19 43	19 38	19 33	19 28
64	03 04	04 10	05 01	19 51	19 51	19 53	19 57
62	03 19	04 19	05 06	19 58	20 02	20 09	20 20
60	03 31	04 26	05 10	20 04	20 12	20 23	20 38
N 58	03 42	04 33	05 13	20 10	20 20	20 34	20 53
56	03 51	04 38	05 17	20 15	20 28	20 44	21 06
54	03 58	04 43	05 20	20 19	20 34	20 53	21 18
52	04 05	04 47	05 22	20 23	20 40	21 01	21 28
50	04 11	04 51	05 24	20 26	20 46	21 09	21 37
45	04 24	04 59	05 29	20 34	20 57	21 24	21 56
N 40	04 34	05 06	05 34	20 41	21 07	21 37	22 11
35	04 41	05 12	05 37	20 46	21 16	21 48	22 25
30	04 48	05 16	05 40	20 51	21 23	21 57	22 36
20	04 58	05 24	05 46	21 00	21 36	22 14	22 56
N 10	05 05	05 29	05 50	21 08	21 47	22 29	23 13
0	05 10	05 34	05 55	21 15	21 58	22 42	23 30
S 10	05 13	05 38	05 59	21 23	22 08	22 56	23 46
20	05 15	05 41	06 03	21 30	22 20	23 11	24 04
30	05 16	05 44	06 08	21 39	22 33	23 28	24 24
35	05 16	05 45	06 10	21 45	22 41	23 38	24 36
40	05 15	05 46	06 13	21 51	22 50	23 49	24 50
45	05 14	05 47	06 17	21 58	23 00	24 03	00 03
S 50	05 11	05 49	06 21	22 06	23 12	24 19	00 19
52	05 10	05 49	06 23	22 10	23 18	24 27	00 27
54	05 09	05 49	06 25	22 14	23 25	24 36	00 36
56	05 07	05 50	06 27	22 19	23 32	24 46	00 46
58	05 05	05 50	06 29	22 24	23 40	24 57	00 57
S 60	05 03	05 51	06 32	22 30	23 49	25 10	01 10

Sunset / Twilight / Moonset

Lat.	Sunset	Civil	Naut.	Moonset 6	7	8	9
°	h m	h m	h m	h m	h m	h m	h m
N 72	19 20	20 38	23 10	10 38	12 36	15 10	▭
N 70	19 11	20 19	22 05	10 26	12 12	14 12	▭
68	19 04	20 05	21 31	10 16	11 54	13 39	15 40
66	18 58	19 53	21 07	10 08	11 39	13 14	14 56
64	18 53	19 43	20 49	10 01	11 27	12 56	14 27
62	18 48	19 35	20 34	09 55	11 17	12 40	14 05
60	18 44	19 28	20 22	09 50	11 08	12 28	13 48
N 58	18 41	19 21	20 12	09 46	11 01	12 17	13 33
56	18 38	19 16	20 03	09 42	10 54	12 07	13 20
54	18 35	19 11	19 56	09 38	10 48	11 59	13 10
52	18 33	19 07	19 49	09 35	10 43	11 51	13 00
50	18 30	19 03	19 43	09 32	10 38	11 44	12 51
45	18 25	18 55	19 31	09 26	10 28	11 30	12 33
N 40	18 21	18 49	19 21	09 21	10 19	11 18	12 18
35	18 18	18 43	19 14	09 16	10 12	11 08	12 06
30	18 15	18 39	19 07	09 12	10 05	10 59	11 55
20	18 10	18 32	18 58	09 05	09 54	10 44	11 36
N 10	18 05	18 26	18 51	08 59	09 45	10 31	11 20
0	18 01	18 22	18 46	08 54	09 35	10 19	11 05
S 10	17 57	18 18	18 43	08 48	09 26	10 07	10 50
20	17 53	18 15	18 41	08 42	09 17	09 54	10 34
30	17 48	18 12	18 40	08 36	09 06	09 39	10 15
35	17 46	18 11	18 40	08 32	09 00	09 30	10 05
40	17 43	18 10	18 41	08 27	08 53	09 20	09 52
45	17 40	18 09	18 43	08 22	08 44	09 09	09 38
S 50	17 36	18 08	18 45	08 16	08 35	08 55	09 20
52	17 34	18 08	18 47	08 14	08 30	08 49	09 12
54	17 32	18 07	18 48	08 11	08 25	08 42	09 03
56	17 30	18 07	18 50	08 07	08 19	08 34	08 53
58	17 27	18 06	18 52	08 04	08 13	08 25	08 41
S 60	17 25	18 06	18 55	08 00	08 06	08 15	08 27

SUN and MOON

Day	Eqn. of Time 00ʰ	12ʰ	Mer. Pass.	Mer. Pass. Upper	Lower	Age	Phase
d	m s	m s	h m	h m	h m	d	%
6	01 39	01 49	11 58	02 44	15 04	18	84
7	01 59	02 09	11 58	03 25	15 47	19	76
8	02 20	02 30	11 57	04 08	16 31	20	68

UT	ARIES GHA	VENUS −4.2 GHA	Dec	MARS −2.0 GHA	Dec	JUPITER −2.5 GHA	Dec	SATURN +0.4 GHA	Dec	Name	SHA	Dec
9 00	348 30.0	223 35.0	N18 14.3	320 50.5	N 6 50.6	59 33.0	S22 42.9	50 47.8	S21 17.8	Acamar	315 14.3	S40 13.2
01	3 32.5	238 34.6	13.9	335 53.0	50.7	74 35.5	42.9	65 50.4	17.8	Achernar	335 22.5	S57 07.8
02	18 35.0	253 34.2	13.4	350 55.4	50.7	89 38.0	42.9	80 52.9	17.8	Acrux	173 04.5	S63 12.7
03	33 37.4	268 33.8	.. 13.0	5 57.9	.. 50.7	104 40.5	.. 42.9	95 55.4	.. 17.8	Adhara	255 08.8	S28 59.8
04	48 39.9	283 33.5	12.6	21 00.3	50.7	119 42.9	42.9	110 58.0	17.8	Aldebaran	290 43.6	N16 33.0
05	63 42.4	298 33.1	12.1	36 02.7	50.8	134 45.4	42.9	126 00.5	17.9			
W 06	78 44.8	313 32.7	N18 11.7	51 05.2	N 6 50.8	149 47.9	S22 42.9	141 03.1	S21 17.9	Alioth	166 16.7	N55 51.2
E 07	93 47.3	328 32.3	11.2	66 07.6	50.8	164 50.4	42.9	156 05.6	17.9	Alkaid	152 55.2	N49 13.0
D 08	108 49.8	343 31.9	10.8	81 10.1	50.8	179 52.9	42.9	171 08.2	17.9	Alnair	27 36.9	S46 51.7
N 09	123 52.2	358 31.5	.. 10.3	96 12.5	.. 50.9	194 55.4	.. 42.9	186 10.7	.. 17.9	Alnilam	275 41.3	S 1 11.3
E 10	138 54.7	13 31.1	09.9	111 15.0	50.9	209 57.9	42.9	201 13.3	17.9	Alphard	217 51.5	S 8 44.7
S 11	153 57.1	28 30.7	09.5	126 17.4	50.9	225 00.4	42.9	216 15.8	18.0			
D 12	168 59.6	43 30.3	N18 09.0	141 19.9	N 6 50.9	240 02.9	S22 42.9	231 18.4	S21 18.0	Alphecca	126 06.9	N26 39.1
A 13	184 02.1	58 29.9	08.6	156 22.4	51.0	255 05.4	42.9	246 20.9	18.0	Alpheratz	357 38.0	N29 12.2
Y 14	199 04.5	73 29.5	08.1	171 24.8	51.0	270 07.9	42.9	261 23.5	18.0	Altair	62 03.2	N 8 55.6
15	214 07.0	88 29.1	.. 07.7	186 27.3	.. 51.0	285 10.4	.. 43.0	276 26.0	.. 18.0	Ankaa	353 10.3	S42 11.6
16	229 09.5	103 28.7	07.2	201 29.7	51.0	300 12.9	43.0	291 28.6	18.1	Antares	112 20.2	S26 28.6
17	244 11.9	118 28.3	06.8	216 32.2	51.0	315 15.4	43.0	306 31.1	18.1			
18	259 14.4	133 27.9	N18 06.3	231 34.7	N 6 51.1	330 17.9	S22 43.0	321 33.7	S21 18.1	Arcturus	145 51.4	N19 04.8
19	274 16.9	148 27.6	05.8	246 37.1	51.1	345 20.4	43.0	336 36.2	18.1	Atria	107 17.5	S69 04.0
20	289 19.3	163 27.2	05.4	261 39.6	51.1	0 22.9	43.0	351 38.7	18.1	Avior	234 16.5	S59 34.3
21	304 21.8	178 26.8	.. 04.9	276 42.1	.. 51.1	15 25.3	.. 43.0	6 41.3	.. 18.1	Bellatrix	278 26.7	N 6 22.1
22	319 24.2	193 26.4	04.5	291 44.5	51.1	30 27.8	43.0	21 43.8	18.2	Betelgeuse	270 55.9	N 7 24.7
23	334 26.7	208 26.0	04.0	306 47.0	51.2	45 30.3	43.0	36 46.4	18.2			
10 00	349 29.2	223 25.6	N18 03.6	321 49.5	N 6 51.2	60 32.8	S22 43.0	51 48.9	S21 18.2	Canopus	263 54.1	S52 42.1
01	4 31.6	238 25.2	03.1	336 51.9	51.2	75 35.3	43.0	66 51.5	18.2	Capella	280 27.1	N46 00.9
02	19 34.1	253 24.8	02.6	351 54.4	51.2	90 37.8	43.0	81 54.0	18.2	Deneb	49 27.8	N45 21.4
03	34 36.6	268 24.4	.. 02.2	6 56.9	.. 51.2	105 40.3	.. 43.0	96 56.6	.. 18.2	Denebola	182 28.9	N14 27.6
04	49 39.0	283 24.0	01.7	21 59.4	51.2	120 42.8	43.0	111 59.1	18.2	Diphda	348 50.5	S17 52.3
05	64 41.5	298 23.6	01.3	37 01.9	51.3	135 45.3	43.0	127 01.6	18.3			
T 06	79 44.0	313 23.2	N18 00.8	52 04.3	N 6 51.3	150 47.8	S22 43.0	142 04.2	S21 18.3	Dubhe	193 46.1	N61 38.5
H 07	94 46.4	328 22.8	18 00.3	67 06.8	51.3	165 50.2	43.0	157 06.7	18.3	Elnath	278 06.3	N28 37.4
U 08	109 48.9	343 22.4	17 59.9	82 09.3	51.3	180 52.7	43.0	172 09.3	18.3	Eltanin	90 43.7	N51 29.5
R 09	124 51.4	358 22.0	.. 59.4	97 11.8	.. 51.3	195 55.2	.. 43.0	187 11.8	.. 18.3	Enif	33 41.9	N 9 58.3
S 10	139 53.8	13 21.6	58.9	112 14.3	51.3	210 57.7	43.0	202 14.4	18.3	Fomalhaut	15 18.1	S29 30.7
D 11	154 56.3	28 21.2	58.5	127 16.8	51.3	226 00.2	43.1	217 16.9	18.4			
A 12	169 58.7	43 20.8	N17 58.0	142 19.3	N 6 51.4	241 02.7	S22 43.1	232 19.4	S21 18.4	Gacrux	171 56.0	S57 13.6
Y 13	185 01.2	58 20.4	57.5	157 21.8	51.4	256 05.2	43.1	247 22.0	18.4	Gienah	175 47.5	S17 39.2
14	200 03.7	73 20.0	57.1	172 24.2	51.4	271 07.6	43.1	262 24.5	18.4	Hadar	148 41.3	S60 28.3
15	215 06.1	88 19.6	.. 56.6	187 26.7	.. 51.4	286 10.1	.. 43.1	277 27.1	.. 18.4	Hamal	327 54.9	N23 33.5
16	230 08.6	103 19.2	56.1	202 29.2	51.4	301 12.6	43.1	292 29.6	18.4	Kaus Aust.	83 37.0	S34 22.5
17	245 11.1	118 18.8	55.6	217 31.7	51.4	316 15.1	43.1	307 32.2	18.5			
18	260 13.5	133 18.4	N17 55.2	232 34.2	N 6 51.4	331 17.6	S22 43.1	322 34.7	S21 18.5	Kochab	137 20.6	N74 04.6
19	275 16.0	148 18.0	54.7	247 36.7	51.4	346 20.1	43.1	337 37.2	18.5	Markab	13 33.0	N15 19.0
20	290 18.5	163 17.6	54.2	262 39.2	51.4	1 22.6	43.1	352 39.8	18.5	Menkar	314 09.6	N 4 10.2
21	305 20.9	178 17.2	.. 53.7	277 41.7	.. 51.4	16 25.0	.. 43.1	7 42.3	.. 18.5	Menkent	148 02.0	S36 28.2
22	320 23.4	193 16.9	53.3	292 44.2	51.5	31 27.5	43.1	22 44.9	18.5	Miaplacidus	221 39.6	S69 47.9
23	335 25.9	208 16.5	52.8	307 46.8	51.5	46 30.0	43.1	37 47.4	18.6			
11 00	350 28.3	223 16.1	N17 52.3	322 49.3	N 6 51.5	61 32.5	S22 43.1	52 49.9	S21 18.6	Mirfak	308 33.0	N49 55.8
01	5 30.8	238 15.7	51.8	337 51.8	51.5	76 35.0	43.1	67 52.5	18.6	Nunki	75 52.0	S26 16.2
02	20 33.2	253 15.3	51.4	352 54.3	51.5	91 37.4	43.1	82 55.0	18.6	Peacock	53 10.9	S56 40.2
03	35 35.7	268 14.9	.. 50.9	7 56.8	.. 51.5	106 39.9	.. 43.1	97 57.6	.. 18.6	Pollux	243 21.8	N27 58.5
04	50 38.2	283 14.5	50.4	22 59.3	51.5	121 42.4	43.1	113 00.1	18.6	Procyon	244 54.7	N 5 10.4
05	65 40.6	298 14.1	49.9	38 01.8	51.5	136 44.9	43.1	128 02.6	18.7			
F 06	80 43.1	313 13.7	N17 49.4	53 04.3	N 6 51.5	151 47.4	S22 43.1	143 05.2	S21 18.7	Rasalhague	96 01.8	N12 33.0
R 07	95 45.6	328 13.3	48.9	68 06.9	51.5	166 49.8	43.1	158 07.7	18.7	Regulus	207 38.5	N11 52.1
I 08	110 48.0	343 12.9	48.4	83 09.4	51.5	181 52.3	43.1	173 10.3	18.7	Rigel	281 07.2	S 8 10.6
D 09	125 50.5	358 12.5	.. 48.0	98 11.9	.. 51.5	196 54.8	.. 43.1	188 12.8	.. 18.7	Rigil Kent.	139 45.4	S60 55.2
A 10	140 53.0	13 12.1	47.5	113 14.4	51.5	211 57.3	43.2	203 15.3	18.7	Sabik	102 06.8	S15 44.9
Y 11	155 55.4	28 11.7	47.0	128 17.0	51.5	226 59.8	43.2	218 17.9	18.7			
12	170 57.9	43 11.3	N17 46.5	143 19.5	N 6 51.5	242 02.2	S22 43.2	233 20.4	S21 18.8	Schedar	349 34.4	N56 38.9
13	186 00.3	58 10.9	46.0	158 22.0	51.5	257 04.7	43.2	248 23.0	18.8	Shaula	96 15.1	S37 07.1
14	201 02.8	73 10.5	45.5	173 24.5	51.5	272 07.2	43.2	263 25.5	18.8	Sirius	258 29.4	S16 44.5
15	216 05.3	88 10.1	.. 45.0	188 27.1	.. 51.5	287 09.7	.. 43.2	278 28.0	.. 18.8	Spica	158 26.2	S11 15.9
16	231 07.7	103 09.7	44.5	203 29.6	51.5	302 12.1	43.2	293 30.6	18.8	Suhail	222 49.2	S43 30.7
17	246 10.2	118 09.3	44.0	218 32.1	51.5	317 14.6	43.2	308 33.1	18.8			
18	261 12.7	133 08.9	N17 43.5	233 34.7	N 6 51.5	332 17.1	S22 43.2	323 35.6	S21 18.9	Vega	80 35.4	N38 48.5
19	276 15.1	148 08.5	43.0	248 37.2	51.5	347 19.6	43.2	338 38.2	18.9	Zuben'ubi	137 00.1	S16 07.5
20	291 17.6	163 08.1	42.6	263 39.8	51.5	2 22.0	43.2	353 40.7	18.9			
21	306 20.1	178 07.7	.. 42.1	278 42.3	.. 51.5	17 24.5	.. 43.2	8 43.3	.. 18.9			
22	321 22.5	193 07.3	41.6	293 44.8	51.5	32 27.0	43.2	23 45.8	18.9			
23	336 25.0	208 06.9	41.1	308 47.4	51.5	47 29.5	43.2	38 48.3	18.9			
Mer. Pass.	h m 0 41.9	v −0.4	d 0.5	v 2.5	d 0.0	v 2.5	d 0.0	v 2.5	d 0.0			

	SHA	Mer. Pass.
	° ′	h m
Venus	233 56.4	9 07
Mars	332 20.3	2 32
Jupiter	71 03.6	19 55
Saturn	62 19.7	20 29

UT	SUN GHA	SUN Dec	MOON GHA	MOON v	MOON Dec	MOON d	MOON HP	Lat.	Twilight Naut.	Twilight Civil	Sunrise	Moonrise 9	Moonrise 10	Moonrise 11	Moonrise 12
d h	° ′	° ′	° ′	′	° ′	′	′	°	h m	h m	h m	h m	h m	h m	h m
9 00	180 40.3	N 5 13.3	288 55.2	13.1	N18 24.4	8.3	54.6	N 72	01 20	03 30	04 46	▭	▭	▭	▭
01	195 40.5	12.3	303 27.3	13.0	18 32.7	8.3	54.6	N 70	02 08	03 47	04 54	▭	▭	▭	▭
02	210 40.7	11.4	317 59.3	12.9	18 41.0	8.2	54.6	68	02 37	04 00	05 00	18 43	▭	▭	▭
03	225 40.9	10.4	332 31.2	12.9	18 49.2	8.1	54.7	66	02 59	04 11	05 05	19 28	19 20	▭	20 07
04	240 41.1	09.5	347 03.1	12.8	18 57.3	8.1	54.7	64	03 15	04 20	05 10	19 57	20 08	20 36	21 37
05	255 41.3	08.5	1 34.9	12.7	19 05.4	7.9	54.7	62	03 29	04 27	05 14	20 20	20 39	21 14	22 14
06	270 41.6	N 5 07.6	16 06.6	12.7	N19 13.3	7.9	54.7	60	03 40	04 34	05 17	20 38	21 02	21 41	22 41
W 07	285 41.8	06.6	30 38.3	12.6	19 21.2	7.8	54.7	N 58	03 50	04 39	05 20	20 53	21 21	22 03	23 02
E 08	300 42.0	05.7	45 09.9	12.5	19 29.0	7.7	54.8	56	03 58	04 44	05 23	21 06	21 37	22 20	23 19
D 09	315 42.2	04.7	59 41.4	12.5	19 36.7	7.7	54.8	54	04 05	04 49	05 25	21 18	21 50	22 35	23 33
N 10	330 42.4	03.8	74 12.9	12.3	19 44.4	7.5	54.8	52	04 11	04 53	05 27	21 28	22 02	22 48	23 46
E 11	345 42.7	02.9	88 44.2	12.3	19 51.9	7.5	54.8	50	04 17	04 56	05 29	21 37	22 13	23 00	23 57
S 12	0 42.9	N 5 01.9	103 15.5	12.3	N19 59.4	7.4	54.8	45	04 28	05 03	05 33	21 56	22 35	23 22	24 20
D 13	15 43.1	01.0	117 46.8	12.1	20 06.8	7.2	54.9	N 40	04 37	05 09	05 37	22 11	22 53	23 41	24 39
A 14	30 43.3	5 00.0	132 17.9	12.1	20 14.0	7.3	54.9	35	04 44	05 14	05 39	22 25	23 07	23 57	24 54
Y 15	45 43.5	4 59.1	146 49.0	12.0	20 21.3	7.1	54.9	30	04 50	05 18	05 42	22 36	23 20	24 11	00 11
16	60 43.7	58.1	161 20.0	12.0	20 28.4	7.0	54.9	20	04 58	05 24	05 46	22 56	23 43	24 34	00 34
17	75 44.0	57.2	175 51.0	11.9	20 35.4	6.9	54.9	N 10	05 05	05 29	05 50	23 13	24 02	00 02	00 55
18	90 44.2	N 4 56.2	190 21.9	11.8	N20 42.3	6.9	55.0	0	05 09	05 33	05 54	23 30	24 20	00 20	01 14
19	105 44.4	55.3	204 52.7	11.7	20 49.2	6.7	55.0	S 10	05 11	05 36	05 57	23 46	24 38	00 38	01 33
20	120 44.6	54.3	219 23.4	11.6	20 55.9	6.7	55.0	20	05 13	05 38	06 00	24 04	00 04	00 58	01 53
21	135 44.8	53.4	233 54.0	11.6	21 02.6	6.6	55.0	30	05 12	05 40	06 04	24 24	00 24	01 21	02 17
22	150 45.1	52.4	248 24.6	11.5	21 09.2	6.5	55.1	35	05 12	05 41	06 06	24 36	00 36	01 34	02 31
23	165 45.3	51.5	262 55.1	11.5	21 15.7	6.3	55.1	40	05 10	05 41	06 08	24 50	00 50	01 49	02 47
10 00	180 45.5	N 4 50.6	277 25.6	11.3	N21 22.0	6.3	55.1	45	05 08	05 42	06 11	00 03	01 06	02 08	03 06
01	195 45.7	49.6	291 55.9	11.3	21 28.3	6.2	55.1	S 50	05 05	05 42	06 14	00 19	01 26	02 30	03 30
02	210 45.9	48.7	306 26.2	11.2	21 34.5	6.1	55.1	52	05 03	05 42	06 16	00 27	01 36	02 41	03 41
03	225 46.1	47.7	320 56.4	11.2	21 40.6	6.0	55.2	54	05 01	05 42	06 17	00 36	01 46	02 54	03 54
04	240 46.4	46.8	335 26.6	11.0	21 46.6	5.9	55.2	56	04 59	05 42	06 19	00 46	01 59	03 08	04 10
05	255 46.6	45.8	349 56.6	11.0	21 52.5	5.8	55.2	58	04 57	05 42	06 21	00 57	02 13	03 25	04 27
06	270 46.8	N 4 44.9	4 26.6	10.9	N21 58.3	5.7	55.2	S 60	04 54	05 42	06 23	01 10	02 30	03 46	04 49

UT	SUN GHA	SUN Dec	MOON GHA	MOON v	MOON Dec	MOON d	MOON HP	Lat.	Sunset	Twilight Civil	Twilight Naut.	Moonset 9	Moonset 10	Moonset 11	Moonset 12
	° ′	° ′	° ′	′	° ′	′	′	°	h m	h m	h m	h m	h m	h m	h m
07	285 47.0	43.9	18 56.5	10.9	22 04.0	5.6	55.3	N 72	19 05	20 19	22 22	▭	▭	▭	▭
T 08	300 47.2	43.0	33 26.4	10.7	22 09.6	5.5	55.3	N 70	18 57	20 03	21 39	▭	▭	▭	▭
H 09	315 47.5	42.0	47 56.1	10.7	22 15.1	5.3	55.3	68	18 51	19 50	21 12	15 40	▭	▭	▭
U 10	330 47.7	41.1	62 25.8	10.7	22 20.4	5.3	55.4	66	18 46	19 40	20 51	14 56	16 47	▭	19 46
R 11	345 47.9	40.1	76 55.5	10.5	22 25.7	5.2	55.4	64	18 42	19 31	20 35	14 27	15 59	17 21	18 15
S 12	0 48.1	N 4 39.2	91 25.0	10.5	N22 30.9	5.1	55.4	62	18 38	19 24	20 22	14 05	15 29	16 43	17 38
D 13	15 48.3	38.2	105 54.5	10.4	22 36.0	4.9	55.4	60	18 35	19 18	20 11	13 48	15 06	16 16	17 11
A 14	30 48.6	37.3	120 23.9	10.3	22 40.9	4.9	55.5	N 58	18 32	19 13	20 02	13 33	14 47	15 55	16 50
Y 15	45 48.8	36.3	134 53.2	10.3	22 45.8	4.7	55.5	56	18 30	19 08	19 54	13 20	14 32	15 38	16 33
16	60 49.0	35.4	149 22.5	10.2	22 50.5	4.6	55.5	54	18 28	19 04	19 47	13 10	14 19	15 23	16 18
17	75 49.2	34.4	163 51.7	10.1	22 55.1	4.5	55.5	52	18 26	19 00	19 41	13 00	14 07	15 10	16 06
18	90 49.4	N 4 33.5	178 20.8	10.0	N22 59.6	4.4	55.6	50	18 24	18 56	19 36	12 51	13 57	14 59	15 54
19	105 49.7	32.5	192 49.8	10.0	23 04.0	4.3	55.6	45	18 20	18 49	19 25	12 33	13 36	14 36	15 31
20	120 49.9	31.6	207 18.8	9.9	23 08.3	4.2	55.6	N 40	18 16	18 44	19 16	12 18	13 18	14 17	15 12
21	135 50.1	30.6	221 47.7	9.8	23 12.5	4.1	55.7	35	18 14	18 39	19 09	12 06	13 04	14 01	14 56
22	150 50.3	29.7	236 16.5	9.8	23 16.6	3.9	55.7	30	18 11	18 35	19 03	11 55	12 51	13 48	14 43
23	165 50.5	28.7	250 45.3	9.7	23 20.5	3.9	55.7	20	18 07	18 29	18 55	11 36	12 30	13 24	14 19
11 00	180 50.8	N 4 27.8	265 14.0	9.6	N23 24.4	3.7	55.8	N 10	18 03	18 24	18 49	11 20	12 11	13 04	13 59
01	195 51.0	26.8	279 42.6	9.5	23 28.1	3.6	55.8	0	18 00	18 21	18 45	11 05	11 54	12 46	13 40
02	210 51.2	25.9	294 11.1	9.5	23 31.7	3.5	55.8	S 10	17 57	18 18	18 42	10 50	11 36	12 27	13 21
03	225 51.4	24.9	308 39.6	9.4	23 35.2	3.3	55.8	20	17 54	18 16	18 41	10 34	11 18	12 07	13 01
04	240 51.6	24.0	323 08.0	9.4	23 38.5	3.3	55.9	30	17 50	18 14	18 42	10 15	10 57	11 44	12 37
05	255 51.9	23.0	337 36.4	9.2	23 41.8	3.1	55.9	35	17 48	18 13	18 43	10 05	10 44	11 30	12 23
06	270 52.1	N 4 22.1	352 04.6	9.3	N23 44.9	3.0	55.9	40	17 46	18 13	18 44	09 52	10 30	11 14	12 07
F 07	285 52.3	21.1	6 32.9	9.1	23 47.9	2.8	56.0	45	17 43	18 12	18 46	09 38	10 13	10 56	11 48
R 08	300 52.5	20.2	21 01.0	9.1	23 50.7	2.8	56.0	S 50	17 40	18 12	18 50	09 20	09 52	10 33	11 24
I 09	315 52.7	19.2	35 29.1	9.0	23 53.5	2.6	56.0	52	17 39	18 12	18 52	09 12	09 42	10 21	11 13
D 10	330 53.0	18.2	49 57.1	8.9	23 56.1	2.5	56.1	54	17 37	18 12	18 54	09 03	09 31	10 09	11 00
A 11	345 53.2	17.3	64 25.0	8.9	23 58.6	2.4	56.1	56	17 36	18 13	18 56	08 53	09 18	09 54	10 45
Y 12	0 53.4	N 4 16.3	78 52.9	8.9	N24 01.0	2.2	56.1	58	17 34	18 13	18 59	08 41	09 04	09 37	10 27
13	15 53.6	15.4	93 20.8	8.7	24 03.2	2.2	56.2	S 60	17 32	18 13	19 02	08 27	08 46	09 17	10 05
14	30 53.8	14.4	107 48.5	8.7	24 05.4	2.0	56.2								
15	45 54.1	13.5	122 16.2	8.7	24 07.4	1.8	56.2								
16	60 54.3	12.5	136 43.9	8.5	24 09.2	1.7	56.3								
17	75 54.5	11.6	151 11.4	8.6	24 10.9	1.6	56.3								
18	90 54.7	N 4 10.6	165 39.0	8.4	N24 12.5	1.5	56.3								
19	105 54.9	09.7	180 06.4	8.4	24 14.0	1.4	56.4								
20	120 55.2	08.7	194 33.8	8.4	24 15.4	1.2	56.4								
21	135 55.4	07.8	209 01.2	8.3	24 16.6	1.0	56.4								
22	150 55.6	06.8	223 28.5	8.2	24 17.6	1.0	56.5								
23	165 55.8	05.9	237 55.7	8.2	N24 18.6	0.8	56.5								
	SD 15.9	d 0.9	SD 14.9		15.1		15.3									

	SUN			MOON			
Day	Eqn. of Time 00h	Eqn. of Time 12h	Mer. Pass.	Mer. Pass. Upper	Mer. Pass. Lower	Age	Phase
d	m s	m s	h m	h m	h m	d	%
9	02 41	02 51	11 57	04 53	17 17	21	59
10	03 02	03 12	11 57	05 42	18 07	22	49
11	03 23	03 33	11 56	06 33	19 00	23	39

UT	ARIES GHA	VENUS −4·2 GHA	Dec	MARS −2·1 GHA	Dec	JUPITER −2·5 GHA	Dec	SATURN +0·4 GHA	Dec	STARS Name	SHA	Dec
12 00	351 27.5	223 06.5	N17 40.6	323 49.9	N 6 51.5	62 31.9	S22 43.2	53 50.9	S21 18.9	Acamar	315 14.2	S40 13.2
01	6 29.9	238 06.1	40.1	338 52.5	51.5	77 34.4	43.2	68 53.4	19.0	Achernar	335 22.4	S57 07.8
02	21 32.4	253 05.7	39.6	353 55.0	51.5	92 36.9	43.2	83 55.9	19.0	Acrux	173 04.5	S63 12.7
03	36 34.8	268 05.3 ..	39.1	8 57.6 ..	51.5	107 39.3 ..	43.2	98 58.5 ..	19.0	Adhara	255 08.7	S28 59.8
04	51 37.3	283 04.9	38.5	24 00.1	51.5	122 41.8	43.2	114 01.0	19.0	Aldebaran	290 43.6	N16 33.0
05	66 39.8	298 04.5	38.0	39 02.7	51.5	137 44.3	43.2	129 03.6	19.0			
06	81 42.2	313 04.1	N17 37.5	54 05.2	N 6 51.5	152 46.8	S22 43.2	144 06.1	S21 19.0	Alioth	166 16.7	N55 51.1
S 07	96 44.7	328 03.7	37.0	69 07.8	51.5	167 49.2	43.2	159 08.6	19.1	Alkaid	152 55.2	N49 12.9
A 08	111 47.2	343 03.3	36.5	84 10.3	51.5	182 51.7	43.2	174 11.2	19.1	Alnair	27 36.9	S46 51.7
T 09	126 49.6	358 02.9 ..	36.0	99 12.9 ..	51.5	197 54.2 ..	43.2	189 13.7 ..	19.1	Alnilam	275 41.3	S 1 11.3
U 10	141 52.1	13 02.5	35.5	114 15.4	51.5	212 56.6	43.2	204 16.2	19.1	Alphard	217 51.5	S 8 44.7
R 11	156 54.6	28 02.1	35.0	129 18.0	51.5	227 59.1	43.2	219 18.8	19.1			
D 12	171 57.0	43 01.7	N17 34.5	144 20.6	N 6 51.5	243 01.6	S22 43.2	234 21.3	S21 19.1	Alphecca	126 06.9	N26 39.1
A 13	186 59.5	58 01.3	34.0	159 23.1	51.5	258 04.0	43.2	249 23.8	19.1	Alpheratz	357 38.0	N29 12.3
Y 14	202 02.0	73 00.9	33.5	174 25.7	51.5	273 06.5	43.2	264 26.4	19.2	Altair	62 03.2	N 8 55.6
15	217 04.4	88 00.5 ..	33.0	189 28.3 ..	51.5	288 09.0 ..	43.2	279 28.9 ..	19.2	Ankaa	353 10.3	S42 11.6
16	232 06.9	103 00.1	32.4	204 30.8	51.5	303 11.4	43.2	294 31.4	19.2	Antares	112 20.2	S26 28.6
17	247 09.3	117 59.7	31.9	219 33.4	51.4	318 13.9	43.2	309 34.0	19.2			
18	262 11.8	132 59.3	N17 31.4	234 36.0	N 6 51.4	333 16.4	S22 43.2	324 36.5	S21 19.2	Arcturus	145 51.4	N19 04.8
19	277 14.3	147 58.9	30.9	249 38.6	51.4	348 18.8	43.2	339 39.0	19.2	Atria	107 17.6	S69 04.0
20	292 16.7	162 58.5	30.4	264 41.1	51.4	3 21.3	43.3	354 41.6	19.2	Avior	234 16.5	S59 34.3
21	307 19.2	177 58.0 ..	29.9	279 43.7 ..	51.4	18 23.8 ..	43.3	9 44.1 ..	19.3	Bellatrix	278 26.6	N 6 22.1
22	322 21.7	192 57.6	29.3	294 46.3	51.4	33 26.2	43.3	24 46.6	19.3	Betelgeuse	270 55.9	N 7 24.7
23	337 24.1	207 57.2	28.8	309 48.9	51.4	48 28.7	43.3	39 49.2	19.3			
13 00	352 26.6	222 56.8	N17 28.3	324 51.4	N 6 51.4	63 31.2	S22 43.3	54 51.7	S21 19.3	Canopus	263 54.1	S52 42.1
01	7 29.1	237 56.4	27.8	339 54.0	51.4	78 33.6	43.3	69 54.2	19.3	Capella	280 27.0	N46 00.9
02	22 31.5	252 56.0	27.3	354 56.6	51.3	93 36.1	43.3	84 56.8	19.3	Deneb	49 27.8	N45 21.5
03	37 34.0	267 55.6 ..	26.7	9 59.2 ..	51.3	108 38.6 ..	43.3	99 59.3 ..	19.3	Denebola	182 28.9	N14 27.6
04	52 36.5	282 55.2	26.2	25 01.8	51.3	123 41.0	43.3	115 01.8	19.4	Diphda	348 50.5	S17 52.3
05	67 38.9	297 54.8	25.7	40 04.4	51.3	138 43.5	43.3	130 04.4	19.4			
06	82 41.4	312 54.4	N17 25.2	55 07.0	N 6 51.3	153 46.0	S22 43.3	145 06.9	S21 19.4	Dubhe	193 46.1	N61 38.5
S 07	97 43.8	327 54.0	24.6	70 09.6	51.3	168 48.4	43.3	160 09.4	19.4	Elnath	278 06.3	N28 37.4
U 08	112 46.3	342 53.6	24.1	85 12.1	51.3	183 50.9	43.3	175 12.0	19.4	Eltanin	90 43.7	N51 29.5
N 09	127 48.8	357 53.2 ..	23.6	100 14.7 ..	51.2	198 53.3 ..	43.3	190 14.5 ..	19.4	Enif	33 41.9	N 9 58.3
D 10	142 51.2	12 52.8	23.1	115 17.3	51.2	213 55.8	43.3	205 17.0	19.4	Fomalhaut	15 18.1	S29 30.7
A 11	157 53.7	27 52.4	22.5	130 19.9	51.2	228 58.3	43.3	220 19.6	19.5			
Y 12	172 56.2	42 52.0	N17 22.0	145 22.5	N 6 51.2	244 00.7	S22 43.3	235 22.1	S21 19.5	Gacrux	171 56.0	S57 13.6
13	187 58.6	57 51.6	21.5	160 25.1	51.2	259 03.2	43.3	250 24.6	19.5	Gienah	175 47.5	S17 39.2
14	203 01.1	72 51.2	20.9	175 27.7	51.2	274 05.6	43.3	265 27.1	19.5	Hadar	148 41.3	S60 28.3
15	218 03.6	87 50.8 ..	20.4	190 30.3 ..	51.1	289 08.1 ..	43.3	280 29.7 ..	19.5	Hamal	327 54.9	N23 33.5
16	233 06.0	102 50.4	19.9	205 32.9	51.1	304 10.6	43.3	295 32.2	19.5	Kaus Aust.	83 37.1	S34 22.5
17	248 08.5	117 50.0	19.3	220 35.5	51.1	319 13.0	43.3	310 34.7	19.5			
18	263 11.0	132 49.6	N17 18.8	235 38.2	N 6 51.1	334 15.5	S22 43.3	325 37.3	S21 19.6	Kochab	137 20.7	N74 04.6
19	278 13.4	147 49.2	18.3	250 40.8	51.1	349 17.9	43.3	340 39.8	19.6	Markab	13 33.0	N15 19.0
20	293 15.9	162 48.8	17.7	265 43.4	51.1	4 20.4	43.3	355 42.3	19.6	Menkar	314 09.6	N 4 10.2
21	308 18.3	177 48.4 ..	17.2	280 46.0 ..	51.0	19 22.8 ..	43.3	10 44.9 ..	19.6	Menkent	148 02.0	S36 28.2
22	323 20.8	192 48.0	16.6	295 48.6	51.0	34 25.3	43.3	25 47.4	19.6	Miaplacidus	221 39.6	S69 47.9
23	338 23.3	207 47.6	16.1	310 51.2	51.0	49 27.8	43.3	40 49.9	19.6			
14 00	353 25.7	222 47.2	N17 15.6	325 53.8	N 6 51.0	64 30.2	S22 43.3	55 52.4	S21 19.6	Mirfak	308 33.0	N49 55.8
01	8 28.2	237 46.8	15.0	340 56.5	51.0	79 32.7	43.3	70 55.0	19.7	Nunki	75 52.0	S26 16.2
02	23 30.7	252 46.4	14.5	355 59.1	50.9	94 35.1	43.3	85 57.5	19.7	Peacock	53 10.9	S56 40.2
03	38 33.1	267 46.0 ..	13.9	11 01.7 ..	50.9	109 37.6 ..	43.3	101 00.0 ..	19.7	Pollux	243 21.8	N27 58.5
04	53 35.6	282 45.6	13.4	26 04.3	50.9	124 40.0	43.3	116 02.6	19.7	Procyon	244 54.7	N 5 10.4
05	68 38.1	297 45.2	12.8	41 06.9	50.9	139 42.5	43.3	131 05.1	19.7			
06	83 40.5	312 44.8	N17 12.3	56 09.6	N 6 50.8	154 44.9	S22 43.3	146 07.6	S21 19.7	Rasalhague	96 01.8	N12 33.0
07	98 43.0	327 44.3	11.8	71 12.2	50.8	169 47.4	43.3	161 10.1	19.7	Regulus	207 38.5	N11 52.1
08	113 45.4	342 43.9	11.2	86 14.8	50.8	184 49.8	43.3	176 12.7	19.7	Rigel	281 07.2	S 8 10.6
M 09	128 47.9	357 43.5 ..	10.7	101 17.5 ..	50.8	199 52.3 ..	43.3	191 15.2 ..	19.8	Rigil Kent.	139 45.4	S60 55.2
O 10	143 50.4	12 43.1	10.1	116 20.1	50.7	214 54.7	43.3	206 17.7	19.8	Sabik	102 06.8	S15 44.9
N 11	158 52.8	27 42.7	09.6	131 22.7	50.7	229 57.2	43.3	221 20.2	19.8			
D 12	173 55.3	42 42.3	N17 09.0	146 25.4	N 6 50.7	244 59.6	S22 43.3	236 22.8	S21 19.8	Schedar	349 34.4	N56 38.9
A 13	188 57.8	57 41.9	08.5	161 28.0	50.7	260 02.1	43.3	251 25.3	19.8	Shaula	96 15.1	S37 07.1
Y 14	204 00.2	72 41.5	07.9	176 30.6	50.6	275 04.5	43.3	266 27.8	19.8	Sirius	258 29.4	S16 44.5
15	219 02.7	87 41.1 ..	07.4	191 33.3 ..	50.6	290 07.0 ..	43.3	281 30.3 ..	19.8	Spica	158 26.2	S11 15.9
16	234 05.2	102 40.7	06.8	206 35.9	50.6	305 09.4	43.3	296 32.9	19.9	Suhail	222 49.2	S43 30.7
17	249 07.6	117 40.3	06.2	221 38.6	50.6	320 11.9	43.3	311 35.4	19.9			
18	264 10.1	132 39.9	N17 05.7	236 41.2	N 6 50.5	335 14.3	S22 43.3	326 37.9	S21 19.9	Vega	80 35.4	N38 48.5
19	279 12.6	147 39.5	05.1	251 43.8	50.5	350 16.8	43.3	341 40.5	19.9	Zuben'ubi	137 00.1	S16 07.5
20	294 15.0	162 39.1	04.6	266 46.5	50.5	5 19.2	43.3	356 43.0	19.9		SHA	Mer. Pass.
21	309 17.5	177 38.7 ..	04.0	281 49.1 ..	50.4	20 21.7 ..	43.3	11 45.5 ..	19.9		° ′	h m
22	324 19.9	192 38.3	03.5	296 51.8	50.4	35 24.1	43.3	26 48.0	19.9	Venus	230 30.2	9 08
23	339 22.4	207 37.9	02.9	311 54.4	50.4	50 26.6	43.3	41 50.6	19.9	Mars	332 24.8	2 20
	h m									Jupiter	71 04.6	19 43
Mer. Pass. 0 30.1		v −0.4 d 0.5		v 2.6 d 0.0		v 2.5 d 0.0		v 2.5 d 0.0		Saturn	62 25.1	20 17

SUN and MOON

UT	SUN GHA	SUN Dec	MOON GHA	v	MOON Dec	d	HP
12 00	180 56.0	N 4 04.9	252 22.9	8.2	N24 19.4	0.6	56.5
01	195 56.3	03.9	266 50.1	8.0	24 20.0	0.6	56.6
02	210 56.5	03.0	281 17.1	8.1	24 20.6	0.4	56.6
03	225 56.7	.. 02.0	295 44.2	8.0	24 21.0	0.2	56.7
04	240 56.9	01.1	310 11.2	7.9	24 21.2	0.2	56.7
05	255 57.2	4 00.1	324 38.1	7.9	24 21.4	0.1	56.7
06	270 57.4	N 3 59.2	339 05.0	7.8	N24 21.3	0.1	56.8
07	285 57.6	58.2	353 31.8	7.8	24 21.2	0.3	56.8
S 08	300 57.8	57.3	7 58.6	7.8	24 20.9	0.4	56.8
A 09	315 58.0	.. 56.3	22 25.4	7.7	24 20.5	0.6	56.9
T 10	330 58.3	55.4	36 52.1	7.6	24 19.9	0.7	56.9
U 11	345 58.5	54.4	51 18.7	7.6	24 19.2	0.9	56.9
R 12	0 58.7	N 3 53.4	65 45.3	7.6	N24 18.3	1.0	57.0
D 13	15 58.9	52.5	80 11.9	7.6	24 17.3	1.1	57.0
A 14	30 59.1	51.5	94 38.5	7.5	24 16.2	1.3	57.1
Y 15	45 59.4	.. 50.6	109 05.0	7.4	24 14.9	1.4	57.1
16	60 59.6	49.6	123 31.4	7.5	24 13.5	1.6	57.1
17	75 59.8	48.7	137 57.9	7.4	24 11.9	1.7	57.2
18	91 00.0	N 3 47.7	152 24.3	7.3	N24 10.2	1.9	57.2
19	106 00.2	46.7	166 50.6	7.3	24 08.3	2.0	57.2
20	121 00.5	45.8	181 16.9	7.3	24 06.3	2.1	57.3
21	136 00.7	.. 44.8	195 43.2	7.3	24 04.2	2.3	57.3
22	151 00.9	43.9	210 09.5	7.2	24 01.9	2.5	57.4
23	166 01.1	42.9	224 35.7	7.3	23 59.4	2.6	57.4
13 00	181 01.4	N 3 42.0	239 02.0	7.1	N23 56.8	2.7	57.4
01	196 01.6	41.0	253 28.1	7.2	23 54.1	2.9	57.5
02	211 01.8	40.0	267 54.3	7.1	23 51.2	3.0	57.5
03	226 02.0	.. 39.1	282 20.4	7.2	23 48.2	3.2	57.6
04	241 02.2	38.1	296 46.6	7.0	23 45.0	3.3	57.6
05	256 02.5	37.2	311 12.6	7.1	23 41.7	3.4	57.6
06	271 02.7	N 3 36.2	325 38.7	7.1	N23 38.3	3.6	57.7
07	286 02.9	35.3	340 04.8	7.0	23 34.7	3.8	57.7
S 08	301 03.1	34.3	354 30.8	7.0	23 30.9	3.9	57.8
U 09	316 03.3	.. 33.3	8 56.8	7.0	23 27.0	4.1	57.8
N 10	331 03.6	32.4	23 22.8	7.0	23 22.9	4.2	57.8
D 11	346 03.8	31.4	37 48.8	7.0	23 18.7	4.3	57.9
A 12	1 04.0	N 3 30.5	52 14.8	6.9	N23 14.4	4.5	57.9
Y 13	16 04.2	29.5	66 40.7	7.0	23 09.9	4.6	57.9
14	31 04.5	28.5	81 06.7	6.9	23 05.3	4.8	58.0
15	46 04.7	.. 27.6	95 32.6	7.0	23 00.5	5.0	58.0
16	61 04.9	26.6	109 58.6	6.9	22 55.5	5.0	58.1
17	76 05.1	25.7	124 24.5	6.9	22 50.5	5.3	58.1
18	91 05.3	N 3 24.7	138 50.4	6.9	N22 45.2	5.3	58.1
19	106 05.6	23.8	153 16.3	6.9	22 39.9	5.5	58.2
20	121 05.8	22.8	167 42.2	7.0	22 34.4	5.7	58.2
21	136 06.0	.. 21.8	182 08.2	6.9	22 28.7	5.8	58.3
22	151 06.2	20.9	196 34.1	6.9	22 22.9	6.0	58.3
23	166 06.5	19.9	211 00.0	6.9	22 16.9	6.1	58.3
14 00	181 06.7	N 3 19.0	225 25.9	6.9	N22 10.8	6.2	58.4
01	196 06.9	18.0	239 51.8	6.9	22 04.6	6.4	58.4
02	211 07.1	17.0	254 17.7	6.9	21 58.2	6.6	58.5
03	226 07.3	.. 16.1	268 43.6	6.9	21 51.6	6.6	58.5
04	241 07.6	15.1	283 09.5	7.0	21 45.0	6.9	58.5
05	256 07.8	14.2	297 35.5	6.9	21 38.1	6.9	58.6
06	271 08.0	N 3 13.2	312 01.4	6.9	N21 31.2	7.1	58.6
07	286 08.2	12.2	326 27.3	7.0	21 24.1	7.3	58.7
M 08	301 08.5	11.3	340 53.3	6.9	21 16.8	7.4	58.7
O 09	316 08.7	.. 10.3	355 19.3	6.9	21 09.4	7.5	58.7
N 10	331 08.9	09.3	9 45.2	7.0	21 01.9	7.7	58.8
D 11	346 09.1	08.4	24 11.2	6.9	20 54.2	7.8	58.8
A 12	1 09.3	N 3 07.4	38 37.2	7.0	N20 46.4	7.9	58.8
Y 13	16 09.6	06.5	53 03.2	7.0	20 38.5	8.1	58.9
14	31 09.8	05.5	67 29.2	7.1	20 30.4	8.3	58.9
15	46 10.0	.. 04.5	81 55.3	7.0	20 22.1	8.3	59.0
16	61 10.2	03.6	96 21.3	7.1	20 13.8	8.5	59.0
17	76 10.5	02.6	110 47.4	7.1	20 05.3	8.7	59.0
18	91 10.7	N 3 01.7	125 13.5	7.1	N19 56.6	8.8	59.1
19	106 10.9	3 00.7	139 39.6	7.1	19 47.8	8.9	59.1
20	121 11.1	2 59.7	154 05.7	7.2	19 38.9	9.0	59.1
21	136 11.3	.. 58.8	168 31.9	7.1	19 29.9	9.2	59.2
22	151 11.6	57.8	182 58.0	7.2	19 20.7	9.3	59.2
23	166 11.8	56.8	197 24.2	7.2	N19 11.4	9.4	59.3
	SD 15.9	d 1.0	SD 15.5		15.8		16.0

Twilight / Moonrise

Lat.	Twilight Naut.	Civil	Sunrise	Moonrise 12	13	14	15
N 72	01 53	03 47	05 00	□	□	□	□
N 70	02 29	04 01	05 06	□	□	23 05	25 56
68	02 54	04 12	05 11	□	□	00 02	00 02
66	03 12	04 22	05 15	20 07	22 29	24 35	00 35
64	03 27	04 29	05 18	21 37	23 11	24 59	00 59
62	03 39	04 36	05 21	22 14	23 39	25 18	01 18
60	03 49	04 41	05 24	22 41	24 00	00 00	01 33
N 58	03 57	04 46	05 26	23 02	24 18	00 18	01 46
56	04 05	04 51	05 28	23 19	24 33	00 33	01 58
54	04 11	04 54	05 30	23 33	24 45	00 45	02 08
52	04 17	04 58	05 32	23 46	24 56	00 56	02 16
50	04 22	05 01	05 33	23 57	25 06	01 06	02 24
45	04 32	05 07	05 37	24 20	00 20	01 27	02 41
N 40	04 40	05 12	05 39	24 39	00 39	01 44	02 55
35	04 46	05 16	05 42	24 54	00 54	01 58	03 06
30	04 51	05 20	05 44	00 11	01 08	02 10	03 16
20	04 59	05 25	05 47	00 34	01 31	02 31	03 33
N 10	05 04	05 29	05 50	00 55	01 51	02 49	03 48
0	05 08	05 32	05 52	01 14	02 09	03 06	04 02
S 10	05 10	05 34	05 55	01 33	02 28	03 23	04 16
20	05 10	05 36	05 58	01 53	02 48	03 41	04 31
30	05 09	05 36	06 00	02 17	03 11	04 01	04 48
35	05 07	05 37	06 02	02 31	03 24	04 13	04 58
40	05 05	05 37	06 04	02 47	03 40	04 27	05 09
45	05 02	05 36	06 06	03 06	03 58	04 44	05 22
S 50	04 58	05 36	06 08	03 30	04 21	05 04	05 38
52	04 56	05 35	06 09	03 41	04 32	05 13	05 46
54	04 54	05 35	06 10	03 54	04 45	05 24	05 54
56	04 51	05 34	06 11	04 10	04 59	05 36	06 03
58	04 48	05 34	06 13	04 27	05 16	05 50	06 13
S 60	04 44	05 33	06 14	04 49	05 36	06 06	06 25

Sunset / Twilight / Moonset

Lat.	Sunset	Twilight Civil	Naut.	Moonset 12	13	14	15
N 72	18 49	20 01	21 50	□	□	□	20 25
N 70	18 43	19 47	21 17	□	□	20 46	19 52
68	18 39	19 36	20 54	□	□	19 49	19 28
66	18 35	19 28	20 36	19 46	19 21	19 14	19 09
64	18 31	19 20	20 22	18 15	18 40	18 49	18 53
62	18 29	19 14	20 10	17 38	18 11	18 30	18 41
60	18 26	19 08	20 01	17 11	17 49	18 13	18 29
N 58	18 24	19 04	19 52	16 50	17 31	18 00	18 20
56	18 22	19 00	19 45	16 33	17 16	17 48	18 11
54	18 20	18 56	19 39	16 18	17 03	17 37	18 04
52	18 19	18 53	19 33	16 06	16 51	17 28	17 57
50	18 17	18 50	19 29	15 54	16 41	17 20	17 51
45	18 14	18 44	19 19	15 31	16 20	17 02	17 37
N 40	18 11	18 39	19 11	15 12	16 02	16 47	17 26
35	18 09	18 35	19 04	14 56	15 48	16 35	17 17
30	18 07	18 31	18 59	14 43	15 35	16 24	17 08
20	18 04	18 26	18 52	14 19	15 13	16 05	16 54
N 10	18 01	18 22	18 47	13 59	14 54	15 48	16 41
0	17 59	18 20	18 44	13 40	14 36	15 33	16 29
S 10	17 57	18 18	18 42	13 21	14 18	15 17	16 17
20	17 54	18 16	18 42	13 01	13 59	15 01	16 04
30	17 52	18 16	18 43	12 37	13 37	14 41	15 48
35	17 50	18 15	18 45	12 23	13 24	14 30	15 40
40	17 49	18 16	18 47	12 07	13 09	14 17	15 30
45	17 47	18 16	18 50	11 48	12 51	14 01	15 18
S 50	17 45	18 17	18 54	11 24	12 28	13 42	15 03
52	17 44	18 17	18 56	11 13	12 17	13 33	14 56
54	17 42	18 18	18 59	11 00	12 05	13 23	14 49
56	17 41	18 18	19 02	10 45	11 51	13 11	14 40
58	17 40	18 19	19 05	10 27	11 35	12 58	14 30
S 60	17 39	18 20	19 09	10 05	11 15	12 42	14 19

SUN and MOON

Day	Eqn. of Time 00h	12h	Mer. Pass.	Mer. Pass. Upper	Lower	Age	Phase
d	m s	m s	h m	h m	h m	d	%
12	03 44	03 54	11 56	07 27	19 55	24	29
13	04 05	04 16	11 56	08 23	20 51	25	20
14	04 26	04 37	11 55	09 19	21 48	26	12

UT (d h)	ARIES GHA	VENUS −4·2 GHA	Dec	MARS −2·2 GHA	Dec	JUPITER −2·5 GHA	Dec	SATURN +0·4 GHA	Dec	STARS Name	SHA	Dec
15 00	354 24.9	222 37.5	N17 02.3	326 57.1	N 6 50.3	65 29.0	S22 43.3	56 53.1	S21 20.0	Acamar	315 14.2	S40 13.2
01	9 27.3	237 37.1	. . 01.8	341 59.7	. . 50.3	80 31.5	43.3	71 55.6	20.0	Achernar	335 22.4	S57 07.8
02	24 29.8	252 36.7	01.2	357 02.4	50.3	95 33.9	43.3	86 58.1	20.0	Acrux	173 04.5	S63 12.7
03	39 32.3	267 36.3	. . 00.6	12 05.1	. . 50.3	110 36.4	. . 43.3	102 00.6	. . 20.0	Adhara	255 08.7	S28 59.8
04	54 34.7	282 35.9	17 00.1	27 07.7	50.2	125 38.8	43.3	117 03.2	20.0	Aldebaran	290 43.5	N16 33.0
05	69 37.2	297 35.5	16 59.5	42 10.4	50.2	140 41.3	43.3	132 05.7	20.0			
06	84 39.7	312 35.0	N16 59.0	57 13.0	N 6 50.2	155 43.7	S22 43.3	147 08.2	S21 20.0	Alioth	166 16.7	N55 51.1
07	99 42.1	327 34.6	58.4	72 15.7	50.1	170 46.2	43.3	162 10.7	20.0	Alkaid	152 55.3	N49 12.9
T 08	114 44.6	342 34.2	57.8	87 18.4	50.1	185 48.6	43.3	177 13.3	20.1	Alnair	27 36.9	S46 51.7
U 09	129 47.1	357 33.8	. . 57.2	102 21.0	. . 50.1	200 51.0	. . 43.3	192 15.8	. . 20.1	Alnilam	275 41.3	S 1 11.3
E 10	144 49.5	12 33.4	56.7	117 23.7	50.0	215 53.5	43.3	207 18.3	20.1	Alphard	217 51.4	S 8 44.7
S 11	159 52.0	27 33.0	56.1	132 26.4	50.0	230 55.9	43.3	222 20.8	20.1			
D 12	174 54.4	42 32.6	N16 55.5	147 29.0	N 6 49.9	245 58.4	S22 43.3	237 23.4	S21 20.1	Alphecca	126 06.9	N26 39.0
A 13	189 56.9	57 32.2	55.0	162 31.7	49.9	261 00.8	43.3	252 25.9	20.1	Alpheratz	357 38.0	N29 12.3
Y 14	204 59.4	72 31.8	54.4	177 34.4	49.9	276 03.3	43.3	267 28.4	20.1	Altair	62 03.2	N 8 55.6
15	220 01.8	87 31.4	. . 53.8	192 37.1	. . 49.8	291 05.7	. . 43.3	282 30.9	. . 20.1	Ankaa	353 10.3	S42 11.6
16	235 04.3	102 31.0	53.2	207 39.7	49.8	306 08.1	43.3	297 33.4	20.2	Antares	112 20.2	S26 28.6
17	250 06.8	117 30.6	52.7	222 42.4	49.8	321 10.6	43.3	312 36.0	20.2			
18	265 09.2	132 30.2	N16 52.1	237 45.1	N 6 49.7	336 13.0	S22 43.3	327 38.5	S21 20.2	Arcturus	145 51.4	N19 04.8
19	280 11.7	147 29.8	51.5	252 47.8	49.7	351 15.5	43.3	342 41.0	20.2	Atria	107 17.6	S69 04.0
20	295 14.2	162 29.4	50.9	267 50.5	49.7	6 17.9	43.3	357 43.5	20.2	Avior	234 16.5	S59 34.2
21	310 16.6	177 29.0	. . 50.4	282 53.2	. . 49.6	21 20.3	. . 43.3	12 46.1	. . 20.2	Bellatrix	278 26.6	N 6 22.1
22	325 19.1	192 28.6	49.8	297 55.8	49.6	36 22.8	43.3	27 48.6	20.2	Betelgeuse	270 55.9	N 7 24.7
23	340 21.5	207 28.2	49.2	312 58.5	49.6	51 25.2	43.3	42 51.1	20.2			
16 00	355 24.0	222 27.8	N16 48.6	328 01.2	N 6 49.5	66 27.7	S22 43.3	57 53.6	S21 20.3	Canopus	263 54.0	S52 42.1
01	10 26.5	237 27.4	48.0	343 03.9	49.5	81 30.1	43.3	72 56.1	20.3	Capella	280 27.0	N46 00.9
02	25 28.9	252 26.9	47.5	358 06.6	49.4	96 32.5	43.3	87 58.7	20.3	Deneb	49 27.8	N45 21.5
03	40 31.4	267 26.5	. . 46.9	13 09.3	. . 49.4	111 35.0	. . 43.3	103 01.2	. . 20.3	Denebola	182 28.9	N14 27.6
04	55 33.9	282 26.1	46.3	28 12.0	49.3	126 37.4	43.3	118 03.7	20.3	Diphda	348 50.5	S17 52.3
05	70 36.3	297 25.7	45.7	43 14.7	49.3	141 39.8	43.3	133 06.2	20.3			
06	85 38.8	312 25.3	N16 45.1	58 17.4	N 6 49.2	156 42.3	S22 43.3	148 08.7	S21 20.3	Dubhe	193 46.1	N61 38.5
W 07	100 41.3	327 24.9	44.5	73 20.1	49.2	171 44.7	43.3	163 11.3	20.3	Elnath	278 06.3	N28 37.4
E 08	115 43.7	342 24.5	43.9	88 22.8	49.2	186 47.1	43.3	178 13.8	20.4	Eltanin	90 43.8	N51 29.5
D 09	130 46.2	357 24.1	. . 43.4	103 25.5	. . 49.1	201 49.6	. . 43.3	193 16.3	. . 20.4	Enif	33 41.9	N 9 58.3
N 10	145 48.7	12 23.7	42.8	118 28.2	49.1	216 52.0	43.3	208 18.8	20.4	Fomalhaut	15 18.0	S29 30.7
E 11	160 51.1	27 23.3	42.2	133 30.9	49.0	231 54.4	43.3	223 21.3	20.4			
S 12	175 53.6	42 22.9	N16 41.6	148 33.6	N 6 49.0	246 56.9	S22 43.3	238 23.8	S21 20.4	Gacrux	171 56.0	S57 13.6
D 13	190 56.0	57 22.5	41.0	163 36.3	48.9	261 59.3	43.3	253 26.4	20.4	Gienah	175 47.5	S17 39.2
A 14	205 58.5	72 22.1	40.4	178 39.0	48.9	277 01.7	43.3	268 28.9	20.4	Hadar	148 41.4	S60 28.3
Y 15	221 01.0	87 21.7	. . 39.8	193 41.7	. . 48.9	292 04.2	. . 43.3	283 31.4	. . 20.4	Hamal	327 54.8	N23 33.5
16	236 03.4	102 21.3	39.2	208 44.4	48.8	307 06.6	43.3	298 33.9	20.5	Kaus Aust.	83 37.1	S34 22.5
17	251 05.9	117 20.9	38.6	223 47.2	48.8	322 09.0	43.3	313 36.4	20.5			
18	266 08.4	132 20.5	N16 38.0	238 49.9	N 6 48.7	337 11.5	S22 43.3	328 39.0	S21 20.5	Kochab	137 20.7	N74 04.6
19	281 10.8	147 20.1	37.4	253 52.6	48.7	352 13.9	43.3	343 41.5	20.5	Markab	13 33.0	N15 19.0
20	296 13.3	162 19.7	36.8	268 55.3	48.6	7 16.3	43.3	358 44.0	20.5	Menkar	314 09.6	N 4 10.2
21	311 15.8	177 19.3	. . 36.2	283 58.0	. . 48.6	22 18.8	. . 43.3	13 46.5	. . 20.5	Menkent	148 02.0	S36 28.2
22	326 18.2	192 18.8	35.6	299 00.7	48.5	37 21.2	43.3	28 49.0	20.5	Miaplacidus	221 39.6	S69 47.8
23	341 20.7	207 18.4	35.0	314 03.5	48.5	52 23.6	43.2	43 51.5	20.5			
17 00	356 23.1	222 18.0	N16 34.4	329 06.2	N 6 48.4	67 26.1	S22 43.2	58 54.1	S21 20.5	Mirfak	308 32.9	N49 55.8
01	11 25.6	237 17.6	33.8	344 08.9	48.4	82 28.5	43.2	73 56.6	20.6	Nunki	75 52.0	S26 16.2
02	26 28.1	252 17.2	33.2	359 11.6	48.3	97 30.9	43.2	88 59.1	20.6	Peacock	53 10.9	S56 40.2
03	41 30.5	267 16.8	. . 32.6	14 14.4	. . 48.3	112 33.3	. . 43.2	104 01.6	. . 20.6	Pollux	243 21.8	N27 58.5
04	56 33.0	282 16.4	32.0	29 17.1	48.2	127 35.8	43.2	119 04.1	20.6	Procyon	244 54.6	N 5 10.4
05	71 35.5	297 16.0	31.4	44 19.8	48.2	142 38.2	43.2	134 06.6	20.6			
06	86 37.9	312 15.6	N16 30.8	59 22.6	N 6 48.1	157 40.6	S22 43.2	149 09.1	S21 20.6	Rasalhague	96 01.8	N12 33.0
07	101 40.4	327 15.2	30.2	74 25.3	48.1	172 43.1	43.2	164 11.7	20.6	Regulus	207 38.5	N11 52.1
T 08	116 42.9	342 14.8	29.6	89 28.0	48.0	187 45.5	43.2	179 14.2	20.6	Rigel	281 07.2	S 8 10.6
H 09	131 45.3	357 14.4	. . 29.0	104 30.8	. . 48.0	202 47.9	. . 43.2	194 16.7	. . 20.6	Rigil Kent.	139 45.5	S60 55.2
U 10	146 47.8	12 14.0	28.4	119 33.5	47.9	217 50.3	43.2	209 19.2	20.7	Sabik	102 06.8	S15 44.9
R 11	161 50.3	27 13.6	27.8	134 36.3	47.9	232 52.8	43.2	224 21.7	20.7			
S 12	176 52.7	42 13.2	N16 27.1	149 39.0	N 6 47.8	247 55.2	S22 43.2	239 24.2	S21 20.7	Schedar	349 34.3	N56 38.9
D 13	191 55.2	57 12.8	26.5	164 41.7	47.8	262 57.6	43.2	254 26.7	20.7	Shaula	96 15.1	S37 07.1
A 14	206 57.6	72 12.4	25.9	179 44.5	47.7	278 00.0	43.2	269 29.3	20.7	Sirius	258 29.4	S16 44.5
Y 15	222 00.1	87 12.0	. . 25.3	194 47.2	. . 47.6	293 02.5	. . 43.2	284 31.8	. . 20.7	Spica	158 26.3	S11 15.9
16	237 02.6	102 11.6	24.7	209 50.0	47.6	308 04.9	43.2	299 34.3	20.7	Suhail	222 49.2	S43 30.7
17	252 05.0	117 11.1	24.1	224 52.7	47.5	323 07.3	43.2	314 36.8	20.7			
18	267 07.5	132 10.7	N16 23.5	239 55.5	N 6 47.5	338 09.7	S22 43.2	329 39.3	S21 20.7	Vega	80 35.5	N38 48.5
19	282 10.0	147 10.3	22.8	254 58.2	47.4	353 12.2	43.2	344 41.8	20.8	Zuben'ubi	137 00.1	S16 07.5
20	297 12.4	162 09.9	22.2	270 01.0	47.4	8 14.6	43.2	359 44.3	20.8			
21	312 14.9	177 09.5	. . 21.6	285 03.8	. . 47.3	23 17.0	. . 43.2	14 46.9	. . 20.8			
22	327 17.4	192 09.1	21.0	300 06.5	47.3	38 19.4	43.2	29 49.4	20.8			
23	342 19.7	207 08.7	20.4	315 09.3	47.2	53 21.8	43.2	44 51.9	20.8			
Mer. Pass. h m 0 18.3		v −0.4	d 0.6	v 2.7	d 0.0	v 2.4	d 0.0	v 2.5	d 0.0			

	SHA	Mer. Pass.
	° ′	h m
Venus	227 03.7	9 10
Mars	332 37.2	2 08
Jupiter	71 03.6	19 31
Saturn	62 29.6	20 05

UT	SUN GHA	SUN Dec	MOON GHA	v	Dec	d	HP
d h	° ′	° ′	° ′	′	° ′	′	′
15 00	181 12.0	N 2 55.9	211 50.4	7.3	N19 02.0	9.6	59.3
01	196 12.2	54.9	226 16.7	7.2	18 52.4	9.7	59.3
02	211 12.5	54.0	240 42.9	7.3	18 42.7	9.8	59.4
03	226 12.7 ..	53.0	255 09.2	7.3	18 32.9	10.0	59.4
04	241 12.9	52.0	269 35.5	7.3	18 22.9	10.1	59.4
05	256 13.1	51.1	284 01.8	7.4	18 12.8	10.2	59.5
06	271 13.3	N 2 50.1	298 28.2	7.4	N18 02.6	10.3	59.5
07	286 13.6	49.1	312 54.6	7.4	17 52.3	10.5	59.5
T 08	301 13.8	48.2	327 21.0	7.4	17 41.8	10.6	59.6
U 09	316 14.0 ..	47.2	341 47.4	7.5	17 31.2	10.7	59.6
E 10	331 14.2	46.3	356 13.9	7.5	17 20.5	10.8	59.6
S 11	346 14.5	45.3	10 40.4	7.5	17 09.7	10.9	59.7
D 12	1 14.7	N 2 44.3	25 06.9	7.5	N16 58.8	11.1	59.7
A 13	16 14.9	43.4	39 33.4	7.6	16 47.7	11.2	59.7
Y 14	31 15.1	42.4	54 00.0	7.6	16 36.5	11.3	59.8
15	46 15.3 ..	41.4	68 26.6	7.6	16 25.2	11.4	59.8
16	61 15.6	40.5	82 53.2	7.7	16 13.8	11.5	59.8
17	76 15.8	39.5	97 19.9	7.7	16 02.3	11.6	59.9
18	91 16.0	N 2 38.5	111 46.6	7.7	N15 50.7	11.8	59.9
19	106 16.2	37.6	126 13.3	7.7	15 38.9	11.8	59.9
20	121 16.5	36.6	140 40.0	7.8	15 27.1	12.0	60.0
21	136 16.7 ..	35.7	155 06.8	7.8	15 15.1	12.0	60.0
22	151 16.9	34.7	169 33.6	7.8	15 03.1	12.2	60.0
23	166 17.1	33.7	184 00.4	7.9	14 50.9	12.3	60.1
16 00	181 17.3	N 2 32.8	198 27.3	7.9	N14 38.6	12.4	60.1
01	196 17.6	31.8	212 54.2	7.9	14 26.2	12.5	60.1
02	211 17.8	30.8	227 21.1	8.0	14 13.7	12.6	60.1
03	226 18.0 ..	29.9	241 48.1	8.0	14 01.1	12.6	60.2
04	241 18.2	28.9	256 15.1	8.0	13 48.5	12.8	60.2
05	256 18.5	27.9	270 42.1	8.0	13 35.7	12.9	60.2
06	271 18.7	N 2 27.0	285 09.1	8.1	N13 22.8	13.0	60.3
W 07	286 18.9	26.0	299 36.2	8.1	13 09.8	13.0	60.3
E 08	301 19.1	25.0	314 03.3	8.2	12 56.8	13.2	60.3
D 09	316 19.3 ..	24.1	328 30.5	8.1	12 43.6	13.3	60.3
N 10	331 19.6	23.1	342 57.6	8.2	12 30.3	13.3	60.4
E 11	346 19.8	22.1	357 24.8	8.2	12 17.0	13.4	60.4
S 12	1 20.0	N 2 21.2	11 52.0	8.3	N12 03.6	13.5	60.4
D 13	16 20.2	20.2	26 19.3	8.3	11 50.1	13.6	60.4
A 14	31 20.5	19.2	40 46.6	8.3	11 36.5	13.7	60.5
Y 15	46 20.7 ..	18.3	55 13.9	8.3	11 22.8	13.8	60.5
16	61 20.9	17.3	69 41.2	8.4	11 09.0	13.8	60.5
17	76 21.1	16.3	84 08.6	8.4	10 55.2	13.9	60.5
18	91 21.4	N 2 15.4	98 36.0	8.4	N10 41.3	14.0	60.6
19	106 21.6	14.4	113 03.4	8.4	10 27.3	14.1	60.6
20	121 21.8	13.4	127 30.8	8.5	10 13.2	14.1	60.6
21	136 22.0 ..	12.5	141 58.3	8.5	9 59.1	14.2	60.6
22	151 22.2	11.5	156 25.8	8.5	9 44.9	14.3	60.6
23	166 22.5	10.5	170 53.3	8.6	9 30.6	14.3	60.7
17 00	181 22.7	N 2 09.6	185 20.9	8.6	N 9 16.3	14.5	60.7
01	196 22.9	08.6	199 48.5	8.6	9 01.8	14.4	60.7
02	211 23.1	07.6	214 16.1	8.6	8 47.4	14.6	60.7
03	226 23.4 ..	06.7	228 43.7	8.6	8 32.8	14.6	60.7
04	241 23.6	05.7	243 11.3	8.7	8 18.2	14.7	60.8
05	256 23.8	04.7	257 39.0	8.7	8 03.5	14.7	60.8
06	271 24.0	N 2 03.8	272 06.7	8.7	N 7 48.8	14.7	60.8
07	286 24.2	02.8	286 34.4	8.7	7 34.1	14.9	60.8
T 08	301 24.5	01.8	301 02.1	8.8	7 19.2	14.9	60.8
H 09	316 24.7	2 00.9	315 29.9	8.8	7 04.3	14.9	60.8
U 10	331 24.9	1 59.9	329 57.7	8.8	6 49.4	15.0	60.9
R 11	346 25.1	58.9	344 25.5	8.8	6 34.4	15.0	60.9
S 12	1 25.4	N 1 58.0	358 53.3	8.8	N 6 19.4	15.1	60.9
D 13	16 25.6	57.0	13 21.1	8.9	6 04.3	15.1	60.9
A 14	31 25.8	56.0	27 49.0	8.8	5 49.2	15.2	60.9
Y 15	46 26.0 ..	55.1	42 16.8	8.9	5 34.0	15.2	60.9
16	61 26.2	54.1	56 44.7	8.9	5 18.8	15.2	60.9
17	76 26.5	53.1	71 12.6	8.9	5 03.6	15.3	61.0
18	91 26.7	N 1 52.2	85 40.5	9.0	N 4 48.3	15.3	61.0
19	106 26.9	51.2	100 08.5	8.9	4 33.0	15.3	61.0
20	121 27.1	50.2	114 36.4	8.9	4 17.7	15.4	61.0
21	136 27.4 ..	49.3	129 04.3	9.0	4 02.3	15.4	61.0
22	151 27.6	48.3	143 32.3	9.0	3 46.9	15.4	61.0
23	166 27.8	47.3	158 00.3	9.0	N 3 31.5	15.5	61.0
	SD 15.9	d 1.0	SD 16.3		16.5		16.6

Twilight and Moonrise:

Lat.	Naut.	Civil	Sunrise	Moonrise 15	16	17	18
°	h m	h m	h m	h m	h m	h m	h m
N 72	02 19	04 02	05 13	▭	01 25	04 03	06 26
N 70	02 48	04 14	05 18	25 56	01 56	04 16	06 28
68	03 09	04 24	05 21	00 02	02 19	04 27	06 30
66	03 25	04 32	05 24	00 35	02 37	04 35	06 32
64	03 38	04 38	05 27	00 59	02 51	04 42	06 33
62	03 48	04 44	05 29	01 18	03 03	04 48	06 34
60	03 57	04 49	05 31	01 33	03 13	04 54	06 35
N 58	04 05	04 53	05 33	01 46	03 21	04 58	06 35
56	04 11	04 57	05 34	01 58	03 29	05 02	06 36
54	04 17	05 00	05 36	02 08	03 36	05 06	06 37
52	04 22	05 03	05 37	02 16	03 42	05 09	06 37
50	04 27	05 05	05 38	02 24	03 47	05 12	06 38
45	04 36	05 11	05 40	02 41	03 59	05 19	06 39
N 40	04 43	05 15	05 42	02 55	04 09	05 24	06 40
35	04 49	05 18	05 44	03 06	04 17	05 29	06 41
30	04 53	05 21	05 45	03 16	04 24	05 33	06 42
20	05 00	05 26	05 48	03 33	04 37	05 40	06 43
N 10	05 04	05 29	05 50	03 48	04 48	05 46	06 44
0	05 07	05 31	05 51	04 02	04 58	05 52	06 45
S 10	05 08	05 32	05 53	04 16	05 08	05 58	06 46
20	05 07	05 33	05 55	04 31	05 19	06 04	06 48
30	05 05	05 33	05 57	04 48	05 31	06 11	06 49
35	05 03	05 32	05 58	04 58	05 38	06 15	06 50
40	05 00	05 32	05 59	05 09	05 46	06 19	06 51
45	04 57	05 31	06 00	05 22	05 55	06 25	06 52
S 50	04 52	05 29	06 01	05 38	06 06	06 31	06 53
52	04 49	05 28	06 02	05 46	06 12	06 34	06 54
54	04 46	05 27	06 03	05 54	06 17	06 37	06 54
56	04 43	05 26	06 03	06 03	06 24	06 40	06 55
58	04 39	05 25	06 04	06 13	06 31	06 44	06 56
S 60	04 35	05 24	06 05	06 25	06 38	06 48	06 56

Twilight and Moonset:

Lat.	Sunset	Civil	Naut.	Moonset 15	16	17	18
°	h m	h m	h m	h m	h m	h m	h m
N 72	18 33	19 44	21 24	20 25	19 43	19 14	18 48
N 70	18 29	19 32	20 57	19 52	19 27	19 08	18 50
68	18 26	19 23	20 37	19 28	19 14	19 03	18 52
66	18 23	19 15	20 22	19 09	19 04	18 59	18 54
64	18 21	19 09	20 09	18 53	18 55	18 55	18 55
62	18 19	19 04	19 59	18 41	18 47	18 52	18 57
60	18 17	18 59	19 50	18 29	18 41	18 50	18 58
N 58	18 15	18 55	19 43	18 20	18 35	18 47	18 59
56	18 14	18 51	19 36	18 11	18 30	18 45	18 59
54	18 13	18 48	19 31	18 04	18 25	18 43	19 00
52	18 12	18 45	19 26	17 57	18 21	18 41	19 01
50	18 11	18 43	19 21	17 51	18 17	18 40	19 02
45	18 08	18 38	19 12	17 37	18 08	18 36	19 03
N 40	18 07	18 34	19 05	17 26	18 01	18 33	19 04
35	18 05	18 30	19 00	17 17	17 55	18 31	19 05
30	18 04	18 28	18 56	17 08	17 50	18 28	19 06
20	18 01	18 23	18 49	16 54	17 40	18 24	19 08
N 10	18 00	18 21	18 45	16 41	17 32	18 21	19 09
0	17 58	18 19	18 43	16 29	17 24	18 17	19 10
S 10	17 56	18 17	18 42	16 17	17 16	18 14	19 12
20	17 55	18 17	18 42	16 04	17 07	18 10	19 13
30	17 53	18 17	18 45	15 48	16 57	18 06	19 14
35	17 52	18 18	18 47	15 40	16 51	18 03	19 15
40	17 51	18 18	18 50	15 30	16 44	18 00	19 16
45	17 50	18 20	18 54	15 18	16 37	17 57	19 17
S 50	17 49	18 21	18 59	15 03	16 27	17 53	19 18
52	17 48	18 22	19 01	14 56	16 23	17 51	19 19
54	17 48	18 23	19 04	14 49	16 18	17 49	19 20
56	17 47	18 24	19 08	14 40	16 13	17 47	19 20
58	17 46	18 26	19 12	14 30	16 07	17 44	19 21
S 60	17 46	18 27	19 16	14 19	16 00	17 41	19 22

	SUN Eqn. of Time 00h	SUN 12h	SUN Mer. Pass.	MOON Mer. Pass. Upper	MOON Mer. Pass. Lower	Age	Phase
Day	m s	m s	h m	h m	h m	d	%
15	04 48	04 58	11 55	10 16	22 43	27	6
16	05 09	05 20	11 55	11 11	23 38	28	2
17	05 30	05 41	11 54	12 05	24 31	00	0

UT	ARIES	VENUS −4.2		MARS −2.3		JUPITER −2.4		SATURN +0.4		STARS		
	GHA	GHA	Dec	GHA	Dec	GHA	Dec	GHA	Dec	Name	SHA	Dec
d h	° ′	° ′	° ′	° ′	° ′	° ′	° ′	° ′	° ′		° ′	° ′
18 00	357 22.3	222 08.3	N16 19.7	330 12.0	N 6 47.1	68 24.3	S22 43.2	59 54.4	S21 20.8	Acamar	315 14.2	S40 13.2
01	12 24.7	237 07.9	19.1	345 14.8	47.1	83 26.7	43.2	74 56.9	20.8	Achernar	335 22.4	S57 07.8
02	27 27.2	252 07.5	18.5	0 17.5	47.0	98 29.1	43.2	89 59.4	20.8	Acrux	173 04.5	S63 12.7
03	42 29.7	267 07.1	.. 17.9	15 20.3	.. 47.0	113 31.5	.. 43.2	105 01.9	.. 20.8	Adhara	255 08.7	S28 59.8
04	57 32.1	282 06.7	17.3	30 23.1	46.9	128 33.9	43.2	120 04.4	20.9	Aldebaran	290 43.5	N16 33.0
05	72 34.6	297 06.3	16.6	45 25.8	46.8	143 36.4	43.2	135 07.0	20.9			
06	87 37.1	312 05.9	N16 16.0	60 28.6	N 6 46.8	158 38.8	S22 43.2	150 09.5	S21 20.9	Alioth	166 16.7	N55 51.1
07	102 39.5	327 05.5	15.4	75 31.4	46.7	173 41.2	43.2	165 12.0	20.9	Alkaid	152 55.3	N49 12.9
08	117 42.0	342 05.1	14.8	90 34.2	46.7	188 43.6	43.1	180 14.5	20.9	Alnair	27 36.9	S46 51.7
F 09	132 44.5	357 04.7	.. 14.1	105 36.9	.. 46.6	203 46.0	.. 43.1	195 17.0	.. 20.9	Alnilam	275 41.3	S 1 11.3
R 10	147 46.9	12 04.3	13.5	120 39.7	46.5	218 48.5	43.1	210 19.5	20.9	Alphard	217 51.4	S 8 44.7
I 11	162 49.4	27 03.9	12.9	135 42.5	46.5	233 50.9	43.1	225 22.0	20.9			
D 12	177 51.9	42 03.5	N16 12.2	150 45.3	N 6 46.4	248 53.3	S22 43.1	240 24.5	S21 20.9	Alphecca	126 06.9	N26 39.0
A 13	192 54.3	57 03.1	11.6	165 48.0	46.4	263 55.7	43.1	255 27.0	20.9	Alpheratz	357 38.0	N29 12.3
Y 14	207 56.8	72 02.6	11.0	180 50.8	46.3	278 58.1	43.1	270 29.5	21.0	Altair	62 03.2	N 8 55.6
15	222 59.2	87 02.2	.. 10.3	195 53.6	.. 46.2	294 00.5	.. 43.1	285 32.1	.. 21.0	Ankaa	353 10.2	S42 11.6
16	238 01.7	102 01.8	09.7	210 56.4	46.2	309 02.9	43.1	300 34.6	21.0	Antares	112 20.2	S26 28.6
17	253 04.2	117 01.4	09.1	225 59.2	46.1	324 05.4	43.1	315 37.1	21.0			
18	268 06.6	132 01.0	N16 08.4	241 01.9	N 6 46.0	339 07.8	S22 43.1	330 39.6	S21 21.0	Arcturus	145 51.4	N19 04.8
19	283 09.1	147 00.6	07.8	256 04.7	46.0	354 10.2	43.1	345 42.1	21.0	Atria	107 17.7	S69 04.0
20	298 11.6	162 00.2	07.2	271 07.5	45.9	9 12.6	43.1	0 44.6	21.0	Avior	234 16.5	S59 34.2
21	313 14.0	176 59.8	.. 06.5	286 10.3	.. 45.8	24 15.0	.. 43.1	15 47.1	.. 21.0	Bellatrix	278 26.6	N 6 22.1
22	328 16.5	191 59.4	05.9	301 13.1	45.8	39 17.4	43.1	30 49.6	21.0	Betelgeuse	270 55.9	N 7 24.7
23	343 19.0	206 59.0	05.2	316 15.9	45.7	54 19.8	43.1	45 52.1	21.0			
19 00	358 21.4	221 58.6	N16 04.6	331 18.7	N 6 45.6	69 22.3	S22 43.1	60 54.6	S21 21.1	Canopus	263 54.0	S52 42.1
01	13 23.9	236 58.2	04.0	346 21.5	45.6	84 24.7	43.1	75 57.1	21.1	Capella	280 27.0	N46 00.9
02	28 26.4	251 57.8	03.3	1 24.3	45.5	99 27.1	43.1	90 59.6	21.1	Deneb	49 27.8	N45 21.5
03	43 28.8	266 57.4	.. 02.7	16 27.1	.. 45.4	114 29.5	.. 43.1	106 02.2	.. 21.1	Denebola	182 28.9	N14 27.6
04	58 31.3	281 57.0	02.0	31 29.9	45.4	129 31.9	43.1	121 04.7	21.1	Diphda	348 50.5	S17 52.3
05	73 33.7	296 56.6	01.4	46 32.7	45.3	144 34.3	43.1	136 07.2	21.1			
06	88 36.2	311 56.2	N16 00.7	61 35.5	N 6 45.2	159 36.7	S22 43.1	151 09.7	S21 21.1	Dubhe	193 46.1	N61 38.5
07	103 38.7	326 55.8	16 00.1	76 38.3	45.2	174 39.1	43.0	166 12.2	21.1	Elnath	278 06.2	N28 37.4
08	118 41.1	341 55.4	15 59.4	91 41.1	45.1	189 41.5	43.0	181 14.7	21.1	Eltanin	90 43.8	N51 29.5
S 09	133 43.6	356 55.0	.. 58.8	106 43.9	.. 45.0	204 44.0	.. 43.0	196 17.2	.. 21.1	Enif	33 41.9	N 9 58.3
A 10	148 46.1	11 54.6	58.2	121 46.7	45.0	219 46.4	43.0	211 19.7	21.2	Fomalhaut	15 18.1	S29 30.8
T 11	163 48.5	26 54.2	57.5	136 49.5	44.9	234 48.8	43.0	226 22.2	21.2			
U 12	178 51.0	41 53.8	N15 56.9	151 52.3	N 6 44.8	249 51.2	S22 43.0	241 24.7	S21 21.2	Gacrux	171 56.0	S57 13.6
R 13	193 53.5	56 53.4	56.2	166 55.1	44.7	264 53.6	43.0	256 27.2	21.2	Gienah	175 47.5	S17 39.2
D 14	208 55.9	71 52.9	55.6	181 58.0	44.7	279 56.0	43.0	271 29.7	21.2	Hadar	148 41.4	S60 28.3
A 15	223 58.4	86 52.5	.. 54.9	197 00.8	.. 44.6	294 58.4	.. 43.0	286 32.2	.. 21.2	Hamal	327 54.8	N23 33.5
Y 16	239 00.8	101 52.1	54.2	212 03.6	44.5	310 00.8	43.0	301 34.7	21.2	Kaus Aust.	83 37.1	S34 22.5
17	254 03.3	116 51.7	53.6	227 06.4	44.5	325 03.2	43.0	316 37.2	21.2			
18	269 05.8	131 51.3	N15 52.9	242 09.2	N 6 44.4	340 05.6	S22 43.0	331 39.7	S21 21.2	Kochab	137 20.7	N74 04.6
19	284 08.2	146 50.9	52.3	257 12.1	44.3	355 08.0	43.0	346 42.2	21.2	Markab	13 33.0	N15 19.1
20	299 10.7	161 50.5	51.6	272 14.9	44.2	10 10.4	43.0	1 44.7	21.2	Menkar	314 09.6	N 4 10.2
21	314 13.2	176 50.1	.. 51.0	287 17.7	.. 44.2	25 12.8	.. 43.0	16 47.3	.. 21.3	Menkent	148 02.0	S36 28.2
22	329 15.6	191 49.7	50.3	302 20.5	44.1	40 15.2	43.0	31 49.8	21.3	Miaplacidus	221 39.5	S69 47.8
23	344 18.1	206 49.3	49.6	317 23.3	44.0	55 17.6	43.0	46 52.3	21.3			
20 00	359 20.6	221 48.9	N15 49.0	332 26.2	N 6 43.9	70 20.0	S22 43.0	61 54.8	S21 21.3	Mirfak	308 32.9	N49 55.8
01	14 23.0	236 48.5	48.3	347 29.0	43.9	85 22.4	43.0	76 57.3	21.3	Nunki	75 52.0	S26 16.2
02	29 25.5	251 48.1	47.7	2 31.8	43.8	100 24.8	43.0	91 59.8	21.3	Peacock	53 10.9	S56 40.2
03	44 28.0	266 47.7	.. 47.0	17 34.7	.. 43.7	115 27.2	.. 42.9	107 02.3	.. 21.3	Pollux	243 21.8	N27 58.5
04	59 30.4	281 47.3	46.3	32 37.5	43.6	130 29.7	42.9	122 04.8	21.3	Procyon	244 54.6	N 5 10.4
05	74 32.9	296 46.9	45.7	47 40.3	43.6	145 32.1	42.9	137 07.3	21.3			
06	89 35.3	311 46.5	N15 45.0	62 43.2	N 6 43.5	160 34.5	S22 42.9	152 09.8	S21 21.3	Rasalhague	96 01.8	N12 33.0
07	104 37.8	326 46.1	44.3	77 46.0	43.4	175 36.9	42.9	167 12.3	21.3	Regulus	207 38.5	N11 52.1
08	119 40.3	341 45.7	43.7	92 48.9	43.3	190 39.3	42.9	182 14.8	21.4	Rigel	281 07.2	S 8 10.6
S 09	134 42.7	356 45.3	.. 43.0	107 51.7	.. 43.3	205 41.7	.. 42.9	197 17.3	.. 21.4	Rigil Kent.	139 45.5	S60 55.2
U 10	149 45.2	11 44.9	42.3	122 54.5	43.2	220 44.1	42.9	212 19.8	21.4	Sabik	102 06.8	S15 44.9
N 11	164 47.7	26 44.5	41.7	137 57.4	43.1	235 46.5	42.9	227 22.3	21.4			
D 12	179 50.1	41 44.1	N15 41.0	153 00.2	N 6 43.0	250 48.9	S22 42.9	242 24.8	S21 21.4	Schedar	349 34.3	N56 38.9
A 13	194 52.6	56 43.7	40.3	168 03.1	42.9	265 51.3	42.9	257 27.3	21.4	Shaula	96 15.1	S37 07.1
Y 14	209 55.1	71 43.3	39.7	183 05.9	42.9	280 53.7	42.9	272 29.8	21.4	Sirius	258 29.4	S16 44.5
15	224 57.5	86 42.9	.. 39.0	198 08.8	.. 42.8	295 56.1	.. 42.9	287 32.3	.. 21.4	Spica	158 26.3	S11 15.9
16	240 00.0	101 42.5	38.3	213 11.6	42.7	310 58.4	42.9	302 34.8	21.4	Suhail	222 49.1	S43 30.7
17	255 02.4	116 42.1	37.7	228 14.5	42.6	326 00.8	42.9	317 37.3	21.4			
18	270 04.9	131 41.7	N15 37.0	243 17.3	N 6 42.5	341 03.2	S22 42.9	332 39.8	S21 21.4	Vega	80 35.5	N38 48.5
19	285 07.4	146 41.3	36.3	258 20.2	42.5	356 05.6	42.8	347 42.3	21.5	Zuben'ubi	137 00.1	S16 07.5
20	300 09.8	161 40.9	35.6	273 23.0	42.4	11 08.0	42.8	2 44.8	21.5		SHA	Mer. Pass.
21	315 12.3	176 40.5	.. 35.0	288 25.9	.. 42.3	26 10.4	.. 42.8	17 47.3	.. 21.5		° ′	h m
22	330 14.8	191 40.0	34.3	303 28.7	42.2	41 12.8	42.8	32 49.8	21.5	Venus	223 37.2	9 12
23	345 17.2	206 39.6	33.6	318 31.6	42.1	56 15.2	42.8	47 52.3	21.5	Mars	332 57.3	1 54
	h m									Jupiter	71 00.8	19 19
Mer. Pass. 0 06.6		v −0.4	d 0.7	v 2.8	d 0.1	v 2.4	d 0.0	v 2.5	d 0.0	Saturn	62 33.2	19 53

UT	SUN GHA	SUN Dec	MOON GHA	v	MOON Dec	d	HP
d h	° ′	° ′	° ′	′	° ′	′	′
18 00	181 28.0	N 1 46.4	172 28.3	9.0	N 3 16.0	15.5	61.0
01	196 28.2	45.4	186 56.3	9.0	3 00.5	15.5	61.0
02	211 28.5	44.4	201 24.3	9.0	2 45.0	15.5	61.0
03	226 28.7	.. 43.5	215 52.3	9.0	2 29.5	15.5	61.0
04	241 28.9	42.5	230 20.3	9.1	2 14.0	15.6	61.0
05	256 29.1	41.5	244 48.4	9.0	1 58.4	15.6	61.0
06	271 29.4	N 1 40.5	259 16.4	9.1	N 1 42.8	15.5	61.0
07	286 29.6	39.6	273 44.5	9.0	1 27.3	15.6	61.1
08	301 29.8	38.6	288 12.5	9.1	1 11.7	15.6	61.1
F 09	316 30.0	.. 37.6	302 40.6	9.0	0 56.1	15.6	61.1
R 10	331 30.2	36.7	317 08.6	9.1	0 40.5	15.6	61.1
I 11	346 30.5	35.7	331 36.7	9.0	0 24.9	15.7	61.1
D 12	1 30.7	N 1 34.7	346 04.7	9.1	N 0 09.2	15.6	61.1
A 13	16 30.9	33.8	0 32.8	9.1	S 0 06.4	15.6	61.1
Y 14	31 31.1	32.8	15 00.9	9.0	0 22.0	15.6	61.1
15	46 31.4	.. 31.8	29 28.9	9.1	0 37.6	15.6	61.1
16	61 31.6	30.9	43 57.0	9.0	0 53.2	15.6	61.1
17	76 31.8	29.9	58 25.1	9.0	1 08.8	15.6	61.1
18	91 32.0	N 1 28.9	72 53.1	9.1	S 1 24.4	15.6	61.1
19	106 32.2	27.9	87 21.2	9.0	1 40.0	15.6	61.1
20	121 32.5	27.0	101 49.2	9.1	1 55.6	15.5	61.1
21	136 32.7	.. 26.0	116 17.3	9.0	2 11.1	15.6	61.1
22	151 32.9	25.0	130 45.3	9.0	2 26.7	15.5	61.0
23	166 33.1	24.1	145 13.3	9.1	2 42.2	15.5	61.0
19 00	181 33.4	N 1 23.1	159 41.4	9.0	S 2 57.7	15.5	61.0
01	196 33.6	22.1	174 09.4	9.0	3 13.2	15.5	61.0
02	211 33.8	21.2	188 37.4	9.0	3 28.7	15.4	61.0
03	226 34.0	.. 20.2	203 05.4	9.0	3 44.1	15.4	61.0
04	241 34.2	19.2	217 33.4	8.9	3 59.5	15.4	61.0
05	256 34.5	18.2	232 01.3	9.0	4 14.9	15.4	61.0
06	271 34.7	N 1 17.3	246 29.3	9.0	S 4 30.3	15.3	61.0
07	286 34.9	16.3	260 57.3	8.9	4 45.6	15.3	61.0
S 08	301 35.1	15.3	275 25.2	8.9	5 00.9	15.2	61.0
A 09	316 35.3	.. 14.4	289 53.1	8.9	5 16.1	15.2	61.0
T 10	331 35.6	13.4	304 21.0	8.9	5 31.3	15.2	61.0
U 11	346 35.8	12.4	318 48.9	8.9	5 46.5	15.2	60.9
R 12	1 36.0	N 1 11.5	333 16.8	8.9	S 6 01.7	15.1	60.9
D 13	16 36.2	10.5	347 44.7	8.8	6 16.8	15.0	60.9
A 14	31 36.5	09.5	2 12.5	8.8	6 31.8	15.0	60.9
Y 15	46 36.7	.. 08.5	16 40.3	8.8	6 46.8	15.0	60.9
16	61 36.9	07.6	31 08.1	8.8	7 01.8	14.9	60.9
17	76 37.1	06.6	45 35.9	8.8	7 16.7	14.8	60.9
18	91 37.3	N 1 05.6	60 03.7	8.7	S 7 31.5	14.8	60.9
19	106 37.6	04.7	74 31.4	8.7	7 46.3	14.8	60.8
20	121 37.8	03.7	88 59.1	8.7	8 01.1	14.7	60.8
21	136 38.0	.. 02.7	103 26.8	8.7	8 15.8	14.6	60.8
22	151 38.2	01.7	117 54.5	8.7	8 30.4	14.6	60.8
23	166 38.5	1 00.8	132 22.2	8.6	8 45.0	14.5	60.8
20 00	181 38.7	N 0 59.8	146 49.8	8.6	S 8 59.5	14.5	60.8
01	196 38.9	58.8	161 17.4	8.6	9 14.0	14.3	60.7
02	211 39.1	57.9	175 45.0	8.5	9 28.3	14.4	60.7
03	226 39.3	.. 56.9	190 12.5	8.5	9 42.7	14.2	60.7
04	241 39.6	55.9	204 40.0	8.5	9 56.9	14.2	60.7
05	256 39.8	55.0	219 07.5	8.5	10 11.1	14.1	60.7
06	271 40.0	N 0 54.0	233 35.0	8.4	S10 25.2	14.0	60.7
07	286 40.2	53.0	248 02.4	8.5	10 39.2	14.0	60.6
08	301 40.4	52.0	262 29.9	8.3	10 53.2	13.9	60.6
S 09	316 40.7	.. 51.1	276 57.2	8.4	11 07.1	13.8	60.6
U 10	331 40.9	50.1	291 24.6	8.3	11 20.9	13.7	60.6
N 11	346 41.1	49.1	305 51.9	8.3	11 34.6	13.7	60.6
D 12	1 41.3	N 0 48.1	320 19.2	8.3	S11 48.3	13.5	60.5
A 13	16 41.6	47.2	334 46.5	8.2	12 01.8	13.5	60.5
Y 14	31 41.8	46.2	349 13.7	8.2	12 15.3	13.4	60.5
15	46 42.0	.. 45.2	3 40.9	8.2	12 28.7	13.3	60.5
16	61 42.2	44.3	18 08.1	8.1	12 42.0	13.3	60.4
17	76 42.4	43.3	32 35.2	8.1	12 55.3	13.1	60.4
18	91 42.7	N 0 42.3	47 02.3	8.1	S13 08.4	13.0	60.4
19	106 42.9	41.3	61 29.4	8.1	13 21.4	13.0	60.4
20	121 43.1	40.4	75 56.5	8.0	13 34.4	12.8	60.4
21	136 43.3	.. 39.4	90 23.5	7.9	13 47.2	12.8	60.3
22	151 43.5	38.4	104 50.4	8.0	14 00.0	12.6	60.3
23	166 43.8	37.5	119 17.4	7.9	S14 12.6	12.6	60.3
	SD 15.9	d 1.0	SD 16.6		16.6		16.5

Twilight / Sunrise / Moonrise

Lat.	Naut.	Civil	Sunrise	18	19	20	21
°	h m	h m	h m	h m	h m	h m	h m
N 72	02 41	04 17	05 27	06 26	08 48	11 17	14 38
N 70	03 05	04 27	05 30	06 28	08 40	10 56	13 29
68	03 23	04 35	05 32	06 30	08 33	10 39	12 52
66	03 37	04 42	05 34	06 32	08 28	10 25	12 27
64	03 48	04 47	05 35	06 33	08 23	10 14	12 07
62	03 57	04 52	05 37	06 34	08 19	10 05	11 51
60	04 05	04 56	05 38	06 35	08 16	09 57	11 38
N 58	04 12	05 00	05 39	06 35	08 13	09 50	11 27
56	04 18	05 03	05 40	06 36	08 10	09 44	11 17
54	04 23	05 05	05 41	06 37	08 08	09 38	11 08
52	04 28	05 08	05 42	06 37	08 06	09 34	11 00
50	04 32	05 10	05 42	06 38	08 04	09 29	10 54
45	04 40	05 14	05 44	06 39	07 59	09 20	10 39
N 40	04 46	05 18	05 45	06 40	07 56	09 12	10 27
35	04 51	05 21	05 46	06 41	07 53	09 05	10 16
30	04 55	05 23	05 47	06 42	07 50	08 59	10 08
20	05 01	05 26	05 48	06 43	07 46	08 49	09 52
N 10	05 04	05 28	05 49	06 44	07 42	08 40	09 39
0	05 06	05 30	05 50	06 45	07 38	08 32	09 27
S 10	05 06	05 30	05 51	06 46	07 35	08 24	09 14
20	05 05	05 30	05 52	06 48	07 31	08 15	09 01
30	05 01	05 29	05 53	06 49	07 27	08 05	08 47
35	04 59	05 28	05 53	06 50	07 24	08 00	08 38
40	04 55	05 27	05 54	06 51	07 22	07 54	08 29
45	04 51	05 25	05 54	06 52	07 18	07 46	08 17
S 50	04 45	05 23	05 55	06 53	07 15	07 38	08 04
52	04 42	05 21	05 55	06 54	07 13	07 34	07 58
54	04 38	05 20	05 55	06 54	07 11	07 29	07 51
56	04 35	05 18	05 55	06 55	07 09	07 25	07 43
58	04 30	05 17	05 56	06 56	07 07	07 19	07 34
S 60	04 25	05 15	05 56	06 56	07 04	07 13	07 25

Sunset / Twilight / Moonset

Lat.	Sunset	Civil	Naut.	18	19	20	21
°	h m	h m	h m	h m	h m	h m	h m
N 72	18 18	19 27	21 01	18 48	18 21	17 45	16 21
N 70	18 15	19 17	20 38	18 50	18 32	18 10	17 32
68	18 13	19 09	20 21	18 52	18 41	18 28	18 10
66	18 12	19 03	20 08	18 54	18 49	18 43	18 37
64	18 10	18 58	19 57	18 55	18 55	18 56	18 58
62	18 09	18 53	19 48	18 57	19 01	19 06	19 14
60	18 08	18 49	19 40	18 58	19 06	19 16	19 29
N 58	18 07	18 46	19 33	18 59	19 10	19 24	19 41
56	18 06	18 43	19 28	18 59	19 14	19 31	19 51
54	18 05	18 41	19 23	19 00	19 18	19 37	20 01
52	18 05	18 38	19 18	19 01	19 21	19 43	20 09
50	18 04	18 36	19 14	19 02	19 24	19 48	20 16
45	18 03	18 32	19 06	19 03	19 30	19 59	20 33
N 40	18 02	18 29	19 00	19 04	19 35	20 09	20 46
35	18 01	18 26	18 55	19 05	19 40	20 17	20 57
30	18 00	18 24	18 52	19 06	19 44	20 24	21 07
20	17 59	18 21	18 46	19 08	19 51	20 36	21 24
N 10	17 58	18 19	18 43	19 09	19 58	20 47	21 39
0	17 57	18 18	18 42	19 10	20 03	20 58	21 53
S 10	17 56	18 17	18 41	19 12	20 09	21 08	22 07
20	17 55	18 17	18 43	19 13	20 16	21 19	22 22
30	17 55	18 19	18 47	19 14	20 23	21 32	22 40
35	17 55	18 20	18 49	19 15	20 27	21 39	22 50
40	17 54	18 21	18 53	19 16	20 32	21 47	23 02
45	17 54	18 23	18 57	19 17	20 37	21 57	23 15
S 50	17 53	18 26	19 04	19 18	20 44	22 09	23 32
52	17 53	18 27	19 07	19 19	20 47	22 15	23 40
54	17 53	18 28	19 10	19 20	20 51	22 21	23 49
56	17 53	18 30	19 14	19 20	20 55	22 28	23 59
58	17 53	18 32	19 19	19 21	20 59	22 36	24 11
S 60	17 53	18 34	19 24	19 22	21 03	22 44	24 24

SUN / MOON

Day	Eqn. of Time 00h	Eqn. of Time 12h	Mer. Pass.	Mer. Pass. Upper	Mer. Pass. Lower	Age	Phase
d	m s	m s	h m	h m	h m	d	%
18	05 52	06 02	11 54	12 58	00 31	01	2
19	06 13	06 24	11 54	13 51	01 24	02	6
20	06 34	06 45	11 53	14 45	02 18	03	13

UT	ARIES	VENUS −4.1		MARS −2.3		JUPITER −2.4		SATURN +0.4		STARS		
d h	GHA	GHA	Dec	GHA	Dec	GHA	Dec	GHA	Dec	Name	SHA	Dec
21 00	0 19.7	221 39.2	N15 32.9	333 34.5	N 6 42.0	71 17.6	S22 42.8	62 54.8	S21 21.5	Acamar	315 14.2	S40 13.2
01	15 22.2	236 38.8	32.2	348 37.3	42.0	86 20.0	42.8	77 57.3	21.5	Achernar	335 22.4	S57 07.8
02	30 24.6	251 38.4	31.6	3 40.2	41.9	101 22.4	42.8	92 59.8	21.5	Acrux	173 04.5	S63 12.7
03	45 27.1	266 38.0 ..	30.9	18 43.1 ..	41.8	116 24.8 ..	42.8	108 02.3 ..	21.5	Adhara	255 08.7	S28 59.8
04	60 29.6	281 37.6	30.2	33 45.9	41.7	131 27.2	42.8	123 04.8	21.5	Aldebaran	290 43.5	N16 33.0
05	75 32.0	296 37.2	29.5	48 48.8	41.6	146 29.6	42.8	138 07.3	21.5			
M 06	90 34.5	311 36.8	N15 28.8	63 51.7	N 6 41.5	161 32.0	S22 42.8	153 09.8	S21 21.6	Alioth	166 16.7	N55 51.1
O 07	105 36.9	326 36.4	28.1	78 54.5	41.5	176 34.4	42.8	168 12.3	21.6	Alkaid	152 55.3	N49 12.9
N 08	120 39.4	341 36.0	27.5	93 57.4	41.4	191 36.8	42.8	183 14.8	21.6	Alnair	27 37.0	S46 51.7
D 09	135 41.9	356 35.6 ..	26.8	109 00.3 ..	41.3	206 39.2 ..	42.8	198 17.3 ..	21.6	Alnilam	275 41.2	S 1 11.3
A 10	150 44.3	11 35.2	26.1	124 03.2	41.2	221 41.5	42.7	213 19.8	21.6	Alphard	217 51.4	S 8 44.7
Y 11	165 46.8	26 34.8	25.4	139 06.0	41.1	236 43.9	42.7	228 22.3	21.6			
12	180 49.3	41 34.4	N15 24.7	154 08.9	N 6 41.0	251 46.3	S22 42.7	243 24.8	S21 21.6	Alphecca	126 06.9	N26 39.0
13	195 51.7	56 34.0	24.0	169 11.8	40.9	266 48.7	42.7	258 27.3	21.6	Alpheratz	357 38.0	N29 12.3
14	210 54.2	71 33.6	23.3	184 14.7	40.9	281 51.1	42.7	273 29.8	21.6	Altair	62 03.2	N 8 55.6
15	225 56.7	86 33.2 ..	22.6	199 17.6 ..	40.8	296 53.5 ..	42.7	288 32.3 ..	21.6	Ankaa	353 10.2	S42 11.6
16	240 59.1	101 32.8	21.9	214 20.4	40.7	311 55.9	42.7	303 34.8	21.6	Antares	112 20.2	S26 28.6
17	256 01.6	116 32.4	21.3	229 23.3	40.6	326 58.3	42.7	318 37.3	21.6			
18	271 04.1	131 32.0	N15 20.6	244 26.2	N 6 40.5	342 00.7	S22 42.7	333 39.8	S21 21.6	Arcturus	145 51.4	N19 04.8
19	286 06.5	146 31.6	19.9	259 29.1	40.4	357 03.1	42.7	348 42.3	21.6	Atria	107 17.7	S69 04.0
20	301 09.0	161 31.2	19.2	274 32.0	40.3	12 05.4	42.7	3 44.7	21.7	Avior	234 16.4	S59 34.2
21	316 11.4	176 30.8 ..	18.5	289 34.9 ..	40.2	27 07.8 ..	42.7	18 47.2 ..	21.7	Bellatrix	278 26.6	N 6 22.1
22	331 13.9	191 30.4	17.8	304 37.8	40.1	42 10.2	42.7	33 49.7	21.7	Betelgeuse	270 55.9	N 7 24.7
23	346 16.4	206 30.0	17.1	319 40.7	40.1	57 12.6	42.6	48 52.2	21.7			
22 00	1 18.8	221 29.6	N15 16.4	334 43.6	N 6 40.0	72 15.0	S22 42.6	63 54.7	S21 21.7	Canopus	263 54.0	S52 42.1
01	16 21.3	236 29.2	15.7	349 46.4	39.9	87 17.4	42.6	78 57.2	21.7	Capella	280 26.9	N46 00.9
02	31 23.8	251 28.8	15.0	4 49.3	39.8	102 19.8	42.6	93 59.7	21.7	Deneb	49 27.8	N45 21.5
03	46 26.2	266 28.4 ..	14.3	19 52.2 ..	39.7	117 22.1 ..	42.6	109 02.2 ..	21.7	Denebola	182 28.9	N14 27.6
04	61 28.7	281 28.0	13.6	34 55.1	39.6	132 24.5	42.6	124 04.7	21.7	Diphda	348 50.5	S17 52.4
05	76 31.2	296 27.6	12.9	49 58.0	39.5	147 26.9	42.6	139 07.2	21.7			
T 06	91 33.6	311 27.2	N15 12.2	65 00.9	N 6 39.4	162 29.3	S22 42.6	154 09.7	S21 21.7	Dubhe	193 46.1	N61 38.4
U 07	106 36.1	326 26.8	11.5	80 03.8	39.3	177 31.7	42.6	169 12.2	21.7	Elnath	278 06.2	N28 37.4
E 08	121 38.5	341 26.4	10.8	95 06.7	39.2	192 34.1	42.6	184 14.7	21.7	Eltanin	90 43.8	N51 29.5
S 09	136 41.0	356 26.0 ..	10.1	110 09.7 ..	39.1	207 36.5 ..	42.6	199 17.2 ..	21.8	Enif	33 41.9	N 9 58.3
D 10	151 43.5	11 25.6	09.4	125 12.6	39.0	222 38.8	42.6	214 19.7	21.8	Fomalhaut	15 18.1	S29 30.8
A 11	166 45.9	26 25.2	08.7	140 15.5	39.0	237 41.2	42.6	229 22.2	21.8			
Y 12	181 48.4	41 24.8	N15 08.0	155 18.4	N 6 38.9	252 43.6	S22 42.5	244 24.7	S21 21.8	Gacrux	171 56.0	S57 13.6
13	196 50.9	56 24.4	07.2	170 21.3	38.8	267 46.0	42.5	259 27.1	21.8	Gienah	175 47.5	S17 39.2
14	211 53.3	71 24.0	06.5	185 24.2	38.7	282 48.4	42.5	274 29.6	21.8	Hadar	148 41.4	S60 28.3
15	226 55.8	86 23.6 ..	05.8	200 27.1 ..	38.6	297 50.7 ..	42.5	289 32.1 ..	21.8	Hamal	327 54.8	N23 33.5
16	241 58.3	101 23.2	05.1	215 30.0	38.5	312 53.1	42.5	304 34.6	21.8	Kaus Aust.	83 37.1	S34 22.5
17	257 00.7	116 22.8	04.4	230 32.9	38.4	327 55.5	42.5	319 37.1	21.8			
18	272 03.2	131 22.4	N15 03.7	245 35.9	N 6 38.3	342 57.9	S22 42.5	334 39.6	S21 21.8	Kochab	137 20.8	N74 04.5
19	287 05.7	146 22.0	03.0	260 38.8	38.2	358 00.3	42.5	349 42.1	21.8	Markab	13 33.0	N15 19.1
20	302 08.1	161 21.6	02.3	275 41.7	38.1	13 02.6	42.5	4 44.6	21.8	Menkar	314 09.6	N 4 10.2
21	317 10.6	176 21.2 ..	01.6	290 44.6 ..	38.0	28 05.0 ..	42.5	19 47.1 ..	21.8	Menkent	148 02.0	S36 28.2
22	332 13.0	191 20.8	00.8	305 47.5	37.9	43 07.4	42.5	34 49.6	21.8	Miaplacidus	221 39.5	S69 47.8
23	347 15.5	206 20.4	15 00.1	320 50.5	37.8	58 09.8	42.4	49 52.1	21.9			
23 00	2 18.0	221 20.0	N14 59.4	335 53.4	N 6 37.7	73 12.2	S22 42.4	64 54.6	S21 21.9	Mirfak	308 32.9	N49 55.8
01	17 20.4	236 19.6	58.7	350 56.3	37.6	88 14.5	42.4	79 57.0	21.9	Nunki	75 52.0	S26 16.2
02	32 22.9	251 19.2	58.0	5 59.3	37.5	103 16.9	42.4	94 59.5	21.9	Peacock	53 10.9	S56 40.2
03	47 25.4	266 18.8 ..	57.3	21 02.2 ..	37.4	118 19.3 ..	42.4	110 02.0 ..	21.9	Pollux	243 21.7	N27 58.5
04	62 27.8	281 18.4	56.5	36 05.1	37.3	133 21.7	42.4	125 04.5	21.9	Procyon	244 54.6	N 5 10.4
05	77 30.3	296 18.0	55.8	51 08.0	37.2	148 24.0	42.4	140 07.0	21.9			
W 06	92 32.8	311 17.6	N14 55.1	66 11.0	N 6 37.1	163 26.4	S22 42.4	155 09.5	S21 21.9	Rasalhague	96 01.8	N12 33.0
E 07	107 35.2	326 17.2	54.4	81 13.9	37.0	178 28.8	42.4	170 12.0	21.9	Regulus	207 38.4	N11 52.1
D 08	122 37.7	341 16.8	53.7	96 16.8	36.9	193 31.2	42.4	185 14.5	21.9	Rigel	281 07.2	S 8 10.6
N 09	137 40.2	356 16.4 ..	52.9	111 19.8 ..	36.8	208 33.5 ..	42.4	200 17.0 ..	21.9	Rigil Kent.	139 45.5	S60 55.2
E 10	152 42.6	11 16.0	52.2	126 22.7	36.7	223 35.9	42.4	215 19.5	21.9	Sabik	102 06.8	S15 44.9
S 11	167 45.1	26 15.6	51.5	141 25.7	36.6	238 38.3	42.3	230 21.9	21.9			
D 12	182 47.5	41 15.2	N14 50.8	156 28.6	N 6 36.5	253 40.7	S22 42.3	245 24.4	S21 21.9	Schedar	349 34.3	N56 39.0
A 13	197 50.0	56 14.8	50.0	171 31.5	36.4	268 43.0	42.3	260 26.9	21.9	Shaula	96 15.1	S37 07.1
Y 14	212 52.5	71 14.4	49.3	186 34.5	36.3	283 45.4	42.3	275 29.4	22.0	Sirius	258 29.4	S16 44.5
15	227 54.9	86 14.0 ..	48.6	201 37.4 ..	36.2	298 47.8 ..	42.3	290 31.9 ..	22.0	Spica	158 26.3	S11 15.9
16	242 57.4	101 13.6	47.8	216 40.4	36.1	313 50.2	42.3	305 34.4	22.0	Suhail	222 49.1	S43 30.7
17	257 59.9	116 13.2	47.1	231 43.3	36.0	328 52.5	42.3	320 36.9	22.0			
18	273 02.3	131 12.8	N14 46.4	246 46.3	N 6 35.9	343 54.9	S22 42.3	335 39.4	S21 22.0	Vega	80 35.5	N38 48.5
19	288 04.8	146 12.4	45.7	261 49.2	35.8	358 57.3	42.3	350 41.8	22.0	Zuben'ubi	137 00.1	S16 07.5
20	303 07.3	161 12.0	44.9	276 52.2	35.7	13 59.6	42.3	5 44.3	22.0		SHA	Mer. Pass.
21	318 09.7	176 11.6 ..	44.2	291 55.1 ..	35.6	29 02.0 ..	42.2	20 46.8 ..	22.0	Venus	220 10.8	9 14
22	333 12.2	191 11.2	43.5	306 58.1	35.5	44 04.4	42.2	35 49.3	22.0	Mars	333 24.7	1 41
23	348 14.7	206 10.9	42.7	322 01.0	35.4	59 06.7	42.2	50 51.8	22.0	Jupiter	70 56.2	19 08
Mer. Pass. 23 50.8		v −0.4	d 0.7	v 2.9	d 0.1	v 2.4	d 0.0	v 2.5	d 0.0	Saturn	62 35.9	19 41

UT	SUN		MOON					Lat.	Twilight		Sunrise	Moonrise			
									Naut.	Civil		21	22	23	24
	GHA	Dec	GHA	v	Dec	d	HP								
d h	° ′	° ′	° ′	′	° ′	′	′	°	h m	h m	h m	h m	h m	h m	h m
21 00	181 44.0	N 0 36.5	133 44.3	7.9	S14 25.2	12.5	60.3	N 72	03 01	04 32	05 40	14 38	▬▬	▬▬	▬▬
01	196 44.2	35.5	148 11.2	7.8	14 37.7	12.3	60.2	N 70	03 21	04 40	05 41	13 29	▬▬	▬▬	▬▬
02	211 44.4	34.5	162 38.0	7.8	14 50.0	12.3	60.2	68	03 36	04 46	05 42	12 52	15 33	▬▬	▬▬
03	226 44.6	.. 33.6	177 04.8	7.8	15 02.3	12.1	60.2	66	03 48	04 52	05 43	12 27	14 34	16 57	▬▬
04	241 44.9	32.6	191 31.6	7.7	15 14.4	12.1	60.2	64	03 58	04 56	05 44	12 07	14 00	15 46	17 07
05	256 45.1	31.6	205 58.3	7.7	15 26.5	11.9	60.1	62	04 06	05 00	05 45	11 51	13 35	15 10	16 24
06	271 45.3	N 0 30.7	220 25.0	7.7	S15 38.4	11.9	60.1	60	04 13	05 03	05 45	11 38	13 16	14 44	15 55
07	286 45.5	29.7	234 51.7	7.6	15 50.3	11.7	60.1	N 58	04 19	05 06	05 46	11 27	13 00	14 24	15 32
08	301 45.7	28.7	249 18.3	7.6	16 02.0	11.6	60.0	56	04 24	05 09	05 46	11 17	12 46	14 07	15 14
M 09	316 46.0	.. 27.7	263 44.9	7.6	16 13.6	11.5	60.0	54	04 29	05 11	05 46	11 08	12 34	13 53	14 59
O 10	331 46.2	26.8	278 11.5	7.5	16 25.1	11.4	60.0	52	04 33	05 13	05 47	11 00	12 24	13 41	14 46
N 11	346 46.4	25.8	292 38.0	7.5	16 36.5	11.3	60.0	50	04 36	05 15	05 47	10 54	12 15	13 30	14 34
D 12	1 46.6	N 0 24.8	307 04.5	7.5	S16 47.8	11.1	59.9	45	04 44	05 18	05 47	10 39	11 55	13 07	14 10
A 13	16 46.8	23.8	321 31.0	7.4	16 58.9	11.1	59.9	N 40	04 49	05 21	05 48	10 27	11 40	12 49	13 51
Y 14	31 47.1	22.9	335 57.4	7.4	17 10.0	10.9	59.9	35	04 53	05 23	05 48	10 16	11 27	12 33	13 35
15	46 47.3	.. 21.9	350 23.8	7.4	17 20.9	10.8	59.8	30	04 57	05 25	05 48	10 08	11 15	12 20	13 21
16	61 47.5	20.9	4 50.2	7.3	17 31.7	10.7	59.8	20	05 01	05 27	05 49	09 52	10 56	11 58	12 57
17	76 47.7	20.0	19 16.5	7.3	17 42.4	10.5	59.8	N 10	05 04	05 28	05 49	09 39	10 39	11 38	12 36
18	91 48.0	N 0 19.0	33 42.8	7.3	S17 52.9	10.5	59.8	0	05 05	05 29	05 49	09 27	10 23	11 20	12 17
19	106 48.2	18.0	48 09.1	7.2	18 03.4	10.3	59.7	S 10	05 04	05 28	05 49	09 14	10 07	11 02	11 58
20	121 48.4	17.0	62 35.3	7.2	18 13.7	10.2	59.7	20	05 02	05 27	05 49	09 01	09 51	10 43	11 38
21	136 48.6	.. 16.1	77 01.5	7.2	18 23.9	10.1	59.7	30	04 57	05 25	05 49	08 47	09 32	10 21	11 14
22	151 48.8	15.1	91 27.7	7.1	18 34.0	9.9	59.6	35	04 54	05 24	05 49	08 38	09 21	10 08	11 01
23	166 49.1	14.1	105 53.8	7.1	18 43.9	9.8	59.6	40	04 50	05 22	05 49	08 29	09 08	09 53	10 45
22 00	181 49.3	N 0 13.1	120 19.9	7.1	S18 53.7	9.7	59.6	45	04 45	05 19	05 48	08 17	08 53	09 36	10 26
01	196 49.5	12.2	134 46.0	7.0	19 03.4	9.6	59.5	S 50	04 38	05 16	05 48	08 04	08 35	09 14	10 02
02	211 49.7	11.2	149 12.0	7.0	19 13.0	9.4	59.5	52	04 34	05 14	05 48	07 58	08 27	09 04	09 51
03	226 49.9	.. 10.2	163 38.0	7.0	19 22.4	9.3	59.5	54	04 31	05 12	05 48	07 51	08 17	08 52	09 38
04	241 50.2	09.3	178 04.0	7.0	19 31.7	9.1	59.4	56	04 26	05 10	05 47	07 43	08 07	08 39	09 23
05	256 50.4	08.3	192 30.0	6.9	19 40.8	9.1	59.4	58	04 21	05 08	05 47	07 34	07 55	08 24	09 06
06	271 50.6	N 0 07.3	206 55.9	6.9	S19 49.9	8.9	59.4	S 60	04 16	05 05	05 47	07 25	07 41	08 05	08 44

UT	SUN		MOON					Lat.	Sunset	Twilight		Moonset			
										Civil	Naut.	21	22	23	24
d h	° ′	° ′	° ′	′	° ′	′	′	°	h m	h m	h m	h m	h m	h m	h m
07	286 50.8	06.3	221 21.8	6.9	19 58.8	8.7	59.4	N 72	18 02	19 10	20 40	16 21	▬▬	▬▬	▬▬
T 08	301 51.0	05.4	235 47.7	6.8	20 07.5	8.7	59.3	N 70	18 01	19 03	20 21	17 32	▬▬	▬▬	▬▬
U 09	316 51.2	.. 04.4	250 13.5	6.8	20 16.2	8.4	59.3	68	18 01	18 56	20 06	18 10	17 28	▬▬	▬▬
E 10	331 51.5	03.4	264 39.3	6.8	20 24.6	8.4	59.3	66	18 00	18 51	19 54	18 37	18 28	18 05	▬▬
S 11	346 51.7	02.4	279 05.1	6.8	20 33.0	8.2	59.2	64	17 59	18 47	19 45	18 58	19 03	19 17	19 55
D 12	1 51.9	N 0 01.5	293 30.9	6.8	S20 41.2	8.1	59.2	62	17 59	18 43	19 37	19 14	19 28	19 53	20 38
A 13	16 52.1	N 00.5	307 56.7	6.7	20 49.3	7.9	59.2	60	17 59	18 40	19 30	19 29	19 48	20 19	21 07
Y 14	31 52.3	S 00.5	322 22.4	6.7	20 57.2	7.8	59.1	N 58	17 58	18 37	19 24	19 41	20 05	20 39	21 29
15	46 52.6	.. 01.5	336 48.1	6.7	21 05.0	7.7	59.1	56	17 58	18 35	19 19	19 51	20 19	20 56	21 47
16	61 52.8	02.4	351 13.8	6.6	21 12.7	7.5	59.1	54	17 58	18 33	19 15	20 01	20 31	21 11	22 03
17	76 53.0	03.4	5 39.4	6.7	21 20.2	7.4	59.0	52	17 58	18 31	19 11	20 09	20 42	21 23	22 16
18	91 53.2	S 0 04.4	20 05.1	6.6	S21 27.6	7.2	59.0	50	17 58	18 29	19 07	20 16	20 51	21 35	22 28
19	106 53.4	05.3	34 30.7	6.6	21 34.8	7.1	59.0	45	17 57	18 26	19 00	20 33	21 12	21 58	22 52
20	121 53.7	06.3	48 56.3	6.6	21 41.9	6.9	58.9	N 40	17 57	18 24	18 55	20 46	21 28	22 16	23 11
21	136 53.9	.. 07.3	63 21.9	6.6	21 48.8	6.8	58.9	35	17 56	18 22	18 51	20 57	21 42	22 32	23 27
22	151 54.1	08.3	77 47.5	6.5	21 55.6	6.7	58.9	30	17 56	18 20	18 48	21 07	21 54	22 46	23 41
23	166 54.3	09.2	92 13.0	6.6	22 02.3	6.5	58.8	20	17 56	18 18	18 43	21 24	22 15	23 09	24 05
23 00	181 54.5	S 0 10.2	106 38.6	6.5	S22 08.8	6.3	58.8	N 10	17 56	18 17	18 41	21 39	22 33	23 29	24 25
01	196 54.8	11.2	121 04.1	6.5	22 15.1	6.2	58.8	0	17 56	18 16	18 41	21 53	22 50	23 48	24 44
02	211 55.0	12.2	135 29.6	6.5	22 21.3	6.1	58.7	S 10	17 56	18 17	18 41	22 07	23 07	24 06	00 06
03	226 55.2	.. 13.1	149 55.1	6.5	22 27.4	5.9	58.7	20	17 56	18 18	18 44	22 22	23 25	24 26	00 26
04	241 55.4	14.1	164 20.6	6.5	22 33.3	5.8	58.7	30	17 56	18 20	18 48	22 40	23 46	24 50	00 50
05	256 55.6	15.1	178 46.1	6.5	22 39.1	5.6	58.6	35	17 57	18 22	18 52	22 50	23 59	25 03	01 03
06	271 55.8	S 0 16.1	193 11.6	6.5	S22 44.7	5.5	58.6	40	17 57	18 24	18 56	23 02	24 13	00 13	01 19
W 07	286 56.1	17.0	207 37.1	6.4	22 50.2	5.3	58.6	45	17 57	18 27	19 01	23 15	24 30	00 30	01 38
E 08	301 56.3	18.0	222 02.5	6.5	22 55.5	5.2	58.5	S 50	17 58	18 30	19 08	23 32	24 51	00 51	02 01
D 09	316 56.5	.. 19.0	236 28.0	6.4	23 00.7	5.1	58.5	52	17 58	18 32	19 12	23 40	25 01	01 01	02 12
N 10	331 56.7	19.9	250 53.4	6.5	23 05.8	4.8	58.5	54	17 59	18 34	19 16	23 49	25 12	01 12	02 25
E 11	346 56.9	20.9	265 18.9	6.5	23 10.6	4.8	58.4	56	17 59	18 36	19 20	23 59	25 25	01 25	02 40
S 12	1 57.2	S 0 21.9	279 44.4	6.4	S23 15.4	4.5	58.4	58	17 59	18 38	19 26	24 11	00 11	01 40	02 57
D 13	16 57.4	22.9	294 09.8	6.5	23 19.9	4.5	58.4	S 60	18 00	18 41	19 31	24 24	00 24	01 58	03 18
A 14	31 57.6	23.8	308 35.3	6.4	23 24.4	4.3	58.3								
Y 15	46 57.8	.. 24.8	323 00.7	6.5	23 28.7	4.1	58.3								
16	61 58.0	25.8	337 26.2	6.5	23 32.8	4.0	58.3								
17	76 58.3	26.8	351 51.7	6.4	23 36.8	3.8	58.2								

								Day	SUN			MOON			
									Eqn. of Time		Mer.	Mer. Pass.		Age	Phase
									00ʰ	12ʰ	Pass.	Upper	Lower		
18	91 58.5	S 0 27.7	6 17.1	6.5	S23 40.6	3.7	58.2	d	m s	m s	h m	h m	h m	d %	
19	106 58.7	28.7	20 42.6	6.5	23 44.3	3.5	58.2	21	06 55	07 06	11 53	15 40	03 12	04 23	
20	121 58.9	29.7	35 08.1	6.5	23 47.8	3.4	58.1	22	07 17	07 27	11 53	16 36	04 08	05 33	
21	136 59.1	.. 30.7	49 33.6	6.5	23 51.2	3.2	58.1	23	07 38	07 48	11 52	17 34	05 05	06 44	
22	151 59.3	31.6	63 59.1	6.5	23 54.4	3.1	58.1								
23	166 59.6	32.6	78 24.6	6.6	S23 57.5	2.9	58.0								
	SD 16.0	d 1.0	SD 16.3		16.1		15.9									

UT	ARIES GHA	VENUS −4.1 GHA	Dec	MARS −2.4 GHA	Dec	JUPITER −2.4 GHA	Dec	SATURN +0.4 GHA	Dec	STARS Name	SHA	Dec
d h	° ′	° ′	° ′	° ′	° ′	° ′	° ′	° ′	° ′		° ′	° ′
24 00	3 17.1	221 10.5	N14 42.0	337 04.0	N 6 35.3	74 09.1	S22 42.2	65 54.3	S21 22.0	Acamar	315 14.2	S40 13.2
01	18 19.6	236 10.1	41.3	352 06.9	35.2	89 11.5	42.2	80 56.8	22.0	Achernar	335 22.4	S57 07.8
02	33 22.0	251 09.7	40.5	7 09.9	35.1	104 13.9	42.2	95 59.2	22.0	Acrux	173 04.5	S63 12.7
03	48 24.5	266 09.3 ..	39.8	22 12.9 ..	35.0	119 16.2 ..	42.2	111 01.7 ..	22.0	Adhara	255 08.7	S28 59.8
04	63 27.0	281 08.9	39.0	37 15.8	34.9	134 18.6	42.2	126 04.2	22.0	Aldebaran	290 43.5	N16 33.0
05	78 29.4	296 08.5	38.3	52 18.8	34.8	149 21.0	42.2	141 06.7	22.0			
06	93 31.9	311 08.1	N14 37.6	67 21.8	N 6 34.6	164 23.3	S22 42.2	156 09.2	S21 22.1	Alioth	166 16.7	N55 51.1
07	108 34.4	326 07.7	36.8	82 24.7	34.5	179 25.7	42.1	171 11.7	22.1	Alkaid	152 55.3	N49 12.9
T 08	123 36.8	341 07.3	36.1	97 27.7	34.4	194 28.1	42.1	186 14.2	22.1	Alnair	27 37.0	S46 51.7
H 09	138 39.3	356 06.9 ..	35.3	112 30.6 ..	34.3	209 30.4 ..	42.1	201 16.6 ..	22.1	Alnilam	275 41.2	S 1 11.3
U 10	153 41.8	11 06.5	34.6	127 33.6	34.2	224 32.8	42.1	216 19.1	22.1	Alphard	217 51.4	S 8 44.7
R 11	168 44.2	26 06.1	33.9	142 36.6	34.1	239 35.2	42.1	231 21.6	22.1			
S 12	183 46.7	41 05.7	N14 33.1	157 39.6	N 6 34.0	254 37.5	S22 42.1	246 24.1	S21 22.1	Alphecca	126 06.9	N26 39.0
D 13	198 49.1	56 05.3	32.4	172 42.5	33.9	269 39.9	42.1	261 26.6	22.1	Alpheratz	357 38.0	N29 12.3
A 14	213 51.6	71 04.9	31.6	187 45.5	33.8	284 42.2	42.1	276 29.1	22.1	Altair	62 03.2	N 8 55.6
Y 15	228 54.1	86 04.5 ..	30.9	202 48.5 ..	33.7	299 44.6 ..	42.1	291 31.6 ..	22.1	Ankaa	353 10.2	S42 11.6
16	243 56.5	101 04.1	30.1	217 51.5	33.6	314 47.0	42.1	306 34.0	22.1	Antares	112 20.2	S26 28.6
17	258 59.0	116 03.7	29.4	232 54.4	33.5	329 49.3	42.0	321 36.5	22.1			
18	274 01.5	131 03.3	N14 28.6	247 57.4	N 6 33.3	344 51.7	S22 42.0	336 39.0	S21 22.1	Arcturus	145 51.4	N19 04.8
19	289 03.9	146 02.9	27.9	263 00.4	33.2	359 54.1	42.0	351 41.5	22.1	Atria	107 17.7	S69 04.0
20	304 06.4	161 02.5	27.1	278 03.4	33.1	14 56.4	42.0	6 44.0	22.1	Avior	234 16.4	S59 34.2
21	319 08.9	176 02.1 ..	26.4	293 06.3 ..	33.0	29 58.8 ..	42.0	21 46.4 ..	22.1	Bellatrix	278 26.5	N 6 22.1
22	334 11.3	191 01.7	25.6	308 09.3	32.9	45 01.1	42.0	36 48.9	22.1	Betelgeuse	270 55.8	N 7 24.7
23	349 13.8	206 01.3	24.9	323 12.3	32.8	60 03.5	42.0	51 51.4	22.1			
25 00	4 16.3	221 00.9	N14 24.1	338 15.3	N 6 32.7	75 05.9	S22 42.0	66 53.9	S21 22.2	Canopus	263 53.9	S52 42.1
01	19 18.7	236 00.5	23.4	353 18.3	32.6	90 08.2	42.0	81 56.4	22.2	Capella	280 26.9	N46 00.9
02	34 21.2	251 00.2	22.6	8 21.3	32.5	105 10.6	41.9	96 58.9	22.2	Deneb	49 27.8	N45 21.5
03	49 23.6	265 59.8 ..	21.9	23 24.3 ..	32.4	120 13.0 ..	41.9	112 01.3 ..	22.2	Denebola	182 28.8	N14 27.6
04	64 26.1	280 59.4	21.1	38 27.3	32.2	135 15.3	41.9	127 03.8	22.2	Diphda	348 50.5	S17 52.4
05	79 28.6	295 59.0	20.4	53 30.2	32.1	150 17.7	41.9	142 06.3	22.2			
06	94 31.0	310 58.6	N14 19.6	68 33.2	N 6 32.0	165 20.0	S22 41.9	157 08.8	S21 22.2	Dubhe	193 46.0	N61 38.4
07	109 33.5	325 58.2	18.8	83 36.2	31.9	180 22.4	41.9	172 11.3	22.2	Elnath	278 06.2	N28 37.4
08	124 36.0	340 57.8	18.1	98 39.2	31.8	195 24.7	41.9	187 13.7	22.2	Eltanin	90 43.8	N51 29.5
F 09	139 38.4	355 57.4 ..	17.3	113 42.2 ..	31.7	210 27.1 ..	41.9	202 16.2 ..	22.2	Enif	33 41.9	N 9 58.3
R 10	154 40.9	10 57.0	16.6	128 45.2	31.6	225 29.5	41.9	217 18.7	22.2	Fomalhaut	15 18.1	S29 30.8
I 11	169 43.4	25 56.6	15.8	143 48.2	31.4	240 31.8	41.8	232 21.2	22.2			
D 12	184 45.8	40 56.2	N14 15.0	158 51.2	N 6 31.3	255 34.2	S22 41.8	247 23.7	S21 22.2	Gacrux	171 56.0	S57 13.6
A 13	199 48.3	55 55.8	14.3	173 54.2	31.2	270 36.5	41.8	262 26.1	22.2	Gienah	175 47.5	S17 39.2
Y 14	214 50.8	70 55.4	13.5	188 57.2	31.1	285 38.9	41.8	277 28.6	22.2	Hadar	148 41.4	S60 28.3
15	229 53.2	85 55.0 ..	12.8	204 00.2 ..	31.0	300 41.2 ..	41.8	292 31.1 ..	22.2	Hamal	327 54.8	N23 33.6
16	244 55.7	100 54.6	12.0	219 03.2	30.9	315 43.6	41.8	307 33.6	22.2	Kaus Aust.	83 37.1	S34 22.5
17	259 58.1	115 54.2	11.2	234 06.2	30.8	330 46.0	41.8	322 36.1	22.2			
18	275 00.6	130 53.8	N14 10.5	249 09.2	N 6 30.6	345 48.3	S22 41.8	337 38.5	S21 22.2	Kochab	137 20.8	N74 04.5
19	290 03.1	145 53.4	09.7	264 12.3	30.5	0 50.7	41.7	352 41.0	22.2	Markab	13 33.0	N15 19.1
20	305 05.5	160 53.1	08.9	279 15.3	30.4	15 53.0	41.7	7 43.5	22.3	Menkar	314 09.5	N 4 10.3
21	320 08.0	175 52.7 ..	08.2	294 18.3 ..	30.3	30 55.4 ..	41.7	22 46.0 ..	22.3	Menkent	148 02.0	S36 28.2
22	335 10.5	190 52.3	07.4	309 21.3	30.2	45 57.7	41.7	37 48.5	22.3	Miaplacidus	221 39.4	S69 47.8
23	350 12.9	205 51.9	06.6	324 24.3	30.1	61 00.1	41.7	52 50.9	22.3			
26 00	5 15.4	220 51.5	N14 05.8	339 27.3	N 6 29.9	76 02.4	S22 41.7	67 53.4	S21 22.3	Mirfak	308 32.8	N49 55.9
01	20 17.9	235 51.1	05.1	354 30.3	29.8	91 04.8	41.7	82 55.9	22.3	Nunki	75 52.0	S26 16.2
02	35 20.3	250 50.7	04.3	9 33.3	29.7	106 07.1	41.7	97 58.4	22.3	Peacock	53 11.0	S56 40.2
03	50 22.8	265 50.3 ..	03.5	24 36.4 ..	29.6	121 09.5 ..	41.7	113 00.8 ..	22.3	Pollux	243 21.7	N27 58.5
04	65 25.3	280 49.9	02.8	39 39.4	29.5	136 11.8	41.6	128 03.3	22.3	Procyon	244 54.6	N 5 10.4
05	80 27.7	295 49.5	02.0	54 42.4	29.4	151 14.2	41.6	143 05.8	22.3			
06	95 30.2	310 49.1	N14 01.2	69 45.4	N 6 29.2	166 16.5	S22 41.6	158 08.3	S21 22.3	Rasalhague	96 01.8	N12 33.0
07	110 32.6	325 48.7	14 00.4	84 48.4	29.1	181 18.9	41.6	173 10.7	22.3	Regulus	207 38.4	N11 52.1
S 08	125 35.1	340 48.3	13 59.7	99 51.5	29.0	196 21.2	41.6	188 13.2	22.3	Rigel	281 07.1	S 8 10.6
A 09	140 37.6	355 47.9 ..	58.9	114 54.5 ..	28.9	211 23.6 ..	41.6	203 15.7 ..	22.3	Rigil Kent.	139 45.5	S60 55.2
T 10	155 40.0	10 47.6	58.1	129 57.5	28.8	226 25.9	41.6	218 18.2	22.3	Sabik	102 06.9	S15 44.9
U 11	170 42.5	25 47.2	57.3	145 00.5	28.6	241 28.3	41.6	233 20.7	22.3			
R 12	185 45.0	40 46.8	N13 56.5	160 03.6	N 6 28.5	256 30.6	S22 41.5	248 23.1	S21 22.3	Schedar	349 34.3	N56 39.0
D 13	200 47.4	55 46.4	55.8	175 06.6	28.4	271 33.0	41.5	263 25.6	22.3	Shaula	96 15.1	S37 07.1
A 14	215 49.9	70 46.0	55.0	190 09.6	28.3	286 35.3	41.5	278 28.1	22.3	Sirius	258 29.3	S16 44.5
Y 15	230 52.4	85 45.6 ..	54.2	205 12.7 ..	28.2	301 37.7 ..	41.5	293 30.6 ..	22.3	Spica	158 26.3	S11 15.9
16	245 54.8	100 45.2	53.4	220 15.7	28.0	316 40.0	41.5	308 33.0	22.3	Suhail	222 49.1	S43 30.7
17	260 57.3	115 44.8	52.6	235 18.7	27.9	331 42.4	41.5	323 35.5	22.3			
18	275 59.7	130 44.4	N13 51.9	250 21.8	N 6 27.8	346 44.7	S22 41.5	338 38.0	S21 22.3	Vega	80 35.5	N38 48.5
19	291 02.2	145 44.0	51.1	265 24.8	27.7	1 47.1	41.5	353 40.5	22.4	Zuben'ubi	137 00.1	S16 07.5
20	306 04.7	160 43.6	50.3	280 27.8	27.5	16 49.4	41.4	8 42.9	22.4		SHA	Mer.Pass.
21	321 07.1	175 43.2 ..	49.5	295 30.9 ..	27.4	31 51.7 ..	41.4	23 45.4 ..	22.4		° ′	h m
22	336 09.6	190 42.9	48.7	310 33.9	27.3	46 54.1	41.4	38 47.9	22.4	Venus	216 44.7	9 16
23	351 12.1	205 42.5	47.9	325 36.9	27.2	61 56.4	41.4	53 50.3	22.4	Mars	333 59.0	1 27
	h m									Jupiter	70 49.6	18 57
Mer.Pass.	23 39.0	v −0.4	d 0.8	v 3.0	d 0.1	v 2.4	d 0.0	v 2.5	d 0.0	Saturn	62 37.6	19 29

UT	SUN GHA	SUN Dec	MOON GHA	v	MOON Dec	d	HP
d h	° ′	° ′	° ′	′	° ′	′	′
24 00	181 59.8	S 0 33.6	92 50.2	6.5	S24 00.4	2.8	58.0
01	197 00.0	34.5	107 15.7	6.6	24 03.2	2.6	58.0
02	212 00.2	35.5	121 41.3	6.6	24 05.8	2.5	57.9
03	227 00.4 ..	36.5	136 06.9	6.6	24 08.3	2.3	57.9
04	242 00.6	37.5	150 32.5	6.6	24 10.6	2.2	57.9
05	257 00.9	38.4	164 58.1	6.6	24 12.8	2.0	57.8
06	272 01.1	S 0 39.4	179 23.7	6.7	S24 14.8	1.9	57.8
T 07	287 01.3	40.4	193 49.4	6.7	24 16.7	1.7	57.8
H 08	302 01.5	41.4	208 15.1	6.7	24 18.4	1.6	57.7
U 09	317 01.7 ..	42.3	222 40.8	6.7	24 20.0	1.4	57.7
R 10	332 01.9	43.3	237 06.5	6.8	24 21.4	1.3	57.7
S 11	347 02.2	44.3	251 32.3	6.8	24 22.7	1.1	57.6
D 12	2 02.4	S 0 45.3	265 58.1	6.8	S24 23.8	1.0	57.6
A 13	17 02.6	46.2	280 23.9	6.9	24 24.8	0.8	57.6
Y 14	32 02.8	47.2	294 49.8	6.9	24 25.6	0.7	57.5
15	47 03.0 ..	48.2	309 15.7	6.9	24 26.3	0.5	57.5
16	62 03.3	49.2	323 41.6	7.0	24 26.8	0.4	57.5
17	77 03.5	50.1	338 07.6	7.0	24 27.2	0.3	57.4
18	92 03.7	S 0 51.1	352 33.6	7.0	S24 27.5	0.1	57.4
19	107 03.9	52.1	6 59.6	7.1	24 27.6	0.1	57.4
20	122 04.1	53.0	21 25.7	7.1	24 27.5	0.2	57.3
21	137 04.3 ..	54.0	35 51.8	7.2	24 27.3	0.3	57.3
22	152 04.5	55.0	50 18.0	7.2	24 27.0	0.5	57.3
23	167 04.8	56.0	64 44.2	7.2	24 26.5	0.6	57.3
25 00	182 05.0	S 0 56.9	79 10.4	7.3	S24 25.9	0.8	57.2
01	197 05.2	57.9	93 36.7	7.3	24 25.1	0.9	57.2
02	212 05.4	58.9	108 03.0	7.4	24 24.2	1.0	57.2
03	227 05.6	0 59.9	122 29.4	7.4	24 23.2	1.2	57.1
04	242 05.8	1 00.8	136 55.8	7.5	24 22.0	1.4	57.1
05	257 06.1	01.8	151 22.3	7.5	24 20.6	1.4	57.1
06	272 06.3	S 1 02.8	165 48.8	7.6	S24 19.2	1.6	57.0
F 07	287 06.5	03.8	180 15.4	7.6	24 17.6	1.8	57.0
R 08	302 06.7	04.7	194 42.0	7.7	24 15.8	1.9	57.0
I 09	317 06.9 ..	05.7	209 08.7	7.7	24 13.9	2.0	57.0
D 10	332 07.1	06.7	223 35.4	7.8	24 11.9	2.2	56.9
A 11	347 07.4	07.7	238 02.2	7.9	24 09.7	2.3	56.9
Y 12	2 07.6	S 1 08.6	252 29.1	7.9	S24 07.4	2.4	56.9
13	17 07.8	09.6	266 56.0	7.9	24 05.0	2.6	56.8
14	32 08.0	10.6	281 22.9	8.0	24 02.4	2.7	56.8
15	47 08.2 ..	11.5	295 49.9	8.1	23 59.7	2.8	56.8
16	62 08.4	12.5	310 17.0	8.2	23 56.9	3.0	56.7
17	77 08.6	13.5	324 44.2	8.2	23 53.9	3.1	56.7
18	92 08.9	S 1 14.5	339 11.4	8.2	S23 50.8	3.2	56.7
19	107 09.1	15.4	353 38.6	8.4	23 47.6	3.4	56.7
20	122 09.3	16.4	8 06.0	8.4	23 44.2	3.4	56.6
21	137 09.5 ..	17.4	22 33.4	8.4	23 40.8	3.7	56.6
22	152 09.7	18.4	37 00.8	8.5	23 37.1	3.7	56.6
23	167 09.9	19.3	51 28.3	8.6	23 33.4	3.9	56.5
26 00	182 10.1	S 1 20.3	65 55.9	8.7	S23 29.5	4.0	56.5
01	197 10.4	21.3	80 23.6	8.7	23 25.5	4.1	56.5
02	212 10.6	22.3	94 51.3	8.8	23 21.4	4.2	56.5
03	227 10.8 ..	23.2	109 19.1	8.8	23 17.2	4.4	56.4
04	242 11.0	24.2	123 46.9	9.0	23 12.8	4.5	56.4
05	257 11.2	25.2	138 14.9	9.0	23 08.3	4.6	56.4
06	272 11.4	S 1 26.1	152 42.9	9.0	S23 03.7	4.7	56.3
S 07	287 11.6	27.1	167 10.9	9.2	22 59.0	4.9	56.3
A 08	302 11.9	28.1	181 39.1	9.2	22 54.1	5.0	56.3
T 09	317 12.1 ..	29.1	196 07.3	9.3	22 49.1	5.0	56.3
U 10	332 12.3	30.0	210 35.6	9.3	22 44.1	5.2	56.3
R 11	347 12.5	31.0	225 03.9	9.4	22 38.9	5.4	56.2
D 12	2 12.7	S 1 32.0	239 32.3	9.5	S22 33.5	5.4	56.2
A 13	17 12.9	33.0	254 00.8	9.6	22 28.1	5.6	56.2
Y 14	32 13.1	33.9	268 29.4	9.7	22 22.5	5.6	56.1
15	47 13.4 ..	34.9	282 58.1	9.7	22 16.9	5.7	56.1
16	62 13.6	35.9	297 26.8	9.8	22 11.1	5.9	56.1
17	77 13.8	36.9	311 55.6	9.8	22 05.2	6.0	56.1
18	92 14.0	S 1 37.8	326 24.4	10.0	S21 59.2	6.1	56.0
19	107 14.2	38.8	340 53.4	10.0	21 53.1	6.2	56.0
20	122 14.4	39.8	355 22.4	10.1	21 46.9	6.3	56.0
21	137 14.6 ..	40.7	9 51.5	10.2	21 40.6	6.4	56.0
22	152 14.8	41.7	24 20.7	10.2	21 34.2	6.5	55.9
23	167 15.1	42.7	38 49.9	10.4	S21 27.7	6.7	55.9
	SD 16.0 d 1.0		SD 15.7		15.5		15.3

Moonrise

Lat.	Twilight Naut.	Civil	Sunrise	24	25	26	27
°	h m	h m	h m	h m	h m	h m	h m
N 72	03 19	04 46	05 54	■■	■■	■■	■■
N 70	03 35	04 52	05 53	■■	■■	■■	19 48
68	03 49	04 57	05 53	■■	■■	19 56	19 00
66	03 59	05 02	05 53	■■	19 05	18 37	18 28
64	04 08	05 05	05 53	17 07	17 46	18 00	18 05
62	04 15	05 08	05 52	16 24	17 09	17 33	17 46
60	04 21	05 11	05 52	15 55	16 43	17 13	17 31
N 58	04 26	05 13	05 52	15 32	16 22	16 55	17 18
56	04 31	05 15	05 52	15 14	16 05	16 41	17 06
54	04 35	05 16	05 52	14 59	15 50	16 28	16 56
52	04 38	05 18	05 52	14 46	15 38	16 17	16 47
50	04 41	05 19	05 51	14 34	15 27	16 08	16 39
45	04 47	05 22	05 51	14 10	15 03	15 47	16 22
N 40	04 52	05 24	05 51	13 51	14 45	15 30	16 08
35	04 56	05 25	05 50	13 35	14 29	15 16	15 56
30	04 58	05 26	05 50	13 21	14 15	15 04	15 46
20	05 02	05 28	05 50	12 57	13 52	14 42	15 28
N 10	05 04	05 28	05 49	12 36	13 32	14 24	15 12
0	05 04	05 28	05 48	12 17	13 13	14 07	14 57
S 10	05 02	05 26	05 47	11 58	12 55	13 50	14 42
20	04 59	05 25	05 47	11 38	12 34	13 31	14 26
30	04 54	05 21	05 45	11 14	12 11	13 10	14 08
35	04 50	05 19	05 45	11 01	11 58	12 57	13 57
40	04 45	05 17	05 44	10 45	11 42	12 43	13 45
45	04 39	05 13	05 43	10 26	11 23	12 26	13 31
S 50	04 31	05 09	05 41	10 02	11 00	12 04	13 13
52	04 27	05 07	05 41	09 51	10 48	11 54	13 04
54	04 23	05 05	05 40	09 38	10 35	11 43	12 55
56	04 18	05 02	05 39	09 23	10 21	11 29	12 44
58	04 12	04 59	05 39	09 06	10 03	11 14	12 32
S 60	04 06	04 56	05 38	08 44	09 42	10 56	12 18

Moonset

Lat.	Sunset	Twilight Civil	Naut.	24	25	26	27
°	h m	h m	h m	h m	h m	h m	h m
N 72	17 47	18 54	20 20	■■	■■	■■	■■
N 70	17 48	18 48	20 04	■■	■■	■■	22 44
68	17 48	18 43	19 51	■■	■■	20 52	23 32
66	17 48	18 39	19 41	■■	19 53	22 10	24 02
64	17 49	18 36	19 33	19 55	21 11	22 47	24 25
62	17 49	18 33	19 26	20 38	21 48	23 13	24 43
60	17 50	18 31	19 20	21 07	22 14	23 34	24 57
N 58	17 50	18 29	19 15	21 29	22 35	23 50	25 10
56	17 50	18 27	19 11	21 47	22 51	24 04	00 04
54	17 50	18 25	19 07	22 03	23 06	24 16	00 16
52	17 50	18 24	19 04	22 16	23 18	24 27	00 27
50	17 51	18 23	19 01	22 28	23 29	24 36	00 36
45	17 51	18 20	18 55	22 52	23 52	24 56	00 56
N 40	17 52	18 19	18 50	23 11	24 10	00 10	01 12
35	17 52	18 17	18 47	23 27	24 26	00 26	01 26
30	17 52	18 16	18 44	23 41	24 39	00 39	01 38
20	17 53	18 15	18 41	24 05	00 05	01 02	01 58
N 10	17 54	18 15	18 39	24 25	00 25	01 21	02 15
0	17 55	18 15	18 39	24 44	00 44	01 39	02 31
S 10	17 56	18 17	18 41	00 06	01 03	01 57	02 47
20	17 57	18 19	18 44	00 26	01 24	02 17	03 05
30	17 58	18 22	18 50	00 50	01 47	02 39	03 24
35	17 59	18 24	18 54	01 03	02 01	02 52	03 36
40	18 00	18 27	18 59	01 19	02 17	03 07	03 49
45	18 01	18 30	19 05	01 38	02 36	03 25	04 04
S 50	18 03	18 35	19 13	02 01	03 00	03 47	04 23
52	18 03	18 37	19 17	02 12	03 11	03 57	04 32
54	18 04	18 39	19 22	02 25	03 24	04 09	04 41
56	18 05	18 42	19 27	02 40	03 39	04 22	04 53
58	18 06	18 45	19 33	02 57	03 56	04 38	05 05
S 60	18 07	18 49	19 39	03 18	04 18	04 56	05 20

Day	SUN Eqn. of Time 00h	12h	Mer. Pass.	MOON Mer. Pass. Upper	Lower	Age	Phase
d	m s	m s	h m	h m	h m	d	%
24	07 59	08 09	11 52	18 31	06 03	07	55
25	08 19	08 30	11 52	19 26	06 59	08	65
26	08 40	08 50	11 51	20 19	07 53	09	75

UT	ARIES GHA	VENUS −4.1 GHA	Dec	MARS −2.4 GHA	Dec	JUPITER −2.4 GHA	Dec	SATURN +0.5 GHA	Dec	STARS Name	SHA	Dec
d h	° ′	° ′	° ′	° ′	° ′	° ′	° ′	° ′	° ′		° ′	° ′
27 00	6 14.5	220 42.1	N13 47.1	340 40.0	N 6 27.1	76 58.8	S22 41.4	68 52.8	S21 22.4	Acamar	315 14.1	S40 13.2
01	21 17.0	235 41.7	46.3	355 43.0	26.9	92 01.1	41.4	83 55.3	22.4	Achernar	335 22.3	S57 07.9
02	36 19.5	250 41.3	45.6	10 46.1	26.8	107 03.5	41.4	98 57.8	22.4	Acrux	173 04.5	S63 12.7
03	51 21.9	265 40.9 ..	44.8	25 49.1 ..	26.7	122 05.8 ..	41.3	114 00.2 ..	22.4	Adhara	255 08.6	S28 59.8
04	66 24.4	280 40.5	44.0	40 52.2	26.6	137 08.1	41.3	129 02.7	22.4	Aldebaran	290 43.4	N16 33.0
05	81 26.9	295 40.1	43.2	55 55.2	26.4	152 10.5	41.3	144 05.2	22.4			
06	96 29.3	310 39.7	N13 42.4	70 58.3	N 6 26.3	167 12.8	S22 41.3	159 07.7	S21 22.4	Alioth	166 16.7	N55 51.1
07	111 31.8	325 39.3	41.6	86 01.3	26.2	182 15.2	41.3	174 10.1	22.4	Alkaid	152 55.3	N49 12.9
08	126 34.2	340 38.9	40.8	101 04.4	26.1	197 17.5	41.3	189 12.6	22.4	Alnair	27 37.0	S46 51.7
S 09	141 36.7	355 38.6 ..	40.0	116 07.4 ..	25.9	212 19.9 ..	41.3	204 15.1 ..	22.4	Alnilam	275 41.2	S 1 11.3
U 10	156 39.2	10 38.2	39.2	131 10.5	25.8	227 22.2	41.3	219 17.5	22.4	Alphard	217 51.4	S 8 44.7
N 11	171 41.6	25 37.8	38.4	146 13.5	25.7	242 24.5	41.2	234 20.0	22.4			
D 12	186 44.1	40 37.4	N13 37.6	161 16.6	N 6 25.6	257 26.9	S22 41.2	249 22.5	S21 22.4	Alphecca	126 07.0	N26 39.0
A 13	201 46.6	55 37.0	36.8	176 19.6	25.4	272 29.2	41.2	264 25.0	22.4	Alpheratz	357 38.0	N29 12.3
Y 14	216 49.0	70 36.6	36.0	191 22.7	25.3	287 31.6	41.2	279 27.4	22.4	Altair	62 03.2	N 8 55.6
15	231 51.5	85 36.2 ..	35.2	206 25.7 ..	25.2	302 33.9 ..	41.2	294 29.9 ..	22.4	Ankaa	353 10.2	S42 11.6
16	246 54.0	100 35.8	34.4	221 28.8	25.1	317 36.2	41.2	309 32.4	22.4	Antares	112 20.3	S26 28.6
17	261 56.4	115 35.4	33.6	236 31.9	24.9	332 38.6	41.2	324 34.8	22.4			
18	276 58.9	130 35.0	N13 32.8	251 34.9	N 6 24.8	347 40.9	S22 41.1	339 37.3	S21 22.4	Arcturus	145 51.4	N19 04.8
19	292 01.4	145 34.7	32.0	266 38.0	24.7	2 43.2	41.1	354 39.8	22.4	Atria	107 17.8	S69 04.0
20	307 03.8	160 34.3	31.2	281 41.0	24.5	17 45.6	41.1	9 42.2	22.4	Avior	234 16.4	S59 34.2
21	322 06.3	175 33.9 ..	30.4	296 44.1 ..	24.4	32 47.9 ..	41.1	24 44.7 ..	22.4	Bellatrix	278 26.5	N 6 22.1
22	337 08.7	190 33.5	29.6	311 47.2	24.3	47 50.3	41.1	39 47.2	22.4	Betelgeuse	270 55.8	N 7 24.7
23	352 11.2	205 33.1	28.8	326 50.2	24.2	62 52.6	41.1	54 49.7	22.5			
28 00	7 13.7	220 32.7	N13 28.0	341 53.3	N 6 24.0	77 54.9	S22 41.1	69 52.1	S21 22.5	Canopus	263 53.9	S52 42.1
01	22 16.1	235 32.3	27.2	356 56.4	23.9	92 57.3	41.0	84 54.6	22.5	Capella	280 26.9	N46 00.9
02	37 18.6	250 31.9	26.4	11 59.4	23.8	107 59.6	41.0	99 57.1	22.5	Deneb	49 27.9	N45 21.5
03	52 21.1	265 31.6 ..	25.6	27 02.5 ..	23.6	123 01.9 ..	41.0	114 59.5 ..	22.5	Denebola	182 28.8	N14 27.6
04	67 23.5	280 31.2	24.8	42 05.6	23.5	138 04.3	41.0	130 02.0	22.5	Diphda	348 50.5	S17 52.4
05	82 26.0	295 30.8	24.0	57 08.7	23.4	153 06.6	41.0	145 04.5	22.5			
06	97 28.5	310 30.4	N13 23.2	72 11.7	N 6 23.3	168 08.9	S22 41.0	160 06.9	S21 22.5	Dubhe	193 46.0	N61 38.4
07	112 30.9	325 30.0	22.4	87 14.8	23.1	183 11.3	41.0	175 09.4	22.5	Elnath	278 06.2	N28 37.4
08	127 33.4	340 29.6	21.5	102 17.9	23.0	198 13.6	40.9	190 11.9	22.5	Eltanin	90 43.9	N51 29.5
M 09	142 35.8	355 29.2 ..	20.7	117 21.0 ..	22.9	213 15.9 ..	40.9	205 14.3 ..	22.5	Enif	33 41.9	N 9 58.3
O 10	157 38.3	10 28.8	19.9	132 24.0	22.7	228 18.3	40.9	220 16.8	22.5	Fomalhaut	15 18.1	S29 30.8
N 11	172 40.8	25 28.4	19.1	147 27.1	22.6	243 20.6	40.9	235 19.3	22.5			
D 12	187 43.2	40 28.1	N13 18.3	162 30.2	N 6 22.5	258 22.9	S22 40.9	250 21.7	S21 22.5	Gacrux	171 56.0	S57 13.6
A 13	202 45.7	55 27.7	17.5	177 33.3	22.3	273 25.3	40.9	265 24.2	22.5	Gienah	175 47.5	S17 39.2
Y 14	217 48.2	70 27.3	16.7	192 36.4	22.2	288 27.6	40.9	280 26.7	22.5	Hadar	148 41.4	S60 28.3
15	232 50.6	85 26.9 ..	15.9	207 39.4 ..	22.1	303 29.9 ..	40.8	295 29.1 ..	22.5	Hamal	327 54.8	N23 33.6
16	247 53.1	100 26.5	15.0	222 42.5	21.9	318 32.3	40.8	310 31.6	22.5	Kaus Aust.	83 37.1	S34 22.5
17	262 55.6	115 26.1	14.2	237 45.6	21.8	333 34.6	40.8	325 34.1	22.5			
18	277 58.0	130 25.7	N13 13.4	252 48.7	N 6 21.7	348 36.9	S22 40.8	340 36.5	S21 22.5	Kochab	137 20.9	N74 04.5
19	293 00.5	145 25.4	12.6	267 51.8	21.5	3 39.2	40.8	355 39.0	22.5	Markab	13 33.0	N15 19.1
20	308 03.0	160 25.0	11.8	282 54.9	21.4	18 41.6	40.8	10 41.5	22.5	Menkar	314 09.5	N 4 10.3
21	323 05.4	175 24.6 ..	10.9	297 58.0 ..	21.3	33 43.9 ..	40.8	25 43.9 ..	22.5	Menkent	148 02.0	S36 28.1
22	338 07.9	190 24.2	10.1	313 01.1	21.1	48 46.2	40.7	40 46.4	22.5	Miaplacidus	221 39.4	S69 47.8
23	353 10.3	205 23.8	09.3	328 04.1	21.0	63 48.6	40.7	55 48.9	22.5			
29 00	8 12.8	220 23.4	N13 08.5	343 07.2	N 6 20.9	78 50.9	S22 40.7	70 51.3	S21 22.5	Mirfak	308 32.8	N49 55.9
01	23 15.3	235 23.0	07.7	358 10.3	20.7	93 53.2	40.7	85 53.8	22.5	Nunki	75 52.0	S26 16.2
02	38 17.7	250 22.6	06.8	13 13.4	20.6	108 55.5	40.7	100 56.3	22.5	Peacock	53 11.0	S56 40.2
03	53 20.2	265 22.3 ..	06.0	28 16.5 ..	20.5	123 57.9 ..	40.7	115 58.7 ..	22.5	Pollux	243 21.7	N27 58.5
04	68 22.7	280 21.9	05.2	43 19.6	20.3	139 00.2	40.6	131 01.2	22.5	Procyon	244 54.6	N 5 10.4
05	83 25.1	295 21.5	04.4	58 22.7	20.2	154 02.5	40.6	146 03.6	22.5			
06	98 27.6	310 21.1	N13 03.5	73 25.8	N 6 20.1	169 04.8	S22 40.6	161 06.1	S21 22.5	Rasalhague	96 01.8	N12 33.0
07	113 30.1	325 20.7	02.7	88 28.9	19.9	184 07.2	40.6	176 08.6	22.5	Regulus	207 38.4	N11 52.1
T 08	128 32.5	340 20.3	01.9	103 32.0	19.8	199 09.5	40.6	191 11.0	22.5	Rigel	281 07.1	S 8 10.6
U 09	143 35.0	355 19.9 ..	01.1	118 35.1 ..	19.7	214 11.8 ..	40.6	206 13.5 ..	22.5	Rigil Kent.	139 45.5	S60 55.2
E 10	158 37.4	10 19.6	13 00.2	133 38.2	19.5	229 14.1	40.6	221 16.0	22.5	Sabik	102 06.9	S15 44.9
S 11	173 39.9	25 19.2	12 59.4	148 41.3	19.4	244 16.5	40.5	236 18.4	22.5			
D 12	188 42.4	40 18.8	N12 58.6	163 44.4	N 6 19.3	259 18.8	S22 40.5	251 20.9	S21 22.5	Schedar	349 34.3	N56 39.0
A 13	203 44.8	55 18.4	57.7	178 47.5	19.1	274 21.1	40.5	266 23.4	22.5	Shaula	96 15.2	S37 07.1
Y 14	218 47.3	70 18.0	56.9	193 50.6	19.0	289 23.4	40.5	281 25.8	22.5	Sirius	258 29.3	S16 44.5
15	233 49.8	85 17.6 ..	56.1	208 53.7 ..	18.9	304 25.8 ..	40.5	296 28.3 ..	22.5	Spica	158 26.3	S11 15.9
16	248 52.2	100 17.3	55.2	223 56.8	18.7	319 28.1	40.5	311 30.7	22.6	Suhail	222 49.1	S43 30.7
17	263 54.7	115 16.9	54.4	239 00.0	18.6	334 30.4	40.4	326 33.2	22.6			
18	278 57.2	130 16.5	N12 53.6	254 03.1	N 6 18.4	349 32.7	S22 40.4	341 35.7	S21 22.6	Vega	80 35.5	N38 48.5
19	293 59.6	145 16.1	52.7	269 06.2	18.3	4 35.0	40.4	356 38.1	22.6	Zuben'ubi	137 00.1	S16 07.5
20	309 02.1	160 15.7	51.9	284 09.3	18.2	19 37.4	40.4	11 40.6	22.6		SHA	Mer. Pass.
21	324 04.6	175 15.3 ..	51.1	299 12.4 ..	18.0	34 39.7 ..	40.4	26 43.0 ..	22.6		° ′	h m
22	339 07.0	190 14.9	50.2	314 15.5	17.9	49 42.0	40.4	41 45.5	22.6	Venus	213 19.0	9 18
23	354 09.5	205 14.6	49.4	329 18.6	17.8	64 44.3	40.3	56 48.0	22.6	Mars	334 39.6	1 12
	h m									Jupiter	70 41.3	18 45
Mer. Pass. 23 27.2		v −0.4 d 0.8		v 3.1 d 0.1		v 2.3 d 0.0		v 2.5 d 0.0		Saturn	62 38.5	19 17

UT	SUN		MOON					Lat.	Twilight		Sunrise	Moonrise			
									Naut.	Civil		27	28	29	30
	GHA	Dec	GHA	v	Dec	d	HP								
d h	° ′	° ′	° ′	′	° ′	′	′	°	h m	h m	h m	h m	h m	h m	h m
								N 72	03 35	05 00	06 07	▬	19 38	18 59	18 33
27 00	182 15.3	S 1 43.7	53 19.3	10.4	S21 21.0	6.7	55.9	N 70	03 50	05 04	06 05	19 48	19 05	18 42	18 24
01	197 15.5	44.6	67 48.7	10.4	21 14.3	6.9	55.9	68	04 01	05 08	06 04	19 00	18 41	18 28	18 17
02	212 15.7	45.6	82 18.1	10.6	21 07.4	6.9	55.9	66	04 10	05 11	06 02	18 28	18 22	18 16	18 11
03	227 15.9	.. 46.6	96 47.7	10.6	21 00.5	7.0	55.8	64	04 17	05 14	06 01	18 05	18 06	18 06	18 06
04	242 16.1	47.6	111 17.3	10.7	20 53.5	7.2	55.8	62	04 23	05 16	06 00	17 46	17 54	17 58	18 01
05	257 16.3	48.5	125 47.0	10.8	20 46.3	7.2	55.8	60	04 29	05 18	05 59	17 31	17 43	17 51	17 57
06	272 16.5	S 1 49.5	140 16.8	10.9	S20 39.1	7.3	55.8	N 58	04 33	05 19	05 58	17 18	17 33	17 45	17 54
07	287 16.8	50.5	154 46.7	10.9	20 31.8	7.5	55.7	56	04 37	05 21	05 58	17 06	17 25	17 39	17 51
08	302 17.0	51.4	169 16.6	11.0	20 24.3	7.5	55.7	54	04 40	05 22	05 57	16 56	17 17	17 34	17 48
S 09	317 17.2	.. 52.4	183 46.6	11.1	20 16.8	7.6	55.7	52	04 43	05 23	05 56	16 47	17 10	17 29	17 45
U 10	332 17.4	53.4	198 16.7	11.2	20 09.2	7.7	55.7	50	04 46	05 24	05 56	16 39	17 04	17 25	17 43
N 11	347 17.6	54.4	212 46.9	11.2	20 01.5	7.8	55.6	45	04 51	05 25	05 55	16 22	16 51	17 16	17 38
D 12	2 17.8	S 1 55.3	227 17.1	11.3	S19 53.7	7.9	55.6	N 40	04 55	05 27	05 54	16 08	16 40	17 08	17 34
A 13	17 18.0	56.3	241 47.4	11.4	19 45.8	8.0	55.6	35	04 58	05 27	05 53	15 56	16 31	17 02	17 30
Y 14	32 18.2	57.3	256 17.8	11.5	19 37.8	8.1	55.6	30	05 00	05 28	05 52	15 46	16 23	16 56	17 27
15	47 18.5	.. 58.3	270 48.3	11.5	19 29.7	8.2	55.6	20	05 03	05 28	05 50	15 28	16 09	16 46	17 21
16	62 18.7	1 59.2	285 18.8	11.7	19 21.5	8.2	55.5	N 10	05 03	05 28	05 49	15 12	15 56	16 37	17 16
17	77 18.9	2 00.2	299 49.5	11.7	19 13.3	8.3	55.5	0	05 03	05 27	05 47	14 57	15 44	16 29	17 11
18	92 19.1	S 2 01.2	314 20.2	11.7	S19 05.0	8.5	55.5	S 10	05 00	05 25	05 46	14 42	15 33	16 20	17 06
19	107 19.3	02.1	328 50.9	11.9	18 56.5	8.5	55.5	20	04 56	05 22	05 44	14 26	15 20	16 11	17 01
20	122 19.5	03.1	343 21.8	11.9	18 48.0	8.6	55.5	30	04 50	05 18	05 42	14 08	15 05	16 01	16 55
21	137 19.7	.. 04.1	357 52.7	12.0	18 39.4	8.6	55.4	35	04 45	05 15	05 40	13 57	14 57	15 55	16 52
22	152 19.9	05.1	12 23.7	12.1	18 30.8	8.8	55.4	40	04 40	05 12	05 39	13 45	14 47	15 49	16 48
23	167 20.1	06.0	26 54.8	12.1	18 22.0	8.8	55.4	45	04 33	05 08	05 37	13 31	14 36	15 41	16 44
28 00	182 20.3	S 2 07.0	41 25.9	12.2	S18 13.2	8.9	55.4	S 50	04 24	05 02	05 35	13 13	14 22	15 31	16 39
01	197 20.6	08.0	55 57.1	12.3	18 04.3	9.0	55.4	52	04 20	05 00	05 34	13 04	14 16	15 27	16 36
02	212 20.8	08.9	70 28.4	12.4	17 55.3	9.1	55.3	54	04 15	04 57	05 33	12 55	14 09	15 22	16 33
03	227 21.0	.. 09.9	84 59.8	12.4	17 46.2	9.1	55.3	56	04 09	04 54	05 31	12 44	14 01	15 16	16 30
04	242 21.2	10.9	99 31.2	12.5	17 37.1	9.2	55.3	58	04 03	04 51	05 30	12 32	13 52	15 10	16 27
05	257 21.4	11.9	114 02.7	12.6	17 27.9	9.3	55.3	S 60	03 55	04 47	05 29	12 18	13 41	15 03	16 23
06	272 21.6	S 2 12.8	128 34.3	12.6	S17 18.6	9.4	55.3	Lat.	Sunset	Twilight		Moonset			
07	287 21.8	13.8	143 05.9	12.8	17 09.2	9.4	55.2			Civil	Naut.	27	28	29	30
08	302 22.0	14.8	157 37.7	12.8	16 59.8	9.5	55.2								
M 09	317 22.2	.. 15.8	172 09.5	12.8	16 50.3	9.6	55.2	°	h m	h m	h m	h m	h m	h m	h m
O 10	332 22.4	16.7	186 41.3	12.9	16 40.7	9.7	55.2	N 72	17 32	18 39	20 02	▬	▬	00 33	02 43
N 11	347 22.7	17.7	201 13.2	13.0	16 31.0	9.7	55.2	N 70	17 34	18 34	19 48	22 44	25 04	01 04	02 58
D 12	2 22.9	S 2 18.7	215 45.2	13.1	S16 21.3	9.8	55.1	68	17 36	18 31	19 37	23 32	25 27	01 27	03 10
A 13	17 23.1	19.6	230 17.3	13.1	16 11.5	9.8	55.1	66	17 37	18 28	19 29	24 02	00 02	01 44	03 20
Y 14	32 23.3	20.6	244 49.5	13.2	16 01.7	9.9	55.1	64	17 38	18 25	19 22	24 25	00 25	01 59	03 29
15	47 23.5	.. 21.6	259 21.7	13.2	15 51.8	10.0	55.1	62	17 39	18 23	19 16	24 43	00 43	02 11	03 36
16	62 23.7	22.6	273 53.9	13.4	15 41.8	10.1	55.1	60	17 40	18 22	19 11	24 57	00 57	02 21	03 42
17	77 23.9	23.5	288 26.3	13.4	15 31.7	10.1	55.0	N 58	17 41	18 20	19 06	25 10	01 10	02 29	03 47
18	92 24.1	S 2 24.5	302 58.7	13.4	S15 21.6	10.1	55.0	56	17 42	18 19	19 02	00 04	01 21	02 37	03 52
19	107 24.3	25.5	317 31.1	13.6	15 11.5	10.3	55.0	54	17 43	18 18	18 59	00 16	01 30	02 44	03 56
20	122 24.5	26.4	332 03.7	13.6	15 01.2	10.3	55.0	52	17 44	18 17	18 56	00 27	01 38	02 50	04 00
21	137 24.7	.. 27.4	346 36.3	13.6	14 50.9	10.3	55.0	50	17 44	18 16	18 54	00 36	01 46	02 56	04 04
22	152 24.9	28.4	1 08.9	13.8	14 40.6	10.4	55.0	45	17 45	18 15	18 49	00 56	02 02	03 07	04 11
23	167 25.2	29.4	15 41.7	13.8	14 30.2	10.5	54.9	N 40	17 47	18 14	18 45	01 12	02 15	03 17	04 18
29 00	182 25.4	S 2 30.3	30 14.5	13.8	S14 19.7	10.5	54.9	35	17 48	18 13	18 42	01 26	02 26	03 25	04 23
01	197 25.6	31.3	44 47.3	13.9	14 09.2	10.6	54.9	30	17 49	18 13	18 40	01 38	02 36	03 33	04 28
02	212 25.8	32.3	59 20.2	14.0	13 58.6	10.6	54.9	20	17 50	18 12	18 38	01 58	02 52	03 45	04 36
03	227 26.0	.. 33.2	73 53.2	14.0	13 48.0	10.7	54.9	N 10	17 52	18 13	18 37	02 15	03 07	03 56	04 43
04	242 26.2	34.2	88 26.2	14.1	13 37.3	10.7	54.9	0	17 54	18 14	18 38	02 31	03 20	04 06	04 49
05	257 26.4	35.2	102 59.3	14.2	13 26.6	10.8	54.8	S 10	17 55	18 17	18 41	02 47	03 34	04 16	04 56
06	272 26.6	S 2 36.2	117 32.5	14.2	S13 15.8	10.8	54.8	20	17 57	18 20	18 45	03 05	03 48	04 27	05 03
07	287 26.8	37.1	132 05.7	14.2	13 05.0	10.9	54.8	30	18 00	18 24	18 52	03 24	04 04	04 39	05 11
T 08	302 27.0	38.1	146 38.9	14.4	12 54.1	11.0	54.8	35	18 01	18 27	18 56	03 36	04 13	04 46	05 15
U 09	317 27.2	.. 39.1	161 12.3	14.3	12 43.1	10.9	54.8	40	18 03	18 30	19 02	03 49	04 24	04 54	05 20
E 10	332 27.4	40.0	175 45.6	14.5	12 32.2	11.1	54.8	45	18 05	18 34	19 09	04 04	04 36	05 03	05 26
S 11	347 27.6	41.0	190 19.1	14.5	12 21.1	11.1	54.8	S 50	18 07	18 40	19 18	04 23	04 51	05 14	05 33
D 12	2 27.9	S 2 42.0	204 52.6	14.5	S12 10.0	11.1	54.7	52	18 08	18 42	19 23	04 32	04 58	05 19	05 36
A 13	17 28.1	42.9	219 26.1	14.6	11 58.9	11.1	54.7	54	18 09	18 45	19 28	04 41	05 06	05 24	05 40
Y 14	32 28.3	43.9	233 59.7	14.7	11 47.8	11.2	54.7	56	18 11	18 48	19 34	04 53	05 14	05 31	05 44
15	47 28.5	.. 44.9	248 33.4	14.7	11 36.6	11.3	54.7	58	18 12	18 52	19 40	05 05	05 24	05 37	05 48
16	62 28.7	45.9	263 07.1	14.7	11 25.3	11.3	54.7	S 60	18 14	18 56	19 48	05 20	05 35	05 45	05 53
17	77 28.9	46.8	277 40.8	14.8	11 14.0	11.3	54.7								
18	92 29.1	S 2 47.8	292 14.6	14.9	S11 02.7	11.4	54.7		SUN			MOON			
19	107 29.3	48.8	306 48.5	14.9	10 51.3	11.4	54.6	Day	Eqn. of Time		Mer.	Mer. Pass.		Age	Phase
20	122 29.5	49.7	321 22.4	14.9	10 39.9	11.5	54.6		00ʰ	12ʰ	Pass.	Upper	Lower		
21	137 29.7	.. 50.7	335 56.3	15.0	10 28.4	11.5	54.6	d	m s	m s	h m	h m	h m	d %	
22	152 29.9	51.7	350 30.3	15.1	10 16.9	11.5	54.6	27	09 01	09 11	11 51	21 09	08 44	10 83	
23	167 30.1	52.7	5 04.4	15.1	S10 05.4	11.6	54.6	28	09 21	09 31	11 50	21 55	09 32	11 90	
	SD 16.0	d 1.0	SD 15.2		15.0		14.9	29	09 41	09 51	11 50	22 39	10 17	12 95	

UT	ARIES GHA	VENUS −4.1 GHA	Dec	MARS −2.5 GHA	Dec	JUPITER −2.4 GHA	Dec	SATURN +0.5 GHA	Dec	STARS Name	SHA	Dec
30 00	9 11.9	220 14.2	N12 48.5	344 21.7	N 6 17.6	79 46.6	S22 40.3	71 50.4	S21 22.6	Acamar	315 14.1	S40 13.2
01	24 14.4	235 13.8	47.7	359 24.9	17.5	94 49.0	40.3	86 52.9	22.6	Achernar	335 22.3	S57 07.9
02	39 16.9	250 13.4	46.9	14 28.0	17.3	109 51.3	40.3	101 55.3	22.6	Acrux	173 04.5	S63 12.7
03	54 19.3	265 13.0 ..	46.0	29 31.1 ..	17.2	124 53.6 ..	40.3	116 57.8 ..	22.6	Adhara	255 08.6	S28 59.8
04	69 21.8	280 12.6	45.2	44 34.2	17.1	139 55.9	40.3	132 00.3	22.6	Aldebaran	290 43.4	N16 33.0
05	84 24.3	295 12.3	44.3	59 37.3	16.9	154 58.2	40.2	147 02.7	22.6			
06	99 26.7	310 11.9	N12 43.5	74 40.5	N 6 16.8	170 00.5	S22 40.2	162 05.2	S21 22.6	Alioth	166 16.7	N55 51.0
W 07	114 29.2	325 11.5	42.7	89 43.6	16.6	185 02.9	40.2	177 07.6	22.6	Alkaid	152 55.3	N49 12.9
E 08	129 31.7	340 11.1	41.8	104 46.7	16.5	200 05.2	40.2	192 10.1	22.6	Alnair	27 37.0	S46 51.7
D 09	144 34.1	355 10.7 ..	41.0	119 49.8 ..	16.4	215 07.5 ..	40.2	207 12.6 ..	22.6	Alnilam	275 41.2	S 1 11.3
N 10	159 36.6	10 10.3	40.1	134 53.0	16.2	230 09.8	40.2	222 15.0	22.6	Alphard	217 51.4	S 8 44.7
E 11	174 39.1	25 10.0	39.3	149 56.1	16.1	245 12.1	40.1	237 17.5	22.6			
S 12	189 41.5	40 09.6	N12 38.4	164 59.2	N 6 15.9	260 14.4	S22 40.1	252 19.9	S21 22.6	Alphecca	126 07.0	N26 39.0
D 13	204 44.0	55 09.2	37.6	180 02.3	15.8	275 16.8	40.1	267 22.4	22.6	Alpheratz	357 38.0	N29 12.3
A 14	219 46.4	70 08.8	36.7	195 05.5	15.7	290 19.1	40.1	282 24.9	22.6	Altair	62 03.2	N 8 55.6
Y 15	234 48.9	85 08.4 ..	35.9	210 08.6 ..	15.5	305 21.4 ..	40.1	297 27.3 ..	22.6	Ankaa	353 10.2	S42 11.6
16	249 51.4	100 08.1	35.0	225 11.7	15.4	320 23.7	40.1	312 29.8	22.6	Antares	112 20.3	S26 28.6
17	264 53.8	115 07.7	34.2	240 14.9	15.2	335 26.0	40.0	327 32.2	22.6			
18	279 56.3	130 07.3	N12 33.3	255 18.0	N 6 15.1	350 28.3	S22 40.0	342 34.7	S21 22.6	Arcturus	145 51.4	N19 04.8
19	294 58.8	145 06.9	32.5	270 21.1	15.0	5 30.6	40.0	357 37.1	22.6	Atria	107 17.8	S69 04.0
20	310 01.2	160 06.5	31.6	285 24.3	14.8	20 33.0	40.0	12 39.6	22.6	Avior	234 16.3	S59 34.2
21	325 03.7	175 06.1 ..	30.8	300 27.4 ..	14.7	35 35.3 ..	40.0	27 42.1 ..	22.6	Bellatrix	278 26.5	N 6 22.1
22	340 06.2	190 05.8	29.9	315 30.5	14.5	50 37.6	40.0	42 44.5	22.6	Betelgeuse	270 55.8	N 7 24.7
23	355 08.6	205 05.4	29.1	330 33.7	14.4	65 39.9	39.9	57 47.0	22.6			
1 00	10 11.1	220 05.0	N12 28.2	345 36.8	N 6 14.3	80 42.2	S22 39.9	72 49.4	S21 22.6	Canopus	263 53.9	S52 42.1
01	25 13.5	235 04.6	27.4	0 39.9	14.1	95 44.5	39.9	87 51.9	22.6	Capella	280 26.8	N46 00.9
02	40 16.0	250 04.2	26.5	15 43.1	14.0	110 46.8	39.9	102 54.3	22.6	Deneb	49 27.9	N45 21.5
03	55 18.5	265 03.9 ..	25.7	30 46.2 ..	13.8	125 49.1 ..	39.9	117 56.8 ..	22.6	Denebola	182 28.9	N14 27.6
04	70 20.9	280 03.5	24.8	45 49.4	13.7	140 51.4	39.8	132 59.2	22.6	Diphda	348 50.5	S17 52.4
05	85 23.4	295 03.1	23.9	60 52.5	13.5	155 53.8	39.8	148 01.7	22.6			
06	100 25.9	310 02.7	N12 23.1	75 55.7	N 6 13.4	170 56.1	S22 39.8	163 04.2	S21 22.6	Dubhe	193 46.0	N61 38.4
T 07	115 28.3	325 02.3	22.2	90 58.8	13.3	185 58.4	39.8	178 06.6	22.6	Elnath	278 06.1	N28 37.4
H 08	130 30.8	340 02.0	21.4	106 01.9	13.1	201 00.7	39.8	193 09.1	22.6	Eltanin	90 43.9	N51 29.5
U 09	145 33.3	355 01.6 ..	20.5	121 05.1 ..	13.0	216 03.0 ..	39.8	208 11.5 ..	22.6	Enif	33 42.0	N 9 58.3
R 10	160 35.7	10 01.2	19.6	136 08.2	12.8	231 05.3	39.7	223 14.0	22.6	Fomalhaut	15 18.1	S29 30.8
S 11	175 38.2	25 00.8	18.8	151 11.4	12.7	246 07.6	39.7	238 16.4	22.6			
D 12	190 40.7	40 00.4	N12 17.9	166 14.5	N 6 12.5	261 09.9	S22 39.7	253 18.9	S21 22.6	Gacrux	171 56.0	S57 13.6
A 13	205 43.1	55 00.1	17.0	181 17.7	12.4	276 12.2	39.7	268 21.3	22.6	Gienah	175 47.5	S17 39.2
Y 14	220 45.6	69 59.7	16.2	196 20.8	12.2	291 14.5	39.7	283 23.8	22.6	Hadar	148 41.4	S60 28.3
15	235 48.0	84 59.3 ..	15.3	211 24.0 ..	12.1	306 16.8 ..	39.7	298 26.2 ..	22.6	Hamal	327 54.8	N23 33.6
16	250 50.5	99 58.9	14.5	226 27.1	12.0	321 19.1	39.6	313 28.7	22.6	Kaus Aust.	83 37.1	S34 22.5
17	265 53.0	114 58.5	13.6	241 30.3	11.8	336 21.4	39.6	328 31.1	22.6			
18	280 55.4	129 58.2	N12 12.7	256 33.4	N 6 11.7	351 23.7	S22 39.6	343 33.6	S21 22.6	Kochab	137 20.9	N74 04.5
19	295 57.9	144 57.8	11.9	271 36.6	11.5	6 26.0	39.6	358 36.0	22.6	Markab	13 33.0	N15 19.1
20	311 00.4	159 57.4	11.0	286 39.7	11.4	21 28.4	39.6	13 38.5	22.6	Menkar	314 09.5	N 4 10.3
21	326 02.8	174 57.0 ..	10.1	301 42.9 ..	11.2	36 30.7 ..	39.5	28 41.0 ..	22.6	Menkent	148 02.0	S36 28.1
22	341 05.3	189 56.6	09.2	316 46.1	11.1	51 33.0	39.5	43 43.4	22.6	Miaplacidus	221 39.4	S69 47.8
23	356 07.8	204 56.3	08.4	331 49.2	10.9	66 35.3	39.5	58 45.9	22.6			
2 00	11 10.2	219 55.9	N12 07.5	346 52.4	N 6 10.8	81 37.6	S22 39.5	73 48.3	S21 22.6	Mirfak	308 32.8	N49 55.9
01	26 12.7	234 55.5	06.6	1 55.5	10.7	96 39.9	39.5	88 50.8	22.6	Nunki	75 52.0	S26 16.2
02	41 15.1	249 55.1	05.8	16 58.7	10.5	111 42.2	39.5	103 53.2	22.6	Peacock	53 11.0	S56 40.3
03	56 17.6	264 54.7 ..	04.9	32 01.9 ..	10.4	126 44.5 ..	39.4	118 55.7 ..	22.6	Pollux	243 21.7	N27 58.5
04	71 20.1	279 54.4	04.0	47 05.0	10.2	141 46.8	39.4	133 58.1	22.6	Procyon	244 54.5	N 5 10.4
05	86 22.5	294 54.0	03.1	62 08.2	10.1	156 49.1	39.4	149 00.6	22.6			
06	101 25.0	309 53.6	N12 02.3	77 11.3	N 6 09.9	171 51.4	S22 39.4	164 03.0	S21 22.6	Rasalhague	96 01.9	N12 33.0
07	116 27.5	324 53.2	01.4	92 14.5	09.8	186 53.7	39.4	179 05.5	22.6	Regulus	207 38.4	N11 52.1
F 08	131 29.9	339 52.9	12 00.5	107 17.7	09.6	201 56.0	39.3	194 07.9	22.6	Rigel	281 07.1	S 8 10.6
R 09	146 32.4	354 52.5	11 59.6	122 20.8 ..	09.5	216 58.3 ..	39.3	209 10.4 ..	22.6	Rigil Kent.	139 45.6	S60 55.1
I 10	161 34.9	9 52.1	58.8	137 24.0	09.3	232 00.6	39.3	224 12.8	22.6	Sabik	102 06.9	S15 44.9
11	176 37.3	24 51.7	57.9	152 27.2	09.2	247 02.9	39.3	239 15.3	22.6			
D 12	191 39.8	39 51.3	N11 57.0	167 30.3	N 6 09.0	262 05.2	S22 39.3	254 17.7	S21 22.6	Schedar	349 34.3	N56 39.0
A 13	206 42.3	54 51.0	56.1	182 33.5	08.9	277 07.5	39.2	269 20.2	22.6	Shaula	96 15.2	S37 07.1
Y 14	221 44.7	69 50.6	55.3	197 36.7	08.7	292 09.8	39.2	284 22.6	22.6	Sirius	258 29.3	S16 44.5
15	236 47.2	84 50.2 ..	54.4	212 39.8 ..	08.6	307 12.1 ..	39.2	299 25.1 ..	22.6	Spica	158 26.3	S11 15.9
16	251 49.6	99 49.8	53.5	227 43.0	08.4	322 14.4	39.2	314 27.5	22.6	Suhail	222 49.1	S43 30.7
17	266 52.1	114 49.5	52.6	242 46.2	08.3	337 16.7	39.2	329 30.0	22.6			
18	281 54.6	129 49.1	N11 51.7	257 49.4	N 6 08.1	352 19.0	S22 39.1	344 32.4	S21 22.6	Vega	80 35.6	N38 48.5
19	296 57.0	144 48.7	50.8	272 52.5	08.0	7 21.3	39.1	359 34.9	22.6	Zuben'ubi	137 00.1	S16 07.5
20	311 59.5	159 48.3	50.0	287 55.7	07.9	22 23.6	39.1	14 37.3	22.6		SHA	Mer.Pass.
21	327 02.0	174 48.0 ..	49.1	302 58.9 ..	07.7	37 25.9 ..	39.1	29 39.7 ..	22.6	Venus	209 53.9	9 20
22	342 04.4	189 47.6	48.2	318 02.1	07.6	52 28.2	39.1	44 42.2	22.6	Mars	335 25.7	0 57
23	357 06.9	204 47.2	47.3	333 05.2	07.4	67 30.4	39.0	59 44.6	22.6	Jupiter	70 31.1	18 34
Mer.Pass. 23 15.4		v −0.4	d 0.9	v 3.1	d 0.1	v 2.3	d 0.0	v 2.5	d 0.0	Saturn	62 38.3	19 06

UT	SUN GHA	SUN Dec	MOON GHA	v	MOON Dec	d	HP
d h	° ′	° ′	° ′	′	° ′	′	′
30 00	182 30.3	S 2 53.6	19 38.5	15.1	S 9 53.8	11.6	54.6
01	197 30.5	54.6	34 12.6	15.2	9 42.2	11.6	54.6
02	212 30.7	55.6	48 46.8	15.2	9 30.6	11.7	54.5
03	227 30.9	.. 56.5	63 21.0	15.3	9 18.9	11.7	54.5
04	242 31.1	57.5	77 55.3	15.3	9 07.2	11.7	54.5
05	257 31.3	58.5	92 29.6	15.4	8 55.5	11.7	54.5
06	272 31.6	S 2 59.4	107 04.0	15.4	S 8 43.8	11.8	54.5
W 07	287 31.8	3 00.4	121 38.4	15.4	8 32.0	11.9	54.5
E 08	302 32.0	01.4	136 12.8	15.5	8 20.1	11.8	54.5
D 09	317 32.2	.. 02.4	150 47.3	15.5	8 08.3	11.9	54.5
N 10	332 32.4	03.3	165 21.8	15.5	7 56.4	11.9	54.5
E 11	347 32.6	04.3	179 56.3	15.6	7 44.5	11.9	54.4
S 12	2 32.8	S 3 05.3	194 30.9	15.6	S 7 32.6	12.0	54.4
D 13	17 33.0	06.2	209 05.5	15.7	7 20.6	12.0	54.4
A 14	32 33.2	07.2	223 40.2	15.7	7 08.6	12.0	54.4
Y 15	47 33.4	.. 08.2	238 14.9	15.7	6 56.6	12.0	54.4
16	62 33.6	09.1	252 49.6	15.8	6 44.6	12.0	54.4
17	77 33.8	10.1	267 24.4	15.8	6 32.6	12.1	54.4
18	92 34.0	S 3 11.1	281 59.2	15.8	S 6 20.5	12.1	54.4
19	107 34.2	12.0	296 34.0	15.9	6 08.4	12.1	54.3
20	122 34.4	13.0	311 08.9	15.9	5 56.3	12.1	54.3
21	137 34.6	.. 14.0	325 43.8	15.9	5 44.2	12.2	54.3
22	152 34.8	14.9	340 18.7	15.9	5 32.0	12.1	54.3
23	167 35.0	15.9	354 53.6	16.0	5 19.9	12.2	54.3
1 00	182 35.2	S 3 16.9	9 28.6	16.0	S 5 07.7	12.2	54.3
01	197 35.4	17.9	24 03.6	16.0	4 55.5	12.2	54.3
02	212 35.6	18.8	38 38.6	16.1	4 43.3	12.3	54.3
03	227 35.8	.. 19.8	53 13.7	16.0	4 31.0	12.2	54.3
04	242 36.0	20.8	67 48.7	16.1	4 18.8	12.3	54.3
05	257 36.2	21.7	82 23.8	16.2	4 06.5	12.2	54.3
06	272 36.4	S 3 22.7	96 59.0	16.1	S 3 54.3	12.3	54.2
T 07	287 36.6	23.7	111 34.1	16.2	3 42.0	12.3	54.2
H 08	302 36.8	24.6	126 09.3	16.2	3 29.7	12.3	54.2
U 09	317 37.0	.. 25.6	140 44.5	16.2	3 17.4	12.3	54.2
R 10	332 37.2	26.6	155 19.7	16.2	3 05.1	12.3	54.2
S 11	347 37.4	27.5	169 54.9	16.2	2 52.8	12.3	54.2
D 12	2 37.6	S 3 28.5	184 30.1	16.3	S 2 40.5	12.3	54.2
A 13	17 37.8	29.5	199 05.4	16.3	2 28.2	12.4	54.2
Y 14	32 38.0	30.4	213 40.7	16.3	2 15.8	12.3	54.2
15	47 38.2	.. 31.4	228 16.0	16.3	2 03.5	12.4	54.2
16	62 38.4	32.4	242 51.3	16.3	1 51.1	12.3	54.2
17	77 38.6	33.3	257 26.6	16.3	1 38.8	12.4	54.2
18	92 38.8	S 3 34.3	272 01.9	16.4	S 1 26.4	12.3	54.1
19	107 39.0	35.3	286 37.3	16.3	1 14.1	12.4	54.1
20	122 39.2	36.2	301 12.6	16.4	1 01.7	12.3	54.1
21	137 39.4	.. 37.2	315 48.0	16.3	0 49.4	12.4	54.1
22	152 39.6	38.2	330 23.3	16.4	0 37.0	12.4	54.1
23	167 39.8	39.1	344 58.7	16.4	0 24.6	12.3	54.1
2 00	182 40.0	S 3 40.1	359 34.1	16.4	S 0 12.3	12.4	54.1
01	197 40.2	41.1	14 09.5	16.4	N 0 00.1	12.3	54.1
02	212 40.4	42.0	28 44.9	16.4	0 12.4	12.4	54.1
03	227 40.6	.. 43.0	43 20.3	16.5	0 24.8	12.3	54.1
04	242 40.8	44.0	57 55.8	16.4	0 37.1	12.4	54.1
05	257 41.0	44.9	72 31.2	16.4	0 49.5	12.3	54.1
06	272 41.2	S 3 45.9	87 06.6	16.4	N 1 01.8	12.3	54.1
07	287 41.4	46.9	101 42.0	16.5	1 14.1	12.4	54.1
08	302 41.6	47.8	116 17.5	16.4	1 26.4	12.4	54.1
F 09	317 41.8	.. 48.8	130 52.9	16.4	1 38.8	12.3	54.1
R 10	332 42.0	49.8	145 28.3	16.5	1 51.1	12.3	54.0
I 11	347 42.2	50.7	160 03.8	16.4	2 03.4	12.3	54.0
D 12	2 42.4	S 3 51.7	174 39.2	16.4	N 2 15.6	12.3	54.0
A 13	17 42.6	52.7	189 14.6	16.4	2 27.9	12.3	54.0
Y 14	32 42.8	53.6	203 50.0	16.5	2 40.2	12.2	54.0
15	47 43.0	.. 54.6	218 25.5	16.4	2 52.4	12.3	54.0
16	62 43.2	55.6	233 00.9	16.4	3 04.7	12.2	54.0
17	77 43.4	56.5	247 36.3	16.4	3 16.9	12.2	54.0
18	92 43.6	S 3 57.5	262 11.7	16.4	N 3 29.1	12.2	54.0
19	107 43.8	58.5	276 47.1	16.4	3 41.3	12.2	54.0
20	122 44.0	3 59.4	291 22.5	16.4	3 53.5	12.2	54.0
21	137 44.2	4 00.4	305 57.9	16.3	4 05.7	12.1	54.0
22	152 44.4	01.4	320 33.2	16.4	4 17.8	12.2	54.0
23	167 44.6	02.3	335 08.6	16.3	N 4 30.0	12.1	54.0
	SD 16.0	d 1.0	SD 14.8		14.8		14.7

Lat.	Twilight Naut.	Twilight Civil	Sunrise	Moonrise 30	1	2	3
°	h m	h m	h m	h m	h m	h m	h m
N 72	03 51	05 13	06 21	18 33	18 11	17 49	17 26
N 70	04 03	05 16	06 17	18 24	18 09	17 54	17 38
68	04 13	05 19	06 14	18 17	18 07	17 58	17 48
66	04 20	05 21	06 12	18 11	18 06	18 01	17 56
64	04 26	05 22	06 10	18 06	18 05	18 03	18 02
62	04 32	05 24	06 08	18 01	18 04	18 06	18 08
60	04 36	05 25	06 06	17 57	18 03	18 08	18 13
N 58	04 40	05 26	06 05	17 54	18 02	18 10	18 18
56	04 43	05 27	06 04	17 51	18 01	18 11	18 22
54	04 46	05 27	06 03	17 48	18 00	18 13	18 26
52	04 49	05 28	06 01	17 45	18 00	18 14	18 29
50	04 51	05 28	06 01	17 43	17 59	18 15	18 32
45	04 55	05 29	05 58	17 38	17 58	18 18	18 38
N 40	04 58	05 30	05 57	17 34	17 57	18 20	18 44
35	05 00	05 30	05 55	17 30	17 56	18 22	18 49
30	05 02	05 30	05 54	17 27	17 56	18 24	18 53
20	05 03	05 29	05 51	17 21	17 54	18 27	19 00
N 10	05 03	05 28	05 49	17 16	17 53	18 30	19 07
0	05 02	05 26	05 46	17 11	17 52	18 32	19 13
S 10	04 58	05 23	05 44	17 06	17 51	18 35	19 19
20	04 53	05 19	05 41	17 01	17 50	18 38	19 26
30	04 46	05 14	05 38	16 55	17 49	18 41	19 34
35	04 41	05 11	05 36	16 52	17 48	18 43	19 38
40	04 35	05 07	05 34	16 48	17 47	18 45	19 43
45	04 27	05 02	05 31	16 44	17 46	18 48	19 49
S 50	04 17	04 56	05 28	16 39	17 45	18 51	19 56
52	04 12	04 53	05 27	16 36	17 44	18 52	20 00
54	04 07	04 50	05 25	16 33	17 44	18 54	20 03
56	04 00	04 46	05 22	16 30	17 43	18 55	20 07
58	03 53	04 42	05 22	16 27	17 42	18 57	20 12
S 60	03 45	04 37	05 19	16 23	17 42	18 59	20 17

Lat.	Sunset	Twilight Civil	Twilight Naut.	Moonset 30	1	2	3
°	h m	h m	h m	h m	h m	h m	h m
N 72	17 16	18 23	19 44	02 43	04 36	06 25	08 14
N 70	17 20	18 20	19 33	02 58	04 43	06 23	08 04
68	17 23	18 18	19 24	03 10	04 48	06 22	07 57
66	17 26	18 16	19 17	03 20	04 52	06 21	07 50
64	17 28	18 15	19 11	03 29	04 55	06 20	07 45
62	17 30	18 14	19 05	03 36	04 58	06 20	07 40
60	17 31	18 13	19 01	03 42	05 01	06 19	07 36
N 58	17 33	18 12	18 58	03 47	05 03	06 18	07 33
56	17 34	18 11	18 54	03 52	05 06	06 18	07 30
54	17 35	18 11	18 52	03 56	05 07	06 17	07 27
52	17 37	18 10	18 49	04 00	05 09	06 17	07 25
50	17 38	18 10	18 47	04 04	05 11	06 17	07 22
45	17 40	18 09	18 43	04 11	05 14	06 16	07 17
N 40	17 42	18 09	18 40	04 18	05 17	06 15	07 13
35	17 43	18 09	18 38	04 23	05 19	06 15	07 10
30	17 45	18 09	18 37	04 28	05 21	06 14	07 07
20	17 48	18 10	18 35	04 36	05 25	06 13	07 01
N 10	17 50	18 11	18 36	04 43	05 28	06 12	06 56
0	17 53	18 13	18 38	04 49	05 31	06 12	06 52
S 10	17 55	18 16	18 41	04 56	05 34	06 11	06 48
20	17 58	18 20	18 46	05 03	05 37	06 10	06 43
30	18 02	18 26	18 54	05 11	05 40	06 09	06 38
35	18 04	18 29	18 59	05 15	05 42	06 08	06 35
40	18 06	18 33	19 05	05 20	05 44	06 08	06 31
45	18 08	18 38	19 13	05 26	05 47	06 07	06 27
S 50	18 12	18 44	19 23	05 33	05 50	06 06	06 22
52	18 13	18 47	19 28	05 36	05 51	06 06	06 20
54	18 15	18 51	19 34	05 40	05 53	06 05	06 18
56	18 17	18 54	19 40	05 44	05 55	06 05	06 15
58	18 19	18 59	19 48	05 48	05 56	06 04	06 12
S 60	18 21	19 04	19 56	05 53	05 58	06 04	06 09

Day	SUN Eqn. of Time 00h	SUN Eqn. of Time 12h	SUN Mer. Pass.	MOON Mer. Pass. Upper	MOON Mer. Pass. Lower	Age	Phase
d	m s	m s	h m	h m	h m	d	%
30	10 01	10 11	11 50	23 21	11 00	13	98
1	10 20	10 30	11 50	24 02	11 41	14	100
2	10 40	10 49	11 49	00 02	12 22	15	99

UT	ARIES GHA	VENUS −4.1 GHA	Dec	MARS −2.5 GHA	Dec	JUPITER −2.3 GHA	Dec	SATURN +0.5 GHA	Dec	STARS Name	SHA	Dec
3 00	12 09.4	219 46.8	N11 46.4	348 08.4	N 6 07.3	82 32.7	S22 39.0	74 47.1	S21 22.6	Acamar	315 14.1	S40 13.2
01	27 11.8	234 46.5	45.5	3 11.6	07.1	97 35.0	39.0	89 49.5	22.6	Achernar	335 22.3	S57 07.9
02	42 14.3	249 46.1	44.6	18 14.8	07.0	112 37.3	39.0	104 52.0	22.6	Acrux	173 04.5	S63 12.6
03	57 16.7	264 45.7 ..	43.8	33 18.0 ..	06.8	127 39.6 ..	39.0	119 54.4 ..	22.6	Adhara	255 08.6	S28 59.8
04	72 19.2	279 45.3	42.9	48 21.1	06.7	142 41.9	38.9	134 56.9	22.6	Aldebaran	290 43.4	N16 33.0
05	87 21.7	294 45.0	42.0	63 24.3	06.5	157 44.2	38.9	149 59.3	22.6			
06	102 24.1	309 44.6	N11 41.1	78 27.5	N 6 06.4	172 46.5	S22 38.9	165 01.8	S21 22.6	Alioth	166 16.7	N55 51.0
07	117 26.6	324 44.2	40.2	93 30.7	06.2	187 48.8	38.9	180 04.2	22.6	Alkaid	152 55.3	N49 12.8
S 08	132 29.1	339 43.8	39.3	108 33.9	06.1	202 51.1	38.9	195 06.7	22.6	Alnair	27 37.0	S46 51.8
A 09	147 31.5	354 43.5 ..	38.4	123 37.0 ..	05.9	217 53.4 ..	38.8	210 09.1 ..	22.6	Alnilam	275 41.1	S 1 11.3
T 10	162 34.0	9 43.1	37.5	138 40.2	05.8	232 55.7	38.8	225 11.6	22.6	Alphard	217 51.4	S 8 44.7
U 11	177 36.5	24 42.7	36.6	153 43.4	05.6	247 58.0	38.8	240 14.0	22.6			
R 12	192 38.9	39 42.3	N11 35.7	168 46.6	N 6 05.5	263 00.3	S22 38.8	255 16.4	S21 22.6	Alphecca	126 07.0	N26 39.0
D 13	207 41.4	54 42.0	34.8	183 49.8	05.3	278 02.5	38.8	270 18.9	22.6	Alpheratz	357 38.0	N29 12.3
A 14	222 43.9	69 41.6	33.9	198 53.0	05.2	293 04.8	38.7	285 21.3	22.6	Altair	62 03.2	N 8 55.6
Y 15	237 46.3	84 41.2 ..	33.1	213 56.2 ..	05.0	308 07.1 ..	38.7	300 23.8 ..	22.6	Ankaa	353 10.2	S42 11.6
16	252 48.8	99 40.8	32.2	229 59.4	04.9	323 09.4	38.7	315 26.2	22.6	Antares	112 20.3	S26 28.6
17	267 51.2	114 40.5	31.3	244 02.5	04.7	338 11.7	38.7	330 28.7	22.6			
18	282 53.7	129 40.1	N11 30.4	259 05.7	N 6 04.6	353 14.0	S22 38.7	345 31.1	S21 22.6	Arcturus	145 51.4	N19 04.8
19	297 56.2	144 39.7	29.5	274 08.9	04.4	8 16.3	38.6	0 33.6	22.6	Atria	107 17.8	S69 04.0
20	312 58.6	159 39.3	28.6	289 12.1	04.3	23 18.6	38.6	15 36.0	22.6	Avior	234 16.3	S59 34.2
21	328 01.1	174 39.0 ..	27.7	304 15.3 ..	04.1	38 20.9 ..	38.6	30 38.4 ..	22.6	Bellatrix	278 26.5	N 6 22.1
22	343 03.6	189 38.6	26.8	319 18.5	04.0	53 23.1	38.6	45 40.9	22.6	Betelgeuse	270 55.8	N 7 24.7
23	358 06.0	204 38.2	25.9	334 21.7	03.8	68 25.4	38.6	60 43.3	22.6			
4 00	13 08.5	219 37.8	N11 25.0	349 24.9	N 6 03.6	83 27.7	S22 38.5	75 45.8	S21 22.6	Canopus	263 53.9	S52 42.1
01	28 11.0	234 37.5	24.1	4 28.1	03.5	98 30.0	38.5	90 48.2	22.6	Capella	280 26.8	N46 00.9
02	43 13.4	249 37.1	23.2	19 31.3	03.3	113 32.3	38.5	105 50.7	22.6	Deneb	49 27.9	N45 21.5
03	58 15.9	264 36.7 ..	22.3	34 34.5 ..	03.2	128 34.6 ..	38.5	120 53.1 ..	22.6	Denebola	182 28.8	N14 27.6
04	73 18.3	279 36.3	21.4	49 37.7	03.0	143 36.9	38.5	135 55.5	22.6	Diphda	348 50.5	S17 52.4
05	88 20.8	294 36.0	20.4	64 40.9	02.9	158 39.2	38.4	150 58.0	22.5			
06	103 23.3	309 35.6	N11 19.5	79 44.1	N 6 02.7	173 41.4	S22 38.4	166 00.4	S21 22.6	Dubhe	193 46.0	N61 38.4
07	118 25.7	324 35.2	18.6	94 47.3	02.6	188 43.7	38.4	181 02.9	22.5	Elnath	278 06.1	N28 37.4
S 08	133 28.2	339 34.9	17.7	109 50.5	02.4	203 46.0	38.4	196 05.3	22.5	Eltanin	90 43.9	N51 29.5
U 09	148 30.7	354 34.5 ..	16.8	124 53.7 ..	02.3	218 48.3 ..	38.3	211 07.7 ..	22.5	Enif	33 42.0	N 9 58.3
N 10	163 33.1	9 34.1	15.9	139 56.9	02.1	233 50.6	38.3	226 10.2	22.5	Fomalhaut	15 18.1	S29 30.8
D 11	178 35.6	24 33.7	15.0	155 00.1	02.0	248 52.9	38.3	241 12.6	22.5			
A 12	193 38.1	39 33.4	N11 14.1	170 03.3	N 6 01.8	263 55.1	S22 38.3	256 15.1	S21 22.5	Gacrux	171 56.0	S57 13.5
Y 13	208 40.5	54 33.0	13.2	185 06.5	01.7	278 57.4	38.3	271 17.5	22.5	Gienah	175 47.5	S17 39.2
14	223 43.0	69 32.6	12.3	200 09.7	01.5	293 59.7	38.2	286 19.9	22.5	Hadar	148 41.4	S60 28.3
15	238 45.5	84 32.2 ..	11.4	215 12.9 ..	01.4	309 02.0 ..	38.2	301 22.4 ..	22.5	Hamal	327 54.8	N23 33.6
16	253 47.9	99 31.9	10.5	230 16.1	01.2	324 04.3	38.2	316 24.8	22.5	Kaus Aust.	83 37.2	S34 22.5
17	268 50.4	114 31.5	09.5	245 19.3	01.1	339 06.5	38.2	331 27.3	22.5			
18	283 52.8	129 31.1	N11 08.6	260 22.5	N 6 00.9	354 08.8	S22 38.2	346 29.7	S21 22.5	Kochab	137 20.9	N74 04.5
19	298 55.3	144 30.8	07.7	275 25.7	00.8	9 11.1	38.1	1 32.1	22.5	Markab	13 33.0	N15 19.1
20	313 57.8	159 30.4	06.8	290 28.9	00.6	24 13.4	38.1	16 34.6	22.5	Menkar	314 09.5	N 4 10.3
21	329 00.2	174 30.0 ..	05.9	305 32.1 ..	00.4	39 15.7 ..	38.1	31 37.0 ..	22.5	Menkent	148 02.0	S36 28.1
22	344 02.7	189 29.6	05.0	320 35.3	00.3	54 18.0	38.1	46 39.5	22.5	Miaplacidus	221 39.3	S69 47.8
23	359 05.2	204 29.3	04.1	335 38.6	00.1	69 20.2	38.1	61 41.9	22.5			
5 00	14 07.6	219 28.9	N11 03.1	350 41.8	N 6 00.0	84 22.5	S22 38.0	76 44.3	S21 22.5	Mirfak	308 32.8	N49 55.9
01	29 10.1	234 28.5	02.2	5 45.0	5 59.8	99 24.8	38.0	91 46.8	22.5	Nunki	75 52.1	S26 16.2
02	44 12.6	249 28.2	01.3	20 48.2	59.7	114 27.1	38.0	106 49.2	22.5	Peacock	53 11.0	S56 40.3
03	59 15.0	264 27.8	11 00.4	35 51.4 ..	59.5	129 29.3 ..	38.0	121 51.7 ..	22.5	Pollux	243 21.7	N27 58.5
04	74 17.5	279 27.4	10 59.5	50 54.6	59.4	144 31.6	37.9	136 54.1	22.5	Procyon	244 54.5	N 5 10.4
05	89 20.0	294 27.1	58.6	65 57.8	59.2	159 33.9	37.9	151 56.5	22.5			
06	104 22.4	309 26.7	N10 57.6	81 01.0	N 5 59.1	174 36.2	S22 37.9	166 59.0	S21 22.5	Rasalhague	96 01.9	N12 33.0
07	119 24.9	324 26.3	56.7	96 04.3	58.9	189 38.5	37.9	182 01.4	22.5	Regulus	207 38.4	N11 52.1
M 08	134 27.3	339 25.9	55.8	111 07.5	58.8	204 40.7	37.9	197 03.8	22.5	Rigel	281 07.1	S 8 10.6
O 09	149 29.8	354 25.6 ..	54.9	126 10.7 ..	58.6	219 43.0 ..	37.8	212 06.3 ..	22.5	Rigil Kent.	139 45.6	S60 55.1
N 10	164 32.3	9 25.2	54.0	141 13.9	58.4	234 45.3	37.8	227 08.7	22.5	Sabik	102 06.9	S15 44.9
D 11	179 34.7	24 24.8	53.0	156 17.1	58.3	249 47.6	37.8	242 11.2	22.5			
A 12	194 37.2	39 24.5	N10 52.1	171 20.3	N 5 58.1	264 49.8	S22 37.8	257 13.6	S21 22.5	Schedar	349 34.3	N56 39.0
Y 13	209 39.7	54 24.1	51.2	186 23.6	58.0	279 52.1	37.7	272 16.0	22.5	Shaula	96 15.2	S37 07.1
14	224 42.1	69 23.7	50.3	201 26.8	57.8	294 54.4	37.7	287 18.5	22.5	Sirius	258 29.3	S16 44.5
15	239 44.6	84 23.4 ..	49.3	216 30.0 ..	57.7	309 56.7 ..	37.7	302 20.9 ..	22.5	Spica	158 26.3	S11 15.9
16	254 47.1	99 23.0	48.4	231 33.2	57.5	324 58.9	37.7	317 23.3	22.5	Suhail	222 49.0	S43 30.6
17	269 49.5	114 22.6	47.5	246 36.4	57.4	340 01.2	37.7	332 25.8	22.5			
18	284 52.0	129 22.3	N10 46.6	261 39.7	N 5 57.2	355 03.5	S22 37.6	347 28.2	S21 22.5	Vega	80 35.6	N38 48.5
19	299 54.4	144 21.9	45.6	276 42.9	57.1	10 05.7	37.6	2 30.6	22.5	Zuben'ubi	137 00.1	S16 07.5
20	314 56.9	159 21.5	44.7	291 46.1	56.9	25 08.0	37.6	17 33.1	22.5		SHA	Mer. Pass.
21	329 59.4	174 21.1 ..	43.8	306 49.3 ..	56.7	40 10.3 ..	37.6	32 35.5 ..	22.5		° ′	h m
22	345 01.8	189 20.8	42.8	321 52.5	56.6	55 12.6	37.5	47 37.9	22.4	Venus	206 29.3	
23	0 04.3	204 20.4	41.9	336 55.8	56.4	70 14.8	37.5	62 40.4	22.4	Mars	336 16.4	0 42
	h m									Jupiter	70 19.2	18 23
Mer. Pass.	23 03.6	v −0.4	d 0.9	v 3.2	d 0.2	v 2.3	d 0.0	v 2.4	d 0.0	Saturn	62 37.3	18 54

UT	SUN GHA	SUN Dec	MOON GHA	v	MOON Dec	d	HP
d h	° ′	° ′	° ′	′	° ′	′	′
3 00	182 44.8	S 4 03.3	349 43.9	16.4	N 4 42.1	12.1	54.0
01	197 45.0	04.3	4 19.3	16.3	4 54.2	12.1	54.0
02	212 45.2	05.2	18 54.6	16.3	5 06.3	12.0	54.0
03	227 45.4	.. 06.2	33 29.9	16.3	5 18.3	12.1	54.0
04	242 45.6	07.2	48 05.2	16.3	5 30.4	12.0	54.0
05	257 45.8	08.1	62 40.5	16.3	5 42.4	12.0	54.0
S 06	272 45.9	S 4 09.1	77 15.8	16.2	N 5 54.4	11.9	54.0
A 07	287 46.1	10.1	91 51.0	16.2	6 06.3	12.0	54.0
T 08	302 46.3	11.0	106 26.2	16.3	6 18.3	11.9	54.0
U 09	317 46.5	.. 12.0	121 01.5	16.2	6 30.2	11.9	54.0
R 10	332 46.7	12.9	135 36.7	16.1	6 42.1	11.9	54.0
D 11	347 46.9	13.9	150 11.8	16.2	6 54.0	11.8	54.0
A 12	2 47.1	S 4 14.9	164 47.0	16.1	N 7 05.8	11.8	54.0
Y 13	17 47.3	15.8	179 22.1	16.2	7 17.6	11.8	54.0
14	32 47.5	16.8	193 57.3	16.0	7 29.4	11.8	54.0
15	47 47.7	.. 17.8	208 32.3	16.1	7 41.2	11.7	54.0
16	62 47.9	18.7	223 07.4	16.1	7 52.9	11.7	54.0
17	77 48.1	19.7	237 42.5	16.0	8 04.6	11.7	54.0
18	92 48.3	S 4 20.7	252 17.5	16.0	N 8 16.3	11.6	54.0
19	107 48.5	21.6	266 52.5	15.9	8 27.9	11.7	54.0
20	122 48.7	22.6	281 27.4	16.0	8 39.6	11.5	54.0
21	137 48.9	.. 23.6	296 02.4	15.9	8 51.1	11.6	54.0
22	152 49.0	24.5	310 37.3	15.9	9 02.7	11.5	54.0
23	167 49.2	25.5	325 12.2	15.9	9 14.2	11.4	54.0
4 00	182 49.4	S 4 26.4	339 47.1	15.8	N 9 25.6	11.5	54.0
01	197 49.6	27.4	354 21.9	15.8	9 37.1	11.4	54.0
02	212 49.8	28.4	8 56.7	15.7	9 48.5	11.3	54.0
03	227 50.0	.. 29.3	23 31.4	15.8	9 59.8	11.4	54.0
04	242 50.2	30.3	38 06.2	15.7	10 11.2	11.3	54.0
05	257 50.4	31.3	52 40.9	15.6	10 22.5	11.2	54.0
S 06	272 50.6	S 4 32.2	67 15.5	15.7	N10 33.7	11.2	54.0
U 07	287 50.8	33.2	81 50.2	15.6	10 44.9	11.2	54.0
N 08	302 51.0	34.1	96 24.8	15.5	10 56.1	11.1	54.0
D 09	317 51.2	.. 35.1	110 59.3	15.6	11 07.2	11.1	54.0
A 10	332 51.3	36.1	125 33.9	15.5	11 18.3	11.0	54.0
Y 11	347 51.5	37.0	140 08.4	15.4	11 29.3	11.0	54.0
12	2 51.7	S 4 38.0	154 42.8	15.4	N11 40.3	11.0	54.0
13	17 51.9	39.0	169 17.2	15.4	11 51.3	10.9	54.0
14	32 52.1	39.9	183 51.6	15.3	12 02.2	10.8	54.0
15	47 52.3	.. 40.9	198 25.9	15.3	12 13.0	10.8	54.0
16	62 52.5	41.8	213 00.2	15.3	12 23.8	10.8	54.0
17	77 52.7	42.8	227 34.5	15.2	12 34.6	10.7	54.0
18	92 52.9	S 4 43.8	242 08.7	15.2	N12 45.3	10.7	54.0
19	107 53.0	44.7	256 42.9	15.1	12 56.0	10.6	54.0
20	122 53.2	45.7	271 17.0	15.1	13 06.6	10.6	54.0
21	137 53.4	.. 46.6	285 51.1	15.0	13 17.2	10.5	54.0
22	152 53.6	47.6	300 25.1	15.0	13 27.7	10.5	54.0
23	167 53.8	48.6	314 59.1	15.0	13 38.2	10.4	54.0
5 00	182 54.0	S 4 49.5	329 33.1	14.9	N13 48.6	10.4	54.0
01	197 54.2	50.5	344 07.0	14.8	13 59.0	10.3	54.1
02	212 54.4	51.4	358 40.8	14.9	14 09.3	10.2	54.1
03	227 54.6	.. 52.4	13 14.7	14.7	14 19.5	10.2	54.1
04	242 54.7	53.4	27 48.4	14.7	14 29.7	10.1	54.1
05	257 54.9	54.3	42 22.1	14.7	14 39.8	10.1	54.1
M 06	272 55.1	S 4 55.3	56 55.8	14.6	N14 49.9	10.1	54.1
O 07	287 55.3	56.2	71 29.4	14.6	15 00.0	9.9	54.1
N 08	302 55.5	57.2	86 03.0	14.5	15 09.9	9.9	54.1
D 09	317 55.7	.. 58.2	100 36.5	14.5	15 19.8	9.9	54.1
A 10	332 55.9	4 59.1	115 10.0	14.4	15 29.7	9.8	54.1
Y 11	347 56.1	5 00.1	129 43.4	14.4	15 39.5	9.7	54.1
12	2 56.2	S 5 01.0	144 16.8	14.3	N15 49.2	9.7	54.1
13	17 56.4	02.0	158 50.1	14.2	15 58.9	9.6	54.1
14	32 56.6	03.0	173 23.3	14.2	16 08.5	9.5	54.1
15	47 56.8	.. 03.9	187 56.5	14.2	16 18.0	9.5	54.2
16	62 57.0	04.9	202 29.7	14.1	16 27.5	9.4	54.2
17	77 57.2	05.8	217 02.8	14.0	16 36.9	9.3	54.2
18	92 57.4	S 5 06.8	231 35.8	14.0	N16 46.2	9.3	54.2
19	107 57.5	07.8	246 08.8	13.9	16 55.5	9.2	54.2
20	122 57.7	08.7	260 41.7	13.9	17 04.7	9.1	54.2
21	137 57.9	.. 09.7	275 14.6	13.8	17 13.8	9.1	54.2
22	152 58.1	10.6	289 47.4	13.8	17 22.9	9.0	54.2
23	167 58.3	11.6	304 20.2	13.7	N17 31.9	8.9	54.2
	SD 16.0	d 1.0	SD 14.7		14.7		14.7

Lat.	Twilight Naut.	Twilight Civil	Sunrise	Moonrise 3	Moonrise 4	Moonrise 5	Moonrise 6
°	h m	h m	h m	h m	h m	h m	h m
N 72	04 06	05 27	06 34	17 26	16 58	16 11	▭
N 70	04 16	05 28	06 29	17 38	17 20	16 54	15 50
68	04 24	05 29	06 25	17 48	17 37	17 22	17 01
66	04 30	05 30	06 21	17 56	17 50	17 45	17 38
64	04 35	05 31	06 18	18 02	18 02	18 02	18 04
62	04 40	05 32	06 16	18 08	18 12	18 17	18 25
60	04 44	05 32	06 14	18 13	18 20	18 29	18 42
N 58	04 47	05 32	06 11	18 18	18 27	18 39	18 56
56	04 49	05 33	06 10	18 22	18 34	18 49	19 08
54	04 52	05 33	06 08	18 26	18 40	18 57	19 19
52	04 54	05 33	06 07	18 29	18 45	19 04	19 28
50	04 55	05 33	06 05	18 32	18 50	19 11	19 37
45	04 59	05 33	06 02	18 38	19 01	19 26	19 55
N 40	05 01	05 32	06 00	18 44	19 09	19 38	20 10
35	05 03	05 32	05 57	18 49	19 17	19 48	20 22
30	05 04	05 31	05 55	18 53	19 24	19 57	20 34
20	05 04	05 30	05 52	19 00	19 35	20 12	20 53
N 10	05 03	05 27	05 48	19 07	19 45	20 26	21 09
0	05 00	05 25	05 45	19 13	19 55	20 39	21 25
S 10	04 56	05 21	05 42	19 19	20 05	20 52	21 41
20	04 51	05 16	05 38	19 26	20 15	21 06	21 57
30	04 42	05 10	05 34	19 34	20 27	21 22	22 17
35	04 36	05 06	05 32	19 38	20 34	21 31	22 28
40	04 30	05 02	05 29	19 43	20 42	21 42	22 41
45	04 21	04 56	05 26	19 49	20 51	21 54	22 57
S 50	04 10	04 49	05 22	19 56	21 03	22 10	23 16
52	04 04	04 46	05 20	20 00	21 08	22 17	23 25
54	03 58	04 42	05 18	20 03	21 14	22 25	23 36
56	03 51	04 38	05 16	20 07	21 20	22 34	23 47
58	03 43	04 33	05 13	20 12	21 28	22 44	24 01
S 60	03 34	04 28	05 10	20 17	21 36	22 56	24 17

Lat.	Sunset	Twilight Civil	Twilight Naut.	Moonset 3	Moonset 4	Moonset 5	Moonset 6
°	h m	h m	h m	h m	h m	h m	h m
N 72	17 01	18 08	19 28	08 14	10 09	12 26	▭
N 70	17 06	18 07	19 18	08 04	09 49	11 44	14 22
68	17 10	18 06	19 11	07 57	09 34	11 17	13 12
66	17 14	18 05	19 05	07 50	09 21	10 56	12 36
64	17 17	18 04	19 00	07 45	09 11	10 39	12 10
62	17 20	18 04	18 55	07 40	09 02	10 26	11 51
60	17 22	18 04	18 52	07 36	08 55	10 14	11 34
N 58	17 24	18 04	18 49	07 33	08 48	10 04	11 21
56	17 26	18 03	18 46	07 30	08 42	09 55	11 09
54	17 28	18 03	18 44	07 27	08 37	09 48	10 59
52	17 30	18 03	18 42	07 25	08 32	09 41	10 50
50	17 31	18 03	18 41	07 22	08 28	09 35	10 42
45	17 34	18 04	18 37	07 17	08 19	09 22	10 24
N 40	17 37	18 04	18 35	07 13	08 12	09 11	10 10
35	17 39	18 05	18 34	07 10	08 05	09 01	09 58
30	17 41	18 05	18 33	07 07	08 00	08 53	09 48
20	17 45	18 07	18 33	07 01	07 50	08 39	09 30
N 10	17 49	18 10	18 34	06 56	07 41	08 27	09 15
0	17 52	18 13	18 37	06 52	07 33	08 16	09 01
S 10	17 55	18 16	18 41	06 48	07 25	08 05	08 46
20	17 59	18 21	18 47	06 43	07 17	07 53	08 31
30	18 03	18 27	18 56	06 38	07 07	07 39	08 14
35	18 06	18 31	19 01	06 35	07 02	07 31	08 04
40	18 09	18 36	19 08	06 31	06 55	07 22	07 52
45	18 12	18 42	19 17	06 27	06 48	07 12	07 38
S 50	18 16	18 49	19 29	06 22	06 40	06 59	07 22
52	18 18	18 53	19 34	06 20	06 36	06 53	07 14
54	18 20	18 57	19 40	06 18	06 31	06 47	07 06
56	18 23	19 01	19 48	06 15	06 26	06 39	06 56
58	18 25	19 06	19 56	06 12	06 21	06 31	06 45
S 60	18 28	19 11	20 05	06 09	06 15	06 22	06 33

	SUN			MOON			
Day	Eqn. of Time 00ʰ	12ʰ	Mer. Pass.	Mer. Pass. Upper	Lower	Age	Phase
d	m s	m s	h m	h m	h m	d	%
3	10 59	11 08	11 49	00 42	13 03	16	98
4	11 17	11 27	11 49	01 23	13 44	17	94
5	11 36	11 45	11 48	02 05	14 27	18	89

UT	ARIES GHA	VENUS −4·1 GHA	Dec	MARS −2·6 GHA	Dec	JUPITER −2·3 GHA	Dec	SATURN +0·5 GHA	Dec	STARS Name	SHA	Dec
6 00	15 06.8	219 20.0	N10 41.0	351 59.0	N 5 56.3	85 17.1	S22 37.5	77 42.8	S21 22.4	Acamar	315 14.1	S40 13.2
01	30 09.2	234 19.7	40.0	7 02.2	56.1	100 19.4	37.5	92 45.2	22.4	Achernar	335 22.3	S57 07.9
02	45 11.7	249 19.3	39.1	22 05.4	56.0	115 21.7	37.4	107 47.7	22.4	Acrux	173 04.5	S63 12.6
03	60 14.2	264 18.9	.. 38.2	37 08.7	.. 55.8	130 23.9	.. 37.4	122 50.1	.. 22.4	Adhara	255 08.6	S28 59.8
04	75 16.6	279 18.6	37.2	52 11.9	55.6	145 26.2	37.4	137 52.5	22.4	Aldebaran	290 43.4	N16 33.0
05	90 19.1	294 18.2	36.3	67 15.1	55.5	160 28.5	37.4	152 55.0	22.4			
06	105 21.6	309 17.8	N10 35.4	82 18.4	N 5 55.3	175 30.7	S22 37.4	167 57.4	S21 22.4	Alioth	166 16.7	N55 51.0
07	120 24.0	324 17.5	34.4	97 21.6	55.2	190 33.0	37.3	182 59.8	22.4	Alkaid	152 55.3	N49 12.8
T 08	135 26.5	339 17.1	33.5	112 24.8	55.0	205 35.3	37.3	198 02.3	22.4	Alnair	27 37.0	S46 51.8
U 09	150 28.9	354 16.7	.. 32.6	127 28.0	.. 54.9	220 37.5	.. 37.3	213 04.7	.. 22.4	Alnilam	275 41.1	S 1 11.3
E 10	165 31.4	9 16.4	31.6	142 31.3	54.7	235 39.8	37.3	228 07.1	22.4	Alphard	217 51.3	S 8 44.7
S 11	180 33.9	24 16.0	30.7	157 34.5	54.6	250 42.1	37.2	243 09.6	22.4			
D 12	195 36.3	39 15.6	N10 29.8	172 37.7	N 5 54.4	265 44.3	S22 37.2	258 12.0	S21 22.4	Alphecca	126 07.0	N26 39.0
A 13	210 38.8	54 15.3	28.8	187 41.0	54.3	280 46.6	37.2	273 14.4	22.4	Alpheratz	357 38.0	N29 12.3
Y 14	225 41.3	69 14.9	27.9	202 44.2	54.1	295 48.9	37.2	288 16.9	22.4	Altair	62 03.3	N 8 55.6
15	240 43.7	84 14.5	.. 26.9	217 47.4	.. 53.9	310 51.1	.. 37.1	303 19.3	.. 22.4	Ankaa	353 10.2	S42 11.6
16	255 46.2	99 14.2	26.0	232 50.7	53.8	325 53.4	37.1	318 21.7	22.4	Antares	112 20.3	S26 28.6
17	270 48.7	114 13.8	25.1	247 53.9	53.6	340 55.7	37.1	333 24.2	22.4			
18	285 51.1	129 13.4	N10 24.1	262 57.1	N 5 53.5	355 57.9	S22 37.1	348 26.6	S21 22.4	Arcturus	145 51.4	N19 04.7
19	300 53.6	144 13.1	23.2	278 00.4	53.3	11 00.2	37.0	3 29.0	22.4	Atria	107 17.9	S69 04.0
20	315 56.1	159 12.7	22.2	293 03.6	53.2	26 02.5	37.0	18 31.5	22.4	Avior	234 16.3	S59 34.2
21	330 58.5	174 12.3	.. 21.3	308 06.8	.. 53.0	41 04.7	.. 37.0	33 33.9	.. 22.4	Bellatrix	278 26.5	N 6 22.1
22	346 01.0	189 12.0	20.4	323 10.1	52.8	56 07.0	37.0	48 36.3	22.4	Betelgeuse	270 55.7	N 7 24.7
23	1 03.4	204 11.6	19.4	338 13.3	52.7	71 09.3	37.0	63 38.7	22.4			
7 00	16 05.9	219 11.2	N10 18.5	353 16.5	N 5 52.5	86 11.5	S22 36.9	78 41.2	S21 22.4	Canopus	263 53.8	S52 42.1
01	31 08.4	234 10.9	17.5	8 19.8	52.4	101 13.8	36.9	93 43.6	22.4	Capella	280 26.8	N46 00.9
02	46 10.8	249 10.5	16.6	23 23.0	52.2	116 16.0	36.9	108 46.0	22.3	Deneb	49 27.9	N45 21.5
03	61 13.3	264 10.1	.. 15.6	38 26.3	.. 52.1	131 18.3	.. 36.9	123 48.5	.. 22.3	Denebola	182 28.8	N14 27.6
04	76 15.8	279 09.8	14.7	53 29.5	51.9	146 20.6	36.8	138 50.9	22.3	Diphda	348 50.5	S17 52.4
05	91 18.2	294 09.4	13.7	68 32.7	51.8	161 22.8	36.8	153 53.3	22.3			
06	106 20.7	309 09.0	N10 12.8	83 36.0	N 5 51.6	176 25.1	S22 36.8	168 55.8	S21 22.3	Dubhe	193 46.0	N61 38.4
W 07	121 23.2	324 08.7	11.8	98 39.2	51.4	191 27.4	36.8	183 58.2	22.3	Elnath	278 06.1	N28 37.4
E 08	136 25.6	339 08.3	10.9	113 42.4	51.3	206 29.6	36.7	199 00.6	22.3	Eltanin	90 43.9	N51 29.5
D 09	151 28.1	354 07.9	.. 09.9	128 45.7	.. 51.1	221 31.9	.. 36.7	214 03.0	.. 22.3	Enif	33 42.0	N 9 58.3
N 10	166 30.5	9 07.6	09.0	143 48.9	51.0	236 34.1	36.7	229 05.5	22.3	Fomalhaut	15 18.1	S29 30.8
E 11	181 33.0	24 07.2	08.0	158 52.2	50.8	251 36.4	36.7	244 07.9	22.3			
S 12	196 35.5	39 06.9	N10 07.1	173 55.4	N 5 50.7	266 38.7	S22 36.6	259 10.3	S21 22.3	Gacrux	171 56.0	S57 13.5
D 13	211 37.9	54 06.5	06.1	188 58.7	50.5	281 40.9	36.6	274 12.7	22.3	Gienah	175 47.5	S17 39.2
A 14	226 40.4	69 06.1	05.2	204 01.9	50.3	296 43.2	36.6	289 15.2	22.3	Hadar	148 41.4	S60 28.2
Y 15	241 42.9	84 05.8	.. 04.2	219 05.1	.. 50.2	311 45.4	.. 36.6	304 17.6	.. 22.3	Hamal	327 54.7	N23 33.6
16	256 45.3	99 05.4	03.3	234 08.4	50.0	326 47.7	36.5	319 20.0	22.3	Kaus Aust.	83 37.2	S34 22.5
17	271 47.8	114 05.0	02.3	249 11.6	49.9	341 49.9	36.5	334 22.5	22.3			
18	286 50.3	129 04.7	N10 01.4	264 14.9	N 5 49.7	356 52.2	S22 36.5	349 24.9	S21 22.3	Kochab	137 21.0	N74 04.5
19	301 52.7	144 04.3	10 00.4	279 18.1	49.6	11 54.5	36.5	4 27.3	22.3	Markab	13 33.0	N15 19.1
20	316 55.2	159 03.9	9 59.5	294 21.4	49.4	26 56.7	36.4	19 29.7	22.3	Menkar	314 09.5	N 4 10.3
21	331 57.7	174 03.6	.. 58.5	309 24.6	.. 49.2	41 59.0	.. 36.4	34 32.2	.. 22.3	Menkent	148 02.0	S36 28.1
22	347 00.1	189 03.2	57.5	324 27.9	49.1	57 01.2	36.4	49 34.6	22.3	Miaplacidus	221 39.3	S69 47.8
23	2 02.6	204 02.9	56.6	339 31.1	48.9	72 03.5	36.4	64 37.0	22.3			
8 00	17 05.0	219 02.5	N 9 55.6	354 34.3	N 5 48.8	87 05.7	S22 36.3	79 39.4	S21 22.2	Mirfak	308 32.8	N49 55.9
01	32 07.5	234 02.1	54.7	9 37.6	48.6	102 08.0	36.3	94 41.9	22.2	Nunki	75 52.1	S26 16.2
02	47 10.0	249 01.8	53.7	24 40.8	48.5	117 10.3	36.3	109 44.3	22.2	Peacock	53 11.0	S56 40.3
03	62 12.4	264 01.4	.. 52.7	39 44.1	.. 48.3	132 12.5	.. 36.3	124 46.7	.. 22.2	Pollux	243 21.6	N27 58.5
04	77 14.9	279 01.0	51.8	54 47.3	48.2	147 14.8	36.2	139 49.1	22.2	Procyon	244 54.5	N 5 10.4
05	92 17.4	294 00.7	50.8	69 50.6	48.0	162 17.0	36.2	154 51.6	22.2			
06	107 19.8	309 00.3	N 9 49.9	84 53.8	N 5 47.9	177 19.3	S22 36.2	169 54.0	S21 22.2	Rasalhague	96 01.9	N12 33.0
07	122 22.3	324 00.0	48.9	99 57.1	47.7	192 21.5	36.2	184 56.4	22.2	Regulus	207 38.4	N11 52.1
T 08	137 24.8	338 59.6	47.9	115 00.3	47.5	207 23.8	36.1	199 58.8	22.2	Rigel	281 07.1	S 8 10.6
H 09	152 27.2	353 59.2	.. 47.0	130 03.6	.. 47.4	222 26.0	.. 36.1	215 01.3	.. 22.2	Rigil Kent.	139 45.6	S60 55.1
U 10	167 29.7	8 58.9	46.0	145 06.8	47.2	237 28.3	36.1	230 03.7	22.2	Sabik	102 06.9	S15 44.9
R 11	182 32.2	23 58.5	45.0	160 10.1	47.1	252 30.5	36.1	245 06.1	22.2			
S 12	197 34.6	38 58.1	N 9 44.1	175 13.3	N 5 46.9	267 32.8	S22 36.0	260 08.5	S21 22.2	Schedar	349 34.3	N56 39.0
D 13	212 37.1	53 57.8	43.1	190 16.6	46.7	282 35.0	36.0	275 10.9	22.2	Shaula	96 15.2	S37 07.1
A 14	227 39.5	68 57.4	42.1	205 19.8	46.6	297 37.3	36.0	290 13.4	22.2	Sirius	258 29.3	S16 44.5
Y 15	242 42.0	83 57.1	.. 41.2	220 23.1	.. 46.4	312 39.5	.. 36.0	305 15.8	.. 22.2	Spica	158 26.3	S11 15.9
16	257 44.5	98 56.7	40.2	235 26.3	46.3	327 41.8	35.9	320 18.2	22.2	Suhail	222 49.0	S43 30.6
17	272 46.9	113 56.3	39.2	250 29.6	46.1	342 44.0	35.9	335 20.6	22.2			
18	287 49.4	128 56.0	N 9 38.3	265 32.8	N 5 46.0	357 46.3	S22 35.9	350 23.1	S21 22.2	Vega	80 35.6	N38 48.5
19	302 51.9	143 55.6	37.3	280 36.1	45.8	12 48.5	35.9	5 25.5	22.2	Zuben'ubi	137 00.1	S16 07.5
20	317 54.3	158 55.2	36.3	295 39.4	45.6	27 50.8	35.8	20 27.9	22.2		SHA	Mer. Pass.
21	332 56.8	173 54.9	.. 35.4	310 42.6	.. 45.5	42 53.0	.. 35.8	35 30.3	.. 22.1		° ′	h m
22	347 59.3	188 54.5	34.4	325 45.9	45.3	57 55.3	35.8	50 32.7	22.1	Venus	203 05.3	9 23
23	3 01.7	203 54.2	33.4	340 49.1	45.2	72 57.5	35.7	65 35.2	22.1	Mars	337 10.6	0 27
	h m									Jupiter	70 05.6	18 12
Mer. Pass. 22 51.9	v −0.4 d 1.0			v 3.2 d 0.2		v 2.3 d 0.0		v 2.4 d 0.0		Saturn	62 35.3	18 42

	UT	SUN GHA	SUN Dec	MOON GHA	MOON v	MOON Dec	MOON d	MOON HP
	d h	° ′	° ′	° ′	′	° ′	′	′
	6 00	182 58.5	S 5 12.6	318 52.9	13.6	N17 40.8	8.9	54.2
	01	197 58.6	13.5	333 25.5	13.6	17 49.7	8.8	54.3
	02	212 58.8	14.5	347 58.1	13.5	17 58.5	8.7	54.3
	03	227 59.0	. . 15.4	2 30.6	13.5	18 07.2	8.6	54.3
	04	242 59.2	16.4	17 03.1	13.4	18 15.8	8.6	54.3
	05	257 59.4	17.3	31 35.5	13.3	18 24.4	8.4	54.3
	06	272 59.6	S 5 18.3	46 07.8	13.3	N18 32.8	8.5	54.3
	07	287 59.7	19.3	60 40.1	13.2	18 41.3	8.3	54.3
T	08	302 59.9	20.2	75 12.3	13.2	18 49.6	8.2	54.3
U	09	318 00.1	. . 21.2	89 44.5	13.1	18 57.8	8.2	54.4
E	10	333 00.3	22.1	104 16.6	13.0	19 06.0	8.1	54.4
S	11	348 00.5	23.1	118 48.6	13.0	19 14.1	8.0	54.4
D	12	3 00.7	S 5 24.0	133 20.6	12.9	N19 22.1	8.0	54.4
A	13	18 00.8	25.0	147 52.5	12.9	19 30.1	7.8	54.4
Y	14	33 01.0	26.0	162 24.4	12.8	19 37.9	7.8	54.4
	15	48 01.2	. . 26.9	176 56.2	12.7	19 45.7	7.7	54.4
	16	63 01.4	27.9	191 27.9	12.7	19 53.4	7.6	54.4
	17	78 01.6	28.8	205 59.6	12.6	20 01.0	7.5	54.5
	18	93 01.7	S 5 29.8	220 31.2	12.5	N20 08.5	7.4	54.5
	19	108 01.9	30.7	235 02.7	12.5	20 15.9	7.3	54.5
	20	123 02.1	31.7	249 34.2	12.4	20 23.2	7.3	54.5
	21	138 02.3	. . 32.7	264 05.6	12.3	20 30.5	7.2	54.5
	22	153 02.5	33.6	278 36.9	12.3	20 37.7	7.0	54.5
	23	168 02.7	34.6	293 08.2	12.2	20 44.7	7.0	54.6
	7 00	183 02.8	S 5 35.5	307 39.4	12.2	N20 51.7	6.9	54.6
	01	198 03.0	36.5	322 10.6	12.1	20 58.6	6.8	54.6
	02	213 03.2	37.4	336 41.7	12.0	21 05.4	6.7	54.6
	03	228 03.4	. . 38.4	351 12.7	11.9	21 12.1	6.6	54.6
	04	243 03.5	39.3	5 43.6	11.9	21 18.7	6.6	54.6
	05	258 03.7	40.3	20 14.5	11.9	21 25.3	6.4	54.7
	06	273 03.9	S 5 41.2	34 45.4	11.7	N21 31.7	6.3	54.7
W	07	288 04.1	42.2	49 16.1	11.7	21 38.0	6.3	54.7
E	08	303 04.3	43.2	63 46.8	11.7	21 44.3	6.1	54.7
D	09	318 04.4	. . 44.1	78 17.5	11.6	21 50.4	6.0	54.7
N	10	333 04.6	45.1	92 48.1	11.5	21 56.4	6.0	54.7
E	11	348 04.8	46.0	107 18.6	11.4	22 02.4	5.8	54.8
S	12	3 05.0	S 5 47.0	121 49.0	11.4	N22 08.2	5.8	54.8
D	13	18 05.2	47.9	136 19.4	11.3	22 14.0	5.6	54.8
A	14	33 05.3	48.9	150 49.7	11.3	22 19.6	5.6	54.8
Y	15	48 05.5	. . 49.8	165 20.0	11.1	22 25.2	5.4	54.8
	16	63 05.7	50.8	179 50.1	11.2	22 30.6	5.3	54.9
	17	78 05.9	51.7	194 20.3	11.0	22 35.9	5.3	54.9
	18	93 06.0	S 5 52.7	208 50.3	11.0	N22 41.2	5.1	54.9
	19	108 06.2	53.6	223 20.3	11.0	22 46.3	5.0	54.9
	20	123 06.4	54.6	237 50.3	10.8	22 51.3	4.9	54.9
	21	138 06.6	. . 55.6	252 20.1	10.9	22 56.2	4.8	55.0
	22	153 06.7	56.5	266 50.0	10.7	23 01.0	4.7	55.0
	23	168 06.9	57.5	281 19.7	10.7	23 05.7	4.6	55.0
	8 00	183 07.1	S 5 58.4	295 49.4	10.6	N23 10.3	4.5	55.0
	01	198 07.3	5 59.4	310 19.0	10.6	23 14.8	4.3	55.1
	02	213 07.4	6 00.3	324 48.6	10.5	23 19.1	4.3	55.1
	03	228 07.6	. . 01.3	339 18.1	10.4	23 23.4	4.1	55.1
	04	243 07.8	02.2	353 47.5	10.4	23 27.5	4.1	55.1
	05	258 08.0	03.2	8 16.9	10.3	23 31.6	3.9	55.1
	06	273 08.1	S 6 04.1	22 46.2	10.3	N23 35.5	3.8	55.2
T	07	288 08.3	05.1	37 15.5	10.2	23 39.3	3.7	55.2
H	08	303 08.5	06.0	51 44.7	10.2	23 43.0	3.5	55.2
U	09	318 08.7	. . 07.0	66 13.9	10.0	23 46.5	3.5	55.2
R	10	333 08.8	07.9	80 42.9	10.1	23 50.0	3.3	55.3
S	11	348 09.0	08.9	95 12.0	10.0	23 53.3	3.3	55.3
D	12	3 09.2	S 6 09.8	109 41.0	9.9	N23 56.6	3.1	55.3
A	13	18 09.4	10.8	124 09.9	9.8	23 59.7	2.9	55.3
Y	14	33 09.5	11.7	138 38.7	9.8	24 02.6	2.9	55.4
	15	48 09.7	. . 12.7	153 07.5	9.8	24 05.5	2.7	55.4
	16	63 09.9	13.6	167 36.3	9.7	24 08.2	2.7	55.4
	17	78 10.0	14.6	182 05.0	9.6	24 10.9	2.5	55.4
	18	93 10.2	S 6 15.5	196 33.6	9.6	N24 13.4	2.4	55.5
	19	108 10.4	16.5	211 02.2	9.6	24 15.8	2.2	55.5
	20	123 10.6	17.4	225 30.8	9.5	24 18.0	2.1	55.5
	21	138 10.7	. . 18.4	239 59.3	9.4	24 20.1	2.0	55.6
	22	153 10.9	19.3	254 27.7	9.4	24 22.1	1.9	55.6
	23	168 11.1	20.3	268 56.1	9.3	N24 24.0	1.8	55.6
		SD 16.0	*d* 1.0	SD 14.8		14.9		15.1

Lat.	Twilight Naut.	Twilight Civil	Sunrise	Moonrise 6	Moonrise 7	Moonrise 8	Moonrise 9
°	h m	h m	h m	h m	h m	h m	h m
N 72	04 21	05 40	06 48	☐	☐	☐	☐
N 70	04 29	05 40	06 41	15 50	☐	☐	☐
68	04 35	05 40	06 36	17 01	☐	☐	☐
66	04 40	05 40	06 31	17 38	17 29	☐	☐
64	04 44	05 40	06 27	18 04	18 11	18 28	19 12
62	04 48	05 39	06 24	18 25	18 39	19 06	19 54
60	04 51	05 39	06 21	18 42	19 01	19 33	20 22
N 58	04 53	05 39	06 18	18 56	19 19	19 54	20 44
56	04 55	05 39	06 16	19 08	19 34	20 11	21 02
54	04 57	05 38	06 14	19 19	19 47	20 26	21 17
52	04 59	05 38	06 12	19 28	19 59	20 39	21 30
50	05 00	05 37	06 10	19 37	20 09	20 50	21 42
45	05 03	05 36	06 06	19 55	20 30	21 14	22 06
N 40	05 04	05 35	06 03	20 10	20 48	21 33	22 25
35	05 05	05 34	06 00	20 22	21 02	21 48	22 41
30	05 05	05 33	05 57	20 34	21 15	22 02	22 55
20	05 05	05 30	05 52	20 53	21 37	22 26	23 19
N 10	05 03	05 27	05 48	21 09	21 56	22 46	23 39
0	05 00	05 24	05 44	21 25	22 14	23 05	23 58
S 10	04 55	05 19	05 40	21 41	22 31	23 24	24 17
20	04 48	05 14	05 36	21 57	22 51	23 44	24 38
30	04 38	05 07	05 31	22 17	23 13	24 08	00 08
35	04 32	05 02	05 28	22 28	23 26	24 22	00 22
40	04 24	04 57	05 24	22 41	23 41	24 38	00 38
45	04 15	04 50	05 20	22 57	23 59	24 57	00 57
S 50	04 03	04 42	05 15	23 16	24 21	00 21	01 21
52	03 57	04 39	05 13	23 25	24 32	00 32	01 33
54	03 50	04 34	05 11	23 36	24 44	00 44	01 46
56	03 42	04 30	05 08	23 47	24 58	00 58	02 02
58	03 34	04 24	05 05	24 01	00 01	01 14	02 20
S 60	03 23	04 18	05 01	24 17	00 17	01 34	02 42

Lat.	Sunset	Twilight Civil	Twilight Naut.	Moonset 6	Moonset 7	Moonset 8	Moonset 9
°	h m	h m	h m	h m	h m	h m	h m
N 72	16 45	17 53	19 12	☐	☐	☐	☐
N 70	16 52	17 53	19 04	14 22	☐	☐	☐
68	16 58	17 54	18 58	13 12	☐	☐	☐
66	17 03	17 54	18 53	12 36	14 25	☐	☐
64	17 07	17 54	18 49	12 10	13 43	15 11	16 17
62	17 10	17 55	18 46	11 51	13 15	14 33	15 35
60	17 13	17 55	18 43	11 34	12 53	14 07	15 07
N 58	17 16	17 55	18 41	11 21	12 36	13 46	14 45
56	17 19	17 56	18 39	11 09	12 21	13 29	14 27
54	17 21	17 56	18 37	10 59	12 08	13 14	14 12
52	17 23	17 57	18 36	10 50	11 57	13 01	13 59
50	17 25	17 57	18 34	10 42	11 47	12 50	13 47
45	17 29	17 58	18 32	10 24	11 27	12 27	13 23
N 40	17 32	17 59	18 31	10 10	11 10	12 08	13 04
35	17 35	18 00	18 30	09 58	10 56	11 53	12 48
30	17 38	18 02	18 30	09 48	10 44	11 39	12 34
20	17 43	18 05	18 30	09 30	10 23	11 16	12 10
N 10	17 47	18 08	18 32	09 15	10 05	10 57	11 50
0	17 51	18 12	18 36	09 01	09 48	10 38	11 30
S 10	17 55	18 16	18 41	08 46	09 31	10 19	11 11
20	18 00	18 22	18 48	08 31	09 13	10 00	10 51
30	18 05	18 29	18 58	08 14	08 53	09 37	10 27
35	18 08	18 34	19 04	08 04	08 41	09 23	10 13
40	18 12	18 39	19 12	07 52	08 27	09 08	09 56
45	18 16	18 46	19 22	07 38	08 10	08 50	09 37
S 50	18 21	18 54	19 34	07 22	07 50	08 27	09 13
52	18 23	18 58	19 40	07 14	07 41	08 16	09 01
54	18 26	19 02	19 47	07 06	07 30	08 03	08 48
56	18 29	19 07	19 55	06 56	07 18	07 49	08 32
58	18 32	19 13	20 04	06 45	07 04	07 32	08 14
S 60	18 36	19 19	20 14	06 33	06 48	07 12	07 52

Day	SUN Eqn. of Time 00^h	SUN Eqn. of Time 12^h	SUN Mer. Pass.	MOON Mer. Pass. Upper	MOON Mer. Pass. Lower	MOON Age	Phase
d	m s	m s	h m	h m	h m	d %	
6	11 53	12 02	11 48	02 50	15 13	19 82	
7	12 11	12 20	11 48	03 36	16 01	20 74	
8	12 28	12 36	11 47	04 26	16 51	21 65	

UT	ARIES GHA	VENUS −4.1 GHA	Dec	MARS −2.6 GHA	Dec	JUPITER −2.3 GHA	Dec	SATURN +0.5 GHA	Dec	STARS Name	SHA	Dec
9 00	18 04.2	218 53.8	N 9 32.5	355 52.4	N 5 45.0	87 59.8	S22 35.7	80 37.6	S21 22.1	Acamar	315 14.1	S40 13.2
01	33 06.7	233 53.4	31.5	10 55.6	44.9	103 02.0	35.7	95 40.0	22.1	Achernar	335 22.3	S57 07.9
02	48 09.1	248 53.1	30.5	25 58.9	44.7	118 04.3	35.7	110 42.4	22.1	Acrux	173 04.4	S63 12.6
03	63 11.6	263 52.7 ..	29.5	41 02.1 ..	44.5	133 06.5 ..	35.6	125 44.9 ..	22.1	Adhara	255 08.5	S28 59.8
04	78 14.0	278 52.4	28.6	56 05.4	44.4	148 08.8	35.6	140 47.3	22.1	Aldebaran	290 43.4	N16 33.0
05	93 16.5	293 52.0	27.6	71 08.7	44.3	163 11.0	35.6	155 49.7	22.1			
06	108 19.0	308 51.6	N 9 26.6	86 11.9	N 5 44.1	178 13.3	S22 35.5	170 52.1	S21 22.1	Alioth	166 16.7	N55 51.0
07	123 21.4	323 51.3	25.6	101 15.2	43.9	193 15.5	35.5	185 54.5	22.1	Alkaid	152 55.3	N49 12.8
08	138 23.9	338 50.9	24.7	116 18.4	43.8	208 17.8	35.5	200 57.0	22.1	Alnair	27 37.0	S46 51.8
F 09	153 26.4	353 50.6 ..	23.7	131 21.7 ..	43.6	223 20.0 ..	35.5	215 59.4 ..	22.1	Alnilam	275 41.1	S 1 11.3
R 10	168 28.8	8 50.2	22.7	146 24.9	43.5	238 22.2	35.5	231 01.8	22.1	Alphard	217 51.3	S 8 44.7
I 11	183 31.3	23 49.8	21.7	161 28.2	43.3	253 24.5	35.4	246 04.2	22.1			
D 12	198 33.8	38 49.5	N 9 20.8	176 31.5	N 5 43.1	268 26.7	S22 35.4	261 06.6	S21 22.1	Alphecca	126 07.0	N26 39.0
A 13	213 36.2	53 49.1	19.8	191 34.7	43.0	283 29.0	35.4	276 09.0	22.1	Alpheratz	357 38.0	N29 12.3
Y 14	228 38.7	68 48.8	18.8	206 38.0	42.8	298 31.2	35.3	291 11.5	22.0	Altair	62 03.3	N 8 55.6
15	243 41.1	83 48.4 ..	17.8	221 41.2 ..	42.7	313 33.5 ..	35.3	306 13.9 ..	22.0	Ankaa	353 10.2	S42 11.7
16	258 43.6	98 48.0	16.8	236 44.5	42.5	328 35.7	35.3	321 16.3	22.0	Antares	112 20.3	S26 28.5
17	273 46.1	113 47.7	15.9	251 47.8	42.4	343 37.9	35.3	336 18.7	22.0			
18	288 48.5	128 47.3	N 9 14.9	266 51.0	N 5 42.2	358 40.2	S22 35.2	351 21.1	S21 22.0	Arcturus	145 51.4	N19 04.7
19	303 51.0	143 47.0	13.9	281 54.3	42.0	13 42.4	35.2	6 23.6	22.0	Atria	107 17.9	S69 03.9
20	318 53.5	158 46.6	12.9	296 57.5	41.9	28 44.7	35.2	21 26.0	22.0	Avior	234 16.2	S59 34.2
21	333 55.9	173 46.3 ..	11.9	312 00.8 ..	41.7	43 46.9 ..	35.2	36 28.4 ..	22.0	Bellatrix	278 26.4	N 6 22.1
22	348 58.4	188 45.9	10.9	327 04.1	41.6	58 49.2	35.1	51 30.8	22.0	Betelgeuse	270 55.7	N 7 24.7
23	4 00.9	203 45.5	10.0	342 07.3	41.4	73 51.4	35.1	66 33.2	22.0			
10 00	19 03.3	218 45.2	N 9 09.0	357 10.6	N 5 41.3	88 53.6	S22 35.1	81 35.6	S21 22.0	Canopus	263 53.8	S52 42.1
01	34 05.8	233 44.8	08.0	12 13.8	41.1	103 55.9	35.1	96 38.1	22.0	Capella	280 26.8	N46 00.9
02	49 08.3	248 44.5	07.0	27 17.1	41.0	118 58.1	35.0	111 40.5	22.0	Deneb	49 27.9	N45 21.5
03	64 10.7	263 44.1 ..	06.0	42 20.4 ..	40.8	134 00.4 ..	35.0	126 42.9 ..	22.0	Denebola	182 28.8	N14 27.6
04	79 13.2	278 43.7	05.0	57 23.6	40.6	149 02.6	35.0	141 45.3	22.0	Diphda	348 50.5	S17 52.4
05	94 15.6	293 43.4	04.0	72 26.9	40.5	164 04.8	34.9	156 47.7	22.0			
06	109 18.1	308 43.0	N 9 03.1	87 30.1	N 5 40.3	179 07.1	S22 34.9	171 50.1	S21 22.0	Dubhe	193 45.9	N61 38.3
07	124 20.6	323 42.7	02.1	102 33.4	40.2	194 09.3	34.9	186 52.6	21.9	Elnath	278 06.1	N28 37.4
S 08	139 23.0	338 42.3	01.1	117 36.7	40.0	209 11.5	34.9	201 55.0	21.9	Eltanin	90 44.0	N51 29.5
A 09	154 25.5	353 42.0	9 00.1	132 39.9 ..	39.9	224 13.8 ..	34.8	216 57.4 ..	21.9	Enif	33 42.0	N 9 58.3
T 10	169 28.0	8 41.6	8 59.1	147 43.2	39.7	239 16.0	34.8	231 59.8	21.9	Fomalhaut	15 18.1	S29 30.8
U 11	184 30.4	23 41.2	58.1	162 46.5	39.6	254 18.3	34.8	247 02.2	21.9			
R 12	199 32.9	38 40.9	N 8 57.1	177 49.7	N 5 39.4	269 20.5	S22 34.7	262 04.6	S21 21.9	Gacrux	171 55.9	S57 13.5
D 13	214 35.4	53 40.5	56.1	192 53.0	39.2	284 22.7	34.7	277 07.0	21.9	Gienah	175 47.4	S17 39.2
A 14	229 37.8	68 40.2	55.1	207 56.3	39.1	299 25.0	34.7	292 09.5	21.9	Hadar	148 41.4	S60 28.2
Y 15	244 40.3	83 39.8 ..	54.1	222 59.5 ..	38.9	314 27.2 ..	34.6	307 11.9 ..	21.9	Hamal	327 54.7	N23 33.6
16	259 42.8	98 39.5	53.2	238 02.8	38.8	329 29.4	34.6	322 14.3	21.9	Kaus Aust.	83 37.2	S34 22.5
17	274 45.2	113 39.1	52.2	253 06.0	38.6	344 31.7	34.6	337 16.7	21.9			
18	289 47.7	128 38.7	N 8 51.2	268 09.3	N 5 38.5	359 33.9	S22 34.6	352 19.1	S21 21.9	Kochab	137 21.0	N74 04.5
19	304 50.1	143 38.4	50.2	283 12.6	38.3	14 36.1	34.6	7 21.5	21.9	Markab	13 33.0	N15 19.1
20	319 52.6	158 38.0	49.2	298 15.8	38.2	29 38.4	34.5	22 23.9	21.9	Menkar	314 09.5	N 4 10.3
21	334 55.1	173 37.7 ..	48.2	313 19.1 ..	38.0	44 40.6 ..	34.5	37 26.3 ..	21.9	Menkent	148 02.0	S36 28.1
22	349 57.5	188 37.3	47.2	328 22.4	37.8	59 42.8	34.5	52 28.8	21.8	Miaplacidus	221 39.2	S69 47.8
23	5 00.0	203 37.0	46.2	343 25.6	37.7	74 45.1	34.4	67 31.2	21.8			
11 00	20 02.5	218 36.6	N 8 45.2	358 28.9	N 5 37.5	89 47.3	S22 34.4	82 33.6	S21 21.8	Mirfak	308 32.7	N49 55.9
01	35 04.9	233 36.3	44.2	13 32.2	37.4	104 49.5	34.4	97 36.0	21.8	Nunki	75 52.1	S26 16.2
02	50 07.4	248 35.9	43.2	28 35.4	37.2	119 51.8	34.4	112 38.4	21.8	Peacock	53 11.1	S56 40.3
03	65 09.9	263 35.5 ..	42.2	43 38.7 ..	37.1	134 54.0 ..	34.3	127 40.8 ..	21.8	Pollux	243 21.6	N27 58.5
04	80 12.3	278 35.2	41.2	58 42.0	36.9	149 56.2	34.3	142 43.2	21.8	Procyon	244 54.5	N 5 10.4
05	95 14.8	293 34.8	40.2	73 45.2	36.8	164 58.5	34.3	157 45.6	21.8			
06	110 17.3	308 34.5	N 8 39.2	88 48.5	N 5 36.6	180 00.7	S22 34.2	172 48.1	S21 21.8	Rasalhague	96 01.9	N12 33.0
07	125 19.7	323 34.1	38.2	103 51.8	36.5	195 02.9	34.2	187 50.5	21.8	Regulus	207 38.4	N11 52.1
08	140 22.2	338 33.8	37.2	118 55.0	36.3	210 05.2	34.2	202 52.9	21.8	Rigel	281 07.0	S 8 10.6
S 09	155 24.6	353 33.4 ..	36.2	133 58.3 ..	36.1	225 07.4 ..	34.2	217 55.3 ..	21.8	Rigil Kent.	139 45.6	S60 55.1
U 10	170 27.1	8 33.1	35.2	149 01.6	36.0	240 09.6	34.1	232 57.7	21.8	Sabik	102 06.9	S15 44.9
N 11	185 29.6	23 32.7	34.2	164 04.8	35.8	255 11.8	34.1	248 00.1	21.8			
D 12	200 32.0	38 32.3	N 8 33.2	179 08.1	N 5 35.7	270 14.1	S22 34.1	263 02.5	S21 21.7	Schedar	349 34.3	N56 39.1
A 13	215 34.5	53 32.0	32.2	194 11.4	35.5	285 16.3	34.0	278 04.9	21.7	Shaula	96 15.2	S37 07.1
Y 14	230 37.0	68 31.6	31.2	209 14.6	35.4	300 18.5	34.0	293 07.3	21.7	Sirius	258 29.2	S16 44.5
15	245 39.4	83 31.3 ..	30.2	224 17.9 ..	35.2	315 20.8 ..	34.0	308 09.7 ..	21.7	Spica	158 26.3	S11 15.9
16	260 41.9	98 30.9	29.2	239 21.2	35.1	330 23.0	33.9	323 12.2	21.7	Suhail	222 49.0	S43 30.6
17	275 44.4	113 30.6	28.2	254 24.4	34.9	345 25.2	33.9	338 14.6	21.7			
18	290 46.8	128 30.2	N 8 27.2	269 27.7	N 5 34.8	0 27.4	S22 33.9	353 17.0	S21 21.7	Vega	80 35.6	N38 48.5
19	305 49.3	143 29.9	26.2	284 31.0	34.6	15 29.7	33.9	8 19.4	21.7	Zuben'ubi	137 00.1	S16 07.5
20	320 51.7	158 29.5	25.2	299 34.2	34.5	30 31.9	33.8	23 21.8	21.7			
21	335 54.2	173 29.2 ..	24.1	314 37.5 ..	34.3	45 34.1 ..	33.8	38 24.2 ..	21.7		SHA	Mer. Pass.
22	350 56.7	188 28.8	23.1	329 40.8	34.2	60 36.3	33.8	53 26.6	21.7	Venus	199 41.9	h m
23	5 59.1	203 28.4	22.1	344 44.0	34.0	75 38.6	33.7	68 29.0	21.7	Mars	338 07.3	0 11
Mer. Pass.	22 40.1	v −0.4	d 1.0	v 3.3	d 0.2	v 2.2	d 0.0	v 2.4	d 0.0	Jupiter	69 50.3	18 02
										Saturn	62 32.3	18 31

SUN / MOON

UT (d h)	SUN GHA	SUN Dec	MOON GHA	v	MOON Dec	d	HP
9 00	183 11.2	S 6 21.2	283 24.4	9.3	N24 25.8	1.6	55.6
01	198 11.4	22.2	297 52.7	9.3	24 27.4	1.5	55.7
02	213 11.6	23.1	312 21.0	9.2	24 28.9	1.4	55.7
03	228 11.8	.. 24.1	326 49.2	9.1	24 30.3	1.3	55.7
04	243 11.9	25.0	341 17.3	9.1	24 31.6	1.1	55.8
05	258 12.1	26.0	355 45.4	9.1	24 32.7	1.0	55.8
06	273 12.3	S 6 26.9	10 13.5	9.0	N24 33.7	0.8	55.8
07	288 12.4	27.9	24 41.5	8.9	24 34.5	0.8	55.8
08	303 12.6	28.8	39 09.4	9.0	24 35.3	0.6	55.9
F 09	318 12.8	.. 29.8	53 37.4	8.9	24 35.9	0.4	55.9
R 10	333 12.9	30.7	68 05.3	8.8	24 36.3	0.4	55.9
I 11	348 13.1	31.7	82 33.1	8.8	24 36.7	0.2	56.0
D 12	3 13.3	S 6 32.6	97 00.9	8.8	N24 36.9	0.1	56.0
A 13	18 13.4	33.6	111 28.7	8.7	24 37.0	0.1	56.0
Y 14	33 13.6	34.5	125 56.4	8.7	24 36.9	0.3	56.1
15	48 13.8	.. 35.4	140 24.1	8.6	24 36.7	0.3	56.1
16	63 13.9	36.4	154 51.7	8.7	24 36.4	0.4	56.1
17	78 14.1	37.3	169 19.4	8.5	24 36.0	0.6	56.2
18	93 14.3	S 6 38.3	183 46.9	8.6	N24 35.4	0.8	56.2
19	108 14.4	39.2	198 14.5	8.5	24 34.6	0.8	56.2
20	123 14.6	40.2	212 42.0	8.5	24 33.8	1.0	56.3
21	138 14.8	.. 41.1	227 09.5	8.4	24 32.8	1.1	56.3
22	153 14.9	42.1	241 36.9	8.5	24 31.7	1.3	56.3
23	168 15.1	43.0	256 04.4	8.4	24 30.4	1.4	56.4
10 00	183 15.3	S 6 44.0	270 31.8	8.3	N24 29.0	1.6	56.4
01	198 15.4	44.9	284 59.1	8.4	24 27.4	1.6	56.4
02	213 15.6	45.9	299 26.5	8.3	24 25.8	1.9	56.5
03	228 15.8	.. 46.8	313 53.8	8.3	24 23.9	1.9	56.5
04	243 15.9	47.7	328 21.1	8.2	24 22.0	2.1	56.5
05	258 16.1	48.7	342 48.3	8.3	24 19.9	2.2	56.6
06	273 16.3	S 6 49.6	357 15.6	8.2	N24 17.7	2.4	56.6
S 07	288 16.4	50.6	11 42.8	8.2	24 15.3	2.5	56.6
A 08	303 16.6	51.5	26 10.0	8.1	24 12.8	2.6	56.7
T 09	318 16.8	.. 52.5	40 37.1	8.2	24 10.2	2.8	56.7
U 10	333 16.9	53.4	55 04.3	8.1	24 07.4	2.9	56.7
R 11	348 17.1	54.4	69 31.4	8.1	24 04.5	3.1	56.8
D 12	3 17.2	S 6 55.3	83 58.5	8.1	N24 01.4	3.2	56.8
A 13	18 17.4	56.2	98 25.6	8.1	23 58.2	3.4	56.8
Y 14	33 17.6	57.2	112 52.7	8.1	23 54.8	3.4	56.9
15	48 17.7	.. 58.1	127 19.8	8.1	23 51.4	3.6	56.9
16	63 17.9	6 59.1	141 46.9	8.0	23 47.8	3.8	56.9
17	78 18.1	7 00.0	156 13.9	8.0	23 44.0	3.9	57.0
18	93 18.2	S 7 01.0	170 40.9	8.0	N23 40.1	4.0	57.0
19	108 18.4	01.9	185 07.9	8.1	23 36.1	4.2	57.1
20	123 18.5	02.8	199 35.0	8.0	23 31.9	4.3	57.1
21	138 18.7	.. 03.8	214 02.0	8.0	23 27.6	4.5	57.1
22	153 18.9	04.7	228 29.0	7.9	23 23.1	4.6	57.2
23	168 19.0	05.7	242 55.9	8.0	23 18.5	4.7	57.2
11 00	183 19.2	S 7 06.6	257 22.9	8.0	N23 13.8	4.9	57.2
01	198 19.3	07.6	271 49.9	8.0	23 08.9	5.0	57.3
02	213 19.5	08.5	286 16.9	7.9	23 03.9	5.2	57.3
03	228 19.7	.. 09.4	300 43.8	8.0	22 58.7	5.3	57.4
04	243 19.8	10.4	315 10.8	7.9	22 53.4	5.4	57.4
05	258 20.0	11.3	329 37.7	8.0	22 48.0	5.6	57.4
06	273 20.1	S 7 12.3	344 04.7	8.0	N22 42.4	5.7	57.5
07	288 20.3	13.2	358 31.7	7.9	22 36.7	5.8	57.5
08	303 20.5	14.1	12 58.6	8.0	22 30.9	6.0	57.6
S 09	318 20.6	.. 15.1	27 25.6	7.9	22 24.9	6.1	57.6
U 10	333 20.8	16.0	41 52.5	8.0	22 18.8	6.3	57.6
N 11	348 20.9	17.0	56 19.5	8.0	22 12.5	6.4	57.7
D 12	3 21.1	S 7 17.9	70 46.5	7.9	N22 06.1	6.5	57.7
A 13	18 21.2	18.8	85 13.4	8.0	21 59.6	6.7	57.8
Y 14	33 21.4	19.8	99 40.4	8.0	21 52.9	6.8	57.8
15	48 21.6	.. 20.7	114 07.4	8.0	21 46.1	6.9	57.8
16	63 21.7	21.7	128 34.4	8.0	21 39.2	7.1	57.9
17	78 21.9	22.6	143 01.4	8.0	21 32.1	7.2	57.9
18	93 22.0	S 7 23.5	157 28.4	8.0	N21 24.9	7.4	58.0
19	108 22.2	24.5	171 55.4	8.0	21 17.5	7.5	58.0
20	123 22.3	25.4	186 22.4	8.1	21 10.0	7.6	58.0
21	138 22.5	.. 26.3	200 49.5	8.0	21 02.4	7.7	58.1
22	153 22.7	27.3	215 16.5	8.0	20 54.7	7.9	58.1
23	168 22.8	28.2	229 43.5	8.1	N20 46.8	8.0	58.2
SD	16.0	d 0.9	SD 15.3		15.5		15.7

Twilight / Moonrise

Lat.	Naut.	Civil	Sunrise	9	10	11	12
N 72	04 35	05 53	07 02	▢	▢	▢	21 48
N 70	04 41	05 52	06 54	▢	▢	20 52	22 47
68	04 46	05 50	06 47	▢	▢	21 19	23 21
66	04 50	05 49	06 41	▢	19 33	21 44	23 46
64	04 53	05 48	06 36	19 12	20 34	22 16	24 05
62	04 56	05 47	06 32	19 54	21 07	22 39	24 20
60	04 58	05 46	06 28	20 22	21 32	22 58	24 33
N 58	05 00	05 45	06 25	20 44	21 52	23 14	24 44
56	05 01	05 44	06 22	21 02	22 08	23 27	24 54
54	05 03	05 44	06 19	21 17	22 22	23 38	25 02
52	05 04	05 43	06 17	21 30	22 34	23 48	25 10
50	05 05	05 42	06 14	21 42	22 45	23 57	25 16
45	05 06	05 40	06 10	22 06	23 07	24 16	00 16
N 40	05 07	05 38	06 06	22 25	23 25	24 32	00 32
35	05 07	05 37	06 02	22 41	23 40	24 45	00 45
30	05 07	05 35	05 59	22 55	23 53	24 56	00 56
20	05 06	05 31	05 53	23 19	24 16	00 16	01 15
N 10	05 03	05 27	05 48	23 39	24 35	00 35	01 32
0	04 59	05 23	05 44	23 58	24 53	00 53	01 48
S 10	04 53	05 18	05 39	24 17	00 17	01 11	02 03
20	04 45	05 11	05 33	24 38	00 38	01 30	02 20
30	04 35	05 03	05 27	00 08	01 02	01 52	02 39
35	04 28	04 58	05 24	00 22	01 16	02 05	02 50
40	04 19	04 52	05 19	00 38	01 32	02 20	03 03
45	04 09	04 45	05 15	00 57	01 51	02 38	03 18
S 50	03 55	04 36	05 09	01 21	02 15	02 59	03 36
52	03 49	04 31	05 07	01 33	02 26	03 10	03 44
54	03 42	04 27	05 03	01 46	02 39	03 22	03 54
56	03 33	04 21	05 00	02 02	02 55	03 35	04 05
58	03 24	04 15	04 56	02 20	03 12	03 51	04 17
S 60	03 12	04 08	04 52	02 42	03 34	04 09	04 31

Sunset / Twilight / Moonset

Lat.	Sunset	Civil	Naut.	9	10	11	12
N 72	16 30	17 38	18 56	▢	▢	▢	19 28
N 70	16 38	17 40	18 50	▢	▢	▢	18 27
68	16 45	17 41	18 46	▢	▢	18 27	17 52
66	16 51	17 43	18 42	▢	17 50	17 34	17 26
64	16 56	17 44	18 39	16 17	16 49	17 02	17 06
62	17 01	17 45	18 36	15 35	16 15	16 37	16 50
60	17 05	17 46	18 34	15 07	15 50	16 18	16 36
N 58	17 08	17 47	18 32	14 45	15 30	16 02	16 24
56	17 11	17 48	18 31	14 27	15 14	15 48	16 14
54	17 14	17 49	18 30	14 12	14 59	15 36	16 05
52	17 16	17 50	18 29	13 59	14 47	15 26	15 57
50	17 18	17 51	18 28	13 47	14 36	15 17	15 49
45	17 23	17 53	18 27	13 23	14 13	14 57	15 34
N 40	17 28	17 55	18 26	13 04	13 55	14 40	15 21
35	17 31	17 57	18 26	12 48	13 39	14 27	15 09
30	17 34	17 58	18 26	12 34	13 26	14 15	15 00
20	17 40	18 02	18 28	12 10	13 03	13 54	14 43
N 10	17 45	18 06	18 31	11 50	12 43	13 36	14 28
0	17 50	18 11	18 35	11 30	12 24	13 19	14 14
S 10	17 55	18 16	18 41	11 11	12 06	13 02	14 00
20	18 01	18 23	18 49	10 51	11 46	12 44	13 45
30	18 07	18 31	19 00	10 27	11 22	12 23	13 27
35	18 11	18 36	19 07	10 13	11 09	12 11	13 17
40	18 15	18 43	19 15	09 56	10 53	11 56	13 05
45	18 20	18 50	19 26	09 37	10 34	11 39	12 51
S 50	18 26	18 58	19 40	09 13	10 10	11 18	12 34
52	18 29	19 04	19 46	09 01	09 59	11 08	12 26
54	18 32	19 08	19 54	08 48	09 46	10 57	12 17
56	18 35	19 14	20 02	08 32	09 31	10 44	12 07
58	18 39	19 20	20 12	08 14	09 13	10 28	11 55
S 60	18 43	19 27	20 24	07 52	08 51	10 10	11 42

SUN / MOON

Day	Eqn. of Time 00h	Eqn. of Time 12h	Mer. Pass.	Mer. Pass. Upper	Mer. Pass. Lower	Age	Phase
	m s	m s	h m	h m	h m	d	%
9	12 45	12 53	11 47	05 18	17 44	22	55
10	13 01	13 09	11 47	06 11	18 39	23	45
11	13 16	13 24	11 47	07 06	19 34	24	35

UT	ARIES GHA	VENUS −4.0 GHA	Dec	MARS −2.6 GHA	Dec	JUPITER −2.3 GHA	Dec	SATURN +0.5 GHA	Dec	STARS Name	SHA	Dec
12 00	21 01.6	218 28.1	N 8 21.1	359 47.3	N 5 33.8	90 40.8	S22 33.7	83 31.4	S21 21.7	Acamar	315 14.1	S40 13.2
01	36 04.1	233 27.7	20.1	14 50.6	33.7	105 43.0	33.7	98 33.8	21.6	Achernar	335 22.3	S57 07.9
02	51 06.5	248 27.4	19.1	29 53.8	33.5	120 45.2	33.7	113 36.2	21.6	Acrux	173 04.4	S63 12.6
03	66 09.0	263 27.0	.. 18.1	44 57.1	.. 33.4	135 47.5	.. 33.6	128 38.6	.. 21.6	Adhara	255 08.5	S28 59.8
04	81 11.5	278 26.7	17.1	60 00.4	33.2	150 49.7	33.6	143 41.1	21.6	Aldebaran	290 43.3	N16 33.0
05	96 13.9	293 26.3	16.1	75 03.7	33.1	165 51.9	33.6	158 43.5	21.6			
06	111 16.4	308 26.0	N 8 15.1	90 06.9	N 5 32.9	180 54.1	S22 33.5	173 45.9	S21 21.6	Alioth	166 16.7	N55 51.0
M 07	126 18.9	323 25.6	14.0	105 10.2	32.8	195 56.4	33.5	188 48.3	21.6	Alkaid	152 55.3	N49 12.8
O 08	141 21.3	338 25.3	13.0	120 13.5	32.6	210 58.6	33.5	203 50.7	21.6	Alnair	27 37.0	S46 51.8
N 09	156 23.8	353 24.9	.. 12.0	135 16.7	.. 32.5	226 00.8	.. 33.4	218 53.1	.. 21.6	Alnilam	275 41.1	S 1 11.3
D 10	171 26.2	8 24.6	11.0	150 20.0	32.3	241 03.0	33.4	233 55.5	21.6	Alphard	217 51.3	S 8 44.7
A 11	186 28.7	23 24.2	10.0	165 23.3	32.2	256 05.2	33.4	248 57.9	21.6			
Y 12	201 31.2	38 23.9	N 8 09.0	180 26.5	N 5 32.0	271 07.5	S22 33.4	264 00.3	S21 21.6	Alphecca	126 07.0	N26 39.0
13	216 33.6	53 23.5	08.0	195 29.8	31.9	286 09.7	33.3	279 02.7	21.5	Alpheratz	357 38.0	N29 12.4
14	231 36.1	68 23.1	06.9	210 33.1	31.7	301 11.9	33.3	294 05.1	21.5	Altair	62 03.3	N 8 55.6
15	246 38.6	83 22.8	.. 05.9	225 36.3	.. 31.6	316 14.1	.. 33.3	309 07.5	.. 21.5	Ankaa	353 10.2	S42 11.7
16	261 41.0	98 22.4	04.9	240 39.6	31.4	331 16.4	33.2	324 09.9	21.5	Antares	112 20.3	S26 28.5
17	276 43.5	113 22.1	03.9	255 42.9	31.3	346 18.6	33.2	339 12.3	21.5			
18	291 46.0	128 21.7	N 8 02.9	270 46.1	N 5 31.1	1 20.8	S22 33.2	354 14.7	S21 21.5	Arcturus	145 51.4	N19 04.7
19	306 48.4	143 21.4	01.9	285 49.4	31.0	16 23.0	33.1	9 17.1	21.5	Atria	107 17.9	S69 03.9
20	321 50.9	158 21.0	8 00.8	300 52.7	30.8	31 25.2	33.1	24 19.5	21.5	Avior	234 16.2	S59 34.2
21	336 53.4	173 20.7	7 59.8	315 55.9	.. 30.7	46 27.4	.. 33.1	39 22.0	.. 21.5	Bellatrix	278 26.4	N 6 22.1
22	351 55.8	188 20.3	58.8	330 59.2	30.5	61 29.7	33.1	54 24.4	21.5	Betelgeuse	270 55.7	N 7 24.7
23	6 58.3	203 20.0	57.8	346 02.5	30.4	76 31.9	33.0	69 26.8	21.5			
13 00	22 00.7	218 19.6	N 7 56.8	1 05.7	N 5 30.2	91 34.1	S22 33.0	84 29.2	S21 21.5	Canopus	263 53.8	S52 42.1
01	37 03.2	233 19.3	55.7	16 09.0	30.1	106 36.3	33.0	99 31.6	21.4	Capella	280 26.7	N46 00.9
02	52 05.7	248 18.9	54.7	31 12.3	29.9	121 38.5	32.9	114 34.0	21.4	Deneb	49 28.0	N45 21.5
03	67 08.1	263 18.6	.. 53.7	46 15.5	.. 29.8	136 40.8	.. 32.9	129 36.4	.. 21.4	Denebola	182 28.8	N14 27.6
04	82 10.6	278 18.2	52.7	61 18.8	29.6	151 43.0	32.9	144 38.8	21.4	Diphda	348 50.5	S17 52.4
05	97 13.1	293 17.9	51.7	76 22.1	29.5	166 45.2	32.8	159 41.2	21.4			
06	112 15.5	308 17.5	N 7 50.6	91 25.4	N 5 29.3	181 47.4	S22 32.8	174 43.6	S21 21.4	Dubhe	193 45.9	N61 38.3
T 07	127 18.0	323 17.2	49.6	106 28.6	29.2	196 49.6	32.8	189 46.0	21.4	Elnath	278 06.0	N28 37.4
U 08	142 20.5	338 16.8	48.6	121 31.9	29.0	211 51.8	32.7	204 48.4	21.4	Eltanin	90 44.0	N51 29.5
E 09	157 22.9	353 16.5	.. 47.6	136 35.2	.. 28.9	226 54.0	.. 32.7	219 50.8	.. 21.4	Enif	33 42.0	N 9 58.3
S 10	172 25.4	8 16.1	46.5	151 38.4	28.7	241 56.3	32.7	234 53.2	21.4	Fomalhaut	15 18.1	S29 30.8
D 11	187 27.8	23 15.8	45.5	166 41.7	28.6	256 58.5	32.6	249 55.6	21.4			
A 12	202 30.3	38 15.4	N 7 44.5	181 45.0	N 5 28.4	272 00.7	S22 32.6	264 58.0	S21 21.4	Gacrux	171 55.9	S57 13.5
Y 13	217 32.8	53 15.1	43.5	196 48.2	28.3	287 02.9	32.6	280 00.4	21.3	Gienah	175 47.4	S17 39.2
14	232 35.2	68 14.7	42.4	211 51.5	28.1	302 05.1	32.6	295 02.8	21.3	Hadar	148 41.4	S60 28.2
15	247 37.7	83 14.4	.. 41.4	226 54.8	.. 28.0	317 07.3	.. 32.5	310 05.2	.. 21.3	Hamal	327 54.7	N23 33.6
16	262 40.2	98 14.0	40.4	241 58.0	27.8	332 09.5	32.5	325 07.6	21.3	Kaus Aust.	83 37.2	S34 22.5
17	277 42.6	113 13.7	39.3	257 01.3	27.7	347 11.8	32.5	340 10.0	21.3			
18	292 45.1	128 13.3	N 7 38.3	272 04.6	N 5 27.5	2 14.0	S22 32.4	355 12.4	S21 21.3	Kochab	137 21.0	N74 04.4
19	307 47.6	143 13.0	37.3	287 07.8	27.4	17 16.2	32.4	10 14.8	21.3	Markab	13 33.0	N15 19.1
20	322 50.0	158 12.6	36.3	302 11.1	27.2	32 18.4	32.4	25 17.2	21.3	Menkar	314 09.5	N 4 10.3
21	337 52.5	173 12.3	.. 35.2	317 14.4	.. 27.1	47 20.6	.. 32.3	40 19.6	.. 21.3	Menkent	148 02.0	S36 28.1
22	352 55.0	188 11.9	34.2	332 17.6	26.9	62 22.8	32.3	55 22.0	21.3	Miaplacidus	221 39.2	S69 47.8
23	7 57.4	203 11.6	33.2	347 20.9	26.8	77 25.0	32.3	70 24.4	21.3			
14 00	22 59.9	218 11.2	N 7 32.1	2 24.2	N 5 26.6	92 27.2	S22 32.2	85 26.8	S21 21.2	Mirfak	308 32.7	N49 55.9
01	38 02.3	233 10.9	31.1	17 27.4	26.5	107 29.4	32.2	100 29.2	21.2	Nunki	75 52.1	S26 16.2
02	53 04.8	248 10.5	30.1	32 30.7	26.3	122 31.6	32.2	115 31.6	21.2	Peacock	53 11.1	S56 40.3
03	68 07.3	263 10.2	.. 29.0	47 34.0	.. 26.2	137 33.9	.. 32.1	130 34.0	.. 21.2	Pollux	243 21.6	N27 58.5
04	83 09.7	278 09.8	28.0	62 37.2	26.0	152 36.1	32.1	145 36.4	21.2	Procyon	244 54.5	N 5 10.4
05	98 12.2	293 09.5	27.0	77 40.5	25.9	167 38.3	32.1	160 38.8	21.2			
06	113 14.7	308 09.1	N 7 25.9	92 43.7	N 5 25.8	182 40.5	S22 32.0	175 41.2	S21 21.2	Rasalhague	96 01.9	N12 33.0
W 07	128 17.1	323 08.8	24.9	107 47.0	25.6	197 42.7	32.0	190 43.6	21.2	Regulus	207 38.3	N11 52.1
E 08	143 19.6	338 08.4	23.9	122 50.3	25.5	212 44.9	32.0	205 46.0	21.2	Rigel	281 07.0	S 8 10.6
D 09	158 22.1	353 08.1	.. 22.8	137 53.5	.. 25.3	227 47.1	.. 32.0	220 48.4	.. 21.2	Rigil Kent.	139 45.6	S60 55.1
N 10	173 24.5	8 07.7	21.8	152 56.8	25.2	242 49.3	31.9	235 50.8	21.1	Sabik	102 06.9	S15 44.9
E 11	188 27.0	23 07.4	20.8	168 00.1	25.0	257 51.5	31.9	250 53.2	21.1			
S 12	203 29.4	38 07.0	N 7 19.7	183 03.3	N 5 24.9	272 53.7	S22 31.9	265 55.6	S21 21.1	Schedar	349 34.3	N56 39.1
D 13	218 31.9	53 06.7	18.7	198 06.6	24.7	287 55.9	31.8	280 58.0	21.1	Shaula	96 15.2	S37 07.1
A 14	233 34.4	68 06.3	17.6	213 09.9	24.6	302 58.1	31.8	296 00.4	21.1	Sirius	258 29.2	S16 44.5
Y 15	248 36.8	83 06.0	.. 16.6	228 13.1	.. 24.4	318 00.3	.. 31.8	311 02.8	.. 21.1	Spica	158 26.3	S11 15.9
16	263 39.3	98 05.6	15.6	243 16.4	24.3	333 02.5	31.7	326 05.2	21.1	Suhail	222 49.0	S43 30.6
17	278 41.8	113 05.3	14.5	258 19.7	24.2	348 04.8	31.7	341 07.6	21.1			
18	293 44.2	128 04.9	N 7 13.5	273 22.9	N 5 24.0	3 07.0	S22 31.7	356 10.0	S21 21.1	Vega	80 35.6	N38 48.5
19	308 46.7	143 04.6	12.4	288 26.2	23.9	18 09.2	31.6	11 12.3	21.1	Zuben'ubi	137 00.1	S16 07.5
20	323 49.2	158 04.2	11.4	303 29.4	23.7	33 11.4	31.6	26 14.7	21.1		SHA	Mer. Pass.
21	338 51.6	173 03.9	.. 10.4	318 32.7	.. 23.6	48 13.6	.. 31.6	41 17.1	.. 21.0			
22	353 54.1	188 03.5	09.3	333 36.0	23.4	63 15.8	31.5	56 19.5	21.0	Venus	196 18.9	9 27
23	8 56.6	203 03.2	08.3	348 39.2	23.3	78 18.0	31.5	71 21.9	21.0	Mars	339 05.0	23 50
Mer. Pass. 22 28.3		v −0.4	d 1.0	v 3.3	d 0.1	v 2.2	d 0.0	v 2.4	d 0.0	Jupiter	69 33.4	17 51
										Saturn	62 28.4	18 19

UT	SUN GHA	SUN Dec	MOON GHA	v	Dec	d	HP
d h	° ′	° ′	° ′	′	° ′	′	′
12 00	183 23.0	S 7 29.2	244 10.6	8.1	N20 38.8	8.2	58.2
01	198 23.1	30.1	258 37.7	8.1	20 30.6	8.3	58.2
02	213 23.3	31.0	273 04.8	8.1	20 22.3	8.4	58.3
03	228 23.4	.. 32.0	287 31.9	8.1	20 13.9	8.5	58.3
04	243 23.6	32.9	301 59.0	8.1	20 05.4	8.7	58.4
05	258 23.7	33.8	316 26.1	8.1	19 56.7	8.8	58.4
M 06	273 23.9	S 7 34.8	330 53.2	8.2	N19 47.9	8.9	58.4
O 07	288 24.0	35.7	345 20.4	8.2	19 39.0	9.1	58.5
N 08	303 24.2	36.7	359 47.6	8.2	19 29.9	9.2	58.5
D 09	318 24.4	.. 37.6	14 14.8	8.2	19 20.7	9.3	58.6
A 10	333 24.5	38.5	28 42.0	8.2	19 11.4	9.4	58.6
Y 11	348 24.7	39.5	43 09.2	8.2	19 02.0	9.6	58.6
12	3 24.8	S 7 40.4	57 36.4	8.3	N18 52.4	9.7	58.7
13	18 25.0	41.3	72 03.7	8.2	18 42.7	9.8	58.7
14	33 25.1	42.3	86 30.9	8.3	18 32.9	9.9	58.8
15	48 25.3	.. 43.2	100 58.2	8.3	18 23.0	10.1	58.8
16	63 25.4	44.1	115 25.5	8.3	18 12.9	10.2	58.8
17	78 25.6	45.1	129 52.8	8.4	18 02.7	10.2	58.9
18	93 25.7	S 7 46.0	144 20.2	8.3	N17 52.5	10.5	58.9
19	108 25.9	46.9	158 47.5	8.4	17 42.0	10.5	59.0
20	123 26.0	47.9	173 14.9	8.4	17 31.5	10.7	59.0
21	138 26.2	.. 48.8	187 42.3	8.4	17 20.8	10.7	59.0
22	153 26.3	49.7	202 09.7	8.5	17 10.1	10.9	59.1
23	168 26.5	50.7	216 37.2	8.4	16 59.2	11.0	59.1
13 00	183 26.6	S 7 51.6	231 04.6	8.5	N16 48.2	11.1	59.2
01	198 26.8	52.5	245 32.1	8.5	16 37.1	11.3	59.2
02	213 26.9	53.5	259 59.6	8.5	16 25.8	11.3	59.2
03	228 27.1	.. 54.4	274 27.1	8.5	16 14.5	11.5	59.3
04	243 27.2	55.3	288 54.6	8.6	16 03.0	11.5	59.3
05	258 27.4	56.3	303 22.2	8.5	15 51.5	11.7	59.3
06	273 27.5	S 7 57.2	317 49.7	8.6	N15 39.8	11.8	59.4
T 07	288 27.7	58.1	332 17.3	8.6	15 28.0	11.9	59.4
U 08	303 27.8	7 59.1	346 44.9	8.7	15 16.1	12.0	59.5
E 09	318 28.0	8 00.0	1 12.6	8.6	15 04.1	12.1	59.5
S 10	333 28.1	00.9	15 40.2	8.7	14 52.0	12.2	59.5
D 11	348 28.2	01.9	30 07.9	8.6	14 39.8	12.3	59.6
A 12	3 28.4	S 8 02.8	44 35.5	8.7	N14 27.5	12.4	59.6
Y 13	18 28.5	03.7	59 03.2	8.8	14 15.1	12.5	59.7
14	33 28.7	04.7	73 31.0	8.7	14 02.6	12.6	59.7
15	48 28.8	.. 05.6	87 58.7	8.7	13 50.0	12.7	59.7
16	63 29.0	06.5	102 26.4	8.8	13 37.3	12.8	59.8
17	78 29.1	07.5	116 54.2	8.8	13 24.5	12.9	59.8
18	93 29.3	S 8 08.4	131 22.0	8.8	N13 11.6	13.0	59.8
19	108 29.4	09.3	145 49.8	8.8	12 58.6	13.1	59.9
20	123 29.6	10.2	160 17.6	8.9	12 45.5	13.2	59.9
21	138 29.7	.. 11.2	174 45.5	8.8	12 32.3	13.3	59.9
22	153 29.8	12.1	189 13.3	8.9	12 19.0	13.3	60.0
23	168 30.0	13.0	203 41.2	8.9	12 05.7	13.5	60.0
14 00	183 30.1	S 8 14.0	218 09.1	8.9	N11 52.2	13.5	60.0
01	198 30.3	14.9	232 37.0	8.9	11 38.7	13.7	60.1
02	213 30.4	15.8	247 04.9	8.9	11 25.0	13.7	60.1
03	228 30.6	.. 16.7	261 32.8	8.9	11 11.3	13.7	60.2
04	243 30.7	17.7	276 00.7	9.0	10 57.6	13.9	60.2
05	258 30.9	18.6	290 28.7	9.0	10 43.7	14.0	60.2
W 06	273 31.0	S 8 19.5	304 56.6	9.0	N10 29.7	14.0	60.3
E 07	288 31.1	20.5	319 24.6	9.0	10 15.7	14.1	60.3
D 08	303 31.3	21.4	333 52.6	9.0	10 01.6	14.2	60.3
N 09	318 31.4	.. 22.3	348 20.6	9.0	9 47.4	14.2	60.3
E 10	333 31.6	23.2	2 48.6	9.0	9 33.2	14.4	60.4
S 11	348 31.7	24.2	17 16.6	9.1	9 18.8	14.4	60.4
D 12	3 31.8	S 8 25.1	31 44.7	9.0	N 9 04.4	14.4	60.4
A 13	18 32.0	26.0	46 12.7	9.1	8 50.0	14.6	60.5
Y 14	33 32.1	26.9	60 40.7	9.1	8 35.4	14.6	60.5
15	48 32.3	.. 27.9	75 08.8	9.1	8 20.8	14.7	60.5
16	63 32.4	28.8	89 36.9	9.0	8 06.1	14.7	60.6
17	78 32.5	29.7	104 04.9	9.1	7 51.4	14.8	60.6
18	93 32.7	S 8 30.6	118 33.0	9.1	N 7 36.6	14.8	60.6
19	108 32.8	31.6	133 01.1	9.1	7 21.8	15.0	60.6
20	123 33.0	32.5	147 29.2	9.0	7 06.8	14.9	60.7
21	138 33.1	.. 33.4	161 57.2	9.1	6 51.9	15.1	60.7
22	153 33.2	34.3	176 25.3	9.1	6 36.8	15.0	60.7
23	168 33.4	35.3	190 53.4	9.1	N 6 21.8	15.2	60.8
	SD 16.1	d 0.9	SD 16.0		16.2		16.5

Moonrise

Lat.	Twilight Naut.	Twilight Civil	Sunrise	Moonrise 12	13	14	15
°	h m	h m	h m	h m	h m	h m	h m
N 72	04 48	06 06	07 16	21 48	24 54	00 54	03 22
N 70	04 53	06 03	07 06	22 47	25 15	01 15	03 30
68	04 56	06 01	06 58	23 21	25 31	01 31	03 36
66	04 59	05 59	06 51	23 46	25 44	01 44	03 41
64	05 02	05 57	06 45	24 05	00 05	01 55	03 46
62	05 04	05 55	06 40	24 20	00 20	02 04	03 49
60	05 05	05 53	06 35	24 33	00 33	02 12	03 52
N 58	05 06	05 52	06 31	24 44	00 44	02 19	03 55
56	05 07	05 50	06 28	24 54	00 54	02 25	03 58
54	05 08	05 49	06 25	25 02	01 02	02 30	04 00
52	05 09	05 48	06 22	25 10	01 10	02 35	04 02
50	05 09	05 47	06 19	25 16	01 16	02 39	04 04
45	05 10	05 44	06 14	00 16	01 31	02 49	04 08
N 40	05 10	05 41	06 09	00 32	01 43	02 56	04 11
35	05 10	05 39	06 05	00 45	01 53	03 03	04 14
30	05 09	05 37	06 01	00 56	02 02	03 09	04 17
20	05 06	05 32	05 54	01 15	02 17	03 19	04 21
N 10	05 03	05 27	05 48	01 32	02 30	03 28	04 25
0	04 58	05 22	05 43	01 48	02 42	03 36	04 29
S 10	04 51	05 16	05 37	02 03	02 54	03 44	04 32
20	04 43	05 09	05 31	02 20	03 07	03 53	04 36
30	04 31	04 59	05 24	02 39	03 22	04 02	04 41
35	04 23	04 54	05 20	02 50	03 31	04 08	04 43
40	04 14	04 47	05 15	03 03	03 41	04 15	04 46
45	04 03	04 39	05 09	03 18	03 52	04 22	04 49
S 50	03 48	04 29	05 03	03 36	04 06	04 31	04 53
52	03 41	04 24	04 59	03 44	04 12	04 35	04 55
54	03 33	04 19	04 56	03 54	04 19	04 39	04 57
56	03 24	04 13	04 52	04 05	04 27	04 44	04 59
58	03 13	04 06	04 48	04 17	04 36	04 50	05 02
S 60	03 01	03 59	04 43	04 31	04 46	04 56	05 04

Moonset

Lat.	Sunset	Twilight Civil	Twilight Naut.	Moonset 12	13	14	15
°	h m	h m	h m	h m	h m	h m	h m
N 72	16 14	17 24	18 41	19 28	18 16	17 41	17 13
N 70	16 24	17 27	18 37	18 27	17 53	17 30	17 11
68	16 33	17 30	18 34	17 52	17 35	17 21	17 10
66	16 40	17 32	18 31	17 26	17 20	17 14	17 08
64	16 46	17 34	18 29	17 06	17 08	17 08	17 07
62	16 51	17 36	18 27	16 50	16 57	17 02	17 06
60	16 56	17 38	18 26	16 36	16 48	16 58	17 05
N 58	17 00	17 39	18 25	16 24	16 41	16 53	17 04
56	17 03	17 41	18 24	16 14	16 34	16 50	17 04
54	17 07	17 42	18 23	16 05	16 27	16 46	17 03
52	17 09	17 43	18 22	15 57	16 22	16 43	17 02
50	17 12	17 45	18 22	15 49	16 17	16 40	17 02
45	17 18	17 48	18 21	15 34	16 06	16 34	17 01
N 40	17 23	17 50	18 22	15 21	15 56	16 29	17 00
35	17 27	17 53	18 22	15 09	15 48	16 24	16 59
30	17 31	17 55	18 23	15 00	15 41	16 20	16 58
20	17 38	18 00	18 26	14 43	15 29	16 13	16 56
N 10	17 44	18 05	18 29	14 28	15 18	16 07	16 55
0	17 49	18 10	18 35	14 14	15 08	16 01	16 54
S 10	17 55	18 16	18 41	14 00	14 57	15 55	16 53
20	18 02	18 24	18 50	13 45	14 46	15 48	16 51
30	18 09	18 33	19 02	13 27	14 33	15 41	16 49
35	18 13	18 39	19 10	13 17	14 26	15 37	16 49
40	18 18	18 46	19 19	13 05	14 17	15 32	16 47
45	18 24	18 54	19 31	12 51	14 07	15 26	16 46
S 50	18 31	19 04	19 45	12 34	13 55	15 19	16 45
52	18 34	19 09	19 53	12 26	13 50	15 16	16 44
54	18 37	19 15	20 01	12 17	13 43	15 12	16 43
56	18 41	19 21	20 10	12 07	13 36	15 08	16 42
58	18 46	19 28	20 21	11 55	13 28	15 04	16 41
S 60	18 50	19 36	20 34	11 42	13 19	14 59	16 40

Day	SUN Eqn. of Time 00h	SUN Eqn. of Time 12h	SUN Mer. Pass.	MOON Mer. Pass. Upper	MOON Mer. Pass. Lower	Age	Phase
d	m s	m s	h m	h m	h m	d	%
12	13 32	13 39	11 46	08 01	20 28	25	25
13	13 46	13 53	11 46	08 55	21 22	26	16
14	14 00	14 07	11 46	09 48	22 15	27	8

UT	ARIES	VENUS −4·0		MARS −2·6		JUPITER −2·3		SATURN +0·5	
d h	GHA	GHA	Dec	GHA	Dec	GHA	Dec	GHA	Dec
15 00	23 59.0	218 02.9 N 7 07.2		3 42.5 N 5 23.1		93 20.2 S22 31.5		86 24.3 S21 21.0	
01	39 01.5	233 02.5 06.2		18 45.8 23.0		108 22.4 31.4		101 26.7 21.0	
02	54 03.9	248 02.2 05.2		33 49.0 22.9		123 24.6 31.4		116 29.1 21.0	
03	69 06.4	263 01.8 . . 04.1		48 52.3 . . 22.7		138 26.8 . . 31.4		131 31.5 . . 21.0	
04	84 08.9	278 01.5 03.1		63 55.5 22.6		153 29.0 31.3		146 33.9 21.0	
05	99 11.3	293 01.1 02.0		78 58.8 22.4		168 31.2 31.3		161 36.3 21.0	
06	114 13.8	308 00.8 N 7 01.0		94 02.1 N 5 22.3		183 33.4 S22 31.2		176 38.7 S21 20.9	
07	129 16.3	323 00.4 6 59.9		109 05.3 22.1		198 35.6 31.2		191 41.1 20.9	
T 08	144 18.7	338 00.1 58.9		124 08.6 22.0		213 37.8 31.2		206 43.5 20.9	
H 09	159 21.2	352 59.7 . . 57.8		139 11.8 . . 21.9		228 40.0 . . 31.2		221 45.9 . . 20.9	
U 10	174 23.7	7 59.4 56.8		154 15.1 21.7		243 42.2 31.1		236 48.3 20.9	
R 11	189 26.1	22 59.0 55.7		169 18.4 21.6		258 44.4 31.1		251 50.7 20.9	
S 12	204 28.6	37 58.7 N 6 54.7		184 21.6 N 5 21.4		273 46.6 S22 31.1		266 53.0 S21 20.9	
D 13	219 31.1	52 58.3 53.6		199 24.9 21.3		288 48.8 31.0		281 55.4 20.9	
A 14	234 33.5	67 58.0 52.6		214 28.1 21.2		303 51.0 31.0		296 57.8 20.9	
Y 15	249 36.0	82 57.6 . . 51.6		229 31.4 . . 21.0		318 53.2 . . 31.0		312 00.2 . . 20.9	
16	264 38.4	97 57.3 50.5		244 34.7 20.9		333 55.4 30.9		327 02.6 20.8	
17	279 40.9	112 57.0 49.5		259 37.9 20.7		348 57.6 30.9		342 05.0 20.8	
18	294 43.4	127 56.6 N 6 48.4		274 41.2 N 5 20.6		3 59.8 S22 30.9		357 07.4 S21 20.8	
19	309 45.8	142 56.3 47.4		289 44.4 20.5		19 02.0 30.8		12 09.8 20.8	
20	324 48.3	157 55.9 46.3		304 47.7 20.3		34 04.2 30.8		27 12.2 20.8	
21	339 50.8	172 55.6 . . 45.2		319 50.9 . . 20.2		49 06.4 . . 30.8		42 14.6 . . 20.8	
22	354 53.2	187 55.2 44.2		334 54.2 20.0		64 08.6 30.7		57 17.0 20.8	
23	9 55.7	202 54.9 43.1		349 57.4 19.9		79 10.8 30.7		72 19.4 20.8	
16 00	24 58.2	217 54.5 N 6 42.1		5 00.7 N 5 19.8		94 13.0 S22 30.7		87 21.7 S21 20.8	
01	40 00.6	232 54.2 41.0		20 04.0 19.6		109 15.2 30.6		102 24.1 20.7	
02	55 03.1	247 53.8 40.0		35 07.2 19.5		124 17.3 30.6		117 26.5 20.7	
03	70 05.5	262 53.5 . . 38.9		50 10.5 . . 19.3		139 19.5 . . 30.6		132 28.9 . . 20.7	
04	85 08.0	277 53.2 37.9		65 13.7 19.2		154 21.7 30.5		147 31.3 20.7	
05	100 10.5	292 52.8 36.8		80 17.0 19.1		169 23.9 30.5		162 33.7 20.7	
06	115 12.9	307 52.5 N 6 35.8		95 20.2 N 5 18.9		184 26.1 S22 30.4		177 36.1 S21 20.7	
07	130 15.4	322 52.1 34.7		110 23.5 18.8		199 28.3 30.4		192 38.5 20.7	
08	145 17.9	337 51.8 33.7		125 26.7 18.7		214 30.5 30.4		207 40.9 20.7	
F 09	160 20.3	352 51.4 . . 32.6		140 30.0 . . 18.5		229 32.7 . . 30.3		222 43.3 . . 20.7	
R 10	175 22.8	7 51.1 31.5		155 33.2 18.4		244 34.9 30.3		237 45.6 20.6	
I 11	190 25.3	22 50.7 30.5		170 36.5 18.2		259 37.1 30.3		252 48.0 20.6	
D 12	205 27.7	37 50.4 N 6 29.4		185 39.7 N 5 18.1		274 39.3 S22 30.2		267 50.4 S21 20.6	
A 13	220 30.2	52 50.0 28.4		200 43.0 18.0		289 41.5 30.2		282 52.8 20.6	
Y 14	235 32.7	67 49.7 27.3		215 46.2 17.8		304 43.7 30.2		297 55.2 20.6	
15	250 35.1	82 49.4 . . 26.3		230 49.5 . . 17.7		319 45.9 . . 30.1		312 57.6 . . 20.6	
16	265 37.6	97 49.0 25.2		245 52.8 17.6		334 48.0 30.1		328 00.0 20.6	
17	280 40.0	112 48.7 24.1		260 56.0 17.4		349 50.2 30.1		343 02.4 20.6	
18	295 42.5	127 48.3 N 6 23.1		275 59.2 N 5 17.3		4 52.4 S22 30.0		358 04.7 S21 20.6	
19	310 45.0	142 48.0 22.0		291 02.5 17.2		19 54.6 30.0		13 07.1 20.5	
20	325 47.4	157 47.6 21.0		306 05.7 17.0		34 56.8 30.0		28 09.5 20.5	
21	340 49.9	172 47.3 . . 19.9		321 09.0 . . 16.9		49 59.0 . . 29.9		43 11.9 . . 20.5	
22	355 52.4	187 46.9 18.8		336 12.2 16.7		65 01.2 29.9		58 14.3 20.5	
23	10 54.8	202 46.6 17.8		351 15.5 16.6		80 03.4 29.9		73 16.7 20.5	
17 00	25 57.3	217 46.3 N 6 16.7		6 18.7 N 5 16.5		95 05.6 S22 29.8		88 19.1 S21 20.5	
01	40 59.8	232 45.9 15.6		21 22.0 16.3		110 07.7 29.8		103 21.5 20.5	
02	56 02.2	247 45.6 14.6		36 25.2 16.2		125 09.9 29.8		118 23.8 20.5	
03	71 04.7	262 45.2 . . 13.5		51 28.5 . . 16.1		140 12.1 . . 29.7		133 26.2 . . 20.5	
04	86 07.1	277 44.9 12.5		66 31.7 15.9		155 14.3 29.7		148 28.6 20.4	
05	101 09.6	292 44.5 11.4		81 35.0 15.8		170 16.5 29.6		163 31.0 20.4	
06	116 12.1	307 44.2 N 6 10.3		96 38.2 N 5 15.7		185 18.7 S22 29.6		178 33.4 S21 20.4	
07	131 14.5	322 43.8 09.3		111 41.5 15.5		200 20.9 29.6		193 35.8 20.4	
S 08	146 17.0	337 43.5 08.2		126 44.7 15.4		215 23.1 29.5		208 38.2 20.4	
A 09	161 19.5	352 43.2 . . 07.1		141 47.9 . . 15.3		230 25.2 . . 29.5		223 40.5 . . 20.4	
T 10	176 21.9	7 42.8 06.1		156 51.2 15.2		245 27.4 29.5		238 42.9 20.4	
U 11	191 24.4	22 42.5 05.0		171 54.4 15.0		260 29.6 29.4		253 45.3 20.4	
R 12	206 26.9	37 42.1 N 6 03.9		186 57.7 N 5 14.9		275 31.8 S22 29.4		268 47.7 S21 20.3	
D 13	221 29.3	52 41.8 02.9		202 00.9 14.8		290 34.0 29.4		283 50.1 20.3	
A 14	236 31.8	67 41.4 01.8		217 04.2 14.6		305 36.2 29.3		298 52.5 20.3	
Y 15	251 34.3	82 41.1 6 00.7		232 07.4 . . 14.5		320 38.3 . . 29.3		313 54.8 . . 20.3	
16	266 36.7	97 40.8 5 59.7		247 10.6 14.4		335 40.5 29.3		328 57.2 20.3	
17	281 39.2	112 40.4 58.6		262 13.9 14.2		350 42.7 29.2		343 59.6 20.3	
18	296 41.6	127 40.1 N 5 57.5		277 17.1 N 5 14.1		5 44.9 S22 29.2		359 02.0 S21 20.3	
19	311 44.1	142 39.7 56.5		292 20.4 14.0		20 47.1 29.1		14 04.4 20.3	
20	326 46.6	157 39.4 55.4		307 23.6 13.8		35 49.3 29.1		29 06.8 20.2	
21	341 49.0	172 39.0 . . 54.3		322 26.8 . . 13.7		50 51.4 . . 29.1		44 09.1 . . 20.2	
22	356 51.5	187 38.7 53.2		337 30.1 13.6		65 53.6 29.0		59 11.5 20.2	
23	11 54.0	202 38.4 52.2		352 33.3 13.5		80 55.8 29.0		74 13.9 20.2	
Mer. Pass.	22 16.5	v −0.3 d 1.1		v 3.3 d 0.1		v 2.2 d 0.0		v 2.4 d 0.0	

STARS

Name	SHA	Dec
Acamar	315 14.0	S40 13.2
Achernar	335 22.3	S57 07.9
Acrux	173 04.4	S63 12.6
Adhara	255 08.5	S28 59.8
Aldebaran	290 43.3	N16 33.0
Alioth	166 16.7	N55 51.0
Alkaid	152 55.3	N49 12.8
Alnair	27 37.0	S46 51.8
Alnilam	275 41.1	S 1 11.3
Alphard	217 51.3	S 8 44.7
Alphecca	126 07.0	N26 39.0
Alpheratz	357 38.0	N29 12.4
Altair	62 03.3	N 8 55.6
Ankaa	353 10.2	S42 11.7
Antares	112 20.3	S26 28.5
Arcturus	145 51.4	N19 04.7
Atria	107 18.0	S69 03.9
Avior	234 16.2	S59 34.2
Bellatrix	278 26.4	N 6 22.1
Betelgeuse	270 55.7	N 7 24.7
Canopus	263 53.7	S52 42.1
Capella	280 26.7	N46 00.9
Deneb	49 28.0	N45 21.5
Denebola	182 28.8	N14 27.6
Diphda	348 50.5	S17 52.4
Dubhe	193 45.9	N61 38.3
Elnath	278 06.0	N28 37.4
Eltanin	90 44.0	N51 29.5
Enif	33 42.0	N 9 58.3
Fomalhaut	15 18.1	S29 30.8
Gacrux	171 55.9	S57 13.5
Gienah	175 47.4	S17 39.2
Hadar	148 41.4	S60 28.2
Hamal	327 54.7	N23 33.6
Kaus Aust.	83 37.2	S34 22.5
Kochab	137 21.1	N74 04.4
Markab	13 33.1	N15 19.1
Menkar	314 09.5	N 4 10.3
Menkent	148 02.0	S36 28.1
Miaplacidus	221 39.2	S69 47.8
Mirfak	308 32.7	N49 55.9
Nunki	75 52.1	S26 16.2
Peacock	53 11.1	S56 40.3
Pollux	243 21.6	N27 58.5
Procyon	244 54.4	N 5 10.4
Rasalhague	96 01.9	N12 32.9
Regulus	207 38.3	N11 52.1
Rigel	281 07.0	S 8 10.6
Rigil Kent.	139 45.6	S60 55.1
Sabik	102 06.9	S15 44.9
Schedar	349 34.3	N56 39.1
Shaula	96 15.3	S37 07.1
Sirius	258 29.2	S16 44.5
Spica	158 26.3	S11 15.9
Suhail	222 48.9	S43 30.6
Vega	80 35.7	N38 48.5
Zuben'ubi	137 00.1	S16 07.5

	SHA	Mer. Pass.
Venus	192 56.4	9 29
Mars	340 02.5	23 35
Jupiter	69 14.8	17 41
Saturn	62 23.6	18 08

UT	SUN GHA	SUN Dec	MOON GHA	v	MOON Dec	d	HP
d h	° ′	° ′	° ′	′	° ′	′	′
15 00	183 33.5	S 8 36.2	205 21.5	9.1	N 6 06.6	15.2	60.8
01	198 33.6	37.1	219 49.6	9.1	5 51.4	15.2	60.8
02	213 33.8	38.0	234 17.7	9.1	5 36.2	15.3	60.8
03	228 33.9	.. 39.0	248 45.8	9.1	5 20.9	15.3	60.9
04	243 34.1	39.9	263 13.9	9.1	5 05.6	15.4	60.9
05	258 34.2	40.8	277 42.0	9.1	4 50.2	15.4	60.9
06	273 34.3	S 8 41.7	292 10.1	9.1	N 4 34.8	15.4	60.9
07	288 34.5	42.7	306 38.2	9.1	4 19.4	15.5	61.0
08	303 34.6	43.6	321 06.3	9.1	4 03.9	15.5	61.0
09	318 34.7	.. 44.5	335 34.4	9.0	3 48.4	15.6	61.0
10	333 34.9	45.4	350 02.4	9.1	3 32.8	15.6	61.0
11	348 35.0	46.3	4 30.5	9.1	3 17.2	15.6	61.0
12	3 35.1	S 8 47.3	18 58.6	9.0	N 3 01.6	15.7	61.1
13	18 35.3	48.2	33 26.6	9.1	2 45.9	15.7	61.1
14	33 35.4	49.1	47 54.7	9.0	2 30.2	15.7	61.1
15	48 35.6	.. 50.0	62 22.7	9.0	2 14.5	15.7	61.1
16	63 35.7	50.9	76 50.7	9.0	1 58.8	15.8	61.1
17	78 35.8	51.9	91 18.7	9.0	1 43.0	15.7	61.2
18	93 36.0	S 8 52.8	105 46.7	9.0	N 1 27.3	15.8	61.2
19	108 36.1	53.7	120 14.7	9.0	1 11.5	15.8	61.2
20	123 36.2	54.6	134 42.7	9.0	0 55.7	15.9	61.2
21	138 36.3	.. 55.5	149 10.7	8.9	0 39.8	15.8	61.2
22	153 36.5	56.5	163 38.6	8.9	0 24.0	15.9	61.2
23	168 36.6	57.4	178 06.6	8.9	N 0 08.1	15.8	61.3
16 00	183 36.7	S 8 58.3	192 34.5	8.9	S 0 07.7	15.9	61.3
01	198 36.9	8 59.2	207 02.4	8.8	0 23.6	15.9	61.3
02	213 37.0	9 00.1	221 30.2	8.9	0 39.5	15.8	61.3
03	228 37.1	.. 01.1	235 58.1	8.9	0 55.3	15.9	61.3
04	243 37.3	02.0	250 26.0	8.8	1 11.2	15.9	61.3
05	258 37.4	02.9	264 53.8	8.8	1 27.1	15.9	61.3
06	273 37.5	S 9 03.8	279 21.6	8.8	S 1 43.0	15.8	61.3
07	288 37.7	04.7	293 49.4	8.7	1 58.8	15.9	61.4
08	303 37.8	05.6	308 17.1	8.7	2 14.7	15.8	61.4
09	318 37.9	.. 06.6	322 44.8	8.7	2 30.5	15.9	61.4
10	333 38.1	07.5	337 12.6	8.6	2 46.4	15.8	61.4
11	348 38.2	08.4	351 40.2	8.7	3 02.2	15.8	61.4
12	3 38.3	S 9 09.3	6 07.9	8.6	S 3 18.0	15.8	61.4
13	18 38.4	10.2	20 35.5	8.6	3 33.8	15.8	61.4
14	33 38.6	11.1	35 03.1	8.6	3 49.6	15.8	61.4
15	48 38.7	.. 12.1	49 30.7	8.6	4 05.4	15.7	61.4
16	63 38.8	13.0	63 58.3	8.5	4 21.1	15.8	61.4
17	78 38.9	13.9	78 25.8	8.5	4 36.9	15.6	61.4
18	93 39.1	S 9 14.8	92 53.3	8.4	S 4 52.5	15.7	61.4
19	108 39.2	15.7	107 20.7	8.4	5 08.2	15.6	61.4
20	123 39.3	16.6	121 48.1	8.4	5 23.8	15.6	61.4
21	138 39.5	.. 17.5	136 15.5	8.4	5 39.4	15.6	61.4
22	153 39.6	18.5	150 42.9	8.3	5 55.0	15.6	61.4
23	168 39.7	19.4	165 10.2	8.3	6 10.5	15.5	61.4
17 00	183 39.8	S 9 20.3	179 37.5	8.3	S 6 26.0	15.5	61.4
01	198 40.0	21.2	194 04.8	8.2	6 41.5	15.4	61.4
02	213 40.1	22.1	208 32.0	8.2	6 56.9	15.4	61.4
03	228 40.2	.. 23.0	222 59.2	8.1	7 12.3	15.3	61.4
04	243 40.3	23.9	237 26.3	8.1	7 27.6	15.3	61.4
05	258 40.5	24.9	251 53.4	8.1	7 42.9	15.2	61.4
06	273 40.6	S 9 25.8	266 20.5	8.0	S 7 58.1	15.2	61.4
07	288 40.7	26.7	280 47.5	8.0	8 13.3	15.1	61.4
08	303 40.8	27.6	295 14.5	7.9	8 28.4	15.1	61.4
09	318 41.0	.. 28.5	309 41.4	8.0	8 43.5	15.0	61.4
10	333 41.1	29.4	324 08.4	7.8	8 58.5	14.9	61.4
11	348 41.2	30.3	338 35.2	7.9	9 13.4	14.9	61.4
12	3 41.3	S 9 31.2	353 02.1	7.7	S 9 28.3	14.8	61.4
13	18 41.4	32.1	7 28.8	7.8	9 43.1	14.8	61.4
14	33 41.6	33.1	21 55.6	7.7	9 57.9	14.7	61.4
15	48 41.7	.. 34.0	36 22.3	7.6	10 12.6	14.6	61.4
16	63 41.8	34.9	50 48.9	7.7	10 27.2	14.5	61.4
17	78 41.9	35.8	65 15.6	7.5	10 41.7	14.5	61.3
18	93 42.1	S 9 36.7	79 42.1	7.5	S10 56.2	14.4	61.3
19	108 42.2	37.6	94 08.6	7.5	11 10.6	14.3	61.3
20	123 42.3	38.5	108 35.1	7.5	11 24.9	14.3	61.3
21	138 42.4	.. 39.4	123 01.6	7.3	11 39.2	14.1	61.3
22	153 42.5	40.3	137 27.9	7.4	11 53.3	14.1	61.3
23	168 42.7	41.2	151 54.3	7.3	S12 07.4	14.0	61.3
	SD 16.1	d 0.9	SD 16.6		16.7		16.7

Lat.	Naut.	Civil	Sunrise	Moonrise 15	16	17	18
°	h m	h m	h m	h m	h m	h m	h m
N 72	05 01	06 20	07 31	03 22	05 45	08 12	11 02
N 70	05 05	06 15	07 19	03 30	05 42	07 58	10 26
68	05 07	06 11	07 09	03 36	05 40	07 47	10 01
66	05 09	06 08	07 01	03 41	05 38	07 37	09 41
64	05 10	06 05	06 54	03 46	05 37	07 30	09 26
62	05 11	06 03	06 48	03 49	05 35	07 23	09 13
60	05 12	06 00	06 43	03 52	05 34	07 17	09 02
N 58	05 13	05 58	06 38	03 55	05 33	07 13	08 53
56	05 13	05 56	06 34	03 58	05 32	07 08	08 45
54	05 14	05 55	06 30	04 00	05 32	07 04	08 38
52	05 14	05 53	06 27	04 02	05 31	07 01	08 31
50	05 14	05 52	06 24	04 04	05 30	06 57	08 25
45	05 14	05 48	06 17	04 08	05 29	06 51	08 13
N 40	05 13	05 45	06 12	04 11	05 28	06 45	08 03
35	05 12	05 41	06 07	04 14	05 27	06 40	07 54
30	05 11	05 39	06 03	04 17	05 26	06 36	07 46
20	05 07	05 33	05 55	04 21	05 24	06 28	07 33
N 10	05 03	05 27	05 49	04 25	05 23	06 22	07 22
0	04 57	05 21	05 42	04 29	05 22	06 16	07 12
S 10	04 50	05 14	05 36	04 32	05 21	06 10	07 01
20	04 40	05 06	05 29	04 36	05 20	06 04	06 50
30	04 27	04 56	05 20	04 41	05 18	05 57	06 38
35	04 19	04 50	05 16	04 43	05 18	05 53	06 30
40	04 09	04 42	05 10	04 46	05 17	05 48	06 22
45	03 57	04 34	05 04	04 49	05 16	05 43	06 13
S 50	03 41	04 23	04 56	04 53	05 15	05 37	06 02
52	03 33	04 17	04 53	04 55	05 14	05 34	05 56
54	03 25	04 11	04 49	04 57	05 14	05 31	05 51
56	03 15	04 05	04 45	04 59	05 13	05 28	05 44
58	03 03	03 57	04 40	05 02	05 13	05 24	05 37
S 60	02 49	03 49	04 34	05 04	05 12	05 20	05 29

Lat.	Sunset	Civil	Naut.	Moonset 15	16	17	18
°	h m	h m	h m	h m	h m	h m	h m
N 72	15 58	17 09	18 27	17 13	16 47	16 15	15 24
N 70	16 10	17 14	18 24	17 11	16 53	16 32	16 02
68	16 20	17 18	18 22	17 10	16 58	16 45	16 29
66	16 29	17 21	18 20	17 08	17 03	16 57	16 50
64	16 36	17 24	18 19	17 07	17 07	17 06	17 06
62	16 42	17 27	18 18	17 06	17 10	17 14	17 20
60	16 47	17 29	18 17	17 05	17 13	17 21	17 32
N 58	16 52	17 32	18 17	17 04	17 15	17 27	17 42
56	16 56	17 34	18 16	17 04	17 18	17 33	17 51
54	17 00	17 35	18 16	17 03	17 20	17 38	17 59
52	17 03	17 37	18 16	17 02	17 22	17 42	18 07
50	17 06	17 39	18 16	17 02	17 23	17 47	18 13
45	17 13	17 42	18 16	17 01	17 27	17 56	18 27
N 40	17 18	17 46	18 17	17 00	17 30	18 03	18 39
35	17 23	17 49	18 18	16 59	17 33	18 09	18 49
30	17 28	17 52	18 20	16 58	17 36	18 15	18 58
20	17 35	17 58	18 23	16 56	17 40	18 25	19 13
N 10	17 42	18 03	18 28	16 55	17 44	18 34	19 26
0	17 49	18 10	18 34	16 54	17 47	18 42	19 39
S 10	17 55	18 17	18 42	16 53	17 51	18 50	19 51
20	18 03	18 25	18 51	16 51	17 55	18 59	20 05
30	18 11	18 35	19 04	16 49	17 59	19 09	20 20
35	18 16	18 42	19 13	16 49	18 01	19 15	20 29
40	18 21	18 49	19 23	16 47	18 04	19 22	20 40
45	18 28	18 58	19 35	16 46	18 07	19 30	20 52
S 50	18 36	19 10	19 51	16 45	18 11	19 39	21 06
52	18 39	19 15	19 59	16 44	18 13	19 43	21 13
54	18 43	19 21	20 08	16 43	18 15	19 48	21 21
56	18 48	19 28	20 18	16 42	18 17	19 54	21 30
58	18 53	19 35	20 30	16 41	18 20	20 00	21 40
S 60	18 58	19 44	20 45	16 40	18 22	20 06	21 51

	SUN			MOON			
Day	Eqn. of Time 00h	Eqn. of Time 12h	Mer. Pass.	Mer. Pass. Upper	Mer. Pass. Lower	Age	Phase
d	m s	m s	h m	h m	h m	d	%
15	14 14	14 20	11 46	10 41	23 08	28	3
16	14 27	14 33	11 45	11 35	24 02	29	0
17	14 39	14 45	11 45	12 29	00 02	01	1

UT	ARIES	VENUS −4·0		MARS −2·5		JUPITER −2·2		SATURN +0·5	
d h	GHA	GHA	Dec	GHA	Dec	GHA	Dec	GHA	Dec
18 00	26 56.4	217 38.0	N 5 51.1	7 36.5	N 5 13.3	95 58.0	S22 29.0	89 16.3	S21 20.2
01	41 58.9	232 37.7	50.0	22 39.8	13.2	111 00.2	28.9	104 18.7	20.2
02	57 01.4	247 37.3	49.0	37 43.0	13.1	126 02.3	28.9	119 21.1	20.2
03	72 03.8	262 37.0	.. 47.9	52 46.3	.. 12.9	141 04.5	.. 28.9	134 23.4	.. 20.2
04	87 06.3	277 36.6	46.8	67 49.5	12.8	156 06.7	28.8	149 25.8	20.1
05	102 08.8	292 36.3	45.7	82 52.7	12.7	171 08.9	28.8	164 28.2	20.1
06	117 11.2	307 36.0	N 5 44.7	97 56.0	N 5 12.6	186 11.1	S22 28.7	179 30.6	S21 20.1
07	132 13.7	322 35.6	43.6	112 59.2	12.4	201 13.2	28.7	194 33.0	20.1
08	147 16.1	337 35.3	42.5	128 02.4	12.3	216 15.4	28.7	209 35.3	20.1
S 09	162 18.6	352 34.9	.. 41.4	143 05.7	.. 12.2	231 17.6	.. 28.6	224 37.7	.. 20.1
U 10	177 21.1	7 34.6	40.4	158 08.9	12.1	246 19.8	28.6	239 40.1	20.1
N 11	192 23.5	22 34.3	39.3	173 12.1	11.9	261 22.0	28.6	254 42.5	20.1
D 12	207 26.0	37 33.9	N 5 38.2	188 15.4	N 5 11.8	276 24.1	S22 28.5	269 44.9	S21 20.0
A 13	222 28.5	52 33.6	37.1	203 18.6	11.7	291 26.3	28.5	284 47.2	20.0
Y 14	237 30.9	67 33.2	36.1	218 21.8	11.6	306 28.5	28.4	299 49.6	20.0
15	252 33.4	82 32.9	.. 35.0	233 25.0	.. 11.4	321 30.7	.. 28.4	314 52.0	.. 20.0
16	267 35.9	97 32.5	33.9	248 28.3	11.3	336 32.8	28.4	329 54.4	20.0
17	282 38.3	112 32.2	32.8	263 31.5	11.2	351 35.0	28.3	344 56.8	20.0
18	297 40.8	127 31.9	N 5 31.7	278 34.7	N 5 11.1	6 37.2	S22 28.3	359 59.1	S21 20.0
19	312 43.2	142 31.5	30.7	293 38.0	10.9	21 39.4	28.3	15 01.5	20.0
20	327 45.7	157 31.2	29.6	308 41.2	10.8	36 41.5	28.2	30 03.9	19.9
21	342 48.2	172 30.8	.. 28.5	323 44.4	.. 10.7	51 43.7	.. 28.2	45 06.3	.. 19.9
22	357 50.6	187 30.5	27.4	338 47.6	10.6	66 45.9	28.2	60 08.6	19.9
23	12 53.1	202 30.2	26.3	353 50.9	10.4	81 48.1	28.1	75 11.0	19.9
19 00	27 55.6	217 29.8	N 5 25.3	8 54.1	N 5 10.3	96 50.2	S22 28.1	90 13.4	S21 19.9
01	42 58.0	232 29.5	24.2	23 57.3	10.2	111 52.4	28.0	105 15.8	19.9
02	58 00.5	247 29.1	23.1	39 00.5	10.0	126 54.6	28.0	120 18.2	19.9
03	73 03.0	262 28.8	.. 22.0	54 03.7	.. 10.0	141 56.8	.. 28.0	135 20.5	.. 19.9
04	88 05.4	277 28.4	20.9	69 07.0	09.8	156 58.9	27.9	150 22.9	19.8
05	103 07.9	292 28.1	19.9	84 10.2	09.7	172 01.1	27.9	165 25.3	19.8
06	118 10.4	307 27.8	N 5 18.8	99 13.4	N 5 09.6	187 03.3	S22 27.8	180 27.7	S21 19.8
07	133 12.8	322 27.4	17.7	114 16.6	09.5	202 05.5	27.8	195 30.0	19.8
08	148 15.3	337 27.1	16.6	129 19.9	09.4	217 07.6	27.8	210 32.4	19.8
M 09	163 17.7	352 26.7	.. 15.5	144 23.1	.. 09.2	232 09.8	.. 27.7	225 34.8	.. 19.8
O 10	178 20.2	7 26.4	14.4	159 26.3	09.1	247 12.0	27.7	240 37.2	19.8
N 11	193 22.7	22 26.1	13.4	174 29.5	09.0	262 14.1	27.7	255 39.5	19.7
D 12	208 25.1	37 25.7	N 5 12.3	189 32.7	N 5 08.9	277 16.3	S22 27.6	270 41.9	S21 19.7
A 13	223 27.6	52 25.4	11.2	204 35.9	08.8	292 18.5	27.6	285 44.3	19.7
Y 14	238 30.1	67 25.0	10.1	219 39.2	08.6	307 20.6	27.5	300 46.7	19.7
15	253 32.5	82 24.7	.. 09.0	234 42.4	.. 08.5	322 22.8	.. 27.5	315 49.0	.. 19.7
16	268 35.0	97 24.4	07.9	249 45.6	08.4	337 25.0	27.5	330 51.4	19.7
17	283 37.5	112 24.0	06.8	264 48.8	08.3	352 27.2	27.4	345 53.8	19.7
18	298 39.9	127 23.7	N 5 05.8	279 52.0	N 5 08.2	7 29.3	S22 27.4	0 56.2	S21 19.6
19	313 42.4	142 23.3	04.7	294 55.2	08.1	22 31.5	27.4	15 58.5	19.6
20	328 44.9	157 23.0	03.6	309 58.4	07.9	37 33.7	27.3	31 00.9	19.6
21	343 47.3	172 22.7	.. 02.5	325 01.7	.. 07.8	52 35.8	.. 27.3	46 03.3	.. 19.6
22	358 49.8	187 22.3	01.4	340 04.9	07.7	67 38.0	27.3	61 05.7	19.6
23	13 52.2	202 22.0	5 00.3	355 08.1	07.6	82 40.2	27.2	76 08.0	19.6
20 00	28 54.7	217 21.6	N 4 59.2	10 11.3	N 5 07.5	97 42.3	S22 27.2	91 10.4	S21 19.6
01	43 57.2	232 21.3	58.1	25 14.5	07.4	112 44.5	27.1	106 12.8	19.5
02	58 59.6	247 21.0	57.0	40 17.7	07.3	127 46.7	27.1	121 15.2	19.5
03	74 02.1	262 20.6	.. 56.0	55 20.9	.. 07.1	142 48.8	.. 27.0	136 17.5	.. 19.5
04	89 04.6	277 20.3	54.9	70 24.1	07.0	157 51.0	27.0	151 19.9	19.5
05	104 07.0	292 19.9	53.8	85 27.3	06.9	172 53.2	27.0	166 22.3	19.5
06	119 09.5	307 19.6	N 4 52.7	100 30.5	N 5 06.8	187 55.3	S22 26.9	181 24.7	S21 19.5
07	134 12.0	322 19.3	51.6	115 33.7	06.7	202 57.5	26.9	196 27.0	19.5
08	149 14.4	337 18.9	50.5	130 36.9	06.6	217 59.7	26.8	211 29.4	19.4
T 09	164 16.9	352 18.6	.. 49.4	145 40.2	.. 06.5	233 01.8	.. 26.8	226 31.8	.. 19.4
U 10	179 19.4	7 18.2	48.3	160 43.4	06.3	248 04.0	26.8	241 34.1	19.4
E 11	194 21.8	22 17.9	47.2	175 46.6	06.2	263 06.2	26.7	256 36.5	19.4
S 12	209 24.3	37 17.6	N 4 46.1	190 49.8	N 5 06.1	278 08.3	S22 26.7	271 38.9	S21 19.4
D 13	224 26.7	52 17.2	45.0	205 53.0	06.0	293 10.5	26.7	286 41.3	19.4
A 14	239 29.2	67 16.9	43.9	220 56.2	05.9	308 12.6	26.6	301 43.6	19.4
Y 15	254 31.7	82 16.5	.. 42.9	235 59.4	.. 05.8	323 14.8	.. 26.6	316 46.0	.. 19.3
16	269 34.1	97 16.2	41.8	251 02.6	05.7	338 17.0	26.5	331 48.4	19.3
17	284 36.6	112 15.9	40.7	266 05.8	05.6	353 19.1	26.5	346 50.7	19.3
18	299 39.1	127 15.5	N 4 39.6	281 09.0	N 5 05.5	8 21.3	S22 26.5	1 53.1	S21 19.3
19	314 41.5	142 15.2	38.5	296 12.2	05.3	23 23.5	26.4	16 55.5	19.3
20	329 44.0	157 14.8	37.4	311 15.4	05.2	38 25.6	26.4	31 57.9	19.3
21	344 46.5	172 14.5	.. 36.3	326 18.5	.. 05.1	53 27.8	.. 26.3	47 00.2	.. 19.3
22	359 48.9	187 14.2	35.2	341 21.7	05.0	68 29.9	26.3	62 02.6	19.2
23	14 51.4	202 13.8	34.1	356 24.9	04.9	83 32.1	26.3	77 05.0	19.2
Mer.Pass.	h m 22 04.7	v −0.3	d 1.1	v 3.2	d 0.1	v 2.2	d 0.0	v 2.4	d 0.0

STARS

Name	SHA	Dec
Acamar	315 14.0	S40 13.3
Achernar	335 22.3	S57 08.0
Acrux	173 04.4	S63 12.6
Adhara	255 08.5	S28 59.8
Aldebaran	290 43.3	N16 33.0
Alioth	166 16.7	N55 50.9
Alkaid	152 55.3	N49 12.8
Alnair	27 37.1	S46 51.8
Alnilam	275 41.0	S 1 11.3
Alphard	217 51.3	S 8 44.7
Alphecca	126 07.0	N26 39.0
Alpheratz	357 38.0	N29 12.4
Altair	62 03.3	N 8 55.6
Ankaa	353 10.2	S42 11.7
Antares	112 20.3	S26 28.5
Arcturus	145 51.4	N19 04.7
Atria	107 18.0	S69 03.9
Avior	234 16.1	S59 34.2
Bellatrix	278 26.4	N 6 22.1
Betelgeuse	270 55.7	N 7 24.7
Canopus	263 53.7	S52 42.1
Capella	280 26.7	N46 00.9
Deneb	49 28.0	N45 21.5
Denebola	182 28.8	N14 27.5
Diphda	348 50.5	S17 52.4
Dubhe	193 45.9	N61 38.3
Elnath	278 06.0	N28 37.4
Eltanin	90 44.0	N51 29.5
Enif	33 42.0	N 9 58.3
Fomalhaut	15 18.1	S29 30.8
Gacrux	171 55.9	S57 13.5
Gienah	175 47.4	S17 39.2
Hadar	148 41.4	S60 28.2
Hamal	327 54.7	N23 33.6
Kaus Aust.	83 37.2	S34 22.5
Kochab	137 21.1	N74 04.4
Markab	13 33.1	N15 19.1
Menkar	314 09.4	N 4 10.3
Menkent	148 02.0	S36 28.1
Miaplacidus	221 39.1	S69 47.7
Mirfak	308 32.7	N49 55.9
Nunki	75 52.1	S26 16.2
Peacock	53 11.1	S56 40.3
Pollux	243 21.5	N27 58.5
Procyon	244 54.4	N 5 10.4
Rasalhague	96 01.9	N12 32.9
Regulus	207 38.3	N11 52.1
Rigel	281 07.0	S 8 10.6
Rigil Kent.	139 45.6	S60 55.1
Sabik	102 06.9	S15 44.9
Schedar	349 34.3	N56 39.1
Shaula	96 15.3	S37 07.1
Sirius	258 29.2	S16 44.5
Spica	158 26.2	S11 15.9
Suhail	222 48.9	S43 30.6
Vega	80 35.7	N38 48.5
Zuben'ubi	137 00.1	S16 07.5

	SHA	Mer. Pass.
Venus	189 34.2	9 30
Mars	340 58.5	23 19
Jupiter	68 54.7	17 30
Saturn	62 17.8	17 56

UT	SUN GHA	SUN Dec	MOON GHA	v	MOON Dec	d	HP
d h	° '	° '	° '	'	° '	'	'
18 00	183 42.8	S 9 42.1	166 20.6	7.2	S12 21.4	13.9	61.3
01	198 42.9	43.0	180 46.8	7.2	12 35.3	13.9	61.2
02	213 43.0	44.0	195 13.0	7.2	12 49.2	13.7	61.2
03	228 43.1	.. 44.9	209 39.2	7.1	13 02.9	13.6	61.2
04	243 43.2	45.8	224 05.3	7.1	13 16.5	13.6	61.2
05	258 43.4	46.7	238 31.4	7.0	13 30.1	13.4	61.2
06	273 43.5	S 9 47.6	252 57.4	7.0	S13 43.5	13.4	61.2
07	288 43.6	48.5	267 23.4	6.9	13 56.9	13.2	61.2
08	303 43.7	49.4	281 49.3	6.9	14 10.1	13.2	61.1
S 09	318 43.8	.. 50.3	296 15.2	6.8	14 23.3	13.0	61.1
U 10	333 44.0	51.2	310 41.0	6.8	14 36.3	13.0	61.1
N 11	348 44.1	52.1	325 06.8	6.7	14 49.3	12.8	61.1
D 12	3 44.2	S 9 53.0	339 32.5	6.7	S15 02.1	12.8	61.1
A 13	18 44.3	53.9	353 58.2	6.7	15 14.9	12.6	61.0
Y 14	33 44.4	54.8	8 23.9	6.5	15 27.5	12.5	61.0
15	48 44.5	.. 55.7	22 49.4	6.6	15 40.0	12.4	61.0
16	63 44.6	56.6	37 15.0	6.5	15 52.4	12.3	61.0
17	78 44.8	57.5	51 40.5	6.5	16 04.7	12.2	60.9
18	93 44.9	S 9 58.4	66 06.0	6.4	S16 16.9	12.0	60.9
19	108 45.0	9 59.3	80 31.4	6.3	16 28.9	12.0	60.9
20	123 45.1	10 00.2	94 56.7	6.4	16 40.9	11.8	60.9
21	138 45.2	.. 01.1	109 22.1	6.2	16 52.7	11.7	60.9
22	153 45.3	02.0	123 47.3	6.3	17 04.4	11.6	60.8
23	168 45.4	02.9	138 12.6	6.2	17 16.0	11.4	60.8
19 00	183 45.6	S10 03.8	152 37.8	6.1	S17 27.4	11.4	60.8
01	198 45.7	04.8	167 02.9	6.1	17 38.8	11.2	60.8
02	213 45.8	05.7	181 28.0	6.1	17 50.0	11.0	60.7
03	228 45.9	.. 06.6	195 53.1	6.0	18 01.0	11.0	60.7
04	243 46.0	07.5	210 18.1	6.0	18 12.0	10.8	60.7
05	258 46.1	08.4	224 43.1	5.9	18 22.8	10.6	60.6
06	273 46.2	S10 09.3	239 08.0	5.9	S18 33.4	10.6	60.6
07	288 46.3	10.2	253 32.9	5.8	18 44.0	10.4	60.6
08	303 46.5	11.1	267 57.7	5.9	18 54.4	10.3	60.6
M 09	318 46.6	.. 12.0	282 22.6	5.7	19 04.7	10.1	60.5
O 10	333 46.7	12.9	296 47.3	5.8	19 14.8	10.0	60.5
N 11	348 46.8	13.8	311 12.1	5.7	19 24.8	9.8	60.5
D 12	3 46.9	S10 14.7	325 36.8	5.7	S19 34.6	9.7	60.4
A 13	18 47.0	15.5	340 01.5	5.6	19 44.3	9.6	60.4
Y 14	33 47.1	16.4	354 26.1	5.6	19 53.9	9.4	60.4
15	48 47.2	.. 17.3	8 50.7	5.6	20 03.3	9.3	60.3
16	63 47.3	18.2	23 15.3	5.5	20 12.6	9.2	60.3
17	78 47.4	19.1	37 39.8	5.5	20 21.8	8.9	60.3
18	93 47.5	S10 20.0	52 04.3	5.5	S20 30.7	8.9	60.2
19	108 47.7	20.9	66 28.8	5.4	20 39.6	8.7	60.2
20	123 47.8	21.8	80 53.2	5.4	20 48.3	8.5	60.2
21	138 47.9	.. 22.7	95 17.6	5.4	20 56.8	8.4	60.1
22	153 48.0	23.6	109 42.0	5.4	21 05.2	8.2	60.1
23	168 48.1	24.5	124 06.4	5.4	21 13.4	8.1	60.1
20 00	183 48.2	S10 25.4	138 30.8	5.3	S21 21.5	8.0	60.0
01	198 48.3	26.3	152 55.1	5.3	21 29.5	7.8	60.0
02	213 48.4	27.2	167 19.4	5.2	21 37.3	7.6	60.0
03	228 48.5	.. 28.1	181 43.6	5.3	21 44.9	7.5	59.9
04	243 48.6	29.0	196 07.9	5.2	21 52.4	7.3	59.9
05	258 48.7	29.9	210 32.1	5.3	21 59.7	7.1	59.9
06	273 48.8	S10 30.8	224 56.4	5.2	S22 06.8	7.0	59.8
07	288 48.9	31.7	239 20.6	5.2	22 13.8	6.9	59.8
08	303 49.0	32.6	253 44.8	5.2	22 20.7	6.7	59.8
T 09	318 49.1	.. 33.5	268 09.0	5.2	22 27.4	6.5	59.7
U 10	333 49.2	34.4	282 33.1	5.2	22 33.9	6.4	59.7
E 11	348 49.3	35.2	296 57.3	5.1	22 40.3	6.2	59.7
S 12	3 49.4	S10 36.1	311 21.4	5.2	S22 46.5	6.0	59.6
D 13	18 49.5	37.0	325 45.6	5.1	22 52.5	5.9	59.6
A 14	33 49.7	37.9	340 09.7	5.1	22 58.4	5.7	59.5
Y 15	48 49.8	.. 38.8	354 33.8	5.2	23 04.1	5.6	59.5
16	63 49.9	39.7	8 58.0	5.1	23 09.7	5.4	59.5
17	78 50.0	40.6	23 22.1	5.1	23 15.1	5.2	59.4
18	93 50.1	S10 41.5	37 46.2	5.2	S23 20.3	5.1	59.4
19	108 50.2	42.4	52 10.4	5.1	23 25.4	4.9	59.4
20	123 50.3	43.3	66 34.5	5.1	23 30.3	4.8	59.3
21	138 50.4	.. 44.2	80 58.6	5.2	23 35.1	4.6	59.3
22	153 50.5	45.0	95 22.8	5.1	23 39.7	4.4	59.2
23	168 50.6	45.9	109 46.9	5.2	S23 44.1	4.3	59.2
	SD 16.1	d 0.9	SD 16.6		16.5		16.2

Twilight / Sunrise / Moonrise

Lat.	Naut.	Civil	Sunrise	Moonrise 18	19	20	21
°	h m	h m	h m	h m	h m	h m	h m
N 72	05 14	06 33	07 46	11 02	■	■	■
N 70	05 16	06 27	07 32	10 26	■	■	■
68	05 17	06 22	07 20	10 01	12 32	■	■
66	05 18	06 17	07 11	09 41	11 52	14 15	■
64	05 19	06 14	07 03	09 26	11 24	13 21	15 01
62	05 19	06 10	06 56	09 13	11 04	12 49	14 16
60	05 19	06 07	06 50	09 02	10 47	12 25	13 47
N 58	05 19	06 05	06 45	08 53	10 32	12 05	13 24
56	05 19	06 02	06 40	08 45	10 20	11 50	13 06
54	05 19	06 00	06 36	08 38	10 10	11 36	12 50
52	05 19	05 58	06 32	08 31	10 00	11 24	12 37
50	05 18	05 56	06 29	08 25	09 52	11 14	12 25
45	05 17	05 52	06 21	08 13	09 34	10 52	12 01
N 40	05 16	05 48	06 15	08 03	09 20	10 34	11 42
35	05 14	05 44	06 10	07 54	09 08	10 19	11 25
30	05 13	05 41	06 05	07 46	08 57	10 06	11 11
20	05 08	05 34	05 56	07 33	08 39	09 45	10 48
N 10	05 03	05 27	05 49	07 22	08 24	09 26	10 27
0	04 56	05 21	05 42	07 12	08 09	09 08	10 08
S 10	04 48	05 13	05 34	07 01	07 55	08 51	09 49
20	04 38	05 04	05 26	06 50	07 40	08 33	09 29
30	04 24	04 53	05 17	06 38	07 22	08 11	09 05
35	04 15	04 46	05 12	06 30	07 12	07 59	08 51
40	04 04	04 38	05 06	06 22	07 01	07 45	08 36
45	03 51	04 28	04 59	06 13	06 47	07 28	08 17
S 50	03 34	04 16	04 50	06 02	06 31	07 07	07 53
52	03 26	04 10	04 46	05 56	06 23	06 58	07 42
54	03 16	04 04	04 42	05 51	06 15	06 47	07 29
56	03 05	03 57	04 37	05 44	06 06	06 34	07 15
58	02 52	03 49	04 32	05 37	05 55	06 20	06 57
S 60	02 37	03 39	04 26	05 29	05 43	06 03	06 37

Sunset / Twilight / Moonset

Lat.	Sunset	Civil	Naut.	Moonset 18	19	20	21
°	h m	h m	h m	h m	h m	h m	h m
N 72	15 42	16 55	18 13	15 24	■	■	■
N 70	15 56	17 01	18 12	16 02	■	■	■
68	16 08	17 06	18 11	16 29	16 00	■	■
66	16 17	17 11	18 10	16 50	16 40	16 22	■
64	16 26	17 15	18 10	17 06	17 09	17 16	17 41
62	16 32	17 18	18 09	17 20	17 30	17 49	18 26
60	16 38	17 21	18 09	17 32	17 48	18 14	18 56
N 58	16 44	17 24	18 09	17 42	18 03	18 33	19 18
56	16 48	17 26	18 10	17 51	18 16	18 50	19 37
54	16 53	17 29	18 10	17 59	18 27	19 04	19 52
52	16 57	17 31	18 10	18 07	18 37	19 16	20 06
50	17 00	17 33	18 10	18 14	18 46	19 27	20 18
45	17 08	17 38	18 12	18 27	19 05	19 49	20 42
N 40	17 14	17 42	18 13	18 39	19 20	20 07	21 02
35	17 20	17 45	18 15	18 49	19 33	20 23	21 18
30	17 25	17 49	18 17	18 58	19 44	20 36	21 32
20	17 33	17 56	18 21	19 13	20 04	20 59	21 56
N 10	17 41	18 02	18 27	19 26	20 21	21 18	22 17
0	17 48	18 09	18 34	19 39	20 37	21 37	22 36
S 10	17 56	18 17	18 42	19 51	20 53	21 55	22 56
20	18 04	18 26	18 53	20 05	21 11	22 15	23 16
30	18 13	18 38	19 07	20 20	21 30	22 38	23 40
35	18 18	18 45	19 16	20 29	21 42	22 51	23 54
40	18 25	18 53	19 26	20 40	21 56	23 07	24 10
45	18 32	19 03	19 40	20 52	22 11	23 25	24 30
S 50	18 40	19 15	19 57	21 06	22 31	23 48	24 54
52	18 45	19 21	20 06	21 13	22 40	23 59	25 06
54	18 49	19 27	20 16	21 21	22 51	24 12	00 12
56	18 54	19 35	20 27	21 30	23 03	24 26	00 26
58	19 00	19 43	20 40	21 40	23 17	24 43	00 43
S 60	19 06	19 53	20 56	21 51	23 33	25 04	01 04

SUN and MOON

Day	Eqn. of Time 00ʰ	12ʰ	Mer. Pass.	Mer. Pass. Upper	Lower	Age	Phase
d	m s	m s	h m	h m	h m	d %	
18	14 51	14 57	11 45	13 25	00 57	02 4	
19	15 02	15 07	11 45	14 23	01 54	03 11	
20	15 13	15 18	11 45	15 23	02 53	04 19	

UT	ARIES GHA	VENUS GHA	Dec	MARS GHA	Dec	JUPITER GHA −2.2	Dec	SATURN GHA +0.6	Dec	Star Name	SHA	Dec
21 00	29 53.8	217 13.5	N 4 33.0	11 28.1	N 5 04.8	98 34.3	S22 26.2	92 07.3	S21 19.2	Acamar	315 14.0	S40 13.3
01	44 56.3	232 13.1	31.9	26 31.3	04.7	113 36.4	26.2	107 09.7	19.2	Achernar	335 22.3	S57 08.0
02	59 58.8	247 12.8	30.8	41 34.5	04.6	128 38.6	26.1	122 12.1	19.2	Acrux	173 04.4	S63 12.6
03	75 01.2	262 12.5 ..	29.7	56 37.7 ..	04.5	143 40.7 ..	26.1	137 14.4 ..	19.2	Adhara	255 08.4	S28 59.8
04	90 03.7	277 12.1	28.6	71 40.9	04.4	158 42.9	26.1	152 16.8	19.2	Aldebaran	290 43.3	N16 33.0
05	105 06.2	292 11.8	27.5	86 44.1	04.1	173 45.1	26.0	167 19.2	19.1			
W 06	120 08.6	307 11.4	N 4 26.4	101 47.3	N 5 04.2	188 47.2	S22 26.0	182 21.5	S21 19.1	Alioth	166 16.7	N55 50.9
E 07	135 11.1	322 11.1	25.3	116 50.5	04.1	203 49.4	25.9	197 23.9	19.1	Alkaid	152 55.3	N49 12.7
D 08	150 13.6	337 10.8	24.2	131 53.7	04.0	218 51.5	25.9	212 26.3	19.1	Alnair	27 37.1	S46 51.8
N 09	165 16.0	352 10.4 ..	23.1	146 56.8 ..	03.8	233 53.7 ..	25.9	227 28.6 ..	19.1	Alnilam	275 41.0	S 1 11.3
E 10	180 18.5	7 10.1	22.0	162 00.0	03.7	248 55.8	25.8	242 31.0	19.1	Alphard	217 51.2	S 8 44.7
S 11	195 21.0	22 09.8	20.9	177 03.2	03.6	263 58.0	25.8	257 33.4	19.1			
D 12	210 23.4	37 09.4	N 4 19.8	192 06.4	N 5 03.5	279 00.2	S22 25.7	272 35.7	S21 19.0	Alphecca	126 07.0	N26 39.0
A 13	225 25.9	52 09.1	18.7	207 09.6	03.4	294 02.3	25.7	287 38.1	19.0	Alpheratz	357 38.0	N29 12.4
Y 14	240 28.3	67 08.7	17.6	222 12.8	03.3	309 04.5	25.7	302 40.5	19.0	Altair	62 03.3	N 8 55.6
15	255 30.8	82 08.4 ..	16.5	237 16.0 ..	03.2	324 06.6 ..	25.6	317 42.8 ..	19.0	Ankaa	353 10.2	S42 11.7
16	270 33.3	97 08.1	15.4	252 19.1	03.1	339 08.8	25.6	332 45.2	19.0	Antares	112 20.3	S26 28.5
17	285 35.7	112 07.7	14.3	267 22.3	03.0	354 10.9	25.5	347 47.6	19.0			
18	300 38.2	127 07.4	N 4 13.2	282 25.5	N 5 02.9	9 13.1	S22 25.5	2 49.9	S21 18.9	Arcturus	145 51.4	N19 04.7
19	315 40.7	142 07.0	12.1	297 28.7	02.8	24 15.2	25.4	17 52.3	18.9	Atria	107 18.0	S69 03.9
20	330 43.1	157 06.7	11.0	312 31.9	02.7	39 17.4	25.4	32 54.7	18.9	Avior	234 16.1	S59 34.2
21	345 45.6	172 06.4 ..	09.9	327 35.0 ..	02.6	54 19.6 ..	25.4	47 57.0 ..	18.9	Bellatrix	278 26.4	N 6 22.1
22	0 48.1	187 06.0	08.8	342 38.2	02.5	69 21.7	25.3	62 59.4	18.9	Betelgeuse	270 55.6	N 7 24.7
23	15 50.5	202 05.7	07.7	357 41.4	02.4	84 23.9	25.3	78 01.8	18.9			
22 00	30 53.0	217 05.3	N 4 06.6	12 44.6	N 5 02.3	99 26.0	S22 25.2	93 04.1	S21 18.9	Canopus	263 53.7	S52 42.1
01	45 55.5	232 05.0	05.5	27 47.7	02.2	114 28.2	25.2	108 06.5	18.8	Capella	280 26.6	N46 00.9
02	60 57.9	247 04.7	04.4	42 50.9	02.1	129 30.3	25.2	123 08.9	18.8	Deneb	49 28.0	N45 21.5
03	76 00.4	262 04.3 ..	03.3	57 54.1 ..	02.0	144 32.5 ..	25.1	138 11.2 ..	18.8	Denebola	182 28.8	N14 27.5
04	91 02.8	277 04.0	02.2	72 57.3	01.9	159 34.6	25.1	153 13.6	18.8	Diphda	348 50.5	S17 52.4
05	106 05.3	292 03.7	4 01.0	88 00.4	01.8	174 36.8	25.0	168 16.0	18.8			
T 06	121 07.8	307 03.3	N 3 59.9	103 03.6	N 5 01.7	189 38.9	S22 25.0	183 18.3	S21 18.8	Dubhe	193 45.8	N61 38.3
H 07	136 10.2	322 03.0	58.8	118 06.8	01.6	204 41.1	25.0	198 20.7	18.7	Elnath	278 06.0	N28 37.4
U 08	151 12.7	337 02.6	57.7	133 09.9	01.5	219 43.2	24.9	213 23.1	18.7	Eltanin	90 44.1	N51 29.5
R 09	166 15.2	352 02.3 ..	56.6	148 13.1 ..	01.4	234 45.4 ..	24.9	228 25.4 ..	18.7	Enif	33 42.0	N 9 58.3
S 10	181 17.6	7 02.0	55.5	163 16.3	01.3	249 47.5	24.8	243 27.8	18.7	Fomalhaut	15 18.1	S29 30.8
D 11	196 20.1	22 01.6	54.4	178 19.5	01.2	264 49.7	24.8	258 30.1	18.7			
A 12	211 22.6	37 01.3	N 3 53.3	193 22.6	N 5 01.1	279 51.8	S22 24.7	273 32.5	S21 18.7	Gacrux	171 55.9	S57 13.5
Y 13	226 25.0	52 00.9	52.2	208 25.8	01.0	294 54.0	24.7	288 34.9	18.7	Gienah	175 47.4	S17 39.2
14	241 27.5	67 00.6	51.1	223 29.0	00.9	309 56.1	24.7	303 37.2	18.6	Hadar	148 41.4	S60 28.2
15	256 30.0	82 00.3 ..	50.0	238 32.1 ..	00.8	324 58.3 ..	24.6	318 39.6 ..	18.6	Hamal	327 54.7	N23 33.6
16	271 32.4	96 59.9	48.9	253 35.3	00.8	340 00.4	24.6	333 42.0	18.6	Kaus Aust.	83 37.2	S34 22.5
17	286 34.9	111 59.6	47.8	268 38.4	00.7	355 02.6	24.5	348 44.3	18.6			
18	301 37.3	126 59.3	N 3 46.6	283 41.6	N 5 00.6	10 04.7	S22 24.5	3 46.7	S21 18.6	Kochab	137 21.1	N74 04.4
19	316 39.8	141 58.9	45.5	298 44.8	00.5	25 06.9	24.5	18 49.0	18.6	Markab	13 33.1	N15 19.1
20	331 42.3	156 58.6	44.4	313 47.9	00.4	40 09.0	24.4	33 51.4	18.5	Menkar	314 09.4	N 4 10.3
21	346 44.7	171 58.2 ..	43.3	328 51.1 ..	00.3	55 11.2 ..	24.4	48 53.8 ..	18.5	Menkent	148 02.0	S36 28.1
22	1 47.2	186 57.9	42.2	343 54.2	00.2	70 13.3	24.3	63 56.1	18.5	Miaplacidus	221 39.1	S69 47.7
23	16 49.7	201 57.6	41.1	358 57.4	00.1	85 15.5	24.3	78 58.5	18.5			
23 00	31 52.1	216 57.2	N 3 40.0	14 00.6	N 5 00.0	100 17.6	S22 24.2	94 00.9	S21 18.5	Mirfak	308 32.6	N49 56.0
01	46 54.6	231 56.9	38.9	29 03.7	4 59.9	115 19.8	24.2	109 03.2	18.5	Nunki	75 52.1	S26 16.2
02	61 57.1	246 56.6	37.8	44 06.9	59.8	130 21.9	24.2	124 05.6	18.4	Peacock	53 11.2	S56 40.3
03	76 59.5	261 56.2 ..	36.6	59 10.0 ..	59.7	145 24.0 ..	24.1	139 07.9 ..	18.4	Pollux	243 21.5	N27 58.5
04	92 02.0	276 55.9	35.5	74 13.2	59.6	160 26.2	24.1	154 10.3	18.4	Procyon	244 54.4	N 5 10.4
05	107 04.5	291 55.5	34.4	89 16.3	59.6	175 28.3	24.0	169 12.7	18.4			
F 06	122 06.9	306 55.2	N 3 33.3	104 19.5	N 4 59.5	190 30.5	S22 24.0	184 15.0	S21 18.4	Rasalhague	96 01.9	N12 32.9
R 07	137 09.4	321 54.9	32.2	119 22.6	59.4	205 32.6	23.9	199 17.4	18.4	Regulus	207 38.3	N11 52.1
I 08	152 11.8	336 54.5	31.1	134 25.8	59.3	220 34.8	23.9	214 19.7	18.3	Rigel	281 07.0	S 8 10.6
D 09	167 14.3	351 54.2 ..	30.0	149 28.9 ..	59.2	235 36.9 ..	23.9	229 22.1 ..	18.3	Rigil Kent.	139 45.6	S60 55.1
A 10	182 16.8	6 53.8	28.9	164 32.1	59.1	250 39.1	23.8	244 24.5	18.3	Sabik	102 07.0	S15 44.9
Y 11	197 19.2	21 53.5	27.7	179 35.2	59.0	265 41.2	23.8	259 26.8	18.3			
12	212 21.7	36 53.2	N 3 26.6	194 38.4	N 4 58.8	280 43.3	S22 23.7	274 29.2	S21 18.3	Schedar	349 34.3	N56 39.1
13	227 24.2	51 52.8	25.5	209 41.5	58.8	295 45.5	23.7	289 31.5	18.3	Shaula	96 15.3	S37 07.1
14	242 26.6	66 52.5	24.4	224 44.7	58.8	310 47.6	23.6	304 33.9	18.2	Sirius	258 29.1	S16 44.5
15	257 29.1	81 52.2 ..	23.3	239 47.8 ..	58.7	325 49.8 ..	23.6	319 36.2 ..	18.2	Spica	158 26.2	S11 15.9
16	272 31.6	96 51.8	22.2	254 50.9	58.6	340 51.9	23.6	334 38.6	18.2	Suhail	222 48.9	S43 30.6
17	287 34.0	111 51.5	21.0	269 54.1	58.5	355 54.1	23.5	349 41.0	18.2			
18	302 36.5	126 51.1	N 3 19.9	284 57.2	N 4 58.4	10 56.2	S22 23.5	4 43.3	S21 18.2	Vega	80 35.7	N38 48.5
19	317 38.9	141 50.8	18.8	300 00.4	58.3	25 58.3	23.4	19 45.7	18.2	Zuben'ubi	137 00.1	S16 07.5
20	332 41.4	156 50.5	17.7	315 03.5	58.2	41 00.5	23.4	34 48.0	18.1			
21	347 43.9	171 50.1 ..	16.6	330 06.6 ..	58.2	56 02.6 ..	23.3	49 50.4 ..	18.1		SHA	Mer.Pass.
22	2 46.3	186 49.8	15.5	345 09.8	58.1	71 04.8	23.3	64 52.7	18.1	Venus	186 12.4	9 32
23	17 48.8	201 49.5	14.3	0 12.9	58.0	86 06.9	23.3	79 55.1	18.1	Mars	341 51.6	23 04
Mer.Pass.	21 52.9	v −0.3	d 1.1	v 3.2	d 0.1	v 2.1	d 0.0	v 2.4	d 0.0	Jupiter	68 33.0	17 20
										Saturn	62 11.2	17 45

UT	SUN GHA	SUN Dec	MOON GHA	v	MOON Dec	d	HP
d h	o ′	o ′	o ′	′	o ′	′	′
21 00	183 50.7	S10 46.8	124 11.1	5.2	S23 48.4	4.1	59.2
01	198 50.8	47.7	138 35.3	5.2	23 52.5	3.9	59.1
02	213 50.9	48.6	152 59.5	5.2	23 56.4	3.8	59.1
03	228 51.0 ..	49.5	167 23.7	5.2	·24 00.2	3.6	59.1
04	243 51.1	50.4	181 47.9	5.2	24 03.8	3.5	59.0
05	258 51.2	51.3	196 12.1	5.3	24 07.3	3.2	59.0
06	273 51.3	S10 52.1	210 36.4	5.3	S24 10.5	3.2	58.9
W 07	288 51.4	53.0	225 00.7	5.3	24 13.7	2.9	58.9
E 08	303 51.5	53.9	239 25.0	5.3	24 16.6	2.8	58.9
D 09	318 51.5 ..	54.8	253 49.3	5.3	24 19.4	2.7	58.8
N 10	333 51.6	55.7	268 13.6	5.4	24 22.1	2.4	58.8
E 11	348 51.7	56.6	282 38.0	5.4	24 24.5	2.4	58.7
S 12	3 51.8	S10 57.5	297 02.4	5.4	S24 26.9	2.1	58.7
D 13	18 51.9	58.3	311 26.8	5.5	24 29.0	2.0	58.7
A 14	33 52.0	10 59.2	325 51.3	5.5	24 31.0	1.8	58.6
Y 15	48 52.1	11 00.1	340 15.8	5.6	24 32.8	1.7	58.6
16	63 52.2	01.0	354 40.4	5.5	24 34.5	1.5	58.5
17	78 52.3	01.9	9 04.9	5.7	24 36.0	1.4	58.5
18	93 52.4	S11 02.8	23 29.6	5.6	S24 37.4	1.1	58.5
19	108 52.5	03.7	37 54.2	5.7	24 38.5	1.1	58.4
20	123 52.6	04.5	52 18.9	5.7	24 39.6	0.8	58.4
21	138 52.7 ..	05.4	66 43.6	5.8	24 40.4	0.8	58.3
22	153 52.8	06.3	81 08.4	5.9	24 41.2	0.5	58.3
23	168 52.9	07.2	95 33.3	5.8	24 41.7	0.4	58.3
22 00	183 53.0	S11 08.1	109 58.1	6.0	S24 42.1	0.3	58.2
01	198 53.1	08.9	124 23.1	5.9	24 42.4	0.1	58.2
02	213 53.2	09.8	138 48.0	6.1	24 42.5	0.1	58.2
03	228 53.3 ..	10.7	153 13.1	6.1	24 42.4	0.2	58.1
04	243 53.3	11.6	167 38.2	6.1	24 42.2	0.4	58.1
05	258 53.4	12.5	182 03.3	6.2	24 41.8	0.5	58.0
06	273 53.5	S11 13.4	196 28.5	6.2	S24 41.3	0.7	58.0
T 07	288 53.6	14.2	210 53.7	6.4	24 40.6	0.8	58.0
H 08	303 53.7	15.1	225 19.1	6.3	24 39.8	1.0	57.9
U 09	318 53.8 ..	16.0	239 44.4	6.5	24 38.8	1.2	57.9
R 10	333 53.9	16.9	254 09.9	6.5	24 37.6	1.2	57.8
S 11	348 54.0	17.7	268 35.4	6.5	24 36.4	1.5	57.8
D 12	3 54.1	S11 18.6	283 00.9	6.6	S24 34.9	1.5	57.8
A 13	18 54.2	19.5	297 26.5	6.7	24 33.4	1.8	57.7
Y 14	33 54.2	20.4	311 52.2	6.8	24 31.6	1.8	57.7
15	48 54.3 ..	21.3	326 18.0	6.8	24 29.8	2.0	57.6
16	63 54.4	22.1	340 43.8	6.9	24 27.8	2.2	57.6
17	78 54.5	23.0	355 09.7	7.0	24 25.6	2.3	57.6
18	93 54.6	S11 23.9	9 35.7	7.0	S24 23.3	2.4	57.5
19	108 54.7	24.8	24 01.7	7.1	24 20.9	2.6	57.5
20	123 54.8	25.6	38 27.8	7.2	24 18.3	2.7	57.5
21	138 54.9 ..	26.5	52 54.0	7.3	24 15.6	2.9	57.4
22	153 54.9	27.4	67 20.3	7.3	24 12.7	3.0	57.4
23	168 55.0	28.3	81 46.6	7.4	24 09.7	3.2	57.3
23 00	183 55.1	S11 29.1	96 13.0	7.5	S24 06.5	3.2	57.3
01	198 55.2	30.0	110 39.5	7.6	24 03.3	3.4	57.3
02	213 55.3	30.9	125 06.1	7.6	23 59.9	3.6	57.2
03	228 55.4 ..	31.8	139 32.7	7.7	23 56.3	3.7	57.2
04	243 55.5	32.6	153 59.4	7.8	23 52.6	3.8	57.2
05	258 55.5	33.5	168 26.2	7.9	23 48.8	3.9	57.1
06	273 55.6	S11 34.4	182 53.1	8.0	S23 44.9	4.1	57.1
07	288 55.7	35.3	197 20.1	8.0	23 40.8	4.2	57.1
08	303 55.8	36.1	211 47.1	8.2	23 36.6	4.3	57.0
F 09	318 55.9 ..	37.0	226 14.3	8.2	23 32.3	4.5	57.0
R 10	333 56.0	37.9	240 41.5	8.3	23 27.8	4.6	56.9
I 11	348 56.0	38.7	255 08.8	8.4	23 23.2	4.7	56.9
D 12	3 56.1	S11 39.6	269 36.2	8.4	S23 18.5	4.8	56.9
A 13	18 56.2	40.5	284 03.6	8.6	23 13.7	5.0	56.8
Y 14	33 56.3	41.4	298 31.2	8.6	23 08.7	5.0	56.8
15	48 56.4 ..	42.2	312 58.8	8.8	23 03.7	5.2	56.8
16	63 56.5	43.1	327 26.6	8.8	22 58.5	5.3	56.7
17	78 56.5	44.0	341 54.4	8.9	22 53.2	5.5	56.7
18	93 56.6	S11 44.8	356 22.3	9.0	S22 47.7	5.5	56.7
19	108 56.7	45.7	10 50.3	9.1	22 42.2	5.7	56.6
20	123 56.8	46.6	25 18.4	9.1	22 36.5	5.8	56.6
21	138 56.9 ..	47.4	39 46.5	9.3	22 30.7	5.9	56.6
22	153 56.9	48.3	54 14.8	9.3	22 24.8	6.0	56.5
23	168 57.0	49.2	68 43.1	9.5	S22 18.8	6.1	56.5
	SD 16.1	d 0.9	SD 16.0		15.7		15.5

Lat.	Twilight Naut.	Twilight Civil	Sunrise	Moonrise 21	Moonrise 22	Moonrise 23	Moonrise 24
o	h m	h m	h m	h m	h m	h m	h m
N 72	05 27	06 46	08 02	■■■	■■■	■■■	■■■
N 70	05 27	06 39	07 45	■■■	■■■	■■■	■■■
68	05 27	06 32	07 32	■■■	■■■	■■■	17 27
66	05 27	06 27	07 21	■■■	■■■	17 02	16 47
64	05 27	06 22	07 12	15 01	15 56	16 14	16 20
62	05 26	06 18	07 04	14 16	15 14	15 43	15 58
60	05 26	06 14	06 58	13 47	14 45	15 20	15 41
N 58	05 25	06 11	06 52	13 24	14 22	15 01	15 26
56	05 25	06 08	06 47	13 06	14 04	14 46	15 14
54	05 24	06 06	06 42	12 50	13 49	14 32	15 03
52	05 24	06 03	06 38	12 37	13 36	14 20	14 53
50	05 23	06 01	06 34	12 25	13 24	14 10	14 44
45	05 21	05 55	06 25	12 01	13 00	13 48	14 26
N 40	05 19	05 51	06 18	11 42	12 41	13 30	14 11
35	05 17	05 46	06 12	11 25	12 24	13 15	13 58
30	05 14	05 42	06 07	11 11	12 10	13 02	13 46
20	05 09	05 35	05 57	10 48	11 46	12 40	13 27
N 10	05 03	05 28	05 49	10 27	11 26	12 20	13 10
0	04 55	05 20	05 41	10 08	11 06	12 02	12 54
S 10	04 46	05 12	05 33	09 49	10 47	11 44	12 38
20	04 35	05 02	05 24	09 29	10 27	11 25	12 21
30	04 20	04 50	05 14	09 05	10 03	11 02	12 02
35	04 11	04 42	05 08	08 51	09 49	10 49	11 50
40	03 59	04 33	05 02	08 36	09 33	10 34	11 37
45	03 45	04 23	04 54	08 17	09 13	10 16	11 22
S 50	03 27	04 10	04 44	07 53	08 49	09 53	11 02
52	03 18	04 03	04 40	07 42	08 37	09 43	10 53
54	03 07	03 57	04 35	07 29	08 24	09 30	10 43
56	02 56	03 49	04 30	07 15	08 09	09 16	10 31
58	02 42	03 40	04 24	06 57	07 51	09 00	10 18
S 60	02 25	03 29	04 17	06 37	07 29	08 40	10 02

Lat.	Sunset	Twilight Civil	Twilight Naut.	Moonset 21	Moonset 22	Moonset 23	Moonset 24
o	h m	h m	h m	h m	h m	h m	h m
N 72	15 25	16 41	17 59	■■■	■■■	■■■	■■■
N 70	15 42	16 49	18 00	■■■	■■■	■■■	■■■
68	15 55	16 55	18 00	■■■	■■■	■■■	20 58
66	16 06	17 01	18 00	■■■	■■■	19 36	21 37
64	16 15	17 05	18 01	17 41	18 47	20 23	22 04
62	16 23	17 09	18 01	18 26	19 30	20 54	22 25
60	16 30	17 13	18 02	18 56	19 58	21 17	22 41
N 58	16 36	17 17	18 02	19 18	20 20	21 35	22 56
56	16 41	17 20	18 03	19 37	20 38	21 51	23 08
54	16 46	17 22	18 03	19 52	20 54	22 04	23 18
52	16 50	17 25	18 04	20 06	21 07	22 15	23 27
50	16 54	17 27	18 05	20 18	21 18	22 25	23 36
45	17 03	17 33	18 07	20 42	21 42	22 47	23 53
N 40	17 10	17 38	18 09	21 02	22 01	23 04	24 07
35	17 16	17 42	18 11	21 18	22 17	23 18	24 20
30	17 22	17 46	18 14	21 32	22 31	23 31	24 30
20	17 31	17 54	18 19	21 56	22 54	23 52	24 48
N 10	17 40	18 01	18 26	22 17	23 15	24 11	00 11
0	17 48	18 08	18 33	22 36	23 34	24 28	00 28
S 10	17 56	18 17	18 42	22 56	23 52	24 45	00 45
20	18 05	18 27	18 54	23 16	24 12	00 12	01 03
30	18 15	18 40	19 09	23 40	24 36	00 36	01 24
35	18 21	18 48	19 19	23 54	24 49	00 49	01 36
40	18 28	18 56	19 30	24 10	00 10	01 05	01 50
45	18 36	19 07	19 45	24 30	00 30	01 23	02 06
S 50	18 45	19 20	20 04	24 54	00 54	01 46	02 26
52	18 50	19 27	20 13	25 06	01 06	01 57	02 36
54	18 55	19 34	20 23	00 12	01 19	02 10	02 47
56	19 00	19 42	20 35	00 26	01 34	02 24	02 59
58	19 07	19 51	20 50	00 43	01 52	02 41	03 13
S 60	19 14	20 02	21 08	01 04	02 15	03 01	03 29

Day	SUN Eqn. of Time 00h	SUN Eqn. of Time 12h	SUN Mer. Pass.	MOON Mer. Pass. Upper	MOON Mer. Pass. Lower	Age	Phase
d	m s	m s	h m	h m	h m	d	%
21	15 22	15 27	11 45	16 22	03 53	05	29
22	15 32	15 36	11 44	17 20	04 51	06	39
23	15 40	15 44	11 44	18 15	05 48	07	50

UT	ARIES	VENUS −4.0		MARS −2.3		JUPITER −2.2		SATURN +0.6		STARS		
	GHA	GHA	Dec	GHA	Dec	GHA	Dec	GHA	Dec	Name	SHA	Dec
d h	° ′	° ′	° ′	° ′	° ′	° ′	° ′	° ′	° ′		° ′	° ′
24 00	32 51.3	216 49.1 N 3 13.2		15 16.1 N 4 57.9		101 09.0 S22 23.2		94 57.5 S21 18.1		Acamar	315 14.0 S40 13.3	
01	47 53.7	231 48.8	12.1	30 19.2	57.8	116 11.2	23.2	109 59.8	18.1	Achernar	335 22.3 S57 08.0	
02	62 56.2	246 48.4	11.0	45 22.3	57.7	131 13.3	23.1	125 02.2	18.0	Acrux	173 04.4 S63 12.6	
03	77 58.7	261 48.1 . .	09.9	60 25.5 . .	57.6	146 15.5 . .	23.1	140 04.5 . .	18.0	Adhara	255 08.4 S28 59.8	
04	93 01.1	276 47.8	08.8	75 28.6	57.6	161 17.6	23.0	155 06.9	18.0	Aldebaran	290 43.3 N16 33.0	
05	108 03.6	291 47.4	07.6	90 31.7	57.5	176 19.7	23.0	170 09.2	18.0			
06	123 06.1	306 47.1 N 3 06.5		105 34.9 N 4 57.4		191 21.9 S22 23.0		185 11.6 S21 18.0		Alioth	166 16.6 N55 50.9	
07	138 08.5	321 46.7	05.4	120 38.0	57.3	206 24.0	22.9	200 14.0	18.0	Alkaid	152 55.3 N49 12.7	
S 08	153 11.0	336 46.4	04.3	135 41.1	57.3	221 26.2	22.9	215 16.3	17.9	Alnair	27 37.1 S46 51.8
A 09	168 13.4	351 46.1 . .	03.2	150 44.2 . .	57.2	236 28.3 . .	22.8	230 18.7 . .	17.9	Alnilam	275 41.0 S 1 11.3	
T 10	183 15.9	6 45.7	02.0	165 47.4	57.1	251 30.4	22.8	245 21.0	17.9	Alphard	217 51.2 S 8 44.7	
U 11	198 18.4	21 45.4	3 00.9	180 50.5	57.0	266 32.6	22.7	260 23.4	17.9			
R 12	213 20.8	36 45.1 N 2 59.8		195 53.6 N 4 56.9		281 34.7 S22 22.7		275 25.7 S21 17.9		Alphecca	126 07.0 N26 38.9	
D 13	228 23.3	51 44.7	58.7	210 56.7	56.9	296 36.8	22.7	290 28.1	17.9	Alpheratz	357 38.0 N29 12.4	
A 14	243 25.8	66 44.4	57.6	225 59.9	56.8	311 39.0	22.6	305 30.4	17.8	Altair	62 03.3 N 8 55.6	
Y 15	258 28.2	81 44.0 . .	56.4	241 03.0 . .	56.7	326 41.1 . .	22.6	320 32.8 . .	17.8	Ankaa	353 10.2 S42 11.7	
16	273 30.7	96 43.7	55.3	256 06.1	56.6	341 43.2	22.5	335 35.1	17.8	Antares	112 20.3 S26 28.5	
17	288 33.2	111 43.4	54.2	271 09.2	56.5	356 45.4	22.5	350 37.5	17.8			
18	303 35.6	126 43.0 N 2 53.1		286 12.4 N 4 56.5		11 47.5 S22 22.4		5 39.9 S21 17.8		Arcturus	145 51.4 N19 04.7	
19	318 38.1	141 42.7	51.9	301 15.5	56.4	26 49.6	22.4	20 42.2	17.7	Atria	107 18.0 S69 03.9	
20	333 40.6	156 42.4	50.8	316 18.6	56.3	41 51.8	22.3	35 44.6	17.7	Avior	234 16.0 S59 34.2	
21	348 43.0	171 42.0 . .	49.7	331 21.7 . .	56.2	56 53.9 . .	22.3	50 46.9 . .	17.7	Bellatrix	278 26.3 N 6 22.1	
22	3 45.5	186 41.7	48.6	346 24.8	56.2	71 56.1	22.3	65 49.3	17.7	Betelgeuse	270 55.6 N 7 24.7	
23	18 47.9	201 41.3	47.5	1 27.9	56.1	86 58.2	22.2	80 51.6	17.7			
25 00	33 50.4	216 41.0 N 2 46.3		16 31.0 N 4 56.0		102 00.3 S22 22.2		95 54.0 S21 17.7		Canopus	263 53.6 S52 42.1	
01	48 52.9	231 40.7	45.2	31 34.2	55.9	117 02.5	22.1	110 56.3	17.6	Capella	280 26.6 N46 00.9	
02	63 55.3	246 40.3	44.1	46 37.3	55.9	132 04.6	22.1	125 58.7	17.6	Deneb	49 28.0 N45 21.5	
03	78 57.8	261 40.0 . .	43.0	61 40.4 . .	55.8	147 06.7 . .	22.0	141 01.0 . .	17.6	Denebola	182 28.7 N14 27.5	
04	94 00.3	276 39.6	41.8	76 43.5	55.7	162 08.8	22.0	156 03.4	17.6	Diphda	348 50.5 S17 52.4	
05	109 02.7	291 39.3	40.7	91 46.6	55.7	177 11.0	21.9	171 05.7	17.6			
06	124 05.2	306 39.0 N 2 39.6		106 49.7 N 4 55.6		192 13.1 S22 21.9		186 08.1 S21 17.6		Dubhe	193 45.8 N61 38.3	
07	139 07.7	321 38.6	38.5	121 52.8	55.5	207 15.2	21.8	201 10.4	17.5	Elnath	278 05.9 N28 37.4	
08	154 10.1	336 38.3	37.3	136 55.9	55.4	222 17.4	21.8	216 12.8	17.5	Eltanin	90 44.1 N51 29.5	
S 09	169 12.6	351 38.0 . .	36.2	151 59.0 . .	55.4	237 19.5 . .	21.8	231 15.1 . .	17.5	Enif	33 42.0 N 9 58.3	
U 10	184 15.0	6 37.6	35.1	167 02.1	55.3	252 21.6	21.7	246 17.5	17.5	Fomalhaut	15 18.1 S29 30.8	
N 11	199 17.5	21 37.3	33.9	182 05.2	55.2	267 23.8	21.7	261 19.8	17.5			
D 12	214 20.0	36 36.9 N 2 32.8		197 08.3 N 4 55.2		282 25.9 S22 21.6		276 22.2 S21 17.4		Gacrux	171 55.9 S57 13.5	
A 13	229 22.4	51 36.6	31.7	212 11.4	55.1	297 28.0	21.6	291 24.5	17.4	Gienah	175 47.4 S17 39.2	
Y 14	244 24.9	66 36.3	30.6	227 14.5	55.0	312 30.2	21.5	306 26.9	17.4	Hadar	148 41.4 S60 28.2	
15	259 27.4	81 35.9 . .	29.4	242 17.6 . .	55.0	327 32.3 . .	21.5	321 29.2 . .	17.4	Hamal	327 54.7 N23 33.6	
16	274 29.8	96 35.6	28.3	257 20.7	54.9	342 34.4	21.4	336 31.6	17.4	Kaus Aust.	83 37.3 S34 22.5	
17	289 32.3	111 35.2	27.2	272 23.8	54.8	357 36.5	21.4	351 33.9	17.4			
18	304 34.8	126 34.9 N 2 26.1		287 26.9 N 4 54.7		12 38.7 S22 21.4		6 36.3 S21 17.3		Kochab	137 21.1 N74 04.4	
19	319 37.2	141 34.6	24.9	302 30.0	54.7	27 40.8	21.3	21 38.6	17.3	Markab	13 33.1 N15 19.1	
20	334 39.7	156 34.2	23.8	317 33.1	54.6	42 42.9	21.3	36 41.0	17.3	Menkar	314 09.4 N 4 10.3	
21	349 42.2	171 33.9 . .	22.7	332 36.2 . .	54.5	57 45.1 . .	21.2	51 43.3 . .	17.3	Menkent	148 02.0 S36 28.1	
22	4 44.6	186 33.6	21.5	347 39.3	54.5	72 47.2	21.2	66 45.7	17.3	Miaplacidus	221 39.0 S69 47.7	
23	19 47.1	201 33.2	20.4	2 42.4	54.4	87 49.3	21.1	81 48.0	17.2			
26 00	34 49.5	216 32.9 N 2 19.3		17 45.5 N 4 54.4		102 51.4 S22 21.1		96 50.4 S21 17.2		Mirfak	308 32.6 N49 56.0	
01	49 52.0	231 32.5	18.2	32 48.6	54.3	117 53.6	21.0	111 52.7	17.2	Nunki	75 52.1 S26 16.2	
02	64 54.5	246 32.2	17.0	47 51.7	54.2	132 55.7	21.0	126 55.1	17.2	Peacock	53 11.2 S56 39.3	
03	79 56.9	261 31.9 . .	15.9	62 54.8 . .	54.2	147 57.8 . .	20.9	141 57.4 . .	17.2	Pollux	243 21.5 N27 58.5	
04	94 59.4	276 31.5	14.8	77 57.8	54.1	162 59.9	20.9	156 59.8	17.1	Procyon	244 54.4 N 5 10.4	
05	110 01.9	291 31.2	13.6	93 00.9	54.0	178 02.1	20.9	172 02.1	17.1			
06	125 04.3	306 30.8 N 2 12.5		108 04.0 N 4 54.0		193 04.2 S22 20.8		187 04.5 S21 17.1		Rasalhague	96 02.0 N12 32.9	
07	140 06.8	321 30.5	11.4	123 07.1	53.9	208 06.3	20.8	202 06.8	17.1	Regulus	207 38.3 N11 52.1	
08	155 09.3	336 30.2	10.2	138 10.2	53.8	223 08.4	20.7	217 09.2	17.1	Rigel	281 06.9 S 8 10.6	
M 09	170 11.7	351 29.8 . .	09.1	153 13.3 . .	53.8	238 10.6 . .	20.7	232 11.5 . .	17.1	Rigil Kent.	139 45.6 S60 55.1	
O 10	185 14.2	6 29.5	08.0	168 16.3	53.7	253 12.7	20.6	247 13.9	17.0	Sabik	102 07.0 S15 44.9	
N 11	200 16.7	21 29.1	06.8	183 19.4	53.7	268 14.8	20.6	262 16.2	17.0			
D 12	215 19.1	36 28.8 N 2 05.7		198 22.5 N 4 53.6		283 16.9 S22 20.5		277 18.6 S21 17.0		Schedar	349 34.3 N56 39.1	
A 13	230 21.6	51 28.5	04.6	213 25.6	53.5	298 19.1	20.5	292 20.9	17.0	Shaula	96 15.3 S37 07.1	
Y 14	245 24.0	66 28.1	03.4	228 28.6	53.5	313 21.2	20.4	307 23.3	17.0	Sirius	258 29.1 S16 44.5	
15	260 26.5	81 27.8 . .	02.3	243 31.7 . .	53.4	328 23.3 . .	20.4	322 25.6 . .	16.9	Spica	158 26.2 S11 15.9	
16	275 29.0	96 27.5	01.2	258 34.8	53.4	343 25.4	20.3	337 27.9	16.9	Suhail	222 48.9 S43 30.6	
17	290 31.4	111 27.1	2 00.0	273 37.9	53.3	358 27.6	20.3	352 30.3	16.9			
18	305 33.9	126 26.8 N 1 58.9		288 40.9 N 4 53.2		13 29.7 S22 20.3		7 32.6 S21 16.9		Vega	80 35.7 N38 48.5	
19	320 36.4	141 26.4	57.8	303 44.0	53.2	28 31.8	20.2	22 35.0	16.9	Zuben'ubi	137 00.1 S16 07.5	
20	335 38.8	156 26.1	56.6	318 47.1	53.1	43 33.9	20.2	37 37.3	16.8		SHA	Mer. Pass.
21	350 41.3	171 25.8 . .	55.5	333 50.2 . .	53.1	58 36.0 . .	20.1	52 39.7 . .	16.8		° ′	h m
22	5 43.8	186 25.4	54.4	348 53.2	53.0	73 38.2	20.1	67 42.0	16.8	Venus	182 50.6	9 33
23	20 46.2	201 25.1	53.2	3 56.3	53.0	88 40.3	20.0	82 44.4	16.8	Mars	342 40.6	22 49
	h m									Jupiter	68 09.9	17 10
Mer. Pass. 21 41.1		v −0.3	d 1.1	v 3.1	d 0.1	v 2.1	d 0.0	v 2.4	d 0.0	Saturn	62 03.6	17 34

UT	SUN GHA	SUN Dec	MOON GHA	v	MOON Dec	d	HP
d h	° ′	° ′	° ′	′	° ′	′	′
24 00	183 57.1	S11 50.0	83 11.6	9.5	S22 12.7	6.2	56.5
01	198 57.2	50.9	97 40.1	9.6	22 06.5	6.4	56.4
02	213 57.3	51.8	112 08.7	9.7	22 00.1	6.4	56.4
03	228 57.3	.. 52.6	126 37.4	9.8	21 53.7	6.6	56.4
04	243 57.4	53.5	141 06.2	9.9	21 47.1	6.7	56.3
05	258 57.5	54.4	155 35.1	9.9	21 40.4	6.7	56.3
06	273 57.6	S11 55.2	170 04.0	10.1	S21 33.7	6.9	56.3
07	288 57.6	56.1	184 33.1	10.2	21 26.8	7.0	56.2
S 08	303 57.7	57.0	199 02.3	10.2	21 19.8	7.0	56.2
A 09	318 57.8	.. 57.8	213 31.5	10.3	21 12.8	7.2	56.2
T 10	333 57.9	58.7	228 00.8	10.4	21 05.6	7.3	56.1
U 11	348 57.9	11 59.6	242 30.2	10.5	20 58.3	7.4	56.1
R 12	3 58.0	S12 00.4	256 59.7	10.6	S20 50.9	7.4	56.1
D 13	18 58.1	01.3	271 29.3	10.7	20 43.5	7.6	56.1
A 14	33 58.2	02.2	285 59.0	10.8	20 35.9	7.7	56.0
Y 15	48 58.2	.. 03.0	300 28.8	10.8	20 28.2	7.7	56.0
16	63 58.3	03.9	314 58.6	11.0	20 20.5	7.9	56.0
17	78 58.4	04.7	329 28.6	11.0	20 12.6	7.9	55.9
18	93 58.5	S12 05.6	343 58.6	11.1	S20 04.7	8.0	55.9
19	108 58.5	06.5	358 28.7	11.2	19 56.7	8.2	55.9
20	123 58.6	07.3	12 58.9	11.3	19 48.5	8.2	55.9
21	138 58.7	.. 08.2	27 29.2	11.4	19 40.3	8.3	55.8
22	153 58.8	09.0	41 59.6	11.5	19 32.0	8.3	55.8
23	168 58.8	09.9	56 30.1	11.5	19 23.7	8.5	55.8
25 00	183 58.9	S12 10.8	71 00.6	11.7	S19 15.2	8.6	55.7
01	198 59.0	11.6	85 31.3	11.7	19 06.6	8.6	55.7
02	213 59.0	12.5	100 02.0	11.8	18 58.0	8.7	55.7
03	228 59.1	.. 13.3	114 32.8	11.9	18 49.3	8.8	55.7
04	243 59.2	14.2	129 03.7	12.0	18 40.5	8.9	55.6
05	258 59.3	15.1	143 34.7	12.1	18 31.6	8.9	55.6
06	273 59.3	S12 15.9	158 05.8	12.1	S18 22.7	9.1	55.6
07	288 59.4	16.8	172 36.9	12.2	18 13.6	9.1	55.5
08	303 59.5	17.6	187 08.1	12.3	18 04.5	9.1	55.5
S 09	318 59.5	.. 18.5	201 39.4	12.4	17 55.4	9.3	55.5
U 10	333 59.6	19.3	216 10.8	12.5	17 46.1	9.3	55.5
N 11	348 59.7	20.2	230 42.3	12.5	17 36.8	9.4	55.4
D 12	3 59.7	S12 21.1	245 13.8	12.7	S17 27.4	9.5	55.4
A 13	18 59.8	21.9	259 45.5	12.7	17 17.9	9.6	55.4
Y 14	33 59.9	22.8	274 17.2	12.7	17 08.3	9.6	55.4
15	48 59.9	.. 23.6	288 48.9	12.9	16 58.7	9.7	55.3
16	64 00.0	24.5	303 20.8	12.9	16 49.0	9.7	55.3
17	79 00.1	25.3	317 52.7	13.1	16 39.3	9.8	55.3
18	94 00.1	S12 26.2	332 24.8	13.0	S16 29.5	9.9	55.3
19	109 00.2	27.0	346 56.8	13.2	16 19.6	10.0	55.3
20	124 00.3	27.9	1 29.0	13.2	16 09.6	10.0	55.2
21	139 00.3	.. 28.7	16 01.2	13.4	15 59.6	10.1	55.2
22	154 00.4	29.6	30 33.6	13.3	15 49.5	10.1	55.2
23	169 00.4	30.4	45 05.9	13.5	15 39.4	10.2	55.2
26 00	184 00.5	S12 31.3	59 38.4	13.5	S15 29.2	10.3	55.1
01	199 00.6	32.2	74 10.9	13.6	15 18.9	10.3	55.1
02	214 00.7	33.0	88 43.5	13.7	15 08.6	10.3	55.1
03	229 00.7	.. 33.9	103 16.2	13.7	14 58.3	10.5	55.1
04	244 00.8	34.7	117 48.9	13.9	14 47.8	10.5	55.0
05	259 00.9	35.6	132 21.8	13.8	14 37.3	10.5	55.0
06	274 00.9	S12 36.4	146 54.6	14.0	S14 26.8	10.6	55.0
07	289 01.0	37.3	161 27.6	14.0	14 16.2	10.7	55.0
08	304 01.0	38.1	176 00.6	14.1	14 05.5	10.7	55.0
M 09	319 01.1	.. 38.9	190 33.7	14.1	13 54.8	10.7	54.9
O 10	334 01.2	39.8	205 06.8	14.2	13 44.1	10.8	54.9
N 11	349 01.2	40.6	219 40.0	14.3	13 33.3	10.9	54.9
D 12	4 01.3	S12 41.5	234 13.3	14.3	S13 22.4	10.9	54.9
A 13	19 01.3	42.3	248 46.6	14.4	13 11.5	10.9	54.9
Y 14	34 01.4	43.2	263 20.0	14.4	13 00.6	11.0	54.8
15	49 01.5	.. 44.0	277 53.4	14.5	12 49.6	11.1	54.8
16	64 01.5	44.9	292 26.9	14.6	12 38.5	11.1	54.8
17	79 01.6	45.7	307 00.5	14.6	12 27.4	11.1	54.8
18	94 01.6	S12 46.6	321 34.1	14.7	S12 16.3	11.2	54.8
19	109 01.7	47.4	336 07.8	14.8	12 05.1	11.2	54.8
20	124 01.8	48.3	350 41.6	14.8	11 53.9	11.3	54.7
21	139 01.8	.. 49.1	5 15.4	14.8	11 42.6	11.3	54.7
22	154 01.9	49.9	19 49.2	14.9	11 31.3	11.3	54.7
23	169 01.9	50.8	34 23.1	15.0	S11 20.0	11.4	54.7
	SD 16.1 d 0.9		SD 15.3	15.1	15.0		

Twilight / Sunrise / Moonrise

Lat.	Naut.	Civil	Sunrise	Moonrise 24	25	26	27
°	h m	h m	h m	h m	h m	h m	h m
N 72	05 40	07 00	08 18	■	18 16	17 24	16 55
N 70	05 38	06 50	07 59	■	17 31	17 03	16 43
68	05 37	06 43	07 44	17 27	17 01	16 46	16 34
66	05 36	06 36	07 32	16 47	16 39	16 32	16 26
64	05 35	06 31	07 21	16 20	16 21	16 21	16 20
62	05 34	06 26	07 13	15 58	16 06	16 11	16 14
60	05 33	06 22	07 05	15 41	15 54	16 03	16 09
N 58	05 32	06 18	06 59	15 26	15 43	15 55	16 04
56	05 31	06 14	06 53	15 14	15 34	15 49	16 01
54	05 30	06 11	06 48	15 03	15 25	15 43	15 57
52	05 29	06 08	06 43	14 53	15 18	15 37	15 54
50	05 28	06 05	06 39	14 44	15 11	15 33	15 51
45	05 25	05 59	06 29	14 26	14 56	15 22	15 44
N 40	05 22	05 54	06 22	14 11	14 44	15 13	15 39
35	05 19	05 49	06 15	13 58	14 34	15 06	15 34
30	05 16	05 44	06 09	13 46	14 25	14 59	15 30
20	05 10	05 36	05 59	13 27	14 09	14 48	15 23
N 10	05 03	05 28	05 49	13 10	13 56	14 37	15 17
0	04 55	05 19	05 41	12 54	13 43	14 28	15 11
S 10	04 45	05 10	05 32	12 38	13 30	14 18	15 05
20	04 33	05 00	05 22	12 21	13 16	14 08	14 58
30	04 17	04 46	05 11	12 02	13 00	13 56	14 51
35	04 07	04 38	05 05	11 50	12 51	13 50	14 47
40	03 55	04 29	04 58	11 37	12 40	13 42	14 42
45	03 39	04 18	04 49	11 22	12 28	13 33	14 36
S 50	03 20	04 03	04 39	11 02	12 12	13 22	14 29
52	03 10	03 57	04 34	10 53	12 05	13 17	14 26
54	02 59	03 49	04 28	10 43	11 57	13 11	14 23
56	02 46	03 41	04 23	10 31	11 48	13 05	14 19
58	02 30	03 31	04 16	10 18	11 38	12 57	14 15
S 60	02 11	03 20	04 08	10 02	11 26	12 49	14 10

Sunset / Twilight / Moonset

Lat.	Sunset	Civil	Naut.	Moonset 24	25	26	27
°	h m	h m	h m	h m	h m	h m	h m
N 72	15 08	16 27	17 46	■	21 51	24 14	00 14
N 70	15 28	16 36	17 48	■	22 34	24 34	00 34
68	15 43	16 44	17 49	20 58	23 03	24 50	00 50
66	15 55	16 50	17 50	21 37	23 24	25 02	01 02
64	16 05	16 56	17 52	22 04	23 41	25 12	01 12
62	16 14	17 01	17 53	22 25	23 54	25 21	01 21
60	16 22	17 05	17 54	22 41	24 06	00 06	01 28
N 58	16 28	17 09	17 55	22 56	24 16	00 16	01 35
56	16 34	17 13	17 56	23 08	24 25	00 25	01 41
54	16 40	17 16	17 57	23 18	24 33	00 33	01 46
52	16 44	17 19	17 59	23 27	24 39	00 39	01 50
50	16 49	17 22	18 00	23 36	24 46	00 46	01 54
45	16 58	17 28	18 02	23 53	24 59	00 59	02 03
N 40	17 06	17 34	18 05	24 07	00 07	01 10	02 11
35	17 13	17 39	18 08	24 20	00 20	01 19	02 17
30	17 19	17 43	18 11	24 30	00 30	01 27	02 23
20	17 29	17 52	18 18	24 48	00 48	01 41	02 32
N 10	17 39	18 00	18 25	00 11	01 04	01 54	02 41
0	17 47	18 09	18 33	00 28	01 18	02 05	02 49
S 10	17 56	18 18	18 43	00 45	01 32	02 16	02 56
20	18 06	18 29	18 55	01 03	01 48	02 28	03 05
30	18 17	18 42	19 12	01 24	02 05	02 42	03 14
35	18 24	18 50	19 22	01 36	02 15	02 49	03 19
40	18 31	19 00	19 34	01 50	02 27	02 58	03 25
45	18 40	19 11	19 50	02 06	02 40	03 08	03 32
S 50	18 51	19 26	20 10	02 26	02 57	03 21	03 41
52	18 55	19 33	20 20	02 36	03 05	03 27	03 44
54	19 01	19 40	20 31	02 47	03 13	03 33	03 49
56	19 07	19 49	20 45	03 00	03 23	03 40	03 53
58	19 14	19 59	21 00	03 13	03 33	03 48	03 58
S 60	19 21	20 11	21 20	03 29	03 46	03 57	04 04

SUN / MOON

Day	Eqn. of Time 00ʰ	Eqn. of Time 12ʰ	Mer. Pass.	Mer. Pass. Upper	Mer. Pass. Lower	Age	Phase
d	m s	m s	h m	h m	h m	d	%
24	15 48	15 52	11 44	19 06	06 41	08	60
25	15 55	15 59	11 44	19 54	07 31	09	69
26	16 02	16 05	11 44	20 38	08 16	10	78

UT	ARIES	VENUS −4.0		MARS −2.3		JUPITER −2.2		SATURN +0.6		STARS		
	GHA	GHA	Dec	GHA	Dec	GHA	Dec	GHA	Dec	Name	SHA	Dec
d h	° ′	° ′	° ′	° ′	° ′	° ′	° ′	° ′	° ′		° ′	° ′
27 00	35 48.7	216 24.7 N 1 52.1		18 59.4 N 4 52.9		103 42.4 S22 20.0		97 46.7 S21 16.8		Acamar	315 14.0	S40 13.3
01	50 51.1	231 24.4	51.0	34 02.4	52.9	118 44.5	19.9	112 49.1	16.7	Achernar	335 22.3	S57 08.0
02	65 53.6	246 24.1	49.8	49 05.5	52.8	133 46.6	19.9	127 51.4	16.7	Acrux	173 04.3	S63 12.5
03	80 56.1	261 23.7 . .	48.7	64 08.5 . .	52.7	148 48.8 . .	19.8	142 53.7 . .	16.7	Adhara	255 08.4	S28 59.8
04	95 58.5	276 23.4	47.6	79 11.6	52.7	163 50.9	19.8	157 56.1	16.7	Aldebaran	290 43.3	N16 33.0
05	111 01.0	291 23.0	46.4	94 14.7	52.6	178 53.0	19.7	172 58.4	16.7			
06	126 03.5	306 22.7 N 1 45.3		109 17.7 N 4 52.6		193 55.1 S22 19.7		188 00.8 S21 16.7		Alioth	166 16.6	N55 50.9
07	141 05.9	321 22.4	44.2	124 20.8	52.5	208 57.2	19.6	203 03.1	16.6	Alkaid	152 55.3	N49 12.7
T 08	156 08.4	336 22.0	43.0	139 23.8	52.5	223 59.4	19.6	218 05.5	16.6	Alnair	27 37.1	S46 51.8
U 09	171 10.9	351 21.7 . .	41.9	154 26.9 . .	52.4	239 01.5 . .	19.5	233 07.8 . .	16.6	Alnilam	275 41.0	S 1 11.3
E 10	186 13.3	6 21.3	40.8	169 30.0	52.4	254 03.6	19.5	248 10.1	16.6	Alphard	217 51.2	S 8 44.7
S 11	201 15.8	21 21.0	39.6	184 33.0	52.3	269 05.7	19.5	263 12.5	16.6			
D 12	216 18.3	36 20.7 N 1 38.5		199 36.1 N 4 52.3		284 07.8 S22 19.4		278 14.8 S21 16.5		Alphecca	126 07.0	N26 38.9
A 13	231 20.7	51 20.3	37.3	214 39.1	52.2	299 09.9	19.4	293 17.2	16.5	Alpheratz	357 38.0	N29 12.4
Y 14	246 23.2	66 20.0	36.2	229 42.2	52.2	314 12.1	19.3	308 19.5	16.5	Altair	62 03.3	N 8 55.6
15	261 25.6	81 19.6 . .	35.1	244 45.2 . .	52.1	329 14.2 . .	19.3	323 21.9 . .	16.5	Ankaa	353 10.2	S42 11.7
16	276 28.1	96 19.3	33.9	259 48.3	52.1	344 16.3	19.2	338 24.2	16.5	Antares	112 20.3	S26 28.5
17	291 30.6	111 19.0	32.8	274 51.3	52.0	359 18.4	19.2	353 26.5	16.4			
18	306 33.0	126 18.6 N 1 31.7		289 54.4 N 4 52.0		14 20.5 S22 19.1		8 28.9 S21 16.4		Arcturus	145 51.4	N19 04.7
19	321 35.5	141 18.3	30.5	304 57.4	51.9	29 22.6	19.1	23 31.2	16.4	Atria	107 18.0	S69 03.9
20	336 38.0	156 17.9	29.4	320 00.4	51.9	44 24.8	19.0	38 33.6	16.4	Avior	234 16.0	S59 34.2
21	351 40.4	171 17.6 . .	28.2	335 03.5 . .	51.8	59 26.9 . .	19.0	53 35.9 . .	16.4	Bellatrix	278 26.3	N 6 22.1
22	6 42.9	186 17.3	27.1	350 06.5	51.8	74 29.0	18.9	68 38.2	16.3	Betelgeuse	270 55.6	N 7 24.7
23	21 45.4	201 16.9	26.0	5 09.6	51.7	89 31.1	18.9	83 40.6	16.3			
28 00	36 47.8	216 16.6 N 1 24.8		20 12.6 N 4 51.7		104 33.2 S22 18.8		98 42.9 S21 16.3		Canopus	263 53.6	S52 42.1
01	51 50.3	231 16.2	23.7	35 15.7	51.7	119 35.3	18.8	113 45.3	16.3	Capella	280 26.6	N46 00.9
02	66 52.7	246 15.9	22.5	50 18.7	51.6	134 37.4	18.7	128 47.6	16.3	Deneb	49 28.1	N45 21.5
03	81 55.2	261 15.6 . .	21.4	65 21.7 . .	51.6	149 39.6 . .	18.7	143 50.0 . .	16.2	Denebola	182 28.7	N14 27.5
04	96 57.7	276 15.2	20.3	80 24.8	51.5	164 41.7	18.6	158 52.3	16.2	Diphda	348 50.5	S17 52.4
05	112 00.1	291 14.9	19.1	95 27.8	51.5	179 43.8	18.6	173 54.6	16.2			
06	127 02.6	306 14.5 N 1 18.0		110 30.8 N 4 51.4		194 45.9 S22 18.5		188 57.0 S21 16.2		Dubhe	193 45.8	N61 38.2
W 07	142 05.1	321 14.2	16.8	125 33.9	51.4	209 48.0	18.5	203 59.3	16.2	Elnath	278 05.9	N28 37.4
E 08	157 07.5	336 13.9	15.7	140 36.9	51.3	224 50.1	18.4	219 01.6	16.1	Eltanin	90 44.1	N51 29.5
D 09	172 10.0	351 13.5 . .	14.6	155 39.9 . .	51.3	239 52.2 . .	18.4	234 04.0 . .	16.1	Enif	33 42.0	N 9 58.3
N 10	187 12.5	6 13.2	13.4	170 43.0	51.3	254 54.3	18.3	249 06.3	16.1	Fomalhaut	15 18.1	S29 30.8
E 11	202 14.9	21 12.8	12.3	185 46.0	51.2	269 56.5	18.3	264 08.7	16.1			
S 12	217 17.4	36 12.5 N 1 11.1		200 49.0 N 4 51.2		284 58.6 S22 18.3		279 11.0 S21 16.1		Gacrux	171 55.9	S57 13.5
D 13	232 19.9	51 12.1	10.0	215 52.0	51.1	300 00.7	18.2	294 13.3	16.0	Gienah	175 47.4	S17 39.2
A 14	247 22.3	66 11.8	08.9	230 55.1	51.1	315 02.8	18.2	309 15.7	16.0	Hadar	148 41.4	S60 28.2
Y 15	262 24.8	81 11.5 . .	07.7	245 58.1 . .	51.1	330 04.9 . .	18.1	324 18.0 . .	16.0	Hamal	327 54.7	N23 33.6
16	277 27.2	96 11.1	06.6	261 01.1	51.0	345 07.0	18.1	339 20.4	16.0	Kaus Aust.	83 37.3	S34 22.5
17	292 29.7	111 10.8	05.4	276 04.1	51.0	0 09.1	18.0	354 22.7	16.0			
18	307 32.2	126 10.4 N 1 04.3		291 07.1 N 4 50.9		15 11.2 S22 18.0		9 25.0 S21 15.9		Kochab	137 21.1	N74 04.3
19	322 34.6	141 10.1	03.1	306 10.2	50.9	30 13.3	17.9	24 27.4	15.9	Markab	13 33.1	N15 19.1
20	337 37.1	156 09.8	02.0	321 13.2	50.9	45 15.5	17.9	39 29.7	15.9	Menkar	314 09.4	N 4 10.3
21	352 39.6	171 09.4	1 00.9	336 16.2 . .	50.8	60 17.6 . .	17.8	54 32.0 . .	15.9	Menkent	148 02.0	S36 28.1
22	7 42.0	186 09.1	0 59.7	351 19.2	50.8	75 19.7	17.8	69 34.4	15.8	Miaplacidus	221 39.0	S69 47.7
23	22 44.5	201 08.7	58.6	6 22.2	50.8	90 21.8	17.7	84 36.7	15.8			
29 00	37 47.0	216 08.4 N 0 57.4		21 25.2 N 4 50.7		105 23.9 S22 17.7		99 39.1 S21 15.8		Mirfak	308 32.6	N49 56.0
01	52 49.4	231 08.0	56.3	36 28.3	50.7	120 26.0	17.6	114 41.4	15.8	Nunki	75 52.2	S26 16.2
02	67 51.9	246 07.7	55.1	51 31.3	50.7	135 28.1	17.6	129 43.7	15.8	Peacock	53 11.2	S56 40.3
03	82 54.3	261 07.4 . .	54.0	66 34.3 . .	50.6	150 30.2 . .	17.5	144 46.1 . .	15.7	Pollux	243 21.4	N27 58.5
04	97 56.8	276 07.0	52.9	81 37.3	50.6	165 32.3	17.5	159 48.4	15.7	Procyon	244 54.3	N 5 10.4
05	112 59.3	291 06.7	51.7	96 40.3	50.6	180 34.4	17.4	174 50.7	15.7			
06	128 01.7	306 06.3 N 0 50.6		111 43.3 N 4 50.5		195 36.5 S22 17.4		189 53.1 S21 15.7		Rasalhague	96 02.0	N12 32.9
07	143 04.2	321 06.0	49.4	126 46.3	50.5	210 38.6	17.3	204 55.4	15.7	Regulus	207 38.2	N11 52.0
T 08	158 06.7	336 05.7	48.3	141 49.3	50.5	225 40.7	17.3	219 57.7	15.6	Rigel	281 06.9	S 8 10.6
H 09	173 09.1	351 05.3 . .	47.1	156 52.3 . .	50.4	240 42.8 . .	17.2	235 00.1 . .	15.6	Rigil Kent.	139 45.6	S60 55.0
U 10	188 11.6	6 05.0	46.0	171 55.3	50.4	255 45.0	17.2	250 02.4	15.6	Sabik	102 07.0	S15 44.9
R 11	203 14.1	21 04.6	44.8	186 58.3	50.4	270 47.1	17.1	265 04.7	15.6			
S 12	218 16.5	36 04.3 N 0 43.7		202 01.3 N 4 50.3		285 49.2 S22 17.1		280 07.1 S21 15.6		Schedar	349 34.3	N56 39.1
D 13	233 19.0	51 03.9	42.5	217 04.3	50.3	300 51.3	17.0	295 09.4	15.5	Shaula	96 15.3	S37 07.1
A 14	248 21.5	66 03.6	41.4	232 07.3	50.3	315 53.4	17.0	310 11.8	15.5	Sirius	258 29.1	S16 44.5
Y 15	263 23.9	81 03.3 . .	40.3	247 10.3 . .	50.2	330 55.5 . .	16.9	325 14.1 . .	15.5	Spica	158 26.2	S11 15.9
16	278 26.4	96 02.9	39.1	262 13.3	50.2	345 57.6	16.9	340 16.4	15.5	Suhail	222 48.8	S43 30.6
17	293 28.8	111 02.6	38.0	277 16.3	50.2	0 59.7	16.8	355 18.8	15.4			
18	308 31.3	126 02.2 N 0 36.8		292 19.3 N 4 50.2		16 01.8 S22 16.8		10 21.1 S21 15.4		Vega	80 35.7	N38 48.5
19	323 33.8	141 01.9	35.7	307 22.3	50.1	31 03.9	16.7	25 23.4	15.4	Zuben'ubi	137 00.1	S16 07.5
20	338 36.2	156 01.5	34.5	322 25.3	50.1	46 06.0	16.7	40 25.8	15.4		SHA	Mer.Pass.
21	353 38.7	171 01.2 . .	33.4	337 28.3 . .	50.1	61 08.1 . .	16.6	55 28.1 . .	15.4		° ′	h m
22	8 41.2	186 00.9	32.2	352 31.3	50.1	76 10.2	16.6	70 30.4	15.3	Venus	179 28.8	9 35
23	23 43.6	201 00.5	31.1	7 34.2	50.0	91 12.3	16.5	85 32.8	15.3	Mars	343 24.8	22 35
	h m									Jupiter	67 45.4	16 59
Mer.Pass. 21 29.3		v −0.3	d 1.1	v 3.0	d 0.0	v 2.1	d 0.0	v 2.3	d 0.0	Saturn	61 55.1	17 22

UT	SUN GHA	SUN Dec	MOON GHA	MOON v	MOON Dec	MOON d	MOON HP
d h	° '	° '	° '	'	° '	'	'
27 00	184 02.0	S12 51.6	48 57.1	15.0	S11 08.6	11.5	54.7
01	199 02.0	52.5	63 31.1	15.1	10 57.1	11.4	54.7
02	214 02.1	53.3	78 05.2	15.1	10 45.7	11.5	54.6
03	229 02.2	. . 54.2	92 39.3	15.1	10 34.2	11.6	54.6
04	244 02.2	55.0	107 13.4	15.2	10 22.6	11.5	54.6
05	259 02.3	55.8	121 47.6	15.3	10 11.1	11.7	54.6
06	274 02.3	S12 56.7	136 21.9	15.3	S 9 59.4	11.6	54.6
07	289 02.4	57.5	150 56.2	15.4	9 47.8	11.7	54.6
T 08	304 02.4	58.4	165 30.6	15.4	9 36.1	11.7	54.5
U 09	319 02.5	12 59.2	180 05.0	15.4	9 24.4	11.7	54.5
E 10	334 02.5	13 00.0	194 39.4	15.5	9 12.7	11.8	54.5
S 11	349 02.6	00.9	209 13.9	15.5	9 00.9	11.8	54.5
D 12	4 02.6	S13 01.7	223 48.4	15.6	S 8 49.1	11.8	54.5
A 13	19 02.7	02.6	238 23.0	15.6	8 37.3	11.9	54.5
Y 14	34 02.7	03.4	252 57.6	15.7	8 25.4	11.9	54.5
15	49 02.8	. . 04.2	267 32.3	15.7	8 13.5	11.9	54.4
16	64 02.8	05.1	282 07.0	15.7	8 01.6	11.9	54.4
17	79 02.9	05.9	296 41.7	15.8	7 49.7	12.0	54.4
18	94 03.0	S13 06.8	311 16.5	15.8	S 7 37.7	12.0	54.4
19	109 03.0	07.6	325 51.3	15.8	7 25.7	12.0	54.4
20	124 03.1	08.4	340 26.1	15.9	7 13.7	12.1	54.4
21	139 03.1	. . 09.3	355 01.0	15.9	7 01.6	12.0	54.4
22	154 03.2	10.1	9 35.9	15.9	6 49.6	12.1	54.4
23	169 03.2	10.9	24 10.8	16.0	6 37.5	12.1	54.3
28 00	184 03.3	S13 11.8	38 45.8	16.0	S 6 25.4	12.1	54.3
01	199 03.3	12.6	53 20.8	16.1	6 13.3	12.2	54.3
02	214 03.3	13.4	67 55.9	16.0	6 01.1	12.2	54.3
03	229 03.4	. . 14.3	82 30.9	16.1	5 48.9	12.1	54.3
04	244 03.4	15.1	97 06.0	16.1	5 36.8	12.2	54.3
05	259 03.5	15.9	111 41.1	16.2	5 24.6	12.3	54.3
06	274 03.5	S13 16.8	126 16.3	16.2	S 5 12.3	12.2	54.3
W 07	289 03.6	17.6	140 51.5	16.2	5 00.1	12.2	54.3
E 08	304 03.6	18.4	155 26.7	16.2	4 47.9	12.3	54.2
D 09	319 03.7	. . 19.3	170 01.9	16.2	4 35.6	12.3	54.2
N 10	334 03.7	20.1	184 37.1	16.3	4 23.3	12.3	54.2
E 11	349 03.8	20.9	199 12.4	16.3	4 11.0	12.3	54.2
S 12	4 03.8	S13 21.8	213 47.7	16.3	S 3 58.7	12.3	54.2
D 13	19 03.9	22.6	228 23.0	16.4	3 46.4	12.3	54.2
A 14	34 03.9	23.4	242 58.4	16.3	3 34.1	12.4	54.2
Y 15	49 03.9	. . 24.2	257 33.7	16.4	3 21.7	12.3	54.2
16	64 04.0	25.1	272 09.1	16.4	3 09.4	12.4	54.2
17	79 04.0	25.9	286 44.5	16.4	2 57.0	12.3	54.2
18	94 04.1	S13 26.7	301 19.9	16.4	S 2 44.7	12.4	54.1
19	109 04.1	27.6	315 55.3	16.4	2 32.3	12.4	54.1
20	124 04.2	28.4	330 30.7	16.5	2 19.9	12.4	54.1
21	139 04.2	. . 29.2	345 06.2	16.4	2 07.5	12.4	54.1
22	154 04.2	30.0	359 41.6	16.5	1 55.1	12.4	54.1
23	169 04.3	30.9	14 17.1	16.5	1 42.7	12.4	54.1
29 00	184 04.3	S13 31.7	28 52.6	16.5	S 1 30.3	12.4	54.1
01	199 04.4	32.5	43 28.1	16.5	1 17.9	12.4	54.1
02	214 04.4	33.3	58 03.6	16.5	1 05.5	12.4	54.1
03	229 04.5	. . 34.2	72 39.1	16.5	0 53.1	12.4	54.1
04	244 04.5	35.0	87 14.6	16.5	0 40.7	12.4	54.1
05	259 04.5	35.8	101 50.1	16.6	0 28.3	12.4	54.1
06	274 04.6	S13 36.6	116 25.7	16.5	S 0 15.9	12.4	54.1
07	289 04.6	37.5	131 01.2	16.6	S 0 03.5	12.5	54.1
T 08	304 04.6	38.3	145 36.8	16.5	N 0 09.0	12.4	54.1
H 09	319 04.7	. . 39.1	160 12.3	16.6	0 21.4	12.4	54.0
U 10	334 04.7	39.9	174 47.9	16.5	0 33.8	12.4	54.0
R 11	349 04.8	40.8	189 23.4	16.6	0 46.2	12.4	54.0
S 12	4 04.8	S13 41.6	203 59.0	16.5	N 0 58.6	12.4	54.0
D 13	19 04.8	42.4	218 34.5	16.6	1 11.0	12.4	54.0
A 14	34 04.9	43.2	233 10.1	16.5	1 23.4	12.3	54.0
Y 15	49 04.9	. . 44.0	247 45.6	16.5	1 35.7	12.4	54.0
16	64 04.9	44.9	262 21.1	16.6	1 48.1	12.4	54.0
17	79 05.0	45.7	276 56.7	16.5	2 00.5	12.3	54.0
18	94 05.0	S13 46.5	291 32.2	16.6	N 2 12.8	12.4	54.0
19	109 05.0	47.3	306 07.8	16.5	2 25.2	12.3	54.0
20	124 05.1	48.1	320 43.3	16.5	2 37.5	12.4	54.0
21	139 05.1	. . 49.0	335 18.8	16.5	2 49.9	12.3	54.0
22	154 05.2	49.8	349 54.3	16.5	3 02.2	12.3	54.0
23	169 05.2	50.6	4 29.8	16.5	N 3 14.5	12.3	54.0
	SD 16.1	d 0.8	SD 14.8		14.8		14.7

Lat.	Twilight Naut.	Twilight Civil	Sunrise	Moonrise 27	Moonrise 28	Moonrise 29	Moonrise 30
°	h m	h m	h m	h m	h m	h m	h m
N 72	05 52	07 13	08 35	16 55	16 31	16 09	15 47
N 70	05 49	07 02	08 13	16 43	16 27	16 12	15 56
68	05 47	06 53	07 56	16 34	16 24	16 14	16 03
66	05 45	06 46	07 42	16 26	16 21	16 15	16 10
64	05 43	06 39	07 31	16 20	16 18	16 17	16 15
62	05 41	06 34	07 21	16 14	16 16	16 18	16 20
60	05 40	06 29	07 13	16 09	16 14	16 19	16 24
N 58	05 38	06 24	07 06	16 04	16 12	16 20	16 27
56	05 36	06 20	06 59	16 01	16 11	16 21	16 31
54	05 35	06 16	06 54	15 57	16 10	16 21	16 34
52	05 33	06 13	06 48	15 54	16 08	16 22	16 36
50	05 32	06 10	06 44	15 51	16 07	16 23	16 39
45	05 29	06 03	06 33	15 44	16 05	16 24	16 44
N 40	05 25	05 57	06 25	15 39	16 03	16 25	16 49
35	05 22	05 52	06 18	15 34	16 01	16 26	16 52
30	05 18	05 47	06 11	15 30	15 59	16 27	16 56
20	05 11	05 37	06 00	15 23	15 56	16 29	17 02
N 10	05 03	05 28	05 50	15 17	15 54	16 30	17 07
0	04 54	05 19	05 40	15 11	15 52	16 32	17 12
S 10	04 44	05 09	05 31	15 05	15 49	16 33	17 17
20	04 31	04 58	05 20	14 58	15 47	16 35	17 23
30	04 14	04 43	05 08	14 51	15 44	16 36	17 29
35	04 03	04 35	05 02	14 47	15 42	16 37	17 33
40	03 50	04 25	04 54	14 42	15 41	16 39	17 37
45	03 34	04 13	04 44	14 36	15 38	16 40	17 42
S 50	03 13	03 57	04 33	14 29	15 36	16 42	17 47
52	03 02	03 50	04 28	14 26	15 35	16 42	17 50
54	02 50	03 42	04 22	14 23	15 33	16 43	17 53
56	02 36	03 33	04 15	14 19	15 32	16 44	17 56
58	02 19	03 22	04 08	14 15	15 30	16 45	18 00
S 60	01 58	03 10	04 00	14 10	15 29	16 46	18 04

Lat.	Sunset	Twilight Civil	Twilight Naut.	Moonset 27	Moonset 28	Moonset 29	Moonset 30
°	h m	h m	h m	h m	h m	h m	h m
N 72	14 51	16 13	17 34	00 14	02 12	04 02	05 50
N 70	15 13	16 24	17 36	00 34	02 21	04 03	05 43
68	15 30	16 33	17 39	00 50	02 29	04 04	05 38
66	15 44	16 41	17 41	01 02	02 35	04 04	05 33
64	15 55	16 47	17 43	01 12	02 40	04 05	05 30
62	16 05	16 53	17 45	01 21	02 44	04 05	05 26
60	16 14	16 58	17 47	01 28	02 48	04 06	05 23
N 58	16 21	17 02	17 49	01 35	02 51	04 06	05 21
56	16 27	17 06	17 50	01 41	02 54	04 07	05 19
54	16 33	17 10	17 52	01 46	02 57	04 07	05 17
52	16 38	17 14	17 53	01 50	02 59	04 07	05 15
50	16 43	17 17	17 55	01 54	03 02	04 08	05 13
45	16 53	17 24	17 58	02 03	03 06	04 08	05 10
N 40	17 02	17 30	18 02	02 11	03 10	04 09	05 07
35	17 09	17 35	18 05	02 17	03 14	04 09	05 04
30	17 16	17 41	18 09	02 23	03 17	04 09	05 02
20	17 27	17 50	18 16	02 32	03 22	04 10	04 58
N 10	17 38	17 59	18 24	02 41	03 26	04 10	04 54
0	17 47	18 08	18 33	02 49	03 30	04 11	04 51
S 10	17 57	18 19	18 44	02 56	03 35	04 11	04 48
20	18 07	18 30	18 57	03 05	03 39	04 12	04 45
30	18 19	18 45	19 14	03 14	03 44	04 12	04 41
35	18 27	18 53	19 25	03 19	03 47	04 13	04 38
40	18 35	19 04	19 38	03 25	03 50	04 13	04 36
45	18 44	19 16	19 55	03 32	03 54	04 13	04 33
S 50	18 56	19 31	20 16	03 41	03 58	04 14	04 30
52	19 01	19 39	20 27	03 44	04 00	04 14	04 28
54	19 07	19 47	20 39	03 49	04 02	04 14	04 26
56	19 13	19 56	20 53	03 54	04 04	04 14	04 24
58	19 21	20 07	21 11	03 58	04 07	04 15	04 22
S 60	19 29	20 20	21 34	04 04	04 10	04 15	04 20

	SUN	SUN	SUN	MOON	MOON	MOON	MOON
Day	Eqn. of Time 00h	Eqn. of Time 12h	Mer. Pass.	Mer. Pass. Upper	Mer. Pass. Lower	Age	Phase
d	m s	m s	h m	h m	h m	d	%
27	16 08	16 10	11 44	21 21	09 00	11	85
28	16 13	16 15	11 44	22 01	09 41	12	91
29	16 17	16 19	11 44	22 42	10 21	13	96

2020 OCT. 30, 31, NOV. 1 (FRI., SAT., SUN.)

UT	ARIES GHA	VENUS −4·0 GHA	VENUS Dec	MARS −2·2 GHA	MARS Dec	JUPITER −2·2 GHA	JUPITER Dec	SATURN +0·6 GHA	SATURN Dec	STARS Name	SHA	Dec
30 00	38 46.1	216 00.2	N 0 29.9	22 37.2	N 4 50.0	106 14.4	S22 16.5	100 35.1	S21 15.3	Acamar	315 14.0	S40 13.3
01	53 48.6	230 59.8	28.8	37 40.2	50.0	121 16.5	16.4	115 37.4	15.3	Achernar	335 22.3	S57 08.0
02	68 51.0	245 59.5	27.6	52 43.2	50.0	136 18.6	16.4	130 39.8	15.3	Acrux	173 04.3	S63 12.5
03	83 53.5	260 59.1 ··	26.5	67 46.2 ··	49.9	151 20.7 ··	16.3	145 42.1 ··	15.2	Adhara	255 08.4	S28 59.8
04	98 56.0	275 58.8	25.3	82 49.2	49.9	166 22.8	16.3	160 44.4	15.2	Aldebaran	290 43.2	N16 33.0
05	113 58.4	290 58.4	24.2	97 52.1	49.9	181 24.9	16.2	175 46.7	15.2			
06	129 00.9	305 58.1	N 0 23.1	112 55.1	N 4 49.9	196 27.0	S22 16.2	190 49.1	S21 15.2	Alioth	166 16.6	N55 50.9
07	144 03.3	320 57.8	21.9	127 58.1	49.8	211 29.1	16.1	205 51.4	15.1	Alkaid	152 55.3	N49 12.7
08	159 05.8	335 57.4	20.8	143 01.1	49.8	226 31.2	16.1	220 53.7	15.1	Alnair	27 37.1	S46 51.8
F 09	174 08.3	350 57.1 ··	19.6	158 04.1 ··	49.8	241 33.3 ··	16.0	235 56.1 ··	15.1	Alnilam	275 41.0	S 1 11.3
R 10	189 10.7	5 56.7	18.5	173 07.0	49.8	256 35.4	16.0	250 58.4	15.1	Alphard	217 51.2	S 8 44.7
I 11	204 13.2	20 56.4	17.3	188 10.0	49.8	271 37.5	15.9	266 00.7	15.1			
D 12	219 15.7	35 56.0	N 0 16.2	203 13.0	N 4 49.7	286 39.6	S22 15.9	281 03.1	S21 15.0	Alphecca	126 07.0	N26 38.9
A 13	234 18.1	50 55.7	15.0	218 16.0	49.7	301 41.7	15.8	296 05.4	15.0	Alpheratz	357 38.0	N29 12.4
Y 14	249 20.6	65 55.3	13.9	233 18.9	49.7	316 43.8	15.8	311 07.7	15.0	Altair	62 03.4	N 8 55.6
15	264 23.1	80 55.0 ··	12.7	248 21.9 ··	49.7	331 45.9 ··	15.7	326 10.1 ··	15.0	Ankaa	353 10.2	S42 11.7
16	279 25.5	95 54.7	11.6	263 24.9	49.7	346 48.0	15.7	341 12.4	15.0	Antares	112 20.4	S26 28.5
17	294 28.0	110 54.3	10.4	278 27.8	49.6	1 50.1	15.6	356 14.7	14.9			
18	309 30.4	125 54.0	N 0 09.3	293 30.8	N 4 49.6	16 52.2	S22 15.5	11 17.0	S21 14.9	Arcturus	145 51.4	N19 04.7
19	324 32.9	140 53.6	08.1	308 33.8	49.6	31 54.3	15.5	26 19.4	14.9	Atria	107 18.1	S69 03.9
20	339 35.4	155 53.3	07.0	323 36.7	49.6	46 56.4	15.4	41 21.7	14.9	Avior	234 16.0	S59 34.2
21	354 37.8	170 52.9 ··	05.8	338 39.7 ··	49.6	61 58.5 ··	15.4	56 24.0 ··	14.8	Bellatrix	278 26.3	N 6 22.1
22	9 40.3	185 52.6	04.7	353 42.6	49.6	77 00.6	15.3	71 26.4	14.8	Betelgeuse	270 55.6	N 7 24.7
23	24 42.8	200 52.2	03.5	8 45.6	49.5	92 02.7	15.3	86 28.7	14.8			
31 00	39 45.2	215 51.9	N 0 02.4	23 48.6	N 4 49.5	107 04.8	S22 15.2	101 31.0	S21 14.8	Canopus	263 53.6	S52 42.2
01	54 47.7	230 51.5	01.2	38 51.5	49.5	122 06.9	15.2	116 33.4	14.8	Capella	280 26.6	N46 00.9
02	69 50.2	245 51.2	N ·· 00.1	53 54.5	49.5	137 09.0	15.1	131 35.7	14.7	Deneb	49 28.1	N45 21.5
03	84 52.6	260 50.9	S ·· 01.1	68 57.4 ··	49.5	152 11.1 ··	15.1	146 38.0	14.7	Denebola	182 28.7	N14 27.5
04	99 55.1	275 50.5	02.2	84 00.4	49.5	167 13.2	15.0	161 40.3	14.7	Diphda	348 50.5	S17 52.4
05	114 57.6	290 50.2	03.4	99 03.3	49.5	182 15.2	15.0	176 42.7	14.7			
06	130 00.0	305 49.8	S 0 04.5	114 06.3	N 4 49.4	197 17.3	S22 14.9	191 45.0	S21 14.6	Dubhe	193 45.7	N61 38.2
07	145 02.5	320 49.5	05.7	129 09.2	49.4	212 19.4	14.9	206 47.3	14.6	Elnath	278 05.9	N28 37.4
S 08	160 04.9	335 49.1	06.8	144 12.2	49.1	227 21.5	14.8	221 49.6	14.6	Eltanin	90 44.1	N51 29.5
A 09	175 07.4	350 48.8 ··	08.0	159 15.1 ··	49.4	242 23.6 ··	14.8	236 52.0 ··	14.6	Enif	33 42.1	N 9 58.3
T 10	190 09.9	5 48.4	09.1	174 18.1	49.4	257 25.7	14.7	251 54.3	14.5	Fomalhaut	15 18.1	S29 30.9
U 11	205 12.3	20 48.1	10.3	189 21.0	49.4	272 27.8	14.7	266 56.6	14.5			
R 12	220 14.8	35 47.7	S 0 11.5	204 24.0	N 4 49.4	287 29.9	S22 14.6	281 59.0	S21 14.5	Gacrux	171 55.8	S57 13.4
D 13	235 17.3	50 47.4	12.6	219 26.9	49.4	302 32.0	14.6	297 01.3	14.5	Gienah	175 47.4	S17 39.2
A 14	250 19.7	65 47.0	13.8	234 29.8	49.4	317 34.1	14.5	312 03.6	14.5	Hadar	148 41.4	S60 28.1
Y 15	265 22.2	80 46.7 ··	14.9	249 32.8 ··	49.4	332 36.2 ··	14.5	327 05.9 ··	14.4	Hamal	327 54.7	N23 33.6
16	280 24.7	95 46.3	16.1	264 35.7	49.3	347 38.3	14.4	342 08.3	14.4	Kaus Aust.	83 37.3	S34 22.5
17	295 27.1	110 46.0	17.2	279 38.7	49.3	2 40.4	14.4	357 10.6	14.4			
18	310 29.6	125 45.7	S 0 18.4	294 41.6	N 4 49.3	17 42.5	S22 14.3	12 12.9	S21 14.4	Kochab	137 21.1	N74 04.3
19	325 32.0	140 45.3	19.5	309 44.5	49.3	32 44.5	14.2	27 15.2	14.3	Markab	13 33.1	N15 19.1
20	340 34.5	155 45.0	20.7	324 47.5	49.3	47 46.6	14.2	42 17.6	14.3	Menkar	314 09.4	N 4 10.3
21	355 37.0	170 44.6 ··	21.8	339 50.4 ··	49.3	62 48.7 ··	14.1	57 19.9 ··	14.3	Menkent	148 02.0	S36 28.1
22	10 39.4	185 44.3	23.0	354 53.3	49.3	77 50.8	14.1	72 22.2	14.3	Miaplacidus	221 38.9	S69 47.7
23	25 41.9	200 43.9	24.1	9 56.3	49.3	92 52.9	14.0	87 24.5	14.3			
1 00	40 44.4	215 43.6	S 0 25.3	24 59.2	N 4 49.3	107 55.0	S22 14.0	102 26.9	S21 14.2	Mirfak	308 32.6	N49 56.0
01	55 46.8	230 43.2	26.4	40 02.1	49.3	122 57.1	13.9	117 29.2	14.2	Nunki	75 52.2	S26 16.2
02	70 49.3	245 42.9	27.6	55 05.0	49.3	137 59.2	13.9	132 31.5	14.2	Peacock	53 11.2	S56 40.3
03	85 51.8	260 42.5 ··	28.7	70 08.0 ··	49.3	153 01.3 ··	13.8	147 33.8 ··	14.2	Pollux	243 21.4	N27 58.5
04	100 54.2	275 42.1	29.9	85 10.9	49.3	168 03.4	13.8	162 36.2	14.1	Procyon	244 54.3	N 5 10.4
05	115 56.7	290 41.8	31.0	100 13.8	49.3	183 05.4	13.7	177 38.5	14.1			
06	130 59.2	305 41.5	S 0 32.2	115 16.7	N 4 49.3	198 07.5	S22 13.7	192 40.8	S21 14.1	Rasalhague	96 02.0	N12 32.9
07	146 01.6	320 41.1	33.4	130 19.7	49.3	213 09.6	13.6	207 43.1	14.1	Regulus	207 38.2	N11 52.0
08	161 04.1	335 40.8	34.5	145 22.6	49.3	228 11.7	13.6	222 45.5	14.0	Rigel	281 06.9	S 8 10.6
S 09	176 06.5	350 40.4 ··	35.7	160 25.5 ··	49.3	243 13.8 ··	13.5	237 47.8 ··	14.0	Rigil Kent.	139 45.6	S60 55.0
U 10	191 09.0	5 40.1	36.8	175 28.4	49.3	258 15.9	13.5	252 50.1	14.0	Sabik	102 07.0	S15 44.9
N 11	206 11.5	20 39.7	38.0	190 31.3	49.3	273 18.0	13.4	267 52.4	14.0			
D 12	221 13.9	35 39.4	S 0 39.1	205 34.2	N 4 49.3	288 20.1	S22 13.3	282 54.8	S21 13.9	Schedar	349 34.3	N56 39.2
A 13	236 16.4	50 39.0	40.3	220 37.2	49.3	303 22.1	13.3	297 57.1	13.9	Shaula	96 15.3	S37 07.1
Y 14	251 18.9	65 38.7	41.4	235 40.1	49.3	318 24.2	13.2	312 59.4	13.9	Sirius	258 29.1	S16 44.5
15	266 21.3	80 38.3 ··	42.6	250 43.0 ··	49.3	333 26.3 ··	13.2	328 01.7 ··	13.9	Spica	158 26.2	S11 15.9
16	281 23.8	95 38.0	43.7	265 45.9	49.3	348 28.4	13.1	343 04.0	13.9	Suhail	222 48.8	S43 30.6
17	296 26.3	110 37.6	44.9	280 48.8	49.3	3 30.5	13.1	358 06.4	13.8			
18	311 28.7	125 37.3	S 0 46.1	295 51.7	N 4 49.3	18 32.6	S22 13.0	13 08.7	S21 13.8	Vega	80 35.7	N38 48.5
19	326 31.2	140 36.9	47.2	310 54.6	49.3	33 34.7	13.0	28 11.0	13.8	Zuben'ubi	137 00.1	S16 07.5
20	341 33.7	155 36.6	48.4	325 57.5	49.3	48 36.7	12.9	43 13.3	13.8		SHA	Mer. Pass.
21	356 36.1	170 36.2 ··	49.5	341 00.4 ··	49.3	63 38.8 ··	12.9	58 15.7 ··	13.7			
22	11 38.6	185 35.9	50.7	356 03.3	49.3	78 40.9	12.8	73 18.0	13.7	Venus	176 06.7	9 37
23	26 41.0	200 35.5	51.8	11 06.2	49.3	93 43.0	12.8	88 20.3	13.7	Mars	344 03.3	22 20
Mer. Pass.	21 17.5	v −0.3	d 1.2	v 2.9	d 0.0	v 2.1	d 0.1	v 2.3	d 0.0	Jupiter	67 19.5	16 49
										Saturn	61 45.8	17 11

UT	SUN GHA	SUN Dec	MOON GHA	MOON v	MOON Dec	MOON d	MOON HP
d h	° '	° '	° '	'	° '	'	'
30 00	184 05.2	S13 51.4	19 05.3	16.5	N 3 26.8	12.3	54.0
01	199 05.3	52.2	33 40.8	16.5	3 39.1	12.2	54.0
02	214 05.3	53.0	48 16.3	16.4	3 51.3	12.3	54.0
03	229 05.3 ..	53.9	62 51.7	16.5	4 03.6	12.2	54.0
04	244 05.3	54.7	77 27.2	16.4	4 15.8	12.2	54.0
05	259 05.4	55.5	92 02.6	16.5	4 28.0	12.2	54.0
06	274 05.4	S13 56.3	106 38.1	16.4	N 4 40.2	12.2	54.0
07	289 05.4	57.1	121 13.5	16.4	4 52.4	12.2	54.0
08	304 05.5	57.9	135 48.9	16.3	5 04.6	12.2	54.0
F 09	319 05.5 ..	58.7	150 24.2	16.3	5 16.8	12.1	54.0
R 10	334 05.5	13 59.6	164 59.6	16.3	5 28.9	12.1	54.0
I 11	349 05.6	14 00.4	179 34.9	16.4	5 41.0	12.1	54.0
D 12	4 05.6	S14 01.2	194 10.3	16.3	N 5 53.1	12.1	54.0
A 13	19 05.6	02.0	208 45.6	16.2	6 05.2	12.0	54.0
Y 14	34 05.6	02.8	223 20.8	16.3	6 17.2	12.0	54.0
15	49 05.7 ..	03.6	237 56.1	16.2	6 29.2	12.0	54.0
16	64 05.7	04.4	252 31.3	16.3	6 41.2	12.0	54.0
17	79 05.7	05.2	267 06.6	16.2	6 53.2	12.0	54.0
18	94 05.8	S14 06.0	281 41.8	16.1	N 7 05.2	11.9	54.0
19	109 05.8	06.9	296 16.9	16.2	7 17.1	11.9	54.0
20	124 05.8	07.7	310 52.1	16.1	7 29.0	11.9	54.0
21	139 05.8 ..	08.5	325 27.2	16.1	7 40.9	11.8	54.0
22	154 05.9	09.3	340 02.3	16.0	7 52.7	11.8	54.0
23	169 05.9	10.1	354 37.3	16.1	8 04.5	11.8	54.0
31 00	184 05.9	S14 10.9	9 12.4	16.0	N 8 16.3	11.8	54.0
01	199 05.9	11.7	23 47.4	16.0	8 28.1	11.7	54.0
02	214 06.0	12.5	38 22.4	15.9	8 39.8	11.7	54.0
03	229 06.0 ..	13.3	52 57.3	15.9	8 51.5	11.6	54.0
04	244 06.0	14.1	67 32.2	15.9	9 03.1	11.7	54.0
05	259 06.0	14.9	82 07.1	15.9	9 14.8	11.5	54.0
06	274 06.1	S14 15.7	96 42.0	15.8	N 9 26.3	11.6	54.0
S 07	289 06.1	16.5	111 16.8	15.8	9 37.9	11.5	54.0
A 08	304 06.1	17.3	125 51.6	15.8	9 49.4	11.5	54.0
T 09	319 06.1 ..	18.2	140 26.4	15.7	10 00.9	11.5	54.0
U 10	334 06.1	19.0	155 01.1	15.7	10 12.4	11.4	54.0
R 11	349 06.2	19.8	169 35.8	15.6	10 23.8	11.3	54.0
D 12	4 06.2	S14 20.6	184 10.4	15.6	N10 35.1	11.4	54.0
A 13	19 06.2	21.4	198 45.0	15.6	10 46.5	11.3	54.0
Y 14	34 06.2	22.2	213 19.6	15.5	10 57.8	11.2	54.0
15	49 06.2 ..	23.0	227 54.1	15.5	11 09.0	11.2	54.0
16	64 06.3	23.8	242 28.6	15.5	11 20.2	11.2	54.0
17	79 06.3	24.6	257 03.1	15.4	11 31.4	11.1	54.0
18	94 06.3	S14 25.4	271 37.5	15.4	N11 42.5	11.1	54.0
19	109 06.3	26.2	286 11.9	15.3	11 53.6	11.0	54.0
20	124 06.3	27.0	300 46.2	15.3	12 04.6	11.0	54.0
21	139 06.4 ..	27.8	315 20.5	15.2	12 15.6	11.0	54.0
22	154 06.4	28.6	329 54.7	15.2	12 26.6	10.9	54.0
23	169 06.4	29.4	344 29.0	15.1	12 37.5	10.8	54.0
1 00	184 06.4	S14 30.2	359 03.1	15.1	N12 48.3	10.8	54.0
01	199 06.4	31.0	13 37.2	15.1	12 59.1	10.8	54.0
02	214 06.4	31.8	28 11.3	15.0	13 09.9	10.7	54.0
03	229 06.5 ..	32.6	42 45.3	15.0	13 20.6	10.6	54.0
04	244 06.5	33.4	57 19.3	14.9	13 31.2	10.6	54.0
05	259 06.5	34.2	71 53.2	14.9	13 41.8	10.6	54.0
06	274 06.5	S14 34.9	86 27.1	14.9	N13 52.4	10.5	54.0
07	289 06.5	35.7	101 01.0	14.7	14 02.9	10.4	54.0
08	304 06.5	36.5	115 34.7	14.8	14 13.3	10.4	54.1
S 09	319 06.5 ..	37.3	130 08.5	14.7	14 23.7	10.3	54.1
U 10	334 06.6	38.1	144 42.2	14.6	14 34.0	10.3	54.1
N 11	349 06.6	38.9	159 15.8	14.6	14 44.3	10.2	54.1
D 12	4 06.6	S14 39.7	173 49.4	14.5	N14 54.5	10.2	54.1
A 13	19 06.6	40.5	188 22.9	14.5	15 04.7	10.1	54.1
Y 14	34 06.6	41.3	202 56.4	14.5	15 14.8	10.1	54.1
15	49 06.6 ..	42.1	217 29.9	14.3	15 24.8	10.0	54.1
16	64 06.6	42.9	232 03.2	14.4	15 34.8	9.9	54.1
17	79 06.6	43.7	246 36.6	14.2	15 44.7	9.9	54.1
18	94 06.7	S14 44.5	261 09.8	14.3	N15 54.6	9.8	54.1
19	109 06.7	45.3	275 43.1	14.1	16 04.4	9.7	54.1
20	124 06.7	46.0	290 16.2	14.1	16 14.1	9.6	54.1
21	139 06.7 ..	46.8	304 49.3	14.1	16 23.7	9.6	54.1
22	154 06.7	47.6	319 22.4	14.0	16 33.3	9.6	54.2
23	169 06.7	48.4	333 55.4	13.9	N16 42.9	9.4	54.2
	SD 16.1	d 0.8	SD 14.7		14.7		14.7

Lat.	Twilight Naut.	Twilight Civil	Sunrise	Moonrise 30	Moonrise 31	Moonrise 1	Moonrise 2
°	h m	h m	h m	h m	h m	h m	h m
N 72	06 04	07 27	08 53	15 47	15 20	14 41	▭
N 70	06 00	07 14	08 28	15 56	15 38	15 14	14 31
68	05 57	07 04	08 08	16 03	15 52	15 39	15 19
66	05 54	06 55	07 53	16 10	16 04	15 58	15 51
64	05 51	06 48	07 40	16 15	16 13	16 13	16 14
62	05 48	06 41	07 30	16 20	16 22	16 26	16 33
60	05 46	06 36	07 21	16 24	16 30	16 37	16 48
N 58	05 44	06 31	07 13	16 27	16 36	16 47	17 01
56	05 42	06 26	07 06	16 31	16 42	16 55	17 13
54	05 40	06 22	06 59	16 34	16 47	17 03	17 23
52	05 38	06 18	06 54	16 36	16 52	17 10	17 32
50	05 37	06 15	06 49	16 39	16 56	17 16	17 40
45	05 32	06 07	06 38	16 44	17 05	17 29	17 57
N 40	05 28	06 00	06 28	16 49	17 13	17 40	18 11
35	05 24	05 54	06 20	16 52	17 20	17 50	18 23
30	05 20	05 49	06 13	16 56	17 26	17 58	18 33
20	05 12	05 38	06 01	17 02	17 36	18 12	18 51
N 10	05 04	05 29	05 50	17 07	17 45	18 25	19 07
0	04 54	05 19	05 40	17 12	17 54	18 37	19 22
S 10	04 43	05 08	05 30	17 17	18 02	18 49	19 37
20	04 29	04 56	05 19	17 23	18 12	19 02	19 53
30	04 11	04 41	05 06	17 29	18 22	19 16	20 12
35	03 59	04 32	04 58	17 33	18 28	19 25	20 23
40	03 45	04 21	04 50	17 37	18 35	19 35	20 35
45	03 28	04 08	04 40	17 42	18 44	19 47	20 50
S 50	03 06	03 51	04 28	17 47	18 54	20 01	21 08
52	02 54	03 44	04 22	17 50	18 58	20 07	21 17
54	02 41	03 35	04 16	17 53	19 03	20 15	21 26
56	02 26	03 25	04 09	17 56	19 09	20 23	21 37
58	02 07	03 13	04 01	18 00	19 15	20 32	21 50
S 60	01 43	03 00	03 52	18 04	19 23	20 43	22 05

Lat.	Sunset	Twilight Civil	Twilight Naut.	Moonset 30	Moonset 31	Moonset 1	Moonset 2
°	h m	h m	h m	h m	h m	h m	h m
N 72	14 33	15 59	17 21	05 50	07 43	09 51	▭
N 70	14 58	16 12	17 26	05 43	07 27	09 19	11 35
68	15 18	16 22	17 29	05 38	07 14	08 56	10 48
66	15 33	16 31	17 32	05 33	07 04	08 38	10 17
64	15 46	16 38	17 35	05 30	06 55	08 23	09 55
62	15 56	16 45	17 38	05 26	06 48	08 11	09 37
60	16 06	16 51	17 40	05 23	06 42	08 01	09 22
N 58	16 14	16 56	17 42	05 21	06 36	07 52	09 09
56	16 21	17 00	17 44	05 19	06 31	07 45	08 59
54	16 27	17 04	17 46	05 17	06 27	07 38	08 49
52	16 33	17 08	17 48	05 15	06 23	07 31	08 41
50	16 38	17 12	17 50	05 13	06 19	07 26	08 33
45	16 49	17 20	17 54	05 10	06 11	07 14	08 17
N 40	16 58	17 26	17 58	05 07	06 05	07 04	08 04
35	17 06	17 33	18 02	05 04	05 59	06 56	07 53
30	17 13	17 38	18 06	05 02	05 55	06 48	07 43
20	17 26	17 48	18 15	04 58	05 46	06 36	07 26
N 10	17 37	17 58	18 23	04 54	05 39	06 25	07 12
0	17 47	18 08	18 33	04 51	05 32	06 14	06 58
S 10	17 57	18 19	18 45	04 48	05 25	06 04	06 45
20	18 09	18 32	18 59	04 45	05 18	05 53	06 31
30	18 22	18 47	19 17	04 41	05 10	05 41	06 14
35	18 29	18 56	19 29	04 38	05 05	05 33	06 05
40	18 38	19 07	19 43	04 36	05 00	05 25	05 54
45	18 48	19 20	20 00	04 33	04 53	05 16	05 41
S 50	19 01	19 37	20 23	04 30	04 46	05 04	05 26
52	19 06	19 45	20 35	04 28	04 43	04 59	05 19
54	19 13	19 54	20 48	04 26	04 39	04 53	05 11
56	19 20	20 04	21 04	04 24	04 35	04 47	05 02
58	19 28	20 16	21 23	04 22	04 30	04 40	04 52
S 60	19 37	20 30	21 48	04 20	04 25	04 32	04 40

Day	SUN Eqn. of Time 00h	SUN Eqn. of Time 12h	SUN Mer. Pass.	MOON Mer. Pass. Upper	MOON Mer. Pass. Lower	MOON Age	MOON Phase
d	m s	m s	h m	h m	h m	d	%
30	16 21	16 22	11 44	23 22	11 02	14	99
31	16 24	16 25	11 44	24 04	11 43	15	100
1	16 26	16 26	11 44	00 04	12 25	16	99

UT	ARIES	VENUS −4·0		MARS −2·1		JUPITER −2·2		SATURN +0·6		STARS		
	GHA	GHA	Dec	GHA	Dec	GHA	Dec	GHA	Dec	Name	SHA	Dec
d h	° ′	° ′	° ′	° ′	° ′	° ′	° ′	° ′	° ′		° ′	° ′
2 00	41 43.5	215 35.2	S 0 53.0	26 09.1	N 4 49.3	108 45.1	S22 12.7	103 22.6	S21 13.7	Acamar	315 14.0	S40 13.3
01	56 46.0	230 34.8	54.1	41 12.0	49.3	123 47.2	12.6	118 24.9	13.6	Achernar	335 22.3	S57 08.0
02	71 48.4	245 34.5	55.3	56 14.9	49.3	138 49.3	12.6	133 27.3	13.6	Acrux	173 04.3	S63 12.5
03	86 50.9	260 34.1	. . 56.5	71 17.8	. . 49.3	153 51.3	. . 12.5	148 29.6	. . 13.6	Adhara	255 08.4	S28 59.8
04	101 53.4	275 33.8	57.6	86 20.7	49.3	168 53.4	12.5	163 31.9	13.6	Aldebaran	290 43.2	N16 33.0
05	116 55.8	290 33.4	58.8	101 23.6	49.4	183 55.5	12.4	178 34.2	13.5			
06	131 58.3	305 33.1	S 0 59.9	116 26.5	N 4 49.4	198 57.6	S22 12.4	193 36.5	S21 13.5	Alioth	166 16.6	N55 50.9
07	147 00.8	320 32.7	1 01.1	131 29.4	49.4	213 59.7	12.3	208 38.9	13.5	Alkaid	152 55.3	N49 12.7
08	162 03.2	335 32.4	02.2	146 32.3	49.4	229 01.7	12.3	223 41.2	13.5	Alnair	27 37.1	S46 51.8
M 09	177 05.7	350 32.0	. . 03.4	161 35.2	. . 49.4	244 03.8	. . 12.2	238 43.5	. . 13.5	Alnilam	275 40.9	S 1 11.3
O 10	192 08.1	5 31.7	04.5	176 38.1	49.4	259 05.9	12.2	253 45.8	13.4	Alphard	217 51.1	S 8 44.7
N 11	207 10.6	20 31.3	05.7	191 40.9	49.4	274 08.0	12.1	268 48.1	13.4			
D 12	222 13.1	35 31.0	S 1 06.9	206 43.8	N 4 49.4	289 10.1	S22 12.0	283 50.5	S21 13.4	Alphecca	126 07.0	N26 38.9
A 13	237 15.5	50 30.6	08.0	221 46.7	49.4	304 12.2	12.0	298 52.8	13.4	Alpheratz	357 38.0	N29 12.4
Y 14	252 18.0	65 30.3	09.2	236 49.6	49.5	319 14.2	11.9	313 55.1	13.3	Altair	62 03.4	N 8 55.6
15	267 20.5	80 29.9	. . 10.3	251 52.5	. . 49.5	334 16.3	. . 11.9	328 57.4	. . 13.3	Ankaa	353 10.2	S42 11.8
16	282 22.9	95 29.6	11.5	266 55.4	49.5	349 18.4	11.8	343 59.7	13.3	Antares	112 20.4	S26 28.5
17	297 25.4	110 29.2	12.6	281 58.2	49.5	4 20.5	11.8	359 02.1	13.3			
18	312 27.9	125 28.8	S 1 13.8	297 01.1	N 4 49.5	19 22.6	S22 11.7	14 04.4	S21 13.2	Arcturus	145 51.4	N19 04.6
19	327 30.3	140 28.5	15.0	312 04.0	49.5	34 24.6	11.7	29 06.7	13.2	Atria	107 18.1	S69 03.9
20	342 32.8	155 28.1	16.1	327 06.9	49.5	49 26.7	11.6	44 09.0	13.2	Avior	234 15.9	S59 34.2
21	357 35.3	170 27.8	. . 17.3	342 09.7	. . 49.6	64 28.8	. . 11.6	59 11.3	. . 13.2	Bellatrix	278 26.3	N 6 22.1
22	12 37.7	185 27.4	18.4	357 12.6	49.6	79 30.9	11.5	74 13.6	13.1	Betelgeuse	270 55.6	N 7 24.6
23	27 40.2	200 27.1	19.6	12 15.5	49.6	94 33.0	11.4	89 16.0	13.1			
3 00	42 42.6	215 26.7	S 1 20.7	27 18.4	N 4 49.6	109 35.0	S22 11.4	104 18.3	S21 13.1	Canopus	263 53.6	S52 42.2
01	57 45.1	230 26.4	21.9	42 21.2	49.6	124 37.1	11.3	119 20.6	13.1	Capella	280 26.5	N46 01.0
02	72 47.6	245 26.0	23.1	57 24.1	49.6	139 39.2	11.3	134 22.9	13.0	Deneb	49 28.1	N45 21.5
03	87 50.0	260 25.7	. . 24.2	72 27.0	. . 49.7	154 41.3	. . 11.2	149 25.2	. . 13.0	Denebola	182 28.7	N14 27.5
04	102 52.5	275 25.3	25.4	87 29.8	49.7	169 43.3	11.2	164 27.5	13.0	Diphda	348 50.5	S17 52.4
05	117 55.0	290 25.0	26.5	102 32.7	49.7	184 45.4	11.1	179 29.9	13.0			
06	132 57.4	305 24.6	S 1 27.7	117 35.5	N 4 49.7	199 47.5	S22 11.1	194 32.2	S21 12.9	Dubhe	193 45.7	N61 38.2
07	147 59.9	320 24.2	28.8	132 38.4	49.7	214 49.6	11.0	209 34.5	12.9	Elnath	278 05.9	N28 37.4
T 08	163 02.4	335 23.9	30.0	147 41.3	49.8	229 51.6	10.9	224 36.8	12.9	Eltanin	90 44.1	N51 29.5
U 09	178 04.8	350 23.5	. . 31.2	162 44.1	. . 49.8	244 53.7	. . 10.9	239 39.1	. . 12.9	Enif	33 42.1	N 9 58.3
E 10	193 07.3	5 23.2	32.3	177 47.0	49.8	259 55.8	10.8	254 41.4	12.8	Fomalhaut	15 18.1	S29 30.9
S 11	208 09.8	20 22.8	33.5	192 49.8	49.8	274 57.9	10.8	269 43.8	12.8			
D 12	223 12.2	35 22.5	S 1 34.6	207 52.7	N 4 49.8	289 59.9	S22 10.7	284 46.1	S21 12.8	Gacrux	171 55.8	S57 13.4
A 13	238 14.7	50 22.1	35.8	222 55.5	49.9	305 02.0	10.7	299 48.4	12.8	Gienah	175 47.3	S17 39.2
Y 14	253 17.1	65 21.8	36.9	237 58.4	49.9	320 04.1	10.6	314 50.7	12.7	Hadar	148 41.4	S60 28.1
15	268 19.6	80 21.4	. . 38.1	253 01.3	. . 49.9	335 06.2	. . 10.5	329 53.0	. . 12.7	Hamal	327 54.7	N23 33.6
16	283 22.1	95 21.0	39.3	268 04.1	49.9	350 08.2	10.5	344 55.3	12.7	Kaus Aust.	83 37.3	S34 22.5
17	298 24.5	110 20.7	40.4	283 06.9	50.0	5 10.3	10.4	359 57.6	12.7			
18	313 27.0	125 20.3	S 1 41.6	298 09.8	N 4 50.0	20 12.4	S22 10.4	15 00.0	S21 12.6	Kochab	137 21.1	N74 04.3
19	328 29.5	140 20.0	42.7	313 12.6	50.0	35 14.5	10.3	30 02.3	12.6	Markab	13 33.1	N15 19.1
20	343 31.9	155 19.6	43.9	328 15.5	50.0	50 16.5	10.3	45 04.6	12.6	Menkar	314 09.4	N 4 10.2
21	358 34.4	170 19.3	. . 45.1	343 18.3	. . 50.1	65 18.6	. . 10.2	60 06.9	. . 12.6	Menkent	148 02.0	S36 28.1
22	13 36.9	185 18.9	46.2	358 21.2	50.1	80 20.7	10.2	75 09.2	12.5	Miaplacidus	221 38.9	S69 47.7
23	28 39.3	200 18.6	47.4	13 24.0	50.1	95 22.8	10.1	90 11.5	12.5			
4 00	43 41.8	215 18.2	S 1 48.5	28 26.9	N 4 50.1	110 24.8	S22 10.0	105 13.8	S21 12.5	Mirfak	308 32.6	N49 56.0
01	58 44.3	230 17.8	49.7	43 29.7	50.2	125 26.9	10.0	120 16.2	12.5	Nunki	75 52.2	S26 16.2
02	73 46.7	245 17.5	50.8	58 32.5	50.2	140 29.0	09.9	135 18.5	12.4	Peacock	53 11.3	S56 40.3
03	88 49.2	260 17.1	. . 52.0	73 35.4	. . 50.2	155 31.1	. . 09.9	150 20.8	. . 12.4	Pollux	243 21.4	N27 58.5
04	103 51.6	275 16.8	53.2	88 38.2	50.3	170 33.1	09.8	165 23.1	12.4	Procyon	244 54.3	N 5 10.3
05	118 54.1	290 16.4	54.3	103 41.0	50.3	185 35.2	09.8	180 25.4	12.4			
06	133 56.6	305 16.0	S 1 55.5	118 43.9	N 4 50.3	200 37.3	S22 09.7	195 27.7	S21 12.3	Rasalhague	96 02.0	N12 32.9
W 07	148 59.0	320 15.7	56.6	133 46.7	50.3	215 39.3	09.6	210 30.0	12.3	Regulus	207 38.2	N11 52.0
E 08	164 01.5	335 15.3	57.8	148 49.5	50.4	230 41.4	09.6	225 32.3	12.3	Rigel	281 06.9	S 8 10.6
D 09	179 04.0	350 15.0	1 59.0	163 52.4	. . 50.4	245 43.5	. . 09.5	240 34.7	. . 12.3	Rigil Kent.	139 45.6	S60 55.0
N 10	194 06.4	5 14.6	2 00.1	178 55.2	50.4	260 45.5	09.5	255 37.0	12.2	Sabik	102 07.0	S15 44.9
E 11	209 08.9	20 14.3	01.3	193 58.0	50.5	275 47.6	09.4	270 39.3	12.2			
S 12	224 11.4	35 13.9	S 2 02.4	209 00.8	N 4 50.5	290 49.7	S22 09.4	285 41.6	S21 12.2	Schedar	349 34.3	N56 39.2
D 13	239 13.8	50 13.5	03.6	224 03.7	50.5	305 51.8	09.3	300 43.9	12.2	Shaula	96 15.3	S37 07.1
A 14	254 16.3	65 13.2	04.8	239 06.5	50.6	320 53.8	09.2	315 46.2	12.1	Sirius	258 29.1	S16 44.5
Y 15	269 18.7	80 12.8	. . 05.9	254 09.3	. . 50.6	335 55.9	. . 09.2	330 48.5	. . 12.1	Spica	158 26.2	S11 15.9
16	284 21.2	95 12.5	07.1	269 12.1	50.6	350 58.0	09.1	345 50.8	12.1	Suhail	222 48.8	S43 30.6
17	299 23.7	110 12.1	08.2	284 14.9	50.7	6 00.0	09.1	0 53.1	12.1			
18	314 26.1	125 11.7	S 2 09.4	299 17.7	N 4 50.7	21 02.1	S22 09.0	15 55.5	S21 12.0	Vega	80 35.8	N38 48.5
19	329 28.6	140 11.4	10.5	314 20.6	50.7	36 04.2	09.0	30 57.8	12.0	Zuben'ubi	137 00.1	S16 07.5
20	344 31.1	155 11.0	11.7	329 23.4	50.8	51 06.2	08.9	46 00.1	12.0		SHA	Mer. Pass.
21	359 33.5	170 10.7	. . 12.9	344 26.2	. . 50.8	66 08.3	. . 08.8	61 02.4	. . 12.0		° ′	h m
22	14 36.0	185 10.3	14.0	359 29.0	50.8	81 10.4	08.8	76 04.7	11.9	Venus	172 44.1	9 38
23	29 38.5	200 09.9	15.2	14 31.8	50.9	96 12.4	08.7	91 07.0	11.9	Mars	344 35.7	22 07
	h m									Jupiter	66 52.4	16 39
Mer. Pass. 21 05.7		v −0.4	d 1.2	v 2.9	d 0.0	v 2.1	d 0.1	v 2.3	d 0.0	Saturn	61 35.6	17 00

SUN / MOON

UT (d h)	SUN GHA	SUN Dec	MOON GHA	v	MOON Dec	d	HP
2 00	184 06.7	S14 49.2	348 28.3	13.9	N16 52.3	9.4	54.2
01	199 06.7	50.0	3 01.2	13.9	17 01.7	9.4	54.2
02	214 06.7	50.8	17 34.1	13.7	17 11.1	9.2	54.2
03	229 06.7	.. 51.6	32 06.8	13.8	17 20.3	9.2	54.2
04	244 06.7	52.3	46 39.6	13.6	17 29.5	9.1	54.2
05	259 06.7	53.1	61 12.2	13.6	17 38.6	9.1	54.2
M 06	274 06.8	S14 53.9	75 44.8	13.6	N17 47.7	8.9	54.2
O 07	289 06.8	54.7	90 17.4	13.4	17 56.6	8.9	54.2
N 08	304 06.8	55.5	104 49.8	13.5	18 05.5	8.9	54.2
D 09	319 06.8	.. 56.3	119 22.3	13.3	18 14.4	8.7	54.2
A 10	334 06.8	57.1	133 54.6	13.3	18 23.1	8.7	54.3
Y 11	349 06.8	57.8	148 26.9	13.3	18 31.8	8.6	54.3
12	4 06.8	S14 58.6	162 59.2	13.2	N18 40.4	8.5	54.3
13	19 06.8	14 59.4	177 31.4	13.1	18 48.9	8.4	54.3
14	34 06.8	15 00.2	192 03.5	13.0	18 57.3	8.4	54.3
15	49 06.8	.. 01.0	206 35.6	13.0	19 05.7	8.3	54.3
16	64 06.8	01.8	221 07.6	12.9	19 14.0	8.2	54.3
17	79 06.8	02.5	235 39.5	12.9	19 22.2	8.1	54.3
18	94 06.8	S15 03.3	250 11.4	12.8	N19 30.3	8.0	54.3
19	109 06.8	04.1	264 43.2	12.8	19 38.3	8.0	54.3
20	124 06.8	04.9	279 15.0	12.7	19 46.3	7.8	54.3
21	139 06.8	.. 05.7	293 46.7	12.7	19 54.1	7.8	54.4
22	154 06.8	06.4	308 18.4	12.5	20 01.9	7.7	54.4
23	169 06.8	07.2	322 49.9	12.6	20 09.6	7.6	54.4
3 00	184 06.8	S15 08.0	337 21.5	12.4	N20 17.2	7.5	54.4
01	199 06.8	08.8	351 52.9	12.4	20 24.7	7.4	54.4
02	214 06.8	09.5	6 24.3	12.3	20 32.1	7.4	54.4
03	229 06.8	.. 10.3	20 55.6	12.3	20 39.5	7.2	54.4
04	244 06.8	11.1	35 26.9	12.2	20 46.7	7.2	54.4
05	259 06.8	11.9	49 58.1	12.2	20 53.9	7.1	54.5
T 06	274 06.8	S15 12.7	64 29.3	12.1	N21 01.0	6.9	54.5
U 07	289 06.8	13.4	79 00.4	12.0	21 07.9	6.9	54.5
E 08	304 06.8	14.2	93 31.4	12.0	21 14.8	6.8	54.5
S 09	319 06.8	.. 15.0	108 02.4	11.9	21 21.6	6.7	54.5
D 10	334 06.8	15.7	122 33.3	11.8	21 28.3	6.6	54.5
A 11	349 06.8	16.5	137 04.1	11.8	21 34.9	6.5	54.5
Y 12	4 06.8	S15 17.3	151 34.9	11.7	N21 41.4	6.4	54.5
13	19 06.8	18.1	166 05.6	11.7	21 47.8	6.3	54.6
14	34 06.8	18.8	180 36.3	11.6	21 54.1	6.2	54.6
15	49 06.8	.. 19.6	195 06.9	11.6	22 00.3	6.1	54.6
16	64 06.7	20.4	209 37.5	11.5	22 06.4	6.0	54.6
17	79 06.7	21.2	224 08.0	11.4	22 12.4	5.9	54.6
18	94 06.7	S15 21.9	238 38.4	11.3	N22 18.3	5.8	54.6
19	109 06.7	22.7	253 08.7	11.4	22 24.1	5.7	54.6
20	124 06.7	23.5	267 39.1	11.2	22 29.8	5.6	54.7
21	139 06.7	.. 24.2	282 09.3	11.2	22 35.4	5.5	54.7
22	154 06.7	25.0	296 39.5	11.1	22 40.9	5.3	54.7
23	169 06.7	25.8	311 09.6	11.1	22 46.2	5.3	54.7
4 00	184 06.7	S15 26.5	325 39.7	11.0	N22 51.5	5.2	54.7
01	199 06.7	27.3	340 09.7	11.0	22 56.7	5.1	54.7
02	214 06.7	28.1	354 39.7	10.9	23 01.8	4.9	54.8
03	229 06.7	.. 28.8	9 09.6	10.9	23 06.7	4.9	54.8
04	244 06.6	29.6	23 39.5	10.8	23 11.6	4.7	54.8
05	259 06.6	30.4	38 09.3	10.7	23 16.3	4.6	54.8
W 06	274 06.6	S15 31.1	52 39.0	10.7	N23 20.9	4.5	54.8
E 07	289 06.6	31.9	67 08.7	10.6	23 25.4	4.4	54.8
D 08	304 06.6	32.7	81 38.3	10.6	23 29.8	4.3	54.9
N 09	319 06.6	.. 33.4	96 07.9	10.5	23 34.1	4.2	54.9
E 10	334 06.6	34.2	110 37.4	10.5	23 38.3	4.1	54.9
S 11	349 06.6	35.0	125 06.9	10.4	23 42.4	3.9	54.9
D 12	4 06.5	S15 35.7	139 36.3	10.4	N23 46.3	3.9	54.9
A 13	19 06.5	36.5	154 05.7	10.3	23 50.2	3.7	54.9
Y 14	34 06.5	37.2	168 35.0	10.3	23 53.9	3.6	55.0
15	49 06.5	.. 38.0	183 04.3	10.2	23 57.5	3.5	55.0
16	64 06.5	38.8	197 33.5	10.2	24 01.0	3.3	55.0
17	79 06.5	39.5	212 02.7	10.1	24 04.3	3.3	55.0
18	94 06.5	S15 40.3	226 31.8	10.1	N24 07.6	3.1	55.0
19	109 06.5	41.0	241 00.9	10.0	24 10.7	3.0	55.0
20	124 06.4	41.8	255 29.9	10.0	24 13.7	2.9	55.1
21	139 06.4	.. 42.6	269 58.9	9.9	24 16.6	2.8	55.1
22	154 06.4	43.3	284 27.8	9.9	24 19.4	2.6	55.1
23	169 06.4	44.1	298 56.7	9.9	N24 22.0	2.6	55.1
	SD 16.2 d 0.8		SD 14.8		14.9		15.0

Twilight / Sunrise / Moonrise

Lat.	Naut.	Civil	Sunrise	2	3	4	5
N 72	06 16	07 40	09 12	□	□	□	□
N 70	06 10	07 26	08 43	14 31	□	□	□
68	06 06	07 14	08 21	15 19	14 26	□	□
66	06 02	07 04	08 04	15 51	15 41	15 13	□
64	05 59	06 56	07 50	16 14	16 18	16 29	17 00
62	05 56	06 49	07 38	16 33	16 44	17 05	17 44
60	05 53	06 43	07 28	16 48	17 05	17 31	18 13
N 58	05 50	06 37	07 20	17 01	17 22	17 52	18 36
56	05 48	06 32	07 12	17 13	17 36	18 09	18 54
54	05 45	06 27	07 05	17 23	17 49	18 23	19 10
52	05 43	06 23	06 59	17 32	18 00	18 36	19 23
50	05 41	06 19	06 54	17 40	18 09	18 47	19 35
45	05 36	06 11	06 42	17 57	18 30	19 10	19 59
N 40	05 31	06 03	06 32	18 11	18 47	19 29	20 18
35	05 27	05 57	06 23	18 23	19 01	19 45	20 35
30	05 22	05 51	06 16	18 33	19 13	19 58	20 49
20	05 14	05 40	06 03	18 51	19 34	20 21	21 13
N 10	05 04	05 29	05 51	19 07	19 53	20 42	21 33
0	04 54	05 19	05 40	19 22	20 10	21 01	21 53
S 10	04 42	05 07	05 29	19 37	20 28	21 19	22 12
20	04 27	04 54	05 17	19 53	20 46	21 40	22 33
30	04 08	04 38	05 03	20 12	21 08	22 03	22 57
35	03 56	04 28	04 55	20 23	21 20	22 17	23 11
40	03 41	04 17	04 46	20 35	21 35	22 33	23 28
45	03 23	04 03	04 35	20 50	21 53	22 52	23 47
S 50	02 59	03 46	04 22	21 08	22 14	23 16	24 12
52	02 47	03 37	04 16	21 17	22 25	23 28	24 24
54	02 33	03 28	04 09	21 26	22 36	23 41	24 37
56	02 16	03 17	04 02	21 37	22 50	23 56	24 53
58	01 55	03 05	03 53	21 50	23 06	24 14	00 14
S 60	01 27	02 50	03 44	22 05	23 24	24 37	00 37

Sunset / Twilight / Moonset

Lat.	Sunset	Civil	Naut.	2	3	4	5
N 72	14 13	15 45	17 10	□	□	□	□
N 70	14 43	16 00	17 15	11 35	□	□	□
68	15 05	16 12	17 20	10 48	13 19	□	□
66	15 22	16 22	17 24	10 17	12 05	14 16	□
64	15 36	16 30	17 27	09 55	11 29	13 01	14 18
62	15 48	16 37	17 30	09 37	11 03	12 25	13 34
60	15 58	16 44	17 33	09 22	10 43	11 59	13 04
N 58	16 07	16 49	17 36	09 09	10 26	11 39	12 42
56	16 14	16 54	17 39	08 59	10 12	11 22	12 24
54	16 21	16 59	17 41	08 49	10 00	11 08	12 08
52	16 27	17 03	17 43	08 41	09 49	10 55	11 55
50	16 33	17 07	17 45	08 33	09 40	10 44	11 43
45	16 45	17 16	17 50	08 17	09 20	10 22	11 19
N 40	16 55	17 23	17 55	08 04	09 04	10 03	11 00
35	17 04	17 30	18 00	07 53	08 51	09 48	10 43
30	17 11	17 36	18 04	07 43	08 39	09 35	10 29
20	17 24	17 47	18 13	07 26	08 19	09 12	10 05
N 10	17 36	17 58	18 23	07 12	08 01	08 52	09 45
0	17 47	18 08	18 33	06 58	07 45	08 34	09 26
S 10	17 58	18 20	18 46	06 45	07 29	08 16	09 06
20	18 10	18 33	19 01	06 31	07 12	07 56	08 46
30	18 24	18 50	19 20	06 14	06 52	07 34	08 22
35	18 32	18 59	19 32	06 05	06 40	07 21	08 08
40	18 42	19 11	19 47	05 54	06 27	07 06	07 51
45	18 53	19 25	20 05	05 41	06 11	06 48	07 32
S 50	19 06	19 43	20 30	05 26	05 52	06 25	07 08
52	19 12	19 51	20 42	05 19	05 43	06 15	06 56
54	19 19	20 01	20 57	05 11	05 33	06 03	06 43
56	19 27	20 12	21 14	05 02	05 22	05 49	06 27
58	19 35	20 24	21 36	04 52	05 09	05 33	06 09
S 60	19 45	20 39	22 05	04 40	04 53	05 14	05 47

SUN / MOON

Day	Eqn. of Time 00h	12h	Mer. Pass.	Mer. Pass. Upper	Lower	Age	Phase %
2	16 27	16 27	11 44	00 48	13 10	17	97
3	16 27	16 27	11 44	01 34	13 57	18	93
4	16 27	16 26	11 44	02 22	14 47	19	87

2020 NOVEMBER 5, 6, 7 (THURS., FRI., SAT.)

UT	ARIES	VENUS −4.0		MARS −2.0		JUPITER −2.1		SATURN +0.6		STARS		
	GHA	GHA	Dec	GHA	Dec	GHA	Dec	GHA	Dec	Name	SHA	Dec
d h	° ′	° ′	° ′	° ′	° ′	° ′	° ′	° ′	° ′		° ′	° ′
5 00	44 40.9	215 09.6	S 2 16.3	29 34.6	N 4 50.9	111 14.5	S22 08.7	106 09.3	S21 11.9	Acamar	315 14.0	S40 13.3
01	59 43.4	230 09.2	17.5	44 37.4	51.0	126 16.6	08.6	121 11.6	11.8	Achernar	335 22.3	S57 08.0
02	74 45.9	245 08.9	18.7	59 40.2	51.0	141 18.6	08.6	136 13.9	11.8	Acrux	173 04.3	S63 12.5
03	89 48.3	260 08.5	.. 19.8	74 43.0	.. 51.1	156 20.7	.. 08.5	151 16.2	.. 11.8	Adhara	255 08.3	S28 59.8
04	104 50.8	275 08.1	21.0	89 45.8	51.1	171 22.8	08.4	166 18.6	11.8	Aldebaran	290 43.2	N16 33.0
05	119 53.2	290 07.8	22.1	104 48.6	51.1	186 24.8	08.4	181 20.9	11.7			
T 06	134 55.7	305 07.4	S 2 23.3	119 51.4	N 4 51.2	201 26.9	S22 08.3	196 23.2	S21 11.7	Alioth	166 16.6	N55 50.8
H 07	149 58.2	320 07.0	24.5	134 54.2	51.2	216 29.0	08.3	211 25.5	11.7	Alkaid	152 55.3	N49 12.7
U 08	165 00.6	335 06.7	25.6	149 57.0	51.3	231 31.0	08.2	226 27.8	11.7	Alnair	27 37.1	S46 51.8
R 09	180 03.1	350 06.3	.. 26.8	164 59.8	.. 51.3	246 33.1	.. 08.1	241 30.1	.. 11.6	Alnilam	275 40.9	S 1 11.3
S 10	195 05.6	5 06.0	27.9	180 02.6	51.4	261 35.2	08.1	256 32.4	11.6	Alphard	217 51.1	S 8 44.7
D 11	210 08.0	20 05.6	29.1	195 05.4	51.4	276 37.2	08.0	271 34.7	11.6			
A 12	225 10.5	35 05.2	S 2 30.3	210 08.2	N 4 51.4	291 39.3	S22 08.0	286 37.0	S21 11.6	Alphecca	126 07.0	N26 38.9
Y 13	240 13.0	50 04.9	31.4	225 11.0	51.5	306 41.4	07.9	301 39.3	11.5	Alpheratz	357 38.0	N29 12.4
14	255 15.4	65 04.5	32.6	240 13.8	51.5	321 43.4	07.9	316 41.6	11.5	Altair	62 03.4	N 8 55.5
15	270 17.9	80 04.1	.. 33.7	255 16.6	.. 51.6	336 45.5	.. 07.8	331 43.9	.. 11.5	Ankaa	353 10.3	S42 11.8
16	285 20.4	95 03.8	34.9	270 19.4	51.6	351 47.5	07.7	346 46.3	11.5	Antares	112 20.3	S26 28.5
17	300 22.8	110 03.4	36.1	285 22.2	51.7	6 49.6	07.7	1 48.6	11.4			
18	315 25.3	125 03.1	S 2 37.2	300 25.0	N 4 51.7	21 51.7	S22 07.6	16 50.9	S21 11.4	Arcturus	145 51.4	N19 04.6
19	330 27.7	140 02.7	38.4	315 27.7	51.8	36 53.7	07.6	31 53.2	11.4	Atria	107 18.1	S69 03.9
20	345 30.2	155 02.3	39.5	330 30.5	51.8	51 55.8	07.5	46 55.5	11.3	Avior	234 15.9	S59 34.2
21	0 32.7	170 02.0	.. 40.7	345 33.3	.. 51.9	66 57.9	.. 07.4	61 57.8	.. 11.3	Bellatrix	278 26.3	N 6 22.1
22	15 35.1	185 01.6	41.9	0 36.1	51.9	81 59.9	07.4	77 00.1	11.3	Betelgeuse	270 55.5	N 7 24.6
23	30 37.6	200 01.2	43.0	15 38.9	52.0	97 02.0	07.3	92 02.4	11.3			
6 00	45 40.1	215 00.9	S 2 44.2	30 41.6	N 4 52.0	112 04.0	S22 07.3	107 04.7	S21 11.2	Canopus	263 53.5	S52 42.2
01	60 42.5	230 00.5	45.3	45 44.4	52.1	127 06.1	07.2	122 07.0	11.2	Capella	280 26.5	N46 01.0
02	75 45.0	245 00.1	46.5	60 47.2	52.1	142 08.2	07.2	137 09.3	11.2	Deneb	49 28.1	N45 21.5
03	90 47.5	259 59.8	.. 47.7	75 50.0	.. 52.2	157 10.2	.. 07.1	152 11.6	.. 11.2	Denebola	182 28.7	N14 27.5
04	105 49.9	274 59.4	48.8	90 52.7	52.2	172 12.3	07.0	167 13.9	11.1	Diphda	348 50.5	S17 52.4
05	120 52.4	289 59.0	50.0	105 55.5	52.3	187 14.3	07.0	182 16.2	11.1			
06	135 54.9	304 58.7	S 2 51.1	120 58.3	N 4 52.3	202 16.4	S22 06.9	197 18.5	S21 11.1	Dubhe	193 45.7	N61 38.2
07	150 57.3	319 58.3	52.3	136 01.0	52.4	217 18.5	06.9	212 20.8	11.1	Elnath	278 05.9	N28 37.4
F 08	165 59.8	334 57.9	53.4	151 03.8	52.4	232 20.5	06.8	227 23.1	11.0	Eltanin	90 44.2	N51 29.4
R 09	181 02.2	349 57.6	.. 54.6	166 06.6	.. 52.5	247 22.6	.. 06.7	242 25.5	.. 11.0	Enif	33 42.1	N 9 58.3
I 10	196 04.7	4 57.2	55.8	181 09.3	52.5	262 24.6	06.7	257 27.8	11.0	Fomalhaut	15 18.1	S29 30.9
D 11	211 07.2	19 56.8	56.9	196 12.1	52.6	277 26.7	06.6	272 30.1	10.9			
A 12	226 09.6	34 56.5	S 2 58.1	211 14.9	N 4 52.6	292 28.8	S22 06.6	287 32.4	S21 10.9	Gacrux	171 55.8	S57 13.4
Y 13	241 12.1	49 56.1	2 59.2	226 17.6	52.7	307 30.8	06.5	302 34.7	10.9	Gienah	175 47.3	S17 39.2
14	256 14.6	64 55.7	3 00.4	241 20.4	52.7	322 32.9	06.4	317 37.0	10.9	Hadar	148 41.4	S60 28.1
15	271 17.0	79 55.4	.. 01.6	256 23.1	.. 52.8	337 34.9	.. 06.4	332 39.3	.. 10.8	Hamal	327 54.7	N23 33.6
16	286 19.5	94 55.0	02.7	271 25.9	52.9	352 37.0	06.3	347 41.6	10.8	Kaus Aust.	83 37.3	S34 22.5
17	301 22.0	109 54.6	03.9	286 28.7	52.9	7 39.0	06.3	2 43.9	10.8			
18	316 24.4	124 54.3	S 3 05.0	301 31.4	N 4 53.0	22 41.1	S22 06.2	17 46.2	S21 10.8	Kochab	137 21.2	N74 04.3
19	331 26.9	139 53.9	06.2	316 34.2	53.0	37 43.2	06.1	32 48.5	10.7	Markab	13 33.1	N15 19.1
20	346 29.4	154 53.5	07.4	331 36.9	53.1	52 45.2	06.1	47 50.8	10.7	Menkar	314 09.4	N 4 10.2
21	1 31.8	169 53.2	.. 08.5	346 39.7	.. 53.1	67 47.3	.. 06.0	62 53.1	.. 10.7	Menkent	148 02.0	S36 28.1
22	16 34.3	184 52.8	09.7	1 42.4	53.2	82 49.3	06.0	77 55.4	10.6	Miaplacidus	221 38.8	S69 47.7
23	31 36.7	199 52.4	10.8	16 45.2	53.3	97 51.4	05.9	92 57.7	10.6			
7 00	46 39.2	214 52.1	S 3 12.0	31 47.9	N 4 53.3	112 53.4	S22 05.8	108 00.0	S21 10.6	Mirfak	308 32.6	N49 56.0
01	61 41.7	229 51.7	13.2	46 50.7	53.4	127 55.5	05.8	123 02.3	10.6	Nunki	75 52.2	S26 16.2
02	76 44.1	244 51.3	14.3	61 53.4	53.4	142 57.5	05.7	138 04.6	10.5	Peacock	53 11.3	S56 40.3
03	91 46.6	259 51.0	.. 15.5	76 56.1	.. 53.5	157 59.6	.. 05.7	153 06.9	.. 10.5	Pollux	243 21.4	N27 58.5
04	106 49.1	274 50.6	16.6	91 58.9	53.6	173 01.7	05.6	168 09.2	10.5	Procyon	244 54.3	N 5 10.3
05	121 51.5	289 50.2	17.8	107 01.6	53.6	188 03.7	05.6	183 11.5	10.5			
06	136 54.0	304 49.8	S 3 19.0	122 04.4	N 4 53.7	203 05.8	S22 05.5	198 13.8	S21 10.4	Rasalhague	96 02.0	N12 32.9
07	151 56.5	319 49.5	20.1	137 07.1	53.8	218 07.8	05.4	213 16.1	10.4	Regulus	207 38.2	N11 52.0
S 08	166 58.9	334 49.1	21.3	152 09.8	53.8	233 09.9	05.4	228 18.4	10.4	Rigel	281 06.9	S 8 10.6
A 09	182 01.4	349 48.7	.. 22.4	167 12.6	.. 53.9	248 11.9	.. 05.3	243 20.7	.. 10.3	Rigil Kent.	139 45.6	S60 55.0
T 10	197 03.8	4 48.4	23.6	182 15.3	53.9	263 14.0	05.2	258 23.0	10.3	Sabik	102 07.0	S15 44.9
U 11	212 06.3	19 48.0	24.8	197 18.0	54.0	278 16.0	05.2	273 25.3	10.3			
R 12	227 08.8	34 47.6	S 3 25.9	212 20.8	N 4 54.1	293 18.1	S22 05.1	288 27.6	S21 10.3	Schedar	349 34.3	N56 39.2
D 13	242 11.2	49 47.2	27.1	227 23.5	54.1	308 20.1	05.1	303 29.9	10.2	Shaula	96 15.3	S37 07.1
A 14	257 13.7	64 46.9	28.2	242 26.2	54.2	323 22.2	05.0	318 32.2	10.2	Sirius	258 29.0	S16 44.6
Y 15	272 16.2	79 46.5	.. 29.4	257 28.9	.. 54.3	338 24.2	.. 04.9	333 34.5	.. 10.2	Spica	158 26.2	S11 15.9
16	287 18.6	94 46.1	30.5	272 31.7	54.3	353 26.3	04.9	348 36.8	10.1	Suhail	222 48.8	S43 30.6
17	302 21.1	109 45.8	31.7	287 34.4	54.4	8 28.3	04.8	3 39.1	10.1			
18	317 23.6	124 45.4	S 3 32.9	302 37.1	N 4 54.5	23 30.4	S22 04.7	18 41.4	S21 10.1	Vega	80 35.8	N38 48.4
19	332 26.0	139 45.0	34.0	317 39.8	54.6	38 32.5	04.7	33 43.7	10.1	Zuben'ubi	137 00.1	S16 07.5
20	347 28.5	154 44.6	35.2	332 42.6	54.6	53 34.5	04.6	48 46.0	10.0		SHA	Mer.Pass.
21	2 31.0	169 44.3	.. 36.3	347 45.3	.. 54.7	68 36.6	.. 04.6	63 48.3	.. 10.0		° ′	h m
22	17 33.4	184 43.9	37.5	2 48.0	54.8	83 38.6	04.5	78 50.6	10.0	Venus	169 20.8	9 40
23	32 35.9	199 43.5	38.7	17 50.7	54.8	98 40.7	04.4	93 52.9	10.0	Mars	345 01.6	21 53
	h m									Jupiter	66 24.0	16 29
Mer. Pass. 20 53.9		v −0.4	d 1.2	v 2.8	d 0.1	v 2.1	d 0.1	v 2.3	d 0.0	Saturn	61 24.6	16 49

UT	SUN GHA	SUN Dec	MOON GHA	v	MOON Dec	d	HP
d h	° '	° '	° '	'	° '	'	'
5 00	184 06.4	S15 44.8	313 25.6	9.8	N24 24.6	2.4	55.1
01	199 06.3	45.6	327 54.4	9.7	24 27.0	2.3	55.2
02	214 06.3	46.3	342 23.1	9.8	24 29.3	2.1	55.2
03	229 06.3	.. 47.1	356 51.9	9.6	24 31.4	2.1	55.2
04	244 06.3	47.9	11 20.5	9.7	24 33.5	1.9	55.2
05	259 06.3	48.6	25 49.2	9.6	24 35.4	1.8	55.2
06	274 06.3	S15 49.4	40 17.8	9.6	N24 37.2	1.6	55.3
T 07	289 06.2	50.1	54 46.4	9.5	24 38.8	1.6	55.3
H 08	304 06.2	50.9	69 14.9	9.5	24 40.4	1.4	55.3
U 09	319 06.2	.. 51.6	83 43.4	9.4	24 41.8	1.3	55.3
R 10	334 06.2	52.4	98 11.8	9.4	24 43.1	1.1	55.4
S 11	349 06.1	53.1	112 40.2	9.4	24 44.2	1.1	55.4
D 12	4 06.1	S15 53.9	127 08.6	9.4	N24 45.3	0.9	55.4
A 13	19 06.1	54.6	141 37.0	9.3	24 46.2	0.7	55.4
Y 14	34 06.1	55.4	156 05.3	9.3	24 46.9	0.7	55.4
15	49 06.1	.. 56.1	170 33.6	9.2	24 47.6	0.5	55.5
16	64 06.0	56.9	185 01.8	9.3	24 48.1	0.5	55.5
17	79 06.0	57.6	199 30.1	9.2	24 48.5	0.3	55.5
18	94 06.0	S15 58.4	213 58.3	9.1	N24 48.8	0.1	55.5
19	109 06.0	59.1	228 26.4	9.2	24 48.9	0.0	55.6
20	124 05.9	15 59.9	242 54.6	9.1	24 48.9	0.1	55.6
21	139 05.9	16 00.6	257 22.7	9.1	24 48.8	0.3	55.6
22	154 05.9	01.4	271 50.8	9.1	24 48.5	0.4	55.6
23	169 05.9	02.1	286 18.9	9.0	24 48.1	0.5	55.7
6 00	184 05.8	S16 02.9	300 46.9	9.0	N24 47.6	0.7	55.7
01	199 05.8	03.6	315 14.9	9.0	24 46.9	0.8	55.7
02	214 05.8	04.4	329 42.9	9.0	24 46.1	0.9	55.7
03	229 05.8	.. 05.1	344 10.9	9.0	24 45.2	1.0	55.7
04	244 05.7	05.8	358 38.9	8.9	24 44.2	1.2	55.8
05	259 05.7	06.6	13 06.8	9.0	24 43.0	1.3	55.8
06	274 05.7	S16 07.3	27 34.8	8.9	N24 41.7	1.5	55.8
F 07	289 05.6	08.1	42 02.7	8.9	24 40.2	1.6	55.9
R 08	304 05.6	08.8	56 30.6	8.9	24 38.6	1.7	55.9
I 09	319 05.6	.. 09.6	70 58.5	8.8	24 36.9	1.8	55.9
D 10	334 05.6	10.3	85 26.3	8.9	24 35.1	2.0	55.9
A 11	349 05.5	11.0	99 54.2	8.8	24 33.1	2.1	56.0
Y 12	4 05.5	S16 11.8	114 22.0	8.9	N24 31.0	2.3	56.0
13	19 05.5	12.5	128 49.9	8.8	24 28.7	2.3	56.0
14	34 05.4	13.3	143 17.7	8.8	24 26.4	2.6	56.0
15	49 05.4	.. 14.0	157 45.5	8.8	24 23.8	2.6	56.1
16	64 05.4	14.7	172 13.3	8.8	24 21.2	2.8	56.1
17	79 05.3	15.5	186 41.1	8.8	24 18.4	2.9	56.1
18	94 05.3	S16 16.2	201 08.9	8.8	N24 15.5	3.1	56.1
19	109 05.3	17.0	215 36.7	8.8	24 12.4	3.1	56.2
20	124 05.2	17.7	230 04.5	8.8	24 09.3	3.4	56.2
21	139 05.2	.. 18.4	244 32.3	8.7	24 05.9	3.4	56.2
22	154 05.2	19.2	259 00.0	8.8	24 02.5	3.6	56.3
23	169 05.1	19.9	273 27.8	8.8	23 58.9	3.7	56.3
7 00	184 05.1	S16 20.6	287 55.6	8.8	N23 55.2	3.9	56.3
01	199 05.1	21.4	302 23.4	8.8	23 51.3	3.9	56.3
02	214 05.0	22.1	316 51.2	8.7	23 47.4	4.2	56.4
03	229 05.0	.. 22.8	331 18.9	8.8	23 43.2	4.2	56.4
04	244 04.9	23.6	345 46.7	8.8	23 39.0	4.4	56.4
05	259 04.9	24.3	0 14.5	8.8	23 34.6	4.5	56.5
06	274 04.9	S16 25.0	14 42.3	8.8	N23 30.1	4.7	56.5
S 07	289 04.8	25.8	29 10.1	8.8	23 25.4	4.7	56.5
A 08	304 04.8	26.5	43 37.9	8.8	23 20.7	4.9	56.6
T 09	319 04.8	.. 27.2	58 05.7	8.8	23 15.8	5.1	56.6
U 10	334 04.7	28.0	72 33.5	8.9	23 10.7	5.2	56.6
R 11	349 04.7	28.7	87 01.4	8.8	23 05.5	5.3	56.6
D 12	4 04.6	S16 29.4	101 29.2	8.8	N23 00.2	5.4	56.7
A 13	19 04.6	30.1	115 57.0	8.9	22 54.8	5.6	56.7
Y 14	34 04.6	30.9	130 24.9	8.8	22 49.2	5.7	56.7
15	49 04.5	.. 31.6	144 52.7	8.9	22 43.5	5.8	56.8
16	64 04.5	32.3	159 20.6	8.9	22 37.7	6.0	56.8
17	79 04.4	33.1	173 48.5	8.9	22 31.7	6.1	56.8
18	94 04.4	S16 33.8	188 16.4	8.9	N22 25.6	6.2	56.9
19	109 04.3	34.5	202 44.3	8.9	22 19.4	6.3	56.9
20	124 04.3	35.2	217 12.2	9.0	22 13.1	6.5	56.9
21	139 04.3	.. 36.0	231 40.2	8.9	22 06.6	6.6	57.0
22	154 04.2	36.7	246 08.1	9.0	22 00.0	6.7	57.0
23	169 04.2	37.4	260 36.1	9.0	N21 53.3	6.9	57.0
	SD 16.2	d 0.7	SD 15.1		15.3		15.4

Twilight / Moonrise

Lat.	Naut.	Civil	Sunrise	Moonrise 5	6	7	8
°	h m	h m	h m	h m	h m	h m	h m
N 72	06 27	07 54	09 34	□	□	□	□
N 70	06 21	07 38	08 59	□	□	□	19 38
68	06 15	07 24	08 34	□	□	□	20 33
66	06 11	07 14	08 15	□	□	19 04	21 06
64	06 06	07 04	08 00	17 00	18 09	19 45	21 30
62	06 03	06 56	07 47	17 44	18 48	20 13	21 49
60	05 59	06 49	07 36	18 13	19 15	20 34	22 04
N 58	05 56	06 43	07 27	18 36	19 37	20 52	22 17
56	05 53	06 38	07 18	18 54	19 54	21 07	22 28
54	05 50	06 33	07 11	19 10	20 09	21 19	22 38
52	05 48	06 28	07 05	19 23	20 21	21 30	22 47
50	05 45	06 24	06 59	19 35	20 33	21 40	22 55
45	05 40	06 15	06 46	19 59	20 56	22 01	23 11
N 40	05 34	06 07	06 35	20 18	21 15	22 18	23 25
35	05 29	06 00	06 26	20 35	21 31	22 32	23 36
30	05 23	05 53	06 18	20 49	21 44	22 44	23 46
20	05 15	05 41	06 04	21 13	22 07	23 05	24 03
N 10	05 05	05 30	05 52	21 33	22 27	23 23	24 18
0	04 54	05 19	05 40	21 53	22 46	23 40	24 32
S 10	04 41	05 06	05 28	22 12	23 05	23 56	24 46
20	04 25	04 53	05 16	22 33	23 25	24 14	00 14
30	04 05	04 36	05 01	22 57	23 48	24 35	00 35
35	03 52	04 25	04 53	23 11	24 01	00 01	00 47
40	03 37	04 13	04 43	23 28	24 17	00 17	01 00
45	03 18	03 59	04 31	23 47	24 35	00 35	01 17
S 50	02 52	03 40	04 17	24 12	00 12	00 59	01 37
52	02 39	03 31	04 11	24 24	00 24	01 10	01 46
54	02 24	03 21	04 04	24 37	00 37	01 22	01 57
56	02 06	03 10	03 55	24 53	00 53	01 36	02 09
58	01 42	02 56	03 46	00 14	01 11	01 53	02 22
S 60	01 09	02 40	03 36	00 37	01 34	02 14	02 39

Sunset / Twilight / Moonset

Lat.	Sunset	Civil	Naut.	Moonset 5	6	7	8
°	h m	h m	h m	h m	h m	h m	h m
N 72	13 52	15 32	16 58	□	□	□	□
N 70	14 27	15 48	17 05	□	□	□	17 15
68	14 52	16 02	17 11	□	□	□	16 19
66	15 11	16 13	17 15	□	□	15 57	15 45
64	15 27	16 22	17 20	14 18	15 00	15 15	15 20
62	15 39	16 30	17 24	13 34	14 20	14 46	15 01
60	15 50	16 37	17 27	13 04	13 53	14 24	14 44
N 58	16 00	16 43	17 30	12 42	13 31	14 06	14 31
56	16 09	16 49	17 33	12 24	13 14	13 51	14 19
54	16 15	16 54	17 36	12 08	12 59	13 38	14 08
52	16 22	16 58	17 39	11 55	12 46	13 27	13 59
50	16 28	17 03	17 41	11 43	12 34	13 17	13 51
45	16 41	17 12	17 47	11 19	12 11	12 55	13 33
N 40	16 52	17 20	17 52	11 00	11 52	12 38	13 19
35	17 01	17 27	17 57	10 43	11 36	12 23	13 06
30	17 09	17 34	18 02	10 29	11 22	12 11	12 55
20	17 23	17 46	18 12	10 05	10 58	11 49	12 37
N 10	17 35	17 57	18 22	09 45	10 38	11 30	12 20
0	17 47	18 09	18 34	09 26	10 18	11 12	12 05
S 10	17 59	18 21	18 47	09 06	09 59	10 54	11 49
20	18 12	18 35	19 02	08 46	09 39	10 35	11 33
30	18 27	18 52	19 23	08 22	09 15	10 12	11 13
35	18 35	19 03	19 36	08 08	09 01	09 59	11 02
40	18 45	19 15	19 51	07 51	08 44	09 44	10 49
45	18 57	19 30	20 11	07 32	08 25	09 26	10 34
S 50	19 11	19 48	20 37	07 08	08 01	09 04	10 15
52	19 18	19 57	20 50	06 56	07 49	08 53	10 06
54	19 25	20 08	21 06	06 43	07 35	08 40	09 56
56	19 33	20 19	21 25	06 27	07 20	08 26	09 44
58	19 43	20 33	21 49	06 09	07 01	08 10	09 31
S 60	19 53	20 49	22 24	05 47	06 38	07 50	09 15

SUN / MOON

Day	Eqn. of Time 00ʰ	12ʰ	Mer. Pass.	Mer. Pass. Upper	Lower	Age	Phase
d	m s	m s	h m	h m	h m	d	%
5	16 26	16 25	11 44	03 13	15 39	20	80
6	16 23	16 22	11 44	04 06	16 32	21	71
7	16 20	16 19	11 44	04 59	17 26	22	61

UT	ARIES GHA	VENUS −4.0 GHA	Dec	MARS −1.9 GHA	Dec	JUPITER −2.1 GHA	Dec	SATURN +0.6 GHA	Dec	STARS Name	SHA	Dec
d h	° ′	° ′	° ′	° ′	° ′	° ′	° ′	° ′	° ′		° ′	° ′
8 00	47 38.3	214 43.1	S 3 39.8	32 53.4	N 4 54.9	113 42.7	S22 04.4	108 55.2	S21 09.9	Acamar	315 14.0	S40 13.3
01	62 40.8	229 42.8	41.0	47 56.1	55.0	128 44.8	04.3	123 57.5	09.9	Achernar	335 22.3	S57 08.1
02	77 43.3	244 42.4	42.1	62 58.9	55.0	143 46.8	04.3	138 59.8	09.9	Acrux	173 04.2	S63 12.5
03	92 45.7	259 42.0 ..	43.3	78 01.6 ..	55.1	158 48.9 ..	04.2	154 02.1 ..	09.8	Adhara	255 08.3	S28 59.8
04	107 48.2	274 41.6	44.4	93 04.3	55.2	173 50.9	04.1	169 04.4	09.8	Aldebaran	290 43.2	N16 33.0
05	122 50.7	289 41.3	45.6	108 07.0	55.3	188 53.0	04.1	184 06.7	09.8			
06	137 53.1	304 40.9	S 3 46.8	123 09.7	N 4 55.3	203 55.0	S22 04.0	199 09.0	S21 09.8	Alioth	166 16.6	N55 50.8
07	152 55.6	319 40.5	47.9	138 12.4	55.4	218 57.1	04.0	214 11.3	09.7	Alkaid	152 55.2	N49 12.6
08	167 58.1	334 40.1	49.1	153 15.1	55.5	233 59.1	03.9	229 13.6	09.7	Alnair	27 37.2	S46 51.8
S 09	183 00.5	349 39.8 ..	50.2	168 17.8 ..	55.5	249 01.1 ..	03.8	244 15.9 ..	09.7	Alnilam	275 40.9	S 1 11.3
U 10	198 03.0	4 39.4	51.4	183 20.5	55.6	264 03.2	03.8	259 18.2	09.6	Alphard	217 51.1	S 8 44.7
N 11	213 05.5	19 39.0	52.6	198 23.2	55.7	279 05.2	03.7	274 20.5	09.6			
D 12	228 07.9	34 38.6	S 3 53.7	213 25.9	N 4 55.8	294 07.3	S22 03.6	289 22.8	S21 09.6	Alphecca	126 07.0	N26 38.9
A 13	243 10.4	49 38.3	54.9	228 28.6	55.9	309 09.3	03.6	304 25.1	09.6	Alpheratz	357 38.0	N29 12.4
Y 14	258 12.8	64 37.9	56.0	243 31.3	55.9	324 11.4	03.5	319 27.4	09.5	Altair	62 03.4	N 8 55.5
15	273 15.3	79 37.5 ..	57.2	258 34.0 ..	56.0	339 13.4 ..	03.5	334 29.7 ..	09.5	Ankaa	353 10.3	S42 11.8
16	288 17.8	94 37.1	58.3	273 36.7	56.1	354 15.5	03.4	349 32.0	09.5	Antares	112 20.3	S26 28.5
17	303 20.2	109 36.8	3 59.5	288 39.4	56.2	9 17.5	03.3	4 34.3	09.4			
18	318 22.7	124 36.4	S 4 00.7	303 42.1	N 4 56.3	24 19.6	S22 03.3	19 36.6	S21 09.4	Arcturus	145 51.4	N19 04.6
19	333 25.2	139 36.0	01.8	318 44.8	56.3	39 21.6	03.2	34 38.9	09.4	Atria	107 18.1	S69 03.8
20	348 27.6	154 35.6	03.0	333 47.4	56.4	54 23.7	03.1	49 41.2	09.4	Avior	234 15.9	S59 34.2
21	3 30.1	169 35.2 ..	04.1	348 50.1 ..	56.5	69 25.7 ..	03.1	64 43.5 ..	09.3	Bellatrix	278 26.2	N 6 22.1
22	18 32.6	184 34.9	05.3	3 52.8	56.6	84 27.8	03.0	79 45.7	09.3	Betelgeuse	270 55.5	N 7 24.6
23	33 35.0	199 34.5	06.4	18 55.5	56.7	99 29.8	03.0	94 48.0	09.3			
9 00	48 37.5	214 34.1	S 4 07.6	33 58.2	N 4 56.7	114 31.8	S22 02.9	109 50.3	S21 09.2	Canopus	263 53.5	S52 42.2
01	63 40.0	229 33.7	08.8	49 00.9	56.8	129 33.9	02.8	124 52.6	09.2	Capella	280 26.5	N46 01.0
02	78 42.4	244 33.3	09.9	64 03.5	56.9	144 35.9	02.8	139 54.9	09.2	Deneb	49 28.1	N45 21.5
03	93 44.9	259 33.0 ..	11.1	79 06.2 ..	57.0	159 38.0 ..	02.7	154 57.2 ..	09.2	Denebola	182 28.6	N14 27.5
04	108 47.3	274 32.6	12.2	94 08.9	57.1	174 40.0	02.6	169 59.5	09.1	Diphda	348 50.5	S17 52.4
05	123 49.8	289 32.2	13.4	109 11.6	57.2	189 42.1	02.6	185 01.8	09.1			
06	138 52.3	304 31.8	S 4 14.5	124 14.3	N 4 57.2	204 44.1	S22 02.5	200 04.1	S21 09.1	Dubhe	193 45.6	N61 38.2
07	153 54.7	319 31.4	15.7	139 16.9	57.3	219 46.2	02.5	215 06.4	09.0	Elnath	278 05.8	N28 37.4
08	168 57.2	334 31.1	16.9	154 19.6	57.4	234 48.2	02.4	230 08.7	09.0	Eltanin	90 44.2	N51 29.4
M 09	183 59.7	349 30.7 ..	18.0	169 22.3 ..	57.5	249 50.2 ..	02.3	245 11.0 ..	09.0	Enif	33 42.1	N 9 58.3
O 10	199 02.1	4 30.3	19.2	184 24.9	57.6	264 52.3	02.3	260 13.3	08.9	Fomalhaut	15 18.2	S29 30.9
N 11	214 04.6	19 29.9	20.3	199 27.6	57.7	279 54.3	02.2	275 15.6	08.9			
D 12	229 07.1	34 29.5	S 4 21.5	214 30.3	N 4 57.8	294 56.4	S22 02.1	290 17.9	S21 08.9	Gacrux	171 55.8	S57 13.4
A 13	244 09.5	49 29.2	22.6	229 32.9	57.8	309 58.4	02.1	305 20.2	08.9	Gienah	175 47.3	S17 39.2
Y 14	259 12.0	64 28.8	23.8	244 35.6	57.9	325 00.5	02.0	320 22.5	08.8	Hadar	148 41.4	S60 28.1
15	274 14.4	79 28.4 ..	25.0	259 38.3 ..	58.0	340 02.5 ..	01.9	335 24.7 ..	08.8	Hamal	327 54.7	N23 33.6
16	289 16.9	94 28.0	26.1	274 40.9	58.1	355 04.5	01.9	350 27.0	08.8	Kaus Aust.	83 37.3	S34 22.5
17	304 19.4	109 27.6	27.3	289 43.6	58.2	10 06.6	01.8	5 29.3	08.7			
18	319 21.8	124 27.3	S 4 28.4	304 46.2	N 4 58.3	25 08.6	S22 01.8	20 31.6	S21 08.7	Kochab	137 21.1	N74 04.3
19	334 24.3	139 26.9	29.6	319 48.9	58.4	40 10.7	01.7	35 33.9	08.7	Markab	13 33.1	N15 19.1
20	349 26.8	154 26.5	30.7	334 51.6	58.5	55 12.7	01.6	50 36.2	08.7	Menkar	314 09.4	N 4 10.2
21	4 29.2	169 26.1 ..	31.9	349 54.2 ..	58.6	70 14.7 ..	01.6	65 38.5 ..	08.6	Menkent	148 02.0	S36 28.1
22	19 31.7	184 25.7	33.0	4 56.9	58.7	85 16.8	01.5	80 40.8	08.6	Miaplacidus	221 38.8	S69 47.7
23	34 34.2	199 25.3	34.2	19 59.5	58.7	100 18.8	01.4	95 43.1	08.6			
10 00	49 36.6	214 24.9	S 4 35.4	35 02.2	N 4 58.8	115 20.9	S22 01.4	110 45.4	S21 08.5	Mirfak	308 32.5	N49 56.0
01	64 39.1	229 24.6	36.5	50 04.8	58.9	130 22.9	01.3	125 47.7	08.5	Nunki	75 52.2	S26 16.2
02	79 41.6	244 24.2	37.7	65 07.5	59.0	145 24.9	01.2	140 50.0	08.5	Peacock	53 11.3	S56 40.3
03	94 44.0	259 23.8 ..	38.8	80 10.1 ..	59.1	160 27.0 ..	01.2	155 52.2 ..	08.4	Pollux	243 21.3	N27 58.5
04	109 46.5	274 23.4	40.0	95 12.8	59.2	175 29.0	01.1	170 54.5	08.4	Procyon	244 54.3	N 5 10.3
05	124 48.9	289 23.0	41.1	110 15.4	59.3	190 31.1	01.1	185 56.8	08.4			
06	139 51.4	304 22.6	S 4 42.3	125 18.1	N 4 59.4	205 33.1	S22 01.0	200 59.1	S21 08.4	Rasalhague	96 02.0	N12 32.9
07	154 53.9	319 22.3	43.4	140 20.7	59.5	220 35.1	00.9	216 01.4	08.3	Regulus	207 38.1	N11 52.0
T 08	169 56.3	334 21.9	44.6	155 23.3	59.6	235 37.2	00.9	231 03.7	08.3	Rigel	281 06.8	S 8 10.6
U 09	184 58.8	349 21.5 ..	45.8	170 26.0 ..	59.7	250 39.2 ..	00.8	246 06.0 ..	08.3	Rigil Kent.	139 45.5	S60 55.0
E 10	200 01.3	4 21.1	46.9	185 28.6	59.8	265 41.2	00.7	261 08.3	08.2	Sabik	102 07.0	S15 44.9
S 11	215 03.7	19 20.7	48.1	200 31.2	4 59.9	280 43.3	00.7	276 10.6	08.2			
D 12	230 06.2	34 20.3	S 4 49.2	215 33.9	N 5 00.0	295 45.3	S22 00.6	291 12.9	S21 08.2	Schedar	349 34.3	N56 39.2
A 13	245 08.7	49 19.9	50.4	230 36.5	00.1	310 47.4	00.5	306 15.1	08.2	Shaula	96 15.3	S37 07.1
Y 14	260 11.1	64 19.5	51.5	245 39.1	00.2	325 49.4	00.5	321 17.4	08.1	Sirius	258 29.0	S16 44.6
15	275 13.6	79 19.2 ..	52.7	260 41.8 ..	00.3	340 51.4 ..	00.4	336 19.7 ..	08.1	Spica	158 26.2	S11 15.9
16	290 16.1	94 18.8	53.8	275 44.4	00.4	355 53.5	00.3	351 22.0	08.1	Suhail	222 48.7	S43 30.7
17	305 18.5	109 18.4	55.0	290 47.0	00.5	10 55.5	00.3	6 24.3	08.0			
18	320 21.0	124 18.0	S 4 56.1	305 49.7	N 5 00.6	25 57.5	S22 00.2	21 26.6	S21 08.0	Vega	80 35.8	N38 48.4
19	335 23.4	139 17.6	57.3	320 52.3	00.7	40 59.6	00.2	36 28.9	08.0	Zuben'ubi	137 00.1	S16 07.5
20	350 25.9	154 17.2	58.5	335 54.9	00.8	56 01.6	00.1	51 31.2	07.9		SHA	Mer.Pass.
21	5 28.4	169 16.8	4 59.6	350 57.5 ..	00.9	71 03.6 ..	00.0	66 33.5 ..	07.9		° ′	h m
22	20 30.8	184 16.4	5 00.8	6 00.2	01.0	86 05.7	22 00.0	81 35.7	07.9	Venus	165 56.6	9 42
23	35 33.3	199 16.0	S 5 01.9	21 02.8	01.1	101 07.7	S21 59.9	96 38.0	07.8	Mars	345 20.7	21 40
Mer.Pass.	20 42.1 (h m)	v −0.4	d 1.2	v 2.7	d 0.1	v 2.0	d 0.1	v 2.3	d 0.0	Jupiter	65 54.4	16 20
										Saturn	61 12.8	16 38

UT	SUN GHA	SUN Dec	MOON GHA	v	MOON Dec	d	HP
d h	° ′	° ′	° ′	′	° ′	′	′
8 00	184 04.1	S16 38.1	275 04.1	9.0	N21 46.4	7.0	57.1
01	199 04.1	38.9	289 32.1	9.0	21 39.4	7.1	57.1
02	214 04.0	39.6	304 00.1	9.1	21 32.3	7.2	57.1
03	229 04.0 ..	40.3	318 28.2	9.0	21 25.1	7.4	57.2
04	244 03.9	41.0	332 56.2	9.1	21 17.7	7.5	57.2
05	259 03.9	41.7	347 24.3	9.1	21 10.2	7.6	57.2
06	274 03.9	S16 42.5	1 52.4	9.1	N21 02.6	7.7	57.3
07	289 03.8	43.2	16 20.5	9.1	20 54.9	7.9	57.3
S 08	304 03.8	43.9	30 48.6	9.2	20 47.0	8.0	57.3
U 09	319 03.7 ..	44.6	45 16.8	9.1	20 39.0	8.1	57.4
N 10	334 03.7	45.3	59 44.9	9.2	20 30.9	8.2	57.4
11	349 03.6	46.1	74 13.1	9.3	20 22.7	8.3	57.4
D 12	4 03.6	S16 46.8	88 41.4	9.2	N20 14.4	8.5	57.5
A 13	19 03.5	47.5	103 09.6	9.2	20 05.9	8.6	57.5
Y 14	34 03.5	48.2	117 37.8	9.3	19 57.3	8.7	57.5
15	49 03.4 ..	48.9	132 06.1	9.3	19 48.6	8.8	57.6
16	64 03.4	49.6	146 34.4	9.3	19 39.8	9.0	57.6
17	79 03.3	50.4	161 02.7	9.4	19 30.8	9.1	57.6
18	94 03.3	S16 51.1	175 31.1	9.3	N19 21.7	9.1	57.7
19	109 03.2	51.8	189 59.4	9.4	19 12.6	9.3	57.7
20	124 03.2	52.5	204 27.8	9.4	19 03.3	9.4	57.7
21	139 03.1 ..	53.2	218 56.2	9.5	18 53.9	9.6	57.8
22	154 03.1	53.9	233 24.7	9.4	18 44.3	9.6	57.8
23	169 03.0	54.6	247 53.1	9.5	18 34.7	9.8	57.8
9 00	184 03.0	S16 55.3	262 21.6	9.5	N18 24.9	9.8	57.9
01	199 02.9	56.1	276 50.1	9.5	18 15.1	10.0	57.9
02	214 02.8	56.8	291 18.6	9.5	18 05.1	10.1	58.0
03	229 02.8 ..	57.5	305 47.1	9.6	17 55.0	10.2	58.0
04	244 02.7	58.2	320 15.7	9.6	17 44.8	10.3	58.0
05	259 02.7	58.9	334 44.3	9.6	17 34.5	10.4	58.1
06	274 02.6	S16 59.6	349 12.9	9.6	N17 24.1	10.6	58.1
07	289 02.6	17 00.3	3 41.5	9.7	17 13.5	10.6	58.1
M 08	304 02.5	01.0	18 10.2	9.7	17 02.9	10.8	58.2
O 09	319 02.5 ..	01.7	32 38.9	9.6	16 52.1	10.8	58.2
N 10	334 02.4	02.4	47 07.5	9.8	16 41.3	11.0	58.2
11	349 02.3	03.1	61 36.3	9.7	16 30.3	11.0	58.3
D 12	4 02.3	S17 03.8	76 05.0	9.8	N16 19.3	11.2	58.3
A 13	19 02.2	04.6	90 33.8	9.7	16 08.1	11.3	58.3
Y 14	34 02.2	05.3	105 02.5	9.8	15 56.8	11.3	58.4
15	49 02.1 ..	06.0	119 31.3	9.9	15 45.5	11.5	58.4
16	64 02.1	06.7	134 00.2	9.8	15 34.0	11.6	58.5
17	79 02.0	07.4	148 29.0	9.9	15 22.4	11.6	58.5
18	94 01.9	S17 08.1	162 57.9	9.8	N15 10.8	11.8	58.5
19	109 01.9	08.8	177 26.7	9.9	14 59.0	11.9	58.6
20	124 01.8	09.5	191 55.6	9.9	14 47.1	11.9	58.6
21	139 01.7 ..	10.2	206 24.5	10.0	14 35.2	12.1	58.6
22	154 01.7	10.9	220 53.5	9.9	14 23.1	12.1	58.7
23	169 01.6	11.6	235 22.4	10.0	14 11.0	12.2	58.7
10 00	184 01.6	S17 12.3	249 51.4	10.0	N13 58.8	12.4	58.7
01	199 01.5	13.0	264 20.4	10.0	13 46.4	12.4	58.8
02	214 01.4	13.7	278 49.4	10.0	13 34.0	12.5	58.8
03	229 01.4 ..	14.4	293 18.4	10.0	13 21.5	12.6	58.9
04	244 01.3	15.1	307 47.4	10.1	13 08.9	12.7	58.9
05	259 01.2	15.8	322 16.5	10.0	12 56.2	12.8	58.9
06	274 01.2	S17 16.5	336 45.5	10.1	N12 43.4	12.9	59.0
07	289 01.1	17.2	351 14.6	10.1	12 30.5	12.9	59.0
T 08	304 01.1	17.9	5 43.7	10.1	12 17.6	13.0	59.1
U 09	319 01.0 ..	18.6	20 12.8	10.1	12 04.6	13.2	59.1
E 10	334 00.9	19.2	34 41.9	10.1	11 51.4	13.2	59.1
S 11	349 00.9	19.9	49 11.0	10.2	11 38.2	13.2	59.1
D 12	4 00.8	S17 20.6	63 40.2	10.1	N11 25.0	13.4	59.2
A 13	19 00.7	21.3	78 09.3	10.2	11 11.6	13.4	59.2
Y 14	34 00.7	22.0	92 38.5	10.1	10 58.2	13.6	59.2
15	49 00.6 ..	22.7	107 07.6	10.2	10 44.6	13.5	59.3
16	64 00.5	23.4	121 36.8	10.2	10 31.1	13.7	59.3
17	79 00.4	24.1	136 06.0	10.2	10 17.4	13.7	59.4
18	94 00.4	S17 24.8	150 35.2	10.2	N10 03.7	13.9	59.4
19	109 00.3	25.5	165 04.4	10.2	9 49.8	13.8	59.4
20	124 00.2	26.2	179 33.6	10.2	9 36.0	14.0	59.5
21	139 00.2 ..	26.9	194 02.8	10.2	9 22.0	14.0	59.5
22	154 00.1	27.5	208 32.0	10.2	9 08.0	14.1	59.5
23	169 00.0	28.2	223 01.2	10.2	N 8 53.9	14.2	59.6
	SD 16.2	d 0.7	SD 15.7		15.9		16.1

Lat.	Twilight Naut.	Twilight Civil	Sunrise	Moonrise 8	Moonrise 9	Moonrise 10	Moonrise 11
°	h m	h m	h m	h m	h m	h m	h m
N 72	06 39	08 08	09 57	▭	21 50	24 22	00 22
N 70	06 31	07 49	09 15	19 38	22 22	24 36	00 36
68	06 24	07 35	08 47	20 33	22 44	24 47	00 47
66	06 19	07 23	08 26	21 06	23 02	24 56	00 56
64	06 14	07 13	08 09	21 30	23 16	25 03	01 03
62	06 09	07 04	07 55	21 49	23 28	25 09	01 09
60	06 06	06 56	07 44	22 04	23 38	25 15	01 15
N 58	06 02	06 50	07 34	22 17	23 47	25 20	01 20
56	05 59	06 44	07 25	22 28	23 55	25 24	01 24
54	05 55	06 38	07 17	22 38	24 02	00 02	01 28
52	05 53	06 33	07 10	22 47	24 08	00 08	01 31
50	05 50	06 29	07 04	22 55	24 13	00 13	01 34
45	05 43	06 19	06 50	23 11	24 25	00 25	01 41
N 40	05 38	06 10	06 39	23 25	24 35	00 35	01 47
35	05 32	06 02	06 29	23 36	24 43	00 43	01 51
30	05 27	05 55	06 20	23 46	24 50	00 50	01 56
20	05 16	05 43	06 06	24 03	00 03	01 03	02 03
N 10	05 05	05 31	05 53	24 18	00 18	01 14	02 09
0	04 54	05 19	05 40	24 32	00 32	01 24	02 15
S 10	04 40	05 06	05 28	24 46	00 46	01 34	02 21
20	04 24	04 51	05 15	00 14	01 01	01 45	02 28
30	04 03	04 33	04 59	00 35	01 18	01 57	02 35
35	03 49	04 23	04 50	00 47	01 27	02 04	02 39
40	03 33	04 10	04 40	01 00	01 39	02 13	02 44
45	03 13	03 54	04 28	01 17	01 52	02 22	02 49
S 50	02 46	03 35	04 13	01 37	02 07	02 33	02 55
52	02 32	03 25	04 06	01 46	02 15	02 38	02 58
54	02 15	03 15	03 58	01 57	02 23	02 44	03 02
56	01 55	03 02	03 49	02 09	02 32	02 50	03 05
58	01 28	02 48	03 39	02 22	02 43	02 57	03 09
S 60	00 47	02 31	03 28	02 39	02 54	03 05	03 13

Lat.	Sunset	Twilight Civil	Twilight Naut.	Moonset 8	Moonset 9	Moonset 10	Moonset 11
°	h m	h m	h m	h m	h m	h m	h m
N 72	13 29	15 18	16 47	▭	16 54	16 10	15 40
N 70	14 11	15 37	16 55	17 15	16 21	15 54	15 34
68	14 39	15 52	17 02	16 19	15 56	15 41	15 29
66	15 01	16 04	17 08	15 45	15 37	15 31	15 24
64	15 17	16 14	17 13	15 20	15 22	15 22	15 21
62	15 31	16 23	17 17	15 01	15 09	15 14	15 17
60	15 43	16 31	17 21	14 44	14 58	15 07	15 14
N 58	15 53	16 37	17 25	14 31	14 48	15 01	15 12
56	16 02	16 43	17 28	14 19	14 39	14 56	15 10
54	16 11	16 49	17 31	14 08	14 32	14 51	15 07
52	16 17	16 54	17 34	13 59	14 25	14 47	15 06
50	16 24	16 58	17 37	13 51	14 19	14 43	15 04
45	16 37	17 09	17 44	13 33	14 05	14 34	15 00
N 40	16 49	17 17	17 50	13 19	13 54	14 27	14 57
35	16 58	17 25	17 55	13 06	13 45	14 20	14 54
30	17 07	17 32	18 01	12 55	13 37	14 15	14 51
20	17 22	17 45	18 11	12 37	13 22	14 05	14 47
N 10	17 35	17 57	18 22	12 20	13 09	13 57	14 43
0	17 47	18 09	18 34	12 05	12 57	13 48	14 39
S 10	18 00	18 22	18 48	11 49	12 45	13 40	14 35
20	18 13	18 37	19 04	11 33	12 32	13 31	14 32
30	18 29	18 55	19 26	11 13	12 17	13 21	14 27
35	18 38	19 06	19 39	11 02	12 08	13 15	14 24
40	18 49	19 19	19 55	10 49	11 58	13 09	14 21
45	19 01	19 34	20 16	10 34	11 46	13 01	14 18
S 50	19 16	19 54	20 44	10 15	11 32	12 51	14 13
52	19 23	20 04	20 58	10 06	11 25	12 47	14 11
54	19 31	20 15	21 15	09 56	11 17	12 42	14 09
56	19 40	20 27	21 36	09 44	11 09	12 37	14 07
58	19 50	20 42	22 03	09 31	10 59	12 31	14 04
S 60	20 02	21 00	22 49	09 15	10 48	12 24	14 01

	SUN Eqn. of Time 00h	SUN Eqn. of Time 12h	SUN Mer. Pass.	MOON Mer. Pass. Upper	MOON Mer. Pass. Lower	Age	Phase
Day	m s	m s	h m	h m	h m	d	%
8	16 17	16 14	11 44	05 52	18 19	23	51
9	16 12	16 09	11 44	06 45	19 11	24	40
10	16 06	16 03	11 44	07 36	20 02	25	29

UT	ARIES GHA	VENUS −3.9 GHA	Dec	MARS −1.8 GHA	Dec	JUPITER −2.1 GHA	Dec	SATURN +0.6 GHA	Dec
11 00	50 35.8	214 15.7	S 5 03.1	36 05.4	N 5 01.2	116 09.7	S21 59.8	111 40.3	S21 07.8
01	65 38.2	229 15.3	04.2	51 08.0	01.3	131 11.8	59.8	126 42.6	07.8
02	80 40.7	244 14.9	05.4	66 10.6	01.4	146 13.8	59.7	141 44.9	07.8
03	95 43.2	259 14.5 ..	06.5	81 13.2 ..	01.5	161 15.8 ..	59.6	156 47.2 ..	07.7
04	110 45.6	274 14.1	07.7	96 15.9	01.6	176 17.9	59.6	171 49.5	07.7
05	125 48.1	289 13.7	08.8	111 18.5	01.7	191 19.9	59.5	186 51.8	07.7
W 06	140 50.5	304 13.3	S 5 10.0	126 21.1	N 5 01.8	206 21.9	S21 59.4	201 54.0	S21 07.6
E 07	155 53.0	319 12.9	11.1	141 23.7	01.9	221 24.0	59.4	216 56.3	07.6
D 08	170 55.5	334 12.5	12.3	156 26.3	02.0	236 26.0	59.3	231 58.6	07.6
N 09	185 57.9	349 12.1 ..	13.4	171 28.9 ..	02.2	251 28.0 ..	59.2	247 00.9 ..	07.5
E 10	201 00.4	4 11.7	14.6	186 31.5	02.3	266 30.1	59.2	262 03.2	07.5
S 11	216 02.9	19 11.4	15.7	201 34.1	02.4	281 32.1	59.1	277 05.5	07.5
D 12	231 05.3	34 11.0	S 5 16.9	216 36.7	N 5 02.5	296 34.1	S21 59.0	292 07.8	S21 07.5
A 13	246 07.8	49 10.6	18.0	231 39.3	02.6	311 36.2	59.0	307 10.1	07.4
Y 14	261 10.3	64 10.2	19.2	246 41.9	02.7	326 38.2	58.9	322 12.3	07.4
15	276 12.7	79 09.8 ..	20.3	261 44.5 ..	02.8	341 40.2 ..	58.8	337 14.6 ..	07.4
16	291 15.2	94 09.4	21.5	276 47.1	02.9	356 42.3	58.8	352 16.9	07.3
17	306 17.7	109 09.0	22.6	291 49.7	03.0	11 44.3	58.7	7 19.2	07.3
18	321 20.1	124 08.6	S 5 23.8	306 52.3	N 5 03.1	26 46.3	S21 58.6	22 21.5	S21 07.3
19	336 22.6	139 08.2	25.0	321 54.9	03.3	41 48.4	58.6	37 23.8	07.2
20	351 25.0	154 07.8	26.1	336 57.5	03.4	56 50.4	58.5	52 26.0	07.2
21	6 27.5	169 07.4 ..	27.3	352 00.1 ..	03.5	71 52.4 ..	58.4	67 28.3 ..	07.2
22	21 30.0	184 07.0	28.4	7 02.7	03.6	86 54.4	58.4	82 30.6	07.1
23	36 32.4	199 06.6	29.6	22 05.3	03.7	101 56.5	58.3	97 32.9	07.1
12 00	51 34.9	214 06.2	S 5 30.7	37 07.8	N 5 03.8	116 58.5	S21 58.2	112 35.2	S21 07.1
01	66 37.4	229 05.8	31.9	52 10.4	03.9	132 00.5	58.2	127 37.5	07.1
02	81 39.8	244 05.4	33.0	67 13.0	04.0	147 02.6	58.1	142 39.8	07.0
03	96 42.3	259 05.0 ..	34.2	82 15.6 ..	04.2	162 04.6 ..	58.0	157 42.0 ..	07.0
04	111 44.8	274 04.6	35.3	97 18.2	04.3	177 06.6	58.0	172 44.3	07.0
05	126 47.2	289 04.2	36.5	112 20.8	04.4	192 08.6	57.9	187 46.6	06.9
T 06	141 49.7	304 03.8	S 5 37.6	127 23.3	N 5 04.5	207 10.7	S21 57.8	202 48.9	S21 06.9
H 07	156 52.1	319 03.4	38.8	142 25.9	04.6	222 12.7	57.8	217 51.2	06.9
U 08	171 54.6	334 03.1	39.9	157 28.5	04.7	237 14.7	57.7	232 53.5	06.8
R 09	186 57.1	349 02.7 ..	41.1	172 31.1 ..	04.9	252 16.8 ..	57.6	247 55.7 ..	06.8
S 10	201 59.5	4 02.3	42.2	187 33.6	05.0	267 18.8	57.6	262 58.0	06.8
D 11	217 02.0	19 01.9	43.3	202 36.2	05.1	282 20.8	57.5	278 00.3	06.7
A 12	232 04.5	34 01.5	S 5 44.5	217 38.8	N 5 05.2	297 22.8	S21 57.4	293 02.6	S21 06.7
Y 13	247 06.9	49 01.1	45.6	232 41.4	05.3	312 24.9	57.4	308 04.9	06.7
14	262 09.4	64 00.7	46.8	247 43.9	05.5	327 26.9	57.3	323 07.2	06.6
15	277 11.9	79 00.3 ..	47.9	262 46.5 ..	05.6	342 28.9 ..	57.2	338 09.4 ..	06.6
16	292 14.3	93 59.9	49.1	277 49.1	05.7	357 30.9	57.2	353 11.7	06.6
17	307 16.8	108 59.5	50.2	292 51.6	05.8	12 33.0	57.1	8 14.0	06.6
18	322 19.3	123 59.1	S 5 51.4	307 54.2	N 5 05.9	27 35.0	S21 57.0	23 16.3	S21 06.5
19	337 21.7	138 58.7	52.5	322 56.7	06.1	42 37.0	57.0	38 18.6	06.5
20	352 24.2	153 58.3	53.7	337 59.3	06.2	57 39.0	56.9	53 20.8	06.5
21	7 26.6	168 57.9 ..	54.8	353 01.9 ..	06.3	72 41.1 ..	56.8	68 23.1 ..	06.4
22	22 29.1	183 57.5	56.0	8 04.4	06.4	87 43.1	56.8	83 25.4	06.4
23	37 31.6	198 57.1	57.1	23 07.0	06.6	102 45.1	56.7	98 27.7	06.4
13 00	52 34.0	213 56.7	S 5 58.3	38 09.5	N 5 06.7	117 47.1	S21 56.6	113 30.0	S21 06.3
01	67 36.5	228 56.2	5 59.4	53 12.1	06.8	132 49.2	56.6	128 32.2	06.3
02	82 39.0	243 55.8	6 00.6	68 14.6	06.9	147 51.2	56.5	143 34.5	06.3
03	97 41.4	258 55.4 ..	01.7	83 17.2 ..	07.1	162 53.2 ..	56.4	158 36.8 ..	06.2
04	112 43.9	273 55.0	02.9	98 19.7	07.2	177 55.2	56.4	173 39.1	06.2
05	127 46.4	288 54.6	04.0	113 22.3	07.3	192 57.3	56.3	188 41.4	06.2
F 06	142 48.8	303 54.2	S 6 05.1	128 24.8	N 5 07.5	207 59.3	S21 56.2	203 43.6	S21 06.1
R 07	157 51.3	318 53.8	06.3	143 27.4	07.6	223 01.3	56.2	218 45.9	06.1
I 08	172 53.8	333 53.4	07.4	158 29.9	07.7	238 03.3	56.1	233 48.2	06.1
D 09	187 56.2	348 53.0 ..	08.6	173 32.5 ..	07.8	253 05.3 ..	56.0	248 50.5 ..	06.0
A 10	202 58.7	3 52.6	09.7	188 35.0	08.0	268 07.4	56.0	263 52.8	06.0
Y 11	218 01.1	18 52.2	10.9	203 37.5	08.1	283 09.4	55.9	278 55.0	06.0
12	233 03.6	33 51.8	S 6 12.0	218 40.1	N 5 08.2	298 11.4	S21 55.8	293 57.3	S21 05.9
13	248 06.1	48 51.4	13.2	233 42.6	08.4	313 13.4	55.8	308 59.6	05.9
14	263 08.5	63 51.0	14.3	248 45.2	08.5	328 15.5	55.7	324 01.9	05.9
15	278 11.0	78 50.6 ..	15.5	263 47.7 ..	08.6	343 17.5 ..	55.6	339 04.2 ..	05.8
16	293 13.5	93 50.2	16.6	278 50.2	08.8	358 19.5	55.5	354 06.4	05.8
17	308 15.9	108 49.8	17.7	293 52.8	08.9	13 21.5	55.5	9 08.7	05.8
18	323 18.4	123 49.4	S 6 18.9	308 55.3	N 5 09.0	28 23.5	S21 55.4	24 11.0	S21 05.8
19	338 20.9	138 49.0	20.0	323 57.8	09.1	43 25.6	55.3	39 13.3	05.7
20	353 23.3	153 48.6	21.2	339 00.3	09.3	58 27.6	55.3	54 15.6	05.7
21	8 25.8	168 48.1 ..	22.3	354 02.9 ..	09.4	73 29.6 ..	55.2	69 17.8 ..	05.7
22	23 28.2	183 47.7	23.5	9 05.4	09.6	88 31.6	55.1	84 20.1	05.6
23	38 30.7	198 47.3	24.6	24 07.9	09.7	103 33.6	55.1	99 22.4	05.6
Mer. Pass.	20 30.3	v −0.4	d 1.1	v 2.6	d 0.1	v 2.0	d 0.1	v 2.3	d 0.0

STARS

Name	SHA	Dec
Acamar	315 14.0	S40 13.4
Achernar	335 22.3	S57 08.1
Acrux	173 04.2	S63 12.5
Adhara	255 08.3	S28 59.8
Aldebaran	290 43.2	N16 33.0
Alioth	166 16.5	N55 50.8
Alkaid	152 55.2	N49 12.6
Alnair	27 37.2	S46 51.8
Alnilam	275 40.9	S 1 11.3
Alphard	217 51.1	S 8 44.8
Alphecca	126 07.0	N26 38.9
Alpheratz	357 38.0	N29 12.4
Altair	62 03.4	N 8 55.5
Ankaa	353 10.3	S42 11.8
Antares	112 20.4	S26 28.5
Arcturus	145 51.4	N19 04.6
Atria	107 18.1	S69 03.8
Avior	234 15.8	S59 34.2
Bellatrix	278 26.2	N 6 22.1
Betelgeuse	270 55.5	N 7 24.6
Canopus	263 53.5	S52 42.2
Capella	280 26.5	N46 01.0
Deneb	49 28.2	N45 21.5
Denebola	182 28.6	N14 27.5
Diphda	348 50.5	S17 52.4
Dubhe	193 45.6	N61 38.2
Elnath	278 05.8	N28 37.4
Eltanin	90 44.2	N51 29.4
Enif	33 42.1	N 9 58.3
Fomalhaut	15 18.2	S29 30.9
Gacrux	171 55.7	S57 13.4
Gienah	175 47.3	S17 39.2
Hadar	148 41.3	S60 28.1
Hamal	327 54.7	N23 33.6
Kaus Aust.	83 37.3	S34 22.5
Kochab	137 21.1	N74 04.2
Markab	13 33.1	N15 19.1
Menkar	314 09.4	N 4 10.2
Menkent	148 02.0	S36 28.1
Miaplacidus	221 38.7	S69 47.8
Mirfak	308 32.5	N49 56.0
Nunki	75 52.2	S26 16.2
Peacock	53 11.3	S56 40.3
Pollux	243 21.3	N27 58.5
Procyon	244 54.2	N 5 10.3
Rasalhague	96 02.0	N12 32.9
Regulus	207 38.1	N11 52.0
Rigel	281 06.8	S 8 10.6
Rigil Kent.	139 45.5	S60 55.0
Sabik	102 07.0	S15 44.9
Schedar	349 34.3	N56 39.2
Shaula	96 15.3	S37 07.1
Sirius	258 29.0	S16 44.6
Spica	158 26.2	S11 16.0
Suhail	222 48.7	S43 30.7
Vega	80 35.8	N38 48.4
Zuben'ubi	137 00.1	S16 07.5

	SHA	Mer. Pass.
Venus	162 31.3	9 44
Mars	345 32.9	21 28
Jupiter	65 23.6	16 10
Saturn	61 00.3	16 27

UT	SUN GHA	SUN Dec	MOON GHA	v	MOON Dec	d	HP
d h	° ′	° ′	° ′	′	° ′	′	′
11 00	184 00.0	S17 28.9	237 30.4	10.2	N 8 39.7	14.2	59.6
01	198 59.9	29.6	251 59.6	10.2	8 25.5	14.3	59.6
02	213 59.8	30.3	266 28.8	10.2	8 11.2	14.3	59.7
03	228 59.7	.. 31.0	280 58.0	10.3	7 56.9	14.4	59.7
04	243 59.7	31.7	295 27.3	10.2	7 42.5	14.5	59.7
05	258 59.6	32.3	309 56.5	10.2	7 28.0	14.5	59.8
06	273 59.5	S17 33.0	324 25.7	10.2	N 7 13.5	14.6	59.8
W 07	288 59.4	33.7	338 54.9	10.2	6 58.9	14.7	59.8
E 08	303 59.4	34.4	353 24.1	10.2	6 44.2	14.7	59.9
D 09	318 59.3	.. 35.1	7 53.3	10.2	6 29.5	14.7	59.9
N 10	333 59.2	35.8	22 22.5	10.2	6 14.8	14.8	59.9
E 11	348 59.1	36.4	36 51.7	10.1	6 00.0	14.9	60.0
S 12	3 59.1	S17 37.1	51 20.8	10.2	N 5 45.1	14.9	60.0
D 13	18 59.0	37.8	65 50.0	10.2	5 30.2	14.9	60.0
A 14	33 58.9	38.5	80 19.2	10.1	5 15.3	15.0	60.1
Y 15	48 58.8	.. 39.2	94 48.3	10.2	5 00.3	15.1	60.1
16	63 58.8	39.8	109 17.5	10.1	4 45.2	15.0	60.1
17	78 58.7	40.5	123 46.6	10.1	4 30.2	15.2	60.1
18	93 58.6	S17 41.2	138 15.7	10.1	N 4 15.0	15.1	60.2
19	108 58.5	41.9	152 44.8	10.1	3 59.9	15.2	60.2
20	123 58.4	42.6	167 13.9	10.0	3 44.7	15.3	60.2
21	138 58.4	.. 43.2	181 42.9	10.1	3 29.4	15.2	60.3
22	153 58.3	43.9	196 12.0	10.0	3 14.2	15.4	60.3
23	168 58.2	44.6	210 41.0	10.0	2 58.8	15.3	60.3
12 00	183 58.1	S17 45.3	225 10.0	10.0	N 2 43.5	15.4	60.4
01	198 58.0	45.9	239 39.0	10.0	2 28.1	15.4	60.4
02	213 58.0	46.6	254 08.0	10.0	2 12.7	15.4	60.4
03	228 57.9	.. 47.3	268 37.0	9.9	1 57.3	15.5	60.4
04	243 57.8	47.9	283 05.9	9.9	1 41.8	15.5	60.5
05	258 57.7	48.6	297 34.8	9.9	1 26.3	15.5	60.5
06	273 57.6	S17 49.3	312 03.7	9.8	N 1 10.8	15.5	60.5
T 07	288 57.6	50.0	326 32.5	9.9	0 55.3	15.6	60.5
H 08	303 57.5	50.6	341 01.4	9.8	0 39.7	15.5	60.6
U 09	318 57.4	.. 51.3	355 30.2	9.8	0 24.2	15.6	60.6
R 10	333 57.3	52.0	9 59.0	9.7	N 0 08.6	15.6	60.6
S 11	348 57.2	52.6	24 27.7	9.7	S 0 07.0	15.6	60.6
D 12	3 57.1	S17 53.3	38 56.4	9.7	S 0 22.6	15.6	60.7
A 13	18 57.1	54.0	53 25.1	9.7	0 38.2	15.7	60.7
Y 14	33 57.0	54.6	67 53.8	9.6	0 53.9	15.6	60.7
15	48 56.9	.. 55.3	82 22.4	9.6	1 09.5	15.7	60.7
16	63 56.8	56.0	96 51.0	9.5	1 25.2	15.6	60.8
17	78 56.7	56.6	111 19.5	9.5	1 40.8	15.7	60.8
18	93 56.6	S17 57.3	125 48.0	9.5	S 1 56.5	15.6	60.8
19	108 56.5	58.0	140 16.5	9.4	2 12.1	15.7	60.8
20	123 56.4	58.6	154 44.9	9.4	2 27.8	15.6	60.8
21	138 56.4	17 59.3	169 13.3	9.4	2 43.4	15.7	60.9
22	153 56.3	18 00.0	183 41.7	9.3	2 59.1	15.6	60.9
23	168 56.2	00.6	198 10.0	9.3	3 14.7	15.7	60.9
13 00	183 56.1	S18 01.3	212 38.3	9.2	S 3 30.4	15.6	60.9
01	198 56.0	02.0	227 06.5	9.2	3 46.0	15.6	60.9
02	213 55.9	02.6	241 34.7	9.2	4 01.6	15.6	61.0
03	228 55.8	.. 03.3	256 02.9	9.1	4 17.2	15.6	61.0
04	243 55.7	03.9	270 31.0	9.0	4 32.8	15.6	61.0
05	258 55.6	04.6	284 59.0	9.1	4 48.4	15.5	61.0
06	273 55.5	S18 05.2	299 27.1	8.9	S 5 03.9	15.5	61.0
07	288 55.5	05.9	313 55.0	8.9	5 19.4	15.5	61.0
08	303 55.4	06.6	328 22.9	8.9	5 34.9	15.5	61.1
F 09	318 55.3	.. 07.2	342 50.8	8.8	5 50.4	15.5	61.1
R 10	333 55.2	07.9	357 18.6	8.8	6 05.9	15.4	61.1
I 11	348 55.1	08.5	11 46.4	8.7	6 21.3	15.4	61.1
D 12	3 55.0	S18 09.2	26 14.1	8.7	S 6 36.7	15.3	61.1
A 13	18 54.9	09.8	40 41.8	8.6	6 52.0	15.3	61.1
Y 14	33 54.8	10.5	55 09.4	8.5	7 07.4	15.2	61.1
15	48 54.7	.. 11.2	69 36.9	8.5	7 22.6	15.3	61.2
16	63 54.6	11.8	84 04.4	8.4	7 37.9	15.2	61.2
17	78 54.5	12.5	98 31.8	8.4	7 53.1	15.2	61.2
18	93 54.4	S18 13.1	112 59.2	8.4	S 8 08.3	15.1	61.2
19	108 54.3	13.8	127 26.6	8.2	8 23.4	15.1	61.2
20	123 54.2	14.4	141 53.8	8.2	8 38.5	15.0	61.2
21	138 54.1	.. 15.1	156 21.0	8.2	8 53.5	15.0	61.2
22	153 54.0	15.7	170 48.2	8.1	9 08.5	14.9	61.2
23	168 53.9	16.4	185 15.3	8.0	S 9 23.4	14.9	61.2
	SD 16.2	d 0.7	SD 16.3		16.5		16.7

Twilight / Sunrise / Moonrise

Lat.	Naut.	Civil	Sunrise	Moonrise 11	12	13	14
°	h m	h m	h m	h m	h m	h m	h m
N 72	06 50	08 22	10 26	00 22	02 42	05 03	07 36
N 70	06 41	08 01	09 33	00 36	02 45	04 55	07 14
68	06 33	07 45	09 01	00 47	02 47	04 49	06 58
66	06 27	07 32	08 37	00 56	02 49	04 44	06 45
64	06 21	07 21	08 19	01 03	02 50	04 40	06 34
62	06 16	07 11	08 04	01 09	02 52	04 36	06 25
60	06 12	07 03	07 51	01 15	02 53	04 33	06 17
N 58	06 08	06 56	07 41	01 20	02 54	04 30	06 10
56	06 04	06 49	07 31	01 24	02 55	04 28	06 04
54	06 00	06 43	07 23	01 28	02 56	04 26	05 58
52	05 57	06 38	07 15	01 31	02 56	04 24	05 53
50	05 54	06 33	07 08	01 34	02 57	04 22	05 49
45	05 47	06 22	06 54	01 41	02 59	04 18	05 40
N 40	05 41	06 13	06 42	01 47	03 00	04 15	05 32
35	05 35	06 05	06 32	01 51	03 01	04 12	05 25
30	05 29	05 58	06 23	01 56	03 02	04 10	05 19
20	05 18	05 44	06 07	02 03	03 04	04 06	05 09
N 10	05 06	05 32	05 54	02 09	03 05	04 02	05 01
0	04 54	05 19	05 41	02 15	03 06	03 59	04 53
S 10	04 39	05 05	05 28	02 21	03 08	03 55	04 45
20	04 22	04 50	05 14	02 28	03 09	03 52	04 36
30	04 04	04 31	04 57	02 35	03 11	03 48	04 27
35	03 46	04 20	04 48	02 39	03 12	03 46	04 21
40	03 29	04 07	04 37	02 44	03 13	03 43	04 15
45	03 08	03 50	04 24	02 49	03 15	03 40	04 08
S 50	02 39	03 30	04 08	02 55	03 16	03 37	03 59
52	02 24	03 20	04 01	02 58	03 17	03 35	03 56
54	02 07	03 08	03 53	03 02	03 18	03 34	03 51
56	01 44	02 55	03 43	03 05	03 18	03 32	03 47
58	01 14	02 40	03 33	03 09	03 19	03 30	03 41
S 60	00 14	02 21	03 21	03 13	03 20	03 27	03 36

Sunset / Twilight / Moonset

Lat.	Sunset	Civil	Naut.	Moonset 11	12	13	14
°	h m	h m	h m	h m	h m	h m	h m
N 72	13 01	15 05	16 37	15 40	15 14	14 45	14 08
N 70	13 54	15 26	16 46	15 34	15 16	14 56	14 32
68	14 27	15 42	16 54	15 29	15 17	15 05	14 50
66	14 50	15 56	17 00	15 24	15 18	15 12	15 05
64	15 09	16 07	17 06	15 21	15 19	15 18	15 18
62	15 24	16 16	17 11	15 17	15 20	15 24	15 28
60	15 36	16 24	17 16	15 14	15 21	15 28	15 37
N 58	15 47	16 32	17 20	15 12	15 22	15 33	15 45
56	15 57	16 38	17 24	15 10	15 23	15 36	15 52
54	16 05	16 44	17 27	15 07	15 23	15 40	15 59
52	16 13	16 50	17 31	15 06	15 24	15 43	16 04
50	16 21	16 55	17 34	15 04	15 24	15 46	16 10
45	16 34	17 05	17 41	15 00	15 25	15 52	16 21
N 40	16 46	17 15	17 47	14 57	15 26	15 57	16 30
35	16 56	17 23	17 53	14 54	15 27	16 01	16 38
30	17 05	17 30	17 59	14 51	15 28	16 05	16 46
20	17 21	17 44	18 11	14 47	15 29	16 12	16 58
N 10	17 35	17 57	18 22	14 43	15 30	16 18	17 09
0	17 48	18 09	18 35	14 39	15 31	16 24	17 19
S 10	18 01	18 23	18 49	14 36	15 32	16 30	17 29
20	18 15	18 39	19 06	14 32	15 33	16 36	17 41
30	18 31	18 57	19 29	14 27	15 34	16 43	17 53
35	18 41	19 09	19 43	14 24	15 35	16 47	18 01
40	18 52	19 22	20 00	14 21	15 35	16 51	18 09
45	19 05	19 39	20 22	14 18	15 36	16 57	18 19
S 50	19 21	20 00	20 51	14 13	15 37	17 03	18 31
52	19 29	20 10	21 06	14 11	15 37	17 06	18 36
54	19 37	20 22	21 24	14 09	15 38	17 09	18 42
56	19 46	20 35	21 47	14 07	15 38	17 13	18 49
58	19 57	20 51	22 20	14 04	15 39	17 17	18 57
S 60	20 10	21 10	////	14 01	15 40	17 21	19 06

SUN / MOON

Day	Eqn. of Time 00h	Eqn. of Time 12h	Mer. Pass.	Mer. Pass. Upper	Mer. Pass. Lower	Age	Phase
d	m s	m s	h m	h m	h m	d	%
11	16 00	15 56	11 44	08 27	20 53	26	19
12	15 53	15 49	11 44	09 19	21 45	27	11
13	15 45	15 40	11 44	10 11	22 38	28	5

UT	ARIES GHA	VENUS −3.9 GHA	VENUS Dec	MARS −1.7 GHA	MARS Dec	JUPITER −2.1 GHA	JUPITER Dec	SATURN +0.6 GHA	SATURN Dec	STARS Name	SHA	Dec
14 00	53 33.2	213 46.9	S 6 25.7	39 10.4	N 5 09.8	118 35.7	S21 55.0	114 24.7	S21 05.6	Acamar	315 14.0	S40 13.4
01	68 35.6	228 46.5	26.9	54 13.0	10.0	133 37.7	54.9	129 26.9	05.5	Achernar	335 22.3	S57 08.1
02	83 38.1	243 46.1	28.0	69 15.5	10.1	148 39.7	54.9	144 29.2	05.5	Acrux	173 04.2	S63 12.5
03	98 40.6	258 45.7	.. 29.2	84 18.0	.. 10.2	163 41.7	.. 54.8	159 31.5	.. 05.5	Adhara	255 08.3	S28 59.9
04	113 43.0	273 45.3	30.3	99 20.5	10.4	178 43.7	54.7	174 33.8	05.4	Aldebaran	290 43.2	N16 33.0
05	128 45.5	288 44.9	31.5	114 23.0	10.5	193 45.7	54.7	189 36.0	05.4			
06	143 48.0	303 44.5	S 6 32.6	129 25.5	N 5 10.6	208 47.8	S21 54.6	204 38.3	S21 05.4	Alioth	166 16.5	N55 50.8
07	158 50.4	318 44.1	33.7	144 28.1	10.8	223 49.8	54.5	219 40.6	05.3	Alkaid	152 55.2	N49 12.6
S 08	173 52.9	333 43.6	34.9	159 30.6	10.9	238 51.8	54.4	234 42.9	05.3	Alnair	27 37.2	S46 51.8
A 09	188 55.4	348 43.2	.. 36.0	174 33.1	.. 11.1	253 53.8	.. 54.4	249 45.2	.. 05.3	Alnilam	275 40.9	S 1 11.3
T 10	203 57.8	3 42.8	37.2	189 35.6	11.2	268 55.8	54.3	264 47.4	05.2	Alphard	217 51.1	S 8 44.8
U 11	219 00.3	18 42.4	38.3	204 38.1	11.3	283 57.9	54.2	279 49.7	05.2			
R 12	234 02.7	33 42.0	S 6 39.4	219 40.6	N 5 11.5	298 59.9	S21 54.2	294 52.0	S21 05.2	Alphecca	126 07.0	N26 38.9
D 13	249 05.2	48 41.6	40.6	234 43.1	11.6	314 01.9	54.1	309 54.3	05.1	Alpheratz	357 38.0	N29 12.4
A 14	264 07.7	63 41.2	41.7	249 45.6	11.8	329 03.9	54.0	324 56.5	05.1	Altair	62 03.4	N 8 55.5
Y 15	279 10.1	78 40.8	.. 42.9	264 48.1	.. 11.9	344 05.9	.. 54.0	339 58.8	.. 05.1	Ankaa	353 10.3	S42 11.8
16	294 12.6	93 40.3	44.0	279 50.6	12.1	359 07.9	53.9	355 01.1	05.0	Antares	112 20.3	S26 28.5
17	309 15.1	108 39.9	45.1	294 53.1	12.2	14 10.0	53.8	10 03.4	05.0			
18	324 17.5	123 39.5	S 6 46.3	309 55.6	N 5 12.3	29 12.0	S21 53.7	25 05.6	S21 05.0	Arcturus	145 51.4	N19 04.6
19	339 20.0	138 39.1	47.4	324 58.1	12.5	44 14.0	53.7	40 07.9	04.9	Atria	107 18.1	S69 03.8
20	354 22.5	153 38.7	48.6	340 00.6	12.6	59 16.0	53.6	55 10.2	04.9	Avior	234 15.8	S59 34.2
21	9 24.9	168 38.3	.. 49.7	355 03.1	.. 12.8	74 18.0	.. 53.5	70 12.5	.. 04.9	Bellatrix	278 26.2	N 6 22.1
22	24 27.4	183 37.9	50.8	10 05.6	12.9	89 20.0	53.5	85 14.7	04.8	Betelgeuse	270 55.5	N 7 24.6
23	39 29.9	198 37.4	52.0	25 08.1	13.1	104 22.0	53.4	100 17.0	04.8			
15 00	54 32.3	213 37.0	S 6 53.1	40 10.6	N 5 13.2	119 24.1	S21 53.3	115 19.3	S21 04.8	Canopus	263 53.5	S52 42.2
01	69 34.8	228 36.6	54.3	55 13.1	13.4	134 26.1	53.3	130 21.6	04.7	Capella	280 26.4	N46 01.0
02	84 37.2	243 36.2	55.4	70 15.6	13.5	149 28.1	53.2	145 23.8	04.7	Deneb	49 28.2	N45 21.5
03	99 39.7	258 35.8	.. 56.5	85 18.0	.. 13.7	164 30.1	.. 53.1	160 26.1	.. 04.7	Denebola	182 28.6	N14 27.4
04	114 42.2	273 35.4	57.7	100 20.5	13.8	179 32.1	53.0	175 28.4	04.6	Diphda	348 50.5	S17 52.5
05	129 44.6	288 34.9	58.8	115 23.0	13.9	194 34.1	53.0	190 30.6	04.6			
06	144 47.1	303 34.5	S 6 59.9	130 25.5	N 5 14.1	209 36.1	S21 52.9	205 32.9	S21 04.6	Dubhe	193 45.6	N61 38.2
07	159 49.6	318 34.1	7 01.1	145 28.0	14.2	224 38.1	52.8	220 35.2	04.5	Elnath	278 05.8	N28 37.4
S 08	174 52.0	333 33.7	02.2	160 30.5	14.4	239 40.2	52.8	235 37.5	04.5	Eltanin	90 44.2	N51 29.4
U 09	189 54.5	348 33.3	.. 03.4	175 32.9	.. 14.5	254 42.2	.. 52.7	250 39.7	.. 04.5	Enif	33 42.1	N 9 58.3
N 10	204 57.0	3 32.9	04.5	190 35.4	14.7	269 44.2	52.6	265 42.0	04.4	Fomalhaut	15 18.2	S29 30.9
D 11	219 59.4	18 32.4	05.6	205 37.9	14.8	284 46.2	52.6	280 44.3	04.4			
A 12	235 01.9	33 32.0	S 7 06.8	220 40.4	N 5 15.0	299 48.2	S21 52.5	295 46.6	S21 04.4	Gacrux	171 55.7	S57 13.4
Y 13	250 04.3	48 31.6	07.9	235 42.8	15.2	314 50.2	52.4	310 48.8	04.3	Gienah	175 47.3	S17 39.2
14	265 06.8	63 31.2	09.0	250 45.3	15.3	329 52.2	52.3	325 51.1	04.3	Hadar	148 41.3	S60 28.1
15	280 09.3	78 30.8	.. 10.2	265 47.8	.. 15.5	344 54.2	.. 52.3	340 53.4	.. 04.3	Hamal	327 54.7	N23 33.6
16	295 11.7	93 30.3	11.3	280 50.3	15.6	359 56.3	52.2	355 55.6	04.2	Kaus Aust.	83 37.3	S34 22.5
17	310 14.2	108 29.9	12.4	295 52.7	15.8	14 58.3	52.1	10 57.9	04.2			
18	325 16.7	123 29.5	S 7 13.6	310 55.2	N 5 15.9	30 00.3	S21 52.1	26 00.2	S21 04.2	Kochab	137 21.1	N74 04.2
19	340 19.1	138 29.1	14.7	325 57.7	16.1	45 02.3	52.0	41 02.5	04.1	Markab	13 33.1	N15 19.1
20	355 21.6	153 28.7	15.8	341 00.1	16.2	60 04.3	51.9	56 04.7	04.1	Menkar	314 09.4	N 4 10.2
21	10 24.1	168 28.2	.. 17.0	356 02.6	.. 16.4	75 06.3	.. 51.8	71 07.0	.. 04.1	Menkent	148 02.0	S36 28.1
22	25 26.5	183 27.8	18.1	11 05.0	16.5	90 08.3	51.8	86 09.3	04.0	Miaplacidus	221 38.7	S69 47.8
23	40 29.0	198 27.4	19.3	26 07.5	16.7	105 10.3	51.7	101 11.5	04.0			
16 00	55 31.5	213 27.0	S 7 20.4	41 10.0	N 5 16.9	120 12.3	S21 51.6	116 13.8	S21 04.0	Mirfak	308 32.5	N49 56.0
01	70 33.9	228 26.5	21.5	56 12.4	17.0	135 14.3	51.6	131 16.1	03.9	Nunki	75 52.2	S26 16.2
02	85 36.4	243 26.1	22.7	71 14.9	17.2	150 16.4	51.5	146 18.4	03.9	Peacock	53 11.3	S56 40.3
03	100 38.8	258 25.7	.. 23.8	86 17.3	.. 17.3	165 18.4	.. 51.4	161 20.6	.. 03.9	Pollux	243 21.3	N27 58.5
04	115 41.3	273 25.3	24.9	101 19.8	17.5	180 20.4	51.3	176 22.9	03.8	Procyon	244 54.2	N 5 10.3
05	130 43.8	288 24.9	26.0	116 22.2	17.6	195 22.4	51.3	191 25.2	03.8			
06	145 46.2	303 24.4	S 7 27.2	131 24.7	N 5 17.8	210 24.4	S21 51.2	206 27.4	S21 03.8	Rasalhague	96 02.0	N12 32.9
07	160 48.7	318 24.0	28.3	146 27.1	18.0	225 26.4	51.1	221 29.7	03.7	Regulus	207 38.1	N11 52.0
08	175 51.2	333 23.6	29.4	161 29.6	18.1	240 28.4	51.1	236 32.0	03.7	Rigel	281 06.8	S 8 10.6
M 09	190 53.6	348 23.2	.. 30.6	176 32.0	.. 18.3	255 30.4	.. 51.0	251 34.2	.. 03.7	Rigil Kent.	139 45.5	S60 55.0
O 10	205 56.1	3 22.7	31.7	191 34.5	18.4	270 32.4	50.9	266 36.5	03.6	Sabik	102 07.0	S15 44.9
N 11	220 58.6	18 22.3	32.8	206 36.9	18.6	285 34.4	50.8	281 38.8	03.6			
D 12	236 01.0	33 21.9	S 7 34.0	221 39.4	N 5 18.8	300 36.4	S21 50.8	296 41.0	S21 03.6	Schedar	349 34.4	N56 39.2
A 13	251 03.5	48 21.4	35.1	236 41.8	18.9	315 38.4	50.7	311 43.3	03.5	Shaula	96 15.3	S37 07.1
Y 14	266 06.0	63 21.0	36.2	251 44.2	19.1	330 40.4	50.6	326 45.6	03.5	Sirius	258 29.0	S16 44.6
15	281 08.4	78 20.6	.. 37.4	266 46.7	.. 19.3	345 42.5	.. 50.6	341 47.9	.. 03.4	Spica	158 26.1	S11 16.0
16	296 10.9	93 20.2	38.5	281 49.1	19.4	0 44.5	50.5	356 50.1	03.4	Suhail	222 48.7	S43 30.7
17	311 13.3	108 19.7	39.6	296 51.6	19.6	15 46.5	50.4	11 52.4	03.4			
18	326 15.8	123 19.3	S 7 40.7	311 54.0	N 5 19.7	30 48.5	S21 50.3	26 54.7	S21 03.3	Vega	80 35.8	N38 48.4
19	341 18.3	138 18.9	41.9	326 56.4	19.9	45 50.5	50.3	41 56.9	03.3	Zuben'ubi	137 00.1	S16 07.5
20	356 20.7	153 18.5	43.0	341 58.9	20.1	60 52.5	50.2	56 59.2	03.3		SHA	Mer. Pass.
21	11 23.2	168 18.0	.. 44.1	357 01.3	.. 20.2	75 54.5	.. 50.1	72 01.5	.. 03.2			h m
22	26 25.7	183 17.6	45.3	12 03.7	20.4	90 56.5	50.0	87 03.7	03.2	Venus	159 04.7	9 46
23	41 28.1	198 17.2	46.4	27 06.1	20.6	105 58.5	50.0	102 06.0	03.2	Mars	345 38.3	21 16
	h m									Jupiter	64 51.7	16 00
Mer. Pass. 20 18.5	v −0.4 d 1.1	v 2.5 d 0.2		v 2.0 d 0.1		v 2.3 d 0.0				Saturn	60 47.0	16 16

SUN / MOON

UT	SUN GHA	SUN Dec	MOON GHA	v	MOON Dec	d	HP
d h	° ′	° ′	° ′	′	° ′	′	′
14 00	183 53.8	S18 17.0	199 42.3	8.0	S 9 38.3	14.8	61.2
01	198 53.7	17.7	214 09.3	7.9	9 53.1	14.8	61.2
02	213 53.6	18.3	228 36.2	7.8	10 07.9	14.6	61.3
03	228 53.5	. . 19.0	243 03.0	7.8	10 22.5	14.7	61.3
04	243 53.4	19.6	257 29.8	7.7	10 37.2	14.5	61.3
05	258 53.3	20.2	271 56.5	7.7	10 51.7	14.6	61.3
06	273 53.2	S18 20.9	286 23.2	7.6	S11 06.3	14.4	61.3
07	288 53.1	21.5	300 49.8	7.5	11 20.7	14.4	61.3
S 08	303 53.0	22.2	315 16.3	7.5	11 35.1	14.2	61.3
A 09	318 52.9	. . 22.8	329 42.8	7.4	11 49.3	14.3	61.3
T 10	333 52.8	23.5	344 09.2	7.3	12 03.6	14.1	61.3
U 11	348 52.7	24.1	358 35.5	7.3	12 17.7	14.1	61.3
R 12	3 52.6	S18 24.8	13 01.8	7.2	S12 31.8	13.9	61.3
D 13	18 52.5	25.4	27 28.0	7.1	12 45.7	13.9	61.3
A 14	33 52.4	26.0	41 54.1	7.1	12 59.6	13.9	61.3
Y 15	48 52.3	. . 26.7	56 20.2	7.0	13 13.5	13.7	61.3
16	63 52.2	27.3	70 46.2	6.9	13 27.2	13.6	61.3
17	78 52.1	28.0	85 12.1	6.9	13 40.8	13.6	61.3
18	93 52.0	S18 28.6	99 38.0	6.8	S13 54.4	13.4	61.3
19	108 51.9	29.2	114 03.8	6.7	14 07.8	13.4	61.3
20	123 51.8	29.9	128 29.5	6.6	14 21.2	13.3	61.3
21	138 51.7	. . 30.5	142 55.1	6.6	14 34.5	13.1	61.3
22	153 51.6	31.1	157 20.7	6.6	14 47.6	13.1	61.2
23	168 51.5	31.8	171 46.3	6.4	15 00.7	13.0	61.2
15 00	183 51.4	S18 32.4	186 11.7	6.4	S15 13.7	12.8	61.2
01	198 51.3	33.0	200 37.1	6.3	15 26.5	12.8	61.2
02	213 51.1	33.7	215 02.4	6.3	15 39.3	12.7	61.2
03	228 51.0	. . 34.3	229 27.7	6.2	15 52.0	12.5	61.2
04	243 50.9	34.9	243 52.9	6.1	16 04.5	12.4	61.2
05	258 50.8	35.6	258 18.0	6.1	16 16.9	12.3	61.2
06	273 50.7	S18 36.2	272 43.1	6.0	S16 29.2	12.2	61.2
07	288 50.6	36.8	287 08.1	5.9	16 41.4	12.1	61.2
08	303 50.5	37.5	301 33.0	5.8	16 53.5	12.0	61.2
S 09	318 50.4	. . 38.1	315 57.8	5.8	17 05.5	11.8	61.1
U 10	333 50.3	38.7	330 22.6	5.8	17 17.3	11.8	61.1
N 11	348 50.2	39.4	344 47.4	5.6	17 29.1	11.6	61.1
D 12	3 50.0	S18 40.0	359 12.0	5.6	S17 40.7	11.4	61.1
A 13	18 49.9	40.6	13 36.6	5.6	17 52.1	11.4	61.1
Y 14	33 49.8	41.2	28 01.2	5.4	18 03.5	11.2	61.1
15	48 49.7	. . 41.9	42 25.6	5.5	18 14.7	11.1	61.1
16	63 49.6	42.5	56 50.1	5.3	18 25.8	11.0	61.1
17	78 49.5	43.1	71 14.4	5.3	18 36.8	10.8	61.1
18	93 49.4	S18 43.7	85 38.7	5.2	S18 47.6	10.7	61.0
19	108 49.3	44.4	100 02.9	5.2	18 58.3	10.5	61.0
20	123 49.1	45.0	114 27.1	5.1	19 08.8	10.4	61.0
21	138 49.0	. . 45.6	128 51.2	5.1	19 19.2	10.3	61.0
22	153 48.9	46.2	143 15.3	5.0	19 29.5	10.1	60.9
23	168 48.8	46.9	157 39.3	5.0	19 39.6	10.0	60.9
16 00	183 48.7	S18 47.5	172 03.3	4.9	S19 49.6	9.9	60.9
01	198 48.6	48.1	186 27.2	4.8	19 59.5	9.7	60.9
02	213 48.4	48.7	200 51.0	4.8	20 09.2	9.5	60.9
03	228 48.3	. . 49.3	215 14.8	4.8	20 18.7	9.4	60.8
04	243 48.2	50.0	229 38.6	4.7	20 28.1	9.3	60.8
05	258 48.1	50.6	244 02.3	4.6	20 37.4	9.1	60.8
06	273 48.0	S18 51.2	258 25.9	4.6	S20 46.5	8.9	60.7
07	288 47.9	51.8	272 49.5	4.6	20 55.4	8.8	60.7
08	303 47.7	52.4	287 13.1	4.5	21 04.2	8.6	60.7
M 09	318 47.6	. . 53.1	301 36.6	4.4	21 12.8	8.5	60.7
O 10	333 47.5	53.7	316 00.0	4.5	21 21.3	8.3	60.7
N 11	348 47.4	54.3	330 23.5	4.4	21 29.6	8.2	60.7
D 12	3 47.3	S18 54.9	344 46.9	4.3	S21 37.8	8.0	60.6
A 13	18 47.1	55.5	359 10.2	4.3	21 45.8	7.9	60.6
Y 14	33 47.0	56.1	13 33.5	4.3	21 53.7	7.7	60.6
15	48 46.9	. . 56.7	27 56.8	4.3	22 01.4	7.5	60.5
16	63 46.8	57.3	42 20.1	4.2	22 08.9	7.3	60.5
17	78 46.6	58.0	56 43.3	4.2	22 16.2	7.2	60.5
18	93 46.5	S18 58.6	71 06.5	4.1	S22 23.4	7.1	60.5
19	108 46.4	59.2	85 29.6	4.2	22 30.5	6.8	60.4
20	123 46.3	18 59.8	99 52.8	4.1	22 37.3	6.7	60.4
21	138 46.2	19 00.4	114 15.9	4.1	22 44.0	6.6	60.4
22	153 46.0	01.0	128 39.0	4.0	22 50.6	6.3	60.3
23	168 45.9	01.6	143 02.0	4.1	S22 56.9	6.2	60.3
	SD 16.2	d 0.6	SD 16.7		16.7		16.5

Twilight / Sunrise / Moonrise

Lat.	Twilight Naut.	Twilight Civil	Sunrise	Moonrise 14	Moonrise 15	Moonrise 16	Moonrise 17
°	h m	h m	h m	h m	h m	h m	h m
N 72	07 01	08 36	11 11	07 36	11 20	■■■	■■■
N 70	06 51	08 13	09 52	07 14	09 58	■■■	■■■
68	06 42	07 55	09 15	06 58	09 19	12 37	■■■
66	06 35	07 41	08 49	06 45	08 53	11 12	■■■
64	06 28	07 29	08 29	06 34	08 33	10 35	12 31
62	06 23	07 19	08 12	06 25	08 16	10 08	11 51
60	06 18	07 10	07 59	06 17	08 03	09 48	11 23
N 58	06 13	07 02	07 47	06 10	07 51	09 31	11 01
56	06 09	06 55	07 37	06 04	07 41	09 17	10 44
54	06 05	06 49	07 28	05 58	07 32	09 04	10 29
52	06 02	06 43	07 21	05 53	07 24	08 54	10 16
50	05 58	06 38	07 13	05 49	07 17	08 44	10 04
45	05 51	06 26	06 58	05 40	07 02	08 24	09 41
N 40	05 44	06 16	06 46	05 32	06 50	08 08	09 22
35	05 37	06 08	06 35	05 25	06 40	07 54	09 06
30	05 31	06 00	06 25	05 19	06 31	07 43	08 52
20	05 19	05 46	06 09	05 09	06 15	07 22	08 29
N 10	05 07	05 33	05 55	05 01	06 02	07 05	08 09
0	04 54	05 19	05 41	04 53	05 49	06 49	07 50
S 10	04 39	05 05	05 27	04 45	05 37	06 33	07 32
20	04 21	04 49	05 13	04 36	05 24	06 16	07 12
30	03 58	04 30	04 56	04 27	05 09	05 56	06 49
35	03 44	04 18	04 46	04 21	05 01	05 45	06 36
40	03 26	04 04	04 34	04 15	04 51	05 32	06 21
45	03 04	03 47	04 21	04 08	04 39	05 17	06 03
S 50	02 33	03 25	04 04	03 59	04 26	04 58	05 40
52	02 17	03 14	03 56	03 56	04 20	04 50	05 30
54	01 58	03 02	03 48	03 51	04 13	04 40	05 17
56	01 33	02 48	03 38	03 47	04 05	04 29	05 04
58	00 57	02 32	03 26	03 41	03 56	04 17	04 48
S 60	////	02 11	03 13	03 36	03 46	04 02	04 28

Sunset / Twilight / Moonset

Lat.	Sunset	Twilight Civil	Twilight Naut.	Moonset 14	Moonset 15	Moonset 16	Moonset 17
°	h m	h m	h m	h m	h m	h m	h m
N 72	12 17	14 52	16 27	14 08	12 25	■■■	■■■
N 70	13 36	15 15	16 38	14 32	13 49	■■■	■■■
68	14 14	15 33	16 46	14 50	14 29	13 17	■■■
66	14 40	15 48	16 54	15 05	14 57	14 43	■■■
64	15 00	16 00	17 00	15 18	15 18	15 21	15 34
62	15 16	16 10	17 06	15 28	15 35	15 48	16 15
60	15 30	16 19	17 11	15 37	15 50	16 09	16 43
N 58	15 41	16 27	17 15	15 45	16 02	16 27	17 05
56	15 51	16 34	17 19	15 52	16 13	16 42	17 23
54	16 00	16 40	17 23	15 59	16 22	16 54	17 38
52	16 08	16 46	17 27	16 04	16 31	17 05	17 51
50	16 15	16 51	17 30	16 10	16 39	17 15	18 02
45	16 31	17 03	17 38	16 21	16 55	17 36	18 27
N 40	16 43	17 12	17 45	16 30	17 09	17 53	18 46
35	16 54	17 21	17 52	16 38	17 20	18 08	19 02
30	17 04	17 29	17 58	16 46	17 30	18 20	19 16
20	17 20	17 43	18 10	16 58	17 48	18 42	19 40
N 10	17 35	17 57	18 22	17 09	18 03	19 01	20 01
0	17 48	18 10	18 35	17 19	18 17	19 18	20 20
S 10	18 02	18 24	18 50	17 29	18 32	19 36	20 39
20	18 17	18 40	19 08	17 41	18 47	19 54	21 00
30	18 34	19 00	19 32	17 53	19 05	20 16	21 23
35	18 44	19 12	19 47	18 01	19 15	20 29	21 38
40	18 56	19 26	20 04	18 09	19 27	20 43	21 54
45	19 09	19 44	20 27	18 19	19 41	21 01	22 13
S 50	19 26	20 05	20 58	18 31	19 59	21 23	22 37
52	19 34	20 16	21 14	18 36	20 07	21 33	22 49
54	19 43	20 28	21 34	18 42	20 16	21 45	23 02
56	19 53	20 43	22 00	18 49	20 26	21 58	23 18
58	20 04	21 00	22 38	18 57	20 38	22 14	23 36
S 60	20 18	21 21	////	19 06	20 52	22 33	23 58

SUN / MOON

Day	Eqn. of Time 00h	Eqn. of Time 12h	Mer. Pass.	Mer. Pass. Upper	Mer. Pass. Lower	Age	Phase
d	m s	m s	h m	h m	h m	d	%
14	15 36	15 31	11 44	11 06	23 34	29	1
15	15 26	15 20	11 45	12 03	24 33	00	0
16	15 15	15 09	11 45	13 03	00 33	01	2

UT	ARIES GHA	VENUS −3·9 GHA	VENUS Dec	MARS −1·6 GHA	MARS Dec	JUPITER −2·1 GHA	JUPITER Dec	SATURN +0·6 GHA	SATURN Dec	STARS Name	SHA	Dec
d h	° ′	° ′	° ′	° ′	° ′	° ′	° ′	° ′	° ′		° ′	° ′
17 00	56 30.6	213 16.7	S 7 47.5	42 08.6	N 5 20.7	121 00.5	S21 49.9	117 08.3	S21 03.1	Acamar	315 14.0	S40 13.4
01	71 33.1	228 16.3	48.6	57 11.0	20.9	136 02.5	49.8	132 10.5	03.1	Achernar	335 22.3	S57 08.1
02	86 35.5	243 15.9	49.8	72 13.4	21.1	151 04.5	49.8	147 12.8	03.1	Acrux	173 04.1	S63 12.5
03	101 38.0	258 15.4	.. 50.9	87 15.8	.. 21.2	166 06.5	.. 49.7	162 15.1	.. 03.0	Adhara	255 08.2	S28 59.9
04	116 40.5	273 15.0	52.0	102 18.3	21.4	181 08.5	49.6	177 17.3	03.0	Aldebaran	290 43.1	N16 33.0
05	131 42.9	288 14.6	53.2	117 20.7	21.6	196 10.5	49.5	192 19.6	03.0			
06	146 45.4	303 14.1	S 7 54.3	132 23.1	N 5 21.8	211 12.5	S21 49.5	207 21.9	S21 02.9	Alioth	166 16.5	N55 50.8
07	161 47.8	318 13.7	55.4	147 25.5	21.9	226 14.5	49.4	222 24.1	02.9	Alkaid	152 55.2	N49 12.6
T 08	176 50.3	333 13.3	56.5	162 27.9	22.1	241 16.5	49.3	237 26.4	02.9	Alnair	27 37.2	S46 51.9
U 09	191 52.8	348 12.9	.. 57.7	177 30.4	.. 22.3	256 18.5	.. 49.2	252 28.7	.. 02.8	Alnilam	275 40.9	S 1 11.3
E 10	206 55.2	3 12.4	58.8	192 32.8	22.4	271 20.5	49.2	267 30.9	02.8	Alphard	217 51.0	S 8 44.8
S 11	221 57.7	18 12.0	7 59.9	207 35.2	22.6	286 22.5	49.1	282 33.2	02.8			
D 12	237 00.2	33 11.6	S 8 01.0	222 37.6	N 5 22.8	301 24.5	S21 49.0	297 35.5	S21 02.7	Alphecca	126 07.0	N26 38.8
A 13	252 02.6	48 11.1	02.2	237 40.0	23.0	316 26.5	48.9	312 37.7	02.7	Alpheratz	357 38.0	N29 12.4
Y 14	267 05.1	63 10.7	03.3	252 42.4	23.1	331 28.5	48.9	327 40.0	02.6	Altair	62 03.4	N 8 55.5
15	282 07.6	78 10.2	.. 04.4	267 44.8	.. 23.3	346 30.5	.. 48.8	342 42.3	.. 02.6	Ankaa	353 10.3	S42 11.8
16	297 10.0	93 09.8	05.5	282 47.2	23.5	1 32.6	48.7	357 44.5	02.6	Antares	112 20.3	S26 28.5
17	312 12.5	108 09.4	06.7	297 49.6	23.7	16 34.6	48.7	12 46.8	02.5			
18	327 15.0	123 08.9	S 8 07.8	312 52.0	N 5 23.8	31 36.6	S21 48.6	27 49.1	S21 02.5	Arcturus	145 51.4	N19 04.6
19	342 17.4	138 08.5	08.9	327 54.4	24.0	46 38.6	48.5	42 51.3	02.5	Atria	107 18.1	S69 03.8
20	357 19.9	153 08.1	10.0	342 56.8	24.2	61 40.6	48.4	57 53.6	02.4	Avior	234 15.8	S59 34.2
21	12 22.3	168 07.6	.. 11.1	357 59.2	.. 24.4	76 42.6	.. 48.4	72 55.8	.. 02.4	Bellatrix	278 26.2	N 6 22.1
22	27 24.8	183 07.2	12.3	13 01.6	24.5	91 44.6	48.3	87 58.1	02.4	Betelgeuse	270 55.5	N 7 24.6
23	42 27.3	198 06.8	13.4	28 04.0	24.7	106 46.6	48.2	103 00.4	02.3			
18 00	57 29.7	213 06.3	S 8 14.5	43 06.4	N 5 24.9	121 48.6	S21 48.1	118 02.6	S21 02.3	Canopus	263 53.4	S52 42.2
01	72 32.2	228 05.9	15.6	58 08.8	25.1	136 50.6	48.1	133 04.9	02.3	Capella	280 26.4	N46 01.0
02	87 34.7	243 05.4	16.8	73 11.2	25.2	151 52.6	48.0	148 07.2	02.2	Deneb	49 28.2	N45 21.5
03	102 37.1	258 05.0	.. 17.9	88 13.6	.. 25.4	166 54.6	.. 47.9	163 09.4	.. 02.2	Denebola	182 28.6	N14 27.4
04	117 39.6	273 04.6	19.0	103 16.0	25.6	181 56.6	47.8	178 11.7	02.2	Diphda	348 50.5	S17 52.5
05	132 42.1	288 04.1	20.1	118 18.4	25.8	196 58.6	47.8	193 14.0	02.1			
06	147 44.5	303 03.7	S 8 21.2	133 20.8	N 5 26.0	212 00.6	S21 47.7	208 16.2	S21 02.1	Dubhe	193 45.5	N61 38.2
W 07	162 47.0	318 03.2	22.4	148 23.2	26.1	227 02.6	47.6	223 18.5	02.0	Elnath	278 05.8	N28 37.4
E 08	177 49.5	333 02.8	23.5	163 25.5	26.3	242 04.5	47.5	238 20.7	02.0	Eltanin	90 44.2	N51 29.4
D 09	192 51.9	348 02.4	.. 24.6	178 27.9	.. 26.5	257 06.5	.. 47.5	253 23.0	.. 02.0	Enif	33 42.1	N 9 58.3
N 10	207 54.4	3 01.9	25.7	193 30.3	26.7	272 08.5	47.4	268 25.3	01.9	Fomalhaut	15 18.2	S29 30.9
E 11	222 56.8	18 01.5	26.8	208 32.7	26.9	287 10.5	47.3	283 27.5	01.9			
S 12	237 59.3	33 01.0	S 8 28.0	223 35.1	N 5 27.0	302 12.5	S21 47.2	298 29.8	S21 01.9	Gacrux	171 55.7	S57 13.4
D 13	253 01.8	48 00.6	29.1	238 37.5	27.2	317 14.5	47.2	313 32.1	01.8	Gienah	175 47.2	S17 39.2
A 14	268 04.2	63 00.2	30.2	253 39.8	27.4	332 16.5	47.1	328 34.3	01.8	Hadar	148 41.3	S60 28.1
Y 15	283 06.7	77 59.7	.. 31.3	268 42.2	.. 27.6	347 18.5	.. 47.0	343 36.6	.. 01.8	Hamal	327 54.7	N23 33.7
16	298 09.2	92 59.3	32.4	283 44.6	27.8	2 20.5	46.9	358 38.8	01.7	Kaus Aust.	83 37.3	S34 22.5
17	313 11.6	107 58.8	33.5	298 47.0	28.0	17 22.5	46.9	13 41.1	01.7			
18	328 14.1	122 58.4	S 8 34.7	313 49.3	N 5 28.2	32 24.5	S21 46.8	28 43.4	S21 01.7	Kochab	137 21.1	N74 04.2
19	343 16.6	137 57.9	35.8	328 51.7	28.3	47 26.5	46.7	43 45.6	01.6	Markab	13 33.1	N15 19.1
20	358 19.0	152 57.5	36.9	343 54.1	28.5	62 28.5	46.6	58 47.9	01.6	Menkar	314 09.4	N 4 10.2
21	13 21.5	167 57.1	.. 38.0	358 56.4	.. 28.7	77 30.5	.. 46.6	73 50.2	.. 01.5	Menkent	148 01.9	S36 28.1
22	28 23.9	182 56.6	39.1	13 58.8	28.9	92 32.5	46.5	88 52.4	01.5	Miaplacidus	221 38.6	S69 47.8
23	43 26.4	197 56.2	40.2	29 01.2	29.1	107 34.5	46.4	103 54.7	01.5			
19 00	58 28.9	212 55.7	S 8 41.3	44 03.5	N 5 29.3	122 36.5	S21 46.3	118 56.9	S21 01.4	Mirfak	308 32.5	N49 56.0
01	73 31.3	227 55.3	42.5	59 05.9	29.5	137 38.5	46.3	133 59.2	01.4	Nunki	75 52.2	S26 16.2
02	88 33.8	242 54.8	43.6	74 08.3	29.6	152 40.5	46.2	149 01.5	01.4	Peacock	53 11.3	S56 40.3
03	103 36.3	257 54.4	.. 44.7	89 10.6	.. 29.8	167 42.5	.. 46.1	164 03.7	.. 01.3	Pollux	243 21.3	N27 58.4
04	118 38.7	272 53.9	45.8	104 13.0	30.0	182 44.5	46.0	179 06.0	01.3	Procyon	244 54.2	N 5 10.3
05	133 41.2	287 53.5	46.9	119 15.3	30.2	197 46.5	46.0	194 08.2	01.3			
06	148 43.7	302 53.0	S 8 48.0	134 17.7	N 5 30.4	212 48.5	S21 45.9	209 10.5	S21 01.2	Rasalhague	96 02.0	N12 32.9
07	163 46.1	317 52.6	49.1	149 20.1	30.6	227 50.5	45.8	224 12.8	01.2	Regulus	207 38.1	N11 52.0
T 08	178 48.6	332 52.1	50.3	164 22.4	30.8	242 52.5	45.7	239 15.0	01.2	Rigel	281 06.8	S 8 10.7
H 09	193 51.1	347 51.7	.. 51.4	179 24.8	.. 31.0	257 54.4	.. 45.7	254 17.3	.. 01.1	Rigil Kent.	139 45.5	S60 55.0
U 10	208 53.5	2 51.2	52.5	194 27.1	31.2	272 56.4	45.6	269 19.5	01.1	Sabik	102 07.0	S15 44.9
R 11	223 56.0	17 50.8	53.6	209 29.5	31.4	287 58.4	45.5	284 21.8	01.0			
S 12	238 58.4	32 50.3	S 8 54.7	224 31.8	N 5 31.6	303 00.4	S21 45.4	299 24.1	S21 01.0	Schedar	349 34.4	N56 39.2
D 13	254 00.9	47 49.9	55.8	239 34.2	31.7	318 02.4	45.4	314 26.3	01.0	Shaula	96 15.3	S37 07.1
A 14	269 03.4	62 49.4	56.9	254 36.5	31.9	333 04.4	45.3	329 28.6	00.9	Sirius	258 28.9	S16 44.6
Y 15	284 05.8	77 49.0	.. 58.0	269 38.9	.. 32.1	348 06.4	.. 45.2	344 30.8	.. 00.9	Spica	158 26.1	S11 16.0
16	299 08.3	92 48.5	8 59.2	284 41.2	32.3	3 08.4	45.1	359 33.1	00.9	Suhail	222 48.6	S43 30.7
17	314 10.8	107 48.1	9 00.3	299 43.5	32.5	18 10.4	45.1	14 35.3	00.8			
18	329 13.2	122 47.6	S 9 01.4	314 45.9	N 5 32.7	33 12.4	S21 45.0	29 37.6	S21 00.8	Vega	80 35.8	N38 48.4
19	344 15.7	137 47.2	02.5	329 48.2	32.9	48 14.4	44.9	44 39.9	00.8	Zuben'ubi	137 00.1	S16 07.5
20	359 18.2	152 46.7	03.6	344 50.6	33.1	63 16.4	44.8	59 42.1	00.7		SHA	Mer. Pass.
21	14 20.6	167 46.3	.. 04.7	359 52.9	.. 33.3	78 18.4	.. 44.8	74 44.4	.. 00.7		° ′	h m
22	29 23.1	182 45.8	05.8	14 55.2	33.5	93 20.4	44.7	89 46.6	00.6	Venus	155 36.6	9 48
23	44 25.6	197 45.4	06.9	29 57.6	33.7	108 22.3	44.6	104 48.9	00.6	Mars	345 36.7	21 04
	h m									Jupiter	64 18.8	15 51
Mer. Pass. 20 06.7	v −0.4 d 1.1	v 2.4 d 0.2		v 2.0 d 0.1		v 2.3 d 0.0				Saturn	60 32.9	16 05

UT	SUN GHA	SUN Dec	MOON GHA	v	MOON Dec	d	HP
d h	° ′	° ′	° ′	′	° ′	′	′
17 00	183 45.8	S19 02.2	157 25.1	4.0	S23 03.1	6.0	60.3
01	198 45.7	02.8	171 48.1	4.0	23 09.1	5.9	60.3
02	213 45.5	03.4	186 11.1	4.0	23 15.0	5.7	60.2
03	228 45.4 ..	04.0	200 34.1	4.0	23 20.7	5.5	60.2
04	243 45.3	04.6	214 57.1	4.0	23 26.2	5.3	60.2
05	258 45.2	05.3	229 20.1	3.9	23 31.5	5.2	60.1
06	273 45.0	S19 05.9	243 43.0	4.0	S23 36.7	5.0	60.1
07	288 44.9	06.5	258 06.0	4.0	23 41.7	4.8	60.1
08	303 44.8	07.1	272 29.0	3.9	23 46.5	4.7	60.0
09	318 44.6 ..	07.7	286 51.9	4.0	23 51.2	4.5	60.0
10	333 44.5	08.3	301 14.9	3.9	23 55.7	4.3	60.0
11	348 44.4	08.9	315 37.8	4.0	24 00.0	4.1	59.9
12	3 44.3	S19 09.5	330 00.8	4.0	S24 04.1	4.0	59.9
13	18 44.1	10.1	344 23.8	4.0	24 08.1	3.7	59.9
14	33 44.0	10.7	358 46.8	4.0	24 11.8	3.7	59.8
15	48 43.9 ..	11.3	13 09.8	4.0	24 15.5	3.4	59.8
16	63 43.7	11.9	27 32.8	4.0	24 18.9	3.3	59.8
17	78 43.6	12.5	41 55.8	4.0	24 22.2	3.1	59.7
18	93 43.5	S19 13.1	56 18.8	4.1	S24 25.3	2.9	59.7
19	108 43.3	13.7	70 41.9	4.1	24 28.2	2.7	59.6
20	123 43.2	14.3	85 05.0	4.1	24 30.9	2.6	59.6
21	138 43.1 ..	14.8	99 28.1	4.1	24 33.5	2.4	59.6
22	153 43.0	15.4	113 51.2	4.2	24 35.9	2.2	59.5
23	168 42.8	16.0	128 14.4	4.2	24 38.1	2.0	59.5
18 00	183 42.7	S19 16.6	142 37.6	4.2	S24 40.1	1.9	59.5
01	198 42.6	17.2	157 00.8	4.2	24 42.0	1.7	59.4
02	213 42.4	17.8	171 24.0	4.3	24 43.7	1.6	59.4
03	228 42.3 ..	18.4	185 47.3	4.4	24 45.3	1.3	59.3
04	243 42.2	19.0	200 10.7	4.3	24 46.6	1.2	59.3
05	258 42.0	19.6	214 34.0	4.4	24 47.8	1.0	59.3
06	273 41.9	S19 20.2	228 57.4	4.5	S24 48.8	0.9	59.2
07	288 41.7	20.8	243 20.9	4.5	24 49.7	0.7	59.2
08	303 41.6	21.3	257 44.4	4.5	24 50.4	0.5	59.2
09	318 41.5 ..	21.9	272 07.9	4.6	24 50.9	0.3	59.1
10	333 41.3	22.5	286 31.5	4.7	24 51.2	0.2	59.1
11	348 41.2	23.1	300 55.2	4.7	24 51.4	0.0	59.0
12	3 41.1	S19 23.7	315 18.9	4.7	S24 51.4	0.1	59.0
13	18 40.9	24.3	329 42.6	4.9	24 51.3	0.4	59.0
14	33 40.8	24.9	344 06.5	4.8	24 50.9	0.6	58.9
15	48 40.6 ..	25.5	358 30.3	5.0	24 50.4	0.6	58.9
16	63 40.5	26.0	12 54.3	5.0	24 49.8	0.8	58.8
17	78 40.4	26.6	27 18.3	5.0	24 49.0	1.0	58.8
18	93 40.2	S19 27.2	41 42.3	5.2	S24 48.0	1.1	58.8
19	108 40.1	27.8	56 06.5	5.2	24 46.9	1.3	58.7
20	123 40.0	28.4	70 30.7	5.2	24 45.6	1.5	58.7
21	138 39.8 ..	28.9	84 54.9	5.4	24 44.1	1.6	58.6
22	153 39.7	29.5	99 19.3	5.4	24 42.5	1.8	58.6
23	168 39.5	30.1	113 43.7	5.5	24 40.7	1.9	58.6
19 00	183 39.4	S19 30.7	128 08.2	5.5	S24 38.8	2.1	58.5
01	198 39.2	31.3	142 32.7	5.7	24 36.7	2.2	58.5
02	213 39.1	31.8	156 57.4	5.7	24 34.5	2.4	58.4
03	228 39.0 ..	32.4	171 22.1	5.8	24 32.1	2.6	58.4
04	243 38.8	33.0	185 46.9	5.9	24 29.5	2.7	58.4
05	258 38.7	33.6	200 11.8	5.9	24 26.8	2.8	58.3
06	273 38.5	S19 34.1	214 36.7	6.1	S24 24.0	3.0	58.3
07	288 38.4	34.7	229 01.8	6.1	24 21.0	3.2	58.2
08	303 38.2	35.3	243 26.9	6.2	24 17.8	3.3	58.2
09	318 38.1 ..	35.9	257 52.1	6.3	24 14.5	3.4	58.2
10	333 38.0	36.4	272 17.4	6.4	24 11.1	3.6	58.1
11	348 37.8	37.0	286 42.8	6.5	24 07.5	3.7	58.1
12	3 37.7	S19 37.6	301 08.3	6.6	S24 03.8	3.9	58.0
13	18 37.5	38.1	315 33.9	6.6	23 59.9	4.0	58.0
14	33 37.4	38.7	329 59.5	6.8	23 55.9	4.1	58.0
15	48 37.2 ..	39.3	344 25.3	6.8	23 51.8	4.3	57.9
16	63 37.1	39.9	358 51.1	7.0	23 47.5	4.5	57.9
17	78 36.9	40.4	13 17.1	7.0	23 43.0	4.5	57.8
18	93 36.8	S19 41.0	27 43.1	7.2	S23 38.5	4.7	57.8
19	108 36.6	41.6	42 09.3	7.2	23 33.8	4.8	57.8
20	123 36.5	42.1	56 35.5	7.3	23 29.0	5.0	57.7
21	138 36.3 ..	42.7	71 01.8	7.5	23 24.0	5.1	57.7
22	153 36.2	43.3	85 28.3	7.5	23 18.9	5.2	57.6
23	168 36.0	43.8	99 54.8	7.6	S23 13.7	5.4	57.6
	SD 16.2	d 0.6	SD 16.3		16.1		15.8

Lat.	Twilight Naut.	Twilight Civil	Sunrise	Moonrise 17	18	19	20
°	h m	h m	h m	h m	h m	h m	h m
N 72	07 11	08 50	■■	■■	■■	■■	■■
N 70	07 00	08 25	10 14	■■	■■	■■	■■
68	06 50	08 05	09 29	■■	■■	■■	16 09
66	06 42	07 50	09 00	■■	■■	15 47	15 08
64	06 35	07 37	08 38	12 31	13 55	14 26	14 34
62	06 29	07 26	08 21	11 51	13 07	13 48	14 08
60	06 24	07 16	08 06	11 23	12 36	13 22	13 48
N 58	06 19	07 08	07 54	11 01	12 12	13 01	13 32
56	06 14	07 00	07 43	10 44	11 54	12 44	13 18
54	06 10	06 54	07 34	10 29	11 38	12 29	13 06
52	06 06	06 48	07 26	10 16	11 24	12 17	12 55
50	06 03	06 42	07 18	10 04	11 12	12 05	12 45
45	05 54	06 30	07 02	09 41	10 47	11 42	12 25
N 40	05 47	06 20	06 49	09 22	10 27	11 23	12 09
35	05 40	06 11	06 38	09 06	10 11	11 07	11 55
30	05 33	06 02	06 28	08 52	09 57	10 54	11 43
20	05 21	05 47	06 11	08 29	09 32	10 30	11 22
N 10	05 08	05 34	05 56	08 09	09 11	10 10	11 04
0	04 54	05 20	05 42	07 50	08 52	09 51	10 47
S 10	04 39	05 05	05 27	07 32	08 32	09 32	10 30
20	04 20	04 48	05 12	07 12	08 11	09 12	10 11
30	03 56	04 28	04 54	06 49	07 47	08 49	09 50
35	03 41	04 16	04 44	06 36	07 33	08 35	09 38
40	03 23	04 01	04 32	06 21	07 17	08 19	09 24
45	02 59	03 43	04 18	06 03	06 57	08 00	09 07
S 50	02 27	03 21	04 00	05 40	06 33	07 36	08 46
52	02 10	03 09	03 52	05 30	06 21	07 25	08 36
54	01 49	02 57	03 43	05 17	06 08	07 12	08 25
56	01 22	02 42	03 33	05 04	05 52	06 57	08 12
58	00 36	02 24	03 21	04 48	05 34	06 39	07 57
S 60	////	02 02	03 07	04 28	05 12	06 17	07 39

Lat.	Sunset	Twilight Civil	Twilight Naut.	Moonset 17	18	19	20
°	h m	h m	h m	h m	h m	h m	h m
N 72	■■	14 39	16 18	■■	■■	■■	■■
N 70	13 16	15 05	16 29	■■	■■	■■	■■
68	14 00	15 24	16 39	■■	■■	■■	18 02
66	14 30	15 40	16 47	■■	■■	16 29	19 01
64	14 51	15 53	16 54	15 34	16 18	17 50	19 35
62	15 09	16 04	17 00	16 15	17 07	18 27	20 00
60	15 23	16 14	17 06	16 43	17 37	18 53	20 19
N 58	15 36	16 22	17 11	17 05	18 01	19 13	20 35
56	15 46	16 29	17 16	17 23	18 19	19 30	20 49
54	15 56	16 36	17 20	17 38	18 35	19 45	21 01
52	16 04	16 42	17 24	17 51	18 49	19 57	21 11
50	16 12	16 48	17 27	18 02	19 01	20 08	21 20
45	16 28	17 00	17 36	18 27	19 26	20 31	21 39
N 40	16 41	17 10	17 43	18 46	19 45	20 49	21 55
35	16 53	17 20	17 50	19 02	20 02	21 05	22 08
30	17 02	17 28	17 57	19 16	20 16	21 18	22 20
20	17 20	17 43	18 10	19 40	20 40	21 41	22 39
N 10	17 35	17 57	18 23	20 01	21 01	22 00	22 56
0	17 49	18 11	18 36	20 20	21 21	22 18	23 12
S 10	18 03	18 26	18 52	20 39	21 40	22 36	23 27
20	18 19	18 42	19 11	21 00	22 01	22 56	23 44
30	18 37	19 03	19 35	21 23	22 25	23 18	24 03
35	18 47	19 15	19 51	21 38	22 39	23 31	24 14
40	18 59	19 30	20 08	21 54	22 55	23 45	24 27
45	19 13	19 48	20 32	22 13	23 14	24 03	00 03
S 50	19 31	20 11	21 05	22 37	23 38	24 25	00 25
52	19 39	20 22	21 22	22 49	23 50	24 35	00 35
54	19 49	20 35	21 44	23 02	24 03	00 03	00 47
56	19 59	20 50	22 13	23 18	24 18	00 18	01 00
58	20 11	21 09	23 03	23 36	24 36	00 36	01 15
S 60	20 26	21 32	////	23 58	24 58	00 58	01 34

Day	SUN Eqn. of Time 00ʰ	SUN Eqn. of Time 12ʰ	Mer. Pass.	MOON Mer. Pass. Upper	MOON Mer. Pass. Lower	Age	Phase
d	m s	m s	h m	h m	h m	d	%
17	15 03	14 57	11 45	14 05	01 34	02	7
18	14 51	14 45	11 45	15 06	02 36	03	15
19	14 38	14 31	11 45	16 05	03 36	04	23

UT	ARIES	VENUS −3.9		MARS −1.5		JUPITER −2.1		SATURN +0.6		STARS		
	GHA	GHA	Dec	GHA	Dec	GHA	Dec	GHA	Dec	Name	SHA	Dec
d h	° ′	° ′	° ′	° ′	° ′	° ′	° ′	° ′	° ′		° ′	° ′
20 00	59 28.0	212 44.9	S 9 08.0	44 59.9	N 5 33.9	123 24.3	S21 44.5	119 51.2	S21 00.6	Acamar	315 14.0	S40 13.4
01	74 30.5	227 44.5	09.1	60 02.2	34.1	138 26.3	44.4	134 53.4	00.5	Achernar	335 22.3	S57 08.1
02	89 32.9	242 44.0	10.2	75 04.6	34.3	153 28.3	44.4	149 55.7	00.5	Acrux	173 04.1	S63 12.5
03	104 35.4	257 43.5	. . 11.3	90 06.9	. . 34.5	168 30.3	. . 44.3	164 57.9	. . 00.5	Adhara	255 08.2	S28 59.9
04	119 37.9	272 43.1	12.4	105 09.2	34.7	183 32.3	44.2	180 00.2	00.4	Aldebaran	290 43.1	N16 33.0
05	134 40.3	287 42.6	13.6	120 11.6	34.9	198 34.3	44.1	195 02.4	00.4			
06	149 42.8	302 42.2	S 9 14.7	135 13.9	N 5 35.1	213 36.3	S21 44.1	210 04.7	S21 00.3	Alioth	166 16.5	N55 50.7
07	164 45.3	317 41.7	15.8	150 16.2	35.3	228 38.3	44.0	225 07.0	00.3	Alkaid	152 55.2	N49 12.6
08	179 47.7	332 41.3	16.9	165 18.5	35.5	243 40.3	43.9	240 09.2	00.3	Alnair	27 37.2	S46 51.9
F 09	194 50.2	347 40.8	. . 18.0	180 20.9	. . 35.7	258 42.2	. . 43.8	255 11.5	. . 00.2	Alnilam	275 40.8	S 1 11.3
R 10	209 52.7	2 40.4	19.1	195 23.2	35.9	273 44.2	43.8	270 13.7	00.2	Alphard	217 51.0	S 8 44.8
I 11	224 55.1	17 39.9	20.2	210 25.5	36.1	288 46.2	43.7	285 16.0	00.2			
D 12	239 57.6	32 39.4	S 9 21.3	225 27.8	N 5 36.3	303 48.2	S21 43.6	300 18.2	S21 00.1	Alphecca	126 07.0	N26 38.8
A 13	255 00.1	47 39.0	22.4	240 30.1	36.5	318 50.2	43.5	315 20.5	00.1	Alpheratz	357 38.0	N29 12.4
Y 14	270 02.5	62 38.5	23.5	255 32.4	36.7	333 52.2	43.4	330 22.7	00.1	Altair	62 03.4	N 8 55.5
15	285 05.0	77 38.1	. . 24.6	270 34.8	. . 36.9	348 54.2	. . 43.4	345 25.0	. . 00.0	Ankaa	353 10.3	S42 11.8
16	300 07.4	92 37.6	25.7	285 37.1	37.1	3 56.2	43.3	0 27.3	21 00.0	Antares	112 20.3	S26 28.5
17	315 09.9	107 37.1	26.8	300 39.4	37.3	18 58.2	43.2	15 29.5	20 59.9			
18	330 12.4	122 36.7	S 9 27.9	315 41.7	N 5 37.5	34 00.1	S21 43.1	30 31.8	S20 59.9	Arcturus	145 51.3	N19 04.6
19	345 14.8	137 36.2	29.0	330 44.0	37.7	49 02.1	43.1	45 34.0	59.9	Atria	107 18.1	S69 03.8
20	0 17.3	152 35.8	30.1	345 46.3	37.9	64 04.1	43.0	60 36.3	59.8	Avior	234 15.7	S59 34.2
21	15 19.8	167 35.3	. . 31.2	0 48.6	. . 38.1	79 06.1	. . 42.9	75 38.5	. . 59.8	Bellatrix	278 26.2	N 6 22.1
22	30 22.2	182 34.8	32.3	15 50.9	38.3	94 08.1	42.8	90 40.8	59.8	Betelgeuse	270 55.4	N 7 24.6
23	45 24.7	197 34.4	33.4	30 53.2	38.6	109 10.1	42.7	105 43.0	59.7			
21 00	60 27.2	212 33.9	S 9 34.5	45 55.5	N 5 38.8	124 12.1	S21 42.7	120 45.3	S20 59.7	Canopus	263 53.4	S52 42.2
01	75 29.6	227 33.4	35.6	60 57.8	39.0	139 14.1	42.6	135 47.6	59.6	Capella	280 26.4	N46 01.0
02	90 32.1	242 33.0	36.7	76 00.1	39.2	154 16.0	42.5	150 49.8	59.6	Deneb	49 28.2	N45 21.5
03	105 34.6	257 32.5	. . 37.8	91 02.4	. . 39.4	169 18.0	. . 42.4	165 52.1	. . 59.6	Denebola	182 28.6	N14 27.4
04	120 37.0	272 32.1	38.9	106 04.7	39.6	184 20.0	42.4	180 54.3	59.5	Diphda	348 50.5	S17 52.5
05	135 39.5	287 31.6	40.0	121 07.0	39.8	199 22.0	42.3	195 56.6	59.5			
06	150 41.9	302 31.1	S 9 41.1	136 09.3	N 5 40.0	214 24.0	S21 42.2	210 58.8	S20 59.5	Dubhe	193 45.5	N61 38.1
07	165 44.4	317 30.7	42.2	151 11.6	40.2	229 26.0	42.1	226 01.1	59.4	Elnath	278 05.8	N28 37.4
S 08	180 46.9	332 30.2	43.3	166 13.9	40.4	244 28.0	42.0	241 03.3	59.4	Eltanin	90 44.2	N51 29.4
A 09	195 49.3	347 29.7	. . 44.4	181 16.2	. . 40.6	259 29.9	. . 42.0	256 05.6	. . 59.3	Enif	33 42.1	N 9 58.3
T 10	210 51.8	2 29.3	45.5	196 18.5	40.9	274 31.9	41.9	271 07.8	59.3	Fomalhaut	15 18.2	S29 30.9
U 11	225 54.3	17 28.8	46.6	211 20.8	41.1	289 33.9	41.8	286 10.1	59.3			
R 12	240 56.7	32 28.3	S 9 47.7	226 23.1	N 5 41.3	304 35.9	S21 41.7	301 12.3	S20 59.2	Gacrux	171 55.6	S57 13.4
D 13	255 59.2	47 27.9	48.8	241 25.4	41.5	319 37.9	41.7	316 14.6	59.2	Gienah	175 47.2	S17 39.2
A 14	271 01.7	62 27.4	49.9	256 27.7	41.7	334 39.9	41.6	331 16.8	59.2	Hadar	148 41.3	S60 28.1
Y 15	286 04.1	77 26.9	. . 51.0	271 30.0	. . 41.9	349 41.8	. . 41.5	346 19.1	. . 59.1	Hamal	327 54.7	N23 33.7
16	301 06.6	92 26.5	52.1	286 32.2	42.1	4 43.8	41.4	1 21.4	59.1	Kaus Aust.	83 37.3	S34 22.4
17	316 09.0	107 26.0	53.2	301 34.5	42.3	19 45.8	41.3	16 23.6	59.0			
18	331 11.5	122 25.5	S 9 54.3	316 36.8	N 5 42.6	34 47.8	S21 41.3	31 25.9	S20 59.0	Kochab	137 21.1	N74 04.2
19	346 14.0	137 25.0	55.3	331 39.1	42.8	49 49.8	41.2	46 28.1	59.0	Markab	13 33.1	N15 19.1
20	1 16.4	152 24.6	56.4	346 41.4	43.0	64 51.8	41.1	61 30.4	58.9	Menkar	314 09.3	N 4 10.2
21	16 18.9	167 24.1	. . 57.5	1 43.6	. . 43.2	79 53.7	. . 41.0	76 32.6	. . 58.9	Menkent	148 01.9	S36 28.1
22	31 21.4	182 23.6	58.6	16 45.9	43.4	94 55.7	40.9	91 34.9	58.9	Miaplacidus	221 38.5	S69 47.8
23	46 23.8	197 23.2	9 59.7	31 48.2	43.6	109 57.7	40.9	106 37.1	58.8			
22 00	61 26.3	212 22.7	S10 00.8	46 50.5	N 5 43.9	124 59.7	S21 40.8	121 39.4	S20 58.8	Mirfak	308 32.5	N49 56.1
01	76 28.8	227 22.2	01.9	61 52.7	44.1	140 01.7	40.7	136 41.6	58.7	Nunki	75 52.2	S26 16.2
02	91 31.2	242 21.7	03.0	76 55.0	44.3	155 03.7	40.6	151 43.9	58.7	Peacock	53 11.4	S56 40.3
03	106 33.7	257 21.3	. . 04.1	91 57.3	. . 44.5	170 05.6	. . 40.6	166 46.1	. . 58.7	Pollux	243 21.2	N27 58.4
04	121 36.2	272 20.8	05.2	106 59.5	44.7	185 07.6	40.5	181 48.4	58.6	Procyon	244 54.2	N 5 10.3
05	136 38.6	287 20.3	06.3	122 01.8	44.9	200 09.6	40.4	196 50.6	58.6			
06	151 41.1	302 19.8	S10 07.4	137 04.1	N 5 45.2	215 11.6	S20 40.3	211 52.9	S20 58.5	Rasalhague	96 02.0	N12 32.9
07	166 43.5	317 19.4	08.4	152 06.3	45.4	230 13.6	40.2	226 55.1	58.5	Regulus	207 38.0	N11 52.0
08	181 46.0	332 18.9	09.5	167 08.6	45.6	245 15.5	40.2	241 57.4	58.5	Rigel	281 06.8	S 8 10.7
S 09	196 48.5	347 18.4	. . 10.6	182 10.9	. . 45.8	260 17.5	. . 40.1	256 59.6	. . 58.4	Rigil Kent.	139 45.5	S60 55.0
U 10	211 50.9	2 17.9	11.7	197 13.1	46.0	275 19.5	40.0	272 01.9	58.4	Sabik	102 07.0	S15 44.9
N 11	226 53.4	17 17.5	12.8	212 15.4	46.3	290 21.5	39.9	287 04.1	58.4			
D 12	241 55.9	32 17.0	S10 13.9	227 17.7	N 5 46.5	305 23.5	S21 39.8	302 06.4	S20 58.3	Schedar	349 34.4	N56 39.2
A 13	256 58.3	47 16.5	15.0	242 19.9	46.7	320 25.4	39.8	317 08.6	58.3	Shaula	96 15.3	S37 07.0
Y 14	272 00.8	62 16.0	16.1	257 22.2	46.9	335 27.4	39.7	332 10.9	58.2	Sirius	258 28.9	S16 44.6
15	287 03.3	77 15.6	. . 17.1	272 24.4	. . 47.2	350 29.4	. . 39.6	347 13.1	. . 58.2	Spica	158 26.1	S11 16.0
16	302 05.7	92 15.1	18.2	287 26.7	47.4	5 31.4	39.5	2 15.4	58.2	Suhail	222 48.6	S43 30.7
17	317 08.2	107 14.6	19.3	302 28.9	47.6	20 33.4	39.4	17 17.6	58.1			
18	332 10.7	122 14.1	S10 20.4	317 31.2	N 5 47.8	35 35.3	S21 39.4	32 19.9	S20 58.1	Vega	80 35.8	N38 48.4
19	347 13.1	137 13.7	21.5	332 33.4	48.0	50 37.3	39.3	47 22.1	58.0	Zuben'ubi	137 00.1	S16 07.5
20	2 15.6	152 13.2	22.6	347 35.7	48.3	65 39.3	39.2	62 24.4	58.0		SHA	Mer.Pass.
21	17 18.0	167 12.7	. . 23.7	2 37.9	. . 48.5	80 41.3	. . 39.1	77 26.6	. . 58.0		° ′	h m
22	32 20.5	182 12.2	24.7	17 40.2	48.7	95 43.3	39.0	92 28.9	57.9	Venus	152 06.7	9 50
23	47 23.0	197 11.7	25.8	32 42.4	48.9	110 45.2	39.0	107 31.1	57.9	Mars	345 28.4	20 53
	h m									Jupiter	63 44.9	15 41
Mer. Pass. 19 54.9		v −0.5	d 1.1	v 2.3	d 0.2	v 2.0	d 0.1	v 2.3	d 0.0	Saturn	60 18.1	15 55

UT	SUN GHA	SUN Dec	MOON GHA	v	MOON Dec	d	HP
	° ′	° ′	° ′	′	° ′	′	′
20 00	183 35.9	S19 44.4	114 21.4	7.7	S23 08.3	5.4	57.6
01	198 35.7	44.9	128 48.1	7.9	23 02.9	5.6	57.5
02	213 35.6	45.5	143 15.0	7.9	22 57.3	5.8	57.5
03	228 35.4	.. 46.1	157 41.9	8.0	22 51.5	5.8	57.5
04	243 35.3	46.6	172 08.9	8.1	22 45.7	6.0	57.4
05	258 35.1	47.2	186 36.0	8.3	22 39.7	6.1	57.4
06	273 35.0	S19 47.8	201 03.3	8.3	S22 33.6	6.2	57.3
07	288 34.8	48.3	215 30.6	8.4	22 27.4	6.3	57.3
08	303 34.7	48.9	229 58.0	8.6	22 21.1	6.4	57.2
F 09	318 34.5	.. 49.4	244 25.6	8.6	22 14.7	6.6	57.2
R 10	333 34.4	50.0	258 53.2	8.8	22 08.1	6.7	57.2
I 11	348 34.2	50.5	273 21.0	8.8	22 01.4	6.7	57.1
D 12	3 34.1	S19 51.1	287 48.8	9.0	S21 54.7	6.9	57.1
A 13	18 33.9	51.7	302 16.8	9.0	21 47.8	7.0	57.0
Y 14	33 33.7	52.2	316 44.8	9.2	21 40.8	7.1	57.0
15	48 33.6	.. 52.8	331 13.0	9.3	21 33.7	7.2	57.0
16	63 33.4	53.3	345 41.3	9.3	21 26.5	7.4	56.9
17	78 33.3	53.9	0 09.6	9.5	21 19.1	7.4	56.9
18	93 33.1	S19 54.4	14 38.1	9.6	S21 11.7	7.5	56.9
19	108 33.0	55.0	29 06.7	9.7	21 04.2	7.7	56.8
20	123 32.8	55.5	43 35.4	9.7	20 56.5	7.7	56.8
21	138 32.7	.. 56.1	58 04.1	9.9	20 48.8	7.8	56.7
22	153 32.5	56.6	72 33.0	10.0	20 41.0	7.9	56.7
23	168 32.3	57.2	87 02.0	10.1	20 33.1	8.1	56.7
21 00	183 32.2	S19 57.7	101 31.1	10.2	S20 25.0	8.1	56.6
01	198 32.0	58.3	116 00.3	10.3	20 16.9	8.2	56.6
02	213 31.9	58.8	130 29.6	10.4	20 08.7	8.3	56.6
03	228 31.7	.. 59.4	144 59.0	10.5	20 00.4	8.4	56.5
04	243 31.5	19 59.9	159 28.5	10.6	19 52.0	8.5	56.5
05	258 31.4	20 00.5	173 58.1	10.7	19 43.5	8.5	56.5
06	273 31.2	S20 01.0	188 27.8	10.8	S19 35.0	8.7	56.4
07	288 31.1	01.5	202 57.6	10.9	19 26.3	8.7	56.4
S 08	303 30.9	02.1	217 27.5	11.0	19 17.6	8.9	56.4
A 09	318 30.7	.. 02.6	231 57.5	11.0	19 08.7	8.9	56.3
T 10	333 30.6	03.2	246 27.5	11.2	18 59.8	9.0	56.3
U 11	348 30.4	03.7	260 57.7	11.3	18 50.8	9.1	56.2
R 12	3 30.3	S20 04.3	275 28.0	11.4	S18 41.7	9.1	56.2
D 13	18 30.1	04.8	289 58.4	11.5	18 32.6	9.2	56.2
A 14	33 29.9	05.3	304 28.9	11.6	18 23.4	9.4	56.1
Y 15	48 29.8	.. 05.9	318 59.5	11.7	18 14.0	9.4	56.1
16	63 29.6	06.4	333 30.2	11.7	18 04.6	9.4	56.1
17	78 29.4	07.0	348 00.9	11.9	17 55.2	9.6	56.0
18	93 29.3	S20 07.5	2 31.8	12.0	S17 45.6	9.6	56.0
19	108 29.1	08.0	17 02.8	12.0	17 36.0	9.7	56.0
20	123 29.0	08.6	31 33.8	12.1	17 26.3	9.7	56.0
21	138 28.8	.. 09.1	46 04.9	12.3	17 16.6	9.8	55.9
22	153 28.6	09.6	60 36.2	12.3	17 06.8	9.9	55.9
23	168 28.5	10.2	75 07.5	12.4	16 56.9	10.0	55.9
22 00	183 28.3	S20 10.7	89 38.9	12.5	S16 46.9	10.0	55.8
01	198 28.1	11.2	104 10.4	12.6	16 36.9	10.1	55.8
02	213 28.0	11.8	118 42.0	12.7	16 26.8	10.2	55.7
03	228 27.8	.. 12.3	133 13.7	12.7	16 16.6	10.2	55.7
04	243 27.6	12.8	147 45.4	12.9	16 06.4	10.2	55.7
05	258 27.5	13.4	162 17.3	12.9	15 56.2	10.4	55.7
06	273 27.3	S20 13.9	176 49.2	13.1	S15 45.8	10.4	55.6
07	288 27.1	14.4	191 21.3	13.1	15 35.4	10.4	55.6
08	303 26.9	14.9	205 53.4	13.1	15 25.0	10.6	55.6
S 09	318 26.8	.. 15.5	220 25.5	13.3	15 14.4	10.5	55.6
U 10	333 26.6	16.0	234 57.8	13.4	15 03.9	10.7	55.5
N 11	348 26.4	16.5	249 30.2	13.4	14 53.2	10.6	55.5
D 12	3 26.3	S20 17.0	264 02.6	13.5	S14 42.6	10.8	55.5
A 13	18 26.1	17.6	278 35.1	13.6	14 31.8	10.8	55.4
Y 14	33 25.9	18.1	293 07.7	13.6	14 21.0	10.8	55.4
15	48 25.8	.. 18.6	307 40.3	13.8	14 10.2	10.9	55.4
16	63 25.6	19.1	322 13.1	13.8	13 59.3	10.9	55.4
17	78 25.4	19.7	336 45.9	13.9	13 48.4	11.0	55.3
18	93 25.2	S20 20.2	351 18.8	13.9	S13 37.4	11.1	55.3
19	108 25.1	20.7	5 51.7	14.1	13 26.3	11.1	55.3
20	123 24.9	21.2	20 24.8	14.1	13 15.2	11.1	55.3
21	138 24.7	.. 21.7	34 57.9	14.1	13 04.1	11.2	55.2
22	153 24.5	22.3	49 31.0	14.3	12 52.9	11.2	55.2
23	168 24.4	22.8	64 04.3	14.3	S12 41.7	11.3	55.2
	SD 16.2	d 0.5	SD 15.6		15.3		15.1

Twilight / Moonrise

Lat.	Naut.	Civil	Sunrise	Moonrise 20	21	22	23
°	h m	h m	h m	h m	h m	h m	h m
N 72	07 22	09 05	■	■	17 32	15 54	15 19
N 70	07 09	08 36	10 39	■	16 04	15 26	15 04
68	06 58	08 15	09 44	16 09	15 24	15 05	14 52
66	06 50	07 58	09 12	15 08	14 57	14 49	14 42
64	06 42	07 44	08 48	14 34	14 35	14 35	14 34
62	06 35	07 33	08 29	14 08	14 18	14 24	14 27
60	06 29	07 22	08 14	13 48	14 04	14 14	14 21
N 58	06 24	07 14	08 01	13 32	13 52	14 05	14 15
56	06 19	07 06	07 49	13 18	13 41	13 57	14 10
54	06 15	06 59	07 39	13 06	13 31	13 51	14 06
52	06 10	06 52	07 31	12 55	13 23	13 44	14 02
50	06 07	06 46	07 23	12 45	13 15	13 39	13 58
45	05 58	06 34	07 06	12 25	12 59	13 27	13 50
N 40	05 50	06 23	06 52	12 09	12 46	13 17	13 44
35	05 42	06 13	06 41	11 55	12 34	13 08	13 38
30	05 36	06 05	06 30	11 43	12 24	13 01	13 33
20	05 22	05 49	06 13	11 22	12 07	12 47	13 24
N 10	05 09	05 35	05 57	11 04	11 52	12 36	13 16
0	04 55	05 20	05 42	10 47	11 38	12 25	13 09
S 10	04 39	05 05	05 28	10 30	11 24	12 14	13 02
20	04 20	04 48	05 12	10 11	11 08	12 02	12 54
30	03 55	04 27	04 53	09 50	10 51	11 49	12 45
35	03 39	04 14	04 42	09 38	10 41	11 41	12 40
40	03 20	03 59	04 30	09 24	10 29	11 32	12 34
45	02 56	03 40	04 15	09 07	10 15	11 22	12 27
S 50	02 22	03 17	03 57	08 46	09 58	11 09	12 18
52	02 04	03 05	03 48	08 36	09 50	11 03	12 15
54	01 41	02 51	03 39	08 25	09 41	10 57	12 10
56	01 09	02 36	03 28	08 12	09 31	10 49	12 06
58	////	02 16	03 15	07 57	09 19	10 41	12 00
S 60	////	01 52	03 00	07 39	09 06	10 32	11 54

Sunset / Twilight / Moonset

Lat.	Sunset	Civil	Naut.	Moonset 20	21	22	23
°	h m	h m	h m	h m	h m	h m	h m
N 72	■	14 26	16 09	■	18 25	21 39	23 44
N 70	12 52	14 55	16 22	■	19 51	22 05	23 57
68	13 47	15 16	16 33	18 02	20 30	22 24	24 07
66	14 20	15 33	16 41	19 01	20 57	22 40	24 15
64	14 44	15 47	16 49	19 35	21 17	22 52	24 22
62	15 02	15 59	16 56	20 00	21 33	23 03	24 28
60	15 18	16 09	17 02	20 19	21 47	23 12	24 33
N 58	15 31	16 18	17 07	20 35	21 58	23 19	24 37
56	15 42	16 26	17 12	20 49	22 08	23 26	24 41
54	15 52	16 33	17 17	21 01	22 17	23 32	24 45
52	16 01	16 39	17 21	21 11	22 25	23 38	24 48
50	16 09	16 45	17 25	21 20	22 32	23 43	24 51
45	16 25	16 58	17 34	21 39	22 47	23 53	24 57
N 40	16 39	17 09	17 42	21 55	23 00	24 02	00 02
35	16 51	17 18	17 49	22 08	23 10	24 10	00 10
30	17 01	17 27	17 56	22 20	23 19	24 16	00 16
20	17 19	17 43	18 10	22 39	23 35	24 27	00 27
N 10	17 35	17 57	18 23	22 56	23 48	24 37	00 37
0	17 50	18 12	18 37	23 12	24 01	00 01	00 46
S 10	18 04	18 27	18 53	23 27	24 14	00 14	00 56
20	18 21	18 44	19 13	23 44	24 27	00 27	01 05
30	18 39	19 06	19 38	24 03	00 03	00 42	01 16
35	18 49	19 19	19 53	24 14	00 14	00 51	01 22
40	19 03	19 34	20 13	24 27	00 27	01 01	01 29
45	19 18	19 53	20 37	00 03	00 42	01 12	01 38
S 50	19 36	20 17	21 12	00 25	01 00	01 26	01 48
52	19 45	20 28	21 30	00 35	01 08	01 33	01 52
54	19 54	20 42	21 54	00 47	01 18	01 40	01 57
56	20 05	20 58	22 27	01 00	01 28	01 48	02 03
58	20 18	21 18	////	01 15	01 40	01 57	02 09
S 60	20 33	21 43	////	01 34	01 54	02 07	02 16

SUN / MOON

Day	Eqn. of Time 00h	Eqn. of Time 12h	Mer. Pass.	Mer. Pass. Upper	Lower	Age	Phase
d	m s	m s	h m	h m	h m	d	%
20	14 24	14 17	11 46	16 59	04 33	05	33
21	14 09	14 01	11 46	17 50	05 25	06	43
22	13 53	13 45	11 46	18 36	06 13	07	53

UT	ARIES GHA	VENUS −3.9 GHA	Dec	MARS −1.3 GHA	Dec	JUPITER −2.1 GHA	Dec	SATURN +0.6 GHA	Dec
23 00	62 25.4	212 11.3	S10 26.9	47 44.7	N 5 49.2	125 47.2	S21 38.9	122 33.4	S20 57.9
01	77 27.9	227 10.8	28.0	62 46.9	49.4	140 49.2	38.8	137 35.6	57.8
02	92 30.4	242 10.3	29.1	77 49.2	49.6	155 51.2	38.7	152 37.9	57.8
03	107 32.8	257 09.8	.. 30.1	92 51.4	.. 49.9	170 53.1	.. 38.6	167 40.1	.. 57.7
04	122 35.3	272 09.3	31.2	107 53.6	50.1	185 55.1	38.6	182 42.4	57.7
05	137 37.8	287 08.8	32.3	122 55.9	50.3	200 57.1	38.5	197 44.6	57.7
06	152 40.2	302 08.4	S10 33.4	137 58.1	N 5 50.5	215 59.1	S21 38.4	212 46.9	S20 57.6
07	167 42.7	317 07.9	34.5	153 00.3	50.8	231 01.1	38.3	227 49.1	57.6
08	182 45.1	332 07.4	35.6	168 02.6	51.0	246 03.0	38.2	242 51.3	57.5
M 09	197 47.6	347 06.9	.. 36.6	183 04.8	.. 51.2	261 05.0	.. 38.2	257 53.6	.. 57.5
O 10	212 50.1	2 06.4	37.7	198 07.1	51.5	276 07.0	38.1	272 55.8	57.5
N 11	227 52.5	17 05.9	38.8	213 09.3	51.7	291 09.0	38.0	287 58.1	57.4
D 12	242 55.0	32 05.4	S10 39.9	228 11.5	N 5 51.9	306 10.9	S21 37.9	303 00.3	S20 57.4
A 13	257 57.5	47 05.0	40.9	243 13.7	52.1	321 12.9	37.8	318 02.6	57.3
Y 14	272 59.9	62 04.5	42.0	258 16.0	52.4	336 14.9	37.7	333 04.8	57.3
15	288 02.4	77 04.0	.. 43.1	273 18.2	.. 52.6	351 16.9	.. 37.7	348 07.1	.. 57.3
16	303 04.9	92 03.5	44.2	288 20.4	52.8	6 18.8	37.6	3 09.3	57.2
17	318 07.3	107 03.0	45.3	303 22.6	53.1	21 20.8	37.5	18 11.6	57.2
18	333 09.8	122 02.5	S10 46.3	318 24.9	N 5 53.3	36 22.8	S21 37.4	33 13.8	S20 57.2
19	348 12.3	137 02.0	47.4	333 27.1	53.5	51 24.8	37.3	48 16.1	57.1
20	3 14.7	152 01.5	48.5	348 29.3	53.8	66 26.7	37.3	63 18.3	57.1
21	18 17.2	167 01.1	.. 49.6	3 31.5	.. 54.0	81 28.7	.. 37.2	78 20.6	.. 57.0
22	33 19.6	182 00.6	50.6	18 33.7	54.2	96 30.7	37.1	93 22.8	57.0
23	48 22.1	197 00.1	51.7	33 36.0	54.5	111 32.7	37.0	108 25.0	57.0
24 00	63 24.6	211 59.6	S10 52.8	48 38.2	N 5 54.7	126 34.6	S21 36.9	123 27.3	S20 56.9
01	78 27.0	226 59.1	53.8	63 40.4	55.0	141 36.6	36.9	138 29.5	56.9
02	93 29.5	241 58.6	54.9	78 42.6	55.2	156 38.6	36.8	153 31.8	56.8
03	108 32.0	256 58.1	.. 56.0	93 44.8	.. 55.5	171 40.6	.. 36.7	168 34.0	.. 56.8
04	123 34.4	271 57.6	57.1	108 47.0	55.7	186 42.5	36.6	183 36.3	56.8
05	138 36.9	286 57.1	58.1	123 49.2	55.9	201 44.5	36.5	198 38.5	56.7
06	153 39.4	301 56.6	S10 59.2	138 51.5	N 5 56.1	216 46.5	S21 36.4	213 40.8	S20 56.7
07	168 41.8	316 56.1	11 00.3	153 53.7	56.4	231 48.5	36.4	228 43.0	56.6
08	183 44.3	331 55.6	01.3	168 55.9	56.6	246 50.4	36.3	243 45.3	56.6
T 09	198 46.8	346 55.2	.. 02.4	183 58.1	.. 56.8	261 52.4	.. 36.2	258 47.5	.. 56.5
U 10	213 49.2	1 54.7	03.5	199 00.3	57.1	276 54.4	36.1	273 49.7	56.5
E 11	228 51.7	16 54.2	04.6	214 02.5	57.3	291 56.3	36.0	288 52.0	56.5
S 12	243 54.1	31 53.7	S11 05.6	229 04.7	N 5 57.6	306 58.3	S21 36.0	303 54.2	S20 56.4
D 13	258 56.6	46 53.2	06.7	244 06.9	57.8	322 00.3	35.9	318 56.5	56.4
A 14	273 59.1	61 52.7	07.8	259 09.1	58.0	337 02.3	35.8	333 58.7	56.4
Y 15	289 01.5	76 52.2	.. 08.8	274 11.3	.. 58.3	352 04.2	.. 35.7	349 01.0	.. 56.3
16	304 04.0	91 51.7	09.9	289 13.5	58.5	7 06.2	35.6	4 03.2	56.3
17	319 06.5	106 51.2	11.0	304 15.7	58.8	22 08.2	35.5	19 05.4	56.2
18	334 08.9	121 50.7	S11 12.0	319 17.9	N 5 59.0	37 10.1	S21 35.5	34 07.7	S20 56.2
19	349 11.4	136 50.2	13.1	334 20.1	59.3	52 12.1	35.4	49 09.9	56.2
20	4 13.9	151 49.7	14.2	349 22.3	59.5	67 14.1	35.3	64 12.2	56.1
21	19 16.3	166 49.2	.. 15.2	4 24.4	5 59.7	82 16.1	.. 35.2	79 14.4	.. 56.1
22	34 18.8	181 48.7	16.3	19 26.6	6 00.0	97 18.0	35.1	94 16.7	56.0
23	49 21.2	196 48.2	17.3	34 28.8	00.2	112 20.0	35.0	109 18.9	56.0
25 00	64 23.7	211 47.7	S11 18.4	49 31.0	N 6 00.5	127 22.0	S21 35.0	124 21.1	S20 56.0
01	79 26.2	226 47.2	19.5	64 33.2	00.7	142 23.9	34.9	139 23.4	55.9
02	94 28.6	241 46.7	20.5	79 35.4	01.0	157 25.9	34.8	154 25.6	55.9
03	109 31.1	256 46.2	.. 21.6	94 37.6	.. 01.2	172 27.9	.. 34.7	169 27.9	.. 55.8
04	124 33.6	271 45.7	22.7	109 39.8	01.5	187 29.8	34.6	184 30.1	55.8
05	139 36.0	286 45.2	23.7	124 41.9	01.7	202 31.8	34.5	199 32.4	55.8
06	154 38.5	301 44.7	S11 24.8	139 44.1	N 6 01.9	217 33.8	S21 34.5	214 34.6	S20 55.7
07	169 41.0	316 44.2	25.8	154 46.3	02.2	232 35.8	34.4	229 36.8	55.7
W 08	184 43.4	331 43.7	26.9	169 48.5	02.4	247 37.7	34.3	244 39.1	55.6
E 09	199 45.9	346 43.2	.. 28.0	184 50.6	.. 02.7	262 39.7	.. 34.2	259 41.3	.. 55.6
D 10	214 48.4	1 42.7	29.0	199 52.8	02.9	277 41.7	34.1	274 43.6	55.6
N 11	229 50.8	16 42.2	30.1	214 55.0	03.2	292 43.6	34.0	289 45.8	55.5
E 12	244 53.3	31 41.7	S11 31.1	229 57.2	N 6 03.4	307 45.6	S21 34.0	304 48.0	S20 55.5
S 13	259 55.7	46 41.1	32.2	244 59.3	03.7	322 47.6	33.9	319 50.3	55.4
D 14	274 58.2	61 40.6	33.3	260 01.5	03.9	337 49.5	33.8	334 52.5	55.4
A 15	290 00.7	76 40.1	.. 34.3	275 03.7	.. 04.2	352 51.5	.. 33.7	349 54.8	.. 55.4
Y 16	305 03.1	91 39.6	35.4	290 05.9	04.4	7 53.5	33.6	4 57.0	55.3
17	320 05.6	106 39.1	36.4	305 08.0	04.7	22 55.4	33.5	19 59.3	55.3
18	335 08.1	121 38.6	S11 37.5	320 10.2	N 6 04.9	37 57.4	S21 33.5	35 01.5	S20 55.2
19	350 10.5	136 38.1	38.5	335 12.4	05.2	52 59.4	33.4	50 03.7	55.2
20	5 13.0	151 37.6	39.6	350 14.5	05.4	68 01.3	33.3	65 06.0	55.2
21	20 15.5	166 37.1	.. 40.6	5 16.7	.. 05.7	83 03.3	.. 33.2	80 08.2	.. 55.1
22	35 17.9	181 36.6	41.7	20 18.8	05.9	98 05.3	33.1	95 10.5	55.1
23	50 20.4	196 36.1	42.8	35 21.0	06.2	113 07.2	33.0	110 12.7	55.0
Mer. Pass.	19 43.1	v −0.5	d 1.1	v 2.2	d 0.2	v 2.0	d 0.1	v 2.2	d 0.0

STARS

Name	SHA	Dec
Acamar	315 14.0	S40 13.4
Achernar	335 22.4	S57 08.1
Acrux	173 04.0	S63 12.5
Adhara	255 08.2	S28 59.9
Aldebaran	290 43.1	N16 33.0
Alioth	166 16.4	N55 50.7
Alkaid	152 55.2	N49 12.5
Alnair	27 37.2	S46 51.9
Alnilam	275 40.8	S 1 11.3
Alphard	217 51.0	S 8 44.8
Alphecca	126 07.0	N26 38.8
Alpheratz	357 38.0	N29 12.4
Altair	62 03.4	N 8 55.5
Ankaa	353 10.3	S42 11.8
Antares	112 20.3	S26 28.5
Arcturus	145 51.3	N19 04.6
Atria	107 18.1	S69 03.8
Avior	234 15.7	S59 34.3
Bellatrix	278 26.2	N 6 22.1
Betelgeuse	270 55.4	N 7 24.6
Canopus	263 53.4	S52 42.3
Capella	280 26.4	N46 01.0
Deneb	49 28.2	N45 21.5
Denebola	182 28.5	N14 27.4
Diphda	348 50.5	S17 52.5
Dubhe	193 45.4	N61 38.1
Elnath	278 05.7	N28 37.4
Eltanin	90 44.2	N51 29.4
Enif	33 42.1	N 9 58.3
Fomalhaut	15 18.2	S29 30.9
Gacrux	171 55.6	S57 13.4
Gienah	175 47.2	S17 39.2
Hadar	148 41.2	S60 28.1
Hamal	327 54.7	N23 33.7
Kaus Aust.	83 37.3	S34 22.4
Kochab	137 21.1	N74 04.2
Markab	13 33.2	N15 19.1
Menkar	314 09.3	N 4 10.2
Menkent	148 01.9	S36 28.1
Miaplacidus	221 38.5	S69 47.8
Mirfak	308 32.5	N49 56.1
Nunki	75 52.2	S26 16.2
Peacock	53 11.4	S56 40.3
Pollux	243 21.2	N27 58.4
Procyon	244 54.1	N 5 10.3
Rasalhague	96 02.0	N12 32.9
Regulus	207 38.0	N11 52.0
Rigel	281 06.8	S 8 10.7
Rigil Kent.	139 45.5	S60 55.0
Sabik	102 07.0	S15 44.9
Schedar	349 34.4	N56 39.2
Shaula	96 15.3	S37 07.0
Sirius	258 28.9	S16 44.6
Spica	158 26.1	S11 16.0
Suhail	222 48.6	S43 30.7
Vega	80 35.8	N38 48.4
Zuben'ubi	137 00.1	S16 07.5

	SHA	Mer. Pass.
Venus	148 35.0	9 52
Mars	345 13.6	20 42
Jupiter	63 10.1	15 32
Saturn	60 02.7	15 44

UT	SUN GHA	SUN Dec	MOON GHA	v	MOON Dec	d	HP
d h	° ′	° ′	° ′	′	° ′	′	′
23 00	183 24.2	S20 23.3	78 37.6	14.4	S12 30.4	11.3	55.2
01	198 24.0	23.8	93 11.0	14.4	12 19.1	11.3	55.1
02	213 23.9	24.3	107 44.4	14.5	12 07.8	11.4	55.1
03	228 23.7	.. 24.8	122 17.9	14.6	11 56.4	11.4	55.1
04	243 23.5	25.4	136 51.5	14.7	11 45.0	11.5	55.1
05	258 23.3	25.9	151 25.2	14.7	11 33.5	11.5	55.0
06	273 23.1	S20 26.4	165 58.9	14.7	S11 22.0	11.5	55.0
07	288 23.0	26.9	180 32.6	14.9	11 10.5	11.6	55.0
08	303 22.8	27.4	195 06.5	14.9	10 58.9	11.6	55.0
M 09	318 22.6	.. 27.9	209 40.4	14.9	10 47.3	11.7	54.9
O 10	333 22.4	28.4	224 14.3	15.0	10 35.6	11.7	54.9
N 11	348 22.3	29.0	238 48.3	15.1	10 23.9	11.7	54.9
D 12	3 22.1	S20 29.5	253 22.4	15.1	S10 12.2	11.7	54.9
A 13	18 21.9	30.0	267 56.5	15.1	10 00.5	11.8	54.9
Y 14	33 21.7	30.5	282 30.6	15.3	9 48.7	11.8	54.8
15	48 21.5	.. 31.0	297 04.9	15.2	9 36.9	11.9	54.8
16	63 21.4	31.5	311 39.1	15.4	9 25.0	11.8	54.8
17	78 21.2	32.0	326 13.5	15.4	9 13.2	11.9	54.8
18	93 21.0	S20 32.5	340 47.9	15.4	S 9 01.3	11.9	54.8
19	108 20.8	33.0	355 22.3	15.5	8 49.4	12.0	54.7
20	123 20.6	33.5	9 56.8	15.5	8 37.4	12.0	54.7
21	138 20.5	.. 34.0	24 31.3	15.6	8 25.4	12.0	54.7
22	153 20.3	34.5	39 05.9	15.6	8 13.4	12.0	54.7
23	168 20.1	35.0	53 40.5	15.6	8 01.4	12.1	54.7
24 00	183 19.9	S20 35.5	68 15.1	15.7	S 7 49.3	12.0	54.6
01	198 19.7	36.0	82 49.8	15.8	7 37.3	12.1	54.6
02	213 19.6	36.5	97 24.6	15.8	7 25.2	12.1	54.6
03	228 19.4	.. 37.0	111 59.4	15.8	7 13.1	12.2	54.6
04	243 19.2	37.5	126 34.2	15.9	7 00.9	12.1	54.6
05	258 19.0	38.0	141 09.1	15.9	6 48.8	12.2	54.6
06	273 18.8	S20 38.5	155 44.0	15.9	S 6 36.6	12.2	54.5
07	288 18.6	39.0	170 18.9	16.0	6 24.4	12.2	54.5
T 08	303 18.5	39.5	184 53.9	16.0	6 12.2	12.3	54.5
U 09	318 18.3	.. 40.0	199 28.9	16.1	5 59.9	12.2	54.5
E 10	333 18.1	40.5	214 04.0	16.0	5 47.7	12.3	54.5
S 11	348 17.9	41.0	228 39.0	16.2	5 35.4	12.3	54.5
D 12	3 17.7	S20 41.5	243 14.2	16.1	S 5 23.1	12.3	54.4
A 13	18 17.5	42.0	257 49.3	16.2	5 10.8	12.4	54.4
Y 14	33 17.3	42.5	272 24.5	16.2	4 58.5	12.3	54.4
15	48 17.2	.. 43.0	286 59.7	16.2	4 46.2	12.3	54.4
16	63 17.0	43.5	301 34.9	16.3	4 33.9	12.4	54.4
17	78 16.8	44.0	316 10.2	16.3	4 21.5	12.3	54.4
18	93 16.6	S20 44.4	330 45.5	16.3	S 4 09.2	12.4	54.4
19	108 16.4	44.9	345 20.8	16.3	3 56.8	12.4	54.4
20	123 16.2	45.4	359 56.1	16.4	3 44.4	12.4	54.3
21	138 16.0	.. 45.9	14 31.5	16.4	3 32.0	12.4	54.3
22	153 15.8	46.4	29 06.9	16.4	3 19.6	12.4	54.3
23	168 15.6	46.9	43 42.3	16.4	3 07.2	12.4	54.3
25 00	183 15.5	S20 47.4	58 17.7	16.4	S 2 54.8	12.4	54.3
01	198 15.3	47.9	72 53.1	16.5	2 42.4	12.4	54.3
02	213 15.1	48.3	87 28.6	16.5	2 30.0	12.5	54.3
03	228 14.9	.. 48.8	102 04.1	16.5	2 17.5	12.4	54.3
04	243 14.7	49.3	116 39.6	16.5	2 05.1	12.4	54.2
05	258 14.5	49.8	131 15.1	16.5	1 52.7	12.5	54.2
06	273 14.3	S20 50.3	145 50.6	16.5	S 1 40.2	12.4	54.2
W 07	288 14.1	50.7	160 26.1	16.6	1 27.8	12.5	54.2
E 08	303 13.9	51.2	175 01.7	16.6	1 15.3	12.4	54.2
D 09	318 13.7	.. 51.7	189 37.3	16.5	1 02.9	12.5	54.2
N 10	333 13.5	52.2	204 12.8	16.6	0 50.4	12.4	54.2
E 11	348 13.3	52.7	218 48.4	16.6	0 38.0	12.5	54.2
S 12	3 13.2	S20 53.1	233 24.0	16.6	S 0 25.5	12.4	54.2
D 13	18 13.0	53.6	247 59.6	16.6	0 13.1	12.5	54.2
A 14	33 12.8	54.1	262 35.2	16.6	S 0 00.6	12.4	54.1
Y 15	48 12.6	.. 54.6	277 10.8	16.6	N 0 11.8	12.4	54.1
16	63 12.4	55.0	291 46.4	16.6	0 24.2	12.5	54.1
17	78 12.2	55.5	306 22.0	16.7	0 36.7	12.4	54.1
18	93 12.0	S20 56.0	320 57.7	16.6	N 0 49.1	12.4	54.1
19	108 11.8	56.5	335 33.3	16.6	1 01.5	12.5	54.1
20	123 11.6	56.9	350 08.9	16.6	1 14.0	12.4	54.1
21	138 11.4	.. 57.4	4 44.5	16.6	1 26.4	12.4	54.1
22	153 11.2	57.9	19 20.1	16.7	1 38.8	12.4	54.1
23	168 11.0	58.4	33 55.8	16.6	N 1 51.2	12.4	54.1
SD	16.2	d 0.5	SD 15.0		14.8		14.8

Lat.	Twilight Naut.	Civil	Sunrise	Moonrise 23	24	25	26
°	h m	h m	h m	h m	h m	h m	h m
N 72	07 31	09 19	■■■	15 19	14 53	14 30	14 08
N 70	07 18	08 48	11 18	15 04	14 46	14 31	14 15
68	07 06	08 24	10 00	14 52	14 41	14 31	14 20
66	06 57	08 06	09 23	14 42	14 36	14 31	14 25
64	06 48	07 52	08 57	14 34	14 32	14 31	14 29
62	06 41	07 39	08 37	14 27	14 29	14 31	14 32
60	06 35	07 28	08 21	14 21	14 26	14 31	14 35
N 58	06 29	07 19	08 07	14 15	14 23	14 31	14 38
56	06 24	07 11	07 55	14 10	14 21	14 31	14 40
54	06 19	07 04	07 45	14 06	14 19	14 31	14 42
52	06 15	06 57	07 36	14 02	14 17	14 31	14 44
50	06 10	06 51	07 27	13 58	14 15	14 31	14 46
45	06 01	06 37	07 10	13 50	14 11	14 31	14 50
N 40	05 53	06 26	06 56	13 44	14 08	14 31	14 53
35	05 45	06 16	06 43	13 38	14 05	14 31	14 56
30	05 38	06 07	06 33	13 33	14 02	14 31	14 59
20	05 24	05 51	06 14	13 24	13 58	14 31	15 03
N 10	05 10	05 36	05 58	13 16	13 54	14 31	15 07
0	04 55	05 21	05 43	13 09	13 50	14 31	15 11
S 10	04 39	05 05	05 28	13 02	13 47	14 31	15 15
20	04 19	04 47	05 11	12 54	13 43	14 31	15 19
30	03 54	04 26	04 52	12 45	13 39	14 31	15 23
35	03 37	04 12	04 41	12 40	13 36	14 31	15 26
40	03 18	03 57	04 28	12 34	13 33	14 31	15 29
45	02 52	03 38	04 13	12 27	13 30	14 31	15 33
S 50	02 17	03 13	03 54	12 18	13 26	14 32	15 37
52	01 57	03 01	03 45	12 15	13 24	14 32	15 39
54	01 32	02 46	03 35	12 10	13 22	14 32	15 41
56	00 56	02 30	03 23	12 06	13 19	14 32	15 44
58	////	02 09	03 10	12 00	13 17	14 32	15 46
S 60	////	01 43	02 54	11 54	13 14	14 32	15 49

Lat.	Sunset	Twilight Civil	Naut.	Moonset 23	24	25	26
°	h m	h m	h m	h m	h m	h m	h m
N 72	■■■	14 14	16 01	23 44	25 36	01 36	03 24
N 70	12 15	14 45	16 15	23 57	25 40	01 40	03 21
68	13 33	15 08	16 27	24 07	00 07	01 43	03 18
66	14 10	15 27	16 36	24 15	00 15	01 46	03 15
64	14 36	15 41	16 44	24 22	00 22	01 48	03 13
62	14 56	15 54	16 52	24 28	00 28	01 50	03 11
60	15 12	16 05	16 58	24 33	00 33	01 52	03 09
N 58	15 26	16 14	17 04	24 37	00 37	01 53	03 08
56	15 38	16 22	17 09	24 41	00 41	01 54	03 06
54	15 48	16 30	17 14	24 45	00 45	01 55	03 05
52	15 58	16 36	17 19	24 48	00 48	01 57	03 04
50	16 06	16 43	17 23	24 51	00 51	01 57	03 03
45	16 23	16 56	17 32	24 57	00 57	02 00	03 01
N 40	16 38	17 07	17 41	00 02	01 02	02 01	02 59
35	16 50	17 17	17 48	00 10	01 07	02 03	02 58
30	17 01	17 26	17 56	00 16	01 11	02 04	02 56
20	17 19	17 43	18 10	00 27	01 18	02 06	02 54
N 10	17 35	17 58	18 23	00 37	01 24	02 08	02 52
0	17 50	18 13	18 38	00 46	01 29	02 10	02 50
S 10	18 06	18 28	18 55	00 56	01 35	02 12	02 48
20	18 22	18 46	19 15	01 05	01 40	02 14	02 46
30	18 42	19 08	19 40	01 16	01 47	02 16	02 44
35	18 53	19 21	19 57	01 22	01 51	02 17	02 43
40	19 06	19 37	20 17	01 29	01 55	02 18	02 41
45	19 21	19 57	20 43	01 38	02 00	02 20	02 39
S 50	19 41	20 22	21 19	01 48	02 06	02 22	02 37
52	19 50	20 34	21 38	01 52	02 08	02 23	02 36
54	20 00	20 49	22 04	01 57	02 11	02 23	02 35
56	20 11	21 06	22 42	02 03	02 14	02 24	02 34
58	20 25	21 26	////	02 09	02 18	02 26	02 33
S 60	20 41	21 54	////	02 16	02 22	02 27	02 31

Day	SUN Eqn. of Time 00h	12h	Mer. Pass.	MOON Mer. Pass. Upper	Lower	Age	Phase
d	m s	m s	h m	h m	h m	d	%
23	13 37	13 29	11 47	19 19	06 58	08	63
24	13 20	13 11	11 47	20 00	07 40	09	72
25	13 02	12 53	11 47	20 41	08 20	10	80

UT	ARIES GHA	VENUS −3.9 GHA	VENUS Dec	MARS −1.2 GHA	MARS Dec	JUPITER −2.0 GHA	JUPITER Dec	SATURN +0.6 GHA	SATURN Dec
26 00	65 22.8	211 35.6	S11 43.8	50 23.2	N 6 06.4	128 09.2	S21 33.0	125 14.9	S20 55.0
01	80 25.3	226 35.0	44.9	65 25.3	06.7	143 11.2	32.9	140 17.2	55.0
02	95 27.8	241 34.5	45.9	80 27.5	06.9	158 13.1	32.8	155 19.4	54.9
03	110 30.2	256 34.0 ..	47.0	95 29.6 ..	07.2	173 15.1 ..	32.7	170 21.6 ..	54.9
04	125 32.7	271 33.5	48.0	110 31.8	07.5	188 17.1	32.6	185 23.9	54.8
05	140 35.2	286 33.0	49.1	125 34.0	07.7	203 19.0	32.5	200 26.1	54.8
06	155 37.6	301 32.5	S11 50.1	140 36.1	N 6 08.0	218 21.0	S21 32.4	215 28.4	S20 54.7
07	170 40.1	316 32.0	51.2	155 38.3	08.2	233 23.0	32.4	230 30.6	54.7
08	185 42.6	331 31.5	52.2	170 40.4	08.5	248 24.9	32.3	245 32.8	54.7
09	200 45.0	346 30.9 ..	53.3	185 42.6 ..	08.7	263 26.9 ..	32.2	260 35.1 ..	54.6
10	215 47.5	1 30.4	54.3	200 44.7	09.0	278 28.9	32.1	275 37.3	54.6
11	230 50.0	16 29.9	55.4	215 46.9	09.2	293 30.8	32.0	290 39.6	54.5
12	245 52.4	31 29.4	S11 56.4	230 49.0	N 6 09.5	308 32.8	S21 31.9	305 41.8	S20 54.5
13	260 54.9	46 28.9	57.5	245 51.1	09.8	323 34.7	31.9	320 44.0	54.5
14	275 57.3	61 28.4	58.5	260 53.3	10.0	338 36.7	31.8	335 46.3	54.4
15	290 59.8	76 27.8	11 59.5	275 55.4 ..	10.3	353 38.7 ..	31.7	350 48.5 ..	54.4
16	306 02.3	91 27.3	12 00.6	290 57.6	10.5	8 40.6	31.6	5 50.7	54.3
17	321 04.7	106 26.8	01.6	305 59.7	10.8	23 42.6	31.5	20 53.0	54.3
18	336 07.2	121 26.3	S12 02.7	321 01.9	N 6 11.1	38 44.6	S21 31.4	35 55.2	S20 54.3
19	351 09.7	136 25.8	03.7	336 04.0	11.3	53 46.5	31.3	50 57.5	54.2
20	6 12.1	151 25.3	04.8	351 06.1	11.6	68 48.5	31.3	65 59.7	54.2
21	21 14.6	166 24.7 ..	05.8	6 08.3 ..	11.8	83 50.4 ..	31.2	81 01.9 ..	54.1
22	36 17.1	181 24.2	06.9	21 10.4	12.1	98 52.4	31.1	96 04.2	54.1
23	51 19.5	196 23.7	07.9	36 12.5	12.4	113 54.4	31.0	111 06.4	54.0
27 00	66 22.0	211 23.2	S12 08.9	51 14.7	N 6 12.6	128 56.3	S21 30.9	126 08.6	S20 54.0
01	81 24.5	226 22.7	10.0	66 16.8	12.9	143 58.3	30.8	141 10.9	54.0
02	96 26.9	241 22.1	11.0	81 18.9	13.1	159 00.3	30.7	156 13.1	53.9
03	111 29.4	256 21.6 ..	12.1	96 21.1 ..	13.4	174 02.2 ..	30.7	171 15.4 ..	53.9
04	126 31.8	271 21.1	13.1	111 23.2	13.7	189 04.2	30.6	186 17.6	53.8
05	141 34.3	286 20.6	14.1	126 25.3	13.9	204 06.1	30.5	201 19.8	53.8
06	156 36.8	301 20.0	S12 15.2	141 27.4	N 6 14.2	219 08.1	S21 30.4	216 22.1	S20 53.8
07	171 39.2	316 19.5	16.2	156 29.6	14.5	234 10.1	30.3	231 24.3	53.7
08	186 41.7	331 19.0	17.3	171 31.7	14.7	249 12.0	30.2	246 26.5	53.7
09	201 44.2	346 18.5 ..	18.3	186 33.8 ..	15.0	264 14.0 ..	30.1	261 28.8 ..	53.6
10	216 46.6	1 17.9	19.3	201 35.9	15.2	279 16.0	30.1	276 31.0	53.6
11	231 49.1	16 17.4	20.4	216 38.1	15.5	294 17.9	30.0	291 33.2	53.5
12	246 51.6	31 16.9	S12 21.4	231 40.2	N 6 15.8	309 19.9	S21 29.9	306 35.5	S20 53.5
13	261 54.0	46 16.4	22.4	246 42.3	16.0	324 21.8	29.8	321 37.7	53.5
14	276 56.5	61 15.8	23.5	261 44.4	16.3	339 23.8	29.7	336 39.9	53.4
15	291 58.9	76 15.3 ..	24.5	276 46.5 ..	16.6	354 25.8 ..	29.6	351 42.2 ..	53.4
16	307 01.4	91 14.8	25.6	291 48.6	16.8	9 27.7	29.5	6 44.4	53.3
17	322 03.9	106 14.2	26.6	306 50.7	17.1	24 29.7	29.5	21 46.7	53.3
18	337 06.3	121 13.7	S12 27.6	321 52.9	N 6 17.4	39 31.6	S21 29.4	36 48.9	S20 53.3
19	352 08.8	136 13.2	28.7	336 55.0	17.6	54 33.6	29.3	51 51.1	53.2
20	7 11.3	151 12.7	29.7	351 57.1	17.9	69 35.5	29.2	66 53.4	53.2
21	22 13.7	166 12.1 ..	30.7	6 59.2 ..	18.2	84 37.5 ..	29.1	81 55.6 ..	53.1
22	37 16.2	181 11.6	31.7	22 01.3	18.5	99 39.5	29.0	96 57.8	53.1
23	52 18.7	196 11.1	32.8	37 03.4	18.7	114 41.4	28.9	112 00.1	53.0
28 00	67 21.1	211 10.5	S12 33.8	52 05.5	N 6 19.0	129 43.4	S21 28.9	127 02.3	S20 53.0
01	82 23.6	226 10.0	34.8	67 07.6	19.3	144 45.3	28.8	142 04.5	53.0
02	97 26.1	241 09.5	35.9	82 09.7	19.5	159 47.3	28.7	157 06.8	52.9
03	112 28.5	256 08.9 ..	36.9	97 11.8 ..	19.8	174 49.3 ..	28.6	172 09.0 ..	52.9
04	127 31.0	271 08.4	37.9	112 13.9	20.1	189 51.2	28.5	187 11.2	52.8
05	142 33.4	286 07.9	39.0	127 16.0	20.3	204 53.2	28.4	202 13.5	52.8
06	157 35.9	301 07.3	S12 40.0	142 18.1	N 6 20.6	219 55.1	S21 28.3	217 15.7	S20 52.8
07	172 38.4	316 06.8	41.0	157 20.2	20.9	234 57.1	28.2	232 17.9	52.7
08	187 40.8	331 06.3	42.0	172 22.3	21.2	249 59.0	28.2	247 20.2	52.7
09	202 43.3	346 05.7 ..	43.1	187 24.4 ..	21.4	265 01.0 ..	28.1	262 22.4 ..	52.6
10	217 45.8	1 05.2	44.1	202 26.5	21.7	280 03.0	28.0	277 24.6	52.6
11	232 48.2	16 04.7	45.1	217 28.6	22.0	295 04.9	27.9	292 26.9	52.5
12	247 50.7	31 04.1	S12 46.1	232 30.7	N 6 22.2	310 06.9	S21 27.8	307 29.1	S20 52.5
13	262 53.2	46 03.6	47.2	247 32.8	22.5	325 08.8	27.7	322 31.3	52.5
14	277 55.6	61 03.0	48.2	262 34.9	22.8	340 10.8	27.6	337 33.6	52.4
15	292 58.1	76 02.5 ..	49.2	277 37.0 ..	23.1	355 12.7 ..	27.5	352 35.8 ..	52.4
16	308 00.6	91 02.0	50.2	292 39.1	23.3	10 14.7	27.5	7 38.0	52.3
17	323 03.0	106 01.4	51.2	307 41.1	23.6	25 16.7	27.4	22 40.3	52.3
18	338 05.5	121 00.9	S12 52.3	322 43.2	N 6 23.9	40 18.6	S21 27.3	37 42.5	S20 52.2
19	353 07.9	136 00.3	53.3	337 45.3	24.2	55 20.6	27.2	52 44.7	52.2
20	8 10.4	150 59.8	54.3	352 47.4	24.5	70 22.5	27.1	67 47.0	52.2
21	23 12.9	165 59.3 ..	55.3	7 49.5 ..	24.7	85 24.5 ..	27.0	82 49.2 ..	52.1
22	38 15.3	180 58.7	56.4	22 51.6	25.0	100 26.4	26.9	97 51.4	52.1
23	53 17.8	195 58.2	57.4	37 53.7	25.3	115 28.4	26.8	112 53.6	52.0
Mer. Pass.	19 31.3	v −0.5	d 1.0	v 2.1	d 0.3	v 2.0	d 0.1	v 2.2	d 0.0

STARS

Name	SHA	Dec
Acamar	315 14.0	S40 13.4
Achernar	335 22.4	S57 08.1
Acrux	173 04.0	S63 12.5
Adhara	255 08.2	S28 59.9
Aldebaran	290 43.1	N16 33.0
Alioth	166 16.4	N55 50.7
Alkaid	152 55.2	N49 12.5
Alnair	27 37.3	S46 51.9
Alnilam	275 40.8	S 1 11.3
Alphard	217 51.0	S 8 44.8
Alphecca	126 07.0	N26 38.8
Alpheratz	357 38.0	N29 12.4
Altair	62 03.4	N 8 55.5
Ankaa	353 10.3	S42 11.8
Antares	112 20.3	S26 28.5
Arcturus	145 51.3	N19 04.5
Atria	107 18.1	S69 03.8
Avior	234 15.7	S59 34.3
Bellatrix	278 26.2	N 6 22.1
Betelgeuse	270 55.4	N 7 24.6
Canopus	263 53.4	S52 42.3
Capella	280 26.4	N46 01.0
Deneb	49 28.2	N45 21.5
Denebola	182 28.5	N14 27.4
Diphda	348 50.5	S17 52.5
Dubhe	193 45.4	N61 38.1
Elnath	278 05.7	N28 37.4
Eltanin	90 44.3	N51 29.3
Enif	33 42.1	N 9 58.3
Fomalhaut	15 18.2	S29 30.9
Gacrux	171 55.6	S57 13.4
Gienah	175 47.2	S17 39.2
Hadar	148 41.2	S60 28.1
Hamal	327 54.7	N23 33.7
Kaus Aust.	83 37.3	S34 22.4
Kochab	137 21.1	N74 04.1
Markab	13 33.2	N15 19.1
Menkar	314 09.3	N 4 10.2
Menkent	148 01.9	S36 28.1
Miaplacidus	221 38.5	S69 47.8
Mirfak	308 32.5	N49 56.1
Nunki	75 52.2	S26 16.2
Peacock	53 11.4	S56 40.3
Pollux	243 21.2	N27 58.4
Procyon	244 54.1	N 5 10.3
Rasalhague	96 02.0	N12 32.8
Regulus	207 38.0	N11 52.0
Rigel	281 06.8	S 8 10.7
Rigil Kent.	139 45.4	S60 54.9
Sabik	102 07.0	S15 44.9
Schedar	349 34.4	N56 39.3
Shaula	96 15.3	S37 07.0
Sirius	258 28.9	S16 44.6
Spica	158 26.1	S11 16.0
Suhail	222 48.6	S43 30.7
Vega	80 35.9	N38 48.4
Zuben'ubi	137 00.0	S16 07.5

	SHA	Mer. Pass.
Venus	145 01.2	9 55
Mars	344 52.7	20 32
Jupiter	62 34.3	15 22
Saturn	59 46.7	15 33

UT	SUN GHA	SUN Dec	MOON GHA	v	MOON Dec	d	HP
26 00	183 10.8	S20 58.8	48 31.4	16.6	N 2 03.6	12.4	54.1
01	198 10.6	59.3	63 07.0	16.6	2 16.0	12.3	54.1
02	213 10.4	20 59.8	77 42.6	16.6	2 28.3	12.4	54.1
03	228 10.2	21 00.2	92 18.2	16.6	2 40.7	12.4	54.1
04	243 10.0	00.7	106 53.8	16.6	2 53.1	12.3	54.1
05	258 09.8	01.2	121 29.4	16.5	3 05.4	12.3	54.1
T 06	273 09.6	S21 01.6	136 04.9	16.6	N 3 17.7	12.4	54.1
H 07	288 09.4	02.1	150 40.5	16.6	3 30.1	12.3	54.1
U 08	303 09.2	02.6	165 16.1	16.5	3 42.4	12.3	54.1
R 09	318 09.0	.. 03.0	179 51.6	16.6	3 54.7	12.2	54.0
S 10	333 08.8	03.5	194 27.2	16.6	4 06.9	12.3	54.0
D 11	348 08.6	03.9	209 02.7	16.5	4 19.2	12.2	54.0
A 12	3 08.4	S21 04.4	223 38.2	16.5	N 4 31.4	12.3	54.0
Y 13	18 08.2	04.9	238 13.7	16.4	4 43.7	12.2	54.0
14	33 08.0	05.3	252 49.1	16.5	4 55.9	12.2	54.0
15	48 07.8	.. 05.8	267 24.6	16.4	5 08.1	12.1	54.0
16	63 07.6	06.2	282 00.0	16.5	5 20.2	12.2	54.0
17	78 07.4	06.7	296 35.5	16.4	5 32.4	12.1	54.0
18	93 07.2	S21 07.2	311 10.9	16.4	N 5 44.5	12.1	54.0
19	108 07.0	07.6	325 46.3	16.3	5 56.6	12.1	54.0
20	123 06.8	08.1	340 21.6	16.4	6 08.7	12.1	54.0
21	138 06.6	.. 08.5	354 57.0	16.3	6 20.8	12.1	54.0
22	153 06.4	09.0	9 32.3	16.3	6 32.9	12.0	54.0
23	168 06.2	09.4	24 07.6	16.2	6 44.9	12.0	54.0
27 00	183 06.0	S21 09.9	38 42.8	16.3	N 6 56.9	12.0	54.0
01	198 05.8	10.3	53 18.1	16.2	7 08.9	11.9	54.0
02	213 05.6	10.8	67 53.3	16.2	7 20.8	11.9	54.0
03	228 05.4	.. 11.2	82 28.5	16.1	7 32.7	11.9	54.0
04	243 05.2	11.7	97 03.6	16.2	7 44.6	11.9	54.0
05	258 04.9	12.1	111 38.8	16.1	7 56.5	11.9	54.0
06	273 04.7	S21 12.6	126 13.9	16.1	N 8 08.4	11.8	54.0
07	288 04.5	13.0	140 49.0	16.0	8 20.2	11.7	54.0
08	303 04.3	13.5	155 24.0	16.0	8 31.9	11.8	54.0
F 09	318 04.1	.. 13.9	169 59.0	16.0	8 43.7	11.7	54.0
R 10	333 03.9	14.4	184 34.0	15.9	8 55.4	11.7	54.0
I 11	348 03.7	14.8	199 08.9	15.9	9 07.1	11.7	54.0
D 12	3 03.5	S21 15.3	213 43.8	15.9	N 9 18.8	11.6	54.0
A 13	18 03.3	15.7	228 18.7	15.8	9 30.4	11.6	54.0
Y 14	33 03.1	16.1	242 53.5	15.8	9 42.0	11.5	54.0
15	48 02.9	.. 16.6	257 28.3	15.8	9 53.5	11.6	54.0
16	63 02.7	17.0	272 03.1	15.7	10 05.1	11.5	54.0
17	78 02.4	17.5	286 37.8	15.7	10 16.5	11.5	54.0
18	93 02.2	S21 17.9	301 12.5	15.7	N10 28.0	11.4	54.1
19	108 02.0	18.4	315 47.2	15.6	10 39.4	11.4	54.1
20	123 01.8	18.8	330 21.8	15.5	10 50.8	11.3	54.1
21	138 01.6	.. 19.2	344 56.3	15.6	11 02.1	11.3	54.1
22	153 01.4	19.7	359 30.9	15.4	11 13.4	11.3	54.1
23	168 01.2	20.1	14 05.3	15.5	11 24.7	11.2	54.1
28 00	183 01.0	S21 20.5	28 39.8	15.4	N11 35.9	11.1	54.1
01	198 00.8	21.0	43 14.2	15.3	11 47.0	11.2	54.1
02	213 00.5	21.4	57 48.5	15.3	11 58.2	11.0	54.1
03	228 00.3	.. 21.8	72 22.8	15.3	12 09.2	11.1	54.1
04	243 00.1	22.3	86 57.1	15.2	12 20.3	11.0	54.1
05	257 59.9	22.7	101 31.3	15.1	12 31.3	11.0	54.1
06	272 59.7	S21 23.1	116 05.4	15.2	N12 42.2	10.9	54.1
07	287 59.5	23.6	130 39.6	15.0	12 53.1	10.8	54.1
S 08	302 59.3	24.0	145 13.6	15.0	13 03.9	10.8	54.1
A 09	317 59.0	.. 24.4	159 47.6	15.0	13 14.7	10.8	54.1
T 10	332 58.8	24.9	174 21.6	14.9	13 25.5	10.7	54.1
U 11	347 58.6	25.3	188 55.5	14.9	13 36.2	10.7	54.1
R 12	2 58.4	S21 25.7	203 29.4	14.8	N13 46.9	10.6	54.1
D 13	17 58.2	26.1	218 03.2	14.7	13 57.5	10.6	54.1
A 14	32 58.0	26.6	232 36.9	14.8	14 08.0	10.5	54.2
Y 15	47 57.8	.. 27.0	247 10.7	14.6	14 18.5	10.4	54.2
16	62 57.5	27.4	261 44.3	14.6	14 28.9	10.4	54.2
17	77 57.3	27.8	276 17.9	14.5	14 39.3	10.3	54.2
18	92 57.1	S21 28.3	290 51.4	14.5	N14 49.6	10.3	54.2
19	107 56.9	28.7	305 24.9	14.5	14 59.9	10.2	54.2
20	122 56.7	29.1	319 58.4	14.3	15 10.1	10.2	54.2
21	137 56.4	.. 29.5	334 31.7	14.3	15 20.3	10.1	54.2
22	152 56.2	30.0	349 05.0	14.3	15 30.4	10.0	54.2
23	167 56.0	30.4	3 38.3	14.2	N15 40.4	10.0	54.2
	SD 16.2 d 0.4		SD 14.7		14.7		14.8

Twilight / Moonrise

Lat.	Naut.	Civil	Sunrise	Moonrise 26	27	28	29
N 72	07 41	09 33	■■	14 08	13 43	13 10	11 56
N 70	07 26	08 58	■■	14 15	13 58	13 36	13 03
68	07 13	08 34	10 16	14 20	14 09	13 57	13 40
66	07 03	08 14	09 34	14 25	14 19	14 13	14 06
64	06 54	07 59	09 06	14 29	14 27	14 26	14 26
62	06 47	07 45	08 45	14 32	14 34	14 37	14 43
60	06 40	07 34	08 27	14 35	14 40	14 47	14 57
N 58	06 34	07 24	08 13	14 38	14 46	14 56	15 08
56	06 28	07 16	08 01	14 40	14 51	15 03	15 19
54	06 23	07 08	07 50	14 42	14 55	15 10	15 28
52	06 19	07 01	07 40	14 44	14 59	15 16	15 36
50	06 14	06 55	07 32	14 46	15 03	15 21	15 44
45	06 04	06 41	07 14	14 50	15 11	15 33	15 59
N 40	05 56	06 29	06 59	14 53	15 17	15 43	16 13
35	05 48	06 19	06 46	14 56	15 23	15 52	16 24
30	05 40	06 09	06 35	14 59	15 28	15 59	16 33
20	05 26	05 53	06 16	15 03	15 37	16 12	16 50
N 10	05 11	05 37	06 00	15 07	15 45	16 24	17 05
0	04 56	05 22	05 44	15 11	15 52	16 34	17 19
S 10	04 39	05 06	05 28	15 15	15 59	16 45	17 33
20	04 19	04 47	05 11	15 19	16 07	16 57	17 48
30	03 53	04 25	04 52	15 23	16 16	17 10	18 06
35	03 36	04 11	04 40	15 26	16 22	17 18	18 16
40	03 15	03 55	04 27	15 29	16 28	17 27	18 27
45	02 49	03 35	04 11	15 33	16 35	17 38	18 41
S 50	02 12	03 10	03 51	15 37	16 43	17 50	18 58
52	01 51	02 57	03 42	15 39	16 47	17 56	19 06
54	01 24	02 42	03 31	15 41	16 52	18 03	19 15
56	00 41	02 24	03 19	15 44	16 56	18 10	19 25
58	////	02 03	03 06	15 46	17 02	18 19	19 37
S 60	////	01 33	02 49	15 49	17 08	18 28	19 50

Sunset / Twilight / Moonset

Lat.	Sunset	Civil	Naut.	Moonset 26	27	28	29
N 72	■■	14 01	15 54	03 24	05 15	07 16	10 02
N 70	■■	14 36	16 09	03 21	05 03	06 51	08 56
68	13 19	15 01	16 21	03 18	04 53	06 32	08 20
66	14 01	15 21	16 32	03 15	04 45	06 17	07 55
64	14 29	15 36	16 40	03 13	04 38	06 05	07 36
62	14 50	15 49	16 48	03 11	04 32	05 55	07 20
60	15 08	16 01	16 55	03 09	04 27	05 46	07 07
N 58	15 22	16 11	17 01	03 08	04 22	05 38	06 56
56	15 34	16 19	17 07	03 06	04 19	05 32	06 46
54	15 45	16 27	17 12	03 05	04 15	05 26	06 37
52	15 55	16 34	17 16	03 04	04 12	05 20	06 30
50	16 03	16 40	17 21	03 03	04 09	05 15	06 23
45	16 22	16 54	17 31	03 01	04 03	05 05	06 08
N 40	16 36	17 06	17 40	02 59	03 57	04 56	05 56
35	16 49	17 17	17 48	02 58	03 53	04 49	05 46
30	17 00	17 27	17 55	02 56	03 49	04 42	05 37
20	17 19	17 43	18 10	02 54	03 42	04 31	05 22
N 10	17 36	17 58	18 24	02 52	03 36	04 21	05 08
0	17 51	18 14	18 39	02 50	03 31	04 12	04 56
S 10	18 07	18 30	18 57	02 48	03 25	04 03	04 43
20	18 24	18 48	19 17	02 46	03 19	03 53	04 30
30	18 44	19 11	19 43	02 44	03 12	03 42	04 15
35	18 56	19 25	20 00	02 43	03 09	03 36	04 06
40	19 09	19 41	20 21	02 41	03 04	03 29	03 56
45	19 25	20 01	20 47	02 39	02 59	03 21	03 45
S 50	19 45	20 27	21 25	02 37	02 53	03 11	03 31
52	19 54	20 40	21 46	02 36	02 50	03 06	03 24
54	20 05	20 55	22 14	02 35	02 47	03 01	03 17
56	20 17	21 13	23 00	02 34	02 44	02 55	03 09
58	20 31	21 35	////	02 33	02 40	02 49	03 00
S 60	20 48	22 05	////	02 31	02 36	02 42	02 50

SUN / MOON

Day	Eqn. of Time 00h	Eqn. of Time 12h	Mer. Pass.	Mer. Pass. Upper	Mer. Pass. Lower	Age	Phase %
	m s	m s	h m	h m	h m	d	%
26	12 44	12 34	11 47	21 21	09 01	11	87
27	12 24	12 14	11 48	22 02	09 41	12	93
28	12 04	11 54	11 48	22 45	10 23	13	97

UT	ARIES GHA	VENUS −3.9 GHA	Dec	MARS −1.2 GHA	Dec	JUPITER −2.0 GHA	Dec	SATURN +0.6 GHA	Dec	STARS Name	SHA	Dec
29 00	68 20.3	210 57.6	S12 58.4	52 55.7	N 6 25.6	130 30.3	S21 26.8	127 55.9	S20 52.0	Acamar	315 14.0	S40 13.4
01	83 22.7	225 57.1	12 59.4	67 57.8	25.8	145 32.3	26.7	142 58.1	51.9	Achernar	335 22.4	S57 08.1
02	98 25.2	240 56.6	13 00.4	82 59.9	26.1	160 34.2	26.6	158 00.3	51.9	Acrux	173 04.0	S63 12.5
03	113 27.7	255 56.0	.. 01.4	98 02.0	.. 26.4	175 36.2	.. 26.5	173 02.6	.. 51.9	Adhara	255 08.2	S28 59.9
04	128 30.1	270 55.5	02.5	113 04.0	26.7	190 38.2	26.4	188 04.8	51.8	Aldebaran	290 43.1	N16 33.0
05	143 32.6	285 54.9	03.5	128 06.1	27.0	205 40.1	26.3	203 07.0	51.8			
06	158 35.0	300 54.4	S13 04.5	143 08.2	N 6 27.2	220 42.1	S21 26.2	218 09.3	S20 51.7	Alioth	166 16.4	N55 50.7
07	173 37.5	315 53.8	05.5	158 10.3	27.5	235 44.0	26.1	233 11.5	51.7	Alkaid	152 55.1	N49 12.5
08	188 40.0	330 53.3	06.5	173 12.3	27.8	250 46.0	26.0	248 13.7	51.6	Alnair	27 37.3	S46 51.9
S 09	203 42.4	345 52.7	.. 07.5	188 14.4	.. 28.1	265 47.9	.. 26.0	263 16.0	.. 51.6	Alnilam	275 40.8	S 1 11.4
U 10	218 44.9	0 52.2	08.5	203 16.5	28.4	280 49.9	25.9	278 18.2	51.6	Alphard	217 50.9	S 8 44.8
N 11	233 47.4	15 51.6	09.6	218 18.5	28.6	295 51.8	25.8	293 20.4	51.5			
D 12	248 49.8	30 51.1	S13 10.6	233 20.6	N 6 28.9	310 53.8	S21 25.7	308 22.6	S20 51.5	Alphecca	126 07.0	N26 38.8
A 13	263 52.3	45 50.5	11.6	248 22.7	29.2	325 55.7	25.6	323 24.9	51.4	Alpheratz	357 38.0	N29 12.4
Y 14	278 54.8	60 50.0	12.6	263 24.7	29.5	340 57.7	25.5	338 27.1	51.4	Altair	62 03.4	N 8 55.5
15	293 57.2	75 49.4	.. 13.6	278 26.8	.. 29.8	355 59.6	.. 25.4	353 29.3	.. 51.3	Ankaa	353 10.3	S42 11.8
16	308 59.7	90 48.9	14.6	293 28.9	30.0	11 01.6	25.3	8 31.6	51.3	Antares	112 20.3	S26 28.5
17	324 02.2	105 48.3	15.6	308 30.9	30.3	26 03.5	25.3	23 33.8	51.3			
18	339 04.6	120 47.8	S13 16.6	323 33.0	N 6 30.6	41 05.5	S21 25.2	38 36.0	S20 51.2	Arcturus	145 51.3	N19 04.5
19	354 07.1	135 47.2	17.6	338 35.0	30.9	56 07.5	25.1	53 38.3	51.2	Atria	107 18.1	S69 03.8
20	9 09.5	150 46.7	18.6	353 37.1	31.2	71 09.4	25.0	68 40.5	51.1	Avior	234 15.6	S59 34.3
21	24 12.0	165 46.1	.. 19.7	8 39.2	.. 31.5	86 11.4	.. 24.9	83 42.7	.. 51.1	Bellatrix	278 26.1	N 6 22.1
22	39 14.5	180 45.6	20.7	23 41.2	31.7	101 13.3	24.8	98 44.9	51.0	Betelgeuse	270 55.4	N 7 24.6
23	54 16.9	195 45.0	21.7	38 43.3	32.0	116 15.3	24.7	113 47.2	51.0			
30 00	69 19.4	210 44.5	S13 22.7	53 45.3	N 6 32.3	131 17.2	S21 24.6	128 49.4	S20 51.0	Canopus	263 53.4	S52 42.3
01	84 21.9	225 43.9	23.7	68 47.4	32.6	146 19.2	24.5	143 51.6	50.9	Capella	280 26.3	N46 01.0
02	99 24.3	240 43.4	24.7	83 49.4	32.9	161 21.1	24.4	158 53.9	50.9	Deneb	49 28.3	N45 21.5
03	114 26.8	255 42.8	.. 25.7	98 51.5	.. 33.2	176 23.1	.. 24.4	173 56.1	.. 50.8	Denebola	182 28.5	N14 27.4
04	129 29.3	270 42.3	26.7	113 53.5	33.5	191 25.0	24.3	188 58.3	50.8	Diphda	348 50.5	S17 52.5
05	144 31.7	285 41.7	27.7	128 55.6	33.7	206 27.0	24.2	204 00.5	50.7			
06	159 34.2	300 41.1	S13 28.7	143 57.6	N 6 34.0	221 28.9	S21 24.1	219 02.8	S20 50.7	Dubhe	193 45.4	N61 38.1
07	174 36.7	315 40.6	29.7	158 59.7	34.3	236 30.9	24.0	234 05.0	50.6	Elnath	278 05.7	N28 37.4
08	189 39.1	330 40.0	30.7	174 01.7	34.6	251 32.8	23.9	249 07.2	50.6	Eltanin	90 44.3	N51 29.3
M 09	204 41.6	345 39.5	.. 31.7	189 03.8	.. 34.9	266 34.8	.. 23.8	264 09.4	.. 50.5	Enif	33 42.2	N 9 58.3
O 10	219 44.0	0 38.9	32.7	204 05.8	35.2	281 36.7	23.7	279 11.7	50.5	Fomalhaut	15 18.2	S29 30.9
N 11	234 46.5	15 38.4	33.7	219 07.9	35.5	296 38.7	23.6	294 13.9	50.5			
D 12	249 49.0	30 37.8	S13 34.7	234 09.9	N 6 35.8	311 40.6	S21 23.6	309 16.1	S20 50.4	Gacrux	171 55.5	S57 13.4
A 13	264 51.4	45 37.2	35.7	249 11.9	36.1	326 42.6	23.5	324 18.4	50.4	Gienah	175 47.2	S17 39.2
Y 14	279 53.9	60 36.7	36.7	264 14.0	36.3	341 44.5	23.4	339 20.6	50.3	Hadar	148 41.2	S60 28.1
15	294 56.4	75 36.1	.. 37.7	279 16.0	.. 36.6	356 46.5	.. 23.3	354 22.8	.. 50.3	Hamal	327 54.7	N23 33.7
16	309 58.8	90 35.6	38.7	294 18.1	36.9	11 48.4	23.2	9 25.0	50.3	Kaus Aust.	83 37.3	S34 22.4
17	325 01.3	105 35.0	39.7	309 20.1	37.2	26 50.4	23.1	24 27.3	50.2			
18	340 03.8	120 34.4	S13 40.7	324 22.1	N 6 37.5	41 52.3	S21 23.0	39 29.5	S20 50.2	Kochab	137 21.1	N74 04.1
19	355 06.2	135 33.9	41.7	339 24.2	37.8	56 54.3	22.9	54 31.7	50.1	Markab	13 33.2	N15 19.1
20	10 08.7	150 33.3	42.7	354 26.2	38.1	71 56.2	22.8	69 33.9	50.1	Menkar	314 09.3	N 4 10.2
21	25 11.2	165 32.7	.. 43.7	9 28.2	.. 38.4	86 58.1	.. 22.7	84 36.2	.. 50.0	Menkent	148 01.9	S36 28.1
22	40 13.6	180 32.2	44.7	24 30.3	38.7	102 00.1	22.7	99 38.4	50.0	Miaplacidus	221 38.4	S69 47.8
23	55 16.1	195 31.6	45.7	39 32.3	39.0	117 02.0	22.6	114 40.6	49.9			
1 00	70 18.5	210 31.0	S13 46.6	54 34.3	N 6 39.3	132 04.0	S21 22.5	129 42.8	S20 49.9	Mirfak	308 32.5	N49 56.1
01	85 21.0	225 30.5	47.6	69 36.3	39.6	147 05.9	22.4	144 45.1	49.9	Nunki	75 52.2	S26 16.2
02	100 23.5	240 29.9	48.6	84 38.4	39.8	162 07.9	22.3	159 47.3	49.8	Peacock	53 11.4	S56 40.3
03	115 25.9	255 29.4	.. 49.6	99 40.4	.. 40.1	177 09.8	.. 22.2	174 49.5	.. 49.8	Pollux	243 21.2	N27 58.4
04	130 28.4	270 28.8	50.6	114 42.4	40.4	192 11.8	22.1	189 51.8	49.7	Procyon	244 54.1	N 5 10.3
05	145 30.9	285 28.2	51.6	129 44.4	40.7	207 13.7	22.0	204 54.0	49.7			
06	160 33.3	300 27.6	S13 52.6	144 46.5	N 6 41.0	222 15.7	S21 21.9	219 56.2	S20 49.6	Rasalhague	96 02.0	N12 32.8
07	175 35.8	315 27.1	53.6	159 48.5	41.3	237 17.6	21.8	234 58.4	49.6	Regulus	207 38.0	N11 51.9
T 08	190 38.3	330 26.5	54.6	174 50.5	41.6	252 19.6	21.7	250 00.7	49.6	Rigel	281 06.8	S 8 10.7
U 09	205 40.7	345 25.9	.. 55.6	189 52.5	.. 41.8	267 21.5	.. 21.7	265 02.9	.. 49.5	Rigil Kent.	139 45.4	S60 54.9
E 10	220 43.2	0 25.4	56.5	204 54.5	42.2	282 23.5	21.6	280 05.1	49.5	Sabik	102 07.0	S15 44.9
S 11	235 45.7	15 24.8	57.5	219 56.6	42.5	297 25.4	21.5	295 07.3	49.4			
D 12	250 48.1	30 24.2	S13 58.5	234 58.6	N 6 42.8	312 27.3	S21 21.4	310 09.6	S20 49.4	Schedar	349 34.4	N56 39.3
A 13	265 50.6	45 23.7	13 59.5	250 00.6	43.1	327 29.3	21.3	325 11.8	49.3	Shaula	96 15.3	S37 07.0
Y 14	280 53.0	60 23.1	14 00.5	265 02.6	43.4	342 31.2	21.2	340 14.0	49.3	Sirius	258 28.9	S16 44.6
15	295 55.5	75 22.5	.. 01.5	280 04.6	.. 43.7	357 33.2	.. 21.1	355 16.2	.. 49.2	Spica	158 26.1	S11 16.0
16	310 58.0	90 21.9	02.4	295 06.6	44.0	12 35.1	21.0	10 18.4	49.2	Suhail	222 48.5	S43 30.7
17	326 00.4	105 21.4	03.4	310 08.7	44.3	27 37.1	20.9	25 20.7	49.2			
18	341 02.9	120 20.8	S14 04.4	325 10.7	N 6 44.6	42 39.0	S21 20.8	40 22.9	S20 49.1	Vega	80 35.9	N38 48.4
19	356 05.4	135 20.2	05.4	340 12.7	44.9	57 41.0	20.7	55 25.1	49.1	Zuben'ubi	137 00.0	S16 07.5
20	11 07.8	150 19.6	06.4	355 14.7	45.2	72 42.9	20.6	70 27.3	49.0		SHA	Mer.Pass.
21	26 10.3	165 19.1	.. 07.4	10 16.7	.. 45.5	87 44.9	.. 20.6	85 29.6	.. 49.0		° '	h m
22	41 12.8	180 18.5	08.3	25 18.7	45.8	102 46.8	20.5	100 31.8	48.9	Venus	141 25.1	9 57
23	56 15.2	195 17.9	09.3	40 20.7	46.1	117 48.7	20.4	115 34.0	48.9	Mars	344 25.9	20 22
	h m									Jupiter	61 57.8	15 13
Mer.Pass. 19 19.5		v −0.6	d 1.0	v 2.0	d 0.3	v 1.9	d 0.1	v 2.2	d 0.0	Saturn	59 30.0	15 22

UT	SUN GHA	SUN Dec	MOON GHA	v	MOON Dec	d	HP
d h	° ′	° ′	° ′	′	° ′	′	′
29 00	182 55.8	S21 30.8	18 11.5	14.2	N15 50.4	9.9	54.2
01	197 55.6	31.2	32 44.7	14.0	16 00.3	9.8	54.2
02	212 55.3	31.6	47 17.7	14.1	16 10.1	9.8	54.2
03	227 55.1	.. 32.1	61 50.8	13.9	16 19.9	9.7	54.3
04	242 54.9	32.5	76 23.7	13.9	16 29.6	9.7	54.3
05	257 54.7	32.9	90 56.6	13.9	16 39.3	9.6	54.3
06	272 54.5	S21 33.3	105 29.5	13.8	N16 48.9	9.5	54.3
07	287 54.2	33.7	120 02.3	13.7	16 58.4	9.5	54.3
08	302 54.0	34.1	134 35.0	13.7	17 07.9	9.3	54.3
S 09	317 53.8	.. 34.5	149 07.7	13.5	17 17.2	9.4	54.3
U 10	332 53.6	35.0	163 40.2	13.6	17 26.6	9.2	54.3
N 11	347 53.4	35.4	178 12.8	13.5	17 35.8	9.2	54.3
D 12	2 53.1	S21 35.8	192 45.3	13.4	N17 45.0	9.1	54.3
A 13	17 52.9	36.2	207 17.7	13.3	17 54.1	9.0	54.4
Y 14	32 52.7	36.6	221 50.0	13.3	18 03.1	8.9	54.4
15	47 52.5	.. 37.0	236 22.3	13.2	18 12.0	8.9	54.4
16	62 52.2	37.4	250 54.5	13.2	18 20.9	8.8	54.4
17	77 52.0	37.8	265 26.7	13.1	18 29.7	8.8	54.4
18	92 51.8	S21 38.2	279 58.8	13.0	N18 38.5	8.6	54.4
19	107 51.6	38.6	294 30.8	13.0	18 47.1	8.6	54.4
20	122 51.3	39.0	309 02.8	12.9	18 55.7	8.5	54.4
21	137 51.1	.. 39.4	323 34.7	12.8	19 04.2	8.4	54.4
22	152 50.9	39.8	338 06.5	12.8	19 12.6	8.3	54.4
23	167 50.7	40.2	352 38.3	12.7	19 20.9	8.2	54.5
30 00	182 50.4	S21 40.6	7 10.0	12.6	N19 29.1	8.2	54.5
01	197 50.2	41.0	21 41.6	12.6	19 37.3	8.1	54.5
02	212 50.0	41.5	36 13.2	12.5	19 45.4	8.0	54.5
03	227 49.8	.. 41.9	50 44.7	12.4	19 53.4	7.9	54.5
04	242 49.5	42.2	65 16.1	12.4	20 01.3	7.8	54.5
05	257 49.3	42.6	79 47.5	12.3	20 09.1	7.7	54.5
06	272 49.1	S21 43.0	94 18.8	12.3	N20 16.8	7.7	54.5
07	287 48.8	43.4	108 50.1	12.1	20 24.5	7.5	54.6
08	302 48.6	43.8	123 21.2	12.2	20 32.0	7.5	54.6
M 09	317 48.4	.. 44.2	137 52.4	12.0	20 39.5	7.4	54.6
O 10	332 48.2	44.6	152 23.4	12.0	20 46.9	7.3	54.6
N 11	347 47.9	45.0	166 54.4	11.9	20 54.2	7.1	54.6
D 12	2 47.7	S21 45.4	181 25.3	11.9	N21 01.3	7.1	54.6
A 13	17 47.5	45.8	195 56.2	11.7	21 08.4	7.0	54.6
Y 14	32 47.2	46.2	210 26.9	11.8	21 15.4	6.9	54.6
15	47 47.0	.. 46.6	224 57.7	11.6	21 22.3	6.9	54.7
16	62 46.8	47.0	239 28.3	11.6	21 29.2	6.7	54.7
17	77 46.5	47.4	253 58.9	11.5	21 35.9	6.6	54.7
18	92 46.3	S21 47.8	268 29.4	11.5	N21 42.5	6.5	54.7
19	107 46.1	48.2	282 59.9	11.4	21 49.0	6.4	54.7
20	122 45.9	48.5	297 30.3	11.4	21 55.4	6.3	54.7
21	137 45.6	.. 48.9	312 00.7	11.2	22 01.7	6.2	54.7
22	152 45.4	49.3	326 30.9	11.2	22 07.9	6.1	54.7
23	167 45.2	49.7	341 01.1	11.2	22 14.0	6.1	54.8
1 00	182 44.9	S21 50.1	355 31.3	11.1	N22 20.1	5.9	54.8
01	197 44.7	50.5	10 01.4	11.0	22 26.0	5.8	54.8
02	212 44.5	50.9	24 31.4	11.0	22 31.8	5.7	54.8
03	227 44.2	.. 51.2	39 01.4	10.9	22 37.5	5.5	54.8
04	242 44.0	51.6	53 31.3	10.8	22 43.0	5.5	54.8
05	257 43.8	52.0	68 01.1	10.8	22 48.5	5.4	54.8
06	272 43.5	S21 52.4	82 30.9	10.7	N22 53.9	5.3	54.9
07	287 43.3	52.8	97 00.6	10.7	22 59.2	5.1	54.9
T 08	302 43.0	53.1	111 30.3	10.6	23 04.3	5.1	54.9
U 09	317 42.8	.. 53.5	125 59.9	10.6	23 09.4	4.9	54.9
E 10	332 42.6	53.9	140 29.5	10.5	23 14.3	4.8	54.9
S 11	347 42.3	54.3	154 59.0	10.4	23 19.1	4.7	54.9
D 12	2 42.1	S21 54.6	169 28.4	10.4	N23 23.8	4.6	55.0
A 13	17 41.9	55.0	183 57.8	10.3	23 28.4	4.5	55.0
Y 14	32 41.6	55.4	198 27.1	10.3	23 32.9	4.4	55.0
15	47 41.4	.. 55.8	212 56.4	10.2	23 37.3	4.2	55.0
16	62 41.2	56.1	227 25.6	10.2	23 41.5	4.1	55.0
17	77 40.9	56.5	241 54.8	10.1	23 45.6	4.1	55.0
18	92 40.7	S21 56.9	256 23.9	10.0	N23 49.7	3.9	55.0
19	107 40.4	57.3	270 52.9	10.1	23 53.6	3.7	55.1
20	122 40.2	57.6	285 22.0	9.9	23 57.3	3.7	55.1
21	137 40.0	.. 58.0	299 50.9	9.9	24 01.0	3.5	55.1
22	152 39.7	58.4	314 19.8	9.9	24 04.5	3.5	55.1
23	167 39.5	58.7	328 48.7	9.8	N24 08.0	3.3	55.1
	SD 16.2	d 0.4	SD 14.8		14.9		15.0

Twilight / Sunrise / Moonrise

Lat.	Naut.	Civil	Sunrise	Moonrise 29	30	1	2
°	h m	h m	h m	h m	h m	h m	h m
N 72	07 49	09 48	■■	11 56	□	□	□
N 70	07 33	09 09	■■	13 03	□	□	□
68	07 20	08 42	10 33	13 40	13 07	□	
66	07 09	08 22	09 45	14 06	13 57	13 39	□
64	07 00	08 05	09 14	14 26	14 28	14 35	14 57
62	06 52	07 51	08 52	14 43	14 52	15 09	15 41
60	06 45	07 40	08 34	14 57	15 11	15 33	16 10
N 58	06 38	07 29	08 19	15 08	15 26	15 53	16 32
56	06 33	07 20	08 06	15 19	15 40	16 09	16 50
54	06 27	07 12	07 55	15 28	15 52	16 23	17 06
52	06 22	07 05	07 45	15 36	16 02	16 35	17 19
50	06 18	06 59	07 36	15 44	16 11	16 46	17 31
45	06 07	06 44	07 17	15 59	16 31	17 09	17 55
N 40	05 58	06 32	07 02	16 13	16 47	17 27	18 15
35	05 50	06 21	06 49	16 24	17 00	17 42	18 31
30	05 42	06 12	06 38	16 33	17 12	17 56	18 45
20	05 27	05 55	06 18	16 50	17 32	18 18	19 09
N 10	05 13	05 39	06 01	17 05	17 50	18 38	19 30
0	04 57	05 23	05 45	17 19	18 07	18 57	19 49
S 10	04 39	05 06	05 29	17 33	18 23	19 15	20 08
20	04 19	04 47	05 12	17 48	18 41	19 35	20 29
30	03 52	04 24	04 51	18 06	19 02	19 58	20 54
35	03 35	04 10	04 39	18 16	19 14	20 12	21 08
40	03 14	03 54	04 26	18 27	19 28	20 28	21 24
45	02 46	03 33	04 09	18 41	19 45	20 47	21 44
S 50	02 07	03 07	03 49	18 58	20 06	21 10	22 09
52	01 46	02 54	03 39	19 06	20 15	21 21	22 21
54	01 16	02 38	03 28	19 15	20 27	21 34	22 34
56	00 22	02 20	03 16	19 25	20 39	21 49	22 50
58	////	01 56	03 02	19 37	20 54	22 07	23 09
S 60	////	01 25	02 44	19 50	21 12	22 28	23 32

Sunset / Twilight / Moonset

Lat.	Sunset	Civil	Naut.	Moonset 29	30	1	2
°	h m	h m	h m	h m	h m	h m	h m
N 72	■■	13 49	15 47	10 02	□	□	□
N 70	■■	14 28	16 04	08 56	□	□	□
68	13 04	14 55	16 17	08 20	10 30	□	
66	13 52	15 15	16 28	07 55	09 41	11 42	□
64	14 23	15 32	16 37	07 36	09 10	10 46	12 11
62	14 45	15 46	16 45	07 20	08 47	10 13	11 28
60	15 03	15 58	16 52	07 07	08 29	09 48	10 59
N 58	15 19	16 08	16 59	06 56	08 14	09 29	10 37
56	15 31	16 17	17 05	06 46	08 01	09 13	10 19
54	15 43	16 25	17 10	06 37	07 49	08 59	10 03
52	15 53	16 32	17 15	06 30	07 39	08 47	09 50
50	16 01	16 39	17 19	06 23	07 31	08 37	09 39
45	16 20	16 53	17 30	06 08	07 12	08 15	09 14
N 40	16 35	17 05	17 39	05 56	06 57	07 57	08 55
35	16 48	17 16	17 47	05 46	06 44	07 42	08 39
30	17 00	17 26	17 55	05 37	06 33	07 29	08 25
20	17 19	17 43	18 10	05 22	06 14	07 07	08 01
N 10	17 36	17 59	18 25	05 08	05 57	06 48	07 41
0	17 52	18 15	18 41	04 54	05 42	06 31	07 22
S 10	18 09	18 32	18 58	04 43	05 26	06 13	07 03
20	18 26	18 50	19 19	04 30	05 10	05 54	06 42
30	18 47	19 14	19 46	04 15	04 51	05 32	06 18
35	18 59	19 28	20 03	04 06	04 40	05 19	06 05
40	19 12	19 44	20 25	03 56	04 28	05 05	05 49
45	19 29	20 05	20 52	03 45	04 13	04 47	05 29
S 50	19 49	20 32	21 32	03 31	03 55	04 26	05 05
52	19 59	20 45	21 54	03 24	03 47	04 16	04 54
54	20 10	21 01	22 24	03 17	03 37	04 04	04 41
56	20 23	21 20	23 25	03 09	03 27	03 51	04 26
58	20 37	21 43	////	03 00	03 15	03 36	04 08
S 60	20 55	22 16	////	02 50	03 01	03 18	03 46

SUN / MOON

Day	Eqn. of Time 00h	Eqn. of Time 12h	Mer. Pass.	Mer. Pass. Upper	Mer. Pass. Lower	Age	Phase
d	m s	m s	h m	h m	h m	d	%
29	11 44	11 33	11 48	23 30	11 07	14	99
30	11 22	11 11	11 49	24 19	11 54	15	100
1	11 00	10 49	11 49	00 19	12 44	16	99

UT	ARIES GHA	VENUS −3.9 GHA	VENUS Dec	MARS −1.1 GHA	MARS Dec	JUPITER −2.0 GHA	JUPITER Dec	SATURN +0.6 GHA	SATURN Dec	STARS Name	SHA	Dec
2 00	71 17.7	210 17.3	S14 10.3	55 22.7	N 6 46.4	132 50.7	S21 20.3	130 36.2	S20 48.8	Acamar	315 14.0	S40 13.4
01	86 20.1	225 16.8	11.3	70 24.7	46.7	147 52.6	20.2	145 38.5	48.8	Achernar	335 22.4	S57 08.2
02	101 22.6	240 16.2	12.3	85 26.7	47.0	162 54.6	20.1	160 40.7	48.7	Acrux	173 03.9	S63 12.5
03	116 25.1	255 15.6	.. 13.2	100 28.7	.. 47.3	177 56.5	.. 20.0	175 42.9	.. 48.7	Adhara	255 08.1	S28 59.9
04	131 27.5	270 15.0	14.2	115 30.7	47.6	192 58.5	19.9	190 45.1	48.7	Aldebaran	290 43.1	N16 33.0
05	146 30.0	285 14.5	15.2	130 32.7	47.9	208 00.4	19.8	205 47.4	48.6			
W 06	161 32.5	300 13.9	S14 16.2	145 34.7	N 6 48.2	223 02.3	S21 19.7	220 49.6	S20 48.6	Alioth	166 16.4	N55 50.7
E 07	176 34.9	315 13.3	17.1	160 36.7	48.5	238 04.3	19.6	235 51.8	48.5	Alkaid	152 55.1	N49 12.5
D 08	191 37.4	330 12.7	18.1	175 38.7	48.8	253 06.2	19.5	250 54.0	48.5	Alnair	27 37.3	S46 51.9
N 09	206 39.9	345 12.1	.. 19.1	190 40.7	.. 49.1	268 08.2	.. 19.5	265 56.2	.. 48.4	Alnilam	275 40.8	S 1 11.4
E 10	221 42.3	0 11.6	20.1	205 42.7	49.4	283 10.1	19.4	280 58.5	48.4	Alphard	217 50.9	S 8 44.8
S 11	236 44.8	15 11.0	21.0	220 44.7	49.7	298 12.1	19.3	296 00.7	48.3			
D 12	251 47.3	30 10.4	S14 22.0	235 46.7	N 6 50.0	313 14.0	S21 19.2	311 02.9	S20 48.3	Alphecca	126 07.0	N26 38.8
A 13	266 49.7	45 09.8	23.0	250 48.7	50.3	328 15.9	19.1	326 05.1	48.3	Alpheratz	357 38.1	N29 12.4
Y 14	281 52.2	60 09.2	23.9	265 50.7	50.6	343 17.9	19.0	341 07.4	48.2	Altair	62 03.5	N 8 55.5
15	296 54.6	75 08.6	.. 24.9	280 52.6	.. 50.9	358 19.8	.. 18.9	356 09.6	.. 48.2	Ankaa	353 10.3	S42 11.8
16	311 57.1	90 08.1	25.9	295 54.6	51.2	13 21.8	18.8	11 11.8	48.1	Antares	112 20.3	S26 28.5
17	326 59.6	105 07.5	26.8	310 56.6	51.5	28 23.7	18.7	26 14.0	48.1			
18	342 02.0	120 06.9	S14 27.8	325 58.6	N 6 51.8	43 25.7	S21 18.6	41 16.2	S20 48.0	Arcturus	145 51.3	N19 04.5
19	357 04.5	135 06.3	28.8	341 00.6	52.1	58 27.6	18.5	56 18.5	48.0	Atria	107 18.1	S69 03.7
20	12 07.0	150 05.7	29.7	356 02.6	52.4	73 29.5	18.4	71 20.7	47.9	Avior	234 15.6	S59 34.3
21	27 09.4	165 05.1	.. 30.7	11 04.6	.. 52.8	88 31.5	.. 18.3	86 22.9	.. 47.9	Bellatrix	278 26.1	N 6 22.1
22	42 11.9	180 04.5	31.7	26 06.5	53.1	103 33.4	18.2	101 25.1	47.9	Betelgeuse	270 55.4	N 7 24.6
23	57 14.4	195 03.9	32.6	41 08.5	53.4	118 35.4	18.2	116 27.3	47.8			
3 00	72 16.8	210 03.4	S14 33.6	56 10.5	N 6 53.7	133 37.3	S21 18.1	131 29.6	S20 47.8	Canopus	263 53.3	S52 42.3
01	87 19.3	225 02.8	34.6	71 12.5	54.0	148 39.2	18.0	146 31.8	47.7	Capella	280 26.3	N46 01.0
02	102 21.8	240 02.2	35.5	86 14.5	54.3	163 41.2	17.9	161 34.0	47.7	Deneb	49 28.3	N45 21.5
03	117 24.2	255 01.6	.. 36.5	101 16.4	.. 54.6	178 43.1	.. 17.8	176 36.2	.. 47.6	Denebola	182 28.5	N14 27.4
04	132 26.7	270 01.0	37.5	116 18.4	54.9	193 45.1	17.7	191 38.4	47.6	Diphda	348 50.5	S17 52.5
05	147 29.1	285 00.4	38.4	131 20.4	55.2	208 47.0	17.6	206 40.7	47.5			
T 06	162 31.6	299 59.8	S14 39.4	146 22.4	N 6 55.5	223 48.9	S21 17.5	221 42.9	S20 47.4	Dubhe	193 45.3	N61 38.1
H 07	177 34.1	314 59.2	40.3	161 24.3	55.8	238 50.9	17.4	236 45.1	47.4	Elnath	278 05.7	N28 37.4
U 08	192 36.5	329 58.6	41.3	176 26.3	56.1	253 52.8	17.3	251 47.3	47.4	Eltanin	90 44.3	N51 29.3
R 09	207 39.0	344 58.0	.. 42.3	191 28.3	.. 56.5	268 54.8	.. 17.2	266 49.5	.. 47.4	Enif	33 42.2	N 9 58.3
S 10	222 41.5	359 57.4	43.2	206 30.3	56.8	283 56.7	17.1	281 51.8	47.3	Fomalhaut	15 18.2	S29 30.9
D 11	237 43.9	14 56.9	44.2	221 32.2	57.1	298 58.6	17.0	296 54.0	47.3			
A 12	252 46.4	29 56.3	S14 45.1	236 34.2	N 6 57.4	314 00.6	S21 16.9	311 56.2	S20 47.2	Gacrux	171 55.5	S57 13.4
Y 13	267 48.9	44 55.7	46.1	251 36.2	57.7	329 02.5	16.8	326 58.4	47.2	Gienah	175 47.1	S17 39.2
14	282 51.3	59 55.1	47.0	266 38.1	58.0	344 04.5	16.8	342 00.6	47.1	Hadar	148 41.1	S60 28.1
15	297 53.8	74 54.5	.. 48.0	281 40.1	.. 58.3	359 06.4	.. 16.7	357 02.9	.. 47.1	Hamal	327 54.7	N23 33.7
16	312 56.3	89 53.9	49.0	296 42.1	58.6	14 08.3	16.6	12 05.1	47.0	Kaus Aust.	83 37.3	S34 22.4
17	327 58.7	104 53.3	49.9	311 44.0	58.9	29 10.3	16.5	27 07.3	47.0			
18	343 01.2	119 52.7	S14 50.9	326 46.0	N 6 59.3	44 12.2	S21 16.4	42 09.5	S20 46.9	Kochab	137 21.0	N74 04.1
19	358 03.6	134 52.1	51.8	341 47.9	59.6	59 14.1	16.3	57 11.7	46.9	Markab	13 33.2	N15 19.1
20	13 06.1	149 51.5	52.8	356 49.9	6 59.9	74 16.1	16.2	72 14.0	46.8	Menkar	314 09.3	N 4 10.2
21	28 08.6	164 50.9	.. 53.7	11 51.9	7 00.2	89 18.0	.. 16.1	87 16.2	.. 46.8	Menkent	148 01.8	S36 28.1
22	43 11.0	179 50.3	54.7	26 53.8	00.5	104 20.0	16.0	102 18.4	46.8	Miaplacidus	221 38.3	S69 47.8
23	58 13.5	194 49.7	55.6	41 55.8	00.8	119 21.9	15.9	117 20.6	46.7			
4 00	73 16.0	209 49.1	S14 56.6	56 57.7	N 7 01.1	134 23.8	S21 15.8	132 22.8	S20 46.7	Mirfak	308 32.5	N49 56.1
01	88 18.4	224 48.5	57.5	71 59.7	01.4	149 25.8	15.7	147 25.0	46.6	Nunki	75 52.2	S26 16.2
02	103 20.9	239 47.9	58.5	87 01.7	01.8	164 27.7	15.6	162 27.3	46.6	Peacock	53 11.4	S56 40.3
03	118 23.4	254 47.3	14 59.4	102 03.6	.. 02.1	179 29.6	.. 15.5	177 29.5	.. 46.5	Pollux	243 21.1	N27 58.4
04	133 25.8	269 46.7	15 00.4	117 05.6	02.4	194 31.6	15.4	192 31.7	46.5	Procyon	244 54.1	N 5 10.3
05	148 28.3	284 46.1	01.3	132 07.5	02.7	209 33.5	15.3	207 33.9	46.4			
06	163 30.8	299 45.5	S15 02.3	147 09.5	N 7 03.0	224 35.5	S21 15.2	222 36.1	S20 46.4	Rasalhague	96 02.0	N12 32.8
07	178 33.2	314 44.9	03.2	162 11.4	03.3	239 37.4	15.1	237 38.4	46.3	Regulus	207 37.9	N11 51.9
08	193 35.7	329 44.3	04.1	177 13.4	03.7	254 39.3	15.1	252 40.6	46.3	Rigel	281 06.7	S 8 10.7
F 09	208 38.1	344 43.7	.. 05.1	192 15.3	.. 04.0	269 41.3	.. 15.0	267 42.8	.. 46.3	Rigil Kent.	139 45.4	S60 54.9
R 10	223 40.6	359 43.1	06.0	207 17.3	04.3	284 43.2	14.9	282 45.0	46.2	Sabik	102 07.0	S15 44.9
I 11	238 43.1	14 42.5	07.0	222 19.2	04.6	299 45.1	14.8	297 47.2	46.2			
D 12	253 45.5	29 41.8	S15 07.9	237 21.1	N 7 04.9	314 47.1	S21 14.7	312 49.4	S20 46.1	Schedar	349 34.4	N56 39.3
A 13	268 48.0	44 41.2	08.9	252 23.1	05.2	329 49.0	14.6	327 51.7	46.1	Shaula	96 15.3	S37 07.0
Y 14	283 50.5	59 40.6	09.8	267 25.0	05.6	344 50.9	14.5	342 53.9	46.0	Sirius	258 28.9	S16 44.7
15	298 52.9	74 40.0	.. 10.7	282 27.0	.. 05.9	359 52.9	.. 14.4	357 56.1	.. 46.0	Spica	158 26.0	S11 16.0
16	313 55.4	89 39.4	11.7	297 28.9	06.2	14 54.8	14.3	12 58.3	45.9	Suhail	222 48.5	S43 30.7
17	328 57.9	104 38.8	12.6	312 30.9	06.5	29 56.7	14.2	28 00.5	45.9			
18	344 00.3	119 38.2	S15 13.6	327 32.8	N 7 06.8	44 58.7	S21 14.1	43 02.7	S20 45.8	Vega	80 35.9	N38 48.3
19	359 02.8	134 37.6	14.5	342 34.7	07.2	60 00.6	14.0	58 05.0	45.8	Zuben'ubi	137 00.0	S16 07.5
20	14 05.3	149 37.0	15.4	357 36.7	07.5	75 02.5	13.9	73 07.2	45.7		SHA	Mer. Pass.
21	29 07.7	164 36.4	.. 16.4	12 38.6	.. 07.8	90 04.5	.. 13.8	88 09.4	.. 45.7	Venus	137 46.5	10 00
22	44 10.2	179 35.8	17.3	27 40.5	08.1	105 06.4	13.7	103 11.6	45.7	Mars	343 53.7	20 13
23	59 12.6	194 35.1	18.2	42 42.5	08.4	120 08.4	13.6	118 13.8	45.6	Jupiter	61 20.5	15 04
Mer. Pass. 19 07.7		v −0.6	d 1.0	v 2.0	d 0.3	v 1.9	d 0.1	v 2.2	d 0.0	Saturn	59 12.7	15 12

SUN and MOON

UT	SUN GHA	SUN Dec	MOON GHA	v	MOON Dec	d	HP
2 00	182 39.2	S21 59.1	343 17.5	9.8	N24 11.3	3.2	55.1
01	197 39.0	59.5	357 46.3	9.7	24 14.5	3.0	55.2
02	212 38.8	21 59.8	12 15.0	9.7	24 17.5	2.9	55.2
03	227 38.5	22 00.2	26 43.7	9.6	24 20.4	2.9	55.2
04	242 38.3	00.6	41 12.3	9.6	24 23.3	2.6	55.2
05	257 38.0	00.9	55 40.9	9.5	24 25.9	2.6	55.2
W 06	272 37.8	S22 01.3	70 09.4	9.6	N24 28.5	2.5	55.2
E 07	287 37.6	01.7	84 38.0	9.4	24 31.0	2.3	55.3
D 08	302 37.3	02.0	99 06.4	9.4	24 33.3	2.2	55.3
N 09	317 37.1	02.4	113 34.8	9.4	24 35.5	2.0	55.3
E 10	332 36.8	02.7	128 03.2	9.4	24 37.5	2.0	55.3
S 11	347 36.6	03.1	142 31.6	9.3	24 39.5	1.8	55.3
D 12	2 36.4	S22 03.5	156 59.9	9.3	N24 41.3	1.6	55.3
A 13	17 36.1	03.8	171 28.2	9.2	24 42.9	1.6	55.4
Y 14	32 35.9	04.2	185 56.4	9.2	24 44.5	1.4	55.4
15	47 35.6	04.5	200 24.6	9.2	24 45.9	1.3	55.4
16	62 35.4	04.9	214 52.8	9.2	24 47.2	1.2	55.4
17	77 35.1	05.2	229 21.0	9.1	24 48.4	1.0	55.4
18	92 34.9	S22 05.6	243 49.1	9.1	N24 49.4	0.9	55.5
19	107 34.6	05.9	258 17.2	9.0	24 50.3	0.8	55.5
20	122 34.4	06.3	272 45.2	9.1	24 51.1	0.6	55.5
21	137 34.2	06.6	287 13.3	9.0	24 51.7	0.5	55.5
22	152 33.9	07.0	301 41.3	9.0	24 52.2	0.4	55.5
23	167 33.7	07.3	316 09.3	8.9	24 52.6	0.3	55.5
3 00	182 33.4	S22 07.7	330 37.2	9.0	N24 52.9	0.1	55.6
01	197 33.2	08.0	345 05.2	8.9	24 53.0	0.0	55.6
02	212 32.9	08.4	359 33.1	8.9	24 53.0	0.2	55.6
03	227 32.7	08.7	14 01.0	8.9	24 52.8	0.3	55.6
04	242 32.4	09.1	28 28.9	8.8	24 52.5	0.4	55.6
05	257 32.2	09.4	42 56.7	8.9	24 52.1	0.5	55.7
T 06	272 31.9	S22 09.8	57 24.6	8.8	N24 51.6	0.7	55.7
H 07	287 31.7	10.1	71 52.4	8.8	24 50.9	0.8	55.7
U 08	302 31.4	10.5	86 20.2	8.8	24 50.1	1.0	55.7
R 09	317 31.2	10.8	100 48.0	8.8	24 49.1	1.0	55.7
S 10	332 30.9	11.2	115 15.8	8.8	24 48.1	1.3	55.8
D 11	347 30.7	11.5	129 43.6	8.7	24 46.8	1.3	55.8
A 12	2 30.4	S22 11.8	144 11.3	8.8	N24 45.5	1.5	55.8
Y 13	17 30.2	12.2	158 39.1	8.8	24 44.0	1.6	55.8
14	32 29.9	12.5	173 06.9	8.7	24 42.4	1.8	55.8
15	47 29.7	12.9	187 34.6	8.8	24 40.6	1.9	55.9
16	62 29.4	13.2	202 02.4	8.7	24 38.7	2.0	55.9
17	77 29.2	13.5	216 30.1	8.7	24 36.7	2.1	55.9
18	92 28.9	S22 13.9	230 57.8	8.8	N24 34.6	2.3	55.9
19	107 28.7	14.2	245 25.6	8.7	24 32.3	2.4	55.9
20	122 28.4	14.5	259 53.3	8.7	24 29.9	2.6	56.0
21	137 28.2	14.9	274 21.0	8.8	24 27.3	2.7	56.0
22	152 27.9	15.2	288 48.8	8.7	24 24.6	2.8	56.0
23	167 27.7	15.5	303 16.5	8.7	24 21.8	3.0	56.0
4 00	182 27.4	S22 15.9	317 44.2	8.8	N24 18.8	3.1	56.0
01	197 27.2	16.2	332 12.0	8.7	24 15.7	3.2	56.1
02	212 26.9	16.5	346 39.7	8.8	24 12.5	3.3	56.1
03	227 26.7	16.9	1 07.5	8.8	24 09.2	3.5	56.1
04	242 26.4	17.2	15 35.3	8.7	24 05.7	3.7	56.1
05	257 26.2	17.5	30 03.0	8.8	24 02.0	3.7	56.1
F 06	272 25.9	S22 17.8	44 30.8	8.8	N23 58.3	3.9	56.2
R 07	287 25.7	18.2	58 58.6	8.8	23 54.4	4.0	56.2
I 08	302 25.4	18.5	73 26.4	8.8	23 50.4	4.2	56.2
D 09	317 25.2	18.8	87 54.2	8.9	23 46.2	4.3	56.2
A 10	332 24.9	19.1	102 22.1	8.8	23 41.9	4.4	56.3
Y 11	347 24.6	19.5	116 49.9	8.9	23 37.5	4.5	56.3
12	2 24.4	S22 19.8	131 17.8	8.9	N23 33.0	4.7	56.3
13	17 24.1	20.1	145 45.7	8.9	23 28.3	4.8	56.3
14	32 23.9	20.4	160 13.6	8.9	23 23.5	4.9	56.3
15	47 23.6	20.8	174 41.5	8.9	23 18.6	5.1	56.4
16	62 23.4	21.1	189 09.4	9.0	23 13.5	5.2	56.4
17	77 23.1	21.4	203 37.4	8.9	23 08.3	5.3	56.4
18	92 22.8	S22 21.7	218 05.3	9.0	N23 03.0	5.5	56.4
19	107 22.6	22.0	232 33.3	9.1	22 57.5	5.6	56.5
20	122 22.3	22.3	247 01.4	9.0	22 51.9	5.7	56.5
21	137 22.1	22.7	261 29.4	9.1	22 46.2	5.8	56.5
22	152 21.8	23.0	275 57.5	9.1	22 40.4	6.0	56.5
23	167 21.6	23.3	290 25.6	9.1	N22 34.4	6.1	56.6
	SD 16.3	d 0.3	SD 15.1		15.2		15.3

Twilight, Sunrise and Moonrise

Lat.	Naut.	Civil	Sunrise	Moonrise 2	3	4	5
N 72	07 57	10 01	■	□	□	□	□
N 70	07 40	09 19	■	□	□	□	□
68	07 27	08 50	10 52	□	□	□	17 56
66	07 15	08 28	09 55	□	□	16 33	18 39
64	07 05	08 11	09 22	14 57	15 54	17 25	19 07
62	06 57	07 57	08 59	15 41	16 37	17 57	19 29
60	06 49	07 45	08 40	16 10	17 06	18 20	19 47
N 58	06 43	07 34	08 24	16 32	17 28	18 39	20 01
56	06 37	07 25	08 11	16 50	17 46	18 55	20 14
54	06 31	07 16	07 59	17 06	18 01	19 09	20 24
52	06 26	07 09	07 49	17 19	18 14	19 20	20 34
50	06 21	07 02	07 40	17 31	18 26	19 31	20 43
45	06 10	06 47	07 21	17 55	18 50	19 53	21 01
N 40	06 01	06 35	07 05	18 15	19 09	20 10	21 15
35	05 52	06 24	06 52	18 31	19 25	20 25	21 28
30	05 44	06 14	06 40	18 45	19 39	20 38	21 39
20	05 29	05 56	06 20	19 09	20 03	20 59	21 57
N 10	05 14	05 40	06 03	19 30	20 23	21 18	22 13
0	04 58	05 24	05 46	19 49	20 42	21 36	22 28
S 10	04 40	05 07	05 30	20 08	21 02	21 53	22 43
20	04 19	04 48	05 12	20 29	21 22	22 12	22 59
30	03 51	04 24	04 51	20 54	21 46	22 34	23 17
35	03 34	04 10	04 39	21 08	21 59	22 46	23 28
40	03 12	03 53	04 25	21 24	22 15	23 01	23 40
45	02 44	03 32	04 08	21 44	22 35	23 18	23 54
S 50	02 04	03 04	03 47	22 09	22 58	23 39	24 11
52	01 41	02 51	03 37	22 21	23 10	23 49	24 20
54	01 08	02 35	03 26	22 34	23 23	24 00	00 00
56	////	02 15	03 13	22 50	23 38	24 13	00 13
58	////	01 51	02 58	23 09	23 56	24 28	00 28
S 60	////	01 16	02 40	23 32	24 17	00 17	00 46

Sunset, Twilight and Moonset

Lat.	Sunset	Civil	Naut.	Moonset 2	3	4	5
N 72	■	13 38	15 42	□	□	□	□
N 70	■	14 21	15 59	□	□	□	□
68	12 48	14 49	16 13	□	□	□	14 46
66	13 44	15 11	16 24	□	□	14 19	14 02
64	14 17	15 28	16 34	12 11	13 05	13 26	13 33
62	14 41	15 43	16 43	11 28	12 22	12 54	13 11
60	15 00	15 55	16 50	10 59	11 53	12 30	12 53
N 58	15 16	16 05	16 57	10 37	11 31	12 11	12 38
56	15 29	16 15	17 03	10 19	11 13	11 55	12 25
54	15 41	16 23	17 08	10 03	10 58	11 41	12 13
52	15 51	16 31	17 14	09 50	10 44	11 29	12 03
50	16 00	16 38	17 18	09 39	10 33	11 18	11 54
45	16 19	16 52	17 29	09 14	10 09	10 56	11 35
N 40	16 35	17 05	17 39	08 55	09 49	10 37	11 20
35	16 48	17 16	17 47	08 39	09 33	10 22	11 06
30	17 00	17 26	17 55	08 25	09 19	10 09	10 55
20	17 20	17 44	18 11	08 01	08 55	09 46	10 35
N 10	17 37	18 00	18 26	07 41	08 34	09 27	10 17
0	17 54	18 16	18 42	07 22	08 15	09 09	10 01
S 10	18 10	18 33	19 00	07 03	07 55	08 50	09 45
20	18 28	18 52	19 21	06 42	07 34	08 30	09 27
30	18 49	19 16	19 49	06 18	07 10	08 07	09 07
35	19 01	19 30	20 06	06 05	06 56	07 53	08 55
40	19 15	19 48	20 28	05 49	06 40	07 38	08 41
45	19 32	20 09	20 57	05 29	06 20	07 19	08 24
S 50	19 53	20 36	21 37	05 05	05 55	06 55	08 04
52	20 03	20 50	22 01	04 54	05 43	06 44	07 54
54	20 15	21 06	22 34	04 41	05 30	06 31	07 44
56	20 28	21 26	////	04 26	05 14	06 17	07 31
58	20 43	21 51	////	04 08	04 55	05 59	07 17
S 60	21 01	22 27	////	03 46	04 32	05 38	06 59

SUN and MOON

Day	Eqn. of Time 00h	Eqn. of Time 12h	Mer. Pass.	Mer. Pass. Upper	Mer. Pass. Lower	Age	Phase
2	10 37	10 26	11 50	01 09	13 35	17	96
3	10 14	10 02	11 50	02 02	14 29	18	91
4	09 50	09 38	11 50	02 55	15 22	19	84

UT	ARIES	VENUS −3.9		MARS −1.0		JUPITER −2.0		SATURN +0.6		STARS		
d h	GHA	GHA	Dec	GHA	Dec	GHA	Dec	GHA	Dec	Name	SHA	Dec
5 00	74 15.1	209 34.5 S15 19.2		57 44.4 N 7 08.8		135 10.3 S21 13.5		133 16.0 S20 45.6		Acamar	315 14.0	S40 13.5
01	89 17.6	224 33.9	20.1	72 46.3	09.1	150 12.2	13.4	148 18.3	45.5	Achernar	335 22.4	S57 08.2
02	104 20.0	239 33.3	21.0	87 48.3	09.4	165 14.2	13.3	163 20.5	45.5	Acrux	173 03.9	S63 12.5
03	119 22.5	254 32.7 ..	22.0	102 50.2 ..	09.7	180 16.1 ..	13.2	178 22.7 ..	45.4	Adhara	255 08.1	S28 59.9
04	134 25.0	269 32.1	22.9	117 52.1	10.0	195 18.0	13.1	193 24.9	45.4	Aldebaran	290 43.1	N16 33.0
05	149 27.4	284 31.5	23.8	132 54.1	10.4	210 20.0	13.1	208 27.1	45.3			
06	164 29.9	299 30.8 S15 24.8		147 56.0 N 7 10.7		225 21.9 S21 13.0		223 29.3 S20 45.3		Alioth	166 16.3	N55 50.7
07	179 32.4	314 30.2	25.7	162 57.9	11.0	240 23.8	12.9	238 31.5	45.2	Alkaid	152 55.1	N49 12.5
S 08	194 34.8	329 29.6	26.6	177 59.8	11.3	255 25.8	12.8	253 33.8	45.2	Alnair	27 37.3	S46 51.9
A 09	209 37.3	344 29.0 ..	27.5	193 01.8 ..	11.7	270 27.7 ..	12.7	268 36.0 ..	45.1	Alnilam	275 40.8	S 1 11.4
T 10	224 39.7	359 28.4	28.5	208 03.7	12.0	285 29.6	12.6	283 38.2	45.1	Alphard	217 50.9	S 8 44.8
U 11	239 42.2	14 27.8	29.4	223 05.6	12.3	300 31.6	12.5	298 40.4	45.0			
R 12	254 44.7	29 27.1 S15 30.3		238 07.5 N 7 12.6		315 33.5 S21 12.4		313 42.6 S20 45.0		Alphecca	126 07.0	N26 38.7
D 13	269 47.1	44 26.5	31.3	253 09.5	13.0	330 35.4	12.3	328 44.8	45.0	Alpheratz	357 38.1	N29 12.4
A 14	284 49.6	59 25.9	32.2	268 11.4	13.3	345 37.3	12.2	343 47.0	44.9	Altair	62 03.5	N 8 55.5
Y 15	299 52.1	74 25.3 ..	33.1	283 13.3 ..	13.6	0 39.3 ..	12.1	358 49.3 ..	44.9	Ankaa	353 10.4	S42 11.8
16	314 54.5	89 24.7	34.0	298 15.2	13.9	15 41.2	12.0	13 51.5	44.8	Antares	112 20.3	S26 28.5
17	329 57.0	104 24.0	35.0	313 17.1	14.3	30 43.1	11.9	28 53.7	44.8			
18	344 59.5	119 23.4 S15 35.9		328 19.1 N 7 14.6		45 45.1 S21 11.8		43 55.9 S20 44.7		Arcturus	145 51.3	N19 04.5
19	0 01.9	134 22.8	36.8	343 21.0	14.9	60 47.0	11.7	58 58.1	44.7	Atria	107 18.0	S69 03.7
20	15 04.4	149 22.2	37.7	358 22.9	15.2	75 48.9	11.6	74 00.3	44.6	Avior	234 15.6	S59 34.3
21	30 06.9	164 21.6 ..	38.6	13 24.8 ..	15.6	90 50.9 ..	11.5	89 02.5 ..	44.6	Bellatrix	278 26.1	N 6 22.1
22	45 09.3	179 20.9	39.6	28 26.7	15.9	105 52.8	11.4	104 04.8	44.5	Betelgeuse	270 55.4	N 7 24.6
23	60 11.8	194 20.3	40.5	43 28.6	16.2	120 54.7	11.3	119 07.0	44.5			
6 00	75 14.2	209 19.7 S15 41.4		58 30.5 N 7 16.5		135 56.7 S21 11.2		134 09.2 S20 44.4		Canopus	263 53.3	S52 42.3
01	90 16.7	224 19.1	42.3	73 32.4	16.9	150 58.6	11.1	149 11.4	44.4	Capella	280 26.3	N46 01.0
02	105 19.2	239 18.4	43.2	88 34.4	17.2	166 00.5	11.0	164 13.6	44.3	Deneb	49 28.3	N45 21.5
03	120 21.6	254 17.8 ..	44.1	103 36.3 ..	17.5	181 02.5 ..	10.9	179 15.8 ..	44.3	Denebola	182 28.4	N14 27.4
04	135 24.1	269 17.2	45.1	118 38.2	17.9	196 04.4	10.8	194 18.0	44.2	Diphda	348 50.5	S17 52.5
05	150 26.6	284 16.6	46.0	133 40.1	18.2	211 06.3	10.7	209 20.3	44.2			
06	165 29.0	299 15.9 S15 46.9		148 42.0 N 7 18.5		226 08.2 S21 10.6		224 22.5 S20 44.2		Dubhe	193 45.3	N61 38.1
07	180 31.5	314 15.3	47.8	163 43.9	18.8	241 10.2	10.5	239 24.7	44.1	Elnath	278 05.7	N28 37.4
S 08	195 34.0	329 14.7	48.7	178 45.8	19.2	256 12.1	10.4	254 26.9	44.1	Eltanin	90 44.3	N51 29.3
U 09	210 36.4	344 14.0 ..	49.6	193 47.7 ..	19.5	271 14.0 ..	10.3	269 29.1 ..	44.0	Enif	33 42.2	N 9 58.3
N 10	225 38.9	359 13.4	50.5	208 49.6	19.8	286 16.0	10.3	284 31.3	44.0	Fomalhaut	15 18.2	S29 30.9
D 11	240 41.4	14 12.8	51.5	223 51.5	20.2	301 17.9	10.2	299 33.5	43.9			
A 12	255 43.8	29 12.1 S15 52.4		238 53.4 N 7 20.5		316 19.8 S21 10.1		314 35.7 S20 43.9		Gacrux	171 55.5	S57 13.4
Y 13	270 46.3	44 11.5	53.3	253 55.3	20.8	331 21.7	10.0	329 38.0	43.8	Gienah	175 47.1	S17 39.2
14	285 48.7	59 10.9	54.2	268 57.2	21.2	346 23.7	09.9	344 40.2	43.8	Hadar	148 41.1	S60 28.1
15	300 51.2	74 10.3 ..	55.1	283 59.1 ..	21.5	1 25.6 ..	09.8	359 42.4 ..	43.7	Hamal	327 54.7	N23 33.7
16	315 53.7	89 09.6	56.0	299 01.0	21.8	16 27.5	09.7	14 44.6	43.7	Kaus Aust.	83 37.3	S34 22.4
17	330 56.1	104 09.0	56.9	314 02.9	22.1	31 29.5	09.6	29 46.8	43.6			
18	345 58.6	119 08.4 S15 57.8		329 04.8 N 7 22.5		46 31.4 S21 09.5		44 49.0 S20 43.6		Kochab	137 21.0	N74 04.1
19	1 01.1	134 07.7	58.7	344 06.7	22.8	61 33.3	09.4	59 51.2	43.5	Markab	13 33.2	N15 19.1
20	16 03.5	149 07.1 15 59.6		359 08.6	23.1	76 35.2	09.3	74 53.4	43.5	Menkar	314 09.3	N 4 10.2
21	31 06.0	164 06.4 16 00.5		14 10.4 ..	23.5	91 37.2 ..	09.2	89 55.6 ..	43.4	Menkent	148 01.8	S36 28.1
22	46 08.5	179 05.8	01.4	29 12.3	23.8	106 39.1	09.1	104 57.9	43.4	Miaplacidus	221 38.3	S69 47.8
23	61 10.9	194 05.2	02.3	44 14.2	24.1	121 41.0	09.0	120 00.1	43.3			
7 00	76 13.4	209 04.5 S16 03.2		59 16.1 N 7 24.5		136 43.0 S21 08.9		135 02.3 S20 43.3		Mirfak	308 32.5	N49 56.1
01	91 15.9	224 03.9	04.1	74 18.0	24.8	151 44.9	08.8	150 04.5	43.2	Nunki	75 52.2	S26 16.2
02	106 18.3	239 03.3	05.0	89 19.9	25.1	166 46.8	08.7	165 06.7	43.2	Peacock	53 11.4	S56 40.3
03	121 20.8	254 02.6 ..	05.9	104 21.8 ..	25.5	181 48.7 ..	08.6	180 08.9 ..	43.2	Pollux	243 21.1	N27 58.4
04	136 23.2	269 02.0	06.8	119 23.7	25.8	196 50.7	08.5	195 11.1	43.1	Procyon	244 54.1	N 5 10.3
05	151 25.7	284 01.3	07.7	134 25.5	26.2	211 52.6	08.4	210 13.3	43.1			
06	166 28.2	299 00.7 S16 08.6		149 27.4 N 7 26.5		226 54.5 S21 08.3		225 15.5 S20 43.0		Rasalhague	96 02.0	N12 32.8
07	181 30.6	314 00.1	09.5	164 29.3	26.8	241 56.4	08.2	240 17.8	43.0	Regulus	207 37.9	N11 51.9
08	196 33.1	328 59.4	10.4	179 31.2	27.2	256 58.4	08.1	255 20.0	42.9	Rigel	281 06.7	S 8 10.7
M 09	211 35.6	343 58.8 ..	11.3	194 33.1 ..	27.5	272 00.3 ..	08.0	270 22.2 ..	42.9	Rigil Kent.	139 45.3	S60 54.9
O 10	226 38.0	358 58.1	12.2	209 35.0	27.8	287 02.2	07.9	285 24.4	42.8	Sabik	102 07.0	S15 44.9
N 11	241 40.5	13 57.5	13.1	224 36.8	28.2	302 04.2	07.8	300 26.6	42.8			
D 12	256 43.0	28 56.9 S16 14.0		239 38.7 N 7 28.5		317 06.1 S21 07.7		315 28.8 S20 42.7		Schedar	349 34.4	N56 39.3
A 13	271 45.4	43 56.2	14.9	254 40.6	28.8	332 08.0	07.6	330 31.0	42.7	Shaula	96 15.3	S37 07.0
Y 14	286 47.9	58 55.6	15.8	269 42.5	29.2	347 09.9	07.5	345 33.2	42.6	Sirius	258 28.8	S16 44.7
15	301 50.3	73 54.9 ..	16.7	284 44.3 ..	29.5	2 11.9 ..	07.4	0 35.4 ..	42.6	Spica	158 26.0	S11 16.0
16	316 52.8	88 54.3	17.6	299 46.2	29.9	17 13.8	07.3	15 37.6	42.5	Suhail	222 48.5	S43 30.7
17	331 55.3	103 53.6	18.5	314 48.1	30.2	32 15.7	07.2	30 39.8	42.5			
18	346 57.7	118 53.0 S16 19.3		329 50.0 N 7 30.5		47 17.6 S21 07.1		45 42.1 S20 42.4		Vega	80 35.9	N38 48.3
19	2 00.2	133 52.3	20.2	344 51.8	30.9	62 19.6	07.0	60 44.3	42.4	Zuben'ubi	137 00.0	S16 07.5
20	17 02.7	148 51.7	21.1	359 53.7	31.2	77 21.5	06.9	75 46.5	42.3		SHA	Mer. Pass.
21	32 05.1	163 51.0 ..	22.0	14 55.6 ..	31.5	92 23.4 ..	06.8	90 48.7 ..	42.3		° ′	h m
22	47 07.6	178 50.4	22.9	29 57.4	31.9	107 25.3	06.7	105 50.9	42.2	Venus	134 05.4	10 03
23	62 10.1	193 49.7	23.8	44 59.3	32.2	122 27.3	06.6	120 53.1	42.2	Mars	343 16.3	20 03
	h m									Jupiter	60 42.4	14 54
Mer. Pass. 18 55.9	v −0.6 　 d 0.9			v 1.9 　 d 0.3		v 1.9 　 d 0.1		v 2.2 　 d 0.0		Saturn	58 54.9	15 01

UT	SUN GHA	Dec	MOON GHA	v	Dec	d	HP
d h	° ′	° ′	° ′	′	° ′	′	′
5 00	182 21.3	S22 23.6	304 53.7	9.1	N22 28.3	6.2	56.6
01	197 21.0	23.9	319 21.8	9.2	22 22.1	6.3	56.6
02	212 20.8	24.2	333 50.0	9.2	22 15.8	6.5	56.6
03	227 20.5 ..	24.5	348 18.2	9.2	22 09.3	6.6	56.6
04	242 20.3	24.9	2 46.4	9.2	22 02.7	6.7	56.7
05	257 20.0	25.2	17 14.6	9.3	21 56.0	6.8	56.7
06	272 19.7	S22 25.5	31 42.9	9.3	N21 49.2	7.0	56.7
07	287 19.5	25.8	46 11.2	9.3	21 42.2	7.0	56.7
S 08	302 19.2	26.1	60 39.5	9.4	21 35.2	7.2	56.8
A 09	317 19.0 ..	26.4	75 07.9	9.4	21 28.0	7.4	56.8
T 10	332 18.7	26.7	89 36.3	9.4	21 20.6	7.4	56.8
U 11	347 18.4	27.0	104 04.7	9.5	21 13.2	7.6	56.8
R 12	2 18.2	S22 27.3	118 33.2	9.5	N21 05.6	7.6	56.8
D 13	17 17.9	27.6	133 01.7	9.5	20 58.0	7.8	56.9
A 14	32 17.7	27.9	147 30.2	9.6	20 50.2	8.0	56.9
Y 15	47 17.4 ..	28.2	161 58.8	9.5	20 42.2	8.0	56.9
16	62 17.1	28.5	176 27.3	9.7	20 34.2	8.1	56.9
17	77 16.9	28.8	190 56.0	9.6	20 26.1	8.3	57.0
18	92 16.6	S22 29.1	205 24.6	9.7	N20 17.8	8.4	57.0
19	107 16.3	29.4	219 53.3	9.7	20 09.4	8.5	57.0
20	122 16.1	29.7	234 22.0	9.8	20 00.9	8.6	57.0
21	137 15.8 ..	30.0	248 50.8	9.8	19 52.3	8.7	57.1
22	152 15.6	30.3	263 19.6	9.8	19 43.6	8.8	57.1
23	167 15.3	30.6	277 48.4	9.9	19 34.8	9.0	57.1
6 00	182 15.0	S22 30.9	292 17.2	9.9	N19 25.8	9.0	57.1
01	197 14.8	31.2	306 46.1	9.9	19 16.8	9.2	57.2
02	212 14.5	31.5	321 15.0	10.0	19 07.6	9.2	57.2
03	227 14.2 ..	31.8	335 44.0	10.0	18 58.4	9.4	57.2
04	242 14.0	32.1	350 13.0	10.0	18 49.0	9.5	57.2
05	257 13.7	32.4	4 42.0	10.1	18 39.5	9.6	57.3
06	272 13.4	S22 32.7	19 11.1	10.1	N18 29.9	9.7	57.3
07	287 13.2	33.0	33 40.2	10.1	18 20.2	9.8	57.3
S 08	302 12.9	33.3	48 09.3	10.2	18 10.4	9.9	57.4
U 09	317 12.6 ..	33.5	62 38.5	10.2	18 00.5	10.0	57.4
N 10	332 12.4	33.8	77 07.7	10.2	17 50.5	10.1	57.4
D 11	347 12.1	34.1	91 36.9	10.3	17 40.4	10.2	57.4
A 12	2 11.8	S22 34.4	106 06.2	10.3	N17 30.2	10.3	57.5
Y 13	17 11.6	34.7	120 35.5	10.3	17 19.9	10.4	57.5
14	32 11.3	35.0	135 04.8	10.4	17 09.5	10.6	57.5
15	47 11.0 ..	35.3	149 34.2	10.4	16 58.9	10.6	57.5
16	62 10.8	35.5	164 03.6	10.4	16 48.3	10.7	57.6
17	77 10.5	35.8	178 33.0	10.5	16 37.6	10.8	57.6
18	92 10.2	S22 36.1	193 02.5	10.5	N16 26.8	10.9	57.6
19	107 10.0	36.4	207 32.0	10.5	16 15.9	11.0	57.6
20	122 09.7	36.7	222 01.5	10.6	16 04.9	11.1	57.7
21	137 09.4 ..	36.9	236 31.1	10.6	15 53.8	11.1	57.7
22	152 09.2	37.2	251 00.7	10.6	15 42.7	11.3	57.7
23	167 08.9	37.5	265 30.3	10.7	15 31.4	11.4	57.7
7 00	182 08.6	S22 37.8	280 00.0	10.7	N15 20.0	11.4	57.8
01	197 08.4	38.1	294 29.7	10.7	15 08.6	11.6	57.8
02	212 08.1	38.3	308 59.4	10.8	14 57.0	11.6	57.8
03	227 07.8 ..	38.6	323 29.2	10.7	14 45.4	11.7	57.9
04	242 07.5	38.9	337 58.9	10.8	14 33.7	11.8	57.9
05	257 07.3	39.2	352 28.7	10.9	14 21.9	11.9	57.9
06	272 07.0	S22 39.4	6 58.6	10.8	N14 10.0	12.0	57.9
07	287 06.7	39.7	21 28.4	10.9	13 58.0	12.0	58.0
08	302 06.5	40.0	35 58.3	10.9	13 46.0	12.2	58.0
M 09	317 06.2 ..	40.2	50 28.2	11.0	13 33.8	12.2	58.0
O 10	332 05.9	40.5	64 58.2	10.9	13 21.6	12.3	58.0
N 11	347 05.6	40.8	79 28.1	11.0	13 09.3	12.4	58.1
D 12	2 05.4	S22 41.1	93 58.1	11.0	N12 56.9	12.4	58.1
A 13	17 05.1	41.3	108 28.1	11.1	12 44.5	12.6	58.1
Y 14	32 04.8	41.6	122 58.2	11.0	12 31.9	12.6	58.2
15	47 04.6 ..	41.9	137 28.2	11.1	12 19.3	12.7	58.2
16	62 04.3	42.1	151 58.3	11.1	12 06.6	12.7	58.2
17	77 04.0	42.4	166 28.4	11.1	11 53.9	12.9	58.2
18	92 03.7	S22 42.6	180 58.5	11.2	N11 41.0	12.9	58.3
19	107 03.5	42.9	195 28.7	11.1	11 28.1	12.9	58.3
20	122 03.2	43.2	209 58.8	11.2	11 15.2	13.1	58.3
21	137 02.9 ..	43.4	224 29.0	11.2	11 02.1	13.1	58.4
22	152 02.6	43.7	238 59.2	11.2	10 49.0	13.2	58.4
23	167 02.4	43.9	253 29.4	11.3	N10 35.8	13.2	58.4
	SD 16.3	d 0.3	SD 15.5		15.7		15.8

Lat.	Twilight Naut.	Civil	Sunrise	Moonrise 5	6	7	8
°	h m	h m	h m	h m	h m	h m	h m
N 72	08 05	10 15	■■	▨	18 58	21 40	23 58
N 70	07 47	09 28	■■	▨	19 43	21 59	24 04
68	07 32	08 57	11 14	17 56	20 13	22 14	24 10
66	07 20	08 35	10 05	18 39	20 35	22 26	24 15
64	07 10	08 17	09 30	19 07	20 52	22 36	24 19
62	07 01	08 02	09 05	19 29	21 06	22 44	24 22
60	06 54	07 49	08 45	19 47	21 18	22 51	24 25
N 58	06 47	07 38	08 29	20 01	21 28	22 57	24 27
56	06 40	07 29	08 15	20 14	21 37	23 03	24 30
54	06 35	07 20	08 03	20 24	21 45	23 08	24 32
52	06 29	07 12	07 53	20 34	21 52	23 12	24 34
50	06 24	07 05	07 43	20 43	21 58	23 16	24 35
45	06 13	06 50	07 24	21 01	22 12	23 25	24 39
N 40	06 04	06 37	07 08	21 15	22 23	23 32	24 42
35	05 55	06 26	06 54	21 28	22 33	23 38	24 45
30	05 46	06 16	06 42	21 39	22 41	23 44	24 47
20	05 31	05 58	06 22	21 57	22 55	23 53	24 51
N 10	05 15	05 42	06 04	22 13	23 08	24 01	00 01
0	04 59	05 25	05 47	22 28	23 19	24 09	00 09
S 10	04 41	05 08	05 31	22 43	23 31	24 17	00 17
20	04 19	04 48	05 12	22 59	23 43	24 25	00 25
30	03 51	04 24	04 51	23 17	23 57	24 34	00 34
35	03 33	04 10	04 39	23 28	24 05	00 05	00 39
40	03 11	03 52	04 25	23 40	24 14	00 14	00 45
45	02 42	03 31	04 07	23 54	24 25	00 25	00 52
S 50	02 01	03 03	03 46	24 11	00 11	00 38	01 00
52	01 36	02 49	03 36	24 20	00 20	00 44	01 04
54	01 01	02 32	03 24	00 00	00 29	00 50	01 08
56	////	02 12	03 11	00 13	00 39	00 58	01 13
58	////	01 46	02 55	00 28	00 50	01 06	01 18
S 60	////	01 08	02 37	00 46	01 03	01 15	01 24

Lat.	Sunset	Twilight Civil	Naut.	Moonset 5	6	7	8
°	h m	h m	h m	h m	h m	h m	h m
N 72	■■	13 27	15 37	▨	15 34	14 37	14 05
N 70	■■	14 14	15 55	▨	14 47	14 16	13 55
68	12 28	14 45	16 10	14 46	14 17	14 00	13 47
66	13 37	15 07	16 22	14 02	13 53	13 46	13 40
64	14 12	15 25	16 32	13 33	13 35	13 35	13 34
62	14 37	15 40	16 41	13 11	13 20	13 26	13 29
60	14 57	15 53	16 49	12 53	13 07	13 17	13 25
N 58	15 13	16 04	16 55	12 38	12 56	13 10	13 21
56	15 27	16 13	17 02	12 25	12 47	13 03	13 17
54	15 39	16 22	17 08	12 13	12 38	12 58	13 14
52	15 49	16 30	17 13	12 03	12 30	12 52	13 11
50	15 59	16 37	17 18	11 54	12 23	12 48	13 09
45	16 18	16 52	17 29	11 35	12 08	12 37	13 03
N 40	16 35	17 05	17 39	11 20	11 56	12 28	12 58
35	16 48	17 16	17 48	11 06	11 46	12 21	12 54
30	17 00	17 26	17 56	10 55	11 36	12 14	12 50
20	17 20	17 44	18 12	10 35	11 20	12 03	12 44
N 10	17 38	18 01	18 27	10 17	11 06	11 53	12 38
0	17 55	18 17	18 43	10 01	10 53	11 43	12 32
S 10	18 12	18 35	19 02	09 45	10 39	11 33	12 27
20	18 30	18 54	19 23	09 27	10 25	11 23	12 21
30	18 51	19 18	19 51	09 07	10 08	11 11	12 14
35	19 04	19 33	20 09	08 55	09 59	11 04	12 10
40	19 18	19 51	20 32	08 41	09 48	10 56	12 05
45	19 35	20 12	21 01	08 24	09 34	10 47	12 00
S 50	19 57	20 40	21 43	08 04	09 18	10 35	11 54
52	20 07	20 55	22 08	07 54	09 11	10 30	11 51
54	20 19	21 11	22 44	07 44	09 02	10 24	11 47
56	20 32	21 32	////	07 31	08 53	10 18	11 44
58	20 48	21 58	////	07 17	08 42	10 10	11 40
S 60	21 07	22 37	////	06 59	08 29	10 02	11 35

Day	SUN Eqn. of Time 00h	12h	Mer. Pass.	MOON Mer. Pass. Upper	Lower	Age	Phase
d	m s	m s	h m	h m	h m	d %	
5	09 26	09 13	11 51	03 49	16 15	20 76	
6	09 01	08 48	11 51	04 41	17 06	21 66	◗
7	08 35	08 22	11 52	05 31	17 56	22 56	

UT	ARIES GHA	VENUS −3.9 GHA	Dec	MARS −0.9 GHA	Dec	JUPITER −2.0 GHA	Dec	SATURN +0.6 GHA	Dec	STARS Name	SHA	Dec
8 00	77 12.5	208 49.1	S16 24.7	60 01.2	N 7 32.6	137 29.2	S21 06.5	135 55.3	S20 42.1	Acamar	315 14.0	S40 13.5
01	92 15.0	223 48.5	25.5	75 03.0	32.9	152 31.1	06.4	150 57.5	42.1	Achernar	335 22.4	S57 08.2
02	107 17.5	238 47.8	26.4	90 04.9	33.2	167 33.0	06.3	165 59.7	42.0	Acrux	173 03.8	S63 12.5
03	122 19.9	253 47.1	.. 27.3	105 06.8	.. 33.6	182 35.0	.. 06.2	181 01.9	.. 42.0	Adhara	255 08.1	S29 00.0
04	137 22.4	268 46.5	28.2	120 08.6	33.9	197 36.9	06.1	196 04.1	42.0	Aldebaran	290 43.1	N16 33.0
05	152 24.8	283 45.8	29.1	135 10.5	34.3	212 38.8	06.0	211 06.4	41.9			
06	167 27.3	298 45.2	S16 30.0	150 12.3	N 7 34.7	227 40.7	S21 05.9	226 08.6	S20 41.9	Alioth	166 16.3	N55 50.7
07	182 29.8	313 44.5	30.8	165 14.2	35.0	242 42.7	05.8	241 10.8	41.8	Alkaid	152 55.1	N49 12.5
08	197 32.2	328 43.9	31.7	180 16.1	35.3	257 44.6	05.7	256 13.0	41.8	Alnair	27 37.3	S46 51.9
09	212 34.7	343 43.2	.. 32.6	195 17.9	.. 35.6	272 46.5	.. 05.6	271 15.2	.. 41.7	Alnilam	275 40.8	S 1 11.4
10	227 37.2	358 42.6	33.5	210 19.8	36.0	287 48.4	05.5	286 17.4	41.7	Alphard	217 50.9	S 8 44.8
11	242 39.6	13 41.9	34.3	225 21.6	36.3	302 50.3	05.4	301 19.6	41.6			
12	257 42.1	28 41.3	S16 35.2	240 23.5	N 7 36.7	317 52.3	S21 05.3	316 21.8	S20 41.6	Alphecca	126 06.9	N26 38.7
13	272 44.6	43 40.6	36.1	255 25.4	37.0	332 54.2	05.2	331 24.0	41.5	Alpheratz	357 38.1	N29 12.4
14	287 47.0	58 40.0	37.0	270 27.2	37.3	347 56.1	05.1	346 26.2	41.5	Altair	62 03.5	N 8 55.5
15	302 49.5	73 39.3	.. 37.8	285 29.1	.. 37.7	2 58.0	.. 05.0	1 28.4	.. 41.4	Ankaa	353 10.4	S42 11.9
16	317 52.0	88 38.6	38.7	300 30.9	38.0	18 00.0	04.9	16 30.6	41.4	Antares	112 20.3	S26 28.5
17	332 54.4	103 38.0	39.6	315 32.8	38.4	33 01.9	04.8	31 32.8	41.3			
18	347 56.9	118 37.3	S16 40.5	330 34.6	N 7 38.7	48 03.8	S21 04.7	46 35.0	S20 41.3	Arcturus	145 51.2	N19 04.5
19	2 59.3	133 36.7	41.3	345 36.5	39.1	63 05.7	04.6	61 37.3	41.2	Atria	107 18.0	S69 03.7
20	18 01.8	148 36.0	42.2	0 38.3	39.4	78 07.6	04.5	76 39.5	41.2	Avior	234 15.5	S59 34.3
21	33 04.3	163 35.3	.. 43.1	15 40.2	.. 39.8	93 09.6	.. 04.4	91 41.7	.. 41.1	Bellatrix	278 26.1	N 6 22.1
22	48 06.7	178 34.7	43.9	30 42.0	40.1	108 11.5	04.3	106 43.9	41.1	Betelgeuse	270 55.3	N 7 24.6
23	63 09.2	193 34.0	44.8	45 43.9	40.4	123 13.4	04.2	121 46.1	41.0			
9 00	78 11.7	208 33.4	S16 45.7	60 45.7	N 7 40.8	138 15.3	S21 04.1	136 48.3	S20 41.0	Canopus	263 53.3	S52 42.3
01	93 14.1	223 32.7	46.5	75 47.5	41.1	153 17.3	04.0	151 50.5	40.9	Capella	280 26.3	N46 01.0
02	108 16.6	238 32.0	47.4	90 49.4	41.5	168 19.2	03.9	166 52.7	40.9	Deneb	49 28.3	N45 21.5
03	123 19.1	253 31.4	.. 48.3	105 51.2	.. 41.8	183 21.1	.. 03.8	181 54.9	.. 40.8	Denebola	182 28.4	N14 27.4
04	138 21.5	268 30.7	49.1	120 53.1	42.2	198 23.0	03.7	196 57.1	40.8	Diphda	348 50.5	S17 52.5
05	153 24.0	283 30.0	50.0	135 54.9	42.5	213 24.9	03.6	211 59.3	40.7			
06	168 26.4	298 29.4	S16 50.9	150 56.7	N 7 42.9	228 26.9	S21 03.5	227 01.5	S20 40.7	Dubhe	193 45.2	N61 38.1
07	183 28.9	313 28.7	51.7	165 58.6	43.2	243 28.8	03.4	242 03.7	40.6	Elnath	278 05.7	N28 37.4
08	198 31.4	328 28.1	52.6	181 00.4	43.6	258 30.7	03.3	257 05.9	40.6	Eltanin	90 44.3	N51 29.3
09	213 33.8	343 27.4	.. 53.4	196 02.3	.. 43.9	273 32.6	.. 03.2	272 08.1	.. 40.5	Enif	33 42.2	N 9 58.3
10	228 36.3	358 26.7	54.3	211 04.1	44.3	288 34.5	03.1	287 10.3	40.5	Fomalhaut	15 18.3	S29 30.9
11	243 38.8	13 26.1	55.2	226 05.9	44.6	303 36.5	03.0	302 12.6	40.4			
12	258 41.2	28 25.4	S16 56.0	241 07.8	N 7 45.0	318 38.4	S21 02.9	317 14.8	S20 40.3	Gacrux	171 55.4	S57 13.4
13	273 43.7	43 24.7	56.9	256 09.6	45.3	333 40.3	02.8	332 17.0	40.3	Gienah	175 47.1	S17 39.2
14	288 46.2	58 24.0	57.7	271 11.4	45.7	348 42.2	02.7	347 19.2	40.3	Hadar	148 41.1	S60 28.1
15	303 48.6	73 23.4	.. 58.6	286 13.3	.. 46.0	3 44.1	.. 02.6	2 21.4	.. 40.2	Hamal	327 54.7	N23 33.7
16	318 51.1	88 22.7	16 59.4	301 15.1	46.4	18 46.1	02.5	17 23.6	40.2	Kaus Aust.	83 37.3	S34 22.4
17	333 53.6	103 22.0	17 00.3	316 16.9	46.7	33 48.0	02.4	32 25.8	40.1			
18	348 56.0	118 21.4	S17 01.2	331 18.8	N 7 47.1	48 49.9	S21 02.3	47 28.0	S20 40.1	Kochab	137 21.0	N74 04.1
19	3 58.5	133 20.7	02.0	346 20.6	47.4	63 51.8	02.2	62 30.2	40.0	Markab	13 33.2	N15 19.1
20	19 00.9	148 20.0	02.9	1 22.4	47.8	78 53.7	02.1	77 32.4	40.0	Menkar	314 09.3	N 4 10.2
21	34 03.4	163 19.4	.. 03.7	16 24.2	.. 48.1	93 55.7	.. 02.0	92 34.6	.. 39.9	Menkent	148 01.8	S36 28.1
22	49 05.9	178 18.7	04.6	31 26.1	48.5	108 57.6	01.9	107 36.8	39.9	Miaplacidus	221 38.3	S69 47.8
23	64 08.3	193 18.0	05.4	46 27.9	48.8	123 59.5	01.8	122 39.0	39.8			
10 00	79 10.8	208 17.3	S17 06.3	61 29.7	N 7 49.2	139 01.4	S21 01.7	137 41.2	S20 39.8	Mirfak	308 32.5	N49 56.1
01	94 13.3	223 16.7	07.1	76 31.5	49.5	154 03.3	01.6	152 43.4	39.7	Nunki	75 52.2	S26 16.2
02	109 15.7	238 16.0	08.0	91 33.4	49.9	169 05.2	01.5	167 45.6	39.7	Peacock	53 11.5	S56 40.2
03	124 18.2	253 15.3	.. 08.8	106 35.2	.. 50.2	184 07.2	.. 01.4	182 47.8	.. 39.6	Pollux	243 21.1	N27 58.4
04	139 20.7	268 14.6	09.6	121 37.0	50.6	199 09.1	01.3	197 50.0	39.6	Procyon	244 54.0	N 5 10.3
05	154 23.1	283 14.0	10.5	136 38.8	50.9	214 11.0	01.2	212 52.2	39.5			
06	169 25.6	298 13.3	S17 11.3	151 40.6	N 7 51.3	229 12.9	S21 01.1	227 54.4	S20 39.5	Rasalhague	96 02.0	N12 32.8
07	184 28.0	313 12.6	12.2	166 42.5	51.6	244 14.8	01.0	242 56.6	39.4	Regulus	207 37.9	N11 51.9
08	199 30.5	328 11.9	13.0	181 44.3	52.0	259 16.8	00.9	257 58.8	39.4	Rigel	281 06.7	S 8 10.7
09	214 33.0	343 11.2	.. 13.9	196 46.1	.. 52.3	274 18.7	.. 00.8	273 01.0	.. 39.3	Rigil Kent.	139 45.3	S60 54.9
10	229 35.4	358 10.6	14.7	211 47.9	52.7	289 20.6	00.7	288 03.2	39.3	Sabik	102 07.0	S15 44.9
11	244 37.9	13 09.9	15.5	226 49.7	53.0	304 22.5	00.6	303 05.5	39.2			
12	259 40.4	28 09.2	S17 16.4	241 51.5	N 7 53.4	319 24.4	S21 00.5	318 07.7	S20 39.2	Schedar	349 34.5	N56 39.3
13	274 42.8	43 08.5	17.2	256 53.3	53.8	334 26.3	00.3	333 09.9	39.1	Shaula	96 15.3	S37 07.0
14	289 45.3	58 07.8	18.1	271 55.2	54.1	349 28.3	00.2	348 12.1	39.1	Sirius	258 28.8	S16 44.7
15	304 47.8	73 07.2	.. 18.9	286 57.0	.. 54.5	4 30.2	.. 00.1	3 14.3	.. 39.0	Spica	158 26.0	S11 16.0
16	319 50.2	88 06.5	19.7	301 58.8	54.8	19 32.1	21 00.0	18 16.5	39.0	Suhail	222 48.4	S43 30.8
17	334 52.7	103 05.8	20.6	317 00.6	55.2	34 34.0	20 59.9	33 18.7	38.9			
18	349 55.2	118 05.1	S17 21.4	332 02.4	N 7 55.5	49 35.9	S20 59.8	48 20.9	S20 38.9	Vega	80 35.9	N38 48.3
19	4 57.6	133 04.4	22.2	347 04.2	55.9	64 37.8	59.7	63 23.1	38.8	Zuben'ubi	137 00.0	S16 07.5
20	20 00.1	148 03.7	23.1	2 06.0	56.2	79 39.8	59.6	78 25.3	38.8		SHA	Mer.Pass.
21	35 02.5	163 03.1	.. 23.9	17 07.8	.. 56.6	94 41.7	.. 59.5	93 27.5	.. 38.7		° ′	h m
22	50 05.0	178 02.4	24.7	32 09.6	57.0	109 43.6	59.4	108 29.7	38.7	Venus	130 21.7	10 06
23	65 07.5	193 01.7	25.6	47 11.4	57.3	124 45.5	59.3	123 31.9	38.6	Mars	342 34.0	19 55
	h m									Jupiter	60 03.7	14 45
Mer.Pass. 18 44.1	v −0.7	d 0.9	v 1.8	d 0.3	v 1.9	d 0.1	v 2.2	d 0.0	Saturn	58 36.6	14 51

UT	SUN GHA	SUN Dec	MOON GHA	MOON v	MOON Dec	MOON d	MOON HP
d h	° ′	° ′	° ′	′	° ′	′	′
8 00	182 02.1	S22 44.2	267 59.7	11.2	N10 22.6	13.4	58.4
01	197 01.8	44.5	282 29.9	11.3	10 09.2	13.4	58.5
02	212 01.5	44.7	297 00.2	11.2	9 55.8	13.4	58.5
03	227 01.3 . .	45.0	311 30.4	11.3	9 42.4	13.5	58.5
04	242 01.0	45.2	326 00.7	11.3	9 28.9	13.6	58.5
05	257 00.7	45.5	340 31.0	11.3	9 15.3	13.6	58.6
06	272 00.4	S22 45.7	355 01.3	11.3	N 9 01.7	13.7	58.6
07	287 00.2	46.0	9 31.6	11.4	8 48.0	13.8	58.6
T 08	301 59.9	46.3	24 02.0	11.3	8 34.2	13.8	58.7
U 09	316 59.6 . .	46.5	38 32.3	11.4	8 20.4	13.8	58.7
E 10	331 59.3	46.8	53 02.7	11.3	8 06.6	14.0	58.7
S 11	346 59.1	47.0	67 33.0	11.4	7 52.6	13.9	58.7
D 12	1 58.8	S22 47.3	82 03.4	11.3	N 7 38.7	14.1	58.8
A 13	16 58.5 .	47.5	96 33.7	11.4	7 24.6	14.0	58.8
Y 14	31 58.2	47.8	111 04.1	11.3	7 10.6	14.2	58.8
15	46 57.9 . .	48.0	125 34.4	11.4	6 56.4	14.1	58.8
16	61 57.7	48.2	140 04.8	11.4	6 42.3	14.3	58.9
17	76 57.4	48.5	154 35.2	11.4	6 28.0	14.2	58.9
18	91 57.1	S22 48.7	169 05.6	11.3	N 6 13.8	14.4	58.9
19	106 56.8	49.0	183 35.9	11.4	5 59.4	14.3	59.0
20	121 56.6	49.2	198 06.3	11.3	5 45.1	14.4	59.0
21	136 56.3 . .	49.5	212 36.6	11.4	5 30.7	14.5	59.0
22	151 56.0	49.7	227 07.0	11.4	5 16.2	14.5	59.0
23	166 55.7	49.9	241 37.4	11.3	5 01.7	14.5	59.1
9 00	181 55.4	S22 50.2	256 07.7	11.3	N 4 47.2	14.6	59.1
01	196 55.2	50.4	270 38.0	11.4	4 32.6	14.6	59.1
02	211 54.9	50.7	285 08.4	11.3	4 18.0	14.6	59.1
03	226 54.6 . .	50.9	299 38.7	11.3	4 03.4	14.7	59.2
04	241 54.3	51.1	314 09.0	11.3	3 48.7	14.7	59.2
05	256 54.0	51.4	328 39.3	11.3	3 34.0	14.8	59.2
06	271 53.8	S22 51.6	343 09.6	11.3	N 3 19.2	14.7	59.2
W 07	286 53.5	51.8	357 39.9	11.2	3 04.5	14.9	59.3
E 08	301 53.2	52.1	12 10.1	11.3	2 49.6	14.8	59.3
D 09	316 52.9 . .	52.3	26 40.4	11.2	2 34.8	14.8	59.3
N 10	331 52.6	52.5	41 10.6	11.2	2 20.0	14.9	59.4
E 11	346 52.3	52.8	55 40.8	11.2	2 05.1	14.9	59.4
S 12	1 52.1	S22 53.0	70 11.0	11.1	N 1 50.2	15.0	59.4
D 13	16 51.8	53.2	84 41.1	11.2	1 35.2	14.9	59.4
A 14	31 51.5	53.5	99 11.3	11.1	1 20.3	15.0	59.5
Y 15	46 51.2 . .	53.7	113 41.4	11.1	1 05.3	15.0	59.5
16	61 50.9	53.9	128 11.5	11.0	0 50.3	15.0	59.5
17	76 50.7	54.2	142 41.6	11.0	0 35.3	15.0	59.5
18	91 50.4	S22 54.4	157 11.6	11.1	N 0 20.3	15.1	59.6
19	106 50.1	54.6	171 41.7	11.0	N 0 05.2	15.1	59.6
20	121 49.8	54.8	186 11.7	10.9	S 0 09.9	15.0	59.6
21	136 49.5 . .	55.1	200 41.6	11.0	0 24.9	15.1	59.6
22	151 49.2	55.3	215 11.6	10.9	0 40.0	15.1	59.6
23	166 48.9	55.5	229 41.5	10.9	0 55.1	15.1	59.7
10 00	181 48.7	S22 55.7	244 11.4	10.8	S 1 10.2	15.1	59.7
01	196 48.4	55.9	258 41.2	10.8	1 25.3	15.1	59.7
02	211 48.1	56.2	273 11.0	10.8	1 40.4	15.1	59.7
03	226 47.8 . .	56.4	287 40.8	10.7	1 55.5	15.1	59.8
04	241 47.5	56.6	302 10.5	10.7	2 10.6	15.2	59.8
05	256 47.2	56.8	316 40.2	10.7	2 25.8	15.1	59.8
06	271 47.0	S22 57.0	331 09.9	10.6	S 2 40.9	15.1	59.8
07	286 46.7	57.2	345 39.5	10.5	2 56.0	15.1	59.9
T 08	301 46.4	57.5	0 09.0	10.6	3 11.1	15.1	59.9
H 09	316 46.1 . .	57.7	14 38.6	10.5	3 26.2	15.1	59.9
U 10	331 45.8	57.9	29 08.1	10.4	3 41.3	15.1	59.9
R 11	346 45.5	58.1	43 37.5	10.4	3 56.4	15.1	59.9
S 12	1 45.2	S22 58.3	58 06.9	10.4	S 4 11.5	15.0	60.0
D 13	16 45.0	58.5	72 36.3	10.3	4 26.5	15.1	60.0
A 14	31 44.7	58.7	87 05.6	10.2	4 41.6	15.0	60.0
Y 15	46 44.4 . .	58.9	101 34.8	10.2	4 56.6	15.0	60.0
16	61 44.1	59.2	116 04.0	10.2	5 11.6	15.0	60.0
17	76 43.8	59.4	130 33.2	10.1	5 26.6	15.0	60.1
18	91 43.5	S22 59.6	145 02.3	10.0	S 5 41.6	15.0	60.1
19	106 43.2	22 59.8	159 31.3	10.0	5 56.6	14.9	60.1
20	121 42.9	23 00.0	174 00.3	10.0	6 11.5	14.9	60.1
21	136 42.7 . .	00.2	188 29.3	9.9	6 26.4	14.9	60.1
22	151 42.4	00.4	202 58.2	9.8	6 41.3	14.9	60.2
23	166 42.1	00.6	217 27.0	9.8	S 6 56.2	14.8	60.2
	SD 16.3	d 0.2	SD 16.0		16.2		16.3

Lat.	Twilight Naut.	Twilight Civil	Sunrise	Moonrise 8	9	10	11
°	h m	h m	h m	h m	h m	h m	h m
N 72	08 11	10 27	■■	23 58	26 11	02 11	04 31
N 70	07 52	09 36	■■	24 04	00 04	02 08	04 17
68	07 37	09 04	■■	24 10	00 10	02 06	04 06
66	07 25	08 40	10 14	24 15	00 15	02 04	03 57
64	07 14	08 22	09 36	24 19	00 19	02 03	03 50
62	07 05	08 06	09 10	24 22	00 22	02 01	03 44
60	06 57	07 53	08 50	24 25	00 25	02 00	03 38
N 58	06 50	07 42	08 33	24 27	00 27	01 59	03 33
56	06 44	07 32	08 19	24 30	00 30	01 58	03 29
54	06 38	07 24	08 07	24 32	00 32	01 57	03 25
52	06 32	07 16	07 56	24 34	00 34	01 57	03 22
50	06 27	07 09	07 47	24 35	00 35	01 56	03 19
45	06 16	06 53	07 27	24 39	00 39	01 55	03 12
N 40	06 06	06 40	07 10	24 42	00 42	01 53	03 07
35	05 57	06 28	06 57	24 45	00 45	01 52	03 02
30	05 48	06 18	06 44	24 47	00 47	01 51	02 58
20	05 33	06 00	06 24	24 51	00 51	01 50	02 50
N 10	05 17	05 43	06 06	00 01	00 55	01 49	02 44
0	05 00	05 26	05 49	00 09	00 58	01 47	02 38
S 10	04 42	05 09	05 32	00 17	01 01	01 46	02 33
20	04 20	04 49	05 13	00 25	01 05	01 45	02 27
30	03 51	04 24	04 52	00 34	01 09	01 44	02 20
35	03 33	04 10	04 39	00 39	01 11	01 43	02 16
40	03 11	03 52	04 24	00 45	01 14	01 42	02 12
45	02 41	03 30	04 07	00 52	01 17	01 41	02 07
S 50	01 58	03 01	03 45	01 00	01 20	01 40	02 01
52	01 33	02 47	03 35	01 04	01 22	01 39	01 58
54	00 54	02 30	03 23	01 08	01 24	01 39	01 55
56	////	02 09	03 09	01 13	01 26	01 38	01 51
58	////	01 42	02 53	01 18	01 28	01 38	01 48
S 60	////	01 00	02 34	01 24	01 30	01 37	01 44

Lat.	Sunset	Twilight Civil	Twilight Naut.	Moonset 8	9	10	11
°	h m	h m	h m	h m	h m	h m	h m
N 72	■■	13 17	15 34	14 05	13 38	13 12	12 41
N 70	■■	14 09	15 52	13 55	13 36	13 18	12 57
68	■■	14 41	16 07	13 47	13 35	13 23	13 10
66	13 31	15 04	16 20	13 40	13 34	13 28	13 21
64	14 08	15 23	16 30	13 34	13 33	13 31	13 30
62	14 35	15 38	16 39	13 29	13 32	13 35	13 38
60	14 55	15 51	16 47	13 25	13 31	13 38	13 45
N 58	15 12	16 03	16 55	13 21	13 30	13 40	13 51
56	15 26	16 12	17 01	13 17	13 30	13 42	13 56
54	15 38	16 21	17 07	13 14	13 29	13 44	14 01
52	15 49	16 29	17 13	13 11	13 29	13 46	14 06
50	15 58	16 36	17 18	13 09	13 28	13 48	14 10
45	16 18	16 52	17 29	13 03	13 27	13 52	14 18
N 40	16 35	17 05	17 39	12 58	13 26	13 55	14 25
35	16 48	17 16	17 48	12 54	13 26	13 58	14 32
30	17 00	17 27	17 56	12 50	13 25	14 00	14 37
20	17 21	17 45	18 12	12 44	13 24	14 04	14 47
N 10	17 39	18 02	18 28	12 38	13 22	14 08	14 55
0	17 56	18 19	18 45	12 32	13 21	14 11	15 03
S 10	18 13	18 36	19 03	12 27	13 20	14 15	15 11
20	18 32	18 56	19 25	12 21	13 19	14 19	15 20
30	18 53	19 21	19 54	12 14	13 18	14 23	15 30
35	19 06	19 36	20 12	12 10	13 17	14 25	15 36
40	19 21	19 53	20 35	12 05	13 16	14 28	15 42
45	19 38	20 15	21 04	12 00	13 15	14 31	15 50
S 50	20 00	20 44	21 48	11 54	13 13	14 35	15 59
52	20 11	20 59	22 14	11 51	13 13	14 37	16 03
54	20 23	21 16	22 53	11 47	13 12	14 39	16 08
56	20 36	21 37	////	11 44	13 11	14 41	16 13
58	20 52	22 05	////	11 40	13 11	14 43	16 19
S 60	21 12	22 47	////	11 35	13 10	14 46	16 25

Day	SUN Eqn. of Time 00ʰ	SUN Eqn. of Time 12ʰ	SUN Mer. Pass.	MOON Mer. Pass. Upper	MOON Mer. Pass. Lower	Age	Phase
d	m s	m s	h m	h m	h m	d	%
8	08 09	07 56	11 52	06 21	18 45	23	45
9	07 42	07 29	11 53	07 10	19 34	24	34
10	07 15	07 02	11 53	07 59	20 25	25	23

UT (d h)	ARIES GHA	VENUS −3.9 GHA	Dec	MARS −0.8 GHA	Dec	JUPITER −2.0 GHA	Dec	SATURN +0.6 GHA	Dec
11 00	80 09.9	208 01.0	S17 26.4	62 13.2	N 7 57.7	139 47.4	S20 59.2	138 34.1	S20 38.6
01	95 12.4	223 00.3	27.2	77 15.0	58.0	154 49.3	59.1	153 36.3	38.5
02	110 14.9	237 59.6	28.1	92 16.8	58.4	169 51.3	59.0	168 38.5	38.5
03	125 17.3	252 58.9 ..	28.9	107 18.6 ..	58.7	184 53.2 ..	58.9	183 40.7 ..	38.4
04	140 19.8	267 58.2	29.7	122 20.4	59.1	199 55.1	58.8	198 42.9	38.4
05	155 22.3	282 57.6	30.5	137 22.2	59.5	214 57.0	58.7	213 45.1	38.3
06	170 24.7	297 56.9	S17 31.4	152 24.0	N 7 59.8	229 58.9	S20 58.6	228 47.3	S20 38.3
07	185 27.2	312 56.2	32.2	167 25.8	8 00.2	245 00.8	58.5	243 49.5	38.2
08	200 29.7	327 55.5	33.0	182 27.6	00.5	260 02.7	58.4	258 51.7	38.2
F 09	215 32.1	342 54.8 ..	33.8	197 29.4 ..	00.9	275 04.7 ..	58.3	273 53.9 ..	38.1
R 10	230 34.6	357 54.1	34.7	212 31.2	01.3	290 06.6	58.2	288 56.1	38.1
I 11	245 37.0	12 53.4	35.5	227 33.0	01.6	305 08.5	58.1	303 58.3	38.0
D 12	260 39.5	27 52.7	S17 36.3	242 34.8	N 8 02.0	320 10.4	S20 58.0	319 00.5	S20 38.0
A 13	275 42.0	42 52.0	37.1	257 36.6	02.3	335 12.3	57.9	334 02.7	37.9
Y 14	290 44.4	57 51.3	37.9	272 38.4	02.7	350 14.2	57.8	349 04.9	37.9
15	305 46.9	72 50.6 ..	38.8	287 40.2 ..	03.1	5 16.1 ..	57.7	4 07.1 ..	37.8
16	320 49.4	87 49.9	39.6	302 42.0	03.4	20 18.1	57.6	19 09.3	37.8
17	335 51.8	102 49.2	40.4	317 43.8	03.8	35 20.0	57.5	34 11.5	37.7
18	350 54.3	117 48.5	S17 41.2	332 45.5	N 8 04.1	50 21.9	S20 57.4	49 13.7	S20 37.7
19	5 56.8	132 47.9	42.0	347 47.3	04.5	65 23.8	57.2	64 15.9	37.6
20	20 59.2	147 47.2	42.8	2 49.1	04.9	80 25.7	57.1	79 18.1	37.6
21	36 01.7	162 46.5 ..	43.7	17 50.9 ..	05.2	95 27.6 ..	57.0	94 20.3 ..	37.5
22	51 04.2	177 45.8	44.5	32 52.7	05.6	110 29.5	56.9	109 22.5	37.5
23	66 06.6	192 45.1	45.3	47 54.5	06.0	125 31.4	56.8	124 24.7	37.4
12 00	81 09.1	207 44.4	S17 46.1	62 56.3	N 8 06.3	140 33.4	S20 56.7	139 26.9	S20 37.4
01	96 11.5	222 43.7	46.9	77 58.0	06.7	155 35.3	56.6	154 29.1	37.3
02	111 14.0	237 43.0	47.7	92 59.8	07.0	170 37.2	56.5	169 31.3	37.3
03	126 16.5	252 42.3 ..	48.5	108 01.6 ..	07.4	185 39.1 ..	56.4	184 33.5 ..	37.2
04	141 18.9	267 41.6	49.3	123 03.4	07.8	200 41.0	56.3	199 35.7	37.2
05	156 21.4	282 40.9	50.1	138 05.2	08.1	215 42.9	56.2	214 37.9	37.1
06	171 23.9	297 40.2	S17 50.9	153 06.9	N 8 08.5	230 44.8	S20 56.1	229 40.1	S20 37.1
07	186 26.3	312 39.5	51.7	168 08.7	08.9	245 46.7	56.0	244 42.3	37.0
S 08	201 28.8	327 38.8	52.6	183 10.5	09.2	260 48.7	55.9	259 44.5	37.0
A 09	216 31.3	342 38.1 ..	53.4	198 12.3 ..	09.6	275 50.6 ..	55.8	274 46.7 ..	36.9
T 10	231 33.7	357 37.3	54.2	213 14.0	10.0	290 52.5	55.7	289 48.9	36.9
U 11	246 36.2	12 36.6	55.0	228 15.8	10.3	305 54.4	55.6	304 51.1	36.8
R 12	261 38.6	27 35.9	S17 55.8	243 17.6	N 8 10.7	320 56.3	S20 55.5	319 53.3	S20 36.8
D 13	276 41.1	42 35.2	56.6	258 19.4	11.1	335 58.2	55.4	334 55.5	36.7
A 14	291 43.6	57 34.5	57.4	273 21.1	11.4	351 00.1	55.3	349 57.7	36.7
Y 15	306 46.0	72 33.8 ..	58.2	288 22.9 ..	11.8	6 02.0 ..	55.2	4 59.9 ..	36.6
16	321 48.5	87 33.1	59.0	303 24.7	12.1	21 04.0	55.0	20 02.1	36.6
17	336 51.0	102 32.4	17 59.8	318 26.4	12.5	36 05.9	54.9	35 04.3	36.5
18	351 53.4	117 31.7	S18 00.6	333 28.2	N 8 12.9	51 07.8	S20 54.8	50 06.5	S20 36.5
19	6 55.9	132 31.0	01.3	348 30.0	13.2	66 09.7	54.7	65 08.7	36.4
20	21 58.4	147 30.3	02.1	3 31.7	13.6	81 11.6	54.6	80 10.9	36.4
21	37 00.8	162 29.6 ..	02.9	18 33.5 ..	14.0	96 13.5 ..	54.5	95 13.1 ..	36.3
22	52 03.3	177 28.9	03.7	33 35.3	14.4	111 15.4	54.4	110 15.3	36.3
23	67 05.8	192 28.1	04.5	48 37.0	14.7	126 17.3	54.3	125 17.5	36.2
13 00	82 08.2	207 27.4	S18 05.3	63 38.8	N 8 15.1	141 19.2	S20 54.2	140 19.7	S20 36.2
01	97 10.7	222 26.7	06.1	78 40.6	15.5	156 21.1	54.1	155 21.9	36.1
02	112 13.1	237 26.0	06.9	93 42.3	15.8	171 23.1	54.0	170 24.1	36.1
03	127 15.6	252 25.3 ..	07.7	108 44.1 ..	16.2	186 25.0 ..	53.9	185 26.3 ..	36.0
04	142 18.1	267 24.6	08.5	123 45.8	16.6	201 26.9	53.8	200 28.5	36.0
05	157 20.5	282 23.9	09.3	138 47.6	16.9	216 28.8	53.7	215 30.7	35.9
06	172 23.0	297 23.2	S18 10.0	153 49.4	N 8 17.3	231 30.7	S20 53.6	230 32.9	S20 35.9
07	187 25.5	312 22.4	10.8	168 51.1	17.7	246 32.6	53.5	245 35.0	35.8
08	202 27.9	327 21.7	11.6	183 52.9	18.0	261 34.5	53.4	260 37.2	35.8
S 09	217 30.4	342 21.0 ..	12.4	198 54.6 ..	18.4	276 36.4 ..	53.2	275 39.4 ..	35.7
U 10	232 32.9	357 20.3	13.2	213 56.4	18.8	291 38.3	53.1	290 41.6	35.6
N 11	247 35.3	12 19.6	14.0	228 58.1	19.1	306 40.2	53.0	305 43.8	35.6
D 12	262 37.8	27 18.9	S18 14.7	243 59.9	N 8 19.5	321 42.1	S20 52.9	320 46.0	S20 35.5
A 13	277 40.3	42 18.1	15.5	259 01.6	19.9	336 44.1	52.8	335 48.2	35.5
Y 14	292 42.7	57 17.4	16.3	274 03.4	20.3	351 46.0	52.7	350 50.4	35.4
15	307 45.2	72 16.7 ..	17.1	289 05.1 ..	20.6	6 47.9 ..	52.6	5 52.6 ..	35.4
16	322 47.6	87 16.0	17.9	304 06.9	21.0	21 49.8	52.5	20 54.8	35.3
17	337 50.1	102 15.3	18.6	319 08.6	21.4	36 51.7	52.4	35 57.0	35.3
18	352 52.6	117 14.5	S18 19.4	334 10.4	N 8 21.7	51 53.6	S20 52.3	50 59.2	S20 35.2
19	7 55.0	132 13.8	20.2	349 12.1	22.1	66 55.5	52.2	66 01.4	35.2
20	22 57.5	147 13.1	21.0	4 13.9	22.5	81 57.4	52.1	81 03.6	35.1
21	38 00.0	162 12.4 ..	21.7	19 15.6 ..	22.9	96 59.3 ..	52.0	96 05.8 ..	35.1
22	53 02.4	177 11.7	22.5	34 17.4	23.2	112 01.2	51.9	111 08.0	35.0
23	68 04.9	192 10.9	23.3	49 19.1	23.6	127 03.1	51.8	126 10.2	35.0
Mer. Pass.	18 32.3	v −0.7	d 0.8	v 1.8	d 0.4	v 1.9	d 0.1	v 2.2	d 0.1

STARS

Name	SHA	Dec
Acamar	315 14.0	S40 13.5
Achernar	335 22.5	S57 08.2
Acrux	173 03.8	S63 12.5
Adhara	255 08.1	S29 00.0
Aldebaran	290 43.1	N16 33.0
Alioth	166 16.3	N55 50.6
Alkaid	152 55.0	N49 12.4
Alnair	27 37.3	S46 51.9
Alnilam	275 40.8	S 1 11.4
Alphard	217 50.8	S 8 44.8
Alphecca	126 06.9	N26 38.7
Alpheratz	357 38.1	N29 12.4
Altair	62 03.5	N 8 55.5
Ankaa	353 10.4	S42 11.9
Antares	112 20.3	S26 28.5
Arcturus	145 51.2	N19 04.5
Atria	107 18.0	S69 03.7
Avior	234 15.5	S59 34.3
Bellatrix	278 26.1	N 6 22.0
Betelgeuse	270 55.3	N 7 24.6
Canopus	263 53.3	S52 42.4
Capella	280 26.3	N46 01.0
Deneb	49 28.3	N45 21.5
Denebola	182 28.4	N14 27.3
Diphda	348 50.5	S17 52.5
Dubhe	193 45.2	N61 38.1
Elnath	278 05.7	N28 37.4
Eltanin	90 44.3	N51 29.3
Enif	33 42.2	N 9 58.3
Fomalhaut	15 18.3	S29 30.9
Gacrux	171 55.4	S57 13.4
Gienah	175 47.1	S17 39.2
Hadar	148 41.0	S60 28.0
Hamal	327 54.7	N23 33.7
Kaus Aust.	83 37.3	S34 22.4
Kochab	137 20.9	N74 04.1
Markab	13 33.2	N15 19.1
Menkar	314 09.3	N 4 10.2
Menkent	148 01.8	S36 28.1
Miaplacidus	221 38.2	S69 47.8
Mirfak	308 32.5	N49 56.1
Nunki	75 52.2	S26 16.2
Peacock	53 11.5	S56 40.2
Pollux	243 21.1	N27 58.4
Procyon	244 54.0	N 5 10.3
Rasalhague	96 02.0	N12 32.8
Regulus	207 37.9	N11 51.9
Rigel	281 06.7	S 8 10.7
Rigil Kent.	139 45.3	S60 54.9
Sabik	102 06.9	S15 44.9
Schedar	349 34.5	N56 39.3
Shaula	96 15.3	S37 07.0
Sirius	258 28.8	S16 44.7
Spica	158 26.0	S11 16.0
Suhail	222 48.4	S43 30.8
Vega	80 35.9	N38 48.3
Zuben'ubi	137 00.0	S16 07.5

	SHA	Mer. Pass.
Venus	126 35.3	10 10
Mars	341 47.2	19 46
Jupiter	59 24.3	14 36
Saturn	58 17.8	14 40

UT	SUN GHA	SUN Dec	MOON GHA	v	MOON Dec	d	HP
d h	° '	° '	° '	'	° '	'	'
11 00	181 41.8	S23 00.8	231 55.8	9.7	S 7 11.0	14.8	60.2
01	196 41.5	01.0	246 24.5	9.6	7 25.8	14.8	60.2
02	211 41.2	01.2	260 53.1	9.6	7 40.6	14.7	60.2
03	226 40.9	.. 01.4	275 21.7	9.6	7 55.3	14.7	60.2
04	241 40.6	01.6	289 50.3	9.4	8 10.0	14.7	60.3
05	256 40.3	01.8	304 18.7	9.4	8 24.7	14.6	60.3
06	271 40.1	S23 02.0	318 47.1	9.4	S 8 39.3	14.6	60.3
07	286 39.8	02.2	333 15.5	9.3	8 53.9	14.5	60.3
08	301 39.5	02.4	347 43.8	9.2	9 08.4	14.5	60.3
F 09	316 39.2	.. 02.6	2 12.0	9.1	9 22.9	14.4	60.3
R 10	331 38.9	02.8	16 40.1	9.1	9 37.3	14.4	60.4
I 11	346 38.6	03.0	31 08.2	9.0	9 51.7	14.4	60.4
D 12	1 38.3	S23 03.2	45 36.2	8.9	S10 06.1	14.2	60.4
A 13	16 38.0	03.4	60 04.1	8.9	10 20.3	14.3	60.4
Y 14	31 37.7	03.6	74 32.0	8.8	10 34.6	14.2	60.4
15	46 37.4	.. 03.7	88 59.8	8.7	10 48.8	14.1	60.4
16	61 37.1	03.9	103 27.5	8.7	11 02.9	14.0	60.4
17	76 36.9	04.1	117 55.2	8.6	11 16.9	14.0	60.4
18	91 36.6	S23 04.3	132 22.8	8.5	S11 30.9	14.0	60.5
19	106 36.3	04.5	146 50.3	8.4	11 44.9	13.9	60.5
20	121 36.0	04.7	161 17.7	8.4	11 58.8	13.8	60.5
21	136 35.7	.. 04.9	175 45.1	8.2	12 12.6	13.7	60.5
22	151 35.4	05.1	190 12.3	8.2	12 26.3	13.7	60.5
23	166 35.1	05.2	204 39.5	8.2	12 40.0	13.6	60.5
12 00	181 34.8	S23 05.4	219 06.7	8.0	S12 53.6	13.5	60.5
01	196 34.5	05.6	233 33.7	8.0	13 07.1	13.4	60.5
02	211 34.2	05.8	248 00.7	7.9	13 20.5	13.4	60.5
03	226 33.9	.. 06.0	262 27.6	7.8	13 33.9	13.3	60.5
04	241 33.6	06.1	276 54.4	7.8	13 47.2	13.2	60.5
05	256 33.3	06.3	291 21.2	7.6	14 00.4	13.1	60.6
06	271 33.0	S23 06.5	305 47.8	7.6	S14 13.5	13.0	60.6
07	286 32.8	06.7	320 14.4	7.5	14 26.5	13.0	60.6
S 08	301 32.5	06.9	334 40.9	7.4	14 39.5	12.9	60.6
A 09	316 32.2	.. 07.0	349 07.3	7.4	14 52.4	12.8	60.6
T 10	331 31.9	07.2	3 33.7	7.2	15 05.1	12.7	60.6
U 11	346 31.6	07.4	17 59.9	7.2	15 17.8	12.6	60.6
R 12	1 31.3	S23 07.6	32 26.1	7.1	S15 30.4	12.5	60.6
D 13	16 31.0	07.7	46 52.2	7.0	15 42.9	12.4	60.6
A 14	31 30.7	07.9	61 18.2	7.0	15 55.3	12.2	60.6
Y 15	46 30.4	.. 08.1	75 44.2	6.8	16 07.5	12.2	60.6
16	61 30.1	08.3	90 10.0	6.8	16 19.7	12.1	60.6
17	76 29.8	08.4	104 35.8	6.7	16 31.8	12.0	60.6
18	91 29.5	S23 08.6	119 01.5	6.6	S16 43.8	11.9	60.6
19	106 29.2	08.8	133 27.1	6.6	16 55.7	11.7	60.6
20	121 28.9	08.9	147 52.7	6.4	17 07.4	11.7	60.6
21	136 28.6	.. 09.1	162 18.1	6.4	17 19.1	11.5	60.6
22	151 28.3	09.3	176 43.5	6.4	17 30.6	11.4	60.6
23	166 28.0	09.4	191 08.8	6.2	17 42.0	11.3	60.6
13 00	181 27.7	S23 09.6	205 34.0	6.2	S17 53.3	11.2	60.6
01	196 27.4	09.8	219 59.2	6.0	18 04.5	11.1	60.6
02	211 27.1	09.9	234 24.2	6.0	18 15.6	10.9	60.6
03	226 26.8	.. 10.1	248 49.2	5.9	18 26.5	10.8	60.6
04	241 26.6	10.2	263 14.1	5.9	18 37.3	10.7	60.6
05	256 26.3	10.4	277 39.0	5.7	18 48.0	10.6	60.6
06	271 26.0	S23 10.6	292 03.7	5.7	S18 58.6	10.5	60.6
07	286 25.7	10.7	306 28.4	5.6	19 09.1	10.3	60.6
08	301 25.4	10.9	320 53.0	5.5	19 19.4	10.1	60.6
S 09	316 25.1	.. 11.0	335 17.5	5.5	19 29.5	10.1	60.6
U 10	331 24.8	11.2	349 42.0	5.4	19 39.6	9.9	60.6
N 11	346 24.5	11.3	4 06.4	5.3	19 49.5	9.8	60.6
D 12	1 24.2	S23 11.5	18 30.7	5.2	S19 59.3	9.6	60.6
A 13	16 23.9	11.7	32 54.9	5.2	20 08.9	9.5	60.5
Y 14	31 23.6	11.8	47 19.1	5.1	20 18.4	9.4	60.5
15	46 23.3	.. 12.0	61 43.2	5.0	20 27.8	9.2	60.5
16	61 23.0	12.1	76 07.2	5.0	20 37.0	9.0	60.5
17	76 22.7	12.3	90 31.2	4.9	20 46.0	9.0	60.5
18	91 22.4	S23 12.4	104 55.1	4.8	S20 55.0	8.7	60.5
19	106 22.1	12.6	119 18.9	4.8	21 03.7	8.7	60.5
20	121 21.8	12.7	133 42.7	4.7	21 12.4	8.4	60.5
21	136 21.5	.. 12.9	148 06.4	4.6	21 20.8	8.4	60.5
22	151 21.2	13.0	162 30.0	4.6	21 29.2	8.1	60.5
23	166 20.9	13.1	176 53.6	4.6	S21 37.3	8.1	60.5
	SD 16.3	d 0.2	SD 16.5		16.5		16.5

Lat.	Twilight Naut.	Twilight Civil	Sunrise	Moonrise 11	Moonrise 12	Moonrise 13	Moonrise 14
°	h m	h m	h m	h m	h m	h m	h m
N 72	08 16	10 38	■	04 31	07 14	■	■
N 70	07 57	09 43	■	04 17	06 40	10 14	■
68	07 42	09 09	■	04 06	06 16	08 46	■
66	07 29	08 45	10 22	03 57	05 58	08 08	10 37
64	07 18	08 26	09 42	03 50	05 43	07 41	09 42
62	07 09	08 10	09 15	03 44	05 30	07 21	09 10
60	07 01	07 57	08 54	03 38	05 20	07 04	08 45
N 58	06 53	07 46	08 37	03 33	05 11	06 50	08 26
56	06 47	07 36	08 23	03 29	05 03	06 38	08 10
54	06 41	07 27	08 10	03 25	04 56	06 28	07 57
52	06 35	07 19	07 59	03 22	04 50	06 19	07 45
50	06 30	07 11	07 50	03 19	04 44	06 10	07 34
45	06 18	06 56	07 29	03 12	04 32	05 53	07 12
N 40	06 08	06 42	07 13	03 07	04 22	05 39	06 55
35	05 59	06 31	06 59	03 02	04 13	05 27	06 40
30	05 50	06 20	06 47	02 58	04 06	05 16	06 27
20	05 34	06 02	06 26	02 50	03 53	04 59	06 05
N 10	05 18	05 45	06 07	02 44	03 42	04 43	05 46
0	05 02	05 28	05 50	02 38	03 32	04 29	05 29
S 10	04 43	05 10	05 33	02 33	03 22	04 15	05 12
20	04 20	04 50	05 14	02 27	03 11	04 00	04 53
30	03 52	04 25	04 52	02 20	02 59	03 42	04 32
35	03 33	04 10	04 40	02 16	02 52	03 33	04 20
40	03 11	03 52	04 25	02 12	02 44	03 21	04 05
45	02 41	03 30	04 07	02 07	02 35	03 08	03 49
S 50	01 56	03 01	03 45	02 01	02 24	02 52	03 28
52	01 30	02 46	03 34	01 58	02 19	02 45	03 18
54	00 49	02 29	03 22	01 55	02 13	02 36	03 08
56	////	02 07	03 08	01 51	02 07	02 27	02 55
58	////	01 39	02 52	01 48	02 00	02 17	02 41
S 60	////	00 54	02 32	01 44	01 52	02 05	02 24

Lat.	Sunset	Twilight Civil	Twilight Naut.	Moonset 11	Moonset 12	Moonset 13	Moonset 14
°	h m	h m	h m	h m	h m	h m	h m
N 72	■	13 09	15 31	12 41	11 52	■	■
N 70	■	14 05	15 51	12 57	12 28	10 55	■
68	■	14 38	16 06	13 10	12 53	12 24	■
66	13 26	15 03	16 19	13 21	13 13	13 03	12 41
64	14 05	15 22	16 29	13 30	13 30	13 31	13 37
62	14 33	15 37	16 39	13 38	13 43	13 52	14 10
60	14 54	15 51	16 47	13 45	13 55	14 10	14 34
N 58	15 11	16 02	16 54	13 51	14 05	14 24	14 54
56	15 25	16 12	17 01	13 56	14 14	14 37	15 10
54	15 37	16 21	17 07	14 01	14 21	14 48	15 24
52	15 48	16 29	17 13	14 06	14 28	14 58	15 37
50	15 58	16 36	17 18	14 10	14 35	15 06	15 47
45	16 18	16 52	17 29	14 18	14 49	15 25	16 10
N 40	16 35	17 05	17 39	14 25	15 00	15 40	16 28
35	16 49	17 17	17 49	14 32	15 10	15 53	16 44
30	17 01	17 27	17 57	14 37	15 18	16 05	16 57
20	17 22	17 46	18 14	14 47	15 33	16 24	17 20
N 10	17 40	18 03	18 30	14 55	15 46	16 41	17 40
0	17 58	18 20	18 46	15 03	15 59	16 57	17 58
S 10	18 15	18 38	19 05	15 11	16 11	17 13	18 17
20	18 34	18 58	19 27	15 20	16 24	17 30	18 37
30	18 56	19 23	19 56	15 30	16 39	17 50	19 00
35	19 08	19 38	20 15	15 36	16 48	18 02	19 13
40	19 23	19 56	20 37	15 42	16 58	18 15	19 29
45	19 41	20 18	21 08	15 50	17 10	18 31	19 47
S 50	20 03	20 47	21 52	16 00	17 25	18 50	20 11
52	20 14	21 02	22 19	16 03	17 31	18 59	20 22
54	20 26	21 20	23 01	16 08	17 39	19 10	20 34
56	20 40	21 42	////	16 13	17 48	19 22	20 49
58	20 56	22 10	////	16 19	17 57	19 35	21 06
S 60	21 16	22 56	////	16 25	18 08	19 52	21 27

Day	SUN Eqn. of Time 00h	SUN Eqn. of Time 12h	SUN Mer. Pass.	MOON Mer. Pass. Upper	MOON Mer. Pass. Lower	Age	Phase
d	m s	m s	h m	h m	h m	d	%
11	06 48	06 34	11 53	08 51	21 18	26	14
12	06 20	06 06	11 54	09 45	22 14	27	7
13	05 52	05 37	11 54	10 43	23 13	28	2

UT	ARIES GHA	VENUS −3.9 GHA	Dec	MARS −0.7 GHA	Dec	JUPITER −2.0 GHA	Dec	SATURN +0.6 GHA	Dec	STARS Name	SHA	Dec
14 00	83 07.4	207 10.2	S18 24.1	64 20.9	N 8 24.0	142 05.0	S20 51.6	141 12.4	S20 34.9	Acamar	315 14.0	S40 13.5
01	98 09.8	222 09.5	24.8	79 22.6	24.4	157 07.0	51.5	156 14.6	34.9	Achernar	335 22.5	S57 08.2
02	113 12.3	237 08.8	25.6	94 24.3	24.7	172 08.9	51.4	171 16.8	34.8	Acrux	173 03.7	S63 12.5
03	128 14.8	252 08.0	.. 26.4	109 26.1	.. 25.1	187 10.8	.. 51.3	186 19.0	.. 34.8	Adhara	255 08.1	S29 00.0
04	143 17.2	267 07.3	27.1	124 27.8	25.5	202 12.7	51.2	201 21.2	34.7	Aldebaran	290 43.1	N16 33.0
05	158 19.7	282 06.6	27.9	139 29.6	25.9	217 14.6	51.1	216 23.4	34.7			
M 06	173 22.1	297 05.9	S18 28.7	154 31.3	N 8 26.2	232 16.5	S20 51.0	231 25.6	S20 34.6	Alioth	166 16.2	N55 50.6
O 07	188 24.6	312 05.1	29.4	169 33.0	26.6	247 18.4	50.9	246 27.8	34.6	Alkaid	152 55.0	N49 12.4
N 08	203 27.1	327 04.4	30.2	184 34.8	27.0	262 20.3	50.8	261 29.9	34.5	Alnair	27 37.3	S46 51.9
D 09	218 29.5	342 03.7	.. 31.0	199 36.5	.. 27.4	277 22.2	.. 50.7	276 32.1	.. 34.5	Alnilam	275 40.7	S 1 11.4
A 10	233 32.0	357 02.9	31.7	214 38.2	27.7	292 24.1	50.6	291 34.3	34.4	Alphard	217 50.8	S 8 44.9
Y 11	248 34.5	12 02.2	32.5	229 40.0	28.1	307 26.0	50.5	306 36.5	34.4			
12	263 36.9	27 01.5	S18 33.2	244 41.7	N 8 28.5	322 27.9	S20 50.4	321 38.7	S20 34.3	Alphecca	126 06.9	N26 38.7
13	278 39.4	42 00.8	34.0	259 43.4	28.9	337 29.8	50.3	336 40.9	34.2	Alpheratz	357 38.1	N29 12.4
14	293 41.9	57 00.0	34.8	274 45.2	29.2	352 31.7	50.1	351 43.1	34.2	Altair	62 03.5	N 8 55.5
15	308 44.3	71 59.3	.. 35.5	289 46.9	.. 29.6	7 33.6	.. 50.0	6 45.3	.. 34.1	Ankaa	353 10.4	S42 11.9
16	323 46.8	86 58.6	36.3	304 48.6	30.0	22 35.6	49.9	21 47.5	34.1	Antares	112 20.2	S26 28.5
17	338 49.3	101 57.8	37.0	319 50.4	30.4	37 37.5	49.8	36 49.7	34.0			
18	353 51.7	116 57.1	S18 37.8	334 52.1	N 8 30.7	52 39.4	S20 49.7	51 51.9	S20 34.0	Arcturus	145 51.2	N19 04.5
19	8 54.2	131 56.4	38.5	349 53.8	31.1	67 41.3	49.6	66 54.1	33.9	Atria	107 18.0	S69 03.7
20	23 56.6	146 55.6	39.3	4 55.6	31.5	82 43.2	49.5	81 56.3	33.9	Avior	234 15.5	S59 34.4
21	38 59.1	161 54.9	.. 40.0	19 57.3	.. 31.9	97 45.1	.. 49.4	96 58.5	.. 33.8	Bellatrix	278 26.1	N 6 22.0
22	54 01.6	176 54.2	40.8	34 59.0	32.2	112 47.0	49.3	112 00.7	33.8	Betelgeuse	270 55.3	N 7 24.6
23	69 04.0	191 53.4	41.5	50 00.7	32.6	127 48.9	49.2	127 02.9	33.7			
15 00	84 06.5	206 52.7	S18 42.3	65 02.5	N 8 33.0	142 50.8	S20 49.1	142 05.1	S20 33.7	Canopus	263 53.3	S52 42.4
01	99 09.0	221 52.0	43.0	80 04.2	33.4	157 52.7	49.0	157 07.2	33.6	Capella	280 26.3	N46 01.1
02	114 11.4	236 51.2	43.8	95 05.9	33.8	172 54.6	48.8	172 09.4	33.6	Deneb	49 28.3	N45 21.5
03	129 13.9	251 50.5	.. 44.5	110 07.6	.. 34.1	187 56.5	.. 48.7	187 11.6	.. 33.5	Denebola	182 28.4	N14 27.3
04	144 16.4	266 49.7	45.3	125 09.3	34.5	202 58.4	48.6	202 13.8	33.5	Diphda	348 50.5	S17 52.5
05	159 18.8	281 49.0	46.0	140 11.1	34.9	218 00.3	48.5	217 16.0	33.4			
T 06	174 21.3	296 48.3	S18 46.8	155 12.8	N 8 35.3	233 02.2	S20 48.4	232 18.2	S20 33.4	Dubhe	193 45.1	N61 38.1
U 07	189 23.8	311 47.5	47.5	170 14.5	35.7	248 04.1	48.3	247 20.4	33.3	Elnath	278 05.7	N28 37.4
E 08	204 26.2	326 46.8	48.3	185 16.2	36.0	263 06.0	48.2	262 22.6	33.2	Eltanin	90 44.3	N51 29.2
S 09	219 28.7	341 46.1	.. 49.0	200 17.9	.. 36.4	278 07.9	.. 48.1	277 24.8	.. 33.2	Enif	33 42.2	N 9 58.3
D 10	234 31.1	356 45.3	49.8	215 19.7	36.8	293 09.8	48.0	292 27.0	33.1	Fomalhaut	15 18.3	S29 30.9
A 11	249 33.6	11 44.6	50.5	230 21.4	37.2	308 11.7	47.9	307 29.2	33.1			
Y 12	264 36.1	26 43.8	S18 51.2	245 23.1	N 8 37.6	323 13.6	S20 47.8	322 31.4	S20 33.0	Gacrux	171 55.3	S57 13.4
13	279 38.5	41 43.1	52.0	260 24.8	37.9	338 15.5	47.7	337 33.6	33.0	Gienah	175 47.0	S17 39.3
14	294 41.0	56 42.3	52.7	275 26.5	38.3	353 17.5	47.5	352 35.8	32.9	Hadar	148 41.0	S60 28.0
15	309 43.5	71 41.6	.. 53.4	290 28.2	.. 38.7	8 19.4	.. 47.4	7 37.9	.. 32.9	Hamal	327 54.7	N23 33.7
16	324 45.9	86 40.9	54.2	305 29.9	39.1	23 21.3	47.3	22 40.1	32.8	Kaus Aust.	83 37.3	S34 22.4
17	339 48.4	101 40.1	54.9	320 31.6	39.5	38 23.2	47.2	37 42.3	32.8			
18	354 50.9	116 39.4	S18 55.7	335 33.4	N 8 39.8	53 25.1	S20 47.1	52 44.5	S20 32.7	Kochab	137 20.9	N74 04.0
19	9 53.3	131 38.6	56.4	350 35.1	40.2	68 27.0	47.0	67 46.7	32.7	Markab	13 33.2	N15 19.1
20	24 55.8	146 37.9	57.1	5 36.8	40.6	83 28.9	46.9	82 48.9	32.6	Menkar	314 09.3	N 4 10.2
21	39 58.3	161 37.1	.. 57.8	20 38.5	.. 41.0	98 30.8	.. 46.8	97 51.1	.. 32.6	Menkent	148 01.7	S36 28.1
22	55 00.7	176 36.4	58.6	35 40.2	41.4	113 32.7	46.7	112 53.3	32.5	Miaplacidus	221 38.2	S69 47.9
23	70 03.2	191 35.6	18 59.3	50 41.9	41.8	128 34.6	46.6	127 55.5	32.5			
16 00	85 05.6	206 34.9	S19 00.0	65 43.6	N 8 42.1	143 36.5	S20 46.5	142 57.7	S20 32.4	Mirfak	308 32.5	N49 56.1
01	100 08.1	221 34.1	00.8	80 45.3	42.5	158 38.4	46.3	157 59.9	32.4	Nunki	75 52.2	S26 16.2
02	115 10.6	236 33.4	01.5	95 47.0	42.9	173 40.3	46.2	173 02.1	32.3	Peacock	53 11.5	S56 40.2
03	130 13.0	251 32.6	.. 02.2	110 48.7	.. 43.3	188 42.2	.. 46.1	188 04.2	.. 32.2	Pollux	243 21.0	N27 58.4
04	145 15.5	266 31.9	02.9	125 50.4	43.7	203 44.1	46.0	203 06.4	32.2	Procyon	244 54.0	N 5 10.2
05	160 18.0	281 31.1	03.7	140 52.1	44.1	218 46.0	45.9	218 08.6	32.1			
W 06	175 20.4	296 30.4	S19 04.4	155 53.8	N 8 44.4	233 47.9	S20 45.8	233 10.8	S20 32.1	Rasalhague	96 02.0	N12 32.8
E 07	190 22.9	311 29.6	05.1	170 55.5	44.8	248 49.8	45.7	248 13.0	32.0	Regulus	207 37.8	N11 51.9
D 08	205 25.4	326 28.9	05.8	185 57.2	45.2	263 51.7	45.6	263 15.2	32.0	Rigel	281 06.7	S 8 10.7
N 09	220 27.8	341 28.1	.. 06.6	200 58.9	.. 45.6	278 53.6	.. 45.5	278 17.4	.. 31.9	Rigil Kent.	139 45.2	S60 54.9
E 10	235 30.3	356 27.4	07.3	216 00.6	46.0	293 55.5	45.4	293 19.6	31.9	Sabik	102 06.9	S15 44.9
S 11	250 32.7	11 26.6	08.0	231 02.3	46.4	308 57.4	45.2	308 21.8	31.8			
D 12	265 35.2	26 25.9	S19 08.7	246 04.0	N 8 46.8	323 59.3	S20 45.1	323 24.0	S20 31.8	Schedar	349 34.5	N56 39.3
A 13	280 37.7	41 25.1	09.4	261 05.7	47.1	339 01.2	45.0	338 26.2	31.7	Shaula	96 15.3	S37 07.0
Y 14	295 40.1	56 24.4	10.1	276 07.4	47.5	354 03.1	44.9	353 28.3	31.7	Sirius	258 28.8	S16 44.7
15	310 42.6	71 23.6	.. 10.9	291 09.1	.. 47.9	9 05.0	.. 44.8	8 30.5	.. 31.6	Spica	158 25.9	S11 16.0
16	325 45.1	86 22.9	11.6	306 10.8	48.3	24 06.9	44.7	23 32.7	31.6	Suhail	222 48.4	S43 30.8
17	340 47.5	101 22.1	12.3	321 12.5	48.7	39 08.8	44.6	38 34.9	31.5			
18	355 50.0	116 21.3	S19 13.0	336 14.2	N 8 49.1	54 10.7	S20 44.5	53 37.1	S20 31.4	Vega	80 35.9	N38 48.3
19	10 52.5	131 20.6	13.7	351 15.8	49.5	69 12.6	44.4	68 39.3	31.4	Zuben'ubi	136 59.9	S16 07.5
20	25 54.9	146 19.8	14.4	6 17.5	49.8	84 14.5	44.3	83 41.5	31.3		SHA	Mer. Pass.
21	40 57.4	161 19.1	.. 15.1	21 19.2	.. 50.2	99 16.4	.. 44.1	98 43.7	.. 31.3		° '	h m
22	55 59.9	176 18.3	15.8	36 20.9	50.6	114 18.3	44.0	113 45.9	31.2	Venus	122 46.2	10 13
23	71 02.3	191 17.6	16.6	51 22.6	51.0	129 20.2	43.9	128 48.1	31.2	Mars	340 56.0	19 38
Mer. Pass.	18 20.6	v −0.7	d 0.7	v 1.7	d 0.4	v 1.9	d 0.1	v 2.2	d 0.1	Jupiter	58 44.3	14 27
										Saturn	57 58.6	14 30

SUN / MOON

UT	SUN GHA	SUN Dec	MOON GHA	v	MOON Dec	d	HP
d h	° ′	° ′	° ′	′	° ′	′	′
14 00	181 20.6	S23 13.3	191 17.2	4.4	S21 45.4	7.8	60.4
01	196 20.3	13.4	205 40.6	4.5	21 53.2	7.7	60.4
02	211 20.0	13.6	220 04.1	4.3	22 00.9	7.6	60.4
03	226 19.7 ..	13.7	234 27.4	4.3	22 08.5	7.4	60.4
04	241 19.4	13.9	248 50.7	4.3	22 15.9	7.2	60.4
05	256 19.1	14.0	263 14.0	4.2	22 23.1	7.1	60.4
06	271 18.8	S23 14.1	277 37.2	4.2	S22 30.2	6.9	60.4
07	286 18.5	14.3	292 00.4	4.1	22 37.1	6.7	60.3
08	301 18.2	14.4	306 23.5	4.1	22 43.8	6.6	60.3
M 09	316 17.9 ..	14.6	320 46.6	4.0	22 50.4	6.4	60.3
O 10	331 17.6	14.7	335 09.6	4.0	22 56.8	6.3	60.3
N 11	346 17.3	14.8	349 32.6	4.0	23 03.1	6.0	60.3
D 12	1 17.0	S23 15.0	3 55.6	3.9	S23 09.1	6.0	60.3
A 13	16 16.7	15.1	18 18.5	3.9	23 15.1	5.7	60.2
Y 14	31 16.4	15.2	32 41.4	3.9	23 20.8	5.6	60.2
15	46 16.1 ..	15.4	47 04.3	3.8	S23 26.4	5.4	60.2
16	61 15.8	15.5					
17	76 15.5	15.6					
18	91 15.2	S23 15.8					
19	106 14.9	15.9					
20	121 14.6	16.0					
21	136 14.3 ..	16.2					
22	151 14.0	16.3	147 43.6	3.7	S24 00.6	4.2	60.1
23	166 13.7	16.4	162 06.3	3.7	24 04.8	4.0	60.0
15 00	181 13.4	S23 16.5	176 29.0	3.6	S24 08.8	3.9	60.0
01	196 13.1	16.7	190 51.6	3.7	24 12.7	3.7	60.0
02	211 12.8	16.8	205 14.3	3.7	24 16.4	3.5	60.0
03	226 12.5 ..	16.9	219 37.0	3.6	24 19.9	3.3	59.9
04	241 12.2	17.0	233 59.6	3.6	24 23.2	3.1	59.9
05	256 11.9	17.2	248 22.2	3.7	24 26.3	3.0	59.9
06	271 11.5	S23 17.3	262 44.9	3.7	S24 29.3	2.8	59.9
07	286 11.2	17.4	277 07.6	3.6	24 32.1	2.6	59.8
T 08	301 10.9	17.5	291 30.2	3.7	24 34.7	2.4	59.8
U 09	316 10.6 ..	17.6	305 52.9	3.7	24 37.1	2.3	59.8
E 10	331 10.3	17.8	320 15.6	3.7	24 39.4	2.1	59.8
S 11	346 10.0	17.9	334 38.3	3.7	24 41.5	1.9	59.7
D 12	1 09.7	S23 18.0	349 01.0	3.7	S24 43.4	1.7	59.7
A 13	16 09.4	18.1	3 23.7	3.7	24 45.1	1.6	59.7
Y 14	31 09.1	18.2	17 46.4	3.8	24 46.7	1.4	59.6
15	46 08.8 ..	18.3	32 09.2	3.8	24 48.1	1.2	59.6
16	61 08.5	18.4	46 32.0	3.8	24 49.3	1.0	59.6
17	76 08.2	18.6	60 54.8	3.9	24 50.3	0.8	59.6
18	91 07.9	S23 18.7	75 17.7	3.9	S24 51.1	0.7	59.5
19	106 07.6	18.8	89 40.6	3.9	24 51.8	0.5	59.5
20	121 07.3	18.9	104 03.5	3.9	24 52.3	0.4	59.5
21	136 07.0 ..	19.0	118 26.4	4.0	24 52.7	0.1	59.4
22	151 06.7	19.1	132 49.4	4.1	24 52.8	0.0	59.4
23	166 06.4	19.2	147 12.5	4.1	24 52.8	0.2	59.4
16 00	181 06.1	S23 19.3	161 35.6	4.1	S24 52.6	0.3	59.4
01	196 05.8	19.4	175 58.7	4.2	24 52.3	0.6	59.3
02	211 05.5	19.5	190 21.9	4.2	24 51.7	0.7	59.3
03	226 05.2 ..	19.6	204 45.1	4.3	24 51.0	0.8	59.3
04	241 04.9	19.7	219 08.4	4.3	24 50.2	1.1	59.2
05	256 04.6	19.8	233 31.7	4.4	24 49.1	1.2	59.2
06	271 04.2	S23 19.9	247 55.1	4.4	S24 47.9	1.4	59.2
W 07	286 03.9	20.0	262 18.5	4.5	24 46.5	1.5	59.1
E 08	301 03.6	20.1	276 42.0	4.6	24 45.0	1.7	59.1
D 09	316 03.3 ..	20.2	291 05.6	4.6	24 43.3	1.9	59.1
N 10	331 03.0	20.3	305 29.2	4.7	24 41.4	2.0	59.0
E 11	346 02.7	20.4	319 52.9	4.8	24 39.4	2.2	59.0
S 12	1 02.4	S23 20.5	334 16.7	4.9	S24 37.2	2.4	59.0
D 13	16 02.1	20.6	348 40.6	4.9	24 34.8	2.5	58.9
A 14	31 01.8	20.7	3 04.5	5.0	24 32.3	2.7	58.9
Y 15	46 01.5 ..	20.8	17 28.5	5.0	24 29.6	2.8	58.9
16	61 01.2	20.9	31 52.5	5.2	24 26.8	3.0	58.8
17	76 00.9	21.0	46 16.7	5.2	24 23.8	3.2	58.8
18	91 00.6	S23 21.1	60 40.9	5.3	S24 20.6	3.3	58.8
19	106 00.3	21.2	75 05.2	5.3	24 17.3	3.4	58.7
20	121 00.0	21.3	89 29.5	5.5	24 13.9	3.7	58.7
21	135 59.7 ..	21.4	103 54.0	5.6	24 10.2	3.7	58.7
22	150 59.4	21.5	118 18.6	5.6	24 06.5	3.9	58.6
23	165 59.0	21.5	132 43.2	5.7	S24 02.6	4.1	58.6
	SD 16.3	d 0.1	SD 16.4		16.3		16.1

Note (in MOON column, Monday 16–20h): A total eclipse of the Sun occurs on this date. See page 5.

Twilight / Moonrise

Lat.	Twilight Naut.	Twilight Civil	Sunrise	Moonrise 14	15	16	17
°	h m	h m	h m	h m	h m	h m	h m
N 72	08 21	10 48	■	■	■	■	■
N 70	08 01	09 48	■	■■	■■	■■	■■
68	07 45	09 14	■	■■	■■	■■	■■
66	07 32	08 49	10 28	10 37	■	■	13 31
64	07 21	08 29	09 47	09 42	11 30	12 28	12 44
62	07 12	08 14	09 19	09 10	10 43	11 43	12 13
60	07 03	08 00	08 58	08 45	10 13	11 14	11 50
N 58	06 56	07 48	08 40	08 26	09 49	10 51	11 31
56	06 49	07 38	08 26	08 10	09 31	10 33	11 15
54	06 43	07 29	08 13	07 57	09 15	10 17	11 02
52	06 37	07 21	08 02	07 45	09 02	10 04	10 50
50	06 32	07 14	07 52	07 34	08 50	09 52	10 39
45	06 21	06 58	07 32	07 12	08 25	09 27	10 17
N 40	06 10	06 44	07 15	06 55	08 06	09 08	10 00
35	06 01	06 33	07 01	06 40	07 49	08 51	09 45
30	05 52	06 22	06 48	06 27	07 35	08 37	09 32
20	05 36	06 03	06 27	06 05	07 11	08 13	09 09
N 10	05 20	05 46	06 09	05 46	06 50	07 52	08 50
0	05 03	05 29	05 52	05 29	06 31	07 33	08 32
S 10	04 44	05 11	05 34	05 12	06 12	07 13	08 14
20	04 21	04 51	05 15	04 53	05 51	06 53	07 54
30	03 53	04 26	04 53	04 32	05 28	06 28	07 32
35	03 34	04 11	04 40	04 20	05 14	06 14	07 19
40	03 11	03 53	04 25	04 05	04 58	05 58	07 03
45	02 41	03 30	04 08	03 49	04 39	05 38	06 45
S 50	01 56	03 01	03 45	03 28	04 15	05 14	06 23
52	01 28	02 46	03 34	03 18	04 04	05 02	06 12
54	00 44	02 28	03 22	03 08	03 51	04 49	06 00
56	////	02 06	03 08	02 55	03 36	04 33	05 45
58	////	01 37	02 51	02 41	03 19	04 15	05 29
S 60	////	00 49	02 31	02 24	02 58	03 52	05 09

Sunset / Twilight / Moonset

Lat.	Sunset	Twilight Civil	Twilight Naut.	Moonset 14	15	16	17
°	h m	h m	h m	h m	h m	h m	h m
N 72	■	13 03	15 30	■	■	■	■
N 70	■	14 02	15 50	■	■	■	■
68	■	14 37	16 05	■	■	■	■
66	13 23	15 02	16 18	12 41	■	■	16 09
64	14 04	15 21	16 29	13 37	13 59	15 10	16 56
62	14 32	15 37	16 39	14 10	14 47	15 54	17 26
60	14 53	15 50	16 47	14 34	15 17	16 24	17 49
N 58	15 10	16 02	16 55	14 54	15 40	16 46	18 07
56	15 25	16 12	17 01	15 10	15 59	17 05	18 22
54	15 38	16 21	17 07	15 24	16 15	17 20	18 35
52	15 49	16 29	17 13	15 37	16 28	17 33	18 47
50	15 58	16 37	17 18	15 47	16 40	17 45	18 57
45	16 19	16 53	17 30	16 10	17 05	18 09	19 18
N 40	16 36	17 06	17 40	16 28	17 25	18 28	19 35
35	16 50	17 18	17 50	16 44	17 41	18 44	19 50
30	17 02	17 28	17 58	16 57	17 56	18 58	20 02
20	17 23	17 47	18 15	17 20	18 20	19 22	20 23
N 10	17 42	18 05	18 31	17 40	18 41	19 42	20 42
0	17 59	18 22	18 51	17 58	19 01	20 01	20 59
S 10	18 17	18 40	19 07	18 17	19 20	20 20	21 16
20	18 35	19 00	19 29	18 37	19 41	20 41	21 34
30	18 57	19 25	19 58	19 00	20 05	21 04	21 54
35	19 10	19 40	20 17	19 13	20 19	21 17	22 06
40	19 25	19 58	20 40	19 29	20 36	21 33	22 20
45	19 43	20 21	21 10	19 47	20 55	21 52	22 36
S 50	20 06	20 50	21 55	20 11	21 20	22 15	22 56
52	20 17	21 05	22 23	20 22	21 32	22 26	23 06
54	20 29	21 23	23 08	20 34	21 45	22 39	23 16
56	20 43	21 45	////	20 49	22 01	22 53	23 28
58	21 00	22 15	////	21 06	22 19	23 10	23 42
S 60	21 20	23 04	////	21 27	22 42	23 30	23 58

SUN / MOON

Day	SUN Eqn. of Time 00h	12h	Mer. Pass.	MOON Mer. Pass. Upper	Lower	Age	Phase
d	m s	m s	h m	h m	h m	d	%
14	05 23	05 09	11 55	11 44	24 15	29	0
15	04 54	04 40	11 55	12 46	00 15	01	1
16	04 25	04 10	11 56	13 47	01 17	02	5

UT	ARIES GHA	VENUS −3.9 GHA	Dec	MARS −0.6 GHA	Dec	JUPITER −2.0 GHA	Dec	SATURN +0.6 GHA	Dec	STARS Name	SHA	Dec
17 00	86 04.8	206 16.8	S19 17.3	66 24.3	N 8 51.4	144 22.1	S20 43.8	143 50.2	S20 31.1	Acamar	315 14.0	S40 13.5
01	101 07.2	221 16.0	18.0	81 26.0	51.8	159 24.0	43.7	158 52.4	31.1	Achernar	335 22.5	S57 08.2
02	116 09.7	236 15.3	18.7	96 27.7	52.2	174 25.9	43.6	173 54.6	31.0	Acrux	173 03.7	S63 12.5
03	131 12.2	251 14.5	.. 19.4	111 29.3	.. 52.6	189 27.8	.. 43.5	188 56.8	.. 31.0	Adhara	255 08.1	S29 00.0
04	146 14.6	266 13.8	20.1	126 31.0	52.9	204 29.7	43.4	203 59.0	30.9	Aldebaran	290 43.1	N16 33.0
05	161 17.1	281 13.0	20.8	141 32.7	53.3	219 31.6	43.3	219 01.2	30.9			
06	176 19.6	296 12.2	S19 21.5	156 34.4	N 8 53.7	234 33.5	S20 43.1	234 03.4	S20 30.8	Alioth	166 16.2	N55 50.6
07	191 22.0	311 11.5	22.2	171 36.1	54.1	249 35.4	43.0	249 05.6	30.8	Alkaid	152 55.0	N49 12.4
T 08	206 24.5	326 10.7	22.9	186 37.7	54.5	264 37.3	42.9	264 07.8	30.7	Alnair	27 37.3	S46 51.8
H 09	221 27.0	341 09.9	.. 23.6	201 39.4	.. 54.9	279 39.2	.. 42.8	279 10.0	.. 30.6	Alnilam	275 40.7	S 1 11.4
U 10	236 29.4	356 09.2	24.3	216 41.1	55.3	294 41.1	42.7	294 12.1	30.6	Alphard	217 50.8	S 8 44.9
R 11	251 31.9	11 08.4	25.0	231 42.8	55.7	309 43.0	42.6	309 14.3	30.5			
S 12	266 34.4	26 07.6	S19 25.7	246 44.5	N 8 56.1	324 44.9	S20 42.5	324 16.5	S20 30.5	Alphecca	126 06.9	N26 38.7
D 13	281 36.8	41 06.9	26.4	261 46.1	56.4	339 46.8	42.4	339 18.7	30.4	Alpheratz	357 38.1	N29 12.4
A 14	296 39.3	56 06.1	27.1	276 47.8	56.8	354 48.7	42.3	354 20.9	30.4	Altair	62 03.5	N 8 55.5
Y 15	311 41.7	71 05.3	.. 27.8	291 49.5	.. 57.2	9 50.6	.. 42.1	9 23.1	.. 30.3	Ankaa	353 10.4	S42 11.9
16	326 44.2	86 04.6	28.4	306 51.2	57.6	24 52.5	42.0	24 25.3	30.3	Antares	112 20.2	S26 28.5
17	341 46.7	101 03.8	29.1	321 52.8	58.0	39 54.4	41.9	39 27.5	30.2			
18	356 49.1	116 03.0	S19 29.8	336 54.5	N 8 58.4	54 56.3	S20 41.8	54 29.7	S20 30.2	Arcturus	145 51.2	N19 04.4
19	11 51.6	131 02.3	30.5	351 56.2	58.8	69 58.2	41.7	69 31.8	30.1	Atria	107 17.9	S69 03.7
20	26 54.1	146 01.5	31.2	6 57.9	59.2	85 00.1	41.6	84 34.0	30.1	Avior	234 15.4	S59 34.4
21	41 56.5	161 00.7	.. 31.9	21 59.5	8 59.6	100 02.0	.. 41.5	99 36.2	.. 30.0	Bellatrix	278 26.1	N 6 22.0
22	56 59.0	176 00.0	32.6	37 01.2	9 00.0	115 03.9	41.4	114 38.4	29.9	Betelgeuse	270 55.3	N 7 24.6
23	72 01.5	190 59.2	33.3	52 02.9	00.4	130 05.8	41.3	129 40.6	29.9			
18 00	87 03.9	205 58.4	S19 34.0	67 04.5	N 9 00.8	145 07.7	S20 41.1	144 42.8	S20 29.8	Canopus	263 53.3	S52 42.4
01	102 06.4	220 57.6	34.6	82 06.2	01.1	160 09.6	41.0	159 45.0	29.8	Capella	280 26.3	N46 01.1
02	117 08.9	235 56.9	35.3	97 07.9	01.5	175 11.5	40.9	174 47.2	29.7	Deneb	49 28.3	N45 21.4
03	132 11.3	250 56.1	.. 36.0	112 09.5	.. 01.9	190 13.4	.. 40.8	189 49.3	.. 29.7	Denebola	182 28.3	N14 27.3
04	147 13.8	265 55.3	36.7	127 11.2	02.3	205 15.3	40.7	204 51.5	29.6	Diphda	348 50.5	S17 52.5
05	162 16.2	280 54.6	37.4	142 12.9	02.7	220 17.2	40.6	219 53.7	29.6			
06	177 18.7	295 53.8	S19 38.0	157 14.5	N 9 03.1	235 19.1	S20 40.5	234 55.9	S20 29.5	Dubhe	193 45.1	N61 38.1
07	192 21.2	310 53.0	38.7	172 16.2	03.5	250 21.0	40.4	249 58.1	29.5	Elnath	278 05.6	N28 37.4
08	207 23.6	325 52.2	39.4	187 17.9	03.9	265 22.9	40.2	265 00.3	29.4	Eltanin	90 44.3	N51 29.2
F 09	222 26.1	340 51.5	.. 40.1	202 19.5	.. 04.3	280 24.8	.. 40.1	280 02.5	.. 29.3	Enif	33 42.2	N 9 58.3
R 10	237 28.6	355 50.7	40.8	217 21.2	04.7	295 26.6	40.0	295 04.7	29.3	Fomalhaut	15 18.3	S29 30.9
I 11	252 31.0	10 49.9	41.4	232 22.8	05.1	310 28.5	39.9	310 06.8	29.2			
D 12	267 33.5	25 49.1	S19 42.1	247 24.5	N 9 05.5	325 30.4	S20 39.8	325 09.0	S20 29.2	Gacrux	171 55.3	S57 13.4
A 13	282 36.0	40 48.3	42.8	262 26.2	05.9	340 32.3	39.7	340 11.2	29.1	Gienah	175 47.0	S17 39.3
Y 14	297 38.4	55 47.6	43.4	277 27.8	06.3	355 34.2	39.6	355 13.4	29.1	Hadar	148 41.0	S60 28.0
15	312 40.9	70 46.8	.. 44.1	292 29.5	.. 06.7	10 36.1	.. 39.5	10 15.6	.. 29.0	Hamal	327 54.7	N23 33.7
16	327 43.4	85 46.0	44.8	307 31.1	07.1	25 38.0	39.3	25 17.8	29.0	Kaus Aust.	83 37.3	S34 22.4
17	342 45.8	100 45.2	45.5	322 32.8	07.4	40 39.9	39.2	40 20.0	28.9			
18	357 48.3	115 44.5	S19 46.1	337 34.4	N 9 07.8	55 41.8	S20 39.1	55 22.1	S20 28.9	Kochab	137 20.9	N74 04.0
19	12 50.7	130 43.7	46.8	352 36.1	08.2	70 43.7	39.0	70 24.3	28.8	Markab	13 33.2	N15 19.1
20	27 53.2	145 42.9	47.5	7 37.7	08.6	85 45.6	38.9	85 26.5	28.7	Menkar	314 09.3	N 4 10.2
21	42 55.7	160 42.1	.. 48.1	22 39.4	.. 09.0	100 47.5	.. 38.8	100 28.7	.. 28.7	Menkent	148 01.7	S36 28.1
22	57 58.1	175 41.3	48.8	37 41.1	09.4	115 49.4	38.7	115 30.9	28.6	Miaplacidus	221 38.1	S69 47.9
23	73 00.6	190 40.5	49.4	52 42.7	09.8	130 51.3	38.6	130 33.1	28.6			
19 00	88 03.1	205 39.8	S19 50.1	67 44.4	N 9 10.2	145 53.2	S20 38.4	145 35.3	S20 28.5	Mirfak	308 32.5	N49 56.1
01	103 05.5	220 39.0	50.8	82 46.0	10.6	160 55.1	38.3	160 37.5	28.5	Nunki	75 52.2	S26 16.2
02	118 08.0	235 38.2	51.4	97 47.7	11.0	175 57.0	38.2	175 39.6	28.4	Peacock	53 11.5	S56 40.2
03	133 10.5	250 37.4	.. 52.1	112 49.3	.. 11.4	190 58.9	.. 38.1	190 41.8	.. 28.4	Pollux	243 21.0	N27 58.4
04	148 12.9	265 36.6	52.7	127 51.0	11.8	206 00.8	38.0	205 44.0	28.3	Procyon	244 54.0	N 5 10.2
05	163 15.4	280 35.8	53.4	142 52.6	12.2	221 02.7	37.9	220 46.2	28.3			
06	178 17.8	295 35.1	S19 54.1	157 54.2	N 9 12.6	236 04.6	S20 37.8	235 48.4	S20 28.2	Rasalhague	96 02.0	N12 32.8
07	193 20.3	310 34.3	54.7	172 55.9	13.0	251 06.5	37.6	250 50.6	28.1	Regulus	207 37.8	N11 51.9
S 08	208 22.8	325 33.5	55.4	187 57.5	13.4	266 08.4	37.5	265 52.8	28.1	Rigel	281 06.7	S 8 10.7
A 09	223 25.2	340 32.7	.. 56.0	202 59.2	.. 13.8	281 10.2	.. 37.4	280 54.9	.. 28.0	Rigil Kent.	139 45.2	S60 54.9
T 10	238 27.7	355 31.9	56.7	218 00.8	14.2	296 12.1	37.3	295 57.1	28.0	Sabik	102 06.9	S15 44.9
U 11	253 30.2	10 31.1	57.3	233 02.5	14.6	311 14.0	37.2	310 59.3	27.9			
R 12	268 32.6	25 30.3	S19 58.0	248 04.1	N 9 15.0	326 15.9	S20 37.1	326 01.5	S20 27.9	Schedar	349 34.5	N56 39.3
D 13	283 35.1	40 29.5	58.6	263 05.8	15.4	341 17.8	37.0	341 03.7	27.8	Shaula	96 15.3	S37 07.0
A 14	298 37.6	55 28.8	59.3	278 07.4	15.8	356 19.7	36.8	356 05.9	27.8	Sirius	258 28.8	S16 44.7
Y 15	313 40.0	70 28.0	19 59.9	293 09.0	.. 16.2	11 21.6	.. 36.7	11 08.1	.. 27.7	Spica	158 25.9	S11 16.0
16	328 42.5	85 27.2	20 00.6	308 10.7	16.6	26 23.5	36.6	26 10.2	27.7	Suhail	222 48.4	S43 30.8
17	343 45.0	100 26.4	01.2	323 12.3	17.0	41 25.4	36.5	41 12.4	27.6			
18	358 47.4	115 25.6	S20 01.9	338 13.9	N 9 17.4	56 27.3	S20 36.4	56 14.6	S20 27.5	Vega	80 35.9	N38 48.3
19	13 49.9	130 24.8	02.5	353 15.6	17.8	71 29.2	36.3	71 16.8	27.5	Zuben'ubi	136 59.9	S16 07.5
20	28 52.3	145 24.0	03.1	8 17.2	18.2	86 31.1	36.2	86 19.0	27.4		SHA	Mer.Pass.
21	43 54.8	160 23.2	.. 03.8	23 18.9	.. 18.6	101 33.0	.. 36.1	101 21.2	.. 27.4	Venus	118 54.5	10 17
22	58 57.3	175 22.4	04.4	38 20.5	19.0	116 34.9	35.9	116 23.3	27.3	Mars	340 00.6	19 30
23	73 59.7	190 21.6	05.1	53 22.1	19.4	131 36.8	35.8	131 25.5	27.3	Jupiter	58 03.8	14 14
Mer. Pass. 18 08.8		v −0.8	d 0.7	v 1.7	d 0.4	v 1.9	d 0.1	v 2.2	d 0.1	Saturn	57 38.9	14 19

UT	SUN GHA	SUN Dec	MOON GHA	v	MOON Dec	d	HP
d h	° ′	° ′	° ′	′	° ′	′	′
17 00	180 58.7	S23 21.6	147 07.9	5.8	S23 58.5	4.2	58.5
01	195 58.4	21.7	161 32.7	5.9	23 54.3	4.4	58.5
02	210 58.1	21.8	175 57.6	6.0	23 49.9	4.5	58.5
03	225 57.8 ..	21.9	190 22.6	6.1	23 45.4	4.7	58.4
04	240 57.5	22.0	204 47.7	6.2	23 40.7	4.8	58.4
05	255 57.2	22.1	219 12.9	6.3	23 35.9	4.9	58.4
06	270 56.9	S23 22.1	233 38.2	6.3	S23 31.0	5.1	58.3
07	285 56.6	22.2	248 03.5	6.5	23 25.9	5.2	58.3
T 08	300 56.3	22.3	262 29.0	6.6	23 20.7	5.3	58.3
H 09	315 56.0 ..	22.4	276 54.6	6.6	23 15.4	5.5	58.2
U 10	330 55.7	22.5	291 20.2	6.8	23 09.9	5.7	58.2
R 11	345 55.4	22.5	305 46.0	6.9	23 04.2	5.7	58.1
S 12	0 55.1	S23 22.6	320 11.9	7.0	S22 58.5	5.9	58.1
D 13	15 54.7	22.7	334 37.9	7.0	22 52.6	6.0	58.1
A 14	30 54.4	22.8	349 03.9	7.2	22 46.6	6.2	58.0
Y 15	45 54.1 ..	22.8	3 30.1	7.3	22 40.4	6.3	58.0
16	60 53.8	22.9	17 56.4	7.4	22 34.1	6.4	58.0
17	75 53.5	23.0	32 22.8	7.5	22 27.7	6.5	57.9
18	90 53.2	S23 23.1	46 49.3	7.6	S22 21.2	6.6	57.9
19	105 52.9	23.1	61 15.9	7.7	22 14.6	6.8	57.8
20	120 52.6	23.2	75 42.6	7.8	22 07.8	6.9	57.8
21	135 52.3 ..	23.3	90 09.4	7.9	22 00.9	7.0	57.8
22	150 52.0	23.3	104 36.3	8.0	21 53.9	7.1	57.7
23	165 51.7	23.4	119 03.3	8.2	21 46.8	7.3	57.7
18 00	180 51.4	S23 23.5	133 30.5	8.2	S21 39.5	7.4	57.7
01	195 51.1	23.5	147 57.7	8.3	21 32.1	7.4	57.6
02	210 50.7	23.6	162 25.0	8.5	21 24.7	7.6	57.6
03	225 50.4 ..	23.7	176 52.5	8.6	21 17.1	7.7	57.5
04	240 50.1	23.7	191 20.1	8.6	21 09.4	7.8	57.5
05	255 49.8	23.8	205 47.7	8.8	21 01.6	7.9	57.5
06	270 49.5	S23 23.9	220 15.5	8.9	S20 53.7	8.0	57.4
07	285 49.2	23.9	234 43.4	9.0	20 45.7	8.1	57.4
F 08	300 48.9	24.0	249 11.4	9.1	20 37.6	8.2	57.4
R 09	315 48.6 ..	24.0	263 39.5	9.2	20 29.4	8.4	57.3
I 10	330 48.3	24.1	278 07.7	9.4	20 21.0	8.4	57.3
D 11	345 48.0	24.2	292 36.1	9.4	20 12.6	8.5	57.3
A 12	0 47.7	S23 24.2	307 04.5	9.5	S20 04.1	8.6	57.2
Y 13	15 47.3	24.3	321 33.0	9.7	19 55.5	8.7	57.2
14	30 47.0	24.3	336 01.7	9.8	19 46.8	8.8	57.1
15	45 46.7 ..	24.4	350 30.5	9.8	19 38.0	8.9	57.1
16	60 46.4	24.4	4 59.3	10.0	19 29.1	9.0	57.1
17	75 46.1	24.5	19 28.3	10.1	19 20.1	9.1	57.0
18	90 45.8	S23 24.5	33 57.4	10.2	S19 11.0	9.1	57.0
19	105 45.5	24.6	48 26.6	10.3	19 01.9	9.3	57.0
20	120 45.2	24.7	62 55.9	10.4	18 52.6	9.3	56.9
21	135 44.9 ..	24.7	77 25.3	10.5	18 43.3	9.4	56.9
22	150 44.6	24.8	91 54.8	10.6	18 33.9	9.5	56.9
23	165 44.3	24.8	106 24.4	10.7	18 24.4	9.6	56.8
19 00	180 43.9	S23 24.8	120 54.1	10.8	S18 14.8	9.7	56.8
01	195 43.6	24.9	135 23.9	10.9	18 05.1	9.7	56.7
02	210 43.3	24.9	149 53.8	11.1	17 55.4	9.8	56.7
03	225 43.0 ..	25.0	164 23.9	11.1	17 45.6	9.9	56.7
04	240 42.7	25.0	178 54.0	11.2	17 35.7	10.0	56.6
05	255 42.4	25.1	193 24.2	11.4	17 25.7	10.0	56.6
06	270 42.1	S23 25.1	207 54.6	11.4	S17 15.7	10.1	56.6
07	285 41.8	25.2	222 25.0	11.5	17 05.6	10.2	56.5
S 08	300 41.5	25.2	236 55.5	11.7	16 55.4	10.3	56.5
A 09	315 41.2 ..	25.2	251 26.2	11.7	16 45.1	10.3	56.5
T 10	330 40.8	25.3	265 56.9	11.8	16 34.8	10.4	56.4
U 11	345 40.5	25.3	280 27.7	11.9	16 24.4	10.4	56.4
R 12	0 40.2	S23 25.4	294 58.6	12.1	S16 14.0	10.5	56.4
D 13	15 39.9	25.4	309 29.7	12.1	16 03.5	10.6	56.3
A 14	30 39.6	25.4	324 00.8	12.2	15 52.9	10.7	56.3
Y 15	45 39.3 ..	25.5	338 32.0	12.3	15 42.2	10.7	56.3
16	60 39.0	25.5	353 03.3	12.4	15 31.5	10.7	56.2
17	75 38.7	25.5	7 34.7	12.5	15 20.8	10.8	56.2
18	90 38.4	S23 25.6	22 06.2	12.5	S15 10.0	10.9	56.2
19	105 38.1	25.6	36 37.7	12.7	14 59.1	10.9	56.1
20	120 37.7	25.6	51 09.4	12.8	14 48.2	11.0	56.1
21	135 37.4 ..	25.7	65 41.2	12.8	14 37.2	11.1	56.1
22	150 37.1	25.7	80 13.0	13.0	14 26.1	11.0	56.0
23	165 36.8	25.7	94 45.0	13.0	S14 15.1	11.2	56.0
	SD 16.3 d 0.1		SD 15.8		15.6		15.4

Lat.	Twilight Naut.	Twilight Civil	Sunrise	Moonrise 17	Moonrise 18	Moonrise 19	Moonrise 20
°	h m	h m	h m	h m	h m	h m	h m
N 72	08 24	10 55	■■	■■	■■	14 30	13 44
N 70	08 04	09 52	■■	■■	15 01	13 52	13 25
68	07 48	09 17	■■	■■	13 51	13 25	13 10
66	07 35	08 52	10 32	13 31	13 14	13 05	12 57
64	07 24	08 32	09 50	12 44	12 48	12 48	12 47
62	07 14	08 16	09 22	12 13	12 27	12 34	12 38
60	07 06	08 03	09 00	11 50	12 10	12 23	12 31
N 58	06 58	07 51	08 43	11 31	11 56	12 12	12 24
56	06 51	07 41	08 28	11 15	11 44	12 03	12 18
54	06 45	07 31	08 15	11 02	11 33	11 55	12 12
52	06 40	07 23	08 04	10 50	11 23	11 48	12 08
50	06 34	07 16	07 54	10 39	11 15	11 42	12 03
45	06 22	07 00	07 34	10 17	10 57	11 28	11 53
N 40	06 12	06 46	07 17	10 00	10 42	11 16	11 45
35	06 03	06 34	07 03	09 45	10 29	11 07	11 39
30	05 54	06 24	06 50	09 32	10 18	10 58	11 32
20	05 38	06 05	06 29	09 09	09 59	10 43	11 22
N 10	05 21	05 48	06 10	08 50	09 42	10 30	11 12
0	05 04	05 31	05 53	08 32	09 27	10 17	11 04
S 10	04 45	05 12	05 35	08 14	09 11	10 05	10 55
20	04 23	04 52	05 17	07 54	08 54	09 52	10 45
30	03 54	04 27	04 54	07 32	08 35	09 36	10 34
35	03 35	04 12	04 41	07 19	08 24	09 27	10 28
40	03 12	03 54	04 26	07 03	08 11	09 17	10 21
45	02 41	03 31	04 08	06 45	07 55	09 05	10 13
S 50	01 56	03 01	03 46	06 23	07 36	08 51	10 03
52	01 28	02 46	03 35	06 12	07 27	08 44	09 58
54	00 42	02 28	03 23	06 00	07 17	08 36	09 53
56	////	02 06	03 08	05 45	07 06	08 28	09 47
58	////	01 36	02 52	05 29	06 53	08 18	09 40
S 60	////	00 46	02 31	05 09	06 37	08 07	09 33

Lat.	Sunset	Twilight Civil	Twilight Naut.	Moonset 17	Moonset 18	Moonset 19	Moonset 20
°	h m	h m	h m	h m	h m	h m	h m
N 72	■■	12 59	15 30	■■	■■	18 48	21 08
N 70	■■	14 01	15 50	■■	16 33	19 24	21 25
68	■■	14 36	16 06	■■	17 42	19 50	21 39
66	13 21	15 02	16 19	16 09	18 18	20 09	21 49
64	14 03	15 21	16 30	16 56	18 43	20 24	21 58
62	14 32	15 37	16 39	17 26	19 03	20 37	22 06
60	14 53	15 51	16 48	17 49	19 19	20 48	22 13
N 58	15 11	16 03	16 55	18 07	19 33	20 57	22 19
56	15 26	16 13	17 02	18 22	19 44	21 06	22 24
54	15 38	16 22	17 08	18 35	19 55	21 13	22 28
52	15 49	16 30	17 14	18 47	20 04	21 19	22 32
50	15 59	16 38	17 19	18 57	20 12	21 25	22 36
45	16 20	16 54	17 31	19 18	20 29	21 38	22 44
N 40	16 37	17 07	17 41	19 35	20 43	21 48	22 51
35	16 51	17 19	17 51	19 50	20 55	21 57	22 56
30	17 03	17 30	18 00	20 02	21 05	22 05	23 01
20	17 25	17 49	18 16	20 23	21 22	22 18	23 10
N 10	17 43	18 06	18 32	20 42	21 37	22 29	23 18
0	18 01	18 23	18 49	20 59	21 52	22 40	23 25
S 10	18 18	18 41	19 08	21 16	22 06	22 51	23 32
20	18 37	19 02	19 31	21 34	22 20	23 02	23 39
30	18 59	19 27	20 00	21 54	22 37	23 15	23 47
35	19 12	19 42	20 19	22 06	22 47	23 22	23 52
40	19 27	20 00	20 42	22 20	22 58	23 30	23 57
45	19 45	20 23	21 13	22 36	23 12	23 40	24 04
S 50	20 08	20 53	21 58	22 56	23 27	23 51	24 11
52	20 19	21 08	22 26	23 06	23 35	23 57	24 14
54	20 31	21 26	23 13	23 16	23 43	24 03	00 03
56	20 45	21 48	////	23 28	23 52	24 09	00 09
58	21 02	22 18	////	23 42	24 03	00 03	00 17
S 60	21 23	23 09	////	23 58	24 15	00 15	00 25

Day	SUN Eqn. of Time 00ʰ	SUN Eqn. of Time 12ʰ	SUN Mer. Pass.	MOON Mer. Pass. Upper	MOON Mer. Pass. Lower	Age	Phase
d	m s	m s	h m	h m	h m	d	%
17	03 56	03 41	11 56	14 45	02 17	03	10
18	03 26	03 11	11 57	15 39	03 13	04	18
19	02 56	02 42	11 57	16 29	04 05	05	26

UT	ARIES GHA	VENUS −3·9 GHA	VENUS Dec	MARS −0·5 GHA	MARS Dec	JUPITER −2·0 GHA	JUPITER Dec	SATURN +0·6 GHA	SATURN Dec	STARS Name	SHA	Dec
20 00	89 02.2	205 20.8	S20 05.7	68 23.8	N 9 19.8	146 38.7	S20 35.7	146 27.7	S20 27.2	Acamar	315 14.0	S40 13.5
01	104 04.7	220 20.0	06.3	83 25.4	20.2	161 40.5	35.6	161 29.9	27.2	Achernar	335 22.5	S57 08.2
02	119 07.1	235 19.2	07.0	98 27.0	20.6	176 42.4	35.5	176 32.1	27.1	Acrux	173 03.7	S63 12.5
03	134 09.6	250 18.5 . .	07.6	113 28.7 . .	21.0	191 44.3 . .	35.4	191 34.3 . .	27.0	Adhara	255 08.1	S29 00.0
04	149 12.1	265 17.7	08.2	128 30.3	21.4	206 46.2	35.3	206 36.5	27.0	Aldebaran	290 43.1	N16 33.0
05	164 14.5	280 16.9	08.9	143 31.9	21.8	221 48.1	35.1	221 38.6	26.9			
06	179 17.0	295 16.1	S20 09.5	158 33.5	N 9 22.2	236 50.0	S20 35.0	236 40.8	S20 26.9	Alioth	166 16.1	N55 50.6
07	194 19.5	310 15.3	10.1	173 35.2	22.6	251 51.9	34.9	251 43.0	26.8	Alkaid	152 54.9	N49 12.4
S 08	209 21.9	325 14.5	10.8	188 36.8	23.0	266 53.8	34.8	266 45.2	26.8	Alnair	27 37.4	S46 51.8
U 09	224 24.4	340 13.7 . .	11.4	203 38.4 . .	23.4	281 55.7 . .	34.7	281 47.4 . .	26.7	Alnilam	275 40.7	S 1 11.4
N 10	239 26.8	355 12.9	12.0	218 40.1	23.8	296 57.6	34.6	296 49.6	26.7	Alphard	217 50.8	S 8 44.9
11	254 29.3	10 12.1	12.7	233 41.7	24.2	311 59.5	34.4	311 51.7	26.6			
D 12	269 31.8	25 11.3	S20 13.3	248 43.3	N 9 24.6	327 01.4	S20 34.3	326 53.9	S20 26.6	Alphecca	126 06.9	N26 38.7
A 13	284 34.2	40 10.5	13.9	263 44.9	25.0	342 03.3	34.2	341 56.1	26.5	Alpheratz	357 38.1	N29 12.4
Y 14	299 36.7	55 09.7	14.5	278 46.6	25.4	357 05.2	34.1	356 58.3	26.4	Altair	62 03.5	N 8 55.5
15	314 39.2	70 08.9 . .	15.2	293 48.2 . .	25.8	12 07.0 . .	34.0	12 00.5 . .	26.4	Ankaa	353 10.4	S42 11.9
16	329 41.6	85 08.1	15.8	308 49.8	26.2	27 08.9	33.9	27 02.7	26.3	Antares	112 20.2	S26 28.5
17	344 44.1	100 07.3	16.4	323 51.4	26.6	42 10.8	33.8	42 04.8	26.3			
18	359 46.6	115 06.5	S20 17.0	338 53.0	N 9 27.0	57 12.7	S20 33.6	57 07.0	S20 26.2	Arcturus	145 51.2	N19 04.4
19	14 49.0	130 05.7	17.7	353 54.7	27.4	72 14.6	33.5	72 09.2	26.2	Atria	107 17.9	S69 03.7
20	29 51.5	145 04.9	18.3	8 56.3	27.8	87 16.5	33.4	87 11.4	26.1	Avior	234 15.4	S59 34.4
21	44 54.0	160 04.1 . .	18.9	23 57.9 . .	28.2	102 18.4 . .	33.3	102 13.6 . .	26.1	Bellatrix	278 26.1	N 6 22.0
22	59 56.4	175 03.3	19.5	38 59.5	28.6	117 20.3	33.2	117 15.8	26.0	Betelgeuse	270 55.3	N 7 24.6
23	74 58.9	190 02.4	20.1	54 01.1	29.0	132 22.2	33.1	132 17.9	25.9			
21 00	90 01.3	205 01.6	S20 20.7	69 02.8	N 9 29.4	147 24.1	S20 33.0	147 20.1	S20 25.9	Canopus	263 53.3	S52 42.4
01	105 03.8	220 00.8	21.4	84 04.4	29.8	162 26.0	32.8	162 22.3	25.8	Capella	280 26.3	N46 01.1
02	120 06.3	235 00.0	22.0	99 06.0	30.2	177 27.8	32.7	177 24.5	25.8	Deneb	49 28.4	N45 21.4
03	135 08.7	249 59.2 . .	22.6	114 07.6 . .	30.7	192 29.7 . .	32.6	192 26.7 . .	25.7	Denebola	182 28.3	N14 27.3
04	150 11.2	264 58.4	23.2	129 09.2	31.1	207 31.6	32.5	207 28.8	25.7	Diphda	348 50.6	S17 52.5
05	165 13.7	279 57.6	23.8	144 10.8	31.5	222 33.5	32.4	222 31.0	25.6			
06	180 16.1	294 56.8	S20 24.4	159 12.4	N 9 31.9	237 35.4	S20 32.3	237 33.2	S20 25.5	Dubhe	193 45.0	N61 38.1
07	195 18.6	309 56.0	25.0	174 14.1	32.3	252 37.3	32.1	252 35.4	25.5	Elnath	278 05.6	N28 37.4
08	210 21.1	324 55.2	25.6	189 15.7	32.7	267 39.2	32.0	267 37.6	25.4	Eltanin	90 44.3	N51 29.2
M 09	225 23.5	339 54.4 . .	26.2	204 17.3 . .	33.1	282 41.1 . .	31.9	282 39.8 . .	25.4	Enif	33 42.2	N 9 58.3
O 10	240 26.0	354 53.6	26.8	219 18.9	33.5	297 43.0	31.8	297 41.9	25.3	Fomalhaut	15 18.3	S29 30.9
N 11	255 28.4	9 52.8	27.4	234 20.5	33.9	312 44.9	31.7	312 44.1	25.3			
D 12	270 30.9	24 51.9	S20 28.0	249 22.1	N 9 34.3	327 46.8	S20 31.6	327 46.3	S20 25.2	Gacrux	171 55.3	S57 13.4
A 13	285 33.4	39 51.1	28.6	264 23.7	34.7	342 48.6	31.4	342 48.5	25.2	Gienah	175 47.0	S17 39.3
Y 14	300 35.8	54 50.3	29.2	279 25.3	35.1	357 50.5	31.3	357 50.7	25.1	Hadar	148 40.9	S60 28.0
15	315 38.3	69 49.5 . .	29.8	294 26.9 . .	35.5	12 52.4 . .	31.2	12 52.9 . .	25.0	Hamal	327 54.7	N23 33.7
16	330 40.8	84 48.7	30.4	309 28.5	35.9	27 54.3	31.1	27 55.0	25.0	Kaus Aust.	83 37.3	S34 22.4
17	345 43.2	99 47.9	31.0	324 30.1	36.3	42 56.2	31.0	42 57.2	24.9			
18	0 45.7	114 47.1	S20 31.6	339 31.7	N 9 36.7	57 58.1	S20 30.9	57 59.4	S20 24.9	Kochab	137 20.8	N74 04.0
19	15 48.2	129 46.3	32.2	354 33.3	37.2	73 00.0	30.7	73 01.6	24.8	Markab	13 33.2	N15 19.1
20	30 50.6	144 45.4	32.8	9 34.9	37.6	88 01.9	30.6	88 03.8	24.8	Menkar	314 09.3	N 4 10.2
21	45 53.1	159 44.6 . .	33.4	24 36.6 . .	38.0	103 03.8 . .	30.5	103 05.9 . .	24.7	Menkent	148 01.7	S36 28.1
22	60 55.6	174 43.8	34.0	39 38.2	38.4	118 05.7	30.4	118 08.1	24.7	Miaplacidus	221 38.1	S69 47.9
23	75 58.0	189 43.0	34.6	54 39.8	38.8	133 07.5	30.3	133 10.3	24.6			
22 00	91 00.5	204 42.2	S20 35.2	69 41.4	N 9 39.2	148 09.4	S20 30.2	148 12.5	S20 24.5	Mirfak	308 32.5	N49 56.2
01	106 02.9	219 41.4	35.8	84 43.0	39.6	163 11.3	30.0	163 14.7	24.5	Nunki	75 52.2	S26 16.2
02	121 05.4	234 40.5	36.4	99 44.6	40.0	178 13.2	29.9	178 16.8	24.4	Peacock	53 11.5	S56 40.2
03	136 07.9	249 39.7 . .	37.0	114 46.2 . .	40.4	193 15.1 . .	29.8	193 19.0 . .	24.4	Pollux	243 21.0	N27 58.4
04	151 10.3	264 38.9	37.5	129 47.7	40.8	208 17.0	29.7	208 21.2	24.3	Procyon	244 54.0	N 5 10.2
05	166 12.8	279 38.1	38.1	144 49.3	41.2	223 18.9	29.6	223 23.4	24.3			
06	181 15.3	294 37.3	S20 38.7	159 50.9	N 9 41.6	238 20.8	S20 29.5	238 25.6	S20 24.2	Rasalhague	96 02.0	N12 32.8
07	196 17.7	309 36.5	39.3	174 52.5	42.0	253 22.7	29.3	253 27.8	24.1	Regulus	207 37.8	N11 51.9
T 08	211 20.2	324 35.6	39.9	189 54.1	42.5	268 24.5	29.2	268 29.9	24.1	Rigel	281 06.7	S 8 10.7
U 09	226 22.7	339 34.8 . .	40.5	204 55.7 . .	42.9	283 26.4 . .	29.1	283 32.1 . .	24.0	Rigil Kent.	139 45.2	S60 54.9
E 10	241 25.1	354 34.0	41.0	219 57.3	43.3	298 28.3	29.0	298 34.3	24.0	Sabik	102 06.9	S15 44.9
S 11	256 27.6	9 33.2	41.6	234 58.9	43.7	313 30.2	28.9	313 36.5	23.9			
D 12	271 30.0	24 32.4	S20 42.2	250 00.5	N 9 44.1	328 32.1	S20 28.8	328 38.7	S20 23.9	Schedar	349 34.5	N56 39.3
A 13	286 32.5	39 31.5	42.8	265 02.1	44.5	343 34.0	28.6	343 40.8	23.8	Shaula	96 15.3	S37 07.0
Y 14	301 35.0	54 30.7	43.4	280 03.7	44.9	358 35.9	28.5	358 43.0	23.8	Sirius	258 28.8	S16 44.7
15	316 37.4	69 29.9 . .	43.9	295 05.3 . .	45.3	13 37.8 . .	28.4	13 45.2 . .	23.7	Spica	158 25.9	S11 16.1
16	331 39.9	84 29.1	44.5	310 06.9	45.7	28 39.6	28.3	28 47.4	23.6	Suhail	222 48.3	S43 30.8
17	346 42.4	99 28.2	45.1	325 08.5	46.1	43 41.5	28.2	43 49.6	23.6			
18	1 44.8	114 27.4	S20 45.7	340 10.0	N 9 46.6	58 43.4	S20 28.1	58 51.7	S20 23.5	Vega	80 35.9	N38 48.2
19	16 47.3	129 26.6	46.2	355 11.6	47.0	73 45.3	27.9	73 53.9	23.5	Zuben'ubi	136 59.9	S16 07.5
20	31 49.8	144 25.8	46.8	10 13.2	47.4	88 47.2	27.8	88 56.1	23.4		SHA	Mer.Pass.
21	46 52.2	159 24.9 . .	47.4	25 14.8 . .	47.8	103 49.1 . .	27.7	103 58.3 . .	23.4		° ′	h m
22	61 54.7	174 24.1	47.9	40 16.4	48.2	118 51.0	27.6	119 00.5	23.3	Venus	115 00.3	10 20
23	76 57.2	189 23.3	48.5	55 18.0	48.6	133 52.9	27.5	134 02.6	23.2	Mars	339 01.4	19 22
	h m									Jupiter	57 22.7	14 09
Mer.Pass. 17 57.0		v −0.8	d 0.6	v 1.6	d 0.4	v 1.9	d 0.1	v 2.2	d 0.1	Saturn	57 18.8	14 09

UT	SUN GHA	Dec	MOON GHA	v	Dec	d	HP
d h	° ′	° ′	° ′	′	° ′	′	′
20 00	180 36.5	S23 25.8	109 17.0	13.1	S14 03.9	11.2	56.0
01	195 36.2	25.8	123 49.1	13.2	13 52.7	11.2	55.9
02	210 35.9	25.8	138 21.3	13.2	13 41.5	11.3	55.9
03	225 35.6 ..	25.8	152 53.5	13.4	13 30.2	11.3	55.9
04	240 35.3	25.9	167 25.9	13.4	13 18.9	11.4	55.8
05	255 34.9	25.9	181 58.3	13.6	13 07.5	11.5	55.8
06	270 34.6	S23 25.9	196 30.9	13.6	S12 56.0	11.4	55.8
07	285 34.3	25.9	211 03.5	13.6	12 44.6	11.5	55.8
08	300 34.0	25.9	225 36.1	13.8	12 33.1	11.6	55.7
S 09	315 33.7 ..	26.0	240 08.9	13.8	12 21.5	11.6	55.7
U 10	330 33.4	26.0	254 41.7	13.9	12 09.9	11.6	55.7
N 11	345 33.1	26.0	269 14.6	14.0	11 58.3	11.7	55.6
D 12	0 32.8	S23 26.0	283 47.6	14.1	S11 46.6	11.7	55.6
A 13	15 32.5	26.0	298 20.7	14.1	11 34.9	11.7	55.6
Y 14	30 32.2	26.1	312 53.8	14.2	11 23.2	11.8	55.5
15	45 31.8 ..	26.1	327 27.0	14.3	11 11.4	11.8	55.5
16	60 31.5	26.1	342 00.3	14.3	10 59.6	11.9	55.5
17	75 31.2	26.1	356 33.6	14.4	10 47.7	11.9	55.5
18	90 30.9	S23 26.1	11 07.0	14.5	S10 35.8	11.9	55.4
19	105 30.6	26.1	25 40.5	14.5	10 23.9	11.9	55.4
20	120 30.3	26.1	40 14.0	14.7	10 12.0	12.0	55.4
21	135 30.0 ..	26.2	54 47.7	14.6	10 00.0	12.0	55.4
22	150 29.7	26.2	69 21.3	14.8	9 48.0	12.1	55.3
23	165 29.4	26.2	83 55.1	14.8	9 35.9	12.0	55.3
21 00	180 29.0	S23 26.2	98 28.9	14.8	S 9 23.9	12.1	55.3
01	195 28.7	26.2	113 02.7	14.9	9 11.8	12.1	55.3
02	210 28.4	26.2	127 36.6	15.0	8 59.7	12.2	55.2
03	225 28.1 ..	26.2	142 10.6	15.1	8 47.5	12.1	55.2
04	240 27.8	26.2	156 44.7	15.0	8 35.4	12.2	55.2
05	255 27.5	26.2	171 18.7	15.2	8 23.2	12.2	55.2
06	270 27.2	S23 26.2	185 52.9	15.2	S 8 11.0	12.3	55.1
07	285 26.9	26.2	200 27.1	15.3	7 58.7	12.2	55.1
08	300 26.6	26.2	215 01.4	15.3	7 46.5	12.3	55.1
M 09	315 26.2 ..	26.2	229 35.7	15.3	7 34.2	12.3	55.1
O 10	330 25.9	26.2	244 10.0	15.4	7 21.9	12.3	55.0
N 11	345 25.6	26.2	258 44.4	15.5	7 09.6	12.4	55.0
D 12	0 25.3	S23 26.2	273 18.9	15.5	S 6 57.2	12.3	55.0
A 13	15 25.0	26.2	287 53.4	15.6	6 44.9	12.4	55.0
Y 14	30 24.7	26.2	302 27.9	15.6	6 32.5	12.3	54.9
15	45 24.4 ..	26.2	317 02.5	15.7	6 20.2	12.4	54.9
16	60 24.1	26.2	331 37.2	15.7	6 07.8	12.4	54.9
17	75 23.8	26.2	346 11.9	15.7	5 55.4	12.5	54.9
18	90 23.4	S23 26.2	0 46.6	15.8	S 5 42.9	12.4	54.9
19	105 23.1	26.2	15 21.4	15.8	5 30.5	12.5	54.8
20	120 22.8	26.2	29 56.2	15.8	5 18.0	12.4	54.8
21	135 22.5 ..	26.2	44 31.0	15.9	5 05.6	12.5	54.8
22	150 22.2	26.2	59 05.9	15.9	4 53.1	12.5	54.8
23	165 21.9	26.2	73 40.8	16.0	4 40.6	12.4	54.8
22 00	180 21.6	S23 26.1	88 15.8	16.0	S 4 28.2	12.5	54.7
01	195 21.3	26.1	102 50.8	16.0	4 15.7	12.5	54.7
02	210 21.0	26.1	117 25.8	16.1	4 03.2	12.6	54.7
03	225 20.6 ..	26.1	132 00.9	16.1	3 50.6	12.5	54.7
04	240 20.3	26.1	146 36.0	16.1	3 38.1	12.5	54.7
05	255 20.0	26.1	161 11.1	16.1	3 25.6	12.5	54.7
06	270 19.7	S23 26.0	175 46.2	16.2	S 3 13.1	12.6	54.6
07	285 19.4	26.0	190 21.4	16.2	3 00.5	12.5	54.6
T 08	300 19.1	26.0	204 56.6	16.2	2 48.0	12.5	54.6
U 09	315 18.8 ..	26.0	219 31.8	16.3	2 35.5	12.6	54.6
E 10	330 18.5	26.0	234 07.1	16.3	2 22.9	12.5	54.6
S 11	345 18.2	26.0	248 42.4	16.3	2 10.4	12.6	54.6
D 12	0 17.8	S23 26.0	263 17.7	16.3	S 1 57.8	12.5	54.5
A 13	15 17.5	25.9	277 53.0	16.3	1 45.3	12.6	54.5
Y 14	30 17.2	25.9	292 28.3	16.4	1 32.7	12.5	54.5
15	45 16.9 ..	25.9	307 03.7	16.4	1 20.2	12.5	54.5
16	60 16.6	25.9	321 39.1	16.4	1 07.7	12.6	54.5
17	75 16.3	25.8	336 14.5	16.4	0 55.1	12.5	54.5
18	90 16.0	S23 25.8	350 49.9	16.4	S 0 42.6	12.6	54.4
19	105 15.7	25.8	5 25.3	16.5	0 30.0	12.5	54.4
20	120 15.4	25.8	20 00.8	16.4	0 17.5	12.5	54.4
21	135 15.1 ..	25.7	34 36.2	16.5	S 0 05.0	12.5	54.4
22	150 14.7	25.7	49 11.7	16.5	N 0 07.5	12.6	54.4
23	165 14.4	25.7	63 47.2	16.5	N 0 20.1	12.5	54.4
	SD 16.3 d 0.0		SD 15.2	15.0		14.9	

Lat.	Twilight Naut.	Twilight Civil	Sunrise	Moonrise 20	21	22	23
°	h m	h m	h m	h m	h m	h m	h m
N 72	08 26	10 58	■■	13 44	13 15	12 51	12 29
N 70	08 06	09 55	■■	13 25	13 06	12 49	12 33
68	07 50	09 19	■■	13 10	12 58	12 47	12 37
66	07 37	08 54	10 35	12 57	12 51	12 45	12 39
64	07 26	08 34	09 52	12 47	12 46	12 44	12 42
62	07 16	08 18	09 24	12 38	12 41	12 44	12 44
60	07 07	08 04	09 02	12 31	12 36	12 41	12 46
N 58	07 00	07 53	08 45	12 24	12 33	12 40	12 48
56	06 53	07 42	08 30	12 18	12 29	12 39	12 49
54	06 47	07 33	08 17	12 12	12 26	12 39	12 50
52	06 41	07 25	08 06	12 08	12 24	12 38	12 52
50	06 36	07 18	07 56	12 03	12 21	12 37	12 53
45	06 24	07 01	07 35	11 53	12 16	12 36	12 55
N 40	06 14	06 48	07 18	11 45	12 11	12 34	12 57
35	06 04	06 36	07 04	11 39	12 07	12 33	12 59
30	05 56	06 25	06 52	11 32	12 03	12 32	13 01
20	05 39	06 07	06 31	11 22	11 57	12 31	13 03
N 10	05 23	05 49	06 12	11 12	11 52	12 29	13 06
0	05 06	05 32	05 55	11 04	11 47	12 28	13 08
S 10	04 47	05 14	05 37	10 55	11 42	12 27	13 11
20	04 24	04 53	05 18	10 45	11 36	12 25	13 13
30	03 55	04 28	04 56	10 34	11 30	12 24	13 16
35	03 36	04 13	04 43	10 28	11 26	12 23	13 18
40	03 13	03 55	04 28	10 21	11 22	12 22	13 20
45	02 42	03 32	04 10	10 13	11 17	12 20	13 22
S 50	01 57	03 02	03 47	10 03	11 12	12 19	13 25
52	01 29	02 47	03 36	09 58	11 09	12 18	13 26
54	00 41	02 29	03 24	09 53	11 06	12 17	13 27
56	////	02 07	03 10	09 47	11 03	12 17	13 29
58	////	01 37	02 53	09 40	10 59	12 16	13 31
S 60	////	00 45	02 32	09 33	10 55	12 15	13 33

Lat.	Sunset	Twilight Civil	Twilight Naut.	Moonset 20	21	22	23
°	h m	h m	h m	h m	h m	h m	h m
N 72	■■	12 59	15 31	21 08	23 06	24 56	00 56
N 70	■■	14 02	15 51	21 25	23 13	24 55	00 55
68	■■	14 37	16 07	21 39	23 19	24 54	00 54
66	13 22	15 03	16 20	21 49	23 23	24 54	00 54
64	14 04	15 22	16 31	21 58	23 27	24 53	00 53
62	14 33	15 39	16 41	22 06	23 31	24 53	00 53
60	14 54	15 52	16 49	22 13	23 34	24 52	00 52
N 58	15 12	16 04	16 57	22 19	23 36	24 52	00 52
56	15 27	16 14	17 03	22 24	23 39	24 52	00 52
54	15 39	16 23	17 10	22 28	23 41	24 51	00 51
52	15 51	16 32	17 15	22 32	23 43	24 51	00 51
50	16 01	16 39	17 21	22 36	23 44	24 51	00 51
45	16 21	16 55	17 32	22 44	23 48	24 50	00 50
N 40	16 38	17 09	17 43	22 51	23 51	24 50	00 50
35	16 52	17 21	17 52	22 56	23 54	24 49	00 49
30	17 05	17 31	18 01	23 01	23 56	24 49	00 49
20	17 26	17 50	18 18	23 10	24 00	00 00	00 48
N 10	17 45	18 07	18 34	23 18	24 03	00 03	00 48
0	18 02	18 25	18 51	23 25	24 07	00 07	00 47
S 10	18 20	18 43	19 10	23 32	24 10	00 10	00 47
20	18 39	19 03	19 33	23 39	24 13	00 13	00 46
30	19 01	19 28	20 02	23 47	24 17	00 17	00 46
35	19 14	19 44	20 20	23 52	24 19	00 19	00 45
40	19 29	20 02	20 44	23 57	24 22	00 22	00 45
45	19 47	20 24	21 14	24 04	00 04	00 25	00 44
S 50	20 10	20 54	22 00	24 11	00 11	00 28	00 44
52	20 20	21 09	22 28	24 14	00 14	00 30	00 44
54	20 33	21 27	23 15	00 03	00 18	00 31	00 43
56	20 47	21 50	////	00 09	00 22	00 33	00 43
58	21 04	22 20	////	00 17	00 27	00 35	00 43
S 60	21 24	23 11	////	00 25	00 32	00 37	00 42

Day	SUN Eqn. of Time 00h	12h	Mer. Pass.	MOON Mer. Pass. Upper	Lower	Age	Phase
d	m s	m s	h m	h m	h m	d	%
20	02 27	02 12	11 58	17 14	04 52	06	36
21	01 57	01 42	11 58	17 57	05 36	07	45
22	01 27	01 12	11 59	18 38	06 17	08	55

2020 DECEMBER 23, 24, 25 (WED., THURS., FRI.)

UT	ARIES GHA	VENUS −3.9 GHA	VENUS Dec	MARS −0.4 GHA	MARS Dec	JUPITER −2.0 GHA	JUPITER Dec	SATURN +0.6 GHA	SATURN Dec	Star Name	SHA	Dec
23 00	91 59.6	204 22.5	S20 49.1	70 19.6	N 9 49.0	148 54.7	S20 27.3	149 04.8	S20 23.2	Acamar	315 14.0	S40 13.5
01	107 02.1	219 21.6	.. 49.6	85 21.1	.. 49.4	163 56.6	.. 27.2	164 07.0	.. 23.1	Achernar	335 22.5	S57 08.2
02	122 04.5	234 20.8	.. 50.2	100 22.7	.. 49.8	178 58.5	.. 27.1	179 09.2	.. 23.1	Acrux	173 03.6	S63 12.5
03	137 07.0	249 20.0	.. 50.8	115 24.3	.. 50.3	194 00.4	.. 27.0	194 11.4	.. 23.0	Adhara	255 08.0	S29 00.0
04	152 09.5	264 19.2	.. 51.3	130 25.9	.. 50.7	209 02.3	.. 26.9	209 13.5	.. 23.0	Aldebaran	290 43.1	N16 33.0
05	167 11.9	279 18.3	.. 51.9	145 27.5	.. 51.1	224 04.2	.. 26.8	224 15.7	.. 22.9			
W 06	182 14.4	294 17.5	S20 52.4	160 29.1	N 9 51.5	239 06.1	S20 26.6	239 17.9	S20 22.8	Alioth	166 16.1	N55 50.6
E 07	197 16.9	309 16.7	.. 53.0	175 30.6	.. 51.9	254 08.0	.. 26.5	254 20.1	.. 22.8	Alkaid	152 54.9	N49 12.4
D 08	212 19.3	324 15.8	.. 53.6	190 32.2	.. 52.3	269 09.8	.. 26.4	269 22.2	.. 22.7	Alnair	27 37.4	S46 51.8
N 09	227 21.8	339 15.0	.. 54.1	205 33.8	.. 52.7	284 11.7	.. 26.3	284 24.4	.. 22.7	Alnilam	275 40.7	S 1 11.4
E 10	242 24.3	354 14.2	.. 54.7	220 35.4	.. 53.1	299 13.6	.. 26.2	299 26.6	.. 22.6	Alphard	217 50.7	S 8 44.9
S 11	257 26.7	9 13.3	.. 55.2	235 36.9	.. 53.6	314 15.5	.. 26.0	314 28.8	.. 22.6			
D 12	272 29.2	24 12.5	S20 55.8	250 38.5	N 9 54.0	329 17.4	S20 25.9	329 31.0	S20 22.5	Alphecca	126 06.9	N26 38.7
A 13	287 31.7	39 11.7	.. 56.3	265 40.1	.. 54.4	344 19.3	.. 25.8	344 33.1	.. 22.4	Alpheratz	357 38.1	N29 12.4
Y 14	302 34.1	54 10.8	.. 56.9	280 41.7	.. 54.8	359 21.2	.. 25.7	359 35.3	.. 22.4	Altair	62 03.5	N 8 55.4
15	317 36.6	69 10.0	.. 57.4	295 43.2	.. 55.2	14 23.0	.. 25.6	14 37.5	.. 22.3	Ankaa	353 10.4	S42 11.9
16	332 39.0	84 09.2	.. 58.0	310 44.8	.. 55.6	29 24.9	.. 25.5	29 39.7	.. 22.3	Antares	112 20.2	S26 28.5
17	347 41.5	99 08.3	.. 58.5	325 46.4	.. 56.0	44 26.8	.. 25.3	44 41.9	.. 22.2			
18	2 44.0	114 07.5	S20 59.1	340 48.0	N 9 56.5	59 28.7	S20 25.2	59 44.0	S20 22.2	Arcturus	145 51.1	N19 04.4
19	17 46.4	129 06.7	20 59.6	355 49.5	.. 56.9	74 30.6	.. 25.1	74 46.2	.. 22.1	Atria	107 17.9	S69 03.7
20	32 48.9	144 05.8	21 00.2	10 51.1	.. 57.3	89 32.5	.. 25.0	89 48.4	.. 22.0	Avior	234 15.4	S59 34.4
21	47 51.4	159 05.0	.. 00.7	25 52.7	.. 57.7	104 34.4	.. 24.9	104 50.6	.. 22.0	Bellatrix	278 26.1	N 6 22.0
22	62 53.8	174 04.2	.. 01.3	40 54.3	.. 58.1	119 36.2	.. 24.7	119 52.8	.. 21.9	Betelgeuse	270 55.3	N 7 24.6
23	77 56.3	189 03.3	.. 01.8	55 55.8	.. 58.5	134 38.1	.. 24.6	134 54.9	.. 21.9			
24 00	92 58.8	204 02.5	S21 02.3	70 57.4	N 9 58.9	149 40.0	S20 24.5	149 57.1	S20 21.8	Canopus	263 53.3	S52 42.4
01	108 01.2	219 01.7	.. 02.9	85 59.0	.. 59.4	164 41.9	.. 24.4	164 59.3	.. 21.8	Capella	280 26.3	N46 01.1
02	123 03.7	234 00.8	.. 03.4	101 00.5	9 59.8	179 43.8	.. 24.3	180 01.5	.. 21.7	Deneb	49 28.4	N45 21.4
03	138 06.1	249 00.0	.. 04.0	116 02.1	10 00.2	194 45.7	.. 24.1	195 03.6	.. 21.6	Denebola	182 28.3	N14 27.3
04	153 08.6	263 59.1	.. 04.5	131 03.7	.. 00.6	209 47.6	.. 24.0	210 05.8	.. 21.6	Diphda	348 50.6	S17 52.5
05	168 11.1	278 58.3	.. 05.0	146 05.2	.. 01.0	224 49.4	.. 23.9	225 08.0	.. 21.5			
T 06	183 13.5	293 57.5	S21 05.6	161 06.8	N10 01.4	239 51.3	S20 23.8	240 10.2	S20 21.5	Dubhe	193 45.0	N61 38.1
H 07	198 16.0	308 56.6	.. 06.1	176 08.4	.. 01.8	254 53.2	.. 23.7	255 12.4	.. 21.4	Elnath	278 05.6	N28 37.4
U 08	213 18.5	323 55.8	.. 06.6	191 09.9	.. 02.3	269 55.1	.. 23.5	270 14.5	.. 21.4	Eltanin	90 44.3	N51 29.2
R 09	228 20.9	338 54.9	.. 07.2	206 11.5	.. 02.7	284 57.0	.. 23.4	285 16.7	.. 21.3	Enif	33 42.2	N 9 58.3
S 10	243 23.4	353 54.1	.. 07.7	221 13.0	.. 03.1	299 58.9	.. 23.3	300 18.9	.. 21.2	Fomalhaut	15 18.3	S29 30.9
D 11	258 25.9	8 53.3	.. 08.2	236 14.6	.. 03.5	315 00.8	.. 23.2	315 21.1	.. 21.2			
A 12	273 28.3	23 52.4	S21 08.8	251 16.2	N10 03.9	330 02.6	S20 23.1	330 23.2	S20 21.1	Gacrux	171 55.2	S57 13.4
Y 13	288 30.8	38 51.6	.. 09.3	266 17.7	.. 04.3	345 04.5	.. 22.9	345 25.4	.. 21.1	Gienah	175 47.0	S17 39.3
14	303 33.3	53 50.7	.. 09.8	281 19.3	.. 04.8	0 06.4	.. 22.8	0 27.6	.. 21.0	Hadar	148 40.9	S60 28.0
15	318 35.7	68 49.9	.. 10.3	296 20.8	.. 05.2	15 08.3	.. 22.7	15 29.8	.. 21.0	Hamal	327 54.7	N23 33.7
16	333 38.2	83 49.1	.. 10.9	311 22.4	.. 05.6	30 10.2	.. 22.6	30 31.9	.. 20.9	Kaus Aust.	83 37.3	S34 22.4
17	348 40.6	98 48.2	.. 11.4	326 24.0	.. 06.0	45 12.1	.. 22.5	45 34.1	.. 20.8			
18	3 43.1	113 47.4	S21 11.9	341 25.5	N10 06.4	60 13.9	S20 22.3	60 36.3	S20 20.8	Kochab	137 20.8	N74 04.0
19	18 45.6	128 46.5	.. 12.4	356 27.1	.. 06.8	75 15.8	.. 22.2	75 38.5	.. 20.7	Markab	13 33.2	N15 19.1
20	33 48.0	143 45.7	.. 12.9	11 28.6	.. 07.3	90 17.7	.. 22.1	90 40.7	.. 20.7	Menkar	314 09.3	N 4 10.2
21	48 50.5	158 44.8	.. 13.5	26 30.2	.. 07.7	105 19.6	.. 22.0	105 42.8	.. 20.6	Menkent	148 01.7	S36 28.1
22	63 53.0	173 44.0	.. 14.0	41 31.7	.. 08.1	120 21.5	.. 21.9	120 45.0	.. 20.6	Miaplacidus	221 38.1	S69 47.9
23	78 55.4	188 43.1	.. 14.5	56 33.3	.. 08.5	135 23.4	.. 21.7	135 47.2	.. 20.5			
25 00	93 57.9	203 42.3	S21 15.0	71 34.8	N10 08.9	150 25.2	S20 21.6	150 49.4	S20 20.4	Mirfak	308 32.5	N49 56.2
01	109 00.4	218 41.4	.. 15.5	86 36.4	.. 09.4	165 27.1	.. 21.5	165 51.5	.. 20.4	Nunki	75 52.2	S26 16.2
02	124 02.8	233 40.6	.. 16.0	101 38.0	.. 09.8	180 29.0	.. 21.4	180 53.7	.. 20.3	Peacock	53 11.5	S56 40.2
03	139 05.3	248 39.7	.. 16.6	116 39.5	.. 10.2	195 30.9	.. 21.3	195 55.9	.. 20.3	Pollux	243 21.0	N27 58.4
04	154 07.8	263 38.9	.. 17.1	131 41.1	.. 10.6	210 32.8	.. 21.1	210 58.1	.. 20.2	Procyon	244 54.0	N 5 10.2
05	169 10.2	278 38.1	.. 17.6	146 42.6	.. 11.0	225 34.7	.. 21.0	226 00.2	.. 20.2			
F 06	184 12.7	293 37.2	S21 18.1	161 44.2	N10 11.4	240 36.5	S20 20.9	241 02.4	S20 20.1	Rasalhague	96 01.9	N12 32.7
R 07	199 15.1	308 36.4	.. 18.6	176 45.7	.. 11.9	255 38.4	.. 20.8	256 04.6	.. 20.0	Regulus	207 37.8	N11 51.9
I 08	214 17.6	323 35.5	.. 19.1	191 47.3	.. 12.3	270 40.3	.. 20.7	271 06.8	.. 20.0	Rigel	281 06.7	S 8 10.8
D 09	229 20.1	338 34.7	.. 19.6	206 48.8	.. 12.7	285 42.2	.. 20.5	286 09.0	.. 19.9	Rigil Kent.	139 45.1	S60 54.9
A 10	244 22.5	353 33.8	.. 20.1	221 50.3	.. 13.1	300 44.1	.. 20.4	301 11.1	.. 19.9	Sabik	102 06.9	S15 44.9
Y 11	259 25.0	8 33.0	.. 20.6	236 51.9	.. 13.5	315 46.0	.. 20.3	316 13.3	.. 19.8			
12	274 27.5	23 32.1	S21 21.1	251 53.4	N10 14.0	330 47.8	S20 20.2	331 15.5	S20 19.7	Schedar	349 34.6	N56 39.3
13	289 29.9	38 31.2	.. 21.6	266 55.0	.. 14.4	345 49.7	.. 20.1	346 17.7	.. 19.7	Shaula	96 15.3	S37 07.0
14	304 32.4	53 30.4	.. 22.1	281 56.5	.. 14.8	0 51.6	.. 19.9	1 19.8	.. 19.6	Sirius	258 28.8	S16 44.7
15	319 34.9	68 29.5	.. 22.6	296 58.1	.. 15.2	15 53.5	.. 19.8	16 22.0	.. 19.6	Spica	158 25.9	S11 16.1
16	334 37.3	83 28.7	.. 23.1	311 59.6	.. 15.6	30 55.4	.. 19.7	31 24.2	.. 19.5	Suhail	222 48.3	S43 30.8
17	349 39.8	98 27.8	.. 23.6	327 01.2	.. 16.1	45 57.3	.. 19.6	46 26.4	.. 19.5			
18	4 42.2	113 27.0	S21 24.1	342 02.7	N10 16.5	60 59.1	S20 19.5	61 28.5	S20 19.4	Vega	80 35.9	N38 48.2
19	19 44.7	128 26.1	.. 24.6	357 04.2	.. 16.9	76 01.0	.. 19.3	76 30.7	.. 19.3	Zuben'ubi	136 59.9	S16 07.5
20	34 47.2	143 25.3	.. 25.1	12 05.8	.. 17.3	91 02.9	.. 19.2	91 32.9	.. 19.3			
21	49 49.6	158 24.4	.. 25.6	27 07.3	.. 17.7	106 04.8	.. 19.1	106 35.1	.. 19.2			
22	64 52.1	173 23.6	.. 26.1	42 08.9	.. 18.2	121 06.7	.. 19.0	121 37.2	.. 19.2			
23	79 54.6	188 22.7	.. 26.6	57 10.4	.. 18.6	136 08.5	.. 18.8	136 39.4	.. 19.1			
Mer. Pass.	h m 17 45.2	v −0.8	d 0.5	v 1.6	d 0.4	v 1.9	d 0.1	v 2.2	d 0.1			

	SHA	Mer. Pass.
	° ′	h m
Venus	111 03.7	10 24
Mars	337 58.6	19 14
Jupiter	56 41.3	14 00
Saturn	56 58.4	13 58

SUN and MOON

UT (d h)	SUN GHA	SUN Dec	MOON GHA	v	Dec	d	HP
23 00	180 14.1	S23 25.6	78 22.7	16.5	N 0 32.6	12.5	54.4
01	195 13.8	25.6	92 58.2	16.5	0 45.1	12.5	54.4
02	210 13.5	25.6	107 33.7	16.5	0 57.6	12.4	54.4
03	225 13.2	.. 25.5	122 09.2	16.5	1 10.0	12.5	54.3
04	240 12.9	25.5	136 44.7	16.5	1 22.5	12.5	54.3
05	255 12.6	25.5	151 20.2	16.6	1 35.0	12.5	54.3
W 06	270 12.3	S23 25.4	165 55.8	16.5	N 1 47.5	12.4	54.3
E 07	285 11.9	25.4	180 31.3	16.5	1 59.9	12.4	54.3
D 08	300 11.6	25.4	195 06.8	16.6	2 12.3	12.5	54.3
N 09	315 11.3	.. 25.3	209 42.4	16.5	2 24.8	12.4	54.3
E 10	330 11.0	25.3	224 17.9	16.5	2 37.2	12.4	54.3
S 11	345 10.7	25.2	238 53.4	16.6	2 49.6	12.4	54.3
D 12	0 10.4	S23 25.2	253 29.0	16.5	N 3 02.0	12.3	54.3
A 13	15 10.1	25.2	268 04.5	16.5	3 14.3	12.4	54.2
Y 14	30 09.8	25.1	282 40.0	16.5	3 26.7	12.3	54.2
15	45 09.5	.. 25.1	297 15.5	16.5	3 39.0	12.4	54.2
16	60 09.1	25.0	311 51.0	16.5	3 51.4	12.3	54.2
17	75 08.8	25.0	326 26.5	16.5	4 03.7	12.2	54.2
18	90 08.5	S23 24.9	341 02.0	16.5	N 4 15.9	12.3	54.2
19	105 08.2	24.9	355 37.5	16.5	4 28.2	12.3	54.2
20	120 07.9	24.9	10 13.0	16.4	4 40.5	12.2	54.2
21	135 07.6	.. 24.8	24 48.4	16.5	4 52.7	12.2	54.2
22	150 07.3	24.8	39 23.9	16.4	5 04.9	12.2	54.2
23	165 07.0	24.7	53 59.3	16.4	5 17.1	12.2	54.2
24 00	180 06.7	S23 24.7	68 34.7	16.4	N 5 29.3	12.1	54.2
01	195 06.4	24.6	83 10.1	16.4	5 41.4	12.2	54.2
02	210 06.0	24.6	97 45.5	16.4	5 53.6	12.1	54.2
03	225 05.7	.. 24.5	112 20.9	16.3	6 05.7	12.1	54.2
04	240 05.4	24.4	126 56.2	16.4	6 17.8	12.0	54.2
05	255 05.1	24.4	141 31.6	16.3	6 29.8	12.1	54.2
T 06	270 04.8	S23 24.3	156 06.9	16.3	N 6 41.9	12.0	54.2
H 07	285 04.5	24.3	170 42.2	16.2	6 53.9	12.0	54.2
U 08	300 04.2	24.2	185 17.4	16.3	7 05.9	11.9	54.1
R 09	315 03.9	.. 24.2	199 52.7	16.2	7 17.8	11.9	54.1
S 10	330 03.6	24.1	214 27.9	16.2	7 29.7	11.9	54.1
D 11	345 03.3	24.0	229 03.1	16.1	7 41.7	11.8	54.1
A 12	0 02.9	S23 24.0	243 38.2	16.2	N 7 53.5	11.9	54.1
Y 13	15 02.6	23.9	258 13.4	16.1	8 05.4	11.8	54.1
14	30 02.3	23.9	272 48.5	16.1	8 17.2	11.8	54.1
15	45 02.0	.. 23.8	287 23.6	16.0	8 29.0	11.7	54.1
16	60 01.7	23.7	301 58.6	16.1	8 40.7	11.7	54.1
17	75 01.4	23.7	316 33.7	16.0	8 52.4	11.7	54.1
18	90 01.1	S23 23.6	331 08.7	15.9	N 9 04.1	11.7	54.1
19	105 00.8	23.5	345 43.6	15.9	9 15.8	11.6	54.1
20	120 00.5	23.5	0 18.5	15.9	9 27.4	11.6	54.1
21	135 00.2	.. 23.4	14 53.4	15.9	9 39.0	11.5	54.1
22	149 59.8	23.3	29 28.3	15.8	9 50.5	11.6	54.1
23	164 59.5	23.3	44 03.1	15.8	10 02.1	11.4	54.1
25 00	179 59.2	S23 23.2	58 37.9	15.7	N10 13.5	11.5	54.1
01	194 58.9	23.1	73 12.6	15.8	10 25.0	11.4	54.1
02	209 58.6	23.1	87 47.4	15.6	10 36.4	11.4	54.2
03	224 58.3	.. 23.0	102 22.0	15.7	10 47.8	11.3	54.2
04	239 58.0	22.9	116 56.7	15.5	10 59.1	11.3	54.2
05	254 57.7	22.8	131 31.2	15.6	11 10.4	11.2	54.2
F 06	269 57.4	S23 22.8	146 05.8	15.5	N11 21.6	11.2	54.2
R 07	284 57.1	22.7	160 40.3	15.4	11 32.8	11.2	54.2
I 08	299 56.8	22.6	175 14.7	15.5	11 44.0	11.1	54.2
D 09	314 56.4	.. 22.5	189 49.2	15.3	11 55.1	11.1	54.2
A 10	329 56.1	22.5	204 23.5	15.4	12 06.2	11.0	54.2
Y 11	344 55.8	22.4	218 57.9	15.2	12 17.2	11.0	54.2
12	359 55.5	S23 22.3	233 32.1	15.3	N12 28.2	10.9	54.2
13	14 55.2	22.2	248 06.4	15.1	12 39.1	10.9	54.2
14	29 54.9	22.1	262 40.5	15.2	12 50.0	10.9	54.2
15	44 54.6	.. 22.1	277 14.7	15.0	13 00.9	10.8	54.2
16	59 54.3	22.0	291 48.7	15.1	13 11.7	10.7	54.2
17	74 54.0	21.9	306 22.8	15.0	13 22.4	10.7	54.2
18	89 53.7	S23 21.8	320 56.8	14.9	N13 33.1	10.7	54.2
19	104 53.4	21.7	335 30.7	14.9	13 43.8	10.6	54.2
20	119 53.1	21.6	350 04.6	14.8	13 54.4	10.5	54.2
21	134 52.7	.. 21.5	4 38.4	14.7	14 04.9	10.5	54.2
22	149 52.4	21.5	19 12.1	14.8	14 15.4	10.4	54.3
23	164 52.1	21.4	33 45.9	14.6	N14 25.8	10.4	54.3
	SD 16.3	d 0.1	SD 14.8		14.8	14.8	

Twilight — Sunrise — Moonrise

Lat.	Naut.	Civil	Sunrise	23	24	25	26
N 72	08 27	10 57	■■	12 29	12 06	11 37	10 49
N 70	08 07	09 55	■■	12 33	12 17	11 58	11 31
68	07 51	09 20		12 37	12 26	12 14	11 59
66	07 38	08 55	10 35	12 39	12 34	12 28	12 21
64	07 27	08 35	09 53	12 42	12 40	12 39	12 38
62	07 17	08 19	09 25	12 44	12 46	12 49	12 53
60	07 09	08 06	09 03	12 46	12 51	12 57	13 05
N 58	07 01	07 54	08 46	12 48	12 55	13 04	13 16
56	06 54	07 44	08 31	12 49	12 59	13 11	13 25
54	06 48	07 35	08 18	12 50	13 03	13 16	13 33
52	06 43	07 26	08 07	12 52	13 06	13 22	13 40
50	06 38	07 19	07 57	12 53	13 09	13 26	13 47
45	06 26	07 03	07 37	12 55	13 15	13 37	14 01
N 40	06 15	06 49	07 20	12 57	13 21	13 45	14 13
35	06 06	06 37	07 06	12 59	13 25	13 53	14 24
30	05 57	06 27	06 53	13 01	13 29	13 59	14 32
20	05 40	06 08	06 32	13 03	13 36	14 11	14 48
N 10	05 24	05 51	06 13	13 06	13 43	14 21	15 02
0	05 07	05 33	05 56	13 08	13 49	14 31	15 14
S 10	04 48	05 15	05 38	13 11	13 55	14 40	15 27
20	04 26	04 55	05 19	13 13	14 01	14 50	15 41
30	03 57	04 30	04 57	13 16	14 09	15 02	15 57
35	03 38	04 15	04 44	13 18	14 13	15 09	16 06
40	03 15	03 56	04 29	13 20	14 18	15 17	16 17
45	02 44	03 34	04 11	13 22	14 24	15 26	16 29
S 50	01 58	03 04	03 49	13 25	14 31	15 37	16 45
52	01 31	02 49	03 38	13 26	14 34	15 42	16 52
54	00 44	02 31	03 26	13 27	14 37	15 48	17 00
56	////	02 09	03 11	13 29	14 41	15 55	17 09
58	////	01 39	02 54	13 31	14 46	16 02	17 19
S 60	////	00 48	02 34	13 33	14 51	16 10	17 31

Sunset — Twilight — Moonset

Lat.	Sunset	Civil	Naut.	23	24	25	26
N 72	■■	13 02	15 33	00 56	02 45	04 41	06 58
N 70	■■	14 04	15 53	00 55	02 36	04 21	06 18
68		14 40	16 09	00 54	02 29	04 06	05 50
66	13 24	15 05	16 22	00 54	02 23	03 54	05 30
64	14 07	15 24	16 33	00 53	02 18	03 44	05 13
62	14 35	15 41	16 43	00 53	02 14	03 36	05 00
60	14 56	15 54	16 51	00 52	02 10	03 28	04 49
N 58	15 14	16 06	16 58	00 52	02 07	03 22	04 39
56	15 29	16 16	17 05	00 52	02 04	03 16	04 30
54	15 41	16 25	17 11	00 51	02 01	03 11	04 23
52	15 52	16 33	17 17	00 51	01 59	03 07	04 16
50	16 02	16 41	17 22	00 51	01 57	03 03	04 10
45	16 23	16 57	17 34	00 50	01 52	02 54	03 57
N 40	16 40	17 10	17 44	00 50	01 48	02 46	03 46
35	16 54	17 22	17 54	00 49	01 45	02 40	03 37
30	17 06	17 33	18 03	00 49	01 42	02 34	03 28
20	17 28	17 52	18 19	00 48	01 36	02 25	03 15
N 10	17 46	18 09	18 35	00 48	01 32	02 17	03 03
0	18 04	18 26	18 52	00 47	01 28	02 09	02 51
S 10	18 21	18 44	19 11	00 47	01 24	02 01	02 40
20	18 40	19 05	19 34	00 46	01 19	01 53	02 28
30	19 02	19 30	20 03	00 46	01 14	01 43	02 15
35	19 14	19 45	20 22	00 45	01 11	01 38	02 07
40	19 30	20 03	20 45	00 45	01 08	01 32	01 58
45	19 48	20 26	21 15	00 44	01 04	01 25	01 48
S 50	20 11	20 55	22 01	00 44	00 59	01 16	01 35
52	20 22	21 10	22 29	00 44	00 57	01 12	01 29
54	20 34	21 28	23 15	00 43	00 55	01 08	01 23
56	20 48	21 51	////	00 43	00 50	01 03	01 16
58	21 05	22 20	////	00 43	00 50	00 58	01 08
S 60	21 25	23 11	////	00 42	00 47	00 52	00 59

SUN and MOON

Day	Eqn. of Time 00h	Eqn. of Time 12h	Mer. Pass.	Mer. Pass. Upper	Mer. Pass. Lower	Age	Phase
23	00 57	00 42	11 59	19 18	06 58	09	64
24	00 27	00 12	12 00	19 59	07 38	10	73
25	00 02	00 17	12 00	20 41	08 20	11	81

UT	ARIES GHA	VENUS −3.9 GHA	VENUS Dec	MARS −0.4 GHA	MARS Dec	JUPITER −2.0 GHA	JUPITER Dec	SATURN +0.6 GHA	SATURN Dec	STARS Name	SHA	Dec
26 00	94 57.0	203 21.8	S21 27.1	72 11.9	N10 19.0	151 10.4	S20 18.7	151 41.6	S20 19.1	Acamar	315 14.0	S40 13.5
01	109 59.5	218 21.0	27.6	87 13.5	19.4	166 12.3	18.6	166 43.8	19.0	Achernar	335 22.6	S57 08.2
02	125 02.0	233 20.1	28.1	102 15.0	19.8	181 14.2	18.5	181 45.9	18.9	Acrux	173 03.6	S63 12.5
03	140 04.4	248 19.3 ..	28.5	117 16.6 ..	20.3	196 16.1 ..	18.4	196 48.1 ..	18.9	Adhara	255 08.0	S29 00.0
04	155 06.9	263 18.4	29.0	132 18.1	20.7	211 18.0	18.2	211 50.3	18.8	Aldebaran	290 43.1	N16 33.0
05	170 09.4	278 17.6	29.5	147 19.6	21.1	226 19.8	18.1	226 52.5	18.8			
06	185 11.8	293 16.7	S21 30.0	162 21.2	N10 21.5	241 21.7	S20 18.0	241 54.6	S20 18.7	Alioth	166 16.1	N55 50.6
07	200 14.3	308 15.8	30.5	177 22.7	22.0	256 23.6	17.9	256 56.8	18.6	Alkaid	152 54.9	N49 12.4
S 08	215 16.7	323 15.0	31.0	192 24.2	22.4	271 25.5	17.8	271 59.0	18.6	Alnair	27 37.4	S46 51.8
A 09	230 19.2	338 14.1 ..	31.4	207 25.8 ..	22.8	286 27.4 ..	17.6	287 01.2 ..	18.5	Alnilam	275 40.7	S 1 11.4
T 10	245 21.7	353 13.3	31.9	222 27.3	23.2	301 29.2	17.5	302 03.3	18.5	Alphard	217 50.7	S 8 44.9
U 11	260 24.1	8 12.4	32.4	237 28.8	23.6	316 31.1	17.4	317 05.5	18.4			
R 12	275 26.6	23 11.5	S21 32.9	252 30.4	N10 24.1	331 33.0	S20 17.3	332 07.7	S20 18.4	Alphecca	126 06.8	N26 38.6
D 13	290 29.1	38 10.7	33.3	267 31.9	24.5	346 34.9	17.1	347 09.9	18.3	Alpheratz	357 38.1	N29 12.4
A 14	305 31.5	53 09.8	33.8	282 33.4	24.9	1 36.8	17.0	2 12.0	18.2	Altair	62 03.5	N 8 55.4
Y 15	320 34.0	68 09.0 ..	34.3	297 34.9 ..	25.3	16 38.6 ..	16.9	17 14.2 ..	18.2	Ankaa	353 10.5	S42 11.9
16	335 36.5	83 08.1	34.8	312 36.5	25.8	31 40.5	16.8	32 16.4	18.1	Antares	112 20.2	S26 28.5
17	350 38.9	98 07.2	35.2	327 38.0	26.2	46 42.4	16.7	47 18.6	18.1			
18	5 41.4	113 06.4	S21 35.7	342 39.5	N10 26.6	61 44.3	S20 16.5	62 20.7	S20 18.0	Arcturus	145 51.1	N19 04.4
19	20 43.9	128 05.5	36.2	357 41.1	27.0	76 46.2	16.4	77 22.9	17.9	Atria	107 17.9	S69 03.7
20	35 46.3	143 04.6	36.6	12 42.6	27.4	91 48.0	16.3	92 25.1	17.9	Avior	234 15.4	S59 34.4
21	50 48.8	158 03.8 ..	37.1	27 44.1 ..	27.9	106 49.9 ..	16.2	107 27.3 ..	17.8	Bellatrix	278 26.1	N 6 22.0
22	65 51.2	173 02.9	37.6	42 45.6	28.3	121 51.8	16.0	122 29.4	17.8	Betelgeuse	270 55.3	N 7 24.6
23	80 53.7	188 02.0	38.0	57 47.2	28.7	136 53.7	15.9	137 31.6	17.7			
27 00	95 56.2	203 01.2	S21 38.5	72 48.7	N10 29.1	151 55.6	S20 15.8	152 33.8	S20 17.7	Canopus	263 53.3	S52 42.4
01	110 58.6	218 00.3	39.0	87 50.2	29.6	166 57.4	15.7	167 36.0	17.6	Capella	280 26.2	N46 01.1
02	126 01.1	232 59.4	39.4	102 51.7	30.0	181 59.3	15.6	182 38.1	17.5	Deneb	49 28.4	N45 21.4
03	141 03.6	247 58.6 ..	39.9	117 53.2 ..	30.4	197 01.2 ..	15.4	197 40.3 ..	17.5	Denebola	182 28.3	N14 27.3
04	156 06.0	262 57.7	40.4	132 54.8	30.8	212 03.1	15.3	212 42.5	17.4	Diphda	348 50.6	S17 52.5
05	171 08.5	277 56.8	40.8	147 56.3	31.3	227 05.0	15.2	227 44.6	17.4			
06	186 11.0	292 56.0	S21 41.3	162 57.8	N10 31.7	242 06.8	S20 15.1	242 46.8	S20 17.3	Dubhe	193 44.9	N61 38.1
07	201 13.4	307 55.1	41.7	177 59.3	32.1	257 08.7	14.9	257 49.0	17.2	Elnath	278 05.6	N28 37.4
S 08	216 15.9	322 54.2	42.2	193 00.8	32.5	272 10.6	14.8	272 51.2	17.2	Eltanin	90 44.3	N51 29.2
U 09	231 18.4	337 53.4 ..	42.6	208 02.4 ..	33.0	287 12.5 ..	14.7	287 53.3 ..	17.1	Enif	33 42.2	N 9 58.3
N 10	246 20.8	352 52.5	43.1	223 03.9	33.4	302 14.4	14.6	302 55.5	17.1	Fomalhaut	15 18.3	S29 30.9
11	261 23.3	7 51.6	43.5	238 05.4	33.8	317 16.2	14.4	317 57.7	17.0			
D 12	276 25.7	22 50.8	S21 44.0	253 06.9	N10 34.2	332 18.1	S20 14.3	332 59.9	S20 16.9	Gacrux	171 55.2	S57 13.4
A 13	291 28.2	37 49.9	44.4	268 08.4	34.7	347 20.0	14.2	348 02.0	16.9	Gienah	175 46.9	S17 39.3
Y 14	306 30.7	52 49.0	44.9	283 10.0	35.1	2 21.9	14.1	3 04.2	16.8	Hadar	148 40.8	S60 28.0
15	321 33.1	67 48.1 ..	45.3	298 11.5 ..	35.5	17 23.8 ..	14.0	18 06.4 ..	16.8	Hamal	327 54.7	N23 33.7
16	336 35.6	82 47.3	45.8	313 13.0	35.9	32 25.6	13.8	33 08.6	16.7	Kaus Aust.	83 37.3	S34 22.4
17	351 38.1	97 46.4	46.2	328 14.5	36.4	47 27.5	13.7	48 10.7	16.7			
18	6 40.5	112 45.5	S21 46.7	343 16.0	N10 36.8	62 29.4	S20 13.6	63 12.9	S20 16.6	Kochab	137 20.7	N74 04.0
19	21 43.0	127 44.7	47.1	358 17.5	37.2	77 31.3	13.5	78 15.1	16.5	Markab	13 33.3	N15 19.1
20	36 45.5	142 43.8	47.6	13 19.0	37.6	92 33.2	13.3	93 17.2	16.5	Menkar	314 09.4	N 4 10.2
21	51 47.9	157 42.9 ..	48.0	28 20.5 ..	38.1	107 35.0 ..	13.2	108 19.4 ..	16.4	Menkent	148 01.6	S36 28.1
22	66 50.4	172 42.0	48.4	43 22.1	38.5	122 36.9	13.1	123 21.6	16.4	Miaplacidus	221 38.0	S69 47.9
23	81 52.8	187 41.2	48.9	58 23.6	38.9	137 38.8	13.0	138 23.8	16.3			
28 00	96 55.3	202 40.3	S21 49.3	73 25.1	N10 39.3	152 40.7	S20 12.8	153 25.9	S20 16.2	Mirfak	308 32.5	N49 56.2
01	111 57.8	217 39.4	49.7	88 26.6	39.8	167 42.5	12.7	168 28.1	16.2	Nunki	75 52.2	S26 16.2
02	127 00.2	232 38.5	50.2	103 28.1	40.2	182 44.4	12.6	183 30.3	16.1	Peacock	53 11.5	S56 40.2
03	142 02.7	247 37.7 ..	50.6	118 29.6 ..	40.6	197 46.3 ..	12.5	198 32.5 ..	16.1	Pollux	243 21.0	N27 58.4
04	157 05.2	262 36.8	51.0	133 31.1	41.0	212 48.2	12.3	213 34.6	16.0	Procyon	244 53.9	N 5 10.2
05	172 07.6	277 35.9	51.5	148 32.6	41.5	227 50.1	12.2	228 36.8	15.9			
06	187 10.1	292 35.0	S21 51.9	163 34.1	N10 41.9	242 51.9	S20 12.1	243 39.0	S20 15.9	Rasalhague	96 01.9	N12 32.7
07	202 12.6	307 34.2	52.3	178 35.6	42.3	257 53.8	12.0	258 41.1	15.8	Regulus	207 37.8	N11 51.9
M 08	217 15.0	322 33.3	52.8	193 37.1	42.7	272 55.7	11.8	273 43.3	15.8	Rigel	281 06.7	S 8 10.8
O 09	232 17.5	337 32.4 ..	53.2	208 38.6 ..	43.2	287 57.6 ..	11.7	288 45.5 ..	15.7	Rigil Kent.	139 45.1	S60 54.9
N 10	247 20.0	352 31.5	53.6	223 40.1	43.6	302 59.5	11.6	303 47.7	15.6	Sabik	102 06.9	S15 44.9
11	262 22.4	7 30.6	54.0	238 41.6	44.0	318 01.3	11.5	318 49.8	15.6			
D 12	277 24.9	22 29.8	S21 54.5	253 43.1	N10 44.5	333 03.2	S20 11.4	333 52.0	S20 15.5	Schedar	349 34.6	N56 39.3
A 13	292 27.3	37 28.9	54.9	268 44.6	44.9	348 05.1	11.2	348 54.2	15.5	Shaula	96 15.2	S37 07.0
Y 14	307 29.8	52 28.0	55.3	283 46.1	45.3	3 07.0	11.1	3 56.3	15.4	Sirius	258 28.8	S16 44.7
15	322 32.3	67 27.1 ..	55.7	298 47.6 ..	45.7	18 08.8 ..	11.0	18 58.5 ..	15.3	Spica	158 25.8	S11 16.1
16	337 34.7	82 26.2	56.2	313 49.1	46.2	33 10.7	10.9	34 00.7	15.3	Suhail	222 48.3	S43 30.8
17	352 37.2	97 25.4	56.6	328 50.6	46.6	48 12.6	10.7	49 02.9	15.2			
18	7 39.7	112 24.5	S21 57.0	343 52.1	N10 47.0	63 14.5	S20 10.6	64 05.0	S20 15.2	Vega	80 35.9	N38 48.2
19	22 42.1	127 23.6	57.4	358 53.6	47.5	78 16.4	10.5	79 07.2	15.1	Zuben'ubi	136 59.9	S16 07.5
20	37 44.6	142 22.7	57.8	13 55.1	47.9	93 18.2	10.4	94 09.4	15.1			
21	52 47.1	157 21.8 ..	58.2	28 56.6 ..	48.3	108 20.1 ..	10.2	109 11.5 ..	15.0			
22	67 49.5	172 21.0	58.6	43 58.1	48.7	123 22.0	10.1	124 13.7	14.9			
23	82 52.0	187 20.1	59.1	58 59.6	49.2	138 23.9	10.0	139 15.9	14.9			

	SHA	Mer. Pass.
	° ′	h m
Venus	107 05.0	10 29
Mars	336 52.5	19 07
Jupiter	55 59.4	13 51
Saturn	56 37.6	13 48

	ARIES	VENUS	MARS	JUPITER	SATURN
Mer. Pass.	h m 17 33.4	v −0.9 d 0.5	v 1.5 d 0.4	v 1.9 d 0.1	v 2.2 d 0.1

UT	SUN GHA	SUN Dec	MOON GHA	v	MOON Dec	d	HP
d h	° ′	° ′	° ′	′	° ′	′	′
26 00	179 51.8	S23 21.3	48 19.5	14.6	N14 36.2	10.4	54.3
01	194 51.5	21.2	62 53.1	14.6	14 46.6	10.2	54.3
02	209 51.2	21.1	77 26.7	14.4	14 56.8	10.3	54.3
03	224 50.9	.. 21.0	92 00.1	14.5	15 07.1	10.1	54.3
04	239 50.6	20.9	106 33.6	14.3	15 17.2	10.1	54.3
05	254 50.3	20.8	121 06.9	14.3	15 27.3	10.1	54.3
06	269 50.0	S23 20.7	135 40.2	14.3	N15 37.4	9.9	54.3
07	284 49.7	20.6	150 13.5	14.2	15 47.3	10.0	54.3
08	299 49.4	20.5	164 46.7	14.1	15 57.3	9.8	54.3
09	314 49.0	.. 20.4	179 19.8	14.1	16 07.1	9.8	54.3
10	329 48.7	20.3	193 52.9	14.0	16 16.9	9.8	54.3
11	344 48.4	20.2	208 25.9	13.9	16 26.7	9.6	54.4
12	359 48.1	S23 20.1	222 58.8	13.9	N16 36.3	9.6	54.4
13	14 47.8	20.0	237 31.7	13.8	16 45.9	9.6	54.4
14	29 47.5	19.9	252 04.5	13.7	16 55.5	9.4	54.4
15	44 47.2	.. 19.8	266 37.2	13.7	17 04.9	9.4	54.4
16	59 46.9	19.7	281 09.9	13.6	17 14.3	9.4	54.4
17	74 46.6	19.6	295 42.5	13.6	17 23.7	9.2	54.4
18	89 46.3	S23 19.5	310 15.1	13.5	N17 32.9	9.2	54.4
19	104 46.0	19.4	324 47.6	13.4	17 42.1	9.2	54.5
20	119 45.7	19.3	339 20.0	13.3	17 51.3	9.0	54.5
21	134 45.4	.. 19.2	353 52.3	13.3	18 00.3	9.0	54.5
22	149 45.1	19.1	8 24.6	13.2	18 09.3	8.9	54.5
23	164 44.7	19.0	22 56.8	13.2	18 18.2	8.8	54.5
27 00	179 44.4	S23 18.9	37 29.0	13.1	N18 27.0	8.8	54.5
01	194 44.1	18.8	52 01.1	13.0	18 35.8	8.7	54.5
02	209 43.8	18.7	66 33.1	12.9	18 44.5	8.6	54.5
03	224 43.5	.. 18.6	81 05.0	12.9	18 53.1	8.5	54.6
04	239 43.2	18.4	95 36.9	12.8	19 01.6	8.4	54.6
05	254 42.9	18.3	110 08.7	12.7	19 10.0	8.4	54.6
06	269 42.6	S23 18.2	124 40.4	12.7	N19 18.4	8.3	54.6
07	284 42.3	18.1	139 12.1	12.6	19 26.7	8.2	54.6
08	299 42.0	18.0	153 43.7	12.5	19 34.9	8.1	54.6
09	314 41.7	.. 17.9	168 15.2	12.4	19 43.0	8.0	54.6
10	329 41.4	17.8	182 46.6	12.4	19 51.0	8.0	54.6
11	344 41.1	17.6	197 18.0	12.3	19 59.0	7.8	54.7
12	359 40.8	S23 17.5	211 49.3	12.3	N20 06.8	7.8	54.7
13	14 40.5	17.4	226 20.6	12.1	20 14.6	7.7	54.7
14	29 40.2	17.3	240 51.7	12.1	20 22.3	7.6	54.7
15	44 39.9	.. 17.2	255 22.8	12.0	20 29.9	7.5	54.7
16	59 39.5	17.0	269 53.8	12.0	20 37.4	7.4	54.7
17	74 39.2	16.9	284 24.8	11.9	20 44.8	7.3	54.8
18	89 38.9	S23 16.8	298 55.7	11.8	N20 52.1	7.3	54.8
19	104 38.6	16.7	313 26.5	11.7	20 59.4	7.1	54.8
20	119 38.3	16.5	327 57.2	11.7	21 06.5	7.1	54.8
21	134 38.0	.. 16.4	342 27.9	11.6	21 13.6	6.9	54.8
22	149 37.7	16.3	356 58.5	11.5	21 20.5	6.9	54.8
23	164 37.4	16.2	11 29.0	11.5	21 27.4	6.7	54.8
28 00	179 37.1	S23 16.0	25 59.5	11.3	N21 34.1	6.7	54.9
01	194 36.8	15.9	40 29.8	11.3	21 40.8	6.6	54.9
02	209 36.5	15.8	55 00.1	11.3	21 47.4	6.4	54.9
03	224 36.2	.. 15.6	69 30.4	11.2	21 53.8	6.4	54.9
04	239 35.9	15.5	84 00.6	11.1	22 00.2	6.3	54.9
05	254 35.6	15.4	98 30.7	11.0	22 06.5	6.1	54.9
06	269 35.3	S23 15.2	113 00.7	11.0	N22 12.6	6.1	55.0
07	284 35.0	15.1	127 30.7	10.8	22 18.7	5.9	55.0
08	299 34.7	15.0	142 00.5	10.9	22 24.6	5.9	55.0
09	314 34.4	.. 14.8	156 30.4	10.7	22 30.5	5.7	55.0
10	329 34.1	14.7	171 00.1	10.7	22 36.2	5.6	55.0
11	344 33.8	14.6	185 29.8	10.6	22 41.8	5.6	55.1
12	359 33.5	S23 14.3	199 59.4	10.6	N22 47.4	5.4	55.1
13	14 33.2	14.3	214 29.0	10.5	22 52.8	5.3	55.1
14	29 32.9	14.1	228 58.5	10.4	22 58.1	5.2	55.1
15	44 32.5	.. 14.0	243 27.9	10.4	23 03.3	5.1	55.1
16	59 32.2	13.9	257 57.3	10.3	23 08.4	4.9	55.1
17	74 31.9	13.7	272 26.6	10.2	23 13.3	4.9	55.2
18	89 31.6	S23 13.6	286 55.8	10.1	N23 18.2	4.8	55.2
19	104 31.3	13.4	301 24.9	10.1	23 23.0	4.6	55.2
20	119 31.0	13.3	315 54.0	10.1	23 27.6	4.5	55.2
21	134 30.7	.. 13.1	330 23.1	10.0	23 32.1	4.4	55.2
22	149 30.4	13.0	344 52.1	9.9	23 36.5	4.3	55.3
23	164 30.1	12.9	359 21.0	9.8	N23 40.8	4.2	55.3
SD	16.3	d 0.1	SD 14.8		14.9		15.0

Saturday (26), **Sunday** (27), **Monday** (28) — as marked vertically beside the hour blocks.

Lat.	Twilight Naut.	Twilight Civil	Sunrise	Moonrise 26	27	28	29
°	h m	h m	h m	h m	h m	h m	h m
N 72	08 27	10 54	■	10 49	□	□	□
N 70	08 07	09 54	■	11 31	10 23	□	□
68	07 51	09 20	■	11 59	11 36	□	□
66	07 38	08 55	10 34	12 21	12 13	12 01	□
64	07 27	08 35	09 53	12 38	12 40	12 44	12 59
62	07 18	08 20	09 25	12 53	13 00	13 14	13 39
60	07 09	08 06	09 04	13 05	13 17	13 36	14 07
N 58	07 02	07 54	08 46	13 16	13 31	13 54	14 29
56	06 55	07 44	08 32	13 25	13 44	14 10	14 47
54	06 49	07 35	08 19	13 33	13 54	14 23	15 02
52	06 43	07 27	08 08	13 40	14 04	14 34	15 15
50	06 38	07 20	07 58	13 47	14 12	14 45	15 26
45	06 27	07 04	07 38	14 01	14 31	15 06	15 50
N 40	06 16	06 50	07 21	14 13	14 46	15 24	16 09
35	06 07	06 39	07 07	14 24	14 58	15 38	16 25
30	05 58	06 28	06 54	14 32	15 09	15 51	16 39
20	05 42	06 09	06 33	14 48	15 28	16 13	17 03
N 10	05 26	05 52	06 15	15 02	15 45	16 32	17 23
0	05 09	05 35	05 58	15 14	16 01	16 50	17 43
S 10	04 50	05 17	05 40	15 27	16 17	17 08	18 02
20	04 27	04 57	05 21	15 41	16 34	17 28	18 22
30	03 58	04 32	04 59	15 57	16 53	17 50	18 46
35	03 40	04 17	04 46	16 06	17 05	18 03	19 01
40	03 17	03 58	04 31	16 17	17 18	18 18	19 17
45	02 46	03 36	04 13	16 29	17 33	18 37	19 36
S 50	02 01	03 06	03 51	16 45	17 53	18 59	20 01
52	01 34	02 51	03 40	16 52	18 02	19 10	20 13
54	00 49	02 34	03 28	17 00	18 12	19 22	20 26
56	////	02 12	03 14	17 09	18 24	19 37	20 42
58	////	01 42	02 57	17 19	18 38	19 53	21 00
S 60	////	00 53	02 37	17 31	18 54	20 13	21 23

Lat.	Sunset	Twilight Civil	Twilight Naut.	Moonset 26	27	28	29
°	h m	h m	h m	h m	h m	h m	h m
N 72	■	13 09	15 36	06 58	□	□	□
N 70	■	14 09	15 56	06 18	09 01	□	□
68	■	14 43	16 12	05 50	07 49	□	□
66	13 29	15 08	16 25	05 30	07 12	09 06	□
64	14 10	15 27	16 36	05 13	06 47	08 22	09 55
62	14 38	15 43	16 45	05 00	06 27	07 54	09 15
60	14 59	15 57	16 53	04 49	06 10	07 32	08 47
N 58	15 16	16 08	17 01	04 39	05 57	07 14	08 26
56	15 31	16 18	17 07	04 30	05 45	06 59	08 08
54	15 44	16 27	17 14	04 23	05 35	06 46	07 53
52	15 55	16 36	17 19	04 16	05 26	06 35	07 40
50	16 04	16 43	17 24	04 10	05 17	06 25	07 29
45	16 25	16 59	17 36	03 57	05 00	06 04	07 06
N 40	16 42	17 12	17 46	03 46	04 46	05 47	06 47
35	16 56	17 24	17 56	03 37	04 34	05 33	06 31
30	17 08	17 35	18 04	03 28	04 24	05 20	06 17
20	17 29	17 53	18 21	03 15	04 06	04 59	05 54
N 10	17 48	18 10	18 37	03 03	03 51	04 41	05 34
0	18 05	18 28	18 54	02 51	03 36	04 24	05 15
S 10	18 23	18 46	19 13	02 40	03 22	04 07	04 56
20	18 41	19 06	19 35	02 28	03 07	03 49	04 36
30	19 03	19 31	20 04	02 15	02 49	03 29	04 13
35	19 16	19 46	20 23	02 07	02 39	03 16	04 00
40	19 31	20 04	20 46	01 58	02 28	03 03	03 44
45	19 49	20 26	21 16	01 48	02 14	02 46	03 25
S 50	20 11	20 56	21 58	01 35	01 58	02 26	03 02
52	20 22	21 11	22 28	01 29	01 50	02 16	02 51
54	20 34	21 29	23 12	01 23	01 41	02 06	02 39
56	20 48	21 51	////	01 16	01 32	01 54	02 24
58	21 05	22 20	////	01 08	01 21	01 40	02 07
S 60	21 25	23 08	////	00 59	01 08	01 23	01 47

Day	SUN Eqn. of Time 00h	SUN Eqn. of Time 12h	SUN Mer. Pass.	MOON Mer. Pass. Upper	MOON Mer. Pass. Lower	Age	Phase %
d	m s	m s	h m	h m	h m	d	%
26	00 32	00 47	12 01	21 25	09 03	12	88
27	01 02	01 16	12 01	22 13	09 49	13	93
28	01 31	01 46	12 02	23 03	10 37	14	97

UT	ARIES	VENUS −3.9		MARS −0.3		JUPITER −2.0		SATURN +0.6		STARS		
	GHA	GHA	Dec	GHA	Dec	GHA	Dec	GHA	Dec	Name	SHA	Dec
d h	° ′	° ′	° ′	° ′	° ′	° ′	° ′	° ′	° ′		° ′	° ′
29 00	97 54.5	202 19.2	S21 59.5	74 01.1	N10 49.6	153 25.7	S20 09.9	154 18.1	S20 14.8	Acamar	315 14.0	S40 13.5
01	112 56.9	217 18.3	21 59.9	89 02.6	50.0	168 27.6	09.7	169 20.2	14.8	Achernar	335 22.6	S57 08.2
02	127 59.4	232 17.4	22 00.3	104 04.1	50.5	183 29.5	09.6	184 22.4	14.7	Acrux	173 03.5	S63 12.5
03	143 01.8	247 16.5	.. 00.7	119 05.6	.. 50.9	198 31.4	.. 09.5	199 24.6	.. 14.6	Adhara	255 08.0	S29 00.1
04	158 04.3	262 15.7	01.1	134 07.1	51.3	213 33.2	09.4	214 26.7	14.6	Aldebaran	290 43.0	N16 33.0
05	173 06.8	277 14.8	01.5	149 08.6	51.7	228 35.1	09.2	229 28.9	14.5			
06	188 09.2	292 13.9	S22 01.9	164 10.1	N10 52.2	243 37.0	S20 09.1	244 31.1	S20 14.5	Alioth	166 16.0	N55 50.6
07	203 11.7	307 13.0	02.3	179 11.6	52.6	258 38.9	09.0	259 33.3	14.4	Alkaid	152 54.8	N49 12.4
T 08	218 14.2	322 12.1	02.7	194 13.1	53.0	273 40.8	08.9	274 35.4	14.3	Alnair	27 37.4	S46 51.8
U 09	233 16.6	337 11.2	.. 03.1	209 14.6	.. 53.5	288 42.6	.. 08.7	289 37.6	.. 14.3	Alnilam	275 40.7	S 1 11.4
E 10	248 19.1	352 10.3	03.5	224 16.1	53.9	303 44.5	08.6	304 39.8	14.2	Alphard	217 50.7	S 8 44.9
S 11	263 21.6	7 09.5	03.9	239 17.5	54.3	318 46.4	08.5	319 41.9	14.2			
D 12	278 24.0	22 08.6	S22 04.3	254 19.0	N10 54.7	333 48.3	S20 08.4	334 44.1	S20 14.1	Alphecca	126 06.8	N26 38.6
A 13	293 26.5	37 07.7	04.7	269 20.5	55.2	348 50.1	08.2	349 46.3	14.0	Alpheratz	357 38.1	N29 12.4
Y 14	308 29.0	52 06.8	05.1	284 22.0	55.6	3 52.0	08.1	4 48.5	14.0	Altair	62 03.5	N 8 55.4
15	323 31.4	67 05.9	.. 05.5	299 23.5	.. 56.0	18 53.9	.. 08.0	19 50.6	.. 13.9	Ankaa	353 10.5	S42 11.9
16	338 33.9	82 05.0	05.9	314 25.0	56.5	33 55.8	07.8	34 52.8	13.9	Antares	112 20.2	S26 28.5
17	353 36.3	97 04.1	06.3	329 26.5	56.9	48 57.6	07.7	49 55.0	13.8			
18	8 38.8	112 03.2	S22 06.7	344 28.0	N10 57.3	63 59.5	S20 07.6	64 57.1	S20 13.7	Arcturus	145 51.1	N19 04.4
19	23 41.3	127 02.4	07.1	359 29.4	57.8	79 01.4	07.5	79 59.3	13.7	Atria	107 17.8	S69 03.6
20	38 43.7	142 01.5	07.4	14 30.9	58.2	94 03.3	07.3	95 01.5	13.6	Avior	234 15.4	S59 34.4
21	53 46.2	157 00.6	.. 07.8	29 32.4	.. 58.6	109 05.1	.. 07.2	110 03.7	.. 13.6	Bellatrix	278 26.1	N 6 22.0
22	68 48.7	171 59.7	08.2	44 33.9	59.0	124 07.0	07.1	125 05.8	13.5	Betelgeuse	270 55.3	N 7 24.6
23	83 51.1	186 58.8	08.6	59 35.4	59.5	139 08.9	07.0	140 08.0	13.4			
30 00	98 53.6	201 57.9	S22 09.0	74 36.9	N10 59.9	154 10.8	S20 06.8	155 10.2	S20 13.4	Canopus	263 53.3	S52 42.5
01	113 56.1	216 57.0	09.4	89 38.3	11 00.3	169 12.6	06.7	170 12.3	13.3	Capella	280 26.2	N46 01.1
02	128 58.5	231 56.1	09.7	104 39.8	00.8	184 14.5	06.6	185 14.5	13.3	Deneb	49 28.4	N45 21.4
03	144 01.0	246 55.2	.. 10.1	119 41.3	.. 01.2	199 16.4	.. 06.5	200 16.7	.. 13.2	Denebola	182 28.2	N14 27.3
04	159 03.5	261 54.3	10.5	134 42.8	01.6	214 18.3	06.3	215 18.8	13.1	Diphda	348 50.6	S17 52.5
05	174 05.9	276 53.4	10.9	149 44.3	02.1	229 20.1	06.2	230 21.0	13.1			
06	189 08.4	291 52.5	S22 11.3	164 45.7	N11 02.5	244 22.0	S20 06.1	245 23.2	S20 13.0	Dubhe	193 44.9	N61 38.1
W 07	204 10.8	306 51.7	11.6	179 47.2	02.9	259 23.9	06.0	260 25.4	13.0	Elnath	278 05.6	N28 37.4
E 08	219 13.3	321 50.8	12.0	194 48.7	03.4	274 25.8	05.8	275 27.5	12.9	Eltanin	90 44.2	N51 29.2
D 09	234 15.8	336 49.9	.. 12.4	209 50.2	.. 03.8	289 27.6	.. 05.7	290 29.7	.. 12.8	Enif	33 42.2	N 9 58.2
N 10	249 18.2	351 49.0	12.8	224 51.6	04.2	304 29.5	05.6	305 31.9	12.8	Fomalhaut	15 18.3	S29 30.9
E 11	264 20.7	6 48.1	13.1	239 53.1	04.7	319 31.4	05.5	320 34.0	12.7			
S 12	279 23.2	21 47.2	S22 13.5	254 54.6	N11 05.1	334 33.3	S20 05.3	335 36.2	S20 12.7	Gacrux	171 55.1	S57 13.4
D 13	294 25.6	36 46.3	13.9	269 56.1	05.5	349 35.1	05.2	350 38.4	12.6	Gienah	175 46.9	S17 39.3
A 14	309 28.1	51 45.4	14.2	284 57.5	05.9	4 37.0	05.1	5 40.5	12.5	Hadar	148 40.8	S60 28.0
Y 15	324 30.6	66 44.5	.. 14.6	299 59.0	.. 06.4	19 38.9	.. 04.9	20 42.7	.. 12.5	Hamal	327 54.7	N23 33.7
16	339 33.0	81 43.6	15.0	315 00.5	06.8	34 40.8	04.8	35 44.9	12.4	Kaus Aust.	83 37.3	S34 22.4
17	354 35.5	96 42.7	15.3	330 02.0	07.2	49 42.6	04.7	50 47.0	12.4			
18	9 38.0	111 41.8	S22 15.7	345 03.4	N11 07.7	64 44.5	S20 04.6	65 49.2	S20 12.3	Kochab	137 20.7	N74 04.0
19	24 40.4	126 40.9	16.0	0 04.9	08.1	79 46.4	04.4	80 51.4	12.2	Markab	13 33.3	N15 19.1
20	39 42.9	141 40.0	16.4	15 06.4	08.5	94 48.3	04.3	95 53.6	12.2	Menkar	314 09.4	N 4 10.2
21	54 45.3	156 39.1	.. 16.8	30 07.8	.. 09.0	109 50.1	.. 04.2	110 55.7	.. 12.1	Menkent	148 01.6	S36 28.1
22	69 47.8	171 38.2	17.1	45 09.3	09.4	124 52.0	04.1	125 57.9	12.1	Miaplacidus	221 38.0	S69 47.9
23	84 50.3	186 37.3	17.5	60 10.8	09.8	139 53.9	03.9	141 00.1	12.0			
31 00	99 52.7	201 36.4	S22 17.8	75 12.3	N11 10.3	154 55.8	S20 03.8	156 02.2	S20 11.9	Mirfak	308 32.5	N49 56.2
01	114 55.2	216 35.5	18.2	90 13.7	10.7	169 57.6	03.7	171 04.4	11.9	Nunki	75 52.2	S26 16.2
02	129 57.7	231 34.6	18.5	105 15.2	11.1	184 59.5	03.5	186 06.6	11.8	Peacock	53 11.5	S56 40.2
03	145 00.1	246 33.7	.. 18.9	120 16.7	.. 11.6	200 01.4	.. 03.4	201 08.7	.. 11.8	Pollux	243 21.0	N27 58.4
04	160 02.6	261 32.8	19.2	135 18.1	12.0	215 03.3	03.3	216 10.9	11.7	Procyon	244 53.9	N 5 10.2
05	175 05.1	276 31.9	19.6	150 19.6	12.4	230 05.1	03.2	231 13.1	11.6			
06	190 07.5	291 31.0	S22 19.9	165 21.1	N11 12.9	245 07.0	S20 03.0	246 15.2	S20 11.6	Rasalhague	96 01.9	N12 32.7
07	205 10.0	306 30.1	20.3	180 22.5	13.3	260 08.9	02.9	261 17.4	11.5	Regulus	207 37.7	N11 51.9
T 08	220 12.5	321 29.2	20.6	195 24.0	13.7	275 10.8	02.8	276 19.6	11.4	Rigel	281 06.7	S 8 10.8
H 09	235 14.9	336 28.3	.. 21.0	210 25.5	.. 14.2	290 12.6	.. 02.7	291 21.8	.. 11.4	Rigil Kent.	139 45.0	S60 54.9
U 10	250 17.4	351 27.4	21.3	225 26.9	14.6	305 14.5	02.5	306 23.9	11.3	Sabik	102 06.9	S15 44.9
R 11	265 19.8	6 26.5	21.7	240 28.4	15.0	320 16.4	02.4	321 26.1	11.3			
S 12	280 22.3	21 25.6	S22 22.0	255 29.8	N11 15.5	335 18.2	S20 02.3	336 28.3	S20 11.2	Schedar	349 34.6	N56 39.3
D 13	295 24.8	36 24.7	22.4	270 31.3	15.9	350 20.1	02.1	351 30.4	11.1	Shaula	96 15.2	S37 07.0
A 14	310 27.2	51 23.8	22.7	285 32.8	16.3	5 22.0	02.0	6 32.6	11.1	Sirius	258 28.8	S16 44.8
Y 15	325 29.7	66 22.9	.. 23.0	300 34.2	.. 16.8	20 23.9	.. 01.9	21 34.8	.. 11.0	Spica	158 25.8	S11 16.1
16	340 32.2	81 22.0	23.4	315 35.7	17.2	35 25.7	01.8	36 36.9	11.0	Suhail	222 48.3	S43 30.9
17	355 34.6	96 21.1	23.7	330 37.1	17.6	50 27.6	01.6	51 39.1	10.9			
18	10 37.1	111 20.2	S22 24.0	345 38.6	N11 18.1	65 29.5	S20 01.5	66 41.3	S20 10.8	Vega	80 35.9	N38 48.2
19	25 39.6	126 19.3	24.4	0 40.1	18.5	80 31.4	01.4	81 43.4	10.8	Zuben'ubi	136 59.8	S16 07.5
20	40 42.0	141 18.4	24.7	15 41.5	18.9	95 33.2	01.3	96 45.6	10.7		SHA	Mer. Pass.
21	55 44.5	156 17.5	.. 25.0	30 43.0	.. 19.4	110 35.1	.. 01.1	111 47.8	.. 10.7		° ′	h m
22	70 46.9	171 16.6	25.4	45 44.4	19.8	125 37.0	01.0	126 49.9	10.6	Venus	103 04.3	10 33
23	85 49.4	186 15.7	25.7	60 45.9	20.3	140 38.8	00.9	141 52.1	10.5	Mars	335 43.3	19 00
	h m									Jupiter	55 17.2	13 42
Mer. Pass. 17 21.6		v −0.9	d 0.4	v 1.5	d 0.4	v 1.9	d 0.1	v 2.2	d 0.1	Saturn	56 16.6	13 37

SUN / MOON

UT	SUN GHA	SUN Dec	MOON GHA	v	MOON Dec	d	HP
d h	° ′	° ′	° ′	′	° ′	′	′
29 00	179 29.8	S23 12.7	13 49.8	9.8	N23 45.0	4.0	55.3
01	194 29.5	12.6	28 18.6	9.8	23 49.0	3.9	55.3
02	209 29.2	12.4	42 47.4	9.6	23 52.9	3.9	55.3
03	224 28.9	12.3	57 16.0	9.7	23 56.8	3.6	55.3
04	239 28.6	12.1	71 44.7	9.5	24 00.4	3.6	55.4
05	254 28.3	12.0	86 13.2	9.5	24 04.0	3.5	55.4
06	269 28.0	S23 11.8	100 41.7	9.5	N24 07.5	3.3	55.4
07	284 27.7	11.7	115 10.2	9.4	24 10.8	3.2	55.4
08	299 27.4	11.5	129 38.6	9.4	24 14.0	3.0	55.4
09	314 27.1	11.3	144 07.0	9.2	24 17.0	3.0	55.5
10	329 26.8	11.2	158 35.2	9.3	24 20.0	2.8	55.5
11	344 26.5	11.0	173 03.5	9.2	24 22.8	2.7	55.5
12	359 26.2	S23 10.9	187 31.7	9.1	N24 25.5	2.6	55.5
13	14 25.9	10.7	201 59.8	9.1	24 28.1	2.4	55.5
14	29 25.6	10.6	216 27.9	9.1	24 30.5	2.3	55.6
15	44 25.3	10.4	230 56.0	9.0	24 32.8	2.2	55.6
16	59 25.0	10.2	245 24.0	9.0	24 35.0	2.1	55.6
17	74 24.7	10.1	259 52.0	8.9	24 37.1	1.9	55.6
18	89 24.4	S23 09.9	274 19.9	8.9	N24 39.0	1.8	55.6
19	104 24.1	09.7	288 47.8	8.8	24 40.8	1.7	55.7
20	119 23.8	09.6	303 15.6	8.8	24 42.5	1.5	55.7
21	134 23.5	09.4	317 43.4	8.7	24 44.0	1.4	55.7
22	149 23.2	09.3	332 11.1	8.8	24 45.4	1.3	55.7
23	164 22.9	09.1	346 38.9	8.7	24 46.7	1.1	55.7
30 00	179 22.6	S23 08.9	1 06.6	8.6	N24 47.8	1.0	55.8
01	194 22.3	08.8	15 34.2	8.6	24 48.8	0.9	55.8
02	209 22.0	08.6	30 01.8	8.6	24 49.7	0.7	55.8
03	224 21.7	08.4	44 29.4	8.5	24 50.4	0.6	55.8
04	239 21.4	08.2	58 56.9	8.6	24 51.0	0.5	55.8
05	254 21.1	08.1	73 24.5	8.5	24 51.5	0.3	55.9
06	269 20.8	S23 07.9	87 52.0	8.4	N24 51.8	0.2	55.9
07	284 20.5	07.7	102 19.4	8.4	24 52.0	0.0	55.9
08	299 20.2	07.6	116 46.8	8.5	24 52.0	0.1	55.9
09	314 19.9	07.4	131 14.3	8.3	24 51.9	0.2	55.9
10	329 19.6	07.2	145 41.6	8.4	24 51.7	0.3	56.0
11	344 19.3	07.0	160 09.0	8.4	24 51.4	0.5	56.0
12	359 19.0	S23 06.8	174 36.4	8.3	N24 50.9	0.7	56.0
13	14 18.7	06.7	189 03.7	8.3	24 50.2	0.7	56.0
14	29 18.4	06.5	203 31.0	8.3	24 49.5	0.9	56.0
15	44 18.1	06.3	217 58.3	8.2	24 48.6	1.1	56.1
16	59 17.8	06.1	232 25.5	8.3	24 47.5	1.2	56.1
17	74 17.5	06.0	246 52.8	8.2	24 46.3	1.3	56.1
18	89 17.2	S23 05.8	261 20.0	8.3	N24 45.0	1.4	56.1
19	104 16.9	05.6	275 47.3	8.2	24 43.6	1.6	56.1
20	119 16.6	05.4	290 14.5	8.2	24 42.0	1.8	56.2
21	134 16.3	05.2	304 41.7	8.2	24 40.2	1.8	56.2
22	149 16.0	05.0	319 08.9	8.2	24 38.4	2.0	56.2
23	164 15.7	04.9	333 36.1	8.2	24 36.4	2.2	56.2
31 00	179 15.4	S23 04.7	348 03.3	8.2	N24 34.2	2.3	56.2
01	194 15.1	04.5	2 30.5	8.2	24 31.9	2.4	56.3
02	209 14.8	04.3	16 57.7	8.2	24 29.5	2.6	56.3
03	224 14.5	04.1	31 24.9	8.2	24 26.9	2.7	56.3
04	239 14.2	03.9	45 52.1	8.1	24 24.2	2.8	56.3
05	254 13.9	03.7	60 19.2	8.2	24 21.4	3.0	56.3
06	269 13.6	S23 03.5	74 46.4	8.2	N24 18.4	3.1	56.4
07	284 13.3	03.3	89 13.6	8.2	24 15.3	3.3	56.4
08	299 13.1	03.1	103 40.8	8.2	24 12.0	3.4	56.4
09	314 12.8	03.0	118 08.0	8.2	24 08.6	3.5	56.4
10	329 12.5	02.8	132 35.2	8.3	24 05.1	3.7	56.5
11	344 12.2	02.6	147 02.5	8.2	24 01.4	3.8	56.5
12	359 11.9	S23 02.4	161 29.7	8.2	N23 57.6	3.9	56.5
13	14 11.6	02.2	175 56.9	8.3	23 53.7	4.1	56.5
14	29 11.3	02.0	190 24.2	8.3	23 49.6	4.2	56.5
15	44 11.0	01.8	204 51.5	8.3	23 45.4	4.4	56.6
16	59 10.7	01.6	219 18.7	8.3	23 41.0	4.5	56.6
17	74 10.4	01.4	233 46.0	8.4	23 36.5	4.6	56.6
18	89 10.1	S23 01.2	248 13.4	8.3	N23 31.9	4.8	56.6
19	104 09.8	01.0	262 40.7	8.4	23 27.1	4.8	56.6
20	119 09.5	00.8	277 08.1	8.3	23 22.3	5.1	56.7
21	134 09.2	00.6	291 35.4	8.4	23 17.2	5.1	56.7
22	149 08.9	00.4	306 02.8	8.5	23 12.1	5.3	56.7
23	164 08.6	00.2	320 30.3	8.4	N23 06.8	5.4	56.7
SD	16.3	d 0.2	SD 15.1		15.3		15.4

Day labels: 29 = TUESDAY, 30 = WEDNESDAY, 31 = THURSDAY

Twilight / Moonrise

Lat.	Twilight Naut.	Twilight Civil	Sunrise	Moonrise 29	Moonrise 30	Moonrise 31	Moonrise 1
°	h m	h m	h m	h m	h m	h m	h m
N 72	08 25	10 47	■■	□	□	□	□
N 70	08 06	09 52	■■	□	□	□	□
68	07 51	09 18	■■	□	□	□	15 16
66	07 38	08 54	10 30	□	□	13 56	16 14
64	07 27	08 35	09 51	12 59	13 43	15 06	16 48
62	07 18	08 19	09 24	13 39	14 27	15 41	17 12
60	07 09	08 06	09 03	14 07	14 57	16 07	17 32
N 58	07 02	07 55	08 46	14 29	15 19	16 27	17 48
56	06 56	07 44	08 32	14 47	15 38	16 44	18 01
54	06 50	07 36	08 19	15 02	15 53	16 58	18 13
52	06 44	07 28	08 08	15 15	16 07	17 10	18 23
50	06 39	07 20	07 59	15 26	16 18	17 21	18 32
45	06 27	07 04	07 38	15 50	16 43	17 44	18 52
N 40	06 17	06 51	07 22	16 09	17 02	18 02	19 07
35	06 08	06 40	07 08	16 25	17 18	18 17	19 21
30	05 59	06 29	06 55	16 39	17 32	18 31	19 32
20	05 43	06 11	06 34	17 03	17 56	18 53	19 52
N 10	05 27	05 53	06 16	17 23	18 17	19 13	20 09
0	05 10	05 36	05 59	17 43	18 36	19 31	20 25
S 10	04 52	05 19	05 42	18 02	18 56	19 49	20 40
20	04 29	04 58	05 23	18 22	19 17	20 09	20 57
30	04 00	04 34	05 01	18 46	19 41	20 31	21 17
35	03 42	04 19	04 48	19 01	19 55	20 44	21 28
40	03 19	04 01	04 33	19 17	20 11	20 59	21 41
45	02 49	03 38	04 16	19 36	20 30	21 17	21 56
S 50	02 05	03 09	03 53	20 01	20 55	21 39	22 14
52	01 38	02 54	03 43	20 13	21 06	21 50	22 23
54	00 56	02 37	03 31	20 26	21 20	22 02	22 33
56	////	02 15	03 17	20 42	21 35	22 15	22 44
58	////	01 47	03 00	21 00	21 54	22 31	22 56
S 60	////	01 01	02 40	21 23	22 16	22 50	23 11

Sunset / Twilight / Moonset

Lat.	Sunset	Twilight Civil	Twilight Naut.	Moonset 29	Moonset 30	Moonset 31	Moonset 1
°	h m	h m	h m	h m	h m	h m	h m
N 72	■■	13 19	15 41	□	□	□	□
N 70	■■	14 14	16 00	□	□	□	□
68	■■	14 47	16 15	□	□	□	13 17
66	13 35	15 12	16 28	□	□	12 44	12 18
64	14 15	15 31	16 39	09 55	11 03	11 34	11 44
62	14 42	15 47	16 48	09 15	10 18	10 58	11 19
60	15 03	16 00	16 56	08 47	09 49	10 32	10 59
N 58	15 20	16 11	17 03	08 26	09 26	10 11	10 42
56	15 34	16 21	17 10	08 08	09 08	09 54	10 28
54	15 47	16 30	17 16	07 53	08 52	09 40	10 16
52	15 57	16 38	17 22	07 40	08 39	09 27	10 05
50	16 07	16 45	17 27	07 29	08 27	09 16	09 56
45	16 27	17 01	17 38	07 06	08 03	08 53	09 36
N 40	16 44	17 14	17 48	06 47	07 43	08 34	09 19
35	16 58	17 26	17 58	06 31	07 27	08 19	09 05
30	17 10	17 36	18 06	06 17	07 13	08 05	08 53
20	17 31	17 55	18 22	05 54	06 49	07 42	08 32
N 10	17 49	18 12	18 38	05 34	06 28	07 22	08 14
0	18 06	18 29	18 55	05 15	06 08	07 03	07 57
S 10	18 24	18 47	19 14	04 56	05 49	06 44	07 40
20	18 42	19 07	19 36	04 36	05 28	06 23	07 21
30	19 04	19 32	20 05	04 13	05 04	06 00	07 00
35	19 17	19 47	20 23	04 00	04 50	05 46	06 47
40	19 32	20 04	20 46	03 44	04 33	05 30	06 33
45	19 50	20 27	21 16	03 25	04 14	05 11	06 15
S 50	20 12	20 56	22 00	03 02	03 49	04 47	05 54
52	20 22	21 11	22 26	02 51	03 37	04 35	05 44
54	20 34	21 28	23 08	02 39	03 23	04 22	05 32
56	20 48	21 49	////	02 24	03 08	04 07	05 19
58	21 04	22 18	////	02 07	02 49	03 48	05 03
S 60	21 24	23 02	////	01 47	02 26	03 26	04 45

SUN / MOON (Eqn. of Time etc.)

Day	Eqn. of Time 00h	Eqn. of Time 12h	Mer. Pass.	Mer. Pass. Upper	Mer. Pass. Lower	Age	Phase
d	m s	m s	h m	h m	h m	d %	
29	02 00	02 15	12 02	23 55	11 29	15 100	
30	02 29	02 43	12 03	24 50	12 22	16 100	○
31	02 58	03 12	12 03	00 50	13 17	17 98	

EXPLANATION

PRINCIPLE AND ARRANGEMENT

1. *Object.* The object of this Almanac is to provide, in a convenient form, the data required for the practice of astronomical navigation at sea.

2. *Principle.* The main contents of the Almanac consist of data from which the *Greenwich Hour Angle* (GHA) and the *Declination* (Dec) of all the bodies used for navigation can be obtained for any instant of *Universal Time* (UT, specifically UT1, or previously Greenwich Mean Time (GMT)).

The *Local Hour Angle* (LHA) can then be obtained by means of the formula:

$$LHA = GHA \; {\textstyle {-\; west \atop +\; east}} \; longitude$$

The remaining data consist of: times of rising and setting of the Sun and Moon, and times of twilight; miscellaneous calendarial and planning data and auxiliary tables, including a list of Standard Times; corrections to be applied to observed altitude.

For the Sun, Moon, and planets, the GHA and Dec are tabulated directly for each hour of UT throughout the year. For the stars, the *Sidereal Hour Angle* (SHA) is given, and the GHA is obtained from:

$$GHA \; Star = GHA \; Aries + SHA \; Star$$

The SHA and Dec of the stars change slowly and may be regarded as constant over periods of several days. GHA Aries, or the Greenwich Hour Angle of the first point of Aries (the Vernal Equinox), is tabulated for each hour. Permanent tables give the appropriate increments and corrections to the tabulated hourly values of GHA and Dec for the minutes and seconds of UT.

The six-volume series of *Sight Reduction Tables for Marine Navigation* (published in U.S.A. as Pub. No. 229) has been designed for the solution of the navigational triangle and is intended for use with *The Nautical Almanac*.

Two alternative procedures for sight reduction are described on pages 277–318. The first requires the use of programmable calculators or computers, while the second uses a set of concise tables that is given on pages 286–317.

The tabular accuracy is $0\!\!\cdot\!\!1$ throughout. The time argument on the daily pages of this Almanac is UT1 denoted throughout by UT. This scale may differ from the broadcast time signals (UTC) by an amount which, if ignored, will introduce an error of up to $0\!\!\cdot\!\!2$ in longitude determined from astronomical observations. The difference arises because the time argument depends on the variable rate of rotation of the Earth while the broadcast time signals are based on an atomic time-scale. Step adjustments of exactly one second are made to the time signals as required (normally at 24^h on December 31 and June 30) so that the difference between the time signals and UT, as used in this Almanac, may not exceed 0^s9. Those who require to reduce observations to a precision of better than 1^s must therefore obtain the correction (DUT1) to the time signals from coding in the signal, or from other sources; the required time is given by UT1=UTC+DUT1 to a precision of 0^s1. Alternatively, the longitude, when determined from astronomical observations, may be corrected by the corresponding amount shown in the following table:

Correction to time signals	Correction to longitude
-0^s9 to -0^s7	$0\!\!\cdot\!\!2$ to east
-0^s6 to -0^s3	$0\!\!\cdot\!\!1$ to east
-0^s2 to $+0^s2$	no correction
$+0^s3$ to $+0^s6$	$0\!\!\cdot\!\!1$ to west
$+0^s7$ to $+0^s9$	$0\!\!\cdot\!\!2$ to west

3. *Lay-out.* The ephemeral data for three days are presented on an opening of two pages: the left-hand page contains the data for the planets and stars; the right-hand page contains the data for the Sun and Moon, together with times of twilight, sunrise, sunset, moonrise and moonset.

The remaining contents are arranged as follows: for ease of reference the altitude-correction tables are given on pages A2, A3, A4, xxxiv and xxxv; calendar, Moon's phases, eclipses, and planet notes (i.e. data of general interest) precede the main tabulations. The Explanation is followed by information on standard times, star charts and list of star positions, sight reduction procedures and concise sight reduction tables, polar phenomena information and graphs, tables of increments and corrections and other auxiliary tables that are frequently used.

MAIN DATA

4. *Daily pages.* The daily pages give the GHA of Aries, the GHA and Dec of the Sun, Moon, and the four navigational planets, for each hour of UT. For the Moon, values of v and d are also tabulated for each hour to facilitate the correction of GHA and Dec to intermediate times; v and d for the Sun and planets change so slowly that they are given, at the foot of the appropriate columns, once only on the page; v is zero for Aries and negligible for the Sun, and is omitted. The SHA and Dec of the 57 selected stars, arranged in alphabetical order of proper name, are also given.

5. *Stars.* The SHA and Dec of 173 stars, including the 57 selected stars, are tabulated for each month on pages 268–273; no interpolation is required and the data can be used in precisely the same way as those for the selected stars on the daily pages. The stars are arranged in order of SHA.

The list of 173 includes all stars down to magnitude 3·0, together with a few fainter ones to fill the larger gaps. The 57 selected stars have been chosen from amongst these on account of brightness and distribution in the sky; they will suffice for the majority of observations.

The 57 selected stars are known by their proper names, but they are also numbered in descending order of SHA. In the list of 173 stars, the constellation names are always given on the left-hand page; on the facing page proper names are given where well-known names exist. Numbers for the selected stars are given in both columns.

An index to the selected stars, containing lists in both alphabetical and numerical order, is given on page xxxiii and is also reprinted on the bookmark.

6. *Increments and corrections.* The tables printed on tinted paper (pages ii–xxxi) at the back of the Almanac provide the increments and corrections for minutes and seconds to be applied to the hourly values of GHA and Dec. They consist of sixty tables, one for each minute, separated into two parts: increments to GHA for Sun and planets, Aries, and Moon for every minute and second; and, for each minute, corrections to be applied to GHA and Dec corresponding to the values of v and d given on the daily pages.

The increments are based on the following adopted hourly rates of increase of the GHA: Sun and planets, $15°$ precisely; Aries, $15°\ 02'\!\cdot\!46$; Moon, $14°\ 19'\!\cdot\!0$. The values of v on the daily pages are the excesses of the actual hourly motions over the adopted values; they are generally positive, except for Venus. The tabulated hourly values of the Sun's GHA have been adjusted to reduce to a minimum the error caused by treating v as negligible. The values of d on the daily pages are the hourly differences of the Dec. For the Moon, the true values of v and d are given for each hour; otherwise mean values are given for the three days on the page.

7. *Method of entry.* The UT of an observation is expressed as a day and hour, followed by a number of minutes and seconds. The tabular values of GHA and Dec, and, where necessary, the corresponding values of v and d, are taken directly from the daily pages for the day and hour of UT; this hour is always *before* the time of observation. SHA and Dec of the selected stars are also taken from the daily pages.

The table of Increments and Corrections for the minute of UT is then selected. For the GHA, the increment for minutes and seconds is taken from the appropriate column opposite the seconds of UT; the v-correction is taken from the second part of the same table opposite the value of v as given on the daily pages. Both increment and v-correction are to be added to the GHA, except for Venus when v is prefixed by a minus sign and the v-correction is to be subtracted. For the Dec there is no increment, but a d-correction is applied in the same way as the v-correction; d is given without sign on the daily pages and the sign of the correction is to be supplied by inspection of the Dec column. In many cases the correction may be applied mentally.

8. *Examples.* (a) Sun and Moon. Required the GHA and Dec of the Sun and Moon on 2020 February 4 at 15^h 47^m 13^s UT.

		SUN			MOON			
		GHA	Dec	d	GHA	v	Dec	d
		° ′	° ′	′	° ′	′	° ′	′
Daily page, February 4^d 15^h		41 31·9	S 16 15·6	0·7	285 43·1	9·4	N 20 30·2	6·3
Increments for	47^m 13^s	11 48·3			11 16·0			
v or d corrections for	47^m		−0·6		+7·4		+5·0	
Sum for February 4^d 15^h 47^m 13^s		53 20·2	S 16 15·0		297 06·5		N 20 35·2	

(b) Planets. Required the LHA and Dec of (i) Venus on 2020 February 4 at 13^h 50^m 00^s UT in longitude E 77° 14′; (ii) Jupiter on 2020 February 4 at 11^h 07^m 39^s UT in longitude W 87° 59′.

		VENUS					JUPITER			
		GHA	v	Dec	d		GHA	v	Dec	d
		° ′	′	° ′	′		° ′	′	° ′	′
Daily page, Feb. 4^d	(13^h)	332 27·4	−0·2	S2 10·1	1·3	(11^h)	13 26·1	1·9	S22 37·3	0·1
Increments (planets)	(50^m 00^s)	12 30·0				(07^m 39^s)	1 54·8			
v or d corrections for	(50^m)	−0·2		−1·1		(07^m)	+0·2		+0·0	
Sum = GHA and Dec.		344 57·2		S2 09·0			15 21·1		S22 37·3	
Longitude	(east)	+ 77 14·0				(west)	− 87 59·0			
Multiples of 360°		−360					+360			
LHA planet		62 11·2					287 22·1			

(c) Stars. Required the GHA and Dec of (i) *Aldebaran* on 2020 February 4 at 19^h 42^m 37^s UT; (ii) *Vega* on 2020 February 4 at 6^h 55^m 31^s UT.

		Aldebaran			Vega	
		GHA	Dec		GHA	Dec
		° ′	° ′		° ′	° ′
Daily page (SHA and Dec)		290 44·0	N 16 32.8		80 36·2	N 38 48.0
Daily page (GHA Aries)	(19^h)	59 24·6		(6^h)	223 52·6	
Increments (Aries)	(42^m 37^s)	10 41·0		(55^m 31^s)	13 55·0	
Sum = GHA star		360 49·6			318 23·8	
Multiples of 360°		−360				
GHA star		0 49·6			318 23·8	

9. *Polaris (Pole Star) tables.* The tables on pages 274–276 provide means by which the latitude can be deduced from an observed altitude of *Polaris*, and they also give its azimuth; their use is explained and illustrated on those pages. They are based on the following formula:

$$\text{Latitude} - H_O = -p \cos h + \tfrac{1}{2} p \sin p \sin^2 h \tan(\text{latitude})$$

where

$H_O =$ Apparent altitude (corrected for refraction)

$p =$ polar distance of *Polaris* $= 90° - \text{Dec}$

$h =$ local hour angle of *Polaris* $= \text{LHA Aries} + \text{SHA}$

a_0, which is a function of LHA Aries only, is the value of both terms of the above formula calculated for mean values of the SHA (315° 38′) and Dec (N 89° 21′.0) of *Polaris*, for a mean latitude of 50°, and adjusted by the addition of a constant (58′.8).

a_1, which is a function of LHA Aries and latitude, is the excess of the value of the second term over its mean value for latitude $50°$, increased by a constant (0.6) to make it always positive. a_2, which is a function of LHA Aries and date, is the correction to the first term for the variation of *Polaris* from its adopted mean position; it is increased by a constant (0.6) to make it positive. The sum of the added constants is $1°$, so that:

$$\text{Latitude} = \text{Apparent altitude (corrected for refraction)} - 1° + a_0 + a_1 + a_2$$

RISING AND SETTING PHENOMENA

10. *General.* On the right-hand daily pages are given the times of sunrise and sunset, of the beginning and end of civil and nautical twilights, and of moonrise and moonset for a range of latitudes from N $72°$ to S $60°$. These times, which are given to the nearest minute, are strictly the UT of the phenomena on the Greenwich meridian; they are given for every day for moonrise and moonset, but only for the middle day of the three on each page for the solar phenomena.

They are approximately the Local Mean Times (LMT) of the corresponding phenomena on other meridians; they can be formally interpolated if desired. The UT of a phenomenon is obtained from the LMT by:

$$\text{UT} = \text{LMT} \genfrac{}{}{0pt}{}{+ \text{ west}}{- \text{ east}} \text{ longitude}$$

in which the longitude must first be converted to time by the table on page i or otherwise. Interpolation for latitude can be done mentally or with the aid of Table I on page xxxii.

The following symbols are used to indicate the conditions under which, in high latitudes, some of the phenomena do not occur:

☐ Sun or Moon remains continuously above the horizon;

■ Sun or Moon remains continuously below the horizon;

//// twilight lasts all night.

Basis of the tabulations. At sunrise and sunset $16'$ is allowed for semi-diameter and $34'$ for horizontal refraction, so that at the times given the Sun's upper limb is on the visible horizon; all times refer to phenomena as seen from sea level with a clear horizon.

At the times given for the beginning and end of twilight, the Sun's zenith distance is $96°$ for civil, and $102°$ for nautical twilight. The degree of illumination at the times given for civil twilight (in good conditions and in the absence of other illumination) is such that the brightest stars are visible and the horizon is clearly defined. At the times given for nautical twilight, the horizon is in general not visible, and it is too dark for observation with a marine sextant.

Times corresponding to other depressions of the Sun may be obtained by interpolation or, for depressions of more than $12°$, less reliably, by extrapolation; times so obtained will be subject to considerable uncertainty near extreme conditions.

At moonrise and moonset, allowance is made for semi-diameter, parallax, and refraction ($34'$), so that at the times given the Moon's upper limb is on the visible horizon as seen from sea level.

Polar phenomena. Information and graphs concerning the rising and setting of the Sun and Moon and the duration of civil twilight for high latitudes are given on pages 320–325.

11. *Sunrise, sunset, twilight.* The tabulated times may be regarded, without serious error, as the LMT of the phenomena on any of the three days on the page and in any longitude. Precise times may normally be obtained by interpolating the tabular values for latitude and to the correct day and longitude, the latter being expressed as a fraction of a day by dividing it by $360°$, positive for west and negative for east longitudes. In the extreme conditions near ☐, ■ or //// interpolation may not be possible in one direction, but accurate times are of little value in these circumstances.

Examples. Required the UT of (a) the beginning of morning twilights and sunrise on 2020 January 13 for latitude S $48°$ $55'$, longitude E $75°$ $18'$; (b) sunset and the end of evening twilights on 2020 January 15 for latitude N $67°$ $10'$, longitude W $168°$ $05'$.

	(a)	Twilight Nautical	Twilight Civil	Sunrise	(b)	Sunset	Twilight Civil	Twilight Nautical
From p. 19		d h m	d h m	d h m		d h m	d h m	d h m
LMT for Lat	S 45°	13 03 08	13 03 55	13 04 31	N 66°	15 14 21	15 15 41	15 16 52
Corr. to	S 48° 55′	−30	−20	−16	N 67° 10′	−24	−12	−6
(p. xxxii, Table I)								
Long (p. i)	E 75° 18′	−5 01	−5 01	−5 01	W 168° 05′	+11 12	+11 12	+11 12
UT		12 21 37	12 22 34	12 23 14		16 01 09	16 02 41	16 03 58

The LMT are strictly for January 14 (middle date on page) and 0° longitude; for more precise times it is necessary to interpolate, but rounding errors may accumulate to about 2^m.

(a) to January $13^d − 75°/360° =$ Jan. 12^d8, i.e. $\frac{1}{3}(1·2) = 0·4$ backwards towards the data for the same latitude interpolated similarly from page 17; the corrections are $−2^m$ to nautical twilight, $−2^m$ to civil twilight and $−2^m$ to sunrise.

(b) to January $15^d + 168°/360° =$ Jan. 15^d5, i.e. $\frac{1}{3}(1·5) = 0·5$ forwards towards the data for the same latitude interpolated similarly from page 21; the corrections are $+8^m$ to sunset, $+4^m$ to civil twilight, and $+4^m$ to nautical twilight.

12. *Moonrise, moonset.* Precise times of moonrise and moonset are rarely needed; a glance at the tables will generally give sufficient indication of whether the Moon is available for observation and of the hours of rising and setting. If needed, precise times may be obtained as follows. Interpolate for latitude, using Table I on page xxxii, on the day wanted and also on the preceding day in east longitudes or the following day in west longitudes; take the difference between these times and interpolate for longitude by applying to the time for the day wanted the correction from Table II on page xxxii, so that the resulting time is between the two times used. In extreme conditions near ▢ or ■ interpolation for latitude or longitude may be possible only in one direction; accurate times are of little value in these circumstances.

To facilitate this interpolation, the times of moonrise and moonset are given for four days on each page; where no phenomenon occurs during a particular day (as happens once a month) the time of the phenomenon on the following day, increased by 24^h, is given; extra care must be taken when interpolating between two values, when one of those values exceeds 24^h. In practice it suffices to use the daily difference between the times for the nearest tabular latitude, and generally, to enter Table II with the nearest tabular arguments as in the examples below.

Examples. Required the UT of moonrise and moonset in latitude S 47° 10′, longitudes E 124° 00′ and W 78° 31′ on 2020 January 5.

	Longitude E 124° 00′ Moonrise	Longitude E 124° 00′ Moonset	Longitude W 78° 31′ Moonrise	Longitude W 78° 31′ Moonset
	d h m	d h m	d h m	d h m
LMT for Lat. S 45°	5 14 28	5 00 43	5 14 28	5 00 43
Lat correction (p. xxxii, Table I)	+04	−02	+04	−02
Long correction (p. xxxii, Table II)	−23	−07	+16	+04
Correct LMT	5 14 09	5 00 34	5 14 48	5 00 45
Longitude (p. i)	−8 16	−8 16	+5 14	+5 14
UT	5 05 53	4 16 18	5 20 02	5 05 59

ALTITUDE CORRECTION TABLES

13. *General.* In general, two corrections are given for application to altitudes observed with a marine sextant; additional corrections are required for Venus and Mars and also for very low altitudes.

Tables of the correction for dip of the horizon, due to height of eye above sea level, are given on pages A2 and xxxiv. Strictly this correction should be applied first and subtracted from the sextant altitude to give apparent altitude, which is the correct argument for the other tables.

Separate tables are given of the second correction for the Sun, for stars and planets (on pages A2 and A3), and for the Moon (on pages xxxiv and xxxv). For the Sun, values are given for both lower and upper limbs, for two periods of the year. The star tables are used for the planets, but additional corrections for parallax (page A2) are required for Venus and Mars. The Moon tables are in two parts: the main correction is a function of apparent altitude only and is tabulated for the lower limb (30′ must be subtracted to obtain the correction for the upper limb); the other, which is given for both lower and upper limbs, depends also on the horizontal parallax, which has to be taken from the daily pages.

An additional correction, given on page A4, is required for the change in the refraction, due to variations of pressure and temperature from the adopted standard conditions; it may generally be ignored for altitudes greater than 10°, except possibly in extreme conditions. The correction tables for the Sun, stars, and planets are in two parts; only those for altitudes greater than 10° are reprinted on the bookmark.

14. *Critical tables.* Some of the altitude correction tables are arranged as critical tables. In these, an interval of apparent altitude (or height of eye) corresponds to a single value of the correction; no interpolation is required. At a "critical" entry the upper of the two possible values of the correction is to be taken. For example, in the table of dip, a correction of −4′1 corresponds to all values of the height of eye from 5·3 to 5·5 metres (17·5 to 18·3 feet) inclusive.

15. *Examples.* The following examples illustrate the use of the altitude correction tables; the sextant altitudes given are assumed to be taken on 2020 March 11 with a marine sextant at height 5·4 metres (18 feet), temperature −3°C and pressure 982 mb, the Moon sights being taken at about 10^h UT.

	SUN lower limb	SUN upper limb	MOON lower limb	MOON upper limb	VENUS	*Polaris*
	° ′	° ′	° ′	° ′	° ′	° ′
Sextant altitude	21 19·7	3 20·2	33 27·6	26 06·7	4 32·6	49 36·5
Dip, height 5·4 metres (18 feet)	−4·1	−4·1	−4·1	−4·1	−4·1	−4·1
Main correction	+13·8	−29·4	+57·3	+60·5	−10·7	−0·8
−30′ for upper limb (Moon)	—	—	—	−30·0	—	—
L, U correction for Moon	—	—	+9·0	+6·2	—	—
Additional correction for Venus	—	—	—	—	+0·2	—
Additional refraction correction	−0·1	−0·6	−0·1	−0·1	−0·5	0·0
Corrected sextant altitude	21 29·3	2 46·1	34 29·7	26 39·2	4 17·5	49 31·6

The main corrections have been taken out with apparent altitude (sextant altitude corrected for index error and dip) as argument, interpolating where possible. These refinements are rarely necessary.

16. *Composition of the Corrections.* The table for the dip of the sea horizon is based on the formula:

Correction for dip $= −1′76\sqrt{\text{(height of eye in metres)}} = −0′97\sqrt{\text{(height of eye in feet)}}$

The correction table for the Sun includes the effects of semi-diameter, parallax and mean refraction.

The correction tables for the stars and planets allow for the effect of mean refraction.

The phase correction for Venus has been incorporated in the tabulations for GHA and Dec, and no correction for phase is required. The additional corrections for Venus and Mars allow for parallax. Alternatively, the correction for parallax may be calculated from $p \cos H$, where p is the parallax and H is the altitude. In 2020 the values for p are:

	Jan. 1	Feb. 17	Apr. 9	May 2	May 18	June 19	July 5	July 28	Sept. 17	Dec. 31
Venus	0′1	0′2	0′3	0′4	0′5	0′4	0′3	0′2	0′1	

	Jan. 1	June 5	Aug. 11	Sept. 29	Oct. 13	Nov. 23	Dec. 31
Mars	0′1	0′2	0′3	0′4	0′3	0′2	

The correction table for the Moon includes the effect of semi-diameter, parallax, augmentation and mean refraction.

Mean refraction is calculated for a temperature of 10°C (50°F), a pressure of 1010 mb (29·83 inches), humidity of 80% and wavelength 0·50169 μm.

17. *Bubble sextant observations.* When observing with a bubble sextant, no correction is necessary for dip, semi-diameter, or augmentation. The altitude corrections for the stars and planets on page A2 and on the bookmark should be used for the Sun as well as for the stars and planets; for the Moon, it is easiest to take the mean of the corrections for lower and upper limbs and subtract 15′ from the altitude; the correction for dip must not be applied.

AUXILIARY AND PLANNING DATA

18. *Sun and Moon.* On the daily pages are given: hourly values of the horizontal parallax of the Moon; the semi-diameters and the times of meridian passage of both Sun and Moon over the Greenwich meridian; the equation of time; the age of the Moon, the percent (%) illuminated and a symbol indicating the phase. The times of the phases of the Moon are given in UT on page 4. For the Moon, the semi-diameters for each of the three days are given at the foot of the column; for the Sun a single value is sufficient. Table II on page xxxii may be used for interpolating the time of the Moon's meridian passage for longitude. The equation of time is given daily at 00^h and 12^h UT. The sign is *positive* for unshaded values and *negative* for shaded values. To obtain apparent time add the equation of time to mean time when the sign is *positive*. Subtract the equation of time from mean time when the sign is *negative*. At 12^h UT, when the sign is *positive*, meridian passage of the Sun occurs *before* 12^h UT, otherwise it occurs *after* 12^h UT.

19. *Planets.* The magnitudes of the planets are given immediately following their names in the headings on the daily pages; also given, for the middle day of the three on the page, are their SHA at 00^h UT and their times of meridian passage.

The planet notes and diagram on pages 8 and 9 provide descriptive information as to the suitability of the planets for observation during the year, and of their positions and movements.

20. *Stars.* The time of meridian passage of the first point of Aries over the Greenwich meridian is given on the daily pages, for the middle day of the three on the page, to 0^{m}1. The interval between successive meridian passages is 23^h 56^{m}1 (24^h less 3^{m}9), so that times for intermediate days and other meridians can readily be derived. If a precise time is required, it may be obtained by finding the UT at which LHA Aries is zero.

The meridian passage of a star occurs when its LHA is zero, that is when LHA Aries + SHA = 360°. An approximate time can be obtained from the planet diagram on page 9.

The star charts on pages 266 and 267 are intended to assist identification. They show the relative positions of the stars in the sky as seen from the Earth and include all 173 stars used in the Almanac, together with a few others to complete the main constellation configurations. The local meridian at any time may be located on the chart by means of its SHA which is 360° − LHA Aries, or west longitude − GHA Aries.

21. *Star globe.* To set a star globe on which is printed a scale of LHA Aries, first set the globe for latitude and then rotate about the polar axis until the scale under the edge of the meridian circle reads LHA Aries.

To mark the positions of the Sun, Moon, and planets on the star globe, take the difference GHA Aries − GHA body and use this along the LHA Aries scale, in conjunction with the declination, to plot the position. GHA Aries − GHA body is most conveniently found by taking the difference when the GHA of the body is small (less than 15°), which happens once a day.

22. *Calendar.* On page 4 are given lists of ecclesiastical festivals, and of the principal anniversaries and holidays in the United Kingdom and the United States of America. The calendar on page 5 includes the day of the year as well as the day of the week.

Brief particulars are given, at the foot of page 5, of the solar and lunar eclipses occurring during the year; the times given are in UT. The principal features of the more important solar eclipses are shown on the maps on pages 6 and 7.

23. *Standard times.* The lists on pages 262–265 give the standard times used in most countries. In general no attempt is made to give details of the beginning and end of summer time, since they are liable to frequent changes at short notice. For the latest information consult Admiralty List of Radio Signals Volume 2 (NP 282) corrected by Section VI of the weekly edition of Admiralty Notices to Mariners.

The Date or Calendar Line is an arbitrary line, on either side of which the date differs by one day; when crossing this line on a westerly course, the date must be advanced one day; when crossing it on an easterly course, the date must be put back one day. The line is a modification of the line of the 180th meridian, and is drawn so as to include, as far as possible, islands of any one group, etc., on the same side of the line. It may be traced by starting at the South Pole and joining up to the following positions:

Lat	S	51·0	S	45·0	S	15·0	S	5·0	N	48·0	N	53·0	N	65·5
Long		180·0	W	172·5	W	172·5		180·0		180·0	E	170·0	W	169·0

thence through the middle of the Diomede Islands to Lat N 68°0, Long W 169°0, passing east of Ostrov Vrangelya (Wrangel Island) to Lat N 75°0, Long 180°0, and thence to the North Pole.

ACCURACY

24. *Main data.* The quantities tabulated in this Almanac are generally correct to the nearest 0′·1; the exception is the Sun's GHA which is deliberately adjusted by up to 0′·15 to reduce the error due to ignoring the v-correction. The GHA and Dec at intermediate times cannot be obtained to this precision, since at least two quantities must be added; moreover, the v- and d-corrections are based on mean values of v and d and are taken from tables for the whole minute only. The largest error that can occur in the GHA or Dec of any body other than the Sun or Moon is less than 0′·2; it may reach 0′·25 for the GHA of the Sun and 0′·3 for that of the Moon.

In practice, it may be expected that only one third of the values of GHA and Dec taken out will have errors larger than 0′·05 and less than one tenth will have errors larger than 0′·1.

25. *Altitude corrections.* The errors in the altitude corrections are nominally of the same order as those in GHA and Dec, as they result from the addition of several quantities each correctly rounded off to 0′·1. But the actual values of the dip and of the refraction at low altitudes may, in extreme atmospheric conditions, differ considerably from the mean values used in the tables.

USE OF THIS ALMANAC IN 2021

This Almanac may be used for the Sun and stars in 2021 in the following manner.

For the Sun, take out the GHA and Dec for the same date but, for January and February, for a time $18^h 12^m 00^s$ *later* and, for March to December, for a time $5^h 48^m 00^s$ *earlier* than the UT of observation; in both cases add 87° 00′ to the GHA so obtained. The error, mainly due to planetary perturbations of the Earth, is unlikely to exceed 0′·4.

For the stars, calculate the GHA and Dec for the same date and the same time, but for January and February *add* 44′·0 and for March to December *subtract* 15′·1 from the GHA so found. The error due to incomplete correction for precession and nutation is unlikely to exceed 0′·4. If preferred, the same result can be obtained by using a time $18^h 12^m 00^s$ later for January and February, and $5^h 48^m 00^s$ earlier for March to December, than the UT of observation (as for the Sun) and adding 86° 59′·2 to the GHA (or adding 87° as for the Sun and subtracting 0′·8, for precession, from the SHA of the star).

The Almanac cannot be so used for the Moon or planets.

LIST I — PLACES FAST ON UTC (mainly those EAST OF GREENWICH)

The times given } *added* to UTC to give Standard Time
below should be } *subtracted* from Standard Time to give UTC.

	h	m		h	m
Admiralty Islands	10		Denmark*†	01	
Afghanistan	04	30	Djibouti	03	
Albania*	01		Egypt, Arab Republic of	02	
Algeria	01		Equatorial Guinea, Republic of	01	
Amirante Islands	04		Bioko	01	
Andaman Islands	05	30	Eritrea	03	
Angola	01		Estonia*†	02	
Armenia	04		Eswatini	02	
Australia			Ethiopia	03	
Australian Capital Territory*	10		Fiji*	12	
New South Wales*[1]	10		Finland*†	02	
Northern Territory	09	30	France*†	01	
Queensland	10		Gabon	01	
South Australia*	09	30	Georgia	04	
Tasmania*	10		Germany*†	01	
Victoria*	10		Gibraltar*	01	
Western Australia	08		Greece*†	02	
Whitsunday Islands	10		Guam	10	
Austria*†	01		Hong Kong	08	
Azerbaijan	04		Hungary*†	01	
Bahrain	03		India	05	30
Balearic Islands*†	01		Indonesia, Republic of		
Bangladesh	06		Bangka, Billiton, Java, West and		
Belarus	03		Central Kalimantan, Madura, Sumatra	07	
Belgium*†	01		Bali, Flores, South, North and East		
Benin	01		Kalimantan, Lombok, Sulawesi,		
Bosnia and Herzegovina*	01		Sumba, Sumbawa, West Timor ...	08	
Botswana, Republic of	02		Aru, Irian Jaya, Kai, Moluccas		
Brunei	08		Tanimbar	09	
Bulgaria*†	02		Iran*	03	30
Burma (Myanmar)	06	30	Iraq	03	
Burundi	02		Israel*	02	
Cambodia	07		Italy*†	01	
Cameroon Republic	01		Jan Mayen Island*	01	
Caroline Islands[2]	10		Japan	09	
Central African Republic	01		Jordan*	02	
Chad	01		Kazakhstan		
Chagos Archipelago & Diego Garcia	06		Western: Aktau, Uralsk, Atyrau ...	05	
Chatham Islands*	12	45	Eastern & Central: Kzyl-Orda, Astana	06	
China, People's Republic of	08		Kenya	03	
Christmas Island, Indian Ocean ...	07		Kerguelen Islands	05	
Cocos (Keeling) Islands	06	30	Kiribati Republic		
Comoro Islands (Comoros)	03		Gilbert Islands	12	
Congo, Democratic Republic			Phoenix Islands[3]	13	
West: Kinshasa, Equateur	01		Line Islands[3]	14	
East: Orientale, Kasai, Kivu, Shaba	02		Korea, North	09	
Congo Republic	01		Korea, South	09	
Corsica*†	01		Kuwait	03	
Crete*†	02		Kyrgyzstan	06	
Croatia*†	01		Laccadive Islands	05	30
Cyprus†: Ercan*, Larnaca*	02		Laos	07	
Czech Republic*†	01				

* Daylight-saving time may be kept in these places.   † For Summer time dates see List II footnotes.
[1] Except Broken Hill Area* which keeps 09[h] 30[m].
[2] Except Pohnpei, Pingelap and Kosrae which keep 11[h] and Palau which keeps 09[h].
[3] The Line and Phoenix Is. not part of the Kiribati Republic may keep other time zones.

LIST I — (continued)

	h	m
Latvia*†	02	
Lebanon*	02	
Lesotho	02	
Libya	02	
Liechtenstein*	01	
Lithuania*†	02	
Lord Howe Island*	10	30
Luxembourg*†	01	
Macau	08	
Macedonia*, former Yugoslav Republic	01	
Madagascar, Democratic Republic of	03	
Malawi	02	
Malaysia, Malaya, Sabah, Sarawak ...	08	
Maldives, Republic of The	05	
Malta*†	01	
Mariana Islands	10	
Marshall Islands	12	
Mauritius	04	
Moldova*	02	
Monaco*	01	
Mongolia	08	
Montenegro*	01	
Morocco	01	
Mozambique	02	
Namibia	02	
Nauru	12	
Nepal	05	45
Netherlands, The*†	01	
New Caledonia	11	
New Zealand*	12	
Nicobar Islands	05	30
Niger	01	
Nigeria, Republic of	01	
Norfolk Island	11	
Norway*	01	
Novaya Zemlya	03	
Okinawa	09	
Oman	04	
Pagalu (Annobon Islands)	01	
Pakistan	05	
Palau Islands	09	
Papua New Guinea[4]	10	
Pescadores Islands	08	
Philippine Republic	08	
Poland*†	01	
Qatar	03	
Reunion	04	
Romania*†	02	
Russia[5]		
Kaliningrad	02	
Moscow, St. Petersburg, Arkhangelsk	03	
Samara, Astrakhan, Saratov, ...		
Volgograd	04	
Ekaterinburg, Ufa, Perm, Novyy Port	05	
Omsk	06	

	h	m
Norilsk, Krasnoyarsk, Dikson,		
Novosibirsk, Tomsk	07	
Irkutsk, Bratsk, Ulan-Ude	08	
Tiksi, Yakutsk, Chita	09	
Vladivostok, Khabarovsk, Okhotsk	10	
Severo-Kurilsk, Magadan,		
Sakhalin Island	11	
Petropavlovsk-K., Anadyr	12	
Rwanda	02	
Ryukyu Islands	09	
Samoa*	13	
Santa Cruz Islands	11	
São Tomé	01	
Sardinia*†	01	
Saudi Arabia	03	
Schouten Islands	09	
Serbia*	01	
Seychelles	04	
Sicily*†	01	
Singapore	08	
Slovakia*†	01	
Slovenia*†	01	
Socotra	03	
Solomon Islands	11	
Somalia Republic	03	
South Africa, Republic of	02	
South Sudan	03	
Spain*†	01	
Spanish Possessions in North Africa*	01	
Spitsbergen (Svalbard)*	01	
Sri Lanka	05	30
Sudan, Republic of	02	
Sweden*†	01	
Switzerland*	01	
Syria (Syrian Arab Republic)*	02	
Taiwan	08	
Tajikistan	05	
Tanzania	03	
Thailand	07	
Timor-Leste	09	
Tonga	13	
Tunisia	01	
Turkey	03	
Turkmenistan	05	
Tuvalu	12	
Uganda	03	
Ukraine*	02	
United Arab Emirates	04	
Uzbekistan	05	
Vanuatu, Republic of	11	
Vietnam, Socialist Republic of	07	
Yemen	03	
Zambia, Republic of	02	
Zimbabwe	02	

* Daylight-saving time may be kept in these places.   † For Summer time dates see List II footnotes.
[4] Excluding the Autonomous Region of Bougainville which keeps 11ʰ.
[5] The boundaries between the zones are irregular; listed are chief towns in each zone.

LIST II — PLACES NORMALLY KEEPING UTC

Ascension Island	Ghana	Irish Republic*†	Portugal*†	Tristan da Cunha
Burkina-Faso	Great Britain†	Ivory Coast	Principe	
Canary Islands*†	Guinea-Bissau	Liberia	St. Helena	
Channel Islands†	Guinea Republic	Madeira*†	Senegal	
Faeroes*, The	Iceland	Mali	Sierra Leone	
Gambia, The	Ireland, Northern†	Mauritania	Togo Republic	

* Daylight-saving time may be kept in these places.

† Summer time (daylight-saving time), one hour in advance of UTC, will be kept from 2020 March 29^d 01^h to October 25^d 01^h UTC (Ninth Summer Time Directive of the European Union). Ratification by member countries has not been verified.

LIST III — PLACES SLOW ON UTC (WEST OF GREENWICH)

The times given } *subtracted* from UTC to give Standard Time
below should be { *added* to Standard Time to give UTC.

	h	m		h	m
American Samoa	11		Canada (*continued*)		
Argentina	03		Prince Edward Island*	04	
Austral (Tubuai) Islands[1]	10		Quebec, east of long. W. 63°	04	
Azores*†	01		west of long. W. 63°*	05	
			Saskatchewan	06	
Bahamas*	05		Yukon*	08	
Barbados	04		Cape Verde Islands	01	
Belize	06		Cayman Islands	05	
Bermuda*	04		Chile		
Bolivia	04		General*	04	
Brazil			Magallanes and Chilean Antarctic	03	
Fernando de Noronha I., Trindade I.,			Colombia	05	
Oceanic Is.	02		Cook Islands	10	
N and NE coastal states, Tocantins,			Costa Rica	06	
Minas Gerais*, Goiás*, Brasilia*,			Cuba*	05	
S and E coastal states*	03		Curaçao Island	04	
Amazonas[2], Mato Grosso do Sul*,					
Mato Grosso*, Rondônia, Roraima	04		Dominican Republic	04	
Acre	05				
British Antarctic Territory[3,4]	03		Easter Island (I. de Pascua)*	06	
			Ecuador	05	
Canada[4‡]			El Salvador	06	
Alberta*	07				
British Columbia*	08		Falkland Islands	03	
Labrador*	04		Fernando de Noronha Island	02	
Manitoba*	06		French Guiana	03	
New Brunswick*	04				
Newfoundland*	03	30	Galápagos Islands	06	
Nunavut*			Greenland		
east of long. W. 85°	05		Danmarkshavn, Mesters Vig	00	
long. W. 85° to W. 102°	06		General*	03	
west of long. W. 102°	07		Scoresby Sound*	01	
Northwest Territories*	07		Thule*, Pituffik*	04	
Nova Scotia*	04		Grenada	04	
Ontario, east of long. W. 90°*	05		Guadeloupe	04	
Ontario, west of long. W. 90°*	06		Guatemala	06	
			Guyana, Republic of	04	

* Daylight-saving time may be kept in these places.   ‡ Dates for DST are given at the end of List III.
[1] This is the legal standard time, but local mean time is generally used.
[2] Except the cities of Eirunepe, Benjamin Constant and Tabatinga which keep 05^h.
[3] Stations may use UTC.
[4] Some areas may keep another time zone.

LIST III — (continued)

	h	m
Haiti*	05	
Honduras	06	
Jamaica	05	
Johnston Island	10	
Juan Fernandez Islands*	04	
Leeward Islands	04	
Marquesas Islands	09	30
Martinique	04	
Mexico		
General*	06	
Quintana Roo	05	
Baja California Sur*, Chihuahua*		
Nayarit*, Sinaloa* and Sonara ...	07	
Baja California Norte*	08	
Midway Islands	11	
Nicaragua	06	
Niue	11	
Panama, Republic of	05	
Paraguay*	04	
Peru	05	
Pitcairn Island	08	
Puerto Rico	04	
St. Pierre and Miquelon*	03	
Society Islands	10	
South Georgia	02	
Suriname	03	
Trindade Island, South Atlantic ...	02	
Trinidad and Tobago	04	
Tuamotu Archipelago	10	
Tubuai (Austral) Islands	10	
Turks and Caicos Islands*	05	
United States of America‡		
Alabama	06	
Alaska	09	
Aleutian Islands, east of W. 169° 30′	09	
Aleutian Islands, west of W. 169° 30′	10	
Arizona[5]	07	
Arkansas	06	
California	08	
Colorado	07	
Connecticut	05	
Delaware	05	
District of Columbia	05	
Florida[6]	05	
Georgia	05	
Hawaii[5]	10	

	h	m
United States of America‡(continued)		
Idaho, southern part	07	
northern part	08	
Illinois	06	
Indiana[6]	05	
Iowa	06	
Kansas[6]	06	
Kentucky, eastern part	05	
western part	06	
Louisiana	06	
Maine	05	
Maryland	05	
Massachusetts	05	
Michigan[6]	05	
Minnesota	06	
Mississippi	06	
Missouri	06	
Montana	07	
Nebraska, eastern part	06	
western part	07	
Nevada	08	
New Hampshire	05	
New Jersey	05	
New Mexico	07	
New York	05	
North Carolina	05	
North Dakota, eastern part	06	
western part	07	
Ohio	05	
Oklahoma	06	
Oregon[6]	08	
Pennsylvania	05	
Rhode Island	05	
South Carolina	05	
South Dakota, eastern part	06	
western part	07	
Tennessee, eastern part	05	
western part	06	
Texas[6]	06	
Utah	07	
Vermont	05	
Virginia	05	
Washington D.C.	05	
Washington	08	
West Virginia	05	
Wisconsin	06	
Wyoming	07	
Uruguay	03	
Venezuela	04	
Virgin Islands	04	
Windward Islands	04	

* Daylight-saving time may be kept in these places.

‡ Daylight-saving (Summer) time, one hour fast on the time given, is kept during 2020 from March 8 (second Sunday) to November 1 (first Sunday), changing at $02^h 00^m$ local clock time.

[5] Exempt from keeping daylight-saving time, except for a portion of Arizona.

[6] A small portion of the state is in another time zone.

STAR CHARTS

NORTHERN STARS

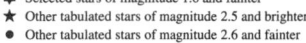
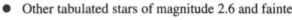

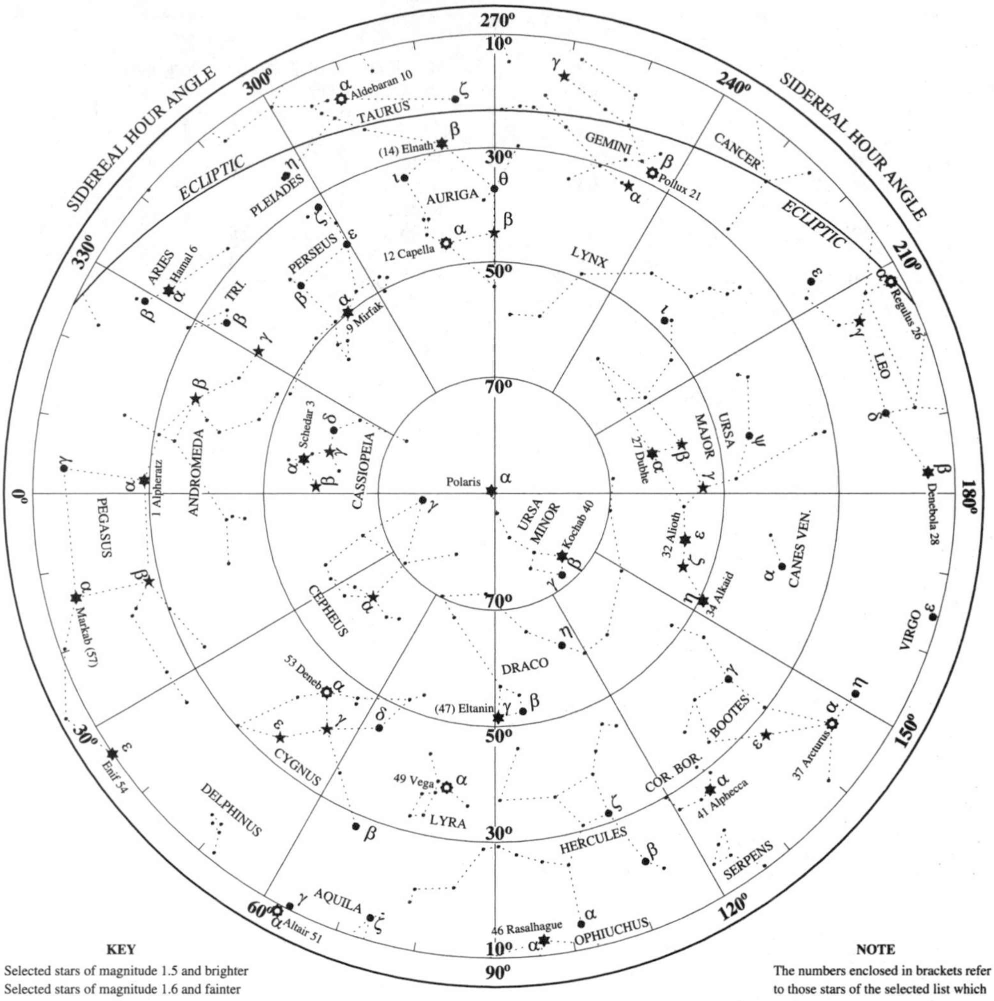

KEY

✿ Selected stars of magnitude 1.5 and brighter
✶ Selected stars of magnitude 1.6 and fainter
★ Other tabulated stars of magnitude 2.5 and brighter
● Other tabulated stars of magnitude 2.6 and fainter
· Untabulated stars

NOTE

The numbers enclosed in brackets refer
to those stars of the selected list which
are not used in Sight Reduction Tables
A.P. 3270, N.P. 303.

EQUATORIAL STARS (SHA 0° to 180°)

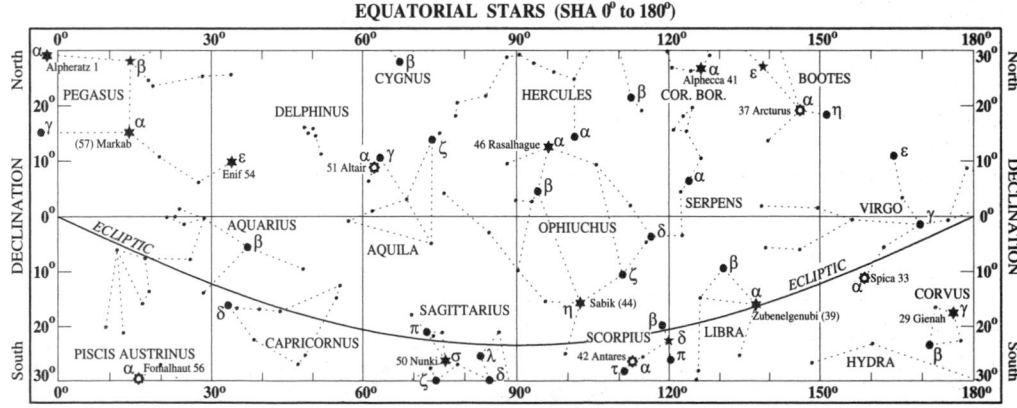

SIDEREAL HOUR ANGLE

SOUTHERN STARS

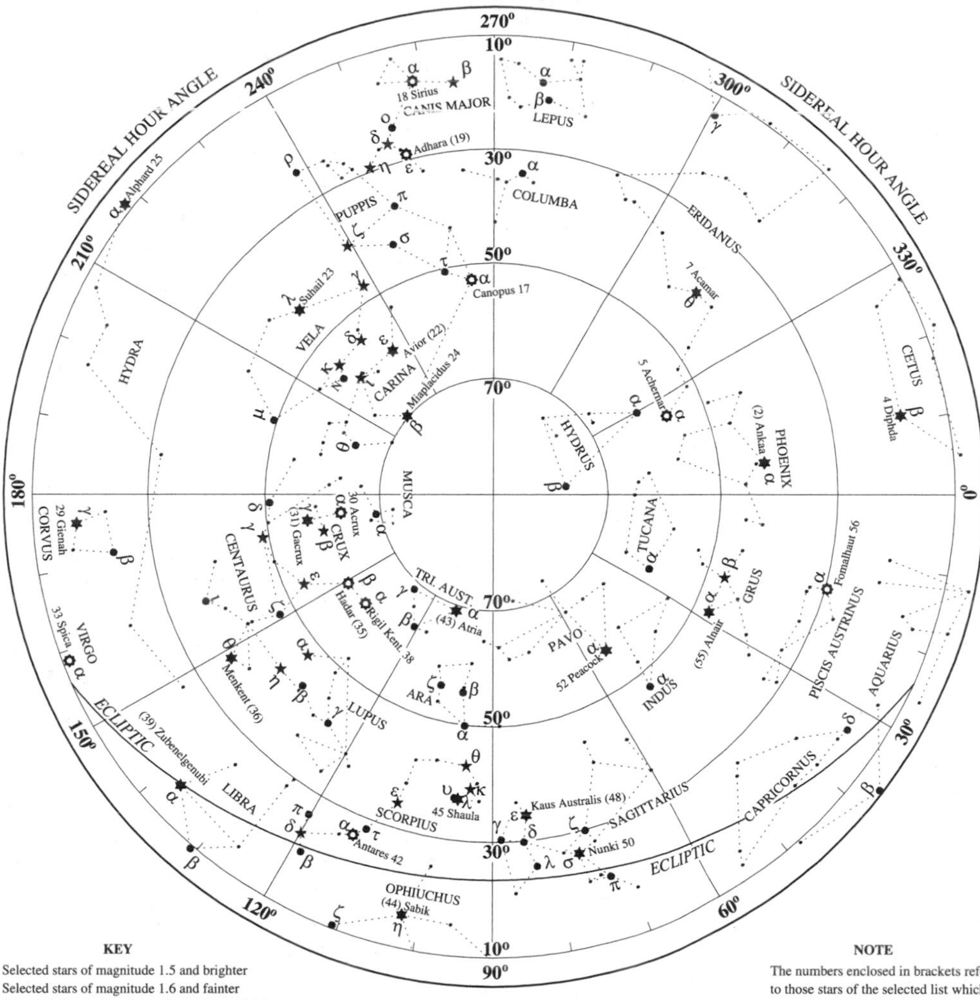

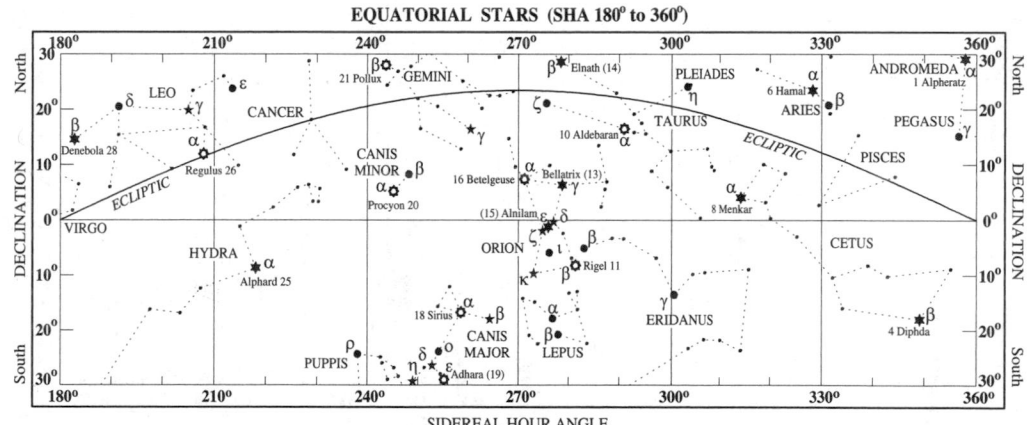

- ✪ Selected stars of magnitude 1.5 and brighter
- ✴ Selected stars of magnitude 1.6 and fainter
- ★ Other tabulated stars of magnitude 2.5 and brighter
- ● Other tabulated stars of magnitude 2.6 and fainter
- · Untabulated stars

NOTE

The numbers enclosed in brackets refer to those stars of the selected list which are not used in Sight Reduction Tables A.P. 3270, N.P. 303.

EQUATORIAL STARS (SHA 180° to 360°)

SIDEREAL HOUR ANGLE

Mag.	Name and Number			SHA							Declination						
				JAN.	FEB.	MAR.	APR.	MAY	JUNE			JAN.	FEB.	MAR.	APR.	MAY	JUNE
			°	′	′	′	′	′	′		°	′	′	′	′	′	′
3·2	γ Cephei		4	58·0	58·6	58·8	58·5	57·9	57·1	N	77	44·8	44·7	44·6	44·4	44·3	44·3
2·5	α Pegasi	57	13	34·0	34·1	34·0	33·9	33·7	33·5	N	15	18·7	18·7	18·6	18·6	18·6	18·7
2·4	β Pegasi		13	49·2	49·3	49·3	49·1	48·9	48·7	N	28	11·5	11·4	11·3	11·3	11·3	11·4
1·2	α Piscis Aust.	56	15	19·2	19·2	19·2	19·1	18·8	18·6	S	29	31·2	31·2	31·1	31·0	30·9	30·8
2·1	β Gruis		19	02·8	02·8	02·8	02·6	02·3	02·0	S	46	47·1	47·0	46·9	46·7	46·6	46·5
2·9	α Tucanæ		25	03·0	03·0	02·9	02·6	02·3	01·9	S	60	09·8	09·7	09·6	09·4	09·3	09·2
1·7	α Gruis	55	27	38·4	38·4	38·3	38·1	37·8	37·5	S	46	52·1	52·0	51·8	51·7	51·6	51·5
2·9	δ Capricorni		32	58·4	58·4	58·3	58·1	57·9	57·6	S	16	02·3	02·3	02·3	02·2	02·1	02·0
2·4	ε Pegasi	54	33	43·0	43·0	42·9	42·7	42·5	42·2	N	9	58·0	57·9	57·9	57·9	57·9	58·0
2·9	β Aquarii		36	51·4	51·3	51·2	51·0	50·8	50·6	S	5	29·1	29·1	29·1	29·0	29·0	28·9
2·4	α Cephei		40	14·9	14·9	14·8	14·5	14·1	13·7	N	62	40·3	40·1	40·0	39·9	39·9	40·0
2·5	ε Cygni		48	15·2	15·2	15·0	14·8	14·6	14·3	N	34	02·7	02·6	02·5	02·5	02·5	02·6
1·3	α Cygni	53	49	28·9	28·8	28·7	28·4	28·2	27·9	N	45	21·1	21·0	20·9	20·8	20·9	21·0
3·1	α Indi		50	16·3	16·2	16·0	15·7	15·4	15·1	S	47	13·4	13·3	13·2	13·1	13·0	13·0
1·9	α Pavonis	52	53	12·7	12·6	12·3	11·9	11·5	11·2	S	56	40·3	40·2	40·1	40·0	39·9	39·9
2·2	γ Cygni		54	16·4	16·3	16·2	15·9	15·6	15·4	N	40	19·3	19·1	19·0	19·0	19·0	19·2
0·8	α Aquilæ	51	62	04·2	04·1	03·9	03·7	03·4	03·3	N	8	55·3	55·2	55·2	55·2	55·2	55·3
2·7	γ Aquilæ		63	12·4	12·3	12·1	11·9	11·7	11·5	N	10	39·7	39·6	39·6	39·6	39·7	39·8
2·9	δ Cygni		63	36·6	36·5	36·3	36·0	35·8	35·5	N	45	10·8	10·6	10·5	10·5	10·6	10·7
3·1	β Cygni		67	07·6	07·5	07·3	07·1	06·9	06·7	N	27	60·1	60·0	59·9	59·9	60·0	60·1
2·9	π Sagittarii		72	16·3	16·2	16·0	15·7	15·5	15·3	S	20	59·5	59·5	59·4	59·4	59·4	59·4
3·0	ζ Aquilæ		73	25·6	25·5	25·3	25·0	24·8	24·7	N	13	53·6	53·5	53·5	53·5	53·5	53·6
2·6	ζ Sagittarii		74	02·4	02·3	02·0	01·8	01·5	01·3	S	29	51·0	51·0	51·0	50·9	50·9	50·9
2·0	σ Sagittarii	50	75	53·1	52·9	52·7	52·4	52·2	52·0	S	26	16·2	16·2	16·2	16·2	16·2	16·2
0·0	α Lyræ	49	80	36·3	36·2	35·9	35·7	35·4	35·3	N	38	48·1	48·0	47·9	47·9	48·0	48·1
2·8	λ Sagittarii		82	42·6	42·4	42·1	41·9	41·6	41·5	S	25	24·5	24·5	24·5	24·5	24·5	24·5
1·9	ε Sagittarii	48	83	38·2	38·0	37·7	37·5	37·2	37·0	S	34	22·4	22·4	22·3	22·3	22·3	22·4
2·7	δ Sagittarii		84	26·5	26·3	26·1	25·8	25·6	25·4	S	29	49·1	49·0	49·0	49·0	49·0	49·0
3·0	γ Sagittarii		88	14·2	14·0	13·8	13·5	13·3	13·1	S	30	25·3	25·3	25·3	25·3	25·3	25·3
2·2	γ Draconis	47	90	44·5	44·3	44·0	43·7	43·5	43·4	N	51	29·1	29·0	28·9	28·9	29·0	29·2
2·8	β Ophiuchi		93	53·6	53·4	53·2	53·0	52·8	52·7	N	4	33·6	33·5	33·5	33·5	33·5	33·6
2·4	κ Scorpii		94	02·6	02·3	02·1	01·8	01·5	01·4	S	39	02·2	02·2	02·2	02·2	02·3	02·3
1·9	θ Scorpii		95	19·4	19·1	18·8	18·5	18·2	18·1	S	43	00·4	00·4	00·4	00·4	00·5	00·5
2·1	α Ophiuchi	46	96	02·6	02·4	02·1	01·9	01·7	01·6	N	12	32·8	32·7	32·6	32·6	32·7	32·8
1·6	λ Scorpii	45	96	16·1	15·9	15·6	15·3	15·1	14·9	S	37	06·9	06·9	06·9	06·9	07·0	07·0
3·0	α Aræ		96	39·9	39·6	39·3	39·0	38·7	38·5	S	49	53·3	53·2	53·2	53·3	53·3	53·4
2·7	υ Scorpii		96	58·8	58·5	58·3	58·0	57·7	57·6	S	37	18·5	18·5	18·5	18·5	18·6	18·6
2·8	β Draconis		97	17·3	17·1	16·8	16·4	16·2	16·1	N	52	17·1	17·0	16·9	17·0	17·1	17·2
2·8	β Aræ		98	16·4	16·0	15·7	15·3	15·0	14·8	S	55	32·6	32·6	32·6	32·6	32·7	32·8
Var.‡	α Herculis		101	07·1	06·9	06·7	06·4	06·3	06·2	N	14	22·1	22·0	21·9	22·0	22·0	22·1
2·4	η Ophiuchi	44	102	07·6	07·4	07·2	07·0	06·8	06·7	S	15	44·8	44·9	44·9	44·9	44·9	44·9
3·1	ζ Aræ		104	56·6	56·2	55·9	55·5	55·2	55·0	S	56	01·0	01·0	01·0	01·0	01·1	01·2
2·3	ε Scorpii		107	08·7	08·4	08·1	07·9	07·7	07·6	S	34	19·5	19·6	19·6	19·6	19·7	19·7
1·9	α Triang. Aust.	43	107	19·2	18·6	18·1	17·5	17·1	16·9	S	69	03·5	03·4	03·4	03·5	03·6	03·8
2·8	ζ Herculis		109	29·9	29·6	29·4	29·2	29·0	28·9	N	31	33·9	33·8	33·8	33·8	33·9	34·1
2·6	ζ Ophiuchi		110	26·6	26·3	26·1	25·9	25·7	25·6	S	10	36·3	36·4	36·4	36·4	36·4	36·4
2·8	τ Scorpii		110	43·6	43·3	43·1	42·8	42·7	42·6	S	28	15·2	15·3	15·3	15·3	15·4	15·4
2·8	β Herculis		112	14·2	14·0	13·8	13·6	13·4	13·4	N	21	26·7	26·6	26·6	26·7	26·7	26·8
1·0	α Scorpii	42	112	21·0	20·7	20·5	20·2	20·1	20·0	S	26	28·4	28·4	28·5	28·5	28·5	28·5
2·7	η Draconis		113	56·6	56·2	55·8	55·5	55·3	55·3	N	61	28·0	27·9	27·8	27·9	28·1	28·2
2·7	δ Ophiuchi		116	09·5	09·3	09·1	08·9	08·7	08·7	S	3	44·6	44·7	44·8	44·8	44·7	44·7
2·6	β Scorpii		118	21·4	21·2	20·9	20·7	20·6	20·5	S	19	51·4	51·5	51·5	51·6	51·6	51·6
2·3	δ Scorpii		119	37·7	37·4	37·2	37·0	36·8	36·8	S	22	40·5	40·6	40·6	40·7	40·7	40·7
2·9	π Scorpii		119	59·5	59·2	59·0	58·8	58·6	58·6	S	26	10·1	10·1	10·2	10·2	10·3	10·3
2·8	β Trianguli Aust.		120	47·0	46·5	46·0	45·7	45·4	45·3	S	63	29·1	29·1	29·2	29·3	29·4	29·6
2·6	α Serpentis		123	41·6	41·4	41·1	41·0	40·8	40·8	N	6	21·8	21·7	21·7	21·7	21·8	21·8
2·8	γ Lupi		125	53·3	53·0	52·7	52·5	52·4	52·3	S	41	13·7	13·8	13·8	13·9	14·0	14·1
2·2	α Coronæ Bor.	41	126	07·4	07·1	06·9	06·7	06·6	06·6	N	26	38·8	38·7	38·7	38·7	38·8	39·0

‡ 2·9 — 3·6

Mag.	Name and Number			SHA							Declination						
			°	JULY '	AUG. '	SEPT. '	OCT. '	NOV. '	DEC. '	°		JULY '	AUG. '	SEPT. '	OCT. '	NOV. '	DEC. '
3·2	γ Cephei		4	56·4	55·8	55·6	55·7	56·2	56·9	N	77	44·4	44·6	44·8	45·0	45·1	45·2
2·5	*Markab*	57	13	33·3	33·1	33·0	33·1	33·1	33·2	N	15	18·8	19·0	19·0	19·1	19·1	19·1
2·4	*Scheat*		13	48·4	48·3	48·2	48·2	48·3	48·4	N	28	11·5	11·6	11·7	11·8	11·9	11·9
1·2	*Fomalhaut*	56	15	18·3	18·1	18·1	18·1	18·2	18·3	S	29	30·7	30·7	30·7	30·8	30·9	30·9
2·1	β Gruis		19	01·7	01·5	01·4	01·5	01·6	01·8	S	46	46·5	46·5	46·6	46·7	46·8	46·8
2·9	α Tucanæ		25	01·5	01·2	01·2	01·3	01·5	01·8	S	60	09·3	09·3	09·5	09·6	09·6	09·6
1·7	*Alnair*	55	27	37·2	37·0	36·9	37·0	37·2	37·3	S	46	51·5	51·6	51·7	51·8	51·8	51·9
2·9	δ Capricorni		32	57·4	57·3	57·3	57·3	57·4	57·5	S	16	02·0	02·0	02·0	02·0	02·0	02·1
2·4	*Enif*	54	33	42·0	41·9	41·9	42·0	42·1	42·2	N	9	58·1	58·2	58·3	58·3	58·3	58·3
2·9	β Aquarii		36	50·4	50·3	50·3	50·4	50·5	50·5	S	5	28·8	28·8	28·7	28·7	28·8	28·8
2·4	*Alderamin*		40	13·5	13·4	13·5	13·8	14·1	14·4	N	62	40·2	40·4	40·5	40·7	40·7	40·7
2·5	ε Cygni		48	14·2	14·1	14·2	14·3	14·5	14·6	N	34	02·8	02·9	03·1	03·1	03·1	03·0
1·3	*Deneb*	53	49	27·7	27·7	27·8	28·0	28·2	28·3	N	45	21·2	21·3	21·5	21·5	21·5	21·5
3·1	α Indi		50	14·8	14·7	14·8	14·9	15·1	15·2	S	47	13·1	13·1	13·2	13·3	13·3	13·3
1·9	*Peacock*	52	53	10·9	10·8	10·9	11·1	11·3	11·5	S	56	40·0	40·1	40·2	40·3	40·3	40·2
2·2	γ Cygni		54	15·3	15·2	15·3	15·5	15·7	15·8	N	40	19·3	19·5	19·6	19·7	19·6	19·6
0·8	*Altair*	51	62	03·1	03·1	03·2	03·3	03·4	03·5	N	8	55·4	55·5	55·6	55·6	55·5	55·5
2·7	γ Aquilæ		63	11·4	11·3	11·4	11·5	11·7	11·7	N	10	39·9	40·0	40·0	40·0	40·0	39·9
2·9	δ Cygni		63	35·4	35·5	35·6	35·8	36·0	36·1	N	45	10·9	11·0	11·1	11·2	11·1	11·0
3·1	*Albireo*		67	06·6	06·6	06·7	06·8	07·0	07·1	N	28	00·2	00·4	00·4	00·5	00·4	00·3
2·9	π Sagittarii		72	15·2	15·2	15·2	15·4	15·5	15·5	S	20	59·3	59·4	59·4	59·4	59·4	59·4
3·0	ζ Aquilæ		73	24·6	24·6	24·7	24·8	24·9	25·0	N	13	53·7	53·8	53·9	53·9	53·8	53·8
2·6	ζ Sagittarii		74	01·2	01·2	01·3	01·4	01·5	01·5	S	29	50·9	51·0	51·0	51·0	51·0	51·0
2·0	*Nunki*	50	75	51·9	51·9	52·0	52·1	52·2	52·2	S	26	16·2	16·2	16·2	16·2	16·2	16·2
0·0	*Vega*	49	80	35·2	35·3	35·5	35·7	35·8	35·9	N	38	48·3	48·4	48·5	48·5	48·4	48·3
2·8	λ Sagittarii		82	41·4	41·4	41·5	41·6	41·7	41·7	S	25	24·5	24·5	24·6	24·6	24·6	24·5
1·9	*Kaus Australis*	48	83	36·9	36·9	37·1	37·2	37·3	37·3	S	34	22·4	22·4	22·5	22·5	22·5	22·4
2·7	δ Sagittarii		84	25·3	25·3	25·5	25·6	25·7	25·7	S	29	49·1	49·1	49·1	49·1	49·1	49·1
3·0	γ Sagittarii		88	13·0	13·1	13·2	13·3	13·4	13·4	S	30	25·3	25·4	25·4	25·4	25·4	25·3
2·2	*Eltanin*	47	90	43·4	43·5	43·7	44·0	44·2	44·3	N	51	29·4	29·5	29·5	29·5	29·4	29·2
2·8	β Ophiuchi		93	52·6	52·7	52·8	52·9	53·0	53·0	N	4	33·7	33·7	33·8	33·7	33·7	33·6
2·4	κ Scorpii		94	01·3	01·4	01·5	01·7	01·8	01·7	S	39	02·4	02·4	02·4	02·4	02·4	02·3
1·9	θ Scorpii		95	18·0	18·1	18·2	18·4	18·5	18·5	S	43	00·6	00·6	00·7	00·6	00·6	00·5
2·1	*Rasalhague*	46	96	01·6	01·7	01·8	01·9	02·0	02·0	N	12	32·9	33·0	33·0	32·9	32·9	32·8
1·6	*Shaula*	45	96	14·9	15·0	15·1	15·2	15·3	15·3	S	37	07·0	07·1	07·1	07·1	07·1	07·0
3·0	α Aræ		96	38·5	38·5	38·7	38·9	39·0	39·0	S	49	53·5	53·5	53·6	53·6	53·5	53·4
2·7	υ Scorpii		96	57·5	57·6	57·7	57·9	58·0	57·9	S	37	18·7	18·7	18·7	18·7	18·6	18·6
2·8	β Draconis		97	16·2	16·3	16·6	16·8	17·0	17·1	N	52	17·4	17·5	17·5	17·5	17·4	17·2
2·8	β Aræ		98	14·7	14·8	15·1	15·3	15·4	15·4	S	55	32·9	33·0	33·0	33·0	32·9	32·8
Var.‡	α Herculis		101	06·2	06·2	06·4	06·5	06·6	06·5	N	14	22·2	22·3	22·3	22·3	22·2	22·1
2·4	*Sabik*	44	102	06·6	06·7	06·8	06·9	07·0	06·9	S	15	44·9	44·9	44·9	44·9	44·9	44·9
3·1	ζ Aræ		104	55·0	55·2	55·4	55·6	55·7	55·6	S	56	01·3	01·4	01·4	01·4	01·3	01·2
2·3	ε Scorpii		107	07·6	07·6	07·8	07·9	08·0	07·9	S	34	19·8	19·8	19·8	19·8	19·7	19·7
1·9	*Atria*	43	107	16·9	17·2	17·6	17·9	18·1	18·0	S	69	03·9	04·0	04·0	03·9	03·8	03·7
2·8	ζ Herculis		109	29·0	29·1	29·3	29·4	29·5	29·4	N	31	34·2	34·2	34·3	34·2	34·1	33·9
2·6	ζ Ophiuchi		110	25·6	25·7	25·8	25·9	26·0	25·9	S	10	36·4	36·4	36·4	36·4	36·4	36·4
2·8	τ Scorpii		110	42·6	42·6	42·8	42·9	42·9	42·8	S	28	15·4	15·4	15·4	15·4	15·4	15·4
2·8	β Herculis		112	13·4	13·5	13·6	13·8	13·8	13·8	N	21	26·9	27·0	27·0	26·9	26·8	26·7
1·0	*Antares*	42	112	20·0	20·1	20·2	20·3	20·4	20·3	S	26	28·6	28·6	28·6	28·5	28·5	28·5
2·7	η Draconis		113	55·5	55·8	56·1	56·4	56·6	56·6	N	61	28·4	28·4	28·4	28·3	28·2	28·0
2·7	δ Ophiuchi		116	08·7	08·8	08·9	09·0	09·0	08·9	S	3	44·7	44·6	44·6	44·6	44·7	44·8
2·6	β Scorpii		118	20·5	20·6	20·8	20·9	20·9	20·8	S	19	51·6	51·6	51·6	51·6	51·6	51·6
2·3	*Dschubba*		119	36·8	36·9	37·0	37·1	37·1	37·0	S	22	40·7	40·7	40·7	40·7	40·7	40·7
2·9	π Scorpii		119	58·6	58·7	58·8	58·9	58·9	58·8	S	26	10·3	10·3	10·3	10·3	10·2	10·2
2·8	β Trianguli Aust.		120	45·4	45·7	46·0	46·2	46·3	46·1	S	63	29·7	29·7	29·7	29·6	29·5	29·4
2·6	α Serpentis		123	40·8	40·9	41·0	41·1	41·1	41·0	N	6	21·9	21·9	21·9	21·9	21·8	21·7
2·8	γ Lupi		125	52·4	52·5	52·6	52·8	52·8	52·6	S	41	14·1	14·1	14·1	14·1	14·0	14·0
2·2	*Alphecca*	41	126	06·6	06·8	06·9	07·0	07·0	06·9	N	26	39·0	39·1	39·1	39·0	38·9	38·7

‡ 2·9 — 3·6

Mag.		Name and Number		SHA	JAN.	FEB.	MAR.	APR.	MAY	JUNE		Declination	JAN.	FEB.	MAR.	APR.	MAY	JUNE
				°	′	′	′	′	′	′		°	′	′	′	′	′	′
2·9	γ	Trianguli Aust.		129	48·7	48·2	47·6	47·2	47·0	47·0	S	68	44·7	44·8	44·9	45·0	45·1	45·3
3·1	γ	Ursæ Minoris		129	49·9	49·3	48·8	48·4	48·3	48·4	N	71	45·5	45·5	45·5	45·6	45·8	45·9
2·6	β	Libræ		130	29·1	28·9	28·6	28·5	28·4	28·3	S	9	27·3	27·3	27·4	27·4	27·4	27·4
2·7	β	Lupi		135	02·7	02·4	02·1	01·9	01·8	01·8	S	43	12·5	12·6	12·7	12·8	12·9	13·0
2·1	β	Ursæ Minoris	40	137	20·5	19·8	19·2	18·9	18·8	19·1	N	74	04·2	04·1	04·2	04·3	04·5	04·6
2·8	α	Libræ	39	136	60·5	60·3	60·1	59·9	59·8	59·8	S	16	07·3	07·4	07·5	07·5	07·5	07·5
2·4	ε	Bootis		138	32·4	32·2	32·0	31·8	31·7	31·8	N	26	59·4	59·3	59·3	59·4	59·5	59·6
2·3	α	Lupi		139	11·4	11·1	10·8	10·6	10·5	10·5	S	47	28·1	28·2	28·3	28·4	28·5	28·6
−0·3	α	Centauri	38	139	45·8	45·4	45·0	44·8	44·7	44·8	S	60	54·6	54·7	54·8	55·0	55·1	55·2
2·3	η	Centauri		140	48·6	48·3	48·1	47·9	47·8	47·8	S	42	14·4	14·5	14·6	14·7	14·8	14·9
3·0	γ	Bootis		141	47·1	46·8	46·6	46·4	46·4	46·4	N	38	13·1	13·1	13·1	13·2	13·3	13·4
0·0	α	Bootis	37	145	51·7	51·4	51·2	51·1	51·1	51·1	N	19	04·7	04·6	04·6	04·6	04·7	04·8
2·1	θ	Centauri	36	148	02·3	02·0	01·8	01·7	01·6	01·7	S	36	27·8	27·9	28·0	28·1	28·2	28·2
0·6	β	Centauri	35	148	41·6	41·2	40·9	40·6	40·6	40·7	S	60	27·7	27·8	28·0	28·1	28·3	28·4
2·6	ζ	Centauri		150	48·3	48·0	47·8	47·6	47·6	47·7	S	47	22·9	22·9	23·1	23·2	23·3	23·4
2·7	η	Bootis		151	05·7	05·5	05·3	05·2	05·1	05·2	N	18	17·8	17·8	17·7	17·8	17·9	17·9
1·9	η	Ursæ Majoris	34	152	55·3	55·0	54·8	54·7	54·7	54·8	N	49	12·6	12·6	12·7	12·8	12·9	13·0
2·3	ε	Centauri		154	42·8	42·4	42·2	42·0	42·0	42·1	S	53	33·7	33·8	33·9	34·1	34·2	34·3
1·0	α	Virginis	33	158	26·5	26·2	26·1	26·0	26·0	26·0	S	11	16·0	16·0	16·0	16·0	16·0	16·0
2·3	ζ	Ursæ Majoris		158	49·3	48·9	48·7	48·6	48·6	48·8	N	54	49·1	49·1	49·1	49·3	49·4	49·5
2·8	ι	Centauri		159	34·3	34·0	33·8	33·7	33·7	33·8	S	36	48·8	48·9	49·0	49·1	49·2	49·3
2·8	ε	Virginis		164	12·6	12·4	12·2	12·2	12·2	12·2	N	10	51·1	51·0	51·0	51·0	51·1	51·1
2·9	α	Canum Venat.		165	45·7	45·5	45·3	45·2	45·3	45·4	N	38	12·5	12·5	12·5	12·6	12·7	12·8
1·8	ε	Ursæ Majoris	32	166	16·6	16·2	16·0	15·9	16·0	16·2	N	55	50·9	50·9	51·0	51·1	51·2	51·3
1·3	β	Crucis		167	46·5	46·2	46·0	45·9	46·0	46·1	S	59	47·5	47·6	47·8	48·0	48·1	48·2
2·9	γ	Virginis		169	20·0	19·8	19·7	19·6	19·7	19·7	S	1	33·5	33·6	33·6	33·6	33·6	33·6
2·2	γ	Centauri		169	20·7	20·4	20·2	20·1	20·2	20·3	S	49	03·8	04·0	04·1	04·3	04·4	04·4
2·7	α	Muscæ		170	24·0	23·6	23·3	23·2	23·4	23·7	S	69	14·3	14·5	14·6	14·8	15·0	15·1
2·7	β	Corvi		171	08·5	08·3	08·2	08·1	08·1	08·2	S	23	30·2	30·4	30·5	30·6	30·6	30·6
1·6	γ	Crucis	31	171	55·7	55·4	55·2	55·2	55·3	55·4	S	57	13·2	13·3	13·5	13·6	13·7	13·8
1·3	α	Crucis	30	173	04·1	03·7	03·5	03·5	03·6	03·8	S	63	12·2	12·4	12·5	12·7	12·9	12·9
2·6	γ	Corvi	29	175	47·5	47·3	47·2	47·2	47·2	47·3	S	17	39·0	39·1	39·2	39·3	39·3	39·3
2·6	δ	Centauri		177	39·0	38·7	38·6	38·6	38·6	38·8	S	50	49·7	49·9	50·0	50·2	50·3	50·3
2·4	γ	Ursæ Majoris		181	16·9	16·6	16·5	16·5	16·6	16·8	N	53	34·8	34·9	35·0	35·1	35·2	35·2
2·1	β	Leonis	28	182	28·9	28·7	28·6	28·6	28·6	28·7	N	14	27·6	27·5	27·5	27·6	27·6	27·6
2·6	δ	Leonis		191	12·5	12·3	12·2	12·2	12·3	12·4	N	20	24·8	24·7	24·8	24·8	24·9	24·9
3·0	ψ	Ursæ Majoris		192	18·3	18·1	18·0	18·0	18·1	18·3	N	44	23·2	23·3	23·3	23·4	23·5	23·6
1·8	α	Ursæ Majoris	27	193	45·7	45·4	45·3	45·4	45·6	45·8	N	61	38·4	38·5	38·6	38·7	38·8	38·8
2·4	β	Ursæ Majoris		194	14·4	14·1	14·0	14·1	14·3	14·5	N	56	16·3	16·4	16·5	16·6	16·7	16·7
2·7	μ	Velorum		198	05·3	05·1	05·1	05·2	05·3	05·5	S	49	31·3	31·5	31·7	31·8	31·9	31·9
2·8	θ	Carinæ		199	04·5	04·2	04·2	04·4	04·7	05·0	S	64	29·7	29·9	30·1	30·2	30·3	30·3
2·3	γ	Leonis		204	43·9	43·7	43·7	43·8	43·9	43·9	N	19	44·3	44·3	44·3	44·4	44·4	44·4
1·4	α	Leonis	26	207	38·4	38·3	38·3	38·3	38·4	38·5	N	11	52·1	52·1	52·1	52·1	52·1	52·1
3·0	ε	Leonis		213	15·2	15·1	15·1	15·1	15·2	15·3	N	23	40·8	40·8	40·8	40·9	40·9	40·9
3·1	N	Velorum		217	02·1	02·0	02·1	02·3	02·6	02·8	S	57	07·2	07·4	07·6	07·7	07·7	07·7
2·0	α	Hydræ	25	217	51·4	51·3	51·3	51·4	51·5	51·6	S	8	44·7	44·8	44·9	44·9	44·9	44·9
2·5	κ	Velorum		219	18·6	18·5	18·6	18·8	19·0	19·3	S	55	05·6	05·8	06·0	06·1	06·1	06·1
2·2	ι	Carinæ		220	35·1	35·0	35·2	35·4	35·7	36·0	S	59	21·4	21·6	21·8	21·9	21·9	21·9
1·7	β	Carinæ	24	221	37·9	37·9	38·1	38·5	39·0	39·4	S	69	47·8	48·0	48·2	48·3	48·3	48·3
2·2	λ	Velorum	23	222	48·7	48·7	48·7	48·9	49·1	49·2	S	43	30·7	30·9	31·0	31·1	31·1	31·1
3·1	ι	Ursæ Majoris		224	51·3	51·2	51·3	51·4	51·6	51·7	N	47	57·6	57·7	57·8	57·9	57·9	57·9
2·0	δ	Velorum		228	40·7	40·7	40·8	41·0	41·3	41·5	S	54	46·9	47·0	47·2	47·3	47·3	47·2
1·9	ε	Carinæ	22	234	15·6	15·6	15·8	16·1	16·4	16·5	S	59	34·4	34·6	34·7	34·8	34·8	34·7
1·8	γ	Velorum		237	27·4	27·4	27·5	27·7	28·0	28·1	S	47	23·7	23·9	24·0	24·1	24·1	24·0
2·8	ρ	Puppis		237	53·9	53·8	53·9	54·1	54·2	54·3	S	24	21·8	21·9	22·0	22·0	22·0	21·9
2·3	ζ	Puppis		238	55·4	55·4	55·5	55·7	55·9	56·0	S	40	03·6	03·8	03·9	03·9	03·9	03·8
1·1	β	Geminorum	21	243	21·8	21·8	21·9	22·0	22·1	22·2	N	27	58·5	58·6	58·6	58·6	58·6	58·6
0·4	α	Canis Minoris	20	244	54·7	54·7	54·7	54·9	55·0	55·0	N	5	10·3	10·3	10·2	10·2	10·3	10·3

Mag.	Name and Number		SHA °	JULY	AUG.	SEPT.	OCT.	NOV.	DEC.	Dec.	JULY	AUG.	SEPT.	OCT.	NOV.	DEC.
2·9	γ	Trianguli Aust.	129	47·2	47·5	47·9	48·1	48·2	47·9	S 68	45·4	45·4	45·4	45·3	45·1	45·0
3·1	γ	Ursæ Minoris	129	48·8	49·3	49·8	50·2	50·4	50·2	N 71	46·0	46·0	46·0	45·8	45·6	45·4
2·6	β	Libræ	130	28·4	28·5	28·6	28·7	28·6	28·5	S 9	27·4	27·4	27·3	27·3	27·4	27·4
2·7	β	Lupi	135	01·9	02·0	02·2	02·2	02·2	02·0	S 43	13·0	13·0	13·0	12·9	12·8	12·8
2·1		Kochab 40	137	19·6	20·1	20·7	21·0	21·1	20·9	N 74	04·7	04·7	04·6	04·4	04·2	04·0
2·8		Zubenelgenubi 39	136	59·9	60·0	60·1	60·1	60·1	59·9	S 16	07·5	07·5	07·5	07·5	07·5	07·5
2·4	ε	Bootis	138	31·8	32·0	32·1	32·2	32·1	32·0	N 26	59·6	59·6	59·6	59·5	59·4	59·2
2·3	α	Lupi	139	10·6	10·7	10·9	11·0	11·0	10·7	S 47	28·6	28·6	28·6	28·5	28·4	28·3
−0·3		Rigil Kent. 38	139	44·9	45·2	45·5	45·6	45·5	45·2	S 60	55·3	55·3	55·2	55·1	55·0	54·9
2·3	η	Centauri	140	47·9	48·0	48·2	48·2	48·2	48·0	S 42	14·9	14·9	14·8	14·8	14·7	14·7
3·0	γ	Bootis	141	46·5	46·7	46·8	46·9	46·8	46·7	N 38	13·5	13·5	13·4	13·3	13·1	13·0
0·0		Arcturus 37	145	51·2	51·3	51·4	51·4	51·4	51·2	N 19	04·8	04·8	04·8	04·7	04·6	04·5
2·1		Menkent 36	148	01·8	01·9	02·0	02·0	02·0	01·7	S 36	28·3	28·2	28·2	28·1	28·1	28·1
0·6		Hadar 35	148	40·9	41·1	41·3	41·4	41·3	41·0	S 60	28·4	28·4	28·3	28·2	28·1	28·0
2·6	ζ	Centauri	150	47·8	47·9	48·1	48·1	48·0	47·8	S 47	23·4	23·4	23·3	23·2	23·1	23·1
2·7	η	Bootis	151	05·3	05·4	05·4	05·5	05·4	05·2	N 18	18·0	18·0	17·9	17·9	17·8	17·6
1·9		Alkaid 34	152	54·9	55·1	55·2	55·3	55·2	55·0	N 49	13·1	13·0	12·9	12·8	12·6	12·4
2·3	ε	Centauri	154	42·2	42·4	42·6	42·6	42·5	42·2	S 53	34·3	34·3	34·2	34·1	34·0	34·0
1·0		Spica 33	158	26·1	26·2	26·3	26·3	26·1	25·9	S 11	16·0	16·0	15·9	15·9	16·0	16·0
2·3		Mizar	158	49·0	49·2	49·3	49·3	49·2	49·0	N 54	49·5	49·5	49·4	49·2	49·0	48·8
2·8	ι	Centauri	159	33·9	34·0	34·1	34·1	34·0	33·8	S 36	49·3	49·2	49·1	49·1	49·0	49·0
2·8	ε	Virginis	164	12·3	12·4	12·4	12·4	12·3	12·1	N 10	51·2	51·2	51·2	51·1	51·0	50·9
2·9		Cor Caroli	165	45·5	45·6	45·7	45·7	45·5	45·3	N 38	12·8	12·8	12·7	12·6	12·4	12·3
1·8		Alioth 32	166	16·4	16·6	16·7	16·7	16·5	16·2	N 55	51·3	51·3	51·1	51·0	50·8	50·6
1·3		Mimosa	167	46·4	46·6	46·7	46·7	46·5	46·1	S 59	48·2	48·1	48·0	47·9	47·8	47·8
2·9	γ	Virginis	169	19·8	19·9	19·9	19·9	19·7	19·5	S 1	33·6	33·5	33·5	33·6	33·6	33·7
2·2		Muhlifain	169	20·5	20·6	20·7	20·7	20·5	20·2	S 49	04·4	04·4	04·3	04·2	04·1	04·1
2·7	α	Muscæ	170	24·0	24·4	24·6	24·6	24·3	23·8	S 69	15·1	15·0	14·9	14·8	14·6	14·6
2·7	β	Corvi	171	08·3	08·4	08·4	08·4	08·2	08·0	S 23	30·6	30·5	30·5	30·4	30·4	30·5
1·6		Gacrux 31	171	55·7	55·9	56·0	55·9	55·7	55·4	S 57	13·8	13·7	13·6	13·5	13·4	13·4
1·3		Acrux 30	173	04·1	04·3	04·5	04·4	04·2	03·8	S 63	12·9	12·9	12·7	12·6	12·5	12·5
2·6		Gienah 29	175	47·4	47·5	47·5	47·4	47·3	47·0	S 17	39·3	39·2	39·2	39·2	39·2	39·3
2·6	δ	Centauri	177	39·0	39·1	39·2	39·1	38·9	38·6	S 50	50·3	50·2	50·1	50·0	49·9	50·0
2·4		Phecda	181	16·9	17·1	17·1	17·0	16·8	16·4	N 53	35·2	35·1	35·0	34·8	34·7	34·5
2·1		Denebola 28	182	28·8	28·9	28·9	28·8	28·6	28·4	N 14	27·7	27·7	27·6	27·6	27·5	27·3
2·6	δ	Leonis	191	12·5	12·5	12·5	12·4	12·2	11·9	N 20	24·9	24·9	24·8	24·7	24·6	24·5
3·0	ψ	Ursæ Majoris	192	18·4	18·4	18·4	18·3	18·0	17·7	N 44	23·5	23·5	23·3	23·2	23·1	22·9
1·8		Dubhe 27	193	46·0	46·1	46·1	45·9	45·6	45·1	N 61	38·8	38·6	38·5	38·3	38·2	38·1
2·4		Merak	194	14·6	14·7	14·7	14·5	14·2	13·8	N 56	16·7	16·6	16·4	16·3	16·1	16·0
2·7	μ	Velorum	198	05·7	05·8	05·7	05·6	05·3	05·0	S 49	31·8	31·7	31·6	31·5	31·4	31·5
2·8	θ	Carinæ	199	05·3	05·4	05·4	05·2	04·8	04·4	S 64	30·2	30·1	30·0	29·8	29·8	29·8
2·3		Algieba	204	44·0	44·0	43·9	43·8	43·5	43·3	N 19	44·4	44·4	44·4	44·3	44·2	44·1
1·4		Regulus 26	207	38·6	38·6	38·5	38·3	38·1	37·9	N 11	52·2	52·2	52·1	52·1	52·0	51·9
3·0	ε	Leonis	213	15·4	15·3	15·2	15·1	14·8	14·6	N 23	40·9	40·9	40·9	40·8	40·7	40·6
3·1	N	Velorum	217	03·0	03·0	02·9	02·7	02·3	02·0	S 57	07·6	07·4	07·3	07·2	07·2	07·3
2·0		Alphard 25	217	51·6	51·6	51·4	51·3	51·1	50·8	S 8	44·8	44·7	44·7	44·7	44·8	44·9
2·5	κ	Velorum	219	19·4	19·4	19·3	19·1	18·7	18·4	S 55	06·0	05·8	05·7	05·6	05·6	05·7
2·2	ι	Carinæ	220	36·1	36·0	35·9	35·7	35·4	35·0	S 59	21·7	21·6	21·4	21·4	21·4	21·5
1·7		Miaplacidus 24	221	39·7	39·7	39·6	39·2	38·7	38·2	S 69	48·2	48·0	47·8	47·8	47·8	47·9
2·2		Suhail 23	222	49·3	49·3	49·2	49·0	48·7	48·4	S 43	31·0	30·8	30·7	30·6	30·7	30·8
3·1	ι	Ursæ Majoris	224	51·7	51·6	51·5	51·2	50·9	50·5	N 47	57·8	57·7	57·6	57·5	57·4	57·4
2·0	δ	Velorum	228	41·6	41·6	41·4	41·2	40·8	40·5	S 54	47·1	46·9	46·8	46·7	46·8	46·9
1·9		Avior 22	234	16·7	16·7	16·5	16·2	15·8	15·5	S 59	34·5	34·4	34·2	34·2	34·2	34·4
1·8	γ	Velorum	237	28·1	28·1	27·9	27·6	27·3	27·1	S 47	23·8	23·7	23·6	23·5	23·6	23·7
2·8	ρ	Puppis	237	54·3	54·2	54·0	53·8	53·6	53·4	S 24	21·8	21·7	21·6	21·6	21·7	21·8
2·3	ζ	Puppis	238	56·0	55·9	55·8	55·5	55·2	55·0	S 40	03·7	03·5	03·4	03·4	03·4	03·6
1·1		Pollux 21	243	22·1	22·0	21·8	21·6	21·3	21·1	N 27	58·6	58·6	58·5	58·5	58·5	58·4
0·4		Procyon 20	244	55·0	54·8	54·7	54·4	54·2	54·0	N 5	10·4	10·4	10·4	10·4	10·3	10·2

Mag.	Name and Number	No.	SHA	JAN.	FEB.	MAR.	APR.	MAY	JUNE	Declination	JAN.	FEB.	MAR.	APR.	MAY	JUNE
1·6	α Geminorum		246	01·8	01·8	01·9	02·0	02·1	02·2	N 31	50·5	50·6	50·6	50·6	50·6	50·6
3·3	σ Puppis		247	31·7	31·7	31·9	32·1	32·3	32·4	S 43	20·6	20·7	20·8	20·9	20·8	20·7
2·9	β Canis Minoris		247	56·4	56·4	56·4	56·6	56·7	56·7	N 8	14·8	14·8	14·8	14·8	14·8	14·8
2·4	η Canis Majoris		248	46·5	46·5	46·6	46·8	46·9	47·0	S 29	20·6	20·8	20·8	20·8	20·8	20·7
2·7	π Puppis		250	32·0	32·0	32·2	32·3	32·5	32·6	S 37	08·1	08·2	08·3	08·3	08·3	08·2
1·8	δ Canis Majoris		252	41·7	41·7	41·9	42·0	42·1	42·2	S 26	25·6	25·7	25·8	25·8	25·8	25·7
3·0	o Canis Majoris		254	01·9	01·9	02·1	02·2	02·3	02·4	S 23	51·9	52·0	52·1	52·1	52·0	51·9
1·5	ε Canis Majoris	19	255	08·6	08·6	08·8	08·9	09·1	09·1	S 29	00·1	00·2	00·3	00·3	00·2	00·1
2·9	τ Puppis		257	23·1	23·2	23·4	23·7	23·9	24·0	S 50	38·4	38·6	38·7	38·7	38·6	38·4
−1·5	α Canis Majoris	18	258	29·4	29·4	29·6	29·7	29·8	29·8	S 16	44·8	44·9	44·9	44·9	44·8	44·8
1·9	γ Geminorum		260	16·9	16·9	17·0	17·2	17·3	17·3	N 16	22·8	22·8	22·8	22·8	22·8	22·8
−0·7	α Carinæ	17	263	53·6	53·7	54·0	54·3	54·5	54·6	S 52	42·6	42·7	42·8	42·7	42·7	42·5
2·0	β Canis Majoris		264	06·1	06·2	06·3	06·4	06·5	06·6	S 17	58·1	58·2	58·2	58·2	58·2	58·1
2·6	θ Aurigæ		269	43·6	43·7	43·8	44·0	44·0	44·0	N 37	12·7	12·8	12·8	12·8	12·8	12·7
1·9	β Aurigæ		269	44·9	45·0	45·2	45·3	45·4	45·4	N 44	56·9	56·9	57·0	57·0	56·9	56·8
Var.‡	α Orionis	16	270	56·1	56·1	56·2	56·4	56·4	56·4	N 7	24·5	24·5	24·5	24·5	24·5	24·5
2·1	κ Orionis		272	49·3	49·4	49·5	49·6	49·7	49·7	S 9	39·9	40·0	40·0	40·0	39·9	39·9
1·9	ζ Orionis		274	33·4	33·4	33·6	33·7	33·7	33·7	S 1	56·1	56·1	56·2	56·1	56·1	56·0
2·6	α Columbæ		274	54·2	54·3	54·5	54·6	54·7	54·7	S 34	04·0	04·1	04·2	04·1	04·0	03·9
3·0	ζ Tauri		275	17·3	17·4	17·5	17·6	17·7	17·6	N 21	09·2	09·2	09·2	09·2	09·2	09·2
1·7	ε Orionis	15	275	41·5	41·5	41·7	41·8	41·8	41·8	S 1	11·5	11·6	11·6	11·6	11·5	11·5
2·8	ι Orionis		275	53·7	53·8	53·9	54·0	54·1	54·1	S 5	54·0	54·0	54·1	54·0	54·0	53·9
2·6	α Leporis		276	35·7	35·8	35·9	36·0	36·1	36·1	S 17	48·7	48·8	48·8	48·8	48·7	48·6
2·2	δ Orionis		276	44·5	44·5	44·7	44·8	44·8	44·8	S 0	17·2	17·3	17·3	17·3	17·2	17·2
2·8	β Leporis		277	43·3	43·4	43·5	43·7	43·8	43·7	S 20	44·8	44·9	44·9	44·9	44·8	44·7
1·7	β Tauri	14	278	06·6	06·6	06·8	06·9	07·0	06·9	N 28	37·3	37·4	37·4	37·4	37·3	37·3
1·6	γ Orionis	13	278	26·9	26·9	27·0	27·2	27·2	27·2	N 6	21·9	21·9	21·9	21·9	21·9	22·0
0·1	α Aurigæ	12	280	27·3	27·4	27·6	27·8	27·9	27·8	N 46	01·0	01·1	01·1	01·1	01·0	00·9
0·1	β Orionis	11	281	07·4	07·5	07·6	07·7	07·8	07·8	S 8	10·9	11·0	11·0	11·0	10·9	10·8
2·8	β Eridani		282	47·4	47·5	47·6	47·7	47·8	47·7	S 5	03·8	03·9	03·9	03·9	03·8	03·7
2·7	ι Aurigæ		285	25·5	25·6	25·7	25·8	25·9	25·8	N 33	11·8	11·8	11·8	11·8	11·7	11·7
0·9	α Tauri	10	290	43·9	44·0	44·1	44·2	44·3	44·2	N 16	32·8	32·8	32·8	32·8	32·8	32·8
2·9	ε Persei		300	12·0	12·1	12·3	12·4	12·4	12·3	N 40	04·0	04·1	04·0	04·0	03·9	03·9
3·0	γ Eridani		300	15·5	15·6	15·8	15·9	15·9	15·8	S 13	27·4	27·4	27·4	27·3	27·3	27·1
2·9	ζ Persei		301	09·1	09·2	09·4	09·5	09·5	09·3	N 31	56·5	56·5	56·5	56·5	56·4	56·4
2·9	η Tauri		302	49·9	50·0	50·1	50·2	50·2	50·1	N 24	09·9	09·9	09·9	09·9	09·9	09·9
1·8	α Persei	9	308	33·6	33·8	34·0	34·1	34·1	33·9	N 49	56·0	56·0	55·9	55·9	55·8	55·7
Var.§	β Persei		312	37·9	38·1	38·2	38·3	38·2	38·1	N 41	02·0	02·0	01·9	01·8	01·8	01·8
2·5	α Ceti	8	314	10·2	10·3	10·4	10·4	10·4	10·3	N 4	09·9	09·9	09·9	09·9	09·9	10·0
3·2	θ Eridani	7	315	14·7	14·9	15·0	15·1	15·1	15·0	S 40	13·9	13·9	13·8	13·7	13·5	13·4
2·0	α Ursæ Minoris		315	37·7	51·3	63·5	70·6	69·9	62·1	N 89	21·1	21·1	21·1	21·0	20·8	20·7
3·0	β Trianguli		327	19·1	19·2	19·3	19·3	19·2	19·0	N 35	04·9	04·9	04·8	04·8	04·7	04·7
2·0	α Arietis	6	327	55·6	55·7	55·8	55·8	55·7	55·5	N 23	33·4	33·3	33·3	33·2	33·2	33·3
2·3	γ Andromedæ		328	43·1	43·3	43·4	43·5	43·4	43·1	N 42	25·6	25·5	25·5	25·4	25·3	25·3
2·9	α Hydri		330	09·1	09·4	09·6	09·7	09·6	09·4	S 61	28·8	28·8	28·7	28·5	28·3	28·1
2·6	β Arietis		331	03·9	04·1	04·1	04·2	04·1	03·9	N 20	54·3	54·2	54·2	54·2	54·2	54·2
0·5	α Eridani	5	335	23·3	23·6	23·7	23·8	23·7	23·4	S 57	08·6	08·5	08·4	08·2	08·0	07·9
2·7	δ Cassiopeiæ		338	13·1	13·4	13·6	13·6	13·4	13·1	N 60	20·5	20·4	20·3	20·2	20·1	20·1
2·1	β Andromedæ		342	17·4	17·5	17·6	17·6	17·4	17·2	N 35	43·6	43·6	43·5	43·4	43·4	43·4
Var.‖	γ Cassiopeiæ		345	31·3	31·6	31·7	31·7	31·5	31·1	N 60	49·6	49·6	49·5	49·3	49·2	49·2
2·0	β Ceti	4	348	51·4	51·5	51·5	51·5	51·4	51·1	S 17	52·9	52·9	52·8	52·7	52·6	52·5
2·2	α Cassiopeiæ	3	349	35·5	35·7	35·8	35·8	35·6	35·2	N 56	39·0	38·9	38·8	38·6	38·6	38·6
2·4	α Phœnicis	2	353	11·3	11·4	11·5	11·4	11·2	11·0	S 42	12·2	12·1	12·0	11·9	11·7	11·6
2·8	β Hydri		353	19·1	19·6	19·8	19·7	19·3	18·6	S 77	08·9	08·8	08·7	08·5	08·3	08·2
2·8	γ Pegasi		356	26·3	26·4	26·4	26·3	26·2	25·9	N 15	17·6	17·6	17·5	17·5	17·5	17·6
2·3	β Cassiopeiæ		357	26·5	26·8	26·8	26·8	26·5	26·1	N 59	15·8	15·7	15·5	15·4	15·3	15·3
2·1	α Andromedæ	1	357	39·0	39·0	39·1	39·0	38·8	38·6	N 29	12·1	12·0	11·9	11·9	11·9	11·9

‡ 0·1 — 1·2   § 2·1 — 3·4   ‖ Irregular variable; 2018 mag. 2·2

Mag.	Name and Number		SHA °	SHA JULY	AUG.	SEPT.	OCT.	NOV.	DEC.	Dec. °	Decl. JULY	AUG.	SEPT.	OCT.	NOV.	DEC.
1·6	*Castor*		246	02·1	02·0	01·8	01·5	01·2	01·0	N 31	50·6	50·5	50·5	50·5	50·4	50·4
3·3	σ Puppis		247	32·4	32·3	32·1	31·8	31·5	31·3	S 43	20·6	20·4	20·3	20·3	20·4	20·5
2·9	β Canis Minoris		247	56·6	56·5	56·3	56·1	55·9	55·7	N 8	14·9	14·9	14·9	14·9	14·8	14·8
2·4	η Canis Majoris		248	47·0	46·8	46·7	46·4	46·2	46·0	S 29	20·6	20·4	20·4	20·4	20·4	20·6
2·7	π Puppis		250	32·6	32·4	32·2	32·0	31·7	31·5	S 37	08·0	07·9	07·8	07·8	07·9	08·0
1·8	*Wezen*		252	42·2	42·0	41·8	41·6	41·4	41·2	S 26	25·5	25·4	25·3	25·3	25·4	25·5
3·0	o Canis Majoris		254	02·3	02·2	02·0	01·8	01·5	01·4	S 23	51·8	51·7	51·6	51·6	51·7	51·8
1·5	*Adhara*	19	255	09·1	08·9	08·7	08·5	08·3	08·1	S 28	60·0	59·9	59·9	59·8	59·9	60·0
2·9	τ Puppis		257	24·0	23·8	23·5	23·3	23·0	22·8	S 50	38·3	38·1	38·0	38·0	38·1	38·3
−1·5	*Sirius*	18	258	29·8	29·6	29·4	29·2	29·0	28·8	S 16	44·6	44·6	44·5	44·5	44·6	44·7
1·9	*Alhena*		260	17·2	17·0	16·8	16·6	16·3	16·1	N 16	22·8	22·9	22·9	22·9	22·8	22·8
−0·7	*Canopus*	17	263	54·5	54·3	54·1	53·7	53·5	53·3	S 52	42·3	42·2	42·1	42·1	42·2	42·4
2·0	*Mirzam*		264	06·5	06·3	06·1	05·9	05·7	05·5	S 17	58·0	57·9	57·8	57·8	57·9	58·0
2·6	θ Aurigæ		269	43·9	43·7	43·4	43·1	42·9	42·7	N 37	12·7	12·7	12·7	12·7	12·7	12·7
1·9	*Menkalinan*		269	45·3	45·0	44·7	44·4	44·1	43·9	N 44	56·8	56·8	56·7	56·7	56·8	56·8
Var.‡	*Betelgeuse*	16	270	56·3	56·1	55·9	55·7	55·5	55·3	N 7	24·6	24·6	24·7	24·7	24·6	24·6
2·1	κ Orionis		272	49·6	49·4	49·2	49·0	48·8	48·6	S 9	39·8	39·7	39·6	39·6	39·7	39·8
1·9	*Alnitak*		274	33·6	33·4	33·2	33·0	32·8	32·7	S 1	55·9	55·9	55·8	55·8	55·9	56·0
2·6	*Phact*		274	54·6	54·4	54·2	54·0	53·8	53·6	S 34	03·7	03·6	03·6	03·6	03·7	03·8
3·0	ζ Tauri		275	17·5	17·3	17·1	16·8	16·6	16·5	N 21	09·2	09·2	09·2	09·2	09·2	09·2
1·7	*Alnilam*	15	275	41·7	41·5	41·3	41·1	40·9	40·7	S 1	11·4	11·3	11·3	11·3	11·3	11·4
2·8	ι Orionis		275	54·0	53·8	53·5	53·3	53·1	53·0	S 5	53·8	53·7	53·7	53·7	53·8	53·8
2·6	α Leporis		276	36·0	35·8	35·6	35·3	35·2	35·0	S 17	48·5	48·3	48·3	48·3	48·4	48·5
2·2	δ Orionis		276	44·7	44·5	44·3	44·1	43·9	43·7	S 0	17·1	17·0	17·0	17·0	17·0	17·1
2·8	β Leporis		277	43·6	43·4	43·2	43·0	42·8	42·7	S 20	44·6	44·5	44·4	44·4	44·5	44·6
1·7	*Elnath*	14	278	06·8	06·5	06·3	06·0	05·8	05·7	N 28	37·3	37·3	37·4	37·4	37·4	37·4
1·6	*Bellatrix*	13	278	27·0	26·8	26·6	26·4	26·2	26·1	N 6	22·0	22·1	22·1	22·1	22·1	22·0
0·1	*Capella*	12	280	27·6	27·3	27·0	26·7	26·4	26·3	N 46	00·9	00·9	00·9	00·9	01·0	01·0
0·1	*Rigel*	11	281	07·6	07·4	07·2	07·0	06·8	06·7	S 8	10·7	10·6	10·6	10·6	10·6	10·7
2·8	β Eridani		282	47·6	47·4	47·2	47·0	46·8	46·7	S 5	03·6	03·6	03·5	03·5	03·6	03·6
2·7	ι Aurigæ		285	25·6	25·4	25·1	24·9	24·6	24·5	N 33	11·7	11·7	11·8	11·8	11·8	11·9
0·9	*Aldebaran*	10	290	44·0	43·8	43·5	43·3	43·2	43·1	N 16	32·9	32·9	33·0	33·0	33·0	33·0
2·9	ε Persei		300	12·0	11·7	11·4	11·2	11·0	10·9	N 40	03·9	03·9	04·0	04·1	04·1	04·2
3·0	γ Eridani		300	15·6	15·4	15·2	15·0	14·8	14·8	S 13	27·0	26·9	26·9	26·9	27·0	27·1
2·9	ζ Persei		301	09·1	08·9	08·6	08·4	08·2	08·1	N 31	56·4	56·5	56·5	56·6	56·7	56·7
2·9	*Alcyone*		302	49·9	49·6	49·4	49·2	49·0	49·0	N 24	09·9	10·0	10·0	10·1	10·1	10·1
1·8	*Mirfak*	9	308	33·6	33·3	32·9	32·7	32·5	32·5	N 49	55·7	55·7	55·8	55·9	56·0	56·1
Var.§	*Algol*		312	37·8	37·5	37·2	37·0	36·9	36·9	N 41	01·8	01·8	01·9	02·0	02·1	02·2
2·5	*Menkar*	8	314	10·1	09·8	09·6	09·5	09·4	09·3	N 4	10·1	10·2	10·2	10·3	10·3	10·4
3·2	*Acamar*	7	315	14·8	14·5	14·2	14·1	14·0	14·0	S 40	13·2	13·2	13·2	13·2	13·4	13·5
2·0	*Polaris*		315	49·1	33·8	20·0	09·9	05·3	09·0	N 89	20·6	20·7	20·8	20·9	21·1	21·3
3·0	β Trianguli		327	18·8	18·5	18·3	18·1	18·1	18·1	N 35	04·8	04·9	05·0	05·1	05·2	05·2
2·0	*Hamal*	6	327	55·3	55·1	54·8	54·7	54·7	54·7	N 23	33·3	33·4	33·5	33·6	33·6	33·7
2·3	*Almach*		328	42·9	42·6	42·3	42·2	42·1	42·1	N 42	25·4	25·5	25·6	25·7	25·8	25·9
2·9	α Hydri		330	09·0	08·6	08·3	08·1	08·1	08·3	S 61	28·0	28·0	28·0	28·2	28·3	28·4
2·6	*Sheratan*		331	03·6	03·4	03·2	03·1	03·0	03·0	N 20	54·3	54·4	54·5	54·5	54·6	54·6
0·5	*Achernar*	5	335	23·1	22·7	22·4	22·3	22·3	22·5	S 57	07·8	07·7	07·8	07·9	08·1	08·2
2·7	*Ruchbah*		338	12·7	12·3	12·0	11·8	11·8	12·0	N 60	20·1	20·2	20·3	20·4	20·7	20·8
2·1	*Mirach*		342	16·9	16·7	16·5	16·4	16·4	16·4	N 35	43·5	43·6	43·7	43·8	43·9	44·0
Var.||	γ Cassiopeiæ		345	30·7	30·4	30·1	30·0	30·1	30·2	N 60	49·3	49·4	49·6	49·7	49·9	50·0
2·0	*Diphda*	4	348	50·9	50·7	50·5	50·5	50·5	50·5	S 17	52·4	52·3	52·3	52·4	52·5	52·5
2·2	*Schedar*	3	349	34·9	34·6	34·4	34·3	34·4	34·5	N 56	38·6	38·8	38·9	39·1	39·2	39·3
2·4	*Ankaa*	2	353	10·7	10·4	10·3	10·2	10·3	10·4	S 42	11·5	11·5	11·6	11·7	11·8	11·9
2·8	β Hydri		353	17·8	17·0	16·6	16·5	16·9	17·5	S 77	08·1	08·2	08·3	08·4	08·6	08·6
2·8	*Algenib*		356	25·7	25·5	25·4	25·3	25·4	25·4	N 15	17·7	17·8	17·9	18·0	18·0	18·0
2·3	*Caph*		357	25·8	25·4	25·3	25·3	25·4	25·6	N 59	15·4	15·6	15·7	15·9	16·0	16·1
2·1	*Alpheratz*	1	357	38·3	38·1	38·0	38·0	38·0	38·1	N 29	12·0	12·1	12·3	12·4	12·4	12·4

‡ 0·1 — 1·2   § 2·1 — 3·4 || Irregular variable; 2018 mag. 2·2

POLARIS (POLE STAR) TABLES, 2020
FOR DETERMINING LATITUDE FROM SEXTANT ALTITUDE AND FOR AZIMUTH

LHA ARIES	0° – 9°	10° – 19°	20° – 29°	30° – 39°	40° – 49°	50° – 59°	60° – 69°	70° – 79°	80° – 89°	90° – 99°	100° – 109°	110° – 119°
°	a_0	a_0	a_0	a_0	a_0	a_0	a_0	a_0	a_0	a_0	a_0	a_0
0	0 31·0	0 26·7	0 23·3	0 21·0	0 19·9	0 20·0	0 21·3	0 23·7	0 27·2	0 31·7	0 37·0	0 42·9
1	30·6	26·3	23·0	20·9	19·9	20·1	21·5	24·0	27·6	32·2	37·5	43·6
2	30·1	25·9	22·8	20·7	19·8	20·2	21·7	24·3	28·0	32·7	38·1	44·2
3	29·6	25·6	22·5	20·6	19·8	20·2	21·9	24·6	28·4	33·2	38·7	44·8
4	29·2	25·2	22·3	20·4	19·8	20·4	22·1	25·0	28·9	33·7	39·3	45·5
5	0 28·8	0 24·9	0 22·0	0 20·3	0 19·8	0 20·5	0 22·3	0 25·3	0 29·3	0 34·2	0 39·9	0 46·1
6	28·3	24·5	21·8	20·2	19·8	20·6	22·6	25·7	29·8	34·8	40·5	46·7
7	27·9	24·2	21·6	20·1	19·8	20·8	22·8	26·0	30·2	35·3	41·1	47·4
8	27·5	23·9	21·4	20·0	19·9	20·9	23·1	26·4	30·7	35·8	41·7	48·1
9	27·1	23·6	21·2	20·0	19·9	21·1	23·4	26·8	31·2	36·4	42·3	48·7
10	0 26·7	0 23·3	0 21·0	0 19·9	0 20·0	0 21·3	0 23·7	0 27·2	0 31·7	0 37·0	0 42·9	0 49·4

Lat.	a_1	a_1	a_1	a_1	a_1	a_1	a_1	a_1	a_1	a_1	a_1	a_1
°												
0	0·5	0·5	0·6	0·6	0·6	0·6	0·6	0·5	0·5	0·4	0·4	0·4
10	·5	·5	·6	·6	·6	·6	·6	·5	·5	·5	·4	·4
20	·5	·6	·6	·6	·6	·6	·6	·6	·6	·5	·5	·4
30	·5	·6	·6	·6	·6	·6	·6	·6	·5	·5	·5	·5
40	0·6	0·6	0·6	0·6	0·6	0·6	0·6	0·6	0·6	0·6	0·5	0·5
45	·6	·6	·6	·6	·6	·6	·6	·6	·6	·6	·6	·6
50	·6	·6	·6	·6	·6	·6	·6	·6	·6	·6	·6	·6
55	·6	·6	·6	·6	·6	·6	·6	·6	·6	·6	·6	·6
60	·6	·6	·6	·6	·6	·6	·6	·6	·7	·7	·7	·7
62	0·7	0·6	0·6	0·6	0·6	0·6	0·6	0·6	0·7	0·7	0·7	0·7
64	·7	·6	·6	·6	·6	·6	·6	·6	·7	·7	·7	·8
66	·7	·7	·6	·6	·6	·6	·6	·7	·7	·7	·8	·8
68	0·7	0·7	0·6	0·6	0·6	0·6	0·6	0·7	0·7	0·8	0·8	0·9

Month	a_2	a_2	a_2	a_2	a_2	a_2	a_2	a_2	a_2	a_2	a_2	a_2
Jan.	0·7	0·7	0·7	0·7	0·7	0·7	0·7	0·7	0·7	0·7	0·6	0·6
Feb.	·6	·6	·7	·7	·7	·8	·8	·8	·8	·8	·8	·8
Mar.	·5	·5	·6	·6	·7	·7	·8	·8	·8	·9	·9	·9
Apr.	0·3	0·4	0·4	0·5	0·6	0·6	0·7	0·7	0·8	0·9	0·9	0·9
May	·2	·3	·3	·4	·4	·5	·5	·6	·7	·8	·8	·9
June	·2	·2	·2	·2	·3	·3	·4	·5	·5	·6	·7	·8
July	0·2	0·2	0·2	0·2	0·2	0·3	0·3	0·4	0·4	0·5	0·5	0·6
Aug.	·4	·3	·3	·3	·3	·3	·3	·3	·3	·3	·4	·4
Sept.	·5	·5	·4	·4	·4	·3	·3	·3	·3	·3	·3	·3
Oct.	0·7	0·7	0·6	0·6	0·5	0·5	0·4	0·4	0·3	0·3	0·3	0·3
Nov.	0·9	0·9	0·8	·7	·7	·6	·6	·5	·4	·4	·3	·3
Dec.	1·0	1·0	1·0	0·9	0·9	0·8	0·7	0·7	0·6	0·5	0·4	0·4

Lat.	AZIMUTH											
°	°	°	°	°	°	°	°	°	°	°	°	°
0	0·4	0·3	0·2	0·1	0·0	359·9	359·8	359·7	359·6	359·5	359·4	359·4
20	0·4	0·3	0·2	0·1	0·0	359·9	359·8	359·6	359·5	359·5	359·4	359·3
40	0·5	0·4	0·3	0·1	0·0	359·8	359·7	359·6	359·4	359·3	359·3	359·2
50	0·6	0·5	0·3	0·2	0·0	359·8	359·6	359·5	359·3	359·2	359·1	359·0
55	0·7	0·6	0·4	0·2	0·0	359·8	359·6	359·4	359·3	359·1	359·0	358·9
60	0·8	0·6	0·4	0·2	0·0	359·8	359·5	359·3	359·1	359·0	358·9	358·8
65	1·0	0·8	0·5	0·3	0·0	359·7	359·4	359·2	359·0	358·8	358·6	358·5

Latitude = Apparent altitude (corrected for refraction) $-1° + a_0 + a_1 + a_2$

The table is entered with LHA Aries to determine the column to be used; each column refers to a range of 10°. a_0 is taken, with mental interpolation, from the upper table with the units of LHA Aries in degrees as argument; a_1, a_2 are taken, without interpolation, from the second and third tables with arguments latitude and month respectively. a_0, a_1, a_2, are always positive. The final table gives the azimuth of *Polaris*.

FOR DETERMINING LATITUDE FROM SEXTANT ALTITUDE AND FOR AZIMUTH

LHA ARIES	120°–129°	130°–139°	140°–149°	150°–159°	160°–169°	170°–179°	180°–189°	190°–199°	200°–209°	210°–219°	220°–229°	230°–239°
	a_0	a_0	a_0	a_0	a_0	a_0	a_0	a_0	a_0	a_0	a_0	a_0
°	° ′	° ′	° ′	° ′	° ′	° ′	° ′	° ′	° ′	° ′	° ′	° ′
0	0 49·4	0 56·1	1 02·9	1 09·6	1 15·9	1 21·7	1 26·8	1 31·1	1 34·4	1 36·6	1 37·7	1 37·6
1	50·0	56·8	03·6	10·2	16·5	22·2	27·3	31·5	34·6	36·8	37·7	37·5
2	50·7	57·5	04·2	10·9	17·1	22·8	27·7	31·8	34·9	36·9	37·8	37·5
3	51·4	58·1	04·9	11·5	17·7	23·3	28·2	32·2	35·2	37·0	37·8	37·4
4	52·0	58·8	05·6	12·1	18·3	23·8	28·6	32·5	35·4	37·2	37·8	37·3
5	0 52·7	0 59·5	1 06·3	1 12·8	1 18·9	1 24·3	1 29·1	1 32·9	1 35·6	1 37·3	1 37·8	1 37·1
6	53·4	1 00·2	06·9	13·4	19·4	24·9	29·5	33·2	35·8	37·4	37·8	37·0
7	54·1	00·9	07·6	14·0	20·0	25·4	29·9	33·5	36·0	37·5	37·8	36·9
8	54·7	01·5	08·2	14·7	20·6	25·8	30·3	33·8	36·2	37·6	37·7	36·7
9	55·4	02·2	08·9	15·3	21·1	26·3	30·7	34·1	36·4	37·6	37·7	36·6
10	0 56·1	1 02·9	1 09·6	1 15·9	1 21·7	1 26·8	1 31·1	1 34·4	1 36·6	1 37·7	1 37·6	1 36·4

Lat.	a_1	a_1	a_1	a_1	a_1	a_1	a_1	a_1	a_1	a_1	a_1	a_1
°	′	′	′	′	′	′	′	′	′	′	′	′
0	0·3	0·3	0·3	0·4	0·4	0·4	0·5	0·5	0·6	0·6	0·6	0·6
10	·4	·4	·4	·4	·4	·5	·5	·5	·6	·6	·6	·6
20	·4	·4	·4	·4	·5	·5	·5	·6	·6	·6	·6	·6
30	·5	·5	·5	·5	·5	·5	·5	·6	·6	·6	·6	·6
40	0·5	0·5	0·5	0·5	0·5	0·6	0·6	0·6	0·6	0·6	0·6	0·6
45	·6	·6	·6	·6	·6	·6	·6	·6	·6	·6	·6	·6
50	·6	·6	·6	·6	·6	·6	·6	·6	·6	·6	·6	·6
55	·7	·7	·7	·6	·6	·6	·6	·6	·6	·6	·6	·6
60	·7	·7	·7	·7	·7	·7	·6	·6	·6	·6	·6	·6
62	0·7	0·8	0·7	0·7	0·7	0·7	0·7	0·6	0·6	0·6	0·6	0·6
64	·8	·8	·8	·8	·7	·7	·7	·6	·6	·6	·6	·6
66	·8	·8	·8	·8	·8	·7	·7	·7	·6	·6	·6	·6
68	0·9	0·9	0·9	0·8	0·8	0·8	0·7	0·7	0·6	0·6	0·6	0·6

Month	a_2	a_2	a_2	a_2	a_2	a_2	a_2	a_2	a_2	a_2	a_2	a_2
	′	′	′	′	′	′	′	′	′	′	′	′
Jan.	0·6	0·6	0·6	0·6	0·5	0·5	0·5	0·5	0·5	0·5	0·5	0·5
Feb.	·8	·7	·7	·7	·7	·6	·6	·6	·5	·5	·5	·4
Mar.	0·9	0·9	0·9	0·8	·8	·8	·7	·7	·6	·6	·5	·5
Apr.	1·0	1·0	1·0	1·0	0·9	0·9	0·9	0·8	0·8	0·7	0·6	0·6
May	0·9	1·0	1·0	1·0	1·0	1·0	1·0	0·9	0·9	0·8	·8	·7
June	·8	0·9	0·9	1·0	1·0	1·0	1·0	1·0	1·0	1·0	0·9	·9
July	0·7	0·7	0·8	0·8	0·9	0·9	1·0	1·0	1·0	1·0	1·0	0·9
Aug.	·5	·6	·6	·7	·7	·8	0·8	0·9	0·9	0·9	0·9	·9
Sept.	·4	·4	·4	·5	·5	·6	·7	·7	·8	·8	·8	·9
Oct.	0·3	0·3	0·3	0·3	0·4	0·4	0·5	0·5	0·6	0·6	0·7	0·7
Nov.	·3	·2	·2	·2	·2	·3	·3	·3	·4	·5	·5	·6
Dec.	0·3	0·3	0·2	0·2	0·2	0·2	0·2	0·2	0·2	0·3	0·3	0·4

Lat.	AZIMUTH											
°	°	°	°	°	°	°	°	°	°	°	°	°
0	359·4	359·4	359·4	359·4	359·4	359·5	359·6	359·7	359·8	359·9	0·0	0·1
20	359·3	359·3	359·3	359·4	359·4	359·5	359·6	359·7	359·8	359·9	0·0	0·1
40	359·2	359·2	359·2	359·2	359·3	359·4	359·5	359·6	359·7	359·9	0·0	0·2
50	359·0	359·0	359·0	359·1	359·1	359·2	359·4	359·5	359·7	359·8	0·0	0·2
55	358·9	358·9	358·9	358·9	359·0	359·1	359·3	359·5	359·6	359·8	0·0	0·2
60	358·7	358·7	358·7	358·8	358·9	359·0	359·2	359·4	359·6	359·8	0·0	0·2
65	358·5	358·5	358·5	358·6	358·7	358·9	359·0	359·3	359·5	359·8	0·0	0·3

ILLUSTRATION	From the daily pages:			H_0	49 31·6
On 2020 April 21 at 23ʰ 18ᵐ 56ˢ UT in longitude W 37° 14′, the apparent altitude (corrected for refraction), H_0, of Polaris was 49° 31′·6	GHA Aries (23ʰ)	195	28·1	a_0 (argument 162° 59′)	1 17·7
	Increment (18ᵐ 56ˢ)	4	44·8	a_1 (Lat 50° approx.)	0·6
	Longitude (west)	−37	14	a_2 (April)	0·9
	LHA Aries	162	59	Sum − 1° = Lat =	49 50·8

POLARIS (POLE STAR) TABLES, 2020
FOR DETERMINING LATITUDE FROM SEXTANT ALTITUDE AND FOR AZIMUTH

LHA ARIES	240° – 249°	250° – 259°	260° – 269°	270° – 279°	280° – 289°	290° – 299°	300° – 309°	310° – 319°	320° – 329°	330° – 339°	340° – 349°	350° – 359°
	a_0	a_0	a_0	a_0	a_0	a_0	a_0	a_0	a_0	a_0	a_0	a_0
°	° ′	° ′	° ′	° ′	° ′	° ′	° ′	° ′	° ′	° ′	° ′	° ′
0	I 36·4	I 34·0	I 30·6	I 26·2	I 21·0	I 15·1	I 08·7	I 02·0	0 55·2	0 48·5	0 42·1	0 36·3
1	36·2	33·7	30·2	25·7	20·4	14·5	08·1	01·4	54·6	47·9	41·5	35·7
2	36·0	33·4	29·8	25·2	19·9	13·9	07·4	00·7	53·9	47·2	40·9	35·2
3	35·8	33·1	29·4	24·7	19·3	13·2	06·7	I 00·0	53·2	46·6	40·3	34·6
4	35·6	32·8	28·9	24·2	18·7	12·6	06·1	0 59·3	52·5	45·9	39·7	34·1
5	I 35·3	I 32·4	I 28·5	I 23·7	I 18·1	I 12·0	I 05·4	0 58·6	0 51·9	0 45·3	0 39·1	0 33·6
6	35·1	32·1	28·1	23·2	17·5	11·3	04·7	58·0	51·2	44·6	38·5	33·0
7	34·8	31·7	27·6	22·6	16·9	10·7	04·1	57·3	50·5	44·0	38·0	32·5
8	34·6	31·4	27·2	22·1	16·3	10·0	03·4	56·6	49·9	43·4	37·4	32·0
9	34·3	31·0	26·7	21·5	15·7	09·4	02·7	55·9	49·2	42·8	36·8	31·5
10	I 34·0	I 30·6	I 26·2	I 21·0	I 15·1	I 08·7	I 02·0	0 55·2	0 48·5	0 42·1	0 36·3	0 31·0

Lat.	a_1	a_1	a_1	a_1	a_1	a_1	a_1	a_1	a_1	a_1	a_1	a_1
°	′	′	′	′	′	′	′	′	′	′	′	′
0	0·6	0·5	0·5	0·4	0·4	0·4	0·3	0·3	0·3	0·4	0·4	0·4
10	·6	·5	·5	·5	·4	·4	·4	·4	·4	·4	·4	·5
20	·6	·6	·5	·5	·5	·4	·4	·4	·4	·4	·5	·5
30	·6	·6	·5	·5	·5	·5	·5	·5	·5	·5	·5	·5
40	0·6	0·6	0·6	0·6	0·5	0·5	0·5	0·5	0·5	0·5	0·5	0·6
45	·6	·6	·6	·6	·6	·6	·6	·6	·6	·6	·6	·6
50	·6	·6	·6	·6	·6	·6	·6	·6	·6	·6	·6	·6
55	·6	·6	·6	·6	·6	·6	·7	·7	·7	·6	·6	·6
60	·6	·6	·7	·7	·7	·7	·7	·7	·7	·7	·7	·7
62	0·6	0·6	0·7	0·7	0·7	0·7	0·7	0·8	0·7	0·7	0·7	0·7
64	·6	·6	·7	·7	·7	·8	·8	·8	·8	·8	·7	·7
66	·6	·7	·7	·7	·8	·8	·8	·8	·8	·8	·8	·7
68	0·6	0·7	0·7	0·8	0·8	0·9	0·9	0·9	0·9	0·8	0·8	0·8

Month	a_2	a_2	a_2	a_2	a_2	a_2	a_2	a_2	a_2	a_2	a_2	a_2
	′	′	′	′	′	′	′	′	′	′	′	′
Jan.	0·5	0·5	0·5	0·5	0·6	0·6	0·6	0·6	0·6	0·6	0·7	0·7
Feb.	·4	·4	·4	·4	·4	·4	·4	·5	·5	·5	·5	·6
Mar.	·4	·4	·4	·3	·3	·3	·3	·3	·3	·4	·4	·4
Apr.	0·5	0·5	0·4	0·3	0·3	0·3	0·2	0·2	0·2	0·2	0·3	0·3
May	·7	·6	·5	·4	·4	·3	·3	·2	·2	·2	·2	·2
June	·8	·7	·7	·6	·5	·4	·4	·3	·3	·2	·2	·2
July	0·9	0·8	0·8	0·7	0·7	0·6	0·5	0·5	0·4	0·4	0·3	0·3
Aug.	·9	·9	·9	·9	·8	·8	·7	·6	·6	·5	·5	·4
Sept.	·9	·9	·9	·9	·9	·9	·8	·8	·8	·7	·7	·6
Oct.	0·8	0·8	0·9	0·9	0·9	0·9	0·9	0·9	0·9	0·9	0·8	0·8
Nov.	·6	·7	·8	·8	·9	·9	·9	1·0	1·0	1·0	1·0	0·9
Dec.	0·5	0·5	0·6	0·7	0·8	0·8	0·9	0·9	1·0	1·0	1·0	1·0

Lat.	AZIMUTH											
°	°	°	°	°	°	°	°	°	°	°	°	°
0	0·2	0·3	0·4	0·5	0·6	0·6	0·6	0·6	0·6	0·6	0·6	0·5
20	0·2	0·4	0·4	0·5	0·6	0·7	0·7	0·7	0·7	0·6	0·6	0·5
40	0·3	0·4	0·5	0·7	0·7	0·8	0·8	0·8	0·8	0·8	0·7	0·6
50	0·4	0·5	0·7	0·8	0·9	0·9	1·0	1·0	1·0	1·0	0·9	0·8
55	0·4	0·6	0·7	0·9	1·0	1·1	1·1	1·1	1·1	1·1	1·0	0·9
60	0·4	0·7	0·8	1·0	1·1	1·2	1·3	1·3	1·3	1·2	1·1	1·0
65	0·5	0·8	1·0	1·2	1·3	1·4	1·5	1·5	1·5	1·5	1·3	1·2

$$\text{Latitude} = \text{Apparent altitude (corrected for refraction)} -1° + a_0 + a_1 + a_2$$

The table is entered with LHA Aries to determine the column to be used; each column refers to a range of 10°. a_0 is taken, with mental interpolation, from the upper table with the units of LHA Aries in degrees as argument; a_1, a_2 are taken, without interpolation, from the second and third tables with arguments latitude and month respectively. a_0, a_1, a_2, are always positive. The final table gives the azimuth of *Polaris*.

SIGHT REDUCTION PROCEDURES
METHODS AND FORMULAE FOR DIRECT COMPUTATION

1. *Introduction.* In this section, formulae and methods are provided for *calculating* position at sea from observed altitudes taken with a marine sextant using a computer or programmable calculator.

The method uses analogous concepts and similar terminology as that used in *manual* methods of astro-navigation, where position is found by plotting position lines from their intercept and azimuth on a marine chart.

The algorithms are presented in standard algebra suitable for translating into the programming language of the user's computer. The basic ephemeris data may be taken directly from the main tabular pages of a current version of *The Nautical Almanac*. Formulae are given for calculating altitude and azimuth from the *GHA* and *Dec* of a body, and the estimated position of the observer. Formulae are also given for reducing sextant observations to observed altitudes by applying the corrections for dip, refraction, parallax and semi-diameter.

The intercept and azimuth obtained from each observation determine a position line, and the observer should lie on or close to each position line. The method of least squares is used to calculate the fix by finding the position where the sum of the squares of the distances from the position lines is a minimum. The use of least squares has other advantages. For example, it is possible to improve the estimated position at the time of fix by repeating the calculation. It is also possible to include more observations in the solution and to reject doubtful ones.

2. *Notation.*

GHA = Greenwich hour angle. The range of *GHA* is from 0° to 360° starting at 0° on the Greenwich meridian increasing to the west, back to 360° on the Greenwich meridian.

SHA = sidereal hour angle. The range is 0° to 360°.

Dec = declination. The sign convention for declination is north is positive, south is negative. The range is from −90° at the south celestial pole to +90° at the north celestial pole.

Long = longitude. The sign convention is east is positive, west is negative. The range is −180° to +180°.

Lat = latitude. The sign convention is north is positive, south is negative. The range is from −90° to +90°.

LHA = *GHA* + *Long* = local hour angle. The *LHA* increases to the west from 0° on the local meridian to 360°.

H_C = calculated altitude. Above the horizon is positive, below the horizon is negative. The range is from −90° in the nadir to +90° in the zenith.

H_S = sextant altitude.

H = apparent altitude = sextant altitude corrected for instrumental error and dip.

H_O = observed altitude = apparent altitude corrected for refraction and, in appropriate cases, corrected for parallax and semi-diameter.

Z = Z_n = true azimuth. Z is measured from true north through east, south, west and back to north. The range is from 0° to 360°.

I = sextant index error.

D = dip of horizon.

R = atmospheric refraction.

HP = horizontal parallax of the Sun, Moon, Venus or Mars.
PA = parallax in altitude of the Sun, Moon, Venus or Mars.
SD = semi-diameter of the Sun or Moon.
p = intercept = $H_O - H_C$. Towards is positive, away is negative.
T = course or track, measured as for azimuth from the north.
V = speed in knots.

3. *Entering Basic Data.*   When quantities such as GHA are entered, which in *The Nautical Almanac* are given in degrees and minutes, convert them to degrees and decimals of a degree by dividing the minutes by 60 and adding to the degrees; for example, if $GHA = 123° 45!6$, enter the two numbers 123 and 45·6 into the memory and set $GHA = 123 + 45 \cdot 6/60 = 123°7600$. Although four decimal places of a degree are shown in the examples, it is assumed that full precision is maintained in the calculations.

When using a computer or programmable calculator, write a subroutine to convert degrees and minutes to degrees and decimals. Scientific calculators usually have a special key for this purpose. For quantities like Dec which require a minus sign for southern declination, change the sign from plus to minus after the value has been converted to degrees and decimals, *e.g.* $Dec = S 0° 12!3 = S 0°2050 = -0°2050$. Other quantities which require conversion are semi-diameter, horizontal parallax, longitude and latitude.

4. *Interpolation of GHA and Dec*   The GHA and Dec of the Sun, Moon and planets are interpolated to the time of observation by direct calculation as follows: If the universal time is $a^h\ b^m\ c^s$, form the interpolation factor $x = b/60 + c/3600$. Enter the tabular value GHA_0 for the preceding hour (a) and the tabular value GHA_1 for the following hour $(a+1)$ then the interpolated value GHA is given by

$$GHA = GHA_0 + x(GHA_1 - GHA_0)$$

If the GHA passes through 360° between tabular values, add 360° to GHA_1 before interpolation. If the interpolated value exceeds 360°, subtract 360° from GHA.

Similarly for declination, enter the tabular value Dec_0 for the preceding hour (a) and the tabular value Dec_1 for the following hour $(a+1)$, then the interpolated value Dec is given by
$$Dec = Dec_0 + x(Dec_1 - Dec_0)$$

5. *Example.* (a) Find the GHA and Dec of the Sun on 2020 February 4 at $0^h\ 47^m\ 13^s$ UT.

The interpolation factor $x = 47/60 + 13/3600 = 0^h7869$

page 33 $0^h\ GHA_0 = 176°\ 32!8 = 176°5467$

$1^h\ GHA_1 = 191°\ 32!8 = 191°5467$

$0^h7869\ GHA = 176 \cdot 5467 + 0 \cdot 7869(191 \cdot 5467 - 176 \cdot 5467) = 188°3508$

$0^h\ Dec_0 = S\ 16°\ 26!8 = -16°4467$

$1^h\ Dec_1 = S\ 16°\ 26!0 = -16°4333$

$0^h7869\ Dec = -16 \cdot 4467 + 0 \cdot 7869(-16 \cdot 4333 + 16 \cdot 4467) = -16°4362$

GHA Aries is interpolated in the same way as GHA of a body. For a star the SHA and Dec are taken from the tabular page and do not require interpolation, then

$$GHA = GHA\ \text{Aries} + SHA$$

where GHA Aries is interpolated to the time of observation.

(b) Find the *GHA* and *Dec* of *Vega* on 2020 February 4 at $0^h\ 47^m\ 13^s$ UT.

The interpolation factor $x = 0^h7869$ as in the previous example

page 32 0^h *GHA* Aries$_0$ = 133° 37.8 = 133°6300

1^h *GHA* Aries$_1$ = 148° 40.2 = 148°6700   (360° added)

0^h7869 *GHA* Aries = 133·6300 + 0·7869(148·6700 − 133·6300) = 145°4656

SHA = 80° 36.2 = 80°6033

GHA = *GHA* Aries + *SHA* = 226°0690   (multiple of 360° removed)

Dec = N 38° 48.0 = +38°8000

6. *The calculated altitude and azimuth.* The calculated altitude H_C and true azimuth Z are determined from the *GHA* and *Dec* interpolated to the time of observation and from the *Long* and *Lat* estimated at the time of observation as follows:

Step 1.   Calculate the local hour angle

$$LHA = GHA + Long$$

Add or subtract multiples of 360° to set *LHA* in the range 0° to 360°.

Step 2.   Calculate S, C and the altitude H_C from

$$S = \sin Dec$$
$$C = \cos Dec \cos LHA$$
$$H_C = \sin^{-1}(S \sin Lat + C \cos Lat)$$

where $\sin^{-1}$ is the inverse function of sine.

Step 3.   Calculate X and A from

$$X = (S \cos Lat - C \sin Lat)/\cos H_C$$
$$\text{If } X > +1 \quad \text{set} \quad X = +1$$
$$\text{If } X < -1 \quad \text{set} \quad X = -1$$
$$A = \cos^{-1} X$$

where $\cos^{-1}$ is the inverse function of cosine.

Step 4.   Determine the azimuth Z

$$\text{If } LHA > 180° \quad \text{then} \quad Z = A$$
$$\text{Otherwise} \quad Z = 360° - A$$

7. *Example.* Find the calculated altitude H_C and azimuth Z when

$$GHA = 53° \quad Dec = S\,15° \quad Lat = N\,32° \quad Long = W\,16°$$

For the calculation

$$GHA = 53°0000 \quad Dec = -15°0000 \quad Lat = +32°0000 \quad Long = -16°0000$$

Step 1. $LHA = 53·0000 - 16·0000 = 37·0000$

Step 2. $S = -0·2588$

$C = +0·9659 \times 0·7986 = 0·7714$

$\sin H_C = -0·2588 \times 0·5299 + 0·7714 \times 0·8480 = 0·5171$

$H_C = 31°1346$

Step 3. $$X = (-0{\cdot}2588 \times 0{\cdot}8480 - 0{\cdot}7714 \times 0{\cdot}5299)/0{\cdot}8560 = -0{\cdot}7340$$
$$A = 137{\cdot}2239$$

Step 4.   Since $LHA \leq 180°$ then $Z = 360° - A = 222{\cdot}7761$

     8. *Reduction from sextant altitude to observed altitude.*   The sextant altitude H_S is corrected for both dip and index error to produce the apparent altitude. The observed altitude H_O is calculated by applying a correction for refraction. For the Sun, Moon, Venus and Mars a correction for parallax is also applied to H, and for the Sun and Moon a further correction for semi-diameter is required. The corrections are calculated as follows:

Step 1.   Calculate dip

$$D = 0{\cdot}0293\sqrt{h}$$

where h is the height of eye above the horizon in metres.

Step 2.   Calculate apparent altitude

$$H = H_S + I - D$$

where I is the sextant index error.

Step 3.   Calculate refraction (R) at a standard temperature of 10° Celsius (C) and pressure of 1010 millibars (mb)

$$R_0 = 0{\cdot}0167/\tan(H + 7{\cdot}32/(H + 4{\cdot}32))$$

If the temperature $T°\,C$ and pressure P mb are known calculate the refraction from

$$R = fR_0 \qquad \text{where} \qquad f = 0{\cdot}28P/(T + 273)$$
$$\text{otherwise set} \qquad R = R_0$$

Step 4.   Calculate the parallax in altitude (PA) from the horizontal parallax (HP) and the apparent altitude (H) for the Sun, Moon, Venus and Mars as follows:

$$PA = HP\cos H$$

For the Sun $HP = 0{\cdot}0024$. This correction is very small and could be ignored.

For the Moon HP is taken for the nearest hour from the main tabular page and converted to degrees.

For Venus and Mars the HP is taken from the critical table at the bottom of page 259 and converted to degrees.

For the navigational stars and the remaining planets, Jupiter and Saturn set $PA = 0$.

If an error of $0{\cdot}2$ is significant the expression for the parallax in altitude for the Moon should include a small correction OB for the oblateness of the Earth as follows:

$$PA = HP\cos H + OB$$
$$\text{where} \quad OB = -0{\cdot}0032\sin^2 Lat \cos H + 0{\cdot}0032\sin(2Lat)\cos Z \sin H$$

At mid-latitudes and for altitudes of the Moon below 60° a simple approximation to OB is

$$OB = -0{\cdot}0017\cos H$$

Step 5. Calculate the semi-diameter for the Sun and Moon as follows:

Sun: *SD* is taken from the main tabular page and converted to degrees.

Moon: $SD = 0°2724HP$ where HP is taken for the nearest hour from the main tabular page and converted to degrees.

Step 6. Calculate the observed altitude

$$H_O = H - R + PA \pm SD$$

where the plus sign is used if the lower limb of the Sun or Moon was observed and the minus sign if the upper limb was observed.

9. *Example.* The following example illustrates how to use a calculator to reduce the sextant altitude (H_S) to observed altitude (H_O); the sextant altitudes given are assumed to be taken on 2020 March 11 with a marine sextant, zero index error, at height 5·4 m, temperature $-3°$ C and pressure 982 mb, the Moon sights are assumed to be taken at 10^h UT.

Body limb	Sun lower	Sun upper	Moon lower	Moon upper	Venus —	*Polaris* —
Sextant altitude: H_S	21·3283	3·3367	33·4600	26·1117	4·5433	49·6083
Step 1. Dip: $D = 0·0293\sqrt{h}$	0·0681	0·0681	0·0681	0·0681	0·0681	0·0681
Step 2. Apparent altitude: $H = H_S + I - D$	21·2602	3·2686	33·3919	26·0436	4·4752	49·5402
Step 3. Refraction: R_0	0·0423	0·2256	0·0251	0·0338	0·1798	0·0142
f	1·0184	1·0184	1·0184	1·0184	1·0184	1·0184
$R = fR_0$	0·0431	0·2298	0·0256	0·0344	0·1831	0·0144
Step 4. Parallax: HP	0·0024	0·0024	(61′2) 1·0200	(61′2) 1·0200	(0′2) 0·0033	—
Parallax in altitude: $PA = HP \cos H$	0·0022	0·0024	0·8516	0·9164	0·0033	—
Step 5. Semi-diameter: Sun : $SD = 16·1/60$	0·2683	0·2683	—	—	—	—
Moon : $SD = 0·2724HP$	—	—	0·2778	0·2778	—	—
Step 6. Observed altitude: $H_O = H - R + PA \pm SD$	21·4877	2·7729	34·4958	26·6478	4·2955	49·5258

Note that for the Moon the correction for the oblateness of the Earth of about $-0°0017\cos H$, which equals $-0°0014$ for the lower limb and $-0°0015$ for the upper limb, has been ignored in the above calculation.

10. *Position from intercept and azimuth using a chart.* An estimate is made of the position at the adopted time of fix. The position at the time of observation is then calculated by dead reckoning from the time of fix. For example, if the course (track) T and the speed V (in knots) of the observer are constant, then *Long* and *Lat* at the time of observation are calculated from

$$Long = L_F + t\,(V/60)\sin T\,/\cos B_F$$
$$Lat = B_F + t\,(V/60)\cos T$$

where L_F and B_F are the estimated longitude and latitude at the time of fix and t is the time interval in hours from the time of fix to the time of observation, t is positive if the time of observation is after the time of fix and negative if it was before.

The position line of an observation is plotted on a chart using the intercept

$$p = H_O - H_c$$

and azimuth Z with origin at the calculated position (*Long, Lat*) at the time of observation, where H_c and Z are calculated using the method in section 6, page 279. Starting from this calculated position a line is drawn on the chart along the direction of the azimuth to the body. Convert p to nautical miles by multiplying by 60. The position line is drawn at right angles to the azimuth line, distance p from (*Long, Lat*) towards the body if p is positive and distance p away from the body if p is negative. Provided there are no gross errors, the navigator should be somewhere on or near the position line at the time of observation. Two or more position lines are required to determine a fix.

11. *Position from intercept and azimuth by calculation.* The position of the fix may be calculated from two or more sextant observations as follows.

If p_1, Z_1, are the intercept and azimuth of the first observation, p_2, Z_2, of the second observation and so on, form the summations

$$A = \cos^2 Z_1 + \cos^2 Z_2 + \cdots$$
$$B = \cos Z_1 \sin Z_1 + \cos Z_2 \sin Z_2 + \cdots$$
$$C = \sin^2 Z_1 + \sin^2 Z_2 + \cdots$$
$$D = p_1 \cos Z_1 + p_2 \cos Z_2 + \cdots$$
$$E = p_1 \sin Z_1 + p_2 \sin Z_2 + \cdots$$

where the number of terms in each summation is equal to the number of observations.

With $G = A\,C - B^2$, an improved estimate of the position at the time of fix (L_I, B_I) is given by

$$L_I = L_F + (A\,E - B\,D)/(G\cos B_F), \qquad B_I = B_F + (C\,D - B\,E)/G$$

Calculate the distance d between the initial estimated position (L_F, B_F) at the time of fix and the improved estimated position (L_I, B_I) in nautical miles from

$$d = 60\sqrt{((L_I - L_F)^2 \cos^2 B_F + (B_I - B_F)^2)}$$

If d exceeds about 20 nautical miles set $L_F = L_I$, $B_F = B_I$ and repeat the calculation until d, the distance between the position at the previous estimate and the improved estimate, is less than about 20 nautical miles.

12. *Example of direct computation.* Using the method described above, calculate the position of a ship on 2020 July 6 at $21^h\,00^m\,00^s$ UT from the marine sextant observations of the three stars *Regulus* (No. 26) at $20^h\,39^m\,23^s$ UT, *Antares* (No. 42) at $20^h\,45^m\,47^s$ UT and *Kochab* (No. 40) at $21^h\,10^m\,34^s$ UT, where the observed altitudes of the three stars corrected for the effects of refraction, dip and instrumental error, are $24°\!9810$, $26°\!8969$ and $47°\!4869$ respectively. The ship was travelling at a constant speed of 20 knots on a course of 325° during the period of observation, and the position of the ship at the time of fix $21^h\,00^m\,00^s$ UT is only known to the nearest whole degree W 15°, N 32°.

Intermediate values for the first iteration are shown in the table. *GHA* Aries was interpolated from the nearest tabular values on page 134. For the first iteration set $L_F = -15°0000$, $B_F = +32°0000$ at the time of fix at $21^h 00^m 00^s$ UT.

First Iteration

Body No.	Regulus 26	Antares 42	Kochab 40
time of observation	$20^h 39^m 23^s$	$20^h 45^m 47^s$	$21^h 10^m 34^s$
H_O	24·9810	26·8969	47·4869
interpolation factor	0·6564	0·7631	0·1761
GHA Aries	235·1282	236·7326	242·9454
SHA (page 134)	207·6433	112·3333	137·3233
GHA	82·7715	349·0660	20·2687
Dec (page 134)	+11·8700	−26·4767	+74·0783
t	−0·3436	−0·2369	+0·1761
Long	−14·9225	−14·9466	−15·0397
Lat	+31·9062	+31·9353	+32·0481
Z	268·7103	154·0916	357·8634
H_C	24·9579	26·5911	47·8870
p	+0·0231	+0·3058	−0·4001

$A = 1·8082 \quad B = −0·4078 \quad C = 1·1918 \quad D = −0·6754 \quad E = 0·1254 \quad G = 1·9887$

$(AE − BD)/(G\cos B_F) = −0·0288, \quad (CD − BE)/G = −0·3790$

An improved estimate of the position at the time of fix is

$$L_I = L_F − 0·0288 = −15·0288 \quad \text{and} \quad B_I = B_F − 0·3790 = +31·6210$$

Since the distance between the previous estimated position and the improved estimate is $d = 22·8$ nautical miles, set $L_F = −15·0288$, and $B_F = +31·6210$ and repeat the calculation. The table shows the intermediate values of the calculation for the second iteration. In each iteration the quantities H_O, *GHA*, *Dec* and t do not change.

Second Iteration

Body No.	Regulus 26	Antares 42	Kochab 40
Long	−14·9517	−14·9756	−15·0684
Lat	+31·5271	+31·5563	+31·6691
Z	268·8713	153·9815	357·8905
H_C	24·9907	26·9211	47·5091
p	−0·0097	−0·0242	−0·0222

$A = 1·8066 \quad B = −0·4113 \quad C = 1·1934 \quad D = −0·0003 \quad E = −0·0001 \quad G = 1·9868$

$(AE − BD)/(G\cos B_F) = −0·0002, \quad (CD − BE)/G = −0·0002$

An improved estimate of the position at the time of fix is

$$L_I = L_F − 0·0002 = −15·0290 \quad \text{and} \quad B_I = B_F − 0·0002 = +31·6208$$

The distance between the previous estimated position and the improved estimated position, $d = 0·02$ nautical miles, is so small that a third iteration would produce a negligible improvement to the estimate of the position.

USE OF CONCISE SIGHT REDUCTION TABLES

1. *Introduction.* The concise sight reduction tables given on pages 286 to 317 are intended for use when neither more extensive tables nor electronic computing aids are available. These "NAO sight reduction tables" provide for the reduction of the local hour angle and declination of a celestial object to azimuth and altitude, referred to an assumed position on the Earth, for use in the intercept method of celestial navigation which is now standard practice.

2. *Form of tables.* Entries in the reduction table are at a fixed interval of one degree for all latitudes and hour angles. A compact arrangement results from division of the navigational triangle into two right spherical triangles, so that the table has to be entered twice. Assumed latitude and local hour angle are the arguments for the first entry. The reduction table responds with the intermediate arguments A, B, and Z_1, where A is used as one of the arguments for the second entry to the table, B has to be incremented by the declination to produce the quantity F, and Z_1 is a component of the azimuth angle. The reduction table is then reentered with A and F and yields H, P, and Z_2 where H is the altitude, P is the complement of the parallactic angle, and Z_2 is the second component of the azimuth angle. It is usually necessary to adjust the tabular altitude for the fractional parts of the intermediate entering arguments to derive computed altitude, and an auxiliary table is provided for the purpose. Rules governing signs of the quantities which must be added or subtracted are given in the instructions and summarized on each tabular page. Azimuth angle is the sum of two components and is converted to true azimuth by familiar rules, repeated at the bottom of the tabular pages.

Tabular altitude and intermediate quantities are given to the nearest minute of arc, although errors of $2'$ in computed altitude may accrue during adjustment for the minutes parts of entering arguments. Components of azimuth angle are stated to $0°.1$; for derived true azimuth, only whole degrees are warranted. Since objects near the zenith are difficult to observe with a marine sextant, they should be avoided; altitudes greater than about $80°$ are not suited to reduction by this method.

In many circumstances, the accuracy provided by these tables is sufficient. However, to maintain the full accuracy ($0'.1$) of the ephemeral data in the almanac throughout their reduction to altitude and azimuth, more extensive tables or a calculator should be used.

3. *Use of Tables.*

Step 1.   Determine the Greenwich hour angle (*GHA*) and Declination (*Dec*) of the body from the almanac. Select an assumed latitude (*Lat*) of integral degrees nearest to the estimated latitude. Choose an assumed longitude nearest to the estimated longitude such that the local hour angle

$$LHA = GHA \; {{- \text{ west}} \atop {+ \text{ east}}} \; \text{longitude}$$

has integral degrees.

Step 2.   Enter the reduction table with *Lat* and *LHA* as arguments. Record the quantities A, B and Z_1. Apply the rules for the sign of B and Z_1: B is minus if $90° < LHA < 270°$: Z_1 has the same sign as B. Set $A° =$ nearest whole degree of A and $A' =$ minutes part of A. This step may be repeated for all reductions before leaving the latitude opening of the table.

Step 3.   Record the declination *Dec*. Apply the rules for the sign of *Dec*: *Dec* is minus if the name of *Dec* (*i.e.* N or S) is contrary to latitude. Add B and *Dec* algebraically to produce F. If F is negative, the object is below the horizon (in sight reduction, this can occur when the objects are close to the horizon). Regard F as positive until step 7. Set $F° =$ nearest whole degree of F and $F' =$ minutes part of F.

Step 4. Enter the reduction table a second time with $A°$ and $F°$ as arguments and record H, P, and Z_2. Set $P° = $ nearest whole degree of P and $Z_2° = $ nearest whole degree of Z_2.

Step 5. Enter the auxiliary table with F' and $P°$ as arguments to obtain $corr_1$ to H for F'. Apply the rule for the sign of $corr_1$: $corr_1$ is minus if $F < 90°$ and $F' > 29'$ or if $F > 90°$ and $F' < 30'$, otherwise $corr_1$ is plus.

Step 6. Enter the auxiliary table with A' and $Z_2°$ as arguments to obtain $corr_2$ to H for A'. Apply the rule for the sign of $corr_2$: $corr_2$ is minus if $A' < 30'$, otherwise $corr_2$ is plus.

Step 7. Calculate the computed altitude H_C as the sum of H, $corr_1$ and $corr_2$. Apply the rule for the sign of H_C: H_C is minus if F is negative.

Step 8. Apply the rule for the sign of Z_2: Z_2 is minus if $F > 90°$. If F is negative, replace Z_2 by $180° - Z_2$. Set the azimuth angle Z equal to the algebraic sum of Z_1 and Z_2 and ignore the resulting sign. Obtain the true azimuth Z_n from the rules

$$\begin{array}{lll} \text{For N latitude, if} & LHA > 180° & Z_n = Z \\ \text{if} & LHA < 180° & Z_n = 360° - Z \\ \\ \text{For S latitude, if} & LHA > 180° & Z_n = 180° - Z \\ \text{if} & LHA < 180° & Z_n = 180° + Z \end{array}$$

Observed altitude H_O is compared with H_C to obtain the altitude difference, which, with Z_n, is used to plot the position line.

4. *Example.* (a) Required the altitude and azimuth of *Schedar* on 2020 February 4 at UT 06^h 33^m from the estimated position N 53°, E 5°.

1. Assumed latitude $Lat = $ 53° N
    From the almanac $GHA = $ 221° 45′
    Assumed longitude   5° 15′ E
    Local hour angle $LHA = $ 227

2. Reduction table, 1st entry
    $(Lat, LHA) = (53, 227)$ $A = $ 26   07 $A° = 26, A' = 7$
                                   $B = -27$ 12 $Z_1 = -49.4,$ $90° < LHA < 270°$
3. From the almanac $Dec = +56$ 39   *Lat* and *Dec* same
    $Sum = B + Dec$ $F = +29$ 27 $F° = 29, F' = 27$

4. Reduction table, 2nd entry
    $(A°, F°) = (26, 29)$ $H = $ 25   50 $P° = 61$
                                                $Z_2 = 76.3, Z_2° = 76$

5. Auxiliary table, 1st entry
    $(F', P°) = (27, 61)$ $corr_1 = $ $+24$ $F < 90°, F' < 29'$
    Sum   26   14
6. Auxiliary table, 2nd entry
    $(A', Z_2°) = (7, 76)$ $corr_2 = $ -2 $A' < 30'$
7. Sum = computed altitude $H_C = +26°$ 12′ $F > 0°$

8. Azimuth, first component $Z_1 = -49.4$ same sign as B
            second component $Z_2 = +76.3$ $F < 90°, F > 0°$
    Sum = azimuth angle $Z = $ 26.9

    True azimuth $Z_n = 027°$ N *Lat*, $LHA > 180°$

continued on page 318

SIGHT REDUCTION TABLE

B: (−) for 90° < LHA < 270°
Dec:(−) for Lat. contrary name

Z₁: same sign as B
Z₂:(−) for F > 90°

Lat./A LHA/F		0° A/H	0° B/P	0° Z₁/Z₂	1° A/H	1° B/P	1° Z₁/Z₂	2° A/H	2° B/P	2° Z₁/Z₂	3° A/H	3° B/P	3° Z₁/Z₂	4° A/H	4° B/P	4° Z₁/Z₂	5° A/H	5° B/P	5° Z₁/Z₂	Lat./A	LHA
0	180	0 00	90 00	90.0	0 00	89 00	90.0	0 00	88 00	90.0	0 00	87 00	90.0	0 00	86 00	90.0	0 00	85 00	90.0	180	360
1	179	1 00	90 00	90.0	1 00	89 00	90.0	1 00	88 00	90.0	1 00	87 00	89.9	1 00	86 00	89.9	1 00	85 00	89.9	181	359
2	178	2 00	90 00	90.0	2 00	89 00	90.0	2 00	88 00	89.9	2 00	87 00	89.9	2 00	86 00	89.9	2 00	85 00	89.8	182	358
3	177	3 00	90 00	90.0	3 00	89 00	89.9	3 00	88 00	89.9	3 00	87 00	89.9	3 00	86 00	89.8	2 59	85 00	89.8	183	357
4	176	4 00	90 00	90.0	4 00	89 00	89.9	4 00	88 00	89.9	4 00	87 00	89.8	3 59	85 59	89.8	3 59	84 59	89.7	184	356
5	175	5 00	90 00	90.0	5 00	89 00	89.9	5 00	88 00	89.8	5 00	86 59	89.7	4 59	85 59	89.7	4 59	84 59	89.6	185	355
6	174	6 00	90 00	90.0	6 00	89 00	89.9	6 00	88 00	89.8	6 00	86 59	89.7	5 59	85 59	89.6	5 59	84 58	89.5	186	354
7	173	7 00	90 00	90.0	7 00	89 00	89.9	7 00	87 59	89.8	6 59	86 58	89.6	6 59	85 58	89.6	6 58	84 58	89.5	187	353
8	172	8 00	90 00	90.0	8 00	88 59	89.9	8 00	87 59	89.7	7 59	86 58	89.6	7 59	85 58	89.5	7 58	84 57	89.4	188	352
9	171	9 00	90 00	90.0	9 00	88 59	89.8	9 00	87 59	89.7	8 59	86 58	89.5	8 59	85 57	89.4	8 58	84 56	89.3	189	351
10	170	10 00	90 00	90.0	10 00	88 59	89.8	10 00	87 58	89.6	9 59	86 58	89.5	9 58	85 56	89.4	9 58	84 55	89.2	190	350
11	169	11 00	90 00	90.0	11 00	88 59	89.8	11 00	87 58	89.6	10 59	86 57	89.4	10 58	85 55	89.3	10 57	84 54	89.1	191	349
12	168	12 00	90 00	90.0	12 00	88 59	89.8	12 00	87 57	89.6	11 59	86 56	89.4	11 58	85 54	89.2	11 57	84 53	89.0	192	348
13	167	13 00	90 00	90.0	13 00	88 58	89.8	13 00	87 57	89.5	12 59	86 55	89.3	12 58	85 53	89.1	12 57	84 52	88.9	193	347
14	166	14 00	90 00	90.0	14 00	88 58	89.7	13 59	87 56	89.5	13 59	86 55	89.3	13 58	85 52	89.1	13 57	84 51	88.8	194	346
15	165	15 00	90 00	90.0	15 00	88 58	89.7	14 59	87 55	89.5	14 59	86 54	89.2	14 58	85 50	89.0	14 56	84 49	88.8	195	345
16	164	16 00	90 00	90.0	16 00	88 58	89.7	15 59	87 55	89.4	15 59	86 53	89.2	15 58	85 49	89.0	15 56	84 48	88.7	196	344
17	163	17 00	90 00	90.0	17 00	88 57	89.7	16 59	87 55	89.4	16 59	86 52	89.1	16 57	85 48	88.9	16 56	84 46	88.6	197	343
18	162	18 00	90 00	90.0	18 00	88 57	89.7	17 59	87 54	89.4	17 58	86 51	89.0	17 57	85 46	88.7	17 56	84 45	88.4	198	342
19	161	19 00	90 00	90.0	19 00	88 57	89.7	18 59	87 53	89.3	18 58	86 50	89.0	18 57	85 45	88.6	18 55	84 43	88.3	199	341
20	160	20 00	90 00	90.0	20 00	88 56	89.6	19 59	87 52	89.3	19 58	86 48	88.9	19 57	85 43	88.5	19 55	84 41	88.2	200	340
21	159	21 00	90 00	90.0	21 00	88 56	89.6	20 59	87 51	89.2	20 58	86 47	88.8	20 57	85 41	88.4	20 55	84 39	88.1	201	339
22	158	22 00	90 00	90.0	22 00	88 55	89.6	21 59	87 51	89.2	21 58	86 46	88.8	21 56	85 39	88.4	21 54	84 37	88.1	202	338
23	157	23 00	90 00	90.0	23 00	88 55	89.6	22 59	87 50	89.2	22 58	86 44	88.7	22 56	85 37	88.3	22 54	84 34	87.9	203	337
24	156	24 00	90 00	90.0	24 00	88 54	89.6	23 59	87 49	89.1	23 58	86 43	88.7	23 56	85 35	88.2	23 54	84 32	87.8	204	336
25	155	25 00	90 00	90.0	25 00	88 54	89.5	24 59	87 48	89.1	24 58	86 41	88.6	24 56	85 33	88.1	24 54	84 29	87.7	205	335
26	154	26 00	90 00	90.0	26 00	88 53	89.5	25 59	87 47	89.0	25 58	86 40	88.5	25 56	85 31	88.1	25 53	84 26	87.6	206	334
27	153	27 00	90 00	90.0	27 00	88 53	89.5	26 59	87 45	89.0	26 58	86 38	88.5	26 55	85 28	88.0	26 53	84 24	87.5	207	333
28	152	28 00	90 00	90.0	28 00	88 52	89.5	27 59	87 44	88.9	27 57	86 36	88.4	27 55	85 26	87.9	27 53	84 20	87.3	208	332
29	151	29 00	90 00	90.0	29 00	88 51	89.4	28 59	87 43	88.9	28 57	86 34	88.3	28 55	85 23	87.8	28 53	84 17	87.2	209	331
30	150	30 00	90 00	90.0	30 00	88 51	89.4	29 59	87 41	88.8	29 57	86 32	88.3	29 55	85 20	87.7	29 52	84 14	87.1	210	330
31	149	31 00	90 00	90.0	31 00	88 50	89.4	30 59	87 40	88.8	30 57	86 30	88.2	30 55	85 17	87.6	30 52	84 10	87.0	211	329
32	148	32 00	90 00	90.0	32 00	88 49	89.4	31 59	87 39	88.7	31 57	86 28	88.1	31 54	85 14	87.5	31 52	84 07	86.9	212	328
33	147	33 00	90 00	90.0	33 00	88 48	89.4	32 59	87 37	88.7	32 57	86 25	88.1	32 54	85 11	87.4	32 51	84 03	86.8	213	327
34	146	34 00	90 00	90.0	34 00	88 48	89.3	33 59	87 35	88.6	33 57	86 23	88.0	33 54	85 07	87.3	33 51	83 59	86.6	214	326
35	145	35 00	90 00	90.0	35 00	88 47	89.3	34 59	87 34	88.6	34 57	86 20	87.9	34 54	85 04	87.2	34 51	83 54	86.5	215	325
36	144	36 00	90 00	90.0	36 00	88 46	89.3	35 58	87 32	88.5	35 57	86 18	87.8	35 54	85 00	87.1	35 51	83 50	86.4	216	324
37	143	37 00	90 00	90.0	37 00	88 45	89.2	36 58	87 30	88.4	36 56	86 15	87.7	36 53	84 56	87.0	36 50	83 45	86.2	217	323
38	142	38 00	90 00	90.0	38 00	88 44	89.2	37 58	87 28	88.4	37 56	86 12	87.7	37 53	84 52	86.9	37 50	83 40	86.1	218	322
39	141	39 00	90 00	90.0	39 00	88 43	89.2	38 58	87 26	88.3	38 56	86 09	87.6	38 53	84 47	86.8	38 50	83 35	86.0	219	321
40	140	40 00	90 00	90.0	40 00	88 42	89.2	39 58	87 23	88.3	39 56	86 05	87.5	39 53	84 42	86.7	39 49	83 29	85.8	220	320
41	139	41 00	90 00	90.0	41 00	88 41	89.1	40 58	87 21	88.2	40 56	86 02	87.4	40 53	84 37	86.5	40 49	83 23	85.7	221	319
42	138	42 00	90 00	90.0	42 00	88 39	89.1	41 58	87 19	88.2	41 56	85 58	87.3	41 52	84 32	86.4	41 48	83 17	85.5	222	318
43	137	43 00	90 00	90.0	43 00	88 38	89.1	42 58	87 16	88.1	42 56	85 54	87.2	42 52	84 27	86.3	42 48	83 11	85.4	223	317
44	136	44 00	90 00	90.0	43 59	88 37	89.0	43 58	87 13	88.1	43 55	85 50	87.1	43 52	84 21	86.1	43 47	83 04	85.2	224	316
45	135	45 00	90 00	90.0	44 59	88 35	89.0	44 58	87 10	88.0	44 55	85 46	87.0	44 52	84 16	86.0	44 47	82 57	85.0	225	315

LHA/F	A	0° A/H	0° B/P	0° Z_1/Z_2	1° A/H	1° B/P	1° Z_1/Z_2	2° A/H	2° B/P	2° Z_1/Z_2	3° A/H	3° B/P	3° Z_1/Z_2	4° A/H	4° B/P	4° Z_1/Z_2	5° A/H	5° B/P	5° Z_1/Z_2	LHA	A
45	135	45 00	90 00	90·0	44 59	88 35	89·0	44 58	87 10	88·0	44 55	85 46	87·0	44 52	84 21	86·0	44 47	82 57	85·0	225	315
46	134	46 00	90 00	90·0	45 59	88 34	89·0	45 58	87 07	87·9	45 55	85 41	86·9	45 51	84 15	85·9	45 46	82 49	84·8	226	314
47	133	47 00	90 00	90·0	46 59	88 32	88·9	46 58	87 04	87·9	46 55	85 36	86·8	46 51	84 09	85·8	46 46	82 41	84·7	227	313
48	132	48 00	90 00	90·0	47 59	88 30	88·9	47 58	87 01	87·8	47 55	85 31	86·7	47 51	84 02	85·6	47 46	82 33	84·5	228	312
49	131	49 00	90 00	90·0	48 59	88 29	88·9	48 58	86 57	87·7	48 55	85 26	86·6	48 51	83 55	85·4	48 45	82 24	84·3	229	311
50	130	50 00	90 00	90·0	49 59	88 27	88·8	49 58	86 53	87·6	49 54	85 20	86·4	49 50	83 47	85·2	49 44	82 15	84·1	230	310
51	129	51 00	90 00	90·0	50 59	88 25	88·8	50 57	86 49	87·5	50 54	85 14	86·3	50 50	83 40	85·1	50 44	82 05	83·9	231	309
52	128	52 00	90 00	90·0	51 59	88 23	88·7	51 57	86 45	87·4	51 54	85 08	86·2	51 49	83 31	84·9	51 43	81 55	83·6	232	308
53	127	53 00	90 00	90·0	52 59	88 21	88·7	52 57	86 41	87·3	52 54	85 01	86·0	52 49	83 22	84·7	52 43	81 44	83·4	233	307
54	126	54 00	90 00	90·0	53 59	88 18	88·6	53 57	86 36	87·2	53 54	84 54	85·9	53 49	83 13	84·5	53 42	81 32	83·2	234	306
55	125	55 00	90 00	90·0	54 59	88 15	88·6	54 57	86 31	87·1	54 53	84 47	85·7	54 48	83 03	84·3	54 41	81 20	82·9	235	305
56	124	56 00	90 00	90·0	55 59	88 13	88·5	55 57	86 26	87·0	55 53	84 39	85·6	55 48	82 52	84·1	55 41	81 06	82·6	236	304
57	123	57 00	90 00	90·0	56 59	88 10	88·4	56 57	86 20	86·9	56 53	84 30	85·4	56 47	82 41	83·9	56 40	80 52	82·4	237	303
58	122	58 00	90 00	90·0	57 59	88 07	88·4	57 57	86 14	86·8	57 53	84 21	85·2	57 47	82 29	83·6	57 39	80 38	82·1	238	302
59	121	59 00	90 00	90·0	58 59	88 04	88·3	58 57	86 07	86·7	58 52	84 11	85·0	58 46	82 16	83·4	58 38	80 22	81·7	239	301
60	120	60 00	90 00	90·0	59 59	88 00	88·3	59 56	86 00	86·5	59 52	84 01	84·8	59 46	82 02	83·1	59 37	80 05	81·4	240	300
61	119	61 00	90 00	90·0	60 59	87 56	88·2	60 56	85 53	86·4	60 52	83 50	84·6	60 45	81 48	82·8	60 36	79 46	81·1	241	299
62	118	62 00	90 00	90·0	61 59	87 52	88·1	61 56	85 45	86·2	61 51	83 38	84·4	61 44	81 32	82·5	61 35	79 27	80·7	242	298
63	117	63 00	90 00	90·0	62 59	87 48	88·0	62 56	85 36	86·1	62 51	83 25	84·1	62 44	81 15	82·2	62 35	79 06	80·3	243	297
64	116	64 00	90 00	90·0	63 59	87 43	87·9	63 56	85 27	85·9	63 50	83 11	83·9	63 43	80 56	81·9	63 33	78 43	79·9	244	296
65	115	65 00	90 00	90·0	64 59	87 37	87·9	64 56	85 17	85·7	64 50	82 55	83·6	64 42	80 36	81·5	64 32	78 18	79·4	245	295
66	114	66 00	90 00	90·0	65 59	87 33	87·8	65 55	85 06	85·5	65 49	82 39	83·3	65 41	80 15	81·1	65 31	77 52	78·9	246	294
67	113	67 00	90 00	90·0	66 59	87 27	87·6	66 55	84 54	85·3	66 49	82 22	83·0	66 40	79 51	80·7	66 29	77 23	78·4	247	293
68	112	68 00	90 00	90·0	67 59	87 20	87·5	67 55	84 40	85·1	67 48	82 02	82·6	67 39	79 26	80·2	67 28	76 51	77·8	248	292
69	111	69 00	90 00	90·0	68 59	87 13	87·4	68 55	84 26	84·8	68 48	81 41	82·2	68 38	78 58	79·7	68 26	76 17	77·2	249	291
70	110	70 00	90 00	90·0	69 59	87 05	87·3	69 54	84 10	84·5	69 47	81 17	81·8	69 37	78 27	79·2	69 25	75 39	76·5	250	290
71	109	71 00	90 00	90·0	70 58	86 56	87·1	70 54	83 53	84·2	70 46	80 51	81·4	70 36	77 53	78·5	70 23	74 58	75·8	251	289
72	108	72 00	90 00	90·0	71 58	86 46	86·9	71 54	83 33	83·9	71 46	80 21	80·8	71 35	77 15	77·9	71 20	74 12	75·0	252	288
73	107	73 00	90 00	90·0	72 58	86 35	86·7	72 53	83 11	83·5	72 45	79 50	80·3	72 33	76 33	77·1	72 18	73 20	74·1	253	287
74	106	74 00	90 00	90·0	73 58	86 23	86·5	73 53	82 47	83·1	73 44	79 14	79·7	73 31	75 46	76·3	73 15	72 23	73·1	254	286
75	105	75 00	90 00	90·0	74 58	86 09	86·3	74 52	82 19	82·6	74 43	78 33	78·9	74 29	74 53	75·4	74 12	71 19	72·0	255	285
76	104	76 00	90 00	90·0	75 58	85 52	86·0	75 52	81 47	82·0	75 41	77 47	78·1	75 27	73 53	74·4	75 07	70 07	70·7	256	284
77	103	77 00	90 00	90·0	76 58	85 34	85·7	76 51	81 11	81·4	76 40	76 53	77·2	76 25	72 44	73·2	76 05	68 45	69·3	257	283
78	102	78 00	90 00	90·0	77 58	85 12	85·3	77 50	80 28	80·7	77 38	75 51	76·2	77 22	71 25	71·8	77 01	67 11	67·7	258	282
79	101	79 00	90 00	90·0	78 57	84 46	84·9	78 49	79 38	79·8	78 36	74 39	74·9	78 18	69 52	70·3	77 56	65 22	65·8	259	281
80	100	80 00	90 00	90·0	79 57	84 16	84·3	79 48	78 38	78·8	79 34	73 12	73·5	79 14	68 04	68·4	78 50	63 16	63·7	260	280
81	99	81 00	90 00	90·0	80 57	83 38	83·7	80 47	77 25	77·6	80 31	71 29	71·7	80 09	65 55	66·2	79 43	60 47	61·2	261	279
82	98	82 00	90 00	90·0	81 56	82 51	82·9	81 45	75 55	76·1	81 28	69 22	69·6	81 04	63 19	63·6	80 34	57 51	58·2	262	278
83	97	83 00	90 00	90·0	82 56	81 51	81·9	82 43	74 01	74·1	82 23	66 44	66·9	81 58	60 09	60·4	81 24	54 04	54·6	263	277
84	96	84 00	90 00	90·0	83 55	80 31	80·6	83 41	71 32	71·6	83 18	63 22	63·5	82 48	56 13	56·4	82 12	50 04	50·3	264	276
85	95	85 00	90 00	90·0	84 54	78 40	78·7	84 37	68 10	68·3	84 10	58 59	59·1	83 36	51 16	51·4	82 56	44 53	45·1	265	275
86	94	86 00	90 00	90·0	85 53	75 57	76·0	85 24	63 24	63·5	85 00	53 05	53·2	84 21	44 56	45·1	83 36	38 34	38·7	266	274
87	93	87 00	90 00	90·0	86 50	71 33	71·6	86 24	56 17	56·3	85 45	44 58	45·0	85 00	36 49	36·9	84 10	30 53	31·0	267	273
88	92	88 00	90 00	90·0	87 46	63 26	63·4	87 10	44 59	45·0	86 24	33 40	33·7	85 32	26 01	26·0	84 37	21 45	21·8	268	272
89	91	89 00	90 00	90·0	88 35	45 00	45·0	87 46	26 33	26·6	86 50	18 25	18·4	85 53	14 01	14·0	84 54	11 17	11·3	269	271
90	90	90 00	90 00	90·0	89 00	0 00	0·0	88 00	0 00	0·0	87 00	0 00	0·0	86 00	0 00	0·0	85 00	0 00	0·0	270	270

N. Lat.: for LHA > 180° ... $Z_n = Z$
for LHA < 180° ... $Z_n = 360° - Z$

S. Lat.: for LHA > 180° ... $Z_n = 180° - Z$
for LHA < 180° ... $Z_n = 180° + Z$

SIGHT REDUCTION TABLE

B: (−) for 90° < LHA < 270°
Dec:(−) for Lat. contrary name

Z1: same sign as B
Z2: (−) for F > 90°

LHA/F	6° A/H	6° B/P	6° Z1/Z2	7° A/H	7° B/P	7° Z1/Z2	8° A/H	8° B/P	8° Z1/Z2	9° A/H	9° B/P	9° Z1/Z2	10° A/H	10° B/P	10° Z1/Z2	11° A/H	11° B/P	11° Z1/Z2	LHA
0	0 00	84 00	90.0	0 00	83 00	90.0	0 00	82 00	90.0	0 00	81 00	90.0	0 00	80 00	90.0	0 00	79 00	90.0	180
1	1 00	84 00	89.9	1 00	83 00	89.9	0 59	82 00	89.9	0 59	81 00	89.8	0 59	80 00	89.8	0 59	79 00	89.8	181
2	1 59	84 00	89.8	1 59	83 00	89.8	1 59	82 00	89.8	1 59	81 00	89.7	1 58	80 00	89.7	1 58	79 00	89.6	182
3	2 59	84 00	89.7	2 59	82 59	89.7	2 58	81 59	89.6	2 58	80 59	89.6	2 57	79 59	89.5	2 57	78 58	89.4	183
4	3 59	83 59	89.6	3 58	82 59	89.6	3 58	81 59	89.5	3 57	80 59	89.4	3 56	79 59	89.3	3 56	78 58	89.2	184
5	4 58	83 59	89.5	4 58	82 58	89.4	4 57	81 58	89.3	4 56	80 58	89.2	4 55	79 58	89.0	4 54	78 58	89.0	185
6	5 58	83 58	89.4	5 57	82 58	89.3	5 56	81 57	89.2	5 56	80 57	89.1	5 55	79 57	89.0	5 53	78 56	88.9	186
7	6 58	83 57	89.3	6 57	82 57	89.1	6 56	81 56	89.0	6 55	80 56	89.0	6 54	79 56	88.8	6 52	78 55	88.7	187
8	7 57	83 56	89.2	7 56	82 57	89.0	7 55	81 55	88.8	7 54	80 55	88.7	7 53	79 54	88.5	7 51	78 54	88.5	188
9	8 57	83 56	89.1	8 56	82 55	89.0	8 55	81 54	88.7	8 53	80 53	88.6	8 52	79 53	88.3	8 50	78 52	88.3	189
10	9 57	83 54	88.9	9 55	82 54	88.8	9 54	81 53	88.6	9 53	80 52	88.4	9 51	79 51	88.2	9 49	78 50	88.1	190
11	10 56	83 53	88.8	10 55	82 52	88.6	10 53	81 51	88.5	10 52	80 50	88.3	10 50	79 49	88.1	10 48	78 48	87.9	191
12	11 56	83 52	88.7	11 55	82 51	88.5	11 53	81 49	88.3	11 51	80 48	88.1	11 49	79 47	87.9	11 47	78 46	87.7	192
13	12 56	83 51	88.6	12 54	82 49	88.4	12 52	81 48	88.2	12 50	80 46	87.9	12 48	79 45	87.7	12 45	78 43	87.5	193
14	13 55	83 49	88.5	13 54	82 47	88.3	13 52	81 46	88.0	13 49	80 44	87.8	13 47	79 42	87.5	13 44	78 40	87.3	194
15	14 55	83 47	88.4	14 53	82 45	88.1	14 51	81 43	87.9	14 48	80 41	87.6	14 46	79 39	87.3	14 43	78 37	87.1	195
16	15 55	83 46	88.3	15 53	82 43	88.0	15 50	81 41	87.7	15 48	80 39	87.4	15 45	79 36	87.1	15 42	78 34	86.9	196
17	16 54	83 44	88.2	16 52	82 41	87.9	16 50	81 38	87.6	16 47	80 36	87.3	16 44	79 33	87.0	16 41	78 31	86.7	197
18	17 54	83 42	88.1	17 52	82 39	87.7	17 49	81 36	87.4	17 46	80 33	87.1	17 43	79 30	86.8	17 39	78 27	86.5	198
19	18 54	83 40	87.9	18 51	82 37	87.6	18 48	81 33	87.3	18 45	80 29	86.9	18 42	79 26	86.6	18 37	78 23	86.3	199
20	19 53	83 37	87.8	19 51	82 33	87.5	19 48	81 30	87.1	19 45	80 26	86.7	19 41	79 22	86.4	19 36	78 19	86.0	200
21	20 53	83 35	87.7	20 50	82 30	87.3	20 47	81 26	86.9	20 44	80 22	86.6	20 40	79 18	86.2	20 35	78 14	85.8	201
22	21 52	83 32	87.6	21 50	82 27	87.2	21 46	81 23	86.8	21 43	80 18	86.4	21 39	79 14	86.0	21 33	78 10	85.6	202
23	22 52	83 29	87.5	22 49	82 24	87.0	22 46	81 19	86.6	22 42	80 14	86.2	22 38	79 09	85.8	22 32	78 05	85.4	203
24	23 52	83 26	87.3	23 49	82 21	86.9	23 45	81 15	86.5	23 41	80 10	86.0	23 37	79 05	85.6	23 31	77 59	85.1	204
25	24 51	83 23	87.2	24 48	82 17	86.7	24 44	81 11	86.3	24 40	80 05	85.8	24 36	78 59	85.4	24 29	77 54	84.9	205
26	25 51	83 20	87.1	25 48	82 13	86.6	25 44	81 07	86.1	25 39	80 00	85.6	25 35	78 54	85.2	25 27	77 48	84.7	206
27	26 50	83 16	87.0	26 47	82 09	86.4	26 43	81 02	85.9	26 38	79 55	85.4	26 33	78 48	85.0	26 26	77 42	84.4	207
28	27 50	83 13	86.8	27 46	82 05	86.3	27 42	80 57	85.8	27 37	79 50	85.2	27 32	78 42	84.9	27 24	77 35	84.2	208
29	28 50	83 09	86.7	28 46	82 01	86.1	28 41	80 52	85.6	28 36	79 44	85.0	28 31	78 36	84.7	28 22	77 28	84.0	209
30	29 49	83 05	86.5	29 45	81 56	86.0	29 41	80 46	85.4	29 35	79 38	84.8	29 30	78 29	84.2	29 24	77 21	83.7	210
31	30 49	83 01	86.4	30 45	81 51	85.8	30 40	80 41	85.2	30 34	79 32	84.6	30 29	78 23	84.0	30 22	77 13	83.5	211
32	31 48	82 56	86.3	31 44	81 46	85.6	31 39	80 35	85.0	31 33	79 25	84.4	31 27	78 15	83.8	31 21	77 05	83.2	212
33	32 48	82 51	86.1	32 43	81 41	85.5	32 38	80 29	84.8	32 32	79 18	84.2	32 26	78 08	83.6	32 19	76 57	82.9	213
34	33 47	82 46	86.0	33 43	81 35	85.3	33 37	80 23	84.6	33 31	79 11	84.0	33 25	78 00	83.3	33 18	76 48	82.7	214
35	34 47	82 41	85.8	34 42	81 29	85.1	34 37	80 16	84.4	34 30	79 03	83.8	34 24	77 51	83.1	34 16	76 39	82.4	215
36	35 46	82 36	85.7	35 41	81 22	84.9	35 36	80 09	84.2	35 29	78 55	83.5	35 22	77 42	82.8	35 14	76 29	82.1	216
37	36 46	82 30	85.5	36 40	81 16	84.8	36 35	80 01	84.0	36 28	78 48	83.3	36 21	77 33	82.5	36 13	76 19	81.8	217
38	37 45	82 24	85.3	37 40	81 09	84.6	37 34	79 53	83.8	37 27	78 38	83.0	37 19	77 23	82.3	37 11	76 09	81.5	218
39	38 45	82 18	85.2	38 39	81 01	84.4	38 33	79 45	83.6	38 26	78 29	82.8	38 18	77 13	82.0	38 09	75 57	81.2	219
40	39 44	82 11	85.0	39 39	80 54	84.2	39 32	79 36	83.3	39 25	78 19	82.5	39 16	77 02	81.7	39 07	75 46	80.9	220
41	40 44	82 04	84.8	40 38	80 46	84.0	40 31	79 27	83.1	40 23	78 09	82.3	40 15	76 51	81.4	40 05	75 33	80.6	221
42	41 43	81 57	84.6	41 37	80 37	83.7	41 30	79 17	82.9	41 22	77 58	82.0	41 13	76 39	81.1	41 04	75 21	80.3	222
43	42 42	81 49	84.4	42 36	80 28	83.5	42 29	79 07	82.6	42 21	77 47	81.7	42 12	76 27	80.8	42 02	75 07	79.9	223
44	43 42	81 41	84.2	43 35	80 19	83.3	43 28	78 57	82.3	43 19	77 35	81.4	43 10	76 14	80.5	43 00	74 53	79.6	224
45	44 41	81 33	84.0	44 34	80 09	83.1	44 27	78 46	82.1	44 18	77 22	81.1	44 08	76 00	80.1	43 57	74 38	79.2	225

Lat. / A · LHA/F		6° A/H	6° B/P	6° Z_1/Z_2	7° A/H	7° B/P	7° Z_1/Z_2	8° A/H	8° B/P	8° Z_1/Z_2	9° A/H	9° B/P	9° Z_1/Z_2	10° A/H	10° B/P	10° Z_1/Z_2	11° A/H	11° B/P	11° Z_1/Z_2	Lat. / A · LHA	
45	135	44 41	81 33	84·0	44 34	80 09	83·1	44 27	78 46	82·1	44 18	77 22	81·1	44 08	76 00	80·1	43 57	74 38	79·2	225	315
46	134	45 41	81 24	83·8	45 34	79 59	82·8	45 26	78 34	81·8	45 16	77 09	80·8	45 06	75 45	79·8	44 55	74 22	78·8	226	314
47	133	46 40	81 14	83·6	46 33	79 48	82·6	46 24	78 21	81·6	46 15	76 56	80·5	46 04	75 30	79·5	45 53	74 05	78·4	227	313
48	132	47 39	81 04	83·4	47 32	79 36	82·3	47 23	78 08	81·2	47 13	76 41	80·1	47 03	75 14	79·1	46 51	73 48	78·0	228	312
49	131	48 38	80 54	83·1	48 31	79 24	82·0	48 21	77 55	80·9	48 12	76 26	79·8	48 01	74 57	78·7	47 48	73 30	77·6	229	311
50	130	49 38	80 43	82·9	49 30	79 11	81·7	49 20	77 40	80·6	49 10	76 09	79·4	48 58	74 40	78·3	48 46	73 10	77·2	230	310
51	129	50 37	80 31	82·6	50 29	78 58	81·4	50 19	77 25	80·2	50 08	75 52	79·1	49 56	74 21	77·9	49 43	72 50	76·7	231	309
52	128	51 36	80 19	82·4	51 27	78 43	81·1	51 18	77 08	79·9	51 06	75 34	78·7	50 54	74 01	77·5	50 40	72 29	76·3	232	308
53	127	52 35	80 06	82·1	52 26	78 28	80·8	52 16	76 51	79·5	52 04	75 15	78·3	51 52	73 40	77·0	51 37	72 06	75·8	233	307
54	126	53 34	79 52	81·8	53 25	78 12	80·5	53 14	76 33	79·2	53 02	74 55	77·8	52 49	73 18	76·6	52 35	71 42	75·3	234	306
55	125	54 33	79 37	81·5	54 24	77 55	80·1	54 13	76 14	78·8	54 00	74 34	77·4	53 47	72 55	76·1	53 31	71 17	74·8	235	305
56	124	55 32	79 21	81·2	55 22	77 37	79·8	55 11	75 54	78·3	54 58	74 11	76·9	54 44	72 30	75·6	54 28	70 50	74·2	236	304
57	123	56 31	79 05	80·9	56 21	77 18	79·4	56 09	75 32	77·9	55 56	73 47	76·5	55 41	72 04	75·0	55 25	70 22	73·6	237	303
58	122	57 30	78 47	80·5	57 19	76 58	79·0	57 07	75 09	77·4	56 53	73 22	75·9	56 38	71 36	74·4	56 21	69 51	73·0	238	302
59	121	58 29	78 28	80·1	58 18	76 35	78·5	58 05	74 44	77·0	57 51	72 54	75·4	57 35	71 06	73·9	57 17	69 19	72·4	239	301
60	120	59 28	78 08	79·7	59 16	76 12	78·1	59 02	74 18	76·4	58 48	72 25	74·8	58 32	70 34	73·3	58 13	68 45	71·7	240	300
61	119	60 26	77 46	79·3	60 14	75 47	77·6	60 00	73 50	75·9	59 45	71 54	74·2	59 28	70 01	72·6	59 09	68 09	71·0	241	299
62	118	61 25	77 23	78·9	61 12	75 21	77·1	60 58	73 20	75·3	60 42	71 21	73·6	60 24	69 25	71·9	60 05	67 31	70·3	242	298
63	117	62 23	76 58	78·4	62 10	74 52	76·5	61 56	72 48	74·7	61 39	70 46	72·9	61 20	68 46	71·2	61 00	66 49	69·5	243	297
64	116	63 22	76 31	77·9	63 08	74 21	76·0	62 53	72 13	74·1	62 35	70 08	72·2	62 16	68 05	70·4	61 55	66 05	68·6	244	296
65	115	64 20	76 02	77·4	64 06	73 48	75·4	63 50	71 36	73·4	63 32	69 28	71·5	63 12	67 21	69·6	62 50	65 18	67·7	245	295
66	114	65 18	75 31	76·8	65 03	73 12	74·7	64 47	70 56	72·6	64 28	68 43	70·6	64 07	66 34	68·7	63 44	64 27	66·8	246	294
67	113	66 16	74 57	76·2	66 01	72 33	74·0	65 43	70 13	71·8	65 23	67 56	69·8	65 02	65 43	67·8	64 38	63 33	65·8	247	293
68	112	67 14	74 20	75·5	66 58	71 51	73·2	66 40	69 26	71·0	66 19	67 05	68·8	65 56	64 48	66·7	65 32	62 35	64·7	248	292
69	111	68 12	73 39	74·8	67 55	71 05	72·4	67 36	68 35	70·1	67 14	66 09	67·8	66 50	63 48	65·7	66 25	61 31	63·6	249	291
70	110	69 09	72 55	74·0	68 51	70 15	71·5	68 31	67 40	69·1	68 09	65 09	66·7	67 44	62 44	64·5	67 17	60 23	62·3	250	290
71	109	70 07	72 06	73·1	69 48	69 20	70·5	69 27	66 39	68·0	69 03	64 03	65·6	68 37	61 34	63·2	68 09	59 10	61·0	251	289
72	108	71 03	71 13	72·2	70 44	68 20	69·4	70 22	65 30	66·8	69 57	62 52	64·3	69 29	60 17	61·9	69 00	57 50	59·6	252	288
73	107	72 00	70 14	71·1	71 39	67 13	68·3	71 16	64 20	65·5	70 50	61 33	62·9	70 21	58 54	60·4	69 50	56 23	58·0	253	287
74	106	72 56	69 08	70·0	72 34	65 59	67·0	72 09	62 59	64·1	71 42	60 07	61·4	71 12	57 24	58·8	70 40	54 49	56·4	254	286
75	105	73 52	67 54	68·7	73 29	64 37	65·5	73 03	61 30	62·6	72 34	58 32	59·7	72 02	55 44	57·1	71 28	53 06	54·5	255	285
76	104	74 48	66 31	67·3	74 23	63 05	64·0	73 55	59 51	60·8	73 23	56 47	57·9	72 51	53 55	55·1	72 16	51 13	52·6	256	284
77	103	75 42	64 57	65·6	75 16	61 22	62·2	74 46	58 00	58·9	74 14	54 51	55·9	73 39	51 55	53·1	73 02	49 10	50·4	257	283
78	102	76 36	63 09	63·8	76 08	59 24	60·2	75 37	55 57	56·8	75 02	52 42	53·6	74 26	49 42	50·8	73 47	46 56	48·1	258	282
79	101	77 29	61 09	61·7	76 59	57 14	57·9	76 26	53 38	54·4	75 49	50 18	51·2	75 11	47 16	48·2	74 30	44 28	45·5	259	281
80	100	78 21	58 49	59·3	77 49	54 44	55·3	77 13	51 01	51·7	76 35	47 38	48·4	75 54	44 34	45·4	75 11	41 47	42·7	260	280
81	99	79 12	56 06	56·6	78 37	51 52	52·4	77 59	48 04	48·7	77 18	44 39	45·4	76 35	41 35	42·4	75 49	38 50	39·7	261	279
82	98	80 01	52 56	53·4	79 23	48 35	49·1	78 42	44 43	45·3	77 59	41 18	41·9	77 13	38 17	39·0	76 26	35 36	36·4	262	278
83	97	80 47	49 13	49·6	80 07	44 47	45·2	79 23	40 56	41·4	78 38	37 35	38·1	77 49	34 40	35·3	76 59	32 05	32·8	263	277
84	96	81 31	44 51	45·2	80 47	40 24	40·8	80 01	36 38	37·1	79 12	33 25	33·9	78 21	30 40	31·2	77 29	28 16	28·6	264	276
85	95	82 12	39 40	39·9	81 24	35 22	35·7	80 34	31 48	32·2	79 43	28 49	29·2	78 50	26 18	26·7	77 56	24 09	24·6	265	275
86	94	82 48	33 34	33·8	81 57	29 36	29·8	81 04	26 24	26·7	80 09	23 46	24·1	79 14	21 35	21·9	78 18	19 44	20·1	266	274
87	93	83 18	26 28	26·6	82 23	23 23	23·0	81 28	20 25	20·6	80 31	18 17	18·5	79 34	16 32	16·8	78 36	15 04	15·4	267	273
88	92	83 41	18 22	18·5	82 43	15 52	16·0	81 45	13 57	14·1	80 47	12 26	12·6	79 48	11 12	11·4	78 49	10 11	10·4	268	272
89	91	83 55	9 26	9·5	82 56	8 05	8·2	81 56	7 05	7·1	80 57	6 17	6·4	79 57	5 39	5·7	78 57	5 08	5·2	269	271
90	90	84 00	0 00	0·0	83 00	0 00	0·0	82 00	0 00	0·0	81 00	0 00	0·0	80 00	0 00	0·0	79 00	0 00	0·0	270	270

N. Lat: for LHA > 180° ... $Z_n = Z$
for LHA < 180° ... $Z_n = 360° - Z$

S. Lat: for LHA > 180° ... $Z_n = 180° - Z$
for LHA < 180° ... $Z_n = 180° + Z$

SIGHT REDUCTION TABLE

B: (−) for 90° < LHA < 270°
Dec:(−) for Lat. contrary name

Z₁: same sign as B
Z₂: (−) for F > 90°

LHA/F	Lat./A	12° A/H	12° B/P	12° Z₁/Z₂	13° A/H	13° B/P	13° Z₁/Z₂	14° A/H	14° B/P	14° Z₁/Z₂	15° A/H	15° B/P	15° Z₁/Z₂	16° A/H	16° B/P	16° Z₁/Z₂	17° A/H	17° B/P	17° Z₁/Z₂	Lat./A	LHA
0	180	0 00	78 00	90·0	0 00	77 00	90·0	0 00	76 00	90·0	0 00	75 00	90·0	0 00	74 00	90·0	0 00	73 00	90·0	180	360
1	179	0 59	78 00	89·8	0 58	77 00	89·8	0 58	76 00	89·8	0 58	75 00	89·7	0 58	74 00	89·7	0 57	73 00	89·7	181	359
2	178	1 57	78 00	89·6	1 57	77 00	89·5	1 56	76 00	89·5	1 56	75 00	89·5	1 55	73 59	89·4	1 55	72 59	89·4	182	358
3	177	2 56	77 59	89·4	2 55	76 59	89·3	2 55	75 59	89·3	2 54	74 59	89·2	2 53	73 59	89·2	2 52	72 59	89·1	183	357
4	176	3 55	77 58	89·2	3 54	76 58	89·1	3 53	75 58	89·1	3 52	74 58	89·0	3 51	73 58	88·9	3 49	72 58	88·8	184	356
5	175	4 53	77 57	89·0	4 52	76 57	88·9	4 51	75 57	88·8	4 50	74 57	88·7	4 48	73 57	88·6	4 47	72 56	88·5	185	355
6	174	5 52	77 56	88·7	5 51	76 56	88·6	5 49	75 56	88·6	5 48	74 55	88·4	5 46	73 55	88·3	5 44	72 55	88·2	186	354
7	173	6 51	77 55	88·5	6 49	76 54	88·4	6 47	75 55	88·4	6 46	74 54	88·2	6 44	73 53	88·1	6 42	72 53	87·9	187	353
8	172	7 49	77 53	88·3	7 48	76 53	88·2	7 46	75 52	88·1	7 44	74 52	87·9	7 41	73 51	87·8	7 39	72 51	87·6	188	352
9	171	8 48	77 51	88·1	8 46	76 51	88·0	8 44	75 50	87·8	8 41	74 49	87·7	8 39	73 49	87·5	8 36	72 49	87·3	189	351
10	170	9 47	77 49	87·9	9 44	76 48	87·7	9 42	75 47	87·6	9 39	74 47	87·4	9 37	73 46	87·2	9 34	72 45	87·0	190	350
11	169	10 45	77 47	87·7	10 43	76 46	87·5	10 40	75 45	87·3	10 37	74 44	87·1	10 34	73 43	86·9	10 31	72 42	86·7	191	349
12	168	11 44	77 44	87·5	11 41	76 43	87·3	11 38	75 42	87·1	11 35	74 41	86·9	11 32	73 40	86·6	11 28	72 39	86·4	192	348
13	167	12 43	77 42	87·3	12 40	76 40	87·0	12 36	75 39	86·8	12 33	74 37	86·6	12 29	73 36	86·4	12 25	72 35	86·1	193	347
14	166	13 41	77 39	87·0	13 38	76 37	86·8	13 35	75 35	86·5	13 31	74 34	86·3	13 27	73 32	86·1	13 23	72 31	85·8	194	346
15	165	14 40	77 35	86·8	14 36	76 33	86·6	14 33	75 32	86·3	14 29	74 30	86·0	14 24	73 28	85·8	14 20	72 26	85·5	195	345
16	164	15 38	77 32	86·6	15 35	76 30	86·3	15 31	75 28	86·0	15 26	74 25	85·8	15 22	73 23	85·5	15 17	72 23	85·2	196	344
17	163	16 37	77 28	86·4	16 33	76 26	86·1	16 29	75 23	85·8	16 24	74 21	85·5	16 19	73 19	85·2	16 14	72 16	84·9	197	343
18	162	17 36	77 24	86·1	17 31	76 21	85·8	17 27	75 19	85·5	17 22	74 16	85·2	17 17	73 13	84·9	17 11	72 11	84·6	198	342
19	161	18 34	77 20	85·9	18 30	76 17	85·6	18 25	75 14	85·2	18 20	74 11	84·9	18 14	73 08	84·6	18 08	72 05	84·3	199	341
20	160	19 33	77 15	85·7	19 28	76 12	85·3	19 23	75 08	85·0	19 17	74 05	84·6	19 12	73 02	84·3	19 05	71 59	83·9	200	340
21	159	20 31	77 10	85·4	20 26	76 07	85·1	20 21	75 03	84·7	20 15	73 59	84·3	20 09	72 56	84·0	20 02	71 52	83·6	201	339
22	158	21 30	77 05	85·2	21 24	76 01	84·8	21 19	74 57	84·4	21 13	73 53	84·0	21 06	72 49	83·6	21 00	71 45	83·3	202	338
23	157	22 28	77 00	85·0	22 23	75 55	84·5	22 17	74 51	84·1	22 10	73 46	83·7	22 04	72 42	83·3	21 56	71 38	82·9	203	337
24	156	23 27	76 54	84·7	23 21	75 49	84·3	23 15	74 44	83·9	23 08	73 39	83·4	23 01	72 34	83·0	22 53	71 30	82·6	204	336
25	155	24 25	76 48	84·5	24 19	75 43	84·0	24 13	74 37	83·6	24 06	73 32	83·1	23 58	72 27	82·7	23 50	71 22	82·2	205	335
26	154	25 23	76 42	84·2	25 17	75 36	83·7	25 10	74 30	83·3	25 03	73 24	82·8	24 55	72 18	82·3	24 47	71 13	81·9	206	334
27	153	26 22	76 35	84·0	26 15	75 28	83·5	26 08	74 22	83·0	26 01	73 16	82·5	25 52	72 10	82·0	25 44	71 04	81·5	207	333
28	152	27 20	76 28	83·7	27 13	75 21	83·2	27 06	74 14	82·7	26 58	73 07	82·2	26 50	72 00	81·7	26 41	70 54	81·2	208	332
29	151	28 18	76 20	83·4	28 11	75 13	82·9	28 04	74 05	82·4	27 55	72 58	81·8	27 47	71 51	81·3	27 37	70 44	80·8	209	331
30	150	29 17	76 13	83·2	29 09	75 04	82·6	29 01	73 56	82·0	28 53	72 48	81·5	28 44	71 41	81·0	28 34	70 33	80·4	210	330
31	149	30 15	76 04	82·9	30 07	74 56	82·3	29 59	73 47	81·7	29 50	72 38	81·2	29 41	71 30	80·6	29 30	70 22	80·0	211	329
32	148	31 13	75 56	82·6	31 05	74 46	82·0	30 57	73 37	81·4	30 47	72 28	80·8	30 37	71 19	80·2	30 27	70 11	79·6	212	328
33	147	32 11	75 47	82·3	32 03	74 37	81·7	31 54	73 27	81·1	31 44	72 17	80·5	31 34	71 07	79·9	31 23	69 58	79·2	213	327
34	146	33 10	75 37	82·0	33 01	74 26	81·4	32 52	73 16	80·7	32 42	72 05	80·1	32 31	70 55	79·5	32 20	69 45	78·8	214	326
35	145	34 08	75 27	81·7	33 59	74 16	81·0	33 49	73 04	80·4	33 39	71 53	79·7	33 28	70 42	79·1	33 16	69 32	78·4	215	325
36	144	35 06	75 17	81·4	34 56	74 04	80·7	34 46	72 52	80·0	34 36	71 40	79·4	34 24	70 29	78·7	34 12	69 18	78·0	216	324
37	143	36 04	75 06	81·1	35 54	73 53	80·4	35 43	72 40	79·7	35 33	71 27	79·0	35 21	70 15	78·3	35 08	69 03	77·6	217	323
38	142	37 02	74 54	80·8	36 52	73 40	80·0	36 41	72 27	79·3	36 29	71 13	78·6	36 17	70 00	77·8	36 04	68 48	77·1	218	322
39	141	38 00	74 42	80·4	37 49	73 27	79·7	37 38	72 13	78·9	37 26	70 59	78·2	37 13	69 45	77·4	37 00	68 32	76·7	219	321
40	140	38 57	74 30	80·1	38 47	73 14	79·3	38 35	71 58	78·5	38 23	70 43	77·7	38 10	69 29	77·0	37 56	68 15	76·2	220	320
41	139	39 55	74 16	79·8	39 44	72 59	78·9	39 32	71 43	78·1	39 19	70 27	77·3	39 06	69 12	76·5	38 51	67 57	75·7	221	319
42	138	40 53	74 02	79·4	40 41	72 45	78·5	40 29	71 27	77·7	40 16	70 10	76·9	40 02	68 54	76·1	39 47	67 38	75·3	222	318
43	137	41 51	73 48	79·0	41 39	72 29	78·2	41 26	71 11	77·3	41 12	69 53	76·4	40 58	68 35	75·6	40 42	67 19	74·7	223	317
44	136	42 48	73 32	78·6	42 36	72 12	77·7	42 23	70 53	76·9	42 09	69 34	76·0	41 54	68 16	75·1	41 38	66 58	74·2	224	316
45	135	43 46	73 16	78·3	43 33	71 55	77·3	43 19	70 35	76·4	43 05	69 15	75·5	42 49	67 56	74·6	42 33	66 37	73·7	225	315

Lat. / A	LHA/F	12° A/H	12° B/P	12° Z1/Z2	13° A/H	13° B/P	13° Z1/Z2	14° A/H	14° B/P	14° Z1/Z2	15° A/H	15° B/P	15° Z1/Z2	16° A/H	16° B/P	16° Z1/Z2	17° A/H	17° B/P	17° Z1/Z2	LHA	LHA
45	135	43 46	73 16	78·3	43 33	71 55	77·3	43 19	70 35	76·4	43 05	69 15	75·5	42 49	67 56	74·6	42 33	66 37	73·7	225	315
46	134	44 43	72 59	77·8	44 30	71 37	76·9	44 16	70 15	75·9	44 01	68 54	75·0	43 45	67 34	74·1	43 28	66 15	73·2	226	314
47	133	45 40	72 41	77·4	45 27	71 18	76·4	45 12	69 55	75·5	44 57	68 33	74·6	44 40	67 12	73·5	44 23	65 51	72·6	227	313
48	132	46 38	72 23	77·0	46 24	70 58	76·0	46 09	69 34	75·0	45 53	68 11	74·0	45 35	66 48	73·0	45 17	65 27	72·0	228	312
49	131	47 35	72 03	76·5	47 20	70 37	75·5	47 05	69 11	74·4	46 48	67 47	73·4	46 30	66 23	72·4	46 12	65 01	71·4	229	311
50	130	48 32	71 42	76·1	48 17	70 15	75·0	48 01	68 48	73·9	47 44	67 22	72·9	47 25	65 58	71·8	47 06	64 34	70·8	230	310
51	129	49 29	71 20	75·6	49 13	69 51	74·5	48 57	68 23	73·4	48 39	66 56	72·3	48 20	65 30	71·2	48 00	64 05	70·1	231	309
52	128	50 25	70 57	75·1	50 09	69 27	73·9	49 52	67 57	72·8	49 34	66 29	71·7	49 15	65 02	70·6	48 54	63 35	69·5	232	308
53	127	51 22	70 33	74·6	51 06	69 01	73·4	50 48	67 30	72·2	50 29	66 00	71·0	50 09	64 31	69·9	49 48	63 04	68·8	233	307
54	126	52 19	70 07	74·0	52 02	68 33	72·8	51 43	67 01	71·6	51 24	65 30	70·4	51 03	64 00	69·2	50 41	62 31	68·1	234	306
55	125	53 15	69 40	73·5	52 57	68 04	72·2	52 38	66 30	70·9	52 18	64 58	69·7	51 57	63 26	68·5	51 34	61 56	67·3	235	305
56	124	54 11	69 11	72·9	53 53	67 34	71·6	53 33	65 58	70·3	53 12	64 24	69·0	52 50	62 51	67·8	52 27	61 20	66·6	236	304
57	123	55 07	68 41	72·2	54 48	67 02	70·9	54 28	65 24	69·6	54 06	63 48	68·3	53 43	62 14	67·0	53 19	60 42	65·8	237	303
58	122	56 03	68 09	71·6	55 43	66 28	70·2	55 22	64 48	68·8	55 00	63 11	67·5	54 36	61 35	66·2	54 12	60 01	64·9	238	302
59	121	56 59	67 34	70·9	56 38	65 52	69·5	56 16	64 10	68·1	55 53	62 31	66·7	55 28	60 54	65·4	55 05	59 18	64·1	239	301
60	120	57 54	66 58	70·2	57 33	65 13	68·7	57 10	63 30	67·3	56 46	61 49	65·9	56 21	60 10	64·5	55 55	58 33	63·1	240	300
61	119	58 49	66 20	69·4	58 27	64 32	67·9	58 04	62 47	66·4	57 39	61 04	65·0	57 13	59 24	63·6	56 46	57 46	62·2	241	299
62	118	59 44	65 38	68·6	59 21	63 49	67·1	58 57	62 02	65·5	58 31	60 17	64·0	58 05	58 35	62·6	57 36	56 56	61·2	242	298
63	117	60 38	64 55	67·8	60 15	63 03	66·2	59 50	61 13	64·6	59 23	59 27	63·1	58 55	57 43	61·6	58 26	56 03	60·2	243	297
64	116	61 32	64 08	66·9	61 08	62 14	65·2	60 42	60 22	63·6	60 15	58 34	62·0	59 46	56 49	60·5	59 16	55 06	59·1	244	296
65	115	62 26	63 18	66·0	62 01	61 21	64·2	61 34	59 28	62·6	61 06	57 37	60·9	60 37	55 51	59·4	60 05	54 07	57·9	245	295
66	114	63 20	62 25	65·0	62 53	60 25	63·2	62 26	58 30	61·5	61 56	56 37	59·8	61 25	54 49	58·2	60 53	53 04	56·7	246	294
67	113	64 13	61 27	63·9	63 45	59 25	62·1	63 16	57 27	60·3	62 46	55 34	58·6	62 14	53 44	57·0	61 41	51 57	55·4	247	293
68	112	65 05	60 26	62·8	64 37	58 21	60·9	64 07	56 21	59·1	63 35	54 25	57·4	63 02	52 34	55·7	62 27	50 47	54·1	248	292
69	111	65 57	59 20	61·6	65 27	57 13	59·6	64 56	55 10	57·8	64 23	53 13	56·0	63 49	51 20	54·3	63 14	49 32	52·7	249	291
70	110	66 48	58 08	60·3	66 18	55 59	58·3	65 45	53 55	56·4	65 11	51 55	54·6	64 36	50 01	52·9	63 59	48 12	51·2	250	290
71	109	67 39	56 52	58·9	67 07	54 40	56·8	66 33	52 33	54·9	65 58	50 33	53·1	65 21	48 38	51·3	64 43	46 48	49·7	251	289
72	108	68 29	55 29	57·4	67 55	53 15	55·3	67 20	51 06	53·3	66 44	49 04	51·5	66 06	47 09	49·7	65 26	45 18	48·0	252	288
73	107	69 18	54 00	55·8	68 43	51 42	53·7	68 07	49 33	51·6	67 29	47 30	49·8	66 49	45 33	48·0	66 09	43 43	46·3	253	287
74	106	70 06	52 22	54·1	69 30	50 03	51·9	68 52	47 52	49·8	68 12	45 49	47·9	67 31	43 52	46·1	66 49	42 02	44·4	254	286
75	105	70 53	50 36	52·2	70 15	48 16	50·0	69 36	46 04	47·9	68 55	44 00	46·0	68 12	42 04	44·2	67 29	40 15	42·5	255	285
76	104	71 38	48 42	50·2	70 59	46 20	47·9	70 18	44 08	45·9	69 36	42 05	44·0	68 52	40 07	42·1	68 07	38 21	40·5	256	284
77	103	72 23	46 37	48·0	71 42	44 14	45·7	70 59	42 03	43·7	70 15	40 01	41·7	69 30	38 07	39·9	68 43	36 13	38·3	257	283
78	102	73 06	44 25	45·6	72 23	42 00	43·4	71 38	39 49	41·3	70 53	37 49	39·4	70 06	35 57	37·6	69 18	34 13	36·0	258	282
79	101	73 47	41 55	43·1	73 02	39 34	40·8	72 16	37 26	38·8	71 28	35 27	36·9	70 40	33 38	35·2	69 50	31 58	33·6	259	281
80	100	74 26	39 15	40·3	73 39	36 57	38·1	72 51	34 51	36·1	72 02	32 57	34·3	71 12	31 12	32·6	70 21	29 36	31·1	260	280
81	99	75 02	36 21	37·3	74 14	34 07	35·1	73 24	32 06	33·2	72 34	30 17	31·5	71 42	28 37	29·9	70 50	27 06	28·4	261	279
82	98	75 37	33 13	34·1	74 46	31 05	32·0	73 55	29 10	30·2	73 03	27 27	28·5	72 09	25 53	27·0	71 16	24 29	25·7	262	278
83	97	76 08	29 50	30·6	75 16	27 50	28·6	74 23	26 03	26·9	73 30	24 27	25·4	72 34	23 02	24·0	71 39	21 44	22·8	263	277
84	96	76 36	26 11	26·8	75 42	24 22	25·0	74 48	22 45	23·5	73 52	21 19	22·1	72 56	20 02	20·9	72 00	18 53	19·8	264	276
85	95	77 01	22 18	22·8	76 05	20 41	21·3	75 09	19 16	19·9	74 12	18 01	18·7	73 15	16 54	17·6	72 18	15 55	16·7	265	275
86	94	77 22	18 10	18·6	76 25	16 49	17·3	75 27	15 38	16·1	74 29	14 36	15·1	73 31	13 40	14·2	72 33	12 51	13·5	266	274
87	93	77 38	13 50	14·1	76 40	12 46	13·1	75 41	11 51	12·2	74 43	11 03	11·4	73 44	10 21	10·8	72 45	9 43	10·2	267	273
88	92	77 50	9 19	9·5	76 51	8 36	8·8	75 52	7 58	8·2	74 52	7 25	7·7	73 53	6 56	7·2	72 53	6 31	6·8	268	272
89	91	77 58	4 42	4·8	76 58	4 19	4·4	75 58	4 00	4·1	74 58	3 44	3·9	73 58	3 29	3·6	72 58	3 16	3·4	269	271
90	90	78 00	0 00	0·0	77 00	0 00	0·0	76 00	0 00	0·0	75 00	0 00	0·0	74 00	0 00	0·0	73 00	0 00	0·0	270	270

N. Lat: for LHA > 180° .... $Z_n = Z$
for LHA < 180° .... $Z_n = 360° - Z$

S. Lat.: for LHA > 180° .... $Z_n = 180° - Z$
for LHA < 180° .... $Z_n = 180° + Z$

SIGHT REDUCTION TABLE

B: (−) for 90° < LHA < 270°
Dec:(−) for Lat. contrary name

Z₁: same sign as B
Z₂: (−) for F > 90°

Lat./A	LHA/F	18° A/H	18° B/P	18° Z₁/Z₂	19° A/H	19° B/P	19° Z₁/Z₂	20° A/H	20° B/P	20° Z₁/Z₂	21° A/H	21° B/P	21° Z₁/Z₂	22° A/H	22° B/P	22° Z₁/Z₂	23° A/H	23° B/P	23° Z₁/Z₂	Lat./A	LHA
180	0	0 00	72 00	90.0	0 00	71 00	90.0	0 00	70 00	90.0	0 00	69 00	90.0	0 00	68 00	90.0	0 00	67 00	90.0	180	360
179	1	0 57	72 00	89.7	0 57	71 00	89.7	0 56	70 00	89.7	0 56	69 00	89.6	0 56	68 00	89.6	0 55	67 00	89.6	181	359
178	2	1 54	71 59	89.4	1 53	70 59	89.3	1 53	69 59	89.3	1 52	68 59	89.3	1 51	67 59	89.3	1 50	66 59	89.2	182	358
177	3	2 51	71 59	89.1	2 50	70 59	89.0	2 49	69 58	89.0	2 48	68 58	88.9	2 47	67 58	88.9	2 46	66 58	88.8	183	357
176	4	3 48	71 58	88.8	3 47	70 57	88.7	3 46	69 57	88.6	3 44	68 57	88.6	3 42	67 57	88.5	3 41	66 57	88.4	184	356
175	5	4 45	71 56	88.5	4 44	70 56	88.4	4 42	69 56	88.3	4 40	68 56	88.2	4 38	67 55	88.1	4 36	66 55	88.0	185	355
174	6	5 42	71 54	88.1	5 40	70 54	87.9	5 38	69 54	87.9	5 36	68 54	87.8	5 34	67 53	87.7	5 31	66 53	87.6	186	354
173	7	6 39	71 52	87.8	6 37	70 52	87.7	6 35	69 52	87.6	6 32	68 51	87.5	6 29	67 51	87.4	6 26	66 51	87.3	187	353
172	8	7 36	71 50	87.5	7 34	70 50	87.4	7 31	69 49	87.2	7 28	68 49	87.1	7 25	67 48	87.0	7 22	66 48	86.9	188	352
171	9	8 33	71 47	87.2	8 30	70 47	87.0	8 27	69 46	86.9	8 24	68 46	86.8	8 20	67 45	86.6	8 17	66 45	86.5	189	351
170	10	9 30	71 44	86.9	9 27	70 44	86.7	9 23	69 43	86.5	9 16	68 39	86.4	9 16	67 42	86.2	9 12	66 41	86.1	190	350
169	11	10 27	71 41	86.6	10 24	70 40	86.4	10 20	69 39	86.2	10 16	68 39	86.0	10 11	67 38	85.8	10 07	66 37	85.7	191	349
168	12	11 24	71 37	86.2	11 20	70 36	86.0	11 16	69 35	85.8	11 12	68 34	85.6	11 07	67 33	85.4	11 02	66 32	85.3	192	348
167	13	12 21	71 33	85.9	12 17	70 32	85.7	12 12	69 31	85.5	12 07	68 30	85.3	12 02	67 29	85.1	11 57	66 28	84.8	193	347
166	14	13 18	71 29	85.6	13 13	70 28	85.4	13 08	69 26	85.1	13 03	68 25	84.9	12 58	67 24	84.7	12 52	66 22	84.4	194	346
165	15	14 15	71 24	85.3	14 10	70 23	85.0	14 04	69 21	84.8	13 59	68 20	84.5	13 53	67 18	84.3	13 47	66 17	84.0	195	345
164	16	15 12	71 19	84.9	15 06	70 18	84.7	15 01	69 16	84.4	14 55	68 14	84.1	14 48	67 12	83.9	14 42	66 10	83.6	196	344
163	17	16 09	71 14	84.6	16 03	70 12	84.3	15 57	69 10	84.0	15 50	68 08	83.7	15 44	67 06	83.5	15 37	66 04	83.2	197	343
162	18	17 05	71 08	84.3	16 59	70 06	84.0	16 53	69 03	83.7	16 46	68 01	83.4	16 39	66 59	83.1	16 32	65 57	82.8	198	342
161	19	18 02	71 02	83.9	17 56	69 59	83.6	17 49	68 57	83.3	17 42	67 54	83.0	17 34	66 52	82.7	17 27	65 49	82.3	199	341
160	20	18 59	70 56	83.6	18 52	69 53	83.2	18 45	68 50	82.9	18 37	67 47	82.6	18 29	66 44	82.2	18 21	65 41	81.9	200	340
159	21	19 56	70 49	83.2	19 48	69 45	82.9	19 41	68 42	82.5	19 33	67 39	82.2	19 24	66 36	81.9	19 16	65 33	81.5	201	339
158	22	20 52	70 41	82.9	20 45	69 38	82.5	20 37	68 34	82.1	20 29	67 31	81.8	20 19	66 27	81.5	20 10	65 24	81.0	202	338
157	23	21 49	70 33	82.5	21 41	69 29	82.1	21 32	68 26	81.7	21 24	67 22	81.4	21 14	66 18	81.0	21 05	65 15	80.6	203	337
156	24	22 45	70 25	82.2	22 37	69 21	81.8	22 28	68 17	81.3	22 19	67 12	80.9	22 09	66 09	80.5	21 59	65 05	80.1	204	336
155	25	23 42	70 17	81.8	23 33	69 12	81.4	23 24	68 07	80.9	23 14	67 03	80.5	23 04	65 58	80.1	22 54	64 54	79.7	205	335
154	26	24 38	70 07	81.4	24 29	69 02	81.0	24 20	67 57	80.5	24 09	66 52	80.1	23 59	65 48	79.6	23 48	64 43	79.2	206	334
153	27	25 35	69 58	81.1	25 25	68 52	80.6	25 15	67 47	80.1	25 05	66 42	79.6	24 54	65 36	79.2	24 42	64 32	78.7	207	333
152	28	26 31	69 48	80.7	26 21	68 42	80.2	26 11	67 36	79.7	26 00	66 30	79.2	25 48	65 25	78.7	25 36	64 19	78.3	208	332
151	29	27 27	69 37	80.3	27 17	68 31	79.8	27 06	67 24	79.3	26 55	66 18	78.8	26 43	65 12	78.3	26 30	64 07	77.8	209	331
150	30	28 24	69 26	79.9	28 13	68 19	79.4	28 01	67 12	78.8	27 50	66 06	78.3	27 37	64 59	77.8	27 24	63 53	77.3	210	330
149	31	29 20	69 14	79.5	29 09	68 07	78.9	28 57	67 00	78.4	28 44	65 53	77.8	28 31	64 46	77.3	28 18	63 39	76.8	211	329
148	32	30 16	69 02	79.1	30 04	67 54	78.5	29 52	66 46	77.9	29 39	65 39	77.4	29 26	64 32	76.8	29 12	63 25	76.3	212	328
147	33	31 12	68 49	78.7	31 00	67 41	78.1	30 47	66 32	77.5	30 33	65 25	76.9	30 20	64 17	76.3	30 05	63 09	75.8	213	327
146	34	32 08	68 36	78.2	31 55	67 27	77.6	31 42	66 18	77.0	31 28	65 09	76.4	31 14	64 01	75.8	30 59	62 53	75.2	214	326
145	35	33 04	68 22	77.8	32 51	67 12	77.2	32 37	66 03	76.5	32 23	64 54	75.9	32 08	63 45	75.3	31 52	62 36	74.7	215	325
144	36	33 59	68 07	77.3	33 46	66 57	76.7	33 32	65 47	76.0	33 17	64 37	75.4	33 01	63 28	74.8	32 45	62 19	74.2	216	324
143	37	34 55	67 52	76.9	34 41	66 41	76.2	34 26	65 30	75.5	34 11	64 20	74.8	33 55	63 11	74.2	33 38	62 01	73.6	217	323
142	38	35 50	67 36	76.4	35 36	66 24	75.7	35 21	65 13	75.0	35 05	64 02	74.4	34 48	62 51	73.7	34 31	61 41	73.0	218	322
141	39	36 46	67 19	76.0	36 31	66 06	75.2	36 15	64 54	74.5	35 59	63 43	73.8	35 42	62 32	73.1	35 24	61 21	72.4	219	321
140	40	37 41	67 01	75.5	37 26	65 48	74.7	37 10	64 35	74.0	36 53	63 23	73.3	36 35	62 12	72.6	36 17	61 01	71.8	220	320
139	41	38 36	66 42	75.0	38 20	65 29	74.2	38 04	64 15	73.4	37 46	63 02	72.7	37 28	61 50	72.0	37 09	60 39	71.2	221	319
138	42	39 31	66 23	74.5	39 15	65 08	73.7	38 58	63 54	72.9	38 40	62 41	72.1	38 21	61 28	71.4	38 01	60 16	70.6	222	318
137	43	40 26	66 03	73.9	40 09	64 47	73.1	39 51	63 33	72.3	39 33	62 18	71.5	39 13	61 05	70.7	38 53	59 52	70.0	223	317
136	44	41 21	65 42	73.4	41 03	64 25	72.5	40 45	63 10	71.7	40 26	61 55	70.9	40 06	60 41	70.1	39 45	59 27	69.3	224	316
135	45	42 16	65 19	72.8	41 57	64 02	72.0	41 38	62 46	71.1	41 19	61 30	70.3	40 58	60 15	69.5	40 37	59 01	68.7	225	315

Lat. / A		18°			19°			20°			21°			22°			23°			Lat. / A	
LHA/F		A/H	B/P	Z₁/Z₂	A/H	B/P	Z₁/Z₂	A/H	B/P	Z₁/Z₂	A/H	B/P	Z₁/Z₂	A/H	B/P	Z₁/Z₂	A/H	B/P	Z₁/Z₂		LHA
45	135	42 16	65 19	72·8	41 57	64 02	72·0	41 38	62 46	71·1	41 19	61 30	70·3	40 58	60 15	69·5	40 37	59 01	68·7	225	315
46	134	43 10	64 56	72·3	42 51	63 38	71·4	42 32	62 21	70·5	42 11	61 05	69·6	41 50	59 49	68·8	41 28	58 34	68·0	226	314
47	133	44 04	64 32	71·7	43 45	63 13	70·8	43 25	61 55	69·9	43 04	60 38	69·0	42 42	59 21	68·1	42 19	58 06	67·3	227	313
48	132	44 58	64 06	71·1	44 38	62 46	70·1	44 18	61 27	69·2	43 56	60 09	68·3	43 33	58 53	67·4	43 10	57 37	66·5	228	312
49	131	45 52	63 39	70·4	45 32	62 18	69·5	45 10	60 59	68·5	44 48	59 40	67·6	44 24	58 22	66·7	44 00	57 06	65·8	229	311
50	130	46 46	63 11	69·8	46 25	61 49	68·8	46 03	60 29	67·8	45 39	59 09	66·9	45 15	57 51	66·0	44 50	56 34	65·0	230	310
51	129	47 39	62 42	69·1	47 17	61 19	68·1	46 55	59 57	67·1	46 31	58 37	66·1	46 06	57 18	65·2	45 40	56 00	64·2	231	309
52	128	48 33	62 11	68·4	48 10	60 47	67·4	47 46	59 25	66·4	47 22	58 03	65·4	46 56	56 44	64·4	46 30	55 25	63·4	232	308
53	127	49 25	61 38	67·7	49 02	60 13	66·6	48 38	58 50	65·6	48 13	57 28	64·6	47 46	56 07	63·6	47 19	54 48	62·6	233	307
54	126	50 18	61 04	67·0	49 54	59 38	65·9	49 29	58 14	64·8	49 03	56 51	63·7	48 36	55 30	62·7	48 08	54 10	61·7	234	306
55	125	51 10	60 28	66·2	50 46	59 01	65·1	50 20	57 36	64·0	49 53	56 12	62·9	49 25	54 50	61·9	48 56	53 30	60·8	235	305
56	124	52 03	59 50	65·4	51 37	58 23	64·2	51 10	56 56	63·1	50 43	55 32	62·0	50 14	54 09	61·0	49 44	52 48	59·9	236	304
57	123	52 54	59 11	64·6	52 28	57 42	63·4	52 00	56 15	62·2	51 32	54 49	61·1	51 02	53 26	60·0	50 32	52 04	59·0	237	303
58	122	53 46	58 31	63·7	53 18	56 59	62·5	52 50	55 31	61·3	52 21	54 05	60·2	51 50	52 41	59·1	51 19	51 18	58·0	238	302
59	121	54 37	57 45	62·8	54 08	56 14	61·5	53 39	54 45	60·4	53 09	53 18	59·2	52 38	51 53	58·1	52 06	50 30	57·0	239	301
60	120	55 27	56 59	61·8	54 58	55 27	60·6	54 28	53 57	59·4	53 57	52 29	58·2	53 25	51 04	57·0	52 52	49 40	55·9	240	300
61	119	56 17	56 10	60·9	55 48	54 37	59·6	55 16	53 06	58·3	54 44	51 38	57·1	54 11	50 12	55·9	53 37	48 48	54·8	241	299
62	118	57 07	55 19	59·8	56 36	53 45	58·5	56 04	52 13	57·2	55 31	50 44	56·0	54 57	49 17	54·8	54 22	47 53	53·7	242	298
63	117	57 56	54 25	58·8	57 24	52 49	57·4	56 51	51 17	56·1	56 17	49 47	54·9	55 42	48 20	53·7	55 06	46 55	52·5	243	297
64	116	58 44	53 27	57·6	58 12	51 51	56·3	57 38	50 18	55·0	57 03	48 48	53·7	56 27	47 20	52·5	55 50	45 55	51·3	244	296
65	115	59 32	52 23	56·5	58 59	50 45	55·1	58 24	49 16	53·7	57 47	47 45	52·5	57 10	46 11	51·2	56 32	44 53	50·0	245	295
66	114	60 19	51 23	55·2	59 45	49 37	53·8	59 09	48 11	52·5	58 32	46 39	51·2	57 53	45 11	49·9	57 14	43 47	48·7	246	294
67	113	61 06	50 15	53·9	60 30	48 37	52·5	59 53	47 02	51·1	59 15	45 30	49·8	58 36	44 02	48·6	57 55	42 38	47·4	247	293
68	112	61 52	49 04	52·6	61 15	47 25	51·1	60 36	45 50	49·8	59 57	44 18	48·4	59 17	42 50	47·2	58 36	41 26	46·0	248	292
69	111	62 37	47 48	51·2	61 58	46 09	49·7	61 19	44 33	48·3	60 39	43 02	47·0	59 57	41 34	45·7	59 15	40 10	44·5	249	291
70	110	63 21	46 28	49·7	62 41	44 48	48·2	62 01	43 13	46·8	61 19	41 42	45·4	60 36	40 15	44·2	59 53	38 52	43·0	250	290
71	109	64 04	45 03	48·1	63 23	43 24	46·6	62 41	41 49	45·2	61 58	40 18	43·9	61 15	38 52	42·6	60 30	37 29	41·4	251	289
72	108	64 45	43 34	46·4	64 04	41 54	44·9	63 21	40 20	43·5	62 37	38 50	42·2	61 52	37 25	40·9	61 06	36 03	39·7	252	288
73	107	65 26	41 59	44·7	64 43	40 20	43·2	63 59	38 46	41·8	63 14	37 18	40·5	62 27	35 53	39·2	61 41	34 34	38·0	253	287
74	106	66 06	40 19	42·9	65 21	38 41	41·4	64 36	37 08	40·0	63 49	35 41	38·7	63 02	34 18	37·4	62 14	33 00	36·3	254	286
75	105	66 44	38 32	40·9	65 58	36 56	39·5	65 11	35 25	38·1	64 23	33 59	36·8	63 35	32 39	35·6	62 46	31 22	34·4	255	285
76	104	67 20	36 40	38·9	66 33	35 05	37·4	65 45	33 37	36·1	64 56	32 13	34·8	64 07	30 55	33·6	63 16	29 41	32·5	256	284
77	103	67 55	34 42	36·8	67 07	33 09	35·3	66 18	31 43	34·0	65 27	30 22	32·8	64 37	29 06	31·6	63 45	27 55	30·6	257	283
78	102	68 29	32 37	34·5	67 39	31 07	33·1	66 48	29 44	31·9	65 57	28 26	30·7	65 05	27 14	29·6	64 13	26 06	28·5	258	282
79	101	69 00	30 25	32·2	68 09	29 00	30·8	67 17	27 40	29·6	66 25	26 26	28·5	65 32	25 17	27·4	64 38	24 12	26·4	259	281
80	100	69 29	28 07	29·7	68 37	26 46	28·4	67 44	25 30	27·3	66 50	24 20	26·2	65 56	23 15	25·2	65 02	22 15	24·3	260	280
81	99	69 57	25 43	27·1	69 03	24 26	25·9	68 09	23 15	24·8	67 14	22 10	23·8	66 19	21 10	22·9	65 23	20 14	22·1	261	279
82	98	70 21	23 11	24·5	69 27	22 00	23·3	68 31	20 56	22·3	67 36	19 56	21·4	66 40	19 00	20·6	65 43	18 09	19·8	262	278
83	97	70 44	20 34	21·7	69 48	19 29	20·7	68 51	18 31	19·7	67 55	17 37	18·9	66 58	16 47	18·1	66 01	16 01	17·4	263	277
84	96	71 03	17 50	18·8	70 07	16 53	17·9	69 09	16 01	17·1	68 12	15 14	16·3	67 14	14 30	15·7	66 16	13 50	15·1	264	276
85	95	71 20	15 01	15·8	70 23	14 12	15·0	69 25	13 28	14·3	68 26	12 48	13·7	67 28	12 10	13·1	66 29	11 36	12·6	265	275
86	94	71 35	12 07	12·8	70 36	11 27	12·1	69 37	10 51	11·6	68 38	10 18	11·0	67 39	9 48	10·6	66 40	9 20	10·1	266	274
87	93	71 46	9 09	9·6	70 46	8 39	9·1	69 47	8 11	8·7	68 48	7 46	8·3	67 48	7 23	8·0	66 49	7 02	7·6	267	273
88	92	71 54	6 08	6·4	70 54	5 47	6·1	69 54	5 29	5·8	68 55	5 12	5·6	67 55	4 56	5·3	66 55	4 42	5·1	268	272
89	91	71 58	3 04	3·2	70 58	2 54	3·1	69 59	2 45	2·9	68 59	2 36	2·8	67 59	2 28	2·7	66 59	2 21	2·6	269	271
90	90	72 00	0 00	0·0	71 00	0 00	0·0	70 00	0 00	0·0	69 00	0 00	0·0	68 00	0 00	0·0	67 00	0 00	0·0	270	270

N. Lat: for LHA > 180° ... $Z_n = Z$
for LHA < 180° ... $Z_n = 360° - Z$

S. Lat.: for LHA > 180° ... $Z_n = 180° - Z$
for LHA < 180° ... $Z_n = 180° + Z$

SIGHT REDUCTION TABLE

B: (−) for 90° < LHA < 270°
Dec:(−) for Lat. contrary name

Z₁: same sign as B
Z₂: (−) for F > 90°

LHA/F	Lat./A	24° A/H	24° B/P	24° Z₁/Z₂	25° A/H	25° B/P	25° Z₁/Z₂	26° A/H	26° B/P	26° Z₁/Z₂	27° A/H	27° B/P	27° Z₁/Z₂	28° A/H	28° B/P	28° Z₁/Z₂	29° A/H	29° B/P	29° Z₁/Z₂	Lat./A	LHA
0	180	0 00	66 00	90.0	0 00	65 00	90.0	0 00	64 00	90.0	0 00	63 00	90.0	0 00	62 00	90.0	0 00	61 00	90.0	180	360
1	179	0 55	66 00	89.6	0 54	65 00	89.6	0 54	64 00	89.6	0 53	63 00	89.5	0 53	62 00	89.5	0 52	61 00	89.5	181	359
2	178	1 50	65 59	89.2	1 49	64 59	89.2	1 48	63 59	89.1	1 47	62 59	89.1	1 46	61 59	89.1	1 45	60 59	89.0	182	358
3	177	2 44	65 58	88.8	2 43	64 58	88.8	2 42	63 58	88.7	2 40	62 58	88.7	2 39	61 58	88.6	2 37	60 58	88.5	183	357
4	176	3 39	65 57	88.4	3 37	64 57	88.3	3 36	63 57	88.2	3 34	62 57	88.2	3 32	61 57	88.1	3 30	60 56	88.1	184	356
5	175	4 34	65 55	88.0	4 32	64 55	87.9	4 30	63 55	87.8	4 27	62 55	87.7	4 25	61 55	87.6	4 22	60 54	87.6	185	355
6	174	5 29	65 53	87.6	5 26	64 53	87.5	5 23	63 53	87.4	5 21	62 52	87.3	5 18	61 52	87.2	5 15	60 52	87.1	186	354
7	173	6 24	65 50	87.1	6 20	64 50	87.1	6 17	63 50	86.9	6 14	62 50	86.8	6 11	61 49	86.7	6 07	60 49	86.6	187	353
8	172	7 18	65 47	86.7	7 15	64 47	86.6	7 11	63 47	86.5	7 07	62 46	86.3	7 04	61 46	86.2	6 59	60 46	86.1	188	352
9	171	8 13	65 44	86.3	8 09	64 44	86.2	8 05	63 43	86.0	8 01	62 43	85.9	7 56	61 42	85.7	7 52	60 42	85.6	189	351
10	170	9 08	65 40	85.9	9 03	64 40	85.7	8 59	63 39	85.6	8 54	62 39	85.4	8 49	61 38	85.3	8 44	60 38	85.1	190	350
11	169	10 02	65 36	85.5	9 57	64 35	85.3	9 52	63 35	85.1	9 47	62 34	85.0	9 42	61 33	84.8	9 36	60 33	84.6	191	349
12	168	10 57	65 32	85.1	10 52	64 31	84.9	10 46	63 30	84.7	10 41	62 29	84.5	10 35	61 28	84.3	10 29	60 28	84.1	192	348
13	167	11 52	65 27	84.6	11 46	64 26	84.4	11 40	63 25	84.2	11 34	62 24	84.0	11 27	61 23	83.8	11 21	60 22	83.6	193	347
14	166	12 46	65 21	84.2	12 40	64 20	84.0	12 34	63 19	83.8	12 27	62 18	83.5	12 20	61 17	83.3	12 13	60 16	83.1	194	346
15	165	13 41	65 15	83.8	13 34	64 14	83.5	13 27	63 13	83.3	13 20	62 11	83.1	13 13	61 10	82.8	13 05	60 09	82.6	195	345
16	164	14 35	65 09	83.3	14 28	64 07	83.1	14 21	63 06	82.8	14 13	62 04	82.6	14 05	61 03	82.3	13 57	60 02	82.1	196	344
17	163	15 29	65 02	82.9	15 22	64 00	82.6	15 14	62 59	82.4	15 06	61 57	82.1	14 58	60 56	81.8	14 49	59 54	81.6	197	343
18	162	16 24	64 55	82.5	16 16	63 53	82.2	16 08	62 51	81.9	15 59	61 49	81.6	15 50	60 47	81.3	15 41	59 46	81.0	198	342
19	161	17 18	64 47	82.0	17 10	63 45	81.7	17 01	62 43	81.4	16 52	61 41	81.1	16 42	60 39	80.8	16 33	59 37	80.5	199	341
20	160	18 12	64 39	81.6	18 03	63 36	81.3	17 54	62 34	80.9	17 45	61 32	80.6	17 35	60 30	80.3	17 24	59 28	80.0	200	340
21	159	19 07	64 30	81.1	18 57	63 28	80.8	18 47	62 25	80.4	18 37	61 23	80.1	18 27	60 20	79.8	18 16	59 18	79.5	201	339
22	158	20 01	64 21	80.7	19 51	63 18	80.3	19 41	62 15	80.0	19 30	61 13	79.6	19 19	60 10	79.3	19 08	59 08	78.9	202	338
23	157	20 55	64 11	80.2	20 44	63 08	79.8	20 34	62 05	79.5	20 22	61 02	79.1	20 11	59 59	78.7	19 59	58 57	78.4	203	337
24	156	21 49	64 01	79.7	21 38	62 58	79.3	21 27	61 54	79.0	21 15	60 51	78.6	21 03	59 48	78.2	20 50	58 45	77.8	204	336
25	155	22 43	63 50	79.3	22 31	62 46	78.9	22 19	61 43	78.4	22 07	60 39	78.0	21 55	59 36	77.7	21 42	58 33	77.3	205	335
26	154	23 36	63 39	78.8	23 25	62 35	78.4	23 12	61 31	77.9	22 59	60 27	77.5	22 46	59 24	77.1	22 33	58 20	76.7	206	334
27	153	24 30	63 27	78.3	24 18	62 22	77.8	24 05	61 18	77.4	23 52	60 14	77.0	23 38	59 10	76.5	23 24	58 07	76.1	207	333
28	152	25 24	63 14	77.8	25 11	62 10	77.3	24 57	61 05	76.9	24 44	60 01	76.4	24 29	58 57	76.0	24 15	57 53	75.5	208	332
29	151	26 17	63 01	77.3	26 04	61 56	76.8	25 50	60 51	76.3	25 36	59 47	75.9	25 21	58 42	75.4	25 05	57 38	75.0	209	331
30	150	27 11	62 48	76.8	26 57	61 42	76.3	26 42	60 37	75.8	26 27	59 32	75.3	26 12	58 27	74.8	25 56	57 23	74.4	210	330
31	149	28 04	62 33	76.3	27 50	61 27	75.8	27 35	60 22	75.2	27 19	59 16	74.7	27 03	58 11	74.2	26 46	57 07	73.8	211	329
32	148	28 57	62 18	75.7	28 42	61 12	75.2	28 27	60 06	74.7	28 10	59 00	74.2	27 54	57 55	73.7	27 37	56 50	73.1	212	328
33	147	29 50	62 02	75.2	29 35	60 56	74.7	29 19	59 49	74.1	29 01	58 43	73.6	28 45	57 38	73.0	28 27	56 33	72.5	213	327
34	146	30 43	61 46	74.7	30 27	60 39	74.1	30 10	59 32	73.5	29 53	58 26	73.0	29 35	57 20	72.4	29 17	56 14	71.9	214	326
35	145	31 36	61 28	74.1	31 19	60 21	73.5	31 02	59 14	72.9	30 44	58 07	72.4	30 26	57 01	71.8	30 07	55 55	71.2	215	325
36	144	32 29	61 10	73.5	32 11	60 02	72.9	31 53	58 55	72.3	31 35	57 48	71.7	31 16	56 41	71.2	30 56	55 35	70.6	216	324
37	143	33 21	60 52	73.0	33 03	59 43	72.3	32 45	58 35	71.7	32 26	57 28	71.1	32 06	56 21	70.5	31 46	55 15	69.9	217	323
38	142	34 13	60 32	72.4	33 55	59 23	71.7	33 36	58 15	71.1	33 16	57 07	70.5	32 56	55 59	69.9	32 35	54 53	69.3	218	322
39	141	35 06	60 11	71.8	34 47	59 02	71.1	34 27	57 53	70.5	34 06	56 45	69.8	33 45	55 37	69.2	33 24	54 30	68.6	219	321
40	140	35 58	59 50	71.2	35 38	58 40	70.5	35 17	57 31	69.8	34 56	56 22	69.2	34 35	55 14	68.5	34 12	54 07	67.9	220	320
41	139	36 49	59 28	70.5	36 29	58 17	69.8	36 08	57 08	69.1	35 46	55 59	68.5	35 24	54 50	67.8	35 01	53 42	67.1	221	319
42	138	37 41	59 04	69.9	37 20	57 54	69.2	36 58	56 43	68.5	36 36	55 34	67.8	36 13	54 25	67.1	35 49	53 17	66.4	222	318
43	137	38 32	58 40	69.2	38 11	57 29	68.5	37 48	56 18	67.8	37 25	55 08	67.1	37 02	53 59	66.4	36 37	52 50	65.7	223	317
44	136	39 23	58 15	68.6	39 01	57 03	67.8	38 38	55 52	67.1	38 14	54 41	66.3	37 50	53 32	65.6	37 25	52 23	64.9	224	316
45	135	40 14	57 48	67.9	39 51	56 36	67.1	39 28	55 24	66.3	39 03	54 13	65.6	38 38	53 04	64.9	38 12	51 54	64.1	225	315

Lat./A (F)	LHA	24° A/H	24° B/P	24° Z1/Z2	25° A/H	25° B/P	25° Z1/Z2	26° A/H	26° B/P	26° Z1/Z2	27° A/H	27° B/P	27° Z1/Z2	28° A/H	28° B/P	28° Z1/Z2	29° A/H	29° B/P	29° Z1/Z2	LHA	Lat./A
135	45	40 14	57 48	67.9	39 51	56 36	67.1	39 28	55 24	66.3	39 03	54 13	65.6	38 38	53 04	64.9	38 12	51 54	64.1	225	315
134	46	41 05	57 21	67.2	40 41	56 08	66.4	40 17	54 56	65.6	39 52	53 44	64.8	39 26	52 34	64.1	38 59	51 25	63.3	226	314
133	47	41 55	56 52	66.4	41 31	55 38	65.6	41 06	54 26	64.8	40 40	53 14	64.0	40 13	52 04	63.3	39 46	50 54	62.5	227	313
132	48	42 45	56 22	65.7	42 20	55 08	64.9	41 54	53 55	64.0	41 28	52 43	63.2	41 00	51 32	62.5	40 32	50 22	61.7	228	312
131	49	43 35	55 50	64.9	43 09	54 36	64.1	42 43	53 22	63.2	42 15	52 10	62.4	41 47	51 00	61.6	41 18	49 48	60.9	229	311
130	50	44 25	55 17	64.1	43 58	54 02	63.3	43 31	52 49	62.4	43 03	51 36	61.6	42 34	50 24	60.8	42 04	49 14	60.0	230	310
129	51	45 14	54 43	63.3	44 47	53 28	62.5	44 18	52 13	61.6	43 49	51 00	60.7	43 20	49 48	59.9	42 49	48 38	59.1	231	309
128	52	46 03	54 08	62.5	45 35	52 52	61.6	45 06	51 37	60.7	44 36	50 23	59.8	44 05	49 11	59.0	43 34	48 00	58.2	232	308
127	53	46 51	53 30	61.6	46 22	52 14	60.7	45 52	50 59	59.8	45 22	49 45	58.9	44 51	48 32	58.1	44 18	47 21	57.2	233	307
126	54	47 39	52 51	60.8	47 09	51 34	59.8	46 38	50 19	58.9	46 07	49 05	58.0	45 35	47 52	57.1	45 02	46 41	56.3	234	306
125	55	48 27	52 11	59.8	47 56	50 53	58.9	47 25	49 37	58.0	46 52	48 23	57.1	46 19	47 10	56.2	45 46	45 59	55.3	235	305
124	56	49 14	51 28	58.9	48 43	50 11	57.9	48 10	48 54	57.0	47 37	47 40	56.1	47 03	46 27	55.2	46 29	45 15	54.3	236	304
123	57	50 01	50 44	57.9	49 28	49 26	56.9	48 55	48 09	56.0	48 21	46 54	55.0	47 46	45 41	54.1	47 11	44 30	53.3	237	303
122	58	50 47	49 58	56.9	50 14	48 39	55.9	49 40	47 22	54.9	49 05	46 07	54.0	48 29	44 54	53.1	47 53	43 43	52.2	238	302
121	59	51 33	49 09	55.9	50 58	47 51	54.9	50 23	46 34	53.9	49 48	45 18	52.9	49 11	44 05	52.0	48 34	42 54	51.1	239	301
120	60	52 18	48 19	54.8	51 43	47 00	53.8	51 07	45 43	52.8	50 30	44 28	51.8	49 53	43 14	50.9	49 14	42 03	50.0	240	300
119	61	53 02	47 26	53.7	52 26	46 07	52.7	51 49	44 50	51.7	51 12	43 35	50.6	50 33	42 22	49.7	49 54	41 10	48.8	241	299
118	62	53 46	46 31	52.6	53 09	45 12	51.5	52 31	43 54	50.5	51 53	42 39	49.5	51 13	41 27	48.6	50 33	40 16	47.6	242	298
117	63	54 29	45 33	51.4	53 51	44 14	50.3	53 13	42 57	49.3	52 33	41 42	48.3	51 53	40 30	47.3	51 12	39 19	46.4	243	297
116	64	55 12	44 33	50.2	54 33	43 14	49.1	53 53	41 57	48.1	53 13	40 42	47.1	52 31	39 30	46.1	51 49	38 20	45.2	244	296
115	65	55 53	43 30	48.9	55 13	42 11	47.8	54 33	40 55	46.8	53 51	39 40	45.8	53 09	38 29	44.8	52 26	37 16	43.9	245	295
114	66	56 34	42 25	47.6	55 52	41 06	46.5	55 12	39 50	45.4	54 29	38 36	44.5	53 46	37 25	43.5	53 02	36 11	42.6	246	294
113	67	57 14	41 16	46.2	56 32	39 58	45.1	55 50	38 42	44.1	55 06	37 29	43.1	54 22	36 19	42.1	53 37	35 11	41.2	247	293
112	68	57 53	40 05	44.8	57 10	38 47	43.7	56 27	37 32	42.7	55 42	36 19	41.7	54 57	35 10	40.7	54 11	34 03	39.8	248	292
111	69	58 32	38 50	43.3	57 47	37 33	42.2	57 03	36 18	41.2	56 17	35 07	40.2	55 31	33 59	39.3	54 44	32 53	38.4	249	291
110	70	59 09	37 32	41.8	58 24	36 16	40.7	57 38	35 02	39.7	56 51	33 52	38.7	56 04	32 45	37.8	55 16	31 41	36.9	250	290
109	71	59 45	36 11	40.2	58 58	34 55	39.2	58 12	33 43	38.1	57 24	32 35	37.2	56 36	31 29	36.3	55 47	30 26	35.4	251	289
108	72	60 19	34 46	38.6	59 32	33 32	37.6	58 44	32 21	36.5	57 56	31 14	35.6	57 07	30 10	34.7	56 17	29 08	33.8	252	288
107	73	60 53	33 18	36.9	60 04	32 05	35.9	59 16	30 56	34.9	58 26	29 51	34.0	57 36	28 48	33.1	56 46	27 48	32.2	253	287
106	74	61 25	31 46	35.2	60 36	30 35	34.2	59 46	29 28	33.2	58 55	28 25	32.3	58 05	27 24	31.4	57 13	26 26	30.6	254	286
105	75	61 56	30 10	33.4	61 06	29 02	32.4	60 15	27 57	31.4	59 23	26 56	30.5	58 31	25 57	29.7	57 39	25 02	28.9	255	285
104	76	62 26	28 31	31.5	61 34	27 25	30.5	60 42	26 23	29.6	59 50	25 24	28.8	58 57	24 28	28.0	58 04	23 35	27.2	256	284
103	77	62 53	26 48	29.6	62 01	25 45	28.6	61 08	24 46	27.8	60 15	23 49	27.0	59 21	22 56	26.2	58 28	22 05	25.5	257	283
102	78	63 20	25 02	27.6	62 26	24 02	26.7	61 32	23 05	25.9	60 38	22 12	25.1	59 44	21 21	24.4	58 49	20 34	23.7	258	282
101	79	63 44	23 12	25.5	62 50	22 15	24.7	61 55	21 22	23.9	61 00	20 32	23.1	60 05	19 44	22.5	59 09	19 00	21.8	259	281
100	80	64 07	21 18	23.4	63 12	20 25	22.6	62 16	19 36	21.9	61 20	18 49	21.2	60 24	18 05	20.6	59 28	17 24	20.0	260	280
99	81	64 28	19 22	21.3	63 32	18 33	20.5	62 35	17 47	19.9	61 39	17 04	19.2	60 42	16 24	18.6	59 45	15 46	18.1	261	279
98	82	64 47	17 22	19.1	63 50	16 37	18.4	62 53	15 56	17.8	61 56	15 17	17.2	60 58	14 40	16.7	60 01	14 06	16.2	262	278
97	83	65 03	15 18	16.8	64 06	14 39	16.2	63 08	14 02	15.6	62 10	13 27	15.1	61 12	12 55	14.7	60 14	12 25	14.2	263	277
96	84	65 18	13 13	14.5	64 20	12 38	14.0	63 22	12 06	13.3	62 25	11 36	13.0	61 25	11 07	12.6	60 26	10 41	12.2	264	276
95	85	65 31	11 05	12.1	64 32	10 35	11.7	63 33	10 08	11.3	62 35	9 42	10.9	61 36	9 19	10.6	60 37	8 56	10.2	265	275
94	86	65 41	8 54	9.8	64 42	8 30	9.4	63 43	8 08	9.1	62 44	7 48	8.8	61 44	7 28	8.5	60 45	7 10	8.2	266	274
93	87	65 49	6 42	7.3	64 50	6 24	7.1	63 50	6 07	6.8	62 51	5 52	6.6	61 51	5 37	6.4	60 52	5 24	6.2	267	273
92	88	65 55	4 29	4.9	64 56	4 17	4.7	63 56	4 06	4.6	62 56	3 55	4.4	61 56	3 45	4.3	60 56	3 36	4.2	268	272
91	89	65 59	2 15	2.5	64 59	2 09	2.4	63 59	2 03	2.3	62 59	1 58	2.2	61 59	1 53	2.1	60 59	1 48	2.1	269	271
90	90	66 00	0 00	0.0	65 00	0 00	0.0	64 00	0 00	0.0	63 00	0 00	0.0	62 00	0 00	0.0	61 00	0 00	0.0	270	270

N. Lat: for LHA > 180° .... Zn = Z
for LHA < 180° .... Zn = 360° − Z

S. Lat: for LHA > 180° .... Zn = 180° − Z
for LHA < 180° .... Zn = 180° + Z

SIGHT REDUCTION TABLE

B: (−) for 90° < LHA < 270°
Dec:(−) for Lat. contrary name

Z₁: same sign as B
Z₂: (−) for F > 90°

Lat./A		30°			31°			32°			33°			34°			35°			Lat./A	
LHA/F	A	A/H	B/P	Z_1/Z_2	A/H	B/P	Z_1/Z_2	A/H	B/P	Z_1/Z_2	A/H	B/P	Z_1/Z_2	A/H	B/P	Z_1/Z_2	A/H	B/P	Z_1/Z_2	LHA	A
0	180	0 00	60 00	90.0	0 00	59 00	90.0	0 00	58 00	90.0	0 00	57 00	90.0	0 00	56 00	90.0	0 00	55 00	90.0	180	360
1	179	0 52	60 00	89.0	0 51	59 00	89.5	0 51	58 00	89.5	0 50	57 00	89.5	0 50	56 00	89.4	0 49	55 00	89.4	181	359
2	178	1 44	59 59	89.0	1 43	58 59	89.0	1 42	57 59	88.9	1 41	56 59	88.9	1 39	55 59	88.9	1 38	54 59	88.9	182	358
3	177	2 36	59 58	88.5	2 34	58 58	88.5	2 33	57 58	88.4	2 31	56 58	88.4	2 29	55 58	88.4	2 27	54 58	88.3	183	357
4	176	3 28	59 56	88.0	3 26	58 56	87.9	3 23	57 56	87.9	3 21	56 56	87.9	3 19	55 56	87.8	3 17	54 56	87.7	184	356
5	175	4 20	59 54	87.5	4 17	58 54	87.4	4 14	57 54	87.3	4 12	56 54	87.3	4 09	55 54	87.2	4 06	54 54	87.1	185	355
6	174	5 12	59 52	87.0	5 08	58 52	86.9	5 05	57 52	86.8	5 02	56 51	86.7	4 58	55 51	86.6	4 55	54 51	86.6	186	354
7	173	6 04	59 49	86.5	6 00	58 49	86.4	5 56	57 49	86.3	5 52	56 48	86.2	5 48	55 48	86.1	5 44	54 48	86.0	187	353
8	172	6 55	59 45	86.0	6 51	58 45	85.9	6 47	57 45	85.7	6 42	56 45	85.7	6 38	55 44	85.5	6 33	54 44	85.4	188	352
9	171	7 47	59 42	85.5	7 42	58 41	85.3	7 37	57 41	85.2	7 32	56 40	85.1	7 27	55 40	84.9	7 22	54 40	84.8	189	351
10	170	8 39	59 37	85.0	8 34	58 37	84.8	8 28	57 36	84.7	8 22	56 36	84.5	8 17	55 36	84.4	8 11	54 35	84.2	190	350
11	169	9 31	59 32	84.4	9 25	58 32	84.3	9 18	57 31	84.1	9 13	56 31	84.0	9 06	55 30	83.8	9 00	54 30	83.6	191	349
12	168	10 22	59 27	83.9	10 16	58 26	83.8	10 09	57 26	83.6	10 03	56 25	83.4	9 56	55 25	83.2	9 48	54 24	83.0	192	348
13	167	11 14	59 21	83.4	11 07	58 20	83.2	11 00	57 20	83.0	10 52	56 19	82.8	10 45	55 18	82.6	10 37	54 18	82.5	193	347
14	166	12 06	59 15	82.9	11 58	58 13	82.7	11 50	57 13	82.5	11 42	56 12	82.3	11 34	55 12	82.1	11 26	54 11	81.9	194	346
15	165	12 57	59 08	82.4	12 49	58 07	82.1	12 41	57 06	81.9	12 32	56 05	81.7	12 23	55 04	81.5	12 14	54 04	81.3	195	345
16	164	13 49	59 01	81.8	13 40	57 59	81.6	13 31	56 58	81.4	13 22	55 57	81.1	13 13	54 57	80.9	13 03	53 56	80.7	196	344
17	163	14 40	58 53	81.3	14 31	57 51	81.1	14 21	56 50	80.8	14 12	55 49	80.5	14 02	54 48	80.3	13 51	53 47	80.1	197	343
18	162	15 31	58 44	80.8	15 22	57 43	80.5	15 12	56 42	80.2	15 01	55 40	80.0	14 51	54 39	79.7	14 40	53 38	79.4	198	342
19	161	16 23	58 35	80.2	16 12	57 34	79.9	16 02	56 32	79.6	15 51	55 31	79.4	15 40	54 30	79.1	15 28	53 29	78.8	199	341
20	160	17 14	58 26	79.7	17 03	57 24	79.4	16 52	56 23	79.1	16 40	55 21	78.8	16 28	54 20	78.5	16 16	53 19	78.2	200	340
21	159	18 05	58 16	79.1	17 53	57 14	78.8	17 42	56 12	78.5	17 29	55 11	78.2	17 17	54 09	77.9	17 04	53 08	77.6	201	339
22	158	18 56	58 05	78.6	18 44	57 03	78.2	18 31	56 01	77.9	18 19	55 00	77.6	18 06	53 58	77.3	17 52	52 56	77.0	202	338
23	157	19 47	57 54	78.0	19 34	56 52	77.7	19 21	55 50	77.3	19 08	54 48	77.0	18 54	53 46	76.6	18 40	52 44	76.3	203	337
24	156	20 37	57 42	77.4	20 24	56 40	77.1	20 11	55 38	76.7	19 57	54 36	76.4	19 42	53 34	76.0	19 28	52 32	75.7	204	336
25	155	21 28	57 30	76.9	21 14	56 27	76.5	21 00	55 25	76.1	20 46	54 23	75.7	20 31	53 21	75.4	20 15	52 19	75.0	205	335
26	154	22 19	57 17	76.3	22 04	56 14	75.9	21 49	55 12	75.5	21 35	54 09	75.1	21 19	53 07	74.7	21 03	52 05	74.4	206	334
27	153	23 09	57 03	75.7	22 54	56 00	75.3	22 39	54 57	74.9	22 23	53 55	74.5	22 07	52 52	74.1	21 50	51 50	73.7	207	333
28	152	23 59	56 49	75.1	23 44	55 46	74.7	23 28	54 43	74.3	23 11	53 40	73.8	22 54	52 37	73.4	22 37	51 35	73.0	208	332
29	151	24 50	56 34	74.5	24 33	55 31	74.1	24 17	54 27	73.6	23 59	53 24	73.2	23 42	52 22	72.8	23 24	51 19	72.4	209	331
30	150	25 40	56 19	73.9	25 23	55 15	73.4	25 05	54 11	73.0	24 48	53 08	72.5	24 29	52 05	72.1	24 11	51 03	71.7	210	330
31	149	26 29	56 02	73.3	26 12	54 58	72.8	25 54	53 54	72.3	25 35	52 51	71.9	25 17	51 48	71.4	24 57	50 45	71.0	211	329
32	148	27 19	55 45	72.6	27 01	54 41	72.2	26 42	53 37	71.7	26 23	52 33	71.2	26 04	51 30	70.7	25 44	50 27	70.3	212	328
33	147	28 09	55 27	72.0	27 50	54 23	71.5	27 31	53 19	71.0	27 11	52 15	70.5	26 50	51 12	70.0	26 30	50 08	69.6	213	327
34	146	28 58	55 09	71.4	28 38	54 04	70.8	28 19	53 00	70.3	27 58	51 56	69.8	27 37	50 52	69.3	27 16	49 49	68.8	214	326
35	145	29 47	54 49	70.7	29 27	53 44	70.2	29 06	52 40	69.6	28 45	51 36	69.1	28 24	50 32	68.6	28 01	49 29	68.1	215	325
36	144	30 36	54 29	70.0	30 15	53 24	69.5	29 54	52 19	68.9	29 32	51 15	68.4	29 10	50 11	67.9	28 47	49 07	67.4	216	324
37	143	31 25	54 08	69.4	31 03	53 03	68.8	30 41	51 57	68.1	30 19	50 53	67.7	29 56	49 49	67.2	29 32	48 45	66.6	217	323
38	142	32 13	53 46	68.7	31 51	52 40	68.1	31 28	51 35	67.5	31 05	50 30	66.9	30 41	49 26	66.4	30 17	48 23	65.9	218	322
39	141	33 02	53 23	68.0	32 39	52 17	67.4	32 15	51 12	66.8	31 51	50 07	66.2	31 27	49 03	65.6	31 02	47 59	65.1	219	321
40	140	33 50	53 00	67.2	33 26	51 53	66.6	33 02	50 48	66.0	32 37	49 43	65.4	32 12	48 38	64.9	31 46	47 34	64.3	220	320
41	139	34 37	52 35	66.5	34 13	51 29	65.9	33 48	50 23	65.3	33 23	49 17	64.7	32 57	48 13	64.1	32 30	47 09	63.5	221	319
42	138	35 25	52 09	65.8	35 00	51 03	65.1	34 34	49 56	64.5	34 08	48 51	63.9	33 42	47 46	63.3	33 14	46 42	62.7	222	318
43	137	36 12	51 43	65.0	35 46	50 36	64.3	35 20	49 29	63.7	34 53	48 24	63.1	34 26	47 19	62.5	33 58	46 15	61.9	223	317
44	136	36 59	51 15	64.2	36 33	50 08	63.6	36 06	49 01	62.9	35 38	47 55	62.3	35 10	46 51	61.6	34 41	45 46	61.0	224	316
45	135	37 46	50 46	63.4	37 19	49 39	62.7	36 51	48 32	62.1	36 22	47 26	61.4	35 53	46 21	60.8	35 24	45 17	60.2	225	315

Lat./A	LHA/F	30° A/H	30° B/P	30° Z₁/Z₂	31° A/H	31° B/P	31° Z₁/Z₂	32° A/H	32° B/P	32° Z₁/Z₂	33° A/H	33° B/P	33° Z₁/Z₂	34° A/H	34° B/P	34° Z₁/Z₂	35° A/H	35° B/P	35° Z₁/Z₂	Lat./A	LHA
45	135	37 46	50 46	63.4	37 19	49 39	62.7	36 51	48 32	62.1	36 22	47 26	61.4	35 53	46 21	60.8	35 24	45 17	60.2	225	315
46	134	38 32	50 16	62.6	38 04	49 08	61.9	37 36	48 02	61.2	37 06	46 56	60.6	36 37	45 51	59.9	36 06	44 46	59.3	226	314
47	133	39 18	49 45	61.8	38 49	48 37	61.1	38 20	47 30	60.4	37 50	46 24	59.7	37 19	45 19	59.1	36 48	44 15	58.4	227	313
48	132	40 04	49 13	61.0	39 34	48 05	60.2	39 04	46 58	59.5	38 33	45 51	58.9	38 02	44 46	58.2	37 30	43 42	57.5	228	312
49	131	40 49	48 39	60.1	40 19	47 31	59.4	39 48	46 24	58.6	39 16	45 18	57.9	38 44	44 12	57.2	38 11	43 08	56.6	229	311
50	130	41 34	48 04	59.2	41 03	46 56	58.5	40 31	45 49	57.7	39 59	44 42	57.0	39 26	43 37	56.3	38 52	42 33	55.6	230	310
51	129	42 18	47 28	58.3	41 46	46 20	57.5	41 14	45 12	56.8	40 41	44 06	56.1	40 07	43 01	55.4	39 32	41 57	54.7	231	309
52	128	43 02	46 50	57.4	42 29	45 42	56.6	41 56	44 34	55.8	41 23	43 28	55.1	40 47	42 23	54.4	40 12	41 19	53.7	232	308
53	127	43 46	46 11	56.4	43 12	45 03	55.6	42 38	43 55	54.9	42 03	42 49	54.1	41 28	41 44	53.4	40 52	40 41	52.7	233	307
54	126	44 29	45 31	55.5	43 54	44 22	54.7	43 19	43 15	53.9	42 44	42 09	53.1	42 07	41 04	52.4	41 30	40 01	51.7	234	306
55	125	45 11	44 49	54.5	44 36	43 40	53.7	44 00	42 33	52.9	43 24	41 27	52.1	42 46	40 23	51.4	42 09	39 19	50.7	235	305
56	124	45 53	44 05	53.5	45 17	42 57	52.6	44 40	41 50	51.8	44 03	40 44	51.1	43 25	39 40	50.3	42 46	38 37	49.6	236	304
57	123	46 35	43 20	52.4	45 58	42 11	51.6	45 20	41 05	50.8	44 42	39 59	50.0	44 03	38 55	49.3	43 24	37 53	48.5	237	303
58	122	47 16	42 33	51.3	46 38	41 25	50.5	45 59	40 18	49.7	45 20	39 13	48.9	44 40	38 09	48.2	44 00	37 07	47.5	238	302
59	121	47 56	41 44	50.2	47 17	40 36	49.4	46 38	39 30	48.6	45 58	38 26	47.8	45 17	37 22	47.1	44 36	36 21	46.3	239	301
60	120	48 35	40 54	49.1	47 56	39 46	48.3	47 16	38 40	47.5	46 35	37 36	46.7	45 53	36 33	45.9	45 11	35 32	45.2	240	300
61	119	49 14	40 01	47.9	48 34	38 54	47.1	47 53	37 48	46.3	47 11	36 45	45.5	46 29	35 42	44.7	45 46	34 42	44.0	241	299
62	118	49 53	39 07	46.8	49 11	38 00	45.9	48 29	36 55	45.1	47 46	35 52	44.3	47 03	34 50	43.6	46 19	33 50	42.8	242	298
63	117	50 30	38 11	45.5	49 48	37 04	44.7	49 05	36 00	43.9	48 21	34 57	43.1	47 37	33 57	42.3	46 53	32 57	41.6	243	297
64	116	51 07	37 13	44.3	50 23	36 07	43.4	49 40	35 03	42.6	48 55	34 01	41.8	48 10	33 01	41.1	47 25	32 03	40.4	244	296
65	115	51 43	36 12	43.0	50 58	35 07	42.2	50 14	34 04	41.3	49 28	33 03	40.6	48 43	32 03	39.8	47 56	31 07	39.1	245	295
66	114	52 18	35 10	41.7	51 33	34 02	40.8	50 47	33 04	40.0	50 01	32 04	39.3	49 14	31 05	38.5	48 27	30 09	37.8	246	294
67	113	52 52	34 05	40.3	52 06	33 00	39.5	51 19	32 01	38.7	50 32	31 02	37.9	49 44	30 05	37.2	48 56	29 10	36.5	247	293
68	112	53 25	32 59	38.9	52 38	31 56	38.1	51 50	30 57	37.3	51 02	29 59	36.6	50 14	29 03	35.8	49 25	28 09	35.2	248	292
69	111	53 57	31 50	37.5	53 09	30 49	36.7	52 21	29 50	35.9	51 32	28 53	35.2	50 43	27 59	34.5	49 53	27 06	33.8	249	291
70	110	54 28	30 39	36.1	53 39	29 39	35.2	52 50	28 41	34.5	52 00	27 46	33.7	51 10	26 53	33.1	50 20	26 02	32.4	250	290
71	109	54 58	29 25	34.6	54 08	28 27	33.8	53 18	27 31	33.0	52 28	26 38	32.3	51 37	25 46	31.6	50 46	24 56	31.0	251	289
72	108	55 27	28 09	33.0	54 37	27 13	32.2	53 46	26 19	31.5	52 54	25 27	30.8	52 03	24 37	30.2	51 10	23 49	29.5	252	288
73	107	55 55	26 51	31.4	55 04	25 57	30.7	54 12	25 05	30.0	53 19	24 14	29.3	52 27	23 26	28.7	51 34	22 40	28.1	253	287
74	106	56 21	25 31	29.8	55 29	24 39	29.1	54 36	23 48	28.4	53 43	23 00	27.8	52 50	22 14	27.1	51 57	21 29	26.6	254	286
75	105	56 46	24 09	28.2	55 53	23 18	27.5	55 00	22 30	26.8	54 06	21 44	26.2	53 12	21 00	25.6	52 18	20 17	25.0	255	285
76	104	57 10	22 44	26.5	56 16	21 56	25.8	55 22	21 10	25.2	54 28	20 26	24.6	53 33	19 44	24.0	52 38	19 04	23.5	256	284
77	103	57 33	21 17	24.8	56 38	20 31	24.1	55 43	19 48	23.5	54 48	19 06	23.0	53 53	18 27	22.4	52 57	17 49	21.9	257	283
78	102	57 54	19 48	23.0	56 59	19 05	22.4	56 03	18 24	21.9	55 07	17 45	21.3	54 11	17 08	20.8	53 15	16 32	20.3	258	282
79	101	58 13	18 17	21.2	57 17	17 37	20.7	56 21	16 59	20.1	55 25	16 22	19.6	54 28	15 48	19.2	53 31	15 15	18.7	259	281
80	100	58 32	16 44	19.4	57 35	16 07	18.9	56 38	15 32	18.4	55 41	14 58	17.9	54 44	14 26	17.5	53 47	13 55	17.1	260	280
81	99	58 48	15 10	17.6	57 51	14 36	17.1	56 53	14 03	16.6	55 56	13 33	16.2	54 58	13 03	15.8	54 00	12 36	15.4	261	279
82	98	59 03	13 33	15.7	58 05	13 02	15.3	57 07	12 33	14.9	56 09	12 06	14.5	55 11	11 40	14.1	54 13	11 14	13.8	262	278
83	97	59 16	11 55	13.8	58 18	11 28	13.4	57 19	11 02	13.0	56 21	10 38	12.7	55 22	10 16	12.4	54 24	9 52	12.1	263	277
84	96	59 28	10 16	11.9	58 29	9 52	11.5	57 30	9 30	11.2	56 31	9 09	10.9	55 32	8 49	10.6	54 33	8 29	10.4	264	276
85	95	59 37	8 35	9.9	58 38	8 15	9.6	57 39	7 56	9.4	56 40	7 39	9.1	55 41	7 22	8.9	54 41	7 06	8.7	265	275
86	94	59 46	6 53	8.0	58 46	6 37	7.7	57 47	6 22	7.5	56 47	6 08	7.3	55 48	5 54	7.1	54 48	5 41	7.0	266	274
87	93	59 52	5 11	6.0	58 52	4 59	5.8	57 52	4 47	5.6	56 53	4 36	5.5	55 53	4 26	5.4	54 53	4 16	5.2	267	273
88	92	59 56	3 28	4.0	58 57	3 19	3.9	57 56	3 12	3.8	56 57	3 05	3.7	55 57	2 58	3.6	54 57	2 51	3.5	268	272
89	91	59 59	1 44	2.0	58 59	1 40	1.9	57 59	1 36	1.9	56 59	1 32	1.8	55 59	1 29	1.8	54 59	1 26	1.7	269	271
90	90	60 00	0 00	0.0	59 00	0 00	0.0	58 00	0 00	0.0	57 00	0 00	0.0	56 00	0 00	0.0	55 00	0 00	0.0	270	270

N. Lat.: for LHA > 180° ... $Z_n = Z$
for LHA < 180° ... $Z_n = 360° - Z$

S. Lat.: for LHA > 180° ... $Z_n = 180° - Z$
for LHA < 180° ... $Z_n = 180° + Z$

SIGHT REDUCTION TABLE

B: (−) for 90° < LHA < 270°
Dec:(−) for Lat. contrary name

Z₁: same sign as B → Z_1: same sign as B
Z_2: (−) for F > 90°

Lat./A LHA/F	36° A/H	36° B/P	36° Z_1/Z_2	37° A/H	37° B/P	37° Z_1/Z_2	38° A/H	38° B/P	38° Z_1/Z_2	39° A/H	39° B/P	39° Z_1/Z_2	40° A/H	40° B/P	40° Z_1/Z_2	41° A/H	41° B/P	41° Z_1/Z_2	Lat./A LHA
0	0 00	54 00	90·0	0 00	53 00	90·0	0 00	52 00	90·0	0 00	51 00	90·0	0 00	50 00	90·0	0 00	49 00	90·0	180
1	0 49	54 00	89·4	0 48	53 00	89·4	0 47	52 00	89·4	0 47	51 00	89·4	0 46	50 00	89·4	0 45	49 00	89·3	181
2	1 37	53 59	88·8	1 36	52 59	88·8	1 35	51 59	88·8	1 33	50 59	88·7	1 32	49 59	88·7	1 31	48 59	88·7	182
3	2 26	53 58	88·2	2 24	52 58	88·2	2 22	51 58	88·2	2 20	50 58	88·1	2 18	49 58	88·1	2 16	48 58	88·0	183
4	3 14	53 56	87·6	3 12	52 56	87·6	3 09	51 56	87·5	3 06	50 56	87·5	3 04	49 56	87·4	3 01	48 56	87·4	184
5	4 03	53 54	87·1	3 59	52 54	87·0	3 56	51 54	86·9	3 53	50 54	86·8	3 50	49 54	86·8	3 46	48 54	86·7	185
6	4 51	53 51	86·5	4 47	52 51	86·4	4 43	51 51	86·3	4 40	50 51	86·2	4 36	49 51	86·1	4 31	48 51	86·1	186
7	5 39	53 48	85·9	5 35	52 48	85·8	5 31	51 48	85·7	5 26	50 47	85·5	5 21	49 47	85·5	5 17	48 47	85·4	187
8	6 28	53 44	85·3	6 23	52 44	85·2	6 18	51 44	85·1	6 13	50 44	84·9	6 07	49 43	84·8	6 02	48 43	84·7	188
9	7 16	53 40	84·7	7 11	52 39	84·6	7 05	51 39	84·4	6 59	50 39	84·3	6 53	49 39	84·2	6 47	48 39	84·1	189
10	8 05	53 35	84·1	7 58	52 35	83·9	7 52	51 34	83·8	7 45	50 34	83·7	7 39	49 34	83·5	7 32	48 34	83·4	190
11	8 53	53 30	83·5	8 46	52 29	83·3	8 39	51 29	83·2	8 32	50 29	83·0	8 24	49 29	82·9	8 17	48 28	82·7	191
12	9 41	53 24	82·9	9 33	52 23	82·7	9 26	51 23	82·5	9 18	50 23	82·4	9 10	49 23	82·2	9 02	48 22	82·1	192
13	10 29	53 17	82·3	10 21	52 17	82·1	10 13	51 17	81·9	10 04	50 16	81·7	9 55	49 16	81·6	9 46	48 16	81·4	193
14	11 17	53 10	81·7	11 08	52 10	81·5	10 59	51 10	81·3	10 50	50 09	81·1	10 41	49 09	80·9	10 31	48 09	80·7	194
15	12 05	53 03	81·0	11 56	52 02	80·8	11 46	51 02	80·6	11 36	50 02	80·4	11 26	49 01	80·2	11 16	48 01	80·0	195
16	12 53	52 55	80·4	12 43	51 54	80·2	12 33	50 54	80·0	12 22	49 53	79·8	12 11	48 53	79·6	12 00	47 53	79·3	196
17	13 41	52 46	79·8	13 30	51 46	79·6	13 19	50 45	79·3	13 08	49 45	79·1	12 57	48 44	78·9	12 45	47 44	78·7	197
18	14 29	52 37	79·2	14 17	51 37	78·9	14 06	50 36	78·7	13 54	49 35	78·4	13 42	48 35	78·2	13 29	47 34	78·0	198
19	15 16	52 28	78·6	15 04	51 27	78·3	14 52	50 26	78·0	14 39	49 25	77·8	14 27	48 25	77·5	14 13	47 24	77·3	199
20	16 04	52 17	77·9	15 51	51 16	77·6	15 38	50 16	77·4	15 25	49 15	77·1	15 11	48 15	76·8	14 58	47 14	76·6	200
21	16 51	52 07	77·3	16 38	51 05	77·0	16 24	50 05	76·7	16 10	49 04	76·4	15 56	48 03	76·1	15 42	47 03	75·9	201
22	17 39	51 55	76·6	17 24	50 54	76·3	17 10	49 53	76·0	16 56	48 52	75·7	16 41	47 51	75·4	16 25	46 51	75·2	202
23	18 26	51 43	76·0	18 11	50 42	75·7	17 56	49 41	75·4	17 41	48 40	75·0	17 25	47 39	74·7	17 09	46 38	74·4	203
24	19 13	51 30	75·3	18 57	50 29	75·0	18 42	49 28	74·7	18 26	48 27	74·3	18 09	47 26	74·0	17 53	46 25	73·7	204
25	20 00	51 17	74·7	19 44	50 15	74·3	19 27	49 14	74·0	19 10	48 13	73·6	18 53	47 12	73·3	18 36	46 11	73·0	205
26	20 46	51 03	74·0	20 30	50 01	73·6	20 13	49 00	73·3	19 55	47 59	72·9	19 37	46 58	72·6	19 19	45 57	72·3	206
27	21 33	50 48	73·3	21 15	49 47	73·0	20 58	48 45	72·6	20 40	47 44	72·2	20 21	46 43	71·9	20 02	45 42	71·5	207
28	22 19	50 32	72·6	22 01	49 31	72·3	21 43	48 30	71·9	21 24	47 28	71·5	21 05	46 28	71·2	20 45	45 27	70·8	208
29	23 06	50 17	72·0	22 47	49 15	71·6	22 28	48 14	71·2	22 08	47 12	70·8	21 48	46 11	70·4	21 28	45 11	70·0	209
30	23 52	50 00	71·3	23 32	48 58	70·8	23 12	47 57	70·4	22 52	46 55	70·0	22 31	45 54	69·6	22 10	44 54	69·3	210
31	24 37	49 43	70·5	24 17	48 41	70·1	23 57	47 39	69·7	23 36	46 38	69·3	23 14	45 37	68·9	22 52	44 36	68·5	211
32	25 23	49 25	69·8	25 02	48 23	69·4	24 41	47 21	69·0	24 19	46 19	68·5	23 57	45 18	68·1	23 34	44 17	67·7	212
33	26 09	49 06	69·1	25 47	48 04	68·7	25 25	47 02	68·2	25 02	46 00	67·8	24 40	44 59	67·3	24 16	43 59	66·9	213
34	26 54	48 46	68·4	26 32	47 44	67·9	26 09	46 42	67·4	25 45	45 40	67·0	25 22	44 39	66·6	24 58	43 39	66·1	214
35	27 39	48 26	67·6	27 16	47 23	67·1	26 52	46 21	66·7	26 28	45 20	66·2	26 04	44 19	65·8	25 39	43 18	65·3	215
36	28 24	48 04	66·9	28 00	47 02	66·4	27 36	46 00	65·9	27 11	44 58	65·4	26 46	43 57	65·0	26 20	42 57	64·5	216
37	29 08	47 42	66·1	28 44	46 40	65·6	28 19	45 38	65·1	27 53	44 36	64·6	27 27	43 35	64·2	27 01	42 34	63·7	217
38	29 52	47 19	65·3	29 27	46 17	64·8	29 01	45 15	64·3	28 35	44 13	63·8	28 08	43 12	63·3	27 41	42 12	62·9	218
39	30 36	46 56	64·5	30 10	45 53	64·0	29 44	44 51	63·5	29 17	43 49	63·0	28 49	42 48	62·5	28 21	41 48	62·0	219
40	31 20	46 31	63·7	30 53	45 28	63·2	30 26	44 26	62·7	29 58	43 25	62·2	29 30	42 24	61·7	29 01	41 23	61·2	220
41	32 03	46 05	62·9	31 36	45 03	62·4	31 08	44 01	61·8	30 39	42 59	61·3	30 10	41 58	60·8	29 41	40 58	60·3	221
42	32 46	45 39	62·1	32 18	44 36	61·5	31 49	43 34	61·0	31 20	42 33	60·5	30 50	41 32	59·9	30 20	40 32	59·4	222
43	33 29	45 11	61·3	33 00	44 09	60·7	32 30	43 07	60·1	32 00	42 05	59·6	31 30	41 05	59·1	30 59	40 05	58·5	223
44	34 12	44 43	60·4	33 42	43 40	59·8	33 11	42 38	59·3	32 41	41 37	58·7	32 09	40 36	58·2	31 37	39 36	57·6	224
45	34 54	44 13	59·6	34 23	43 11	59·0	33 52	42 09	58·4	33 20	41 08	57·8	32 48	40 07	57·3	32 15	39 08	56·7	225

Lat./A		36°			37°			38°			39°			40°			41°			Lat./A	
LHA	F	A/H	B/P	Z_1/Z_2	A/H	B/P	Z_1/Z_2	A/H	B/P	Z_1/Z_2	A/H	B/P	Z_1/Z_2	A/H	B/P	Z_1/Z_2	A/H	B/P	Z_1/Z_2	A	LHA
45	135	34 54	44 13	59·6	34 23	43 11	59·0	33 52	42 09	58·4	33 20	41 08	57·8	32 48	40 07	57·3	32 15	39 08	56·7	315	225
46	134	35 35	43 43	58·7	35 04	42 40	58·1	34 32	41 38	57·5	33 59	40 37	56·9	33 26	39 37	56·4	32 53	38 38	55·8	314	226
47	133	36 17	43 11	57·8	35 44	42 09	57·2	35 12	41 07	56·6	34 38	40 06	56·0	34 04	39 06	55·4	33 30	38 07	54·9	313	227
48	132	36 57	42 39	56·9	36 24	41 36	56·2	35 51	40 35	55·6	35 17	39 34	55·0	34 42	38 34	54·5	34 07	37 35	53·9	312	228
49	131	37 38	42 05	55·9	37 04	41 03	55·3	36 30	40 01	54·7	35 55	39 01	54·1	35 19	38 01	53·5	34 43	37 03	53·0	311	229
50	130	38 18	41 30	55·0	37 43	40 28	54·4	37 08	39 27	53·7	36 32	38 27	53·1	35 56	37 27	52·5	35 19	36 29	52·0	310	230
51	129	38 57	40 54	54·0	38 22	39 52	53·4	37 46	38 51	52·8	37 09	37 51	52·1	36 32	36 52	51·6	35 55	35 54	51·0	309	231
52	128	39 36	40 17	53·0	39 00	39 15	52·4	38 23	38 14	51·8	37 46	37 15	51·1	37 08	36 16	50·6	36 30	35 18	50·0	308	232
53	127	40 15	39 38	52·0	39 38	38 37	51·4	39 00	37 36	50·8	38 22	36 37	50·1	37 43	35 39	49·5	37 04	34 42	49·0	307	233
54	126	40 53	38 58	51·0	40 15	37 57	50·4	39 36	36 57	49·7	38 57	35 58	49·1	38 18	35 01	48·5	37 38	34 04	47·9	306	234
55	125	41 30	38 17	50·0	40 52	37 17	49·3	40 12	36 17	48·7	39 32	35 19	48·1	38 52	34 21	47·4	38 11	33 25	46·9	305	235
56	124	42 07	37 35	48·9	41 28	36 35	48·3	40 47	35 36	47·6	40 07	34 38	47·0	39 26	33 41	46·4	38 44	32 45	45·8	304	236
57	123	42 44	36 51	47·9	42 03	35 51	47·2	41 22	34 53	46·5	40 41	33 55	45·9	39 59	32 59	45·3	39 16	32 04	44·7	303	237
58	122	43 19	36 06	46·8	42 38	35 07	46·1	41 56	34 09	45·4	41 14	33 12	44·8	40 31	32 16	44·2	39 48	31 22	43·6	302	238
59	121	43 54	35 20	45·6	43 12	34 21	45·0	42 29	33 24	44·3	41 46	32 27	43·7	41 03	31 32	43·1	40 19	30 39	42·5	301	239
60	120	44 29	34 32	44·5	43 46	33 34	43·8	43 02	32 37	43·2	42 18	31 42	42·5	41 34	30 47	41·9	40 49	29 54	41·3	300	240
61	119	45 02	33 43	43·3	44 18	32 45	42·6	43 34	31 49	42·0	42 49	30 55	41·4	42 04	30 01	40·8	41 18	29 08	40·2	299	241
62	118	45 35	32 52	42·1	44 51	31 55	41·5	44 05	31 00	40·8	43 20	30 06	40·2	42 34	29 14	39·6	41 47	28 22	39·0	298	242
63	117	46 07	32 00	40·9	45 22	31 04	40·3	44 36	30 10	39·6	43 49	29 17	39·0	43 03	28 25	38·4	42 15	27 35	37·8	297	243
64	116	46 39	31 06	39·7	45 52	30 11	39·0	45 06	29 18	38·4	44 18	28 26	37·8	43 31	27 35	37·2	42 43	26 46	36·6	296	244
65	115	47 09	30 11	38·4	46 22	29 17	37·8	45 35	28 25	37·1	44 47	27 34	36·5	43 58	26 44	36·0	43 09	25 56	35·4	295	245
66	114	47 39	29 14	37·1	46 51	28 21	36·5	46 03	27 30	35·9	45 14	26 40	35·2	44 25	25 52	34·7	43 35	25 04	34·2	294	246
67	113	48 08	28 16	35·8	47 19	27 24	35·2	46 30	26 34	34·6	45 40	25 45	34·0	44 50	24 58	33·4	44 00	24 12	32·9	293	247
68	112	48 36	27 17	34·5	47 46	26 26	33·9	46 56	25 37	33·3	46 06	24 50	32·7	45 15	24 03	32·2	44 24	23 19	31·6	292	248
69	111	49 03	26 15	33·1	48 13	25 26	32·5	47 22	24 38	31·9	46 31	23 52	31·4	45 39	23 08	30·8	44 48	22 24	30·3	291	249
70	110	49 29	25 13	31·8	48 38	24 24	31·1	47 47	23 39	30·6	46 55	22 54	30·0	46 02	22 11	29·5	45 10	21 29	29·0	290	250
71	109	49 54	24 08	30·4	49 02	23 22	29·8	48 10	22 37	29·2	47 17	21 54	28·7	46 25	21 12	28·2	45 32	20 32	27·7	289	251
72	108	50 18	23 02	28·9	49 25	22 18	28·4	48 33	21 35	27·8	47 39	20 53	27·3	46 46	20 13	26·8	45 52	19 34	26·3	288	252
73	107	50 41	21 55	27·5	49 48	21 12	26·9	48 54	20 31	26·4	48 00	19 51	25·9	47 06	19 13	25·4	46 12	18 34	25·0	287	253
74	106	51 03	20 47	26·0	50 09	20 06	25·5	49 15	19 26	25·0	48 20	18 48	24·5	47 25	18 11	24·0	46 30	17 36	23·6	286	254
75	105	51 24	19 36	24·5	50 29	18 57	24·0	49 34	18 20	23·5	48 39	17 43	23·1	47 44	17 09	22·6	46 48	16 35	22·2	285	255
76	104	51 43	18 25	23·0	50 48	17 48	22·5	49 52	17 12	22·0	48 57	16 38	21·6	48 01	16 05	21·2	47 05	15 33	20·8	284	256
77	103	52 02	17 12	21·4	51 06	16 37	21·0	50 09	16 04	20·6	49 13	15 31	20·1	48 17	15 01	19·8	47 20	14 31	19·4	283	257
78	102	52 19	15 58	19·9	51 22	15 25	19·5	50 25	14 54	19·0	49 29	14 24	18·7	48 32	13 55	18·3	47 35	13 27	18·0	282	258
79	101	52 35	14 43	18·3	51 37	14 13	17·9	50 40	13 43	17·5	49 43	13 16	17·2	48 46	12 49	16·8	47 48	12 23	16·5	281	259
80	100	52 49	13 27	16·7	51 52	12 59	16·3	50 54	12 32	16·0	49 56	12 06	15·7	48 58	11 42	15·3	48 01	11 18	15·0	280	260
81	99	53 02	12 09	15·1	52 04	11 44	14·7	51 06	11 19	14·4	50 08	10 56	14·1	49 10	10 34	13·8	48 12	10 12	13·6	279	261
82	98	53 14	10 51	13·4	52 16	10 28	13·1	51 18	10 06	12·9	50 19	9 45	12·6	49 20	9 25	12·3	48 22	9 06	12·1	278	262
83	97	53 25	9 31	11·8	52 26	9 11	11·5	51 27	8 52	11·3	50 29	8 34	11·0	49 30	8 16	10·8	48 31	7 59	10·6	277	263
84	96	53 34	8 11	10·1	52 35	7 54	9·9	51 36	7 37	9·7	50 37	7 21	9·5	49 38	7 06	9·3	48 38	6 51	9·1	276	264
85	95	53 42	6 50	8·5	52 42	6 36	8·3	51 43	6 22	8·1	50 44	6 09	7·9	49 44	5 56	7·8	48 45	5 44	7·6	275	265
86	94	53 49	5 29	6·8	52 49	5 17	6·6	51 49	5 06	6·5	50 50	4 55	6·3	49 50	4 45	6·2	48 50	4 35	6·1	274	266
87	93	53 54	4 07	5·1	52 54	3 58	5·0	51 54	3 50	4·9	50 54	3 42	4·8	49 54	3 34	4·7	48 55	3 27	4·6	273	267
88	92	53 57	2 45	3·4	52 57	2 39	3·3	51 57	2 33	3·2	50 57	2 28	3·2	49 58	2 23	3·1	48 58	2 18	3·0	272	268
89	91	53 59	1 23	1·7	52 59	1 20	1·7	51 59	1 17	1·6	50 59	1 14	1·6	49 59	1 11	1·6	48 59	1 09	1·5	271	269
90	90	54 00	0 00	0·0	53 00	0 00	0·0	52 00	0 00	0·0	51 00	0 00	0·0	50 00	0 00	0·0	49 00	0 00	0·0	270	270

N. Lat: for LHA > 180° ... $Z_n = Z$
for LHA < 180° ... $Z_n = 360° − Z$

S. Lat: for LHA > 180° ... $Z_n = 180° − Z$
for LHA < 180° ... $Z_n = 180° + Z$

SIGHT REDUCTION TABLE

B: (–) for 90° < LHA < 270°
Dec:(–) for Lat. contrary name

Z₁: same sign as B
Z₂: (–) for F > 90°

LHA/F	F	42° A/H	42° B/P	42° Z₁/Z₂	43° A/H	43° B/P	43° Z₁/Z₂	44° A/H	44° B/P	44° Z₁/Z₂	45° A/H	45° B/P	45° Z₁/Z₂	46° A/H	46° B/P	46° Z₁/Z₂	47° A/H	47° B/P	47° Z₁/Z₂	LHA	LHA
0	180	0 00	48 00	90·0	0 00	47 00	90·0	0 00	46 00	90·0	0 00	45 00	90·0	0 00	44 00	90·0	0 00	43 00	90·0	180	360
1	179	0 45	48 00	89·3	0 44	47 00	89·3	0 43	46 00	89·3	0 42	45 00	89·3	0 42	44 00	89·3	0 41	43 00	89·3	181	359
2	178	1 29	47 59	88·7	1 28	46 59	88·7	1 26	45 59	88·7	1 25	44 59	88·6	1 23	43 59	88·6	1 22	42 59	88·5	182	358
3	177	2 14	47 58	88·0	2 12	46 58	88·0	2 09	45 58	87·9	2 07	44 58	87·9	2 05	43 58	87·8	2 03	42 58	87·8	183	357
4	176	2 58	47 56	87·3	2 55	46 56	87·3	2 53	45 56	87·2	2 50	44 56	87·2	2 47	43 56	87·1	2 44	42 56	87·1	184	356
5	175	3 43	47 53	86·6	3 39	46 53	86·6	3 36	45 53	86·5	3 32	44 53	86·5	3 28	43 53	86·4	3 24	42 53	86·3	185	355
6	174	4 27	47 51	86·0	4 23	46 51	85·9	4 19	45 51	85·8	4 14	44 51	85·7	4 10	43 51	85·7	4 05	42 51	85·6	186	354
7	173	5 12	47 47	85·3	5 07	46 47	85·2	5 02	45 47	85·1	4 57	44 47	85·0	4 51	43 47	85·0	4 46	42 47	84·9	187	353
8	172	5 56	47 43	84·6	5 51	46 43	84·5	5 45	45 43	84·4	5 39	44 43	84·3	5 33	43 43	84·2	5 27	42 43	84·1	188	352
9	171	6 41	47 37	84·0	6 34	46 39	83·8	6 28	45 39	83·7	6 21	44 39	83·6	6 14	43 39	83·5	6 07	42 39	83·4	189	351
10	170	7 25	47 34	83·3	7 18	46 34	83·1	7 11	45 34	83·0	7 03	44 34	82·9	6 56	43 34	82·8	6 48	42 34	82·7	190	350
11	169	8 09	47 28	82·6	8 01	46 28	82·4	7 53	45 28	82·3	7 45	44 28	82·2	7 37	43 28	82·0	7 29	42 28	81·9	191	349
12	168	8 53	47 22	81·9	8 45	46 22	81·8	8 36	45 22	81·6	8 27	44 22	81·5	8 18	43 22	81·3	8 09	42 22	81·2	192	348
13	167	9 37	47 16	81·1	9 28	46 15	81·1	9 19	45 15	80·9	9 09	44 15	80·7	8 59	43 15	80·6	8 49	42 16	80·4	193	347
14	166	10 21	47 08	80·5	10 11	46 08	80·3	10 01	45 08	80·2	9 51	44 08	80·0	9 40	43 08	79·8	9 30	42 08	79·7	194	346
15	165	11 05	47 01	79·8	10 55	46 00	79·6	10 44	45 00	79·5	10 33	44 00	79·3	10 21	43 00	79·1	10 10	42 01	78·9	195	345
16	164	11 49	46 52	79·1	11 38	45 52	78·8	11 26	44 52	78·7	11 14	43 52	78·5	11 02	42 52	78·3	10 50	41 52	78·2	196	344
17	163	12 33	46 43	78·4	12 21	45 43	78·1	12 08	44 43	78·0	11 56	43 43	77·8	11 43	42 43	77·6	11 30	41 44	77·4	197	343
18	162	13 17	46 34	77·7	13 04	45 34	77·5	12 51	44 34	77·3	12 37	43 34	77·1	12 24	42 34	76·8	12 10	41 34	76·6	198	342
19	161	14 00	46 24	77·0	13 46	45 24	76·8	13 33	44 24	76·5	13 19	43 24	76·3	13 04	42 24	76·1	12 50	41 24	75·9	199	341
20	160	14 43	46 13	76·3	14 29	45 13	76·1	14 15	44 13	75·8	14 00	43 13	75·6	13 45	42 13	75·3	13 29	41 14	75·1	200	340
21	159	15 27	46 02	75·6	15 12	45 02	75·3	14 56	44 02	75·1	14 41	43 02	74·8	14 25	42 02	74·6	14 09	41 03	74·3	201	339
22	158	16 10	45 50	74·9	15 54	44 50	74·6	15 38	43 50	74·3	15 22	42 50	74·1	15 05	41 50	73·8	14 48	40 51	73·5	202	338
23	157	16 53	45 38	74·1	16 36	44 38	73·9	16 19	43 38	73·6	16 02	42 38	73·3	15 45	41 38	73·0	15 27	40 39	72·8	203	337
24	156	17 36	45 25	73·4	17 18	44 25	73·1	17 01	43 25	72·8	16 43	42 25	72·5	16 25	41 25	72·2	16 06	41 34	72·0	204	336
25	155	18 18	45 11	72·7	18 00	44 11	72·4	17 42	43 11	72·1	17 23	42 11	71·8	17 04	41 12	71·5	16 45	40 26	71·2	205	335
26	154	19 01	44 57	71·9	18 42	43 57	71·6	18 23	42 57	71·3	18 03	41 57	71·0	17 44	40 57	70·7	17 24	39 58	70·4	206	334
27	153	19 43	44 42	71·2	19 24	43 42	70·8	19 04	42 42	70·5	18 43	41 42	70·2	18 23	40 43	69·9	18 02	39 48	69·6	207	333
28	152	20 25	44 26	70·4	20 05	43 26	70·1	19 44	42 26	69·7	19 23	41 27	69·4	19 02	40 27	69·1	18 40	39 48	68·8	208	332
29	151	21 07	44 10	69·6	20 46	43 10	69·3	20 25	42 10	68·9	20 03	41 10	68·6	19 41	40 11	68·3	19 18	39 12	67·9	209	331
30	150	21 49	43 53	68·9	21 27	42 53	68·5	21 05	41 53	68·1	20 42	40 54	67·8	20 19	39 54	67·4	19 56	38 55	67·1	210	330
31	149	22 30	43 35	68·1	22 08	42 35	67·7	21 45	41 36	67·3	21 21	40 36	66·9	20 58	39 37	66·6	20 34	38 38	66·3	211	329
32	148	23 11	43 17	67·3	22 48	42 17	66·9	22 24	41 17	66·5	22 00	40 18	66·2	21 36	39 19	65·8	21 11	38 20	65·4	212	328
33	147	23 53	42 58	66·5	23 28	41 58	66·1	23 04	40 58	65·7	22 39	39 59	65·3	22 14	39 00	65·0	21 48	38 02	64·6	213	327
34	146	24 34	42 38	65·7	24 08	41 38	65·3	23 43	40 39	64·9	23 17	39 40	64·5	22 51	38 41	64·1	22 25	37 42	63·7	214	326
35	145	25 14	42 18	64·9	24 48	41 18	64·5	24 22	40 18	64·1	23 56	39 19	63·7	23 29	38 21	63·3	23 02	37 23	62·9	215	325
36	144	25 54	41 56	64·1	25 28	40 57	63·6	25 01	39 57	63·2	24 34	38 58	62·8	24 06	38 00	62·4	23 38	37 02	62·0	216	324
37	143	26 34	41 34	63·2	26 07	40 35	62·8	25 39	39 35	62·4	25 11	38 37	61·9	24 43	37 38	61·5	24 14	36 41	61·1	217	323
38	142	27 14	41 11	62·4	26 46	40 12	61·9	26 17	39 13	61·5	25 48	38 14	61·1	25 19	37 16	60·7	24 50	36 19	60·3	218	322
39	141	27 53	40 48	61·5	27 24	39 48	61·1	26 55	38 50	60·6	26 25	37 51	60·2	25 55	36 53	59·8	25 25	35 56	59·4	219	321
40	140	28 32	40 23	60·7	28 02	39 24	60·2	27 32	38 25	59·8	27 02	37 27	59·3	26 31	36 30	58·9	26 00	35 32	58·5	220	320
41	139	29 11	39 58	59·8	28 40	38 59	59·3	28 10	38 01	58·9	27 38	37 03	58·4	27 07	36 05	58·0	26 35	35 08	57·6	221	319
42	138	29 49	39 32	58·9	29 18	38 33	58·4	28 46	37 35	58·0	28 14	36 37	57·5	27 42	35 40	57·1	27 09	34 43	56·6	222	318
43	137	30 27	39 05	58·0	29 55	38 06	57·5	29 23	37 08	57·1	28 50	36 11	56·6	28 17	35 14	56·1	27 43	34 18	55·7	223	317
44	136	31 05	38 37	57·1	30 32	37 39	56·6	29 59	36 41	56·1	29 25	35 44	55·7	28 51	34 47	55·2	28 17	33 51	54·8	224	316
45	135	31 42	38 09	56·2	31 08	37 10	55·7	30 34	36 13	55·2	30 00	35 16	54·7	29 25	34 20	54·3	28 50	33 24	53·8	225	315

Lat./A LHA/F	A	42° A/H	42° B/P	42° Z₁/Z₂	43° A/H	43° B/P	43° Z₁/Z₂	44° A/H	44° B/P	44° Z₁/Z₂	45° A/H	45° B/P	45° Z₁/Z₂	46° A/H	46° B/P	46° Z₁/Z₂	47° A/H	47° B/P	47° Z₁/Z₂	Lat./A LHA	A
45	135	31 42	38 09	56.2	31 08	37 10	55.7	30 34	36 13	55.2	30 00	35 16	54.7	29 25	34 20	54.3	28 50	33 24	53.8	225	315
46	134	32 19	37 39	55.3	31 45	36 41	54.8	31 10	35 44	54.3	30 34	34 47	53.8	29 59	33 51	53.3	29 23	32 56	52.9	226	314
47	133	32 55	37 08	54.3	32 20	36 11	53.8	31 45	35 14	53.3	31 08	34 18	52.8	30 32	33 22	52.4	29 55	32 27	51.9	227	313
48	132	33 31	36 37	53.4	32 55	35 40	52.9	32 19	34 43	52.3	31 42	33 47	51.9	31 05	32 52	51.4	30 27	31 58	50.9	228	312
49	131	34 07	36 05	52.4	33 30	35 08	51.9	32 53	34 11	51.4	32 15	33 16	50.9	31 37	32 21	50.4	30 59	31 27	49.9	229	311
50	130	34 42	35 31	51.4	34 04	34 35	50.9	33 26	33 39	50.4	32 48	32 44	49.9	32 09	31 50	49.4	31 30	30 56	48.9	230	310
51	129	35 17	34 57	50.4	34 38	34 01	49.9	33 59	33 05	49.4	33 20	32 11	48.9	32 40	31 17	48.4	32 00	30 24	47.9	231	309
52	128	35 51	34 22	49.4	35 12	33 26	48.9	34 32	32 31	48.4	33 52	31 37	47.9	33 11	30 44	47.4	32 30	29 52	46.9	232	308
53	127	36 24	33 45	48.4	35 45	32 50	47.9	35 04	31 56	47.3	34 24	31 02	46.9	33 42	30 10	46.3	33 00	29 18	45.9	233	307
54	126	36 57	33 08	47.4	36 17	32 13	46.8	35 35	31 20	46.3	34 54	30 27	45.8	34 12	29 35	45.3	33 29	28 44	44.8	234	306
55	125	37 30	32 30	46.3	36 48	31 36	45.8	36 06	30 43	45.2	35 24	29 50	44.7	34 41	28 59	44.2	33 58	28 08	43.8	235	305
56	124	38 02	31 51	45.2	37 19	30 57	44.7	36 37	30 04	44.2	35 53	29 13	43.6	35 10	28 22	43.2	34 26	27 32	42.7	236	304
57	123	38 33	31 10	44.1	37 50	30 17	43.6	37 06	29 25	43.1	36 21	28 34	42.6	35 38	27 45	42.1	34 53	26 56	41.6	237	303
58	122	39 04	30 29	43.0	38 20	29 36	42.5	37 36	28 45	42.0	36 51	27 55	41.5	36 06	27 06	41.0	35 20	26 18	40.5	238	302
59	121	39 34	29 46	41.9	38 49	28 55	41.4	38 04	28 04	40.9	37 19	27 15	40.4	36 33	26 27	39.9	35 46	25 39	39.4	239	301
60	120	40 04	29 03	40.8	39 18	28 12	40.2	38 32	27 22	39.7	37 46	26 34	39.2	36 59	25 46	38.8	36 12	25 00	38.3	240	300
61	119	40 32	28 18	39.6	39 46	27 28	39.1	38 59	26 39	38.6	38 12	25 52	38.1	37 25	25 05	37.6	36 37	24 20	37.2	241	299
62	118	41 00	27 32	38.5	40 13	26 43	37.9	39 26	25 56	37.4	38 38	25 09	36.9	37 50	24 23	36.5	37 02	23 39	36.0	242	298
63	117	41 28	26 45	37.3	40 40	25 58	36.8	39 52	25 11	36.3	39 03	24 25	35.8	38 14	23 40	35.3	37 25	22 57	34.9	243	297
64	116	41 54	25 58	36.1	41 06	25 11	35.6	40 17	24 25	35.1	39 28	23 40	34.6	38 38	22 57	34.1	37 48	22 14	33.7	244	296
65	115	42 20	25 09	34.9	41 31	24 23	34.4	40 41	23 38	33.9	39 51	22 55	33.4	39 01	22 12	33.0	38 11	21 31	32.5	245	295
66	114	42 45	24 19	33.6	41 55	23 34	33.1	41 05	22 50	32.7	40 14	22 08	32.2	39 23	21 27	31.8	38 32	20 46	31.3	246	294
67	113	43 10	23 28	32.4	42 19	22 44	31.9	41 28	22 02	31.4	40 37	21 21	31.0	39 45	20 40	30.5	38 53	20 01	30.1	247	293
68	112	43 33	22 35	31.1	42 42	21 53	30.6	41 50	21 12	30.2	40 58	20 32	29.7	40 06	19 53	29.3	39 13	19 15	28.9	248	292
69	111	43 56	21 42	29.8	43 04	21 01	29.4	42 11	20 22	28.9	41 19	19 43	28.5	40 26	19 05	28.1	39 33	18 29	27.7	249	291
70	110	44 18	20 48	28.5	43 25	20 08	28.1	42 32	19 30	27.7	41 38	18 53	27.2	40 45	18 17	26.8	39 51	17 41	26.5	250	290
71	109	44 38	19 53	27.2	43 45	19 15	26.8	42 52	18 38	26.4	41 57	18 02	26.0	41 03	17 27	25.6	40 09	16 53	25.2	251	289
72	108	44 58	18 57	25.9	44 04	18 20	25.5	43 10	17 45	25.1	42 16	17 10	24.7	41 21	16 37	24.3	40 26	16 05	24.0	252	288
73	107	45 17	17 59	24.6	44 23	17 24	24.1	43 28	16 51	23.8	42 33	16 18	23.4	41 38	15 46	23.0	40 42	15 15	22.7	253	287
74	106	45 35	17 01	23.2	44 40	16 28	22.8	43 45	15 56	22.4	42 49	15 25	22.1	41 54	14 54	21.7	40 58	14 25	21.4	254	286
75	105	45 53	16 02	21.8	44 57	15 31	21.4	44 01	15 00	21.1	43 05	14 31	20.8	42 09	14 02	20.4	41 12	13 34	20.1	255	285
76	104	46 09	15 02	20.4	45 12	14 34	20.1	44 16	14 04	19.7	43 19	13 36	19.4	42 23	13 09	19.1	41 26	12 43	18.8	256	284
77	103	46 24	14 02	19.0	45 27	13 34	18.7	44 30	13 07	18.4	43 33	12 41	18.1	42 36	12 15	17.8	41 39	11 51	17.5	257	283
78	102	46 38	13 00	17.6	45 40	12 34	17.3	44 43	12 09	17.0	43 46	11 45	16.7	42 48	11 21	16.5	41 51	10 58	16.2	258	282
79	101	46 51	11 58	16.2	45 53	11 34	15.9	44 55	11 11	15.6	43 57	10 48	15.4	43 00	10 26	15.1	42 02	10 05	14.9	259	281
80	100	47 03	10 55	14.8	46 04	10 33	14.5	45 06	10 12	14.2	44 08	9 51	14.0	43 10	9 31	13.8	42 12	9 12	13.6	260	280
81	99	47 13	9 51	13.3	46 15	9 31	13.1	45 16	9 12	12.8	44 18	8 53	12.6	43 19	8 35	12.4	42 21	8 18	12.2	261	279
82	98	47 23	8 47	11.9	46 24	8 28	11.6	45 26	8 12	11.4	44 27	7 55	11.2	43 28	7 39	11.1	42 29	7 24	10.9	262	278
83	97	47 32	7 42	10.4	46 33	7 27	10.2	45 34	7 12	10.0	44 34	6 57	9.9	43 35	6 43	9.5	42 36	6 29	9.5	263	277
84	96	47 39	6 37	8.9	46 40	6 24	8.8	45 41	6 11	8.6	44 41	5 58	8.5	43 42	5 46	8.3	42 42	5 34	8.2	264	276
85	95	47 46	5 32	7.4	46 46	5 20	7.3	45 46	5 09	7.1	44 47	4 59	7.1	43 47	4 49	6.9	42 48	4 39	6.8	265	275
86	94	47 51	4 26	6.0	46 51	4 17	5.9	45 51	4 08	5.7	44 52	3 59	5.6	43 52	3 51	5.6	42 52	3 43	5.5	266	274
87	93	47 55	3 20	4.5	46 55	3 13	4.4	45 55	3 06	4.3	44 55	3 00	4.2	43 55	2 54	4.2	42 56	2 48	4.1	267	273
88	92	47 58	2 13	3.0	46 58	2 09	2.9	45 58	2 04	2.9	44 58	2 00	2.8	43 58	1 56	2.8	42 58	1 52	2.7	268	272
89	91	47 59	1 07	1.5	46 59	1 04	1.5	45 59	1 02	1.4	44 59	1 00	1.4	43 59	0 58	1.4	42 59	0 56	1.4	269	271
90	90	48 00	0 00	0.0	47 00	0 00	0.0	46 00	0 00	0.0	45 00	0 00	0.0	44 00	0 00	0.0	43 00	0 00	0.0	270	270

N. Lat.: for LHA > 180° .... $Z_n = Z$
       for LHA < 180° .... $Z_n = 360° − Z$

S. Lat.: for LHA > 180° .... $Z_n = 180° − Z$
       for LHA < 180° .... $Z_n = 180° + Z$

SIGHT REDUCTION TABLE

B: (−) for 90° < LHA < 270°
Dec:(−) for Lat. contrary name

Z₁: same sign as B
Z₂: (−) for F > 90°

LHA/F	F	48° A/H	48° B/P	48° Z_1/Z_2	49° A/H	49° B/P	49° Z_1/Z_2	50° A/H	50° B/P	50° Z_1/Z_2	51° A/H	51° B/P	51° Z_1/Z_2	52° A/H	52° B/P	52° Z_1/Z_2	53° A/H	53° B/P	53° Z_1/Z_2	LHA	Lat./A
0	180	0 00	42 00	90.0	0 00	41 00	90.0	0 00	40 00	90.0	0 00	39 00	90.0	0 00	38 00	90.0	0 00	37 00	90.0	180	360
1	179	0 40	42 00	89.3	0 39	41 00	89.2	0 39	40 00	89.2	0 38	39 00	89.2	0 37	38 00	89.2	0 36	37 00	89.2	181	359
2	178	1 20	41 59	88.5	1 19	40 59	88.5	1 17	39 59	88.5	1 16	38 59	88.4	1 14	37 59	88.4	1 12	36 59	88.4	182	358
3	177	2 00	41 58	87.8	1 58	40 58	87.7	1 56	39 58	87.7	1 53	38 58	87.7	1 51	37 58	87.6	1 48	36 58	87.6	183	357
4	176	2 41	41 56	87.0	2 37	40 56	87.0	2 34	39 56	86.9	2 31	38 56	86.9	2 28	37 56	86.8	2 24	36 56	86.8	184	356
5	175	3 21	41 53	86.3	3 17	40 54	86.2	3 13	39 54	86.2	3 09	38 54	86.1	3 05	37 54	86.1	3 00	36 54	86.0	185	355
6	174	4 01	41 51	85.5	3 56	40 51	85.5	3 51	39 51	85.4	3 46	38 51	85.3	3 41	37 51	85.3	3 36	36 51	85.2	186	354
7	173	4 41	41 47	84.8	4 36	40 47	84.7	4 30	39 47	84.6	4 24	38 47	84.6	4 18	37 48	84.5	4 12	36 48	84.4	187	353
8	172	5 21	41 43	84.0	5 14	40 43	83.9	5 08	39 43	83.9	5 01	38 44	83.8	4 55	37 44	83.7	4 48	36 44	83.6	188	352
9	171	6 01	41 39	83.3	5 53	40 39	83.2	5 46	39 39	83.1	5 39	38 39	83.0	5 32	37 39	82.9	5 24	36 40	82.8	189	351
10	170	6 40	41 34	82.5	6 33	40 34	82.4	6 25	39 34	82.3	6 16	38 34	82.2	6 08	37 35	82.1	6 00	36 35	82.0	190	350
11	169	7 20	41 28	81.8	7 11	40 28	81.7	7 03	39 29	81.5	6 54	38 29	81.4	6 45	37 29	81.3	6 36	36 29	81.2	191	349
12	168	8 00	41 22	81.0	7 50	40 22	80.9	7 41	39 23	80.8	7 31	38 23	80.6	7 21	37 23	80.5	7 11	36 24	80.4	192	348
13	167	8 39	41 16	80.3	8 29	40 16	80.1	8 19	39 16	80.0	8 08	38 16	79.8	7 58	37 17	79.7	7 47	36 17	79.6	193	347
14	166	9 19	41 09	79.5	9 08	40 09	79.3	8 57	39 09	79.2	8 45	38 09	79.0	8 34	37 10	78.9	8 22	36 10	78.7	194	346
15	165	9 58	41 01	78.7	9 47	40 01	78.6	9 35	39 02	78.4	9 22	38 02	78.2	9 10	37 02	78.1	8 58	36 03	77.9	195	345
16	164	10 38	40 53	78.0	10 25	39 53	77.8	10 12	38 53	77.6	9 59	37 54	77.4	9 46	36 54	77.3	9 33	35 55	77.1	196	344
17	163	11 17	40 44	77.2	11 04	39 44	77.0	10 50	38 45	76.8	10 36	37 45	76.6	10 22	36 46	76.5	10 08	35 47	76.3	197	343
18	162	11 56	40 34	76.4	11 42	39 35	76.2	11 27	38 35	76.0	11 13	37 36	75.8	10 58	36 37	75.6	10 43	35 38	75.5	198	342
19	161	12 35	40 25	75.6	12 20	39 25	75.4	12 05	38 26	75.2	11 49	37 26	75.0	11 34	36 27	74.8	11 18	35 28	74.6	199	341
20	160	13 14	40 14	74.9	12 58	39 15	74.6	12 42	38 15	74.4	12 26	37 16	74.2	12 09	36 17	74.0	11 53	35 18	73.8	200	340
21	159	13 52	40 03	74.1	13 36	39 04	73.8	13 19	38 04	73.6	13 02	37 05	73.4	12 45	36 06	73.2	12 27	35 06	73.0	201	339
22	158	14 31	39 51	73.3	14 14	38 52	73.0	13 56	37 53	72.8	13 38	36 54	72.6	13 20	35 55	72.3	13 02	34 56	72.1	202	338
23	157	15 09	39 39	72.5	14 51	38 40	72.2	14 33	37 41	72.0	14 14	36 42	71.7	13 55	35 43	71.5	13 36	34 45	71.3	203	337
24	156	15 48	39 26	71.7	15 29	38 27	71.4	15 09	37 28	71.2	14 50	36 30	70.9	14 30	35 31	70.7	14 10	34 33	70.4	204	336
25	155	16 25	39 13	70.9	16 06	38 14	70.6	15 46	37 15	70.3	15 25	36 17	70.1	15 05	35 18	69.8	14 44	34 20	69.6	205	335
26	154	17 03	38 59	70.1	16 43	38 00	69.8	16 22	37 01	69.5	16 01	36 03	69.2	15 39	35 05	69.0	15 18	34 07	68.7	206	334
27	153	17 41	38 44	69.3	17 20	37 46	69.0	16 58	36 47	68.7	16 36	35 49	68.4	16 14	34 51	68.1	15 51	33 53	67.9	207	333
28	152	18 19	38 28	68.4	17 56	37 30	68.1	17 34	36 32	67.8	17 11	35 34	67.5	16 48	34 36	67.3	16 25	33 38	67.0	208	332
29	151	18 56	38 13	67.6	18 33	37 15	67.3	18 09	36 16	67.0	17 46	35 18	66.7	17 22	34 21	66.4	16 58	33 23	66.1	209	331
30	150	19 33	37 57	66.8	19 09	36 58	66.5	18 45	36 00	66.1	18 20	35 03	65.8	17 56	34 05	65.5	17 31	33 08	65.2	210	330
31	149	20 10	37 40	65.9	19 45	36 41	65.6	19 20	35 44	65.3	18 55	34 46	65.0	18 29	33 49	64.7	18 03	32 52	64.4	211	329
32	148	20 46	37 23	65.1	20 21	36 23	64.8	19 55	35 26	64.4	19 29	34 29	64.1	19 02	33 32	63.8	18 36	32 35	63.5	212	328
33	147	21 22	37 03	64.2	20 56	36 06	63.9	20 30	35 08	63.6	20 03	34 11	63.2	19 35	33 14	62.9	19 08	32 18	62.6	213	327
34	146	21 58	36 44	63.4	21 31	35 47	63.0	21 04	34 49	62.7	20 36	33 53	62.3	20 08	32 56	62.0	19 40	32 00	61.7	214	326
35	145	22 34	36 25	62.5	22 06	35 27	62.1	21 38	34 30	61.8	21 10	33 33	61.4	20 41	32 37	61.1	20 12	31 41	60.8	215	325
36	144	23 10	36 04	61.6	22 41	35 07	61.3	22 12	34 10	60.9	21 43	33 14	60.5	21 13	32 18	60.2	20 43	31 22	59.9	216	324
37	143	23 45	35 43	60.8	23 15	34 46	60.4	22 45	33 50	60.0	22 15	32 53	59.6	21 45	31 58	59.3	21 14	31 02	59.0	217	323
38	142	24 20	35 21	59.9	23 49	34 25	59.5	23 19	33 28	59.1	22 48	32 33	58.7	22 16	31 37	58.4	21 45	30 42	58.0	218	322
39	141	24 54	34 59	59.0	24 23	34 02	58.7	23 52	33 07	58.2	23 20	32 11	57.8	22 48	31 16	57.5	22 15	30 21	57.1	219	321
40	140	25 28	34 36	58.1	24 57	33 40	57.7	24 24	32 44	57.3	23 52	31 49	56.9	23 19	30 54	56.5	22 45	30 00	56.2	220	320
41	139	26 02	34 12	57.1	25 30	33 16	56.7	24 57	32 21	56.3	24 23	31 26	56.0	23 49	30 32	55.6	23 15	29 38	55.2	221	319
42	138	26 36	33 47	56.2	26 02	32 52	55.8	25 28	31 57	55.4	24 54	31 02	55.0	24 20	30 08	54.6	23 45	29 15	54.3	222	318
43	137	27 09	33 22	55.3	26 35	32 27	54.9	26 00	31 32	54.5	25 25	30 38	54.1	24 50	29 45	53.7	24 14	28 52	53.3	223	317
44	136	27 42	32 56	54.3	27 07	32 01	53.9	26 31	31 07	53.5	25 55	30 13	53.1	25 19	29 20	52.7	24 43	28 28	52.4	224	316
45	135	28 14	32 29	53.4	27 38	31 35	53.0	27 02	30 41	52.5	26 25	29 48	52.1	25 48	28 55	51.8	25 11	28 03	51.4	225	315

Lat. / A	48°			49°			50°			51°			52°			53°			Lat. / A
LHA/F	A/H	B/P	Z₁/Z₂	A/H	B/P	Z₁/Z₂	A/H	B/P	Z₁/Z₂	A/H	B/P	Z₁/Z₂	A/H	B/P	Z₁/Z₂	A/H	B/P	Z₁/Z₂	LHA
135	28 14	32 29	53.4	27 38	31 35	53.0	27 02	30 41	52.5	26 25	29 48	52.1	25 48	28 55	51.8	25 11	28 03	51.4	225
134	28 46	32 01	52.4	28 10	31 08	52.0	27 32	30 14	51.6	26 55	29 22	51.2	26 17	28 29	50.8	25 39	27 38	50.4	226
133	29 18	31 31	51.4	28 40	30 40	51.0	28 02	29 47	50.6	27 25	28 55	50.2	26 46	28 03	49.8	26 07	27 12	49.4	227
132	29 49	31 04	50.5	29 11	30 11	50.0	28 32	29 19	49.6	27 53	28 27	49.2	27 14	27 36	48.8	26 34	26 46	48.4	228
131	30 20	30 34	49.5	29 41	29 42	49.0	29 01	28 50	48.6	28 21	27 59	48.2	27 41	27 08	47.8	27 01	26 18	47.4	229
130	30 50	30 04	48.5	30 10	29 12	48.0	29 30	28 20	47.6	28 49	27 30	47.2	28 08	26 40	46.8	27 27	25 51	46.4	230
129	31 20	29 32	47.5	30 39	28 41	47.0	29 58	27 50	46.6	29 17	27 00	46.2	28 35	26 11	45.8	27 53	25 22	45.4	231
128	31 49	29 00	46.4	31 08	28 09	46.0	30 26	27 19	45.6	29 44	26 30	45.2	29 01	25 41	44.8	28 19	24 53	44.4	232
127	32 18	28 27	45.4	31 36	27 37	45.0	30 53	26 48	44.5	30 10	25 59	44.1	29 27	25 11	43.7	28 44	24 24	43.3	233
126	32 46	27 53	44.4	32 03	27 04	43.9	31 20	26 15	43.5	30 36	25 27	43.1	29 52	24 40	42.7	29 08	23 53	42.3	234
125	33 14	27 19	43.3	32 30	26 30	42.9	31 46	25 42	42.4	31 02	24 55	42.0	30 17	24 08	41.6	29 32	23 23	41.2	235
124	33 42	26 44	42.2	32 57	25 55	41.8	32 12	25 08	41.4	31 27	24 22	41.0	30 41	23 36	40.6	29 56	22 51	40.2	236
123	34 08	26 07	41.1	33 23	25 20	40.7	32 37	24 34	40.3	31 51	23 48	39.9	31 05	23 03	39.5	30 19	22 19	39.1	237
122	34 34	25 30	40.1	33 48	24 44	39.6	33 02	23 58	39.2	32 15	23 14	38.8	31 28	22 29	38.4	30 41	21 46	38.0	238
121	35 00	24 53	39.0	34 13	24 07	38.5	33 26	23 22	38.1	32 39	22 38	37.7	31 51	21 55	37.3	31 03	21 13	37.0	239
120	35 25	24 14	37.8	34 37	23 30	37.4	33 50	22 46	37.0	33 02	22 03	36.6	32 13	21 20	36.2	31 25	20 39	35.9	240
119	35 49	23 35	36.7	35 01	22 51	36.3	34 14	22 08	35.9	33 24	21 26	35.5	32 35	20 45	35.1	31 46	20 04	34.8	241
118	36 13	22 55	35.6	35 24	22 12	35.2	34 35	21 30	34.8	33 45	20 49	34.4	32 56	20 09	34.0	32 06	19 29	33.7	242
117	36 36	22 14	34.4	35 46	21 32	34.0	34 56	20 51	33.6	34 06	20 11	33.3	33 16	19 32	32.9	32 26	18 53	32.5	243
116	36 58	21 32	33.3	36 08	20 52	32.9	35 17	20 12	32.5	34 27	19 33	32.1	33 36	18 54	31.8	32 45	18 17	31.4	244
115	37 20	20 50	32.1	36 29	20 10	31.7	35 38	19 32	31.3	34 47	18 54	31.0	33 55	18 16	30.6	33 03	17 40	30.3	245
114	37 41	20 07	30.9	36 49	19 28	30.5	35 58	18 51	30.2	35 06	18 14	29.8	34 13	17 38	29.5	33 21	17 02	29.1	246
113	38 01	19 23	29.7	37 09	18 46	29.4	36 17	18 09	29.0	35 24	17 33	28.6	34 31	16 59	28.3	33 38	16 24	28.0	247
112	38 21	18 38	28.5	37 28	18 02	28.2	36 35	17 27	27.8	35 42	16 53	27.5	34 48	16 19	27.1	33 55	15 46	26.8	248
111	38 40	17 53	27.3	37 46	17 18	27.0	36 53	16 44	26.6	35 59	16 11	26.3	35 05	15 38	26.0	34 11	15 07	25.7	249
110	38 58	17 07	26.1	38 04	16 33	25.7	37 10	16 01	25.4	36 15	15 29	25.1	35 21	14 58	24.8	34 26	14 27	24.5	250
109	39 15	16 20	24.9	38 20	15 48	24.5	37 26	15 17	24.2	36 31	14 46	23.9	35 36	14 16	23.6	34 41	13 47	23.3	251
108	39 31	15 33	23.6	38 36	15 02	23.3	37 41	14 32	23.0	36 46	14 03	22.7	35 50	13 34	22.4	34 55	13 07	22.1	252
107	39 47	14 45	22.4	38 51	14 16	22.1	37 56	13 47	21.8	37 00	13 19	21.5	36 04	12 52	21.2	35 08	12 25	20.9	253
106	40 02	13 56	21.1	39 06	13 28	20.8	38 10	13 01	20.5	37 13	12 35	20.3	36 17	12 09	20.0	35 21	11 44	19.8	254
105	40 16	13 07	19.8	39 19	12 41	19.5	38 23	12 15	19.3	37 26	11 50	19.0	36 29	11 26	18.8	35 33	11 02	18.5	255
104	40 29	12 17	18.5	39 32	11 53	18.3	38 35	11 28	18.0	37 38	11 05	17.6	36 41	10 42	17.6	35 44	10 20	17.3	256
103	40 41	11 27	17.3	39 44	11 04	17.0	38 47	10 41	16.8	37 49	10 19	16.5	36 52	9 58	16.3	35 54	9 37	16.1	257
102	40 53	10 36	16.0	39 55	10 15	15.7	38 57	9 54	15.5	38 00	9 33	15.3	37 02	9 14	15.1	36 04	8 54	14.9	258
101	41 04	9 45	14.7	40 05	9 25	14.4	39 07	9 06	14.2	38 09	8 47	14.0	37 11	8 29	13.9	36 13	8 11	13.7	259
100	41 13	8 53	13.3	40 15	8 35	13.2	39 16	8 17	13.0	38 18	8 00	12.8	37 19	7 44	12.6	36 21	7 27	12.5	260
99	41 22	8 01	12.0	40 23	7 45	11.9	39 25	7 29	11.7	38 26	7 13	11.5	37 27	6 58	11.4	36 28	6 43	11.2	261
98	41 30	7 09	10.7	40 31	6 54	10.5	39 32	6 40	10.4	38 33	6 26	10.3	37 34	6 12	10.1	36 35	5 59	10.0	262
97	41 37	6 16	9.4	40 38	6 03	9.2	39 40	5 50	9.1	38 40	5 38	9.0	37 40	5 26	8.7	36 41	5 15	8.7	263
96	41 43	5 23	8.1	40 44	5 12	7.9	39 44	5 01	7.8	38 45	4 50	7.7	37 45	4 40	7.5	36 46	4 30	7.5	264
95	41 48	4 29	6.7	40 49	4 20	6.6	39 49	4 11	6.5	38 49	4 02	6.4	37 50	3 54	6.3	36 50	3 45	6.3	265
94	41 52	3 36	5.4	40 53	3 28	5.3	39 53	3 21	5.2	38 53	3 14	5.1	37 53	3 07	5.1	36 54	3 01	5.0	266
93	41 56	2 42	4.0	40 56	2 36	4.0	39 56	2 31	3.9	38 56	2 26	3.9	37 56	2 20	3.8	36 56	2 16	3.8	267
92	41 58	1 48	2.7	40 58	1 44	2.6	39 58	1 41	2.6	38 58	1 37	2.6	37 58	1 34	2.5	36 58	1 30	2.5	268
91	42 00	0 54	1.3	41 00	0 52	1.3	40 00	0 50	1.3	39 00	0 49	1.3	38 00	0 47	1.3	37 00	0 45	1.3	269
90	42 00	0 00	0.0	41 00	0 00	0.0	40 00	0 00	0.0	39 00	0 00	0.0	38 00	0 00	0.0	37 00	0 00	0.0	270

N. Lat: for LHA > 180° ... $Z_n = Z$
for LHA < 180° ... $Z_n = 360° − Z$

S. Lat: for LHA > 180° ... $Z_n = 180° − Z$
for LHA < 180° ... $Z_n = 180° + Z$

SIGHT REDUCTION TABLE

B: (−) for 90° < LHA < 270°
Dec:(−) for Lat. contrary name

Z₁: same sign as B
Z₂: (−) for F > 90°

Lat./A LHA/F	54° A/H	54° B/P	54° Z₁/Z₂	55° A/H	55° B/P	55° Z₁/Z₂	56° A/H	56° B/P	56° Z₁/Z₂	57° A/H	57° B/P	57° Z₁/Z₂	58° A/H	58° B/P	58° Z₁/Z₂	59° A/H	59° B/P	59° Z₁/Z₂	Lat./A LHA
0 / 180	0 00	36 00	90.0	0 00	35 00	90.0	0 00	34 00	90.0	0 00	33 00	90.0	0 00	32 00	90.0	0 00	31 00	90.0	180 / 360
1 / 179	0 35	36 00	89.2	0 34	35 00	89.2	0 34	34 00	89.2	0 33	33 00	89.2	0 32	32 00	89.2	0 31	31 00	89.1	181 / 359
2 / 178	1 11	35 59	88.4	1 09	34 59	88.4	1 07	33 59	88.4	1 05	32 59	88.3	1 04	31 59	88.3	1 02	30 59	88.3	182 / 358
3 / 177	1 46	35 58	87.6	1 43	34 58	87.5	1 41	33 58	87.5	1 38	32 58	87.5	1 35	31 58	87.5	1 33	30 59	87.4	183 / 357
4 / 176	2 21	35 56	86.8	2 18	34 56	86.7	2 14	33 56	86.7	2 11	32 56	86.6	2 07	31 56	86.6	2 04	30 56	86.6	184 / 356
5 / 175	2 56	35 54	86.0	2 52	34 54	85.9	2 48	33 54	85.9	2 43	32 54	85.8	2 39	31 54	85.8	2 34	30 54	85.7	185 / 355
6 / 174	3 31	35 51	85.1	3 26	34 51	85.1	3 21	33 51	85.0	3 16	32 51	85.0	3 11	31 52	84.9	3 05	30 52	84.9	186 / 354
7 / 173	4 06	35 48	84.3	4 00	34 48	84.3	3 54	33 48	84.3	3 48	32 48	84.1	3 42	31 49	84.0	3 36	30 49	84.0	187 / 353
8 / 172	4 42	35 44	83.5	4 35	34 44	83.4	4 28	33 44	83.4	4 21	32 45	83.3	4 14	31 45	83.2	4 07	30 45	83.1	188 / 352
9 / 171	5 17	35 40	82.7	5 09	34 40	82.6	5 01	33 40	82.6	4 53	32 41	82.4	4 45	31 41	82.3	4 37	30 41	82.3	189 / 351
10 / 170	5 51	35 35	81.9	5 43	34 35	81.8	5 34	33 36	81.8	5 26	32 36	81.6	5 17	31 36	81.5	5 08	30 37	81.4	190 / 350
11 / 169	6 26	35 30	81.1	6 17	34 30	81.0	6 08	33 31	81.0	5 58	32 31	80.7	5 48	31 31	80.6	5 38	30 32	80.5	191 / 349
12 / 168	7 01	35 24	80.2	6 51	34 24	80.1	6 41	33 25	80.1	6 30	32 25	79.9	6 20	31 26	79.8	6 09	30 27	79.7	192 / 348
13 / 167	7 36	35 18	79.4	7 25	34 18	79.3	7 14	33 19	79.3	7 02	32 19	79.0	6 51	31 14	78.9	6 39	30 21	78.8	193 / 347
14 / 166	8 11	35 12	78.6	7 59	34 12	78.5	7 46	33 12	78.5	7 34	32 13	78.2	7 22	31 07	78.1	7 09	30 15	77.9	194 / 346
15 / 165	8 45	35 04	77.8	8 32	34 04	77.6	8 19	33 05	77.6	8 06	32 06	77.3	7 53	31 00	77.2	7 40	30 08	77.1	195 / 345
16 / 164	9 20	34 56	76.9	9 06	33 57	76.8	8 52	32 58	76.8	8 38	31 58	76.5	8 24	30 52	76.3	8 10	30 01	76.2	196 / 344
17 / 163	9 54	34 47	76.1	9 39	33 48	75.9	9 25	32 49	75.9	9 10	31 50	75.6	8 55	30 52	75.5	8 40	29 53	75.3	197 / 343
18 / 162	10 28	34 39	75.3	10 13	33 40	75.1	9 57	32 41	75.1	9 41	31 42	74.8	9 25	30 43	74.6	9 09	29 45	74.4	198 / 342
19 / 161	11 02	34 29	74.4	10 46	33 30	74.2	10 29	32 32	74.2	10 13	31 33	73.9	9 56	30 35	73.7	9 39	29 36	73.6	199 / 341
20 / 160	11 36	34 19	73.6	11 19	33 21	73.4	11 02	32 22	73.4	10 44	31 24	73.0	10 27	30 25	72.8	10 09	29 27	72.7	200 / 340
21 / 159	12 10	34 09	72.7	11 52	33 10	72.5	11 34	32 12	72.5	11 15	31 14	72.2	10 57	30 15	72.0	10 38	29 17	71.8	201 / 339
22 / 158	12 43	33 58	71.9	12 24	33 00	71.7	12 06	32 01	71.7	11 46	31 03	71.3	11 27	30 05	71.1	11 07	29 07	70.9	202 / 338
23 / 157	13 17	33 46	71.0	12 57	32 48	70.8	12 37	31 50	70.8	12 17	30 52	70.4	11 57	29 54	70.2	11 37	28 57	70.0	203 / 337
24 / 156	13 50	33 34	70.2	13 29	32 36	70.0	13 09	31 38	70.0	12 48	30 41	69.5	12 27	29 43	69.3	12 06	28 46	69.1	204 / 336
25 / 155	14 23	33 22	69.3	14 02	32 24	69.1	13 40	31 26	69.1	13 19	30 29	68.6	12 56	29 31	68.4	12 34	28 34	68.2	205 / 335
26 / 154	14 56	33 09	68.5	14 34	32 11	68.2	14 11	31 14	68.2	13 49	30 16	67.7	13 26	29 19	67.5	13 03	28 22	67.3	206 / 334
27 / 153	15 29	32 55	67.6	15 06	31 58	67.3	14 42	31 00	67.3	14 19	30 03	66.9	13 55	29 06	66.6	13 31	28 10	66.4	207 / 333
28 / 152	16 01	32 41	66.7	15 37	31 44	66.5	15 13	30 47	66.5	14 49	29 50	66.0	14 24	28 53	65.7	14 00	27 57	65.5	208 / 332
29 / 151	16 33	32 26	65.8	16 09	31 29	65.6	15 44	30 32	65.6	15 19	29 36	65.1	14 53	28 39	64.8	14 28	27 43	64.6	209 / 331
30 / 150	17 05	32 11	65.0	16 40	31 14	64.7	16 14	30 17	64.4	15 48	29 21	64.2	15 22	28 25	63.9	14 55	27 29	63.7	210 / 330
31 / 149	17 37	31 55	64.1	17 11	30 58	63.8	16 44	30 02	63.5	16 17	29 06	63.3	15 50	28 10	63.0	15 23	27 15	62.7	211 / 329
32 / 148	18 09	31 39	63.2	17 42	30 42	62.9	17 14	29 46	62.6	16 47	28 51	62.3	16 19	27 55	62.1	15 50	27 00	61.8	212 / 328
33 / 147	18 40	31 21	62.3	18 12	30 25	62.0	17 44	29 30	61.7	17 15	28 34	61.4	16 47	27 39	61.2	16 17	26 45	60.9	213 / 327
34 / 146	19 11	31 04	61.4	18 42	30 08	61.1	18 13	29 13	60.8	17 44	28 18	60.5	17 14	27 23	60.2	16 44	26 29	60.0	214 / 326
35 / 145	19 42	30 46	60.5	19 12	29 50	60.2	18 42	28 55	59.9	18 12	28 01	59.6	17 42	27 06	59.3	17 11	26 12	59.0	215 / 325
36 / 144	20 13	30 27	59.6	19 42	29 32	59.2	19 11	28 37	59.0	18 40	27 43	58.7	18 09	26 49	58.4	17 37	25 55	58.1	216 / 324
37 / 143	20 43	30 07	58.6	20 12	29 13	58.3	19 40	28 19	58.0	19 08	27 25	57.7	18 36	26 31	57.4	18 03	25 38	57.1	217 / 323
38 / 142	21 13	29 48	57.7	20 41	28 53	57.4	20 08	27 59	57.1	19 35	27 06	56.8	19 02	26 13	56.5	18 29	25 20	56.2	218 / 322
39 / 141	21 43	29 27	56.8	21 10	28 33	56.4	20 36	27 40	56.1	20 03	26 47	55.8	19 29	25 54	55.5	18 55	25 02	55.2	219 / 321
40 / 140	22 12	29 06	55.8	21 38	28 13	55.5	21 04	27 20	55.2	20 30	26 27	54.9	19 55	25 35	54.6	19 20	24 43	54.3	220 / 320
41 / 139	22 41	28 44	54.9	22 06	27 51	54.5	21 31	26 59	54.2	20 56	26 07	53.9	20 21	25 15	53.6	19 45	24 24	53.3	221 / 319
42 / 138	23 10	28 22	53.9	22 34	27 29	53.6	21 58	26 37	53.3	21 22	25 46	52.9	20 46	24 55	52.6	20 10	24 04	52.3	222 / 318
43 / 137	23 38	27 59	53.0	23 02	27 07	52.6	22 25	26 15	52.3	21 48	25 24	52.0	21 11	24 34	51.7	20 34	23 43	51.4	223 / 317
44 / 136	24 06	27 36	52.0	23 29	26 44	51.7	22 51	25 53	51.3	22 14	25 02	51.0	21 36	24 12	50.7	20 58	23 23	50.4	224 / 316
45 / 135	24 34	27 11	51.0	23 56	26 20	50.7	23 17	25 30	50.3	22 39	24 40	50.0	22 00	23 50	49.7	21 21	23 01	49.4	225 / 315

Lat.	LHA/F	54° A/H	54° B/P	54° Z_1/Z_2	55° A/H	55° B/P	55° Z_1/Z_2	56° A/H	56° B/P	56° Z_1/Z_2	57° A/H	57° B/P	57° Z_1/Z_2	58° A/H	58° B/P	58° Z_1/Z_2	59° A/H	59° B/P	59° Z_1/Z_2	LHA	LHA
45	135	24 34	27 11	51.0	23 56	26 20	50.7	23 17	25 30	50.3	22 39	24 40	50.0	22 00	23 50	49.7	21 21	23 01	49.4	225	315
46	134	25 01	26 47	50.0	24 22	25 56	49.7	23 43	25 06	49.4	23 04	24 17	49.0	22 25	23 28	48.7	21 45	22 39	48.4	226	314
47	133	25 28	26 22	49.1	24 48	25 32	48.7	24 08	24 42	48.4	23 28	23 53	48.0	22 48	23 05	47.7	22 08	22 17	47.4	227	313
48	132	25 54	25 56	48.1	25 14	25 06	47.7	24 33	24 17	47.4	23 53	23 29	47.0	23 11	22 41	46.7	22 30	21 54	46.4	228	312
49	131	26 20	25 30	47.1	25 39	24 40	46.7	24 58	23 52	46.4	24 16	23 05	46.0	23 34	22 17	45.7	22 52	21 31	45.4	229	311
50	130	26 46	25 02	46.0	26 04	24 14	45.7	25 22	23 26	45.3	24 40	22 39	45.0	23 57	21 53	44.7	23 14	21 07	44.4	230	310
51	129	27 11	24 34	45.0	26 28	23 47	44.7	25 45	23 00	44.3	25 02	22 14	44.0	24 19	21 28	43.7	23 36	20 43	43.4	231	309
52	128	27 36	24 06	44.0	26 52	23 19	43.6	26 09	22 33	43.3	25 25	21 48	43.0	24 41	21 03	42.7	23 57	20 18	42.3	232	308
53	127	28 00	23 37	43.0	27 16	22 51	42.6	26 32	22 06	42.3	25 47	21 21	41.9	25 02	20 37	41.6	24 17	19 53	41.3	233	307
54	126	28 24	23 07	41.9	27 39	22 22	41.6	26 54	21 38	41.2	26 09	20 54	40.9	25 23	20 10	40.6	24 37	19 27	40.3	234	306
55	125	28 47	22 37	40.9	28 01	21 53	40.5	27 16	21 09	40.2	26 30	20 26	39.9	25 44	19 43	39.5	24 57	19 01	39.2	235	305
56	124	29 10	22 07	39.8	28 24	21 23	39.5	27 37	20 40	39.1	26 50	19 57	38.8	26 04	19 16	38.5	25 17	18 34	38.2	236	304
57	123	29 32	21 35	38.8	28 45	20 52	38.4	27 58	20 10	38.1	27 11	19 29	37.8	26 23	18 48	37.4	25 35	18 07	37.1	237	303
58	122	29 54	21 03	37.7	29 06	20 21	37.3	28 19	19 40	37.0	27 31	18 59	36.7	26 42	18 19	36.4	25 54	17 40	36.1	238	302
59	121	30 15	20 31	36.6	29 27	19 50	36.3	28 38	19 09	35.9	27 50	18 30	35.6	27 01	17 50	35.3	26 12	17 12	35.0	239	301
60	120	30 36	19 58	35.5	29 47	19 18	35.2	28 58	18 38	34.9	28 09	17 59	34.5	27 19	17 21	34.2	26 29	16 43	34.0	240	300
61	119	30 56	19 24	34.4	30 07	18 45	34.1	29 17	18 06	33.8	28 27	17 29	33.5	27 37	16 51	33.2	26 46	16 14	32.9	241	299
62	118	31 16	18 50	33.3	30 26	18 12	33.0	29 35	17 34	32.7	28 45	16 57	32.4	27 54	16 21	32.1	27 03	15 45	31.8	242	298
63	117	31 35	18 15	32.2	30 44	17 38	31.9	29 53	17 02	31.6	29 02	16 26	31.3	28 10	15 50	31.0	27 19	15 15	30.7	243	297
64	116	31 53	17 40	31.1	31 02	17 04	30.8	30 10	16 28	30.5	29 19	15 53	30.2	28 26	15 19	29.9	27 35	14 45	29.6	244	296
65	115	32 11	17 04	30.0	31 19	16 29	29.7	30 27	15 55	29.4	29 35	15 21	29.1	28 42	14 48	28.8	27 50	14 15	28.5	245	295
66	114	32 29	16 28	28.8	31 36	15 54	28.5	30 43	15 20	28.2	29 50	14 48	28.0	28 57	14 16	27.7	28 04	13 44	27.4	246	294
67	113	32 45	15 51	27.7	31 52	15 18	27.4	30 59	14 46	27.1	30 05	14 14	26.8	29 12	13 43	26.6	28 18	13 13	26.3	247	293
68	112	33 01	15 14	26.5	32 08	14 42	26.3	31 14	14 11	26.0	30 20	13 40	25.7	29 26	13 10	25.5	28 31	12 41	25.2	248	292
69	111	33 17	14 36	25.4	32 23	14 05	25.1	31 28	13 35	24.8	30 34	13 06	24.6	29 39	12 37	24.4	28 44	12 09	24.1	249	291
70	110	33 32	13 57	24.2	32 37	13 28	24.0	31 42	12 59	23.7	30 47	12 31	23.5	29 52	12 04	23.2	28 57	11 37	23.0	250	290
71	109	33 46	13 18	23.1	32 51	12 51	22.8	31 55	12 23	22.6	31 00	11 56	22.3	30 04	11 30	22.1	29 09	11 04	21.9	251	289
72	108	33 59	12 39	21.9	33 04	12 13	21.6	32 08	11 46	21.4	31 12	11 21	21.2	30 16	10 56	21.0	29 20	10 31	20.8	252	288
73	107	34 12	12 00	20.7	33 16	11 34	20.5	32 20	11 09	20.2	31 23	10 45	20.0	30 27	10 21	19.8	29 30	9 58	19.6	253	287
74	106	34 24	11 19	19.5	33 28	10 55	19.3	32 31	10 32	19.1	31 34	10 09	18.9	30 37	9 46	18.7	29 41	9 24	18.5	254	286
75	105	34 36	10 39	18.3	33 39	10 16	18.1	32 42	9 54	17.9	31 44	9 32	17.7	30 47	9 11	17.5	29 50	8 50	17.4	255	285
76	104	34 46	9 58	17.1	33 49	9 37	16.9	32 52	9 16	16.7	31 54	8 56	16.6	30 57	8 36	16.4	29 59	8 16	16.2	256	284
77	103	34 56	9 17	15.9	33 59	8 57	15.7	33 01	8 38	15.6	32 03	8 19	15.4	31 05	8 00	15.2	30 07	7 42	15.1	257	283
78	102	35 06	8 35	14.7	34 08	8 17	14.5	33 10	7 59	14.4	32 11	7 41	14.2	31 13	7 24	14.1	30 15	7 07	13.9	258	282
79	101	35 14	7 53	13.5	34 16	7 37	13.3	33 18	7 20	13.2	32 19	7 04	13.0	31 21	6 48	12.9	30 22	6 32	12.8	259	281
80	100	35 22	7 11	12.3	34 24	6 56	12.1	33 25	6 41	12.0	32 26	6 26	11.9	31 27	6 12	11.7	30 29	5 57	11.6	260	280
81	99	35 29	6 29	11.1	34 30	6 15	10.9	33 32	6 01	10.8	32 33	5 48	10.7	31 34	5 35	10.6	30 35	5 22	10.5	261	279
82	98	35 36	5 46	9.9	34 37	5 33	9.7	33 37	5 22	9.6	32 38	5 10	9.5	31 39	4 58	9.4	30 40	4 47	9.3	262	278
83	97	35 41	5 04	8.6	34 42	4 53	8.5	33 43	4 42	8.4	32 43	4 32	8.3	31 44	4 21	8.2	30 45	4 11	8.2	263	277
84	96	35 46	4 21	7.4	34 47	4 11	7.3	33 47	4 02	7.2	32 48	3 53	7.1	31 48	3 44	7.1	30 49	3 36	7.0	264	276
85	95	35 51	3 37	6.2	34 51	3 30	6.1	33 51	3 22	6.0	32 52	3 14	6.0	31 52	3 07	5.9	30 52	3 00	5.8	265	275
86	94	35 54	2 54	4.9	34 54	2 48	4.9	33 54	2 42	4.8	32 55	2 36	4.8	31 55	2 30	4.7	30 55	2 24	4.7	266	274
87	93	35 57	2 11	3.7	34 57	2 06	3.7	33 57	2 01	3.6	32 57	1 57	3.6	31 57	1 52	3.5	30 57	1 48	3.5	267	273
88	92	35 58	1 27	2.5	34 59	1 24	2.4	33 59	1 21	2.4	32 59	1 18	2.4	31 59	1 15	2.4	30 59	1 12	2.3	268	272
89	91	36 00	0 44	1.2	35 00	0 42	1.2	34 00	0 40	1.2	33 00	0 39	1.2	32 00	0 37	1.2	31 00	0 36	1.2	269	271
90	90	36 00	0 00	0.0	35 00	0 00	0.0	34 00	0 00	0.0	33 00	0 00	0.0	32 00	0 00	0.0	31 00	0 00	0.0	270	270

N. Lat.: for LHA > 180° .... $Z_n = Z$
for LHA < 180° .... $Z_n = 360° − Z$

S. Lat.: for LHA > 180° .... $Z_n = 180° − Z$
for LHA < 180° .... $Z_n = 180° + Z$

SIGHT REDUCTION TABLE

B: (−) for 90° < LHA < 270°
Dec: (−) for Lat. contrary name

Z_1: same sign as B
Z_2: (−) for F > 90°

LHA/F	Lat./A	60° A/H	60° B/P	60° Z_1/Z_2	61° A/H	61° B/P	61° Z_1/Z_2	62° A/H	62° B/P	62° Z_1/Z_2	63° A/H	63° B/P	63° Z_1/Z_2	64° A/H	64° B/P	64° Z_1/Z_2	65° A/H	65° B/P	65° Z_1/Z_2	Lat./A	LHA
0	180	0 00	30 00	90·0	0 00	29 00	90·0	0 00	28 00	90·0	0 00	27 00	90·0	0 00	26 00	90·0	0 00	25 00	90·0	180	360
1	179	0 30	30 00	89·1	0 29	29 00	89·1	0 28	28 00	89·1	0 27	27 00	89·1	0 26	26 00	89·1	0 25	25 00	89·1	181	359
2	178	1 00	29 59	88·3	0 58	28 59	88·3	0 56	27 59	88·2	0 54	26 59	88·2	0 53	25 59	88·2	0 51	24 59	88·2	182	358
3	177	1 30	29 58	87·4	1 27	28 58	87·4	1 24	27 59	87·4	1 22	26 58	87·3	1 19	25 58	87·3	1 16	24 58	87·3	183	357
4	176	2 00	29 56	86·5	1 56	28 56	86·5	1 53	27 57	86·5	1 49	26 57	86·4	1 45	25 57	86·4	1 41	24 57	86·4	184	356
5	175	2 30	29 54	85·7	2 25	28 54	85·7	2 21	27 55	85·6	2 16	26 55	85·5	2 11	25 55	85·5	2 07	24 55	85·5	185	355
6	174	3 00	29 52	84·8	2 54	28 52	84·7	2 49	27 52	84·7	2 43	26 52	84·6	2 38	25 53	84·6	2 32	24 53	84·6	186	354
7	173	3 30	29 49	83·9	3 23	28 49	83·9	3 17	27 49	83·8	3 10	26 50	83·8	3 04	25 50	83·7	2 57	24 50	83·7	187	353
8	172	3 59	29 45	83·1	3 52	28 46	83·0	3 45	27 46	82·9	3 37	26 46	82·9	3 30	25 47	82·8	3 22	24 47	82·7	188	352
9	171	4 29	29 42	82·2	4 21	28 42	82·1	4 13	27 42	82·1	4 04	26 43	82·0	3 56	25 43	81·9	3 47	24 44	81·8	189	351
10	170	4 59	29 37	81·3	4 50	28 38	81·2	4 41	27 38	81·2	4 31	26 39	81·1	4 22	25 39	81·0	4 13	24 40	80·9	190	350
11	169	5 28	29 33	80·4	5 18	28 33	80·4	5 08	27 34	80·3	4 58	26 34	80·2	4 48	25 35	80·1	4 38	24 36	80·0	191	349
12	168	5 58	29 27	79·6	5 47	28 28	79·5	5 36	27 29	79·4	5 25	26 29	79·3	5 14	25 30	79·2	5 02	24 31	79·1	192	348
13	167	6 27	29 22	78·7	6 16	28 22	78·6	6 04	27 23	78·5	5 52	26 24	78·4	5 40	25 25	78·3	5 27	24 26	78·2	193	347
14	166	6 57	29 15	77·8	6 44	28 16	77·7	6 31	27 17	77·6	6 18	26 18	77·5	6 05	25 20	77·4	5 52	24 21	77·3	194	346
15	165	7 26	29 09	76·9	7 13	28 10	76·8	6 59	27 11	76·7	6 45	26 12	76·6	6 31	25 14	76·5	6 17	24 15	76·4	195	345
16	164	7 55	29 02	76·1	7 41	28 03	75·9	7 26	27 04	75·8	7 11	26 06	75·7	6 56	25 07	75·6	6 41	24 09	75·4	196	344
17	163	8 24	28 54	75·2	8 09	27 55	75·0	7 53	26 57	74·9	7 38	25 59	74·8	7 22	25 00	74·6	7 06	24 02	74·5	197	343
18	162	8 53	28 46	74·3	8 37	27 48	74·1	8 20	26 50	74·0	8 04	25 51	73·9	7 47	24 53	73·7	7 30	23 55	73·6	198	342
19	161	9 22	28 38	73·4	9 05	27 40	73·2	8 48	26 41	73·1	8 30	25 43	72·9	8 12	24 45	72·8	7 55	23 48	72·7	199	341
20	160	9 51	28 29	72·5	9 33	27 31	72·3	9 14	26 33	72·2	8 56	25 35	72·0	8 37	24 37	71·9	8 19	23 40	71·7	200	340
21	159	10 19	28 19	71·6	10 00	27 21	71·4	9 41	26 24	71·3	9 22	25 26	71·1	9 02	24 29	71·0	8 43	23 32	70·8	201	339
22	158	10 48	28 10	70·7	10 28	27 12	70·5	10 08	26 15	70·4	9 48	25 17	70·2	9 27	24 20	70·0	9 07	23 23	69·9	202	338
23	157	11 16	27 59	69·8	10 55	27 02	69·6	10 34	26 05	69·5	10 13	25 08	69·3	9 52	24 11	69·1	9 30	23 14	69·0	203	337
24	156	11 44	27 49	68·9	11 22	26 51	68·7	11 00	25 54	68·5	10 38	24 58	68·4	10 16	24 01	68·2	9 54	23 04	68·0	204	336
25	155	12 12	27 37	68·0	11 49	26 40	67·8	11 27	25 44	67·6	11 04	24 47	67·4	10 41	23 51	67·1	10 17	22 55	67·1	205	335
26	154	12 40	27 26	67·1	12 16	26 29	66·9	11 53	25 33	66·7	11 29	24 36	66·5	11 05	23 40	66·3	10 41	22 44	66·2	206	334
27	153	13 07	27 13	66·2	12 43	26 17	66·0	12 18	25 21	65·8	11 54	24 25	65·6	11 29	23 29	65·4	11 04	22 34	65·2	207	333
28	152	13 35	27 01	65·3	13 09	26 05	65·1	12 44	25 09	64·9	12 18	24 13	64·7	11 53	23 18	64·5	11 27	22 23	64·3	208	332
29	151	14 02	26 48	64·4	13 36	25 52	64·1	13 09	24 56	63·9	12 43	24 01	63·7	12 16	23 06	63·5	11 49	22 11	63·3	209	331
30	150	14 29	26 34	63·4	14 02	25 39	63·2	13 35	24 43	63·0	13 07	23 49	62·8	12 40	22 54	62·6	12 12	21 59	62·4	210	330
31	149	14 55	26 20	62·5	14 28	25 25	62·3	14 00	24 30	62·1	13 31	23 36	61·8	13 03	22 41	61·6	12 34	21 47	61·4	211	329
32	148	15 22	26 05	61·6	14 53	25 11	61·3	14 24	24 16	61·1	13 55	23 22	60·9	13 26	22 28	60·7	12 56	21 35	60·5	212	328
33	147	15 48	25 50	60·6	15 19	24 56	60·4	14 49	24 02	60·2	14 19	23 08	59·9	13 49	22 15	59·7	13 18	21 22	59·5	213	327
34	146	16 14	25 35	59·7	15 44	24 41	59·5	15 13	23 47	59·2	14 42	22 54	59·0	14 11	22 01	58·8	13 40	21 08	58·6	214	326
35	145	16 40	25 19	58·8	16 09	24 25	58·5	15 37	23 32	58·3	15 06	22 39	58·0	14 34	21 47	57·8	14 02	20 54	57·6	215	325
36	144	17 05	25 02	57·8	16 33	24 09	57·6	16 01	23 17	57·3	15 29	22 24	57·1	14 56	21 32	56·9	14 23	20 40	56·6	216	324
37	143	17 31	24 45	56·9	16 58	23 53	56·6	16 25	23 00	56·4	15 51	22 09	56·1	15 18	21 17	55·9	14 44	20 26	55·7	217	323
38	142	17 56	24 28	55·9	17 22	23 36	55·7	16 48	22 44	55·4	16 14	21 53	55·2	15 39	21 01	54·9	15 05	20 11	54·7	218	322
39	141	18 20	24 10	55·0	17 46	23 18	54·7	17 11	22 27	54·4	16 36	21 36	54·2	16 01	20 46	54·0	15 25	19 56	53·7	219	321
40	140	18 45	23 52	54·0	18 09	23 00	53·7	17 34	22 10	53·5	16 58	21 19	53·2	16 22	20 29	53·0	15 46	19 39	52·7	220	320
41	139	19 09	23 33	53·0	18 33	22 42	52·8	17 56	21 52	52·5	17 20	21 02	52·2	16 43	20 13	51·9	16 06	19 23	51·8	221	319
42	138	19 33	23 13	52·1	18 56	22 23	51·8	18 19	21 34	51·5	17 41	20 44	51·3	17 03	19 55	51·0	16 26	19 07	50·8	222	318
43	137	19 56	22 54	51·1	19 18	22 04	50·8	18 40	21 15	50·5	18 02	20 26	50·3	17 24	19 38	50·0	16 45	18 50	49·8	223	317
44	136	20 19	22 33	50·1	19 41	21 44	49·8	19 02	20 56	49·5	18 23	20 08	49·3	17 44	19 20	49·0	17 04	18 33	48·8	224	316
45	135	20 42	22 12	49·1	20 03	21 24	48·8	19 23	20 36	48·6	18 43	19 49	48·3	18 03	19 02	48·1	17 23	18 15	47·8	225	315

LHA/F	Lat./A	60° A/H	60° B/P	60° Z₁/Z₂	61° A/H	61° B/P	61° Z₁/Z₂	62° A/H	62° B/P	62° Z₁/Z₂	63° A/H	63° B/P	63° Z₁/Z₂	64° A/H	64° B/P	64° Z₁/Z₂	65° A/H	65° B/P	65° Z₁/Z₂	LHA	Lat./A
45	135	20 42	22 12	49.1	20 03	21 24	48.8	19 23	20 36	48.6	18 43	19 49	48.3	18 03	19 02	48.1	17 23	18 15	47.8	225	315
46	134	21 05	21 51	48.1	20 25	21 04	47.8	19 44	20 16	47.6	19 04	19 29	47.3	18 23	18 43	47.1	17 42	17 57	46.8	226	314
47	133	21 27	21 30	47.1	20 46	20 43	46.8	20 05	19 56	46.6	19 24	19 10	46.3	18 42	18 24	46.1	18 00	17 39	45.8	227	313
48	132	21 49	21 07	46.1	21 07	20 21	45.8	20 25	19 35	45.6	19 43	18 50	45.3	19 01	18 04	45.1	18 18	17 20	44.8	228	312
49	131	22 10	20 45	45.1	21 28	19 59	44.8	20 45	19 14	44.6	20 02	18 29	44.3	19 19	17 45	44.0	18 36	17 01	43.8	229	311
50	130	22 31	20 22	44.1	21 48	19 37	43.8	21 05	18 52	43.5	20 21	18 08	43.3	19 37	17 24	43.0	18 53	16 41	42.8	230	310
51	129	22 52	19 58	43.1	22 08	19 14	42.8	21 24	18 30	42.5	20 40	17 47	42.3	19 55	17 04	42.0	19 10	16 21	41.8	231	309
52	128	23 12	19 34	42.1	22 28	18 51	41.8	21 43	18 08	41.5	20 58	17 25	41.3	20 13	16 43	41.0	19 27	16 01	40.8	232	308
53	127	23 32	19 10	41.0	22 47	18 27	40.7	22 01	17 45	40.5	21 15	17 03	40.2	20 30	16 21	40.0	19 44	15 41	39.7	233	307
54	126	23 52	18 45	40.0	23 06	18 03	39.7	22 19	17 21	39.4	21 33	16 40	39.2	20 46	16 00	39.0	20 00	15 20	38.7	234	306
55	125	24 11	18 19	39.0	23 24	17 38	38.7	22 37	16 58	38.4	21 50	16 17	38.2	21 03	15 38	37.9	20 15	14 58	37.7	235	305
56	124	24 29	17 54	37.9	23 42	17 13	37.6	22 54	16 34	37.3	22 07	15 54	37.1	21 19	15 15	36.9	20 31	14 37	36.7	236	304
57	123	24 48	17 27	36.9	23 59	16 48	36.6	23 11	16 09	36.3	22 23	15 31	36.1	21 34	14 53	35.8	20 46	14 15	35.6	237	303
58	122	25 05	17 01	35.8	24 17	16 22	35.5	23 28	15 44	35.3	22 39	15 07	35.0	21 49	14 29	34.8	21 00	13 53	34.6	238	302
59	121	25 23	16 34	34.8	24 33	15 56	34.5	23 44	15 19	34.2	22 54	14 42	34.0	22 04	14 06	33.8	21 14	13 30	33.5	239	301
60	120	25 40	16 06	33.7	24 50	15 29	33.4	23 59	14 53	33.2	23 09	14 18	32.9	22 19	13 42	32.7	21 28	13 07	32.5	240	300
61	119	25 56	15 38	32.6	25 05	15 03	32.4	24 15	14 27	32.1	23 24	13 53	31.9	22 33	13 18	31.7	21 42	12 44	31.5	241	299
62	118	26 12	15 10	31.5	25 21	14 35	31.3	24 29	14 01	31.1	23 38	13 27	30.8	22 46	12 54	30.6	21 55	12 21	30.4	242	298
63	117	26 27	14 41	30.5	25 36	14 08	30.2	24 44	13 34	30.0	23 52	13 01	29.8	22 59	12 29	29.5	22 07	11 57	29.3	243	297
64	116	26 42	14 12	29.4	25 50	13 39	29.1	24 57	13 07	29.0	24 05	12 35	28.7	23 12	12 04	28.5	22 19	11 33	28.3	244	296
65	115	26 57	13 43	28.3	26 04	13 11	28.1	25 11	12 40	27.9	24 18	12 09	27.6	23 25	11 39	27.4	22 31	11 09	27.2	245	295
66	114	27 11	13 13	27.2	26 17	12 42	27.0	25 24	12 12	26.8	24 30	11 43	26.6	23 36	11 13	26.4	22 43	10 44	26.2	246	294
67	113	27 24	12 43	26.1	26 30	12 13	25.9	25 36	11 44	25.7	24 42	11 16	25.5	23 48	10 47	25.3	22 54	10 20	25.1	247	293
68	112	27 37	12 12	25.0	26 43	11 44	24.8	25 48	11 16	24.6	24 54	10 48	24.4	23 59	10 21	24.2	23 04	9 55	24.0	248	292
69	111	27 50	11 41	23.9	26 55	11 14	23.7	26 00	10 47	23.5	25 05	10 21	23.3	24 09	9 55	23.1	23 14	9 29	23.0	249	291
70	110	28 01	11 10	22.8	27 06	10 44	22.6	26 11	10 18	22.4	25 15	9 53	22.2	24 20	9 28	22.0	23 24	9 03	21.9	250	290
71	109	28 13	10 39	21.7	27 17	10 14	21.5	26 21	9 49	21.3	25 25	9 25	21.1	24 29	9 01	20.9	23 33	8 38	20.8	251	289
72	108	28 24	10 07	20.6	27 27	9 43	20.4	26 31	9 20	20.2	25 35	8 57	20.0	24 38	8 34	19.9	23 42	8 12	19.7	252	288
73	107	28 34	9 35	19.4	27 37	9 12	19.3	26 41	8 50	19.1	25 44	8 28	18.9	24 47	8 07	18.8	23 50	7 46	18.6	253	287
74	106	28 44	9 03	18.3	27 47	8 41	18.2	26 50	8 20	18.0	25 52	8 00	17.8	24 55	7 39	17.7	23 58	7 19	17.6	254	286
75	105	28 53	8 30	17.2	27 55	8 10	17.0	26 58	7 50	16.9	26 01	7 31	16.7	25 03	7 12	16.6	24 06	6 53	16.5	255	285
76	104	29 01	7 57	16.1	28 04	7 38	15.9	27 06	7 20	15.8	26 08	7 02	15.6	25 10	6 44	15.5	24 13	6 26	15.4	256	284
77	103	29 09	7 24	14.9	28 11	7 06	14.8	27 13	6 49	14.7	26 15	6 32	14.5	25 17	6 16	14.4	24 19	5 59	14.3	257	283
78	102	29 17	6 51	13.8	28 18	6 34	13.7	27 20	6 19	13.5	26 22	6 03	13.4	25 23	5 47	13.3	24 25	5 32	13.2	258	282
79	101	29 24	6 17	12.7	28 25	6 02	12.5	27 27	5 48	12.4	26 28	5 33	12.3	25 29	5 19	12.2	24 31	5 05	12.1	259	281
80	100	29 30	5 44	11.5	28 31	5 30	11.4	27 32	5 17	11.3	26 33	5 03	11.2	25 35	4 50	11.1	24 36	4 38	11.0	260	280
81	99	29 36	5 10	10.4	28 37	4 57	10.3	27 38	4 45	10.2	26 38	4 33	10.1	25 39	4 22	10.0	24 40	4 10	9.9	261	279
82	98	29 41	4 36	9.2	28 41	4 25	9.1	27 42	4 14	9.0	26 43	4 03	9.0	25 44	3 53	8.9	24 44	3 43	8.8	262	278
83	97	29 45	4 01	8.1	28 46	3 52	8.0	27 46	3 42	7.9	26 47	3 33	7.8	25 48	3 24	7.8	24 48	3 15	7.7	263	277
84	96	29 49	3 27	6.9	28 50	3 19	6.9	27 50	3 11	6.8	26 50	3 03	6.7	25 51	2 55	6.7	24 51	2 47	6.6	264	276
85	95	29 52	2 53	5.8	28 53	2 46	5.7	27 53	2 39	5.7	26 53	2 33	5.6	25 54	2 26	5.6	24 54	2 20	5.5	265	275
86	94	29 55	2 18	4.6	28 55	2 13	4.6	27 56	2 07	4.5	26 56	2 02	4.5	25 56	1 57	4.4	24 56	1 52	4.4	266	274
87	93	29 57	1 44	3.5	28 57	1 40	3.4	27 57	1 36	3.4	26 58	1 32	3.4	25 58	1 28	3.3	24 58	1 24	3.3	267	273
88	92	29 59	1 09	2.3	28 59	1 06	2.3	27 59	1 04	2.3	26 59	1 01	2.2	25 59	0 59	2.2	24 59	0 56	2.2	268	272
89	91	30 00	0 35	1.2	29 00	0 33	1.1	28 00	0 32	1.1	27 00	0 31	1.1	26 00	0 29	1.1	25 00	0 28	1.1	269	271
90	90	30 00	0 00	0.0	29 00	0 00	0.0	28 00	0 00	0.0	27 00	0 00	0.0	26 00	0 00	0.0	25 00	0 00	0.0	270	270

N. Lat.: for LHA > 180° … $Z_n = Z$
for LHA < 180° … $Z_n = 360° - Z$

S. Lat.: for LHA > 180° … $Z_n = 180° - Z$
for LHA < 180° … $Z_n = 180° + Z$

SIGHT REDUCTION TABLE

B: (−) for 90° < LHA < 270°
Dec:(−) for Lat. contrary name

Z1: same sign as B
Z2: (−) for F > 90°

Lat. / A		66°			67°			68°			69°			70°			71°			Lat. / A
LHA/F		A/H	B/P	Z1/Z2	A/H	B/P	Z1/Z2	A/H	B/P	Z1/Z2	A/H	B/P	Z1/Z2	A/H	B/P	Z1/Z2	A/H	B/P	Z1/Z2		LHA
0	180	0 00	24 00	90.0	0 00	23 00	90.0	0 00	22 00	90.0	0 00	21 00	90.0	0 00	20 00	90.0	0 00	19 00	90.0	180	360
1	179	0 24	24 00	89.1	0 23	23 00	89.1	0 22	22 00	89.1	0 22	21 00	89.1	0 21	20 00	89.1	0 20	19 00	89.1	181	359
2	178	0 49	23 59	88.2	0 47	22 59	88.2	0 45	21 59	88.2	0 43	20 59	88.2	0 41	19 59	88.1	0 39	18 59	88.1	182	358
3	177	1 13	23 58	87.3	1 10	22 58	87.2	1 07	21 58	87.2	1 04	20 58	87.2	1 02	19 58	87.2	0 59	18 59	87.2	183	357
4	176	1 38	23 57	86.3	1 34	22 57	86.3	1 30	21 57	86.3	1 26	20 57	86.3	1 22	19 57	86.2	1 18	18 58	86.2	184	356
5	175	2 02	23 55	85.4	1 57	22 55	85.4	1 52	21 55	85.4	1 47	20 56	85.3	1 42	19 56	85.3	1 38	18 56	85.3	185	355
6	174	2 26	23 53	84.5	2 20	22 53	84.5	2 15	21 53	84.4	2 09	20 54	84.4	2 03	19 54	84.4	1 57	18 54	84.3	186	354
7	173	2 50	23 50	83.6	2 44	22 51	83.6	2 37	21 51	83.5	2 30	20 51	83.5	2 23	19 52	83.4	2 16	18 52	83.4	187	353
8	172	3 15	23 48	82.7	3 07	22 48	82.6	2 59	21 48	82.6	2 52	20 49	82.5	2 44	19 49	82.5	2 36	18 50	82.4	188	352
9	171	3 39	23 44	81.8	3 30	22 45	81.7	3 22	21 45	81.7	3 13	20 46	81.6	3 04	19 46	81.5	2 55	18 47	81.5	189	351
10	170	4 03	23 41	80.8	3 53	22 41	80.8	3 44	21 42	80.7	3 34	20 42	80.7	3 24	19 43	80.6	3 14	18 44	80.5	190	350
11	169	4 27	23 36	79.9	4 17	22 37	79.9	4 06	21 38	79.8	3 55	20 39	79.7	3 45	19 40	79.6	3 34	18 41	79.6	191	349
12	168	4 51	23 32	79.0	4 40	22 33	78.9	4 28	21 34	78.9	4 16	20 35	78.8	4 05	19 36	78.7	3 53	18 37	78.6	192	348
13	167	5 15	23 27	78.1	5 03	22 28	78.0	4 50	21 29	77.9	4 37	20 30	77.8	4 25	19 32	77.8	4 12	18 33	77.7	193	347
14	166	5 39	23 22	77.2	5 25	22 23	77.1	5 12	21 24	77.0	4 58	20 26	76.9	4 45	19 27	76.8	4 31	18 28	76.7	194	346
15	165	6 03	23 16	76.2	5 48	22 18	76.1	5 34	21 19	76.0	5 19	20 21	76.0	5 05	19 22	75.9	4 50	18 24	75.8	195	345
16	164	6 26	23 10	75.3	6 11	22 12	75.2	5 56	21 13	75.1	5 40	20 15	75.0	5 25	19 17	74.9	5 09	18 19	74.8	196	344
17	163	6 50	23 04	74.4	6 34	22 06	74.3	6 17	21 08	74.2	6 01	20 09	74.0	5 44	19 11	74.0	5 28	18 14	73.9	197	343
18	162	7 13	22 57	73.5	6 56	21 59	73.3	6 39	21 01	73.2	6 21	20 03	73.1	6 04	19 06	73.0	5 46	18 08	72.9	198	342
19	161	7 37	22 50	72.5	7 19	21 52	72.4	7 00	20 54	72.3	6 42	19 57	72.2	6 24	18 59	72.1	6 05	18 02	72.0	199	341
20	160	8 00	22 42	71.6	7 41	21 45	71.5	7 22	20 47	71.4	7 02	19 50	71.2	6 43	18 53	71.1	6 24	17 56	71.0	200	340
21	159	8 23	22 34	70.7	8 03	21 37	70.5	7 43	20 40	70.4	7 23	19 43	70.2	7 02	18 46	70.2	6 42	17 49	70.1	201	339
22	158	8 46	22 26	69.7	8 25	21 29	69.6	8 04	20 32	69.5	7 43	19 35	69.3	7 22	18 39	69.2	7 00	17 42	69.1	202	338
23	157	9 09	22 17	68.8	8 47	21 21	68.7	8 25	20 24	68.5	8 03	19 28	68.4	7 41	18 31	68.3	7 19	17 35	68.1	203	337
24	156	9 31	22 08	67.9	9 09	21 12	67.7	8 46	20 16	67.6	8 23	19 19	67.4	8 00	18 24	67.3	7 37	17 28	67.2	204	336
25	155	9 54	21 58	66.9	9 30	21 03	66.8	9 07	20 07	66.6	8 43	19 11	66.5	8 19	18 15	66.3	7 55	17 20	66.2	205	335
26	154	10 16	21 49	66.0	9 52	20 53	65.8	9 27	19 57	65.7	9 02	19 02	65.5	8 37	18 07	65.4	8 12	17 12	65.2	206	334
27	153	10 38	21 38	65.0	10 13	20 43	64.9	9 48	19 48	64.7	9 22	18 53	64.6	8 56	17 58	64.4	8 30	17 03	64.3	207	333
28	152	11 00	21 28	64.1	10 34	20 33	63.9	10 08	19 38	63.8	9 41	18 43	63.6	9 14	17 49	63.5	8 48	16 55	63.3	208	332
29	151	11 22	21 17	63.1	10 55	20 22	63.0	10 28	19 28	62.8	10 00	18 34	62.6	9 33	17 39	62.5	9 05	16 46	62.3	209	331
30	150	11 44	21 05	62.2	11 16	20 11	62.0	10 48	19 17	61.8	10 19	18 23	61.7	9 51	17 30	61.5	9 22	16 36	61.4	210	330
31	149	12 06	20 53	61.2	11 37	20 00	61.1	11 07	19 06	60.9	10 38	18 13	60.7	10 09	17 20	60.5	9 39	16 27	60.4	211	329
32	148	12 27	20 41	60.3	11 57	19 48	60.1	11 27	18 55	59.9	10 57	18 02	59.7	10 27	17 09	59.6	9 56	16 16	59.4	212	328
33	147	12 48	20 29	59.3	12 17	19 36	59.1	11 46	18 43	58.9	11 15	17 51	58.8	10 44	16 58	58.6	10 13	16 06	58.4	213	327
34	146	13 09	20 16	58.4	12 37	19 23	58.2	12 06	18 31	58.0	11 34	17 39	57.8	11 02	16 47	57.6	10 29	15 56	57.5	214	326
35	145	13 29	20 02	57.4	12 57	19 10	57.2	12 24	18 19	57.0	11 52	17 27	56.8	11 19	16 36	56.7	10 46	15 45	56.5	215	325
36	144	13 50	19 49	56.4	13 17	18 57	56.2	12 43	18 06	56.0	12 10	17 15	55.9	11 36	16 24	55.7	11 02	15 34	55.5	216	324
37	143	14 10	19 34	55.5	13 36	18 44	55.3	13 02	17 53	55.1	12 27	17 03	54.9	11 53	16 12	54.7	11 18	15 23	54.5	217	323
38	142	14 30	19 20	54.5	13 55	18 30	54.3	13 20	17 40	54.1	12 45	16 50	53.9	12 09	16 00	53.7	11 34	15 11	53.5	218	322
39	141	14 50	19 05	53.5	14 14	18 15	53.3	13 38	17 26	53.1	13 02	16 37	52.9	12 26	15 48	52.7	11 49	14 59	52.6	219	321
40	140	15 09	18 50	52.5	14 33	18 01	52.3	13 56	17 12	52.1	13 19	16 23	51.9	12 42	15 35	51.7	12 05	14 47	51.6	220	320
41	139	15 29	18 34	51.5	14 51	17 46	51.3	14 14	16 57	51.1	13 36	16 09	50.9	12 58	15 22	50.8	12 20	14 34	50.6	221	319
42	138	15 48	18 18	50.6	15 09	17 30	50.3	14 31	16 43	50.1	13 52	15 55	49.9	13 14	15 08	49.8	12 35	14 21	49.6	222	318
43	137	16 06	18 02	49.6	15 27	17 15	49.4	14 48	16 28	49.2	14 09	15 41	49.0	13 29	14 54	48.8	12 50	14 08	48.6	223	317
44	136	16 25	17 46	48.6	15 45	16 59	48.4	15 05	16 12	48.2	14 25	15 26	48.0	13 45	14 40	47.8	13 04	13 55	47.6	224	316
45	135	16 43	17 29	47.6	16 02	16 42	47.4	15 22	15 57	47.2	14 41	15 11	47.0	14 00	14 26	46.8	13 19	13 41	46.6	225	315

Lat./A	LHA/F	66° A/H	66° B/P	66° Z₁/Z₂	67° A/H	67° B/P	67° Z₁/Z₂	68° A/H	68° B/P	68° Z₁/Z₂	69° A/H	69° B/P	69° Z₁/Z₂	70° A/H	70° B/P	70° Z₁/Z₂	71° A/H	71° B/P	71° Z₁/Z₂	LHA	Lat./A
135	45	16 43	17 29	47·6	16 02	16 42	47·4	15 22	15 57	47·2	14 41	15 11	47·0	14 00	14 26	46·8	13 19	13 41	46·6	225	315
134	46	17 01	17 11	46·6	16 20	16 26	46·4	15 38	15 41	46·2	14 57	14 56	46·0	14 15	14 11	45·8	13 33	13 27	45·6	226	314
133	47	17 18	16 53	45·6	16 36	16 09	45·4	15 54	15 24	45·2	15 12	14 40	45·0	14 29	13 56	44·8	13 46	13 13	44·6	227	313
132	48	17 36	16 35	44·6	16 53	15 51	44·4	16 10	15 08	44·2	15 27	14 24	44·0	14 43	13 41	43·8	14 00	12 58	43·6	228	312
131	49	17 53	16 17	43·6	17 09	15 34	43·4	16 25	14 51	43·2	15 42	14 08	43·0	14 58	13 26	42·8	14 13	12 44	42·6	229	311
130	50	18 09	15 58	42·6	17 25	15 16	42·4	16 41	14 33	42·1	15 56	13 52	41·9	15 11	13 10	41·8	14 27	12 29	41·6	230	310
129	51	18 26	15 39	41·6	17 41	14 57	41·3	16 56	14 16	41·1	16 10	13 35	40·9	15 25	12 54	40·8	14 39	12 14	40·6	231	309
128	52	18 42	15 20	40·5	17 56	14 39	40·3	17 11	13 58	40·1	16 24	13 18	39·9	15 38	12 38	39·7	14 52	11 58	39·6	232	308
127	53	18 57	15 00	39·5	18 11	14 20	39·3	17 24	13 40	39·1	16 38	13 00	38·9	15 51	12 21	38·7	15 04	11 42	38·6	233	307
126	54	19 13	14 40	38·5	18 26	14 01	38·3	17 39	13 22	38·1	16 51	12 43	37·9	16 04	12 05	37·7	15 16	11 26	37·5	234	306
125	55	19 28	14 20	37·5	18 40	13 41	37·3	17 52	13 03	37·1	17 04	12 25	36·9	16 16	11 48	36·7	15 28	11 10	36·5	235	305
124	56	19 42	13 59	36·4	18 54	13 21	36·2	18 06	12 44	36·0	17 17	12 07	35·8	16 28	11 30	35·7	15 40	10 54	35·5	236	304
123	57	19 57	13 38	35·4	19 08	13 01	35·2	18 19	12 25	35·0	17 29	11 49	34·8	16 40	11 13	34·6	15 51	10 37	34·5	237	303
122	58	20 11	13 17	34·4	19 21	12 41	34·2	18 31	12 05	34·0	17 42	11 30	33·8	16 52	10 55	33·6	16 02	10 20	33·5	238	302
121	59	20 24	12 55	33·3	19 34	12 20	33·1	18 44	11 45	32·9	17 53	11 11	32·8	17 03	10 37	32·6	16 12	10 03	32·4	239	301
120	60	20 37	12 33	32·3	19 47	11 59	32·1	18 56	11 25	31·9	18 05	10 52	31·7	17 14	10 19	31·6	16 23	9 46	31·4	240	300
119	61	20 50	12 11	31·2	19 59	11 38	31·1	19 08	11 05	30·9	18 16	10 33	30·7	17 24	10 00	30·5	16 33	9 29	30·4	241	299
118	62	21 03	11 48	30·2	20 11	11 16	30·0	19 19	10 44	29·8	18 27	10 13	29·7	17 35	9 42	29·5	16 42	9 11	29·4	242	298
117	63	21 15	11 26	29·2	20 23	10 54	29·0	19 30	10 24	28·8	18 37	9 53	28·6	17 45	9 23	28·5	16 52	8 53	28·3	243	297
116	64	21 27	11 03	28·1	20 34	10 32	27·9	19 41	10 03	27·7	18 47	9 33	27·6	17 54	9 04	27·4	17 01	8 35	27·3	244	296
115	65	21 38	10 39	27·0	20 44	10 10	26·9	19 51	9 41	26·7	18 57	9 13	26·5	18 03	8 45	26·4	17 10	8 17	26·3	245	295
114	66	21 49	10 16	26·0	20 55	9 48	25·8	20 01	9 20	25·7	19 07	8 52	25·5	18 12	8 25	25·4	17 18	7 58	25·2	246	294
113	67	21 59	9 52	24·9	21 05	9 25	24·8	20 10	8 58	24·6	19 16	8 32	24·5	18 21	8 06	24·3	17 26	7 40	24·2	247	293
112	68	22 09	9 28	23·9	21 14	9 02	23·7	20 19	8 36	23·5	19 24	8 11	23·4	18 29	7 46	23·3	17 34	7 21	23·1	248	292
111	69	22 19	9 04	22·8	21 24	8 39	22·8	20 28	8 14	22·5	19 33	7 50	22·4	18 37	7 26	22·2	17 42	7 02	22·1	249	291
110	70	22 28	8 39	21·7	21 32	8 16	21·7	20 37	7 52	21·4	19 41	7 29	21·3	18 45	7 06	21·2	17 49	6 43	21·1	250	290
109	71	22 37	8 15	20·7	21 41	7 52	20·7	20 45	7 30	20·4	19 48	7 07	20·2	18 52	6 45	20·1	17 56	6 24	20·0	251	289
108	72	22 45	7 50	19·6	21 49	7 28	19·6	20 52	7 07	19·3	19 56	6 46	19·2	18 59	6 25	19·1	18 02	6 04	19·0	252	288
107	73	22 53	7 25	18·5	21 56	7 04	18·4	21 00	6 44	18·2	20 03	6 24	18·1	19 05	6 04	18·0	18 08	5 45	17·9	253	287
106	74	23 01	7 00	17·4	22 04	6 40	17·4	21 06	6 21	17·2	20 09	6 02	17·1	19 12	5 44	17·0	18 14	5 25	16·9	254	286
105	75	23 08	6 34	16·3	22 10	6 16	16·3	21 13	5 58	16·1	20 15	5 40	16·0	19 17	5 23	15·9	18 20	5 06	15·8	255	285
104	76	23 15	6 09	15·3	22 17	5 52	15·3	21 19	5 35	15·1	20 21	5 18	15·0	19 23	5 02	14·9	18 25	4 46	14·8	256	284
103	77	23 21	5 43	14·2	22 23	5 27	14·1	21 24	5 12	14·0	20 26	4 56	13·9	19 28	4 41	13·8	18 30	4 26	13·7	257	283
102	78	23 27	5 17	13·1	22 28	5 03	13·1	21 30	4 48	12·9	20 31	4 34	12·8	19 33	4 20	12·7	18 34	4 06	12·7	258	282
101	79	23 32	4 51	12·0	22 33	4 38	12·0	21 35	4 24	11·8	20 36	4 11	11·8	19 37	3 58	11·7	18 38	3 46	11·6	259	281
100	80	23 37	4 25	10·9	22 38	4 13	10·9	21 39	4 01	10·8	20 40	3 49	10·7	19 41	3 37	10·6	18 42	3 25	10·6	260	280
99	81	23 41	3 59	9·8	22 42	3 48	9·8	21 43	3 37	9·7	20 44	3 26	9·6	19 45	3 16	9·6	18 45	3 05	9·5	261	279
98	82	23 45	3 33	8·7	22 46	3 23	8·7	21 46	3 13	8·6	20 47	3 03	8·6	19 48	2 54	8·5	18 48	2 45	8·5	262	278
97	83	23 49	3 06	7·7	22 49	2 58	7·6	21 50	2 49	7·5	20 50	2 41	7·5	19 51	2 32	7·4	18 51	2 24	7·4	263	277
96	84	23 52	2 40	6·6	22 52	2 32	6·5	21 52	2 25	6·5	20 53	2 18	6·4	19 53	2 11	6·4	18 54	2 04	6·3	264	276
95	85	23 54	2 13	5·5	22 54	2 07	5·4	21 55	2 01	5·4	20 55	1 55	5·4	19 55	1 49	5·3	18 55	1 43	5·3	265	275
94	86	23 56	1 47	4·4	22 56	1 42	4·3	21 57	1 37	4·3	20 57	1 32	4·3	19 57	1 27	4·2	18 57	1 23	4·2	266	274
93	87	23 58	1 20	3·3	22 58	1 16	3·3	21 58	1 13	3·2	20 58	1 09	3·2	19 58	1 05	3·2	18 58	1 02	3·2	267	273
92	88	23 59	0 53	2·2	22 59	0 51	2·2	21 59	0 48	2·2	20 59	0 46	2·1	19 59	0 44	2·1	18 59	0 41	2·1	268	272
91	89	24 00	0 27	1·1	23 00	0 25	1·1	22 00	0 24	1·1	21 00	0 23	1·1	20 00	0 22	1·1	19 00	0 21	1·1	269	271
90	90	24 00	0 00	0·0	23 00	0 00	0·0	22 00	0 00	0·0	21 00	0 00	0·0	20 00	0 00	0·0	19 00	0 00	0·0	270	270

N. Lat.: for LHA > 180° .... Z_n = Z
for LHA < 180° .... Z_n = 360° − Z

S. Lat.: for LHA > 180° .... Z_n = 180° − Z
for LHA < 180° .... Z_n = 180° + Z

SIGHT REDUCTION TABLE

B: (−) for 90° < LHA < 270°
Dec:(−) for Lat. contrary name

Z₁: same sign as B
Z₂: (−) for F > 90°

Lat./A LHA/F	72° A/H	72° B/P	72° Z₁/Z₂	73° A/H	73° B/P	73° Z₁/Z₂	74° A/H	74° B/P	74° Z₁/Z₂	75° A/H	75° B/P	75° Z₁/Z₂	76° A/H	76° B/P	76° Z₁/Z₂	77° A/H	77° B/P	77° Z₁/Z₂	Lat./A LHA
0 / 180	0 00	18 00	90·0	0 00	17 00	90·0	0 00	16 00	90·0	0 00	15 00	90·0	0 00	14 00	90·0	0 00	13 00	90·0	180 / 360
1 / 179	0 19	18 00	89·0	0 18	17 00	89·0	0 17	16 00	89·0	0 16	15 00	89·0	0 15	14 00	89·0	0 13	13 00	89·0	181 / 359
2 / 178	0 37	17 59	88·1	0 35	16 59	88·1	0 33	15 59	88·1	0 31	14 59	88·1	0 29	13 59	88·1	0 27	12 59	88·1	182 / 358
3 / 177	0 56	17 59	87·1	0 53	16 59	87·1	0 50	15 59	87·1	0 47	14 59	87·1	0 44	13 59	87·1	0 40	12 58	87·1	183 / 357
4 / 176	1 14	17 58	86·2	1 10	16 58	86·2	1 06	15 58	86·1	1 02	14 58	86·1	0 58	13 58	86·1	0 54	12 58	86·1	184 / 356
5 / 175	1 33	17 57	85·2	1 28	16 56	85·2	1 23	15 57	85·2	1 18	14 57	85·2	1 12	13 57	85·1	1 07	12 57	85·1	185 / 355
6 / 174	1 51	17 54	84·3	1 45	16 55	84·3	1 39	15 55	84·2	1 33	14 55	84·2	1 27	13 56	84·2	1 21	12 56	84·2	186 / 354
7 / 173	2 09	17 52	83·3	2 03	16 53	83·3	1 56	15 53	83·3	1 48	14 54	83·2	1 41	13 54	83·2	1 34	12 54	83·2	187 / 353
8 / 172	2 28	17 50	82·4	2 20	16 51	82·3	2 12	15 51	82·3	2 04	14 52	82·3	1 56	13 52	82·2	1 48	12 53	82·2	188 / 352
9 / 171	2 46	17 48	81·4	2 37	16 48	81·4	2 28	15 49	81·3	2 19	14 49	81·3	2 10	13 50	81·3	2 01	12 51	81·2	189 / 351
10 / 170	3 05	17 45	80·5	2 55	16 45	80·4	2 45	15 46	80·4	2 35	14 47	80·3	2 24	13 48	80·3	2 14	12 49	80·3	190 / 350
11 / 169	3 23	17 41	79·5	3 12	16 42	79·5	3 01	15 43	79·4	2 50	14 44	79·3	2 39	13 45	79·3	2 28	12 46	79·3	191 / 349
12 / 168	3 41	17 38	78·6	3 29	16 39	78·5	3 17	15 40	78·4	3 05	14 41	78·4	2 53	13 42	78·3	2 41	12 44	78·3	192 / 348
13 / 167	3 59	17 34	77·6	3 46	16 35	77·5	3 33	15 37	77·5	3 20	14 38	77·4	3 07	13 39	77·4	2 54	12 41	77·3	193 / 347
14 / 166	4 17	17 30	76·7	4 03	16 31	76·6	3 49	15 33	76·5	3 35	14 34	76·4	3 21	13 36	76·4	3 07	12 38	76·3	194 / 346
15 / 165	4 35	17 25	75·7	4 20	16 27	75·6	4 05	15 29	75·5	3 50	14 31	75·5	3 35	13 32	75·4	3 20	12 34	75·4	195 / 345
16 / 164	4 53	17 21	74·7	4 37	16 23	74·7	4 21	15 25	74·6	4 05	14 27	74·5	3 49	13 29	74·4	3 33	12 31	74·4	196 / 344
17 / 163	5 11	17 16	73·8	4 54	16 18	73·7	4 37	15 20	73·6	4 20	14 22	73·5	4 03	13 25	73·5	3 46	12 27	73·4	197 / 343
18 / 162	5 29	17 10	72·8	5 11	16 13	72·7	4 53	15 15	72·7	4 35	14 18	72·6	4 17	13 20	72·5	3 59	12 23	72·4	198 / 342
19 / 161	5 46	17 05	71·9	5 28	16 07	71·8	5 09	15 10	71·7	4 50	14 13	71·6	4 31	13 16	71·5	4 12	12 19	71·5	199 / 341
20 / 160	6 04	16 59	70·9	5 44	16 02	70·8	5 25	15 05	70·7	5 05	14 08	70·6	4 45	13 11	70·5	4 25	12 14	70·5	200 / 340
21 / 159	6 21	16 52	69·9	6 01	15 56	69·8	5 40	14 59	69·8	5 19	14 03	69·7	4 58	13 06	69·6	4 37	12 10	69·5	201 / 339
22 / 158	6 39	16 46	69·0	6 17	15 50	68·9	5 56	14 53	68·8	5 34	13 57	68·7	5 12	13 01	68·6	4 50	12 05	68·5	202 / 338
23 / 157	6 56	16 39	68·0	6 34	15 43	67·9	6 11	14 47	67·8	5 48	13 51	67·7	5 25	12 56	67·6	5 03	12 00	67·5	203 / 337
24 / 156	7 13	16 32	67·1	6 50	15 36	66·9	6 26	14 41	66·8	6 03	13 45	66·7	5 39	12 50	66·6	5 15	11 55	66·5	204 / 336
25 / 155	7 30	16 25	66·1	7 06	15 29	66·0	6 41	14 34	65·9	6 17	13 39	65·8	5 52	12 44	65·6	5 27	11 49	65·5	205 / 335
26 / 154	7 47	16 17	65·1	7 22	15 22	65·0	6 56	14 27	64·9	6 31	13 32	64·8	6 05	12 38	64·7	5 40	11 43	64·6	206 / 334
27 / 153	8 04	16 09	64·1	7 38	15 14	64·0	7 11	14 20	63·9	6 45	13 26	63·8	6 18	12 32	63·7	5 52	11 37	63·6	207 / 333
28 / 152	8 21	16 00	63·2	7 53	15 06	63·0	7 26	14 12	62·9	6 59	13 19	62·8	6 31	12 25	62·7	6 04	11 31	62·6	208 / 332
29 / 151	8 37	15 52	62·2	8 09	14 58	62·1	7 41	14 05	61·9	7 13	13 11	61·8	6 44	12 18	61·7	6 16	11 25	61·6	209 / 331
30 / 150	8 53	15 43	61·2	8 24	14 50	61·1	7 55	13 57	61·0	7 26	13 04	60·9	6 57	12 11	60·7	6 27	11 18	60·6	210 / 330
31 / 149	9 09	15 34	60·3	8 40	14 41	60·1	8 10	13 49	60·0	7 40	12 56	59·9	7 09	12 04	59·8	6 39	11 12	59·7	211 / 329
32 / 148	9 25	15 24	59·3	8 55	14 32	59·1	8 24	13 40	59·1	7 53	12 48	58·9	7 22	11 56	58·8	6 51	11 05	58·7	212 / 328
33 / 147	9 41	15 15	58·3	9 09	14 23	58·2	8 38	13 31	58·2	8 06	12 40	58·0	7 34	11 49	57·8	7 02	10 57	57·7	213 / 327
34 / 146	9 57	15 05	57·3	9 25	14 13	57·2	8 52	13 22	57·1	8 19	12 31	57·0	7 46	11 41	56·8	7 14	10 50	56·7	214 / 326
35 / 145	10 13	14 54	56·3	9 39	14 04	56·2	9 06	13 13	56·1	8 32	12 23	55·9	7 59	11 33	55·8	7 25	10 43	55·7	215 / 325
36 / 144	10 28	14 44	55·4	9 54	13 54	55·2	9 19	13 04	55·1	8 45	12 14	54·9	8 11	11 24	54·8	7 36	10 35	54·7	216 / 324
37 / 143	10 43	14 33	54·4	10 08	13 43	54·2	9 33	12 54	54·1	8 58	12 05	53·9	8 22	11 16	53·8	7 47	10 27	53·7	217 / 323
38 / 142	10 58	14 22	53·4	10 22	13 33	53·2	9 46	12 44	53·1	9 10	11 55	53·0	8 34	11 07	52·8	7 58	10 19	52·7	218 / 322
39 / 141	11 13	14 10	52·4	10 36	13 22	52·2	9 59	12 34	52·1	9 22	11 46	51·9	8 45	10 58	51·7	8 08	10 10	51·7	219 / 321
40 / 140	11 27	13 59	51·4	10 50	13 11	51·3	10 12	12 23	51·1	9 35	11 36	51·0	8 57	10 49	50·8	8 19	10 02	50·7	220 / 320
41 / 139	11 42	13 47	50·4	11 04	13 00	50·3	10 25	12 13	50·1	9 47	11 26	50·0	9 08	10 39	49·9	8 29	9 53	49·7	221 / 319
42 / 138	11 56	13 34	49·4	11 17	12 48	49·3	10 38	12 02	49·1	9 58	11 16	49·0	9 19	10 30	48·9	8 39	9 44	48·7	222 / 318
43 / 137	12 10	13 22	48·4	11 30	12 36	48·3	10 50	11 51	48·1	10 10	11 05	48·0	9 30	10 20	47·9	8 49	9 35	47·7	223 / 317
44 / 136	12 24	13 09	47·4	11 43	12 24	47·3	11 02	11 39	47·1	10 21	10 55	47·0	9 40	10 10	46·9	8 59	9 26	46·7	224 / 316
45 / 135	12 37	12 56	46·4	11 56	12 12	46·3	11 14	11 28	46·1	10 33	10 44	46·0	9 51	10 00	45·9	9 09	9 16	45·7	225 / 315

LHA/F	A	72° A/H	72° B/P	72° Z_1/Z_2	73° A/H	73° B/P	73° Z_1/Z_2	74° A/H	74° B/P	74° Z_1/Z_2	75° A/H	75° B/P	75° Z_1/Z_2	76° A/H	76° B/P	76° Z_1/Z_2	77° A/H	77° B/P	77° Z_1/Z_2	LHA	A
135	45	12 37	12 56	46·4	11 56	12 12	46·3	11 14	11 28	46·1	10 33	10 44	46·0	9 51	10 00	45·9	9 09	9 16	45·7	315	225
134	46	12 51	12 43	45·4	12 08	11 59	45·3	11 26	11 16	45·1	10 44	10 33	45·0	10 01	9 50	44·9	9 19	9 07	44·7	314	226
133	47	13 04	12 30	44·4	12 21	11 47	44·3	11 38	11 04	44·1	10 55	10 21	44·0	10 11	9 39	43·9	9 28	8 57	43·7	313	227
132	48	13 17	12 16	43·4	12 33	11 34	43·3	11 49	10 52	43·1	11 05	10 10	43·0	10 21	9 28	42·9	9 37	8 47	42·7	312	228
131	49	13 29	12 02	42·4	12 45	11 21	42·3	12 00	10 39	42·1	11 16	9 58	42·0	10 31	9 17	41·9	9 46	8 37	41·7	311	229
130	50	13 42	11 48	41·4	12 57	11 07	41·3	12 11	10 27	41·1	11 26	9 46	41·0	10 41	9 06	40·9	9 55	8 26	40·7	310	230
129	51	13 54	11 33	40·4	13 08	10 53	40·3	12 22	10 14	40·1	11 36	9 34	40·0	10 50	8 55	39·8	10 04	8 16	39·7	309	231
128	52	14 06	11 19	39·4	13 19	10 40	39·2	12 32	10 01	39·1	11 46	9 22	39·0	10 59	8 44	38·8	10 13	8 05	38·7	308	232
127	53	14 17	11 04	38·4	13 30	10 26	38·2	12 43	9 47	38·1	11 56	9 10	38·0	11 08	8 32	37·8	10 21	7 55	37·7	307	233
126	54	14 29	10 49	37·4	13 41	10 11	37·2	12 53	9 34	37·1	12 05	8 57	36·9	11 17	8 20	36·8	10 29	7 44	36·7	306	234
125	55	14 40	10 33	36·4	13 51	9 57	36·2	13 03	9 20	36·1	12 14	8 44	35·9	11 26	8 08	35·8	10 37	7 33	35·7	305	235
124	56	14 51	10 18	35·3	14 02	9 42	35·2	13 13	9 07	35·1	12 23	8 31	34·9	11 34	7 56	34·8	10 45	7 21	34·7	304	236
123	57	15 01	10 02	34·3	14 12	9 27	34·2	13 22	8 53	34·0	12 32	8 18	33·9	11 42	7 44	33·8	10 52	7 10	33·7	303	237
122	58	15 12	9 46	33·3	14 21	9 12	33·2	13 31	8 38	33·0	12 41	8 05	32·9	11 50	7 32	32·8	11 00	6 58	32·7	302	238
121	59	15 21	9 30	32·3	14 31	8 57	32·1	13 40	8 24	32·0	12 49	7 51	31·9	11 58	7 19	31·8	11 07	6 47	31·7	301	239
120	60	15 31	9 14	31·3	14 40	8 41	31·1	13 49	8 10	31·0	12 57	7 38	30·9	12 06	7 06	30·8	11 14	6 35	30·6	300	240
119	61	15 41	8 57	30·2	14 49	8 26	30·1	13 57	7 55	30·0	13 05	7 24	29·8	12 13	6 54	29·7	11 21	6 23	29·6	299	241
118	62	15 50	8 40	29·2	14 58	8 10	29·1	14 05	7 40	28·9	13 13	7 10	28·8	12 20	6 41	28·7	11 27	6 11	28·6	298	242
117	63	15 59	8 23	28·2	15 06	7 54	28·0	14 13	7 25	27·9	13 20	6 56	27·8	12 27	6 27	27·7	11 34	5 59	27·6	297	243
116	64	16 08	8 06	27·2	15 14	7 38	27·0	14 21	7 10	26·9	13 27	6 42	26·8	12 34	6 14	26·7	11 40	5 47	26·6	296	244
115	65	16 16	7 49	26·1	15 22	7 22	26·0	14 28	6 55	25·9	13 34	6 28	25·8	12 40	6 01	25·7	11 46	5 34	25·6	295	245
114	66	16 24	7 32	25·1	15 29	7 05	25·0	14 35	6 39	24·9	13 41	6 13	24·7	12 46	5 47	24·6	11 52	5 22	24·6	294	246
113	67	16 32	7 14	24·1	15 37	6 49	23·9	14 42	6 24	23·8	13 47	5 59	23·7	12 52	5 34	23·6	11 57	5 09	23·5	293	247
112	68	16 39	6 56	23·0	15 44	6 32	22·9	14 48	6 08	22·8	13 53	5 44	22·7	12 58	5 20	22·6	12 02	4 57	22·5	292	248
111	69	16 46	6 38	22·0	15 50	6 15	21·9	14 55	5 52	21·8	13 59	5 29	21·7	13 03	5 06	21·6	12 07	4 44	21·5	291	249
110	70	16 53	6 20	20·9	15 57	5 58	20·8	15 01	5 36	20·7	14 04	5 14	20·6	13 08	4 52	20·6	12 12	4 31	20·5	290	250
109	71	16 59	6 02	19·9	16 03	5 41	19·8	15 06	5 20	19·7	14 10	4 59	19·6	13 13	4 38	19·5	12 17	4 18	19·5	289	251
108	72	17 05	5 44	18·9	16 09	5 24	18·8	15 12	5 04	18·7	14 15	4 44	18·6	13 18	4 24	18·5	12 21	4 05	18·4	288	252
107	73	17 11	5 26	17·8	16 14	5 06	17·7	15 17	4 48	17·6	14 20	4 29	17·6	13 23	4 10	17·5	12 25	3 52	17·4	287	253
106	74	17 17	5 07	16·8	16 19	4 49	16·7	15 22	4 31	16·6	14 24	4 13	16·5	13 27	3 56	16·5	12 29	3 38	16·4	286	254
105	75	17 22	4 48	15·7	16 24	4 31	15·7	15 26	4 15	15·6	14 29	3 58	15·5	13 31	3 42	15·4	12 33	3 25	15·4	285	255
104	76	17 27	4 30	14·7	16 29	4 14	14·6	15 31	3 58	14·5	14 33	3 43	14·5	13 35	3 27	14·4	12 36	3 12	14·4	284	256
103	77	17 31	4 11	13·6	16 33	3 56	13·6	15 35	3 41	13·5	14 36	3 27	13·4	13 38	3 13	13·4	12 40	2 59	13·3	283	257
102	78	17 36	3 52	12·6	16 37	3 38	12·5	15 38	3 25	12·5	14 40	3 11	12·4	13 41	2 58	12·4	12 43	2 45	12·3	282	258
101	79	17 39	3 33	11·6	16 41	3 20	11·5	15 42	3 08	11·4	14 43	2 56	11·4	13 44	2 43	11·3	12 45	2 31	11·3	281	259
100	80	17 43	3 14	10·5	16 44	3 02	10·4	15 45	2 51	10·4	14 46	2 40	10·3	13 47	2 29	10·3	12 48	2 18	10·3	280	260
99	81	17 46	2 55	9·5	16 47	2 44	9·4	15 48	2 34	9·4	14 49	2 24	9·3	13 49	2 14	9·3	12 50	2 04	9·2	279	261
98	82	17 49	2 35	8·4	16 50	2 26	8·4	15 50	2 17	8·3	14 51	2 08	8·3	13 52	1 59	8·2	12 52	1 50	8·2	278	262
97	83	17 52	2 16	7·4	16 52	2 08	7·3	15 53	2 00	7·3	14 53	1 52	7·2	13 54	1 44	7·2	12 54	1 37	7·2	277	263
96	84	17 54	1 57	6·3	16 54	1 50	6·3	15 55	1 43	6·2	14 55	1 36	6·2	13 55	1 30	6·2	12 56	1 23	6·2	276	264
95	85	17 56	1 37	5·3	16 56	1 32	5·2	15 56	1 26	5·2	14 56	1 20	5·2	13 57	1 15	5·2	12 57	1 09	5·1	275	265
94	86	17 57	1 18	4·2	16 57	1 13	4·2	15 58	1 09	4·2	14 58	1 04	4·1	13 58	1 00	4·1	12 58	0 55	4·1	274	266
93	87	17 58	0 58	3·2	16 59	0 55	3·1	15 59	0 52	3·1	14 59	0 48	3·1	13 59	0 45	3·1	12 59	0 42	3·1	273	267
92	88	17 59	0 39	2·1	16 59	0 37	2·1	15 59	0 34	2·1	14 59	0 32	2·1	13 59	0 30	2·1	12 59	0 28	2·1	272	268
91	89	18 00	0 19	1·1	17 00	0 18	1·0	16 00	0 17	1·0	15 00	0 16	1·0	14 00	0 15	1·0	13 00	0 14	1·0	271	269
90	90	18 00	0 00	0·0	17 00	0 00	0·0	16 00	0 00	0·0	15 00	0 00	0·0	14 00	0 00	0·0	13 00	0 00	0·0	270	270

N. Lat.: for LHA > 180°... $Z_n = Z$
        for LHA < 180°... $Z_n = 360° - Z$

S. Lat.: for LHA > 180°... $Z_n = 180° - Z$
       for LHA < 180°... $Z_n = 180° + Z$

SIGHT REDUCTION TABLE

B: (−) for 90° < LHA < 270°
Dec: (−) for Lat. contrary name

Z₁: same sign as B
Z₂: (−) for F > 90°

LHA/F	Lat./A	78° A/H	78° B/P	78° Z₁/Z₂	79° A/H	79° B/P	79° Z₁/Z₂	80° A/H	80° B/P	80° Z₁/Z₂	81° A/H	81° B/P	81° Z₁/Z₂	82° A/H	82° B/P	82° Z₁/Z₂	83° A/H	83° B/P	83° Z₁/Z₂	Lat./A	LHA
0	180	0 00	12 00	90·0	0 00	11 00	90·0	0 00	10 00	90·0	0 00	9 00	90·0	0 00	8 00	90·0	0 00	7 00	90·0	360	180
1	179	0 12	12 00	89·0	0 11	11 00	89·0	0 10	10 00	89·0	0 09	9 00	89·0	0 08	8 00	89·0	0 07	7 00	89·0	359	181
2	178	0 25	12 00	88·0	0 23	11 00	88·0	0 21	10 00	88·0	0 19	9 00	88·0	0 17	8 00	88·0	0 15	7 00	88·0	358	182
3	177	0 37	11 58	87·1	0 34	10 59	87·1	0 31	9 59	87·0	0 28	8 59	87·0	0 25	7 59	87·0	0 22	6 59	87·0	357	183
4	176	0 50	11 58	86·1	0 46	10 58	86·1	0 42	9 59	86·1	0 38	8 59	86·0	0 33	7 59	86·0	0 29	6 59	86·0	356	184
5	175	1 02	11 57	85·1	0 57	10 58	85·1	0 52	9 58	85·1	0 47	8 58	85·1	0 42	7 58	85·0	0 37	6 58	85·0	355	185
6	174	1 15	11 56	84·1	1 09	10 56	84·1	1 02	9 57	84·1	0 56	8 57	84·1	0 50	7 57	84·1	0 44	6 58	84·0	354	186
7	173	1 27	11 55	83·2	1 20	10 55	83·1	1 12	9 56	83·1	1 06	8 56	83·1	0 58	7 56	83·1	0 51	6 57	83·1	353	187
8	172	1 39	11 53	82·2	1 31	10 54	82·1	1 23	9 54	82·1	1 15	8 55	82·1	1 07	7 55	82·1	0 58	6 56	82·1	352	188
9	171	1 52	11 51	81·2	1 43	10 52	81·2	1 33	9 53	81·1	1 24	8 53	81·1	1 15	7 54	81·1	1 06	6 55	81·1	351	189
10	170	2 04	11 49	80·2	1 54	10 50	80·2	1 44	9 51	80·2	1 33	8 52	80·1	1 23	7 53	80·1	1 13	6 54	80·1	350	190
11	169	2 16	11 47	79·2	2 05	10 48	79·2	1 54	9 49	79·2	1 43	8 50	79·1	1 31	7 51	79·1	1 20	6 52	79·1	349	191
12	168	2 29	11 45	78·3	2 16	10 46	78·2	2 04	9 47	78·2	1 52	8 48	78·1	1 39	7 50	78·1	1 27	6 51	78·1	348	192
13	167	2 41	11 42	77·3	2 28	10 43	77·2	2 14	9 45	77·2	2 01	8 46	77·2	1 48	7 48	77·1	1 34	6 49	77·1	347	193
14	166	2 53	11 39	76·3	2 39	10 41	76·2	2 24	9 43	76·2	2 10	8 44	76·2	1 56	7 46	76·1	1 41	6 48	76·1	346	194
15	165	3 05	11 36	75·3	2 50	10 38	75·3	2 35	9 40	75·2	2 19	8 42	75·2	2 04	7 44	75·1	1 48	6 46	75·1	345	195
16	164	3 17	11 33	74·3	3 01	10 35	74·3	2 45	9 37	74·2	2 28	8 39	74·2	2 12	7 42	74·2	1 56	6 44	74·1	344	196
17	163	3 29	11 29	73·4	3 12	10 32	73·3	2 55	9 34	73·2	2 37	8 37	73·2	2 20	7 39	73·2	2 03	6 42	73·1	343	197
18	162	3 41	11 26	72·4	3 23	10 28	72·3	3 05	9 31	72·3	2 46	8 34	72·2	2 28	7 37	72·2	2 09	6 40	72·1	342	198
19	161	3 53	11 22	71·4	3 34	10 25	71·3	3 14	9 28	71·3	2 55	8 31	71·3	2 36	7 34	71·2	2 16	6 37	71·1	341	199
20	160	4 05	11 18	70·4	3 45	10 21	70·3	3 24	9 24	70·3	3 04	8 28	70·3	2 44	7 31	70·2	2 23	6 35	70·1	340	200
21	159	4 16	11 13	69·4	3 55	10 17	69·4	3 34	9 21	69·3	3 13	8 25	69·3	2 52	7 28	69·2	2 30	6 32	69·1	339	201
22	158	4 28	11 09	68·4	4 06	10 13	68·4	3 44	9 17	68·3	3 22	8 21	68·3	2 59	7 25	68·2	2 37	6 30	68·1	338	202
23	157	4 40	11 04	67·5	4 17	10 09	67·4	3 53	9 13	67·3	3 30	8 18	67·3	3 07	7 22	67·2	2 44	6 27	67·2	337	203
24	156	4 51	10 59	66·5	4 27	10 04	66·4	4 03	9 09	66·4	3 39	8 14	66·3	3 15	7 19	66·2	2 50	6 24	66·2	336	204
25	155	5 02	10 54	65·5	4 38	9 59	65·4	4 13	9 05	65·4	3 47	8 10	65·3	3 22	7 16	65·2	2 57	6 21	65·2	335	205
26	154	5 14	10 49	64·5	4 48	9 55	64·4	4 22	9 00	64·4	3 56	8 06	64·3	3 30	7 12	64·2	3 04	6 18	64·2	334	206
27	153	5 25	10 43	63·5	4 58	9 50	63·5	4 31	8 56	63·4	4 04	8 02	63·3	3 37	7 08	63·2	3 10	6 15	63·2	333	207
28	152	5 36	10 38	62·5	5 08	9 44	62·5	4 41	8 51	62·4	4 13	7 58	62·4	3 45	7 04	62·2	3 17	6 11	62·2	332	208
29	151	5 47	10 32	61·5	5 18	9 39	61·5	4 50	8 46	61·4	4 21	7 53	61·4	3 52	7 00	61·2	3 23	6 08	61·2	331	209
30	150	5 58	10 26	60·5	5 28	9 33	60·5	4 59	8 41	60·4	4 29	7 49	60·4	3 59	6 56	60·2	3 30	6 04	60·2	330	210
31	149	6 09	10 20	59·6	5 38	9 28	59·6	5 08	8 36	59·4	4 37	7 44	59·4	4 07	6 52	59·2	3 36	6 00	59·2	329	211
32	148	6 20	10 13	58·6	5 48	9 22	58·5	5 17	8 30	58·4	4 45	7 39	58·4	4 14	6 48	58·3	3 42	5 57	58·2	328	212
33	147	6 30	10 06	57·6	5 58	9 16	57·5	5 26	8 25	57·5	4 53	7 34	57·4	4 21	6 43	57·3	3 48	5 53	57·2	327	213
34	146	6 41	10 00	56·6	6 08	9 09	56·5	5 34	8 19	56·5	5 01	7 29	56·4	4 28	6 39	56·3	3 54	5 49	56·2	326	214
35	145	6 51	9 53	55·6	6 17	9 03	55·5	5 43	8 13	55·5	5 09	7 24	55·4	4 35	6 34	55·3	4 00	5 45	55·2	325	215
36	144	7 01	9 45	54·6	6 26	8 56	54·5	5 51	8 07	54·5	5 17	7 18	54·4	4 42	6 29	54·3	4 06	5 40	54·2	324	216
37	143	7 11	9 38	53·6	6 36	8 49	53·6	6 00	8 01	53·5	5 24	7 13	53·4	4 48	6 24	53·3	4 12	5 36	53·2	323	217
38	142	7 21	9 31	52·6	6 45	8 43	52·6	6 08	7 55	52·5	5 32	7 07	52·4	4 55	6 19	52·3	4 18	5 32	52·2	322	218
39	141	7 31	9 23	51·6	6 54	8 35	51·6	6 16	7 48	51·5	5 39	7 01	51·4	5 01	6 14	51·3	4 24	5 27	51·2	321	219
40	140	7 41	9 15	50·6	7 03	8 28	50·6	6 25	7 42	50·5	5 46	6 55	50·4	5 08	6 09	50·3	4 30	5 22	50·2	320	220
41	139	7 50	9 07	49·6	7 11	8 21	49·6	6 32	7 35	49·5	5 53	6 49	49·4	5 14	6 03	49·3	4 35	5 18	49·2	319	221
42	138	8 00	8 59	48·6	7 20	8 13	48·5	6 40	7 28	48·5	6 01	6 43	48·4	5 21	5 58	48·3	4 41	5 13	48·2	318	222
43	137	8 09	8 50	47·6	7 29	8 05	47·5	6 48	7 21	47·5	6 07	6 36	47·4	5 27	5 52	47·3	4 46	5 08	47·2	317	223
44	136	8 18	8 42	46·6	7 37	7 58	46·5	6 56	7 14	46·5	6 14	6 30	46·4	5 33	5 46	46·3	4 51	5 03	46·2	316	224
45	135	8 27	8 33	45·6	7 45	7 50	45·5	7 03	7 06	45·5	6 21	6 23	45·4	5 39	5 41	45·3	4 57	4 58	45·2	315	225

A	LHA	83° A/H	83° B/P	83° Z_1/Z_2	82° A/H	82° B/P	82° Z_1/Z_2	81° A/H	81° B/P	81° Z_1/Z_2	80° A/H	80° B/P	80° Z_1/Z_2	79° A/H	79° B/P	79° Z_1/Z_2	78° A/H	78° B/P	78° Z_1/Z_2	LHA/F	A
315	225	4 57	4 58	45.2	5 39	5 41	45.3	6 21	6 23	45.4	7 03	7 06	45.4	7 45	7 50	45.5	8 27	8 33	45.6	135	45
314	226	5 02	4 53	44.2	5 45	5 35	44.3	6 28	6 17	44.4	7 11	6 59	44.4	7 53	7 41	44.5	8 36	8 24	44.6	134	46
313	227	5 07	4 47	43.2	5 51	5 28	43.3	6 34	6 10	43.4	7 18	6 51	43.4	8 01	7 33	43.5	8 45	8 15	43.6	133	47
312	228	5 12	4 42	42.2	5 56	5 22	42.3	6 41	6 03	42.4	7 25	6 44	42.4	8 09	7 25	42.5	8 53	8 06	42.6	132	48
311	229	5 17	4 36	41.2	6 02	5 16	41.3	6 47	5 56	41.4	7 32	6 36	41.4	8 17	7 16	41.5	9 02	7 56	41.6	131	49
310	230	5 21	4 31	40.2	6 07	5 10	40.3	6 53	5 49	40.3	7 39	6 28	40.4	8 24	7 07	40.5	9 10	7 47	40.6	130	50
309	231	5 26	4 25	39.2	6 13	5 03	39.3	6 59	5 42	39.3	7 45	6 20	39.4	8 32	6 58	39.5	9 18	7 37	39.6	129	51
308	232	5 31	4 19	38.2	6 18	4 57	38.3	7 05	5 34	38.3	7 52	6 12	38.4	8 39	6 49	38.5	9 26	7 27	38.6	128	52
307	233	5 35	4 14	37.2	6 23	4 50	37.3	7 11	5 27	37.3	7 58	6 03	37.4	8 46	6 40	37.5	9 33	7 17	37.6	127	53
306	234	5 39	4 08	36.2	6 28	4 43	36.3	7 16	5 19	36.3	8 05	5 55	36.4	8 53	6 31	36.5	9 41	7 07	36.6	126	54
305	235	5 44	4 02	35.2	6 33	4 37	35.3	7 22	5 11	35.3	8 11	5 47	35.4	9 00	6 22	35.5	9 48	6 57	35.6	125	55
304	236	5 48	3 56	34.2	6 38	4 30	34.3	7 27	5 04	34.3	8 17	5 38	34.4	9 06	6 12	34.5	9 56	6 47	34.6	124	56
303	237	5 52	3 50	33.2	6 42	4 23	33.3	7 32	4 56	33.3	8 22	5 29	33.4	9 13	6 03	33.5	10 03	6 36	33.6	123	57
302	238	5 56	3 43	32.2	6 47	4 16	32.3	7 37	4 48	32.3	8 28	5 20	32.4	9 19	5 53	32.5	10 09	6 26	32.6	122	58
301	239	6 00	3 37	31.2	6 51	4 08	31.2	7 42	4 40	31.3	8 34	5 11	31.4	9 25	5 43	31.5	10 16	6 15	31.6	121	59
300	240	6 04	3 31	30.2	6 55	4 01	30.2	7 47	4 32	30.3	8 39	5 02	30.4	9 31	5 33	30.5	10 22	6 04	30.6	120	60
299	241	6 07	3 24	29.2	6 59	3 54	29.2	7 52	4 23	29.3	8 44	4 53	29.4	9 36	5 23	29.5	10 29	5 53	29.5	119	61
298	242	6 11	3 18	28.2	7 04	3 46	28.2	7 56	4 15	28.3	8 49	4 44	28.4	9 42	5 13	28.4	10 35	5 42	28.5	118	62
297	243	6 14	3 11	27.2	7 07	3 39	27.2	8 01	4 07	27.3	8 54	4 35	27.4	9 47	5 03	27.4	10 41	5 31	27.5	117	63
296	244	6 17	3 05	26.2	7 11	3 32	26.2	8 05	3 58	26.3	8 59	4 25	26.3	9 52	4 52	26.4	10 46	5 19	26.5	116	64
295	245	6 20	2 58	25.2	7 15	3 24	25.2	8 09	3 50	25.3	9 03	4 16	25.3	9 57	4 42	25.4	10 52	5 08	25.5	115	65
294	246	6 24	2 52	24.2	7 18	3 16	24.2	8 13	3 41	24.3	9 08	4 06	24.3	10 02	4 31	24.4	10 57	4 56	24.5	114	66
293	247	6 26	2 45	23.2	7 22	3 09	23.2	8 17	3 32	23.3	9 12	3 56	23.3	10 07	4 21	23.4	11 02	4 45	23.5	113	67
292	248	6 29	2 38	22.1	7 25	3 01	22.2	8 20	3 24	22.2	9 16	3 47	22.3	10 11	4 10	22.4	11 07	4 33	22.4	112	68
291	249	6 32	2 31	21.1	7 28	2 53	21.2	8 24	3 15	21.2	9 20	3 37	21.3	10 16	3 59	21.4	11 12	4 21	21.4	111	69
290	250	6 35	2 24	20.1	7 31	2 45	20.2	8 27	3 06	20.2	9 23	3 27	20.3	10 20	3 48	20.3	11 16	4 09	20.4	110	70
289	251	6 37	2 17	19.1	7 34	2 37	19.2	8 30	2 57	19.2	9 27	3 17	19.3	10 24	3 37	19.3	11 20	3 58	19.4	109	71
288	252	6 39	2 10	18.1	7 36	2 29	18.2	8 33	2 48	18.2	9 30	3 07	18.3	10 27	3 26	18.3	11 24	3 45	18.4	108	72
287	253	6 42	2 03	17.1	7 39	2 21	17.2	8 36	2 39	17.2	9 34	2 57	17.2	10 31	3 15	17.3	11 28	3 33	17.4	107	73
286	254	6 44	1 56	16.1	7 41	2 13	16.1	8 39	2 30	16.2	9 37	2 47	16.2	10 34	3 04	16.3	11 32	3 21	16.3	106	74
285	255	6 46	1 49	15.1	7 44	2 05	15.1	8 41	2 21	15.1	9 39	2 37	15.2	10 37	2 53	15.3	11 35	3 09	15.3	105	75
284	256	6 47	1 42	14.1	7 46	1 57	14.1	8 44	2 12	14.1	9 42	2 27	14.2	10 40	2 42	14.3	11 38	2 57	14.3	104	76
283	257	6 49	1 35	13.1	7 48	1 49	13.1	8 46	2 02	13.1	9 44	2 16	13.2	10 43	2 30	13.2	11 41	2 44	13.3	103	77
282	258	6 51	1 28	12.1	7 49	1 40	12.1	8 48	1 53	12.1	9 47	2 06	12.2	10 45	2 19	12.2	11 44	2 32	12.3	102	78
281	259	6 52	1 21	11.1	7 51	1 32	11.1	8 50	1 44	11.1	9 49	1 56	11.2	10 48	2 07	11.2	11 47	2 19	11.2	101	79
280	260	6 54	1 13	10.1	7 53	1 24	10.1	8 52	1 35	10.1	9 51	1 45	10.2	10 50	1 56	10.2	11 49	2 07	10.2	100	80
279	261	6 55	1 06	9.1	7 54	1 16	9.1	8 53	1 25	9.1	9 53	1 35	9.1	10 52	1 45	9.1	11 51	1 54	9.2	99	81
278	262	6 56	0 59	8.1	7 55	1 07	8.1	8 55	1 16	8.1	9 54	1 24	8.1	10 53	1 33	8.1	11 53	1 42	8.2	98	82
277	263	6 57	0 51	7.1	7 56	0 59	7.1	8 56	1 06	7.1	9 55	1 14	7.1	10 55	1 21	7.1	11 55	1 29	7.2	97	83
276	264	6 58	0 44	6.0	7 57	0 50	6.1	8 57	0 57	6.1	9 57	1 03	6.1	10 56	1 10	6.1	11 56	1 16	6.1	96	84
275	265	6 58	0 37	5.0	7 58	0 42	5.1	8 58	0 47	5.1	9 58	0 53	5.1	10 57	0 58	5.1	11 57	1 04	5.1	95	85
274	266	6 59	0 29	4.0	7 59	0 34	4.0	8 59	0 38	4.0	9 59	0 42	4.1	10 58	0 47	4.1	11 58	0 51	4.1	94	86
273	267	6 59	0 22	3.0	7 59	0 25	3.0	8 59	0 28	3.0	9 59	0 32	3.0	10 59	0 35	3.1	11 59	0 38	3.1	93	87
272	268	7 00	0 15	2.0	8 00	0 17	2.0	9 00	0 19	2.0	10 00	0 21	2.0	11 00	0 23	2.0	12 00	0 26	2.0	92	88
271	269	7 00	0 07	1.0	8 00	0 08	1.0	9 00	0 10	1.0	10 00	0 11	1.0	11 00	0 12	1.0	12 00	0 13	1.0	91	89
270	270	7 00	0 00	0.0	8 00	0 00	0.0	9 00	0 00	0.0	10 00	0 00	0.0	11 00	0 00	0.0	12 00	0 00	0.0	90	90

N. Lat.: for LHA > 180° .... $Z_n = Z$
for LHA < 180° .... $Z_n = 360° - Z$

S. Lat.: for LHA > 180° .... $Z_n = 180° - Z$
for LHA < 180° .... $Z_n = 180° + Z$

SIGHT REDUCTION TABLE

B: (−) for 90° < LHA < 270°
Dec:(−) for Lat. contrary name

Z₁: same sign as B
Z₂: (−) for F > 90°

LHA/F	84° A/H	84° B/P	84° Z₁/Z₂	85° A/H	85° B/P	85° Z₁/Z₂	86° A/H	86° B/P	86° Z₁/Z₂	87° A/H	87° B/P	87° Z₁/Z₂	88° A/H	88° B/P	88° Z₁/Z₂	89° A/H	89° B/P	89° Z₁/Z₂	Z₁/Z₂	LHA
0 / 180	0 00	6 00	90.0	0 00	5 00	90.0	0 00	4 00	90.0	0 00	3 00	90.0	0 00	2 00	90.0	0 00	1 00	90.0	90.0	180 / 360
1 / 179	0 06	6 00	89.0	0 05	5 00	89.0	0 04	4 00	89.0	0 03	3 00	89.0	0 02	2 00	89.0	0 01	1 00	89.0	89.0	181 / 359
2 / 178	0 13	6 00	88.0	0 10	5 00	88.0	0 08	4 00	88.0	0 06	3 00	88.0	0 04	2 00	88.0	0 02	1 00	88.0	88.0	182 / 358
3 / 177	0 19	6 00	87.0	0 16	5 00	87.0	0 13	4 00	87.0	0 09	3 00	87.0	0 06	2 00	87.0	0 03	1 00	87.0	87.0	183 / 357
4 / 176	0 25	5 59	86.0	0 21	4 59	86.0	0 17	3 59	86.0	0 13	3 00	86.0	0 08	2 00	86.0	0 04	1 00	86.0	86.0	184 / 356
5 / 175	0 31	5 59	85.0	0 26	4 59	85.0	0 21	3 59	85.0	0 16	2 59	85.0	0 10	2 00	85.0	0 05	1 00	85.0	85.0	185 / 355
6 / 174	0 38	5 58	84.0	0 31	4 58	84.0	0 25	3 59	84.0	0 19	2 59	84.0	0 13	1 59	84.0	0 06	1 00	84.0	84.0	186 / 354
7 / 173	0 44	5 58	83.0	0 37	4 58	83.0	0 29	3 58	83.0	0 22	2 59	83.0	0 15	1 59	83.0	0 07	1 00	83.0	83.0	187 / 353
8 / 172	0 50	5 57	82.0	0 42	4 57	82.0	0 33	3 58	82.0	0 25	2 58	82.0	0 17	1 59	82.0	0 08	0 59	82.0	82.0	188 / 352
9 / 171	0 56	5 56	81.0	0 47	4 56	81.0	0 38	3 57	81.0	0 28	2 58	81.0	0 19	1 58	81.0	0 09	0 59	81.0	81.0	189 / 351
10 / 170	1 02	5 55	80.1	0 52	4 55	80.1	0 42	3 56	80.0	0 31	2 57	80.0	0 21	1 58	80.0	0 10	0 59	80.0	80.0	190 / 350
11 / 169	1 09	5 53	79.1	0 57	4 55	79.1	0 46	3 56	79.0	0 34	2 57	79.0	0 23	1 58	79.0	0 11	0 59	79.0	79.0	191 / 349
12 / 168	1 15	5 52	78.1	1 02	4 53	78.0	0 50	3 55	78.0	0 37	2 56	78.0	0 25	1 57	78.0	0 12	0 59	78.0	78.0	192 / 348
13 / 167	1 21	5 51	77.1	1 07	4 52	77.1	0 54	3 54	77.0	0 40	2 55	77.0	0 27	1 57	77.0	0 13	0 58	77.0	77.0	193 / 347
14 / 166	1 27	5 49	76.1	1 12	4 51	76.1	0 58	3 53	76.1	0 44	2 55	76.0	0 29	1 56	76.0	0 15	0 58	76.0	76.0	194 / 346
15 / 165	1 33	5 48	75.1	1 18	4 50	75.1	1 02	3 52	75.0	0 47	2 54	75.0	0 31	1 56	75.0	0 16	0 58	75.0	75.0	195 / 345
16 / 164	1 39	5 46	74.1	1 23	4 48	74.1	1 06	3 51	74.0	0 50	2 53	74.0	0 33	1 56	74.0	0 17	0 58	74.0	74.0	196 / 344
17 / 163	1 45	5 44	73.1	1 28	4 47	73.1	1 10	3 50	73.0	0 53	2 52	73.0	0 35	1 55	73.0	0 18	0 57	73.0	73.0	197 / 343
18 / 162	1 51	5 42	72.1	1 33	4 45	72.1	1 14	3 48	72.0	0 56	2 51	72.0	0 37	1 54	72.0	0 19	0 57	72.0	72.0	198 / 342
19 / 161	1 57	5 41	71.1	1 38	4 44	71.1	1 18	3 47	71.0	0 59	2 50	71.0	0 39	1 53	71.0	0 20	0 57	71.0	71.0	199 / 341
20 / 160	2 03	5 38	70.1	1 42	4 42	70.1	1 22	3 46	70.1	1 02	2 49	70.0	0 41	1 53	70.0	0 21	0 56	70.0	70.0	200 / 340
21 / 159	2 09	5 36	69.1	1 47	4 40	69.1	1 26	3 44	69.1	1 04	2 48	69.0	0 43	1 52	69.0	0 22	0 56	69.0	69.0	201 / 339
22 / 158	2 15	5 34	68.1	1 52	4 38	68.1	1 30	3 43	68.1	1 07	2 47	68.0	0 45	1 52	68.0	0 22	0 56	68.0	68.0	202 / 338
23 / 157	2 20	5 32	67.1	1 57	4 36	67.1	1 34	3 41	67.1	1 10	2 46	67.0	0 47	1 51	67.0	0 23	0 55	67.0	67.0	203 / 337
24 / 156	2 26	5 29	66.1	2 02	4 34	66.1	1 38	3 39	66.1	1 13	2 44	66.0	0 49	1 50	66.0	0 24	0 55	66.0	66.0	204 / 336
25 / 155	2 32	5 26	65.1	2 07	4 32	65.1	1 41	3 38	65.1	1 16	2 43	65.0	0 51	1 49	65.0	0 25	0 54	65.0	65.0	205 / 335
26 / 154	2 38	5 24	64.1	2 11	4 30	64.1	1 45	3 36	64.1	1 19	2 42	64.0	0 53	1 48	64.0	0 26	0 54	64.0	64.0	206 / 334
27 / 153	2 43	5 21	63.1	2 16	4 27	63.1	1 49	3 34	63.1	1 22	2 40	63.0	0 54	1 47	63.0	0 27	0 53	63.0	63.0	207 / 333
28 / 152	2 49	5 18	62.1	2 21	4 25	62.1	1 53	3 32	62.1	1 24	2 39	62.0	0 56	1 46	62.0	0 28	0 53	62.0	62.0	208 / 332
29 / 151	2 54	5 15	61.1	2 25	4 23	61.1	1 56	3 30	61.1	1 27	2 37	61.0	0 58	1 45	61.0	0 29	0 52	61.0	61.0	209 / 331
30 / 150	3 00	5 12	60.1	2 30	4 20	60.1	2 00	3 28	60.1	1 30	2 36	60.0	1 00	1 44	60.0	0 30	0 52	60.0	60.0	210 / 330
31 / 149	3 05	5 09	59.1	2 34	4 17	59.1	2 04	3 26	59.1	1 33	2 34	59.0	1 02	1 43	59.0	0 31	0 51	59.0	59.0	211 / 329
32 / 148	3 11	5 06	58.1	2 39	4 15	58.1	2 07	3 24	58.1	1 35	2 33	58.0	1 04	1 42	58.0	0 32	0 51	58.0	58.0	212 / 328
33 / 147	3 16	5 02	57.1	2 43	4 12	57.1	2 11	3 21	57.1	1 38	2 31	57.0	1 05	1 41	57.0	0 33	0 50	57.0	57.0	213 / 327
34 / 146	3 21	4 59	56.1	2 48	4 09	56.1	2 14	3 19	56.1	1 41	2 29	56.0	1 07	1 39	56.0	0 34	0 50	56.0	56.0	214 / 326
35 / 145	3 26	4 55	55.1	2 52	4 06	55.1	2 18	3 17	55.1	1 43	2 27	55.0	1 09	1 38	55.0	0 34	0 49	55.0	55.0	215 / 325
36 / 144	3 31	4 52	54.1	2 56	4 03	54.1	2 21	3 14	54.1	1 46	2 26	54.0	1 11	1 37	54.0	0 35	0 49	54.0	54.0	216 / 324
37 / 143	3 36	4 48	53.2	3 00	4 00	53.1	2 24	3 12	53.1	1 48	2 24	53.0	1 12	1 36	53.0	0 36	0 48	53.0	53.0	217 / 323
38 / 142	3 41	4 44	52.2	3 05	3 57	52.2	2 28	3 09	52.1	1 51	2 22	52.0	1 14	1 35	52.0	0 37	0 47	52.0	52.0	218 / 322
39 / 141	3 46	4 40	51.2	3 09	3 53	51.2	2 31	3 07	51.1	1 53	2 20	51.0	1 16	1 33	51.0	0 38	0 47	51.0	51.0	219 / 321
40 / 140	3 51	4 36	50.2	3 13	3 50	50.2	2 34	3 04	50.1	1 56	2 18	50.0	1 17	1 32	50.0	0 39	0 46	50.0	50.0	220 / 320
41 / 139	3 56	4 32	49.2	3 17	3 47	49.1	2 37	3 01	49.1	1 58	2 16	49.0	1 19	1 31	49.0	0 39	0 45	49.0	49.0	221 / 319
42 / 138	4 01	4 28	48.2	3 21	3 43	48.1	2 41	2 58	48.1	2 00	2 14	48.0	1 20	1 29	48.0	0 40	0 45	48.0	48.0	222 / 318
43 / 137	4 05	4 24	47.2	3 24	3 40	47.1	2 44	2 56	47.1	2 03	2 12	47.0	1 22	1 28	47.0	0 41	0 44	47.0	47.0	223 / 317
44 / 136	4 10	4 19	46.2	3 28	3 36	46.1	2 47	2 53	46.1	2 05	2 10	46.0	1 23	1 26	46.0	0 42	0 43	46.0	46.0	224 / 316
45 / 135	4 14	4 15	45.2	3 32	3 32	45.1	2 50	2 50	45.1	2 07	2 07	45.0	1 25	1 25	45.0	0 42	0 42	45.0	45.0	225 / 315

Lat./A	LHA/F	84° A/H	84° B/P	84° Z₁/Z₂	85° A/H	85° B/P	85° Z₁/Z₂	86° A/H	86° B/P	86° Z₁/Z₂	87° A/H	87° B/P	87° Z₁/Z₂	88° A/H	88° B/P	88° Z₁/Z₂	89° A/H	89° B/P	89° Z₁/Z₂	LHA	Lat./A
45	135	4 14	4 15	45·2	3 32	3 32	45·1	2 50	2 50	45·1	2 07	2 07	45·0	1 25	1 25	45·0	0 42	0 42	45·0	225	315
46	134	4 19	4 11	44·2	3 36	3 29	44·1	2 53	2 47	44·1	2 09	2 05	44·0	1 26	1 23	44·0	0 43	0 42	44·0	226	314
47	133	4 23	4 06	43·2	3 39	3 25	43·1	2 55	2 44	43·1	2 12	2 03	43·0	1 28	1 22	43·0	0 44	0 41	43·0	227	313
48	132	4 27	4 01	42·2	3 43	3 21	42·1	2 58	2 41	42·1	2 14	2 01	42·0	1 29	1 20	42·0	0 45	0 40	42·0	228	312
49	131	4 31	3 57	41·2	3 46	3 17	41·1	3 01	2 38	41·1	2 16	1 58	41·0	1 31	1 19	41·0	0 45	0 39	41·0	229	311
50	130	4 36	3 52	40·2	3 50	3 13	40·1	3 04	2 34	40·1	2 18	1 56	40·0	1 32	1 17	40·0	0 46	0 39	40·0	230	310
51	129	4 40	3 47	39·2	3 53	3 09	39·1	3 06	2 31	39·1	2 20	1 53	39·0	1 33	1 16	39·0	0 47	0 38	39·0	231	309
52	128	4 43	3 42	38·2	3 56	3 05	38·1	3 09	2 28	38·1	2 22	1 51	38·0	1 35	1 14	38·0	0 47	0 37	38·0	232	308
53	127	4 47	3 37	37·2	3 59	3 01	37·1	3 12	2 25	37·1	2 24	1 48	37·0	1 36	1 12	37·0	0 48	0 36	37·0	233	307
54	126	4 51	3 32	36·1	4 03	2 57	36·1	3 14	2 21	36·1	2 26	1 46	36·0	1 37	1 11	36·0	0 49	0 35	36·0	234	306
55	125	4 55	3 27	35·1	4 06	2 52	35·1	3 17	2 18	35·1	2 27	1 43	35·0	1 38	1 09	35·0	0 49	0 34	35·0	235	305
56	124	4 58	3 22	34·1	4 09	2 48	34·1	3 19	2 14	34·1	2 29	1 41	34·0	1 39	1 07	34·0	0 50	0 34	34·0	236	304
57	123	5 02	3 17	33·1	4 12	2 44	33·1	3 21	2 11	33·1	2 31	1 38	33·0	1 41	1 05	33·0	0 50	0 33	33·0	237	303
58	122	5 05	3 11	32·1	4 14	2 39	32·1	3 23	2 07	32·1	2 33	1 35	32·0	1 42	1 04	32·0	0 51	0 32	32·0	238	302
59	121	5 08	3 06	31·1	4 17	2 35	31·1	3 26	2 04	31·1	2 34	1 33	31·0	1 43	1 02	31·0	0 51	0 31	31·0	239	301
60	120	5 12	3 00	30·1	4 20	2 30	30·1	3 28	2 00	30·1	2 36	1 30	30·0	1 44	1 00	30·0	0 52	0 30	30·0	240	300
61	119	5 15	2 55	29·1	4 22	2 26	29·1	3 30	1 56	29·1	2 37	1 27	29·0	1 45	0 58	29·0	0 52	0 29	29·0	241	299
62	118	5 18	2 49	28·1	4 25	2 21	28·1	3 32	1 53	28·1	2 39	1 25	28·0	1 46	0 56	28·0	0 53	0 28	28·0	242	298
63	117	5 21	2 44	27·1	4 27	2 16	27·1	3 34	1 49	27·1	2 40	1 22	27·0	1 47	0 54	27·0	0 53	0 27	27·0	243	297
64	116	5 23	2 38	26·1	4 30	2 12	26·1	3 36	1 45	26·1	2 42	1 19	26·0	1 48	0 53	26·0	0 54	0 26	26·0	244	296
65	115	5 26	2 33	25·1	4 32	2 07	25·1	3 37	1 42	25·1	2 43	1 16	25·0	1 49	0 51	25·0	0 54	0 25	25·0	245	295
66	114	5 29	2 27	24·1	4 34	2 02	24·1	3 39	1 38	24·1	2 44	1 13	24·0	1 50	0 49	24·0	0 55	0 24	24·0	246	294
67	113	5 31	2 21	23·1	4 36	1 57	23·1	3 41	1 34	23·1	2 46	1 10	23·0	1 50	0 47	23·0	0 55	0 23	23·0	247	293
68	112	5 34	2 15	22·1	4 38	1 53	22·1	3 42	1 30	22·1	2 47	1 07	22·0	1 51	0 45	22·0	0 56	0 22	22·0	248	292
69	111	5 36	2 09	21·1	4 40	1 48	21·1	3 44	1 26	21·1	2 48	1 05	21·0	1 52	0 43	21·0	0 56	0 22	21·0	249	291
70	110	5 38	2 04	20·1	4 43	1 43	20·1	3 46	1 22	20·0	2 49	1 02	20·0	1 53	0 41	20·0	0 56	0 21	20·0	250	290
71	109	5 40	1 58	19·1	4 44	1 38	19·1	3 47	1 18	19·0	2 50	0 59	19·0	1 53	0 39	19·0	0 57	0 20	19·0	251	289
72	108	5 42	1 52	18·1	4 45	1 33	18·1	3 48	1 14	18·0	2 51	0 56	18·0	1 54	0 37	18·0	0 57	0 19	18·0	252	288
73	107	5 44	1 46	17·1	4 47	1 28	17·1	3 49	1 10	17·0	2 52	0 53	17·0	1 55	0 35	17·0	0 57	0 18	17·0	253	287
74	106	5 46	1 40	16·1	4 48	1 23	16·1	3 51	1 06	16·0	2 53	0 50	16·0	1 55	0 33	16·0	0 58	0 17	16·0	254	286
75	105	5 48	1 33	15·1	4 50	1 18	15·1	3 52	1 02	15·0	2 54	0 47	15·0	1 56	0 31	15·0	0 58	0 16	15·0	255	285
76	104	5 49	1 27	14·1	4 51	1 13	14·1	3 53	0 58	14·0	2 55	0 44	14·0	1 56	0 29	14·0	0 58	0 15	14·0	256	284
77	103	5 51	1 21	13·1	4 52	1 08	13·0	3 54	0 54	13·0	2 56	0 41	13·0	1 57	0 27	13·0	0 59	0 13	13·0	257	283
78	102	5 52	1 15	12·1	4 53	1 03	12·0	3 55	0 50	12·0	2 56	0 37	12·0	1 57	0 25	12·0	0 59	0 12	12·0	258	282
79	101	5 53	1 09	11·1	4 54	0 57	11·0	3 56	0 46	11·0	2 57	0 34	11·0	1 58	0 23	11·0	0 59	0 11	11·0	259	281
80	100	5 55	1 03	10·1	4 55	0 52	10·0	3 56	0 42	10·0	2 57	0 31	10·0	1 58	0 21	10·0	0 59	0 10	10·0	260	280
81	99	5 56	0 57	9·0	4 56	0 47	9·0	3 57	0 38	9·0	2 58	0 28	9·0	1 59	0 19	9·0	0 59	0 09	9·0	261	279
82	98	5 56	0 50	8·0	4 57	0 42	8·0	3 58	0 33	8·0	2 58	0 25	8·0	1 59	0 17	8·0	0 59	0 08	8·0	262	278
83	97	5 57	0 44	7·0	4 58	0 37	7·0	3 58	0 29	7·0	2 59	0 22	7·0	1 59	0 15	7·0	1 00	0 07	7·0	263	277
84	96	5 58	0 38	6·0	4 58	0 31	6·0	3 59	0 25	6·0	2 59	0 19	6·0	1 59	0 13	6·0	1 00	0 06	6·0	264	276
85	95	5 59	0 31	5·0	4 59	0 26	5·0	3 59	0 21	5·0	2 59	0 16	5·0	2 00	0 10	5·0	1 00	0 05	5·0	265	275
86	94	5 59	0 25	4·0	4 59	0 21	4·0	3 59	0 17	4·0	3 00	0 13	4·0	2 00	0 08	4·0	1 00	0 04	4·0	266	274
87	93	6 00	0 19	3·0	5 00	0 16	3·0	4 00	0 13	3·0	3 00	0 09	3·0	2 00	0 06	3·0	1 00	0 03	3·0	267	273
88	92	6 00	0 13	2·0	5 00	0 10	2·0	4 00	0 08	2·0	3 00	0 06	2·0	2 00	0 04	2·0	1 00	0 02	2·0	268	272
89	91	6 00	0 06	1·0	5 00	0 05	1·0	4 00	0 04	1·0	3 00	0 03	1·0	2 00	0 02	1·0	1 00	0 01	1·0	269	271
90	90	6 00	0 00	0·0	5 00	0 00	0·0	4 00	0 00	0·0	3 00	0 00	0·0	2 00	0 00	0·0	1 00	0 00	0·0	270	270

N. Lat: for LHA > 180° ... Zn = Z
　　　　for LHA < 180° ... Zn = 360° − Z

S. Lat.: for LHA > 180° ... Zn = 180° − Z
　　　　for LHA < 180° ... Zn = 180° + Z

AUXILIARY TABLE

Sign for $corr_2$ for A'. → $-/+$ A' Z°_2

Sign of $corr_1$ for F'. *Reverse sign if $F > 90^\circ$.* → F' $+/-$ P°

P°	Z°	1/59	2/58	3/57	4/56	5/55	6/54	7/53	8/52	9/51	10/50	11/49	12/48	13/47	14/46	15/45	16/44	17/43	18/42	19/41	20/40	21/39	22/38	23/37	24/36	25/35	26/34	27/33	28/32	29/31	30/□
1	89	0	0	0	0	0	0	0	0	0	0	0	0	0	0	0	0	0	0	0	0	0	0	0	0	0	0	0	0	1	1
2	88	0	0	0	0	0	0	0	0	0	0	0	0	0	0	0	1	1	1	1	1	1	1	1	1	1	1	1	1	1	1
3	87	0	0	0	0	0	0	0	0	0	1	1	1	1	1	1	1	1	1	1	1	1	1	1	1	1	1	1	1	2	2
4	86	0	0	0	0	0	0	0	0	0	1	1	1	1	1	1	1	1	1	1	1	1	2	2	2	2	2	2	2	2	2
5	85	0	0	0	0	0	0	1	1	1	1	1	1	1	1	1	1	1	2	2	2	2	2	2	2	2	2	2	2	3	3
6	84	0	0	0	0	0	1	1	1	1	1	1	1	1	1	1	2	2	2	2	2	2	2	2	3	3	3	3	3	3	3
7	83	0	0	0	0	1	1	1	1	1	1	2	2	2	2	2	2	2	2	2	2	3	3	3	3	3	3	3	3	4	4
8	82	0	0	0	1	1	1	1	1	1	2	2	2	2	2	2	2	2	3	3	3	3	3	3	3	4	4	4	3	4	4
9	81	0	0	0	1	1	1	1	1	1	2	2	2	2	2	2	3	3	3	3	3	3	3	4	4	4	4	4	4	5	5
10	80	0	0	1	1	1	1	1	1	2	2	2	2	2	2	2	3	3	3	3	3	4	4	4	4	5	5	5	5	5	5
11	79	0	0	1	1	1	1	1	2	2	2	2	2	2	3	3	3	3	3	4	4	4	4	4	5	5	5	5	5	6	6
12	78	0	0	1	1	1	1	1	2	2	2	2	2	3	3	3	3	4	4	4	4	4	5	5	5	5	5	6	6	6	6
13	77	0	0	1	1	1	1	2	2	2	2	3	3	3	3	3	4	4	4	4	4	5	5	5	5	6	6	6	6	7	7
14	76	0	0	1	1	1	1	2	2	2	2	3	3	3	3	4	4	4	4	5	5	5	5	6	6	6	6	7	7	7	7
15	75	0	1	1	1	1	2	2	2	2	3	3	3	3	4	4	4	4	5	5	5	5	6	6	6	6	7	7	7	8	8
16	74	0	1	1	1	1	2	2	2	3	3	3	3	4	4	4	4	5	5	5	6	6	6	6	7	7	7	7	8	8	8
17	73	0	1	1	1	1	2	2	2	3	3	3	4	4	4	4	5	5	5	6	6	6	6	7	7	7	8	8	8	8	9
18	72	0	1	1	1	2	2	2	2	3	3	4	4	4	4	5	5	5	6	6	6	6	7	7	7	8	8	8	9	9	9
19	71	0	1	1	1	2	2	2	3	3	3	4	4	4	5	5	5	6	6	6	7	7	7	7	8	8	8	9	9	9	10
20	70	0	1	1	1	2	2	2	3	3	3	4	4	4	5	5	5	6	6	6	7	7	8	8	8	9	9	9	10	10	10
21	69	0	1	1	2	2	2	3	3	3	4	4	4	5	5	5	6	6	6	7	7	8	8	8	9	9	9	10	10	10	11
22	68	0	1	1	2	2	2	3	3	3	4	4	5	5	5	6	6	6	7	7	8	8	8	9	9	9	10	10	10	11	11
23	67	0	1	1	2	2	2	3	3	4	4	4	5	5	5	6	6	7	7	7	8	8	9	9	9	10	10	11	11	11	12
24	66	0	1	1	2	2	2	3	3	4	4	5	5	5	6	6	7	7	7	8	8	9	9	9	10	10	11	11	11	12	12
25	65	0	1	1	2	2	2	3	3	4	4	5	5	5	6	6	7	7	8	8	9	9	9	10	10	11	11	11	12	12	13
26	64	0	1	1	2	2	3	3	3	4	4	5	5	6	6	7	7	7	8	8	9	9	10	10	11	11	11	12	12	13	13
27	63	0	1	1	2	2	3	3	4	4	5	5	5	6	6	7	7	8	8	9	9	10	10	10	11	11	12	12	13	13	14
28	62	0	1	1	2	2	3	3	4	4	5	5	6	6	7	7	8	8	8	9	10	10	10	11	11	12	12	13	13	14	14
29	61	1	1	1	2	2	3	3	4	4	5	5	6	6	7	7	8	8	9	9	10	10	11	11	12	12	13	13	14	14	15
30	60	1	1	1	2	2	3	3	4	4	5	5	6	6	7	7	8	8	9	9	10	10	11	11	12	12	13	13	14	14	15
31	59	1	1	2	2	2	3	4	4	5	5	6	6	7	7	8	8	9	9	10	10	11	11	12	12	13	13	14	14	15	15
32	58	1	1	2	2	3	3	4	4	5	5	6	6	7	7	8	8	9	10	10	11	11	12	12	13	13	14	14	15	15	16
33	57	1	1	2	2	3	3	4	4	5	5	6	7	7	8	8	9	9	10	11	11	12	12	13	13	14	14	15	15	16	16
34	56	1	1	2	3	3	3	4	4	5	6	6	7	7	8	8	9	10	10	11	11	12	13	13	13	14	15	15	16	16	17
35	55	1	1	2	3	3	3	4	5	5	6	6	7	7	8	9	9	10	11	11	12	12	13	13	14	14	15	15	16	17	17
36	54	1	1	2	2	3	3	4	5	5	6	6	7	8	8	9	9	10	11	11	12	12	13	14	14	15	15	16	16	17	18
37	53	1	1	2	2	3	3	4	5	5	6	7	7	8	8	9	10	10	11	12	12	13	13	14	14	15	16	16	17	17	18
38	52	1	1	2	2	3	4	4	5	6	6	7	7	8	9	9	10	11	11	12	13	13	14	14	15	15	16	17	17	18	18
39	51	1	1	2	3	3	4	4	5	6	6	7	8	8	9	9	10	11	11	12	13	13	14	15	15	16	16	17	18	18	19
40	50	1	1	2	3	3	4	4	5	6	6	7	8	8	9	10	10	11	12	12	13	13	14	15	15	16	17	17	18	19	19

F′ +	1	2	3	4	5	6	7	8	9	10	11	12	13	14	15	16	17	18	19	20	21	22	23	24	25	26	27	28	29	□	− A′
F′ −	59	58	57	56	55	54	53	52	51	50	49	48	47	46	45	44	43	42	41	40	39	38	37	36	35	34	33	32	31	30	+ A′
P°	′	′	′	′	′	′	′	′	′	′	′	′	′	′	′	′	′	′	′	′	′	′	′	′	′	′	′	′	′	′	Z_2°
41	1	1	2	3	3	4	5	5	6	7	7	8	9	9	10	10	11	12	12	13	14	14	15	16	16	17	18	18	19	20	49
42	1	1	2	3	3	4	5	5	6	7	7	8	9	9	10	11	11	12	13	13	14	15	15	16	17	17	18	19	19	20	48
43	1	1	2	3	3	4	5	5	6	7	8	8	9	10	10	11	12	12	13	14	14	15	16	16	17	18	18	19	20	20	47
44	1	1	2	3	3	4	5	6	6	7	8	8	9	10	10	11	12	13	13	14	15	15	16	17	17	18	19	19	20	21	46
45	1	1	2	3	4	4	5	6	6	7	8	8	9	10	11	11	12	13	13	14	15	16	16	17	18	18	19	20	21	21	45
46	1	1	2	3	4	4	5	6	6	7	8	9	9	10	11	12	12	13	14	14	15	16	17	17	18	19	19	20	21	22	44
47	1	1	2	3	4	4	5	6	7	7	8	9	10	10	11	12	12	13	14	15	15	16	17	18	18	19	20	20	21	22	43
48	1	1	2	3	4	4	5	6	7	7	8	9	10	10	11	12	13	13	14	15	16	16	17	18	19	19	20	21	22	22	42
49	1	2	2	3	4	5	5	6	7	8	8	9	10	11	11	12	13	14	14	15	16	17	17	18	19	20	20	21	22	23	41
50	1	2	2	3	4	5	5	6	7	8	8	9	10	11	11	12	13	14	15	15	16	17	18	18	19	20	21	21	22	23	40
51	1	2	2	3	4	5	5	6	7	8	9	9	10	11	12	12	13	14	15	16	16	17	18	19	19	20	21	22	23	23	39
52	1	2	2	3	4	5	6	6	7	8	9	9	10	11	12	13	13	14	15	16	17	17	18	19	20	20	21	22	23	24	38
53	1	2	2	3	4	5	6	6	7	8	9	10	10	11	12	13	14	14	15	16	17	18	18	19	20	21	22	22	23	24	37
54	1	2	2	3	4	5	6	6	7	8	9	10	11	11	12	13	14	15	15	16	17	18	19	19	20	21	22	23	23	24	36
55	1	2	2	3	4	5	6	7	7	8	9	10	11	11	12	13	14	15	16	16	17	18	19	20	20	21	22	23	24	25	35
56	1	2	2	3	4	5	6	7	7	8	9	10	11	12	12	13	14	15	16	17	17	18	19	20	21	22	22	23	24	25	34
57	1	2	3	3	4	5	6	7	8	8	9	10	11	12	13	13	14	15	16	17	18	18	19	20	21	22	23	23	24	25	33
58	1	2	3	3	4	5	6	7	8	8	9	10	11	12	13	14	14	15	16	17	18	19	20	20	21	22	23	24	25	25	32
59	1	2	3	3	4	5	6	7	8	9	9	10	11	12	13	14	15	15	16	17	18	19	20	21	21	22	23	24	25	26	31
60	1	2	3	3	4	5	6	7	8	9	10	10	11	12	13	14	15	16	16	17	18	19	20	21	22	23	23	24	25	26	30
61	1	2	3	3	4	5	6	7	8	9	10	10	11	12	13	14	15	16	17	17	18	19	20	21	22	23	24	24	25	26	29
62	1	2	3	4	4	5	6	7	8	9	10	11	11	12	13	14	15	16	17	18	19	19	20	21	22	23	24	25	26	26	28
63	1	2	3	4	4	5	6	7	8	9	10	11	12	12	13	14	15	16	17	18	19	20	20	21	22	23	24	25	26	27	27
64	1	2	3	4	4	5	6	7	8	9	10	11	12	13	13	14	15	16	17	18	19	20	21	22	22	23	24	25	26	27	26
65	1	2	3	4	5	5	6	7	8	9	10	11	12	13	14	15	15	16	17	18	19	20	21	22	23	24	24	25	26	27	25
66	1	2	3	4	5	5	6	7	8	9	10	11	12	13	14	15	16	16	17	18	19	20	21	22	23	24	25	26	26	27	24
67	1	2	3	4	5	6	6	7	8	9	10	11	12	13	14	15	16	17	17	18	19	20	21	22	23	24	25	26	27	28	23
68	1	2	3	4	5	6	6	7	8	9	10	11	12	13	14	15	16	17	18	19	19	20	21	22	23	24	25	26	27	28	22
69	1	2	3	4	5	6	7	7	8	9	10	11	12	13	14	15	16	17	18	19	20	21	21	22	23	24	25	26	27	28	21
70	1	2	3	4	5	6	7	8	8	9	10	11	12	13	14	15	16	17	18	19	20	21	22	23	23	24	25	26	27	28	20
71	1	2	3	4	5	6	7	8	9	9	10	11	12	13	14	15	16	17	18	19	20	21	22	23	24	25	26	26	27	28	19
72	1	2	3	4	5	6	7	8	9	10	10	11	12	13	14	15	16	17	18	19	20	21	22	23	24	25	26	27	28	29	18
73	1	2	3	4	5	6	7	8	9	10	11	11	12	13	14	15	16	17	18	19	20	21	22	23	24	25	26	27	28	29	17
74	1	2	3	4	5	6	7	8	9	10	11	12	12	13	14	15	16	17	18	19	20	21	22	23	24	25	26	27	28	29	16
75	1	2	3	4	5	6	7	8	9	10	11	12	13	14	14	15	16	17	18	19	20	21	22	23	24	25	26	27	28	29	15
76	1	2	3	4	5	6	7	8	9	10	11	12	13	14	15	16	16	17	18	19	20	21	22	23	24	25	26	27	28	29	14
77	1	2	3	4	5	6	7	8	9	10	11	12	13	14	15	16	17	18	19	19	20	21	22	23	24	25	26	27	28	29	13
78	1	2	3	4	5	6	7	8	9	10	11	12	13	14	15	16	17	18	19	20	21	22	22	23	24	25	26	27	28	29	12
79	1	2	3	4	5	6	7	8	9	10	11	12	13	14	15	16	17	18	19	20	21	22	23	24	25	26	27	27	28	29	11
80	1	2	3	4	5	6	7	8	9	10	11	12	13	14	15	16	17	18	19	20	21	22	23	24	25	26	27	28	29	30	10

For P > 80°, use 80°

For $Z_2 < 10°$, use 10°

USE OF CONCISE SIGHT REDUCTION TABLES (continued)

4. *Example.* (b) Required the altitude and azimuth of *Vega* on 2020 July 29 at UT 04^h 47^m from the estimated position S 15°, W 152°.

1. Assumed latitude $Lat =$ 15° S
   From the almanac $GHA =$ 99° 38′
   Assumed longitude   151° 38′ W

   Local hour angle $LHA =$ 308

2. Reduction table, 1st entry
   $(Lat, LHA) = (15, 308)$ $A =$ 49   34 $A° = 50$, $A' = 34$
                             $B = +66$ 29 $Z_1 = +71.7$, $LHA > 270°$

3. From the almanac $Dec = -38$ 48   *Lat* and *Dec* contrary

   Sum $= B + Dec$ $F = +27$ 41 $F° = 28$, $F' = 41$

4. Reduction table, 2nd entry
   $(A°, F°) = (50, 28)$ $H =$ 17   34 $P° = 37$
                                            $Z_2 = 67.8, Z_2° = 68$

5. Auxiliary table, 1st entry
   $(F', P°) = (41, 37)$ $corr_1 =$ -11 $F < 90°$, $F' > 29'$
   Sum   17   23

6. Auxiliary table, 2nd entry
   $(A', Z_2°) = (34, 68)$ $corr_2 =$ $+10$ $A' > 30'$

7. Sum = computed altitude $H_c = +17° 33'$ $F > 0°$

8. Azimuth,   first component $Z_1 = +71.7$ same sign as B
            second component $Z_2 = +67.8$ $F < 90°$, $F > 0°$
   Sum = azimuth angle $Z =$ 139.5

   True azimuth $Z_n =$ 040°   S *Lat*, $LHA > 180°$

5. *Form for use with the Concise Sight Reduction Tables.* The form on the following page lays out the procedure explained on pages 284-285. Each step is shown, with notes and rules to ensure accuracy, rather than speed, throughout the calculation. The form is mainly intended for the calculation of star positions. It therefore includes the formation of the Greenwich hour of Aries (*GHA* Aries), and thus the Greenwich hour angle of the star (*GHA*) from its tabular sidereal hour angle (*SHA*). These calculations, included in step 1 of the form, can easily be replaced by the interpolation of *GHA* and *Dec* for the Sun, Moon or planets.

The form may be freely copied; however, acknowledgement of the source is requested.

Date & UT of observation	Body	Estimated Latitude & Longitude
h m s		° ' ° '

Step	Calculate Altitude & Azimuth	Summary of Rules & Notes
Assumed latitude	$Lat =$ °	Nearest estimated latitude, integral number of degrees.
Assumed longitude	$Long =$ ° '	Choose *Long* so that *LHA* has integral number of degrees.
1. From the almanac:	$Dec =$ ° '	Record the *Dec* for use in Step 3.
GHA Aries ^{h}	$=$ ° '	Needed if using *SHA*. Tabular value.
Increment ^{m} ^{s}	$=$ ° '	for minutes and seconds of time.
SHA	$SHA =$ ° '	
GHA = GHA Aries + SHA	$GHA =$ ° '	Remove multiples of 360°.
Assumed longitude	$Long =$ ° '	West longitudes are negative.
LHA = GHA + Long	$LHA =$ °	Remove multiples of 360°.
2. Reduction table, 1ˢᵗ entry $(Lat, LHA) = ($ °, °$)$ record A, B and Z_1.	$A =$ ° ' $A° =$ °	nearest whole degree of A.
	$A' =$ '	minutes part of A.
	$B =$ ° '	B is minus if $90° < LHA < 270°$.
	$Z_1 =$ °	Z_1 has the same sign as B.
3. From step 1	$Dec =$ ° '	*Dec* is minus if contrary to *Lat*.
$F = B + Dec$	$F =$ ° '	Regard F as positive until step 7.
	$F° =$ °	nearest whole degree of F.
	$F' =$ '	minutes part of F.
4. Reduction table, 2ⁿᵈ entry $(A°, F°) = ($ °, °$)$ record H, P and Z_2.	$H =$ ° ' $P° =$ °	nearest whole degree of P.
	$Z_2 =$ °	
5. Auxiliary table, 1ˢᵗ entry $(F', P°) = ($ ', °$)$ record $corr_1$	$corr_1 =$ '	$corr_1$ is minus if $F < 90°$ & $F' > 29'$, or if $F > 90°$ & $F' < 30'$.
6. Auxiliary table, 2ⁿᵈ entry $(A', Z_2°) = ($ ', °$)$ record $corr_2$	$corr_2 =$ '	$Z_2°$ nearest whole degree of Z_2. $corr_2$ is minus if $A' < 30'$.
7. Calculated altitude = $H_c = H + corr_1 + corr_2$	$H_c =$ ° '	H_c is minus if F is negative, and object is below the horizon.
8. Azimuth, 1ˢᵗ component	$Z_1 =$ °	Z_1 has the same sign as B.
2ⁿᵈ component	$Z_2 =$ °	Z_2 is minus if $F > 90°$. If F is negative, $Z_2 = 180° - Z_2$
$Z = Z_1 + Z_2$	$Z =$ °	Ignore the sign of Z.
	N *Lat*:	If $LHA > 180°$, $Z_n = Z$, or if $LHA < 180°$, $Z_n = 360° - Z$,
	S *Lat*:	If $LHA > 180°$, $Z_n = 180° - Z$, or if $LHA < 180°$, $Z_n = 180° + Z$.
True azimuth	$Z_n =$ °	©HMNAO

For use with *The Nautical Almanac's* Concise Sight Reduction Tables pages 284-318.

POLAR PHENOMENA
EXPLANATION

1. *Introduction.* The graphs on pages 322-325 give data concerning the rising and setting of the Sun and Moon and the duration of civil twilight for high latitudes. Graphs are given instead of tables for high latitudes because they give a clearer picture of the phenomena and of the attainable accuracy in any given case. In the regions of the graph that are difficult to read accurately, the phenomenon itself is generally uncertain.

2. *Semiduration of sunlight.* The graphs for the semiduration of sunlight (page 322) give for latitudes north of N 65° the number of hours from sunrise to meridian passage or from meridian passage to sunset. There is continuous daylight in an area marked "Sun above horizon", and no direct sunlight in an area marked "Sun below horizon". The figures near the top indicate, for several convenient dates, the local mean times of meridian passage; with the aid of the intermediate dots the LMT on any given day may be obtained to the nearest minute. The LMT of sunrise may be found by subtracting the semiduration from the time of meridian passage, and the time of sunset by adding. The equation of time is given by subtracting the time of meridian passage from noon.

Examples. (a) Estimate the time of sunrise and sunset on 2020 March 10 at latitude N 78°. The semiduration of sunlight (page 322) is about $5^h 00^m$. The time of meridian passage is $12^h 10^m$, and hence the LMT of sunrise is $07^h 10^m$, and of sunset $17^h 10^m$. (b) Estimate the dates, for the first half of 2020, when the Sun is continuously below and above the horizon at latitude N 80°. The semiduration of sunlight graph (page 322) indicates the Sun is continuously below the horizon until about February 21, and is continuously above the horizon after April 14.

3. *Duration of civil twilight.* The graphs for the duration of twilight (page 322) give the interval from the beginning of morning civil twilight (Sun 6° below the horizon) to the time of sunrise or from the time of sunset to the end of evening civil twilight. In a region marked "No twilight or sunlight", the Sun is continuously below the horizon by more than 6°. In a region marked "Continuous twilight or sunlight", the Sun never goes lower than 6° below the horizon.

Adjacent to a region marked "No twilight or sunlight" is a region in which the Sun is continuously below the horizon, but so near to the horizon during a portion of the day that there is twilight. This area is the shaded region. The value given by the graph in this shaded region is the interval from the beginning of morning twilight to meridian passage of the Sun, or from meridian passage to the end of evening twilight, the total duration of twilight being twice the value given by the graph. The border between this shaded region and the remainder of the graph indicates that the Sun only just rises at meridian passage at the date and latitude shown. The remainder of the graph gives the total duration of civil twilight.

Examples. (a) Estimate the time of the beginning of morning civil twilight at latitude N 78° on 2020 March 10. The duration of twilight (page 322) is about $1^h 40^m$. Applying this to the time of sunrise, $07^h 10^m$, found in the preceding example, the beginning of morning civil twilight is $05^h 30^m$ LMT. (b) Estimate, for the first half of 2020, the limiting dates of civil twilight and sunlight at latitude N 80°. The graphs (page 322) indicate there is no sunlight or twilight till about February 6, there is twilight but no sunlight from February 6 until February 21, sunlight and twilight till March 31, continuous twilight or sunlight till April 14, and then continuous sunlight. (c) Estimate the time of the beginning and end of civil twilight on 2020 February 14 at latitude N 80°. The graph (page 322) indicates there is no direct sunlight at this date and latitude, but three hours of twilight before and after meridian passage occurring at $12^h 14^m$. Thus civil twilight begins at about $09^h 14^m$ and ends at about $15^h 14^m$ LMT.

4. *Semiduration of moonlight* The graphs, for each month, for the semiduration of moonlight give for the Moon the same data as the graphs for the semiduration of sunlight give for the Sun. The scale near the top gives the LMT of meridian passage. In addition, the phase symbols are placed on the graphs to show the day on which each phase occurs. Since the times of meridian passage and the semiduration change more rapidly from day to day for the Moon than for the Sun, special care will be required in reading the graphs accurately.

For most purposes, in these high latitudes, a rough idea of the time of moonrise or moonset is all that is required, and this may be obtained by a glance at the graph.

Example. Estimate the moon phase and the time of moonrise and moonset on 2020 June 13 at latitude N 75°. The phase is found from pages 323-325 to be near last quarter, and the Moon crosses the meridian at 06^h LMT. The semiduration of moonlight taken for the time of meridian passage is 4 hours, giving moonrise at 02^h LMT on June 13 and moonset at 10^h on June 13.

If greater accuracy is required, it is necessary to read the graph for the UT of each phenomenon at the desired meridian. The dates indicated on the graph are for 00^h UT, and intermediate values of the UT may be located by estimation.

Example. Required to improve the results obtained in the preceding example, assuming the observer to be in longitude W 90° (6^h) west.

The values found previously were:

			d	h				d	h	
Time of meridian passage	2020	June	13	06	LMT	=	June	13	12	UT
Semiduration of moonlight				4						
Time of moonrise		June	13	02	LMT	=	June	13	08	UT
Time of moonset		June	13	10	LMT	=	June	13	16	UT

Returning to the graphs (pages 323-325) with these three values of the UT, the following results are obtained:

			d	h	m				d	h	m	
Time of meridian passage	2020	June	13	06	10	LMT	=	June	13	12	10	UT
Semiduration for moonrise				04	10							
Time of moonrise		June	13	02	00	LMT	=	June	13	08	00	UT
Semiduration for moonset				04	40							
Time of moonset		June	13	10	50	LMT	=	June	13	16	50	UT

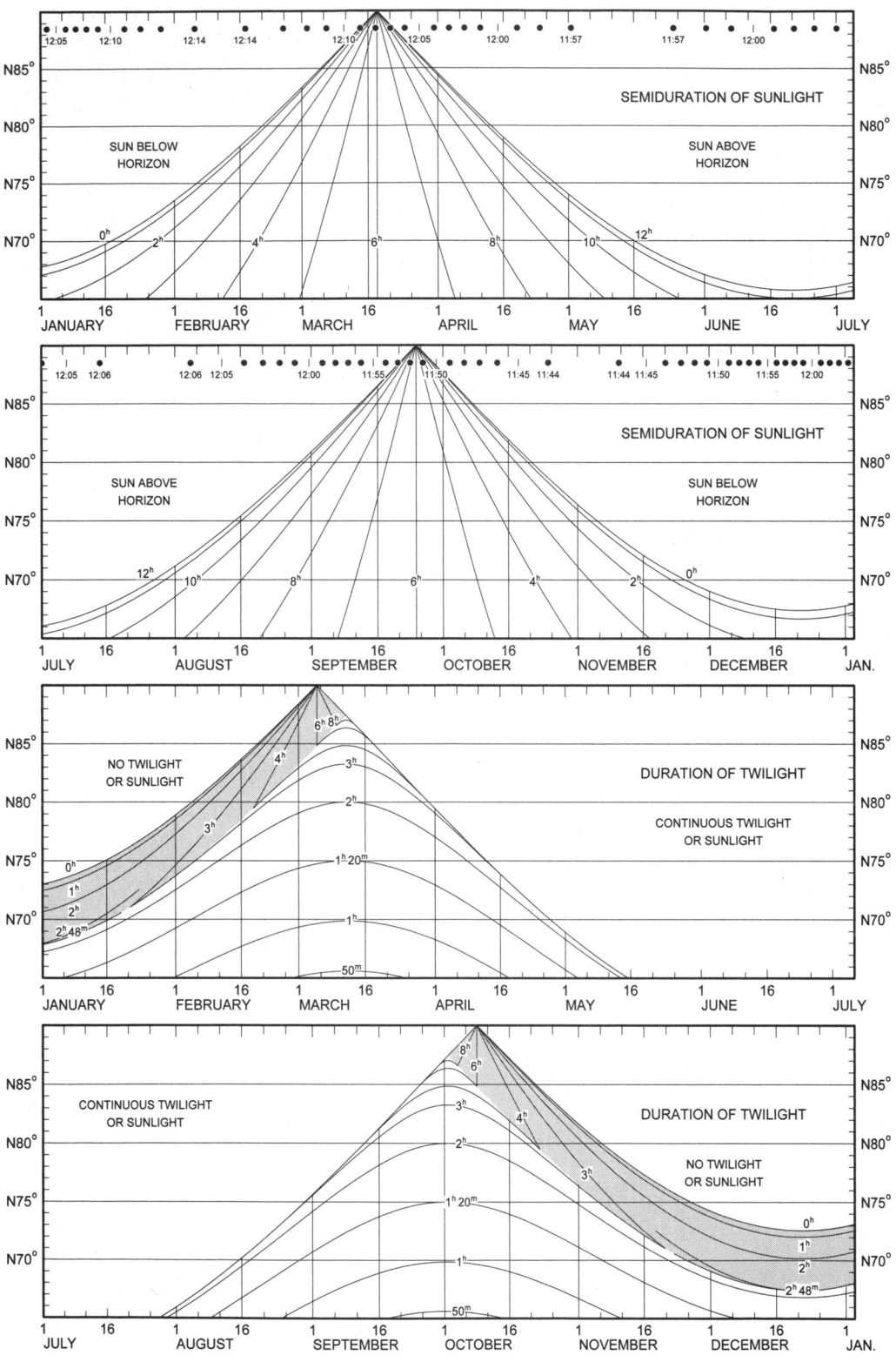

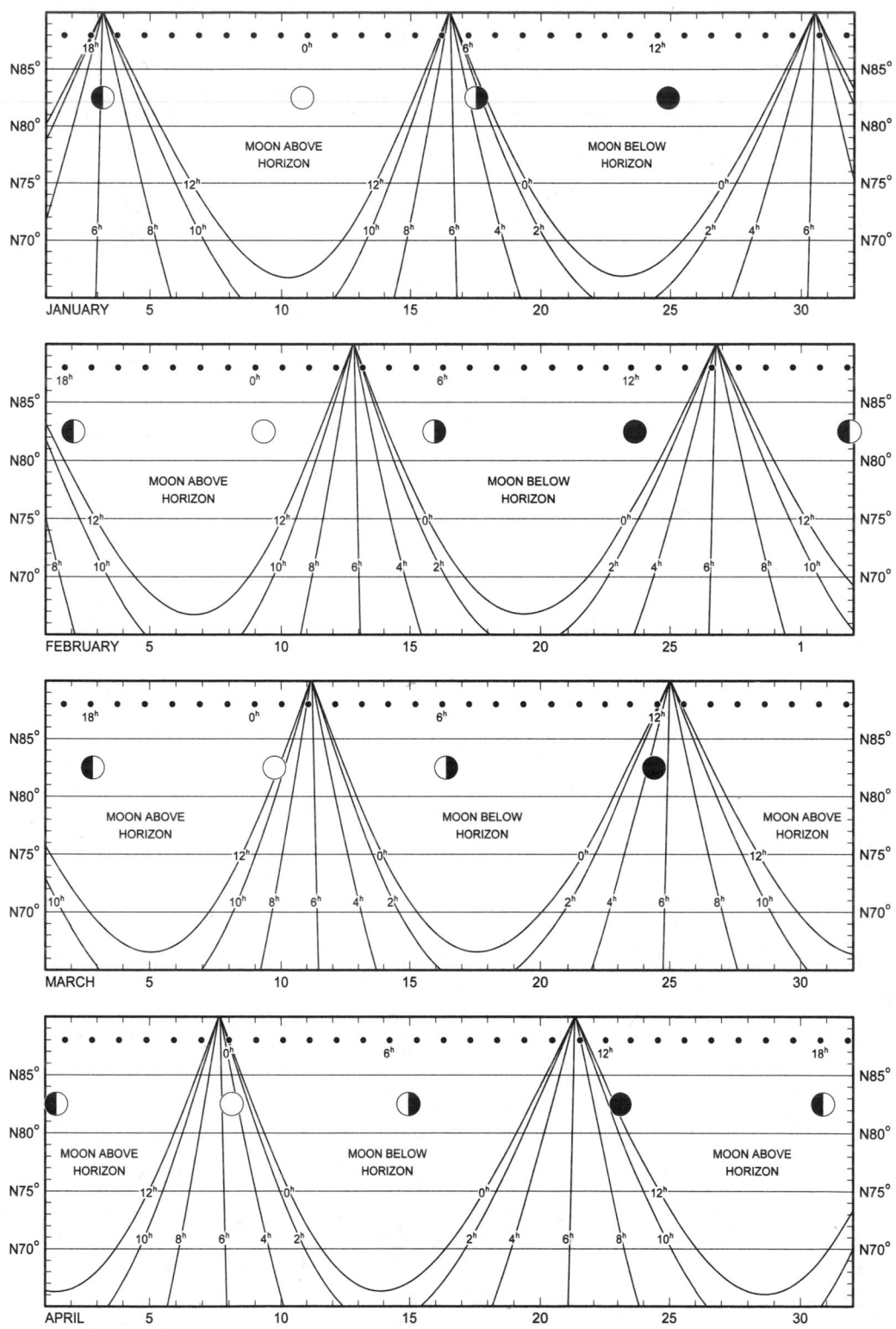

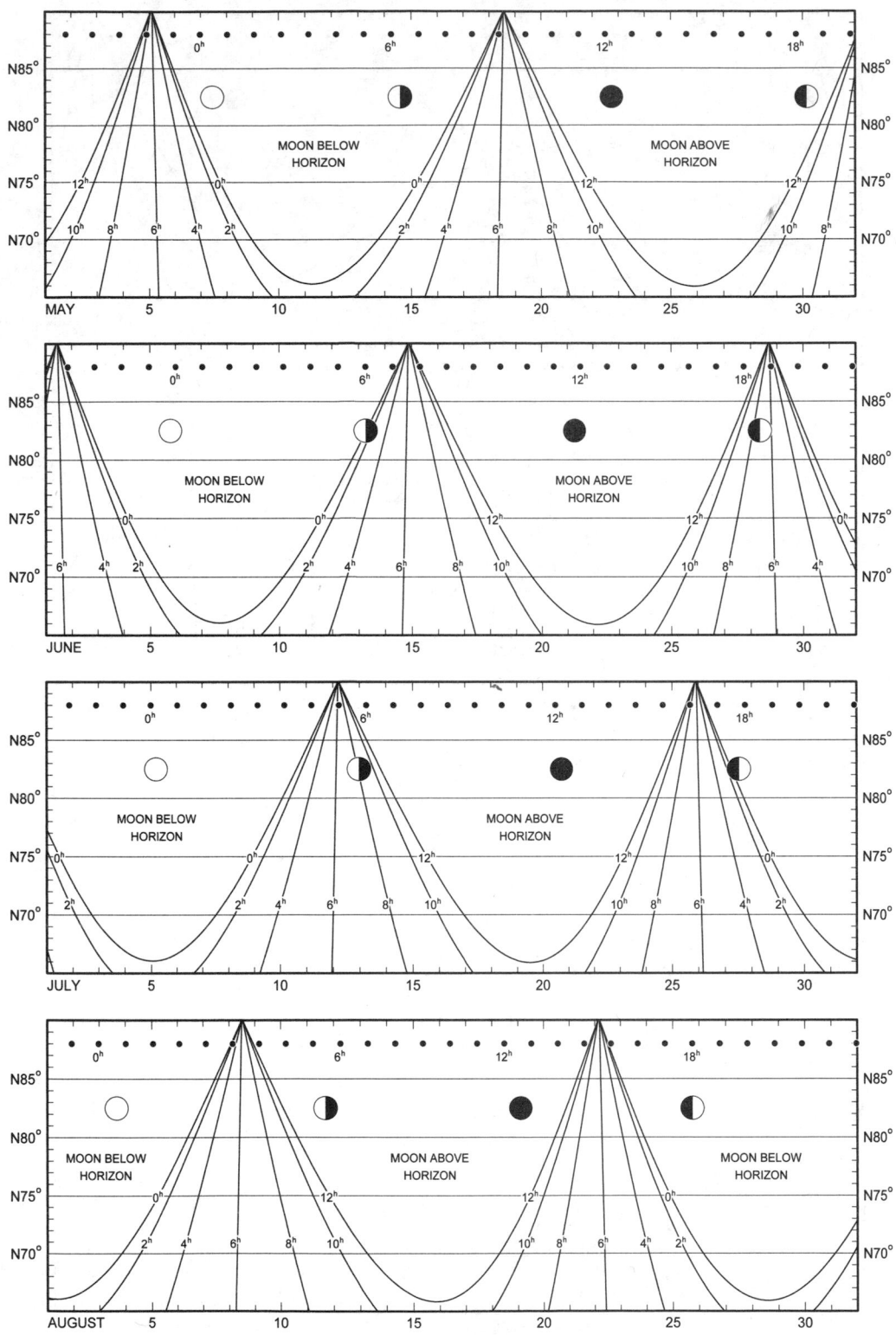

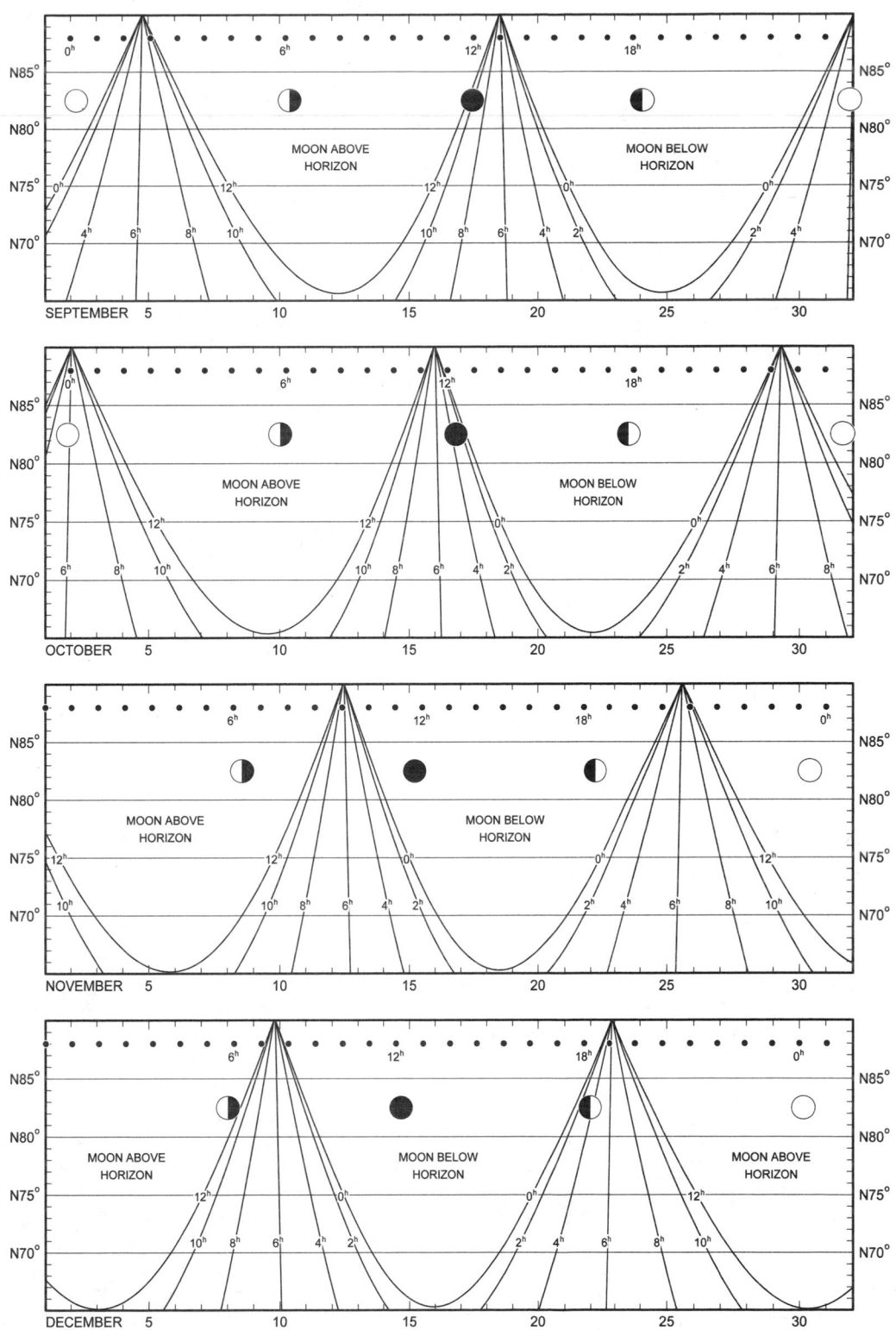

NOTES

CONVERSION OF ARC TO TIME

°	h m	°	h m	°	h m	°	h m	°	h m	°	h m	′	0′·00 m s	0′·25 m s	0′·50 m s	0′·75 m s
0	0 00	60	4 00	120	8 00	180	12 00	240	16 00	300	20 00	0	0 00	0 01	0 02	0 03
1	0 04	61	4 04	121	8 04	181	12 04	241	16 04	301	20 04	1	0 04	0 05	0 06	0 07
2	0 08	62	4 08	122	8 08	182	12 08	242	16 08	302	20 08	2	0 08	0 09	0 10	0 11
3	0 12	63	4 12	123	8 12	183	12 12	243	16 12	303	20 12	3	0 12	0 13	0 14	0 15
4	0 16	64	4 16	124	8 16	184	12 16	244	16 16	304	20 16	4	0 16	0 17	0 18	0 19
5	0 20	65	4 20	125	8 20	185	12 20	245	16 20	305	20 20	5	0 20	0 21	0 22	0 23
6	0 24	66	4 24	126	8 24	186	12 24	246	16 24	306	20 24	6	0 24	0 25	0 26	0 27
7	0 28	67	4 28	127	8 28	187	12 28	247	16 28	307	20 28	7	0 28	0 29	0 30	0 31
8	0 32	68	4 32	128	8 32	188	12 32	248	16 32	308	20 32	8	0 32	0 33	0 34	0 35
9	0 36	69	4 36	129	8 36	189	12 36	249	16 36	309	20 36	9	0 36	0 37	0 38	0 39
10	0 40	70	4 40	130	8 40	190	12 40	250	16 40	310	20 40	10	0 40	0 41	0 42	0 43
11	0 44	71	4 44	131	8 44	191	12 44	251	16 44	311	20 44	11	0 44	0 45	0 46	0 47
12	0 48	72	4 48	132	8 48	192	12 48	252	16 48	312	20 48	12	0 48	0 49	0 50	0 51
13	0 52	73	4 52	133	8 52	193	12 52	253	16 52	313	20 52	13	0 52	0 53	0 54	0 55
14	0 56	74	4 56	134	8 56	194	12 56	254	16 56	314	20 56	14	0 56	0 57	0 58	0 59
15	1 00	75	5 00	135	9 00	195	13 00	255	17 00	315	21 00	15	1 00	1 01	1 02	1 03
16	1 04	76	5 04	136	9 04	196	13 04	256	17 04	316	21 04	16	1 04	1 05	1 06	1 07
17	1 08	77	5 08	137	9 08	197	13 08	257	17 08	317	21 08	17	1 08	1 09	1 10	1 11
18	1 12	78	5 12	138	9 12	198	13 12	258	17 12	318	21 12	18	1 12	1 13	1 14	1 15
19	1 16	79	5 16	139	9 16	199	13 16	259	17 16	319	21 16	19	1 16	1 17	1 18	1 19
20	1 20	80	5 20	140	9 20	200	13 20	260	17 20	320	21 20	20	1 20	1 21	1 22	1 23
21	1 24	81	5 24	141	9 24	201	13 24	261	17 24	321	21 24	21	1 24	1 25	1 26	1 27
22	1 28	82	5 28	142	9 28	202	13 28	262	17 28	322	21 28	22	1 28	1 29	1 30	1 31
23	1 32	83	5 32	143	9 32	203	13 32	263	17 32	323	21 32	23	1 32	1 33	1 34	1 35
24	1 36	84	5 36	144	9 36	204	13 36	264	17 36	324	21 36	24	1 36	1 37	1 38	1 39
25	1 40	85	5 40	145	9 40	205	13 40	265	17 40	325	21 40	25	1 40	1 41	1 42	1 43
26	1 44	86	5 44	146	9 44	206	13 44	266	17 44	326	21 44	26	1 44	1 45	1 46	1 47
27	1 48	87	5 48	147	9 48	207	13 48	267	17 48	327	21 48	27	1 48	1 49	1 50	1 51
28	1 52	88	5 52	148	9 52	208	13 52	268	17 52	328	21 52	28	1 52	1 53	1 54	1 55
29	1 56	89	5 56	149	9 56	209	13 56	269	17 56	329	21 56	29	1 56	1 57	1 58	1 59
30	2 00	90	6 00	150	10 00	210	14 00	270	18 00	330	22 00	30	2 00	2 01	2 02	2 03
31	2 04	91	6 04	151	10 04	211	14 04	271	18 04	331	22 04	31	2 04	2 05	2 06	2 07
32	2 08	92	6 08	152	10 08	212	14 08	272	18 08	332	22 08	32	2 08	2 09	2 10	2 11
33	2 12	93	6 12	153	10 12	213	14 12	273	18 12	333	22 12	33	2 12	2 13	2 14	2 15
34	2 16	94	6 16	154	10 16	214	14 16	274	18 16	334	22 16	34	2 16	2 17	2 18	2 19
35	2 20	95	6 20	155	10 20	215	14 20	275	18 20	335	22 20	35	2 20	2 21	2 22	2 23
36	2 24	96	6 24	156	10 24	216	14 24	276	18 24	336	22 24	36	2 24	2 25	2 26	2 27
37	2 28	97	6 28	157	10 28	217	14 28	277	18 28	337	22 28	37	2 28	2 29	2 30	2 31
38	2 32	98	6 32	158	10 32	218	14 32	278	18 32	338	22 32	38	2 32	2 33	2 34	2 35
39	2 36	99	6 36	159	10 36	219	14 36	279	18 36	339	22 36	39	2 36	2 37	2 38	2 39
40	2 40	100	6 40	160	10 40	220	14 40	280	18 40	340	22 40	40	2 40	2 41	2 42	2 43
41	2 44	101	6 44	161	10 44	221	14 44	281	18 44	341	22 44	41	2 44	2 45	2 46	2 47
42	2 48	102	6 48	162	10 48	222	14 48	282	18 48	342	22 48	42	2 48	2 49	2 50	2 51
43	2 52	103	6 52	163	10 52	223	14 52	283	18 52	343	22 52	43	2 52	2 53	2 54	2 55
44	2 56	104	6 56	164	10 56	224	14 56	284	18 56	344	22 56	44	2 56	2 57	2 58	2 59
45	3 00	105	7 00	165	11 00	225	15 00	285	19 00	345	23 00	45	3 00	3 01	3 02	3 03
46	3 04	106	7 04	166	11 04	226	15 04	286	19 04	346	23 04	46	3 04	3 05	3 06	3 07
47	3 08	107	7 08	167	11 08	227	15 08	287	19 08	347	23 08	47	3 08	3 09	3 10	3 11
48	3 12	108	7 12	168	11 12	228	15 12	288	19 12	348	23 12	48	3 12	3 13	3 14	3 15
49	3 16	109	7 16	169	11 16	229	15 16	289	19 16	349	23 16	49	3 16	3 17	3 18	3 19
50	3 20	110	7 20	170	11 20	230	15 20	290	19 20	350	23 20	50	3 20	3 21	3 22	3 23
51	3 24	111	7 24	171	11 24	231	15 24	291	19 24	351	23 24	51	3 24	3 25	3 26	3 27
52	3 28	112	7 28	172	11 28	232	15 28	292	19 28	352	23 28	52	3 28	3 29	3 30	3 31
53	3 32	113	7 32	173	11 32	233	15 32	293	19 32	353	23 32	53	3 32	3 33	3 34	3 35
54	3 36	114	7 36	174	11 36	234	15 36	294	19 36	354	23 36	54	3 36	3 37	3 38	3 39
55	3 40	115	7 40	175	11 40	235	15 40	295	19 40	355	23 40	55	3 40	3 41	3 42	3 43
56	3 44	116	7 44	176	11 44	236	15 44	296	19 44	356	23 44	56	3 44	3 45	3 46	3 47
57	3 48	117	7 48	177	11 48	237	15 48	297	19 48	357	23 48	57	3 48	3 49	3 50	3 51
58	3 52	118	7 52	178	11 52	238	15 52	298	19 52	358	23 52	58	3 52	3 53	3 54	3 55
59	3 56	119	7 56	179	11 56	239	15 56	299	19 56	359	23 56	59	3 56	3 57	3 58	3 59

The above table is for converting expressions in arc to their equivalent in time; its main use in this Almanac is for the conversion of longitude for application to LMT (*added* if *west*, *subtracted* if *east*) to give UT or vice versa, particularly in the case of sunrise, sunset, etc.

0ᵐ

s	SUN PLANETS	ARIES	MOON	v or d	Corrⁿ	v or d	Corrⁿ	v or d	Corrⁿ
00	0 00.0	0 00.0	0 00.0	0.0	0.0	6.0	0.1	12.0	0.1
01	0 00.3	0 00.3	0 00.2	0.1	0.0	6.1	0.1	12.1	0.1
02	0 00.5	0 00.5	0 00.5	0.2	0.0	6.2	0.1	12.2	0.1
03	0 00.8	0 00.8	0 00.7	0.3	0.0	6.3	0.1	12.3	0.1
04	0 01.0	0 01.0	0 01.0	0.4	0.0	6.4	0.1	12.4	0.1
05	0 01.3	0 01.3	0 01.2	0.5	0.0	6.5	0.1	12.5	0.1
06	0 01.5	0 01.5	0 01.4	0.6	0.0	6.6	0.1	12.6	0.1
07	0 01.8	0 01.8	0 01.7	0.7	0.0	6.7	0.1	12.7	0.1
08	0 02.0	0 02.0	0 01.9	0.8	0.0	6.8	0.1	12.8	0.1
09	0 02.3	0 02.3	0 02.1	0.9	0.0	6.9	0.1	12.9	0.1
10	0 02.5	0 02.5	0 02.4	1.0	0.0	7.0	0.1	13.0	0.1
11	0 02.8	0 02.8	0 02.6	1.1	0.0	7.1	0.1	13.1	0.1
12	0 03.0	0 03.0	0 02.9	1.2	0.0	7.2	0.1	13.2	0.1
13	0 03.3	0 03.3	0 03.1	1.3	0.0	7.3	0.1	13.3	0.1
14	0 03.5	0 03.5	0 03.3	1.4	0.0	7.4	0.1	13.4	0.1
15	0 03.8	0 03.8	0 03.6	1.5	0.0	7.5	0.1	13.5	0.1
16	0 04.0	0 04.0	0 03.8	1.6	0.0	7.6	0.1	13.6	0.1
17	0 04.3	0 04.3	0 04.1	1.7	0.0	7.7	0.1	13.7	0.1
18	0 04.5	0 04.5	0 04.3	1.8	0.0	7.8	0.1	13.8	0.1
19	0 04.8	0 04.8	0 04.5	1.9	0.0	7.9	0.1	13.9	0.1
20	0 05.0	0 05.0	0 04.8	2.0	0.0	8.0	0.1	14.0	0.1
21	0 05.3	0 05.3	0 05.0	2.1	0.0	8.1	0.1	14.1	0.1
22	0 05.5	0 05.5	0 05.2	2.2	0.0	8.2	0.1	14.2	0.1
23	0 05.8	0 05.8	0 05.5	2.3	0.0	8.3	0.1	14.3	0.1
24	0 06.0	0 06.0	0 05.7	2.4	0.0	8.4	0.1	14.4	0.1
25	0 06.3	0 06.3	0 06.0	2.5	0.0	8.5	0.1	14.5	0.1
26	0 06.5	0 06.5	0 06.2	2.6	0.0	8.6	0.1	14.6	0.1
27	0 06.8	0 06.8	0 06.4	2.7	0.0	8.7	0.1	14.7	0.1
28	0 07.0	0 07.0	0 06.7	2.8	0.0	8.8	0.1	14.8	0.1
29	0 07.3	0 07.3	0 06.9	2.9	0.0	8.9	0.1	14.9	0.1
30	0 07.5	0 07.5	0 07.2	3.0	0.0	9.0	0.1	15.0	0.1
31	0 07.8	0 07.8	0 07.4	3.1	0.0	9.1	0.1	15.1	0.1
32	0 08.0	0 08.0	0 07.6	3.2	0.0	9.2	0.1	15.2	0.1
33	0 08.3	0 08.3	0 07.9	3.3	0.0	9.3	0.1	15.3	0.1
34	0 08.5	0 08.5	0 08.1	3.4	0.0	9.4	0.1	15.4	0.1
35	0 08.8	0 08.8	0 08.4	3.5	0.0	9.5	0.1	15.5	0.1
36	0 09.0	0 09.0	0 08.6	3.6	0.0	9.6	0.1	15.6	0.1
37	0 09.3	0 09.3	0 08.8	3.7	0.0	9.7	0.1	15.7	0.1
38	0 09.5	0 09.5	0 09.1	3.8	0.0	9.8	0.1	15.8	0.1
39	0 09.8	0 09.8	0 09.3	3.9	0.0	9.9	0.1	15.9	0.1
40	0 10.0	0 10.0	0 09.5	4.0	0.0	10.0	0.1	16.0	0.1
41	0 10.3	0 10.3	0 09.8	4.1	0.0	10.1	0.1	16.1	0.1
42	0 10.5	0 10.5	0 10.0	4.2	0.0	10.2	0.1	16.2	0.1
43	0 10.8	0 10.8	0 10.3	4.3	0.0	10.3	0.1	16.3	0.1
44	0 11.0	0 11.0	0 10.5	4.4	0.0	10.4	0.1	16.4	0.1
45	0 11.3	0 11.3	0 10.7	4.5	0.0	10.5	0.1	16.5	0.1
46	0 11.5	0 11.5	0 11.0	4.6	0.0	10.6	0.1	16.6	0.1
47	0 11.8	0 11.8	0 11.2	4.7	0.0	10.7	0.1	16.7	0.1
48	0 12.0	0 12.0	0 11.5	4.8	0.0	10.8	0.1	16.8	0.1
49	0 12.3	0 12.3	0 11.7	4.9	0.0	10.9	0.1	16.9	0.1
50	0 12.5	0 12.5	0 11.9	5.0	0.0	11.0	0.1	17.0	0.1
51	0 12.8	0 12.8	0 12.2	5.1	0.0	11.1	0.1	17.1	0.1
52	0 13.0	0 13.0	0 12.4	5.2	0.0	11.2	0.1	17.2	0.1
53	0 13.3	0 13.3	0 12.6	5.3	0.0	11.3	0.1	17.3	0.1
54	0 13.5	0 13.5	0 12.9	5.4	0.0	11.4	0.1	17.4	0.1
55	0 13.8	0 13.8	0 13.1	5.5	0.0	11.5	0.1	17.5	0.1
56	0 14.0	0 14.0	0 13.4	5.6	0.0	11.6	0.1	17.6	0.1
57	0 14.3	0 14.3	0 13.6	5.7	0.0	11.7	0.1	17.7	0.1
58	0 14.5	0 14.5	0 13.8	5.8	0.0	11.8	0.1	17.8	0.1
59	0 14.8	0 14.8	0 14.1	5.9	0.0	11.9	0.1	17.9	0.1
60	0 15.0	0 15.0	0 14.3	6.0	0.1	12.0	0.1	18.0	0.2

1ᵐ

s	SUN PLANETS	ARIES	MOON	v or d	Corrⁿ	v or d	Corrⁿ	v or d	Corrⁿ
00	0 15.0	0 15.0	0 14.3	0.0	0.0	6.0	0.2	12.0	0.3
01	0 15.3	0 15.3	0 14.6	0.1	0.0	6.1	0.2	12.1	0.3
02	0 15.5	0 15.5	0 14.8	0.2	0.0	6.2	0.2	12.2	0.3
03	0 15.8	0 15.8	0 15.0	0.3	0.0	6.3	0.2	12.3	0.3
04	0 16.0	0 16.0	0 15.3	0.4	0.0	6.4	0.2	12.4	0.3
05	0 16.3	0 16.3	0 15.5	0.5	0.0	6.5	0.2	12.5	0.3
06	0 16.5	0 16.5	0 15.7	0.6	0.0	6.6	0.2	12.6	0.3
07	0 16.8	0 16.8	0 16.0	0.7	0.0	6.7	0.2	12.7	0.3
08	0 17.0	0 17.0	0 16.2	0.8	0.0	6.8	0.2	12.8	0.3
09	0 17.3	0 17.3	0 16.5	0.9	0.0	6.9	0.2	12.9	0.3
10	0 17.5	0 17.5	0 16.7	1.0	0.0	7.0	0.2	13.0	0.3
11	0 17.8	0 17.8	0 16.9	1.1	0.0	7.1	0.2	13.1	0.3
12	0 18.0	0 18.0	0 17.2	1.2	0.0	7.2	0.2	13.2	0.3
13	0 18.3	0 18.3	0 17.4	1.3	0.0	7.3	0.2	13.3	0.3
14	0 18.5	0 18.6	0 17.7	1.4	0.0	7.4	0.2	13.4	0.3
15	0 18.8	0 18.8	0 17.9	1.5	0.0	7.5	0.2	13.5	0.3
16	0 19.0	0 19.1	0 18.1	1.6	0.0	7.6	0.2	13.6	0.3
17	0 19.3	0 19.3	0 18.4	1.7	0.0	7.7	0.2	13.7	0.3
18	0 19.5	0 19.6	0 18.6	1.8	0.0	7.8	0.2	13.8	0.3
19	0 19.8	0 19.8	0 18.9	1.9	0.0	7.9	0.2	13.9	0.3
20	0 20.0	0 20.1	0 19.1	2.0	0.1	8.0	0.2	14.0	0.4
21	0 20.3	0 20.3	0 19.3	2.1	0.1	8.1	0.2	14.1	0.4
22	0 20.5	0 20.6	0 19.6	2.2	0.1	8.2	0.2	14.2	0.4
23	0 20.8	0 20.8	0 19.8	2.3	0.1	8.3	0.2	14.3	0.4
24	0 21.0	0 21.1	0 20.0	2.4	0.1	8.4	0.2	14.4	0.4
25	0 21.3	0 21.3	0 20.3	2.5	0.1	8.5	0.2	14.5	0.4
26	0 21.5	0 21.6	0 20.5	2.6	0.1	8.6	0.2	14.6	0.4
27	0 21.8	0 21.8	0 20.8	2.7	0.1	8.7	0.2	14.7	0.4
28	0 22.0	0 22.1	0 21.0	2.8	0.1	8.8	0.2	14.8	0.4
29	0 22.3	0 22.3	0 21.2	2.9	0.1	8.9	0.2	14.9	0.4
30	0 22.5	0 22.6	0 21.5	3.0	0.1	9.0	0.2	15.0	0.4
31	0 22.8	0 22.8	0 21.7	3.1	0.1	9.1	0.2	15.1	0.4
32	0 23.0	0 23.1	0 22.0	3.2	0.1	9.2	0.2	15.2	0.4
33	0 23.3	0 23.3	0 22.2	3.3	0.1	9.3	0.2	15.3	0.4
34	0 23.5	0 23.6	0 22.4	3.4	0.1	9.4	0.2	15.4	0.4
35	0 23.8	0 23.8	0 22.7	3.5	0.1	9.5	0.2	15.5	0.4
36	0 24.0	0 24.1	0 22.9	3.6	0.1	9.6	0.2	15.6	0.4
37	0 24.3	0 24.3	0 23.1	3.7	0.1	9.7	0.2	15.7	0.4
38	0 24.5	0 24.6	0 23.4	3.8	0.1	9.8	0.2	15.8	0.4
39	0 24.8	0 24.8	0 23.6	3.9	0.1	9.9	0.2	15.9	0.4
40	0 25.0	0 25.1	0 23.9	4.0	0.1	10.0	0.3	16.0	0.4
41	0 25.3	0 25.3	0 24.1	4.1	0.1	10.1	0.3	16.1	0.4
42	0 25.5	0 25.6	0 24.3	4.2	0.1	10.2	0.3	16.2	0.4
43	0 25.8	0 25.8	0 24.6	4.3	0.1	10.3	0.3	16.3	0.4
44	0 26.0	0 26.1	0 24.8	4.4	0.1	10.4	0.3	16.4	0.4
45	0 26.3	0 26.3	0 25.1	4.5	0.1	10.5	0.3	16.5	0.4
46	0 26.5	0 26.6	0 25.3	4.6	0.1	10.6	0.3	16.6	0.4
47	0 26.8	0 26.8	0 25.5	4.7	0.1	10.7	0.3	16.7	0.4
48	0 27.0	0 27.1	0 25.8	4.8	0.1	10.8	0.3	16.8	0.4
49	0 27.3	0 27.3	0 26.0	4.9	0.1	10.9	0.3	16.9	0.4
50	0 27.5	0 27.6	0 26.2	5.0	0.1	11.0	0.3	17.0	0.4
51	0 27.8	0 27.8	0 26.5	5.1	0.1	11.1	0.3	17.1	0.4
52	0 28.0	0 28.1	0 26.7	5.2	0.1	11.2	0.3	17.2	0.4
53	0 28.3	0 28.3	0 27.0	5.3	0.1	11.3	0.3	17.3	0.4
54	0 28.5	0 28.6	0 27.2	5.4	0.1	11.4	0.3	17.4	0.4
55	0 28.8	0 28.8	0 27.4	5.5	0.1	11.5	0.3	17.5	0.4
56	0 29.0	0 29.1	0 27.7	5.6	0.1	11.6	0.3	17.6	0.4
57	0 29.3	0 29.3	0 27.9	5.7	0.1	11.7	0.3	17.7	0.4
58	0 29.5	0 29.6	0 28.2	5.8	0.1	11.8	0.3	17.8	0.4
59	0 29.8	0 29.8	0 28.4	5.9	0.1	11.9	0.3	17.9	0.4
60	0 30.0	0 30.1	0 28.6	6.0	0.2	12.0	0.3	18.0	0.5

2	SUN PLANETS	ARIES	MOON	v or Corr^n d		v or Corr^n d		v or Corr^n d	
s	° ′	° ′	° ′	′	′	′	′	′	′
00	0 30·0	0 30·1	0 28·6	0·0	0·0	6·0	0·3	12·0	0·5
01	0 30·3	0 30·3	0 28·9	0·1	0·0	6·1	0·3	12·1	0·5
02	0 30·5	0 30·6	0 29·1	0·2	0·0	6·2	0·3	12·2	0·5
03	0 30·8	0 30·8	0 29·3	0·3	0·0	6·3	0·3	12·3	0·5
04	0 31·0	0 31·1	0 29·6	0·4	0·0	6·4	0·3	12·4	0·5
05	0 31·3	0 31·3	0 29·8	0·5	0·0	6·5	0·3	12·5	0·5
06	0 31·5	0 31·6	0 30·1	0·6	0·0	6·6	0·3	12·6	0·5
07	0 31·8	0 31·8	0 30·3	0·7	0·0	6·7	0·3	12·7	0·5
08	0 32·0	0 32·1	0 30·5	0·8	0·0	6·8	0·3	12·8	0·5
09	0 32·3	0 32·3	0 30·8	0·9	0·0	6·9	0·3	12·9	0·5
10	0 32·5	0 32·6	0 31·0	1·0	0·0	7·0	0·3	13·0	0·5
11	0 32·8	0 32·8	0 31·3	1·1	0·0	7·1	0·3	13·1	0·5
12	0 33·0	0 33·1	0 31·5	1·2	0·1	7·2	0·3	13·2	0·6
13	0 33·3	0 33·3	0 31·7	1·3	0·1	7·3	0·3	13·3	0·6
14	0 33·5	0 33·6	0 32·0	1·4	0·1	7·4	0·3	13·4	0·6
15	0 33·8	0 33·8	0 32·2	1·5	0·1	7·5	0·3	13·5	0·6
16	0 34·0	0 34·1	0 32·5	1·6	0·1	7·6	0·3	13·6	0·6
17	0 34·3	0 34·3	0 32·7	1·7	0·1	7·7	0·3	13·7	0·6
18	0 34·5	0 34·6	0 32·9	1·8	0·1	7·8	0·3	13·8	0·6
19	0 34·8	0 34·8	0 33·2	1·9	0·1	7·9	0·3	13·9	0·6
20	0 35·0	0 35·1	0 33·4	2·0	0·1	8·0	0·3	14·0	0·6
21	0 35·3	0 35·3	0 33·6	2·1	0·1	8·1	0·3	14·1	0·6
22	0 35·5	0 35·6	0 33·9	2·2	0·1	8·2	0·3	14·2	0·6
23	0 35·8	0 35·8	0 34·1	2·3	0·1	8·3	0·3	14·3	0·6
24	0 36·0	0 36·1	0 34·4	2·4	0·1	8·4	0·4	14·4	0·6
25	0 36·3	0 36·3	0 34·6	2·5	0·1	8·5	0·4	14·5	0·6
26	0 36·5	0 36·6	0 34·8	2·6	0·1	8·6	0·4	14·6	0·6
27	0 36·8	0 36·9	0 35·1	2·7	0·1	8·7	0·4	14·7	0·6
28	0 37·0	0 37·1	0 35·3	2·8	0·1	8·8	0·4	14·8	0·6
29	0 37·3	0 37·4	0 35·6	2·9	0·1	8·9	0·4	14·9	0·6
30	0 37·5	0 37·6	0 35·8	3·0	0·1	9·0	0·4	15·0	0·6
31	0 37·8	0 37·9	0 36·0	3·1	0·1	9·1	0·4	15·1	0·6
32	0 38·0	0 38·1	0 36·3	3·2	0·1	9·2	0·4	15·2	0·6
33	0 38·3	0 38·4	0 36·5	3·3	0·1	9·3	0·4	15·3	0·6
34	0 38·5	0 38·6	0 36·7	3·4	0·1	9·4	0·4	15·4	0·6
35	0 38·8	0 38·9	0 37·0	3·5	0·1	9·5	0·4	15·5	0·6
36	0 39·0	0 39·1	0 37·2	3·6	0·2	9·6	0·4	15·6	0·7
37	0 39·3	0 39·4	0 37·5	3·7	0·2	9·7	0·4	15·7	0·7
38	0 39·5	0 39·6	0 37·7	3·8	0·2	9·8	0·4	15·8	0·7
39	0 39·8	0 39·9	0 37·9	3·9	0·2	9·9	0·4	15·9	0·7
40	0 40·0	0 40·1	0 38·2	4·0	0·2	10·0	0·4	16·0	0·7
41	0 40·3	0 40·4	0 38·4	4·1	0·2	10·1	0·4	16·1	0·7
42	0 40·5	0 40·6	0 38·7	4·2	0·2	10·2	0·4	16·2	0·7
43	0 40·8	0 40·9	0 38·9	4·3	0·2	10·3	0·4	16·3	0·7
44	0 41·0	0 41·1	0 39·1	4·4	0·2	10·4	0·4	16·4	0·7
45	0 41·3	0 41·4	0 39·4	4·5	0·2	10·5	0·4	16·5	0·7
46	0 41·5	0 41·6	0 39·6	4·6	0·2	10·6	0·4	16·6	0·7
47	0 41·8	0 41·9	0 39·8	4·7	0·2	10·7	0·4	16·7	0·7
48	0 42·0	0 42·1	0 40·1	4·8	0·2	10·8	0·5	16·8	0·7
49	0 42·3	0 42·4	0 40·3	4·9	0·2	10·9	0·5	16·9	0·7
50	0 42·5	0 42·6	0 40·6	5·0	0·2	11·0	0·5	17·0	0·7
51	0 42·8	0 42·9	0 40·8	5·1	0·2	11·1	0·5	17·1	0·7
52	0 43·0	0 43·1	0 41·0	5·2	0·2	11·2	0·5	17·2	0·7
53	0 43·3	0 43·4	0 41·3	5·3	0·2	11·3	0·5	17·3	0·7
54	0 43·5	0 43·6	0 41·5	5·4	0·2	11·4	0·5	17·4	0·7
55	0 43·8	0 43·9	0 41·8	5·5	0·2	11·5	0·5	17·5	0·7
56	0 44·0	0 44·1	0 42·0	5·6	0·2	11·6	0·5	17·6	0·7
57	0 44·3	0 44·4	0 42·2	5·7	0·2	11·7	0·5	17·7	0·7
58	0 44·5	0 44·6	0 42·5	5·8	0·2	11·8	0·5	17·8	0·7
59	0 44·8	0 44·9	0 42·7	5·9	0·2	11·9	0·5	17·9	0·7
60	0 45·0	0 45·1	0 43·0	6·0	0·3	12·0	0·5	18·0	0·8

3	SUN PLANETS	ARIES	MOON	v or Corr^n d		v or Corr^n d		v or Corr^n d	
s	° ′	° ′	° ′	′	′	′	′	′	′
00	0 45·0	0 45·1	0 43·0	0·0	0·0	6·0	0·4	12·0	0·7
01	0 45·3	0 45·4	0 43·2	0·1	0·0	6·1	0·4	12·1	0·7
02	0 45·5	0 45·6	0 43·4	0·2	0·0	6·2	0·4	12·2	0·7
03	0 45·8	0 45·9	0 43·7	0·3	0·0	6·3	0·4	12·3	0·7
04	0 46·0	0 46·1	0 43·9	0·4	0·0	6·4	0·4	12·4	0·7
05	0 46·3	0 46·4	0 44·1	0·5	0·0	6·5	0·4	12·5	0·7
06	0 46·5	0 46·6	0 44·4	0·6	0·0	6·6	0·4	12·6	0·7
07	0 46·8	0 46·9	0 44·6	0·7	0·0	6·7	0·4	12·7	0·7
08	0 47·0	0 47·1	0 44·9	0·8	0·0	6·8	0·4	12·8	0·7
09	0 47·3	0 47·4	0 45·1	0·9	0·1	6·9	0·4	12·9	0·8
10	0 47·5	0 47·6	0 45·3	1·0	0·1	7·0	0·4	13·0	0·8
11	0 47·8	0 47·9	0 45·6	1·1	0·1	7·1	0·4	13·1	0·8
12	0 48·0	0 48·1	0 45·8	1·2	0·1	7·2	0·4	13·2	0·8
13	0 48·3	0 48·4	0 46·1	1·3	0·1	7·3	0·4	13·3	0·8
14	0 48·5	0 48·6	0 46·3	1·4	0·1	7·4	0·4	13·4	0·8
15	0 48·8	0 48·9	0 46·5	1·5	0·1	7·5	0·4	13·5	0·8
16	0 49·0	0 49·1	0 46·8	1·6	0·1	7·6	0·4	13·6	0·8
17	0 49·3	0 49·4	0 47·0	1·7	0·1	7·7	0·4	13·7	0·8
18	0 49·5	0 49·6	0 47·2	1·8	0·1	7·8	0·5	13·8	0·8
19	0 49·8	0 49·9	0 47·5	1·9	0·1	7·9	0·5	13·9	0·8
20	0 50·0	0 50·1	0 47·7	2·0	0·1	8·0	0·5	14·0	0·8
21	0 50·3	0 50·4	0 48·0	2·1	0·1	8·1	0·5	14·1	0·8
22	0 50·5	0 50·6	0 48·2	2·2	0·1	8·2	0·5	14·2	0·8
23	0 50·8	0 50·9	0 48·4	2·3	0·1	8·3	0·5	14·3	0·8
24	0 51·0	0 51·1	0 48·7	2·4	0·1	8·4	0·5	14·4	0·8
25	0 51·3	0 51·4	0 48·9	2·5	0·1	8·5	0·5	14·5	0·8
26	0 51·5	0 51·6	0 49·2	2·6	0·2	8·6	0·5	14·6	0·9
27	0 51·8	0 51·9	0 49·4	2·7	0·2	8·7	0·5	14·7	0·9
28	0 52·0	0 52·1	0 49·6	2·8	0·2	8·8	0·5	14·8	0·9
29	0 52·3	0 52·4	0 49·9	2·9	0·2	8·9	0·5	14·9	0·9
30	0 52·5	0 52·6	0 50·1	3·0	0·2	9·0	0·5	15·0	0·9
31	0 52·8	0 52·9	0 50·3	3·1	0·2	9·1	0·5	15·1	0·9
32	0 53·0	0 53·1	0 50·6	3·2	0·2	9·2	0·5	15·2	0·9
33	0 53·3	0 53·4	0 50·8	3·3	0·2	9·3	0·5	15·3	0·9
34	0 53·5	0 53·6	0 51·1	3·4	0·2	9·4	0·5	15·4	0·9
35	0 53·8	0 53·9	0 51·3	3·5	0·2	9·5	0·6	15·5	0·9
36	0 54·0	0 54·1	0 51·5	3·6	0·2	9·6	0·6	15·6	0·9
37	0 54·3	0 54·4	0 51·8	3·7	0·2	9·7	0·6	15·7	0·9
38	0 54·5	0 54·6	0 52·0	3·8	0·2	9·8	0·6	15·8	0·9
39	0 54·8	0 54·9	0 52·3	3·9	0·2	9·9	0·6	15·9	0·9
40	0 55·0	0 55·2	0 52·5	4·0	0·2	10·0	0·6	16·0	0·9
41	0 55·3	0 55·4	0 52·7	4·1	0·2	10·1	0·6	16·1	0·9
42	0 55·5	0 55·7	0 53·0	4·2	0·2	10·2	0·6	16·2	0·9
43	0 55·8	0 55·9	0 53·2	4·3	0·3	10·3	0·6	16·3	1·0
44	0 56·0	0 56·2	0 53·4	4·4	0·3	10·4	0·6	16·4	1·0
45	0 56·3	0 56·4	0 53·7	4·5	0·3	10·5	0·6	16·5	1·0
46	0 56·5	0 56·7	0 53·9	4·6	0·3	10·6	0·6	16·6	1·0
47	0 56·8	0 56·9	0 54·2	4·7	0·3	10·7	0·6	16·7	1·0
48	0 57·0	0 57·2	0 54·4	4·8	0·3	10·8	0·6	16·8	1·0
49	0 57·3	0 57·4	0 54·6	4·9	0·3	10·9	0·6	16·9	1·0
50	0 57·5	0 57·7	0 54·9	5·0	0·3	11·0	0·6	17·0	1·0
51	0 57·8	0 57·9	0 55·1	5·1	0·3	11·1	0·6	17·1	1·0
52	0 58·0	0 58·2	0 55·4	5·2	0·3	11·2	0·7	17·2	1·0
53	0 58·3	0 58·4	0 55·6	5·3	0·3	11·3	0·7	17·3	1·0
54	0 58·5	0 58·7	0 55·8	5·4	0·3	11·4	0·7	17·4	1·0
55	0 58·8	0 58·9	0 56·1	5·5	0·3	11·5	0·7	17·5	1·0
56	0 59·0	0 59·2	0 56·3	5·6	0·3	11·6	0·7	17·6	1·0
57	0 59·3	0 59·4	0 56·6	5·7	0·3	11·7	0·7	17·7	1·0
58	0 59·5	0 59·7	0 56·8	5·8	0·3	11·8	0·7	17·8	1·0
59	0 59·8	0 59·9	0 57·0	5·9	0·3	11·9	0·7	17·9	1·0
60	1 00·0	1 00·2	0 57·3	6·0	0·4	12·0	0·7	18·0	1·1

4 s	SUN PLANETS	ARIES	MOON	v or d / Corrn	v or d / Corrn	v or d / Corrn
00	1 00·0	1 00·2	0 57·3	0·0 0·0	6·0 0·5	12·0 0·9
01	1 00·3	1 00·4	0 57·5	0·1 0·0	6·1 0·5	12·1 0·9
02	1 00·5	1 00·7	0 57·7	0·2 0·0	6·2 0·5	12·2 0·9
03	1 00·8	1 00·9	0 58·0	0·3 0·0	6·3 0·5	12·3 0·9
04	1 01·0	1 01·2	0 58·2	0·4 0·0	6·4 0·5	12·4 0·9
05	1 01·3	1 01·4	0 58·5	0·5 0·0	6·5 0·5	12·5 0·9
06	1 01·5	1 01·7	0 58·7	0·6 0·0	6·6 0·5	12·6 0·9
07	1 01·8	1 01·9	0 58·9	0·7 0·1	6·7 0·5	12·7 1·0
08	1 02·0	1 02·2	0 59·2	0·8 0·1	6·8 0·5	12·8 1·0
09	1 02·3	1 02·4	0 59·4	0·9 0·1	6·9 0·5	12·9 1·0
10	1 02·5	1 02·7	0 59·7	1·0 0·1	7·0 0·5	13·0 1·0
11	1 02·8	1 02·9	0 59·9	1·1 0·1	7·1 0·5	13·1 1·0
12	1 03·0	1 03·2	1 00·1	1·2 0·1	7·2 0·5	13·2 1·0
13	1 03·3	1 03·4	1 00·4	1·3 0·1	7·3 0·5	13·3 1·0
14	1 03·5	1 03·7	1 00·6	1·4 0·1	7·4 0·6	13·4 1·0
15	1 03·8	1 03·9	1 00·8	1·5 0·1	7·5 0·6	13·5 1·0
16	1 04·0	1 04·2	1 01·1	1·6 0·1	7·6 0·6	13·6 1·0
17	1 04·3	1 04·4	1 01·3	1·7 0·1	7·7 0·6	13·7 1·0
18	1 04·5	1 04·7	1 01·6	1·8 0·1	7·8 0·6	13·8 1·0
19	1 04·8	1 04·9	1 01·8	1·9 0·1	7·9 0·6	13·9 1·0
20	1 05·0	1 05·2	1 02·0	2·0 0·2	8·0 0·6	14·0 1·1
21	1 05·3	1 05·4	1 02·3	2·1 0·2	8·1 0·6	14·1 1·1
22	1 05·5	1 05·7	1 02·5	2·2 0·2	8·2 0·6	14·2 1·1
23	1 05·8	1 05·9	1 02·8	2·3 0·2	8·3 0·6	14·3 1·1
24	1 06·0	1 06·2	1 03·0	2·4 0·2	8·4 0·6	14·4 1·1
25	1 06·3	1 06·4	1 03·2	2·5 0·2	8·5 0·6	14·5 1·1
26	1 06·5	1 06·7	1 03·5	2·6 0·2	8·6 0·6	14·6 1·1
27	1 06·8	1 06·9	1 03·7	2·7 0·2	8·7 0·7	14·7 1·1
28	1 07·0	1 07·2	1 03·9	2·8 0·2	8·8 0·7	14·8 1·1
29	1 07·3	1 07·4	1 04·2	2·9 0·2	8·9 0·7	14·9 1·1
30	1 07·5	1 07·7	1 04·4	3·0 0·2	9·0 0·7	15·0 1·1
31	1 07·8	1 07·9	1 04·7	3·1 0·2	9·1 0·7	15·1 1·1
32	1 08·0	1 08·2	1 04·9	3·2 0·2	9·2 0·7	15·2 1·1
33	1 08·3	1 08·4	1 05·1	3·3 0·2	9·3 0·7	15·3 1·1
34	1 08·5	1 08·7	1 05·4	3·4 0·3	9·4 0·7	15·4 1·2
35	1 08·8	1 08·9	1 05·6	3·5 0·3	9·5 0·7	15·5 1·2
36	1 09·0	1 09·2	1 05·9	3·6 0·3	9·6 0·7	15·6 1·2
37	1 09·3	1 09·4	1 06·1	3·7 0·3	9·7 0·7	15·7 1·2
38	1 09·5	1 09·7	1 06·3	3·8 0·3	9·8 0·7	15·8 1·2
39	1 09·8	1 09·9	1 06·6	3·9 0·3	9·9 0·7	15·9 1·2
40	1 10·0	1 10·2	1 06·8	4·0 0·3	10·0 0·8	16·0 1·2
41	1 10·3	1 10·4	1 07·0	4·1 0·3	10·1 0·8	16·1 1·2
42	1 10·5	1 10·7	1 07·3	4·2 0·3	10·2 0·8	16·2 1·2
43	1 10·8	1 10·9	1 07·5	4·3 0·3	10·3 0·8	16·3 1·2
44	1 11·0	1 11·2	1 07·8	4·4 0·3	10·4 0·8	16·4 1·2
45	1 11·3	1 11·4	1 08·0	4·5 0·3	10·5 0·8	16·5 1·2
46	1 11·5	1 11·7	1 08·2	4·6 0·3	10·6 0·8	16·6 1·2
47	1 11·8	1 11·9	1 08·5	4·7 0·4	10·7 0·8	16·7 1·3
48	1 12·0	1 12·2	1 08·7	4·8 0·4	10·8 0·8	16·8 1·3
49	1 12·3	1 12·4	1 09·0	4·9 0·4	10·9 0·8	16·9 1·3
50	1 12·5	1 12·7	1 09·2	5·0 0·4	11·0 0·8	17·0 1·3
51	1 12·8	1 12·9	1 09·4	5·1 0·4	11·1 0·8	17·1 1·3
52	1 13·0	1 13·2	1 09·7	5·2 0·4	11·2 0·8	17·2 1·3
53	1 13·3	1 13·5	1 09·9	5·3 0·4	11·3 0·8	17·3 1·3
54	1 13·5	1 13·7	1 10·2	5·4 0·4	11·4 0·9	17·4 1·3
55	1 13·8	1 14·0	1 10·4	5·5 0·4	11·5 0·9	17·5 1·3
56	1 14·0	1 14·2	1 10·6	5·6 0·4	11·6 0·9	17·6 1·3
57	1 14·3	1 14·5	1 10·9	5·7 0·4	11·7 0·9	17·7 1·3
58	1 14·5	1 14·7	1 11·1	5·8 0·4	11·8 0·9	17·8 1·3
59	1 14·8	1 15·0	1 11·3	5·9 0·4	11·9 0·9	17·9 1·3
60	1 15·0	1 15·2	1 11·6	6·0 0·5	12·0 0·9	18·0 1·4

5 s	SUN PLANETS	ARIES	MOON	v or d / Corrn	v or d / Corrn	v or d / Corrn
00	1 15·0	1 15·2	1 11·6	0·0 0·0	6·0 0·6	12·0 1·1
01	1 15·3	1 15·5	1 11·8	0·1 0·0	6·1 0·6	12·1 1·1
02	1 15·5	1 15·7	1 12·1	0·2 0·0	6·2 0·6	12·2 1·1
03	1 15·8	1 16·0	1 12·3	0·3 0·0	6·3 0·6	12·3 1·1
04	1 16·0	1 16·2	1 12·5	0·4 0·0	6·4 0·6	12·4 1·1
05	1 16·3	1 16·5	1 12·8	0·5 0·0	6·5 0·6	12·5 1·1
06	1 16·5	1 16·7	1 13·0	0·6 0·1	6·6 0·6	12·6 1·2
07	1 16·8	1 17·0	1 13·3	0·7 0·1	6·7 0·6	12·7 1·2
08	1 17·0	1 17·2	1 13·5	0·8 0·1	6·8 0·6	12·8 1·2
09	1 17·3	1 17·5	1 13·7	0·9 0·1	6·9 0·6	12·9 1·2
10	1 17·5	1 17·7	1 14·0	1·0 0·1	7·0 0·6	13·0 1·2
11	1 17·8	1 18·0	1 14·2	1·1 0·1	7·1 0·7	13·1 1·2
12	1 18·0	1 18·2	1 14·4	1·2 0·1	7·2 0·7	13·2 1·2
13	1 18·3	1 18·5	1 14·7	1·3 0·1	7·3 0·7	13·3 1·2
14	1 18·5	1 18·7	1 14·9	1·4 0·1	7·4 0·7	13·4 1·2
15	1 18·8	1 19·0	1 15·2	1·5 0·1	7·5 0·7	13·5 1·2
16	1 19·0	1 19·2	1 15·4	1·6 0·1	7·6 0·7	13·6 1·2
17	1 19·3	1 19·5	1 15·6	1·7 0·2	7·7 0·7	13·7 1·3
18	1 19·5	1 19·7	1 15·9	1·8 0·2	7·8 0·7	13·8 1·3
19	1 19·8	1 20·0	1 16·1	1·9 0·2	7·9 0·7	13·9 1·3
20	1 20·0	1 20·2	1 16·4	2·0 0·2	8·0 0·7	14·0 1·3
21	1 20·3	1 20·5	1 16·6	2·1 0·2	8·1 0·7	14·1 1·3
22	1 20·5	1 20·7	1 16·8	2·2 0·2	8·2 0·8	14·2 1·3
23	1 20·8	1 21·0	1 17·1	2·3 0·2	8·3 0·8	14·3 1·3
24	1 21·0	1 21·2	1 17·3	2·4 0·2	8·4 0·8	14·4 1·3
25	1 21·3	1 21·5	1 17·5	2·5 0·2	8·5 0·8	14·5 1·3
26	1 21·5	1 21·7	1 17·8	2·6 0·2	8·6 0·8	14·6 1·3
27	1 21·8	1 22·0	1 18·0	2·7 0·2	8·7 0·8	14·7 1·3
28	1 22·0	1 22·2	1 18·3	2·8 0·3	8·8 0·8	14·8 1·4
29	1 22·3	1 22·5	1 18·5	2·9 0·3	8·9 0·8	14·9 1·4
30	1 22·5	1 22·7	1 18·7	3·0 0·3	9·0 0·8	15·0 1·4
31	1 22·8	1 23·0	1 19·0	3·1 0·3	9·1 0·8	15·1 1·4
32	1 23·0	1 23·2	1 19·2	3·2 0·3	9·2 0·8	15·2 1·4
33	1 23·3	1 23·5	1 19·5	3·3 0·3	9·3 0·9	15·3 1·4
34	1 23·5	1 23·7	1 19·7	3·4 0·3	9·4 0·9	15·4 1·4
35	1 23·8	1 24·0	1 19·9	3·5 0·3	9·5 0·9	15·5 1·4
36	1 24·0	1 24·2	1 20·2	3·6 0·3	9·6 0·9	15·6 1·4
37	1 24·3	1 24·5	1 20·4	3·7 0·3	9·7 0·9	15·7 1·4
38	1 24·5	1 24·7	1 20·7	3·8 0·3	9·8 0·9	15·8 1·4
39	1 24·8	1 25·0	1 20·9	3·9 0·4	9·9 0·9	15·9 1·5
40	1 25·0	1 25·2	1 21·1	4·0 0·4	10·0 0·9	16·0 1·5
41	1 25·3	1 25·5	1 21·4	4·1 0·4	10·1 0·9	16·1 1·5
42	1 25·5	1 25·7	1 21·6	4·2 0·4	10·2 0·9	16·2 1·5
43	1 25·8	1 26·0	1 21·8	4·3 0·4	10·3 0·9	16·3 1·5
44	1 26·0	1 26·2	1 22·1	4·4 0·4	10·4 1·0	16·4 1·5
45	1 26·3	1 26·5	1 22·3	4·5 0·4	10·5 1·0	16·5 1·5
46	1 26·5	1 26·7	1 22·6	4·6 0·4	10·6 1·0	16·6 1·5
47	1 26·8	1 27·0	1 22·8	4·7 0·4	10·7 1·0	16·7 1·5
48	1 27·0	1 27·2	1 23·0	4·8 0·4	10·8 1·0	16·8 1·5
49	1 27·3	1 27·5	1 23·3	4·9 0·4	10·9 1·0	16·9 1·5
50	1 27·5	1 27·7	1 23·5	5·0 0·5	11·0 1·0	17·0 1·6
51	1 27·8	1 28·0	1 23·8	5·1 0·5	11·1 1·0	17·1 1·6
52	1 28·0	1 28·2	1 24·0	5·2 0·5	11·2 1·0	17·2 1·6
53	1 28·3	1 28·5	1 24·2	5·3 0·5	11·3 1·0	17·3 1·6
54	1 28·5	1 28·7	1 24·5	5·4 0·5	11·4 1·0	17·4 1·6
55	1 28·8	1 29·0	1 24·7	5·5 0·5	11·5 1·1	17·5 1·6
56	1 29·0	1 29·2	1 24·9	5·6 0·5	11·6 1·1	17·6 1·6
57	1 29·3	1 29·5	1 25·2	5·7 0·5	11·7 1·1	17·7 1·6
58	1 29·5	1 29·7	1 25·4	5·8 0·5	11·8 1·1	17·8 1·6
59	1 29·8	1 30·0	1 25·7	5·9 0·5	11·9 1·1	17·9 1·6
60	1 30·0	1 30·2	1 25·9	6·0 0·6	12·0 1·1	18·0 1·7

6ᵐ

6 s	SUN PLANETS	ARIES	MOON	v or d	Corrⁿ	v or d	Corrⁿ	v or d	Corrⁿ
00	1 30·0	1 30·2	1 25·9	0·0	0·0	6·0	0·7	12·0	1·3
01	1 30·3	1 30·5	1 26·1	0·1	0·0	6·1	0·7	12·1	1·3
02	1 30·5	1 30·7	1 26·4	0·2	0·0	6·2	0·7	12·2	1·3
03	1 30·8	1 31·0	1 26·6	0·3	0·0	6·3	0·7	12·3	1·3
04	1 31·0	1 31·2	1 26·9	0·4	0·0	6·4	0·7	12·4	1·3
05	1 31·3	1 31·5	1 27·1	0·5	0·1	6·5	0·7	12·5	1·4
06	1 31·5	1 31·8	1 27·3	0·6	0·1	6·6	0·7	12·6	1·4
07	1 31·8	1 32·0	1 27·6	0·7	0·1	6·7	0·7	12·7	1·4
08	1 32·0	1 32·3	1 27·8	0·8	0·1	6·8	0·7	12·8	1·4
09	1 32·3	1 32·5	1 28·0	0·9	0·1	6·9	0·7	12·9	1·4
10	1 32·5	1 32·8	1 28·3	1·0	0·1	7·0	0·8	13·0	1·4
11	1 32·8	1 33·0	1 28·5	1·1	0·1	7·1	0·8	13·1	1·4
12	1 33·0	1 33·3	1 28·8	1·2	0·1	7·2	0·8	13·2	1·4
13	1 33·3	1 33·5	1 29·0	1·3	0·1	7·3	0·8	13·3	1·4
14	1 33·5	1 33·8	1 29·2	1·4	0·2	7·4	0·8	13·4	1·5
15	1 33·8	1 34·0	1 29·5	1·5	0·2	7·5	0·8	13·5	1·5
16	1 34·0	1 34·3	1 29·7	1·6	0·2	7·6	0·8	13·6	1·5
17	1 34·3	1 34·5	1 30·0	1·7	0·2	7·7	0·8	13·7	1·5
18	1 34·5	1 34·8	1 30·2	1·8	0·2	7·8	0·8	13·8	1·5
19	1 34·8	1 35·0	1 30·4	1·9	0·2	7·9	0·9	13·9	1·5
20	1 35·0	1 35·3	1 30·7	2·0	0·2	8·0	0·9	14·0	1·5
21	1 35·3	1 35·5	1 30·9	2·1	0·2	8·1	0·9	14·1	1·5
22	1 35·5	1 35·8	1 31·1	2·2	0·2	8·2	0·9	14·2	1·5
23	1 35·8	1 36·0	1 31·4	2·3	0·2	8·3	0·9	14·3	1·5
24	1 36·0	1 36·3	1 31·6	2·4	0·3	8·4	0·9	14·4	1·6
25	1 36·3	1 36·5	1 31·9	2·5	0·3	8·5	0·9	14·5	1·6
26	1 36·5	1 36·8	1 32·1	2·6	0·3	8·6	0·9	14·6	1·6
27	1 36·8	1 37·0	1 32·3	2·7	0·3	8·7	0·9	14·7	1·6
28	1 37·0	1 37·3	1 32·6	2·8	0·3	8·8	1·0	14·8	1·6
29	1 37·3	1 37·5	1 32·8	2·9	0·3	8·9	1·0	14·9	1·6
30	1 37·5	1 37·8	1 33·1	3·0	0·3	9·0	1·0	15·0	1·6
31	1 37·8	1 38·0	1 33·3	3·1	0·3	9·1	1·0	15·1	1·6
32	1 38·0	1 38·3	1 33·5	3·2	0·3	9·2	1·0	15·2	1·6
33	1 38·3	1 38·5	1 33·8	3·3	0·4	9·3	1·0	15·3	1·7
34	1 38·5	1 38·8	1 34·0	3·4	0·4	9·4	1·0	15·4	1·7
35	1 38·8	1 39·0	1 34·3	3·5	0·4	9·5	1·0	15·5	1·7
36	1 39·0	1 39·3	1 34·5	3·6	0·4	9·6	1·0	15·6	1·7
37	1 39·3	1 39·5	1 34·7	3·7	0·4	9·7	1·1	15·7	1·7
38	1 39·5	1 39·8	1 35·0	3·8	0·4	9·8	1·1	15·8	1·7
39	1 39·8	1 40·0	1 35·2	3·9	0·4	9·9	1·1	15·9	1·7
40	1 40·0	1 40·3	1 35·4	4·0	0·4	10·0	1·1	16·0	1·7
41	1 40·3	1 40·5	1 35·7	4·1	0·4	10·1	1·1	16·1	1·7
42	1 40·5	1 40·8	1 35·9	4·2	0·5	10·2	1·1	16·2	1·8
43	1 40·8	1 41·0	1 36·2	4·3	0·5	10·3	1·1	16·3	1·8
44	1 41·0	1 41·3	1 36·4	4·4	0·5	10·4	1·1	16·4	1·8
45	1 41·3	1 41·5	1 36·6	4·5	0·5	10·5	1·1	16·5	1·8
46	1 41·5	1 41·8	1 36·9	4·6	0·5	10·6	1·1	16·6	1·8
47	1 41·8	1 42·0	1 37·1	4·7	0·5	10·7	1·2	16·7	1·8
48	1 42·0	1 42·3	1 37·4	4·8	0·5	10·8	1·2	16·8	1·8
49	1 42·3	1 42·5	1 37·6	4·9	0·5	10·9	1·2	16·9	1·8
50	1 42·5	1 42·8	1 37·8	5·0	0·5	11·0	1·2	17·0	1·8
51	1 42·8	1 43·0	1 38·1	5·1	0·6	11·1	1·2	17·1	1·9
52	1 43·0	1 43·3	1 38·3	5·2	0·6	11·2	1·2	17·2	1·9
53	1 43·3	1 43·5	1 38·5	5·3	0·6	11·3	1·2	17·3	1·9
54	1 43·5	1 43·8	1 38·8	5·4	0·6	11·4	1·2	17·4	1·9
55	1 43·8	1 44·0	1 39·0	5·5	0·6	11·5	1·2	17·5	1·9
56	1 44·0	1 44·3	1 39·3	5·6	0·6	11·6	1·3	17·6	1·9
57	1 44·3	1 44·5	1 39·5	5·7	0·6	11·7	1·3	17·7	1·9
58	1 44·5	1 44·8	1 39·7	5·8	0·6	11·8	1·3	17·8	1·9
59	1 44·8	1 45·0	1 40·0	5·9	0·6	11·9	1·3	17·9	1·9
60	1 45·0	1 45·3	1 40·2	6·0	0·7	12·0	1·3	18·0	2·0

7ᵐ

7 s	SUN PLANETS	ARIES	MOON	v or d	Corrⁿ	v or d	Corrⁿ	v or d	Corrⁿ
00	1 45·0	1 45·3	1 40·2	0·0	0·0	6·0	0·8	12·0	1·5
01	1 45·3	1 45·5	1 40·5	0·1	0·0	6·1	0·8	12·1	1·5
02	1 45·5	1 45·8	1 40·7	0·2	0·0	6·2	0·8	12·2	1·5
03	1 45·8	1 46·0	1 40·9	0·3	0·0	6·3	0·8	12·3	1·5
04	1 46·0	1 46·3	1 41·2	0·4	0·1	6·4	0·8	12·4	1·6
05	1 46·3	1 46·5	1 41·4	0·5	0·1	6·5	0·8	12·5	1·6
06	1 46·5	1 46·8	1 41·6	0·6	0·1	6·6	0·8	12·6	1·6
07	1 46·8	1 47·0	1 41·9	0·7	0·1	6·7	0·8	12·7	1·6
08	1 47·0	1 47·3	1 42·1	0·8	0·1	6·8	0·9	12·8	1·6
09	1 47·3	1 47·5	1 42·4	0·9	0·1	6·9	0·9	12·9	1·6
10	1 47·5	1 47·8	1 42·6	1·0	0·1	7·0	0·9	13·0	1·6
11	1 47·8	1 48·0	1 42·8	1·1	0·1	7·1	0·9	13·1	1·6
12	1 48·0	1 48·3	1 43·1	1·2	0·2	7·2	0·9	13·2	1·7
13	1 48·3	1 48·5	1 43·3	1·3	0·2	7·3	0·9	13·3	1·7
14	1 48·5	1 48·8	1 43·6	1·4	0·2	7·4	0·9	13·4	1·7
15	1 48·8	1 49·0	1 43·8	1·5	0·2	7·5	0·9	13·5	1·7
16	1 49·0	1 49·3	1 44·0	1·6	0·2	7·6	1·0	13·6	1·7
17	1 49·3	1 49·5	1 44·3	1·7	0·2	7·7	1·0	13·7	1·7
18	1 49·5	1 49·8	1 44·5	1·8	0·2	7·8	1·0	13·8	1·7
19	1 49·8	1 50·1	1 44·8	1·9	0·2	7·9	1·0	13·9	1·7
20	1 50·0	1 50·3	1 45·0	2·0	0·3	8·0	1·0	14·0	1·8
21	1 50·3	1 50·6	1 45·2	2·1	0·3	8·1	1·0	14·1	1·8
22	1 50·5	1 50·8	1 45·5	2·2	0·3	8·2	1·0	14·2	1·8
23	1 50·8	1 51·1	1 45·7	2·3	0·3	8·3	1·0	14·3	1·8
24	1 51·0	1 51·3	1 45·9	2·4	0·3	8·4	1·1	14·4	1·8
25	1 51·3	1 51·6	1 46·2	2·5	0·3	8·5	1·1	14·5	1·8
26	1 51·5	1 51·8	1 46·4	2·6	0·3	8·6	1·1	14·6	1·8
27	1 51·8	1 52·1	1 46·7	2·7	0·3	8·7	1·1	14·7	1·8
28	1 52·0	1 52·3	1 46·9	2·8	0·4	8·8	1·1	14·8	1·9
29	1 52·3	1 52·6	1 47·1	2·9	0·4	8·9	1·1	14·9	1·9
30	1 52·5	1 52·8	1 47·4	3·0	0·4	9·0	1·1	15·0	1·9
31	1 52·8	1 53·1	1 47·6	3·1	0·4	9·1	1·1	15·1	1·9
32	1 53·0	1 53·3	1 47·9	3·2	0·4	9·2	1·2	15·2	1·9
33	1 53·3	1 53·6	1 48·1	3·3	0·4	9·3	1·2	15·3	1·9
34	1 53·5	1 53·8	1 48·3	3·4	0·4	9·4	1·2	15·4	1·9
35	1 53·8	1 54·1	1 48·6	3·5	0·4	9·5	1·2	15·5	1·9
36	1 54·0	1 54·3	1 48·8	3·6	0·5	9·6	1·2	15·6	2·0
37	1 54·3	1 54·6	1 49·0	3·7	0·5	9·7	1·2	15·7	2·0
38	1 54·5	1 54·8	1 49·3	3·8	0·5	9·8	1·2	15·8	2·0
39	1 54·8	1 55·1	1 49·5	3·9	0·5	9·9	1·2	15·9	2·0
40	1 55·0	1 55·3	1 49·8	4·0	0·5	10·0	1·3	16·0	2·0
41	1 55·3	1 55·6	1 50·0	4·1	0·5	10·1	1·3	16·1	2·0
42	1 55·5	1 55·8	1 50·2	4·2	0·5	10·2	1·3	16·2	2·0
43	1 55·8	1 56·1	1 50·5	4·3	0·5	10·3	1·3	16·3	2·0
44	1 56·0	1 56·3	1 50·7	4·4	0·6	10·4	1·3	16·4	2·1
45	1 56·3	1 56·6	1 51·0	4·5	0·6	10·5	1·3	16·5	2·1
46	1 56·5	1 56·8	1 51·2	4·6	0·6	10·6	1·3	16·6	2·1
47	1 56·8	1 57·1	1 51·4	4·7	0·6	10·7	1·3	16·7	2·1
48	1 57·0	1 57·3	1 51·7	4·8	0·6	10·8	1·4	16·8	2·1
49	1 57·3	1 57·6	1 51·9	4·9	0·6	10·9	1·4	16·9	2·1
50	1 57·5	1 57·8	1 52·1	5·0	0·6	11·0	1·4	17·0	2·1
51	1 57·8	1 58·1	1 52·4	5·1	0·6	11·1	1·4	17·1	2·1
52	1 58·0	1 58·3	1 52·6	5·2	0·7	11·2	1·4	17·2	2·2
53	1 58·3	1 58·6	1 52·9	5·3	0·7	11·3	1·4	17·3	2·2
54	1 58·5	1 58·8	1 53·1	5·4	0·7	11·4	1·4	17·4	2·2
55	1 58·8	1 59·1	1 53·3	5·5	0·7	11·5	1·4	17·5	2·2
56	1 59·0	1 59·3	1 53·6	5·6	0·7	11·6	1·5	17·6	2·2
57	1 59·3	1 59·6	1 53·8	5·7	0·7	11·7	1·5	17·7	2·2
58	1 59·5	1 59·8	1 54·1	5·8	0·7	11·8	1·5	17·8	2·2
59	1 59·8	2 00·1	1 54·3	5·9	0·7	11·9	1·5	17·9	2·2
60	2 00·0	2 00·3	1 54·5	6·0	0·8	12·0	1·5	18·0	2·3

8ᵐ

8 s	SUN PLANETS	ARIES	MOON	v or d / Corrⁿ	v or d / Corrⁿ	v or d / Corrⁿ
00	2 00·0	2 00·3	1 54·5	0·0 0·0	6·0 0·9	12·0 1·7
01	2 00·3	2 00·6	1 54·8	0·1 0·0	6·1 0·9	12·1 1·7
02	2 00·5	2 00·8	1 55·0	0·2 0·0	6·2 0·9	12·2 1·7
03	2 00·8	2 01·1	1 55·2	0·3 0·0	6·3 0·9	12·3 1·7
04	2 01·0	2 01·3	1 55·5	0·4 0·1	6·4 0·9	12·4 1·8
05	2 01·3	2 01·6	1 55·7	0·5 0·1	6·5 0·9	12·5 1·8
06	2 01·5	2 01·8	1 56·0	0·6 0·1	6·6 0·9	12·6 1·8
07	2 01·8	2 02·1	1 56·2	0·7 0·1	6·7 0·9	12·7 1·8
08	2 02·0	2 02·3	1 56·4	0·8 0·1	6·8 1·0	12·8 1·8
09	2 02·3	2 02·6	1 56·7	0·9 0·1	6·9 1·0	12·9 1·8
10	2 02·5	2 02·8	1 56·9	1·0 0·1	7·0 1·0	13·0 1·8
11	2 02·8	2 03·1	1 57·2	1·1 0·2	7·1 1·0	13·1 1·9
12	2 03·0	2 03·3	1 57·4	1·2 0·2	7·2 1·0	13·2 1·9
13	2 03·3	2 03·6	1 57·6	1·3 0·2	7·3 1·0	13·3 1·9
14	2 03·5	2 03·8	1 57·9	1·4 0·2	7·4 1·0	13·4 1·9
15	2 03·8	2 04·1	1 58·1	1·5 0·2	7·5 1·1	13·5 1·9
16	2 04·0	2 04·3	1 58·4	1·6 0·2	7·6 1·1	13·6 1·9
17	2 04·3	2 04·6	1 58·6	1·7 0·2	7·7 1·1	13·7 1·9
18	2 04·5	2 04·8	1 58·8	1·8 0·3	7·8 1·1	13·8 2·0
19	2 04·8	2 05·1	1 59·1	1·9 0·3	7·9 1·1	13·9 2·0
20	2 05·0	2 05·3	1 59·3	2·0 0·3	8·0 1·1	14·0 2·0
21	2 05·3	2 05·6	1 59·5	2·1 0·3	8·1 1·1	14·1 2·0
22	2 05·5	2 05·8	1 59·8	2·2 0·3	8·2 1·2	14·2 2·0
23	2 05·8	2 06·1	2 00·0	2·3 0·3	8·3 1·2	14·3 2·0
24	2 06·0	2 06·3	2 00·3	2·4 0·3	8·4 1·2	14·4 2·0
25	2 06·3	2 06·6	2 00·5	2·5 0·4	8·5 1·2	14·5 2·1
26	2 06·5	2 06·8	2 00·7	2·6 0·4	8·6 1·2	14·6 2·1
27	2 06·8	2 07·1	2 01·0	2·7 0·4	8·7 1·2	14·7 2·1
28	2 07·0	2 07·3	2 01·2	2·8 0·4	8·8 1·2	14·8 2·1
29	2 07·3	2 07·6	2 01·5	2·9 0·4	8·9 1·3	14·9 2·1
30	2 07·5	2 07·8	2 01·7	3·0 0·4	9·0 1·3	15·0 2·1
31	2 07·8	2 08·1	2 01·9	3·1 0·4	9·1 1·3	15·1 2·1
32	2 08·0	2 08·4	2 02·2	3·2 0·5	9·2 1·3	15·2 2·2
33	2 08·3	2 08·6	2 02·4	3·3 0·5	9·3 1·3	15·3 2·2
34	2 08·5	2 08·9	2 02·6	3·4 0·5	9·4 1·3	15·4 2·2
35	2 08·8	2 09·1	2 02·9	3·5 0·5	9·5 1·3	15·5 2·2
36	2 09·0	2 09·4	2 03·1	3·6 0·5	9·6 1·4	15·6 2·2
37	2 09·3	2 09·6	2 03·4	3·7 0·5	9·7 1·4	15·7 2·2
38	2 09·5	2 09·9	2 03·6	3·8 0·5	9·8 1·4	15·8 2·2
39	2 09·8	2 10·1	2 03·8	3·9 0·6	9·9 1·4	15·9 2·3
40	2 10·0	2 10·4	2 04·1	4·0 0·6	10·0 1·4	16·0 2·3
41	2 10·3	2 10·6	2 04·3	4·1 0·6	10·1 1·4	16·1 2·3
42	2 10·5	2 10·9	2 04·6	4·2 0·6	10·2 1·4	16·2 2·3
43	2 10·8	2 11·1	2 04·8	4·3 0·6	10·3 1·5	16·3 2·3
44	2 11·0	2 11·4	2 05·0	4·4 0·6	10·4 1·5	16·4 2·3
45	2 11·3	2 11·6	2 05·3	4·5 0·6	10·5 1·5	16·5 2·3
46	2 11·5	2 11·9	2 05·5	4·6 0·7	10·6 1·5	16·6 2·4
47	2 11·8	2 12·1	2 05·7	4·7 0·7	10·7 1·5	16·7 2·4
48	2 12·0	2 12·4	2 06·0	4·8 0·7	10·8 1·5	16·8 2·4
49	2 12·3	2 12·6	2 06·2	4·9 0·7	10·9 1·5	16·9 2·4
50	2 12·5	2 12·9	2 06·5	5·0 0·7	11·0 1·6	17·0 2·4
51	2 12·8	2 13·1	2 06·7	5·1 0·7	11·1 1·6	17·1 2·4
52	2 13·0	2 13·4	2 06·9	5·2 0·7	11·2 1·6	17·2 2·4
53	2 13·3	2 13·6	2 07·2	5·3 0·8	11·3 1·6	17·3 2·5
54	2 13·5	2 13·9	2 07·4	5·4 0·8	11·4 1·6	17·4 2·5
55	2 13·8	2 14·1	2 07·7	5·5 0·8	11·5 1·6	17·5 2·5
56	2 14·0	2 14·4	2 07·9	5·6 0·8	11·6 1·6	17·6 2·5
57	2 14·3	2 14·6	2 08·1	5·7 0·8	11·7 1·7	17·7 2·5
58	2 14·5	2 14·9	2 08·4	5·8 0·8	11·8 1·7	17·8 2·5
59	2 14·8	2 15·1	2 08·6	5·9 0·8	11·9 1·7	17·9 2·5
60	2 15·0	2 15·4	2 08·9	6·0 0·9	12·0 1·7	18·0 2·6

9ᵐ

9 s	SUN PLANETS	ARIES	MOON	v or d / Corrⁿ	v or d / Corrⁿ	v or d / Corrⁿ
00	2 15·0	2 15·4	2 08·9	0·0 0·0	6·0 1·0	12·0 1·9
01	2 15·3	2 15·6	2 09·1	0·1 0·0	6·1 1·0	12·1 1·9
02	2 15·5	2 15·9	2 09·3	0·2 0·0	6·2 1·0	12·2 1·9
03	2 15·8	2 16·1	2 09·6	0·3 0·0	6·3 1·0	12·3 1·9
04	2 16·0	2 16·4	2 09·8	0·4 0·1	6·4 1·0	12·4 2·0
05	2 16·3	2 16·6	2 10·0	0·5 0·1	6·5 1·0	12·5 2·0
06	2 16·5	2 16·9	2 10·3	0·6 0·1	6·6 1·0	12·6 2·0
07	2 16·8	2 17·1	2 10·5	0·7 0·1	6·7 1·1	12·7 2·0
08	2 17·0	2 17·4	2 10·8	0·8 0·1	6·8 1·1	12·8 2·0
09	2 17·3	2 17·6	2 11·0	0·9 0·1	6·9 1·1	12·9 2·0
10	2 17·5	2 17·9	2 11·2	1·0 0·2	7·0 1·1	13·0 2·1
11	2 17·8	2 18·1	2 11·5	1·1 0·2	7·1 1·1	13·1 2·1
12	2 18·0	2 18·4	2 11·7	1·2 0·2	7·2 1·1	13·2 2·1
13	2 18·3	2 18·6	2 12·0	1·3 0·2	7·3 1·2	13·3 2·1
14	2 18·5	2 18·9	2 12·2	1·4 0·2	7·4 1·2	13·4 2·1
15	2 18·8	2 19·1	2 12·4	1·5 0·2	7·5 1·2	13·5 2·1
16	2 19·0	2 19·4	2 12·7	1·6 0·3	7·6 1·2	13·6 2·2
17	2 19·3	2 19·6	2 12·9	1·7 0·3	7·7 1·2	13·7 2·2
18	2 19·5	2 19·9	2 13·1	1·8 0·3	7·8 1·2	13·8 2·2
19	2 19·8	2 20·1	2 13·4	1·9 0·3	7·9 1·3	13·9 2·2
20	2 20·0	2 20·4	2 13·6	2·0 0·3	8·0 1·3	14·0 2·2
21	2 20·3	2 20·6	2 13·9	2·1 0·3	8·1 1·3	14·1 2·2
22	2 20·5	2 20·9	2 14·1	2·2 0·3	8·2 1·3	14·2 2·2
23	2 20·8	2 21·1	2 14·3	2·3 0·4	8·3 1·3	14·3 2·3
24	2 21·0	2 21·4	2 14·6	2·4 0·4	8·4 1·3	14·4 2·3
25	2 21·3	2 21·6	2 14·8	2·5 0·4	8·5 1·3	14·5 2·3
26	2 21·5	2 21·9	2 15·1	2·6 0·4	8·6 1·4	14·6 2·3
27	2 21·8	2 22·1	2 15·3	2·7 0·4	8·7 1·4	14·7 2·3
28	2 22·0	2 22·4	2 15·5	2·8 0·4	8·8 1·4	14·8 2·3
29	2 22·3	2 22·6	2 15·8	2·9 0·5	8·9 1·4	14·9 2·4
30	2 22·5	2 22·9	2 16·0	3·0 0·5	9·0 1·4	15·0 2·4
31	2 22·8	2 23·1	2 16·2	3·1 0·5	9·1 1·4	15·1 2·4
32	2 23·0	2 23·4	2 16·5	3·2 0·5	9·2 1·5	15·2 2·4
33	2 23·3	2 23·6	2 16·7	3·3 0·5	9·3 1·5	15·3 2·4
34	2 23·5	2 23·9	2 17·0	3·4 0·5	9·4 1·5	15·4 2·4
35	2 23·8	2 24·1	2 17·2	3·5 0·6	9·5 1·5	15·5 2·5
36	2 24·0	2 24·4	2 17·4	3·6 0·6	9·6 1·5	15·6 2·5
37	2 24·3	2 24·6	2 17·7	3·7 0·6	9·7 1·5	15·7 2·5
38	2 24·5	2 24·9	2 17·9	3·8 0·6	9·8 1·6	15·8 2·5
39	2 24·8	2 25·1	2 18·2	3·9 0·6	9·9 1·6	15·9 2·5
40	2 25·0	2 25·4	2 18·4	4·0 0·6	10·0 1·6	16·0 2·5
41	2 25·3	2 25·6	2 18·6	4·1 0·6	10·1 1·6	16·1 2·5
42	2 25·5	2 25·9	2 18·9	4·2 0·7	10·2 1·6	16·2 2·6
43	2 25·8	2 26·1	2 19·1	4·3 0·7	10·3 1·6	16·3 2·6
44	2 26·0	2 26·4	2 19·3	4·4 0·7	10·4 1·6	16·4 2·6
45	2 26·3	2 26·7	2 19·6	4·5 0·7	10·5 1·7	16·5 2·6
46	2 26·5	2 26·9	2 19·8	4·6 0·7	10·6 1·7	16·6 2·6
47	2 26·8	2 27·2	2 20·1	4·7 0·7	10·7 1·7	16·7 2·6
48	2 27·0	2 27·4	2 20·3	4·8 0·8	10·8 1·7	16·8 2·7
49	2 27·3	2 27·7	2 20·5	4·9 0·8	10·9 1·7	16·9 2·7
50	2 27·5	2 27·9	2 20·8	5·0 0·8	11·0 1·7	17·0 2·7
51	2 27·8	2 28·2	2 21·0	5·1 0·8	11·1 1·8	17·1 2·7
52	2 28·0	2 28·4	2 21·3	5·2 0·8	11·2 1·8	17·2 2·7
53	2 28·3	2 28·7	2 21·5	5·3 0·8	11·3 1·8	17·3 2·7
54	2 28·5	2 28·9	2 21·7	5·4 0·9	11·4 1·8	17·4 2·8
55	2 28·8	2 29·2	2 22·0	5·5 0·9	11·5 1·8	17·5 2·8
56	2 29·0	2 29·4	2 22·2	5·6 0·9	11·6 1·8	17·6 2·8
57	2 29·3	2 29·7	2 22·5	5·7 0·9	11·7 1·9	17·7 2·8
58	2 29·5	2 29·9	2 22·7	5·8 0·9	11·8 1·9	17·8 2·8
59	2 29·8	2 30·2	2 22·9	5·9 0·9	11·9 1·9	17·9 2·8
60	2 30·0	2 30·4	2 23·2	6·0 1·0	12·0 1·9	18·0 2·9

m 10	SUN PLANETS	ARIES	MOON	v or d Corrⁿ	v or d Corrⁿ	v or d Corrⁿ
s	° ′	° ′	° ′	′ ′	′ ′	′ ′
00	2 30·0	2 30·4	2 23·2	0·0 0·0	6·0 1·1	12·0 2·1
01	2 30·3	2 30·7	2 23·4	0·1 0·0	6·1 1·1	12·1 2·1
02	2 30·5	2 30·9	2 23·6	0·2 0·0	6·2 1·1	12·2 2·1
03	2 30·8	2 31·2	2 23·9	0·3 0·1	6·3 1·1	12·3 2·2
04	2 31·0	2 31·4	2 24·1	0·4 0·1	6·4 1·1	12·4 2·2
05	2 31·3	2 31·7	2 24·4	0·5 0·1	6·5 1·1	12·5 2·2
06	2 31·5	2 31·9	2 24·6	0·6 0·1	6·6 1·2	12·6 2·2
07	2 31·8	2 32·2	2 24·8	0·7 0·1	6·7 1·2	12·7 2·2
08	2 32·0	2 32·4	2 25·1	0·8 0·1	6·8 1·2	12·8 2·2
09	2 32·3	2 32·7	2 25·3	0·9 0·2	6·9 1·2	12·9 2·3
10	2 32·5	2 32·9	2 25·6	1·0 0·2	7·0 1·2	13·0 2·3
11	2 32·8	2 33·2	2 25·8	1·1 0·2	7·1 1·2	13·1 2·3
12	2 33·0	2 33·4	2 26·0	1·2 0·2	7·2 1·3	13·2 2·3
13	2 33·3	2 33·7	2 26·3	1·3 0·2	7·3 1·3	13·3 2·3
14	2 33·5	2 33·9	2 26·5	1·4 0·2	7·4 1·3	13·4 2·3
15	2 33·8	2 34·2	2 26·7	1·5 0·3	7·5 1·3	13·5 2·4
16	2 34·0	2 34·4	2 27·0	1·6 0·3	7·6 1·3	13·6 2·4
17	2 34·3	2 34·7	2 27·2	1·7 0·3	7·7 1·3	13·7 2·4
18	2 34·5	2 34·9	2 27·5	1·8 0·3	7·8 1·4	13·8 2·4
19	2 34·8	2 35·2	2 27·7	1·9 0·3	7·9 1·4	13·9 2·4
20	2 35·0	2 35·4	2 27·9	2·0 0·4	8·0 1·4	14·0 2·5
21	2 35·3	2 35·7	2 28·2	2·1 0·4	8·1 1·4	14·1 2·5
22	2 35·5	2 35·9	2 28·4	2·2 0·4	8·2 1·4	14·2 2·5
23	2 35·8	2 36·2	2 28·7	2·3 0·4	8·3 1·5	14·3 2·5
24	2 36·0	2 36·4	2 28·9	2·4 0·4	8·4 1·5	14·4 2·5
25	2 36·3	2 36·7	2 29·1	2·5 0·4	8·5 1·5	14·5 2·5
26	2 36·5	2 36·9	2 29·4	2·6 0·5	8·6 1·5	14·6 2·6
27	2 36·8	2 37·2	2 29·6	2·7 0·5	8·7 1·5	14·7 2·6
28	2 37·0	2 37·4	2 29·8	2·8 0·5	8·8 1·5	14·8 2·6
29	2 37·3	2 37·7	2 30·1	2·9 0·5	8·9 1·6	14·9 2·6
30	2 37·5	2 37·9	2 30·3	3·0 0·5	9·0 1·6	15·0 2·6
31	2 37·8	2 38·2	2 30·6	3·1 0·5	9·1 1·6	15·1 2·6
32	2 38·0	2 38·4	2 30·8	3·2 0·6	9·2 1·6	15·2 2·7
33	2 38·3	2 38·7	2 31·0	3·3 0·6	9·3 1·6	15·3 2·7
34	2 38·5	2 38·9	2 31·3	3·4 0·6	9·4 1·6	15·4 2·7
35	2 38·8	2 39·2	2 31·5	3·5 0·6	9·5 1·7	15·5 2·7
36	2 39·0	2 39·4	2 31·8	3·6 0·6	9·6 1·7	15·6 2·7
37	2 39·3	2 39·7	2 32·0	3·7 0·6	9·7 1·7	15·7 2·7
38	2 39·5	2 39·9	2 32·2	3·8 0·7	9·8 1·7	15·8 2·8
39	2 39·8	2 40·2	2 32·5	3·9 0·7	9·9 1·7	15·9 2·8
40	2 40·0	2 40·4	2 32·7	4·0 0·7	10·0 1·8	16·0 2·8
41	2 40·3	2 40·7	2 32·9	4·1 0·7	10·1 1·8	16·1 2·8
42	2 40·5	2 40·9	2 33·2	4·2 0·7	10·2 1·8	16·2 2·8
43	2 40·8	2 41·2	2 33·4	4·3 0·8	10·3 1·8	16·3 2·9
44	2 41·0	2 41·4	2 33·7	4·4 0·8	10·4 1·8	16·4 2·9
45	2 41·3	2 41·7	2 33·9	4·5 0·8	10·5 1·8	16·5 2·9
46	2 41·5	2 41·9	2 34·1	4·6 0·8	10·6 1·9	16·6 2·9
47	2 41·8	2 42·2	2 34·4	4·7 0·8	10·7 1·9	16·7 2·9
48	2 42·0	2 42·4	2 34·6	4·8 0·8	10·8 1·9	16·8 2·9
49	2 42·3	2 42·7	2 34·9	4·9 0·9	10·9 1·9	16·9 3·0
50	2 42·5	2 42·9	2 35·1	5·0 0·9	11·0 1·9	17·0 3·0
51	2 42·8	2 43·2	2 35·3	5·1 0·9	11·1 1·9	17·1 3·0
52	2 43·0	2 43·4	2 35·6	5·2 0·9	11·2 2·0	17·2 3·0
53	2 43·3	2 43·7	2 35·8	5·3 0·9	11·3 2·0	17·3 3·0
54	2 43·5	2 43·9	2 36·1	5·4 0·9	11·4 2·0	17·4 3·0
55	2 43·8	2 44·2	2 36·3	5·5 1·0	11·5 2·0	17·5 3·1
56	2 44·0	2 44·4	2 36·5	5·6 1·0	11·6 2·0	17·6 3·1
57	2 44·3	2 44·7	2 36·8	5·7 1·0	11·7 2·0	17·7 3·1
58	2 44·5	2 45·0	2 37·0	5·8 1·0	11·8 2·1	17·8 3·1
59	2 44·8	2 45·2	2 37·2	5·9 1·0	11·9 2·1	17·9 3·1
60	2 45·0	2 45·5	2 37·5	6·0 1·1	12·0 2·1	18·0 3·2

m 11	SUN PLANETS	ARIES	MOON	v or d Corrⁿ	v or d Corrⁿ	v or d Corrⁿ
s	° ′	° ′	° ′	′ ′	′ ′	′ ′
00	2 45·0	2 45·5	2 37·5	0·0 0·0	6·0 1·2	12·0 2·3
01	2 45·3	2 45·7	2 37·7	0·1 0·0	6·1 1·2	12·1 2·3
02	2 45·5	2 46·0	2 38·0	0·2 0·0	6·2 1·2	12·2 2·3
03	2 45·8	2 46·2	2 38·2	0·3 0·1	6·3 1·2	12·3 2·4
04	2 46·0	2 46·5	2 38·4	0·4 0·1	6·4 1·2	12·4 2·4
05	2 46·3	2 46·7	2 38·7	0·5 0·1	6·5 1·2	12·5 2·4
06	2 46·5	2 47·0	2 38·9	0·6 0·1	6·6 1·3	12·6 2·4
07	2 46·8	2 47·2	2 39·2	0·7 0·1	6·7 1·3	12·7 2·4
08	2 47·0	2 47·5	2 39·4	0·8 0·2	6·8 1·3	12·8 2·5
09	2 47·3	2 47·7	2 39·6	0·9 0·2	6·9 1·3	12·9 2·5
10	2 47·5	2 48·0	2 39·9	1·0 0·2	7·0 1·3	13·0 2·5
11	2 47·8	2 48·2	2 40·1	1·1 0·2	7·1 1·4	13·1 2·5
12	2 48·0	2 48·5	2 40·3	1·2 0·2	7·2 1·4	13·2 2·5
13	2 48·3	2 48·7	2 40·6	1·3 0·2	7·3 1·4	13·3 2·5
14	2 48·5	2 49·0	2 40·8	1·4 0·3	7·4 1·4	13·4 2·6
15	2 48·8	2 49·2	2 41·1	1·5 0·3	7·5 1·4	13·5 2·6
16	2 49·0	2 49·5	2 41·3	1·6 0·3	7·6 1·5	13·6 2·6
17	2 49·3	2 49·7	2 41·5	1·7 0·3	7·7 1·5	13·7 2·6
18	2 49·5	2 50·0	2 41·8	1·8 0·3	7·8 1·5	13·8 2·6
19	2 49·8	2 50·2	2 42·0	1·9 0·4	7·9 1·5	13·9 2·7
20	2 50·0	2 50·5	2 42·3	2·0 0·4	8·0 1·5	14·0 2·7
21	2 50·3	2 50·7	2 42·5	2·1 0·4	8·1 1·6	14·1 2·7
22	2 50·5	2 51·0	2 42·7	2·2 0·4	8·2 1·6	14·2 2·7
23	2 50·8	2 51·2	2 43·0	2·3 0·4	8·3 1·6	14·3 2·7
24	2 51·0	2 51·5	2 43·2	2·4 0·5	8·4 1·6	14·4 2·8
25	2 51·3	2 51·7	2 43·4	2·5 0·5	8·5 1·6	14·5 2·8
26	2 51·5	2 52·0	2 43·7	2·6 0·5	8·6 1·6	14·6 2·8
27	2 51·8	2 52·2	2 43·9	2·7 0·5	8·7 1·7	14·7 2·8
28	2 52·0	2 52·5	2 44·2	2·8 0·5	8·8 1·7	14·8 2·8
29	2 52·3	2 52·7	2 44·4	2·9 0·6	8·9 1·7	14·9 2·9
30	2 52·5	2 53·0	2 44·6	3·0 0·6	9·0 1·7	15·0 2·9
31	2 52·8	2 53·2	2 44·9	3·1 0·6	9·1 1·7	15·1 2·9
32	2 53·0	2 53·5	2 45·1	3·2 0·6	9·2 1·8	15·2 2·9
33	2 53·3	2 53·7	2 45·4	3·3 0·6	9·3 1·8	15·3 2·9
34	2 53·5	2 54·0	2 45·6	3·4 0·7	9·4 1·8	15·4 3·0
35	2 53·8	2 54·2	2 45·8	3·5 0·7	9·5 1·8	15·5 3·0
36	2 54·0	2 54·5	2 46·1	3·6 0·7	9·6 1·8	15·6 3·0
37	2 54·3	2 54·7	2 46·3	3·7 0·7	9·7 1·9	15·7 3·0
38	2 54·5	2 55·0	2 46·6	3·8 0·7	9·8 1·9	15·8 3·0
39	2 54·8	2 55·2	2 46·8	3·9 0·7	9·9 1·9	15·9 3·0
40	2 55·0	2 55·5	2 47·0	4·0 0·8	10·0 1·9	16·0 3·1
41	2 55·3	2 55·7	2 47·3	4·1 0·8	10·1 1·9	16·1 3·1
42	2 55·5	2 56·0	2 47·5	4·2 0·8	10·2 2·0	16·2 3·1
43	2 55·8	2 56·2	2 47·7	4·3 0·8	10·3 2·0	16·3 3·1
44	2 56·0	2 56·5	2 48·0	4·4 0·8	10·4 2·0	16·4 3·1
45	2 56·3	2 56·7	2 48·2	4·5 0·9	10·5 2·0	16·5 3·2
46	2 56·5	2 57·0	2 48·5	4·6 0·9	10·6 2·0	16·6 3·2
47	2 56·8	2 57·2	2 48·7	4·7 0·9	10·7 2·1	16·7 3·2
48	2 57·0	2 57·5	2 48·9	4·8 0·9	10·8 2·1	16·8 3·2
49	2 57·3	2 57·7	2 49·2	4·9 0·9	10·9 2·1	16·9 3·2
50	2 57·5	2 58·0	2 49·4	5·0 1·0	11·0 2·1	17·0 3·3
51	2 57·8	2 58·2	2 49·7	5·1 1·0	11·1 2·1	17·1 3·3
52	2 58·0	2 58·5	2 49·9	5·2 1·0	11·2 2·1	17·2 3·3
53	2 58·3	2 58·7	2 50·1	5·3 1·0	11·3 2·2	17·3 3·3
54	2 58·5	2 59·0	2 50·4	5·4 1·0	11·4 2·2	17·4 3·3
55	2 58·8	2 59·2	2 50·6	5·5 1·1	11·5 2·2	17·5 3·4
56	2 59·0	2 59·5	2 50·8	5·6 1·1	11·6 2·2	17·6 3·4
57	2 59·3	2 59·7	2 51·1	5·7 1·1	11·7 2·2	17·7 3·4
58	2 59·5	3 00·0	2 51·3	5·8 1·1	11·8 2·3	17·8 3·4
59	2 59·8	3 00·2	2 51·6	5·9 1·1	11·9 2·3	17·9 3·4
60	3 00·0	3 00·5	2 51·8	6·0 1·2	12·0 2·3	18·0 3·5

12 m s	SUN PLANETS	ARIES	MOON	v or Corrⁿ d	v or Corrⁿ d	v or Corrⁿ d
	° ′	° ′	° ′	′ ′	′ ′	′ ′
00	3 00·0	3 00·5	2 51·8	0·0 0·0	6·0 1·3	12·0 2·5
01	3 00·3	3 00·7	2 52·0	0·1 0·0	6·1 1·3	12·1 2·5
02	3 00·5	3 01·0	2 52·3	0·2 0·0	6·2 1·3	12·2 2·5
03	3 00·8	3 01·2	2 52·5	0·3 0·1	6·3 1·3	12·3 2·6
04	3 01·0	3 01·5	2 52·8	0·4 0·1	6·4 1·3	12·4 2·6
05	3 01·3	3 01·7	2 53·0	0·5 0·1	6·5 1·4	12·5 2·6
06	3 01·5	3 02·0	2 53·2	0·6 0·1	6·6 1·4	12·6 2·6
07	3 01·8	3 02·2	2 53·5	0·7 0·1	6·7 1·4	12·7 2·6
08	3 02·0	3 02·5	2 53·7	0·8 0·2	6·8 1·4	12·8 2·7
09	3 02·3	3 02·7	2 53·9	0·9 0·2	6·9 1·4	12·9 2·7
10	3 02·5	3 03·0	2 54·2	1·0 0·2	7·0 1·5	13·0 2·7
11	3 02·8	3 03·3	2 54·4	1·1 0·2	7·1 1·5	13·1 2·7
12	3 03·0	3 03·5	2 54·7	1·2 0·3	7·2 1·5	13·2 2·8
13	3 03·3	3 03·8	2 54·9	1·3 0·3	7·3 1·5	13·3 2·8
14	3 03·5	3 04·0	2 55·1	1·4 0·3	7·4 1·5	13·4 2·8
15	3 03·8	3 04·3	2 55·4	1·5 0·3	7·5 1·6	13·5 2·8
16	3 04·0	3 04·5	2 55·6	1·6 0·3	7·6 1·6	13·6 2·8
17	3 04·3	3 04·8	2 55·9	1·7 0·4	7·7 1·6	13·7 2·9
18	3 04·5	3 05·0	2 56·1	1·8 0·4	7·8 1·6	13·8 2·9
19	3 04·8	3 05·3	2 56·3	1·9 0·4	7·9 1·6	13·9 2·9
20	3 05·0	3 05·5	2 56·6	2·0 0·4	8·0 1·7	14·0 2·9
21	3 05·3	3 05·8	2 56·8	2·1 0·4	8·1 1·7	14·1 2·9
22	3 05·5	3 06·0	2 57·0	2·2 0·5	8·2 1·7	14·2 3·0
23	3 05·8	3 06·3	2 57·3	2·3 0·5	8·3 1·7	14·3 3·0
24	3 06·0	3 06·5	2 57·5	2·4 0·5	8·4 1·8	14·4 3·0
25	3 06·3	3 06·8	2 57·8	2·5 0·5	8·5 1·8	14·5 3·0
26	3 06·5	3 07·0	2 58·0	2·6 0·5	8·6 1·8	14·6 3·0
27	3 06·8	3 07·3	2 58·2	2·7 0·6	8·7 1·8	14·7 3·1
28	3 07·0	3 07·5	2 58·5	2·8 0·6	8·8 1·8	14·8 3·1
29	3 07·3	3 07·8	2 58·7	2·9 0·6	8·9 1·9	14·9 3·1
30	3 07·5	3 08·0	2 59·0	3·0 0·6	9·0 1·9	15·0 3·1
31	3 07·8	3 08·3	2 59·2	3·1 0·6	9·1 1·9	15·1 3·1
32	3 08·0	3 08·5	2 59·4	3·2 0·7	9·2 1·9	15·2 3·2
33	3 08·3	3 08·8	2 59·7	3·3 0·7	9·3 1·9	15·3 3·2
34	3 08·5	3 09·0	2 59·9	3·4 0·7	9·4 2·0	15·4 3·2
35	3 08·8	3 09·3	3 00·2	3·5 0·7	9·5 2·0	15·5 3·2
36	3 09·0	3 09·5	3 00·4	3·6 0·8	9·6 2·0	15·6 3·3
37	3 09·3	3 09·8	3 00·6	3·7 0·8	9·7 2·0	15·7 3·3
38	3 09·5	3 10·0	3 00·9	3·8 0·8	9·8 2·0	15·8 3·3
39	3 09·8	3 10·3	3 01·1	3·9 0·8	9·9 2·1	15·9 3·3
40	3 10·0	3 10·5	3 01·3	4·0 0·8	10·0 2·1	16·0 3·3
41	3 10·3	3 10·8	3 01·6	4·1 0·9	10·1 2·1	16·1 3·4
42	3 10·5	3 11·0	3 01·8	4·2 0·9	10·2 2·1	16·2 3·4
43	3 10·8	3 11·3	3 02·1	4·3 0·9	10·3 2·1	16·3 3·4
44	3 11·0	3 11·5	3 02·3	4·4 0·9	10·4 2·2	16·4 3·4
45	3 11·3	3 11·8	3 02·5	4·5 0·9	10·5 2·2	16·5 3·4
46	3 11·5	3 12·0	3 02·8	4·6 1·0	10·6 2·2	16·6 3·5
47	3 11·8	3 12·3	3 03·0	4·7 1·0	10·7 2·2	16·7 3·5
48	3 12·0	3 12·5	3 03·3	4·8 1·0	10·8 2·3	16·8 3·5
49	3 12·3	3 12·8	3 03·5	4·9 1·0	10·9 2·3	16·9 3·5
50	3 12·5	3 13·0	3 03·7	5·0 1·0	11·0 2·3	17·0 3·5
51	3 12·8	3 13·3	3 04·0	5·1 1·1	11·1 2·3	17·1 3·6
52	3 13·0	3 13·5	3 04·2	5·2 1·1	11·2 2·3	17·2 3·6
53	3 13·3	3 13·8	3 04·4	5·3 1·1	11·3 2·4	17·3 3·6
54	3 13·5	3 14·0	3 04·7	5·4 1·1	11·4 2·4	17·4 3·6
55	3 13·8	3 14·3	3 04·9	5·5 1·1	11·5 2·4	17·5 3·6
56	3 14·0	3 14·5	3 05·2	5·6 1·2	11·6 2·4	17·6 3·7
57	3 14·3	3 14·8	3 05·4	5·7 1·2	11·7 2·4	17·7 3·7
58	3 14·5	3 15·0	3 05·6	5·8 1·2	11·8 2·5	17·8 3·7
59	3 14·8	3 15·3	3 05·9	5·9 1·2	11·9 2·5	17·9 3·7
60	3 15·0	3 15·5	3 06·1	6·0 1·3	12·0 2·5	18·0 3·8

13 m s	SUN PLANETS	ARIES	MOON	v or Corrⁿ d	v or Corrⁿ d	v or Corrⁿ d
	° ′	° ′	° ′	′ ′	′ ′	′ ′
00	3 15·0	3 15·5	3 06·1	0·0 0·0	6·0 1·4	12·0 2·7
01	3 15·3	3 15·8	3 06·4	0·1 0·0	6·1 1·4	12·1 2·7
02	3 15·5	3 16·0	3 06·6	0·2 0·0	6·2 1·4	12·2 2·7
03	3 15·8	3 16·3	3 06·8	0·3 0·1	6·3 1·4	12·3 2·8
04	3 16·0	3 16·5	3 07·1	0·4 0·1	6·4 1·4	12·4 2·8
05	3 16·3	3 16·8	3 07·3	0·5 0·1	6·5 1·5	12·5 2·8
06	3 16·5	3 17·0	3 07·5	0·6 0·1	6·6 1·5	12·6 2·8
07	3 16·8	3 17·3	3 07·8	0·7 0·2	6·7 1·5	12·7 2·9
08	3 17·0	3 17·5	3 08·0	0·8 0·2	6·8 1·5	12·8 2·9
09	3 17·3	3 17·8	3 08·3	0·9 0·2	6·9 1·6	12·9 2·9
10	3 17·5	3 18·0	3 08·5	1·0 0·2	7·0 1·6	13·0 2·9
11	3 17·8	3 18·3	3 08·7	1·1 0·2	7·1 1·6	13·1 2·9
12	3 18·0	3 18·5	3 09·0	1·2 0·3	7·2 1·6	13·2 3·0
13	3 18·3	3 18·8	3 09·2	1·3 0·3	7·3 1·6	13·3 3·0
14	3 18·5	3 19·0	3 09·5	1·4 0·3	7·4 1·7	13·4 3·0
15	3 18·8	3 19·3	3 09·7	1·5 0·3	7·5 1·7	13·5 3·0
16	3 19·0	3 19·5	3 09·9	1·6 0·4	7·6 1·7	13·6 3·1
17	3 19·3	3 19·8	3 10·2	1·7 0·4	7·7 1·7	13·7 3·1
18	3 19·5	3 20·0	3 10·4	1·8 0·4	7·8 1·8	13·8 3·1
19	3 19·8	3 20·3	3 10·7	1·9 0·4	7·9 1·8	13·9 3·1
20	3 20·0	3 20·5	3 10·9	2·0 0·5	8·0 1·8	14·0 3·2
21	3 20·3	3 20·8	3 11·1	2·1 0·5	8·1 1·8	14·1 3·2
22	3 20·5	3 21·0	3 11·4	2·2 0·5	8·2 1·8	14·2 3·2
23	3 20·8	3 21·3	3 11·6	2·3 0·5	8·3 1·9	14·3 3·2
24	3 21·0	3 21·6	3 11·8	2·4 0·5	8·4 1·9	14·4 3·2
25	3 21·3	3 21·8	3 12·1	2·5 0·6	8·5 1·9	14·5 3·3
26	3 21·5	3 22·1	3 12·3	2·6 0·6	8·6 1·9	14·6 3·3
27	3 21·8	3 22·3	3 12·6	2·7 0·6	8·7 2·0	14·7 3·3
28	3 22·0	3 22·6	3 12·8	2·8 0·6	8·8 2·0	14·8 3·3
29	3 22·3	3 22·8	3 13·0	2·9 0·7	8·9 2·0	14·9 3·4
30	3 22·5	3 23·1	3 13·3	3·0 0·7	9·0 2·0	15·0 3·4
31	3 22·8	3 23·3	3 13·5	3·1 0·7	9·1 2·0	15·1 3·4
32	3 23·0	3 23·6	3 13·8	3·2 0·7	9·2 2·1	15·2 3·4
33	3 23·3	3 23·8	3 14·0	3·3 0·7	9·3 2·1	15·3 3·4
34	3 23·5	3 24·1	3 14·2	3·4 0·8	9·4 2·1	15·4 3·5
35	3 23·8	3 24·3	3 14·5	3·5 0·8	9·5 2·1	15·5 3·5
36	3 24·0	3 24·6	3 14·7	3·6 0·8	9·6 2·2	15·6 3·5
37	3 24·3	3 24·8	3 14·9	3·7 0·8	9·7 2·2	15·7 3·5
38	3 24·5	3 25·1	3 15·2	3·8 0·9	9·8 2·2	15·8 3·6
39	3 24·8	3 25·3	3 15·4	3·9 0·9	9·9 2·2	15·9 3·6
40	3 25·0	3 25·6	3 15·7	4·0 0·9	10·0 2·3	16·0 3·6
41	3 25·3	3 25·8	3 15·9	4·1 0·9	10·1 2·3	16·1 3·6
42	3 25·5	3 26·1	3 16·1	4·2 0·9	10·2 2·3	16·2 3·6
43	3 25·8	3 26·3	3 16·4	4·3 1·0	10·3 2·3	16·3 3·7
44	3 26·0	3 26·6	3 16·6	4·4 1·0	10·4 2·3	16·4 3·7
45	3 26·3	3 26·8	3 16·9	4·5 1·0	10·5 2·4	16·5 3·7
46	3 26·5	3 27·1	3 17·1	4·6 1·0	10·6 2·4	16·6 3·7
47	3 26·8	3 27·3	3 17·3	4·7 1·1	10·7 2·4	16·7 3·8
48	3 27·0	3 27·6	3 17·6	4·8 1·1	10·8 2·4	16·8 3·8
49	3 27·3	3 27·8	3 17·8	4·9 1·1	10·9 2·5	16·9 3·8
50	3 27·5	3 28·1	3 18·0	5·0 1·1	11·0 2·5	17·0 3·8
51	3 27·8	3 28·3	3 18·3	5·1 1·1	11·1 2·5	17·1 3·8
52	3 28·0	3 28·6	3 18·5	5·2 1·2	11·2 2·5	17·2 3·9
53	3 28·3	3 28·8	3 18·8	5·3 1·2	11·3 2·5	17·3 3·9
54	3 28·5	3 29·1	3 19·0	5·4 1·2	11·4 2·6	17·4 3·9
55	3 28·8	3 29·3	3 19·2	5·5 1·2	11·5 2·6	17·5 3·9
56	3 29·0	3 29·6	3 19·5	5·6 1·3	11·6 2·6	17·6 4·0
57	3 29·3	3 29·8	3 19·7	5·7 1·3	11·7 2·6	17·7 4·0
58	3 29·5	3 30·1	3 20·0	5·8 1·3	11·8 2·7	17·8 4·0
59	3 29·8	3 30·3	3 20·2	5·9 1·3	11·9 2·7	17·9 4·0
60	3 30·0	3 30·6	3 20·4	6·0 1·4	12·0 2·7	18·0 4·1

14^m

14^m s	SUN PLANETS	ARIES	MOON	v or d / Corr^n	v or d / Corr^n	v or d / Corr^n
00	3 30.0	3 30.6	3 20.4	0.0 0.0	6.0 1.5	12.0 2.9
01	3 30.3	3 30.8	3 20.7	0.1 0.0	6.1 1.5	12.1 2.9
02	3 30.5	3 31.1	3 20.9	0.2 0.0	6.2 1.5	12.2 2.9
03	3 30.8	3 31.3	3 21.1	0.3 0.1	6.3 1.5	12.3 3.0
04	3 31.0	3 31.6	3 21.4	0.4 0.1	6.4 1.5	12.4 3.0
05	3 31.3	3 31.8	3 21.6	0.5 0.1	6.5 1.6	12.5 3.0
06	3 31.5	3 32.1	3 21.9	0.6 0.1	6.6 1.6	12.6 3.0
07	3 31.8	3 32.3	3 22.1	0.7 0.2	6.7 1.6	12.7 3.1
08	3 32.0	3 32.6	3 22.3	0.8 0.2	6.8 1.6	12.8 3.1
09	3 32.3	3 32.8	3 22.6	0.9 0.2	6.9 1.7	12.9 3.1
10	3 32.5	3 33.1	3 22.8	1.0 0.2	7.0 1.7	13.0 3.1
11	3 32.8	3 33.3	3 23.1	1.1 0.3	7.1 1.7	13.1 3.2
12	3 33.0	3 33.6	3 23.3	1.2 0.3	7.2 1.7	13.2 3.2
13	3 33.3	3 33.8	3 23.5	1.3 0.3	7.3 1.8	13.3 3.2
14	3 33.5	3 34.1	3 23.8	1.4 0.3	7.4 1.8	13.4 3.2
15	3 33.8	3 34.3	3 24.0	1.5 0.4	7.5 1.8	13.5 3.3
16	3 34.0	3 34.6	3 24.3	1.6 0.4	7.6 1.8	13.6 3.3
17	3 34.3	3 34.8	3 24.5	1.7 0.4	7.7 1.9	13.7 3.3
18	3 34.5	3 35.1	3 24.7	1.8 0.4	7.8 1.9	13.8 3.3
19	3 34.8	3 35.3	3 25.0	1.9 0.5	7.9 1.9	13.9 3.4
20	3 35.0	3 35.6	3 25.2	2.0 0.5	8.0 1.9	14.0 3.4
21	3 35.3	3 35.8	3 25.4	2.1 0.5	8.1 2.0	14.1 3.4
22	3 35.5	3 36.1	3 25.7	2.2 0.5	8.2 2.0	14.2 3.4
23	3 35.8	3 36.3	3 25.9	2.3 0.6	8.3 2.0	14.3 3.5
24	3 36.0	3 36.6	3 26.2	2.4 0.6	8.4 2.0	14.4 3.5
25	3 36.3	3 36.8	3 26.4	2.5 0.6	8.5 2.1	14.5 3.5
26	3 36.5	3 37.1	3 26.6	2.6 0.6	8.6 2.1	14.6 3.5
27	3 36.8	3 37.3	3 26.9	2.7 0.7	8.7 2.1	14.7 3.6
28	3 37.0	3 37.6	3 27.1	2.8 0.7	8.8 2.1	14.8 3.6
29	3 37.3	3 37.8	3 27.4	2.9 0.7	8.9 2.2	14.9 3.6
30	3 37.5	3 38.1	3 27.6	3.0 0.7	9.0 2.2	15.0 3.6
31	3 37.8	3 38.3	3 27.8	3.1 0.7	9.1 2.2	15.1 3.6
32	3 38.0	3 38.6	3 28.1	3.2 0.8	9.2 2.2	15.2 3.7
33	3 38.3	3 38.8	3 28.3	3.3 0.8	9.3 2.3	15.3 3.7
34	3 38.5	3 39.1	3 28.5	3.4 0.8	9.4 2.3	15.4 3.7
35	3 38.8	3 39.3	3 28.8	3.5 0.8	9.5 2.3	15.5 3.7
36	3 39.0	3 39.6	3 29.0	3.6 0.9	9.6 2.3	15.6 3.8
37	3 39.3	3 39.9	3 29.3	3.7 0.9	9.7 2.3	15.7 3.8
38	3 39.5	3 40.1	3 29.5	3.8 0.9	9.8 2.4	15.8 3.8
39	3 39.8	3 40.4	3 29.7	3.9 0.9	9.9 2.4	15.9 3.8
40	3 40.0	3 40.6	3 30.0	4.0 1.0	10.0 2.4	16.0 3.9
41	3 40.3	3 40.9	3 30.2	4.1 1.0	10.1 2.4	16.1 3.9
42	3 40.5	3 41.1	3 30.5	4.2 1.0	10.2 2.5	16.2 3.9
43	3 40.8	3 41.4	3 30.7	4.3 1.0	10.3 2.5	16.3 3.9
44	3 41.0	3 41.6	3 30.9	4.4 1.1	10.4 2.5	16.4 4.0
45	3 41.3	3 41.9	3 31.2	4.5 1.1	10.5 2.5	16.5 4.0
46	3 41.5	3 42.1	3 31.4	4.6 1.1	10.6 2.6	16.6 4.0
47	3 41.8	3 42.4	3 31.6	4.7 1.1	10.7 2.6	16.7 4.0
48	3 42.0	3 42.6	3 31.9	4.8 1.2	10.8 2.6	16.8 4.1
49	3 42.3	3 42.9	3 32.1	4.9 1.2	10.9 2.6	16.9 4.1
50	3 42.5	3 43.1	3 32.4	5.0 1.2	11.0 2.7	17.0 4.1
51	3 42.8	3 43.4	3 32.6	5.1 1.2	11.1 2.7	17.1 4.1
52	3 43.0	3 43.6	3 32.8	5.2 1.3	11.2 2.7	17.2 4.2
53	3 43.3	3 43.9	3 33.1	5.3 1.3	11.3 2.7	17.3 4.2
54	3 43.5	3 44.1	3 33.3	5.4 1.3	11.4 2.8	17.4 4.2
55	3 43.8	3 44.4	3 33.6	5.5 1.3	11.5 2.8	17.5 4.2
56	3 44.0	3 44.6	3 33.8	5.6 1.4	11.6 2.8	17.6 4.3
57	3 44.3	3 44.9	3 34.0	5.7 1.4	11.7 2.8	17.7 4.3
58	3 44.5	3 45.1	3 34.3	5.8 1.4	11.8 2.9	17.8 4.3
59	3 44.8	3 45.4	3 34.5	5.9 1.4	11.9 2.9	17.9 4.3
60	3 45.0	3 45.6	3 34.8	6.0 1.5	12.0 2.9	18.0 4.4

15^m

15^m s	SUN PLANETS	ARIES	MOON	v or d / Corr^n	v or d / Corr^n	v or d / Corr^n
00	3 45.0	3 45.6	3 34.8	0.0 0.0	6.0 1.6	12.0 3.1
01	3 45.3	3 45.9	3 35.0	0.1 0.0	6.1 1.6	12.1 3.1
02	3 45.5	3 46.1	3 35.2	0.2 0.1	6.2 1.6	12.2 3.2
03	3 45.8	3 46.4	3 35.5	0.3 0.1	6.3 1.6	12.3 3.2
04	3 46.0	3 46.6	3 35.7	0.4 0.1	6.4 1.7	12.4 3.2
05	3 46.3	3 46.9	3 35.9	0.5 0.1	6.5 1.7	12.5 3.2
06	3 46.5	3 47.1	3 36.2	0.6 0.2	6.6 1.7	12.6 3.3
07	3 46.8	3 47.4	3 36.4	0.7 0.2	6.7 1.7	12.7 3.3
08	3 47.0	3 47.6	3 36.7	0.8 0.2	6.8 1.8	12.8 3.3
09	3 47.3	3 47.9	3 36.9	0.9 0.2	6.9 1.8	12.9 3.3
10	3 47.5	3 48.1	3 37.1	1.0 0.3	7.0 1.8	13.0 3.4
11	3 47.8	3 48.4	3 37.4	1.1 0.3	7.1 1.8	13.1 3.4
12	3 48.0	3 48.6	3 37.6	1.2 0.3	7.2 1.9	13.2 3.4
13	3 48.3	3 48.9	3 37.9	1.3 0.3	7.3 1.9	13.3 3.4
14	3 48.5	3 49.1	3 38.1	1.4 0.4	7.4 1.9	13.4 3.5
15	3 48.8	3 49.4	3 38.3	1.5 0.4	7.5 1.9	13.5 3.5
16	3 49.0	3 49.6	3 38.6	1.6 0.4	7.6 2.0	13.6 3.5
17	3 49.3	3 49.9	3 38.8	1.7 0.4	7.7 2.0	13.7 3.5
18	3 49.5	3 50.1	3 39.0	1.8 0.5	7.8 2.0	13.8 3.6
19	3 49.8	3 50.4	3 39.3	1.9 0.5	7.9 2.0	13.9 3.6
20	3 50.0	3 50.6	3 39.5	2.0 0.5	8.0 2.1	14.0 3.6
21	3 50.3	3 50.9	3 39.8	2.1 0.5	8.1 2.1	14.1 3.6
22	3 50.5	3 51.1	3 40.0	2.2 0.6	8.2 2.1	14.2 3.7
23	3 50.8	3 51.4	3 40.2	2.3 0.6	8.3 2.1	14.3 3.7
24	3 51.0	3 51.6	3 40.5	2.4 0.6	8.4 2.2	14.4 3.7
25	3 51.3	3 51.9	3 40.7	2.5 0.6	8.5 2.2	14.5 3.7
26	3 51.5	3 52.1	3 41.0	2.6 0.7	8.6 2.2	14.6 3.8
27	3 51.8	3 52.4	3 41.2	2.7 0.7	8.7 2.2	14.7 3.8
28	3 52.0	3 52.6	3 41.4	2.8 0.7	8.8 2.3	14.8 3.8
29	3 52.3	3 52.9	3 41.7	2.9 0.7	8.9 2.3	14.9 3.8
30	3 52.5	3 53.1	3 41.9	3.0 0.8	9.0 2.3	15.0 3.9
31	3 52.8	3 53.4	3 42.1	3.1 0.8	9.1 2.4	15.1 3.9
32	3 53.0	3 53.6	3 42.4	3.2 0.8	9.2 2.4	15.2 3.9
33	3 53.3	3 53.9	3 42.6	3.3 0.9	9.3 2.4	15.3 4.0
34	3 53.5	3 54.1	3 42.9	3.4 0.9	9.4 2.4	15.4 4.0
35	3 53.8	3 54.4	3 43.1	3.5 0.9	9.5 2.5	15.5 4.0
36	3 54.0	3 54.6	3 43.3	3.6 0.9	9.6 2.5	15.6 4.0
37	3 54.3	3 54.9	3 43.6	3.7 1.0	9.7 2.5	15.7 4.1
38	3 54.5	3 55.1	3 43.8	3.8 1.0	9.8 2.5	15.8 4.1
39	3 54.8	3 55.4	3 44.1	3.9 1.0	9.9 2.6	15.9 4.1
40	3 55.0	3 55.6	3 44.3	4.0 1.0	10.0 2.6	16.0 4.1
41	3 55.3	3 55.9	3 44.5	4.1 1.1	10.1 2.6	16.1 4.2
42	3 55.5	3 56.1	3 44.8	4.2 1.1	10.2 2.6	16.2 4.2
43	3 55.8	3 56.4	3 45.0	4.3 1.1	10.3 2.7	16.3 4.2
44	3 56.0	3 56.6	3 45.2	4.4 1.1	10.4 2.7	16.4 4.2
45	3 56.3	3 56.9	3 45.5	4.5 1.2	10.5 2.7	16.5 4.3
46	3 56.5	3 57.1	3 45.7	4.6 1.2	10.6 2.7	16.6 4.3
47	3 56.8	3 57.4	3 46.0	4.7 1.2	10.7 2.8	16.7 4.3
48	3 57.0	3 57.6	3 46.2	4.8 1.2	10.8 2.8	16.8 4.3
49	3 57.3	3 57.9	3 46.4	4.9 1.3	10.9 2.8	16.9 4.4
50	3 57.5	3 58.2	3 46.7	5.0 1.3	11.0 2.8	17.0 4.4
51	3 57.8	3 58.4	3 46.9	5.1 1.3	11.1 2.9	17.1 4.4
52	3 58.0	3 58.7	3 47.2	5.2 1.3	11.2 2.9	17.2 4.4
53	3 58.3	3 58.9	3 47.4	5.3 1.4	11.3 2.9	17.3 4.5
54	3 58.5	3 59.2	3 47.6	5.4 1.4	11.4 2.9	17.4 4.5
55	3 58.8	3 59.4	3 47.9	5.5 1.4	11.5 3.0	17.5 4.5
56	3 59.0	3 59.7	3 48.1	5.6 1.4	11.6 3.0	17.6 4.5
57	3 59.3	3 59.9	3 48.4	5.7 1.5	11.7 3.0	17.7 4.6
58	3 59.5	4 00.2	3 48.6	5.8 1.5	11.8 3.0	17.8 4.6
59	3 59.8	4 00.4	3 48.8	5.9 1.5	11.9 3.1	17.9 4.6
60	4 00.0	4 00.7	3 49.1	6.0 1.6	12.0 3.1	18.0 4.7

16ᵐ	SUN PLANETS	ARIES	MOON	v or d Corrⁿ	v or d Corrⁿ	v or d Corrⁿ	17ᵐ	SUN PLANETS	ARIES	MOON	v or d Corrⁿ	v or d Corrⁿ	v or d Corrⁿ
s	° ′	° ′	° ′	′ ′	′ ′	′ ′	s	° ′	° ′	° ′	′ ′	′ ′	′ ′
00	4 00·0	4 00·7	3 49·1	0·0 0·0	6·0 1·7	12·0 3·3	00	4 15·0	4 15·7	4 03·4	0·0 0·0	6·0 1·8	12·0 3·5
01	4 00·3	4 00·9	3 49·3	0·1 0·0	6·1 1·7	12·1 3·3	01	4 15·3	4 15·9	4 03·6	0·1 0·0	6·1 1·8	12·1 3·5
02	4 00·5	4 01·2	3 49·5	0·2 0·1	6·2 1·7	12·2 3·4	02	4 15·5	4 16·2	4 03·9	0·2 0·1	6·2 1·8	12·2 3·6
03	4 00·8	4 01·4	3 49·8	0·3 0·1	6·3 1·7	12·3 3·4	03	4 15·8	4 16·5	4 04·1	0·3 0·1	6·3 1·8	12·3 3·6
04	4 01·0	4 01·7	3 50·0	0·4 0·1	6·4 1·8	12·4 3·4	04	4 16·0	4 16·7	4 04·3	0·4 0·1	6·4 1·9	12·4 3·6
05	4 01·3	4 01·9	3 50·3	0·5 0·1	6·5 1·8	12·5 3·4	05	4 16·3	4 17·0	4 04·6	0·5 0·1	6·5 1·9	12·5 3·6
06	4 01·5	4 02·2	3 50·5	0·6 0·2	6·6 1·8	12·6 3·5	06	4 16·5	4 17·2	4 04·8	0·6 0·2	6·6 1·9	12·6 3·7
07	4 01·8	4 02·4	3 50·7	0·7 0·2	6·7 1·8	12·7 3·5	07	4 16·8	4 17·5	4 05·1	0·7 0·2	6·7 2·0	12·7 3·7
08	4 02·0	4 02·7	3 51·0	0·8 0·2	6·8 1·9	12·8 3·5	08	4 17·0	4 17·7	4 05·3	0·8 0·2	6·8 2·0	12·8 3·7
09	4 02·3	4 02·9	3 51·2	0·9 0·2	6·9 1·9	12·9 3·5	09	4 17·3	4 18·0	4 05·5	0·9 0·3	6·9 2·0	12·9 3·8
10	4 02·5	4 03·2	3 51·5	1·0 0·3	7·0 1·9	13·0 3·6	10	4 17·5	4 18·2	4 05·8	1·0 0·3	7·0 2·0	13·0 3·8
11	4 02·8	4 03·4	3 51·7	1·1 0·3	7·1 2·0	13·1 3·6	11	4 17·8	4 18·5	4 06·0	1·1 0·3	7·1 2·1	13·1 3·8
12	4 03·0	4 03·7	3 51·9	1·2 0·3	7·2 2·0	13·2 3·6	12	4 18·0	4 18·7	4 06·2	1·2 0·4	7·2 2·1	13·2 3·9
13	4 03·3	4 03·9	3 52·2	1·3 0·4	7·3 2·0	13·3 3·7	13	4 18·3	4 19·0	4 06·5	1·3 0·4	7·3 2·1	13·3 3·9
14	4 03·5	4 04·2	3 52·4	1·4 0·4	7·4 2·0	13·4 3·7	14	4 18·5	4 19·2	4 06·7	1·4 0·4	7·4 2·2	13·4 3·9
15	4 03·8	4 04·4	3 52·6	1·5 0·4	7·5 2·1	13·5 3·7	15	4 18·8	4 19·5	4 07·0	1·5 0·4	7·5 2·2	13·5 3·9
16	4 04·0	4 04·7	3 52·9	1·6 0·4	7·6 2·1	13·6 3·7	16	4 19·0	4 19·7	4 07·2	1·6 0·5	7·6 2·2	13·6 4·0
17	4 04·3	4 04·9	3 53·1	1·7 0·5	7·7 2·1	13·7 3·8	17	4 19·3	4 20·0	4 07·4	1·7 0·5	7·7 2·2	13·7 4·0
18	4 04·5	4 05·2	3 53·4	1·8 0·5	7·8 2·1	13·8 3·8	18	4 19·5	4 20·2	4 07·7	1·8 0·5	7·8 2·3	13·8 4·0
19	4 04·8	4 05·4	3 53·6	1·9 0·5	7·9 2·2	13·9 3·8	19	4 19·8	4 20·5	4 07·9	1·9 0·6	7·9 2·3	13·9 4·1
20	4 05·0	4 05·7	3 53·8	2·0 0·6	8·0 2·2	14·0 3·9	20	4 20·0	4 20·7	4 08·2	2·0 0·6	8·0 2·3	14·0 4·1
21	4 05·3	4 05·9	3 54·1	2·1 0·6	8·1 2·2	14·1 3·9	21	4 20·3	4 21·0	4 08·4	2·1 0·6	8·1 2·4	14·1 4·1
22	4 05·5	4 06·2	3 54·3	2·2 0·6	8·2 2·3	14·2 3·9	22	4 20·5	4 21·2	4 08·6	2·2 0·6	8·2 2·4	14·2 4·1
23	4 05·8	4 06·4	3 54·6	2·3 0·6	8·3 2·3	14·3 3·9	23	4 20·8	4 21·5	4 08·9	2·3 0·7	8·3 2·4	14·3 4·2
24	4 06·0	4 06·7	3 54·8	2·4 0·7	8·4 2·3	14·4 4·0	24	4 21·0	4 21·7	4 09·1	2·4 0·7	8·4 2·5	14·4 4·2
25	4 06·3	4 06·9	3 55·0	2·5 0·7	8·5 2·3	14·5 4·0	25	4 21·3	4 22·0	4 09·3	2·5 0·7	8·5 2·5	14·5 4·2
26	4 06·5	4 07·2	3 55·3	2·6 0·7	8·6 2·4	14·6 4·0	26	4 21·5	4 22·2	4 09·6	2·6 0·8	8·6 2·5	14·6 4·3
27	4 06·8	4 07·4	3 55·5	2·7 0·7	8·7 2·4	14·7 4·0	27	4 21·8	4 22·5	4 09·8	2·7 0·8	8·7 2·5	14·7 4·3
28	4 07·0	4 07·7	3 55·7	2·8 0·8	8·8 2·4	14·8 4·1	28	4 22·0	4 22·7	4 10·1	2·8 0·8	8·8 2·6	14·8 4·3
29	4 07·3	4 07·9	3 56·0	2·9 0·8	8·9 2·4	14·9 4·1	29	4 22·3	4 23·0	4 10·3	2·9 0·8	8·9 2·6	14·9 4·3
30	4 07·5	4 08·2	3 56·2	3·0 0·8	9·0 2·5	15·0 4·1	30	4 22·5	4 23·2	4 10·5	3·0 0·9	9·0 2·6	15·0 4·4
31	4 07·8	4 08·4	3 56·5	3·1 0·9	9·1 2·5	15·1 4·2	31	4 22·8	4 23·5	4 10·8	3·1 0·9	9·1 2·7	15·1 4·4
32	4 08·0	4 08·7	3 56·7	3·2 0·9	9·2 2·5	15·2 4·2	32	4 23·0	4 23·7	4 11·0	3·2 0·9	9·2 2·7	15·2 4·4
33	4 08·3	4 08·9	3 56·9	3·3 0·9	9·3 2·6	15·3 4·2	33	4 23·3	4 24·0	4 11·3	3·3 1·0	9·3 2·7	15·3 4·5
34	4 08·5	4 09·2	3 57·2	3·4 0·9	9·4 2·6	15·4 4·2	34	4 23·5	4 24·2	4 11·5	3·4 1·0	9·4 2·7	15·4 4·5
35	4 08·8	4 09·4	3 57·4	3·5 1·0	9·5 2·6	15·5 4·3	35	4 23·8	4 24·5	4 11·7	3·5 1·0	9·5 2·8	15·5 4·5
36	4 09·0	4 09·7	3 57·7	3·6 1·0	9·6 2·6	15·6 4·3	36	4 24·0	4 24·7	4 12·0	3·6 1·1	9·6 2·8	15·6 4·6
37	4 09·3	4 09·9	3 57·9	3·7 1·0	9·7 2·7	15·7 4·3	37	4 24·3	4 25·0	4 12·2	3·7 1·1	9·7 2·8	15·7 4·6
38	4 09·5	4 10·2	3 58·1	3·8 1·0	9·8 2·7	15·8 4·3	38	4 24·5	4 25·2	4 12·5	3·8 1·1	9·8 2·9	15·8 4·6
39	4 09·8	4 10·4	3 58·4	3·9 1·1	9·9 2·7	15·9 4·4	39	4 24·8	4 25·5	4 12·7	3·9 1·1	9·9 2·9	15·9 4·6
40	4 10·0	4 10·7	3 58·6	4·0 1·1	10·0 2·8	16·0 4·4	40	4 25·0	4 25·7	4 12·9	4·0 1·2	10·0 2·9	16·0 4·7
41	4 10·3	4 10·9	3 58·8	4·1 1·1	10·1 2·8	16·1 4·4	41	4 25·3	4 26·0	4 13·2	4·1 1·2	10·1 2·9	16·1 4·7
42	4 10·5	4 11·2	3 59·1	4·2 1·2	10·2 2·8	16·2 4·5	42	4 25·5	4 26·2	4 13·4	4·2 1·2	10·2 3·0	16·2 4·7
43	4 10·8	4 11·4	3 59·3	4·3 1·2	10·3 2·8	16·3 4·5	43	4 25·8	4 26·5	4 13·6	4·3 1·3	10·3 3·0	16·3 4·8
44	4 11·0	4 11·7	3 59·6	4·4 1·2	10·4 2·9	16·4 4·5	44	4 26·0	4 26·7	4 13·9	4·4 1·3	10·4 3·0	16·4 4·8
45	4 11·3	4 11·9	3 59·8	4·5 1·2	10·5 2·9	16·5 4·5	45	4 26·3	4 27·0	4 14·1	4·5 1·3	10·5 3·1	16·5 4·8
46	4 11·5	4 12·2	4 00·0	4·6 1·3	10·6 2·9	16·6 4·6	46	4 26·5	4 27·2	4 14·4	4·6 1·3	10·6 3·1	16·6 4·8
47	4 11·8	4 12·4	4 00·3	4·7 1·3	10·7 2·9	16·7 4·6	47	4 26·8	4 27·5	4 14·6	4·7 1·4	10·7 3·1	16·7 4·9
48	4 12·0	4 12·7	4 00·5	4·8 1·3	10·8 3·0	16·8 4·6	48	4 27·0	4 27·7	4 14·8	4·8 1·4	10·8 3·2	16·8 4·9
49	4 12·3	4 12·9	4 00·8	4·9 1·3	10·9 3·0	16·9 4·6	49	4 27·3	4 28·0	4 15·1	4·9 1·4	10·9 3·2	16·9 4·9
50	4 12·5	4 13·2	4 01·0	5·0 1·4	11·0 3·0	17·0 4·7	50	4 27·5	4 28·2	4 15·3	5·0 1·5	11·0 3·2	17·0 5·0
51	4 12·8	4 13·4	4 01·2	5·1 1·4	11·1 3·1	17·1 4·7	51	4 27·8	4 28·5	4 15·6	5·1 1·5	11·1 3·2	17·1 5·0
52	4 13·0	4 13·7	4 01·5	5·2 1·4	11·2 3·1	17·2 4·7	52	4 28·0	4 28·7	4 15·8	5·2 1·5	11·2 3·3	17·2 5·0
53	4 13·3	4 13·9	4 01·7	5·3 1·5	11·3 3·1	17·3 4·8	53	4 28·3	4 29·0	4 16·0	5·3 1·5	11·3 3·3	17·3 5·0
54	4 13·5	4 14·2	4 02·0	5·4 1·5	11·4 3·1	17·4 4·8	54	4 28·5	4 29·2	4 16·3	5·4 1·6	11·4 3·3	17·4 5·1
55	4 13·8	4 14·4	4 02·2	5·5 1·5	11·5 3·2	17·5 4·8	55	4 28·8	4 29·5	4 16·5	5·5 1·6	11·5 3·4	17·5 5·1
56	4 14·0	4 14·7	4 02·4	5·6 1·5	11·6 3·2	17·6 4·8	56	4 29·0	4 29·7	4 16·7	5·6 1·6	11·6 3·4	17·6 5·1
57	4 14·3	4 14·9	4 02·7	5·7 1·6	11·7 3·2	17·7 4·9	57	4 29·3	4 30·0	4 17·0	5·7 1·7	11·7 3·4	17·7 5·2
58	4 14·5	4 15·2	4 02·9	5·8 1·6	11·8 3·2	17·8 4·9	58	4 29·5	4 30·2	4 17·2	5·8 1·7	11·8 3·4	17·8 5·2
59	4 14·8	4 15·4	4 03·1	5·9 1·6	11·9 3·3	17·9 4·9	59	4 29·8	4 30·5	4 17·5	5·9 1·7	11·9 3·5	17·9 5·2
60	4 15·0	4 15·7	4 03·4	6·0 1·7	12·0 3·3	18·0 5·0	60	4 30·0	4 30·7	4 17·7	6·0 1·8	12·0 3·5	18·0 5·3

18	SUN PLANETS	ARIES	MOON	v or Corrⁿ d	v or Corrⁿ d	v or Corrⁿ d	19	SUN PLANETS	ARIES	MOON	v or Corrⁿ d	v or Corrⁿ d	v or Corrⁿ d
s	° ′	° ′	° ′	′ ′	′ ′	′ ′	s	° ′	° ′	° ′	′ ′	′ ′	′ ′
00	4 30·0	4 30·7	4 17·7	0·0 0·0	6·0 1·9	12·0 3·7	00	4 45·0	4 45·8	4 32·0	0·0 0·0	6·0 2·0	12·0 3·9
01	4 30·3	4 31·0	4 17·9	0·1 0·0	6·1 1·9	12·1 3·7	01	4 45·3	4 46·0	4 32·3	0·1 0·0	6·1 2·0	12·1 3·9
02	4 30·5	4 31·2	4 18·2	0·2 0·1	6·2 1·9	12·2 3·8	02	4 45·5	4 46·3	4 32·5	0·2 0·1	6·2 2·0	12·2 4·0
03	4 30·8	4 31·5	4 18·4	0·3 0·1	6·3 1·9	12·3 3·8	03	4 45·8	4 46·5	4 32·7	0·3 0·1	6·3 2·0	12·3 4·0
04	4 31·0	4 31·7	4 18·7	0·4 0·1	6·4 2·0	12·4 3·8	04	4 46·0	4 46·8	4 33·0	0·4 0·1	6·4 2·1	12·4 4·0
05	4 31·3	4 32·0	4 18·9	0·5 0·2	6·5 2·0	12·5 3·9	05	4 46·3	4 47·0	4 33·2	0·5 0·2	6·5 2·1	12·5 4·1
06	4 31·5	4 32·2	4 19·1	0·6 0·2	6·6 2·0	12·6 3·9	06	4 46·5	4 47·3	4 33·4	0·6 0·2	6·6 2·1	12·6 4·1
07	4 31·8	4 32·5	4 19·4	0·7 0·2	6·7 2·1	12·7 3·9	07	4 46·8	4 47·5	4 33·7	0·7 0·2	6·7 2·2	12·7 4·1
08	4 32·0	4 32·7	4 19·6	0·8 0·2	6·8 2·1	12·8 3·9	08	4 47·0	4 47·8	4 33·9	0·8 0·3	6·8 2·2	12·8 4·2
09	4 32·3	4 33·0	4 19·8	0·9 0·3	6·9 2·1	12·9 4·0	09	4 47·3	4 48·0	4 34·2	0·9 0·3	6·9 2·2	12·9 4·2
10	4 32·5	4 33·2	4 20·1	1·0 0·3	7·0 2·2	13·0 4·0	10	4 47·5	4 48·3	4 34·4	1·0 0·3	7·0 2·3	13·0 4·2
11	4 32·8	4 33·5	4 20·3	1·1 0·3	7·1 2·2	13·1 4·0	11	4 47·8	4 48·5	4 34·6	1·1 0·4	7·1 2·3	13·1 4·3
12	4 33·0	4 33·7	4 20·6	1·2 0·4	7·2 2·2	13·2 4·1	12	4 48·0	4 48·8	4 34·9	1·2 0·4	7·2 2·3	13·2 4·3
13	4 33·3	4 34·0	4 20·8	1·3 0·4	7·3 2·3	13·3 4·1	13	4 48·3	4 49·0	4 35·1	1·3 0·4	7·3 2·4	13·3 4·3
14	4 33·5	4 34·2	4 21·0	1·4 0·4	7·4 2·3	13·4 4·1	14	4 48·5	4 49·3	4 35·4	1·4 0·5	7·4 2·4	13·4 4·4
15	4 33·8	4 34·5	4 21·3	1·5 0·5	7·5 2·3	13·5 4·2	15	4 48·8	4 49·5	4 35·6	1·5 0·5	7·5 2·4	13·5 4·4
16	4 34·0	4 34·8	4 21·5	1·6 0·5	7·6 2·3	13·6 4·2	16	4 49·0	4 49·8	4 35·8	1·6 0·5	7·6 2·5	13·6 4·4
17	4 34·3	4 35·0	4 21·8	1·7 0·5	7·7 2·4	13·7 4·2	17	4 49·3	4 50·0	4 36·1	1·7 0·6	7·7 2·5	13·7 4·5
18	4 34·5	4 35·3	4 22·0	1·8 0·6	7·8 2·4	13·8 4·3	18	4 49·5	4 50·3	4 36·3	1·8 0·6	7·8 2·5	13·8 4·5
19	4 34·8	4 35·5	4 22·2	1·9 0·6	7·9 2·4	13·9 4·3	19	4 49·8	4 50·5	4 36·6	1·9 0·6	7·9 2·6	13·9 4·5
20	4 35·0	4 35·8	4 22·5	2·0 0·6	8·0 2·5	14·0 4·3	20	4 50·0	4 50·8	4 36·8	2·0 0·7	8·0 2·6	14·0 4·6
21	4 35·3	4 36·0	4 22·7	2·1 0·6	8·1 2·5	14·1 4·3	21	4 50·3	4 51·0	4 37·0	2·1 0·7	8·1 2·6	14·1 4·6
22	4 35·5	4 36·3	4 22·9	2·2 0·7	8·2 2·5	14·2 4·4	22	4 50·5	4 51·3	4 37·3	2·2 0·7	8·2 2·7	14·2 4·6
23	4 35·8	4 36·5	4 23·2	2·3 0·7	8·3 2·6	14·3 4·4	23	4 50·8	4 51·5	4 37·5	2·3 0·7	8·3 2·7	14·3 4·6
24	4 36·0	4 36·8	4 23·4	2·4 0·7	8·4 2·6	14·4 4·4	24	4 51·0	4 51·8	4 37·7	2·4 0·8	8·4 2·7	14·4 4·7
25	4 36·3	4 37·0	4 23·7	2·5 0·8	8·5 2·6	14·5 4·5	25	4 51·3	4 52·0	4 38·0	2·5 0·8	8·5 2·8	14·5 4·7
26	4 36·5	4 37·3	4 23·9	2·6 0·8	8·6 2·7	14·6 4·5	26	4 51·5	4 52·3	4 38·2	2·6 0·8	8·6 2·8	14·6 4·7
27	4 36·8	4 37·5	4 24·1	2·7 0·8	8·7 2·7	14·7 4·5	27	4 51·8	4 52·5	4 38·5	2·7 0·9	8·7 2·8	14·7 4·8
28	4 37·0	4 37·8	4 24·4	2·8 0·9	8·8 2·7	14·8 4·6	28	4 52·0	4 52·8	4 38·7	2·8 0·9	8·8 2·9	14·8 4·8
29	4 37·3	4 38·0	4 24·6	2·9 0·9	8·9 2·7	14·9 4·6	29	4 52·3	4 53·1	4 38·9	2·9 0·9	8·9 2·9	14·9 4·8
30	4 37·5	4 38·3	4 24·9	3·0 0·9	9·0 2·8	15·0 4·6	30	4 52·5	4 53·3	4 39·2	3·0 1·0	9·0 2·9	15·0 4·9
31	4 37·8	4 38·5	4 25·1	3·1 1·0	9·1 2·8	15·1 4·7	31	4 52·8	4 53·6	4 39·4	3·1 1·0	9·1 3·0	15·1 4·9
32	4 38·0	4 38·8	4 25·3	3·2 1·0	9·2 2·8	15·2 4·7	32	4 53·0	4 53·8	4 39·7	3·2 1·0	9·2 3·0	15·2 4·9
33	4 38·3	4 39·0	4 25·6	3·3 1·0	9·3 2·9	15·3 4·7	33	4 53·3	4 54·1	4 39·9	3·3 1·1	9·3 3·0	15·3 5·0
34	4 38·5	4 39·3	4 25·8	3·4 1·0	9·4 2·9	15·4 4·7	34	4 53·5	4 54·3	4 40·1	3·4 1·1	9·4 3·1	15·4 5·0
35	4 38·8	4 39·5	4 26·1	3·5 1·1	9·5 2·9	15·5 4·8	35	4 53·8	4 54·6	4 40·4	3·5 1·1	9·5 3·1	15·5 5·0
36	4 39·0	4 39·8	4 26·3	3·6 1·1	9·6 3·0	15·6 4·8	36	4 54·0	4 54·8	4 40·6	3·6 1·2	9·6 3·1	15·6 5·1
37	4 39·3	4 40·0	4 26·5	3·7 1·1	9·7 3·0	15·7 4·8	37	4 54·3	4 55·1	4 40·8	3·7 1·2	9·7 3·2	15·7 5·1
38	4 39·5	4 40·3	4 26·8	3·8 1·2	9·8 3·0	15·8 4·9	38	4 54·5	4 55·3	4 41·1	3·8 1·2	9·8 3·2	15·8 5·1
39	4 39·8	4 40·5	4 27·0	3·9 1·2	9·9 3·1	15·9 4·9	39	4 54·8	4 55·6	4 41·3	3·9 1·3	9·9 3·2	15·9 5·2
40	4 40·0	4 40·8	4 27·2	4·0 1·2	10·0 3·1	16·0 4·9	40	4 55·0	4 55·8	4 41·6	4·0 1·3	10·0 3·3	16·0 5·2
41	4 40·3	4 41·0	4 27·5	4·1 1·3	10·1 3·1	16·1 5·0	41	4 55·3	4 56·1	4 41·8	4·1 1·3	10·1 3·3	16·1 5·2
42	4 40·5	4 41·3	4 27·7	4·2 1·3	10·2 3·1	16·2 5·0	42	4 55·5	4 56·3	4 42·0	4·2 1·4	10·2 3·3	16·2 5·3
43	4 40·8	4 41·5	4 28·0	4·3 1·3	10·3 3·2	16·3 5·0	43	4 55·8	4 56·6	4 42·3	4·3 1·4	10·3 3·3	16·3 5·3
44	4 41·0	4 41·8	4 28·2	4·4 1·4	10·4 3·2	16·4 5·1	44	4 56·0	4 56·8	4 42·5	4·4 1·4	10·4 3·4	16·4 5·3
45	4 41·3	4 42·0	4 28·4	4·5 1·4	10·5 3·2	16·5 5·1	45	4 56·3	4 57·1	4 42·8	4·5 1·5	10·5 3·4	16·5 5·4
46	4 41·5	4 42·3	4 28·7	4·6 1·4	10·6 3·3	16·6 5·1	46	4 56·5	4 57·3	4 43·0	4·6 1·5	10·6 3·4	16·6 5·4
47	4 41·8	4 42·5	4 28·9	4·7 1·4	10·7 3·3	16·7 5·1	47	4 56·8	4 57·6	4 43·2	4·7 1·5	10·7 3·5	16·7 5·4
48	4 42·0	4 42·8	4 29·2	4·8 1·5	10·8 3·3	16·8 5·2	48	4 57·0	4 57·8	4 43·5	4·8 1·6	10·8 3·5	16·8 5·5
49	4 42·3	4 43·0	4 29·4	4·9 1·5	10·9 3·4	16·9 5·2	49	4 57·3	4 58·1	4 43·7	4·9 1·6	10·9 3·5	16·9 5·5
50	4 42·5	4 43·3	4 29·6	5·0 1·5	11·0 3·4	17·0 5·2	50	4 57·5	4 58·3	4 43·9	5·0 1·6	11·0 3·6	17·0 5·5
51	4 42·8	4 43·5	4 29·9	5·1 1·6	11·1 3·4	17·1 5·3	51	4 57·8	4 58·6	4 44·2	5·1 1·7	11·1 3·6	17·1 5·6
52	4 43·0	4 43·8	4 30·1	5·2 1·6	11·2 3·5	17·2 5·3	52	4 58·0	4 58·8	4 44·4	5·2 1·7	11·2 3·6	17·2 5·6
53	4 43·3	4 44·0	4 30·3	5·3 1·6	11·3 3·5	17·3 5·3	53	4 58·3	4 59·1	4 44·7	5·3 1·7	11·3 3·7	17·3 5·6
54	4 43·5	4 44·3	4 30·6	5·4 1·7	11·4 3·5	17·4 5·4	54	4 58·5	4 59·3	4 44·9	5·4 1·8	11·4 3·7	17·4 5·7
55	4 43·8	4 44·5	4 30·8	5·5 1·7	11·5 3·5	17·5 5·4	55	4 58·8	4 59·6	4 45·1	5·5 1·8	11·5 3·7	17·5 5·7
56	4 44·0	4 44·8	4 31·1	5·6 1·7	11·6 3·6	17·6 5·4	56	4 59·0	4 59·8	4 45·4	5·6 1·8	11·6 3·8	17·6 5·7
57	4 44·3	4 45·0	4 31·3	5·7 1·8	11·7 3·6	17·7 5·5	57	4 59·3	5 00·1	4 45·6	5·7 1·9	11·7 3·8	17·7 5·8
58	4 44·5	4 45·3	4 31·5	5·8 1·8	11·8 3·6	17·8 5·5	58	4 59·5	5 00·3	4 45·9	5·8 1·9	11·8 3·8	17·8 5·8
59	4 44·8	4 45·5	4 31·8	5·9 1·8	11·9 3·7	17·9 5·5	59	4 59·8	5 00·6	4 46·1	5·9 1·9	11·9 3·9	17·9 5·8
60	4 45·0	4 45·8	4 32·0	6·0 1·9	12·0 3·7	18·0 5·6	60	5 00·0	5 00·8	4 46·3	6·0 2·0	12·0 3·9	18·0 5·9

20ᵐ

s	SUN PLANETS	ARIES	MOON	v or d	Corrⁿ	v or d	Corrⁿ	v or d	Corrⁿ
00	5 00·0	5 00·8	4 46·3	0·0	0·0	6·0	2·1	12·0	4·1
01	5 00·3	5 01·1	4 46·6	0·1	0·0	6·1	2·1	12·1	4·1
02	5 00·5	5 01·3	4 46·8	0·2	0·1	6·2	2·1	12·2	4·2
03	5 00·8	5 01·6	4 47·0	0·3	0·1	6·3	2·2	12·3	4·2
04	5 01·0	5 01·8	4 47·3	0·4	0·1	6·4	2·2	12·4	4·2
05	5 01·3	5 02·1	4 47·5	0·5	0·2	6·5	2·2	12·5	4·3
06	5 01·5	5 02·3	4 47·8	0·6	0·2	6·6	2·3	12·6	4·3
07	5 01·8	5 02·6	4 48·0	0·7	0·2	6·7	2·3	12·7	4·3
08	5 02·0	5 02·8	4 48·2	0·8	0·3	6·8	2·3	12·8	4·4
09	5 02·3	5 03·1	4 48·5	0·9	0·3	6·9	2·4	12·9	4·4
10	5 02·5	5 03·3	4 48·7	1·0	0·3	7·0	2·4	13·0	4·4
11	5 02·8	5 03·6	4 49·0	1·1	0·4	7·1	2·4	13·1	4·5
12	5 03·0	5 03·8	4 49·2	1·2	0·4	7·2	2·5	13·2	4·5
13	5 03·3	5 04·1	4 49·4	1·3	0·4	7·3	2·5	13·3	4·5
14	5 03·5	5 04·3	4 49·7	1·4	0·5	7·4	2·5	13·4	4·6
15	5 03·8	5 04·6	4 49·9	1·5	0·5	7·5	2·6	13·5	4·6
16	5 04·0	5 04·8	4 50·2	1·6	0·5	7·6	2·6	13·6	4·6
17	5 04·3	5 05·1	4 50·4	1·7	0·6	7·7	2·6	13·7	4·7
18	5 04·5	5 05·3	4 50·6	1·8	0·6	7·8	2·7	13·8	4·7
19	5 04·8	5 05·6	4 50·9	1·9	0·6	7·9	2·7	13·9	4·7
20	5 05·0	5 05·8	4 51·1	2·0	0·7	8·0	2·7	14·0	4·8
21	5 05·3	5 06·1	4 51·3	2·1	0·7	8·1	2·8	14·1	4·8
22	5 05·5	5 06·3	4 51·6	2·2	0·8	8·2	2·8	14·2	4·9
23	5 05·8	5 06·6	4 51·8	2·3	0·8	8·3	2·8	14·3	4·9
24	5 06·0	5 06·8	4 52·1	2·4	0·8	8·4	2·9	14·4	4·9
25	5 06·3	5 07·1	4 52·3	2·5	0·9	8·5	2·9	14·5	5·0
26	5 06·5	5 07·3	4 52·5	2·6	0·9	8·6	2·9	14·6	5·0
27	5 06·8	5 07·6	4 52·8	2·7	0·9	8·7	3·0	14·7	5·0
28	5 07·0	5 07·8	4 53·0	2·8	1·0	8·8	3·0	14·8	5·1
29	5 07·3	5 08·1	4 53·3	2·9	1·0	8·9	3·0	14·9	5·1
30	5 07·5	5 08·3	4 53·5	3·0	1·0	9·0	3·1	15·0	5·1
31	5 07·8	5 08·6	4 53·7	3·1	1·1	9·1	3·1	15·1	5·2
32	5 08·0	5 08·8	4 54·0	3·2	1·1	9·2	3·1	15·2	5·2
33	5 08·3	5 09·1	4 54·2	3·3	1·1	9·3	3·2	15·3	5·2
34	5 08·5	5 09·3	4 54·4	3·4	1·2	9·4	3·2	15·4	5·3
35	5 08·8	5 09·6	4 54·7	3·5	1·2	9·5	3·2	15·5	5·3
36	5 09·0	5 09·8	4 54·9	3·6	1·2	9·6	3·3	15·6	5·3
37	5 09·3	5 10·1	4 55·2	3·7	1·3	9·7	3·3	15·7	5·4
38	5 09·5	5 10·3	4 55·4	3·8	1·3	9·8	3·3	15·8	5·4
39	5 09·8	5 10·6	4 55·6	3·9	1·3	9·9	3·4	15·9	5·4
40	5 10·0	5 10·8	4 55·9	4·0	1·4	10·0	3·4	16·0	5·5
41	5 10·3	5 11·1	4 56·1	4·1	1·4	10·1	3·5	16·1	5·5
42	5 10·5	5 11·4	4 56·4	4·2	1·4	10·2	3·5	16·2	5·5
43	5 10·8	5 11·6	4 56·6	4·3	1·5	10·3	3·5	16·3	5·6
44	5 11·0	5 11·9	4 56·8	4·4	1·5	10·4	3·6	16·4	5·6
45	5 11·3	5 12·1	4 57·1	4·5	1·5	10·5	3·6	16·5	5·6
46	5 11·5	5 12·4	4 57·3	4·6	1·6	10·6	3·6	16·6	5·7
47	5 11·8	5 12·6	4 57·5	4·7	1·6	10·7	3·7	16·7	5·7
48	5 12·0	5 12·9	4 57·8	4·8	1·6	10·8	3·7	16·8	5·7
49	5 12·3	5 13·1	4 58·0	4·9	1·7	10·9	3·7	16·9	5·8
50	5 12·5	5 13·4	4 58·3	5·0	1·7	11·0	3·8	17·0	5·8
51	5 12·8	5 13·6	4 58·5	5·1	1·7	11·1	3·8	17·1	5·8
52	5 13·0	5 13·9	4 58·7	5·2	1·8	11·2	3·8	17·2	5·9
53	5 13·3	5 14·1	4 59·0	5·3	1·8	11·3	3·9	17·3	5·9
54	5 13·5	5 14·4	4 59·2	5·4	1·8	11·4	3·9	17·4	5·9
55	5 13·8	5 14·6	4 59·5	5·5	1·9	11·5	3·9	17·5	6·0
56	5 14·0	5 14·9	4 59·7	5·6	1·9	11·6	4·0	17·6	6·0
57	5 14·3	5 15·1	4 59·9	5·7	1·9	11·7	4·0	17·7	6·0
58	5 14·5	5 15·4	5 00·2	5·8	2·0	11·8	4·0	17·8	6·1
59	5 14·8	5 15·6	5 00·4	5·9	2·0	11·9	4·1	17·9	6·1
60	5 15·0	5 15·9	5 00·7	6·0	2·1	12·0	4·1	18·0	6·2

21ᵐ

s	SUN PLANETS	ARIES	MOON	v or d	Corrⁿ	v or d	Corrⁿ	v or d	Corrⁿ
00	5 15·0	5 15·9	5 00·7	0·0	0·0	6·0	2·2	12·0	4·3
01	5 15·3	5 16·1	5 00·9	0·1	0·0	6·1	2·2	12·1	4·3
02	5 15·5	5 16·4	5 01·1	0·2	0·1	6·2	2·2	12·2	4·4
03	5 15·8	5 16·6	5 01·4	0·3	0·1	6·3	2·3	12·3	4·4
04	5 16·0	5 16·9	5 01·6	0·4	0·1	6·4	2·3	12·4	4·4
05	5 16·3	5 17·1	5 01·8	0·5	0·2	6·5	2·3	12·5	4·5
06	5 16·5	5 17·4	5 02·1	0·6	0·2	6·6	2·4	12·6	4·5
07	5 16·8	5 17·6	5 02·3	0·7	0·3	6·7	2·4	12·7	4·6
08	5 17·0	5 17·9	5 02·6	0·8	0·3	6·8	2·4	12·8	4·6
09	5 17·3	5 18·1	5 02·8	0·9	0·3	6·9	2·5	12·9	4·6
10	5 17·5	5 18·4	5 03·0	1·0	0·4	7·0	2·5	13·0	4·7
11	5 17·8	5 18·6	5 03·3	1·1	0·4	7·1	2·5	13·1	4·7
12	5 18·0	5 18·9	5 03·5	1·2	0·4	7·2	2·6	13·2	4·7
13	5 18·3	5 19·1	5 03·8	1·3	0·5	7·3	2·6	13·3	4·8
14	5 18·5	5 19·4	5 04·0	1·4	0·5	7·4	2·7	13·4	4·8
15	5 18·8	5 19·6	5 04·2	1·5	0·5	7·5	2·7	13·5	4·8
16	5 19·0	5 19·9	5 04·5	1·6	0·6	7·6	2·7	13·6	4·9
17	5 19·3	5 20·1	5 04·7	1·7	0·6	7·7	2·8	13·7	4·9
18	5 19·5	5 20·4	5 04·9	1·8	0·6	7·8	2·8	13·8	4·9
19	5 19·8	5 20·6	5 05·2	1·9	0·7	7·9	2·8	13·9	5·0
20	5 20·0	5 20·9	5 05·4	2·0	0·7	8·0	2·9	14·0	5·0
21	5 20·3	5 21·1	5 05·7	2·1	0·8	8·1	2·9	14·1	5·1
22	5 20·5	5 21·4	5 05·9	2·2	0·8	8·2	2·9	14·2	5·1
23	5 20·8	5 21·6	5 06·1	2·3	0·8	8·3	3·0	14·3	5·1
24	5 21·0	5 21·9	5 06·4	2·4	0·9	8·4	3·0	14·4	5·2
25	5 21·3	5 22·1	5 06·6	2·5	0·9	8·5	3·0	14·5	5·2
26	5 21·5	5 22·4	5 06·9	2·6	0·9	8·6	3·1	14·6	5·2
27	5 21·8	5 22·6	5 07·1	2·7	1·0	8·7	3·1	14·7	5·3
28	5 22·0	5 22·9	5 07·3	2·8	1·0	8·8	3·2	14·8	5·3
29	5 22·3	5 23·1	5 07·6	2·9	1·0	8·9	3·2	14·9	5·3
30	5 22·5	5 23·4	5 07·8	3·0	1·1	9·0	3·2	15·0	5·4
31	5 22·8	5 23·6	5 08·0	3·1	1·1	9·1	3·3	15·1	5·4
32	5 23·0	5 23·9	5 08·3	3·2	1·1	9·2	3·3	15·2	5·4
33	5 23·3	5 24·1	5 08·5	3·3	1·2	9·3	3·3	15·3	5·5
34	5 23·5	5 24·4	5 08·8	3·4	1·2	9·4	3·4	15·4	5·5
35	5 23·8	5 24·6	5 09·0	3·5	1·3	9·5	3·4	15·5	5·6
36	5 24·0	5 24·9	5 09·2	3·6	1·3	9·6	3·4	15·6	5·6
37	5 24·3	5 25·1	5 09·5	3·7	1·3	9·7	3·5	15·7	5·6
38	5 24·5	5 25·4	5 09·7	3·8	1·4	9·8	3·5	15·8	5·7
39	5 24·8	5 25·6	5 10·0	3·9	1·4	9·9	3·5	15·9	5·7
40	5 25·0	5 25·9	5 10·2	4·0	1·4	10·0	3·6	16·0	5·7
41	5 25·3	5 26·1	5 10·4	4·1	1·5	10·1	3·6	16·1	5·8
42	5 25·5	5 26·4	5 10·7	4·2	1·5	10·2	3·7	16·2	5·8
43	5 25·8	5 26·6	5 10·9	4·3	1·5	10·3	3·7	16·3	5·8
44	5 26·0	5 26·9	5 11·1	4·4	1·6	10·4	3·7	16·4	5·9
45	5 26·3	5 27·1	5 11·4	4·5	1·6	10·5	3·8	16·5	5·9
46	5 26·5	5 27·4	5 11·6	4·6	1·6	10·6	3·8	16·6	5·9
47	5 26·8	5 27·6	5 11·9	4·7	1·7	10·7	3·8	16·7	6·0
48	5 27·0	5 27·9	5 12·1	4·8	1·7	10·8	3·9	16·8	6·0
49	5 27·3	5 28·1	5 12·3	4·9	1·8	10·9	3·9	16·9	6·1
50	5 27·5	5 28·4	5 12·6	5·0	1·8	11·0	3·9	17·0	6·1
51	5 27·8	5 28·6	5 12·8	5·1	1·8	11·1	4·0	17·1	6·1
52	5 28·0	5 28·9	5 13·1	5·2	1·9	11·2	4·0	17·2	6·2
53	5 28·3	5 29·1	5 13·3	5·3	1·9	11·3	4·1	17·3	6·2
54	5 28·5	5 29·4	5 13·5	5·4	1·9	11·4	4·1	17·4	6·2
55	5 28·8	5 29·7	5 13·8	5·5	2·0	11·5	4·1	17·5	6·3
56	5 29·0	5 29·9	5 14·0	5·6	2·0	11·6	4·2	17·6	6·3
57	5 29·3	5 30·2	5 14·3	5·7	2·0	11·7	4·2	17·7	6·3
58	5 29·5	5 30·4	5 14·5	5·8	2·1	11·8	4·2	17·8	6·4
59	5 29·8	5 30·7	5 14·7	5·9	2·1	11·9	4·3	17·9	6·4
60	5 30·0	5 30·9	5 15·0	6·0	2·2	12·0	4·3	18·0	6·5

22ᵐ

22ᵐ s	SUN PLANETS ° ′	ARIES ° ′	MOON ° ′	v or d ′	Corrⁿ ′	v or d ′	Corrⁿ ′	v or d ′	Corrⁿ ′
00	5 30·0	5 30·9	5 15·0	0·0	0·0	6·0	2·3	12·0	4·5
01	5 30·3	5 31·2	5 15·2	0·1	0·0	6·1	2·3	12·1	4·5
02	5 30·5	5 31·4	5 15·4	0·2	0·1	6·2	2·3	12·2	4·6
03	5 30·8	5 31·7	5 15·7	0·3	0·1	6·3	2·4	12·3	4·6
04	5 31·0	5 31·9	5 15·9	0·4	0·2	6·4	2·4	12·4	4·7
05	5 31·3	5 32·2	5 16·2	0·5	0·2	6·5	2·4	12·5	4·7
06	5 31·5	5 32·4	5 16·4	0·6	0·2	6·6	2·5	12·6	4·7
07	5 31·8	5 32·7	5 16·6	0·7	0·3	6·7	2·5	12·7	4·8
08	5 32·0	5 32·9	5 16·9	0·8	0·3	6·8	2·6	12·8	4·8
09	5 32·3	5 33·2	5 17·1	0·9	0·3	6·9	2·6	12·9	4·8
10	5 32·5	5 33·4	5 17·4	1·0	0·4	7·0	2·6	13·0	4·9
11	5 32·8	5 33·7	5 17·6	1·1	0·4	7·1	2·7	13·1	4·9
12	5 33·0	5 33·9	5 17·8	1·2	0·5	7·2	2·7	13·2	5·0
13	5 33·3	5 34·2	5 18·1	1·3	0·5	7·3	2·7	13·3	5·0
14	5 33·5	5 34·4	5 18·3	1·4	0·5	7·4	2·8	13·4	5·0
15	5 33·8	5 34·7	5 18·5	1·5	0·6	7·5	2·8	13·5	5·1
16	5 34·0	5 34·9	5 18·8	1·6	0·6	7·6	2·9	13·6	5·1
17	5 34·3	5 35·2	5 19·0	1·7	0·6	7·7	2·9	13·7	5·1
18	5 34·5	5 35·4	5 19·3	1·8	0·7	7·8	2·9	13·8	5·2
19	5 34·8	5 35·7	5 19·5	1·9	0·7	7·9	3·0	13·9	5·2
20	5 35·0	5 35·9	5 19·7	2·0	0·8	8·0	3·0	14·0	5·3
21	5 35·3	5 36·2	5 20·0	2·1	0·8	8·1	3·0	14·1	5·3
22	5 35·5	5 36·4	5 20·2	2·2	0·8	8·2	3·1	14·2	5·3
23	5 35·8	5 36·7	5 20·5	2·3	0·9	8·3	3·1	14·3	5·4
24	5 36·0	5 36·9	5 20·7	2·4	0·9	8·4	3·2	14·4	5·4
25	5 36·3	5 37·2	5 20·9	2·5	0·9	8·5	3·2	14·5	5·4
26	5 36·5	5 37·4	5 21·2	2·6	1·0	8·6	3·2	14·6	5·5
27	5 36·8	5 37·7	5 21·4	2·7	1·0	8·7	3·3	14·7	5·5
28	5 37·0	5 37·9	5 21·6	2·8	1·0	8·8	3·3	14·8	5·6
29	5 37·3	5 38·2	5 21·9	2·9	1·1	8·9	3·3	14·9	5·6
30	5 37·5	5 38·4	5 22·1	3·0	1·1	9·0	3·4	15·0	5·6
31	5 37·8	5 38·7	5 22·4	3·1	1·2	9·1	3·4	15·1	5·7
32	5 38·0	5 38·9	5 22·6	3·2	1·2	9·2	3·5	15·2	5·7
33	5 38·3	5 39·2	5 22·8	3·3	1·2	9·3	3·5	15·3	5·7
34	5 38·5	5 39·4	5 23·1	3·4	1·3	9·4	3·5	15·4	5·8
35	5 38·8	5 39·7	5 23·3	3·5	1·3	9·5	3·6	15·5	5·8
36	5 39·0	5 39·9	5 23·6	3·6	1·4	9·6	3·6	15·6	5·9
37	5 39·3	5 40·2	5 23·8	3·7	1·4	9·7	3·6	15·7	5·9
38	5 39·5	5 40·4	5 24·0	3·8	1·4	9·8	3·7	15·8	5·9
39	5 39·8	5 40·7	5 24·3	3·9	1·5	9·9	3·7	15·9	6·0
40	5 40·0	5 40·9	5 24·5	4·0	1·5	10·0	3·8	16·0	6·0
41	5 40·3	5 41·2	5 24·7	4·1	1·5	10·1	3·8	16·1	6·0
42	5 40·5	5 41·4	5 25·0	4·2	1·6	10·2	3·8	16·2	6·1
43	5 40·8	5 41·7	5 25·2	4·3	1·6	10·3	3·9	16·3	6·1
44	5 41·0	5 41·9	5 25·5	4·4	1·7	10·4	3·9	16·4	6·1
45	5 41·3	5 42·2	5 25·7	4·5	1·7	10·5	3·9	16·5	6·2
46	5 41·5	5 42·4	5 25·9	4·6	1·7	10·6	4·0	16·6	6·2
47	5 41·8	5 42·7	5 26·2	4·7	1·8	10·7	4·0	16·7	6·3
48	5 42·0	5 42·9	5 26·4	4·8	1·8	10·8	4·1	16·8	6·3
49	5 42·3	5 43·2	5 26·7	4·9	1·8	10·9	4·1	16·9	6·3
50	5 42·5	5 43·4	5 26·9	5·0	1·9	11·0	4·1	17·0	6·4
51	5 42·8	5 43·7	5 27·1	5·1	1·9	11·1	4·2	17·1	6·4
52	5 43·0	5 43·9	5 27·4	5·2	2·0	11·2	4·2	17·2	6·5
53	5 43·3	5 44·2	5 27·6	5·3	2·0	11·3	4·2	17·3	6·5
54	5 43·5	5 44·4	5 27·9	5·4	2·0	11·4	4·3	17·4	6·5
55	5 43·8	5 44·7	5 28·1	5·5	2·1	11·5	4·3	17·5	6·6
56	5 44·0	5 44·9	5 28·3	5·6	2·1	11·6	4·4	17·6	6·6
57	5 44·3	5 45·2	5 28·6	5·7	2·1	11·7	4·4	17·7	6·6
58	5 44·5	5 45·4	5 28·8	5·8	2·2	11·8	4·4	17·8	6·7
59	5 44·8	5 45·7	5 29·0	5·9	2·2	11·9	4·5	17·9	6·7
60	5 45·0	5 45·9	5 29·3	6·0	2·3	12·0	4·5	18·0	6·8

23ᵐ

23ᵐ s	SUN PLANETS ° ′	ARIES ° ′	MOON ° ′	v or d ′	Corrⁿ ′	v or d ′	Corrⁿ ′	v or d ′	Corrⁿ ′
00	5 45·0	5 45·9	5 29·3	0·0	0·0	6·0	2·4	12·0	4·7
01	5 45·3	5 46·2	5 29·5	0·1	0·0	6·1	2·4	12·1	4·7
02	5 45·5	5 46·4	5 29·8	0·2	0·1	6·2	2·4	12·2	4·8
03	5 45·8	5 46·7	5 30·0	0·3	0·1	6·3	2·5	12·3	4·8
04	5 46·0	5 46·9	5 30·2	0·4	0·2	6·4	2·5	12·4	4·9
05	5 46·3	5 47·2	5 30·5	0·5	0·2	6·5	2·5	12·5	4·9
06	5 46·5	5 47·4	5 30·7	0·6	0·2	6·6	2·6	12·6	4·9
07	5 46·8	5 47·7	5 31·0	0·7	0·3	6·7	2·6	12·7	5·0
08	5 47·0	5 48·0	5 31·2	0·8	0·3	6·8	2·7	12·8	5·0
09	5 47·3	5 48·2	5 31·4	0·9	0·4	6·9	2·7	12·9	5·1
10	5 47·5	5 48·5	5 31·7	1·0	0·4	7·0	2·7	13·0	5·1
11	5 47·8	5 48·7	5 31·9	1·1	0·4	7·1	2·8	13·1	5·1
12	5 48·0	5 49·0	5 32·1	1·2	0·5	7·2	2·8	13·2	5·2
13	5 48·3	5 49·2	5 32·4	1·3	0·5	7·3	2·9	13·3	5·2
14	5 48·5	5 49·5	5 32·6	1·4	0·5	7·4	2·9	13·4	5·2
15	5 48·8	5 49·7	5 32·9	1·5	0·6	7·5	2·9	13·5	5·3
16	5 49·0	5 50·0	5 33·1	1·6	0·6	7·6	3·0	13·6	5·3
17	5 49·3	5 50·2	5 33·3	1·7	0·7	7·7	3·0	13·7	5·4
18	5 49·5	5 50·5	5 33·6	1·8	0·7	7·8	3·1	13·8	5·4
19	5 49·8	5 50·7	5 33·8	1·9	0·7	7·9	3·1	13·9	5·4
20	5 50·0	5 51·0	5 34·1	2·0	0·8	8·0	3·1	14·0	5·5
21	5 50·3	5 51·2	5 34·3	2·1	0·8	8·1	3·2	14·1	5·5
22	5 50·5	5 51·5	5 34·5	2·2	0·9	8·2	3·2	14·2	5·6
23	5 50·8	5 51·7	5 34·8	2·3	0·9	8·3	3·3	14·3	5·6
24	5 51·0	5 52·0	5 35·0	2·4	0·9	8·4	3·3	14·4	5·6
25	5 51·3	5 52·2	5 35·2	2·5	1·0	8·5	3·3	14·5	5·7
26	5 51·5	5 52·5	5 35·5	2·6	1·0	8·6	3·4	14·6	5·7
27	5 51·8	5 52·7	5 35·7	2·7	1·1	8·7	3·4	14·7	5·8
28	5 52·0	5 53·0	5 36·0	2·8	1·1	8·8	3·4	14·8	5·8
29	5 52·3	5 53·2	5 36·2	2·9	1·1	8·9	3·5	14·9	5·8
30	5 52·5	5 53·5	5 36·4	3·0	1·2	9·0	3·5	15·0	5·9
31	5 52·8	5 53·7	5 36·7	3·1	1·2	9·1	3·6	15·1	5·9
32	5 53·0	5 54·0	5 36·9	3·2	1·3	9·2	3·6	15·2	6·0
33	5 53·3	5 54·2	5 37·2	3·3	1·3	9·3	3·6	15·3	6·0
34	5 53·5	5 54·5	5 37·4	3·4	1·3	9·4	3·7	15·4	6·0
35	5 53·8	5 54·7	5 37·6	3·5	1·4	9·5	3·7	15·5	6·1
36	5 54·0	5 55·0	5 37·9	3·6	1·4	9·6	3·8	15·6	6·1
37	5 54·3	5 55·2	5 38·1	3·7	1·4	9·7	3·8	15·7	6·1
38	5 54·5	5 55·5	5 38·4	3·8	1·5	9·8	3·8	15·8	6·2
39	5 54·8	5 55·7	5 38·6	3·9	1·5	9·9	3·9	15·9	6·2
40	5 55·0	5 56·0	5 38·8	4·0	1·6	10·0	3·9	16·0	6·3
41	5 55·3	5 56·2	5 39·1	4·1	1·6	10·1	4·0	16·1	6·3
42	5 55·5	5 56·5	5 39·3	4·2	1·6	10·2	4·0	16·2	6·3
43	5 55·8	5 56·7	5 39·5	4·3	1·7	10·3	4·0	16·3	6·4
44	5 56·0	5 57·0	5 39·8	4·4	1·7	10·4	4·1	16·4	6·4
45	5 56·3	5 57·2	5 40·0	4·5	1·8	10·5	4·1	16·5	6·5
46	5 56·5	5 57·5	5 40·3	4·6	1·8	10·6	4·2	16·6	6·5
47	5 56·8	5 57·7	5 40·5	4·7	1·8	10·7	4·2	16·7	6·5
48	5 57·0	5 58·0	5 40·7	4·8	1·9	10·8	4·2	16·8	6·6
49	5 57·3	5 58·2	5 41·0	4·9	1·9	10·9	4·3	16·9	6·6
50	5 57·5	5 58·5	5 41·2	5·0	2·0	11·0	4·3	17·0	6·7
51	5 57·8	5 58·7	5 41·5	5·1	2·0	11·1	4·3	17·1	6·7
52	5 58·0	5 59·0	5 41·7	5·2	2·0	11·2	4·4	17·2	6·7
53	5 58·3	5 59·2	5 41·9	5·3	2·1	11·3	4·4	17·3	6·8
54	5 58·5	5 59·5	5 42·2	5·4	2·1	11·4	4·5	17·4	6·8
55	5 58·8	5 59·7	5 42·4	5·5	2·2	11·5	4·5	17·5	6·9
56	5 59·0	6 00·0	5 42·6	5·6	2·2	11·6	4·5	17·6	6·9
57	5 59·3	6 00·2	5 42·9	5·7	2·2	11·7	4·6	17·7	6·9
58	5 59·5	6 00·5	5 43·1	5·8	2·3	11·8	4·6	17·8	7·0
59	5 59·8	6 00·7	5 43·4	5·9	2·3	11·9	4·7	17·9	7·0
60	6 00·0	6 01·0	5 43·6	6·0	2·4	12·0	4·7	18·0	7·1

24^m	SUN PLANETS	ARIES	MOON	v or d Corrⁿ		v or d Corrⁿ		v or d Corrⁿ	
s	° ′	° ′	° ′	′	′	′	′	′	′
00	6 00·0	6 01·0	5 43·6	0·0	0·0	6·0	2·5	12·0	4·9
01	6 00·3	6 01·2	5 43·8	0·1	0·0	6·1	2·5	12·1	4·9
02	6 00·5	6 01·5	5 44·1	0·2	0·1	6·2	2·5	12·2	5·0
03	6 00·8	6 01·7	5 44·3	0·3	0·1	6·3	2·6	12·3	5·0
04	6 01·0	6 02·0	5 44·6	0·4	0·2	6·4	2·6	12·4	5·1
05	6 01·3	6 02·2	5 44·8	0·5	0·2	6·5	2·7	12·5	5·1
06	6 01·5	6 02·5	5 45·0	0·6	0·2	6·6	2·7	12·6	5·1
07	6 01·8	6 02·7	5 45·3	0·7	0·3	6·7	2·7	12·7	5·2
08	6 02·0	6 03·0	5 45·5	0·8	0·3	6·8	2·8	12·8	5·2
09	6 02·3	6 03·2	5 45·7	0·9	0·4	6·9	2·8	12·9	5·3
10	6 02·5	6 03·5	5 46·0	1·0	0·4	7·0	2·9	13·0	5·3
11	6 02·8	6 03·7	5 46·2	1·1	0·4	7·1	2·9	13·1	5·3
12	6 03·0	6 04·0	5 46·5	1·2	0·5	7·2	2·9	13·2	5·4
13	6 03·3	6 04·2	5 46·7	1·3	0·5	7·3	3·0	13·3	5·4
14	6 03·5	6 04·5	5 46·9	1·4	0·6	7·4	3·0	13·4	5·5
15	6 03·8	6 04·7	5 47·2	1·5	0·6	7·5	3·1	13·5	5·5
16	6 04·0	6 05·0	5 47·4	1·6	0·7	7·6	3·1	13·6	5·6
17	6 04·3	6 05·2	5 47·7	1·7	0·7	7·7	3·1	13·7	5·6
18	6 04·5	6 05·5	5 47·9	1·8	0·7	7·8	3·2	13·8	5·6
19	6 04·8	6 05·7	5 48·1	1·9	0·8	7·9	3·2	13·9	5·7
20	6 05·0	6 06·0	5 48·4	2·0	0·8	8·0	3·3	14·0	5·7
21	6 05·3	6 06·3	5 48·6	2·1	0·9	8·1	3·3	14·1	5·8
22	6 05·5	6 06·5	5 48·8	2·2	0·9	8·2	3·3	14·2	5·8
23	6 05·8	6 06·8	5 49·1	2·3	0·9	8·3	3·4	14·3	5·8
24	6 06·0	6 07·0	5 49·3	2·4	1·0	8·4	3·4	14·4	5·9
25	6 06·3	6 07·3	5 49·6	2·5	1·0	8·5	3·5	14·5	5·9
26	6 06·5	6 07·5	5 49·8	2·6	1·1	8·6	3·5	14·6	6·0
27	6 06·8	6 07·8	5 50·0	2·7	1·1	8·7	3·6	14·7	6·0
28	6 07·0	6 08·0	5 50·3	2·8	1·1	8·8	3·6	14·8	6·0
29	6 07·3	6 08·3	5 50·5	2·9	1·2	8·9	3·6	14·9	6·1
30	6 07·5	6 08·5	5 50·8	3·0	1·2	9·0	3·7	15·0	6·1
31	6 07·8	6 08·8	5 51·0	3·1	1·3	9·1	3·7	15·1	6·2
32	6 08·0	6 09·0	5 51·2	3·2	1·3	9·2	3·8	15·2	6·2
33	6 08·3	6 09·3	5 51·5	3·3	1·3	9·3	3·8	15·3	6·2
34	6 08·5	6 09·5	5 51·7	3·4	1·4	9·4	3·8	15·4	6·3
35	6 08·8	6 09·8	5 52·0	3·5	1·4	9·5	3·9	15·5	6·3
36	6 09·0	6 10·0	5 52·2	3·6	1·5	9·6	3·9	15·6	6·4
37	6 09·3	6 10·3	5 52·4	3·7	1·5	9·7	4·0	15·7	6·4
38	6 09·5	6 10·5	5 52·7	3·8	1·6	9·8	4·0	15·8	6·5
39	6 09·8	6 10·8	5 52·9	3·9	1·6	9·9	4·0	15·9	6·5
40	6 10·0	6 11·0	5 53·1	4·0	1·6	10·0	4·1	16·0	6·5
41	6 10·3	6 11·3	5 53·4	4·1	1·7	10·1	4·1	16·1	6·6
42	6 10·5	6 11·5	5 53·6	4·2	1·7	10·2	4·2	16·2	6·6
43	6 10·8	6 11·8	5 53·9	4·3	1·8	10·3	4·2	16·3	6·7
44	6 11·0	6 12·0	5 54·1	4·4	1·8	10·4	4·2	16·4	6·7
45	6 11·3	6 12·3	5 54·3	4·5	1·8	10·5	4·3	16·5	6·7
46	6 11·5	6 12·5	5 54·6	4·6	1·9	10·6	4·3	16·6	6·8
47	6 11·8	6 12·8	5 54·8	4·7	1·9	10·7	4·4	16·7	6·8
48	6 12·0	6 13·0	5 55·1	4·8	2·0	10·8	4·4	16·8	6·9
49	6 12·3	6 13·3	5 55·3	4·9	2·0	10·9	4·5	16·9	6·9
50	6 12·5	6 13·5	5 55·5	5·0	2·0	11·0	4·5	17·0	6·9
51	6 12·8	6 13·8	5 55·8	5·1	2·1	11·1	4·5	17·1	7·0
52	6 13·0	6 14·0	5 56·0	5·2	2·1	11·2	4·6	17·2	7·0
53	6 13·3	6 14·3	5 56·2	5·3	2·2	11·3	4·6	17·3	7·1
54	6 13·5	6 14·5	5 56·5	5·4	2·2	11·4	4·7	17·4	7·1
55	6 13·8	6 14·8	5 56·7	5·5	2·2	11·5	4·7	17·5	7·1
56	6 14·0	6 15·0	5 57·0	5·6	2·3	11·6	4·7	17·6	7·2
57	6 14·3	6 15·3	5 57·2	5·7	2·3	11·7	4·8	17·7	7·2
58	6 14·5	6 15·5	5 57·4	5·8	2·4	11·8	4·8	17·8	7·3
59	6 14·8	6 15·8	5 57·7	5·9	2·4	11·9	4·9	17·9	7·3
60	6 15·0	6 16·0	5 57·9	6·0	2·5	12·0	4·9	18·0	7·4

25^m	SUN PLANETS	ARIES	MOON	v or d Corrⁿ		v or d Corrⁿ		v or d Corrⁿ	
s	° ′	° ′	° ′	′	′	′	′	′	′
00	6 15·0	6 16·0	5 57·9	0·0	0·0	6·0	2·6	12·0	5·1
01	6 15·3	6 16·3	5 58·2	0·1	0·0	6·1	2·6	12·1	5·1
02	6 15·5	6 16·5	5 58·4	0·2	0·1	6·2	2·6	12·2	5·2
03	6 15·8	6 16·8	5 58·6	0·3	0·1	6·3	2·7	12·3	5·2
04	6 16·0	6 17·0	5 58·9	0·4	0·2	6·4	2·7	12·4	5·3
05	6 16·3	6 17·3	5 59·1	0·5	0·2	6·5	2·8	12·5	5·3
06	6 16·5	6 17·5	5 59·3	0·6	0·3	6·6	2·8	12·6	5·4
07	6 16·8	6 17·8	5 59·6	0·7	0·3	6·7	2·8	12·7	5·4
08	6 17·0	6 18·0	5 59·8	0·8	0·3	6·8	2·9	12·8	5·4
09	6 17·3	6 18·3	6 00·1	0·9	0·4	6·9	2·9	12·9	5·5
10	6 17·5	6 18·5	6 00·3	1·0	0·4	7·0	3·0	13·0	5·5
11	6 17·8	6 18·8	6 00·5	1·1	0·5	7·1	3·0	13·1	5·6
12	6 18·0	6 19·0	6 00·8	1·2	0·5	7·2	3·1	13·2	5·6
13	6 18·3	6 19·3	6 01·0	1·3	0·6	7·3	3·1	13·3	5·7
14	6 18·5	6 19·5	6 01·3	1·4	0·6	7·4	3·1	13·4	5·7
15	6 18·8	6 19·8	6 01·5	1·5	0·6	7·5	3·2	13·5	5·7
16	6 19·0	6 20·0	6 01·7	1·6	0·7	7·6	3·2	13·6	5·8
17	6 19·3	6 20·3	6 02·0	1·7	0·7	7·7	3·3	13·7	5·8
18	6 19·5	6 20·5	6 02·2	1·8	0·8	7·8	3·3	13·8	5·9
19	6 19·8	6 20·8	6 02·5	1·9	0·8	7·9	3·4	13·9	5·9
20	6 20·0	6 21·0	6 02·7	2·0	0·9	8·0	3·4	14·0	6·0
21	6 20·3	6 21·3	6 02·9	2·1	0·9	8·1	3·4	14·1	6·0
22	6 20·5	6 21·5	6 03·2	2·2	0·9	8·2	3·5	14·2	6·0
23	6 20·8	6 21·8	6 03·4	2·3	1·0	8·3	3·5	14·3	6·1
24	6 21·0	6 22·0	6 03·6	2·4	1·0	8·4	3·6	14·4	6·1
25	6 21·3	6 22·3	6 03·9	2·5	1·1	8·5	3·6	14·5	6·2
26	6 21·5	6 22·5	6 04·1	2·6	1·1	8·6	3·7	14·6	6·2
27	6 21·8	6 22·8	6 04·4	2·7	1·1	8·7	3·7	14·7	6·2
28	6 22·0	6 23·0	6 04·6	2·8	1·2	8·8	3·7	14·8	6·3
29	6 22·3	6 23·3	6 04·8	2·9	1·2	8·9	3·8	14·9	6·3
30	6 22·5	6 23·5	6 05·1	3·0	1·3	9·0	3·8	15·0	6·4
31	6 22·8	6 23·8	6 05·3	3·1	1·3	9·1	3·9	15·1	6·4
32	6 23·0	6 24·0	6 05·6	3·2	1·4	9·2	3·9	15·2	6·5
33	6 23·3	6 24·3	6 05·8	3·3	1·4	9·3	4·0	15·3	6·5
34	6 23·5	6 24·5	6 06·0	3·4	1·4	9·4	4·0	15·4	6·5
35	6 23·8	6 24·8	6 06·3	3·5	1·5	9·5	4·0	15·5	6·6
36	6 24·0	6 25·1	6 06·5	3·6	1·5	9·6	4·1	15·6	6·6
37	6 24·3	6 25·3	6 06·7	3·7	1·6	9·7	4·1	15·7	6·7
38	6 24·5	6 25·6	6 07·0	3·8	1·6	9·8	4·2	15·8	6·7
39	6 24·8	6 25·8	6 07·2	3·9	1·7	9·9	4·2	15·9	6·8
40	6 25·0	6 26·1	6 07·5	4·0	1·7	10·0	4·3	16·0	6·8
41	6 25·3	6 26·3	6 07·7	4·1	1·7	10·1	4·3	16·1	6·8
42	6 25·5	6 26·6	6 07·9	4·2	1·8	10·2	4·3	16·2	6·9
43	6 25·8	6 26·8	6 08·2	4·3	1·8	10·3	4·4	16·3	6·9
44	6 26·0	6 27·1	6 08·4	4·4	1·9	10·4	4·4	16·4	7·0
45	6 26·3	6 27·3	6 08·7	4·5	1·9	10·5	4·5	16·5	7·0
46	6 26·5	6 27·6	6 08·9	4·6	2·0	10·6	4·5	16·6	7·1
47	6 26·8	6 27·8	6 09·1	4·7	2·0	10·7	4·5	16·7	7·1
48	6 27·0	6 28·1	6 09·4	4·8	2·0	10·8	4·6	16·8	7·1
49	6 27·3	6 28·3	6 09·6	4·9	2·1	10·9	4·6	16·9	7·2
50	6 27·5	6 28·6	6 09·8	5·0	2·1	11·0	4·7	17·0	7·2
51	6 27·8	6 28·8	6 10·1	5·1	2·2	11·1	4·7	17·1	7·3
52	6 28·0	6 29·1	6 10·3	5·2	2·2	11·2	4·8	17·2	7·3
53	6 28·3	6 29·3	6 10·6	5·3	2·3	11·3	4·8	17·3	7·4
54	6 28·5	6 29·6	6 10·8	5·4	2·3	11·4	4·8	17·4	7·4
55	6 28·8	6 29·8	6 11·0	5·5	2·3	11·5	4·9	17·5	7·4
56	6 29·0	6 30·1	6 11·3	5·6	2·4	11·6	4·9	17·6	7·5
57	6 29·3	6 30·3	6 11·5	5·7	2·4	11·7	5·0	17·7	7·5
58	6 29·5	6 30·6	6 11·8	5·8	2·5	11·8	5·0	17·8	7·6
59	6 29·8	6 30·8	6 12·0	5·9	2·5	11·9	5·1	17·9	7·6
60	6 30·0	6 31·1	6 12·2	6·0	2·6	12·0	5·1	18·0	7·7

26	SUN PLANETS	ARIES	MOON	v or Corrⁿ d		v or Corrⁿ d		v or Corrⁿ d	
s	° ′	° ′	° ′	′	′	′	′	′	′
00	6 30.0	6 31.1	6 12.2	0.0	0.0	6.0	2.7	12.0	5.3
01	6 30.3	6 31.3	6 12.5	0.1	0.0	6.1	2.7	12.1	5.3
02	6 30.5	6 31.6	6 12.7	0.2	0.1	6.2	2.7	12.2	5.4
03	6 30.8	6 31.8	6 12.9	0.3	0.1	6.3	2.8	12.3	5.4
04	6 31.0	6 32.1	6 13.2	0.4	0.2	6.4	2.8	12.4	5.5
05	6 31.3	6 32.3	6 13.4	0.5	0.2	6.5	2.9	12.5	5.5
06	6 31.5	6 32.6	6 13.7	0.6	0.3	6.6	2.9	12.6	5.6
07	6 31.8	6 32.8	6 13.9	0.7	0.3	6.7	3.0	12.7	5.6
08	6 32.0	6 33.1	6 14.1	0.8	0.4	6.8	3.0	12.8	5.7
09	6 32.3	6 33.3	6 14.4	0.9	0.4	6.9	3.0	12.9	5.7
10	6 32.5	6 33.6	6 14.6	1.0	0.4	7.0	3.1	13.0	5.7
11	6 32.8	6 33.8	6 14.9	1.1	0.5	7.1	3.1	13.1	5.8
12	6 33.0	6 34.1	6 15.1	1.2	0.5	7.2	3.2	13.2	5.8
13	6 33.3	6 34.3	6 15.3	1.3	0.6	7.3	3.2	13.3	5.9
14	6 33.5	6 34.6	6 15.6	1.4	0.6	7.4	3.3	13.4	5.9
15	6 33.8	6 34.8	6 15.8	1.5	0.7	7.5	3.3	13.5	6.0
16	6 34.0	6 35.1	6 16.1	1.6	0.7	7.6	3.4	13.6	6.0
17	6 34.3	6 35.3	6 16.3	1.7	0.8	7.7	3.4	13.7	6.1
18	6 34.5	6 35.6	6 16.5	1.8	0.8	7.8	3.4	13.8	6.1
19	6 34.8	6 35.8	6 16.8	1.9	0.8	7.9	3.5	13.9	6.1
20	6 35.0	6 36.1	6 17.0	2.0	0.9	8.0	3.5	14.0	6.2
21	6 35.3	6 36.3	6 17.2	2.1	0.9	8.1	3.6	14.1	6.2
22	6 35.5	6 36.6	6 17.5	2.2	1.0	8.2	3.6	14.2	6.3
23	6 35.8	6 36.8	6 17.7	2.3	1.0	8.3	3.7	14.3	6.3
24	6 36.0	6 37.1	6 18.0	2.4	1.1	8.4	3.7	14.4	6.4
25	6 36.3	6 37.3	6 18.2	2.5	1.1	8.5	3.8	14.5	6.4
26	6 36.5	6 37.6	6 18.4	2.6	1.1	8.6	3.8	14.6	6.4
27	6 36.8	6 37.8	6 18.7	2.7	1.2	8.7	3.8	14.7	6.5
28	6 37.0	6 38.1	6 18.9	2.8	1.2	8.8	3.9	14.8	6.5
29	6 37.3	6 38.3	6 19.2	2.9	1.3	8.9	3.9	14.9	6.6
30	6 37.5	6 38.6	6 19.4	3.0	1.3	9.0	4.0	15.0	6.6
31	6 37.8	6 38.8	6 19.6	3.1	1.4	9.1	4.0	15.1	6.7
32	6 38.0	6 39.1	6 19.9	3.2	1.4	9.2	4.1	15.2	6.7
33	6 38.3	6 39.3	6 20.1	3.3	1.5	9.3	4.1	15.3	6.8
34	6 38.5	6 39.6	6 20.3	3.4	1.5	9.4	4.2	15.4	6.8
35	6 38.8	6 39.8	6 20.6	3.5	1.5	9.5	4.2	15.5	6.8
36	6 39.0	6 40.1	6 20.8	3.6	1.6	9.6	4.2	15.6	6.9
37	6 39.3	6 40.3	6 21.1	3.7	1.6	9.7	4.3	15.7	6.9
38	6 39.5	6 40.6	6 21.3	3.8	1.7	9.8	4.3	15.8	7.0
39	6 39.8	6 40.8	6 21.5	3.9	1.7	9.9	4.4	15.9	7.0
40	6 40.0	6 41.1	6 21.8	4.0	1.8	10.0	4.4	16.0	7.1
41	6 40.3	6 41.3	6 22.0	4.1	1.8	10.1	4.5	16.1	7.1
42	6 40.5	6 41.6	6 22.3	4.2	1.9	10.2	4.5	16.2	7.2
43	6 40.8	6 41.8	6 22.5	4.3	1.9	10.3	4.5	16.3	7.2
44	6 41.0	6 42.1	6 22.7	4.4	1.9	10.4	4.6	16.4	7.2
45	6 41.3	6 42.3	6 23.0	4.5	2.0	10.5	4.6	16.5	7.3
46	6 41.5	6 42.6	6 23.2	4.6	2.0	10.6	4.7	16.6	7.3
47	6 41.8	6 42.8	6 23.4	4.7	2.1	10.7	4.7	16.7	7.4
48	6 42.0	6 43.1	6 23.7	4.8	2.1	10.8	4.8	16.8	7.4
49	6 42.3	6 43.4	6 23.9	4.9	2.2	10.9	4.8	16.9	7.5
50	6 42.5	6 43.6	6 24.2	5.0	2.2	11.0	4.9	17.0	7.5
51	6 42.8	6 43.9	6 24.4	5.1	2.3	11.1	4.9	17.1	7.6
52	6 43.0	6 44.1	6 24.6	5.2	2.3	11.2	4.9	17.2	7.6
53	6 43.3	6 44.4	6 24.9	5.3	2.3	11.3	5.0	17.3	7.6
54	6 43.5	6 44.6	6 25.1	5.4	2.4	11.4	5.0	17.4	7.7
55	6 43.8	6 44.9	6 25.4	5.5	2.4	11.5	5.1	17.5	7.7
56	6 44.0	6 45.1	6 25.6	5.6	2.5	11.6	5.1	17.6	7.8
57	6 44.3	6 45.4	6 25.8	5.7	2.5	11.7	5.2	17.7	7.8
58	6 44.5	6 45.6	6 26.1	5.8	2.6	11.8	5.2	17.8	7.9
59	6 44.8	6 45.9	6 26.3	5.9	2.6	11.9	5.3	17.9	7.9
60	6 45.0	6 46.1	6 26.6	6.0	2.7	12.0	5.3	18.0	8.0

27	SUN PLANETS	ARIES	MOON	v or Corrⁿ d		v or Corrⁿ d		v or Corrⁿ d	
s	° ′	° ′	° ′	′	′	′	′	′	′
00	6 45.0	6 46.1	6 26.6	0.0	0.0	6.0	2.8	12.0	5.5
01	6 45.3	6 46.4	6 26.8	0.1	0.0	6.1	2.8	12.1	5.5
02	6 45.5	6 46.6	6 27.0	0.2	0.1	6.2	2.8	12.2	5.6
03	6 45.8	6 46.9	6 27.3	0.3	0.1	6.3	2.9	12.3	5.6
04	6 46.0	6 47.1	6 27.5	0.4	0.2	6.4	2.9	12.4	5.7
05	6 46.3	6 47.4	6 27.7	0.5	0.2	6.5	3.0	12.5	5.7
06	6 46.5	6 47.6	6 28.0	0.6	0.3	6.6	3.0	12.6	5.8
07	6 46.8	6 47.9	6 28.2	0.7	0.3	6.7	3.1	12.7	5.8
08	6 47.0	6 48.1	6 28.5	0.8	0.4	6.8	3.1	12.8	5.9
09	6 47.3	6 48.4	6 28.7	0.9	0.4	6.9	3.2	12.9	5.9
10	6 47.5	6 48.6	6 28.9	1.0	0.5	7.0	3.2	13.0	6.0
11	6 47.8	6 48.9	6 29.2	1.1	0.5	7.1	3.3	13.1	6.0
12	6 48.0	6 49.1	6 29.4	1.2	0.6	7.2	3.3	13.2	6.1
13	6 48.3	6 49.4	6 29.7	1.3	0.6	7.3	3.3	13.3	6.1
14	6 48.5	6 49.6	6 29.9	1.4	0.6	7.4	3.4	13.4	6.1
15	6 48.8	6 49.9	6 30.1	1.5	0.7	7.5	3.4	13.5	6.2
16	6 49.0	6 50.1	6 30.4	1.6	0.7	7.6	3.5	13.6	6.2
17	6 49.3	6 50.4	6 30.6	1.7	0.8	7.7	3.5	13.7	6.3
18	6 49.5	6 50.6	6 30.8	1.8	0.8	7.8	3.6	13.8	6.3
19	6 49.8	6 50.9	6 31.1	1.9	0.9	7.9	3.6	13.9	6.4
20	6 50.0	6 51.1	6 31.3	2.0	0.9	8.0	3.7	14.0	6.4
21	6 50.3	6 51.4	6 31.6	2.1	1.0	8.1	3.7	14.1	6.5
22	6 50.5	6 51.6	6 31.8	2.2	1.0	8.2	3.8	14.2	6.5
23	6 50.8	6 51.9	6 32.0	2.3	1.1	8.3	3.8	14.3	6.6
24	6 51.0	6 52.1	6 32.3	2.4	1.1	8.4	3.9	14.4	6.6
25	6 51.3	6 52.4	6 32.5	2.5	1.1	8.5	3.9	14.5	6.6
26	6 51.5	6 52.6	6 32.8	2.6	1.2	8.6	3.9	14.6	6.7
27	6 51.8	6 52.9	6 33.0	2.7	1.2	8.7	4.0	14.7	6.7
28	6 52.0	6 53.1	6 33.2	2.8	1.3	8.8	4.0	14.8	6.8
29	6 52.3	6 53.4	6 33.5	2.9	1.3	8.9	4.1	14.9	6.8
30	6 52.5	6 53.6	6 33.7	3.0	1.4	9.0	4.1	15.0	6.9
31	6 52.8	6 53.9	6 33.9	3.1	1.4	9.1	4.2	15.1	6.9
32	6 53.0	6 54.1	6 34.2	3.2	1.5	9.2	4.2	15.2	7.0
33	6 53.3	6 54.4	6 34.4	3.3	1.5	9.3	4.3	15.3	7.0
34	6 53.5	6 54.6	6 34.7	3.4	1.6	9.4	4.3	15.4	7.1
35	6 53.8	6 54.9	6 34.9	3.5	1.6	9.5	4.4	15.5	7.1
36	6 54.0	6 55.1	6 35.1	3.6	1.7	9.6	4.4	15.6	7.2
37	6 54.3	6 55.4	6 35.4	3.7	1.7	9.7	4.4	15.7	7.2
38	6 54.5	6 55.6	6 35.6	3.8	1.7	9.8	4.5	15.8	7.2
39	6 54.8	6 55.9	6 35.9	3.9	1.8	9.9	4.5	15.9	7.3
40	6 55.0	6 56.1	6 36.1	4.0	1.8	10.0	4.6	16.0	7.3
41	6 55.3	6 56.4	6 36.3	4.1	1.9	10.1	4.6	16.1	7.4
42	6 55.5	6 56.6	6 36.6	4.2	1.9	10.2	4.7	16.2	7.4
43	6 55.8	6 56.9	6 36.8	4.3	2.0	10.3	4.7	16.3	7.5
44	6 56.0	6 57.1	6 37.0	4.4	2.0	10.4	4.8	16.4	7.5
45	6 56.3	6 57.4	6 37.3	4.5	2.1	10.5	4.8	16.5	7.6
46	6 56.5	6 57.6	6 37.5	4.6	2.1	10.6	4.9	16.6	7.6
47	6 56.8	6 57.9	6 37.8	4.7	2.2	10.7	4.9	16.7	7.7
48	6 57.0	6 58.1	6 38.0	4.8	2.2	10.8	5.0	16.8	7.7
49	6 57.3	6 58.4	6 38.2	4.9	2.2	10.9	5.0	16.9	7.7
50	6 57.5	6 58.6	6 38.5	5.0	2.3	11.0	5.0	17.0	7.8
51	6 57.8	6 58.9	6 38.7	5.1	2.3	11.1	5.1	17.1	7.8
52	6 58.0	6 59.1	6 39.0	5.2	2.4	11.2	5.1	17.2	7.9
53	6 58.3	6 59.4	6 39.2	5.3	2.4	11.3	5.2	17.3	7.9
54	6 58.5	6 59.6	6 39.4	5.4	2.5	11.4	5.2	17.4	8.0
55	6 58.8	6 59.9	6 39.7	5.5	2.5	11.5	5.3	17.5	8.0
56	6 59.0	7 00.1	6 39.9	5.6	2.6	11.6	5.3	17.6	8.1
57	6 59.3	7 00.4	6 40.2	5.7	2.6	11.7	5.4	17.7	8.1
58	6 59.5	7 00.6	6 40.4	5.8	2.7	11.8	5.4	17.8	8.2
59	6 59.8	7 00.9	6 40.6	5.9	2.7	11.9	5.5	17.9	8.2
60	7 00.0	7 01.1	6 40.9	6.0	2.8	12.0	5.5	18.0	8.3

28ᵐ

28	SUN PLANETS	ARIES	MOON	v or Corrⁿ d	v or Corrⁿ d	v or Corrⁿ d
s	° ′	° ′	° ′	′ ′	′ ′	′ ′
00	7 00.0	7 01.1	6 40.9	0.0 0.0	6.0 2.9	12.0 5.7
01	7 00.3	7 01.4	6 41.1	0.1 0.0	6.1 2.9	12.1 5.7
02	7 00.5	7 01.7	6 41.3	0.2 0.1	6.2 2.9	12.2 5.8
03	7 00.8	7 01.9	6 41.6	0.3 0.1	6.3 3.0	12.3 5.8
04	7 01.0	7 02.2	6 41.8	0.4 0.2	6.4 3.0	12.4 5.9
05	7 01.3	7 02.4	6 42.1	0.5 0.2	6.5 3.1	12.5 5.9
06	7 01.5	7 02.7	6 42.3	0.6 0.3	6.6 3.1	12.6 6.0
07	7 01.8	7 02.9	6 42.5	0.7 0.3	6.7 3.2	12.7 6.0
08	7 02.0	7 03.2	6 42.8	0.8 0.4	6.8 3.2	12.8 6.1
09	7 02.3	7 03.4	6 43.0	0.9 0.4	6.9 3.3	12.9 6.1
10	7 02.5	7 03.7	6 43.3	1.0 0.5	7.0 3.3	13.0 6.2
11	7 02.8	7 03.9	6 43.5	1.1 0.5	7.1 3.4	13.1 6.2
12	7 03.0	7 04.2	6 43.7	1.2 0.6	7.2 3.4	13.2 6.3
13	7 03.3	7 04.4	6 44.0	1.3 0.6	7.3 3.5	13.3 6.3
14	7 03.5	7 04.7	6 44.2	1.4 0.7	7.4 3.5	13.4 6.4
15	7 03.8	7 04.9	6 44.4	1.5 0.7	7.5 3.6	13.5 6.4
16	7 04.0	7 05.2	6 44.7	1.6 0.8	7.6 3.6	13.6 6.5
17	7 04.3	7 05.4	6 44.9	1.7 0.8	7.7 3.7	13.7 6.5
18	7 04.5	7 05.7	6 45.2	1.8 0.9	7.8 3.7	13.8 6.6
19	7 04.8	7 05.9	6 45.4	1.9 0.9	7.9 3.8	13.9 6.6
20	7 05.0	7 06.2	6 45.6	2.0 1.0	8.0 3.8	14.0 6.7
21	7 05.3	7 06.4	6 45.9	2.1 1.0	8.1 3.8	14.1 6.7
22	7 05.5	7 06.7	6 46.1	2.2 1.0	8.2 3.9	14.2 6.7
23	7 05.8	7 06.9	6 46.4	2.3 1.1	8.3 3.9	14.3 6.8
24	7 06.0	7 07.2	6 46.6	2.4 1.1	8.4 4.0	14.4 6.8
25	7 06.3	7 07.4	6 46.8	2.5 1.2	8.5 4.0	14.5 6.9
26	7 06.5	7 07.7	6 47.1	2.6 1.2	8.6 4.1	14.6 6.9
27	7 06.8	7 07.9	6 47.3	2.7 1.3	8.7 4.1	14.7 7.0
28	7 07.0	7 08.2	6 47.5	2.8 1.3	8.8 4.2	14.8 7.0
29	7 07.3	7 08.4	6 47.8	2.9 1.4	8.9 4.2	14.9 7.1
30	7 07.5	7 08.7	6 48.0	3.0 1.4	9.0 4.3	15.0 7.1
31	7 07.8	7 08.9	6 48.3	3.1 1.5	9.1 4.3	15.1 7.2
32	7 08.0	7 09.2	6 48.5	3.2 1.5	9.2 4.4	15.2 7.2
33	7 08.3	7 09.4	6 48.7	3.3 1.6	9.3 4.4	15.3 7.3
34	7 08.5	7 09.7	6 49.0	3.4 1.6	9.4 4.5	15.4 7.3
35	7 08.8	7 09.9	6 49.2	3.5 1.7	9.5 4.5	15.5 7.4
36	7 09.0	7 10.2	6 49.5	3.6 1.7	9.6 4.6	15.6 7.4
37	7 09.3	7 10.4	6 49.7	3.7 1.8	9.7 4.6	15.7 7.5
38	7 09.5	7 10.7	6 49.9	3.8 1.8	9.8 4.7	15.8 7.5
39	7 09.8	7 10.9	6 50.2	3.9 1.9	9.9 4.7	15.9 7.6
40	7 10.0	7 11.2	6 50.4	4.0 1.9	10.0 4.8	16.0 7.6
41	7 10.3	7 11.4	6 50.6	4.1 1.9	10.1 4.8	16.1 7.6
42	7 10.5	7 11.7	6 50.9	4.2 2.0	10.2 4.8	16.2 7.7
43	7 10.8	7 11.9	6 51.1	4.3 2.0	10.3 4.9	16.3 7.7
44	7 11.0	7 12.2	6 51.4	4.4 2.1	10.4 4.9	16.4 7.8
45	7 11.3	7 12.4	6 51.6	4.5 2.1	10.5 5.0	16.5 7.8
46	7 11.5	7 12.7	6 51.8	4.6 2.2	10.6 5.0	16.6 7.9
47	7 11.8	7 12.9	6 52.1	4.7 2.2	10.7 5.1	16.7 7.9
48	7 12.0	7 13.2	6 52.3	4.8 2.3	10.8 5.1	16.8 8.0
49	7 12.3	7 13.4	6 52.6	4.9 2.3	10.9 5.2	16.9 8.0
50	7 12.5	7 13.7	6 52.8	5.0 2.4	11.0 5.2	17.0 8.1
51	7 12.8	7 13.9	6 53.0	5.1 2.4	11.1 5.3	17.1 8.1
52	7 13.0	7 14.2	6 53.3	5.2 2.5	11.2 5.3	17.2 8.2
53	7 13.3	7 14.4	6 53.5	5.3 2.5	11.3 5.4	17.3 8.2
54	7 13.5	7 14.7	6 53.8	5.4 2.6	11.4 5.4	17.4 8.3
55	7 13.8	7 14.9	6 54.0	5.5 2.6	11.5 5.5	17.5 8.3
56	7 14.0	7 15.2	6 54.2	5.6 2.7	11.6 5.5	17.6 8.4
57	7 14.3	7 15.4	6 54.5	5.7 2.7	11.7 5.6	17.7 8.4
58	7 14.5	7 15.7	6 54.7	5.8 2.8	11.8 5.6	17.8 8.5
59	7 14.8	7 15.9	6 54.9	5.9 2.8	11.9 5.7	17.9 8.5
60	7 15.0	7 16.2	6 55.2	6.0 2.9	12.0 5.7	18.0 8.6

29ᵐ

29	SUN PLANETS	ARIES	MOON	v or Corrⁿ d	v or Corrⁿ d	v or Corrⁿ d
s	° ′	° ′	° ′	′ ′	′ ′	′ ′
00	7 15.0	7 16.2	6 55.2	0.0 0.0	6.0 3.0	12.0 5.9
01	7 15.3	7 16.4	6 55.4	0.1 0.0	6.1 3.0	12.1 5.9
02	7 15.5	7 16.7	6 55.7	0.2 0.1	6.2 3.0	12.2 6.0
03	7 15.8	7 16.9	6 55.9	0.3 0.1	6.3 3.1	12.3 6.0
04	7 16.0	7 17.2	6 56.1	0.4 0.2	6.4 3.1	12.4 6.1
05	7 16.3	7 17.4	6 56.4	0.5 0.2	6.5 3.2	12.5 6.1
06	7 16.5	7 17.7	6 56.6	0.6 0.3	6.6 3.2	12.6 6.2
07	7 16.8	7 17.9	6 56.9	0.7 0.3	6.7 3.3	12.7 6.2
08	7 17.0	7 18.2	6 57.1	0.8 0.4	6.8 3.3	12.8 6.3
09	7 17.3	7 18.4	6 57.3	0.9 0.4	6.9 3.4	12.9 6.3
10	7 17.5	7 18.7	6 57.6	1.0 0.5	7.0 3.4	13.0 6.4
11	7 17.8	7 18.9	6 57.8	1.1 0.5	7.1 3.5	13.1 6.4
12	7 18.0	7 19.2	6 58.0	1.2 0.6	7.2 3.5	13.2 6.5
13	7 18.3	7 19.4	6 58.3	1.3 0.6	7.3 3.6	13.3 6.5
14	7 18.5	7 19.7	6 58.5	1.4 0.7	7.4 3.6	13.4 6.6
15	7 18.8	7 20.0	6 58.8	1.5 0.7	7.5 3.7	13.5 6.6
16	7 19.0	7 20.2	6 59.0	1.6 0.8	7.6 3.7	13.6 6.7
17	7 19.3	7 20.5	6 59.2	1.7 0.8	7.7 3.8	13.7 6.7
18	7 19.5	7 20.7	6 59.5	1.8 0.9	7.8 3.8	13.8 6.8
19	7 19.8	7 21.0	6 59.7	1.9 0.9	7.9 3.9	13.9 6.8
20	7 20.0	7 21.2	7 00.0	2.0 1.0	8.0 3.9	14.0 6.9
21	7 20.3	7 21.5	7 00.2	2.1 1.0	8.1 4.0	14.1 6.9
22	7 20.5	7 21.7	7 00.4	2.2 1.1	8.2 4.0	14.2 7.0
23	7 20.8	7 22.0	7 00.7	2.3 1.1	8.3 4.1	14.3 7.0
24	7 21.0	7 22.2	7 00.9	2.4 1.2	8.4 4.1	14.4 7.1
25	7 21.3	7 22.5	7 01.1	2.5 1.2	8.5 4.2	14.5 7.1
26	7 21.5	7 22.7	7 01.4	2.6 1.3	8.6 4.2	14.6 7.2
27	7 21.8	7 23.0	7 01.6	2.7 1.3	8.7 4.3	14.7 7.2
28	7 22.0	7 23.2	7 01.9	2.8 1.4	8.8 4.3	14.8 7.3
29	7 22.3	7 23.5	7 02.1	2.9 1.4	8.9 4.4	14.9 7.3
30	7 22.5	7 23.7	7 02.3	3.0 1.5	9.0 4.4	15.0 7.4
31	7 22.8	7 24.0	7 02.6	3.1 1.5	9.1 4.5	15.1 7.4
32	7 23.0	7 24.2	7 02.8	3.2 1.6	9.2 4.5	15.2 7.5
33	7 23.3	7 24.5	7 03.1	3.3 1.6	9.3 4.6	15.3 7.5
34	7 23.5	7 24.7	7 03.3	3.4 1.7	9.4 4.6	15.4 7.6
35	7 23.8	7 25.0	7 03.5	3.5 1.7	9.5 4.7	15.5 7.6
36	7 24.0	7 25.2	7 03.8	3.6 1.8	9.6 4.7	15.6 7.7
37	7 24.3	7 25.5	7 04.0	3.7 1.8	9.7 4.8	15.7 7.7
38	7 24.5	7 25.7	7 04.3	3.8 1.9	9.8 4.8	15.8 7.8
39	7 24.8	7 26.0	7 04.5	3.9 1.9	9.9 4.9	15.9 7.8
40	7 25.0	7 26.2	7 04.7	4.0 2.0	10.0 4.9	16.0 7.9
41	7 25.3	7 26.5	7 05.0	4.1 2.0	10.1 5.0	16.1 7.9
42	7 25.5	7 26.7	7 05.2	4.2 2.1	10.2 5.0	16.2 8.0
43	7 25.8	7 27.0	7 05.4	4.3 2.1	10.3 5.1	16.3 8.0
44	7 26.0	7 27.2	7 05.7	4.4 2.2	10.4 5.1	16.4 8.1
45	7 26.3	7 27.5	7 05.9	4.5 2.2	10.5 5.2	16.5 8.1
46	7 26.5	7 27.7	7 06.2	4.6 2.3	10.6 5.2	16.6 8.2
47	7 26.8	7 28.0	7 06.4	4.7 2.3	10.7 5.3	16.7 8.2
48	7 27.0	7 28.2	7 06.6	4.8 2.4	10.8 5.3	16.8 8.3
49	7 27.3	7 28.5	7 06.9	4.9 2.4	10.9 5.4	16.9 8.3
50	7 27.5	7 28.7	7 07.1	5.0 2.5	11.0 5.4	17.0 8.4
51	7 27.8	7 29.0	7 07.4	5.1 2.5	11.1 5.5	17.1 8.4
52	7 28.0	7 29.2	7 07.6	5.2 2.6	11.2 5.5	17.2 8.5
53	7 28.3	7 29.5	7 07.8	5.3 2.6	11.3 5.6	17.3 8.5
54	7 28.5	7 29.7	7 08.1	5.4 2.7	11.4 5.6	17.4 8.6
55	7 28.8	7 30.0	7 08.3	5.5 2.7	11.5 5.7	17.5 8.6
56	7 29.0	7 30.2	7 08.5	5.6 2.8	11.6 5.7	17.6 8.7
57	7 29.3	7 30.5	7 08.8	5.7 2.8	11.7 5.8	17.7 8.7
58	7 29.5	7 30.7	7 09.0	5.8 2.9	11.8 5.8	17.8 8.8
59	7 29.8	7 31.0	7 09.3	5.9 2.9	11.9 5.9	17.9 8.8
60	7 30.0	7 31.2	7 09.5	6.0 3.0	12.0 5.9	18.0 8.9

30m

30 (s)	SUN PLANETS	ARIES	MOON	v or d	Corrn	v or d	Corrn	v or d	Corrn
00	7 30·0	7 31·2	7 09·5	0·0	0·0	6·0	3·1	12·0	6·1
01	7 30·3	7 31·5	7 09·7	0·1	0·1	6·1	3·1	12·1	6·2
02	7 30·5	7 31·7	7 10·0	0·2	0·1	6·2	3·2	12·2	6·2
03	7 30·8	7 32·0	7 10·2	0·3	0·2	6·3	3·2	12·3	6·3
04	7 31·0	7 32·2	7 10·5	0·4	0·2	6·4	3·3	12·4	6·3
05	7 31·3	7 32·5	7 10·7	0·5	0·3	6·5	3·3	12·5	6·4
06	7 31·5	7 32·7	7 10·9	0·6	0·3	6·6	3·4	12·6	6·4
07	7 31·8	7 33·0	7 11·2	0·7	0·4	6·7	3·4	12·7	6·5
08	7 32·0	7 33·2	7 11·4	0·8	0·4	6·8	3·5	12·8	6·5
09	7 32·3	7 33·5	7 11·6	0·9	0·5	6·9	3·5	12·9	6·6
10	7 32·5	7 33·7	7 11·9	1·0	0·5	7·0	3·6	13·0	6·6
11	7 32·8	7 34·0	7 12·1	1·1	0·6	7·1	3·6	13·1	6·7
12	7 33·0	7 34·2	7 12·4	1·2	0·6	7·2	3·7	13·2	6·7
13	7 33·3	7 34·5	7 12·6	1·3	0·7	7·3	3·7	13·3	6·8
14	7 33·5	7 34·7	7 12·8	1·4	0·7	7·4	3·8	13·4	6·8
15	7 33·8	7 35·0	7 13·1	1·5	0·8	7·5	3·8	13·5	6·9
16	7 34·0	7 35·2	7 13·3	1·6	0·8	7·6	3·9	13·6	6·9
17	7 34·3	7 35·5	7 13·6	1·7	0·9	7·7	3·9	13·7	7·0
18	7 34·5	7 35·7	7 13·8	1·8	0·9	7·8	4·0	13·8	7·0
19	7 34·8	7 36·0	7 14·0	1·9	1·0	7·9	4·0	13·9	7·1
20	7 35·0	7 36·2	7 14·3	2·0	1·0	8·0	4·1	14·0	7·1
21	7 35·3	7 36·5	7 14·5	2·1	1·1	8·1	4·1	14·1	7·2
22	7 35·5	7 36·7	7 14·7	2·2	1·1	8·2	4·2	14·2	7·2
23	7 35·8	7 37·0	7 15·0	2·3	1·2	8·3	4·2	14·3	7·3
24	7 36·0	7 37·2	7 15·2	2·4	1·2	8·4	4·3	14·4	7·3
25	7 36·3	7 37·5	7 15·5	2·5	1·3	8·5	4·3	14·5	7·4
26	7 36·5	7 37·7	7 15·7	2·6	1·3	8·6	4·4	14·6	7·4
27	7 36·8	7 38·0	7 15·9	2·7	1·4	8·7	4·4	14·7	7·5
28	7 37·0	7 38·3	7 16·2	2·8	1·4	8·8	4·5	14·8	7·5
29	7 37·3	7 38·5	7 16·4	2·9	1·5	8·9	4·5	14·9	7·6
30	7 37·5	7 38·8	7 16·7	3·0	1·5	9·0	4·6	15·0	7·6
31	7 37·8	7 39·0	7 16·9	3·1	1·6	9·1	4·6	15·1	7·7
32	7 38·0	7 39·3	7 17·1	3·2	1·6	9·2	4·7	15·2	7·7
33	7 38·3	7 39·5	7 17·4	3·3	1·7	9·3	4·7	15·3	7·8
34	7 38·5	7 39·8	7 17·6	3·4	1·7	9·4	4·8	15·4	7·8
35	7 38·8	7 40·0	7 17·9	3·5	1·8	9·5	4·8	15·5	7·9
36	7 39·0	7 40·3	7 18·1	3·6	1·8	9·6	4·9	15·6	7·9
37	7 39·3	7 40·5	7 18·3	3·7	1·9	9·7	4·9	15·7	8·0
38	7 39·5	7 40·8	7 18·6	3·8	1·9	9·8	5·0	15·8	8·0
39	7 39·8	7 41·0	7 18·8	3·9	2·0	9·9	5·0	15·9	8·1
40	7 40·0	7 41·3	7 19·0	4·0	2·0	10·0	5·1	16·0	8·1
41	7 40·3	7 41·5	7 19·3	4·1	2·1	10·1	5·1	16·1	8·2
42	7 40·5	7 41·8	7 19·5	4·2	2·1	10·2	5·2	16·2	8·2
43	7 40·8	7 42·0	7 19·8	4·3	2·2	10·3	5·2	16·3	8·3
44	7 41·0	7 42·3	7 20·0	4·4	2·2	10·4	5·3	16·4	8·3
45	7 41·3	7 42·5	7 20·2	4·5	2·3	10·5	5·3	16·5	8·4
46	7 41·5	7 42·8	7 20·5	4·6	2·3	10·6	5·4	16·6	8·4
47	7 41·8	7 43·0	7 20·7	4·7	2·4	10·7	5·4	16·7	8·5
48	7 42·0	7 43·3	7 21·0	4·8	2·4	10·8	5·5	16·8	8·5
49	7 42·3	7 43·5	7 21·2	4·9	2·5	10·9	5·5	16·9	8·6
50	7 42·5	7 43·8	7 21·4	5·0	2·5	11·0	5·6	17·0	8·6
51	7 42·8	7 44·0	7 21·7	5·1	2·6	11·1	5·6	17·1	8·7
52	7 43·0	7 44·3	7 21·9	5·2	2·6	11·2	5·7	17·2	8·7
53	7 43·3	7 44·5	7 22·1	5·3	2·7	11·3	5·7	17·3	8·8
54	7 43·5	7 44·8	7 22·4	5·4	2·7	11·4	5·8	17·4	8·8
55	7 43·8	7 45·0	7 22·6	5·5	2·8	11·5	5·8	17·5	8·9
56	7 44·0	7 45·3	7 22·9	5·6	2·8	11·6	5·9	17·6	8·9
57	7 44·3	7 45·5	7 23·1	5·7	2·9	11·7	5·9	17·7	9·0
58	7 44·5	7 45·8	7 23·3	5·8	2·9	11·8	6·0	17·8	9·0
59	7 44·8	7 46·0	7 23·6	5·9	3·0	11·9	6·0	17·9	9·1
60	7 45·0	7 46·3	7 23·8	6·0	3·1	12·0	6·1	18·0	9·2

31m

31 (s)	SUN PLANETS	ARIES	MOON	v or d	Corrn	v or d	Corrn	v or d	Corrn
00	7 45·0	7 46·3	7 23·8	0·0	0·0	6·0	3·2	12·0	6·3
01	7 45·3	7 46·5	7 24·1	0·1	0·1	6·1	3·2	12·1	6·4
02	7 45·5	7 46·8	7 24·3	0·2	0·1	6·2	3·3	12·2	6·4
03	7 45·8	7 47·0	7 24·5	0·3	0·2	6·3	3·3	12·3	6·5
04	7 46·0	7 47·3	7 24·8	0·4	0·2	6·4	3·4	12·4	6·5
05	7 46·3	7 47·5	7 25·0	0·5	0·3	6·5	3·4	12·5	6·6
06	7 46·5	7 47·8	7 25·2	0·6	0·3	6·6	3·5	12·6	6·6
07	7 46·8	7 48·0	7 25·5	0·7	0·4	6·7	3·5	12·7	6·7
08	7 47·0	7 48·3	7 25·7	0·8	0·4	6·8	3·6	12·8	6·7
09	7 47·3	7 48·5	7 26·0	0·9	0·5	6·9	3·6	12·9	6·8
10	7 47·5	7 48·8	7 26·2	1·0	0·5	7·0	3·7	13·0	6·8
11	7 47·8	7 49·0	7 26·4	1·1	0·6	7·1	3·7	13·1	6·9
12	7 48·0	7 49·3	7 26·7	1·2	0·6	7·2	3·8	13·2	6·9
13	7 48·3	7 49·5	7 26·9	1·3	0·7	7·3	3·8	13·3	7·0
14	7 48·5	7 49·8	7 27·2	1·4	0·7	7·4	3·9	13·4	7·0
15	7 48·8	7 50·0	7 27·4	1·5	0·8	7·5	3·9	13·5	7·1
16	7 49·0	7 50·3	7 27·6	1·6	0·8	7·6	4·0	13·6	7·1
17	7 49·3	7 50·5	7 27·9	1·7	0·9	7·7	4·0	13·7	7·2
18	7 49·5	7 50·8	7 28·1	1·8	0·9	7·8	4·1	13·8	7·2
19	7 49·8	7 51·0	7 28·4	1·9	1·0	7·9	4·1	13·9	7·3
20	7 50·0	7 51·3	7 28·6	2·0	1·1	8·0	4·2	14·0	7·4
21	7 50·3	7 51·5	7 28·8	2·1	1·1	8·1	4·3	14·1	7·4
22	7 50·5	7 51·8	7 29·1	2·2	1·2	8·2	4·3	14·2	7·5
23	7 50·8	7 52·0	7 29·3	2·3	1·2	8·3	4·4	14·3	7·5
24	7 51·0	7 52·3	7 29·5	2·4	1·3	8·4	4·4	14·4	7·6
25	7 51·3	7 52·5	7 29·8	2·5	1·3	8·5	4·5	14·5	7·6
26	7 51·5	7 52·8	7 30·0	2·6	1·4	8·6	4·5	14·6	7·7
27	7 51·8	7 53·0	7 30·3	2·7	1·4	8·7	4·6	14·7	7·7
28	7 52·0	7 53·3	7 30·5	2·8	1·5	8·8	4·6	14·8	7·8
29	7 52·3	7 53·5	7 30·7	2·9	1·5	8·9	4·7	14·9	7·8
30	7 52·5	7 53·8	7 31·0	3·0	1·6	9·0	4·7	15·0	7·9
31	7 52·8	7 54·0	7 31·2	3·1	1·6	9·1	4·8	15·1	7·9
32	7 53·0	7 54·3	7 31·5	3·2	1·7	9·2	4·8	15·2	8·0
33	7 53·3	7 54·5	7 31·7	3·3	1·7	9·3	4·9	15·3	8·0
34	7 53·5	7 54·8	7 31·9	3·4	1·8	9·4	4·9	15·4	8·1
35	7 53·8	7 55·0	7 32·2	3·5	1·8	9·5	5·0	15·5	8·1
36	7 54·0	7 55·3	7 32·4	3·6	1·9	9·6	5·0	15·6	8·2
37	7 54·3	7 55·5	7 32·6	3·7	1·9	9·7	5·1	15·7	8·2
38	7 54·5	7 55·8	7 32·9	3·8	2·0	9·8	5·1	15·8	8·3
39	7 54·8	7 56·0	7 33·1	3·9	2·0	9·9	5·2	15·9	8·3
40	7 55·0	7 56·3	7 33·4	4·0	2·1	10·0	5·3	16·0	8·4
41	7 55·3	7 56·6	7 33·6	4·1	2·2	10·1	5·3	16·1	8·5
42	7 55·5	7 56·8	7 33·8	4·2	2·2	10·2	5·4	16·2	8·5
43	7 55·8	7 57·1	7 34·1	4·3	2·3	10·3	5·4	16·3	8·6
44	7 56·0	7 57·3	7 34·3	4·4	2·3	10·4	5·5	16·4	8·6
45	7 56·3	7 57·6	7 34·6	4·5	2·4	10·5	5·5	16·5	8·7
46	7 56·5	7 57·8	7 34·8	4·6	2·4	10·6	5·6	16·6	8·7
47	7 56·8	7 58·1	7 35·0	4·7	2·5	10·7	5·6	16·7	8·8
48	7 57·0	7 58·3	7 35·3	4·8	2·5	10·8	5·7	16·8	8·8
49	7 57·3	7 58·6	7 35·5	4·9	2·6	10·9	5·7	16·9	8·9
50	7 57·5	7 58·8	7 35·7	5·0	2·6	11·0	5·8	17·0	8·9
51	7 57·8	7 59·1	7 36·0	5·1	2·7	11·1	5·8	17·1	9·0
52	7 58·0	7 59·3	7 36·2	5·2	2·7	11·2	5·9	17·2	9·0
53	7 58·3	7 59·6	7 36·5	5·3	2·8	11·3	5·9	17·3	9·1
54	7 58·5	7 59·8	7 36·7	5·4	2·8	11·4	6·0	17·4	9·1
55	7 58·8	8 00·1	7 36·9	5·5	2·9	11·5	6·0	17·5	9·2
56	7 59·0	8 00·3	7 37·2	5·6	2·9	11·6	6·1	17·6	9·2
57	7 59·3	8 00·6	7 37·4	5·7	3·0	11·7	6·1	17·7	9·3
58	7 59·5	8 00·8	7 37·7	5·8	3·0	11·8	6·2	17·8	9·3
59	7 59·8	8 01·1	7 37·9	5·9	3·1	11·9	6·2	17·9	9·4
60	8 00·0	8 01·3	7 38·1	6·0	3·2	12·0	6·3	18·0	9·5

32ᵐ

32 s	SUN PLANETS	ARIES	MOON	v or d Corrⁿ	v or d Corrⁿ	v or d Corrⁿ
00	8 00·0	8 01·3	7 38·1	0·0 0·0	6·0 3·3	12·0 6·5
01	8 00·3	8 01·6	7 38·4	0·1 0·1	6·1 3·3	12·1 6·6
02	8 00·5	8 01·8	7 38·6	0·2 0·1	6·2 3·4	12·2 6·6
03	8 00·8	8 02·1	7 38·8	0·3 0·2	6·3 3·4	12·3 6·7
04	8 01·0	8 02·3	7 39·1	0·4 0·2	6·4 3·5	12·4 6·7
05	8 01·3	8 02·6	7 39·3	0·5 0·3	6·5 3·5	12·5 6·8
06	8 01·5	8 02·8	7 39·6	0·6 0·3	6·6 3·6	12·6 6·8
07	8 01·8	8 03·1	7 39·8	0·7 0·4	6·7 3·6	12·7 6·9
08	8 02·0	8 03·3	7 40·0	0·8 0·4	6·8 3·7	12·8 6·9
09	8 02·3	8 03·6	7 40·3	0·9 0·5	6·9 3·7	12·9 7·0
10	8 02·5	8 03·8	7 40·5	1·0 0·5	7·0 3·8	13·0 7·0
11	8 02·8	8 04·1	7 40·8	1·1 0·6	7·1 3·8	13·1 7·1
12	8 03·0	8 04·3	7 41·0	1·2 0·7	7·2 3·9	13·2 7·2
13	8 03·3	8 04·6	7 41·2	1·3 0·7	7·3 4·0	13·3 7·2
14	8 03·5	8 04·8	7 41·5	1·4 0·8	7·4 4·0	13·4 7·3
15	8 03·8	8 05·1	7 41·7	1·5 0·8	7·5 4·1	13·5 7·3
16	8 04·0	8 05·3	7 42·0	1·6 0·9	7·6 4·1	13·6 7·4
17	8 04·3	8 05·6	7 42·2	1·7 0·9	7·7 4·2	13·7 7·4
18	8 04·5	8 05·8	7 42·4	1·8 1·0	7·8 4·2	13·8 7·5
19	8 04·8	8 06·1	7 42·7	1·9 1·0	7·9 4·3	13·9 7·5
20	8 05·0	8 06·3	7 42·9	2·0 1·1	8·0 4·3	14·0 7·6
21	8 05·3	8 06·6	7 43·1	2·1 1·1	8·1 4·4	14·1 7·6
22	8 05·5	8 06·8	7 43·4	2·2 1·2	8·2 4·4	14·2 7·7
23	8 05·8	8 07·1	7 43·6	2·3 1·2	8·3 4·5	14·3 7·7
24	8 06·0	8 07·3	7 43·9	2·4 1·3	8·4 4·6	14·4 7·8
25	8 06·3	8 07·6	7 44·1	2·5 1·4	8·5 4·6	14·5 7·9
26	8 06·5	8 07·8	7 44·3	2·6 1·4	8·6 4·7	14·6 7·9
27	8 06·8	8 08·1	7 44·6	2·7 1·5	8·7 4·7	14·7 8·0
28	8 07·0	8 08·3	7 44·8	2·8 1·5	8·8 4·8	14·8 8·0
29	8 07·3	8 08·6	7 45·1	2·9 1·6	8·9 4·8	14·9 8·1
30	8 07·5	8 08·8	7 45·3	3·0 1·6	9·0 4·9	15·0 8·1
31	8 07·8	8 09·1	7 45·5	3·1 1·7	9·1 4·9	15·1 8·2
32	8 08·0	8 09·3	7 45·8	3·2 1·7	9·2 5·0	15·2 8·2
33	8 08·3	8 09·6	7 46·0	3·3 1·8	9·3 5·0	15·3 8·3
34	8 08·5	8 09·8	7 46·2	3·4 1·8	9·4 5·1	15·4 8·3
35	8 08·8	8 10·1	7 46·5	3·5 1·9	9·5 5·1	15·5 8·4
36	8 09·0	8 10·3	7 46·7	3·6 2·0	9·6 5·2	15·6 8·5
37	8 09·3	8 10·6	7 47·0	3·7 2·0	9·7 5·3	15·7 8·5
38	8 09·5	8 10·8	7 47·2	3·8 2·1	9·8 5·3	15·8 8·6
39	8 09·8	8 11·1	7 47·4	3·9 2·1	9·9 5·4	15·9 8·6
40	8 10·0	8 11·3	7 47·7	4·0 2·2	10·0 5·4	16·0 8·7
41	8 10·3	8 11·6	7 47·9	4·1 2·2	10·1 5·5	16·1 8·7
42	8 10·5	8 11·8	7 48·2	4·2 2·3	10·2 5·5	16·2 8·8
43	8 10·8	8 12·1	7 48·4	4·3 2·3	10·3 5·6	16·3 8·8
44	8 11·0	8 12·3	7 48·6	4·4 2·4	10·4 5·6	16·4 8·9
45	8 11·3	8 12·6	7 48·9	4·5 2·4	10·5 5·7	16·5 8·9
46	8 11·5	8 12·8	7 49·1	4·6 2·5	10·6 5·7	16·6 9·0
47	8 11·8	8 13·1	7 49·3	4·7 2·5	10·7 5·8	16·7 9·0
48	8 12·0	8 13·3	7 49·6	4·8 2·6	10·8 5·9	16·8 9·1
49	8 12·3	8 13·6	7 49·8	4·9 2·7	10·9 5·9	16·9 9·2
50	8 12·5	8 13·8	7 50·1	5·0 2·7	11·0 6·0	17·0 9·2
51	8 12·8	8 14·1	7 50·3	5·1 2·8	11·1 6·0	17·1 9·3
52	8 13·0	8 14·3	7 50·5	5·2 2·8	11·2 6·1	17·2 9·3
53	8 13·3	8 14·6	7 50·8	5·3 2·9	11·3 6·1	17·3 9·4
54	8 13·5	8 14·9	7 51·0	5·4 2·9	11·4 6·2	17·4 9·4
55	8 13·8	8 15·1	7 51·3	5·5 3·0	11·5 6·2	17·5 9·5
56	8 14·0	8 15·4	7 51·5	5·6 3·0	11·6 6·3	17·6 9·5
57	8 14·3	8 15·6	7 51·7	5·7 3·1	11·7 6·3	17·7 9·6
58	8 14·5	8 15·9	7 52·0	5·8 3·1	11·8 6·4	17·8 9·6
59	8 14·8	8 16·1	7 52·2	5·9 3·2	11·9 6·4	17·9 9·7
60	8 15·0	8 16·4	7 52·5	6·0 3·3	12·0 6·5	18·0 9·8

33ᵐ

33 s	SUN PLANETS	ARIES	MOON	v or d Corrⁿ	v or d Corrⁿ	v or d Corrⁿ
00	8 15·0	8 16·4	7 52·5	0·0 0·0	6·0 3·4	12·0 6·7
01	8 15·3	8 16·6	7 52·7	0·1 0·1	6·1 3·4	12·1 6·8
02	8 15·5	8 16·9	7 52·9	0·2 0·1	6·2 3·5	12·2 6·8
03	8 15·8	8 17·1	7 53·2	0·3 0·2	6·3 3·5	12·3 6·9
04	8 16·0	8 17·4	7 53·4	0·4 0·2	6·4 3·6	12·4 6·9
05	8 16·3	8 17·6	7 53·6	0·5 0·3	6·5 3·6	12·5 7·0
06	8 16·5	8 17·9	7 53·9	0·6 0·3	6·6 3·7	12·6 7·0
07	8 16·8	8 18·1	7 54·1	0·7 0·4	6·7 3·7	12·7 7·1
08	8 17·0	8 18·4	7 54·4	0·8 0·4	6·8 3·8	12·8 7·1
09	8 17·3	8 18·6	7 54·6	0·9 0·5	6·9 3·9	12·9 7·2
10	8 17·5	8 18·9	7 54·8	1·0 0·6	7·0 3·9	13·0 7·3
11	8 17·8	8 19·1	7 55·1	1·1 0·6	7·1 4·0	13·1 7·3
12	8 18·0	8 19·4	7 55·3	1·2 0·7	7·2 4·0	13·2 7·4
13	8 18·3	8 19·6	7 55·6	1·3 0·7	7·3 4·1	13·3 7·4
14	8 18·5	8 19·9	7 55·8	1·4 0·8	7·4 4·1	13·4 7·5
15	8 18·8	8 20·1	7 56·0	1·5 0·8	7·5 4·2	13·5 7·5
16	8 19·0	8 20·4	7 56·3	1·6 0·9	7·6 4·2	13·6 7·6
17	8 19·3	8 20·6	7 56·5	1·7 0·9	7·7 4·3	13·7 7·6
18	8 19·5	8 20·9	7 56·7	1·8 1·0	7·8 4·4	13·8 7·7
19	8 19·8	8 21·1	7 57·0	1·9 1·1	7·9 4·4	13·9 7·8
20	8 20·0	8 21·4	7 57·2	2·0 1·1	8·0 4·5	14·0 7·8
21	8 20·3	8 21·6	7 57·5	2·1 1·2	8·1 4·5	14·1 7·9
22	8 20·5	8 21·9	7 57·7	2·2 1·2	8·2 4·6	14·2 7·9
23	8 20·8	8 22·1	7 57·9	2·3 1·3	8·3 4·6	14·3 8·0
24	8 21·0	8 22·4	7 58·2	2·4 1·3	8·4 4·7	14·4 8·0
25	8 21·3	8 22·6	7 58·4	2·5 1·4	8·5 4·7	14·5 8·1
26	8 21·5	8 22·9	7 58·7	2·6 1·5	8·6 4·8	14·6 8·2
27	8 21·8	8 23·1	7 58·9	2·7 1·5	8·7 4·9	14·7 8·2
28	8 22·0	8 23·4	7 59·1	2·8 1·6	8·8 4·9	14·8 8·3
29	8 22·3	8 23·6	7 59·4	2·9 1·6	8·9 5·0	14·9 8·3
30	8 22·5	8 23·9	7 59·6	3·0 1·7	9·0 5·0	15·0 8·4
31	8 22·8	8 24·1	7 59·8	3·1 1·7	9·1 5·1	15·1 8·4
32	8 23·0	8 24·4	8 00·1	3·2 1·8	9·2 5·1	15·2 8·5
33	8 23·3	8 24·6	8 00·3	3·3 1·8	9·3 5·2	15·3 8·5
34	8 23·5	8 24·9	8 00·6	3·4 1·9	9·4 5·2	15·4 8·6
35	8 23·8	8 25·1	8 00·8	3·5 2·0	9·5 5·3	15·5 8·7
36	8 24·0	8 25·4	8 01·0	3·6 2·0	9·6 5·4	15·6 8·7
37	8 24·3	8 25·6	8 01·3	3·7 2·1	9·7 5·4	15·7 8·8
38	8 24·5	8 25·9	8 01·5	3·8 2·1	9·8 5·5	15·8 8·8
39	8 24·8	8 26·1	8 01·8	3·9 2·2	9·9 5·5	15·9 8·9
40	8 25·0	8 26·4	8 02·0	4·0 2·2	10·0 5·6	16·0 8·9
41	8 25·3	8 26·6	8 02·2	4·1 2·3	10·1 5·6	16·1 9·0
42	8 25·5	8 26·9	8 02·5	4·2 2·3	10·2 5·7	16·2 9·0
43	8 25·8	8 27·1	8 02·7	4·3 2·4	10·3 5·8	16·3 9·1
44	8 26·0	8 27·4	8 02·9	4·4 2·5	10·4 5·8	16·4 9·2
45	8 26·3	8 27·6	8 03·2	4·5 2·5	10·5 5·9	16·5 9·2
46	8 26·5	8 27·9	8 03·4	4·6 2·6	10·6 5·9	16·6 9·3
47	8 26·8	8 28·1	8 03·7	4·7 2·6	10·7 6·0	16·7 9·3
48	8 27·0	8 28·4	8 03·9	4·8 2·7	10·8 6·0	16·8 9·4
49	8 27·3	8 28·6	8 04·1	4·9 2·7	10·9 6·1	16·9 9·4
50	8 27·5	8 28·9	8 04·4	5·0 2·8	11·0 6·1	17·0 9·5
51	8 27·8	8 29·1	8 04·6	5·1 2·8	11·1 6·2	17·1 9·5
52	8 28·0	8 29·4	8 04·9	5·2 2·9	11·2 6·3	17·2 9·6
53	8 28·3	8 29·6	8 05·1	5·3 3·0	11·3 6·3	17·3 9·7
54	8 28·5	8 29·9	8 05·3	5·4 3·0	11·4 6·4	17·4 9·7
55	8 28·8	8 30·1	8 05·6	5·5 3·1	11·5 6·4	17·5 9·8
56	8 29·0	8 30·4	8 05·8	5·6 3·1	11·6 6·5	17·6 9·8
57	8 29·3	8 30·6	8 06·1	5·7 3·2	11·7 6·5	17·7 9·9
58	8 29·5	8 30·9	8 06·3	5·8 3·2	11·8 6·6	17·8 9·9
59	8 29·8	8 31·1	8 06·5	5·9 3·3	11·9 6·6	17·9 10·0
60	8 30·0	8 31·4	8 06·8	6·0 3·4	12·0 6·7	18·0 10·1

34ᵐ

s	SUN PLANETS	ARIES	MOON	v or d	Corrⁿ	v or d	Corrⁿ	v or d	Corrⁿ
	° ′	° ′	° ′	′	′	′	′	′	′
00	8 30.0	8 31.4	8 06.8	0.0	0.0	6.0	3.5	12.0	6.9
01	8 30.3	8 31.6	8 07.0	0.1	0.1	6.1	3.5	12.1	7.0
02	8 30.5	8 31.9	8 07.2	0.2	0.1	6.2	3.6	12.2	7.0
03	8 30.8	8 32.1	8 07.5	0.3	0.2	6.3	3.6	12.3	7.1
04	8 31.0	8 32.4	8 07.7	0.4	0.2	6.4	3.7	12.4	7.1
05	8 31.3	8 32.6	8 08.0	0.5	0.3	6.5	3.7	12.5	7.2
06	8 31.5	8 32.9	8 08.2	0.6	0.3	6.6	3.8	12.6	7.2
07	8 31.8	8 33.2	8 08.4	0.7	0.4	6.7	3.9	12.7	7.3
08	8 32.0	8 33.4	8 08.7	0.8	0.5	6.8	3.9	12.8	7.4
09	8 32.3	8 33.7	8 08.9	0.9	0.5	6.9	4.0	12.9	7.4
10	8 32.5	8 33.9	8 09.2	1.0	0.6	7.0	4.0	13.0	7.5
11	8 32.8	8 34.2	8 09.4	1.1	0.6	7.1	4.1	13.1	7.5
12	8 33.0	8 34.4	8 09.6	1.2	0.7	7.2	4.1	13.2	7.6
13	8 33.3	8 34.7	8 09.9	1.3	0.7	7.3	4.2	13.3	7.6
14	8 33.5	8 34.9	8 10.1	1.4	0.8	7.4	4.3	13.4	7.7
15	8 33.8	8 35.2	8 10.3	1.5	0.9	7.5	4.3	13.5	7.8
16	8 34.0	8 35.4	8 10.6	1.6	0.9	7.6	4.4	13.6	7.8
17	8 34.3	8 35.7	8 10.8	1.7	1.0	7.7	4.4	13.7	7.9
18	8 34.5	8 35.9	8 11.1	1.8	1.0	7.8	4.5	13.8	7.9
19	8 34.8	8 36.2	8 11.3	1.9	1.1	7.9	4.5	13.9	8.0
20	8 35.0	8 36.4	8 11.5	2.0	1.2	8.0	4.6	14.0	8.1
21	8 35.3	8 36.7	8 11.8	2.1	1.2	8.1	4.7	14.1	8.1
22	8 35.5	8 36.9	8 12.0	2.2	1.3	8.2	4.7	14.2	8.2
23	8 35.8	8 37.2	8 12.3	2.3	1.3	8.3	4.8	14.3	8.2
24	8 36.0	8 37.4	8 12.5	2.4	1.4	8.4	4.8	14.4	8.3
25	8 36.3	8 37.7	8 12.7	2.5	1.4	8.5	4.9	14.5	8.3
26	8 36.5	8 37.9	8 13.0	2.6	1.5	8.6	4.9	14.6	8.4
27	8 36.8	8 38.2	8 13.2	2.7	1.6	8.7	5.0	14.7	8.5
28	8 37.0	8 38.4	8 13.4	2.8	1.6	8.8	5.1	14.8	8.5
29	8 37.3	8 38.7	8 13.7	2.9	1.7	8.9	5.1	14.9	8.6
30	8 37.5	8 38.9	8 13.9	3.0	1.7	9.0	5.2	15.0	8.6
31	8 37.8	8 39.2	8 14.2	3.1	1.8	9.1	5.2	15.1	8.7
32	8 38.0	8 39.4	8 14.4	3.2	1.8	9.2	5.3	15.2	8.7
33	8 38.3	8 39.7	8 14.6	3.3	1.9	9.3	5.3	15.3	8.8
34	8 38.5	8 39.9	8 14.9	3.4	2.0	9.4	5.4	15.4	8.9
35	8 38.8	8 40.2	8 15.1	3.5	2.0	9.5	5.5	15.5	8.9
36	8 39.0	8 40.4	8 15.4	3.6	2.1	9.6	5.5	15.6	9.0
37	8 39.3	8 40.7	8 15.6	3.7	2.1	9.7	5.6	15.7	9.0
38	8 39.5	8 40.9	8 15.8	3.8	2.2	9.8	5.6	15.8	9.1
39	8 39.8	8 41.2	8 16.1	3.9	2.2	9.9	5.7	15.9	9.1
40	8 40.0	8 41.4	8 16.3	4.0	2.3	10.0	5.8	16.0	9.2
41	8 40.3	8 41.7	8 16.5	4.1	2.4	10.1	5.8	16.1	9.3
42	8 40.5	8 41.9	8 16.8	4.2	2.4	10.2	5.9	16.2	9.3
43	8 40.8	8 42.2	8 17.0	4.3	2.5	10.3	5.9	16.3	9.4
44	8 41.0	8 42.4	8 17.3	4.4	2.5	10.4	6.0	16.4	9.4
45	8 41.3	8 42.7	8 17.5	4.5	2.6	10.5	6.0	16.5	9.5
46	8 41.5	8 42.9	8 17.7	4.6	2.6	10.6	6.1	16.6	9.5
47	8 41.8	8 43.2	8 18.0	4.7	2.7	10.7	6.2	16.7	9.6
48	8 42.0	8 43.4	8 18.2	4.8	2.8	10.8	6.2	16.8	9.7
49	8 42.3	8 43.7	8 18.5	4.9	2.8	10.9	6.3	16.9	9.7
50	8 42.5	8 43.9	8 18.7	5.0	2.9	11.0	6.3	17.0	9.8
51	8 42.8	8 44.2	8 18.9	5.1	2.9	11.1	6.4	17.1	9.8
52	8 43.0	8 44.4	8 19.2	5.2	3.0	11.2	6.4	17.2	9.9
53	8 43.3	8 44.7	8 19.4	5.3	3.0	11.3	6.5	17.3	9.9
54	8 43.5	8 44.9	8 19.7	5.4	3.1	11.4	6.6	17.4	10.0
55	8 43.8	8 45.2	8 19.9	5.5	3.2	11.5	6.6	17.5	10.1
56	8 44.0	8 45.4	8 20.1	5.6	3.2	11.6	6.7	17.6	10.1
57	8 44.3	8 45.7	8 20.4	5.7	3.3	11.7	6.7	17.7	10.2
58	8 44.5	8 45.9	8 20.6	5.8	3.3	11.8	6.8	17.8	10.2
59	8 44.8	8 46.2	8 20.8	5.9	3.4	11.9	6.8	17.9	10.3
60	8 45.0	8 46.4	8 21.1	6.0	3.5	12.0	6.9	18.0	10.4

35ᵐ

s	SUN PLANETS	ARIES	MOON	v or d	Corrⁿ	v or d	Corrⁿ	v or d	Corrⁿ
	° ′	° ′	° ′	′	′	′	′	′	′
00	8 45.0	8 46.4	8 21.1	0.0	0.0	6.0	3.6	12.0	7.1
01	8 45.3	8 46.7	8 21.3	0.1	0.1	6.1	3.6	12.1	7.2
02	8 45.5	8 46.9	8 21.6	0.2	0.1	6.2	3.7	12.2	7.2
03	8 45.8	8 47.2	8 21.8	0.3	0.2	6.3	3.7	12.3	7.3
04	8 46.0	8 47.4	8 22.0	0.4	0.2	6.4	3.8	12.4	7.3
05	8 46.3	8 47.7	8 22.3	0.5	0.3	6.5	3.8	12.5	7.4
06	8 46.5	8 47.9	8 22.5	0.6	0.4	6.6	3.9	12.6	7.5
07	8 46.8	8 48.2	8 22.8	0.7	0.4	6.7	4.0	12.7	7.5
08	8 47.0	8 48.4	8 23.0	0.8	0.5	6.8	4.0	12.8	7.6
09	8 47.3	8 48.7	8 23.2	0.9	0.5	6.9	4.1	12.9	7.6
10	8 47.5	8 48.9	8 23.5	1.0	0.6	7.0	4.1	13.0	7.7
11	8 47.8	8 49.2	8 23.7	1.1	0.7	7.1	4.2	13.1	7.8
12	8 48.0	8 49.4	8 23.9	1.2	0.7	7.2	4.3	13.2	7.8
13	8 48.3	8 49.7	8 24.2	1.3	0.8	7.3	4.3	13.3	7.9
14	8 48.5	8 49.9	8 24.4	1.4	0.8	7.4	4.4	13.4	7.9
15	8 48.8	8 50.2	8 24.7	1.5	0.9	7.5	4.4	13.5	8.0
16	8 49.0	8 50.4	8 24.9	1.6	0.9	7.6	4.5	13.6	8.0
17	8 49.3	8 50.7	8 25.1	1.7	1.0	7.7	4.6	13.7	8.1
18	8 49.5	8 50.9	8 25.4	1.8	1.1	7.8	4.6	13.8	8.2
19	8 49.8	8 51.2	8 25.6	1.9	1.1	7.9	4.7	13.9	8.2
20	8 50.0	8 51.5	8 25.9	2.0	1.2	8.0	4.7	14.0	8.3
21	8 50.3	8 51.7	8 26.1	2.1	1.2	8.1	4.8	14.1	8.3
22	8 50.5	8 52.0	8 26.3	2.2	1.3	8.2	4.9	14.2	8.4
23	8 50.8	8 52.2	8 26.6	2.3	1.4	8.3	4.9	14.3	8.5
24	8 51.0	8 52.5	8 26.8	2.4	1.4	8.4	5.0	14.4	8.5
25	8 51.3	8 52.7	8 27.0	2.5	1.5	8.5	5.0	14.5	8.6
26	8 51.5	8 53.0	8 27.3	2.6	1.5	8.6	5.1	14.6	8.6
27	8 51.8	8 53.2	8 27.5	2.7	1.6	8.7	5.1	14.7	8.7
28	8 52.0	8 53.5	8 27.8	2.8	1.7	8.8	5.2	14.8	8.8
29	8 52.3	8 53.7	8 28.0	2.9	1.7	8.9	5.3	14.9	8.8
30	8 52.5	8 54.0	8 28.2	3.0	1.8	9.0	5.3	15.0	8.9
31	8 52.8	8 54.2	8 28.5	3.1	1.8	9.1	5.4	15.1	8.9
32	8 53.0	8 54.5	8 28.7	3.2	1.9	9.2	5.4	15.2	9.0
33	8 53.3	8 54.7	8 29.0	3.3	2.0	9.3	5.5	15.3	9.1
34	8 53.5	8 55.0	8 29.2	3.4	2.0	9.4	5.6	15.4	9.1
35	8 53.8	8 55.2	8 29.4	3.5	2.1	9.5	5.6	15.5	9.2
36	8 54.0	8 55.5	8 29.7	3.6	2.1	9.6	5.7	15.6	9.2
37	8 54.3	8 55.7	8 29.9	3.7	2.2	9.7	5.7	15.7	9.3
38	8 54.5	8 56.0	8 30.2	3.8	2.2	9.8	5.8	15.8	9.3
39	8 54.8	8 56.2	8 30.4	3.9	2.3	9.9	5.9	15.9	9.4
40	8 55.0	8 56.5	8 30.6	4.0	2.4	10.0	5.9	16.0	9.5
41	8 55.3	8 56.7	8 30.9	4.1	2.4	10.1	6.0	16.1	9.5
42	8 55.5	8 57.0	8 31.1	4.2	2.5	10.2	6.0	16.2	9.6
43	8 55.8	8 57.2	8 31.3	4.3	2.5	10.3	6.1	16.3	9.6
44	8 56.0	8 57.5	8 31.6	4.4	2.6	10.4	6.2	16.4	9.7
45	8 56.3	8 57.7	8 31.8	4.5	2.7	10.5	6.2	16.5	9.8
46	8 56.5	8 58.0	8 32.1	4.6	2.7	10.6	6.3	16.6	9.8
47	8 56.8	8 58.2	8 32.3	4.7	2.8	10.7	6.3	16.7	9.9
48	8 57.0	8 58.5	8 32.5	4.8	2.8	10.8	6.4	16.8	9.9
49	8 57.3	8 58.7	8 32.8	4.9	2.9	10.9	6.4	16.9	10.0
50	8 57.5	8 59.0	8 33.0	5.0	3.0	11.0	6.5	17.0	10.1
51	8 57.8	8 59.2	8 33.3	5.1	3.0	11.1	6.6	17.1	10.1
52	8 58.0	8 59.5	8 33.5	5.2	3.1	11.2	6.6	17.2	10.2
53	8 58.3	8 59.7	8 33.7	5.3	3.1	11.3	6.7	17.3	10.2
54	8 58.5	9 00.0	8 34.0	5.4	3.2	11.4	6.7	17.4	10.3
55	8 58.8	9 00.2	8 34.2	5.5	3.3	11.5	6.8	17.5	10.4
56	8 59.0	9 00.5	8 34.4	5.6	3.3	11.6	6.9	17.6	10.4
57	8 59.3	9 00.7	8 34.7	5.7	3.4	11.7	6.9	17.7	10.5
58	8 59.5	9 01.0	8 34.9	5.8	3.4	11.8	7.0	17.8	10.5
59	8 59.8	9 01.2	8 35.2	5.9	3.5	11.9	7.0	17.9	10.6
60	9 00.0	9 01.5	8 35.4	6.0	3.6	12.0	7.1	18.0	10.7

36ᵐ

s	SUN PLANETS ° ′	ARIES ° ′	MOON ° ′	v or d	Corrⁿ	v or d	Corrⁿ	v or d	Corrⁿ
00	9 00·0	9 01·5	8 35·4	0·0	0·0	6·0	3·7	12·0	7·3
01	9 00·3	9 01·7	8 35·6	0·1	0·1	6·1	3·7	12·1	7·4
02	9 00·5	9 02·0	8 35·9	0·2	0·1	6·2	3·8	12·2	7·4
03	9 00·8	9 02·2	8 36·1	0·3	0·2	6·3	3·8	12·3	7·5
04	9 01·0	9 02·5	8 36·4	0·4	0·2	6·4	3·9	12·4	7·5
05	9 01·3	9 02·7	8 36·6	0·5	0·3	6·5	4·0	12·5	7·6
06	9 01·5	9 03·0	8 36·8	0·6	0·4	6·6	4·0	12·6	7·7
07	9 01·8	9 03·2	8 37·1	0·7	0·4	6·7	4·1	12·7	7·7
08	9 02·0	9 03·5	8 37·3	0·8	0·5	6·8	4·1	12·8	7·8
09	9 02·3	9 03·7	8 37·5	0·9	0·5	6·9	4·2	12·9	7·8
10	9 02·5	9 04·0	8 37·8	1·0	0·6	7·0	4·3	13·0	7·9
11	9 02·8	9 04·2	8 38·0	1·1	0·7	7·1	4·3	13·1	8·0
12	9 03·0	9 04·5	8 38·3	1·2	0·7	7·2	4·4	13·2	8·0
13	9 03·3	9 04·7	8 38·5	1·3	0·8	7·3	4·4	13·3	8·1
14	9 03·5	9 05·0	8 38·7	1·4	0·8	7·4	4·5	13·4	8·2
15	9 03·8	9 05·2	8 39·0	1·5	0·9	7·5	4·6	13·5	8·2
16	9 04·0	9 05·5	8 39·2	1·6	1·0	7·6	4·6	13·6	8·3
17	9 04·3	9 05·7	8 39·5	1·7	1·0	7·7	4·7	13·7	8·3
18	9 04·5	9 06·0	8 39·7	1·8	1·1	7·8	4·7	13·8	8·4
19	9 04·8	9 06·2	8 39·9	1·9	1·2	7·9	4·8	13·9	8·5
20	9 05·0	9 06·5	8 40·2	2·0	1·2	8·0	4·9	14·0	8·5
21	9 05·3	9 06·7	8 40·4	2·1	1·3	8·1	4·9	14·1	8·6
22	9 05·5	9 07·0	8 40·6	2·2	1·3	8·2	5·0	14·2	8·6
23	9 05·8	9 07·2	8 40·9	2·3	1·4	8·3	5·0	14·3	8·7
24	9 06·0	9 07·5	8 41·1	2·4	1·5	8·4	5·1	14·4	8·8
25	9 06·3	9 07·7	8 41·4	2·5	1·5	8·5	5·2	14·5	8·8
26	9 06·5	9 08·0	8 41·6	2·6	1·6	8·6	5·2	14·6	8·9
27	9 06·8	9 08·2	8 41·8	2·7	1·6	8·7	5·3	14·7	8·9
28	9 07·0	9 08·5	8 42·1	2·8	1·7	8·8	5·4	14·8	9·0
29	9 07·3	9 08·7	8 42·3	2·9	1·8	8·9	5·4	14·9	9·1
30	9 07·5	9 09·0	8 42·6	3·0	1·8	9·0	5·5	15·0	9·1
31	9 07·8	9 09·2	8 42·8	3·1	1·9	9·1	5·5	15·1	9·2
32	9 08·0	9 09·5	8 43·0	3·2	1·9	9·2	5·6	15·2	9·2
33	9 08·3	9 09·8	8 43·3	3·3	2·0	9·3	5·7	15·3	9·3
34	9 08·5	9 10·0	8 43·5	3·4	2·1	9·4	5·7	15·4	9·4
35	9 08·8	9 10·3	8 43·8	3·5	2·1	9·5	5·8	15·5	9·4
36	9 09·0	9 10·5	8 44·0	3·6	2·2	9·6	5·8	15·6	9·5
37	9 09·3	9 10·8	8 44·2	3·7	2·3	9·7	5·9	15·7	9·6
38	9 09·5	9 11·0	8 44·5	3·8	2·3	9·8	6·0	15·8	9·6
39	9 09·8	9 11·3	8 44·7	3·9	2·4	9·9	6·0	15·9	9·7
40	9 10·0	9 11·5	8 44·9	4·0	2·4	10·0	6·1	16·0	9·7
41	9 10·3	9 11·8	8 45·2	4·1	2·5	10·1	6·1	16·1	9·8
42	9 10·5	9 12·0	8 45·4	4·2	2·6	10·2	6·2	16·2	9·9
43	9 10·8	9 12·3	8 45·7	4·3	2·6	10·3	6·3	16·3	9·9
44	9 11·0	9 12·5	8 45·9	4·4	2·7	10·4	6·3	16·4	10·0
45	9 11·3	9 12·8	8 46·1	4·5	2·7	10·5	6·4	16·5	10·0
46	9 11·5	9 13·0	8 46·4	4·6	2·8	10·6	6·4	16·6	10·1
47	9 11·8	9 13·3	8 46·6	4·7	2·9	10·7	6·5	16·7	10·2
48	9 12·0	9 13·5	8 46·9	4·8	2·9	10·8	6·6	16·8	10·2
49	9 12·3	9 13·8	8 47·1	4·9	3·0	10·9	6·6	16·9	10·3
50	9 12·5	9 14·0	8 47·3	5·0	3·0	11·0	6·7	17·0	10·3
51	9 12·8	9 14·3	8 47·6	5·1	3·1	11·1	6·8	17·1	10·4
52	9 13·0	9 14·5	8 47·8	5·2	3·2	11·2	6·8	17·2	10·5
53	9 13·3	9 14·8	8 48·0	5·3	3·2	11·3	6·9	17·3	10·5
54	9 13·5	9 15·0	8 48·3	5·4	3·3	11·4	6·9	17·4	10·6
55	9 13·8	9 15·3	8 48·5	5·5	3·3	11·5	7·0	17·5	10·6
56	9 14·0	9 15·5	8 48·8	5·6	3·4	11·6	7·1	17·6	10·7
57	9 14·3	9 15·8	8 49·0	5·7	3·5	11·7	7·1	17·7	10·8
58	9 14·5	9 16·0	8 49·2	5·8	3·5	11·8	7·2	17·8	10·8
59	9 14·8	9 16·3	8 49·5	5·9	3·6	11·9	7·2	17·9	10·9
60	9 15·0	9 16·5	8 49·7	6·0	3·7	12·0	7·3	18·0	11·0

37ᵐ

s	SUN PLANETS ° ′	ARIES ° ′	MOON ° ′	v or d	Corrⁿ	v or d	Corrⁿ	v or d	Corrⁿ
00	9 15·0	9 16·5	8 49·7	0·0	0·0	6·0	3·8	12·0	7·5
01	9 15·3	9 16·8	8 50·0	0·1	0·1	6·1	3·8	12·1	7·6
02	9 15·5	9 17·0	8 50·2	0·2	0·1	6·2	3·9	12·2	7·6
03	9 15·8	9 17·3	8 50·4	0·3	0·2	6·3	3·9	12·3	7·7
04	9 16·0	9 17·5	8 50·7	0·4	0·3	6·4	4·0	12·4	7·8
05	9 16·3	9 17·8	8 50·9	0·5	0·3	6·5	4·1	12·5	7·8
06	9 16·5	9 18·0	8 51·1	0·6	0·4	6·6	4·1	12·6	7·9
07	9 16·8	9 18·3	8 51·4	0·7	0·4	6·7	4·2	12·7	7·9
08	9 17·0	9 18·5	8 51·6	0·8	0·5	6·8	4·3	12·8	8·0
09	9 17·3	9 18·8	8 51·9	0·9	0·6	6·9	4·3	12·9	8·1
10	9 17·5	9 19·0	8 52·1	1·0	0·6	7·0	4·4	13·0	8·1
11	9 17·8	9 19·3	8 52·3	1·1	0·7	7·1	4·4	13·1	8·2
12	9 18·0	9 19·5	8 52·6	1·2	0·8	7·2	4·5	13·2	8·3
13	9 18·3	9 19·8	8 52·8	1·3	0·8	7·3	4·6	13·3	8·3
14	9 18·5	9 20·0	8 53·1	1·4	0·9	7·4	4·6	13·4	8·4
15	9 18·8	9 20·3	8 53·3	1·5	0·9	7·5	4·7	13·5	8·4
16	9 19·0	9 20·5	8 53·5	1·6	1·0	7·6	4·8	13·6	8·5
17	9 19·3	9 20·8	8 53·8	1·7	1·1	7·7	4·8	13·7	8·6
18	9 19·5	9 21·0	8 54·0	1·8	1·1	7·8	4·9	13·8	8·6
19	9 19·8	9 21·3	8 54·3	1·9	1·2	7·9	4·9	13·9	8·7
20	9 20·0	9 21·5	8 54·5	2·0	1·3	8·0	5·0	14·0	8·8
21	9 20·3	9 21·8	8 54·7	2·1	1·3	8·1	5·1	14·1	8·8
22	9 20·5	9 22·0	8 55·0	2·2	1·4	8·2	5·1	14·2	8·9
23	9 20·8	9 22·3	8 55·2	2·3	1·4	8·3	5·2	14·3	8·9
24	9 21·0	9 22·5	8 55·4	2·4	1·5	8·4	5·3	14·4	9·0
25	9 21·3	9 22·8	8 55·7	2·5	1·6	8·5	5·3	14·5	9·1
26	9 21·5	9 23·0	8 55·9	2·6	1·6	8·6	5·4	14·6	9·1
27	9 21·8	9 23·3	8 56·2	2·7	1·7	8·7	5·4	14·7	9·2
28	9 22·0	9 23·5	8 56·4	2·8	1·8	8·8	5·5	14·8	9·3
29	9 22·3	9 23·8	8 56·6	2·9	1·8	8·9	5·6	14·9	9·3
30	9 22·5	9 24·0	8 56·9	3·0	1·9	9·0	5·6	15·0	9·4
31	9 22·8	9 24·3	8 57·1	3·1	1·9	9·1	5·7	15·1	9·4
32	9 23·0	9 24·5	8 57·4	3·2	2·0	9·2	5·8	15·2	9·5
33	9 23·3	9 24·8	8 57·6	3·3	2·1	9·3	5·8	15·3	9·6
34	9 23·5	9 25·0	8 57·8	3·4	2·1	9·4	5·9	15·4	9·6
35	9 23·8	9 25·3	8 58·1	3·5	2·2	9·5	5·9	15·5	9·7
36	9 24·0	9 25·5	8 58·3	3·6	2·3	9·6	6·0	15·6	9·8
37	9 24·3	9 25·8	8 58·5	3·7	2·3	9·7	6·1	15·7	9·8
38	9 24·5	9 26·0	8 58·8	3·8	2·4	9·8	6·1	15·8	9·9
39	9 24·8	9 26·3	8 59·0	3·9	2·4	9·9	6·2	15·9	9·9
40	9 25·0	9 26·5	8 59·3	4·0	2·5	10·0	6·3	16·0	10·0
41	9 25·3	9 26·8	8 59·5	4·1	2·6	10·1	6·3	16·1	10·1
42	9 25·5	9 27·0	8 59·7	4·2	2·6	10·2	6·4	16·2	10·1
43	9 25·8	9 27·3	9 00·0	4·3	2·7	10·3	6·4	16·3	10·2
44	9 26·0	9 27·5	9 00·2	4·4	2·8	10·4	6·5	16·4	10·3
45	9 26·3	9 27·8	9 00·5	4·5	2·8	10·5	6·6	16·5	10·3
46	9 26·5	9 28·1	9 00·7	4·6	2·9	10·6	6·6	16·6	10·4
47	9 26·8	9 28·3	9 00·9	4·7	2·9	10·7	6·7	16·7	10·4
48	9 27·0	9 28·6	9 01·2	4·8	3·0	10·8	6·8	16·8	10·5
49	9 27·3	9 28·8	9 01·4	4·9	3·1	10·9	6·8	16·9	10·6
50	9 27·5	9 29·1	9 01·6	5·0	3·1	11·0	6·9	17·0	10·6
51	9 27·8	9 29·3	9 01·9	5·1	3·2	11·1	6·9	17·1	10·7
52	9 28·0	9 29·6	9 02·1	5·2	3·3	11·2	7·0	17·2	10·8
53	9 28·3	9 29·8	9 02·4	5·3	3·3	11·3	7·1	17·3	10·8
54	9 28·5	9 30·1	9 02·6	5·4	3·4	11·4	7·1	17·4	10·9
55	9 28·8	9 30·3	9 02·8	5·5	3·4	11·5	7·2	17·5	10·9
56	9 29·0	9 30·6	9 03·1	5·6	3·5	11·6	7·3	17·6	11·0
57	9 29·3	9 30·8	9 03·3	5·7	3·6	11·7	7·3	17·7	11·1
58	9 29·5	9 31·1	9 03·6	5·8	3·6	11·8	7·4	17·8	11·1
59	9 29·8	9 31·3	9 03·8	5·9	3·7	11·9	7·4	17·9	11·2
60	9 30·0	9 31·6	9 04·0	6·0	3·8	12·0	7·5	18·0	11·3

38ᵐ

38 s	SUN PLANETS	ARIES	MOON	v or d	Corrⁿ	v or d	Corrⁿ	v or d	Corrⁿ
00	9 30.0	9 31.6	9 04.0	0.0	0.0	6.0	3.9	12.0	7.7
01	9 30.3	9 31.8	9 04.3	0.1	0.1	6.1	3.9	12.1	7.8
02	9 30.5	9 32.1	9 04.5	0.2	0.1	6.2	4.0	12.2	7.8
03	9 30.8	9 32.3	9 04.7	0.3	0.2	6.3	4.0	12.3	7.9
04	9 31.0	9 32.6	9 05.0	0.4	0.3	6.4	4.1	12.4	8.0
05	9 31.3	9 32.8	9 05.2	0.5	0.3	6.5	4.2	12.5	8.0
06	9 31.5	9 33.1	9 05.5	0.6	0.4	6.6	4.2	12.6	8.1
07	9 31.8	9 33.3	9 05.7	0.7	0.4	6.7	4.3	12.7	8.1
08	9 32.0	9 33.6	9 05.9	0.8	0.5	6.8	4.4	12.8	8.2
09	9 32.3	9 33.8	9 06.2	0.9	0.6	6.9	4.4	12.9	8.3
10	9 32.5	9 34.1	9 06.4	1.0	0.6	7.0	4.5	13.0	8.3
11	9 32.8	9 34.3	9 06.7	1.1	0.7	7.1	4.6	13.1	8.4
12	9 33.0	9 34.6	9 06.9	1.2	0.8	7.2	4.6	13.2	8.5
13	9 33.3	9 34.8	9 07.1	1.3	0.8	7.3	4.7	13.3	8.5
14	9 33.5	9 35.1	9 07.4	1.4	0.9	7.4	4.7	13.4	8.6
15	9 33.8	9 35.3	9 07.6	1.5	1.0	7.5	4.8	13.5	8.7
16	9 34.0	9 35.6	9 07.9	1.6	1.0	7.6	4.9	13.6	8.7
17	9 34.3	9 35.8	9 08.1	1.7	1.1	7.7	4.9	13.7	8.8
18	9 34.5	9 36.1	9 08.3	1.8	1.2	7.8	5.0	13.8	8.9
19	9 34.8	9 36.3	9 08.6	1.9	1.2	7.9	5.1	13.9	8.9
20	9 35.0	9 36.6	9 08.8	2.0	1.3	8.0	5.1	14.0	9.0
21	9 35.3	9 36.8	9 09.0	2.1	1.3	8.1	5.2	14.1	9.0
22	9 35.5	9 37.1	9 09.3	2.2	1.4	8.2	5.3	14.2	9.1
23	9 35.8	9 37.3	9 09.5	2.3	1.5	8.3	5.3	14.3	9.2
24	9 36.0	9 37.6	9 09.8	2.4	1.5	8.4	5.4	14.4	9.2
25	9 36.3	9 37.8	9 10.0	2.5	1.6	8.5	5.5	14.5	9.3
26	9 36.5	9 38.1	9 10.2	2.6	1.7	8.6	5.5	14.6	9.4
27	9 36.8	9 38.3	9 10.5	2.7	1.7	8.7	5.6	14.7	9.4
28	9 37.0	9 38.6	9 10.7	2.8	1.8	8.8	5.6	14.8	9.5
29	9 37.3	9 38.8	9 11.0	2.9	1.9	8.9	5.7	14.9	9.6
30	9 37.5	9 39.1	9 11.2	3.0	1.9	9.0	5.8	15.0	9.6
31	9 37.8	9 39.3	9 11.4	3.1	2.0	9.1	5.8	15.1	9.7
32	9 38.0	9 39.6	9 11.7	3.2	2.1	9.2	5.9	15.2	9.8
33	9 38.3	9 39.8	9 11.9	3.3	2.1	9.3	6.0	15.3	9.8
34	9 38.5	9 40.1	9 12.1	3.4	2.2	9.4	6.0	15.4	9.9
35	9 38.8	9 40.3	9 12.4	3.5	2.2	9.5	6.1	15.5	9.9
36	9 39.0	9 40.6	9 12.6	3.6	2.3	9.6	6.2	15.6	10.0
37	9 39.3	9 40.8	9 12.9	3.7	2.4	9.7	6.2	15.7	10.1
38	9 39.5	9 41.1	9 13.1	3.8	2.4	9.8	6.3	15.8	10.1
39	9 39.8	9 41.3	9 13.3	3.9	2.5	9.9	6.4	15.9	10.2
40	9 40.0	9 41.6	9 13.6	4.0	2.6	10.0	6.4	16.0	10.3
41	9 40.3	9 41.8	9 13.8	4.1	2.6	10.1	6.5	16.1	10.3
42	9 40.5	9 42.1	9 14.1	4.2	2.7	10.2	6.5	16.2	10.4
43	9 40.8	9 42.3	9 14.3	4.3	2.8	10.3	6.6	16.3	10.5
44	9 41.0	9 42.6	9 14.5	4.4	2.8	10.4	6.7	16.4	10.5
45	9 41.3	9 42.8	9 14.8	4.5	2.9	10.5	6.7	16.5	10.6
46	9 41.5	9 43.1	9 15.0	4.6	3.0	10.6	6.8	16.6	10.7
47	9 41.8	9 43.3	9 15.2	4.7	3.0	10.7	6.9	16.7	10.7
48	9 42.0	9 43.6	9 15.5	4.8	3.1	10.8	6.9	16.8	10.8
49	9 42.3	9 43.8	9 15.7	4.9	3.1	10.9	7.0	16.9	10.8
50	9 42.5	9 44.1	9 16.0	5.0	3.2	11.0	7.1	17.0	10.9
51	9 42.8	9 44.3	9 16.2	5.1	3.3	11.1	7.1	17.1	11.0
52	9 43.0	9 44.6	9 16.4	5.2	3.3	11.2	7.2	17.2	11.0
53	9 43.3	9 44.8	9 16.7	5.3	3.4	11.3	7.3	17.3	11.1
54	9 43.5	9 45.1	9 16.9	5.4	3.5	11.4	7.3	17.4	11.2
55	9 43.8	9 45.3	9 17.2	5.5	3.5	11.5	7.4	17.5	11.2
56	9 44.0	9 45.6	9 17.4	5.6	3.6	11.6	7.4	17.6	11.3
57	9 44.3	9 45.8	9 17.6	5.7	3.7	11.7	7.5	17.7	11.4
58	9 44.5	9 46.1	9 17.9	5.8	3.7	11.8	7.6	17.8	11.4
59	9 44.8	9 46.4	9 18.1	5.9	3.8	11.9	7.6	17.9	11.5
60	9 45.0	9 46.6	9 18.4	6.0	3.9	12.0	7.7	18.0	11.6

39ᵐ

39 s	SUN PLANETS	ARIES	MOON	v or d	Corrⁿ	v or d	Corrⁿ	v or d	Corrⁿ
00	9 45.0	9 46.6	9 18.4	0.0	0.0	6.0	4.0	12.0	7.9
01	9 45.3	9 46.9	9 18.6	0.1	0.1	6.1	4.0	12.1	8.0
02	9 45.5	9 47.1	9 18.8	0.2	0.1	6.2	4.1	12.2	8.0
03	9 45.8	9 47.4	9 19.1	0.3	0.2	6.3	4.1	12.3	8.1
04	9 46.0	9 47.6	9 19.3	0.4	0.3	6.4	4.2	12.4	8.2
05	9 46.3	9 47.9	9 19.5	0.5	0.3	6.5	4.3	12.5	8.2
06	9 46.5	9 48.1	9 19.8	0.6	0.4	6.6	4.3	12.6	8.3
07	9 46.8	9 48.4	9 20.0	0.7	0.5	6.7	4.4	12.7	8.4
08	9 47.0	9 48.6	9 20.3	0.8	0.5	6.8	4.5	12.8	8.4
09	9 47.3	9 48.9	9 20.5	0.9	0.6	6.9	4.5	12.9	8.5
10	9 47.5	9 49.1	9 20.7	1.0	0.7	7.0	4.6	13.0	8.6
11	9 47.8	9 49.4	9 21.0	1.1	0.7	7.1	4.7	13.1	8.6
12	9 48.0	9 49.6	9 21.2	1.2	0.8	7.2	4.7	13.2	8.7
13	9 48.3	9 49.9	9 21.5	1.3	0.9	7.3	4.8	13.3	8.8
14	9 48.5	9 50.1	9 21.7	1.4	0.9	7.4	4.9	13.4	8.8
15	9 48.8	9 50.4	9 21.9	1.5	1.0	7.5	4.9	13.5	8.9
16	9 49.0	9 50.6	9 22.2	1.6	1.1	7.6	5.0	13.6	9.0
17	9 49.3	9 50.9	9 22.4	1.7	1.1	7.7	5.1	13.7	9.0
18	9 49.5	9 51.1	9 22.6	1.8	1.2	7.8	5.1	13.8	9.1
19	9 49.8	9 51.4	9 22.9	1.9	1.3	7.9	5.2	13.9	9.2
20	9 50.0	9 51.6	9 23.1	2.0	1.3	8.0	5.3	14.0	9.2
21	9 50.3	9 51.9	9 23.4	2.1	1.4	8.1	5.3	14.1	9.3
22	9 50.5	9 52.1	9 23.6	2.2	1.4	8.2	5.4	14.2	9.3
23	9 50.8	9 52.4	9 23.8	2.3	1.5	8.3	5.5	14.3	9.4
24	9 51.0	9 52.6	9 24.1	2.4	1.6	8.4	5.5	14.4	9.5
25	9 51.3	9 52.9	9 24.3	2.5	1.6	8.5	5.6	14.5	9.5
26	9 51.5	9 53.1	9 24.6	2.6	1.7	8.6	5.7	14.6	9.6
27	9 51.8	9 53.4	9 24.8	2.7	1.8	8.7	5.7	14.7	9.7
28	9 52.0	9 53.6	9 25.0	2.8	1.8	8.8	5.8	14.8	9.7
29	9 52.3	9 53.9	9 25.3	2.9	1.9	8.9	5.9	14.9	9.8
30	9 52.5	9 54.1	9 25.5	3.0	2.0	9.0	5.9	15.0	9.9
31	9 52.8	9 54.4	9 25.7	3.1	2.0	9.1	6.0	15.1	9.9
32	9 53.0	9 54.6	9 26.0	3.2	2.1	9.2	6.1	15.2	10.0
33	9 53.3	9 54.9	9 26.2	3.3	2.2	9.3	6.1	15.3	10.1
34	9 53.5	9 55.1	9 26.5	3.4	2.2	9.4	6.2	15.4	10.1
35	9 53.8	9 55.4	9 26.7	3.5	2.3	9.5	6.3	15.5	10.2
36	9 54.0	9 55.6	9 26.9	3.6	2.4	9.6	6.3	15.6	10.3
37	9 54.3	9 55.9	9 27.2	3.7	2.4	9.7	6.4	15.7	10.3
38	9 54.5	9 56.1	9 27.4	3.8	2.5	9.8	6.5	15.8	10.4
39	9 54.8	9 56.4	9 27.7	3.9	2.6	9.9	6.5	15.9	10.5
40	9 55.0	9 56.6	9 27.9	4.0	2.6	10.0	6.6	16.0	10.5
41	9 55.3	9 56.9	9 28.1	4.1	2.7	10.1	6.6	16.1	10.6
42	9 55.5	9 57.1	9 28.4	4.2	2.8	10.2	6.7	16.2	10.7
43	9 55.8	9 57.4	9 28.6	4.3	2.8	10.3	6.8	16.3	10.8
44	9 56.0	9 57.6	9 28.8	4.4	2.9	10.4	6.8	16.4	10.8
45	9 56.3	9 57.9	9 29.1	4.5	3.0	10.5	6.9	16.5	10.9
46	9 56.5	9 58.1	9 29.3	4.6	3.0	10.6	7.0	16.6	10.9
47	9 56.8	9 58.4	9 29.6	4.7	3.1	10.7	7.0	16.7	11.0
48	9 57.0	9 58.6	9 29.8	4.8	3.2	10.8	7.1	16.8	11.1
49	9 57.3	9 58.9	9 30.0	4.9	3.2	10.9	7.2	16.9	11.1
50	9 57.5	9 59.1	9 30.3	5.0	3.3	11.0	7.2	17.0	11.2
51	9 57.8	9 59.4	9 30.5	5.1	3.4	11.1	7.3	17.1	11.3
52	9 58.0	9 59.6	9 30.8	5.2	3.4	11.2	7.4	17.2	11.3
53	9 58.3	9 59.9	9 31.0	5.3	3.5	11.3	7.4	17.3	11.4
54	9 58.5	10 00.1	9 31.2	5.4	3.6	11.4	7.5	17.4	11.5
55	9 58.8	10 00.4	9 31.5	5.5	3.6	11.5	7.6	17.5	11.5
56	9 59.0	10 00.6	9 31.7	5.6	3.7	11.6	7.6	17.6	11.6
57	9 59.3	10 00.9	9 31.9	5.7	3.8	11.7	7.7	17.7	11.7
58	9 59.5	10 01.1	9 32.2	5.8	3.8	11.8	7.8	17.8	11.7
59	9 59.8	10 01.4	9 32.4	5.9	3.9	11.9	7.8	17.9	11.8
60	10 00.0	10 01.6	9 32.7	6.0	4.0	12.0	7.9	18.0	11.9

m 40	SUN PLANETS	ARIES	MOON	v or d Corrⁿ	v or d Corrⁿ	v or d Corrⁿ
s	° ′	° ′	° ′	′ ′	′ ′	′ ′
00	10 00·0	10 01·6	9 32·7	0·0 0·0	6·0 4·1	12·0 8·1
01	10 00·3	10 01·9	9 32·9	0·1 0·1	6·1 4·1	12·1 8·2
02	10 00·5	10 02·1	9 33·1	0·2 0·1	6·2 4·2	12·2 8·2
03	10 00·8	10 02·4	9 33·4	0·3 0·2	6·3 4·3	12·3 8·3
04	10 01·0	10 02·6	9 33·6	0·4 0·3	6·4 4·3	12·4 8·4
05	10 01·3	10 02·9	9 33·9	0·5 0·3	6·5 4·4	12·5 8·4
06	10 01·5	10 03·1	9 34·1	0·6 0·4	6·6 4·5	12·6 8·5
07	10 01·8	10 03·4	9 34·3	0·7 0·5	6·7 4·5	12·7 8·6
08	10 02·0	10 03·6	9 34·6	0·8 0·5	6·8 4·6	12·8 8·6
09	10 02·3	10 03·9	9 34·8	0·9 0·6	6·9 4·7	12·9 8·7
10	10 02·5	10 04·1	9 35·1	1·0 0·7	7·0 4·7	13·0 8·8
11	10 02·8	10 04·4	9 35·3	1·1 0·7	7·1 4·8	13·1 8·8
12	10 03·0	10 04·7	9 35·5	1·2 0·8	7·2 4·9	13·2 8·9
13	10 03·3	10 04·9	9 35·8	1·3 0·9	7·3 4·9	13·3 9·0
14	10 03·5	10 05·2	9 36·0	1·4 0·9	7·4 5·0	13·4 9·0
15	10 03·8	10 05·4	9 36·2	1·5 1·0	7·5 5·1	13·5 9·1
16	10 04·0	10 05·7	9 36·5	1·6 1·1	7·6 5·1	13·6 9·2
17	10 04·3	10 05·9	9 36·7	1·7 1·1	7·7 5·2	13·7 9·2
18	10 04·5	10 06·2	9 37·0	1·8 1·2	7·8 5·3	13·8 9·3
19	10 04·8	10 06·4	9 37·2	1·9 1·3	7·9 5·3	13·9 9·4
20	10 05·0	10 06·7	9 37·4	2·0 1·4	8·0 5·4	14·0 9·5
21	10 05·3	10 06·9	9 37·7	2·1 1·4	8·1 5·5	14·1 9·5
22	10 05·5	10 07·2	9 37·9	2·2 1·5	8·2 5·5	14·2 9·6
23	10 05·8	10 07·4	9 38·2	2·3 1·6	8·3 5·6	14·3 9·7
24	10 06·0	10 07·7	9 38·4	2·4 1·6	8·4 5·7	14·4 9·7
25	10 06·3	10 07·9	9 38·6	2·5 1·7	8·5 5·7	14·5 9·8
26	10 06·5	10 08·2	9 38·9	2·6 1·8	8·6 5·8	14·6 9·9
27	10 06·8	10 08·4	9 39·1	2·7 1·8	8·7 5·9	14·7 9·9
28	10 07·0	10 08·7	9 39·3	2·8 1·9	8·8 5·9	14·8 10·0
29	10 07·3	10 08·9	9 39·6	2·9 2·0	8·9 6·0	14·9 10·1
30	10 07·5	10 09·2	9 39·8	3·0 2·0	9·0 6·1	15·0 10·1
31	10 07·8	10 09·4	9 40·1	3·1 2·1	9·1 6·1	15·1 10·2
32	10 08·0	10 09·7	9 40·3	3·2 2·2	9·2 6·2	15·2 10·3
33	10 08·3	10 09·9	9 40·5	3·3 2·2	9·3 6·3	15·3 10·3
34	10 08·5	10 10·2	9 40·8	3·4 2·3	9·4 6·3	15·4 10·4
35	10 08·8	10 10·4	9 41·0	3·5 2·4	9·5 6·4	15·5 10·5
36	10 09·0	10 10·7	9 41·3	3·6 2·4	9·6 6·5	15·6 10·5
37	10 09·3	10 10·9	9 41·5	3·7 2·5	9·7 6·5	15·7 10·6
38	10 09·5	10 11·2	9 41·7	3·8 2·6	9·8 6·6	15·8 10·7
39	10 09·8	10 11·4	9 42·0	3·9 2·6	9·9 6·7	15·9 10·7
40	10 10·0	10 11·7	9 42·2	4·0 2·7	10·0 6·8	16·0 10·8
41	10 10·3	10 11·9	9 42·4	4·1 2·8	10·1 6·8	16·1 10·9
42	10 10·5	10 12·2	9 42·7	4·2 2·8	10·2 6·9	16·2 10·9
43	10 10·8	10 12·4	9 42·9	4·3 2·9	10·3 7·0	16·3 11·0
44	10 11·0	10 12·7	9 43·2	4·4 3·0	10·4 7·0	16·4 11·1
45	10 11·3	10 12·9	9 43·4	4·5 3·0	10·5 7·1	16·5 11·1
46	10 11·5	10 13·2	9 43·6	4·6 3·1	10·6 7·2	16·6 11·2
47	10 11·8	10 13·4	9 43·9	4·7 3·2	10·7 7·2	16·7 11·3
48	10 12·0	10 13·7	9 44·1	4·8 3·2	10·8 7·3	16·8 11·6
49	10 12·3	10 13·9	9 44·4	4·9 3·3	10·9 7·4	16·9 11·4
50	10 12·5	10 14·2	9 44·6	5·0 3·4	11·0 7·4	17·0 11·5
51	10 12·8	10 14·4	9 44·8	5·1 3·4	11·1 7·5	17·1 11·5
52	10 13·0	10 14·7	9 45·1	5·2 3·5	11·2 7·6	17·2 11·6
53	10 13·3	10 14·9	9 45·3	5·3 3·6	11·3 7·6	17·3 11·7
54	10 13·5	10 15·2	9 45·6	5·4 3·6	11·4 7·7	17·4 11·7
55	10 13·8	10 15·4	9 45·8	5·5 3·7	11·5 7·8	17·5 11·8
56	10 14·0	10 15·7	9 46·0	5·6 3·8	11·6 7·8	17·6 11·9
57	10 14·3	10 15·9	9 46·3	5·7 3·8	11·7 7·9	17·7 11·9
58	10 14·5	10 16·2	9 46·5	5·8 3·9	11·8 8·0	17·8 12·0
59	10 14·8	10 16·4	9 46·7	5·9 4·0	11·9 8·0	17·9 12·1
60	10 15·0	10 16·7	9 47·0	6·0 4·1	12·0 8·1	18·0 12·2

m 41	SUN PLANETS	ARIES	MOON	v or d Corrⁿ	v or d Corrⁿ	v or d Corrⁿ
s	° ′	° ′	° ′	′ ′	′ ′	′ ′
00	10 15·0	10 16·7	9 47·0	0·0 0·0	6·0 4·2	12·0 8·3
01	10 15·3	10 16·9	9 47·2	0·1 0·1	6·1 4·2	12·1 8·4
02	10 15·5	10 17·2	9 47·5	0·2 0·1	6·2 4·3	12·2 8·4
03	10 15·8	10 17·4	9 47·7	0·3 0·2	6·3 4·4	12·3 8·5
04	10 16·0	10 17·7	9 47·9	0·4 0·3	6·4 4·4	12·4 8·6
05	10 16·3	10 17·9	9 48·2	0·5 0·3	6·5 4·5	12·5 8·6
06	10 16·5	10 18·2	9 48·4	0·6 0·4	6·6 4·6	12·6 8·7
07	10 16·8	10 18·4	9 48·7	0·7 0·5	6·7 4·6	12·7 8·8
08	10 17·0	10 18·7	9 48·9	0·8 0·6	6·8 4·7	12·8 8·9
09	10 17·3	10 18·9	9 49·1	0·9 0·6	6·9 4·8	12·9 8·9
10	10 17·5	10 19·2	9 49·4	1·0 0·7	7·0 4·8	13·0 9·0
11	10 17·8	10 19·4	9 49·6	1·1 0·8	7·1 4·9	13·1 9·1
12	10 18·0	10 19·7	9 49·8	1·2 0·8	7·2 5·0	13·2 9·1
13	10 18·3	10 19·9	9 50·1	1·3 0·9	7·3 5·0	13·3 9·2
14	10 18·5	10 20·2	9 50·3	1·4 1·0	7·4 5·1	13·4 9·3
15	10 18·8	10 20·4	9 50·6	1·5 1·0	7·5 5·2	13·5 9·3
16	10 19·0	10 20·7	9 50·8	1·6 1·1	7·6 5·3	13·6 9·4
17	10 19·3	10 20·9	9 51·0	1·7 1·2	7·7 5·3	13·7 9·5
18	10 19·5	10 21·2	9 51·3	1·8 1·2	7·8 5·4	13·8 9·5
19	10 19·8	10 21·4	9 51·5	1·9 1·3	7·9 5·5	13·9 9·6
20	10 20·0	10 21·7	9 51·8	2·0 1·4	8·0 5·5	14·0 9·7
21	10 20·3	10 21·9	9 52·0	2·1 1·5	8·1 5·6	14·1 9·8
22	10 20·5	10 22·2	9 52·2	2·2 1·5	8·2 5·7	14·2 9·8
23	10 20·8	10 22·4	9 52·5	2·3 1·6	8·3 5·7	14·3 9·9
24	10 21·0	10 22·7	9 52·7	2·4 1·7	8·4 5·8	14·4 10·0
25	10 21·3	10 23·0	9 52·9	2·5 1·7	8·5 5·9	14·5 10·0
26	10 21·5	10 23·2	9 53·2	2·6 1·8	8·6 5·9	14·6 10·1
27	10 21·8	10 23·5	9 53·4	2·7 1·9	8·7 6·0	14·7 10·2
28	10 22·0	10 23·7	9 53·7	2·8 1·9	8·8 6·1	14·8 10·2
29	10 22·3	10 24·0	9 53·9	2·9 2·0	8·9 6·2	14·9 10·3
30	10 22·5	10 24·2	9 54·1	3·0 2·1	9·0 6·2	15·0 10·4
31	10 22·8	10 24·5	9 54·4	3·1 2·1	9·1 6·3	15·1 10·4
32	10 23·0	10 24·7	9 54·6	3·2 2·2	9·2 6·4	15·2 10·5
33	10 23·3	10 25·0	9 54·9	3·3 2·3	9·3 6·4	15·3 10·6
34	10 23·5	10 25·2	9 55·1	3·4 2·4	9·4 6·5	15·4 10·7
35	10 23·8	10 25·5	9 55·3	3·5 2·4	9·5 6·6	15·5 10·7
36	10 24·0	10 25·7	9 55·6	3·6 2·5	9·6 6·6	15·6 10·8
37	10 24·3	10 26·0	9 55·8	3·7 2·6	9·7 6·7	15·7 10·9
38	10 24·5	10 26·2	9 56·1	3·8 2·6	9·8 6·8	15·8 10·9
39	10 24·8	10 26·5	9 56·3	3·9 2·7	9·9 6·8	15·9 11·0
40	10 25·0	10 26·7	9 56·5	4·0 2·8	10·0 6·9	16·0 11·1
41	10 25·3	10 27·0	9 56·8	4·1 2·8	10·1 7·0	16·1 11·1
42	10 25·5	10 27·2	9 57·0	4·2 2·9	10·2 7·1	16·2 11·2
43	10 25·8	10 27·5	9 57·2	4·3 3·0	10·3 7·1	16·3 11·3
44	10 26·0	10 27·7	9 57·5	4·4 3·0	10·4 7·2	16·4 11·3
45	10 26·3	10 28·0	9 57·7	4·5 3·1	10·5 7·3	16·5 11·4
46	10 26·5	10 28·2	9 58·0	4·6 3·2	10·6 7·3	16·6 11·5
47	10 26·8	10 28·5	9 58·2	4·7 3·3	10·7 7·4	16·7 11·6
48	10 27·0	10 28·7	9 58·4	4·8 3·3	10·8 7·5	16·8 11·6
49	10 27·3	10 29·0	9 58·7	4·9 3·4	10·9 7·5	16·9 11·7
50	10 27·5	10 29·2	9 58·9	5·0 3·5	11·0 7·6	17·0 11·8
51	10 27·8	10 29·5	9 59·2	5·1 3·5	11·1 7·7	17·1 11·8
52	10 28·0	10 29·7	9 59·4	5·2 3·6	11·2 7·7	17·2 11·9
53	10 28·3	10 30·0	9 59·6	5·3 3·7	11·3 7·8	17·3 12·0
54	10 28·5	10 30·2	9 59·9	5·4 3·7	11·4 7·9	17·4 12·0
55	10 28·8	10 30·5	10 00·1	5·5 3·8	11·5 8·0	17·5 12·1
56	10 29·0	10 30·7	10 00·3	5·6 3·9	11·6 8·0	17·6 12·2
57	10 29·3	10 31·0	10 00·6	5·7 3·9	11·7 8·1	17·7 12·2
58	10 29·5	10 31·2	10 00·8	5·8 4·0	11·8 8·2	17·8 12·3
59	10 29·8	10 31·5	10 01·1	5·9 4·1	11·9 8·2	17·9 12·4
60	10 30·0	10 31·7	10 01·3	6·0 4·2	12·0 8·3	18·0 12·5

42^m	SUN PLANETS	ARIES	MOON	v or d Corr^n	v or d Corr^n	v or d Corr^n	43^m	SUN PLANETS	ARIES	MOON	v or d Corr^n	v or d Corr^n	v or d Corr^n
s	° ′	° ′	° ′	′ ′	′ ′	′ ′	s	° ′	° ′	° ′	′ ′	′ ′	′ ′
00	10 30·0	10 31·7	10 01·3	0·0 0·0	6·0 4·3	12·0 8·5	00	10 45·0	10 46·8	10 15·6	0·0 0·0	6·0 4·4	12·0 8·7
01	10 30·3	10 32·0	10 01·5	0·1 0·1	6·1 4·3	12·1 8·6	01	10 45·3	10 47·0	10 15·9	0·1 0·1	6·1 4·4	12·1 8·8
02	10 30·5	10 32·2	10 01·8	0·2 0·1	6·2 4·4	12·2 8·6	02	10 45·5	10 47·3	10 16·1	0·2 0·1	6·2 4·5	12·2 8·8
03	10 30·8	10 32·5	10 02·0	0·3 0·2	6·3 4·5	12·3 8·7	03	10 45·8	10 47·5	10 16·3	0·3 0·2	6·3 4·6	12·3 8·9
04	10 31·0	10 32·7	10 02·3	0·4 0·3	6·4 4·5	12·4 8·8	04	10 46·0	10 47·8	10 16·6	0·4 0·3	6·4 4·6	12·4 9·0
05	10 31·3	10 33·0	10 02·5	0·5 0·4	6·5 4·6	12·5 8·9	05	10 46·3	10 48·0	10 16·8	0·5 0·4	6·5 4·7	12·5 9·1
06	10 31·5	10 33·2	10 02·7	0·6 0·4	6·6 4·7	12·6 8·9	06	10 46·5	10 48·3	10 17·0	0·6 0·4	6·6 4·8	12·6 9·1
07	10 31·8	10 33·5	10 03·0	0·7 0·5	6·7 4·7	12·7 9·0	07	10 46·8	10 48·5	10 17·3	0·7 0·5	6·7 4·9	12·7 9·2
08	10 32·0	10 33·7	10 03·2	0·8 0·6	6·8 4·8	12·8 9·1	08	10 47·0	10 48·8	10 17·5	0·8 0·6	6·8 4·9	12·8 9·3
09	10 32·3	10 34·0	10 03·4	0·9 0·6	6·9 4·9	12·9 9·1	09	10 47·3	10 49·0	10 17·8	0·9 0·7	6·9 5·0	12·9 9·4
10	10 32·5	10 34·2	10 03·7	1·0 0·7	7·0 5·0	13·0 9·2	10	10 47·5	10 49·3	10 18·0	1·0 0·7	7·0 5·1	13·0 9·4
11	10 32·8	10 34·5	10 03·9	1·1 0·8	7·1 5·0	13·1 9·3	11	10 47·8	10 49·5	10 18·2	1·1 0·8	7·1 5·1	13·1 9·5
12	10 33·0	10 34·7	10 04·2	1·2 0·9	7·2 5·1	13·2 9·4	12	10 48·0	10 49·8	10 18·5	1·2 0·9	7·2 5·2	13·2 9·6
13	10 33·3	10 35·0	10 04·4	1·3 0·9	7·3 5·2	13·3 9·4	13	10 48·3	10 50·0	10 18·7	1·3 0·9	7·3 5·3	13·3 9·6
14	10 33·5	10 35·2	10 04·6	1·4 1·0	7·4 5·2	13·4 9·5	14	10 48·5	10 50·3	10 19·0	1·4 1·0	7·4 5·4	13·4 9·7
15	10 33·8	10 35·5	10 04·9	1·5 1·1	7·5 5·3	13·5 9·6	15	10 48·8	10 50·5	10 19·2	1·5 1·1	7·5 5·4	13·5 9·8
16	10 34·0	10 35·7	10 05·1	1·6 1·1	7·6 5·4	13·6 9·6	16	10 49·0	10 50·8	10 19·4	1·6 1·2	7·6 5·5	13·6 9·9
17	10 34·3	10 36·0	10 05·4	1·7 1·2	7·7 5·5	13·7 9·7	17	10 49·3	10 51·0	10 19·7	1·7 1·2	7·7 5·6	13·7 9·9
18	10 34·5	10 36·2	10 05·6	1·8 1·3	7·8 5·5	13·8 9·8	18	10 49·5	10 51·3	10 19·9	1·8 1·3	7·8 5·7	13·8 10·0
19	10 34·8	10 36·5	10 05·8	1·9 1·3	7·9 5·6	13·9 9·8	19	10 49·8	10 51·5	10 20·2	1·9 1·4	7·9 5·7	13·9 10·1
20	10 35·0	10 36·7	10 06·1	2·0 1·4	8·0 5·7	14·0 9·9	20	10 50·0	10 51·8	10 20·4	2·0 1·5	8·0 5·8	14·0 10·2
21	10 35·3	10 37·0	10 06·3	2·1 1·5	8·1 5·7	14·1 10·0	21	10 50·3	10 52·0	10 20·6	2·1 1·5	8·1 5·9	14·1 10·2
22	10 35·5	10 37·2	10 06·5	2·2 1·6	8·2 5·8	14·2 10·1	22	10 50·5	10 52·3	10 20·9	2·2 1·6	8·2 5·9	14·2 10·3
23	10 35·8	10 37·5	10 06·8	2·3 1·6	8·3 5·9	14·3 10·1	23	10 50·8	10 52·5	10 21·1	2·3 1·7	8·3 6·0	14·3 10·4
24	10 36·0	10 37·7	10 07·0	2·4 1·7	8·4 6·0	14·4 10·2	24	10 51·0	10 52·8	10 21·3	2·4 1·7	8·4 6·1	14·4 10·4
25	10 36·3	10 38·0	10 07·3	2·5 1·8	8·5 6·0	14·5 10·3	25	10 51·3	10 53·0	10 21·6	2·5 1·8	8·5 6·2	14·5 10·5
26	10 36·5	10 38·2	10 07·5	2·6 1·8	8·6 6·1	14·6 10·3	26	10 51·5	10 53·3	10 21·8	2·6 1·9	8·6 6·2	14·6 10·6
27	10 36·8	10 38·5	10 07·7	2·7 1·9	8·7 6·2	14·7 10·4	27	10 51·8	10 53·5	10 22·1	2·7 2·0	8·7 6·3	14·7 10·7
28	10 37·0	10 38·7	10 08·0	2·8 2·0	8·8 6·2	14·8 10·5	28	10 52·0	10 53·8	10 22·3	2·8 2·0	8·8 6·4	14·8 10·7
29	10 37·3	10 39·0	10 08·2	2·9 2·1	8·9 6·3	14·9 10·6	29	10 52·3	10 54·0	10 22·5	2·9 2·1	8·9 6·5	14·9 10·8
30	10 37·5	10 39·2	10 08·5	3·0 2·1	9·0 6·4	15·0 10·6	30	10 52·5	10 54·3	10 22·8	3·0 2·2	9·0 6·5	15·0 10·9
31	10 37·8	10 39·5	10 08·7	3·1 2·2	9·1 6·4	15·1 10·7	31	10 52·8	10 54·5	10 23·0	3·1 2·2	9·1 6·6	15·1 10·9
32	10 38·0	10 39·7	10 08·9	3·2 2·3	9·2 6·5	15·2 10·8	32	10 53·0	10 54·8	10 23·3	3·2 2·3	9·2 6·7	15·2 11·0
33	10 38·3	10 40·0	10 09·2	3·3 2·3	9·3 6·6	15·3 10·8	33	10 53·3	10 55·0	10 23·5	3·3 2·4	9·3 6·7	15·3 11·1
34	10 38·5	10 40·2	10 09·4	3·4 2·4	9·4 6·7	15·4 10·9	34	10 53·5	10 55·3	10 23·7	3·4 2·5	9·4 6·8	15·4 11·2
35	10 38·8	10 40·5	10 09·7	3·5 2·5	9·5 6·7	15·5 11·0	35	10 53·8	10 55·5	10 24·0	3·5 2·5	9·5 6·9	15·5 11·2
36	10 39·0	10 40·7	10 09·9	3·6 2·6	9·6 6·8	15·6 11·1	36	10 54·0	10 55·8	10 24·2	3·6 2·6	9·6 7·0	15·6 11·3
37	10 39·3	10 41·0	10 10·1	3·7 2·6	9·7 6·9	15·7 11·1	37	10 54·3	10 56·0	10 24·4	3·7 2·7	9·7 7·0	15·7 11·4
38	10 39·5	10 41·3	10 10·4	3·8 2·7	9·8 6·9	15·8 11·2	38	10 54·5	10 56·3	10 24·7	3·8 2·8	9·8 7·1	15·8 11·5
39	10 39·8	10 41·5	10 10·6	3·9 2·8	9·9 7·0	15·9 11·3	39	10 54·8	10 56·5	10 24·9	3·9 2·8	9·9 7·2	15·9 11·5
40	10 40·0	10 41·8	10 10·8	4·0 2·8	10·0 7·1	16·0 11·3	40	10 55·0	10 56·8	10 25·2	4·0 2·9	10·0 7·3	16·0 11·6
41	10 40·3	10 42·0	10 11·1	4·1 2·9	10·1 7·2	16·1 11·4	41	10 55·3	10 57·0	10 25·4	4·1 3·0	10·1 7·3	16·1 11·7
42	10 40·5	10 42·3	10 11·3	4·2 3·0	10·2 7·2	16·2 11·5	42	10 55·5	10 57·3	10 25·6	4·2 3·0	10·2 7·4	16·2 11·7
43	10 40·8	10 42·5	10 11·6	4·3 3·0	10·3 7·3	16·3 11·5	43	10 55·8	10 57·5	10 25·9	4·3 3·1	10·3 7·5	16·3 11·8
44	10 41·0	10 42·8	10 11·8	4·4 3·1	10·4 7·4	16·4 11·6	44	10 56·0	10 57·8	10 26·1	4·4 3·2	10·4 7·5	16·4 11·9
45	10 41·3	10 43·0	10 12·0	4·5 3·2	10·5 7·4	16·5 11·7	45	10 56·3	10 58·0	10 26·4	4·5 3·3	10·5 7·6	16·5 12·0
46	10 41·5	10 43·3	10 12·3	4·6 3·3	10·6 7·5	16·6 11·8	46	10 56·5	10 58·3	10 26·6	4·6 3·3	10·6 7·7	16·6 12·0
47	10 41·8	10 43·5	10 12·5	4·7 3·3	10·7 7·6	16·7 11·8	47	10 56·8	10 58·5	10 26·8	4·7 3·4	10·7 7·8	16·7 12·1
48	10 42·0	10 43·8	10 12·8	4·8 3·4	10·8 7·7	16·8 11·9	48	10 57·0	10 58·8	10 27·1	4·8 3·5	10·8 7·8	16·8 12·2
49	10 42·3	10 44·0	10 13·0	4·9 3·5	10·9 7·7	16·9 12·0	49	10 57·3	10 59·0	10 27·3	4·9 3·6	10·9 7·9	16·9 12·3
50	10 42·5	10 44·3	10 13·2	5·0 3·5	11·0 7·8	17·0 12·0	50	10 57·5	10 59·3	10 27·5	5·0 3·6	11·0 8·0	17·0 12·3
51	10 42·8	10 44·5	10 13·5	5·1 3·6	11·1 7·9	17·1 12·1	51	10 57·8	10 59·6	10 27·8	5·1 3·7	11·1 8·0	17·1 12·4
52	10 43·0	10 44·8	10 13·7	5·2 3·7	11·2 7·9	17·2 12·2	52	10 58·0	10 59·8	10 28·0	5·2 3·8	11·2 8·1	17·2 12·5
53	10 43·3	10 45·0	10 13·9	5·3 3·8	11·3 8·0	17·3 12·2	53	10 58·3	11 00·1	10 28·3	5·3 3·8	11·3 8·2	17·3 12·5
54	10 43·5	10 45·3	10 14·2	5·4 3·8	11·4 8·1	17·4 12·3	54	10 58·5	11 00·3	10 28·5	5·4 3·9	11·4 8·3	17·4 12·6
55	10 43·8	10 45·5	10 14·4	5·5 3·9	11·5 8·1	17·5 12·4	55	10 58·8	11 00·6	10 28·7	5·5 4·0	11·5 8·3	17·5 12·7
56	10 44·0	10 45·8	10 14·7	5·6 4·0	11·6 8·2	17·6 12·5	56	10 59·0	11 00·8	10 29·0	5·6 4·1	11·6 8·4	17·6 12·8
57	10 44·3	10 46·0	10 14·9	5·7 4·0	11·7 8·3	17·7 12·5	57	10 59·3	11 01·1	10 29·2	5·7 4·1	11·7 8·5	17·7 12·8
58	10 44·5	10 46·3	10 15·1	5·8 4·1	11·8 8·4	17·8 12·6	58	10 59·5	11 01·3	10 29·5	5·8 4·2	11·8 8·6	17·8 12·9
59	10 44·8	10 46·5	10 15·4	5·9 4·2	11·9 8·4	17·9 12·7	59	10 59·8	11 01·6	10 29·7	5·9 4·3	11·9 8·6	17·9 13·0
60	10 45·0	10 46·8	10 15·6	6·0 4·3	12·0 8·5	18·0 12·8	60	11 00·0	11 01·8	10 29·9	6·0 4·4	12·0 8·7	18·0 13·1

44ᵐ

44 s	SUN PLANETS	ARIES	MOON	v or d	Corrⁿ	v or d	Corrⁿ	v or d	Corrⁿ
00	11 00·0	11 01·8	10 29·9	0·0	0·0	6·0	4·5	12·0	8·9
01	11 00·3	11 02·1	10 30·2	0·1	0·1	6·1	4·5	12·1	9·0
02	11 00·5	11 02·3	10 30·4	0·2	0·1	6·2	4·6	12·2	9·0
03	11 00·8	11 02·6	10 30·6	0·3	0·2	6·3	4·7	12·3	9·1
04	11 01·0	11 02·8	10 30·9	0·4	0·3	6·4	4·7	12·4	9·2
05	11 01·3	11 03·1	10 31·1	0·5	0·4	6·5	4·8	12·5	9·3
06	11 01·5	11 03·3	10 31·4	0·6	0·4	6·6	4·9	12·6	9·3
07	11 01·8	11 03·6	10 31·6	0·7	0·5	6·7	5·0	12·7	9·4
08	11 02·0	11 03·8	10 31·8	0·8	0·6	6·8	5·0	12·8	9·5
09	11 02·3	11 04·1	10 32·1	0·9	0·7	6·9	5·1	12·9	9·6
10	11 02·5	11 04·3	10 32·3	1·0	0·7	7·0	5·2	13·0	9·6
11	11 02·8	11 04·6	10 32·6	1·1	0·8	7·1	5·3	13·1	9·7
12	11 03·0	11 04·8	10 32·8	1·2	0·9	7·2	5·3	13·2	9·8
13	11 03·3	11 05·1	10 33·0	1·3	1·0	7·3	5·4	13·3	9·9
14	11 03·5	11 05·3	10 33·3	1·4	1·0	7·4	5·5	13·4	9·9
15	11 03·8	11 05·6	10 33·5	1·5	1·1	7·5	5·6	13·5	10·0
16	11 04·0	11 05·8	10 33·8	1·6	1·2	7·6	5·6	13·6	10·1
17	11 04·3	11 06·1	10 34·0	1·7	1·3	7·7	5·7	13·7	10·2
18	11 04·5	11 06·3	10 34·2	1·8	1·3	7·8	5·8	13·8	10·2
19	11 04·8	11 06·6	10 34·5	1·9	1·4	7·9	5·9	13·9	10·3
20	11 05·0	11 06·8	10 34·7	2·0	1·5	8·0	5·9	14·0	10·4
21	11 05·3	11 07·1	10 34·9	2·1	1·6	8·1	6·0	14·1	10·5
22	11 05·5	11 07·3	10 35·2	2·2	1·6	8·2	6·1	14·2	10·5
23	11 05·8	11 07·6	10 35·4	2·3	1·7	8·3	6·2	14·3	10·6
24	11 06·0	11 07·8	10 35·7	2·4	1·8	8·4	6·2	14·4	10·7
25	11 06·3	11 08·1	10 35·9	2·5	1·9	8·5	6·3	14·5	10·8
26	11 06·5	11 08·3	10 36·1	2·6	1·9	8·6	6·4	14·6	10·8
27	11 06·8	11 08·6	10 36·4	2·7	2·0	8·7	6·5	14·7	10·9
28	11 07·0	11 08·8	10 36·6	2·8	2·1	8·8	6·5	14·8	11·0
29	11 07·3	11 09·1	10 36·9	2·9	2·2	8·9	6·6	14·9	11·1
30	11 07·5	11 09·3	10 37·1	3·0	2·2	9·0	6·7	15·0	11·1
31	11 07·8	11 09·6	10 37·3	3·1	2·3	9·1	6·7	15·1	11·2
32	11 08·0	11 09·8	10 37·6	3·2	2·4	9·2	6·8	15·2	11·3
33	11 08·3	11 10·1	10 37·8	3·3	2·4	9·3	6·9	15·3	11·3
34	11 08·5	11 10·3	10 38·0	3·4	2·5	9·4	7·0	15·4	11·4
35	11 08·8	11 10·6	10 38·3	3·5	2·6	9·5	7·0	15·5	11·5
36	11 09·0	11 10·8	10 38·5	3·6	2·7	9·6	7·1	15·6	11·6
37	11 09·3	11 11·1	10 38·8	3·7	2·7	9·7	7·2	15·7	11·6
38	11 09·5	11 11·3	10 39·0	3·8	2·8	9·8	7·3	15·8	11·7
39	11 09·8	11 11·6	10 39·2	3·9	2·9	9·9	7·3	15·9	11·8
40	11 10·0	11 11·8	10 39·5	4·0	3·0	10·0	7·4	16·0	11·9
41	11 10·3	11 12·1	10 39·7	4·1	3·0	10·1	7·5	16·1	11·9
42	11 10·5	11 12·3	10 40·0	4·2	3·1	10·2	7·6	16·2	12·0
43	11 10·8	11 12·6	10 40·2	4·3	3·2	10·3	7·6	16·3	12·1
44	11 11·0	11 12·8	10 40·4	4·4	3·3	10·4	7·7	16·4	12·2
45	11 11·3	11 13·1	10 40·7	4·5	3·3	10·5	7·8	16·5	12·2
46	11 11·5	11 13·3	10 40·9	4·6	3·4	10·6	7·9	16·6	12·3
47	11 11·8	11 13·6	10 41·1	4·7	3·5	10·7	7·9	16·7	12·4
48	11 12·0	11 13·8	10 41·4	4·8	3·6	10·8	8·0	16·8	12·5
49	11 12·3	11 14·1	10 41·6	4·9	3·6	10·9	8·1	16·9	12·5
50	11 12·5	11 14·3	10 41·9	5·0	3·7	11·0	8·2	17·0	12·6
51	11 12·8	11 14·6	10 42·1	5·1	3·8	11·1	8·2	17·1	12·7
52	11 13·0	11 14·8	10 42·3	5·2	3·9	11·2	8·3	17·2	12·8
53	11 13·3	11 15·1	10 42·6	5·3	3·9	11·3	8·4	17·3	12·8
54	11 13·5	11 15·3	10 42·8	5·4	4·0	11·4	8·5	17·4	12·9
55	11 13·8	11 15·6	10 43·1	5·5	4·1	11·5	8·5	17·5	13·0
56	11 14·0	11 15·8	10 43·3	5·6	4·2	11·6	8·6	17·6	13·1
57	11 14·3	11 16·1	10 43·5	5·7	4·2	11·7	8·7	17·7	13·1
58	11 14·5	11 16·3	10 43·8	5·8	4·3	11·8	8·8	17·8	13·2
59	11 14·8	11 16·6	10 44·0	5·9	4·4	11·9	8·8	17·9	13·3
60	11 15·0	11 16·8	10 44·3	6·0	4·5	12·0	8·9	18·0	13·4

45ᵐ

45 s	SUN PLANETS	ARIES	MOON	v or d	Corrⁿ	v or d	Corrⁿ	v or d	Corrⁿ
00	11 15·0	11 16·8	10 44·3	0·0	0·0	6·0	4·6	12·0	9·1
01	11 15·3	11 17·1	10 44·5	0·1	0·1	6·1	4·6	12·1	9·2
02	11 15·5	11 17·3	10 44·7	0·2	0·2	6·2	4·7	12·2	9·3
03	11 15·8	11 17·6	10 45·0	0·3	0·2	6·3	4·8	12·3	9·3
04	11 16·0	11 17·9	10 45·2	0·4	0·3	6·4	4·9	12·4	9·4
05	11 16·3	11 18·1	10 45·4	0·5	0·4	6·5	4·9	12·5	9·5
06	11 16·5	11 18·4	10 45·7	0·6	0·5	6·6	5·0	12·6	9·6
07	11 16·8	11 18·6	10 45·9	0·7	0·5	6·7	5·1	12·7	9·6
08	11 17·0	11 18·9	10 46·2	0·8	0·6	6·8	5·2	12·8	9·7
09	11 17·3	11 19·1	10 46·4	0·9	0·7	6·9	5·2	12·9	9·8
10	11 17·5	11 19·4	10 46·6	1·0	0·8	7·0	5·3	13·0	9·9
11	11 17·8	11 19·6	10 46·9	1·1	0·8	7·1	5·4	13·1	9·9
12	11 18·0	11 19·9	10 47·1	1·2	0·9	7·2	5·5	13·2	10·0
13	11 18·3	11 20·1	10 47·4	1·3	1·0	7·3	5·5	13·3	10·1
14	11 18·5	11 20·4	10 47·6	1·4	1·1	7·4	5·6	13·4	10·2
15	11 18·8	11 20·6	10 47·8	1·5	1·1	7·5	5·7	13·5	10·2
16	11 19·0	11 20·9	10 48·1	1·6	1·2	7·6	5·8	13·6	10·3
17	11 19·3	11 21·1	10 48·3	1·7	1·3	7·7	5·8	13·7	10·4
18	11 19·5	11 21·4	10 48·5	1·8	1·4	7·8	5·9	13·8	10·5
19	11 19·8	11 21·6	10 48·8	1·9	1·4	7·9	6·0	13·9	10·5
20	11 20·0	11 21·9	10 49·0	2·0	1·5	8·0	6·1	14·0	10·6
21	11 20·3	11 22·1	10 49·3	2·1	1·6	8·1	6·1	14·1	10·7
22	11 20·5	11 22·4	10 49·5	2·2	1·7	8·2	6·2	14·2	10·8
23	11 20·8	11 22·6	10 49·7	2·3	1·7	8·3	6·3	14·3	10·8
24	11 21·0	11 22·9	10 50·0	2·4	1·8	8·4	6·4	14·4	10·9
25	11 21·3	11 23·1	10 50·2	2·5	1·9	8·5	6·4	14·5	11·0
26	11 21·5	11 23·4	10 50·5	2·6	2·0	8·6	6·5	14·6	11·1
27	11 21·8	11 23·6	10 50·7	2·7	2·0	8·7	6·6	14·7	11·1
28	11 22·0	11 23·9	10 50·9	2·8	2·1	8·8	6·7	14·8	11·2
29	11 22·3	11 24·1	10 51·2	2·9	2·2	8·9	6·7	14·9	11·3
30	11 22·5	11 24·4	10 51·4	3·0	2·3	9·0	6·8	15·0	11·4
31	11 22·8	11 24·6	10 51·6	3·1	2·4	9·1	6·9	15·1	11·5
32	11 23·0	11 24·9	10 51·9	3·2	2·4	9·2	7·0	15·2	11·5
33	11 23·3	11 25·1	10 52·1	3·3	2·5	9·3	7·1	15·3	11·6
34	11 23·5	11 25·4	10 52·4	3·4	2·6	9·4	7·1	15·4	11·7
35	11 23·8	11 25·6	10 52·6	3·5	2·7	9·5	7·2	15·5	11·8
36	11 24·0	11 25·9	10 52·8	3·6	2·7	9·6	7·3	15·6	11·8
37	11 24·3	11 26·1	10 53·1	3·7	2·8	9·7	7·4	15·7	11·9
38	11 24·5	11 26·4	10 53·3	3·8	2·9	9·8	7·4	15·8	12·0
39	11 24·8	11 26·6	10 53·6	3·9	3·0	9·9	7·5	15·9	12·1
40	11 25·0	11 26·9	10 53·8	4·0	3·0	10·0	7·6	16·0	12·1
41	11 25·3	11 27·1	10 54·0	4·1	3·1	10·1	7·7	16·1	12·2
42	11 25·5	11 27·4	10 54·3	4·2	3·2	10·2	7·7	16·2	12·3
43	11 25·8	11 27·6	10 54·5	4·3	3·3	10·3	7·8	16·3	12·4
44	11 26·0	11 27·9	10 54·7	4·4	3·3	10·4	7·9	16·4	12·4
45	11 26·3	11 28·1	10 55·0	4·5	3·4	10·5	8·0	16·5	12·5
46	11 26·5	11 28·4	10 55·2	4·6	3·5	10·6	8·0	16·6	12·6
47	11 26·8	11 28·6	10 55·5	4·7	3·6	10·7	8·1	16·7	12·7
48	11 27·0	11 28·9	10 55·7	4·8	3·6	10·8	8·2	16·8	12·7
49	11 27·3	11 29·1	10 55·9	4·9	3·7	10·9	8·3	16·9	12·8
50	11 27·5	11 29·4	10 56·2	5·0	3·8	11·0	8·3	17·0	12·9
51	11 27·8	11 29·6	10 56·4	5·1	3·9	11·1	8·4	17·1	13·0
52	11 28·0	11 29·9	10 56·7	5·2	3·9	11·2	8·5	17·2	13·0
53	11 28·3	11 30·1	10 56·9	5·3	4·0	11·3	8·6	17·3	13·1
54	11 28·5	11 30·4	10 57·1	5·4	4·1	11·4	8·6	17·4	13·2
55	11 28·8	11 30·6	10 57·4	5·5	4·2	11·5	8·7	17·5	13·3
56	11 29·0	11 30·9	10 57·6	5·6	4·2	11·6	8·8	17·6	13·3
57	11 29·3	11 31·1	10 57·9	5·7	4·3	11·7	8·9	17·7	13·4
58	11 29·5	11 31·4	10 58·1	5·8	4·4	11·8	8·9	17·8	13·5
59	11 29·8	11 31·6	10 58·3	5·9	4·5	11·9	9·0	17·9	13·6
60	11 30·0	11 31·9	10 58·6	6·0	4·6	12·0	9·1	18·0	13·7

46	SUN PLANETS	ARIES	MOON	v or d	Corrⁿ	v or d	Corrⁿ	v or d	Corrⁿ
s	° ′	° ′	° ′	′	′	′	′	′	′
00	11 30·0	11 31·9	10 58·6	0·0	0·0	6·0	4·7	12·0	9·3
01	11 30·3	11 32·1	10 58·8	0·1	0·1	6·1	4·7	12·1	9·4
02	11 30·5	11 32·4	10 59·0	0·2	0·2	6·2	4·8	12·2	9·5
03	11 30·8	11 32·6	10 59·3	0·3	0·2	6·3	4·9	12·3	9·5
04	11 31·0	11 32·9	10 59·5	0·4	0·3	6·4	5·0	12·4	9·6
05	11 31·3	11 33·1	10 59·8	0·5	0·4	6·5	5·0	12·5	9·7
06	11 31·5	11 33·4	11 00·0	0·6	0·5	6·6	5·1	12·6	9·8
07	11 31·8	11 33·6	11 00·2	0·7	0·5	6·7	5·2	12·7	9·8
08	11 32·0	11 33·9	11 00·5	0·8	0·6	6·8	5·3	12·8	9·9
09	11 32·3	11 34·1	11 00·7	0·9	0·7	6·9	5·3	12·9	10·0
10	11 32·5	11 34·4	11 01·0	1·0	0·8	7·0	5·4	13·0	10·1
11	11 32·8	11 34·6	11 01·2	1·1	0·9	7·1	5·5	13·1	10·2
12	11 33·0	11 34·9	11 01·4	1·2	0·9	7·2	5·6	13·2	10·2
13	11 33·3	11 35·1	11 01·7	1·3	1·0	7·3	5·7	13·3	10·3
14	11 33·5	11 35·4	11 01·9	1·4	1·1	7·4	5·7	13·4	10·4
15	11 33·8	11 35·6	11 02·1	1·5	1·2	7·5	5·8	13·5	10·5
16	11 34·0	11 35·9	11 02·4	1·6	1·2	7·6	5·9	13·6	10·5
17	11 34·3	11 36·2	11 02·6	1·7	1·3	7·7	6·0	13·7	10·6
18	11 34·5	11 36·4	11 02·9	1·8	1·4	7·8	6·0	13·8	10·7
19	11 34·8	11 36·7	11 03·1	1·9	1·5	7·9	6·1	13·9	10·8
20	11 35·0	11 36·9	11 03·3	2·0	1·6	8·0	6·2	14·0	10·9
21	11 35·3	11 37·2	11 03·6	2·1	1·6	8·1	6·3	14·1	10·9
22	11 35·5	11 37·4	11 03·8	2·2	1·7	8·2	6·4	14·2	11·0
23	11 35·8	11 37·7	11 04·1	2·3	1·8	8·3	6·4	14·3	11·1
24	11 36·0	11 37·9	11 04·3	2·4	1·9	8·4	6·5	14·4	11·2
25	11 36·3	11 38·2	11 04·5	2·5	1·9	8·5	6·6	14·5	11·2
26	11 36·5	11 38·4	11 04·8	2·6	2·0	8·6	6·7	14·6	11·3
27	11 36·8	11 38·7	11 05·0	2·7	2·1	8·7	6·7	14·7	11·4
28	11 37·0	11 38·9	11 05·2	2·8	2·2	8·8	6·8	14·8	11·5
29	11 37·3	11 39·2	11 05·5	2·9	2·2	8·9	6·9	14·9	11·5
30	11 37·5	11 39·4	11 05·7	3·0	2·3	9·0	7·0	15·0	11·6
31	11 37·8	11 39·7	11 06·0	3·1	2·4	9·1	7·1	15·1	11·7
32	11 38·0	11 39·9	11 06·2	3·2	2·5	9·2	7·1	15·2	11·8
33	11 38·3	11 40·2	11 06·4	3·3	2·6	9·3	7·2	15·3	11·9
34	11 38·5	11 40·4	11 06·7	3·4	2·6	9·4	7·3	15·4	11·9
35	11 38·8	11 40·7	11 06·9	3·5	2·7	9·5	7·4	15·5	12·0
36	11 39·0	11 40·9	11 07·2	3·6	2·8	9·6	7·4	15·6	12·1
37	11 39·3	11 41·2	11 07·4	3·7	2·9	9·7	7·5	15·7	12·2
38	11 39·5	11 41·4	11 07·6	3·8	2·9	9·8	7·6	15·8	12·2
39	11 39·8	11 41·7	11 07·9	3·9	3·0	9·9	7·7	15·9	12·3
40	11 40·0	11 41·9	11 08·1	4·0	3·1	10·0	7·8	16·0	12·4
41	11 40·3	11 42·2	11 08·3	4·1	3·2	10·1	7·8	16·1	12·5
42	11 40·5	11 42·4	11 08·6	4·2	3·3	10·2	7·9	16·2	12·6
43	11 40·8	11 42·7	11 08·8	4·3	3·3	10·3	8·0	16·3	12·6
44	11 41·0	11 42·9	11 09·1	4·4	3·4	10·4	8·1	16·4	12·7
45	11 41·3	11 43·2	11 09·3	4·5	3·5	10·5	8·1	16·5	12·8
46	11 41·5	11 43·4	11 09·5	4·6	3·6	10·6	8·2	16·6	12·9
47	11 41·8	11 43·7	11 09·8	4·7	3·6	10·7	8·3	16·7	12·9
48	11 42·0	11 43·9	11 10·0	4·8	3·7	10·8	8·4	16·8	13·0
49	11 42·3	11 44·2	11 10·3	4·9	3·8	10·9	8·4	16·9	13·1
50	11 42·5	11 44·4	11 10·5	5·0	3·9	11·0	8·5	17·0	13·2
51	11 42·8	11 44·7	11 10·7	5·1	4·0	11·1	8·6	17·1	13·3
52	11 43·0	11 44·9	11 11·0	5·2	4·0	11·2	8·7	17·2	13·3
53	11 43·3	11 45·2	11 11·2	5·3	4·1	11·3	8·8	17·3	13·4
54	11 43·5	11 45·4	11 11·5	5·4	4·2	11·4	8·8	17·4	13·5
55	11 43·8	11 45·7	11 11·7	5·5	4·3	11·5	8·9	17·5	13·6
56	11 44·0	11 45·9	11 11·9	5·6	4·3	11·6	9·0	17·6	13·6
57	11 44·3	11 46·2	11 12·2	5·7	4·4	11·7	9·1	17·7	13·7
58	11 44·5	11 46·4	11 12·4	5·8	4·5	11·8	9·1	17·8	13·8
59	11 44·8	11 46·7	11 12·6	5·9	4·6	11·9	9·2	17·9	13·9
60	11 45·0	11 46·9	11 12·9	6·0	4·7	12·0	9·3	18·0	14·0

47	SUN PLANETS	ARIES	MOON	v or d	Corrⁿ	v or d	Corrⁿ	v or d	Corrⁿ
s	° ′	° ′	° ′	′	′	′	′	′	′
00	11 45·0	11 46·9	11 12·9	0·0	0·0	6·0	4·8	12·0	9·5
01	11 45·3	11 47·2	11 13·1	0·1	0·1	6·1	4·8	12·1	9·6
02	11 45·5	11 47·4	11 13·4	0·2	0·2	6·2	4·9	12·2	9·7
03	11 45·8	11 47·7	11 13·6	0·3	0·2	6·3	5·0	12·3	9·7
04	11 46·0	11 47·9	11 13·8	0·4	0·3	6·4	5·1	12·4	9·8
05	11 46·3	11 48·2	11 14·1	0·5	0·4	6·5	5·1	12·5	9·9
06	11 46·5	11 48·4	11 14·3	0·6	0·5	6·6	5·2	12·6	10·0
07	11 46·8	11 48·7	11 14·6	0·7	0·6	6·7	5·3	12·7	10·1
08	11 47·0	11 48·9	11 14·8	0·8	0·6	6·8	5·4	12·8	10·1
09	11 47·3	11 49·2	11 15·0	0·9	0·7	6·9	5·5	12·9	10·2
10	11 47·5	11 49·4	11 15·3	1·0	0·8	7·0	5·5	13·0	10·3
11	11 47·8	11 49·7	11 15·5	1·1	0·9	7·1	5·6	13·1	10·4
12	11 48·0	11 49·9	11 15·7	1·2	1·0	7·2	5·7	13·2	10·5
13	11 48·3	11 50·2	11 16·0	1·3	1·0	7·3	5·8	13·3	10·5
14	11 48·5	11 50·4	11 16·2	1·4	1·1	7·4	5·9	13·4	10·6
15	11 48·8	11 50·7	11 16·5	1·5	1·2	7·5	5·9	13·5	10·7
16	11 49·0	11 50·9	11 16·7	1·6	1·3	7·6	6·0	13·6	10·8
17	11 49·3	11 51·2	11 16·9	1·7	1·3	7·7	6·1	13·7	10·8
18	11 49·5	11 51·4	11 17·2	1·8	1·4	7·8	6·2	13·8	10·9
19	11 49·8	11 51·7	11 17·4	1·9	1·5	7·9	6·3	13·9	11·0
20	11 50·0	11 51·9	11 17·7	2·0	1·6	8·0	6·3	14·0	11·1
21	11 50·3	11 52·2	11 17·9	2·1	1·7	8·1	6·4	14·1	11·2
22	11 50·5	11 52·4	11 18·1	2·2	1·7	8·2	6·5	14·2	11·2
23	11 50·8	11 52·7	11 18·4	2·3	1·8	8·3	6·6	14·3	11·3
24	11 51·0	11 52·9	11 18·6	2·4	1·9	8·4	6·7	14·4	11·4
25	11 51·3	11 53·2	11 18·8	2·5	2·0	8·5	6·7	14·5	11·5
26	11 51·5	11 53·4	11 19·1	2·6	2·1	8·6	6·8	14·6	11·6
27	11 51·8	11 53·7	11 19·3	2·7	2·1	8·7	6·9	14·7	11·6
28	11 52·0	11 53·9	11 19·6	2·8	2·2	8·8	7·0	14·8	11·7
29	11 52·3	11 54·2	11 19·8	2·9	2·3	8·9	7·0	14·9	11·8
30	11 52·5	11 54·5	11 20·0	3·0	2·4	9·0	7·1	15·0	11·9
31	11 52·8	11 54·7	11 20·3	3·1	2·5	9·1	7·2	15·1	12·0
32	11 53·0	11 55·0	11 20·5	3·2	2·5	9·2	7·3	15·2	12·0
33	11 53·3	11 55·2	11 20·8	3·3	2·6	9·3	7·4	15·3	12·1
34	11 53·5	11 55·5	11 21·0	3·4	2·7	9·4	7·4	15·4	12·2
35	11 53·8	11 55·7	11 21·2	3·5	2·8	9·5	7·5	15·5	12·3
36	11 54·0	11 56·0	11 21·5	3·6	2·9	9·6	7·6	15·6	12·4
37	11 54·3	11 56·2	11 21·7	3·7	2·9	9·7	7·7	15·7	12·4
38	11 54·5	11 56·5	11 22·0	3·8	3·0	9·8	7·8	15·8	12·5
39	11 54·8	11 56·7	11 22·2	3·9	3·1	9·9	7·8	15·9	12·6
40	11 55·0	11 57·0	11 22·4	4·0	3·2	10·0	7·9	16·0	12·7
41	11 55·3	11 57·2	11 22·7	4·1	3·2	10·1	8·0	16·1	12·7
42	11 55·5	11 57·5	11 22·9	4·2	3·3	10·2	8·1	16·2	12·8
43	11 55·8	11 57·7	11 23·1	4·3	3·4	10·3	8·2	16·3	12·9
44	11 56·0	11 58·0	11 23·4	4·4	3·5	10·4	8·2	16·4	13·0
45	11 56·3	11 58·2	11 23·6	4·5	3·6	10·5	8·3	16·5	13·1
46	11 56·5	11 58·5	11 23·9	4·6	3·6	10·6	8·4	16·6	13·1
47	11 56·8	11 58·7	11 24·1	4·7	3·7	10·7	8·5	16·7	13·2
48	11 57·0	11 59·0	11 24·3	4·8	3·8	10·8	8·6	16·8	13·3
49	11 57·3	11 59·2	11 24·6	4·9	3·9	10·9	8·6	16·9	13·4
50	11 57·5	11 59·5	11 24·8	5·0	4·0	11·0	8·7	17·0	13·5
51	11 57·8	11 59·7	11 25·1	5·1	4·0	11·1	8·8	17·1	13·5
52	11 58·0	12 00·0	11 25·3	5·2	4·1	11·2	8·9	17·2	13·6
53	11 58·3	12 00·2	11 25·5	5·3	4·2	11·3	8·9	17·3	13·7
54	11 58·5	12 00·5	11 25·8	5·4	4·3	11·4	9·0	17·4	13·8
55	11 58·8	12 00·7	11 26·0	5·5	4·4	11·5	9·1	17·5	13·9
56	11 59·0	12 01·0	11 26·2	5·6	4·4	11·6	9·2	17·6	13·9
57	11 59·3	12 01·2	11 26·5	5·7	4·5	11·7	9·3	17·7	14·0
58	11 59·5	12 01·5	11 26·7	5·8	4·6	11·8	9·3	17·8	14·1
59	11 59·8	12 01·7	11 27·0	5·9	4·7	11·9	9·4	17·9	14·2
60	12 00·0	12 02·0	11 27·2	6·0	4·8	12·0	9·5	18·0	14·3

48ᵐ

48 s	SUN PLANETS	ARIES	MOON	v or d Corrⁿ	v or d Corrⁿ	v or d Corrⁿ
00	12 00·0	12 02·0	11 27·2	0·0 0·0	6·0 4·9	12·0 9·7
01	12 00·3	12 02·2	11 27·4	0·1 0·1	6·1 4·9	12·1 9·8
02	12 00·5	12 02·5	11 27·7	0·2 0·2	6·2 5·0	12·2 9·9
03	12 00·8	12 02·7	11 27·9	0·3 0·2	6·3 5·1	12·3 9·9
04	12 01·0	12 03·0	11 28·2	0·4 0·3	6·4 5·2	12·4 10·0
05	12 01·3	12 03·2	11 28·4	0·5 0·4	6·5 5·3	12·5 10·1
06	12 01·5	12 03·5	11 28·6	0·6 0·5	6·6 5·3	12·6 10·2
07	12 01·8	12 03·7	11 28·9	0·7 0·6	6·7 5·4	12·7 10·3
08	12 02·0	12 04·0	11 29·1	0·8 0·6	6·8 5·5	12·8 10·3
09	12 02·3	12 04·2	11 29·3	0·9 0·7	6·9 5·6	12·9 10·4
10	12 02·5	12 04·5	11 29·6	1·0 0·8	7·0 5·7	13·0 10·5
11	12 02·8	12 04·7	11 29·8	1·1 0·9	7·1 5·7	13·1 10·6
12	12 03·0	12 05·0	11 30·1	1·2 1·0	7·2 5·8	13·2 10·7
13	12 03·3	12 05·2	11 30·3	1·3 1·1	7·3 5·9	13·3 10·8
14	12 03·5	12 05·5	11 30·5	1·4 1·1	7·4 6·0	13·4 10·8
15	12 03·8	12 05·7	11 30·8	1·5 1·2	7·5 6·1	13·5 10·9
16	12 04·0	12 06·0	11 31·0	1·6 1·3	7·6 6·1	13·6 11·0
17	12 04·3	12 06·2	11 31·3	1·7 1·4	7·7 6·2	13·7 11·1
18	12 04·5	12 06·5	11 31·5	1·8 1·5	7·8 6·3	13·8 11·2
19	12 04·8	12 06·7	11 31·7	1·9 1·5	7·9 6·4	13·9 11·2
20	12 05·0	12 07·0	11 32·0	2·0 1·6	8·0 6·5	14·0 11·3
21	12 05·3	12 07·2	11 32·2	2·1 1·7	8·1 6·5	14·1 11·4
22	12 05·5	12 07·5	11 32·4	2·2 1·8	8·2 6·6	14·2 11·5
23	12 05·8	12 07·7	11 32·7	2·3 1·9	8·3 6·7	14·3 11·6
24	12 06·0	12 08·0	11 32·9	2·4 1·9	8·4 6·8	14·4 11·6
25	12 06·3	12 08·2	11 33·2	2·5 2·0	8·5 6·9	14·5 11·7
26	12 06·5	12 08·5	11 33·4	2·6 2·1	8·6 7·0	14·6 11·8
27	12 06·8	12 08·7	11 33·6	2·7 2·2	8·7 7·0	14·7 11·9
28	12 07·0	12 09·0	11 33·9	2·8 2·3	8·8 7·1	14·8 12·0
29	12 07·3	12 09·2	11 34·1	2·9 2·3	8·9 7·2	14·9 12·0
30	12 07·5	12 09·5	11 34·4	3·0 2·4	9·0 7·3	15·0 12·1
31	12 07·8	12 09·7	11 34·6	3·1 2·5	9·1 7·4	15·1 12·2
32	12 08·0	12 10·0	11 34·8	3·2 2·6	9·2 7·4	15·2 12·3
33	12 08·3	12 10·2	11 35·1	3·3 2·7	9·3 7·5	15·3 12·4
34	12 08·5	12 10·5	11 35·3	3·4 2·7	9·4 7·6	15·4 12·4
35	12 08·8	12 10·7	11 35·6	3·5 2·8	9·5 7·7	15·5 12·5
36	12 09·0	12 11·0	11 35·8	3·6 2·9	9·6 7·8	15·6 12·6
37	12 09·3	12 11·2	11 36·0	3·7 3·0	9·7 7·8	15·7 12·7
38	12 09·5	12 11·5	11 36·3	3·8 3·1	9·8 7·9	15·8 12·8
39	12 09·8	12 11·7	11 36·5	3·9 3·2	9·9 8·0	15·9 12·9
40	12 10·0	12 12·0	11 36·7	4·0 3·2	10·0 8·1	16·0 12·9
41	12 10·3	12 12·2	11 37·0	4·1 3·3	10·1 8·2	16·1 13·0
42	12 10·5	12 12·5	11 37·2	4·2 3·4	10·2 8·2	16·2 13·1
43	12 10·8	12 12·8	11 37·5	4·3 3·5	10·3 8·3	16·3 13·2
44	12 11·0	12 13·0	11 37·7	4·4 3·6	10·4 8·4	16·4 13·3
45	12 11·3	12 13·3	11 37·9	4·5 3·6	10·5 8·5	16·5 13·3
46	12 11·5	12 13·5	11 38·2	4·6 3·7	10·6 8·6	16·6 13·4
47	12 11·8	12 13·8	11 38·4	4·7 3·8	10·7 8·6	16·7 13·5
48	12 12·0	12 14·0	11 38·7	4·8 3·9	10·8 8·7	16·8 13·6
49	12 12·3	12 14·3	11 38·9	4·9 4·0	10·9 8·8	16·9 13·7
50	12 12·5	12 14·5	11 39·1	5·0 4·0	11·0 8·9	17·0 13·7
51	12 12·8	12 14·8	11 39·4	5·1 4·1	11·1 9·0	17·1 13·8
52	12 13·0	12 15·0	11 39·6	5·2 4·2	11·2 9·1	17·2 13·9
53	12 13·3	12 15·3	11 39·8	5·3 4·3	11·3 9·1	17·3 14·0
54	12 13·5	12 15·5	11 40·1	5·4 4·4	11·4 9·2	17·4 14·1
55	12 13·8	12 15·8	11 40·3	5·5 4·4	11·5 9·3	17·5 14·1
56	12 14·0	12 16·0	11 40·6	5·6 4·5	11·6 9·4	17·6 14·2
57	12 14·3	12 16·3	11 40·8	5·7 4·6	11·7 9·5	17·7 14·3
58	12 14·5	12 16·5	11 41·0	5·8 4·7	11·8 9·5	17·8 14·4
59	12 14·8	12 16·8	11 41·3	5·9 4·8	11·9 9·6	17·9 14·5
60	12 15·0	12 17·0	11 41·5	6·0 4·9	12·0 9·7	18·0 14·6

49ᵐ

49 s	SUN PLANETS	ARIES	MOON	v or d Corrⁿ	v or d Corrⁿ	v or d Corrⁿ
00	12 15·0	12 17·0	11 41·5	0·0 0·0	6·0 5·0	12·0 9·9
01	12 15·3	12 17·3	11 41·8	0·1 0·1	6·1 5·0	12·1 10·0
02	12 15·5	12 17·5	11 42·0	0·2 0·2	6·2 5·1	12·2 10·1
03	12 15·8	12 17·8	11 42·2	0·3 0·2	6·3 5·2	12·3 10·1
04	12 16·0	12 18·0	11 42·5	0·4 0·3	6·4 5·3	12·4 10·2
05	12 16·3	12 18·3	11 42·7	0·5 0·4	6·5 5·4	12·5 10·3
06	12 16·5	12 18·5	11 42·9	0·6 0·5	6·6 5·4	12·6 10·4
07	12 16·8	12 18·8	11 43·2	0·7 0·6	6·7 5·5	12·7 10·5
08	12 17·0	12 19·0	11 43·4	0·8 0·7	6·8 5·6	12·8 10·6
09	12 17·3	12 19·3	11 43·7	0·9 0·7	6·9 5·7	12·9 10·6
10	12 17·5	12 19·5	11 43·9	1·0 0·8	7·0 5·8	13·0 10·7
11	12 17·8	12 19·8	11 44·1	1·1 0·9	7·1 5·9	13·1 10·8
12	12 18·0	12 20·0	11 44·4	1·2 1·0	7·2 5·9	13·2 10·9
13	12 18·3	12 20·3	11 44·6	1·3 1·1	7·3 6·0	13·3 11·0
14	12 18·5	12 20·5	11 44·9	1·4 1·2	7·4 6·1	13·4 11·1
15	12 18·8	12 20·8	11 45·1	1·5 1·2	7·5 6·2	13·5 11·1
16	12 19·0	12 21·0	11 45·3	1·6 1·3	7·6 6·3	13·6 11·2
17	12 19·3	12 21·3	11 45·6	1·7 1·4	7·7 6·4	13·7 11·3
18	12 19·5	12 21·5	11 45·8	1·8 1·5	7·8 6·4	13·8 11·4
19	12 19·8	12 21·8	11 46·1	1·9 1·6	7·9 6·5	13·9 11·5
20	12 20·0	12 22·0	11 46·3	2·0 1·7	8·0 6·6	14·0 11·6
21	12 20·3	12 22·3	11 46·5	2·1 1·7	8·1 6·7	14·1 11·6
22	12 20·5	12 22·5	11 46·8	2·2 1·8	8·2 6·8	14·2 11·7
23	12 20·8	12 22·8	11 47·0	2·3 1·9	8·3 6·8	14·3 11·8
24	12 21·0	12 23·0	11 47·2	2·4 2·0	8·4 6·9	14·4 11·9
25	12 21·3	12 23·3	11 47·5	2·5 2·1	8·5 7·0	14·5 12·0
26	12 21·5	12 23·5	11 47·7	2·6 2·1	8·6 7·1	14·6 12·0
27	12 21·8	12 23·8	11 48·0	2·7 2·2	8·7 7·2	14·7 12·1
28	12 22·0	12 24·0	11 48·2	2·8 2·3	8·8 7·3	14·8 12·2
29	12 22·3	12 24·3	11 48·4	2·9 2·4	8·9 7·3	14·9 12·3
30	12 22·5	12 24·5	11 48·7	3·0 2·5	9·0 7·4	15·0 12·4
31	12 22·8	12 24·8	11 48·9	3·1 2·6	9·1 7·5	15·1 12·5
32	12 23·0	12 25·0	11 49·2	3·2 2·6	9·2 7·6	15·2 12·5
33	12 23·3	12 25·3	11 49·4	3·3 2·7	9·3 7·7	15·3 12·6
34	12 23·5	12 25·5	11 49·6	3·4 2·8	9·4 7·8	15·4 12·7
35	12 23·8	12 25·8	11 49·9	3·5 2·9	9·5 7·8	15·5 12·8
36	12 24·0	12 26·0	11 50·1	3·6 3·0	9·6 7·9	15·6 12·9
37	12 24·3	12 26·3	11 50·3	3·7 3·1	9·7 8·0	15·7 13·0
38	12 24·5	12 26·5	11 50·6	3·8 3·1	9·8 8·1	15·8 13·0
39	12 24·8	12 26·8	11 50·8	3·9 3·2	9·9 8·2	15·9 13·1
40	12 25·0	12 27·0	11 51·1	4·0 3·3	10·0 8·3	16·0 13·2
41	12 25·3	12 27·3	11 51·3	4·1 3·4	10·1 8·3	16·1 13·3
42	12 25·5	12 27·5	11 51·5	4·2 3·5	10·2 8·4	16·2 13·4
43	12 25·8	12 27·8	11 51·8	4·3 3·5	10·3 8·5	16·3 13·4
44	12 26·0	12 28·0	11 52·0	4·4 3·6	10·4 8·6	16·4 13·5
45	12 26·3	12 28·3	11 52·3	4·5 3·7	10·5 8·7	16·5 13·6
46	12 26·5	12 28·5	11 52·5	4·6 3·8	10·6 8·7	16·6 13·7
47	12 26·8	12 28·8	11 52·7	4·7 3·9	10·7 8·8	16·7 13·8
48	12 27·0	12 29·0	11 53·0	4·8 4·0	10·8 8·9	16·8 13·9
49	12 27·3	12 29·3	11 53·2	4·9 4·0	10·9 9·0	16·9 13·9
50	12 27·5	12 29·5	11 53·4	5·0 4·1	11·0 9·1	17·0 14·0
51	12 27·8	12 29·8	11 53·7	5·1 4·2	11·1 9·2	17·1 14·1
52	12 28·0	12 30·0	11 53·9	5·2 4·3	11·2 9·2	17·2 14·2
53	12 28·3	12 30·3	11 54·2	5·3 4·4	11·3 9·3	17·3 14·3
54	12 28·5	12 30·5	11 54·4	5·4 4·5	11·4 9·4	17·4 14·4
55	12 28·8	12 30·8	11 54·6	5·5 4·5	11·5 9·5	17·5 14·4
56	12 29·0	12 31·1	11 54·9	5·6 4·6	11·6 9·6	17·6 14·5
57	12 29·3	12 31·3	11 55·1	5·7 4·7	11·7 9·7	17·7 14·6
58	12 29·5	12 31·6	11 55·4	5·8 4·8	11·8 9·7	17·8 14·7
59	12 29·8	12 31·8	11 55·6	5·9 4·9	11·9 9·8	17·9 14·8
60	12 30·0	12 32·1	11 55·8	6·0 5·0	12·0 9·9	18·0 14·9

50 s	SUN PLANETS	ARIES	MOON	v or d	Corrⁿ	v or d	Corrⁿ	v or d	Corrⁿ	51 s	SUN PLANETS	ARIES	MOON	v or d	Corrⁿ	v or d	Corrⁿ	v or d	Corrⁿ
00	12 30·0	12 32·1	11 55·8	0·0	0·0	6·0	5·1	12·0	10·1	00	12 45·0	12 47·1	12 10·2	0·0	0·0	6·0	5·2	12·0	10·3
01	12 30·3	12 32·3	11 56·1	0·1	0·1	6·1	5·1	12·1	10·2	01	12 45·3	12 47·3	12 10·4	0·1	0·1	6·1	5·2	12·1	10·4
02	12 30·5	12 32·6	11 56·3	0·2	0·2	6·2	5·2	12·2	10·3	02	12 45·5	12 47·6	12 10·6	0·2	0·2	6·2	5·3	12·2	10·5
03	12 30·8	12 32·8	11 56·5	0·3	0·3	6·3	5·3	12·3	10·4	03	12 45·8	12 47·8	12 10·9	0·3	0·3	6·3	5·4	12·3	10·6
04	12 31·0	12 33·1	11 56·8	0·4	0·3	6·4	5·4	12·4	10·4	04	12 46·0	12 48·1	12 11·1	0·4	0·3	6·4	5·5	12·4	10·6
05	12 31·3	12 33·3	11 57·0	0·5	0·4	6·5	5·5	12·5	10·5	05	12 46·3	12 48·3	12 11·3	0·5	0·4	6·5	5·6	12·5	10·7
06	12 31·5	12 33·6	11 57·3	0·6	0·5	6·6	5·6	12·6	10·6	06	12 46·5	12 48·6	12 11·6	0·6	0·5	6·6	5·7	12·6	10·8
07	12 31·8	12 33·8	11 57·5	0·7	0·6	6·7	5·6	12·7	10·7	07	12 46·8	12 48·8	12 11·8	0·7	0·6	6·7	5·8	12·7	10·9
08	12 32·0	12 34·1	11 57·7	0·8	0·7	6·8	5·7	12·8	10·8	08	12 47·0	12 49·1	12 12·1	0·8	0·7	6·8	5·8	12·8	11·0
09	12 32·3	12 34·3	11 58·0	0·9	0·8	6·9	5·8	12·9	10·9	09	12 47·3	12 49·4	12 12·3	0·9	0·8	6·9	5·9	12·9	11·1
10	12 32·5	12 34·6	11 58·2	1·0	0·8	7·0	5·9	13·0	10·9	10	12 47·5	12 49·6	12 12·5	1·0	0·9	7·0	6·0	13·0	11·2
11	12 32·8	12 34·8	11 58·5	1·1	0·9	7·1	6·0	13·1	11·0	11	12 47·8	12 49·9	12 12·8	1·1	0·9	7·1	6·1	13·1	11·2
12	12 33·0	12 35·1	11 58·7	1·2	1·0	7·2	6·1	13·2	11·1	12	12 48·0	12 50·1	12 13·0	1·2	1·0	7·2	6·2	13·2	11·3
13	12 33·3	12 35·3	11 58·9	1·3	1·1	7·3	6·1	13·3	11·2	13	12 48·3	12 50·4	12 13·3	1·3	1·1	7·3	6·3	13·3	11·4
14	12 33·5	12 35·6	11 59·2	1·4	1·2	7·4	6·2	13·4	11·3	14	12 48·5	12 50·6	12 13·5	1·4	1·2	7·4	6·4	13·4	11·5
15	12 33·8	12 35·8	11 59·4	1·5	1·3	7·5	6·3	13·5	11·4	15	12 48·8	12 50·9	12 13·7	1·5	1·3	7·5	6·4	13·5	11·6
16	12 34·0	12 36·1	11 59·7	1·6	1·4	7·6	6·4	13·6	11·5	16	12 49·0	12 51·1	12 14·0	1·6	1·4	7·6	6·5	13·6	11·7
17	12 34·3	12 36·3	11 59·9	1·7	1·4	7·7	6·5	13·7	11·5	17	12 49·3	12 51·4	12 14·2	1·7	1·5	7·7	6·6	13·7	11·8
18	12 34·5	12 36·6	12 00·1	1·8	1·5	7·8	6·6	13·8	11·6	18	12 49·5	12 51·6	12 14·4	1·8	1·5	7·8	6·7	13·8	11·8
19	12 34·8	12 36·8	12 00·4	1·9	1·6	7·9	6·6	13·9	11·7	19	12 49·8	12 51·9	12 14·7	1·9	1·6	7·9	6·8	13·9	11·9
20	12 35·0	12 37·1	12 00·6	2·0	1·7	8·0	6·7	14·0	11·8	20	12 50·0	12 52·1	12 14·9	2·0	1·7	8·0	6·9	14·0	12·0
21	12 35·3	12 37·3	12 00·8	2·1	1·8	8·1	6·8	14·1	11·9	21	12 50·3	12 52·4	12 15·2	2·1	1·8	8·1	7·0	14·1	12·1
22	12 35·5	12 37·6	12 01·1	2·2	1·9	8·2	6·9	14·2	12·0	22	12 50·5	12 52·6	12 15·4	2·2	1·9	8·2	7·0	14·2	12·2
23	12 35·8	12 37·8	12 01·3	2·3	1·9	8·3	7·0	14·3	12·0	23	12 50·8	12 52·9	12 15·6	2·3	2·0	8·3	7·1	14·3	12·3
24	12 36·0	12 38·1	12 01·6	2·4	2·0	8·4	7·1	14·4	12·1	24	12 51·0	12 53·1	12 15·9	2·4	2·1	8·4	7·2	14·4	12·4
25	12 36·3	12 38·3	12 01·8	2·5	2·1	8·5	7·2	14·5	12·2	25	12 51·3	12 53·4	12 16·1	2·5	2·1	8·5	7·3	14·5	12·4
26	12 36·5	12 38·6	12 02·0	2·6	2·2	8·6	7·2	14·6	12·3	26	12 51·5	12 53·6	12 16·4	2·6	2·2	8·6	7·4	14·6	12·5
27	12 36·8	12 38·8	12 02·3	2·7	2·3	8·7	7·3	14·7	12·4	27	12 51·8	12 53·9	12 16·6	2·7	2·3	8·7	7·5	14·7	12·6
28	12 37·0	12 39·1	12 02·5	2·8	2·4	8·8	7·4	14·8	12·5	28	12 52·0	12 54·1	12 16·8	2·8	2·4	8·8	7·6	14·8	12·7
29	12 37·3	12 39·3	12 02·8	2·9	2·4	8·9	7·5	14·9	12·5	29	12 52·3	12 54·4	12 17·1	2·9	2·5	8·9	7·6	14·9	12·8
30	12 37·5	12 39·6	12 03·0	3·0	2·5	9·0	7·6	15·0	12·6	30	12 52·5	12 54·6	12 17·3	3·0	2·6	9·0	7·7	15·0	12·9
31	12 37·8	12 39·8	12 03·2	3·1	2·6	9·1	7·7	15·1	12·7	31	12 52·8	12 54·9	12 17·5	3·1	2·7	9·1	7·8	15·1	13·0
32	12 38·0	12 40·1	12 03·5	3·2	2·7	9·2	7·7	15·2	12·8	32	12 53·0	12 55·1	12 17·8	3·2	2·7	9·2	7·9	15·2	13·0
33	12 38·3	12 40·3	12 03·7	3·3	2·8	9·3	7·8	15·3	12·9	33	12 53·3	12 55·4	12 18·0	3·3	2·8	9·3	8·0	15·3	13·1
34	12 38·5	12 40·6	12 03·9	3·4	2·9	9·4	7·9	15·4	13·0	34	12 53·5	12 55·6	12 18·3	3·4	2·9	9·4	8·1	15·4	13·2
35	12 38·8	12 40·8	12 04·2	3·5	2·9	9·5	8·0	15·5	13·0	35	12 53·8	12 55·9	12 18·5	3·5	3·0	9·5	8·2	15·5	13·3
36	12 39·0	12 41·1	12 04·4	3·6	3·0	9·6	8·1	15·6	13·1	36	12 54·0	12 56·1	12 18·7	3·6	3·1	9·6	8·2	15·6	13·4
37	12 39·3	12 41·3	12 04·7	3·7	3·1	9·7	8·2	15·7	13·2	37	12 54·3	12 56·4	12 19·0	3·7	3·2	9·7	8·3	15·7	13·5
38	12 39·5	12 41·6	12 04·9	3·8	3·2	9·8	8·2	15·8	13·3	38	12 54·5	12 56·6	12 19·2	3·8	3·3	9·8	8·4	15·8	13·6
39	12 39·8	12 41·8	12 05·1	3·9	3·3	9·9	8·3	15·9	13·4	39	12 54·8	12 56·9	12 19·5	3·9	3·3	9·9	8·5	15·9	13·6
40	12 40·0	12 42·1	12 05·4	4·0	3·4	10·0	8·4	16·0	13·5	40	12 55·0	12 57·1	12 19·7	4·0	3·4	10·0	8·6	16·0	13·7
41	12 40·3	12 42·3	12 05·6	4·1	3·5	10·1	8·5	16·1	13·6	41	12 55·3	12 57·4	12 19·9	4·1	3·5	10·1	8·7	16·1	13·8
42	12 40·5	12 42·6	12 05·9	4·2	3·5	10·2	8·6	16·2	13·6	42	12 55·5	12 57·6	12 20·2	4·2	3·6	10·2	8·8	16·2	13·9
43	12 40·8	12 42·8	12 06·1	4·3	3·6	10·3	8·7	16·3	13·7	43	12 55·8	12 57·9	12 20·4	4·3	3·7	10·3	8·8	16·3	14·0
44	12 41·0	12 43·1	12 06·3	4·4	3·7	10·4	8·8	16·4	13·8	44	12 56·0	12 58·1	12 20·6	4·4	3·8	10·4	8·9	16·4	14·1
45	12 41·3	12 43·3	12 06·6	4·5	3·8	10·5	8·8	16·5	13·9	45	12 56·3	12 58·4	12 20·9	4·5	3·9	10·5	9·0	16·5	14·2
46	12 41·5	12 43·6	12 06·8	4·6	3·9	10·6	8·9	16·6	14·0	46	12 56·5	12 58·6	12 21·1	4·6	3·9	10·6	9·1	16·6	14·2
47	12 41·8	12 43·8	12 07·0	4·7	4·0	10·7	9·0	16·7	14·1	47	12 56·8	12 58·9	12 21·4	4·7	4·0	10·7	9·2	16·7	14·3
48	12 42·0	12 44·1	12 07·3	4·8	4·0	10·8	9·1	16·8	14·1	48	12 57·0	12 59·1	12 21·6	4·8	4·1	10·8	9·3	16·8	14·4
49	12 42·3	12 44·3	12 07·5	4·9	4·1	10·9	9·2	16·9	14·2	49	12 57·3	12 59·4	12 21·8	4·9	4·2	10·9	9·4	16·9	14·5
50	12 42·5	12 44·6	12 07·8	5·0	4·2	11·0	9·3	17·0	14·3	50	12 57·5	12 59·6	12 22·1	5·0	4·3	11·0	9·4	17·0	14·6
51	12 42·8	12 44·8	12 08·0	5·1	4·3	11·1	9·3	17·1	14·4	51	12 57·8	12 59·9	12 22·3	5·1	4·4	11·1	9·5	17·1	14·7
52	12 43·0	12 45·1	12 08·2	5·2	4·4	11·2	9·4	17·2	14·5	52	12 58·0	13 00·1	12 22·6	5·2	4·5	11·2	9·6	17·2	14·8
53	12 43·3	12 45·3	12 08·5	5·3	4·5	11·3	9·5	17·3	14·6	53	12 58·3	13 00·4	12 22·8	5·3	4·5	11·3	9·7	17·3	14·8
54	12 43·5	12 45·6	12 08·7	5·4	4·5	11·4	9·6	17·4	14·6	54	12 58·5	13 00·6	12 23·0	5·4	4·6	11·4	9·8	17·4	14·9
55	12 43·8	12 45·8	12 09·0	5·5	4·6	11·5	9·7	17·5	14·7	55	12 58·8	13 00·9	12 23·3	5·5	4·7	11·5	9·9	17·5	15·0
56	12 44·0	12 46·1	12 09·2	5·6	4·7	11·6	9·8	17·6	14·8	56	12 59·0	13 01·1	12 23·5	5·6	4·8	11·6	10·0	17·6	15·1
57	12 44·3	12 46·3	12 09·4	5·7	4·8	11·7	9·8	17·7	14·9	57	12 59·3	13 01·4	12 23·8	5·7	4·9	11·7	10·0	17·7	15·2
58	12 44·5	12 46·6	12 09·7	5·8	4·9	11·8	9·9	17·8	15·0	58	12 59·5	13 01·6	12 24·0	5·8	5·0	11·8	10·1	17·8	15·3
59	12 44·8	12 46·8	12 09·9	5·9	5·0	11·9	10·0	17·9	15·1	59	12 59·8	13 01·9	12 24·2	5·9	5·1	11·9	10·2	17·9	15·4
60	12 45·0	12 47·1	12 10·2	6·0	5·1	12·0	10·1	18·0	15·2	60	13 00·0	13 02·1	12 24·5	6·0	5·2	12·0	10·3	18·0	15·5

52 (m)	SUN PLANETS	ARIES	MOON	v or Corrⁿ d	v or Corrⁿ d	v or Corrⁿ d
s	° ′	° ′	° ′	′ ′	′ ′	′ ′
00	13 00·0	13 02·1	12 24·5	0·0 0·0	6·0 5·3	12·0 10·5
01	13 00·3	13 02·4	12 24·7	0·1 0·1	6·1 5·3	12·1 10·6
02	13 00·5	13 02·6	12 24·9	0·2 0·2	6·2 5·4	12·2 10·7
03	13 00·8	13 02·9	12 25·2	0·3 0·3	6·3 5·5	12·3 10·8
04	13 01·0	13 03·1	12 25·4	0·4 0·4	6·4 5·6	12·4 10·9
05	13 01·3	13 03·4	12 25·7	0·5 0·4	6·5 5·7	12·5 10·9
06	13 01·5	13 03·6	12 25·9	0·6 0·5	6·6 5·8	12·6 11·0
07	13 01·8	13 03·9	12 26·1	0·7 0·6	6·7 5·9	12·7 11·1
08	13 02·0	13 04·1	12 26·4	0·8 0·7	6·8 6·0	12·8 11·2
09	13 02·3	13 04·4	12 26·6	0·9 0·8	6·9 6·0	12·9 11·3
10	13 02·5	13 04·6	12 26·9	1·0 0·9	7·0 6·1	13·0 11·4
11	13 02·8	13 04·9	12 27·1	1·1 1·0	7·1 6·2	13·1 11·5
12	13 03·0	13 05·1	12 27·3	1·2 1·1	7·2 6·3	13·2 11·6
13	13 03·3	13 05·4	12 27·6	1·3 1·1	7·3 6·4	13·3 11·6
14	13 03·5	13 05·6	12 27·8	1·4 1·2	7·4 6·5	13·4 11·7
15	13 03·8	13 05·9	12 28·0	1·5 1·3	7·5 6·6	13·5 11·8
16	13 04·0	13 06·1	12 28·3	1·6 1·4	7·6 6·7	13·6 11·9
17	13 04·3	13 06·4	12 28·5	1·7 1·5	7·7 6·7	13·7 12·0
18	13 04·5	13 06·6	12 28·8	1·8 1·6	7·8 6·8	13·8 12·1
19	13 04·8	13 06·9	12 29·0	1·9 1·7	7·9 6·9	13·9 12·2
20	13 05·0	13 07·1	12 29·2	2·0 1·8	8·0 7·0	14·0 12·3
21	13 05·3	13 07·4	12 29·5	2·1 1·8	8·1 7·1	14·1 12·3
22	13 05·5	13 07·7	12 29·7	2·2 1·9	8·2 7·2	14·2 12·4
23	13 05·8	13 07·9	12 30·0	2·3 2·0	8·3 7·3	14·3 12·5
24	13 06·0	13 08·2	12 30·2	2·4 2·1	8·4 7·4	14·4 12·6
25	13 06·3	13 08·4	12 30·4	2·5 2·2	8·5 7·4	14·5 12·7
26	13 06·5	13 08·7	12 30·7	2·6 2·3	8·6 7·5	14·6 12·8
27	13 06·8	13 08·9	12 30·9	2·7 2·4	8·7 7·6	14·7 12·9
28	13 07·0	13 09·2	12 31·1	2·8 2·5	8·8 7·7	14·8 13·0
29	13 07·3	13 09·4	12 31·4	2·9 2·5	8·9 7·8	14·9 13·0
30	13 07·5	13 09·7	12 31·6	3·0 2·6	9·0 7·9	15·0 13·1
31	13 07·8	13 09·9	12 31·9	3·1 2·7	9·1 8·0	15·1 13·2
32	13 08·0	13 10·2	12 32·1	3·2 2·8	9·2 8·0	15·2 13·3
33	13 08·3	13 10·4	12 32·3	3·3 2·9	9·3 8·1	15·3 13·4
34	13 08·5	13 10·7	12 32·6	3·4 3·0	9·4 8·2	15·4 13·5
35	13 08·8	13 10·9	12 32·8	3·5 3·1	9·5 8·3	15·5 13·6
36	13 09·0	13 11·2	12 33·1	3·6 3·2	9·6 8·4	15·6 13·7
37	13 09·3	13 11·4	12 33·3	3·7 3·2	9·7 8·5	15·7 13·7
38	13 09·5	13 11·7	12 33·5	3·8 3·3	9·8 8·6	15·8 13·8
39	13 09·8	13 11·9	12 33·8	3·9 3·4	9·9 8·7	15·9 13·9
40	13 10·0	13 12·2	12 34·0	4·0 3·5	10·0 8·8	16·0 14·0
41	13 10·3	13 12·4	12 34·2	4·1 3·6	10·1 8·8	16·1 14·1
42	13 10·5	13 12·7	12 34·5	4·2 3·7	10·2 8·9	16·2 14·2
43	13 10·8	13 12·9	12 34·7	4·3 3·8	10·3 9·0	16·3 14·3
44	13 11·0	13 13·2	12 35·0	4·4 3·9	10·4 9·1	16·4 14·3
45	13 11·3	13 13·4	12 35·2	4·5 3·9	10·5 9·2	16·5 14·4
46	13 11·5	13 13·7	12 35·4	4·6 4·0	10·6 9·3	16·6 14·5
47	13 11·8	13 13·9	12 35·7	4·7 4·1	10·7 9·4	16·7 14·6
48	13 12·0	13 14·2	12 35·9	4·8 4·2	10·8 9·5	16·8 14·7
49	13 12·3	13 14·4	12 36·2	4·9 4·3	10·9 9·5	16·9 14·8
50	13 12·5	13 14·7	12 36·4	5·0 4·4	11·0 9·6	17·0 14·9
51	13 12·8	13 14·9	12 36·6	5·1 4·5	11·1 9·7	17·1 15·0
52	13 13·0	13 15·2	12 36·9	5·2 4·6	11·2 9·8	17·2 15·1
53	13 13·3	13 15·4	12 37·1	5·3 4·6	11·3 9·9	17·3 15·1
54	13 13·5	13 15·7	12 37·4	5·4 4·7	11·4 10·0	17·4 15·2
55	13 13·8	13 15·9	12 37·6	5·5 4·8	11·5 10·1	17·5 15·3
56	13 14·0	13 16·2	12 37·8	5·6 4·9	11·6 10·2	17·6 15·4
57	13 14·3	13 16·4	12 38·1	5·7 5·0	11·7 10·2	17·7 15·5
58	13 14·5	13 16·7	12 38·3	5·8 5·1	11·8 10·3	17·8 15·6
59	13 14·8	13 16·9	12 38·5	5·9 5·2	11·9 10·4	17·9 15·7
60	13 15·0	13 17·2	12 38·8	6·0 5·3	12·0 10·5	18·0 15·8

53 (m)	SUN PLANETS	ARIES	MOON	v or Corrⁿ d	v or Corrⁿ d	v or Corrⁿ d
s	° ′	° ′	° ′	′ ′	′ ′	′ ′
00	13 15·0	13 17·2	12 38·8	0·0 0·0	6·0 5·4	12·0 10·7
01	13 15·3	13 17·4	12 39·0	0·1 0·1	6·1 5·4	12·1 10·8
02	13 15·5	13 17·7	12 39·3	0·2 0·2	6·2 5·5	12·2 10·9
03	13 15·8	13 17·9	12 39·5	0·3 0·3	6·3 5·6	12·3 11·0
04	13 16·0	13 18·2	12 39·7	0·4 0·4	6·4 5·7	12·4 11·1
05	13 16·3	13 18·4	12 40·0	0·5 0·4	6·5 5·8	12·5 11·1
06	13 16·5	13 18·7	12 40·2	0·6 0·5	6·6 5·9	12·6 11·2
07	13 16·8	13 18·9	12 40·5	0·7 0·6	6·7 6·0	12·7 11·3
08	13 17·0	13 19·2	12 40·7	0·8 0·7	6·8 6·1	12·8 11·4
09	13 17·3	13 19·4	12 40·9	0·9 0·8	6·9 6·2	12·9 11·5
10	13 17·5	13 19·7	12 41·2	1·0 0·9	7·0 6·2	13·0 11·6
11	13 17·8	13 19·9	12 41·4	1·1 1·0	7·1 6·3	13·1 11·7
12	13 18·0	13 20·2	12 41·6	1·2 1·1	7·2 6·4	13·2 11·8
13	13 18·3	13 20·4	12 41·9	1·3 1·2	7·3 6·5	13·3 11·9
14	13 18·5	13 20·7	12 42·1	1·4 1·2	7·4 6·6	13·4 11·9
15	13 18·8	13 20·9	12 42·4	1·5 1·3	7·5 6·7	13·5 12·0
16	13 19·0	13 21·2	12 42·6	1·6 1·4	7·6 6·8	13·6 12·1
17	13 19·3	13 21·4	12 42·8	1·7 1·5	7·7 6·9	13·7 12·2
18	13 19·5	13 21·7	12 43·1	1·8 1·6	7·8 7·0	13·8 12·3
19	13 19·8	13 21·9	12 43·3	1·9 1·7	7·9 7·0	13·9 12·4
20	13 20·0	13 22·2	12 43·6	2·0 1·8	8·0 7·1	14·0 12·5
21	13 20·3	13 22·4	12 43·8	2·1 1·9	8·1 7·2	14·1 12·6
22	13 20·5	13 22·7	12 44·0	2·2 2·0	8·2 7·3	14·2 12·7
23	13 20·8	13 22·9	12 44·3	2·3 2·1	8·3 7·4	14·3 12·8
24	13 21·0	13 23·2	12 44·5	2·4 2·1	8·4 7·5	14·4 12·8
25	13 21·3	13 23·4	12 44·7	2·5 2·2	8·5 7·6	14·5 12·9
26	13 21·5	13 23·7	12 45·0	2·6 2·3	8·6 7·7	14·6 13·0
27	13 21·8	13 23·9	12 45·2	2·7 2·4	8·7 7·8	14·7 13·1
28	13 22·0	13 24·2	12 45·5	2·8 2·5	8·8 7·8	14·8 13·2
29	13 22·3	13 24·4	12 45·7	2·9 2·6	8·9 7·9	14·9 13·3
30	13 22·5	13 24·7	12 45·9	3·0 2·7	9·0 8·0	15·0 13·4
31	13 22·8	13 24·9	12 46·2	3·1 2·8	9·1 8·1	15·1 13·5
32	13 23·0	13 25·2	12 46·4	3·2 2·9	9·2 8·2	15·2 13·6
33	13 23·3	13 25·4	12 46·7	3·3 2·9	9·3 8·3	15·3 13·6
34	13 23·5	13 25·7	12 46·9	3·4 3·0	9·4 8·4	15·4 13·7
35	13 23·8	13 26·0	12 47·1	3·5 3·1	9·5 8·5	15·5 13·8
36	13 24·0	13 26·2	12 47·4	3·6 3·2	9·6 8·6	15·6 13·9
37	13 24·3	13 26·5	12 47·6	3·7 3·3	9·7 8·6	15·7 14·0
38	13 24·5	13 26·7	12 47·9	3·8 3·4	9·8 8·7	15·8 14·1
39	13 24·8	13 27·0	12 48·1	3·9 3·5	9·9 8·8	15·9 14·2
40	13 25·0	13 27·2	12 48·3	4·0 3·6	10·0 8·9	16·0 14·3
41	13 25·3	13 27·5	12 48·6	4·1 3·7	10·1 9·0	16·1 14·4
42	13 25·5	13 27·7	12 48·8	4·2 3·7	10·2 9·1	16·2 14·4
43	13 25·8	13 28·0	12 49·0	4·3 3·8	10·3 9·2	16·3 14·5
44	13 26·0	13 28·2	12 49·3	4·4 3·9	10·4 9·3	16·4 14·6
45	13 26·3	13 28·5	12 49·5	4·5 4·0	10·5 9·4	16·5 14·7
46	13 26·5	13 28·7	12 49·8	4·6 4·1	10·6 9·5	16·6 14·8
47	13 26·8	13 29·0	12 50·0	4·7 4·2	10·7 9·5	16·7 14·9
48	13 27·0	13 29·2	12 50·2	4·8 4·3	10·8 9·6	16·8 15·0
49	13 27·3	13 29·5	12 50·5	4·9 4·4	10·9 9·7	16·9 15·1
50	13 27·5	13 29·7	12 50·7	5·0 4·5	11·0 9·8	17·0 15·2
51	13 27·8	13 30·0	12 51·0	5·1 4·5	11·1 9·9	17·1 15·2
52	13 28·0	13 30·2	12 51·2	5·2 4·6	11·2 10·0	17·2 15·3
53	13 28·3	13 30·5	12 51·4	5·3 4·7	11·3 10·1	17·3 15·4
54	13 28·5	13 30·7	12 51·7	5·4 4·8	11·4 10·2	17·4 15·5
55	13 28·8	13 31·0	12 51·9	5·5 4·9	11·5 10·3	17·5 15·6
56	13 29·0	13 31·2	12 52·1	5·6 5·0	11·6 10·3	17·6 15·7
57	13 29·3	13 31·5	12 52·4	5·7 5·1	11·7 10·4	17·7 15·8
58	13 29·5	13 31·7	12 52·6	5·8 5·2	11·8 10·5	17·8 15·9
59	13 29·8	13 32·0	12 52·9	5·9 5·3	11·9 10·6	17·9 16·0
60	13 30·0	13 32·2	12 53·1	6·0 5·4	12·0 10·7	18·0 16·1

54ᵐ s	SUN PLANETS	ARIES	MOON	v or d / Corrⁿ	v or d / Corrⁿ	v or d / Corrⁿ
	° ′	° ′	° ′	′ ′	′ ′	′ ′
00	13 30.0	13 32.2	12 53.1	0.0 0.0	6.0 5.5	12.0 10.9
01	13 30.3	13 32.5	12 53.3	0.1 0.1	6.1 5.5	12.1 11.0
02	13 30.5	13 32.7	12 53.6	0.2 0.2	6.2 5.6	12.2 11.1
03	13 30.8	13 33.0	12 53.8	0.3 0.3	6.3 5.7	12.3 11.2
04	13 31.0	13 33.2	12 54.1	0.4 0.4	6.4 5.8	12.4 11.3
05	13 31.3	13 33.5	12 54.3	0.5 0.5	6.5 5.9	12.5 11.4
06	13 31.5	13 33.7	12 54.5	0.6 0.5	6.6 6.0	12.6 11.4
07	13 31.8	13 34.0	12 54.8	0.7 0.6	6.7 6.1	12.7 11.5
08	13 32.0	13 34.2	12 55.0	0.8 0.7	6.8 6.2	12.8 11.6
09	13 32.3	13 34.5	12 55.2	0.9 0.8	6.9 6.3	12.9 11.7
10	13 32.5	13 34.7	12 55.5	1.0 0.9	7.0 6.4	13.0 11.8
11	13 32.8	13 35.0	12 55.7	1.1 1.0	7.1 6.4	13.1 11.9
12	13 33.0	13 35.2	12 56.0	1.2 1.1	7.2 6.5	13.2 12.0
13	13 33.3	13 35.5	12 56.2	1.3 1.2	7.3 6.6	13.3 12.1
14	13 33.5	13 35.7	12 56.4	1.4 1.3	7.4 6.7	13.4 12.2
15	13 33.8	13 36.0	12 56.7	1.5 1.4	7.5 6.8	13.5 12.3
16	13 34.0	13 36.2	12 56.9	1.6 1.5	7.6 6.9	13.6 12.4
17	13 34.3	13 36.5	12 57.2	1.7 1.5	7.7 7.0	13.7 12.4
18	13 34.5	13 36.7	12 57.4	1.8 1.6	7.8 7.1	13.8 12.5
19	13 34.8	13 37.0	12 57.6	1.9 1.7	7.9 7.2	13.9 12.6
20	13 35.0	13 37.2	12 57.9	2.0 1.8	8.0 7.3	14.0 12.7
21	13 35.3	13 37.5	12 58.1	2.1 1.9	8.1 7.4	14.1 12.8
22	13 35.5	13 37.7	12 58.3	2.2 2.0	8.2 7.4	14.2 12.9
23	13 35.8	13 38.0	12 58.6	2.3 2.1	8.3 7.5	14.3 13.0
24	13 36.0	13 38.2	12 58.8	2.4 2.2	8.4 7.6	14.4 13.1
25	13 36.3	13 38.5	12 59.1	2.5 2.3	8.5 7.7	14.5 13.2
26	13 36.5	13 38.7	12 59.3	2.6 2.4	8.6 7.8	14.6 13.3
27	13 36.8	13 39.0	12 59.5	2.7 2.5	8.7 7.9	14.7 13.4
28	13 37.0	13 39.2	12 59.8	2.8 2.5	8.8 8.0	14.8 13.4
29	13 37.3	13 39.5	13 00.0	2.9 2.6	8.9 8.1	14.9 13.5
30	13 37.5	13 39.7	13 00.3	3.0 2.7	9.0 8.2	15.0 13.6
31	13 37.8	13 40.0	13 00.5	3.1 2.8	9.1 8.3	15.1 13.7
32	13 38.0	13 40.2	13 00.7	3.2 2.9	9.2 8.4	15.2 13.8
33	13 38.3	13 40.5	13 01.0	3.3 3.0	9.3 8.4	15.3 13.9
34	13 38.5	13 40.7	13 01.2	3.4 3.1	9.4 8.5	15.4 14.0
35	13 38.8	13 41.0	13 01.5	3.5 3.2	9.5 8.6	15.5 14.1
36	13 39.0	13 41.2	13 01.7	3.6 3.3	9.6 8.7	15.6 14.2
37	13 39.3	13 41.5	13 01.9	3.7 3.4	9.7 8.8	15.7 14.3
38	13 39.5	13 41.7	13 02.2	3.8 3.5	9.8 8.9	15.8 14.4
39	13 39.8	13 42.0	13 02.4	3.9 3.5	9.9 9.0	15.9 14.4
40	13 40.0	13 42.2	13 02.6	4.0 3.6	10.0 9.1	16.0 14.5
41	13 40.3	13 42.5	13 02.9	4.1 3.7	10.1 9.2	16.1 14.6
42	13 40.5	13 42.7	13 03.1	4.2 3.8	10.2 9.3	16.2 14.7
43	13 40.8	13 43.0	13 03.4	4.3 3.9	10.3 9.4	16.3 14.8
44	13 41.0	13 43.2	13 03.6	4.4 4.0	10.4 9.4	16.4 14.9
45	13 41.3	13 43.5	13 03.8	4.5 4.1	10.5 9.5	16.5 15.0
46	13 41.5	13 43.7	13 04.1	4.6 4.2	10.6 9.6	16.6 15.1
47	13 41.8	13 44.0	13 04.3	4.7 4.3	10.7 9.7	16.7 15.2
48	13 42.0	13 44.3	13 04.6	4.8 4.4	10.8 9.8	16.8 15.3
49	13 42.3	13 44.5	13 04.8	4.9 4.5	10.9 9.9	16.9 15.4
50	13 42.5	13 44.8	13 05.0	5.0 4.5	11.0 10.0	17.0 15.4
51	13 42.8	13 45.0	13 05.3	5.1 4.6	11.1 10.1	17.1 15.5
52	13 43.0	13 45.3	13 05.5	5.2 4.7	11.2 10.2	17.2 15.6
53	13 43.3	13 45.5	13 05.7	5.3 4.8	11.3 10.3	17.3 15.7
54	13 43.5	13 45.8	13 06.0	5.4 4.9	11.4 10.4	17.4 15.8
55	13 43.8	13 46.0	13 06.2	5.5 5.0	11.5 10.4	17.5 15.9
56	13 44.0	13 46.3	13 06.5	5.6 5.1	11.6 10.5	17.6 16.0
57	13 44.3	13 46.5	13 06.7	5.7 5.2	11.7 10.6	17.7 16.1
58	13 44.5	13 46.8	13 06.9	5.8 5.3	11.8 10.7	17.8 16.2
59	13 44.8	13 47.0	13 07.2	5.9 5.4	11.9 10.8	17.9 16.3
60	13 45.0	13 47.3	13 07.4	6.0 5.5	12.0 10.9	18.0 16.4

55ᵐ s	SUN PLANETS	ARIES	MOON	v or d / Corrⁿ	v or d / Corrⁿ	v or d / Corrⁿ
	° ′	° ′	° ′	′ ′	′ ′	′ ′
00	13 45.0	13 47.3	13 07.4	0.0 0.0	6.0 5.6	12.0 11.1
01	13 45.3	13 47.5	13 07.7	0.1 0.1	6.1 5.6	12.1 11.2
02	13 45.5	13 47.8	13 07.9	0.2 0.2	6.2 5.7	12.2 11.3
03	13 45.8	13 48.0	13 08.1	0.3 0.3	6.3 5.8	12.3 11.4
04	13 46.0	13 48.3	13 08.4	0.4 0.4	6.4 5.9	12.4 11.5
05	13 46.3	13 48.5	13 08.6	0.5 0.5	6.5 6.0	12.5 11.6
06	13 46.5	13 48.8	13 08.8	0.6 0.6	6.6 6.1	12.6 11.7
07	13 46.8	13 49.0	13 09.1	0.7 0.6	6.7 6.2	12.7 11.7
08	13 47.0	13 49.3	13 09.3	0.8 0.7	6.8 6.3	12.8 11.8
09	13 47.3	13 49.5	13 09.6	0.9 0.8	6.9 6.4	12.9 11.9
10	13 47.5	13 49.8	13 09.8	1.0 0.9	7.0 6.5	13.0 12.0
11	13 47.8	13 50.0	13 10.0	1.1 1.0	7.1 6.6	13.1 12.1
12	13 48.0	13 50.3	13 10.3	1.2 1.1	7.2 6.7	13.2 12.2
13	13 48.3	13 50.5	13 10.5	1.3 1.2	7.3 6.8	13.3 12.3
14	13 48.5	13 50.8	13 10.8	1.4 1.3	7.4 6.8	13.4 12.4
15	13 48.8	13 51.0	13 11.0	1.5 1.4	7.5 6.9	13.5 12.5
16	13 49.0	13 51.3	13 11.2	1.6 1.5	7.6 7.0	13.6 12.6
17	13 49.3	13 51.5	13 11.5	1.7 1.6	7.7 7.1	13.7 12.7
18	13 49.5	13 51.8	13 11.7	1.8 1.7	7.8 7.2	13.8 12.8
19	13 49.8	13 52.0	13 12.0	1.9 1.8	7.9 7.3	13.9 12.9
20	13 50.0	13 52.3	13 12.2	2.0 1.9	8.0 7.4	14.0 13.0
21	13 50.3	13 52.5	13 12.4	2.1 1.9	8.1 7.5	14.1 13.0
22	13 50.5	13 52.8	13 12.7	2.2 2.0	8.2 7.6	14.2 13.1
23	13 50.8	13 53.0	13 12.9	2.3 2.1	8.3 7.7	14.3 13.2
24	13 51.0	13 53.3	13 13.1	2.4 2.2	8.4 7.8	14.4 13.3
25	13 51.3	13 53.5	13 13.4	2.5 2.3	8.5 7.9	14.5 13.4
26	13 51.5	13 53.8	13 13.6	2.6 2.4	8.6 8.0	14.6 13.5
27	13 51.8	13 54.0	13 13.9	2.7 2.5	8.7 8.0	14.7 13.6
28	13 52.0	13 54.3	13 14.1	2.8 2.6	8.8 8.1	14.8 13.7
29	13 52.3	13 54.5	13 14.3	2.9 2.7	8.9 8.2	14.9 13.8
30	13 52.5	13 54.8	13 14.6	3.0 2.8	9.0 8.3	15.0 13.9
31	13 52.8	13 55.0	13 14.8	3.1 2.9	9.1 8.4	15.1 14.0
32	13 53.0	13 55.3	13 15.1	3.2 3.0	9.2 8.5	15.2 14.1
33	13 53.3	13 55.5	13 15.3	3.3 3.1	9.3 8.6	15.3 14.2
34	13 53.5	13 55.8	13 15.5	3.4 3.1	9.4 8.7	15.4 14.2
35	13 53.8	13 56.0	13 15.8	3.5 3.2	9.5 8.8	15.5 14.3
36	13 54.0	13 56.3	13 16.0	3.6 3.3	9.6 8.9	15.6 14.4
37	13 54.3	13 56.5	13 16.2	3.7 3.4	9.7 9.0	15.7 14.5
38	13 54.5	13 56.8	13 16.5	3.8 3.5	9.8 9.1	15.8 14.6
39	13 54.8	13 57.0	13 16.7	3.9 3.6	9.9 9.2	15.9 14.7
40	13 55.0	13 57.3	13 17.0	4.0 3.7	10.0 9.3	16.0 14.8
41	13 55.3	13 57.5	13 17.2	4.1 3.8	10.1 9.3	16.1 14.9
42	13 55.5	13 57.8	13 17.4	4.2 3.9	10.2 9.4	16.2 15.0
43	13 55.8	13 58.0	13 17.7	4.3 4.0	10.3 9.5	16.3 15.1
44	13 56.0	13 58.3	13 17.9	4.4 4.1	10.4 9.6	16.4 15.2
45	13 56.3	13 58.5	13 18.2	4.5 4.2	10.5 9.7	16.5 15.3
46	13 56.5	13 58.8	13 18.4	4.6 4.3	10.6 9.8	16.6 15.4
47	13 56.8	13 59.0	13 18.6	4.7 4.3	10.7 9.9	16.7 15.4
48	13 57.0	13 59.3	13 18.9	4.8 4.4	10.8 10.0	16.8 15.5
49	13 57.3	13 59.5	13 19.1	4.9 4.5	10.9 10.1	16.9 15.6
50	13 57.5	13 59.8	13 19.3	5.0 4.6	11.0 10.2	17.0 15.7
51	13 57.8	14 00.0	13 19.6	5.1 4.7	11.1 10.3	17.1 15.8
52	13 58.0	14 00.3	13 19.8	5.2 4.8	11.2 10.4	17.2 15.9
53	13 58.3	14 00.5	13 20.1	5.3 4.9	11.3 10.5	17.3 16.0
54	13 58.5	14 00.8	13 20.3	5.4 5.0	11.4 10.5	17.4 16.1
55	13 58.8	14 01.0	13 20.5	5.5 5.1	11.5 10.6	17.5 16.2
56	13 59.0	14 01.3	13 20.8	5.6 5.2	11.6 10.7	17.6 16.3
57	13 59.3	14 01.5	13 21.0	5.7 5.3	11.7 10.8	17.7 16.4
58	13 59.5	14 01.8	13 21.3	5.8 5.4	11.8 10.9	17.8 16.5
59	13 59.8	14 02.0	13 21.5	5.9 5.5	11.9 11.0	17.9 16.6
60	14 00.0	14 02.3	13 21.7	6.0 5.6	12.0 11.1	18.0 16.7

56ᵐ

s	SUN PLANETS	ARIES	MOON	v or d	Corrⁿ	v or d	Corrⁿ	v or d	Corrⁿ
00	14 00·0	14 02·3	13 21·7	0·0	0·0	6·0	5·7	12·0	11·3
01	14 00·3	14 02·6	13 22·0	0·1	0·1	6·1	5·7	12·1	11·4
02	14 00·5	14 02·8	13 22·2	0·2	0·2	6·2	5·8	12·2	11·5
03	14 00·8	14 03·1	13 22·4	0·3	0·3	6·3	5·9	12·3	11·6
04	14 01·0	14 03·3	13 22·7	0·4	0·4	6·4	6·0	12·4	11·7
05	14 01·3	14 03·6	13 22·9	0·5	0·5	6·5	6·1	12·5	11·8
06	14 01·5	14 03·8	13 23·2	0·6	0·6	6·6	6·2	12·6	11·9
07	14 01·8	14 04·1	13 23·4	0·7	0·7	6·7	6·3	12·7	12·0
08	14 02·0	14 04·3	13 23·6	0·8	0·8	6·8	6·4	12·8	12·1
09	14 02·3	14 04·6	13 23·9	0·9	0·9	6·9	6·5	12·9	12·1
10	14 02·5	14 04·8	13 24·1	1·0	0·9	7·0	6·6	13·0	12·2
11	14 02·8	14 05·1	13 24·4	1·1	1·0	7·1	6·7	13·1	12·3
12	14 03·0	14 05·3	13 24·6	1·2	1·1	7·2	6·8	13·2	12·4
13	14 03·3	14 05·6	13 24·8	1·3	1·2	7·3	6·9	13·3	12·5
14	14 03·5	14 05·8	13 25·1	1·4	1·3	7·4	7·0	13·4	12·6
15	14 03·8	14 06·1	13 25·3	1·5	1·4	7·5	7·1	13·5	12·7
16	14 04·0	14 06·3	13 25·6	1·6	1·5	7·6	7·2	13·6	12·8
17	14 04·3	14 06·6	13 25·8	1·7	1·6	7·7	7·3	13·7	12·9
18	14 04·5	14 06·8	13 26·0	1·8	1·7	7·8	7·3	13·8	13·0
19	14 04·8	14 07·1	13 26·3	1·9	1·8	7·9	7·4	13·9	13·1
20	14 05·0	14 07·3	13 26·5	2·0	1·9	8·0	7·5	14·0	13·2
21	14 05·3	14 07·6	13 26·7	2·1	2·0	8·1	7·6	14·1	13·3
22	14 05·5	14 07·8	13 27·0	2·2	2·1	8·2	7·7	14·2	13·4
23	14 05·8	14 08·1	13 27·2	2·3	2·2	8·3	7·8	14·3	13·5
24	14 06·0	14 08·3	13 27·5	2·4	2·3	8·4	7·9	14·4	13·6
25	14 06·3	14 08·6	13 27·7	2·5	2·4	8·5	8·0	14·5	13·7
26	14 06·5	14 08·8	13 27·9	2·6	2·4	8·6	8·1	14·6	13·7
27	14 06·8	14 09·1	13 28·2	2·7	2·5	8·7	8·2	14·7	13·8
28	14 07·0	14 09·3	13 28·4	2·8	2·6	8·8	8·3	14·8	13·9
29	14 07·3	14 09·6	13 28·7	2·9	2·7	8·9	8·4	14·9	14·0
30	14 07·5	14 09·8	13 28·9	3·0	2·8	9·0	8·5	15·0	14·1
31	14 07·8	14 10·1	13 29·1	3·1	2·9	9·1	8·6	15·1	14·2
32	14 08·0	14 10·3	13 29·4	3·2	3·0	9·2	8·7	15·2	14·3
33	14 08·3	14 10·6	13 29·6	3·3	3·1	9·3	8·8	15·3	14·4
34	14 08·5	14 10·8	13 29·8	3·4	3·2	9·4	8·9	15·4	14·5
35	14 08·8	14 11·1	13 30·1	3·5	3·3	9·5	8·9	15·5	14·6
36	14 09·0	14 11·3	13 30·3	3·6	3·4	9·6	9·0	15·6	14·7
37	14 09·3	14 11·6	13 30·6	3·7	3·5	9·7	9·1	15·7	14·8
38	14 09·5	14 11·8	13 30·8	3·8	3·6	9·8	9·2	15·8	14·9
39	14 09·8	14 12·1	13 31·0	3·9	3·7	9·9	9·3	15·9	15·0
40	14 10·0	14 12·3	13 31·3	4·0	3·8	10·0	9·4	16·0	15·1
41	14 10·3	14 12·6	13 31·5	4·1	3·9	10·1	9·5	16·1	15·2
42	14 10·5	14 12·8	13 31·8	4·2	4·0	10·2	9·6	16·2	15·3
43	14 10·8	14 13·1	13 32·0	4·3	4·0	10·3	9·7	16·3	15·3
44	14 11·0	14 13·3	13 32·2	4·4	4·1	10·4	9·8	16·4	15·4
45	14 11·3	14 13·6	13 32·5	4·5	4·2	10·5	9·9	16·5	15·5
46	14 11·5	14 13·8	13 32·7	4·6	4·3	10·6	10·0	16·6	15·6
47	14 11·8	14 14·1	13 32·9	4·7	4·4	10·7	10·1	16·7	15·7
48	14 12·0	14 14·3	13 33·2	4·8	4·5	10·8	10·2	16·8	15·8
49	14 12·3	14 14·6	13 33·4	4·9	4·6	10·9	10·3	16·9	15·9
50	14 12·5	14 14·8	13 33·7	5·0	4·7	11·0	10·4	17·0	16·0
51	14 12·8	14 15·1	13 33·9	5·1	4·8	11·1	10·5	17·1	16·1
52	14 13·0	14 15·3	13 34·1	5·2	4·9	11·2	10·5	17·2	16·2
53	14 13·3	14 15·6	13 34·4	5·3	5·0	11·3	10·6	17·3	16·3
54	14 13·5	14 15·8	13 34·6	5·4	5·1	11·4	10·7	17·4	16·4
55	14 13·8	14 16·1	13 34·9	5·5	5·2	11·5	10·8	17·5	16·5
56	14 14·0	14 16·3	13 35·1	5·6	5·3	11·6	10·9	17·6	16·6
57	14 14·3	14 16·6	13 35·3	5·7	5·4	11·7	11·0	17·7	16·7
58	14 14·5	14 16·8	13 35·6	5·8	5·5	11·8	11·1	17·8	16·8
59	14 14·8	14 17·1	13 35·8	5·9	5·6	11·9	11·2	17·9	16·9
60	14 15·0	14 17·3	13 36·1	6·0	5·7	12·0	11·3	18·0	17·0

57ᵐ

s	SUN PLANETS	ARIES	MOON	v or d	Corrⁿ	v or d	Corrⁿ	v or d	Corrⁿ
00	14 15·0	14 17·3	13 36·1	0·0	0·0	6·0	5·8	12·0	11·5
01	14 15·3	14 17·6	13 36·3	0·1	0·1	6·1	5·8	12·1	11·6
02	14 15·5	14 17·8	13 36·5	0·2	0·2	6·2	5·9	12·2	11·7
03	14 15·8	14 18·1	13 36·8	0·3	0·3	6·3	6·0	12·3	11·8
04	14 16·0	14 18·3	13 37·0	0·4	0·4	6·4	6·1	12·4	11·9
05	14 16·3	14 18·6	13 37·2	0·5	0·5	6·5	6·2	12·5	12·0
06	14 16·5	14 18·8	13 37·5	0·6	0·6	6·6	6·3	12·6	12·1
07	14 16·8	14 19·1	13 37·7	0·7	0·7	6·7	6·4	12·7	12·2
08	14 17·0	14 19·3	13 38·0	0·8	0·8	6·8	6·5	12·8	12·3
09	14 17·3	14 19·6	13 38·2	0·9	0·9	6·9	6·6	12·9	12·4
10	14 17·5	14 19·8	13 38·4	1·0	1·0	7·0	6·7	13·0	12·5
11	14 17·8	14 20·1	13 38·7	1·1	1·1	7·1	6·8	13·1	12·6
12	14 18·0	14 20·3	13 38·9	1·2	1·2	7·2	6·9	13·2	12·7
13	14 18·3	14 20·6	13 39·2	1·3	1·2	7·3	7·0	13·3	12·7
14	14 18·5	14 20·9	13 39·4	1·4	1·3	7·4	7·1	13·4	12·8
15	14 18·8	14 21·1	13 39·6	1·5	1·4	7·5	7·2	13·5	12·9
16	14 19·0	14 21·4	13 39·9	1·6	1·5	7·6	7·3	13·6	13·0
17	14 19·3	14 21·6	13 40·1	1·7	1·6	7·7	7·4	13·7	13·1
18	14 19·5	14 21·9	13 40·3	1·8	1·7	7·8	7·5	13·8	13·2
19	14 19·8	14 22·1	13 40·6	1·9	1·8	7·9	7·6	13·9	13·3
20	14 20·0	14 22·4	13 40·8	2·0	1·9	8·0	7·7	14·0	13·4
21	14 20·3	14 22·6	13 41·1	2·1	2·0	8·1	7·8	14·1	13·5
22	14 20·5	14 22·9	13 41·3	2·2	2·1	8·2	7·9	14·2	13·6
23	14 20·8	14 23·1	13 41·5	2·3	2·2	8·3	8·0	14·3	13·7
24	14 21·0	14 23·4	13 41·8	2·4	2·3	8·4	8·1	14·4	13·8
25	14 21·3	14 23·6	13 42·0	2·5	2·4	8·5	8·1	14·5	13·9
26	14 21·5	14 23·9	13 42·3	2·6	2·5	8·6	8·2	14·6	14·0
27	14 21·8	14 24·1	13 42·5	2·7	2·6	8·7	8·3	14·7	14·1
28	14 22·0	14 24·4	13 42·7	2·8	2·7	8·8	8·4	14·8	14·2
29	14 22·3	14 24·6	13 43·0	2·9	2·8	8·9	8·5	14·9	14·3
30	14 22·5	14 24·9	13 43·2	3·0	2·9	9·0	8·6	15·0	14·4
31	14 22·8	14 25·1	13 43·4	3·1	3·0	9·1	8·7	15·1	14·5
32	14 23·0	14 25·4	13 43·7	3·2	3·1	9·2	8·8	15·2	14·6
33	14 23·3	14 25·6	13 43·9	3·3	3·2	9·3	8·9	15·3	14·7
34	14 23·5	14 25·9	13 44·2	3·4	3·3	9·4	9·0	15·4	14·8
35	14 23·8	14 26·1	13 44·4	3·5	3·4	9·5	9·1	15·5	14·9
36	14 24·0	14 26·4	13 44·6	3·6	3·5	9·6	9·2	15·6	15·0
37	14 24·3	14 26·6	13 44·9	3·7	3·5	9·7	9·3	15·7	15·0
38	14 24·5	14 26·9	13 45·1	3·8	3·6	9·8	9·4	15·8	15·1
39	14 24·8	14 27·1	13 45·4	3·9	3·7	9·9	9·5	15·9	15·2
40	14 25·0	14 27·4	13 45·6	4·0	3·8	10·0	9·6	16·0	15·3
41	14 25·3	14 27·6	13 45·8	4·1	3·9	10·1	9·7	16·1	15·4
42	14 25·5	14 27·9	13 46·1	4·2	4·0	10·2	9·8	16·2	15·5
43	14 25·8	14 28·1	13 46·3	4·3	4·1	10·3	9·9	16·3	15·6
44	14 26·0	14 28·4	13 46·5	4·4	4·2	10·4	10·0	16·4	15·7
45	14 26·3	14 28·6	13 46·8	4·5	4·3	10·5	10·1	16·5	15·8
46	14 26·5	14 28·9	13 47·0	4·6	4·4	10·6	10·2	16·6	15·9
47	14 26·8	14 29·1	13 47·3	4·7	4·5	10·7	10·3	16·7	16·0
48	14 27·0	14 29·4	13 47·5	4·8	4·6	10·8	10·4	16·8	16·1
49	14 27·3	14 29·6	13 47·7	4·9	4·7	10·9	10·4	16·9	16·2
50	14 27·5	14 29·9	13 48·0	5·0	4·8	11·0	10·5	17·0	16·3
51	14 27·8	14 30·1	13 48·2	5·1	4·9	11·1	10·6	17·1	16·4
52	14 28·0	14 30·4	13 48·5	5·2	5·0	11·2	10·7	17·2	16·5
53	14 28·3	14 30·6	13 48·7	5·3	5·1	11·3	10·8	17·3	16·6
54	14 28·5	14 30·9	13 48·9	5·4	5·2	11·4	10·9	17·4	16·7
55	14 28·8	14 31·1	13 49·2	5·5	5·3	11·5	11·0	17·5	16·8
56	14 29·0	14 31·4	13 49·4	5·6	5·4	11·6	11·1	17·6	16·9
57	14 29·3	14 31·6	13 49·7	5·7	5·5	11·7	11·2	17·7	17·0
58	14 29·5	14 31·9	13 49·9	5·8	5·6	11·8	11·3	17·8	17·1
59	14 29·8	14 32·1	13 50·1	5·9	5·7	11·9	11·4	17·9	17·2
60	14 30·0	14 32·4	13 50·4	6·0	5·8	12·0	11·5	18·0	17·3

58ᵐ

58	SUN PLANETS	ARIES	MOON	v or d	Corrⁿ	v or d	Corrⁿ	v or d	Corrⁿ
s	° ′	° ′	° ′	′	′	′	′	′	′
00	14 30·0	14 32·4	13 50·4	0·0	0·0	6·0	5·9	12·0	11·7
01	14 30·3	14 32·6	13 50·6	0·1	0·1	6·1	5·9	12·1	11·8
02	14 30·5	14 32·9	13 50·8	0·2	0·2	6·2	6·0	12·2	11·9
03	14 30·8	14 33·1	13 51·1	0·3	0·3	6·3	6·1	12·3	12·0
04	14 31·0	14 33·4	13 51·3	0·4	0·4	6·4	6·2	12·4	12·1
05	14 31·3	14 33·6	13 51·6	0·5	0·5	6·5	6·3	12·5	12·2
06	14 31·5	14 33·9	13 51·8	0·6	0·6	6·6	6·4	12·6	12·3
07	14 31·8	14 34·1	13 52·0	0·7	0·7	6·7	6·5	12·7	12·4
08	14 32·0	14 34·4	13 52·3	0·8	0·8	6·8	6·6	12·8	12·5
09	14 32·3	14 34·6	13 52·5	0·9	0·9	6·9	6·7	12·9	12·6
10	14 32·5	14 34·9	13 52·8	1·0	1·0	7·0	6·8	13·0	12·7
11	14 32·8	14 35·1	13 53·0	1·1	1·1	7·1	6·9	13·1	12·8
12	14 33·0	14 35·4	13 53·2	1·2	1·2	7·2	7·0	13·2	12·9
13	14 33·3	14 35·6	13 53·5	1·3	1·3	7·3	7·1	13·3	13·0
14	14 33·5	14 35·9	13 53·7	1·4	1·4	7·4	7·2	13·4	13·1
15	14 33·8	14 36·1	13 53·9	1·5	1·5	7·5	7·3	13·5	13·2
16	14 34·0	14 36·4	13 54·2	1·6	1·6	7·6	7·4	13·6	13·3
17	14 34·3	14 36·6	13 54·4	1·7	1·7	7·7	7·5	13·7	13·4
18	14 34·5	14 36·9	13 54·7	1·8	1·8	7·8	7·6	13·8	13·5
19	14 34·8	14 37·1	13 54·9	1·9	1·9	7·9	7·7	13·9	13·6
20	14 35·0	14 37·4	13 55·1	2·0	2·0	8·0	7·8	14·0	13·7
21	14 35·3	14 37·6	13 55·4	2·1	2·0	8·1	7·9	14·1	13·7
22	14 35·5	14 37·9	13 55·6	2·2	2·1	8·2	8·0	14·2	13·8
23	14 35·8	14 38·1	13 55·9	2·3	2·2	8·3	8·1	14·3	13·9
24	14 36·0	14 38·4	13 56·1	2·4	2·3	8·4	8·2	14·4	14·0
25	14 36·3	14 38·6	13 56·3	2·5	2·4	8·5	8·3	14·5	14·1
26	14 36·5	14 38·9	13 56·6	2·6	2·5	8·6	8·4	14·6	14·2
27	14 36·8	14 39·2	13 56·8	2·7	2·6	8·7	8·5	14·7	14·3
28	14 37·0	14 39·4	13 57·0	2·8	2·7	8·8	8·6	14·8	14·4
29	14 37·3	14 39·7	13 57·3	2·9	2·8	8·9	8·7	14·9	14·5
30	14 37·5	14 39·9	13 57·5	3·0	2·9	9·0	8·8	15·0	14·6
31	14 37·8	14 40·2	13 57·8	3·1	3·0	9·1	8·9	15·1	14·7
32	14 38·0	14 40·4	13 58·0	3·2	3·1	9·2	9·0	15·2	14·8
33	14 38·3	14 40·7	13 58·2	3·3	3·2	9·3	9·1	15·3	14·9
34	14 38·5	14 40·9	13 58·5	3·4	3·3	9·4	9·2	15·4	15·0
35	14 38·8	14 41·2	13 58·7	3·5	3·4	9·5	9·3	15·5	15·1
36	14 39·0	14 41·4	13 59·0	3·6	3·5	9·6	9·4	15·6	15·2
37	14 39·3	14 41·7	13 59·2	3·7	3·6	9·7	9·5	15·7	15·3
38	14 39·5	14 41·9	13 59·4	3·8	3·7	9·8	9·6	15·8	15·4
39	14 39·8	14 42·2	13 59·7	3·9	3·8	9·9	9·7	15·9	15·5
40	14 40·0	14 42·4	13 59·9	4·0	3·9	10·0	9·8	16·0	15·6
41	14 40·3	14 42·7	14 00·1	4·1	4·0	10·1	9·8	16·1	15·7
42	14 40·5	14 42·9	14 00·4	4·2	4·1	10·2	9·9	16·2	15·8
43	14 40·8	14 43·2	14 00·6	4·3	4·2	10·3	10·0	16·3	15·9
44	14 41·0	14 43·4	14 00·9	4·4	4·3	10·4	10·1	16·4	16·0
45	14 41·3	14 43·7	14 01·1	4·5	4·4	10·5	10·2	16·5	16·1
46	14 41·5	14 43·9	14 01·3	4·6	4·5	10·6	10·3	16·6	16·2
47	14 41·8	14 44·2	14 01·6	4·7	4·6	10·7	10·4	16·7	16·3
48	14 42·0	14 44·4	14 01·8	4·8	4·7	10·8	10·5	16·8	16·4
49	14 42·3	14 44·7	14 02·1	4·9	4·8	10·9	10·6	16·9	16·5
50	14 42·5	14 44·9	14 02·3	5·0	4·9	11·0	10·7	17·0	16·6
51	14 42·8	14 45·2	14 02·5	5·1	5·0	11·1	10·8	17·1	16·7
52	14 43·0	14 45·4	14 02·8	5·2	5·1	11·2	10·9	17·2	16·8
53	14 43·3	14 45·7	14 03·0	5·3	5·2	11·3	11·0	17·3	16·9
54	14 43·5	14 45·9	14 03·3	5·4	5·3	11·4	11·1	17·4	17·0
55	14 43·8	14 46·2	14 03·5	5·5	5·4	11·5	11·2	17·5	17·1
56	14 44·0	14 46·4	14 03·7	5·6	5·5	11·6	11·3	17·6	17·2
57	14 44·3	14 46·7	14 04·0	5·7	5·6	11·7	11·4	17·7	17·3
58	14 44·5	14 46·9	14 04·2	5·8	5·7	11·8	11·5	17·8	17·4
59	14 44·8	14 47·2	14 04·4	5·9	5·8	11·9	11·6	17·9	17·5
60	14 45·0	14 47·4	14 04·7	6·0	5·9	12·0	11·7	18·0	17·6

59ᵐ

59	SUN PLANETS	ARIES	MOON	v or d	Corrⁿ	v or d	Corrⁿ	v or d	Corrⁿ
s	° ′	° ′	° ′	′	′	′	′	′	′
00	14 45·0	14 47·4	14 04·7	0·0	0·0	6·0	6·0	12·0	11·9
01	14 45·3	14 47·7	14 04·9	0·1	0·1	6·1	6·0	12·1	12·0
02	14 45·5	14 47·9	14 05·2	0·2	0·2	6·2	6·1	12·2	12·1
03	14 45·8	14 48·2	14 05·4	0·3	0·3	6·3	6·2	12·3	12·2
04	14 46·0	14 48·4	14 05·6	0·4	0·4	6·4	6·3	12·4	12·3
05	14 46·3	14 48·7	14 05·9	0·5	0·5	6·5	6·4	12·5	12·4
06	14 46·5	14 48·9	14 06·1	0·6	0·6	6·6	6·5	12·6	12·5
07	14 46·8	14 49·2	14 06·4	0·7	0·7	6·7	6·6	12·7	12·6
08	14 47·0	14 49·4	14 06·6	0·8	0·8	6·8	6·7	12·8	12·7
09	14 47·3	14 49·7	14 06·8	0·9	0·9	6·9	6·8	12·9	12·8
10	14 47·5	14 49·9	14 07·1	1·0	1·0	7·0	6·9	13·0	12·9
11	14 47·8	14 50·2	14 07·3	1·1	1·1	7·1	7·0	13·1	13·0
12	14 48·0	14 50·4	14 07·5	1·2	1·2	7·2	7·1	13·2	13·1
13	14 48·3	14 50·7	14 07·8	1·3	1·3	7·3	7·2	13·3	13·2
14	14 48·5	14 50·9	14 08·0	1·4	1·4	7·4	7·3	13·4	13·3
15	14 48·8	14 51·2	14 08·3	1·5	1·5	7·5	7·4	13·5	13·4
16	14 49·0	14 51·4	14 08·5	1·6	1·6	7·6	7·5	13·6	13·5
17	14 49·3	14 51·7	14 08·7	1·7	1·7	7·7	7·6	13·7	13·6
18	14 49·5	14 51·9	14 09·0	1·8	1·8	7·8	7·7	13·8	13·7
19	14 49·8	14 52·2	14 09·2	1·9	1·9	7·9	7·8	13·9	13·8
20	14 50·0	14 52·4	14 09·5	2·0	2·0	8·0	7·9	14·0	13·9
21	14 50·3	14 52·7	14 09·7	2·1	2·1	8·1	8·0	14·1	14·0
22	14 50·5	14 52·9	14 09·9	2·2	2·2	8·2	8·1	14·2	14·1
23	14 50·8	14 53·2	14 10·2	2·3	2·3	8·3	8·2	14·3	14·2
24	14 51·0	14 53·4	14 10·4	2·4	2·4	8·4	8·3	14·4	14·3
25	14 51·3	14 53·7	14 10·6	2·5	2·5	8·5	8·4	14·5	14·4
26	14 51·5	14 53·9	14 10·9	2·6	2·6	8·6	8·5	14·6	14·5
27	14 51·8	14 54·2	14 11·1	2·7	2·7	8·7	8·6	14·7	14·6
28	14 52·0	14 54·4	14 11·4	2·8	2·8	8·8	8·7	14·8	14·7
29	14 52·3	14 54·7	14 11·6	2·9	2·9	8·9	8·8	14·9	14·8
30	14 52·5	14 54·9	14 11·8	3·0	3·0	9·0	8·9	15·0	14·9
31	14 52·8	14 55·2	14 12·1	3·1	3·1	9·1	9·0	15·1	15·0
32	14 53·0	14 55·4	14 12·3	3·2	3·2	9·2	9·1	15·2	15·1
33	14 53·3	14 55·7	14 12·6	3·3	3·3	9·3	9·2	15·3	15·2
34	14 53·5	14 55·9	14 12·8	3·4	3·4	9·4	9·3	15·4	15·3
35	14 53·8	14 56·2	14 13·0	3·5	3·5	9·5	9·4	15·5	15·4
36	14 54·0	14 56·4	14 13·3	3·6	3·6	9·6	9·5	15·6	15·5
37	14 54·3	14 56·7	14 13·5	3·7	3·7	9·7	9·6	15·7	15·6
38	14 54·5	14 56·9	14 13·8	3·8	3·8	9·8	9·7	15·8	15·7
39	14 54·8	14 57·2	14 14·0	3·9	3·9	9·9	9·8	15·9	15·8
40	14 55·0	14 57·5	14 14·2	4·0	4·0	10·0	9·9	16·0	15·9
41	14 55·3	14 57·7	14 14·5	4·1	4·1	10·1	10·0	16·1	16·0
42	14 55·5	14 58·0	14 14·7	4·2	4·2	10·2	10·1	16·2	16·1
43	14 55·8	14 58·2	14 14·9	4·3	4·3	10·3	10·2	16·3	16·2
44	14 56·0	14 58·5	14 15·2	4·4	4·4	10·4	10·3	16·4	16·3
45	14 56·3	14 58·7	14 15·4	4·5	4·5	10·5	10·4	16·5	16·4
46	14 56·5	14 59·0	14 15·7	4·6	4·6	10·6	10·5	16·6	16·5
47	14 56·8	14 59·2	14 15·9	4·7	4·7	10·7	10·6	16·7	16·6
48	14 57·0	14 59·5	14 16·1	4·8	4·8	10·8	10·7	16·8	16·7
49	14 57·3	14 59·7	14 16·4	4·9	4·9	10·9	10·8	16·9	16·8
50	14 57·5	15 00·0	14 16·6	5·0	5·0	11·0	10·9	17·0	16·9
51	14 57·8	15 00·2	14 16·9	5·1	5·1	11·1	11·0	17·1	17·0
52	14 58·0	15 00·5	14 17·1	5·2	5·2	11·2	11·1	17·2	17·1
53	14 58·3	15 00·7	14 17·3	5·3	5·3	11·3	11·2	17·3	17·2
54	14 58·5	15 01·0	14 17·6	5·4	5·4	11·4	11·3	17·4	17·3
55	14 58·8	15 01·2	14 17·8	5·5	5·5	11·5	11·4	17·5	17·4
56	14 59·0	15 01·5	14 18·0	5·6	5·6	11·6	11·5	17·6	17·5
57	14 59·3	15 01·7	14 18·3	5·7	5·7	11·7	11·6	17·7	17·6
58	14 59·5	15 02·0	14 18·5	5·8	5·8	11·8	11·7	17·8	17·7
59	14 59·8	15 02·2	14 18·8	5·9	5·9	11·9	11·8	17·9	17·8
60	15 00·0	15 02·5	14 19·0	6·0	6·0	12·0	11·9	18·0	17·9

TABLES FOR INTERPOLATING SUNRISE, MOONRISE, ETC.
TABLE I—FOR LATITUDE

Tabular Interval 10°	5°	2°	5ᵐ	10ᵐ	15ᵐ	20ᵐ	25ᵐ	30ᵐ	35ᵐ	40ᵐ	45ᵐ	50ᵐ	55ᵐ	60ᵐ	1ʰ05ᵐ	1ʰ10ᵐ	1ʰ15ᵐ	1ʰ20ᵐ
0 30	0 15	0 06	0	0	1	1	1	1	1	2	2	2	2	2	0 02	0 02	0 02	0 02
1 00	0 30	0 12	0	1	1	2	2	3	3	3	4	4	4	5	05	05	05	05
1 30	0 45	0 18	1	1	2	3	3	4	4	5	5	6	7	7	07	07	07	07
2 00	1 00	0 24	1	2	3	4	5	5	6	7	7	8	9	10	10	10	10	10
2 30	1 15	0 30	1	2	4	5	6	7	8	9	9	10	11	12	12	13	13	13
3 00	1 30	0 36	1	3	4	6	7	8	9	10	11	12	13	14	0 15	0 15	0 16	0 16
3 30	1 45	0 42	2	3	5	7	8	10	11	12	13	14	16	17	18	18	19	19
4 00	2 00	0 48	2	4	6	8	9	11	13	14	15	16	18	19	20	21	22	22
4 30	2 15	0 54	2	4	7	9	11	13	15	16	18	19	21	22	23	24	25	26
5 00	2 30	1 00	2	5	7	10	12	14	16	18	20	22	23	25	26	27	28	29
5 30	2 45	1 06	3	5	8	11	13	16	18	20	22	24	26	28	0 29	0 30	0 31	0 32
6 00	3 00	1 12	3	6	9	12	14	17	20	22	24	26	29	31	32	33	34	36
6 30	3 15	1 18	3	6	10	13	16	19	22	24	26	29	31	34	36	37	38	40
7 00	3 30	1 24	3	7	10	14	17	20	23	26	29	31	34	37	39	41	42	44
7 30	3 45	1 30	4	7	11	15	18	22	25	28	31	34	37	40	43	44	46	48
8 00	4 00	1 36	4	8	12	16	20	23	27	30	34	37	41	44	0 47	0 48	0 51	0 53
8 30	4 15	1 42	4	8	13	17	21	25	29	33	36	40	44	48	0 51	0 53	0 56	0 58
9 00	4 30	1 48	4	9	13	18	22	27	31	35	39	43	47	52	0 55	0 58	1 01	1 04
9 30	4 45	1 54	5	9	14	19	24	28	33	38	42	47	51	56	1 00	1 04	1 08	1 12
10 00	5 00	2 00	5	10	15	20	25	30	35	40	45	50	55	60	1 05	1 10	1 15	1 20

Table I is for interpolating the LMT of sunrise, twilight, moonrise, etc., for latitude. It is to be entered, in the appropriate column on the left, with the difference between true latitude and the nearest tabular latitude which is *less* than the true latitude; and with the argument at the top which is the nearest value of the difference between the times for the tabular latitude and the next higher one; the correction so obtained is applied to the time for the tabular latitude; the sign of the correction can be seen by inspection. It is to be noted that the interpolation is not linear, so that when using this table it is essential to take out the tabular phenomenon for the latitude *less* than the true latitude.

TABLE II—FOR LONGITUDE

Long. East or West	10ᵐ	20ᵐ	30ᵐ	40ᵐ	50ᵐ	60ᵐ	1ʰ+10ᵐ	20ᵐ	30ᵐ	1ʰ+40ᵐ	50ᵐ	60ᵐ	2ʰ10ᵐ	2ʰ20ᵐ	2ʰ30ᵐ	2ʰ40ᵐ	2ʰ50ᵐ	3ʰ00ᵐ
0	0	0	0	0	0	0	0	0	0	0	0	0	0 00	0 00	0 00	0 00	0 00	0 00
10	0	1	1	1	1	2	2	2	2	3	3	3	04	04	04	04	05	05
20	1	1	2	2	3	3	4	4	5	6	6	7	07	08	08	09	09	10
30	1	2	2	3	4	5	6	7	7	8	9	10	11	12	12	13	14	15
40	1	2	3	4	6	7	8	9	10	11	12	13	14	16	17	18	19	20
50	1	3	4	6	7	8	10	11	12	14	15	17	0 18	0 19	0 21	0 22	0 24	0 25
60	2	3	5	7	8	10	12	13	15	17	18	20	22	23	25	27	28	30
70	2	4	6	8	10	12	14	16	17	19	21	23	25	27	29	31	33	35
80	2	4	7	9	11	13	16	18	20	22	24	27	29	31	33	36	38	40
90	2	5	7	10	12	15	17	20	22	25	27	30	32	35	37	40	42	45
100	3	6	8	11	14	17	19	22	25	28	31	33	0 36	0 39	0 42	0 44	0 47	0 50
110	3	6	9	12	15	18	21	24	27	31	34	37	40	43	46	49	0 52	0 55
120	3	7	10	13	17	20	23	27	30	33	37	40	43	47	50	53	0 57	1 00
130	4	7	11	14	18	22	25	29	32	36	40	43	47	51	54	0 58	1 01	1 05
140	4	8	12	16	19	23	27	31	35	39	43	47	51	54	0 58	1 02	1 06	1 10
150	4	8	13	17	21	25	29	33	38	42	46	50	0 54	0 58	1 03	1 07	1 11	1 15
160	4	9	13	18	22	27	31	36	40	44	49	53	0 58	1 02	1 07	1 11	1 16	1 20
170	5	9	14	19	24	28	33	38	42	47	52	57	1 01	1 06	1 11	1 16	1 20	1 25
180	5	10	15	20	25	30	35	40	45	50	55	60	1 05	1 10	1 15	1 20	1 25	1 30

Difference between the times for given date and preceding date (for east longitude) or for given date and following date (for west longitude)

Table II is for interpolating the LMT of moonrise, moonset and the Moon's meridian passage for longitude. It is entered with longitude and with the difference between the times for the given date and for the preceding date (in east longitudes) or following date (in west longitudes). The correction is normally *added* for west longitudes and *subtracted* for east longitudes, but if, as occasionally happens, the times become earlier each day instead of later, the signs of the corrections must be reversed.

INDEX TO SELECTED STARS, 2020

Name	No	Mag	SHA	Dec
			°	°
Acamar	7	3·2	315	S 40
Achernar	5	0·5	335	S 57
Acrux	30	1·3	173	S 63
Adhara	19	1·5	255	S 29
Aldebaran	10	0·9	291	N 17
Alioth	32	1·8	166	N 56
Alkaid	34	1·9	153	N 49
Alnair	55	1·7	28	S 47
Alnilam	15	1·7	276	S 1
Alphard	25	2·0	218	S 9
Alphecca	41	2·2	126	N 27
Alpheratz	1	2·1	358	N 29
Altair	51	0·8	62	N 9
Ankaa	2	2·4	353	S 42
Antares	42	1·0	112	S 26
Arcturus	37	0·0	146	N 19
Atria	43	1·9	107	S 69
Avior	22	1·9	234	S 60
Bellatrix	13	1·6	278	N 6
Betelgeuse	16	Var.*	271	N 7
Canopus	17	−0·7	264	S 53
Capella	12	0·1	280	N 46
Deneb	53	1·3	49	N 45
Denebola	28	2·1	182	N 14
Diphda	4	2·0	349	S 18
Dubhe	27	1·8	194	N 62
Elnath	14	1·7	278	N 29
Eltanin	47	2·2	91	N 51
Enif	54	2·4	34	N 10
Fomalhaut	56	1·2	15	S 30
Gacrux	31	1·6	172	S 57
Gienah	29	2·6	176	S 18
Hadar	35	0·6	149	S 60
Hamal	6	2·0	328	N 24
Kaus Australis	48	1·9	84	S 34
Kochab	40	2·1	137	N 74
Markab	57	2·5	14	N 15
Menkar	8	2·5	314	N 4
Menkent	36	2·1	148	S 36
Miaplacidus	24	1·7	222	S 70
Mirfak	9	1·8	309	N 50
Nunki	50	2·0	76	S 26
Peacock	52	1·9	53	S 57
Pollux	21	1·1	243	N 28
Procyon	20	0·4	245	N 5
Rasalhague	46	2·1	96	N 13
Regulus	26	1·4	208	N 12
Rigel	11	0·1	281	S 8
Rigil Kentaurus	38	−0·3	140	S 61
Sabik	44	2·4	102	S 16
Schedar	3	2·2	350	N 57
Shaula	45	1·6	96	S 37
Sirius	18	−1·5	258	S 17
Spica	33	1·0	158	S 11
Suhail	23	2·2	223	S 44
Vega	49	0·0	81	N 39
Zubenelgenubi	39	2·8	137	S 16

No	Name	Mag	SHA	Dec
			°	°
1	Alpheratz	2·1	358	N 29
2	Ankaa	2·4	353	S 42
3	Schedar	2·2	350	N 57
4	Diphda	2·0	349	S 18
5	Achernar	0·5	335	S 57
6	Hamal	2·0	328	N 24
7	Acamar	3·2	315	S 40
8	Menkar	2·5	314	N 4
9	Mirfak	1·8	309	N 50
10	Aldebaran	0·9	291	N 17
11	Rigel	0·1	281	S 8
12	Capella	0·1	280	N 46
13	Bellatrix	1·6	278	N 6
14	Elnath	1·7	278	N 29
15	Alnilam	1·7	276	S 1
16	Betelgeuse	Var.*	271	N 7
17	Canopus	−0·7	264	S 53
18	Sirius	−1·5	258	S 17
19	Adhara	1·5	255	S 29
20	Procyon	0·4	245	N 5
21	Pollux	1·1	243	N 28
22	Avior	1·9	234	S 60
23	Suhail	2·2	223	S 44
24	Miaplacidus	1·7	222	S 70
25	Alphard	2·0	218	S 9
26	Regulus	1·4	208	N 12
27	Dubhe	1·8	194	N 62
28	Denebola	2·1	182	N 14
29	Gienah	2·6	176	S 18
30	Acrux	1·3	173	S 63
31	Gacrux	1·6	172	S 57
32	Alioth	1·8	166	N 56
33	Spica	1·0	158	S 11
34	Alkaid	1·9	153	N 49
35	Hadar	0·6	149	S 60
36	Menkent	2·1	148	S 36
37	Arcturus	0·0	146	N 19
38	Rigil Kentaurus	−0·3	140	S 61
39	Zubenelgenubi	2·8	137	S 16
40	Kochab	2·1	137	N 74
41	Alphecca	2·2	126	N 27
42	Antares	1·0	112	S 26
43	Atria	1·9	107	S 69
44	Sabik	2·4	102	S 16
45	Shaula	1·6	96	S 37
46	Rasalhague	2·1	96	N 13
47	Eltanin	2·2	91	N 51
48	Kaus Australis	1·9	84	S 34
49	Vega	0·0	81	N 39
50	Nunki	2·0	76	S 26
51	Altair	0·8	62	N 9
52	Peacock	1·9	53	S 57
53	Deneb	1·3	49	N 45
54	Enif	2·4	34	N 10
55	Alnair	1·7	28	S 47
56	Fomalhaut	1·2	15	S 30
57	Markab	2·5	14	N 15

*0·1 — 1·2   xxxiii

App. Alt.	0°–4° Corrⁿ	5°–9° Corrⁿ	10°–14° Corrⁿ	15°–19° Corrⁿ	20°–24° Corrⁿ	25°–29° Corrⁿ	30°–34° Corrⁿ	App. Alt.
00	**0** 34·5	**5** 58·2	**10** 62·1	**15** 62·8	**20** 62·2	**25** 60·8	**30** 58·9	00
10	36·5	58·5	62·2	62·8	62·2	60·8	58·8	10
20	38·3	58·7	62·2	62·8	62·1	60·7	58·8	20
30	40·0	58·9	62·3	62·8	62·1	60·7	58·7	30
40	41·5	59·1	62·3	62·8	62·0	60·6	58·6	40
50	42·9	59·3	62·4	62·7	62·0	60·6	58·5	50
00	**1** 44·2	**6** 59·5	**11** 62·4	**16** 62·7	**21** 62·0	**26** 60·5	**31** 58·5	00
10	45·4	59·7	62·4	62·7	61·9	60·4	58·4	10
20	46·5	59·9	62·5	62·7	61·9	60·4	58·3	20
30	47·5	60·0	62·5	62·7	61·9	60·3	58·2	30
40	48·4	60·2	62·5	62·7	61·8	60·3	58·2	40
50	49·3	60·3	62·6	62·7	61·8	60·2	58·1	50
00	**2** 50·1	**7** 60·5	**12** 62·6	**17** 62·7	**22** 61·7	**27** 60·1	**32** 58·0	00
10	50·8	60·6	62·6	62·6	61·7	60·1	57·9	10
20	51·5	60·7	62·6	62·6	61·6	60·0	57·8	20
30	52·2	60·9	62·7	62·6	61·6	59·9	57·8	30
40	52·8	61·0	62·7	62·6	61·6	59·9	57·7	40
50	53·4	61·1	62·7	62·6	61·5	59·8	57·6	50
00	**3** 53·9	**8** 61·2	**13** 62·7	**18** 62·5	**23** 61·5	**28** 59·7	**33** 57·5	00
10	54·4	61·3	62·7	62·5	61·4	59·7	57·4	10
20	54·9	61·4	62·7	62·5	61·4	59·6	57·4	20
30	55·3	61·5	62·8	62·5	61·3	59·5	57·3	30
40	55·7	61·6	62·8	62·4	61·3	59·5	57·2	40
50	56·1	61·6	62·8	62·4	61·2	59·4	57·1	50
00	**4** 56·4	**9** 61·7	**14** 62·8	**19** 62·4	**24** 61·2	**29** 59·3	**34** 57·0	00
10	56·8	61·8	62·8	62·4	61·1	59·3	56·9	10
20	57·1	61·9	62·8	62·3	61·1	59·2	56·9	20
30	57·4	61·9	62·8	62·3	61·0	59·1	56·8	30
40	57·7	62·0	62·8	62·3	61·0	59·1	56·7	40
50	58·0	62·1	62·8	62·2	60·9	59·0	56·6	50

HP	L U	L U	L U	L U	L U	L U	L U	HP
54·0	0·3 0·9	0·3 0·9	0·4 1·0	0·5 1·1	0·6 1·2	0·7 1·3	0·9 1·5	54·0
54·3	0·7 1·1	0·7 1·2	0·8 1·2	0·9 1·4	0·9 1·4	1·1 1·5	1·2 1·7	54·3
54·6	1·1 1·4	1·1 1·4	1·1 1·4	1·2 1·5	1·3 1·6	1·4 1·7	1·5 1·8	54·6
54·9	1·4 1·6	1·5 1·6	1·5 1·6	1·6 1·7	1·6 1·8	1·8 1·9	1·9 2·0	54·9
55·2	1·8 1·8	1·8 1·8	1·9 1·8	1·9 1·9	2·0 2·0	2·1 2·1	2·2 2·2	55·2
55·5	2·2 2·0	2·2 2·0	2·3 2·1	2·3 2·1	2·4 2·2	2·4 2·3	2·5 2·4	55·5
55·8	2·6 2·2	2·6 2·2	2·6 2·3	2·7 2·3	2·7 2·4	2·8 2·4	2·9 2·5	55·8
56·1	3·0 2·4	3·0 2·5	3·0 2·5	3·0 2·5	3·1 2·6	3·1 2·6	3·2 2·7	56·1
56·4	3·3 2·7	3·4 2·7	3·4 2·7	3·4 2·7	3·4 2·8	3·5 2·8	3·5 2·9	56·4
56·7	3·7 2·9	3·7 2·9	3·8 2·9	3·8 2·9	3·8 3·0	3·8 3·0	3·9 3·0	56·7
57·0	4·1 3·1	4·1 3·1	4·1 3·1	4·1 3·1	4·2 3·2	4·2 3·2	4·2 3·2	57·0
57·3	4·5 3·3	4·5 3·3	4·5 3·3	4·5 3·3	4·5 3·3	4·5 3·4	4·6 3·4	57·3
57·6	4·9 3·5	4·9 3·5	4·9 3·5	4·9 3·5	4·9 3·5	4·9 3·5	4·9 3·6	57·6
57·9	5·3 3·8	5·3 3·8	5·2 3·8	5·2 3·7	5·2 3·7	5·2 3·7	5·2 3·7	57·9
58·2	5·6 4·0	5·6 4·0	5·6 4·0	5·6 4·0	5·6 3·9	5·6 3·9	5·6 3·9	58·2
58·5	6·0 4·2	6·0 4·2	6·0 4·2	6·0 4·2	6·0 4·1	5·9 4·1	5·9 4·1	58·5
58·8	6·4 4·4	6·4 4·4	6·4 4·4	6·3 4·4	6·3 4·3	6·3 4·3	6·2 4·2	58·8
59·1	6·8 4·6	6·8 4·6	6·7 4·6	6·7 4·6	6·7 4·5	6·6 4·5	6·6 4·4	59·1
59·4	7·2 4·8	7·1 4·8	7·1 4·8	7·1 4·8	7·0 4·7	7·0 4·7	6·9 4·6	59·4
59·7	7·5 5·1	7·5 5·0	7·5 5·0	7·5 5·0	7·4 4·9	7·3 4·8	7·2 4·8	59·7
60·0	7·9 5·3	7·9 5·3	7·9 5·2	7·8 5·2	7·8 5·1	7·7 5·0	7·6 4·9	60·0
60·3	8·3 5·5	8·3 5·5	8·2 5·4	8·2 5·4	8·1 5·3	8·0 5·2	7·9 5·1	60·3
60·6	8·7 5·7	8·7 5·7	8·6 5·7	8·6 5·6	8·5 5·5	8·4 5·4	8·2 5·3	60·6
60·9	9·1 5·9	9·0 5·9	9·0 5·9	8·9 5·8	8·8 5·7	8·7 5·6	8·6 5·4	60·9
61·2	9·5 6·2	9·4 6·1	9·4 6·1	9·3 6·0	9·2 5·9	9·1 5·8	8·9 5·6	61·2
61·5	9·8 6·4	9·8 6·3	9·7 6·3	9·7 6·2	9·5 6·1	9·4 5·9	9·2 5·8	61·5

DIP

Ht. of Eye	Corrⁿ	Ht. of Eye	Ht. of Eye	Corrⁿ	Ht. of Eye
m		ft.	m		ft.
2·4	−2·8	8·0	9·5	−5·5	31·5
2·6	−2·9	8·6	9·9	−5·6	32·7
2·8	−3·0	9·2	10·3	−5·7	33·9
3·0	−3·1	9·8	10·6	−5·8	35·1
3·2	−3·2	10·5	11·0	−5·9	36·3
3·4	−3·3	11·2	11·4	−6·0	37·6
3·6	−3·4	11·9	11·8	−6·1	38·9
3·8	−3·5	12·6	12·2	−6·2	40·1
4·0	−3·6	13·3	12·6	−6·3	41·5
4·3	−3·7	14·1	13·0	−6·4	42·8
4·5	−3·8	14·9	13·4	−6·5	44·2
4·7	−3·9	15·7	13·8	−6·6	45·5
5·0	−4·0	16·5	14·2	−6·7	46·9
5·2	−4·1	17·4	14·7	−6·8	48·4
5·5	−4·2	18·3	15·1	−6·9	49·8
5·8	−4·3	19·1	15·5	−7·0	51·3
6·1	−4·4	20·1	16·0	−7·1	52·8
6·3	−4·5	21·0	16·5	−7·2	54·3
6·6	−4·6	22·0	16·9	−7·3	55·8
6·9	−4·7	22·9	17·4	−7·4	57·4
7·2	−4·8	23·9	17·9	−7·5	58·9
7·5	−4·9	24·9	18·4	−7·6	60·5
7·9	−5·0	26·0	18·8	−7·7	62·1
8·2	−5·1	27·1	19·3	−7·8	63·8
8·5	−5·2	28·1	19·8	−7·9	65·4
8·8	−5·3	29·2	20·4	−8·0	67·1
9·2	−5·4	30·4	20·9	−8·1	68·8
9·5		31·5	21·4		70·5

MOON CORRECTION TABLE

The correction is in two parts; the first correction is taken from the upper part of the table with argument apparent altitude, and the second from the lower part, with argument HP, in the same column as that from which the first correction was taken. Separate corrections are given in the lower part for lower (L) and upper(U) limbs. All corrections are to be **added** to apparent altitude, *but 30′ is to be subtracted from the altitude of the upper limb.*

For corrections for pressure and temperature see page A4.

For bubble sextant observations ignore dip, take the mean of upper and lower limb corrections and subtract 15′ from the altitude.

App. Alt. = Apparent altitude = Sextant altitude corrected for index error and dip.

ALTITUDE CORRECTION TABLES 35°–90°— MOON

App. Alt.	35°–39° Corrⁿ	40°–44° Corrⁿ	45°–49° Corrⁿ	50°–54° Corrⁿ	55°–59° Corrⁿ	60°–64° Corrⁿ	65°–69° Corrⁿ	70°–74° Corrⁿ	75°–79° Corrⁿ	80°–84° Corrⁿ	85°–89° Corrⁿ	App. Alt.
00	35 56.5	40 53.7	45 50.5	50 46.9	55 43.1	60 38.9	65 34.6	70 30.0	75 25.3	80 20.5	85 15.6	00
10	56.4	53.6	50.4	46.8	42.9	38.8	34.4	29.9	25.2	20.4	15.5	10
20	56.3	53.5	50.2	46.7	42.8	38.7	34.3	29.7	25.0	20.2	15.3	20
30	56.2	53.4	50.1	46.5	42.7	38.5	34.1	29.6	24.9	20.0	15.1	30
40	56.2	53.3	50.0	46.4	42.5	38.4	34.0	29.4	24.7	19.9	15.0	40
50	56.1	53.2	49.9	46.3	42.4	38.2	33.8	29.3	24.5	19.7	14.8	50
00	36 56.0	41 53.1	46 49.8	51 46.2	56 42.3	61 38.1	66 33.7	71 29.1	76 24.4	81 19.6	86 14.6	00
10	55.9	53.0	49.7	46.0	42.1	37.9	33.5	29.0	24.2	19.4	14.5	10
20	55.8	52.9	49.5	45.9	42.0	37.8	33.4	28.8	24.1	19.2	14.3	20
30	55.7	52.8	49.4	45.8	41.9	37.7	33.2	28.7	23.9	19.1	14.2	30
40	55.6	52.6	49.3	45.7	41.7	37.5	33.1	28.5	23.8	18.9	14.0	40
50	55.5	52.5	49.2	45.5	41.6	37.4	32.9	28.3	23.6	18.7	13.8	50
00	37 55.4	42 52.4	47 49.1	52 45.4	57 41.4	62 37.2	67 32.8	72 28.2	77 23.4	82 18.6	87 13.7	00
10	55.3	52.3	49.0	45.3	41.3	37.1	32.6	28.0	23.3	18.4	13.5	10
20	55.2	52.2	48.8	45.2	41.2	36.9	32.5	27.9	23.1	18.2	13.3	20
30	55.1	52.1	48.7	45.0	41.0	36.8	32.3	27.7	22.9	18.1	13.2	30
40	55.0	52.0	48.6	44.9	40.9	36.6	32.2	27.6	22.8	17.9	13.0	40
50	55.0	51.9	48.5	44.8	40.8	36.5	32.0	27.4	22.6	17.8	12.8	50
00	38 54.9	43 51.8	48 48.4	53 44.6	58 40.6	63 36.4	68 31.9	73 27.2	78 22.5	83 17.6	88 12.7	00
10	54.8	51.7	48.3	44.5	40.5	36.2	31.7	27.1	22.3	17.4	12.5	10
20	54.7	51.6	48.1	44.4	40.3	36.1	31.6	26.9	22.1	17.3	12.3	20
30	54.6	51.5	48.0	44.2	40.2	35.9	31.4	26.8	22.0	17.1	12.2	30
40	54.5	51.4	47.9	44.1	40.1	35.8	31.3	26.6	21.8	16.9	12.0	40
50	54.4	51.2	47.8	44.0	39.9	35.6	31.1	26.5	21.7	16.8	11.8	50
00	39 54.3	44 51.1	49 47.7	54 43.9	59 39.8	64 35.5	69 31.0	74 26.3	79 21.5	84 16.6	89 11.7	00
10	54.2	51.0	47.5	43.7	39.6	35.3	30.8	26.1	21.3	16.4	11.5	10
20	54.1	50.9	47.4	43.6	39.5	35.2	30.7	26.0	21.2	16.3	11.4	20
30	54.0	50.8	47.3	43.5	39.4	35.0	30.5	25.8	21.0	16.1	11.2	30
40	53.9	50.7	47.2	43.3	39.2	34.9	30.4	25.7	20.9	16.0	11.0	40
50	53.8	50.6	47.0	43.2	39.1	34.7	30.2	25.5	20.7	15.8	10.9	50

HP	L U	L U	L U	L U	L U	L U	L U	L U	L U	L U	L U	HP
54.0	1.1 1.7	1.3 1.9	1.5 2.1	1.7 2.4	2.0 2.6	2.3 2.9	2.6 3.2	2.9 3.5	3.2 3.8	3.5 4.1	3.8 4.5	54.0
54.3	1.4 1.8	1.6 2.0	1.8 2.2	2.0 2.5	2.2 2.7	2.5 3.0	2.8 3.2	3.1 3.5	3.3 3.8	3.6 4.1	3.9 4.4	54.3
54.6	1.7 2.0	1.9 2.2	2.1 2.4	2.3 2.6	2.5 2.8	2.7 3.0	3.0 3.3	3.2 3.5	3.5 3.8	3.8 4.0	4.0 4.3	54.6
54.9	2.0 2.2	2.2 2.3	2.3 2.5	2.5 2.7	2.7 2.9	2.9 3.1	3.2 3.3	3.4 3.5	3.6 3.8	3.9 4.0	4.1 4.3	54.9
55.2	2.3 2.3	2.5 2.5	2.6 2.6	2.8 2.8	3.0 2.9	3.2 3.1	3.4 3.3	3.6 3.5	3.8 3.7	4.0 4.0	4.2 4.2	55.2
55.5	2.7 2.5	2.8 2.6	2.9 2.7	3.1 2.9	3.2 3.0	3.4 3.2	3.6 3.4	3.7 3.5	3.9 3.7	4.1 3.9	4.3 4.1	55.5
55.8	3.0 2.6	3.1 2.7	3.2 2.8	3.3 3.0	3.5 3.1	3.6 3.3	3.8 3.4	3.9 3.6	4.1 3.7	4.2 3.9	4.4 4.0	55.8
56.1	3.3 2.8	3.4 2.9	3.5 3.0	3.6 3.1	3.7 3.2	3.8 3.3	4.0 3.4	4.1 3.6	4.2 3.7	4.4 3.8	4.5 4.0	56.1
56.4	3.6 2.9	3.7 3.0	3.8 3.1	3.9 3.2	3.9 3.3	4.0 3.4	4.1 3.5	4.3 3.6	4.4 3.7	4.5 3.8	4.6 3.9	56.4
56.7	3.9 3.1	4.0 3.1	4.1 3.2	4.1 3.3	4.2 3.3	4.3 3.4	4.3 3.5	4.4 3.6	4.5 3.7	4.6 3.8	4.7 3.8	56.7
57.0	4.3 3.2	4.3 3.3	4.3 3.3	4.4 3.4	4.4 3.4	4.5 3.5	4.5 3.5	4.6 3.6	4.7 3.6	4.7 3.7	4.8 3.8	57.0
57.3	4.6 3.4	4.6 3.4	4.6 3.4	4.6 3.5	4.7 3.5	4.7 3.5	4.7 3.6	4.8 3.6	4.8 3.6	4.8 3.7	4.9 3.7	57.3
57.6	4.9 3.6	4.9 3.6	4.9 3.6	4.9 3.6	4.9 3.6	4.9 3.6	4.9 3.6	4.9 3.6	5.0 3.6	5.0 3.6	5.0 3.6	57.6
57.9	5.2 3.7	5.2 3.7	5.2 3.7	5.2 3.7	5.2 3.7	5.1 3.6	5.1 3.6	5.1 3.6	5.1 3.6	5.1 3.6	5.1 3.6	57.9
58.2	5.5 3.9	5.5 3.8	5.5 3.8	5.4 3.8	5.4 3.7	5.4 3.7	5.3 3.7	5.3 3.6	5.2 3.6	5.2 3.5	5.2 3.5	58.2
58.5	5.9 4.0	5.8 4.0	5.8 3.9	5.7 3.9	5.6 3.8	5.6 3.8	5.5 3.7	5.5 3.6	5.4 3.6	5.3 3.5	5.3 3.4	58.5
58.8	6.2 4.2	6.1 4.1	6.0 4.1	5.9 4.0	5.9 3.9	5.8 3.8	5.7 3.7	5.6 3.6	5.5 3.5	5.4 3.5	5.3 3.4	58.8
59.1	6.5 4.3	6.4 4.3	6.3 4.2	6.2 4.1	6.1 4.0	6.0 3.9	5.9 3.8	5.8 3.6	5.6 3.5	5.6 3.4	5.4 3.3	59.1
59.4	6.8 4.5	6.7 4.4	6.6 4.3	6.5 4.2	6.4 4.1	6.2 3.9	6.1 3.8	6.0 3.7	5.8 3.5	5.7 3.4	5.5 3.2	59.4
59.7	7.1 4.7	7.0 4.5	6.9 4.4	6.8 4.3	6.6 4.1	6.5 4.0	6.3 3.8	6.1 3.7	6.0 3.5	5.8 3.3	5.6 3.2	59.7
60.0	7.5 4.8	7.3 4.7	7.2 4.5	7.0 4.4	6.9 4.2	6.7 4.0	6.5 3.9	6.3 3.7	6.1 3.5	5.9 3.3	5.7 3.1	60.0
60.3	7.8 5.0	7.6 4.8	7.5 4.7	7.3 4.5	7.1 4.3	6.9 4.1	6.7 3.9	6.5 3.7	6.3 3.5	6.0 3.2	5.8 3.0	60.3
60.6	8.1 5.1	7.9 5.0	7.7 4.8	7.6 4.6	7.3 4.4	7.1 4.2	6.9 3.9	6.7 3.7	6.4 3.4	6.2 3.2	5.9 2.9	60.6
60.9	8.4 5.3	8.2 5.1	8.0 4.9	7.8 4.7	7.6 4.5	7.3 4.2	7.1 4.0	6.8 3.7	6.6 3.4	6.3 3.2	6.0 2.9	60.9
61.2	8.7 5.4	8.5 5.2	8.3 5.0	8.1 4.8	7.8 4.5	7.6 4.3	7.3 4.0	7.0 3.7	6.7 3.4	6.4 3.1	6.1 2.8	61.2
61.5	9.1 5.6	8.8 5.4	8.6 5.1	8.3 4.9	8.1 4.6	7.8 4.3	7.5 4.0	7.2 3.7	6.9 3.4	6.5 3.1	6.2 2.7	61.5

DISCOVER
A NEW WORLD
OF GEAR, VOYAGING TIPS & DESTINATIONS
OCEAN NAVIGATOR
MARINE NAVIGATION AND OCEAN VOYAGING
WWW.OCEANNAVIGATOR.COM
SUBSCRIBE NOW
AND SAVE 37% OFF THE NEWSSTAND PRICE

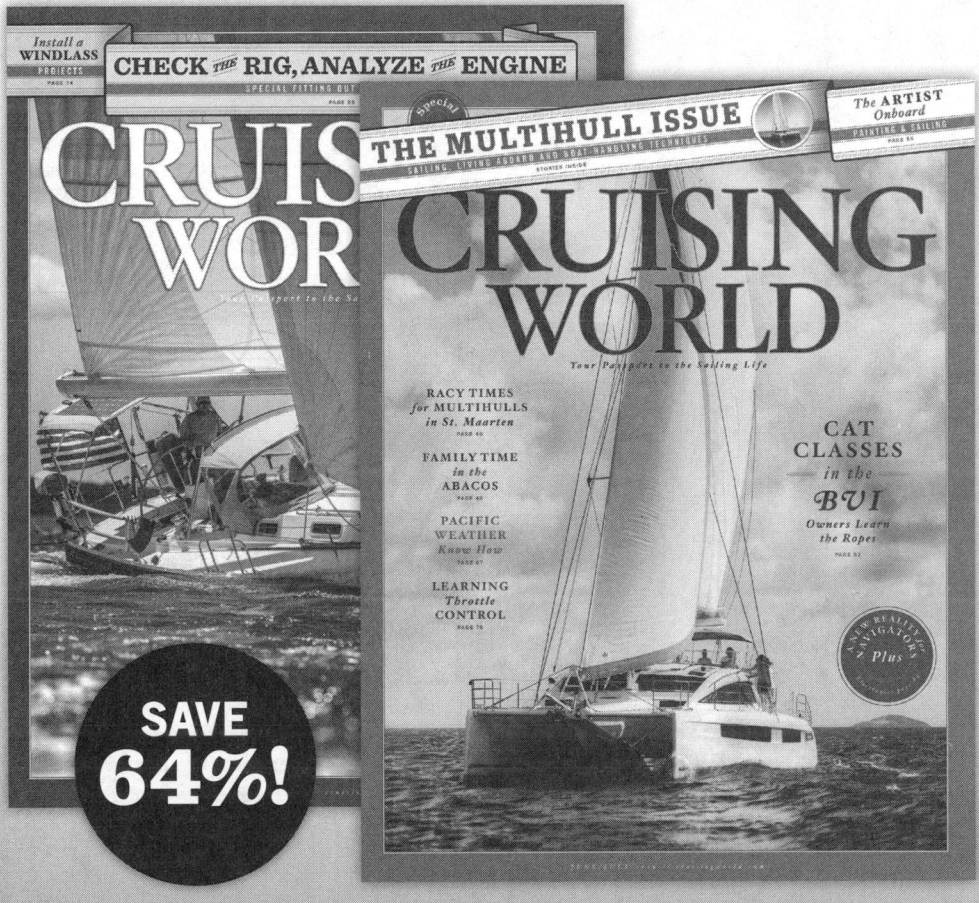

INDUMAR

CHARTS & PUBLICATIONS

Charts & Publications

Paper and digital format, Print On Demand service, CNTA active member.

- ADMIRALTY
- OceanGrafix
- SEMAR Mexico
- IMO
- Witherbys
- Marisec
- Shipping guides LTD
- I.C. Brindle & Co.
- ITU

Marine Electronic Services

Installation and maintenance of navigation & communication equipment.

Class inspections approved by: BV · DNV GL · LR · RINA · ABS · CLASS NK

- Sperry Marine
- Consilium
- Jotron
- Simrad
- JRC
- Entel
- Cobham Sailor
- Kelvin Hughes
- Tokyo Keiki
- Danelec
- Wärtsilä
- Yokogawa

Maritime Products

SOLAS approved signage, safety equipment, nautical instruments & more.

- DHR lights
- PC Maritime
- Annin Flags
- Maritime Progress
- Weems & Plath
- Datrex

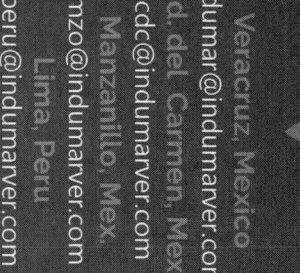

Four Locations to Meet Your Needs

Seattle
206-285-5010

Bellingham
360-734-2400

Kodiak
907-486-5752

Naknek
907-246-4230
(Seasonal, April - August)

b2b.seamar.com • seamar.com

Islamorada

NAVIGATIONAL SUPPLIES & SERVICE I TELS: (507)228-4348 / 228-6069

Business Office: Bldg 808 Balboa Road, (former Canal Zone), Republic of Panama

Business Hours: 0800 - 1700 hours (Local) or 1300 - 2200 hours (UTC). Fax: 507-228-1234

Islamorada is the appointed Admiralty chart agent in the Republic of Panama, and the largest nautical bookstore in Latin America. Located in Balboa, and on the Panama Canal, Islamorada is ideally positioned to provide products and services to ships in transit through the Isthmus, as well as to other countries throughout the region.

| Digital Charts | Paper Charts | Nautical Publications | Maritime Software | Instruments | Flags & Pennants | IMO Signs |

Nautical Books

Navigation, Seamanship

Towing & Salvage

Ship Design & Naval Architecture

Yachting & Leisure

Marine Engineering

Cargo Work

Log Books

Maritime Business, Maritime Law

Publications

Almanacs & Sight Reduction Tables

ITU - Call Signs, Ship Stations, Coastal Stations, MMS

Shipping Guides - Atlas, Guide to Port Entry

IMO - Solas, Marpol, STCW95
(Wide Range of Stock)

Plotting Instrument

Binoculars & Magnifying Glasses

Sextants

Weather Instruments

Clocks & Chronometers

Global Positioning Systems (GPS)

Iridium Satellite Telephones

Brands

C. Plath

B. Cooke & Sons

Blundell Harley

ACR

Admiralty

Oceangrafix

Maui Jim

Reactor Watches

Davis Instruments

and more.

Software For:

Electronic Chart Viewers and ECDIS Software/Hardware

Interactive Diesel Engine Training

Tide Tables & Tidal Current Tables

Electronic Charts

Port Guides

Vessel Traffic Services

Superyacht operations

Fleet Tracking

Nautical Surveys

Because of our strategic location, we are able to provide fast delivery of charts and other important products to ships calling on ports throughout Latin America and the Caribbean Basin.

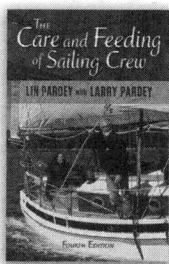

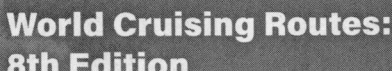

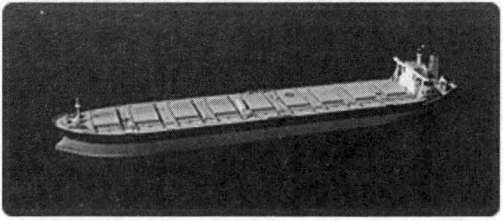

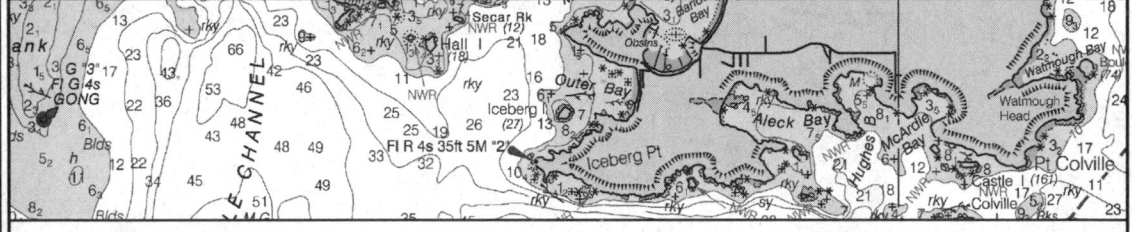